THE WORLD ALMANAC

& BOOK OF FACTS

1975

THE AUTHORITY SINCE 1868

Published Annually by
NEWSPAPER ENTERPRISE ASSOCIATION, INC.
New York, Cleveland

"The fact is the sweetest dream that labor knows."
Robert Frost, "Mowing"

Publisher: Edward R. Kennedy
Executive Editor: George E. Delury
Managing Editor: Vincent P. Bannan
Associate Editor: Kenneth C. Johnston
Assistant Editors: Thomas J. McGuire,
Hana Umlauf
Senior Assistants: Florence Byrnes,
Clive Louden
Assistant to Executive Editor:
Juliana Zankowich

Senior Editor, Canada: Dr. Paul W. Fox
Assistant Editor: Glenda M. Patrick

The editors acknowledge with thanks the many letters of helpful comment and criticism from users of THE WORLD ALMANAC, and invite further suggestions and observations. Because of the volume of mail directed to the editorial offices, it is not possible personally to reply to each letter writer. However, every communication will be read by the editors and all comments and suggestions will receive careful attention.

THE WORLD ALMANAC is published annually in November.

Inquiries regarding contents and purchase orders should be sent to: World Almanac, 230 Park Avenue, New York, N.Y. 10017.

THE WORLD ALMANAC does not decide wagers.

The first edition of THE WORLD ALMANAC, a 120-page hand-set volume with 12 pages of advertising, was published by the *New York World* in 1868, 107 years ago. Annual publication was suspended in 1876. Joseph Pulitzer, publisher of the *New York World*, revived THE WORLD ALMANAC in 1886 with the goal of making it a "compendium of universal knowledge." It has been published annually since then. In 1931, it was acquired by the Scripps-Howard Newspapers; until 1951, it bore the imprint of the *New York World-Telegram* and thereafter, until 1967, that of the *New York World Telegram and Sun.* It is now published in paper and clothbound editions by Newspaper Enterprise Association, Inc., a Scripps-Howard company.

THE WORLD ALMANAC
& BOOK OF FACTS
1975

Copyright© Newspaper Enterprise Association, Inc. 1974

Library of Congress Catalog Card Number 4-3781

International Standard Serial Number (ISSN) 0084-1382

Hard-Cover Edition: Doubleday and Co., Inc.
ISBN 0-385-07724-6

Soft-Cover Edition: Newspaper Enterprise Association, Inc.
ISBN 0-911818-03-0

California State Adoption Code Number 50/3657

Microform Edition since 1868: Bell and Howell Co.

Printed in the United States of America

NEWSPAPER ENTERPRISE ASSOCIATION, INC., 230 Park Avenue, New York, NY 10017; 1200 West Third Street, Cleveland, OH 44113. Robert Roy Metz, president; Earl H. Anderson, vice president and general manager; Edward R. Kennedy, vice president — publications.

General Index

3

Late News, Addenda, Changes

U.S. Administration (Pp 767-768)

White House Staff

Assistant to the President: Donald Rumsfeld.
Presidential press secretary: Ron Nessen.

Executive Agencies

Federal Energy Council: Interior Secretary Rogers C.B. Morton, chairman.

Federal Energy Administration: Andrew B. Gibson succeeded John C. Sawhill, Oct. 29, 1974.

Economic Policy Board: Secretary of the Treasury William E. Simon, chairman.

Council of Economic Advisers: Alan Greenspan, chairman.

Council on International Economic Policy: William O. Eberle, executive director.

Council on Wage and Price Stability: Albert Rees, director.

Department of State

Deputy Secretary: Robert S. Ingersoll was confirmed.
Under Secretary for Security Assistance: Carlyle E. Maw, confirmed.

Department of the Army

Chief of Staff: Gen. Frederick C. Weyand was named after the death of Gen. Creighton W. Abrams.

Dep't. of Health, Education and Welfare

Alcohol, Drug Abuse and Mental Health Administration: Robert L. Dupont Jr., nominated.

National Defense (P 465)

Gen. Alexander M. Haig Jr. was named supren e allied commander, Europe (NATO), and head of the U.S. European Command, Sept. 16, 1974, to replace Gen. Andrew J. Goodpaster in both posts.
The Army chief of staff is Gen. Frederick C. Weyand.

Pay scale: Effective Oct. 1, 1974, base rates were increased about 12%, varying according to pay grade and years of service.

Heads of State (Pp 591-592)

Egypt: Abdel Aziz Hegazi was named premier by President Anwar el-Sadat, Sept. 25, 1974.
Ethiopia: Emperor Haile Selassie, ruler for 58 years, was deposed Sept. 12, 1974; Gen. Aman Michael Andom headed a new military government.
Guinea-Bissau: Luiz de Almeida Cabral, 42, became the new nation's first president Sept. 10, 1974.
Italy: Aldo Moro, a Christian Democrat, was named Oct. 29, 1974, to try to form a new cabinet.
Lebanon: Rashid al Solh became premier Oct. 31, 1974.
New Zealand: Wallace Edward Rowling became prime minister Sept. 6, 1974, following the death of Norman E. Kirk Aug. 31.
Nicaragua: Gen. Anastasio Somoza Debayle, 48, was elected president Sept. 1, 1974, to take office Dec. 1.
Portugal: Gen. Antonio de Spinola resigned as president Sept. 30, 1974, and Gen. Francisco da Costa Gomes became president.

Ambassadors (Pp 593-594)

New ambassadors, named by the president and confirmed by the Senate, included:
People's Republic of China: George Bush.
France: Kenneth Rush.
x Ghana: Shirley Temple Black.
Portugal: Frank C. Carlucci 3d was nominated Nov. 1, 1974.
Great Britain: Walter H. Annenberg retired as ambassador in Oct. 1974.
U.S. Mission to NATO: David K.E. Bruce.
The nomination of Staunton D. Anderson to be ambassador to Costa Rica was withdrawn at his own request.
With establishment of diplomatic relations between the Democratic Republic of (East) Germany and the U.S., Sept. 4, 1974, ambassadors were named by the 2 nations, their first to each other: John Sherman Cooper from the U.S., Rolf Sieber to the U.S.

Sports (Pp 821-914)

Boxing: Muhammad Ali regained the world heavyweight championship Oct. 30, 1974, by knocking out champion George Foreman in 2 minutes, 58 seconds of the 8th round in Kinshasa, Zaire.
Horse Racing: The French filly Dahlia won the $152,750 Canadian International Championship Stakes in the record time of 2:40 for the 1 and 5/8 mi. race Oct. 27, 1974.
Baseball: Jim (Catfish) Hunter of the Oakland A's won the American League Cy Young Award for 1974.
Hockey: The Soviet National team won the last of an 8-game series, Oct. 6, 1974, defeating a team of Canadian World Hockey Assn. pros 4 games to 1 with 3 tied.
Olympics: Moscow was named Oct. 23, 1974, as the site of the Summer Olympics in 1980 and Lake Placid, N.Y., for the Winter Olympics.

1974 Awards, Prizes (Pp 381-392)

Nobel Prize for Peace: Former Japanese Premier Eisaku Sato and Sean MacBride of Ireland, UN Commissioner for South-West Africa (Namibia).
Nobel Prize in Chemistry: Dr. Paul J. Flory, U.S., for his work with plastics.
Nobel Prize in Physics: Dr. Martin Ryle, Great Britain, for radiotelescope developments, and Dr. Antony Hewish, Great Britain, for discovering pulsars.
Nobel Prize in Literature: Eyvind Johnson and Harry Edmund Martinson, both Sweden.
Nobel Prize in Physiology-Medicine: Dr. Albert Claude, Luxembourg-U.S.; Dr. George Emil Palade, Romania-U.S., and Dr. Christian Rene de Duve, Belgium; all for contributions to cell biology science.
Nobel Memorial Prize in Economics: Dr. Gunnar Myrdal, Sweden, and Dr. Friedrich A. von Hayek, Austria, for socio-economic studies.
Maria Moors Cabot Awards: Fernando Pedreira, O Estado de Sao Paulo; Don Bohning and William D. Montalbano, the Miami Herald, and prizes to both newspapers.
Artur Rubinstein Piano Award: Emanuel Ax, U.S.
Emmy Documentary Awards: "Journey to the Outer Limits" and "Fire," ABC; "The Rockefellers" and "Solzhenitsyn," CBS; "American Nerve Gas Arsenal," NBC. Independently produced and public TV programs included: "The World at War," "Gift of Tears" (This Is the Life), Henry Steele Commager and "A Question of Impeachment" (Bill Moyers Journal), "The Runaways," "Make a Wish," "Inside Out," "Electric Company," the Muppets (Sesame Street), The Adversaries.

New York, N.Y. (P 632)

Officers of the Daily and Sunday News should read: Chairman of the board F.M. Flynn, president and publisher W.H. James, editor and senior vice president Floyd Barger, executive editor and vice president Michael J. O'Neill, managing editor William J. Brink, treasurer and vice president R.J. Rohrbach, general manager, vice president and secretary V.E. Palmer.

World Cities (P 21)

The latitude of Tokyo should be 35°45' N.

U.S. Bicentennial—1976

The 200th anniversary of the independence of the United States will be celebrated in 1976. Observances are planned in each of the 50 states and many communities, including reenactments of historic events and varied cultural and scientific projects.

The World Almanac

and Book of Facts for 1975

Some Major Events and Trends of 1974

See Chronology and consult Index for more complete reports.

After 18 months of denials and countercharges, Richard Nixon practically admitted his participation in a conspiracy to obstruct justice in the Watergate case and resigned as President of the United States. The resignation followed a bipartisan recommendation of impeachment by the House Judiciary Committee and a report to Nixon by Republican Congressional leaders that he had lost nearly all support in both Houses.

Less than one month later, Nixon accepted a pardon granted him by his successor in office, Gerald R. Ford, the nation's first unelected president. Ford's popularity, which had been strengthened by post-Watergate euphoria, fell to a bare majority in national polls.

Led by oil price increases, food shortages, and public and private debt, two-digit inflation became almost worldwide. At the same time, the collapse of several banks in Europe and the U.S. after unsuccessful currency speculation, the declining growth of most national economies, and increasing balance of payments deficits among oil-importing nations led to fears of a global economic crisis and an economic depression.

Elections for the 94th U.S. Congress resulted in a Democratic party landslide as Republicans suffered a net loss of about 47 seats in the House and Senate. The Democratic victory was attributed to voters' anger over inflation and Watergate.

Turkey invaded Cyprus after Greek army officers attached to the Cypriot national guard brought down the government of Archbishop Makarios. Discredited by Turkey's successful invasion, the military junta which had ruled Greece since 1967 returned the Greek government to civilian control.

The Portuguese civilian dictatorship, in power since 1932, was overthrown by junior army officers. The new regime moved quickly to establish full civil liberties in Portugal and to make peace with national liberation movements in the African colonies of Guinea-Bissau, Mozambique and Angola.

Egypt, Syria and Israel, led by the indefatigable diplomacy of U.S. Secretary of State Henry Kissinger, signed disengagement agreements requiring a partial Israeli pullback along the Syrian border and in Sinai. International teams began to clear debris from the Suez Canal, blocked since 1967.

British and Canadian elections, the kidnapping and conversion of Patricia Hearst by political terrorists in California, India's explosion of an atomic device, the resignation of West German Chancellor Willy Brandt, and the exile of Russian author Alexander Solzhenitsyn were among other top news stories of 1974.

THE WATERGATE RECORD

For further details on Watergate and related events, see Chronology, page 915.

It was a remarkable year. Between October 1973 and October 1974, the United States witnessed 5 unthinkable "firsts":
—the first resignation of a vice president in face of criminal charges, Oct. 10, 1973.
—the inauguration of the first vice president to be chosen under Article 25 of the Constitution, Dec. 6, 1973.
—the first resignation of a president, Aug. 9, 1974.
—the inauguration of the first president not chosen in a national election, Aug. 9, 1974.
—the first pardon of a president for alleged criminal acts, Sept. 8, 1974.

Shortly before Spiro Agnew resigned as vice president, President Nixon remarked to Attorney General Elliot Richardson, "Now that we have disposed of that matter (Agnew's resignation), we can go ahead and get rid of (Archibald) Cox (the Watergate special prosecutor)." Ten days later, Cox was fired. The attorney general resigned and his assistant was sacked when they refused to participate in the firing — which was later ruled illegal by Federal District Court Judge Gerhard A. Gesell.

In the "firestorm" of public outrage that followed, the House of Representatives began its first formal moves toward impeachment. On Nov. 1, Nixon was forced to name a new special prosecutor, Leon Jaworski, who now had firm congressional, judicial, and public support for his independence. On the same day, Congress opened hearings on the nomination of Gerald R. Ford for Vice President. The hearings paid far more attention to Ford's presidential qualifications than might have been expected under normal circumstances.

By the end of May 1974, the special prosecutor and the president were again at loggerheads over subpoenaed presidential tapes and documents. The prosecutor took his case to the Supreme Court. There, in oral arguments on July 8, the president's lawyer, James D. St. Clair, argued that the principle of "separation of powers" forbade the court to interfere in a dispute between the executive and an employee of the executive branch. Furthermore, argued the lawyer, the president's tapes and documents were not subject to subpoena because they were protected by the principle of "executive privilege."

On July 24, The Supreme Court ruled unanimously against Richard Nixon. The decision, read by Nixon appointee Chief Justice Warren E. Burger, contained no stirring rhetoric, but it carefully and soberly marked a limit to presidential power.

From the Supreme Court's Decision

...Notwithstanding the deference each branch must accord the others, the "judicial power of the United States" vested in the Federal courts by Art. 111, Section 1 of the Constitution can no more be shared with the executive branch than the chief executive, for example, can share with the judiciary the veto power, or the Congress share with the judiciary the power to override a Presidential veto. Any other conclusion would be contrary to the basic concept of separation of powers and the checks and balances that flow from the scheme of a tripartite Government....

In this case we must weigh the importance of the general privilege of confidentiality of Presidential communications in performance of his responsibilities against the inroads of such a privilege on the fair administration of criminal justice. The interest in preserving confidentiality is weighty indeed and entitled to great respect. However we cannot conclude that advisers will be moved to temper the candor of their remarks by the infrequent occasions of disclosure because of the possibility that such conversations will be called for in the context of a criminal prosecution.

On the other hand, the allowance of the privilege to withold evidence that is demonstrably relevant in a criminal trial would cut deeply into the guarantee of due process of law and gravely impair the basic function of the courts. A President's acknowledged need for confidentiality in the communications of his office is general in nature, whereas the constitutional need for production of relevant evidence in a criminal proceeding is specific and central to the fair adjudication of a particular criminal case in the administration of justice....

We conclude that when the ground for asserting privilege as to subpoenaed materials sought for use in a criminal trial is based only on the generalized interest in confidentiality, it cannot prevail over the fundamental demands of due process of law in the fair administration of criminal justice. The generalized assertion of privilege must yield to the demonstrated, specific need for evidence in a pending criminal trial.

Hours after the Supreme Court ruling was announced, the House Committee on the Judiciary opened public, televised hearings on proposed articles of impeachment. The hearings followed more than 6 months of investigation and the amassing of over 30 volumes of evidence. Within a week, the committee had approved, with bipartisan support, 2 articles of impeachment to be submitted to the full House for consideration.

The Articles of Impeachment

Article I
(Obstruction of Justice)

In his conduct of the office of President of the United States, Richard M. Nixon, in violation of his constitutional oath faithfully to execute the office of President of the United States and, to the best of his ability, preserve, protect, and defend the Constitution of the United States, and in violation of his constitutional duty to take care that the laws be faithfully executed, has prevented, obstructed, and impeded the administration of justice, in that:

On June 17, 1972, and prior thereto, agents of the Committee for the Re-Election of the President committed unlawful entry of the headquarters of the Democratic National Committee in Washington, District of Columbia, for the purpose of securing political intelligence. Subsequent thereto, Richard M. Nixon, using the powers of his high office, engaged personally and through his subordinates and agents in a course of conduct or plan designed to delay, impede and obstruct investigations of such unlawful entry; to cover up, conceal and protect those responsible and to conceal the existence and scope of other unlawful covert activities.

The means used to implement this course of conduct or plan have included one or more of the following:

(1) Making or causing to be made false or misleading statements to lawfully authorized investigative officers and employes of the United States.

(2) Withholding relevant and material evidence or information from lawfully authorized investigative officers and employes of the United States.

(3) Approving, condoning, acquiescing in, and counseling witnesses with respect to the giving of false or misleading statements to lawfully authorized investigative officers and employes of the United States and false or misleading testimony in fully instituted judicial and congressional proceedings.

(4) Interfering, or endeavoring to interfere with the conduct of investigations by the Department of Justice of the United States, the Federal Bureau of Investigation, the office of the Watergate Special Prosecution Force and congressional committees.

(5) Approving, condoning, and acquiescing in, the surreptitious payment of substantial sums of money for the purpose of obtaining the silence or influencing the testimony of witnesses, potential witnesses or individuals who participated in such unlawful entry and other illegal activities.

(6) Endeavoring to misuse the Central Intelligence Agency, an agency of the United States.

(7) Disseminating information received from officers of the Department of Justice of the United States to subjects of investigations conducted by lawfully authorized investigative officers and employes of the United States for the purpose of aiding and assisting such subjects in their attempts to avoid criminal liability.

(8) Making false or misleading public statements for the purpose of deceiving the people of the United States into believing that a thorough and complete investigation has been conducted with respect to allegations of misconduct on the part of personnel of the

Executive Branch of the United States and personnel of the Committee for the Re-Election of the President, and that there was no involvement of such personnel in such misconduct; or

(9) Endeavoring to cause prospective defendants, and individuals duly tried and convicted, to expect favored treatment and consideration in return for their silence or false testimony, or rewarding individuals for their silence or false testimony.

In all of this, Richard M. Nixon has acted in a manner contrary to his trust as President and subversive of constitutional government, to the great prejudice of the cause of law and justice and to the manifest injury of the people of the United States.

Wherefore Richard M. Nixon, by such conduct, warrants impeachment and trial, and removal from office.

Members of the Committee and their votes on Article I were: Ayes—Chairman Peter W. Rodino Jr. (D-N.J.), Harold D. Donohue (D-Mass.), Jack Brooks (D-Tex.), Robert W. Kastenmeir (D-Wisc.), Don Edwards (D-Cal.), Wm. L. Hungate (D-Mo.), John R. Conyers Jr. (D-Mich.), Joshua Eilberg (D-Pa.), Jerome R. Waldie (D-Cal.), Walter Flowers (D-Ala.), James R. Mann (D-S.C.), Paul S. Sarbanes (D-Md.), John F. Seiberling (D-Ohio), George E. Danielson (D-Cal.), Robert F. Drinan (D-Mass.), Charles B. Rangel (D-N.Y.), Barbara Jordan (D-Tex.), Ray Thornton (D-Ark.), Elizabeth Holtzman (D-N.Y.), Wayne W. Owens (D-Utah), Edward Mezvinsky (D-Ia.), Tom Railsback (R-Ill.), Hamilton Fish Jr. (R-N.Y.), Lawrence J. Hogan (R-Md.), M. Caldwell Butler (R-Va.), Wm. S. Cohen (R-Me.), Harold V. Froelich (R-Wisc.); Nays—Edward Hutchinson (R-Mich.), Robert McClory (R-Ill.), Henry P. Smith III (R-N.Y.), Chas. W. Sandman (R-N.J.), Chas. E. Wiggins (R-Cal.), David W. Dennis (R-Ind.), Wiley Mayne (R-Ia.), Trent Lott (R-Miss.), Carlos J. Moorehead (R-Cal.), Joseph J. Maraziti (R-N.J.), Delbert L. Latta (R-Ohio); 27 to 11.

Article II
(Abuse of Power)

Using the power of the office of President of the United States, Richard M. Nixon, in violation of his constitutional oath faithfully to execute the office of President of the United States and, to the best of his ability, preserve, protect, and defend the Constitution of the United States, and in disregard of his constitutional duty to take care that the laws be faithfully executed, has repeatedly engaged in conduct violating the constitutional rights of citizens, impairing the due and proper administration of justice and the conduct of lawful inquiries, or contravening the laws governing agencies of the executive branch and the purposes of these agencies.

This conduct has included one or more of the following:

(1) He has, acting personally and through his subordinates and agents, endeavored to obtain from the Internal Revenue Service, in violation of the constitutional rights of citizens, confidential information contained in income tax returns for purposes not authorized by law, and to cause, in violation of the constitutional rights of citizens, income tax audits or other income tax investigations to be initiated or conducted in a discriminatory manner.

(2) He misused the Federal Bureau of Investigation, the Secret Service, and other executive personnel, in violation or disregard of the constitutional right of citizens, by directing, or authorizing such agencies or personnel to conduct or continue electronic surveillance or other investigations for purposes unrelated to national security, the enforcement of laws, or any other lawful function of his office; he did direct, authorize, or permit the use of information obtained thereby for purposes unrelated to national security, the enforcement of laws, or any other lawful function of his office; and he did direct the concealment of certain records made by the Federal Bureau of Investigation of electronic surveillance.

(3) He has, acting personally and through his subordinates and agents, in violation or disregard of the constitutional rights of citizens, authorized and permitted to be maintained a secret investigative unit within the office of the President, financed in part with money derived from campaign contributions to him, which unlawfully utilized the resources of the Central Intelligence Agency, engaged in covert and unlawful activities, and attempted to prejudice the constitutional right of an accused to a fair trial.

(4) He has failed to take care that the laws were faithfully executed by failing to act when he knew or had reason to know that his close subordinates endeavored to impede and frustrate lawful inquiries by duly constituted executive, judicial, and legislative entities concerning the unlawful entry into the headquarters of the Democratic National Committee, and the cover-up thereof, and concerning other unlawful activities including those relating to the confirmation of Richard Kleindienst as attorney general of the United States, the electronic surveillance of private citizens, the break-in into the office of Dr. Lewis Fielding, and the campaign financing practices of the Committee to Re-elect the President.

(5) In disregard of the rule of law he knowingly misused the executive power by interfering with agencies of the executive branch, including the Federal Bureau of Investigation, the Criminal Division and the Office of Watergate Special Prosecution Force of the Department of Justice, and the Central Intelligence Agency, in violation of his duty to take care that the laws be faithfully executed.

In all of this, Richard M. Nixon has acted in a manner contrary to his trust as President and subversive of constitutional government, to the great prejudice of the cause of law and justice and to the manifest injury of the people of the United States.

Wherefore Richard M. Nixon, by such conduct, warrants impeachment and trial, and removal from office.

The vote on Article II was the same as on Article I except for McClory who voted aye; 28 to 10.

Article III
(Contempt of Congress)

In his conduct of the office of President of the United States, Richard M. Nixon, contrary to his oath faithfully to execute the office of the President of the United States, and to the best of his ability preserve, protect and defend the Constitution of the United States, and in violation of his constitutional duty to take care that the laws be faithfully executed, has failed without lawful cause or excuse, to produce papers and things as directed by duly authorized subpoenas issued by the Committee on the Judiciary of the House of Representatives, on April 11, 1974, May 15, 1974, May 30, 1974, and June 24, 1974, and willfully disobeyed such subpoenas. The subpoenaed papers and things were deemed necessary by the Committee in order to resolve by direct evidence fundamental, factual questions relating to Presidential direction, knowledge or approval of actions demonstrated by other evidence to be substantial grounds for impeachment of the President. In refusing to produce these papers and things, Richard M. Nixon, substituting his judgement as to what materials were necessary for the inquiry, interposed the powers of the Presidency against the lawful subpoenas of the House of Representatives, thereby assuming to himself functions and judgments necessary to the exercise of the sole power of impeachment vested by the Constitution in the House of Representatives.

In all this, Richard M. Nixon has acted in a manner contrary to his trust as President and subversive of constitutional government, to the great prejudice of the cause of law and justice, and to the manifest injury of the people of the United States. Wherefore, Richard M. Nixon, by such conduct, warrants impeachment and trial and removal from office.

The vote on Article III was: Ayes — Republicans McClory and Hogan and all Democrats except Flowers and Mann; 21 to 17.

On Aug. 5, under pressure from his attorney, Nixon released transcripts of 3 subpoenaed tapes of conversations with his former chief aide, H. R. Haldeman, on June 23, 1972, only 5 days after the Watergate break-in. Nixon also released a statement explaining his new disclosures.

From the Nixon Statement

. . . In May, I made a preliminary review of some of the 64 taped conversations subpoenaed by the special prosecutor.

Among the conversations I listened to at that time were two of those of June 23. Although I recognized that these presented potential problems, I did not inform my staff or my counsel of it, or those arguing my case, nor did I amend my submission to the Judiciary Committee in order to include and reflect it. At the time, I did not realize the extent of the implications which these conversations might now appear to have. As a result, those arguing my case, as well as those passing judgement on the case, did so with information that was incomplete and in some respects erroneous. This was a serious act of ommission for which I take full responsibility and which I deeply regret. . . .

The June 23 tapes clearly show . . . that at the time I gave those instructions [to have the CIA halt the FBI investigation of the money found on the Watergate burglars] I also discussed the political aspects of the situation, and that I was aware of the advantages this course of action would have with respect to limiting possible public exposure of involvement by persons connected with the re-election committee . . . .

I am firmly convinced that the record, in its entirety, does not justify the extreme step of impeachment and removal of a President.

From the Transcript of the First Meeting on July 23, 1972

. . . Haldeman: Now, on the investigation, you know the Democratic break-in thing, we're back in the problem area because the FBI is not under control, because Gray doesn't exactly know how to control it and they have — their investigation is now leading into some productive areas — because they've been able to trace the money — not through the money itself— but through the bank sources — the banker. And, and it goes in some directions we don't want it to go. . . .

Haldeman: And the proposal would be that Ehrlichman and I call them (CIA officials) in, and say . . . .

President: When you get in — when you get in (unintelligible) people, say, "Look the problem is that this will open the whole, the whole Bay of Pigs thing, and the President just feels that ah, without going into details — don't, don't lie to them to the extent to say no involvement, but just say this is a comedy of errors, without getting into it, the President believes that it is going to open the whole Bay of Pigs thing up again. And, ah, because these people are plugging for (unintelligible) and that they should call the FBI in and (unintelligible) don't go any further into this case period!

With this revelation, Nixon's support collapsed. His defenders on the House Judiciary Committee declared unanimously that they would now vote for impeachment on the first article, and Republican Senators Scott and Goldwater informed Nixon that he could count on no more than 15 of the 34 votes required to escape conviction in the Senate. In a televised speech the evening of Aug. 8, Nixon's 2-year struggle to preserve his presidency and his reputation came to an end. He announced he would resign.

From Nixon's Resignation Speech

. . . Throughout the long and difficult period of Watergate, I have felt it was my duty to persevere; to make every possible effort to complete the term of office to which you elected me.

In the past few days, however, it has become evident to me that I no longer have a strong enough political base in the Congress to justify continuing that effort.

As long as there was such a base, I felt strongly that it was necessary to see the constitutional process through to its conclusion; that to do otherwise would be unfaithful to the spirit of that deliberately difficult process, and a dangerously destabilizing precedent for the future.

But with the disappearance of that base, I now believe that the constitutional purpose has been served. And there is no longer a need for the process to be prolonged.

I would have preferred to carry through to the finish whatever the personal agony it would have involved, and my family unanimously urged me to do so. . . .

I have never been a quitter.

To leave office before my term is completed is opposed to every instinct in my body. But as President I must put the interest of America first.

America needs a full-time President and a full-time Congress, particularly at this time with problems we face at home and abroad.

To continue to fight through the months ahead for my personal vindication would almost totally absorb the time and attention of both the President and the

Congress in a period when our entire focus should be on the great issues of peace abroad and prosperity without inflation at home.

Therefore, I shall resign the Presidency effective at noon tomorrow....

I regret deeply any injuries that may have been done in the course of the events that led to this decision. I would say only that if some of my judgments were wrong — and some were wrong — they were made in what I believed at the time to be the best interests of the nation....

When I first took the oath of office as President five and a half years ago, I made this sacred commitment: to consecrate my office, my energies and all the wisdom I can summon to the cause of peace among nations.

I've done my very best in all the days since to be true to that pledge.

As a result of these efforts, I am confident that the world is a safer place today, not only for the people of America but for the people of all nations, and that all of our children have a better chance than before of living in peace rather than dying in war.

The following day, shortly after noon, Gerald R. Ford was sworn in as the 38th president of the United States. Only 10 months before, he had been the Republican leader in the House and had thought to remain there to the end of his political career.

From President Ford's Inaugural Address

... I assume the Presidency under extraordinary circumstances never before experienced by Americans. This is an hour of history that troubles our minds and hurts our hearts....

I am acutely aware that you have not elected me as your President by your ballots. So I ask you to confirm me as your President with your prayers.

If you have not chosen me by secret ballot, neither have I gained office by any secret promises. I have not subscribed to any partisan platform. I am indebted to no man....

My fellow Americans, our long national nightmare is over. Our Constitution works. Our great republic is a government of laws and not of men. Here, the people rule....

On Aug. 22, the House Judiciary Committee released its report, which would have become the basis for impeachment if Nixon had not resigned. Besides the long report of the majority who had voted for the articles of impeachment, the committee members who had voted against them added a minority report stating they would now vote for Article I.

From the Majority Report

On Article II

... In considering this Article the Committee has relied on evidence of acts directly attributable to Richard M. Nixon himself. He had repeatedly attempted to deceive and mislead the American people about his own responsibility. He governed behind closed doors, directing the operation of the executive branch through close subordinates, and sought to conceal his knowledge of what they did illegally on his behalf. Although the Committee finds it unnecessary in this case to take any position on whether the President should be held accountable, through exercise of the power of impeachment, for the actions of his immediate subordinates, undertaken on his behalf, when his personal authorization and knowledge of them cannot be proved, it is appropriate to call attention to the dangers inherent in the performance of the highest public office in the land in an air of secrecy and concealment....

On Article III

There can be no question that in refusing to comply with limited, narrowly drawn subpoenas — issued only after the Committee was satisfied that there was other evidence pointing to the existence of impeachable offenses—the President interfered with the exercise of the House's function as the "Grand Inquest of the Nation." Unless the defiance of the Committee's subpoenas under these circumstances is considered grounds for impeachment, it is difficult to conceive of any President acknowledging that he is obligated to supply the relevant evidence necessary for Congress to exercise its constitutional responsibility in an impeachment proceeding. If this were to occur, the impeachment power would be drained of its vitality. Article III, therefore, seeks to preserve the integrity of the impeachment process itself and the ability of Congress to act as the ultimate safeguard against improper presidential conduct.

From the Minority Report

... Our gratitude of his having by his resignation spared the Nation additional agony should no obscure for history our judgment that Richard Nixon, as President, committed certain acts for which he should have been impeached and removed from office. Likewise, having effectively admitted guilt of one ipeachable offense—obstruction of justice in connection with the Watergate investigation—Richard Nixon is not consequently to be presumed guilty of all other offenses with which he was charged by the majority of the Committee....

(1) With respect to proposed Article I, we believe that the charges of conspiracy to obstruct justice, and obstruction of justice, which are contained in the Article in essence, if not in terms, may be taken as substantially confessed by Mr. Nixon on August 5, 1974, and corroborated by ample other evidence in the record....

(2) With respect to proposed Article II, we find sufficient evidence to warrant a belief that isolated instances of unlawful conduct by presidential aides and subordinates did occur during the five-and-one-half years of the Nixon Administration, with varying degrees of direct personal knowledge or involvement of the President in these respective illegal episodes...

Moreover, even as to those acts which we would concur in characterizing as abusive and which the President appeared to direct or countenance, neither singly nor in the aggregate do they impress us as being offenses for which Richard Nixon, or any President, should be impeached or removed from office, when considered, as they must be, on their own footing....

(3) Likewise, with respect to proposed Article III, we believe that this charge, standing alone, affords insufficient grounds for impeachment....

We know that it has been said, and perhaps some will continue to say, that Richard Nixon was "hounded from office" by his political opponents and media critics. We feel constrained to point out, however, that it was Richard Nixon who impeded the FBI's investigation of the Watergate affair by wrongfully attempting to implicate the Central Intelligence Agency; it was Richard Nixon, who created and preserved the evidence of that transgression and who, knowing that it had been subpoenaed by this Committee and the Special Prosecutor, concealed its

terrible import, even from his own counsel, until he could do so no longer. And it was a unanimous Supreme Court of the United States which, in an opinion authored by the Chief Justice whom he appointed, ordered Richard Nixon to surrender that evidence to the Special Prosecutor, to further the ends of justice. The tragedy that finally engulfed Richard Nixon had many facets. One was the very self-inflicted nature of the harm....

In the month following Ford's inauguration, a mild euphoria of relief and goodwill seized the nation. As the President had said, the "long national nightmare is over." Then, on Sunday morning, Sept. 8, in one of the boldest acts in the history of the presidency, Ford granted his predecessor "a full, free and absolute pardon."

Proclamation of Pardon

Richard Nixon became the thirty-seventh President of the United States on January 20, 1969, and was re-elected in 1972 for a second term by the electors of forty-nine of fifty states. His term in office continued until his resignation on August 9, 1974.

Pursuant to resolutions of the House of Representatives, its Committee on the Judiciary conducted an inquiry and investigation on the impeachment of the President extending over more than eight months. The hearings of the committee and its deliberations, which received wide national publicity over television, radio, and in printed media, resulted in votes adverse to Richard Nixon on recommended Articles of Impeachment.

As a result of certain acts or omissions occurring before his resignation from the office of President, Richard Nixon has become liable to possible indictment and trial for offenses against the United States. Whether or not he shall be so prosecuted depends on findings of the appropriate grand jury and on the discretion of the authorized prosecutor. Should an indictment ensue, the accused shall then be entitled to a fair trial by an impartial jury, as guaranteed to

every individual by the Constitution.

It is believed that a trial of Richard Nixon, if it became necessary, could not fairly begin until a year or more has elapsed. In the meantime, the tranquility to which this nation has been restored by the events of recent weeks could be irreparably lost by the prospects of bringing to trial a former President of the United States. The prospects of such trial will cause prolonged and divisive debate over the propriety of exposing to further punishment and degradation a man who has already paid the unprecedented penalty of relinquishing the highest office in the United States.

NOW, THEREFORE, I, Gerald R. Ford, President of the United States, pursuant to the pardon power conferred upon me by Article II, Section 2, of the Constitution, have granted and by these presents do grant a full, free, and absolute pardon unto Richard Nixon for all offenses against the United States which he, Richard Nixon, has committed or may have committed or taken part in during the period from January 20, 1969, through August 9, 1974.

From the President's Announcement of the Pardon

... As we are a nation under God, so I am sworn to uphold our laws with the help of God. And I have sought such guidance and searched my own conscience with special diligence to determine the right thing for me to do with respect to my predecessor in this place, Richard Nixon, and his loyal wife and family.

played a part, It can go on and on, or someone must write "The End" to it.

I have concluded that only I can do that. And if I can, I must....

It is common knowledge that serious allegations and accusations hang like a sword over our former president's head and threaten his health as he tries to

reshape his life, a great part of which was spent in service of this country and by the mandate of its people.

After years of bitter controversy and divisive national debate, I have been advised and am compelled to conclude that many months and perhaps more years will have to pass before Richard Nixon could hope to obtain a fair trial by jury in any jurisdiction of the United States....

Finally, I feel that Richard Nixon and his loved ones have suffered enough, and will continue to suffer no matter what I do, no matter what we as a great and good nation can do together to make his goal of peace come true.

From Richard Nixon's Response to the Pardon

... Looking back on what is still in my mind a complex and confusing maze of events, decisions, pressures, and personalities, one thing I can see clearly now is that I was wrong in not acting more decisively and more forthrightly in dealing with Watergate, particularly when it reached the stage of judicial proceedings and grew from a political scandal into a national tragedy.

No words can describe the depths of my regret and pain at the anguish my mistakes over Watergate have

caused the nation and the Presidency, a nation I so deeply love and an institution I so greatly respect.

I know that many fair-minded people believe that my motivation and actions in the Watergate affair were intentionally self-serving and illegal. I now understand how my own mistakes and misjudgments have contributed to that belief and seemed to support it. This burden is the heaviest one of all to bear. That the way I tried to deal with Watergate was the wrong way is a burden I shall bear for every day of the life that is left to me.

Once again, a large portion of the public protested this arbitrary exercise of presidential power; but the outcry was quickly stilled in face of the wholly legal and irrevocable character of the pardon. By the time the trial of Nixon's top associates for obstruction of justice opened on Sept. 30, the numbed national consciousness appeared to have settled into the wary hope that there were no further shocks to come in the concluding scenes of the Watergate tragedy.

Democrats Win Big In 1974 Elections

Restless voters, roused by Watergate, inflation and the specter of recession, dealt the Republican party a series of punishing blows on Election Day, Nov. 5, 1974. But the voters displayed a strong sense of selectivity, electing Republicans in a number of important races.

Democrats boosted their big majorities in the Senate and the House and in governors' mansions.

In the House, where all 435 seats were at stake, Democrats captured a total of more than two-thirds. In the Senate, with only 35 of the 100 seats up for grabs, the Democrats came only a few short of the two-thirds mark.

In the governorships, the Democrats took the 2 giant prizes, California and New York, as well as 5 others away from the GOP. But Republicans took 2 state houses away from the Democrats, Ohio and South Carolina. An independent won the previously Democratic post in Maine.

All that gave the Democrats a net gain of 4 governorships, a total of 36 compared to their old total of 32.

Republican Victories

Some of the Republican victories were surprises as in Ohio where a former governor, Republican James A. Rhodes, upset Democratic Gov. John J. Gilligan while former astronaut John Glenn, a Democrat, won a Senate seat in a landslide over Cleveland Republican Mayor Ralph J. Perk.

Despite the overall Democratic sweep, the election had its mixed-bag aspect, well typified in New York State. A little-known Congressman from Brooklyn, Hugh Carey, soundly defeated Nelson Rockefeller's hand-picked successor, Gov. Malcolm Wilson, and carried into the lieutenant governorship Mary Anne Krupsak, first woman to hold statewide office. But 2 Republican stalwarts won re-election, Sen. Jacob K. Javits by a wide margin and Attorney General Louis Lefkowitz narrowly. Democrats took over the Assembly, the GOP held on to the State Senate.

Connecticut voters elected the first woman to be governor of any state in the northeast, overwhelmingly choosing Ella T. Grasso, 55-year-old Democratic congresswoman, and soundly re-electing Sen. Abraham A. Ribicoff.

In California, Democrat Edmund G. Brown Jr., son of the man Ronald Reagan defeated 8 years earlier, won the governorship by defeating Republican Houston I. Flournoy in a close race. Democratic Sen. Alan Cranston was soundly re-elected over H. L. Richardson, Republican and former John Birch Society official.

California Congressman and former Olympic hero Bob Mathias was among the losing Republicans despite last-minute personal assistance from President Ford. Democrat John Krebs defeated Mathias in a newly-apportioned district containing many more Democrats than previously.

Ford failed to save a majority of the Republicans he campaigned for in a 19-state, 16,685-mile mission. Most of them had been apparent losers before his month-long effort.

Judiciary Committee Losers

Four Republican Congressmen who voted against impeaching Richard Nixon in the House Judiciary Committee were defeated in bids for re-election:

Charles W. Sandman, caustic critic of Nixon opponents on the committee, lost his New Jersey seat to William J. Hughes, whom he had defeated

in a previous election. Joseph J. Maraziti, also in New Jersey, lost out to Helen Meyner, wife of a former Democratic governor. The other losers were Wiley Mayne, Iowa and David Dennis of Indiana.

One Republican on the committee, Harold Froehlich of Wisconsin, had voted for 2 articles of impeachment, but was defeated anyway by Roman Catholic priest Robert J. Cornell. Froehlich had defeated him with 52% of the vote in 1970. Another casualty of the impeachment process, perhaps, was Wayne Owens of Utah. A Democrat, he had supported the impeachment drive. He resigned his House seat to run for the Senate, but was roundly beaten by Jake Garn, Republican.

All other committee members who ran for re-election were victorious. Charles Wiggins, one of Nixon's chief defenders on the committee, won by a narrow margin in a staunchly Republican district; and Robert McClory, Republican, who voted twice for impeachment, just barely won his 7th term in the House.

Ethnic minorities gained additional representation as blacks added a new member to their Congressional delegation, Harold Ford in Tennessee, and 2 black lieutenant governors. Two Spanish-surnamed governors were elected, Jerry Apodaca, Democrat, in New Mexico and Raul Castro, Democrat, in Arizona.

Blacks also picked up 11 seats in the Alabama House for a total there of 13, and also elected 2 to the State Senate.

Candidates of Oriental descent swept all major offices in Hawaii.

Women Win, Lose

Women, who had about 300 representatives in races major and minor around the country, had varied success.

Top gains included the Grasso win in Connecticut and the Krupsak victory in New York.

In Tennessee, Marilyn Lloyd bested Republican Congressman Lamar Baker to become the first woman ever elected in the state to a full Congressional term. Jane Grey Hayes, a Democrat, was elected the first female mayor of a city of over 500,000 population.

But Louise Gore, Republican, was defeated by Gov. Marvin Mandel, who won re-election in Maryland. Democrat Betty Roberts failed to unseat Republican Senator Robert Packwood in Oregon.

Fredi Wechsler, elections analyst for the National Women's Political Caucus, estimated from incomplete results that women increased their numbers in state legislatures from the present 470 to more than 750 — a 70% gain.

Based on those estimates, she said, the feminist movement now believes it may win ratification of the equal rights amendment, which would prohibit statutory discrimination against women. The amendment has been ratified in 33 of the required 38 states.

Independents

The lone independent elected governor was James Longley, who made history by winning the governorship of Maine with 40% of the vote, barely besting the favored Democrat, who had 37%, and the Republican, who garnered 23%. A 50-year-old insurance executive, Longley promised to run the state "like a business."

Other independents and 3d party candidates had less success. In New York, Barbara Keating, personable Conservative candidate for senator, got 16% of the vote but failed to hurt Republican Javits, whose 45% also topped former U.S. Attorney General Ramsey Clark's 39%.

Democrats did well in the once Republican stronghold of Vermont, electing Patrick J. Leahy to be the state's first Democratic senator and giving Democratic Gov. Thomas Salmon his 2d term.

By contrast, a Republican won the governorship in South Carolina, the first to win that post since the post-Civil War reconstruction days. State Sen. James B. Edwards defeated Democratic Congressman William Jennings Bryan Dorn for the gubernatorial post. Dorn had been a last-minute nominee, selected after Charles D. Ravenel was disqualified from the race because he had not been a state resident a full 5 years.

Democrats in the South

The South, where former President Nixon had scored many gains, turned against the Republicans in many cases.

Tennessee turned over the governorship and control of the 8-member Congressional delegation to the Democrats. Former White House aide Lamar Alexander lost his bid to succeed Republican Gov. Winfield Dunn as Democrat Ray Blanton won a hard fought race in which Alexander had been the early favorite.

In Memphis, 4-term Republican Congressman Dan Kuykendall was defeated by Harold Ford who became the first black sent to Congress from Tennessee since reconstruction.

In North Carolina, veteran GOP Congressman Wilmer "Vinegar Bend" Mizell, oldtime baseball hero, went down to defeat, as did veterans Joel T. Broyhill and Stanford E. Parris in Virginia, and Republican Congressmen Bob Price in Texas and Ken Blackburn in Georgia.

State Legislatures

In state legislatures, the Democrats made gains matching their successes in the U.S. Senate and House races. They won control from Republicans of the upper or lower houses, or both, in a dozen states.

Republicans lost control of both the House and Senate in Illinois, Iowa and Connecticut. Democrats won Senate majorities in Wisconsin, which had not had a Democratic Senate since 1893, and in Ohio and Arizona. Democrats already controlled the lower houses in the 3 states.

Democrats wrested control of the lower houses in New York, Colorado, Utah, Indiana, Maine and Pennsylvania. The Republicans retained control of the Senate in all 6, except Pennsylvania.

In states in which Democratic representation was already strong, such as Maryland, Florida, West Virginia, California and Texas, the GOP lost more seats.

Special Issues

A host of propositions, referendums, constitutional changes and other issues, some attracting more attention than many of the candidates, were decided by the voters.

In New Jersey they decided that Atlantic City will not become "Las Vegas East," beating down a proposal to allow casino gambling in the coast resort. Church groups and many law-enforcement officers spent only about $20,000 fighting the proposal while its proponents were reported to have used $500,000 boosting it.

Michigan voters approved a proposal to give a $650, one-time bonus to state veterans who served in the armed forces between 1961 and 1973.

In Oregon, an anti-pornography measure aimed at bookstores, theaters and massage parlors won approval. In adjoining Washington, a proposed state-operated lottery was voted down.

Maryland voters, while re-electing Gov. Mandel, refused to raise his salary from its current $25,000 to $45,000.

New Yorkers approved a $250 million rail bond issue to improve commuter, high-speed and freight train service.

In Other States

In Colorado, last state to execute a person, the voters decided to reinstate the death penalty and to ban underground nuclear tests without voter approval.

In addition to the nuclear test ban, Colorado voters took other action showing their interest in environmental matters by electing Richard Lamm, an ardent environmentalist who helped keep the Winter Olympics out of Denver, in a stunning upset victory over incumbent Republican governor John D. Vanderhoof.

Colorado voters also elected a new senator, Gary Hart, who 2 years earlier had been presidential campaign manager for Sen. George McGovern. He defeated Republican Sen. Peter Dominick with a landslide vote. They also elected the state's first black lieutenant governor, George Brown, but approved a constitutional amendment banning forced busing to achieve school integration.

Results in Michigan were mixed. Republican Gov. William G. Milliken turned back a close challenge by Democrat Sander M. Levin. But Congressman Richard Vanderveen, a Democrat, easily defeated Republican Paul Goebel Jr. to retain President Ford's old House seat in Grand Rapids, to which Vanderveen was named earlier in the year in a special election.

In Kentucky, Sen. Marlow Cook, ranking Republican on the Senate Rules Committee, which handled the hearings on Gerald Ford's vice-presidential confirmation, was overwhelmed by Democratic Gov. Wendell B. Ford in the Senate race.

In Indiana, Democratic Sen. Birch Bayh was re-elected, but only by a narrow margin, defeating Richard Lugar, Republican mayor of Indianapolis, whom former President Nixon once called his "favorite mayor."

Indiana Democrats took 9 of the state's 11 Congressional seats, a gain of 5. Among the Democrats re-elected was Ray J. Madden, 82-year-old chairman of the House Rules Committee.

"New Faces"

Six of the "new" faces elected to the House were familiar ones: all had been members in the past and in 1974 made successful comebacks. They were New York Democrat-Liberals James H. Scheuer and Richard L. Ottinger; Democrats Abner Mikva of Illinois, Andrew Jacobs Jr. of Indiana and Robert Duncan of Oregon, and Republican George Hansen of Idaho.

But 5 other comeback hopefuls failed: New York Democrats John Dow and Allard K. Loewenstein; Democrats Peter F. Mack of Illinois and Paul H. Todd Jr. of Michigan, and Republican C. D. Carlson of Illinois.

Democrats were jubilant over their successes. But Sen. McGovern, once the standard-bearer of their party, said of the big sweep in the House and Senate: "It places a heavy responsibility on the Democrats in Congress to grapple with the problems of the future."

The Ninety-Fourth Congress
The Senate

Terms are for 6 years and end January 3 of the year preceding name. Annual salary $42,500. To be eligible for the U.S. Senate, a person must be at least 30 years of age, a citizen of the United States for at least 9 years, and a resident of the state from which he is chosen. The Congress must meet annually on Jan. 3, unless it has, by law, appointed a different day.

Senate officials: Pres. Pro Tempore, James O. Eastland; Secretary, Francis R. Valeo; Sgt. at Arms, William H. Wannall; Chaplain, L.R. Elson, S.T.D.

Dem., 62; Rep., 38; 1 Undecided. Total, 100. * Asterisk designates senior senator.

Terms Expire	SENATORS	Home	Terms Expire	SENATORS	Home
	ALABAMA			**MONTANA**	
1979	John Sparkman*............	Dem., Huntsville	1977	Mike Mansfield*...........	Dem., Missoula
1981	James B. Allen.............	Dem., Gadsden	1979	Lee Metcalf................	Dem., Helena
	ALASKA			**NEBRASKA**	
1979	Ted Stevens*..............	Rep., Anchorage	1977	Roman L. Hruska*..........	Rep., Omaha
1981	Mike Gravel...............	Dem., Anchorage	1979	Carl T. Curtis..............	Rep., Minden
	ARIZONA			**NEVADA**	
1977	Paul J. Fannin*............	Rep., Phoenix	1977	Howard W. Cannon*........	Dem., Las Vegas
1981	Barry Goldwater...........	Rep., Scottsdale	1981	Paul Laxalt................	Rep., Carson City
	ARKANSAS			**NEW HAMPSHIRE**	
1977	John L. McClellan*.........	Dem., Little Rock	1979	Thomas J. McIntyre*........	Dem., Laconia
1981	Dale Bumpers.............	Dem., Charleston	1981	Louis C. Wyman............	Rep., Manchester
	CALIFORNIA			**NEW JERSEY**	
1977	John V. Tunney*...........	Dem., Riverside	1977	Harrison Williams, Jr.......	Dem., Westfield
1981	Alan Cranston*............	Dem., Palm Springs	1979	Clifford P. Case*...........	Rep., Rahway
	COLORADO			**NEW MEXICO**	
1979	Flody K. Haskell*..........	Dem., Denver	1977	Joseph M. Montoya*........	Dem., Santa Fe
1981	Gary Hart.................	Dem., Denver	1979	Pete V. Domenici...........	Rep., Albuquerque
	CONNECTICUT			**NEW YORK**	
1977	Lowell P. Weicker, Jr.......	Rep., Greenwich	1977	James L. Buckley...........	Con., New York
1981	Abraham A. Ribicoff*.......	Dem., Hartford	1981	Jacob K. Javits*...........	Rep., New York
	DELAWARE			**NORTH CAROLINA**	
1977	William V. Roth, Jr.*.......	Rep., Wilmington	1979	Jesse A. Helms*...........	Rep., Raleigh
1979	Joseph R. Biden, Jr........	Dem., Faulkland	1981	Robert Morgan.............	Dem., Lillington
	FLORIDA			**NORTH DAKOTA**	
1977	Lawton Chiles*............	Dem., Lakeland	1977	Quentin N. Burdick.........	Dem., Fargo
1981	Richard Stone.............	Dem., Tallahassee	1981	William L. Guy*...........	Dem., Casselton
	GEORGIA				Milton R. Young*..........	Rep., La Moure
1979	Sam Nunn.................	Dem., Perry		**OHIO**	
1981	Herman E. Talmadge*......	Dem., Lovejoy	1977	Robert Taft, Jr.*..........	Rep., Cincinnati
	HAWAII		1981	John Glenn................	Dem., Columbus
1977	Hiram L. Fong*............	Rep., Honolulu		**OKLAHOMA**	
1981	Daniel K. Inouye...........	Dem., Honolulu	1979	Dewey F. Bartlett..........	Rep., Tulsa
	IDAHO		1981	Henry Bellmon............	Rep., Red Rock
1979	James A. McClure..........	Rep., Payette		**OREGON**	
1981	Frank Church*.............	Dem., Boise	1979	Mark O. Hatfield*..........	Rep., Salem
	ILLINOIS		1981	Robert W. Packwood........	Rep., Lake Oswego
1979	Charles H. Percy*..........	Rep., Kenilworth		**PENNSYLVANIA**	
1981	Adlai E. Stevenson 3d......	Dem., Chicago	1977	Hugh Scott*..............	Rep., Philadelphia
	INDIANA		1981	Richard S. Schweicker.......	Rep., Worcester
1977	Vance Hartke*.............	Dem., Evansville		**RHODE ISLAND**	
1981	Birch Bayh................	Dem., Indianapolis	1977	John O. Pastore*...........	Dem., Providence
	IOWA		1979	Claiborne Pell.............	Dem., Newport
1979	Dick Clark*...............	Dem., Marion		**SOUTH CAROLINA**	
1981	John C. Culver............	Dem., Cedar Rapids	1979	Strom Thurmond*..........	Rep., Aiken
	KANSAS		1981	Ernest F. Hollings.........	Dem., Columbia
1979	James B. Pearson*.........	Rep., Prairie Village		**SOUTH DAKOTA**	
1981	Robert J. Dole.............	Rep., Russell	1979	James Abourezk...........	Dem., Rapid City
	KENTUCKY		1981	George McGovern*.........	Dem., Mitchell
1979	Walter Huddleston*........	Dem., Elizabethtown		**TENNESSEE**	
1981	Wendell H. Ford...........	Dem., Owensboro	1977	William E. Brock, 3rd.......	Rep., Chattanooga
	LOUISIANA		1979	Howard H. Baker, Jr.*......	Rep., Knoxville
1979	J. Bennett Johnston, Jr......	Dem., Shreveport		**TEXAS**	
1981	Russell B. Long*...........	Dem., Baton Rouge	1977	Lloyd M. Bentsen..........	Dem., Houston
	MAINE		1979	John G. Tower*............	Rep., Wichita Falls
1977	Edmund S. Muskie*........	Dem., Waterville		**UTAH**	
1979	William D. Hathaway........	Dem., Auburn	1977	Frank E. Moss*............	Dem., Salt Lake City
	MARYLAND		1981	Jake Garn.................	Rep., Salt Lake City
1977	J. Glenn Beall, Jr..........	Rep., Frostburg		**VERMONT**	
1981	Charles McC.Mathias*......	Rep., Frederick	1977	Robert T. Stafford*........	Rep., Rutland
	MASSACHUSETTS		1981	Patrick J. Leahy...........	Dem., Burlington
1977	Edward M. Kennedy*.......	Dem., Boston		**VIRGINIA**	
1979	Edward W. Brooke.........	Rep., Newton Center	1977	Harry F. Byrd, Jr.*.........	Ind., Winchester
	MICHIGAN		1979	William Lloyd Scott.........	Rep., Fairfax
1977	Philip A. Hart*............	Dem., Mackinac Is.		**WASHINGTON**	
1979	Robert P. Griffin..........	Rep., Traverse City	1977	Henry M. Jackson*.........	Dem., Everett
	MINNESOTA		1981	Warren G. Magnuson*.......	Dem., Seattle
1977	Hubert Humphrey*.........	Dem., Waverly		**WEST VIRGINIA**	
1979	Walter F. Mondale*........	Dem., Minneapolis	1977	Robert C. Byrd...........	Dem., Sophia
	MISSISSIPPI		1979	Jennings Randolph*........	Dem., Elkins
1977	John Stennis..............	Dem., De Kalb		**WISCONSIN**	
1979	James O. Eastland*........	Dem., Doddsville	1977	William Proxmire*..........	Dem., Madison
	MISSOURI		1981	Gaylord A. Nelson..........	Dem., Madison
1977	Stuart Symington*.........	Dem., St. Louis		**WYOMING**	
1981	Thomas F. Eagleton........	Dem., St. Louis	1977	Gale W. McGee*...........	Dem., Laramie
			1979	Clifford P. Hansen.........	Rep., Jackson

The House of Representatives

Members' terms to Jan. 3, 1977. Annual salary $42,500; House Speaker $62,500 and $10,000 expenses, all taxable. To be eligible for membership, a person must be at least 25, a U.S. citizen for at least 7 years, and a resident of the state from which he is chosen.

(Those marked * served in the 93rd Congress.)

94th Congress House Officials

Parliamentarian, Lewis Deschler; Chaplain, Rev. Edward G. Latch; Sergeant at Arms, Kenneth Harding; Clerk, W. Pat Jennings; Doorkeeper, William M. Miller; Postmaster, Robert V. Rota.

Democrats, 290, Republicans, 144, Total, 435; 1 undecided race.

District	Representative	Home

Alabama

1 Jack Edwards*. . . . . Rep., Mobile
2 William L. Dickinson*. . . . . Rep., Montgomery
3 Bill Nichols*. . . . . Dem., Sylacauga
4 Tom Bevill*. . . . . Dem., Jasper
5 Bob Jones*. . . . . Dem., Scottsboro
6 John H. Buchanan Jr.*. . . . Rep., Birmingham

Alaska - At Large

Don Young*. . . . . Rep., Fort Yukon

Arizona

1 John J. Rhodes*. . . . . Rep., Mesa
2 Morris K. Udall*. . . . . Dem., Tucson
3 Sam Steiger*. . . . . Rep., Prescott
4 John B. Conlan*. . . . . Rep., Paradise Valley

Arkansas

1 Bill Alexander*. . . . . Dem., Osceola
2 Wilbur D. Mills*. . . . . Dem., Kensett
3 John Paul
 Hammerschmidt*. . . . . . . Rep., Harrison
4 Ray Thornton*. . . . . Dem., Sheridan

California

1 Harold T. Johnson*. . . . . . Dem., Roseville
2 Don H. Clausen*. . . . . Rep., Crescent City
3 John E. Moss*. . . . . Dem., Sacramento
4 Robert L. Leggett*. . . . . . . Dem., Suisun City
5 John Burton*. . . . . Dem., San Francisco
6 Phillip Burton*. . . . . Dem., San Francisco
7 George Miller. . . . . Dem., Martinez
8 Ronald V. Dellums*. . . . . . Dem., Berkeley
9 Fortney H. Stark*. . . . . Dem., Danville
10 Don Edwards*. . . . . Dem., San Jose
11 Leo J. Ryan*. . . . . Dem., S. San Francisco
 Paul N. McCloskey Jr.*. . . Rep., Menlo Park
13 Norman Y. Mineta . . . . . . Dem., San Jose
14 John J. McFall*. . . . . Dem., Manteca
15 B. F. Sisk*. . . . . Dem., Fresno
16 Burt L. Talcott*. . . . . Rep., Salinas
17 John Krebs. . . . . Dem., Fresno
18 William M. Ketchum*. . . . . Rep., Bakersfield
19 Robert J. Lagomarsino*. . . Rep., Ojai
20 Barry Goldwater Jr.*. . . . . . Rep., Burbank
21 James C. Corman*. . . . . . . Dem., Reseda
22 Carlos J. Moorhead*. . . . . Rep., Glendale
23 Thomas M. Rees*. . . . . . . Dem., Beverly Hills
24 Henry A. Waxman . . . . . . Dem., Los Angeles
25 Edward R. Roybal*. . . . . . . Dem., Los Angeles
26 John Rousselot*. . . . . Rep., San Marino
27 Alphonzo Bell*. . . . . Rep., Marina Del Rey
28 Yvonne Brathwaite
 Burke*. . . . . Dem., Los Angeles
29 Augustus F. Hawkins*. . . . Dem., Los Angeles
30 George E. Danielson*. . . . Dem., Monterey Park
31 Charles H. Wilson*. . . . . . Dem., Hawthorne
32 Glenn M. Anderson*. . . . . Dem., Harbor City
33 Del Clawson*. . . . . Rep., Downey
34 Mark W. Hannaford . . . . . Dem., Lakewood
35 Jim Lloyd . . . . Dem., West Covina
36 George E. Brown Jr.*. . . . . Dem., Colton

37 Jerry L. Pettis*. . . . . Rep., Loma Linda
38 Jerry M. Patterson. . . . . . . Dem., Santa Ana
39 Charles E. Wiggins*. . . . . . Rep., Fullerton
40 Andrew Hinshaw*. . . . . . . Rep., Newport Beach
41 Bob Wilson*. . . . . Rep., San Diego
42 Lionel Van Deerlin*. . . . . . Dem., Chula Vista
43 Clair W. Burgener*. . . . . . . Rep., Rancho Santa Fe

Colorado

1 Pat Schroeder*. . . . . Dem., Denver
2 Timothy E. Wirth. . . . . Dem., Denver
3 Frank E. Evans*. . . . . Dem., Beulah
4 James P. Johnson*. . . . . . Rep., Fort Collins
5 William L. Armstrong*. . . . Rep., Aurora

Connecticut

1 William R. Cotter*. . . . . . . Dem., Hartford
2 Christopher J. Dodd . . . . . Dem., North Stonington
3 Robert Giaimo*. . . . . Dem., North Haven
4 Stewart B. McKinney*. . . . Rep., Fairfield
5 Ronald A. Sarasin*. . . . . . . Rep., Beacon Falls
6 Anthony Toby Moffett . . . . Dem., Unionville

Delaware - At Large

Pierre S. du Pont 4th*. . . . . Rep., Wilmington

Florida

1 Bob Sikes*. . . . . Dem., Crestview
2 Don Fuqua*. . . . . Dem., Altha
3 Charles E. Bennett*. . . . . . Dem., Jacksonville
4 Bill Chappell Jr.*. . . . . Dem., Ocala
5 Richard Kelly. . . . . Rep., Holiday
6 C. W. Bill Young*. . . . . Rep., St. Petersburg
7 Sam M. Gibbons*. . . . . . . Dem., Tampa
8 James A. Haley*. . . . . Dem., Sarasota
9 Lou Frey Jr.*. . . . . Rep., Winter Park
10 L.A. Bafalis*. . . . . Rep., Ft. Myers Beach
11 Paul G. Rogers*. . . . . Dem., West Palm Beach
12 J. Herbert Burke*. . . . . Rep., Hollywood
13 William Lehman*. . . . . Dem., North Miami
14 Claude Pepper*. . . . . Dem., Miami Beach
15 Dante B. Fascell*. . . . . Dem., Miami

Georgia

1 Bo Ginn*. . . . . Dem., Millen
2 Dawson Mathis*. . . . . Dem., Albany
3 Jack Brinkley*. . . . . Dem., Columbus
4 Elliott H. Levitas. . . . . Dem., Atlanta
5 Andrew Young*. . . . . Dem., Atlanta
6 John J. Flynt Jr.*. . . . . Dem., Griffin
7 Larry McDonald. . . . . Dem., Marietta
 Quincy Collins. . . . . Rep., Marietta
8 W. S. Stuckey Jr.*. . . . . . . Dem., Eastman
9 Phil Landrum*. . . . . Dem., Jasper
10 Robert G. Stephens Jr.*. . . Dem., Athens

Hawaii

1 Spark M. Matsunaga*. . . . Dem., Honolulu
2 Patsy Takemoto Mink*. . . . Dem., Waipahu

District	Representative	Home

Idaho
1 Steven D. Symms*....... Rep., Caldwell
2 George Hansen......... Rep., Pocatello

Illinois
1 Ralph H. Metcalfe*...... Dem., Chicago
2 Morgan F. Murphy*...... Dem., Chicago
3 Martin A.. Russo........ Dem., Calumet Park
4 Edward J. Derwinski*..... Rep., Flossmoor
5 John C. Kluczynski*..... Dem., Chicago
6 Henry J. Hyde........ Rep., Port Ridge
7 Cardiss Collins*........ Dem., Chicago
8 Daniel D.
   Rostenkowski*......... Dem., Chicago
9 Sidney R. Yates*....... Dem., Chicago
10 Abner J. Mikva......... Dem., Evanston
11 Frank Annunzio*........ Dem., Chicago
12 Philip M. Crane*........ Rep., Mount Prospect
13 Robert McClory*........ Rep., Lake Bluff
14 John N. Erlenborn*...... Rep., Glen Ellyn
15 Tim L. Hall............. Dem., Dwight
16 John B. Anderson*...... Rep., Rockford
17 George M. O'Brien*...... Rep., Joliet
18 Robert H. Michel*...... Rep., Peoria
19 Tom Railsback*........ Rep., Moline
20 Paul Findley*.......... Rep., Pittsfield
21 Edward R. Madigan*..... Rep., Lincoln
22 George E. Shipley*...... Dem., Olney
23 Melvin Price*.......... Dem., East St. Louis
24 Paul Simon............ Dem., Carbondale

Indiana
1 Ray J. Madden*........ Dem., Gary
2 Floyd J. Fithian........ Dem., Lafayette
3 John Brademas*........ Dem., South Bend
4 J. Edward Roush*....... Dem., Huntington
5 Elwood H. Hillis*....... Rep., Kokomo
6 David Walter Evans...... Dem., Indianapolis
7 John T. Myers*......... Rep., Covington
8 Philip H. Hayes........ Dem., Evansville
9 Lee H. Hamilton*....... Dem., Columbus
10 Philip R. Sharp........ Dem., Muncie
11 Andrew Jacobs Jr........ Dem., Indianapolis

Iowa
1 Edward Mezvinsky*...... Dem., Iowa City
2 Michael T. Blouin........ Dem., Dubuque
3 Charles E. Grassley...... Rep., New Hartford
4 Neal Smith*........... Dem., Altoona
5 Tom Harkin............. Dem., Ames
6 Berkley Bedell.......... Dem., Spirit Lake

Kansas
1 Keith G. Sebelius*....... Rep., Norton
2 Martha Keys........... Dem., Manhattan
3 Larry Winn Jr.*........ Rep., Overland Park
4 Garner E. Shriver*...... Rep., Wichita
5 Joe Skubitz*........... Rep., Pittsburg

Kentucky
1 Carroll Hubbard Jr....... Dem., Mayfield
2 William H. Natcher*...... Dem., Bowling Green
3 Romano L. Mazzoli*..... Dem., Louisville
4 Marion Gene Snyder*.... Rep., Brownsboro Farms
5 Tim Lee Carter*........ Rep., Tompkinsville
6 John B. Breckinridge*.... Dem., Lexington
7 Carl D. Perkins*........ Dem., Hindman

Louisiana
1 F. Edward Hebert*...... Dem., New Orleans
2 Lindy (Mrs. Hale) Boggs*.. Dem., New Orleans
3 David C. Treen*........ Rep., Metairie
4 Joe D. Waggoner Jr.*..... Dem., Plain Dealing
5 Otto E. Passman*....... Dem., Monroe
6 W. Henson Moore....... Rep., Baton Rouge
7 John B. Breaux*....... Dem., Crowley
8 Gillis W. Long*......... Dem., Alexandria

Maine
1 David F. Emery......... Rep., Rockland
  William S. Cohen*....... Rep., Bangor

Maryland
1 Robert E. Bauman*...... Rep., Easton
2 Clarence D. Long*...... Dem., Towson
3 Paul S. Sarbanes*...... Dem., Baltimore
4 Marjorie S. Holt*........ Rep., Severna Park
5 Gladys Noon Spellman.... Dem., Laurel
6 Goodloe E. Byron*...... Dem., Frederick
7 Parren J. Mitchell*...... Dem., Baltimore
8 Gilbert Gude*......... Rep., Bethesda

Massachusetts
1 Silvio O. Conte*........ Rep., Pittsfield
2 Edward P. Boland*...... Dem., Springfield
3 Joseph D. Early*....... Dem., Worcester
4 Robert F. Drinan*....... Dem., Newton
5 Paul E. Tsongas........ Dem., Lowell
6 Michael J. Harrington*.... Dem., Beverly
7 Torbert H. Macdonald*.... Dem., Malden
8 Thomas P. O'Neill Jr.*.... Dem., Cambridge
9 John Joseph Moakley*.... Dem., Boston
10 Margaret M. Heckler*.... Rep., Wellesley
11 James A. Burke*....... Dem., Milton
12 Gary E. Studds*........ Dem., Cohasset

Michigan
1 John Conyers Jr.*....... Dem., Detroit
2 Marvin L. Esch*........ Rep., Ann Arbor
3 Garry Brown*......... Rep., Schoolcraft
4 Edward Hutchinson*..... Rep., St. Joseph
5 Richard F. VanderVeen*.. Dem., Grand Rapids
6 Bob Carr............. Dem., East Lansing
7 Donald W. Riegle Jr.*.... Dem., Flint
8 Bob Traxler*.......... Dem., Bay City
9 Guy A. Vander Jagt*..... Rep., Luther
10 Elford A. Cederberg*..... Rep., Midland
11 Philip E. Ruppe*....... Rep., Houghton
12 James G. O'Hara*...... Dem., Utica
13 Charles C. Diggs Jr.*..... Dem., Detroit
14 Lucien N. Nedzi*....... Dem., Detroit
15 William D. Ford*....... Dem., Taylor
16 John D. Dingell*........ Dem., Trenton
17 William M. Brodhead..... Dem., Detroit
18 James J. Blanchard...... Dem., Pleasant Ridge
19 William S. Broomfield*.... Rep., Birmingham

Minnesota
1 Albert H. Quie*........ Rep., Dennison
2 Tom Hagedorn......... Rep., Truman
3 Bill Frenzel*.......... Rep., Golden Valley
4 Joseph E. Karth*....... Dem., St. Paul
5 Donald Fraser *........ Dem., Minneapolis
6 Richard Nolan......... Dem., Waite Park
7 Bob Bergland.......... Dem., Roseau
8 James L. Oberstar....... Dem., Chisholm

Mississippi
1 Jamie L. Whitten*....... Dem., Charleston
2 David R. Bowen*....... Dem., Cleveland
3 G.V. Montgomery*...... Dem., Meridian
4 Thad Cochran*........ Rep., Jackson
5 Trent Lott*........... Rep., Pascagoula

Missouri
1 William Clay*.......... Dem., St. Louis
2 James W. Symington*.... Dem., Ladue
3 Leonor K. Sullivan*...... Dem., St. Louis
4 Wm. J. Randall*........ Dem., Independence
5 Richard Bolling*........ Dem., Kansas City
6 Jerry Litton........... Dem., Chillicothe
7 Gene Taylor*.......... Rep., Sarcoxie
8 Richard H. Ichord*...... Dem., Houston
9 William L. Hungate*..... Dem., Troy
10 Bill D. Burlison*........ Dem., Cape Girardeau

Montana
1 Max S. Baucus*........ Dem., Missoula
2 John Melcher*.......... Dem., Forsyth

District	Representative	Home

Nebraska

1 Charles Thone* . . . . Rep., Lincoln
2 John Y. McCollister* . . . . . . Rep., Omaha
3 Virginia Smith . . . . Rep., Chappell

Nevada - At Large

Jim Santini . . . . Dem., Las Vegas

New Hampshire

1 Norman E. D'Amours . . . . . Dem., Manchester
2 James C. Cleveland* . . . . . Rep., New London

New Jersey

1 James J. Florio . . . . Dem., Camden
2 William J. Hughes . . . . Dem., Ocean City
3 James J. Howard* . . . . Dem., Spring Lake Hts.
4 Frank Thompson Jr.* . . . . . Dem., Trenton
5 Millicent Fenwick . . . . Rep., Bernardsville
6 Edwin B. Forsythe* . . . . . . Rep., Moorestown
7 Andrew Maguire . . . . Dem., Ridgewood
8 Robert A. Roe* . . . . Dem., Wayne
9 Henry Helstoski* . . . . Dem., Rutherford
10 Peter W. Rodino Jr.* . . . . . Dem., Newark
11 Joseph G. Minish* . . . . Dem., West Orange
12 Matthew J. Rinaldo* . . . . . . Rep., Union
13 Helen S. Meyner . . . . Dem., Phillipsburg
14 Dominick V. Daniels* . . . . . Dem., Union City
15 Edward J. Patten* . . . . Dem., Perth Amboy

New Mexico

1 Manuel Lujan Jr.* . . . . Rep., Albuquerque
2 Harold Runnels* . . . . Dem., Lovington

New York

1 Otis G. Pike* . . . . Dem., Riverhead
2 Thomas J. Downey . . . . . . Dem., W. Islip
3 Jerome Ambro Jr. . . . . Dem., East Northport
4 Norman F. Lent* . . . . Rep., Baldwin
5 John W. Wydler* . . . . Rep., Mineola
6 Lester L. Wolff* . . . . Dem., Great Neck
7 Joseph P. Addabbo* . . . . . Dem., Ozone Park
8 Benjamin S. Rosenthal* . . . Dem., Flushing
9 James J. Delaney* . . . . . . Dem., L.I. City
10 Mario Biaggi* . . . . Dem., Bronx
11 James H. Scheuer . . . . . . Dem., Floral Park
12 Shirley A. Chisholm* . . . . . Dem., Brooklyn
13 Stephen J. Solarz . . . . Dem., Brooklyn
14 Frederick W. Richmond . . . Dem., Brooklyn
15 Leo C. Zeferetti . . . . Dem., Brooklyn
16 Elizabeth Holtzman* . . . . . Dem., Brooklyn
17 John M. Murphy* . . . . Dem., Staten Island
18 Edward I Koch* . . . . Dem., New York
19 Charles B. Rangel* . . . . . . Dem., New York
20 Bella S. Abzug* . . . . Dem., New York
21 Herman Badillo* . . . . Dem., Bronx
22 Jonathan B. Bingham* . . . . Dem., Bronx
23 Peter A. Peyser* . . . . Rep., Irvington
24 Richard L. Ottinger . . . . . . Dem., Pleasantville
25 Hamilton Fish Jr.* . . . . Rep., Millbrook
26 Benjamin A. Gilman* . . . . . Rep., Middletown
27 Matthew F. McHugh . . . . . Dem., Ithaca
28 Samuel S. Stratton* . . . . . Dem., Amsterdam
29 Edward W. Pattison . . . . . . Dem., W. Sand Lake
30 Robert C. McEwen* . . . . . Rep., Ogdensburg
31 Donald J. Mitchell* . . . . . . Rep., Herkimer
32 James M. Hanley* . . . . Dem., Syracuse
33 William F. Walsh* . . . . Rep., Syracuse
34 Frank Horton* . . . . Rep., Rochester
35 Barber B. Conable Jr.* . . . . Rep., Alexander
36 John J. LaFalce . . . . Dem., Kenmore
37 Henry J. Nowak . . . . Dem., Buffalo
38 Jack F. Kemp* . . . . Rep., Hamburg
39 James F. Hastings* . . . . . . Rep., Caneadea

North Carolina

1 Walter B. Jones* . . . . Dem., Farmville
2 L.H. Fountain* . . . . Dem., Tarboro
3 David N. Henderson* . . . . . Dem., Wallace
4 Ike Andrews* . . . . Dem., Siler City

5 Stephen L. Neal . . . . Dem., Winston-Salem
6 Richardson Preyer* . . . . . . Dem., Greensboro
7 Charles Rose* . . . . Dem., Fayetteville
8 W. G. Hefner . . . . Dem., Concord
9 James G. Martin* . . . . Rep., Davisson
10 James T. Broyhill* . . . . Rep., Lenoir
11 Roy A. Taylor* . . . . Dem., Asheville

North Dakota—at large

Mark Andrews* . . . . Rep., Mapleton

Ohio

1 Willis D. Gradison Jr. . . . . . Rep., Cincinnati
2 Donald D. Clancy* . . . . . . Rep., Cincinnati
3 Charles W. Whalen Jr.* . . . Rep., Dayton
4 Tennyson Guyer* . . . . Rep., Findlay
5 Delbert L. Latta* . . . . Rep., Bowling Green
6 William H. Harsha* . . . . . . Rep., Portsmouth
7 Clarence J. Brown* . . . . . . Rep., Urbana
8 Thomas N. Kindness . . . . . Rep., Hamilton
9 Thomas Ludlow Ashley* . . Dem., Maumee
10 Clarence E. Miller* . . . . . . Rep., Lancaster
11 J. William Stanton* . . . . . . Rep., Painesville
12 Samuel L. Devine* . . . . . . Rep., Columbus
13 Charles A. Mosher* . . . . . . Rep., Oberlin
14 John F. Seiberling* . . . . . . Dem., Akron
15 Chalmers P. Wylie* . . . . . . Rep., Worthington
16 Ralph S. Regula* . . . . Rep., Navarre
17 John M. Ashbrook* . . . . . . Rep., Johnstown
18 Wayne L. Hays* . . . . Dem., Flushing
19 Charles J. Carney* . . . . . . Dem., Youngstown
20 James V. Stanton* . . . . . . Dem., Cleveland
21 Louis Stokes* . . . . Dem., Cleveland
22 Charles A. Vanik* . . . . Dem., Euclid
23 Ronald M. Mottl . . . . Dem., Parma

Oklahoma

1 James R. Jones* . . . . Dem., Tulsa
2 Theodore M. Risenhoover . Dem., Tahlequah
3 Carl Albert* . . . . Dem., McAlester
4 Tom Steed* . . . . Dem., Shawnee
5 John Jarman* . . . . Dem., Oklahoma City
6 Glenn English . . . . Dem., Cordell

Oregon

1 Les AuCoin . . . . Dem., Forest Grove
2 Al Ullman* . . . . Dem., Baker
3 Robert Duncan . . . . Dem., Gresham
4 James Weaver . . . . Dem., Eugene

Pennsylvania

1 William A. Barrett* . . . . Dem., Philadelphia
2 Robert N.C. Nix* . . . . Dem., Philadelphia
3 William J. Green* . . . . Dem., Philadelphia
4 Joshua Eilberg* . . . . Dem., Philadelphia
5 Richard T. Schulze . . . . . . Rep., Malvern
6 Gus Yatron* . . . . Dem., Reading
7 Robert W. Edgar . . . . Dem., Broomall
8 Edward G. Biester Jr.* . . . . Rep., Furlong
9 E. G. Shuster* . . . . Rep., Everett
10 Joseph M. McDade* . . . . . Rep., Scranton
11 Daniel J. Flood* . . . . Dem., Wilkes-Barre
12 John P. Murtha* . . . . Dem., Johnstown
13 Lawrence Coughlin* . . . . . Rep., Villanova
14 William S. Moorhead* . . . . Dem., Pittsburgh
15 Fred B. Rooney* . . . . Dem., Bethlehem
16 Edwin D. Eshleman* . . . . . Rep., Lancaster
17 Herman T. Schneebeli* . . . Rep., Williamsport
18 H. John Heinz 3d* . . . . Rep., Pittsburgh
19 William F. Goodling . . . . . . Rep., Jacobus
20 Joseph M. Gaydos* . . . . . Dem., McKeesport
21 John H. Dent* . . . . Dem., Ligonier
22 Thomas E. Morgan* . . . . . Dem., Fredericktown
23 Albert W. Johnson* . . . . . . Rep., Smethport
24 Joseph P. Vigorito* . . . . . . Dem., Erie
25 Gary A. Myers . . . . Rep., Butler

Rhode Island

1 Fernard J. St. Germain* . . . Dem., Woonsocket
2 Edward P. Beard . . . . Dem., Cranston

District	Representative	Home

South Carolina
1 Mendel J. Davis* . . . . Dem., Charleston
2 Floyd Spence* . . . . Rep., Lexington
3 Butler Derrick . . . . Dem., Edgefield
4 James R. Mann* . . . . Dem., Greenville
5 Kenneth L. Holland . . . . Dem., Camden
6 John W. Jenrette Jr. . . . . . . Dem., N. Myrtle Beach

South Dakota
1 Larry Pressler . . . . Rep., Humboldt
2 James Abdnor* . . . . Rep., Kennebec

Tennessee
1 James J. Quillen* . . . . Rep., Kingsport
2 John Duncan* . . . . Rep., Knoxville
3 Marilyn Lloyd* . . . . Dem., Chattanooga
4 Joe L. Evins* . . . . Dem., Smithville
5 Richard Fulton* . . . . Dem., Goodlettsville
6 Robin Beard* . . . . Rep., Brentwood
7 Ed Jones* . . . . Dem., Yorkville
8 Harold E. Ford . . . . Dem., Memphis

Texas
1 Wright Patman* . . . . Dem., Texarkana
2 Charles Wilson* . . . . Dem., Lufkin
3 James M. Collins* . . . . . .l. . Rep., Dallas
4 Ray Roberts* . . . . Dem., McKinney
5 Alan Steelman* . . . . Rep., Dallas
6 Olin E. Teague* . . . . Dem., College Station
7 Bill Archer* . . . . Rep., Houston
8 Bob Eckhardt* . . . . Dem., Houston
9 Jack Brooks* . . . . Dem., Beaumont
10 J. J. Pickle* . . . . Dem., Austin
11 W. R. Paoge* . . . . Dem., Waco
12 James C. Wright Jr* . . . . . Dem., Fort Worth
13 Jack Hightower . . . . Dem., Vernon
14 John Young* . . . . Dem., Corpus Christi
15 E. de la Garza* . . . . Dem., Mission
16 Richard C. White* . . . . Dem., El Paso
17 Omar Burleson* . . . . Dem., Anson
18 Barbara Jordan* . . . . Dem., Houston
19 George Mahon* . . . . Dem., Lubbock
20 Henry B. Gonzalez* . . . . . Dem., San Antonio
21 Robert Krueger . . . . Dem., New Braunfels
22 Bob Casey* . . . . Dem., Pasadena
23 Abraham Kazen Jr* . . . . . . Dem., Laredo
24 Dale Milford* . . . . Dem., Grand Prairie

District	Representative	Home

Utah
1 K. Gunn McKay* . . . . Dem., Huntsville
2 Allen T. Howe . . . . Dem., Salt Lake City

Vermont—at Large
James M. Jeffords . . . . Rep., Montpelier

Virginia
1 Thomas N. Downing* . . . . . Dem., Newport News
2 G. William Whitehurst* . . . . Rep., Norfolk
3 David E. Satterfield 3d* . . . Dem., Richmond
4 Robert W. Daniel Jr.* . . . . . Rep., Spring Grove
5 W. D. Daniel* . . . . Dem., Danville
6 M. Caldwell Butler* . . . . Rep., Roanoke
7 J. Kenneth Robinson* . . . . Rep., Winchester
8 Herbert E. Harris 2d . . . . . . Dem., Alexandria
9 William C. Wampler* . . . . . Rep., Bristol
10 Joseph L. Fisher . . . . Dem., Arlington

Washington
1 Joel Pritchard* . . . . Rep., Seattle
2 Lloyd Meeds* . . . . Dem., Everett
3 Don Bonker . . . . Dem., Ridgefield
4 Mike McCormack* . . . . Dem., Richland
5 Thomas S. Foley* . . . . Dem., Spokane
6 Floyd V. Hicks* . . . . Dem., Tacoma
7 Brock Adams* . . . . Dem., Seattle

West Virginia
1 Robert H. Mollohan* . . . . . . Dem., Fairmont
2 Harley O. Staggers* . . . . . . Dem., Keyser
3 John M. Slack* . . . . Dem., Charleston
4 Ken Hechler* . . . . Dem., Huntington

Wisconsin
1 Les Aspin* . . . . Dem., Racine
2 Robert W. Kastenmeier* . . Dem., Sun Prairie
3 Alvin Baldus . . . . Dem., Menominie
4 Clement J. Zablocki* . . . . . Dem., Milwaukee
5 Henry S. Reuss* . . . . Dem., Milwaukee
6 William A. Steiger* . . . . Rep., Oshkosh
7 David R. Obey* . . . . Dem., Wausau
8 Robert J. Cornell . . . . Dem., DePere
9 Robert W. Kasten Jr. . . . . . Rep., Milwaukee

Wyoming—at Large
Teno Roncalio* . . . . Dem., Cheyenne

Non-Voting Delegates
District of Columbia . . . . Walter E. Fauntroy*

Longevity of Male Government Officials to end of 1968

By Period of Initial Entry into Office (Compared to white males in U.S. population)

Source: Statistical Bulletin, Metropolitan Life

Period of 1st Entry to Office	Number at Entry	Avg. Age at Entry	No. Died By end of 1968	Avg. Years Lived From Entry to End '68 or Prior Death	Differ- entials
Representatives					
1861-1900	2,434	45.4	2,434	23.8	0.1
1901-1930	1,582	46.1	1,520	24.6	0.4
1931-1968	1,659	45.7	585	17.0	0.2
Senators					
1861-1900	392	49.5	392	21.7	0.8
1901-1930	319	52.3	310	21.0	1.1
1931-1968	339	51.5	148	15.7	0.4
State Governors					
1901-1930	415	49.5	412	22.1	0.7
1931-1968	441	49.6	179	15.5	0.5
Cabinet Officers					
1789-1860	118	47.8	118	21.4	-0.2
1861-1900	108	53.1	108	20.0	1.4
1901-1930	73	52.9	73	21.1	1.8
1931-1968	92	52.7	38	12.2	-0.7
Supreme Court Justices					
1789-1900	57	51.2	57	20.2	0.2
1901-1968	39	54.3	25	17.2	1.4

*The difference between (a) the average number of years actually lived from entry into office to end of 1968 or prior death and (b) the average life expectancy of contemporaneous cohorts of white males in the general population of the United States observed for the same periods.

Governors of States and Possessions

State	Capital	Governor	Party	Term Years	Term Expires	Annual Salary
Alabama	Montgomery	George C. Wallace	Dem.	4	Jan. 1979	$25,000
Alaska*	Juneau	William A. Egan	Dem.	4	Dec. 1978	40,000
		Jay Hammond	Rep.			
Arizona	Phoenix	Raul Castro	Dem.	4	Jan. 1979	35,000
Arkansas	Little Rock	David Pryor	Dem.	2	Jan. 1977	10,000
California	Sacramento	Edmund G. Brown Jr.	Dem.	4	Jan. 1979	49,100
Colorado	Denver	Richard D. Lamm	Dem.	4	Jan. 1979	40,000
Connecticut	Hartford	Ella T. Grasso	Dem.	4	Jan. 1979	35,000
Delaware	Dover	Sherman W. Tribbitt	Dem.	4	Jan. 1977	35,000
Florida	Tallahassee	Reubin Askew	Dem.	4	Jan. 1979	40,000
Georgia	Atlanta	George Busbee	Dem.	4	Jan. 1979	50,000
Hawaii	Honolulu	George R. Ariyoshi	Dem.	4	Dec. 1978	42,000
Idaho	Boise	Cecil D. Andrus	Dem.	4	Jan. 1979	30,000
Illinois	Springfield	Daniel Walker	Dem.	4	Jan. 1977	50,000
Indiana	Indianapolis	Otis R. Bowen	Rep.	4	Jan. 1977	36,000
Iowa	Des Moines	Robert D. Ray	Rep.	4	Jan. 1979	40,000
Kansas	Topeka	Robert F. Bennett	Rep.	4	Jan. 1979	20,000
Kentucky	Frankfort	Wendell H. Ford	Dem.	4	Dec. 1975	30,000
Louisiana	Baton Rouge	Edwin W. Edwards	Dem.	4	May 1976	28,374
Maine	Augusta	James Longley	Ind.	4	Jan. 1979	35,000
Maryland	Annapolis	Marvin Mandel	Dem.	4	Jan. 1979	25,000
Massachusetts	Boston	Michael S. Dukakis	Dem.	4	Jan. 1979	40,000
Michigan	Lansing	William G. Milliken	Rep.	4	Jan. 1979	45,000
Minnesota	St. Paul	Wendell R. Anderson	Dem.	4	Jan. 1979	41,000
Mississippi	Jackson	William L. Waller	Dem.	4	Jan. 1976	35,000
Missouri	Jefferson City	Christopher S. Bond	Rep.	4	Jan. 1977	37,500
Montana	Helena	Thomas L. Judge	Dem.	4	Jan. 1977	25,000
Nebraska	Lincoln	J. James Exon	Dem.	4	Jan. 1979	25,000
Nevada	Carson City	Mike O'Callaghan	Dem.	4	Jan. 1979	30,000
New Hampshire	Concord	Meldrim Thomson Jr.	Rep.	2	Jan. 1977	32,760
New Jersey	Trenton	Brendan T. Byrne	Dem.	4	Jan. 1978	50,000
New Mexico	Santa Fe	Jerry Apodaca	Dem.	4	Jan. 1979	26,000
New York	Albany	Hugh L. Carey	Dem.	4	Jan. 1979	85,000
North Carolina	Raleigh	James E. Holshouser Jr.	Rep.	4	Jan. 1977	35,000
North Dakota	Bismarck	Arthur A. Link	Dem.	4	Jan. 1977	18,000
Ohio	Columbus	James A. Rhodes	Rep.	4	Jan. 1979	50,000
Oklahoma	Oklahoma City	David Boren	Dem.	4	Jan. 1979	35,000
Oregon	Salem	Robert Straub	Dem.	4	Jan. 1979	35,000
Pennsylvania	Harrisburg	Milton J. Shapp	Dem.	4	Jan. 1979	45,000
Rhode Island	Providence	Philip W. Noel	Dem.	2	Jan. 1977	42,500
South Carolina	Columbia	James B. Edwards	Rep.	4	Jan. 1979	35,000
South Dakota	Pierre	Richard F. Kneip	Dem.	4	Jan. 1979	25,000
Tennessee	Nashville	Ray Blanton	Dem.	4	Jan. 1979	50,000
Texas	Austin	Dolph Briscoe	Dem.	4	Jan. 1979	63,000
Utah	Salt Lake City	Calvin L. Rampton	Dem.	4	Jan. 1977	33,000
Vermont	Montpelier	Thomas P. Salmon	Dem.	2	Jan. 1977	35,000
Virginia	Richmond	Mills E. Godwin Jr.	Rep.	4	Jan. 1978	35,000
Washington	Olympia	Daniel J. Evans	Rep.	4	Jan. 1977	34,300
West Virginia	Charleston	Arch A. Moore Jr.	Rep.	4	Jan. 1977	35,000
Wisconsin	Madison	Patrick J. Lucey	Dem.	4	Jan. 1979	25,000
Wyoming	Cheyenne	Ed Herschler	Dem.	4	Jan. 1979	37,500

*Race undecided at press time

Possessions

Guam	Agana	Carlos G. Camacho	Rep.	4	Jan. 1977	35,000
Puerto Rico	San Juan	Rafael Hernandez Colon	Pop.	4	Jan. 1977	35,000
Virgin Isls.	Charlotte Amalie	Melvin Evans	Rep.	4	Jan. 1977	35,505

Women Governors in U.S. History

Ella Tamburri Grasso, as Democratic candidate in Connecticut, became the 4th woman governor in U.S. history. Her 3 predecessors were also Democrats but, unlike Mrs. Grasso, had been preceded in office by their husbands. First was Nellie Tayloe Ross of Wyoming; her husband, William, died in office. Elected to fill his unexpired 4-year term, she took office Jan. 5, 1925. A few days later, Miriam Wallace (Ma) Fergu-

son, also elected in 1924, became governor of Texas and served, like Mrs. Ross, 1925-27; she served again, 1933-35. (Her husband, James, was removed from the governorship in 1917.) Lurleen Burns Wallace, elected 1966, became Alabama governor Jan. 16, 1967, succeeding her husband George. She died of cancer May 7, 1968.

Mayors and City Managers of Larger North American Cities
as of Nov. 5 elections, 1974

*Asterisk before name denotes city manager. All others are mayors. For mayors, dates are those of expiration of term, for city managers, they are dates of appointment.

D., Democrat: R., Republican; N-P, Non-Partisan.

City	Name	Term
Abilene, Tex.	*Fred Sandlin	1974, May
Abington, Pa.	*Fred Schaefer	1958, June
Akron, Ohio.	John S. Ballard, R.	1975, Dec.
Alameda, Calif.	*John Goss	1973, Dec.
Albany, Ga.	*S. A. Roos	1961, Aug.
Albany, N.Y.	Erastus Corning, 2nd, D.	1975, Dec.
Albuquerque N.M.	Harry Kinney, N-P	1977, Dec.
Alexandria, La.	John K. Snyder, D.	1977, June
Alexandria, Va.	*Keith Mulrooney	1974, Nov.
Alhambra, Calif.	*Harry S. Scott	1968, Sept.
Allen Park, Mich.	Frank J. Lada, N-P	1975, Nov.
Allentown, Pa.	Joseph Daddona, D.	1978, Jan.
Alton, Ill.	Paul A. Lenz, N-P	1977, Apr.
Altoona, Pa.	William C. Stouffer, R.	1976, Jan.
Amarillo, Tex.	*John S. Stiff	1963, Sept.
Ames, Iowa.	*J. R. Castner	1964, Oct.
Anaheim, Calif.	*Keith A. Murdoch	1950, Oct.
Anchorage, Alas.	*Douglas G. Weiford	1974, May
Anderson, Ind.	Robert Rock, D.	1976, Jan.
Anderson, S.C.	*Charles B. Martin	1973, Mar.
Ann Arbor, Mich.	*Sylvester Murray	1973, July
Appleton, Wis.	Jas. P. Sutherland, N-P	1976, Apr.
Arcadia, Calif.	*Lyman H. Cozad	1966, Aug.
Arlington, Mass.	*Donald R. Marquis	1966, Nov.
Arlington, Tex.	*Ross Calhoun	1973, Feb.
Arlingt n, Va.	*Bert Johnson	1962, Dec.
Arlington Hts. Ill.	*L. A. Hanson	1958, Oct.
Arvada, Colo.	*Vacant	
Asheville, N.C.	*Ernest J. Ward.	1972, Sept.
Athens, Ga.	Julius Bishop, D.	1975, Nov.
Atlanta, Ga.	Maynard Jackson, D.	1977, Oct.
Atlantic City, N.J.	Joseph Bradway, Jr., N-P	1976, May
Auburn, N.Y.	*Bruce L. Clifford.	1966, Aug.
Augusta, Ga.	Lewis A. Newman	1975, Dec.
Aurora, Colo.	*W. Robert Semple	1972, Feb.
Aurora, Ill.	Albert D. McCoy, N-P	1977, Apr.
Austin, Tex.	*Dan H. Davidson	1972, Sept.
Bakersfield, Cal.	*Harold E. Bergen	1966, July
Baldwin Park, Cal.	*James S. Mocalis	1971, Dec.
Baltimore, Md.	William Schaefer, D.	1975, Dec.
Bangor, Me.	*Merle F. Goff.	1966, Dec.
Baton Rouge, La.	W. W. Dumas, D.	1976, Dec.
Battle Creek, Mich.	*Aaron Marsh.	1971, Aug.
Bay City, Mich.	*E. J. Redmond.	1973, July
Baytown, Tex.	*Fritz Lanham	1972, May
Beaumont, Tex.	*Charles Hill	1970, Sept.
Belleville, Ill.	Chas. E. Nichols, N-P	1977, Apr.
Belleville, N.J.	Joseph F. McGreevy, N-P	1975, May
Bellevue, Wash.	*L. Joe Miller.	1961, Jan.
Bellflower, Calif.	*Peter B. Feenstra	1968, Oct.
Bellingham, Wash.	Reginald Williams, N-P	1976, Jan.
Beloit, Wisc.	*H. Herbert Holt.	1971, Mar.
Berkeley, Calif.	*John L. Taylor.	1974, Feb.
Berwyn, Ill.	Emil Vacin, D.	1977, Apr.
Bessemer, Ala.	Ed Porter, D.	1978, Oct.
Bethlehem, Pa.	Gordon Mowrer, D.	1977, Dec.
Beverly, Mass.	James Vitale.	1975, Dec.
Billings, Mont.	Joseph Leone, D.	1977, May
Biloxi, Miss.	Jerry O'Keefe, D.	1977, July
Binghamton, N.Y.	Alfred J. Libous, R.	1977, Dec.
Birmingham, Ala.	George Seibels, R.	1975, Nov.
Bloomfield, N.J.	*H. Joseph North.	1967, Oct.
Bloomington, Ill.	*Richard Blodgett.	1970, June
Bloomington, Ind.	Francis X. McCloskey, D.	1975, Dec.
Bloomington, Minn.	*John Pidgeon	1967, Dec.
Boise, Idaho.	Dick Eardlay, N-P	1977, Dec.
Bossier City, La.	James Cathey, D.	1977, June
Boston, Mass.	Kevin White, D.	1975, Dec.
Boulder, Colo.	*Archie J. Twitchell.	1973, June
Bowie, Md.	*A. Louis Hayward	1968, July
Bowling Green, Ky.	*Paul McCauley	1973, Jan.
Braintree, Mass.	Board of Selectmen	
Bridgeport, Conn.	Nicholas A. Panuzio, R.	1975, Nov.
Bristol, Conn.	Frank Longo, D.	1975, Nov.
Brockton, Mass.	David L. Crosby	1975, Dec.
Brookfield, Wisc.	Franklin Wirth, R.	1976, Apr.
Brookline, Mass.	Board of Selectmen	
Brooklyn Center, Minn.	*Donald G. Poss	1966, June
Brownsville, Tex.	*Kirby Lilljedahl	1970, Mar.
Bryan, Texas	*J. Louis Odle.	1974, May
Buffalo, N.Y.	Stanley M. Makowsky, D.	1977, Dec.
Burbank, Calif.	*Joseph N. Baker.	1968, Mar.
Burlington, Vt.	Gordon H. Paquette, D.	1975, Apr.
Calumet City, Ill.	Robert C. Stefaniak, D.	1977, Apr.
Cambridge, Mass.	*James L. Stullivan	1968, July
Camden, N.J.	Angelo Errichetti	1975, July
Canton, Ohio.	Stanley A. Cmich, R.	1975, Dec.
Cape Girardeau, Mo.	*W. G. Lawley	1970, July
Carson, Calif.	*E. Frederick Bien	1968, Aug.
Casper, Wyo.	*Kenneth Erickson	1969, Oct.
Cedar Rapids, Iowa	Donald J. Canney, N-P	1975, Dec.
Champaign, Ill.	*Eugene Miller	1974, Sept.
Charleston, S.C.	J. Palmer Gailliard, D.	1975, Dec.
Charleston, W. Va.	*H. Hugh Bosely.	1973, Apr.
Charlotte, N.C.	*David A. Burkhalter.	1971, May
Charlottesville, Va.	*Cole Hendrix.	1971, Jan.
Chattanooga, Tenn.	Robert Kirk Walker, D.	1975, Apr.
Chesapeake, Va.	*Durwood S. Curling	1971, Jan.
Chester, Pa.	John Nacrelli, R.	1976, Jan.
Cheyenne, Wyo.	Bill Nation, N-P	1976, Dec.
Chicago, Ill.	Richard J. Daley, D.	1975, Apr.
Chicopee, Mass.	Edward Ziemba	1976, Jan.
Chula Vista, Calif.	*John R. Thomson	1970, Aug.
Cicero, Ill.	John Karner, R.	1976, Apr.
Cincinnati, Ohio	*E. Robert Turner	1972, June
Clarksville, Tenn.	Charles W. Crow, D.	1979, Jan.
Clearwater, Fla.	*Merrett R. Stierheim	1967, Nov.
Cleveland, Ohio.	Ralph J. Perk, R.	1975, Nov.
Cleveland Heights.	*William C. Lahman	1964, Oct.
Clifton, N.J.	*William Holster	1957, Jan.
Colo. Spgs., Colo.	*George H. Fellows.	1966, July
Columbia, Mo.	*Terry Novak.	1974, Feb.
Columbia, S.C.	*Graydon V. Olive, Jr.	1970, Mar.
Columbus, Ga.	*Franklyn Lambert	1971, Jan.
Columbus, Ohio.	Tom Moody, R.	1976, Jan.
Commerce, Calif.	*Robert Hinderliter.	1973, Sept.
Compton, Calif.	*James S. Wilson, Jr.	1974, Feb.
Concord, Calif.	*F. A. Stewart.	1960, Apr.
Concord, N.H.	*James E. Henchey	1968, Jan.
Coon Rapids, Minn.	*John K. Cottingham	1969, July
Coral Gables, Fla.	*L. W. Robinson, Jr.	1959, Jan.
Corpus Christi, Tex.	*R. Marvin Townsend.	1968, July
Corvallis, Ore.	*C. Dean Smith.	1968, Jan.
Costa Mesa, Calif.	*Fred Sorsabel.	1970, Nov.
Council Bluffs, Ia.	*M. Don Harmon.	1968, Feb.
Covington, Ky.	Bernard A. Grimm, D.	1975, Dec.
Cranston, R.I.	James L. Taft, Jr., R.	1979, Jan.
Crystal, Minn.	*John Irving.	1963, Sept.
Culver City, Cal.	*H. Dale Jones.	1969, Aug.
Cuyahoga Falls. O.	Robert Quirk, D.	1977, Dec.
Dallas, Tex.	*George R. Schrader	1972, Dec.
Daly City, Calif.	*David R. Rowe.	1969, Aug.
Danbury, Conn.	Charles A. Ducibella, D.	1975, Dec.
Danville, Ill.	Rolland Craig, R.	1975, Apr.
Danville, Va.	*James W. Lord	1971, Nov.
Davenport, Ia.	Kathryn Kirschbaum, D.	1975, Dec.
Dayton, Ohio.	*James Alloway	1973, Feb.
Daytona Bch., Fla.	*Charles E. Jackson.	1966, Aug.
Dearborn, Mich.	Orville L. Hubbard, N-P.	1978, Jan.
Decatur, Ala.	Russell Bolding, N-P.	1976, Sept.
Decatur, Ill.	*Leslie T. Allen.	1972, Sept.
Denton, Tex.	*Jim White.	1968, May
Denver, Colo.	William H. McNichols, D.	1975, July
Des Moines, Ia.	*Richard A. Wilkey.	1974, Mar.
Des Plaines, Ill.	Herbert Behrel, R.	1977, Apr.
Detroit, Mich.	Coleman A. Young, N-P.	1978, Jan.
Dotham, Ala.	James W. Grant.	1977, Oct.
Downers Grove, Ill.	*James R. Griesemer.	1972, Sept.
Dubuque, Ia.	*Gilbert D. Chavenelle.	1960, July
Duluth, Minn.	Ben Boo, R.	1976, Jan.
Durham, N.C.	*I. Harding Hughes, Jr.	1963, Feb.

City	Name	Term
E. Chicago, Ind.	Robert A. Pastrick, D.	1975, Dec.
E. Cleveland, O.	*Curtis Hall	1972, Jan.
E. Detroit, Mich.	*Vacant.	
E. Hartford, Conn.	Richard H. Blackstone, D.	1975, Nov.
E. Lansing, Mich.	*John Patriarche	1948, Jan.
E. Orange, N.J.	William S. Hart, D.	1977, Dec.
E. Point, Ga.	Bruce Bannister, N-P.	1976, Dec.
E. Providence, R.I.	*Paul A. Flynn	1972, July
E. St. Louis, Ill.	James E. Williams, N-P.	1975, Apr.
Eau Claire, Wis.	*Ray E. Wachs	1970, June
Edina, Minn.	*Warren Hyde	1955, May
Edison, N.J.	*John Delesandro	1965, Feb.
El Cajon, Calif.	*Robert M. Applegate	1958, Sept.
Elgin, Ill.	*Leo Nelson	1972, Dec.
Elizabeth, N.J.	Thomas G. Dunn, D.	1976, Dec.
Elkhart, Ind.	Daniel Hayes, D.	1975, Dec.
Elmhurst, Ill.	*Robert T. Palmer	1953, Aug.
Elmira, N.Y.	*Joseph E. Sartori	1972, June
El Monte, Calif.	*Kenneth Botts	1969, Aug.
El Paso, Tex.	Fred Hervey, R.	1975, Apr.
Elyria, O.	L. P. Reichlin, D.	1975, Dec.
Enfield, Conn.	*C. Samuel Kissinger	1968, June
Enid, Okla.	*Tom Sailors, Jr.	1969, Oct.
Erie, Pa.	Louis J. Tullio, D.	1977, Dec.
Escondido, Calif.	*George Patterson	1970, May
Euclid, Ohio	Harry Knuth, R.	1975, Dec.
Eugene, Ore.	*Hugh McKinley	1960, Oct.
Evanston, Ill.	*Edward A. Martin	1971, Mar.
Evansville, Ind.	Russell Lloyd, R.	1976, Jan.
Everett, Mass.	George R. McCarthy, D.	1975, Dec.
Everett, Wash.	Robert C. Anderson, N-P.	1978, Jan.
Fairborn, Ohio	*Claude Malone, Jr.	1970, July
Fairfield, Calif.	*B. Gale Wilson	1956, Mar.
Fairfield, Conn.	John J. Sullivan, D.	1975, Nov.
Fair Lawn, N.J.	*George Pellack	1959, June
Fall River, Mass.	Wilfred C. Driscoll, D.	1975, Dec.
Fayetteville, Ark.	*Donald Grimes	1972, Apr.
Fayetteville, N.C.	*J. Guy Smith	1970, Oct.
Fitchburg, Mass.	Hedley Bray, D.	1976, Jan.
Flagstaff, Ariz.	*Charles McClain	1973, Nov.
Flint, Mich.	*Daniel Bogi an Jr.	1974, June
Florissant, Mo.	James J. Eagen, D.	1975, Apr.
Fond du Lac, Wisc.	*Myron J. Medin, Jr.	1967, Nov.
Ft. Collins, Colo.	*Robert L. Brunton	1972, Oct.
Ft. Lauderdale, Fla.	*Robert H. Bubier	1962, Dec.
Ft. Lee, N.J.	*James J Mulcare	1973, Jan.
Ft. Smith, Ark.	*Ray A. Riley	1972, Dec.
Ft. Wayne, Ind.	Ivan Lebamoff, D.	1975, Dec.
Ft. Worth, Tex.	*Roger Line	1971, Apr.
Fremont, Calif.	*Don Driggs	1968, July
Fresno, Calif.	*Ralph W. Hanley	1973, Sept.
Fullerton, Calif.	*W. F. Cornett, Jr.	1966, Oct.
Gadsden, Ala.	Steve Means, D.	1978, Oct.
Gainesville, Fla.	*B. Harold Farmer	1968, Nov.
Galesburg, Ill.	*Thomas B. Herring	1960, Nov.
Galveston, Tex.	*Philip Lohec	1973, Nov.
Gardena, Calif.	*Harvery Hurlburt	1973, Mar.
Garden Grove, Calif.	*Richard R. Powers	1972, Apr.
Garfield Hts., Ohio	Raymond Stachewicz, D.	1975, Dec.
Garland, Tex.	*C. E. Duckworth	1965, Jan.
Gary, Ind.	R. G. Hatcher, D.	1975, Nov.
Gastonia, N.C.	*Gary Hicks	1973, Dec.
Glendale, Ariz.	*S. F. Van de Putte	1960, Aug.
Glendale, Calif.	*C. E. Perkins	1952, Apr.
Gr. Forks, N.D.	Cyril P. O'Neill, D.	1976, Apr.
Gr. Island, Nebr.	*John M. Carpenter	1964, Aug.
Gr. Prairie, Tex.	*Clifford A. Johnson	1962, Oct.
Gr. Rapids, Mich.	*Joseph R Grassie	1970, June
Granite City, Ill.	Paul Schuler, D.	1977, Apr.
Great Falls, Mont.	*Richard D. Thomas	1973, Apr.
Green Bay, Wis.	Thomas Atkinson, N-P.	1975, Apr.
Greensboro, N.C.	*Thomas Z. Osborne	1973, Jan.
Greenville, Miss.	Patrick Dunne, D.	1976, Jan.
Greensville, S.C.	*John J. Dullea	1971, Oct.
Greenwich, Conn.	William B. Lewis, R.	1975, Dec.
Gulfport, Miss.	C. L. Bullock, D.	1977, July
Hackensack, N.J.	*Joseph J. Squillace.	1964, Oct.
Hagerstown, Md.	Varner L. Paddack, R.	1977, Mar.
Hamden, Conn.	Lucien A. DiMeo, R.	1975, Nov.
Hamilton, Ohio	*Edward C. Sm th	1971, June
Hammond, Ind.	Joseph E. Klen, D.	1975,Dec.
Hampton, Va.	*C. E. Johnson	1958, May
Harlingen, Tex.	*George Adkins	1972, Aug.
Harrisburg, Pa.	Harold Swenson, D.	1978, Jan.

City	Name	Term
Hartford, Conn.	*Edward Curtin.	1971, June
Harvey, Ill.	James A. Haines.	1975, Apr.
Hattiesburg, Miss.	A. L. Gerrard Jr., D.	1977, July
Haverhill, Mass.	George Kay Katsaros, R.	1975, Dec.
Hawthorne, Calif.	*Donald W. Mansfield	1972, Jan.
Hayward, Calif.	*William C. Hanley	1972, Feb.
Hempstead, N.Y.	Dalton R. Miller, R.	1977, Apr.
Hialeah, Fla.	Dale Bennett, D.	1975, Dec.
High Point, N.C.	*Harold R. Cheek	1960, Mar.
Highland Pk., Ill.	*Vacant.	
Hoboken, N.J.	Steve Cappiello, N-P.	1977, July
Holyoke, Mass	William Taupier, D.	1976, Jan.
Hollywood, Fla.	*F. T. Kain.	1971, June
Honolulu, Hawaii.	Frank F. Fasi, D.	1976, Dec.
Hot Springs, Ark.	Tom Ellsworth, N-P.	1978, Dec.
Houston, Tex.	Fred Holheinz, D.	1976, Jan.
Huntington, W. Va.	*Barry R. Evans.	1973, Mar.
Huntington Beach, Calif.	*David D. Rowlands	1972, Feb.
Huntsville, Ala.	Joe W. Davis, N-P.	1976, Oct.
Hutchinson, Kan.	*George W. Pyle.	1967, Sept.
Independence, Mo.	*Lyle Alberg	1968, Sept.
Indianapolis, Ind.	Richard Lugar, R.	1975, Dec.
Inglewood, Calif.	*Douglas W. Ayres.	1968, Apr.
Inkster, Mich.	*David S. Williams.	1973, Oct.
Iowa City, Iowa	*Ray S. Wells.	1972, May
Irving, Tex.	*Darwin McGill.	1973, June
Irvington, N.J.	Robert Miller, N-P.	1978, July
Jackson, Mich.	*S. W. McAllister Jr.	1974, Mar.
Jackson, Miss.	Russell C. Davis, D.	1977, July
Jackson, Tenn.	Bob Conger, D.	1975, July
Jacksonville, Fla.	Hans Tanzler Jr., D.	1975, June
Jamestown, N.Y.	Stanley Lundine, D.	1975, Dec.
Janesville, Wis.	*Robert O. Bailey.	1971, Jan.
Jefferson City, Mo.	John G. Christy, D.	1975, Apr.
Jersey City, N.J.	Paul Jordan, D.	1977, July
Johnson City, Tenn.	Kyle Chinouth, R.	1975, May
Johnstown, Pa.	Herbert Pfuhl, R.	1978, Jan.
Joliet, Ill.	*Lynn Neuhart.	1972, Feb.
Joplin, Mo.	*Robert E. Metzinger.	1968, Mar.
Kalamazoo, Mich.	*James Caplinger	1968, July
Kansas City, Kan.	Richard F. Walsh, R.	1975, Apr.
Kansas City, Mo.	*John L. Taylor.	1968, Feb.
Kearney, N.J.	David C. Rowlands, N-P.	1975, Dec.
Kenosha, Wis.	Wallace E. Burkee, N-P.	1976, Apr.
Kettering, O.	*Ervin L. Welch.	1954, Dec.
Key West, Fla.	*Robert J. Stack.	1974, June
Killeen, Tex.	*Robert Brockman.	1972, Jan.
Knoxville, Tenn.	Kyle C. Testerman, R.	1975, Dec.
Kokomo, Ind.	John Peacock, D.	1976, Jan.
LaCrosse, Wis.	Peter Gilberton, N-P.	1975, Apr.
Lafayette, Ind.	James Riehle, D.	1975, Dec.
Lafayette, La.	Kenneth Bowen, D.	1976, June
La Habra, Calif.	*Lee Risner.	1971, Nov.
La Mesa, Calif.	*Donald P. Wolfer.	1972, July
La Mirada, Calif.	*Claude J. Klug.	1971, Aug.
Lake Charles, La.	William E. Boyer, D.	1977, June
Lakeland, Fla.	*Robert V. Youkey.	1960, Jan.
Lakewood, Calif.	*Milton R. Farrell.	1972, Dec.
Lakewood, Colo.	*Ray Wells.	1974, Sept.
Lakewood, Ohio.	Robert M. Lawther, R.	1975, Dec.
Lancaster, Pa.	Richard M. Scott, R.	1978, Jan.
Lansing, Mich.	Gerald Graves, N-P.	1977, Dec.
Laredo, Tex.	J. C. Martin Jr., N-P.	1978, May
Las Cruces, N.M.	*J. W. Harrington, Acting.	1974, July
Las Vegas, Nev.	*Arthur R. Trelease.	1965, Jan.
Lawrence, Kan.	*Buford M. Watson Jr.	1970, Jan.
Lawrence, Mass.	John J. Buckley, N-P.	1975, Dec.
Lawton, Okla.	*Vacant.	
Lewiston, Me.	John C. Orestis, D.	1976, Jan.
Lexington, Ky.	H. Foster Pettit, N-P.	1978, Jan.
Lima, Ohio.	Harry Moyer, R.	1977, Nov.
Lincoln, Nebr.	Sam Schwartzkop, D.	1975, May
Lincoln Pk., Mich.	Max S. Schiebold, N-P.	1975, Dec.
Linden, N.J.	John Gregorio, D.	1978, Dec.
Little Rock, Ark.	*Carleton E. McMullin.	1973, Nov.
Livermore, Calif.	*William H. Parness.	1957, Oct.
Livonia, Mich.	E. H. McNamara, N-P.	1976, Jan.
Lombard, Ill.	*Paul L. White.	1969, July
Long Beach, Cal.	*John R. Mansell.	1961, Mar.
Long Beach, N.Y.	*Richard Bowen.	1974, Apr.
Longview Tex.	*Harry G. Mosley.	1952, July
Lorain, Ohio.	Joseph J. Zahorec, D.	1975, Dec.
Los Angeles, Cal.	Thomas Bradley, D.	1977, June

City	Name	Term	City	Name	Term
Louisville, Ky.	Harvey Sloane, D.	1978, Dec.	Oak Park, Ill.	*Lee A. Ellis.	1971, Sept.
Lowell, Mass.	*Paul Sheehy	1974, May	Oak Pk., Mich	*James B. Thompson.	1970, Sept.
L. Merion, Pa.	*Thomas B. Fulweiler.	1968, Jan.	Oakland, Calif.	*Cecil S. Riley.	1972, Sept.
Lubbock, Tex.	*N. B. McCullough.	1971, Oct.	Oak Ridge, Tenn.	*William N. Haddock (act.).	1973, Oct.
Lynchburg, Va.	*David B. Norman.	1970, Dec.	Oceanside, Calif.	*Lawrence M. Bagley.	1970,July
Lynn, Mass.	Donald Phillips.	1976, Jan.	Odessa, Tex.	*Ronald J. Neighbors.	1968, Nov.
Lynwood, Calif.	*Stephen Wright.	1972, Dec.	Ogden, Utah	*R. L. Larsen.	1972, Feb.
			Okla. City, Okla.	*Howard McMahon.	1974, Jan.
Macon, Ga.	Ronnie Thompson, R.	1975, Nov.	Omaha, Nebr.	Edward Zorinsky, N-P.	1977, May
Madison, Wisc.	Paul Soglin, N-P.	1975, Mar.	Ontario, Calif.	*H.K. Hunter.	1966, Jan.
Malden, Mass.	Walter J. Kelliher, D.	1976, Jan.	Orange, Calif.	*Gifford Miller.	1968, Dec.
Manchester, Conn.	*Robert B. Weiss.	1966, Jan.	Orange, N.J.	Carmine Capone, R.	1978, May
Manchester, N.H.	Silvio Dupuis, D.	1976, Jan.	Orlando, Fla.	Carl Langford, D	1976, Oct.
Manitowoc, Wisc.	Anthony V. Dufek, D.	1975, Apr.	Oshkosh, Wis.	*Gordon Jaeger.	1970, Dec.
Mansfield, Ohio.	Richard A. Porter, R.	1975, Dec.	Owensboro, Ky.	*Max N. Rhoads.	1958, Sept.
Maple Hts., Ohio.	Emil J. Lisy Jr. N-P.	1975, Dec.	Oxnard, Calif.	*Paul E. Wolven.	1953, Feb.
Marion, Ind.	W. Ray Burns, D.	1976, Jan.			
Marion, Ohio	Don Quaintance, R.	1975, Dec.	Pacifica, Calif.	*David J. Thompson.	1972, Nov.
McKeesport, Pa.	John E. Pribanic, D.	1977, Dec.	Palo Alto, Cal.	*George Sipel.	1972, Feb.
Medford, Mass.	*James Nicholson.	1970, Oct.	Parkersburg, W. Va.	William Nicely, R.	1977, Dec.
Melbourne, Fla.	*Ernest E. Watkins.	1963, Oct.	Parma, Ohio	John Petruska, D.	1975, Dec.
Memphis, Tenn.	Wyeth Chandler, N-P.	1975, Dec.	Pasadena, Calif.	*Donald F. McIntyre.	1973, June
Mentor, Ohio.	*Arthur V. Dickard.	1969, Sept.	Pasadena, Tex.	John Ray Harrison, D.	1977, Apr.
Meridian, Miss	*Joel W. Forrester.	1973, July	Passaic, N.J.	Gerald Goldman, R.	1977, June
Mesa, Ariz.	*J. A. Petrie.	1952, June	Paterson, N.J.	*Larry Worth.	1974, Sept.
Mesquite, Tex.	*Billy G. York.	1969, Oct.	Pawtucket, R.I.	Dennis Lynch, D.	1976, Jan.
Miami, Fla.	*P. W. Andrews.	1973, Aug.	Pekin, Ill.	William L. Waldmeier.	1975, May
Miami Beach, Fla.	*Frack Spence.	1972, Nov.	Pensacola, Fla.	*Frank A. Faison.	1971, Apr.
Michigan City, Ind.	Randall C. Miller, R.	1975, Dec.	Peoria, Ill.	*Robert O. Wright.	1970, Oct.
Middletown, O.	*Dale F. Helsel.	1970, Oct.	Perth Amboy, N.J.	*Robert J. Cabana.	1973, July
Midland, Tex.	*James W. Brown	1964, Nov.	Petersburg, Va.	*Roy F. Ash.	1950, Jan.
Midwest City, Okla.	*W. D. Baker.	1966, June	Philadelphia, Pa.	Frank L. Rizzo, D.	1976, Jan.
Milford, Conn.	Joel Baldwin, D.	1975, Nov.	Phoenix, Ariz.	*John B. Wentz.	1970, July
Milwaukee, Wis.	Henry W. Maier, D.	1976, Apr.	Pico Rivera, Cal.	*Howard Schroyer.	1970, July
Minneapolis.	Albert J. Hofstede, D.	1976, Jan.	Pittsburgh, Pa.	Peter Flaherty, D.	1977, Dec.
Minnetonka, Minn.	*Carsten D. Leikvold.	1972, Dec.	Pittsfield, Mass.	Evan S. Dobelle.	1976, Jan.
Minot, N.D.	*John Arnold.	1972, Oct.	Plainfield, N.J.	*Kennedy Shaw.	1969, Feb.
Mishawaka, Ind.	Margaret H. Prickett, R.	1975, Dec.	Pocatello, Idaho.	*Charles W. Moss.	1970, Sept.
Mobile, Ala.	Gary A. Greenough.	1975, Feb.	Pompona, Claif.	*Jerrold R. Gonce.	1973, Oct.
Modesto, Calif.	*Garth Lipsky.	1974, Jan.	Pompano Bch., Fla.	*John Cartwright	1972,
Moline, Ill	Earl Wendt, R.	1977, May	Pontiac, Mich.	*Frank Smiley	1972, Jan.
Monroe, La.	Ralph T. Troy, D.	1976, June	Portage, Mich.	*Donald P. Ziemke.	1974, Sept.
Montebello, Cal.	*Roy Pederson	1969, Jan.	Port Arthur, Tex.	*George E. Dibrell.	1962, Oct.
Monterey Park, Cal.	*Gerald C. Weeks.	1970, Aug.	Port Huron, Mich.	*Gerald R. Bouchard.	1965, June
Montgomery, Ala.	Jim Robinson, N-P.	1975, Oct.	Portland, Me.	*John Menario.	1967, June
Mt. Prospect, Ill.	*Robert J. Eppley.	1971, Aug.	Portland, Ore.	Neil Goldschmidt, N-P.	1976, Jan.
Mt. Vernon, N.Y.	August Petrillo, R.	1975, Dec.	Portsmouth, O.	*C. Scott Johnson.	1974, Feb.
Mt. View, Cal.	*Richard De Long.	1973, Oct.	Portsmouth, Va.	*Phin Horton.	1974, Apr.
Munice, Ind.	Paul Cooley, D.	1975, Dec.	Poughkeepsie, N.Y.	*John Geib.	1974, Oct.
Mundelein, Ill	Maurice A. Noll, N-P.	1977, Apr.	Providence, R.I.	Vincent Cianci, R (subject to recount)	
Muskegon, Mich.	*Paul F. Frederick	1970, June	Provo, Utah.	Russell D. Grange, N-P.	1977, Dec.
Muskogee, Okla.	*W. T. Smith.	1971, Oct.	Pueblo, Colo.	*Fred E. Weisbrod.	1967, Feb.
			Quincy, Ill.	Don Nicholson, D.	1977, May
Napa, Calif.	*Lee M. Roberts.	1952, Feb.	Quincy, Mass.	Walter Hannon, N-P	1977, Jan.
Nashua, N.H.	Dennis Sullivan, D.	1975, Dec.			
Nashville, Tenn.	C. Beverly Briley, D.	1975, Sept.	Racine, Wis.	Stephen Olson, N-P.	1975, Apr.
National City, Cal.	*Cleo Osburn.	1965, July	Raleigh, N.C.	*L. P. Zachary Jr.	1974, Nov.
New Albany, Ind.	Warren V. Nash, D.	1975, Dec.	Rapid City, S.D.	Don Barnett, N-P.	1975, May
New Bedford, Mass	John Markey, D.	1976, Jan.	Raytown, Mo.	Willard H. Ross, R.	1975, Apr.
New Britain, Conn.	Stanley J. Pac, D.	1975, Nov.	Reading, Pa.	Eugene L. Shirk, R.	1976, Jan.
New Brunswick,N.J.	Richard Mulligan, N-P.	1979, Jan.	Redlands, Calif.	*R. P. Merritt, Jr.	1964, Mar.
New Castle, Pa.	Francis J. Rogan, D.	1975, Dec.	Redondo Beach, Cal.	*Joseph P. Leach.	1973, Feb.
New Haven, Conn.	Bartholomew Guida, D.	1976, Jan.	Redwood City, Cal.	*James M. Fales Jr.	1971, Aug.
N. Kensington, Pa.	Verle N. Bevan, D.	1977, Dec.	Reno, Nev.	*Joe Latimore.	1960, Oct.
New Orleans, La.	Moon Landrieu, D.	1978, Apr.	Revere, Mass.	William Reinstein.	1976, Jan.
New Rochelle, N.Y.	*James E. Malone.	1974, May	Richardson, Tex.	*Bob Hughey.	1974, Jan.
New York, N.Y.	Abraham Beame, D.	1977, Dec.	Richfield, Minn.	*Wayne Burggraaff.	1968, Dec.
Newark, N.J.	Kenneth Gibson, D.	1978, July	Richmond, Calif.	*Kenneth Smith.	1967, Sept.
Newark, Ohio.	Richard Baker, R.	1975, Dec.	Richmond, Ind.	Byron E. Klute, D.	1975, Dec.
Newport, R.I.	*B. Cowles Mallory.	1968, Feb.	Richmond, Va.	*William J. Leidinger.	1972, June
Newport Beach, Calif.	*Robert L. Wynn.	1971, Aug.	Riverside, Calif.	*Daniel E. Stone.	1970, July
Newport News	*W. E. Lawson Jr.	1965, Sept.	Roanoke, Va.	*Byron E. Haner.	1973, Jan.
Newton, Mass.	Theodore Mann	1977, Dec.	Rochester, Minn.	*Robert W. Freson.	1974, July
Niagara Falls	*Morton Abramowitz	1970, Jan.	Rochester, N.Y.	*Elisha Freedman.	1974, Jan.
Niles, Ill.	*Kenneth Scheel.	1973, May	Rock Hill, S.C.	*Max Holland.	1965, Mar.
Niles, Ohio.	W. A. Thorp, R.	1975, Dec.	Rock Island, Ill.	*Raymond P. Botch.	1961, Feb.
Norfolk, Va.	*G. Robert House.	1971, Jan.	Rockford, Ill.	Robert McGaw, D.	1977, May
Norman, Okla.	*Richard Gray	1972, Nov.	Rockville, Md.	*Larry N. Blick.	1972, Nov.
North Chicago, Ill.	Leo F. Kukla, D.	1977, Apr.	Rome, N.Y.	Wm. A. Valentine, R.	1975, Dec.
No. Little Rock, Ark.	Robert L. (Bob)Rosamond	1976, Dec.	Rosemead, Calif.	*Lee Gunn.	1969, May
No. Olmstead, Ohio	Ralph Christman, R.	1975, Dec.	Roseville, Mich.	*James F. Andre.	1974, May
Norristown, Pa.	*Vacant.		Roseville, Minn.	*Burke Raymond.	1969, Apr.
Norwalk, Calif.	*William H. Kraus.	1973, May	Roswell, N.M.	*Robert J. Owen.	1973, Oct.
Norwalk, Conn.	Donald J. Irwin, D.	1975, Nov.	Royal Oak, Mich.	*Bruce W. Love.	1961, June
Norwich, Conn	*Charles Whitty	1973, June			
Novato, Calif.	*Charles A. Brown.	1968, Dec.	Sacramento, Calif.	*R. L. Rathfon.	1969, Jan.
Oak Lawn, Ill.	*Kenneth M. McDonald.	1973, Dec.	Saginaw, Mich.	*E. H. Potthoff, Jr.	1961, July

City	Name	Term
St. Clair Shores, Mich.	*Donald J. Harm.	1962, Jan.
St. Joseph, Mo.	W. J. Bennett, D.	1978, Apr.
St. Louis, Mo.	John Poelker, D.	1977, Apr.
St. Louis Pk., Minn.	*Chris Cherches.	1968, Oct.
St. Paul, Minn.	*Frank Marzitelli.	1971, Nov.
St. Petersburg, Fla.	*R. E. Harbaugh.	1970, May
Salem, Mass.	Gene Levesque.	1976, Jan.
Salem, Ore.	*Robert S. Moore.	1968, Aug.
Salina, Kan.	*Norris D. Olson.	1963, May
Salinas, Calif.	*Robert Christofferson.	1972, Dec.
Salt Lake City.	Jake Garn, N-P.	1976, Jan.
San Angelo, Tex.	*H. D. Howard.	1958, May
San Antonio, Tex.	*Sam Granata, Jr.	1973, May
San Bernardino.	*Marshall Julian	1971, Nov.
San Diego, Calif.	*Kimball H. Moore.	1971, Dec.
San Francisco.	Joseph Alioto, D.	1976, Jan.
San Jose, Calif.	*Ted Tedesco	1973, Feb.
San Leandro, Calif.	*Wesley McCure.	1948, May
San Mateo, Calif.	*John Lilly.	1974, Apr.
San Rafael, Cal.	*William, J. Bielser	1973, Jan.
Sandusky, Ohio.	*Frank Link.	1972, Jan.
Santa Ana, Calif.	*Bruce C. Spragg.	1972, Sept.
Santa Barbara.	*John L. Scott.	1973, Mar.
Santa Cruz, Calif.	*David C. Koester.	1962, Oct.
Santa Fe, N.M.	*Philip Baca	1972, Aug.
Santa Maria, Cal.	*Robert Grogan.	1963, Jan.
Santa Monica.	*James D. Williams.	1973, Oct.
Santa Rosa, Calif.	*Kenneth R. Blackman.	1970, July
Sarasota, Fla.	*Kenneth Thompson.	1950, Feb.
Savannah, Ga.	*Arthur A. Mendonsa.	1971, Sept.
Schenectady, N.Y.	*Peter Caputo.	1973, Oct.
Scottsdale, Ariz.	*Dale Carter.	1971, Nov.
Scranton, Pa.	Eugene J. Peters, R.	1977, Dec.
Seattle, Wash.	Wesley C. Uhlman, N-P.	1977, Dec.
Shaker Hghts., O.	Walter C. Kelley.	1975, Dec.
Sheboygan, Wis.	Richard Suscha, R.	1977, Apr.
Shreveport, La.	L. Calhoun Allen Jr., D.	1978, Nov.
Simi Valley, Calif.	*Bruce A. Altman.	1970, Jan.
Sioux City, Ia.	*Gary F. Pokorny.	1974, Jan.
Sioux Falls, S.D.	Rick Knobe, R.	1979, May
Skokie, Ill.	*John N. Matzer Jr.	1970, Jan.
Somerville, Mass.	L. Lester Ralph.	1976, Jan.
South Bend, Ind.	Jerry Miller, D.	1975, Dec.
So. Gate, Calif.	Harold Prukop, D.	1975, Mar.
So. S. F., Calif.	*Edward G. Alario.	1973, Nov.
Southfield, Mich.	*Peter Cristiano.	1968, July
Southgate, Mich.	*William Valusek.	1972, Feb.
Spartanburg, S.C.	*Lott T. Rogers.	1958, Oct.
Spokane, Wash.	*F. Sylvin Fulwiler	1963, Aug.
Springfield, Ill.	William C. Telford, N-P.	1975, Apr.
Springfield, Mass.	William Sullivan	1976, Jan.
Springfield, Mo.	*Don G. Busch	1971, Oct.
Springfield, Ohio.	*Alfred Strozdas.	1968, Nov.
Stamford, Conn.	Frederick P. Lenz, D.	1975, Nov.
Sterling Hts., Mich.	*Kenneth Johnson.	1974, July
Stillwater, Okla.	*Lawrence Gish.	1966
Stockton, Calif.	*Elder Gunter.	1969, July
Stratford, Conn.	*Joseph W. Venables.	1970, Apr.
Sunnyvale, Cal.	*John E. Dever.	1967, Aug.
Syracuse, N.Y.	Lee Alexander, D.	1977, Dec.
Tacoma, Wash.	*William V. Donaldson	1971, Apr.
Tallahassee, Fla.	*Daniel A. Kleman.	1974, Aug.
Tampa, Fla.	Dick Greco Jr., D.	1975, Sept.
Taunton, Mass.	Theodore Aleixo	1975, Dec.
Taylor, Mich.	S. Richard Marshall, N-P.	1975, Dec.
Teaneck, N.J.	*Werner H. Shmid.	1959, Mar.
Tempe, Ariz.	*Kenneth A. McDonald.	1968, June
Terre Haute, Ind.	William Brighton, D.	1975, Dec.
Thousand Oaks, Cal.	*Glenn Kendall.	1966
Titusville, Fla.	*Lee Ayres	1969, Apr.
Toledo, Ohio.	*James B. Daken.	1971, Mar.
Topeka, Kan.	William McCormick, N-P.	1975, Apr.
Torrance, Calif.	*Edward J. Ferraro.	1964, Mar.
Trenton, N.J.	Arthur Holland, D.	1978, July
Troy, Mich.	*Frank, Gerstenecker.	1970, Feb.
Troy, N.Y.	*John P. Buckley.	1972, June
Tuscon, Ariz.	*Joel Valdez.	1974, Apr.
Tulsa, Okla.	Robert La Fortune, R.	1976, May
Tuscaloosa, Ala.	C. Snow Hinton, D.	1977, Oct.
Tyler, Tex.	*Ed Wagoner.	1972, Nov.
Univ. City, Mo.	*Charles T. Henry	1959, Jan.
Upland, Calif.	*S. Lee Travers.	1974, June
Upper Arlington, O.	*H. W. Hyrne.	1968, May
Urbana, Ill.	Hiram Paley, D.	1977, May
Utica, N.Y.	Edward Hanna, N-P.	1975, Dec.

City	Name	Term
Vallejo, Calif.	*Gerald R. Davis	1973, Aug.
Vancouver, Wash.	*Alan Harvey.	1969, Mar.
Ventura, Calif.	*Edward E. McCombs.	1970, Mar.
Victoria, Tex.	*John Lee.	1959, Sept.
Vineland, N.J.	Joseph D'Ippolito, R.	1976, June
Virginia Beach, Va.	*Roger Scott.	1968, July
Waco, Tex.	*David F. Smith Jr.	1972, Sept.
Walnut Creek, Cal.	*Thomas G. Dunne	1972, May
Waltham, Mass.	Arthur J. Clark.	1976, Jan.
Warren, Mich.	Ted Bates, N-P.	1975, Apr.
Wash., D.C.	Walter Washington, D.	1978, Dec.
Waterbury, Conn.	Victor A. Mambruno, D.	1975, Dec.
Waterloo, Ia.	Leo Rooff, N-P.	1976, Jan.
Waukegan, Ill.	Robert Sabonjian, R.	1977, Apr.
Waukesha, Wisc.	Paul Vrakas, N-P.	1976, Apr.
Wauwatosa, Wisc.	*J. William Little.	1972, Mar.
West Allis, Wisc.	Urban Ganser, N-P.	1975, Apr.
W. Covina, Cal.	*George Aiassa.	1958, May
W. Hartford, Conn.	*Richard H. Custer.	1972, Sept.
W. Haven, Conn.	Robert A. Johson, D.	1975, Dec.
W. New York, N.J.	Anthony De Fino, D.	1975, May
W. Orange, N.J.	William F. Cuozzi, N-P.	1978, June
W. Palm Beach.	*Richard Simmons.	1969, Sept.
Westland, Mich.	Eugene McKinney, N-P	1975, Dec.
Westminster, Cal.	*Robert J. Huntley.	1967, July
Weymouth, Mass.	Board of Selectmen.	
Wheeling, W. Va.	*Charles Steele.	1973, Jan.
White Plains, N.Y.	Michael J. Keating, D.	1976, Jan.
Wichita, Kan.	*Ralph Wulz.	1968, Sept.
Wichita Falls, Tex.	*Gerald G. Fox.	1969, Feb.
Wheaton, Ill.	*William E. Kirchhoff.	1973, May
Wilkes-Barre, Pa.	*Bernard J. Gallagher	1972, June
Williamsport, Pa.	John R. Coder, R.	1976, Jan.
Wilmington, Del.	Thomas Maloney, D.	1977, Jan.
Wilmington, N.C.	*John A. Jones.	1971, Sept.
Winston-Salem.	*Orville W. Powell.	1972, Nov.
Woodbridge, N.J.	*Stephen Cuccio.	1974, Apr.
Woodbridge, N.J.	John J. Cassidy, R.	1975, Dec.
Woonsocket, R.I.	John A. Cummings, D.	1975, Nov.
Worcester, Mass.	*Francis J. McGrath.	1951, Apr.
Wyandotte, Mich.	William Sullivan, N-P.	1975, Apr.
Wyoming, Mich.	*William P. Von Houten.	1972, May
Yakima, Wash.	*Craign McMicken.	1967, Sept.
Yonkers, N.Y.	*J.E. Casey.	1974, July
Youngstown, O.	Jack Hunter, R.	1975, Dec.
York, Pa.	John D. Krout, R.	1978, Jan.
Zanesville, Ohio.	*Frank Patrizio.	1974, Aug.

Canadian Cities

City	Name	Term
Calgary, Alta.	Rod Sykes.	1974, Oct.
Dartmouth, N.S.	Eileen Stubbs.	1975, Dec.
Edmonton, Alta.	I.G. Dent.	
Guelph, Ont.	N. Jary.	1974, Dec.
Halifax, N.S.	Walter R. Fitzgerald.	1974, Nov.
Hamilton, Ont.	Victor K. Copps.	1976, Jan.
Hull, Que.	Gilles Rocheleau.	1974, Nov.
Kingston, Ont.	George N. Speal.	1974, Dec.
Kitchener, Ont.	Sid McLennan.	1974, Dec.
Lachine, Que.	Guy Descary.	1977, Nov.
La Salle, Que.	Gerald Raymond.	1975, Nov.
Laval, Que.	Lucien Paiement.	1977, Nov.
London, Ont.	Mrs. Jane Bigelow.	1974, Dec.
Moncton, N.B.	Leonard Jones.	
Montreal, Que.	Jean Drapeau.	1974, Oct.
Oshawa, Ont.	J.H. Potticary.	1976, Dec.
Ottawa, Ont.	Pierre Benoit.	1974, Dec.
Peterborough, Ont.	P.H. Turner.	1974, Dec.
Quebec, Que.	J. Gilles Lamontagne.	1977, Nov.
Regina, Sask.	H.G.R. Walter.	1976, Oct.
St. John, N.B.	Mrs. Dorothy Wyatt.	
Saskatoon, Sask.	Herbert S. Sears.	1976, Oct.
Sault Ste. Marie, Ont.	R.A. Irwin.	1974, Dec.
Sherbrooke, Que.	Marc Bureau.	1977, Nov.
Sudbury, Ont.	Joseph J. Fabbro.	1974, Dec.
Toronto, Ont.	David Crombie.	1974, Dec.
Vancouver, B.C.	Art Phillips.	1974, Dec.
Victoria, B.C.	Peter A. Pollen.	1974, Nov.
Waterloo, Ont.	Donovan Meston.	1974, Dec.
Windsor, Ont.	F. Wansbrough.	1974, Dec.
Winnipeg, Man.	Stephen Juba.	1974, Oct.

Off-Beat News in 1974

If those "sinister forces" which perpetrated shortages, crises of a hundred sorts, wars, Watergate and inflation thought they could throw humanity offstride in 1974, they fell short. All they managed was to throw people off-beat, for off-beat was the tempo in 1974.

In the spring more than young men's fancy was aired as the phenomenon of streaking thrust itself onto the world vista. Begun as a campus rite of spring, the streak was soon embraced by an appreciative, bad-news-weary world.

A Streak of Baring

Lone streakers and highly-organized streak teams bared all coast-to-coast, during televised events including the Academy Awards broadcast, on trains, in planes, while ski-jumping in Missoula, Montana, waterskiing in Hong Kong and even at St. Peter's Square in the Vatican. Even a barish stock broker turned in a Wall Street streak. And, completing some sort of cycle, 20 members of a soccer club in Coventry, England dashed *au naturel* through the town which had given the world Lady Godiva.

Streaking never caught on in China, perhaps because Chinese youth were too busy singing one of the top popular songs there: How I Love To Carry Fertilizer Up the Mountainside for the Commune.

At the other end of the fertilizer business, cows in Atsugi, Japan were fed newspapers as part of a government experiment seeking cheap hay substitutes. The cows continued to produce good milk and it seemed likely newspapers would be headed for greater ends than birdcage bottoms.

While the cows were busy digesting the news of the day, bulls in Madrid, Spain were awaiting their first mortal confrontation with women. Government officials there decreed an end to discriminatory laws which prevented women from killing bulls publicly. Thrice-gored Latin American bullfighter Angela Hernandez, who had fought for the right to fight in Spain, declared the sport "superbly suited for modern woman."

Crime Capers

Economic pinches did nothing to improve the crime situation, except perhaps in Milan, Italy, where thieves loaded a truck with cartons of stolen loot; sped away and promptly ran out of gas.

An armed robber fared even worse in Miami when he jumped into what he thought was his getaway car — actually an unmarked patrol car which took him, and his getaway driver, to jail.

The tables were turned in Key Largo, Florida, where a sheriff's deputy pursuing a speeding car discovered he was chasing his own auto. The deputy reported the thief piqued, to say the least, at his choice of wheels.

No more piqued, but more surprised, was a Houston prisoner who, wriggling his way toward freedom through the county jail's air conditioning ducts, fell through a weak spot and crashed to the courtroom below.

But no thief was more surprised than the unknown purloiner of a sack taken from the back seat of a Miami auto. Inside the bag was a seven-foot rattlesnake.

Crooked moxie of the year honors, though, must go to the burglar who entered an empty courtroom in the Columbus, Ohio, police headquarters and slipped away with just about everything that wasn't nailed down — including the presiding judge's nameplate, which was.

Emphasizing the value of a college degree was a Sante Fe, N.M., prison inmate, serving a 30- to 150-year sentence, who earned a two-year diploma through a special rehabilitation program. At commencement exercises the prisoner picked up his sheepskin — and vanished.

But at least one among the lawless saw the light. He wrote Canadian tax authorities: "I haven't been able to sleep since cheating on my income tax. I enclose a check for $500. If still unable to sleep, will send you the balance."

No Shortage of Shortages

Shortages, real and imagined, were prominent in the news of the year. With high-priced gasoline in short supply at the end of long gas lines, walking and bicycling took on greater appeal.

One group of bicyclists saved time, as well as money and fuel, in a 21-mile trip to Lake Geneva, Wisconsin. The amateur bicyclists challenged, and beat, a commuter train over the last stretch of the Chicago to Lake Geneva route.

Highway fatality figures in California were reduced because of the high cost of gassing-up. In this case it was the lack of saloon gassing-up that diminished the accidents. According to the State Highway Patrol Commissioner the rising cost of the price of a drink is driving the drinking drivers out of their taverns and into their homes where their own bottles may be consumed more economically — and more safely.

Drinkers in Warsaw, Poland, too were driven — into the moonshine business. With vodka rising in price by 23 per cent, sales dropped by one-fourth. Coincidentally, sugar and yeast sales began to boom.

Some citizens in Leningrad had more trouble with drink than the price as they first built, then destroyed a neighborhood recreation spot. Tables and chairs arranged for chess playing, reading and lounging soon attracted vodka-laden drunks. When all attempts to dislodge them failed, an outraged citizen took an ax to the tables. Now the neighborhood is without a chess center, but the drunks remain, drinking on their feet — where the tables had been — until they collapse.

Whether or not a shortage prompted his all-out effort to produce a four and one-quarter pound tomato is unknown, but an Eastport, England man did reveal his technique: he said he put earphones around the jumbo tomato and played stereo music to it.

Sheepish

Once again in Katmandu, Nepal, the government announced that worshippers could not sacrifice any more local animals during the Hindu festival to the goddess Durga Bhawani. Since animal sacrifice outstrips supply at festival time, 10,000 sheep and mountain goats were imported.

The number of sheep in Spokane, Washington was reduced by eight this year when a pack of dogs jumped a 12-foot fence to attack and eat the experimental animals. The sheep were part of a state-funded study on ways to train coyotes not to eat sheep.

Perhaps the most notable shortage in the off-beat news-of-the-year was no shortage at all. Following a congressman's news release warning of a possible shortage of toilet paper, complicated by newspaper and television emphasis on the supposed shortage, a run began on the tissue. Millions of Americans stripped tens of millions of rolls of toilet paper off the grocery shelves. In the end, apparently, the shortage was simply a rumor. Supplies were soon replenished and, it seems, the tissue issue is behind us.

And finally, to cheer any soul bearing even the smallest spark of vengefulness, the weather forecaster's annual picnic in Seattle was cancelled this year, due to rain.

Deaths, Nov. 1, 1973 - Nov. 1, 1974

A

Abbot, Charles Greeley, 101; astrophysicist, former secretary of the Smithsonian Institution; Riverdale, Md., Dec. 17.

Abbott, Bud, 78; straight man in the "Abbott and Costello" comedy team; Woodland Hills, Cal., Apr. 24.

Abrams, Gen. Creighton W., 59; Army Chief of Staff; former commander of U.S. forces in Vietnam; Washington, D.C., Sept. 4.

Akeman, David, 57; TV comedian known as "Stringbean" on "Grand Ole Opry" and "Hee Haw"; Nashville, Nov. 11.

Aldrich, Winthrop W., 88; banker and former U.S. ambassador to Britain; New York, Feb. 25.

Allen, Dr. Forrest (Phog) 88; basketball coach at Univ. of Kansas for almost 40 years; intrumental in beginning the NCAA tournaments; Lawrence, Kansas, Sept. 16.

Alsop, Stewart, 60; political columnist and writer; Wash., D.C., May 26.

Amrine, Michael, 55; science writer aided in the creation of the Atomic Energy Comm.; Wash., D.C., Feb. 17.

Anokhin, Dr. Pyotr K., 76; Soviet brain specialist and physiologist; Moscow, Mar. 6.

Apostoli, Fred, 59; former middleweight boxing champion; San Francisco, Nov. 29.

Arquette, Cliff, 68; comic actor appeared as Charlie Weaver on TVs "Hollywood Squares"; Los Angeles, Sept. 23.

Asturias, Miguel Angel, 74; Guatemalan novelist won 1967 Nobel prize; Madrid, June 9.

Ayub Khan, Field Marshall Mohammad, 67; President of Pakistan, 1958-69; Karachi, Pakistan, Apr. 20.

B

Baclanova, Olga, 74; Russian-born stage and film actress; Vevey, Switzerland, Sept. 6.

Bates, H.E., British novelist wrote over 50 books, "Darling Buds of May"; Kent, England, Jan. 29.

Ben-Gurion, David, 87; first Premier of Israel; Tel Aviv, Dec. 1.

Best, Edna, 74; British stage and film actress; Geneva, Sept. 18.

Biddle, George, 88; muralist and portrait painter; Croton-on Hudson, N.Y.

Bieber, Isidor, 87; race horse owner-breeder; Hollywood, Fla., Aug. 29.

Biossat, Bruce, 64; chief Washington correspondent for Newspaper Enterprise Association; Washington, D.C., May 27.

Blackett, Patrick Lord, 76; British scientist won Nobel prize for physics in 1948; London, July 13.

Blunden, Edmund, 77; British poet and biographer; Sudbury, Eng., Jan. 20.

Bohlen, Charles E., 69; diplomat, a top expert on Russia; Washington, D.C., Jan. 2.

Bose, Satyendranath, 80; theoretical physicist influenced the work of Einstein; Calcutta, Feb. 4.

Bowen, Catherine Drinker, 76; award winning biographer; Haverford, Pa., Nov. 1.

Boyle, Hal, 63; AP columnist won Pulitzer prize in 1945; New York, Apr. 2.

Brennan, Walter, 80; veteran film and TV actor won 3 Academy awards for supporting actor; Oxnard, Cal., Sept. 21.

Britton, Pamela, 50; actress starred in the "Blondie" TV series; Arlington Heights, Ill., June 17.

Burckhardt, Dr. Carl, 82; Swiss historian and diplomat; Geneva, Mar. 3.

Bush, Vannevar, 84; engineer marshalled American technology for world war 2, founded National Defense Research Comm., Belmont, Mass., June 28.

Butts, Wally, 68; Univ. of Georgia football coach, 1939-1960; Athens, Ga., Dec. 17.

C

Cannon, Jimmy, 63; syndicated sports columnist; New York, Dec. 5.

Cassels, Louis, 52; religion columnist for UPI; Aiken, S.C., Jan. 23.

Chadwick, Sir James, 82; British physicist won Nobel prize for discovery of the neutron; Cambridge, Eng., July 24.

Chenery, William L., 90; head of Collier's magazine for 25 years; Monterey, Cal., Aug. 18.

Chotiner, Murray, 64; key advisor to President Nixon for 25 years; Washington, D.C., Jan. 30.

Cicognani, Amleto Cardinal, 90; Dean of the Sacred College of Cardinals; Rome, Dec. 17.

Clapp, Margaret, 64; Pulitzer prize winning biographer and president of Wellesley College, 1949-66; Tyringham, Mass., May 3.

Cole, Jack, 60; dance choreographer; Los Angeles, Feb. 17.

Condon, Dr. Edward, 72; physicist was leader in the World War II atomic bomb and radar programs; Boulder, Colo., Mar. 26.

Cooley, Harold D., 76; North Carolina Democrat served in House for 16 terms, 1935-1966; Wilson, N.C., Jan. 15.

Cord, Errett, 79; designer of the Cord automobile of the 30's; Reno, Nev., Jan. 2.

Cornell, Katharine, 81; foremost actress of the American theater; Vineyard Haven, Mass., June 8.

Cortines, Adolfo Ruiz, 82; President of Mexico, 1952-58; Mexico City, Dec. 3.

Cox, James M., 71; led newspaper and broadcasting corporations; Miami, Oct. 27.

Crisp, Donald, 93; character actor won Oscar for "How Green Was My Valley"; Van Nuys, Cal., May 26.

Curran, Rev. Edward Lodge, 75; anticommunist priest supported Father Coughlin, Joseph McCarthy; Port Jefferson, N.Y., Feb. 14.

D

Daley, Arthur, 69; N.Y. Times sports columnist won Pulitzer prize; New York, Jan. 3.

Darin, Bobby, 37; pop singer, "Mack the Knife"; Los Angeles, Dec. 20.

Darvas, Lili, 72; Hungarian actress had career spanning 50 years; New York, July 22.

Daugherty, James, 84; artist; children's book author; Boston, Feb. 21.

Davis, Adelle, 70; nutritionist whose books sold millions; Palos Verdes Es-

tates, Cal., May 31.

Davis, Johanna, 36; author of "Life Signs"; New York, July 25.

Dean, Jay Hanna (Dizzy), 63; Hall of Fame pitcher and baseball broadcaster; Reno, Nev., July 17.

Deane, Martha (Marian Young Taylor), 66; radio interview hostess for 32 years; New York, Dec. 9.

DeSalvo, Albert, 40; widely known as the "Boston Strangler"; Walpole State Prison, Nov. 27.

de Seversky, Alexander P., 80; strategic air power proponent whose inventions were major contributions to military and commercial flying; New York, Aug. 24.

Dewey, Bradley, 87; industrialist and inventor; New London, N.H., Oct. 14.

DeWolfe, Billy, 67; stage and movie comedian and actor; Los Angeles, Mar. 5.

Dilworth, Richardson K., 75; Mayor of Philadelphia, 1955-62; Philadelphia, Jan. 23.

Dumbrille, Douglass, 84; character actor appeared in hundreds of roles in TV, films and the stage; Woodland Hills, Cal., Apr. 2.

Dunn, Alan, 73; cartoonist for the New Yorker for 40 years; New York, May 20.

Dunn, Leslie, 80; geneticist renowned for research into heredity and evolution; No. Tarrytown, N.Y., Mar. 19.

E

Eisendrath, Rabbi Maurice N., 71; leader of reform Judaism in the United States; New York, Nov. 9.

Ellington, Duke, 75; jazz composer and musician; New York, May 24.

Elliot, "Mama" Cass, 33; pop singer, gained fame with "Mamas and Papas" group; London, July 29.

Emmet, Christopher T., 73; political writer active in opposition to totalitarianism; New York, Feb. 11.

Esterel, Jacques, 56; Paris couturier specialized in avant-garde clothes and novelty items; Paris, Apr. 14.

Ewing, Dr. Maurice, 67; earth scientist; Galveston, Tex., May 4.

F

Ferger, Roger, 80; former president and publisher of the Cincinnati Enquirer; West Palm Beach, Fla., Apr. 8.

Fields, Dorothy, 68; lyricist wrote over 400 songs, "The Way You Look Tonight"; "I'm in the Mood for Love"; New York, Mar. 28.

Flynn, Joe, 49; actor made numerous film and TV appearances; best known for TVs "McHale's Navy"; Hollywood, July 18.

Fouchet, Christian, 63; French diplomat; Geneva, Aug. 11.

Freed, Fred, 53; producer of documentaries won 7 Emmy awards; New York, Mar. 31.

Fremont-Smith, Dr. Frank, 78; mental health leader; Massapequa, N.Y., Feb. 27.

Fryxell, Dr. Roald, 40; anthropologist discovered the oldest documented human remains in the Pacific Northwest; Othello, Wash., May 18.

Fuller, Alfred C., 88; the original "Fuller Brush Man," founded company that now employs 25,000 salesmen; Hartford, Conn., Dec. 4.

Furtseva, Yekaterina, 63; Soviet Minister of Culture promoted cultural exchanges with the West; USSR, Oct. 25.

G

Garand, John C., 86; inventor of the M-1 rifle; Springfield, Mass., Feb. 16.

Gaylord, E.K., 101; publisher of the Daily Oklahoman; Oklahoma City, May 31.

Gerber, Daniel, 75; introduced strained baby foods to a mass market; Fremont, Mich., Mar. 16.

Ginott, Dr. Haim, 51; child psychologist wrote the best seller "Between Parent and Child"; New York, Nov. 4.

Gloucester, Duke of, 74; last surviving son of King George V; Northamptonshire, Eng., June 10.

Goldwyn, Samuel, 91; Hollywood producer of over 70 films; won Oscar in 1947 for "The Best Years of Our Lives"; Los Angeles, Jan. 31.

Golenpaul, Dan, 73; creator of the radio quiz show "Information Please"; publisher of almanac of same name; New York, Feb. 13.

Gordon, Kitty, 96; actress for whom Victor Herbert composed the musical "The Enchantress"; Brentwood, N.Y., May 27.

Gottlieb, Adolph, 70; abstract expressionist; New York, Mar. 4.

Grivas, Gen. George, 75; Greek Cypriot underground leader; Jan. 27, Limassol, Cyprus.

Gruenberg, Sidonie, 91; authority on children; New York, Mar. 11.

Gruening, Ernest, 87; former Senator from Alaska was among the first to oppose U.S. involvement in Vietnam; Washington, D.C., June 26.

Guthrie, Ramon, 77;poet; Hanover, N.H., Nov. 22.

Guttmacher, Dr. Alan F., 75; pioneer in the birth-control movement; New York, Mar. 18.

H

Harris, Dr. Seymour E., 77; political economist advised Presidents Kennedy and Johnson; San Diego, Oct. 27.

Handwerker, Nathan, 83; frankfurter king founded Nathan's Famous chain; Sarasota, Fla., Mar. 24.

Harvey, Laurence, 45; actor often played a cad in films, "Room at the Top", "Butterfield 8"; London, Nov. 25.

Hayakawa, Sessue, 83; Japanese actor appeared in 120 films, "The Bridge on the River Kwai"; Nov. 23, Tokyo.

Heyer, Georgette, 71; novelist wrote over 50 historical novels set in Regency England; London, July 4.

Hobler, Atherton W., 83; advertising pioneer; Princeton, N.J., Jan. 3.

Hodges, Luther, 76; former Secy. of Commerce and Governor of North Carolina; Chapel Hill, N.C., Oct. 6.

Hoerter, Charles, 67; sports editor of the N.Y. Daily News, 1957-67; Palm Beach, Fla., Mar. 18.

Hoffman, Paul G., 83; administer of the Marshall Plan and other aid programs; New York, Oct. 8.

Hogan, Frank S., 72; District Attorney for New York County for 32 years; New York, Apr. 2.

Horton, Tim, 44; star defenseman in the National Hockey League for 23 seasons; Ontario, Feb. 21.

Hull, Warren, 71; radio-TV host of "Strike It Rich" quiz show; Waterbury, Conn., Sept. 14.

Huntley, Chet, 62; newscaster was half of the Huntley-Brinkley team for 15 years on NBC-TV; Bozeman, Mont., Mar. 20.

Hurok, Sol, 85; famed impresario produced concerts, ballet and opera; New York, Mar. 5.

I

Inonu, Ismet, 89; first Premier of modern Turkey; Ankara, Turkey, Dec. 25.

J

Jenkins, Allen, 74; character actor in over 175 films; Santa Monica, Cal., July 20.

Johnson, Earl J., 73; editor of United Press International for 30 years; Tucson, Jan. 3.

Jonas, Franz, 74; President of Austria since 1956; Vienna, Apr. 23.

Jordan, Sen. B. Everett, 77; No. Carolina Democrat served in Senate 1958-72; headed Bobby Baker inquiry; Saxaphaw, N.C., Mar. 15.

Judge, Arline, 61; much married film star of the 30s; Hollywood, Feb. 7.

K

Kahn, Louis I., 73; major American architect; New York, Mar. 17.

Kallen, Dr. Horace, 91; philosopher and educator; founded New School for Social Research; Palm Beach, Fla., Feb. 16.

Kannon, Jackie, 48; comedian; New York, Feb. 1.

Kartveli, Alexander, 77; designer of the P-47 and F-105 aircraft; Huntington, N.Y., July 20.

Kase, Max, 75; sports editor of the N.Y. Journal-American; broke college basketball fix story in 1951; Yonkers, N.Y., Mar. 19.

Keightley, Gen. Sir Charles, 72; Commander in Chief of the Anglo-French invasion of Suez in 1956; Salisbury, Eng., June 17.

Kelly, George, 87; Pulitzer prize winning playwright, "Craig's Wife"; Bryn Mawr, Pa., June 18.

King, Cecil, 76; Democratic Congressman from Cal., 1942-68; Inglewood, Cal., Mar. 17.

King, Mrs. Martin Luther, Sr., 69; mother of the late civil rights leader; Atlanta, June 30.

Kirk, Norman E., 51; Prime Minister of New Zealand; Wellington, N.Z., Aug. 31.

Kleberg, Robert Jr., 78; owner of the King Ranch, the country's largest single producer of beef cattle; Houston, Oct. 13.

Klein, Anne, 51; fashion designer famed for the All-American look in sportswear; New York, Mar. 19.

Knowland, William F., 65; former Republican leader in the Senate; publisher of the Oakland Tribune; Guerneville, Cal., Feb. 23.

Krips, Josef, 72; Austrian orchestra conductor; Geneva, Oct. 12.

Krock, Arthur, 87; leading American journalist for 60 years; won 3 Pulitzer prizes; Washington, D.C., Apr. 12.

Kruger, Otto, 89; suave stage and screen actor; Los Angeles, Sept. 6.

Kuiper, Gerard, Dr., 68; astronomer played a key role in early U.S. space program; Mexico City, Dec. 23.

L

Lagerkvist, Per, 83; Swedish novelist, poet and playwright won Nobel prize in 1951; Sweden, July 11.

Lee, Harold B., 74; President of the Mormon Church; Salt Lake City, Dec. 26.

Leech, Margaret, 80; historian, won Pulitzer prizes in 1942 and 1960; New York, Feb. 24.

Lentz, Arthur G., 65; executive director of the U. S. Olympic Committee, 1965-73; New York, Jan. 25.

Lewis, John Henry, 59; light-heavyweight boxing champion of the 30s; Berkeley, Cal., Apr. 19.

Lindbergh, Charles A., 72; first man to fly the Atlantic solo nonstop (1927); Kipahulu, Maui, Hawaii, Aug. 26.

Link, Theodore C., 69; crime reporter for the St. Louis Post-Dispatch; aided Kefauver committee; St. Louis, Feb. 14.

Lovejoy, Clarence E., 79; creator of "Lovejoys College Guide"; Red Bank, N.J., Jan. 16.

Lowdermilk, Walter Clay, 86; international authority on conservation; Berkeley Cal., May 6.

M

Maganini, Quinto, 77; composer, conductor won Pulitzer prize for music in 1927; Greenwich, Conn., Mar. 10.

Mangrum, Lloyd, 59; one of the top pro golfers in 40s and 50s; Apple Valley, Cal., Nov. 17.

Marie, Andre, 76; former French Premier and cabinet minister; Rouen, France, June 12.

Marsh, Bruce, 48; Canadian broadcaster; Los Angeles, Mar. 17.

Mason, Edith, 80; lyric soprano sang at the Metropolitan and Chicago operas; San Diego, Nov. 26.

Massey, Ilona, 62; film actress; Bethesda, Md., Aug. 20.

McCafferty, Don, 53; head coach of the Detroit Lions; Pontiac, Mich., July 28.

McGee, Frank, 52; TV newsman hosted NBC's "Today" program; New York, Apr. 17.

McKeldin, Theodore R., 73; major figure in Maryland politics for 25 years; Baltimore, Aug. 10.

Menon, V. K. Krishna, 77; former Defense Minister of India; New Delhi, Oct. 6.

Merrow, Chester, 67; member of Congress (R.-N.H.) for 20 years; Wolfeboro, N.H., Feb. 10.

Meyer, Dr. Karl F., 89; veterinarian scientist and public health leader; San Francisco, Apr. 27.

Milhaud, Darius, 81; French composer; Geneva, June 24.

Mitchell, Stephen A., 71; Democratic National Chairman in the 50s; Taos, N.M., Apr. 23.

Mohr, Hal, 79; cinematographer made first sound film "The Jazz Singer"; won 2 Oscars; Santa Monica, Cal, May 10.

Molyneux, Capt. Edward, 79; British fashion designer; Monte Carlo, Mar. 22.

Moorehead, Agnes, 67; character actress starred in stage, films and TV; nominated for 5 Oscars; Rochester, Minn., Apr. 30.

Morgan, Claudia, 62; actress best known as Nora Charles on radio's "The Thin Man"; New York, Sept. 17.

Morris, Arthur J., 92; banker pioneered personal loans under his Morris Plan; No. Tarrytown, N.Y., Nov. 18.

Morris, Glenn, 62; Olympic decathlon winner in 1936; played Tarzan in films; Palo Alto, Cal., Jan. 31.

Morse, Sen. Wayne, 73; represented Oregon in the Senate for 24 years; an early critic of the Vietnam war; Portland, Ore., July 22.

Mundt, Sen. Karl, 74; anti-communist Senator from So. Dakota figured in the Hiss and McCarthy hearings; Washington, D.C., Aug. 16.

Munro, Sir Leslie, 72; New Zealand diplomat; president of the UN General Assembly 1957-58; Hamilton, N.Z., Feb. 13.

N

Nilsson, Anna Q., 85; Swedish born film actress; Hemet, Cal., Feb. 11.

Notestein, Ada Comstock, 97; president of Radcliffe, 1923-1943; New Haven, Dec. 11.

Nourse, Edwin, 90; first chairman of the President's Council of Economic Advisors; Bethesda, Md., Apr. 7.

O

O'Brien, Kate, 76; Irish novelist and playwright; Kent, Eng., Aug. 13.

Odria, Gen. Manuel, 77; President of Peru, 1948-56; Lima, Peru, Feb. 18.

Oistrakh, David, 65; Soviet violinist; Amsterdam, Oct. 24.

O'Shaughnessy, Ignatius, 88; oilman and philanthropist; Miami, Nov. 21.

O'Shea, Michael, 67; stage, film and television actor; Dallas, Dec. 4.

P

Pagnol, Marcel, 79; French film director and playwright; Paris, Apr. 18.

Patrick, Van, 58; broadcaster for the Detroit Lions (football) and Tigers (baseball); South Bend, Ind., Sept. 29.

Pelly, Thomas M., 71; former congressman (R-Wash.) for 20 years, opposed foreign aid; Ojai, Cal., Nov. 21.

Peron, Juan, 78; President of Argentina; Argentina, July 1.

Platt, Ed, 58; actor who played the Chief in "Get Smart" TV series; Santa Monica, Cal., Mar. 20.

Pompidou, Georges, 62; President of France; Paris, Apr. 2.

Pope-Hennessy, James, 57; British biographer; London, Jan. 25.

Prouty, Olive Higgins, 92; author of "Stella Dallas"; Brookline, Mass., Mar. 24.

Pryer, Roger, 72; bandleader and actor; Puerta Vallarta, Mexico, Jan. 31.

Pusser, Buford, 36; crusading sheriff whose exploits were related in the film "Walking Tall"; Selmar, Tenn., Aug. 21.

Q

Quayle, Oliver, 52; public-opinion poll specialist; Hanover, N.H., Apr. 14.

R

Ransom, John Crowe, 86; poet and critic; Gambier, Ohio, July 5.

Reese, Ben, 85; Pulitzer prize winning editor of St. Louis Post-Dispatch; Neptune, N.J., June 10.

Revson, Peter, 35; American racing driver; Johannesburg, So. Africa, Mar. 22.

Rice, Sam, 84; member of the Baseball Hall of Fame; Rossmor, Md., Oct. 13.

Ritter, Tex, 68; singing cowboy of movies and records; Nashville, Jan. 2.

Romer, Dr. Alfred, 78; authority on evolution; Cambridge, Mass., Nov. 5.

Rosay, Francoise, 82; French film and stage actress; Paris, Mar. 28.

Rounesville, Robert, 60; tenor appeared in opera and on the stage; New York, Aug. 6.

Ruby, Harry, 79; song writer, "Three Little Words", "Who's Sorry Now?"; Woodland Hills, Cal., Feb. 23.

Ruskin, Leonard, 51; producer; a founder of "TV Guide"; Miami Beach, Dec. 22.

S

Saillant, Louis, 73; head of the World Federation of Trade Union for 24 years; Paris, Oct. 28.

Santos, Eduardo, 86; President of Colombia, 1938-42; founder of the newspaper "El Tiempo"; Colombia, Mar. 27.

Saunders, Carl M., 83; editor, won Pulitzer prize in 1949 for editorial suggesting National Day of Prayer; Grand Rapids, Mich., Oct. 2.

Schlag, Felix, 82; designer of the Jefferson nickel; Owosso, Mich., Mar. 9.

Seaton, Fred A., 64; Secretary of the Interior, 1956-1961; Minneapolis, Jan. 16.

Secunda, Sholom, 79; composer of some 60 operettas and 1,000 songs "Bei Mir Bist du Schoen"; New York, June 13.

Seeley, Blossom, 82; vaudeville star; New York, Apr. 17.

Sessions, Almira, 85; character actress of stage, films, and television; Los Angeles, Aug. 3.

Sexton, Anne, 45; poet won Pulitzer prize in 1967; Weston, Mass., Oct. 4.

Shaw, Clay, 60; New Orleans businessman acquitted in 1969 of plotting the assassination of President Kennedy; New Orleans, Aug. 15.

Shazar, Zalman, 84; President of Israel, 1963-73; Jerusalem, Oct. 5.

Shecter, Leonard, 47; sportswriter and author, "The Jocks", "Ball Four"; New York, Jan. 19.

Shelley, John F., 68; labor leader, Congressman, and Mayor of San Francisco, 1964-67; San Francisco, Sept. 1.

Sherman, Allan, 48; entertainer wrote comic lyrics to well known tunes; Los Angeles, Nov. 20.

Shute, Denny, 69; golfer, won PGA championship in 1936 and 1937; Akron, Ohio, May 13.

Simonds, Gen. Guy, 71; a leading Canadian field commander in World War II; Toronto, May 15.

Siqueiros, David Alfaro, 77; Mexican muralist; Cuernavaca, Mexico, Jan. 6.

Smithwick, A. P. (Paddy), 46; steeplechase jockey won national championship 5 times; Baltimore, Nov. 14.

Smrkovsky, Josef, 62; President of Czech National Assembly during 1968 Czech reform; Prague, Jan. 14.

Sokolova, Lydia, 77; ballerina was protegee of Diaghilev; Kent, Eng., Feb. 2.

Soyer, Moses, 74; Russian born painter; New York, Sept. 2.

Spaatz, Gen. Carl A., 83; first Chief of Staff of the Air Force and commander of strategic bombing forces in World War II; Washington, D.C., July 14.

Stone, Harvey, 61; nightclub comedian; at sea, Mar. 4.

Stouffer, Vernon B., 72; president of restaurant chain; owner of Cleveland Indians; Lakewood, Ohio, July 26.

Strauss, Lewis L., 77; chairman of Atomic Energy Commission, 1950-1958; Brandy Station, Va., Jan. 21.

Sullivan, Ed, 73; hosted long-running TV variety show; Broadway columnist; New York, Oct. 13.

Susann, Jacqueline, 53; novelist wrote "Valley of the Dolls," world's best selling novel; New York, Sept. 21.

Sutherland, Dr. Earl W. Jr., 58; biologist, won 1971 Nobel prize for research on hormones; Miami, Mar. 9.

Sutton, Frank, 51; actor, played Sgt. Carter in "Gomer Pyle" TV series; Shreveport, La., June 28.

Swinnerton, James, 98; pioneer newspaper cartoonist, "Little Jimmy," "The Canyon Kiddies"; Palm Springs, Cal., Sept. 5.

T

Talmadge, Constance, 73; actress in silent films; Los Angeles, Nov. 23.

Teague, Charles M., 64; Congressman from Cal., was serving 10th term; Santa Paula, Cal., Jan. 1.

Tikhonravov, Mikhail, 73; Soviet pioneer in rocketry and space; USSR, Mar. 4.

Topping, Dan, 61; former Yankee baseball co-owner whose teams won 10 championships; Miami, May 18.

Tourel, Jennie, 63; opera and concert mezzo-soprano; New York, Nov. 23.

Troisgros, Jean-Baptiste, 77; renowned French restaurateur; France, Oct. 23.

V

Vanderbilt, Jr., Cornelius, 76; author and newspaperman; Miami Beach, July 7.

Virtanen, Prof. Artturi, 78; Finnish chemist won Nobel prize in 1945; Helsinki, Nov. 11.

Volkov, Leon, 59; Soviet affairs specialist for Newsweek magazine for 20 years; Bethesda, Md., Jan. 2.

W

Wahl, Jean, 88; existentialist philosopher and poet; Paris, June 19.

Warren, Earl, 83; Chief Justice of the Supreme Court for 16 years; known for liberal decisions in social issues; Washington, D.C., July 9.

Watson-Watt, Sir Robert, 81; developed world's first practical radar system which helped repulse Germany in the Battle of Britain; Inverness, Scotland, Dec. 5.

Watts, Alan, 58; philosopher whose writings influenced the "beat" and "hippie" generations and helped popularize Zen Buddhism; Mill Valley, Cal., Nov. 16.

Weaver, Charlie, see *Arquette, Cliff.*

Webb, Del, 75; former part owner of the N. Y. Yankees; Rochester, Minn., July 4.

Weiu, Billy, 41; former pro bowler was a member of ABC-TV sports staff; Houston, May 16.

Wheeler, Sir Charles, 82; British sculptor; Sussex, Eng., Aug. 23.

Whittaker, Charles Evans, 72; Supreme Court Justice, 1957-62; Kansas City, Nov. 26.

Wilder, Robert, 73; author of many popular novels, "Written on the Wind"; La Jolla, Cal., Aug. 22.

Wolfson, Harry, 86; philosopher and leading scholar on comparative religion; Cambridge, Mass., Sept. 19.

Y

Yarnell, Bruce, 35; singer and actor; Los Angeles, Nov. 30.

Yonkman, Dr. Frederick, 72; developer of one of the first tranquilizers; New Brunswick, Canada, Sept. 16.

Yurka, Blanche, 86; actress for over 50 years; New York, June 6.

Z

Zhukov, Marshall Georgi, 77; Russian military leader in World War II; led Red Army into Berlin; USSR, June 18.

Zwicky, Dr. Fritz, 74; astronomer and inventor; leading expert on jet propulsion; Pasadena, Cal., Feb. 8.

PERSONAL FINANCE
The Bite of Inflation

Jerome Shuchter, Editor, Jeremiad
Box 36496, Los Angeles, CA 90036

Most of us engage, each week or so, in the dull business of dividing our paychecks among many claimants — landlord or mortgagor, food market, department store, car payments, and a dozen more. Having traded hard labor for dollars, we now cheerlessly trade the dollars for the means of living. We do so week after week, until the process is ingrained, such a commonplace that we shove it into the background, the merest means to an end.

With inflation rampant, all that changes. When prices rise by as much as 1% each month, money transactions come roaring up front as a pressing central problem. The clutch of dollars loses its innocence; it no longer figures as a smooth way to transact personal business. In normal times life style adjusts slowly and methodically to moderate income shifts and to modest changes in the prices of goods and services; now the needed changes may appear suddenly, demanding immediate attention. In place of an easygoing attitude toward money, many find both income and outgo suddenly flaring into financial emergency — fires to put out — adjustments to be made. In such an environment, some elementary concepts may be clarifying.

The Arithmetic of Inflation

Wherever you find a dollar, there inflation attacks. It undermines the flow of income, the wage or salary, pension or welfare check. It goes on to attack accumulations of wealth in the various forms taken by savings. How can an individual take the measure of his own income and savings as inflation takes its toll?

To measure the impact of inflation, the indispensable tool is the Consumer Price Index (CPI) published monthly by the Bureau of Labor Statistics. The index

Average Consumer Price Indexes

Source: Bureau of Labor Statistics, United States Department of Labor

The Consumer Price Index measures the average change in prices of goods and services purchased by urban wage-earner and clerical-worker families and single workers living alone. Data for 56 large, medium size, and small cities are combined for the all-city average.
(1967 — 100)

Year and month	All items	Food	Housing Total	Rent	Gas and electricity	Fuel and utilities	Household furnishings & operation	Apparel and upkeep	Transportation	Medical care	Personal care	Reading and recreation	Other goods and services
1965	94.5	94.4	94.9	96.9	99.4	98.3	95.3	93.7	95.9	89.5	95.2	95.9	94.2
1970	116.3	114.9	118.9	110.1	107.3	107.6	113.4	116.1	112.7	120.6	113.2	113.4	116.0
1971	121.3	118.4	124.3	115.2	114.7	115.1	118.1	119.8	118.6	128.4	116.8	119.3	120.9
1972	125.3	123.5	129.2	119.2	120.5	120.1	121.0	122.3	119.9	132.5	119.8	122.8	125.5
1973 (All)	133.1	141.4	135.0	124.2	126.4	126.9	124.9	126.8	123.8	137.7	125.2	125.9	129.0
1974 Jan.	139.7	153.7	142.2	127.3	134.3	140.8	129.0	128.8	128.1	142.2	129.8	128.3	131.8
Feb.	141.5	157.6	143.4	128.0	137.3	143.5	130.1	130.4	129.3	143.4	130.8	128.9	132.3
Mar.	143.1	159.1	144.9	128.4	140.0	144.9	132.6	132.2	132.0	144.8	131.8	129.5	132.8
Apr.	144.0	158.6	146.0	128.8	141.9	146.9	134.0	133.6	134.4	145.6	131.1	130.4	133.6
May	145.6	159.7	147.6	129.3	143.9	148.6	137.0	135.0	137.6	147.2	134.9	130.2	134.4
June	147.1	160.3	149.2	129.8	144.5	149.4	139.2	135.7	140.7	149.4	136.5	133.5	135.8
July	148.3	160.5	150.9	130.3	146.2	150.9	141.4	135.3	142.6	151.4	137.8	134.6	137.7

Indexes of Retail Prices of Foods

Source: Bureau of Labor Statistics, United States Department of Labor (1967=100)

Year and Month	All Food	Food Away From Home	Food Prepared at Home — Food at Home	Cereals, Bakery	Beef, Veal	Pork	Other Meats	Poultry	Fish	Dairy Products	Fruits, Vegetables	Other Foods	Nonalcoholic Beverages
1968	103.6		103.2	100.4						103.3	107.9	102.6	
1969	108.9		108.2	103.3						106.7	109.3	107.9	
1970	114.9		113.7	108.9						111.8	113.4	114.1	
1971	118.4	126.1	116.4	113.9	124.9	105.0	115.6	109.0	130.2	115.3	119.1	115.9	121.6
1972	123.5	131.1	121.6	114.7	136.6	121.6	124.0	110.4	141.9	117.1	125.0	116.7	121.3
1973	141.4	141.4	141.4	127.7	161.1	161.7	154.4	154.8	162.8	127.9	142.5	130.3	130.2
1974 Jan.	153.7	151.6	154.3	149.7	169.9	173.5	168.1	157.0	180.4	146.3	149.7	143.9	137.3
Feb.	157.6	152.6	159.0	154.4	176.3	174.0	168.8	154.7	182.6	149.3	155.9	148.0	139.1
Mar.	159.1	153.7	160.6	158.6	173.1	169.0	167.6	152.0	185.2	151.5	162.5	150.2	142.0
Apr.	158.6	155.6	159.4	161.4	164.8	158.2	162.8	147.0	186.9	153.7	163.0	151.8	145.7
May	159.7	157.1	160.4	164.3	158.7	148.8	157.1	138.7	187.1	154.6	177.7	151.2	149.3
June	160.3	158.6	160.9	165.3	154.8	141.2	154.1	135.8	187.1	153.8	183.1	154.4	153.8
July	160.5	160.4	160.6	166.7	154.0	145.9	150.2	136.2	188.2	151.6	178.7	158.4	158.1

has been specifically designed to apply to a worker family's pattern of purchases. Unless your own budget is markedly different from this norm, you should be able to employ the CPI to interpret your own affairs. The index is reported each month by most of the news media, often specifically for your own city, and what follows tells, step by step, how to employ the figures to analyze your own financial affairs.

The CPI emerges each month as a single number. In June 1974 it stood at 147.1, meaning that all the goods and services it measured cost 47.1% more that month than they did in the base year 1967. It can be considered this way: the 1967 value was 100.0%; by June 1974 another 47.1% had been added to living costs. The total comes to 147.1, the term "index" having the same sense as percent, merely omitting the percent sign.

Using the CPI

Thousands of detailed price readings enter into the calculation of the price index, and these are combined into sub-groups, such as food, clothing, shelter, and so on. CPI data are available separately also for many of the principal cities of the U.S. It may seem to be a great oversimplification to evaluate your personal earnings in terms of the entire nation's price index. Users have found that there is considerable uniformity in the way inflation takes shape everywhere. Unions, for example, normally employ the national CPI as the basis for their multi-city contracts or a local CPI when a contract affects a single city for which an index is available. It is possible to apply the CPI in this way to your own needs, but we will consider only the use of the national CPI for all goods and services.

The change in the price level for consumer goods and services can be calculated by comparing the CPI readings in one period against another. The June 1974 CPI of 147.1 may be compared to the June reading for 1973 of 132.4. Dividing 147.1 by 132.4, the excess over 1 is the percentage increase over the 12-month period; in this case, 11.1%. A similar year-to-year comparison may be made each month — indeed, these percentage changes often figure in the news releases when the month's CPI is announced. In the next sections we show how to evaluate your earnings by comparison to the CPI.

Income flow

Most forms of income have shown some increase as price inflation proceeded, but in recent years white collar and blue collar wages and salaries have not kept pace with prices. The common result has been that even with higher paychecks working people could not buy the goods and services they bought before. The worker's standard of living fell. Or, if he or she persisted in buying about the same mix of goods and services as before, that required going into debt or reducing savings.

The inflationary processes take place invisibly and may appear insidious and complex. To come to grips with them, we need to measure the actual dimensions of the change. We determined above that the CPI increased by 11.1% between June 1973 and June 1974. Did your income do the same? To make the comparison you might dig out your paycheck stubs for the same months and follow the arithmetic below.

The comparison can be made in terms of your base pay — your basic rate of earnings — or in terms of what you actually take home after standard deductions. Both gross and takehome comparisons are likely to be of interest to you, but take care to compare

Indexes By Cities, All Items and Food (1967 = 100)

| City | Annual Average | | | | City | Annual Average | | | |
| | All Items | | Food | | | All Items | | Food | |
	1972	1973	1972	1973		1972	1973	1972	1973
U.S. City Average	125.3	133.1	123.5	141.4	Los Angeles, Ca if.	122.3	129.2	120.4	136.5
Atlanta, Ga.	125.5	133.7	124.4	144.0	Milwaukee, Wis.	123.7	131.5	120.6	138.4
Baltimore, Md.	126.3	134.9	124.7	143.8	Minneapolis, Minn.	125.5	133.0	124.4	142.0
Boston, Mass.	127.1	134.7	123.7	140.1	New York, N.Y.	131.4	139.7	128.6	145.4
Buffalo, N.Y.	126.6	134.8	123.5	141.0	Philadelphia, Pa.	127.0	135.5	124.4	142.7
Chicago, Ill.	124.3	132.0	123.9	142.7	Pittsburgh, Pa.	125.3	132.9	122.8	141.7
Cincinnati, Ohio	124.7	132.1	124.5	142.9	Portland, Ore.	119.5	127.3	118.0	133.7
Cleveland, Ohio	126.5	134.1	123.3	142.1	St. Louis, Mo.	122.3	129.3	122.5	140.2
Dallas, Texas.	124.9	132.0	123.0	140.1	San Diego, Calif.	124.4	132.5	123.3	139.6
Detroit, Mich.	126.2	134.5	122.9	143.6	San Francisco, Calif.	124.3	131.5	121.4	138.0
Honolulu, Hawaii.	122.8	128.3	123.2	135.2	Scranton, Pa.	125.9	134.7	123.4	141.9
Houston, Tex.	125.2	132.3	125.0	143.3	Seattle, Wash.	119.7	127.5	120.7	136.3
Kansas City, Mo.	124.0	130.3	123.6	141.4	Washington, D. C.	126.9	135.0	125.8	145.5

Latest Month, 1974[1]

City	All Items (Month)	Food (July)	City	All Items (Month)	Food (July)
U. S. City Average	148.3 (7)	160.5	Los Angeles, Calif.	143.3 (7)	155.5
Atlanta, Ga.	147.5 (6)	162.7	Milwaukee, Wis.	142.1 (5)	154.8
Baltimore, Md.	151.7 (6)	163.1	Minneapolis, Minn.	149.0 (7)	162.9
Boston, Mass.	149.9 (7)	161.6	New York, N.Y.	154.6 (7)	165.0
Buffalo, N.Y.	147.7 (5)	159.9	Philadelphia, Pa.	152.1 (7)	164.5
Chicago, Ill.	146.5 (7)	160.4	Pittsburgh, Pa.	148.6 (7)	162.9
Cincinnati, Ohio	146.1 (6)	163.2	Portland, Ore.	143.7 (7)	154.8
Cleveland, Ohio	146.2 (5)	159.2	St. Louis, Mo.	141.1 (6)	157.6
Dallas, Texas.	143.3 (5)	155.7	San Diego, Calif.	145.3 (5)	159.2
Detroit, Mich.	149.8 (7)	162.6	San Francisco, Calif.	144.4 (6)	154.8
Honolulu, Hawaii.	141.4 (6)	156.9	Scranton, Pa.	148.1 (5)	159.3[2]
Houston, Tex.	148.2 (7)	162.7	Seattle, Wash.	139.5 (5)	155.3
Kansas City, Mo.	143.6 (6)	160.7	Washington, D.C.	147.7 (5)	164.4

[1]All items indexes are computed monthly in 5 areas and on a rotating cycle in other areas: (7)=July, (6)=June, (5)=May.
[2]In May.

Purchasing Power of the Dollar

Source: U.S. Department of Labor, Bureau of Labor Statistics

1967=$1.00

Beginning 1961, wholesale prices include data for Alaska and Hawaii; and, beginning 1964 consumer prices include them. Obtained by dividing the average price index for 1967 base period (100.0) by the price index for given period and expressing the result in dollars and cents.

Year	Monthly average as measured by— Wholesale prices	Con- sumer prices	Year	Monthly average as measured by— Wholesale prices	Con- sumer prices
1940	$2.469	$2.381	1964	$1.056	$1.076
1950	1.222	1.387	1965	1.035	1.058
1955	1.139	1.247	1966	1.002	1.029
1956	1.103	1.229	1967	1.000	1.000
1957	1.072	1.186	1968	.976	.960
1958	1.057	1.155	1969	.939	.911
1959	1.055	1.145	1970	.906	.860
1960	1.054	1.127	1971	.878	.824
1961	1.058	1.116	1972	.840	.799
1962	1.055	1.104	1973	.744	.752
1963	1.058	1.091	1974, July	.618	.674

equals. Overtime pay should be omitted. When dealing with takehome pay, look out for changes in deductions which are unrelated to inflation, such as added exemptions, credit union deductions, payroll bonds, and the like.

Measuring Your Paycheck

A. To compare the year-to-year earnings in percent form, divide your June 1974 earnings by your June 1973 earnings and express the result as a percent. If you earned the wage of the average U.S. worker, for example, your paycheck showed $154.66 per week in June 1974 as compared with $144.74 in June 1973, an increase of 6.9%. Since prices rose by 11.1% during the same 12-month period, the average worker's pay fell 4.2% short of keeping pace with inflation.

B. Another way of dealing with the same figures takes a dollar form. For this calculation, assume your wage in June 1973 was $144.74 per week. Prices increased by 11.1% in the following 12 months, according to the CPI. To match that pace, your wage should have gone to $160.81 ($144.74 times .111) by June 1974. However, if your earnings ran only $154.66, as did the average worker's, you lost $6.15 per week to inflation.

Single readings on a weekly or monthly basis could be misleading; the inflation rate changes rapidly, earnings are affected by special situations unrelated to inflation. Repeated readings over a period of months provide a broader look. For this purpose you may consider an entire year as the appropriate period for measuring the total impact of inflation on your earnings.

The CPI provides us with an index of 125.3 for the year 1972 as a whole and 133.1 for 1973. Dividing 133.1 by 125.3, we get 1.062; the excess over 1 shows price increases of 6.2% over the year. If you compare your earnings for the same years by the methods we have described, your shortfall due to inflation can be ascertained in percent or dollar form. You can readily determine your annual earnings on your income tax return or from your W-2 statements. At the time of writing it appears that 1974 prices will wind up 10.7% ahead of 1973, taking the year as a whole, and an early estimate of your earnings status for 1974 can be made on that basis.

The figures cited above measure an individual's progress as compared with the rate of inflation, as if matching the rate were the sole target. Nothing is said about your personal capacity for advancement or of the commonly accepted view that earnings should grow on the order of 3% a year to take account

ormal growth in productivity. In that sense, figuring your loss to inflation is only the first step of the reckoning, a way to true up your income figures so you can check your real progress and advancement.

Savings

Less visible to the average individual than the loss on earnings is the attrition inflation brings to his savings. Narrowly considered, savings are the funds salted away in some savings institution. Although such funds earn interest, it is clear that during double-digit inflation of 10% to 12%, interest rates of 5% to 8% cause a real loss in the value of the savings. It is a glaring injustice of public policy that government regulations place an artificial barrier on the rate of interest paid to the public, while far higher interest earnings are available to the wealthy and to business firms. It lends credence to the view that inflation is hardly neutral, its specific function to dry up the worker's income and savings.

The apparent loss in the value of savings — the amount of goods and services the funds will ultimately buy — should be considered in terms of a broadened view of savings. In addition to funds placed at interest, savings would include the paid-up value of a home or insurance policy and the value of savings bonds. In each case the loss to inflation can be measured by calculating the shrinkage due to the rise of the CPI. If you had $10,000 in all forms of savings in June 1973, the buying power of such funds will decline by 11.1% by June 1974 due to inflation — that is, by $1,110, to $8,890, in terms of 1973 dollars. Meanwhile you may have collected some $500 in interest, which would reduce your loss to $610. In addition you will have lost even a nominal real return on your savings.

Debt is the opposite side of savings, and debtors have been favored by inflation. If you have old debts, a mortgage for example, particularly one with pre-inflationary interest rates, you will be repaying it now with cheaper dollars. For illustration, suppose you owed $1,000 in June 1973 and made no payments against the debt all year. The debt would still run $1,000, but by June 1974 you would be repaying with shrunken dollars, each worth about 90 cents. Despite the gain to debtors, true interest rates on debts are so often far in excess of the rate of inflation that debt is hardly an escape hatch from inflation's ravages.

To sum up, inflation will have a damaging effect on your wealth, your dollar savings, which can be measured by use of the CPI. The total loss you experience in dollar terms will be offset by the interest you collect and by possible gains from the reduced pain of old debts. Taken in conjunction with losses in the flow of income, such losses fill out the total picture of the inroads inflation makes on your financial well-being.

The Escalator

Dr. Julius Shiskin, Commissioner of the Bureau of Labor Statistics, has "estimated' that 5.1 million workers are covered by collective bargaining contracts which provide for increases in wage rates when the CPI rises." The number is growing and, in addition, millions of others on Social Security or in retirement have their income tied to the CPI, some 44 million affected in all. Such is the degree of escalation today.

Union contracts ordinarily include a general negotiated wage increase, and then may go on to provide for further wage adjustment to track inflation. The central idea of the cost of living escalator is to protect the negotiated wage.

Two general forms of escalation are in common use. One, the percent form, simply matches the percent increase in the CPI by a corresponding percent adjustment in the base wage; the other employs a point formula ("a cost of living adjustment equal to 1ᶜ per hour for each full .4 of a point change in the CPI", reads one such contract). The two approaches can be made roughly equivalent, but the point formula might conceivably be outrun by events.

Escalator clauses rarely provide full protection to workers against inflation simply because time elapses between the price rise itself, the time it takes for the Bureau of Labor Statistics to measure and publish the fact, and the time it takes to install the revised wage rates. In one study of such lags, Jack Frye of the Labor Bureau of Middle West checked a bus driver contract over a 2-year period. He found the total loss to inflation had amounted to $648, of which only $440 was recovered through escalation, leaving a loss to each driver of $208. Such losses often figure in the next wage negotiation.

A New Idea—Indexation

The escalator concept figured in the news in 1974 when the well-known conservative economist Milton Friedman, of the University of Chicago, espoused the policy of near-universal escalation — his term for it was "indexation." In addition to wages a wide variety of incomes, including taxes, rents, bank and mortgage interest rates, would be tied into the CPI and varied according to the degree of inflation. Professor Friedman's view was that since none would then gain or lose by virtue of inflation, the government would be freed to take the most restrictive measures against inflation to subdue it, measures which might otherwise be politically impossible.

Average Weekly Earnings of Production Workers[1]
Source: Bureau of Labor Statistics

	Private nonagricultural workers				Manufacturing workers			
	Spendable average weekly earnings[2]				Spendable average weekly earnings[2]			
	Workers with no dependents		Worker with 3 dependents		Worker with no dependents		Workers with 3 dependents	
	Current dollars	1967 dollars	Current dollars	1967 dollars	Current dollars	1967 dollars	Current dollars	1967 dollars
1965.............	78.99	83.59	86.30	91.32	89.08	94.26	96.78	102.41
1969.............	90.96	82.84	99.99	91.07	101.90	92.81	111.14	101.49
1970.............	95.94	92.49	104.61	89.95	106.62	91.68	115.90	99.66
1971.............	103.51	85.33	112.12	92.43	114.68	94.54	123.93	102.17
1972.............	111.37	88.88	120.79	96.40	125.32	100.02	135.56	108.19
1973..............	116.73	87.70	126.55	95.08	132.00	99.17	142.90	107.36
1974 January	118.20	84.61	128.10	91.70	134.00	95.92	145.01	103.80
February	119.32	84.33	129.28	91.36	134.30	94.91	145.34	102.71
March	119.86	83.76	129.85	90.74	135.82	94.91	146.94	102.68
April	119.23	82.80	129.19	89.72	132.38	91.93	143.29	99.51
May	122.00	83.79	132.11	90.73	138.49	95.12	149.77	102.89
June (p)	124.29	84.49	134.53	91.45	140.30	95.38	151.68	103.11
July (p)	125.44	84.59	135.79	91.56	139.92	94.35	151.28	102.01

[1]Data relate to production workers in mining and manufacturing; to construction workers in contract construction; and to non-supervisory workers in transportation and public utilities; wholesale and retail trade; finance, insurance, and real estate; and services.
[2]Spendable average weekly earnings are based on gross average weekly earnings less the estimated amount of the worker's Federal social security and income taxes. (p)—preliminary.

Net Public and Private Debt
Source: Office of Economic Analysis, U.S. Dept. of Commerce (In billions of dollars)

| End of year | Public and private total | Public | | | Total private | Corporate | Private Individual and noncorporate | | | | | |
| | | Total public | Federal[1] | State and Local | | | Farm | | Nonfarm Mortgage | | Other nonfarm | |
							Production	Mortgage	1-4 family residential	Multifamily residential & commercial	Commercial	Financial	Consumer
1965...	1,243.0	373.7	266.4	98.3	870.0	454.3	18.1	21.2	208.7	28.1	27.0	22.7	89.9
1970...	1,868.9	484.9	301.1	145.0	1,384.0	797.7	27.5	31.2	278.9	53.2	35.0	33.3	127.2
1971...	2,045.8	528.2	325.9	162.4	1,517.6	869.3	30.3	32.9	305.2	68.2	37.2	36.2	138.4
1972...	2,270.2	557.6	341.2	175.0	1,712.7	978.3	32.4	35.4	339.8	86.2	40.5	42.4	157.6
1973...	2,525.8	593.4	349.1	184.5	1,932.4	1,111.1	37.7	39.6	374.6	105.5	43.0	40.4	180.5

(1.) Net Federal Government debt is the outstanding debt held by the public, as defined in the Budget of the U.S. Govt., Fiscal Year 1974.

Federal Individual Income Tax
Source: Tax Foundation: Internal Revenue Service, Treasury Dept.

Who Must File

Every individual under 65 years of age who resided in the United States and had a gross income of $2,050 or more during the year must file a Federal income tax return. Anyone 65 or older on the last day of the tax year is not required to file a return unless he had gross income of $2,800 or more during the year. A married couple both 65 or older, need not file unless their gross income exceeds $4,300.

A taxpayer with gross income of less than $2,050 (or less than $2,800 if 65 or older) should file a return to claim the refund of any taxes withheld, even if he is listed as a dependent by another taxpayer.

Forms to Use

A taxpayer may, at his election, file Form 1040 and let IRS compute his tax if his income is $20,000 or less and consists only of wages or salaries and tips, dividends, interest, pensions and annuities and he chooses the standard deductions.

However, a taxpayer may generally use short Form 1040A if all his income is from wages, tips, and interest income and he is taking the standard deduction.

Deductions

A taxpayer may either itemize deductions or choose one of the two types of standard deduction — the percentage standard deduction or the low-income allowance. For taxpayers with adjusted gross income of $10,000 or more, the percentage standard deduction is 15% of adjusted gross income up to a maximum of $2,000 ($1,000 for married persons filing separate returns). The low-income allowance of up to $1,300 is built into the tax tables; it is available only with adjusted gross incomes below $10,000.

Dates For Filing Returns

For individuals using the calendar year, Apr. 15 is final date (unless it falls on a Saturday, Sunday or a legal holiday) for filing income tax returns and for payment of any tax due, and the first quarterly installment of the estimated tax. Other installments of estimated tax to be paid June 15, Sept. 15 and Jan. 15.

Apr. 15 is final date for filing declaration of estimated tax. Amended declarations may be filed June 15, Sept. 15, and Jan. 15.

Instead of paying the 4th installment a final income return may be filed Jan. 31. Farmers may file a final return Mar. 1 to satisfy estimated tax requirements.

Joint Return

A husband and wife may make a return jointly, even if one has no income personally. Their tax will be twice the tax imposed if the income were cut in half and taxed at the married filing separate rate.

One provision stipulates that if one spouse dies, the survivor may compute his tax using joint return rates for the first two taxable years following, provided he or she also was entitled to file a joint return the year of the death, and furnishes over half the cost of maintaining in his household a home for a dependent child or stepchild. If the taxpayer remarries before the end of the taxable year these privileges are lost but he is permitted to file a joint return with his new spouse. An individual legally separated or divorced is not considered married.

Estimated Tax

If total tax exceeds withheld tax by at least $100, declarations of estimated tax are required from (1) single individuals, heads of a household or surviving spouses, or a married person entitled to file a joint return whose spouse does not receive wages, who expects a gross income over $20,000; (2) married individuals with over $10,000 where both spouses receive wages; (3) married individuals with over $5,000 not entitled to file a joint return; and (4) individuals whose gross income can reasonably be expected to include more than $500 from sources other than wages subject to withholdings.

Exemptions

Personal exemption is $750.

Every individual has an exemption of $750, to be deducted from gross income. A husband and a wife are each entitled to a $750 exemption. A taxpayer 65 or over on the last day of the year gets another exemption of $750. A person blind on the last day of the year gets another exemption of $750.

Exemption for dependents, over one-half of whose total support comes from the taxpayer and for whom the other dependency tests have been met, is $750. This applies to a child, stepchild or adopted child as well as certain other relatives with less than $750 gross income; also to a child, stepchild, or adopted child of the taxpayer who is under 19 at the end of the year or was a full-time student during 5 months of the year even if he makes $750 or more. A dependent can be a non-relative if a member of the taxpayer's household and living there all year.

Taxpayer gets the exemption for his child who is a student regardless of the student's age or earnings, provided the taxpayer provides over half of the student's total support. If the student gets a scholarship, this is not counted as support.

Child and Disabled Dependent Care

Taxpayers with adjusted gross income of $18,000 or less may be able to deduct up to $400 per month for household and dependent care expenses.

To qualify, a taxpayer must be employed and provide over one-half the cost of maintaining a household for a dependent child under 15, a disabled dependent of any age, or a disabled spouse.

Household expenses incurred to permit a taxpayer to be gainfully employed may be deducted. Expenses incurred outside the home for the care of a child under 15 also qualify but the deduction for these expenses is limited to $200 per month for one child, $300 for two children and $400 for three or more.

Life Insurance

Life insurance paid to survivors is not taxed as income. Interest on life insurance left with the insurance company and paid to survivors at intervals is taxable when available. Surviving spouse has an exclusion of the prorata amount of principal payable at death plus up to $1,000 per year of interest earned when life insurance proceeds are payable in installments.

Regular payments under the Railroad Retirement Act, and those received as social security, are exempt.

Dividends

The first $100 in dividends can be excluded from income. If husband and wife both receive $100 on their joint return they can exclude $200.

The exclusion does not apply to dividends from tax-exempt corporations, mutual savings banks, building and loan associations and several others.

Dividends paid in stock or in stock rights are generally exempt from tax, except when paid in place of preferred stock dividends of the current or preceding year, or when the stockholder has an option to take stock or property or when the stock distribution is disproportionate.

Deductible Medical Expenses

Expenses for medical care, not compensated for by insurance or other payment for taxpayer, spouse, and dependents, in excess of 3% of adjusted gross income are deductible. This rule also applies to taxpayers 65 or over and dependent parents 65 or over. Previously these persons were not subject to the percentage limitations. There is no limit to the maximum amount of medical expense that can be deducted.

Medical care includes diagnosis, treatment and prevention of disease or for the purpose of affecting any structure or function of the body, and amounts paid for insurance to reimburse for hospitalization, surgical fees and other medical expenses.

Only medicine and drugs in excess of 1% of adjusted gross income may be included in medical expenses.

One-half the cost of medical care insurance premiums up to $150 can be deducted without regard to the 3% limitation. The other half plus any excess over $150 is included with other medical expenses subject to the 3% limit.

Medical expenses for a decedent paid by his estate within one year after his death may be treated as expenses of the decedent taxpayer.

Medical and hospital benefits provided by the employer may be exempt from individual income tax. Wages paid as "sick pay" are exempt up to $100 a week after a certain waiting period.

Deductions For Contributions

Deductions up to 50% of taxpayers' adjusted gross income may be taken for contribution to most publicly supported charitable organizations, including churches or associations of churches, tax-exempt educational institutions, tax-exempt hospitals, and medical research organizations associated with a hospital, and nonprofit cemeteries. The deduction is generally limited to 20% for such organizations as private foundations.

Taxpayers also are permitted to carry over for five years certain contributions, generally to publicly supported organizations, which exceed the 50% allowable deduction the year the contribution was made.

Also permissible is the deduction as a charitable contribution of unreimbursed amounts up to $50 a month spent to maintain an elementary or high school student, other than a dependent or relative, in taxpayer's home.

Deductions for Interest Paid

Interest paid by the taxpayer is deductible.

If personal property is bought under a contract

1973 Income Tax Rate Schedules*

(A.) Married Individuals Filing Joint Returns and Certain Surviving Spouses.

If taxable income is: | | | The tax is:
Not over $1,000 . . . . 14% of the taxable income.

Over	But not over			Of excess over
$1,000—	$2,000	. . . . . . $140,	plus 15%	$1,000
$2,000—	$3,000	. . . . . . $290,	plus 16%	$2,000
$3,000—	$4,000	. . . . . . $450,	plus 17%	$3,000
$4,000—	$8,000	. . . . . . $620,	plus 19%	$4,000
$8,000—	$12,000	. . $1,380,	plus 22%	$8,000
$12,000—	$16,000	. . $2,260,	plus 25%	$12,000
$16,000—	$20,000	. . $3,260,	plus 28%	$16,000
$20,000—	$24,000	. . $4,380,	plus 32%	$20,000
$24,000—	$28,000	. . $5,660,	plus 36%	$24,000
$28,000—	$32,000	. . $7,100,	plus 39%	$28,000
$32,000—	$36,000	. . $8,660,	plus 42%	$32,000
$36,000—	$40,000	. . $10,340,	plus 45%	$36,000
$40,000—	$44,000	. . $12,140,	plus 48%	$40,000
$44,000—	$52,000	. . $14,060,	plus 50%	$44,000
$52,000—	$64,000	. . $18,060,	plus 53%	$52,000
$64,000—	$76,000	. . $24,420,	plus 55%	$64,000
$76,000—	$88,000	. . $31,020,	plus 58%	$76,000
$88,000—	$100,000	. . $37,980,	plus 60%	$88,000
$100,000—	$120,000	. . $45,180,	plus 62%	$100,000
$120,000—	$140,000	. . $57,580,	plus 64%	$120,000
$140,000—	$160,000	. . $70,380,	plus 66%	$140,000
$160,000—	$180,000	. . $83,580,	plus 68%	$160,000
$180,000—	$200,000	. . $97,180,	plus 69%	$180,000
$200,000—	. . . .	. . $10,980,	plus 70%	$200,000

(B.) Certain Heads of Households

Not over $1,000 . . . . 14% of the taxable income.

Over	But not over			Of excess over
$1,000—	$2,000	. . . . . . $140,	plus 16%	$1,000
$2,000—	$4,000	. . . . . . $300,	plus 18%	$2,000
$4,000—	$6,000	. . . . . . $660,	plus 19%	$4,000
$6,000—	$8,000	. . $1,040,	plus 22%	$6,000
$8,000—	$10,000	. . $1,480,	plus 23%	$8,000
$10,000—	$12,000	. . $1,940,	plus 25%	$10,000
$12,000—	$14,000	. . $2,440,	plus 27%	$12,000
$14,000—	$16,000	. . $2,980,	plus 28%	$14,000
$16,000—	$18,000	. . $3,540,	plus 31%	$16,000
$18,000—	$20,000	. . $4,160,	plus 32%	$18,000
$20,000—	$22,000	. . $4,800,	plus 35%	$20,000
$22,000—	$24,000	. . $5,500,	plus 36%	$22,000
$24,000—	$26,000	. . $6,220,	plus 38%	$24,000
$26,000—	$28,000	. . $6,980,	plus 41%	$26,000
$28,000—	$32,000	. . $7,800,	plus 42%	$28,000
$32,000—	$36,000	. . $9,480,	plus 45%	$32,000
$36,000—	$38,000	. . $11,280,	plus 48%	$36,000
$38,000—	$40,000	. . $12,240,	plus 51%	$38,000
$40,000—	$44,000	. . $13,260,	plus 52%	$40,000
$44,000—	$50,000	. . $15,340,	plus 55%	$44,000
$50,000—	$52,000	. . $18,640,	plus 56%	$50,000
$52,000—	$64,000	. . $19,760,	plus 58%	$52,000
$64,000—	$70,000	. . $26,720,	plus 59%	$64,000
$70,000—	$76,000	. . $30,260,	plus 61%	$70,000
$76,000—	$80,000	. . $33,920,	plus 62%	$76,000
$80,000—	$88,000	. . $36,400,	plus 63%	$80,000
$88,000—	$100,000	. . $41,440,	plus 64%	$88,000
$100,000—	$120,000	. . $49,120,	plus 66% . . .	$100,000
$120,000—	$140,000	. . $62,320,	plus 67% . . .	$120,000

$140,000—	$160,000	. . $75,720,	plus 68% . . .	$140,000
$160,000—	$180,000	. . $89,320,	plus 69% . . .	$160,000
$180,000—		. . $103,120,	plus 70% . . .	$180,000

(C.) Married Individuals Filing Separate Returns

If Taxable income is: | | | The tax is:
Not over $500 . . . . 14% of the taxable income.

Over	But not over			Of excess over
$500—	$1,000	. . . . . . $70,	plus 15%	$500
$1,000—	$1,500	. . . . . . $145,	plus 16%	$1,000
$1,500—	$2,000	. . . . . . $225,	plus 17%	$1,500
$2,000—	$4,000	. . . . . . $310,	plus 19%	$2,000
$4,000—	$6,000	. . . . . . $690,	plus 22%	$4,000
$6,000—	$8,000	. . $1,130,	plus 25%	$6,000
$8,000—	$10,000	. . $1,630,	plus 28%	$8,000
$10,000—	$12,000	. . $2,190,	plus 32%	$10,000
$12,000—	$14,000	. . $2,830,	plus 36%	$12,000
$14,000—	$16,000	. . $3,550,	plus 39%	$14,000
$16,000—	$18,000	. . $4,330,	plus 42%	$16,000
$18,000—	$20,000	. . $5,170,	plus 45%	$18,000
$20,000—	$22,000	. . $6,070,	plus 48%	$20,000
$22,000—	$26,000	. . $7,030,	plus 50%	$22,000
$26,000—	$32,000	. . $9,030,	plus 53%	$26,000
$32,000—	$38,000	. . $12,210,	plus 55%	$32,000
$38,000—	$44,000	. . $15,510,	plus 58%	$38,000
$44,000—	$50,000	. . $18,990,	plus 60%	$44,000
$50,000—	$60,000	. . $22,590,	plus 62%	$50,000
$60,000—	$70,000	. . $28,790,	plus 64%	$60,000
$70,000—	$80,000	. . $35,190,	plus 66%	$70,000
$80,000—	$90,000	. . $41,790,	plus 68%	$80,000
$90,000—	$100,000	. . $48,590,	plus 69%	$90,000
$100,000—		. . $55,490,	plus 70%	$100,000

(D.) Unmarried Individuals (Other Than Certain Surviving Spouse and Heads of Households).

Not over $500 . . . . 14% of the taxable income.

Over	But not over			Of excess over
$500—	$1,000	. . . . . . $70,	plus 15%	$500
$1,000—	$1,500	. . . . . . $145,	plus 16%	$1,000
$1,500—	$2,000	. . . . . . $225,	plus 17%	$1,500
$2,000—	$4,000	. . . . . . $310,	plus 19%	$2,000
$4,000—	$6,000	. . . . . . $690,	plus 21%	$4,000
$6,000—	$8,000	. . $1,110,	plus 24%	$6,000
$8,000—	$10,000	. . $1,590,	plus 25%	$8,000
$10,000—	$12,000	. . $2,090,	plus 27%	$10,000
$12,000—	$14,000	. . $2,630,	plus 29%	$12,000
$14,000—	$16,000	. . $3,210,	plus 31%	$14,000
$16,000—	$18,000	. . $3,830,	plus 34%	$16,000
$18,000—	$20,000	. . $4,510,	plus 36%	$18,000
$20,000—	$22,000	. . $5,230,	plus 38%	$20,000
$22,000—	$26,000	. . $5,990,	plus 40%	$22,000
$26,000—	$32,000	. . $7,590,	plus 45%	$26,000
$32,000—	$38,000	. . $10,290,	plus 50%	$32,000
$38,000—	$44,000	. . $13,290,	plus 55%	$38,000
$44,000—	$50,000	. . $16,590,	plus 60%	$44,000
$50,000—	$60,000	. . $20,190,	plus 62%	$50,000
$60,000—	$70,000	. . $26,390,	plus 64%	$60,000
$70,000—	$80,000	. . $32,790,	plus 66%	$70,000
$80,000—	$90,000	. . $39,390,	plus 68%	$80,000
$90,000—	$100,000	. . $46,190,	plus 69%	$90,000
$100,000—		. . $53,090,	plus 70%	$100,000

*Under the tax reform act of 1969 the maximum rate of earned income is 50% for single taxpayers earning taxable income in excess of $50,000 and for married persons filing jointly with taxable income in excess of $100,000.

providing for payment by installments, and in which carrying charges are stated but interest is not ascertainable, then subject to limitation payments are held to include interest equal to 6% on average unpaid balance.

However, the amount charged to a customer's revolving charge account is solely for the privilege of deferring payment and is interest.

Prizes and Awards

All prizes and awards must be reported in gross income, except when received without action by the recipient. To be exempt, awards must be received primarily in recognition of religious, charitable, scientific, educational, artistic, literary, or civic achievement. (Nobel and Pulitzer prizes exempt.)

Deductions for Employees

An employee may take the standard deduction and deduct as well the following if in connection with his employment: transportation, except commuting; automobile expense, including gas, oil and depreciation; however, meals and lodging are deductible as traveling expense only if the employee is away from home overnight.

An outside salesman—a salesman who works fulltime outside the office, using the latter only for incidentals—may deduct both the standard deduction and all his business expenses.

An employee who is reimbursed and is required to account to his employer for his business expenses will not be required to report either the reimbursement or the expenses on his tax return. Any allowance to the employee in excess of his expenses must be included in gross income. If he claims a deduction for an excess of expenses over reimbursement he will have to report the reimbursement and claim actual expenses.

An employee who is not required to account to his employer must report on his return the total amounts of reimbursements and expenses for travel, transportation, entertainment, etc., that he incurs under a reimbursement arrangement with his employer.

The expense of moving to a new place of employment may be deducted under certain circumstances regardless of whether the taxpayer is a new or continuing employee, or whether he pays his own expenses or is reimbursed by his employer. Reimbursement must be reported as income.

Retirement Income Credit

A credit against the tax otherwise due, of 15% of retirement income up to $1,524 included in gross income, is allowed to persons 65 and over. Persons under 65 and retired under a public retirement system (firemen, policemen, teachers, federal employees) are allowed the same credit on income from pensions and annuities paid under the system, but not on dividends, interests and rent. Included in public systems are funds for members of the Armed Forces for 1955 and subsequent years. Any pension or annuity received under the Social Security Act or the Railroad Retirement Act reduces the $1,524. Compensation in excess of $900 received by an individual under 62 and compensation in excess of $1,200 for one over 62 but under 72 will reduce the $1,524 by varying amounts. No reduction if the individual is 72 or older.

Net Capital Losses

An individual taxpayer may deduct capital losses up to $1,000 against his ordinary income. However, it takes $2 of net long-term capital loss to get $1 of offset against other income. He may carry the rest over to subsequent years at the same rate, no legal limit on the number of years.

Income Averaging

Individuals with large fluctuations in their annual income may be able to take advantage of averaging provisions available to taxpayers whose income for a particular year exceeds 120% of their average income for the prior 4 years, if the excess is more than $3,000.

Individual Income Tax Returns (1972)

Source: Internal Revenue Service
(*Money amounts in thousands of dollars*)

Size of Adjusted Gross Incomes	All Returns	Number	Adjusted Gross Income*	Taxable Income*	Tax After Credit*	Average Tax
Total..........................	77,674,818	60,920,327	$717,743,764	$444,810,174	$93,366,531	$ 1,536
No adjusted gross income............	433,606	1,561	-155,366			
$1 under $1,000.............	5,703,532	16,335	15,084	1,294	176	16
$1,000 under $2,000.............	5,866,364	152,635	254,139	59,749	8,482	57
$2,000 under $3,000.............	4,987,094	3,035,565	7,663,808	1,422,448	202,676	67
$3,000 under $4,000.............	4,963,911	3,680,118	12,954,122	4,343,117	641,311	174
$4,000 under $5,000.............	5,057,835	4,333,940	19,481,474	8,079,648	1,251,517	289
$5,000 under $6,000.............	4,739,391	4,364,837	24,000,529	11,169,264	1,788,085	410
$6,000 under $7,000.............	4,252,284	4,049,177	26,331,556	13,318,914	2,171,867	536
$7,000 under $8,000.............	4,273,911	4,124,416	30,901,737	16,480,854	2,744,138	665
$8,000 under $9,000.............	4,038,289	3,966,965	33,684,601	18,618,431	3,148,952	794
$9,000 under $10,000.............	3,892,863	3,841,278	36,444,670	20,464,161	3,500,948	911
$10,000 under $11,000.............	3,644,984	3,619,997	37,996,352	22,123,624	3,834,706	1,059
$11,000 under $12,000.............	3,469,497	3,450,465	39,658,661	23,313,496	4,074,023	1,181
$12,000 under $13,000.............	3,111,318	3,095,123	38,668,028	23,173,465	4,092,751	1,322
$13,000 under $14,000.............	2,786,630	2,776,160	37,411,551	22,944,509	4,108,741	1,480
$14,000 under $15,000.............	2,377,919	2,369,596	34,311,213	21,520,419	3,911,246	1,651
$15,000 under $20,000.............	7,776,311	7,758,867	133,009,446	87,956,629	16,687,034	2,151
$20,000 under $25,000.............	3,098,369	3,092,215	68,415,527	48,029,594	9,836,522	3,182
$25,000 under $30,000.............	1,267,623	1,263,045	34,324,722	24,830,156	5,484,100	4,343
$30,000 under $50,000.............	1,335,813	1,332,645	49,361,514	36,591,683	9,400,770	7,061
$50,000 under $100,000.............	482,964	481,479	31,821,883	24,424,494	8,495,987	17,696
$100,000 under $200,000...........	91,423	91,120	11,907,457	9,197,333	4,090,559	45,268
$200,000 under $500,000...........	19,230	19,147	5,387,798	4,014,122	2,159,264	115,099
$500,000 under $1,000,000.........	2,646	2,634	1,768,178	1,279,383	780,830	306,037
$1,000,000 or more.................	1,011	1,007	2,125,080	1,453,387	951,846	995,930

Excise Taxes On Selected Items

Source: Tax Foundation (As of Sept. 1, 1974)

Gasoline, diesel fuel, benzol, naphtha, for vehicle propulsion are taxed at 4c a gallon scheduled through Sept. 30, 1977, and at 1.5c thereafter.

Liquor taxes:
Distilled spirits.................$10.50 per proof gallon
Still wines: Not over 14% alcohol.... 17c per wine gallon
Not over 21% alcohol... 67c per wine gallon
Not over 24% alcohol ...$2.25 per wine gallon

Beer and fermented liquors: (Beer, ale, porter, etc., containing 1% or more of alcohol) ....$9.00 per barrel
Tires and tubes (per lb.)............................10c
Tobacco-small cigarettes weighing less than 3 lbs. per thousand, $4.00 per thousand
Air travel tickets (domestic)........................8%
Telephone: Local and toll service 10%, to be reduced to 9% in 1973; and by 1% annually until rate reaches 1% in 1981.

Canada: Taxable Returns by Income
Source: Taxation Statistics

Total income $ 1972	Number	%	Total income (millions)	%	Taxed income (millions)	Federal Tax[1] (millions)	%
0–2,000	249,929	3.09	423.7	.67	45.1	8.8	.11
2,000–2,500	331,253	4.10	746.0	1.19	171.4	26.8	.35
2,500–3,000	378,217	4.68	1,041.6	1.66	324.7	52.1	.67
3,000–3,500	427,007	5.29	1,388.2	2.20	515.6	83.4	1.07
3,500–4,000	453,003	5.60	1,700.7	2.71	713.6	116.7	1.49
4,000–6,000	1,767,874	21.88	8,785.1	13.96	4,412.9	745.3	9.56
6,000–8,000	1,472,794	18.22	10,268.4	16.33	6,010.5	1,055.9	13.55
8,000–10,000	1,172,472	14.51	10,476.1	16.65	6,627.7	1,218.5	15.62
10,000–15,000	1,297,754	16.06	15,471.5	24.60	10,589.8	2,077.9	26.66
15,000–20,000	306,426	3.79	5,199.2	8.26	3,787.0	811.5	10.40
20,000–50,000	199,635	2.47	5,492.2	8.73	4,282.3	1,073.6	13.77
50,000–100,000	21,157	.27	1,381.7	2.20	1,192.8	369.3	4.74
100,000–200,000	3,015	.03	385.5	.61	341.8	117.3	1.51
200,000 & over	479	.01	143.5	.23	118.0	39.5	.51
Total..........	8,081,015	100.00	62,903.4	100.00	39,133.2	7,796.6	100.00

(1) Federal taxes include income taxes, social development tax and old age security tax.

Effective Federal Tax Rates

Selected total incomes, 1972	Rate on total income	Rate on taxed income	Selected total incomes	Rate on total income	Rate on taxed income
1,600 to 1,700	.87	20.79	9,000 to 9,500	11.78	18.46
2,000 to 2,100	2.70	15.80	10,000 to 11,000	12.61	19.00
2,500 to 2,600	4.81	16.12	13,000 to 14,000	14.08	20.09
3,000 to 3,100	5.58	16.15	15,000 to 16,000	14.94	20.77
3,500 to 3,600	6.60	16.26	17,000 to 18,000	15.70	21.57
4,000 to 4,500	7.57	16.58	20,000 to 25,000	17.48	23.26
5,000 to 5,500	8.74	17.01	30,000 to 40,000	21.10	26.32
6,000 to 6,500	9.67	17.30	50,000 to 100,000	26.73	30.96
7,000 to 7,500	10.50	17.64	100,000 to 200,000	30.44	34.33
8,000 to 8,500	11.14	18.09	200,000 & over	27.53	33.47

City Income Tax in Cities Over 50,000
Compiled by Tax Foundation from Commerce Clearing House data and other sources.

City	Rates% 1974	Orig.	Year Start	City	Rates% 1974	Orig.	Year start
Cities with 500,000 or more inhabitants				**Cities with 50,000 to 99,000 inhabitants**			
Baltimore, Md............	(50% of state tax)	1.0	1966	Toledo, Ohio.............	1.5	1.0	1946
Cleveland, Ohio...........	1.0	.5	1967	Youngstown, Ohio..........	1.5	.3	1948
Columbus, Ohio...........	1.5	.5	1947	Altoona, Pa..............	1.0	1.0	1948
Detroit, Mich.............	2.0	1.0	1964	Bethlehem, Pa...........	1.0	1.0	1957
Kansas City, Mo...........	1.0	.5	1964	Chester, Pa.............	1.0	1.0	1956
New York, N.Y.............	.7-3.5	.4-2.0	1966	Covington, Ky...........	2.5	1.0	1956
Philadelphia, Pa..........	3.125	1.5	1939	Euclid, Ohio............	1.0	.5	1967
St. Louis, Mo.............	1.0	.25	1948	Gadsden, Ala............	2.0	1.0	1956
Cities with 100,000 to 499,000 inhabitants				Hamilton, Ohio..........	1.5	.8	1960
Akron, Ohio..............	1.5	1.0	1963	Harrisburg, Pa..........	1.0	1.0	1966
Allentown, Pa............	1.0	1.0	1958	Johnstown, Pa...........	1.0	1.0	1948
Birmingham, Ala..........	1.0	1.0	1970	Kettering, Ohio.........	1.0	1.0	1968
Canton, Ohio............	1.5	.6	1954	Lakewood, Ohio..........	1.0	1.0	1968
Cincinnati, Ohio..........	2.0	1.0	1954	Lancaster, Pa...........	1.0	.5	1959
Dayton, Ohio............	1.0	.5	1949	Lima, Ohio.............	1.0	.75	1959
Erie, Pa.................	1.0	1.0	1948	Lorain, Ohio............	1.0	.5	1967
Flint, Mich..............	1.0	1.0	1965	Pontiac, Mich...........	1.0	1.0	1968
Grand Rapids, Mich........	1.0	1.0	1967	Saginaw, Mich...........	1.0	1.0	1965
Lansing, Mich............	1.0	1.0	1968	Springfield, Ohio.......	1.5	1.0	1948
Lexington, Ky............	2.0	1.0	1952	Warren, Ohio...........	1.0	.5	1952
Louisville, Ky............	2.0	1.0	1948	Wilkes-Barre, Pa........	0.5	1.0	1966
Parma, Ohio.............	1.0	.5	1967	York, Pa...............	1.0	1.0	1965
Scranton, Pa.............	2.0	1.0	1948	Wilmington, Del.........	1.25	.5	1970

Taxable Returns by Income, 1950-1972*
Source: Taxation Statistics

Year	Under $2,000	$2,000 -3,000	$3,000 -4,000	$4,000 -5,000	$5,000 -10,000	$10,000 -25,000	$25,000 and over	Total
1950	747,060	889,900	434,200	134,380	125,420	36,890	6,390	2,374,240
1955	730,490	983,900	947,930	459,540	360,430	65,660	10,700	3,558,650
1960	653,920	876,235	998,741	805,264	913,885	124,032	17,689	4,389,766
1965	695,135	932,921	999,015	945,585	1,860,115	263,900	32,271	5,728,942
1966	742,443	940,942	1,044,646	967,104	2,195,334	347,761	38,349	6,276,579
1967	745,413	920,507	1,026,477	977,456	2,490,063	447,690	48,077	6,655,683
1968	748,896	881,808	1,011,641	918,082	2,778,210	570,866	57,411	6,966,914
1969	767,097	895,280	983,011	905,489	2,985,437	757,336	70,313	7,363,963
1970	758,066	868,765	935,225	887,984	3,127,045	984,231	80,415	7,641,731
1971	280,151	767,941	872,520	873,113	3,220,092	1,264,272	94,482	7,372,571
1972	249,929	709,470	880,010	925,901	3,487,239	1,704,056	124,410	8,081,015

*Income class based on total income.

State Inheritance Tax Rates and Exemptions

Source: Compiled by Tax Foundation from Commerce Clearing House data
As of Sept. 1, 1974

State (a)	Rates (per cent)(b)			Max. Rate applies above ($1,000)	Exemptions (c) ($1,000)			
	Spouse Child or parent	Brother or sister	Other than relative		Spouse	Child or parent	Brother or sister	Other than relative
California	3-14	6-20	10-24	$400	$5 (d)	$5 (e)	$2	$.3
Colorado (f)	2-8	3-10	10-19	500	20	10	2	.5 (h)
Connecticut (i)	2-8	4-10	8-14	1,000	50	10	3	.5
Delaware	1-6	5-10	10-16	200	20	3	1	None
Dist. of Col.	1-8	5-23	5-23	1,000	5	5	1	1
Hawaii	1.5-7.5	3.5-9	3.5-9	250	20	5	.5	.5
Idaho	2-15	4-20	8-30	500	10 (d, g)	4 (e)	1	None
Illinois	2-14	2-14	10-30	500	20	20	10	.1
Indiana	1-10	5-15	7-20	1,500	15	2 (e)	.5	.1
Iowa	1-8	5-10	10-15	150	40	10 (e)	None	None
Kansas	.5-5	3-12.5	10-15	500	75	15	5	.2 (h)
Kentucky	2-10	4-16	6-16	500	10 (g)	5 (e)	1	.5
Louisiana	2-3	5-7	5-10	25	5	5	1	.5
Maine	2-6	8-12	12-18	250	15	10	.5	.5
Maryland (k)	1	7.5	7.5	(l)	.15 (h)	.15 (h)	.15 (h)	.15 (h)
Massachusetts (m)	1.8-11.8	5.5-19.3	8-19.3	1,000	30 (h)	15 (n)	5 (n)	5 (n)
Michigan	2-8(o)	2-8 (o)	10-15 (o)	750	30 (e)	5	5	None
Minnesota	1.5-10	6-25	8-30	1,000	30 (g)	6 (e)	1.5	.5
Missouri	1-6	3-18	5-30	400	20 (p)	5 (e)	.5	.1 (h)
Montana	2-8	4-16	8-32	100	20	2 (e)	.5	None
Nebraska	1	1	6-18	60	10	10	10	.5
New Hampshire	(q)	15	15	(l)	(q)	(q)	None	None
New Jersey	1-16	11-16	15-16	3,200	5	5	.5 (h)	.5 (h)
New Mexico	1	5	5	(l)	(r)	(r)	(r)	(r)
North Carolina	1-12	4-16	8-17	3,000	10	2 (e)	None	None
Oregon (a)	2-10	2-10 (r)	2-10 (r)	500	(r)	(r)	3	.5
Pennsylvania	6	15	15	(l)	None (s)	None (s)	None	None
Rhode Island	2-9	3-10	8-15	1,000	10	10	5	1
South Dakota (a)	(t)	4-16	6-24	100	60	3 (e)	.5	.1
Tennessee	5.5-9.5	6.5-20	6.5-20	500	60	60	1	1
Texas	1-6	3-10	5-20	1,000	25 (d)	25	10	.5
Virginia	1-5	2-10	5-15	1,000	5	5	2	1
Washington	1-10	3-20	10-25	500	10 (d)	10	1	None
West Virginia (a)	3-13	4-18	10-30	1,000	15	5	None	None
Wisconsin	1.25-12.5	5-25	10-30	500	50	4	1	.5
Wyoming	2	2	6	(l)	10	10	10	None

(a) In addition to an inheritance tax, all states listed also levy an estate tax, generally to assure full absorption of the Federal credit. Exceptions are Ore., S. D., and W. Va.

(b) Rates generally apply to excess above graduated absolute amounts.

(c) Generally, transfers to governments or to solely charitable, educational, scientific, religious, literary, public, and other similar organizations in the U.S. are wholly exempt. Some states grant additional exemptions either for insurance, homestead, joint deposits, support allowance, disinherited minor children, orphaned, incompetent or blind children, and for previously or later taxed transfers. In many states, exemptions are deducted from the first bracket only. Adopted children generally receive the same consideration as natural children.

(d) Community property state in which, in general, either all community property to the surviving spouse is exempt, or only one-half of the community property is taxable on the death of either spouse.

(e) Exemption for child (in thousands); $15 in Iowa; and $10 in S. D. Exemption for minor child is (in thousands): $12 in Calif.; $10 in Idaho; $5 in Ind.; $10 in Ky.; $15 in Minn.; $5 in Mont.; $5 in N.C. In Mo. the exemption for an insane, blind or otherwise incapacitated lineal descendant is (thousands) $15. In Mich. a widow receives $5,000 for every minor child to whom no property is transferred in addition to the normal exception for a spouse.

(f) Colo. imposes an additional tax of 10% upon the amount of tax computed at above rates.

(g) Exemption for widower differs in the following states (thousands): Idaho, $4; Ky., $5; Minn., $6.

(h) No exemption if share exceeds amount stated.

(i) On estates an additional inheritance tax equal to 30% of the basic tax is imposed.

(j) Estates over $3,000,000 are not subject to the inheritance tax but are subject to an estate tax equal to the amount of the Federal credit.

(k) Where property of a decedent subject to administration in Md. is $2,000 or less, no inheritance taxes are due.

(l) Rate applies to entire share.

(m) Mass. imposes a 14% surtax in addition to the inheritance tax on all property or interests.

(n) No exemption if share exceeds amount stated except that the tax shall not reduce the share below the amount of the exemption. In addition there are certain exemptions for the spouse's home.

(o) There is no tax on the share of any beneficiary if the value of the share is less than $100.

(p) In addition, an exemption of one-half of the decedent's estate, or one-third if decedent is survived by lineal descendants.

(q) Spouses, minor children and minor adopted children in the decedent's line of succession are entirely exempt. Parents have no exemption and are taxable at the flat rate of 15%.

(r) An additional tax of 2-20% is levied on all beneficiaries other than grandparents, parents, spouse, children, stepchildren or lineal descendants. These categories of beneficiaries are exempt from the additional taxes.

(s) However, the $1,500 family exemption is specifically allowed as a deduction.

(t) The rates range from 1.5-6% for a spouse or a child and from 3-12% for parents.

Federal Estate Tax

Source: Tax Foundation

An estate tax tax return must be filed for every citizen or resident of the United States whose gross estate exceeds $60,000 in value at the time of his death. In general, the tax must be paid within 15 mos. from the date of death. Extensions may be granted in hardship cases. A return must be filed for a non-resident, not a citizen, if his gross estate in the U.S. exceeds $30,000 in value.

An estate gets credit for state death taxes, according to a graduated table; also deductions for funeral expenses, administration, claims, and bequests to religious, charitable and fraternal organizations or government welfare agencies.

Life insurance payable to named beneficiaries is not to be included in the gross estate if the insured retained no incidents of ownership in the policy. A reversionary inter-est which exceeds 5 per cent of the value of the policy is considered an incident of ownership in the policy.

The marital deduction provides that the value of the tax-able estate "shall be determined by deducting from the value of the gross estate an amount equal to the value of any interest in property which passes or has passed from the decedent to his surviving spouse." Thus the deduction applies when the surviving spouse has a right to the income for life from all or only a part of the property, as well as power to appoint all, or the part in which the survivor has income rights, whether or not the property is held in trust. If the spouse has control only over part, the deduction is limited proportionately. The deduction is limited, however, to the value of one-half of the adjusted gross estate.

Estate Tax Rate

The tax is computed under the rates listed below on the net taxable estate of the decedent, citizen or resident of the United States after allowing for the specific exemption of $60,000 and deduction for debts, expenses, charitable, marital deductions. There is a credit allowance for state death taxes.

If the taxable estate is:			The tax shall be:	
Not over $5,000			3% of the taxable estate	
Over	$5,000	but not over	$10,000	$150, plus 7% of excess over	$5,000
Over	$10,000	but not over	$20,000	$500, plus 11% of excess over	$10,000
Over	$20,000	but not over	$30,000	$1,600, plus 14% of excess over	$20,000
Over	$30,000	but not over	$40,000	$3,000, plus 18% of excess over	$30,000
Over	$40,000	but not over	$50,000	$4,800, plus 22% of excess over	$40,000
Over	$50,000	but not over	$60,000	$7,000, plus 25% of excess over	$50,000
Over	$60,000	but not over	$100,000	$9,500, plus 28% of excess over	$60,000
Over	$100,000	but not over	$250,000	$20,700, plus 30% of excess over	$100,000
Over	$250,000	but not over	$500,000	$65,700, plus 32% of excess over	$250,000
Over	$500,000	but not over	$750,000	$145,700, plus 35% of excess over	$500,000
Over	$750,000	but not over	$1,000,000	$233,200, plus 37% of excess over	$750,000
Over	$1,000,000	but not over	$1,250,000	$325,700, plus 39% of excess over	$1,000,000
Over	$1,250,000	but not over	$1,500,000	$423,200, plus 42% of excess over	$1,250,000
Over	$1,500,000	but not over	$2,000,000	$528,200, plus 45% of excess over	$1,500,000
Over	$2,000,000	but not over	$2,500,000	$753,200, plus 49% of excess over	$2,000,000
Over	$2,500,000	but not over	$3,000,000	$998,200, plus 53% of excess over	$2,500,000
Over	$3,000,000	but not over	$3,500,000	$1,263,200. plus 56% of excess over	$3,000,000
Over	$3,500,000	but not over	$4,000,000	$1,543,200, plus 59% of excess over	$3,500,000
Over	$4,000,000	but not over	$5,000,000	$1,838,200, plus 63% of excess over	$4,000,000
Over	$5,000,000	but not over	$6,000,000	$2,468,200, plus 67% of excess over	$5,000,000
Over	$6,000,000	but not over	$7,000,000	$3,138,200, plus 70% of excess over	$6,000,000
Over	$7,000,000	but not over	$8,000,000	$3,838,200, plus 73% of excess over	$7,000,000
Over	$8,000,000	but not over	$10,000,000	$4,568,200, plus 76% of excess over	$8,000,000
Over	$10,000,000			$6,088,200, plus 77% of excess over	$10,000,000

State Estate Tax Rates and Exemptions*

Source: Compiled by Tax Foundation from Commerce Clearing House Data

As of Sept. 1, 1974. *See Index for state inheritance tax rates and exemptions.

State (a)	Rates (on net estate After exemptions) (b)	Maximum rate applies above	Exemption	
Alabama	Maximum Federal Credit (c, d)	$10,040,000	$60,000	
Alaska	Maximum Federal Credit (c, d)	10,040,000	60,000	
Arizona	0.8% on first $50,000 to 16% (e)	10,000,000	100,000	(f, g)
Arkansas	Maximum Federal Credit (c, d)	10,040,000	60,000	(g)
Florida	Maximum Federal Credit (c, d)	10,040,000	60,000	
Georgia	Maximum Federal Credit (c, d)	10,040,000	60,000	
Mississippi	1% on first $60,000 to 16%	10,000,000	60,000	(f, g)
New York	2% on first $50,000 to 21% (e, h)	10,100,000		(f, g, i)
North Dakota	2% on first $25,000 to 23%	1,500,000	20,000	(g, j)
Ohio	2% on first $40,000 to 7% (e)	500,000	5,000	(g, k)
Oklahoma	1% on first $10,000 to 10% (e)	10,000,000	15,000	(g, l)
South Carolina	4% on first $40,000 to 6%	100,000	60,000	(g)
Utah	5% of first $35,000 to 10% (e)	85,000	60,000	(g)

(a) Excludes states shown in table on page 65 which levy an estate tax, in addition to their inheritance taxes, to assure full absorption of the Federal credit.

(b) The rates generally are in addition to graduated absolute amounts.

(c) Maximum Federal credit allowed under the 1954 code for state estate taxes paid is expressed as a percentage of the taxable estate (after $60,000 exemption) in excess of $40,000, plus a graduated absolute amount.

(d) A tax on nonresident estates is imposed on the proportionate share of the net estate which the property located in the state bears to the entire estate wherever situated.

(e) An additional estate tax is imposed to assure full absorption of the Federal credit.

(f) Insurance receives special treatment.

(g) Transfers to religious, charitable, educational, and munici-pal corporations are fully exempt. Limited in Mississippi to those located in U.S

(h) On net estate before exemption.

(i) The specific exemptions ($20,000 of the net estate transferred to spouse and $5,000 to lineal ancestors and descendants and certain other named relatives are allowed in an amount equal to 2% of the first $50,000 and 3% of the next $100,000.

(j) A marital deduction of 50% of adjusted gross estate is allowed instead, if larger. Exemption for a lineal descendant, if a minor, is $7,000; for other lineal descendants and ancestors, $2,000.

(k) Property is exempt to the extent transferred to surviving spouse not exceeding $20,000; for a child under 18, $5,000 and for each child 18 or over, $3,000.

(l) An estate valued at $100 or less is exempt.

State Individual Income Taxes: Rates, Exemptions

Source: Office of Tax Analysis, Treasury Dept. Data as of July 1, 1974

State	Net income after pers'l. exemption	Percentage rates	Net income after pers'l. exemption	Percentage rates	Personal Exemp. Single	Married family head	Credit Depends.
Alabama[1]	First $1,000 1,001- 3,000	1.5 3	$3,001-$5,000 Over 5,000	4.5 5	$1,500	$3,000	$300
Alaska		16% of Federal income tax			Federal exemptions		
Arizona[1][2]	First 1,0000 1,001- 2,000 2,001- 3,000	2 3 4	3,001- 4,000 4,001- 5,000 5,001- 6,000	5 6 7	1,000 Over 6,000 8	2,000	600
Arkansas[3]	First 3,000 3,001- 6,000 6,001- 9,000	1 2.5 3.5	9,001-15,000 15,001-25,000 Over 25,000	4.5 6 7	17.50 (tax credit)	35	6
California[1][2]	First 2,000 2,001- 3,500 3,501- 5,000 5,001- 6,500 6,501- 8,000	1 2 3 4 5	8,001- 9,500 9,501-11,000 11,001-12,500 12,501-14,000 14,001-15,500	6 7 8 9 10	(tax credit) 25 Heads of households have slightly lower tax rates. Over 15,500 11	50	8
Colorado[1][4]	First 1,000 1,001- 2,000 2,001- 3,000 3,001- 4,000 4,001- 5,000 5,001- 6,000	3 3.5 4 4.5 5 5.5	6,001- 7,000 7,001- 8,000 8,001- 9,000 9,001-10,000 Over 10,000	6 6.5 7 7.5 8	750 Surtax on intangible income over $5,000, 2%. A credit equal to ½ of 1% of net taxation is allowed for income under $9,000.	1,500	750
Connecticut	Capital gains	6					
Delaware[3]	First 1,000 1,001- 2,000 2,001- 3,000 3,001- 4,000 4,001- 5,000 5,001- 6,000	1.6 2.2 3.3 4.4 5.5 6.6	6,001- 8,000 8,001-20,000 20,001-25,000 25,001-30,000 30,001-40,000 40,001-50,000	7.7 8.8 9.3 9.9 12.1 13.2	600	1,200 50,000-75,000 75,001-100,000 Over 100,000	600 15.4 16.5 19.8
Dist. of Col.[1][4]	First 1,000 1,001- 2,000 2,001- 3,000 3,001- 5,000 5,001- 8,000	2 3 4 5 6	8,001-12,000 12,001-17,000 17,001-25,000 Over 25,000	7 8 9 10	1,000 A tax credit is provided for low-income taxpayers (adjusted gross not over $6,000) for increased sales tax on food ($2 to $6 credit per exemption). A refund is allowed if the credit exceeds tax liability.	2,000	500
Georgia[3][5]	First 750 751- 2,250 2,251- 3,750 3,751- 5,250	1 2 3 4	5,251- 7,000 Over 7,000	5 6	1,500 Students above high school level and handicapped or retarded children under 21 are allowed a $1,400 exemption.	3,000	700
Hawaii[1][4]	First 500 501- 1,000 1,001- 500 1,501- 2,000 2,001- 3,000 3,001- 5,000	2.25 3.25 4.5 5 6.5 7.5	5,001-10,000 10,001-14,000 14,001-20,000 20,001-30,000 Over 30,000	8.5 9.5 10 10.5 11	750 Special tax rates for heads of households.	1,500	750
Idaho[2][3][4]	First 1,000 1,001- 2,000 2,001- 3,000	2 4 4.5	3,001- 4,000 4,001- 5,000 Over 5,000	5.5 6.5 7.5	Federal exemptions		
Illinois	Net taxable income	2.5			1,000	2,000	1,000
Indiana[4]	Adjusted gross	2			1,000	*2,000	500

*Lesser of $1,000 or adjusted gross income of each spouse, but not less than $500.

State	Net income after pers'l. exemption	Percentage rates	Net income after pers'l. exemption	Percentage rates	Personal Exemp. Single	Married family head	Credit Depends.
Iowa[1]	First 1,000 1,001- 2,000 2,001- 3,000	.75 1.5 3	3,001- 4,000 4,001- 7,000 7,001- 9,000	4 5 6	(Tax Credit) 15 Incomes $3,000 or less are exempt. Over 9,000 7	30	10
Kansas[1][4]	First 2,000 2,001- 3,000 3,001- 5,000	2 3.5 4	5,001- 7,000 Over 7,000	5 6.5	600	1,200	600
Kentucky[1]	First 3,000 3,001- 4,000	2 3	4,001- 5,000 5,001- 8,000	4 5	(Tax Credit) 20 Over 8,000 6	40	20

State	Net income after pers'l. exemption	Percentage rates	Net income after pers'l. exemption	Percentage rates	Personal Exemp. Single	Married family head	Credit Depends.
Louisiana[2] [3]	First 10,000 10,001-50,000	2 4	Over 50,000	6	2,500	5,000	400
Credits are allowed new income which is taxed at 2%; additional $1,000 exemp. for blindness allowed for dependents.								
Maine	First 2,000 2,001- 5,000 5,001-10,000	1 2 3	10,001-25,000 25,000-50,000 Over 50,000	4 5 6	1,000	2,000	1,000
Maryland[1] [4]	First 1,000 1,001- 2,000	2 3	2,001- 3,000 Over 3,000	4 5	800	1,600	800
An additional exemption of $800 is allowed for each dependent 65 or over.								
Massachusetts[4] .	Earned and business income: Interest, divs., capital gains on intangibles:	5 9			2,000	2,600-4,600	600
The exemptions shown are those allowed against business income, including salaries and wages. A specific exemption of $2,000 is allowed for each taxpayer. In addition, a dependency exemption of $600 is allowed for a dependent spouse who has income from all sources of less than $2,000. In the case of a joint return, the exemption is the smaller of (1) $4,600 or (2) $2,600 plus the income of the spouse having the smaller income. The exemption allowed against annuity income is the amount of any unused business income exemptions. Married persons must file a joint return in order to obtain any non-business income exemption.								
Michigan[4]			All taxable income	3.9	1,500	3,000	1,500
Minnesota[1] [4] . . .	First 500 501-1,000 1,001- 2,000 2,001- 3,000 3,001- 4,000 4,001- 5,000	1.6 2.2 3.5 5.8 7.3 8.8	5,001- 7,000 7,001- 9,000 9,001-12,500 12,501-20,000 Over 20,000	10.2 11.5 12.8 14 15	21 An additional tax credit of $21 is allowed for each taxpayer 65 years old.	42	21
Mississippi[3]	First 5,000	3	Over 5,000	4	4,500	6,500	750
Missouri[1]	First 1,000 1,001- 2,000 2,001- 3,000 3,001- 4,000 4,001- 5,000	1.5 2 2.5 3 3.5	5,001- 6,000 6,001- 7,000 7,001- 8,000 8,001- 9,000 Over 9,000	4 4.5 5 5.5 6	1,200	2,400	400
Montana[3]	First 1,000 1,001-2,000 2,001-4,000 4,001-6,000 6,001-8,000	2 3 4 5 6	8,001-10,000 10,001-14,000 14,001-20,000 20,001-35,000 Over 35,000	7 8 9 10 11	650	1,300	650
Nebraska[4]							Federal exemptions
The tax is imposed as a % of the taxpayer's Fed. income tax liability (not including surtax) before credits, with limited adjustments. For the year 1973 the rate was set at 13% by State Board of Equalization and Assessment.								
New Hampshire.	Interest and dividends (except interest on savings accounts).	4.25	4% commuter tax		600	600-1,200	
Joint returns are not pemitted; each spouse with taxable income is allowed a $600 exemption.								
New Jersey[3]	First 1,000 1,001-3,000 3,001-5,000 5,001-7,000 7,001-9,000 9,001-11,000 11,001-13,000	2 3 4 5 6 7 8	13,001-15,000 15,001-17,000 17,001-19,000 19,001-21,000 21,001-23,000 23,001-25,000 Over 25,000	9 10 11 12 13 14 15	650	1,300	650
minimum tax on tax preference items. The surtax is computed before the allowance of any applicable credits and is effective through the 1976 calendar year. The rate of tax on minimum taxable income is 6%. The Tax is imposed on the net income derived from New York sources by New Jersey residents. The rates are the same as those in effect in New York. A surtax of 2.5% is imposed on both the regular income tax and								
New Mexico[2] [3] . . .	First 500 501-1,000 1,001-1,500 1,501-2,000 2,001-3,000 3,001-4,000 4,001-5,000 5,001-6,000	0.9 1.1 1.3 1.5 1.6 1.9 2.3 2.4	6,001-7,000 7,001-8,000 8,001-10,000 10,001-12,000 12,001-20,000 20,001-50,000 50,001-100,000 Over 100,000	3.0 3.3 3.6 4.3 6.1 8.0 8.5 9.0	Federal exemptions The income classes reported are for individuals. For joint returns and heads of households, a separate rate schedule is provided. A credit is allowed for state and local taxes for gross income of less than $6,000.		
New York[1]	First 1,000 1,001- 3,000 3,001- 5,000 5,001- 7,000 7,001- 9,000 9,001-11,000 11,001-13,000	2 3 4 5 6 7 8	13,001-15,000 15,001-17,000 17,001-19,000 19,001-21,000 21,001-23,000 23,001-25,000 Over 25,000	9 10 11 12 13 14 15	650	1,300	650
taxed at 5½%. The following credit is allowed: $100 or less-full amount; $100-200-difference between $200 and amount of tax; $200 or more, no credit. A 2.5% surtax is imposed. Tax credits of $12.50 for single persons, $12.50 for married persons filing separately, and $25 for married persons filing jointly and heads of households are allowed. Income from unincorporated business is								

State	Net Income after pers'l. exemption	Percentage rates	Net Income after pers'l. exemption	Percentage rates	Personal Single	Exemp. Married family head	Credit Depends.
North Carolina³	First 2,000	3	6,001-10,000	6	1,000	2,000	600
	2,001-4,000	4	Over 10,000	7		3,000	
	4,000-6,000	5					

An additional exemption of $1,000 is allowed a married woman with a separate income; joint returns are not permitted.

State							
North Dakota³	First 1,000	1	6,001-8,000	7.5		Federal Exemptions	
	1,001-3,000	2	Over 8,000	10			
	3,001-5,000	3					
	5,001-6,000	5					

An additional 1% tax is imposed on net incomes of individuals, estates, trusts and corporations (minimum $2.50, maximum $12.50).

State							
Ohio⁴	First 5,000	0.5	15,001-20,000	2.5	500	1,000	500
	5,001-10,000	1	20,001-40,000	3			
	10,001-15,000	2	Over 40,000	3.5			

Maximum personal exemption is $3,000 per return. Taxpayers age 65 or older are allowed a $25 credit, or if they have received a lump sum distribution from a pension, retirement or profit sharing plan during the tax year, they are allowed a credit equal to $25 times the taxpayer's expected remaining life. Credit may not exceed tax otherwise due. Credit is also allowed for an amount paid during the school year for elementary and secondary education or instruction or training of dependents who do not have a high school diploma.

State							
Oklahoma¹	First 1,000	0.5	5,001-6,250	4	750	1,500	750
	1,001-2,500	1	6,251-7,500	5			
	2,501-3,750	2	Over 7,500	6			
	3,751-5,000	3					

For joint returns the rates shown apply to income classes twice as large. Rates of heads of households range from ½% on the first $1,500 to 6% on taxable income over $11,250. Non-residents are taxed at a flat rate of 6% of Oklahoma taxable income.

State							
Oregon¹	First $500	4	3,001-4,000	8			
	501-1,000	5	4,001-5,000	9			
	1,001-2,000	6	Over 5,000	10			
	2,001-3,000	7					

A credit is provided in an amount and equal to 25% of the Federal retirement income tax credit to the extent that such a credit is based on Oregon taxable income.

State		
Pennsylvania	Modified Federal taxable income 2	

Pennsylvania residents working in New Jersey are subject to a flat 2.3% commuter's tax on their New Jersey Income.

State		
Rhode Island	Federal income tax liability 15	Federal Exemptions.

State							
South Carolina¹	First 2,000	2	6,001- 8,000	5	800	1,600	800
	2,001-4,000	3	8,001-10,000	6			
	4,001-6,000	4	Over 10,000	7			

State		
Tennessee	Interest and dividends	6

Dividends from corporations, 75% of whose property is taxable in Tenn., are taxed at 4%.

State						
Utah³	First 750	2	2,251-3,000	5	Federal exemptions	
	751-1,500	3	3,001-3,750	6		
	1,501-2,250	4	Over 3,750	7.25		

State	
Vermont	Federal Exemptions.

The tax is imposed at a rate of 25% of the Fed. income tax liability of the taxpayer for the taxable year after certain credits (retirement income, investment, foreign tax and tax-free covenant bonds) but before any surtax on Fed. liability, reduced by a % equal to the % of the taxpayer's adjusted gross income for the taxable year which is not Vermont income. A 9% surcharge is imposed for 1974, and thereafter

State							
Virginia³	First 2,000	2	5,001-12,000	5	600	1,200	600
	3,001-5,000	3	Over 12,000	5.75			

State							
West Virginia¹	First 2,000	2.1	26,001-32,000	6.5	600	1,200	600
	2,001-4,000	2.3	32,001-38,000	6.8			
	4,001-6,000	2.8	38,001-44,000	7.2			
	6,001-8,000	3.2	44,001-50,000	7.5			
	8,001-10,000	3.5	50,001-60,000	7.9			
	10,001-12,000	4	60,001-70,000	8.2			
	12,001-14,000	4.6	70,001-80,000	8.6			
	14,001-16,000	4.9	80,001-90,000	8.8			
	16,001-18,000	5.3	90,001-100,000	9.1			
	18,001-20,000	5.4	100,001-150,000	9.3			
	20,001-22,000	6	150,001-200,000	9.5			
	22,001-26,000	6.1	Over 200,000	9.6			

For joint returns and a return of a surviving spouse, a separate rate schedule is provided.

State							
Wisconsin¹⁴	First 1,000	3.1	8,001-9,000	8.2	(Tax Credit) 20	40	20
	1,001-2,000	3.4	9,001-10,000	8.8			
	2,001-3,000	3.6	10,001-11,000	9.3			
	3,001-4,000	4.8	11,001-12,000	9.9			
	4,001-5,000	5.4	12,001-13,000	10.5			
	5,001-6,000	5.9	13,001-14,000	11.1			
	6,001-7,000	6.5	Over 14,000	11.4			
	7,001-8,000	7.6					

(1) A standard deduction and optional tax table are provided.

(2) Community property state in which, in general, one-half of the community income is taxable to each spouse.

(3) A standard deduction is allowed.

(4) A limited tax credit is allowed for sales taxes in Colorado, the District of Columbia, Hawaii, Idaho, Indiana, Massachusetts, Nebraska, and Vermont; for property taxes on homesteads of the elderly in Colorado, Kansas, Michigan, Minnesota, Vermont, and Wisconsin; for property taxes and city income taxes in Michigan; and for personal property taxes in Maryland.

(5) Tax credits are allowed: $15 for single person or married person filing separately if AGI is $3,000 or less. (For each dollar by which the Federal AGI exceeds $3,000, the credit is reduced by $1 until no credit is allowed if Federal AGI is $3,015 or more.) $30 for heads of households or married persons filing jointly with $6,000 or less AGI. (For each dollar by which Federal AGI exceeds $6,000, credit is reduced by $1 until no credit is allowed if Federal AGI is $6,030 or more.)

State Retail Sales Taxes; Types and Rates

Source: Analysis Staff, Tax Division, Treasury Dept. Data as of July 1, 1974

| State | Tangible Personal Property | Admissions | Selected Service | | Public Utilities | Rates on other services and nonretail business |
			Rest. Meals	Trans- ient Lodging		
Alabama[2]	4%[3] agric., mining and mfg. mach., 1.5%.	4%	4%	4%	. . .	Gross rcpts of amus't operators, 4%
Arizona[2]	4 al, 3%.	4	4	3	4	Timbering, 1.5%; storage, apt., office rent-
Arkansas[2]	3 from coin-operated dev.; repair services incl. auto and elect., 3%.	3	3	3	3	Printing, photographic services; rcpts,
California[2]	4.75[5] processing, printing, 4.75%.	. . .	4.75	. . .	. . .	Renting, leasing, producing, fabricating,
Colorado[2]	3	. . .	3	3	3	
Connecticut	6 property items, 6%.	. . .	6[7]	6[10]	6[14]	Storing for use or consumption of personal
D. of C.	5[3] lic stenographic services, 5%; sales of food for off-premise consumption, nonprescription medicines, 2%.	5	6	6	5	Duplicating, mailing, addressing and pub-
Florida	4	4	4	4	. . .	Rental income of amus't. mach., 4%.
Georgia	3	3	3	3	3	Levies on amus't dev., 3%.
Hawaii[1]	4 selected businesses, 1/2%: insur. solicitors, 2%; contractors, sales rep., professions, radio stations, 4%[6].	4	4	4	. . .	Sugar processors, pineapple farmers and
Idaho[6]	3	3	3	3	. . .	Closed circuit tv boxing, wrestling, 5%.
Illinois[2]	4 service, 4%; remodeling, repairing and reconditioning of tangible personal property, 4%.	. . .	4			Property sold in connection with a sale of
Indiana	4	. . .	4	4	4	
Iowa	3 cold storage, photography, printing, repairs, barber and beauty parlor services, advt., dry cleaning equip. rentals and gross rcpts. from amus't dev., 3%.	3	3	3	3	Laundry, dry cleaning, automobile and
Kansas[2]	3 ated devices; commer. an.us't, 3%.	3	3	3	3	Gross rcpts. from operation of coin-oper-
Kentucky	5 photo fin., 5%; ticket sales to boxing or wrestling on closed circuit tv 5% of gross rcpts; tax also applies to pay'ts for right to broadcast matches.	5	5	5	5	Storage, sewer services, photog. and
Louisiana[2]	3	3	3	3	. . .	Food and prescpt'n. drugs, 2%.
Maine	5	. . .	5	5	5	Proceeds from closed circuit tv, 5%.
Maryland	4[9] that used in generation of electricity or in R.&S. sold to mfrs., 2%; watercraft, 3%.	12	4[7]	4	4	Farm equip., 2%; mfg. equip., including
Mass.	3	. . .	7	5[10]		
Michigan	4	. . .	4	4	4	
Minnesota[2]	4 coin-operated vending mach., 3% of gross sales.	4	4	4	4	Food, medicines and clothing are exempt;
Mississippi[1]	5[3] sales of meat for human consumption; 5% on beer, alc. bevs., soft drinks and motor fuel); extracting or mining of minerals, specified miscellaneous bus. incl. bowling, pool halls, warehouses, laundry and dry cleaning, pest control services, specified repair services, 5%; cotton ginning, 15¢ per bale; sales of materials to railroads for use in track structures, 3%; tractors, indust. fuel and mfg. mach. sales over $500, 1%.	5	5	5	5	Wholesaling, 11/16% (one-half of 1% on
Missouri[2]	3	3	3	3	3	
Nebraska[2]	2.5	2.5	2.5	2.5	2.5	
Nevada[2]	3[11]	. . .	3	. . .	. . .	

State	Tangible Personal Property	Admissions	Selected Service			Rates on other services and nonretail business
			Rest. Meals	Transient Lodging	Public Utilities	
New Jersey[1]	5	5[12]	5	5[10]	...	
N.M.[1-2]	4[3]	4	4	4	4	
N.Y.[2]	4	4[12]	4[7]	4[10]	4	Safe deposit rentals, 4%.
N.C.[2]	3[3]	...	3	3	...	Farm and industrial machinery, 1% ($80 max.); airplanes, boats and locomotives, 2% ($120 max.); sales of horses and mules, 1%.
N.D.	4	4	4	4	4	Severance of sand or gravel from the soil, 4%.
Ohio[2]	4	...	4	4	...	
Okla.[2]	2[3]	2	2	2	2	Advert. (exclusive of newspapers, periodicals, billboards), printing, auto storage, gross proceeds from amusement dev., 2%.
Penn.[2]	6	...	6[7]	6	6	Cleaning, polishing, lubr. and insp. motor vehicles, rental income of coin-operated amuse. dev., 6%.
R.I.	5	...	5	5	5	
S.C.	4	...	4	4	4	
S.D.[1-2]	4[3]	3	4	3	3	Farm mach. and agric. irrigation equip., 2%; gross rcpts. from professions (other than medical), 4%.
Tenn.[2-9]	3.5	...	3.5	3.5	3.5	Vending machines, 1.5% (except tobacco products, 2.5%); industrial, farm equipment and machinery, 1%.
Texas[2]	4[3]	...	4	...	...	
Utah[2]	4	4	4	4	4	
Vt.	3	...	3[13]	3[13]	3	
Va.[2]	3[3]	...	3	3	...	Closed cir. tv, 5% of gross.
Wash.[1-2]	4.5	4.5	4.5	4.5		Rentals, auto, parking, other specified services, amusements, recreations, 4.5% (unless subject to county or city adm. taxes, when they remain taxable under the state business, occupation levy, 1%).
W. Va.[1]	3[3]	3	3	3	...	All services except public util. and pers., prof., 3%.
Wis.	4	4[12]	4	4	4	
Wyo.	3	3	3	3	3	

(1) All but a few States levy sales taxes of the single-stage retail type. Hi. and Miss. levy multiple-stage sales taxes. The N.M. and S.D. taxes have broad bases with respect to taxable services but they are not multiple-stage taxes. Wash. and W.Va. levy gross receipts taxes on all business, distinct from their sales taxes. Alaska also levies a gross receipts tax on businesses. The rates applicable to retailers, with exceptions, under these gross receipts taxes are as follows: Alaska, ½% on gross receipts of $20,000-$100,000 and ¼% on gross receipts in excess of $100,000; Wash., 44/100%; and W. Va., 55/100%. N.J. imposes a tax of 1/20 of 1% on retail stores with income in excess of $150,000, and an unincorporated business tax at the rate of ¼ of 1% if gross receipts exceed $5,000.

(2) In addition to the State tax, sales taxes are also levied by certain cities and/or counties.

(3) Motor vehicles are taxed at the general sales tax rates with the following exceptions: Ala., 1½%; Miss., 3%; and N.C., 2% ($120 maximum) Motor vehicles are exempt from the general sales and use taxes but are taxed under motor vehicle tax laws in Md., 4%; Minn., 4%; N.M., 2%; N.D. 4%; Okla., 2%; S.D. and W.Va., 3%; Tex., 4%; Va., 2%; and the D.C., 4%.

(4) Ariz. and Miss. also tax the transportation of oil and gas by pipeline. Ga., Mo., Okla. and Utah do not tax transportation of property. Miss. taxes taxicab transportation at the rate of 2%. Okla. does not tax fares of 15c or less on local transportation. Utah does not tax street railway fares.

(5) "Lease" excludes the use of tangible personal property for a period of less than one day for a charge of less than $10 when the privilege of using the property is restricted to use on the premises or at a business location of the grantor.

(6) A limited credit (or refund) in the form of a flat dollar amount per personal exemption is allowed against the personal income tax to compensate for (1) sales taxes paid on food in Colo., D.C. and Neb.; and (2) all sales taxes paid in Hi., Idaho, Mass. and Vt. Low-income taxpayers (adjusted gross income not over $6,000) are allowed a credit against D.C. tax liability ranging from $2 to $6 per personal exemption, depending on taxpayer's income bracket. A refund is allowed if credit exceeds tax liability.

(7) Restaurant meals below a specified price are exempt: Conn. and Md. less than $1; N.Y. less than $1 (when alcoholic beverages are sold, meals are taxable regardless of price); and Penn., 50c or less. In Mass., restaurant meals ($1 or more) which are taxed at 5% under the meals excise tax are exempt.

(8) Conn., exempts clothing for children under 10 years of age. Penn. and Wisc. exempt clothing with certain exceptions.

(9) In Tenn., the 3½% rate is effective through 6/30/75, thereafter reverting to 3%.

(10) In Del. a 6% hotel occupancy tax is imposed. In Colo. and Conn., the first 30 consecutive days of rental or occupancy of rooms is taxable. Over 30 days is exempt. In Mass., transient lodging (in excess of $2 a day) is subject to a 5.7% (5% plus 14% surtax) room occupancy excise tax. In N.J. and N.Y., rooms which rent for $2 a day or less are exempt.

(11) Includes a statewide mandatory 1% county sales tax collected by the state and paid to the counties for support of local school districts.

(12) Md. taxes at ½ of 1% gross receipts derived from charges for rentals of sporting or recreational equipment, and admissions, cover charges for tables, services or merchandise at any roof garden or cabaret. In N.J., admissions to a place of amusement are taxable if the charge is in excess of 75c. N.Y. taxes admissions when the charge is over 10c; exempt are participating sports (such as bowling and swimming), motion picture theaters, race tracks, boxing, wrestling, and live dramatic or musical performances. In Wisc., sales of admissions to motion picture theaters costing 75c or less are exempt.

(13) Meals and rooms are exempt from sales tax, but are subject to a special excise tax of 5%.

(14) Gas, water, electricity, telephone and telegraph services provided to consumers through mains, lines or pipes are exempt. Gas and electric energy used for domestic heating are exempt. Interstate telephone calls are exempt, as are calls from coin-operated telephones.

Savings by Individuals in the United States

Source: Federal Reserve System
(Billions of Dollars)* Indicates less than $50 million

	1969	1970	1971	1972	1973	1974'
Incr. in financial assets	61.3	79.6	99.9	124.9	132.4	123.5
Currency and demand deposits	1.6	9.6	11.0	12.9	15.1	3.3
Savings accounts	6.0	44.4	70.5	75.8	67.1	86.8
Securities	29.7	-2.3	-14.7	5.1	14.2	-5.3
U. S. Savings bonds	-.4	.3	2.4	3.3	2.7	3.0
Other U. S. Treasury Sec.	9.8	10.7	-11.7	1.5	7.6	2.8
U.S.G. agency securities	2.8	2.7	-3.5	-.5	8.4	-3.5
State & local obligations	9.6	-.5	-.9	1.3	1.7	-.1
Corporation & foreign bonds	7.4	10.1	8.2	4.9	.8	2.7
Commercial paper	4.8	-1.5	-3.9	.4	3.3	5.2
Investment company shares	4.8	2.6	1.2	-.6	-1.6	-1.7
Other corporate stock	-9.0	-5.2	-6.6	-5.2	-8.8	-13.5
Private life insurance reserves	4.9	5.1	6.1	7.2	7.7	7.6
Private insured pension reserves	2.9	3.3	5.2	4.6	5.0	5.8
Private noninsured pension reserves	6.3	7.1	7.3	5.7	7.9	9.1
Government ins. & pension reserves	6.6	8.8	9.7	10.5	9.8	10.1
Miscellaneous financial assets	3.1	3.6	4.9	3.1	5.7	6.1
Gross investment in tangible assets	143.0	140.2	165.8	190.5	213.6	198.7
Nonfarm homes	22.0	19.6	26.8	34.3	40.0	35.0
Noncorporate business construction & equipment	29.2	30.4	34.3	39.5	41.7	41.0
Consumer durables	90.8	91.3	103.5	117.4	130.8	124.5
Inventories	1.1	-1.1	1.1	-.8	1.1	-1.8
Capital consumption al owances	104.5	112.4	121.3	130.6	142.0	149.3
Nonfarm homes	8.7	9.0	9.4	10.2	10.4	10.7
Noncorporate business plant and equipment	21.3	22.6	24.4	26.7	28.6	29.6
Consumer durables	74.6	80.7	87.5	93.8	103.0	109.0
Net investment in tangible assets	38.5	27.8	44.5	59.8	71.6	49.4
Nonfarm homes	13.3	10.6	17.4	24.1	29.5	24.2
Noncorporate business construction and equipment	7.9	7.7	9.9	12.8	13.1	11.4
Consumer durables	16.2	10.6	16.0	23.6	27.9	15.5
Inventories	1.1	-1.1	1.1	-.8	1.1	-1.8
Increase in debt	39.8	30.6	54.6	85.1	90.8	66.5
Mortgage debt on nonfarm homes	16.1	12.5	24.1	38.4	43.0	35.7
Noncorporate business mortgage debt	7.0	8.0	11.2	13.2	13.8	9.4
Consumer credit	10.4	6.0	11.2	19.2	22.9	8.2
Security credit	-3.4	-1.8	2.6	4.7	-4.6	.3
Policy loans	2.6	2.3	1.0	.9	2.1	2.0
Other debt	7.1	3.6	4.4	8.6	13.5	10.8
Individual saving	60.1	76.8	89.8	99.7	113.2	106.4
Less-Govt. Ins. & Pen Reserves	6.6	8.8	9.7	10.5	9.8	10.1
Net inv. in cons. dur.	16.2	10.6	16.0	23.6	27.9	15.5
Capital gains dividends from invest. cos.	2.5	.9	.8	1.4	.9	.1
Net savings by farm corps.	*	-.1	*	*	-.1	-.1
Equals pers. saving, F/F basis	34.7	56.6	63.3	64.2	74.6	80.7
Personal saving, NIA basis	38.2	56.2	60.2	49.7	54.8	60.6
Difference	-3.5	.4	3.2	14.4	19.9	20.1

(1.) First quarter of 1974.

Federal Gift Tax

Any citizen or resident who within the calendar year makes gifts in excess of $3,000 to any one individual, or any gift of a future interest regardless of value, must file a gift tax return on or before April 15 of the following year. In addition to the annual $3,000 exclusion for each person to whom gifts are made, each donor also has a specific lifetime exemption of $30,000, and this

may be taken all at one time or spread over years.

When a husband or wife transfers by gift an interest in property to his or her spouse a deduction in computing gift tax will be allowed to the extent of one-half of the value of the gift. Also gifts to a third party by either husband or wife may be treated as made one-half by each. Tax Foundation.

If the taxable gifts are:			The tax will be:
Not over $5,000			2¼% of the taxable gifts
Over	$5,000 but not over	$10,000	$112.50, plus 5¼% of excess over $5,000
Over	$10,000 but not over	$20,000	$375, plus 8¼% of excess over $10,000
Over	$20,000 but not over	$30,000	$1,200, plus 10½% of excess over $20,000
Over	$30,000 but not over	$40,000	$2,250, plus 13½% of excess over $30,000
Over	$40,000 but not over	$50,000	$3,600, plus 16½% of excess over $40,000
Over	$50,000 but not over	$60,000	$5,250, plus 18¾% of excess over $50,000
Over	$60,000 but not over	$100,000	$7,125, plus 21 % of excess over $60,000
Over	$100,000 but not over	$250,000	$15,525, plus 22½% of excess over $100,000
Over	$250,000 but not over	$500,000	$49,275, plus 24 % of excess over $250,000
Over	$500,000 but not over	$750,000	$109,275, plus 26¼% of excess over $500,000
Over	$750,000 but not over	$1,000,000	$174,900, plus 27¾% of excess over $750,000
Over	$1,000,000 but not over	$1,250,000	$244,275, plus 29¼% of excess over $1,000,000
Over	$1,250,000 but not over	$1,500,000	$317,400, plus 31½% of excess over $1,250,000
Over	$1,500,000 but not over	$2,000,000	$396,150, plus 33¾% of excess over $1,500,000
Over	$2,000,000 but not over	$2,500,000	$564,900, plus 36¾% of excess over $2,000,000
Over	$2,500,000 but not over	$3,000,000	$748,650, plus 39¾% of excess over $2,500,000
Over	$3,000,000 but not over	$3,500,000	$947,400, plus 42 % of excess over $3,000,000
Over	$3,500,000 but not over	$4,000,000	$1,157,400, plus 44¼% of excess over $3,500,000
Over	$4,000,000 but not over	$5,000,000	$1,378,650, plus 47¼% of excess over $4,000,000
Over	$5,000,000 but not over	$6,000,000	$1,851,150, plus 50¼% of excess over $5,000,000
Over	$6,000,000 but not over	$7,000,000	$2,353,650, plus 52½% of excess over $6,000,000
Over	$7,000,000 but not over	$8,000,000	$2,878,650, plus 54¾% of excess over $7,000,000
Over	$8,000,000 but not over	$10,000,000	$3,426,150, plus 57 % of excess over $8,000,000
Over	$10,000,000		$4,566,150, plus 57¾% of excess over $10,000,000

Social Security Programs

Source: Office of Research and Statistics, Social Security Administration, Dept. of Health, Education and Welfare

Medicare; Old-Age, Survivors and Disability Insurance; Supplemental Security Income

Amendments, signed Dec. 31, 1973, included (1) an 11-percent increase in regular monthly benefits and special payments to those aged 72 and over, with 7 percent of the rise effective for March 1974 and the remainder payable for June 1974; (2) for the special minimum, a rise to $9 in the added amount payable for each year of coverage above 10 and up to 30; (3) a shift to June 1975 for the first possible automatic increase in benefits, based on the cost-of-living rise from the second quarter of 1974 through the first quarter of 1975; (4) for those aged 72 and over, suspension of their special benefits if they receive supplemental security income payments; (5) a rise to $13,200 in the maximum amount of annual earnings counted for contribution and benefit computation purposes, effective for 1974. In the supplemental security income program, payment levels were raised to $140 a month for an individual and to $210 per couple, effective for January 1974, with a further rise to $146 for an individual and $219 for a couple scheduled for July 1974; the amount added to the payment level for an "essential" person was lifted to $70 for January 1974 and to $73 beginning July 1974; food-stamp eligibility for supplemental security income recipients was liberalized temporarily. Under Medicare, certain reimbursement provisions and some technical provisions were amended.

Legislation in 1974 amended the supplemental security income program to extend the food-stamp eligibility liberalization for a year and to provide for automatic cost-of-living increases in payment levels whenever automatic increases in social security benefits occur, with the same percentage increase applying in both programs. Under another 1974 provision, farm rental income is not to be covered under the social security program unless the landowner materially participates in the farm's operation. The 1973 provision on Medicare reimbursement of teaching-physician's services was extended.

The Commissioner of Social Security is James B. Cardwell. There are 635 district offices, with 477 branches and 156 metropolitan branch offices, where the public may obtain information about benefit rights.

Medicare
Health Insurance for Aged

Under Medicare, protection against the costs of hospital care is provided for social security and railroad retirement beneficiaries aged 65 and over (beginning July 1966) and, effective July 1973, for persons entitled for 24 months to receive a social security disability benefit, certain persons with chronic kidney disease and their dependents, and, on a voluntary basis with payment of a special premium, persons aged 65 and over not otherwise eligible for hospital benefits; all those eligible for hospital benefits may enroll for medical benefits and pay a monthly premium and so may persons aged 65 and over who are not eligible for hospital benefits.

Persons eligible for both hospital and medical insurance or for medical insurance only may choose to have their covered services provided through a Health Maintenance Organization (a prepaid group health or other capitation plan that meets prescribed standards).

Hospital insurance. — In the 8th year of operation (July 1973-June 1974) about $7.8 billion was withdrawn from the hospital insurance trust fund for hospital and related benefits. About 21,600,000 persons were enrolled as of July 1973.

The hospital insurance program pays the cost of covered services for hospital and posthospital care as follows:
• Up to 90 days of hospital care during a benefit period (spell of illness, starting on the 1st day of care as a bed-patient is received in a hospital or skilled nursing facility and ending when the individual has not been a bed-patient for 60 consecutive days). For the first 60 days, the hospital insurance pays for all but the first $92 of expenses; for the 61st day to 90th day, the program pays all but $23 a day for covered services. In addition, each person has a 60-day lifetime reserve that can be used after the 90 days of hospital care in a benefit period are exhausted, and all but $46 a day of expenses during the reserve days are paid. Once used the reserve days are not replaced. (Payment for care in a mental hospital is limited to 190 days.)
• Up to 100 days' care in a skilled nursing facility (skilled nursing home) in each benefit period. Hospital insurance pays for all covered services for the first 20 days and $11.50 daily for the next 80 days. At least 3 day's hospital stay must precede these services, and the skilled nursing facility must be entered within 14 days after leaving the hospital. (The 1972 law permits more than 14 days in certain circumstances).
• Up to 100 visits by nurses or other health workers (not doctors) from a home health agency in the 365 days after release from a hospital or extended-care facility.

Money to pay these benefits comes from special contributions paid by workers, their employers, and the self-employed. The 1975 rate is 0.9% on earnings up to $13,200 (the maximum taxable for that year).

Medical insurance—Aged persons can receive benefits under this supplementary program only if they sign up for them and agree to a monthly premium ($6.70 to July 1975). The Federal Government pays the rest of the cost. In December of each year the Secretary of Health, Education, and Welfare announces the amount of the premium payable starting in July of the following year. The premiums are to be increased only when there is a general benefit increase in the year and it will rise no more than the percent by which the cash benefits have been increased since the last premium increase.

Benefit payments under the medical insurance program from July 1973 through June 1974 totaled $2.9 billion. As of July 1973, 20,900,000 persons were enrolled.

The medical insurance program pays 80% of the reasonable charges (after the first $60 in each calendar year) for the following services:
• Physicians' surgeons' services, whether in the doctor's office, a clinic, or hospital or at home (but physician's charges for X-ray or clinical laboratory services for hospital bed-patients are paid in full and without meeting the deductible).
• Other medical and health services, such as diagnostic tests, surgical dressings and splints, and rental or purchase of medical equipment. Beginning July 1, 1973, services of a physical therapist in independent practice, furnished in his office or the patient's home. Beginning Jan. 1, 1973, a hospital or extended-care facility may provide covered outpatient physical therapy services under the medical insurance program to its patients who have exhausted their hospital insurance coverage.
• Physical therapy services furnished under the supervision of a practicing hospital, clinic, skilled nursing facility, or agency.
• Certain services by podiatrists.
• All outpatient services of a participating hospital (including diagnostic tests).
• Beginning Jan. 1, 1973, under the 1972 amendments, outpatient speech pathology services, under the same requirements as physical therapy.

- Services of licensed chiropractors who meet uniform standards, but only for treatment by means of manual manipulation of the spine and treatment of subluxation of the spine demonstrated by X-ray.
- Supplies related to colostomies are considered prosthetic devices and payable under the program. Home health services even without a hospital stay (up to 100 visits a year) are paid up to 100%.

To get medical insurance protection, persons approaching age 65 may enroll in the 7-month period that includes 3 months before the 65th birthday, the month of the birthday, and 3 months after the birthday, but if they wish coverage to begin in the month they reach 65 they must enroll in the 3 months **before** their birthday. Persons not enrolling within their first enrollment period may enroll later, during the first 3 months of each year but their premium is 10% higher for each 12-month period elapsed since they first could have enrolled.

The monthly premium is deducted from the cash benefit for persons receiving social security, railroad retirement, or civil service retirement benefits. Income from the medical premiums and the Federal matching payments are put in a Supplementary Medical Insurance Trust Fund, from which benefits and administrative expenses are paid.

Medicare card. Persons qualifying for hospital insurance under social security receive a health insurance card similar to cards now used by Blue Cross and other health agencies. The card indicates whether the individual has taken out medical insurance protection. It is to be shown to the hospital, skilled nursing facility, home health agency, doctor, or whoever provides the covered services.

Payments are made only in the 50 States, Puerto Rico, the Virgin Islands, Guam, and American Samoa, except that hospital services may be provided in border areas immediately outside the U.S. if comparable services are not accessible in the U.S. for a beneficiary who becomes ill or is injured in the U.S.

Old-Age Survivors, and Disability Insurance

Retired and disabled workers and their families and the survivors of deceased workers received $55.2 billion in social security cash benefits in the 12 months ended in June 1974. In that month the average benefit being received by a retired worker was about $186; for retired workers just coming on the rolls, the average benefit award was about $190. For a disabled worker, the average June check was $205 and new disabled-worker beneficiaries were awarded $215, on the average.

Old-age, survivors, and disability insurance covers almost all jobs in which people work for wages or salaries, as well as most work of self-employed persons, whether in a city job, or in business, or on a farm.

Old-age, survivors, and disability insurance is paid for by a tax on earnings (for 1974 up to $13,200 and at least $13,200 for 1975; the taxable earnings base is now subject to adjustment when cost-of-living benefit increases have been made). The employed worker and his employer share the tax equally, (cash tips count as covered wages if they amount to $20 or more from one place of employment. The worker reports them to his employer, who includes them in his social security tax reports, but only the worker pays contributions on the amount of the tips).

The employer deducts the tax each payday and sends it, with an equal amount as his own share, to the District Director of Internal Revenue. The collected taxes are deposited in the Federal Old-Age and Survivors Insurance Trust Fund and the Federal Disability Insurance Trust Fund; they can be used only to pay benefits, the costs of rehabilitation services, and administrative expenses.

Amount of Work Required

To qualify for benefits for himself and his family, the worker must have been in covered employment long enough to become insured. Just how long depends on his date of birth (or if he dies or becomes disabled, the date of his death or disability).

A person is fully covered if he has one quarter of coverage for every year after 1950 (or year he reaches age 21) up to but not including the year in which he reaches age 62 or dies.

Certain provisions in the law permit special monthly payments under the social security program to persons aged 72 and over who are not eligible for regular social security benefits since they had little or no opportunity to earn social security work credits during their working lifetime.

To get disability benefits, the worker must also have credit for 5 out of 10 years before he becomes disabled. Persons disabled before age 31 can qualify with a briefer period of coverage.

Work Years Required

The following table shows the number of work years required to be fully insured for old-age or survivors benefits, according to the year worker reaches retirement age or dies.

Work credit for retirement benefits:

If you reach 62 in	Years men need	Years women need
1971	5³/₄	5
1972	6	5¹/₄
1973	6	5¹/₂
1974	6	5³/₄
1975	6	6
1977	6¹/₂	6¹/₂
1979	7	7
1981	7¹/₂	7¹/₂
1983	8	8
1987	9	9
1991 or later	10	10

Work credit for survivors checks

Born after 1929, die at	Born before 1930, die before age 62	Years you need
28 or younger		1¹/₂
30		2
32		2¹/₂
34		3
36		3¹/₂
38		4
40		4¹/₂
42		5
44	1973	5¹/₂
46	1975	6
48	1977	6¹/₂
50	1979	7
52	1981	7¹/₂
54	1983	8
56	1985	8¹/₂
58	1987	9
60	1989	9¹/₂
62 or older	1991 or later	10

Self-Employed

A self-employed person who has earnings of $400 or more in a year must report his earnings for income tax and social security tax purposes. If he is not a farmer he reports only net returns from his business. He need not add income from real estate, savings, dividends, loans, pensions or insurance policies if these are not part of his business.

A self-employed person who has net earnings of $400 or more in a year gets 4 quarters of coverage for that year. If his earnings are less than $400 in a year they do not count toward social security credits. The nonfarm self-employed person must make estimated payments of his social security taxes, on a quarterly basis, for taxable years after 1966, if combined estimated income tax and social security tax amount to at least $40.

The self-employed now have the option, comparable to that for farm workers, of reporting their earnings as ²/₃ of their gross income from self-employment but not more than $1,600 a year. This option can be used only if actual net earnings from self-employment income is less than $1,600 and less than ²/₃ of gross income and may be used only 5 times.

When a person has both taxable wages and earnings from self-employment, only as much of the self-employment income as will bring total earnings up to the current taxable maximum is subject to tax for social security purposes. A self-employed person pays the tax at a lower rate than the combined rate for an employee and his employer — about 1½ times what the employee alone pays.

Farm Owners and Hands

Self-employed farmers whose gross annual earnings from farming are under $2,400 may report ²/₃ of their gross earnings instead of net earnings for social security purposes. Cash or crop shares received from a tenant or share farmer count if the owner participated materially in production or management. The self-employed farmer pays contributions at the same rate as other self-employed, but he may make his tax returns annually.

Farm Workers. Earnings from farm work count toward benefits (1) if the employer pays $150 or more in cash during the year; (2) if the employee works on 20 or more days for cash pay figured on a time basis. Under these rules a person gets credit for one calendar quarter for each $100 in cash pay in a year but no more than four quarters in any one year.

Foreign farm workers admitted to the United States on a temporary basis will not be covered.

Household Workers

Anyone working as maid, cook, laundress, nursemaid, baby-sitter, chauffeur, gardener and at other household tasks in the house of another, is covered by social security if he or she earns $50 or more in cash in three months from any one employer. Room and board do not count, but carefare counts if paid in cash. The job does not have to be regular or fulltime. The employee should get a card at the social security office and show it to the employer.

The employer deducts the amount of the social security tax from the worker's pay, adds an identical amount as his own tax and sends the total amount to the Federal Government, with the number of the employee's social security card.

What Aged Workers Get

When a person has enough work in covered employment and reaches retirement age (65 for full benefit, 62 for reduced benefit), he may retire and get monthly old-age benefits. If he continues to work and has earnings of more than $2,400, $1 in benefits will be withheld for every $2 above $2,400. The amount that can be earned in a month without loss of any benefits is $200. The annual exempt amount and the monthly test will be raised automatically in the future, according to the rise in general earnings levels. The eligible worker who is 72 receives the full amount of benefit, regardless of earnings.

A worker's benefit will be raised by 1% for each year after 1970 for which the worker between 65 and 72 did not receive benefits because of earnings from work. No increases are to be paid to the worker's dependents or survivors under this provision.

A special minimum benefit is payable to persons who worked 20 or more years under social security as an alternative to the regular minimum of $93.80 if a higher amount results. The highest minimum under this provision would be $180 a month for a person ($270 for a couple) with 30 or more years of coverage.

When a person receives old-age benefits, payments can also be made to certain of his dependents including a wife 62 or over, dependent children under 18 or who became totally disabled before age 22 or who are full-time students not yet aged 22, a wife (regardless of age) if caring for an eligible child, and a dependent husband 62 or over.

The special benefit for persons aged 72 or over who do not meet the regular coverage requirements is $64.40 a month ($96.60 for a couple if both members are eligible). Like the monthly benefits, these payments are subject to cost-of-living increases, beginning June 1975. The special payment is not made to persons on the public assistance or supplemental security income rolls.

Social Security benefits are not subject to income taxes.

A woman worker is eligible for a full old-age benefit at age 65, but she may retire at 62 and get 80% of her full benefit for the rest of her life; the nearer she is to 65 when she begins collecting her benefit, the larger it will be. (Benefits for men retiring before 65 are reduced at the same rate as benefits for women retiring before 65.)

A child can get benefits based on his mother's earnings on the same conditions as those entitling a child to benefits based on his father's earnings record.

Benefits for Worker's Wife (or Husband)

The wife of a man who is getting social security retirement or disability payments may become entitled to wife's insurance benefits in a reduced amount when she reaches 62, or she may wait until she reaches 65 and get the entire amount of the wife's benefit, which is one-half of the husband's benefits. Benefits are also payable to the divorced wife of an insured worker if she was married to him for at least 20 years and he was contributing to or was ordered by a court to contribute to her support.

If a woman worker entitled to old-age benefit has a dependent husband aged 65 or over, he may draw a benefit similar to a wife's benefit at 65 (or a reduced benefit at age 62).

Benefits for Children of Retired or Disabled Workers

If a worker has children under 18 when he retires for age or disability they will get a benefit that is half his benefit, and so will his wife, even if she is under 62. Total benefits paid on a worker's earnings record are subject to a maximum and if the total paid to a family exceeds that maximum, the individual dependents' benefits are adjusted downward. (Total benefits paid to the family of a worker who retired in 1974 at age 65 with average yearly earnings of $5,838 could be no higher than $541.)

When his children reach 18, their benefits will stop, except that a child permanently and totally disabled before 22 may get a benefit as long as his disability meets the definition in the law. In addition, child's benefits are payable until the child reaches his 22nd birthday if he is attending school as a full-time student. Benefits may now be paid to a grandchild or step grandchild of a worker or of his spouse, in special circumstances.

What Disabled Worker Gets

If a worker becomes so severely disabled that he is unable to work, he may be eligible to receive a monthly disability benefit that is the same amount he would receive as an old-age benefit if he were 65 at the start of his disability. When he reaches 65, his disability benefit becomes an old-age benefit.

Benefits like those provided for dependents of retired-worker beneficiaries may be paid to dependents of disabled beneficiaries.

Survivor Benefits

If a worker should die while insured, one or more types of benefits would be payable to survivors.

1. A cash payment to cover burial expenses that amounts to 3 times the basic benefit but not more than $255, paid at the death of every insured worker.

2. A benefit for each child until the child reaches 18 (or up to age 22, if he is attending school). The monthly benefit of each child of a worker who has died is three-quarters of the amount the worker would have received if he had lived and drawn retirement benefits. A child with a permanent disability that began before age 22 may receive his benefit after that age.

3. A mother's benefit for the widow, if children under 18 are left in her care. Her benefit is 75% of the basic benefit and she draws it until the youngest child reaches 18. Payments stop then even if the

child's benefit continues because he is attending school. They will start again when she is 62 (or 60), unless she marries. If she marries and the marriage is ended, she regains benefit rights. If she has a disabled child beneficiary aged 18 or over in her care, her benefits also continue.

Disabled widows and widowers qualify for benefits at age 50 at reduced rates that depend on age at entitlement. The widow or widower must have become totally disabled before or within 7 years after the spouse's death.

4. If there are no children entitled to receive benefits, the widow will receive a benefit that is 100% of the husband's basic amount, if it is first payable when she is 65. She may choose to get her benefit when she is 60; her benefit is then reduced by 19/40 of 1% for each month it is paid before she is 65. However, for widows aged 62 and over whose husbands claimed their benefits before 65, the benefit is the reduced amount he would be getting if he were alive but not less than 82½% of his basic benefit. Dependent widowers aged 60 or over are entitled to survivor benefits on same basis as widows.

5. Dependent parents may be eligible for benefits, if they have been receiving at least half their support from the worker before his death, have reached age 62, and (except in certain circumstances) have not remarried since the worker's death. Each parent gets 75% of the basic benefit except that if only one parent survives the benefit is 82½%.

The survivors of a woman worker receive benefits on the same basis as those of men workers.

Maximum Benefits Payable

The illustrative table below shows a column heading for average earnings of $10,800, but the benefit amounts shown in the column are not in general payable yet, since it will be some time before workers can have an average that high (years when the maximum creditable amount of earnings was lower than $10,800 — the 1973 maximum — must currently be included when the average is figured). Benefit amounts larger than those shown in the table will eventually be payable to persons who raise their average yearly earnings for social security purposes by earning, for a sufficient period, the highest creditable amount in years with the higher maximums specified in the law — $13,200 in 1974 and $13,200 in 1975 unless it is raised under the provision for automatic increase, effective for years after 1974.

Examples of Monthly OASDI Cash Payments
(Effective through May 1975)

Average yearly earnings after 1950*	$912	$3,600	$4,800	$6,600	$7,800	$9,000	$10,800
Retired worker claiming benefit at 65 or disabled worker:							
Alone	$93.80	$214.40	$259.00	$320.20	$367.50	$393.50	$426.80
With spouse claiming benefit at—							
65 or over	140.70	321.60	388.50	480.30	551.30	590.30	640.20
62	129.00	294.80	356.20	440.30	505.40	541.10	586.90
With wife and 1 child	140.80	351.70	472.60	579.80	643.10	688.70	747.00
Retired worker claiming benefit at 62:							
Alone	75.10	171.60	207.20	256.20	294.00	314.80	341.50
With spouse claiming benefit at—							
65 or over	122.00	278.80	336.70	416.30	477.80	511.60	554.90
62	110.30	252.00	304.40	376.30	431.90	462.40	501.60
Widow claiming benefit at—							
65 or over	93.80	214.40	259.00	320.20	367.50	393.50	426.80
60	74.90	153.30	185.20	229.00	262.80	281.40	305.20
Disabled widow claiming benefit at 50	56.80	107.30	129.60	160.20	183.80	196.80	213.50
1 surviving child	93.80	160.80	194.30	240.20	275.70	295.20	320.10
Widow 65 and over and 1 child	140.80	351.70	453.30	560.40	643.10	688.70	747.00
Widowed mother and 1 child	140.80	321.60	388.60	480.40	551.40	590.40	640.20
Widowed mother and 2 children	140.80	351.70	472.60	579.80	643.10	688.70	747.00
Maximum family benefit	140.80	351.70	472.60	579.80	643.10	688.70	747.00

*Generally, average earnings are figured over the period from 1951 until the worker reaches retirement age, becomes disabled, or dies. Up to 5 years of low earnings or no earnings can be excluded. The maximum earnings creditable for social security are $3,600 for 1951-1954; $4,200 for 1955-1958; $4,800 for 1959-65; $6,600 for 1966-67; $7,800 for 1968-71; $9,000 for 1972; $10,800 for 1973; and $13,200 for 1974. As the text under the heading "Maximum Benefits Payable" explains, amounts shown in the last column will generally not be payable until later. When a person is entitled to more than one benefit, the amount actually payable is limited to the larger of the benefits.

Contribution Rate for Employees, Employers, and Self-Employed
Percent of Covered Earnings

Years	Employees and employers			Self-employed		
	OASDI Benefits	Hospital Insurance	Total	OASDI Benefits	Hospital Insurance	Total
1974-77	4.95	0.90	5.85	7.0	0.90	7.90
1978-80	4.95	1.10	6.05	7.0	1.10	8.10
1981-85	4.95	1.35	6.30	7.0	1.35	8.35
1986-98	4.95	1.50	6.45	7.0	1.50	8.50
1999-2010*	4.95	(1.50)	(6.45)	7.0	(1.50)	(8.50)
2011 and thereafter	5.95	(1.50)	(7.45)	7.0	(1.50)	(8.50)

*Costs of hospital insurance estimated only through 1997.

Supplemental Security Income

On Jan. 1, 1974, the supplemental security income program established by the 1972 Social Security Act amendments replaced the former Federal grants to States for aid to the needy aged, blind, and disabled in the 50 States and the District of Columbia. The program provides both for Federal payments based on uniform national standards and eligibility requirements and for State supplementary payments varying from State to State. The Social Security Administration administers the Federal payments financed from general funds of the Treasury — and the State supplements as well, if the State elects to have its supplementary program federally administered. The States may supplement the Federal payment for all recipients and must supplement it for persons otherwise adversely affected by the transition from the former public assistance programs. In August 1974, the number of persons receiving Federal payments and federally administered State payments was 3,734,300, and the amount of these payments was $449,110,000. The average amount for all types of payments (federally administered and State-administered) was $64.76 in January 1974 and $71.04 in June 1974.

Social Security Trust Funds
Old-Age and Survivors and Disability Insurance Trust Funds, 1936-1974
(In thousands)

| Period and fiscal year | Receipts | | | Expenditures | | Total asset at period end |
	Net contribution income and transfers	Net interest received	Transfers to RR Retirement Acct.	Benefit payments	Administrative expenses	
1936-37	$265,000	$2,262	....	$27		$267,235
1940-41	688,141	55,958	....	64,342	$26,840	2,397,615
1945-46	1,238,218	147,766	....	320,510	37,427	7,641,428
1950-51	3,124,098	287,392		1,498,088	70,447	1,735,567
1955-56	6,449,809	487,450		5,360,813	124,339	22,593,109
1960-61	12,314,678	591,713	336,882	11,888,527	272,188	23,404,734
1965-66	19,422,599	648,635	468,782	19,794,079	437,159	21,558,397
1969-70	34,554,182	1,572,375	589,257	29,045,046	623,055	37,719,951
1970-71	36,949,617	1,943,206	626,266	34,482,466	741,764	40,739,117
1972-73	47,304,791	2,281,098	802,457	47,373,415	913,984	44,285,368
1973-74	55,182,373	2,521,044	930,912	54,066,729	884,173	46,106,970
Cumulative[1] to June, 1974[2]	464,090,901	23,201,186	8,370,253	423,423,343	9,391,523	46,106,970

(1.)Beginning 1966, includes amounts for rehabilitative services, authorized by 1965 amendments (a total of $205,121,000 from 1965-66 to 1973-74).
(2.)Preliminary.
*Cumulative totals are not totals of columns since several years are omitted.

Hospital Insurance Trust Fund: Status, 1966-74
(In thousands)

| Period | Receipts | | | | Expenditures | | Total assets |
	Net contribution income[1]	Transfers from general revenues[2]	Transfers from railroad retirement account[3]	Net interest[4]	Net hospital and related service benefits[5]	Administrative expenses[6]	
Jan. 1966-June 1974[7]	44,713,095	4,374,106	459,318	1,327,699	41,688,839	1,250,609	7,934,772
Fiscal year:							
1965-66	908,797			5,970		63,564	851,204
1966-67	2,688,684	337,850	16,200	45,903	2,507,773	88,848	1,343,221
1967-68	3,514,049	283,631	43,613	61,091	3,736,322	78,647	1,430,636
1968-69	4,423,236	770,968	53,776	96,063	4,653,976	104,182	2,016,521
1969-70	4,784,789	628,262	61,307	139,423	4,804,242	148,660	2,677,401
1970-71	4,897,979	873,849	63,255	183,027	5,442,971	149,434	3,103,106
1971-72	5,225,891	551,351	63,782	190,105	6,109,139	166,370	2,858,725
1972-73	7,663,119	429,415	61,222	197,844	6,648,819	192,839	4,368,666
1973-74[7]	10,606,551	498,780	96,163	408,273	7,785,596	258,066	7,934,772

(1.)Represents amounts appropriated (estimated tax collections with suitable subsequent adjustments), after deductions for refund of estimated amount of employee-tax overpayment.
(2.)Represents Federal Government transfers from general funds appropriations to meet costs of benefits for persons not insured for cash benefits under OASDHI or railroad retirement and for costs of benefits arising from military wage credits.
(3.)Represents receipts under the financial interchange with railroad retirement account with respect to contributions for hospital insurance coverage of railroad workers.
(4.)Represents interest and profit on investments after transfers of interest on administrative expenses reimbursed to the OASI trust fund and on amounts transferred from railroad accounts.
(5.)Represents (1) payment vouchers on letters of credit issued to fiscal intermediaries under sec. 1816 and (2) direct payments to providers of services under sec. 1815 of the Social Security Act.
(6.)Subject to subsequent adjustment among all 4 social security trust funds, for allocated cost of each operation.
(7.)Preliminary.

Supplementary Medical Insurance Trust Fund: Status, 1966-74
(In thousands)

| Period | Receipts | | | Expenditures | | Total assets |
	Premium income[1]	Transfers from general revenues[2]	Net interest[3]	Net medical service benefits[4]	Administrative expenses[5]	
Jan. 1966-June 1974[6]	8,906,751	9,239,391	236,966	15,228,445	1,879,180	1,275,483
Fiscal year:						
1966-67	646,682	623,000	14,052	664,261	133,682	485,791
1967-68	698,465	634,000	20,677	1,389,622	142,608	306,703
1968-69	902,821	984,287	23,466	1,644,842	194,660	377,774
1969-70	936,000	928,151	11,536	1,979,287	216,993	57,181
1971-72	1,340,052	1,365,295	28,993	2,255,069	288,619	480,709
1972-73	1,462,607	1,430,451	45,049	2,391,232	245,861	745,722
1973-74[6]	1,703,189	2,028,926	75,924	2,869,132	409,146	1,275,483

(1.)Represents voluntary premium payments from and in behalf of insured persons.
(2.)Represents Federal Government transfers from general funds appropriations to match aggregate premiums paid.
(3.)Represents interest and profit on investments after transfer of interest on administrative expenses reimbursed to the OASI trust fund (see footnote 5).
(4.)Represents payment vouchers on letters of credit issued to carriers under section 1842 of the Social Security Act.
(5.)Subject to subsequent adjustment among all 4 social security trust funds for allocated cost of each operation.
(6.)Preliminary.

Employment and Training Services and Unemployment Insurance

Source: Manpower Administration, U.S. Department of Labor

The Federal-State Employment Service consists of the U.S. Employment Service and affiliated state employment services with their network of about 2,400 local offices. During fiscal 1974, these offices made almost 4.8 million placements in nonfarm jobs, an increase of 5.3% over the previous year. The most notable gain was a 23% increase, to 1.5 million, in the number of young workers under 22 who were placed.

The employment service works to refer employable applicants to job openings that use their highest skills and helps the unemployed obtain services or training to make them employable. It gives special attention to the needs of older workers, youth, minorities, the handicapped, migrants, the disadvantaged, and workers who lose jobs because of foreign trade competition. Special efforts are being made to improve manpower services in rural areas.

The employment service helps employers find needed workers and offers many employer services, including job-related personnel assistance. To give employers a wider choice of workers and applicants access to more job openings, it has developed job banks, which provide computerized daily lists of all available jobs in a city or area. Statewide networks of job banks now serve 43 states with over three-quarters of the nation's population. Other activities include enforcing standards on housing, transportation, and other conditions for farm and woods workers recruited for jobs in other states.

Special Veterans Service

Veterans receive special services and absolute preference in placements at all local employment service offices. During the year, these offices placed 600,000 veterans, of whom two-thirds served during the Vietnam era. The requirements that Federal contractors list job openings with the employment service is proving of particular benefit to veterans. The number of veterans placed in jobs listed under this requirement was up more than 30% over the previous year. Continuing efforts included overseas counseling on education, training, and job opportunities, given to nearly 90,000 servicemen in fiscal 1974, and hiring disabled veterans to work with other veterans.

Community Manpower System

The Comprehensive Employment and Training Act of 1973 sets up a new community manpower system to give people training and job-related services and place them in jobs. Under the new system which replaces certain Federal manpower programs, all States and cities, counties, and combinations of local units with populations of 100,000 or more receive Federal grants to plan and run comprehensive manpower programs in their localities. The job-related services provided are much the same as those formerly offered by national programs, but they vary from one area to another, according to local decisions on the needs of the area's workers and the demands of its labor market. Among them are classroom and on-the-job training, education, job referral, needed services like child care and medical aid, transitional public service jobs, and special programs for groups such as youth, migrants, Indians, and persons with limited English. In addition to comprehensive programs in all parts of the country, the new law authorizes transitional public service jobs in areas with an unemployment rate of 6½ percent or higher for 3 consecutive months.

National Manpower Activities

The Federal role under the new system is to provide support and technical assistance to local programs; insure proper use of Federal money; and serve Indians, migrants, ex-offenders, and others with particular job disadvantages. The Federal Government also continues to administer some programs and act as the Federal partner in the employment service system and the unemployment insurance pro-

gram. These responsibilities are carried out by the Department of Labor's Manpower Administration. Continuing national activities include apprenticeship, Job Corps, and the Work Incentive Program. Apprenticeship is conducted by employers, often jointly with labor unions, to train workers in a skilled trade on the job and in related classroom instruction. During the year, the Federal Government continued activities to guide, assist, and improve apprenticeship and give more minority members a chance to become apprentices. Job Corps, which trains disadvantaged youth largely at residential centers, recorded a 93% placement rate for former enrollees available for placement and planned nontraditional training or women leading to union apprenticeship jobs in carpentry, painting, bricklaying, and cement masonry and plastering. The Work Incentive Program helps people on Aid to Families with Dependent Children get and keep jobs. In fiscal 1974, some 353,000 persons became WIN participants, receiving manpower, counseling, or placement services; more than 178,000 were placed in unsubsidized jobs.

Unemployment Insurance

Unlike old-age and survivors insurance, entirely a Federal program, the unemployment insurance program is a Federal-State system which provides insured wage earners with partial replacement of wages lost during involuntary unemployment. The program protects most workers in the industry, but few in agriculture. Some 70,000,000 jobs in commerce, industry, and government, including the Armed Forces, were covered under the Federal-State system during calendar year 1973. In addition, 679,500 railroad workers were insured against unemployment under a system administered by the Railroad Retirement Board.

Each state, as well as the District of Columbia and Puerto Rico, has its own law and operates its own program. The amount and duration of the weekly benefits are determined by state laws, based on prior wages and length of employment. States are required to extend the duration of benefits when unemployment rises to and remains above specified state or national levels; costs of extended benefits are shared by the state and Federal governments.

Under the Federal Unemployment Tax Act, as amended in 1970, the tax rate is 3.2% on the first $4,200 paid to each employee of employers with one or more employees in 20 weeks of the year or a quarterly payroll of $1,500. A credit of up to 2.7% is allowed for taxes paid under state unemployment insurance laws that meet certain criteria, leaving the Federal share at 0.5% of taxable wages, from which the Federal government pays its share of the cost of extended benefits and makes grants to the states to cover the administrative costs of the unemployment insurance and employment service programs. Grants from this source for employment service administrative costs are limited to that proportion of total employment service costs that is attributable to the covered work force.

Social Security Requirement

The Social Security Act requires, as a condition of such grants, prompt payment of due benefits. The Federal Unemployment Tax Act provides safeguards for workers' right to benefits if they refuse jobs that fail to meet certain labor standards. Through the Unemployment Insurance Service of the Manpower Administration, the Secretary of Labor determines whether states qualify for grants and for tax offset credit for employers.

Benefits are financed solely by employer contributions, except in Alaska, Alabama, and New Jersey, where employees also contribute. Benefits are paid through the public employment offices, at which unemployed workers must register for work and to which they must report regularly for referral to a possible job during the time when they are drawing weekly benefit payments. During the 1973 calendar, year, $4.15 billion in benefits were paid under the state unemployment insurance programs to 5,328,600 beneficiaries, representing compensation for 72,643,-800 weeks of unemployment. They received an average weekly payment of $59 (est.) for total unemployment for an average of 13.4 weeks.

Federal Worker Benefits

Title 5, chapter 85 of the U.S. Code provided unemployment insurance protection during calendar year 1973 to about 2,844,000 Federal civilian employees and about 2,202,000 members of the Armed Forces.

Benefits for unemployed Federal workers and ex-servicemen are financed through direct Federal appropriations but are paid by the state agencies as agents of the Federal government.

During calendar year 1973 a total of $121,998,000 was paid to 104,800 unemployed Federal civilian workers for a total of 1,976,000 weeks of unemployment. The average weekly payment was $61.74 and was paid for an average of 18.9 weeks. A total of $201,605,800 was paid to 230,700 unemployed ex-servicemen for 3,187,400 weeks of unemployment. The average weekly benefit was $63.25 and was paid for an average of 13.8 weeks.

Employment Security

Source: Manpower Administration, U.S. Dept. of Labor

Fiscal year 1973-74, State Program Only

State	Insured claimants[1] (1,000)	Benefici-aries[2] (1,000)	Exhaus-tions[3] (1,000)	Initial claims[4] (1,000)	Benefit Payments — Total[5] (1,000)	Avg. weekly b'fit for total unemploy. (dollars)	Funds available for b'fits June 30, 1974[6] (millions)	Employers subj. to state law March 31, 1974 (1,000)
Alabama	101	80	18	174	$ 38,962	48.68	126	53
Alaska	23	21	5	38	22,863	66.10	36	7
Arizona	59	48	11	119	28,854	54.21	161	42
Arkansas	71	46	10	116	24,364	51.39	65	40
California	1,145	856	229	2,075	671,257	61.44	1,245	391
Colorado	52	29	7	88	22,746	71.02	111	48
Connecticut	188	173	31	343	131,482	71.90	40	66
Delaware	27	24	4	59	18,675	67.82	36	12
District of Columbia	25	21	8	31	30,024	80.86	45	17
Florida	151	100	30	263	55,409	51.05	362	155
Georgia	143	89	26	172	46,015	52.73	461	84
Hawaii	42	34	10	57	31,915	70.68	19	16
Idaho	31	27	6	65	15,571	59.17	54	18
Illinois	325	259	66	587	204,838	64.38	475	185
Indiana	194	153	42	323	71,249	49.49	379	81
Iowa	57	41	10	92	30,020	62.95	119	56
Kansas	51	42	9	83	28,394	60.09	125	45
Kentucky	104	88	16	157	47,830	57.94	211	53
Louisiana	106	82	28	187	61,621	54.57	129	60
Maine	48	46	13	105	24,538	52.82	27	21
Maryland	116	89	15	203	61,342	61.55	163	63
Massachusetts	274	267	95	543	264,929	66.98	195	113
Michigan	709	435	100	1,177	317,660	62.21	501	140
Minnesota	123	103	35	192	92,106	64.50	67	69
Mississippi	43	29	5	73	12,120	37.67	120	35
Missouri	185	140	29	383	80,010	55.02	239	83
Montana	27	20	6	49	13,643	51.68	20	18
Nebraska	40	29	9	53	18,470	56.74	58	31
Nevada	34	34	9	87	28,159	65.80	30	14
New Hampshire	45	34	1	60	12,223	57.21	58	18
New Jersey	475	380	132	729	380,332	70.15	120	141
New Mexico	24	22	6	62	15,860	50.02	43	22
New York	828	620	166	1,711	624,545	61.56	1,372	383
North Carolina	146	98	11	272	36,735	43.04	547	92
North Dakota	13	11	3	21	9,127	55.95	17	14
Ohio	288	232	33	564	171,556	68.34	773	180
Oklahoma	54	43	17	101	26,919	45.37	61	48
Oregon	116	91	17	268	63,595	54.99	114	49
Pennsylvania	528	422	66	1,073	385,612	71.00	566	195
Puerto Rico	122	120	60	263	69,007	36.10	19	36
Rhode Island	72	53	18	133	43,018	63.67	25	23
South Carolina	66	42	11	107	24,176	50.89	227	42
South Dakota	9	8	2	16	4,370	50.62	23	15
Tennessee	135	102	20	203	48,002	48.23	316	64
Texas	166	114	42	275	68,532	51.15	344	202
Utah	36	31	8	60	21,511	61.15	51	23
Vermont	21	18	4	40	15,552	61.53	1	11
Virginia	67	41	8	102	21,787	54.87	248	71
Washington	176	162	60	460	138,728	63.49	—13	72
West Virginia	65	57	9	109	25,968	46.08	113	26
Wisconsin	138	113	23	255	92,237	68.82	301	82
Wyoming	5	4	1	8	2,586	54.13	26	10
Total	[7]8,091	6,223	1,600	14,785	$4,797,043	$ 61.41	10,970	3,838

(1) Claimants whose base-period earnings or whose employment — covered by the unemployment insurance program — was sufficient to make them eligible for unemployment insurance benefits as provided by State law. (2) Based on number of first payments. (3) Based on final payments. Some claimants shown, therefore, actually experienced their final week of compensable unemployment toward the end of the previous fiscal year but received their final payments in the current fiscal year. Similarly, some claimants who served their last week of compensable unemployment toward the end of the current fiscal year did not receive their final payment in this fiscal year and hence are not shown. A final week of compensable unemployment in a benefit year results in the exhaustion of benefit rights for the benefit year. Claimants who exhaust their benefit rights in one benefit year may be entitled to further benefits in the following benefit year. (4) Excludes intrastate transitional claims to reflect more nearly instances of new unemployment. Includes claims filed by interstate claimants in the Virgin Islands. (5) Adjusted for voided benefit checks and transfers under interstate combined wage plan. (6) Sum of balance in State clearing accounts, benefit payment accounts, and unemployment trust fund accounts maintained in the U.S. Treasury. (7) Preliminary.

How and Where to Get Help on Consumer Complaints
by Kenneth C. Johnston

Consumers complaining about faulty merchandise or wretched repair services can get help through customer relations offices in many corporations as well as through new or expanded government agencies.

Many big businesses now provide phone numbers (some toll-free) or addresses where complainants can receive courteous consideration and have some hope of action.

New government services are also available to consumers, although Congress again failed, because of a 1974 Senate filibuster, to set up a federal consumer protection agency.

The range of services open to consumers includes Better Business Bureaus, government prosecutors, small claims courts and local government consumer agencies.

There are also industry and trade associations and those newspapers and radio stations which intercede for readers or listeners.

What Corporations Provide

Here's what some big companies suggest you do if you can't get satisfaction from your local dealer:

General Motors: Phone or write GM zone office nearest you (listed in your owner's manual). If still unsatisfied, phone or write Divisional Owner Relations Office (also in manual).

Ford: Phone or write Ford Customer Service Div., district office (see phone book or ask local Ford dealer); or phone 800 648-4848 (free call) for all vehicles made by Ford.

Chrysler: Phone or write Chrysler Corp., Customer Service (ask dealer or see phone book); or write to: Consumer Affairs, Chrysler Corp., P.O. Box 1086, Detroit, Mich. 48231; include your own phone no.

General Electric: Write to Manager of Customer Relations, General Electric Co., 570 Lexington Ave., New York, N.Y. 10022. But, on appliances, the warranty tells customer where to write.

Westinghouse: Phone 800 245-0600 (free call) and ask for Betty Wade, national consumer service manager.

RCA: On any RCA product, phone 212 598-4921 or write Customer Relations, RCA Corp., 30 Rockefeller Plaza, New York, N.Y. 10020.

Union Carbide: The product or the guarantee has address to write to; or write Union Carbide Corp., Consumer Information, 270 Park Ave., New York, N.Y. 10017.

American Motors: Phone 800 521-7500 (free call) or phone or write nearest AM zone customer relations department.

Exxon: Write to John B. Boatwright, Marketing Dept., Exxon, Box 2180, Houston, Tex. 77001, on product, service or credit card complaints.

Gulf Oil: See phone book or dealer for nearest Gulf Oil district office or write Gulf Oil Corp., 1290 Ave. of the Americas, New York, N.Y. 10019, on products or service; for credit card troubles, see address on bill.

Mobil Oil: See dealer or phone book for regional Customer Relations Dept., Mobil Oil Corp., in Chicago, Los Angeles, Philadelphia or Scarsdale, N.Y. For credit card troubles, write Mobil Oil, Credit Card Customer Relations Department, 150 E. 42d St., New York, N.Y. 10017.

Texaco: See dealer or phone book for Texaco, Inc., district office; if not satisfied, write Texaco, Inc., Retail Sales Office, 135 E. 42d St., New York, N.Y. 10017.

ARCO: See phone book or dealer for Atlantic Richfield district office or write to Atlantic Richfield Co., Marketing Manager, P.O. Box 2679 T.A., Los Angeles, Cal. 96051. On credit cards, use free "800" phone no. shown on bill.

Goodyear: See dealer or phone book for Goodyear

Tire & Rubber Co. customer service representative at district office, or write Director of Consumer Affairs, Goodyear Tire & Rubber Co., 1144 E. Market St., Akron, Ohio 44316.

Sears, Roebuck: Ask for Customer Service at the store; then, the store manager; finally, write Sears, Roebuck & Co., Customer Relations, 925 S. Homan Ave., Chicago, Ill. 60607.

J. C. Penney: See manager or, in large stores, Customer Service manager; write Patricia Ludorf, Customer Relations Dept., J. C. Penney Co., 1301 Avenue of the Americas, New York, N.Y. 10019.

Kresge's: See section supervisor; then, store manager; finally, get from manager address of S.S. Kresge Co. regional office, write to Customer Relations there.

Kodak: See phone book under Eastman Kodak Co. for Kodak Consumer Center (in some 35 cities) for free minor adjustments and advice; or for Costumer Equipment Services Division (in 8 cities) for service and repairs; or write Consumer Photo Information Dept., Eastman Kodak Co., 343 State St., Rochester, N.Y. 14650.

A & P: See store manager or phone book under A & P Food Stores or Great Atlantic & Pacific Tea Co. for Customer Relations Dept. (in 32 cities); finally, write Executive Office, A & P Food Stores, 420 Lexington Ave., New York, N.Y. 10017.

Firestone: See dealer or phone book, under Firestone Tire & Rubber Co., for district office, contact consumer affairs representative there (in some 50 cities); write Consumer Affairs Director, Firestone Tire & Rubber Co., 1200 Firestone Parkway, Akron, Ohio 44317.

DuPont: See dealer or phone book under duPont de Nemours, Product Information (in 8 major cities), or write duPont Co., Wilmington, Del. 19898.

General Foods: Write to General Foods Corp., 250 North St., White Plains, N.Y. 10625.

Woolworth's: See store manager for address of Regional Vice President, F.W. Woolworth Co., or write Vice President Public Affairs, F. W. Woolworth Co., 233 Broadway, New York, N.Y. 10007.

Panasonic: Write nearest regional office listed on card accompanying product.

Procter & Gamble: Write Consumer Services, P.O. Box 599, Cincinnati, Ohio 45201. If possible, include your phone number, times you can be reached and name and serial number from the product package.

Admiral Corporation: Toll-free phone to company headquarters is 800 447-1305.

Whirlpool Corporation: Round-the-clock toll-free service through 800 253-1301.

Volkswagen: Try Customer Relations Dep't. at Volkswagen regional office (see owner's manual); or write Customer Relations, Volkswagen of America, Englewood Cliffs, N.J. 07632.

United Van Lines: Call toll-free 800 235-3870, ask for Bette Malone.

Government Agencies

There are numerous government agencies which can be helpful:

Cities: Some have Offices of Consumer Complaints or Depts. of Consumer Affairs (see phone book). In N.Y. City, for example, the department will investigate the complaint, then may try to work out a settlement; it may sue on behalf of a consumer, issue violation notices, hold hearings and fine a company or revoke or suspend a company's license to operate in the city.

Many towns and counties also have consumer protection agencies.

States likewise offer aid to the unhappy consumer. Usually, it is a part of the Attorney General's office.

Write or phone the Attorney General, Attention Consumer Protection Office, in your state.

New Jersey became in 1974 the first state to set up a Public Advocate Department to represent citizens in civil suits as well as criminal.

Nationally, one may write to the Bureau of Consumer Protection, Federal Trade Commission, Washington, D.C. 20580, or the nearest FTC regional office. In 1974 the FTC cracked down on collection agencies using deceptive means to collect allegedly delinquent accounts.

The Consumer Product Safety Commission, a federal agency created in 1973, offers a toll-free number, 800 638-2666, where you can find out if a particular product has been declared unsafe or complain about one you believe is hazardous. If enough complaints are received, the commission will investigate and can order the product banned.

For a complaint against an airline (fares, baggage, service, delays), write Office of Consumer Affairs, Civil Aeronautics Board, Washington, D.C. 20428.

In **Canada**, one may write the Director, Trade Practices Branch, Dept. of Consumer and Corporate Affairs, 219 Laurier Ave. West, Ottawa, Ontario.

Other Industry Aids

Within industry groups there are industry and trade associations which may be helpful. One which claims an excellent record in handling a large number of complaints is MACAP, the **Major Appliance Consumer Action Panel**, 20 North Wacker Drive, Chicago, Ill. 60606. You may write or make a free, collect phone call to 312 236-3165, if you don't get satisfaction from a manufacturer of home laundry equipment, range, refrigerator, freezer, room air conditioner, water heater, dehumidifier, dishwasher, disposer, gas incinerator or humidifier. Give full details.

A similar organization is CRICAP, the **Carpet and Rug Industry Consumer Action Panel**, Box 1568, Dalton, Ga. 30720. Write them, if the dealer and maker won't cooperate, giving full details and your phone number. They will recommend appropriate action to the company involved; they claim good results, especially among firms that are members of the Carpet & Rug Institute.

Among industry complaint centers sponsored by the U.S. Chamber of Commerce are:

American Apparel Manufacturers Assn., 1611 N. Kent St., Arlington, Va. 22209.

American Footwear Manufacturers Assn., 342 Madison Ave., N.Y. 10017.

Direct Mail Advertising Assn., 230 Park Ave., New York, N.Y. 10017.

Master Photo Dealers and Finishers Assn., 603 Lansing Ave., Jackson, Mich. 49202.

Mobile Homes Manufacturing Assn., 14650 Lee Rd., Chantilly, Va. 22021.

National Assn. of Furniture Manufacturers, 8401 Connecticut Ave., Suite 911, Washington, D.C. 20015.

National Employment Assn., 2000 K St. N.W., Washington, D.C. 20006. (For employment agencies.)

Don't Forget

As a complaining consumer you will find it helpful to provide whatever agency you appeal to with copies of receipts and guarantees (not the actual receipts). Be as specific as possible about the dealer's name and address, purchase date, price, name and serial number (if any) of the product, places you may already have sought relief, with dates. Don't forget your name, address and phone number (some companies or agencies may want to serve you as rapidly as possible and may need further information).

The consumer may even return the favor in some cases and help the manufacturer: as a Procter & Gamble spokesman points out, some manufacturers will want the consumer to hold on to the offending product so that the maker can analyze it, find out what went wrong and try to prevent its happening again.

Consumers' Association of Canada

Consumers' Association of Canada is a voluntary, non-profit organization, founded in 1947. CAC's aims are:
(a) to unite the strength of consumers to improve the standards of living in Canadian homes;
(b) to study Consumer problems and make recommendations for their solution;
(c) to bring the views of consumers to the attention of governments, trade and industry, and provide a channel from these two to the consumer;
(d) to obtain and provide for consumers information and council on consumer goods and services and to conduct research and tests for the better accomplishment of the objects of the corporation.

CAC publishes a bi-monthly magazine, CANADIAN CONSUMER which provides test results on consumer products and information on legislation and other consumer concerns.

There are seventy-seven local associations across Canada, and eight provincial representatives.

CAC's achievements in the areas of textile labelling, hazardous products, packaging, selling practices, and food and drug regulations.

National Office is located at 100 Glouster Street, Ottawa, Ontario, K2P2E5.

Consumer Credit Statistics

Source: Federal Reserve System (Estimated amounts outstanding. In millions of dollars)

End of year or month	Total	Installment credit — Total	Automobile paper[1]	Other consumer goods paper[1]	Repair and modernization loans[2]	Personal loans	Noninstallment credit — Total	Single payment loans	Charge Accounts	Service credit
1960.......	56,141	42,968	17,658	11,545	3,148	10,617	13,173	4,507	5,329	3,337
1965.......	89,883	70,893	28,437	18,483	3,736	20,237	18,990	7,671	6,430	4,889
1970.......	127,163	102,064	35,184	31,465	5,070	30,345	25,099	9,675	7,968	7,456
1971.......	138,394	111,295	38,664	34,353	5,413	32,865	27,099	10,585	8,350	8,164
1972.......	157,564	127,332	44,129	40,080	6,201	36,922	30,232	12,256	9,002	8,974
1973.......	180,486	147,437	51,130	47,530	7,352	41,425	33,049	13,241	9,829	9,979
1974, June..	183,425	150,615	51,641	48,099	7,930	42,945	32,810	13,311	9,106	10,393

(1.) Includes all consumer installment credit extended for the purpose of purchasing automobiles and other consumer goods, whether held by retail outlets or financial institutions. Includes credit on purchases by individuals of automobiles or other consumer goods that may be used in part for business.

(2.) Includes only repair and modernization loans held by financial institutions; such loans held by retail outlets are included in "other consumer goods paper."

Interest Laws and Consumer Finance Loan Rates

Source: Revised by Roger S. Barrett of Chicago, Editor Consumer Finance Law Bulletin

Most states have laws regulating interest rates. These laws fix a legal or conventional rate which applies when there is no contract for interest. They also fix a general maximum contract rate, but in many states there are so many exceptions that the general contract maximum actually applies only to exceptional cases.

1. Legal rate of interest. The legal or conventional rate of interest applies to money obligations when no interest rate is contracted for and also to judgments. The rate is usually 6% a year; 5% or 7% in some states.

2. General maximum contract rates. The most common general maximum rate is 8% a year but many states permit 9%, 10%, or 12%. Rhode Island permits 21%. The general maximum is fixed by the State Constitution rather than by statute at 10% per year in Arkansas, California, Tennessee, and Texas. Loans to corporations are frequently exempted or subject to a higher maximum. In recent years, it has also been common to provide special rates for home mortgage loans. Courts generally hold that installment sale charges are not interest, but installment sale charges are limited by laws in many states.

3. Specific enabling acts. In many states special statutes permit industrial loan companies and banks to charge interest and fees without regard to installment payments which yield 1½% a month or more.

Laws regulating charge accounts and credit cards generally limit charges to 1½% per month. Credit unions may generally charge 1% a month. Pawnbrokers' rates vary widely. Building and loan associations, and loans insured by the F.H.A., are also specially regulated.

4. Consumer finance loan statutes. Most consumer finance loan statutes are based on early models drafted by the Russell Sage Foundation (1916-42) to provide small loans to wage earners under license and other protective regulations. Since 1969, however, the model has frequently been the Uniform Consumer Credit Code which applies to credit sales and loans for consumer purposes up to $25,000. In general, licensed lenders may charge 2½% or 3% a month for $300 or less and reduced rates for additional amounts up to $2,000 or more. A number of states permit add-on rates of 17% to 20% ($17 to $20 per $100) a year of the original principal for $300 and lower rates for additional amounts. An add-on of 17% ($17 per $100) per year yields about 2½% per month when the loan is paid in equal monthly installments. In the table below unless otherwise stated, monthly and annual rates are based on reducing principal balances, annual add-on rates are based on the original principal for the full term, and two or more rates apply to different portions of balance or original principal.

The states with consumer finance loan laws and the rates of charge as of October 1, 1973, are as follows:

Maximum rate	Monthly unless otherwise stated	Maximum rate

Ala..... Annual add-on: 15% to $500, 10% to $1,000, 8% to $2,000. Over $2,000, 8% add-on on entire balance. Higher rates for loans up to $300.

Ark.....3% to $400, 2% to $800, 1% to $1,500. 5% for loans up to $50.

Ariz.....3% to $300. 2% to $600. 1¹/₂ to $1,500. 1% to $2,500.

Cal...2¹/₂% to $225, 2% to $625, 1¹/₂% to $1650, 1% to $10,000 (1¹/₂% min.). (eff. 1/1/'75)

Colo...36% per annum to $300. 21% to $1,000, 15% to $25,-000 (18% min.).

Conn... Annual Add-on: 17% to $300. 11% to $1,800.

Del..... Annual Discount: 9% for 1st 36 mos., 6% for remaining months; plus 2% fee.

Fla..... 30% per annum to $300, 24% to $600, 16% to $2,500.

Haw... 3¹/₂% to $100, 2¹/₂% to $300.

Idaho. ..36% per annum to $390, 21% to $1,300, 15% to $32,-500 (18% min.).

Ill...... 3% to $150, 2% to $300, 1% to $800.

Ind..... 36% per annum to $330, 21% to $1,100, 15% to $30,000 (18% min.).

Ia...... 3% to $250, 2% to $400, 1¹/₂% to $1,000.

Kan.... 3% to $300, ⁵/₆% to $25,000; or 18% per annum to $1,000, 14.45% to $25,000 (eff. 1/1/'74).

Ky.....3% to $300, 2% to $1,000, 1% to $1,200; or annual add-on of 20% to $300; 16% to $800, 13% to $1,200.

La.....36% per annum to $800, 27% to $2,000, 21% to $3,500, 15% to $25,000 (18% min.).

Me..... 30% per annum to $300, 21% to $1,000, 15% to $25,-000 (18% min.). (eff. 1/1/75).

Md..... 3% to $300, 2% to $500.

Mass... 2¹/₂% to $200, 2% to $600; 1³/₄% to $1,000, ³/₄% to $3,000.

Mich...2¹/₂% to $400, 1¹/₄% to $1,500.

Minn...2³/₄% to $300, 1¹/₂% to $600, 1¹/₄% to $1200 plus fee of $1 per $100.

Miss. ..36% per annum to $600, 33% to $1800, 2 .% to $4,500, 12% over $4,500.

Mo..... 2.218% to $500, 8% per annum on any remainder.

Mont... Annual add-on; 20% to $300, 16% to $500, 12% to $1,000, 10% to $2,500. Special rate to $90.

Neb.... 30% per annum to $300, 24% to $500, 18% to $1,000, 12% to $3,000.

Nev..... Annual add-on: 9% to $1,000, 8% to $2,500; monthly fee of 1% on first $200 and ¹/₂% on next $200; over $2,500 to $10,000 annual interest is 17.74%.

N.H.....2% to $600, 1¹/₂% to $1,500, 1¹/₂% on larger loans to $5,000.

N.J.....24% per annum to $500, 22% to $1,000.

N.M.... 3% to $150, 2¹/₂% to $300, 1% to $2,500 (1¹/₂% min.).

N.Y.....2¹/₂% to $100, 2% to $300, 1¹/₂% to $900, 1¹/₄% to $2,500.

N.C.....2¹/₂% to $300, 1¹/₂% to $1500. Special rate up to $95.

N.D.....2¹/₂% to $250, 2% to $500, 1³/₄% to $750, 1¹/₂% to $1,000.

Ohio... Annual add-on: 16% to $500, 9% to $1,000, 7% to $2,000; or equivalent simple interest rate.

Okla...30% per annum to $300, 21% to $1,000, 15% to $25,-000. Special rates to $100 (18% min.)

Ore.....3% to $300, 1³/₄% to $1,000, 1¹/₄% to $5,000. Over $5,000, 1¹/₂%.

Pa..... 3% to $150, 2% to $300, 1% to $600.

P.R..... Annual Add-on: 20% to $300, 7% to $600.

R.I..... 3% to $300, 2¹/₂% for loans between $300 and $800; 2% for larger loans to $2,500.

S.C.....Annual add-on: 20% to $100, 18% to $300, 9% to $1,000; 7% for larger loans to $7,500, plus service fee. Special rate to $150.

S.D.....2¹/₂% to $300, 2% to $600, 1¹/₂% to $1,200, 1% to $2,500; $2 minimum.

Tenn... 7¹/₂% per annum discount plus fees; no size limit.

Texas.. Annual add-on: 18% to $300, 8% to $2,500. Special rates to $100.

Utah ... 36% per annum to $390, 21% to $1300, 15% to $32,-500 (18% min.).

Vt..... Annual add-on of 14% to $1,500.

Va..... 2¹/₂% to $500, 1¹/₂% to $1500; annual add-on of 17% to $500, 13% to $1000, 11% to $1,500.

Wash... 3% to $300, 1¹/₂6 to $500, 1% to $1,000; $1 minimum.

W.Va... 36% per year to $200, 24% to $600, 18% to $1,200.

Wis..... Annual Discount: 9¹/₂% on first $1,000, 8% to $3,000 up to 36 months; 18% per annum for larger loans.

Wyo.... 36% per annum to $300, 21% to $1,000, 15% to $25,-000 (18% min.).

ECONOMICS
Boom to Bust
The Story of the Two-Industry Economic Rocket
by Jerome Shuchter, Editor, Jeremiad
Box 36496, Los Angeles, CA 90036

The early 1970s tried out a number of experiments in economics, all largely unsuccessful. We learned the pitfalls of wage and price controls but less in the public eye was the by-play which tapped 2 key industries for a very special role.

The nation languished in the aftermath of the 1970 recession. The economy lacked sparkle. We caught our first glimpse of that mythical monster — no body, all wings — half recession, half inflation. A general disaffection sprouted everywhere which sought release in wage and price controls. It was in August 1971 that the nation took the plunge into a new era of controls, starting with a general freeze. During the ensuing years controls would switch on-again off-again a number of times before expiring in the spring of 1974.

By common consent, controls flopped. Whether from some innate flaw built into the control system, or because of unenthusiastic administration of the program, what is certain is that three years of blunder-prone experiment brought negative results: inflation not only persisted, it even strengthened. So much so that President Gerald R. Ford, seeking new programs in his September 1974 conferences with business, labor and others, ruled out at once only one economic stratagem, wage and price control.

Trickle-down Policy

Other heritages from the August 1971 policy overhaul are almost forgotten. The great hold-down on prices and wages was accompanied by a set of stimuli for industry which were wide-ranging in character. Over a period of several months there were tax breaks for all corporations; a dollar devaluation which made foreign goods more expensive and less salable here while it stimulated U.S. exports (for awhile there was a 10% tax on most imports); and there was a 7% tax credit allowed on new capital investment. Such a range of programs has been described as the "trickle-down" variety, pressuring business to expand and in the process to create employment and good times. Such a strategy contrasts with the more familiar stimulus of preceding administrations which encouraged consumer spending through tax relief, which then "trickles up" to stimulate greater production. The Nixon administration opted for "trickle down."

The program was even more calculated than that. Two industries in particular, housing and automobiles, were delegated to take a lead role in the upturn.

The housing industry received an infusion of subsidies; down payment requirements were cut by over two-thirds; loanable funds at savings and loan institutions were increased; steps were taken to reduce the actual selling price of homes to buyers.

Homebuilding rates skyrocketed, setting two yearly records in a row, the number of new housing units increasing from 1.5 million in 1970 to 2.1 million in 1971 and to a dazzling 2.4 million in 1972.

As Detroit Goes...

The auto industry also won particular favor. It garnered all the benefits provided to industry in general, and in addition won the elimination of a 7% excise tax on auto sales. During the ensuing period it secured another benefit in spite of itself. When it sought higher prices from the price board it was turned down cold. While prices of other products continued to rise, auto prices stayed down, and cars were a relatively good buy.

The sales results were spectacular. In 1970 U.S. automakers had sold only 7.1 million cars; by 1971 the total was up to 8.7 million; by 1972, to 9.3 million; in 1973, to 9.7 million, up more than one-third during the brief span of years.

Huge as housing and autos may themselves be, a notable feature of the two industries is that they form the centerpieces for a host of dependent industries. Not only do they call forth vast quantities of lumber and steel and numberless other ingredients for their production, but when they are complete, a caravan of other industries follow in behind: home furnishings, roads, utilities, and schools thrive when there is homebuilding; auto accessories, service stations, garages and travel networks follow the auto market.

The 1972 Upturn

The outcome: a brilliant, dizzying success. The economic chariot had made a screeching turn into prosperity by 1972, as the administration lashed the outside pair of horses into a frenzy. As they lunged ahead, they pulled the whole of U.S. industry around the turn. In 1972, total production of the nation increased by 7.9% as compared to normal growth averages of about 4%; in 1973 there followed an even stronger advance, by 9.0%. Even as price controls stumbled from shambles to shambles, the nation's production expanded powerfully on a broad basis, inspirited by the two lead industries.

By the end of 1973, just as prices entered a period of almost unbridled growth, the industrial expansion ground to a halt. The index of industrial production for all industry had hit its peak in Nov. 1973, then it declined and ran virtually flat through all of 1974.

The Morning After

Housing led the decline, starting a precipitous drop in mid-1973, finding a plateau for many months at the 1.5 million level, then dropping closer to the one million zone in the fall of 1974. The industry lay in ruins.

Autos, equally over-stimulated, started a downward trajectory at the same time. Early in 1973 domestic cars had sold at a rate of 10 million or better. By year's end the rate was down to 8 million, where it languished through most of 1974.

Clearly, the two lead industries, having opened the way to dazzling peaks in the glory days of 1972 and early 1973 — even before dramatic food and oil shortages struck — started to reverse their course. Now, as they founder, stagnant or still declining, they drag down with them a train of follower industries.

The lumber industry is a case in point. Boom and bust are traditional here, but this was the worst down cycle in years, explained the president of an Oregon lumber company, Paul Ehinger: "What makes this cycle different is that we're coming off a high plateau that extended over a much longer period . . . The drop could be a lot deeper." Because of the outsize housing boom, he expects a matching bust. Similar trends are visible for all housing-related products, including the furniture and the equipment new householders purchase. The same is true for auto's sub-markets.

United States Budget Receipts and Outlays—1973-1974

Source: Treasury Department; each fiscal year ends June 30 (data preliminary)

Classification	Fiscal 1974	Fiscal 1973
Receipts		
Individual income taxes	$142,702,852	$125,112,006
Corporate income taxes	41,788,719	39,045,309
Social insurance taxes and contributions:		
Federal old-age and survivors insurance	48,169,717	41,076,363
Federal disability insurance	6,197,642	5,431,595
Federal hospital insurance	10,648,146	7,658,385
Railroad Retirement Tax Act	1,413,996	1,189,637
Total employment taxes and contributions	**66,429,501**	**55,355,980**
Other insurance and retirement:		
Unemployment	6,932,914	6,070,854
Federal supplementary medical insurance	1,703,189	1,426,607
Federal employees retirement	2,299,864	2,146,407
Civil service retirement and disability	45,628	41,033
Total other insurance and retirement	**4,048,681**	**3,614,046**
Total social insurance taxes and contributions	**77,411,096**	**65,040,280**
Excise taxes	17,151,652	16,572,318
Estate and gift taxes	5,075,353	4,975,862
Customs duties	3,444,059	3,307,821
Deposits of earnings-Federal Reserve Banks	4,845,423	3,495,069
All other miscellaneous receipts	509,868	425,997
Total Budget receipts	**292,929,023**	**257,974,663**
Refunds	28,081,540	25,749,191
Net Budget Receipts	**264,847,484**	**232,225,472**
Outlays		
Legislative Branch	640,197	555,404
The Judiciary	209,029	190,213
Executive Office of the President	70,563	49,164
Funds appropriated to the President:		
Appalachian regional development	288,522	265,073
Disaster relief	250,085	358,252
Economic stabilization activities	73,690	26,405
Emergency fund for the President	435	14
Expansion of defense production	3,352	103,883
Expenses of management improvement	150	548
Foreign assistance-security	4,502,520	3,122,291
Foreign assistance-development	1,711,408	1,607,599
Foreign assistance-contingency fund	25,246	10,535
Office of Economic Opportunity	681,160	800,832
Miscellaneous	—	40
Total funds appropriated to the President	7,785,406	6,295,471
Agriculture Department	18,402,239	21,691,889
Commerce Department	1,582,082	1,462,079
Defense Department:		
Military personnel	23,737,533	23,245,741
Retired military personnel	5,128,078	4,390,097
Operation and maintenance	22,442,197	21,068,608
Procurement	15,240,383	15,654,330
Research and development	8,575,096	8,156,775
Military construction	1,400,926	1,119,269
Family housing	891,415	733,091
Civil Defense	75,321	74,064
Special foreign currency program	3,600	4,374
Revolving and management funds	381,173	-1,008,631
Corps of Engineers	1,676,284	1,706,513
Total Defense Department	**79,909,504**	**74,477,856**
Health, Education and Welfare Department	93,784,607	82,102,688
Housing and Urban Development Department	9,918,615	9,281,237
Interior Department	2,861,963	2,539,144
Justice Department	1,807,297	1,538,806
Labor Department	8,972,375	8,639,882
State Department	739,615	596,625
Transportation Department	8,204,949	8,247,924
Treasury Department-Internal Revenue Service	1,591,635	1,430,700
Interest on the public debt	29,318,933	24,167,493
Total Treasury Department	**36,625,165**	**31,732,647**
Atomic Energy Commission	2,307,791	2,393,483
Environmental Protection Agency	2,031,103	1,114,384
General Services Administration	1,065,370	950,297
National Aeronautics and Space Administration	3,260,255	3,324,391
Veterans Administration	14,801,563	13,781,260
Other independent agencies:		
Action	165,913	152,460
Administrative Conference of the U.S.	528	364
American Battle Monuments Commission	4,158	3,425
Arms Control and Disarmament Agency	8,801	8,686
Civil Aeronautics Board	88,659	86,548
Civil Service Commission	7,708,245	6,516,681
Commission of Fine Arts	135	144
Commission on Civil Rights	6,055	4,624
Consumer Product Safety	18,711	20

Classification **Outlays (cont'd.)**	Fiscal 1974	Fiscal 1973
Corporation for Public Broadcasting.	47,750	35,000
District of Columbia federal payment.	191,533	185,574
Equal Employment Opportunity Commission.	41,098	28,310
Farm Credit Administration.	5,696	5,513
Federal Communications Commission.	38,146	33,888
Federal Deposit Insurance Corporation.	471,421	97,244
Federal Home Loan Bank Board.	50,419	-27,502
Federal Maritime Commission.	6,488	5,385
Federal Mediation and Conciliation Service	11,783	10,641
Federal Power Commission.	26,669	22,473
Federal Trade Commission.	32,364	26,614
Foreign Claims Settlement Commission.	5,630	768
Historical and Memorial Commission.	10,359	7,066
Indian Claims Commission.	1,185	1,060
Intergovernmental Agencies.	174,501	79,830
Interstate Commerce Commission.	38,097	44,915
National Capital Planning Commission.	1,510	1,302
National Council on Indian Opportunity.	314	218
National Credit Union Administration.	12,300	11,759
National Foundation-Arts and Humanities.	92,764	66,935
National Labor Relations Board.	55,312	48,414
National Mediation Board.	2,835	2,814
National Science Foundation.	650,763	584,914
Occupational Safety Commission.	4,593	3,934
Railroad Retirement Board.	2,668,110	2,439,154
Renegotiation Board.	4,709	4,721
Securities and Exchange Commission.	34,603	29,865
Selective Service System.	59,526	78,988
Small Business Administration.	1,233,600	1,745,609
Smithsonian Institution.	83,888	70,554
Subversive Activities Control Board.	11	338
Tariff Commission.	7,079	5,579
Temporary Study Commissions.	7,181	10,712
Tennessee Valley Authority.	1,265,145	1,130,516
United States Information Agency.	214,501	206,524
Water Resources Council.	7,703	6,846
Total-Other independent agencies.	17,463,795	25,496,462
Undistributed intragovernmental transactions.	-9,938,397	-8,378,934
Total Budget Outlays.	**302,505,087**	**289,082,372**
Applicable receipts.	34,162,135	42,556,387
Net Budget Outlays.	**268,342,952**	**246,525,985**
Less net receipts.	264,847,484	232,225,472
Deficit.	**-3,495,468**	**-14,300,514**

United States Net Receipts and Outlays

Source: Treasury Department; annual statements for year ending June 30

Yearly average	Re- ceipts $1,000	Expend- itures $1,000	Yearly average	Re- ceipts $1,000	Expend- itures $1,000	Yearly average	Re- ceipts $1,000	Expend- itures $1,000
1789-1800[1]	5,717	5,776	1871-1875	336,830	287,460	1911-1915	710,227	720,252
1801-1810[2]	13,056	9,086	1876-1880	288,124	255,598	1916-1920[6]	3,483,652	8,065,333
1811-1820[2]	21,032	23,943	1881-1885	366,961	257,691	1921-1925	4,306,673	3,578,989
1821-1830[3]	21,928	16,162	1886-1890	375,448	279,134	1926-1930	4,069,138	3,182,807
1831-1840[3]	30,461	24,495	1891-1895	352,891	363,599	1931-1935[4]	2,770,973	5,214,874
1841-1850[3]	28,545	34,097	1896-1900	434,877	457,451	1936-1940[4]	4,960,614	10,192,367
1851-1860	60,237	60,163	1901-1905	559,481	535,559	1941-1945[4]	25,951,137	66,037,928
1861-1865	160,907	683,785	1906-1910	628,507	639,178	1946-1950[5][7][8]	39,047,243	42,334,534
1866-1870	447,301	377,642						

Fiscal Year	Receipts	Expenditures	Fiscal Year	Receipts	Expenditures
1955.	60,389,743,895	64,569,972,817	1965	93,071,796,891	96,506,904,210
1958.	69,116,717,311	71,936,171,353	1968	153,675,705,000	172,803,186,000
1959.	67,915,348,624	80,342,335,375	1969	187,792,337,000	183,079,841,000
1960.	77,763,460,220	76,539,412,798	1970	193,843,791,000	194,968,258,000
1961.	77,659,424,905	81,515,167,453	1971	188,332,129,000	210,652,667,000
1962.	81,409,092,072	87,786,766,580	1972	215,262,638,670	238,285,906,846
1963.	86,357,020,251	92,589,764,029	1973	232,191,842,000	246,603,359,000
1964.	89,458,664,071	97,684,374,794	1974	264,847,484,000	268,342,952,000

(1) Average for period March 4, 1789, to Dec. 31, 1800.
(2) Years ended Dec. 31, 1801, to 1842; average for 1841-1850 is for the period Jan. 1, 1841, to June 30, 1850.
(3) Receipts from 1937 on have deducted appropriations to Federal old-age and survivors insurance trust fund.
(4) Expenditures for years 1932 through 1946 have been revised to include Government Corps. (wholly owned) etc. (net).
(5) Effective January 3, 1949, amounts refunded by the Government, principally for the overpayment of taxes, are being reported as deductions from total receipts rather than as expenditures. Also, effective July 1, 1948, payments to the Treasury, principally by wholly owned Government corporations for retirement of capital stock and for disposition of earnings, are excluded in reporting both budget receipts and expenditures. Neither of these changes affects the size of the budget surplus or deficit. Beginning 1931 figures in each case have been adjusted accordingly for comparative purposes.
(6) Figures for 1918 through 1946 are revised to exclude statutory debt retirement sinking fund, etc.).
(7) Excludes $3 billion transferred to Foreign Economics Corporation Trust Fund.
(8) Includes $3 billion representing expenditures made from the FEC Trust Fund.
(9) Effective fiscal year 1972 loan repayments and loan disbursements will be netted against expenditures and known as outlays.

Summary of U.S. Receipts by Source and Outlays by Function

Source: U.S. Treasury Department (June 30, 1974 preliminary)

(in thousands)

Net Receipts	Fiscal Year	1974	1973	1972
Individual income taxes		$118,750,071	$103,245,521	$ 94,736,616
Corporation income taxes		38,664,197	36,152,530	32,165,916
Social Insurance taxes and contributions:				
Employment taxes and contributions		65,893,961	54,876,420	46,119,776
Unemployment insurance		6,906,711	6,051,483	4,356,671
Contributions for other insurance and retirement		4,048,681	3,614,046	3,437,322
Excise taxes		16,885,403	16,259,861	15,476,901
Estate and gift taxes		5,009,320	4,917,069	5,435,862
Customs		3,334,127	3,187,980	3,286,906
Miscellaneous		5,355,013	3,920,561	3,632,589
Total		**264,847,484**	**232,225,472**	**208,648,559**
Outlays				
National defense		78,792,890	76,023,290	78,336,072
International affairs and finance		4,175,456	3,132,253	3,785,746
Space research and technology		3,228,146	3,311,000	3,421,763
Agriculture and rural development		5,182,770	6,051,111	7,061,398
Natural resources		- 989,552	559,471	3,759,276
Commerce and transportation		12,549,002	12,505,309	11,196,707
Community development and housing		5,129,221	4,162,197	4,215,694
Education and manpower		10,574,715	10,822,340	10,198,471
Health		21,501,547	18,393,281	16,980,431
Income security		84,075,160	72,949,571	64,557,519
Veterans benefits and services		13,369,846	12,004,029	10,747,366
Interest		28,101,163	22,835,562	20,584,295
General government		6,485,062	5,519,134	4,888,631
General revenue sharing		6,105,922	6,636,369	....
Undistributed intrabudgetary transactions		- 9,938,397	- 8,378,934	7,857,514
Total		**268,342,952**	**246,525,985**	**231,875,854**

United States Customs and Internal Revenue Receipts

Source: Treasury Department

Gross. Not reduced by appropriations to Federal old-age and survivors insurance trust fund or refunds or receipts. Data are for fiscal years.

Year	Customs	Internal Revenue	Year	Customs	Internal Revenue	Year	Customs	Internal Revenue
1930	$587,000,903	$3,039,295,014	1961	1,007,755,214	94,401,086,397	1968	2,113,474,950	153,675,705,000
1935	343,353,034	3,277,690,028	1962	1,171,205,973	99,440,839,244	1969	2,318,962,000	187,792,337,000
1940	348,590,635	5,303,133,988	1963	1,240,537,884	105,925,395,281	1970	2,429,799,000	193,743,251,000
1945	354,775,542	43,902,001,929	1964	1,284,176,379	112,206,115,000	1971	2,589,973,339	188,332,129,000
1950	422,650,329	39,448,607,109	1965	1,477,548,820	114,428,991,753	1972	3,284,922,000	208,595,814,000
1955	606,396,634	66,288,691,586	1966	1,811,170,211	128,842,531,268	1973	3,175,268,000	232,191,842,000
1960	1,123,037,579	91,774,802,823	1967	1,971,799,790	147,899,815,000	1974	3,334,127,000	264,847,484,000

U.S. Direct Investments Abroad, Countries and Industries

Source: Bureau of Economic Analysis, U.S. Dept. of Commerce
(Millions of Dollars)

	Book Value at Year-End		Net Capital Outflows		Reinvested Earnings		Earnings		Income	
	1972	1973	1972	1973	1972	1973	1972	1973	1972	1973
Total	94,337	107,268	3,517	4,872	4,715	8,124	11,485	17,495	6,925	9,415
By area										
Developed countries	64,359	74,084	1,988	3,631	3,710	6,147	6,880	10,330	3,331	4,299
Canada	25,771	28,055	350	540	1,384	1,846	2,251	2,846	989	1,126
Europe	30,817	37,218	1,168	2,939	1,892	3,476	3,721	5,956	1,847	2,470
Japan	2,375	2,733	229	36	183	311	362	548	168	222
Australia, New Zealand and South Africa	5,395	6,079	241	116	250	514	546	981	326	481
Developing countries	25,235	27,867	1,134	1,198	894	1,510	4,110	6,538	3,195	4,932
Latin American Rep. and other Western Hemisphere	16,798	18,452	300	673	732	1,028	1,656	2,628	967	1,622
Other Africa	3,091	2,830	126	-427	99	177	504	618	410	446
Middle East	1,992	2,682	353	588	-22	108	1,391	2,277	1,418	2,172
Other Asia and Pacific	3,354	3,903	355	365	85	198	558	1,014	399	692
International and unallocated	4,743	5,317	395	43	111	467	496	627	400	185
By industry										
Mining and smelting	7,110	7,483	382	201	41	143	419	675	395	548
Petroleum	26,363	29,567	1,603	1,417	563	1,927	3,311	6,183	2,826	4,325
Manufacturing	39,716	45,791	1,100	1,820	2,991	4,408	5,172	7,286	2,144	2,757
Other	21,249	24,427	433	1,434	1,119	1,645	2,583	3,351	1,560	1,785

Public Debt of The United States

Source: Treasury Department (p preliminary subject to revision. r revised)

Fiscal Year	Gross Debt	Per Cap.	Fiscal Year	Gross Debt	Per Cap.	Fiscal Year	Gross Debt	Per Cap.
	Dollars	Dollars		Dollars	Dollars		Dollars	Dollars
1870..	2,436,453,269	61.06	1930..	16,185,309,831	131.51	1968..	347,578,406,426(r)	1,727.72
1880..	2,090,908,872	41.60	1940..	42,967,531,038	367.48	1970..	370,918,706,950(r)	1,811.12
1890..	1,132,396,584	17.80	1950..	257,357,352,351	1,696.67	1971..	398,129,744,455(r)	1,923.12
1900..	1,263,416,913	16.60	1960..	286,330,760,848	1,584.70	1972..	427,260,460,940(p)	2,046.00
1910..	1,146,939,969	12.41	1965..	317,273,898,984	1,630.46	1973..	458,141,605,312(p)	2,177.30
1920..	24,299,321,467	228.23	1966..	319,907,087,795(r)	1,624.66	1974..	475,059,815,732(p)	2,241.81

Appropriations by the Federal Government
Source: Treasury Department (Fiscal Year)

Year	Appropriations	Year	Appropriations	Year	Appropriations	Year	Appropriations
1890..	$ 395,430,284.26	1940..	$ 13,349,202,681.73	1953..	$94,916,821,231.67	1963..	$102,149,886,566.52
1895..	492,477,759.97	1944..	118,411,173,965.24	1954..	74,744,844,304.88	1965..	107,555,087,622.62
1900..	698,912,982.83	1945..	73,067,712,071.39	1955..	54,761,172,461.58	1966..	125,998,173,095.19
1905..	781,288,215.95	1946..	76,597,999,662.67	1956..	63,857,731,203.86	1967..	140,861,235,376.56
1910..	1,044,433,622.64	1947..	40,823,734,061.18	1957..	70,717,305,080.55	1968¹.	195,908,743,535.65
1915..	1,122,471,919.12	1948..	42,098,608,820.42	1958..	77,145,934,082.25	1969..	203,049,351,090.91
1920..	6,454,596,649.56	1949..	47,357,993,957.59	1959..	82,055,863,758.58	1970..	222,200,021,901.52
1925..	3,748,651,750.35	1950..	52,867,672,466.21	1960..	80,169,728,902.87	1971..	247,623,820,964.75
1930..	4,665,236,678.04	1951..	67,966,083,088.46	1961..	89,229,575,129.94	1972..	247,638,104,722.57
1935..	7,527,559,327.66	1952..	127,788,153,262.97	1962..	91,447,827,731.00	1973..	275,554,945,383.88

(1.) This appropriation for 1968 incorporates for the first time the changes in the President's Budget for 1969, in consonance with those recommendations of the President's Commission on Budget Concepts which were adopted and implemented during fiscal year 1968.

Gross National Product, National Income, and Personal Income
Source: Department of Commerce. Office of Economic Analysis
(In millions of dollars) Includes Alaska and Hawaii beginning in 1960

	1950	1960	1970	1971	1972	1973
Gross National product....................	284,769	503,734	977,080	1,055,450	1,155,155	1,294,919
Less: Capital consumption allowances..........	18,342	43,408	87,254	93,834	102,357	110,818
Equals: Net national product...............	266,427	460,326	889,826	961,616	1,052,798	1,184,101
Less: Indirect business tax and nontax liability.....	23,334	45,200	93,461	102,438	109,541	119,191
Business transfer payments................	778	1,878	3,989	4,319	4,610	4,866
Statistical discrepancy....................	1,488	-1,031	-6,392	-3,363	-1,481	-4,957
Plus: Subsidies minus current surplus of government enterprises....................	247	243	1,694	1,227	1,664	589
Equals: National income...................	241,074	414,522	800,462	859,449	941,792	1,065,590
Less: Corporate profits and inventory valuation adjustment......................	37,669	49,904	69,240	80,133	91,120	105,123
Contributions for social insurance...........	6,870	20,672	57,708	64,598	73,729	91,231
Wage accurals less disbursement...........	24	0	0	582	-511	-56
Plus: Government transfer payments to persons . .	14,294	26,609	75,119	88,889	98,343	112,977
Net Interest paid by gov't and consumers......	7,198	15,083	30,988	31,029	32,713	38,327
Dividends..............................	8,838	13,437	24,680	25,142	26,041	29,582
Business transfer payments................	778	1,878	3,989	4,319	4,610	4,866
Equals: Personal income...................	227,619	400,953	808,290	863,575	939,161	1,655,044

National Income by Type of Income
(Millions of dollars)

	1960	1965	1970	1971	1972	1973
Compensation of employees...............	294,226	393,844	603,869	644,103	707,052	785,983
Wage and salaries......................	270,844	358,885	541,976	573,832	627,334	691,620
Private................................	222,108	289,621	426,875	449,711	493,276	545,060
Military...............................	9,894	12,143	19,561	19,419	20,276	20,603
Government, civilian....................	38,842	57,121	95,540	104,702	113,782	125,957
Supplements to wages, sal................	23,382	34,959	61,893	70,271	79,718	94,363
Empl. contrib. soc. ins..................	11,380	16,217	29,717	33,702	39,002	48,407
Other labor income.....................	12,002	18,742	32,176	36,569	40,716	45,956
Empl. contrib. priv. pen.................	9,684	15,623	27,214	31,104	34,672	39,161
Other................................	2,318	3,119	4,962	5,465	6,044	6,795
Proprietors' income......................	46,209	57,253	66,919	68,724	74,227	96,089
Business and professional................	34,244	42,416	50,017	51,893	53,987	57,560
Income unic. enterprises.................	34,263	42,796	50,723	52,552	55,104	59,835
Inventory valuation adj..................	-19	-380	-706	-659	-1,117	-2,275
Farm.................................	11,965	14,837	16,902	16,831	20,240	38,529
Rental income of persons.................	15,822	18,952	23,938	24,530	24,148	26,140
Corp. prof., inv. adjust...................	49,904	76,070	69,240	80,133	91,120	105,123
Corp. profits before tax.................	49,712	77,787	74,041	85,053	98,037	122,702
Corp. profits tax liability.................	23,032	31,326	34,789	37,444	42,687	49,788
Corp. profits after tax..................	26,680	46,461	39,252	47,609	55,350	72,914
Dividends...........................	13,437	19,808	24,680	25,142	26,041	29,582
Undistributed profits..................	13,243	26,653	14,572	22,467	29,309	43,332
Inventory valuation adj................	192	-1,717	-4,801	-4,920	-6,917	-17,579
Net Interest............................	8,361	18,217	36,496	41,959	45,245	52,255
National income........................	414,522	564,336	800,462	859,449	941,792	1,065,590

National Income by Industry

Source: Department of Commerce, Bureau of Economic Analysis
(Millions of dollars)

	1960	1965	1968	1970	1971	1972	1973
Agricul., forestry, fisheries	16,852	21,017	22,080	25,582	26,218	30,395	50,609
Farms	15,857	19,630	20,425	23,639	24,028	27,967	47,878
Agri. services, forestry, fisheries	995	1,417	1,655	1,943	2,190	2,428	2,731
Mining	5,732	6,116	6,702	7,682	7,012	8,246	9,397
Metal mining	817	908	888	1,177	970	1,035	1,210
Coal mining	1,253	1,332	1,429	2,157	2,052	2,375	2,411
Crude petroleum, natural gas	2,734	2,754	3,153	3,048	2,571	3,279	4,006
Nonmetallic min. & quar.	928	1,122	1,232	1,300	1,419	1,557	1,770
Contract construction	20,810	29,116	36,270	42,791	46,692	51,694	57,077
Manufacturing	125,822	172,572	212,672	217,505	226,363	252,589	287,237
Nondurable goods	52,208	66,482	82,069	88,902	91,828	99,881	108,895
Food, kindred products	12,225	14,495	17,130	19,530	19,866	20,774	21,438
Tobacco manufacturers	1,017	1,111	1,359	1,738	1,770	1,805	2,010
Textile mill products	4,488	5,837	7,123	7,419	7,379	8,237	8,734
Appa'l, other fabric prod.	4,953	6,556	8,307	8,634	8,950	9,564	10,279
Paper, allied products	4,707	5,929	7,338	7,970	8,041	9,318	10,440
Ptg., pub., allied indust.	6,655	8,746	10,766	11,929	12,401	13,622	14,887
Chemicals, allied products	9,159	12,648	15,614	16,342	16,827	18,236	21,032
Petroleum refining, related ind.	4,586	5,381	6,680	7,342	7,917	8,634	9,364
Rubber, misc. plastic products	2,809	3,949	5,477	5,776	6,482	7,497	8,364
Leather, leather products	1,609	1,830	2,275	2,222	2,195	2,194	2,347
Durable goods	73,614	106,090	130,603	128,603	134,535	152,708	178,342
Lumber, wood, except furn.	3,255	4,212	5,035	5,135	5,705	7,109	8,740
Furniture and fixtures	2,092	2,870	3,485	3,657	3,735	4,543	4,993
Stone, clay, glass products	4,640	5,713	6,329	6,894	7,517	8,533	9,867
Primary metal industries	11,103	14,735	15,871	15,961	15,325	17,404	22,025
Fabricated metal products	8,113	11,518	14,354	14,635	15,082	17,543	20,297
Machinery, except electrical	11,861	18,357	22,891	24,296	23,596	26,585	32,489
Electrical machinery	10,469	14,850	19,772	20,327	20,614	22,539	26,928
Trans. equip. exc. autos	8,270	11,361	16,435	14,347	13,750	15,066	15,653
Motor vehicles equipment	8,532	15,432	17,156	13,801	19,454	22,555	25,387
Instruments	2,954	4,170	5,742	5,843	5,843	6,477	7,202
Misc. manufacturing	2,325	2,872	3,533	3,707	3,914	4,354	4,761
Transportation	18,177	23,150	26,909	29,824	32,819	36,008	40,381
Railroad	6,718	7,047	6,992	7,358	8,083	8,464	9,587
Local suburban highway pass.	1,639	1,897	2,210	2,285	2,373	2,349	2,522
Motor freight trans., warehous'g.	5,840	8,317	10,326	11,632	13,295	14,924	17,060
Water transportation	1,654	1,990	2,476	2,502	2,341	2,551	2,705
Air transportation	1,400	2,697	3,556	4,374	5,030	5,863	6,343
Pipeline transportation	355	401	414	518	524	555	695
Transportation service	571	801	935	1,155	1,173	1,302	1,469
Communication	8,237	11,241	14,131	16,787	17,826	19,966	21,064
Telephone and telegraph	7,304	9,991	12,594	15,074	16,026	17,907	18,821
Radio broadcasting, television	933	1,250	1,537	1,713	1,800	2,059	2,243
Electric, gas, sanitary services	8,934	11,447	13,291	14,718	16,462	18,167	19,077
Wholesale and retail trade	64,396	84,302	106,069	121,274	130,900	139,682	155,888
Wholesale trade	23,126	30,341	38,394	44,430	46,951	50,531	58,745
Retail trade	41,270	53,961	67,675	76,844	83,949	89,151	97,143
Finance, ins. and real estate	45,940	61,857	77,755	89,948	100,139	107,865	117,821
Banking	7,276	8,989	12,258	16,437	16,855	18,671	20,758
Credit agencies, holding, other investment co.	−435	−505	−1,209	−1,873	−1,480	−2,448	−4,049
Security, commodity brokers	1,243	1,903	4,023	2,675	3,864	4,259	3,364
Insurance carriers	4,641	5,186	6,520	8,544	10,484	11,801	12,018
Insurance agents, brokers, service	1,948	2,671	3,299	3,871	4,334	4,700	5,305
Real estate	31,267	43,613	52,864	60,294	66,082	70,882	80,425
Services	44,371	64,076	85,721	102,876	109,824	120,137	134,570
Hotels, other lodging places	2,111	2,788	3,744	4,236	4,490	5,029	5,654
Personal services	4,608	5,993	7,265	7,433	7,370	7,420	7,830
Misc. business services	5,093	8,413	11,490	13,984	14,508	15,965	18,471
Automobile repair, serv., garages	1,762	2,450	3,106	3,628	4,059	4,473	5,117
Misc. repair services	1,105	1,501	1,866	2,117	2,283	2,503	2,846
Motion pictures	894	1,205	1,535	1,565	1,542	1,624	1,745
Amusement, recreation services	1,661	2,221	2,783	3,244	3,389	3,870	4,278
Medical, other health services	10,724	16,256	23,250	29,942	32,822	36,378	41,127
Legal services	2,636	4,069	5,114	6,443	7,242	8,230	9,270
Education services	2,402	4,191	5,975	7,231	7,818	8,678	9,154
Nonprofit membership org.	3,815	5,306	6,955	8,376	9,024	9,791	10,780
Misc. professional services	3,761	5,719	8,009	9,847	10,318	11,195	13,120
Private households	3,799	3,964	4,629	4,830	4,959	5,021	5,178
Govt., govt. enterprises	52,891	75,233	104,704	126,850	138,242	149,507	164,087
Federal	21,868	33,458	46,058	53,414	56,497	59,677	63,056
General Govt.	25,524	28,450	39,496	45,164	47,563	50,281	52,816
Govt. Enterprises	3,656	5,008	6,562	8,250	8,934	9,396	10,240
State & local	25,615	41,775	58,646	73,436	81,745	89,830	101,031
General Govt.	27,367	39,345	55,434	69,553	77,562	85,145	95,652
Government enterprises	1,752	2,430	3,212	3,883	4,183	4,685	5,379
Rest of the world	2,360	4,179	4,736	4,625	6,952	7,536	8,382
All industries, total	414,522	564,336	711,140	800,462	859,449	941,792	1,065,590

State Finances

Revenues, Expenditures, Debts, Taxes, U.S. Aid, Military Contracts

For fiscal 1973 (year ending June 30, 1973, except: Alabama, Sept. 30; New York, Mar. 31; Texas, Aug. 31).

Sources: Census Bureau, Treasury and Defense Depts. *Military prime contracts. All figures in dollars.

State	Receipts (add 000)	Outlays (add 000)	Total Debt (add 000)	Per Cap Debt	Per Cap Taxes	Per Cap U.S. Aid	*Mltry Cntrcts (add 000)
Ala.	$1,889,867	$1,767,650	$847,846	$239.57	$263.07	$224	$293,883
Alaska	466,556	646,098	434,592	1,316.95	330.43	633	127,170
Ariz.	1,204,886	1,088,399	87,303	42.42	331.37	184	390,014
Ark.	985,720	849,770	109,037	53.53	257.77	229	62,448
Cal.	15,582,635	13,096,164	6,039,292	293.14	355.49	225	6,214,501
Col.	1,450,892	1,229,856	118,537	48.64	273.54	206	237,575
Conn.	1,926,301	1,830,057	2,579,752	838.67	371.45	167	1,004,462
Del.	442,173	492,742	540,258	937.95	460.83	207	66,236
Fla.	3,882,857	3,449,745	1,260,271	164.16	324.06	145	781,959
Ga.	2,514,318	2,344,539	754,971	157.75	284.49	189	437,955
Hawaii	870,396	957,608	986,844	1,186.11	519.98	253	155,393
Idaho	473,122	435,110	37,009	48.06	292.10	226	9,731
Ill.	6,432,161	6,034,221	1,946,237	173.21	327.13	191	476.141
Ind.	2,213,911	2,072,690	611,828	115.07	236.29	126	640,997
Iowa	1,554,028	1,416,285	123,632	42.57	294.20	150	153,332
n.	1,144,418	978,090	203,500	89.29	267.55	172	322,926
Ky.	1,914,060	1,782,288	1,815,647	543.28	305.22	230	104,336
La.	2,321,105	2,230,123	1,213,669	322.44	316.00	250	298,092
Me.	639,694	624,766	358,305	348.55	295.37	235	44,832
Md.	2,514,083	2,556,241	1,587,391	390.02	357.79	192	687,407
Mass.	3,745,822	3,868,186	3,105,048	533.70	353.06	203	1,589,178
Mich.	6,503,617	5,830,839	1,418,459	156.82	390.01	192	493,952
Minn.	2,747,783	2,591,532	634,848	162.91	420.44	199	377,185
Miss.	1,348,448	1,217,098	583,603	255.85	289.91	298	395,905
Mo.	2,086,447	1,848,756	187,694	39.46	256.83	176	1,183,681
Mont.	499,593	439,600	92,090	127.73	259.58	312	17,662
Neb.	689,545	616,116	78,840	51.13	243.27	154	88,752
Nev.	442,489	382,151	51,860	94.64	388.45	225	15,442
N.H.	453,584	419,830	178,587	225.77	197.02	174	157,029
N.J.	4,111,999	3,800,271	2,755,193	374.30	260.75	163	1,042,565
N.M.	819,589	715,930	144,281	130.45	349.61	312	104,293
N.Y.	15,694,079	14,396,384	11,800,574	646.08	447.30	254	3,476,186
N.C.	2,873,534	2,472,679	528,487	100.23	314.33	177	355,370
N.D.	420,146	379,909	59,243	92.57	280.81	255	62,556
Ohio	5,624,679	4,997,249	2,248,470	209.53	249.40	147	952,045
Okla.	1,442,432	1,416,147	766,408	287.80	259.54	220	147,493
Ore.	1,513,963	1,302,693	1,086,572	488.35	268.09	260	41,874
Pa.	7,486,296	7,380,319	4,596,406	386.19	366.95	198	1,241,030
R.I.	656,896	613,623	390,899	401.75	321.40	248	86,455
S.C.	1,489,575	1,332,133	603,108	221.24	302.71	203	131,739
S.D.	356,583	346,758	38,808	56.74	221.19	289	20,594
Tenn.	1,882,304	1,675,600	642,386	155.69	242.94	197	423,606
Tex.	5,254,353	4,498,120	1,621,101	137.45	239.02	174	2,232,444
Utah	783,581	687,347	91,254	78.87	310.71	224	157,102
Vt.	394,176	400,381	420,808	906.91	377.79	517	35,785
Va.	2,619,679	2,446,379	387,789	80.60	291.04	170	782,910
Wash.	2,790,206	2,622,737	1,098,484	320.35	375.37	241	1,050,957
W.Va.	1,256,169	1,206,980	841,841	469.25	317.14	299	87,468
Wis.	3,107,175	2,789,632	923,312	202.08	408.84	169	298,824
Wyo.	282,146	257,924	39,020	110.54	297.94	326	118,199
Total or Average	129,800,71	118,835,745	59,071,399	282.49	325.53	NA	30,065,075

U.S. Money in Circulation, by Denominations

Source: Federal Reserve System
Outside Treasury and Federal Reserve Banks. (In millions of dollars)

End of year	Total in circulation	Coin and small denomination						Large denomination currency					
		Total	Coin	$1	$2	$5	$10	$20	Total	$50	$100	$500	$1,000	$5,000	$10,000
1950	27,741	19,305	1,554	1,113	64	2,049	5,998	8,529	8,438	2,422	5,043	368	588	4	12
1960	32,869	23,521	2,427	1,533	88	2,246	6,691	10,536	9,348	2,815	5,954	249	316	3	10
1970	57,093	39,639	6,281	2,310	136	3,161	9,170	18,581	17,454	4,896	12,084	215	252	3	4
1971	61,068	41,831	6,775	2,408	135	3,273	9,348	19,893	19,237	5,377	13,414	203	237	2	4
1972	66,516	45,105	7,287	2,523	135	3,449	9,827	21,883	21,411	5,868	15,118	193	225	2	4
1973	72,497	48,288	7,759	2,639	135	3,614	10,226	23,915	24,210	6,514	17,288	185	216	2	4

Bureau of the Mint
Source: Bureau of the Mint

The first United States Mint was established in Philadelphia, Pa., then the nation's capital, by the Act of April 2, 1792, which provided for gold, silver and copper coinage. Originally, supervision of the Mint was a function of the Secretary of State, but it became (1799) an independent agency reporting directly to the president. When the Coinage Act of 1873 was passed, all mint and assay office activities were placed under a newly organized Bureau of the Mint in the Department of the Treasury.

The Bureau of the Mint manufactures all U.S. coins and distributes them through the Federal Reserve banks and branches. The Mint also maintains physical custody of the Treasury's monetary stocks of gold and silver, and refines and processes silver bullion. Functions performed by the Mint on a reimbursable basis include: the manufacture and sale of medals of a national character, the production and sale of numismatic coins and coin sets, and, as scheduling permits, the manufacture of foreign coins.

Amendments to the Coinage Act of 1965 (Public Law 91-607, Dec. 31, 1970) authorized the production of dollar coins and provided that the dollar and half dollar coins for general circulation be of the same nonsilver clad composition as the quarter dollars and dimes. The cladding is an alloy of 75 percent copper and 25 percent nickel, bonded to a core of pure copper. The legislation authorized the Secretary of the Treasury to mint and issue not more than 150 million one dollar pieces containing 40-percent silver, for sale to the public at premium prices. The new dollar coins bear the likeness of the late President of the United States, Dwight David Eisenhower, and a design emblematic of the symbolic eagle of the Apollo 11 landing on the moon. The silver-clad and cupronickel dollars and the cupronickel half dollars were first minted and issued during the calendar year 1971. The composition of the five cent and one cent coins remains unchanged. The five cent pieces are 75 percent copper, 25 percent nickel, while the one cent pieces are 95 percent copper and 5 percent zinc.

Calendar year 1973 coinage production for general circulation follows:

Domestic Coinage Executed During Calendar Year 1973

Denomination	Philadelphia	Denver	San Francisco	Total Value	Total Pieces
Dollars—non-silver	$ 2,000,056.00	$ 2,000,000.00	—0—	$ 4,000,056.00	4,000,056
Half dollars	32,482,000.00	41,585,700.00	—0—	74,067,700.00	148,135,400
Quarter dollars	86,731,000.00	58,244,350.00	—0—	144,975,350.00	579,901,400
Dimes	31,567,000.00	45,503,242.60	—0—	77,070,242.60	770,702,426
Five-cent pieces	19,219,800.00	13,070,270.00	—0—	32,290,070.00	645,801,400
One-cent pieces	37,282,450.00	35,495,765.88	$3,199,376.34	75,977,592.22	7,597,759,222

Large Denominations of U.S. Currency Discontinued

The largest denomination of United States currency now being issued is the $100 bill. Issuance of currency in denominations of $500, $1,000, $5,000 and $10,000 has been discontinued because their use has declined sharply over the past two decades. Issuance of $2 bills has also been discontinued because of a lack of public interest.

As large denomination bills reach the Federal Reserve Bank they are removed from circulation. Existing stocks of $2 bills in condition fit for circulation will be circulated as long as the supply lasts.

Because some of the discontinued currency is expected to be in the hands of holders for many years, the descriptions of the various denominations below is continued:

Portraits on U.S. Currency

Amt.	Portrait	Embellishment on Back	Amt.	Portrait	Embellishment on Back
$ 1	Washington	Great Seal of U.S.	$ 100	Franklin	Independence Hall
2	Jefferson	Monticello	* 500	McKinley	Ornate denominational marking
5	Lincoln	Lincoln Memorial	* 1,000	Cleveland	Ornate denominational marking
10	Hamilton	U.S. Treasury	* 5,000	Madison	Ornate denominational marking
20	Jackson	White House	* 10,000	Chase	Ornate denominational marking
50	Grant	U.S. Capitol	*100,000	Wilson	Ornate denominational marking

*For use only in transactions between Federal Reserve System and Treasury Department.

Portraits on U.S. Treasury Bills, Bonds, Notes and Savings Bonds

Denomination	Savings bonds	Treas. bills	Treas. bonds	Treas. notes
25	Washington			
50	Jefferson		Jefferson	
75	Kennedy			
100	Cleveland		Jackson	
200	F.D. Roosevelt			
500	Wilson		Washington	
1,000	Lincoln	H.McCulloch	Lincoln	Lincoln
5,000		J.G. Carlisle	Monroe	Monroe
10,000	T. Roosevelt	J. Sherman	Cleveland	Cleveland
50,000		C. Glass		
100,000		A. Gallatin	Grant	Grant
1,000,000		O. Wolcott	T. Roosevelt	T. Roosevelt
100,000,000				Madison
500,000,000				McKinley

How to Determine the Value of Silver in Coins
Source: Treasury Department

To figure the value of the silver contained in the silver coins issued by the U.S. Treasury prior to the clad or copper sandwiched coins it is necessary to find the value of pure silver. This may be accomplished by taking the market price as listed and dividing by .999 (the fineness of commercial grade silver) to arrive at the price for silver 1,000 fine. Then multiply by the fraction shown under the table beneath. This will give you the value of the silver content in each coin.

	Fine Troy Weight			Fine Troy Weight	
	Oz.	Grain		Oz.	Grain
Dollar	.7734375	371.25	Quarter	.18084375	86.805
Half-Dollar	.3618875	173.61	Dime	.0723375	34.722

For example: The market price on July 8, 1973, was $2.72 per fine troy ounce. Divide $2.72 by .999 the fineness of commercial grade silver - $2.7227 per troy ounce fine. The value of the silver in the dollar is .7734375 x $2.7227, or $2.11.

The silver content of the new silver-copper half dollar is .14789341504 of a fine troy ounce, and this multiplied by the selling price of $2.7227 gives a value for the silver content of 40.3 cents.

U.S. Currency and Coin — June 30, 1974

Source: Treasury Department

Amounts Outstanding and in Circulation

	Total Currency and Coin	Total	Coin[a] Dollars	Fractional Coin
Amounts outstanding	$78,413,597,461	$8,314,819,898	[b]$792,509,898	$7,522,310,000
Less amounts held by:				
The Treasury	167,772,360	57,202,674	11,418,589	45,784,085
The Federal Reserve banks. ...	4,412,709,600	217,990,018	16,135,321	201,854,697
Amounts in circulation	73,833,115,501	8,039,627,206	764,955,988	7,274,671,218

Currency[c]

	Total	Federal Reserve Notes[d]	United States Notes	Currency No Longer Issued
Amounts outstanding ....'	$70,098,777,563	$69,489,265,174	$322,539,016	$286,973,373
Less amounts held by:				
The Treasury	110,569,686	109,395,506	1,063,212	110,968
The Federal Reserve banks. ...	4,194,719,582	4,194,472,871	166,306	80,405
Amounts in circulation	65,793,488,295	65,185,396,797	321,309,498	286,782,000

Currency by Denominations, and Coin, in Circulation

	Total	Federal Reserve Notes[d]	United States Notes	Currency No Longer Issued
One dollar...................	$2,531,942,239	$2,374,362,507	$144,054	$157,435,678
Two dollars..................	135,354,660	....	135,341,214	13,446
Five dollars..................	3,439,429,945	3,277,810,420	118,647,940	42,971,585
Ten dollars	9,878,258,260	9,851,252,630	10,685	26,994,945
Twenty dollars................	24,348,444,304	24,327,691,840	4,030	20,748,434
Fifty dollars.................	6,762,773,500	6,749,958,900	25	12,814,575
One hundred dollars...........	18,295,573,900	18,203,268,000	67,159,550	25,146,350
Five hundred dollars...........	182,475,000	182,258,500	2,000	214,500
One thousand dollars...........	213,026,000	212,779,000	....	247,000
Five thousand dollars..........	2,200,000	2,135,000	....	65,000
Ten thousand dollars..........	4,010,000	3,880,000	....	130,000
Fractional parts	487	....	....	487
Total currency	65,793,488,295	65,185,396,797	321,309,498	286782,000
Total coin	8,039,627,206			
Total currency and coin	73,833,115,501			

Comparative Totals of Money in Circulation — Selected dates

Date	Amounts (in millions)	Per Capita[e]	Date	Amounts (in millions)	Per Capita[e]	Date	Amounts (in millions)	Per Capita[e]
June 30,1974	[f]$73,833.1	$348.44	June 30, 1955	30,229.3	182.90	June 30, 1930	4,522.0	36.74
June 30, 1973	67,771.2	[g]322.11	June 30, 1950	27,156.3	179.03	June 30, 1925	4,815.2	41.56
June 30, 1970	54,351.0	265.39	June 30, 1945	26,746.4	191.14	June 30, 1920	5,467.6	51.36
June 30, 1965	39,719.8	204.14	June 30, 1940	7,847.5	59.40	June 30, 1915	3,319.6	33.01
June 30, 1960	32,064.6	177.47	June 30, 1935	5,567.1	43.75	June 30, 1910	3.148.7	34.07

[a]Excludes coin sold to collectors at premium prices. [b]Includes $481,781,898 in standard silver dollars. [c]Excludes gold certificates, Series of 1934, which are issued only to Federal Reserve banks and do not appear in circulation. [d]Issued on and after July 1, 1929. [e]Based on Bureau of the Census estimates of population. [f]Highest amount to date. [g]Revised.

The requirement for a gold reserve against U.S. notes was repealed by Public Law 90-269 approved Mar. 18, 1968. Silver certificates issued on and after July 1, 1929 became redeemable from the general fund on June 24, 1968. The amount of security after those dates has been reduced accordingly.

*Seigniorage on Coin and Silver Bullion

Source: Fiscal Service, Dept. of Treasury
(Jan. 1, 1935 to June 30, 1974)

	Total	Potential[1]
Fiscal Year Jan. 1, 1935-June 30, 1965, cumulative........................	$2,525,927,763.84	[2]$ 6,560,393.72
1967..	r836,734,039.35	980,037,560.91
1968..	r383,141,339.00	759,844,047.56
1969..	250,170,276.34	700,000,000.00
1970..	274,217,884.01	....
1971..	399,652,811.18	....
1972..	580,586,683.00	....
1973..	399,799,682.00	....
1974..	320,706,638.49	....
Cumulative Jan. 1, 1935-June 30, 1974.	6,619,741,444.00	

*Seigniorage is the profit from coining money; it is the difference between the monetary value of coins and their cost; including the manufacturing expense.
(r.) Revised to include seigniorage on clad coins. (p.) Preliminary.
(1.) Not cumulative, as coinage metals held by the Treasurer of the United States changes, the potential seigniorage changes. Potential seigniorage also changes depending on the denomination of the coins manufactured.
(2.) Represents potential seigniorage as of June 30, 1965.

World Gold Production

Source: Federal Reserve Board. In millions of dollars at $35 per fine troy ounce through 1971, at $38 for 1972.

Year	estimated world prod.	Africa			North and South America					Other			
		South Africa	Ghana	Zaire	United States	Canada	Mexico	Nicaragua	Colombia	Australia	India	Japan	Phil-ippines	All other
1960.	1,175.0	748.4	30.8	11.1	58.8	162.0	10.5	7.0	15.2	38.0	5.6	11.8	14.4	61.4
1965.	1,440.0	1,069.4	26.4	2.3	58.6	125.6	7.6	5.4	11.2	30.7	4.6	18.1	15.3	64.8
1966.	1,445.0	1,080.8	24.0	5.6	63.1	114.6	7.5	5.2	9.8	32.1	4.2	19.4	15.8	62.9
1967.	1,410.0	1.068.7	26.7	5.4	53.4	103.7	5.8	5.2	9.0	28.4	3.4	23.7	17.2	59.4
1968.	1,420.0	1,088.0	25.4	5.9	53.9	94.1	6.2	4.9	8.4	27.6	4.0	21.5	18.5	61.6
1969.	1,420.0	1,090.7	24.8	6.0	60.1	89.1	6.3	3.7	7.7	24.5	3.4	23.7	20.0	60.0
1970.	1,450.0	1,128.0	24.8	6.2	63.5	84.3	6.9	4.0	7.1	21.7	3.7	24.8	21.1	54.1
1971p.		1,098.7	24.4	6.0	52.3	79.1	5.3	3.7	6.6	23.5	4.1	27.0	22.2	
1972p.		1,109.8			54.3	77.2			7.1		4.0	32.2	23.0	

(p) Preliminary.

Gold Reserves of Central Banks and Governments

Source: Federal Reserve Board

Millions of dollars; valued at $35 per ounce through 1971, at $38 for 1972, and $42.22 for 1973.

Dec.	(Est.) total world[1]	Int'l Monetary Fund	United States	Canada	(Est.) rest of world	Belgium	France	Germany Rep. of Fed.	Italy	Neth-er-lands	Swit-zer-land	United King-dom
1960.	40,540	2,439	17,804	885	20,295	1,170	1,641	2,971	2,203	1,451	2,185	2,800
1965.	43,230	1,869	13,806	1,151	27,285	1,558	4,706	4,410	2,404	1,756	3,042	2,265
1969.	41,015	2,310	11,859	872	26,845	1,520	3,547	4,079	2,956	1,720	2,642	1,411
1970.	41,275	4,339	11,072	791	25,865	1,470	3,532	3,980	2,887	1,787	2,732	1,349
1971.	41,175	4,732	10,206	792	26,235	1,544	3,523	4,077	2,884	1,909	2,909	775
1972.	44,890	5,830	10,487	834	28,575	1,638	3,826	4,459	3,130	2,059	3,158	800
1973.	49,850	6,478	11,652	927	31,720	1,781	4,261	4,966	3,483	2,294	3,513	886

(1.) Excludes USSR, other Eastern European countries and China mainland.

Argentina 169, Australia 311, Austria 881, Brazil 56, Colombia 18, Denmark 77, Domincan Republic 4, Ecuador 16, Egypt 103, El Salvador 21, Finland 35, Greece 148, Guatemala 21, India 293, Iran 159, Iraq 173, Ireland 18, Israel 46, Japan 891, Lebanon 389, Mexico 196, Norway 41, Pakistan 67, Peru 42, Philippines 45, Portugal 1,163, South Africa 802, Spain 602, Sweden 244, Thailand 99, Turkey 151, Uruguay 148, Venezuela 472, Yugoslavia 62, B.I.S. (net) 235.

U.S. and World Silver Production

Source: Bureau of Mines

Largest production of silver in the United States in 1915—74,961,075 fine ounces. (r) revised (p) preliminary.

Year (Cal.)	United States Fine ozs.	Value	World Fine ozs.	Year (Cal.)	United States Fine ozs.	Value	World Fine ozs.
1930.	50,748,127	19,538,000	248,708,426	1960	36,000,000	$33,305,858	241,300,000
1935.	45,924,454	33,008,000	220,704,231	1965r	39,806,033	51,469,201	257,415,000
1940.	69,585,734	49,483,000	275,387,000	1970r	45,006,000	79,697,000	310,891,000
1945.	29,063,255	20,667,200	162,000,000	1971r	41,564,000	64,258,000	291,464,000
1950.	42,308,739	38,291,545	203,300,000	1972r	37,233,000	62,737,000	290,564,000
1955.	36,469,610	33,006,839	224,000,000	1973	37,827,000	96,762,000	305,916,000

Bank Rates on Short-Term Business Loans

Source: Reserve System

% per annum. Estimates based on reports from banks in 35 centers. Short-term loans mature within one year.

	Ave. 35 Cities	N.Y. C.	7 Other N.E.	8 No. Cent.	7 S.E.	8 S.W.	4 West	$1-9	$10-99	$100 to 499	$500 to 999	$1,000 and over
1967 Aug. 1-15	5.95	5.66	6.29	5.92	5.92	6.01	6.02	6.58	6.46	6.16	5.89	5.72
Nov. 1-15	5.96	5.71	6.29	5.91	5.94	6.03	6.03	6.60	6.48	6.17	5.90	5.73
1969 Aug. 1-15	8.82	8.65	9.14	8.85	8.46	8.85	8.75	8.99	9.14	8.96	8.84	8.67
Nov. 1-15	8.83	8.66	9.21	8.83	8.58	8.79	8.81	9.05	9.20	9.00	8.84	8.66
1970 Aug. 1-15	8.50	8.24	8.89	8.47	8.49	8.53	8.54	9.15	9.07	8.75	8.46	8.25
Nov. 1-15	8.07	7.74	8.47	8.05	8.15	8.08	8.16	8.89	8.79	8.34	8.09	7.74
1971 Aug.	6.51	6.25	6.77	6.46	6.77	6.64	6.54	7.68	7.27	6.88	6.58	6.27
Nov.	6.18	5.86	6.40	6.13	6.47	6.43	6.21	7.51	7.05	6.51	6.26	5.93
1972 Aug.	5.84	5.55	6.14	5.79	6.06	6.07	5.82	7.27	6.72	6.20	5.91	5.59
Nov.	6.33	6.09	6.61	6.27	6.56	6.36	6.41	7.52	7.10	6.60	6.24	6.14
1973 Aug.	9.24	9.08	9.49	9.24	9.25	9.16	9.25	8.95	9.25	9.50	9.31	9.14
Nov.	10.08	9.90	10.51	10.02	9.96	10.08	10.04	9.80	10.14	10.43	10.18	9.95
1974 Feb.	9.91	9.68	10.28	9.98	9.80	9.93	9.78	9.86	10.09	10.28	10.06	9.75
May	11.15	11.08	11.65	11.09	10.88	10.82	11.19	10.50	11.06	11.41	11.32	11.06

NOTE:—The Quarterly Survey of Interest Rates Charged by Banks on Business Loans has been revised beginning with the survey period of February 1971. The revision incorporates a number of technical changes in coverage, sampling, and interest rate calculations. These include elimination of accounts receivable loans from the survey, shortening the sample period for respondent banks in most districts, and calculation of effective annual interest rates on discounted loans using a revised formula based on annual rather than quarterly compounding of interest. As a result of the above changes, new weights derived from this Survey have been used to calculate the weighted average rates.

U. S. Commercial Banks With Deposits Over One Billion

A compilation of the 300 largest commercial banks in the United States is made twice a year by the American Banker, daily banking newspaper, 525 W. 42 St., New York, N. Y. 10036. Of these the first 80 banks had deposits of more than $1 billion on June 30, 1973. They are listed below. (Copyright 1973, by American Banker)

Rank 6/30/74	June 30, 1974 Deposits	Rank 6/30/74	June 30, 1974 Deposits
1 Bank of America NT&SA, S. F.	$47,377,582,000	41 Bank of New York	$2,085,666,248
2 First National City Bank, N.Y.	41,438,901,000	42 Franklin National Bank, N.Y.	2,085,336,059
3 Chase Manhattan Bank NA, N.Y.	35,156,257,552	43 United States NB of Ore., Portland	2,052,913,345
4 Manufacturers Hanover Trust, N.Y.	21,739,868,322	44 Pittsburgh National Bank	2,046,467,989
5 Morgan Guaranty Trust Co., N.Y.	18,309,055,276	45 Natl. Bank of Commerce, Seattle	1,978,312,283
6 Bankers Trust Co., N.Y.	17,215,410,730	46 Marine Midl'd Bk.—West'n, Buffalo.	1,879,618,382
7 Chemical Bank, N.Y.	16,523,626,000	47 Texas Commerce Bank NA, Houston.	1,855,242,096
8 First National Bank, Chicago.	14,419,643,751	48 First Natl. Bank of Ariz., Phoenix	1,544,457,402
9 Continental Illinois NB&T Co., Chi.	13,585,714,941	49 National City Bank, Cleveland	1,522,679,000
10 Security Pacific Nat'l Bk., L.A.	12,571,391,873	50 Maryland Natl. Bank, Balt.	1,499,379,000
11 Wells Fargo Bank NA, S.F.	8,884,276,270	51 First Union NB of No. Car., Char.	1,492,724,759
12 Irving Trust Co., N.Y.	8,499,164,193	52 Equibank NA, Pitts.	1,484,364,620
13 Crocker National Bank, S.F.	8,327,169,615	53 Industrial NB of R.I., Providence	1,455,418,000
14 United California Bank, L.A.	7,523,303,479	54 Central Natl. Bank, Cleveland.	1,443,750,885
15 Marine Midland Bank—N.Y.	7,473,771,000	55 Security Natl. Bank, Hempstead, N.Y.	1,431,956,000
16 Mellon Bank NA, Pittsburgh.	7,430,681,000	56 Hartford Natl. Bank & Trust Co., Conn.	1,418,768,000
17 First National Bank, Boston.	7,122,379,749	57 Indiana Natl. Bank, Indianapolis.	1,414,496,202
18 National Bank of Detroit.	6,298,853,119	58 Amer. Fletcher NB&T Co., Ind'polis.	1,406,092,877
19 First Pennsylvania Bank NA, Phila.	3,894,483,000	59 Bank of Tokyo Trust Co., N.Y.	1,398,633,732
20 Union Bank, L.A.	3,312,176,000	60 Virginia Natl. Bank, Norfolk	1,394,027,644
21 Northern Trust Co., Chicago	3,263,691,274	61 Conn. Bank & Trust Co., Hartford	1,393,193,821
22 Philadelphia National Bank	3,242,259,770	62 First Natl. Bank, Atlanta, Ga.	1,376,006,247
23 Harris Trust & Savings Bank, Chi.	3,141,234,348	63 First Natl. Bank, Miami, Fla.	1,302,065,589
24 Seattle-First National Bank.	3,135,621,000	64 Michigan Natl. Bank, Lansing.	1,281,073,850
25 First National Bank, Dallas	3,088,656,225	65 Provident Natl. Bank, Phila.	1,245,434,733
26 Republic National Bank, Dallas.	3,087,097,425	66 Trust Co. of Georgia, Atlanta.	1,216,290,000
27 Cleveland Trust Co.	2,812,194,679	67 Riggs Natl. Bank, Wash., D.C.	1,209,898,892
28 Girard Bank, Philadelphia	2,811,046,000	68 Union Commerce Bank, Cleveland.	1,203,219,550
29 N. C. National Bank, Charlotte.	2,785,425,907	69 Manuf. & Traders Trust Co., Buff., N.Y.	1,185,361,037
30 Wachovia B&T NA, Win.-Sal., N.C.	2,634,962,483	70 Mercantile Trust Co. NA, St. Louis, Mo.	1,184,341,262
31 National Bank of No. America, N.Y.	2,430,987,860	71 Natl. Shawmut Bank, Boston	1,173,681,000
32 Detroit Bank & Trust Co.	2,410,795,917	72 First Natl. Bank, St. Louis, Mo.	1,163,296,514
33 Manufacturers Natl. Bank, Detroit	2,395,395,000	73 First Natl. Bank, Minneapolis, Minn.	1,141,860,752
34 Bank of California NA, S.F.	2,373,078,000	74 Northwestern Natl. Bank, Minn'polis.	1,140,811,732
35 Valley Natl. Bank, Phoenix, Ariz.	2,342,891,143	75 American Natl. B&T Co., Chicago.	1,108,567,739
36 First Wis. Natl. Bank, Milw.	2,215,924,160	76 First Western B&T Co., L.A.	1,104,056,875
37 Citizens & Southern NB, Atlanta, Ga.	2,126,345,933	77 State St. Bank & Trust Co., Boston	1,094,815,161
38 First City Natl. Bank, Houston, Tex.	2,097,710,150	78 First Natl. Bank, St. Paul, Minn.	1,054,989,554
39 Fidelity Bank, Philadelphia	2,092,716,050	79 Lincoln First Bank, Roch., N.Y.	1,030,651,456
40 First Natl. Bank of Ore., Portland	2,088,343,193	80 New England Merchants NB, Boston	1,013,367,329

Largest Bank in Each of 38 Foreign Countries

Source: 500 Largest Banks in the Free World, compiled by the American Banker, New York. (Copyright 1974) Based on deposits Jan. 1, 1974, or nearest fiscal year-end. For Canada, see Index.

Banks and Country	Deposits in U.S. $	Banks and Country	Deposits in U.S. $
Argentina, Banco de la Nacion	$ 1,616,323,228	Korea, Korea Exchange Bank	$ 1,343,632,400
Australia, Commonwealth Bkng. Corp.	10,028,354,587	Kuwait, National Bank of	918,646,545
Austria, Creditanstalt- Bankverein	3,695,948,954	Luxembourg, Cie. Luxembourgeoise	1,730,922,000
Belgium, Societe Generale de Banque.	8,879,566,318	Mexico, Banco de Comercio	1,691,361,760
Brazil, Banco do Brasil	10,965,977,208	Netherlands, Cooperatieve Centrale	
Denmark, Copenhagen Handelsbank	1,857,682,947	Raiffeisen-Boerenleenbank	10,343,253,000
Egypt, National Bank of Egypt	2,024,359,399	New Zealand, Bank of	1,633,585,668
England, National Westminster Bank	24,744,185,040	No. Ireland, Northern Bank Ltd.	721,373,840
Finland, Kansallis-Osake Pankki.	1,833,359,470	Norway, Norske Creditbank.	1,225,486,971
France, Banque Nationale de Paris.	29,622,323,153	Pakistan, Habib Bank Ltd.	712,650,820
		Peru, Banco de la Nacion.	1,577,319,078
Germany, Deutsche Bank.	22,849,775,174	Portugal, Banco Portugues do Atlantico.	1,779,417,237
Greece, National Bank of Greece	3,598,496,241	Scotland, Bank of	2,320,761,590
Hong Kong, Hongkong & Shanghai	6,528,916,832	South Africa, Standard Bank of.	2,523,272,265
India, State Bank of India.	3,965,822,000	Spain, Banco Espanol de Credito.	5,911,962,831
Iran, Bank Melli Iran	2,789,966,475	Sweden, Skandinaviska Enskilda Banken.	5,693,819,040
Ireland, Bank of Ireland	2,591,264,836	Switzerland, Union Bank of	11,358,673,507
Israel, Bank of Leurni le-Israel.	5,349,710,062	Taiwan, Bank of.	1,568,099,557
Italy, Banca Nazionale del Lavoro	20,043,768,580	Thailand, Bangkok Bank Ltd.	1,202,614,105
Japan, Dai-Ichi Kangyo Bank Ltd.	22,204,490,246	Turkey, Cumhuriyeti Ziraat Bankasi.	1,586,209,778

Federal Deposit Insurance Corporation (FDIC)

The primary purpose of the Federal Deposit Insurance Corporation (FDIC) is to insure the deposits of all banks entitled to insurance benefits under the Federal Deposit Insurance Act. The major functions of the FDIC are to pay off depositors of insured banks closed without adequate provision having been made to pay depositors' claims, to act as receiver for all national banks placed in receivership or for state banks placed in receivership when appointed receiver by state authorities, and to prevent the continuance or development of unsafe and unsound banking practices. The FDIC's entire income consists of assessments on insured banks and income from investments; it receives no appropriations from Congress. It may borrow from the U. S. Treasury not to exceed $3 billion outstanding at any one time, but has made no such borrowings since it was organized in 1933. The FDIC surplus (Deposit Insurance Fund) as of June 30, 1973, was $5,393,006,060.

Corporations and Stocks

Over 30,900,000 Persons Own Shares in U.S. Corporations

About 30,900,000 persons owned shares in American corporations in 1974, compared to 31,700,000 in 1973 and 8,630,000 in 1956.

The N.Y. Stock Exchange listed 2,071 issues of 1,567 companies for a total of 21.47 billion shares, valued as of Aug. 31, 1974, at $545.45 billion. Average daily trading was 13,365,138 shares through Aug. 31, compared to 14,892,046 in 1973.

The American Stock Exchange listed 1,394 issues of 1,292 companies, totaling 3.45 billion shares, valued Jan. 2, 1974, at $38.7 billion. Average daily volume through Sept. 25, 1974, was 1.87 million shares, compared to 2.87 million a year earlier.

The N.Y. Stock Exchange reported 78 of its listed companies had sales or revenues of over $2 billion in 1973. There were 72 in 1972, 46 in 1968.

U.S. Companies with Largest Annual Sales or Revenues

Top listed firms of N.Y. Stock Exchange for 1973 as shown by its Research Dep't.

Company	Sales or revenues (in millions)	Net profit (in millions)	Company	Sales or revenues (in millions)	Net profit (in millions)
General Motors Corp.	$35,798.3	$2,398.1	Continental Oil Co.	$4,471.5	$242.7
Exxon Corp.	28,022.4	2,443.3	RCA Corp.	4,246.8	183.7
American Tel. & Tel.	23,527.3	2,946.7	Kroger Co.	4,204.7	29.9
Ford Motor Co.	23,015.1	906.5	International Harvester	4,192.5	106.9
Mobil Oil Corp.	12,620.1	849.3	LTV Corp.	4,150.6	32.5
Sears, Roebuck & Co.	12,306.2	679.9	Bethlehem Steel Corp.	4,137.6	206.6
Chrysler Corp.	11,774.4	255.4	Marcor Inc.	4,077.4	96.7
General Electric Co.	11,575.3	585.1	Eastman Kodak Co.	4,035.5	635.5
Texaco Inc.	11,406.9	1,292.4	Esmark Inc.	3,951.0	48.8
Int'l Business Machines	10,993.2	1,575.5	Union Carbide Corp.	3,938.8	290.9
Int'l Tel. & Tel.	10,183.0	521.3	Tenneco Inc.	3,910.5	230.2
Gulf Oil Corp.	9,843.0	800.0	Procter & Gamble Co.	3,906.7	302.1
Standard Oil Co. of Cal.	8,480.0	843.6	Woolworth (F. W.) Co.	3,722.1	93.5
United States Steel	6,951.9	325.8	Kraftco Corp.	3,601.5	103.4
Safeway Stores, Inc.	6,773.7	86.3	Beatrice Foods Co.	3,541.2	117.0
Great A&P Tea Co.	6,747.7	12.2	Occidental Petroleum	3,455.7	79.8
Standard Oil Co. (Ind.)	6,379.4	511.2	Greyhound Corp.	3,421.4	76.4
Penney (J. C.) Co.	6,243.7	185.8	Boeing Co.	3,335.2	51.2
Westinghouse Electric.	5,702.3	161.9	Reynolds (R.J.) Industries	3,294.9	293.6
Shell Oil Co.	5,701.1	332.7	Caterpillar Tractor Co.	3,182.4	246.8
du Pont de Nemours (E.I.)	5,275.6	585.6	Rockwell International	3,179.0	126.2
General Tel. & Electronics	5,105.3	352.1	Firestone Tire & Rubber.	3,154.9	164.9
Goodyear Tire & Rubber.	4,675.3	184.8	American Brands Inc.	3,096.4	131.3
Kresge (S. S.) Co.	4,633.2	138.3	Dow Chemical Co.	3,067.9	271.1
Atlantic Richfield Co.	4,489.1	270.2	Engelhard Mins. & Chem.	3,046.1	52.5

Largest Industrial Companies Outside the U.S.

Reprinted by special permission from the Fortune Directory, as listed for 1973; © 1974, Time Inc.

Company	Sales	Net profit	Company	Sales	Net profit
Royal Dutch Shell, N-B.	$18,672,150	$1,789,248	Nissan Motor, J.	$4,883,494	$150,895
Unilever, B-N.	11,009,559	423,484	Renault, F.	4,655,696	12,902
Philips' Gloeilampenfab, N.	8,108,065	323,096	Bayer, G.	4,653,665	164,866
British Petroleum, B.	7,725,980	760,539	Montedison, I.	4,452,335	57,181
Nippon Steel, J.	7,628,385	195,545	Matsushita Elec Inds, J.	4,409,465	252,434
Volkswagenwerk, G.	6,412,056	73,071	British Steel, B.	4,289,512	120,831
Hitachi, J.	5,971,604	292,071	ENI, I.	4,280,043	64,982
Farbwerke Hoechst, G.	5,590,817	176,330	August Thyssen Hutte, G.	4,243,456	61,240
Daimler-Benz, G.	5,550,899	97,527	AEG Telefunken, G.	4,186,977	30,135
Toyota Motor, J.	5,547,425	277,807	Fiat, I.	4,074,914	450
Siemens, G.	5,522,688	161,897	Cie Francaise Petroles, F.	4,060,034	197,028
BASF (Badische Anilin), G.	5,383,585	194,144	Tokyo Shibaura Electric, J.	4,022,349	66,846
ICI (Imp Chem Ind), B.	5,308,578	449,510	National Iranian Oil, Ir.	4,000,000	155,000
Mitsubishi Heavy Inds, J.	5,226,713	109,596	British Leland Motor, B.	3,827,248	66,802
Nestle, S.	5,205,229	217,783	British-American Tobacco, B.	3,737,305	272,313

Nation of Hqs: N, Netherlands; B, Britain; G, Germany; S, Switzerland; I, Italy; F, France; J, Japan; Ir, Iran

Stocks Most Widely Held by Investment Cos., Insurance Cos., Trust Funds

As listed in 1974 in Growth Leaders on the Big Board, published by the N.Y. Stock Exchange
(In order of number of institutions, etc., which held shares, 1974)

Intnat'l Bus. Mach.	Sears Roebuck	Gen'l. Tel. & Elec.	Amer. Home Prods.	Pfizer Inc.
Exxon Corp.	Minn. Mng. & Mfg.	Merck & Co.	Burroughs Corp.	Warner-Lambert
Eastman Kodak	Citicorp	Phillips Petroleum	Stand. Oil (Cal.)	Procter & Gamble
General Motors	Ford Motor	Gulf Oil	Texas Utilities	Int'l Nickel Can. 'A'
General Electric	duPont (E.I.)	Stand. Oil Indiana	Kresge (S.S.)	Penney (J.C.)
Amer. Tel. & Tel.	Dow Chemical	Westinghouse Elec.	Goodyear T. & Rub.	Southern Co.
Xerox Corp.	Mobil Oil	Union Carbide	Int'l. Tel. & Tel.	Avon Products
Texaco Inc.	Atlantic Richfield	Caterpillar Tractor	Monsanto Co.	Int'l. Paper

N.Y. Stock Exchange Transactions and Seat Prices
Source: New York Stock Exchange

Year	Stock Shares	Bonds Par Values	Seat Price High	Low	Year	Stock Shares	Bonds Par Values	Seat Price High	Low
1900	138,981,000	$579,293,000	$47,500	$37,500	1935	381,635,752	$3,339,458,000	$140,000	$65,000
1905	260,569,000	1,026,254,000	85,000	72,000	1940	207,599,749	1,669,438,000	60,000	33,000
1910	163,705,000	634,863,000	94,000	65,000	1945	377,563,575	2,261,985,110	95,000	49,000
1915	172,497,000	961,700,000	74,000	38,000	1950	524,799,621	1,112,425,170	54,000	46,000
1920	227,636,000	3,868,422,000	115,000	85,000	1960	766,693,818	1,346,419,750	162,000	135,000
1925	459,717,623	3,427,042,210	150,000	99,000	1970	2,937,359,448	4,494,864,600	320,000	130,000
1929	1,124,800,410	2,996,398,000	625,000	550,000	1971	3,891,317,731	*6,563,822,400	300,000	145,000
1930	810,632,546	2,720,301,800	480,000	205,000	1972	*4,138,187,706	5,444,117,100	250,000	150,000
*Record high for trading in stocks and bonds.					1973	4,053,201,306	4,424,671,800	170,000	72,000

American Stock Exchange Transactions and Seat Prices
Source: American Stock Exchange

Year	Stock Shares	Bonds Par Values	Seat Price High	Low	Year	Stock Shares	Bonds Par Values	Seat Price High	Low
1929	476,140,375	$513,551,000	$254,000	$150,000	1965	534,221,999	$146,927,000	$80,000	$55,000
1930	222,270,065	863,541,000	225,000	70,000	1969	1,240,742,012	913,940,000	350,000	150,000
1940	42,928,337	303,902,000	7,250	6,900	1970	843,116,260	641,270,000	180,000	70,000
1945	143,309,392	167,333,000	32,000	12,000	1971	1,070,924,002	867,046,000	150,000	65,000
1950	107,792,340	47,549,000	11,000	6,500	1972	1,117,989,153	728,524,000	145,000	70,000
1960	286,039,982	32,670,000	60,000	51,000	1973	759,840,245	457,940,000	100,000	27,000

U.S. Business Indexes
Source: Federal Reserve System

	Industrial production (Physical volume) 1967 = 100 Manufacturers						Construct'n contracts (value)[1] 1967 = 100			Employment[2] 1967 = 100 Manuf. production workers				Prices 1967 = 100	
	Total	Total	Durable	Non-Durable	Mining	Utilities	Total	Residential	All Other	Non-agricultural	Employment	Payrolls	Consumer	Wholesale commodity
1960.............	66.2	65.4	63.3	68.6	82.7	61.8	69	77	64	82.4	88.0	78.1	88.7	94.9
1965.............	89.2	89.1	88.5	90.0	93.9	86.9	93	109	84	92.3	93.9	93.6	94.5	96.6
1966.............	97.9	98.3	99.0	97.3	98.4	93.6	95	91	97	97.1	99.9	97.8	97.2	99.8
1967.............	100.0	100.0	100.0	100.0	100.0	100	100	100	100.0	100.0	100.0	100.0	100.0	100.0
1968.............	105.7	105.7	105.5	106.0	103.9	109.4	113	117	111	103.1	101.4	106.6	104.2	102.5
1969.............	110.7	110.5	110.0	111.1	107.2	19.5	124	119	126	106.7	103.2	112.7	109.8	106.5
1970.............	106.6	105.2	101.4	110.6	109.7	128.3	123	115	130	107.2	98.0	114.1	116.3	110.4
1971.............	106.8	105.2	99.4	113.5	107.0	133.7	145	163	134	107.3	93.9	116.3	121.3	113.9
1972.............	115.2	114.0	108.4	122.1	108.8	143.4	N.A.	N.A.	N.A.	110.5	96.7	130.2	N.A.	N.A.
1973.............	125.6	125.1	122.0	129.7	110.3	152.6	N.A.	N.A.	N.A.	N.A.	N.A.	N.A.	N.A.	N.A.

(1) Indexes beginning 1960 are based on data from 48 states. (2) Revisions have been made in some figures.

Wholesale Price Indexes
Source: Bureau of Labor Statistics, United States Department of Labor

The Wholesale Primary Market Price Index is designed to show the rate and direction of the composite of price movements, and to measure price changes not influenced by quality, quantity, terms of sale, etc. Wholesale refers to sales in quantities, not to prices received or paid by wholesalers.

Commodity group (1967 = 100)	1974 June	1974 Jan.	1973 Avg.	1972 Avg.
All commodities...	155.7	146.6	134.7	119.1
Farm products, and processed foods, and feeds.........................	161.7	177.8	159.1	122.4
Farm products..	168.6	202.6	176.3	125.0
Processed foods and feeds	157.4	162.1	148.1	120.8
All commodities except farm products	154.2	140.1	129.9	118.4
Industrial commodities..	153.6	135.3	125.9	117.9
Textile products and apparel....................................	141.7	133.8	123.8	113.6
Hides, skins, leather and related products	146.0	142.6	143.1	131.3
Fuels and related products and power	210.5	162.5	134.3	118.6
Chemicals and allied products	142.8	118.2	110.0	104.2
Rubber and plastic products	135.6	117.7	112.4	109.3
Lumber and wood products	192.2	183.7	177.2	144.3
Pulp, paper and allied products	147.5	131.8	122.1	113.4
Metals and metal products	174.0	145.0	132.8	123.5
Machinery and equipment......................................	137.2	126.0	121.7	117.9
Furniture and household durables	126.1	119.0	115.2	111.4
Nonmetallic mineral products	152.3	138.7	130.2	126.1
Transportation equipment (Dec. 1968 = 100)	122.8	118.6	115.1	113.7
Miscellaneous products..	134.3	123.5	119.7	114.6

Civilian Employment of the Federal Government

Source: United States Civil Service Commission, Manpower Statistics Division, data as of June 30, 1974

		United States		Part-Time & Intermittent	Outside United States		
	All Areas	Total	Full-Time		Total	Terri-tories	Foreign Countries
Total, all agencies (a)	2,893,119	2,756,310	2,539,382	216,928	136,809	35,202	101,607
Percent distribution	100	95	88	7	5	1	4
Legislative branch	36,558	36,483	35,700	783	75	...	75
Congress	16,056	16,056	16,056	...	...	...	...
Architect of the Capitol	1,901	1,901	1,775	126	...	...	...
Botanic Garden	62	62	62	...	...	...	...
General Accounting Office	5,220	5,155	5,093	62	65	...	65
Government Printing Office	8,564	8,564	8,152	412	...	...	...
Library of Congress	4,504	4,494	4,316	178	10	...	10
National Study Commission	61	61	56	5	...	...	...
United States Tax Court	190	190	190	...	...	...	...
Judicial branch	9,490	9,403	8,872	531	87	87	...
Executive branch	2,847,071	2,710,424	2,494,810	215,614	136,647	35,115	101,532
Executive Office of the President	5,751	5,751	5,551	200	...	...	...
White House Office	583	583	554	29	...	...	...
Office of the Vice President	30	30	29	1	...	...	...
Office of Management and Budget	688	688	664	24	...	...	...
Council of Economic Advisors	42	42	39	3	...	...	...
Citizens' Advisory Committee on Environmental Quality	1	1	1	...	...	...	...
Cost of Living Council	614	614	570	44	...	...	...
Council on Environmental Quality	61	61	58	3	...	...	...
Council on International Economic Policy	43	43	37	6	...	...	...
Domestic Council	33	33	32	1	...	...	...
Executive Mansion and Grounds	70	70	70	...	...	...	...
Federal Energy Administration	2,203	2,203	2,162	41	...	...	...
National Security Council	85	85	71	14	...	...	...
Office of Economic Opportunity	1,125	1,125	1,110	15	...	...	...
Office of Special Representative for Trade Negotiations	42	42	39	3	...	...	...
Office of Telecommunications Policy	68	68	58	10	...	...	...
Special Action Office for Drug Abuse Prevention	63	63	57	6	...	...	...
Executive Departments	1,746,682	1,636,930	1,584,310	52,620	109,752	15,165	94,587
State (b)	33,396	10,630	10,067	563	22,766	...	22,766
Treasury	116,213	115,328	113,045	2,283	885	586	299
Defense	1,070,004	988,442	976,095	12,347	81,562	11,655	69,907
Office of the Secretary	1,971	1,927	1,853	74	44	...	44
Department of the Army	382,388	349,132	345,094	4,038	33,256	4,226	29,030
Department of the Navy	329,378	302,118	298,562	3,556	27,260	5,239	22,021
Department of the Air Force	280,812	261,665	257,270	4,395	19,147	2,014	17,133
Other defense activities	75,455	73,600	73,316	284	1,855	176	1,679
Justice	50,531	49,740	48,932	808	791	319	472
Interior	76,919	76,484	71,623	4,861	435	370	65
Agriculture	116,203	114,951	94,651	20,300	1,252	632	620
Commerce	35,759	35,439	31,580	3,859	320	124	196
Labor	14,487	14,379	13,831	548	108	96	12
Health, Education, and Welfare	142,159	141,591	136,082	5,509	568	510	58
Housing and Urban Development	17,274	17,095	16,874	221	179	179	...
Transportation	73,737	72,851	71,530	1,321	886	694	192
Independent agencies	1,094,638	1,067,743	904,949	162,794	26,895	19,950	6,945
ACTION	1,797	1,282	1,183	99	515	27	488
Atomic Energy Commission	7,988	7,976	7,784	192	12	...	12
Board of Governors, Federal Reserve System	1,353	1,353	1,328	25	...	...	...
Canal Zone Government	3,286	...	...	...	3,286	3,286	...
Civil Aeronautics Board	721	721	718	3	...	...	...
Civil Service Commission	7,500	7,485	6,585	900	15	15	...
Environmental Protection Agency	10,711	10,695	10,029	666	16	9	7
Federal Communications Commission	2,064	2,057	2,053	4	7	7	...
Federal Power Commission	1,345	1,345	1,320	25	...	...	...
Federal Trade Commission	1,626	1,626	1,602	24	...	...	...
General Services Administration	40,219	40,127	38,823	1,304	92	80	12
Information Agency	9,028	3,310	3,281	29	5,718	...	5,718
Interstate Commerce Commission	2,022	2,022	2,003	19	...	...	...
National Aeronautics and Space Administration	26,686	26,665	26,447	218	21	1	20
National Labor Relations Board	2,504	2,479	2,456	23	25	25	...
Panama Canal Company	11,797	90	90	...	11,707	11,707	...
Securities and Exchange Commission	1,889	1,889	1,879	10	...	...	...
Selective Service System	2,471	2,422	2,287	135	49	49	...
Small Business Administration	4,718	4,646	4,574	72	72	72	...
Tennessee Valley Authority	25,261	25,257	25,000	257	4	...	4
U.S. Postal Service	707,202	704,394	562,435	141,959	2,808	2,808	...
Veterans Administration	202,361	200,320	184,397	15,923	2,041	1,749	292
All other agencies	20,089	19,582	18,675	907	507	115	392

(a) Excludes employees of Central Intelligence Agency, National Security Agency (not reported to the Civil Service Commission), and uncompensated employees. June 1974 total includes 53,346 employees exempted from personnel ceilings in the Youth Programs, Public Service Careers, and Worker Trainee Opportunities Program. (b) Includes 9,278 employees in Agency for International Development (3,129 in the Washington, D.C., metropolitan area): employees in foreign countries include 2,732 paid from local currency trust funds established by foreign governments.

Assets and Liabilities of Insured Commercial Banks

As of December 31, 1973 (In thousands of dollars)

State	Loans and Securities	Total Assets	Total Deposits	Total Liabilities	Reserves and Cap.Accts.	State	Loans and Securities	Total Assets	Total Deposits	Total Liabilities	Reserves and Cap.Accts.
Ala...	7,599,620	8,996,990	7,711,713	8,239,762	757,208	Neb...	5,247,133	6,302,351	5,390,050	5,800,136	502,215
Alask..	767,327	920,266	794,820	847,872	72,394	Nev...	1,685,360	1,974,756	1,752,022	1,831,934	142,822
Ariz...	5,792,954	7,056,939	5,784,841	6,601,323	455,616	N.H...	1,423,764	1,643,392	1,412,357	1,490,098	153,294
Ark...	4,684,352	5,676,722	4,922,101	5,225,334	451,388	N.J...	19,920,324	23,304,543	20,352,217	21,378,946	1,925,597
Calif..	71,866,355	88,157,078	70,849,088	82,358,200	5,798,820	N.M...	2,340,741	2,848,160	2,484,643	2,625,636	222,524
Colo...	6,283,477	7,821,665	6,628,695	7,225,896	595,769	N.Y...	112,915,399	149,721,837	115,054,647	137,181,405	12,540,417
Conn..	6,463,382	7,966,206	6,871,492	7,321,600	644,606	N.C...	11,314,106	14,053,956	11,644,852	12,961,400	1,092,530
Del....	1,977,202	2,256,230	1,786,994	2,075,056	181,174	N.D...	2,037,301	2,293,330	2,038,905	2,110,352	182,978
D.C...	3,359,414	4,066,707	3,437,088	3,707,464	359,243	Ohio..	28,805,820	34,105,736	28,273,675	31,117,963	2,987,628
Fla....	21,781,579	26,347,123	22,855,255	24,278,270	2,068,792	Okla..	7,951,309	9,693,537	8,269,477	8,897,971	795,522
Ga....	11,660,774	14,454,118	11,142,865	13,230,731	1,223,387	Ore...	5,422,129	6,636,664	5,478,529	6,115,723	520,924
Hwii..	2,257,285	2,680,403	2,353,661	2,472,091	208,312	Pa....	41,786,791	49,299,137	39,710,625	45,107,882	4,188,832
Ida...	2,036,056	2,434,242	2,159,954	2,264,700	169,401	R.I....	2,507,861	2,856,153	2,390,590	2,626,457	229,696
Ill.....	54,587,971	63,796,385	51,825,517	58,876,125	4,920,220	S.C...	3,591,576	4,373,146	3,719,926	4,001,513	371,633
Ind....	15,486,949	18,261,004	15,342,302	16,941,441	1,319,562	S.D...	2,303,509	2,639,083	2,367,997	2,430,571	208,512
Ia.....	9,440,991	10,979,902	9,549,318	10,096,281	883,359	Tenn..	11,480,908	13,928,394	11,690,558	12,867,372	1,060,591
Kan...	7,191,350	8,573,975	7,343,979	7,825,604	748,186	Tex...	37,387,873	46,861,936	38,556,977	43,269,197	3,591,985
Ky....	7,755,083	9,193,025	7,828,706	8,446,316	746,709	Utah..	2,535,364	3,169,913	2,707,811	2,924,178	245,654
La....	9,748,230	11,748,144	9,719,532	10,794,661	953,480	Vt....	1,195,628	1,344,671	1,209,695	1,234,466	110,205
Me....	1,726,113	2,005,406	1,743,860	1,835,107	170,299	Va....	12,407,514	14,605,504	12,241,494	13,487,019	1,117,952
Md....	7,563,793	8,887,721	7,535,262	8,133,403	754,318	Wash.	7,895,204	9,735,464	7,667,948	9,071,584	663,856
Mass.	14,140,960	17,549,915	14,098,491	16,099,833	1,450,082	W.Va..	4,557,970	5,210,588	4,361,835	4,751,537	459,051
Mich..	26,896,363	31,626,745	26,922,946	29,139,279	2,487,389	Wis...	13,235,617	15,249,727	13,094,209	14,067,899	1,181,804
Minn..	13,431,956	15,615,225	12,656,855	14,430,660	1,184,565	Wyo...	1,205,651	1,439,679	1,267,730	1,320,553	119,126
Miss..	4,639,567	5,604,022	4,915,834	5,157,504	446,411	*Other	4,252,384	5,577,621	4,261,600	5,323,883	253,738
Mo....	15,451,001	18,377,793	15,041,695	16,855,892	1,521,900	U.S.	682,365,800	832,658,280	681,619,425	767,005,602	65,647,205
Mont..	2,368,460	2,735,051	2,396,192	2,529,522	205,529						

*Includes Guam, Puerto Rico, and Virgin Islands.

Bank Suspensions

Source: Federal Reserve System. The figures for bank suspensions represent banks which, during the periods shown, closed temporarily or permanently on account of financial difficulties; does not include banks whose deposit liabilities were assumed by other banks at the time of closing (in some instances with Federal Deposit Insurance Corp. loans).

Year	Suspensions	Deposits	Year	Suspensions	Deposits	Year	Suspensions	Deposits	Year	Suspensions	Deposits
1929....	659	230,643,000	1938....	55	13,012,000	1954.....	3	2,880,000	1963.....	2	23,256,000
1930...	1,352	853,363,000	1939....	42	34,998,000	1955.....	4	6,498,000	1964.....	8	22,022,000
1931...	2,294	1,690,669,000	1940....	22	5,943,000	1956.....	3	11,881,000	1965.....	7	44,857,000
1932...	1,456	715,626,000	1943.....	4	6,223,000	1957.....	3	12,869,000	1967.....	4	10,802,000
1933*	4,004	3,598,975,000	1944(a)...	1	405,000	1958.....	8	6,287,000	1969.....	4	8,910,000
1934....	57	36,937,000	1947.....	1	167,000	1959.....	3	2,048,000	1970.....	1	149,500
1935....	34	10,015,000	1949.....	4	2,443,000	1960.....	2	7,987,000	1971.....	1	516,000
1936....	44	11,306,000	1950.....	1	42,000	1961.....	9	7,527,000	1972.....	1	20,579
1937....	59	19,723,000	1953.....	4	44,412,000	1962.....	2	1,201,000	1973.....	3	20,626,000

*Figures for 1933 comprise 628 banks with deposits of $360,413,000 suspended before or after the banking holiday (the holiday began March 6 and closed March 15) or placed in receivership during the holiday; 2,124 banks with deposits of $2,520,391,000 which were not licensed following the banking holiday and were placed in liquidation or receivership; and 1,252 banks with deposits of $718,171,000 which had not been licensed by June 30, 1933. (a) No suspensions in years 1945, 1946, 1948 and 1968.

Federal Reserve System

The Federal Reserve System, central banking system of the United States, was established Dec. 23, 1913, by an Act of Congress to give the country an elastic currency, to provide facilities for discounting commercial paper, and to improve supervision of banking. Today it is generally recognized that the primary function of the System is to foster a flow of credit and money that will facilitate orderly economic growth, a stable dollar, and a long-run balance in international payments.

The Federal Reserve System consists of the (1) Board of Governors of the Federal Reserve System; (2) Federal Open Market Committee; (3) 12 Fed. Reserve Banks and 24 branches; (4) member banks; and (5) Fed. Advisory Council.

The 7 members of the Board of Governors in Washington are appointed by the President with the advice and consent of the Senate; Dr. Arthur F. Burns is chairman. One of the Board's principal functions is in the area of monetary policy. The Board has authority to approve changes in discount rates, to change member bank reserve requirements within specified limits, to set margin requirements for certain kinds of stock transactions, and to set maximum interest rates payable on member banks' savings and time deposits. Another important duty of the Board relates to supervision of Federal Reserve Banks, member banks and bank holding companies. Expenses of the Board of Governors are paid out of assessments upon the Reserve Banks.

The Federal Open Market Committee is composed of the 7 members of the Board of Governors and 5 Federal Reserve Bank representatives elected annually. The Committee establishes System open market policy for the purchases and sales of securities and for operations in foreign currencies.

Rather than having one central bank in the political capital, as in central banking systems of most countries, the Federal Reserve System is divided into 12 districts, each with a Federal Reserve Bank—in Boston, New York, Philadelphia, Cleveland, Richmond, Atlanta, Chicago, St. Louis, Minneapolis, Kansas City, Dallas, and San Francisco. Reserve Banks are operated for public service. By statute, their stock is held entirely by member banks, which include all national banks and such state banks and trust companies as have been admitted to membership. Ownership of Reserve Bank stock is in the nature of an obligation incident to membership in the System and does not carry with it the attributes of control and financial interest ordinarily attached to stock ownership in corporations that are operated for profit. The amount of stock that member banks own is specified by law and dividends are limited to 6% per annum. In case of the liquidation of any Reserve Bank, its surplus would be paid entirely to the United States. Each Reserve Bank has 9 directors, 6 of whom are chosen by member banks and 3 by the Board of Governors.

The 12-member Federal Advisory Council is composed of one member selected annually by the directors of each Federal Reserve Bank. The Council meets in Washington at least 4 times a year and advises the Board of Governors on matters within the Board's jurisdiction.

U.S. Balance of International Payments

Source: Bureau of Economic Analysis, Dept. of Commerce

(In millions of dollars. Excludes military transfers under grants. Revised. Credits +; debits-)

	1955	1960	1965	1969	1970	1971	1972	1973
Exports of goods and services	19,948	27,490	39,407	55,501	62,874	66,136	73,462	100,950
Merchandise adjusted.	14,424	19,650	26,438	36,417	41,963	42,770	48,769	70,252
Transfers under U.S. military agency sales contracts. ..	200	335	830	1,512	1,479	1,923	1,166	2,354
Receipts of income on U.S. investments abroad	2,602	3,939	7,092	10,539	11,428	12,900	13,925	13,984
Other services.	2,722	3,567	5,047	7,033	8,004	8,543	9,602	14,360
Imports of goods and services	-17,795	-23,364	-32,277	-53,594	-59,308	65,410	-78,071	-96,407
Merchandise, adjusted.	-11,527	-14,744	-21,496	-35,796	-39,799	-45,459	-55,681	-69,629
Direct defense expenditures	-2,901	-3,087	-2,952	-4,856	-4,852	-4,817	-4,724	-4,555
Payments of income on foreign investments in U.S.	-511	-1,098	-1,798	-4,564	-5,167	-4,905	-6,063	-8,694
Other services.	-2,856	-4,435	-6,033	-8,377	-9,490	-10,229	-11,603	-13,529
Unilateral transfers, net.	-2,498	-2,292	-2,835	-2,947	-3,208	-3,575	-3,744	-3,876
U.S. Government capital flows, net	-310	-1,104	-1,598	-2,193	-1,584	-1,892	-1,576	-2,650
U.S. Private capital flows, net.	-1,255	-3,878	-3,794	-5,424	-6,886	-9,781	-8,534	-14,101
Foreign capital flows, net.	1,357	2,120	383	12,309	5,945	22,381	20,833	18,650
Transaction in U.S. official reserve assets, net	182	2,145	1,222	-1,187	2,477	-2,348	32	209
Allocation of special drawing rights (SDR). ...	-	-	-	-	867	717	710	-
Errors and omissions, net	371	-1,116	-507	-2,876	-1,075	-10,928	-3,112	-2,776
Balance on goods and services	2,153	4,126	7,130	1,907	3,563	727	-4,609	4,543
Balance on goods, services, and remittances. ...	1,556	3,498	6,102	610	2,089	-802	-6,179	2,600
Balance on current account	-345	1,834	4,295	-899	355	-2,847	-8,353	667
Balance on current account and. long-term capital ..	n.a.	-1,155	-1,814	-3,118	-3,061	-9,374	-9,842	-744
Net liquidity balance.	n.a.	-3,655	-2,493	-6,128	-3,851	-21,965	-13,882	-7,796
Official reserve transactions balance	n.a.	-3,403	-1,289	2,696	-9,839	-29,765	-10,340	-5,304
Liquidity balance, excluding SDR.	-1,242	-3,711	-1,335	-6,963	-4,721	-23,994	-15,826	-9,740

Details may not add to total because of rounding. N.A.-Not available.

All Banks in United States—Number, Deposits

Source: Federal Reserve System

Comprises all national banks in the United States and all state commercial banks, trust companies, mutual and stock savings banks, private and industrial banks and special types of institutions that are treated as banks by the Federal bank supervisory agencies.

Date June 30	Number of Banks					Total Deposits (Millions of Dollars)					
	Total All Banks	Member Banks		Nonmember		Total All Banks	Member		Nonmember	
		Total	Nat'l	State	Mutual Savings	Other		Total	Nat'l	State	Mutual Savings	Other
1925.	26,479	9,538	8,066	1,472	621	18,320	51,641	32,457	19,912	12,546	7,089	12,095
1930.	23,855	8,315	7,247	1,068	604	14,936	59,828	38,069	23,235	14,834	9,117	12,642
1935.	16,047	6,410	5,425	985	569	9,068	51,149	34,938	22,477	12,461	9,830	6,381
1940.	14,955	6,398	5,164	1,234	551	8,008	70,770	51,729	33,014	18,715	10,631	8,410
1945.	14,542	6,840	5,015	1,825	539	7,163	151,033	118,378	76,534	41,844	14,413	18,242
1950.	14,674	6,885	4,971	1,914	527	7,262	163,770	122,707	82,430	40,277	19,927	21,137
1955.	14,309	6,611	4,744	1,867	525	7,173	208,850	154,670	98,636	56,034	27,310	26,870
1960.	14,006	6,217	4,542	1,675	513	7,276	249,163	179,519	116,178	63,341	35,316	34,328
1965.	14,295	6,235	4,803	1,432	504	7,556	362,611	259,743	171,528	88,215	50,980	51,889
1970.	14,167	5,803	4,637	1,166	496	7,868	502,658	346,229	254,261	91,967	69,285	87,145
1973.	14,529	5,705	4,629	1,076	483	8,341	726,200	487,145	364,129	123,016	96,447	142,608
1974*.	14,652	5,735	4,659	1,076	481	8,436	779,513	527,188	395,767	131,421	97,159	155,166

*First 6 months of fiscal year—to Dec. 31, 1973.

Bank Clearings in Chief United States Cities

Year (Cal.)	New York	Chicago	Phila.	Los Ang.	Boston	San Fran.	Detroit	Dallas
	$1,000	$1,000	$1,000	$1,000	$1,000	$1,000	$1,000	$1,000
1935.	181,551,008	13,194,988	16,909,000	5,852,244	10,645,822	6,478,835	4,523,167	1,969,290
1940.	160,878,038	16,684,672	21,455,000	7,543,880	11,943,665	6,773,877	6,312,233	2,986,774
1945.	334,432,654	27,279,588	34,710,000	17,144,078	19,589,725	15,743,086	16,472,971	6,634,514
1950.	399,308,634	40,674,983	51,102,000	26,504,731	25,348,336	21,982,689	22,855,273	14,451,332
1955.	530,883,498	52,818,527	59,962,000	42,818,633	32,472,726	31,492,157	36,364,754	21,678,567
1960.	738,604,276	66,651,600	56,716,000	53,635,826	40,759,040	39,787,147	39,101,854	27,811,939
1965.	1,280,402,568	82,507,560	69,116,728	111,587,481	60,318,717	87,095,481	56,068,833	42,414,327
1970.	3,752,515,518	110,219,418	94,003,896	174,153,125	125,033,163	122,929,389	136,965,556	51,886,403
1971.	4,208,890,740	118,508,177	98,275,037	196,698,129	134,930,871	140,478,784	172,079,317	57,320,551
1972.	6,897,248,349	126,959,884	104,819,843	222,499,794	113,515,212	155,684,868	175,620,419	63,336,639

Year (Cal.)	Kan. City	Houston	Pittsburgh	Cleveland	St. Louis	Minneap.	Baltimore	Atlanta
	$1,000	$1,000	$1,000	$1,000	$1,000	$1,000	$1,000	$1,000
1935.	4,348,113	1,420,404	5,245,718	3,417,055	3,940,654	3,044,735	2,910,637	2,204,500
1940.	4,997,593	2,568,518	7,074,775	5,734,407	4,822,016	3,787,088	4,201,985	3,430,900
1945.	10,856,497	5,982,318	12,978,668	11,529,428	9,723,815	8,196,279	8,315,468	8,263,900
1950.	16,707,120	11,922,307	16,782,419	17,683,829	14,896,444	14,113,814	12,154,904	12,910,100
1955.	20,057,800	19,199,929	21,142,527	26,426,614	18,481,105	18,496,868	17,071,914	18,597,100
1960.	24,967,583	21,887,889	23,913,706	32,364,009	21,138,861	25,129,318	20,423,684	22,993,200
1965.	33,936,377	33,938,170	29,070,474	44,600,090	28,399,392	34,029,120	25,893,740	34,371,000
1970.	53,509,523	39,855,427	42,418,973	52,690,067	33,611,932	43,112,445	29,964,761	53,784,237
1971.	52,040,273	43,761,645	40,791,361	54,307,281	39,218,274	46,940,376	31,025,066	66,327,913
1972.	56,063,129	58,312,671	48,606,390	57,634,920	40,485,176	52,798,284	32,179,679	73,475,516

Per Capita Personal Income, by States and Regions

Source: Department of Commerce, Bureau of Economic Analysis. Revised

State and Region	1970	1971	1972	1973
United States	3,966	4,195	4,549	5,041
New England	4,304	4,479	4,774	5,212
Connecticut	4,923	5,067	5,414	5,938
Maine	3,309	3,397	3,664	4,082
Massachusetts	4,347	4,545	4,825	5,253
New Hampshire	3,795	3,978	4,279	4,694
Rhode Island	3,960	4,190	4,513	4,841
Vermont	3,328	3,533	3,703	4,054
Mideast	4,473	4,722	5,075	5,523
Delaware	4,527	5,876	5,222	5,778
District of Columbia	4,938	5,357	5,827	6,337
Maryland	4,350	4,601	5,017	5,489
New Jersey	4,705	4,982	5,379	5,845
New York	4,712	4,962	5,275	5,705
Pennsylvania	3,970	4,187	4,545	4,993
Great Lakes	4,130	4,394	4,766	5,324
Illinois	4,504	4,808	5,162	5,770
Indiana	3,768	4,051	4,364	4,987
Michigan	4,175	4,481	4,982	5,551
Ohio	4,011	4,230	4,572	5,076
Wisconsin	3,809	3,983	4,279	4,750
Plains	3,749	3,949	4,333	5,116
Iowa	3,755	3,866	4,316	5,273
Kansas	3,857	4,097	4,535	5,304
Minnesota	3,839	4,019	4,343	5,137
Missouri	3,775	4,012	4,307	4,841
Nebraska	3,786	3,974	4,451	5,271
North Dakota	3,191	3,559	4,128	5,695
South Dakota	3,101	3,283	3,766	4,713
Southeast	3,260	3,500	3,852	4,282
Alabama	2,947	3,175	3,476	3,871
Arkansas	2,886	3,060	3,345	3,952
Florida	3,741	4,050	4,450	4,923
Georgia	3,357	3,614	3,956	4,395
Kentucky	3,118	3,327	3,624	4,033
Louisiana	3,097	3,299	3,565	3,931
Mississippi	2,630	2,832	3,188	3,556
North Carolina	3,256	3,470	3,868	4,282
South Carolina	2,992	3,181	3,500	3,882
Tennessee	3,124	3,373	3,708	4,095
Virginia	3,707	3,981	4,396	4,886
West Virginia	3,070	3,309	3,624	3,961
Southwest	3,542	3,707	4,033	4,505
Arizona	3,665	3,953	4,273	4,692
New Mexico	3,092	3,256	3,512	3,853
Oklahoma	3,381	3,553	3,837	4,340
Texas	3,600	3,743	4,085	4,571
Rocky Mountain	3,587	3,845	4,200	4,670
Colorado	3,851	4,204	4,600	5,029
Idaho	3,294	3,467	3,711	4,413
Montana	3,504	3,700	4,083	4,682
Utah	3,218	3,434	3,741	4,072
Wyoming	3,816	3,879	4,269	4,695
Far West	4,376	4,582	4,966	5,422
California	4,498	4,699	5,087	5,521
Nevada	4,563	4,880	5,209	5,745
Oregon	3,717	3,979	4,339	4,833
Washington	4,053	4,224	4,601	5,154
Alaska	4,632	4,949	5,222	5,933
Hawaii	4,623	4,836	5,153	5,541

(1.) Per capita personal income for each state is derived by the division of total personal income by total population. Personal income is a measure of the income received from all sources during the calendar year by the residents of each state. It comprises income received by persons in the form of wages and salaries, net income of proprietors (including farmers) dividends, interest, net rents, and other items such as social insurance benefits, relief, veterans pensions and benefits, and allotment payments to dependents of military personnel.

Manufacturing Output and Labor Costs, Industrial Nations

Source: U.S. Bureau of Labor Statistics

Output per Man-Hour

Country	1960	1965	1967	1969	1970	1971	1972	1973
United States	80.5	98.9	100.0	107.3	108.0	115.7	121.8	127.5
Industrial nations	68.9	89.7	100.0	116.2	122.4	128.3	138.5	151.7
Canada	75.4	94.5	100.0	113.2	115.0	121.6	126.9	132.1
Japan	52.5	79.1	100.0	130.0	146.5	151.7	168.1	198.8
Belgium	70.5	78.1	100.0	117.7	128.4	132.4	144.5	N.A.
Denmark	68.2	87.3	100.0	121.0	128.1	137.5	152.6	N.A.
France	69.6	88.7	100.0	115.1	120.9	126.7	134.7	144.2
Germany	66.4	90.4	100.0	113.8	116.7	122.3	130.5	138.9
Italy	65.1	91.5	100.0	112.2	117.3	123.0	133.4	143.3
Netherlands	67.8	87.8	100.0	120.7	130.6	138.0	152.6	N.A.
Sweden	63.1	88.6	100.0	118.8	124.6	130.5	141.0	151.4
Switzerland (wage earners only)	80.4	90.6	100.0	116.0	125.5	132.2	138.8	N.A.
United Kingdom	76.8	92.4	100.0	108.3	109.0	115.0	122.0	132.9
9 European Countries	69.5	90.3	100.0	113.5	117.8	124.1	133.0	142.7
Original EEC	67.4	89.9	100.0	114.4	119.4	125.3	134.4	N.A.

Unit Labor Costs in U.S. Dollars

	1960	1965	1967	1969	1970	1971	1972	1973
United States	95.2	92.3	100.0	106.3	113.2	113.0	114.1	117.6
11 Industrial nations	83.5	97.8	100.0	100.8	111.2	124.1	141.6	168.0
Canada	105.8	91.2	100.0	102.1	111.9	118.2	124.0	128.3
Japan	82.6	102.6	100.0	106.9	112.7	129.9	156.3	184.1
Belgium	77.2	93.6	100.0	97.6	102.7	116.4	135.0	N.A.
Denmark	74.7	91.8	100.0	95.8	101.1	108.1	118.9	N.A.
France	81.3	97.9	100.0	101.1	102.4	110.2	127.4	156.2
Germany	78.1	95.6	100.0	103.1	124.6	142.1	164.6	210.1
Italy	76.5	97.1	100.0	104.3	119.2	137.2	153.7	176.5
Netherlands	65.4	91.8	100.0	102.7	109.1	122.5	136.2	N.A.
Sweden	79.7	92.7	100.0	100.8	106.2	116.1	130.9	149.5
Switzerland (wage earners only)	71.1	95.6	100.0	97.1	99.7	112.1	128.5	N.A.
United Kingdom	86.5	99.6	100.0	93.7	106.9	116.5	128.6	136.5
9 European Countries	80.4	97.0	100.0	100.0	112.0	124.6	141.7	170.6
Original EEC	78.0	96.3	100.0	102.4	115.1	129.1	147.9	N.A.

Average Percent Increase in Earnings

Period and area May 1972 to May 1973	All Industries				Manufacturing			
	Office Clerical	Industrial nurses	Skilled maintenence	Unskilled plant	Office Clerical	Industrial nurses	Skilled maintenence	Unskilled plant
United States	5.3	6.0	6.5	6.4	5.4	5.7	6.2	6.5
Northeast	5.1	5.4	6.6	6.2	5.3	5.5	6.2	6.4
South	5.5	6.4	6.8	6.1	5.7	7.0	6.5	6.8
North Central	5.2	6.2	6.2	6.3	4.9	5.4	5.9	6.4
West	5.7	5.7	7.1	7.3	6.2	5.6	6.4	6.4

U. S. Labor Force, Employment and Unemployment

Source: Bureau of the Census, U. S. Dept. of Commerce; Bureau of Labor Statistics, U. S. Dept. of Labor
(Unemployment by sex, age, color and other characteristics)   **1974**

	1971	1972	1973	Jan.	Feb.	Mar.	Apr.	May	June
					Numbers in thousands				
U.S. Pop. (incl. armed forces overseas)	'207,045	'208,842	'210,396	211,210	211,329	211,432	211,551	211,660	N.A.
Labor Force³									
Labor force, persons 16 years of age and over . . .	86,929	88,991	91,042	91,354	91,692	91,884	91,736	92,158	94,758
Civilian labor force.	84,113	86,542	88,716	89,096	89,434	89,633	89,493	89,929	92,546
Employed, total.	79,120	81,702	84,410	84,088	84,294	84,878	85,192	85,785	87,167
Agriculture.	3,387	3,472	3,453	3,197	3,283	3,334	3,437	3,604	3,895
Nonagriculture Industries.	75,732	78,230	80,957	80,891	81,011	81,544	81,756	82,181	83,272
Unemployed.	4,993	4,840	4,306	5,008	5,140	4,755	4,301	4,144	5,380
Long term, 15 weeks and over.	1,181	1,158	812	789	905	1,051	1,112	970	922
Seasonally adjusted									
Civilian labor force.	. . . . .	. . . . .	. . . . .	90,543	90,556	90,496	90,313	90,679	90,919
Employed total.	. . . . .	. . . . .	. . . . .	85,811	85,803	85,863	85,775	85,971	86,165
Agriculture.	. . . . .	. . . . .	. . . . .	3,794	3,852	3,699	3,511	3,457	3,293
Nonagricultural industries	. . . . .	. . . . .	. . . . .	82,017	81,951	82,164	82,264	82,514	82,872
Unemployed	. . . . .	. . . . .	. . . . .	4,732	4,753	4,633	4,538	4,708	4,754
Long term, 15 weeks and over.	. . . . .	. . . . .	. . . . .	768	830	815	857	877	939
Rates (unemployed in each group as percent of total in the group):									
All civilian workers , ...	5.9	5.6	4.9	5.2	5.2	5.1	5.0	5.2	5.2
Men, 20 years and over.	4.4	4.0	3.2	3.4	3.9	3.4	3.6	3.4	3.5
Women, 20 years and over.	5.7	5.4	4.8	5.2	5.1	5.0	4.9	5.1	5.1
Both sexes, 16-19 years	16.9	16.2	14.5	15.6	15.3	15.0	13.8	15.8	15.6
White	5.4	5.0	4.3	4.7	4.7	4.6	4.5	4.7	4.8
Negro and other races	9.9	10.0	8.9	9.4	9.2	9.4	8.7	9.5	8.8
Household heads.	3.6	3.3	2.9	3.0	3.0	3.0	3.1	3.0	3.1
Married men	3.2	2.8	2.3	2.3	2.4	2.4	2.5	2.2	2.6
Occupation:									
White-collar workers.	3.5	3.4	2.9	3.2	3.2	2.8	2.8	3.2	3.1
Blue-collar workers.	7.4	6.5	5.3	6.0	6.1	6.1	6.4	5.7	6.2
Industry of last job (nonagricultural)									
Private wage and salary workers.	6.2	5.7	4.8	5.3	5.4	5.1	5.3	5.2	5.4
Construction.	10.4	10.3	8.8	9.1	7.9	8.4	10.3	9.6	10.2
Manufacturing	6.8	5.6	4.3	5.1	5.3	5.2	5.0	4.7	5.2
Durable goods.	7.0	5.4	3.9	5.0	5.1	5.0	5.0	4.5	4.8

(1) As of July 1. (2) Effective January 1972, data reflect adjustment to the 1970 Census of Population. For example the civilian labor force and employment totals were increased by a little more than 300,000; unemployment levels and rates were essentially unchanged. A subsequent census adjustment, primarily affecting whites and Negroes and other race groups, was introduced into the survey for March 1973. As a result, the white labor force and employment levels were lowered by about 150,000, while the Negro labor force was raised by 210,000. Consequently, the overall labor force and employment showed a net increase of about 60,000. Unemployment levels and rates were not affected significantly. Comparisons with data prior to these two dates should take these adjustments into account.
N.A.—Not available.

Employed Persons by Major Occupational Groups and Sex

Source: Bureau of Labor Statistics

Annual Averages 1973

OCCUPATIONAL GROUP	Thousands of persons			Percent Distribution		
	Both sexes	Males	Females	Both sexes	Males	Females
Total employed.	84,409	51,963	32,446	100.0	100.0	100.0
White-collar workers.	40,386	20,705	19,681	47.8	39.8	60.7
Professional and technical	11,777	7,066	4,711	14.0	13.6	14.5
Managers and administrators, except farm	8,644	7,054	1,590	10.2	13.6	4.9
Sales workers.	5,415	3,175	2,240	6.4	6.1	6.9
Clerical workers.	14,548	3,409	11,140	17.2	6.6	34.3
Blue-collar workers.	29,869	24,625	5,244	35.4	47.4	16.2
Craftsmen and kindred workers.	11,288	10,826	463	13.4	20.8	1.4
Operatives, except transport.	10,972	6,653	4,319	13.0	12.8	13.3
Transport equipment operatives.	3,297	3,134	163	3.9	6.0	.5
Nonfarm laborers	4,312	4,012	299	5.1	7.7	.9
Service workers	11,128	4,120	7,008	13.2	7.9	21.6
Private household workers.	1,353	23	1,330	1.6	(1)	4.1
Other service workers	9,775	4,097	5,678	11.6	7.9	17.5
Farm workers.	3,027	2,513	514	3.6	4.8	1.6
Farmers and farm managers.	1,664	1,561	103	2.0	3.0	.3
Farm laborers and foremen.	1,363	952	411	1.6	1.8	1.3

Employment and Unemployment in the United States

Civilian Labor Force, Persons 16 Years of Age and Over (in thousands)

Year	Civilian Labor Force	Employed	Unemployed	Year	Civilian Labor Force	Employed	Unemployed
						First Half Average	
1965.	74,455	71,088	3,366	1969.	79,691	76,893	2,798
1969.	80,733	77,902	2,831	1970.	81,907	78,151	3,756
1970.	82,715	78,627	4,088	1971.	83,165	78,064	5,101
1971.	84,113	79,120	4,993	1972.	85,616	80,524	5,090
1972.	86,542	81,702	4,840	1974.	90,022	85,234	4,788
1973.	88,714	84,409	4,304				

Overseas Direct Investment in the United States

Source: U.S. Dept. of Commerce

The value of overseas direct investments in the United States increased $708,000,000 in 1972 to $14,363 billion at year-end. The increase resulted from reinvested earnings of $548 million and net capital inflows of $160 million. *Interest, dividends, and branch profits account for most of the income received by foreign owners from direct investments in the U.S.

(Millions of dollars)	Book Value	Net Cap. inflows	Earnings Total	Int.* div.	Reinv'd.
1972	14,263	383	1,202	687	496
1973 Total (prelim.)	17,748	2,537	1,843	892	945
By country					
Canada	4,003	348	332	96	233
United Kingdom	5,437	573	493	262	243
Netherlands	2,550	81	205	91	112
Switzerland	1,825	211	144	105	47
Other	3,933	1,324	669	338	310

Canadian Labor Force

Source: Statistics Canada (July, 1974, seasonally adjusted)
(thousands of workers)

	Can.	Nfld.	P.E.I.	N.S.	N.B.	Que.	Ont.	Man.	Sask.	Alta.	B.C.
Labor Force	9,657	189	43	295	252	2,617	3,667	422	364	742	1,071
Employed	9,165	157	40	277	229	2,442	3,520	414	356	722	1,006
Unemployed	492	32	...	18	23	175	147	8	8	20	65
Percent unemployed	5.1	16.9	...	6.1	9.1	6.7	4.0	1.9	2.2	2.7	6.1

Canada: Labor Force Characteristics

Source: Statistics Canada

	Labor force (000)	Employed (thousands)					Unem-ployed (000)	Unem-ployed %
		All workers			Paid workers			
		Total	Agri-culture	Non-Agri-culture	Total	Non-Agri culture		
1950	5,163	4,976	1,018	3,958	3,522	3,411	186	3.6
1955	5,610	5,364	819	4,546	4,133	4,027	245	4.4
1960	6,411	5,965	683	5,282	4,843	4,732	446	7.0
1965	7,141	6,862	594	6,268	5,760	5,655	280	3.9
1969	8,162	7,780	535	7,245	6,720	6,625	382	4.7
1970	8,374	7,879	511	7,368	6,839	6,740	495	5.9
1971	8,631	8,079	510	7,569	7,029	6,927	552	6.4
1972	8,891	8,329	481	7,848	7,310	7,211	562	6.3
1973	9,279	8,759	467	8,292	7,757	7,661	520	5.6

Average Weekly Canadian Wages and Salaries, by Province (C$)

Source: Canadian Statistical Review, July, 1974 (p) Preliminary

Year & Month	Canada	Nfld.	P.E.I.	N.S.	N.B.	Que.	Ont.	Man.	Sask.	Alta.	B.C.
1960	117.63	106.00	80.87	94.51	96.80	114.24	121.55	107.67	107.90	117.95	129.35
1970	126.82	117.70	83.82	104.21	104.01	122.38	131.52	115.88	114.87	128.15	137.97
1971	137.64	123.79	89.96	112.82	113.36	132.04	143.02	123.84	121.71	138.78	152.50
1973											
Jan.	155.47	143.29	108.95	131.39	133.25	148.61	161.42	139.21	136.23	155.70	171.00
Mar.	157.09	140.35	109.94	131.92	132.29	149.88	163.19	141.82	137.94	157.71	173.83
1974											
Jan.	167.36	155.20	118.81	142.37	145.29	160.63	172.21	153.21	149.63	168.06	185.63
Mar. (p)	170.65	161.29	119.79	144.44	147.72	163.28	174.61	156.91	154.34	172.40	192.93

Activities of the Unemployment Insurance Commission — Canada

Source: Canadian Statistical Review — July, 1974

Benefits Paid (thousand dollars)

Year and Month	Claims Data Claimants[1][2]	Claims received (000)	Weeks paid (000)	Total[3] Paid	Benefits Paid				
					Regular	Sickness	Maternity	Retirement	Fishing
1972	804	2,470	30,462	1,871,802	1,764,030	58,855	36,431	2,440	20,404
1973	828	2,239	29,537	2,004,211	1,850,928	80,179	66,750	3,690	20,296
1974									
Jan.	981	278	3,368	247,603	226,850	8,481	6,752	396	6,076
Feb.	1,009	170	2,951	220,512	201,737	7,697	5,794	326	5,800
Mar.	984	159	2,952	221,427	202,286	8,588	6,108	295	4,908
Apr.	960	156	2,810	210,937	194,319	7,727	5,580	291	3,508

[1] Persons who have applied for or are in receipt of unemployment insurance benefit at the end of the month.
[2] Annual figures are average of 12 months.
[3] Includes adjustments for cancellation of warrants and collection of overpayments.

Canada: Regional Unemployment Rates, 1974

Source: Statistics Canada

Region	July	June	May	April	Mar.	Feb.	Region	July	June	May	April	Mar.	Feb.
Atlantic	9.5	10.3	10.7	9.2	9.3	9.2	Prairie	2.4	2.7	3.3	2.9	3.0	3.0
Quebec	6.7	6.4	7.8	7.4	7.3	7.6	British Columbia	6.1	5.3	5.4	5.7	5.5	5.8
Ontario	4.0	3.6	3.9	3.6	4.2	4.3	Canada	5.1	4.9	5.5	5.3	5.4	5.5

Total Value of Construction Work Performed in Canada
(thousand dollars)
Source: Statistics Canada

Province	1973 New	Repair	Total	1974 New	Repair	Total
Newfoundland............	418,106	53,307	471,413	452,945	60,820	513,765
Prince Edward Island......	91,143	17,336	108,479	98,231	20,371	118,602
Nova Scotia.............	526,878	96,734	623,612	601,208	108,044	709,252
New Brunswick..........	404,377	89,786	494,163	517,301	103,365	620,666
Quebec.................	3,684,284	673,682	4,357,966	4,315,028	748,593	5,063,621
Ontario.................	6,086,278	1,151,244	7,237,522	6,989,776	1,290,548	8,280,324
Manitoba................	745,196	143,297	888,493	800,910	169,008	969,918
Saskatchewan...........	534,749	171,085	705,834	590,104	189,215	779,319
Alberta.................	1,921,501	351,239	2,272,740	2,265,339	390,105	2,655,444
British Columbia..........	2,548,169	429,891	2,978,060	2,958,843	483,592	3,442,435

Includes residential, commercial, institutional, marine, road, highway and aerodrome, waterworks and sewage systems, and all other construction.

Pulpwood, Wood Pulp and Newsprint—Canada
(thousand tons)
Source: Canadian Statistical Review, July 1974

Year and Month	Pulpwood Production (thousand Units[1])	Wood Pulp Production[2] Total	Mechanical	Chemical	Wood Pulp Exports[3]	News-Print Production	Total	Domestic	Export[4]
1972...	18,805	18,593.3	7,520.8	11,033.9	6,071.2	8,660.8	8,739.4	779.7	7,959.8
1973...	18,435	20,030.0	7,646.5	12,045.8	8,343.6	8,966.1	9,039.2	857.6	8,162.8
1974...									
Jan..	1,524	1,713.6	705.8	1,004.9	624.8	814.9	791.4	73.4	718.1
Feb..	1,496	2,034.6	660.5	1,023.4	568.5	..	..	..	..
Mar..	1,568	1,891.6	718.9	1,172.7	560.2	..	..	..	..
Apr...	984	2,044.4	692.4	1,040.0	576.6	..	..	..	..

(1) 100 cu. ft. of solid wood; pulpwood produced for domestic use and excluding exports, but including receipts of purchased roundwood.

(2) Total pulp production covers "screenings" which are already included in exports. "Screenings" are excluded throughout from mechanical and chemical pulp.

(3) Customs exports.

(4) Mill shipments destined for export.

Telephones in North American Cities With Over 100,000 Telephones
Source: American Telephone and Telegraph Co., and Trans-Canada Telephone Systems (Jan. 1, 1973)

City	Number	City	Number	City	Number	City	Number
Akron............	323,310	Eugene,		Miami...........	867,535	St. Louis..........	568,600
Albany, N.Y......	161,367	Springfield, Ore..	110,308	Milwaukee......	743,568	St. Petersburg....	236,924
Albuquerque.....	224,701	Evansville........	109,712	Minn.-St. Paul...	1,315,800	Salt Lake City....	355,127
Alexandria, Va...	195,767	Flint.............	191,002	Mobile...........	176,228	San Antonio......	369,760
Allentown, Pa. ...	125,672	Ft.Lauderdale....	275,347	Monterrey.......	116,095	San Diego (Area)..	813,484
Amarillo.........	105,870	Fort Wayne......	155,088	Montgomery.....	117,374	San Francisco....	731,577
Anaheim, Calif...	177,257	Fort Worth......	284,446	Montreal........	1,070,673	San Jose.........	445,146
Ann Arbor, Mich..	105,247	Fresno..........	199,983	Mt. Vernon, N.Y..	115,361	Santa Ana.......	282,673
Atlanta, Ga......	778,958	Gary............	114,097	Nashville........	319,274	Santa Barbara...	112,007
Augusta, Ga.....	111,171	Grand Rapids....	250,006	New Haven......	247,469	Savannah.......	115,242
Austin, Tex......	226,965	Greensboro.....	150,945	New Orleans....	588,472	Schenectady....	120,498
Bakersfield, Calif..	130,737	Greenville, N.C....	134,314	New York.......	5,922,128	Seattle..........	544,671
Baltimore........	1,144,495	Halifax..........	115,911	Newark.........	317,402	Shreveport......	167,561
Baton Rouge.....	205,500	Hamilton........	172,905	Newport News...	181,427	Skokie, Ill........	136,153
Birmingham.....	347,934	Harrisburg......	179,588	Norfolk (Area)....	371,706	South Bend......	123,425
Boston..........	501,243	Hartford........	294,960	Oklahoma City...	478,552	Spokane........	177,288
Bridgeport.......	165,150	Hayward, Calif...	118,843	Omaha..........	366,700	Springfield, Ill....	119,981
Buffalo..........	432,187	Hollywood, Fla...	167,100	Orlando.........	203,128	Springfield, Mass.	142,479
Calgary.........	273,850	Honolulu........	305,845	Ottawa.........	346,705	Stockton, Calif....	112,562
Cambridge......	104,143	Houston........	1,058,177	Palo Alto.......	132,147	Syracuse.......	251,034
Canton..........	118,118	Huntsville, Ala...	126,000	Passaic.........	130,548	Tacoma.........	188,204
Charleston, S.C...	153,718	Indianapolis.....	593,164	Paterson........	112,486	Tampa..........	291,393
Charlotte........	273,740	Jackson, Miss....	151,514	Pensacola.......	120,242	Toledo..........	284,889
Chattanooga.....	202,083	Jacksonville.....	354,444	Peoria..........	155,971	Toronto.........	741,425
Chicago.........	2,389,073	Jersey City......	168,054	Philadelphia.....	1,574,692	Tucson.........	233,307
Cincinnati.......	654,450	Kalamazoo......	124,305	Phoenix.........	691,374	Tulsa..........	317,677
Cleveland.......	877,276	Kansas City, Kans	148,466	Pittsburgh.......	736,655	Union City, N.J....	111,246
Colorado Springs.	174,746	Kansas City, Mo..	329,643	Pomona........	137,749	Vancouver......	364,917
Columbia, S.C....	199,932	Knoxville........	167,731	Portland, Ore....	426,678	Victoria.........	107,722
Columbus, Ga....	115,883	Lansing.........	186,957	Providence......	237,660	Warren, Mich....	257,017
Columbus, Ohio..	453,884	Las Vegas......	217,476	Quebec City.....	212,486	Washington, D.C.	955,952
Corpus Christi...	122,284	Lexington.......	128,819	Raleigh.........	142,406	Weston.........	183,993
Dallas..........	685,771	Lincoln.........	118,900	Reading, Pa.....	143,933	West Palm Beach.	215,938
Dayton..........	354,001	Little Rock......	174,785	Richmond, Va....	323,578	Wichita.........	186,891
Denver..........	929,904	Livonia, Mich....	149,441	Riverside, Calif...	123,923	Willowdale......	165,558
Des Moines......	232,900	London.........	141,503	Roanoke, Va.....	106,385	Wilmington, Del...	186,507
Detroit..........	1,414,424	Los Angeles (Area)	5,067,189	Rochester, N.Y...	357,076	Windsor........	109,770
East Orange, N.J..	118,683	Louisville.......	451,304	Rockford, Ill.....	156,207	Winnipeg.......	316,691
Edmonton.......	241,437	Lubbock, Tex.....	124,046	Royal Oak, Mich..	178,455	Winston-Salem...	136,235
El Paso.........	205,951	Madison, Wisc...	161,789	Sacramento.....	398,170	Worcester.......	126,241
Erie............	124,776	Memphis........	470,974	Saginaw, Mich...	109,195	Youngstown.....	169,812
		Mexico City......	1,012,488				

MANUFACTURES AND MINERALS
General Statistics for Major Industry Groups
Source: Bureau of the Census

The estimates for 1972 in the following table are based upon reports from a representative sample of about 65,000 manufacturing establishments.

Industry	All Employees		Production Workers			Value—added by mf'r adj. (Millions)
	Number (1,000)	Payroll (Millions)	Number (1,000)	Man-hours (Millions)	Wages (Millions)	
Food and kindred products	1,559.4	12,854.6	1,076.5	2,151.7	7,993.1	35,332.1
Tobacco manufactures	66.1	500.3	57.2	106.1	399.8	2,630.2
Textile mill products	948.9	6,019.8	831.5	1,713.7	4,779.2	11,558.1
Apparel and other textile products	1,357.5	7,115.7	1,186.0	2,146.8	5,402.8	13,227.1
Lumber and wood products	680.8	4,890.0	584.6	1,147.0	3,827.3	10,101.3
Furniture and fixtures	463.8	3,178.3	381.5	765.6	2,310.1	6,138.0
Paper and allied products	633.0	5,984.9	497.5	1,041.0	4,314.9	12,930.0
Printing and publishing	1,045.7	9,736.1	623.4	1,166.6	5,411.4	20,057.7
Chemicals and allied products	831.2	8,668.7	521.8	1,049.7	4,734.5	32,387.8
Petroleum and coal products	138.7	1,627.5	97.0	199.4	1,057.4	5,800.7
Rubber and plastics products, n.e.c.	617.0	5,158.4	484.0	967.5	3,596.0	12,023.4
Leather and leather products	268.1	1,554.7	235.4	439.9	1,204.3	2,870.5
Stone, clay, and glass products	615.9	5,495.3	485.6	989.4	4,000.7	12,562.5
Primary metal industries	1,138.9	12,137.9	919.2	1,843.4	9,187.4	23,189.8
Fabricated metal products	1,481.4	13,725.1	1,136.4	2,285.5	9,480.4	26,929.9
Machinery, except electrical	1,819.7	18,461.1	1,254.7	2,521.8	11,304.4	37,497.1
Electrical equipment and supplies	1,650.0	15,107.5	1,152.6	2,256.9	8,766.7	30,299.4
Transportation equipment	1,720.1	19,907.5	1,242.6	2,525.0	12,842.2	40,146.1
Instruments and related products	442.6	4,212.4	282.6	557.2	2,187.5	10,452.2
Miscellaneous manufacturing industries	443.8	3,139.6	343.8	652.9	2,055.5	6,697.0
Administrative and auxiliary¹	996.5	13,817.0	—	—	—	—
All industries total	18,919.1	173,292.4	13,393.9	26,527.1	104,900.6	352,830.9

(1) In addition to the employment and payroll for operating manufacturing establishments, manufacturing concerns reported separately for central administrative offices or auxiliary units (e.g., research laboratories, storage warehouses, power plants, garages, repair shops, etc.) which serve the manufacturing establishments of a company rather than the public.

Manufacturing Production Worker Statistics
Source: Bureau of Labor Statistics, U.S. Dept. of Labor (P Preliminary)

Year	All Employees	Production Workers	Payroll index 1967=100	Average Earnings	Avg. Hourly Earnings	Avg. Hrs. Weekly
1955	16,882,000	13,288,000	61.1	75.70	1.86	40.7
1960	16,796,000	12,586,000	68.9	89.72	2.26	39.7
1965	18,062,000	13,434,000	88.1	107.53	2.61	41.2
1968	19,781,000	14,514,000	108.3	122.51	3.01	40.7
1969	20,167,000	14,767,000	116.6	129.51	3.19	40.6
1970	19,349,000	14,020,000	114.1	133.73	3.36	39.8
1971	18,529,000	13,434,000	116.3	142.04	3.56	39.9
1972	18,933,000	13,838,000	130.2	154.69	3.81	40.6
1973	19,820,000	14,575,000	146.9	165.65	4.07	40.7
1974 Jan	19,818,000	14,513,000	148.7	168.40	4.21	40.0
Feb	19,738,000	14,422,000	148.3	168.82	4.21	40.1
Mar	19,726,000	14,405,000	149.6	170.87	4.24	40.3
Apr	19,777,000	14,454,000	146.3	166.18	4.25	39.1
May	19,825,000	14,486,000	153.8	174.50	4.33	40.3
June (p)	20,099,000	14,717,000	158.6	176.95	4.38	40.4
July (p)	19,808,000	14,415,000	155.0	176.44	4.40	40.1

Hourly Earnings in Manufacturing Industries
Source: Bureau of Labor Statistics, U.S. Dept of Labor (P Preliminary)

Year and month (annual average)	Manufacturing		Durable goods		Nondurable goods	
	Gross	Excluding overtime	Gross	Excluding overtime	Gross	Excluding overtime
1950	$1.440	$1.39	$1.519	$1.46	$1.347	$1.31
1955	1.86	1.79	1.99	1.91	1.67	1.62
1960	2.26	2.20	2.43	2.36	2.05	1.99
1965	2.61	2.51	2.79	2.67	2.36	2.27
1968	3.01	2.88	3.19	3.05	2.74	2.63
1969	3.19	3.06	3.38	3.24	2.91	2.79
1970	3.36	3.24	3.55	3.43	3.08	2.97
1971	3.56	3.44	3.79	3.66	3.26	3.14
1972	3.81	3.65	4.05	3.88	3.47	3.33
1973	4.07	3.88	4.32	4.12	3.69	3.53
1974 Jan	4.21	4.04	4.47	4.29	3.83	3.68
Feb	4.21	4.05	4.47	4.29	3.83	3.69
Mar	4.24	4.07	4.50	4.31	3.85	3.70
Apr	4.25	4.11	4.50	4.35	3.87	3.74
May	4.33	4.15	4.60	4.41	3.91	3.77
June (p)	4.38	4.20	4.65	4.45	3.97	3.82
July (p)	4.40	4.23	4.66	4.48	4.02	3.86

General Manufacturing Statistics for States

Source: Bureau of the Census, Census of Manufacturers 1972 preliminary report

Divisions, Regions and States	All employees Number (1,000)	All employees Payroll (millions)	Production workers Number (1,000)	Production workers Man-hrs. (millions)	Production workers Wages (millions)	Value added by mfr. (millions)	Mate-rials (millions)	Capital expend. (millions)
New England Division	1,366.0	11,967.0	937.8	1,850.0	6,749.3	22,732.6	18,728.2	1,261.6
Maine	100.4	699.5	82.6	162.6	512.1	1,396.6	1,482.8	137.7
New Hampshire	90.4	668.1	68.3	132.6	418.2	1,297.4	1,042.7	104.7
Vermont	37.9	320.9	26.8	53.8	182.9	578.9	644.2	36.8
Massachusetts	613.4	5,445.4	410.3	802.1	2,985.7	10,721.5	8,564.5	534.5
Rhode Island	117.8	884.4	91.0	174.9	566.4	1,782.2	1,487.1	103.9
Connecticut	406.1	3,948.7	258.8	524.0	2,084.0	6,956.0	5,506.9	344.0
Middle Atlantic Division	3,952.7	37,120.6	2,636.9	5,097.7	20,431.4	70,625.4	69,140.4	3,912.3
New York	1,691.4	16,216.4	1,076.5	2,078.0	8,196.4	30,774.6	28,043.5	1,495.0
New Jersey	842.7	8,120.5	547.4	1,068.3	4,343.0	16,318.6	16,070.6	931.9
Pennsylvania	1,418.6	12,783.7	1,013.0	1,951.4	7,892.0	23,532.2	25,026.3	1,485.4
East North Central Division	4,929.7	50,935.9	3,481.1	6,991.2	32,093.6	99,638.3	114,798.3	5,752.0
Ohio	1,333.9	13,632.5	933.0	1,873.9	8,655.4	26,910.6	28,392.0	1,579.5
Indiana	706.3	6,911.1	527.2	1,044.0	4,660.2	14,280.4	15,385.0	857.0
Illinois	1,310.1	12,867.3	896.8	1,776.7	7,651.0	25,759.0	28,376.3	1,486.9
Michigan	1,084.5	12,850.0	767.5	1,584.3	8,088.4	23,337.8	30,833.2	1,299.5
Wisconsin	494.9	4,675.0	356.6	712.3	3,038.6	9,350.5	11,811.8	529.1
West North Central Division	1,201.8	10,948.7	834.7	1,646.4	6,598.7	23,519.8	36,508.5	1,306.9
Minnesota	300.0	2,869.2	194.6	381.0	1,546.6	5,551.4	7,454.2	304.1
Iowa	216.5	2,052.5	156.7	311.5	1,357.3	4,730.6	7,987.4	318.4
Missouri	436.2	3,920.0	300.1	585.8	2,311.6	8,178.3	10,780.5	348.9
North Dakota	9.9	76.4	6.9	14.2	47.3	207.5	376.1	13.2
South Dakota	17.2	133.0	12.7	24.7	88.2	272.5	650.4	20.0
Nebraska	84.8	703.3	63.0	127.5	469.1	1,737.9	4,240.6	104.6
Kansas	137.2	1,194.3	100.7	201.7	778.6	2,841.6	5,019.3	197.7
South Atlantic Division	2,723.0	20,451.0	2,092.6	4,193.9	13,345.7	43,918.9	52,903.4	3,742.5
Delaware	70.2	768.9	37.7	73.9	306.4	1,308.5	2,121.9	91.7
Maryland	252.2	2,347.4	174.5	344.0	1,416.8	4,686.4	5,290.5	273.7
District of Columbia	19.6	219.3	9.5	17.0	97.5	385.9	243.8	18.7
Virginia	376.6	2,846.7	292.3	582.5	1,901.0	6,121.8	6,728.9	582.6
West Virginia	118.9	1,075.7	92.1	181.3	762.2	2,632.7	2,379.4	215.7
North Carolina	750.8	5,017.4	604.4	1,214.3	3,436.0	11,023.1	13,314.5	989.4
South Carolina	344.7	2,327.0	281.7	579.9	1,666.0	4,921.0	5,737.3	489.2
Georgia	462.5	3,296.7	364.8	731.5	2,227.5	7,362.2	10,967.6	632.5
Florida	327.5	2,551.9	235.6	469.5	1,531.9	5,477.3	6,119.5	449.0
East South Central Division	1,247.2	9,219.0	990.2	1,961.9	6,450.9	21,336.2	25,575.0	1,518.5
Kentucky	261.7	2,180.2	202.1	397.6	1,494.0	5,800.4	6,872.3	380.4
Tennessee	466.7	3,344.9	364.8	721.6	2,287.5	7,715.7	8,748.2	533.2
Alabama	321.2	2,394.5	260.1	516.7	1,725.3	5,048.5	6,233.8	374.5
Mississippi	197.6	1,299.4	163.2	326.0	944.1	2,771.6	3,720.7	230.4
West South Central Division	1,242.4	10,336.2	893.1	1,787.5	6,352.9	24,832.6	35,236.0	2,311.2
Arkansas	180.0	1,148.0	149.0	297.0	850.5	2,767.1	3,685.1	216.2
Louisiana	181.2	1,619.7	135.0	277.6	1,081.6	4,380.7	7,077.1	578.1
Oklahoma	141.7	1,188.5	93.9	183.2	653.8	2,241.9	3,103.3	225.6
Texas	739.5	6,380.0	515.2	1,029.7	3,767.0	15,442.9	21,370.5	1,291.3
Mountain Division	377.9	3,342.0	265.3	518.7	2,078.7	7,315.3	10,597.5	736.5
Montana	21.1	182.0	16.7	33.2	136.8	457.5	1,122.9	75.4
Idaho	41.3	317.3	33.2	62.6	231.2	749.8	1,193.8	72.8
Wyoming	7.1	58.4	5.1	10.1	40.4	148.4	315.4	23.2
Colorado	125.6	1,201.9	86.5	172.4	752.6	2,455.0	3,376.7	230.2
New Mexico	23.9	162.3	17.2	33.3	98.7	366.2	569.5	30.4
Arizona	94.8	870.5	62.3	122.2	485.8	1,916.9	2,260.5	199.4
Utah	53.9	455.3	37.3	70.9	274.1	1,005.9	1,533.9	80.8
Nevada	10.2	94.3	7.0	14.0	59.1	215.6	224.8	24.3
Pacific Division	1,972.5	19,630.0	1,334.9	2,584.0	11,145.2	40,016.4	42,868.3	2,375.1
Washington	223.2	2,281.9	156.8	299.5	1,390.2	4,570.5	5,732.4	332.7
Oregon	176.2	1,599.9	140.0	269.1	1,157.1	3,471.2	4,049.1	276.3
California	1,540.3	15,474.4	1,014.1	1,969.9	8,422.3	31,382.7	32,323.4	1,697.2
Alaska	8.0	83.6	6.4	12.4	62.6	179.7	219.6	22.3
Hawaii	24.8	190.2	17.6	33.1	113.0	412.3	543.8	46.6
Total	18,919.1	173,292.4	13,393.9	26,527.1	104,900.6	352,830.9	405,057.9	22,917.0

Employees in Non-Agricultural Establishments

Source: Burea of Labor Statistics, U.S. Dept. of Labor (P) Preliminary

Annual Average by Industry Division

(In thousands)

Year	Total	Mining	Contract construc-tion	Manu-factur-ing	Trans. and public utilities	Whole., retail trade	Finance, insur., real estate	Service, miscel-laneous	Govern-ment
1955	50,675	792	2,802	16,882	4,141	10,535	2,335	6,274	6,914
1960	54,234	712	2,885	16,796	4,004	11,391	2,669	7,423	8,353
1965	60,815	632	3,186	18,062	4,036	12,716	3,023	9,087	10,074
1970	70,593	623	3,381	19,349	4,493	14,914	3,688	11,612	12,535
1971	70,645	602	3,411	18,529	4,442	15,142	3,796	11,869	12,856
1972	72,764	607	3,521	18,933	4,495	15,683	3,927	12,309	13,290
1973	75,567	625	3,648	19,820	4,611	16,288	4,053	12,866	13,657
1974 (July)P.	76,830	688	3,741	19,808	4,693	16,579	4,199	13,558	13,564

Profits of Manufacturing Corporations by Industry Groups

Source: Federal Trade Commission and the Securities and Exchange Commission

Industry Group (Amounts estimated in millions of dollars)	Before Income Taxes Pct. of sales			Profits After Taxes Pct. of sales		
	1972	1972	1971	1972	1972	1971
Durable goods	33,602	7.7	6.9	18,488	4.2	3.8
Transportation equipment	8,331	7.5	7.1	4,419	4.0	3.8
Motor vehicles and equipment	6,905	8.9	8.7	3,639	4.7	4.6
Electrical machinery, equipment and supplies	5,571	7.2	6.4	2,999	3.9	3.5
Other machinery	6,614	9.2	8.3	3,481	4.8	4.2
Other fabricated metal products	2,944	6.5	5.7	1,569	3.4	2.9
Primary iron and steel	1,650	5.0	4.1	1,022	3.0	2.6
Primary nonferrous metals	1,050	5.6	4.7	687	3.7	3.3
Stone, clay, and glass products	1,810	7.9	7.8	1,060	4.6	4.5
Furniture and fixtures	690	7.0	5.9	369	3.7	3.0
Other lumber and wood products	1,606	8.0	6.8	1,012	5.0	4.4
Instruments and related products	2,736	14.8	13.3	1,514	8.2	7.2
Miscellaneous manufacturing	598	6.2	6.2	314	3.2	3.2
Nondurable goods	29,649	7.2	7.2	18,019	4.4	4.5
Food and kindred products	5,508	4.6	4.9	3,021	2.5	2.6
Tobacco manufactures	1,246	11.1	11.5	676	6.0	6.1
Textile mill products	1,212	4.7	4.6	659	2.6	2.4
Apparel and other finished products	1,237	4.3	4.3	679	2.3	2.4
Paper and allied products	1,584	6.8	4.3	941	4.0	2.3
Printing and publishing	2,498	8.6	7.8	1,335	4.6	4.1
Chemicals and allied products	7,904	11.2	10.8	4,499	6.4	6.1
Petroleum refining and related products	6,549	8.4	9.5	5,201	6.7	8.2
Petroleum refining[1]	6,455	8.4	9.6	5,151	6.6	8.3
Rubber and miscellaneous plastic products	1,599	7.4	6.6	859	4.0	3.6
Leather and leather products	314	5.1	4.8	148	2.4	2.2
All Manufacturing Corps.	63,249	7.4	7.0	36,467	4.3	4.1

[1]Included in major industry above.

Occupational Earnings in Selected Cities

Source: Bureau of Labor Statistics, Department of Labor

(Average earnings (1) for selected occupations studied in 6 broad industry divisions: Manufacturing; transportation, communication, and other public utilities; wholesale; retail; finance, insurance, and real estate; and services, March-May 1974)

Occupations	Albany-Schenectady-Troy, N.Y.	Worcester, Mass.	Birmingham, Ala.	Houston, Tex.	Toledo, Ohio-Mich.	Albuquerque, N. Mex.	San Francisco-Oakland, Calif.
			Average weekly earnings, straight-time				
Office workers—Men							
Accounting clerks[2]	$177.00	$170.50	$185.00	$180.00	$195.50	—	$186.50
Draftsmen[2]	—	235.00	234.00	242.50	254.00	—	247.00
Messengers (office boys)	115.00	—	104.00	103.00	120.50	$92.50	116.00
Office workers—Women							
Accounting clerks[2]	155.00	160.00	151.50	149.00	162.00	137.00	172.50
Billers (billing machine)	—	121.00	115.50	103.50	—	—	145.50
Bookkeeping-machine operators[2]	144.50	—	132.50	124.00	139.00	133.00	162.50
Keypunch operators[2]	144.00	140.50	134.50	138.50	156.00	117.00	161.50
Nurses, industrial (registered)	190.00	179.00	181.00	193.00	196.00	—	209.00
Messengers (office girls)	116.50	94.00	98.00	98.50	106.00	—	113.50
Payroll clerks	126.00	135.50	128.00	146.00	136.00	117.00	173.00
Secretaries	163.50	153.00	146.50	159.50	169.00	147.00	173.00
Stenographers (general)	133.50	134.00	125.00	135.50	138.50	113.50	135.50
Switchboard operators[2]	143.50	141.00	129.00	141.00	161.00	139.00	151.00
Typists[2]	144.00	117.00	108.50	126.00	136.00	106.50	131.00
			Average hourly earnings, straight-time				
Maintenance, custodial, and material movement workers—Men							
Carpenters	$5.12	$4.56	$5.13	$5.34	$5.60	$4.99	$6.41
Electricians	5.22	5.29	5.57	5.57	5.94	5.04	6.31
Engineers, stationary	4.64	4.94	5.22	4.79	5.64	—	6.55
Helpers, trades	4.05	—	4.24	4.06	4.99	—	5.08
Machinists	5.30	5.02	5.48	5.59	5.76	—	6.48
Mechanics, automotive	5.56	4.92	4.56	5.25	5.92	5.95	7.05
Painters	4.95	—	4.99	4.95	5.40	—	6.72
Guards and watchmen	2.67	2.79	2.24	2.38	2.76	2.68	2.99
Janitors, porters, cleaners	3.48	3.33	2.24	2.28	3.91	2.30	4.04
Laborers, material handling	4.25	3.76	3.06	3.33	4.70	2.94	5.46
Packers, shipping	3.24	4.20	3.90	3.11	4.70	—	5.21
Shipping clerks	3.97	3.89	4.28	3.78	4.60	—	5.25
Truckdrivers, local	5.62	4.96	3.55	4.14	5.69	4.49	6.36

1. Weekly earnings relate to regular straight-time salaries that are paid for standard workweeks. Hourly earnings exclude premium pay for overtime, weekends, holidays, or late shifts.

2. More than one skill level surveyed. Earnings are for the highest level surveyed.

NOTE: Maintenance plumbers are no longer surveyed by the Bureau.

Annual Rates of Profit on Stockholders' Equity

Source: Federal Trade Commission

(Each rate is the arithmetic mean of four quarterly rates, each on an annual basis.)

By industry after taxes: by percent	1950	1960	1965	1968	1969¹	1970	1971	1972
All manufacturing corporations, except newspapers	15.4	9.2	13.0	12.1	11.5	9.3	9.7	10.6
Durable goods industries	16.8	8.6	13.8	12.2	11.4	8.3	9.1	10.8
Metals and metal fabricating industries	16.9	8.6	14.2	12.0	11.2	*	*	*
Transportation equipment	21.5	11.7	18.5	14.7	12.0	6.3	11.2	12.5
Motor vehicles and equipment	25.2	13.5	19.5	15.1	12.6	6.1	13.0	14.6
Aircraft and parts	*	7.4	15.1	14.2	10.6	6.8	5.8	7.9
Electrical machinery, equipment and supplies	20.8	9.5	13.5	12.2	11.1	9.1	9.5	10.8
Machinery, except electrical	14.0	7.6	14.1	12.3	12.2	9.9	8.7	10.6
Metalworking machinery and equipment	*	5.3	14.4	12.4	11.6	8.3	3.8	6.5
Other fabricated metal products	15.9	5.6	13.2	11.7	11.3	8.6	8.3	10.8
Primary metal industries	14.5	7.2	10.6	8.9	9.5	7.0	4.8	6.0
Blast furnaces, steel works and foundries	14.3	7.2	9.8	7.6	7.6	4.3	4.5	6.0
Monferrous metals	15.0	7.1	11.9	10.7	12.2	10.7	5.1	5.9
Other durable goods industries	16.3	8.6	12.2	12.8	12.4	*	*	*
Lumber and wood products, except furniture	17.4	3.6	10.0	14.6	13.2	5.9	11.3	16.2
Furniture and fixtures	15.1	6.5	13.3	12.2	12.6	7.9	9.5	13.3
Stone, clay and glass products	17.6	9.9	10.2	9.2	9.2	6.9	9.1	10.1
Instruments and related products	16.7	11.6	17.5	16.5●	15.6	14.2	13.5	14.8
Miscellaneous manufacturing and ordnance	12.2	9.2	10.7	12.4	11.6	10.0	9.0	10.7
Nondurable goods industries	14.0	9.8	12.2	11.9	11.5	10.3	10.3	10.5
Chemicals; petroleum, rubber and plastics	15.4	10.8	13.0	12.6	12.0	*	*	*
Chemicals and allied products	17.8	12.2	15.2	13.3	12.8	11.5	11.8	12.8
Basic chemicals and related products	*	11.1	14.3	11.0	10.5	8.5	8.7	10.0
Drugs	*	16.8	20.3	18.3	18.4	17.6	17.9	18.4
Petroleum refining and related industries	13.8	10.1	11.8	12.2	11.7	11.0	10.3	8.7
Petroleum refining	*	10.1	11.8	12.3	11.7	11.0	10.3	8.7
Rubber and miscellaneous plastics products	16.7	9.1	11.7	12.2	10.4	7.1	9.6	10.8
Other nondurable goods industries	12.8	8.5	11.1	10.9	10.8	*	*	*
Food and kindred products	12.3	8.7	10.7	10.7	10.9	10.8	11.0	11.0
Dairy products	*	*	10.6	9.8	10.1	10.2	11.1	10.1
Bakery products	*	*	9.3	11.7	8.6	8.8	10.7	10.6
Alcoholic beverages	*	7.1	9.3	10.1	10.3	10.5	10.6	10.7
Tobacco manufacturers	11.5	13.4	13.5	14.4	14.4	15.7	15.7	15.4
Textile mill products	12.6	5.8	10.8	8.8	7.9	5.1	6.6	7.5
Apparel and other fabricated textile products	10.1	7.7	12.6	12.9	11.9	9.3	11.0	11.9
Paper and allied products	16.1	8.5	9.4	9.7	10.1	7.0	4.8	9.0
Printing and publishing, except newspapers	11.5	10.6	14.1	12.6	12.6	11.2	10.7	12.0
Leather and leather products	10.9	6.3	11.6	13.0	9.3	9.4	8.2	9.1

*—Not available. (I.) Includes newspapers for the first time.

Personal Consumption Expenditures for the U.S.

Source: Bureau of Economic Analysis, U.S. Department of Commerce

(In millions of dollars)

	1950	1955	1960	1965	1969	1970	1971	1972
Food and tobacco	58,120	72,236	87,510	107,183	130,707	111,181	148,344	157,892
Clothing, accessories and jewelry	23,709	27,982	33,032	43,318	59,924	62,834	66,961	72,676
Personal care	2,438	3,461	5,324	7,578	9,760	10,420	10,600	11,119
Housing	21,286	33,738	46,305	63,509	84,141	90,926	98,477	105,517
Household operation	29,461	37,322	46,906	61,789	82,294	87,360	93,836	104,830
Medical care	8,788	12,755	19,116	28,082	42,814	47,401	52,015	57,431
Personal business	6,858	10,049	14,974	21,879	33,277	35,314	38,641	41,226
Transportation	24,672	35,574	43,134	58,154	77,772	77,776	90,441	100,159
Recreation	11,147	14,078	18,295	26,298	36,901	40,653	42,652	47,826
Private educ. and research	1,618	2,339	3,718	5,927	9,536	10,363	10,849	12,008
Religious and welfare act.	2,282	3,257	4,748	5,972	8,084	8,601	9,134	10,096
Foreign travel and remittances — net	630	1,590	2,179	3,150	4,247	4,815	5,201	5,726
Total personal consumption Expenditures	191,009	254,381	325,241	432,839	579,457	617,644	667,151	726,506

Work Stoppages (Strikes) in the United States

Source: Bureau of Labor Statistics, U. S. Department of Labor

Year	Number stoppages	Workers involved	Man days idle	Year	Number stoppages	Workers involved	Man days idle
Average 1935 to 1939	2,862	1,130,000	16,900,000	1967	4,595	2,870,000	42,100,000
				1968	5,045	2,649,000	49,018,000
				1969	5,700	2,481,000	42,869,000
War Period Dec. 8, 1941- Aug. 14, 1945	14,371	6,744,000	36,300,000	1970	5,716	3,305,000	66,414,000
				1971	5,138	3,280,000	47,589,000
				1972	5,010	1,714,000	27,066,000
Average				1973(p)	5,600	2,200,000	27,000,000
				1974 Jan.	310	132,000	1,305,000
1947-49	3,573	2,380,000	39,700,000	Feb.	350	102,000	1,142,000
1950	4,843	2,410,000	38,800,000	Mar.	480	163,000	1,973,000
1955	4,320	2,650,000	28,200,000	Apr.	550	211,000	3,542,000
1960	3,333	1,320,000	19,100,000	May	740	391,000	6,267,000
1965	3,963	1,550,000	23,300,000	Jun.	640	474,000	7,345,000

Retail Store Sales, by Kind of Business
Source: Bureau of the Census, U.S. Dept. of Commerce. In millions of dollars

Kinds of business	1972	1973	Kinds of business	1972	1973
All retail stores	448,379	503,317			
Durable goods store	149,659	170,275	Apparel group.	21,993	24,062
Automotive group	88,612	100,661	Men's and boys' wear stores. . .	5,198	5,609
Motor vehicle, other			Women's apparel, accessory		
automotive dealers	81,521	92,768	stores.	8,386	9,119
Tire, battery, accessory			Shoe stores	3,774	4,229
dealers.	7,091	7,895	Food group	95,020	105,731
Furniture and appliance group. . .	21,315	24,030	Grocery stores.	88,340	98,392
Furniture, home furnishings			General merchandise group		
stores.	12,550	14,290	with non stores.	74,903	83,301
Household appliance, radio			Department stores, excl.		
TV stores	7,029	7,904	mail order.	46,560	52,292
Lumber, building, hardware			Mail order (catalog sales).	4,722	5,384
group	20,064	22,766	Variety stores.	7,478	8,212
Lumber, building materials			Eating and drinking places.	33,891	37,925
dealers.	15,973	18,049	Gasoline service stations.	31,044	34,432
Hardware stores	4,081	4,717	Drug and proprietary stores	14,523	15,474
Nondurable goods stores. . .	298,720	333,042	Liquor stores.	9,215	9,602

(1) Sales by jewelry stores, other durable goods stores, other general merchandise stores, and other nondurable goods stores are not shown separately but are included in totals.

Total Retail Stores Sales (In millions of dollars) — (1955) 183,851; (1956) 189,729; (1957) 200,002; (1958) 200,353; (1959) 215,413; (1960) 219,529; (1961) 218,992; (1962) 235,563; (1963) 246,666; (1964) 261,870; (1965) 284,128; (1966) 303,956; (1967) 313,809; (1968) 341,876; (1969) 357,885; (1970) 375,527; (1971) 408,850.

Cotton, Wool, Silk, and Man-Made Fibers Production
Source: Economic Research Service, U.S. Dept. of Agriculture

Cotton and wool from reports of the Dept. of Agriculture; silk, rayon and non-cellulosic man-made fibers from Textile Organon, a publication of the Textile Economics Bureau, Inc.

Year	Cotton[1] U.S. Mil. bales[5]	World Mil. bales[5]	Wool[2] U.S. Mil. lb.	World Mil. lb.	Silk World Mil. lb.	Rayon & Acetate U.S. Mil. lb.	Man-made fibers[3] World Mil.	Non-Cellulosic U.S. Mil.	World Mil.
1940.	12.6	31.2	434.0	4,180	130	471.2	2,485.3	4.6	4.6
1950.	10.0	30.6	249.3	4,000	42	1,259.4	3,552.8	145.9	177.4
1960.	14.2	46.2	298.9	5,615	68	1,028.5	5,749.1	854.2	1,779.1
1964.	15.1	52.9	237.4	5,766	71	1,431.8	7,245.4	1,646.2	4,067.3
1965.	15.0	54.4	224.8	5,836	72	1,527.0	7,359.4	2,062.4	4,928.9
1966.	9.6	49.7	219.2	5,958	72	1,519.0	7,364.2	2,415.2	5,708.9[6]
1967.	7.4	48.8	211.4	6,040	75	1,388.1	7,297.4	2,662.1	6,501.5
1968.	10.9	54.1	197.9	6,295	82	1,594.3	7,780.2	3,632.1	8,524.6
1969.	10.0	52.3	182.8	6,261	86	1,576.2	7,835.6	4,029.3	10,002.5
1970.	10.2	52.2	176.8	6,174	90	1,373.2	7,565.2	4,053.5	11,203.3
1971.	10.5	57.1	172.2	6,027	88	1,392.4	7,613.8	4,761.0	13,231.5
1972.	13.7	59.4	167.0	5,706	88	1,394.3	7,833.1	5,927.3	15,079.2
1973[7].	13.0	59.1	153.9	5,660	87	1,357.0	8,083.0	6,997.9	17,999.6

(1). Year beginning Aug. 1. (2.) Grease basis. (3.) Includes filament yarn and staple and tow fiber. (4.) Includes textile glass fiber. (5.) 480-pound net weight bales, U.S. beginning 1960 and World beginning 1965. (6.) 1966 to date, excludes Olefin. (7.) Preliminary.

World Production of Natural Rubber
Source: Business and Defense Services Administration, U.S. Dept. of Commerce

Long Tons — Estimated

Year	Far East	Tropical America	Africa	Total	Year	Far East	Tropical America	Africa	Total
1940	1,357,000	26,000	16,000	1,399,000	1968	2,396,000	29,958	167,022	2,593,000
1945	170,500	48,000	53,500	272,000	1969	2,630,000	30,500	178,100	2,838,600
1950	1,760,500	27,000	55,000	1,842,500	1970	2,811,500	31,500	209,600	3,052,600
1955	1,787,000	27,500	98,000	1,912,500	1971	2,795,500	33,700	198,800	3,028,000
1960	1,813,267	29,733	147,000	1,990,000	1972	2,820,400	40,150	201,950	3,062,500
1965	2,149,673	35,827	157,000	2,342,500	1973	3,180,250	39,750	216,500	3,436,500

Full-time and Part-time Status of Civilian Labor Force
Source: Bureau of Labor Statistics, U.S. Dept. of Labor (in thousands) (Seasonally adjusted)

Employment Status	1973 July	Aug.	Sept.	Oct.	Nov.	Dec.	1974 Jan.	Feb.	Mar.	April	May	June
Total, 16 years and over												
Full Time												
Civilian Labor Force .	75,966	75,801	76,127	76,583	76,764	76,807	77,458	77,585	77,401	77,661	77,868	77,347
Employed.	72,800	72,631	72,942	73,473	73,439	73,406	73,842	73,958	73,841	74,069	74,291	73,741
Unemployed	3,166	3,170	3,185	3,110	3,325	3,401	3,616	3,627	3,560	3,592	3,597	3,606
Unemployment rate .	4.2	4.2	4.2	4.1	4.3	4.4	4.7	4.7	4.6	4.6	4.6	4.7
Part Time Civilian												
Labor Force	12,612	12,810	13,307	13,186	13,190	13,317	13,171	13,067	13,097	12,845	13,041	13,419
Employed.	11,534	11,770	12,278	12,203	12,228	12,314	12,085	11,975	12,041	11,903	11,893	12,225
Unemployed	1,078	1,040	1,029	983	962	1,003	1,086	1,092	1,056	942	1,148	1,194
Unemployment rate .	8.5	8.1	7.7	7.5	7.3	7.5	8.2	8.4	8.1	7.3	8.8	8.9

Labor Union Membership

Source: AFL-CIO and World Almanac Questionnaire

Unions with a membership of 25,000 or over (Sept., 1973).

Union	Members
Actors and Artists of America, Associated	72,000
Air Line Pilots Association	40,000
Aluminum Workers International Union	25,000
Bakery and Confectionery Workers International Union of America	130,000
Barbers, Hairdressers and Cosmetologists' International Union of America, the Journeymen	50,000
Boilermakers, Iron Ship Builders, Blacksmiths, Forgers and Helpers, International Brotherhood of	115,000
Boot and Shoe Workers' Union	35,000
Bricklayers, Masons, and Plasters International Union of America	134,000
Carpenters and Joiners of America, United Brotherhood of	700,000
Cement, Lime and Gypsum Workers International Union, United.	30,000
Chemical Workers Union, International	70,000
Clothing Workers of America, Amalgamated	257,000
Communications Workers of America	438,000
Dolls, Toys, Playthings, Novelties and Allied Products of the United States and Canada, AFL-CIO, International Union of.	25,000
Electrical, Radio and Machine Workers International Union of	227,000
Electrical Workers, International Brotherhood of	779,000
Engineers, International Union of Operating	300,000
Fire Fighters, International Association of	105,000
Firemen and Oilers, International Brotherhood of	40,000
Furniture Workers of America, United	30,000
Garment Workers of America, United	32,000
Garment Workers Union, International Ladies'	363,000
Glass and Ceramic Workers of North America, United	30,000
Glass Bottle Blowers' Association of the United States and Canada	74,000
Glass Workers Union, American Flint	34,000
Government Employees, American Federation of	270,000
Graphic Arts International Union	99,000
Hotel and Restaurant Employees' and Bartenders' International Union	328,000
Industrial Workers of America, International Union, Allied	88,000
Iron Workers, International Association of Bridge and Structural	160,000
Laborers' International Union of North America	475,000
Leather Goods, Plastics and Novelty Workers Union, International	43,000
Letter Carriers, National Association of	151,000
Lithographers and Photoengravers International Union	46,000
Longshoremen's Association, International	60,000
Machinists and Aerospace Workers, International Association of	698,000
Maintenance of Way Employes, Brotherhood of	71,000
Maritime Union of America, National	43,000
Meat Cutters and Butcher Workmen of North America, Amalgamated	470,000
Mechanics Educational Society of America	26,000
Molders and Allied Workers Union, International	50,000
Musicians, American Federation of	204,000
Newspaper Guild, The	26,000
Office and Professional Employees International Union	68,000
Oil, Chemical and Atomic Workers International Union	145,000
Painters & Allied Trades of the United States and Canada, International Brotherhood of	160,000
Paper Workers International Union, United	266,000
Plasterers' & Cement Masons' International Association of the United States and Canada, Operative	68,000
Plumbing and Pipe Fitting Industry of the United States & Canada, United Association of Journeymen & Apprentices of the	228,000
Postal Workers Union, American	234,000
Printing Pressmen's & Assistants' Union of North America, International	104,000
Railway, Airline and Steamship Clerks, Freight Handlers, Express & Station Employes,	

Union	Members
Brotherhood of	153,000
Railway Carmen of the United States & Canada, Brotherhood	57,000
Retail Clerks International Association	582,000
Retail, Wholesale and Department Store Union	98,000
Roofers, Damp & Waterproof Workers Association, United Slate, Tile & Composition	26,000
Rubber, Cork, Linoleum & Plastic Workers of America, United	169,000
Seafarers International Union of North America	80,000
Service Employees International Union, AFL-CIO	439,000
Sheet Metal Workers International Association	120,000
Shoe Workers of America, United	33,000
Stage Employes & Moving Picture Machine Operators of the United States & Canada, International Alliance of Theatrical	50,000
State, County & Municipal Employees, American Federation of	545,000
Steelworkers of America, United	945,000
Teachers, American Federation of	254,000
Textile Workers of America, United	37,000
Textile Workers Union of America	117,000
Tobacco Workers International Union	25,000
Transit Union, Amalgamated	87,000
Transport Workers Union of America	95,000
Transportation Union, United	134,000
Typographical Union, International	81,000
Upholsterers' International Union of North America	50,000
Utility Workers Union of America	54,000
Woodworkers of America, International	55,000

Independent Unions

Union	Members
Automobile, Aerospace and Agricultural Implement Workers of America, Intl. Union, United	1,400,000
Chemical Workers Union, Int.	86,000
Civil Service Association of Ontario, The	30,499
Distributive Workers of America, Nat'l. Council of	40,000
Electrical, Radio and Machine Workers of America, United.	165,000
Federal Employees, Nat'l. Federation of	100,000
Government Employees, Nat'l. Assn. of	200,000
Internal Revenue Employees, Nat'l. Assn.	26,360
Letter Carriers Assn., Nat'l. Rural	41,192
Locomotive Engineers, Brotherhood of	39,000
Longshoremen's and Warehousemen's Union Int'l.	60,000
Mine Workers of America, United	450,000
Postal Union, National.	80,000
Postal and Federal Employees, Nat'l. Alliance of	45,000
Postal Supervisors, Nat'l. Assn. of	33,000
Postmasters, Nat'l. Assn. of	28,273
Teamsters, Chauffeurs, Warehousemen and Helpers of America, Int'l. Brotherhood of	2,000,000
Telephone Unions, Alliance of Independent	53,098

CNTU Unions

Union	Members
Government Employees' Union, Quebec	30,000
Public Service Employees Inc., Federation of	28,149
Services, Inc., National Federation of	52,307
Steel, Mine and Chemical Workers, Federation of	30,641

CLC Unions

Union	Members
Automobile, Aerospace and Agricultural Implement Workers of America, International Union, United	111,219
Public Employees, Canadian Union of	138,088
Public Service Alliance of Canada— Union of National Defense Employees	28,450
Railway, Transport and General Workers, Canadian Brotherhood of	33,037

Mineral Production in United States[1]

Source: Bureau of Mines

Mineral Fuels	1972 Quantity	1972 Value (thousands)	1973 Quantity	1973 Value (thousands)
Asphalt and related bitumens (native):				
Bituminous limestone & sandstone & gilsonite . . . . short tons	1,995,374	$10,303	2,088,657	$8,464
Carbon dioxide, natural (e). . . . . thousand cubic feet	1,228,741	165	1,134,986	259
Coal: Bituminous and lignite[2]. . . . . .thousand short tons	595,386	4,561,983	591,738	5,049,612
Pennsylvania anthracite. . . . . thousand short tons	7,106[R]	85,251	6,830	90,260
Helium: Crude. . . . . million cubic feet	3,467[R]	41,604[R]	2,558	30,696
Grade A . . . . .million cubic feet	629[R]	15,673[R]	647	16,121
Natural gas. . . . . million cubic feet	22,531,698	4,180,462[R]	22,647,549	4,894,072
Natural gas liquids: Gasoline products. . . . . thousand 42-gal. bbls.	193,480	604,423	187,390	668,784
LP gases . . . . thousand 42-gal. bbls.	444,736	847,810	447,033	1,188,289
Peat. . . . . thousand short tons	607	7,112	621	7,547
Petroleum (crude). . . . . .thousand 42-gal. bbls.	3,455,368	11,706,510	3,360,903	13,057,905
Total mineral fuels.	XX	22,061,000	XX	25,012,000
Non Metals (except fuels)				
Abrasive stones[3]. . . . . short tons	3,241	670	3,466	667
Asbestos. . . . . short tons	131,663	13,408	150,036	16,288
Barite. . . . . thousand short tons	906	14,883	1,104	16,688
Boron minerals. . . . . thousand short tons	1,121	95,882	1,225	113,648
Bromine . . . . thousand pounds	386,864	63,689	418,250	67,131
Calcium-magnesium chloride . . . . short tons	W	W	609,300	17,581
Cement: Portland. thousand short tons	77,973	1,588,290	82,718	1,810,292
Masonry . . . . .thousand short tons	3,777	100,269	4,057	119,547
Natural and slag . . . . .thousand short tons	W	W	W	W
Clays. . . . . .thousand short tons	59,456	303,022	64,351	354,058
Diatomite . . . . short tons	576,089	37,554	608,906	36,083
Feldspar. . . . . short tons	746,212[R]	10,623[R]	791,900	12,830
Fluorspar. . . . . short tons	250,347	17,315	248,601	17,337
Garnet (abrasive). . . . . short tons	18,916	1,957	22,772	2,381
Gem stones (e).	NA	2,728	NA	2,739
Gypsum . . . . thousand short tons	12,328	48,504	13,558	56,650
Lime. . . . . thousand short tons	20,290	339,304	21,090	365,849
Magnesium compounds from sea water and brine				
(except for metals). . . . . short tons, MgO equivalent	729,472	63,915	853,907	77,733
Mica: Scrap. . . . . .thousand short tons	160	4,354	177	6,082
Sheet . . . . pounds	14,280	7	—	—
Perlite . . . . short tons	544,594	6,231	543,683	5,591
Phosphate rock. . . . . thousand short tons	40,831	207,910	42,137	238,667
Potassium salts. . . . . thousand short tons, K₂O equivalent	2,659	106,680	2,603	112,613
Pumice. . . . . thousand short tons	3,813	6,539	3,772	8,770
Pyrites. . . . . thousand long tons	741	6,652	559	4,961
Salt . . . . .thousand short tons	45,022	296,772	43,910	306,103
Sand and gravel. thousand short tons	914,324[R]	1,200,701[R]	983,629	1,359,370
Sodium carbonate (natural) . . . . thousand short tons	3,218	71,689	3,722	94,385
Sodium sulfate (natural). . . . . thousand short tons	701	11,396	672	11,597
Stone[4]. . . . . .thousand short tons	920,423[R]	1,672,293[R]	1,060,124	1,990,463
Sulfur: Frasch process mines. . . . . .thousand long tons	7,613	132,385	7,438	138,578
Talc, soapstone, and pyrophyllite. . . . . short tons	1,107,404	7,828[R]	1,246,534	9,144
Tripoli. . . . . short tons	87,864	797	101,519	930
Vermiculite. . . . . thousand short tons	337	8,092	365	9,464
Value of items that cannot be disclosed: Aplite, brucite, emery, graphite, iodine, kyanite, lithium, minerals, magnesite, greensand marl, olivine, staurolite, wollastonite, and values of nonmetal items indicated by symbol W.				
	XX	39,730	XX	29,196
Total nonmetals.	XX	6,482,000[R]	XX	7,413,000
Metals				
Antimony ore & concentrate, short tons, antimony content	489	386	545	688
Bauxite. . . . . thousand long tons, dried equivalent	1,812	23,238	1,879	26,635
Beryllium concentrate . . . . short tons, gross weight	W	W	W	W
Copper (recoverable content of ores, etc.). . . . . short tons	1,664,840	1,704,796	1,717,940	2,044,346
Gold (recoverable content of ores, etc.). . . . . troy ounces	1,449,943	84,967	1,175,750	115,000
Iron ore, (excluding iron sinter). . . . . . . thousand long tons, gr. wgt.	77,884[R]	950,365[R]	90,654	1,163,710
Lead (recoverable content of ores, etc.). . . . . short tons	618,915	186,046	603,024	196,465
Manganese ore (35% or more Mn). . . . . . . short tons, gross weight	578	W	239	W
Manganiferous ore (5 to 35% Mn). . . . . . . short tons, gross weight	147,161	W	203,055	W
Mercury. . . . . 76-pound flasks	7,333[R]	1,601[R]	2,171	621
Molybdenum (content of concentrate). . . . . thousand pounds	102,197	170,530	135,097	217,701
Nickel (content of ore and concentrate). . . . . short tons	16,864	W	18,272	W
Rare-earth metal concentrates . . . . short tons	19,520	8,479	31,278	13,780
Silver (recoverable content of ores, etc.). . . . . . .thousand troy ozs.	37,233	62,737	37,827	96,762
Titanium concentrate, ilmenite. . . . . short tons, gross weight	739,801[R]	16,739[R]	804,355	19,829
Tungsten ore and concentrate . . . . thousand pounds	7,045[R]	18,104	7,059	19,154
Uranium (recoverable content U₃O₈) . . . . thousand pounds	25,758	162,272	25,820	167,830
Vanadium (recoverable in ore and concentrate) . . . . short tons	4,887	30,867	4,377	26,611
Zinc (recoverable content of ores, etc.). . . . . short tons	478,318	169,803	478,850	197,861
Value of items that cannot be disclosed: symbol W.	XX	50,650[R]	XX	55,212
Total metals	XX	3,642,000[R]	XX	4,362,000
Grand total mineral production.	XX	32,185,000[R]	XX	36,788,000

(e) Estimate. (R) Revised. (NA) Not available. (W) Withheld to avoid disclosing individual company confidential data; included with "Value of items that cannot be disclosed." (XX) Not applicable.
(1) Production as measured by mine shipments, sales, or marketable production (including consumption by producers).
(2) Includes a small quantity of anthracite mined in states other than Pennsylvania.
(3) Grindstones, pulpstones, grinding pebbles, sharpening stones, and tube mill liners.
(4) Excludes abrasive stone, bituminous limestone, bituminous sandstone, and soapstone, all included elsewhere.

Mineral Production in U.S.—Leading States
Source: Bureau of Mines (1972)

State	Value (thousands)	Rank	Percent of U.S. total	Principal minerals, in order of value
Texas...........	$7,211,551	1	22.38	Petroleum, natural gas, natural gas liquids, cement.
Louisiana.......	5,411,543	2	16.80	Petroleum, natural gas, natural gas liquids, sulfur.
California.......	1,851,365	3	5.75	Petroleum, cement, natural gas, sand and gravel.
West Virginia.....	1,430,632	4	4.44	Coal, natural gas, stone, cement.
Pennsylvania.....	1,231,485	5	3.82	Coal, cement, stone, sand and gravel.
Oklahoma.......	1,210,728	6	3.76	Petroleum, natural gas, nat. gas liquids, cement.
New Mexico......	1,097,292	7	3.41	Petroleum, natural gas, copper, potassium salts.
Arizona..........	1,091,004	8	3.39	Copper, molybdenum, sand and gravel, cement.
Kentucky........	976,910	9	3.03	Coal, stone, petroleum, natural gas.
Illinois..........	769,737	10	2.39	Petroleum, natural gas, sodium carbonate, uranium.

Value of Mineral Production in the United States[2]
Source: Bureau of Mines (r-Revised)
(In millions of dollars)

Year[1]	Fuels	Nonmetallic	Metals	Total[3]	Year[1]	Fuels	Nonmetallic	Metals	Total[3]
1930.....	2,500	973	501	3,980	1968......	16,820	5,449	2,698	r24,966
1940.....	2,662	784	752	4,198	1969......	17,965	5,624	3,333	26,921
1950.....	8,689	1,882	1,351	11,862	1970......	20,152	r5,712	3,928	r29,792
1960.....	12,142	3,868	2,022	18,032	1971......	21,247	6,058	6,403	30,708
1965.....	14,047	4,933	2,544	21,524	1972......	22,061	6,482	3,642	32,185
1966.....	15,088	5,176	2,703	22,968	1973......	25,012	7,413	4,362	26,788
1967.....	16,195	5,200	2,327	r23,723					

(1.) Excludes Alaska and Hawaii, 1930-53. (2.) Production as measured by mine shipments sales or marketable production. (3.) Data may not add to total because of rounding figures. (P.) Preliminary.

Copper, Lead and Zinc Production in the U.S.
Source: Bureau of Mines

Year	Copper Mil. lbs.	Copper $1,000	Lead[1] Short Tons	Lead[1] $1,000	Zinc Short tons	Zinc Mil. dol.	Year	Copper Mil. lbs.	Copper $1,000	Lead[1] Short Tons	Lead[1] $1,000	Zinc Short tons	Zinc Mil. dol.
1950	1,823	379,122	418,809	113,078	591,454	167	1970	3,439	1,984,484	571,767	178,609	534,136	164
1960	2,286	733,708	228,899	53,562	334,101	87	1971	3,044	1,583,071	578,550	159,679	491,407	158
1965	2,703	957,028	301,147	93,959	611,153	178	1972	3,330	1,704,796	618,915	186,046	478,318	170
1969	3,089	1,468,400	509,013	151,635	553,124	162	1973	3,436	2,044,346	603,024	196,465	478,850	198

(1.) Production from domestic ores.

United States Pig Iron and Steel Output
Source: American Iron and Steel Institute; figures show net tons

Year	Total pig iron	Pig iron and ferro-alloys	Raw steel	Year	Total pig iron	Pig iron and ferro-alloys	Raw Steel
1940..........	46,071,666	47,398,529	66,982,686	1968..........	88,780,000	91,362,000	131,462,000
1945..........	53,223,169	54,919,029	79,701,648	1969..........	95,017,000	97,593,000	141,262,000
1950..........	64,586,907	66,400,311	96,836,075	1970..........	91,435,000	93,851,000	131,514,000
1955..........	76,857,417	79,263,865	117,036,085	1971..........	81,299,000	83,468,000	120,443,000
1960..........	66,480,648	68,566,384	99,281,601	1972..........	88,942,000	91,338,000	133,241,000
1965..........	88,184,901	90,918,040	131,461,601	1973..........	100,837,000	103,089,000	150,799,000

Steel figures include only that portion of the capacity and production of steel for castings used by foundries which were operated by companies producing steel ingots.

Raw Steel Production
(Thousands of Net Tons)

State	1973
New York....................................	6,401
Pennsylvania................................	33,925
R. I., Conn., N.J., Del., Md.................	7,612
Va., W. Va., Ga., Fla., N. C., S. C...........	5,743
Kentucky...................................	2,688
Ala., Tenn., Miss............................	4,860
Ohio.......................................	26,540
Indiana....................................	23,622
Illinois....................................	13,428
Michigan...................................	10,945
Minn., Mo., Okla., Texas.....................	5,596
Ariz., Colo., Utah, Wash., Ore., Hawaii........	4,990
California..................................	4,479
Total...................................	150,799

1972 Scrap Iron Production and Export
Source: Institute of Scrap Iron & Steel
(net tons 2,000 pounds each)

The United States generated an estimated 95,552,828 tons of ferrous scrap. Of this total, 31,851,000 tons is attributed to "prompt industrial" scrap, the leftovers from the fabrication of new iron and steel products.

Consumption of mill revert and purchased scrap................................	90,404,308
Consumption of purchased scrap only......................	41,766,790 n.t. (est.)
Value of exports..........................	$233,395,596
Sales of scrap amounted to................	$3,154,000,000
Exports of iron and steel scrap............	7,176,222 n.t.
Imports of iron and steel scrap............	312,000 n.t.

(Export and import figures are from Minerals Yearbook, Dept. of Interior)

U.S. Primary Aluminum Production
Source: The Aluminum Association

Year	Short tons	Year	Short tons	Year	Short tons	Year	Short tons
1883-1902....	13,981	1930.........	114,518	1965.........	2,754,478	1970.........	3,976,148
1903-1912....	108,412	1940.........	206,280	1967.........	3,269,259	1971.........	3,925,224
1913-1923....	282,722	1950.........	718,622	1968.........	3,255,042	1972.........	4,122,392
1924-1925....	145,340	1960.........	2,014,498	1969.........	3,793,062	1973.........	4,530,000

Estimated Markets For Total U.S. Aluminum Shipments (Data for 1972)

Market	Thousands of Lbs.	Percent	Market	Thousands of Lbs.	Percent
Building & Construction.....	3,599,000	24.7	Containers & Packaging....	2,057,000	14.1
Transportation.............	2,809,000	19.3	Exports..................	939,000	6.5
Consumer Durables........	1,338,000	9.2	Other...................	870,000	7.0
Electrical..................	1,854,000	12.7			
Machinery & Equipment.....	949,000	6.5	**Total Industry**	14,555,000	100.0

ENERGY

Project Independence?
The Hard Questions Ahead

By Hana Umlauf

After the oil-producing Arab nations embargoed deliveries of oil to the United States last October, Pres. Richard M. Nixon, on Nov. 7, 1973, launched Project Independence. He called on the nation to dedicate itself "in this bicentennial era" to the goal of attaining self-sufficiency in energy supplies by 1980.

Only a year later, most energy experts agree that 1980 is an unrealistic deadline. Some see 1985 as a reasonable deadline. But even that date is under fire. Too many variables and stumbling blocks bestrew the road toward energy self-sufficiency.

What Does Project Independence Mean?

Pres. Nixon envisioned Project Independence as a "national goal, in the spirit of Apollo and with the determination of the Manhattan Project, that by the end of this decade, we will have developed the potential to meet our own energy needs without depending on any foreign enemy — foreign energy sources." The means to the goal are, Nixon said, unleashing the nation's huge known coal reserves, its vast untapped sources of natural gas, oil in the continental shelf, oil shale in western deposits, and "the most advanced nuclear technology known to man."

However, as Project Independence got underway, basic questions immediately arose — how and at what cost? Most top energy planners don't have the answers.

For openers, there is no consensus on what "self-sufficiency" actually means. Richard Pastore, a planning official at AEC, warned, "We could become self-sufficient and not like it very much, because of high economic and social costs and drastically worsened environmental conditions." William E. Simon, when he was energy "czar", talked of the U.S. becoming "reasonably self-sufficient" by ending reliance on any "insecure " (i.e. Arab) foreign sources, but didn't envision ending imports from friendly nations like Canada and Venezuela. Roy L. Ash, director of the Office of Management and Budget, stated Project Independence "does not mean we are going to produce in this country all the energy we need." His office voices great skepticism about a government commitment to a costly long-term spending program toward self-sufficiency. Many feel selling war planes and capital goods to Saudi Arabia in return for oil would be cheaper and better for the balance of payments situation than developing expensive domestic supplies. Recently, Pres. Gerald R. Ford rephrased self-sufficiency to mean independence to the degree necessary to avoid disruption to our economy. "Realistically," said Ford, "this does not mean zero imports."

The Ford Foundation Energy Policy Project, headed by S. David Freeman, in preliminary findings of a 2-year study, attacked the goal of self-sufficiency as carrying too big an environmental and economic price tag. The study group viewed the policy of forsaking all imports as an impractical and simplistic overreaction to the Arab oil embargo. Pointing out that even during the embargo the U.S. continued to import more than 5 million barrels of oil per day, the study recommended greater care and selectivity in planning future oil imports.

The Implications of Self-Sufficiency

Despite general lack of coherence in policy, most energy experts agree on the major implications of attaining self-sufficiency.

For one, energy prices would remain high for an indefinite period of time. Because domestic fuel sources would be developed at considerable cost, the "stable long-term price" of gasoline would be about $.65 per gallon and, if inflation continues at an approximate annual rate of 5%, the price could reach $1.00 per gallon in a decade.

The U.S. government would have to make a considerable investment to encourage energy industries to gamble millions of dollars on commercial development of unproved methods of creating synthetic fuels, a basic element of Project Independence. The investment would take the form of federal subsidies, price guarantees, and insurance against failure.

Another basic implication might be the need for import tariffs or quotas on oil imports to prevent Arabs and other low-cost oil producers from undercutting the considerable cost of a domestic synthetic-fuel industry.

Environmental harm is perhaps the most staggering implication of a determined pursuit of self-sufficiency. Increased burning of high-sulfur coal instead of less-polluting oil, massive strip mining, surface-mining of oil-bearing shale rock, and offshore drilling for oil, as well as increased dependence on nuclear reactors to generate electricity, all bear the stigma of potential environmental harm. Pursuance of any or all of these actions portends bitter conflict with environmentalists and conservationists.

The incredible amount of money needed — estimated by Gulf Oil Corporation Pres. James E. Lee at approximately $500 billion — to attain the 1985 goal might well set off a scramble for funds, increasing competition among borrowers, thereby maintaining upward pressure on interest rates. Federal Reserve Board member Robert C. Holland has said that such borrowing "will probably test the flexibility and responsiveness of our financial system as it has seldom been tested before."

From an international point of view, it is highly likely that U.S. allies might perceive Project Independence as an inward turn toward developing an economically isolationist America. They could respond with protectionist policies that could harm alliances as well as world trade.

Pres. Ford recently tried to reassure the world as to the international implications of Project Independence. He told the Ninth World Energy Conference in Detroit, Mich., that ". . . especially with regard to energy, national sufficiency and international interdependence fit together and actually work together." He explained that Project Independence did not set the U.S. apart from the rest of the world, but rather would enable the U.S. to more effectively do its part in the world's effort to provide more energy. He simultaneously called for the formation of Project

Interdependence, "a comprehensive energy program for the world to develop our resources not just for the benefit of a few, but for all mankind."

Basic Elements of Project Independence

Although a blueprint of Project Independence has not yet been formally presented, its basic elements have emerged, specifically in background papers drawn up by former FEA head William E. Simon.

In the area of coal production, Simon projected that U.S. output by 1980 would increase by 60% over 1973. The number of utilities burning coal would increase by 29% by 1980 as power stations switched from oil to coal. To facilitate the conversion, Simon had recommended a 5-year relaxation of secondary sulfur emission standards, which in the past have curbed electric utilities from using the dirtier fuel.

In development of oil from shale, Project Independence projected an output of at least 500,000 barrels of shale oil daily by 1980.

Another element of Project Independence calls for a tenfold increase in leasing of offshore oil acreage on the outer continental shelf as well as a tenfold increase in nuclear generation of energy.

The project also calls for an Energy Trust Fund which would offer "government loans, grants and guarantees for energy and energy equipment industries." Additional amounts would also be needed to subsidize the oil shale synthetic fuel industries, because of "high initial cost and market uncertainty."

Current Domestic Crude Oil Supply

Why, in its pursuit of energy self-sufficiency, is the U.S. focusing on yet untapped and new sources of energy? What has happened to the traditional domestic energy sources — oil, natural gas and coal?

Oil production in the U.S. peaked in 1971 at 9.5 million barrels of oil per day and has now declined to 9.1 million barrels per day. The American Petroleum Institute reported in March that instead of increasing, as might have been expected due to oil price and profit increases of the past year, proved recoverable crude oil reserves (oil that can be recovered with present technology at a suitable profit) declined from 36.3 billion at the end of 1972 to 35.5 billion at the end of December 1973.

Yet, there is encouraging news. Spurred by high prices, wildcat drilling is picking up for the first time in some 20 years. The number of wells drilled for both oil and natural gas increased by nearly 4% in the last 3 months of 1973 and, in February, the number was 14.2% larger than a year before. The price of newly discovered oil, which is free from price controls, has escalated to about $10 a barrel, keeping pace with the rising price of foreign oil. However, the formidable problem is to overcome declining output of old wells. Even with output increases from newly-discovered oil and oil from Alaska, which by 1977 may provide over 2 million barrels a day, if demand continues to grow at the steady rate of past years, production gains could be wiped out. "For the next few years, we're going to be running just to stand still," says one oil industry official.

To maintain its search for new oil reserves, the industry must also overcome shortages of labor, equipment, and supplies and face the high cost of obtaining these necessities.

In his recent economy plan, Pres. Ford, as part of his energy recommendations, called for increased production of crude oil "in old wells." Under consideration as incentives, according to administration sources, are several policies which would have the effect of also releasing old-well oil from price controls, which in turn would probably lead to higher retail prices for gasoline, heating oil, and other petroleum products.

What About Natural Gas?

Unlike crude oil, production of natural gas has been holding steady. However, the number of wells drilled has declined annually, along with natural gas reserves. There is the prospect of sizeable amounts of gas from Alaska's North Slope but, as yet, no proposed means of bringing the fuel to market has been approved. Once approved, transport facilities would take another 3 to 5 years to complete.

The effort to build up declining reserves of natural gas depends on its price. As prices were kept low for the nation's cleanest and most environmentally desirable fuel, industries and utilities turned to natural gas, instead of oil or coal. Lacking a financial incentive to search for new sources, exploration came to a virtual standstill. Now the search for natural gas is also picking up in anticipation of higher prices. Responding to the situation, Pres. Ford, in his plan to improve the economy, again called for Congress to repeal regulation at the wellhead of natural gas prices.

Oceans of Oil Offshore

Since it appears that drilling for oil and gas inland will barely keep up with escalating demand, many, especially officials at the Interior Department, believe drilling for oil and gas off U.S. shores is the best chance to save Project Independence. Under Secretary John C. Whitaker feels development of new outer continental shelf areas "is the only way to get energy self-sufficiency short of major research and development breakthroughs."

According to conservative government estimates, waters off Alaska and the Atlantic coast alone may hold enough oil to meet U.S. demands for 2 to 4 years and meet gas demands for even longer. The Interior Department estimates that the 1.1 million barrels currently being produced offshore might be increased to 4 million per day by 1980 if new areas in the Gulf of Mexico, the Gulf of Alaska and off the Atlantic were tapped.

As rosy as the picture may look to the Interior Department, the drawbacks to tapping offshore reserves are considerable. For one, the current rush to offshore exploration is being hindered by a shortage of equipment. Currently, little more than 100 mobile off-shore exploration rigs are being built with 84 scheduled for delivery in 1975 and 1976. In addition, shortages of shipyard space, steel, and experienced offshore drilling crews are curbing a bigger exploration boom.

But beyond the supply problem, offshore drilling poses a major environmental issue. The fight between oil men and environmentalists has already begun. Many environmental groups and local politicians argue offshore development is not worth the risk of potential ecological damage. They point to the dangers of oil spills and blowouts as well as the drastic alteration of coastal resort areas.

Leonard C. Meeker, an attorney representing the Sierra Club, points out that most environmental organizations are not actually opposed to the development of the outer continental shelf, but "question the premise of maximum speed in consumption and depletion of (these) resources." New York Rep. Lester L. Wolff argues that the U.S. should develop a definitive energy policy before it begins offshore development in the Atlantic. He also calls for the development of new environmental protection measures "far in excess" of those used so far in the Gulf of Mexico.

The oil industry spokesmen answer that major accidents in the Gulf drilling area have been rare. They also point out that the fish catch in the Gulf of Mexico drilling area has risen steadily during the period of offshore development — 4½ times greater in 1972 than in 1945. This fish catch increase, however, may be due in part to a fivefold increase in tonnage of commercial vessels engaged in fishing activity in the gulf over the past 30 years. They argue new safety precautions and proper planning can minimize dangers to the environment. Administration officials note that since the 1969 oil leak off Santa Barbara, Calif., stricter federal regulations have been introduced and enforcement has been strengthened.

In April 1973, Pres. Nixon said that offshore leasing of federal tracts for oil and gas exploration would be tripled by 1979. At the same time he ordered the Council on Environmental Quality to study the implications of offshore drilling. A year later, in its environmental impact statement, the Council stopped just short of recommending an outright ban of drilling in the Gulf of Alaska, foreseeing a high probability of oil spills washing ashore and of severe storms, earthquakes, and tidal waves wrecking the drilling operations. Conservationists also noted that the gulf is rich in fish and marine animals ranging from pink salmon, king and snow crabs, to sea lions, seals, and otters as well as more than 200 species of birds.

The Environmental Quality Council gave indirect approval to offshore exploration in certain parts of the Atlantic region, but declined to make direct recommendations on drilling in several areas it considered environmentally vulnerable. Environmental Protection Agency Administrator Russel E. Train responded that there should be "very careful advance planning" before leasing began in the Alaska Gulf and along the Atlantic coast. He stated that the EPA expected "to participate and comment on any plans — absolutely." He further said that while some of the exploration recommended by the Council — off the New England shore and in the Maryland-Delaware-New Jersey area — "would be acceptable" if it was "well-planned and strongly regulated" with tough environmental measures, "there are some places where it shouldn't be done."

As the controversy continues, the Interior Department has begun the push for sales of offshore leases off Alaska and in the Atlantic. According to an internal memo, the Interior Department's Bureau of Land Management and its Geological Survey were directed in October to draw up a "firm leasing schedule" aimed at leasing 10 million offshore acres by 1975.

Coal, the Dirty Fuel

The United States has almost half of the coal reserves in the world. However, the bottlenecks to tapping the resource are monumental. Recently, one coal company executive called Project Independence "dead, buried and mortified unless someone at the top in Washington does something" to end uncertainties curbing billions of dollars in capital investment essential to expanding domestic coal use.

Instead of increasing, coal production has been dropping, 17% since 1969. Wildcat strikes, accelerating absenteeism, stagnant technology, inefficient company management and increasingly strict federal health and safety regulations are holding back productivity. Additionally, strip mining firms are running short of diesel fuel, as well as ammonium nitrate (a vital explosive), coal-hauling railway cars, and steel bolts to hold up mine shorings.

An FEA task force reported recently that more than 2 billion tons of coal could be produced by 1985 if "highest priority" were assigned to it, but the report stated that would be "an unlikely development." Those with the money to invest in making coal a primary energy source are not moving because they claim the government hasn't made up its mind on energy issues.

Essential to a significant output of coal by 1985 is the opening of new mines, requiring an investment of about $16 billion plus a substantial capital outlay for mining equipment. Also required would be an increase in selling prices of about 10% above 1973 prices, an increase in employment from 150,000 to about 200,000 miners, and more transportation equipment, such as railroad hopper cars and locomotives, at an additional total cost of some $6.5 billion. The industry is calling for relaxation of air quality standards, specifically the Clean Air Act, for legislation which would give the strip mining industry more leeway in exploiting lands, and for a new policy for leasing coal lands owned by the government.

In his recent plan for the economy, Pres. Ford responded to some of the above imperatives. He called for legislation to modify the Clean Air Act, to compel natural gas and oil-burning utilities to turn to coal and to require new utilities to either burn coal or use nuclear reactors. He also called for action to prepare for leasing of federal coal lands in 1975.

However, beyond governmental waffling, internal mismanagement, supply dislocations, and employee problems, the coal industry faces another major bottleneck: the environmentalists. They have fought for tough strip mining regulation and a strict Clean Air Act and will not graciously bow to government demands for modification of the legislation.

Currently, only 5% of yearly coal output has come from western mines where half of the known recoverable reserves lie, mostly in the Ft. Union formation which extends across Montana, Wyoming, and North Dakota. It is estimated that only 10% of western coal reserves could meet standards set by the Clean Air Act, currently scheduled to go into effect July 1, 1975.

Additionally, most western coal must be surface mined. Although most western states require that stripped land be graded and reclaimed, enforcement of reclamation standards has been weak. A bill setting up minimum reclamation standards is currently tied up in Congress.

Although most environmentalists agree that land can be reclaimed successfully at a high cost to the coal industry, few believe it will really be done. They point out the coal industry spent a mere $9 million on land reclamation research from 1969 to 1973 and that less than half of the land previously strip mined has been reclaimed. Environmentalist Carolyn Anderson's assessment is much harsher: "We're not comforted by assurances of reclamation when in fact there is not one acre of reclaimed land in the Northern Great Plains which has been returned to agricultural production, much less grazing."

Much of the debate over reclamation centers on water, which is essential to developing new vegetation that can be sustained in a natural balance over the long run. Environmentalists argue there is not sufficient water in the already water-scarce western states to insure successful reclamation. While the coal industry wants to continue strip mining in conjunction with experimental reclamation, environmentalists argue successful reclamation must be proved first.

Oil and Gas From Coal

The nation's immense coal reserves — some 300 billion recoverable tons of coal — have focused interest on the development of synthetic fuels from coal as a solution for energy shortages. Although Pres. Nixon, under Project Independence, requested an expenditure of $285 million in fiscal year 1975 for gasification and liquefaction projects, the consensus is that the development of synthetic fuels in quantity is a long-term prospect, not to be realized until 1985 or later. Although the technology already exists, most proven methods to date have been deemed too complex and too expensive. Also, for reasons noted above, the necessary coal mines have not been developed. The synthetic fuel industry also faces many of the same problems associated with coal development; strip mining and reclamation, need for water, and concern about land use. Synthetic fuel complexes, which need to be situated near the mines to cut down on transportation costs, depend on water to clean and prepare coal and to treat coal by-products created in the process. The processes do have one environmental advantage over the direct burning of coal; much of the ash and sulfur is removed from the coal in the gasification and liquefaction process.

Thus, according to recent projections, the U.S., by 1980, will have no more than 4 to 6 coal gasification plants which will meet no more than 2% of the demand for gas. By 1986, the number of plants may rise to 15, fulfilling 4% to 6% of the demand for gas. The estimates for oil flowing from liquefaction are about the same.

Even these conservative estimates may be short-lived. In October, FEA head John C. Sawhill stated that he would advise Pres. Ford against a crash program to develop synthetic fuels in the next 10 years. Noting suggestions that the government finance 20 to 30 liquefaction plants, Sawhill said the nation probably wouldn't need them. Eric R. Zausner, in charge of drafting a blueprint for Project Independence, said that natural gas and oil from the outer continental shelf might cut imports to zero by 1985. "This country has to make some choices," said Zausner, "but it doesn't have to do everything on every front."

Nuclear Power

The Atomic Industrial Forum, Inc. reported in January that a total of 42 nuclear power reactors — first generation light water reactors — were classed as operable at the end of 1973. Their capacity was placed at 25.67 million kilowatts or 5.6% of the nation's total electric generating capacity. A spokesman for the Forum said, "In 1973, this over-promised, under-appreciated source of electricity revealed its true potential as probably one of the two mainstays of the nation's near-term quest for energy self-sufficiency, the other being coal."

Many consider the light-water reactor a keystone in the short-term struggle toward energy self-sufficiency. The Atomic Energy Commission (AEC) has been counting on nuclear energy to double its contribution to the nation's electricity supply from 7.4% to at least 15% by 1980 and to 40% by 1990.

But a recent economic survey on cutbacks of construction budgets by electric utilities showed that AEC aims are highly optimistic. An 18% cutback —

$16.1 million of their projected $88.1 billion construction budget through 1978 — hit particularly hard at nuclear energy plants. The cutback in construction, affecting 132,490,000 kilowatts of projected capacity over the next 4 years, represents half of "the total of all nuclear capacity being planned for the future earlier this year," according to a survey conducted by National Economic Research Associates, Inc. The concern's president, Irving M. Stelzer, told FEA head John C. Sawhill that if the cutbacks were not restored soon, "then our only options five or six years from now will be voluntary conservation or involuntary curtailment of service."

The recent cutback jeopardizes nuclear industry estimates that by 1980 some 140 reactors would be supplying more than 20% of the nation's electrical demand. That estimate came before Pres. Nixon's call for acceleration of nuclear capacity, to reduce the 10-year time span between the order for a new plant and actual operation. Acceleration depends on a retooling of the AEC's present system of operation to permit construction of nuclear power plants on an assembly-line basis. Two proposals to alleviate major bottlenecks are currently under consideration: the setting aside of potential power plant sites on which environmental studies have been made and hearings for local citizens held in advance, and the selection of a small number of standardized plant designs currently being drafted under rules already issued by the AEC.

Nuclear Dangers

The major drawback to a speed up of nuclear power still lies with the industry's critics. Ralph Nader has said, "The underlying point is that no society should rest its energy future in a fragile nuclear-fission basket when risks of accident and sabotage are at a point of catastrophic consequence unparalleled in the history of mankind."

The Union of Concerned Scientists has outlined the major fears about nuclear power plants. Human error or failure of mechanical parts could result in a disastrous nuclear accident. The disposal of waste products, some of which remain radioactive for thousands of years, has not yet been satisfactorily solved, they say. They also fear terrorists could steal fissionable material — such as the by-product plutonium — to make a nuclear bomb.

The AEC denies charges of excessive dangers. AEC head Dixie Lee Ray feels certain today's reactors feature enough built-in safeguards to prevent accidents and to mitigate their consequences should they occur. She points out that the AEC has already spent over half a billion dollars on a nuclear safety research program.

However, adding fuel to critics' arguments, Carl J. Hocevar, formerly a leading nuclear safety expert at AEC, recently quit his job with the following statement: "In spite of the soothing reassurances the AEC gives to the uninformed, misled public, unresolved questions about nuclear power safety are so grave that the United States should consider a complete halt to nuclear power plant construction while we see if these serious questions can, somehow, be resolved." As if in confirmation of his concern, the AEC in September, ordered 21 of its 50 operating nuclear energy plants to close down within 60 days to determine whether cracks were developing in their cooling systems. Although the AEC said cracks discovered in 3 plants did not pose a serious safety hazard, they admitted repair could mean a long shutdown of the plants.

The AEC has concluded, despite protest from critics, that development of the second-generation breeder reactor would expand the nation's generating capacity at a savings of $60 billion in 46 years. But this program also faces setbacks. In September, it was disclosed that the cost of the prototype of the breeder reactor planned for use late in this century has increased more than $1 billion in the past 2 years, due to inflation, additional research requirements and anticipated construction delays. Again environmentalists are concerned about the storage and transport of large amounts of fissionable plutonium-239 that will accumulate in the breeder reactor.

Oil From Shale

In the search for alternative energy sources, many are looking enthusiastically to refining the extensive shale deposits in the west into a burnable oil. The process is not that simple, however. Shale rocks, actually marlstone, must be heated to about 900 degrees F. to cook out a substance called kerogen which, in turn, can be refined into gasoline and other petroleum products. Many industry engineers prefer shale oil over synthetic oil from coal because chemically it is more like petroleum.

On Jan. 8, when the government put up for lease the first 5,120-acre tract of land with shale deposits, Standard Oil of Indiana and the Gulf Oil Corporation jointly submitted an unexpectedly high bid of $210 million for the northwestern Colorado land. Under the prototype plan, the companies would have 3 years to study, test, build pilot plants, and submit a proposal for full-scale extraction of oil from shale. That one tract is believed to contain more oil than is known to exist in the North Slope of Alaska. All told, some 16,500 square miles of Colorado, Utah, and Wyoming are believed to contain oil-bearing shale able to supply 600 billion to 3 trillion barrels of oil, or 2 to 3 times more oil than is known to exist in the rest of the world.

Interior Secretary Rogers C.B. Morton hailed the success of the first of 6 such leasings this year: "The bidding provides one more example that this nation can become self-sufficient in energy. While large amounts of shale oil will not be available for several years, it is encouraging to get such strong evidence that oil shale provides a good insurance policy for the future."

Again, not everyone is so optimistic. Environmental groups predict an ecological nightmare. The oil-extraction process depends on conventional openpit mining with huge daily extractions. The Oil and Gas Journal predicts 99,000 cubic yards of raw shale and processed shale would have to be moved daily to produce 40,000 barrels of oil. The retorting process, in which the oil is cooked out of the shale rock, will pollute air and water, according to ecologists. Also, in the retorting process, the shale expands to twice its original volume, thereby creating a considerable storage problem. Environmentalists also point to the sociological disturbances associated with thousands of workers and their families moving into sparsely inhabited oil shale areas.

Even the Interior Department admits oil shale can play only a small role in future energy needs. Hank Ash, deputy oil shale coordinator, says lack of sufficient water for mining and processing in the tri-state shale area is likely to limit daily production to 3 to 5 million barrels by the year 2000. Given today's annual increase in crude oil consumption, that would account for no more than 7% of the nation's fuel needs.

Given the potential ecological dangers and low energy yield, Jim Moorman, executive director of the

Sierra Club's legal defense fund, concluded, "we think the oil-shale program is far more dangerous than any offshore drilling program, and all for maybe 500,000 barrels of oil per day 10 years from now. It just doesn't make sense."

And most recently, a 24-page environmental impact statement, part of the blueprint for Project Independence, outlined in bleak terms the potential ecological impact of a 1.5 million barrels-per-day production in 1990. The report projected the cumulative agricultural damage at more than $30 million, the creation of a salt desert environment over a wide area with possible permanent climatic changes, and increased salinity in the Colorado River. An FEA source estimated that a viable oil-shale operation might require a fixed oil price as high as $15 per barrel.

Geothermal Power

Geothermal energy, the unleashing of heat in the earth's interior, is considered a potentially feasible means of supplementing other forms of electric generation, particularly on a local scale. Despite the fact that currently geothermal energy is not expected to replace significant amounts of other forms of electric generation, the government had begun competitive leasing of tracts in California for geothermal exploration.

Geothermal energy has attractions. Most environmentalists consider it clean energy, although not without environmental costs. Long-distance power lines would be required to deliver power to urban areas. It is also possible dry rock geothermal fields might be heavy users of water in already water-scarce western areas.

Energy experts, however, feel commercial geothermal energy may be 20 years away. Largely because of many unknowns, the energy-producing life of a geothermal field for one, electric utilities have been wary of spending money on the necessary research. Estimates of geothermal capactiy by the year 2000 range from as low as 1% to more than 20% of total national electric power.

Alternatives to Project Independence

Given the high-cost of attaining energy self-sufficiency, the uncertainties of the time scope for its achievement, and the potential environmental harm, are there alternatives? Some definitely think so.

S. David Freeman's Ford Foundation Energy Project concluded that more emphasis should be put on long-range conservation methods than big development projects. Freeman has pointed out that huge investments in mass transit and the renewal of inner cities would "balance the energy budget" by curbing demand rather than boosting supply. As another step, the project recommended removal of government subsidies which prevent energy prices from reflecting their "full costs to society."

Yale University Economics Prof. William D. Nordhaus views stockpiling of foreign oil imports as a feasible alternative. He believes that whenever the price of foreign oil falls below that of domestic fuels by large enough a margin to cover storage costs, it would pay to stockpile. According to his calculations the cost of continued reliance on foreign oil during the next 20 years would come to $663 billion, while the total for self-sufficiency would amount to $985 billion, a difference of $16 billion per year.

An MIT study, "Energy Self-Sufficiency: An Economic Evaluation," published in May, came to a similar conclusion. The group concluded that the 2 justifications for independence from oil imports —

avoiding oil blackmail and cutting the resource cost of our energy — were, in fact, contradictory if the date for self-sufficiency were set in the early 1980s. Concluding that the cost of additional domestic supplies within that time scale was above the cost of economic imports, the group said too little attention had been given to the option and costs of providing a stockpile of crude oil beyond normal inventories. They said a curtailment of imports would replace a temporary embargo with a permanent embargo which would certainly increase energy prices beyond present levels. The group also underlined that environmental degradation was implicit in moving too quickly toward energy self-sufficiency.

In the long run, historians may well conclude that the idea of U.S. energy independence was an emotional reaction to the shock of Arab blackmail. It is clear that closer study of all the factors — investment, environmental problems, technology — has thrown the Project Independence concept into serious doubt. A nation comprising 6% of the world's population and consuming 33% of the world's energy output must face an almost impossible challenge if it wishes to balance its energy budget without decreasing its spendthrift ways.

U.S. Petroleum and Natural Gas Resources
(onshore and offshore to water depth of 200 meters)
Source: U.S. Geological Survey

Crude Oil and Natural Gas Liquids
(Billions of barrels)

| AREA | PRODUCTION | | | | RESERVES | | | | RESOURCES** | |
| | 1972 | | Cumulative end 1972 | | Measured*** | | Indicated-Inferred | | Undiscovered Recoverable | |
	State	Federal	State	Federal	State	Federal*	State	Federal*	State	Federal
Conterminous states onshore	3.100	0.214	104.200	5.577	29.3	1.7	16.0-27.0	1.0-1.5	100-200	10- 20
Alaska onshore	0.000	0.009	0.000	0.134	9.6	0.1	5.0-10.0	-0.0	20- 40	5- 10
Total onshore	3.100	0.223	104.200	5.711	38.9	1.8	21.0-37.0	1.0-1.5	120-240	15- 30
Atlantic offshore	0.000	0.000	0.000	0.000	0.0	0.0	0.0	0.0	2- 4	8- 16
Gulf of Mexico offshore	0.100	0.390	0.700	2.770	0.5	3.5	0- 0.5	2.0-3.0	2- 4	18- 36
Pacific offshore	0.100	0.020	1.300	0.090	0.7	2.2	0- 0.5	1.0-2.0	1- 2	4- 8
Alaska offshore	0.100	0.000	0.500	0.000	0.7	0.0	0- 0.5	0.0	2- 4	28- 56
Total offshore	0.300	0.410	2.500	2.860	1.9	5.7	0- 1.5	3.0-5.0	7- 14	58-116
Total on- and offshore	3.400	0.630	106.700	8.570	40.8	7.5	21.0-38.5	4.0-6.5	127-254	73-146

Natural Gas
(Trillions of cubic feet)

	State	Federal	State	Federal	State	Federal*	State	Federal*	State	Federal
Conterminous states onshore	17.700	1.001	397.400	16.870	175.7	14.1	86.0-164.0	7.0-13.0	450- 900	50-100
Alaska onshore	0.00	0.056	0.000	0.307	26.4	2.1	13.0- 26.0	1.0- 2.0	80- 160	25- 50
Total onshore	17.700	1.057	397.400	17.177	202.1	16.2	99.0-190.0	8.0-15.0	530-1060	75-150
Atlantic offshore	0.000	0.000	0.000	0.000	0.0	0.0	0.0	0.0	5- 10	50-100
Gulf of Mexico offshore	0.600	3.030	3.900	17.400	6.5	36.8	3.0- 5.0	18.0-36.0	10- 20	150-300
Pacific offshore	0.000	0.010	1.200	0.040	0.7	2.0	0.0- 0.5	1.0- 2.0	5- 10	5- 10
Alaska offshore	0.100	0.000	0.600	0.000	1.8	0.0	1.0- 1.5	0.0	20- 40	150-300
Total offshore	0.700	3.040	5.700	17.440	9.0	38.8	4.0- 7.0	19.0-38.0	40- 80	355-710
Total on- and offshore	18.400	4.100	403.100	34.617	211.1	55.0	103.0-197.0	27.0-53.0	570-1140	430-860

*Distribution between State and Federal is based on assumption that reserves are in the same ratio between the two as recent production. **As shown by the range, unit figures have little significance for individual areas, but merely show the approximate distribution of the rounded total for the United States—200-400 billion barrels of petroleum liquids and 1,000-2,000 trillion cubic feet of natural gas. ***Total U.S. measured reserves derived from American Petroleum Institute and American Gas Association.

Measured Reserves are identified resources from which an energy or mineral commodity can be economically extracted with existing technology, and whose location, quality, and quantity are known from geologic and engineering evidence. **Indicated reserves** are reserves based partly upon specific measurements, samples, or production data and partly from projection for a reasonable distance on geologic evidence. **Inferred Reserves** are the reserves based upon broad geologic knowledge for which quantitative measurements are not available. Such reserves are estimated to be recoverable in the future as a result of extensions, revisions of estimates, and deeper drilling in known fields.)

(**Resources** include undiscovered deposits of the same quality as reserves as well as deposits presently unrecoverable for either economic, technologic, or legal reasons.)

Measuring Energy
Source: House Subcommittee on Energy

The following tables of equivalents contain those figures commonly used to compare different types of energy sources and their various measurements.

Btu - a British thermal unit — the amount of heat required to raise one pound of water one degree Farenheit. Equivalent to 1055 joules or about 252 gram calories. A **therm** is usually 100,000 Btu but is sometimes used to refer to other units.

Calorie - the amount of heat required to raise one gram of water one degree centigrade; abbreviated cal.; equivalent to about .003968 Btu. More common is the kilogram calorie, also called a **kilocalorie** and abbreviated Cal. or Kcal; equivalent to about 3.97 Btu. (One Kcal is equivalent to one food calorie.)

The Btu. and cal., being small amounts of energy, are usually expressed as follows when large numbers are involved.

1×10^3 Btu = 1,000
1×10^6 Btu = 1,000,000
1×10^9 Btu = 1,000,000,000
1×10^{12} Btu = 1 trillion
1×10^{15} Btu = 1 quadrillion
1×10^{18} Btu = 1 quintillion or 1 Q unit
One Q unit = 38.46 billion tons of coal
= 172.4 billion barrels of oil
= 968.9 trillion cubic ft. of natural gas

U.S. energy consumption in 1970 was about one-seventh of a Q unit

Btu Values of Energy Sources
(These are conventional or average values, not precise equivalents.)

Coal (per 2,000 lb. ton):
Anthracite = 25.4×10^6 Btu
Bituminous = 26.2×10^6
Sub-bituminous = 19.0×10^6
Lignite = 13.4×10^6
Average heating value of coal used to generate electricity in 1969 was 27.7×10^6 Btu.

Natural Gas (per cubic foot):
Dry = 1,031 Btu
Wet = 1,103
Liquid (avg.) = 4,100
Electricity— 1 kwh = 3,413 Btu.

Petroleum (per barrel)
Crude oil = 5.60×10^6 Btu
Residual fuel oil = 6.29×10^6
Distillate fuel oil = 5.83×10^6
Gasoline (including av gas) = 5.25×10^6
Jet fuel (kerosene) = 5.67×10^6
Jet fuel (naphtha) = 5.36×10^6

Kerosene = 5.67×10^6 Btu
Nuclear
1 gram of fissioned U-235 — 74,000 Btu

Other Conversion Factors

Electricity— 1 kwh = 0.88 lbs. of coal
= 0.076 gallons of oil
= 10.4 cu. ft. of natural gas

Natural Gas— 1 tcf
(trillion cubic feet) = 39,300 tons of coal
= 184,000 barrels of oil

Coal— 1 mtce
(million tons of coal equivalent) = 4.48×10^6 barrels of oil
= 67 tons of oil
= 25.19×10^{12} cu. ft. of natural gas

Oil— 1 million tons
(6.65×10^6 barrels) = 4×10^9 kwh of electricity (when used to generate power)
= 12×10^9 kwh unconverted
= 1.5×10^6 tons of coal
= 41.2×10^9 cu. ft. of natural gas

Approximate Conversion Factors For Oils

To convert—	Barrels to Metric tons	Metric tons to barrels	Barrels/ days to tons/year	Tons/year to barrels/day
		Multiply by—		
Crude oil	0.136	7.33	49.8	0.0201
Gasoline.....	.118	8.45	43.2	.0232
Kerosene.....	.128	7.80	46.8	.0214
Diesel fuel....	.133	7.50	48.7	.0205
Fuel oil.......	.149	6.70	54.5	.0184

[1] Based on world average gravity (excluding natural gas liquids).

U.S. Energy Consumption — Source, Use, Efficiency

Source: Joint Congressional Committee on Atomic Energy Report — Understanding The "National Energy Dilemma," published by The Center for Strategic and International Studies, September, 1973. The Report converts the figures below into a visual scheme for a 3-dimensional display of energy consumption since 1950 and projected to 1990. The Report and display are available from CSIS, 1800 K Street, Washington, D.C. 20006.
(in millions of barrels per day of oil equivalent[1])

Energy Sources and Uses..	1950	1960	1970	1980[2]
Hydroelectric............	0.2	0.3	0.4	0.6
Gas.....................	2.9	5.9	10.7	12.2[3]
Electricity generation......	0.3	0.8	1.9	1.6
Residential and commercial	0.8	2.0	3.5	5.0
Industrial................	1.6	2.8	4.6	4.7
Transportation...........	0.1	0.2	0.3	0.4
Non-energy..............	0.2	0.2	0.3	0.5
Coal....................	6.5	5.3	7.4	10.3[4]
Electricity generation......	1.1	2.0	3.7	5.2
Residential and commercial	1.4	0.5	0.2	0.1
Industrial................	2.8	2.3	2.5	3.5
Transportation...........	0.8	0.1	—	—
Non-energy..............	0.1	0.1	0.1	0.1
Exports.................	0.4	0.5	0.9	1.4
Oil.....................	6.5	9.7	13.9	21.3[5]
(domestic).............	(5.6)	(7.8)	(10.4)	(11.5)
(imported).............	(0.9)	(1.9)	(3.5)	(10.0)
Electricity generation......	0.3	0.3	1.0	2.0
Residential and commercial	1.2	2.0	2.5	2.0
Industrial................	1.0	1.3	1.6	2.7
Transportation...........	3.2	5.0	7.4	11.5
Non-energy..............	0.4	0.8	1.5	3.1
Exports.................	0.3	0.2	—	—
Nuclear—electric..........	—	—	0.1	3.6
Geothermal—electric......	—	—	0.003	0.2
Electricity generation......	1.9	3.4	7.1	13.2
Residential and commercial	0.2	0.5	1.3	2.8
Industrial................	0.2	0.7	1.2	2.1
Transportation...........	—	—	0.007	0.5
TOTAL INPUT............	16.1	21.2	32.5	48.3

	1950	1960	1970	1980
TOTAL INPUT............	16.1	21.2	32.5	48.3
To: Electricity Generation..	1.9	3.4	7.1	13.2
Used...............	0.5	1.2	2.5	5.4
Lost................	1.4	2.3	4.6	8.1
Residential and Commercial	3.6	5.0	7.5	9.9
Used...............	2.7	3.5	5.6	7.3
Lost................	0.9	1.5	1.9	2.6
Industrial..............	5.6	7.1	9.9	13.0
Used...............	4.2	2.1	7.4	9.6
Lost................	1.4	4.9	2.4	3.4
Transportation..........	4.1	5.3	7.7	12.0
Used...............	1.0	1.2	1.9	3.0
Lost................	1.4	4.0	5.8	9.0
TOTAL USED............	7.9	9.6	15.0	19.9
TOTAL LOST............	6.6	9.9	14.7	23.3[6]

[1] All energy sources have been converted to barrels of oil equivalent (B/DOE) by determining their heat value and converting that Btu figure to barrels of oil, viz.: 5,800,000 Btu = one barrel of crude oil; 3,412 Btu = one kilowatt-hour; 1,000 Btu = 1 cu. ft. of natural gas; 26,000,000 Btu = one ton of coal. Figures may not add to totals due to rounding while converting to B/DOE.
[2] "There are many reasons for the high degree of confidence in the predictability of 1980 .... The Nation has already ordered a large part of the electrical capacity that can be functioning commercially by the year 1980; it has already ordered every major rail-based mass transit system that can be functioning by 1980 ..." etc.
[3] Including gas derived from oil (0.15) and coal (0.13).
[4] Excluding coal (0.2) converted to gas.
[5] Excluding oil (0.2) converted to gas.
[6] Including energy lost (0.12) in oil and coal conversion to gas.

Coal: Strip Mining Increase

Source: Bureau of Mines

Strip Mining by State 1973 (millions of tons)

Alabama	11.5	Kansas	1.1	Oklahoma	2.2
Alaska	.7	Kentucky	55.0	Penn	29.8
Arizona	3.2	Maryland	1.6	Tenn	4.2
Arkansas	.4	Missouri	4.7	Texas	6.9
Colorado	2.8	Montana	10.7	Virginia	8.7
Illinois	29.0	No. Dakota	6.9	Wash	3.3
Indiana	24.5	New Mexico	8.3	W. Virginia	17.7
Iowa	.2	Ohio	28.5	Wyoming	14.5

1964 Total soft coal, 487,000,000 tons; Strip mined 152,000,000 tons; 31%.
1968 Total soft coal, 545,000,000 tons; Strip mined 186,000,000 tons; 34%.
1973 Total soft coal, 591,738,000 tons; Strip mined 276,645,000 tons; 47%.

Coal and Coke Production in the United States

Source: Bureau of Mines

Year	Penn. Anthracite		Bituminous		Year	Penn. Anthracite		Bituminous	
	Production 1,000 net tons	Value $1,000	Production 1,000 net tons	Value $1,000		Production 1,000 net tons	Value $1,000	Production 1,000 net tons	Value $1,000
1945	54,934	323,944	577,617	1,768,204	1966	12,941	100,663	533,881	2,421,293
1950	44,077	392,398	516,311	2,500,374	1967	12,256	96,160	552,026	2,555,377
1955	26,205	206,097	464,633	2,092,383	1968	11,461	97,245	545,245	2,546,340
1960	18,817	147,116	415,512	1,950,421	1969	10,473	100,769	560,505	2,795,509
1962	16,894	134,094	422,149	1,891,555	1970	9,729	105,341	602,932	3,772,662
1963	18,267	153,503	458,928	2,013,390	1971	8,727	103,469	552,192	3,901,496
1964	17,184	148,648	486,998	2,165,582	1972	7,106	85,251	595,386	4,561,983
1965	14,866	122,021	512,088	2,276,022	1973	6,830	90,260	591,738	5,049,612

Coke Production (1,000 net tons—value in $1,000)—(1968) 63,653, $1,157,359; (1969) 64,757, $1,355,260; (1970) 66,525, $1,849,160; (1971) 57,436, $1,745,693; (1972) 60,507, $2,012,486; (1973) 64,325, $2,442,151.
Coke Exports (short tons)—(1968) 791,909; (1969) 1,629,000; (1970) 2,478,338 (1971) 1,508,639; (1972) 1,231,633; (1973) 1,394,980; Imports—(1968) 94,085; (1969) 173,052; (1970) 152,879; (1971) 173,914; (1972) 185,023; (1973) 1,077,737.
Anthracite exports (net tons)—(1966) 766,025; (1967) 594,797; (1968) 518,159; (1969) 627,492; (1970) 789,499; (1971) 671,024; (1972) 743,451; (1973) 716,546.

U.S. Petroleum and Natural Gas Production

Source: Bureau of Mines

Year	Crude oil		Natural gas liquids			Natural gas	
	Production 1,000 bbls.	Value $1,000	Production 1,000 bbls.	Value $1,000	Total 42 gal. bbls.	Marketed Mil. cu. ft.	Value $1,000
1945	1,713,655	2,094,250	112,004	187,564	1,828,539,000	3,944,021	191,006
1950	1,973,574	4,963,380	181,961	419,605	2,155,693,000	6,282,060	408,521
1955	2,484,428	6,870,380	281,371	619,006	2,766,325,000	9,405,351	978,357
1960	2,574,933	7,420,181	340,157	808,385	2,915,365,000	12,771,038	1,789,970
1965	2,848,514	8,158,298	441,556	911,603	3,290,083,000	16,042,753	2,494,542
1969	3,371,751	10,426,680	580,241	1,102,011	3,951,992,000	20,698,240	3,455,615
1970	3,517,450	11,173,726	605,916	1,275,112	4,123,366,000	21,920,642	3,745,680
1971	3,453,914	11,692,998	617,815	1,386,054	4,071,729,000	22,493,012	4,085,482
1972	3,455,368	11,706,510	638,216	1,452,233	4,093,584,000	22,531,698	4,180,462
1973	3,360,903	13,057,905	634,423	1,857,073	3,995,326,000	22,647,549	4,894,072

U. S. Total Fuel Supply and Demand

In thousands of 42-gallon barrels. *Includes special naphtha production. *Includes kerosene type jet fuel.

Year	Gasoline*		Kerosene*		Distillate fuel oil		Residual fuel oil	
	Production	Total Demand	Production	Total Demand	Production	Total Demand	Production	Total Demand
1950	1,024,181	1,019,011	118,512	119,922	398,912	75,435	425,217	570,021
1960²	1,522,497	1,525,126	136,842	133,188	667,050	695,165	332,147	577,934
1965	1,733,258	1,756,419	201,788	219,932	765,071	779,644	268,567	601,893
1970	2,135,838	2,165,395	313,544	358,025	897,097	927,211	257,510	804,288
1971 (rev.)	2,231,157	2,242,921	306,847	364,908	912,097	971,316	274,684	838,045
1972	2,352,310	2,382,293	313,554	379,849	963,625	1,066,049	292,519	925,647
1973	2,434,943	2,464,262	327,818	383,050	1,030,178	1,124,308	354,597	1,019,934

(1) Demand in some cases exceeds the production; in these cases the difference is made up by dipping into stocks or by imports. (2) In the years prior to 1960 figures are on a 48-state basis.

U. S. Motor Fuel Supply[1] and Demand

Source: Bureau of Mines (Figures in 42-gallon barrels)

Year	Supply		Demand		Year	Supply		Demand	
	Production (1,000)	Daily average (1,000)	Domestic (1,000)	Export (1,000)		Production (1,000)	Daily average (1,000)	Domestic (1,000)	Export (1,000)
1945	793,431	2,174	696,333	88,059	1969	2,057,041	5,636	2,072,144	4,468
1950	1,024,481	2,806	994,290	24,721	1970	2,135,838	5,852	2,162,439	2,956
1955	1,373,950	3,764	1,329,788	34,521	1971 (rev.)	2,231,157	6,113	2,242,921	3,104
1960*	1,522,497	4,160	1,511,670	13,456	1972	2,352,310	6,427	2,382,293	2,441
1965	1,733,258	4,749	1,750,028	6,391	1973	2,434,943	6,671	2,484,262	3,318

*Beginning with 1959 Alaska and Hawaii are included. (1.) Includes special naptha.

World Production of Crude Petroleum[1]
Source: Bureau of Mines; in thousands of 42-gallon barrels

Country	1973	1972	Country	1973	1972
North America:			Congo (Brazzaville)	12,713	(E) 2,146
Canada	648,348	560,693	Egypt, Arab Republic of	60,483	78,800
Cuba (E)	775	775	Gabon	55,045	45,671
Mexico[1]	191,482	185,011	Libya	794,094	819,619
Trinidad and Tobago	60,666	51,719	Morocco	320	216
United States[1]	3,360,903	3,455,368	Nigeria	749,820	665,282
South America:			Tunisia	29,828	31,607
Argentina	153,539	158,464	**Asia:**		
Bolivia	17,266	15,967	Bahrain	24,948	25,547
Brazil	62,122	61,088	Brunei	78,673	67,008
Chile	11,429	12,527	Burma	7,514	7,466
Colombia	66,844	71,674	China, People's Rep. of (E) . .	365,000	216,080
Ecuador	76,221	28,579	India	55,388	56,965
Peru	25,767	23,635	Indonesia	488,536	395,581
Venezuela	1,228,594	1,178,487	Iran	2,139,269	1,843,869
Europe:			Iraq	736,607	529,419
Albania	14,345	10,508	Israel (E)[2]	32,193	43,920
Austria	17,982	17,284	Japan	5,142	5,242
Bulgaria	1,460	1,825	Kuwait[3]	1,100,369	1,201,346
Czechoslovakia	1,221	1,322	Malaysia	33,054	33,867
Denmark	1,460	1,281	Mongolia (E)	90	90
France	9,152	10,811	Oman	106,926	103,131
Germany, East.	2,500	1,806	Pakistan	2,871	3,294
Germany, West.	47,944	51,271	Qatar	208,152	176,545
Hungary	15,176	15,084	Saudi Arabia[3]	2,772,733	2,202,049
Italy	7,082	7,850	Syrian Arab Republic	38,170	39,879
Netherlands	10,169	10,885	Taiwan	1,055	732
Norway	11,166	12,078	Thailand	45	(E)112
Poland	2,908	2,574	Turkey	24,273	24,416
Romania	106,578	105,296	**United Arab Emirates**		
Spain	5,932	1,020	Abu Dhabi	479,192	384,190
U.S.S.R.	3,094,350	2,895,900	Dubai	80,207	55,942
United Kingdom[1]	3,296	607	**Oceania:**		
Yugoslavia	24,680	23,709	Australia	142,277	119,516
Africa:			New Zealand[1]	1,290	1,119
Algeria	390,711	384,858	**Total . . . . . .**	**20,357,175**	**18,583,783**
Angola	58,910	43,161			

(E) Estimate. (P) Preliminary. (R) Revised. [1]Includes field condensate. [2]Estimates of Israeli production from Sinai peninsula oilfields included with Israel rather than with United Arab Republic. [3]Data for both Kuwait and Saudi Arabia include those countries' share of production from former Kuwait-Saudi Arabia Neutral Zone.

U.S. Crude Petroleum Production By Chief States
(Figures represent thousands of 42-gallon barrels)

Year	Ark.	Calif.	Ill.	Kans.	La.	Miss.	N.M.	N.D.	Okla.	Texas	Wyo.
1950. . .	31,108	327,607	62,028	107,586	208,965	38,236	47,367	. . . .	164,599	829,874	61,631
1960. . .	30,117	305,352	77,341	113,453	400,832	51,673	107,380	21,992	192,913	927,479	133,910
1965. . .	25,930	316,428	63,708	104,733	594,853	56,183	119,166	26,350	203,441	1,000,749	138,314
1970. . .	18,035	372,191	43,747	84,853	906,907	65,119	128,184	21,998	223,574	1,249,697	160,345
1971. . .	18,263	358,484	39,084	78,532	935,243	64,066	118,412	21,653	213,313	1,222,926	148,114
1972. . .	18,519	347,022	34,874	73,744	891,827	61,100	110,525	20,624	207,633	1,301,685	140,011
1973. . .	18,016	336,075	30,669	66,227	831,524	56,102	100,986	20,235	191,204	1,294,671	141,914

World's Largest Hydroelectric Generating Plants
Source: Bureau of Reclamation
Ultimate capacity of 1,000,000 kilowatts or more. UC - Under construction. NA - Not available. Year - Initial operation.

Name	Present Megawatts	Ultimate Megawatts	Year	Name	Present Megawatts	Ultimate Megawatts	Year
Itaipu, Brazil-Paraguay	...	10,710	U.C.	The Dalles, U.S.	1,291	1,807	1957
Grand Coulee, U.S.	2,161	9,780	1941	Mica, Canada	...	1,740	U.C.
Guri, Venezuela	524	6,500	1967	Kemano, Canada.	813	1,670	1954
Sayansk, USSR.	...	6,400	U.C.	Beauharnois, Canada	1,021	1,670	1950
Krasnoyarsk, USSR.	6,096	6,096	1968	Cheboksary, USSR.	...	1,632	U.C.
Paulo Afonso, Brazil.	1,030	5,942	1955	Inguri, USSR.	...	1,600	U.C.
Churchill Falls, Canada.	1,900	5,225	1971	Kariba, Rhodesia	600	1,500	1959
Bratsk, USSR. . . . . \	4,500	4,600	1964	Liukiahsia, China	...	1,500	1963
Sukhovo, USSR.	...	4,500	U.C.	Tumut-3, Australia.	750	1,500	1972
Ust-Illimsk, USSR.	720	4,300	U.C.	McNary, U.S.	980	1,406	1953
Cabora Basa, Portugal.				Jupia, Brazil.	600	1,400	1966
(Mozambique).	...	4,000	U.C.	Marimbondo, Brazil.	...	1,400	U.C.
Inga, Zaire.	350	3,700	U.C.	Saratov, USSR	...	1,359	1967
Chief Joseph, U.S.	1,024	3,642	1956	Daniel Johnson, Canada.	165	1,353	1970
Ilha Soltena, Brazil	...	3,200	U.C.	Hoover, U.S.	1,345	1,345	1936
John Day, U.S.	2,160	2,700	1968	Wanapum, U.S.	831	1,330	1964
Nurek, USSR.	...	2,700	U.C.	Zeya, USSR.	...	1,290	U.C.
Volga—22nd Congress,.				Priest Rapids, U.S.	789	1,262	1959
USSR.	2,543	2,560	1958	Castaic, U.S.	...	1,250	U.C.
Volga—V.I.Lenin, USSR.	2,100	2,300	1955	Keban, Turkey	620	1,240	U.C.
W.A.C. Bennett, Canada.	1,816	2,270	1969	Kettle Rapids, Canada.	612	1,224	1970
Iron Gate, Romania-Yugo.	500	2,160	U.C.	Sir Adam Beck (#2), Canada. .	1,224	1,224	1954
Saad-El-Aali,				Rocky Beach, U.S.	775	1,215	1961
(High Aswan), Egypt	1,750	2,100	1967	Furnas, Brazil.	900	1,200	1963
Robert Moses-Niagara, U.S. . .	1,950	1,950	1961	Toktogul, USSR.	...	1,200	U.C.
St. Lawrence Power Dam, ...				El Chocon, Argentina.	...	1,200	U.C.
U.S./Canada	1,824	1,824	1958	Manicouagan No. 3, Canada . . .	...	1,176	U.C.

Name	Pres. Mega.	Ult. Mega.	Year	Name	Pres. Mega.	Ult. Mega.	Year
Sanmen-Hsia, China	...	1,100		Manicouagan No. 2, Canada	...	1,015	1965
Nizhne-Kamskaya, U.S.S.R.	...	1,090	U.C.	Votkinsk, U.S.S.R.	...	1,000	1961
Dworshak, U.S.A.	90	1,060	U.C.	Mangla, Pakistan	300	1,000	U.C.
Bersimis No. 1, Canada	912	1,050	1956	Chirkey, U.S.S.R.	...	1,000	U.C.
Bhakra, India	450	1,050	1963	Kaniji, Nigeria	...	1,000	U.C.
Estreito, Brazil	1,050	1,050	1969	Northfield Mountain, U.S.A.	...	1,000	U.C.
Salto Osorio, Brazil	...	1,050	U.C.	Chivor, Colombia	...	1,000	U.C.
Lago Delio, Italy	...	1,016	U.C.	Blenheim-Gilboa, U.S.A.	...	1,000	U.C.

Non-Federal Hydroelectric Plants in U.S.
Capacities of 100,000 Kilowatts or More as of January 1, 1973
Auxiliary and Pumped Storage Units are not included in Hydroelectric Capacities
Source: Federal Power Commission, Bureau of Power

Plant	State	Owner	Kilowatts
Robert Moses, Niagara	N. Y.	Power Authority State of N. Y.	1,953,900
Robert Moses, (Massena)	N. Y.	Power Authority State of N. Y.	912,000
Wanapum	Wash.	Grant County Dist. No. 2	831,250
Priest Rapids	Wash.	Grant County Dist. No. 2	788,500
Wells	Wash.	Douglas County PUD No. 1	774,300
Rocky Reach	Wash.	Chelan County Dist. No. 1	711,550
Boundary	Wash.	Seattle Dept. of Lighting	551,000
Conowingo	Md.	Philadelphia Electric Co.	474,480
Hells Canyon	Ore.	Idaho Power Co.	391,500
Brownlee	Idaho	Idaho Power Co.	360,400
Ross	Wash.	Seattle Dept. of Lighting Co.	360,000
Edward Hyatt	Calif.	Calif. Dept. of Water Resources.	351,000
Cowans Ford	N. C.	Duke Power Co.	350,000
Upper Smith Mt.	Va.	Appalachian Power Co.	300,200
Mossyrock	Wash.	City of Tacoma	300,000
New Colgate	Calif.	Yuba County Water Agency	284,400
Noxon Rapids	Mont.	The Washington Water Power Co.	282,880
Round Butte	Ore.	Portland Gen. Elec. Co.	247,050
Safe Harbor	Pa.	Safe Harbor Water Power Corp.	228,000
Walter Bouldin	Ala.	Alabama Power Co.	225,000
Rock Island	Wash.	Chelan County Dist. No. 1	212,100
Swift No. 1	Wash.	Pacific Power and Light Co.	204,000
Cabinet Gorge	Idaho	The Washington Water Power Co.	200,000
Saluda	S. C.	So. Carolina Electric and Gas Co.	197,500
Oxbow	Oreg.	Idaho Power Co.	190,000
White Rock	Calif.	Sacramento Mun. Utility Dist.	190,000
Caribou No. 1 & 2	Calif.	Pacific Gas and Electric Co.	184,800
Gaston	N. C.	Virginia Electric and Power Co.	177,920
Lay Dam	Ala.	Alabama Power Co.	177,000
Osage	Mo.	Union Electric Co. of Mo.	172,000
Kerr	Mont.	The Montana Power Co.	168,000
Lewis Smith	Ala.	Alabama Power Co.	157,500
James B. Black	Calif.	Pacific Gas and Electric Co.	154,800
Martin Dam	Ala.	Alabama Power Co.	154,200
Camino	Calif.	Sacramento Mun. Utility Dist.	142,500
Pit No. 5	Calif.	Pacific Gas and Electric Co.	140,560
Comerford	N. H.	New England Power Co.	140,400
S. C. Moore	N. H.	New England Power Co.	140,400
Keowee	S. C.	Duke Power Co.	140,000
Gorge	Wash.	Seattle Department of Lighting Co.	137,700
New Don Pedro	Calif.	Turlock Modesto Irr. Dist.	136,515
Merwin	Wash.	Pacific Power and Light Co.	135,000
D. R. Holm	Calif.	San Francisco Utilities Commission.	135,000
Haas	Calif.	Pacific Gas and Electric Co.	135,000
Jaybird	Calif.	Sacramento Mun. Util. Dist.	133,000
Pinopolis	S. C.	So. Carolina Public Service Authority	132,615
Mammoth Pool	Calif.	Southern California Edison Co.	129,360
Logan-Martin	Ala.	Alabama Power Co.	128,250
Balch No. 1 & 2	Calif.	Pacific Gas and Electric	128,200
Keokuk	Iowa	Union Electric Co.	124,800
Poe	Calif.	Pacific Gas and Electric Co.	124,200
Mayfield	Wash.	City of Tacoma	121,500
Calderwood	Tenn.	Tapoco Inc.	121,500
Diablo	Wash.	Seattle Department of Lighting Co.	120,000
Belden	Calif.	Pacific Gas and Electric Co.	117,900
Rock Creek	Calif.	Pacific Gas and Electric Co.	113,400
Cheoah	N. C.	Tapoco Inc.	110,000
Middle Fork American	Calif.	Placer County Water Agency	109,800
Markham Ferry	Okla.	Grand River Dam Auth.	108,000
Walters	N. C.	Carolina Power and Light Co.	108,000
Yale	Wash.	Pacific Power and Light Co.	108,000
Pelton	Oreg.	Portland General Electric Co.	108,000
Holtwood	Pa.	Pennsylvania Power and Light Co.	107,200
Big Creek No. 3	Calif.	Southern California Edison Co.	106,500
Pit No. 7	Calif.	Pacific Gas and Electric Co.	104,400
Hawks Nest	W. Va.	Union Carbide Corp.	102,000
Roanoke Rapids	N. C.	Virginia Electric and Power Co.	100,080
Jordan No. 1	Ala.	Alabama Power Co.	100,000

World Electric Power
Source: Federal Power Commission

Country	Kw[1]	Kwhrs.[2]	Country	Kw[1]	Kwhrs.[2]
United States	332,606	1,552,757	France	36,326	131,583
USSR	153,790	659,210	Italy	31,034	106,329
United Kingdom	61,372	222,295	China (Mainland)	17,000	50,000
Japan	59,482	305,917	India	15,493	55,247
Germany (West)	48,812	210,985	Subtotal	810,291	3,556,596
Canada	54,376	262,273	World Total	1,060,768	4,515,101

(1) As of January 1, 1974; Kilowatts in thousands. (2) Year ended December 31, 1973; kilowatt-hours in millions.

Nuclear Power Reactors in U.S.

Source: U.S. Atomic Energy Commission (June 30, 1974)

State	Site	Plant Name	Capacity (kilowatts)	Utility	Commercial Operation
Alabama	Decatur	Browns Ferry Unit 1	1,065,000	Tennessee Valley Authority	1974
	Decatur	Browns Ferry Unit 2	1,065,000	Tennessee Valley Authority	1974
	Decatur	Browns Ferry Unit 3	1,065,000	Tennessee Valley Authority	1975
	Dothan	Joseph M. Farley	829,000	Alabama Power Co.	1975
Arkansas	Russellville	Arkansas Unit 1	850,000	Ark. Power & Light Co.	1974
California	Humboldt Bay	Humboldt Bay Power Unit 3	65,000	Pacific Gas & Electric Co.	1963
	San Clemente	San Onofre Unit 1	430,000	So. Calif. Ed. & San Diego Gas & El. Co.	1968
	Diablo Canyon	Diablo Canyon Unit 1	1,084,000	Pacific Gas & Electric Co.	1975
	Clay Station	Rancho Seco Station	804,000	Sacramento Mun. Utility District.	1974
Colorado	Platteville	Ft. St. Vrain Station.	330,000	Public Service Co. of Colo.	1974
Connecticut	Haddam Neck	Haddam Neck.	575,000	Conn. Yankee Atomic Power Co.	1968
	Waterford	Millstone Station: Unit 1	652,100	Northeast Utilities	1971
	Waterford	Millstone Station: Unit 2	828,000	Northeast Utilities	1974
Florida	Florida City	Turkey Point Unit 3	693,000	Fla. Power & Light Co.	1972
	Florida City	Turkey Point Unit 4	693,000	Fla. Power & Light Co.	1973
	Red Level	Crystal River Unit 3	825,000	Fla. Power Corp.	1974
	Ft. Pierce	St. Lucie Plant: Unit 1	801,000	Fla. Power & Light Co.	1975
Georgia	Baxley	Edwin I. Hatch Unit 1	786,000	Georgia Power Co.	1974
Illinois	Morris	Dresden Station: Unit 1	200,000	Commonwealth Edison Co.	1960
	Morris	Dresden Station: Unit 2	809,000	Commonwealth Edison Co.	1970
	Morris	Dresden Station: Unit 3	809,000	Commonwealth Edison Co.	1971
	Zion	Zion: Unit 1	1,050,000	Commonwealth Edison Co.	1973
	Zion	Zion: Unit 2	1,050,000	Commonwealth Edison Co.	1974
	Cordova	Quad-Cities Station: Unit 1	800,000	Comm. Ed. Co.-Ia.-Ill. Gas & Elec. Co.	1972
	Cordova	Quad-Cities Station: Unit 2	800,000	Comm. Ed. Co.-Ia.-Ill. Gas & Elec. Co.	1972
Iowa	Palo	Duane Arnold Unit 1	569,000	Iowa Electric Light and Power Co.	1974
Maine	Wiscasset	Maine Yankee Atomic Power	790,000	Me. Yankee Atomic Power Co.	1972
Maryland	Lusby	Calvert Cliffs Unit 1	845,000	Baltimore Gas and Electric Co.	1974
	Lusby	Calvert Cliffs Unit 2	845,000	Baltimore Gas and Electric Co.	1975
Massachusetts	Rowe	Yankee Station	175,000	Yankee Atomic Elec'..c Co.	1961
	Plymouth	Pilgrim Station: Unit 1	664,000	Boston Edison Co.	1972
Michigan	Big Rock Point	Big Rock Point	75,000	Consumers Power Co.	1965
	South Haven	Palisades Station	700,000	Consumers Power Co.	1971
	Bridgman	Donald C. Cook Unit 1	1,060,000	Ind.& Michigan Electric Co.	1974
Minnesota	Monticello	Monticello	545,000	Northern States Power Co.	1971
	Red Wing	Prairie Island Unit 1	530,000	Northern States Power Co.	1973
	Red Wing	Prairie Island Unit 2	530,000	Northern States Power Co.	1974
Nebraska	Fort Calhoun	Ft. Calhoun Unit 1	457,000	Omaha Public Power District	1973
	Brownville	Cooper Station	778,000	Pub. Power Dist. Ia. Power	1974
New Jersey	Toms River	Oyster Creek Unit 1	640,000	Jersey Central Power Co.	1969
New York	Indian Point	Indian Point Unit 1	265,000	Consolidated Edison Co.	1962
	Indian Point	Indian Point Unit 2	873,000	Consolidated Edison Co.	1973
	Indian Point	Indian Point Unit 3	965,000	Consolidated Edison Co.	1974
	Scriba	Nine Mile Point: Unit 1	625,000	Niagara Mohawk Power Co.	1969
	Ontario	R.E. Ginna Unit 1	490,000	Rochester Gas & Electric Co.	1970
	Scriba	James A. Fitzpatrick	821,000	Power Authority of State of N.Y.	1973
North Carolina	Southport	Brunswick Steam Unit 1	821,000	Carolina Power and Light Co.	1975
	Southport	Brunswick Steam Unit 2	821,000	Carolina Power and Light Co.	1974
Oregon	Prescott	Trojan Nuclear: Unit 1	1,130,000	Portland General Electric Co.	1975
Pennsylvania	Peach Bottom	Peach Bottom Unit 1	40,000	Philadelphia Electric Co.	1967
	Peach Bottom	Peach Bottom Unit 2	1,065,000	Philadelphia Electric Co.	1973
	Peach Bottom	Peach Bottom Unit 3	1,065,000	Philadelphia Electric Co.	1974
	Shippingport	Shippingport Unit 1	90,000	Duquesne Light Co.	1957
	Shippingport	Beaver Valley: Unit 1	852,000	Duquesne Light Co.-Ohio Edison Co.	1975
	Goldsboro	Three Mile Island: Unit 1	819,000	Metropolitan Edison Co.	1974
South Carolina	Hartsville	H. B. Robinson Unit 2	700,000	Carolina Power & Light Co.	1971
	Seneca	Oconee Unit 1	886,000	Duke Power Co.	1973
	Seneca	Oconee Unit 2	886,000	Duke Power Co.	1973
	Seneca	Oconee Unit 3	886,000	Duke Power Co.	1974
Tennessee	Daisy	Sequoyah Unit 1	1,140,000	Tennessee Valley Authority	1975
Vermont	Vernon	Vermont Yankee	513,900	Vt. Yankee Nu. Power Corp.	1972
Virginia	Gravel Neck	Surry Power Unit 1	788,000	Va. Electric & Power Co.	1972
	Gravel Neck	Surry Power Unit 2	788,000	Va. Electric & Power Co.	1973
	Mineral	North Anna Unit 1	898,000	Va. Electric & Power Co.	1975
Washington	Richland	N. Rector/WPPSS Steam	800,000	Atomic Energy Commission	1966
Wisconsin	Genoa	Genoa Station	50,000	Dairyland Power Corporation	1971
	Two Creeks	Point Beach Unit 1	497,000	Wis. Mich. Power Co.	1970
	Two Creeks	Point Beach Unit 2	497,000	Wis. Mich. Power Co.	1972
	Carlton	Kewaunee Unit 1	541,000	Wis. Mich. Power Co.	1973

Nuclear plant capacity (kilowatts): In operation 29,123,000, being built 57,970,000; planned (reactors ordered) 115,948,000; total 203,041,000.

Production of Electric Energy in the U. S.

Source: The Federal Power Commission

These amounts include both the privately-owned and publicly-owned utilities.

Calendar Year	Total 1,000 Kw. hrs.	Hydro 1,000 Kw. hrs.	Steam 1,000 Kw. hrs.	Gas Turbine(a) 1,000 Kw. hrs.	Internal Comb'n 1,000 Kw. hrs.	Coal Short tons	Oil 42 Gal. Barrels	Gas 1,000 Cu. ft.
1935	95,287,390	38,372,154	56,144,412		770,824	32,714,761	11,256,565	124,117,769
1940	141,837,010	47,321,278	93,001,735		1,513,997	51,473,881	16,325,122	180,096,185
1945	222,486,283	79,970,312	140,435,268		2,080,703	74,724,956	20,228,215	326,211,969
1950	329,141,343	95,938,317	229,543,366		3,659,660	91,870,770	75,420,490	628,918,834
1955	547,037,985	112,275,069	430,119,086		3,943,830	143,759,195	75,273,863	1,153,279,586
1960	753,350,271	145,516,253	603,341,840		4,492,178	176,633,789	85,340,108	1,724,762,376
1965	1,055,251,929	193,850,643	856,312,128		5,089,198	244,788,119	115,202,583	2,321,100,937
1968	1,329,443,027	222,490,584	1,101,767,366		5,185,000	297,779,069	188,641,862	3,147,908,961
1969	1,442,182,474	250,192,655	1,178,182,761	8,227,148	5,579,910	310,316,640	250,937,800	3,487,642,263
1970	1,531,608,921	247,456,119	1,262,358,866	15,732,082	6,061,854	320,818,141	335,503,752	3,931,996,247
1971 (Prelim.)	1,613,935,744	266,320,232	1,319,291,654	22,072,221	6,251,637	327,926,249	396,237,967	3,992,980,610
1972 (Prelim.)	1,747,322,933	272,733,504	1,438,420,059	29,493,248		351,050,000	493,930,000	3,978,700,000

(a)Data prior to 1969 included under steam.

Notable Steamships and Motorships

Source: Lloyd's Register of Shipping as of May 1, 1974
Gross tonnage is a measurement of enclosed space (1 gross ton - 100 cu. ft.)

World's Largest Passenger Ships
30,000 gross tons and over

Name-registry	Gross ton.	Lgth. Ft.	Bdth. Ft.
France, Fr.	66,348	1035	110
Queen Elizabeth 2, Br.	65,863	963	105
Raffaello, It.	45,933	904	101
Michelangelo, It.	45,911	904	101
Canberra, Br.	44,807	818	102
Oriana, Br.	41,910	804	97
*United States, U.S.	38,216	990	101
Rotterdam, Neth.	37,783	748	94
Nieuw Amsterdam, Neth.	36,982	758	88
Windsor Castle, Br.	36,277	783	92
Leonardo Da Vinci, It.	33,340	767	92
Eugenio C., It.	30,567	713	96
S. A. Vaal, S. Af. (1)	30,213	760	90
Ogden Bridgestone, Pan.	36,125	690	106
Tohbei Maru, Jap.	35,491	806	105
Kazutama Maru, Jap.	34,529	656	103
Antilla Bay, Neth.	34,015	710	105
Dovertown, Br.	34,000	710	106
Japan Ambrose, Jap.	33,287	748	105
Sovietskaya Rossiya, USSR	33,154	713	94
Descartes, Fr.	32,702	721	104
Delta Norte, U.S.	32,325	893	100
Delta Sud, U.S.	32,325	893	100
Delta Mar, U.S.	32,306	893	100
Kosmonaut Gagarin, USSR	32,291	760	101
Garmula, Br.	32,213	679	103
Sovietskaya Ukraina, USSR	32,024	713	94
Providence Multina, Fr.	32,000	710	106
Hampshire, Br.	32,000	679	103
Hoegh Multina, Nor.	31,918	679	103
Hassi R'Mel, Alg.	31,420	656	96
Tatsuno Maru, Jap.	31,083	663	98
Dart Atlantic, Br.	31,036	759	100
Dart Europe, Bel.	31,036	759	100
Dart America, Br.	31,036	759	100

*Remeasured 1972

Container, Liquefied Gas, Misc. Ships
31,000 gross tons and over

Name-registry	Gross ton.	Lgth. Ft.	Bdth. Ft.
Norman Lady, Br.	76,416	818	131
Benjamin Franklin, Fr.	75,000	894	134
Cardigan Bay, Br.	58,899	950	106
Kowloon Bay, Br.	58,889	950	106
Liverpool Bay, Br.	58,889	950	106
Tokyo Bay, Br.	58,889	950	106
Osaka Bay, Br.	58,889	950	106
Nedlloyd Delft, Neth.	58,716	941	106
Nedlloyd Dejima, Neth.	58,716	941	106
City of Edinburgh, Br.	58,440	950	106
Hamburg Express, Ger.	58,088	943	105
Tokio Express, Ger.	58,082	895	105
Benavon, Br.	57,887	950	106
Benalder, Br.	57,887	850	106
Bremen Express, Ger.	57,535	941	106
Hong Kong Express, Ger.	57,535	941	106
Korrigan, Fr.	57,249	946	105
Toyama, Nor.	56,450	902	106
Esso Fuji, Pan.	55,897	807	131
Elbe Maru, Jap.	51,623	882	105
Kitano Maru, Jap.	51,159	856	105
Kurama Maru, Jap.	51,139	856	105
Kamakura Maru, Jap.	51,139	856	105
Rhine Maru, Jap.	51,085	856	105
Nihon, Sw.	50,805	902	105
Jutlandia, Den.	49,890	900	106
Selandia, Den.	49,890	900	106
Gadila, Br.	48,862	842	114
Gadinia, Br.	48,662	842	114
Gari, Br.	48,662	852	114
Yusho Maru, Jap.	47,783	744	114
Amirrosios, Pan.	45,000	666	113
Arctic Tokyo, Lib.	44,089	798	111
Polar Alaska, Lib.	44,089	798	111
Remuera, Br.	42,007	826	105
Kanayama Maru, Jap.	41,939	734	113
Sea-Land Exchange, U.S.	41,555	946	105
Sea-Land Market, U.S.	41,127	946	105
Sea-Land Commerce, U.S.	41,127	946	105
Sea-Land Trade, U.S.	41,127	946	105
Sea-Land Finance, U.S.	41,127	946	105
Sea-Land Resource, U.S.	41,127	946	105
Sea-Land Galloway, U.S.	41,127	946	105
Sea-Land McLean, U.S.	41,127	946	105
Bridgestone Maru V, Jap.	40,934	690	106
Verrazano Bridge, Jap.	39,153	867	105
Izumisan Maru, Jap.	38,872	705	105
New York Maru, Jap.	38,825	862	105
Kiso Maru, Jap.	38,540	857	105
Svendborg Maersk, Den.	38,540	850	105
Kurobe Maru, Jap.	37,845	854	105
New Jersey Maru, Jap.	37,799	863	105
Munchen, Ger.	37,134	857	105
Bilderdyk, Neth.	36,974	857	105
World Rainbow, Pan.	36,917	734	113
Atlantic Forest, Nor.	36,870	857	106
Acadia Forest, Nor.	36,862	857	106
World Bridgestone, Pan.	36,556	690	106

Nuclear Powered Merchant Ships

Name-registry	Gross ton.	Lgth. Ft.	Bdth. Ft.
Otto Hahn, Ger.	16,871	564	76
Savannah, U.S.	15,585	595	78
Lenin, USSR	14,067	439	90
Mutsu, Jap.	8,350	426	62

Oil Tankers
284,000 tons deadweight and over

Deadweight tonnage is the weight (long tons) or cargo, fuel etc., which a vessel is designed to carry safely.

Name-registry	Dwght ton.	Lgth. Ft.	Bdth. Ft.
Globtik London, Br.	476,293	1243	203
Globtik Tokyo, Br.	476,094	1243	203
Nisseki Maru, Jap.	366,813	1138	179
Universe Iran, Lib.	326,933	1132	175
Universe Kuwait, Lib.	326,848	1132	175
Universe Korea, Lib.	326,676	1132	175
Universe Portugal, Lib.	326,676	1132	175
Universe Ireland, Lib.	326,585	1132	175
Universe Japan, Lib.	326,562	1132	175
Venoil, Lib.	320,581	1115	175
Venpet, Lib.	320,499	1115	175
Arteaga, Sp.	317,985	1141	175
Butron, Sp.	317,985	1141	175
Radny, Nor.	286,160	1138	170
Arietta Livanos, Lib.	285,050	1140	170
Eugenie Livanos, Lib.	285,075	1140	170
Richard Maersk, Den.	284,600	1140	170
Rosa Maersk, Den.	284,600	1140	170
Romo Maersk, Den.	284,600	1140	170
Regina Maersk, Den.	284,500	1140	170
Roy Maersk, Den.	284,500	1140	170
Ras Maersk, Den.	284,500	1140	170
Robert Maersk, Den.	284,500	1140	170
Adele, Lib.	284,500	1140	170
Rania Chandris, Lib.	284,500	1140	170

Bulk, Ore, Bulk Oil & Ore Oil Carriers
165,000 tons deadweight and over

Name-registry	Dwght ton.	Lgth. Ft.	Bdth. Ft.
Svealand, Sw.	282,450	1109	179
Docecanyon, Lib.	271,235	1113	180
Tarfala, Sw.	265,000	1099	170
Usa Maru, Jap.	264,523	1105	179
Naess Ambassador, Br.	264,485	1101	176
Lauderdale, Br.	260,424	1101	176
Licorne Atlantique, Fr.	260,417	1101	176
La Loma, Br.	245,288	1069	170
Hoegh Hood, Nor.	244,677	1069	170

Name-registry	Dwght ton.	Lgth. Ft.	Bdth. Ft.	Name-registry	Dwght ton.	Lgth. Ft.	Bdth. Ft.
Hoegh Hill, Nor.	241,447	1069	170	Arafura Maru, Jap.	180,626	1023	156
Havkong, Nor.	231,045	1075	161	Larina, Lib.	175,927	984	157
Falkefjell, Nor.	231,045	1075	160	Romantic, Lib.	174,107	995	151
Andros Atlas, Gr.	224,074	1061	158	Rhetoric, Lib.	173,668	995	151
Berge Brioni, Lib.	223,968	1030	165	Cedros, Lib. (2)	170,418	995	142
Berge Adria, Nor.	223,968	1030	164	Cetra Centaurus, Fr.	170,414	981	143
Berge Istra, Lib.	223,963	1030	165	Bunga Mawar, Malaysia	169,623	918	155
San Giusto, It.	223,819	1901	149	Sir John Hunter, Br.	169,080	965	145
Andros Antares, Gr.	223,808	1061	158	Tyne Bridge, Br.	166,753	965	145
Andros Aries, Gr.	223,808	1061	158	Garden Green, Lib.	166,476	967	155
Sysla, Nor.	223,500	1096	149	English Bridge, Br.	166,417	965	145
Alva Bay, Br.	222,331	1091	149	Hampton Maru, Jap.	166,191	974	155
Alva Sea, Br.	221,457	1090	149	Furness Bridge, Br.	166,064	965	145
Tantalus, Br.	215,680	1075	164	Pacific Maru, Jap.	165,739	974	155
Tartar, Nor.	215,621	1075	164	Bristol Maru, Jap.	165,733	976	155
Atsuta Maru, Jap.	215,600	1075	164	Japan Mimosa, Jap.	165,707	976	155
Jarl Malmros, Sw.	215,500	1075	164	Laura, Lib.	165,636	974	155
Tsurumi Maru, Jap.	215,000	1075	164	(1) Former name. Transvaal Castle, (2) Salt/oil carrier, operates			
Adria Maru, Jap.	108,671	1023	156	as an oil carrier.			

U. S. Exports and Imports of Leading Commodities

Source: Bureau of International Commerce, Dept. of Commerce, (Value in millions of dollars)

Commodity	Exports 1972	Exports 1973	Imports 1972	Imports 1973
Total	$48,979	$70,223	$55,583	$69,121
Food and live animals	5,661	11,931	6,370	7,986
Meat	252	444	1,223	1,668
Dairy products and eggs	143	56	111	156
Cheese	135	242	1,205	1,387
Fish			92	105
Grains and preparations	3,501	8,495		
Wheat and wheat flour	1,452	4,151		
Rice	389	541		
Corn	1,241	2,837		
Fruit and nuts	526	662	496	577
Vegetables	209	307	350	409
Sugar			832	918
Coffee, green			1,182	1,566
Beverages and Tobaccos	908	1,008	1,009	1,213
Alcoholic Beverages			824	996
Tobacco, unmanufactured	639	681	157	187
Crude materials, inedible other than fuels	5,030	8,384	3,860	4,988
Synthetic rubber	161	196		
Ores and metal scrap	508	1,081	1,022	1,291
Coal	984	1,014		
Petroleum and products	444	518	4,300	7,548
Animal and vegetable oils and fats	508	684	180	255
Chemicals	4,133	5,748	2,015	2,437
Medicinal and Pharmaceutical	474	626	149	164
Machinery and transport equipment	21,533	27,842	17,420	20,970
Automotive engines	485	578	846	983
Agricultural machinery	249	346	237	313
Tractors and parts	249	339	211	292
Metalworking machinery	410	489	140	188
Textile and leather machinery	272	375	638	625
Other nonelectrical machinery	1,040	1,300	796	1,052
Electrical apparatus	3,698	5,031	3,377	4,471
Transport equipment	7,971	10,255	9,504	10,876
New motor vehicles	2,064	2,666	5,724	6,479
Aircraft and parts	3,015	4,124	415	554
Other manufactured goods	8,094	11,112	18,332	21,382
Rubber manufactures	231	308		
Paper and manufactures	726	919	1,261	1,457
Diamonds excluding industrial	172	314	637	827
Metals and manufactures	828	1,111	6,004	6,885
Iron and steel-mill products	800	1,258	2,743	2,769
Nonferrous base metals	567	951	1,754	1,994
Textiles other than clothing	779	1,225	1,528	1,568
Clothing	215	254	1,883	2,154
Other transactions	1,560	1,844	1,598	1,790

U.S. Merchandise Exports and Imports, by Continent

Source: International Trade Analysis Division, Dept. of Commerce (Value in millions of dollars)

Year	Exports Western Hemisp.	Exports Europe	Exports Asia & Oceania	Exports Africa	General Imports Western Hemisp.	General Imports Europe	General Imports Asia & Oceania	General Imports Africa
1965	9,932	9,397	7,129	1,071	9,257	6,292	4,999	867
1968	13,411	11,347	8,656	1,221	14,148	10,338	7,640	1,090
1969	14,713	12,642	9,327	1,324	15,547	10,334	9,141	1,008
1970	15,611	14,817	11,294	1,502	16,928	11,395	10,515	1,090
1971	16,850	14,562	11,086	1,631	18,730	12,881	12,694	1,217
1972	19,694	16,180	12,407	1,500	21,930	15,744	16,279	1,578
1973	25,003	23,157	20,395	2,081	27,229	19,687	19,614	2,552

United States Foreign Trade with Leading Countries

Source: Bureau of International Commerce, Dept. of Commerce
(Value in millions of dollars)

Exports from the U.S. to the following areas and countries and imports into the U. S. from those areas and countries:	Exports		Imports	
	1972	1973	1972	1973
Total	$49,778	$71,314	$55,583	$69,121
Western Hemisphere	19,694	25,003	21,930	27,229
Canada	12,415	15,073	14,927	17,670
19 American Republics	6,467	8,921	5,772	7,790
Central American Common Market	439	621	485	685
Latin American Free Trade Ass'n	5,576	7,708	4,949	6,668
Dominican Republic	183	229	232	307
Panama	216	286	55	67
Bahamas	144	208	247	286
Jamaica	221	268	181	176
Netherlands Antilles	122	159	400	733
Trinidad and Tobago	121	133	251	409
Europe	16,180	23,157	15,744	19,687
OECD Countries (Excludes dependencies and Yugoslavia)	15,173	21,094	15,268	18,994
Western Europe	15,361	21,361	15,423	19,167
European Economic Community	11,900	16,746	12,489	15,513
Belgium and Luxembourg	1,138	1,622	968	1,261
France	1,609	2,263	1,369	1,717
Germany, Federal Republic of	2,807	3,756	4,250	5,318
Italy	1,434	2,119	1,757	1,989
Netherlands	1,871	2,860	639	925
United Kingdom	2,658	3,563	2,987	3,642
Denmark	258	404	367	458
Ireland	125	159	152	202
European Free Trade Association	1,775	2,307	1,984	2,500
Austria	96	118	173	228
Finland	91	133	142	178
Iceland	20	26	59	77
Norway	213	297	241	261
Portugal	211	232	149	192
Sweden	472	542	601	753
Switzerland	672	960	619	811
Greece	250	375	90	92
Spain	930	1,319	600	761
Turkey	317	347	106	129
Yugoslavia	169	236	150	167
Eastern Europe	819	1,796	321	519
Asia	11,373	18,651	15,134	18,060
NearEast	1,974	3,041	773	1,370
Egypt	76	225	17	26
Iraq	23	56	9	16
Iran	558	771	199	340
Israel	557	961	222	265
Jordan	65	79	—	—
Kuwait	111	119	49	65
Lebanon	130	162	21	32
Saudi Arabia	314	442	194	507
Japan	4,963	8,312	9,064	9,645
East and South Asia	4,373	6,609	5,264	6,979
China, Republic of (Taiwan)	628	1,168	1,293	1,772
Hong Kong	489	740	1,249	1,444
India	350	525	427	437
Indonesia	308	442	278	499
Korea, Republic of	735	1,242	708	971
Malaysia	128	162	301	417
Singapore	385	684	265	459
Pakistan	183	239	40	39
Philippines	365	495	491	663
Thailand	172	256	116	140
Vietnam, Republic of	318	314	2	3
Oceania	1,034	1,744	1,145	1,554
Australia	842	1,439	807	1,062
New Zealand and Western Samoa	136	249	277	410
Africa	1,500	2,081	1,578	2,552
North Africa excluding Egypt	346	504	309	565
Algeria	98	160	104	215
Ethiopia	24	25	58	79
Libya	85	104	116	216
Morocco	58	113	11	13
Tunisia	55	60	8	33
Western and Equatorial Africa	398	561	674	1,266
Angola	26	38	90	166
Ghana	44	63	80	90
Ivory Coast	22	69	92	108
Liberia	41	46	52	72
Nigeria	114	161	271	650
Central and Southern Africa	754	1,016	594	721
Kenya	24	39	27	26
South Africa, Republic of	602	746	325	374
Zaire	37	115	43	70

Important Waterways and Canals

The St. Lawrence & Great Lakes Waterway, the largest inland navigation system on the continent, extends from the Atlantic Ocean to Duluth at the western end of Lake Superior, a distance of 2,342 miles. With the deepening of channels and locks to 27 ft., ocean carriers are able to penetrate to ports in the Canadian interior and the American midwest.

The major canals are those of the St. Lawrence-Great Lakes waterway — the 3 new canals of the St. Lawrence Seaway, with their 7 locks, providing navigation for vessels of 26 foot draught from Montreal to Lake Ontario; the Welland Ship Canal by-passing the Niagara River between Lake Ontario and Lake Erie with its 8 locks, and the Sault Ste. Marie Canal and lock between Lake Huron and Lake Superior. These 16 locks overcome a drop of 580 ft. from the head of the lakes to Montreal. From Montreal to Lake Ontario the former bottleneck of narrow, shallow canals and of slow passage through 22 locks has been overcome, giving faster and safer movement for larger vessels. The new locks and linking channels now accommodate all but the largest ocean-going vessels and the upper St. Lawrence and Great Lakes are open to 80% of the world's saltwater fleet.

Subsidiary Canadian canals or branches include the St. Peters Canal between Bras d'Or Lakes and the Atlantic Ocean in Nova Scotia; the St. Ours and Chambly Canals on the Richelieu River, Quebec; the Ste. Anne and Carillon Canals on the Ottawa River; the Rideau Canal between the Ottawa River and Lake Ontario, the Trent and Murray Canals between Lake Ontario and Georgian Bay in Ontario and the St. Andrew's Canal on the Red River. The commercial value of these canals is not great but they are maintained to control water levels and permit the passage of small vessels and pleasure craft. The Canso Canal, completed 1957, permits shipping to pass through the causeway connecting Cape Breton Island with the Nova Scotia mainland.

In 1973 the St. Lawrence Seaway carried its greatest volume of traffic since it opened to deep-draft navigation in 1959. Cargo tonnage on the Montreal-Lake Ontario section of the Seaway amounted to 57,600,000 tons, an increase of 7.4% over 1972. General cargo showed a considerable decrease compared to the previous year, but was compensated for by the increase in bulk cargo.

St. Lawrence Seaway provides a navigational channel with a minimum water depth of 27 ft. to link the Great Lakes to the Atlantic Ocean. A vessel entering the Great Lakes from the Atlantic ascends 20 ft. above sea level in the 1,000-mile long reach up the Gulf of St. Lawrence and St. Lawrence River to Montreal, Quebec. At Montreal, the vessel enters the first of 7 new locks, 5 of which are in Canadian waters and 2 within United States waters, which raise or lower shipping a total of 226 ft. in the 182-mile stretch of the St. Lawrence River between Montreal and Lake Ontario. Crossing Lake Ontario, the vessel enters Canada's 28-mile-long Welland Canal, with 8 locks to compensate for the difference in elevation of 326 ft. between Lake Ontario and Lake Erie.

The signing of the Merchant Marine Bill of 1970 removed the major obstacles to the future development of the St. Lawrence Seaway. The bill eliminated interest payments on the Seaway's debt, gave official "fourth seacoast" identity to the Great Lakes-St. Lawrence Waterway, and enabled lake shipbuilders to qualify for federal shipbuilding subsidies.

Richard M. Nixon, President of the U.S. and Pierre E. Trudeau, Prime Minister of Canada, signed the Great Lakes Water Quality Agreement in 1971.

Saint Lawrence Seaway Development Corporation (U.S.), Seaway Circle, Massena, New York, David W. Oberlin, Administrator.

St. Lawrence Seaway Authority (Canada), Ottawa, Ontario, Mr. Paul D. Normandeau, president.

The Welland Canal overcomes the 326-ft. drop of Niagara Falls and the rapids of the Niagara River. It has 8 locks, each 859 ft. long, 80 ft. wide and 30 ft. deep. Regulations permit ships of 730-ft. length and 75-ft. beam to transit.

In 1973 cargo tonnage on the Welland section of the Seaway totalled 67,200,000 tons in comparison with 64,200,000 tons in 1972.

Sault Ste. Marie Canal reported 110,688,294 short tons of freight passed through during the season of 1973 compared with 97,047,762 for 1972.

Panama Canal

The Panama Canal is a lock and lake canal, crossing the Isthmus of Panama from the Caribbean Sea in a southeasterly direction to the Bay of Panama of the Pacific Ocean. It is 50 mi. long from deep water to deep water, at least 500 ft. wide at the bottom of excavated channels, 110 ft. wide in lock chambers, which have a usable length of 1,000 ft. Depth varies, but is not less than 40 ft. Average time in transit is 12 hours.

Gatun Dam blocks the Chagres river near its Atlantic mouth, creating Gatun lake, 23¾ mi. long, 85 ft. above sea level, about 45 ft. deep. Ships ascend to the lake by locks and then pass through Gaillard (formerly Culebra) Cut, 8 mi. long.

Cargo tonnage on the Panama Canal in fiscal 1973 amounted to 127,500,000 compared with 111,100,000 tons in 1972. Transit of oceangoing ships in fiscal 1973 totaled 14,238 compared with 14,238 in fiscal 1972 (same figure). Toll collections in fiscal 1973 were $113,400,000 compared with $101,500,000 in 1972.

Improvements have included the widening of the eight-mile long channel through Gaillard Cut from 300 to 500 feet, costing $60,000,000; illumination of Gaillard Cut and installation of new towing locomotives at the locks costing $8,000,000.

Thatcher Ferry Bridge, opened 1962, spans Panama Canal 201 ft. above the water level near Balboa. It is a steel-arch bridge, about 1 mi. long, with 3 spans and 4 lanes. It cost $20,000,000 authorized by the U.S. Congress in 1956.

Other Foreign Canals

One of the busiest canals in Europe is the Gota, in Sweden, 115 mi. long. Others: Kiel Canal, Germany, connecting the Baltic with the North Sea, 61 mi.; Elbe, Germany, 41 mi.; Amsterdam, Netherlands, 16 mi. Also the Manchester Ship Canal, England, 35.5 mi.

United States Foreign Trade, by Economic Classes

Source: International Trade Analysis Div., Dept. of Commerce, (Value in Millions of dollars)

Year (cal.)	Value of domestic exports					Value of imports				
	Crude Mater'ls	Crude Foods	Manu'd Foods	Semi Manuf's	Finish. Manuf's	Crude Mater'ls	Crude Foods	Manu'd Foods	Semi-Manuf's	Finish. Manuf's
1965	2,887	2,587	1,590	4,114	16,008	3,709	2,008	1,877	4,964	8,871
1970	4,492	2,748	1,921	6,866	26,563	4,126	2,579	3,519	7,263	22,464
1972	5,242	3,738	2,325	6,163	31,500	5,354	2,868	4,320	10,262	32,751
1973	7,826	8,804	3,524	9,250	40,820	7,795	3,552	5,494	13,043	39,238

Total agricultural exports were valued as follows (in millions of dollars): 1965—1,942; 1968—2,177; 1969—2,057; 1970—2,524; 1971—2,884; 1972—3,325; 1973—5,290. Agricultural imports for consumption were valued as follows (in millions of dollars): 1965—864; 1968—834; 1969—909; 1970—797; 1971—685; 1972—801; 1973—1,080.

Shortest Navigable Distances Between Ports

Source: Distances Between Ports, 1965. Defense Mapping Agency Hydrographic Center.

Distances shown are in nautical miles (1,852 meters or about 6,076.115 feet).

To get statute miles, multiply by (one statute mile equals 5,280 feet).

TO	FROM New York	Montreal	Colon[1]	TO	FROM San Fran.	Vancouver	Panama[1]
Algiers, Algeria	3,617	3,600	4,745	Acapulco, Mexico	1,833	2,613	1,426
Amsterdam, Netherlands	3,438	3,162	4,825	Anchorage, Alas.	1,872	1,444	5,093
Baltimore, Md.	417	1,769	1,901	Bombay, India	9,794	9,578	12,962
Barcelona, Spain	3,714	3,697	4,842	Calcutta, India	8,991	8,728	12,154
Boston, Mass.	386	1,308	2,157	Colon, Panama[1]	3,298	4,076	44
Buenos Aires, Argentina	5,817	6,455	5,472	Djakarta, Indonesia	7,641	7,360	10,637
Cape Town, So. Africa[2]	6,786	7,118	6,494	Haiphong, No. Vietnam	6,496	6,231	9,673
Cherbourg, France	3,154	2,878	4,541	Hong Kong	6,044	5,777	9,195
Cobh, Ireland	2,901	2,603	4,308	Honolulu, Hawaii	2,091	2,423	4,685
Copenhagen, Denmark	3,846	3,570	5,233	Los Angeles, Calif.	371	1,161	2,913
Dakar, Senegal	3,335	3,566	3,694	Manila, Philippines	6,221	5,976	9,347
Galveston, Texas	1,882	3,165	1,492	Melbourne, Australia	6,970	7,343	7,928
Gibraltar[3]	3,204	3,187	4,332	Pusan, So. Korea	4,914	4,623	8,074
Glasgow, Scotland	3,086	2,691	4,508	Saigon, So. Vietnam	6,878	6,664	10,017
Halifax, N.S.	600	895	2,295	San Francisco, Calif.		812	3,245
Hamburg, W. Germany	3,674	3,398	5,061	Seattle, Wash.	807	126	4,020
Hamilton, Bermuda	697	1,572	1,659	Shanghai, China	5,396	5,110	8,566
Havana, Cuba	1,186	2,473	998	Singapore	7,353	7,078	10,505
Helsinki, Finland	4,309	4,033	5,696	Suva, Fiji	4,749	5,183	6,325
Istanbul, Turkey	5,001	4,984	6,129	Valparaiso, Chile	5,140	5,915	2,616
Kingston, Jamaica	1,474	2,690	551	Vancouver, B.C.	812		4,032
Lagos, Nigeria	4,883	5,130	5,049	Vladivostok, Sov. Union	4,563	4,378	7,741
Lisbon, Portugal	2,972	2,943	4,152	Yokohama, Japan	4,536	4,262	7,682
Marseille, France	3,891	3,874	5,019				

TO	FROM New York	Montreal	Colon[1]	TO	FROM Port Said	Cape Town[2]	Singapore
Montreal, Quebec	1,460		3,126				
Naples, Italy	4,181	4,164	5,309	Bombay, India	3,049	4,616	2,441
Nassau, Bahamas	962	2,274	1,166	Calcutta, India	4,695	5,638	1,649
New Orleans, La.	1,708	2,991	1,389	Dar es Salaam, Tanzania	3,238	2,365	4,042
New York, N.Y.		1,460	1,974	Djakarta, Indonesia	5,293	5,276	525
Norfolk, Va.	294	1,700	1,779	Hong Kong	6,462	7,006	1,454
Oslo, Norway	3,827	3,165	5,053	Kuwait	3,360	5,176	3,833
Piraeus, Greece	4,688	4,671	5,816	Manila, Philippines	6,348	6,777	1,330
Port Said, Egypt	5,123	5,106	6,251	Melbourne, Australia	7,842	5,963	3,844
Rio de Janeiro, Brazil	4,770	5,354	4,367	Saigon, So. Vietnam	5,667	6,263	649
St. John's, Nfld.	1,093	1,043	2,695	Singapore	5,018	5,614	
San Juan, Puerto Rico	1,399	2,445	993	Yokohama	7,907	8,503	2,889
Southampton, England	3,189	2,913	4,576				

(1) Colon on the Atlantic is 44 nautical miles from Panama (port) on the Pacific. (2) Cape Town is 35 nautical miles northwest of the Cape of Good Hope. (3) Gibraltar (port) is 24 nautical miles east of the Straits of Gribaltar.

Mississippi River System and Gulf Intracoastal Waterway

Source: Corps of Engineers, Department of the Army.

(Note—The Mississippi River System comprises main channels and all tributaries of the Mississippi, Illinois, Missouri and Ohio Rivers. The Gulf Intracoastal Waterway, 1,137 miles long, extends from Apalachee Bay, Florida, to the Mexican border).

Port	1963 Tonnage	1972 Tonnage	1973 Tonnage	Port	1963 Tonnage	1972 Tonnage	1973 Tonnage
Minneapolis	825,429	1,671,323	1,849,783	Lake Providence	Not Compiled	366,387	282,022
St. Paul	4,210,106	5,059,621	5,080,428	Vicksburg	1,258,508	2,571,546	2,787,239
Metropolitan St. Louis	*	22,008,151	18,319,148	Natchez	582,942	898,682	501,433
Memphis	7,024,509	10,612,101	10,392,243	Baton Rouge	30,272,282	52,903,352	53,568,530
Helena	1,740,938	2,672,209	3,224,197	New Orleans	79,130,710	125,719,378	136,104,315
Greenville	1,250,608	2,278,634	2,374,822				

*Port limits expanded in 1972.

Reach

Port	1963 Tonnage	1972 Tonnage	1973 Tonnage	Port	1963 Tonnage	1972 Tonnage	1973 Tonnage
Mississippi R. System	271,319,518	419,805,850	419,942,374	Baton Rouge to			
Minneapolis to the Gulf	157,807,291	271,980,414	276,346,896	N. Orleans	69,913,376	163,345,088	169,849,105
Minneapolis to St. Louis	30,943,237	60,746,385	58,064,198	New Orleans to the Gulf	99,554,315	171,370,861	182,338,659
St. Louis to Cairo	35,726,911	67,545,404	63,385,876	Gulf Intracoastal			
Cairo to Baton Rouge	49,370,417	102,698,573	100,395,636	Waterway	67,320,002	108,999,010	100,767,257

Ton-Mileage of Freight Carried on Inland Waterways

Source: Corps of Engineers, Department of the Army.

System	1972	1971	1970
Atlantic coast waterways	29,238,516,000	28,619,707,000	28,571,788,000
Gulf coast waterways	32,513,287,000	30,473,095,000	28,582,418,000
Pacific coast waterways	9,549,062,000	8,525,013,000	8,397,133,000
Mississippi River system, including Ohio River and tributaries	158,453,365,000	142,385,476,000	138,533,627,000
Great Lakes System includes Alaskan waterways		105,027,016,000	114,475,222,000
Total	108,938,909,000	315,030,307,000	318,560,188,000

Commerce at Principal North American Ports

Excluding Great Lakes Shipping
Source: Corps of Engineers, U.S. Army
Calendar Year 1972. Canadian Ports 1970. In tons of 2,000 pounds.

Ports Handling Over 7,500,000 Tons

Port of New York, N.Y. and N.J.	196,842,857
New Orleans, La.	125,719,378
Houston, Texas	71,430,789
Philadelphia Harbor, Pa.	48,356,885
Norfolk Harbor, Va.	47,781,241
Baltimore Harbor and Channels, Md.	45,798,776
Baton Rouge, La.	52,903,352
Beaumont, Texas	32,391,055
Tampa Harbor, Fla.	43,230,138
Los Angeles Harbor, Calif.	23,836,690
Corpus Christi, Texas	22,300,918
Port Arthur, Texas	21,707,770
Portland Harbor, Me.	30,682,669
Paulsboro, N.J. and Vicinity	25,664,052
Mobile Harbor, Ala.	27,291,063
Boston, Mass.	26,483,438
Marcus Hook, Pa. and Vicinity	23,491,196
Huntington, W. Va.	21,147,502
Lake Charles, La.	17,028,562
Texas City, Tex.	20,355,038
Richmond Harbor, Calif.	15,650,278
Portland, Ore.	17,086,391
Clairton-Elizabeth, Pa.	9,521,480
Seattle Harbor, Wash.	14,662,811
Port of Newport News, Va.	10,549,835
Long Beach, Calif.	20,795,050
Pascagoula Harbor, Miss.	12,434,967
Penn Manor, Pa. and Vicinity	7,795,120
New Castle, Del. and Vicinity	11,380,860
New Haven Harbor, Conn.	13,162,993
Port of Metropolitan St. Louis.	22,008,151
Jacksonville Harbor, Fla.	14,885,935
Cincinnati, Ohio	9,252,158
Providence River and Harbor, R.I.	9,200,386
Pittsburgh, Pa.	8,267,168
Port of Albany, N.Y.	10,252,329
Louisville, Ky.	9,487,006
Memphis, Tenn.	10,612,101
Port Everglades Harbor, Fla.	11,182,662
Vancouver, B.C.	26,517,891
Sept-Iles, P.Q.	24,240,914
Montreal, P.Q.	22,376,281
Thunder Bay, Ont.	20,754,165
Port Cartier, P.Q.	16,017,407
Hamilton, Ont.	2,881,123
Halifax, N.S.	11,072,468
Quebec, P.Q.	8,552,289
Baie Comeau, P.Q.	7,695,715

Other ports Maine to Washington

Searsport Harbor, Maine	1,198,562
Portsmouth Harbor, N.H.	2,188,071
Burlington Harbor, Vt.	524,614
Beverly Harbor, Mass.	251,075
Fall River Harbor, Mass.	4,300,619
Gloucester Harbor, Mass.	351,465
New Bedford, Fairhaven Harbor, Mass.	474,308
Salem Harbor, Mass.	1,562,159
Bridgeport Harbor, Conn.	3,471,623
New London Harbor, Conn.	5,332,989
Norwalk Harbor, Conn.	812,865
Stamford Harbor, Conn.	1,080,615
Hempstead Harbor, N.Y.	4,125,250
Huntington Harbor, N.Y.	398,853
Peekskill Harbor, N.Y.	223,485
Plattsburg, N.Y.	487,066
Port Chester Harbor, N.Y.	499,096
Port Jefferson Harbor, N.Y.	5,488,186
Rondout Harbor, N.Y.	647,009
Tarrytown Harbor, N.Y.	597,487
Camden-Gloucester, N.J.	11,779,298
Trenton Harbor, N.J.	1,176,981
Aliquippa-Rochester, Pa.	5,979,526
Chester, Pa.	608,029
Wilmington Harbor, Del.	3,602,395
Washington Harbor, D.C.	1,961,286
Alexandria, Va.	258,007
Port of Hopewell, Va.	921,560
Port of Richmond, Va.	1,902,441
Morehead City Harbor, N.C.	1,422,933
Port of Wilmington, N.C.	7,589,971
Charleston Harbor, S.C.	7,476,635
Georgetown Harbor, S.C.	1,524,102
Brunswick Harbor, Ga.	1,263,086
Savannah Harbor, Ga.	8,037,171
Canaveral Harbor, Fla.	1,835,329
Charlotte Harbor, Fla.	2,302,392
Fernandina Harbor, Fla.	382,683
Miami Harbor, Fla.	4,483,676
Palm Beach Harbor, Fla.	1,114,865
Panama City Harbor, Fla.	1,662,637
Pensacola Harbor, Fla.	2,014,682

Port St. Joe Harbor, Fla.	668,601
St. Petersburg Harbor, Fla.	506,501
Weedon Island, Fla.	490,424
Guntersville, Ala.	1,462,242
Greenville, Miss.	2,278,634
Gulfport Harbor, Miss.	1,197,621
Natchez, Miss.	898,682
Vicksburg, Miss.	2,571,546
Brownsville, Texas	3,875,289
Freeport Harbor, Texas	5,977,249
Galveston, Texas.	4,273,647
Harbor Island, Texas	3,215,952
Orange, Texas.	1,485,565
Port Isabel, Texas.	478,410
Matagorda Ship Channel, Port Lavaca, Tex.	4,855,803
Sabine Pass Harbor, Texas.	235,323
Victoria, Texas.	2,973,220
Helena, Ark.	2,672,209
Chattanooga, Tenn.	1,657,952
Knoxville, Tenn.	602,029
Nashville, Tenn.	3,571,014
Kansas City, Mo.	1,470,763
Mount Vernon, Ind.	3,496,967
Minneapolis, Minn.	1,671,323
St. Paul, Minn.	5,059,621
Carpinteria, Calif.	529,107
Crescent City Harbor, Calif.	275,701
El Segundo, Calif.	5,757,833
Gaviota, Santa Barbara County, Calif.	236,959
Humboldt Harbor and Bay, Calif.	1,074,126
Moss Landing Harbor, Calif.	278,405
Oakland Harbor, Calif.	5,907,709
Redwood City Harbor, Calif.	959,443
San Diego Harbor, Calif.	1,666,283
San Francisco Harbor, Calif.	2,589,746
San Luis Obispo Harbor, Calif.	1,396,343
Stockton, Calif.	1,514,790
Ventura Harbor, Calif.	2,353,120
Astoria, Ore.	1,921,799
Coos Bay, Ore.	6,543,775
Oregon Slough (No. Portland Hbr.), Ore.	322,020
Anacortes Harbor, Wash.	3,316,013
Bellingham Bay and Harbor, Wash.	2,183,859
Everett Harbor, Wash.	5,218,986
Grays Harbor and Chehalis River, Wash.	3,785,907
Hammersley Inlet, Wash. (Shelton Hbr.).	1,119,264
Longview, Wash.	5,431,193
Olympia Harbor, Wash.	2,027,183
Port Angeles Harbor, Wash.	2,849,121
Port Gamble Harbor, Wash.	860,607
Port Townsend Harbor, Wash.	1,399,092
Tacoma Harbor, Wash.	8,477,318
Vancouver, Wash.	3,188,758
Willapa Riv. & Hbr., Naselle Riv., Wash.	364,389

Alaska, Hawaii, Puerto Rico

Anchorage, Alaska	2,058,199
Ketchikan Harbor, Alaska.	2,186,282
Sitka Harbor, Alaska.	1,243,437
Skagway Harbor, Alaska.	1,387,562
Whittier Harbor, Alaska.	646,609
Wrangell Harbor, Alaska.	1,169,203
Barbers Point, Oahu, Hawaii.	3,420,445
Hilo Harbor, Hawaii, Hawaii.	1,108,067
Honolulu Harbor, Oahu, Hawaii.	7,960,447
Kahului Harbor, Maui, Hawaii.	1,297,829
Kaumalapau Harbor, Lanai, Hawaii.	286,876
Kaunakakai Harbor, Molokai, Hawaii.	751,455
Kawaihae Harbor, Hawaii, Hawaii.	303,116
Nawiliwili Harbor, Kauai, Hawaii.	582,887
Pearl Harbor, Oahu, Hawaii.	728,475
Wake Island Harbor.	199,499
Mayaguez Harbor, P.R.	264,583
Ponce Harbor, P.R.	756,691
San Juan Harbor, P.R.	9,527,784
St. Thomas Harbor, V.I.	377,913
Guam Island, Pacific Ocean	297,237
Corner Brook, Nfld.	1,225,372
St. John's, Nfld.	794,494
Charlottetown, P.E.I.	554,399
Hantsport, N.S.	1,648,191
Sydney, N.S.	1,966,105
Saint John, N.B.	6,400,885
Port Alfred, Que.	4,973,666
Sorel, Que.	6,813,817
Trois Rivieres, Que.	4,954,649
Port Colborne, Ont.	2,259,345
Sarnia, Ont.	7,331,360
Saulte Ste. Marie, Ont.	5,753,245
Toronto, Ont.	5,162,904
Windsor, Ont.	3,550,556
Nanaimo, B.C.	2,492,110
New Westminster, B.C.	4,564,477
Powell River, B.C.	1,783,686
Victoria, B.C.	2,071,342

Commerce at Great Lakes Ports

Source: Corps of Engineers, U.S. Army
Calendar Year 1972, in tons of 2,000 pounds

Duluth-Superior Harbor, Minn. & Wis.	37,895,954	Port Dolomite, Mich.	3,263,721
Silver Bay, Minn.	10,742,092	Port Gypsum, Mich.	341,929
Taconite Harbor, Minn.	12,053,875	Port Huron, Mich.	857,217
Ashland Harbor, Wis.	280,100	Port Inland, Mich.	4,199,020
Green Bay Harbor, Wis.	2,823,604	Port of Detroit, Mich.	29,913,128
Kewaunee Harbor, Wis.	1,205,791	Presque Isle Harbor, Mich.	3,450,111
Manitowoc Harbor, Wis.	1,818,313	St. Clair, Mich.	3,950,487
Milwaukee Harbor, Wis.	5,373,630	St. Ignace, Mich.	130,950
Oak Creek, Wis.	920,766	St. Joseph Harbor, Mich.	475,139
Port Washington Harbor, Wis.	717,312	Sault Ste. Marie, Mich.	97,309
Racine Harbor, Wis.	100,192	Stoneport, Mich.	7,707,485
Sheboygan Harbor, Wis.	221,128	Traverse City Harbor, Mich.	446,244
Two Rivers Harbor, Wis.	99,447	Wells, Mich.	132,781
Alabaster, Mich.	591,227	Port of Chicago, Ill.	46,838,259
Alpena Harbor, Mich.	3,380,410	Waukegan Harbor, Ill.	436,710
Calcite, Mich.	12,805,756	Buffington Harbor, Ind.	1,731,519
Cheboygan Harbor, Mich.	114,919	Gary Harbor, Ind.	8,751,620
Detour, Mich.	209,424	Indiana Harbor, Ind.	17,610,662
Drummond Island, Mich.	1,784,051	Michigan City Harbor, Ind.	371
Escanaba, Mich.	10,954,237	Ashtabula Harbor, Ohio.	12,063,864
Frankfort Harbor, Mich.	1,353,101	Cleveland Harbor, Ohio.	23,865,810
Gladstone Harbor, Mich.	292,031	Conneaut Harbor, Ohio.	14,683,654
Gd. Haven Harbor & Gd. River, Mich.	2,977,109	Fairport Harbor, Ohio.	2,913,317
Holland Harbor, Mich.	261,738	Huron Harbor, Ohio	3,380,742
Lime Island, Mich.	85,474	Lorain Harbor, Ohio.	10,173,023
Ludington Harbor, Mich.	3,368,015	Marblehead, Ohio.	1,866,226
Mackinaw City, Mich.	68,619	Sandusky Harbor, Ohio	5,612,730
Manistee Harbor, Mich.	522,741	Toledo Harbor, Ohio.	25,248,550
Manistique Harbor, Mich.	135	Erie Harbor, Pa.	1,360,244
Marquette Harbor, Mich.	849,253	Ogdensburg Harbor, N. Y.	215,542
Marysville, Mich.	633,656	Oswego Harbor, N.Y.	779,417
Menominee Harbor, Mich. & Wis.	152,568	Port of Buffalo, N.Y.	9,226,253
Muskegon Harbor, Mich.	2,835,823	Rochester (Charlotte) Harbor, N.Y.	366,285
Petoskey Penn Dixie Harbor, Mich.	473,074		

Value of U.S. Merchandise Exports and Imports

Source: International Trade Analysis Division, Dept. of Commerce
Value in Millions of dollars (Revised)

	U.S. exports					U.S. imports		
		Domestic and foreign						
Year	Total	Military aid	Excl. military aid	Domestic merchandise	Foreign merchandise	General	For consumption	Gross merchandise balance[1]
1950	10,279	[2]282	9,997	10,146	133	8,954	8,844	1,043
1955	15,554	1,256	14,298	15,426	128	11,566	11,519	2,732
1960	20,608	949	19,659	20,408	201	15,073	15,069	4,586
1965	27,521	779	26,742	27,178	343	21,427	21,345	5,315
1970	43,224	565	42,659	42,590	634	39,952	39,756	2,707
1972	49,778	560	49,219	48,979	800	55,583	55,310	—6,364
1973	71,314	516	70,798	70,223	1,091	69,121	68,656	1,677

(1.) Balance represents exports exclu ing military grant-aid valued f.a.s. less imports which are valued generally at the market value in the foreign country. Export values include both commercially-financed shipments and shipments under government-financed programs. (2) Includes data from April when shipments under the program began.

Total Exports and Exports Financed by Foreign Aid

Source: Bureau of International Commerce, Dept. of Commerce

(In millions of dollars)	1965	1968	1969	1970	1971	1972	1973
Exports, total.	27,530	34,636	38,006	43,224	44,130	49,778	71,314
Agricultural commodities.	6,306	6,300	6,004	7,349	7,786	9,505	17,855
Nonagricultural commodities.	20,445	27,763	31,328	35,310	35,763	39,714	52,943
Manufactured goods (domestic).	17,439	23,818	26,785	29,343	30,443	33,742	44,702
Military grant—aid.	779	573	674	565	581	560	516
Export financed under P.L. 480	1,323	1,178	1,019	1,021	983	1,064	750
Sales for foreign currency.	899	539	337	276	174	70	4
Donations, including disaster relief.	253	251	256	255	291	376	209
Barter for strategic goods.	19	3	—	—	—	—	—
Long-term dollar credit sales.	152	384	426	490	518	618	537

Merchant Fleets of the World

Source: Maritime Administration, U.S. Dept. of Commerce

Excludes ships operating exclusively on the Great Lakes and inland waterways and special types such as channel ships, icebrakers, cable ships, etc., and merchant ships owned by any military force.

Gross Tons: Volume, not weight; each cargogross ton represents 100 cubic ft. of enclosed space. **Deadweight Tons:** Number of long tons (2,240 lbs. ea.) of cargo, fuel, etc., a ship can carry at maximum draft.

Registry Jan. 1, 1973 (Tonnage in 1,000)	Total No.	Gross tons	Dwt. tons	(Psgr.-Cargo) No.	(Psgr.-Cargo) Dwt.	Freighters No.	Freighters Dwt.	Tankers No.	Tankers Dwt.
Total-All Countries	21,600	275,727	446,370	789	3,443	11,170	90,511	4,813	220,481
United States[1]	1,016	12,775	17,467	116	727	587	7,400	274	8,636
Privately owned	596	9,511	13,717	5	36	320	4,817	241	8,210
Government owned	420	3,264	3,750	111	691	267	2,583	33	426
United Kingdom	1,596	29,405	47,783	32	213	662	6,297	442	26,924
Australia	83	903	1,277	—	—	36	275	13	272
British Colonies	93	1,343	2,181	5	17	36	253	22	1,246
Canada	71	308	383	15	17	26	99	21	183
Cyprus	532	3,138	4,547	6	39	414	2,973	52	903
Ghana	16	118	154	—	—	16	154	—	—
India	264	3,011	4,669	9	56	185	1,962	16	638
Malaysia	21	285	413	2	5	12	124	1	2
New Zealand	39	115	152	—	—	15	142	—	—
Nigeria	15	98	142	—	—	15	142	—	—
Pakistan	58	499	664	7	58	49	576	—	—
Singapore	274	2,173	3,285	17	81	195	1,445	29	754
*Albania	10	147	189	—	—	7	56	—	—
Algeria	19	147	189	—	—	12	71	4	82
Argentina	161	1,255	1,722	9	39	67	575	56	803
Belgium	74	1,121	1,716	2	25	32	412	15	505
Brazil	251	2,042	2,983	8	18	157	1,133	52	1,212
*Bulgaria	110	724	1,043	4	8	58	353	17	308
Burma	10	58	73	2	3	8	70	—	—
Chile	46	374	554	3	5	30	274	5	140
China (Taiwan)	156	1,404	2,139	8	39	95	767	14	606
*China (Communist)	293	1,736	2,368	22	47	210	1,743	34	384
Colombia	42	229	303	—	—	40	271	1	30
*Cuba	59	360	475	2	10	40	361	7	77
*Czechoslovakia	11	103	148	—	—	8	53	—	—
Denmark	299	3,919	6,553	7	16	181	1,430	57	4,120
Ecuador	12	107	152	—	—	5	41	5	98
Ethiopia	5	37	53	—	—	3	17	2	36
Finland	200	1,370	2,019	7	9	126	671	47	1,209
France	413	8,188	13,482	8	39	172	1,675	137	9,731
Germany (West)	702	7,455	11,417	5	17	504	4,153	70	3,228
*Germany (East)	141	1,029	1,430	5	33	105	768	9	290
Greece	1,724	19,852	32,315	60	247	900	8,417	308	12,201
Honduras	11	53	51	—	—	—	—	—	—
*Hungary	18	50	69	—	—	18	69	—	—
Iceland	27	53	74	1	2	18	49	—	—
Indonesia	144	505	616	30	95	92	416	15	82
Iran	23	219	305	—	—	17	217	5	84
Ireland	19	183	276	—	—	8	43	2	3
Israel	67	612	843	—	—	47	313	—	—
Italy	635	8,358	12,832	55	225	198	1,372	220	5,915
Ivory Coast	16	117	161	—	—	14	150	—	—
Japan	2,145	34,389	57,286	32	79	1,004	8,159	485	27,694
Korea (South)	122	1,008	1,647	1	11	77	494	25	809
*Korea (North)[2]	8	30	33	1	2	5	26	—	—
Kuwait	33	653	1,104	—	—	27	314	6	790
Lebanon	39	116	159	1	4	33	140	—	—
Liberia	2,211	51,602	95,315	25	172	495	5,026	864	59,684
Malagasy	13	64	96	—	—	9	50	4	46
Maldives	27	79	102	—	—	23	92	—	—
Mexico	44	385	586	—	—	17	124	23	397
Morocco	16	43	61	—	—	10	46	—	—
Netherlands	434	4,606	6,708	10	79	287	2,409	81	3,420
Norway	1,102	23,894	40,781	34	79	347	2,909	349	21,941
Panama	1,111	9,610	15,246	34	202	696	4,453	209	7,995
Peru	36	274	388	1	12	26	255	5	69
Philippines	157	749	1,050	18	33	99	676	28	200
Poland	257	1,897	2,648	2	7	177	1,483	3	49
Portugal	114	1,108	1,596	16	104	66	525	24	837
*Romania	68	453	632	1	2	46	239	3	91
Saudi Arabia	13	52	66	2	4	7	27	1	28
Somalia	217	1,609	2,337	2	8	178	1,558	11	218
South Africa	52	412	519	—	—	38	304	3	61
Spain	432	4,017	6,545	36	136	209	1,052	110	3,900
Sudan	7	36	44	—	—	6	39	—	—
Sweden	322	5,647	9,239	4	15	137	1,179	75	4,097
Switzerland	26	243	354	—	—	20	213	—	—
Thailand	25	138	230	—	—	14	76	10	152
Tunisia	10	25	34	—	—	7	15	2	15
Turkey	98	744	1,046	15	32	60	491	16	354
United Arab Republic	46	204	264	7	40	30	123	9	101
Uruguay	16	154	238	1	10	7	46	7	179
*USSR[2]	2,262	12,868	16,507	80	210	1,337	8,299	454	5,532
Venezuela	44	409	588	—	—	23	149	17	420
Yugoslavia	199	1,646	2,396	11	60	142	1,276	17	382

British Commonwealth

*Source material limited. (1)Excludes 73 non-merchant type ships which are currently in the National Defense Reserve Fleet. (2) Includes U.S. Government-owned ships transferred to USSR under lend-lease agreements, 42 of which are still under that registry and 2 under North Korean registry.

Notable Ocean Passages by Ships

Time	From	To	Distance Naut. mi.	Date	Ship
		One Hundred Years of Sailing Vessels			
16d	Liverpool......	New York.....	3,150	Nov. 1846	Yorkshire
76d 6h	San Francisco...	Boston.........	. . .	1853	Northern Light
12d 6h	Boston Light...	Light Rock....	. . .	1854	James Baines
89d	New York......	San Francisco...	15,091	1854	Flying Cloud
'89d 20h	New York......	San Francisco...	13,700	1860	Andrew Jackson
63d 18h 15m.	Liverpool......	Melbourne......	. . .	1868-69	Thermopylae
13d 1h 25m..	New York......	Liverpool.......	3,150	. . . .	Red Jacket
36d	50 S. Lat.......	Golden Gate....	. . .	. . . .	Starr King
12d 12h	Equator........	San Francisco...	. . .	. . . .	Golden Fleece
12d 4h 1m ..	Sandy Hook....	England........	3,013	1905	Atlantic
23d	England........	Sandy Hook....	3,013	1928	Atlantic
22d 6h 7m ..	Bishop's Rock...	Boston Light....	. . .	1936	Yankee
		Atlantic Crossings by Power Vessels			
29d 4h	Savannah......	Liverpool......	. . .	May 22, 1819	Savannah (Amer.) (a)
15d	Bristol.........	New York......	. . .	Apr. 1838	Great Western (Br.)
14d 8h	Liverpool......	New York......	3,150	July 1840	Britannia (Br.) (b)
9d 13h	Liverpool......	New York......	3,054	Aug. 1852	Baltic (Amer.)
8d 1h 45m...	Queenstown	New York......	2,780	1856	Persia
8d 2h 48m...	Queenstown	New York......	2,780	1866	Scotia
7d 4h 1m....	Queenstown	New York......	. . .	1867	City of Paris (Br.)
7d 22h 3m...	Queenstown	New York......	2,780	1869	City of Brussels (Br.)
7d 20h 9m...	Queenstown	New York......	2,780	1873	Baltic (Br.)
7d 15h 48m..	Queenstown	New York......	2,780	1875	City of Berlin (Br.)
7d 11h 37m..	Queenstown	New York......	2,780	1876	Germanic (Br.)
7d 10h 53m..	Queenstown	New York......	2,780	1877	Britannic (Br.)
7d 8h 0m ...	New York......	Queenstown.....	. . .	1879	Arizona (Br.)
6d 7h 23m...	Queenstown	New York......	2,780	1880	Arizona (Br.)
6d 18h 37m..	New York......	Queenstown.....	2,780	1882	Alaska (Br.)
6d 21h 40m..	Queenstown	New York......	2,780	1883	Alaska (Br.)
6d 10h 40m..	New York......	Queenstown.....	2,780	1884	Oregon (Br.)
6d 4h 34m...	Queenstown	New York......	2,780	1887	Umbria (Br.)
5d 1h 55m...	Queenstown	New York......	2,780	1888	Etruria (Br.)
5d 22h 50m..	New York......	Queenstown.....	2,780	1889	City of Paris (Br.)
5d 16h 31m..	Queenstown	New York......	2,780	1891	Teutonic (Br.)
5d 14h 24m..	Queenstown	New York......	2,780	1892	City of Paris (Br.)
5d 9h 6m....	Queenstown	New York......	2,780	1893	Campania (Br.)
5d 7h 23m...	Queenstown	New York......	2,780	1894	Lucania (Br.)
5d 15h 20m..	Southampton ...	New York......	3,189	1898	Kaiser Wilhelm Der Grosse (Ger.)
5d 7h 38m...	Sandy Hook....	Plymouth......	3,082	Sept. 1900	Deutschland (Ger.)
4d 11h 42m..	Queenstown	New York......	2,780	1909	Lusitania (Br.)
4d 10h 41m..	Queenstown	New York......	2,780	1910	Mauretania (Br.)
5d 6h 21m...	New York......	Cherbourg......	3,227	Oct. 1924	Leviathan (Amer.)
6d 5h 30m...	Cherbourg.....	Cape Henry.....	3,320	June 1927	U.S.S. Memphis (c)
4d 17h 42m..	Cherbourg.....	Ambrose Lt.....	3,164	July 1929	Bremen (Ger.)*
4d 14h 30m..	New York......	Plymouth......	3,082	July 1929	Bremen (Ger.)
4d 19h 57m..	Ambrose Lt.....	Cherbourg......	3,196	June 1933	Europa (Ger.)
4d 16h 48m..	Cherbourg.....	New York......	3,149	July 1933	Europa (Ger.)
4d 13h 58m..	Gibraltar.......	Ambrose Lt......	3,181	Aug. 1933	Rex (Ital.)
4d 14h 27m..	Cherbourg.....	Ambrose Lt.....	3,092	Nov. 1934	Bremen (Ger.)
4d 12h 24m..	Cherbourg.....	Ambrose Lt.....	3,158	May-June, '36	Queen Mary (Br.)*
3d 23h 02m..	Bishop's Rock..	Ambrose Lt.....	2,906	July-Aug., '37	Normandie (Fr.)
3d 22h 07m..	New York......	Southampton ...	2,936	Aug. 1937	Normandie (Fr.)
3d 20h 42m..	Ambrose Lt.....	Bishop's Rock ..	3,120	Aug. 10-14, '38	Queen Mary (Br.)
3d 21h 48m..	Bishop's Rock..	Ambrose Lt.....	3,120	Aug. 1948	Queen Mary (Br.)
3d 10h 40m..	Ambrose Lt.....	Bishop's Rock ...	2,942	July 3-7, 1952	United States U.S.)* (e)
3d 12h 12m..	Bishop's Rock...	Ambrose Lt.....	2,902	July 11-14, '52	United States (U.S.) (e)
3d 11h 24m..	Bishop's Rock...	Ambrose Lt.....	2,912	Aug. 20, 1973	Sea-Land Exchange (j)
		Other Ocean Passages			
3d 00h 36m..	San Pedro......	Honolulu......	2,226	June 1928	U.S.S. Lexington
3d 2h 30m...	San Francisco...	Oahu, Hawaii ...	2,091	July 16-19, '45	U.S.S. Indianapolis (d)
4d 8h 51m...	Gibraltar.......	Newport News...	3,360	Nov. 26, 1945	U.S.S. Lake Champlain
7d 18h 36m..	Japan..........	San Francisco...	5,000	July-Aug. 4, '50	U.S.S. Boxer
7d 13h......	Yokosuka......	Alameda.......	5,000	June 1-9, 1951	U.S.S. Philippine Sea
8d 11h......	Nantucket......	Portland, Eng....	3,161	Feb.25-Mar. 4, '58	U.S.S. Skate (f)
7d 5h.......	Lizard Head....	Nantucket, Mass.	. . .	Mar. 23-29, '58	U.S.S. Skate (f)
15d	Pearl Harbor....	Iceland (via N. Pole)......	. . .	July 23-Aug. 7, '58	U.S.S. Nautilus (g)
84d	New London.....	Rehoboth, Del...	41,500	Feb. 16-May 10,'60	S.S. Triton (h)
6d..........	Baffin Bay	N. Wk. Passage, Pac...........	850	Aug. 15-20, '60	U.S.S. Seadragon (i)
12d 16h 22m.	New York......	Cape Town.	6,786	Oct. 30-Nov. 11, '62	African Comet*

*Maiden voyage. (a) The Savannah, a fully rigged sailing vessel with steam auxiliary (over 300 tons, 98.5 ft. long, beam 25.8 ft., depth 12.9 ft.), was launched in the East River in 1818. It was the first ship to use steam in crossing any ocean. It was supplied with engines and detachable iron paddle wheels. On its famous voyage it used steam 105 hours during parts of 12 days. The world's first nuclear-powered merchant ship, the N.S. Savannah, was named for the old steamship. (b) First Cunard liner. (c) Carried Charles A. Lindbergh back to the United States after his flight from New York to Paris. (d) Carried Hiroshima atomic bomb in World War II. (e) Set world speed record; average speed eastbound on maiden voyage 35.59 knots (about 41 m.p.h.); westbound, 34.51 knots. (f) First atomic submarine to cross Atlantic both ways submerged. (g) World's first atomic submarine also first to make undersea voyage under polar ice cap, 1,830 mi. from Point Barrow, Alaska, to Atlantic Ocean, Aug. 1-4, 1958, reaching North Pole Aug. 3. Second undersea transit of the North Pole made by submarine USS Skate Aug. 11, 1958, during trip from New London, Conn., and return. (h) World's largest submarine. Nuclear-powered Triton was submerged during nearly all its voyage around the globe. It duplicated the route of Ferdinand Magellan's circuit (1519-1522), 30,708 mi., starting from St. Paul Rocks off the NE coast of Brazil, Feb. 24-Apr. 25, 1960, then sailed to Cadiz, Spain, before returning home. (i) First underwater transit of Northwest Passage. (j) Fastest freighter crossing of Atlantic.

Distances Between Great Lakes Ports
Lake Survey Center, 630 Federal Blvd. Detroit, Mich.

In Statute Miles	St. Lawrence				Erie					St. Clair and Huron				
	Quebec	Montreal	Ogdensburg	Kingston	Buffalo	Prt. Colborne	Erie	Cleveland	Toledo	Detroit	Port Huron	Bay City	Alpena	Collingwood
Quebec, Canada		157	283	346	553	531	596	691	768	775	837	999	994	1095
Montreal, Canada	157		126	189	396	374	439	534	611	618	680	842	837	938
Ogdensburg, New York	283	126		63	270	248	313	408	485	492	554	716	711	812
Kingston, Canada	346	189	63		208	186	251	346	423	430	492	654	649	750
Buffalo, New York	553	396	270	208		22	78	176	254	261	322	484	479	580
Port Colborne, Canada	531	374	248	186	22		65	160	237	244	306	468	463	564
Erie, Pennsylvania	596	439	313	251	78	65		102	185	191	253	415	410	511
Cleveland, Ohio	691	534	408	346	176	160	102		96	96	170	331	326	427
Toledo, Ohio	768	611	485	423	254	237	185	96		54	116	278	273	374
Detroit, Michigan	775	618	492	430	261	244	191	1008	54		62	224	219	320
Port Huron, Michigan	837	680	554	492	322	306	253	170	116	62		162	157	258
Bay City, Michigan	999	842	716	654	484	468	415	331	278	224	162		116	257
Alpena, Michigan	994	837	711	649	479	463	410	326	273	219	157	116		185
Collingwood, Canada	1095	938	812	750	580	564	511	427	374	320	258	257	185	
Oswego, New York	391	234	108	55	190	168	233	328	405	412	474	636	631	732
Rochester, New York	432	275	149	89	139	117	182	277	354	361	423	585	580	681
Toronto, Canada	506	349	223		161	77	55	120	215	292	299	361	523	518
Sault Ste. Marie	1106	949	823	761	592	575	522	438	385	331	269	232	137	259
Marquette, Michigan	1266	1109	983	921	751	735	682	598	545	491	429	391	297	418
Houghton, Michigan	1327	1170	1044	982	813	796	743	659	606	552	490	453	358	480
Ashland, Wisconsin	1455	1298	1172	1110	941	924	871	788	734	680	618	581	486	608
Duluth, Minnesota	1501	1344	1218	1156	986	970	917	833	781	726	664	627	532	653
Thunder Bay, Canada	1379	1222	1096	1034	864	848	795	711	658	604	542	505	410	531
Escanaba, Michigan	1213	1056	930	868	699	682	629	545	492	438	376	339	244	376
Green Bay, Wisconsin	1282	1125	999	937	767	751	698	614	561	507	445	407	313	444
Muskegon, Michigan	1308	1151	1025	963	794	777	724	640	587	533	471	434	339	471
Milwaukee, Wisconsin	1343	1186	1060	998	828	812	759	675	622	568	506	468	374	505
Chicago, Illinois	1408	1251	1125	1063	893	877	824	740	688	633	571	534	439	570

In Statute Miles	Ontario			Superior						Michigan				
	Oswego	Rochester	Toronto	Saulte Ste. Marie	Marquette	Houghton	Ashland	Duluth	Thunder Bay	Escanaba	Green Bay	Muskegon	Milwaukee	Chicago
Quebec, Canada	391	432	506	1106	1266	1327	1455	1501	1379	1213	1282	1308	1343	1408
Montreal, Canada	234	275	349	949	1109	1170	1298	1344	1222	1056	1125	1151	1186	1251
Ogdensburg, New York	108	149	223	823	983	1044	1172	1218	1096	930	999	1025	1060	1125
Kingston, Canada	55	89	161	761	921	982	1110	1156	1034	868	937	963	998	1063
Buffalo, New York	190	139	77	592	751	813	941	986	864	682	751	777	812	893
Port Colborne, Canada	168	117	55	575	735	796	924	970	848	629	698	724	759	824
Erie, Pennsylvania	233	182	120	522	682	743	871	917	795	545	614	640	675	740
Cleveland, Ohio	328	277	215	438	598	659	788	833	711	492	561	587	622	688
Toledo, Ohio	405	354	292	385	545	606	734	781	658	438	507	533	568	633
Detroit, Michigan	412	361	299	331	491	552	680	726	604	376	445	471	506	571
Port Huron, Michigan	474	423	361	269	429	490	618	664	542	339	407	434	468	534
Bay City, Michigan	636	585	523	232	391	453	581	627	505	244	313	339	374	435
Alpena, Michigan	631	580	518	137	297	358	486	532	410					
Collingwood, Canada	732	681	619	259	418	480	608	653	531	376	444	471	505	570
Oswego, New York		59	145	743	903	964	1092	1138	1016	850	919	945	980	1045
Rochester, New York	59		95	692	852	913	1041	1087	965	799	868	894	929	994
Toronto, Canada	145	95		630	790	851	979	1025	903	737	806	832	867	932
Sault Ste. Marie	743	692	630		159	221	349	394	273	219	288	314	349	414
Marquette, Michigan	903	852	790	159		84	213	261	171	378	447	474	508	573
Houghton, Michigan	964	913	851	221	84		131	179	116	440	509	535	570	635
Ashland, Wisconsin	1092	1041	979	349	213	131		93	164	568	637	663	698	763
Duluth, Minnesota	1138	1087	1025	394	261	179	93		195	614	682	709	743	808
Port Arthur, Canada	1016	965	903	273	171	116	164	195		492	560	587	621	686
Escanaba, Michigan	850	799	737	219	378	440	568	614	492		101	181	201	274
Green Bay, Wisconsin	919	868	806	288	447	509	637	682	560	101		171	180	255
Muskegon, Michigan	945	894	832	314	474	535	663	709	587	181	171		80	114
Milwaukee, Wisconsin	980	929	867	349	508	570	698	743	621	201	180	80		85
Chicago, Illinois	1045	994	932	414	573	635	763	808	686	274	255	114	85	

Fastest Scheduled Train Runs in United States and Canada

Source: Donald M. Steffee; figures are based on 1974 timetables

Electric Traction-Passenger-(80 m.p.h. and over)

Railroad	Train	From	To	Dis.	Time	Speed
Amtrak	Metroliners (14)	Baltimore	Wilmington	68.4	44	93.3
Amtrak	Metroliners (11)	Wilmington	Baltimore	68.4	44	93.3
Amtrak	Metroliners (3)	Wilmington	Baltimore	68.4	45	91.2
Amtrak	Metroliner	Newark	Philadelphia	80.5	56	86.2
Amtrak	Metroliner	Newark	North Philadelphia	76.0	53	86.0
Amtrak	Metroliner	Newark	Trenton	48.1	34	84.9
Amtrak	Metroliners (2)	Metro Park	Trenton	33.9	24	84.7
Amtrak	Metroliner	Baltimore	Philadelphia	94.0	67	84.2
Amtrak	Metroliners (2)	Newark	Philadelphia	80.5	58	83.3
Amtrak	Metroliner	No. Philadelphia	Newark	76.0	55	82.9
Amtrak	Metroliners (3)	Metro Park	Philadelphia	66.3	48	82.9
Amtrak	Metroliner	Baltimore	Capital Beltway	30.3	22	82.6
Amtrak	Metroliners (2)	Trenton	Newark	48.1	35	82.4
Amtrak	Metroliners (5)	Philadelphia	Newark	80.5	59	81.9
Amtrak	Metroliner	Newark	Philadelphia	80.5	59	81.9
Amtrak	Metroliner	Philadelphia	Baltimore	94.0	69	81.7
Amtrak	Metroliner	Trenton	Metro Park	33.9	25	81.3
Amtrak	Metroliners (4)	Philadelphia	Metro Park	66.3	49	81.2
Amtrak	Metroliner	Metro Park	Philadelphia	66.3	49	81.2
Amtrak	Metroliner	New York	Trenton	58.1	43	81.1
Amtrak	Metroliner	New York	Philadelphia	90.5	67	81.0

Diesel Traction-Passenger-(75 m.p.h. and over)

Railroad	Train	From	To	Dis.	Time	Speed
Canadian National	Turbotrain	Guildwood	Dorval	310.9	207	90.1
Canadian National	Turbotrain	Dorval	Guildwood	310.9	210	88.8
Canadian National	Rapido	Guildwood	Belleville	100.5	72	83.7
Canadian National	Rapido	Dorval	Brockville	115.3	86	80.4
Amtrak	Illini	Kankakee	Rantoul	57.9	44	79.0
Amtrak	Southwest Limited	Garden City	Lamar	99.9	76	78.9
Amtrak	Panama Limited; Shawnee	Champaign	Mattoon	44.6	34	78.7
Amtrak	Lone Star	Marceline	Carrollton	39.1	30	78.2
Canadian National	Ontarian	Trenton	Cobourg	31.2	24	78.0
Amtrak	Panama Limited; Shawnee	Centralia	Effingham	53.2	41	77.9
Amtrak	Southwest Limited	Dodge City	Hutchinson	120.1	93	77.5
Amtrak	Southwest Limited	Lamar	Garden City	99.9	78	76.8
Amtrak	Illinois Zephyr	Princeton	Kewanee	26.8	21	76.6
Canadian National	Bonaventure	Cobourg	Belleville	43.3	34	76.3
Canadian National	Lakeshore	Prescott	Cornwall	45.8	36	76.3
Amtrak	San Francisco Zephyr	Akron	McCook	143.0	114	75.3
Canadian National	Bonaventure	Brockville	Cornwall	57.6	46	75.1
Canadian National	Bonaventure	Cornwall	Brockville	57.6	46	75.1

Diesel Traction Passenger-(75 m.p.h. and over)

Railroad	Train	From	To	Dis.	Time	Speed
Sante Fe	Super C	Waynoka	Amarillo	205.2	175	70.3
Sante Fe	Super C	Winslow	Gallup	127.2	110	69.4
Sante Fe	Super C	Gallup	Winslow	127.2	110	69.4
Sante Fe	Super C	Vaughn	Clovis	130.8	115	68.3
Sante Fe	Super C	Wellington	Waynoka	106.6	95	67.2
Sante Fe	Super C	Amarillo	Waynoka	205.2	185	66.6
Sante Fe	Super C	Clovis	Vaughn	130.8	120	65.4
Southern Pacific	Blue Streak Merchandise	East Yard	Del Rio	171.2	159	64.6
Sante Fe	Super C	Gallup	Belen	144.4	135	64.2
Sante Fe	Super C	Emporia	Kansas City	112.1	105	64.1
Santa Fe	Super C	Kansas City	Emporia	112.1	105	64.1
Santa Fe	Super C	Waynoka	Wellington	106.6	100	64.0

Some Fast Railway Runs in the United States and Canada

Date	Railroad	Run	Miles	H.	M.	S.	M.P.H.
Aug., 1894	Atlantic Coast Line Route	Jacksonville-Washington	780.9	15	49		49.4
May, 1905	Atlantic City	Camden-Atlantic City	55.5		42	33	78.3
July, 1905	Atchison, Topeka & Santa Fe	Los Angeles-Chicago	2244.5	44	54		50.0
April, 1911	Lake Shore & Michigan Southern	Toledo-Elkhart	133.0	1	46		75.28
May, 1923	Canadian National	Montreal-Toronto	335	6	45	0	49.6
Nov., 1925	Canadian National	Montreal-Vancouver	2937.5	67	0	0	43.8
June, 1927	Pennsylvania	Washington-New York	224.6	3	7		72.1
May, 1934	Chicago, Burlington & Quincy	Denver-Chicago	1015.31	13	5	44	77.6
July, 1934	Chicago, Milwaukee, St. Paul & Pacific	Chicago-Milwaukee	85.0	1	7	35	75.46
Oct., 1934	Union Pacific	Cheyene-Omaha	506.7	6	11	0	81.95
Oct., 1934	Union Pacific, Chicago & North-western, New York Central	Los Angeles-New York	3257.6	56	55		57.2
Jan., 1935	Pennsylvania	Philadelphia-Washington	134.2	1	50		73.2
April, 1935	New York, New Haven & Hartford	Providence-Boston	43.8		32	35	80.6
Oct., 1936	Chicago, Burlington & Quincy	Chicago-Denver	1017.23	12	12	27	83.3
May, 1937	Atchison, Topeka & Santa Fe	Los Angeles-Chicago	2228.6	36	49		60.5
May, 1955	Baltimore & Ohio	Washington-Chicago (Train consisted of 3 Budd Rail Diesel cars)	768.0	12	29	30	61.5
July, 1966	New York Central	Bryan, Ohio (MP 350-345)	5.0		1	39³/₄	181.0*
May, 1967	Pennsylvania	County Tower-Milheim Tower	21.2		11†		115.66†
Jan., 1968	Atchison, Topeka & Santa Fe	Corwith-Hobart Yards (Super C Frgt.)	2202.1	34	35	40	63.6

*The official speed measured by ground instruments was 183.85 mph on passing mile post 347 + 13 over an accurately measured 300 feet of track. This is the highest speed on rails ever recorded in the United States. The run was made by a single Budd Rail Diesel car fitted with two turbo-jet J-47 aircraft engines mounted on forward end. †Time and speed calculated from standing start at County to passing Milheim Tower (end of test track) at 80-mph, after which the train was gradually braked down on regular track to a stop in Trenton passenger station. Between mileposts 46 and 51, speed was 150 mph or over, a momentary peak of 156 mph. was reached in the vicinity of milepost 47.

Fastest Scheduled Train Runs in European Countries

Passenger

Country	Train	From	to	Dis.	Time	Speed
France	Etendard	St. Pierre des Corps	Poitiers	62.9	37	102.0
Great Britain	Six trains	Rugby	Watford	65.1	44	88.8
West Germany	Dompheil; Germaina; Porta Westfalicia	Dortmund	Bielefeld	61.0	42	87.1
Italy	Superrapidos(3); Vesuvio	Rome	Naples	130.3	90	86.9
	Superraidos(2); Vesuvio	Naples	Rome	130.8	90	86.9
Russia	Aurora*	Moscow	Bologoe	205.5	148	83.3

Freight

Great Britain	Freightliner	Carlisle	Wigan	105.3	95	66.5
France	Freight Express	Orange	St.-Rambert-d'Albon	87.6	81	64.9

*Operated during summer months only.

72 Japanese Trains Average Over 100 Miles per Hour

Service between Tokyo and Osaka via the standard-gauged New Tokaido Line is headed by 36 "Hikari" superexpress trains daily in each direction which make the 320.1-mile run, inclusive of stops at Nagoya and Kyoto, in 3 hrs. 10 min. at average overall speed of 101.1 mph.

With opening of the new Sanyo Line on Mar. 15, 1972, westward from Osaka to Okayama, the runs of most of the "Hikari" trains were extended to provide service over the new line. Four trains in each direction cover the 99.9 miles between the two cities in 58 minutes nonstop — at 103.3 mph. Best time between Tokyo and Okayama, 420 miles, is 4 hrs. 10 mins. — 100.8 mph including stops at Nagoya, Kyoto and Osaka.

French Achieve 90-100 Miles Per Hour Speeds On Regular Schedules.

Having upgraded about 80% of its Paris to Bordeaux mainline to a 125-mile an hour standard, French National Railways has quickened the times of a number of trains between the two cities. Below are shown the fastest point-to-point timings in current French timetables.

Train	From	To	Dis.	Time	Speed
L'Etendard	St. Pierre des Corps.	Poitiers	62.93	37	102.0
L'Etendard	Paris	St. Pierre des Corps.	143.4	92	93.5
L'Etendard	Angouleme	Paris	276.3	178	93.1
L'Aquitaine	Angouleme	Poitiers	70.00	46	91.3

American Railway Statistics
Source: Interstate Commerce Commission

Year	Mile-Age Owned	Miles Built	Loco-Mo.'es In Use	Freight Cars In Use	Pass. Cars in Use	Passengers	Freight Carried	Em-ployees	Employees Wages
	Miles	Miles	No.	No.	No.	No.	Tons	No.	Dollars
1960	217,552	21	31,178	1,690,396	25,746	327,171,745	2,409,039,608	793,071	4,956,902,360
1965	211,384	59	30,061	1,515,169	*20,022	305,825,407	2,741,706,964	654,670	4,886,739,954
1970	205,782	80	29,122	1,453,708	11,378	289,468,947	2,798,324,161	577,435	5,646,480,859
1972	202.775	22	29,338	1,410,584	7,763	262,009,545	2,721,519,553	537,038	6,530,643,091

Passenger and Freight Data

Year	Passenger Revenue	Freight Revenue	Miles Traveled by Passenger	Rev. per Pas. Mile	Ave. Trip per Pas.	Fre. Rev. a ton Mile	Miles Traveled by Pas. Trains	Miles Traveled by Freight Trains	Casualties Kill'd	Inj.
	Dollars	Dollars	Thousands	Cts.	Miles	Cts.	Miles.	Miles	No.	No.
1960	641,495.655	8,151,706,391	21,284,084	3.01	65.05	1.42	209,676,995	411,173,556	2,248	19,577
1965	555,985,653	9,036,540.448	17,453,919	3.19	57.07	1.28	173,579,220	430,716,900	2,399	25,789
1970	423,190,535	11,124,128,498	10,785,746	3.92	37.26	1.44	93,575,236	434,584,544	2,225	21,327
1972	408,863,074	12,790,277,197	8,571,552	4.77	32.71	1.63	60,487,534	457,843,421	1,945	17,530

Revenues, Expenses and Dividends

Year	Total Operating Revenues	Operating Expenses	Tax Accruals	Net Railway Operating Income	Net Income	Dividends Declared	Ratio Oper. Exp. to Oper. Rev.
	Dollars	Dollars	Dollars	Dollars	Dollars	Dollars	Pct.
1960	9,641,592,812	7,657,328,712	1,020,471,011	594,618,250	473,174,842	411,649,958	79.42
1965	10,425,052,359	8,002,684,949	949,215,638	980,065,623	865,898,537	532,649,374	76.76
1970	12,209,237,323	9,805,555,323	1,103,988,230	505,669,405	*126,429,274	486,132,169	80.31
1972	13,821,880.051	11,016,037,781	1,198,078,647	705,028,519	*295,294,576	531,907,505	79.70

Values, Stocks, Bonds, and Capital

Year	Investment In Road and Equipment	Common Stock Outstand.[1]	Preferred Stock Outstand.[1]	Funded Debt Outstand.[1]	Tot. Railway Capital Outstand.1	Amount of Stock Pay Dividends
	Dollars	Dollars	Dollars	Dollars	Dollars	Dollars
1960	35,513,350.796	6,185,117,735	1,218,060,497	8,730,551,088	16,133,729,320	5,617,239,155
1965	35,489,328,198	5,579,833,608	1,115,727,381	8,161,792,077	14,857,353,066	4,845,089.946
1970	37,918,381,770	5,604,882,147	718,205,376	8,015,822,800	14,338,910,323	3,594,834,452
1972	37,358,706,778	5,285,241,990	619,572,068	7,063,411,065	12,968,225,123	3,472,045,984

(1.) Data for years prior to 1965 have been revised to represent amounts actually outstanding in order that they may be comparable to those shown for the year 1965.

*After extraordinary and prior period time.

State Automobile Speed Limits
All states 55 mph or as posted. Exceptions are listed below.
Source: American Automobile Assn. Digest of Motor Laws 1974

Alabama: 50 mph, nighttime; residential districts, 25 mph.; business districts, school zones, etc., 15 mph.

Alaska: City streets, 30 mph.

Arizona: Residential areas, business districts, 25 mph. or as posted; school zones, 15 mph.

Arkansas: Urban districts, 30 mph.

California: Residential and business districts, school zones, 25 mph.

Colorado: Residential districts, 30 mph.; business districts, 25 mph.; open mountain highway, 40 mph.; winding mountain highway, 20 mph.

Connecticut: Reasonable and proper for conditions. Posted limits prima facie evidence of reasonable speed; residential and business districts posted locally.

Delaware: Open highways, 2-lane, 50 mph.; residential and business districts, 25 mph.

District of Columbia: Expressways, 45 mph.; school and playground areas, 15 mph.; other roads, 25 mph.

Florida: Residential & business districts, 30 mph.

Georgia: Open highway 50 mph. nighttime; residential, business and school areas, 25 mph.

Hawaii: Open highways, 45 mph.; or as posted. Residential and business districts, local ordinances govern.

Idaho: Urban and business districts, 35 mph.

Illinois: Urban areas, 30 mph.; school zones, 20 mph.

Indiana: Residential district, 30 mph.; school zones as posted.

Iowa: Suburban, 45 mph.; residential and school districts, 25 mph.; business districts, 20 mph.; secondary roads, 50 mph. nighttime.

Kansas: Residential districts, 30 mph.; business districts, 20 mph.; Kansas Turnpike; 40 mph., minimum.

Kentucky: Open highway, 50 mph. nighttime; residential and business districts, 35 mph.

Louisiana: As posted.

Maine: Open highways, 45 mph; residential and business districts, 25 mph.

Maryland: Dual lane highways, 55 mph.; other highways, 50 mph.; residential and business districts, 30 mph.; thinly settled areas, 35 mph., other highways 30 mph.

Massachusetts: Divided highway, 50 mph.; other highways, 40 mph.; residential and business districts, 30 mph.; school zones, 20 mph.

Michigan: Residential, 25 mph.

Minnesota: Urban districts, 30 mph.

Mississippi: Residential districts, 25 mph.; business districts, 20 mph.; school zones, 15 mph.

Missouri: Municipalities, 45 mph.

Montana: Open highways, day, reasonable and prudent unless posted, residential and business districts, 25 mph.

Nebraska: Residential districts, 25 mph.; business districts, 20 mph.; on non-hard surfaced roads, 50 mph.

Nevada: Careful and prudent; residential and business, as posted.

New Hampshire: Rural residential districts, 35 mph.; urban and business districts, 30 mph.; school zones, 20 mph.

New Jersey: Open highways, 50 mph.; residential and business districts, 25 mph.

New Mexico: Residential and business districts, 25 mph.; school zones, 15 mph.

New York: School zones, when children going to and from school as posted.

North Carolina: Residential districts, 35 mph.; business, 20 mph.

Ohio: Open highways, 50 mph. nighttime; within municipal corporations, 25 mph.; school zones, 20 mph.

Oklahoma: School zones, 25 mph.

Oregon: Residential districts, 25 mph.; business and school zones, 20 mph.

Pennsylvania: Residential and business districts, 15 to 40 mph.; school zones, 15 mph.

Rhode Island: Residential and business districts, 25 mph.; elsewhere, 50 mph. daytime, 45 mph. nighttime.

South Carolina: Urban districts 30 mph.

South Dakota: Residential and business districts, 30 mph.; school zones, 15 mph.

Tennessee: School zones, 15 mph.; Interstate highways 75 mph.

Texas: Urban districts, 30 mph.

Utah: Open highways, as posted; residential and business districts, 25 mph.; school zones, 20 mph.

Vermont: Open highways, 50 mph.

Virginia: Residential, business and school areas, 25 mph.

Washington: County roads, 50 mph.; cities and towns, 25 mph.; school zones, 20 mph.

West Virginia: Residential districts, 25 mph.; school zones, 15 mph.

Wisconsin: Residential and business districts, 25 mph.; school zone, 15 mph.

Wyoming: Residential districts, 30 mph.; business and school districts, 20 mph.

Canal Zone: Outside town limits, 40 mph.; within town limits, 25 mph.

Guam: Roads, 45 mph.; school zones when children at recess or going to and from school, 10 mph.

Puerto Rico: Open highways, 45 mph.; urban districts and school zones, 25 mph.

Mobile Homes and Recreational Vehicles Sales
Source: Construction Review, U.S. Dept. of Commerce and Recreational Vehicle Institute

A **mobile home**, or housing-type trailer is a vehicular portable structure built on a chassis and designed to be used without a permanent foundation as a year-round dwelling when connected to utilities. Mobile homes are defined as units 29 feet or longer and weighing over 4,500 pounds. **Travel trailers** are vehicular structures mounted on wheels (2 or 4 wheel units depending on weight), do not require special highway movement permits when towed. **Motor homes** are self-powered and self-contained units built directly on a truck or bus chassis. **Truck campers** are portable structures that are loaded onto or affixed to the bed or chassis of a truck; in most states they do not require special state licenses.

Camping trailers are mounted on wheels with collapsible side walls of fabric, plastic or other pliable material. They unfold into large tent-top structures that will sleep 4 to 8 people. **Pickup covers** are shells which resemble truck campers without the overcab section. They are mostly utilitarian and offer no built-in sleeping or cooking.

Year	Travel Trailers	Motor Homes	Truck Campers	Camping Trailers	Pickup Covers
1970	138,000	30,300	95,900	116,100	91,700
1971	190,800	57,200	107,200	95,800	98,400
1972	250,800	105,500	105,100	110,200	164,600
1973	212,300	129,000	89,800	97,700	223,700

Major North American Turnpikes; Tolls and Speed Limits

Source: American Automobile Association, Washington, D.C. 20006

Speed limits on U.S. turnpikes 55 mph or as posted.

Airport Expressway: Miami International Airport to North—South Expressway interchange, 4.4 miles. Toll 5c per axle.

Atlantic City Expressway: N.J. Freeway at Turnersville to Atlantic City, N.J. 44 miles. Maximum toll $1.25.

Bluegrass Parkway: Fort Springs to Elizabethtown, Ky. 72 miles. Maximum toll $1.30.

Connecticut Turnpike: N.Y. State line near Greenwich, Conn. to R.I. State line at Killingly, Conn., 129 miles. Maximum toll $2.

Dallas-Ft. Worth Turnpike: Dallas to Ft. Worth 30 miles. Maximum toll 60c.

Dallas North tollway 9.8 miles long. Max. toll 20c.

Eastern Townships Autoroute: Montreal to Sherbrooke, Quebec. 75 miles. Speed limit 70 mph. (50 minimum) car and passengers 25c at each toll gate.

Ensenada-Tijuana Tollway: Ensenada to Tijuana, Mexico, 63 miles. Speed limit 65 mph. Max. toll $2.40.

Everett Turnpike: Mass-N.H. state line to Concord, N.H. 40 miles. Toll maximum 50c.

Florida's Turnpike: Miami, Fla., to Wildwood, Fla., 265 miles. Maximum toll $4.80.

Garden State Parkway: Montvale, N.J. to Cape May, N.J. 173 miles. Max. toll $2.75.

H. E. Bailey Turnpike: Oklahoma City to Randlett, Okla., 86.4 miles. Toll max. $1.70.

Hutchinson River Parkway: N.Y.C. to Conn. state line, 15 miles. Speed limit 50 mph. Toll 25c.

Illinois Tollway: Includes Tri-State Tollway from Indiana state line to Deerfield; Northwest Tollway from the Tri-State to Wisconsin state line at So. Beloit, Ill., and East-West Tollway between Chicago and Aurora. 187 miles. Maximum tolls, Tri-State $1.80, Northwest $1.50 and East-West 50c.

Indian Nation Turnpike: Henryetta to Hugo, Okla. 105.2 miles. Maximum toll $2.25.

Indiana Toll Road: Eastpoint (Ohio line) to Westpoint (Illinois line), 157 miles. Maximum toll $3.25.

John F. Kennedy Memorial Highway: Baltimore, d., to Wilmington, Del., 60 miles. Maximum toll 90c Md., 40c Del. portion.

Kansas Turnpike: Kansas City to South Haven, Kan. 236 miles. Maximum toll $5.25.

Kentucky Turnpike: Louisville to Elizabethtown,

Ky. 40 miles. Max. toll 60c.

Maine Turnpike: York, Me., to Augusta, Me., 100 miles. Max. toll $2.15.

Massachusetts Turnpike: Downtown Boston to state line, Mass., (N. Y. border), 135 miles. Max. toll $3.30.

Merritt Parkway: New York-Conn. state line to Housatonic River, Stratford, Conn., 37½ miles. Toll 20c.

Montreal-Laurentian Autoroute: Montreal to Ste. Adele. 45 miles. Speed limit 70 mph. Toll: 25c at each gate.

Mountain Parkway: Winchester to Salyersville, Ky., 76 miles. Maximum toll $1.60.

New Hampshire Turnpike: Mass.-N. H. state line to Portsmouth, N. H., 14.7 miles. Toll 15c to 25c.

New Jersey Turnpike: Deepwater, N. J. to Ridgefield Park, N. J., 141 miles including extensions. (50 mph. on Hudson County extension). Max. toll $1.75.

New York Thruway (Thomas E. Dewey Thruway): Pennsylvania border near Erie to New York City, 559 miles including extensions. Max. toll $8.80.

Ohio Turnpike: Ohio-Pennsylvania line to Ohio-Indiana line, 241 miles. Maximum toll $3.50.

Pennsylvania Turnpike: Gateway (state line near Youngstown, Ohio) to New Jersey line at Levittown, Pa., then to Scranton, 470 miles. Maximum toll $7.10.

Richmond-Petersburg Turnpike: North of Richmond, Va., to south of Petersburg, Va., 34.7 miles. Maximum toll 95c.

Saw Mill River Parkway: New York City to Katonah, N. Y. 30 miles. Speed limit 50 mph. Maximum toll 25c. Trailers not permitted.

Seventeen-Mile Drive: Pacific Grove through Pebble Beach, Monterey, Calif. Maximum toll $3.00.

Spaulding Turnpike: Portsmouth, N. H. to Rochester, N. H., 22.8 miles. Max. toll 10-15c.

Turner Turnpike: Oklahoma City to Tulsa, Okla., 86 miles. Maximum toll $1.60.

Western Kentucky Parkway: Elizabethtown to Princeton, 135 miles. Maximum toll $2.20.

West Virginia Turnpike: Princeton, W. Va., to Charleston, W. Va., 88 miles. Maximum toll $3.00.

Wilbur Cross Parkway: Milford to Meriden, Conn. 29.5 miles. Maximum toll 35c.

Will Rogers Turnpike: Tulsa, Okla., to Joplin, Mo., 88 miles. Maximum toll $1.60.

Provincial Automobile Speed Limits in Canada

Source: Digest of Motor Laws: 1974

Albertac Open highway, 60 mph, day, 50 mph, night; 4-lane highway, 70 mph day, 60 mph night, or as posted; urban areas, 30 mph or as posted; school zone, urban 20 mph, rural, 25 mph.

British Columbia: Open highway, 50 mph or as posted; residential and business districts, 30 mph; school and playground zones, 20 mph, when posted.

Manitoba: Open highway, 60 mph or as posted; urban areas 30 mph or as posted.

New Brunswick: Fixed maximum limits; residential or business districts, 30 mph; open highway, 60 mph where posted; cities and towns, local laws as posted.

Newfoundland: Reasonable and prudent not to exceed 60 mph on paved portions of trans-Canada highway, 50 mph on other paved highways; unpaved roads, 40 mph under all conditions except through settlements, 30 mph; municipalities, school zones and places of public assembly, as posted.

Nova Scotia: Reasonable and prudent with prima facie limits; residential and business districts, curves, intersections and school zones, 30 mph. Max. speed on

any highway, 60 mph or 65 mph when posted.

Ontario: Fixed maximum limits; open highway, 50 mph or as posted; cities, towns, villages and built-up areas, 30 mph or as posted; railway crossings, 20 mph; 70 mph on 4-lane highways.

Prince Edward Island: Reasonable and proper within maximum limits; open highway, 60 mph day, 55 mph night; residential and business districts, 30 mph; school zones, curves and intersections, 20 mph.

Quebec: Fixed maximum limits. Auto routes 70 mph; numbered hard-surfaced highways outside cities, towns and villages, 60 mph; hard-surfaced highways or gravel roads, outside cities, towns and villages, 50 mph; earth roads, outside cities, towns and villages, 40 mph; all speeds reduced at least 5 mph at night or in bad weather, in cities, towns, and villages, 30 mph or as posted; school zones at times when pupils enter or leave school, and at level crossing, 30 mph.

Saskatchewan: Fixed maximum limits as posted. Open highway 50 mph, or as posted. Local speeds set by municipalities.

Highway Mileage Between Selected Cities

Cities In The East*	ALBANY, N.Y.	ATLANTA, GA.	BALTIMORE, MD.	BANGOR, ME.	BIRMINGHAM, ALA.	BOSTON, MASS.	BUFFALO, N.Y.	CHARLESTON, W.VA.	CHICAGO, ILL.	CINCINNATI, OHIO	CLEVELAND, OHIO	DETROIT, MICH.	INDIANAPOLIS, IND.	JACKSON, MISS.	JACKSONVILLE, FLA.
ALBANY		988	321	366	1091	170	283	712	807	707	466	536	766	1379	1117
ATLANTA	988		671	1315	155	1070	876	519	707	467	692	726	539	400	315
BALTIMORE	321	671		632	800	400	366	391	690	497	348	510	565	998	794
BANGOR	366	1315	632		1407	233	652	1018	1174	1094	827	892	1136	1635	1426
BIRMINGHAM	1091	155	800	1407		1210	932	589	661	499	742	743	492	243	427
BOSTON	170	1070	400	233	1210		458	781	974	861	640	707	931	1446	1201
BUFFALO	283	876	366	652	932	458		439	520	428	186	249	486	1115	1080
CHARLESTON	712	519	391	1018	589	781	439		483	202	268	357	301	786	671
CHICAGO	807	707	690	1174	661	974	520	483		294	345	269	188	747	1017
CINCINNATI	707	467	497	1094	499	861	428	202	294		244	251	104	678	783
CLEVELAND	466	692	348	827	742	640	186	268	345	244		168	300	924	971
DETROIT	536	726	510	892	743	707	249	357	269	251	168		277	931	1039
INDIANAPOLIS	766	539	565	1136	492	931	486	301	188	104	300	277		631	852
JACKSON	1379	400	998	1635	243	1446	1115	786	747	678	924	931	631		597
JACKSONVILLE	1117	315	794	1426	427	1201	1080	671	1017	783	971	1039	852	597	
LOUSIVILLE	827	428	602	1198	362	964	537	266	304	108	351	363	114	573	766
MEMPHIS	1217	366	951	1594	247	1340	924	615	548	487	737	726	444	210	672
MIAMI	1468	665	1143	1773	765	1539	1431	1043	1377	1133	1322	1387	1197	920	345
NASHVILLE	1090	251	732	736	201	1126	717	409	452	289	532	544	293	375	577
NEW ORLEANS	1476	517	1153	1747	359	1556	1248	936	929	820	1060	1077	839	182	568
NEW YORK	147	863	192	450	988	211	367	566	828	635	486	626	716	1232	979
NORFOLK	560	592	249	881	753	543	561	397	874	600	531	699	698	996	661
PHILADELPHIA	233	771	99	541	897	303	360	481	758	571	425	578	639	1153	889
PITTSBURGH	457	737	230	819	763	576	220	233	459	278	127	287	355	972	893
PORTLAND, ME.	275	1185	513	128	1325	106	574	895	1089	967	752	817	1037	1552	1293
RICHMOND	472	545	144	773	697	543	473	309	786	512	443	611	620	944	646
ST. LOUIS	1016	553	804	1379	503	1188	723	538	291	338	540	513	239	505	881
TAMPA	1331	464	986	1620	552	1383	1263	884	1187	948	1166	1201	1005	678	194
TRENTON	223	783	128	520	915	289	358	513	780	590	435	594	660	1163	921
WASHINGTON	367	640	39	673	767	440	372	355	687	497	362	516	567	1000	754

	LOUISVILLE, KY.	MEMPHIS, TENN.	MIAMI, FLA.	NASHVILLE, TENN.	NEW ORLEANS, LA.	NEW YORK, N.Y.	NORFOLK, VA.	PHILADELPHIA, PA.	PITTSBURGH, PA.	PORTLAND, ME.	RICHMOND, VA.	ST. LOUIS, MO.	TAMPA, FLA.	TRENTON, N.J.	WASHINGTON, D.C.
ALBANY	827	1217	1468	1090	1476	147	560	233	457	275	472	1016	1331	223	367
ATLANTA	428	366	665	251	517	863	592	771	737	1185	545	553	464	783	640
BALTIMORE	602	951	1143	732	1153	192	249	99	230	513	144	804	986	128	39
BANGOR	1198	1594	1773	736	1747	450	881	541	819	128	773	1379	1620	520	673
BIRMINGHAM	362	247	765	201	359	988	753	897	763	1325	697	503	552	915	767
BOSTON	964	1340	1539	1126	1556	211	543	303	576	106	543	1188	1383	289	440
BUFFALO	537	924	1431	717	1248	367	561	360	220	574	473	723	1263	358	372
CHARLESTON	266	615	1043	409	936	566	397	481	233	895	309	538	884	513	355
CHICAGO	304	548	1377	452	929	828	874	758	459	1089	786	291	1187	780	687
CINCINNATI	108	487	1133	289	820	635	600	571	278	967	512	338	948	590	497
CLEVELAND	351	737	1322	532	1060	486	531	425	127	752	443	540	1166	435	362
DETROIT	363	726	1387	544	1077	626	699	578	287	817	611	513	1201	594	516
INDIANAPOLIS	114	444	1197	293	839	716	698	639	355	1037	620	239	1005	660	567
JACKSON	573	210	920	375	182	1232	996	1153	972	1552	944	505	678	1163	1000
JACKSONVILLE	766	672	345	577	568	979	661	889	893	1293	646	881	194	921	754
LOUISVILLE		365	1078	180	719	759	693	682	398	1070	575	267	865	705	605
MEMPHIS	365		1017	220	399	1142	958	1057	786	1446	845	294	782	1064	917
MIAMI	1078	1017		916	878	1327	1013	1230	1237	1649	994	1222	248	1276	1105
NASHVILLE	180	220	916		536	929	713	838	568	1232	625	295	908	853	697
NEW ORLEANS	719	399	878	536		1353	1101	1239	1113	1655	1057	699	644	1270	1150
NEW YORK	759	1142	1327	929	1353		441	91	363	317	330	961	1176	70	226
NORFOLK	693	958	1013	713	1101	441		348	400	649	88	930	859	359	195
PHILADELPHIA	682	1057	1230	838	1239	91	348		294	409	240	881	1083	32	136
PITTSBURGH	398	786	1237	568	1113	363	400	294		682	312	599	1045	205	229
PORTLAND, ME.	1070	1446	1649	1232	1655	317	649	409	682		649	1294	1488	395	549
RICHMOND	575	845	994	625	1057	330	88	240	312	649		842	842	277	107
ST. LOUIS	267	294	1222	295	699	961	930	881	599	1294	842		1030	897	804
TAMPA	865	782	248	908	644	1176	859	1083	1045	1488	842	1030		1109	947
TRENTON	705	1064	1276	853	1270	70	359	32	205	395	277	897	1109		169
WASHINGTON	605	917	1105	697	1150	226	195	136	229	549	107	804	947	169	

*Directions for Use of Mileage Charts

To measure mileage between the east and west charts there are 5 key cities: Chicago, Jackson (Miss.), Memphis, New Orleans and St. Louis.

Plot your course between the city listed nearest your home town and whichever of the 5 key cities you desire to pass through to the city of your destination.

Add the mileage shown and this will give you the approximate total mileage.

For example: The mileage between Cheyenne and Philadelphia through St. Louis: Philadelphia to St. Louis - 881 miles, St. Louis to Cheyenne - 910; the total is 1,791 miles.

Highway Mileage Between Selected Cities

Cities In The West

	ALBUQUERQUE, N.M.	BOISE, IDAHO	CHEYENNE, WYO.	CHICAGO, ILL.	DALLAS, TEXAS	DENVER, COLO.	DES MOINES, IOWA	FARGO, N.D.	HELENA, MONT.	HOUSTON, TEXAS	JACKSON, MISS.	KANSAS CITY, MO.	LITTLE ROCK, ARK.	LOS ANGELES, CALIF.	MEMPHIS, TENN.
ALBUQUERQUE		980	545	1285	650	432	1032	1310	1111	844	1062	791	901	805	1032
BOISE	980		766	1726	1637	867	1397	1228	494	1825	2063	1446	1833	887	1913
CHEYENNE	545	766		967	880	101	632	823	700	1143	1282	657	1053	1182	1127
CHICAGO	1285	1726	967		936	1018	330	657	1478	1092	747	505	652	2106	548
DALLAS	650	1637	880	936		784	704	1110	1571	245	411	498	330	1410	468
DENVER	432	867	101	1018	784		674	901	792	1028	1219	613	962	1162	1058
DES MOINES	1032	1397	632	330	704	674		491	1162	948	828	207	581	1788	608
FARGO, N.D.	1310	1228	823	657	1110	901	491		822	1364	1271	636	1054	1935	1061
HELENA	1111	494	700	1478	1571	792	1162	822		1813	1922	1261	1666	1234	1720
HOUSTON	844	1825	1143	1092	245	1028	948	1364	1813		433	744	439	1554	572
JACKSON	1062	2063	1282	747	411	1219	828	1271	1922	433		613	257	1864	210
KANSAS CITY	791	1446	657	505	498	613	207	636	1261	744	613		409	1620	467
LITTLE ROCK	901	1833	1053	652	330	962	581	1045	1666	439	257	409		1698	139
LOS ANGELES	805	887	1182	2106	1410	1162	1788	1935	1234	1554	1864	1620	1698		1823
MEMPHIS	1032	1913	1127	548	468	1058	627	1061	1720	572	210	467	139	1823	
MILWAUKEE	1390	1763	1019	87	1063	1039	358	573	1392	1163	826	564	727	2145	632
MINNEAPOLIS	1223	1446	821	418	964	845	254	239	1056	1211	1062	461	833	1996	852
NEW ORLEANS	1145	2140	1376	929	500	1284	1028	1479	2070	358	182	846	434	1916	399
OKLAHOMA CITY	545	1489	702	826	212	616	566	900	1392	458	587	357	350	1353	482
OMAHA	892	1267	491	465	672	537	139	436	1056	917	882	208	623	1698	671
PHOENIX	449	1020	924	1753	1021	826	1449	1726	1147	1158	1456	1238	1337	389	1470
PORTLAND, ORE.	1461	435	1211	2131	2057	1285	1819	1590	657	2282	2506	1901	2284	994	2367
RENO	1036	427	995	1970	1695	1040	1638	1639	905	1888	2104	1665	2030	476	2083
ST. LOUIS	1057	1701	910	291	651	863	349	812	1498	801	505	254	357	1862	294
SALT LAKE CITY	612	363	457	1443	1262	512	1089	1215	500	1453	1685	1118	1444	730	1570
SAN FRANCISCO	1132	654	1209	2183	1773	1267	1851	1873	1134	1955	2203	1893	2032	403	2162
SEATTLE	1511	529	1279	2031	2136	1377	1766	1505	611	2354	2601	1904	2273	1177	2362
SIOUX FALLS	1082	1295	654	525	844	655	282	230	960	1110	1013	390	799	1817	858
TUCSON	454	1191	999	1739	951	845	1462	1746	1270	1070	1362	1255	1278	512	1417
WICHITA	620	1663	590	711	386	512	403	731	1241	629	733	202	472	1384	549

	MILWAUKEE, WIS.	MINNEAPOLIS, MINN.	NEW ORLEANS, LA.	OKLAHOMA CITY, OKLA.	OMAHA, NEB.	PHOENIX, ARIZ.	PORTLAND, ORE.	RENO, NEV.	ST. LOUIS, MO.	SALT LAKE CITY, UTAH	SAN FRANCISCO, CALIF.	SEATTLE, WASH.	SIOUX FALLS, S.D.	TUCSON, ARIZ.	WICHITA, KAN.
ALBUQUERQUE	1390	1223	1145	545	892	449	1461	1036	1057	612	1132	1511	1082	454	620
BOISE	1763	1446	2140	1489	1267	1020	435	427	1701	363	654	525	1295	1191	1663
CHEYENNE	1019	821	1376	702	491	924	1211	995	910	457	1209	1279	654	999	590
CHICAGO	87	418	929	826	465	1753	2131	1970	291	1443	2183	2031	525	1739	711
DALLAS	1063	964	500	212	672	1021	2057	1695	651	1262	1773	2136	844	951	386
DENVER	1039	845	1284	616	537	826	1285	1040	863	512	1267	1377	655	845	512
DES MOINES	358	254	1028	566	139	1449	1819	1638	349	1089	1851	1766	282	1462	403
FARGO, N.D.	573	239	1479	900	436	1726	1590	1639	812	1215	1873	1505	230	1746	731
HELENA	1392	1056	2070	1392	1056	1147	657	905	1498	500	1134	611	960	1270	1241
HOUSTON	1163	1211	358	458	917	1158	2282	1888	801	1453	1955	2354	1110	1070	629
JACKSON	826	1062	182	587	882	1456	2506	2104	505	1685	2203	2601	1013	1362	733
KANSAS CITY	564	461	846	357	208	1238	1901	1665	254	1118	1893	1904	390	1255	202
LITTLE ROCK	727	833	434	350	623	1337	2284	2030	357	1444	2032	2273	799	1278	472
LOS ANGELES	2145	1996	1916	1353	1698	389	994	476	1862	730	403	1177	1817	512	1384
MEMPHIS	632	852	399	482	671	1470	2367	2083	294	1570	2162	2362	858	1417	549
MILWAUKEE		334	1034	905	501	1833	2069	2003	371	1502	2203	2045	507	1819	792
MINNEAPOLIS	334		1251	818	364	1671	1721	1797	553	1246	2001	1673	221	1677	650
NEW ORLEANS	1034	1251		684	1065	1527	2591	2199	699	1773	2278	2645	1265	1436	840
OKLAHOMA CITY	905	818	648		477	989	1926	1529	523	1112	1692	1975	644	941	168
OMAHA	1501	364	1065	477		1325	1700	1500	453	955	1720	1657	187	1341	309
PHOENIX	1833	1671	1527	989	1325		1273	762	1492	688	794	1510	1481	123	1040
PORTLAND, ORE.	2069	1721	2591	1926	1700	1273		566	2113	807	669	173	1580	1396	1854
RENO	2003	1797	2199	1529	1500	762	566		1906	531	227	760	1472	912	1542
ST. LOUIS	371	553	699	523	453	1492	2113	1879		1381	2133	2102	632	1457	460
SALT LAKE CITY	1502	1246	1773	1112	953	688	807	531	1381		755	869	941	820	1020
SAN FRANCISCO	2203	2001	2278	1692	1720	794	669	227	2133	755		858	1696	921	1730
SEATTLE	2045	1673	2645	1975	1657	1510	173	760	2102	869	858		1526	1666	1842
SIOUX FALLS	507	221	1265	644	187	1481	1580	1472	632	941	1696	1526		1536	493
TUCSON	1819	1677	1436	941	1341	123	1396	912	1457	820	921	1666	1536		1074
WICHITA	792	650	840	168	309	1040	1854	1542	460	1020	1730	1842	493	1074	

Highway Mileage Between Selected Canadian and U.S. Cities

	CALGARY	EDMONTON	HALIFAX	LONDON	MONCTON	MONTREAL	OTTAWA	QUEBEC	REGINA	ST. JOHN	SAULT STE. MARIE	THUNDER BAY	TORONTO	VANCOUVER	WINNIPEG
BANGOR, ME.	2592	2595	450	762	287	310	436	241	2115	188	936	1331	651	3250	1760
BOSTON, MASS.	2620	2639	683	675	520	333	458	390	2142	421	958	1403	564	3168	1812
BUFFALO, N.Y.	2106	2125	1141	142	978	383	350	533	1628	879	532	977	102	2878	1377
BUTTE, MONT.	378	561	2950	1859	2787	2309	2033	2470	629	2739	1533	1303	1972	764	875
CALGARY, ALB.		183	3073	2246	2910	2282	2202	2432	478	2862	1601	1271	2142	659	832
DETROIT, MICH.	1915	1934	1336	122	1204	576	475	738	1437	1156	246	691	235	2505	1149
DULUTH, MINN.	1240	1243	1842	777	1679	1051	925	1199	763	1631	425	195	865	1898	408
EDMONTON, ALB.	183		3076	2249	2913	2285	2205	2435	497	2865	1632	1274	2145	842	835
FARGO, N.D.	989	1172	2092	1048	1929	1502	1175	1764	511	1881	675	445	1161	1654	233
HALIFAX, N.S.	3073	3076		1243	163	791	917	657	2596	262	1417	1812	1132	3731	2241
LONDON, ONTARIO	2246	2249	1243		1080	452	359	602	1769	1032	403	985	111	2904	1414
MONCTON, N.B.	2910	2913	163	1080		628	754	494	2433	99	1254	1649	969	3568	2078
MONTREAL, QUE.	2282	2285	791	452	628		126	150	1805	580	626	1021	341	2940	1450
OTTAWA, ONT.	2202	2205	917	359	754	126		274	1725	706	500	941	248	2860	1370
QUEBEC, QUE.	2432	2435	657	602	494	150	274		1955	446	774	1171	491	3090	1600
REGINA, SASK.	478	497	2596	1769	2433	1805	1725	1955		2385	1146	794	1665	1136	355
ST. JOHN, N.B.	2862	2865	262	1032	99	580	706	446	2385		1206	1601	921	3520	2030
SAULT STE. MARIE	1601	1632	1417	403	1254	626	500	774	1146	1206		445	440	2201	797
SEATTLE, WASH.	762	945	3494	2489	3331	2693	2577	2934	1092	3283	2077	1883	2600	146	1444
THUNDER BAY, ONT.	1271	1274	1812	985	1649	1021	941	1171	794	1601	445		881	1929	439
TORONTO, ONT.	2142	2145	1132	111	969	341	248	491	1665	921	440	881		2800	1310
VANCOUVER, B.C.	659	842	3731	2904	3568	2940	2860	3090	1136	3520	2201	1929	2800		1490
WINNIPEG, MAN.	832	835	2241	1414	2078	1450	1370	1600	355	2030	797	439	1310	1490	

Motor Bus Passenger Operations, Intercity Class I Carriers

Source: Interstate Commerce Commission

Year ended December 31	1968	1970	1971	1972	1973
Number of carriers reporting	159	71	72	72	71
Miles of line, regular route	216,668	192,130	193,948	NA	NA
Regular route intercity service revenue (dollars)	484,709,405	509,753,126	540,809,039	534,611,714	563,466,235
Local and suburban revenue (dollars)	16,092,699	13,894,726	13,268,731	11,652,843	12,018,079
Charter or special service bus (dollars)	83,463,349	80,473,873	86,236,590	93,953,690	103,325,461
Total operating revenue (dollars)	685,662,405	722,174,070	760,911,530	768,055,522	813,396,249
Total operating expenses (dollars)	604,808,045	638,435,771	666,541,446	682,458,001	735,979,839
Net operating revenue (dollars)	80,854,360	83,738,299	94,370,084	85,597,521	77,416,410
Bus-miles in intercity line service	814,587,544	745,691,295	729,206,679	698,920,436	706,378,742
Bus-miles in local and suburban service	23,644,551	17,869,121	17,014,044	14,499,911	14,800,065
Bus-miles in charter or special service	125,941,786	111,236,118	114,015,821	121,363,601	127,093,013
Intercity revenue passengers carried	160,692,862	132,041,325	128,329,446	120,899,734	118,862,777
Local and suburban revenue passengers carried	28,871,544	21,782,439	19,479,049	5,500,788	14,832,110
Charter or special revenue passengers carried	27,086,221	19,683,951	19,502,788	20,389,118	22,115,336

Intercity Bus Operations

Source: National Association of Motor Bus Owners

	1970	1971	1972	1973
Operating Companies	1,000	1,000	1,000	1,000
Buses	23,100	23,000	22,500	22,300
Miles of highway served (Dec. 31)[1]	267,000	267,000	270,000	271,000
Employees (Dec. 31)[2]	49,500	50,200	49,100	48,000
Total bus miles	1,209,000,000	1,202,000,000	1,182,000,000	1,175,000,000
Revenue passengers	401,000,000	395,000,000	393,000,000	385,000,000
Revenue passenger-miles	25,300,000,000	25,500,000,000	25,600,000,000	26,400,000,000
Operating revenue, all services	$901,400,000	$953,200,000	$974,400,000	$1,020,700,000
Operating expenses	$812,200,000	$851,800,000	$882,100,000	$935,100,000
Net operating rev. before inc. taxes	$89,200,000	$101,400,000	$92,300,000	$85,600,000
Taxes assignable to operations[3]	$76,700,000	$80,700,000	84,100,000	90,100,000

(1.)Includes duplication between carriers. (2.)Operating companies only. (3.)Excludes income taxes.

Minimum Legal Age for Purchase of Alcoholic Beverages

In the United States and Canada

	Years		Years		Years		Years
Alabama	21	Indiana	21	New Brunswick	21	Quebec	18
Alaska	19	Iowa	18	Newfoundland	21	Rhode Island	18
Alberta	18	Kansas (c)	21	New Hampshire	18	Saskatchewan	18
Arizona	19	Kentucky	21	New Jersey	18	South Carolina (e)	21
Arkansas	21	Louisiana	18	New Mexico	21	South Dakota (g)	21
British Columbia	19	Maine	18	New York	18	Tennessee	18
California	21	Manitoba	18	North Carolina (b)	21	Texas	18
Colorado (c)	21	Maryland	21	North Dakota	21	Utah	21
Connecticut	18	Massachusetts	18	Northwest Territories	19	Vermont	18
Delaware	20	Michigan	18	Nova Scotia	19	Virginia (c)	18
Dist. of Col. (b)	21	Minnesota	21	Ohio (c)	21	Washington	19
Florida	21	Mississippi (h)	21	Oklahoma (d)	21	West Virginia	18
Georgia	18	Missouri	21	Oregon	21	Wisconsin	18
Hawaii	18	Montana	18	Ontario	18	Wyoming	19
Idaho	19	Nebraska	19	Pennsylvania	21	Yukon Territory	19
Illinois	19	Nevada	21	Prince Edward Island	18		

(b) Light wine, beer 18. (c) 3.2 beer 18. (d) 3.2 beer: male 21; female 18 (e) Beer and wine 18. (g) 3.2 beer (h) Beer not over 4% by wt. 18.

Trucking: More Workers, Bigger Payroll
Source: American Trucking Assns.; Dept. of Transportation

1972	Employees	Annual Payroll	Truck Registration New	Total	1972	Employees	Annual Payroll	Truck Registration New	Total
Alabama..	161,800	$1,226,120,400	45,070	454,615	Nebraska..	91,400	$678,279,400	26,842	290,178
Alaska....	14,400	177,854,400	6,165	42,559	Nevada...	42,000	371,112,000	12,673	92,689
Arizona...	114,500	973,250,000	39,095	314,250	N. Hamp...	28,200	213,135,600	12,014	61,982
Arkansas..	134,800	871,482,000	41,566	325,842	N. Jersey..	211,700	1,945,099,600	45,406	338,612
California.	1,184,000	12,627,360,000	268,088	2,157,882	N. Mexico.	66,300	492,144,900	22,473	198,449
Colorado..	145,700	1,237,138,700	50,709	386,935	New York..	407,800	3,902,646,000	96,743	647,934
Conn.....	126,800	1,114,318,400	20,343	143,297	N. Carolina	311,200	2,150,392,000	71,233	617,973
Delaware.	29,800	269,421,800	6,492	49,382	N. Dakota.	37,100	266,971,600	11,222	166,208
Dist. of Col.	15,100	163,231,000	1,976	13,999	Ohio.....	330,800	3,031,120,400	94,549	687,221
Florida...	270,000	2,128,410,000	91,737	653,116	Oklahoma.	167,400	1,315,764,000	NA	535,594
Georgia..	215,700	1,644,281,100	74,012	554,314	Oregon...	119,900	988,095,900	49,633	247,270
Hawaii..	21,000	182,700,000	6,067	50,155	Penna.....	452,000	3,784,144,000	98,672	804,415
Idaho....	49,100	355,975,000	19,533	154,999	R. Island..	35,700	271,819,800	5,433	56,642
Illinois...	340,200	3,230,539,200	93,160	687,708	S. Carolina	144,200	982,867,200	33,169	272,777
Indiana...	322,100	2,805,168,900	68,746	576,575	S. Dakota.	37,600	253,160,800	11,954	140,712
Iowa.....	164,300	1,283,347,300	37,783	438,461	Tenn.....	142,700	1,056,265,400	58,227	446,266
Kansas...	148,100	1,128,522,000	37,858	450,248	Texas....	677,000	5,095,779,000	191,961	1,659,550
Kentucky.	153,600	1,198,848,000	39,738	429,944	Utah.....	59,600	457,310,800	22,912	191,959
Louisiana.	166,500	1,316,182,500	49,758	400,780	Vermont..	18,500	143,449,000	7,847	42,873
Maine....	54,900	384,849,000	14,693	108,260	Virginia...	180,500	1,424,867,000	56,204	406,238
Maryland.	122,200	1,033,689,800	37,172	276,199	Wash.....	193,100	1,743,886,100	47,955	503,882
Mass.....	165,200	1,385,036,800	34,235	247,233	W. Va.....	87,600	749,330,400	27,919	194,433
Michigan.	315,500	3,059,403,500	112,022	692,559	Wisconsin.	155,200	1,301,662,400	42,878	374,929
Minnesota.	190,100	1,594,178,600	43,461	466,759	Wyoming .	30,100	219,639,700	11,522	93,670
Miss.....	105,800	688,334,800	35,938	309,010	**Total....**	**9,050,300**	**77,353,699,200**	**2,513,952**	***20,225,745**
Missouri..	241,000	2,061,514,000	65,081	568,143	**1971**				
Montana ..	50,500	373,599,000	20,374	200,125	**Totals...**	**9,034,000**	**72,405,973,000**	**1,981,294**	**19,802,490**

*Includes 28,725 Federal Govt. Trucks, 64,964 Motor Homes.

745,741,082 Tons of Intercity Freight Moved
Source: American Trucking Associations
Based on operations of 2,343 Class I & II intercity motor carriers. In tons.

Region	1972	1973	Commodity Class	1972	1973
New England	22,329,340	22,809,795	General Freight	247,202,986	275,950,815
Middle Atlantic	145,050,864	155,089,615	Household Goods	2,834,700	3,233,536
Central	178,027,945	202,527,260	Heavy Machinery	7,413,313	8,800,504
Southern	117,380,139	132,357,068	Liquid Petroleum	169,314,381	184,481,002
Northwestern	48,626,198	52,567,553	Refrig. Solids & Liquids	13,430,917	14,298,477
Midwestern	38,774,028	43,823,677	Agricultural Commodities	11,062,592	11,956,809
Southwestern	52,632,722	58,832,344	Motor Vehicles	24,332,885	27,799,659
Rocky Mountain	18,195,089	19,330,878	Building Materials	29,373,117	31,506,301
Pacific	54,127,518	58,402,892	All Other Classes	170,178,952	187,713,909
United States	675,143,843	745,741,082	All Commodities	675,143,843	745,741,082

Automobile Factory Sales
Source: Motor Vehicle Manufacturers Association, Detroit, Mich.—Values, Wholesale

Year	Passenger Cars Number	Value	Motor Trucks, Buses Number	Value	Total Number	Value
1900............	4,192	$4,899,443	...	...	4,190	$4,899,443
1905............	24,250	38,670,000	350	$1,330,000	187,000	225,000,000
1910............	181,000	215,340,000	6,000	9,660,000	187,000	225,000,000
1915............	895,930	575,978,000	74,000	125,800,000	969,930	701,778,000
1920............	1,905,560	1,809,170,963	321,789	423,249,410	2,227,349	2,232,420,373
1925............	3,735,171	2,458,370,026	530,659	458,400,277	4,265,830	2,916,770,303
1930............	2,787,456	1,644,083,152	575,364	390,752,061	3,362,820	2,034,853,213
1935............	3,273,874	1,707,836,325	697,367	380,997,330	3,971,241	2,088,833,655
1940............	3,717,385	2,370,654,083	754,901	567,820,414	4,472,286	2,938,474,497
1945............	69,532	57,254,655	655,683	1,181,955,532	725,215	1,239,210,187
1950............	6,665,863	8,468,137,000	1,337,193	1,707,748,000	8,003,056	10,175,885,000
1955............	7,920,186	12,452,871,000	1,249,106	2,020,973,000	9,169,292	14,473,844,000
1960............	6,674,796	12,164,234,000	1,194,475	2,350,680,000	7,869,271	14,514,914,000
1965............	9,305,561	18,380,036,000	1,751,805	3,733,664,000	11,057,366	22,113,700,000
1970............	6,546,817	14,630,217,000	1,692,440	4,819,752,000	8,239,257	19,449,969,000
1973............	9,657,647	26,239,996,000	2,979,688	9,544,112,000	12,637,335	35,784,108,000

After July 1, 1964 all tactical vehicles are excluded. Federal excise taxes are excluded in all years. *Preliminary.

Automotive Exports from United States
Source: Bureau of Economic Analysis, Dept. of Commerce
(in millions)

	Total Value Vehicles	Automotive*		Total Value Vehicles	Automotive*		Total Value Vehicles	Automotive*
1940	$147	$259	1965.....	$739	$1,929	1970.....	$1,397	$3,652
1950	406	746	1967.....	1,236	2,784	1971.....	1,784	4,397
1955	747	1,276	1968.....	1,415	3,453	1972.....	2,008	5,119
1960	634	1,266	1969.....	1,553	3,887	1973.....	2,651	6,312

*Includes used passenger cars and trucks, trailers, parts for assembly, and garage equipment.

Effect of Speed on Fuel Consumption Rates
(Without use of air conditioning)

Source: U.S. Department of Transportation

Net Car Weight	Miles per gallon at selected speeds				
(pounds)	30	40	50	60	70
2,290	21.55	20.07	19.11.	17.83	16.72
2,400	22.72	21.94	22.22	21.08	17.21
2,450	31.45	35.19	33.05	30.78	22.82
3,500	19.30	18.89	17.29	15.67	13.32
3,540	23.67	24.59	20.46	14.83	13.42
3,820	22.88	19.41	20.28	17.78	14.88
3,975	18.25	20.00	16.32	15.77	13.61
3,990	15.61	14.89	16.98	13.67	11.08
4,530	20.33	20.00	17.50	16.17	14.86
4,880	17.12	17.20	16.11	14.92	13.13
5,250	18.33	19.28	15.62	14.22	12.74

The Effect of the Use of Air Conditioning on Fuel Consumption Rates[1]

Operating Speed, Miles Per Hour	Air Conditioning In Use	Air Conditioning Not in Use	Reduction in Miles Per Gallon	Percent Saving With A.C. Off
	(Miles Per Gallon)	(Miles Per Gallon)		
30	18.14	20.05	1.91	10.53
40	17.51	19.71	2.20	12.56
50	16.42	18.29	1.87	11.39
60	15.00	16.25	1.25	8.33
70	13.17	14.18	1.01	7.67

[1] All cars included in the averages in this table are equipped with air conditioning in good operating condition.

Fewer Cars Need Recalls; Highway Deaths Drop

Recalls of motor vehicles for safety defects dropped dramatically in late 1973 and in 1974, coincidentally with big cuts in the highway death toll.

The 1973 recalls totaled 7,000,996 compared to 12,081,803 in 1972, a slash of 41%. The trend continued at its slowed-down pace in 1974.

Traffic fatalities in 1974 were running an average 1,000 per month fewer than in 1973. And the 1973 toll was down 1,000 from the 1972 total, 56,600.

While authorities credited the decline in deaths to the 55-mile-an-hour speed limit and the early-1974 gasoline shortages, many felt that the 1972-73 recall campaigns, as well as the apparent reduced need for recalls in late 1973-74 were also an important factor in the fewer fatalities.

In addition to safety recalls, initiated by the National Highway Traffic Safety Administration, 1974 saw the first large-scale recalls under Environmental Protection Agency programs, with over a million cars of 4 makes called back for pollution control problems.

The pollution control callbacks involved 825,000 Chrysler cars, 1,000 Chrysler trucks and 282,000 Ford cars. An additional 1.4 million GM, Volkswagen, Ford and Chrysler vehicles were being studied on similar complaints, the EPA announced.

1974 Safety Campaigns

The highway safety agency in 1974 warned 135,000 owners of Ford Pinto station wagons of a built-in danger to rear tires; GM recalled 42,000 trucks and 500 school buses for possible brake defects; Chrysler recalled 12,700 Imperials for a parking brake problem. American Motors called in 20,000 Jeeps because of a suspension system problem.

Nissan Motors, in Aug. 1974, recalled 63,023 Datsuns with a potential hazard in fuel pump covers. British Leyland ordered back all 40,000 Triumph TR-6 sports cars sold in North America for a possible fuel system fire hazard. Porsche Audi recalled 9,000 Porsche 911s.

The 1973 safety recall figures showed GM suffered a big increase to 5,846,937, more than half of all recalls, from 1,346,390 in 1972. Ford Motors, by contrast, dropped from 5,775,514 in 1972 to 319,849 in 1973, sufficient however to make it 2d to GM.

Following GM and Ford in the big parade back to the service stations were 306,883 Chrysler vehicles. The GM cars, suffering a variety of problems, included Chevrolets, Buicks, Pontiacs, Oldsmobiles, Cadillacs, trucks, buses and motor homes. Biggest Ford recalls were Torinos with possible steering control troubles and Fords with a potential brake problem. Half the Chryslers were Plymouths and Dodges with possible fuel leakage in the engine compartments.

In 4th place was Volkswagen with 151,830 callbacks, most for a possibility of fumes in the passenger compartment.

Porsche Audi took 5th place with 73,576 recalls, including Porsches with mirror problems and Audis with a chance of dangerous electric shorts.

In 6th was International Harvester with 51,792 vehicles, mostly trucks afflicted with either possible steering problems or incorrect gas caps.

In 7th were 39,081 Harley-Davidson motorcycles with potential brake or frame troubles. In 8th were 37,072 Peugeots with possible brake, seat belt or windshield problems.

More Foreign Cars

Next came 20,000 Subarus possibly needing seat belt modifications. In 10th place were 17,826 Mercedes-Benz cars with possible brake or throttle troubles. Nissan Motors was 11th with 16,274 Datsuns possibly susceptible to stalling at the wrong time.

In 12th place were 15,087 Honda Civics with possible brake fluid leaks. Oddly, 13th were 13,479 Paccar trucks with potential steering or door lock troubles.

The 14th was Volvo, calling back 12,092 cars with possible fuel injector trouble. Next came 9,145 Checker cars and cabs with potential engine mount trouble.

American Motors, the 4th largest U.S. automaker, had only 4,246 recalls, mostly for a possible steering defect.

Saab-Scania and Toyota emerged from 1973 with clean records — no recalls.

The 1973 recalls brought to over 43 million the total recalls since the National Traffic and Motor Vehicle Safety Act went into effect in Sept. 1966.

Passenger Car Production, U.S. Plants

Source: Motor Vehicle Manufacturers Association of the U.S., Inc.

	1972	1973	1974 4 Mos.		1972	1973	1974 4 Mos.
American Motors Corp.				Lincoln	49,457	57,257	5,543
Gremlin	69,773	93,597	41,378	Mark III/IV	55,561	76,137	11,589
Hornet	83,213	114,839	44,801	**Total Lincoln**	105,018	133,394	17,132
Javelin/AMX	29,105	31,267	8,880	**Total Ford Motor**			
Matador	52,343	72,476	28,059	**Co.**	2,400,871	2,495,853	755,007
Ambassador	44,698	43,676	7,474	**General Motors Corp.**			
Total American				Chevrolet	955,237	866,826	147,971
Motors Corp.	279,132	355,855	130,592	Corvette	27,376	32,616	12,921
Chrysler Corp.				Monte Carlo	186,171	246,533	73,243
Valiant	250,583	335,816	146,693	Chevelle	358,568	314,755	92,590
Barracuda	19,090	21,338	3,939	Camaro	35,943	117,828	57,114
Satellite	75,089	140,745	46,101	Nova	367,733	395,673	155,446
Fury	268,724	245,058	28,010	Vega	368,743	359,882	129,991
Total Plymouth	613,486	742,957	224,743	**Total Chevrolet**	2,299,771	2,334,113	669,276
Chrysler	204,881	205,601	27,917	Pontiac	304,545	345,214	22,071
Imperial	15,393	14,956	4,525	Grand Prix	98,587	168,803	17,490
Total Chrysler-				Le Mans/Tempest	198,41	205,135	32,165
Plymouth	833,760	963,514	257,185	Firebird	15,828	58,296	29,882
Challenger	27,770	30,211	6,063	Ventura	85,200	89,150	36,322
Dart	182,122	239,598	100,041	**Total Pontiac**	702,571	866,598	137,930
Coronet/Charger	178,261	188,584	48,874	Oldsmobile	389,089	383,623	39,758
Dodge	145,441	134,470	18,806	Toronado	51,267	56,468	4,081
Total Dodge	533,594	592,863	173,784	F-85/Cutlass	341,130	422,477	95,734
Total Chrysler Corp.	1,367,354	1,556,377	430,969	Omega	25,708	55,551	22,487
Ford Motor Co.				**Total Oldsmobile**	807,194	918,119	162,060
Ford	812,718	752,468	108,110	Buick	425,813	425,207	37,581
Torino	365,532	298,545	116,530	Riviera	36,210	29,992	4,312
Club Wagon	23,934	23,105	8,399	Century/Skylark	226,534	311,879	51,435
Maverick	165,934	184,810	89,688	Apollo		59,128	18,762
Pinto	322,338	366,748	135,681	**Total Buick**	688,557	826,206	112,090
Mustang	118,972	193,129	135,698	Cadillac	233,456	252,767	51,710
Thunderbird	58,582	90,404	15,249	Eldorado	43,795	54,931	10,474
Total Ford	1,868,010	1,909,209	609,355	**Total Cadillac**	277,251	307,698	62,184
Mercury	150,671	132,896	20,986	**Total General**			
Montego	140,477	146,565	29,573	**Motors Corp.**	4,775,344	5,252,734	1,143,540
Cougar	53,594	70,714	36,046	**Checkers Motors**			
Comet	83,101	103,275	41,915	**Corp.**	5,504	6,333	1,981
Total Mercury	427,843	453,250	128,520	**Total Passenger Cars**	8,828,205	9,667,152	2,462,089

Total Road and Street Mileage in United States

Source: Federal Highway Administration, Dept. of Transportation 1972

State	Rural	Urban	Surfaced	Total	State	Rural	Urban	Surfaced	Total
Ala.	67,423	17,924	77,577	85,347	Neb.	91,667	6,880	77,312	98,547
Alaska	7,240	1,391	5,126	8,631	Nev.	47,738	1,921	16,156	49,659
Ariz.	42,993	6,308	22,760	49,301	N.H.	10,135	4,839	12,383	14,974
Ark.	68,398	9,487	62,526	77,885	N.J.	13,605	18,731	30,459	32,336
Calif.	120,796	45,676	122,276	166,472	N.M.	63,190	4,885	21,238	68,075
Colo.	74,444	7,580	51,883	82,024	N.Y.	66,516	40,779	103,058	107,295
Conn.	5,395	13,229	18,510	18,624	N.C.	72,432	14,179	79,738	86,611
Del.	4,339	797	5,119	5,136	N.D.	103,148	3,168	69,771	106,316
Fla.	71,076	25,698	71,342	96,774	Ohio	85,823	23,724	107,933	109,547
Ga.	85,173	15,067	69,080	100,240	Okla.	93,543	14,338	82,321	107,881
Hawaii	2,697	1,012	3,542	3,709	Ore.	92,964	6,567	62,671	99,531
Idaho	52,834	3,157	30,602	55,991	Pa.	89,915	24,229	98,122	114,144
Ill.	102,439	27,989	124,094	130,428	R.I.	1,022	4,450	5,215	5,472
Ind.	75,344	15,629	86,736	90,973	S.C.	52,919	7,019	41,418	59,938
Iowa	99,162	13,768	106,769	112,930	S.D.	79,812	2,978	60,543	82,790
Kan.	123,361	11,322	101,013	134,683	Tenn.	68,623	11,954	78,835	80,577
Ky.	63,888	5,751	62,253	69,639	Tex.	198,712	51,834	187,127	250,546
La.	42,465	11,180	49,954	53,645	Utah	42,863	4,468	23,405	47,331
Maine	18,923	2,521	19,948	21,444	Vt.	13,556	1,011	12,656	14,567
Md.	22,557	4,180	26,671	26,737	Va.	52,548	9,278	61,077	61,826
Mass.	6,138	23,554	29,323	29,692	Wash.	70,286	9,993	64,288	80,279
Mich.	97,828	20,232	100,654	118,060	W.Va.	32,527	3,643	27,002	36,170
Minn.	110,620	17,444	116,036	128,064	Wis.	89,447	14,375	98,220	103,822
Miss.	59,847	6,977	64,739	66,824	Wyo.	39,342	1,289	17,658	40,631
Mo.	100,054	15,536	108,759	115,590	D. of C.			1,099	1,099
Mon.	75,520	2,386	44,355	77,906	**Total**				

Car, Truck and Bus Drivers in the U.S.

Source: Federal Highway Administration, estimated total licenses in force during 1973.

State	No. of drivers	State	No. of drivers	State	No. of drivers	State	No. of drivers
Alabama	1,851,584	Indiana	2,959,000	Nebraska	1,086,797	South Carolina	1,415,728
Alaska	161,188	Iowa	1,780,781	Nevada	388,842	South Dakota	417,071
Arizona	1,221,771	Kansas	1,593,442	New Hampshire	505,322	Tennessee	2,244,706
Arkansas	1,203,248	Kentucky	1,722,322	New Jersey	4,342,059	Texas	6,973,335
California	12,775,000	Louisiana	2,015,999	New Mexico	665,839	Utah	664,546
Colorado	1,611,341	Maine	595,478	New York	8,545,595	Vermont	292,873
Connecticut	1,807,796	Maryland	2,217,934	North Carolina	3,060,227	Virginia	2,855,948
Delaware	370,704	Massachusetts	3,209,000	North Dakota	353,574	Washington	2,145,283
Florida	4,758,804	Michigan	5,436,121	Ohio	6,294,028	West Virginia	1,051,025
Georgia	3,338,920	Minnesota	2,384,410	Oklahoma	1,673,664	Wisconsin	2,593,838
Hawaii	475,176	Mississippi	1,379,109	Oregon	1,706,982	Wyoming	224,097
Idaho	539,340	Missouri	2,874,676	Pennsylvania	6,573,742	Dist. of Col.	335,388
Illinois	6,124,554	Montana	462,047	Rhode Island	558,127	**Total**	121,838,381

Auto Registrations, Taxes, Gasoline, Drivers' Ages

Source: Federal Highway Adm.

State	Driver's Age Jan. 1, (1) Regular	Driver's Age 1974 (2) Juvenile	Registered autos, buses & trucks est. (1973) Number	State Gas Tax per gal. (1973) Cents	Motor Fuel Gross Tax Collections $1,000 (1973)	Motor Fuel consumption (1973) Highway 1,000 Gallons	Non-highway 1,000 Gallons	Total 1,000 Gallons
Alabama	16		2,353,629	7	154,572	1,845,423	43,009	1,888,432
Alaska	16		160,958	8	9,621	106,678	38,490	145,168
Arizona	16		1,419,452	7	91,145	1,158,608	49,278	1,207,886
Arkansas	16		1,185,423	7.5	106,079	1,132,251	30,484	1,162,735
California	16/18	14	13,412,774	7	748,619	10,314,828	224,340	10,539,168
Colorado	21	16	1,803,167	7	95,036	1,339,563	60,790	1,400,353
Connecticut	16/18		1,890,632	10	146,679	1,363,064	23,315	1,386,379
Delaware	16/18		333,137	8	26,671	304,189	6,191	310,380
Florida	16/18		5,347,245	8	357,425	4,072,726	111,688	4,184,414
Georgia	16		3,170,412	7.5	236,253	2,838,473	49,575	2,888,048
Hawaii	15		477,780	5	13,753	273,261	11,472	284,733
Idaho	16	14	590,126	8.5	41,490	457,288	35,223	492,511
Illinois	18	16	5,951,948	7.5	382,772	4,838,664	306,124	5,144,788
Indiana	16/21		2,978,209	8	245,637	2,721,404	95,103	2,816,507
Iowa	16/18	14	1,978,631	7	116,807	1,493,901	203,978	1,697,879
Kansas	16	14	1,777,799	7	95,880	1,289,920	131,720	1,421,640
Kentucky	16		2,090,748	9	171,734	1,699,782	29,115	1,728,897
Louisiana	17	15	2,057,279	8	154,004	1,737,330	50,745	1,788,075
Maine	15/17	15	596,345	9	51,139	533,046	12,087	545,133
Maryland	16/18		2,258,772	9	180,359	1,873,422	24,531	1,897,953
Massachusetts	18	16½	2,951,795	7.5	181,628	2,395,795	26,413	2,422,208
Michigan	16/18	14	5,239,792	7	396,779	4,557,437	172,522	4,729,959
Minnesota	16/18	15	2,452,616	7	147,830	1,980,187	182,569	2,162,756
Mississippi	15		1,312,445	8	117,453	1,216,484	31,059	1,247,543
Missouri	16		2,744,553	7	197,053	2,625,743	129,665	2,755,408
Montana	15/16		567,056	7	37,430	438,741	35,857	474,598
Nebraska	16	14	1,096,840	8.5	81,056	854,567	54,724	909,291
Nevada	16	14	436,978	6	25,359	377,738	15,792	393,530
New Hampshire	16/18	16	462,140	9	38,091	408,868	6,623	415,491
New Jersey	17	16	4,073,749	8	291,940	3,319,546	58,276	3,377,822
New Mexico	15/16		725,637	7	54,347	679,487	16,111	695,598
New York	17/18	16	7,319,493	8	502,226	5,939,779	244,782	6,184,561
North Carolina	16/18		3,445,377	9	283,258	2,834,535	79,501	2,914,036
North Dakota	16	14	489,442	7	23,795	325,271	105,608	430,879
Ohio	16/18	14	6,678,903	7	372,376	4,964,465	134,941	5,099,406
Oklahoma	16		1,984,145	6.5	112,901	1,569,792	48,870	1,618,662
Oregon	16	14	1,605,880	7	85,663	1,247,367	51,315	1,298,682
Pennsylvania	17/18	16	6,674,740	8	434,237	5,119,071	174,952	5,294,023
Rhode Island	16/18		562,830	8	33,153	380,298	13,170	393,468
South Carolina	16	15	1,601,114	8	135,634	1,482,460	32,934	1,515,394
South Dakota	16	14	486,059	7	30,995	405,865	73,363	479,228
Tennessee	16	14	2,466,821	7	198,295	2,171,725	43,004	2,214,729
Texas	16/18	15	7,815,645	5	383,641	7,105,036	152,329	7,257,365
Utah	16/17		751,313	7	47,351	619,527	25,098	644,625
Vermont	18	16	274,563	9	23,005	251,926	5,892	257,818
Virginia	16/18		2,793,549	9	251,099	2,508,530	51,086	2,559,616
Washington	16/18		2,370,610	9	165,295	1,674,245	56,238	1,730,483
West Virginia	16/18		911,005	8.5	71,981	750,577	9,496	760,073
Wisconsin	16/18	14	2,472,201	7	160,883	2,112,759	124,043	2,236,802
Wyoming	16	14	293,912	7	23,159	264,428	41,378	305,806
District of Columbia	18	16	261,207	8	18,598	228,898	4,684	233,582
Totals			**125,156,876**		**8,352,186**	**102,204,968**	**3,739,553**	**105,944,521**

(1) Unrestricted operation of private passenger car. When 2 ages are shown, license is issued at lower age upon completion of approved driver education course. (2) Juvenile license issued for use between home and school in Cal., Iowa, Kan., Me., Mich., Neb., Nev., N.H., N.D., Oreg. restricted to daylight or curfew hours in Idaho, Ill., La., Mass., Minn., N.Y., Pa., S.C., S.D., Tenn., Wisc.: hardship cases in Ohio and Texas: for agricultural pursuits in N.J. (3) Estimated.

Auto Registrations, Taxes, Gasoline, Drivers' Ages in Canada

Source: Statistics Canada and Digest of Motor Laws, 1974

Province	Driver's Age Min. Minor (1974)		Registered¹ autos, buses, trucks & Motorcycles (1972)	Province Gas Tax per gal. (1972) cents	Motor Fuel Gross Tax Collections 1,000 (1972)	Motor Fuel Consumption (1972)² Public Roads & Highways 1,000 gallons	Non-Highway 1,000 gallons	Total³ 1,000 gallons
Newfoundland	17		140,650	25	25.985	88,045	14,255	102,300
Prince Edward	16	*	45,430	21	6.703	30,015	3,441	33,456
Nova Scotia	16	*	304,028	21	45,725	198,203	10,513	208,716
New Brunswick	18	16-18	235,108	20	37,654	172,317	16,449	188,766
Quebec	17	16	2,589,351	19	342,110	1,511,596	26,494	1,538,090
Ontario	16	-	3,382,497	19	486,660	2,293,403	95,535	2,388,938
Manitoba	16	*	428,360	17	50,947	257,291	78,329	335,620
Saskatchewan	16	-	496,214	19	54,939	243,111	118,949	362,060
Alberta	16	14	864,397	15	90,868	510,382	123,898	634,280
British Columbia	19	16	1,191,953	15	116,906	611,593	107,926	719,519
Yukon & Northwest Territories	—	—	22,779	14	4,929	18,612	4,295	22,907
Total			9,700,767	17.9	1,263,430	5,934,572	600,025	6,534,797

(1) Registrations include: passenger automobiles 7,407,275; motor trucks and truck tractors 1,639,175; buses 42,802; motorcycles 248,501; other motor vehicles (includes farm tractors) 363,014. (2) Refers to gasoline sales only and excludes aviation and aviation turbo fuels. (3) Gasoline for motive purposes only; excludes aviation and aviation turbo fuels.
* No junior permit.

UNITED STATES POPULATION

Population Growth Rate Drops Sharply

By Vincent P. Barabba
Director, Bureau of the Census
Social and Economic Statistics Administration
U.S. Department of Commerce

On January 1, 1974, the U.S. population including Armed Forces overseas was estimated to be 211,210,-000, an increase of 1,505,000, over January 1, 1973. The numerical gain was the lowest since 1945, and the growth rate (7.2 per 1,000 of midyear population) the lowest since 1937.

During 1973 there were an estimated 3,141,000 births, more than half a million under the 1970 figure of 3.7 million, and the lowest number since 1945 when there were 2.9 million births.

Lowest Fertility

Birth and fertility rates dropped to their lowest points in history in 1973. It was the second consecutive year in which new lows were reached. Because of the sharp decline in births, the total fertility rate dropped to 1.9 births per woman, well below the estimated population replacement level of 2.1 children. The total fertility rate is the annual total of births expressed in terms of the implied completed family size of 1,000 women. If the current trend continues, the United States would reach zero population growth sometime in the first half of the 21st century.

In addition the general fertility rate for women age 18 and younger is dropping — from 204 births per 1,000 women among those born in 1935-39 to 104 births per 1,000 women among those born in 1950-55. Also, women are expecting to have fewer children. As recently as 1967, wives 18 to 24 years old anticipated having an average of 2.9 children during their lifetimes. Surveys for 1972 and 1973 show an anticipated average of only 2.3 children.

With immigration averaging more than 350,000 annually since 1960 and birth and fertility rates declining, immigration constitutes a larger proportion of the U.S. population growth than in the past. Twenty-two percent of the 1973 population gain of 1.5 million resulted from a net immigration of 344,000.

Declining birth and fertility rates also resulted in a 2.2 percent drop in elementary school enrollment in 1973. Fall enrollment, both public and private, was 59.4 million, down from 60.1 million a year earlier. High school enrollment has not yet been affected. It was up slightly in 1973 to 15.3 million, and college enrollment was down slightly to 8.2 million.

Because proportionately there are fewer children, older Americans will play an ever more significant future role. Persons age 65 and older made up 9.8 percent of the 1970 population and 10.1 percent in 1973. The proportion of children under age 14 declined from 26.3 percent to 24.5 percent in 1970-73, and the median age of the U.S. population rose from 27.9 years to 28.4 years.

Mobile Americans

A Census Bureau study shows that 31.8 percent of the U.S. population age 3 and older changed residence during the three years ending in March 1973. Central cities of Standard Metropolitan Statistical Areas (SMSA's) had a net loss of 4,021,000 persons in the three years, continuing the pattern of the 1960-70 decade. At the same time, the suburban zone within SMSA's but outside of central cities, had a net migration gain of 3,077,000 persons, not enough to offset a net migration loss of 944,000 persons from SMSA's to nonmetropolitan areas.

Together, the West and South experienced a net migration gain of 1,250,000 persons from the Northeast and North Central regions and during 1970-73, more blacks (198,000) moved to the South from the Northeast and North Central States than the 117,000 who moved from the South to the Northeast and North Central States, a reversal of an historic pattern.

Voter Participation

A Census Bureau survey of voter participation in the 1972 national election showed that, of the approximately 11 million persons, age 18-20 added to the electorate by the 26th Amendment, only 48 percent reported that they voted. But among those enrolled in school, 73 percent reported that they were registered and 64 percent said they voted. Among those not in school, about 50 percent were registered and 40 percent voted.

The survey showed that higher levels of registration and voting were associated with persons who were male, white, middle age (35-64), had at least a high school education, were in families with incomes greater than $10,000, and were white collar workers.

Incomes to Increase

By 1985, median family income in the U.S. would rise to $15,500 measured in terms of 1971 purchasing power, if the 3 percent annual rate of increase of the past 20 years continues, a Census Bureau study shows. This is about 50 percent greater than the 1971 median of $10,300. In 1971 only about 15 percent of the families had incomes greater than $15,500. During the same period, the proportion of families having money income in excess of $25,000 would more than triple, increasing from 5.3 percent in 1971 to 18.5 percent in 1985. The proportion of families with incomes of $4,000 or less would decrease to 6.6 percent, almost one-half of the 13 percent in 1971.

The Nation's Spanish origin population totaled 10.6 million in March 1973. Included in the estimate were 6.3 million persons of Mexican origin, 1.5 million of Puerto Rican origin, 700,000 of Cuban origin, and 2 million of Central or South American or other Spanish origin.

Local Property Tax Revenue Up

Reports from the 1972 Census of Governments show that although local government property tax collections in 1971 ($36.7 billion) were more than twice the 1961 total ($17.4 billion), they constituted a smaller portion of total revenue. They accounted for 36.4 percent of all revenue and 84.6 percent of tax revenue in fiscal 1971, compared with 42.9 percent and 87.7 percent, respectively, in fiscal 1961.

Real property assessments by local officials throughout the Nation averaged 33 percent of sales value in 1971. Residential, commercial, and industrial property assessments averaged 34 percent of sales price, vacant lots about 28 percent, and rural acreage about 21 percent.

Local schools are getting approximately half of local property tax revenue. During fiscal 1972, school districts received $39.3 billion from all sources, 73 percent more than in fiscal 1967. Overall, they expended $39.1 billion in 1971-72, more than half for wages and salaries. Payrolls totaled $26.1 billion, or 75 percent more than five years earlier, reflecting an increase in the total of employees as well as cost of living raises.

At the beginning of 1972 there were 78,269 governmental units in the U.S. The 15,781 local school districts and 23,885 special districts accounted for more than half of the total. The remainder includes the Federal Government, the 50 State governments, 3,044 county, 18,517 city and 16,991 township governments.

Population of the United States, 1960-70

Region, Division and State	1970 census	1960 census	Pct. + or -	1970 census Urban	1970 census Rural	Pct. Urban	Rank 1970	Rank 1960
United States..............	203,235,298	179,323,175	13.3	149,324,930	53,886,996	73.5	...	...
Regions:								
Northeast..............	48,999,999	44,677,819	9.7	39,449,818	9,590,885	80.4	...	...
North Central..........	56,577,067	51,619,139	9.6	40,480,760	16,090,903	71.6	...	...
South................	62,798,347	54,973,113	14.2	40,539,961	22,255,406	64.6	...	...
West.................	34,809,359	28,053,104	24.1	28,854,391	5,949,802	82.9	...	...
New England.......	11,847,186	10,509,367	12.7	9,043,517	2,798,146	76.4	...	...
Maine................	993,663	969,265	2.5	504,157	487,891	50.8	38	36
New Hampshire........	737,681	606,921	21.5	416,040	321,641	56.4	42	45
Vermont.............	444,732	389,881	14.1	142,889	301,441	32.2	49	47
Massachusetts........	5,689,170	5,148,578	10.5	4,810,449	878,721	84.6	10	9
Rhode Island.........	949,723	859,488	10.5	824,930	121,795	87.1	39	39
Connecticut..........	3,032,217	2,535,234	19.6	2,345,052	686,657	77.4	24	25
Middle Atlantic......	37,152,813	34,168,452	8.7	30,406,301	6,792,739	81.7	...	...
New York............	18,241,266	16,782,304	8.4	15,602,486	2,634,481	85.6	2	1
New Jersey..........	7,168,164	6,066,782	18.2	6,373,405	794,759	88.9	8	8
Pennsylvania.........	11,793,909	11,319,366	4.2	8,430,410	3,363,499	71.5	3	3
East North Central......	40,252,678	36,225,024	11.1	30,091,847	10,160,629	74.8	...	...
Ohio................	10,652,017	9,706,397	9.7	8,025,775	2,625,242	75.3	6	5
Indiana.............	5,193,669	4,662,498	11.4	3,372,060	1,821,609	64.9	11	11
Illinois.............	11,113,976	10,081,158	10.2	9,229,821	1,884,155	83.0	5	4
Michigan............	8,875,083	7,823,194	13.4	6,553,773	2,321,310	73.8	7	7
Wisconsin...........	4,417,933	3,951,777	11.8	2,910,418	1,507,313	65.9	16	15
West North Central......	16,324,389	15,394,115	6.0	10,388,913	5,930,274	63.7	...	...
Minnesota...........	3,805,069	3,413,864	11.5	2,527,308	1,277,663	66.4	19	18
Iowa................	2,825,041	2,757,537	2.4	1,616,405	1,207,971	57.2	25	24
Missouri............	4,677,399	4,319,813	8.3	3,277,662	1,398,839	70.1	13	13
North Dakota........	617,781	632,446	-2.3	273,442	344,319	44.3	46	44
South Dakota........	666,257	680,514	-2.1	296,628	368,879	44.6	45	40
Nebraska...........	1,483,791	1,411,330	5.1	912,598	570,895	61.5	35	34
Kansas.............	2,249,071	2,178,611	3.2	1,484,870	761,708	66.1	28	28
South Atlantic........	30,671,337	25,971,732	18.1	19,523,920	11,147,417	63.7	...	...
Delaware............	548,104	446,292	22.8	395,569	152,535	72.2	47	46
Maryland............	3,922,399	3,100,689	26.5	3,003,935	918,464	76.6	18	21
District of Columbia..	756,510	763,956	-1.0	756,510		100.0	41	...
Virginia.............	4,648,494	3,966,949	17.2	2,934,841	1,713,653	63.1	14	14
West Virginia........	1,744,237	1,860,421	-6.2	679,491	1,064,746	39.0	34	30
North Carolina.......	5,082,059	4,556,155	11.5	2,285,168	2,796,891	45.0	12	12
South Carolina.......	2,590,516	2,382,594	8.7	1,232,195	1,358,321	47.6	26	26
Georgia.............	4,589,575	3,943,116	16.4	2,768,074	1,821,501	60.3	15	16
Florida.............	6,789,443	4,951,560	37.1	5,468,137	1,321,306	80.5	9	10
East South Central......	12,804,522	12,050,126	6.3	6,987,943	5,815,527	54.6	...	...
Kentucky............	3,219,311	3,038,156	6.0	1,684,053	1,534,653	52.3	23	22
Tennessee...........	3,924,164	3,567,089	10.0	2,305,307	1,618,380	58.7	17	17
Alabama............	3,444,165	3,266,740	5.4	2,011,941	1,432,224	58.4	21	19
Mississippi..........	2,216,912	2,178,141	1.8	986,642	1,230,270	44.5	29	29
West South Central......	19,322,458	16,951,255	14.0	14,028,098	5,292,462	72.6	...	...
Arkansas............	1,923,295	1,786,272	7.7	960,865	962,430	50.0	32	31
Louisiana...........	3,643,180	3,257,022	11.9	2,406,150	1,235,156	66.1	20	20
Oklahoma...........	2,559,253	2,328,284	9.9	1,740,137	819,092	68.0	27	27
Texas..............	11,196,730	9,579,677	16.9	8,920,946	2,275,784	79.7	4	6
Mountain..........	8,283,585	6,855,060	20.8	6,054,979	2,226,583	73.1	...	...
Montana............	694,409	674,767	2.9	370,676	323,733	53.4	44	41
Idaho..............	713,008	667,191	6.9	385,434	327,133	54.1	43	42
Wyoming...........	332,416	330,066	0.7	201,111	131,305	60.5	50	48
Colorado...........	2,207,259	1,753,947	25.8	1,733,311	473,948	78.5	30	33
New Mexico.........	1,016,000	951,023	6.8	708,775	307,225	69.8	37	37
Arizona............	1,772,482	1,302,161	36.1	1,408,864	362,036	79.5	33	35
Utah...............	1,059,273	890,627	18.9	851,472	207,801	80.4	36	38
Nevada............	488,738	285,278	71.3	395,336	93,402	80.9	48	49
Pacific.............	26,525,774	21,198,044	25.1	22,799,412	3,723,219	86.0	...	...
Washington..........	3,409,169	2,853,214	19.5	2,476,468	932,701	72.6	22	23
Oregon.............	2,091,385	1,768,687	18.2	1,402,704	688,681	67.1	31	32
California...........	19,953,134	15,717,204	27.0	18,136,045	1,817,089	90.9	1	2
Alaska..............	302,173	226,167	33.6	145,512	154,870	48.4	51	50
Hawaii.............	769,913	632,772	21.7	638,683	129,878	83.1	40	43

Urban and rural figures do not equal total 1970 population because of errors discovered by census bureau after tabulation.

Congressional Apportionment

State	1970 Census	1960 Census	State	1970 Census	1960 Census	State	1970 Census	1960 Census	State	1970 Census	1960 Census	State	1970 Census	1960 Census
Ala.....	7	8	Idaho..	2	2	Minn....	8	8	N.D....	1	2	Vt.....	1	1
Alaska.	1	1	Ill......	24	24	Miss.....	5	5	Ohio....	23	24	Va.....	10	10
Ariz....	4	3	Ind.....	11	11	Mo.....	10	10	Okla....	6	6	Wash...	7	7
Ark.....	4	4	Iowa...	6	7	Mont....	2	2	Ore.....	4	4	W.Va...	4	5
Calif...	43	38	Kan....	5	5	Neb.....	3	3	Pa.....	25	27	Wis.....	9	10
Colo....	5	4	Ky.....	7	7	Nev.....	1	1	R.I.....	2	2	Wyo.....	1	1
Conn...	6	6	La......	8	8	N.H.....	2	2	S.C.....	6	6			
Del.....	1	1	Me......	2	2	N.J.....	15	15	S.D.....	2	2	**Totals...**	**435**	**435**
Fla.....	15	12	Md.....	8	8	N.M.....	2	2	Tenn....	8	9			
Ga.....	10	10	Mass...	12	12	N.Y.....	39	41	Texas....	24	23			
Hawaii.	2	2	Mich...	19	19	N.C.....	11	11	Utah....	2	2			

The chief reason why the Constitution provided for a census of the population every 10 years was to give a basis for apportionment of Representatives among the states. This apportionment has largely determined the number of electoral votes allotted to each state.

The number of Representatives of each state in Congress is determined by the state's population, except that each state is entitled to one Representative regardless of population. A Congressional apportionment has been made after each decennial census except that of 1920.

Under provisions of a law that became effective Nov. 15, 1941, apportionment of Representatives is made by the method of equal proportions. In the application of this method, the apportionment is made so that the average population per Representative has the least possible variation between one state and any other. The first House of Representatives, in 1790, had 65 members, or one Representative for each 30,000 of the estimated population, as provided by the Constitution. As the population grew, the number of Representatives was increased but the total membership has been fixed at 435 since 1912.

United States Population (Official Census), 1790-1880

Source: Bureau of the Census

State	1790	1800	1810	1820	1830[1]	1840[1]	1850	1860	1870	1880
Ala.		1,250	9,046	127,901	309,527	590,756	771,623	964,201	996,992	1,262,505
Ariz.									9,658	40,440
Ark.			1,062	14,273	30,388	97,574	209,897	435,450	484,471	802,525
Calif.							92,597	379,994	560,247	864,694
Colo.								34,277	39,864	194,327
Conn.	237,946	251,002	261,942	275,248	297,675	309,978	370,792	460,147	537,454	622,700
Del.	59,096	64,273	72,674	72,749	76,748	78,085	91,532	112,216	125,015	146,608
D.C.		14,093	24,023	33,039	39,834	43,712	51,687	75,080	131,700	177,624
Fla.					34,730	54,477	87,445	140,424	187,748	269,493
Ga.	82,548	162,686	252,433	340,989	516,823	691,392	906,185	1,057,286	1,184,109	1,542,180
Id.									14,999	32,610
Ill.			12,282	55,211	157,445	476,183	851,470	1,711,951	2,539,891	3,077,871
Ind.		5,641	24,520	147,178	343,031	685,866	988,416	1,350,428	1,680,637	1,978,301
Iowa						43,112	192,214	674,913	1,194,020	1,624,615
Kans.								107,206	364,399	996,096
Ky.	73,677	220,995	406,511	564,317	687,917	779,828	982,405	1,155,684	1,321,011	1,648,690
La.			76,556	153,407	215,739	352,411	517,762	708,002	726,915	939,946
Me.	96,540	151,719	228,705	298,335	399,455	501,793	583,169	628,279	626,915	648,936
Md.	319,728	341,548	380,546	407,350	447,040	470,019	583,034	687,049	780,894	934,943
Mass.	378,787	422,845	472,040	523,287	610,408	737,699	994,514	1,231,066	1,457,351	1,783,085
Mich.			4,762	8,896	31,639	212,267	397,654	749,113	1,184,059	1,636,937
Minn.							6,077	172,023	439,706	780,773
Miss.		8,850	40,352	75,448	136,621	375,651	606,526	791,305	827,922	1,131,597
Mo.			19,783	66,586	140,455	383,702	682,044	1,182,012	1,721,295	2,168,380
Mont.									20,595	39,159
Neb.								28,841	122,993	452,402
Nev.								6,857	42,491	62,266
N.H.	141,885	183,858	214,460	244,161	269,328	284,574	317,976	326,073	318,300	346,991
N.J.	184,139	211,149	245,562	277,575	320,823	373,306	489,555	672,035	906,096	1,131,116
N.M.							61,547	93,516	91,874	119,565
N.Y.	340,120	589,051	959,049	1,372,812	1,918,608	2,428,921	3,097,394	3,880,735	4,382,759	5,082,871
N.C.	393,751	478,103	555,500	638,829	737,987	753,419	869,039	992,622	1,071,361	1,399,750
N.D.									*2,405	36,909
Ohio		45,365	230,760	581,434	937,903	1,519,467	1,980,329	2,339,511	2,665,260	3,198,062
Okla.										
Ore.							13,294	52,465	90,923	174,768
Penn.	434,373	602,365	810,091	1,049,458	1,348,233	1,724,033	2,311,786	2,906,215	3,521,951	4,282,891
R.I.	68,825	69,122	76,931	83,059	97,199	108,830	147,545	174,620	217,353	276,531
S.C.	249,073	345,591	415,115	502,741	581,185	594,398	668,507	703,708	705,606	995,577
S.D.									*4,837	98,268
Tenn.	35,691	105,602	261,727	422,823	681,904	829,210	1,002,717	1,109,801	1,258,520	1,542,359
Tex.							212,592	604,215	818,579	1,591,749
Utah							11,380	40,273	86,786	143,963
Vt.	85,425	154,465	217,895	235,981	280,652	291,948	314,120	315,098	330,551	332,286
Va.	821,287	880,200	974,600	1,065,366	1,211,405	1,239,797	1,421,661	1,596,318	1,225,163	1,512,565
Wash.								1,201	11,594	75,116
W. Va.									442,014	618,457
Wis.						30,945	305,391	775,881	1,054,670	1,315,497
Wyo.									9,118	20,789
U.S.	3,929,214	5,308,483	7,239,881	9,638,453	12,866,020	17,069,453	23,191,876	31,443,321	38,558,371	50,155,783

*1860 figure is for Dakota Territory; 1870 figures are for parts of Dakota Territory.
(1.) U.S. TOTAL INCLUDES PERSONS (5,318 in 1830 and 6,100 in 1840) on public ships in the service of the United States not credited to any region, division, or state.

U.S. Center of Population, 1790-1970

Center of population is that point which may be considered as center of population gravity of the U.S. or that point upon which the U.S. would balance if it were a rigid plane without weight and the population distributed thereon with each individual being assumed to have equal weight and to exert an influence on a central point proportional to his distance from that point.

Year	North latitude ° ' "	West longitude ° ' "	Approximate location
1790	39 16 30	76 11 12	23 miles east of Baltimore, Md.
1800	39 16 6	76 56 30	18 miles west of Baltimore, Md.
1810	39 11 30	77 37 12	40 miles northwest by west of Washington, D.C. (in Va.)
1820	39 5 42	78 33 0	16 miles east of Moorefield, W. Va.[1]
1830	38 57 54	79 16 54	19 miles west-southwest of Moorefield, W. Va.[1]
1840	39 2 0	80 18 0	16 miles south of Clarksburg, W. Va.[1]
1850	38 59 0	81 19 0	23 miles southeast of Parkersburg, W. Va.[1]
1860	39 0 24	82 48 48	20 miles south by east of Chillicothe, Ohio.
1870	39 12 0	83 35 42	48 miles east by north of Cincinnati, Ohio.
1880	39 4 8	84 39 40	8 miles west by south of Cincinnati, Ohio (in Ky.)
1890	39 11 56	85 32 53	20 miles east of Columbus, Ind.
1900	39 9 36	85 48 54	6 miles southeast of Columbus, Ind.
1910	39 10 12	86 32 20	In the city of Bloomington, Ind.
1920	39 10 21	86 43 15	8 miles south-southeast of Spencer, Owen County, Ind.
1930	39 3 45	87 8 6	3 miles northeast of Linton, Greene County, Ind.
1940	38 56 54	87 22 35	2 miles southeast by east of Carlisie, Haddon township, Sullivan County, Ind.
1950 (Inc. Alaska & Hawaii)	38 48 15	88 22 8	3 miles northeast of Louisville, Clay County, Ill.
1960 (Inc. Alaska & Hawaii)	38 35 58	89 12 35	6½ miles northwest of Centralia, Ill.
1970 (Inc. Alaska & Hawaii)	38 27 47	89 42 22	5 miles east southeast of Mascoutah, St. Clair County, Ill.

(1) West Virginia was set off from Virginia Dec. 31, 1862, and admitted as a State June 20,1863.

United States Population (Official Census) 1890-1970

Source: Bureau of the Census

State	1890	1900	1910	1920	1930	1940	1950	1960	1970
Alabama	1,513,401	1,828,697	2,138,093	2,348,174	2,646,248	2,832,961	3,061,743	3,266,740	3,444,165
Alaska								226,167	302,173
Arizona	88,243	122,931	204,354	334,162	435,573	499,261	749,587	1,302,161	1,772,482
Arkansas	1,128,211	1,311,564	1,574,449	1,752,204	1,854,482	1,949,387	1,909,511	1,786,272	1,923,295
California	1,213,398	1,485,053	2,377,549	3,426,861	5,677,251	6,907,387	10,586,223	15,717,204	19,953,134
Colorado	413,249	539,700	799,024	939,629	1,035,791	1,123,296	1,325,089	1,753,947	2,207,259
Connecticut	746,258	908,420	1,114,756	1,380,631	1,606,903	1,709,242	2,007,280	2,535,234	3,032,217
Delaware	168,493	184,735	202,322	223,003	238,380	266,505	318,085	446,292	548,104
Dist. of Col	230,392	278,718	331,069	437,571	486,869	663,091	802,178	763,956	756,510
Florida	391,422	528,542	752,619	968,470	1,468,211	1,897,414	2,771,305	4,951,560	6,789,443
Georgia	1,837,353	2,216,331	2,609,121	2,895,832	2,908,506	3,123,723	3,444,578	3,943,116	4,589,575
Hawaii								632,772	769,913
Idaho	88,548	161,772	325,594	431,866	445,032	524,873	588,637	667,191	713,008
Illinois	3,826,352	4,821,550	5,638,591	6,485,280	7,630,654	7,897,241	8,712,176	10,081,158	11,113,976
Indiana	2,192,404	2,516,462	2,700,876	2,930,390	3,238,503	3,427,796	3,934,224	4,662,498	5,193,669
Iowa	1,912,297	2,231,853	2,224,771	2,404,021	2,470,939	2,538,268	2,621,073	2,757,537	2,825,041
Kansas	1,428,108	1,470,495	1,690,949	1,769,257	1,880,999	1,801,028	1,905,299	2,178,611	2,249,071
Kentucky	1,858,635	2,147,174	2,289,905	2,416,630	2,614,589	2,845,627	2,944,806	3,038,156	3,219,311
Louisiana	1,118,588	1,381,625	1,656,388	1,798,509	2,101,593	2,363,880	2,683,516	3,257,022	3,643,180
Maine	661,086	694,466	742,371	768,014	797,423	847,226	913,774	969,265	993,663
Maryland	1,042,390	1,188,044	1,295,346	1,449,661	1,631,526	1,821,244	2,343,001	3,100,689	3,922,399
Massach'ts.	2,238,947	2,805,346	3,366,416	3,852,356	4,249,614	4,316,721	4,690,514	5,148,578	5,689,170
Michigan	2,093,890	2,420,982	2,810,173	3,668,412	4,842,325	5,256,106	6,371,766	7,823,194	8,875,083
Minnesota	1,310,283	1,751,394	2,075,708	2,387,125	2,563,953	2,792,300	2,982,483	3,413,864	3,805,069
Mississippi	1,289,600	1,551,270	1,797,114	1,790,618	2,009,821	2,183,796	2,178,914	2,178,141	2,216,912
Missouri	2,679,185	3,106,665	3,293,335	3,404,055	3,629,367	3,784,664	3,954,653	4,319,813	4,677,399
Montana	142,924	243,329	376,053	548,889	537,606	559,456	591,024	674,767	694,409
Nebraska	1,062,656	1,066,300	1,192,214	1,296,372	1,377,963	1,315,834	1,325,510	1,411,330	1,483,791
Nevada	47,355	42,335	81,875	77,407	91,058	110,247	160,083	285,278	488,738
N. Hamp.	376,530	411,588	430,572	443,083	465,293	491,524	533,242	606,921	737,681
New Jersey	1,444,933	1,883,669	2,537,167	3,155,900	4,041,334	4,160,165	4,835,329	6,066,782	7,168,164
New Mexico	160,282	195,310	327,301	360,350	423,317	531,818	681,187	951,023	1,016,000
New York	6,003,174	7,268,894	9,113,614	10,385,227	12,588,066	13,479,142	14,830,192	16,782,304	18,241,266
No. Carolina	1,617,949	1,893,810	2,206,287	2,559,123	3,170,276	3,571,623	4,061,929	4,556,155	5,082,059
No. Dakota	190,983	319,146	577,056	646,872	680,845	641,935	619,636	632,446	617,761
Ohio	3,672,329	4,157,545	4,767,121	5,759,394	6,646,697	6,907,612	7,946,627	9,706,397	10,652,017
Oklahoma	258,657	790,391	1,657,155	2,028,283	2,396,040	2,336,434	2,233,351	2,328,284	2,559,253
Oregon	317,704	413,536	672,765	783,389	953,786	1,089,684	1,521,341	1,768,687	2,091,385
Penn	5,258,113	6,302,115	7,665,111	8,720,017	9,631,350	9,900,180	10,498,012	11,319,366	11,793,909
Rhode Is	345,506	428,556	542,610	604,397	687,497	713,346	791,896	859,488	949,723
So. Carolina	1,151,149	1,340,316	1,515,400	1,683,724	1,738,765	1,899,804	2,117,027	2,382,594	2,590,516
So. Dakota	348,600	401,570	583,888	636,547	692,849	642,961	652,740	680,514	666,257
Tennessee	1,767,518	2,020,616	2,184,789	2,337,885	2,616,556	2,915,841	3,291,718	3,567,089	3,924,164
Texas	2,235,527	3,048,710	3,896,542	4,663,228	5,824,715	6,414,824	7,711,194	9,579,677	11,196,730
Utah	210,779	276,749	373,351	449,396	507,847	550,310	688,862	890,627	1,059,273
Vermont	332,422	343,641	355,956	352,428	359,611	359,231	377,747	389,881	444,732
Virginia	1,655,980	1,854,184	2,061,612	2,309,187	2,421,851	' 2,677,773	3,318,680	3,966,949	4,648,494
Washington	357,232	518,103	1,141,990	1,356,621	1,563,396	1,736,191	2,378,962	2,853,214	3,409,169
W. Virginia	762,794	958,800	1,221,119	1,463,701	1,729,205	1,901,974	2,005,553	1,860,421	1,744,237
Wisconsin	1,693,330	2,069,042	2,333,860	2,632,067	2,939,006	3,137,587	3,434,575	3,951,777	4,417,933
Wyoming	62,555	92,531	145,965	194,402	225,565	250,742	290,529	330,066	332,416
Tot. U.S.	62,947,714	75,994,575	91,972,266	105,710,620	122,775,046	131,669,275	150,697,361	179,323,175	203,235,298

Members of the Armed Forces overseas or other U.S. nationals overseas are not included.

50 Cities with the Largest Negro Population

Source: Bureau of the Census

City and State	Rank	1970 Number	%	1960 Number
New York, N. Y.	1	1,666,636	21.2	1,087,931
Chicago, Ill.	2	1,102,620	32.7	812,637
Detroit, Mich.	3	660,428	43.7	482,223
Philadelphia, Pa.	4	653,791	33.6	529,240
Washington, D.C.	5	537,712	71.1	411,737
Los Angeles, Calif.	6	503,606	17.9	334,916
Baltimore, Md.	7	420,210	46.4	325,589
Houston, Texas	8	316,551	25.7	215,037
Cleveland, Ohio	9	287,841	38.3	250,818
New Orleans, La.	10	267,308	45.0	233,514
Atlanta, Ga.	11	255,051	51.3	186,464
St. Louis, Mo.	12	254,191	40.9	214,377
Memphis, Tenn.	13	242,513	38.9	184,320
Dallas, Texas	14	210,238	24.9	129,242
Newark, N.J.	15	207,458	54.2	138,035
Indianapolis, Ind.	16	134,320	18.0	98,049
Birmingham, Ala.	17	126,388	42.0	135,113
Cincinnati, Ohio	18	125,070	27.6	108,754
Oakland, Calif.	19	124,710	34.5	83,618
Jacksonville, Fla.	20	118,158	22.3	105,655
Kansas City, Mo.	21	112,005	22.1	83,146
Milwaukee, Wis.	22	105,088	14.7	62,458
Pittsburgh, Pa.	23	104,904	20.2	100,692
Richmond, Va.	24	104,766	42.0	91,972
Boston, Mass.	25	104,707	16.3	63,165
Columbus, Ohio	26	99,627	18.5	77,140
San Francisco, Calif.	27	96,078	13.4	74,383
Buffalo, N.Y.	28	94,329	20.4	70,904
Gary, Ind.	29	92,695	52.8	69,123
Nashville-Davidson, Tenn.	30	87,851	19.6	76,437
Norfolk, Va.	31	87,261	28.3	78,806
Louisville, Ky.	32	86,040	23.8	70,075
Ft. Worth, Texas	33	78,324	19.9	56,440
Miami, Fla.	34	76,156	22.7	65,213
Dayton, Ohio	35	74,284	30.5	57,288
Charlotte, N.C.	36	72,972	30.3	56,248
Mobile, Ala.	37	67,356	35.4	65,619
Shreveport, La.	38	62,152	34.1	56,607
Jackson, Miss.	39	61,063	39.7	51,556
Compton, Calif.	40	55,781	71.0	28,265
Tampa, Fla.	41	54,720	19.7	46,244
Jersey City, N.J.	42	54,595	21.0	36,692
Flint, Mich.	43	54,237	28.1	34,521
Savannah, Ga.	44	53,111	44.9	53,035
San Diego, Calif.	45	52,961	7.6	34,435
Toledo, Ohio	46	52,915	13.8	40,015
Oklahoma City, Okla.	47	50,103	13.7	37,529
San Antonio, Texas	48	50,041	7.6	41,605
Rochester, N.Y.	49	49,647	16.8	23,586
E. St. Louis, Ill.	50	48,368	69.1	36,338

Household and Family Characteristics by Race, for Regions

Source: Bureau of the Census

	Northeast Urban	Northeast Rural	North Central Urban	North Central Rural	South Urban	South Rural	West Urban	West Rural
White Population								
All persons	34,883,058	9,427,446	35,772,964	5,868,219	32,212,232	18,207,876	25,904,986	5,472,194
In households	33,919,080	9,194,848	34,633,956	5,613,024	30,972,359	17,941,478	25,124,710	5,329,398
Head	11,339,522	2,751,979	11,413,201	4,749,933	10,427,974	5,619,044	8,574,651	1,653,070
14 to 24 years	628,661	134,336	926,403	251,702	917,782	361,226	774,936	95,240
25 to 34 years	1,813,323	503,239	2,083,148	807,526	1,991,622	987,740	1,714,363	290,835
35 to 44 years	1,998,345	560,192	2,024,370	864,230	1,929,128	1,025,004	1,601,758	318,790
45 to 64 years	4,503,811	1,042,062	4,122,728	1,750,327	3,654,347	2,072,639	2,979,055	629,661
65 years and over	2,395,382	512,150	2,256,552	1,076,148	1,935,095	1,171,435	1,504,539	318,544
Primary individual: Male	823,787	151,645	807,030	271,093	667,659	259,955	829,374	128,761
Female	1,596,600	232,131	1,596,602	426,444	1,369,490	468,847	1,208,160	131,619
Family head: Male	7,937,024	2,209,587	8,195,368	3,835,580	7,574,885	4,540,683	5,867,227	1,313,562
Female	982,111	158,616	814,201	216,816	815,940	349,559	669,890	79,128
Wife of head	7,652,346	2,146,061	7,985,311	3,727,274	7,389,352	4,410,024	5,702,582	1,278,242
Children Under 18 Years								
All families	8,919,135	2,368,203	9,089,569	4,052,396	8,390,825	4,890,242	6,537,117	1,392,690
With own children under 18 years	4,584,736	1,353,307	4,929,020	2,256,756	4,519,739	2,616,560	3,616,094	773,423
Number of own under 18 yrs	10,274,201	3,258,604	11,370,142	5,624,725	9,645,885	5,796,905	8,093,135	1,884,319
Number of own under 6 yrs	3,091,347	970,872	3,446,997	1,583,268	2,930,580	1,714,273	2,447,638	518,967
Husband-wife families	7,650,541	2,147,190	7,984,914	3,730,584	7,397,548	4,414,290	5,714,742	1,281,210
With own children under 18 yrs	4,103,377	1,259,810	4,469,719	2,125,638	4,038,238	2,422,233	3,137,802	711,254
Number of own under 18 yrs	9,277,376	3,054,156	10,415,342	5,331,450	8,681,504	5,386,887	7,104,987	1,746,002
Number of own under 6 yrs	2,861,268	929,504	3,239,679	1,527,395	2,727,718	1,635,457	2,215,558	490,309
Families with female head	982,111	158,616	814,201	216,816	815,940	349,559	669,890	79,128
With own children under 18 years	422,250	75,841	401,874	104,394	424,036	156,464	423,452	49,388
Number of own under 18 yrs	885,216	168,583	842,258	236,438	855,282	333,381	885,270	112,989
Number of own under 6 yrs	211,287	34,890	189,300	46,409	183,691	64,603	214,217	24,559
Marital Status								
Male, 14 yrs. and over	12,444,611	3,313,507	12,556,025	5,643,203	11,578,384	6,593,397	9,309,611	2,020,714
Single	3,667,887	888,197	3,536,779	1,506,178	3,111,973	1,614,286	2,651,313	546,361
Married, except separated	7,934,969	2,226,080	8,204,714	3,824,546	7,730,080	4,591,228	5,936,659	1,336,333
14 to 19 years	30,276	10,475	35,828	22,606	75,925	44,876	45,153	9,197
20 to 34 years	1,898,608	589,533	2,355,174	973,070	2,369,546	1,265,235	1,793,987	340,711
35 to 64 years	4,889,678	1,344,570	4,752,271	2,236,440	4,316,711	2,605,898	4,390,869	798,569
Female, 14 yrs. and over	14,193,572	3,433,257	14,018,539	5,718,049	12,699,860	6,817,000	9,966,606	1,926,577
Single	3,544,700	722,927	3,264,869	1,122,496	2,547,782	1,185,662	2,112,525	360,334
Married, except separated	7,950,573	2,225,192	8,232,039	3,835,482	7,728,776	4,610,944	5,922,390	1,322,180
14 to 19 years	96,631	33,855	168,125	72,057	223,954	148,661	141,434	28,631
20 to 34 years	2,301,755	713,096	2,752,341	1,182,156	2,694,281	1,507,899	2,069,094	410,960
35 to 64 years	4,775,795	1,283,825	4,581,126	2,177,943	4,157,126	2,520,537	3,215,674	762,703
Negro Population								
All persons	4,214,819	129,334	4,446,946	124,604	8,063,781	3,906,180	1,641,772	52,853
In households	4,113,224	101,853	4,356,720	93,928	7,813,805	3,804,140	1,585,464	36,988
Head	1,252,116	27,332	1,257,211	26,662	2,211,638	898,624	495,961	10,716
14 to 24 years	102,634	1,232	113,019	1,199	171,929	43,647	50,323	697
25 to 34 Years	301,696	4,640	277,381	3,274	429,513	128,908	124,988	1,860
35 to 44 years	289,793	6,129	280,349	4,329	436,296	153,667	110,814	2,174
45 to 64 years	415,546	10,520	424,432	10,231	789,399	351,415	159,703	4,055
65 years and over	142,447	4,811	162,030	7,629	384,501	220,987	50,133	1,930
Primary individual: Male	131,378	2,888	132,412	3,121	197,402	69,421	66,991	1,642
Female	173,301	2,394	149,733	2,859	289,059	77,648	63,335	963
Family head: Male	644,838	18,471	705,305	17,258	1,224,030	591,649	264,712	6,947
Female	302,599	3,579	269,761	3,424	501,147	159,906	100,923	1,164
Wife of head	596,969	16,896	656,384	16,217	1,142,114	550,493	240,529	6,268
Children Under 18 Years								
All families	947,437	22,050	975,066	20,682	1,725,177	751,555	365,635	8,111
With own children under 18 years	596,271	13,209	612,979	11,054	1,025,804	438,689	237,367	4,952
Number of own under 18 yrs	1,497,438	37,370	1,669,460	34,413	2,801,365	1,429,001	606,081	14,548
Number of own under 6 yrs	486,787	10,405	504,337	9,234	833,281	388,688	190,129	4,012
Husband-wife families	602,187	17,434	663,312	16,303	1,144,050	549,920	250,250	6,675
With own children under 18 yrs	365,431	10,522	397,377	8,599	676,726	334,434	153,588	3,956
Number of own under 18 yrs	903,317	29,373	1,057,167	26,434	1,830,076	1,105,648	384,584	11,490
Number of own under 6 yrs	305,037	8,353	333,361	7,264	582,554	315,117	126,918	3,324
Families with female head	302,599	3,579	269,761	3,424	501,147	159,906	100,923	1,164
With own children under 18 years	214,438	2,273	198,712	2,086	317,610	87,662	77,280	853
Number of own under 18 yrs	558,423	6,920	571,991	6,950	897,508	278,616	207,650	2,688
Number of own under 6 yrs	172,578	1,793	161,497	1,720	233,406	63,270	59,944	611
Marital Status								
Male, 14 years and over	1,277,559	53,049	1,372,041	54,551	2,480,076	1,225,388	531,947	26,474
Single	447,194	24,135	461,057	25,764	875,726	484,862	183,549	13,058
Married, except separated	656,462	22,715	712,719	21,376	1,263,589	612,567	270,736	9,809
14 to 19 years	5,552	190	7,587	191	15,919	6,745	2,801	177
20 to 34 years	221,380	6,821	227,474	5,549	403,805	157,508	99,430	3,627
35 to 64 years	373,635	13,137	407,395	11,566	694,912	344,160	149,122	5,041
Female, 18 years and over	1,586,269	40,213	1,593,961	38,286	2,971,088	1,310,701	7,758	13,190
Single	464,496	13,148	431,851	11,661	836,031	413,777	143,257	3,725
Married, except separated	654,616	18,837	705,092	17,953	1,265,790	610,506	257,396	6,875
14 to 19 years	16,998	384	23,842	450	48,514	22,246	8,577	206
20 to 34 years	260,754	5,720	265,367	4,384	466,842	184,828	106,480	2,247
35 to 64 years	343,257	11,262	374,945	10,632	663,376	340,465	130,638	3,843

Two types of household heads are distinguished, the head of a family and a primary individual. A family head is a household head living with one or more persons related to him by blood, marriage, or adoption. A primary individual is a household head living alone or with nonrelatives only.

Rankings of U.S. Standard Metropolitan Statistical Areas

Source: Bureau of the Census

The rankings of areas based on new SMSA definitions in order of population size according to the 1970 Census and a comparison with 1970 ranking. Includes all of the 265 Standard Metropolitan Statistical Areas (SMSA's) as currently defined by the Office of Management and Budget. There are 6 new SMSA's; 12 existing areas were combined into 6 new ones, boundary definitions were changed in 98 areas, and names were changed in 14 others.

The six new areas are Anniston, Alabama; Burlington, North Carolina; Clarksville-Hopkinsville, Tennessee-Kentucky; Fayetteville-Springdale, Arkansas; Kingsport-Bristol, Tennessee-Virginia; and St. Cloud, Minnesota. The 6 new areas resulting from mergers include Charlotte-Gasto-nia, North Carolina; Dallas-Fort Worth, Texas; Greenville-Spartanburg, South Carolina; Raleigh-Durham, North Carolina; Salt Lake City-Ogden, Utah; and northeast Pennsylvania (a combination of the former Scranton and Wilkes-Barre-Hazleton SMSA's).

Nassau-Suffolk, N.Y., replaces Pittsburgh as the ninth largest metropolitan area in the new ranking. The Nassau-Suffolk SMSA was created out of the eastern Long Island counties formerly in the New York SMSA and has a population of 2.6 million.

The combined Dallas-Fort Worth SMSA now ranks 12th and has a population of 2.4 million persons. The former Dallas SMSA ranked 16th.

SMSA	1974 Rank	1974 Pop.	1970 Rank	1970 Pop.
New York, N.Y.-N.J.[3]	1	9,973,577	1	11,571,899
Los Angeles-Long Beach, Calif.	2	7,032,075	2	7,032,075
Chicago, Ill.	3	6,978,947	3	6,978,947
Philadelphia, Pa.-N.J.	4	4,817,914	4	4,817,914
Detroit, Mich.[1]	5	4,431,390	5	4,199,931
San Francisco-Oakland, Calif.	6	3,109,519	6	3,109,519
Washington, D.C.-Md.-Va.[1]	7	2,908,801	7	2,861,123
Boston, Mass.[1]	8	2,899,101	8	2,753,700
Nassau-Suffolk, N.Y.[4]	9	2,553,030		
St. Louis, Mo.-Ill.[1]	10	2,410,163	10	2,363,017
Pittsburgh, Pa.	11	2,401,245	9	2,401,245
Dallas-Fort Worth, Tex.[6]	12	2,377,979	16	1,555,950
Baltimore, Md.	13	2,070,670	11	2,070,670
Cleveland, Ohio	14	2,064,194	12	2,064,194
Newark, N.J.[1]	15	2,054,928	14	1,856,556
Houston, Tex.[1]	16	1,999,316	13	1,985,031
Minneapolis-St. Paul, Minn.-Wis.[3]	17	1,965,159	15	1,813,647
Atlanta, Ga.[1]	18	1,597,816	20	1,390,164
Seattle-Everett, Wash.	19	1,421,869	17	1,421,869
Anaheim-Santa Ana-Garden Grove, Calif	20	1,420,386	18	1,420,386
Milwaukee, Wis.	21	1,403,688	19	1,403,688
Cincinnati, Ohio-Ky.-Ind.	22	1,384,851	21	1,384,851
San Diego, Calif.	23	1,357,854	23	1,357,854
Buffalo, N.Y.	24	1,349,211	24	1,349,211
Kansas City, Mo.-Kans.[1]	25	1,271,515	26	1,253,916
Miami, Fla.	26	1,267,792	25	1,267,792
Denver-Boulder, Colo.[3]	27	1,237,208	27	1,227,529
Riverside-San Bernardino-Ontario, Calif.[2]	28	1,143,146	28	1,143,146
Indianapolis, Ind.	29	1,109,882	29	1,109,882
Tampa-St. Petersburg, Fla.[1]	30	1,088,549	32	1,012,594
San Jose, Calif.	31	1,064,714	30	1,064,714
New Orleans, La.	32	1,045,809	31	1,045,809
Columbus, Ohio[1]	33	1,017,847	35	916,228
Portland, Oreg.-Wash.	34	1,009,129	33	1,009,129
Phoenix, Ariz.	35	967,522	34	967,522
Rochester, N.Y.[1]	36	961,516	37	882,667
Providence-Warwick-Pawtucket, R.I.-Mass.[3]	37	905,558	36	910,781
San Antonio, Tex.[1]	38	888,179	38	864,014
Louisville, Ky.-Ind.[1]	39	867,330	40	826,553
Dayton, Ohio	40	850,266	39	850,266
Memphis, Tenn.-Ark.-Miss.[3]	41	834,006	42	770,120
Sacramento, Calif.[1]	42	800,592	41	800,592
Albany-Schnectady-Troy, N.Y.[1]	43	777,793	45	721,910
Birmingham, Ala.[1]	44	767,230	44	739,274
Toledo, Ohio-Mich.[1]	45	762,741	46	692,571
Norfolk-Virginia Beach-Portsmouth, Va.-N.C.[3]	46	732,600	47	680,600
Greensboro - Winston-Salem - High Point, N.C.[1]	47	723,304	56	603,895
Hartford, Conn.[1]	48	720,581	49	663,891
Salt Lake City-Ogden, Utah[6]	49	705,458	57	557,635
Nashville-Davidson, Tenn.[3]	50	699,144	59	541,108
Oklahoma City, Okla.[1]	51	698,180	50	640,889
Akron, Ohio	52	679,239	48	679,239
Syracuse, N.Y.	53	636,507	51	636,507
Gary-Hammond-E. Chicago, Ind.	54	633,367	52	633,367
Honolulu, Hawaii	55	629,176	53	629,176
Northeast Pennsylvania[6]	56	621,830	87	342,301
Jacksonville, Fla.[1]	57	621,519	64	528,865
Fort Lauderdale-Hollywood, Fla.	58	620,100	54	620,100
Jersey City, N.J.	59	609,266	55	609,266
Allentown-Bethlehem-Easton, Pa.-N.J.[1]	60	594,124	58	543,551
New Brunswick-Perth Amboy Sayreville, N.J.[4]	61	583,813		
Charlotte-Gastonia, N.C.[6]	62	557,785	73	409,370
Tulsa, Okla.[1]	63	550,835	68	476,945
Richmond, Va.[1]	64	542,242	65	518,319
Springfield-Chicopee-Holyoke, Mass-Conn.[1]	65	541,752	63	529,922
Omaha, Nebr.-Iowa	66	540,142	60	540,142
Grand Rapids, Mich.	67	539,225	61	539,225
Youngstown-Warren, Ohio	68	536,003	62	536,003
Flint, Mich.[1]	69	507,416	67	496,658
Wilmington, Del.-N.J.-Md.	70	499,493	66	499,493
Greenville-Spartanburg, S.C.[6]	71	473,226	101	299,502
Paterson-Clifton-Passaic, N.J.[1]	72	460,782	22	1,358,794
Long Branch-Asbury Park, N.J.[4]	73	459,379		
Orlando, Fla.[1]	74	453,270	69	428,003
Lansing-East Lansing, Mich.[3]	75	424,271	77	378,423
Raleigh-Durham, N.C.[6]	76	418,841	135	228,453
New Haven-West Haven, Conn.[3]	77	413,722	83	355,538
Fresno, Calif.	78	413,053	70	413,053
Tacoma, Wash.	79	411,027	71	411,027
Harrisburg, Pa.	80	410,626	72	410,626
Knoxville, Tenn.[1]	81	409,409	74	400,337
Bridgeport, Conn.[1]	82	401,752	76	389,153
Canton, Ohio[1]	83	393,789	80	372,210
Wichita, Kans.	84	389,352	75	389,352
Mobile, Ala.	85	376,690	78	376,690
Oxnard-Simi Valley-Ventura, Calif[2]	86	376,430	79	376,430
Baton Rouge, La.[1]	87	375,628	110	285,167
Worcester, Mass.[1]	88	372,144	86	344,320
Chattanooga, Tenn.-Ga.[1]	89	370,016	97	304,927
Davenport-Rock Island-Moline, Iowa-Ill.	90	362,638	81	362,638
Fort Wayne, Ind.[1]	91	361,984	112	280,455
El Paso, Tex.	92	359,291	82	359,291
Tucson, Ariz.	93	351,667	84	351,667
West Palm Beach-Boca Raton[2]	94	384,753	85	348,753
Beaumont-Port Arthur-Orange, Tex.	95	345,939	95	315,943
Peoria, Ill.	96	341,979	88	341,979
Utica-Rome, N.Y.	97	340,670	89	340,670
Charleston, S.C.[1]	98	336,125	99	303,849
Shreveport, La.[1]	99	334,642	104	294,703
Albuquerque, N.M.[1]	100	333,266	96	315,774
Newport News-Hampton, Va.[1]	101	333,140	105	292,159
York, Pa.	102	329,540	90	329,540
Bakersfield, Calif.	103	329,162	91	329,162
Little Rock-North Little Rock	104	329,296	92	323,296
Austin, Tex.[1]	105	323,158	103	295,516
Columbia, S.C.	106	322,880	93	322,880
Lancaster, Pa.	107	319,693	94	319,693
Des Moines, Iowa[1]	108	313,533	109	286,101
Trenton, N.J.	109	303,968	98	303,968
Binghamton, N.Y.-Pa.	110	302,672	100	302,672
Reading, Pa.	111	296,382	102	296,382
Madison, Wis.	112	290,272	106	290,272
Stockton, Calif.	113	290,208	107	290,208
Spokane, Wash.	114	287,487	108	287,487
Huntington-Ashland, W. Va.-Ky.-Ohio[1]	115	286,935	123	253,743
Evansville, Ind.-Ky.[1]	116	284,959	132	232,775
Corpus Christi, Tex.	117	284,832	111	284,832
Huntsville, Ala.[1]	118	282,450	136	228,239
South Bend, Ind.	119	280,031	113	280,031
Appleton-Oshkosh, Wis.	120	276,891	114	276,891
Augusta, Ga.-S.C.[1]	121	275,787	124	253,460
Las Vegas, Nev.	122	273,288	115	273,288
Rockford, Ill.	123	272,063	116	272,063
Lexington, Ky.[1]	124	266,701	160	174,323

SMSA	1974 Rank	1974 Pop.	1970 Rank	1970 Pop.
Duluth-Superior, Minn.-Wis..	125	265,350	117	265,350
Santa Barbara-Santa Maria-Lompoc, Calif.[7]. ...	126	264,324	118	264,324
Erie, Pa..............	127	263,654	119	263,654
Johnstown, Pa............,...	128	262,822	120	262,822
Jackson, Miss............	129	258,906	121	258,906
Lawrence-Haverhill, Mass.-N.H.[1]...........	130	258,564	133	232,415
Kalamazoo-Portage, Mich.[3].	131	257,723	147	201,550
Charleston, W. Va.[1].......	132	257,140	134	229,515
Lorain-Elyria, Ohio......	133	256,843	122	256,843
Salinas-Seaside-Monterey, Calif.[2]..........	134	250,071	125	250,071
Vallejo-Fairfield-Napa, Calif.[2]	135	249,081	126	249,081
Pensacola, Fla............	136	243,075	127	243,075
New London-Norwich, Conn.-R.I.[3]...........	137	241,556	143	208,412
Kingsport-Bristol, Tenn.-Va.[4]	138	241,123		
Colorado Springs, Colo.[1]....	139	239,288	129	235,972
Columbus, Ga.-Ala........	140	238,584	128	238,584
Ann Arbor, Mich..........	141	234,103	131	234,103
Melbourne-Titusville-Cocoa, Fla.[4]..............	142	230,006		
Lakeland-Winter Haven, Fla.[4]	143	227,222		
Macon, Ga.[1].............	144	226,782	145	206,342
Hamilton-Middletown, Ohio.	145	226,207	137	226,207
Montgomery, Ala.[1]........	146	225,785	148	201,325
Poughkeepsie, N.Y.[4].......	147	222,295		
Saginaw, Mich............	148	219,743	138	219,743
Lowell, Mass.-N.H.[3].......	149	218,268	140	212,860
Waterbury, Conn.[1]........	150	216,808	142	208,956
Eugene-Springfield, Oreg.[2]..	151	213,358	139	213,358
Fayetteville, N.C..........	152	212,042	141	212,042
Lima, Ohio[1].............	153	210,074	161	171,472
Savannah, Ga.[1]..........	154	207,938	152	187,767
Stamford, Conn.	155	206,419	144	206,419
Santa Rosa, Calif..........	156	204,885	146	204,885
Roanoke, Va.[1]...........	157	203,153	156	181,436
Modesto, Calif............	158	194,506	149	194,506
Springfield, Ohio[1]........	159	187,606	172	157,115
Salem, Oreg.............	160	186,658	153	186,658
Wheeling, W. Va.-Ohio-....	161	182,712	154	182,712
McAllen-Pharr-Edinburg, Tex.................	162	181,535	155	181,535
Topeka, Kans.[1]..........	163	180,619	173	155,322
Battle Creek, Mich.[3]......	164	180,129		
Lubbock, Tex.............	165	179,295	157	179,295
Muskegon-Muskegon Heights, Mich.[1].........	166	175,410	171	157,426
Terre Haute, Ind..........	167	175,143	158	175,143
Atlantic City, N.J.........	168	175,043	159	175,043
Springfield, Ill.[1].........	169	171,020	168	161,335
Racine, Wis..............	170	170,838	162	170,838
Portland, Maine[1]	171	170,081	183	141,625
Galveston-Texas City, Tex..	172	169,812	163	169,812
Fall River, Mass.-R.I.[1].....	173	169,549	176	149,976
Daytona Beach, Fla.[4]......	174	169,487		
Springfield, Mo.[1]........	175	168,053	174	152,929
Lincoln, Nebr............	176	167,972	164	167,972
Steubenville-Weirton, Ohio-W. Va..............	177	165,627	165	165,627
Champaign-Urbana-Rantoul, Ill.[2]. .._.......	178	163,281	166	163,281
Cedar Rapids, Iowa.......	179	163,213	167	163,213
New Bedford, Mass.[1]......	180	161,288	175	152,642
Asheville, N.C.[1]..........	181	161,059	180	145,056
Fort Smith, Ark.-Okla.......	182	160,421	169	160,421
Biloxi-Gulfport, Miss.[1].....	183	160,070	188	134,582
Killeen-Temple, Tex.[4]......	184	159,794		
Green Bay, Wis...........	185	158,244	170	158,244
Brockton, Mass.[1].........	186	150,416	151	189,820
Parkersburg-Marietta, W. Va.-Ohio[6]...........	187	148,132		
Waco, Tex...............	188	147,553	177	147,553
Lake Charles, La..........	189	145,415	178	145,415
New Britain, Conn........	190	145,269	179	145,269
Yakima, Wash.[4]..........	191	144,971		
Amarillo, Tex.............	192	144,396	181	144,396
Jackson, Mich............	193	143,274	182	143,274
Brownsville-Harlingen-San. Benito, Tex........	194	140,368	184	140,368
Anderson, Ind............	195	138,451	185	138,451
Provo-Orem, Utah.........	196	137,776	186	137,776
Altoona, Pa..............	197	135,356	187	135,356
St. Cloud, Minn.[4]........	198	134,585		
Lynchburg, Va.[1].........	199	133,258	196	123,474
Waterloo-Cedar Falls, Iowa[2].	200	132,916	189	132,916
Manchester, N.H.[1]........	201	132,512	211	108,461
Alexandria, La.[5]..........	202	131,749		
Mansfield, Ohio...........	203	129,997	190	129,997
Wichita Falls, Tex.[1].......	204	129,941	193	127,621
Muncie, Ind.............	205	129,219	191	129,219
Petersburg-Colonial Heights-Hopewell, Va.[2].	206	128,809	192	128,809
Fayetteville-Springdale, Ark.[4]	207	127,846		
Norwalk, Conn.[1].........	208	127,516	200	120,099
Decatur, Ill..............	209	125,010	195	125,010
Anchorage, Alaska[4]......	210	124,542		
Santa Cruz, Calif.[4]........	211	123,790		
Abilene, Tex[1]............	212	122,164	207	113,959
Vineland-Millville-Bridgeton, N.J.................	213	121,374	197	121,374
Reno, Nev..............	214	121,068	198	121,068
Sarasota, Fla.[4]...........	215	120,413		
Fargo-Moorhead, N. Dak.-Minn...........	216	120,238	199	120,238
Clarksville-Hopkinsville, Tenn.-Ky.[4]............	217	118,945		
Pueblo, Colo.............	218	118,238	201	118,238
Kenosha, Wis............	219	117,917	202	117,917
Florence, Ala[4]...........	220	117,743		
Bay City, Mich...........	221	117,339	203	117,339
Sioux City, Iowa-Nebr......	222	116,189	204	116,189
Tuscaloosa, Ala...........	223	116,029	205	116,029
Danbury, Conn.[1].........	224	115,538	235	78,405
Monroe, La..............	225	115,387	206	115,387
Williamsport, Pa.[4]........	226	113,296		
Texarkana, Tex.-Texarkana, Ark.[3]..............	227	112,392	217	101,198
Boise City, Idaho.........	228	112,230	208	112,230
Lafayette, La............	229	109,716	209	109,716
Lafayette-West Lafayette, Ind.................	230	109,378	210	109,378
Tallahassee, Fla.[1]........	231	109,355	216	103,047
Lawton, Okla............	232	108,144	212	108,144
Wilmington, N.C..........	233	107,219	213	107,219
Fort Myers, Fla.[4].........	234	105,216		
Gainesville, Fla...........	235	104,764	214	104,764
Bloomington-Normal, Ill.....	236	104,389	215	104,389
Anniston, Ala.[4].	237	103,092		
Elmira, N.Y.[4]............	238	101,537		
St. Joseph, Mo.[1].........	239	98,828	226	86,915
Fitchburg-Leominster, Mass...............	240	97,164	218	97,164
Tyler, Tex...............	241	97,096	219	97,096
Pittsfield, Mass.[1].........	242	96,817	233	79,727
Albany, Ga.[1]............	243	96,683	224	89,639
Burlington, N.C.[4].........	244	96,362		
Sioux Falls, S. Dak........	245	95,209	220	95,209
Gadsden, Ala............	246	94,144	221	94,144
Richland-Kennewick, Wash.[4]	247	93,356		
Odessa, Tex.............	248	91,805	222	91,805
Dubuque, Iowa...........	249	90,609	223	90,609
Billings, Mont............	250	87,367	225	87,367
Nashua, N.H.[1]..........	251	86,280	239	66,458
Pine Bluff, Ark...........	252	85,329	227	85,329
Rochester, Minn..........	253	84,104	228	84,104
Sherman-Denison, Tex.....	254	83,225	229	83,225
Great Falls, Mont.........	255	81,804	230	81,804
Columbia, Mo............	256	80,911	231	80,911
La Crosse, Wis...........	257	80,468	232	80,468
Owensboro, Ky...........	258	79,486	234	79,486
Laredo, Tex.............	259	72,859	236	72,859
Lewiston-Auburn, Maine.....	260	72,474	237	72,474
San Angelo, Tex..........	261	71,047	238	71,047
Bristol, Conn.[1]..........	262	69,878	240	65,808
Midland, Tex.............	263	65,433	241	65,433
Bryan-College Station, Tex..	264	57,978	242	57,978
Meriden, Conn.	265	55,959	243	55,959

(1) Change in area definition since 1970 census, without change of title.
(2) Change in title since 1970 census.
(3) Change in area definition since 1970 census, with change of title.
(4) New SMSA established since 1970 census.
(5) New SMSA established in November 1971, and area definition changed in April 1973.
(6) Merger of two existing SMSAs since 1970 census; rank and population given for 1970 definition refer to the larger of the two merged SMSAs.

How the Cities Grew

Source: Bureau of the Census
(Cities over 100,000 in the 1970 census)

Rank	Cities	1970	1960	1950	1900	1850	1790
1	New York, N.Y....	7,895,563	7,781,984	7,891,957	3,437,202	696,115	49,401
	Bronx boro...	1,471,701	1,424,815	1,451,277	200,507	8,032	1,781
	Brooklyn boro...	2,602,012	2,627,319	2,738,175	1,166,582	138,882	4,495
	Manhattan boro...	1,539,233	1,698,281	1,960,101	1,850,093	515,547	33,131
	Queens boro...	1,986,473	1,809,578	1,550,849	152,999	18,593	6,159
	Richmond boro...	295,443	221,991	191,555	67,021	15,061	3,835
2	Chicago, Ill...	3,369,357	3,550,404	3,620,962	1,698,575	29,963	...
3	Los Angeles, Calif.	2,809,813	2,479,015	1,970,358	102,479	1,610	...
4	Phila., Pa.	1,949,996	2,002,512	2,071,605	1,293,697	121,376	28,522
5	Detroit, Mich.	1,513,601	1,670,144	1,849,568	285,704	21,019	...
6	Houston, Tex.	1,232,802	938,219	596,163	44,633	2,396	...
7	Baltimore, Md.	905,787	939,024	949,708	508,957	169,054	13,503
8	Dallas, Tex...	844,401	679,684	434,462	42,638	...	...
9	Washington, D.C...	756,510	763,956	802,178	278,718	40,001	...
10	Cleveland, Ohio.	750,879	876,050	914,808	381,768	17,034	...
11	Indianapolis, Ind.	746,302	476,258	427,173	169,164	8,091	...
12	Milwaukee, Wis..	717,372	741,324	637,392	285,315	20,061	...
13	San Francisco, Calif.	715,674	740,316	775,357	342,782	²34,776	...
14	San Diego, Calif.	697,027	573,224	334,387	17,700	...	...
15	San Antonio, Tex.	654,153	587,718	408,442	53,321	3,488	...
16	Boston, Mass.	641,071	697,197	801,444	560,892	136,881	18,320
17	Memphis, Tenn.	623,530	497,524	396,000	102,320	8,841	...
18	St. Louis, Mo.	622,236	750,026	856,796	575,238	77,860	...
19	New Orleans, La.	593,471	627,525	570,445	287,104	116,375	...
20	Phoenix, Ariz.	581,562	439,170	106,818	5,544	...	...
21	Columbus, Ohio.	540,025	471,316	375,901	125,560	17,882	...
22	Seattle, Wash.	530,831	557,087	467,591	80,671	...	...
23	Jacksonville, Fla.	528,865	201,030	204,517	28,429	1,045	...
24	Pittsburgh, Pa.	520,117	604,332	676,806	321,616	46,601	...
25	Denver, Colo.	514,678	493,887	415,786	133,859	...	...
26	Kansas City, Mo.	507,330	475,539	456,622	163,752	...	...
27	Atlanta, Ga.	497,421	487,455	331,314	89,872	2,572	...
28	Buffalo, N.Y.	462,768	532,759	580,132	352,387	42,261	...
29	Cincinnati, Ohio	451,455	502,550	503,998	325,902	115,435	...
30	Nashville, Tenn³.	447,877	170,874	174,307	80,865	10,165	...
31	San Jose, Calif.	446,537	204,196	95,280	21,500	...	...
32	Minneapolis, Minn.	434,400	482,872	521,718	202,718	...	...
33	Fort Worth, Tex...	393,476	356,263	278,778	26,688	...	...
34	Toledo, Ohio.	383,105	318,003	303,616	131,822	3,829	...
35	Newark, N.J..	381,930	405,220	438,776	246,070	38,894	...
36	Portland, Oreg.	379,967	372,676	373,628	90,426	...	...
37	Oklahoma City, Okla.	368,377	324,253	243,504	10,037	...	...
38	Louisville, Ky.	361,706	390,639	369,129	204,731	43,194	200
39	Oakland, Calif.	361,561	367,548	384,575	66,960	...	...
40	Long Beach, Calif.	358,879	344,168	250,767	2,252	...	...
41	Omaha, Nebr.	346,929	301,598	251,117	102,555	...	...
42	Miami, Fla.	334,859	291,688	249,276	1,681	...	...
43	Tulsa, Okla.	330,350	261,685	182,740	1,390	...	...
44	Honolulu, Hawaii.	324,871	294,194	248,034	39,306	...	...
45	El Paso, Tex.	322,261	276,687	130,485	15,906	...	...
46	St. Paul, Minn.	309,714	313,411	311,349	163,065	1,112	...
47	Norfolk, Va.	307,951	304,869	213,513	46,624	14,326	2,959
48	Birmingham, Ala.	300,910	340,887	326,037	38,415	...	...
49	Rochester, N.Y.	296,233	318,611	332,488	162,608	36,403	...
50	Tampa, Fla.	277,753	274,970	124,681	15,839	...	...
51	Wichita, Kans.	276,554	254,698	168,279	24,671	...	...
52	Akron, Ohio.	275,425	290,351	274,605	42,728	3,266	...
53	Tucson, Ariz.	262,933	212,892	45,454	7,531	...	...
54	Jersey City, N.J.	260,350	276,101	299,017	206,433	6,856	...
55	Sacramento, Calif.	257,105	191,667	137,572	29,282	6,820	...
56	Austin, Tex.	251,808	186,545	132,459	22,258	629	...
57	Richmond, Va.	249,431	219,958	230,310	85,050	27,570	3,761
58	Albuquerque, N. Mex.	243,751	201,189	96,815	6,238	...	...
59	Dayton, Ohio.	242,917	262,332	243,872	85,333	10,977	...
60	Charlotte, N.C.	241,178	201,564	134,042	18,091	1,065	...
61	St. Petersburg, Fla.	216,159	181,298	96,738	1,575	...	...
62	Corpus Christi, Tex.	204,525	167,690	108,287	4,703	...	...
63	Yonkers, N.Y.	204,297	190,634	152,798	47,931	...	...
64	Des Moines, Iowa.	201,404	208,982	177,965	62,139	...	...
65	Grand Rapids, Mich.	197,649	177,313	176,515	87,565	2,686	...
66	Syracuse, N.Y.	197,297	216,038	220,583	103,374	22,271	...
67	Flint, Mich.	193,317	196,940	163,143	13,103	...	...
68	Mobile, Ala.	190,026	194,856	129,009	38,469	20,515	...
69	Shreveport, La.	182,064	164,372	127,206	16,013	1,728	...
70	Warren, Mich.	179,260	89,246	727	350	...	...
71	Providence, R.I.	179,116	207,498	248,674	175,597	41,513	6,380
72	Fort Wayne, Ind.	178,021	161,776	133,607	45,115	4,282	...
73	Worcester, Mass.	176,572	186,587	203,486	118,421	17,049	2,095
74	Salt Lake City, Utah.	175,885	189,454	182,121	53,531	...	...
75	Gary, Ind.	175,415	178,320	133,911	...	...	...
76	Knoxville, Tenn.	174,587	111,827	124,769	32,637	2,076	...

Rank	Cities	1970	1960	1950	1900	1850	1790
77	Virginia Beach, Va.	172,106	8,091	5,390	...	...	...
78	Madison, Wis.	171,769	126,706	96,056	19,164	1,525	...
79	Spokane, Wash.	170,516	181,608	161,721	36,848	...	...
80	Kansas City, Kan.	168,213	121,901	129,553	51,418	...	...
81	Anaheim, Calif.	166,408	104,184	14,556	1,456	...	...
82	Fresno, Calif.	165,972	133,929	91,669	12,470	...	...
83	Baton Rouge, La.	165,921	152,419	125,629	11,269	3,905	...
84	Springfield, Mass.	163,905	174,463	162,399	62,059	11,766	1,574
85	Hartford, Conn.	158,017	162,178	177,397	72,850	13,555	2,683
86	Bridgeport, Conn.	156,542	156,748	158,709	70,996	6,080	...
87	Santa Ana, Calif.	155,762	100,350	45,533	4,933	...	...
88	Columbus, Ga.	155,028	116,779	79,611	17,614	5,942	...
89	Tacoma, Wash.	154,407	147,979	143,673	37,714	...	...
90	Jackson, Miss.	153,968	144,422	98,271	7,816	1,881	...
91	Lincoln, Nebr.	149,518	128,521	98,884	40,159	...	...
92	Lubbock, Tex.	149,101	128,691	71,747	...	...	...
93	Rockford, Ill.	147,370	126,706	92,927	31,051	...	...
94	Paterson, N.J.	144,824	143,663	139,336	105,171	11,334	...
95	Greensboro, N.C.	144,076	119,574	74,389	10,035	...	...
96	Youngstown, Ohio	140,909	166,689	168,330	44,885	...	...
97	Riverside, Calif.	140,089	84,332	46,764	7,973	...	...
98	Fort Lauderdale, Fla.	139,590	83,648	36,328	...	...	...
99	Huntsville, Ala.	139,282	72,365	16,437	8,068	2,863	...
100	Evansville, Ind.	138,764	141,543	128,636	59,007	3,235	...
101	Newport News, Va.	138,177	113,662	42,358	19,635	...	...
102	New Haven, Conn.	137,707	152,048	164,443	108,027	20,345	4,487
103	Colorado Springs, Colo.	135,060	70,194	45,472	21,083	...	...
104	Torrance, Calif.	134,968	100,991	22,241	...	...	...
105	Winston-Salem, N.C.[4]	133,683	111,135	87,811	13,650	...	...
106	Montgomery, Ala.	133,386	134,393	106,525	30,346	8,728	...
107	Glendale, Calif.	132,664	119,442	95,702	...	...	...
108	Little Rock, Ark.	132,483	107,813	102,213	38,307	2,167	...
109	Lansing, Mich.	131,403	107,807	92,129	16,485	...	...
110	Erie, Pa.	129,231	138,440	130,803	52,733	5,858	...
111	Amarillo, Tex.	127,010	137,969	74,246	1,442	...	...
112	Peoria, Ill.	126,963	103,162	111,856	56,100	5,095	...
113	Las Vegas, Nev.	125,787	64,405	24,624	...	...	...
114	South Bend, Ind.	125,580	132,445	115,911	35,999	1,652	...
115	Topeka, Kan.	125,011	119,484	78,791	33,608	...	...
116	Raleigh, N.C.	123,793	93,931	65,679	13,643	4,518	...
117	Macon, Ga.	122,423	69,764	70,252	23,272	5,720	...
118	Garden Grove, Calif.	121,357	84,238	...	...	...	...
119	Hampton, Va.	120,779	89,258	5,966	2,764	...	...
120	Springfield, Mo.	120,096	95,865	66,731	23,267	415	...
121	Chattanooga, Tenn.	119,923	130,009	131,041	30,154	...	...
122	Savannah, Ga.	118,349	149,245	119,638	54,244	15,312	...
123	Beaumont, Tex.	117,548	119,175	94,014	9,427	...	...
124	Berkeley, Calif.	116,716	111,268	113,805	13,214	...	...
125	Huntington Bch., Calif.	115,960	11,492	5,237	...	...	...
126	Albany, N.Y.	115,781	129,726	134,995	94,151	50,763	3,498
127	Columbia, S.C.	113,542	97,433	86,914	21,103	6,060	...
128	Pasadena, Calif.	112,951	116,407	104,577	3,117	...	...
129	Elizabeth, N.J.	112,654	107,698	112,817	52,130	5,583	...
130	Independence, Mo.	111,630	62,328	36,963	6,974	...	...
131	Portsmouth, Va.	110,963	114,773	80,039	17,427	8,626	...
132	Alexandria, Va.	110,927	91,023	61,787	14,528	8,734	2,748
133	Cedar Rapids, Iowa	110,642	92,035	72,296	25,656	...	...
134	Livonia, Mich.	110,109	66,702	17,534	...	...	...
135	Canton, Ohio	110,053	113,631	118,912	30,667	2,603	...
136	Stockton, Calif.	109,963	86,321	70,853	17,506	...	...
137	Allentown, Pa.	109,871	108,347	106,756	35,416	3,779	...
138	Stamford, Conn.	108,798	92,713	74,293	15,997	...	...
139	Lexington, Ky.	108,137	62,810	55,534	26,369	8,159	834
140	Waterbury, Conn.	108,033	107,130	104,477	45,859	...	...
141	Hammond, Ind.	107,885	111,698	87,594	12,376	...	...
142	Hollywood, Fla.	106,873	35,237	14,351	...	...	...
143	San Bernardino, Calif.	106,869	91,922	63,058	6,150	...	...
144	Trenton, N.J.	104,786	114,167	128,009	73,307	6,461	...
145	Dearborn, Mich.	104,199	112,007	94,994	844	...	...
146	Scranton, Pa.	103,564	111,443	125,536	102,026	...	...
147	Camden, N.J.	102,551	117,159	124,555	75,935	9,479	...
148	Hialeah, Fla.	102,452	66,972	19,676	...	...	...
149	New Bedford, Mass.	101,777	102,477	109,189	62,442	16,443	3,313
150	Fremont, Calif.	100,869	43,790	...	...	...	...
151	Duluth, Minn.	100,578	106,884	104,511	52,969	...	...
152	Cambridge, Mass.	100,361	107,716	120,740	91,886	15,215	2,115
153	Parma, Ohio	100,216	82,845	28,897	...	...	...
	San Juan, P.R.	452,749	432,377	224,767	32,048	...	...
	Bayamon, P.R.	147,552	13,109	20,171	2,218	...	...
	Ponce, P.R.	128,233	114,286	99,492	27,952	...	...

(1) Population shown for years prior to 1900 is for New York and its boroughs as constituted under the act of consolidation in 1898. (2) Population shown is for 1862 as given in State census for that year: 1850 returns for San Francisco were destoyed by fire. (3) Figure for 1970 is for the Metropolitan Government of Nashville and Davidson County; figures for previous years are for Nashville city. (4) Winston city and Salem town consolidated as Winston-Salem city between 1910 and 1920. Figure for 1900 represents combined population of Winston and Salem.

Foreign Born and 2d Generation in U.S.; Countries of Origin

Source: Bureau of the Census

The table below shows, state by state, the country of origin of U.S. residents who were either foreign born or had at least one foreign-born parent.

In the table, Germany includes both East and West Germany, West Asia includes European Turkey, and China includes both the mainland and Taiwan.

	Ala.	Alaska	Ariz.	Ark.	Calif.	Colo.	Conn.	Del.	D. of C.	Fla.
Mixed parents	47,742	24,842	219,830	29,269	3,234,089	219,579	708,193	48,710	39,340	695,699
Foreign Born	15,988	7,763	76,570	8,287	1,757,990	60,311	261,614	15,648	33,562	540,284
U.K.	8,944	3,081	19,866	3,797	373,495	26,377	71,532	7,949	5,638	114,870
Ireland	1,912	804	5,670	1,056	109,888	7,804	60,366	4,244	3,553	36,389
Norway	643	2,501	4,745	408	69,278	4,787	5,513	510	504	12,288
Sweden	678	1,565	6,903	1,100	103,913	13,193	23,427	676	773	26,944
Denmark	555	632	3,180	559	61,757	5,508	5,471	231	426	9,944
Netherlands	526	215	2,947	537	63,772	3,609	3,586	485	408	10,800
Switzerland	408	201	1,629	989	44,483	2,419	4,291	309	533	6,909
France	1,799	630	2,972	1,010	63,449	3,695	8,388	686	1,881	14,833
Germany	12,074	3,526	25,653	9,806	360,656	43,172	60,290	5,991	5,642	123,429
Poland	2,097	765	7,930	1,331	115,833	7,882	103,820	7,263	2,787	50,591
Czecho	989	536	3,483	1,170	44,964	5,074	19,871	865	804	16,222
Austria	1,556	603	5,370	1,027	77,382	9,242	24,595	1,819	1,612	35,896
Hungary	819	169	3,144	310	58,097	3,035	21,641	952	847	23,054
Yugo	421	361	2,592	198	53,868	6,079	3,447	331	474	5,728
USSR	1,854	679	8,812	912	221,198	28,023	48,150	3,523	5,597	81,833
Lithuania	415	169	1,591	355	22,063	1,146	20,469	487	953	8,938
Greece	2,092	208	2,009	500	43,645	3,111	10,933	1,117	1,716	11,637
Italy	5,771	866	12,498	2,284	340,675	21,411	227,782	12,112	4,657	84,881
Other Europe	1,358	1,208	6,952	854	189,979	7,252	32,304	1,648	2,368	47,368
Western Asia	1,753	103	2,501	672	64,565	2,272	8,655	457	1,614	13,755
China	554	282	3,162	661	136,860	1,697	2,195	523	2,099	3,110
Japan	1,392	1,203	2,310	625	144,335	6,005	1,492	516	602	4,843
Other Asia	1,797	1,808	3,488	945	222,709	4,418	6,008	1,690	4,084	10,963
Canada	5,232	6,499	26,136	3,016	439,862	21,580	126,305	4,047	3,914	114,615
Mexico	975	766	113,816	862	1,112,008	24,759	1,220	246	611	11,047
Cuba	680	56	505	86	47,699	945	5,772	483	902	252,520
Other Amer	2,146	576	3,586	572	176,586	3,519	18,844	1,239	11,514	44,411

	Ga.	Haw.	Ida.	Ill.	Ind.	Iowa	Kan.	Ky.	La.	Maine
Mixed parents	78,528	180,577	60,972	1,572,843	268,060	257,342	147,206	56,080	100,221	149,746
Foreign Born	32,988	75,595	12,572	628,898	83,198	40,217	27,842	16,553	39,542	43,014
U.K.	14,517	5,114	10,406	115,891	30,039	22,008	15,986	7,619	9,252	12,073
Ireland	3,461	1,056	1,653	101,856	9,931	9,441	4,853	3,156	3,240	6,528
Norway	933	664	3,534	34,922	2,934	20,418	1,920	457	1,331	1,234
Sweden	1,641	841	5,333	98,254	8,274	21,108	9,622	817	1,284	2,740
Denmark	759	532	3,627	22,021	2,269	20,024	3,200	473	729	1,050
Netherlands	971	355	1,568	27,189	6,760	19,213	1,692	555	1,005	448
Switzerland	517	275	1,736	11,827	3,710	3,476	3,256	1,650	608	222
France	2,684	811	865	19,266	5,372	2,911	2,775	1,848	5,420	1,052
Germany	20,951	5,112	9,894	312,070	64,883	101,974	43,252	21,438	14,237	4,488
Poland	4,574	775	684	299,316	34,590	3,323	4,046	2,147	2,771	2,532
Czecho	1,456	385	1,118	88,259	13,681	10,995	4,978	857	977	741
Austria	2,646	746	1,091	65,026	10,441	3,347	5,581	1,627	1,751	826
Hungary	1,286	342	357	35,822	14,108	1,007	938	1,103	1,267	240
Yugo	824	198	421	59,280	14,410	2,202	3,815	451	1,412	133
USSR	5,831	828	3,136	110,321	9,933	4,563	17,664	2,531	3,073	2,878
Lithuania	798	207	151	58,285	4,265	1,226	507	545	358	1,172
Greece	2,984	371	657	48,669	7,852	2,085	965	861	1,560	1,281
Italy	5,220	1,656	1,595	228,898	17,935	7,683	4,552	4,499	29,031	6,083
Other Europe	3,668	8,318	3,966	67,143	15,478	6,160	3,810	2,092	4,149	2,986
Western Asia	2,457	344	177	18,270	4,098	1,670	1,738	1,523	2,758	1,079
China	1,278	20,939	456	11,833	1,976	1,073	786	539	1,117	284
Japan	1,775	105,223	1,322	12,948	1,888	787	2,435	1,056	1,308	226
Other Asia	4,068	79,410	571	28,637	4,948	2,448	3,066	2,324	3,109	922
Canada	10,021	5,865	10,452	80,611	21,920	13,297	10,425	4,823	6,090	136,801
Mexico	1,562	1,159	5,669	117,268	18,325	4,546	13,728	692	4,865	277
Cuba	3,816	235	73	19,649	1,690	382	796	556	6,711	223
Other Amer	3,880	1,371	371	31,276	4,208	1,538	2,011	1,998	18,235	808

	Md.	Mass.	Mich.	Minn.	Miss.	Mo.	Mont.	Neb.	Nev.	N.H.
Mixed parents	329,813	1,397,064	1,259,961	609,218	22,862	245,948	101,688	175,556	50,274	133,502
Foreign Born	124,345	494,660	424,309	98,056	8,125	65,744	19,634	28,796	18,119	37,048
U.K.	40,291	152,741	148,612	25,672	3,910	23,080	11,293	11,083	6,969	14,040
Ireland	18,267	218,798	28,667	11,900	816	15,470	5,274	4,846	1,991	8,436
Norway	3,385	8,969	12,899	114,221	347	2,257	14,595	3,183	1,163	1,219
Sweden	4,546	38,753	33,639	114,512	445	6,274	6,177	17,099	1,670	2,774
Denmark	2,461	5,163	11,951	22,762	294	2,879	4,302	13,202	1,485	593
Netherlands	3,312	5,656	72,763	13,166	237	2,425	2,731	1,754	796	616
Switzerland	2,437	3,845	5,442	4,282	160	5,204	1,225	2,054	1,103	422
France	6,519	12,342	12,149	3,766	733	5,297	1,160	1,296	1,959	1,265
Germany	59,680	54,846	184,192	137,442	4,960	77,748	15,593	62,726	7,023	6,308
Poland	39,334	117,992	214,085	26,931	730	15,469	1,781	8,333	1,578	6,886
Czecho	11,111	6,434	32,176	17,905	377	7,504	2,171	19,551	796	428
Austria	13,516	16,898	40,730	17,266	576	11,755	3,464	3,612	1,483	1,297
Hungary	7,817	5,583	39,202	3,741	266	5,861	828	1,060	751	481
Yugo	3,148	1,776	30,375	12,266	574	6,517	3,020	1,599	957	229
USSR	46,332	104,223	65,606	18,666	534	19,127	11,365	14,160	2,247	2,982
Lithuania	9,090	32,617	16,908	2,445	152	2,168	242	1,428	282	1,929
Greece	12,508	39,669	19,519	2,833	471	4,209	541	859	1,205	5,040

Continued

Continued from previous page

	Md.	Mass.	Mich.	Minn.	Miss.	Mo.	Mont.	Neb.	Nev.	N.H.
Italy	49,619	294,318	117,064	12,910	3,957	30,114	3,415	6,414	7,927	6,465
Other Europe	15,069	117,653	94,603	41,228	954	9,085	4,157	3,823	3,645	3,952
Western Asia	8,124	27,159	31,579	2,411	1,249	3,279	377	771	633	1,281
China	5,975	11,324	5,725	1,998	1,078	2,337	245	543	811	541
Japan	3,784	3,390	4,952	2,206	394	2,618	675	1,106	1,084	370
Other Asia	13,832	10,897	12,925	4,749	945	5,301	746	1,428	2,148	662
Canada	25,300	466,942	353,154	57,604	2,496	15,532	21,106	8,247	7,587	96,834
Mexico	2,714	2,136	31,067	4,575	783	8,353	1,485	5,552	5,760	209
Cuba	4,931	6,915	3,231	765	241	1,131	45	608	1,306	195
Other Amer	19,309	27,299	13,339	3,390	1,427	3,857	426	1,017	1,147	728

	N.J.	N.M.	N.Y.	N.C.	N.D.	Ohio	Okla.	Ore.	Pa.	R.I.
Mixed parents	1,521,045	66,170	3,885,445	65,661	127,689	994,850	72,713	229,357	1,687,145	237,233
Foreign Born	634,818	22,510	2,109,776	28,620	18,437	316,496	20,160	66,149	445,895	74,374
U.K.	172,308	6,000	334,424	12,826	3,537	108,027	9,812	28,525	198,190	34,178
Ireland	122,600	1,718	386,403	2,506	1,248	37,941	2,386	7,175	118,174	21,041
Norway	17,474	872	47,605	773	38,722	4,382	901	18,085	5,251	1,093
Sweden	19,366	1,681	52,058	1,401	8,434	12,539	1,962	17,830	20,370	6,669
Denmark	11,000	721	20,911	728	3,442	4,492	1,396	8,792	4,935	574
Netherlands	28,440	655	32,043	1,444	1,120	6,539	1,101	4,776	5,691	749
Switzerland	13,219	557	23,773	678	426	12,337	1,200	6,816	8,039	522
France	22,152	1,219	56,861	1,820	402	13,640	1,669	3,263	18,484	3,261
Germany	219,178	7,438	516,216	16,614	21,004	188,386	21,475	40,242	202,611	768
Poland	217,509	1,422	557,478	3,037	1,952	116,262	2,670	4,855	243,752	13,389
Czecho	51,599	763	90,641	1,132	2,473	93,187	3,411	4,144	118,855	763
Austria	83,165	1,483	237,836	1,664	2,254	62,829	1,893	5,294	145,815	2,896
Hungary	70,424	687	115,474	1,190	1,590	82,944	793	2,298	62,014	589
Yugo	16,202	899	41,756	449	194	73,843	400	3,220	54,424	278
USSR	143,234	1,725	569,813	2,928	33,177	54,520	5,463	15,709	157,348	11,198
Lithuania	22,658	371	42,863	545	117	13,979	559	778	43,183	1,459
Greece	25,703	747	90,886	3,883	168	22,210	667	3,480	23,198	2,242
Italy	515,889	3,916	1,330,057	4,658	485	166,629	3,531	9,644	444,841	73,255
Other Europe	69,176	1,725	197,966	2,764	4,076	48,002	2,584	13,752	52,748	33,222
Western Asia	23,415	865	87,036	2,536	770	18,246	2,488	2,348	20,191	4,211
China	7,748	506	66,407	1,178	150	4,987	758	4,423	6,010	1,069
Japan	6,064	1,029	17,304	2,988	391	5,169	1,810	3,983	4,480	783
Other Asia	16,085	1,137	51,785	3,583	555	14,066	2,539	5,345	15,248	2,278
Canada	58,720	5,663	286,047	10,334	15,630	63,258	7,811	53,002	47,827	66,003
Mexico	3,301	37,822	12,249	1,770	276	13,349	6,071	7,739	4,707	407
Cuba	71,233	418	98,479	1,330	46	3,593	352	689	5,195	516
Other Amer	54,867	1,484	415,906	3,012	378	11,679	2,114	2,887	20,183	2,788

	S.C.	S.D.	Tenn.	Tex.	Utah	Vt.	Va.	Wash.	W. Va.	Wis.
Mixed parents	35,436	98,147	49,368	889,246	102,036	62,680	179,518	481,586	57,358	617,479
Foreign Born	14,364	10,899	19,024	309,772	29,573	18,482	72,281	156,020	16,662	130,669
U.K.	7,779	4,562	8,682	49,185	28,531	7,008	32,737	60,522	8,259	28,446
Ireland	1,336	1,980	2,087	12,143	1,416	3,071	10,162	13,266	1,742	9,433
Norway	392	18,898	600	5,442	4,113	651	3,077	60,427	191	52,681
Sweden	686	7,790	1,081	10,873	7,477	1,142	4,144	45,251	601	27,352
Denmark	325	6,584	630	4,801	10,464	476	2,195	14,422	170	18,959
Netherlands	516	5,126	698	4,722	7,617	518	2,690	13,297	223	15,315
Switzerland	576	950	802	4,314	3,392	529	1,640	7,675	762	14,316
France	1,069	399	1,333	8,992	1,014	759	6,210	6,145	881	4,457
Germany	9,193	26,792	11,675	104,726	14,179	4,195	32,596	71,353	6,960	234,767
Poland	1,701	1,052	2,789	16,328	904	2,797	9,423	9,821	6,360	71,534
Czecho	704	3,507	776	29,536	668	393	4,675	6,137	2,996	26,465
Austria	935	1,305	1,354	13,397	1,436	614	6,827	10,332	2,572	27,343
Hungary	479	503	995	4,852	394	602	3,814	4,269	2,931	12,448
Yugo	391	280	376	2,992	1,337	84	1,775	7,580	2,549	19,873
USSR	1,661	14,041	3,649	16,149	1,151	1,171	11,129	23,466	1,996	24,246
Lithuania	228	140	388	2,069	112	211	2,040	1,436	602	5,796
Greece	2,188	284	1,563	6,168	3,372	504	5,712	4,061	1,894	4,746
Italy	2,653	616	6,054	26,886	4,688	4,982	18,026	21,422	17,906	30,513
Other Europe	1,658	2,659	1,678	15,713	2,396	1,707	8,005	24,907	2,564	22,142
Western Asia	1,382	523	1,579	9,219	672	652	6,248	3,411	2,522	3,388
China	408	270	1,032	7,606	983	165	2,936	8,107	135	2,141
Japan	892	273	1,352	8,388	2,834	66	4,691	15,777	433	1,871
Other Asia	2,106	403	2,726	12,465	1,533	449	14,060	18,701	1,704	4,928
Canada	4,805	6,617	6,213	35,900	11,194	46,176	24,048	136,546	2,492	36,888
Mexico	668	472	1,036	711,058	7,710	111	3,167	17,892	513	9,160
Cuba	860	58	894	7,749	116	7	4,479	570	110	787
Other Amer	1,405	303	1,593	21,300	1,593	356	10,538	5,173	772	3,834

Wyoming

Mixed parents	31,014	Germany	5,721	Other Europe	1,194
Foreign born	6,989	Poland	1,033	Western Asia	177
U.K.	5,367	Czecho	824	China	177
Ireland	1,066	Austria	1,300	Japan	341
Norway	1,257	Hungary	250	Other Asia	385
Sweden	2,156	Yugo	1,263	Canada	3,069
Denmark	1,505	USSR	2,913	Mexico	2,638
Netherlands	332	Lithuania	82	Cuba	
Switzerland	563	Greece	728	Other Amer	277
France	504	Italy	1,750		

Origin of The Population By Age and Sex

Source: Bureau of the Census

About 102,000,000 of the 205,000,000 persons in the U.S. in a March 1972 survey by the Bureau of the Census reported that their origin or descent was one of 8 specific origin categories. The Spanish category includes persons who reported that they were of Mexican, Puerto Rican, Cuban, Central or South American or other Spanish origin.

Origin	Total population Number	Total population Percent	Under 14	Percent Distribution by age 14 to 24	Percent Distribution by age 25 to 44	Percent Distribution by age 45 to 64	65 and over	Median age (years)
Total	204,840,000	100.0	25.8	20.0	24.0	20.6	9.7	28.0
English, Scottish, Welsh	29,548,000	14.4	23.6	16.2	23.1	23.7	13.3	33.1
French	5,420,000	2.6	28.5	16.1	25.0	20.6	9.8	28.2
German	25,543,000	12.5	28.1	16.3	24.3	20.3	11.1	28.9
Irish	16,408,000	8.0	26.3	16.2	23.7	22.7	11.0	30.9
Italian	8,764,000	4.3	24.2	16.9	23.6	26.3	9.0	32.0
Polish	5,105,000	2.5	23.7	15.5	23.5	27.8	9.5	32.9
Russian	2,188,000	1.1	20.8	13.2	21.3	29.5	15.2	39.7
Spanish	9,178,000	4.5	37.2	20.4	26.0	12.9	3.5	20.1
Other	85,130,000	41.6	26.3	23.7	23.4	18.4	8.2	25.0
Not reported	17,556,000	8.6	18.2	21.6	27.5	22.1	10.7	31.7
Male	99,378,000	100.0	27.1	20.2	24.2	20.2	8.3	26.9
English, Scottish, Welsh	14,302,000	14.4	25.0	16.4	23.6	23.8	11.1	31.2
French	2,572,000	2.6	28.5	16.4	26.0	20.7	8.4	27.9
German	12,812,000	12.9	28.1	16.2	24.7	21.2	9.7	29.0
Irish	7,762,000	7.8	28.6	16.3	23.1	22.7	9.2	28.9
Italian	4,432,000	4.5	24.3	16.9	24.9	25.2	8.7	31.8
Polish	2,424,000	2.4	24.3	16.0	23.7	27.8	8.2	31.8
Russian	1,052,000	1.1	21.2	13.4	22.8	27.3	15.2	38.2
Spanish	4,540,000	4.6	39.4	19.7	25.6	12.3	3.0	18.7
Other	40,850,000	41.1	28.0	24.4	23.1	17.6	6.9	23.7
Not reported	8,631,000	8.7	19.2	21.7	29.0	20.8	9.3	30.6
Female	105,462,000	100.0	24.6	19.7	23.8	21.0	11.0	29.1
English, Scottish, Welsh	15,245,000	14.5	22.3	16.0	22.7	23.6	15.4	35.0
French	2,849,000	2.7	28.6	15.9	24.0	20.4	11.1	28.5
German	12,730,000	12.1	28.0	16.4	23.8	19.4	12.4	28.8
Irish	8,646,000	8.2	24.3	16.1	24.3	22.7	12.6	32.6
Italian	4,333,000	4.1	24.0	17.0	2.2	27.4	9.3	32.1
Polish	2,681,000	2.5	23.2	15.0	23.3	27.8	10.7	34.0
Russian	1,137,000	1.1	20.5	13.1	19.9	31.5	15.1	41.3
Spanish	4,638,000	4.4	35.0	21.1	26.3	13.6	4.0	21.4
Other	44,280,000	42.0	24.7	23.1	23.7	19.2	9.3	26.5
Not reported	8,925,000	8.5	17.3	21.5	26.0	23.3	12.0	33.0

Mother Tongue and Nativity by Age (1970 Census)

	Number	Percent	Under 14	14 to 24	25 to 44	45 to 64	65 and over	Median age
Native	193,591,000	100.0	27.5	19.9	23.5	20.3	8.8	27.2
English	159,019,000	82.1	29.4	21.0	23.0	18.4	8.2	24.8
French	2,188,000	1.1	14.7	15.8	29.4	27.9	12.2	38.3
German	4,892,000	2.5	7.3	7.6	24.4	35.8	24.8	51.0
Italian	3,118,000	1.6	7.3	10.3	33.6	43.3	5.6	44.3
Polish	2,018,000	1.0	4.8	10.4	30.1	47.4	7.3	47.0
Spanish	6,127,000	3.2	38.8	22.9	24.8	11.0	2.5	19.4
Yiddish	1,156,000	0.6	3.8	8.7	26.7	49.8	11.1	49.3
Other	5,851,000	3.0	11.1	10.9	27.7	38.5	11.9	45.2
Not reported	9,222,000	4.8	27.3	20.2	21.1	18.9	12.5	27.4
Foreign born	9,619,000	100.0	5.6	9.5	25.9	27.0	32.0	51.7
English	1,698,000	17.7	6.2	8.2	24.1	30.5	31.0	52.5
French	411,000	4.3	5.7	10.4	30.3	28.3	25.2	47.5
German	1,202,000	12.5	2.2	5.9	28.1	28.7	35.1	
Italian	1,026,000	10.7	2.7	6.0	17.1	28.6	45.7	61.9
Polish	420,000	4.4	1.8	6.8	12.6	30.3	48.4	64.0
Spanish	1,696,000	17.6	12.5	17.1	36.8	22.6	11.0	36.1
Yiddish	438,000	4.6	0.4	3.1	5.2	34.2	57.0	65
Other	2,633,000	27.4	5.0	9.8	27.3	24.5	33.4	51.4
Not reported	96,000	1.0	7.8	10.9	21.5	23.1	36.7	53.5

Density of Population by States

By Square Mile, Land Area Only

State	1920	1960	1970	State	1920	1960	1970	State	1920	1960	1970
Ala	45.8	64.2	67.9	Ky	60.1	76.2	81.2	N.D.	9.2	9.1	8.9
Alaska*	0.1	0.4	0.5	La	39.6	72.2	81.0	Ohio	141.4	236.6	260.0
Ariz	2.9	11.5	15.6	Maine	25.7	31.3	32.1	Okla	29.2	33.8	37.2
Ark	33.4	34.2	37.0	Md	145.8	313.5	396.6	Oregon	8.2	18.4	21.7
Calif	22.0	100.4	127.6	Mass	479.2	657.3	727.0	Pa	194.5	251.4	262.3
Colo	9.1	16.9	21.3	Mich	63.8	137.6	156.2	R.I.	566.4	819.3	905.5
Conn	286.4	520.6	623.7	Minn	29.5	43.0	48.0	S.C.	55.2	78.7	85.7
Del	113.5	225.2	276.5	Miss	38.6	46.0	46.9	S.D.	8.3	9.0	8.8
D.C.	7,292.9	12,523.9	12,401.8	Mo	49.5	62.6	67.8	Tenn	56.1	86.2	94.9
Fla	17.7	91.5	125.5	Mont	3.8	4.6	4.8	Texas	17.8	36.4	42.7
Ga	49.3	67.8	79.0	Neb	16.9	18.4	19.4	Utah	5.5	10.8	12.9
Hawaii*	39.9	98.5	119.8	Nev	.7	2.6	4.4	Vt	38.6	42.0	47.9
Idaho	5.2	8.1	8.6	N.H.	49.1	67.2	81.7	Va	57.4	99.5	116.9
Illinois	115.7	180.4	199.4	N.J.	420.0	805.5	953.1	Wash	20.3	42.8	51.2
Indiana	81.3	128.8	143.9	N.M.	2.9	7.8	8.4	W. Va.	60.9	77.2	72.5
Iowa	43.2	49.2	50.5	N.Y.	217.9	350.6	381.3	Wis.	47.6	72.6	81.1
Kan	21.6	26.6	27.5	N.C.	52.5	93.2	104.1	Wyo	2.0	3.4	3.4
								U.S.	*29.9	50.6	57.5

*For purposes of comparison, Alaska and Hawaii included in above tabulation for 1920 even though not states then.

Number of inhabitants per sq. mi. of Land Area in U.S. (1790) 4.5; (1800) 6.1; (1810) 4.3; (1820) 5.5; (1830) 7.4; (1840) 9.8; (1850) 7.9; (1860) 10.6; (1870) 13.0; (1880) 16.9; (1890) 21.2; (1900) 25.6; (1910) 31.0; (1920) 35.5; (1930) 41.2; (1940) 44.2; (1950) 50.7; (1960) 50.6; (1970) 57.5 (Alaska and Hawaii included in 1960 and 1970.)

Urban and Rural Population by Race and Sex

Source: Bureau of the Census (1970)

	Male Total*	White	Negro	Female Total*	White	Negro
Urban United States	71,958,564	62,210,243	8,657,231	77,366,366	66,562,997	9,710,087
Regions						
Northeast.	18,784,554	16,653,329	1,955,446	20,665,264	18,229,729	2,259,373
North Central	19,487,418	17,247,113	2,111,447	20,993,342	18,525,851	2,335,499
South	19,543,387	15,624,618	3,786,610	20,996,574	16,587,614	4,277,171
West	14,143,205	12,685,183	803,728	14,711,186	13,219,803	838,044
Northeast						
New England	4,316,939	4,114,117	175,407	4,726,578	4,502,322	197,237
Middle Atlantic	14,467,615	12,539,212	1,780,039	15,938,686	13,727,407	2,062,136
North Central						
East North Central	14,506,612	12,621,941	1,793,477	15,585,235	13,505,243	1,986,690
West North Central	4,980,806	4,625,172	317,970	5,408,107	5,020,608	348,809
South						
South Atlantic.	9,415,616	7,359,956	1,999,619	10,108,304	7,809,142	2,244,906
East South Central.	3,333,530	2,595,228	728,948	3,654,413	2,797,862	847,417
West South Central.	6,794,241	5,669,434	1,058,043	7,233,857	5,980,610	1,184,848
West						
Mountain.	2,969,168	2,831,054	86,251	3,085,811	2,946,955	83,810
Pacific.	11,174,037	9,854,129	717,477	11,625,375	10,272,848	754,234
Rural United States	26,953,628	24,510,744	2,091,085	26,933,368	24,464,991	2,121,888
Regions						
Northeast.	4,778,451	4,690,206	71,498	4,812,434	4,737,240	57,836
North Central	8,075,281	7,956,592	70,774	8,015,622	7,911,627	53,830
South	11,044,454	9,059,936	1,915,492	11,210,952	9,147,940	1,990,688
West	3,055,442	2,804,010	33,321	2,894,360	2,668,184	19,532
Northeast						
New England	1,397,940	1,383,636	9,119	1,400,206	1,388,699	6,635
Middle Atlantic	3,380,511	3,306,570	62,379	3,412,228	3,348,541	15,201
North Central						
East North Central	5,095,788	5,024,915	54,096	5,064,841	5,008,036	38,642
West North Central	2,979,493	2,931,677	16,678	2,950,781	2,903,591	15,188
South						
South Atlantic.	5,528,039	4,445,567	1,052,993	5,619,378	4,497,730	1,090,978
East South Central.	2,879,338	2,390,214	484,092	2,936,189	2,419,506	510,834
West South Central.	2,637,077	2,224,155	378,407	2,655,385	2,230,704	388,876
West						
Mountain.	1,132,632	1,029,436	6,454	1,093,951	990,642	3,867
Pacific.	1,922,810	1,774,574	26,867	1,800,409	1,677,542	15,665

*The difference between the total of white and negro represents other races.

United States Area and Population: 1790 to 1970

Source: Bureau of the Census

Area figures represent area on indicated date including in some cases considerable areas not then organized or settled, and not covered by the census. Area figures have been adjusted to bring them into agreement with remeasurements made in 1940. *Changes in land and water area between 1960 and 1970 due to construction of dams and reservoirs. Also total area of Texas reduced approximately one square mile in the Chamizal agreement between U.S. and Mexico.

Census Date	Area (square miles) Gross	Land	Water	Population Number	Per sq. mile of land area	Increase over preceding census No.	%
1790 (Aug. 2).	888,811	864,746	24,065	3,929,214	4.5	(X)	(X)
1800 (Aug. 4).	888,811	864,746	24,065	5,308,483	6.1	1,379,269	35.1
1810 (Aug. 6).	1,716,003	1,681,828	34,175	7,239,881	4.3	1,931,398	36.4
1820 (Aug. 7).	1,788,006	1,749,462	38,544	9,638,453	5.5	2,398,572	33.1
1830 (June 1).	1,788,006	1,749,462	38,544	12,866,020	7.4	3,227,567	33.5
1840(June 1).	1,788,006	1,749,462	38,544	17,069,453	9.8	4,203,433	32.7
1850 (June 1).	2,992,747	2,940,042	52,705	23,191,876	7.9	6,122,423	35.9
1860 (June 1).	3,022,387	2,969,640	52,747	31,443,321	10.6	8,251,445	35.6
1870 (June 1).	3,022,387	2,969,640	52,747	'39,818,449	'13.4	8,375,128	26.6
1880 (June 1).	3,022,387	2,969,640	52,747	50,155,783	16.9	10,337,334	26.0
1890 (June 1).	3,022,387	2,969,640	52,747	62,947,714	21.2	12,791,931	25.5
1900 (June 1).	3,022,387	2,969,834	52,553	75,994,575	25.6	13,046,861	20.7
1910 (Apr. 15).	3,022,387	2,969,565	52,822	91,972,266	31.0	15,977,691	21.0
1920 (Jan. 1).	3,022,387	2,969,451	52,936	105,710,620	35.6	13,738,354	14.9
1930 (Apr. 1).	3,022,387	2,977,128	45,259	122,775,046	41.2	17,064,426	16.1
1940 (Apr. 1).	3,022,387	2,977,128	45,259	131,669,275	44.2	8,894,229	7.2
1950 (Apr. 1)².	3,615,211	3,552,206	63,005	151,325,798	42.6	19,161,229	14.5
1960 (Apr. 1)².	3,615,123	3,540,911	74,212	179,323,175	50.5	27,997,377	18.5
1970* (Apr. 1)².	3,615,122	3,536,855	78,267	203,211,926	57.5	23,888,751	13.3

(X) Not applicable. (1)Revised to include adjustments for underenumeration in Southern States; unrevised number is 38,558,371. (2)includes Alaska and Hawaii.

Incidence of Poverty for Families

Source: Bureau of the Census

(in thousands)

Mar. 1973 Persons below low-income levels	Total	White	Black
U.S. Total	**24,460**	**16,203**	**7,710**
Metropolitan areas	14,508	8,920	5.249
Central Cities	9,179	4,599	4,359
Outside cent. cities	5,329	4,320	889
Nonmetropolitan areas	9,952	7,283	2,461
North and West	**13,532**	**10,230**	**2,908**
Metropolitan areas	9,557	6,525	2,783
Central cities	5,949	3,375	2,401
Outside cent. cities	3,608	3,150	382
Nonmetropolitan areas	3,975	3,705	125
South	**10,928**	**5,973**	**4,802**
Metropolitan areas	4,951	2,395	2,466
Central cities	3,230	1,225	1,958
Outside cent. cities	1,721	1,170	507
Nonmetropolitan areas	5,977	3,578	2,336

Family Status Below Low-income levels	total	White	Black
In families	**19,577**	**12,268**	**6,841**
Male heads	2,917	2,306	558
Female heads	2,158	1,135	972
Members under 18 yrs.[1]	10,082	5,784	4,025
Other family members	4,420	3,043	1,287
Unrelated individuals	4,883	3,935	870
Nonfarm			
In families	**18,319**	**11,275**	**6,594**
Male heads	2,624	2,051	524
Female heads	2,128	1,120	957
Members under 18 yrs.[1]	9,550	5,383	3,904
Other family members	4,017	2,722	1,209
Unrelated individuals	4,749	3,826	845
Farm			
In families	**1,258**	**993**	**246**
Male heads	293	256	34
Female heads	29	15	15
Members under 18 yrs.[1]	532	401	120
Other family members	403	321	78
Unrelated individuals	134	109	25

[1] Other than head or wife.

Family: A group of two or more persons related by blood, marriage, or adoption and residing together.
Head: One person in each family was designated as the head and usually regarded as head by members of the family. Women are not classified as heads if their husbands live with them.

Size of family: Number of persons living together who are related to each other by blood, marriage or adoption.
Unrelated individuals: Persons 14 years or older not living with relatives.

Low-Income Level by Family Size and Sex of Head

Number of family members	Total	Non Farm			Farm		
		Total	Male	Female	Total	Male	Female
1 member	$2,101	$2,109	$2,207	$2,046	$1,774	$1,824	$1,723
Under 65 yrs.	2,163	2,168	2,254	2,085	1,861	1,916	1,772
65 years and over	1,994	2,005	2,025	2,000	1,708	1,722	1,698
2 members	2,703	2,724	2,734	2,670	2,296	2,302	2,197
Head under 65 yrs	2,790	2,808	2,823	2,729	2,393	2,399	2,258
Head 65 & over	2,505	2,530	2,532	2,516	2,153	2,154	2,141
3 members	3,319	3,339	3,356	3,234	2,830	2,838	2,702
4 members	4,247	4,275	4,277	4,254	3,643	3,644	3,598
5 members	5,011	5,044	5,048	4,994	4,302	4,301	4,355
6 members	5,633	5,673	5,679	5,617	4,851	4,849	4,900
7 or more members	6,917	6,983	7,000	6,841	5,947	5,963	5,771

Poverty by Age, Race and Sex

(in thousands)

Age and Sex (Mar., 1973)	White			Black		
	Total	Number of Poor	% of Total	Total	Number of Poor	% of Total
Male[1]	87,593	6,656	7.6	10,847	3,264	30.1
Under 6 years	8,728	968	11.1	1,494	636	42.6
6 to 15 years	17,097	1,750	10.2	2,704	1,183	43.8
16 to 21 years	9,647	765	7.9	1,374	436	31.7
22 to 44 years	26,296	1,336	5.1	2,893	433	15.0
45 to 54 years	10,138	468	4.6	987	150	15.2
55 to 59 years	4,366	232	5.3	386	92	23.8
60 to 64 years	3,751	285	7.6	332	101	30.4
65 years and over	7,570	852	11.3	677	233	34.4
Female[1]	92,462	9,548	10.3	12,257	4,459	37.1
Under 6 years	8,327	947	11.4	1,487	639	43.0
6 to 15 years	16,383	1,653	10.1	2,708	1,182	46.8
16 to 21 years	9,941	1,015	10.2	1,531	557	36.4
22 to 44 years	27,000	2,024	7.5	3,542	1,059	29.9
45 to 54 years	10,878	682	6.3	1,184	308	26.0
55 to 59 years	4,820	434	9.0	453	148	32.7
60 to 64 years	4,344	574	13.2	427	158	37.0
65 years and over	10,769	2,219	20.6	925	408	44.1

[1] Excluding 14 and 15-year-old heads of household and spouses.

The tables above show several interesting facts about poverty in the U.S. In the North and West, poverty tends to be concentrated in the cities, while in the South most poverty is rural.

Among whites less than half the poor are children, while among blacks well over half are children. White persons living apart from relatives constitute a far larger proportion of the white poor than is the case with blacks. This is partly due to the longer life span of whites which tends to create a larger proportion of aged poor whites, as shown in the bottom table.

The middle table shows the upper limit of official poverty standards. A nonfarm family of four with only $4,275 annual income in 1972 was classified as poor.

The bottom table suggests that women are less likely than men to begin their lives in poverty; but in old age, they are far more likely to be poor.

What Price Welfare?

Source: Department of Health Education and Welfare, Social and Rehabilitation Service

State	Per capita inc. 1972	Cost per inhabitant[1]	Federal funding %, FY72[9]	Recipients per 1,000 pop., 12-73	Avg. monthly payment per recipient, Dec.; 1973				
					Old-age	Blind	Disabled	AFDC[2]	GA[3]
Alabama	3,420	40.43	78.3	79.1	72.92	102.54	78.88	21.72	12.50
Alaska	5,141	50.09	25.4	54.0	118.92	178.65	170.49	71.96	40.25
Arizona	4,263	27.05	69.1	47.4	80.16	86.50	89.29	35.00	71.93
Arkansas	3,365	49.70	78.7	80.4	67.74	90.36	81.89	32.51	5.78
California	4,988	97.30	46.9	93.0	115.36	164.84[8]	151.72	65.55	79.41
Colorado	4,574	52.48	54.4	57.1	77.67	112.43	121.82	64.42	76.60
Connecticut	5,328	38.03	45.4	50.6	82.34	110.15	124.02	70.35	63.10
Delaware	5,188	36.56	49.5	65.1	82.78	118.24	111.47	33.10	32.59
Dist. of Col.	6,265	100.44	47.6	167.2	92.60	125.73	115.71	61.20	120.75
Florida	4,378	23.52	67.9	53.7	83.33	91.87	92.67	31.06	(5)
Georgia	3,909	44.55	73.3	98.4	58.56	75.36	69.25	32.22	28.40
Hawaii	5,031	52.21	41.2	80.6	109.23	137.66	148.23	85.39	66.13
Idaho	3,780	30.40	69.5	32.3	70.07	95.37	94.67	58.97	(5)
Illinois	5,140	55.43	45.4	85.3	71.83	112.45	108.29	70.14	98.92
Indiana	4,366	23.53	55.3	36.4	57.09	82.38	60.36	40.84	(5)
Iowa	4,300	33.61	56.4	35.2	66.14	101.09	99.28	60.96	(5)
Kansas	4,455	30.30	51.9	40.0	62.05	79.43	79.71	59.73	80.25
Kentucky	3,609	35.92	74.4	68.1	67.98	93.72	94.27	43.40	(5)
Louisiana	3,543	51.36	73.8	103.4	73.29	80.15	56.55	25.24	51.87
Maine	3,610	51.61	66.3	101.6	75.08	108.55	110.36	39.77	19.23
Maryland	4,882	35.64	44.5	66.2	67.21	100.42	92.27	46.53	89.14
Massachusetts	4,855	71.23	46.1	74.2	121.21	156.53	153.61	95.93[7]	106.49
Michigan	4,881	56.72	45.8	82.2	73.85	113.15	121.56	74.03	122.26
Minnesota	4,298	45.89	52.5	41.9	68.78	106.63	92.86	81.58	51.22
Mississippi	3,137	48.22	82.4	130.3	53.82	65.91	64.72	14.39	12.16
Missouri	4,293	40.43	62.7	79.4	83.46	114.55	86.67	35.80	64.18
Montana	3,999	24.24	56.9	40.6	67.63	96.59	100.77	52.79	29.19
Nebraska	4,355	27.76	59.7	33.1	62.17	102.10	90.26	46.46	(5)
Nevada	5,078	20.36	52.0	28.7	70.86	88.19	(4)	41.99	(5)
New Hampshire	4,241	32.73	57.4	41.2	37.93	69.33	96.62	69.48	31.32
New Jersey	5,232	50.27	47.0	64.9	82.34	101.60	114.33	71.91	137.18
New Mexico	3,564	35.98	74.9	70.8	57.53	75.22	79.54	36.26	62.49
New York	5,242	89.37	43.1	89.8	59.29	132.53	139.89	77.41	84.73
North Carolina	3,799	25.59	72.1	43.6	80.95	93.34	85.05	41.09	12.07
North Dakota	3,738	29.45	70.6	30.6	71.60	101.38	94.84	60.83	19.56
Ohio	4,534	30.85	46.5	59.6	62.58	85.60	87.77	51.60	59.47
Oklahoma	3,795	54.90	68.6	63.2	67.24	106.48	102.71	52.36	7.66
Oregon	4,287	35.94	54.0	47.3	91.30	134.35	114.76	70.63	83.73
Pennsylvania	4,465	50.55	44.4	65.3	53.47	112.76	78.37	65.32	113.34
Puerto Rico	(5)	13.60	27.3	103.1	18.52	13.60	13.37	9.23	(5)
Rhode Island	4,483	50.87	46.8	73.7	71.22	110.26	110.49	62.30	52.06
South Carolina	3,477	16.35	78.5	57.9	56.78	78.83	67.73	24.29	41.12
South Dakota	3,699	28.75	65.0	41.5	66.99	101.17	81.55	54.89	13.25
Tennessee	3,671	33.51	75.2	66.1	54.67	75.87	74.45	31.85	11.47
Texas	3,991	33.61	69.5	54.9	54.44	82.45	75.68	30.78	(5)
Utah	3,728	33.35	68.7	39.6	46.73	87.19	82.45	61.86	73.01
Vermont	3,686	54.65	63.4	56.2	76.61	117.80	118.16	73.09	(5)
Virginia	4,298	25.67	60.2	43.3	81.70	103.48	102.37	50.93	69.11
Washington	4,472	48.16	47.0	58.3	81.61	125.81	130.36	72.75	69.35
West Virginia	3,594	34.01	75.0	52.8	76.67	92.76	86.79	40.67	11.40
Wisconsin	4,255	32.39	51.5	38.0	89.49	92.63	103.08	95.42	56.66
Wyoming	4,330	18.50	56.7	28.1	65.10	(6)	77.81	51.71	24.94
U.S.	4,492	51.09[10]	51.1[10]	69.3[10]	76.16[10]	112.00[10]	109.73[10]	56.95[10]	79.77[10]

(1) Amount expended per inhabitant in money payments to public assistance recipients in fiscal year 1972; does not include medical or miscellaneous payments. (2) Aid to Families with Dependent Children. (3) General Assistance: eligibility criteria vary greatly from state to state. (4) No program. (5) Data not available. (6) Fewer than 50 recipients. (7) Includes special payments for special needs in Mass. (8) Data includes payments made without federal participation. (9) Includes most medical payments. (10) Includes Guam and Virgin Islands.

Recipients and Payments, 1955-1973

	Category	1955, Dec.	1960, Dec.	1965, Dec.	1970, Dec.	1971, Dec.	1972, Dec.	1973, Dec.
Old-age:	Recipients	2,538,000	2,305,000	2,087,000	2,082,000	2,024,000	1,933,000	1,823,000
	Total amt	$127,003,000	$135,759,000	$131,674,000	$161,642,000	$156,585,000	$154,571,000	$138,638,000
	Avg. amt	$50.05	$58.90	$63.10	$77.65	$77.35	$79.95	$76.15
	[1]Avg. real $	53.50	56.70	56.85	56.05	62.85	—	—
AFDC:	Recipients[2]	2,192,000	3,073,000	4,396,000	9,660,000	10,651,000	11,069,000	10,814,000
	Total amt	$51,472,000	$87,051,000	$144,355,000	$486,232,000	$557,003,000	$598,912,000	$615,903,000
	Avg. amt	$23.50	$28.35	$32.85	$49.65	$51.65	$54.10	$56.95
	[1]Avg. real $	25.10	27.25	29.60	35.85	41.95	—	—
Blind:	Recipients	104,000	107,000	85,100	81,000	80,300	79,800	77,900
	Total amt	$5,803,000	$7,215,000	$6,922,000	$8,447,000	$8,548,000	$9,005,000	$8,723,000
	Avg. amt	$55.55	$67.45	$81.35	$104.35	$106.40	$112.85	$112.00
	[1]Avg. real $	59.40	64.95	73.25	75.35	86.45	—	—
Disabled:	Recipients	241,000	369,000	557,000	935,000	1,068,000	1,169,000	1.275,000
	Total amt	$11,750,000	$20,751,000	$37,035,000	$91,325,000	$108,947,000	$124,074,000	$139,903,000
	Avg. amt	$48.75	$56.15	$66.50	$97.65	$101.95	$106.15	$109.75
	[1]Avg. real $	52.15	54.05	59.95	70.50	82.80	—	—

(1) Dollar amounts adjusted to represent actual purchasing power in terms of the average value of the dollar during the period 1957-1959 based on the consumers' price index for moderate-income families in large cities maintained by the Bureau of Labor statistics. (2) Includes as recipients the children and one or both parents or one caretaker relative other than a parent in families in which the requirements of such adults were considered in determining the amount of assistance.

Jewish Population by Countries and Cities

Source: Jewish Statistical Bureau, Dr. H. S. Linfield, Exec. Secy. Figures are latest estimates

North America	6,460,000	Australia and New Zealand	74,100
Central and South America	779,550	Africa	177,550
Europe	4,086,750	**World Total**	14,437,900
Asia	2,859,950		

Europe

Albania	300
Austria	9,000
Belgium	41,000
Bulgaria	7,000
Czechoslovakia	14,000
Denmark	6,000
Finland	1,500
France	550,000
Germany	32,000
Gibraltar	650
Great Britain	410,000
Greece	5,000
Hungary	90,000
Irish Free State	4,500
Italy	35,000
Luxembourg	1,000
Malta	50
Netherlands	30,000
Norway	750
Poland	8,000
Portugal	500
Romania	100,000
Soviet Union	2,654,000
Spain	9,000
Sweden	15,000
Switzerland	20,000
Turkey	35,000
Yugoslavia	7,500

North America

Canada	305,000
United States	6,115,000
Mexico	40,000

Central and South America

Argentina	500,000
Barbados	100
Bolivia	2,000
Brazil	150,000
Chile	32,000
Colombia	13,000
Costa Rica	1,500
Cuba	1,700
Curacao	700
Dominican Rep	100
Dutch Guiana	500
Ecuador	1,000
El Salvador	300
Guatemala	1,500
Haiti	200
Honduras	150
Jamaica	600
Nicaragua	200
Panama	2,000
Paraguay	1,200
Peru	5,500
Trinidad	300
Uruguay	50,000
Venezuela	15,000

Asia

Afghanistan	500
Burma	200
Cyprus	50
China	100
Hong Kong	200
India	14,000
Indonesia	100
Iran	80,000
Iraq	500
Israel	2,755,500
Japan	1,000
Lebanon	2,000
Pakistan	300
Philippines	500
Singapore	500
Syria	4,000
Yemen	500

Africa

Algeria	1,000
Congo	250
Egypt	500
Ethiopia	12,000
Kenya	200
Libya	100
Morocco	30,000
Rhodesia	5,000
Tunisia	8,000
Union of South Africa	120,000
Zambia	500

Australia and New Zealand

Australia	70,000
New Zealand	4,100

Estimated Jewish Population in Foreign Cities

Amsterdam	12,000
Antwerp	13,000
Ascalon[1]	43,100
Ashdod[1]	40,000
Beersheba[1]	84,100
Berlin	6,000
Bet Shean[1]	11,500
Birmingham	6,000
B'nai B'rak	74,100
Bordeaux	6,500
Brussels	24,000
Bucharest	50,000
Budapest	65,000
Buenos Aires	350,000
Casablanca	30,000
Copenhagen	6,500
Czernowitz	70,000
Elat[1]	13,000
Glasgow	13,500
Haifa[1]	219,000
Istanbul	22,000
Jerusalem[1]	304,500
Johannesburg	57,500
Kharkov	80,000
Kiev	220,000
Leeds	18,000
Leningrad	165,000
Liverpool	6,500
Lod (Lydda)[1]	30,500
London (gr.)	280,000
Lyons	25,000
Marseilles	65,000
Manchester and Salford	35,000
Melbourne	30,000
Milan	9,500
Montreal	113,000
Moscow	285,000
Nazareth[1]	33,500
Nazareth Illet[1]	15,000
Nice	20,000
Ottawa	6,000
Paris	300,000
Petach Tikvah	92,500
Ramath Gan[1]	117,500
Rehovoth	39,200
Rio de Janeiro	50,000
Rome	15,000
Safed	13,500
Santiago	32,000
Sao Paulo	65,000
Stockholm	7,500
Strasbourg	12,000
Sydney	25,300
Teheran	50,000
Tel Aviv-Jaffa[1]	363,000
Tiberias[1]	24,000
Toronto	97,000
Toulouse	18,000
Vancouver	8,000
Vienna	9,000
Warsaw	5,000
Winnipeg	21,000
Zurich	6,200

(1.) Includes some Christians, Mohammedans

Estimated Jewish Population in Large U. S. Cities

Albany	13,500
Alexandria, Arlington & Fairfax cos., Va.	13,000
Atlanta	18,000
Atlantic City	10,000
Baltimore	100,000
Bergen County	100,000
Boston	180,000
Bridgeport	14,500
Buffalo	24,000
Camden	18,000
Chicago	270,000
Cincinnati	28,000
Cleveland	80,000
Columbus	13,000
Dallas	20,000
Denver	26,000
Detroit	80,000
Elizabeth	20,000
Hartford	23,000
Hollywood, Fla.	20,000
Houston	22,000
Jersey City	12,000
Kansas City	22,000
Long Beach, Cal.	15,000
Los Angeles*	535,000
Lynn	19,000
Miami*	200,000
Milwaukee	24,000
Minneapolis	22,000
Montg'y Co., Md.	57,000
New Brunswick	13,500
New Haven	20,000
New Orleans	10,000
New York City	1,836,000
Manhattan	250,000
Bronx	395,000
Brooklyn	760,000
Queens	420,000
Richmond	11,000
N.Y. City environs:	
Nassau Co.	372,000
Suffolk Co.	42,000
Westchester Co.	131,000
Newark:	
Essex Co.	100,000
Oakland:	
Alameda and Contra Costa Co.*	19,000
Orange Co. Calif.	30,000
Passaic	10,500
Paterson*	26,000
Philadelphia*	325,000
Phoenix*	14,000
Pittsburgh	45,000
Prince George County, Md.	28,000
Providence*	32,000
Richmond, Va.	10,000
Rochester	21,500
Rockland Co., N.Y.	25,000
St. Louis	60,000
St. Paul	10,000
San Diego	14,000
San Francisco*	75,000
Seattle	12,500
Springfield, Mass.	11,000
Stanford	11,000
Syracuse	11,000
Trenton, N.J.	10,000
Washington	113,000
Worcester *	10,000

*Indicates greater area.

Black Population by States

Source: Bureau of the Census (1970)

Ala.	903,467	Ill.	1,425,674	Mont.	1,995	R. I.	25,338
Alaska	8,911	Ind.	357,464	Neb.	39,911	S. C.	789,041
Ariz.	53,344	Iowa	32,596	Nev.	27,762	S. D.	1,627
Ark.	352,445	Kan.	106,977	N. H.	2,505	Tenn.	621,261
Calif.	1,400,143	Ken.	230,793	N. J.	770,292	Texas.	1,399,005
Colo.	66,411	La.	1,086,832	N. M.	19,555	Utah.	6,617
Conn.	181,177	Maine	2,800	N. Y.	2,168,949	Vt.	761
Del.	78,276	Md.	699,479	N. C.	1,126,478	Va.	861,368
D. of C.	537,712	Mass.	175,817	N. D.	2,494	Wash.	71,308
Fla.	1,401,651	Mich.	991,066	Ohio.	970,477	W. Va.	67,342
Ga.	1,187,149	Minn.	34,868	Okla.	171,892	Wis.	128,224
Hawaii	7,573	Miss.	815,770	Ore.	26,308	Wyo.	2,568
Idaho	2,130	Mo.	480,172	Pa.	1,016,514	**Total**	**22,580,289**

U.S. Places of 5,000 or More Population—with ZIP Codes

Source: U.S. Bureau of the Census; U.S. Postal Service

The listings below show the official urban population of the United States. "Urban population" is defined as all persons living in (a) places of 5,000 inhabitants or more, incorporated as cities, villages, boroughs (except Alaska), and towns (except in New England, New York, New Jersey, Pennsylvania and Wisconsin), but excluding those persons living in the rural portions of extended cities; (b) unincorporated places of 5,000 inhabitants or more; and (c) other territory, incorporated or unincorporated, included in urbanized areas.

The non-urban portion of an extended city contains one or more areas, each at least 5 square miles in extent and with a population density of less than 100 persons per square mile. The area or areas constitute at least 25 percent of the legal city's land area of a total of 25 square miles or more.

In New England, New York, New Jersey, Pennsylvania, and Wisconsin, minor civil divisions called "towns" often include rural areas and one or more urban areas. Only the urban areas of these "towns" are included here, except in the case of New England, where entire town populations, which may include some rural population, are shown in italics. Boroughs in Alaska may contain one or more urban areas which are included here.

Where special censuses were taken after April 1, 1970, the year appears after the name of the place.

The ZIP Code of each place appears before the name of that place, if it is obtainable.

CAUTION—Where an asterisk (*) appears before the ZIP Code, ask your local postmaster for the correct ZIP Code for a specific address within the place listed.

ZIP Code	Place	1970	1960
	Alabama		
35950	Albertville	9,963	8,250
35010	Alexander City	12,358	13,140
36420	Andalusia	10,092	10,263
36201	Anniston	31,533	33,657
	Anniston Northwest	6,509	
35611	Athens	14,360	9,330
36502	Atmore	8,293	8,173
35954	Attalla	7,510	8,257
36830	Auburn	22,767	16,261
36507	Bay Minette	6,727	5,197
35020	Bessemer	33,663	33,054
*35203	Birmingham	300,910	340,887
35226	Bluff Park	12,431	
35957	Boaz	5,635	4,654
36426	Brewton	6,747	6,309
35215	Center Point	15,675	
36611	Chickasaw	8,447	10,002
35045	Clanton	5,868	5,863
35055	Cullman	12,601	10,883
36322	Daleville	5,182	693
35601	Decatur	38,044	29,217
36732	Demopolis	7,651	7,377
36301	Dothan	36,733	31,440
36330	Enterprise	15,591	11,410
36027	Eufaula	9,102	8,357
35064	Fairfield	14,369	15,816
36532	Fairhope	5,720	4,858
35630	Florence	34,031	31,649
35214	Forestdale	6,091	
36201	Fort McClellan	5,334	
35967	Fort Payne	8,435	7,029
36360	Fort Rucker	14,242	
35068	Fultondale	5,163	2,001
*35901	Gadsden	53,928	58,088
35071	Gardendale	6,537	4,712
36037	Greenville	8,033	6,894
35976	Guntersville	6,491	6,592
35640	Hartselle	7,355	5,000
35209	Homewood	21,137	20,289
35020	Hueytown	8,174	5,997
35804	Huntsville	139,282	72,365
36545	Jackson	5,957	4,959
36265	Jacksonville	7,715	5,678
35501	Jasper	10,798	10,799
36863	Lanett	6,908	7,674
35094	Leeds	6,991	6,162
35228	Midfield	6,340	3,556
*36601	Mobile	190,026	194,856
*36104	Montgomery	133,386	134,393
35223	Mountain Brook	19,509	12,680
35660	Muscle Shoals	6,907	4,084
35476	Northport	9,435	5,245
36801	Opelika	19,027	15,678
36467	Opp	6,493	5,535
36360	Ozark	13,555	9,534
35125	Pell City	5,602	4,165
36867	Phenix City	25,281	27,630
36272	Piedmont	5,063	4,794
35127	Pleasant Grove	5,090	3,097
36067	Prattville	13,116	6,616
36610	Prichard	41,578	47,371
36274	Roanoke	5,251	5,288
35653	Russellville	7,814	6,628
36571	Saraland	7,840	4,595
35768	Scottsboro	9,324	6,449
36701	Selma	27,379	28,385
35660	Sheffield	13,115	13,491
35150	Sylacauga	12,255	12,857
35160	Talladega	17,662	17,742
35217	Tarrant City	6,835	7,810
36081	Troy	11,482	10,234
35401	Tuscaloosa	65,773	63,370
35674	Tuscumbia	8,828	8,994
36083	Tuskegee	11,028	7,240
35216	Vestavia Hills	8,311	4,029
36201	West End—Cobb	5,515	5,485
	Alaska		
99502	Anchorage	48,081	44,237
99702	Eielson	6,149	
99506	Elmendorf	6,018	
99701	Fairbanks	14,771	13,311
99505	Fort Richardson	10,751	
99703	Fort Wainwright	9,097	
99801	Juneau	6,050	6,797
99901	Ketchikan	6,994	6,483
99503	Spenard	18,089	9,074
	Arizona		
85321	Ajo	5,881	7,049
85323	Avondale	6,626	6,151
85603	Bisbee	8,328	9,914
85222	Casa Grande	10,536	8,311
85224	Chandler	13,763	9,531
85533	Clifton	5,087	4,191
85228	Coolidge	5,314	4,990
85607	Douglas	12,462	11,925
85231	Eloy	5,381	4,899
86001	Flagstaff	26,117	18,214
85613	Fort Huachuca	6,659	
85301	Glendale	36,228	15,893
85501	Globe	7,333	6,217
86401	Kingman	7,312	4,525
85301	Luke	5,047	
85201	Mesa	62,853	33,772
85621	Nogales	8,946	7,286
85253	Paradise Valley	7,155	
*85026	Phoenix	582,500	439,170
86301	Prescott	13,283	12,861
85546	Safford	5,333	4,648
85251	Scottsdale	67,823	10,026
85635	Sierra Vista	6,689	3,121
85713	South Tucson	6,220	7,004
85351	Sun City	13,670	
85282	Tempe	63,550	24,897
*85726	Tucson	262,933	212,892
85364	West Yuma	5,552	2,781
86047	Winslow	8,066	8,862
85364	Yuma	29,007	23,974
	Arkansas		
71923	Arkadelphia	9,841	8,069
72501	Batesville	7,209	6,207
72015	Benton	16,499	10,399
72712	Bentonville, 1972	6,391	3,649
72315	Blytheville	24,752	20,797
72021	Brinkley	5,275	4,636
71701	Camden	15,147	15,823
72032	Conway 1973	16,772	9,791
71635	Crossett	6,191	5,370
71730	El Dorado	25,283	25,292
72701	Fayetteville 1972	31,915	20,274
72335	Forrest City	12,521	10,544
72901	Fort Smith 1973	65,393	52,991
72601	Harrison	7,239	6,580
72342	Helena 1971	10,201	11,500
71801	Hope	8,830	8,399
71901	Hot Springs	35,631	28,337
72076	Jacksonville 1972	22,392	14,488

ZIP Code	Place	1970	1960
72401	Jonesboro	27,050	21,418
*72201	Little Rock	132,483	107,813
71753	Magnolia 1973	11,527	10,651
72104	Malvern	8,739	9,566*
72360	Marianna	6,196	5,134
71655	Monticello 1972	7,034	4,412
72110	Morrilton	6,814	5,997
72653	Mountain Home 1973	5,028	2,105
72112	Newport	7,725	7,007
*72114	North Little Rock	60,040	58,032
72370	Osceola	7,204	6,189
72450	Paragould	10,639	9,947
71601	Pine Bluff	57,389	44,037
72756	Rogers 1973	13,189	5,700
72801	Russellville	11,750	8,921
72143	Searcy 1973	10,867	7,272
72761	Siloam Springs	6,009	3,953
72204	Southwest Little Rock	13,231	
72764	Springdale 1972	18,848	10,076
72160	Stuttgart	10,477	9,661
75501	Texarkana	21,682	19,788
72472	Trumann	6,023	4,511
72956	Van Buren	8,373	6,787
71671	Warren	6,433	6,752
72390	West Helena 1973	10,838	8,385
72301	West Memphis 1973	28,236	19,374
72396	Wynne	6,696	4,922

California

ZIP Code	Place	1970	1960
94501	Alameda	70,968	63,855
94507	Alamo-Danville	14,059	
94706	Albany	14,674	14,804
91802	Alhambra	62,125	54,807
90249	Alondra Park	12,193	
91001	Altadena	42,415	40,568
95116	Alum Rock	18,355	18,942
*92803	Anaheim	166,408	104,184
96007	Anderson	5,492	4,492
94509	Antioch	28,060	17,305
92307	Apple Valley	6,702	
95003	Aptos	8,704	
91006	Arcadia	45,138	41,005
95521	Arcata	8,985	5,235
95825	Arden-Arcade	82,492	73,352
93420	Arroyo Grande	7,454	3,291
90701	Artesia	14,757	9,993
93203	Arvin	5,199	
94577	Ashland	14,810	
93422	Atascadero	10,290	5,983
94025	Atherton	8,085	7,717
95301	Atwater	11,640	7,318
95603	Auburn	6,570	5,586
92505	August School Area	6,735	
91746	Avocado Heights	9,810	
91702	Azusa	25,217	20,497
*93302	Bakersfield	69,515	56,848
91706	Baldwin Park	47,285	33,951
92220	Banning	12,034	10,250
92311	Barstow	17,442	11,644
95903	Beale East	7,029	
92223	Beaumont	5,484	4,288
90201	Bell	21,836	19,450
90706	Bellflower	51,454	45,909
90201	Bell Gardens	29,308	
94002	Belmont	23,538	15,996
94510	Benicia	7,349	6,070
*94704	Berkeley	116,716	111,268
*90213	Beverly Hills	33,416	30,817
92314	Big Bear	5,268	1,562
92316	Bloomington	11,957	
92225	Blythe	7,047	6,023
92227	Brawley	13,746	12,703
92621	Brea	18,447	8,487
95605	Broderick-Bryte	12,782	
90620	Buena Park	63,646	46,401
*91505	Burbank	88,871	90,155
94010	Burlingame	27,320	24,036
92231	Calexico	10,625	7,992
93745	Calwa	5,191	
93010	Camarillo	19,219	
93010	Camarillo Heights	5,892	1,704
95124	Cambrian Park	5,316	
95008	Campbell	24,770	11,863
95010	Capitola	5,080	2,021
92007	Cardiff-by-the-Sea	5,724	3,149
92008	Carlsbad	14,944	9,253
95608	Carmichael	37,625	20,455
93013	Carpinteria	6,982	
90744	Carson	71,150	
94546	Castro Valley	44,760	37,120
95307	Ceres	6,029	4,406
90701	Cerritos	15,856	3,508
94541	Cherryland	9,969	
95926	Chico	19,580	14,757
95926	Chico North	6,656	
93555	China Lake	11,105	
91710	Chino	20,411	10,305

ZIP Code	Place	1970	1960
*92010	Chula Vista	67,901	42,034
95610	Citrus Heights	21,760	
91711	Claremont	23,464	12,633
93612	Clovis	13,856	5,546
92236	Coachella	8,353	4,854
93210	Coalinga	6,161	5,965
92324	Colton	20,016	18,666
90022	Commerce	10,536	9,555
*90220	Compton	78,547	71,812
*94520	Concord	85,164	36,000
93212	Corcoran	5,249	4,976
91720	Corona	27,519	13,336
92118	Coronado	20,020	18,039
94925	Corte Madera	8,464	5,962
92626	Costa Mesa	72,660	37,550
91722	Covina	30,395	20,124
91730	Cucamonga	5,796	
90201	Cudahy	16,998	
90230	Culver City	34,451	32,163
95014	Cupertino	18,216	3,664
90630	Cypress	31,569	1,753
*94017	Daly City	66,922	44,791
95616	Davis	23,488	8,910
90250	Del Aire	11,930	
93215	Delano	14,559	11,913
91765	Diamond Bar	10,576	
93618	Dinuba	7,917	6,103
90810	Dominguez	5,980	
*90241	Downey	88,442	82,505
91010	Duarte	14,981	13,962
94566	Dublin	13,641	
90020	East Compton	5,853	
90638	East La Mirada	12,339	
90022	East Los Angeles	105,033	104,270
94303	East Palo Alto	18,099	
93523	Edwards	10,331	
92020	El Cajon	52,273	37,618
92243	El Centro 1973	21,134	16,811
94530	El Cerrito	25,190	25,437
93017	El Encanto Heights	6,225	
*91731	El Monte	69,892	13,163
93446	El Paso de Robles	7,168	6,677
93030	El Rio	6,173	6,966
90245	El Segundo	15,620	14,219
92630	El Toro	8,654	
92709	El Toro Station	6,970	
92024	Encinitas	5,375	2,786
96001	Enterprise	11,486*	4,946
92025	Escondido	36,792	16,377
95501	Eureka	24,337	28,137
94930	Fairfax	7,661	5,813
94533	Fairfield	44,146	14,968
95628	Fair Oaks	11,256	
92028	Fallbrook	6,945	4,814
93015	Fillmore	6,285	4,808
90001	Florence-Graham	42,900	38,164
95828	Florin	9,646	
95630	Folsom	5,810	3,925
92335	Fontana	20,673	14,659
94404	Foster City	9,522	
92708	Fountain Valley	31,886	2,068
95019	Freedom	5,563	4,206
*94536	Fremont	100,869	43,790
*93721	Fresno	165,972	133,929
*92631	Fullerton	85,987	56,180
*90247	Gardena	41,021	35,943
95205	Garden Acres	7,870	
*92640	Garden Grove	121,357	84,238
92392	George	7,404	
95020	Gilroy	12,665	7,348
92509	Glen Avon	5,759	3,416
*91209	Glendale	132,664	119,442
91740	Glendora	31,380	20,752
92324	Grand Terrace	5,901	
95945	Grass Valley	5,149	4,876
92041	Grossmont-Mt. Helix	8,723	
93433	Grover City	5,939	5,210
91745	Hacienda Heights	35,969	
93230	Hanford	15,179	10,133
90716	Hawaiian Gardens	9,052	
90250	Hawthorne	53,304	33,035
*94544	Hayward	93,058	72,700
95448	Healdsburg	5,438	4,816
92343	Hemet	12,252	5,416
92343	Hemet East	8,598	1,936
90254	Hermosa Beach	17,412	16,115
92346	Highland	12,699	
94010	Hillsborough	8,753	7,554
95023	Hollister	7,663	6,071
91720	Home Gardens	5,116	1,541
92647	Huntington Beach	115,960	11,492
90255	Huntington Park	33,744	29,920
92032	Imperial Beach	20,244	17,773
92201	Indio	14,459	9,745
*90306	Inglewood	89,985	63,390
93017	Isla Vista	13,441	
94707	Kensington	5,823	
91011	La Canada-Flintridge	20,714	18,338

Zip Code	Place	1970	1960
91214	La Crescenta-Montrose	19,620	
90045	Ladera Heights	6,535	
94549	Lafayette	20,484	7,114
92651	Laguna Beach	14,550	9,288
92653	Laguna Hills	13,676	
90631	La Habra	41,350	25,136
92040	Lakeside	11,991	
*90714	Lakewood	83,025	67,126
92041	La Mesa	39,178	30,441
90638	La Mirada	30,808	22,444
93241	Lamont	7,007	6,177
93534	Lancaster	32,728	26,012
90620	La Palma	9,687	622
*91747	La Puente	31,092	24,723
94939	Larkspur	10,487	5,710
91750	La Verne	12,965	6,516
90260	Lawndale	24,825	21,740
92045	Lemon Grove	19,690	19,348
93245	Lemoore Station	9,210	
90304	Lennox	16,121	31,224
95207	Lincoln Village	6,112	
95901	Linda	7,731	6,129
93247	Lindsay	5,206	5,397
95062	Live Oak (Santa Cruz)	6,443	3,518
94550	Livermore	37,703	16,058
95240	Lodi	28,691	22,229
92354	Loma Linda	9,797	
90717	Lomita	19,784	
93436	Lompoc	25,284	14,415
*90801	Long Beach	358,879	344,168
90720	Los Alamitos	11,346	4,312
94022	Los Altos	24,726	19,696
94022	Los Altos Hills	6,865	3,412
*90052	Los Angeles	2,809,813	2,479,015
93635	Los Banos	9,188	5,272
95030	Los Gatos	23,735	9,036
90262	Lynwood	43,354	31,614
93637	Madera	16,044	14,430
90266	Manhattan Beach	35,352	33,934
95336	Manteca	13,845	8,242
93933	Marina	8,343	3,310
94553	Martinez	16,506	9,604
95901	Marysville	9,353	9,553
95655	Mather	7,027	
90270	Maywood	16,996	14,588
93023	Meiners Oaks-Mira Mone	7,025	
94025	Menlo Park	26,826	26,957
95340	Merced	22,670	20,068
94030	Millbrae	20,792	15,873
94941	Mill Valley	12,942	10,411
95035	Milpitas	27,149	6,572
91752	Mira Loma	8,482	3,982
92675	Mission Viejo	11,933	
*95350	Modesto	61,712	36,585
91016	Monrovia	30,562	27,079
91763	Montclair	22,546	13,546
90640	Montebello	42,807	32,097
93940	Monterey	26,302	22,618
91754	Monterey Park	49,166	37,821
94556	Moraga	14,205	
95037	Morgan Hill	6,485	3,151
93442	Morro Bay	7,109	
94040	Mountain View	54,304	30,889
92505	Muscoy	7,091	
94558	Napa	35,978	22,170
92050	National City	43,184	32,771
94560	Newark	27,153	9,884
91321	Newhall	9,651	4,705
92660	Newport Beach	49,422	26,564
91760	Norco	14,511	
94025	North Fair Oaks	9,740	
95660	North Highlands	31,854	21,271
92135	North Island	6,892	
90650	Norwalk	91,827	88,739
94947	Novato	31,006	17,881
95361	Oakdale	6,594	4,980
*94615	Oakland	361,561	367,548
92054	Oceanside	40,494	24,971
93308	Oildale	20,879	
93023	Ojai	5,591	4,495
95961	Olivehurst	8,100	4,835
91761	Ontario	64,118	46,617
95060	Opal Cliffs	5,425	3,825
*92667	Orange	77,365	26,444
95662	Orangevale	16,493	
93454	Orcutt	8,500	1,414
94563	Orinda	6,790	5,568
95965	Oroville	7,536	6,115
92010	Otay-Castle Park	15,445	
93030	Oxnard	71,225	40,265
94044	Pacifica	36,020	20,995
93950	Pacific Grove	13,505	12,121
93550	Palmdale	8,511	
92260	Palm Desert	6,171	1,295
92262	Palm Springs	20,936	13,468
*94302	Palo Alto	55,835	52,287
90274	Palos Verdes Estates	13,631	9,564
90274	Palos Verdes Peninsula	38,914	

ZIP Code	Place	1970	1960
95969	Paradise	14,539	8,268
90723	Paramount	34,734	27,249
95823	Parkway-Sacramento So	28,574	
*91109	Pasadena	112,951	116,407
92055	Pendleton North	11,803	
92055	Pendleton South	13,692	
94952	Petaluma	24,870	14,035
90660	Pico Rivera	54,170	49,150
94611	Piedmont	10,917	11,117
94564	Pinole	13,266	6,064
94565	Pittsburg	20,651	19,062
92670	Placentia	21,948	5,861
95667	Placerville	5,416	4,439
94523	Pleasant Hill	24,610	23,844
94566	Pleasanton	18,328	4,203
*91766	Pomona	87,384	67,157
93257	Porterville	12,602	7,991
93257	Porterville West	6,200	
93041	Port Hueneme	14,295	11,067
92064	Poway	9,422	1,921
95670	Rancho Cordova	30,451	7,429
95014	Rancho Rinconada	5,149	
96080	Red Bluff	7,676	7,202
96001	Redding	16,659	12,773
92373	Redlands	36,355	26,829
*90277	Redondo Beach	57,451	46,986
*94064	Redwood City	55,686	46,290
93654	Reedley	8,131	5,850
92376	Rialto	28,370	18,567
*94802	Richmond	79,043	71,854
93555	Ridgecrest	7,629	
95673	Rio Linda	7,524	2,189
*92502	Riverside	140,089	84,332
94572	Rodeo	5,356	
94928	Rohnert Park	6,133	
90274	Rolling Hills Estates	6,735	3,941
95401	Roseland	5,105	4,510
91770	Rosemead	40,972	15,476
95678	Roseville	18,221	13,421
90720	Rossmoor	12,922	
91745	Rowland Heights	16,881	
92509	Rubidoux	13,969	
*95813	Sacramento	257,105	191,667
93901	Salinas	58,896	28,957
94960	San Anselmo	13,031	11,584
*92403	San Bernardino	106,869	91,922
94066	San Bruno	36,254	29,063
	San Buenaventura (See Ventura)		
94070	San Carlos	26,053	21,370
92672	San Clemente	17,063	8,527
*92101	San Diego	697,027	573,224
91773	San Dimas	15,692	
*91340	San Fernando	16,571	16,093
*94101	San Francisco	715,674	740,316
91776	San Gabriel	29,336	22,561
93657	Sanger	10,088	8,072
*95125	San Jose	445,779	204,196
*94577	San Leandro	68,698	65,962
94580	San Lorenzo	24,633	23,773
93401	San Luis Obispo	28,036	20,437
91108	San Marino	14,177	13,658
*94402	San Mateo	78,991	69,870
94806	San Pablo	21,461	19,687
*94901	San Rafael	38,977	20,460
*92711	Santa Ana	155,762	100,350
*93102	Santa Barbara	70,215	58,768
*95052	Santa Clara	87,717	58,880
95060	Santa Cruz	32,076	25,596
90670	Santa Fe Springs	14,750	16,342
93454	Santa Maria	32,749	20,027
93454	Santa Maria South	7,129	
*90406	Santa Monica	88,289	83,249
93060	Santa Paula	18,001	13,279
*95402	Santa Rosa	50,006	31,027
92071	Santee	21,107	
95070	Saratoga	27,110	14,861
94965	Sausalito	6,158	5,331
90740	Seal Beach	24,441	6,994
93955	Seaside	35,935	19,353
93662	Selma	7,459	6,934
93263	Shafter	5,327	4,576
91024	Sierra Madre	12,140	9,732
90806	Signal Hill	5,588	4,627
93065	Simi Valley	59,832	
92075	Solana Beach	5,023	
95073	Soquel	5,795	
91733	South El Monte	13,443	4,850
90280	South Gate	56,909	53,831
95705	South Lake Tahoe	12,921	
95350	South Modesto	7,889	5,465
91030	South Pasadena	22,979	19,706
94080	South San Francisco	46,646	39,418
91770	South San Gabriel	5,051	
91744	South San Jose Hills	12,386	
90605	South Whittier	46,641	
95991	South Yuba	5,352	3,200
92077	Spring Valley	29,742	
94305	Stanford	8,691	

ZIP Code	Place	1970	1960
90680	Stanton	18,186	11,163
*95204	Stockton	109,963	86,321
92381	Sun City	5,519	
92388	Sunnymead	6,708	3,404
*94086	Sunnyvale	95,408	52,898
96130	Susanville	6,608	5,598
*91780	Temple City	31,034	
*91360	Thousand Oaks	35,873	
94920	Tiburon	6,209	
*90510	Torrance	134,968	100,991
95376	Tracy	14,724	11,289
93274	Tulare	16,235	13,824
95380	Turlock	13,992	9,116
92680	Tustin	21,180	2,006
92705	Tustin-Foothills	26,598	
92277	Twentynine Palms	5,667	
92278	Twentynine Palms Base	5,647	
95482	Ukiah	10,095	9,900
94587	Union City	14,724	6,618
91786	Upland	32,551	15,918
95688	Vacaville	21,690	10,898
91744	Valinda	18,837	
94590	Vallejo	71,710	60,877
93437	Vandenburg	13,193	
93001	Ventura	57,964	29,114
92392	Victorville	10,845	
90043	View Park-Windsor Hills	12,268	
93277	Visalia	27,268	15,791
92083	Vista	24,688	
91789	Walnut	5,992	934
*94596	Walnut Creek	39,844	9,903
94596	Walnut Creek West	8,330	
90255	Walnut Park	8,925	
93280	Wasco	8,269	6,841
95076	Watsonville	14,569	13,293
90044	West Athens	13,311	
90502	West Carson	15,918	
90247	West Compton	5,605	
*91790	West Covina	68,034	50,645
90069	West Hollywood	34,622	28,870
92683	Westminster	59,874	25,750
95351	West Modesto	6,135	1,897
90047	Westmont	29,310	
94565	West Pittsburg	5,969	5,188
91746	West Puente Valley	20,733	
95691	West Sacramento	12,002	
*90605	West Whittier-Los Nietos	20,845	
*90605	Whittier	72,863	33,663
90222	Willowbrook	32,328	
95695	Woodland	20,677	13,524
92686	Yorba Linda	11,856	
96097	Yreka City	5,394	4,759
95991	Yuba City	13,986	11,507
92399	Yucaipa	19,284	

Colorado

ZIP Code	Place	1970	1960
81101	Alamosa	6,985	6,205
80401	Applewood	8,214	
80001	Arvada	49,083	19,242
80010	Aurora	74,974	48,548
80302	Boulder	66,870	37,718
80601	Brighton	8,309	7,055
80020	Broomfield	7,261	
81212	Canon City	9,206	8,973
*80901	Colorado Springs	135,060	70,194
80022	Commerce City	17,407	8,970
81321	Cortez	6,032	6,764
*80202	Denver	514,678	493,887
80022	Derby	10,206	10,124
81301	Durango	10,333	10,530
80110	Englewood	33,695	33,398
80913	Fort Carson	19,399	
80521	Fort Collins	43,337	25,027
80701	Fort Morgan	7,594	7,379
80401	Golden	9,817	7,118
81501	Grand Junction	20,170	18,694
80631	Greeley	38,902	26,314
81050	La Junta	7,938	8,026
80215	Lakewood	92,743	
81052	Lamar	7,797	7,369
80120	Littleton Southeast	22,899	
80120	Littleton	26,466	13,670
80501	Longmont	23,209	11,489
80537	Loveland	16,220	9,734
81401	Montrose	6,496	5,044
80233	North Glenn	27,937	
81501	Orchard Mesa	5,824	4,956
*81003	Pueblo	97,453	91,181
80911	Security-Widefield	15,297	9,017
80221	Sherrelwood	18,868	
80751	Sterling	10,636	10,751
80906	Stratton Meadows	6,223	
80229	Thornton	13,326	11,353
81082	Trinidad	9,901	10,691
80229	Welby	6,875	
80030	Westminster	19,432	13,850
80221	Westminster East	7,576	
80033	Wheat Ridge	29,778	

ZIP Code	Place	1970	1960
	Connecticut		
	See Note on Page 159		
06401	Ansonia	21,160	19,819
06001	Avon	8,352	5,273
06037	Berlin	14,149	11,250
06801	Bethel	10,945	8,200
06002	Bloomfield	18,301	13,613
06405	Branford	20,444	16,610
*06602	Bridgeport	156,542	156,748
06010	Bristol	55,487	45,499
06804	Brookfield	9,688	3,405
06019	Canton	6,868	4,783
06410	Cheshire	19,051	13,383
06413	Clinton Center	5,957	2,693
06413	Clinton	10,267	4,166
06415	Colchester	6,603	4,648
06340	Conning Towers-Nautilus Park	9,791	3,457
06238	Coventry	8,140	6,356
06416	Cromwell	7,400	6,780
06810	Danbury	50,781	22,928
06820	Darien	20,411	18,437
06418	Derby	12,599	12,132
06424	East Hampton	7,078	5,403
06108	East Hartford	57,583	43,977
06512	East Haven	25,120	21,388
06333	East Lyme	11,399	6,782
06016	East Windsor	8,513	7,500
06029	Ellington	7,707	5,580
06082	Enfield	46,189	31,464
06430	Fairfield	56,487	46,183
06032	Farmington	14,390	10,813
06033	Glastonbury	20,651	14,497
06035	Granby	6,150	4,968
06830	Greenwich	59,755	53,793
06351	Griswold	7,763	6,472
06340	Groton	38,244	29,937
06340	Groton Borough	8,933	10,111
06437	Guilford	12,033	7,913
06514	Hamden	49,357	41,056
*06101	Hartford	158,017	162,178
06239	Killingly	13,573	11,298
06339	Ledyard	14,837	5,395
06759	Litchfield	7,399	6,264
06443	Madison	9,768	4,567
06040	Manchester	47,994	42,102
06250	Mansfield	19,994	14,638
06450	Meriden	55,959	51,850
06762	Middlebury	5,542	4,785
06457	Middletown	36,924	33,250
06460	Milford	50,858	41,662
06468	Monroe	12,047	6,402
06353	Montville	15,662	7,759
06770	Naugatuck	23,034	19,511
*06050	New Britain	83,441	82,201
06840	New Canaan	17,455	13,466
06810	New Fairfield	6,991	3,355
*06501	New Haven	137,707	152,048
06111	Newington	26,037	17,664
06320	New London	31,630	34,182
06776	New Milford	14,601	8,318
06470	Newtown	16,942	11,373
06471	North Branford	10,778	6,771
06473	North Haven	22,194	15,935
06856	Norwalk	79,113	67,775
06360	Norwich	41,739	38,506
06475	Old Saybrook	8,468	5,274
06477	Orange	13,524	8,547
02891	Pawcatuck	5,255	4,389
06374	Plainfield	11,957	8,884
06062	Plainville	16,733	13,149
06782	Plymouth	10,321	8,981
06480	Portland	8,812	7,496
06712	Prospect	6,543	4,367
06260	Putnam	6,918	6,952
	Putnam	8,598	8,412
06875	Redding	5,590	3,359
06877	Ridgefield	5,878	2,954
	Ridgefield	18,188	8,165
06067	Rocky Hill	11,103	7,404
06483	Seymour	12,776	10,100
06484	Shelton	27,165	18,190
	Simsbury	17,475	10,138
06071	Somers	6,983	3,702
06488	Southbury	7,852	5,186
06489	Southington	30,946	22,797
06074	South Windsor	15,553	9,460
06075	Stafford	8,680	7,476
*06904	Stamford	108,798	92,713
06378	Stonington	15,940	13,969
06268	Storrs	10,691	6,054
06497	Stratford	49,775	45,012
06078	Suffield	8,634	6,779
06787	Thomaston	6,233	5,850
06277	Thompson	7,580	6,217
06084	Tolland	7,857	2,950
06790	Torrington	31,952	30,045
06611	Trumbull	31,394	20,379

ZIP Code	Place	1970	1960
06086	Vernon	27,237	16,961
06492	Wallingford	35,714	29,920
*06701	Waterbury	108,033	107,130
06385	Waterford	17,227	15,391
06795	Watertown	18,610	14,837
06107	West Hartford	68,031	62,382
06516	West Haven	52,851	43,002
06880	Weston	7,417	4,039
06880	Westport	27,414	20,955
06109	Wethersfield	26,662	20,561
06226	Willimantic	14,402	13,881
06897	Wilton	13,572	8,026
06094	Winchester	11,106	10,496
06280	Windham	19,626	16,973
06095	Windsor	22,502	19,467
06096	Windsor Locks	15,080	11,411
06098	Winsted	8,954	8,136
06716	Wolcott	12,495	8,889
06525	Woodbridge	7,673	5,182
06798	Woodbury	5,869	3,910

Delaware

ZIP Code	Place	1970	1960
19711	Brookside Park	7,856	
19703	Claymont	6,584	
19901	Dover	17,488	7,250
19901	Dover Base	8,106	
19805	Elsmere	8,415	7,319
19963	Milford	5,314	5,795
19711	Newark	21,298	11,404
19973	Seaford	5,537	4,430
*19899	Wilmington	80,386	95,827
19720	Wilmington Manor —Chelsea—Leedom	10,134	

District of Columbia

ZIP Code	Place	1970	1960
*20013	Washington	756,510	763,956
	Northeast	184,439	197,536
	Northwest	347,337	374,165
	Southeast	194,365	173,988
	Southwest	30,369	18,267

Florida

ZIP Code	Place	1970	1960
33821	Arcadia	5,658	5,889
33823	Auburndale	5,386	5,595
33825	Avon Park	6,712	6,073
32807	Azalea Park	7,367	
33830	Bartow	12,891	12,849
33505	Bayshore Gardens	9,255	2,297
33430	Belle Glade	15,949	11,273
33432	Boca Raton	28,506	6,961
33435	Boynton Beach	18,115	10,467
*33506	Bradenton	21,040	19,380
33511	Brandon	12,749	1,665
33314	Broadview Park-Rock Hill	6,049	
33311	Browardale	17,444	
33142	Browns Village	23,442	
33054	Bunche Park	5,773	
33904	Cape Coral	10,193	
33054	Carol City	27,361	21,749
33023	Carver Ranch Estates	5,515	
32707	Casselberry	9,438	2,463
33505	Cedar Hammock- Bradenton South	10,820	
32324	Chattahoochee	7,944	9,699
33515	Clearwater	52,074	34,653
32922	Cocoa	16,110	12,294
32931	Cocoa Beach	9,952	3,475
32922	Cocoa West	5,779	3,975
33064	Collier Manor-Cresthaven	7,202	
32809	Conway	8,642	
33134	Coral Gables	42,494	34,793
32536	Crestview	7,952	7,467
33157	Cutler Ridge	17,441	7,005
33004	Dania	9,013	7,065
33314	Davie	5,859	
*32015	Daytona Beach	45,327	37,395
33441	Deerfield Beach	16,662	9,573
32720	De Land	11,641	10,775
33444	Delray Beach	19,915	12,230
33528	Dunedin	17,639	8,444
33610	East Lake-Orient Park	5,711	
33940	East Naples	6,152	
32542	Eglin	7,769	
33614	Egypt Lake	7,556	
33533	Englewood	5,108	2,877
32726	Eustis	6,722	6,189
32034	Fernandina Beach	6,955	7,276
33030	Florida City	5,133	4,114
*33310	Fort Lauderdale	139,590	83,648
*33902	Fort Myers	27,351	22,523
33901	Fort Myers Southwest	5,086	
33450	Fort Pierce	29,721	25,256
32548	Fort Walton Beach	19,994	12,147
32601	Gainesville	64,510	29,701
32960	Gifford	5,772	3,509
33170	Goulds	6,690	5,121
33581	Gulf Gate Estates	5,874	
33737	Gulfport	9,976	9,730
33844	Haines City	8,956	9,135
33009	Hallandale	23,849	10,483
*33010	Hialeah	102,452	66,972
32805	Holden Heights	6,206	
32017	Holly Hill	8,191	4,182
*33022	Hollywood	106,873	35,237
33030	Homestead	13,674	9,152
33030	Homestead Base	8,257	
32937	Indian Harbour Beach	5,371	
*32201	Jacksonville	528,865	201,030
33156	Kendall	35,497	
33040	Key West	29,312	33,956
32741	Kissimmee	7,119	6,845
	Lake Carroll	5,577	
32055	Lake City	10,575	9,465
32208	Lake Forest	5,216	
33803	Lake Holloway	6,227	3,172
*33802	Lakeland	41,550	41,350
33612	Lake Magdalene	9,266	
33403	Lake Park	6,993	3,589
33853	Lake Wales	8,240	8,346
33460	Lake Worth	23,714	20,758
33460	Lantana	7,126	5,021
33540	Largo	22,031	5,302
33313	Lauderdale Lakes	10,577	
33313	Lauderhill	8,465	132
32748	Leesburg	11,869	11,172
33614	Leto	8,458	
33064	Lighthouse Point	9,071	2,453
32060	Live Oak	6,830	6,544
32810	Lockhart	5,809	
32751	Maitland	7,157	3,570
33063	Margate	8,867	2,646
32446	Marianna	6,741	7,152
*32901	Melbourne	40,236	11,982
33314	Melrose Park	6,111	
32952	Merritt Island	29,233	3,554
*33101	Miami	334,859	291,688
33139	Miami Beach	87,072	63,145
33153	Miami Shores	9,425	8,865
33166	Miami Springs	13,279	11,229
32570	Milton	5,360	4,108
32754	Mims	8,309	1,307
33023	Miramar	23,997	5,485
32506	Myrtle Grove	16,186	
33940	Naples	12,042	4,655
33552	New Port Richey 1973	7,137	3,520
32069	New Smyrna Beach	10,580	8,781
33308	North Andrews Terrace	7,082	
33903	North Fort Myers	8,798	
33161	North Miami	34,767	28,708
33160	North Miami Beach	30,544	21,405
33403	North Palm Beach	9,035	2,684
33169	Norwood	14,973	
33308	Oakland Park	16,261	5,331
32670	Ocala	22,583	13,598
32548	Ocean City	5,267	
33054	Opa-Locka	11,902	9,810
32073	Orange Park	7,619	2,624
*32802	Orlando	99,006	88,135
32074	Ormond Beach	14,063	8,658
32074	Ormond By-The-Sea	6,002	3,476
33476	Pahokee	5,663	4,709
32077	Palatka	9,444	11,028
32905	Palm Bay	7,176	2,808
33480	Palm Beach	9,086	6,055
33403	Palm Beach Gardens	6,102	1
33561	Palmetto	7,422	5,556
33619	Palm River-Clair Mel	8,536	
32401	Panama City	32,096	33,275
33023	Pembroke Pines	15,496	1,429
*32502	Pensacola	59,507	56,752
33157	Perrine	10,257	6,424
32347	Perry	7,701	8,030
32808	Pine Hills	13,882	
33565	Pinellas Park	22,287	10,848
33566	Plant City	15,451	15,711
33314	Plantation	23,523	4,772
*33060	Pompano Beach	38,587	15,992
33064	Pompano Beach Highlands	5,014	
33950	Port Charlotte	10,769	3,197
32351	Quincy	8,334	8,874
33156	Richmond Heights	6,663	4,311
33312	Riverland Village- Lauderdale Isles	5,512	
33404	Riviera Beach	21,401	13,046
32955	Rockledge	10,523	3,481
32084	St. Augustine	12,352	14,734
32769	St. Cloud	5,041	4,353
*33730	St. Petersburg	216,159	181,298
33706	St. Petersburg Beach	8,024	6,268
32771	Sanford	17,393	19,175
*33578	Sarasota	40,237	34,083
33579	Sarasota Southeast	6,885	

ZIP Code	Place	1970	1960
32937	Satellite Beach	6,558	825
33870	Sebring	7,223	6,939
33143	South Miami	11,780	9,846
33157	South Miami Heights	10,395	
32937	South Patrick Shores	10,313	
32401	Springfield	5,949	4,628
33304	Sunrise 1972	11,693	
33614	Sweetwater Creek	19,453	
*32302	Tallahassee	72,624	48,174
33513	Tamarac	5,078	
*33602	Tampa	277,753	274,970
33589	Tarpon Springs	7,118	6,768
33617	Temple Terrace	7,347	3,812
33905	Tice	7,254	4,377
32780	Titusville	30,515	6,410
33740	Treasure Island	6,120	3,506
33620	University (Hillsborough)	10,039	
32580	Valparaiso	6,504	5,975
33595	Venice	6,648	3,444
32960	Vero Beach	11,908	8,849
32960	Vero Beach South	7,330	
32507	Warrington	15,848	16,752
33505	West Bradenton	6,162	
32446	West End	5,289	3,124
33144	West Miami	5,494	5,296
*33401	West Palm Beach	57,375	56,208
32505	West Pensacola	20,924	
33880	West Winter Haven	7,716	5,050
33165	Westwood Lakes	12,811	22,517
33305	Wilton Manors	10,948	8,257
32787	Winter Garden	5,153	5,513
33880	Winter Haven	16,136	16,277
32789	Winter Park	21,895	17,162

Georgia

ZIP Code	Place	1970	1960
*31702	Albany	72,623	55,890
31709	Americus	16,091	13,472
30601	Athens	44,342	31,355
*30304	Atlanta	497,421	487,455
*30901	Augusta	59,864	70,626
31717	Bainbridge	10,887	12,714
31723	Blakely	5,267	3,580
31520	Brunswick	19,585	21,703
31728	Cairo	8,061	7,427
30117	Carrollton	13,520	10,973
30120	Cartersville	10,138	8,668
30125	Cedartown	9,253	9,340
30341	Chamblee	9,127	6,635
31014	Cochran	5,161	4,714
30337	College Park	18,203	23,469
*31902	Columbus	155,028	116,779
31015	Cordele	10,733	10,609
30209	Covington	10,267	8,167
30720	Dalton	18,872	17,868
31742	Dawson	5,383	5,062
*30030	Decatur	21,943	22,026
31520	Dock Junction	6,009	5,417
30340	Doraville	9,157	4,437
31533	Douglas	10,195	8,736
30134	Douglasville	5,472	4,462
31021	Dublin	15,143	13,814
31023	Eastman	5,416	5,118
30344	East Point	39,315	35,633
30635	Elberton	6,438	7,107
31750	Fitzgerald	8,187	8,781
30050	Forest Park	19,994	14,201
31905	Fort Benning	27,495	
30905	Fort Gordon	15,589	
31030	Fort Valley	9,251	8,310
30501	Gainesville	15,459	16,523
31408	Garden City	5,790	5,451
30223	Griffin	22,734	21,735
30354	Hapeville	9,567	10,082
31545	Jesup	9,091	7,304
30728	La Fayette	6,044	5,588
30240	La Grange	23,301	23,632
30245	Lawrenceville	5,115	3,804
*31201	Macon	122,423	69,764
30060	Marietta	27,216	25,565
31034	Midway-Hardwick	14,047	16,909
31061	Milledgeville	11,601	11,117
30655	Monroe	8,071	6,826
31768	Moultrie	14,400	15,764
30263	Newnan	11,205	12,169
31069	Perry	7,771	6,032
30161	Rome	30,759	32,226
30075	Roswell	5,430	2,963
31522	St. Simons	5,346	3,199
31082	Sandersville	5,546	5,425
*31401	Savannah	118,349	149,245
30080	Smyrna	19,157	10,157
30458	Statesboro	14,616	8,356
30747	Summerville	5,043	4,706
30401	Swainsboro	7,325	5,943
30286	Thomaston	10,024	9,336
31792	Thomasville	18,155	18,246
30824	Thomson	6,503	4,522

ZIP Code	Place	1970	1960
31794	Tifton	12,179	9,903
30577	Toccoa	6,971	7,303
31601	Valdosta	32,303	30,652
30474	Vidalia	9,507	7,569
31093	Warner Robins	33,491	18,633
31501	Waycross	18,996	20,944
30830	Waynesboro	5,530	5,359
30680	Winder	6,605	5,555
31406	Windsor Forest	7,288	

Hawaii

ZIP Code	Place	1970	1960
96701	Aiea	12,560	11,826
96706	Ewa Beach	7,765	4,627
96701	Halawa Heights	5,809	
96824	Hickam Housing	7,352	
96720	Hilo	26,353	25,966
*96813	Honolulu	324,871	294,194
96732	Kahului	8,280	4,223
96734	Kailua	33,783	25,622
96744	Kaneohe	29,903	14,414
96734	Maunawili	5,303	
96734	Mokapu	7,860	
96792	Nanakuli	6,506	2,745
96782	Pacific Palisades	7,846	
96782	Pearl City	19,552	
96786	Schofield Barracks	13,516	
96786	Wahiawa	17,598	15,512
96793	Wailuku	7,979	6,969
96797	Waipahu	24,150	

Idaho

ZIP Code	Place	1970	1960
83221	Blackfoot	8,716	7,378
*83707	Boise City	74,990	34,481
83318	Burley	8,279	7,508
83605	Caldwell	14,219	12,230
83814	Coeur D'Alene	16,228	14,291
83401	Idaho Falls	35,776	33,161
83501	Lewiston	26,068	12,691
83843	Moscow	14,146	11,183
83647	Mountain Home	6,451	5,984
83648	Mountain Home Base	6,038	
83651	Nampa	20,768	18,897
83201	Pocatello	40,036	28,534
83440	Rexburg 1973	9,761	4,767
83301	Twin Falls	21,914	20,126

Illinois

ZIP Code	Place	1970	1960
60101	Addison 1973	25,645	6,741
60658	Alsip	11,141	3,770
62002	Alton	39,700	43,047
*60004	Arlington Heights 1972	69,204	27,878
*60507	Aurora	74,182	63,715
60010	Barrington	8,674	5,434
61607	Bartonville	7,221	7,253
60510	Batavia	8,994	7,496
62618	Beardstown	6,222	6,294
62220	Belleville	41,699	37,264
61104	Bellwood 1971	21,473	20,729
61008	Belvidere	14,061	11,223
60106	Bensenville	12,956	9,141
62812	Benton	6,833	7,023
60162	Berkeley	6,152	5,792
60402	Berwyn	52,502	54,224
62010	Bethalto 1971	7,332	3,235
60108	Bloomingdale 1973	6,426	1,262
61701	Bloomington	39,992	36,271
60406	Blue Island	22,958	19,618
60439	Bolingbrook 1973	20,914	
60914	Bourbonnais	5,909	3,336
60915	Bradley 1972	10,631	8,082
60455	Bridge View 1972	13,495	7,334
60153	Broadview 1971	9,470	8,588
60513	Brookfield	20,284	20,429
60090	Buffalo Grove 1972	15,653	1,492
60459	Burbank	29,900	
62206	Cahokia	20,649	15,829
62914	Cairo	6,277	9,348
60409	Calumet City 1972	35,808	25,000
60643	Calumet Park	10,069	8,448
61520	Canton	14,217	13,588
62901	Carbondale	22,816	14,670
62626	Carlinville	5,675	5,440
62821	Carmi	6,033	6,152
60187	Carol Stream 1973	7,519	836
*60110	Carpentersville	24,059	17,424
62801	Centralia	15,217	13,904
62206	Centreville	11,378	12,769
61820	Champaign	56,532	49,583
61920	Charleston	16,421	10,505
62233	Chester	5,310	4,460
*60607	Chicago	3,369,357	3,550,404
60411	Chicago Heights	40,900	34,331
60415	Chicago Ridge 1971	9,847	5,748
61523	Chillicothe	6,052	3,054
60650	Cicero	67,058	69,130

ZIP Code	Place	1970	1960
60514	Clarendon Hills	6,750	5,885
61727	Clinton	7,570	7,355
62234	Collinsville	17,992	14,217
60077	Country Club Hills	6,920	3,421
60525	Countryside 1973	5,434	
60435	Crest Hill 1973	8,322	5,887
60445	Crestwood 1973	7,557	1,213
61611	Creve Coeur 1973	6,594	6,684
60014	Crystal Lake 1972	16,049	8,314
61832	Danville	42,570	41,856
60559	Darien 1973	9,770	
*62521	Decatur	90,397	78,004
60015	Deerfield 1972	18,867	11,786
60115	De Kalb	32,949	18,486
*60016	Des Plaines 1973	55,594	34,886
61021	Dixon	18,147	19,565
60419	Dolton	25,937	18,746
60515	Downers Grove	32,751	21,154
62832	Du Quoin	6,691	6,558
62024	East Alton	7,309	7,630
60411	East Chicago Heights 1973	6,405	3,270
61244	East Moline	20,832	16,732
61611	East Peoria	18,455	12,310
*62201	East St. Louis	69,996	81,712
62025	Edwardsville	11,070	9,996
62401	Effingham	9,458	8,172
60120	Elgin 1972	56,937	49,447
60007	Elk Grove Village 1972	22,860	6,608
60126	Elmhurst	48,887	36,991
60635	Elmwood Park	26,160	23,866
*60204	Evanston	80,113	79,283
60642	Evergreen Park 1971	25,981	24,178
62837	Fairfield	5,897	6,362
62232	Fairview Heights	8,625	
62839	Flora	5,283	5,331
60422	Flossmoor	7,846	4,624
60130	Forest Park	15,472	14,452
60131	Franklin Park	20,348	18,322
61032	Freeport	27,736	26,628
60030	Gages Lake-Wildwood	5,337	
61401	Galesburg 1971	34,501	37,243
61254	Geneseo	5,840	5,169
60134	Geneva	9,115	7,646
60022	Glencoe	10,675	10,472
60137	Glendale Heights 1973	13,494	173
60137	Glen Ellyn	21,909	15,972
60025	Glenview	24,880	18,132
60425	Glenwood 1972	9,406	882
62040	Granite City	40,685	40,073
60103	Hanover Park 1972	19,609	451
62946	Harrisburg	9,535	9,171
60033	Harvard	5,177	4,248
60426	Harvey	34,636	29,071
60656	Harwood Heights 1971	8,837	5,688
60429	Hazel Crest 1972	11,657	6,205
62948	Herrin	9,623	9,474
60457	Hickory Hills	13,176	2,707
62249	Highland	5,981	4,943
60035	Highland Park	32,263	25,532
60162	Hillside 1971	9,466	7,794
60521	Hinsdale	15,918	12,859
60172	Hoffman Estates 1973	31,833	8,296
60456	Hometown	6,729	7,479
60430	Homewood 1973	20,074	13,371
60942	Hoopeston	6,461	6,606
62650	Jacksonville	20,553	21,690
62052	Jerseyville	7,446	7,420
*60431	Joliet	78,887	66,780
60458	Justice	9,473	2,803
60901	Kankakee	30,944	27,666
61109	Ken Rock	5,945	
61443	Kewanee	15,762	16,324
60525	La Grange	17,814	15,285
60525	La Grange Highlands	6,842	
60525	La Grange Park	15,459	13,793
60044	Lake Bluff	5,008	3,494
60045	Lake Forest	15,642	10,687
60047	Lake Zurich 1972	6,357	3,458
60438	Lansing 1973	28,232	18,098
61301	La Salle	10,736	11,897
62439	Lawrenceville	5,863	5,492
60439	Lemont	5,080	3,397
60048	Libertyville	11,684	8,560
62656	Lincoln	17,582	16,890
60645	Lincolnwood	12,929	11,744
60532	Lisle 1971	6,921	4,219
62056	Litchfield	7,190	7,330
60441	Lockport	9,985	7,560
60148	Lombard 1971	37,052	22,561
61111	Loves Park	12,390	9,086
60534	Lyons	11,124	9,936
60050	McHenry 1972	7,680	3,336
61455	Macomb 1973	22,304	12,135
62060	Madison	7,042	6,861
62959	Marion 1972	12,899	11,274
60426	Markham	15,987	11,704
62258	Mascoutah	5,045	3,625
61938	Mattoon 1972	19,270	19,088

ZIP Code	Place	1970	1960
60153	Maywood	29,019	27,330
*60160	Melrose Park	22,716	22,291
61342	Mendota	6,902	6,154
62960	Metropolis	6,940	7,339
60445	Midlothian	15,939	6,605
61264	Milan 1972	5,053	3,065
61265	Moline	46,237	42,705
61462	Monmouth	11,022	10,372
60450	Morris 1972	8,435	7,935
61550	Morton 1973	12,217	5,325
60053	Morton Grove	26,369	20,533
62863	Mount Carmel	8,096	8,594
60056	Mount Prospect 1973	46,525	18,906
62864	Mount Vernon	16,382	15,566
60060	Mundelein 1972	17,153	10,526
62966	Murphysboro	10,013	8,673
60540	Naperville 1973	27,837	12,933
60648	Niles 1971	32,432	20,393
61761	Normal 1972	31,343	13,357
60656	Norridge 1971	18,043	14,087
60062	Northbrook	27,297	11,635
60064	North Chicago	47,275	22,938
60093	Northfield	5,010	4,005
60164	Northlake	14,212	12,318
61111	North Park	15,679	
60546	North Riverside 1971	7,849	7,989
60452	Oak Forest 1972	20,903	3,724
*60454	Oak Lawn 1972	62,023	27,471
*60301	Oak Park	62,511	61,093
62269	O'Fallon 1973	10,045	4,018
62450	Olney	8,974	8,780
60462	Orland Park 1973	11,219	2,592
61350	Ottawa	18,716	19,408
60067	Palatine 1973	28,807	11,504
60463	Palos Heights 1973	9,879	3,775
60465	Palos Hills 1972	9,778	3,766
62557	Pana	6,326	6,432
61944	Paris	9,971	9,823
60466	Park Forest	30,638	29,993
60068	Park Ridge	42,614	32,659
61554	Pekin	31,375	28,146
*61601	Peoria	126,963	103,162
61614	Peoria Heights	7,943	7,064
61354	Peru	11,772	10,460
61764	Pontiac	10,595	8,435
60469	Posen	5,498	4,517
61356	Princeton	6,959	6,250
60070	Prospect Heights	13,333	
62301	Quincy	45,288	43,793
61866	Rantoul	25,562	22,116
60471	Richton Park 1973	6,551	933
60627	Riverdale	15,806	12,008
60305	River Forest	13,402	12,695
60171	River Grove	11,465	8,464
60546	Riverside	10,432	9,750
60472	Robbins	9,641	7,511
62454	Robinson	7,178	7,226
61068	Rochelle	8,594	7,008
61071	Rock Falls	10,287	10,261
*61101	Rockford	147,370	126,706
61201	Rock Island	50,166	51,863
60008	Rolling Meadows	19,178	10,879
60441	Romeoville 1971	15,336	3,574
60172	Roselle 1973	7,986	3,581
60073	Round Lake Beach 1972	9,425	5,011
60174	St. Charles	12,945	9,269
62881	Salem 1973	6,359	6,165
60548	Sandwich	5,056	3,842
60411	Sauk	7,479	4,687
60172	Schaumburg 1973	32,352	986
60176	Schiller Park	12,712	5,687
62225	Scott	7,871	
61282	Silvis	5,907	3,973
60076	Skokie 1971	68,911	59,364
60473	South Holland 1972	25,220	10,412
60459	South Stickney (see Burbank)		
*62708	Springfield	91,753	83,271
61362	Spring Valley	5,605	5,371
60475	Steger 1973	9,285	6,432
61081	Sterling	16,113	15,688
60402	Stickney	6,601	6,239
60103	Streamwood	18,176	4,821
61364	Streator	15,600	16,868
60501	Summit	11,569	10,374
62221	Swansea	5,432	3,018
60178	Sycamore	7,843	6,961
62568	Taylorville	10,927	8,801
60477	Tinley Park	12,382	6,392
61801	Urbana	32,800	27,294
62471	Vandalia	5,160	5,537
60181	Villa Park 1971	25,546	20,391
61571	Washington 1973	9,466	5,919
62204	Washington Park	9,524	6,601
60970	Watseka	5,294	5,219
60084	Wauconda	5,460	3,227
60085	Waukegan	65,269	55,719
60153	Westchester	20,033	18,092
60185	West Chicago 1972	11,624	6,854

ZIP Code	Place	1970	1960
61102	West End	7,554	
60558	Western Springs	13,029	10,838
62896	West Frankfort	8,854	9,027
60559	Westmont	8,920	5,997
61604	West Peoria	6,873	
60187	Wheaton 1973	36,148	24,312
60090	Wheeling	14,746	7,169
60091	Wilmette	32,134	28,268
60093	Winnetka	13,998	13,368
60191	Wood Dale 1973	10,494	3,071
60515	Woodridge	11,028	542
62095	Wood River	13,186	11,694
60098	Woodstock	10,226	8,897
60482	Worth 1971	12,153	8,196
60099	Zion	17,268	11,941

Indiana

ZIP Code	Place	1970	1960
46001	Alexandria	5,600	5,582
*46011	Anderson	70,787	49,061
46703	Angola	5,117	4,746
46706	Auburn	7,388	6,350
47421	Bedford	13,087	13,024
46107	Beech Grove 1973	14,651	10,973
46408	Black Oak	9,624	
47401	Bloomington	43,262	31,357
46714	Bluffton	8,297	6,238
47601	Boonville	5,736	4,801
47834	Brazil	8,163	8,853
46112	Brownsburg	5,751	4,478
46032	Carmel 1973	10,563	1,442
46303	Cedar Lake	7,589	
47111	Charlestown	5,933	5,726
46304	Chesterton	6,177	4,335
47130	Clarksville	13,806	8,088
47842	Clinton	5,340	5,8 3
47201	Columbus	26,457	20,778
47331	Connersville	17,604	17,698
47933	Crawfordsville	13,842	14,231
46307	Crown Point 1973	13,420	8,443
46733	Decatur	8,445	8,327
46312	East Chicago	46,982	57,669
46405	East Gary	9,858	9,309
46514	Elkhart	43,152	40,274
46036	Elwood	11,196	11,793
*47708	Evansville	138,764	141,543
*46802	Fort Wayne	178,021	161,776
46041	Frankfort	14,956	15,302
46131	Franklin	11,477	9,453
*46401	Gary	175,415	178,320
46933	Gas City	5,742	4,469
46526	Goshen	17,871	13,718
46135	Greencastle	8,852	8,506
46140	Greenfield	10,808	9,049
47240	Greensburg	8,620	7,492
46142	Greenwood	11,408	7,169
46319	Griffith	18,168	9,483
46320	Hammond	107,885	111,698
47348	Hartford City	8,207	8,053
46322	Highland	24,947	16,284
46342	Hobart	21,485	18,680
46750	Huntington	16,217	16,185
*46206	Indianapolis	746,302	476,258
47546	Jasper	8,641	6,737
47130	Jeffersonville	20,008	19,522
46755	Kendallville	6,838	6,765
46901	Kokomo	44,042	47,197
*47901	Lafayette	44,955	42,330
46350	La Porte	22,140	21,157
46226	Lawrence	16,917	10,103
46052	Lebanon	9,766	9,523
47441	Linton	5,450	5,736
46947	Logansport	19,255	21,106
47250	Madison	13,081	10,488
46952	Marion	39,607	37,854
46151	Martinsville	9,723	7,525
46410	Merrillville 1973	25,978	
46360	Michigan City	39,369	36,653
46544	Mishawaka	35,517	33,361
46158	Mooresville	5,800	3,856
47620	Mount Vernon	6,770	5,970
*47302	Muncie	69,082	68,603
46321	Munster	18,894	10,313
47150	New Albany	38,402	37,812
47362	New Castle	21,215	20,349
46774	New Haven	5,728	3,396
46060	Noblesville	7,548	7,664
46962	North Manchester	5,791	4,377
46970	Peru	14,139	14,453
46168	Plainfield	8,211	5,460
46563	Plymouth	7,661	7,558
46368	Portage 1973	20,624	11,822
47371	Portland	7,115	6,999
47670	Princeton	7,431	7,906
47374	Richmond	43,999	44,149
46173	Rushville	6,686	7,264
47167	Salem	5,041	4,546
47274	Seymour	13,352	11,629

ZIP Code	Place	1970	1960
46176	Shelbyville	15,094	14,317
*46624	South Bend	125,580	132,445
46224	Speedway	14,649	9,624
47586	Tell City	7,933	6,609
*47808	Terre Haute	70,335	72,500
46072	Tipton	5,313	5,604
46383	Valparaiso	20,020	15,227
47591	Vincennes	19,867	18,046
46992	Wabash	13,379	12,621
46580	Warsaw	7,506	7,234
47501	Washington	11,358	10,846
46408	West Glen Park	5,940	
47906	West Lafayette	19,157	12,680
46394	Whiting	7,152	8,137
47394	Winchester	5,493	5,742

Iowa

ZIP Code	Place	1970	1960
50511	Algona	6,032	5,702
50010	Ames	39,505	27,003
50021	Ankeny	9,151	2,964
50022	Atlantic	7,306	6,890
52722	Bettendorf	22,126	11,534
50036	Boone	12,468	12,468
52601	Burlington	32,366	32,430
51401	Carroll	8,716	7,682
50613	Cedar Falls	29,597	21,195
*52401	Cedar Rapids	110,642	92,035
52544	Centerville	6,531	6,629
50049	Chariton	5,009	5,042
50616	Charles City	9,268	9,964
51012	Cherokee	7,272	7,724
51632	Clarinda	5,420	5,901
50428	Clear Lake City 1973	6,876	6,158
52732	Clinton	34,719	33,589
52240	Coralville	6,130	2,357
51501	Council Bluffs	60,348	55,641
50801	Creston	8,234	7,667
*52802	Davenport	98,469	88,981
52101	Decorah	7,458	6,435
51442	Denison	6,218	4,930
*50318	Des Moines	201,404	208,982
52001	Dubuque	62,309	56,606
51334	Estherville	8,108	7,927
50707	Evansdale	5,038	5,738
52556	Fairfield	8,715	8,054
50501	Fort Dodge	31,263	28,399
52627	Fort Madison	13,996	15,247
50112	Grinnell	8,402	7,367
51537	Harlan	5,049	4,350
50644	Independence	5,910	5,498
50125	Indianola	8,852	7,062
52240	Iowa City	46,850	33,443
50126	Iowa Falls	6,454	5,565
52632	Keokuk	14,631	16,316
50138	Knoxville	7,755	7,817
51031	Le Mars	8,159	6,767
52060	Maquoketa	5,677	5,909
52302	Marion	18,028	10,882
50158	Marshalltown	26,219	22,521
50401	Mason City	30,379	30,642
52641	Mount Pleasant	7,007	7,339
52761	Muscatine	22,405	20,997
50208	Newton	15,619	15,381
50662	Oelwein	7,735	8,282
52577	Oskaloosa	11,224	11,053
52501	Ottumwa	29,610	33,871
50219	Pella	6,668	5,198
50220	Perry	6,906	6,442
51566	Red Oak	6,210	6,421
51601	Shenandoah	5,968	6,567
*51101	Sioux City	85,925	89,159
51301	Spencer	10,278	8,864
50588	Storm Lake	8,591	7,728
50322	Urbandale	14,434	5,821
52353	Washington	6,317	6,037
*50701	Waterloo	75,533	71,755
50677	Waverly	7,205	6,357
50595	Webster City	8,488	8,520
50265	West Des Moines	16,441	11,949
50311	Windsor Heights	6,303	4,715

Kansas

ZIP Code	Place	1970	1960
67410	Abilene	6,661	6,746
67005	Arkansas City	13,216	14,262
66002	Atchison	12,565	12,529
67010	Augusta	5,977	6,434
66720	Chanute	10,341	10,849
67337	Coffeyville	15,116	17,382
66901	Concordia	7,221	7,022
67037	Derby	7,947	6,458
67801	Dodge City	14,127	13,520
67042	El Dorado	12,308	12,523
66801	Emporia	23,327	18,190
66205	Fairway	5,133	5,398
66027	Fort Leavenworth	8,060	
66701	Fort Scott	8,967	9,410

ZIP Code	Place	1970	1960	ZIP Code	Place	1970	1960
67846	Garden City	14,790	11,811	40383	Versailles	5,679	4,060
67735	Goodland	5,510	4,459	40391	Winchester	13,402	10,187
67530	Great Bend	16,133	16,670				
67601	Hays	15,396	11,947		**Louisiana**		
67060	Haysville	6,483	5,836				
67501	Hutchinson	36,885	37,574	70510	Abbeville	10,996	10,414
67301	Independence	10,347	11,222	71301	Alexandria	41,557	40,279
66749	Iola	6,493	6,885	70714	Baker	8,281	4,823
66441	Junction City	19,018	18,700	71220	Bastrop	14,713	15,193
66110	Kansas City	168,213	121,901	*70821	Baton Rouge	165,963	152,419
66044	Lawrence	45,698	32,858	70360	Bayou Cane	9,077	3,173
66048	Leavenworth	25,147	22,052	70380	Bayou Vista	5,121	
66206	Leawood	10,349	7,466	70427	Bogalusa	18,412	21,423
66215	Lenexa	5,242	2,487	71010	Bossier City	41,595	32,776
67901	Liberal	13,789	13,813	71322	Bunkie	5,395	5,188
67460	McPherson	10,851	9,996	71101	Cooper Road	9,034	
66502	Manhattan	27,575	22,993	70433	Covington	7,170	6,754
66203	Merriam	10,851	5,084	70526	Crowley	16,104	15,617
66222	Mission	8,376	4,626	70726	Denham Springs	6,752	5,991
67114	Newton	15,439	14,877	70634	De Ridder	8,030	7,188
66442	North Fort Riley	12,469		70346	Donaldsonville	7,367	6,082
66061	Olathe	17,917	10,987	70535	Eunice	11,390	11,326
66067	Ottawa	11,036	10,673	71334	Ferriday	5,239	4,563
66204	Overland Park	79,034		70538	Franklin	9,325	8,673
67357	Parsons	13,015	13,929	70053	Gretna	24,875	21,967
66762	Pittsburg	20,171	18,678	70401	Hammond	12,487	10,563
66208	Prairie Village	28,138	25,356	70123	Harahan	13,037	9,275
67124	Pratt	6,736	8,156	70058	Harvey	6,347	
66203	Roeland Park	9,974	8,949	70360	Houma	30,922	22,561
67665	Russell	5,371	6,113	70544	Jeanerette	6,322	5,568
67401	Salina	37,714	43,202	70121	Jefferson Heights	16,489	19,353
*66202	Shawnee	20,482	9,072	70546	Jennings	11,783	11,887
*66601	Topeka	125,011	119,484	71251	Jonesboro	5,072	3,848
67152	Wellington	8,072	8,809	70548	Kaplan	5,540	5,267
*67202	Wichita	276,554	254,698	70062	Kenner	29,858	17,037
67156	Winfield	11,405	11,117	70501	Lafayette	68,908	40,400
				70501	Lafayette Southwest	5,396	6,682
				70601	Lake Charles	77,998	63,392
	Kentucky			71254	Lake Providence	6,183	5,781
				70068	Laplace	5,953	3,541
41101	Ashland	29,245	31,283	71446	Leesville	8,928	4,689
40004	Bardstown	5,816	4,798	70123	Little Farms	15,713	
41073	Bellevue	8,847	9,336	71052	Mansfield	6,432	5,839
40403	Berea	6,956	4,302	70072	Marrero	29,015	
42101	Bowling Green	36,705	28,338	*70080	Metairie	136,477	
40218	Buechel	5,359		71055	Minden	13,996	12,785
42718	Campbellsville	7,598	6,966	71201	Monroe	56,374	52,219
42330	Central City	5,450	3,694	70380	Morgan City	16,586	13,540
40701	Corbin	7,317	7,119	71457	Natchitoches	15,974	13,924
*41011	Covington	52,535	60,376	70560	New Iberia	30,147	29,062
41031	Cynthiana	6,356	5,641	*70113	New Orleans	593,471	627,525
40422	Danville	11,542	9,010	71459	North Fort Polk	7,955	
41074	Dayton	8,751	9,050	71463	Oakdale	7,301	6,618
42701	Elizabethtown	11,748	9,641	70570	Opelousas	20,387	17,417
41018	Elsmere	5,161	4,607	71360	Pineville	8,951	8,636
41018	Erlanger	12,676	7,072	70764	Plaquemine	7,739	7,689
41139	Flatwoods	7,380	3,741	70767	Port Allen	5,728	5,026
41042	Florence	11,661	5,837	70578	Rayne	9,510	8,634
42223	Fort Campbell North	13,616		70084	Reserve	6,381	5,297
40121	Fort Knox	37,608		71270	Ruston	17,365	13,991
41077	Fort Mitchell	6,982	525	70582	St. Martinville	7,153	6,468
41075	Fort Thomas	16,338	14,896	70807	Scotlandville	22,557	
40601	Frankfort	21,902	18,365	*71102	Shreveport	182,064	164,372
42134	Franklin	6,553	5,319	70458	Slidell	16,101	6,356
40324	Georgetown	8,629	6,986	71459	South Fort Polk	15,600	
42141	Glasgow	11,301	10,069	71075	Springhill	6,496	6,437
40330	Harrodsburg	6,741	6,061	70663	Sulphur	14,959	11,429
41701	Hazard	5,459	5,958	71282	Tallulah	9,643	9,413
42420	Henderson	22,976	16,892	71285	Terry	13,382	
42240	Hopkinsville	21,250	19,465	70301	Thibodaux	15,028	13,403
40299	Jeffersontown	9,701	3,431	71373	Vidalia	5,538	4,313
40033	Lebanon	5,528	4,813	70586	Ville Platte	9,692	7,512
*40507	Lexington	108,137	62,810	71291	West Monroe	14,868	15,215
*40201	Louisville	361,706	390,639	70094	Westwego	11,402	9,815
41016	Ludlow	5,815	6,233	71483	Winnfield	7,142	7,022
42431	Madisonville	15,332	13,110	71295	Winnsboro	5,349	4,437
42066	Mayfield	10,724	10,762				
41056	Maysville	7,411	8,484				
40965	Middlesborough	11,878	12,607		**Maine**		
40351	Morehead	7,191	4,170		*See Note on Page 159*		
40353	Mount Sterling	5,083	5,370				
42071	Murray	13,537	9,303	04210	Auburn	24,151	24,449
*41071	Newport	25,998	30,070	04330	Augusta	21,945	21,680
40356	Nicholasville	5,829	4,275	04401	Bangor	33,168	38,912
40219	Okolona	17,643		04530	Bath	9,679	10,717
42301	Owensboro	50,329	42,471	04915	Belfast	5,957	6,140
42001	Paducah	31,627	34,479	04005	Biddeford	19,983	19,255
40361	Paris	7,823	7,791	04412	Brewer	9,300	9,009
41501	Pikeville	5,205	4,754	04011	Brunswick Center	10,867	9,444
40258	Pleasure Ridge Park	28,566	10,612		Brunswick	16,195	15,797
42445	Princeton	6,292	5,618	04107	Cape Elizabeth	7,873	5,505
40160	Radcliff	7,881	3,384	04736	Caribou	10,419	12,464
40475	Richmond	16,861	12,168		Fairfield	5,684	5,829
42276	Russellville	6,456	5,861	04105	Falmouth	6,291	5,976
40207	St. Matthews	13,152	8,738		Farmington	5,657	5,001
40216	Shively	19,139	15,155	04345	Gardiner	6,685	6,897
42501	Somerset	10,436	7,112		Gorham	7,839	5,767
40272	Valley Station	24,471	10,533	04730	Houlton Center	6,760	5,976

ZIP Code	Place	1970	1960
	Houlton	8,111	8,289
	Kennebunk	5,646	4,551
03904	Kittery Center	7,363	8,051
	Kittery	11,028	10,689
04240	Lewiston	41,779	40,804
04750	Limestone	10,360	13,102
04250	Lisbon	6,544	5,042
04750	Loring	7,881	
	Madawaska	5,585	5,507
04462	Millinocket Center	7,558	7,318
	Millinocket	7,742	7,453
04064	Old Orchard Beach Ctr	5,273	4,431
	Old Orchard Beach	5,404	4,580
04468	Old Town	9,057	8,626
04473	Orono Center	9,146	3,234
	Orono	9,989	8,341
*04101	Portland	65,116	72,566
04769	Presque Isle	11,452	12,886
04841	Rockland	8,505	8,769
04276	Rumford	6,198	7,233
	Rumford	9,363	10,005
04072	Saco	11,678	10,515
04073	Sanford Center	10,457	10,936
	Sanford	15,812	14,962
04074	Scarborough	7,845	6,418
04976	Skowhegan Center	6,571	6,667
	Skowhegan	7,601	7,661
04106	South Portland	23,267	22,788
	Topsham	5,022	3,818
04901	Waterville	18,192	19,001
04092	Westbrook	14,444	13,820
04082	Windham	6,593	4,498
04901	Winslow Center	5,389	3,640
	Winslow	7,299	5,891
03909	York	5,690	4,663

Maryland

ZIP Code	Place	1970	1960
21001	Aberdeen	12,375	9,679
21005	Aberdeen Proving Ground	7,403	
20331	Andrews	6,418	
*21401	Annapolis	30,095	23,385
21227	Arbutus	22,745	22,402
20853	Aspen Hill	16,823	
	Avenel-Hilandale	19,520	
21905	Bainbridge Center	5,257	
*21233	Baltimore	905,759	939,024
21014	Bel Air	6,307	4,300
20705	Beltsville	8,912	
20014	Bethesda	71,621	56,527
20021	Birchwood City	13,514	
20710	Bladensburg	7,488	3,103
20715	Bowie	35,028	1,072
21225	Brooklyn	13,896	
20705	Calverton	6,543	
21613	Cambridge	11,595	12,239
20031	Camp Springs	22,776	
20027	Carmody Hills-Pepper Mill	6,335	
21228	Catonsville	54,812	37,372
20027	Chapel Oaks-Cedar Heights	6,049	
20785	Cheverly	6,808	5,223
20015	Chevy Chase	16,424	
20783	Chillum	35,656	
20904	Colesville	9,455	
20740	College Park	26,156	18,482
21043	Columbia	8,815	
20027	Coral Hills	9,058	
21502	Cumberland	29,724	33,415
21222	Defense Heights	6,775	
20028	District Heights	7,659	7,524
21222	Dundalk	85,377	82,428
21601	Easton	6,809	6,337
21219	Edgemere	10,352	11,775
21040	Edgewood	8,551	1,670
21921	Elkton	5,362	5,989
21043	Ellicott	9,435	
21221	Essex	38,193	35,205
21061	Ferndale	9,929	
20028	Forestville	16,188	
20755	Fort Meade	16,699	
21701	Frederick	23,641	21,744
21532	Frostburg	7,327	6,722
20760	Gaithersburg	8,344	3,847
21061	Glen Burnie	38,608	
20801	Good Luck	10,584	
20770	Greenbelt	18,199	7,479
21740	Hagerstown	35,862	36,660
21740	Halfway	6,106	4,256
20852	Halpine	6,118	
21078	Havre De Grace	9,791	8,510
20031	Hillcrest Heights	24,037	15,295
*20780	Hyattsville	14,998	15,168
21085	Joppatowne	9,092	
20904	Kemp Mill	10,037	
20785	Kentland	9,649	
20784	Landover	5,597	
20787	Langley Park	11,564	11,510
20801	Lanham-Seabrook	13,244	

ZIP Code	Place	1970	1960
21227	Lansdowne-Baltimore Highlands	17,770	13,134
20810	Laurel	10,525	8,503
20653	Lexington Pk.-Patuxent River	9,136	
21090	Linthicum	9,775	
21093	Lutherville-Timonium	24,055	12,265
20810	Maryland City	7,102	
21220	Middle River	19,935	10,825
20852	Montrose	5,902	
20822	Mount Rainier	8,180	9,855
20784	New Carrollton	14,870	3,385
20854	North Potomac	12,784	
20012	North Takoma Park	7,373	
21113	Odenton	5,989	1,914
21206	Overlea	13,124	10,795
21117	Owings Mills	7,360	3,810
20021	Oxon Hill	11,974	
20785	Palmer Park	8,172	
21234	Parkville	33,589	27,236
21128	Perry Hall	5,446	
21208	Pikesville	25,395	18,737
20016	Potomac Valley	5,122	
21227	Pumphrey	6,425	
21133	Randallstown	33,683	
20853	Randolph	13,215	
21136	Reisterstown	12,568	4,216
20840	Riverdale	5,724	4,389
20840	Riverdale Hgts.-E. Pine	8,941	
21122	Riviera Beach	7,464	4,902
*20850	Rockville	41,821	26,090
21237	Rosedale	19,417	
21801	Salisbury	15,252	16,302
20027	Seat Pleasant	7,217	5,365
21146	Severna Park	16,358	3,728
*20907	Silver Spring	77,411	66,348
21061	South Gate	9,356	
20795	South Kensington	10,289	
20810	South Laurel	13,345	
20023	Suitland-Silver Hills	30,355	10,300
20012	Takoma Park	18,507	16,799
21204	Towson	77,768	19,090
20601	Waldorf	7,368	1,048
20028	Walker Mill	7,103	
21157	Westminster	7,207	6,123
20902	Wheaton	66,280	54,635
20903	White Oak	19,769	
21207	Woodlawn-Woodmoor	28,821	

Massachusetts
See Note on Page 159

ZIP Code	Place	1970	1960
02351	Abington	12,334	10,607
01720	Acton	14,770	7,238
02743	Acushnet	7,767	5,755
01220	Adams Center	11,256	11,949
	Adams	11,772	12,391
01001	Agawam	21,717	15,718
01913	Amesbury Center	10,088	9,625
	Amesbury	11,388	10,787
01002	Amherst Center	17,926	10,306
	Amherst	26,331	13,718
01810	Andover	23,695	17,134
02174	Arlington	53,534	49,953
01721	Ashland	8,882	7,779
01331	Athol Center	9,723	10,161
	Athol	11,185	11,637
02703	Attleboro	32,907	27,118
01501	Auburn	15,347	14,047
02322	Avon	5,295	4,301
01432	Ayer	7,393	14,927
02630	Barnstable	19,842	13,465
01730	Bedford	13,513	10,969
01007	Belchertown	5,936	5,186
02019	Bellingham	13,967	6,774
02178	Belmont	28,285	28,715
01915	Beverly	38,348	36,108
01821	Billerica	31,648	17,867
01504	Blackstone	6,566	5,130
*02109	Boston	641,071	697,197
02532	Bourne	12,636	14,011
02184	Braintree	35,050	31,069
02324	Bridgewater	11,829	10,276
*02403	Brockton	89,040	72,813
02146	Brookline	58,886	54,044
01803	Burlington	21,980	12,852
*02138	Cambridge	100,361	107,716
02021	Canton	17,100	12,771
01824	Chelmsford	31,432	15,130
02150	Chelsea	30,625	33,749
01021	Chicopee	66,676	61,553
01510	Clinton	13,383	12,848
02025	Cohasset	6,954	5,840
01742	Concord	16,148	12,517
01226	Dalton	7,505	6,436
01923	Danvers	26,151	21,926
02714	Dartmouth	18,800	14,607
02026	Dedham	25,938	23,869
02638	Dennis	6,454	3,727

ZIP Code	Place	1970	1960	ZIP Code	Place	1970	1960
01826	Dracut	18,214	13,674	02062	Norwood	30,815	24,898
01570	Dudley	8,087	6,510	01364	Orange	6,104	6,154
02332	Duxbury	7,636	4,727	01253	Otis	5,596	
02333	East Bridgewater	8,347	6,139	01540	Oxford Center	6,109	6,985
01027	Easthampton	13,012	12,326		Oxford	10,345	9,282
01028	East Longmeadow	13,029	10,294	01069	Palmer	11,680	10,358
02334	Easton	12,157	9,078	01960	Peabody	48,080	32,202
02149	Everett	42,485	43,544	02359	Pembroke	11,193	4,919
02719	Fairhaven	16,332	14,339	01463	Pepperell	5,887	4,336
*02722	Fall River	96,898	99,942	01866	Pinehurst	5,681	1,991
*02540	Falmouth Center	5,806	3,308	01201	Pittsfield	57,020	57,879
	Falmouth	15,942	13,037	02360	Plymouth Center	6,940	6,488
01420	Fitchburg	43,343	43,021		Plymouth	18,606	14,445
01433	Fort Devens	12,019		02169	Quincy	87,966	87,409
02035	Foxborough	14,218	10,136	02368	Randolph	27,035	18,900
01701	Framingham	64,048	44,526	02767	Raynham	6,705	4,150
02038	Franklin Center	8,863	6,391	01867	Reading	22,539	19,259
	Franklin	17,830	10,530	02769	Rehoboth	6,512	4,953
01440	Gardner	19,748	19,038	02151	Revere	43,159	40,080
01833	Georgetown	5,290	3,755	02370	Rockland	15,674	13,119
01930	Gloucester	27,941	25,789	01966	Rockport	5,636	4,616
01519	Grafton	11,659	10,627	01970	Salem	40,556	39,211
01033	Granby	5,473	4,221	02563	Sandwich	5,239	2,082
01230	Great Barrington	7,537	6,624	01906	Saugus	25,110	20,666
01301	Greenfield Center	14,642	14,389	02066	Scituate	16,973	11,214
	Greenfield	18,116	17,690	02771	Seekonk	11,116	8,399
01450	Groton	5,109	3,904	02067	Sharon	12,367	10,070
01834	Groveland	5,382	3,297	01545	Shrewsbury	19,196	16,622
01936	Hamilton	6,373	5,488	02725	Somerset	18,088	12,196
02339	Hanover	10,107	5,923	02143	Somerville	88,779	94,697
02341	Hanson	7,148	4,370	01772	Southborough	5,798	3,996
01451	Harvard	12,494	2,563	01550	Southbridge Center	14,261	15,889
02645	Harwich	5,892	3,747		Southbridge	17,057	16,523
01830	Haverhill	46,120	46,346	01075	South Hadley	17,033	14,956
02043	Hingham	18,845	15,378	01077	Southwick	6,330	5,139
02343	Holbrook	11,775	10,104	02664	South Yarmouth	5,380	2,029
01520	Holden	12,564	10,117	01562	Spencer Center	5,895	5,593
01746	Holliston	12,069	6,222		Spencer	8,779	7,838
01040	Holyoke	50,112	52,689	*01101	Springfield	163,905	174,463
01748	Hopkinton	5,981	4,932	02180	Stoneham	20,725	17,821
01749	Hudson Center	14,283	7,987	02072	Stoughton	23,459	16,328
	Hudson	16,084	9,666	01776	Sudbury	13,506	7,447
02045	Hull	9,961	7,055	01907	Swampscott	13,578	13,294
02601	Hyannis	6,847	5,139	02777	Swansea	12,640	9,916
01938	Ipswich	5,022	4,617	02780	Taunton	43,756	41,132
	Ipswich	10,750	8,544	01468	Templeton	5,863	5,371
02364	Kingston	5,999	4,302	01876	Tewksbury	22,755	15,902
01523	Lancaster	6,095	3,958	01983	Topsfield	5,225	3,351
*01842	Lawrence	66,915	70,933	01376	Turners Falls	5,168	4,917
01238	Lee	6,426	5,271	01569	Uxbridge	8,253	7,789
01524	Leicester	9,140	8,177	01880	Wakefield	25,402	24,295
01240	Lenox	5,804	4,253	02081	Walpole	18,149	14,068
01453	Leominster	32,939	27,929	02154	Waltham	61,582	55,413
02173	Lexington	31,886	27,691	01082	Ware Center	6,509	6,650
01773	Lincoln	7,567	5,613		Ware	8,187	7,517
01460	Littleton	6,380	5,109	02571	Wareham	11,492	9,461
01106	Longmeadow	15,630	10,565	02172	Watertown	39,307	39,092
*01853	Lowell	94,239	92,107	01778	Wayland	13,461	10,444
01056	Ludlow	17,580	13,805	01570	Webster Center	12,432	12,072
01462	Lunenburg	7,419	6,334		Webster	14,917	13,680
*01901	Lynn	90,294	94,478	02181	Wellesley	28,051	26,071
01940	Lynnfield	10,826	8,398	01581	Westborough	12,594	9,599
02148	Malden	56,127	57,676	01583	West Boylston	6,369	5,526
01944	Manchester	5,151	3,932	02379	West Bridgewater	7,152	5,061
02048	Mansfield	9,939	7,773	01085	Westfield	31,433	26,302
01945	Marblehead	21,295	18,521	01886	Westford	10,368	6,261
01752	Marlborough	27,936	18,819	02193	Weston	10,870	8,261
02050	Marshfield	15,223	6,748	02790	Westport	9,791	6,641
01754	Maynard	9,710	7,695	01089	West Springfield	28,461	24,924
02052	Medfield	9,821	6,021	02090	Westwood	12,750	10,354
02155	Medford	64,397	64,971	02188	Weymouth	54,610	48,177
02053	Medway	7,938	5,168	01588	Whitinsville	5,210	5,102
02176	Melrose	33,180	29,619	02382	Whitman	13,059	10,485
01844	Methuen	35,456	28,114		Wilbraham	11,984	7,387
02346	Middleborough Center	6,259	6,003		Williamstown	8,454	7,322
	Middleborough	13,607	11,065	01887	Wilmington	17,102	12,475
01757	Milford Center	13,740	13,722		Winchendon	6,635	6,237
	Milford	19,352	15,749	01890	Winchester	22,269	19,376
01527	Millbury	11,987	9,623	02152	Winthrop	20,335	20,303
02054	Millis	5,686	4,374	01801	Woburn	37,406	31,214
02186	Milton	27,190	26,375	*01613	Worcester	176,572	186,587
01057	Monson	7,355	6,712	02093	Wrentham	7,315	6,685
01351	Montague	8,451	7,836	02675	Yarmouth	12,033	5,504
01760	Natick	31,057	28,831				
02192	Needham	29,748	25,793		**Michigan**		
*02741	New Bedford	101,777	102,477				
01950	Newburyport	15,807	14,004	49221	Adrian	20,382	20,347
02158	Newton	91,066	92,384	49224	Albion	12,112	12,749
01247	North Adams	19,195	19,905	48101	Allen Park	40,747	37,494
01060	Northampton	29,664	30,058	48801	Alma	9,611	8,978
01845	North Andover	16,284	10,908	49707	Alpena	13,805	14,682
*02760	North Attleborough	18,665	14,777	*48106	Ann Arbor	99,797	67,340
01532	Northborough	9,218	6,687	*49016	Battle Creek	38,931	44,169
01534	Northbridge	11,795	10,800	48706	Bay City	49,449	53,604
01864	North Reading	11,264	8,331	48809	Belding	5,121	4,887
02060	North Scituate	5,507	3,421	49022	Benton Central	8,067	
02766	Norton	9,487	6,818	49022	Benton Harbor	16,481	19,136
02061	Norwell	7,796	5,207	48072	Berkley	21,879	23,275

ZIP Code	Place	1970	1960	ZIP Code	Place	1970	1960
48009	Beverly Hills	13,598	8,633	49770	Petoskey	6,342	6,138
49307	Big Rapids	11,995	8,686	48170	Plymouth	11,758	8,766
*48012	Birmingham	26,170	25,525	*48053	Pontiac	85,279	82,233
49601	Cadillac	9,990	10,112	49081	Portage	33,590	
48724	Carrollton	7,300		48060	Port Huron	35,794	36,084
48015	Center Line	10,379	10,164	48024	Quakertown North	7,101	
48813	Charlotte	8,244	7,657	48218	River Rouge	15,947	18,147
49721	Cheboygan	5,553	5,859	48192	Riverview	11,342	7,237
48017	Clawson	17,617	14,795	48063	Rochester	7,054	5,431
49036	Coldwater	9,155	8,880	48066	Roseville	60,529	50,195
49041	Comstock	5,003		*48067	Royal Oak	86,238	80,612
49321	Comstock Park	5,766		*48605	Saginaw	91,849	98,265
49508	Cutlerville	6,267		*48083	St. Clair Shores	88,093	76,657
48423	Davison	5,259	3,761	48879	St. Johns	6,672	5,629
*48120	Dearborn	104,199	112,007	49085	St. Joseph	11,042	11,755
48127	Dearborn Heights	80,069		49783	Sault Ste. Marie	15,136	18,722
*48233	Detroit	1,513,601	1,670,144	*48075	Southfield	69,285	31,501
49047	Dowagiac	6,583	7,208	48192	Southgate	33,909	29,404
48020	Drayton Plains	16,462		49090	South Haven	6,471	6,149
48021	East Detroit	45,920	45,756	*48077	Sterling Heights	61,365	
49506	East Grand Rapids	12,565	10,924	49091	Sturgis	9,295	8,915
48823	East Lansing	47,540	30,198	48180	Taylor	70,020	
49001	Eastwood	9,682		49286	Tecumseh	7,120	7,045
48229	Ecorse	17,515	17,328	49093	Three Rivers	7,355	7,092
49829	Escanaba	15,368	15,391	49684	Traverse City	18,048	18,432
48024	Farmington	10,329	6,881	48183	Trenton	24,127	18,439
48430	Fenton	8,284	6,142	48084	Troy	39,419	19,402
48220	Ferndale	30,850	31,347	49504	Walker	11,492	
48134	Flat Rock	5,643	4,696	*48089	Warren	179,260	89,246
*48502	Flint	193,317	196,940	48184	Wayne	21,054	16,034
48433	Flushing	7,190	3,761	48185	Westland	86,749	
48026	Fraser	11,868	7,027	49007	Westwood	9,143	
48135	Garden City	41,864	38,017	48753	Wurtsmith	6,932	
49837	Gladstone	5,237	5,267	48192	Wyandotte	41,061	43,519
48439	Grand Blanc	5,132	1,565	49509	Wyoming	56,560	45,829
49417	Grand Haven	11,844	11,066	48197	Ypsilanti	29,538	20,957
48837	Grand Ledge	6,032	5,165				
*49501	Grand Rapids	197,649	177,313		**Minnesota**		
49418	Grandville	10,764	7,975				
48838	Greenville	7,493	7,440	56007	Albert Lea	19,418	17,108
48138	Grosse Ile	8,306		56308	Alexandria	6,973	6,713
48236	Grosse Pointe	6,637	6,631	55303	Anoka	13,295	10,562
48236	Grosse Pointe Farms	11,701	12,172	55068	Apple Valley	8,502	
48236	Grosse Pointe Park	15,641	15,457	55112	Arden Hills	5,149	3,930
48236	Grosse Pointe Woods	21,878	18,580	55912	Austin	25,074	27,908
48212	Hamtramck	27,245	34,137	56601	Bemidji	11,490	9,958
48236	Harper Woods	20,186	19,995	55433	Blaine	20,625	7,570
49058	Hastings	6,501	6,375	55420	Bloomington	81,970	50,498
48030	Hazel Park	23,784	25,631	56401	Brainerd	11,667	12,898
48203	Highland Park	35,444	38,063	55429	Brooklyn Center	35,173	24,356
49242	Hillsdale	7,728	7,629	55429	Brooklyn Park 1972	29,945	10,197
49423	Holland	26,479	24,777	55378	Burnsville	19,940	
48842	Holt	6,980	4,818	55316	Champlin 1972	6,298	1,271
49931	Houghton	6,067	3,393	55317	Chanhassen 1971	5,054	244
48843	Howell	5,224	4,861	55318	Chaska 1972	5,398	2,501
48070	Huntington Woods	8,536	8,746	55719	Chisholm	5,913	7,144
48141	Inkster	38,595	39,097	55720	Cloquet	8,699	9,013
48846	Ionia	6,361	6,754	55421	Columbia Heights	23,837	17,533
49801	Iron Mountain	8,702	9,299	55433	Coon Rapids	30,505	14,931
49938	Ironwood	8,711	10,265	55016	Cottage Grove	13,419	
49849	Ishpeming	8,245	8,857	56716	Crookston	8,312	8,546
*49201	Jackson	45,484	50,720	55428	Crystal	30,925	24,283
49428	Jenison	11,266		56501	Detroit Lakes	5,797	5,633
*49001	Kalamazoo	85,555	82,089	*55806	Duluth	100,578	106,884
49508	Kentwood	20,310		56721	East Grand Forks	7,607	6,998
49788	Kincheloe	6,331		55343	Eden Prairie	6,938	
49801	Kingsford	5,276	5,084	55424	Edina	44,046	28,501
49843	K.I. Sawyer	8,224		56031	Fairmont	10,751	9,745
48850	Lakeview	11,391	10,384	55113	Falcon Heights	5,641	5,927
48144	Lambertville	5,711	1,168	55021	Faribault	16,595	16,926
*48924	Lansing	131,403	107,807	56537	Fergus Falls	12,443	13,733
48446	Lapeer	6,314	6,160	55421	Fridley	29,233	15,173
48503	Lapeer Heights	7,130		55427	Golden Valley	24,246	14,559
48146	Lincoln Park	52,984	53,933	55744	Grand Rapids	7,247	7,265
*48150	Livonia	110,109	66,702	55033	Hastings	12,195	8,965
49431	Ludington	9,021	9,421	55746	Hibbing	16,104	17,731
48071	Madison Heights	38,599	33,343	55343	Hopkins	13,428	11,370
49660	Manistee	7,723	8,324	55350	Hutchinson	8,031	6,207
49855	Marquette	21,967	19,824	56649	International Falls	6,439	6,778
49068	Marshall	7,253	6,736	55075	Inver Grove Heights	12,148	
48040	Marysville	5,610	4,065	55044	Lakeville	7,556	924
48854	Mason	5,468	4,522	55355	Litchfield	5,262	5,078
48122	Melvindale	13,862	13,089	56345	Little Falls	7,467	7,551
49858	Menominee	10,748	11,289	56001	Mankato	30,895	23,797
48640	Midland	35,176	27,779	55369	Maple Grove	6,275	2,213
48161	Monroe	23,894	22,968	55109	Maplewood	25,222	18,519
48043	Mount Clemens	20,476	21,016	56258	Marshall	9,886	6,681
48858	Mount Pleasant	20,524	14,875	55118	Mendota Heights	6,165	5,028
*49440	Muskegon	44,631	46,485	*55401	Minneapolis	434,400	482,872
49444	Muskegon Heights	17,304	19,552	55343	Minnetonka	35,737	25,037
49866	Negaunee	5,248	6,126	56265	Montevideo	5,661	5,693
49120	Niles	12,988	13,842	56560	Moorhead	29,687	22,934
48167	Northville	5,400	3,967	56267	Morris	5,366	4,199
49441	Norton Shores	22,271		55364	Mound	7,572	5,440
48050	Novi	9,668	6,390	55112	Mounds View	10,641	6,416
48237	Oak Park	36,762	36,632	55112	New Brighton	19,507	6,448
48864	Okemos	7,770		55428	New Hope	23,180	3,552
48867	Owosso	17,179	17,006	56073	New Ulm	13,051	11,114

ZIP Code	Place	1970	1960
55057	Northfield	10,235	8,707
56001	North Mankato	7,347	5,927
55109	North St. Paul	11,950	8,520
55119	Oakdale	7,304	
55391	Orono	6,787	5,643
55060	Owatonna	15,341	13,409
56164	Pipestone	5,328	5,324
55427	Plymouth	18,077	9,576
55066	Red Wing	10,441	10,528
55423	Richfield	47,231	42,523
55422	Robbinsdale	16,845	16,381
55901	Rochester	53,766	40,663
55113	Roseville	34,438	23,997
55414	St. Anthony	9,239	5,084
56301	St. Cloud	39,691	33,815
55426	St. Louis Park	48,922	43,310
*55101	St. Paul	309,714	313,411
55071	St. Paul Park	5,587	3,267
56082	St. Peter	8,339	8,484
56379	Sauk Rapids	5,051	4,038
55379	Shakopee	6,876	5,201
55112	Shoreview	10,995	7,157
55075	South St. Paul	25,016	22,032
55432	Spring Lake Park	6,417	3,260
55082	Stillwater	10,191	8,310
56701	Thief River Falls	8,618	7,151
55792	Virginia	12,450	14,034
56093	Waseca	6,789	5,898
55118	West St. Paul	18,799	13,101
55110	White Bear Lake	23,313	12,849
56201	Willmar	12,869	10,417
55987	Winona	26,438	24,895
55119	Woodbury	6,184	
56187	Worthington	9,916	9,015

Mississippi

ZIP Code	Place	1970	1960
39730	Aberdeen	6,507	6,450
38821	Amory	7,236	6,474
39520	Bay St. Louis	6,752	5,073
*39530	Biloxi	48,486	44,053
38829	Booneville	5,895	3,480
39601	Brookhaven	10,700	9,885
39046	Canton	10,503	9,707
38614	Clarksdale	21,673	21,105
38732	Cleveland	13,327	10,172
39056	Clinton	7,289	3,438
39429	Columbia	7,587	7,117
39701	Columbus	25,795	24,771
38834	Corinth	11,581	11,453
39532	D'Iberville	7,288	3,005
38701	Greenville	39,648	41,502
38930	Greenwood	22,400	20,436
38901	Grenada	9,944	7,914
39501	Gulfport	40,791	30,204
39401	Hattiesburg	38,277	34,989
38635	Holly Springs	5,728	5,621
38751	Indianola	8,947	6,714
*39205	Jackson	153,968	144,422
39090	Kosciusko	7,266	6,800
39440	Laurel	24,145	27,889
38756	Leland	6,000	6,295
39560	Long Beach	6,170	4,770
39339	Louisville	6,626	5,066
39648	McComb	11,969	12,020
39301	Meridian	45,083	49,374
39563	Moss Point	19,321	6,631
39120	Natchez	19,704	23,791
38652	New Albany	6,426	5,151
39564	Ocean Springs	9,580	5,025
38655	Oxford City	13,846	5,283
39567	Pascagoula	27,264	17,155
39208	Pearl	9,623	5,081
39465	Petal	6,986	4,007
39350	Philadelphia	6,274	5,017
39466	Picayune	10,467	7,834
38671	Southaven	8,931	
39759	Starkville	11,369	9,041
38801	Tupelo	20,471	17,221
39180	Vicksburg	25,478	29,143
39501	West Gulfport	6,996	3,323
39773	West Point	8,714	8,550
38967	Winona	5,521	4,282
39194	Yazoo City	11,688	11,236

Missouri

ZIP Code	Place	1970	1960
63123	Affton	24,264	
65605	Aurora	5,359	4,683
63011	Ballwin	10,656	5,710
63137	Bellefontaine Neighbors	14,084	13,650
63133	Bel-Ridge	5,346	4,395
64012	Belton	12,179	4,897
63134	Berkeley	19,743	18,676
64015	Blue Springs	6,779	2,555
65233	Boonville	7,514	7,090
63114	Breckenridge Hills	7,011	6,299
63144	Brentwood	11,248	12,250
63044	Bridgeton	19,992	7,820
64628	Brookfield	5,491	5,694
63701	Cape Girardeau	31,282	24,947
64836	Carthage	11,035	11,264
63830	Caruthersville	7,350	8,643
63834	Charleston	5,131	5,911
64601	Chillicothe	9,519	9,236
63105	Clayton	16,100	15,245
64735	Clinton	7,504	6,925
65201	Columbia	58,812	36,650
63128	Concord	21,217	
63126	Crestwood	15,123	11,106
63141	Creve Coeur	8,967	5,122
63136	Dellwood	7,137	4,720
63020	De Soto	5,984	5,804
63131	Des Peres	5,333	4,362
63841	Dexter	6,024	5,519
64024	Excelsior Springs	9,411	6,473
63640	Farmington	6,590	5,618
63135	Ferguson	28,759	22,149
63028	Festus	7,530	7,021
63033	Florissant	65,908	38,166
65473	Fort Leonard Wood	33,799	
65251	Fulton	12,248	11,131
64118	Gladstone	23,422	14,502
63122	Glendale	6,981	7,048
64030	Grandview	17,456	6,027
63401	Hannibal	18,698	20,028
64701	Harrisonville	5,052	3,510
*63042	Hazelwood	14,082	6,045
*64051	Independence	111,630	62,328
63755	Jackson	5,896	4,875
65101	Jefferson City	32,407	28,228
63136	Jennings	19,379	19,965
64801	Joplin	39,256	38,958
*64108	Kansas City	507,330	475,539
63857	Kennett	10,000	9,098
63140	Kinloch	5,629	6,501
63501	Kirksville	15,560	13,123
63122	Kirkwood	31,679	29,421
63124	Ladue	10,359	9,466
65536	Lebanon	8,616	8,220
64063	Lee's Summit	16,230	8,267
63125	Lemay	40,516	
64067	Lexington	5,388	4,845
64068	Liberty	13,704	8,909
63552	Macon	5,301	4,547
63863	Malden	5,374	5,007
63011	Manchester	5,031	2,021
63143	Maplewood	12,785	12,552
65340	Marshall	12,051	9,572
63043	Maryland Heights	8,805	
64469	Maryville	9,970	7,807
65265	Mexico	11,807	12,889
65270	Moberly	12,988	13,170
65708	Monett	5,937	5,359
64850	Neosho	7,517	7,452
64772	Nevada	9,736	8,416
63121	Normandy	6,236	4,452
64116	North Kansas City	5,183	5,657
63366	O'Fallon	7,018	3,770
63124	Olivette	9,156	8,257
63114	Overland	24,819	22,763
63133	Pagedale	5,044	5,106
63775	Perryville	5,149	5,117
63120	Pine Lawn	5,745	5,943
63901	Poplar Bluff	16,653	15,926
64133	Raytown	33,306	17,083
63117	Richmond Heights	13,802	15,622
63124	Rock Hill	6,815	6,523
65401	Rolla	13,571	11,132
63074	St. Ann	18,215	12,155
63301	St. Charles	31,834	21,189
63114	St. John	8,960	7,342
*64501	St. Joseph	72,691	79,673
*63155	St. Louis	622,236	750,026
63126	Sappington	10,603	
65301	Sedalia	22,847	23,874
63119	Shrewsbury	5,896	4,730
63801	Sikeston	14,699	13,765
63138	Spanish Lake	15,647	
*65801	Springfield	120,096	95,865
63080	Sullivan	5,111	4,098
64683	Trenton	6,063	6,262
63084	Union	5,183	3,937
63130	University City	47,527	51,249
64093	Warrensburg	13,125	9,689
63090	Washington	8,499	7,961
64870	Webb City	6,923	6,740
63119	Webster Groves	27,457	28,990
63112	Wellston	7,050	7,979
65775	West Plains	6,893	5,836
65301	Whiteman	5,040	
63134	Woodson Terrace	5,880	6,048

Montana

ZIP Code	Place	1970	1960
59711	Anaconda	9,771	12,054

ZIP Code	Place	1970	1960
*59101	Billings	61,581	52,851
59715	Bozeman	18,670	13,361
59701	Butte	23,368	27,877
59701	Floral Park	5,113	4,079
59330	Glendive	6,305	7,058
*59401	Great Falls	60,091	55,244
59501	Havre	10,558	10,740
59601	Helena	22,730	20,227
59901	Kalispell	10,526	10,151
59457	Lewistown	6,437	7,408
59047	Livingston	6,883	8,229
59402	Malmstrom	8,374	
59301	Miles City	9,023	9,665
59801	Missoula	29,497	27,090
59801	Missoula West	9,148	
59701	Silver Bow Park	5,524	4,798

Nebraska

ZIP Code	Place	1970	1960
69301	Alliance	6,862	7,845
68310	Beatrice	12,389	12,132
68005	Bellevue	21,953	8,831
68008	Blair	6,106	4,931
69337	Chadron	5,921	5,079
68601	Columbus	15,471	12,476
68352	Fairbury	5,265	5,572
68355	Falls City	5,444	5,598
68025	Fremont	22,962	19,698
69341	Gering	5,639	4,585
68801	Grand Island	31,269	25,742
68901	Hastings	23,580	21,412
68949	Holdrege	5,635	5,226
68847	Kearney	19,181	14,210
68128	La Vista 1971	6,388	1,004
68850	Lexington	5,654	5,572
*68501	Lincoln	149,518	128,521
69001	McCook	8,285	8,301
68137	Millard	7,460	1,014
68410	Nebraska City	7,441	7,252
68701	Norfolk	16,607	13,640
69101	North Platte	19,447	17,184
68113	Offutt East	5,195	
68113	Offutt West	8,445	
*68108	Omaha	346,929	301,598
68046	Papillion	5,606	2,235
68048	Plattsmouth	6,371	6,244
69361	Scottsbluff	14,507	13,377
68434	Seward	5,294	4,208
69162	Sidney	6,403	8,004
68776	South Sioux City	7,920	7,200
68787	Wayne	5,379	4,217
68467	York	6,778	6,173

Nevada

ZIP Code	Place	1970	1960
89005	Boulder City	5,223	4,059
89701	Carson City	15,468	5,163
89112	East Las Vegas	6,501	
89801	Elko	7,621	6,298
89015	Henderson	16,395	12,525
*89114	Las Vegas	125,787	64,405
89110	Nellis	6,449	
89030	North Las Vegas	36,216	18,422
89109	Paradise	24,477	
*89501	Reno	72,863	51,470
89431	Sparks	24,187	16,618
89110	Sunrise Manor	10,886	
89109	Vegas Creek	8,970	
89101	Winchester	13,981	

New Hampshire
See note on page 159

ZIP Code	Place	1970	1960
03102	Bedford	5,859	3,636
03570	Berlin	15,256	17,821
03743	Claremont	14,221	13,563
03301	Concord	30,022	28,991
03038	Derry	6,090	4,468
03038	Derry	11,712	6,987
03820	Dover	20,850	19,131
03824	Durham	7,221	4,688
	Durham	8,869	5,504
03833	Exeter	6,439	5,896
	Exeter	8,892	7,243
03235	Franklin	7,292	6,742
03045	Goffstown	9,284	7,230
03842	Hampton	5,407	3,281
	Hampton	8,011	5,379
03755	Hanover	6,147	5,649
	Hanover	8,494	7,329
03106	Hooksett	5,564	3,713
03051	Hudson	10,638	5,876
03431	Keene	20,467	17,562
03246	Laconia	14,888	15,288
03766	Lebanon	9,725	9,299
	Littleton	5,290	5,003
03053	Londonderry	5,346	2,457

ZIP Code	Place	1970	1960
*03101	Manchester	87,754	88,282
03054	Merrimack	8,595	2,989
03055	Milford	6,622	4,863
03060	Nashua	55,820	39,096
03773	Newport	5,899	5,458
03076	Pelham	5,408	2,605
03801	Portsmouth	25,717	26,900
03867	Rochester	17,938	15,927
03079	Salem	20,142	9,210
03878	Somersworth	9,026	8,529

New Jersey

ZIP Code	Place	1970	1960
08201	Absecon	6,094	4,320
07401	Allendale	6,240	4,092
07712	Asbury Park	16,533	17,366
*08401	Atlantic City	47,859	59,544
07716	Atlantic Highlands	5,102	4,119
08106	Audubon	10,802	10,440
08007	Barrington	8,409	7,943
07002	Bayonne	72,743	74,215
07109	Belleville	37,629	35,005
08031	Bellmawr	15,618	11,853
07719	Belmar	5,782	5,190
07621	Bergenfield	29,000	27,203
07922	Berkeley Hts. Twp.	13,078	8,721
07924	Bernardsville	6,652	5,515
07003	Bloomfield	52,029	51,867
07403	Bloomingdale	7,797	5,293
07603	Bogota	8,960	7,965
07005	Boonton	9,261	7,981
08805	Bound Brook	10,450	10,263
08723	Brick Twp.	35,057	16,299
08302	Bridgeton	20,435	20,966
08203	Brigantine	6,741	4,201
08015	Browns Mills	7,144	
08016	Burlington	11,991	12,687
07405	Butler	7,05	5,414
07006	Caldwell	8,677	6,942
*08101	Camden	102,551	117,159
08701	Candlewood	5,629	
07072	Carlstadt	6,724	6,042
07008	Carteret	23,137	20,502
07009	Cedar Grove Twp.	15,582	14,603
07928	Chatham	9,566	9,517
08034	Cherry Hill Twp.	64,395	31,522
08077	Cinnaminson Twp.	16,962	8,302
07066	Clark Twp.	18,829	12,195
08312	Clayton	5,193	4,711
07010	Cliffside Park	18,891	17,642
07721	Cliffwood-Cliffwood Beach	7,056	
*07015	Clifton	82,437	82,084
07624	Closter	8,604	7,767
08108	Collingswood	17,422	17,370
07016	Cranford Twp.	27,391	26,424
07626	Cresskill	8,298	7,290
08075	Delran Twp.	10,065	5,327
07627	Demarest	5,133	4,231
07834	Denville Twp.	14,045	10,632
08096	Deptford Twp.	24,232	17,878
07801	Dover	15,039	13,034
07628	Dumont	20,155	18,882
08812	Dunellen	7,072	6,840
08816	East Brunswick Twp.	34,166	19,965
07019	East Orange	75,471	77,259
07407	East Paterson	20,511	19,344
07073	East Rutherford	8,536	7,769
08520	East Windsor Twp.	11,736	2,298
07724	Eatontown	14,619	10,334
08817	Edison Twp.	67,120	44,799
*07207	Elizabeth	112,654	107,698
07630	Emerson	8,428	6,849
07631	Englewood	24,985	26,057
07632	Englewood Cliffs	5,938	2,913
08053	Evesham Twp.	13,477	4,548
08618	Ewing Twp.	32,831	26,628
07006	Fairfield	6,884	
07701	Fair Haven	6,142	5,678
07410	Fair Lawn	37,975	36,421
07022	Fairview	10,698	9,399
07023	Fanwood	8,920	7,963
08518	Florence-Roebling	7,551	
07932	Florham Park	8,094	7,222
08640	Fort Dix	26,290	
07024	Fort Lee	30,631	21,815
07417	Franklin Lakes	7,550	3,316
07728	Freehold	10,545	9,140
07026	Garfield	30,797	29,253
07027	Garwood	5,260	5,426
08028	Glassboro	12,938	10,253
07028	Glen Ridge	8,518	8,322
07452	Glen Rock	13,011	12,896
08030	Gloucester City	14,707	15,511
07093	Guttenberg	5,754	5,118
*07602	Hackensack	36,008	30,521
07840	Hackettstown	9,472	5,276
08108	Haddon Twp.	18,192	17,099
08033	Haddonfield	13,118	13,201

ZIP Code	Place	1970	1960
08035	Haddon Heights	9,365	9,260
07508	Haledon	6,767	6,161
08037	Hammonton	11,464	9,854
07981	Hanover Twp.	10,700	9,329
07029	Harrison	11,811	11,743
07604	Hasbrouck Heights	13,651	13,046
07507	Hawthorne	19,173	17,735
07730	Hazlet Twp.	22,239	15,334
08904	Highland Park	14,385	11,049
08520	Hightstown	5,431	4,317
07642	Hillsdale	11,768	8,734
07205	Hillside Twp.	21,636	22,304
07030	Hoboken	45,380	48,441
07843	Hopatcong	9,052	3,391
08560	Hopewell Twp. (Mercer)	10,030	7,818
07111	Irvington	59,743	59,379
08527	Jackson Twp.	18,276	5,939
*07303	Jersey City	260,350	276,101
07734	Keansburg	9,720	6,854
07032	Kearny	37,585	37,472
08824	Kendall Park	7,412	
07033	Kenilworth	9,165	8,379
07735	Keyport	7,205	6,440
07405	Kinnelon	7,600	4,431
07034	Lake Hiawatha	11,389	
07871	Lake Mohawk	6,262	4,647
07054	Lake Parsippany	7,488	
08701	Lakewood	17,874	13,004
08879	Laurence Harbor	6,715	
07605	Leonia	8,847	8,384
07035	Lincoln Park	9,034	6,048
07036	Linden	41,409	39,931
08021	Lindenwold 1973	16,265	7,335
08221	Linwood	6,159	3,847
07424	Little Falls Twp.	11,727	9,730
07643	Little Ferry	9,064	6,176
07739	Little Silver	6,010	5,202
07039	Livingston Twp.	30,127	23,124
07644	Lodi	25,163	23,502
07740	Long Branch	31,774	26,228
07071	Lyndhurst Twp.	22,729	21,867
07940	Madison	16,710	15,122
08049	Magnolia	5,893	4,199
07430	Mahwah Twp.	10,800	7,376
08835	Manville	13,029	10,995
08052	Maple Shade Twp.	16,464	12,947
07040	Maplewood Twp.	24,932	23,977
08402	Margate City	10,576	9,474
07746	Marlboro Twp.	12,273	8,038
08053	Marlton	10,180	
07747	Matawan	9,136	5,097
07607	Maywood	11,087	11,460
08641	McGuire	10,933	
08619	Mercerville-Hamilton Sq.	24,465	
08840	Metuchen	16,031	14,041
08846	Middlesex	15,038	10,520
07748	Middletown Twp.	54,623	39,675
07432	Midland Park	8,159	7,543
07041	Millburn Twp.	21,089	18,799
08850	Milltown	6,470	5,435
08332	Millville	21,366	19,096
07434	Monroe Twp. (Gloucester)	14,071	9,396
*07042	Montclair	44,043	43,129
07645	Montvale	7,327	3,699
07045	Montville Twp.	11,846	6,772
08057	Moorestown-Lenola	14,179	
07950	Morris Plains	5,540	4,703
07960	Morristown	17,662	17,712
07092	Mountainside	7,520	6,325
08059	Mount Ephraim	5,625	5,447
08060	Mount Holly Twp.	12,713	13,271
07753	Neptune Twp.	27,863	21,487
07753	Neptune City	5,502	4,013
*07102	Newark	381,930	405,220
*08901	New Brunswick	41,885	40,139
08511	New Hanover	27,410	28,528
07646	New Milford	19,149	18,810
07974	New Providence	13,796	10,243
07724	New Shrewsbury	8,395	7,313
07860	Newton	7,297	6,563
07032	North Arlington	18,096	17,477
07047	North Bergen Twp.	47,751	42,387
08902	North Brunswick Twp.	16,691	10,099
07006	North Caldwell	6,733	4,163
08225	Northfield	8,875	5,849
07508	North Haledon	7,614	6,026
07060	North Plainfield	21,796	16,993
07647	Northvale	5,177	2,892
07110	Nutley	31,913	29,513
07755	Oakhurst	5,558	4,374
07436	Oakland	14,420	9,446
08226	Ocean City	10,575	7,618
07757	Oceanport	7,503	4,937
08857	Old Bridge	25,176	
07649	Oradell	8,903	7,487
*07050	Orange	32,566	35,789
07650	Palisades Park	13,351	11,943
08065	Palmyra	6,969	7,036
07652	Paramus	28,381	23,238
07656	Park Ridge	8,709	6,389
07055	Passaic	55,124	53,963
*07510	Paterson	144,824	143,663
08066	Paulsboro	8,084	8,121
08110	Pennsauken Twp	36,394	33,771
08069	Penns Grove	5,727	6,176
08070	Pennsville	11,014	
07440	Pequannock Twp.	14,350	10,553
08861	Perth Amboy	38,798	38,007
08865	Phillipsburg	17,849	18,502
08021	Pine Hill	5,132	3,939
08854	Piscataway Twp.	36,418	19,890
08071	Pitman	10,257	8,644
*07061	Plainfield	46,862	45,330
08232	Pleasantville	13,778	15,172
08742	Point Pleasant	15,968	10,182
07442	Pompton Lakes	11,397	9,445
08540	Princeton	12,331	11,890
08540	Princeton North	5,488	4,506
07508	Prospect Park	5,176	5,201
*07065	Rahway	29,114	27,699
08057	Ramblewood	5,556	
07446	Ramsey	12,571	9,527
07970	Randolph Twp.	13,296	7,295
08869	Raritan	6,691	6,137
07701	Red Bank	12,847	12,482
07657	Ridgefield	11,308	10,788
07660	Ridgefield Park	13,990	12,701
*07451	Ridgewood	27,547	25,391
07456	Ringwood	10,393	4,182
07761	River Edge	12,850	13,264
08075	Riverside Twp.	8,591	8,474
07662	Rochell Park Twp.	6,380	6,119
07866	Rockaway	6,383	5,413
07203	Roselle	22,585	21,032
07204	Rosel e Park	14,227	12,546
07760	Rumson	7,421	6,405
08078	Runnemede	10,475	8,396
*07070	Rutherford	20,802	20,473
07662	Saddle Brook Twp.	15,975	13,834
08079	Salem	7,648	8,941
08872	Sayreville	32,508	22,553
07076	Scotch Plains Twp.	22,279	18,491
07094	Secaucus	13,228	12,154
08083	Somerdale	6,510	4,839
08244	Somers Point	7,919	4,504
08876	Somerville	13,652	12,458
08879	South Amboy	9,338	8,422
07079	South Orange	16,971	16,175
07080	South Plainfield	21,142	17,879
08882	South River	15,428	13,397
07871	Sparta Twp.	10,819	6,717
08884	Spotswood	7,891	5,788
07081	Springfield Twp.	15,740	14,467
08084	Stratford	9,801	4,308
07747	Strathmore	7,674	
07901	Summit	23,620	23,677
07666	Teaneck Twp.	42,355	42,085
07670	Tenafly	14,827	14,264
08753	Toms River	7,303	6,062
07512	Totowa	11,580	10,897
*08608	Trenton	104,786	114,167
07083	Union Twp.	53,077	51,499
07735	Union Beach	6,472	5,862
07087	Union City	57,305	52,180
07458	Upper Saddle River	7,949	3,570
08406	Ventnor City	10,385	8,688
07044	Verona	15,067	13,782
08360	Vineland	47,399	37,685
07463	Waldwick	12,313	10,495
07057	Wallington	10,284	9,261
07465	Wanaque	8,636	7,126
07882	Washington	5,943	5,723
07675	Washington Twp. (Bergen)	10,577	6,654
07470	Wayne Twp.	49,141	29,353
07087	Weehawken Twp.	13,383	13,504
07006	West Caldwell	11,913	8,314
07091	Westfield	33,720	31,447
07764	West Long Branch	6,845	5,337
07480	West Milford Twp.	17,304	8,157
07093	West New York	40,627	35,547
07424	West Orange	43,715	39,895
07424	West Paterson	11,692	7,602
08093	Westville	5,170	4,951
07675	Westwood	11,105	9,046
07885	Wharton	5,535	5,006
08610	White Horse-Yardville	18,680	
07886	White Meadow Lake	8,499	
08046	Willingboro Twp. 1973	44,607	11,861
08095	Winslow Twp.	11,202	9,142
07095	Woodbridge Twp.	98,944	78,846
08096	Woodbury	12,408	12,453
07675	Woodcliff Lake	5,506	2,742
07075	Wood-Ridge	8,311	7,964
07481	Wyckoff Twp.	16,039	11,205

ZIP Code	Place	1970	1960
	New Mexico		
88310	Alamogordo	23,035	21,723
*87101	Albuquerque	243,751	201,189
88210	Artesia	10,315	12,000
88101	Cannon	5,461	
88220	Carlsbad	21,297	25,541
88101	Clovis	28,495	23,713
88030	Deming	8,343	6,764
87401	Farmington	21,979	23,786
87301	Gallup	14,596	14,089
87020	Grants	8,768	10,274
88240	Hobbs	26,025	26,275
88330	Holloman	8,001	
88001	Las Cruces	37,857	29,367
87701	Las Vegas (city)	7,528	7,790
87701	Las Vegas (town)	6,307	6,028
87544	Los Alamos	11,310	12,584
88260	Lovington	8,915	9,660
87107	North Valley	10,366	
88130	Portales	10,554	9,695
87740	Raton	6,962	8,146
88201	Roswell	33,908	39,593
87115	Sandia	6,867	
87501	Santa Fe	41,167	33,394
88061	Silver City	8,557	6,972
87801	Socorro	5,849	5,271
87105	South Valley	29,389	
88401	Tucumcari	7,189	8,143
	New York		
*12207	Albany	115,781	129,726
11507	Albertson	6,825	
14411	Albion	5,122	5,182
11701	Amityville	9,794	8,318
12010	Amsterdam	25,524	28,772
12603	Arlington	11,203	8,317
13021	Auburn	34,599	35,249
*11702	Babylon	12,897	11,062
11510	Baldwin	34,525	30,204
13027	Baldwinsville	6,298	5,985
14020	Batavia	17,338	18,210
14810	Bath	6,053	6,166
11705	Bayport	8,232	
11706	Bay Shore	11,119	
11709	Bayville	6,147	3,962
12508	Beacon	13,255	13,922
11710	Bellmore	18,431	12,784
11714	Bethpage	18,555	
*13902	Binghamton	64,123	75,941
10913	Blauvelt	5,426	
11716	Bohemia	8,926	
11717	Brentwood	28,327	15,387
10510	Briarcliff Manor	6,521	5,105
14420	Brockport	7,878	5,256
10708	Bronxville	6,674	6,744
*14240	Buffalo	462,768	532,759
14424	Canandaigua 1971	10,753	9,370
13032	Canastota	5,033	4,896
13617	Canton	6,398	5,046
11514	Carle Place	6,326	
12414	Catskill	5,317	5,825
11516	Cedarhurst	6,941	6,954
11720	Centereach	9,427	8,524
11722	Central Islip	36,391	
12065	Clifton Knolls	5,771	
12047	Cohoes	18,653	20,129
11724	Cold Spring Harbor	5,450	1,705
12205	Colonie	8,701	6,992
11725	Commack	24,138	9,613
10920	Congers	5,928	
11726	Copiague	19,632	14,081
14830	Corning	15,792	17,085
13045	Cortland	19,621	19,181
10520	Croton-on-Hudson	7,523	6,812
14437	Dansville	5,436	5,460
11729	Deer Park	32,274	16,726
14043	Depew	22,158	13,580
13214	DeWitt	10,032	
11743	Dix Hills	10,050	
10522	Dobbs Ferry	10,353	9,260
14048	Dunkirk	16,855	18,205
14052	East Aurora	7,033	6,791
10709	Eastchester	23,750	
12302	East Glenville	5,898	
11746	East Half Hollow Hills	9,691	
11576	East Hills	8,624	7,184
11730	East Islip	6,861	
11758	East Massapequa	15,926	14,779
11554	East Meadow	46,290	46,036
11743	East Neck	5,221	3,789
11731	East Northport	12,392	8,381
11772	East Patchogue	8,092	
14445	East Rochester	8,347	8,152
11518	East Rockaway	11,795	10,721
13902	East Vestal	10,472	
*14901	Elmira	39,945	46,517

ZIP Code	Place	1970	1960
11003	Elmont	29,363	30,138
11731	Elwood	15,031	
13760	Endicott	16,556	18,775
13760	Endwell	15,999	
13219	Fairmount	15,317	
14450	Fairport	6,474	5,507
12601	Fairview	8,517	8,626
11735	Farmingdale	9,297	6,128
*11001	Floral Park	18,466	17,499
11010	Franklin Square	32,156	32,483
14063	Fredonia	10,326	8,477
11520	Freeport	40,374	34,419
13069	Fulton	14,003	14,261
11530	Garden City	25,373	23,948
11040	Garden City Park	7,488	
14454	Geneseo	5,714	3,284
14456	Geneva	16,793	17,286
11542	Glen Cove	25,770	23,817
12801	Glens Falls	17,222	18,580
12078	Gloversville	19,677	21,741
11022	Great Neck	10,798	10,171
11020	Great Neck Plaza	6,043	4,948
11740	Greenlawn	8,493	5,422
11746	Half Hollow Hills	12,081	
14075	Hamburg	10,215	9,145
10528	Harrison Town	21,544	19,201
10530	Hartsdale	12,226	
10706	Hastings-on-Hudson	9,479	8,979
11787	Hauppauge	13,957	
10927	Haverstraw	8,198	5,771
*11551	Hempstead	39,411	34,641
13350	Herkimer	8,960	9,396
11040	Herricks	9,112	
11557	Hewlett	6,796	
*11802	Hicksville	49,820	50,405
10977	Hillcrest	5,357	
11741	Holbrook-Holtsville	12,103	
14843	Hornell	12,144	13,907
14845	Horseheads Village	7,989	7,207
12534	Hudson	8,940	11,075
12839	Hudson Falls	7,917	7,752
11743	Huntington	12,601	11,255
11746	Huntington Station	28,817	23,438
13357	Ilion	9,808	10,199
11696	Inwood	8,433	10,362
10533	Irvington	5,878	5,494
11558	Island Park	5,396	3,846
11751	Islip	7,692	
14850	Ithaca	26,226	28,799
14701	Jamestown	39,795	41,818
10535	Jefferson Valley-Yorktown	9,008	
11753	Jericho	14,010	10,795
13790	Johnson City	18,025	19,118
12095	Johnstown	10,045	10,390
14217	Kenmore	20,980	21,261
11754	Kings Park	5,555	4,949
11024	Kings Point	5,614	5,410
12401	Kingston	25,544	29,260
14218	Lackawanna	28,657	29,564
11755	Lake Grove	9,133	
11552	Lakeview	5,471	
14086	Lancaster	13,365	12,254
10538	Larchmont	7,203	6,789
12110	Latham	9,661	
11559	Lawrence	6,566	5,907
14482	Le Roy	5,118	4,662
11756	Levittown	65,440	65,276
*11757	Lindenhurst	28,359	20,905
13365	Little Falls	7,629	8,935
14094	Lockport	25,399	26,443
11791	Locust Grove	11,626	11,558
11561	Long Beach	33,127	26,473
12211	Loudonville	9,299	
11563	Lynbrook	23,151	19,881
10541	Mahopac	5,265	1,337
12953	Malone	8,048	8,737
11565	Malverne	10,036	9,968
10543	Mamaroneck	18,909	17,673
11030	Manhasset	8,541	
11050	Manorhaven	5,488	3,566
11758	Massapequa	26,821	32,900
11762	Massapequa Park	22,112	19,904
13662	Massena	14,042	15,478
13211	Mattydale	8,292	
12118	Mechanicville	6,247	6,831
14103	Medina	6,415	6,681
11746	Melville	6,641	
11566	Merrick	25,904	18,789
10940	Middletown	22,607	23,475
11501	Mineola	21,744	20,519
10952	Monsey	8,797	
12701	Monticello	5,991	5,222
10549	Mt. Kisco	6,805	6,805
*10551	Mount Vernon	72,788	76,010
10954	Nanuet	10,447	
11767	Nesconset	10,048	1,964
14513	Newark	11,644	12,868
12550	Newburgh	26,219	30,979

ZIP Code	Place	1970	1960
11590	New Cassel	8,721	
10956	New City	27,344	
11040	New Hyde Park	10,116	10,808
12561	New Paltz	6,058	3,041
*10802	New Rochelle	75,385	76,812
*12550	New Windsor	8,803	4,041
*10001	New York	7,895,563	7,781,984
*10451	Bronx	1,471,701	1,424,815
*11201	Brooklyn	2,602,012	2,627,319
*10001	Manhattan	1,539,233	1,698,281
*(Q)	Queens	1,987,174	1,809,578

(Q)There are 4 Zip Codes for Queens: 11101 for L. I. City; 11691 Far Rockaway; 11351 Flushing and 11431 Jamaica.

ZIP Code	Place	1970	1960
*10314	Richmond	295,443	221,991
*14302	Niagara Falls	85,615	102,394
13901	Nimmonsburg-Chenango Bridge	5,059	
12309	Niskayuna	6,186	
11701	North Amityville	11,936	
11703	North Babylon	39,526	
11710	North Bellmore	22,893	19,639
11713	North Bellport	5,903	
11752	North Great River	12,080	
11757	North Lindenhurst	11,117	
11758	North Massapequa	23,123	
11566	North Merrick	13,650	12,976
11040	North New Hyde Park	18,154	17,929
11772	North Patchogue	5,232	
10803	North Pelham	5,184	5,326
11768	Northport	7,494	5,972
13212	North Syracuse	8,687	7,412
10591	North Tarrytown	8,334	8,818
14120	North Tonawanda	36,012	34,757
11580	North Valley Stream	14,881	17,239
11793	North Wantagh	15,053	
13815	Norwich	8,843	9,175
10960	Nyack	6,659	6,062
11769	Oakdale	7,334	
11572	Oceanside	35,372	30,448
13669	Ogdensburg	14,554	16,122
11804	Old Bethpage	7,084	
14760	Olean	19,169	21,868
13421	Oneida	11,658	11,677
13820	Oneonta	16,030	13,412
10562	Ossining	21,659	18,662
13126	Oswego	20,913	22,155
13827	Owego	5,152	5,417
11771	Oyster Bay	6,822	
11772	Patchogue	11,582	8,838
10965	Pearl River	17,146	
10566	Peekskill	19,283	18,737
10803	Pelham Manor	6,873	6,114
14527	Penn Yan	5,293	5,770
11714	Plainedge	10,759	21,973
11803	Plainview	31,695	27,710
12901	Plattsburgh	18,715	20,172
12903	Plattsburgh Base	7,078	
10570	Pleasantville	7,110	5,877
10573	Port Chester	25,803	24,960
11777	Port Jefferson	5,515	
11776	Port Jefferson Station	7,403	1,041
12771	Port Jervis	8,852	9,268
11050	Port Washington	15,923	15,657
13676	Potsdam	10,303	7,765
*12601	Poughkeepsie	32,029	38,330
12144	Rensselaer	10,136	10,506
11901	Riverhead	7,585	5,830
*14603	Rochester	296,233	318,611
*11570	Rockville Centre	27,444	26,355
12205	Roessleville	5,476	
13440	Rome	50,148	51,646
11779	Ronkonkoma	7,284	4,220
11575	Roosevelt	15,008	12,883
11577	Roslyn Heights	7,242	
12303	Rotterdam	25,214	16,871
10580	Rye	15,869	14,225
11780	St. James	10,500	3,524
14779	Salamanca	7,877	8,480
11754	San Remo	8,302	3,160
12983	Saranac Lake	6,086	6,421
12866	Saratoga Springs	18,845	16,630
11782	Sayville	11,680	
10583	Scarsdale	19,229	17,968
*12305	Schenectady	77,958	81,682
12302	Scotia	7,370	7,625
11579	Sea Cliff	5,890	5,669
11783	Seaford	17,379	14,718
11784	Selden	11,613	1,604
13148	Seneca Falls	7,794	7,439
11733	Setauket-South Setauket	6,857	
11967	Shirley	6,280	
14225	Sloan	5,216	5,803
13209	Solvay	8,280	8,732
11735	South Farmingdale	20,464	16,318
11741	South Holbrook	6,700	

ZIP Code	Place	1970	1960
11746	South Huntington	9,115	7,084
14904	Southport	8,685	6,698
11790	South Stony Brook	15,329	
11581	South Valley Stream	6,595	
11590	South Westbury	10,978	11,977
10977	Spring Valley	18,112	6,538
11790	Stony Brook	6,391	3,548
10980	Stony Point	8,270	3,330
10901	Suffern	8,273	5,094
11791	Syosset	10,084	
*13201	Syracuse	197,297	216,038
10983	Tappan	7,424	
10591	Tarrytown	11,115	11,109
10594	Thornwood	6,874	
14150	Tonawanda	21,898	21,561
*12180	Troy	62,918	67,492
10707	Tuckahoe	6,236	6,423
11553	Uniondale	22,077	20,041
*13503	Utica	91,340	100,410
10989	Valley Cottage	6,007	
*11580	Valley Stream	40,413	38,629
11731	Vernon Valley	7,925	5,998
13850	Vestal-Twin Orchards	8,303	
10901	Viola	5,136	
12586	Walden	5,277	4,851
11793	Wantagh	21,873	34,172
12590	Wappingers Falls	5,607	4,447
13165	Waterloo	5,418	5,098
13601	Watertown	30,787	33,306
12189	Watervliet	12,404	13,917
14892	Waverly	5,261	5,950
14580	Webster	5,037	3,060
14895	Wellsville	5,815	5,967
11701	West Amityville	6,424	
11704	West Babylon	12,893	
11590	Westbury	15,362	14,757
14905	West Elmira	5,901	5,763
10993	West Haverstraw	8,558	5,020
11552	West Hempstead	20,375	
11795	West Islip	17,374	
12203	Westmere	6,364	
10994	West Nyack	5,510	
11796	West Sayville	7,386	
13219	Westvale	7,253	
*10602	White Plains	50,346	50,485
14221	Williamsville	6,835	6,316
11596	Williston Park	9,154	8,255
11598	Woodmere	19,831	14,011
11798	Wyandanch	15,716	
11980	Yaphank	5,460	
*10701	Yonkers	204,297	190,634
10598	Yorktown Heights	6,805	2,478

North Carolina

ZIP Code	Place	1970	1960
27910	Ahoskie	5,105	4,583
28001	Albemarle	11,126	12,261
27203	Asheboro	10,797	9,449
*28801	Asheville	57,681	60,192
28012	Belmont	5,054	5,007
28607	Boone	8,754	3,686
28712	Brevard	5,243	4,857
27215	Burlington	35,930	33,199
28542	Camp Le Jeune Central	34,549	
28716	Canton	5,158	5,068
27510	Carrboro	5,058	1,997
27511	Cary	7,435	3,356
27514	Chapel Hill	25,537	12,573
*28202	Charlotte	241,178	201,564
28533	Cherry Point	12,029	
28021	Cherryville	5,258	3,607
28328	Clinton	7,157	7,461
28025	Concord	18,464	17,799
28334	Dunn	8,302	7,566
*27701	Durham	95,438	78,302
27288	Eden	15,871	
27909	Elizabeth City	14,381	14,062
*28302	Fayetteville	53,510	47,106
28043	Forest City	7,179	6,556
28307	Fort Bragg	46,995	
28052	Gastonia	47,142	37,276
27530	Goldsboro	26,810	28,873
27253	Graham	8,172	7,723
*27420	Greensboro	144,076	119,574
27834	Greenville	29,063	22,860
28532	Havelock	5,283	2,433
27536	Henderson	13,896	12,740
28739	Hendersonville	6,443	5,911
28601	Hickory	20,569	19,328
*27260	High Point	63,259	62,063
28540	Jacksonville	16,289	13,491
28081	Kannapolis	36,293	34,647
28086	Kings Mountain	8,465	8,008
28501	Kinston	23,020	24,819
28352	Laurinburg	8,859	8,242

ZIP Code	Place	1970	1960	ZIP Code	Place	1970	1960
28645	Lenoir	14,705	10,257	45459	Centerville	10,333	3,490
27292	Lexington	17,205	16,093	45211	Cheviot	11,135	10,701
28092	Lincolnton	5,293	5,699	45601	Chillicothe	24,842	24,957
28358	Lumberton	16,961	15,305	44505	Churchill	7,457	
28110	Monroe	11,282	10,882	*45202	Cincinnati	451,455	502,550
28115	Mooresville	8,808	6,918	43113	Circleville	11,687	11,059
28557	Morehead City	5,233	5,583	*44101	Cleveland	750,879	876,050
28655	Morganton	13,625	9,186	44118	Cleveland Heights	60,767	61,813
27030	Mount Airy	7,325	7,055	43410	Clyde	5,503	4,826
28120	Mount Holly	5,107	4,037	*43216	Columbus	540,025	471,316
28560	New Bern	14,660	15,717	44030	Conneaut	14,552	10,557
28540	New River Gieger	8,699		43812	Coshocton	13,747	13,106
28658	Newton	7,857	6,658	45238	Covedale	6,639	
28012	North Belmont	10,672	8,328	44827	Crestline	5,947	5,521
27565	Oxford	7,178	6,978	45341	Crystal Lakes	5,851	1,569
*27611	Raleigh	123,793	93,931	44222	Cuyahoga Falls	49,678	47,922
27320	Reidsville	13,636	14,267	*45401	Dayton	242,917	262,332
27870	Roanoke Rapids	13,508	13,320	45236	Deer Park	7,415	8,423
28379	Rockingham	5,852	5,512	43512	Defiance	16,281	14,553
27801	Rocky Mount	34,284	32,147	43015	Delaware	15,008	13,282
27573	Roxboro	5,370	5,147	45833	Delphos	7,608	6,961
28144	Salisbury	22,515	21,297	44622	Dover	11,516	11,300
27330	Sanford	11,716	12,253	44112	East Cleveland	39,600	37,991
27530	Seymour-Johnson	8,172		44094	Eastlake	19,690	12,467
28150	Shelby	16,328	17,698	43920	East Liverpool	20,020	22,306
27577	Smithfield	6,677	6,117	43920	East Liverpool North	6,223	
28387	Southern Pines	5,937	5,198	44413	East Palestine	5,604	5,232
28677	Statesville	20,007	19,844	45320	Eaton	6,020	5,034
27886	Tarboro	9,425	8,411	44035	Elyria	53,427	43,782
27360	Thomasville	15,230	15,190	45322	Englewood	7,885	1,515
27889	Washington	8,961	9,939	44117	Euclid	71,552	62,998
28786	Waynesville	6,488	6,159	45324	Fairborn	32,267	·19,453
28025	West Concord	5,347	5,510	45014	Fairfield	14,680	9,734
27892	Williamston	6,570	6,924	44313	Fairlawn	6,102	
28401	Wilmington	46,169	44,013	44126	Fairview Park	21,681	14,624
27893	Wilson	29,347	28,753	45840	Findlay	35,800	30,344
*27102	Winston-Salem	133,683	111,135	45405	Forest Park	15,139	
				45426	Fort McKinley	11,536	
	North Dakota			44830	Fostoria	16,037	15,732
58501	Bismarck	34,703	27,670	45005	Franklin	10,075	7,917
58301	Devils Lake	7,078	6,299	43420	Fremont	18,490	18,767
58601	Dickinson	12,405	9,971	43230	Gahanna	12,400	2,717
58102	Fargo	53,365	46,662	44833	Galion	13,123	12,650
58237	Grafton, 1973	5,931	5,885	45631	Gallipolis	7,490	8,775
58201	Grand Forks, 1971	40,060	34,451	44125	Garfield Heights	41,417	38,455
58201	Grand Forks Base	10,474		44041	Geneva	6,449	5,677
58401	Jamestown, 1971	15,078	15,163	44420	Girard	14,119	12,997
58554	Mandan, 1973	11,400	10,525	45237	Golf Manor	5,170	4,648
58701	Minot	32,290	30,604	43212	Grandview Heights	8,460	8,270
58701	Minot Base	12,077		45218	Greenhills	6,092	5,407
58072	Valley City	7,843	7,809	45331	Greenville	12,380	10,585
58075	Wahpeton	7,076	5,876	43123	Grove City	13,911	8,107
58078	West Fargo, 1972	6,437	3,328	*45012	Hamilton	67,865	72,354
58801	Williston	11,280	11,866	43055	Heath	6,768	2,426
				44124	Highland Heights	5,926	2,929
	Ohio			43026	Hilliard	8,369	5,633
45810	Ada	5,309	3,918	45133	Hillsboro	5,584	5,474
*44309	Akron	275,425	290,351	44425	Hubbard	8,583	7,137
44601	Alliance	26,547	28,362	45424	Huber Heights	18,943	
44001	Amherst	9,902	6,750	44839	Huron	6,896	5,197
44805	Ashland	19,872	17,419	44131	Independence	7,034	6,868
44004	Ashtabula	24,313	24,559	45243	Indian Hill	5,651	4,526
45701	Athens	24,168	16,470	45638	Ironton	15,030	15,745
44202	Aurora	6,549	4,049	45640	Jackson	6,843	6,980
44515	Austintown	29,393		44240	Kent	28,183	17,836
44011	Avon	7,214	6,002	43326	Kenton	8,315	8,747
45404	Avondale	5,240		45236	Kenwood	15,789	
44012	Avon Lake	12,261	9,403	45429	Kettering	71,864	54,462
44203	Barberton	33,052	33,805	44094	Kirtland	5,530	
44140	Bay Village	18,163	14,489	45432	Knollwood	5,353	
44122	Beachwood	9,631	6,089	44107	Lakewood	70,173	66,154
44146	Bedford	17,552	15,223	43130	Lancaster	32,911	29,916
44146	Bedford Heights	13,063	5,275	45036	Lebanon	7,934	5,993
43906	Bellaire	9,655	11,502	*45802	Lima	53,734	51,037
43311	Bellefontaine	11,255	11,424	43228	Lincoln	11,215	
44811	Bellevue	8,604	8,286	45215	Lincoln Heights	6,099	7,798
45714	Belpre	7,189	5,418	43217	Lockbourne Base	5,623	
44017	Berea	22,465	16,592	45215	Lockland	5,288	5,292
43209	Bexley	14,888	14,319	43138	Logan	6,269	6,417
43004	Blacklick Estates	8,351		43140	London	6,481	6,379
45242	Blue Ash	8,324	8,341	*44052	Lorain	78,185	68,932
44512	Boardman	30,852		44641	Louisville	6,298	5,116
43402	Bowling Green	21,760	13,574	45140	Loveland	7,144	5,008
44141	Brecksville	9,137	5,435	44124	Lyndhurst	19,749	16,805
45211	Bridgetown	13,352		44056	Macedonia	6,375	
44141	Broadview Heights	11,463	6,209	45243	Madeira	6,713	6,744
44144	Brooklyn	13,142	10,733	44057	Madison North	6,882	
44142	Brook Park	30,774	12,856	*44901	Mansfield	55,047	47,325
44212	Brunswick	15,852	11,725	44137	Maple Heights	34,093	31,667
43506	Bryan	7,008	7,361	45750	Marietta	16,861	16,847
48820	Bucyrus	13,111	12,276	43302	Marion	38,646	37,079
43725	Cambridge	13,656	14,562	43935	Martins Ferry	10,757	11,919
44405	Campbell	12,577	13,406	43040	Marysville	5,744	4,952
*44711	Canton	110,053	113,631	45040	Mason	5,677	4,727
45822	Celina	8,072	7,659	44646	Massillon	32,539	31,236
				44537	Maumee	15,937	12,063
				44124	Mayfield Heights	22,139	13,478
				44256	Medina	10,913	8,235

ZIP Code	Place	1970	1960	ZIP Code	Place	1970	1960
44060	Mentor	36,912	4,354	44890	Willard	5,510	5,457
44060	Mentor-on-the-Lake	6,517	3,290	44094	Willoughby	18,634	15,058
45342	Miamisburg	14,797	9,893	44094	Willoughby Hills	5,247	4,241
44017	Middleburg Heights	12,367	7,282	44094	Willowick	21,237	18,749
45042	Middletown	48,767	42,115	45177	Wilmington	10,051	8,915
43938	Mingo Junction	5,278	4,987	44691	Wooster	18,703	17,046
45242	Montgomery	5,683	3,075	43085	Worthington	15,326	9,239
45231	Mount Healthy	7,446	6,553	45433	Wright-Patterson	10,151	
43050	Mount Vernon	13,373	13,284	45215	Wyoming	9,089	7,736
43545	Napoleon	7,791	6,739	45385	Xenia	25,373	20,445
43055	Newark	41,836	41,790	*44501	Youngstown	140,909	166,689
44344	New Carlisle	6,112	4,107	43701	Zanesville	33,045	39,077
44663	New Philadelphia	15,184	14,241				
44444	Newton Falls	5,378	5,038		**Oklahoma**		
44446	Niles	21,581	19,545				
44720	North Canton	15,228	7,727	74820	Ada	14,859	14,347
45239	North College Hill	12,363	12,035	73521	Altus	23,302	21,225
44070	North Olmsted	34,861	16,290	73717	Alva	7,440	6,258
45414	Northridge	10,084		73005	Anadarko	6,682	6,299
44035	North Ridgeville	13,152	8,057	73401	Ardmore	20,881	20,184
44133	North Royalton	12,807	9,290	74003	Bartlesville	29,683	27,893
44203	Norton	12,308		73008	Bethany	22,694	12,342
44857	Norwalk	13,386	12,900	74631	Blackwell	8,645	9,588
45212	Norwood	30,420	34,580	74012	Broken Arrow	11,787	5,928
45873	Oakwood City	10,095	10,493	73018	Chickasha	14,194	14,866
44074	Oberlin	8,761	8,198	74017	Claremore	9,084	6,639
43616	Oregon	16,563	13,319	73601	Clinton	8,513	9,617
44667	Orrville	7,408	6,511	74023	Cushing	7,529	8,619
45431	Overlook-Page Manor	19,719		73115	Del City	27,133	12,934
45056	Oxford	15,868	7,828	73533	Duncan	19,718	20,009
44077	Painesville	16,536	16,116	74701	Durant	11,118	10,467
44077	Painesville Southwest	5,461		73034	Edmond	16,633	8,577
44129	Parma	100,216	82,845	73644	Elk City	7,323	8,196
44130	Parma Heights	27,192	18,100	73036	El Reno	14,510	11,015
44124	Pepper Pike	5,382	3,217	73701	Enid	44,986	38,859
43551	Perrysburg	7,693	5,519	73503	Fort Sill	21,217	
45356	Piqua	20,741	19,219	73542	Frederick	6,132	5,879
43452	Port Clinton	7,202	6,870	73044	Guthrie	9,575	9,502
45662	Portsmouth	27,633	33,637	73942	Guymon	7,674	5,760
44266	Ravenna	11,780	10,918	74437	Henryetta	6,430	6,551
45215	Reading	14,617	12,832	74848	Holdenville	5,181	5,712
43068	Reynoldsburg	13,921	7,793	74743	Hugo	6,585	6,287
44143	Richmond Heights	9,220	5,068	74745	Idabel	5,946	4,967
44270	Rittman	6,308	5,410	73501	Lawton	74,470	61,697
44116	Rocky River	22,958	18,097	74501	McAlester	18,802	17,419
43460	Rossford	5,302	4,406	74354	Miami	13,880	12,869
45217	St. Bernard	6,080	6,778	73110	Midwest City	48,212	36,058
45885	St. Marys	7,699	7,737	73060	Moore	18,761	1,783
44460	Salem	14,186	13,854	74401	Muskogee	37,331	38,059
44870	Sandusky	32,674	31,989	73069	Norman	52,117	33,412
44870	Sandusky South	8,501	4,724	*73125	Oklahoma City	368,377	324,253
44131	Seven Hills	12,700	5,708	74447	Okmulgee	15,180	15,951
43947	Shadyside	5,070	5,028	73075	Pauls Valley	5,769	6,856
44120	Shaker Heights	36,306	36,460	73077	Perry	5,341	5,210
45241	Sharonville	11,393	3,890	74601	Ponca City	25,940	24,411
44054	Sheffield Lake	8,734	6,884	74953	Poteau	5,500	4,428
44875	Shelby	9,847	9,106	74361	Pryor	7,057	6,476
44878	Shiloh	11,368		74063	Sand Springs	10,565	7,754
45365	Sidney	16,332	14,663	74066	Sapulpa	15,159	14,282
45236	Silverton	6,588	6,682	74868	Seminole	7,878	11,464
44139	Solon	11,519	6,333	74801	Shawnee	25,075	24,326
44121	South Euclid	29,579	27,569	74074	Stillwater	31,126	23,965
45246	Springdale	8,127	3,556	73086	Sulphur	5,158	4,737
*45501	Springfield	81,941	82,723	74464	Tahlequah	9,254	5,840
43952	Steubenville	30,771	32,495	73120	The Village	13,695	12,118
44224	Stow	19,847	12,194	*74101	Tulsa	330,350	261,685
44240	Streetsboro	7,966		74301	Vinita	5,847	6,027
44136	Strongsville	15,182	8,504	73123	Warr Acres	9,887	7,135
44471	Struthers	15,343	15,631	73096	Weatherford	7,959	4,499
43560	Sylvania	12,031	5,187	74884	Wewoka	5,284	5,954
44278	Tallmadge	15,274	10,246	73801	Woodward	9,412	7,747
44883	Tiffin	21,596	21,478	73099	Yukon	8,411	3,076
45371	Tipp City	5,090	4,267				
*43601	Toledo	383,105	318,003		**Oregon**		
43964	Toronto	7,705	7,780				
45067	Trenton	5,278	3,064	97321	Albany	18,181	12,926
45426	Trotwood	6,997	4,992	97601	Altamont	15,746	10,811
45373	Troy	17,186	13,685	97520	Ashland	12,342	9,119
44087	Twinsburg	6,432	4,098	97103	Astoria	10,244	11,239
44683	Uhrichsville	5,731	6,201	97814	Baker	9,354	9,986
44118	University Heights	17,055	16,641	97005	Beaverton	18,577	5,937
43221	Upper Arlington	38,727	28,486	97701	Bend	13,710	11,936
43351	Upper Sandusky	5,645	4,941	97420	Coos Bay	13,466	7,084
43078	Urbana	11,237	10,461	97330	Corvallis	35,056	20,669
45377	Vandalia	10,796	6,342	97424	Cottage Grove	6,004	3,895
45891	Van Wert	11,320	11,323	97338	Dallas	6,361	5,072
44089	Vermilion	9,872	4,785	*97401	Eugene	79,028	50,977
44281	Wadsworth	13,142	10,635	97116	Forest Grove	8,275	5,628
45895	Wapakoneta	7,324	6,756	97301	Four Corners	5,823	4,743
*44481	Warren	63,494	59,648	97027	Gladstone	6,254	3,854
44122	Warrensville Heights	18,925	10,609	97526	Grants Pass	12,455	10,118
43160	Washington	12,495	12,388	97030	Gresham	10,030	3,944
45692	Wellston	5,410	5,728	97303	Hayesville	5,518	4,568
43968	Wellsville	5,891	7,117	97123	Hillsboro	14,675	8,232
45449	West Carrollton	10,748	4,749	97303	Keizer	11,405	5,288
43081	Westerville	12,530	7,011	97601	Klamath Falls	15,775	16,949
44145	Westlake	15,689	12,906	97850	La Grande	9,645	9,014
43213	Whitehall	25,263	20,818				
44092	Wickliffe	21,354	15,760				

ZIP Code	Place	1970	1960
97034	Lake Oswego	14,615	8,906
97355	Lebanon	6,636	5,858
97128	McMinnville	10,125	7,656
97501	Medford	28,454	24,425
97222	Milwaukie	16,444	9,099
97361	Monmouth	5,237	2,229
97132	Newberg	6,507	4,204
97365	Newport	5,188	5,344
97459	North Bend	8,553	7,512
97914	Ontario	6,523	5,101
97045	Oregon City	9,176	7,996
97801	Pendleton	13,197	14,434
97208	Portland	379,967	372,676
97470	Roseburg	14,461	11,467
97051	St. Helens	6,212	5,022
97301	Salem	68,480	49,142
97477	Springfield	26,874	19,616
97058	The Dalles	10,423	10,493
97223	Tigard	5,302	......
97068	West Linn	7,091	3,933
97071	Woodburn	7,495	3,120

Pennsylvania

ZIP Code	Place	1970	1960
19001	Abington	8,594	......
19018	Aldan	5,001	4,324
15001	Aliquippa	22,277	26,369
*18101	Allentown	109,527	108,347
*16603	Altoona	63,115	69,407
19002	Ambler	7,800	6,765
15003	Ambridge	11,324	13,865
18403	Archbald	6,118	5,642
19003	Ardmore	5,131	......
15068	Arnold	8,174	9,437
15202	Avalon	7,010	6,859
15005	Baden	5,536	6,109
19004	Bala-Cynwyd	6,483	......
15234	Baldwin	26,729	24,489
18013	Bangor	5,425	5,766
15009	Beaver	6,100	6,160
15010	Beaver Falls	14,375	16,240
16823	Bellefonte	6,828	6,088
15202	Bellevue	11,586	11,412
18603	Berwick	12,274	13,353
15102	Bethel Park	34,791	23,650
*18016	Bethlehem	72,686	75,408
18847	Blakely	6,391	6,374
17815	Bloomsburg	11,652	10,655
15104	Braddock	8,795	12,337
16701	Bradford	12,672	15,061
19406	Brandywine	11,411	......
15227	Brentwood	13,732	13,706
19405	Bridgeport	5,630	5,306
15017	Bridgeville	6,717	7,112
19007	Bristol	12,085	12,364
19015	Brookhaven 1973	7,262	5,280
19010	Bryn Mawr	5,815	......
16001	Butler	18,691	20,975
15419	California	6,635	5,978
17011	Camp Hill	9,931	8,559
15317	Canonsburg	11,439	11,877
18407	Carbondale	12,808	13,595
17013	Carlisle	18,079	16,623
15106	Carnegie	10,864	11,887
15108	Carnot-Moon	13,093	......
15234	Castle Shannon	11,899	11,836
18032	Catasauqua	5,702	5,062
19095	Cedarbrook-Melrose Park	9,980	......
19428	Cedar Heights	6,326	......
17201	Chambersburg	17,315	17,670
15022	Charleroi	6,723	8,148
19380	Chatwood	7,168	3,621
*19013	Chester	56,331	63,658
19025	Clairton	15,051	18,389
16214	Clarion	6,095	4,958
18411	Clarks Summit	5,376	3,693
16830	Clearfield	8,176	9,270
19018	Clifton Heights	8,348	8,005
19320	Coatesville	12,331	12,971
19023	Collingdale	10,605	10,268
17512	Columbia	11,237	12,075
15425	Connellsville	11,643	12,814
19428	Conshohocken	10,195	10,259
15108	Coraopolis	8,435	9,643
16407	Corry	7,435	7,744
15205	Crafton	8,233	8,418
17821	Danville	6,176	6,889
19023	Darby	13,729	14,059
18519	Dickson City	7,698	7,738
15033	Donora	8,825	11,131
15216	Dormont	12,856	13,098
19335	Downingtown	7,437	5,598
18901	Doylestown	8,270	5,917
15801	Du Bois	10,112	10,667
18512	Dunmore	17,300	18,917
15110	Duquesne	11,410	15,019
18642	Duryea	5,264	5,626

ZIP Code	Place	1970	1960
18042	Easton	29,450	31,955
18301	East Stroudsburg	7,894	7,674
15005	Economy 1973	7,605	5,925
15218	Edgewood	5,138	5,124
18704	Edwardsville	5,633	5,711
17022	Elizabethtown	8,072	6,780
16117	Ellwood City	10,857	12,413
18049	Emmaus	11,511	10,262
17522	Ephrata	9,662	7,688
*16501	Erie	129,231	138,440
15223	Etna	5,819	5,519
16121	Farrell	11,022	13,793
19031	Flourtown	9,149	......
19032	Folcroft	9,610	7,013
15221	Forest Hills	9,561	8,796
18704	Forty Fort	6,114	6,431
18015	Fountain Hill	5,384	5,428
17931	Frackville	5,445	5,654
16323	Franklin	8,629	9,586
15143	Franklin Park	5,310	......
18052	Fullerton	7,908	......
	General Wayne	5,368	......
17325	Gettysburg	7,275	7,960
15045	Glassport	7,450	8,418
19036	Glenolden	8,697	7,249
19038	Glenside	17,353	......
15601	Greensburg	17,077	17,383
15220	Green Tree	6,441	5,226
16125	Greenville	8,704	8,765
16127	Grove City	8,312	8,368
17331	Hanover	15,623	15,538
*17105	Harrisburg	68,061	79,697
19040	Hatboro	8,880	7,315
19044	Hatboro West	13,542	......
18201	Hazelton	30,426	32,056
18055	Hellertown	6,615	6,716
17033	Hershey	7,407	6,851
18042	Highland Park (Northampton)	5,500	......
16648	Hollidaysburg	6,262	6,475
16001	Homeacre-Lyndora	8,415	......
15120	Homestead	6,309	7,502
18431	Honesdale	5,224	5,569
16652	Huntingdon	6,987	7,234
16701	Indiana	16,100	13,005
15644	Jeannette	15,209	16,565
15344	Jefferson	8,512	8,280
19401	Jefferson-Trooper	13,022	......
19046	Jenkintown	5,990	5,017
17740	Jersey Shore	5,322	5,613
18229	Jim Thorpe	5,456	5,945
*15901	Johnstown	42,476	53,949
16735	Kane	5,001	5,380
18704	Kingston	18,325	20,261
16201	Kittanning	6,231	6,793
19444	Lafayette Hills-Plymouth Meeting	8,275	......
*17604	Lancaster	57,690	61,055
19446	Lansdale	18,451	12,612
19050	Lansdowne	14,090	12,601
18232	Lansford	5,168	5,958
15650	Latrobe	11,749	11,932
17042	Lebanon	28,572	30,045
18235	Lehighton	6,095	6,318
17837	Lewisburg	6,376	5,523
17044	Lewistown	11,098	12,640
17543	Lititz	7,072	5,987
17745	Lock Haven	11,427	11,748
15068	Lower Burrell	13,654	11,952
15134	McKeesport	37,977	45,489
15136	McKees Rocks	11,901	13,185
17948	Mahanoy City	7,257	8,536
17545	Manheim	5,434	4,790
16335	Meadville	16,573	16,671
17055	Mechanicsburg	9,385	8,123
*19063	Media	6,444	5,803
19066	Merion	5,686	......
17057	Middletown	9,080	11,182
15059	Midland	5,271	6,425
17551	Millersville	6,396	3,883
15209	Millvale	5,815	6,624
17847	Milton	7,723	7,972
17954	Minersville	6,012	6,606
15061	Monaca	7,486	8,394
15062	Monessen	15,216	18,424
15063	Monongahela	7,113	8,388
15146	Monroeville	29,011	22,446
17754	Montoursville	5,455	5,211
19067	Morrisville	11,309	7,790
17851	Mount Carmel	9,317	10,760
17552	Mount Joy	5,041	3,292
15210	Mount Oliver	5,487	5,980
15666	Mount Pleasant	5,895	6,107
15120	Munhall	16,574	17,312
18634	Nanticoke	14,632	15,601
19072	Narberth	5,151	5,109
18064	Nazareth	5,815	6,209
15066	New Brighton	7,637	8,397
*16101	New Castle	38,559	44,790

ZIP Code	Place	1970	1960
17070	New Cumberland	9,803	9,257
15068	New Kensington	20,312	23,485
*19401	Norristown	38,169	38,925
18067	Northampton	8,389	8,866
19003	North Ardmore	5,856	
15104	North Braddock	10,838	13,204
19038	North Hills-Ardsley	13,096	
19074	Norwood	7,229	6,729
19126	Oak Lane	6,192	
15139	Oakmont	7,550	7,504
19117	Ogontz	5,463	2,254
16301	Oil City	15,033	17,692
18518	Old Forge	9,522	8,928
18447	Olyphant	5,422	5,864
19075	Oreland	9,261	
18071	Palmerton	5,620	5,942
17078	Palmyra	7,615	6,999
19301	Paoli	5,835	
17331	Parkville	5,120	4,516
19004	Pencoyd	6,650	
19401	Penn Sq.-Plymouth Valley	20,238	
19151	Penn Wynne	6,038	
18944	Perkasie	5,451	4,650
*19104	Philadelphia	1,949,996	2,002,512
19460	Phoenixville	14,823	13,797
*15219	Pittsburgh	520,117	604,332
*18640	Pittston	11,113	12,407
18705	Plains	6,606	
15236	Pleasant Hills	10,409	8,573
15239	Plum	21,932	10,241
18651	Plymouth	9,536	10,401
15133	Port Vue	5,862	6,635
19464	Pottstown	25,355	26,144
17901	Pottsville	19,715	21,659
19076	Prospect Park	7,250	6,596
15767	Punxsutawney	7,792	8,805
18951	Quakertown	7,276	6,305
*19603	Reading	87,643	98,177
17356	Red Lion	5,645	5,594
15853	Ridgway	6,022	6,387
19078	Ridley Park	9,025	7,387
19001	Roslyn	18,380	
19046	Rydal	5,083	
15857	St. Marys	7,470	8,065
18840	Sayre	7,473	7,917
17972	Schuylkill Haven	6,125	6,470
15683	Scottdale	5,818	6,244
*18503	Scranton	103,564	111,443
17870	Selinsgrove	5,116	3,948
15143	Sewickley	5,660	6,157
17872	Shamokin	11,719	13,674
16146	Sharon	22,653	25,267
19079	Sharon Hill	7,464	7,123
15215	Sharpsburg	5,453	6,096
16150	Sharpsville	6,126	6,061
17976	Shenandoah	8,287	11,073
19607	Shillington	6,249	5,639
17257	Shippensburg	6,536	6,138
18080	Slatington	4,687	4,316
16057	Slippery Rock	4,949	2,563
15501	Somerset	6,269	6,347
18964	Souderton	6,366	5,381
17701	South Williamsport	7,153	6,972
15144	Springdale	5,202	5,602
16801	State College	33,778	22,409
17113	Steelton	8,556	11,266
18360	Stroudsburg	5,451	6,070
16323	Sugar Creek	5,944	
17801	Sunbury	13,025	13,687
19081	Swarthmore	6,156	5,753
15218	Swissvale	13,819	15,089
18704	Swoyersville	6,786	6,751
18252	Tamaqua	9,246	10,173
15084	Tarentum	7,379	8,232
18517	Taylor	6,977	6,148
16354	Titusville	7,331	8,356
15145	Turtle Creek	8,308	10,607
16686	Tyrone	7,072	7,792
15401	Uniontown	16,282	17,942
15690	Vandergrift	7,889	8,742
16365	Warren	12,998	14,505
15301	Washington	19,827	23,545
17268	Waynes boro	10,011	10,427
15370	Waynesburg	5,152	5,188
19380	West Chester	19,301	15,705
18201	West Hazleton	6,059	6,278
15122	West Mifflin	28,070	27,289
15905	Westmont	6,673	6,573
18643	West Pittston	7,074	6,998
15229	West View	8,312	8,079
17404	West York	5,314	5,526
18052	Whitehall	16,551	16,075
15131	White Oak	9,304	9,047
*18701	Wilkes-Barre	58,856	63,551
15221	Wilkinsburg	26,780	30,066
17701	Williamsport	37,918	41,967
19090	Willow Grove	16,494	
15025	Wilson	8,406	8,465

ZIP Code	Place	1970	1960
15963	Windber	6,332	6,994
19610	Wyomissing	7,136	5,044
19050	Yeadon	12,136	11,610
*17405	York	50,335	54,504

Rhode Island
See Note on Page 159

ZIP Code	Place	1970	1960
02806	Barrington	17,554	13,826
02809	Bristol	17,860	14,570
02830	Burrillville	10,087	9,119
02863	Central Falls	18,716	19,858
02816	Coventry	22,947	15,432
02910	Cranston	74,287	66,766
02864	Cumberland	26,605	18,792
02818	East Greenwich	9,577	6,100
02914	East Providence	48,207	41,955
02814	Glocester	5,160	3,397
02833	Hopkinton	5,392	4,174
02919	Johnston	22,037	17,160
02881	Kingston	5,601	2,616
02865	Lincoln	16,182	13,551
02840	Middletown	29,290	12,675
02882	Narragansett	7,138	3,444
02840	Newport	34,562	47,049
02843	Newport East	10,285	2,643
02852	North Kingstown	29,793	18,977
02908	North Providence	24,337	18,220
02876	North Smithfield	9,349	7,632
*02860	Pawtucket	76,984	81,001
02871	Portsmouth	12,521	8,251
*02904	Providence	179,116	207,498
02857	Scituate	7,489	5,210
02917	Smithfield	13,468	9,442
02879	South Kingstown	16,913	11,942
02878	Tiverton	12,559	9,461
*02880	Wakefield-Peacedale	6,331	5,569
02885	Warren	10,523	8,750
02887	Warwick	83,694	68,504
02891	Westerly Center	13,654	9,698
02891	Westerly	17,248	14,267
02893	West Warwick	24,323	21,414
02895	Woonsocket	46,820	47,080

South Carolina

ZIP Code	Place	1970	1960
29620	Abbeville	5,515	5,436
29801	Aiken	13,436	11,243
29621	Anderson	27,556	41,316
29407	Avondale-Moorland	5,236	
29902	Beaufort	9,434	6,298
29627	Belton	5,257	5,106
29512	Bennettsville	7,468	6,963
29601	Berea	7,186	
29020	Camden	8,532	6,842
29033	Cayce	9,967	8,517
*29401	Charleston	66,945	65,925
29404	Charleston Base	6,238	
29408	Charleston Yard	13,565	
29520	Cheraw	5,627	5,171
29706	Chester	7,045	6,906
29631	Clemson	5,578	1,587
29325	Clinton	8,138	7,937
29201	Columbia	113,542	97,433
29526	Conway	8,151	8,563
29532	Darlington	6,990	6,710
29536	Dillon	6,391	6,173
29640	Easley	11,175	8,283
29501	Florence	25,997	24,722
29206	Forest Acres	6,808	3,842
29340	Gaffney	13,253	10,435
	Gantt	11,386	
29440	Georgetown	10,449	12,261
29602	Greenville	61,436	66,188
29646	Greenwood	21,069	16,644
29651	Greer	10,642	8,967
29410	Hanahan	8,376	
29550	Hartsville	8,017	6,392
29560	Lake City	6,247	6,059
29720	Lancaster	9,186	7,999
29360	Laurens	10,298	9,598
29571	Marion	7,435	7,174
29662	Mauldin 1973	5,480	1,462
29464	Mount Pleasant	6,879	5,116
29574	Mullins	6,006	6,299
29577	Myrtle Beach	9,035	7,834
29108	Newberry	9,218	8,208
29841	North Augusta	12,883	10,348
29115	Orangeburg	13,252	13,852
29905	Parris Island	8,868	
29730	Rock Hill	33,846	29,404
29407	St. Andrews	9,202	
29678	Seneca	6,382	5,227
29150	Shannontown	7,491	7,064
29152	Shaw	5,819	
*29301	Spartanburg	44,546	44,352
29150	Sumter	24,555	23,062
29687	Taylors	6,831	1,071

ZIP Code	Place	1970	1960	ZIP Code	Place	1970	1960
29379	Union	10,775	10,191	*79105	Amarillo	127,010	137,969
29607	Wade-Hampton	17,152		79714	Andrews	8,625	11,135
29488	Walterboro	6,257	5,417	77515	Angleton	9,770	7,312
29169	West Columbia	7,838	6,410	78336	Aransas Pass	5,813	6,956
29745	York	5,081	4,758	*76010	Arlington	90,032	44,775
				75751	Athens	9,582	7,086
	South Dakota			75551	Atlanta	5,007	4,076
				*78710	Austin	251,808	186,545
57401	Aberdeen	26,476	23,073	75149	Balch Springs	10,464	6,821
57006	Brookings	13,717	10,558	77414	Bay City	13,445	11,656
57706	Ellsworth	6,207		77520	Baytown	43,980	28,159
57350	Huron	14,299	14,180	*77704	Beaumont	117,548	119,175
57754	Lead	5,420	6,211	76021	Bedford	10,049	2,706
57042	Madison	6,315	5,420	78102	Beeville	13,506	13,811
57301	Mitchell	13,425	12,555	77401	Bellaire	19,009	19,872
57501	Pierre	9,699	10,088	76705	Bellmead	7,698	5,127
57701	Rapid City	43,836	42,399	76513	Belton	8,696	8,163
*57101	Sioux Falls	72,488	65,466	76126	Benbrook	8,169	3,254
57069	Vermillion	9,128	6,102	79720	Big Spring	28,735	31,230
57201	Watertown	13,388	14,077	75418	Bonham	7,698	7,357
57078	Yankton	11,919	9,279	79007	Borger	14,195	20,911
				76230	Bowie	5,185	4,566
	Tennessee			76825	Brady	5,557	5,338
				76024	Breckenridge	5,944	6,273
37701	Alcoa	7,739	6,395	77833	Brenham	8,922	7,740
37303	Athens	11,790	12,103	77611	Bridge City	8,164	4,677
38008	Bolivar	6,674	3,338	79316	Brownfield	9,647	10,286
37620	Bristol	20,064	17,582	78520	Brownsville	52,522	48,040
38012	Brownsville	7,011	5,424	76801	Brownwood	17,368	16,974
*37401	Chattanooga	119,923	130,009	77801	Bryan	33,7¹9	27,542
37040	Clarksville	31,719	22,021	76354	Burkburnett	9,230	7,621
37311	Cleveland	20,651	16,196	76028	Burleson	7,713	2,345
38401	Columbia	21,471	17,624	76520	Cameron	5,546	5,640
38501	Cookeville	14,270	7,805	79015	Canyon	8,333	5,864
38019	Covington	5,801	5,298	78834	Carrizo Springs	5,374	5,699
38555	Crossville	5,381	4,668	75006	Carrollton	13,855	4,242
37055	Dickson	5,665	5,028	75633	Carthage	5,392	5,262
38024	Dyersburg	14,523	12,499	78213	Castle Hills	5,311	2,622
37801	Eagleton Village	5,345	5,068	79201	Childress	5,408	6,399
37412	East Ridge	21,799	19,570	76031	Cleburne	16,015	15,381
37643	Elizabethton	12,269	10,896	77327	Cleveland	5,627	5,838
37334	Fayetteville	7,030	6,804	77531	Clute City	6,023	4,501
42223	Fort Campbell South	9,279		75834	Coleman	5,608	6,371
37064	Franklin	9,497	6,977	77840	College Station	17,676	11,396
37066	Gallatin	13,253	7,901	79512	Colorado City	5,227	6,457
37075	Greater Hendersonville	11,996		75428	Commerce	9,534	5,789
37743	Greeneville	13,722	11,759	77301	Conroe	11,969	9,192
37748	Harriman	8,734	5,931	76522	Copperas Cove	10,818	4,567
37343	Hixson	6,188		78408	Corpus Christi	204,525	167,690
38343	Humboldt	10,066	8,482	75110	Corsicana	19,972	20,344
38301	Jackson	39,996	34,376	75835	Crockett	6,616	5,356
37760	Jefferson City	5,124	4,550	78839	Crystal City	8,104	9,101
37601	Johnson City	33,770	31,187	77954	Cuero	6,956	7,338
*37662	Kingsport	31,938	26,314	79022	Dalhart	5,705	5,160
37665	Kingsport North	13,118		75221	Dallas	844,401	679,684
*37901	Knoxville	174,587	111,827	77536	Deer Park	12,773	4,865
37766	La Follette	6,902	6,204	78840	Del Rio	21,330	18,612
37416	Lake Hills-Murray Hills	7,806		75020	Denison	24,923	22,748
38464	Lawrenceburg	8,889	8,042	76201	Denton	39,874	26,844
37087	Lebanon	12,492	10,512	75115	De Soto	6,617	1,969
37771	Lenoir City	5,324	4,979	77539	Dickinson	10,776	4,715
37091	Lewisburg	7,207	6,338	78537	Donna	7,365	7,522
38351	Lexington	5,024	3,943	79029	Dumas	9,771	8,477
37110	Mc Minnville	10,662	9,013	75116	Duncanville	14,105	3,774
37355	Manchester	6,208	3,930	78852	Eagle Pass	15,364	12,094
38237	Martin	7,781	4,750	78539	Edinburg	17,163	18,706
37801	Maryville	13,808	10,348	77957	Edna	5,332	5,038
*38101	Memphis	623,530	497,524	77437	El Campo	9,332	7,700
38358	Milan	7,313	5,208	79910	El Paso	322,261	276,687
38053	Millington	21,177	6,059	75119	Ennis	11,046	9,347
37814	Morristown	20,318	21,267	76039	Euless	19,316	4,263
37130	Murfreesboro	26,360	18,991	78355	Falfurrias	6,355	6,515
*37202	Nashville-Davidson	**447,877	170,874	75234	Farmers Branch	27,492	13,441
37821	Newport	7,328	6,448	76119	Forest Hill	8,236	3,221
37830	Oak Ridge	28,319	27,169	79906	Fort Bliss	13,288	
38242	Paris	9,892	9,325	76544	Fort Hood	32,597	
38478	Pulaski	6,989	6,616	78234	Fort Sam Houston	10,553	
37415	Red Bank	12,715	10,777	79735	Fort Stockton	8,283	6,373
37854	Rockwood	5,259	5,345	76101	Fort Worth	393,476	356,268
38372	Savannah	5,576	4,315	78624	Fredericksburg	5,326	4,629
37160	Shelbyville	12,262	10,466	77541	Freeport	11,997	11,619
37167	Smyrna	5,698	3,612	77546	Friendswood	5,675	
37379	Soddy-Daisy	7,569		76240	Gainesville	13,830	13,083
37711	South Cleveland	5,070	1,512	77547	Galena Park	10,479	10,852
37172	Springfield	9,720	9,221	77550	Galveston	61,809	67,175
37388	Tullahoma	15,311	12,242	75040	Garland	81,437	38,501
38261	Union City	11,925	8,837	78626	Georgetown	6,395	5,218
37398	Winchester	5,256	4,760	75647	Gladewater	5,574	5,742
				78629	Gonzales	5,854	5,829

**Comprises the Metropolitan Government of Nashville and Davidson County.

ZIP Code	Place	1970	1960
	76046	Graham	7,477	8,505

	Texas			75050	Grand Prairie	50,904	30,386
				76051	Grapevine	7,023	2,821
				75401	Greenville	22,043	19,087
*79604	Abilene	89,653	90,368	77619	Groves	18,067	17,304
78209	Alamo Heights	6,933	7,552	76117	Haltom City	28,127	23,133
78332	Alice	20,121	20,861	78550	Harlingen	33,503	41,207
79830	Alpine	5,971	4,740	75652	Henderson	10,187	9,666
77511	Alvin	10,671	5,643	79045	Hereford	13,414	7,652

ZIP Code	Place	1970	1960
75205	Highland Park	10,133	10,411
76645	Hillsboro	7,224	7,402
77563	Hitchcock	5,565	5,216
78861	Hondo	5,487	4,992
*77013	Houston	1,232,802	938,219
77340	Huntsville	17,610	11,999
76053	Hurst	27,215	10,165
76367	Iowa Park	5,796	3,295
*75060	Irving	97,260	45,985
77029	Jacinto City	9,563	9,547
75766	Jacksonville	9,734	9,590
75951	Jasper	6,251	4,889
79745	Kermit	7,884	10,465
78028	Kerrville	12,672	8,901
75662	Kilgore	9,495	10,092
76541	Killeen	35,507	23,377
78363	Kingsville	28,915	25,297
78236	Lackland	19,141	......
77566	Lake Jackson	13,376	9,651
77568	La Marque	16,131	13,969
79331	Lamesa	11,559	12,438
76550	Lampasas	5,922	5,061
75146	Lancaster	10,522	7,501
77571	La Porte	7,149	4,512
78040	Laredo	69,024	60,678
77573	League City	10,818	......
79336	Levelland	11,445	10,153
75067	Lewisville	9,264	3,956
77575	Liberty	5,591	6,127
79339	Littlefield	6,738	7,236
78644	Lockhart	6,489	6,084
75601	Longview	45,547	40,050
*79408	Lubbock	149,101	128,691
75901	Lufkin	23,049	17,641
78501	McAllen	37,636	32,728
75069	McKinney	15,193	13,763
76661	Marlin	6,351	6,918
75670	Marshall	22,937	23,846
78368	Mathis	5,351	6,075
78570	Mercedes	9,355	10,943
75149	Mesquite	55,131	27,526
76667	Mexia	5,943	6,121
79701	Midland	59,463	62,625
76067	Mineral Wells	18,411	11,053
78572	Mission	13,043	14,081
79756	Monahans	8,333	8,567
75455	Mount Pleasant	9,459	8,027
75961	Nacogdoches	22,544	12,674
77868	Navasota	5,111	4,937
77627	Nederland	16,810	12,036
78130	New Braunfels	17,859	15,631
76118	North Richland Hills	16,514	8,662
79760	Odessa	78,380	80,338
77630	Orange	24,457	25,605
75801	Palestine	14,525	13,974
79065	Pampa	21,726	24,664
75460	Paris	23,441	20,977
*77501	Pasadena	89,277	58,737
77581	Pearland	6,444	1,497
78061	Pearsall	5,545	4,957
79772	Pecos	12,682	12,728
79070	Perryton	7,810	7,903
78577	Pharr	15,829	14,106
79072	Plainview	19,096	18,735
75074	Plano	17,872	3,695
78064	Pleasanton	5,407	3,467
77640	Port Arthur	57,371	66,676
78374	Portland	7,302	2,538
77979	Port Lavaca	10,491	8,864
77651	Port Neches	10,894	8,696
75475	Randolph	5,329	......
78580	Raymondville	7,987	9,385
75080	Richardson	48,582	16,810
76118	Richland Hills	8,865	7,804
77469	Richmond	5,777	3,668
78582	Rio Grande City	5,676	5,835
77019	River Oaks	8,193	8,444
78380	Robstown	11,217	10,266
77471	Rosenberg	12,098	9,698
76901	San Angelo	63,884	58,815
*78284	San Antonio	654,153	587,718
78586	San Benito	15,176	16,422
78589	San Juan	5,070	4,371
78666	San Marcos	18,860	12,713
78155	Seguin	15,934	14,299
79360	Seminole	5,007	5,737
75090	Sherman	29,061	24,988
77656	Silsbee	7,271	6,277
78387	Sinton	5,563	6,008
79364	Slaton	6,583	6,568
79549	Snyder	11,171	13,850
77587	South Houston	11,527	7,523
76401	Stephenville	9,277	7,359
75482	Sulphur Springs	10,642	9,160
79556	Sweetwater	12,020	13,914
76574	Taylor	9,616	9,434
76501	Temple	33,431	30,419
75160	Terrell	14,182	13,803

ZIP Code	Place	1970	1960
78209	Terrell Hills	5,225	5,572
75501	Texarkana	30,497	30,218
77590	Texas City	38,908	32,065
79088	Tulia	5,294	4,410
75701	Tyler	57,770	51,230
78148	Universal City	7,613	......
76308	University Park	23,498	23,202
78801	Uvalde	10,764	10,293
76384	Vernon	11,454	12,141
77901	Victoria	41,349	33,047
77662	Vidor	9,738	......
*76701	Waco	95,326	97,808
75165	Waxahachie	13,452	12,749
76086	Weatherford	11,750	9,759
78596	Weslaco	15,313	15,649
77005	West University Place	13,317	14,628
77488	Wharton	7,881	5,734
76108	White Settlement	13,449	11,513
*76307	Wichita Falls	96,265	101,724
77995	Yoakum	5,755	5,761

Utah

ZIP Code	Place	1970	1960
84003	American Fork	7,713	6,373
84010	Bountiful	27,751	17,039
84302	Brigham City	14,007	11,728
84720	Cedar City	8,946	7,543
84015	Clearfield	13,316	8,833
84121	Cottonwood	8,431	......
84109	East Millcreek	26,579	......
84119	Granger-Hunter	9,029	......
84106	Granite Park	9,573	......
84117	Holladay	23,014	......
84037	Kaysville	6,192	3,608
84118	Kearns	17,247	17,172
84041	Layton	13,603	9,027
84321	Logan	22,333	18,731
84044	Magna	5,509	6,442
84047	Midvale	7,840	5,802
84117	Mount Olympus	5,909	......
84107	Murray	21,206	16,806
84404	North Ogden	5,257	2,621
*84401	Ogden	69,478	70,197
84057	Orem	25,729	18,394
84062	Pleasant Grove	5,327	4,772
84501	Price	6,218	6,802
84601	Provo	53,131	36,047
84067	Roy	14,356	9,239
84770	St. George	7,097	5,130
*84101	Salt Lake City	175,885	189,454
84070	Sandy City	6,438	3,322
84403	South Ogden	9,991	7,405
84115	South Salt Lake	7,810	9,520
84660	Spanish Fork	7,284	6,472
84663	Springville	8,790	7,913
84015	Sunset	6,268	4,235
84074	Tooele	12,539	9,133
84403	Washington Terrace	7,241	6,441
84070	White City	6,402	......

Vermont

See Note on Page 159

ZIP Code	Place	1970	1960
05641	Barre	10,209	10,387
	Barre	6,509	4,580
05201	Bennington	14,586	13,002
	Bennington	7,950	8,023
05301	Brattleboro	9,055	9,315
	Brattleboro	12,239	11,734
05401	Burlington	38,633	35,531
05446	Colchester	8,776	4,718
05451	Essex	10,951	7,090
05452	Essex Junction	6,511	5,340
05047	Hartford	6,477	6,355
05753	Middlebury	6,532	5,305
05602	Montpelier	8,609	8,782
05101	Rockingham	5,601	5,704
05701	Rutland	19,293	18,325
05478	St. Albans	8,082	8,806
05819	St. Johnsbury	8,409	8,869
05401	South Burlington	10,032	6,903
05156	Springfield	5,632	6,600
	Springfield	10,063	9,934
05401	Williston Road Section	5,376	3,259
05404	Winooski	7,309	7,420

Virginia

ZIP Code	Place	1970	1960
*22313	Alexandria	110,927	91,023
22003	Annandale	27,405	......
*22210	Arlington	174,284	163,401
22041	Bailey's Crossroads	7,295	......
24523	Bedford	6,011	5,921
22307	Belleview	8,299	......
24060	Blacksburg	9,384	7,070
24605	Bluefield	5,286	4,235
23235	Bon Air	10,771	......
24201	Bristol	14,857	17,144
24416	Buena Vista	6,425	6,300

ZIP Code	Place	1970	1960
*22902	Charlottesville	38,880	29,427
*23320	Chesapeake	89,580	
23831	Chester	5,556	1,290
24073	Christiansburg	7,857	3,653
24422	Clifton Forge	5,501	5,268
24078	Collinsville	6,015	3,586
23834	Colonial Heights	15,097	9,587
24426	Covington	10,060	11,062
22701	Culpeper	6,056	2,412
22191	Dale	13,857	
24541	Danville	46,391	46,577
23847	Emporia	5,300	5,535
22030	Fairfax	21,970	13,585
*22046	Falls Church	10,772	10,192
22060	Fort Belvoir	14,591	
22308	Fort Hunt	10,415	
23801	Fort Lee	12,435	
23851	Franklin	6,880	7,264
22401	Fredericksburg	14,450	13,639
22630	Front Royal	8,211	7,949
24333	Galax	6,278	5,254
22306	Groveton	11,761	
23669	Hampton	120,779	89,258
*23369			
22801	Harrisonburg	14,605	11,916
23075	Highland Springs	7,345	
23860	Hopewell	23,471	17,895
22303	Huntington	5,559	
22042	Jefferson	25,432	
22041	Lake Barcroft	11,605	
23228	Lakeside	11,137	
24450	Lexington	7,597	7,537
22312	Lincolnia	10,761	
22030	Long Branch	21,634	
*24505	Lynchburg	54,083	54,790
22110	Manassas	9,164	3,555
22110	Manassas Park	6,844	5,342
22030	Mantua	6,911	
24354	Marion	8,158	8,385
24112	Martinsville	19,653	18,798
22101	McLean	17,698	
23111	Mechanicsville	5,189	
*23607	Newport News	138,177	113,662
*23501	Norfolk	307,951	304,869
22151	North Springfield	8,631	
23803	Petersburg	36,103	36,750
23362	Poquoson	5,441	4,278
*23705	Portsmouth	110,963	114,773
24301	Pulaski	10,279	10,469
22134	Quantico Station	6,213	
24141	Radford	11,596	9,371
22070	Reston	5,723	
*23232	Richmond	249,431	219,958
*24001	Roanoke	92,115	97,110
24281	Rose Hill	14,492	
24153	Salem	21,982	16,058
22044	Seven Corners	5,590	
24592	South Boston	6,889	5,974
*22150	Springfield	11,613	10,783
24401	Staunton	24,504	22,232
22170	Sterling Park	8,321	
23434	Suffolk	9,858	12,609
22180	Vienna	17,146	11,440
24179	Vinton	6,347	3,432
*23458	Virginia Beach	172,106	8,091
22980	Waynesboro	16,707	15,694
22152	West Springfield	14,143	
23185	Williamsburg	9,069	6,832
22601	Winchester	14,643	15,110
22191	Woodbridge-Marumsco	25,412	
24382	Wytheville	6,069	5,634

Washington

ZIP Code	Place	1970	1960
98520	Aberdeen	18,489	18,741
98221	Anacortes	7,701	8,414
98002	Auburn	21,653	11,933
98009	Bellevue	61,196	12,809
98225	Bellingham	39,375	34,688
98011	Bothell	5,420	2,237
98310	Bremerton	35,307	28,922
98607	Camas	5,790	5,666
98531	Centralia	10,054	8,586
98532	Chehalis	5,727	5,199
99004	Cheney	6,358	3,173
99403	Clarkston	6,312	6,209
*99213	Dishman	9,079	
98020	Edmonds	23,998	8,016
98926	Ellensburg	13,568	8,625
98823	Ephrata	5,255	6,548
*98201	Everett	53,622	40,304
99011	Fairchild	6,754	
98466	Fircrest	5,651	3,565
98433	Fort Lewis	38,054	
98550	Hoquiam	10,466	10,762
98626	Kelso	10,296	8,379
99336	Kennewick	15,212	14,244
98031	Kent	16,596	9,017
98033	Kirkland	14,970	6,025
98503	Lacey	9,696	
98499	Lakes District	48,195	
98632	Longview	28,373	23,349
98036	Lynwood	16,919	7,207
98438	McChord	6,515	
98040	Mercer Island	19,047	
98837	Moses Lake	10,310	11,299
98043	Mountlake Terrace	16,600	9,122
98273	Mount Vernon	8,804	7,921
98277	Oak Harbor	9,167	3,942
*98507	Olympia	23,296	18,273
99214	Opportunity	16,604	12,465
98444	Parkland	21,012	
99301	Pasco	13,920	14,522
98362	Port Angeles	16,367	12,653
98368	Port Townsend	5,241	5,074
99163	Pullman	20,509	12,957
98371	Puyallup	14,742	12,063
98052	Redmond	11,020	1,426
98055	Renton	25,878	18,453
99352	Richland	26,290	23,548
*98101	Seattle	530,831	557,087
98584	Shelton	6,515	5,651
98290	Snohomish	5,174	3,894
98387	Spanaway	5,768	
*99210	Spokane	170,516	181,608
98944	Sunnyside	6,751	6,208
*98402	Tacoma	154,407	147,979
98948	Toppenish	5,744	5,667
99268	Town and Country	6,484	
98502	Tumwater	5,373	3,885
98406	University Place	13,230	
*98660	Vancouver	41,859	32,464
99362	Walla Walla	23,619	24,536
98801	Wenatchee	16,912	16,726
*98901	Yakima	45,588	43,284

West Virginia

ZIP Code	Place	1970	1960
25801	Beckley	19,884	18,642
24701	Bluefield	15,921	19,256
26201	Buckhannon	7,261	6,386
*25301	Charleston	71,505	85,796
26301	Clarksburg	24,864	28,112
25064	Dunbar	9,151	11,006
26241	Elkins	8,287	8,307
26554	Fairmont	26,093	27,477
26354	Grafton	6,433	5,791
*25701	Huntington	74,315	83,627
26726	Keyser	6,586	6,192
25401	Martinsburg	14,626	15,179
26505	Morgantown	29,431	22,487
26041	Moundsville	13,560	15,163
26155	New Martinsville	6,528	5,607
25143	Nitro	8,019	6,894
26105	Parkersburg	44,208	44,797
25550	Point Pleasant	6,122	5,785
24740	Princeton	7,253	8,393
25177	St. Albans	14,356	15,103
25303	South Charleston	16,333	19,180
26101	Vienna	11,549	9,381
26062	Weirton	27,131	28,201
26452	Weston	7,323	8,754
26505	Westover	5,086	4,749
26003	Wheeling	48,188	53,400
25661	Williamson	5,831	6,746

Wisconsin

ZIP Code	Place	1970	1960
54301	Allouez	13,753	
54409	Antigo	9,005	9,691
54911	Appleton	56,377	48,411
54806	Ashland	9,615	10,132
54304	Ashwaubenon	9,323	
53913	Baraboo	7,931	7,660
53916	Beaver Dam	14,265	13,118
53511	Beloit	35,729	32,846
54923	Berlin	5,338	4,838
53005	Brookfield	32,140	19,812
53209	Brown Deer	12,582	11,280
53105	Burlington	7,479	5,856
53012	Cedarburg	7,697	5,191
54729	Chippewa Falls	12,351	11,708
53110	Cudahy	22,078	17,975
53115	Delavan	5,526	4,846
54115	De Pere	13,309	10,045
54701	Eau Claire	44,619	37,987
53122	Elm Grove	7,201	4,994
54935	Fond Du Lac	35,515	32,719
53538	Fort Atkinson	9,164	7,908
53217	Fox Point	7,939	7,315
53132	Franklin	12,247	10,006
53022	Germantown	6,974	622
53209	Glendale	13,426	9,537
53024	Grafton 1973	7,169	3,748
*54305	Green Bay	87,809	62,888
53129	Greendale	15,089	6,843
53220	Greenfield	24,424	17,636

ZIP Code	Place	1970	1960	ZIP Code	Place	1970	1960
53130	Hales Corners	7,771	5,549	54971	Ripon	7,053	6,163
53027	Hartford	6,499	5,627	54022	River Falls	7,238	4,857
54016	Hudson 1973	5,322	4,325	53207	St. Francis	10,489	10,065
53545	Janesville	46,426	35,164	54166	Shawano	6,488	6,103
53549	Jefferson	5,429	4,548	53081	Sheboygan	48,484	45,747
54130	Kaukauna	11,308	10,096	53211	Shorewood	15,576	15,990
53140	Kenosha	78,805	67,899	53172	South Milwaukee	23,297	20,307
54136	Kimberly	6,131	5,322	54656	Sparta	6,258	6,080
54601	La Crosse	51,153	47,575	54481	Stevens Point	23,479	17,837
54140	Little Chute	5,522	5,099	53589	Stoughton	6,096	5,555
*53701	Madison	171,769	126,706	54235	Sturgeon Bay 1973	7,202	7,353
54220	Manitowoc	33,430	32,275	53590	Sun Prairie	9,935	4,008
54143	Marinette	12,696	13,329	54880	Superior	32,237	33,563
54449	Marshfield	15,619	14,153	54660	Tomah	5,647	5,321
54952	Menasha	14,836	14,647	54241	Two Rivers	13,553	12,393
53051	Menomonee Falls	31,697	18,276	53094	Watertown	15,683	13,943
54751	Menomonie	11,275	8,624	53186	Waukesha	39,695	30,004
53092	Mequon	12,150	8,543	53963	Waupun	7,946	7,935
54452	Merrill	9,502	9,451	54401	Wausau	32,806	31,943
53562	Middleton	8,286	4,410	54401	Wausau West	6,399	4,105
*53203	Milwaukee	717,372	741,324	53213	Wauwatosa	58,676	56,923
53716	Monona	10,420	8,178	53214	West Allis	71,649	68,157
53566	Monroe	8,654	8,050	53095	West Bend	16,555	9,969
53150	Muskego	11,573		53217	Whitefish Bay	17,402	18,390
54956	Neenah	22,902	18,057	53190	Whitewater	12,038	6,380
53151	New Berlin	26,910	15,788	54494	Wisconsin Rapids	18,587	15,042
54961	New London	5,801	5,288				
53154	Oak Creek	13,928	9,372		**Wyoming**		
53066	Oconomowoc	8,741	6,682				
54901	Oshkosh	53,082	45,110	82601	Casper	39,361	38,930
53511	Perry Go Place	5,912	4,475	82001	Cheyenne	40,914	43,505
53818	Platteville	9,599	6,957	82414	Cody	5,161	4,838
53073	Plymouth	5,810	5,128	82716	Gillette	7,194	3,580
53901	Portage	7,821	7,822	82520	Lander	7,125	4,182
53074	Port Washington	8,752	5,984	82070	Laramie	23,143	17,520
53821	Prairie Du Chien	5,540	5,649	82301	Rawlins	7,855	8,968
*53401	Racine	95,162	89,144	82501	Riverton	7,995	6,845
54501	Rhinelander	8,218	8,790	82901	Rock Springs	11,657	10,371
54868	Rice Lake	7,278	7,303	82801	Sheridan	10,856	11,651
53581	Richland Center	5,086	4,746	82401	Worland	5,055	5,806

1970 Census & Areas of Counties and States

WITH NAMES OF COUNTY SEATS OR COURT HOUSES; LAND AREA IN SQUARE MILES

Source: Bureau of the Census

County	Pop. April 1, 1970	County Seat or Court House	Land Area Sq. Mi.	County	Pop. April 1, 1970	County Seat or Court House	Land Area Sq. Mi.
				Lawrence	27,281	Moulton	685
				Lee	61,268	Opelika	612
				Limestone	41,699	Athens	546
				Lowndes	12,897	Hayneville	715
Alabama				Macon	24,841	Tuskegee	616
				Madison	186,540	Huntsville	803
(67 counties, 50,708 sq. mi. land; pop. 3,444,165)				Marengo	23,819	Linden	978
				Marion	23,788	Hamilton	743
Autauga	24,460	Prattville	599	Marshall	54,211	Guntersville	571
Baldwin	59,382	Bay Minette	1,578	Mobile	317,308	Mobile	1,240
Barbour	22,543	Clayton	891	Monroe	20,883	Monroeville	1,032
Bibb	13,812	Centreville	625	Montgomery	167,790	Montgomery	790
Blount	26,853	Oneonta	639	Morgan	77,306	Decatur	570
Bullock	11,824	Union Springs	615	Perry	15,388	Marion	734
Butler	22,007	Greenville	773	Pickens	20,326	Carrollton	887
Calhoun	103,092	Anniston	611	Pike	25,038	Troy	673
Chambers	36,356	Lafayette	597	Randolph	18,331	Wedowee	581
Cherokee	15,606	Centre	556	Russell	45,394	Phenix City	627
Chilton	25,180	Clanton	699	St. Clair	27,956	Ashville & Pell City	640
Choctaw	16,589	Butler	911	Shelby	38,037	Columbiana	798
Clarke	26,724	Grove Hill	1,232	Sumter	16,974	Livingston	915
Clay	12,636	Ashland	603	Talladega	65,280	Talladega	750
Cleburne	10,996	Heflin	574	Tallapoosa	33,840	Dadeville	704
Coffee	34,872	Elba	677	Tuscaloosa	116,029	Tuscaloosa	1,333
Colbert	49,632	Tuscumbia	596	Walker	56,246	Jasper	805
Conecuh	15,645	Evergreen	850	Washington	16,241	Chatom	1,066
Coosa	10,662	Rockford	650	Wilcox	16,303	Camden	899
Covington	34,079	Andalusia	984	Winston	16,654	Double Springs	615
Crenshaw	13,188	Luverne	611				
Cullman	52,445	Cullman	730				
Dale	52,938	Ozark	559		**Alaska**		
Dallas	55,296	Selma	976				
De Kalb	41,981	Fort Payne	778	*(29 divisions, 566,432 sq. mi. land., pop. 302,173)*			
Elmore	33,661	Wetumpka	624				
Escambia	34,912	Brewton	962				
Etowah	94,144	Gadsden	555			Pop. April 1, 1970	Land Area Sq. Mi.
Fayette	16,252	Fayette	627	**Census Division**			
Franklin	23,933	Russellville	644				
Geneva	21,924	Geneva	577	Aleutian Islands		8,057	14,583
Greene	10,650	Eutaw	627	Anchorage		126,385	927
Hale	15,888	Greensboro	662	Angoon		503	2,825
Henry	13,254	Abbeville	554	Barrow		2,663	57,587
Houston	56,574	Dothan	575				
Jackson	39,202	Scottsboro	1,079				
Jefferson	644,991	Birmingham	1,115				
Lamar	14,335	Vernon	605				
Lauderdale	68,111	Florence	662				

Census Division	Pop. April 1, 1970	Land Area Sq. Mi.
Bethel	7,767	19,642
Bristol Bay Borough	1,147	531
Bristol Bay	3,485	36,565
Cordova-McCarthy	1,857	15,481
Fairbanks	45,864	7,074
Haines	1,504	2,128
Juneau	13,556	1,286
Kenai-Cook Inlet	14,250	12,474
Ketchikan	10,041	1,345
Kobuk	4,434	42,978
Kodiak	9,409	5,375
Kuskokwim	2,306	56,562
Matanuska-Susitna	6,509	25,730
Nome	5,749	24,968
Outer Ketchikan	1,676	3,762
Prince of Wales	2,106	3,485
Seward	2,336	3,727
Sitka	6,106	2,296
Skagway-Yakutat	2,157	8,646
Southeast Fairbanks	4,179	17,713
Upper Yukon	1,684	84,142
Valdez-Chitina-Whittier	3,098	18,619
Wade Hampton	3,917	16,770
Wrangell-Petersburg	4,913	6,178
Yukon-Koyukuk	4,758	73,053

County	Pop. April 1, 1970	County Seats or Court House	Land Area Sq. Mi.

Arizona

(14 counties, 113,417 sq. mi. land; pop. 1,772,482)

County	Pop.	County Seats	Land Area
Apache	32,304	Saint Johns	11,171
Cochise	61,918	Bisbee	6,256
Coconino	48,326	Flagstaff	18,540
Gila	29,255	Globe	4,748
Graham	16,578	Safford	4,618
Greenlee	10,330	Clifton	1,879
Maricopa	968,487	Phoenix	9,155
Mohave	25,857	Kingman	13,217
Navajo	47,559	Holbrook	9,910
Pima	351,667	Tucson	9,240
Pinal	68,579	Florence	5,364
Santa Cruz	13,966	Nogales	1,246
Yavapai	37,005	Prescott	8,091
Yuma	60,827	Yuma	9,983

Arkansas

(75 counties, 51,945 sq. mi. land; pop. 1,923,295)

County	Pop.	County Seats	Land Area
Arkansas	23,347	DeWitt & Stuttgart	1,015
Ashley	24,976	Hamburg	928
Baxter	15,319	Moutain Home	537
Benton	50,476	Bentonville	851
Boone	19,073	Harrison	586
Bradley	12,778	Warren	651
Calhoun	5,573	Hampton	629
Carroll	12,301	Berryville and Eureka Sprg.	626
Chicot	18,164	Lake Village	643
Clark	21,537	Arkadelphia	878
Clay	18,771	Corning; Piggott	639
Cleburne	10,349	Heber Springs	554
Cleveland	6,605	Rison	601
Columbia	25,952	Magnolia	768
Conway	16,805	Morrilton	561
Craighead	52,068	Jonesboro and Lake City	716
Crawford	25,677	Van Buren	596
Crittenden	48,106	Marion	608
Cross	19,783	Wynne	625
Dallas	10,022	Fordyce	672
Desha	18,761	Arkansas City	736
Drew	15,157	Monticello	832
Faulkner	31,578	Conway	641
Franklin	11,301	Charleston and Ozark	613
Fulton	7,699	Salem	608
Garland	54,131	Hot Spgs. Nat'l Pk.	658
Grant	9,711	Sheridan	631
Greene	24,765	Paragould	579
Hempstead	19,308	Hope	726
Hot Spring	21,963	Malvern	621
Howard	11,412	Nashville	569
Independence	22,723	Batesville	752
Izard	7,381	Melbourne	574
Jackson	20,452	Newport	629
Jefferson	85,329	Pine Bluff	873
Johnson	13,630	Clarksville	673
Lafayette	10,018	Lewisville	523

County	Pop. April 1, 1970	County Seats or Court House	Land Area Sq. Mi.
Lee	18,884	Marianna	608
Lincoln	12,913	Star City	563
Little River	11,194	Ashdown	486
Logan	16,789	Booneville & Paris	718
Lonoke	26,249	Lonoke	796
Madison	9,453	Huntsville	832
Marion	7,000	Yellville	584
Miller	33,385	Texarkana	623
Mississippi	62,060	Blytheville and Osceola	904
Monroe	15,657	Clarendon	607
Montgomery	5,821	Mount Ida	775
Nevada	10,111	Prescott	616
Newton	5,844	Jasper	822
Ouachita	30,896	Camden	736
Perry	5,634	Perryville	551
Phillips	40,046	Helena	686
Pike	8,711	Murfreesboro	600
Poinsett	26,843	Harrisburg	760
Polk	13,297	Mena	859
Pope	28,607	Russellville	812
Prairie	10,249	Des Arc and De Valls Bluff	661
Pulaski	287,189	Little Rock	765
Randolph	12,645	Pocahontas	647
St. Francis	30,799	Forest City	635
Saline	36,107	Benton	724
Scott	8,207	Waldron	898
Searcy	7,731	Marshall	664
Sebastian	79,237	Fort Smith; Greenwood	527
Sevier	11,272	De Queen	522
Sharp	8,233	Ash Flat	581
Stone	6,838	Mountain View	608
Union	45,428	El Dorado	1,050
Van Buren	8,275	Clinton	699
Washington	77,370	Fayetteville	958
White	39,253	Searcy	1,041
Woodruff	11,566	Augusta	591
Yell	14,208	Danville and Dardanelle	929

California

(58 counties, 156,361 sq. mi. land; pop. 19,953,134)

County	Pop.	County Seats	Land Area
Alameda	1,073,184	Oakland	733
Alpine	484	Markleeville	727
Amador	11,821	Jackson	583
Butte	101,969	Oroville	1,645
Calaveras	13,585	San Andreas	1,024
Colusa	12,430	Colusa	1,152
Contra Costa	555,805	Martinez	735
Del Norte	14,580	Crescent City	1,007
El Dorado	43,833	Placerville	1,715
Fresno	413,329	Fkresno	5,966
Glenn	17,521	Willows	1,314
Humboldt	99,692	Eureka	3,586
Imperial	74,492	El Centro	4,241
Inyo	15,571	Independence	10,130
Kern	329,281	Bakersfield	8,152
Kings	66,717	Hanford	1,396
Lake	19,548	Lakeport	1,261
Lassen	16,796	Susanville	4,561
Los Angeles	7,040,697	Los Angeles	4,069
Madera	41,519	Madera	2,145
Marin	206,758	San Rafael	520
Mariposa	6,015	Mariposa	1,453
Mendocino	51,101	Ukiah	3,511
Merced	104,629	Merced	1,958
Modoc	7,469	Alturas	4,097
Mono	4,016	Bridgeport	3,027
Monterey	247,450	Salinas	3,324
Napa	79,140	Napa	787
Nevada	26,346	Nevada City	973
Orange	1,420,676	Santa Ana	782
Placer	77,632	Auburn	1,431
Plumas	11,707	Quincy	2,566
Riverside	459,074	Riverside	7,176
Sacramento	634,190	Sacramento	975
San Benito	18,226	Hollister	1,396
San Bernardino	682,233	San Bernardino	20,117
San Diego	1,357,854	San Diego	4,261
San Francisco	715,674	San Francisco	45
San Joaquin	289,564	Stockton	1,412
San Luis Obispo	105,690	San Luis Obispo	3,183
San Mateo	556,605	Redwood City	447
Santa Barbara	264,324	Santa Barbara	2,737
Santa Clara	1,066,174	San Jose	1,300
Santa Cruz	123,790	Santa Cruz	440
Shasta	77,640	Redding	3,788
Sierra	2,365	Downieville	958
Siskiyou	33,225	Yreka	6,262
Solano	171,989	Fairfield	823
Sonoma	204,885	Santa Rosa	1,604
Stanislaus	194,506	Modesto	1,511

County	Pop. April 1, 1970	County Seats or Court House	Land Area Sq. Mi.
Sutter	41,935	Yuba City	603
Tehama	29,517	Red Bluff	2,982
Trinity	7,615	Weaverville	3,173
Tulare	188,322	Visalia	4,812
Tuolumne	22,169	Sonora	2,252
Ventura	378,497	Ventura	1,863
Yolo	91,788	Woodland	1,028
Yuba	44,736	Marysville	639

Colorado

(63 counties, 103,766 sq. mi. land; pop. 2,207,259)

County	Pop.	County Seat	Land
Adams	185,789	Brighton	1,237
Alamosa	11,422	Alamosa	719
Arapahoe	162,142	Littleton	797
Archuleta	2,733	Pagosa Springs	1,364
Baca	5,674	Springfield	2,563
Bent	6,493	Las Animas	1,519
Boulder	131,889	Boulder	748
Chaffee	10,162	Salida	1,038
Cheyenne	2,396	Cheyenne Wells	1,772
Clear Creek	4,819	Georgetown	394
Conejos	7,846	Conejos	1,268
Costilla	3,091	San Luis	1,213
Crowley	3,086	Ordway	802
Custer	1,120	Westcliffe	737
Delta	15,286	Delta	1,154
Denver	514,678	Denver	95
Dolores	1,641	Dove Creek	1,026
Douglas	8,407	Castle Rock	843
Eagle	7,498	Eagle	1,681
Elbert	3,903	Kiowa	1,864
El Paso	235,972	Colorado Springs	2,157
Fremont	21,942	Canon City	1,561
Garfield	14,821	Glenwood Springs	2,996
Gilpin	1,272	Central City	148
Grand	4,107	Hot Sulphur Springs	1,854
Gunnison	7,578	Gunnison	3,220
Hinsdale	202	Lake City	1,054
Huerfano	6,590	Walsenburg	1,574
Jackson	1,811	Walden	1,622
Jefferson	235,300	Golden	783
Kiowa	2,029	Eads	1,767
Kit Carson	7,530	Burlington	2,171
Lake	8,282	Leadville	379
La Plata	19,199	Durango	1,683
Larimer	89,900	Fort Collins	2,611
Las Animas	15,744	Trinidad	4,794
Lincoln	4,836	Hugo	2,593
Logan	18,852	Sterling	1,822
Mesa	54,374	Grand Junction	3,301
Mineral	786	Creede	921
Moffat	6,525	Craig	4,743
Montezuma	12,952	Cortez	2,094
Montrose	18,366	Montrose	2,238
Morgan	20,105	Fort Morgan	1,278
Otero	23,523	LaJunta	1,254
Ouray	1,546	Ouray	540
Park	2,185	Fairplay	2,162
Phillips	4,131	Holyoke	680
Pitkin	6,185	Aspen	973
Prowers	13,258	Lamar	1,621
Pueblo	118,238	Pueblo	2,405
Rio Blanco	4,842	Meeker	3,263
Rio Grande	10,494	Del Norte	915
Routt	6,592	Steamboat Spgs	2,330
Saguache	3,827	Saguache	3,144
San Juan	831	Silverton	391
San Miguel	1,949	Telluride	1,283
Sedgwick	3,405	Julesburg	544
Summit	2,665	Breckenridge	604
Teller	3,316	Cripple Creek	553
Washington	5,550	Akron	2,526
Weld	89,297	Greeley	4,002
Yuma	8,544	Wray	2,379

Connecticut

(8 counties, 4,862 sq. mi. land; pop. 3,032,217)

County	Pop.	County Seat	Land
Fairfield	792,814	Bridgeport	626
Hartford	816,737	Hartford	739
Litchfield	144,091	Litchfield	925
Middlesex	115,018	Middletown	372
New Haven	744,948	New Haven	604
New London	230,654	Norwich	667
Tolland	103,440	Rockville	416
Windham	84,515	Putnam	514

Delaware

(3 counties, 1,982 sq. mi. land; pop. 548,104)

County	Pop.	County Seat	Land
Kent	81,892	Dover	594
New Castle	385,856	Wilmington	438
Sussex	80,356	Georgetown	950

District of Columbia

(61 sq. mi. land; pop. 756,510)

Florida

(67 counties, 54,090 sq. mi. land; pop. 6,789,443)

County	Pop.	County Seat	Land
Alachua	104,764	Gainesville	916
Baker	9,242	Macclenny	585
Bay	75,283	Panama City	747
Bradford	14,625	Starke	294
Brevard	230,006	Titusville	1,011
Broward	620,100	Fort Lauderdale	1,219
Calhoun	7,624	Blountstown	561
Charlotte	27,559	Punta Gorda	703
Citrus	19,196	Inverness	560
Clay	32,059	Green Cove Spgs	593
Collier	38,040	Naples	2,006
Columbia	25,250	Lake City	784
Dade	1,267,792	Miami	2,042
De Soto	13,060	Arcadia	648
Dixie	5,480	Cross City	692
Duval	528,865	Jacksonville	766
Escambia	205,334	Pensacola	665
Flagler	4,454	Bunnell	487
Franklin	7,065	Apalachicola	536
Gadsden	39,184	Quincy	512
Gilchrist	3,551	Trenton	346
Glades	3,669	Moore Haven	753
Gulf	10,096	Port St. Joe	565
Hamilton	7,787	Jasper	514
Hardee	14,889	Wauchula	629
Hendry	11,859	La Belle	1,187
Hernando	17,004	Brooksville	484
Highlands	29,507	Sebring	997
Hillsborough	490,265	Tampa	1,038
Holmes	10,720	Bonifay	482
Indian River	35,992	Vero Beach	506
Jackson	34,434	Marianna	935
Jefferson	8,778	Monticello	605
Lafayette	2,892	Mayo	549
Lake	69,305	Tavares	961
Lee	105,216	Fort Myers	785
Leon	103,047	Tallahassee	670
Levy	12,756	Bronson	1,083
Liberty	3,379	Bristol	839
Madison	13,481	Madison	703
Manatee	97,115	Bradenton	739
Marion	69,030	Ocala	1,600
Martin	28,035	Stuart	556
Monroe	52,586	Key West	1,034
Nassau	20,626	Fernandina Beach	650
Okaloosa	88,187	Crestview	944
Okeechobee	11,233	Okeechobee	777
Orange	344,311	Orlando	910
Osceola	25,267	Kissimmee	1,313
Palm Beach	348,993	West Palm Beach	2,023
Pasco	75,955	Dade City	742
Pinellas	522,329	Clearwater	265
Polk	228,026	Bartow	1,858
Putnam	36,424	Palatka	779
St. Johns	31,035	Saint Augustine	605
St. Lucie	50,836	Fort Pierce	584
Santa Rosa	37,741	Milton	1,032
Sarasota	120,413	Sarasota	587
Seminole	83,692	Sanford	305
Sumter	14,839	Bushnell	555
Suwannee	15,559	Live Oak	686
Taylor	13,641	Perry	1,051
Union	8,112	Lake Butler	241
Volusia	169,487	De Land	1,062
Wakulla	6,308	Crawfordville	601
Walton	16,087	De Funiak Springs	1,053
Washington	11,453	Chipley	585

Georgia

(159 counties, 58,073 sq. mi. land; pop. 4,589,575)

County	Pop.	County Seat	Land
Appling	12,726	Baxley	513
Atkinson	5,879	Pearson	318
Bacon	8,233	Alma	293
Baker	3,875	Newton	355
Baldwin	34,240	Milledgeville	255
Banks	6,833	Homer	231
Barrow	16,859	Winder	171
Bartow	32,911	Cartersville	461
Ben Hill	13,171	Fitzgerald	255
Berrien	11,556	Nashville	468

County	Pop. April 1, 1970	County Seats or Court House	Land Area Sq. Mi.	County	Pop. April 1, 1970	County Seats or Court House	Land Area Sq. Mi.
Bibb	143,418	Macon	254	Paulding	17,520	Dallas	318
Bleckley	10,291	Cochran	219	Peach	15,990	Fort Valley	151
Brantley	5,940	Nahunta	447	Pickens	9,620	Jasper	225
Brooks	13,743	Quitman	491	Pierce	9,281	Blackshear	342
Bryan	6,539	Pembroke	443	Pike	7,316	Zebulon	230
Bulloch	31,585	Statesboro	685	Polk	29,656	Cedartown	312
Burke	18,255	Waynesboro	831	Pulaski	8,066	Hawkinsville	253
Butts	10,560	Jackson	185	Putnam	9,394	Eatonton	339
Calhoun	6,606	Morgan	289	Quitman	2,180	Georgetown	156
Camden	11,334	Woodbine	653	Rabun	8,327	Clayton	368
Candler	6,412	Metter	250	Randolph	8,734	Cuthbert	436
Carroll	45,404	Carrollton	495	Richmond	162,437	Augusta	323
Catoosa	28,271	Ringgold	167	Rockdale	18,152	Conyers	128
Charlton	5,680	Folkston	796	Schley	3,097	Ellaville	162
Chatham	187,816	Savannah	445	Screven	12,591	Sylvania	651
Chattahoochee	25,813	Cusseta	253	Seminole	7,059	Donalsonville	246
Chattooga	20,541	Summerville	317	Spalding	39,514	Griffin	201
Cherokee	31,059	Canton	415	Stephens	20,331	Toccoa	173
Clarke	65,177	Athens	116	Stewart	6,511	Lumpkin	452
Clay	3,636	Fort Gaines	200	Sumter	26,931	Americus	488
Clayton	98,126	Jonesboro	149	Talbot	6,625	Talbotton	390
Clinch	6,405	Homerville	797	Taliaferro	2,423	Crawfordville	195
Cobb	196,793	Marietta	343	Tattnall	16,557	Reidsville	490
Coffee	22,828	Douglas	612	Taylor	7,865	Butler	403
Colquitt	32,298	Moultrie	563	Telfair	11,394	MacRae	440
Columbia	22,327	Appling	290	Terrell	11,416	Dawson	329
Cook	12,129	Adel	233	Thomas	34,562	Thomasville	541
Coweta	32,310	Newnan	442	Tift	27,288	Tifton	266
Crawford	5,748	Knoxville	315	Toombs	19,151	Lyons	368
Crisp	18,087	Cordele	292	Towns	4,565	Hiawassee	166
Dade	9,910	Trenton	168	Treutlen	5,647	Soperton	194
Dawson	3,639	Dawsonville	211	Troup	44,466	La Grange	415
Decatur	22,310	Bainbridge	575	Turner	8,790	Ashburn	293
De Kalb	415,387	Decatur	269	Twiggs	8,222	Jeffersonville	364
Dodge	15,658	Eastman	498	Union	6,811	Blairsville	309
Dooly	10,404	Vienna	395	Upson	23,505	Thomaston	334
Dougherty	89,639	Albany	324	Walker	50,691	La Fayette	445
Douglas	28,659	Douglasville	202	Walton	23,404	Monroe	330
Early	12,682	Blakely	524	Ware	33,525	Waycross	912
Echols	1,924	Statenville	425	Warren	6,669	Warrenton	284
Effingham	13,632	Springfield	480	Washington	17,480	Sandersville	674
Elbert	17,262	Elberton	358	Wayne	17,858	Jesup	645
Emanuel	18,357	Swainsboro	686	Webster	2,362	Preston	195
Evans	7,290	Claxton	186	Wheeler	4,596	Alamo	306
Fannin	13,357	Blue Ridge	394	White	7,742	Cleveland	243
Fayette	11,364	Fayetteville	199	Whitfield	55,108	Dalton	281
Floyd	73,742	Rome	514	Wilcox	6,998	Abbeville	383
Forsyth	16,928	Cumming	219	Wilkes	18,184	Washington	468
Franklin	12,784	Carnesville	263	Wilkinson	9,393	Irwinton	458
Fulton	607,592	Atlanta	530	Worth	14,770	Sylvester	579
Gilmer	8,956	Ellijay	439				
Glascock	2,280	Gibson	143				
Glynn	50,528	Brunswick	412				
Gordon	23,570	Calhoun	358				
Grady	17,826	Cairo	466				
Greene	10,212	Greensboro	403				
Gwinnett	72,349	Lawrenceville	437				
Habersham	20,691	Clarkesville	282				
Hall	59,405	Gainesville	378				
Hancock	9,019	Sparta	478				
Haralson	15,927	Buchanan	285				
Harris	11,520	Hamilton	465				
Hart	15,814	Hartwell	231				
Heard	5,354	Franklin	297				
Henry	23,724	McDonough	331				
Houston	62,924	Perry	380				
Irwin	8,036	Ocilla	372				
Jackson	21,093	Jefferson	346				
Jasper	5,760	Monticello	373				
Jeff Davis	9,425	Hazlehurst	331				
Jefferson	17,174	Louisville	530				
Jenkins	8,332	Millen	351				
Johnson	7,727	Wrightsville	313				
Jones	12,218	Gray	402				
Lamar	10,688	Barnesville	181				
Lanier	5,031	Lakeland	177				
Laurens	32,738	Dublin	810				
Lee	7,044	Leesburg	355				
Liberty	17,569	Hinesville	514				
Lincoln	5,895	Lincolnton	193				
Long	3,746	Ludowici	402				
Lowndes	55,112	Valdosta	508				
Lumpkin	8,728	Dahlonega	292				
McDuffie	15,276	Thomson	253				
McIntosh	7,371	Darien	426				
Macon	12,933	Oglethorpe	403				
Madison	13,517	Danielsville	281				
Marion	5,099	Buena Vista	365				
Meriwether	19,461	Greenville	499				
Miller	6,424	Colquitt	287				
Mitchell	18,956	Camilla	510				
Monroe	10,991	Forsyth	398				
Montgomery	6,099	Mount Vernon	237				
Morgan	9,904	Madison	356				
Murray	12,986	Chatsworth	342				
Muscogee	167,377	Columbus	220				
Newton	26,282	Covington	271				
Oconee	7,915	Watkinsville	186				
Oglethorpe	7,598	Lexington	435				

Hawaii

(4 counties, 6,425 sq. mi. land; pop. 769,913)

County	Pop. April 1, 1970	County Seats or Court House	Land Area Sq. Mi.
Hawaii	63,468	Hilo	4,037
Honolulu	630,528	Honolulu	596
Kauai	29,761	Lihue	619
Maui*	46,156	Wailuku	1,173

*Includes population of Kalawao County (279) shown separately in 1960 but included with Maui County in 1970.

Idaho

(44 counties, 82,677 sq. mi. land; pop. 713,008)

County	Pop. April 1, 1970	County Seats or Court House	Land Area Sq. Mi.
Ada	112,230	Boise	1,043
Adams	2,877	Council	1,371
Bannock	52,200	Pocatello	1,122
Bear Lake	5,801	Paris	984
Benewah	6,230	Saint Maries	788
Bingham	29,167	Blackfoot	2,084
Blaine	5,749	Hailey	2,647
Boise	1,763	Idaho City	1,910
Bonner	15,560	Sandpoint	1,733
Bonneville	52,457	Idaho Falls	1,836
Boundary	5,484	Bonners Ferry	1,275
Butte	2,925	Arco	2,239
Camas	728	Fairfield	1,054
Canyon	61,288	Caldwell	578
Caribou	6,534	Soda Springs	1,746
Cassia	17,017	Burley	2,544
Clark	741	Dubois	1,751
Clearwater	10,871	Orofino	2,521
Custer	2,967	Challis	4,929
Elmore	17,479	Mountain Home	3,048
Franklin	7,373	Preston	664
Fremont	8,710	Saint Anthony	1,864
Gem	9,387	Emmett	555
Gooding	8,645	Gooding	720
Idaho	12,891	Grangeville	8,516
Jefferson	11,740	Rigby	1,096
Jerome	10,253	Jerome	595

County	Pop. April 1, 1970	County Seats or Court House	Land Area Sq. Mi.
Kootenai	35,332	Coeur d'Alene	1,249
Latah	24,898	Moscow	1,090
Lemhi	5,566	Salmon	4,580
Lewis	3,867	Nezperce	476
Lincoln	3,057	Shoshone	1,203
Madison	13,452	Rexburg	473
Minidoka	15,731	Rupert	750
Nez Perce	30,376	Lewiston	844
Oneida	2,864	Malad City	1,191
Owyhee	6,422	Murphy	7,641
Payette	12,401	Payette	402
Power	4,864	American Falls	1,413
Shoshone	19,718	Wallace	2,609
Teton	2,351	Driggs	457
Twin Falls	41,807	Twin Falls	1,947
Valley	3,609	Cascade	3,676
Washington	7,633	Weiser	1,462

Illinois

(102 counties, 55,748 sq. mi. land; pop. 11,113,976)

County	Pop. April 1, 1970	County Seats or Court House	Land Area Sq. Mi.
Adams	70,861	Quincy	862
Alexander	12,015	Cairo	229
Bond	14,012	Greenville	378
Boone	25,440	Belvidere	283
Brown	5,586	Mount Sterling	306
Bureau	38,541	Princeton	866
Calhoun	5,675	Hardin	247
Carroll	19,276	Mount Carroll	456
Cass	14,219	Virginia	371
Champaign	163,281	Urbana	1,000
Christian	35,948	Taylorville	709
Clark	16,216	Marshall	505
Clay	14,735	Louisville	464
Clinton	28,315	Carlyle	434
Coles	47,815	Charleston	506
Cook	5,493,766	Chicago	954
Crawford	19,824	Robinson	443
Cumberland	9,772	Toledo	347
De Kalb	71,654	Sycamore	636
De Witt	16,975	Clinton	399
Douglas	18,997	Tuscola	420
Du Page	490,822	Wheaton	331
Edgar	21,591	Paris	628
Edwards	7,090	Albion	225
Effingham	24,608	Effingham	481
Fayette	20,752	Vandalia	703
Ford	16,382	Paxton	488
Franklin	38,329	Benton	434
Fulton	41,900	Lewiston	877
Gallatin	7,418	Shawneetown	328
Greene	17,014	Carrollton	543
Grundy	26,535	Morris	432
Hamilton	8,665	McLeansboro	435
Hancock	23,664	Carthage	797
Hardin	4,914	Elizabethtown	183
Henderson	8,451	Oquawka	376
Henry	53,217	Cambridge	826
Iroquois	33,532	Watseka	1,122
Jackson	55,008	Murphysboro	605
Jasper	10,741	Newton	495
Jefferson	31,848	Mount Vernon	573
Jersey	18,492	Jerseyville	376
Jo Daviess	21,766	Galena	606
Johnson	7,550	Vienna	345
Kane	251,005	Geneva	520
Kankakee	97,250	Kankakee	678
Kendall	26,374	Yorkville	320
Knox	60,939	Galesburg	728
Lake	382,638	Waukegan	457
La Salle	111,409	Ottawa	1,150
Lawrence	17,522	Lawrenceville	374
Lee	37,947	Dixon	728
Livingston	40,690	Pontiac	1,043
Logan	33,538	Lincoln	622
Mc Donough	36,653	Macomb	582
Mc Henry	111,555	Woodstock	610
Mc Lean	104,389	Bloomington	1,173
Macon	125,010	Decatur	578
Macoupin	44,557	Carlinville	872
Madison	250,911	Edwardsville	733
Marion	38,986	Salem	579
Marshall	13,302	Lacon	391
Mason	16,180	Havana	541
Massac	13,889	Metropolis	245
Menard	9,685	Petersburg	312
Mercer	17,294	Aledo	556
Monroe	18,831	Waterloo	382
Montgomery	30,260	Hillsboro	705
Morgan	36,174	Jacksonville	561
Moultrie	13,263	Sullivan	326
Ogle	42,867	Oregon	758
Peoria	195,318	Peoria	623
Perry	19,757	Pinckneyville	439
Piatt	15,509	Monticello	437
Pike	19,185	Pittsfield	828
Pope	3,857	Golconda	381
Pulaski	8,741	Mound City	204
Putnam	5,007	Hennepin	160
Randolph	31,379	Chester	594
Richland	16,829	Olney	364
Rock Island	166,734	Rock Island	424
St. Clair	285,199	Belleville	673
Saline	25,721	Harrisburg	383
Sangamon	161,335	Springfield	879
Schuyler	8,135	Rushville	434
Scott	6,096	Winchester	251
Shelby	22,589	Shelbyville	752
Stark	7,510	Toulon	291
Stephenson	48,861	Freeport	568
Tazewell	118,649	Pekin	652
Union	16,071	Jonesboro	416
Vermilion	97,047	Danville	899
Wabash	12,841	Mt. Carmel	222
Warren	21,595	Monmouth	541
Washington	13,780	Nashville	564
Wayne	17,004	Fairfield	715
White	17,312	Carmi	502
Whiteside	62,877	Morrison	687
Will	247,825	Joliet	847
Williamson	49,021	Marion	429
Winnebago	246,623	Rockford	519
Woodford	28,012	Eureka	528

Indiana

(92 counties, 36,097 sq. mi. land; pop. 5,193,669)

County	Pop. April 1, 1970	County Seats or Court House	Land Area Sq. Mi.
Adams	26,871	Decatur	345
Allen	280,455	Fort Wayne	671
Bartholomew	57,022	Columbus	402
Benton	11,262	Fowler	409
Blackford	15,888	Hartford City	167
Boone	30,870	Lebanon	427
Brown	9,057	Nashville	319
Carroll	17,734	Delphi	374
Cass	40,456	Logansport	415
Clark	75,876	Jeffersonville	384
Clay	23,933	Brazil	364
Clinton	30,547	Frankfort	407
Crawford	8,033	English	312
Daviess	26,602	Washington	430
Dearborn	29,430	Lawrenceburg	306
Decatur	22,738	Greensburg	370
De Kalb	30,837	Auburn	366
Delaware	129,219	Muncie	396
Dubois	30,934	Jasper	433
Elkhart	126,529	Goshen	468
Fayette	26,216	Connersville	215
Floyd	55,622	New Albany	149
Fountain	18,257	Covington	397
Franklin	16,943	Brookville	394
Fulton	16,984	Rochester	368
Gibson	30,444	Princeton	498
Grant	83,955	Marion	421
Greene	26,894	Bloomfield	549
Hamilton	54,532	Noblesville	401
Hancock	35,096	Greenfield	305
Harrison	20,423	Corydon	479
Hendricks	53,974	Danville	417
Henry	52,603	New Castle	400
Howard	83,198	Kokomo	293
Huntington	34,970	Huntington	369
Jackson	33,187	Brownstown	509
Jasper	20,429	Rensselaer	562
Jay	23,575	Portland	386
Jefferson	27,006	Madison	366
Jennings	19,454	Vernon	377
Johnson	61,138	Franklin	315
Knox	41,546	Vincennes	516
Kosciusko	48,127	Warsaw	540
Lagrange	20,890	Lagrange	381
Lake	546,253	Crown Point	513
La Porte	105,342	La Porte	607
Lawrence	38,038	Bedford	459
Madison	138,522	Anderson	453
Marion	793,769	Indianapolis	392
Marshall	34,986	Plymouth	443
Martin	10,969	Shoals	345
Miami	39,246	Peru	377
Monroe	85,221	Bloomington	386
Montgomery	33,930	Crawfordsville	507
Morgan	44,176	Martinsville	406
Newton	11,606	Kentland	413
Noble	31,382	Albion	412
Ohio	4,289	Rising Sun	87
Orange	16,968	Paoli	405
Owen	12,163	Spencer	390
Parke	14,600	Rockville	445
Perry	19,075	Cannelton	384
Pike	12,281	Petersburg	335
Porter	87,114	Valparaiso	425
Posey	21,740	Mount Vernon	412

County	Pop. April 1, 1970	County Seats or Court House	Land Area Sq. Mi.	County	Pop. April 1, 1970	County Seats or Court House	Land Area Sq. Mi.
Pulaski	12,534	Winamac	433	Marshall	41,076	Marshalltown	574
Putnam	26,932	Greencastle	490	Mills	11,832	Glenwood	447
Randolph	28,915	Winchester	457	Mitchell	13,108	Osage	467
Ripley	21,138	Versailles	442	Monona	12,069	Onawa	699
Rush	20,352	Rushville	409	Monroe	9,357	Albia	435
St. Joseph	245,045	South Bend	466	Montgomery	12,781	Red Oak	422
Scott	17,144	Scottsburg	193	Muscatine	37,181	Muscatine	443
Shelby	37,797	Shelbyville	409	O'Brien	17,522	Primghar	575
Spencer	17,134	Rockport	396	Osceola	8,555	Sibley	398
Starke	19,280	Knox	310	Page	18,537	Clarinda	535
Steuben	20,159	Angola	309	Palo Alto	13,289	Emmetsburg	561
Sullivan	19,889	Sullivan	457	Plymouth	24,322	Le Mars	863
Switzerland	6,306	Vevay	221	Pocahontas	12,793	Pocahontas	581
Tippecanoe	109,378	Lafayette	500	Polk	286,130	Des Moines	578
Tipton	16,650	Tipton	261	Pottawattamie	86,991	Council Bluffs	963
Union	6,582	Liberty	168	Poweshiek	18,803	Montezuma	589
Vanderburgh	168,772	Evansville	241	Ringgold	6,373	Mount Ayr	538
Vermilion	16,793	Newport	263	Sac	15,573	Sac City	578
Vigo	114,528	Terre Haute	415	Scott	142,687	Davenport	454
Wabash	35,553	Wabash	398	Shelby	15,528	Harlan	587
Warren	8,705	Williamsport	368	Sioux	27,996	Orange City	766
Warrick	27,972	Boonville	391	Story	62,783	Nevada	568
Washington	19,278	Salem	516	Tama	20,147	Toledo	720
Wayne	79,190	Richmond	405	Taylor	8,790	Bedford	528
Wells	23,821	Bluffton	368	Union	13,557	Creston	425
White	20,995	Monticello	497	Van Buren	8,643	Keosauqua	487
Whitley	23,395	Columbia City	337	Wapello	42,149	Ottumwa	437
				Warren	27,432	Indianola	558
				Washington	18,967	Washington	568
				Wayne	8,405	Corydon	532
				Webster	48,391	Fort Dodge	718
				Winnebago	12,990	Forest City	401
				Winneshiek	21,758	Decorah	688
				Woodbury	103,052	Sioux City	871
				Worth	8,984	Northwood	400
				Wright	17,294	Clarion	577

Iowa

(99 counties; 55,941 sq. mi. land; pop. 2,825,041)

County	Pop.	County Seat	Land Area
Adair	9,487	Greenfield	569
Adams	6,322	Corning	426
Allamakee	14,968	Waukon	636
Appanoose	15,007	Centerville	523
Audubon	9,595	Audubon	448
Benton	22,885	Vinton	718
Black Hawk	132,916	Waterloo	568
Boone	26,470	Boone	573
Bremer	22,737	Waverly	439
Buchanan	21,762	Independence	568
Buena Vista	20,693	Storm Lake	572
Butler	16,953	Allison	582
Calhoun	14,292	Rockwell City	571
Carroll	22,912	Carroll	574
Cass	17,007	Atlantic	559
Cedar	17,655	Tipton	585
Cerro Gordo	49,223	Mason City	575
Cherokee	17,269	Cherokee	573
Chickasaw	14,969	New Hampton	505
Clarke	7,581	Osceola	429
Clay	18,464	Spencer	580
Clayton	20,606	Elkader	779
Clinton	56,749	Clinton	693
Crawford	19,116	Denison	716
Dallas	26,085	Adel	597
Davis	8,207	Bloomfield	509
Decatur	9,737	Leon	530
Delaware	18,770	Manchester	572
Des Moines	46,982	Burlington	408
Dickinson	12,565	Spirit Lake	380
Dubuque	90,609	Dubuque	612
Emmet	14,009	Estherville	394
Fayette	26,898	West Union	728
Floyd	19,860	Charles City	503
Franklin	13,255	Hampton	586
Fremont	9,282	Sidney	524
Greene	12,716	Jefferson	569
Grundy	14,119	Grundy Center	501
Guthrie	12,243	Guthrie Center	596
Hamilton	18,383	Webster City	577
Hancock	13,506	Garner	570
Hardin	22,248	Eldora	574
Harrison	16,240	Logan	696
Henry	18,114	Mount Pleasant	440
Howard	11,442	Cresco	471
Humboldt	12,519	Dakota City	435
Ida	9,283	Ida Grove	431
Iowa	15,419	Marengo	584
Jackson	20,839	Maquoketa	644
Jasper	35,425	Newton	731
Jefferson	15,774	Fairfield	436
Johnson	72,127	Iowa City	619
Jones	19,868	Anamosa	585
Keokuk	13,943	Sigourney	579
Kossuth	22,937	Algona	979
Lee	42,996	Fort Madison and Keokuk	527
Linn	163,213	Cedar Rapids	717
Louisa	10,682	Wapello	403
Lucas	10,163	Chariton	434
Lyon	13,340	Rock Rapids	588
Madison	11,558	Winterset	564
Mahaska	22,177	Oskaloosa	572
Marion	26,352	Knoxville	498

Kansas

(105 counties, 81,787 sq. mi. land; pop. 2,249,071)

County	Pop.	County Seat	Land Area
Allen	15,043	Iola	506
Anderson	8,501	Garnett	577
Atchison	19,165	Atchison	427
Barber	7,016	Medicine Lodge	1,146
Barton	30,663	Great Bend	894
Bourbon	15,215	Fort Scott	639
Brown	11,685	Hiawatha	577
Butler	38,658	El Dorado	1,442
Chase	3,408	Cottonwood Falls	774
Chautauqua	4,642	Sedan	647
Cherokee	21,549	Columbus	586
Cheyenne	4,256	Saint Francis	1,027
Clark	2,896	Ashland	983
Clay	9,890	Clay Center	635
Cloud	13,466	Concordia	711
Coffey	7,397	Burlington	617
Comanche	2,702	Coldwater	800
Cowley	35,012	Winfield	1,136
Crawford	37,850	Girard	598
Decatur	4,988	Oberlin	899
Dickinson	19,993	Abilene	855
Doniphan	9,107	Troy	388
Douglas	57,932	Lawrence	471
Edwards	4,581	Kinsley	617
Elk	3,858	Howard	647
Ellis	24,730	Hays	900
Ellsworth	6,146	Ellsworth	717
Finney	19,029	Garden City	1,301
Ford	22,587	Dodge City	1,091
Franklin	20,007	Ottawa	577
Geary	28,111	Junction City	374
Gove	2,940	Gove	1,070
Graham	4,751	Hill City	891
Grant	5,961	Ulysses	571
Gray	4,516	Cimarron	872
Greeley	1,819	Tribune	783
Greenwood	9,141	Eureka	1,133
Hamilton	2,747	Syracuse	992
Harper	7,871	Anthony	801
Harvey	27,236	Newton	540
Haskell	3,672	Sublette	580
Hodgeman	2,662	Jetmore	860
Jackson	10,342	Holton	656
Jefferson	11,945	Oskaloosa	510
Jewell	6,099	Mankato	910
Johnson	220,073	Olathe	476
Kearny	3,047	Lakin	855
Kingman	8,886	Kingman	864
Kiowa	4,088	Greensburg	720
Labette	25,775	Oswego	654
Lane	2,707	Dighton	720
Leavenworth	53,340	Leavenworth	466
Lincoln	4,582	Lincoln	725
Linn	7,770	Mound City	606
Logan	3,814	Oakley	1,073

County	Pop. April 1, 1970	County Seats or Court House	Land Area Sq. Mi.
Lyon	32,071	Emporia	841
McPherson	24,778	McPherson	896
Marion	13,935	Marion	945
Marshall	13,139	Marysville	883
Meade	4,912	Meade	979
Miami	19,254	Paola	592
Mitchell	8,010	Beloit	714
Montgomery	39,949	Independence	628
Morris	6,432	Council Grove	697
Morton	3,576	Elkhart	728
Nemaha	11,825	Seneca	708
Neosho	18,812	Erie	587
Ness	4,791	Ness City	1,081
Norton	7,279	Norton	872
Osage	13,352	Lyndon	707
Osborne	6,416	Osborne	886
Ottawa	6,183	Minneapolis	723
Pawnee	8,484	Larned	755
Phillips	7,888	Phillipsburg	897
Pottawatomie	11,755	Westmoreland	820
Pratt	10,056	Pratt	729
Rawlins	4,393	Atwood	1,078
Reno	60,765	Hutchinson	1,260
Republic	8,498	Belleville	718
Rice	12,320	Lyons	725
Riley	56,788	Manhattan	597
Rooks	7,628	Stockton	886
Rush	5,117	LaCrosse	724
Russell	9,428	Russell	867
Saline	46,592	Salina	720
Scott	5,606	Scott City	724
Sedgwick	350,694	Wichita	1,007
Seward	16,062	Liberal	646
Shawnee	155,322	Topeka	548
Sheridan	3,859	Hoxie	893
Sherman	7,792	Goodland	1,055
Smith	6,757	Smith Center	893
Stafford	5,943	Saint John	795
Stanton	2,287	Johnson	676
Stevens	4,198	Hugoton	731
Sumner	23,553	Wellington	1,186
Thomas	7,501	Colby	1,070
Trego	4,436	Wakeeney	901
Wabaunsee	6,397	Alma	792
Wallace	2,215	Sharon Springs	911
Washington	9,249	Washington	891
Wichita	3,274	Leoti	724
Wilson	11,317	Fredonia	574
Woodson	4,789	Yates Center	497
Wyandotte	186,845	Kansas City	152

Kentucky

(120 counties, 39,650 sq. mi. land; pop. 3,219,311)

County	Pop. April 1, 1970	County Seats or Court House	Land Area Sq. Mi.
Adair	13,037	Columbia	370
Allen	12,598	Scottsville	351
Anderson	9,358	Lawrenceburg	206
Ballard	8,276	Wickliffe	259
Barren	28,677	Glasgow	468
Bath	9,235	Owingsville	287
Bell	31,121	Pineville	370
Boone	32,812	Burlington	249
Bourbon	18,476	Paris	300
Boyd	52,376	Catlettsburg	159
Boyle	21,861	Danville	183
Bracken	7,227	Brooksville	204
Breathitt	14,221	Jackson	494
Breckinridge	14,789	Hardinsburg	554
Bullitt	26,090	Shepherdsville	300
Butler	9,723	Morgantown	443
Caldwell	13,179	Princeton	357
Calloway	27,692	Murray	384
Campbell	88,704	Alexandria	149
Carlisle	5,354	Bardwell	195
Carroll	8,523	Carrollton	130
Carter	19,850	Grayson	397
Casey	12,930	Liberty	435
Christian	56,224	Hopkinsville	725
Clark	24,090	Winchester	259
Clay	18,481	Manchester	474
Clinton	8,174	Albany	190
Crittenden	8,493	Marion	365
Cumberland	6,850	Burkesville	310
Daviess	79,486	Owensboro	462
Edmonson	8,751	Brownsville	298
Elliott	5,933	Sandy Hook	240
Estill	12,752	Irvine	260
Fayette	174,323	Lexington	280
Fleming	11,366	Flemingsburg	350
Floyd	35,889	Prestonsburg	399
Franklin	34,481	Frankfort	211
Fulton	10,183	Hickman	203
Gallatin	4,134	Warsaw	100
Garrard	9,457	Lancaster	236
Grant	9,999	Williamstown	249
Graves	30,939	Mayfield	560

County	Pop. April 1, 1970	County Seats or Court House	Land Area Sq. Mi.
Grayson	16,445	Leitchfield	496
Green	10,350	Greensburg	282
Greenup	33,192	Greenup	351
Hancock	7,080	Hawesville	187
Hardin	78,421	Elizabethtown	616
Harlan	37,370	Harlan	469
Harrison	14,158	Cynthiana	308
Hart	13,980	Munfordville	420
Henderson	36,031	Henderson	433
Henry	10,910	New Castle	289
Hickman	6,264	Clinton	246
Hopkins	38,167	Madisonville	553
Jackson	10,005	McKee	337
Jefferson	695,055	Louisville	375
Jessamine	17,430	Nicholasville	177
Johnson	17,539	Paintsville	264
Kenton	129,440	Independence	165
Knott	14,698	Hindman	356
Knox	23,689	Barbourville	373
Larue	10,672	Hodgenville	260
Laurel	27,386	London	446
Lawrence	10,726	Louisa	425
Lee	6,587	Beattyville	210
Leslie	11,623	Hyden	409
Letcher	23,165	Whitesburg	339
Lewis	12,355	Vanceburg	486
Lincoln	16,663	Stanford	340
Livingston	7,596	Smithland	311
Logan	21,793	Russellville	563
Lyon	5,562	Eddyville	216
McCracken	58,281	Paducah	250
McCreary	12,548	Whitley City	418
McLean	9,062	Calhoun	257
Madison	42,730	Richmond	446
Magoffin	10,443	Salyersville	303
Marion	16,714	Lebanon	343
Marshall	20,381	Benton	303
Martin	9,377	Inez	231
Mason	17,273	Maysville	238
Meade	18,796	Brandenburg	305
Menifee	4,050	Frenchburg	210
Mercer	15,960	Harrodsburg	256'
Metcalfe	8,177	Edmonton	296
Monroe	11,642	Tompkinsville	334
Montgomery	15,364	Mount Sterling	204
Morgan	10,019	West Liberty	369
Muhlenberg	27,537	Greenville	481
Nelson	23,477	Bardstown	437
Nicholas	6,508	Carlisle	204
Ohio	18,790	Hartford	596
Oldham	14,687	La Grange	184
Owen	7,470	Owenton	351
Owsley	5,023	Booneville	197
Pendleton	9,949	Falmouth	279
Perry	26,259	Hazard	341
Pike	61,059	Pikeville	782
Powell	7,704	Stanton	173
Pulaski	35,234	Somerset	653
Robertson	2,163	Mount Olivet	101
Rockcastle	12,305	Mount Vernon	311
Rowan	17,010	Morehead	290
Russell	10,542	Jamestown	238
Scott	17,948	Georgetown	284
Shelby	18,999	Shelbyville	383
Simpson	13,054	Franklin	239
Spencer	5,488	Taylorsville	193
Taylor	17,138	Campbellsville	277
Todd	10,823	Elkton	376
Trigg	8,620	Cadiz	408
Trimble	5,349	Bedford	146
Union	15,882	Morganfield	340
Warren	57,884	Bowling Green	546
Washington	10,728	Springfield	307
Wayne	14,268	Monticello	440
Webster	13,282	Dixon	339
Whitley	24,145	Williamsburg	459
Wolfe	5,669	Campton	227
Woodford	14,434	Versailles	193

Louisiana

(64 parishes, 44,930 sq. mi. land; pop. 3,643,180)

County	Pop. April 1, 1970	County Seats or Court House	Land Area Sq. Mi.
Acadia	52,109	Crowley	663
Allen	20,794	Oberlin	774
Ascension	37,086	Donaldsonville	301
Assumption	19,654	Napoleonville	356
Avoyelles	37,751	Marksville	832
Beauregard	22,888	De Ridder	1,181
Bienville	16,024	Arcadia	832
Bossier	63,703	Benton	849
Caddo	230,184	Shreveport	899
Calcasieu	145,415	Lake Charles	1,105
Caldwell	9,354	Columbia	551
Cameron	8,149	Cameron	1,441
Catahoula	11,769	Harrisonburg	742

County	Pop. April 1, 1970	County Seats or Court House	Land Area Sq. Mi.
Claiborne	17,024	Homer	763
Concordia	22,578	Vidalia	718
De Soto	22,764	Mansfield	894
East Baton Rouge	285,167	Baton Rouge	459
East Carroll	12,884	Lake Providence	436
East Feliciana	17,657	Clinton	454
Evangeline	31,932	Ville Platte	669
Franklin	23,946	Winnsboro	648
Grant	13,671	Colfax	670
Iberia	57,397	New Iberia	589
Iberville	30,746	Plaquemine	627
Jackson	15,963	Jonesboro	582
Jefferson	338,229	Gretna	369
Jefferson Davis	29,554	Jennings	658
Lafayette	111,643	Lafayette	283
Lafourche	68,941	Thibodaux	1,141
La Salle	13,295	Jena	643
Lincoln	33,800	Ruston	469
Livingston	36,511	Livingston	654
Madison	15,065	Tallulah	661
Morehouse	32,463	Bastrop	804
Natchitoches	35,219	Natchitoches	1,292
Orleans	593,471	New Orleans	197
Ouachita	115,387	Monroe	638
Plaquemines	25,225	Pointe a la Hache	1,030
Pointe Coupee	22,002	New Roads	563
Rapides	118,078	Alexandria	1,318
Red River	9,226	Coushatta	406
Richland	21,774	Rayville	576
Sabine	18,638	Many	873
St. Bernard	51,185	Chalmette	514
St. Charles	29,550	Hahnville	294
St. Helena	9,937	Greensburg	420
St. James	19,733	Convent	253
St. John The Baptist	23,813	Edgard	227
St. Landry	80,364	Opelousas	932
St. Martin	32,453	Saint Martinville	736
St. Mary	60,752	Franklin	624
St. Tammany	63,585	Covington	887
Tangipahoa	65,875	Amite	808
Tensas	9,732	Saint Joseph	626
Terrebonne	76,049	Houma	1,368
Union	18,447	Farmerville	885
Vermilion	43,071	Abbeville	1,205
Vernon	53,794	Leesville	1,351
Washington	41,987	Franklinton	665
Webster	39,939	Minden	615
West Baton Rouge	16,864	Port Allen	203
West Carroll	13,028	Oak Grove	356
West Feliciana	11,376	Saint Francisville	405
Winn	16,369	Winnfield	950

Maine

(16 counties, 30,920 sq. mi. land; pop. 993,663)

County	Pop. April 1, 1970	County Seats or Court House	Land Area Sq. Mi.
Androscoggin	91,279	Auburn	474
Aroostook	94,078	Houlton	6,821
Cumberland	192,528	Portland	879
Franklin	22,444	Farmington	1,709
Hancock	34,590	Ellsworth	1,536
Kennebec	95,306	Augusta	872
Knox	29,013	Rockland	369
Lincoln	20,537	Wiscasset	454
Oxford	43,457	South Paris	2,080
Penobscot	125,393	Bangor	3,390
Piscataquis	16,285	Dover-Foxcroft	3,892
Sagadahoc	23,452	Bath	257
Somerset	40,597	Skowhegan	3,894
Waldo	23,328	Belfast	737
Washington	29,859	Machias	2,554
York	111,576	Alfred	1,001

Maryland

(23 cos., 1 ind. city, 9,891 sq. mi. land; pop. 3,922,399)

County	Pop. April 1, 1970	County Seats or Court House	Land Area Sq. Mi.
Allegany	84,044	Cumberland	428
Anne Arundel	298,042	Annapolis	423
Baltimore	620,409	Towson	598
Calvert	20,682	Prince Frederick	217
Caroline	19,781	Denton	321
Carroll	69,006	Westminster	456
Cecil	53,291	Elkton	362
Charles	47,678	La Plata	459
Dorchester	29,405	Cambridge	594
Frederick	84,927	Frederick	665
Garrett	21,476	Oakland	659
Harford	115,378	Bel Air	453
Howard	62,394	Ellicott City	251
Kent	16,146	Chestertown	281
Montgomery	522,809	Rockville	495
Prince Georges	661,082	Upper Marlboro	485
Queen Annes	18,422	Centreville	375
St. Marys	47,388	Leonardtown	373

County	Pop. April 1, 1970	County Seats or Court House	Land Area Sq. Mi.
Somerset	18,924	Princess Anne	339
Talbot	23,682	Easton	261
Washington	103,829	Hagerstown	459
Wicomico	54,236	Salisbury	381
Worcester	24,442	Snow Hill	479
Baltimore Independent City	905,787		78

Massachusetts

(14 counties; 7,826 sq. mi. land; pop. 5,689,170)

County	Pop. April 1, 1970	County Seats or Court House	Land Area Sq. Mi.
Barnstable	96,656	Barnstable	393
Berkshire	149,402	Pittsfield	941
Bristol	444,301	Taunton	554
Dukes	6,117	Edgartown	104
Essex	637,887	Salem	494
Franklin	59,210	Greenfield	708
Hampden	459,050	Springfield	619
Hampshire	123,981	Northampton	529
Middlesex	1,397,465	Cambridge	825
Nantucket	3,774	Nantucket	46
Norfolk	604,854	Dedham	394
Plymouth	333,314	Plymouth	654
Suffolk	735,190	Boston	56
Worcester	637,037	Worcester	1,509

Michigan

(83 counties; 56,817 sq. mi. land; pop. 8,875,083)

County	Pop. April 1, 1970	County Seats or Court House	Land Area Sq. Mi.
Alcona	7,113	Harrisville	678
Alger	8,568	Munising	905
Allegan	66,575	Allegan	826
Alpena	30,708	Alpena	565
Antrim	12,612	Bellaire	476
Arenac	11,149	Standish	367
Baraga	7,789	L'Anse	901
Barry	38,166	Hastings	554
Bay	117,339	Bay City	447
Benzie	8,593	Beulah	316
Berrien	163,940	Saint Joseph	580
Branch	37,906	Coldwater	506
Calhoun	141,963	Marshall	709
Cass	43,312	Cassopolis	491
Charlevoix	16,541	Charlevoix	414
Cheboygan	16,573	Cheboygan	721
Chippewa	32,412	Sault Sainte Marie	1,590
Clare	16,695	Harrison	571
Clinton	48,492	Saint Johns	572
Crawford	6,482	Grayling	561
Delta	35,924	Escanaba	1,177
Dickinson	23,753	Iron Mountain	757
Eaton	68,892	Charlotte	571
Emmet	18,331	Petoskey	461
Genesee	445,589	Flint	642
Gladwin	13,471	Gladwin	503
Gogebic	20,676	Bessemer	1,107
Grand Traverse	39,175	Traverse City	462
Gratiot	39,246	Ithaca	566
Hillsdale	37,171	Hillsdale	600
Houghton	34,652	Houghton	1,017
Huron	34,083	Bad Axe	819
Ingham	261,039	Mason	559
Ionia	45,848	Ionia	575
Iosco	24,905	Tawas City	544
Iron	13,813	Crystal Falls	1,171
Isabella	44,594	Mount Pleasant	572
Jackson	143,274	Jackson	698
Kalamazoo	201,550	Kalamazoo	562
Kalkaska	5,272	Kalkaska	566
Kent	411,044	Grand Rapids	857
Keweenaw	2,264	Eagle River	538
Lake	5,661	Baldwin	571
Lapeer	52,361	Lapeer	658
Leelanau	10,872	Leland	345
Lenawee	81,951	Adrian	753
Livingston	58,967	Howell	572
Luce	6,789	Newberry	906
Mackinac	9,660	Saint Ignace	1,014
Macomb	625,309	Mount Clemens	480
Manistee	20,393	Manistee	553
Marquette	64,686	Marquette	1,828
Mason	22,612	Ludington	490
Mecosta	27,992	Big Rapids	560
Menominee	24,587	Menominee	1,038
Midland	63,769	Midland	520
Missaukee	7,126	Lake City	565
Monroe	119,172	Monroe	557
Montcalm	39,660	Stanton	712
Montmorency	5,247	Atlanta	555
Muskegon	157,426	Muskegon	501
Newaygo	27,992	White Cloud	849
Oakland	907,871	Pontiac	867
Oceana	17,984	Hart	536
Ogemaw	11,903	West Branch	571

County	Pop. April 1, 1970	County Seats or Court House	Land Area Sq. Mi.
Ontonagon	10,548	Ontonagon	1,316
Osceola	14,838	Reed City	581
Oscoda	4,726	Mio	563
Otsego	10,422	Gaylord	527
Ottawa	128,181	Grand Haven	563
Presque Isle	12,836	Rogers City	648
Roscommon	9,892	Roscommon	521
Saginaw	219,743	Saginaw	814
St. Clair	120,175	Port Huron	734
St. Joseph	47,392	Centreville	506
Sanilac	35,181	Sandusky	961
Schoolcraft	8,226	Manistique	1,181
Shiawassee	63,075	Corunna	540
Tuscola	48,603	Caro	815
Van Buren	56,173	Paw Paw	603
Washtenaw	234,103	Ann Arbor	711
Wayne	2,670,368	Detroit	605
Wexford	19,717	Cadillac	559

Minnesota

(87 counties; 79,289 sq. mi. land; pop., 3,805,069)

County	Pop. April 1, 1970	County Seats or Court House	Land Area Sq. Mi.
Aitkin	11,403	Aitkin	1,828
Anoka	154,401	Anoka	424
Becker	24,372	Detroit Lakes	1,297
Beltrami	26,373	Bemidji	2,507
Benton	20,841	Foley	402
Big Stone	7,941	Ortonville	490
Blue Earth	52,322	Mankato	737
Brown	28,887	New Ulm	610
Carlton	28,072	Carlton	862
Carver	28,331	Chaska	359
Cass	17,323	Walker	1,998
Chippewa	15,109	Montevideo	582
Chisago	17,492	Center City	419
Clay	46,608	Moorhead	1,045
Clearwater	8,013	Bagley	1,000
Cook	3,423	Grand Marais	1,346
Cottonwood	14,887	Windom	636
Crow Wing	34,826	Brainerd	995
Dakota	139,808	Hastings	576
Dodge	13,037	Mantorville	435
Douglas	22,910	Alexandria	647
Faribault	20,896	Blue Earth	711
Fillmore	21,916	Preston	859
Freeborn	38,064	Albert Lea	701
Goodhue	34,804	Red Wing	753
Grant	7,462	Elbow Lake	546
Hennepin	960,080	Minneapolis	567
Houston	17,556	Caledonia	565
Hubbard	10,583	Park Rapids	932
Isanti	16,560	Cambridge	438
Itasca	35,530	Grand Rapids	2,633
Jackson	14,352	Jackson	696
Kanabec	9,775	Mora	524
Kandiyohi	30,548	Willmar	783
Kittson	6,853	Hallock	1,123
Koochiching	17,131	International Falls	3,127
Lac Qui Parle	11,164	Madison	768
Lake	13,351	Two Harbors	2,062
Lake of the Woods	3,987	Baudette	1,311
Le Sueur	21,332	Le Center	440
Lincoln	8,143	Ivanhoe	531
Lyon	24,273	Marshall	709
McLeod	27,662	Glencoe	488
Mahnomen	5,638	Mahnomen	563
Marshall	13,060	Warren	1,789
Martin	24,316	Fairmont	703
Meeker	18,387	Litchfield	619
Mille Lacs	15,703	Milaca	571
Morrison	26,949	Little Falls	1,127
Mower	43,783	Austin	703
Murray	12,508	Slayton	703
Nicollet	24,518	Saint Peter	432
Nobles	23,208	Worthington	712
Norman	10,008	Ada	885
Olmsted	84,104	Rochester	656
Otter Tail	46,097	Fergus Falls	1,962
Pennington	13,266	Thief River Falls	622
Pine	16,821	Pine City	1,414
Pipestone	12,791	Pipestone	464
Polk	34,435	Crookston	2,013
Pope	11,107	Glenwood	669
Ramsey	476,350	Saint Paul	155
Red Lake	5,388	Red Lake Falls	432
Redwood	20,024	Redwood Falls	874
Renville	21,139	Olivia	979
Rice	41,582	Fairbault	496
Rock	11,346	Luverne	485
Roseau	11,569	Roseau	1,676
St. Louis	220,693	Duluth	6,092
Scott	32,423	Shakopee	353
Sherburne	18,344	Elk River	431
Sibley	15,845	Gaylord	583
Stearns	95,400	Saint Cloud	1,342
Steele	26,931	Owatonna	425

County	Pop. April 1, 1970	County Seats or Court House	Land Area Sq. Mi.
Stevens	11,218	Morris	558
Swift	13,177	Benson	739
Todd	22,114	Long Prairie	942
Traverse	6,254	Wheaton	568
Wabasha	17,224	Wabasha	522
Wadena	12,412	Wadena	536
Waseca	16,663	Waseca	415
Washington	82,948	Stillwater	386
Watonwan	13,298	Saint James	433
Wilkin	9,389	Breckenridge	752
Winona	44,409	Winona	620
Wright	38,933	Buffalo	674
Yellow Medicine	14,523	Granite Falls	753

Mississippi

(82 counties, 47,296 sq. mi. land; pop., 2,216,912)

County	Pop. April 1, 1970	County Seats or Court House	Land Area Sq. Mi.
Adams	37,293	Natchez	449
Alcorn	27,179	Corinth	405
Amite	13,763	Liberty	729
Attala	19,570	Kosciusko	724
Benton	7,505	Ashland	412
Bolivar	49,409	Cleveland and Rosedale	923
Calhoun	14,623	Pittsboro	575
Carroll	9,397	Carrollton & Vaiden	637
Chickasaw	16,805	Houston & Okolona	506
Choctaw	8,440	Ackerman	417
Claiborne	10,086	Port Gibson	489
Clarke	15,049	Quitman	697
Clay	18,840	West Point	414
Coahoma	40,447	Clarksdale	569
Copiah	24,764	Hazlehurst	780
Covington	14,002	Collins	416
De Soto	35,885	Hernando	476
Forrest	57,849	Hattiesburg	468
Franklin	8,011	Meadville	568
George	12,459	Lucedale	481
Greene	8,545	Leakesville	728
Grenada	19,854	Grenada	431
Hancock	17,387	Bay Saint Louis	482
Harrison	134,582	Gulfport	585
Hinds	214,973	Jackson & Raymond	876
Holmes	23,120	Lexington	769
Humphreys	14,601	Belzoni	421
Issaquena	2,737	Mayersville	414
Itawamba	16,847	Fulton	541
Jackson	87,975	Pascagoula	736
Jasper	15,994	Bay Springs & Paulding	683
Jefferson	9,295	Fayette	521
Jefferson Davis	12,936	Prentiss	414
Jones	56,357	Ellisville & Laurel	702
Kemper	10,233	De Kalb	757
Lafayette	24,181	Oxford	668
Lamar	15,209	Purvis	500
Lauderdale	67,087	Meridian	708
Lawrence	11,137	Monticello	433
Leake	17,075	Carthage	586
Lee	46,148	Tupelo	455
Leflore	42,111	Greenwood	592
Lincoln	26,198	Brookhaven	586
Lowndes	49,700	Columbus	508
Madison	29,700	Canton	727
Marion	22,871	Columbia	550
Marshall	24,027	Holly Springs	710
Monroe	34,043	Aberdeen	769
Montgomery	12,918	Winona	403
Neshoba	20,802	Philadelphia	568
Newton	18,983	Decatur	580
Noxubee	14,288	Macon	695
Oktibbeha	28,752	Starkville	454
Panola	26,829	Batesville & Sardis	693
Pearl River	27,802	Poplarville	828
Perry	9,065	New Augusta	653
Pike	31,813	Magnolia	409
Pontotoc	17,363	Pontotoc	501
Prentiss	20,133	Booneville	418
Quitman	15,888	Marks	412
Rankin	43,933	Brandon	775
Scott	21,369	Forest	615
Sharkey	9,937	Rolling Fork	436
Simpson	19,947	Mendenhall	587
Smith	13,561	Raleigh	642
Stone	8,101	Wiggins	448
Sunflower	37,047	Indianola	694
Tallahatchie	19,338	Charleston and Sumner	644
Tate	18,544	Senatobia	405
Tippah	15,852	Ripley	464
Tishomingo	14,940	Iuka	443
Tunica	11,854	Tunica	458
Union	19,096	New Albany	422
Walthall	12,500	Tylertown	403

County	Pop. April 1, 1970	County Seats or Court House	Land Area Sq. Mi.
Warren	44,981	Vicksburg	581
Washington	70,581	Greenville	734
Wayne	16,650	Waynesboro	827
Webster	10,047	Walthall	416
Wilkinson	11,099	Woodville	674
Winston	18,406	Louisville	606
Yalobusha	11,915	Coffeeville and Water Valley	488
Yazoo	27,314	Yazoo City	938

Missouri

(114 cos., 1 ind. city, 68,995 sq. mi. land; pop., 4,677,399)

County	Pop. April 1, 1970	County Seats or Court House	Land Area Sq. Mi.
Adair	22,472	Kirksville	572
Andrew	11,913	Savannah	436
Atchison	9,240	Rockport	549
Audrain	25,362	Mexico	692
Barry	19,597	Cassville	783
Barton	10,431	Lamar	594
Bates	15,468	Butler	841
Benton	9,695	Warsaw	735
Bollinger	8,820	Marble Hill	621
Boone	80,935	Columbia	685
Buchanan	86,915	Saint Joseph	404
Butler	33,529	Poplar Bluff	715
Caldwell	8,351	Kingston	430
Callaway	25,991	Fulton	835
Camden	13,315	Camdenton	640
Cape Girardeau	49,350	Jackson	574
Carroll	12,565	Carrollton	697
Carter	3,878	Van Buren	506
Cass	39,448	Harrisonville	698
Cedar	9,424	Stockton	496
Chariton	11,084	Keytesville	754
Christian	15,124	Ozark	567
Clark	8,260	Kahoka	506
Clay	123,702	Liberty	412
Clinton	12,462	Plattsburg	420
Cole	46,228	Jefferson City	384
Cooper	14,732	Boonville	566
Crawford	14,828	Steelville	760
Dade	6,850	Greenfield	504
Dallas	10,054	Buffalo	537
Daviess	8,420	Gallatin	563
De Kalb	7,305	Maysville	423
Dent	11,457	Salem	756
Douglas	9,268	Ava	809
Dunklin	33,742	Kennett	543
Franklin	55,127	Union	934
Gasconade	11,878	Hermann	519
Gentry	8,060	Albany	488
Greene	152,929	Springfield	677
Grundy	11,819	Trenton	435
Harrison	10,257	Bethany	720
Henry	18,451	Clinton	734
Hickory	4,481	Hermitage	377
Holt	6,654	Oregon	458
Howard	10,561	Fayette	472
Howell	23,521	West Plains	920
Iron	9,529	Ironton	554
Jackson	654,178	Independence	603
Jasper	79,852	Carthage	642
Jefferson	105,248	Hillsboro	668
Johnson	34,172	Warrensburg	826
Knox	5,692	Edina	512
Laclede	19,944	Lebanon	770
Lafayette	26,626	Lexington	632
Lawrence	24,585	Mount Vernon	619
Lewis	10,993	Monticello	508
Lincoln	18,041	Troy	625
Linn	15,125	Linneus	622
Livingston	15,368	Chillicothe	530
McDonald	12,357	Pineville	540
Macon	15,432	Macon	798
Madison	8,641	Fredericktown	496
Maries	6,851	Vienna	525
Marion	28,121	Palmyra	438
Mercer	4,910	Princeton	455
Miller	15,026	Tuscumbia	600
Mississippi	16,647	Charleston	415
Moniteau	10,742	California	419
Monroe	9,542	Paris	669
Montgomery	11,000	Montgomery City	534
Morgan	10,083	Versailles	592
New Madrid	23,420	New Madrid	679
Newton	32,981	Neosho	629
Nodaway	22,467	Maryville	877
Oregon	9,180	Alton	784
Osage	10,994	Linn	608
Ozark	6,226	Gainesville	732
Pemiscot	26,373	Caruthersville	493
Perry	14,393	Perryville	471
Pettis	34,137	Sedalia	679
Phelps	29,567	Rolla	677
Pike	16,928	Bowling Green	681
Platte	32,081	Platte City	427

County	Pop. April 1, 1970	County Seats or Court House	Land Area Sq. Mi.
Polk	15,415	Bolivar	637
Pulaski	53,967	Waynesville	551
Putnam	5,916	Unionville	518
Ralls	7,764	New London	478
Randolph	22,434	Huntsville	473
Ray	17,599	Richmond	573
Reynolds	6,106	Centerville	817
Ripley	9,803	Doniphan	639
St. Charles	92,954	St. Charles	551
St. Clair	7,667	Osceola	697
St. Francois	36,875	Farmington	457
St. Louis	951,671	Clayton	499
Ste. Genevieve	12,867	Ste. Genevieve	499
Saline	24,837	Marshall	757
Schuyler	4,665	Lancaster	306
Scotland	5,499	Memphis	441
Scott	33,250	Benton	421
Shannon	7,196	Eminence	999
Shelby	7,906	Shelbyville	501
Stoddard	25,771	Bloomfield	823
Stone	9,921	Galena	449
Sullivan	7,572	Milan	654
Taney	13,023	Forsyth	615
Texas	18,320	Houston	1,183
Vernon	19,065	Nevada	838
Warren	9,699	Warrenton	426
Washington	15,086	Potosi	760
Wayne	8,546	Greenville	766
Webster	15,562	Marshfield	590
Worth	3,359	Grant City	267
Wright	13,667	Hartville	684
St. Louis Independent City	622,236		61

Montana

(57 counties, 145,587 sq. mi. land; pop., 694,409)

County	Pop. April 1, 1970	County Seats or Court House	Land Area Sq. Mi.
Beaverhead	8,187	Dillon	5,551
Big Horn	10,057	Hardin	5,023
Blaine	6,727	Chinook	4,275
Broadwater	2,526	Townsend	1,193
Carbon	7,080	Red Lodge	2,066
Carter	1,956	Ekalaka	3,313
Cascade	81,804	Great Falls	2,661
Chouteau	6,473	Fort Benton	3,927
Custer	12,174	Miles City	3,756
Daniels	3,083	Scobey	1,443
Dawson	11,269	Glendive	2,370
Deer Lodge	15,652	Anaconda	740
Fallon	4,050	Baker	1,633
Fergus	12,611	Lewistown	4,242
Flathead	39,460	Kalispell	5,137
Gallatin	32,505	Bozeman	2,517
Garfield	1,796	Jordan	4,455
Glacier	10,783	Cut Bank	2,964
Golden Valley	931	Ryegate	1,176
Granite	2,737	Philipsburg	1,733
Hill	17,358	Havre	2,927
Jefferson	5,238	Boulder	1,652
Judith Basin	2,667	Stanford	1,880
Lake	14,445	Polson	1,494
Lewis & Clark	33,281	Helena	3,476
Liberty	2,359	Chester	1,439
Lincoln	18,063	Libby	3,714
McCone	2,875	Circle	2,607
Madison	5,014	Virginia City	3,528
Meagher	2,122	White Sulphur Springs	2,354
Mineral	2,958	Superior	1,222
Missoula	58,263	Missoula	2,612
Musselshell	3,734	Roundup	1,887
Park	11,197	Livingston	2,626
Petroleum	675	Winnett	1,655
Phillips	5,386	Malta	5,213
Pondera	6,611	Conrad	1,645
Powder River	2,862	Broadus	3,288
Powell	6,660	Deer Lodge	2,336
Prairie	1,752	Terry	1,730
Ravalli	14,409	Hamilton	2,382
Richland	9,837	Sidney	2,079
Roosevelt	10,365	Wolf Point	2,385
Rosebud	6,032	Forsyth	5,037
Sanders	7,093	Thompson Falls	2,778
Sheridan	5,779	Plentywood	1,694
Silver Bow	41,981	Butte	715
Stillwater	4,632	Columbus	1,794
Sweet Grass	2,980	Big Timber	1,840
Teton	6,116	Choteau	2,294
Toole	5,839	Shelby	1,950
Treasure	1,069	Hysham	985
Valley	11,471	Glasgow	4,974
Wheatland	2,529	Harlowton	1,420
Wibaux	1,465	Wibaux	890
Yellowstone	87,367	Billings	2,642
Yellowstone Nat. Park	64		269

County	Pop. April 1, 1970	County Seats or Court House	Land Area Sq. Mi.

Nebraska

(93 counties, 76,483 sq. mi. land; pop., 1,483,791)

County	Pop. April 1, 1970	County Seats or Court House	Land Area Sq. Mi.
Adams	30,553	Hastings	562
Antelope	9,047	Neligh	853
Arthur	606	Arthur	704
Banner	1,034	Harrisburg	738
Blaine	847	Brewster	710
Boone	8,190	Albion	683
Box Butte	10,094	Alliance	1,065
Boyd	3,752	Butte	538
Brown	4,021	Ainsworth	1,216
Buffalo	31,222	Kearney	949
Burt	9,247	Tekamah	483
Butler	9,461	David City	582
Cass	18,076	Plattsmouth	555
Cedar	12,192	Hartington	742
Chase	4,129	Imperial	890
Cherry	6,846	Valentine	5,966
Cheyenne	10,778	Sidney	1,186
Clay	8,266	Clay Center	570
Colfax	9,498	Schuyler	406
Cuming	12,034	West Point	571
Custer	14,092	Broken Bow	2,558
Dakota	13,137	Dakota City	255
Dawes	9,761	Chadron	1,386
Dawson	19,771	Lexington	975
Deuel	2,717	Chappell	436
Dixon	7,453	Ponca	475
Dodge	34,782	Fremont	528
Douglas	389,455	Omaha	335
Dundy	2,926	Benkelman	921
Fillmore	8,137	Geneva	577
Franklin	4,566	Franklin	578
Frontier	3,982	Stockville	962
Furnas	6,897	Beaver City	722
Gage	25,731	Beatrice	858
Garden	2,929	Oshkosh	1,678
Garfield	2,411	Burwell	569
Gosper	2,178	Elwood	464
Grant	1,019	Hyannis	764
Greeley	4,000	Greeley	570
Hall	42,851	Grand Island	537
Hamilton	8,867	Aurora	537
Harlan	4,357	Alma	556
Hayes	1,530	Hayes Center	711
Hitchcock	4,051	Trenton	712
Holt	12,933	O'Neil	2,405
Hooker	939	Mullen	722
Howard	6,807	Saint Paul	564
Jefferson	10,436	Fairbury	577
Johnson	5,743	Tecumseh	377
Kearney	6,707	Minden	512
Keith	8,487	Ogallala	1,032
Keya Paha	1,340	Springview	768
Kimball	6,009	Kimball	953
Knox	11,723	Center	1,107
Lancaster	167,972	Lincoln	845
Lincoln	29,538	North Platte	2,522
Logan	991	Stapleton	570
Loup	854	Taylor	574
McPherson	623	Tryon	856
Madison	27,402	Madison	572
Merrick	8,751	Central City	480
Morrill	5,813	Bridgeport	1,402
Nance	5,142	Fullerton	439
Nemaha	8,976	Auburn	400
Nuckolls	7,404	Nelson	579
Otoe	15,576	Nebraska City	619
Pawnee	4,473	Pawnee City	433
Perkins	3,423	Grant	885
Phelps	9,553	Holdrege	544
Pierce	8,493	Pierce	573
Platte	26,544	Columbus	667
Polk	6,468	Osceola	432
Red Willow	12,191	McCook	686
Richardson	12,277	Falls City	550
Rock	2,231	Bassett	1,009
Saline	12,809	Wilber	575
Sarpy	66,200	Papillion	239
Saunders	17,108	Wahoo	759
Scotts Bluff	36,432	Gering	726
Seward	14,460	Seward	571
Sheridan	7,285	Rushville	2,462
Sherman	4,725	Loup City	567
Sioux	2,034	Harrison	2,063
Stanton	5,758	Stanton	431
Thayer	7,779	Hebron	577
Thomas	954	Thedford	716
Thurston	6,942	Pender	388
Valley	5,783	Ord	569
Washington	13,310	Blair	386
Wayne	10,400	Wayne	443
Webster	5,396	Red Cloud	575
Wheeler	1,051	Bartlett	576
York	13,685	York	577

Nevada

(16 cos., 1 ind. city, 109,889 sq. mi. land; pop., 488,738)

County	Pop. April 1, 1970	County Seats or Court House	Land Area Sq. Mi.
Churchill	10,513	Fallon	4,883
Clark	273,288	Las Vegas	7,874
Douglas	6,882	Minden	703
Elko	13,958	Elko	17,162
Esmeralda	629	Goldfield	3,570
Eureka	948	Eureka	4,182
Humboldt	6,375	Winnemucca	9,702
Lander	2,666	Austin	5,621
Lincoln	2,557	Pioche	10,649
Lyon	8,221	Yerington	2,030
Mineral	7,051	Hawthorne	3,765
Nye	5,599	Tonopah	18,064
Pershing	2,670	Lovelock	6,001
Storey	695	Virginia City	262
Washoe	121,068	Reno	6,366
White Pine	10,150	Ely	8,904
Independent City			
Carson City	15,468	Carson City	150

New Hampshire

(10 counties, 9,027 sq. mi. land; pop., 737,681)

County	Pop. April 1, 1970	County Seats or Court House	Land Area Sq. Mi.
Belknap	32,367	Laconia	400
Carroll	18,548	Ossipee	938
Cheshire	52,364	Keene	715
Coos	34,291	Lancaster	1,820
Grafton	54,914	Woodsville	1,732
Hillsborough	223,941	Nashua	887
Merrimack	80,925	Concord	930
Rockingham	138,951	Exeter	691
Stratford	70,431	Dover	376
Sullivan	30,949	Newport	539

New Jersey

(21 counties, 7,521 sq. mi. land; pop. 7,168,164)

County	Pop. April 1, 1970	County Seats or Court House	Land Area Sq. Mi.
Atlantic	175,043	Mays Landing	569
Bergen	897,148	Hackensack	234
Burlington	323,132	Mount Holly	819
Camden	456,291	Camden	221
Cape May	59,554	Cape May Court House	267
Cumberland	121,374	Bridgeton	500
Essex	932,526	Newark	130
Gloucester	172,681	Woodbury	329
Hudson	607,839	Jersey City	47
Hunterdon	69,718	Flemington	423
Mercer	304,116	Trenton	228
Middlesex	583,813	New Brunswick	312
Monmouth	461,849	Freehold	476
Morris	383,454	Morristown	468
Ocean	208,470	Toms River	642
Passaic	460,782	Paterson	192
Salem	60,346	Salem	365
Somerset	198,372	Somerville	307
Sussex	77,528	Newton	527
Union	543,116	Elizabeth	103
Warren	73,960	Belvidere	362

New Mexico

(32 counties, 121,412 sq. mi. land; pop., 1,016,000)

County	Pop. April 1, 1970	County Seats or Court House	Land Area Sq. Mi.
Bernalillo	315,774	Albuquerque	1,169
Catron	2,198	Reserve	6,897
Chaves	43,335	Roswell	6,084
Colfax	12,170	Raton	3,764
Curry	39,517	Clovis	1,403
De Baca	2,547	Fort Sumner	2,356
Dona Ana	69,773	Las Cruces	3,804
Eddy	41,119	Carlsbad	4,167
Grant	22,030	Silver City	3,970
Guadalupe	4,969	Santa Rosa	2,998
Harding	1,348	Mosquero	2,134
Hidalgo	4,734	Lordsburg	3,447
Lea	49,554	Lovington	4,393
Lincoln	7,560	Carrizozo	4,858
Los Alamos	15,198	Los Alamos	108
Luna	11,706	Deming	2,957
McKinley	43,208	Gallup	5,454
Mora	4,673	Mora	1,940
Otero	41,097	Alamogordo	6,638
Quay	10,903	Tucumcari	2,875
Rio Arriba	25,170	Tierra Amarilla	5,843
Roosevelt	16,479	Portales	2,454
Sandoval	17,492	Bernalillo	3,714
San Juan	52,517	Aztec	5,500
San Miguel	21,951	Las Vegas	4,741
Santa Fe	54,774	Santa Fe	1,902
Sierra	7,189	Truth or Consequences	4,166
Socorro	9,763	Socorro	6,603
Taos	17,516	Taos	2,256

County	Pop. April 1, 1970	County Seats or Court House	Land Area Sq. Mi.
Torrance	5,290	Estancia	3,346
Union	4,925	Clayton	3,816
Valencia	40,576	Los Lunas	5,656

New York
(62 counties, 47,831 sq. mi. land; pop., 18,241,266)

County	Pop. April 1, 1970	County Seats or Court House	Land Area Sq. Mi.
Albany	286,742	Albany	526
Allegany	46,458	Belmont	1,047
Bronx	1,471,701	Bronx	41
Broome	221,815	Binghamton	714
Cattaraugus	81,666	Little Valley	1,318
Cayuga	77,439	Auburn	698
Chautauqua	147,305	Mayville	1,081
Chemung	101,537	Elmira	415
Chenango	46,368	Norwich	903
Clinton	72,934	Plattsburgh	1,059
Columbia	51,519	Hudson	645
Cortland	45,894	Cortland	502
Delaware	44,718	Delhi	1,443
Dutchess	222,295	Poughkeepsie	813
Erie	1,113,491	Buffalo	1,058
Essex	34,631	Elizabethtown	1,823
Franklin	43,931	Malone	1,674
Fulton	52,637	Johnstown	498
Genesee	58,722	Batavia	501
Greene	33,136	Catskill	653
Hamilton	4,714	Lake Pleasant	1,735
Herkimer	67,633	Herkimer	1,435
Jefferson	88,508	Watertown	1,294
Kings	2,602,012	Brooklyn	70
Lewis	23,644	Lowville	1,291
Livingston	54,041	Geneseo	638
Madison	62,864	Wampsville	661
Monroe	711,917	Rochester	675
Montgomery	55,883	Fonda	408
Nassau	1,428,838	Mineola	289
New York	1,539,233	New York	23
Niagara	235,720	Lockport	532
Oneida	273,037	Utica	1,223
Onondaga	472,835	Syracuse	794
Ontario	78,849	Canandaigua	651
Orange	221,657	Goshen	833
Orleans	37,305	Albion	396
Oswego	100,897	Oswego	964
Otsego	56,181	Cooperstown	1,013
Putnam	56,696	Carmel	231
Queens	1,987,174	Jamaica	108
Rensselaer	152,510	Troy	665
Richmond	295,443	Saint George	58
Rockland	229,903	New City	176
St. Lawrence	112,309	Canton	2,768
Saratoga	121,764	Ballston Spa	818
Schenectady	161,078	Schenectady	207
Schoharie	24,750	Schoharie	624
Schuyler	16,737	Watkins Glen	330
Seneca	35,083	Ovid & Waterloo	330
Steuben	99,546	Bath	1,410
Suffolk	1,127,030	Riverhead	929
Sullivan	52,580	Monticello	980
Tioga	46,513	Owego	524
Tompkins	77,064	Ithaca	482
Ulster	141,241	Kingston	1,141
Warren	49,402	Lake George	887
Washington	52,725	Hudson Falls	836
Wayne	79,404	Lyons	606
Westchester	894,406	White Plains	443
Wyoming	37,688	Warsaw	598
Yates	19,831	Penn Yan	343

North Carolina
(100 counties, 48,798 sq. mi. land; pop., 5,082,059)

County	Pop. April 1, 1970	County Seats or Court House	Land Area Sq. Mi.
Alamance	96,362	Graham	428
Alexander	19,466	Taylorsville	259
Alleghany	8,134	Sparta	225
Anson	23,488	Wadesboro	533
Ashe	19,571	Jefferson	426
Avery	12,655	Newland	245
Beaufort	35,980	Washington	826
Bertie	20,528	Windsor	698
Bladen	26,477	Elizabethtown	883
Brunswick	24,223	Southport	856
Buncombe	145,056	Asheville	657
Burke	60,364	Morganton	511
Cabarrus	74,629	Concord	363
Caldwell	56,699	Lenoir	469
Camden	5,453	Camden	239
Carteret	31,603	Beaufort	536
Caswell	19,055	Yanceyville	428
Catawba	90,873	Newton	394
Chatham	29,554	Pittsboro	709
Cherokee	16,330	Murphy	452
Chowan	10,764	Edenton	173
Clay	5,180	Hayesville	209
Cleveland	72,556	Shelby	468
Columbus	46,937	Whiteville	945
Craven	62,554	New Bern	699
Cumberland	212,042	Fayetteville	654
Currituck	6,976	Currituck	246
Dare	6,995	Manteo	391
Davidson	95,627	Lexington	549
Davie	18,855	Mocksville	265
Duplin	38,015	Kenansville	815
Durham	132,681	Durham	295
Edgecombe	52,341	Tarboro	510
Forsyth	215,118	Winston-Salem	419
Franklin	26,820	Louisburg	491
Gaston	148,415	Gastonia	356
Gates	8,524	Gatesville	337
Graham	6,562	Robbinsville	292
Granville	32,762	Oxford	537
Greene	14,967	Snow Hill	267
Guilford	288,645	Greensboro	655
Halifax	53,884	Halifax	734
Harnett	49,667	Lillington	603
Haywood	41,710	Waynesville	551
Henderson	42,804	Hendersonville	378
Hertford	23,529	Winton	353
Hoke	16,436	Raeford	389
Hyde	5,571	Swanquarter	613
Iredell	72,197	Statesville	572
Jackson	21,593	Sylva	491
Johnston	61,737	Smithfield	797
Jones	9,779	Trenton	467
Lee	30,467	Sanford	256
Lenoir	55,204	Kinston	400
Lincoln	32,682	Lincolnton	297
McDowell	30,648	Marion	436
Macon	15,788	Franklin	513
Madison	16,003	Marshall	450
Martin	24,730	Williamston	455
Mecklenburg	354,656	Charlotte	530
Mitchell	13,447	Bakersville	215
Montgomery	19,267	Troy	488
Moore	39,048	Carthage	704
Nash	59,122	Nashville	544
New Hanover	82,996	Wilmington	185
Northampton	24,009	Jackson	536
Onslow	103,126	Jacksonville	765
Orange	57,707	Hillsboro	400
Pamlico	9,467	Bayboro	338
Pasquotank	26,824	Elizabeth City	228
Pender	18,149	Burgaw	871
Perquimans	8,351	Hertford	246
Person	25,914	Roxboro	401
Pitt	73,900	Greenville	655
Polk	11,735	Columbus	239
Randolph	76,358	Asheboro	798
Richmond	39,889	Rockingham	475
Robeson	84,842	Lumberton	949
Rockingham	72,402	Wentworth	569
Rowan	90,035	Salisbury	523
Rutherford	47,337	Rutherfordton	563
Sampson	44,954	Clinton	945
Scotland	26,929	Laurinburg	319
Stanly	42,822	Albemarle	398
Stokes	23,782	Danbury	457
Surry	51,415	Dobson	536
Swain	8,835	Bryson City	524
Transylvania	19,713	Brevard	382
Tyrrell	3,806	Columbia	390
Union	54,714	Monroe	639
Vance	32,691	Henderson	249
Wake	229,006	Raleigh	858
Warren	15,810	Warrenton	424
Washington	14,038	Plymouth	343
Watauga	23,404	Boone	317
Wayne	85,408	Goldsboro	557
Wilkes	49,524	Wilkesboro	757
Wilson	57,486	Wilson	375
Yadkin	24,599	Yadkinville	336
Yancey	12,629	Burnsville	312

North Dakota
(53 counties, 69,273 sq. mi. land; pop., 617,761)

County	Pop. April 1, 1970	County Seats or Court House	Land Area Sq. Mi.
Adams	3,832	Hettinger	989
Barnes	14,669	Valley City	1,479
Benson	8,245	Minnewaukan	1,403
Billings	1,198	Medora	1,139
Bottineau	9,496	Bottineau	1,677
Bowman	3,901	Bowman	1,170
Burke	4,739	Bowbells	1,119
Burleigh	40,714	Bismarck	1,625
Cass	73,653	Fargo	1,749
Cavalier (1973)	10,977	Langdon	1,512
Dickey	6,976	Ellendale	1,143
Divide	4,564	Crosby	1,300

County	Pop. April 1, 1970	County Seats or Court House	Land Area Sq. Mi.	County	Pop. April 1, 1970	County Seats or Court House	Land Area Sq. Mi.
Dunn	4,895	Manning	1,992	Medina	82,717	Medina	425
Eddy	4,103	New Rockford	635	Meigs	19,799	Pomeroy	436
Emmons	7,200	Linton	1,503	Mercer	35,558	Celina	444
Foster	4,832	Carrington	645	Miami	84,342	Troy	407
Golden Valley	2,611	Beach	1,014	Monroe	15,739	Woodsfield	456
Grand Forks	61,102	Grand Forks	1,438	Montgomery	608,413	Dayton	459
Grant	5,009	Carson	1,666	Morgan	12,375	McConnelsville	420
Griggs	4,184	Cooperstown	710	Morrow	21,348	Mount Gilead	403
Hettinger	5,075	Mott	1,134	Muskingum	77,826	Zanesville	651
Kidder	4,362	Steele	1,358	Noble	10,428	Caldwell	398
La Moure	7,117	La Moure	1,136	Ottawa	37,099	Port Clinton	261
Logan	4,245	Napoleon	1,001	Paulding	19,329	Paulding	417
McHenry	8,977	Towner	1,879	Perry	27,434	New Lexington	410
McIntosh	5,545	Ashley	992	Pickaway	40,071	Circleville	504
McKenzie	6,127	Watford City	2,735	Pike	19,114	Waverly	443
McLean	11,251	Washburn	2,065	Portage	125,868	Ravenna	495
Mercer	6,175	Stanton	1,042	Preble	34,719	Eaton	427
Morton	20,310	Mandan	1,920	Putnam	31,134	Ottawa	486
Mountrail	8,437	Stanley	1,819	Richland	129,997	Mansfield	496
Nelson	5,807	Lakota	995	Ross	61,211	Chillicothe	687
Oliver	2,322	Center	721	Sandusky	60,983	Fremont	409
Pembina	10,728	Cavalier	1,124	Scioto	76,951	Portsmouth	608
Pierce	6,323	Rugby	1,038	Seneca	60,696	Tiffin	551
Ramsey	12,915	Devils Lake	1,248	Shelby	37,748	Sidney	408
Ransom	7,102	Lisbon	861	Stark	372,210	Canton	576
Renville	3,828	Mohall	886	Summit	553,371	Akron	408
Richland	18,089	Wahpeton	1,449	Trumbull	232,579	Warren	608
Rolette	11,549	Rolla	913	Tuscarawas	77,211	New Philadelphia	569
Sargent	5,937	Forman	853	Union	23,786	Marysville	434
Sheridan	3,232	McClusky	989	Van Wert	29,194	Van Wert	409
Sioux	3,632	Fort Yates	1,103	Vinton	9,420	McArthur	411
Slope	1,484	Amidon	1,225	Warren	85,505	Lebanon	408
Stark	19,613	Dickinson	1,316	Washington	57,160	Marietta	641
Steele	3,749	Finley	710	Wayne	87,123	Wooster	561
Stutsman	23,550	Jamestown	2,264	Williams	33,669	Bryan	421
Towner	4,645	Cando	1,043	Wood	89,722	Bowling Green	619
Traill	9,571	Hillsboro	861	Wyandot	21,826	Upper Sandusky	406
Walsh	16,251	Grafton	1,286				
Ward	58,560	Minot	2,044				
Wells	7,847	Fessenden	1,299				
Williams	19,301	Williston	2,064				

Ohio

(88 counties, 40,975 sq. mi. land; pop., 10,652,017)

County	Pop. April 1, 1970	County Seats or Court House	Land Area Sq. Mi.
Adams	18,957	West Union	587
Allen	111,144	Lima	410
Ashland	43,303	Ashland	424
Ashtabula	98,237	Jefferson	700
Athens	55,747	Athens	504
Auglaize	38,602	Wapakoneta	400
Belmont	80,917	Saint Clairsville	534
Brown	26,635	Georgetown	490
Butler	226,207	Hamilton	471
Carroll	21,579	Carrollton	390
Champaign	30,491	Urbana	432
Clark	157,115	Springfield	402
Clermont	95,887	Batavia	458
Clinton	31,464	Wilmington	410
Columbiana	108,310	Lisbon	534
Coshocton	33,486	Coshocton	562
Crawford	50,364	Bucyrus	404
Cuyahoga	1,720,835	Cleveland	456
Darke	49,141	Greenville	605
Defiance	36,949	Defiance	412
Delaware	42,908	Delaware	450
Erie	75,909	Sandusky	264
Fairfield	73,301	Lancaster	505
Fayette	25,461	Washington, C. H.	404
Franklin	833,249	Columbus	538
Fulton	33,071	Wauseon	407
Gallia	25,239	Gallipolis	471
Geauga	62,977	Chardon	407
Greene	125,057	Xenia	415
Guernsey	37,665	Cambridge	528
Hamilton	923,205	Cincinnati	414
Hancock	61,217	Findlay	532
Hardin	30,813	Kenton	467
Harrison	17,013	Cadiz	401
Henry	27,058	Napoleon	416
Highland	28,996	Hillsboro	549
Hocking	20,322	Logan	421
Holmes	23,024	Millersburg	424
Huron	49,587	Norwalk	497
Jackson	27,174	Jackson	419
Jefferson	96,193	Steubenville	411
Knox	41,795	Mount Vernon	531
Lake	197,200	Painesville	231
Lawrence	56,868	Ironton	456
Licking	107,799	Newark	686
Logan	35,072	Bellefontaine	460
Lorain	256,843	Elyria	495
Lucas	483,594	Toledo	343
Madison	28,318	London	463
Mahoning	304,545	Youngstown	415
Marion	64,724	Marion	405

Oklahoma

(77 counties, 68,782 sq. mi. land; pop., 2,559,253)

County	Pop. April 1, 1970	County Seats or Court House	Land Area Sq. Mi.
Adair	15,141	Stillwell	570
Alfalfa	7,224	Cherokee	868
Atoka	10,972	Atoka	991
Beaver	6,282	Beaver	1,790
Beckham	15,754	Sayre	907
Blaine	11,794	Watonga	917
Bryan	25,552	Durant	889
Caddo	28,931	Anadarko	1,272
Canadian	32,245	El Reno	897
Carter	37,349	Ardmore	830
Cherokee	23,174	Tahlequah	756
Choctaw	15,141	Hugo	778
Cimarron	4,145	Boise City	1,843
Cleveland	81,839	Norman	527
Coal	5,525	Coalgate	526
Comanche	108,144	Lawton	1,084
Cotton	6,832	Walters	651
Craig	14,722	Vinita	764
Creek	45,532	Sapulpa	936
Custer	22,665	Arapaho	980
Delaware	17,767	Jay	707
Dewey	5,656	Taloga	1,018
Ellis	5,129	Arnett	1,242
Garfield	56,343	Enid	1,054
Garvin	24,874	Pauls Valley	814
Grady	29,354	Chickasha	1,096
Grant	7,117	Medford	1,007
Greer	7,979	Mangum	633
Harmon	5,136	Hollis	545
Harper	5,151	Buffalo	1,041
Haskell	9,578	Stigler	602
Hughes	13,228	Holdenville	807
Jackson	30,902	Altus	810
Jefferson	7,125	Waurika	780
Johnston	7,870	Tishomingo	638
Kay	48,791	Newkirk	950
Kingfisher	12,857	Kingfisher	904
Kiowa	12,532	Hobart	1,027
Latimer	8,601	Wilburton	737
Le Flore	32,137	Poteau	1,560
Lincoln	19,482	Chandler	973
Logan	19,645	Guthrie	751
Love	5,637	Marietta	513
McClain	14,157	Purcell	573
McCurtain	28,642	Idabel	1,800
McIntosh	12,472	Eufaula	608
Major	7,529	Fairview	963
Marshall	7,682	Madill	366
Mayes	23,302	Pryor	648
Murray	10,669	Sulphur	423
Muskogee	59,542	Muskogee	818
Noble	10,043	Perry	743
Nowata	9,773	Nowata	537
Okfuskee	10,683	Okemah	637
Oklahoma	527,717	Oklahoma City	700

County	Pop. April 1, 1970	County Seats or Court House	Land Area Sq. Mi.
Okmulgee	35,358	Okmulgee	700
Osage	29,750	Pawhuska	2,272
Ottawa	29,800	Miami	464
Pawnee	11,338	Pawnee	61
Payne	50,654	Stillwater	694
Pittsburg	37,521	McAlester	1,241
Pontotoc	27,867	Ada	714
Pottawatomie	43,134	Shawnee	794
Pushmataha	9,385	Antlers	1,420
Roger Mills	4,452	Cheyenne	1,140
Rogers	28,425	Claremore	685
Seminole	25,144	Wewoka	630
Sequoyah	23,370	Sallisaw	696
Stephens	35,902	Duncan	891
Texas	16,352	Guymon	2,062
Tillman	12,901	Frederick	901
Tulsa	399,982	Tulsa	573
Wagoner	22,163	Wagoner	563
Washington	42,302	Bartlesville	424
Washita	12,141	Cordell	1,009
Woods	11,920	Alva	1,298
Woodward	15,537	Woodward	1,251

Oregon

(36 counties, 96,184 sq. mi. land; pop., 2,091,385)

County	Pop. April 1, 1970	County Seats or Court House	Land Area Sq. Mi.
Baker	14,919	Baker	3,068
Benton	53,776	Corvallis	668
Clackamas	166,088	Oregon City	1,884
Clatsop	28,473	Astoria	805
Columbia	28,790	Saint Helens	639
Coos	56,515	Coquille	1,604
Crook	9,985	Prineville	2,975
Curry	13,006	Gold Beach	1,627
Deschutes	30,442	Bend	3,031
Douglas	71,743	Roseburg	5,063
Gilliam	2,342	Condon	1,208
Grant	6,996	Canyon City	4,530
Harney	7,215	Burns	10,166
Hood River	13,187	Hood River	523
Jackson	94,533	Medford	2,812
Jefferson	8,548	Madras	1,793
Josephine	35,746	Grants Pass	1,625
Klamath	50,021	Klamath Falls	5,970
Lake	6,343	Lakeview	8,231
Lane	215,401	Eugene	4,552
Lincoln	25,755	Newport	986
Linn	71,914	Albany	2,283
Malheur	23,169	Vale	9,859
Marion	151,309	Salem	1,166
Morrow	4,465	Heppner	2,060
Multnomah	554,668	Portland	423
Polk	35,349	Dallas	736
Sherman	2,139	Moro	830
Tillamook	18,034	Tillamook	1,115
Umatilla	44,923	Pendleton	3,227
Union	19,377	La Grande	2,032
Wallowa	6,247	Enterprise	3,178
Wasco	20,133	The Dalles	2,381
Washington	157,920	Hillsboro	716
Wheeler	1,849	Fossil	1,707
Yamhill	40,213	McMinnville	711

Pennsylvania

(67 counties, 44,966 sq. mi. land; pop., 11,793,909)

County	Pop. April 1, 1970	County Seats or Court House	Land Area Sq. Mi.
Adams	56,937	Gettysburg	526
Allegheny	1,605,133	Pittsburgh	728
Armstrong	75,590	Kittanning	652
Beaver	208,418	Beaver	440
Bedford (1973)	43,278	Bedford	1,018
Berks	296,382	Reading	862
Blair	135,356	Hollidaysburg	530
Bradford	57,962	Towanda	1,148
Bucks	416,728	Doylestown	614
Butler	127,941	Butler	794
Cambria	186,785	Ebensburg	692
Cameron	7,096	Emporium	401
Carbon	50,573	Jim Thorpe	404
Centre	99,267	Bellefonte	1,115
Chester	277,746	West Chester	761
Clarion	38,414	Clarion	597
Clearfield	74,619	Clearfield	1,139
Clinton	37,721	Lock Haven	899
Columbia	55,114	Bloomsburg	484
Crawford	81,342	Meadville	1,012
Cumberland	158,177	Carlisle	555
Dauphin	223,713	Harrisburg	518
Delaware	601,715	Media	184
Elk	37,770	Ridgeway	807
Erie	263,654	Erie	813
Fayette	154,667	Uniontown	802
Forest	4,926	Tionesta	419
Franklin	100,833	Chambersburg	754
Fulton	10,776	McConnellsburg	435
Greene	36,090	Waynesburg	578
Huntingdon	39,108	Huntingdon	895
Indiana	79,451	Indiana	825
Jefferson	43,695	Brookville	652
Juniata	16,712	Mifflintown	386
Lackawanna	234,107	Scranton	454
Lancaster	320,079	Lancaster	946
Lawrence	107,374	New Castle	367
Lebanon	99,665	Lebanon	363
Lehigh	255,304	Allentown	348
Luzerne	342,329	Wilkes-Barre	886
Lycoming	113,296	Williamsport	1,216
McKean	51,915	Smethport	992
Mercer	127,225	Mercer	670
Mifflin	45,268	Lewistown	431
Monroe	45,422	Stroudsburg	611
Montgomery	623,956	Norristown	496
Montour	16,508	Danville	130
Northampton	214,545	Easton	376
Northumberland	99,190	Sunbury	453
Perry	28,615	New Bloomfield	551
Philadelphia	1,949,996	Philadelphia	129
Pike	11,818	Milford	542
Potter	16,395	Coudersport	1,092
Schuylkill	160,089	Pottsville	784
Snyder	29,269	Middleburg	327
Somerset	76,037	Somerset	1,078
Sullivan	5,961	Laporte	478
Susquehanna	34,344	Montrose	833
Tioga	39,691	Wellsboro	1,146
Union	28,603	Lewisburg	318
Venango	62,353	Franklin	678
Warren	47,682	Warren	905
Washington	210,876	Washington	857
Wayne	29,581	Honesdale	741
Westmoreland	376,935	Greensburg	1,024
Wyoming	19,082	Tunkhannock	398
York	272,603	York	909

Rhode Island

(5 counties, 1,049 sq. mi. land; pop., 949,723)

County	Pop. April 1, 1970	County Seats or Court House	Land Area Sq. Mi.
Bristol	45,937	Bristol	25
Kent	142,382	East Greenwich	173
Newport	94,228	Newport	115
Providence	581,470	Providence	416
Washington	85,706	West Kingston	321

South Carolina

(46 counties, 30,225 sq. mi. land; pop., 2,590,516)

County	Pop. April 1, 1970	County Seats or Court House	Land Area Sq. Mi.
Abbeville	21,112	Abbeville	506
Aiken	91,023	Aiken	1,087
Allendale	9,783	Allendale	418
Anderson	105,474	Anderson	749
Bamberg	15,950	Bamberg	395
Barnwell	17,176	Barnwell	553
Beaufort	51,136	Beaufort	579
Berkeley	56,199	Moncks Corner	1,110
Calhoun	10,780	Saint Matthews	377
Charleston	247,650	Charleston	939
Cherokee	36,791	Gaffney	394
Chester	29,811	Chester	584
Chesterfield	33,667	Chesterfield	790
Clarendon	25,604	Manning	599
Colleton	27,622	Walterboro	1,049
Darlington	53,442	Darlington	543
Dillon	28,838	Dillon	407
Dorchester	32,276	Saint George	569
Edgefield	15,692	Edgefield	482
Fairfield	19,999	Winnsboro	696
Florence	89,636	Florence	805
Georgetown	33,500	Georgetown	812
Greenville	240,774	Greenville	792
Greenwood	49,686	Greenwood	446
Hampton	15,878	Hampton	562
Horry	69,992	Conway	1,154
Jasper	11,885	Ridgeland	652
Kershaw	34,727	Camden	781
Lancaster	43,328	Lancaster	502
Laurens	49,713	Laurens	711
Lee	18,323	Bishopville	409
Lexington	89,012	Lexington	717
McCormick	7,955	McCormick	360
Marion	30,270	Marion	487
Marlboro	27,151	Bennettsville	483
Newberry	29,273	Newberry	635
Oconee	40,728	Walhalla	654
Orangeburg	69,789	Orangeburg	1,106
Pickens	58,956	Pickens	492
Richland	233,868	Columbia	748
Saluda	14,528	Saluda	458
Spartanburg	173,724	Spartanburg	831
Sumter	79,425	Sumter	672
Union	29,230	Union	514

County	Pop. April 1, 1970	County Seats or Court House	Land Area Sq. Mi.
Williamsburg	34,243	Kingstree	935
York	85,216	York	684

South Dakota

(67 counties, 75,955 sq. mi. land; pop., 666,257)

County	Pop. April 1, 1970	County Seats or Court House	Land Area Sq. Mi.
Aurora	4,183	Plankinton	709
Beadle	20,877	Huron	1,259
Bennett	3,088	Martin	1,181
Bon Homme	8,577	Tyndall	560
Brookings	22,158	Brookings	800
Brown	36,920	Aberdeen	1,674
Brule	5,870	Chamberlain	818
Buffalo	1,739	Gannvalley	482
Butte	7,825	Belle Fourche	2,250
Campbell	2,866	Mound City	732
Charles Mix	9,994	Lake Andes	1,097
Clark	5,515	Clark	964
Clay	12,923	Vermillion	405
Codington	19,140	Watertown	687
Corson	4,994	McIntosh	2,470
Custer	4,698	Custer	1,557
Davison	17,319	Mitchell	432
Day	8,713	Webster	1,030
Deuel	5,686	Clear Lake	639
Dewey	5,170	Timber Lake	2,351
Douglas	4,569	Armour	435
Edmunds	5,548	Ipswich	1,154
Fall River	7,505	Hot Springs	1,743
Faulk	3,893	Faulkton	996
Grant	9,005	Milbank	681
Gregory	6,710	Burke	997
Haakon	2,802	Philip	1,816
Hamlin	5,520	Hayti	511
Hand	5,883	Miller	1,432
Hanson	3,781	Alexandria	430
Harding	1,855	Buffalo	2,682
Hughes	11,632	Pierre	748
Hutchinson	10,379	Olivet	815
Hyde	2,515	Highmore	863
Jackson	1,531	Kadoka	808
Jerauld	3,310	Wessington Spgs.	527
Jones	1,882	Murdo	973
Kingsbury	7,657	De Smet	818
Lake	11,456	Madison	567
Lawrence	17,453	Deadwood	800
Lincoln	11,761	Canton	576
Lyman	4,060	Kennebec	1,683
McCook	7,246	Salem	575
McPherson	5,022	Leola	1,147
Marshall	5,965	Britton	848
Meade	17,020	Sturgis	3,465
Mellette	2,420	White River	1,306
Miner	4,454	Howard	570
Minnehaha	95,209	Sioux Falls	813
Moody	7,622	Flandreau	523
Pennington	59,349	Rapid City	2,779
Perkins	4,769	Bison	2,860
Potter	4,449	Gettysburg	869
Roberts	11,678	Sisseton	1,108
Sanborn	3,697	Woonsocket	570
Shannon	8,198	(Attached to Fall River)	2,100
Spink	10,595	Redfield	1,505
Stanley	2,457	Fort Pierce	1,414
Sully	2,362	Onida	1,004
Todd	6,606	(Attached to Tripp)	1,388
Tripp	8,171	Winner	1,620
Turner	9,872	Parker	612
Union	9,643	Elk Point	452
Walworth	7,842	Selby	718
Washabaugh	1,389	(Attached to Jackson)	1,061
Yankton	19,039	Yankton	519
Zeibach	2,221	Dupree	1,981

Tennessee

(95 counties, 41,328 sq. mi. land; pop., 3,924,164)

County	Pop. April 1, 1970	County Seats or Court House	Land Area Sq. Mi.
Anderson	60,300	Clinton	335
Bedford	25,039	Shelbyville	482
Benton	12,126	Camden	392
Bledsoe	7,643	Pikeville	404
Blount	63,744	Maryville	575
Bradley	50,686	Cleveland	334
Campbell	26,045	Jacksboro	451
Cannon	8,467	Woodbury	271
Carroll	25,741	Huntingdon	596
Carter	43,259	Elizabethton	348
Cheatham	13,199	Ashland City	305
Chester	9,927	Henderson	285
Claiborne	19,420	Tazewell	444
Clay	6,624	Celina	233
Cocke	25,283	Newport	424
Coffee	32,572	Manchester	434

County	Pop. April 1, 1970	County Seats or Court House	Land Area Sq. Mi.
Crockett	14,402	Alamo	269
Cumberland	20,733	Crossville	678
Davidson	447,877	Nashville	508
Decatur	9,457	Decaturville	337
De Kalb	11,151	Smithville	278
Dickson	21,977	Charlotte	485
Dyer	30,427	Dyersburg	529
Fayette	22,692	Somerville	704
Fentress	12,593	Jamestown	498
Franklin	27,289	Winchester	553
Gibson	47,871	Trenton	607
Giles	22,138	Pulaski	619
Grainger	13,948	Rutledge	282
Greene	47,630	Greeneville	613
Grundy	10,631	Altamont	358
Hamblen	38,696	Morristown	155
Hamilton	255,077	Chattanooga	550
Hancock	6,719	Sneedville	230
Hardeman	22,435	Bolivar	656
Hardin	18,212	Savannah	587
Hawkins	33,757	Rogersville	480
Haywood	19,596	Brownsville	519
Henderson	17,360	Lexington	515
Henry	23,749	Paris	567
Hickman	12,096	Centerville	610
Houston	5,853	Erin	201
Humphreys	13,560	Waverly	530
Jackson	8,141	Gainesboro	323
Jefferson	24,940	Dandridge	274
Johnson	11,569	Mountain City	293
Knox	276,293	Knoxville	508
Lake	8,074	Tiptonville	167
Lauderdale	20,271	Ripley	477
Laarence	29,097	Lawrenceburg	634
Lewis	6,761	Hohenwald	285
Lincoln	24,318	Fayetteville	580
Loudon	24,266	Loudon	237
McMinn	35,462	Athens	432
McNairy	18,369	Selmer	569
Macon	12,315	Lafayette	304
Madison	65,774	Jackson	560
Marion	20,577	Jasper	506
Marshall	17,319	Lewisburg	377
Maury	44,028	Columbia	614
Meigs	5,219	Decatur	191
Monroe	23,475	Madisonville	660
Montgomery	62,721	Clarksville	539
Moore	3,568	Lynchburg	124
Morgan	13,619	Wartburg	539
Obion	30,247	Union City	556
Overton	14,866	Livingston	441
Perry	5,238	Linden	411
Pickett	3,774	Byrdstown	158
Polk	11,669	Benton	434
Putnam	35,487	Cookeville	405
Rhea	17,202	Dayton	312
Roane	38,881	Kingston	350
Robertson	29,102	Springfield	476
Rutherford	59,428	Murfreesboro	612
Scott	14,762	Huntsville	544
Sequatchie	6,331	Dunlap	273
Sevier	28,241	Sevierville	597
Shelby	722,111	Memphis	755
Smith	12,509	Carthage	323
Stewart	7,319	Dover	470
Sullivan	127,329	Blountville	413
Sumner	56,266	Gallatin	534
Tipton	28,001	Covington	459
Trousdale	5,155	Hartsville	114
Unicoi	15,254	Erwin	185
Union	9,072	Maynardville	212
Van Buren	3,758	Spencer	254
Warren	26,972	McMinnville	439
Washington	73,924	Jonesboro	323
Wayne	12,365	Waynesboro	739
Weakley	28,827	Dresden	576
White	16,329	Sparta	382
Williamson	34,423	Franklin	593
Wilson	36,999	Lebanon	567

Texas

(254 counties, 262,134 sq. mi. land; pop., 11,196,730)

County	Pop. April 1, 1970	County Seats or Court House	Land Area Sq. Mi.
Anderson	27,789	Palestine	1,072
Andrews	10,372	Andrews	1,504
Angelina	49,349	Lufkin	738
Aransas	8,902	Rockport	275
Archer	5,759	Archer City	913
Armstrong	1,895	Claude	907
Atascosa	18,696	Jourdanton	1,206
Austin	13,831	Bellville	663
Bailey	8,487	Muleshoe	835
Bandera	4,747	Bandera	763
Bastrop	17,297	Bastrop	890
Baylor	5,221	Seymour	845
Bee	22,737	Beeville	842

County	Pop. April 1, 1970	County Seats or Court House	Land Area Sq. Mi.
Bell	124,483	Belton	1,047
Bexar	830,460	San Antonio	1,246
Blanco	3,567	Johnson City	719
Borden	888	Gail	907
Bosque	10,966	Meridian	990
Bowie	67,813	Boston	891
Brazoria	108,312	Angleton	1,423
Brazos	57,978	Bryan	586
Breaster	7,780	Alpine	6,204
Briscoe	2,794	Silverton	874
Brooks	8,005	Falfurrias	904
Brown	25,877	Brownwood	938
Burleson	9,999	Caldwell	670
Burnet	11,420	Burnet	996
Caldwell	21,178	Lockhart	544
Calhoun	17,831	Port Lavanca	527
Callahan	8,205	Baird	856
Cameron	140,368	Brownsville	896
Camp	8,005	Pittsburg	192
Carson	6,358	Panhandle	900
Cass	24,133	Linden	941
Castro	10,394	Dimmitt	880
Chambers	12,187	Anahuac	616
Cherokee	32,008	Rusk	1,049
Childress	6,605	Childress	699
Clay	8,079	Henrietta	1,102
Cochran	5,326	Morton	783
Coke	3,087	Robert Lee	911
Coleman	10,288	Coleman	1,280
Collin	66,920	McKinney	836
Collingsworth	4,755	Wellington	894
Colorado	17,638	Columbus	949
Comal	24,165	New Braunfels	567
Comanche	11,898	Comanche	944
Concho	2,937	Paint Rock	1,004
Cooke	23,471	Gainesville	985
Coryell	35,311	Gatesville	1,043
Cottle	3,204	Paducah	900
Crane	4,172	Crane	795
Crockett	3,885	Ozona	2,794
Crosby	9,085	Crosbyton	911
Culberson	3,429	Van Horn	3,851
Dallam	6,012	Dalhart	1,494
Dallas	1,327,695	Dallas	859
Dawson	16,604	Lamesa	902
Deaf Smith	18,999	Hereford	1,510
Delta	4,927	Cooper	276
Denton	75,633	Denton	911
Dewitt	18,660	Cuero	910
Dickens	3,737	Dickens	931
Dimmit	9,039	Carrizo Springs	1,344
Donley	3,641	Clarendon	905
Duval	11,722	San Diego	1,814
Eastland	18,092	Eastland	952
Ector	91,805	Odessa	907
Edwards	2,107	Rocksprings	2,076
Ellis	46,638	Waxahachie	940
El Paso	359,291	El Paso	1,057
Erath	18,141	Stephenville	1,085
Falls	17,300	Marlin	764
Fannin	22,705	Bonham	905
Fayette	17,650	La Grange	934
Fisher	6,344	Roby	904
Floyd	11,044	Floydada	993
Foard	2,211	Crowell	676
Fort Bend	52,314	Richmond	869
Franklin	5,291	Mount Vernon	293
Freestone	11,116	Fairfield	865
Frio	11,159	Pearsall	1,116
Gaines	11,593	Seminole	1,489
Galveston	169,812	Galveston	399
Garza	5,289	Post	914
Gillespie	10,553	Fredericksburg	1,055
Glasscock	1,155	Garden City	863
Goliad	4,869	Goliad	871
Gonzales	16,375	Gonzales	1,056
Gray	26,949	Pampa	934
Grayson	83,225	Sherman	940
Gregg	75,929	Longview	282
Grimes	11,855	Anderson	801
Guadalupe	33,554	Seguin	714
Hale	34,137	Plainview	979
Hall	6,015	Memphis	885
Hamilton	7,198	Hamilton	844
Hansford	6,351	Spearman	907
Hardeman	6,795	Quanah	687
Hardin	29,996	Kountze	897
Harris	1,741,912	Houston	1,723
Harrison	44,841	Marshall	894
Hartley	2,782	Channing	1,488
Haskell	8,512	Haskell	877
Hays	27,642	San Marcos	650
Hemphill	3,084	Canadian	904
Henderson	26,466	Athens	943
Hidalgo	181,535	Edinburg	1,543
Hill	22,596	Hillsboro	1,010
Hockley	20,396	Levelland	908
Hood	6,368	Granbury	426
Hopkins	20,710	Sulphur Springs	793
Houston	17,855	Crockett	1,237
Howard	37,796	Big Spring	911
Hudspeth	2,392	Sierra Blanca	4,554
Hunt	47,948	Greenville	826
Hutchinson	24,443	Stinnett	875
Irion	1,070	Mertzon	1,073
Jack	6,711	Jacksboro	945
Jackson	12,975	Edna	850
Jasper	24,692	Jasper	907
Jeff Davis	1,527	Fort Davis	2,259
Jefferson	246,402	Beaumont	951
Jim Hogg	4,654	Hebbronville	1,143
Jim Wells	33,032	Alice	845
Johnson	45,769	Cleburne	740
Jones	16,106	Anson	956
Karnes	13,462	Karnes City	758
Kaufman	32,392	Kaufman	815
Kendall	6,964	Boerne	670
Kenedy	678	Sarita	1,394
Kent	1,434	Jayton	880
Kerr	19,454	Kerrville	1,101
Kimble	3,904	Junction	1,274
King	464	Guthrie	944
Kinney	2,006	Brackettville	1,393
Kleberg	33,166	Kingsville	851
Knox	5,972	Benjamin	851
Lamar	36,062	Paris	984
Lamb	17,770	Littlefield	1,022
Lampasas	9,323	Lampasas	726
La Salle	5,014	Cotulla	1,500
Lavaca	17,903	Hallettsville	975
Lee	8,048	Giddings	637
Leon	8,738	Centerville	1,102
Liberty	33,014	Liberty	1,180
Limestone	18,100	Groesbeck	931
Lipscomb	3,486	Lipscomb	934
Live Oak	6,697	George West	1,055
Llano	6,979	Llano	941
Loving	164	Mentone	648
Lubbock	179,295	Lubbock	893
Lynn	9,107	Tahoka	915
McCulloch	8,571	Brady	1,066
McLennan	147,553	Waco	1,000
McMullen	1,095	Tilden	1,159
Madison	7,693	Madisonville	480
Marion	8,517	Jefferson	380
Martin	4,774	Stanton	911
Mason	3,356	Mason	935
Matagorda	27,913	Bay City	1,157
Maverick	18,093	Eagle Pass	1,289
Medina	20,249	Hondo	1,352
Menard	2,646	Menard	914
Midland	65,433	Midland	939
Milam	20,028	Cameron	1,028
Mills	4,212	Goldthwaite	734
Mitchell	9,073	Colorado City	920
Montague	15,326	Montague	932
Montgomery	49,479	Conroe	1,090
Moore	14,060	Dumas	909
Morris	12,310	Daingerfield	260
Motley	2,178	Matador	980
Nacogdoches	36,362	Nacogdoches	902
Navarro	31,150	Corsicana	1,070
Newton	11,657	Newton	949
Nolan	16,220	Sweetwater	922
Nueces	237,544	Corpus Christi	841
Orchiltree	9,704	Perryton	907
Oldham	2,258	Vega	1,478
Orange	71,170	Orange	359
Palo Pinto	28,962	Palo Pinto	948
Panola	15,894	Carthage	869
Parker	33,888	Weatherford	903
Parmer	10,509	Farwell	859
Pecos	13,748	Fort Stockton	4,740
Polk	14,457	Livingston	1,100
Potter	90,511	Amarillo	898
Presidio	4,842	Marfa	3,892
Rains	3,752	Emory	210
Randall	53,885	Canyon	914
Reagan	3,239	Big Lake	1,132
Real	2,013	Leakey	622
Red River	14,298	Clarksville	1,033
Reeves	16,526	Pecos	2,608
Refugio	9,494	Refugio	774
Roberts	967	Miami	899
Robertson	14,389	Franklin	877
Rockwall	7,046	Rockwall	147
Runnels	12,108	Ballinger	1,058
Rusk	34,102	Henderson	939
Sabine	7,187	Hemphill	456
San Augustine	7,858	San Augustine	473
San Jacinto	6,702	Coldspring	624
San Patricio	47,288	Sinton	685
San Saba	5,540	San Saba	1,120
Schleicher	2,277	Eldorado	1,331

County	Pop. April 1, 1970	County Seats or Court House	Land Area Sq. Mi.
Scurry	15,760	Snyder	904
Shackelford	3,323	Albany	887
Shelby	19,672	Center	778
Sherman	3,657	Stratford	916
Smith	97,096	Tyler	934
Somervell	2,793	Glen Rose	197
Starr	17,707	Rio Grande City	1,211
Stephens	8,414	Breckenridge	899
Sterling	1,056	Sterling City	914
Stonewall	2,397	Aspermont	926
Sutton	3,175	Sonora	1,493
Swisher	10,373	Tulia	896
Tarrant	716,317	Fort Worth	861
Taylor	97,853	Abilene	912
Terrell	1,940	Sanderson	2,391
Terry	14,118	Brownfield	899
Throckmorton	2,205	Throckmorton	920
Titus	16,702	Mount Pleasant	418
Tom Green	71,047	San Angelo	1,500
Travis	295,516	Austin	1,012
Trinity	7,628	Groveton	707
Tyler	12,417	Woodville	919
Upshur	20,976	Gilmer	584
Upton	4,697	Rankin	1,312
Uvalde	17,348	Uvalde	1,588
Val Verde	27,471	Del Rio	3,241
Van Zandt	22,155	Canton	845
Victoria	53,766	Victoria	892
Walker	27,680	Huntsville	790
Waller	14,285	Hempstead	509
Ward	13,019	Monahans	827
Washington	18,842	Brenham	594
Webb	72,859	Laredo	3,306
Wharton	36,729	Wharton	1,076
Wheeler	6,434	Wheeler	914
Wichita	120,563	Wichita Falls	611
Wilbarger	15,355	Vernon	952
Willacy	15,570	Raymondville	591
Williamson	37,305	Georgetown	1,104
Wilson	13,041	Floresville	802
Winkler	9,640	Kermit	887
Wise	19,687	Decatur	922
Wood	18,589	Quitman	721
Yoakum	7,344	Plains	830
Young	15,400	Graham	888
Zapata	4,352	Zapata	957
Zavala	11,370	Crystal City	1,291

Utah

(29 counties, 82,096 sq. mi. land; pop. 1,059,273)

County	Pop. April 1, 1970	County Seats or Court House	Land Area Sq. Mi.
Beaver	3,800	Beaver	2,584
Box Elder	28,129	Brigham City	5,603
Cache	42,331	Logan	1,174
Carbon	15,647	Price	1,476
Daggett	666	Manila	682
Davis	99,028	Farmington	297
Duchesne	7,299	Duchesne	3,255
Emery	5,137	Castle Dale	4,439
Garfield	3,157	Panguitch	5,158
Grand	6,688	Moab	3,682
Iron	12,177	Parowan	3,300
Juab	4,574	Nkephi	3,412
Kane	2,421	Kanab	3,904
Millard	6,988	Fillmore	6,793
Morgan	3,983	Morgan	603
Piute	1,164	Junction	754
Rich	1,615	Randolph	1,023
Salt Lake	458,607	Salt Lake City	764
San Juan	9,606	Monticello	7,707
Sanpete	10,976	Manti	1,597
Sevier	10,103	Richfield	1,929
Summit	5,879	Coalville	1,849
Tooele	21,545	Tooele	6,923
Uintah	12,684	Vernal	4,487
Utah	137,776	Provo	2,014
Wasatch	5,863	Heber City	1,191
Washington	13,669	Saint George	2,427
Wayne	1,483	Loa	2,486
Weber	126,278	Ogden	581

Vermont

(14 counties, 9,267 sq. mi. land; pop. 444,732)

County	Pop. April 1, 1970	County Seats or Court House	Land Area Sq. Mi.
Addison	24,266	Middlebury	784
Bennington	29,282	Bennington	672
Caledonia	22,789	Saint Johnsbury	612
Chittenden	99,131	Burlington	533
Essex	5,416	Guildhall	663
Franklin	31,282	Saint Albans	660
Grand Isle	3,574	North Hero	83
Lamoille	13,309	Hyde Park	474
Orange	17,676	Chelsea	690
Orleans	20,153	Newport	715
Rutland	52,637	Rutland	927

County	Pop. April 1, 1970	County Seats or Court House	Land Area Sq. Mi.
Washington	47,659	Montpelier	707
Windham	33,476	Newfane	784
Windsor	44,082	Woodstock	962

Virginia

(96 cos., 38 ind. cities, 39,780 sq. mi.; pop. 4,648,494)

County	Pop. April 1, 1970	County Seats or Court House	Land Area Sq. Mi.
Accomack	29,004	Accomac	476
Albemarle	37,780	Charlottesville	740
Alleghany	12,461	Covington	444
Amelia	7,592	Amelia, C. H.	366
Amherst	26,072	Amherst	470
Appomattox	9,784	Appomattox	345
Arlington	174,284	Arlington	26
Augusta	44,220	Staunton	986
Bath	5,192	Warm Springs	540
Bedford	26,728	Bedford	727
Bland	5,423	Bland	369
Botetourt	18,193	Fincastle	548
Brunswick	16,172	Lawrenceville	579
Buchanan	32,071	Grundy	508
Buckingham	10,597	Buckingham	582
Campbell	43,319	Rustburg	529
Caroline	13,925	Bowling Green	545
Carroll	23,092	Hillsville	494
Charles City	6,158	Charles City	181
Charlotte	12,366	Charlotte Courthouse	470
Chesterfield	77,045	Chesterfield	442
Clarke	8,102	Berryville	174
Craig	3,524	New Castle	336
Culpeper	18,218	Culpeper	389
Cumberland	6,179	Cumberland	291
Dickenson	16,077	Clintwood	332
Dinwiddie	25,046	Dinwiddie	507
Essex	7,099	Tappahannock	250
Fairfax	455,032	Fairfax	399
Fauquier	26,375	Warrenton	660
Floyd	9,775	Floyd	383
Fluvanna	7,621	Palmyra	288
Franklin	28,163	Rocky Mount	716
Frederick	28,893	Winchester	405
Giles	16,741	Pearisburg	363
Gloucester	14,059	Gloucester	228
Goochland	10,069	Goochland	289
Grayson	15,439	Independence	452
Greene	5,248	Stanardsville	153
Greensville	9,604	Emporia	299
Halifax	30,076	Halifax	796
Hanover	37,479	Hanover	465
Henrico	154,364	Richmond	229
Henry	50,901	Martinsville	381
Highland	2,529	Monterey	416
Isle of Wight	18,285	Isle of Wight	317
James City	17,853	Williamsburg	152
King and Queen	5,491	King and Queen	318
King George	8,039	King George	176
King William	7,497	King William	278
Lancaster	9,126	Lancaster	137
Lee	20,321	Jonesville	438
Loudoun	37,150	Leesburg	517
Louisa	14,004	Louisa	517
Lunenburg	11,687	Lunenburg	442
Madison	8,638	Madison	327
Mathews	7,168	Mathews	89
Mecklenburg	29,426	Boydton	612
Middlesex	6,295	Saluda	130
Montgomery	47,157	Christiansburg	394
*Nansemond	35,166	Suffolk	408
Nelson	11,702	Lovingston	471
New Kent	5,300	New Kent	210
Northampton	14,442	Eastville	220
Northumberland	9,239	Heathsville	190
Nottoway	14,260	Nottoway	308
Orange	13,792	Orange	355
Page	16,581	Luray	316
Patrick	15,282	Stuart	464
Pittsylvania	58,789	Chatham	1,001
Powhatan	7,696	Powhatan	269
Prince Edward	14,379	Farmville	357
Prince George	29,092	Prince George	276
Prince William	111,102	Manassas	347
Pulaski	29,564	Pulaski	328
Rappahannock	5,199	Washington	267
Richmond	6,504	Warsaw	190
Roanoke	67,339	Salem	262
Rockbridge	16,637	Lexington	601
Rockingham	47,890	Harrisonburg	865
Russell	24,533	Lebanon	483
Scott	24,376	Gate City	539
Shenandoah	22,852	Woodstock	507
Smyth	31,349	Marion	435
Southampton	18,582	Courtland	602
Spotsylvania	16,424	Spotsylvania	409
Stafford	24,587	Stafford	270
Surry	5,882	Surry	277
Sussex	11,464	Sussex	494
Tazewell	39,816	Tazewell	522

County	Pop. April 1, 1970	County Seats or Court House	Land Area Sq. Mi.
Warren	15,301	Front Royal	219
Washington	40,835	Abingdon	574
Westmoreland	12,142	Montross	229
Wise	35,947	Wise	412
Wythe	22,139	Wytheville	460
York	33,203	Yorktown	129

*1/1/74 merged with ind. city of Suffolk.

Independent Cities

County	Pop. April 1, 1970		Land Area Sq. Mi.
Alexandria	110,927		15
Bedford	6,011		7
Bristol	14,857		4
Buena Vista	6,425		3
Charlottesville	38,880		10
Chesapeake	89,580		341
Clifton Forge	5,501		4
Colonial Heights	15,097		8
Covington	10,060		4
Danville	46,391		17
Emporia	5,300		2
Fairfax	21,970		6
Falls Church	10,772		2
Franklin	6,880		4
Fredericksburg	14,450		6
Galax	6,278		7
Hampton	120,779		55
Harrisonburg	14,605		6
Hopewell	23,471		9
Lexington	7,597		3
Lynchburg	54,083		25
Martinsville	19,653		11
Newport News	138,177		69
Norfolk	307,951		53
Norton	4,172		4
Petersburg	36,103		8
Portsmouth	110,963		29
Radford	11,596		5
Richmond	249,431		60
Roanoke	92,115		27
Salem	21,982		14
South Boston	6,889		9
Staunton	24,504		9
Suffolk	9,858		2
Virginia Beach	172,106		259
Waynesboro	16,707		7
Williamsburg	9,069		5
Winchester	14,643		3

Washington

(39 counties 66,570 sq. mi. land; pop., 3,409,169)

County	Pop. April 1, 1970	County Seats or Court House	Land Area Sq. Mi.
Adams	12,014	Ritzville	1,894
Asotin	13,799	Asotin	633
Benton	67,540	Prosser	1,722
Chelan	41,103	Wenatchee	2,918
Clallam	34,770	Port Angeles	1,753
Clark	128,454	Vancouver	627
Columbia	4,439	Dayton	853
Cowlitz	68,616	Kelso	1,144
Douglas	16,787	Waterville	1,831
Ferry	3,655	Republic	2,202
Franklin	25,816	Pasco	1,253
Garfield	2,911	Pomeroy	709
Grant	41,881	Ephrata	2,675
Grays Harbor	59,553	Montesano	1,910
Island	27,011	Coupeville	212
Jefferson	10,661	Port Townsend	1,805
King	1,159,375	Seattle	2,128
Kitsap	101,732	Port Orchard	393
Kittitas	25,039	Ellensburg	2,317
Klickitat	12,138	Goldendale	1,908
Lewis	45,467	Chehalis	2,423
Lincoln	9,572	Davenport	2,306
Mason	20,918	Shelton	962
Okanogan	25,867	Okanogan	5,301
Pacific	15,796	South Bend	908
Pend Oreille	6,025	Newport	1,402
Pierce	411,027	Tacoma	1,676
San Juan	3,856	Friday Harbor	179
Skagit	52,381	Mount Vernon	1,735
Skamania	5,845	Stevenson	1,672
Snohomish	265,236	Everett	2,098
Spokane	287,487	Spokane	1,758
Stevens	17,405	Colville	2,481
Thurston	76,894	Olympia	714
Wahkiakum	3,592	Cathlamet	261
Walla Walla	42,176	Walla Walla	1,262
Whatcom	81,950	Bellingham	2,126
Whitman	37,900	Colfax	2,153
Yakima	144,971	Yakima	4,268

West Virginia

(55 counties, 24,070 sq. mi. land; pop., 1,744,237)

County	Pop. April 1, 1970	County Seats or Court House	Land Area Sq. Mi.
Barbour	14,030	Philippi	341
Berkeley	36,356	Martinsburg	316
Boone	2,118	Madison	501
Braxton	12,666	Sutton	511
Brooke	29,685	Wellsburg	88
Cabell	106,918	Huntington	279
Calhoun	7,046	Grantsville	281
Clay	9,330	Clay	343
Doddridge	6,389	West Union	319
Fayette	49,332	Fayetteville	663
Gilmer	7,782	Glenville	339
Grant	8,607	Petersburg	478
Greenbrier	32,090	Lewisburg	1,026
Hampshire	11,710	Romney	639
Hancock	39,749	New Cumberland	83
Hardy	8,855	Moorefield	585
Harrison	73,028	Clarksburg	418
Jackson	20,903	Ripley	461
Jefferson	21,280	Charles Town	211
Kanawha	229,515	Charleston	907
Lewis	17,847	Weston	392
Lincoln	18,912	Hamlin	438
Logan	46,269	Logan	456
McDowell	50,666	Welch	533
Marion	61,356	Fairmont	311
Marshall	37,598	Moundsville	304
Mason	24,306	Point Pleasant	433
Mercer	63,206	Princeton	417
Mineral	23,109	Keyser	330
Mingo	32,780	Williamson	423
Monongalia	63,714	Morgantown	365
Monroe	11,272	Union	473
Morgan	8,547	Berkeley Springs	233
Nicholas	22,552	Summersville	642
Ohio	64,197	Wheeling	106
Pendleton	7,031	Franklin	695
Pleasants	7,274	St. Marys	129
Pocahontas	8,870	Marlinton	943
Preston	25,455	Kingwood	645
Putnam	27,625	Winfield	348
Raleigh	70,080	Beckley	605
Randolph	24,596	Elkins	1,036
Ritchie	10,145	Harrisville	452
Roane	14,111	Spencer	486
Summers	13,213	Hinton	350
Taylor	13,878	Grafton	174
Tucker	7,447	Parsons	421
Tyler	9,929	Middlebourne	256
Upshur	19,092	Buckhannon	352
Wayne	37,581	Wayne	513
Webster	9,809	Webster Springs	551
Wetzel	20,314	New Martinsville	363
Wirt	4,154	Elizabeth	235
Wood	86,818	Parkersburg	368
Wyoming	30,095	Pineville	504

Wisconsin

(72 counties, 54,464 sq. mi. land; pop., 4,417,933)

County	Pop. April 1, 1970	County Seats or Court House	Land Area Sq. Mi.
Adams	9,234	Friendship	646
Ashland	16,743	Ashland	1,038
Barron	33,955	Barron	864
Bayfield	11,683	Washburn	1,460
Brown	158,244	Green Bay	524
Buffalo	13,743	Alma	711
Burnett	9,276	Grantsburg	840
Calumet	27,604	Chilton	322
Chippewa	47,717	Chippewa Falls	1,018
Clark	30,361	Neillsville	1,221
Columbia	40,150	Portage	776
Crawford	15,252	Prairie du Chien	568
Dane	290,272	Madison	1,198
Dodge	69,004	Juneau	889
Door	20,106	Sturgeon Bay	492
Douglas	44,657	Superior	1,305
Dunn	29,154	Menomonie	853
Eau Claire	67,219	Eau Claire	647
Florence	3,298	Florence	487
Fond Du Lac	84,567	Fond du Lac	725
Forest (1973)	8,265	Crandon	1,007
Grant	48,398	Lancaster	1,147
Green	26,714	Monroe	585
Green Lake	16,878	Green Lake	354
Iowa	19,306	Dodgeville	762
Iron	6,533	Hurley	747
Jackson	15,325	Black River Falls	999
Jefferson	60,060	Jefferson	564
Juneau	18,455	Mauston	774
Kenosha	117,917	Kenosha	272
Kewaunee	18,961	Kewaunee	330
La Crosse	80,468	La Crosse	451
Lafayette	17,456	Darlington	643
Langlade	19,220	Antigo	856
Lincoln	23,499	Merrill	892
Manitowoc	82,294	Manitowoc	590

County	Pop. April 1, 1970	County Seats or Court House	Land Area Sq. Mi.	County	Pop. April 1, 1970	County Seats or Court House	Land Area Sq. Mi.
Marathon	97,457	Wausau	1,586	Waupaca	37,780	Waupaca	751
Marinette	35,810	Marinette	1,378	Waushara	14,795	Wautoma	627
Marquette	8,865	Montello	455	Winnebago	129,946	Oshkosh	448
Menominee	2,607	Keshena	360	Wood	65,362	Wisconsin Rapids	807
Milwaukee	1,054,249	Milwaukee	237				
Monroe	31,610	Sparta	915				
Oconto	25,553	Oconto	1,001				
Oneida	24,427	Rhinelander	1,112				
Outaramie	119,398	Appleton	634				

Wyoming

(23 counties, 97,203 sq. mi. land; pop., 332,416)

County	Pop. April 1, 1970	County Seats or Court House	Land Area Sq. Mi.
Ozaukee	54,461	Port Washington	236
Pepin	7,319	Durand	235
Pierce	26,652	Ellsworth	590
Polk	26,666	Balsam Lake	931
Portage	47,541	Stevens Point	806
Price	14,520	Phillips	1,260
Racine	170,838	Racine	337
Richland	17,079	Richland Center	583
Rock	131,970	Janesville	721
Rusk	14,238	Ladysmith	906
St. Croix	34,354	Hudson	734
Sauk	39,057	Baraboo	841
Sawyer	9,670	Hayward	1,259
Shawano	32,650	Shawano	919
Sheboygan	96,660	Sheboygan	505
Taylor	16,958	Medford	975
Trempealeau	23,344	Whitehall	735
Vernon	24,557	Viroqua	802
Vilas	10,958	Eagle River	867
Walworth	63,444	Elkhorn	557
Washburn	10,601	Shell Lake	817
Washington	63,839	West Bend	429
Waukesha	231,338	Waukesha	554

County	Pop. April 1, 1970	County Seats or Court House	Land Area Sq. Mi.
Albany	26,431	Laramie	4,248
Big Horn	10,202	Basin	3,157
Campbell	12,957	Gillette	4,756
Carbon	13,354	Rawlins	7,905
Converse	5,938	Douglas	4,281
Crook	4,535	Sundance	2,882
Fremont	28,352	Lander	9,106
Goshen	10,885	Torrington	2,228
Hot Springs	4,952	Thermopolis	2,022
Johnson	5,587	Buffalo	4,175
Laramie	56,360	Cheyenne	2,703
Lincoln	8,640	Kemmerer	4,085
Natrona	51,264	Casper	5,342
Niobrara	2,924	Lusk	2,614
Park	17,752	Cody	6,959
Platte	6,486	Wheatland	2,086
Sheridan	17,852	Sheridan	2,532
Sublette	3,755	Pinedale	4,851
Sweetwater	18,391	Green River	10,429
Teton	4,823	Jackson	4,000
Uinta	7,100	Evanston	2,086
Washakie	7,569	Worland	2,262
Weston	6,307	Newcastle	2,407

1970 Population of Outlying Areas
Source: Bureau of the Census
Puerto Rico

Zip Code	Municipios	Pop. April 1	Land Area Sq. Mile	Zip Code	Municipios	Pop. April 1	Land Area Sq. Mile	Zip Code	Municipios	Pop. April 1	Land Area Sq. Mile
00601	Adjuntas	18,691	66	00653	Guanica	14,889	37	00720	Orocovis	20,201	63
00602	Aguada	25,658	30	00654	Guayama	36,249	65	00723	Patillas	17,828	48
00603	Aguadilla	51,355	36	00656	Guayanilla	18,144	42	00724	Penuelas	15,973	44
00607	Aguas Buenas	18,600	30	00657	Guaynabo	67,042	27	00731	Ponce	158,981	116
00609	Aibonito	20,044	31	00658	Gurabo	18,289	28	00742	Quebradillas	15,582	23
00610	Anasco	19,416	40	00659	Hatillo	21,913	42	00743	Rincon	9,094	14
00612	Arecibo	73,468	127	00660	Hormigueros	10,827	11	00745	Rio Grande	22,032	61
00615	Arroyo	13,033	15	00661	Humacao	36,023	45	00747	Sabana Grande	16,343	37
00617	Barceloneta	20,792	34	00662	Isabela	30,430	56	00751	Salinas	21,837	69
00618	Barranquitas	20,118	33	00664	Jayuya	13,588	39	00753	San German	27,990	54
00619	Bayamon	156,192	44	00665	Juana Diaz	36,270	61	*00936	San Juan	463,242	47
00623	Cabo Rojo	26,060	72	00666	Juncos	21,814	26	00754	San Lorenzo	27,755	53
00625	Caguas	95,661	58	00667	Lajas	16,545	60	00755	San Sebastian	30,157	71
00627	Camuy	19,922	46	00669	Lares	25,263	62	00757	Santa Isabel	16,056	34
00630	Carolina	107,643	48	00670	Las Marias	7,841	44	00758	Toa Alta	18,964	27
00632	Catano	26,459	5	00671	Las Piedras	18,112	33	00759	Toa Baja	46,384	24
00633	Cayey	38,432	50	00672	Loiza	39,062	53	00760	TrujilloAlto	30,669	21
00635	Ceiba	10,312	27	00673	Luquillo	10,390	26	00761	Utuado	35,494	115
00638	Ciales	15,595	66	00701	Manati	30,559	46	00762	Vega Alta	22,810	28
00639	Cidra	23,892	36	00706	Maricao	5,991	37	00763	Vega Baja	35,327	47
00640	Coamo	26,468	77	00707	Maunabo	10,792	21	00765	Vieques	7,767	52
00642	Comerio	18,819	28	00708	Mayaguez	85,857	77	00766	Villalba	18,733	37
00643	Corozal	24,545	42	00716	Moca	22,361	51	00767	Yabucoa	30,165	55
00645	Culebra	732	10	00717	Morovis	19,059	39	00768	Yauco	35,103	68
00646	Dorado	17,388	23	00718	Naguabo	17,996	52				
00648	Fajardo	23,032	31	00719	Naranjito	19,913	28		**Total**	**2,712,033**	**3,421**

Zip Code	Area	Pop. April 1	Land Area Sq. Mile	Zip Code	Area	Pop. April 1	Land Area Sq. Mile	Zip Code	Area	Pop. April 1	Land Area Sq. Mile
	American Samoa				Dededo	10,780	30		**Virgin Islands**		
96920	American Samoa	27,159	76		Inarajan	1,897	19		St. Croix	31,779	80
					Mangilao	3,228	10	00830	St. John	1,729	20
	Canal Zone				Merizo	1,529	6	00801	St. Thomas	28,960	32
	Canal Zone	44,198	362		Mongmong-Too-Maite	6,057	2	00801	Charlotte Amalie	12,220	
	Balboa	32,552	222		Piti	1,284	7	00820	Christiansted	3,020	
	Cristobal	11,646	140		Santa Rita	8,109	17	00840	Frederiksted	1,531	
					Sinajana	3,506	1		**Total**	**62,468**	**132**
	Guam				Talofofo	1,935	17				
96910	Guam	84,996	209		Tamuning	10,218	6		**Trust Territory of Pacific Islands**		
	Agana	2,119	1		Umatac	813	6		Mariana district	9,640	184
	Agana Hts.	3,156	1		Yigo	11,542	35		Marshall district	22,888	70
	Agat	4,308	10		Yona	2,599	20		Palau district	11,210	192
	Asan	2,629	6						Ponape district	18,536	176
	Barrigada	6,356	9						Truk district	21,041	49
	Chalan-Pago-Ordot	2,931	6						Yap district	7,625	46
									Total	**90,940**	**717**

ASTRONOMY AND CALENDAR

Edited by Dr. Kenneth L. Franklin, Astronomer
American Museum-Hayden Planetarium

Celestial Events Highlights, 1975

(All Times are Greenwich Mean Time)

North America this year experiences two total lunar eclipses. In clear skies, a total lunar eclipse is a beautiful and unforgettable experience. Usually, the moon remains visible, bathed in a reddish, coppery light coming from a magnificent sunset and sunrise effect surrounding the earth as seen from the moon. The moon, when viewed in binoculars, seems to be glowing from within like a warm ember in the black, star-studded sky. A lunar eclipse repays a sleepless night.

There are also two partial solar eclipses. In the first case, the conical umbral shadow passes so far from the north polar region that no part of it touches the earth. Substitute "south polar region" in that last sentence, and it's all been said for the second partial solar eclipse.

Of several occultations of planets and Spica, only one, of Mercury, involves North America in any way. Consider notification of occultations, then, as indications that on the days just before and after, the moon will be very close to the other object.

Venus is busy this year. In the spring and early summer it becomes more easily visible in the evening sky. With a little effort, it might be possible to observe the conjunction with Jupiter (0°.2 apart) in February, although twilight makes binoculars useful. In May and June, Venus, Saturn and the moon will be a beautiful evening twilight show; and the dawn sky in late November will bring Venus, the moon, and Spica together. In January, Saturn is in opposition; in October, Jupiter and in December, Mars, all three superior classical planets.

January

Mercury is at greatest eastern elongation on the 23rd, 19° east of the sun in Capricornus. This is not a favorable elongation for easy sighting even though Mercury will be brighter than a zero magnitude star. Stationary on the 29th.

Venus is 6° south of a very thin crescent moon (40 hours past New Moon) on the 14th, appearing as a star of -3.4 magnitude in Capricornus. Only 16° east of the sun, it will be lost in the bright evening twilight.

Mars is 1° south of the waning crescent moon on the 9th. It is a little brighter than a 2d magnitude star but is probably lost in the morning twilight in Ophiuchus.

Jupiter is 7° south of the moon on the 17th in Aquarius. It is slowly fading (down to -1.7), but it is still the brightest planet we can easily see.

Saturn is in opposition on the 6th, 748 million miles away, resembling a zero magnitude star, and found in Gemini. The nearly full moon passes 3° south of it on the 26th. At opposition, a superior planet is at nearly its closest position to earth and thus looks largest in a telescope. In Saturn's case, its rings are most prominent at opposition and nearly at their most "opened" aspect. Saturn is a good object for viewing by any means this entire winter.

Moon passes 1° from Mars on the 9th, Last Quarter, 4th; New Moon, 12th; First Quarter, 20th; Full Moon, 27th. Apogee, 15th (252,300 miles); perigee, 28th (222,200 miles).

Jan. 2 —Earth at perihelion, 91.45 million miles from the sun.

Jan. 3/4 — Quadrantid meteor shower may be weakly visible; the moon rises about midnight just as the shower should begin to appear.

Jan. 6 — Saturn in opposition.

Jan. 19 — Sun enters Capricornus.

February

Mercury is in inferior conjunction on the 8th, 60.8 million miles from Earth, and becomes stationary on the 20th, in Capricornus.

Venus presents an interesting opportunity for astronomical photographers near mid-month. On the evening of the 13th, the very thin crescent moon is seen northeast of bright Venus and northwest of easily seen Jupiter. On the evening of the 17th, Venus is 0°.2 south of Jupiter and is the brighter of the pair. Although they are on the border of Pisces and Aquarius, Venus is 138.6 million miles away and

Jupiter is 544.1 million miles from us.

Mars may be formed as a 1.6 magnitude star 4° south of the waning cresent moon on the 7th. They are in Sagittarius.

Jupiter meets Venus on the 17th.

Saturn, still in Gemini and in retrograde, is 3° north of the gibbous moon on the 22d.

Moon: Last Quarter, 3rd; New Moon, 11th; First Quarter, 19th; Full Moon, 26th in Greenwich, England, 25th in the western hemisphere. Apogee, 12th (252,700 miles); perigee, 25th (221,600 miles). Full moon and perigee are only 3 hours apart. Such close times often result in exceptionally extreme tides.

Feb. 16 — Sun enters Aquarius.

Feb. 17 — Venus and Jupiter are in mutual conjunction, 0°.2 apart.

March

Mercury reaches greatest western elongation (27°) on the 6th. It appears slightly fainter than a zero magnitude star before dawn in the eastern third of Capricornus. This is not a favorable time to find Mercury, because it rises far to the south of east and not sufficiently ahead of the sun.

Venus and the thin crescent moon are beautiful in the twilight sky 3° apart on the 15th.

Mars, in Capricornus, is 6° south of the waning crescent moon on the 9th.

Jupiter is in conjunction on the 22d, 553.8 million miles from the earth, beyond the sun.

Saturn ends its retrograde motion on the 14th in Gemini, appearing as a zero magnitude star.

Moon occults Spica on Mar. 21, but this cannot be seen in the western hemisphere. The night of Mar. 31 (April 1 in Greenwich) the moon occults Neptune. The planet is a little brighter than 8th magnitude, so a telescope is necessary to observe this event. Last Quarter, 4th; New Moon, 13th; First Quarter, 20th; Full Moon, 27th. Apogee, 11th (252,600 miles); perigee, 26th (222,900 miles).

Mar. 11 — Sun enters Pisces.

Mar. 21 — Spring begins in the northern hemisphere at 5:57 GMT (1:57 a.m., EDT). At that moment the Sun will be in the zenith on the equator in the Indian Ocean, south of Calcutta, about dawn on the Prime Meridian through Greenwich.

Mar. 29 — Pluto in opposition, only 2,774 million miles away in Virgo north of Epsilon Virginis. (Numerologists may enjoy the fact that its right

202

ascension is 12h 55m and declination is   12° 55'.)

April

Mercury is in superior conjunction, beyond the sun and 124 million miles from earth on the 18th.

Venus, only 1° to the north, is passed by the crescent moon on the 14th, and passes 7° north of Aldebaran on the 22d, in Taurus.

Mars is 7° south of the waning crescent moon on the 7th. This is the last time the moon will point out this first magnitude "star" in Capricornus. Mars from now on should be interesting to watch as its brightness climbs to its maximum in December, some 7.4 magnitudes brighter than the moon.

Jupiter is still too close to the sun to be seen.

Saturn is 3° north of the thick crescent moon on the 18th (or the evening of the 17th in the eastern hemisphere).

Moon again occults Spica on the 24th for the western hemisphere (2 hours past midnight on the 25th in England). Even though Spica is bright, a telescope or binoculars must be used to watch this because the moon is nearly full. The moon again occults Neptune, 28th. Last Quarter, 3rd; New Moon, 11th; First Quarter, 19th; Full Moon, 25th. Apogee, 7th (252,200 miles); perigee, 23rd (225,700).

Apr. 18 — Sun enters Aries.

Apr. 21 — Uranus in opposition, 1,625 million miles away in Virgo.

May

Mercury is 4° north of the two-day-old crescent moon in the evening twilight of the 13th. Look for a zero magnitude star 8 moon diameters from the moon in Taurus near a line from Aldebaran to El Nath (Beta Tauri), the horn star sometimes associated with Auriga. On the evening of the 16th in the western hemisphere, Mercury will be 22° east of the sun at greatest eastern elongation, still in Taurus and on the line mentioned above, about two-thirds of the way from Aldebaran to El Nath.

Venus is 6° north of the four-day-old moon on the 14th, and 3° north of Saturn on the 24th, all this occuring in Gemini. Notice how Venus moves across Gemini this month. From Taurus, it enters the western boundary of Gemini on the 10th and ends the month 4° south of Pollux on the 31st, passing about 0°.5 south of third magnitude Kappa Geminorum.

Mars, resembling a reddish star of 1st magnitude, the second brightest looking star (after Jupiter) near the border of Pisces and Aquarius, is 7° south of the fading crescent moon in the dawn sky of the 6th.

Jupiter is the brightest looking star in the faint constellation of Pisces. It is 5° south of the thin crescent moon in the dawn sky of the 8th.

Saturn in Gemini is 4° north of the moon on the 15th and 3° south of Venus on the 23rd.

Moon is busy this month. The 11th is the date for a partial eclipse of the sun, seen primarily from Europe. On the 22nd an occultation of Spica will be visible mostly in Antarctica. On the 25th we can see a total eclipse of the moon in its entirety from most of the western hemisphere. About half a day later, the moon occults Neptune, seen from South Africa and the Indian Ocean. Last Quarter on the 3rd; New Moon, 11th; First Quarter, 18th; Full Moon, 25th; Apogee, 5th (251,500 miles); perigee, 20th (228,800 miles).

May 11 — Partial eclipse of the sun.

May 12 — Sun moves into Taurus.

May 14 — The crescent moon is between Venus and Saturn, making a good photo opportunity.

May 24 — Venus-Saturn conjunction. Cameras ready?

May 25 — Total eclipse of the moon, and an occultation of Neptune.

June

Mercury is in inferior conjunction on the 10th, 51 million miles from us.

Venus, east of Saturn in Cancer, is 7° north of the crescent moon on the 13th. It is at greatest eastern elongation from the sun (45°) on the 18th.

Mars is busy in Pisces this month. A little brighter than 1st magnitude, it is 6° south of the moon on the 4th and about 0°.5 south of brilliant Jupiter on the 16th, moving nearly 5 times as fast as the giant planet.

Jupiter is 5° south of the moon on the 5th, and 0°.5 north of Mars on the 16th.

Saturn is becoming lost in the evening twilight, but might be seen in the western hemisphere 4° north of the crescent moon on the 11th. It is a little fainter than a zero magnitude star.

Moon again occults Spica (seen from Antarctica on the 18th) and Neptune (seen from Antarctica on the 22d), and may make its last twilight tableau with Venus and Saturn on the 12th. Last Quarter, 1st; New Moon, 9th; First Quarter, 16th; Full Moon, 23rd. Apogee, 2d (751,100 miles); perigee 14th (229,300 miles); apogee, 29th (251,300 miles).

June 1 — Neptune in opposition, 2,724 million miles away, in Ophiuchus, north of Antares.

June 5 — Check rising times for Mars and Jupiter, add about an hour, and set the alarm. The waning crescent moon will make an interesting arrangement with these planets.

June 12/13 — On these evenings, look into the twilight for the moon with Venus and Saturn close by.

June 16 — See June 5 and follow the instructions there. This time, Mars and Jupiter will be about one moon diameter apart. A good opportunity for a telescope photograph. Mars is only 135 million miles away, but Jupiter is 493 million miles from us.

June 20 — Sun enters Gemini.

June 22 — At Greenwich, at 27 minutes past midnight, the sun makes its most northerly declination and the summer solstice. This same instant translates into June 21, 8:27 p.m., E.D.T.

June 29 — A day or two either side of this date may be included for observation after midnight of the Delta Aquarid meteor shower. The last quarter moon will be a nuisance, however.

July

Mercury is at greatest western elongation (22° from the Sun in eastern Taurus on the 4th. It is occulted by the moon the morning of the 7th, an event visible wherever it is above the horizon in parts of Europe and North America.

Venus in Leo is 0°.4 south of Regulus the evening of the 8th, easily visible to the naked eye. It is 5° north of the crescent moon on the 12th, and achieves greatest brilliancy (magnitude minus 4.2) on the 22d. If you can look through a good amateur telescope or mounted binoculars at this time, you may be surprised to see that brilliant Venus is only a thin crescent.

Mars, barely having quitted Pisces for Aries, is 4° south of the moon on the 3rd.

Jupiter is passed by the moon twice this month in Pisces, first 5° south of the moon on the 2d; then 4° south on the 30th.

Saturn is in conjunction with the sun on the 15th, 936 million miles from us.

Moon occults the 9th magnitude asteroid, Pallas, the morning of the 1st; definitely a telescopic event available to observers in the southern hemisphere. On the 7th, it occults Mercury; on 15th, Spica; and Neptune again on the 19th. Last Quarter, 1st; New Moon, 9th; First Quarter, 15th; Full Moon, 23rd; Last Quarter, 31st. Perigee, 11th (226,500 miles); apogee, 27th (251,900 miles).

July 6 — At 3 hours past midnight at Greenwich, the earth attains its greatest distance from the sun at aphelion, 94.5 million miles.

July 8 — Venus passes less than a moon diameter from Regulus this evening (about 7 p.m. EDT). A telescope will help you see this event which occurs before sunset for most of the western hemisphere.

July 20 — Sun enters Cancer.

August

Mercury is in superior conjunction on the 1st, 125 million miles away.

Venus rapidly moves into the twilight early in the month and arrives at inferior conjunction on the 27th, about 26.7 million miles away.

Mars, brightening noticeably although still a little fainter than a zero magnitude star, is 2° south of the moon on the 1st near the boundary of Aries and Taurus. It is occulted by the moon on the 30th, but not for observers in the western hemisphere. It is still worth watching the close approach, however. The moon has just passed Mars by the time they rise on the night of 29/30.

Jupiter, in Pisces, is 4° south of the moon on the 26th, having begun its retrograde motion on the 15th.

Saturn is still lost in the morning twilight, but may be visible by the end of the month.

Moon occults Venus on the 9th, Spica on the 12th, Neptune on the 15th and Mars on the 30th, but none is visible in North America. Regard these exotic events as opportunities to see the moon make a very close approach to these bodies. New Moon, 7th; First Quarter, 14th; Full Moon, 21st, Last Quarter, 29th. Perigee, 8th (223,700 miles); apogee, 24th (252,400 miles).

Aug. 9 — Sun enters Leo.

Aug. 10-14 — After midnight, when the moon sets, is the most favorable time for the Perseid meteor shower. This is the "Old Faithful" of showers, usually giving a count of about 50 an hour.

September

Mercury is 2° north of the crescent moon in Virgo on the 7th; and at greatest eastern elongation (27° from the sun) on the 13th. Something of a curiosity is a double conjunction of Mercury and Spica this month. On the 24th, in direct motion, it passes 1°.8 south of Spica; is stationary on the 26th; and, now in retrograde, passes 1°.8 south of Spica on the 29th (evening of the 28th for western observers). These events will occur rather low in the southwest twilight.

Venus is stationary in Sextans on the 16th, resuming its direct motion.

Mars starts the month 4° north of Aldebaran on the night of 31/1. Aldebaran, Alpha Tauri, is magnitude 1.1 and Mars is now about +0.3, thus brighter. This is a good time to compare their colors. Try setting binoculars a little out of focus to bring out stellar colors. Mars is 2° north of the moon on the 27th.

Jupiter, still in Pisces, is 4° south of the moon on the 22nd.

Saturn, becoming more visible in the morning sky in faint Cancer, is 5° north of the moon on the 2d and the 30th.

Moon occults only Spica (on the 8th) and Neptune (on the 11th) this month, neither being visible in North America. New Moon, 5th; First Quarter, 12th; Full Moon, 20th; Last Quarter, 28th. Perigee, 6th (222,000 miles); apogee, 20th (252,500 miles).

Sept. 15 — Sun enters Virgo.

Sept. 23 — At 15:55 in Greenwich (11:55 a.m., EDT), the sun crosses the equator over the Amazon jungle, leaving the northern hemisphere for the year. Autumn begins.

October

Mercury is in inferior conjunction on the 9th, 61.4 million miles from us. It is at greatest western elongation (18°) on the 25th.

Venus, occulted by the moon on the 2d, is visible in the southern hemisphere, attaining greatest brilliancy on the 3rd. It is 4° south of Regulus on the 6th, and is 5° north of the moon on the 31st.

Mars, in the confused feet of Gemini, is 4° north of the moon on the 25th.

Jupiter, at magnitude minus 2.5, is in opposition on

the 13th. Only 368 million miles away, it may be found in the rope of Pisces.

Saturn is 5° north of the last quarter moon on the 27th, in Cancer.

Moon occults Venus on the 2d and Neptune on the 9th, events not visible in North America. New Moon, 5th; First Quarter, 12th; Full Moon, 20th; Last Quarter, 27th. Perigee, 4th (222,100 miles); apogee, 17th (257,300 miles).

Oct. 3 — Venus at greatest brilliancy, -4.3 magnitude.

Oct. 13 — Jupiter at opposition.

Oct. 21 — Orionid meteor shower will suffer from a bright waning gibbous moon.

Oct. 29 — Sun enters Libra.

November

Mercury is 5° north of the moon on the 2d, in Virgo, and is 1°.1 north of Uranus on the morning of the 8th. It is in superior conjunction on the 28th, 135 million miles away.

Venus is at the greatest western elongation (47°) in Virgo on the 7th. On the morning of the 29th, Venus, Spica, and the moon are quite close in the morning sky; the Pacific Ocean area can see the occultation of Spica and the conjunction (5°) of Venus and Spica.

Mars, brighter than Sirius by the end of the month, is 5° north of the moon in Gemini on the 21st.

Jupiter, in Pisces, is 5° south of the moon on the 15th.

Saturn stationary in Cancer, begins its retrograde motion on the 15th. On the 24th it is 5° north of the moon.

Moon eclipses the sun partially on the 3rd, visible in Antarctica and southern South America. The moon is in total eclipse on the 18th, again visible over most of North America. The moon occults Spica on the 2d, Neptune on the 5th, and Spica again on the 29th. New Moon, 3rd; First Quarter, 10th; Full Moon, 18th; Last Quarter, 26th. Perigee, 2d (224,100 miles); apogee, 14th (251,800 miles); perigee, 30th (227,400 miles).

Nov. 3 — Partial solar eclipse.

Nov. 18 — Total lunar eclipse.

Nov. 22 — Sun enters Scorpius.

Nov. 29 — Sun enters Ophiuchus.

December

Mercury is left out of the list of events since passing superior conjunction last month. Alone in the evening sky, even the moon cannot catch up to this dizzy little planet.

Venus is 2° north of Uranus on the 11th, and 2° north of the moon on the 29th.

Mars is the star of December and Christmas this year. It is closest to the earth, 52.6 million miles away, on the 9th, and in opposition on the 15th. 52.9 million miles from us in the constellation of Taurus. It is now at magnitude minus 1.6. It is 5° north of the full moon on the 18th.

Jupiter begins its direct motion in Pisces on the 11th, and is 5° south of the moon on the 13th.

Saturn is 5° north of the moon on the 21st.

Moon manages only one occultation, Spica, on the 27th. New moon, 3rd; First Quarter, 10th; Full Moon, 18th; Last Quarter, 25th. Apogee, 11th (251,300 miles); perigee, 26th (230,100 miles).

Dec. 9 — Mars nearest earth.

Dec. 14 — Gemini meteor shower may be a good show in spite of moon.

Dec. 15 — Mars at opposition.

Dec. 18 — Sun enters Sagittarius.

Dec. 22 — At 11:46 GMT (7:46 a.m. EDT), winter begins as the sun stands above the Tropic of Capricorn, and summer begins in the southern hemisphere.

Planets and the Sun

The planets of the solar system, in order of their distance from the sun are Mercury, Venus, Earth, Mars, Jupiter, Saturn, Uranus, Neptune and Pluto. Uranus, Neptune and Pluto are not included in the celestial list because they are too faint to be seen without optical aid. Both Uranus and Neptune are visible through good field glasses, but Pluto is so distant and so small that only large telescopes or long exposure photographs can make it visible.

Since Mercury and Venus are nearer to the sun than is the earth, their motions about the sun are seen from the earth as wide swings first to one side of the sun and then to the other, although they are both passing continuously around the sun in orbits that are almost circular. When their passage takes them either between the earth and the sun, or beyond the sun as seen from the earth, they are invisible to us. Because of the laws which govern the motions of planets about the sun, both Mercury and Venus require much less time to pass between the earth and the sun than around the far aside of the sun so their periods of invisibility are unequal.

The planets that lie farther from the sun than does the earth may be seen for longer periods of time and are invisible only when they are so located in our sky that they rise and set about the same time as the sun when, of course, they are overwhelmed by the sun's great brilliance. None of the planets has any light or exterior heat of its own but each shines only by reflecting sunlight from its surface. Mercury and Venus, because they are between the earth and the sun, show phases very much as the moon does. The planets farther from the sun are always seen as full, although Mars does occasionally present a slightly gibbous phase — like the moon when not quite full.

The planets move rapidly among the stars because they are very much nearer to us than the stars are. The stars are also in motion, some of them at tremendous speeds but they are so far away that their motion does not change their apparent positions in the heavens sufficiently for anyone to perceive that change in a single lifetime. The very nearest star is about 7,000 times as far away as the most distant planet.

Visible Planets of the Solar System

Mercury, Venus, Mars, Jupiter and Saturn

Mercury

Mercury, nearest planet to the sun, is also the smallest of the nine planets known to be orbiting the sun. Its diameter is 3,100 miles and its mean distance from the sun is 36,000,000 miles.

Mercury moves with great speed in its journey about the sun, averaging about 30 miles a second to complete its circuit of the sun in 88 of our days. Radar observations of Mercury by the 1,000-foot radio telescope at Arecibo, Puerto Rico, disclosed that Mercury rotates upon its axis over a period of nearly 59 days, thus exposing all of its surface periodically to the sun. For nearly 100 years, astronomy had accepted a rotational period for Mercury of 88 earth-days, synchronous with its period of revolution. A synchronous rotation-revolution period would have caused the same side of Mercury to face the sun continually and would have produced a temperature of between 750° and 1,000° on the sun-facing surface, while the perpetually dark side would have had a temperature of about — 450° Fahrenheit.

Now, while it is believed that the surface passing before the sun may have a temperature of about 800° F., the temperature on the side turned temporarily away from the sun does not fall as low as might be expected. This night temperature has been described by Russian astronomers as "room temperature" — possibly about 70°. This would contradict the former belief that Mercury did not possess an atmosphere, for some sort of atmosphere would be needed to retain some of the fierce solar radiation that must strike Mercury at its small distance from the sun. A shallow but dense layer of carbon dioxide would produce the "greenhouse" effect in which heat accumulated during exposure to the sun, would not completely escape at night. The actual presence of a carbon dioxide atmosphere is in dispute.

This uncertainty about conditions upon Mercury and its motion arise from its short angular distance from the sun as seen from the earth, for Mercury is always too much in line with the sun to be observed against a dark sky, but is always seen during either morning or evening twilight.

Venus

Venus is slightly smaller than the earth. Its diameter is about 200 miles less than the earth's diameter. Venus moves about the sun at a mean distance of 67,000,000 miles in 225 of our days. Its synodical revolution — its return to the same relationship with the earth and the sun, which is a result of the combination of its own motion and that of the earth — is 584 days. Venus will, then, be nearer to the earth every 19 months than any of the other planets of the solar system. We have never been able to see the surface of Venus because the planet is covered with a dense, white cloudy atmosphere that conceals whatever is below it. This same cloud reflects sunlight efficiently so that when Venus is favorably situated, it is the third brightest object in the sky, exceeded only by the sun and the moon.

Ordinary telescopic observation has been unable to reveal much about the nature of the surface of Venus, nor even its periods of axial rotation. Spectroscopic analysis of light reflected from the clouds indicates only carbon dioxide present above the cloud bank. Infrared spectroscopy from a balloon-borne telescope nearly 20 miles above the earth's surface gave indications of a small amount of water vapor present in the same region of the atmosphere of Venus. In 1956, however, a breakthrough in our knowledge came from radio astronomers at the Naval Research Laboratories in Wash., D. C. Their observations indicated a temperature for Venus of about 600 degrees Fahrenheit, in marked contrast to minus 125 degrees Fahrenheit, previously found at the cloud tops. Subsequent radio work confirmed a high temperature and produced evidence for this temperature to be associated with the solid body of Venus. With this peculiarity in mind, space scientists devised experiments for the U.S. space probe Mariner II to perform when it flew by in 1962. Mariner II confirmed the high temperature and the fact that it pertained to the ground rather than to some special activity of the atmosphere. In addition, Mariner II was unable to detect any radiation belts similar to the earth's so-called Van Allen belts. Nor was it able to detect the existence of a magnetic field even as weak as 1/100,-000 of that of the earth, but it passed about 22,000 miles from the sunward surface.

An international scientific drama occurred in 1966 when a Russian space probe, Venus 4, and the American Mariner V arrived at Venus within a few hours of each other. Venus 4 was unique in that it was designed to allow an instrument package to land gently on the planet's surface via parachute. It ceased transmission of information after 75 minutes when the temperature it read went above 500 degrees Fahrenheit. After considerable controversy, it was agreed several years later that it still had 20 miles to go to reach the surface. In 1969, two more Russian probes dived into Venus' atmosphere, but ended reports after about ¾ hour. The Russians claimed these did make it to the surface and confirmed earlier findings of the Mariner probes. The U.S. probe, Mariner V, went around the dark side of Venus at a distance of about 6,000 miles. Again, it detected no significant magnetic field, but its radio signals passed to earth through Venus' atmosphere twice — once on the night side and once on the day side. The results are startling. Venus' atmosphere is nearly all carbon dioxide and must exert a pressure at the planet's surface of up to 100 times the earth's normal sea-level pressure of one atmosphere. Since the earth and Venus are about the same size, and were presumably formed at the same time by the same general process from the same mixture of chemical elements, one is faced with the question: which is the planet with the unusual history — earth or Venus?

But the apparent strangeness of Venus continues to enlarge. In the last several years, astronomers using radar techniques involving powerful transmitters as well as sensitive receivers and computers have succeeded in determining the rotation period of Venus. It turns out to be 243 days clockwise — in other words, contrary to the spin of most of the other planets and to its own motion around the sun. If it were exactly 243.16 days, Venus would always present the same face toward the earth at every inferior conjunction. This rate and sense of rotation allows a "day" on Venus of 117.4 earth days. Any part of Venus will receive sunlight on its clouds for over 58 days and will be in darkness for 58 days. The atmosphere here must be in sifficient motion to distribute much of the daytime heat to the night side, for little difference in temperature is detected between the two hemispheres. The mysteries of Venus have only been intensified by the knowledge we have recently gained about it.

Mars

Mars is the first planet beyond the earth, away from the sun. Mars' diameter is about 4,200 miles although a determination of the radius and mass of Mars by the space-probe, Mariner IV, which flew by Mars on July 14, 1965 at a distance of less than 6,000 miles, indicated that these dimensions were slightly larger than had been previously estimated. While Mars' orbit is also nearly circular, it is not as nearly centered on the sun as are the orbits of many of the other planets and Mars is more than 30 million miles farther from the sun in some parts of its year than it is at others. Mars takes 687 of our days to make one circuit of the sun, traveling at about 15 miles a second. Mars rotates upon its axis in almost the same period of time that the earth does — 24 hours and 37 minutes. Mars' mean distance from the sun is 141 million miles, so that the temperature on Mars would be lower than that on the earth even if Mars' atmosphere were about the same as ours. The atmosphere is not, however, for Mariner IV reported that

atmosheric pressure on Mars is between 1% and 2% of the earth's atmospheric pressure. This thin atmosphere appears to be largely carbon dioxide. No evidence of free water was found.

There appears to be no magnetic field about Mars. This would eliminate the previous conception of a dangerous radiation belt around Mars similar to the Van Allen Belt around the earth. The same lack of a magnetic field would expose the surface of Mars to an influx of cosmic radiation about 100 times as intense as that on earth.

Deductions from years of telescopic observation indicate that ⅝ths of the surface of Mars is a desert of reddish rock, sand and soil. The rest of Mars is covered by irregular patches that appear generally green in hues that change through the Martian year. These were formerly held to be some sort of primitive vegetation, but with the findings of Mariner IV of a complete lack of water and oxygen, such growth does not appear possible. The nature of the green areas is now unknown. They may be regions covered with volcanic salts whose color changes with changing temperatures and atmospheric conditions, or they may be gray, rather than green. Optical experiments show that when large gray areas are placed beside large red areas, the gray areas will appear green to the eye.

Mars is inclined from a vertical to the plane of its orbit about the sun by about 25° and therefore has seasons as does the earth, except that the Martian seasons are longer because Mars' year is longer. White caps form about the winter pole of Mars, growing through the winter and shrinking in summer. These polar caps were thought to be frozen water which when it melted, nourished the green areas. In view of the negative findings of Mariner IV, however, the caps are thought to be carbon dioxide.

The canals of Mars have become more of a mystery than they were before the voyage of Mariner IV. Markings forming a network of fine lines crossing much of the surface of Mars have been seen there by men who have devoted much of their professional time to the study of the planet, but no canals have shown clearly enough upon previous photographs to be universally accepted. A few of the 21 photographs sent back to earth by Mariner IV covered areas crossed by canals. The pictures show faint, ill-defined, broad, dark markings, but no positive identification of the nature of the markings.

Mariners VI & VII in 1969 sent back many more photographs of higher quality than those of the pioneering Mariner IV. These pictures showed cratering similar to the earlier views, but in addition showed two other types of terrain. Some regions seemed featureless for many square miles, but others were chaotic, showing high relief without apparent organization into mountain chains or craters.

Mariner IX, the first artificial body to be placed in an orbit about Mars, has transmitted over 10,000 photographs covering 100% of the planet's surface. Preliminary study of these photos and other data shows that Mars resembles no other planet we know. Using terrestrial terms, however, scientists describe features that seem to be clearly of volcanic origin. One of these features is Nix Olympica, apparently a caldera over 300 miles in diameter. Some features may have been produced by cracking (faulting) of the surface and the sliding of one region over or past another. Many craters seen to have been produced by impacting bodies such as may have come from the nearby asteroid belt. Features near the south pole may have been produced by glaciers that are no longer present. Flowing water, non-existent on Mars at the present time, probably carved canyons, one 10 times longer and 3 times deeper than the Grand Canyon.

Mars' position in its orbit and its speed around that orbit in relation to the earth's position and speed bring Mars fairly close to the earth on occasions about two years apart and then move Mars and the earth too far apart for accurate observation and photography. Every 15-17 years, the close approaches are especially favorable for an all-out astronomical attack on Mars.

Mars has two satellites. They are small, estimated to be about 5 and 10 miles in diamter if their surfaces have properties similar to that of our moon. They were discovered in 1877 by Asaph Hall. The outer satellite is named Deimos and it revolves around Mars in about 31 hours. The inner satellite, Phobos, whips around Mars in a little more than 7 hours, making three trips around the planet each Martian day.

The Mariner flights of 1969 produced a photograph accidentally taken showing Phobos, silhouetted against the planet. An analysis of the image gives dimensions of Phobos as about 14 miles by 8 miles, proportions resembling those of a potato. The ability of Phobos to reflect light appears to be even less than that of the earth's moon. Mariner IX has confirmed those results and added information that Phobos and Deimos are pitted with large craters and are of irregular shape, suggesting a history of fragmentation.

Jupiter

Jupiter is the largest of the planets. Its equatorial diameter is 88,000 miles, 11 times the diameter of the earth. Its polar diameter is about 6,000 miles shorter. This is caused by the almost fluid condition of its atmosphere and its extremely rapid rate of rotation. Jupiter's day is just under 10 hours long. For a planet of this size, this rotational speed is amazing, and it carries a point on Jupiter's equator along at a speed of 22,000 miles an hour, as compared with 1,000 miles an hour for a point on the earth's equator. Jupiter is at an average distance of 480 million miles from the sun and takes almost 12 of our years to make one complete circuit of the sun.

The only directly observable chemical constituents of Jupiter's atmosphere are methane (CH_4) and ammonia (NH_3), but is reasonable to assume the same mixture of elements available to make Jupiter as to make the sun. This would mean a large fraction of hydrogen and helium must be present also, as well as water, H_2O. The temperature at the tops of the clouds may be about minus 260 degrees Fahrenheit. The clouds are probably ammonia ice crystals, becoming ammonia droplets lower down. There may be a space before water ice crystals show up as clouds; in turn, these become water droplets near the bottom of the entire cloud layer. The total atmosphere may be only a few hundred miles in depth, pulled down by the surface gravity (= 2.64 times earth's) to a relatively thin layer. Of course, the gases become denser with depth until they may turn into a slush or a slurry. Perhaps there is no solid surface—no real interface between solid and gas, but its temperature may approach 1,000 degrees Fahrenheit. Long before the center ith the other elements regarded as impurities—become a fluid metal and perhaps a solid metal near the center. Jupiter's cloudy atmosphere is a fairly good reflector of sunlight and makes it far brighter than any of the stars among which it wanders. An extremely heavy radioactive belt has also been discovered surrounding Jupiter, similar to the earth's Van Allen Belt. This belt was discovered by radio astronomers following the identification of Jupiter as a source of radio emission by B.F. Burke and K.L. Franklin in 1955.

Jupiter has 12 satellites. Four of these are large and bright, rivaling our own moon and the planet Mercury in diameter, and may be seen through a field glass. They move rapidly around Jupiter and their change of position from night to night is extremely interesting to watch. The eight additional satellites are much smaller and in all but one instance, much farther from Jupiter and cannot be seen except through powerful telescopes. The 4 outermost satellites are revolving around Jupiter clockwise as seen from the north, contrary to the motions of the great majority of the satellites in the solar system and to the direction of revolution of the planets around the sun. The reason for this retrograde motion is not known, but one theory is that Jupiter's tremendous gravitational power may have captured 4 of the minor planets or asteroids, that move about the sun between Mars and Jupiter, and that these 4 may be running backwards. Jupiter's mass is more than twice the mass of all the other planets put together, and accounts for Jupiter's tremendous gravitational field and so, probably, for its numerous satellites and its dense atmosphere.

On March 2, 1972, the Pioneer 10 spacecraft was launched on a 21-month trip to Jupiter. Designed to take pictures of the planet and to measure its atmosphere, Pioneer 10 will make a 4-day swing around Jupiter and radio back the information collected before hurtling on into outer space. Some 50 years later, Pioneer 10 will become the first man-made object to leave our solar system. If the space craft is intercepted by intelligent beings in the far reaches of the universe millenia from now, they will find in it a 6x9 in. metal plaque etched with schematic drawings of a man and a woman and a code utilizing the radio properties of pulsars to indicate the location of Planet Earth. On April 5, Pioneer II was launched on a similar mission.

Saturn

Saturn, last of the planets visible to the unaided eye, is almost twice as far from the sun as Jupiter, almost 900 million miles. It is second in size to Jupiter but its mass is much smaller. Saturn's specific gravity is less than that of water. Its diameter is about 71,000 miles at the equator; its rotational speed spins it completely around in a little more than 10 hours, and its atmosphere is much like that of Jupiter, except that its temperature at the top of its cloud layer is at least 100° colder. At about 300° F. below zero, the ammonia would be frozen out of Saturn's clouds. The theoretical construction of Saturn resembles that of Jupiter; it is either all gas, or it has a small dense center surrounded by a layer of ice and a deep atmosphere.

Saturn has ten satellites, the 10th having been discovered by the French astronomer Audouin Dollfus in December, 1966. The newly found satellite is a few thousand miles outside of the edge of Saturn's ring system. Its discovery was made possible by an edgeon presentation of the rings. At such times, the rings virtually disappear to observers on earth. This aspect of the rings reduces their brilliance and permitted the hitherto unknown satellite to be seen.

Saturn's ring system begins about 7,000 miles above the visible disk of Saturn, lying above its equator and extending about 35,000 miles into space. The diameter of the ring system, including Saturn itself, is about 170,000 miles; the rings are estimated to be no thicker than 10 miles. In 1973, radar observation showed the ring particles to be large chunks of material averaging a meter on a side.

The rings cannot be seen except in a telescope of at least 3-inch aperture. Because of Saturn's inclination, as stated above, there are two periods during Saturn's journey around the sun when the rings are presented to us edge-on. At these times, the rings disappear. Nothing that is only 10 miles wide can be seen from a distance of nearly 900 million miles. The rings are approaching a favorable position to be seen. They were edge-on in 1966 and reached maximum visibility again in 1973.

Pioneer II, to pass Jupiter next year, has been guided to pass Jupiter in such a way that Jupiter will swing Pioneer II into an orbit that will bring it near Saturn in 1979. If the space craft is functioning adequately at that time, it will send us the photos and physical data possible only from a close fly-by. This will complete man's initial on-site inspection of the classical planets.

Planetary Configurations, 1975

Greenwich Mean Time

(0 designates midnight; 12 designates noon)

Mo.	d.	h.	m.	
Jan.	2	13	—	⊕at perihelion
	6	09	—☍♄☉	
	9	23	—☌♂☽	♂ 1° S
	13	23	—☌☿☽	☿ 6° S
	14	02	—☌♀☽	♀ 6° S
	17	06	—☌♃☽	♃ 7° S
	23	20	—	☿ gr. elong. E (19°)
	26	03	—☌♄☽	♄ 3° N
Feb.	7	23	—☌♂☽	♂ 4° S
	8	09	—☌☿☉	inferior
	13	15	—☌♀☽	♀ 7° S
	14	00	—☌♃☽	♃ 6° S
	17	19	—☌♀♃	♀ 0°.2 S
	22	11	—☌♄☽	♄ 3° N
Mar.	6	06	—	☿ gr. elong. W (27°)
	9	03	—☌♂☽	♂ 6° S
	10	17	—☌☿☽	☿ 6° S
	15	21	—☌♀☽	♀ 3° S
	21	05	57	☉ enters ♈ spring begins
	21	18	—☌♄☽	♄ 3° N
	22	02	—☌♃☉	
Apr.	6	20	—☌☿♃	☿ 1° S
	7	08	—☌♂☽	♂ 7° S
	10	14	—☌♃☽	♃ 6° S
	14	21	—☌♀☽	♀ 1° N
	18	02	—☌♄☽	♄ 3° N
	18	21	—☌☿☉	superior
May	6	13	—☌♂☽	♂ 7° S
	8	10	—☌♃☽	♃ 5° S
	11	07	—	☉ partial eclipse
	13	01	—☌☿☽	☿ 4° N
	14	18	—☌♀☽	♀ 6° N
	15	12	—☌♄☽	♄ 4° N
	17	00	—	☿ gr. elong. E (22°)
	24	01	—☌♀♄	♀ 3° N
	25	06	—	☽ total eclipse
June	4	16	—☌♂☽	♂ 6° S
	5	05	—☌♃☽	♃ 5° S
	10	18	—☌☿☉	inferior
	12	00	—☌♄☽	♄ 4° N
	13	10	—☌♀☽	♀ 7° N
	16	06	—☌♂♃	♂ 0°.5 S
	18	16	—	♀ gr. elong. E (45°)
	22	00	27	☉ sun enters ♋ summer begins
July	2	21	—☌♃☽	♃ 5° S
	3	16	—☌♂☽	♂ 4° S

Mo.	d.	h.	m.	
	4	14	—	☿ gr. elong. W (22°)
	6	03	—	⊕ aphelion
	7	13	—☌☿☽	☿ 0°.5 S
	12	10	—☌♀☽	♀ 5° N
	15	15	—☌♄☉	
	22	00	—	♀ gr. brilliancy
	30	10	—☌♃☽	♃ 4° S
Aug.	1	09	—☌☿☉	superior
	1	13	—☌♂☽	♂ 2° S
	6	06	—☌♄☽	♄ 4° N
	9	07	—☌♀☽	♀ 0°.7 S
	15	22	—☌☿♀	☿ 9° N
	26	17	—☌♃☽	♃ 4° S
	27	13	—☌♀☉	inferior
	30	05	—☌♂☽	♂ 0°.1 N
Sept.	2	22	—☌♄☽	♄ 5° N
	7	10	—☌☿☽	☿ 2° N
	13	22	—	☿ gr. elong. E (27°)
	22	19	—☌♃☽	♃ 4° S
	23	15	55	☉ enters ♎ autumn begins
	27	14	—☌♂☽	♂ 2° N
	30	12	—☌♄☽	♄ 5° N
Oct.	2	09	—☌♀☽	♀ 1° N
	3	17	—	♀ gr. brilliancy
	9	11	—☌☿☉	inferior
	13	15	—☍♃☉	
	19	18	—☌♃☽	♃ 5° S
	25	01	—	☿ gr. elong. W (18°)
	25	12	—☌♂☽	♂ 4° N
	27	22	—☌♄☽	♄ 5° N
	31	08	—☌♀☽	♀ 5° N
Nov.	2	13	—☌☿☽	☿ 5° N
	3	13	—	☉ partial eclipse
	7	06	—	♀ gr. elong. W (47°)
	15	19	—☌♃☽	♃ 5° S
	18	22	—	☽ total eclipse
	21	17	—☌♂☽	♂ 5° N
	24	04	—☌♂☽	♂ 5° N
	28	21	—☌☿☉	superior
	29	19	—☌♀☽	♀ 5° N
Dec.	9	00	—	♂ nearest ⊕
	13	01	—☌♃☽	♃ 5° S
	15	14	—☍♂☉	
	18	07	—☌♂☽	♂ 5° N
	21	08	—☌♄☽	♄ 5° N
	22	11	46	☉ enters ♑ winter begins
	29	10	—☌♀☽	♀ 2° N

Planetary Configurations, 1976

As a service to those who wish to consult the planetary configurations for early 1976 in the preceding fall, THE WORLD ALMANAC publishes the configurations for January, February, March and April, 1976.

Mo.	d.	h.	m.	
Jan.	4	11	—	⊕ at perihelion
	7	05	—	☿ gr. elong. E (19°)
	20	11	—☍♄☉	
	23	06	—☌☿☉	inferior
Feb.	16	15	—	☿ gr. elong. W (26°)
Mar.	20	11	50	☉ enters ♈ spring begins
Apr.	1	18	—☌☿☉	superior
	12	18	—☌☿♃	☿ 1°.9 north
	27	20	—☌♃☉	
	28	02	—	☿ gr. elong. E (21°)

Moon's Perigee and Apogee, 1975

Greenwich Mean Time in 24 hour clock (0 is midnight; 12 is noon).

Perigee 1975

Day	Hour GMT	Hour EST	Day	Hour GMT	Hour EST
Jan. 28	09	04	July 11	20	15
Feb. 25	22	17	Aug. 8	20	15
Mar. 26	09	04	Sept. 6	04	23*
Apr. 23	13	08	Oct. 4	15	10
May 20	20	15	Nov. 2	01	20*
June 14	22	17	Nov. 30	01	20*
			Dec. 26	04	23*

Apogee 1975

Day	Hour GMT	Hour EST	Day	Hour GMT	Hour EST
Jan. 15	21	16	June 29	23	18
Feb. 12	04	23*	July 27	16	11
Mar. 11	05	00	Aug. 24	04	23*
Apr. 7	16	11	Sept. 20	07	02
May 5	10	5	Oct. 17	11	06
June 2	04	23*	Nov. 14	00	19*
			Dec. 11	19	14

*Previous date.

Four Eclipses in 1975
Greenwich Mean Time

First Eclipse

A **partial eclipse of the sun, May 11.** The umbral shadow of the moon passes about 250 miles over the north polar region without contacting the earth at any point, but the penumbral shadow will cover a wide area. The beginning is seen from North Africa, while the end is seen from Kamchatka. All of Europe and most of Siberia is included, as well as Greenland. Greatest eclipse, when over 86% of the Sun's diameter is covered, is seen at the northern end of Baffin Island. Northern Alaska experiences a small part of the event about sunset.

Circumstances of the Eclipse

Eclipse begins.........	May 11, 05:08.5
Greatest eclipse......	07:16.8
Eclipse ends..........	09:24.8

Second Eclipse

A **total eclipse of the moon, May 24/25.** This eclipse may be seen in its entirety from almost all of the western hemisphere. The beginning of the umbral phase is visible in the western half of Africa and southwestern Europe, South America, Antarctica, the Atlantic Ocean, southern Greenland, North America except the northwestern part, and the eastern Pacific. The end is visible in extreme eastern Australia, New Zealand, the Pacific Ocean, Antarctica, South America, North America except the northern part, and the western Atlantic Ocean. The magnitude is 1.43.

Circumstances of the Eclipse

Moon enters penumbra.	May 25, 02:58.6
Moon enters umbra....	04:00.0
Total eclipse begins....	05:03.4
Middle of eclipse.......	05:48.0
Total eclipse ends......	06:32.6
Moon leaves umbra....	07:36.0
Moon leaves penumbra.	08:37.6

Third Eclipse

A **partial eclipse of the sun, Nov. 3.** As in the first eclipse, the umbral shadow of the moon does not fall on the earth at any point, passing about 100 miles over the south polar region. The penumbral portion of the shadow will fall on almost all of Antarctica and South America south of 30° south latitude. At greatest eclipse, observed from about 70° south latitude and 162° west longitude, 96% of the solar diameter will be covered by the moon.

Circumstances of the Eclipse

Eclipse begins.........	Nov. 3, 11:16.4
Greatest eclipse......	13:16.7
Eclipse ends..........	15:16.7

Fourth Eclipse

A **total eclipse of the moon, Nov. 18/19.** Anything happening to the moon is independent of an observer's location on the earth, hence if the moon is above the observer's horizon, he will see whatever is happening to it at that moment. Thus, the beginning of the umbral phase of this eclipse is visible over most of Asia, the western part of Australia, the Indian Ocean, Indonesia, the arctic regions, Africa, Europe, the eastern part of the Atlantic Ocean, Greenland, the extreme northeastern part of South America, and the eastern part of North America. The end of this eclipse is visible in North America except the western part, most of South America, Greenland, the Atlantic Ocean, Europe, Africa, the western half of Asia, the western part of the Indian Ocean and the arctic regions. Magnitude of the eclipse is 1.07.

Circumstances of the Eclipse

Moon enters penumbra.	Nov. 18, 19:27.1
Moon enters umbra....	20:40.2
Total eclipse begins....	22:04.2
Middle eclipse.........	22:25.0
Total eclipse ends......	22:45.7
Moon leaves umbra....	Nov. 19, 00:09.8
Moon leaves penumbra.	01:22.7

Morning and Evening Stars, 1975
(Greenwich Mean Time)

January:
Morning—Mars
Evening—Mercury, Venus, Jupiter, Saturn

February:
Morning—Mercury (Feb. 8), Mars
Evening—Mercury (Feb. 1-7), Venus, Jupiter, Saturn

March:
Morning—Mercury, Mars, Jupiter (Mar. 22)
Evening—Venus, Jupiter (Mar. 1-21), Saturn

April:
Morning—Mercury (Apr. 1-17), Mars, Jupiter
Evening—Mercury (Apr. 18), Venus, Saturn

May:
Morning—Mars, Jupiter
Evening—Mercury, Venus, Saturn

June:
Morning—Mercury (June 10), Mars, Jupiter
Evening—Mercury (June 1-9), Venus, Saturn

July:
Morning—Mercury, Mars, Jupiter, Saturn (July 15)
Evening—Venus, Saturn (July 1-14)

August:
Morning—Venus (Aug. 27), Mars, Jupiter, Saturn
Evening—Mercury (Aug. 1), Venus (Aug. 1-26)

September:
Morning—Venus, Mars, Jupiter, Saturn
Evening—Mercury

October:
Morning—Mercury (Oct. 9), Venus, Mars, Jupiter (Oct. 1-12), Saturn
Evening—Mercury (Oct. 1-8), Jupiter (Oct. 13)

November:
Morning—Mercury (Nov. 1-27), Venus, Mars, Saturn
Evening—Mercury (Nov. 28), Jupiter

December:
Morning—Venus, Mars (Dec. 1-14), Saturn
Evening—Mercury, Mars (Dec. 15)

Right Ascension of Mean Sun, 1975
0ʰ Greenwich Mean Time

Date	h	m	Date	h	m	Date	h	m	Date	h	m	Date	h	m	Date	h	m
Jan. 1	18	40.1	Mar. 2	22	36.6	May 1	2	33.2	July 10	7	09.2	Sept. 8	11	05.8	Nov. 7	15	02.3
11	19	19.5	12	23	16.1	11	3	12.6	20	7	48.6	18	11	45.2	17	15	41.7
21	19	59.0	22	23	55.5	21	3	52.1	30	8	28.0	28	12	24.6	27	16	21.2
31	20	38.4				31	4	31.5									
Feb. 10	21	17.8	Apr. 1	0	34.9	June 10	5	10.9	Aug. 9	9	07.5	Oct. 8	13	04.0	Dec. 7	17	00.6
20	21	57.2	11	1	14.4	20	5	50.3	19	9	46.9	18	13	43.4	17	17	40.0
			21	1	53.8	30	6	29.8	29	10	26.3	28	14	22.9	27	18	19.4

Largest Telescopes are in Northern Hemisphere

Most of the world's major astronomical installations are in the northern hemisphere, while many of astronomy's major problems are found in the southern sky. This imbalance has long been recognized and is being remedied at this time. For several years, large telescopes have been under construction in South America and Australia. Many of these will soon be in use.

In the northern hemisphere the very large reflectors include 3 in California: at Palomar Mtn., 200 inches; at Lick Observatory, Mt. Hamilton, 120 inches; and at Mt. Wilson Observatory, 100 inches. Also in the U.S. are a 158-inch reflector at Kitt Peak, Arizona dedicated in June 1973 and a 107-inch telescope at the McDonald Observatory on Mt. Locke in Texas. A telescope at the Crimean Astrophysical observatory in the Soviet Union has a 104-inch mirror and the USSR is building one with a mirror 236 inches in diameter which will be placed in operation soon.

At present the largest telescopes in the southern hemisphere are 74-inch reflectors in Pretoria, South Africa, and Mt. Stromlo, Australia. But the U.S. is erecting a 150-inch reflector at Cerro Tololo, in Chile. A 140-inch mirror at La Silla Mountain in Chile will be administered by the European Observatory Group. And Australia is building a telescope with a 150-inch aperture at Siding Spring.

Tremendous advances in the study of the central region of the Milky Way and of the Magellanic Clouds, as well as more detailed studies of many other regions hitherto unavailable to giant telescopes, will be made through the use of these new instruments.

Optical Telescopes

Optical astronomical telescopes are of two kinds, refracting and reflecting. In the first, light passes through a lens which brings the light rays into focus, where the image may be examined after being magnified by a second lens, the eye-piece, or directly photographed.

The reflector consists of a concave parabolic mirror, generally of Pyrex or now of a relatively heat insensitive material, cervit, coated with silver or aluminum, which reflects the light rays back toward the upper end of the telescope, where they are either magnified and observed by the eye-piece or, as in the case of the refractors, photographed. In most reflecting telescopes, the light is reflected again by a secondary mirror and comes to a focus after passing through a hole in the side of the telescope, where the eye-piece or camera is located, or after passing through a hole in center of the primary mirror.

World's Largest Refractors
Location and diameter in inches

Yerkes Obs., Williams Bay, Wisc.	40
Lick Obs., Mt. Hamilton, Calif.	36
Astrophys. Obs., Potsdam, E. Germany	32
Paris Observatory, Meudon, France	32
Allegheny Obs., Pittsburgh, Pa.	30
Univ. of Paris, Nice, France	30
Royal Greenwich Obs., Herstmonceux, England	28
Union Obs., Johannesburg, South Africa	26.5
Universitats-Sternwarte, Vienna, Austria	26.5
University of Virginia	26
Obs., Academy of Sciences Pulkova, USSR	26
Astronomical Obs., Belgrade, Yugoslavia	26
Leander McCormick Obs., Charlottesville, Va.	26

Obs. Mitaka, Tokyo-to, Japan.	26
US Naval Obs., Washington, D.C.	26
Mt. Stromlo Obs., Canberra, Australia	26

The Schmidt Telescopes are strictly cameras and cannot be used for visual observation. Light enters the upper end of the telescope tube, is refracted slightly by a correcting lens and is then reflected from a spherical mirror with a short focus. A camera, placed inside the telescope at the focus of the mirror can photograph large areas of the sky without distortion at the edges of the photograph. The diameters of Schmidt telescopes are given in two figures; first, the diameter of the correcting lens, followed by the diameter of the mirror.

The lists are partial lists including refractors from 26 inches and reflectors of 40-inches aperture or larger.

World's Largest Reflectors

Hale Obs., Palomar Mtn., Calif.	200
Kitt Peak National Obs., Tucson, Ariz.	158
Lick Obs., Mt. Hamilton, Calif.	120
McDonald Obs., Fort Davis, Texas.	107
Crimean Astrophys. Obs., Nauchny, USSR	104
Hale Obs., Mount Wilson, Calif.	100
Royal Greenwich Obs., Herstmonceux, England.	98
Mauna Kea Obs., Univ. of Hawaii, Hawaii.	88
Kitt Peak National Obs., Tucson, Ariz.	84
McDonald Obs., Fort Davis, Texas.	82
Saint Michel l'Observatoire, (Basses Alpes), Fr.	77
Tokyo Obs., Japan.	74
David Dunlap Obs., Ontario, Canada	74
Helwan Obs., Helwan, Egypt.	74
Astrophys. Obs., Kamogata, Okayama-ken, Japan.	74
Radcliffe Obs., Pretoria, South Africa	74
Dominion Astrophys, Obs., Victoria, B.C.	73
Perkins Obs., Flagstaff, Ariz.	72
Agassiz Station Harvard Obs., Cambridge, Mass.	61
National Obs., Bosque Alegre Sta. Argentina	61
Arizona Univ. Obs., Tucson, Ariz.	60
Boyden Obs., Bloemfontein, South Africa.	60
Mt. Wilson Obs., Pasadena, Calif.	60
Observatorium der Deutschen Tautenberg, Germany (Schmidt)	54-80
Mt. Stromlo Obs., Canberra, Australia	50
Observatorio Astronomica, Merate, Como Italy.	50
Sternberg Astronomical Inst., Crimea, USSR.	50
Berlin-Babelsberg, Obs., Germany	49
Obs. Padua Univ., Asiago, Italy.	48
Melbourne, Australia.	48
Astrophy. Obs., Nauchny, Crimea, USSR	48
Dominion Astrophys. Obs., Victoria, B.C.	48
Saint Michel l'Observatoire, (Basses Alpes), Fr.	48
Nizamiah Obs., Osmania Univ., Hyderabad, India.	48
Palomar Obs., Mt. Palomar, Calif. (Schmidt)	48-72
Paris Obs., St. Michel, France	47
Uccle Obs., Belgium. (Schmidt)	33-46
Lowell Obs., Flagstaff, Ariz.	42
Hamburg-Bergedorf Sternwarte, Germany.	40
Kvistaberg Obs., Uppsala U., Swe. (Schmidt)	40-54
Observatoire Geneva, Switzerland.	40
Observatorio Merate, Como, Italy.	40
Royal Obs., Cape of Good Hope, S. Africa.	40
Stockholm Obs., Saltsjobaden, Sweden.	40
US Naval Obs., Flagstaff, Ariz.	40
Pulkovo Obs., Russia.	40
Mt. Stromlo, Canberra Australia.	40

Major Planetariums in the United States

A planetarium projector is perhaps the most complicated instructional device ever made. The first modern planetarium projector was designed and built in 1923 by Walter Bauersfeld of the Zeiss Optical Company. Other instruments had been attempted with only fair success before this time and modern projectors have developed from this beginning. There are now several manufacturers who make elaborate planetarium projectors frequently employing computers and industrial electronic circuitry.

A typical projector for a large auditorium can project the images of nearly 9,000 stars against the reflective surface of a hemispherical dome. In addition, the Milky Way, star clusters, nebulae and other objects sufficiently bright to be seen under ideal conditions by the unaided eye are shown.

Planetarium projectors are usually in the form of two globes, one at either end of a latticed cylinder. The globes contain projectors for the stars, one for the northern hemisphere and the other for the south. In the latticed cylinder are projectors for the sun, the moon and the five planets visible to the eye. The motions of all of these objects are duplicated by the projector with amazing fidelity. First of all, the projector can be set in latitude so that it will produce the sky as it might be seen from any location on earth. The daily motion of the earth, which appears to move the sky throughout the day and night, is the most obvious effect produced. Then there is annual motion, the progress of the sun, moon and planets through the year, including the phasing of the moon. Finally, the precession of the equinoxes, the slow swing of the poles of the earth which is accomplished in 25,800 years and which slowly changes our view of the sky, is also built into the mechanism of these instruments.

The effects of the projector itself are usually supplemented by auxiliary projectors mounted around the edges of the auditorium to produce the color effects of sunrise and sunset, the aurora, clouds, rainbows, eclipses and many other phenomena. Most of the functions of the projector are controlled by the lecturer, who produces them from an array of switches and rheostats mounted in a control console usually situated near the north side of the auditorium.

There are literally hundreds of small planetarium projectors in schools and museums in the United States and several planetariums whose auditoriums will seat hundreds. Some of the major planetariums in the United States are listed below:

Academy Planetarium, U. S. Air Force Academy.
Adler Planetarium, Chicago, Ill.
American Museum-Hayden Planetarium, N. Y. C.
Buhl Planetarium, Pittsburgh, Pa.
Charles Hayden Planetarium, Boston, Mass.
Fels Planetarium, Philadelphia, Pa.
Fernback Science Center Planetarium, Atlanta, Ga.
Griffith Planetarium, Los Angeles, Calif.
La. Arts and Science Planetarium, Baton Rouge, La.
McDonnell Planetarium, St. Louis, Mo.
Morehead Planetarium, Chapel Hill, N.C.
Morrison Planetarium, San Francisco, Calif.
Robert T. Longway Planetarium, Flint, Mich.
Straslenbrugh Planetarium Rochester, N. Y.

Midnight To Dawn Best Time to See Meteors

In the earth's journey around the sun, the side from midnight to noon is the "front" of the earth. The hours from midnight to dawn are best for observing most meteors and meteor showers, for the earth is "running into" the meteoroids. It is common to see 5 to 10 meteors every morning hour. These sporadic meteors are unpredictable, appear in any part of the sky, and move in any direction. A meteor shower involves some organization. Many showers may exhibit 50 or more meteors each hour, but some events of weak showers may be hours apart. Shower meteors are distinguished by noting where the streak of light has come from. After three or more meteors have been traced back to a common point on the sky, one may suspect them of being part of a stream of meteoroids in space. The common point is called the radiant and is geometrically related to the vanishing point in perspective.

About a dozen meteor showers occur each year and the dates on which they take place may be found in the Calendar of Celestial Events. These showers are caused by the earth's passage through streams of meteoroids left in space by comets, of which they were a part. The meteoroids orbit the sun along the path originally followed by the comet and are encountered annually by the earth as it moves about the sun.

Canadian and American researchers have found evidence that the earth has been subjected to heavy bombardment from space on several occasions from 34,000,000 to 700,000 years ago.

The oldest of these catastrophes covered the eastern half of North America, the Atlantic Ocean and the northern half of Africa. Scars in the form of circular pits, sometimes a score of yards in diameter and ofter filled with water, have been located in northern Quebec, and fragments of metallic, stony and glassy objects define the area.

Central Europe received a fall of similar objects about 15,000,000 years ago and the most recent fall, about 700,000 years ago, struck the region including Australia and southeastern Asia.

The stony-metallic fragments are thought to originate in the asteroid belt, a region in space roughly between Mars and Jupiter in which travel thousands of minor planets ranging in size from 480 miles in diameter down to flying mountains a few miles across. Collisions among asteroids are believed to provide fragments, some of which may reach the earth. The glassy fragments, called tektites, were thought to be material resulting from collisions of large objects with the earth or the moon, scattered originally in liquid form and cooling in flight after initial impact into drop-shaped, glassy particles. Rocks recovered from the moon in the Apollo program show such a difference in chemical composition from tektites that most investigators feel that tektites did not come from the moon.

Meteorites

Meteoroids are celestial bodies, possibly associated with comets, that move through space with velocities up to 40 miles per second. Upon reaching the earth's atmosphere, they are vaporized by the heat of the friction of their passage into the atmosphere and are seen as meteors. An unusual number in a short period of time is called a meteor shower. Meteors are popularly known as falling stars or shooting stars. While most of them are consumed, a few fall to earth as fused metal or stone, and are called meteorites.

Many meteorites have been picked up in the United States, most of them small. A huge meteorite may lie embedded in the earth at Meteor Crater on U. S. 6 near Canyon Diablo in Arizona. The crater is 1 mi. in diameter at the surface and over 500 feet deep, and is surrounded by a wall of earth filled with pyrites presumably originating with the meteor. A lake in the Ungava region of northern Quebec fills the Chubb Crater, discovered 1943, which is 7½ mi. around. Vast destruction of timber was caused by a meteorite that hit in the vicinity of Lake Baikal, in Siberia, June 30, 1908. A large meteor that split into fragments of 80 to 820 pounds fell Feb. 17, 1930, 14 mi. sw of Paragould, Ark.

On display in the American Museum-Hayden Planetarium, New York, N. Y. are three meteorites: a 34 ton 85 pound iron-nickel meteorite and another 3-ton one brought from Cape York, Greenland, by Robert E. Peary in 1907 and a 14½ ton meteorite found in the Willamette region of Oregon in 1902.

The Sun

The sun, the controlling body of our solar system, is a star whose dimensions cause it to be classified among stars as average in size, temperature and brightness. Its proximity to the earth makes it appear to us as tremendously large and bright. A series of thermo-nuclear reactions involving the atoms of the elements of which it is composed produces the heat and light that make life possible on the earth.

The sun has a diameter of 864,000 miles and is distant, on the average, 92,900,000 miles from the earth. It is 1.41 times as dense as water. The light of the sun reaches the earth in 499.02 seconds or slightly more than 8 minutes. The average solar surface temperature has been measured by several indirect methods which agree closely on a value of 6,000° Kelvin or about 10,000° Farenheit. The interior temperature of the sun is about 35,000,000° Fahrenheit.

When sunlight is analyzed with a spectroscope, it is found to consist of a continuous spectrum composed of all the colors of the rainbow in order, crossed by many dark lines. The "absorption lines" are produced by gaseous materials in the atmosphere of the sun. More than 60 of the natural terrestrial elements have been identified in the sun, all in gaseous form because of the intense heat of the sun.

Spheres and Corona

The radiating surface of the sun is called the **photosphere,** and just above it is the **chromosphere.** The chromosphere is visible to the naked eye only at times of total solar eclipses, appearing then to be a pinkish-violet layer with occasional great prominences projecting above its general level. With proper instruments the chromosphere can be seen or photographed when ever the sun is visible without waiting for a total eclipse. Above the chromosphere is the **corona,** also visible to the naked eye only at times of total eclipse. Instruments also permit the brighter portions of the corona to be studied whenever conditions are favorable. The pearly light of the corona surges millions of miles from the sun. Iron, nickel and calcium are believed to be principal contributors to the composition of the corona, all in a state of extreme attenuation and high ionization that indicates temperatures on the order of a million degrees, Fahrenheit.

Sunspots

There is an intimate connection between sunspots and the corona. At times of low sunspot activity, the fine streamers of the corona will be much longer above the sun's equator than over the polar regions of the sun, while during high sunspot activity, the corona extends fairly evenly outward from all regions of the sun, but to a much greater distance in space. Sunspots are dark, irregularly-shaped regions whose diameters may reach tens of thousands of miles. The average life of a sunspot group is from two to three weeks, but there have been groups that have lasted for more than a year, being carried repeatedly around as the sun rotated upon its axis. The record for the duration of a sunspot is 18 months. Sunspots reach a low point every 11.3 years, with a peak of activity occurring irregularly between two successive minima.

The sun is 400,000 times as bright as the full moon and gives the earth 6 million times as much light as do all the other stars put together. Actually, most of the stars that can be easily seen on any clear night are brighter than the sun.

The Zodiac

The sun's apparent yearly path among the stars is known as the **ecliptic** The zone 16° wide, 8° on each side of the ecliptic, is known as the **zodiac.** Inside of this zone are the apparent paths of the sun, moon, earth and major planets. Beginning at the point on the ecliptic which marks the position of the sun at the vernal equinox, and thence proceeding eastward, the zodiac is divided into twelve signs of 30° each, as shown herewith.

These signs are named from the twelve constellations of the zodiac with which the signs coincided in the time of the astronomer Hipparchus, about 2,000 years ago. Owing to the precession of the equinoxes, that is to say, to the retrograde motion of the equinoxes along the ecliptic, each sign in the zodiac has, in the course of 2,000 years, moved backward 30° into the constellation west of it; so that the sign Aries is now in the constellation Pisces, and so on. The vernal equinox will move from Pisces into Aquarius about the middle of the 26th Century. The signs of the zodiac with their Latin and English names are as follows:

Spring	1.♈Aries.	The Ram.		5.♌Leo	the Lion.		9.♐Sagittarius.	The Archer.
	2.♉Taurus.	The Bull.		6.♍Virgo.	The Virgin.	**Winter**	10.♑Capricornus.	The Goat.
	3.♊Gemini.	The Twins.	**Autumn**	7.♎Libra.	The Balance.		11.♒Aquarius.	The Water Bearer.
Summer	4.♋Cancer.	The Crab.		8.♏Scorpius.	The Scorpion.		12.♓Pisces	The Fishes.

The Moon

The moon completes a circuit around the earth in a period whose mean or average duration is 27 days 7 hours 43.2 minutes. This is the moon's sidereal period. Because of the motion of the moon in common with the earth around the sun, the mean duration of the lunar month — the period from one new moon to the next new moon — is 29 days 12 hours 44.05 minutes. This is the moon's synodical period.

The mean distance of the moon from the earth according to the American Ephemeris is 238,857 miles. Because the orbit of the moon about the earth is not circular but elliptical, however, the maximum distance from the earth that the moon may reach is 252,710 miles and the least distance is 221,463 miles. All distances are from the center of one obuect to the center of the other.

The moon's diameter is 2,160 miles. If we deduct the radius of the moon, 1,080 miles, and the radius of the earth, 3,963 miles from the monimum distance or perigee, given above, we shall have for the nearest approach of the bodies' surfaces 216,420 miles.

The moon rotates on its axis in a period of time exactly equal to its sidereal revolution about the earth — 27.321666 days. The moon's revolution about the earth is irregular because of its elliptical orbit. The moon's rotation, however, is regular and this produces together with the irregular revolution what is called "libration in longitude" which permits us to see first farther around the east side and then farther around the west side of the moon. The moon's variation north or south of the ecliptic permits us to see farther over first one pole and then the other of the moon and this is "libration in latitude." These two libration effects permit us to see a total of about 60% of the moon's surface over a period of time. The hidden side of the moon was photographed in 1959 by the Soviet space vehicle Lunik III. Since then many excellent pictures of nearly all of the moon's surface have been transmitted to earth by Lunar Orbiters launched by the U.S.

The tides are caused mainly by the moon, because of its proximity to the earth. The ratio of the tide-raising power of the moon to that of the sun is 11 to 5.

Comet Table 1975-1986

Name	Year of Disc.	Due to Return		Period in Years	Peri-helion Dist.	Aphe-lion Dist.	Inclina-tion to Ecliptic Degree	Long. of Ascend. Node Degree	From Asc. Node to Perihelion Degree
Arend.	1951	Mar.	1975	7.98	1.85	6.14	20	356	47
Perrine-Mrkos.	1896	July	1975	6.72	1.27	5.85	18	240	166
Westphal.	1852	Oct.	1975	61.88	1.25	30.03	41	347	57
Gunn.	1970*	Feb.	1976	6.80	2.44	4.74	10	68	197
Wolf.	1884	Feb.	1976	8.43	2.51	5.78	27	204	161
Churyumou-Gerasimenko.	1969*	Mar.	1976	6.55	1.28	5.72	7	50	11
Harrington-Abell.	1955	July	1976	7.19	1.77	5.68	17	146	338
Schaumasse.	1911	Aug.	1976	8.18	1.20	6.92	12	86	52
Klemola.	1965*	Aug.	1976	11.0	1.76	8.1	11	182	148
d'Arrest.	1851	Aug.	1976	6.23	1.17	5.61	17	141	179
Pons-Winnecke.	1819	Nov.	1976	6.34	1.25	5.61	22	93	172
Kojima.	1970	Dec.	1976	6.19	1.63	5.11	4	291	198
Johnson	1949	Jan.	1977	6.77	2.20	4.96	14	118	206
Dutoit-Neujmin.	1941	Feb.	1977	6.31	1.68	5.15	3	188	116
Van Houten.	1961	Feb.	1977	15.75	3.94	8.03	7	23	15
Kopff.	1906	Mar.	1977	6.42	1.57	5.34	5	120	163
Faye.	1843	Mar.	1977	7.39	1.62	5.98	9	199	204
Grigg-Skjellerup.	1902	Apr.	1977	5.12	1.00	4.94	21	213	359
Encke.	1786	Aug.	1977	3.30	0.39	4.10	12	334	186
Temple I.	1867	Jan.	1978	5.50	1.50	4.73	10	68	179
Arend-Rigaux.	1951	Feb.	1978	6.84	1.44	5.76	18	122	329
Temple II.	1873	Feb.	1978	5.26	1.36	4.68	12	119	191
Wolf-Harrington.	1924	Mar.	1978	6.55	1.62	5.38	18	254	187
Whipple.	1933	Mar.	1978	7.47	2.48	5.16	10	188	190
Tschinshan I.	1965	May	1978	6.64	1.50	5.57	10	96	23
Comas-Sola.	1926	May	1978	8.55	1.77	6.60	13	63	40
Daniel.	1909	June	1978	7.09	1.66	5.72	20	68	11
Ashbrook-Jackson.	1948	Aug.	1978	7.43	2.28	5.33	12	2	349
Tschinshan II.	1965	Sept.	1978	6.80	1.78	5.40	7	288	203
Jackson-Neujmin.	1936	Dec.	1978	8.39	1.43	6.83	14	163	196
VanBiesbroeck.	1954	Dec.	1978	12.41	2.41	8.31	7	149	134
Halley.	240BC	May	1986	76.1	0.59	35.3	162	58	112

*One appearance only.

Notes on the Comet Table

Most of the comets in the table will not be seen except by professional astronomers or by well-equipped amateurs. At any given time, these observers may be able to follow about a half dozen comets of which the public is unaware. An easily seen comet is rare, one or two every ten to fifteen years.

Comets are named for their discoverers, up to three independent observers being so honored. If a comet becomes unusual, it may be well-known by these names. Usually, however, a preliminary designation is used. This is the year followed by a letter of the alphabet assigned in the order of discovery during that year. About two years later, after any likely late discoveries, comets are given their permanent designation which states the year of their perihelion passage and a Roman numeral giving the order of passage during that year. Well-known periodic comets will receive these designations at each appearance, but the literature and the Comet Table will continue to identify them by their discoverers' names.

Chronological Eras, 1975

The year 1975 of the Christian Era comprises the latter part of the 199th and the beginning of the 200th year of the independence of the United States of America.

Era	Year	Begins in 1975	Era	Year	Begins in 1975
Byzantine.	7484	Sept. 14	Japanese.	2635	Jan. 1
Jewish.	5736	Sept. 6	Grecian (Seleucidae).	2287	Sept. 14
Olympiads.	2750	July 1			(or Oct. 14
(Third year of Olympiad 688)			Indian (Saka).	1897	Mar. 22
Roman (Ab Urbe Condita).	2728	Jan. 14	Diocletian.	1692	Sept. 12
Nabonassar (Babylonian).	2724	Apr. 30	Mohammedan (Hegira).	1395	Jan. 14

Chronological Cycles, 1975

Dominical Letter . . . . E   Golden Number (Lunar Cycle) . . . 19   Roman Indiction 13
Epact 17   Solar Cycle 24   Julian Period (year in) 6688

Astronomical Constants; Speed of Light

The following astronomical constants were adopted in 1968, in accordance with the resolutions and recommendations of the International Astronomical Union (Hamburg 1964): Velocity of light, 299,792.5 kilometers per second, or about 186,282 statute miles per second; solar parallax, $8''.794$; constant of nutation, $9''.210$; and constant of aberration, $20''.496$.

The Earth: Size, Computation of Time, Seasons

Size and Dimensions

The earth is the fifth largest planet and the third from the sun. Its mass is 6 sextillion, 588 quintillion short tons. Using the parameters of an ellipsoid adopted by the International Astronomical Union in 1964 and recognized by the International Union of Geodesy and Geophysics in 1967, the length of the equator is 24,901.55 miles, the length of a meridian is 24,859.82 miles, the equatorial diameter is 7,926.41 miles, and the area of this reference ellipsoid is approximately 196,938,800 square miles.

The earth is considered a solid, rigid mass with a dense core of magnetic, probably metallic material. The outer part of the core is probably liquid. Around the core is a thick shell or mantle of heavy crystalline rock which in turn is covered by a thin crust forming the solid granite and basalt base of the continents and ocean basins. Over broad areas of the earth's surface the crust has a thin cover of sedimentary rock such as sandstone, shale, and limestone formed by weathering of the earth's surface and deposition of sands, clays, and plant and animal remains.

The temperature in the earth increases about 1°F. with every 100 to 200 feet in depth, in the upper 100 kilometers of the earth, and the temperature near the core is believed to be near the melting point of the core materials under the conditions at that depth. The heat of the earth is believed to be derived from radioactivity in the rocks, pressures developed within the earth, and original heat (if the earth in fact was formed at high temperature).

Atmosphere of the Earth

The earth's atmosphere is a blanket composed of gases and some water vapor. The principal gases are nitrogen, óxygen and argon, in amounts of about 78,21 and 1% by volume. Also present in minute quantities are carbon dioxide, hydrogen, neon, helium, krypton and xenon.

Water vapor displaces other gases and varies from nearly zero to about 4% by volume. The height of the ozone layer varies from approximately 12 to 21 miles above the earth. Traces exist as low as 6 miles and as high as 35 miles. Traces of methane have been found.

The atmosphere rests on the earth's surface with the weight equivalent to a layer of water 34 ft. deep. For about 300,000 ft. upward the gases remain in the proportions stated. Gravity holds the gases to the earth. The weight of the air compresses it at the bottom, so that the greatest density is at the earth's surface. Pressure, as well as density, decreases as height increases because the weight pressing upon any layer is always less than that pressing upon the layers below.

The temperature of the air drops with increased height, until the tropopause is reached. This may vary from 25,000 to 60,000 ft. The atmosphere below the tropopause is the troposphere; the atmosphere for about twenty miles above the tropopause is the stratosphere, where the temperature generally increases with height except at high latitudes in winter. A temperature maximum near the 30-mile level is called the stratopause. Above this boundary is the mesosphere where the temperature decreases with height to a minimum, the mesopause, at a height of 50 miles. Extending above the mesosphere to the outer fringes of the atmosphere is the thermosphere, a region where temperature increases with height to a value measured in thousands of degrees Fahrenheit. The lower portion of this region, extending from 50 to about 400 miles in altitude, is characterized by a high ion density, and is thus called the ionosphere. The outer region is called exosphere; this is the region where gas molecules traveling at high speed may escape into outer space. Above 600 miles.

Latitude, Longitude

Position on the globe is measured by means of meridians and parallels. Meridians, which are imaginary lines drawn around the earth through the poles, determine longitude. The meridian running through Greenwich, England, is the prime meridian of longitude, and all others are either east or west. Parallels, which are imaginary circles parallel with the equator, determine latitude. The length of a degree of longitude varies as the cosine of the latitude. At the equator a degree is 69.171 statute miles; this is gradually reduced toward the poles. Value of a longitude degree at the poles is zero.

Latitude is reckoned by the number of degrees north or south of the equator, an imaginary circle on the earth's surface everywhere equidistant between the two poles. According to the IAU Ellipsoid of 1964, the length of a degree of latitude is 68.708 statute miles at the equator and varies slightly north and south because of the oblate form of the globe; at the poles it is 69.403 statute miles.

Computation of Time

The earth rotates on its axis and follows an ellipitical orbit around the sun. The rotation makes the sun appear to move across the sky from East to West. It determines day and night and the complete rotation, in relation to the sun, is called the apparent or true solar day. This varies but an average determines the mean solar day of 24 hours.

The mean solar day is in universal use for civil purposes. It may be obtained from apparent solar time by correcting observations of the sun for the equation of time, bu when high precision is required, the mean solar time is calculated from its relation to sidereal time. These relations are extremely complicated, but for most practical uses, they may be considered as follows:

Sideral time is the measure of time defined by the diurnal motion of the vernal equinox, and is determined from observation of the meridian transits of stars. One complete rotation of the earth relative to the equinox is called the sidereal day. The mean sideral day is 23 hours, 56 minutes, 4.091 seconds of mean solar time.

The Calendar Year begins at 12 o'clock precisely local clock time, on the night of Dec. 31-Jan. 1. The day and the calendar month also begin at midnight by the clock. The interval required for the earth to make one absolute revolution around the sun is a sidereal year; it consists of 365 days, 6 hours, 9 minutes, and 9.5 seconds of mean solar time (approximately 24 hours per day) in 1900, and is increasing at the rate of 0.0001-second annually.

The Tropical Year, on which the return of the seasons depends, is the interval between two consecutive returns of the sun to the vernal equinox. The tropical year consisted of 365 days, 5 hours, 48 minutes, and 46 seconds. It is decreasing at the rate of 0.530 seconds per century.

In 1956 the unit of time interval was defined to be identical with the second of Ephemeris Time, 1/31,556,925.9747 of the tropical year for 1900 January 0d 12th hour E. T. A physical definition of the second based on a quantum transition of cesium (atomic second) was adopted in 1964. The atomic second is equal to 9,192,631,770 cycles of the emitted radiation. In 1967 this atomic second was adopted as the unit of time interval for the Intern'l System of units.

The Zones and Seasons

The five zones of the earth's surface are the torrid, lying between the Tropics of Cancer and Capricorn; North Temperate, between Cancer and the Arctic Circle; South Temperate, between Capricorn and the

Antarctic Circle; the Frigid Zones, between the polar Circles and the Poles.

The inclination or tilt of the earth's axis with respect to the sun determines the seasons. These are commonly marked in the North Temperate Zone, where spring begins at the vernal equinox, summer at the summer solstice, autumn at the autumnal equinox and winter at the winter solstice.

In the South Temperate Zone, the seasons are reversed. Spring begins at the autumnal equinox, summer at the winter solstice, etc.

If the earth's axis were perpendicular to the plane of the earth's orbit around the sun there would be no change of seasons. Day and night would be of nearly constant length and there would be equable conditions of temperature. But the axis is tilted 23° 27′ away from a perpendicular to the orbit and only in March and September is the axis at right angles to the sun.

The points at which the sun crosses the equator are the equinoxes, when day and night are most nearly equal. The points at which the sun is at a maximum distance from the equator are the solstices. Days and nights are then most unequal.

In June the North Pole is tilted 23° 27′ toward the sun and the days in the northern hemishpere are longer than the nights, while the days in the southern hemisphere are shorter than the nights. In December the North Pole is tilted 23° 27′ away from the sun and the situation is reversed.

The Seasons in 1975

In 1975 the 4 seasons will begin as follows: add one hour to EST for Atlantic Time; subtract one hour for Central, two hours for Mountain, 3 hours for Pacific, 4 hours for Yukon, 5 hours for Alaska-Hawaii and six hours for Bering Time. Also shown in Greenwich Mean Time.

		Date	GMT	EST
Vernal Equinox	**Spring**	Mar. 21	05:57	00:57 am
Summer Solstice	**Summer**	June 22	00:27	7:27 p.m.*
Autumnal Equinox	**Autumn**	Sept. 23	15:55	10:55 am
Winter Solstice	**Winter**	Dec. 22	11:46	6:46 am
*June 21				

Poles and Rotation of the Earth

Poles of The Earth

Source: National Oceanic and Atmospheric Admn.

The geographic (rotation) poles, or points where the earth's axis of rotation cuts the surface, are not absolutely fixed in the body of the earth. The pole of rotation describes an irregular curve about its mean position.

Two periods have been detected in this motion: (1) an annual period due to seasonal changes in barometric pressure, load of ice and snow on the surface and to other phenomena of seasonal character; (2) a period of about 14 months due to the shape and constitution of the Earth.

In addition there are small but as yet unpredictable irregularities. The whole motion is so small that the actual pole at any time remains within a circle of 30 or 40 feet in radius centered at the mean position of the pole.

The pole of rotation for the time being is of course the pole having a latitude of 90° and an indeterminate longitude.

Magnetic Poles

The **north magnetic pole** of the earth is that region where the magnetic force is vertically downward and the **south magnetic pole** that region where the magnetic force is vertically upward. A compass placed at the magnetic poles experiences no directive force.

There are slow changes in the disribution of the earth's magnetic field. These changes were at one time attributed in part to a periodic movement of the magnetic poles around the geographical poles, but later evidence refutes this theory and points, rather, to a slow migration of "disturbance" foci over the earth.

There appear shifts in position of the magnetic poles due to the changes in the earth's magnetic field. The center of the area designated as the north magnetic pole was estimated to be in about latitude 70.5° N and longitude 96° W in 1905; from recent nearby measurements and studies of the secular changes, the position in 1970 is estimated as latitude 76.2° N and longitude 101° W. Improved data rather than actual motion account for at least part of the change.

The position of the south magnetic pole in 1912 was near 71° S and longitude 150° E; the position in 1970 is estimated at latitude 66° S and longitude 139.1° E.

The direction of the horizontal components of the magnetic field at any point is known as magnetic north at that point, and the angle by which it deviates east or west of true north is known as the magnetic declination, or in the mariner's terminology the **variation of the compass.**

A compass without error points in the direction of magnetic north. (In general this is *not* the direction of the magnetic north pole.) If one follows the direction indicated by the north end of the compass, he will travel along a rather irregular curve which eventually reaches the north magnetic pole (though not usually by a great-circle route). However, the action of the compass should not be thought of as due to any influence of the distant pole, but simply as an indication of the distribution of the earth's magnetism at the place of observation.

Rotation of The Earth

Source: U.S. Naval Observatory

The speed of rotation of the earth about its axis has been found to be slightly variable. The variations may be classified as:

(A) **Secular.** Tidal friction acts as a brake on the rotation and causes a slow secular increase in the length of the day, about 1 millisecond per century.

(B) **Irregular.** The speed of rotation may increase for a number of years, about 5 to 10, and then start decreasing. The maximum difference from the mean in the length of the day during a century is about 5 milliseconds. The accumulated difference in time has amounted to approximately 44 seconds since 1900. The cause is probably motion in the interior of the earth.

(C) **Periodic.** Seasonal variations exist with periods of one year and six months. The cumulative effect is such that each year the earth is late about 30 milliseconds near June 1 and is ahead about 30 milliseconds near Oct. 1. The maximum seasonal variation in the length of the day is about 0.5 millisecond. It is believed that the principal cause of the annual variation is the seasonal change in the wind patterns of the Northern and Southern Hemispheres. The semiannual variation is due chiefly to tidal action of the sun, which distorts the shape of the earth slightly.

The secular and irregular variations were discovered by comparing time based on the rotation of the earth with time based on the orbital motion of the moon about the earth and of the planets about the sun. The periodic variation was determined largely with the aid of quartz-crystal clocks. The introduction of the cesium-beam atomic clock in 1955 made it possible to determine in greater detail than before the nature of the irregular and periodic variations.

Star Tables, 1975

These tables include stars of visual magnitude 2.5 and brighter. Co-ordinates are for the epoch Jan. 0.978, 1975. Where no parallax figures are given, the trigonometric parallax figure is smaller than the margin for error and the distance given is obtained by indirect methods. Stars of variable magnitude designated by V.

To find the time when star is on meridian, subtract R.A.M.S. of the sun table on page 209 from the star's right ascension, first adding 24h to the latter, if necessary. Mark this result P.M., if less than 12h; but if greater than 12, subtract 12h and mark the remainder A.M.

Star	Magni-tude	Paral-lax ″	Light Yrs.	Right Ascen. h. m.	Decli-nation ° ′	Star	Magni-tude	Paral-lax ″	Light Yrs.	Right Ascen. h. m.	Decli-nation ° ′
α Andromedae (Alpheratz).......	2.06	0.02	90	0 07.1	+28 57	α Ursae Majoris (Dubhe)........	1.81	0.03	105 11	02.2	+61 53
β Cassiopeiae......	2.26	0.07	45	0 07.8	+59 01	β Leonis (Denebola)..	2.14	0.08	43 11	47.8	+14 43
α Phoenicis.........	2.39	0.04	93	0 25.0	-42 27	γ Ursae Majoris (Phecda).........	2.44	0.02	90 11	52.5	+53 50
α Cassiopeiae (Schedir)........	2.16	0.01	150	0 39.1	+56 24	α Crucis............	1.39		370 12	25.2	+62 58
β Ceti.............	1.02	0.06	57	0 42.3	-18 07	γ Crucis............	1.69		220 12	29.8	-56 58
γ Cassiopeiae.......	2.13v	0.03	96	0 55.2	+60 35	γ Centauri..........	2.17		160 12	40.1	-48 49
β Andromedae......	2.02	0.04	76	1 08.3	+35 29	β Crucis............	1.28		490 12	46.2	-59 33
α Eridani (Achernar)..	0.51	0.02	118	1 36.8	-57 22	ε Ursae Majoris (Alioth)...........	1.79	0.01	68 12	52.9	+56 06
γ Andromedae......	2.14		260	2 02.4	+42 13	ζ Ursae Majoris.....					
α Arietis...........	2.00	0.04	76	2 05.8	+23 21	(Mizar)..........	2.26	0.04	88 13	22.9	+55 03
α Ursae Min. (Pole Star)........	1.99v		680	2 07.4	+89 09	α Virginis (Spica)...	0.91v	0.02	220 13	23.9	-11 02
ο Ceti.............	2.00v	0.01	103	2 18.1	-3 05	ε Centauri..........	2.33		570 13	38.3	-53 20
β Persei (Algol).....	2.06v	0.03	105	3 06.5	+40 52	η Ursae Majoris (Alkaid)..........	1.87		210 13	46.6	+49 26
α Persei...........	1.80	0.03	570	3 22.5	+49 46	β Centauri..........	0.63	0.02	490 14	02.0	-60 15
α Tauri (Aldebaran)..	0.86v	0.05	68	4 34.5	+16 28	θ Centauri..........	2.04	0.06	55 14	05.2	-36 15
β Orionis (Rigel).....	0.14v		900	5 13.3	-8 14	α Bootis (Arcturus)..	0.06	0.09	36 14	14.5	+19 19
α Aurigae (Capella)..	0.05	0.07	45	5 14.8	+45 58	η Centauri..........	2.39v		390 14	35.9	-42 03
γ Orionis (Bellatrix)...	1.64	0.03	470	5 23.8	+6 20	α Centauri..........	0.01	0.75	4.4 14	37.9	-60 44
β Tauri (El Nath)....	1.65	0.02	300	5 24.7	+28 35	α Lupi.............	2.32		430 14	40.3	-47 17
δ Orionis..........	2.20v		1500	5 30.7	-0 19	ε Bootis............	2.37	0.01	103 14	43.9	+27 11
ε Orionis..........	1.70		1600	5 34.9	-1 13	β Ursae Minoris.....	2.04	0.03	105 14	50.8	+74 15
ζ Orionis..........	1.79	0.02	1600	5 39.5	-1 57	α Coronae Borealis...	2.23v	0.04	76 15	33.6	+26 48
κ Orionis..........	2.06		2100	5 46.6	-9 41	δ Scorpii...........	2.34		590 15	58.9	-22 33
α Orionis (Betelgeuse)	0.41v		520	5 53.8	+7 24	α Scorpii (Antares)..	0.92v	0.02	520 16	27.9	-26 23
β Aurigae..........	1.86	0.04	88	5 57.7	+44 57	α Trianguli Australis..	1.93	0.02	82 16	46.0	-68 59
β Canis Majoris.....	1.96	0.01	750	6 21.6	-17 57	ε Scorpii...........	2.28	0.05	66 16	48.5	-34 15
α Carinae (Canopus)..	-0.72	0.02	98	6 23.4	-52 41	η Ophiuchi.........	2.46	0.05	69 17	08.9	-15 42
γ Geminorum.......	1.93	0.03	105	6 36.3	+16 25	λ Scorpii...........	1.60		310 17	31.9	-37 05
α Canis Majoris (Sirius)..........	-1.42	0.38	8.7	6 44.0	-16 41	α Ophiuchi.........	2.09	0.06	58 17	33.8	+12 35
ε Canis Majoris......	1.48		680	6 57.6	-28 56	θ Scorpii...........	1.86	0.02	650 17	35.5	-42 59
δ Canis Majoris......	1.85		2100	7 07.4	-26 21	κ Scorpii.▪.......	2.39		470 17	40.8	-39 01
η Canis Majoris.....	2.46		2700	7 23.1	-29 15	γ Draconis.........	2.21	0.02	108 17	56.0	+51 29
α Geminorum (Castor)	1.97	0.07	45	7 33.0	+31 57	ε Sagittarii.........	1.81	0.02	124 18	22.5	-34 24
α Canis Minoris (Procyon)........	0.37	0.29	11.3	7 38.0	+5 17	α Lyrae (Vega)......	0.04	0.12	26.5 18	36.1	+38 46
β Geminorum (Pollux).	1.16	0.09	35	7 43.8	+28 05	σ Sagittarii.........	2.12		300 18	53.7	-26 20
ζ Puppis...........	2.23		2400	8 02.7	-39 56	α Aquilae (Altair)....	0.77	0.20	16.5 19	49.6	+8 48
γ Velorum.........	1.88		520	8 08.8	-47 16	γ Cygni............	2.22		750 20	21.3	+40 11
ε Carinae..........	1.97		340			α Pavonis..........	1.95		310 20	23.7	-56 49
δ Velorum..........	1.95	0.04	76			α Cygni (Deneb).....	1.26		1600 20	40.6	+45 11
λ Velorum..........	2.24	0.02	750			ε Cygni............	2.46	0.04	75 20	45.2	+33 53
β Carinae........	1.67	0.04	86	9 12.9	-69 37	α Cephei...........	2.44	0.06	52 21	18.0	+62 29
ι Carinae..........	2.25		750	9 16.4	-59 10	ε Pegasi...........	2.31		780 21	43.0	+9 46
κ Velorum..........	2.45	0.01	470	9 21.3	-54 54	α Gruis............	1.76	0.05	64 22	06.7	-47 05
α Hydrae..........	1.98	0.02	94	9 26.4	-8 33	β Gruis............	2.17v		280 22	41.2	-47 01
α Leonis (Regulus)...	1.36	0.04	84	10 07.0	+12 05	α Piscis Austrinis (Fomalhaut).......	1.19	0.14	22.6 22	56.3	-29 45
γ Leonis...........	1.99	0.02	90	10 18.6	+19 58	β Pegasi...........	2.50v	0.02	210 23	02.6	+27 57
β Ursae Majoris (Merak)..........	2.37	0.04	78	11 00.3	+56 31	α Pegasi...........	2.50	0.03	109 23	03.5	+15 04

Pole Star, 1975

Mean time of upper transit 0° Longitude, Greenwich Mean Time

Date	Upper Transit h. m. s.	Polar Dist. ° ′ ″	Date	Upper Transit h. m. s.	Polar Dist. ° ′ ″	Date	Upper Transit h. m. s.	Polar Dist. ° ′ ″
Jan. 1....	19 25 15	0 50 38	May 1....	11 31 41	0 50 56	Sept. 1....	3 30 39	0 51 02
Feb. 1....	17 22 39	0 50 35	June 1....	9 30 11	0 51 04	Oct. 1....	1 33 14	0 50 53
Mar. 1....	15 31 57	0 50 38	July 1....	7 32 53	0 51 08	Nov. 1....	23 27 39	0 50 42
Apr. 1....	13 29 39	0 50 46	Aug. 1....	5 31 47	0 51 07	Dec. 1....	21 29 35	0 50 31

Upper transit of Polaris occurs, on the average, 3m. 56s. earlier each day. The interval between lower and upper transit of Polaris is 11h.58m.2s. The greatest Eastern elongation of Polaris occurs 5h.56m. before upper transit and 6h.2m. after lower transit, while the greatest Western elongation occurs 5h.56m. after upper transit and 6h.2m. before lower transit.

Harvest Moon and Hunter's Moon

The Harvest Moon, the full moon nearest the Autumnal Equinox, ushers in a period of several successive days when the moon rises soon after sunset. This phenomenon gives farmers in temperate latitudes extra hours of light in which to harvest their crops before frost and winter come. The 1975 Harvest Moon falls on Sept. 20. Harvest moon in the south temperate latitudes falls on Mar. 27.

The next full moon after Harvest Moon is called the Hunter's Moon, accompanied by a similar phenomenon but less marked; — Oct. 20, northern hemisphere, Apr. 25, southern hemisphere.

Latitude, Longitude and Altitude of North American Cities

Source: National Ocean Survey (NOAA) for geographic position.
Altitudes U.S. Geological Survey and various sources. *Approx. altitude at downtown business area U.S.; in Canada at tower of major airport.
Source for Canadian Cities: Geodetic Survey of Canada, Dept. of Energy, Mines and Resources.

City	Lat.	Long.	Alt.* Feet	City	Lat.	Long.	Alt.* Feet
Abilene, Texas	32 27 54	99 42 48	1710	Edmonton, Alta.	53 32 45	113 29 15	2,373
Akron, Ohio	41 05 00	81 30 44	874	El Paso, Tex.	31 45 36	106 29 11	3,695
Albany, N.Y.	42 39 01	73 45 01	20	Elizabeth, N.J.	40 39 43	74 12 59	21
Albuquerque, N.M.	35 05 01	106 39 05	4,945	Enid, Okla.	36 23 42	97 52 30	1,240
Allentown, Pa.	40 36 11	75 28 06	255	Erie, Pa.	42 07 15	80 04 57	685
Alert, N.W.T.	82 29 50	62 21 15	95	Eugene, Ore.	44 03 16	123 05 30	422
Altoona, Pa.	40 30 55	78 24 03	1,180	Eureka, Cal.	40 46 54	124 09 24	45
Amarillo, Tex.	35 12 27	101 50 04	3,685	Evansville, Ind.	37 58 20	87 34 21	385
Anchorage, Alaska	61 10 00	149 59 00	118				
Ann Arbor, Mich.	42 16 59	83 44 52	880	Fairbanks, Alaska	64 48 00	147 51 00	448
Asheville, N.C.	35 35 42	82 33 26	1,985	Fall River, Mass.	41 42 06	71 09 18	40
Ashland, Ky.	38 28 36	82 38 23	536	Fargo, N.D.	46 52 30	96 47 18	900
Atlanta, Ga.	33 45 10	84 23 37	1,050	Flagstaff, Ariz.	35 11 36	111 39 06	6,900
Atlantic City, N.J.	39 21 32	74 25 53	10	Flint, Mich.	43 01 18	83 41 00	750
Augusta, Ga.	33 28 20	81 58 00	143	Ft. Smith, Ark.	35 23 06	94 25 06	440
Augusta, Me.	44 18 53	69 46 29	45	Fort Wayne, Ind.	41 04 21	85 08 26	790
Austin, Tex.	30 16 09	97 44 37	505	Fort Worth, Tex.	32 44 55	97 19 44	670
				Fredericton, N.B.	45 57 40	66 38 30	67
Bakersfield, Cal.	35 22 30	119 01 18	400	Fresno, Cal.	36 44 12	119 47 11	285
Baltimore, Md.	39 17 26	76 36 45	20				
Bangor, Me.	44 48 13	68 46 18	20	Gadsden, Ala.	34 00 57	86 00 41	555
Baton Rouge, La.	30 26 58	91 11 00	57	Gainesville, Fla.	29 39 36	82 19 48	175
Battle Creek, Mich.	42 18 58	85 10 48	820	Gallup, N.M.	35 31 30	108 44 30	6,540
Bay City, Mich.	43 36 04	83 53 15	595	Galveston, Tex.	29 18 10	94 47 43	5
Beaumont, Tex.	30 05 20	94 06 09	20	Gary, Ind.	41 36 12	87 20 19	590
Belleville, Ont.	44 09 30	77 22 30	280	Grand Junction, Colo.	39 04 06	108 33 06	4,590
Bellingham, Wash.	48 45 02	122 28 36	60	Grand Rapids, Mich.	42 58 03	85 40 13	610
Berkeley, Cal.	37 52 10	122 16 17	40	Great Falls, Mont.	47 30 06	111 17 06	3,340
Bethlehem, Pa.	40 37 16	75 22 34	235	Green Bay, Wis.	44 30 48	88 00 50	590
Billings, Mont.	45 47 00	108 30 04	3,120	Greensboro, N.C.	36 04 17	79 47 25	839
Biloxi, Miss.	30 23 48	88 53 00	20	Greenville, S.C.	34 50 50	82 24 01	966
Binghamton, N.Y.	42 06 03	75 54 47	865	Guelph, Ont.	43 32 30	80 15 30	1,075
Birmingham, Ala.	33 31 01	86 48 36	600	Gulfport, Miss.	30 22 04	89 05 36	20
Bismarck, N.D.	46 48 23	100 47 17	1,674				
Bloomington, Ill.	40 28 54	88 59 36	800	Halifax, N.S.	44 38 39	63 34 34	476
Boise, Idaho	43 37 07	116 11 58	2,704	Hamilton, Ont.	43 15 17	79 52 28	776
Boston, Mass.	42 21 24	71 03 25	21	Hamilton, Ohio	39 23 59	84 33 47	600
Bowling Green, Ky.	36 59 18	86 27 03	510	Harrisburg, Pa.	40 15 43	76 52 59	365
Brattleboro, Vt.	42 51 06	72 33 48	300	Hartford, Conn.	41 46 12	72 40 49	40
Brandon, Man.	49 51 00	99 57 00	1,265	Helena, Mont.	46 35 33	112 02 24	4,155
Brantford, Ont.	43 07 30	80 15 30	705	Hilo, Hawaii	19 43 30	155 05 24	40
Bridgeport, Conn.	41 10 49	73 11 22	10	Holyoke, Mass.	42 12 29	72 36 36	115
Brockton, Mass.	42 05 02	71 01 25	130	Honolulu, Hawaii	21 18 22	157 51 35	21
Brownsville, Tex.	25 54 07	97 29 58	35	Houston, Tex.	29 45 26	95 21 37	40
Buffalo, N.Y.	42 52 52	78 52 21	585	Hull, Que.	45 26 00	75 44 00	225
Burlington, Ont.	43 18 30	79 46 30	875	Huntington, W.Va.	38 25 12	82 26 33	565
Burlington, Vt.	44 28 34	73 12 46	110	Huntsville, Ala.	34 43 54	86 35 12	640
Butte, Mont.	46 01 06	112 32 11	5,765				
				Indianapolis, Ind.	39 46 07	86 09 46	710
Calgary, Alta.	51 02 46	114 03 24	3,557	Iowa City, Iowa	41 39 37	91 31 53	685
Cambridge, Mass.	42 22 01	71 06 22	20				
Camden, N.J.	39 56 41	75 07 14	30	Jackson, Mich.	42 14 43	84 24 22	940
Canton, Ohio	40 47 50	81 22 37	1,030	Jackson, Miss.	32 17 56	90 11 06	298
Carson City, Nev.	39 10 00	119 46 00	4,680	Jacksonville, Fla.	30 19 44	81 39 42	20
Cedar Rapids, Iowa	41 58 01	91 39 53	730	Jersey City, N.J.	40 43 50	74 03 56	20
Central Islip, N.Y.	40 47 24	73 12 00	80	Johnstown, Pa.	40 19 35	78 55 03	1,185
Champaign, Ill.	40 07 05	88 14 48	740	Joplin, Mo.	37 05 36	94 30 42	990
Charleston, S.C.	32 46 35	79 55 53	9	Juneau, Alaska	58 18 12	134 24 30	50
Charleston, W.Va.	38 21 01	81 37 52	601				
Charlotte, N.C.	35 13 44	80 50 45	720	Kalamazoo, Mich.	42 17 29	85 35 14	755
Charlottetown, P.E.I.	46 14 00	63 07 45	181	Kansas City, Kan.	39 07 04	94 38 24	750
Chattanooga, Tenn.	35 02 41	85 18 32	675	Kansas City, Mo.	39 04 56	94 35 20	750
Cheyenne, Wyo.	41 08 09	104 49 07	6,100	Kenosha, Wis.	42 35 43	87 50 11	610
Chicago, Ill.	41 52 28	87 38 22	595	Key West, Fla.	24 33 30	81 48 12	5
Churchill, Man.	58 45 15	94 10 00	94	Kingston, Ont.	44 13 30	76 30 00	310
Cincinnati, Ohio	39 06 07	84 30 35	550	Kitchener, Ont.	43 26 59	80 29 17	1,031
Cleveland, Ohio	41 29 51	81 41 50	660	Knoxville, Tenn.	35 57 39	83 55 07	890
Colorado Springs	38 50 07	104 49 16	5,980				
Columbia, Mo.	38 57 03	92 19 46	730	Lafayette, Ind.	40 25 11	86 53 39	550
Columbia, S.C.	34 00 02	81 02 00	190	Lancaster, Pa.	40 02 25	76 18 29	355
Columbus, Ga.	32 28 07	84 59 24	265	Lansing, Mich.	42 44 01	84 33 15	830
Columbus, Ohio	39 57 47	83 00 17	780	Laredo, Tex.	27 30 22	99 30 30	440
Concord, N.H.	43 12 22	71 32 25	290	La Salle, Que.	45 25 30	73 38 30	100
Corpus Christi, Tex.	27 47 51	97 23 45	35	Las Vegas, Nev.	36 10 20	115 08 37	2,030
				Laval, Que.	45 35 30	73 45 30	100
Dallas, Tex.	32 47 09	96 47 37	435	Lawrence, Mass.	42 42 16	71 10 08	65
Dartmouth, N.S.	44 38 39	63 34 34	476	Lethbridge, Alta.	49 41 30	112 49 00	2,990
Davenport, Iowa	41 31 19	90 34 33	590	Lexington, Ky.	38 02 50	84 29 46	955
Dawson, Yukon	64 03 30	139 26 00	1,211	Lihue, Hawaii	21 58 48	159 22 30	210
Dayton, Ohio	39 45 32	84 11 43	574	Lima, Ohio	40 44 35	84 06 20	865
Daytona Beach, Fla.	29 12 44	81 01 10	7	Lincoln, Nebr.	40 48 59	96 42 15	1,150
Decatur, Ill.	39 50 42	88 56 47	682	Little Rock, Ark.	34 44 42	92 16 37	286
Denver, Colo.	39 44 58	104 59 22	5,280	London, Ont.	42 59 00	81 15 00	912
Des Moines, Iowa	41 35 14	93 37 00	805	Long Beach, Cal.	33 46 14	118 11 13	35
Detroit, Mich.	42 19 48	83 02 57	585	Lorain, Ohio	41 28 05	82 10 49	610
Dodge City, Kans.	37 45 17	100 01 09	2,480	Los Angeles, Cal.	34 03 15	118 14 28	340
Dubuque, Iowa	42 30 12	90 40 30	620	Louisville, Ky.	38 14 47	85 45 49	450
Duluth, Minn.	46 46 56	92 06 24	610	Lowell, Mass.	42 38 25	71 19 14	100
Durham, N.C.	36 00 00	78 54 45	405	Lubbock, Tex.	33 35 05	101 50 33	3,195
				Macon, Ga.	32 50 12	83 37 36	335
Eau Claire, Wis.	44 48 48	91 29 42	790	Madison, Wis.	43 04 23	89 22 55	860

City	Lat. ° ' "	Long. ° ' "	Alt.* Feet
Manchester, N.H.	42 59 28	71 27 41	175
Marshall, Texas	32 33 00	94 23 00	410
Memphis, Tenn.	35 08 46	90 03 13	275
Meriden, Conn.	41 32 06	72 47 30	190
Mexico City, Mexico	19 25 45	99 7 00	7,347
Miami, Fla.	25 46 37	80 11 32	10
Milwaukee, Wis.	43 02 19	87 54 15	635
Minneapolis, Minn.	44 58 57	93 15 43	815
Minot, N.D.	48 14 18	101 17 48	1,550
Mississauga, Ont.	43 33 00	79 35 00	260
Mobile, Ala.	30 41 36	88 02 33	5
Moline, Ill.	41 30 31	90 30 49	585
Moncton, N.B.	46 05 30	64 47 30	75
Montgomery, Ala.	32 22 33	86 18 31	160
Montpelier, Vt.	44 15 36	72 34 41	485
Montreal, Que.	45 30 30	73 33 20	117
Moose Jaw, Sask.	50 23 30	105 32 30	1,810
Muncie, Ind.	40 11 28	85 23 16	950
Nashville, Tenn.	36 09 33	86 46 55	450
Natchez, Miss.	31 33 48	91 23 30	210
Newark, N.J.	40 44 14	74 10 19	55
New Bedford, Mass.	41 38 13	70 55 41	15
New Britain, Conn.	41 40 08	72 46 59	200
New Haven, Conn.	41 18 25	72 55 30	40
New Orleans, La.	29 56 53	90 04 10	5
New York, N.Y.	40 45 06	73 59 39	55
Niagara Falls, N.Y.	43 05 34	79 03 26	570
Niagara Falls, Ont.	43 05 30	79 03 30	585
Nome, Alaska	64 30 00	165 25 00	25
Norfolk, Va.	36 51 10	76 17 21	10
North Bay, Ont.	46 18 30	79 27 30	925
Oakland, Cal.	37 48 03	122 15 54	25
Ogden, Utah.	41 13 31	111 58 21	4,295
Oklahoma City.	35 28 26	97 31 04	1,195
Omaha, Neb.	41 15 42	95 56 14	1,040
Orlando, Fla.	28 32 42	81 22 38	70
Oshawa, Ont.	43 54 00	78 52 00	350
Ottawa, Ont.	45 25 40	75 42 45	374
Paducah, Ky.	37 05 13	88 35 56	345
Pasadena, Cal.	34 08 44	118 08 41	830
Paterson, N.J.	40 55 01	74 10 21	100
Pensacola, Fla.	30 24 51	87 12 56	15
Peoria, Ill.	40 41 42	89 35 33	470
Peterborough, Ont.	44 18 00	78 19 30	685
Philadelphia, Pa.	39 56 58	75 09 21	100
Phoenix, Ariz.	33 27 12	112 04 28	1,090
Pierre, S.D.	44 22 18	100 20 54	1,480
Pittsburgh, Pa.	40 26 19	80 00 00	745
Pittsfield, Mass.	42 26 53	73 15 14	1,015
Pocatello, Idaho.	42 52 24	112 27 00	4,460
Port Arthur, Texas.	29 52 30	93 56 15	10
Portland, Me.	43 39 33	70 15 19	25
Portland, Ore.	45 31 06	122 40 35	77
Portsmouth, N.H.	43 04 30	70 45 24	20
Portsmouth, Va.	36 50 07	76 18 14	10
Prince Rupert, B.C.	54 19 00	130 19 00	125
Providence, R.I.	41 49 32	71 24 41	80
Provo, Utah	40 14 06	111 39 24	4,550
Pueblo, Col.	38 16 17	104 36 33	4,690
Quebec City, Que.	46 48 46	71 12 20	239
Racine, Wis.	42 43 49	87 47 12	630
Rapid City, S.D.	44 04 48	103 13 42	3,230
Raleigh, N.C.	35 46 38	78 38 21	365
Reading, Pa.	40 20 09	75 55 40	265
Regina, Sask.	50 27 02	104 36 30	1,894
Reno, Nev.	39 31 27	119 48 40	4,490
Richmond, Va.	37 32 15	77 26 09	160
Roanoke, Va.	37 16 13	79 56 44	905
Rochester, Minn.	44 01 21	92 28 03	990
Rochester, N.Y.	43 09 41	77 36 21	515
Rockford, Ill.	42 16 07	89 05 48	715
Sacramento, Cal.	38 34 57	121 29 41	30
Saginaw, Mich.	43 25 52	83 56 05	595
St. Catharines, Ont.	43 09 30	79 14 30	362
Saint John, N.B.	45 16 00	66 04 30	80
St. Cloud, Minn.	45 34 00	94 10 24	1,040
St. John's, Nfld.	47 34 00	52 43 30	200
St. Joseph, Mo.	39 45 57	94 51 02	850
St. Louis, Mo.	38 37 45	90 12 22	455
St. Paul, Minn.	44 57 19	93 06 07	780
St. Petersburg, Fla.	27 46 18	82 38 19	20
Salem, Ore.	44 56 24	123 02 00	155
Salina, Kan.	38 50 06	97 36 30	1,229
Salt Lake City	40 45 23	111 53 26	4,390
San Angelo, Tex.	31 27 39	100 26 03	1,845
San Antonio, Tex.	29 25 37	98 29 06	650
San Bernardino, Cal.	34 06 30	117 17 28	1,080
San Diego, Cal.	32 42 53	117 09 21	20
San Francisco, Cal.	37 46 39	122 24 40	65
San Jose, Cal.	37 20 16	121 53 24	90
San Juan, P.R.	18 27 00	66 04 15	35
Santa Barbara, Cal.	34 25 18	119 41 55	100
Santa Cruz, Cal.	36 58 18	122 01 18	20
Santa Fe, N.M.	35 41 11	105 56 10	6,950
Sarasota, Fla.	27 20 12	82 31 54	20
Saskatoon, Sask.	52 07 50	106 39 41	1,653
Sault Ste. Marie, Ont.	46 31 30	84 20 00	650
Savannah, Ga.	32 04 42	81 05 37	20
Schenectady, N.Y.	42 48 42	73 55 42	245
Scranton, Pa.	41 24 32	75 39 46	725
Seattle, Wash.	47 36 32	122 20 12	10
Sheboygan, Wis.	43 45 36	87 44 54	630
Sherbrooke, Que.	45 24 00	71 53 30	625
Sheridan, Wyo.	44 47 48	106 57 42	3,740
Shreveport, La.	32 30 46	93 44 58	204
Sioux City, Iowa	42 29 46	96 24 30	1,110
Sioux Falls, S.D.	43 32 35	96 43 35	1,395
Somerville, Mass.	42 23 15	71 06 07	13
South Bend, Ind.	41 40 33	86 15 01	710
Spartanburg, S.C.	34 57 03	81 56 06	875
Spokane, Wash.	47 39 32	117 25 33	1,890
Springfield, Ill.	39 47 58	89 38 51	610
Springfield, Mass.	42 06 21	72 35 32	85
Springfield, Mo.	37 13 03	93 17 32	1,300
Springfield, Ohio.	39 55 38	83 48 29	980
Stamford, Conn.	41 03 09	73 32 24	35
Steubenville, Ohio.	40 21 42	80 36 53	660
Stockton, Cal.	37 57 30	121 17 16	20
Sudbury, Ont.	46 28 30	80 58 30	917
Superior, Wis.	46 43 14	92 06 07	630
Sydney, N.S.	46 08 30	60 11 00	50
Syracuse, N.Y.	43 03 04	76 09 14	400
Tacoma, Wash.	47 14 59	122 26 15	110
Tallahassee, Fla.	30 26 42	84 16 54	150
Tampa, Fla.	27 56 58	82 27 25	15
Terre Haute, Ind.	39 28 03	87 24 26	496
Texarkana, kTexas	33 25 48	94 02 30	324
Thunder Bay, Ont.	48 25 00	89 14 00	650
Toledo, Ohio.	41 39 14	83 32 39	585
Topeka, Kan.	39 03 16	95 40 23	930
Toronto, Ont.	43 39 12	79 23 00	532
Trenton, N.J.	40 13 14	74 46 13	35
Trois-Rivieres, Que.	46 21 00	72 33 00	115
Troy, N.Y.	42 43 45	73 40 58	35
Tucson, Ariz.	32 13 15	110 58 08	2,390
Tulsa, Okla.	36 09 12	95 59 34	804
Urbana, Ill.	40 06 42	88 12 06	
Utica, N.Y.	43 06 12	75 13 33	415
Vancouver, B.C.	49 16 30	123 07 30	388
Victoria, B.C.	48 25 40	123 21 45	...
Waco, Tex.	31 33 12	97 08 00	405
Walla Walla, Wash.	46 04 08	118 20 24	936
Washington, D.C.	38 53 51	77 00 33	25
Waterbury, Conn.	41 33 13	73 02 31	260
Waterloo, Iowa	42 29 40	92 20 20	850
West Palm Beach, Fla.	26 43 00	80 03 12	15
Wheeling W. Va.	40 04 03	80 43 20	650
Whitehorse, Yukon	60 43 15	135 03 15	2,305
White Plains, N.Y.	41 02 00	73 45 48	220
Wichita, Kan.	37 41 30	97 20 16	1,290
Wichita Falls, Tex.	33 54 34	98 29 28	945
Wilkes-Barre, Pa.	41 14 32	75 53 17	640
Wilmington, Del.	39 44 46	75 32 51	135
Wilmington, N.C.	34 14 12	77 55 24	35
Windsor, Ont.	42 19 50	83 03 00	590
Winnipeg, Man.	49 53 56	97 08 20	765
Winston-Salem, N.C.	36 05 52	80 14 42	860
Worcester, Mass.	42 15 37	71 48 17	475
Yakima, Wash.	46 35 42	120 30 48	1,060
Yellowknife, N.W.T.	62 28 15	114 22 00	674
Yonkers, N.Y.	40 55 55	73 53 54	10
York, Pa.	39 57 35	76 43 36	370
Youngstown, Ohio.	41 05 57	80 39 02	840
Yuma, Ariz.	32 42 54	114 37 24	160
Zanesville, Ohio.	39 56 18	82 00 30	720

World Cities

City	Lat. ° ' "	Long. ° ' "	Alt.* Feet
London, UK(Greenwich)	51 30 00	0 0 0	245
Paris, France	48 50 14	2 20 14	300
Berlin, Germany	52 32 00	13 25 00	110
Rome, Italy	41 53 00	12 30 00	95
Warsaw, Poland	52 15 00	21 00 00	360
Moscow, U.S.S.R.	55 45 00	37 42 00	394
Athens, Greece	37 58 00	23 44 00	300
Jerusalem, Israel	31 47 00	35 13 00	2,500
Johannesburg, So. Afr.	26 10 00	28 02 00	5,740
New Delhi, India	28 38 00	77 12 00	770
Peking, China	39 54 00	116 28 00	600
Rio de Janeiro, Brazil	22 53 43	43 13 22	30
Tokyo, Japan	31 41 00	139 45 00	30
Sydney, Australia	33 52 00	151 12 00	25

Calendar Adjustment Tables

The tables below will allow you to determine the approximate time of the rise or set of the sun and moon at your specific location. Rise and set times for your location can be more than one-half hour later than the times given on the following pages.

First find your latitude and longitude or that of a nearby city in the tables on pages 217-218. On the calendar tables look for the time given for the nearest latitude to your south. Compare that time with the time given for the next latitude to your north.

On Table A below, find the difference between the two latitudes in the top row. Run your finger down the column until you reach the row that indicates how far north you are of the southern latitude. Adjust the time given for the southern latitude by the number of minutes shown in Table A.

Now compare the time given for the southern latitude on the day you're seeking and for the next day. Using Table B, find the time difference between the two days. Run your finger down the column until you reach the row that belongs to the longitude nearest you. Add the minutes given there to your previous figure.

Finally, to adjust for local time, you must determine how many degrees of longitude you are from your time zone meridian: Atlantic — 60°, Eastern — 75°, Central — 90°, Mountain — 105°, Pacific — 120° and Alaska-Hawaii — 150°. For every degree of longitude west of the meridian you must add 4 minutes of time; for every degree of longitude east, subtract 4 minutes.

Example: Find the moonrise time for Superior, Wisconsin for March 7, 1975. Superior is at 92° 06' longitude and 46° 43' latitude.
Calendar time given for 40° — 3:05
Calendar time given for 50° — 3:37
Difference — 32 minutes
Table A at 30 min. and 6° 40' — 20 minutes
First adjusted time — 3:25
Time for 40° on March 8 — 3:43
Difference between Mar. 7 and Mar. 8 — 38 minutes
Table B at 40 min. and 90° 00' — 10 minutes
Second adjusted time — 3:35
Local time adjustment 2° x 4 min. — 8 minutes
Moonrise on March 7 — about 3:43 a.m.

Table A: Latitude Adjustment

Diff. in Min. / Lat.	0	20	30	40	50	60	70	80	90	100	110	120
0°20'	0	1	1	1	2	2	2	3	3	3	4	4
40	1	1	2	3	3	4	5	5	6	7	7	8
1 00	1	2	3	4	5	6	7	8	9	10	11	12
20	1	3	4	5	7	8	9	11	12	13	15	16
40	2	3	5	7	8	10	12	13	15	17	18	20
2 00	2	4	6	8	10	12	14	16	18	20	22	24
20	2	5	7	9	12	14	16	19	21	23	26	28
40	3	5	8	11	13	16	19	21	24	27	29	32
3 00	3	6	9	12	15	18	21	24	27	30	33	36
20	3	7	10	13	17	20	23	27	30	33	37	40
40	4	7	11	15	18	22	26	29	33	37	40	44
4 00	4	8	12	16	20	24	28	32	36	40	44	48
20	4	9	13	17	22	26	30	35	39	43	48	52
40	5	9	14	19	23	28	33	37	42	47	51	56
5 00	5	10	15	20	25	30	35	40	45	50	55	60
20	5	11	16	21	27	32	37	43	48	53	59	64
40	6	11	17	23	28	34	40	45	51	57	62	68
6 00	6	12	18	24	30	36	42	48	54	60	66	72
20	6	13	19	25	32	38	44	51	57	63	70	76
40	7	13	20	27	33	40	47	53	60	67	73	80
7 00	7	14	21	28	35	42	49	56	63	70	77	84
20	7	15	22	29	37	44	51	59	66	73	81	88
40	8	15	23	31	38	46	54	61	69	77	84	92
8 00	8	16	24	32	40	48	56	64	72	80	88	96
20	8	17	25	33	42	50	58	67	75	83	92	100
40	9	17	26	35	43	52	61	69	78	87	95	104
9 00	9	18	27	36	45	54	63	72	81	90	99	108
20	9	19	28	37	47	56	65	75	84	93	103	112
40	10	19	29	39	48	58	68	77	87	97	106	116

Table B: Longitude Adjustment

Diff. in Min. / Long.	10	20	30	40	50	60	70	80	90	100	110	120
	1	3	4	6	7	8	10	11	12	14	15	17
55°	2	3	5	6	8	9	11	12	14	15	17	18
60	2	3	5	7	8	10	12	13	15	17	18	20
65	2	4	5	7	9	11	13	14	16	18	20	22
70	2	4	6	8	10	12	14	16	18	19	21	23
75	2	4	6	8	10	12	15	17	19	21	23	25
80	2	4	7	9	11	13	16	18	20	22	24	27
85	2	5	7	9	12	14	16	19	21	24	26	28
90	2	5	8	10	12	15	18	20	22	25	28	30
95	3	5	8	11	13	16	18	21	24	26	29	32
100	3	6	8	11	14	17	19	22	25	28	31	33
105	3	6	9	12	15	18	20	23	26	29	32	35
110	3	6	9	12	15	18	21	24	28	31	34	37
115	3	6	10	13	16	19	22	26	29	32	35	38
120	3	7	10	13	17	20	23	27	30	33	37	40
125	4	7	10	14	17	21	24	28	31	35	38	42
130	4	7	11	14	18	22	25	29	32	36	40	43
135	4	8	11	15	19	22	26	30	34	38	41	45
140	4	8	12	16	19	23	27	31	35	39	43	47
145	4	8	12	16	20	24	28	32	36	40	44	48
150	4	8	12	17	21	25	29	33	38	42	46	50
155	4	9	13	17	22	26	30	34	39	43	47	52
160	4	9	13	18	22	27	31	36	40	44	49	53
165	5	9	14	18	23	28	32	37	41	46	50	55
170	5	9	14	19	24	28	33	38	42	47	52	57

1st Month   January, 1975   31 Days

Greenwich Mean Time

NOTE: Light figures indicate Sun. **Dark** figures indicate **Moon.** *Degrees are North Latitude.*

CAUTION: Must be converted to local time. For instruction see page 219.

Day of month / week / year	Sun on meridian / Moon phase (h m s)	20° Rise Sun/Moon	20° Set Sun/Moon	30° Rise Sun/Moon	30° Set Sun/Moon	40° Rise Sun/Moon	40° Set Sun/Moon	50° Rise Sun/Moon	50° Set Sun/Moon	60° Rise Sun/Moon	60° Set Sun/Moon
1 We	+3 22	6 35	17 31	6 56	17 10	7 22	16 44	7 59	16 07	9 03	15 03
1		21 18	9 12	21 13	9 19	21 07	9 29	20 58	9 41	20 45	9 59
2 Th	+3 50	6 35	17 31	6 56	7 11	7 22	16 45	7 59	16 08	9 03	15 04
2		22 19	9 56	22 18	9 59	22 18	10 02	22 18	10 06	22 18	10 12
3 Fr	+4 18	6 35	17 32	6 56	17 12	7 22	16 46	7 59	16 09	9 02	15 06
3		23 17	10 39	23 22	10 37	23 28	10 34	23 36	10 30	23 49	10 24
4 Sa	+4 45	6 36	17 33	6 56	17 13	7 22	16 47	7 58	16 11	9 01	15 08
4	19 04 ☾		11 21		11 14		11 06		10 54		10 36
5 Su	+5 13	6 36	17 34	6 57	17 14	7 22	16 48	7 58	16 13	9 00	15 10
5		0 15	12 04	0 25	11 53	0 37	11 39	0 53	11 20	1 19	10 50
6 Mo	+5 39	6 36	17 34	6 57	17 14	7 22	16 49	7 58	16 14	8 59	15 12
6		1 13	12 49	1 27	12 33	1 44	12 15	2 07	11 49	2 46	11 07
7 Tu	+6 06	6 37	17 35	6 57	17 15	7 22	16 50	7 57	16 15	8 58	15 14
7		2 10	13 35	2 27	13 17	2 49	12 54	3 19	12 23	4 10	11 30
8 We	+6 32	6 37	17 36	6 57	17 16	7 22	16 51	7 57	16 16	8 57	15 16
8		3 06	14 25	3 26	14 04	3 51	13 39	4 26	13 03	5 27	12 01
9 Th	+6 57	6 37	17 37	6 57	17 17	7 22	16 52	7 56	16 17	8 56	15 18
9		4 01	15 16	4 22	14 55	4 49	14 28	5 26	13 51	6 32	12 44
10 Fr	+7 22	6 37	17 38	6 57	17 18	7 22	16 53	7 56	16 19	8 55	15 20
10		4 53	16 08	5 14	15 48	5 40	15 22	6 18	14 45	7 23	13 41
11 Sa	+7 46	6 37	17 38	6 57	17 18	7 21	16 54	7 55	16 20	8 54	15 22
11		5 42	17 01	6 02	16 42	6 26	16 19	7 01	15 45	7 59	14 48
12 Su	+8 10	6 38	17 39	6 57	17 19	7 21	16 55	7 55	16 21	8 53	15 24
12	10 20 ●	6 27	17 54	6 45	17 37	7 06	17 17	7 36	16 49	8 25	16 02
13 Mo	+8 33	6 38	17 40	6 57	17 20	7 21	16 56	7 54	16 22	8 52	15 26
13		7 09	18 45	7 23	18 32	7 41	18 16	8 05	17 54	8 44	17 18
14 Tu	+8 55	6 38	17 41	6 57	17 21	7 20	16 57	7 54	16 24	8 51	15 28
14		7 47	19 34	7 58	19 25	8 11	19 14	8 29	18 58	8 57	18 34
15 We	+9 17	6 38	17 41	6 57	17 22	7 20	16 59	7 53	16 26	8 49	15 30
15		8 24	20 23	8 31	20 18	8 39	20 11	8 51	20 02	9 09	19 49
16 Th	+9 38	6 38	17 42	6 56	17 22	7 20	17 00	7 53	16 27	8 48	15 32
16		8 58	21 11	9 02	21 10	9 05	21 08	9 11	21 06	9 18	21 03
17 Fr	+9 59	6 38	17 42	6 56	17 23	7 19	17 01	7 52	16 28	8 47	15 34
17		9 33	21 59	9 32	22 02	9 31	22 05	9 30	22 10	9 28	22 17
18 Sa	+10 18	6 38	17 43	6 56	17 24	7 19	17 02	7 51	16 29	8 45	15 36
18		10 07	22 47	10 02	22 54	9 57	23 03	9 49	23 14	9 37	23 33
19 Su	+10 37	6 38	17 43	6 56	17 25	7 18	17 03	7 50	16 31	8 43	15 39
19		10 43	23 38	10 35	23 49	10 24		10 10		9 48	
20 Mo	+10 56	6 38	17 44	6 56	17 26	7 18	17 04	7 49	16 33	8 41	15 42
20	15 14 ☽	11 22		11 09		10 54	0 02	10 33	0 20	10 01	0 50
21 Tu	+11 13	6 38	17 44	6 55	17 27	7 17	17 05	7 48	16 34	8 39	15 44
21		12 04	0 30	11 48	0 45	11 29	1 03	11 02	1 28	10 18	2 09
22 We	+11 30	6 38	17 45	6 55	17 28	7 17	17 06	7 47	16 36	8 37	15 46
22		12 51	1 25	12 32	1 43	12 09	2 05	11 37	2 36	10 43	3 28
23 Th	+11 46	6 37	17 45	6 55	17 29	7 16	17 07	7 46	16 38	8 35	15 48
23		13 43	2 22	13 23	2 42	12 57	3 07	12 21	3 43	11 19	4 44
24 Fr	+12 01	6 37	17 46	6 54	17 30	7 16	17 08	7 45	16 39	8 33	15 51
24		14 41	3 21	14 20	3 42	13 54	4 08	13 17	4 45	12 12	5 50
25 Sa	+12 15	6 37	17 47	6 54	17 31	7 15	17 10	7 44	16 41	8 31	15 54
25		15 44	4 19	15 24	4 40	14 59	5 05	14 25	5 41	13 25	6 42
26 Su	+12 29	6 37	17 47	6 54	17 31	7 15	17 11	7 43	16 42	8 29	15 56
26		16 49	5 16	16 32	5 34	16 11	5 57	15 42	6 28	14 53	7 19
27 Mo	+12 42	6 37	17 48	6 53	17 32	7 14	17 12	7 42	16 44	8 27	15 58
27	15 09 ○	17 55	6 10	17 42	6 25	17 27	6 42	17 05	7 07	16 30	7 45
28 Tu	+12 53	6 36	17 48	6 53	17 33	7 13	17 13	7 41	16 46	8 25	16 01
28		19 00	7 01	18 52	7 11	18 43	7 23	18 30	7 39	18 09	8 04
29 We	+13 05	6 36	17 49	6 53	17 34	7 12	17 14	7 40	16 48	8 23	16 04
29		20 04	7 48	20 01	7 53	19 58	7 59	19 54	8 07	19 47	8 19
30 Th	+13 15	6 36	17 50	6 52	17 35	7 11	17 16	7 38	16 50	8 20	16 07
30		21 06	8 33	21 08	8 33	21 12	8 33	21 16	8 33	21 23	8 32
31 Fr	+13 24	6 36	17 50	6 52	17 36	7 11	17 18	7 37	16 51	8 18	16 09
31		22 06	9 17	22 14	9 12	22 23	9 06	22 36	8 58	22 57	8 45

2nd Month   February, 1975   28 Days

Greenwich Mean Time

NOTE: Light figures indicate Sun. **Dark** figures indicate **Moon.** *Degrees are North Latitude.*

CAUTION: Must be converted to local time. For instruction see page 219.

Day of month / week / year	Sun on meridian / Moon phase (h m s)	20° Rise Sun/Moon	20° Set Sun/Moon	30° Rise Sun/Moon	30° Set Sun/Moon	40° Rise Sun/Moon	40° Set Sun/Moon	50° Rise Sun/Moon	50° Set Sun/Moon	60° Rise Sun/Moon	60° Set Sun/Moon
1 Sa	+13 33	6 35	17 51	6 51	17 37	7 10	17 19	7 36	16 53	8 16	16 11
32		23 06	10 02	23 18	9 52	23 33	9 40	23 54	9 24		8 59
2 Su	+13 41	6 35	17 52	6 51	17 38	7 09	17 20	7 34	16 54	8 14	16 14
33			10 47	-	10 33		10 16		9 53	0 28	9 15
3 Mo	+13 48 / 06 23 ☾	6 35	17 53	6 50	17 39	7 08	17 21	7 32	16 56	8 12	16 17
34		0 05	11 34	0 21	11 16	0 40	10 55	1 08	10 25	1 55	9 37
4 Tu	+13 54	6 35	17 53	6 49	17 39	7 07	17 22	7 30	16 58	8 09	16 20
35		1 02	12 23	1 21	12 03	1 44	11 38	2 18	11 04	3 15	10 05
5 We	+14 00	6 34	17 54	6 49	17 40	7 06	17 24	7 29	17 00	8 07	16 23
36		1 57	13 13	2 18	12 52	2 44	12 26	3 20	11 49	4 24	10 45
6 Th	+14 04	6 34	17 55	6 48	17 41	7 05	17 25	7 27	17 02	8 05	16 26
37		2 50	14 05	3 11	13 44	3 37	13 18	4 14	12 41	5 19	11 36
7 Fr	+14 08	6 34	17 55	6 48	17 42	7 04	17 26	7 25	17 04	8 02	16 29
38		3 39	14 57	3 59	14 38	4 25	14 13	5 00	13 39	6 00	12 40
8 Sa	+14 12	6 33	17 56	6 47	17 43	7 03	17 27	7 24	17 06	7 59	16 32
39		4 25	15 49	4 43	15 32	5 06	15 11	5 37	14 41	6 29	13 50
9 Su	+14 14	6 33	17 56	6 46	17 43	7 01	17 28	7 22	17 07	7 56	16 34
40		5 08	16 40	5 23	16 26	5 42	16 09	6 08	15 44	6 50	15 05
10 Mo	+14 15	6 32	17 57	6 46	17 44	7 00	17 29	7 21	17 09	7 54	16 37
41		5 47	17 30	5 59	17 20	6 14	17 07	6 34	16 49	7 06	16 20
11 Tu	+14 16 / 05 17 ●	6 32	17 57	6 45	17 45	6 59	17 31	7 20	17 11	7 52	16 40
42		6 24	18 19	6 33	18 12	6 43	18 04	6 57	17 53	7 18	17 35
12 We	+14 16	6 31	17 58	6 44	17 46	6 58	17 32	7 18	17 13	7 49	16 43
43		7 00	19 07	7 04	19 04	7 10	19 01	7 17	18 57	7 29	18 50
13 Th	+14 16	6 31	17 58	6 43	17 47	6 57	17 33	7 16	17 14	7 46	16 45
44		7 34	19 55	7 35	19 56	7 35	19 58	7 37	20 00	7 38	20 04
14 Fr	+14 14	6 30	17 59	6 42	17 47	6 55	17 34	7 14	17 15	7 43	16 47
45		8 08	20 43	8 05	20 49	8 01	20 55	7 56	21 04	7 48	21 18
15 Sa	+14 12	6 30	17 59	6 41	17 48	6 54	17 36	7 13	17 17	7 41	16 51
46		8 44	21 33	8 37	21 42	8 28	21 53	8 16	22 09	7 58	22 34
16 Su	+14 09	6 29	18 00	6 40	17 49	6 53	17 37	7 11	17 19	7 38	16 54
47		9 21	22 24	9 10	22 36	8 57	22 53	8 39	23 15	8 10	23 51
17 Mo	+14 05	6 29	18 00	6 39	17 50	6 52	17 38	7 09	17 21	7 35	16 56
48		10 01	23 16	9 47	23 32	9 29	23 53	9 05		8 26	
18 Tu	+14 01	6 28	18 01	6 38	17 51	6 51	17 39	7 07	17 23	7 32	16 58
49		10 45		10 28		10 06		9 36	0 21	8 47	1 08
19 We	+13 55 / 07 39 ☽	6 27	18 01	6 37	17 51	6 49	17 40	7 05	17 24	7 29	17 00
50		11 33	0 11	11 14	0 30	10 49	0 53	10 15	1 27	9 17	2 23
20 Th	+13 50	6 27	18 02	6 36	17 52	6 48	17 41	7 03	17 26	7 27	17 03
51		12 27	1 07	12 06	1 27	11 40	1 53	11 04	2 29	10 00	3 32
21 Fr	+13 43	6 26	18 02	6 35	17 53	6 47	17 42	7 01	17 28	7 24	17 06
52		13 25	2 03	13 05	2 24	12 39	2 50	12 03	3 26	11 01	4 29
22 Sa	+13 36	6 26	18 02	6 34	17 54	6 46	17 43	6 59	17 30	7 21	17 09
53		14 27	2 59	14 08	3 18	13 46	3 42	13 13	4 16	12 19	5 12
23 Su	+13 28	6 25	18 03	6 33	17 55	6 44	17 44	6 57	17 32	7 18	17 11
54		15 31	3 53	15 16	4 10	14 57	4 30	14 32	4 58	13 49	5 43
24 Mo	+13 20	6 24	18 03	6 32	17 55	6 42	17 45	6 55	17 33	7 15	17 13
55		16 36	4 45	16 25	4 57	16 12	5 13	15 55	5 33	15 26	6 06
25 Tu	+13 11	6 24	18 03	6 31	17 56	6 41	17 47	6 53	17 35	7 13	17 16
56		17 41	5 34	17 35	5 42	17 29	5 51	17 19	6 04	17 05	6 23
26 We	+13 01 / 01 15 ○	6 23	18 04	6 30	17 57	6 40	17 48	6 51	17 37	7 10	17 19
57		18 45	6 21	18 45	6 24	18 44	6 27	18 44	6 31	18 44	6 38
27 Th	+12 51	6 22	18 04	6 29	17 58	6 39	17 49	6 49	17 39	7 07	17 22
58		19 48	7 07	19 53	7 04	19 59	7 01	20 08	6 57	20 22	6 51
28 Fr	+12 40	6 21	18 04	6 29	17 59	6 37	17 50	6 47	17 40	7 04	17 24
59		20 50	7 53	21 00	7 45	21 13	7 36	21 30	7 24	21 57	7 06

3rd Month   March, 1975   **31 Days**

Greenwich Mean Time

NOTE: Light figures indicate Sun. **Dark** figures indicate **Moon.** *Degrees are North Latitude.*
CAUTION: Must be converted to local time. For instruction see page 219.

Day of month week year	Sun on meridian Moon phase	20° Rise Sun/Moon	20° Set Sun/Moon	30° Rise Sun/Moon	30° Set Sun/Moon	40° Rise Sun/Moon	40° Set Sun/Moon	50° Rise Sun/Moon	50° Set Sun/Moon	60° Rise Sun/Moon	60° Set Sun/Moon
1 Sa 60	+12 29	6 20	18 05	6 27	17 59	6 35	17 51	6 45	17 41	7 01	17 26
		21 52	8 39	22 06	8 27	22 24	8 13	22 49	7 53	23 29	7 22
2 Su 61	+12 17	6 20	18 05	6 26	18 00	6 34	17 52	6 43	17 42	6 58	17 29
		22 52	9 27	23 10	9 12	23 32	8 52		8 25		7 42
3 Mo 62	+12 05	6 19	18 06	6 25	18 01	6 33	17 53	6 41	17 43	6 55	17 32
		23 52	10 17		9 59		9 35	0 03	9 03	0 55	8 09
4 Tu 63	+11 52 20 20 ☾	6 19	18 06	6 24	18 01	6 31	17 54	6 39	17 45	6 52	17 34
			11 08	0 10	10 48	0 35	10 23	1 10	9 47	2 11	8 45
5 We 64	+11 39	6 18	18 06	6 23	18 02	6 29	17 55	6 37	17 47	6 49	17 36
		0 45	12 01	1 05	11 40	1 31	11 14	2 08	10 37	3 12	9 33
6 Th 65	+11 25	6 17	18 07	6 21	18 02	6 27	17 56	6 35	17 49	6 46	17 38
		1 36	12 53	1 56	12 34	2 22	12 09	2 57	11 34	3 59	10 33
7 Fr 66	+11 11	6 17	18 07	6 20	18 03	6 26	17 57	6 33	17 50	6 43	17 43
		2 23	13 45	2 42	13 28	3 05	13 06	3 37	12 34	4 32	11 42
8 Sa 67	+10 57	6 16	18 07	6 19	18 03	6 25	17 58	6 31	17 51	6 40	17 45
		3 07	14 37	3 23	14 22	3 43	14 03	4 10	13 37	4 55	12 55
9 Su 68	+10 42	6 15	18 08	6 18	18 04	6 23	17 59	6 29	17 53	6 37	17 47
		3 47	15 27	4 00	15 15	4 16	15 01	4 38	14 41	5 13	14 09
10 Mo 69	+10 27	6 14	18 08	6 17	18 04	6 21	18 00	6 27	17 55	6 34	17 49
		4 25	16 16	4 34	16 08	4 46	15 58	5 02	15 45	5 26	15 24
11 Tu 70	+10 11	6 13	18 08	6 16	18 05	6 19	18 02	6 24	17 57	6 31	17 51
		5 01	17 04	5 06	17 00	5 13	16 55	5 23	16 48	5 38	16 38
12 We 71	+9 56 23 47 ●	6 12	18 09	6 15	18 06	6 18	18 03	6 22	17 58	6 28	17 54
		5 35	17 52	5 37	17 52	5 40	17 52	5 43	17 52	5 48	17 52
13 Th 72	+9 40	6 11	18 09	6 14	18 07	6 17	18 04	6 20	17 59	6 25	17 57
		6 10	18 40	6 08	18 44	6 06	18 49	6 03	18 56	5 58	19 06
14 Fr 73	+9 23	6 10	18 09	6 13	18 07	6 15	18 05	6 18	18 01	6 22	17 59
		6 45	19 30	6 40	19 38	6 32	19 47	6 23	20 01	6 08	20 22
15 Sa 74	+9 07	6 09	18 10	6 12	18 08	6 13	18 06	6 16	18 03	6 19	18 01
		7 22	20 20	7 13	20 32	7 01	20 46	6 45	21 06	6 20	21 38
16 Su 75	+8 50	6 08	18 10	6 10	18 08	6 11	18 07	6 13	18 05	6 16	18 03
		8 01	21 12	7 48	21 27	7 32	21 46	7 10	22 12	6 35	22 55
17 Mo 76	+8 33	6 08	18 10	6 09	18 09	6 10	18 08	6 11	18 06	6 13	18 06
		8 44	22 05	8 28	22 23	8 07	22 46	7 40	23 17	6 54	
18 Tu 77	+8 16	6 07	18 11	6 08	18 10	6 09	18 09	6 09	18 07	6 10	18 09
		9 30	23 00	9 11	23 20	8 48	23 45	8 16		7 21	0 10
19 We 78	+7 58	6 06	18 11	6 07	18 11	6 07	18 10	6 07	18 09	6 07	18 11
		10 21	23 55	10 01		9 35		9 00	0 20	7 59	1 20
20 Th 79	+7 40 20 05 ☽	6 05	18 11	6 06	18 12	6 05	18 11	6 05	18 11	6 04	18 13
		11 15		10 55	0 15	10 30	0 41	9 54	1 17	8 52	2 19
21 Fr 80	+7 23	6 04	18 11	6 04	18 12	6 03	18 12	6 02	18 13	6 01	18 15
		12 14	0 49	11 55	1 09	11 31	1 34	10 57	2 08	10 00	3 06
22 Sa 81	+7 05	6 04	18 12	6 03	18 13	6 02	18 13	6 00	18 14	5 58	18 18
		13 14	1 42	12 58	2 00	12 38	2 21	12 09	2 51	11 22	3 41
23 Su 82	+6 47	6 03	18 12	6 02	18 14	6 01	18 14	5 58	18 15	5 55	18 21
		14 16	2 33	14 04	2 47	13 48	3 04	13 27	3 28	12 52	4 06
24 Mo 83	+6 29	6 02	18 12	6 00	18 14	5 59	18 15	5 56	18 17	5 52	18 23
		15 19	3 21	15 11	3 31	15 02	3 43	14 48	4 00	14 27	4 26
25 Tu 84	+6 10	6 01	18 12	5 59	18 15	5 57	18 16	5 54	18 19	5 49	18 25
		16 22	4 08	16 19	4 13	16 16	4 20	16 11	4 28	16 03	4 41
26 We 85	+5 52	6 00	18 13	5 58	18 15	5 55	18 17	5 52	18 21	5 46	18 27
		17 25	4 54	17 28	4 54	17 31	4 54	17 34	4 55	17 40	4 56
27 Th 86	+5 34 10 36 ○	5 59	18 13	5 57	18 16	5 54	18 18	5 50	18 22	5 43	18 30
		18 29	5 40	18 36	5 35	18 45	5 29	18 58	5 22	19 17	5 10
28 Fr 87	+5 15	5 58	18 13	5 56	18 16	5 53	18 19	5 48	18 23	5 40	18 33
		19 32	6 26	19 44	6 17	19 59	6 05	20 20	5 50	20 53	5 25
29 Sa 88	+4 57	5 57	18 13	5 55	18 17	5 51	18 20	5 46	18 25	5 37	18 36
		20 34	7 15	20 50	7 01	21 10	6 44	21 38	6 21	22 24	5 44
30 Su 89	+4 39	5 56	18 14	5 54	18 17	5 49	18 21	5 44	18 27	5 34	18 38
		21 35	8 06	21 54	7 48	22 18	7 27	22 51	6 57	23 48	6 09
31 Mo 90	+4 21	5 55	18 14	5 52	18 18	5 47	18 23	5 41	18 29	5 31	18 40
		22 34	8 58	22 54	8 39	23 19	8 14	23 55	7 40		6 42

4th Month   April, 1975   30 Days

Greenwich Mean Time

NOTE: Light figures indicate Sun. **Dark** figures indicate **Moon.** *Degrees are North Latitude.*

CAUTION: Must be converted to local time. For instruction see page 219.

Day of month / week / year	Sun on meridian / Moon phase (h m s)	20° Rise Sun/Moon	20° Set Sun/Moon	30° Rise Sun/Moon	30° Set Sun/Moon	40° Rise Sun/Moon	40° Set Sun/Moon	50° Rise Sun/Moon	50° Set Sun/Moon	60° Rise Sun/Moon	60° Set Sun/Moon
1 Tu / 91	+4 03	5 54	18 14	5 50	18 18	5 45	18 24	5 38	18 31	5 28	18 43
		23 28	9 52	23 48	9 31		9 06		8 29	0 58	7 27
2 We / 92	+3 45	5 53	18 14	5 49	18 19	5 43	18 25	5 36	18 33	5 25	18 46
			10 46		10 26	0 14	10 01	0 50	9 25	1 52	8 24
3 Th / 93	+3 27 12 25 ☾	5 52	18 15	5 48	18 19	5 41	18 26	5 34	18 35	5 22	18 48
		0 18	11 39	0 37	11 21	1 01	10 58	1 34	10 26	2 30	9 31
4 Fr / 94	+3 09	5 51	18 15	5 47	18 20	5 40	18 27	5 32	18 36	5 19	18 50
		1 04	12 31	1 20	12 16	1 41	11 56	2 10	11 28	2 58	10 43
5 Sa. / 95	+2 52	5 51	18 15	5 46	18 21	5 39	18 28	5 30	18 37	5 16	18 52
		1 45	13 22	1 59	13 09	2 17	12 54	2 40	12 32	3 18	11 57
6 Su / 96	+2 35	5 50	18 15	5 44	18 21	5 37	18 29	5 27	18 39	5 13	18 55
		2 24	14 11	2 35	14 02	2 48	13 51	3 05	13 36	3 33	13 12
7 Mo / 97	+2 18	5 49	18 16	5 43	18 22	5 35	18 30	5 25	18 41	5 10	18 58
		3 00	15 00	3 07	14 55	3 16	14 48	3 28	14 39	3 45	14 25
8 Tu / 98	+2 01	5 48	18 16	5 42	18 22	5 33	18 31	5 23	18 43	5 07	19 00
		3 36	15 48	3 39	15 47	3 43	15 45	3 48	15 43	3 56	15 39
9 We / 99	+1 44	5 47	18 16	5 41	18 23	5 32	18 32	5 21	18 44	5 04	19 02
		4 10	16 36	4 10	16 39	4 09	16 42	4 08	16 47	4 06	16 53
10 Th / 100	+1 28	5 47	18 17	5 40	18 24	5 31	18 33	5 19	18 45	5 01	19 04
		4 46	17 25	4 41	17 32	4 36	17 40	4 28	17 51	4 17	18 09
11 Fr / 101	+1 12 16 39 ●	5 46	18 17	5 38	18 24	5 29	18 34	5 17	18 47	4 58	19 07
		5 22	18 16	5 14	18 26	5 04	18 39	4 50	18 57	4 29	19 25
12 Sa / 102	+0 56	5 45	18 17	5 37	18 25	5 27	18 35	5 15	18 49	4 55	19 10
		6 01	19 08	5 49	19 22	5 34	19 39	5 14	20 03	4 43	20 42
13 Su / 103	+0 41	5 44	18 18	5 36	18 25	5 25	18 36	5 13	18 51	4 52	19 12
		6 43	20 01	6 28	20 18	6 09	20 39	5 43	21 09	5 01	21 58
14 Mo / 104	+0 26	5 43	18 18	5 35	18 26	5 24	18 37	5 11	18 52	4 49	19 14
		7 28	20 56	7 11	21 15	6 48	21 39	6 17	22 13	5 26	23 10
15 Tu / 105	+0 11	5 43	18 18	5 34	18 27	5 23	18 38	5 09	18 53	4 46	19 16
		8 18	21 51	7 58	22 11	7 34	22 36	6 59	23 12	6 01	
16 We / 106	-0 04	5 42	18 19	5 33	18 27	5 21	18 39	5 07	18 55	4 43	19 19
		9 11	22 45	8 51	23 05	8 26	23 30	7 50		6 49	0 13
17 Th / 107	-0 18	5 41	18 19	5 32	18 28	5 19	18 40	5 05	18 57	4 40	19 22
		10 08	23 37	9 49	23 56	9 24		8 50	0 04	7 52	1 04
18 Fr / 108	-0 32	5 40	18 19	5 31	18 28	5 18	18 41	5 03	18 59	4 37	19 25
		11 07		10 49		10 28	0 18	9 58	0 49	9 08	1 41
19 Sa / 109	-0 45 04 41 ☽	5 39	18 20	5 30	18 29	5 17	18 42	5 01	19 00	4 34	19 27
		12 06	0 27	11 53	0 43	11 35	1 02	11 12	1 27	10 33	2 09
20 Su / 110	-0 58	5 39	18 20	5 29	18 30	5 16	18 43	4 59	19 01	4 31	19 29
		13 07	1 15	12 57	1 27	12 45	1 41	12 29	2 00	12 03	2 30
21 Mo / 111	-1 11	5 38	18 20	5 28	18 30	5 14	18 44	4 57	19 03	4 28	19 32
		14 07	2 01	14 02	2 08	13 56	2 17	13 48	2 28	13 35	2 46
22 Tu / 112	-1 23	5 37	18 20	5 27	18 31	5 12	18 45	4 55	19 05	4 25	19 35
		15 08	2 45	15 08	2 48	15 08	2 51	15 08	2 55	15 08	3 01
23 We / 113	-1 35	5 36	18 21	5 26	18 31	5 11	18 46	4 53	19 06	4 22	19 37
		16 10	3 29	16 14	3 27	16 21	3 24	16 29	3 20	16 42	3 14
24 Th / 114	-1 46	5 35	18 21	5 25	18 32	5 10	18 47	4 51	19 07	4 19	19 39
		17 12	4 15	17 21	4 08	17 33	3 59	17 50	3 47	18 16	3 29
25 Fr / 115	-1 57 19 55 ○	5 35	18 21	5 24	18 33	5 09	18 48	4 49	19 08	4 17	19 41
		18 14	5 02	18 28	4 50	18 46	4 36	19 10	4 16	19 50	3 46
26 Sa / 116	-2 08	5 34	18 22	5 23	18 33	5 07	18 49	4 47	19 10	4 14	19 44
		19 16	5 51	19 34	5 36	19 56	5 17	20 26	4 50	21 18	4 08
27 Su / 117	-2 18	5 33	18 22	5 22	18 34	5 05	18 50	4 45	19 12	4 11	19 47
		20 17	6 43	20 37	6 25	21 01	6 02	21 36	5 30	22 36	4 37
28 Mo / 118	-2 27	5 33	18 22	5 21	18 34	5 04	18 51	4 43	19 14	4 08	19 50
		21 15	7 38	21 35	7 18	22 00	6 53	22 37	6 17	23 39	5 17
29 Tu / 119	-2 36	5 32	18 23	5 20	18 35	5 03	18 52	4 41	19 15	4 05	19 52
		22 08	8 33	22 28	8 13	22 52	7 48	23 27	7 12		6 10
30 We / 120	-2 44	5 32	18 23	5 19	18 36	5 02	18 53	4 40	19 16	4 03	19 54
		22 57	9 28	23 14	9 09	23 36	8 45		8 12	0 25	7 14

5th Month   May, 1975   31 Days

Greenwich Mean Time

NOTE: Light figures indicate Sun. **Dark** figures indicate **Moon**. *Degrees are North Latitude.*
CAUTION: Must be converted to local time. For instruction see page 219.

Day of month / week / year	Sun on meridian / Moon phase (h m s)	20° Rise Sun/Moon	20° Set Sun/Moon	30° Rise Sun/Moon	30° Set Sun/Moon	40° Rise Sun/Moon	40° Set Sun/Moon	50° Rise Sun/Moon	50° Set Sun/Moon	60° Rise Sun/Moon	60° Set Sun/Moon
1 Th	-2 52	5 31	18 23	5 18	18 36	5 00	18 54	4 38	19 18	4 00	19 56
121		23 41	10 22	23 56	10 05		9 45	0 07	9 15	0 58	8 26
2 Fr	-2 59	5 31	18 24	5 17	18 37	4 59	18 55	4 36	19 20	3 57	19 58
122			11 14		11 01	0 14	10 44	0 40	10 20	1 21	9 41
3 Sa	-3 06	5 30	18 24	5 16	18 37	4 58	18 56	4 34	19 22	3 54	20 00
123	05 44 ☾	0 21	12 05	0 33	11 55	0 48	11 42	1 07	11 24	1 38	10 56
4 Su	-3 12	5 30	18 24	5 15	18 38	4 57	18 57	4 32	19 23	3 51	20 03
124		0 59	12 54	1 07	12 47	1 17	12 39	1 31	12 28	1 52	12 11
5 Mo	-3 18	5 29	18 25	5 14	18 39	4 56	18 58	4 31	19 24	3 49	20 06
125		1 34	13 42	1 39	13 39	1 45	13 36	1 52	13 31	2 03	13 24
6 Tu	-3 23	5 29	18 25	5 13	18 39	4 55	18 59	4 29	19 25	3 46	20 08
126		2 09	14 30	2 10	14 31	2 11	14 33	2 12	14 35	2 14	14 38
7 We	-3 27	5 28	18 26	5 12	18 40	4 54	19 00	4 27	19 26	3 43	20 10
127		2 44	15 19	2 41	15 24	2 37	15 30	2 32	15 39	2 25	15 53
8 Th	-3 31	5 27	18 26	5 11	18 41	4 53	19 01	4 25	19 27	3 40	20 12
128		3 20	16 09	3 13	16 18	3 05	16 29	2 53	16 44	2 36	17 09
9 Fr	-3 34	5 27	18 26	5 11	18 42	4 52	19 02	4 24	19 29	3 38	20 15
129		3 58	17 00	3 48	17 13	3 35	17 29	3 17	17 51	2 49	18 26
10 Sa	-3 37	5 26	18 27	5 10	18 43	4 51	19 03	4 23	19 31	3 36	20 18
130		4 39	17 54	4 25	18 10	4 08	18 30	3 44	18 58	3 06	19 43
11 Su	-3 39	5 26	18 27	5 09	18 43	4 50	19 04	4 21	19 32	3 33	20 20
131	07 05 ●	5 24	18 49	5 07	19 08	4 46	19 31	4 17	20 03	3 29	20 58
12 Mo	-3 41	5 25	18 28	5 09	18 44	4 49	19 05	4 19	19 33	3 30	20 22
132		6 13	19 45	5 54	20 05	5 30	20 30	4 57	21 05	4 00	22 06
13 Tu	-3 42	5 25	18 28	5 08	18 45	4 48	19 06	4 17	19 34	3 28	20 24
133		7 06	20 41	6 46	21 01	6 21	21 26	5 45	22 01	4 45	23 01
14 We	-3 42	5 24	18 29	5 07	18 45	4 47	19 07	4 16	19 36	3 26	20 27
134		8 03	21 34	7 43	21 53	7 18	22 16	6 44	22 49	5 44	23 43
15 Th	-3 42	5 24	18 29	5 07	18 46	4 46	19 08	4 15	19 38	3 24	20 30
135		9 01	22 25	8 44	22 41	8 21	23 01	7 50	23 29	6 57	
16 Fr	-3 41	5 23	18 29	5 07	18 46	4 45	19 08	4 13	19 39	3 21	20 32
136		10 01	23 13	9 46	23 26	9 28	23 42	9 02		8 20	0 13
17 Sa	-3 40	5 23	18 30	5 06	18 47	4 44	19 09	4 11	19 40	3 19	20 34
137		11 01	23 59	10 50		10 36		10 18	0 03	9 48	0 36
18 Su	-3 38	5 23	18 30	5 05	18 47	4 43	19 10	4 10	19 41	3 17	20 36
138	10 29 ☽	12 00		11 54	0 07	11 46	0 18	11 35	0 32	11 18	0 53
19 Mo	-3 36	5 22	18 30	5 04	18 48	4 42	19 11	4 09	19 43	3 15	20 39
139		12 59	0 43	12 58	0 47	12 55	0 52	12 53	0 58	12 48	1 08
20 Tu	-3 33	5 22	18 31	5 04	18 49	4 41	19 12	4 08	19 45	3 13	20 42
140		13 59	1 26	14 02	1 25	14 05	1 24	14 11	1 23	14 19	1 21
21 We	-3 30	5 22	18 31	5 03	18 49	4 40	19 13	4 07	19 46	3 10	20 44
141		14 58	2 09	15 06	2 04	15 16	1 57	15 29	1 48	15 50	1 35
22 Th	-3 26	5 22	18 32	5 03	18 50	4 39	19 14	4 06	19 47	3 08	20 46
142		15 59	2 54	16 11	2 44	16 26	2 32	16 47	2 16	17 21	1 50
23 Fr	-3 21	5 21	18 32	5 02	18 50	4 38	19 15	4 05	19 48	3 06	20 48
143		17 00	3 41	17 16	3 27	17 36	3 10	18 04	2 47	18 50	2 09
24 Sa	-3 17	5 21	18 33	5 02	18 51	4 37	19 16	4 04	19 50	3 04	20 50
144		18 01	4 31	18 20	4 14	18 43	3 52	19 16	3 23	20 13	2 34
25 Su	-3 11	5 21	18 33	5 02	18 52	4 37	19 17	4 03	19 52	3 02	20 53
145	05 51 ○	19 00	5 24	19 20	5 04	19 45	4 40	20 21	4 06	21 23	3 08
26 Mo	-3 05	5 21	18 33	5 01	18 52	4 36	19 17	4 02	19 53	3 00	20 55
146		19 55	6 19	20 16	5 59	20 41	5 33	21 16	4 57	22 17	3 55
27 Tu	-2 59	5 20	18 34	5 01	18 53	4 36	19 18	4 01	19 54	2 58	20 57
147		20 47	7 15	21 06	6 55	21 29	6 30	22 02	5 55	22 56	4 55
28 We	-2 52	5 20	18 34	5 01	18 54	4 35	19 19	4 00	19 55	2 56	20 59
148		21 34	8 10	21 50	7 52	22 10	7 30	22 38	6 58	23 24	6 05
29 Th	-2 45	5 20	18 35	5 00	18 55	4 35	19 20	3 59	19 56	2 54	21 01
149		22 16	9 04	22 30	8 49	22 46	8 30	23 08	8 04	23 44	7 21
30 Fr	-2 37	5 20	18 35	5 00	18 55	4 34	19 21	3 58	19 57	2 53	21 03
150		22 56	9 56	23 05	9 44	23 17	9 30	23 34	9 09	23 59	8 37
31 Sa	-2 28	5 20	18 35	5 00	18 56	4 34	19 21	3 57	19 58	2 51	21 05
151		23 32	10 46	23 38	10 38	23 46	10 28	23 56	10 14		9 52

6th Month　　　　June, 1975　　　　30 Days

Greenwich Mean Time

NOTE: Light figures indicate Sun. **Dark** figures indicate **Moon**. *Degrees are North Latitude.*

CAUTION: Must be converted to local time. For instruction see page 219.

Day of month week year	Sun on meridian Moon phase h m s	20° Rise Sun Moon h m	20° Set Sun Moon h m	30° Rise Sun Moon h m	30° Set Sun Moon h m	40° Rise Sun Moon h m	40° Set Sun Moon h m	50° Rise Sun Moon h m	50° Set Sun Moon h m	60° Rise Sun Moon h m	60° Set Sun Moon h m
1 Su	-2 20	5 20	18 37	4 59	18 57	4 33	19 23	3 56	20 00	2 49	21 07
152	23 23 (		11 35		11 31		11 25		11 18	0 11	11 07
2 Mo	-2 11	5 20	18 37	4 59	18 57	4 33	19 23	3 55	20 01	2 48	21 09
153		0 07	12 23	0 10	12 23	0 13	12 22	0 16	12 22	0 22	12 21
3 Tu	-2 01	5 20	18 37	4 59	18 58	4 33	19 24	3 54	20 02	2 47	21 10
154		0 42	13 11	0 41	13 15	0 39	13 19	0 36	13 25	0 32	13 34
4 We	-1 51	5 20	18 37	4 59	18 58	4 32	19 24	3 54	20 03	2 46	21 11
155		1 18	14 00	1 12	14 08	1 06	14 17	0 57	14 30	0 43	14 49
5 Th	-1 41	5 20	18 38	4 59	18 59	4 32	19 25	3 53	20 04	2 44	21 13
156		1 55	14 51	1 45	15 02	1 34	15 16	1 19	15 35	0 56	16 06
6 Fr	-1 30	5 20	18 38	4 59	18 59	4 32	19 25	3 53	20 05	2 43	21 15
157		2 34	15 43	2 21	15 58	2 06	16 16	1 44	16 42	1 11	17 23
7 Sa	-1 19	5 20	18 38	4 58	18 59	4 31	19 26	3 53	20 06	2 42	21 17
158		3 17	16 38	3 01	16 56	2 42	17 18	2 14	17 48	1 31	18 40
8 Su	-1 08	5 20	18 38	4 58	19 00	4 31	19 27	3 52	20 07	2 41	21 18
159		4 05	17 34	3 46	17 54	3 23	18 18	2 51	18 53	1 58	19 52
9 Mo	-0 56	5 20	18 39	4 58	19 00	4 31	19 27	3 52	20 07	2 40	21 19
160	18 49 ●	4 57	18 31	4 37	18 51	4 12	19 17	3 37	19 52	2 37	20 53
10 Tu	-0 44	5 20	18 39	4 58	19 00	4 31	19 28	3 52	20 08	2 39	21 20
161		5 53	19 27	5 33	19 46	5 08	20 10	4 32	20 44	3 31	21 41
11 We	-0 32	5 20	18 39	4 58	19 01	4 30	19 28	3 51	20 08	2 38	21 21
162		6 52	20 20	6 34	20 37	6 10	20 59	5 37	21 28	4 42	22 17
12 Th	-0 20	5 20	18 39	4 58	19 01	4 30	19 29	3 51	20 09	2 38	21 22
163		7 53	21 11	7 37	21 24	7 17	21 42	6 50	22 05	6 04	22 42
13 Fr	-0 08	5 20	18 40	4 58	19 01	4 30	19 29	3 51	20 09	2 37	21 23
164		8 55	21 58	8 42	22 08	8 27	22 20	8 06	22 36	7 32	23 01
14 Sa	+0 05	5 20	18 40	4 58	19 02	4 30	19 30	3 50	20 10	2 37	21 24
165		9 55	22 42	9 47	22 48	9 37	22 55	9 24	23 03	9 03	23 17
15 Su	+0 18	5 20	18 40	4 58	19 02	4 30	19 30	3 50	20 10	2 36	21 25
166		10 54	23 26	10 51	23 26	10 47	23 27	10 42	23 29	10 34	23 30
16 Mo	+0 30	5 20	18 40	4 59	19 02	4 30	19 31	3 50	20 11	2 36	21 25
167	14 58 ☽	11 53		11 55		11 57		12 00	23 53	12 04	23 44
17 Tu	+0 43	5 21	18 41	4 59	19 03	4 30	19 31	3 50	20 11	2 36	21 26
168		12 52	0 08	12 58	0 04	13 06	0 00	13 17		13 34	23 58
18 We	+0 56	5 21	18 41	4 59	19 03	4 31	19 31	3 50	20 11	2 35	21 26
169		13 51	0 52	14 02	0 43	14 15	0 33	14 34	0 19	15 03	
19 Th	+1 09	5 21	18 41	4 59	19 03	4 31	19 32	3 50	20 12	2 35	21 27
170		14 51	1 37	15 05	1 24	15 24	1 09	15 49	0 48	16 31	0 15
20 Fr	+1 22	5 21	18 41	4 59	19 04	4 31	19 32	3 50	20 12	2 35	21 27
171		15 50	2 25	16 08	2 09	16 30	1 49	17 01	1 21	17 54	0 37
21 Sa	+1 35	5 21	18 42	4 59	19 04	4 31	19 32	3 50	20 12	2 35	21 27
172		16 49	3 15	17 08	2 57	17 33	2 33	18 08	2 01	19 08	1 06
22 Su	+1 48	5 21	18 42	5 00	19 04	4 31	19 32	3 51	20 12	2 36	21 28
173		17 45	4 08	18 05	3 48	18 31	3 23	19 07	2 48	20 09	1 47
23 Mo	+2 01	5 22	18 42	5 00	19 04	4 32	19 32	3 51	20 12	2 36	21 28
174	16 54 ○	18 38	5 03	18 57	4 43	19 22	4 18	19 56	3 42	20 54	2 40
24 Tu	+2 14	5 22	18 42	5 00	19 05	4 32	19 33	3 51	20 13	2 36	21 28
175		19 26	5 59	19 44	5 40	20 06	5 16	20 36	4 43	21 26	3 46
25 We	+2 27	5 22	18 42	5 00	19 05	4 32	19 33	3 51	20 13	2 37	21 28
176		20 11	6 53	20 26	6 37	20 44	6 16	21 09	5 48	21 49	5 00
26 Th	+2 39	5 22	18 43	5 00	19 05	4 32	19 33	3 52	20 13	2 37	21 28
177		20 52	7 46	21 03	7 33	21 17	7 17	21 36	6 54	22 06	6 16
27 Fr	+2 52	5 22	18 43	5 01	19 05	4 33	19 33	3 52	20 13	2 38	21 28
178		21 30	8 38	21 38	8 28	21 47	8 16	22 00	7 59	22 19	7 33
28 Sa	+3 04	5 23	18 43	5 01	19 05	4 33	19 33	3 52	20 13	2 38	21 27
179		22 06	9 27	22 10	9 21	22 14	9 14	22 21	9 04	22 31	8 48
29 Su	+3 16	5 23	18 43	5 01	19 05	4 33	19 33	3 53	20 13	2 39	21 27
180		22 41	10 16	22 41	10 14	22 41	10 11	22 41	10 08	22 41	10 02
30 Mo	+3 28	5 23	18 43	5 01	19 05	4 34	19 33	3 53	20 13	2 40	21 27
181		23 16	11 04	23 12	11 06	23 07	11 08	23 01	11 11	22 52	11 16

7th Month   July, 1975   31 Days

Greenwich Mean Time

NOTE: Light figures indicate Sun. **Dark** figures indicate **Moon**. *Degrees are North Latitude.*
CAUTION: Must be converted to local time. For instruction see page 219.

Day of month / week / year	Sun on meridian / Moon phase (h m s)	20° Rise Sun / Moon (h m)	20° Set Sun / Moon (h m)	30° Rise Sun / Moon (h m)	30° Set Sun / Moon (h m)	40° Rise Sun / Moon (h m)	40° Set Sun / Moon (h m)	50° Rise Sun / Moon (h m)	50° Set Sun / Moon (h m)	60° Rise Sun / Moon (h m)	60° Set Sun / Moon (h m)
1 Tu	+3 40 16 37 (	5 24	18 44	5 02	19 05	4 34	19 32	3 54	20 12	2 41	21 26
182		23 51	11 52	23 44	11 58	23 35	12 05	23 22	12 15	23 03	12 30
2 We	+3 52	5 24	18 44	5 02	19 05	4 35	19 32	3 54	20 12	2 42	21 25
183			12 41		12 51		13 03	23 46	13 19	23 17	13 45
3 Th	+4 03	5 24	18 44	5 03	19 05	4 35	19 32	3 55	20 12	2 43	21 24
184		0 29	13 32	0 18	13 46	0 04	14 02		14 24	23 34	15 01
4 Fr	+4 14	5 25	18 44	5 03	19 05	4 36	19 32	3 56	20 12	2 44	21 23
185		1 10	14 26	0 56	14 42	0 38	15 02	0 13	15 30	23 57	16 17
5 Sa	+4 25	5 25	18 44	5 04	19 04	4 36	19 32	3 56	20 11	2 45	21 22
186		1 55	15 21	1 38	15 39	1 16	16 03	0 46	16 36		17 31
6 Su	+4 35	5 25	18 44	5 04	19 04	4 37	19 31	3 57	20 11	2 46	21 21
187		2 44	16 17	2 25	16 37	2 01	17 02	1 27	17 38	0 30	18 38
7 Mo	+4 45	5 26	18 44	5 05	19 04	4 37	19 31	3 58	20 10	2 47	21 20
188		3 39	17 14	3 19	17 34	2 54	17 59	2 18	18 34	1 17	19 33
8 Tu	+4 55	5 26	18 44	5 05	19 04	4 38	19 31	3 59	20 10	2 49	21 19
189		4 38	18 09	4 18	18 28	3 54	18 50	3 19	19 22	2 20	20 15
9 We	+5 05	5 27	18 43	5 06	19 04	4 39	19 31	4 00	20 09	2 51	21 17
190	04 10 ●	5 39	19 02	5 22	19 18	5 00	19 37	4 30	20 03	3 39	20 45
10 Th	+5 14	5 27	18 43	5 06	19 03	4 39	19 30	4 01	20 09	2 52	21 16
191		6 42	19 52	6 28	20 04	6 11	20 18	5 46	20 37	5 07	21 07
11 Fr	+5 22	5 27	18 43	5 07	19 03	4 40	19 30	4 02	20 08	2 54	21 15
192		7 45	20 39	7 35	20 46	7 23	20 55	7 06	21 07	6 40	21 25
12 Sa	+5 30	5 28	18 43	5 07	19 03	4 40	19 30	4 03	20 07	2 56	21 14
193		8 46	21 24	8 41	21 27	8 35	21 30	8 27	21 34	8 14	21 40
13 Su	+5 38	5 28	18 43	5 08	19 03	4 41	19 29	4 04	20 06	2 58	21 12
194		9 47	22 08	9 47	22 06	9 47	22 03	9 46	21 59	9 46	21 53
14 Mo	+5 45	5 28	18 43	5 08	19 03	4 42	19 29	4 05	20 05	3 00	21 10
195		10 47	22 52	10 51	22 45	10 57	22 36	11 05	22 25	11 18	22 08
15 Tu	+5 51	5 29	18 42	5 09	19 02	4 42	19 29	4 06	20 05	3 02	21 09
196	19 47)	11 46	23 36	11 55	23 25	12 07	23 11	12 23	22 53	12 48	22 24
16 We	+5 57	5 29	18 42	5 09	19 02	4 43	19 28	4 07	20 04	3 04	21 07
197		12 45		12 59		13 15	23 50	13 39	23 24	14 16	22 44
17 Th	+6 03	5 29	18 42	5 10	19 02	4 44	19 28	4 08	20 03	3 06	21 05
198		13 44	0 23	14 01	0 08	14 22		14 51		15 41	23 10
18 Fr	46 08	5 30	18 42	5 10	19 02	4 45	19 27	4 09	20 02	3 08	21 03
199		14 42	1 12	15 01	0 54	15 25	0 32	15 59	0 01	16 57	23 46
19 Sa	+6 12	5 30	18 42	5 11	19 01	4 46	19 26	4 11	20 01	3 10	21 01
200		15 38	2 03	15 59	1 44	16 24	1 19	17 00	0 44	18 01	
20 Su	+6 16	5 30	18 41	5 11	19 01	4 46	19 26	4 12	20 00	3 12	20 59
201		16 32	2 57	16 51	2 37	17 16	2 11	17 51	1 35	18 51	0 33
21 Mo	+6 20	5 31	18 41	5 12	19 01	4 47	19 25	4 13	19 59	3 14	20 57
202		17 21	3 51	17 40	3 32	18 02	3 07	18 34	2 33	19 27	1 34
22 Tu	+6 22	5 31	18 41	5 12	19 00	4 48	19 24	4 14	19 58	3 16	20 55
203		18 07	4 45	18 23	4 28	18 43	4 06	19 10	3 35	19 53	2 44
23 We	+6 25 05 28 ○	5 31	18 41	5 13	19 00	4 49	19 23	4 15	19 57	3 18	20 53
204		18 49	5 39	19 02	5 24	19 18	5 06	19 39	4 40	20 13	3 59
24 Th	+6 26	5 32	18 41	5 14	18 59	4 50	19 22	4 17	19 55	3 20	20 51
205		19 28	6 30	19 37	6 19	19 49	6 05	20 04	5 46	20 28	5 15
25 Fr	+6 27	5 32	18 40	5 14	18 59	4 51	19 22	4 18	19 54	3 22	20 49
206		20 05	7 21	20 10	7 13	20 17	7 04	20 26	6 51	20 40	6 31
26 Sa	+6 28	5 32	18 40	5 15	18 58	4 52	19 21	4 19	19 53	3 24	20 47
207		20 40	8 10	20 42	8 06	20 44	8 01	20 47	7 55	20 51	7 46
27 Su	+6 28	5 33	18 40	5 15	18 58	4 53	19 20	4 20	19 52	3 26	20 45
208		21 15	8 58	21 13	8 58	21 10	8 58	21 07	8 59	21 02	8 59
28 Mo	+6 27	5 33	18 39	5 16	18 57	4 54	19 19	4 22	19 50	3 29	20 42
209		21 50	9 46	21 44	9 50	21 37	9 55	21 27	10 02	21 13	10 13
29 Tu	+6 26	5 34	18 39	5 17	18 56	4 55	19 18	4 24	19 48	3 32	20 39
210		22 27	10 34	22 17	10 42	22 06	10 52	21 50	11 05	21 25	11 26
30 We	+6 24	5 34	18 39	5 17	18 56	4 55	19 17	4 25	19 47	3 34	20 37
211		23 06	11 24	22 53	11 35	22 37	11 50	22 15	12 09	21 41	12 41
31 Th	+6 21 08 48 (	5 34	18 38	5 18	18 55	4 56	19 16	4 26	19 46	3 36	20 35
212		23 48	12 15	23 32	12 30	23 12	12 48	22 45	13 14	22 01	13 56

8th Month   August, 1975   31 Days

Greenwich Mean Time

NOTE: Light figures indicate Sun. **Dark** figures indicate **Moon**. *Degrees are North Latitude.*

CAUTION: Must be converted to local time. For instruction see page 219.

Day of month week year	Sun on meridian Moon phase h m s	20° Rise Sun/Moon	20° Set Sun/Moon	30° Rise Sun/Moon	30° Set Sun/Moon	40° Rise Sun/Moon	40° Set Sun/Moon	50° Rise Sun/Moon	50° Set Sun/Moon	60° Rise Sun/Moon	60° Set Sun/Moon
1 Fr	+6 18	5 35	18 38	5 19	18 54	4 57	19 15	4 27	19 45	3 38	20 33
213			13 08		13 26	23 53	13 48	23 21	14 18	22 28	15 10
2 Sa	+6 14	5 35	18 37	5 19	18 53	4 58	19 14	4 29	19 43	3 40	20 30
214		0 34	14 03	0 16	14 22		14 47		15 21	23 07	16 19
3 Su	+6 10	5 36	18 36	5 20	18 52	4 59	19 12	4 31	19 41	3 43	20 27
215		1 25	14 59	1 05	15 19	0 41	15 4	0 06	16 19		17 19
4 Mo	+6 05	5 36	18 36	5 20	18 52	5 00	19 11	4 32	19 40	3 45	20 25
216		2 21	15 54	2 01	16 13	1 36	16 37	1 01	17 11	0 01	18 07
5 Tu	+6 00	5 36	18 35	5 21	18 51	5 01	19 10	4 33	19 38	3 47	20 23
217		3 21	16 48	3 02	17 05	2 39	17 26	2 06	17 55	1 11	18 43
6 We	+5 54	5 37	18 35	5 22	18 50	5 02	19 09	4 34	19 36	3 49	20 20
218		4 23	17 40	4 07	17 54	3 48	18 10	3 20	18 33	2 35	19 09
7 Th	+5 47	5 37	18 34	5 22	18 49	5 03	19 08	4 36	19 34	3 52	20 17
219 11 57 ●		5 27	18 30	5 15	18 39	5 00	18 50	4 40	19 06	4 07	19 30
8 Fr	+5 40	5 37	18 34	5 23	18 48	5 04	19 07	4 38	19 32	3 55	20 14
220		6 30	19 17	6 23	19 21	6 14	19 27	6 02	19 35	5 43	19 46
9 Sa	+5 32	5 38	18 33	5 23	18 48	5 05	19 06	4 39	19 31	3 57	20 12
221		7 33	20 03	7 31	20 02	7 28	20 02	7 24	20 02	7 18	20 01
10 Su	+5 24	5 38	18 33	5 24	18 47	5 06	19 05	4 40	19 29	4 00	20 10
222		8 36	20 48	8 38	20 43	8 42	20 37	8 46	20 29	8 53	20 16
11 Mo	+5 15	5 38	18 32	5 25	18 46	5 07	19 04	4 41	19 27	4 03	20 07
223		9 37	21 34	9 45	21 24	9 54	21 12	10 07	20 57	10 27	20 32
12 Tu	+5 05	5 39	18 32	5 25	18 45	5 08	19 02	4 43	19 25	4 05	20 04
224		10 38	22 21	10 50	22 07	11 05	21 51	11 25	21 28	11 58	20 51
13 We	+4 55	5 39	18 31	5 26	18 44	5 09	19 00	4 45	19 23	4 07	20 00
225		11 38	23 10	11 54	22 53	12 14	22 32	12 41	22 03	13 26	21 16
14 Th	+4 44 02 24 ☽	5 39	18 31	5 26	18 43	5 10	18 59	4 46	19 22	4 09	19 59
226		12 37		12 56	23 42	13 19	23 18	13 51	22 45	14 46	21 49
15 Fr	+4 33	5 40	18 30	5 27	18 42	5 11	18 58	4 47	19 20	4 12	19 56
227		13 34	0 01	13 54		14 19		14 54	23 33	15 54	22 33
16 Sa	+4 21	5 40	18 29	5 28	18 41	5 12	18 56	4 49	19 18	4 14	19 53
228		14 28	0 53	14 48	0 34	15 13	0 08	15 48		16 48	23 28
17 Su	+4 09	5 40	18 28	5 29	18 40	5 13	18 55	4 51	19 16	4 16	19 50
229		15 18	1 47	15 37	1 28	16 01	1 03	16 33	0 28	17 28	
18 Mo	+3 56	5 41	18 27	5 29	18 39	5 14	18 54	4 53	19 14	4 19	19 47
230		16 05	2 41	16 22	2 23	16 42	2 00	17 11	1 28	17 58	0 35
19 Tu	+3 43	5 41	18 27	5 29	18 38	5 15	18 53	4 54	19 12	4 21	19 44
231		16 48	3 34	17 02	3 18	17 19	2 59	17 42	2 32	18 19	1 47
20 We	+3 29	5 41	18 26	5 30	18 37	5 16	18 52	4 55	19 10	4 23	19 41
232		17 28	4 26	17 38	4 13	17 51	3 58	18 08	3 36	18 35	3 02
21 Th	+3 14 19 48 ○	5 41	18 25	5 30	18 36	5 16	18 50	4 56	19 08	4 25	19 38
233		18 05	5 16	18 12	5 07	18 20	4 56	18 31	4 41	18 49	4 17
22 Fr	+3 00	5 42	18 24	5 31	18 35	5 17	18 48	4 58	19 08	4 28	19 35
234		18 41	6 05	18 44	6 00	18 48	5 54	18 53	5 45	19 00	5 32
23 Sa	+2 44	5 42	18 23	5 31	18 34	5 18	18 46	5 00	19 04	4 31	19 32
235		19 16	6 54	19 15	6 52	19 14	6 51	19 13	6 49	19 11	6 46
24 Su	+2 28	5 42	18 23	5 32	18 33	5 19	18 45	5 01	19 02	4 33	19 30
236		19 51	7 42	19 46	7 44	19 41	7 47	19 34	7 52	19 23	7 59
25 Mo	+2 12	5 42	18 22	5 32	18 32	5 20	18 43	5 02	19 00	4 35	19 27
237		20 27	8 30	20 19	8 36	20 09	8 44	19 55	8 55	19 35	9 12
26 Tu	+1 56	5 42	18 21	5 33	18 31	5 21	18 41	5 04	18 58	4 37	19 24
238		21 05	9 19	20 53	9 29	20 39	9 41	20 19	9 58	19 49	10 25
27 We	+1 39	5 43	18 20	5 33	18 30	5 22	18 40	5 06	18 56	4 40	19 21
239		21 45	10 09	21 30	10 22	21 12	10 39	20 47	11 02	20 07	11 39
28 Th	+1 21	5 43	18 19	5 34	18 28	5 23	18 39	5 08	18 54	4 43	19 18
240		22 29	11 00	22 11	11 16	21 50	11 37	21 20	12 05	20 31	12 52
29 Fr	+1 04	5 43	18 19	5 34	18 27	5 24	18 38	5 09	18 52	4 45	19 15
241 23 20 ☾		23 16	11 53	22 57	12 11	22 33	12 34	22 00	13 07	21 04	14 02
30 Sa	+0 46	5 43	18 18	5 35	18 26	5 25	18 36	5 10	18 50	4 47	19 12
242			12 47	23 49	13 06		13 31	22 49	14 05	21 50	15 04
31 Su	+0 27	5 43	18 17	5 35	18 25	5 26	18 34	5 11	18 48	4 49	19 09
243		0 08	13 41		14 00		14 24	23 48	14 59	22 51	15 56

9th Month   September, 1975   30 Days

Greenwich Mean Time

NOTE: Light figures indicate Sun. **Dark** figures indicate **Moon.** *Degrees are North Latitude.*

CAUTION: Must be converted to local time. For instruction see page 219.

Day of month / week / year	Sun on meridian / Moon phase (h m s)	20° Rise Sun/Moon (h m)	20° Set Sun/Moon (h m)	30° Rise Sun/Moon	30° Set Sun/Moon	40° Rise Sun/Moon	40° Set Sun/Moon	50° Rise Sun/Moon	50° Set Sun/Moon	60° Rise Sun/Moon	60° Set Sun/Moon
1 Mo	+0 09	5 44	18 16	5 36	18 24	5 27	18 33	5 13	18 46	4 52	19 06
244		1 04	14 34	0 45	14 52	0 22	15 14		15 46		16 37
2 Tu	-0 10	5 44	18 15	5 37	18 22	5 28	18 31	5 15	18 44	4 55	19 03
245		2 04	15 26	1 47	15 41	1 26	16 00	0 56	16 26	0 06	17 07
3 We	-0 29	5 44	18 15	5 37	18 21	5 29	18 30	5 16	18 42	4 57	19 00
246		3 06	16 16	2 52	16 28	2 35	16 42	2 11	17 01	1 32	17 31
4 Th	-0 49	5 45	18 14	5 38	18 20	5 30	18 29	5 17	18 40	4 59	18 57
247		4 09	17 04	3 59	17 11	3 48	17 20	3 31	17 32	3 05	17 50
5 Fr	-1 09, 19 19 ●	5 45	18 13	5 38	18 19	5 31	18 27	5 19	18 38	5 01	18 54
248		5 13	17 51	5 08	17 54	5 02	17 57	4 54	18 00	4 41	18 06
6 Sa	-1 29	5 45	18 12	5 39	18 17	5 32	18 25	5 21	18 36	5 04	18 51
249		6 17	18 38	6 17	18 36	6 17	18 32	6 17	18 28	6 18	18 22
7 Su	-1 49	5 45	18 11	5 40	18 16	5 33	18 23	5 23	18 33	5 07	18 48
250		7 20	19 25	7 25	19 18	7 32	19 09	7 41	18 57	7 54	18 38
8 Mo	-2 09	5 46	18 10	5 40	18 15	5 33	18 22	5 24	18 31	5 09	18 45
251		8 24	20 13	8 34	20 02	8 46	19 47	9 03	19 28	9 30	18 57
c Tu	-2 30	5 46	18 09	5 41	18 14	5 34	18 21	5 25	18 29	5 11	18 42
252		9 26	21 03	9 40	20 48	9 58	20 29	10 22	20 03	11 02	19 20
0 We	-2 50	5 46	18 08	5 41	18 13	5 35	18 19	5 26	18 27	5 13	18 39
253		10 28	21 55	10 45	21 37	11 07	21 15	11 37	20 43	12 28	19 51
11 Th	-3 11	5 46	18 07	5 42	18 12	5 36	18 17	5 28	18 25	5 16	18 36
254		11 27	22 49	11 46	22 29	12 10	22 05	12 44	21 30	13 42	20 32
12 Fr	-3 32, 11 59 ☽	5 47	18 06	5 42	18 10	5 37	18 15	5 30	18 22	5 19	18 33
255		12 23	23 43	12 43	23 23	13 08	22 59	13 43	22 24	14 42	21 25
13 Sa	-3 53	5 47	18 06	5 43	18 09	5 38	18 14	5 31	18 20	5 21	18 30
256		13 15		13 34		13 58	23 56	14 31	23 23	15 27	22 28
14 Su	-4 15	5 47	18 05	5 43	18 08	5 39	18 13	5 32	18 18	5 23	18 27
257		14 03	0 37	14 20	0 19	14 42		15 11		16 00	23 38
15 Mo	-4 36	5 47	18 04	5 44	18 07	5 40	18 11	5 34	18 16	5 25	18 24
258		14 47	1 30	15 02	1 14	15 20	0 54	15 44	0 25	16 24	
16 Tu	-4 57	5 48	18 03	5 44	18 06	5 41	18 09	5 36	18 14	5 28	18 21
259		15 28	2 22	15 39	2 09	15 53	1 52	16 12	1 29	16 42	0 52
17 We	-5 19	5 48	18 02	5 45	18 04	5 42	18 07	5 38	18 11	5 31	18 17
260		16 05	3 13	16 13	3 03	16 23	2 50	16 36	2 34	16 57	2 07
18 Th	-5 40	5 48	18 01	5 45	18 03	5 43	18 06	5 39	18 09	5 33	18 14
261		16 42	4 02	16 46	3 56	16 51	3 48	16 58	3 37	17 09	3 21
19 Fr	-6 02	5 48	18 00	5 46	18 02	5 44	18 05	5 40	18 07	5 35	18 11
262		17 17	4 50	17 17	4 48	17 18	4 45	17 19	4 41	17 21	4 34
20 Sa	-6 23, 11 50 ○	5 48	17 59	5 46	18 01	5 45	18 03	5 41	18 05	5 37	18 08
263		17 52	5 38	17 49	5 40	17 45	5 41	17 40	5 44	17 32	5 47
21 Su	-6 44	5 49	17 58	5 47	17 59	5 46	18 01	5 43	18 03	5 39	18 05
264		18 28	6 27	18 21	6 32	18 13	6 38	18 01	6 47	17 44	7 00
22 Mo	-7 06	5 49	17 57	5 47	17 58	5 47	17 59	5 45	18 00	5 42	18 02
265		19 05	7 15	18 55	7 24	18 42	7 35	18 05	7 50	17 58	8 13
23 Tu	-7 27	5 49	17 56	5 48	17 57	5 48	17 58	5 46	17 58	5 44	17 59
266		19 45	8 05	19 31	8 17	19 14	8 32	18 51	8 53	18 15	9 27
24 We	-7 48	5 49	17 55	5 49	17 56	5 49	17 56	5 47	17 56	5 46	17 56
267		20 27	8 56	20 11	9 11	19 50	9 30	19 23	9 56	18 37	10 40
25 Th	-8 09	5 49	17 54	5 49	17 55	5 50	17 54	5 49	17 54	5 48	17 53
268		21 13	9 48	20 54	10 05	20 32	10 27	20 00	10 58	19 07	11 50
26 Fr	-8 29	5 50	17 53	5 50	17 53	5 51	17 52	5 51	17 52	5 51	17 50
269		22 02	10 40	21 43	10 59	21 19	11 23	20 45	11 57	19 47	12 54
27 Sa	-8 50	5 50	17 52	5 51	17 51	5 52	17 50	5 53	17 49	5 54	17 47
270		22 55	11 33	22 36	11 52	22 12	12 16	21 38	12 50	20 41	13 48
28 Su	-9 10, 11 46 ☾	5 50	17 51	5 51	17 50	5 52	17 49	5 54	17 47	5 56	17 44
271		23 51	12 25	23 34	12 43	23 11	13 06	22 40	13 38	21 48	14 32
29 Mo	-9 30	5 50	17 50	5 51	17 49	5 53	17 48	5 55	17 45	5 58	17 41
272			13 15		13 32		13 52	23 50	14 20	23 06	15 05
30 Tu	-9 50	5 51	17 49	5 52	17 48	5 54	17 46	5 56	17 43	6 00	17 38
273		0 50	14 03	0 34	14 18	0 16	14 34		14 56		15 31

10th Month　　　　October, 1975　　　　31 Days

Greenwich Mean Time

NOTE: Light figures indicate Sun. Dark figures indicate Moon. *Degrees are North Latitude.*
CAUTION: Must be converted to local time. For instruction see page 219.

Day of month week year	Sun on meridian Moon phase h m s	20° Rise Sun Moon h m	20° Set Sun Moon h m	30° Rise Sun Moon h m	30° Set Sun Moon h m	40° Rise Sun Moon h m	40° Set Sun Moon h m	50° Rise Sun Moon h m	50° Set Sun Moon h m	60° Rise Sun Moon h m	60° Set Sun Moon h m
1 We 274	-10 09	5 51	17 49	5 52	17 46	5 55	17 44	5 58	17 41	6 03	17 35
		1 51	14 52	1 39	15 01	1 25	15 13	1 05	15 28	0 33	15 51
2 Th 275	-10 29	5 51	17 48	5 53	17 45	5 56	17 42	6 00	17 38	6 06	17 32
		2 52	15 39	2 45	15 43	2 36	15 49	2 24	15 57	2 04	16 09
3 Fr 276	-10 48	5 51	17 47	5 53	17 43	5 57	17 40	6 01	17 35	6 08	17 29
		3 55	16 25	3 52	16 25	3 49	16 25	3 45	16 25	3 39	16 25
4 Sa 277	-11 06	5 52	17 46	5 54	17 42	5 58	17 38	6 02	17 33	6 10	17 26
		4 58	17 12	5 00	17 07	5 04	17 01	5 08	16 53	5 15	16 41
5 Su 278	-11 24 03 23 ●	5 52	17 45	5 54	17 41	5 59	17 36	6 04	17 31	6 12	17 23
		6 02	18 00	6 09	17 51	6 19	17 39	6 31	17 23	6 51	16 59
6 Mo 279	-11 42	5 52	17 44	5 55	17 40	6 00	17 35	6 06	17 29	6 15	17 20
		7 06	18 51	7 18	18 37	7 33	18 20	7 54	17 57	8 27	17 21
7 Tu 280	-12 00	5 52	17 44	5 56	17 39	6 01	17 34	6 08	17 27	6 18	17 17
		8 11	19 43	8 26	19 27	8 46	19 06	9 13	18 36	9 59	17 49
8 We 281	-12 17	5 53	17 43	5 56	17 37	6 02	17 32	6 09	17 25	6 20	17 14
		9 13	20 38	9 31	20 19	9 54	19 56	10 26	19 22	11 21	18 27
9 Th 282	-12 34	5 53	17 42	5 57	17 36	6 03	17 30	6 10	17 23	6 23	17 11
		10 13	21 34	10 32	21 14	10 56	20 50	11 31	20 15	12 30	19 16
10 Fr 283	-12 50	5 53	17 41	5 58	17 35	6 04	17 28	6 12	17 21	6 24	17 08
		11 08	22 30	11 27	22 11	11 51	21 47	12 25	21 14	13 22	20 18
11 Sa 284	-13 06	5 53	17 40	5 58	17 34	6 05	17 27	6 14	17 19	6 27	17 05
		11 58	23 24	12 16	23 08	12 38	22 46	13 09	22 17	14 00	21 27
12 Su 285	-13 21 01 15 ☽	5 54	17 39	5 59	17 33	6 06	17 26	6 16	17 17	6 30	17 02
		12 44		13 00		13 19	23 46	13 45	23 21	14 27	22 41
13 Mo 286	-13 36	5 54	17 38	5 59	17 32	6 07	17 24	6 17	17 14	6 32	16 59
		13 26	0 17	13 39	0 03	13 54		14 15		14 48	23 56
14 Tu 287	-13 50	5 54	17 37	6 00	17 31	6 08	17 22	6 18	17 12	6 34	16 56
		14 05	1 09	14 14	0 58	14 25	0 44	14 40	0 25	15 03	
15 We 288	-14 04	5 55	17 37	6 01	17 30	6 09	17 21	6 20	17 10	6 36	16 53
		14 42	1 58	14 47	1 51	14 54	1 42	15 03	1 29	15 17	1 10
16 Th 289	-14 18	5 55	17 36	6 02	17 29	6 10	17 20	6 22	17 08	6 39	16 50
		15 18	2 47	15 19	2 43	15 21	2 39	15 24	2 33	15 29	2 23
17 Fr 290	-14 30	5 55	17 36	6 03	17 28	6 12	17 19	6 24	17 06	6 42	16 48
		15 53	3 35	15 51	3 35	15 48	3 35	15 45	3 35	15 40	3 36
18 Sa 291	-14 43	5 56	17 35	6 03	17 27	6 13	17 17	6 25	17 04	6 44	16 45
		16 28	4 23	16 23	4 27	16 16	4 32	16 06	4 38	15 52	4 48
19 Su 292	-14 54	5 56	17 34	6 04	17 26	6 14	17 15	6 26	17 02	6 46	16 42
		17 05	5 12	16 56	5 19	16 45	5 29	16 29	5 41	16 06	6 02
20 Mo 293	-15 05 05 06 ○	5 57	17 33	6 05	17 25	6 15	17 14	6 28	17 00	6 49	16 39
		17 44	6 01	17 32	6 12	17 16	6 26	16 55	6 45	16 22	7 15
21 Tu 294	-15 15	5 57	17 32	6 05	17 24	6 16	17 13	6 30	16 58	6 52	16 36
		18 26	6 52	18 11	7 06	17 51	7 24	17 25	7 49	16 43	8 29
22 We 295	-15 25	5 57	17 32	6 06	17 23	6 17	17 12	6 32	16 57	6 55	16 33
		19 11	7 44	18 53	8 01	18 31	8 22	18 01	8 51	17 10	9 40
23 Th 296	-15 34	5 58	17 31	6 07	17 22	6 18	17 10	6 33	16 55	6 57	16 30
		19 59	8 36	19 40	8 55	19 17	9 18	18 43	9 51	17 47	10 46
24 Fr 297	-15 42	5 58	17 31	6 07	17 21	6 19	17 08	6 34	16 53	6 59	16 27
		20 51	9 29	20 32	9 48	20 08	10 12	19 34	10 46	18 37	11 44
25 Sa 298	-15 50	5 58	17 30	6 08	17 20	6 20	17 07	6 36	16 51	7 01	16 24
		21 46	10 21	21 27	10 39	21 05	11 03	20 33	11 35	19 39	12 30
26 Su 299	-15 57	5 59	17 30	6 09	17 19	6 21	17 06	6 38	16 49	7 03	16 21
		22 42	11 11	22 26	11 28	22 06	11 49	21 38	12 18	20 52	13 06
27 Mo 300	-16 03 22 07 ☾	5 59	17 29	6 10	17 18	6 23	17 05	6 40	16 47	7 07	16 19
		23 40	11 59	23 27	12 13	23 11	12 31	22 49	12 55	22 13	13 34
28 Tu 301	-16 08	5 59	17 28	6 10	17 17	6 24	17 03	6 41	16 45	7 09	16 16
			12 45		12 56		13 09		13 27	23 39	13 55
29 We 302	-16 13	6 00	17 28	6 11	17 16	6 25	17 02	6 42	16 43	7 11	16 13
		0 39	13 31	0 30	13 37	0 19	13 45	0 04	13 56		14 13
30 Th 303	-16 17	6 00	17 27	6 12	17 15	6 26	17 01	6 44	16 41	7 14	16 10
		1 39	14 15	1 34	14 17	1 28	14 20	1 21	14 23	1 09	14 29
31 Fr 304	-16 20	6 00	17 27	6 12	17 14	6 27	17 00	6 46	16 39	7 17	16 08
		2 39	15 00	2 39	14 58	2 40	14 55	2 40	14 50	2 40	14 44

11th Month   November, 1975   30 Days

Greenwich Mean Time

NOTE: Light figures indicate **Sun**. **Dark** figures indicate **Moon**. *Degrees are North Latitude.*
CAUTION: Must be converted to local time. For instruction see page 219.

Day of month week year	Sun on meridian Moon phase	20° Rise Sun/Moon	20° Set Sun/Moon	30° Rise Sun/Moon	30° Set Sun/Moon	40° Rise Sun/Moon	40° Set Sun/Moon	50° Rise Sun/Moon	50° Set Sun/Moon	60° Rise Sun/Moon	60° Set Sun/Moon
1 Sa	-16 22	6 01	17 26	6 13	17 14	6 28	16 59	6 48	16 38	7 20	16 06
305		3 41	15 46	3 46	15 39	3 52	15 31	4 01	15 19	4 14	15 01
2 Su	-16 24	6 01	17 26	6 14	17 13	6 30	16 57	6 50	16 36	7 23	16 03
306		4 44	16 35	4 54	16 24	5 06	16 10	5 22	15 50	5 48	15 20
3 Mo	-16 24	6 02	17 25	6 15	17 12	6 31	16 56	6 52	16 34	7 27	16 00
307	13 05 ●	5 48	17 27	6 02	17 12	6 19	16 53	6 43	16 27	7 22	15 45
4 Tu	-16 24	6 03	17 25	6 16	17 11	6 32	16 55	6 54	16 32	7 29	15 57
308		6 52	18 22	7 09	18 04	7 31	17 41	8 01	17 10	8 51	16 18
5 We	-16 23	6 03	17 24	6 17	17 10	6 33	16 54	6 56	16 31	7 31	15 55
309		7 55	19 18	8 14	18 59	8 38	18 35	9 11	18 01	10 08	17 03
6 Th	-16 21	6 04	17 24	6 17	17 10	6 34	16 53	6 57	16 30	7 33	15 53
310		8 54	20 16	9 13	19 57	9 38	19 33	10 12	18 59	11 10	18 01
7 Fr	-16 18	6 04	17 23	6 18	17 09	6 36	16 52	6 59	16 28	7 46	15 50
311		9 48	21 13	10 07	20 55	10 30	20 33	11 02	20 02	11 56	19 09
8 Sa	-16 15	6 05	17 23	6 19	17 08	6 3	16 51	7 01	16 26	7 39	15 47
312		10 38	22 08	10 54	21 53	11 14	21 34	11 42	21 07	12 28	20 23
9 Su	-16 11	6 05	17 22	6 20	17 08	6 38	16 50	7 03	16 24	7 42	15 45
313		11 22	23 01	11 36	22 49	11 52	22 34	12 15	22 13	12 52	21 40
10 Mo	-16 07	6 06	17 22	6 21	17 07	6 39	16 49	7 04	16 23	7 44	15 43
314	18 21 ☽	12 03	23 52	12 13	23 44	12 26	23 33	12 43	23 18	13 09	22 55
11 Tu	-16 00	6 06	17 22	6 21	17 07	6 40	16 48	7 05	16 22	7 46	15 41
315		12 41		12 48		12 56		13 07		13 24	
12 We	-15 53	6 07	17 21	6 22	17 06	6 41	16 47	7 07	16 20	7 49	15 38
316		13 17	0 42	13 20	0 37	13 24	0 30	13 29	0 22	13 36	0 09
13 Th	-15 46	6 07	17 21	6 23	17 06	6 42	16 46	7 09	16 19	7 52	15 36
317		13 52	1 30	13 51	1 29	13 51	1 27	13 50	1 25	13 48	1 22
14 Fr	-15 37	6 08	17 21	6 24	17 05	6 43	16 45	7 11	16 18	7 55	15 34
318		14 27	2 18	14 23	2 20	14 18	2 24	14 11	2 28	14 00	2 35
15 Sa	-15 27	6 08	17 20	6 25	17 05	6 44	16 44	7 12	16 17	7 57	15 32
319		15 04	3 06	14 56	3 12	14 46	3 20	14 33	3 31	14 13	3 47
16 Su	-15 17	6 09	17 20	6 25	17 04	6 45	16 44	7 13	16 16	7 59	15 30
320		15 42	3 55	15 31	4 05	15 17	4 18	14 58	4 34	14 28	5 01
17 Mo	-15 06	6 10	17 20	6 26	17 04	6 47	16 43	7 15	16 14	8 02	15 28
321		16 23	4 46	16 09	4 59	15 51	5 16	15 26	5 38	14 47	6 15
18 Tu	-14 54	6 10	17 20	6 27	17 03	6 48	16 42	7 17	16 13	8 05	15 26
322	22 28 ○	17 07	5 38	16 50	5 54	16 29	6 14	16 00	6 42	15 12	7 28
19 We	-14 42	6 11	17 19	6 28	17 03	6 49	16 41	7 19	16 12	8 07	15 24
323		17 55	6 31	17 37	6 49	17 13	7 12	16 41	7 43	15 46	8 37
20 Th	-14 28	6 11	17 19	6 29	17 02	6 50	16 40	7 20	16 11	8 09	15 22
324		18 47	7 24	18 28	7 43	18 03	8 08	17 30	8 41	16 32	9 39
21 Fr	-14 14	6 12	17 19	6 29	17 02	6 51	16 40	7 21	16 10	8 11	15 20
325		19 41	8 17	19 23	8 36	18 59	9 00	18 26	9 33	17 31	10 29
22 Sa	-13 59	6 13	17 19	6 30	17 02	6 53	16 39	7 23	16 09	8 14	15 18
326		20 38	9 08	20 21	9 26	20 00	9 48	19 30	10 19	18 42	11 09
23 Su	-13 43	6 13	17 19	6 31	17 02	6 54	16 39	7 25	16 08	8 17	15 16
327		21 35	9 57	21 21	10 13	21 04	10 31	20 40	10 57	20 01	11 39
24 Mo	-13 26	6 14	17 19	6 32	17 01	6 55	16 38	7 27	16 07	8 19	15 14
328		22 33	10 44	22 23	10 56	22 10	11 11	21 52	11 30	21 25	12 02
25 Tu	-13 09	6 14	17 19	6 33	17 01	6 56	16 38	7 28	16 06	8 21	15 12
329		23 31	11 29	23 25	11 37	23 17	11 46	23 07	12 00	22 51	12 20
26 We	-12 51	6 15	17 19	6 34	17 01	6 57	16 37	7 29	16 05	8 23	15 11
330	06 52 ☾		12 12		12 16		12 20		12 27		12 36
27 Th	-12 32	6 16	17 19	6 35	17 01	6 58	16 37	7 31	16 04	8 26	15 09
331		0 29	12 55	0 28	12 54	0 26	12 54	0 23	12 52	0 19	12 51
28 Fr	-12 12	6 16	17 19	6 36	17 00	6 59	16 37	7 33	16 04	8 28	15 07
332		1 28	13 39	1 31	13 34	1 35	13 28	1 40	13 19	1 48	13 06
29 Sa	-11 51	6 17	17 19	6 37	17 00	7 00	16 36	7 34	16 03	8 30	15 06
333		2 29	14 25	2 36	14 15	2 46	14 04	2 59	13 48	3 19	13 23
30 Su	-11 30	6 17	17 19	6 38	17 00	7 01	16 36	7 35	16 03	8 32	15 05
334		3 30	15 14	3 42	15 00	3 57	14 43	4 17	14 21	4 50	13 44

12th Month   December, 1975   31 Days

Greenwich Mean Time

NOTE: Light figures indicate Sun. **Dark** figures indicate **Moon.** *Degrees are North Latitude.*
CAUTION: Must be converted to local time. For instruction see page 219.

Day of month week year	Sun on meridian Moon phase h m s	20° Rise Sun Moon h m	20° Set Sun Moon h m	30° Rise Sun Moon h m	30° Set Sun Moon h m	40° Rise Sun Moon h m	40° Set Sun Moon h m	50° Rise Sun Moon h m	50° Set Sun Moon h m	60° Rise Sun Moon h m	60° Set Sun Moon h m
1 Mo	-11 08	6 18	17 19	6 38	17 00	7 02	16 36	7 36	16 02	8 34	15 04
335		4 33	16 06	4 48	15 49	5 08	15 28	5 35	14 59	6 20	14 12
2 Tu	-10 46	6 18	17 20	6 39	17 00	7 03	16 36	7 38	16 01	8 36	15 02
336		5 35	17 01	5 53	16 42	6 16	16 19	6 48	15 46	7 42	14 50
3 We	-10 22	6 19	17 20	6 40	17 00	7 04	16 36	7 39	16 01	8 38	15 01
337	00 50 ●	6 36	17 58	6 55	17 39	7 20	17 15	7 54	16 40	8 53	15 41
4 Th	-9 59	6 19	17 20	6 41	17 00	7 05	16 35	7 40	16 00	8 40	15 00
338		7 33	18 57	7 52	18 38	8 16	18 15	8 50	17 42	9 47	16 46
5 Fr	-9 34	6 20	17 20	6 42	17 00	7 06	16 35	7 41	16 00	8 42	14 59
339		8 26	19 54	8 44	19 37	9 06	19 17	9 36	18 47	10 26	17 59
6 Sa	-9 09	6 20	17 20	6 42	17 00	7 07	16 35	7 42	15 59	8 43	14 58
340		9 14	20 49	9 29	20 36	9 48	20 19	10 13	19 55	10 54	19 16
7 Su	-8 44	6 21	17 21	6 43	17 00	7 08	16 35	7 44	15 59	8 45	14 57
341		9 58	21 42	10 09	21 32	10 24	21 19	10 44	21 02	11 15	20 34
8 Mo	-8 16	6 22	17 21	6 43	17 01	7 09	16 35	7 45	15 59	8 47	14 56
342		10 37	22 33	10 46	22 27	10 56	22 19	11 09	22 07	11 31	21 50
Tu	-7 51	6 23	17 21	6 44	17 00	7 10	16 35	7 46	15 59	8 49	14 55
343		11 15	23 23	11 19	23 20	11 25	23.16	11 32	23 12	11 44	23 04
10 We	-7 15	6 24	17 21	6 44	17 01	7 11	16 35	7 47	15 58	8 50	14 54
344	14 39 ☽	11 50		11 51		11 52		11 54		11 56	
11 Th	-6 57	6 24	17 22	6 45	17 01	7 11	16 35	7 48	15 58	8 51	14 54
345		12 26	0 11	12 23	0 12	12 19	0 13	12 15	0 15	12 08	0 17
12 Fr	-6 30	6 25	17 22	6 46	17 01	7 12	16 35	7 49	15 58	8 53	14 54
346		13 01	0 59	12 55	1 04	12 47	1 10	12 36	1 18	12 20	1 30
13 Sa	-6 02	6 25	17 22	6 47	17 02	7 13	16 35	7 50	15 58	8 55	14 53
347		13 39	1 48	13 29	1 56	13 16	2 06	13 00	2 21	12 34	2 43
14 Su	-5 33	6 26	17 23	6 48	17 02	7 14	16 36	7 51	15 58	8 56	14 53
348		14 18	2 37	14 05	2 49	13 49	3 04	13 27	3 24	12 51	3 57
15 Mo	-5 05	6 26	17 23	6 49	17 02	7 15	16 36	7 52	15 58	8 57	14 53
349		15 01	3 29	14 45	3 43	14 25	4 02	13 58	4 28	13 14	5 10
16 Tu	-4 36	6 27	17 23	6 49	17 02	7 15	16 36	7 52	15 58	8 58	14 53
350		15 48	4 21	15 30	4 39	15 07	5 00	14 36	5 31	13 44	6 21
17 We	-4 07	6 28	17 24	6 50	17 03	7 16	16 36	7 53	15 59	8 59	14 53
351		16 38	5 15	16 19	5 34	15 55	5 58	15 22	6 31	14 25	7 27
18 Th	-3 38	6 28	17 24	6 50	17 03	7 17	16 37	7 53	15 59	9 00	14 54
352	22 28 ○	17 33	6 09	17 14	6 28	16 50	6 53	16 16	7 26	15 19	8 24
19 Fr	-3 08	6 29	17 24	6 50	17 03	7 17	16 37	7 54	15 59	9 01	14 54
353		18 30	7 02	18 12	7 21	17 50	7 43	17 19	8 15	16 27	9 09
20 Sa	-2 38	6 29	17 25	6 51	17 04	7 18	16 37	7 54	16 00	9 02	14 54
354		19 28	7 53	19 13	8 10	18 54	8 30	18 28	8 57	17 45	9 42
21 Su	-2 09	6 30	17 25	6 51	17 04	7 18	16 38	7 55	16 00	9 02	14 54
355		20 27	8 42	20 16	8 55	20 01	9 11	19 41	9 33	19 10	10 08
22 Mo	-1 39	6 30	17 26	6 52	17 05	7 19	16 38	7 56	16 01	9 03	14 55
356		21 26	9 28	21 19	9 37	21 09	9 49	20 57	10 04	20 37	10 28
23 Tu	-1 09	6 31	17 26	6 52	17 05	7 19	16 39	7 56	16 01	9 03	14 55
357		22 25	10 12	22 21	10 17	22 18	10 24	22 13	10 32	22 05	10 45
24 We	-0 39	6 31	17 27	6 53	17 06	7 19	16 39	7 57	16 02	9 03	14 56
358		23 23	10 55	23 24	10 56	23 26	10 57	23 29	10 58	23 33	11 00
25 Th	-0 09	6 32	17 27	6 53	17 06	7 20	16 40	7 57	16 02	9 04	14 56
359	52 ☾		11 38		11 35		11 30		11 24		11 15
26 Fr	+0 20	6 32	17 28	6 54	17 07	7 20	16 40	7 58	16 03	9 04	14 57
360		0 22	12 22	0 28	12 14	0 35	12 04	0 45	11 51	1 02	11 31
27 Sa	+0 50	6 33	17 28	6 54	17 07	7 20	16 41	7 58	16 03	9 04	14 58
361		1 21	13 09	1 31	12 56	1 44	12 42	2 02	12 21	2 30	11 50
28 Su	+1 20	6 33	17 29	6 54	17 08	7 21	16 41	7 58	16 04	9 04	14 59
362		2 21	13 58	2 35	13 42	2 53	13 23	3 18	12 56	3 58	12 14
29 Mo	+1 49	6 34	17 29	6 55	17 08	7 21	16 42	7 59	16 05	9 03	15 00
363		3 22	14 50	3 39	14 32	4 01	14 09	4 31	13 38	5 21	12 46
30 Tu	+2 18	6 34	17 30	6 55	17 09	7 21	16 43	7 59	16 06	9 03	15 01
364		4 22	15 45	4 41	15 26	5 05	15 01	5 38	14 27	6 36	13 29
31 We	+2 47	6 35	17 31	6 55	17 10	7 22	16 44	7 59	16 07	9 03	15 03
365		5 20	16 42	5 39	16 23	6 04	15 59	6 38	15 25	7 36	14 27

PERPETUAL CALENDAR
(1800-2059)

DIRECTIONS: Pick desired year from box at top left. The number shown with each year indicates what calendar to use for that year.

Julian and Gregorian Calendars; Leap Year

Calendars based on the movements of sun and moon have been used since ancient times, but none has been perfect. The Julian calendar, under which western nations measured time until 1582 A. D., was authorized by Julius Caesar in 46 B.C., the year 709 of Rome. His expert was a Greek, Sosigenes, The Julian calendar, on the assumption that the true year was 365¼ days long, gave every fourth year 366 days. The Venerable Bede, an Anglo-Saxon monk, announced in 730 A.D. that the 365¼-day Julian year was 11 min. 14 sec. too long, making a cumulative error of about a day every 128 years, but nothing was done about it for over 800 years.

By 1582 the accumulated error was estimated to have amounted to 10 days. In that year Pope Gregory XIII decreed that the day following Oct. 4, 1582, should be called Oct. 15, thus dropping 10 days.

However, with common years 365 days and a 366-day leap year every fourth year, the error in the length of the year would have recurred at the rate of a little more than 3 days every 400 years. So 3 of every 4 centesimal years (ending in 00) were made common years, not leap years. Thus 1600 was a leap year, 1700, 1800 and 1900 were not, but 2000 will be. Leap years are those divisible by 4 except centesimal years, which are common unless divisible by 400.

The Gregorian calendar was adopted at once by most predominantly Roman Catholic countries, but many Protestant countries did not accept it until the 18th Century.

The British Government imposed the Gregorian calendar on all its possessions, including the American colonies, in 1752. The British decreed that the day following Sept. 2, 1752, should be called Sept. 14, a loss of 11 days. All dates preceding were marked O.S., for Old Style: the British new year, which started Mar. 25, O.S., was changed to Jan. 1, 1752, New Style, as the switch was made to the Gregorian calendar. George Washington's birth date, which was Feb. 11, 1731, O.S., became Feb. 22, 1732, N.S.

In 1793 the French Revolutionary Government adopted a calendar of 12 months of 30 days each with 5 extra days in September of each common year and a 6th extra day every 4th year. Napoleon reinstated the Gregorian calendar in 1806.

Japan adopted the Gregorian calendar in 1873, the Chinese Republic in 1912, Greece and Greek Orthodox communities in 1924, and Turkey (predominantly Moslem) in 1927.

To change from the Julian to the Gregorian calendar, add 10 days to dates Oct. 5, 1582, through Feb. 28, 1700; after that date add 11 days through Feb. 28, 1800; after that date add 12 days through Feb. 28, 1900; and then 13 days through Feb. 28, 2100.

The Julian Period

How many days have you lived? To determine this, you must multiply your age by 365, add the number of days since your last birthday until today, and account for all the leap years. Chances are your answer would be wrong. Astronomers, however, find it very convenient to express dates and long time intervals in days rather than in years, months, and days. This is accomplished by use of the number of the day in the Julian Period.

In 1582, Joseph Scaliger introduced the Julian Period, an interval that is the least common multiple of 3 periods. The solar cycle is the interval of time between coincidences of Jan. 1 and Sunday. This is 28 Julian Years. The Lunar Cycle, 19 Julian years, is the cycle that brings full moon back to the same day of the year. The Roman Indication is a 15-year cycle that

was used on a rotating basis much as the oriental lunar calendar is used. The Julian Period so determined is 7980 Julian years. Scaliger computed the date when the 3 cycles were in step, i.e., when the full moon fell on Sunday, Jan. 1. This date is Jan. 1, 4713 B.C., long before any reliable astronomical records. Dec. 31, 1973 is Julian Day (JD) 2,442,047 since the beginning of the Julian Period. The JD of any day in 1974 may be found by adding the day of the year given in the calendar tables, pages 238 to 249, to this value. Tables available to astronomers make the conversion of dates to the JD system very simple.

Although this period was introduced in the year when the Gregorian Calendar replaced the Julian Calendar, the Julian Period was not named for Caesar, but for Julius Scaliger, Joseph's father.

Days Between Two Dates

Table covers period of two ordinary years. For leap year, one day must be added after Feb. 28.
Example—Days between Feb. 10, 1973 and Dec. 15, 1974; subtract 41 from 714; answer is 673 days.

Day Mo.	Jan.	Feb.	Mar.	April	May	June	July	Aug.	Sept.	Oct.	Nov.	Dec.
1	1	32	60	91	121	152	182	213	244	274	305	335
2	2	33	61	92	122	153	183	214	245	275	306	336
3	3	34	62	93	123	154	184	215	246	276	307	337
4	4	35	63	94	124	155	185	216	247	277	308	338
5	5	36	64	95	125	156	186	217	248	278	309	339
6	6	37	65	96	126	157	187	218	249	279	310	340
7	7	38	66	97	127	158	188	219	250	280	311	341
8	8	39	67	98	128	159	189	220	251	281	312	342
9	9	40	68	99	129	160	190	221	252	282	313	343
10	10	41	69	100	130	161	191	222	253	283	314	344
11	11	42	70	101	131	162	192	223	254	284	315	345
12	12	43	71	102	132	163	193	224	255	285	316	346
13	13	44	72	103	133	164	194	225	256	286	317	347
14	14	45	73	104	134	165	195	226	257	287	318	348
15	15	46	74	105	135	166	196	227	258	288	319	349
16	16	47	75	106	136	167	197	228	259	289	320	350
17	17	48	76	107	137	168	198	229	260	290	321	351
18	18	49	77	108	138	169	199	230	261	291	322	352
19	19	50	78	109	139	170	200	231	262	292	323	353
20	20	51	79	110	140	171	201	232	263	293	324	354
21	21	52	80	111	141	172	202	233	264	294	325	355
22	22	53	81	112	142	173	203	234	265	295	326	356
23	23	54	82	113	143	174	204	235	266	296	327	357
24	24	55	83	114	144	175	205	236	267	297	328	358
25	25	56	84	115	145	176	206	237	268	298	329	359
26	26	57	85	116	146	177	207	238	269	299	330	360
27	27	58	86	117	147	178	208	239	270	300	331	361
28	28	59	87	118	148	179	209	240	271	301	332	362
29	29	—	88	119	149	180	210	241	272	302	333	363
30	30	—	89	120	150	181	211	242	273	303	334	364
31	31	—	90	—	151	—	212	243	—	304	—	365

Day Mo.	Jan.	Feb.	Mar.	April	May	June	July	Aug.	Sept.	Oct.	Nov.	Dec.
1	366	397	425	456	486	517	547	578	609	639	670	700
2	367	398	426	457	487	518	548	579	610	640	671	701
3	368	399	427	458	488	519	549	580	611	641	672	702
4	369	400	428	459	489	520	550	581	612	642	673	703
5	370	401	429	460	490	521	551	582	613	643	674	704
6	371	402	430	461	491	522	552	583	614	644	675	705
7	372	403	431	462	492	523	553	584	615	645	676	706
8	373	404	432	463	493	524	554	585	616	646	677	707
9	374	405	433	464	494	525	555	586	617	647	678	708
10	375	406	434	465	495	526	556	587	618	648	679	709
11	376	407	435	466	496	527	557	588	619	649	680	710
12	377	408	436	467	497	528	558	589	620	650	681	711
13	378	409	437	468	498	529	559	590	621	651	682	712
14	379	410	438	469	499	530	560	591	622	652	683	713
15	380	411	439	470	500	531	561	592	623	653	684	714
16	381	412	440	471	501	532	562	593	624	654	685	715
17	382	413	441	472	502	533	563	594	625	655	686	716
18	383	414	442	473	503	534	564	595	626	656	687	717
19	384	415	443	474	504	535	565	596	627	657	688	718
20	385	416	444	475	505	536	566	597	628	658	689	719
21	386	417	445	476	506	537	567	598	629	659	690	720
22	387	418	446	477	507	538	568	599	630	660	691	721
23	388	419	447	478	508	539	569	600	631	661	692	722
24	389	420	448	479	509	540	570	601	632	662	693	723
25	390	421	449	480	510	541	571	602	633	663	694	724
26	391	422	450	481	511	542	572	603	634	664	695	725
27	392	423	451	482	512	543	573	604	635	665	696	726
28	393	424	452	483	513	544	574	605	636	666	697	727
29	394	—	453	484	514	545	575	606	637	667	698	728
30	395	—	454	485	515	546	576	607	638	668	699	729
31	396	—	455	—	516	—	577	608	—	669	—	730

Twilight

Date 1975	20° Begin	20° End	30° Begin	30° End	40° Begin	40° End	50° Begin	50° End	60° Begin	60° End
	h m	h m	h m	h m	h m	h m	h m	h m	h m	h m
Jan. 1	5 16	6 50	5 30	6 35	5 45	6 21	6 00	6 07	6 18	5 49
11	5 19	6 56	5 33	6 43	5 46	6 30	6 00	6 17	6 15	6 01
21	5 21	7 01	5 32	6 51	5 43	6 40	5 55	6 30	6 06	6 18
Feb. 1	5 21	7 07	5 29	6 58	5 38	6 51	5 45	6 44	5 51	6 38
11	5 18	7 11	5 24	7 05	5 29	7 01	5 32	6 59	5 32	7 01
21	5 13	7 15	5 17	7 12	5 17	7 12	5 16	7 14	5 09	7 23
Mar. 1	5 08	7 18	5 08	7 19	5 06	7 21	4 59	7 29	4 44	7 45
11	5 00	7 21	4 58	7 24	4 50	7 32	4 38	7 46	4 12	8 12
21	4 52	7 24	4 45	7 32	4 33	7 44	4 14	8 04	3 37	8 43
Apr. 1	4 42	7 28	4 31	7 39	4 14	7 57	3 47	8 25	2 53	9 21
11	4 32	7 32	4 18	7 47	3 56	8 09	3 20	8 47	2 03	10 10
21	4 23	7 36	4 04	7 54	3 37	8 23	2 52	9 11	0 37	11 47
May 1	4 14	7 41	3 52	8 04	3 19	8 37	2 22	9 39		
11	4 08	7 46	3 41	8 13	3 03	8 53	1 49	10 09		
21	4 02	7 52	3 32	8 22	2 48	9 07	1 13	10 46		
June 1	3 58	7 58	3 26	8 30	2 36	9 20	0 21	11 52		
11	3 56	8 03	3 22	8 36	2 29	9 30				
21	3 57	8 06	3 22	8 40	2 28	9 35				
July 1	3 59	8 07	3 25	8 41	2 30	9 35				
11	4 03	8 06	3 30	8 39	2 40	9 30				
21	4 08	8 03	3 39	8 33	2 52	9 18	1 12	11 23		
Aug. 1	4 15	7 56	3 48	8 23	3 09	9 01	1 49	10 20		
11	4 20	7 50	3 56	8 13	3 22	8 46	2 21	9 46		
21	4 24	7 41	4 05	8 01	3 34	8 27	2 47	9 15		
Sept. 1	4 29	7 31	4 14	7 46	3 51	8 08	3 13	8 43	1 40	10 02
11	4 32	7 20	4 20	7 33	4 02	7 50	3 33	8 16	2 36	9 12
21	4 35	7 11	4 26	7 19	4 14	7 31	3 52	7 52	3 11	8 31
Oct. 1	4 38	7 02	4 33	7 05	4 25	7 13	4 10	7 28	3 41	7 54
11	4 40	6 53	4 40	6 53	4 35	6 58	4 26	7 05	4 07	7 23
21	4 43	6 47	4 45	6 44	4 45	6 43	4 41	6 46	4 32	6 55
Nov. 1	4 46	6 41	4 52	6 34	4 56	6 30	4 58	6 27	4 56	6 27
11	4 50	6 38	4 59	6 28	5 06	6 21	5 13	6 14	5 17	6 08
21	4 55	6 36	5 06	6 25	5 16	6 15	5 26	6 04	5 37	5 52
Dec. 1	5 00	6 37	5 13	6 24	5 25	6 11	5 38	5 58	5 53	5 42
11	5 06	6 40	5 20	6 26	5 34	6 12	5 48	5 57	6 06	5 38
21	5 11	6 45	5 25	6 30	5 39	6 16	5 55	6 00	6 15	5 40
31	5 15	6 50	5 30	6 35	5 44	6 21	6 00	6 06	6 18	5 48

Rising and Setting of Sun and Moon; Twilight

The astronomical definition of the time of rising or setting of a body, such as the sun or moon, is the instant when the upper edge of the observable disk (upper limb) is exactly 90 degrees away from the observer's zenith, on the astronomical horizon. These are the times presented in the appropriate tables.

The calculations behind these tables must take into account several important effects. The basic calculations relate to the center of the sun's disk as seen from the center of the earth. Next a correction is applied for the apparent radius of the sun, which varies throughout the year as our distance from the sun changes. This locates the upper limb. The third step changes the viewpoint to the earth's surface where atmospheric refraction is encountered. This has the effect of elevating the upper limb an average of 34 minutes of arc.

The center of the sun's disk is usually about 50 minutes of arc below the astronomical horizon at the instant given for sunrise or sunset. This causes confusion in people's minds at the times of the equinoxes when it is expected that the durations of daylight and dark are equal. Ignoring refraction and the apparent size of the sun, one would find these periods to be equal at those times. Taking into account the proper definitions, the periods of daylight and dark are equal on some date prior to the vernal equinox and after the autumnal equinox, depending on the observer's latitude. At the times of the equinoxes, periods of light are equal all over the earth, and periods of dark are equal, but periods of light are not equal to periods of dark. At these times both poles see the sun continually, although this circumstance changes rapidly.

Users of the tables must remember that the instant sunlight will strike or leave a particular location will depend on that location, its height above sea level and the particular nature of the eastern or western horizon. It may be advisable to make personal observations of the event at the site a few days before the time required. It should be remembered that the direction of the sunrise or set also changes from day to day.

Similar calculations are made with respect to moon-rise and set, but there are important differences. The atmospheric refraction is the same, but viewing the moon from the earth's surface involves a change of about 4,000 miles from the earth's center. This results in an apparent displacement (horizontal parallax) of the moon away from the zenith. This depression nearly cancels the refraction effect, but the parallax and the apparent radius of the moon vary significantly throughout the month, and must be accounted for.

Because the moon moves so rapidly through the sky, users of the tables must make an important adjustment to the given times.

The twilight tables give the times when the center of the sun's disk is 18° below the astronomical horizon, or 108° away from the observer's zenith. At this time, under ideal conditions, an observer should be able to see without optical aid a sixth magnitude star in the zenith. Navigators need to see bright stars and a horizon reference simultaneously. This condition no longer prevails when the sun is beyond 12° below the horizon, the limits of nautical twilight. The limits of civil twilight occur when the sun is greater than 6° below the horizon. The durations of twilight vary with season and latitude.

Rising and Setting of Planets, 1975

Greenwich Mean Time (0 designates midnight)

Venus, 1975

Date	20° N. Latitude Rise	Set	30° N. Latitude Rise	Set	40° N. Latitude Rise	Set	50° N. Latitude Rise	Set	60° N. Latitude Rise	Set
Jan. 1	7:34	18:30	7:54	18:09	8:20	17:44	8:56	17:08	9:58	18:05
15	7:46	18:54	8:02	18:38	8:23	18:17	8:51	17:49	9:38	17:02
Feb. 1	7:51	19:21	8:01	19:11	8:14	18:59	8:31	18:42	8:57	18:16
15	7:51	19:41	7:55	19:37	8:00	19:32	8:06	19:25	8:16	19:15
Mar. 1	7:48	19:59	7:46	20:01	7:43	20:04	7:39	20:08	7:33	20:14
15	7:45	20:17	7:37	20:26	7:26	20:36	7:12	20:50	6:50	21:12
Apr. 1	7:45	20:40	7:30	20:55	7:11	21:14	6:44	21:41	6:01	22:24
15	7:49	21:01	7:28	21:22	7:02	21:47	6:26	22:24	5:21	23:29
May 1	8:03	21:22	7:39	21:45	7:09	22:15	6:25	22:59	5:03	0:18
15	8:17	21:38	7:52	22:02	7:21	22:33	6:36	23:18	5:09	0:44
June 1	8:34	21:48	8:12	22:10	7:45	22:37	7:05	23:17	5:54	0:30
15	8:45	21:46	8:27	22:04	8:04	22:26	7:32	22:58	6:39	23:51
July 1	8:47	21:1	8:35	21:43	8:19	21:59	7:57	22:21	7:23	22:55
15	8:37	21:05	8:29	21:13	8:19	21:23	8:06	21:36	7:45	21:57
Aug. 1	8:00	20:12	7:57	20:15	7:53	20:19	7:47	20:25	7:39	20:33
15	6:58	19:06	6:57	19:07	6:55	19:09	6:52	19:11	6:48	19:15
Sept. 1	5:13	17:23	5:10	17:26	5:06	17:30	5:01	17:35	4:54	17:42
15	3:56	16:14	3:51	16:21	3:44	16:28	4:37	16:37	3:21	16:51
Oct. 1	3:06	15:30	3:00	15:37	2:51	15:46	2:40	15:57	2:22	16:15
15	2:48	15:09	2:42	15:15	2:35	15:23	2:24	15:33	2:09	15:49
Nov. 1	2:44	14:55	2:41	14:58	2:37	15:02	2:32	15:07	2:25	15:14
15	2:47	14:49	2:48	14:48	2:49	14:47	2:49	14:47	2:52	14:45
Dec. 1	2:59	14:43	3:05	14:37	3:12	14:30	3:22	14:21	3:37	14:06
15	3:14	14:42	3:24	14:21	3:37	14:18	3:55	14:01	4:23	13:33

Mars, 1975

Date	20° N. Latitude Rise	Set	30° N. Latitude Rise	Set	40° N. Latitude Rise	Set	50° N. Latitude Rise	Set	60° N. Latitude Rise	Set
Jan. 1	4:47	15:42	5:07	15:21	5:33	14:55	6:10	14:19	7:13	13:15
15	4:36	15:28	4:58	15:06	5:25	14:39	6:04	14:00	7:13	12:51
Feb. 1	4:24	15:15	4:45	14:53	5:13	14:26	5:52	13:47	7:01	12:38
15	4:12	15:06	4:33	14:46	4:59	14:20	5:36	13:43	6:41	12:38
Mar. 1	3:59	14:59	4:18	14:40	4:42	14:16	5:15	13:42	6:12	12:17
15	3:44	14:51	4:00	14:34	4:21	14:14	4:50	13:45	5:38	12:57
Apr. 1	3:23	14:42	3:36	14:29	3:52	14:12	4:15	13:50	4:50	13:14
15	3:03	14:33	3:13	14:23	3:26	14:11	3:42	13:55	4:08	13:29
May 1	2:40	14:23	2:45	14:17	2:53	14:09	3:03	14:00	3:18	13:44
15	2:18	14:13	2:20	14:11	2:23	14:07	2:27	14:03	2:33	13:57
June 1	1:50	14:00	1:49	14:02	1:47	14:04	1:44	14:07	1:39	14:11
15	1:28	13:49	1:22	13:54	1:16	14:01	1:07	14:09	0:54	14:23
July 1	1:02	13:36	0:53	13:45	0:42	13:56	0:27	14:11	0:03	14:34
15	0:39	13:23	0:27	13:35	0:12	13:50	23:52	14:10	23:20	14:43
Aug. 1	0:12	13:07	23:57	13:22	23:38	13:41	23:12	14:07	22:29	14:50
15	23:49	12:52	23:32	13:09	22:41	14:00	22:40	14:01	21:49	14:52
Sept. 1	23:21	12:30	23:01	12:49	22:37	13:14	22:02	13:48	21:02	14:48
15	22:55	12:08	23:34	12:29	22:08	12:55	21:31	13:32	20:26	14:37
Oct. 1	22:21	11:37	22:00	11:59	21:32	12:26	20:53	13:05	19:43	14:15
15	21:45	11:04	21:23	11:26	20:56	11:54	20:15	12:34	19:01	13:48
Nov. 1	20:51	10:11	20:28	10:34	19:59	11:03	19:17	11:45	17:59	13:03
15	19:53	9:16	19:29	9:39	18:59	10:10	18:16	10:53	16:53	17:16
Dec. 1	18:32	7:58	18:08	8:22	17:36	8:54	16:51	9:39	15:21	11:09
15	17:08	6:35	16:43	7:00	16:11	7:32	15:24	8:19	13:50	9:52

Jupiter, 1975

Date	20° N. Latitude Rise	Set	30° N. Latitude Rise	Set	40° N. Latitude Rise	Set	50° N. Latitude Rise	Set	60° N. Latitude Rise	Set
Jan. 1	10:26	22:09	10:32	22:02	10:40	21:55	10:50	21:44	11:06	21:29
15	9:39	21:24	9:44	21:19	9:51	21:12	10:00	21:04	10:13	20:50
Feb. 1	8:43	20:32	8:47	20:28	8:52	20:23	8:59	20:16	9:09	20:06
15	7:57	19:51	8:00	19:47	8:04	19:44	8:09	19:39	8:17	19:31
Mar. 1	7:12	19:10	7:14	19:07	7:17	19:05	7:20	19:02	7:24	19:25
15	6:28	18:29	6:29	18:28	6:30	18:27	6:31	18:26	6:33	18:24
Apr. 1	5:33	17:39	5:33	17:40	5:32	17:40	5:31	17:41	5:29	17:43
15	4:49	16:58	4:47	17:00	4:45	17:02	4:45	17:02	4:38	17:10
May 1	3:57	16:11	3:54	16:14	3:51	16:18	3:46	16:22	3:38	16:30
15	3:12	15:29	3:08	15:33	3:03	15:38	2:57	15:44	2:46	15:55
June 1	2:16	14:37	2:11	14:42	2:05	14:48	1:56	14:56	1:43	15:09
15	1:29	13:52	1:23	13:58	1:16	14:05	1:06	14:30	0:51	14:30
July 1	0:33	12:59	0:27	13:07	0:19	13:14	0:08	13:25	23:51	13:42
15	23:43	12:11	23:36	12:18	23:28	12:27	23:16	12:38	22:58	12:57
Aug. 1	22:41	11:09	22:33	11:17	22:24	11:26	22:12	11:38	21:53	11:57
15	21:47	10:16	21:39	10:23	21:30	10:32	21:18	10:44	20:59	11:04
Sept. 1	20:38	9:07	20:31	9:14	20:23	9:23	20:11	9:35	19:52	9:53
15	19:40	8:07	19:33	8:14	19:25	8:22	19:14	8:33	18:56	8:51
Oct. 1	18:32	6:56	18:25	7:02	18:18	7:10	18:08	7:20	17:51	7:36
15	17:26	5:49	17:21	5:54	17:14	6:01	17:05	6:10	16:50	6:25
Nov. 1	16:13	4:33	16:08	4:38	16:02	4:43	15:54	4:52	15:41	5:04
15	15:13	3:32	15:09	3:36	15:03	3:42	14:56	3:49	14:44	4:00
Dec. 1	14:07	2:25	14:03	2:29	13:58	2:34	13:51	2:41	13:40	2:52
15	13:12	1:30	13:07	1:34	13:02	1:39	12:55	1:46	12:44	1:57

Saturn, 1975

Date	20° N. Lat. Rise	Set	30° N. Lat. Rise	Set	40° N. Lat. Rise	Set	50° N. Lat. Rise	Set	60° N. Lat. Rise	Set
Jan. 1	17:51	7:04	17:31	7:25	17:05	7:51	16:28	8:28	15:22	9:34
15	16:47	6:00	16:26	6:21	16:00	6:47	15:22	7:25	14:16	8:31
Feb. 1	15:34	4:48	15:13	5:09	14:47	5:36	14:09	6:14	13:02	7:21
15	14:35	3:50	14:14	4:11	13:48	4:38	13:10	5:16	12:02	6:24
Mar. 1	13:38	2:53	13:17	3:14	12:50	3:41	12:12	4:19	11:04	5:28
15	12:42	1:58	12:21	2:19	11:55	2:45	11:16	3:24	10:08	4:32
Apr. 1	11:37	0:52	11:16	1:13	10:49	1:40	10:11	2:18	9:02	3:27
15	10:45	0:00	10:24	0:21	9:57	0:48	9:19	1:26	8:10	2:34
May 1	9:47	23:02	9:26	23:22	8:59	23:49	8:21	0:27	7:13	1:35
15	8:57	22:12	8:36	22:32	8:10	22:59	7:32	23:32	6:25	0:44
June 1	7:58	21:12	7:38	21:33	7:12	21:59	6:34	22:36	5:28	23:43
15	7:11	20:24	6:50	20:44	6:24	21:10	5:47	21:47	4:42	22:52
July 1	6:17	19:29	5:57	19:49	5:31	20:15	4:55	20:57	3:51	21:55
15	5:30	18:41	5:10	19:01	4:45	19:26	4:09	20:02	3:06	21:05
Aug. 1	4:33	17:43	4:13	18:02	3:49	18:27	3:14	19:02	2:13	20:03
15	3:46	16:55	3:26	17:14	3:02	17:38	2:28	18:13	1:28	19:12
Sept. 1	2:48	15:55	2:29	16:14	2:05	16:38	1:31	17:12	0:34	18:10
15	1:59	15:06	1:40	15:25	1:17	15:48	0:44	16:21	23:47	17:18
Oct. 1	1:02	14:08	0:44	14:27	0:21	14:50	23:49	15:22	22:53	16:18
15	0;11	13:17	23:53	13:35	23:31	13:58	22:58	14:30	22:04	15:25
Nov. 1	23:08	12:13	22:50	12:31	22:27	12:53	21:55	13:25	21:01	14:19
15	22:13	11:18	21:55	11:36	21:33	11:59	21:01	12:31	20:07	13:25
Dec. 1	21:25	9:59	20:51	10:33	20:29	10:55	19:57	11:27	19:02	12:22
15	20:12	9:17	19:53	9:36	19:30	9:59	18:58	10:31	18:03	11:26

The Planets and the Solar System

Name of Planet	Mean Daily Motion	Orbital Velocity Miles Per Sec.	Sidereal Revolution Days	Synodical Revolution Days	Dist. from Sun in Millions of Miles Max.	Min.	Approx. miles from Earth in Millions Max.	Min.	Light at Peri-helion	Aphe-lion
Mercury....	14732.420	29.75	87.9693	115.9	43.403	28.597	136	50	10.58	4.59
Venus.....	5767.668	21.76	224.7009	583.9	67.726	66.813	161	25	1.94	1.89
Earth......	3548.329	18.51	365.2564	—	94.555	91.445	—	—	1.03	0.97
Mars......	1886.519	14.99	686.9796	779.9	154.936	128.471	248	35	0.524	0.360
Jupiter....	299.167	8.12	4332.0466	398.9	507.046	460.595	600	368	0.0408	0.0336
Saturn.....	120.264	5.99	10775.056	378.1	937.541	838.425	1031	745	0.01230	0.00984
Uranus.....	42.390	4.23	30572.21	369.7	1859.748	1699.331	1953	1606	0.00300	0.00250
Neptune....	21.585	3.38	60050.04	367.5	2821.686	2760.386	2915	2667	0.00114	0.00109
Pluto......	14.404	2.95	89952.8	366.7	4551.386	2756.427	4644	2663	0.00114	0.00042

Light at Perihelion and Aphelion is solar illumination in units of mean illumination at Earth.

Name of Planet	Mean Longitude of:* Ascending Node ° ' "	Perihelion ° ' "	Inclination* of Orbit to Ecliptic ° ' "	Mean Distance*	Eccentricity* of Orbit	Mean Longitude at the Epoch* ° ' "
Mercury....	48 02 18	77 03 57	7 00 15	0.387099	0.205630	269 30 30
Venus.....	76 27 16	131 13 08	3 23 39	0.723332	0.006785	290 56 51
Earth......	—	102 30 35	—	1.000000	0.016720	87 12 49
Mars......	49 21 52	335 35 53	1 50 59	1.523691	0.093382	243 04 42
Jupiter....	100 11 37	13 58 09	1 18 20	5.202343	0.0479995	14 14 49
Saturn.....	113 28 15	91 56 00	2 29 18	9.549694	0.0559478	111 23 14
Uranus.....	73 55 03	168 37 13	0 46 21	19.13383	0.0451022	208 27 25
Neptune....	131 35 38	42 45 33	1 46 15	30.00424	0.0111454	251 27 32
Pluto......	109 58 01	224 06 29	17 08 32	39.28932	0.2456219	203 10 11

*Values for Mercury, Venus, Earth and Mars are consistent at Epoch = 1974 Dec. 19.0; values for Jupiter, Saturn, Uranus, Neptune and Pluto are consistent at Epoch = 1975 Aug. 16.0, Greenwich Mean Time.

Sun and Planets	Semi-Diameter At Unit Distance "	At Mean Least Dist. "	In Miles Mean S.-D.	Volume ⊕=1.	Mass ⊕=1.	Density ⊕=1.	Axial Rotation d.	h.	m.	s.	Gravity at Surface ⊕=1.	Reflecting Power Pct.	Probable Temperature F.
Sun..........	15 59.63		432000	1300000.	332000.	0.26	24	16	48		27.9		+10,000
Mercury........	3.34	5.45	1505	0.056	0.0543	0.68	59				0.38	0.07	+ 600
Venus.........	8.41	30.40	3805	0.910	0.8136	0.94	243	(R)			0.88	0.76	+ 100
Earth.........	—	—	3959	1.000	1.000	1.00		23	56		1.00	0.39	+ 50
Moon.........	2.44	932.58	1080	0.020	0.0120	0.60	27	7	43	12	0.16	0.07	+ 215
Mars.........	4.68	8.94	2070	0.150	0.1069	0.71		24	37	23	0.39	0.15	+ 0
Jupiter........	1 35.19	22.60	43450	1312.	318.35	0.24		9	50		2.65	0.51	- 150
Saturn........	1 18.95	9.24	35750	763.	95.3	0.12		10	14		1.17	0.50	- 250
Uranus........	34.28	1.88	14750	53.	14.54	0.28		10	45	(R)	1.05	0.66	- 350
Neptune.......	36.56	1.26	15750	65.	17.2	0.26		15	48		1.23	0.62	400

The planet Pluto was located by C. W. Tombaugh of Lowell Observatory Mar. 13, 1930. Its mass is about 0.18 of the mass of the Earth. It rotates on its axis in 6 days 9 hours. Its average distance from the sun is 3,664,000-000 miles. On Mar. 19 at 5 hours, GMT, it is in opposition in Virgo at right ascension 12 hrs. 50 mins. 16 secs. and declination, North 13 degrees 12 minutes 10 seconds, northeast of Epsilon Virginis; Pluto will have a magnitude of about 15. (R) Venus and Uranus are in retrograde motion, rotating in opposite direction from other planets.

Standard Time Differences — North American Cities

At 12 o'clock noon Eastern Standard Time, the standard time in N.A. cities is as follows:

Akron, Ohio	12.00 NOON	Fort Worth, Texas	11.00 A.M.	Philadelphia, Pa.	12.00 NOON
Albuquerque, N.Mex.	10.00 A.M.	Frankfort, Ky.	12.00 NOON	*Phoenix, Ariz.	10.00 A.M.
Atlanta, Ga.	12.00 NOON	Galveston, Tex.	11.00 A.M.	Pierre, S. Dak.	11.00 A.M.
Austin, Tex.	11.00 A.M.	Grand Rapids, Mich.	12.00 NOON	Pittsburgh, Pa.	12.00 NOON
Baltimore, Md.	12.00 NOON	Halifax, N.S.	1.00 P.M.	Portland, Me.	12.00 NOON
Birmingham, Ala.	11.00 A.M.	Hartford, Conn.	12.00 NOON	Portland, Oreg.	9.00 A.M.
Bismarck, N. Dak.	11.00 A.M.	Helena, Mont.	10.00 A.M.	Providence, R.I.	12.00 NOON
Boise, Idaho	10.00 A.M.	*Honolulu, Hawaii	7.00 A.M.	*Regina, Man.	11.00 A.M.
Boston, Mass.	12.00 NOON	Houston, Tex.	11.00 A.M.	Reno, Nev.	9.00 A.M.
Buffalo, N.Y.	12.00 NOON	*Indianapolis, Ind.	12.00 NOON	Richmond, Va.	12.00 NOON
Butte, Mont.	10.00 A.M.	Jacksonville, Fla.	12.00 NOON	Rochester, N.Y.	12.00 NOON
Calgary, Alta.	10.00 A.M.	Juneau, Alaska	9.00 A.M.	Sacramento, Calif.	9.00 A.M.
Charleston, S.C.	12.00 NOON	Kansas City, Mo.	11.00 A.M.	St. John's, Nfld.	1.30 P.M.
Charleston, W. Va.	12.00 NOON	Knoxville, Tenn.	12.00 NOON	St. Louis, Mo.	11.00 A.M.
Charlotte, N.C.	12.00 NOON	Lexington, Ky.	12.00 NOON	St. Paul, Minn.	11.00 A.M.
Charlottetown, P.E.I.	1.00 P.M.	Lincoln, Nebr.	11.00 A.M.	Salt Lake City, Utah.	10.00 A.M.
Chattanooga, Tenn.	12.00 NOON	Little Rock, Ark.	11.00 A.M.	San Antonio, Tex.	11.00 A.M.
Cheyenne, Wyo.	10.00 A.M.	Los Angeles, Calif.	9.00 A.M.	San Diego, Calif.	9.00 A.M.
Chicago, Ill.	11.00 A.M.	Louisville, Ky.	12.00 NOON	San Francisco, Calif.	9.00 A.M.
Cleveland, Ohio.	12.00 NOON	*Mexico City	11.00 A.M.	Santa Fe, N.M.	10.00 A.M.
Colorado Spr., Colo.	10.00 A.M.	Memphis, Tenn.	11.00 A.M.	Savannah, Ga.	12.00 NOON
Columbus, Ohio.	12.00 NOON	Miami, Fla.	12.00 NOON	Seattle, Wash.	9.00 A.M.
Dallas, Tex.	11.00 A.M.	Milwaukee, Wis.	11.00 A.M.	Shreveport, La.	11.00 A.M.
*Dawson, Yuk.	8.00 A.M.	Minneapolis, Minn.	11.00 A.M.	Sioux Falls, S. Dak.	11.00 A.M.
Dayton, Ohio.	12.00 NOON	Mobile, Ala.	11.00 A.M.	Spokane, Wash.	9.00 A.M.
Denver, Colo.	10.00 A.M.	Montreal, Que.	12.00 NOON	Tampa, Fla.	12.00 NOON
Des Moines, Iowa.	11.00 A.M.	Nashville, Tenn.	11.00 A.M.	Toledo, Ohio	12.00 NOON
Detroit, Mich.	12.00 NOON	New Haven, Conn.	12.00 NOON	Topeka, Kan.	11.00 A.M.
Duluth, Minn.	11.00 A.M.	New Orleans, La.	11.00 A.M.	*Tucson, Ariz.	10.00 A.M.
El Paso, Tex.	10.00 A.M.	New York, N.Y.	12.00 NOON	Tulsa, Okla.	11.00 A.M.
Erie, Pa.	12.00 NOON	Nome, Alaska	6.00 A.M.	Vancouver, B.C.	9.00 A.M.
Evansville, Ind.	11.00 A.M.	Norfolk, Va.	12.00 NOON	Washington, D.C.	12.00 NOON
Fairbanks, Alaska.	7.00 A.M.	Okla. City, Okla.	11.00 A.M.	Wichita, Kan.	11.00 A.M.
Flint, Mich.	12.00 NOON	Omaha, Nebr.	11.00 A.M.	Wilmington, Del.	12.00 NOON
*Fort Wayne, Ind.	12.00 NOON	Peoria, Ill.	11.00 A.M.	Winnipeg, Man.	11.00 A.M.

*Cities with an asterisk do not observe daylight savings time. It is necessary to add one hour to the cities observing daylight savings to get the proper time relation.

Standard Time Differences — World Cities

By government decree or proclamation Great Britain, Ireland, Spain, France, Netherlands, Portugal, and Belgium have advanced their time from the standard meridian by one hour throughout the year. The time indicated in table is fixed by law and is called the legal time, or, more generally, Standard Time. °Indicates EST morning of the following day. At 12 o'clock noon, the standard time in foreign cities is as follows:

Alexandria.	7:00 P.M.	Copenhagen.	6:00 P.M.	Liverpool	5:00 P.M.	Seoul.	2:00 A.M.°
Amsterdam.	6:00 P.M.	Dacca.	11:00 P.M.	London	5:00 P.M.	Shanghai.	1:00 A.M.°
Athens.	7:00 P.M.	Delhi.	10:30 P.M.	Madrid.	6:00 P.M.	Singapore.	12:30 A.M.°
Auckland.	5:00 A.M.°	Djakarta.	12:00 MID.	Manila.	1:00 A.M.°	Stockholm.	6:00 P.M.
Baghdad.	8:00 P.M.	Dublin.	5:00 P.M.	Melbourne.	3:00 A.M.°	Sydney	
Bangkok.	12:00 MID.	Gdansk.	6:00 P.M.	Montevideo.	2:00 P.M.	(Australia).	3:00 A.M.°
Belfast.	5:00 P.M.	Geneva.	6:00 P.M.	Moscow.	8:00 P.M.	Tashkent.	11:00 P.M.
Berlin.	6:00 P.M.	Havana.	12:00 NOON	Nagasaki.	2:00 A.M.°	Teheran.	8:30 P.M.
Bogota.	12:00 NOON	Helsinki.	7:00 P.M.	Oslo.	6:00 P.M.	Tel Aviv.	7:00 P.M.
Bombay.	10:30 P.M.	Hong Kong.	1:00 A.M.°	Paris.	6:00 P.M.	Tokyo.	2:00 A.M.°
Bremen.	6:00 P.M.	Istanbul.	7:00 P.M.	Peking.	1:00 A.M.°	Valparaiso.	1:00 P.M.
Brussels.	6:00 P.M.	Jerusalem.	7:00 P.M.	Prague.	6:00 P.M.	Vladivostok.	3:00 A.M.°
Bucharest.	7:00 P.M.	Johannesburg	7:00 P.M.	Rangoon.	11:30 P.M.	Vienna.	6:00 P.M.
Budapest.	6:00 P.M.	Karachi.	10:00 P.M.	Rio de Janeiro	2:00 P.M.	Wassaw.	6:00 P.M.
Buenos Aires	2:00 P.M.	Le Havre.	6:00 P.M.	Rome.	6:00 P.M.	Wellington	
Calcutta.	10:30 P.M.	Leningrad.	8:00 P.M.	Saigon.	1:00 A.M.°	(N.Z.).	5:00 A.M.°
Cape Town.	7:00 P.M.	Lima.	12:00 NOON	Santiago		Yokohama.	2:00 A.M.°
Caracas.	1:00 P.M.	Lisbon.	6:00 P.M.	(Chile).	1:00 P.M.	Zurich.	6:00 P.M.

Aurora Borealis and Aurora Australis

The Aurora Borealis, also called the Northern Lights, is a broad display of rather faint light in the northern skies at night. The Aurora Australis, a similar phenomenon, appears at the same time in southern skies. The aurora appears in a wide variety of forms. Sometimes it is seen as a quiet glow, almost foglike in character; sometimes as vertical streamers in which there may be considerable motion; sometimes as a series of luminous expanding arcs. There are many colors, with white, yellow and red predominating.

The auroras are most vivid and most frequently seen at about 20 degrees from the magnetic poles, along the northern coast of the North American continent and the eastern part of the northern coast of Europe. They have been seen as far south as Key West and as far north as Australia and New Zealand, but such occasions are rare.

While the cause of the auroras is not known beyond question, there does seem to be a definite correlation between auroral displays and the sun-spot activity. It is thought that atomic particles expelled from the sun by the forces that cause solar flares speed through space at velocities of 400 to 600 miles per second. These particles are entrapped by the earth's magnetic field, forming what are termed the Van Allen belts. The encounter of these clouds of the solar wind with the earth's magnetic field weakens the field so that previously trapped particles are allowed to impact the upper atmosphere. The collisions between solar and terrestrial atoms result in the glow in the upper atmosphere called the aurora. The glow may be vivid where the lines of magnetic force converge near the magnetic poles.

The auroral displays appear at heights ranging from 50 to about 600 miles and have given us a means of estimating the extent of the earth's atmosphere.

The auroras are often accompanied by magnetic storms whose forces, also guided by the lines of force of the earth's magnetic field, disrupt electrical communication.

Standard Time, Daylight Saving Time and Others

Source: Defense Mapping Agency Hydrographic Center; Department of Transportation; National Bureau of Standards and U. S. Naval Observatory

Standard Time

Standard time is reckoned from Greenwich, England, recognized as the Prime Meridian of Longitude. The world is divided into 24 zones, each 15° of arc, or one hour in time apart. The meridian of Greenwich (0°) extends through the center of the initial zone, and the zones to the eastward are numbered from 1 to 12 with the prefix "minus" indicating the number of hours to be subtracted to obtain Greenwich Time.

Zones westward are similarly numbered, but prefixed "plus" showing the number of hours that must be added to get Greenwich time. While these zones apply generally to sea areas, it should be noted that the Standard Time maintained in many countries does not coincide with zone time. A graphical representation of the zones is shown on the Standard Time Zone Chart of the World published by the Defense Mapping Agency Hydrographic Center, Washington, D.C. 20390.

The United States and possessions are divided into eight Standard Time zones, as set forth by the Uniform Time Act of 1966, which also provides for the use of Daylight Saving Time therein. Each zone is approximately 15° of longitude in width. All places in each zone use, instead of their own local time, the time counted from the transit of the "mean sun" across the Standard Time meridian which passes near the middle of that zone.

These time zones are designated as Atlantic, Eastern, Central, Mountain, Pacific, Yukon, Alaska-Hawaii, and Bering and the time in these zones is basically reckoned from the 60th, 75th, 90th, 105th, 120th, 135th, 150th, 165th meridians west of Greenwich. The line wanders to conform to local geographical regions. The time in the various zones is earlier than Greenwich Time by 4, 5, 6, 7, 8, 9, 10, and 11 hours respectively.

High Precision Time and Frequency are broadcast by U.S. Navy Stations which are maintained on frequency with the aid of Atomic Clocks (cesium beam and atomic hydrogen masers). The stations are as follows: NBA: NSS: NLK: NAA: NPM: NWC: NPN: NPG: NDT: Omega.

Loran-C Navigational Transmissions at 100 KHz of the East Coast, Central Pacific, Mediterranean, Northwest Pacific and the Norwegian sea chains may be used for time and frequency comparisons.

Standard Frequency Stations

The National Bureau of Standards (NBS) radio stations WWV at Fort Collins, Colorado, and WWVH on the island of Kauai, Hawaii, broadcast a number of technical services continuously night and day. These services are: 1. standard radio frequencies, 2.5, 5, 10, 15, w0 and 25 MHz (WWV) and 2.5, 5, 10, 15 and 20 MHz (WWVH); 2. standard time voice announcements (WWV—male, 7.5 seconds before the minute; WWVH — female, 15 seconds before the minute); 3. standard time intervals of one second and one minute; 4. corrections to adjust atomic time to astronomical time; 5. standard audio frequencies of 500 and 600 Hz on alternate minutes and a 440 Hz tone (the musical pitch A above middle C) once each hour; 6. A slow time code at 100 Hz giving the day, hour and minute in binary coded decimal form; 7. hourly radio propagation forecasts; 8. geophysical alerts on events in process and summaries of solar and geophysical events of the last 24 hours; and 9. storm warnings. The NBS also broadcasts time and frequency signals from its low frequency station (60kHz). WWVB, also located at Fort Collins, Colorado.

Each hour there are periods with no tone modulation during which the carrier, seconds ticks, minute time announcements, and 100 Hz time code continue.

They occur during the 16th through the 20th minute on WWVH and the 46th through the 50th minute on WWV.

The National Research council of Canada continually transmits precision time signals from Ottawa over station CHU on 3 frequencies, 3330, 7335, and 14670 kHz.

Storm warnings cover the waters of the Atlantic and Eastern Pacific from WWV and the Pacific from WWVH and are given at the 8th, 10th and 12th minute of each hour from WWV and at the 49th and 51st minute of each hour from WWVH. Times of issue are 0500, 1100, 1600, and 2300 UT from WWV, and 0000, 0600, 1200, and 1800 UT from WWVH.

The time and frequency broadcasts are controlled by the NBS atomic frequency standards, which follow the internationally defined cesium resonance frequency with an accuracy of 2 parts in 10^{12}. (The cesium atom invariably resonates at a little over 9 billion oscillations per second.)

The atomic time scale is uniform and does not reflect the variable rotational speed of the earth. The time signals are adjusted by introducing a leap second about once a year (at the end of June or December) so that the broadcast time never departs more than nine-tenths of a second from mean solar time, determined by the rotational position of the earth.

Special Publication 236 describes in detail the standard frequency and time service of the National Bureau of Standards. Single copies may be obtained upon request from the National Bureau of Standards, Boulder, Colorado, 80302. Quantities may be obtained from the Superintendent of Documents, U.S. Gov. Printing Office, Wash., D.C. 20402, at 25c per copy.

Daylight Saving Time

Under the Uniform Time Act, which became effective in 1967, all states, the District of Columbia and U.S. possessions must observe Daylight Saving Time beginning at 2 a.m. on the last Sunday in April and ending at 2 a.m. on the last Sunday in October. Any state, by law, can exempt itself from the law; Hawaii and American Samoa did so in 1967, Arizona, Puerto Rico, and the Virgin Islands in 1968, and Indiana in 1971. The 1972 amendment to the Uniform Time Act authorizes states split by time zones to take that into consideration in exempting themselves. As a result Indiana's exemption law applies only to the eastern portion of its state. The Dept. of Transportation, which oversees the act, has modified during the last 5 years some boundaries in Kansas, Texas, Florida and Michigan due to local problems. To conserve energy Congress put most of the nation on Daylight Saving Time for two years effective January 6, 1974 through April 27 1975. Alaska and Hawaii were exempted from th requirement. Daylight Saving Time is achieved y advancing the clock one hour.

24-Hour Time

24-hour time is widely used in scientific work throughout the world. In the United States it is used also in operations of the Armed Forces. In Europe it is used in preference to the 12-hour a.m. and p.m. system. With the 24-hour system the day begins at midnight and hours are numbered 0 through 23.

International Date Line

The Date Line is a zig-zag line that approximately coincides with the 180th meridian, and it is where each calendar day begins. The date must be advanced one day when crossing in a westerly direction and set back one day when crossing in an easterly direction. The line is deflected between north latitude 48° and 75°, so that all Asia lies to the west of it.

A Unique Generation

In the six months from November 1973 to April 1974 we have probably learned more about three of the planets than we had gathered in the previous six millenia. Pioneer 10 began to send us data about Jupiter and most of its twelve satellites early in November 1973, and passed about 80,000 miles from Jupiter on December 3. It continued to transmit new information for another month, and the accumulation will provide material for analysis for years to come.

In February, 1974, Mariner 10 flew by Venus with the first high resolution cameras brought close to that planet. Just as a basketball may run around the rim of the basket, so Mariner 10 dipped into the strong gravitational well of Venus and was flipped into a new orbit leading it on to Mercury. By April, it had passed within 700 miles of Mercury, obtaining the first photos ever of this elusive little Messenger of the Gods. Mid-course corrections to the flight path of Mariner 10 allowed it to repeat a pass around Mercury in September, 1974, and it will pass by again in the spring of 1975, permitting more picture coverage.

The Pioneer Probe

Pioneer 10, launched March 3, 1972, in passing unscathed through the asteroid belt, demonstrated that this region may not be the terror that had been expected. It is cleaner and freer of dust and debris than had been supposed, so that Pioneer 10 arrived intact at the region of Jupiter. The outermost satellites are nearly 15 million miles from the planet, and it took Pioneer a month to travel that distance, accelerating all the time. The acceleration, of course, was caused by the gravitational attraction of the mass of Jupiter on the mass of the probe. So accurate were the observations of the change in speed of Pioneer 10, better than a millimeter per second, that the masses of Jupiter's satellites are now known well, and even our accounting of the mass of Jupiter has been increased by about 0.004 percent, equivalent in amount to the mass of the earth's moon.

Jupiter, the giant of the solar system, is even more mighty and unusual in many respects than was expected. A stream of gas emitted by the sun creates a solar wind blowing outward in all directions. Just as a rock causes a disturbance in a flowing stream, so the planets produce bow waves in the solar wind. The bow shock wave of Jupiter is much larger than was expected, being encountered nearly 5 million miles from the planet. Pioneer 10 entered the planet's magnetic field a day earlier than expected, and found the effects of the Jovian Van Allen elts of trapped particles to be a hundred thousand or more times greater than those around the earth. And Jupiter's magnetic field is upside down compared to earth, having the opposite polarity orientation of ours.

The easiest information for the layman to assimilate is in photographs. Even though the pictures returned are excellent, many people may not notice improvement over earth-based photography, since the features observed are all clouds. The details of cloud structure allow an interpretation of Jovian winds and other atmospheric properties. Initially, it seems the dark banks are lower than the bright zones. Only blue and red filtered pictures were obtained. The published color photographs, while attractive, contain no green information, for the blue images are repeated in the green emulsion.

Mariner Mission

As Pioneer 10 began to send us information from close to Jupiter, Mariner 10 was launched toward Venus and Mercury. Passing Venus in early February, 1974, it sent us over 3,000 photographs of our nearest planetary neighbor. We have known for many years that the chief gaseous component of the atmosphere is carbon dioxide, a gas that is best detected optically in ultra violet light. Mariner 10 used UV to detect changes in cloud heights, thus providing longer and shorter lines of sight into the nearby atmosphere.

Because Venus rotates on its axis once in 243 days, and revolves around the sun once in 225 days, the sun can shine on any particular part of the atmosphere for about 60 days. This intense solar heating, accumulated by the carbon dioxide atmosphere, creates high velocity winds and causes spiral cloud patterns reaching to the poles. So efficient is the atmospheric transport of heat that spacecraft instruments detected no great temperature difference between day and night hemispheres. There seem to be at least three layers in the atmosphere, one about 25 miles up, a second around 40 miles, and a third around 45 miles altitude.

Mariner 10 confirmed the lack of a magnetic field and, consequently, of trapped particles in a Van Allen belt system. This implies a direct bombardment of the upper atmosphere of Venus by the solar wind and by cosmic ray particles from the sun and from interstellar space.

Comparison of the atmospheric circulation patterns of rapidly rotating Jupiter and slowly rotating Venus may provide meterologists with a sufficient range of conditions to aid our understanding of our own weather and climate problems.

On March 29, 1974, Mariner 10 swept past Mercury's dark side at a distance of less than 700 miles. The high-resolution cameras on board initially showed craters. As Mariner 10 left Mercury behind, it began to show us more of the illuminated hemisphere, and the presence of craters in great abundance was confirmed. Even to the experienced astronomer, the resemblance to our moon is striking. From information obtained on the first fly-by, no great mare areas (large, flat expanses suggesting "seas") were found, but there was at least one feature reminiscent of Mare Orientale on our satellite. Even rayed craters, like the moon's Copernicus, were seen. The temperatures found were not surprising, but the presence of a weak magnetic field and of gases (including hydrogen and helium) sufficient to constitute an atmosphere were new and unexpected items of information. Since earth-like size and rotation seem to be minimum conditions for establishment of a magnetic field, Mercury's is a puzzle. The atmosphere may be transient gases temporarily subtracted from the solar wind with the aid of the magnetic field.

Into The Future

One or two more passes of Mariner 10 by Mercury — to be made before mid-1975 — may provide us with sufficient information to enable us to define more accurately the problems to be solved.

Pioneer 11 will provide us a second series of observations of Jupiter in November, 1974. In addition, Pioneer 11 is so directed that it will be flipped across the solar system to fly-by Saturn — or even through its rings — in 1978.

In 1975, the Viking project will launch a lander to Mars to begin making observations from the surface in July, 1976. Perhaps it will detect evidence of a history of life on Mars.

Another probe in the Pioneer series will be launched about May 1978 to go into orbit around Venus in December. A second Pioneer will also arrive at the same time to send probes into the atmosphere of Venus.

Probes coming within 26 million miles of the sun are being planned, and an encounter with Encke's comet may come about by 1980.

Thus, in one generation, we will have gone from beeping Sputnik to an intimate observation and even invasion of our neighbor worlds. Professor Carl Sagan of Cornell reminds us that this generation is unique in world history. "All before us have looked at the planets and have wondered. All after us will look at them and know. We are the only generation to wonder and to know."

National Weather Service: National Oceanic and Atmospheric Admn.

The National Weather Service, formerly the Weather Bureau is a component of the National Oceanic and Atmospheric Administration (NOAA), a new agency created in the Dept. of Commerce on Oct. 3, 1970, under a Presidential reorganization plan.

The National Weather Service reports the weather of the U.S. and possessions, provides weather forecasts to the general public, issues warnings against tornadoes, hurricanes, floods, winter storms, and other atmospheric and hydrologic hazards, and provides a broad array of special services to aeronautical, maritime, astronautic, agricultural, and other weather-sensitive activities. These services are supported by a national network of observing and forecasting stations, communications links, aircraft, satellite systems, and computers. Some 300 NWS offices across the land ensure prompt and useful dissemination of weather information. See also National Weather Service Watches and Warnings, Page 243.

The River and Flood Forecasting Service is conducted through about 70 river district offices and 12 river forecasting centers and issues river stage and flood warnings for all the principal rivers and tributaries of the United States. The Water Supply Forecasting Service is conducted through 5 Water Supply Forecasting Centers for the Western and Northeastern United States on a water year or seasonal basis. Rainfall studies conducted in cooperation with the Army Corps of Engineers and the Department of Agriculture Soil Conservation Service assist in planning engineering works for flood control, water utilization, water-shed protection and local drainage design.

Weather service to aviation involves the responsibilities of providing current measurements and of forecasting conditions pertinent to conducting safe and efficient flight operations at airport terminals and along flight routes. Aviation weather forecasts and briefings are provided for transoceanic and domestic operations extending upward from the surface to include operational levels of civil jet aircraft.

The agricultural weather service program provides weather observations from representative agricultural areas, specialized forecasts of weather factors directly affecting agricultural production.

In addition, technical studies of the influence of weather on agriculture are coordinated jointly with agricultural experiment station personnel.

U. S. Department of Agriculture and the National Weather Service cooperate in issuing local weather-crop bulletins on an area basis.

The Fruit-frost Service provides detailed and localized forecasts and warnings to fruit growers on a cooperative basis in those states where winter and spring fruit and vegetable production is a major activity.

The marine weather service provides specialized weather forecasts, warnings, sea heights and data essential to the conduct of marine operations on the high seas and on coastal and inland waterways. In addition, it supplies forecasts for related phenomena, such as seiches and storm surges, for the protection of life and property.

The Weather Service also provides weather support for the U.S. manned space flight program and assists in the weather support to the Nation's other space programs.

The repository for all American and many international weather records and for large-scale tabulation, processing, and publication is the National Climatic Center, operated by NOAA's Environmental Data Service at Asheville, N. C. The Environmental Data Service also has an Agricultural Climatology Service Office which issues the Weekly Weather and Crop Bulletin jointly with the U.S. Dept. of Agriculture.

Is Our Weather Changing?

The high and low temperature records of the National Weather Service used by The World Almanac tend to support the theory that the U.S. climate is cooling off. Through 1972, the last time a new state record for heat was established was in the summer of 1954. But new cold weather records have been set in 8 states in 5 different years since 1957.

This cooling trend reverses a previous trend toward warmer weather through the early 1940s. Since the late 1940s the average temperature of the northern hemisphere has dropped one-half a degree. Some scientists believe this small change is enough to cause important changes in the world's weather and in agriculture. A recent study by the International Federation of Institutes for Advanced Study concluded that the weather change will continue for several decades and will lead to major crop failures during the next 10 years.

A Careful Watch

Weather experts and governments are watching these changes carefully because of their probable effect on world food supplies. Present populations and agricultural methods are highly dependent on the favorable weather trends of 30 years ago. A slight change in weather can lead to devastating famines around the world.

A paradoxical element in the cooling trend is that it can bring hotter and drier weather to some food-producing areas such as sub-Sarahan Africa, central India and, this year, to the American Midwest.

One theory to explain this paradox holds that as the earth cools, the cold air mass over the North Pole expands. This, in turn, pushes southward the great circumpolar air currents which carry moisture into the Midwest, the Mediterranean, and southern Russia.

The southward movement of these currents keeps the monsoon and South Atlantic winds from moving north to bring rain to central Africa and India.

Another theory relating to the drought in the Midwest is that these dry spells come in 20-year cycles. The last drought extended from 1953 to 1956, and the one before that — the worst in this century — ran from 1933 to 1936. One expert forecaster predicts the present drought will last until 1978.

Sunspot Theory

The sunspot theory of weather changes — that great storms on the sun throw streams of solar particles into space and into Earth's atmosphere, thus changing the weather — is supported by some studies which show sunnier, dryer weather during and just after peak sunspot activity. However, since sunspot activity reaches its height about every 11 years, the link between sunspots and drought is not widely accepted.

In the short run, weather changes will add to inflation. As estimates of the 1974 U.S. grain crop drop 10 percent to 30 percent, the price of feed grains for chickens, pigs and cattle will go up. Production of meat will probably decline and prices for good meat will go up. At the same time, other areas of the world will bid up the price of all grains as attempts are made to make up shortages of food in other countries.

Many experts, including specialists in the U.S. Department of Agriculture, maintain that the weather is simply following its normal fluctuations with good crop weather in some areas and bad weather in others. They are not persuaded that there is any major trend toward cooler weather or any permanent shift in rainfall patterns.

Tides and Their Causes
Source: National Ocean Survey (NOAA)

The tides are a natural phenomenon involving the alternating rise and fall in the large fluid bodies of the earth caused by the combined gravitational attraction of the sun and moon. The combination of these two variable force influences, as modified by certain factors such as depth of the water, configuration of the shoreline, and geographic location, produce the complex recurrent cycle of the tides. Tides may occur in both oceans and seas, to a limited extent in large lakes, the atmosphere, and, to a very minute degree, in the earth itself. The period between succeeding tides varies as the result of many factors and force influences.

The tide-generating force represents the difference between (1) the centrifugal force produced by the revolution of the earth around the common center-of-gravity of the earth-moon system and (2) the gravitational attraction of the moon acting upon the earth's overlying waters. Similar tide-producing forces exist in the earth-sun system. Since, on the average, the moon is only 238,857 miles from the earth compared with the sun's much greater distance of 93,000,000 miles, this closer distance outranks the much smaller mass of the moon compared with that of the sun, and the moon's tide-raising force is, accordingly, $2^1/_5$ times that of the sun.

The effect of the tide-generating forces of the moon and sun acting tangentially to the earth's surface (the so-called "tractive force") tends to cause a maximum accumulation of the waters of the oceans at two diameterically opposite positions on the surface of the earth and to withdraw compensating amounts of water from all points 90° removed from the positions of these tidal bulges. The presence of the continents, as well as other factors, prevents the total free movement of water. However, as the earth rotates beneath the maxima and minima of these tide-generating forces, a sequence of two high tides, separated by two low tides, ideally is produced each day.

Twice in each lunar month, when the sun, moon, and earth are directly aligned, with the moon between the earth and the sun (at new moon) or on the opposite side of the earth from the sun (at full moon), the sun and the moon exert their gravitational force in a mutual or addititive fashion. Higher high tides and lower low tides are produced. These are called spring tides. At two positions 90° in between; the gravitational forces of the moon and sun — imposed at right angles—tend to counteract each other to the greatest extent, and the range between high and low tides is reduced. These are called neap tides. This semi-monthly variation between the spring and neap tides is called the phase inequality.

The inclination of the moon's orbit to the equator also produces a difference in the height of succeeding high tides and in the extent of depression of succeeding low tides which is known as the diurnal inequality. In extreme cases this phenomenon can result in only one high tide and one low tide each day. The changing distance of the moon from the earth in each lunar month due to the elliptical orbit of the moon produces a difference in the height of the tides known as the lunar parallactic inequality. The changing distance of the earth from the sun during the earth's anual revolution around the sun similarly introduces the solar parallactic inequality.

The actual amount of the uplift of the waters in the deep ocean may amount to only one or two feet. However, as this tide approaches shoal waters and its effects are augmented, the tidal range may be greatly increased. In Nova Scotia along the narrow channel of the Bay of Fundy, the range of tides or difference between high and low waters, may reach 43½ feet or more (under spring tide conditions) due to resonant amplifications.

At New Orleans, the periodic rise and fall of the tide varies with the state of the Mississippi, being about 10 inches at low stage and zero at high. The Canadian Tide Tables for 1972 gave a maximum range of nearly 50 feet at Leaf Basin, Ungava Bay.

In every case, actual high or low tide can vary considerably from the average due to weather conditions such as strong winds, abrupt barometric pressure changes, or prolonged periods of extreme high or low pressure.

The Average Rise and Fall of Tides
Source: National Ocean Survey (NOAA)

Places	Feet In	Places	Feet In	Places	Feet In
Baltimore, Md.	1 1	Mobile, Ala.	1 6	San Diego, Calif.	4 1
Boston, Mass.	9 6	New London, Conn.	2 7	Sandy Hook, N.J.	4 7
Charleston, S.C.	5 2	Newport, R.I.	3 6	San Francisco, Calif.	4 0
Colon, Panama	1 1	New York, N.Y.	4 6	Savannah, Ga.	7 5
Eastport, Me.	18 2	Old Pt. Comfort, Va.	2 6	Seattle, Wash.	7 7
Galveston, Tex.	1 5	Philadelphia, Pa.	5 11	Tampa, Fla.	2 10
Halifax, N.S.	4 5	Portland, Me.	9 0	Vancouver, B.C.	10 6
Key West, Fla.	1 4	St. John's, Nfld.	2 7	Washington, D.C.	2 11

Astronomical Signs and Symbols

☉	The Sun	⊕	The Earth	♅	Uranus	☐	Quadrature
☾	The Moon	♂	Mars	♆	Neptune	☌	Opposition
☿	Mercury	♃	Jupiter	♇	Pluto	☊	Ascending Node
♀	Venus	♄	Saturn	☌	Conjunction	☋	Descending Node

Two heavenly bodies are in "conjunction"(☌) when they are due north and south of each other, either in Right Ascension (with respect to the north celestial pole) or in Celestial Longitude (with respect to the north ecliptic pole). If the bodies are seen near each other, they will rise and set at nearly the same time. They are in "opposition" (☍) when their Right Ascensions differ by exactly 12 hours, or their Celestial Longitudes differ by 180°. One of the two objects in opposition will rise while the other is setting. "Quadrature" (☐) refers to the arrangement when the coordinates of two bodies differ by exactly 90°. These terms may refer to the relative positions of any two bodies as seen from the earth, but one of the bodies is so frequently the sun that mention of the sun is omitted; otherwise, both bodies are named. The geocentric angular separation betweeen sun and object is termed "elongation". Elongation is limited only for Mercury and Venus; the "greatest elongation" for each of these bodies is noted in the appropriate tables and is approximately the time for longest observation. When a planet is in its "ascending" (☊) or "descending" (☋) node, it is passing northward or southward, respectively, through the plane of the earth's orbit, across the celestial circle called the ecliptic. The term "perihelion" means nearest to the sun, and "aphelion," farthest from the sun. An "occultation" of a planet or star is an eclipse of it by some other body, usually the moon.

National Weather Service Watches and Warnings

National Weather Service forecasters issue a TORNADO WATCH for a specific area where it is reasonably possible that tornadoes may occur during the valid time of the watch. A WATCH is to alert people to watch for tornado activity and listen for a TORNADO WARNING. A TORNADO WARNING means that a tornado has been sighted or indicated by radar, and that safety precautions should be taken at once. The terms HURRICANE WATCH and HURRICANE WARNING are used similarly during hurricane season.

Definitions

Tornado—A violent rotating column of air pendant from a thundercloud, usually recognized as a funnel-shaped vortex accompanied by a loud roar. With rotating winds est. up to 300 mph., it is the most destructive storm. Tornado paths have varied in length from a few feet to nearly 300 miles (avg. 5 mi.); diameter from a few feet to over a mile (average 220 yards); average forward speed, 25-40 mph.

Cyclone—An atmospheric circulation of winds rotating counterclockwise in the northern hemisphere and clockwise in the southern hemisphere. Tornadoes, hurricanes and the LOWS shown on weather maps are all examples of cyclones having various sizes and intensities. Cyclones are usually accompanied by precipitation or stormy weather.

Hurricane—A severe cyclone originating over tropical ocean waters and having winds 74 miles an hour or higher. (In the western Pacific, such storms

are known as typhoons.) The area of strong winds takes the form of a circle or an oval, sometimes as much as 500 miles in diameter. In the lower latitudes hurricanes usually move toward the west or northwest at 10 to 15 mph. When the center approaches 25° to 30° North Latitude, direction of motion often changes to northeast, with increased forward speed.

Blizzard—A severe weather condition characterized by low temperatures and by strong winds bearing a great amount of snow (mostly fine, dry snow picked up from the ground). The National Weather Service specifies, for "blizzard," a wind of 35 miles an hour or higher, temperatures 20°F. or lower, and sufficient falling and/or blowing snow to reduce visibility to less than ¼ of a mile. For "severe blizzard" wind speeds of 45 mph or more, temperature near or below 10°F., and visibility reduced by snow to near zero.

Monsoon—A name for seasonal winds (derived from Arabic "mausim," a season). It was first applied to the winds over the Arabian Sea, which blow for six months from northeast and six months from southwest, but it has been extended to similar winds in other parts of the world. The monsoons are strongest on the southern and eastern sides of Asia.

Flood—The condition that occurs when water overflows the natural or artificial confines of a stream or other body of water, or accumulates by drainage over low-lying areas.

National Weather Service Marine Warning and Advisories

Source: National Weather Service, NOAA, Dept. of Commerce

Small Craft Advisory: A Small Craft Advisory alerts mariners to sustained (exceeding two hours) weather and/or sea conditions either present or forecast, potentially hazardous to small boats. Hazardous conditions may include winds of 18 to 33 knots and/or dangerous wave or inlet conditions. It is the responsibility of the mariner, based on his experience and size or type of boat, to determine if the conditions are hazardous. When a mariner becomes aware of a Small Craft Advisory, he should immediately obtain the latest marine forecast to determine the reason for the Advisory. The visual signal is a **RED** pennant by day, a **RED OVER WHITE** light at night.

Gale Warning: Two **RED** pennants displayed by day and a **WHITE** light **ABOVE** a **RED** light at night to indicate that winds within the range 34 to 47 knots are forecast for the area.

Storm Warning: A single square **RED** flag with a **BLACK** center displayed during daytime and two **RED** lights at night to indicate that winds 48 knots and above, no matter how high the speed, are forecast for the area. However, if the winds are associated with a tropical cyclone (hurricane), the **STORM WARNING** display indicates that winds within the range 48 to 63 knots are forecast.

Hurricane Warning: Displayed only in connection with a hurricane or typhoon. Two square **RED** flags with **BLACK** centers displayed by day and a **WHITE** light between two **RED** lights at night to indicate that winds 64 knots and above are forecast for the area.

Primary source of dissemination are by commercial radio, TV, U.S. Coast Guard Radio stations and NOAA VHF-FM broadcasts. These broadcasts on 162.40 and 162.55 MHz can usually be received 20-40 miles from the transmitting antenna site, depending on terrain and quality of the receiver used. Where transmitting antennas are on high ground, the range is somewhat greater, reaching 60 miles or more.

The frequencies 162.55 and 162.40 MHz require narrow band FM receivers of + 5 kilohertz deviation. In selecting a suitable receiver, special attention should be paid to the manufacturer's rating of the receiver's sensitivity. Generally speaking, a receiver with a sensitivity of 1 microvolt or less should pick up a broadcast at a distance of about 40-50 miles depending upon antenna height and terrain.

Dissemination is also made by means of visual displays (flags, pennants and lights). These are indicated under each warning and advisory category.

Hurricane Names in 1975

The National Weather Service has used girls' names to identify hurricanes in the Atlantic, Caribbean and Gulf of Mexico since 1953. A semi-permanent list of 10 sets of names in aphabetical order was established in 1971. Hurricane season begins June 1 and ends Nov. 30.

Names assigned to hurricanes: **1975** —Amy, Blanche, Caroline, Doris, Eloise, Faye, Gladys, Hallie,

Ingrid, Julia, Kitty, Lilly, Mabel, Niki, Opal, Peggy, Ruby, Sheila, Tilda, Vicky, and Winnie.

Hurricanes and typhoons in the Eastern North Pacific are also identified by girls' names. **1975** — Agatha, Bridget, Carlotta, Denise, Eleanor, Francene, Georgette, Hilary, Ilsa, Jewel, Katrina, Lily, Monica, Nanette, Olivia, Priscilla, Ramona, Sharon, Terry, Veronica, and Winifred.

New Developments in U.S. Weather Satellite System

Source: National Oceanic and Atmospheric Administration

Since the successful launching of ESSA 1 and ESSA 2 (Environmental Survey Satellites) in Feb. 1966, the United States has had an operational weather satellite system providing both global and local cloud-cover pictures at least once every day.

The operational system is now based on the improved TIROS Operational Satellite. The first of these, ITOS-1, was launched Jan. 23, 1970; the second, called NOAA-1 was launched Dec. 11, 1970; the third, NOAA-2, was launched Oct. 15, 1972 and the fourth, NOAA-3, on Nov. 6, 1973. The ITOS system is managed and operated by the National Environmental Satellite Service (NESS) of the National Oceanic and Atmospheric Administration (NOAA).

Although similar in appearance to previous ITOS satellites, NOAA-2 and NOAA-3 have cameras onboard and rely entirely on scanning radiometers for imagery. They also carry a sensor to obtain vertical temperature profile soundings of the atmosphere routinely on a near-global basis.

The 40x40x49-inch box, with a 3-panel solar cell array attached, contains the 2-channel scanning radiometer, the solar proton monitor and the vertical temperature profile radiometer (VTPR) and the very high resolution radiometer (VHRR). Duplication of all sensors in the spacecraft ensures a more reliable service and longer lifetime.

The scanning radiometer system obtains data in both visible and infrared channels. The visible channel observes only sunlit portions of the earth, while the infrared channel furnishes cloud pictures both night and day. The radiometer scans a 2000-nautical mile-wide swath beneath the satellite's path. Picture resolution is 2 nautical miles in the visible channel and 4 nautical miles in the infrared.

The scanning radiometer replaces the 2 types of camera systems formerly carried on operational satellites, by providing both stored picture coverage of the earth's weather and direct transmission of cloud cover photographs from the satellite to more than 50 local receiving stations around the world. Its ability to photograph the dark side of the earth makes nighttime satellite observations available for use in preparing early morning forecasts and will en-sure night as well as daytime coverage of hazardous weather, such as hurricanes and winter storms.

The very high resolution radiometer (VHRR) obtains observations similar to those taken by the scanning radiometer, but with a resolution of ½ mile in contrast to the 2-to-4-mile resolution of the scanning radiometer. In addition to providing images of cloud cover, the scanning radiometer and the VHRR obtain a measure of the sea surface temperature in cloud-free areas.

The vertical temperature profile radiometer, developed by NASA, is an instrument that measures infrared energy radiated at 6 levels of the atmosphere and at the earth's surface or cloud tops. These measurements are used to calculate the vertical temperature distribution of the atmosphere beneath the satellite. The radiometer also provides information on the total moisture content of the atmospheric column observed.

Nimbus III, launched April 14, 1969, carried the first systems for gathering quantitative measurements through the column of atmosphere beneath the spacecraft. Called Satellite Infrared Spectrometer (SIRS), and Infrared Interferometer Spectrometer (IRIS), they provided vertical temperature measurements in the atmosphere, and additional information on atmospheric pressure can be derived from these soundings. NASA's Nimbus IV, launched April 8, 1970, and Nimbus V, launched December 11, 1972 (2:56 AM EST) carried other experiments designed to develop techniques for measuring, on a global basis, parameters needed for mathematical modeling.

The era of weather observation by satellite was inaugurated on April 1, 1960, with the successful launching and operation of the 270-lb. TIROS I.

The prototype satellite in NOAA's Geostationary Operational Environmental Satellite (GOES) system, NASA's Synchronous Meteorological Satellite A (SMS-1) was launched May 17, 1974. A second satellite will follow within several months to complete the two-GOES system capable of viewing the 48 contiguous States and the adjacent waters from Puerto Rico to Hawaii.

NOAA's Ark

The National Oceanic and Atmospheric Administration, a part of the Dept. of Commerce, was created in 1970 to explore and chart the global oceans and their potential use to the nation; to monitor characteristics of the environment and predict changes in the air, sun and sea; to warn against environmental hazards; and to ease the impact of destructive natural events.

Among its many activities, the NOAA reports the weather, prepares and issues aeronautical and nautical charts; conducts geodetic, oceanographic and marine geophysical surveys; predicts tides and currents; provides satellite observation of the environment; and collects and disseminates worldwide environmental data. One of its current projects is the establishment of a system of buoys to monitor the condition of U.S. coastal waters and the world's oceans.

NOAA consists of 6 major offices: National Marine Fisheries Service, National Ocean Survey, National Weather Service, Environmental Data Service, National Environmental Satellite Service, and Environmental Research Laboratories. It also includes the Office of Sea Grant, which administers a variety of grants, and the Office of Coastal Zone Management, which issues grants to states for programs leading to balanced use of the shore areas.

Wind Chill Table

Source: National Oceanic and Atmospheric Administration

Degrees (Fahrenheit) MPH	35	30	25	20	15	10	5	0	—5	—10	—15	—20	—25	—30	—35	—40	—45
Wind Chill Index: (Equivalent temperature) Equivalent in cooling power on exposed flesh under calm conditions.																	
0	35	30	25	20	15	10	5	0	—5	—10	—15	—20	—25	—30	—35	—40	—45
5	33	27	21	16	12	7	1	—6	—11	—15	—20	—26	—31	—35	—41	—47	—54
10	21	16	9	2	—2	—9	—15	—22	—27	—31	—38	—45	—52	—58	—64	—70	—77
15	16	11	1	—6	—11	—18	—25	—33	—40	—45	—51	—60	—65	—70	—78	—85	—90
20	12	3	—4	—9	—17	—24	—32	—40	—46	—52	—60	—68	—76	—81	—88	—96	—103
25	7	0	—7	—15	—22	—29	—37	—45	—52	—58	—67	—75	—83	—89	—96	—104	—112
30	5	—2	—11	—18	—26	—33	—41	—49	—56	—63	—70	—78	—87	—94	—101	—109	—117
35	3	—4	—13	—20	—27	—35	—43	—52	—60	—67	—72	—83	—90	—98	—105	—113	—123
40	1	—4	—15	—22	—29	—36	—45	—54	—62	—69	—76	—87	—94	—101	—107	—116	—128
45	1	—6	—17	—24	—31	—38	—46	—54	—63	—70	—78	—87	—94	—101	—108	—118	—128
50	0	—7	—17	—24	—31	—38	—47	—56	—63	—70	—79	—88	—96	—103	—110	—120	—128

(Wind speeds greater than 40 mph have little additional chilling effect.)

How Cold is Cold? Temperature and wind both affect the heat loss from the surface of the body. The effect of these two factors is expressed as an "equivalent temperature," which approximates the still-air temperature which would have the same cooling effect as the wind and temperature combination. For example, from the table above, with a temperature of 20°F. and a wind of 20 mph, the effect on exposed flesh is the same as —9°F. with no wind.

Monthly Normal Temperature and Precipitation

Source: National Climatic Center, NOAA, Dept. of Commerce

These normals are based on records for the thirty-year period 1941 to 1970 inclusive. See explanation on page 250. For stations that did not have continuous records from the same instrument site for the entire 30 years, the means have been adjusted to the record at the present site.

AP indicates airport station; those not so marked are city office stations.

T, Temperature in Fahrenheit; P, precipitation in inches; L, less than .05 inch.

Stations	Jan.		Feb.		Mar.		Apr.		May		June		July		Aug.		Sept.		Oct.		Nov.		Dec.	
	T.	P.	T.	P.	T.	P.	T.	P.	T.	P.	T.	P.	T.	P.	T.	P.	T.	P.	T.	P.	T.	P.	T.	P.
Albany, N. Y. (AP)	22	2.2	24	2.1	33	2.6	47	2.7	58	3.3	68	3.0	72	3.1	70	2.9	62	3.1	51	2.6	40	2.8	26	2.9
Albuquerque, N. M. (AP)	35	0.3	40	0.4	46	0.5	56	0.5	65	0.5	75	0.5	79	1.4	77	1.3	70	0.8	58	0.8	45	0.3	36	0.5
Anchorage, Alaska (AP)	12	0.8	18	0.8	24	0.6	35	0.6	46	0.6	55	1.1	58	2.1	56	2.3	48	2.4	35	1.4	21	1.0	13	1.1
Asheville, N. C. (AP)	38	3.4	39	3.6	46	4.7	56	3.5	64	3.3	71	4.0	74	4.9	73	4.5	67	3.6	57	3.3	46	2,9	39	3.6
Atlanta, Ga. (AP)	42	4.3	45	4.4	51	5.8	61	4.6	69	3.7	76	3.7	78	4.9	78	3.5	72	3.2	62	2.5	51	3.4	44	4.2
Baltimore, Md. (AP)	42	2.9	44	2.8	53	3.7	65	3.1	75	3.6	83	3.8	87	4.1	85	4.2	79	3,1	68	2.8	56	3.1	44	3.3
Barrow, Alaska (AP)	-15	0.2	-19	0.2	-15	0.2	-1	0.2	19	0.2	33	0.4	39	0.9	38	1.0	30	0.6	15	0.6	-1	0.3	-12	0.2
Birmingham, Ala. (AP)	44	4.8	47	5.3	53	6.2	63	4.6	71	3.6	77	4.0	80	5.2	79	4.3	74	3.6	63	2.6	52	3.7	45	5.2
Bismarck, N. D. (AP)	8	0.5	14	0.4	25	0.7	43	1.4	54	2.2	64	3.6	71	2.2	69	2.0	58	1.3	47	0.8	29	0.6	16	0.5
Boise, Idaho (AP)	29	1.5	36	1.2	41	1.0	49	1.1	57	1.3	65	1.1	75	0.2	72	0.3	63	0.4	52	0.8	40	1.3	32	1.4
Boston, Mass. (AP)	29	3.7	30	3.5	38	4.0	49	3.5	59	3.5	68	3.2	73	2.7	71	3.5	65	3.2	55	3.0	45	4.5	33	4.2
Buffalo, N. Y. (AP)	24	2.9	24	2.6	32	2.9	45	3.2	55	3.0	66	2.2	70	2.9	68	3.5	62	3.3	52	3.0	40	3.7	28	3.0
Burlington, Vt. (AP)	17	1.7	19	1.7	29	1.9	43	2.6	55	3.0	65	3.5	70	3.5	67	3.7	59	3.1	49	2.7	37	2.9	23	2.2
Caribou, Maine (AP)	11	2.0	13	2.1	24	2.2	37	2.4	50	3.0	60	3.4	65	4.0	62	3.8	54	3.5	44	3.3	31	3.5	16	2.6
Charleston, S. C. (AP)	49	2.9	51	3.3	57	4.8	65	3.0	72	3.8	78	6.3	80	8.2	80	6.4	75	5.2	66	3.1	56	2.1	49	3.1
Chicago, Ill. (AP)	24	1.9	27	1.6	37	2.7	50	3.8	60	3.4	71	4.0	75	4.1	74	3.1	66	3.0	55	2.6	40	2.2	29	2.1
Cincinnati, Ohio	32	3.4	34	3.0	43	4.1	55	3.9	64	4.0	73	3.9	76	4.0	75	3.0	68	2.7	58	2.2	45	3.1	34	2.9
Cleveland, Ohio (AP)	27	2.6	28	2.2	36	3.1	48	3.5	58	3.5	68	3.3	71	3.5	70	3.0	64	2.8	54	2.6	42	2.8	30	2.4
Columbus, Ohio (AP)	28	2.9	30	2.3	39	3.4	51	3.7	61	4.1	70	4.1	74	4.2	72	2.9	65	2.4	54	1.9	42	2.7	31	2.4
Dallas, Texas (AP)	45	2.0	49	2.6	56	3.0	66	4.7	74	4.9	82	3.3	86	1.8	86	2.4	78	3.3	68	3.2	56	2.6	48	2.3
Denver, Colo. (AP)	30	0.6	33	0.7	37	1.2	48	1.9	57	2.6	66	1.9	73	1.8	72	1.3	63	1.1	52	1.1	39	0.8	33	0.4
Des Moines, Iowa (AP)	19	1.1	24	1.1	34	2.3	50	2.9	61	4.2	71	4,9	75	3.3	73	3.3	64	3.1	54	2.1	38	1.4	25	1.1
Detroit, Mich. (AP)	26	1.9	27	1.8	35	2.3	48	3.1	58	3.4	69	3.0	73	3.0	72	3.0	65	2.3	54	2.5	41	2.3	30	2.2
Dodge City, Kansas (AP)	31	0.5	35	0.6	41	1.1	54	1.7	64	3.1	74	3.3	79	3.1	78	2.6	69	1.7	58	1.7	43	0.6	33	8.5
Duluth, Minn. (AP)	9	1.2	12	0.9	24	1.8	39	2.6	49	3.4	59	4.4	66	3.7	64	3.8	54	3.1	45	2.3	28	1.7	14	1.4
Eureka, Calif.	47	7.4	48	5.2	48	4.8	50	3.0	53	2.1	55	0.7	56	0.1	57	0.3	57	0.7	54	3.2	52	5.8	49	6.6
Fairbanks, Alaska (AP)	-12	0.6	-3	0.5	10	0.5	29	0.3	47	0.7	59	1.4	61	1.9	55	2.2	44	1.1	25	0.7	3	0.7	-10	0.7
Ft. Worth, Tex. (AP)	45	1.8	49	2.4	55	2.5	65	4.3	73	4.5	81	3.1	85	1.8	85	2.3	78	3.2	68	2.7	56	2.0	48	1.8
Fresno, Calif. (AP)	45	1.8	50	1.7	54	1.6	60	1.2	67	0.3	74	0.1	81	L	78	L	74	0.1	64	0.4	54	1.2	46	1.7
Galveston, Texas	54	3.0	56	2.7	61	2.6	69	2.6	76	3.2	81	4.1	83	4.4	83	4.4	80	5.6	73	2.8	64	3.2	57	3.7
Grand Junction, Colo. (AP)	27	0.6	34	0.6	41	0.8	52	0.8	62	0.6	71	0.6	79	0.5	75	1.1	67	0.8	55	0.9	40	0.6	30	0.6
Gr. Rapids, Mich. (AP)	23	1.9	25	1.5	33	2.5	47	3.4	57	3.2	67	3.4	72	3.1	70	2.5	62	3.3	52	2.6	39	2.8	27	2.2
Helena, Mont. (AP)	18	0.6	25	0.4	31	0.7	43	0.9	52	1.8	59	2.4	68	1.0	66	1.0	56	1.0	45	0.6	32	0.6	23	0.6
Honolulu, Hawaii (AP)	72	4.4	72	2.5	73	3.2	75	1.4	77	1.0	79	0.3	80	0.6	81	0.8	80	0.7	79	1.5	77	3.0	74	3.7
Houston, Tex. (AP)	52	3.6	55	3.5	61	2.7	69	3.5	76	5.1	81	4.5	83	4.1	83	4.4	79	4.7	71	4.1	61	4.0	55	4.0
Huron, S. D. (AP)	13	0.4	18	0.8	29	1.1	46	2.0	57	2.8	67	3.8	74	2.2	72	2.0	61	1.8	50	1.5	32	0.	19	0.5
Indianapolis, Ind. (AP)	28	2.9	31	2.4	40	3.8	52	3.9	62	4.1	72	4.2	75	3.7	73	2.8	66	2.9	56	2.5	42	3.1	31	2.7
Jacksonville, Fla. (AP)	55	2.8	56	3.6	61	3.6	68	3.1	74	3.2	79	6.3	81	7.4	81	7.9	78	7.8	71	4.5	61	1.8	55	2.6
Juneau, Alaska (AP)	24	3.9	28	3.4	32	3.6	39	3.8	47	3.3	53	2.9	56	4.7	54	5.0	49	6.9	42	7.9	33	5.5	27	4.5
Kansas City, Mo. (AP)	28	1.3	33	1.3	41	2.6	55	3.5	65	4.3	74	5.6	79	4.4	77	3.8	69	4.2	59	3.2	44	1.5	32	1.5
Knoxville, Tenn. (AP)	41	4.7	43	4.7	50	4.9	60	3.6	68	3.3	76	3.6	78	4.7	77	3.2	72	2.8	61	2.7	49	3.6	42	4.5
Lander, Wyo. (AP)	20	0.5	26	0.7	31	1.2	43	2.4	53	2.6	61	1.9	71	0.6	69	0.4	58	1.1	47	1.2	32	0.9	23	0.5
Little Rock, Ark. (AP)	40	4.2	43	4.4	50	4.9	62	5.3	70	5.3	78	3.5	81	3.4	81	3.0	73	3.6	62	3.0	50	3.9	42	4.1
Los Angeles, Calif.	57	3.0	48	2.8	59	2.2	62	1.3	65	0.1	68	L	73	L	74	L	73	0.2	68	0.3	63	2.0	58	2.2
Louisville, Ky. (AP)	33	3.5	36	3.5	44	5.1	56	4.1	65	4.2	73	4.1	77	3.8	76	3.0	69	2.9	58	2.4	45	3.3	36	3.3
Marquette, Mich.	18	1.5	20	1.5	27	1.9	40	2.6	50	2.9	60	3.4	66	3.1	66	3.0	57	3.5	49	2.4	34	3.0	24	2.0
Memphis, Tenn. (AP)	41	4.9	44	4.7	51	5.1	63	5.4	71	4.4	79	3.5	82	3.5	80	3.3	74	3.0	63	2.6	51	3.9	43	4.7
Miami, Fla. (AP)	67	2.2	68	2.0	71	2.1	75	3.6	78	6.1	81	9.0	82	6.9	83	6.7	82	8.7	78	8.2	72	2.7	68	1.6
Milwaukee, Wisc. (AP)	19	1.6	23	1.1	31	2.2	45	2.8	54	2.9	65	3.6	70	3.4	69	2.7	61	3.0	51	2.0	37	2.0	24	1.8
Minneapolis, Minn. (AP)	12	0.7	17	0.8	28	1.7	45	2.0	57	3.4	67	3.9	72	3.7	70	3.1	60	2.7	50	1.8	32	1.2	19	0.9
Mobile, Ala. (AP)	51	4.7	54	4.8	59	7.1	68	5.6	75	4.5	80	6.1	82	8.9	82	6.9	78	6.6	69	2.6	59	3.4	53	5.9
Moline, Ill. (AP)	22	1.7	26	1.3	36	2.6	51	3.8	61	3.9	71	4.4	75	4.6	73	3.4	65	3.8	54	2.7	39	1.9	27	1.8
Nashville, Tenn. (AP)	38	4.8	41	4.4	49	5.0	60	4.1	69	4.1	77	3.4	80	3.8	79	3.2	72	3.1	61	2.2	48	3.5	40	4.5
Newark, N. J. (AP)	31	2.9	33	3.0	41	3.9	52	3.4	62	3.6	71	3.0	76	4.0	75	4.3	68	3.4	58	2.8	46	3.6	35	3.5
New Haven, Conn. (AP)	29	3.2	30	3.1	37	4.0	48	3.7	57	3.7	67	2.7	72	3.1	71	3.8	65	3.1	55	3.1	44	4.3	32	4.1
New Orleans, La. (AP)	53	4.5	56	4.8	61	5.5	69	4.2	75	4.2	80	4.7	82	6.7	82	5.3	78	5.6	70	2.3	60	3.9	55	5.1
New York City, N. Y.	32	2.9	33	3.1	41	4.0	52	3.6	62	3.4	72	2.9	77	3.9	75	4.5	68	3.2	58	3.0	47	3.8	35	3.6
Nome, Alaska (AP)	6	0.9	5	0.8	7	0.8	19	0.7	35	0.7	46	1.0	50	2.4	49	3.6	42	2.4	29	1.4	16	1.0	4	0.7
Norfolk, Va. (AP)	41	3.4	41	3.3	48	3.4	58	2.7	67	3.3	75	3.6	78	5.7	77	5.9	72	4.2	62	3.1	52	2.9	42	3.1
Okla. City, Okla. (AP)	37	1.1	41	1.3	48	2.1	60	3.5	68	5.2	77	4.2	82	2.7	81	2.6	73	3.6	62	2.6	49	1.4	40	1.3
Omaha, Nebr. (AP)	23	0.8	28	1.0	37	1.6	52	3.0	63	4.1	72	4.9	77	3.7	76	4.0	66	3.3	56	1.9	40	1.1	28	0.8
Parkersburg, W. Va.	33	3.1	35	2.8	43	3.8	55	3.5	64	3.6	72	4.0	75	4.3	74	3.3	67	2.8	57	2.1	45	2.5	35	2.8
Philadelphia, Pa. (AP)	34	3.9	34	3.0	47	3.5	53	6.7	60	4.1	75	7.9	78	2.4	79	2.0	71	3.4	59	2.2	48	0.6	39	6.3
Phoenix, Ariz. (AP)	51	0.1	58	1.4	57	1.7	67	0.1	81	0.1	88	L	94	1.3	93	L	85	L	74	L	61	1.4	55	L
Pittsburgh, Pa. (AP)	30	2.0	29	1.8	48	3.9	49	4.7	56	5.9	71	3.1	73	2.2	73	3.4	67	3.6	56	4.5	44	2.7	33	2.2
Portland, Me. (AP)	23	2.6	23	2.6	38	2.6	46	9.9	51	6.3	64	4.9	71	1.7	71	3.5	58	2.2	49	3.4	38	2.4	34	9.6
Portland, Ore. (AP)	39	3.7	45	1.9	48	2.5	52	1.3	59	1.4	64	1.5	70	0.1	66	1.4	64	3.3	54	3.1	44	11.6	45	10.0
Providence, R. I. (AP)	28	3.5	29	3.5	37	4.0	47	3.7	57	3.5	66	2.7	72	2.9	70	3.9	63	3.3	54	3.3	43	4.5	32	4.1
Raleigh, N. C. (AP)	41	3.2	42	3.3	49	3.4	60	3.1	67	3.3	74	3.7	78	5.1	77	4.9	71	3.8	60	2.8	50	2.8	41	3.1
Rapid City, S. D. (AP)	22	0.5	26	0.6	31	1.0	45	2.1	55	2.8	64	3.7	73	2.1	72	1.5	61	1.2	50	0.9	35	0.5	27	0.4
Reno, Nevada (AP)	32	1.2	37	0.9	40	0.7	47	0.5	55	0.7	62	0.4	69	0.3	67	0.2	60	0.2	50	0.4	40	0.7	33	1.1
Richmond, Va. (AP)	38	2.9	39	3.0	47	3.4	58	2.8	67	3.4	74	3.5	78	5.6	76	5.1	70	3.6	59	2.9	49	3.2	39	3.2
St. Louis, Mo. (AP)	31	1.9	35	2.1	43	3.0	57	3.9	66	3.9	75	4.4	79	3.7	77	2.9	70	2.9	59	2.8	45	2.5	35	2.0
Salt Lake City, Utah (AP)	20	1.5	32	0.9	42	2.7	48	1.6	62	1.7	70	0.2	77	1.1	77	1.2	62	4.1	54	0.7	41	2.5	33	2.3
San Antonio, Tex. (AP)	51	1.7	55	2.1	61	1.5	70	2.5	76	3.1	82	2.8	84	1.7	85	2.4	79	3.7	71	2.8	60	1.8	53	1.5
San Diego, Calif. (AP)	56	1.7	60	1.6	58	2.3	62	0.1	63	L	68	L	69	L	71	L	69	L	67	L	61	1.6	58	0.2
San Francisco, Calif. (AP)	48	4.4	51	3.0	53	2.5	55	1.6	58	0.4	62	0.1	63	L	63	0.0	64	0.2	61	1.0	55	2.3	50	4.0
San Juan, P. R. (AP)	75	3.7	75	2.5	76	2.0	78	3.4	79	6.5	81	5.6	81	6.4	81	7.0	81	6.1	81	5.6	79	5.5	77	4.7
Sault Ste. Marie, Mich.	14	1.9	15	1.5	24	1.7	38	2.2	49	3.0	59	3.3	64	2.6	63	3.1	55	3.9	46	2.9	33	3.3	20	2.4
Savannah, Ga. (AP)	50	2.9	52	2.9	58	4.4	66	2.9	73	4.2	79	5.9	81	7.9	81	6.5	76	5.6	67	2.8	57	1.9	50	3.3
Sea.-Tac. Wash. (AP)	38	5.8	42	4.2	44	3.6	49	2.5	55	1.7	60	1.5	65	0.7	64	1.1	60	2.0	52	3.9	45	5.9	41	5.9
Spokane, Wash. (AP)	25	2.5	32	1.7	38	1.5	46	1.1	55	1.5	62	1.4	70	0.4	68	0.6	60	0.8	48	1.4	36	2.2	29	2.4
Springfield, Mo. (AP)	33	1.7	37	2.2	44	3.0	57	4.3	65	4.9	74	4.7	78	3.6	77	2.9	69	4.1	59	3.4	46	2.3	36	2.5
Syracuse, N. Y. (AP)	24	2.7	25	2.8	33	3.0	47	3.1	57	3.0	67	3.1	72	3.1	70	3.5	63	2.7	53	3.1	41	3.3	28	3.1
Tampa, Fla. (AP)	60	2.3	62	2.9	66	3.9	72	2.1	77	2.4	81	6.5	82	8.4	82	8.0	81	6.4	75	2.5	67	1.8	62	2.2
Trenton, N.J.	32	2.8	33	2.7	41	3.8	52	3.2	62	3.4	71	3.2	76	4.7	74	4.2	67	3.2	57	2.5	46	3.3	35	3.3
Vicksburg, Miss.	48	4.9	51	5.3	57	.5	66	5.4	73	4.2	79	3.3	82	3.6	81	3.0	76	2.8	67	2.3	56	4.1	50	5.5
Washington, D. C. (AP)	36	2.6	37	2.5	45	3.3	56	2.9	66	3.7	75	3.5	79	4.1	77	4.7	71	3.1	60	2.7	48	2.9	37	3.0
Wilmington, Del. (AP)	32	2.9	34	2.8	42	3.7	52	3.2	62	3.4	71	3.2	76	4.3	74	4.0	68	3.4	57	2.6	46	3.5	35	3.3

Annual Climatological Data

Source: National Oceanic & Atmospheric Administration, National Climatic Center

1973

Station	Elev. ft.	Temp. Highest	Date	Temp. Lowest	Date	Precip. Total (in.)	Greatest 24 hrs	Date	Sleet/snow Total (in.)	Greatest 24 hrs	Date	Wind Fastest MPH	Date	Clear*	Cloudy*	Prec. .01 in. or more	Snow, sleet 1 in. or more
Albany, N.Y.	275	97	7/8	-21	2/18	38.74	3.19	6/29-30	42.8	9.4	12/17	35	1/29	60	193	136	9
Albuquerque, N.M.	5311	102	7/7+	6	12/27	10.88	1.11	3/29-30	34.3	10.7	3/29-30	54	4/18	168	83	74	10
Anchorage, Alaska	114	73	6/21	-27	1/26+	10.68	1.26	8/20-21	50.4	7.3	11/21-22	32	2/19	60	230	95	16
Asheville, N.C.	2140	92	8/9	4	1/13	64.91	4.95	5/27-28	11.6	7.1	1/7-8	40	8/20	90	159	133	4
Atlanta, Ga.	1010	92	9/9+	16	2/17+	55.16	3.91	1/7-8	1.0	1.0	1/7	42	5/19	95	169	105	1
Baltimore, Md.	148	99	8/28	8	2/18	45.83	1.83	4/25-26	9.5	6.9	12/16-17	46	3/17	103	166	120	3
Barrow, Alaska	31	65	7/26	-43	1/30	7.17	0.59	8/1	40.9	3.4	10/11-12	55	12/31	50	201	119	16
Birmingham, Ala.	620	95	9/10	14	1/13	66.11	3.45	12/25-26	T	T	12/20+	58	5/11	81	173	129	0
Bismarck, N.D.	1647	109	7/11	-29	12/31+	11.04	1.49	9/2-3	21.6	4.7	12/13-14	45	12/8	102	157	75	8
Boise, Idaho	2838	103	7/10+	11	1/27	11.97	1.14	4/13-14	21.5	4.9	11/25-26	47	6/22	120	164	93	7
Boston, Mass.	15	99	8/30	1	1/8	42.75	2.76	12/16-17	6.4	1.7	1/4	49	9/6	86	176	125	3
Buffalo, N.Y.	705	90	9/4+	-5	2/17	36.84	1.64	11/15	63.1	5.4	3/17-18	38	12/6+	38	232	181	24
Burlington, Vt.	332	94	7/8	-21	2/18	46.28	1.88	12/20-21	65.3	12.8	12/17-18	38	10/14	49	226	154	15
Charleston, S.C.	40	97	6/17	12	2/12	72.17	10.10	6/10-11	7.1	5.9	2/9-10	58	5/29	106	143	114	2
Charleston, W.Va.	939	95	9/3+	2	2/17	49.32	2.35	11/27-28	18.5	4.0	12/20-21	37	12/5+	55	203	159	7
Chicago, Ill.	607	97	8/27+	-2	12/22	37.99	1.75	10/12-13	42.3	8.3	12/19	42	4/19	78	191	146	15
Cincinnati, Ohio	869	95	9/3	2	2/17	48.66	3.57	7/20-21	NA	NA	NA	29	4/9	NA	NA	NA	NA
Cleveland, Ohio	777	93	9/4+	-1	2/17	41.25	1.97	6/15-16	57.1	10.6	2/15-16	40	3/17	61	210	170	14
Columbus, Ohio	812	94	8/28	0	2/17	46.25	2.16	8/30	21.8	6.3	4/12	42	8/30	62	198	149	7
Concord, N.H.	342	96	6/11	-19	2/1	42.04	3.71	8/2	28.8	9.2	1/28-29	32	4/6+	75	183	116	8
Dallas, Texas	481	101	8/14	14	1/12	47.96	3.38	9/26-27	.....	..	...	44	10/10	125	140	97	...
Denver, Colo.	5283	103	7/6	-7	12/31+	22.96	3.55	5/5-6	98.4	11.8	12/23-24	49	12/12	121	129	112	22
Des Moines, Iowa	938	95	6/8	-10	1/9	45.18	3.07	9/27-28	44.6	10.4	4/8-9	49	6/16	93	186	129	13
Detroit, Mich.	619	96	8/28	1	2/17	NA	NA	NA	33.0	NA	NA	35	12/2+	NA	NA	NA	NA
Dodge City, Kansas	2582	106	8/25	-4	1/9	32.42	2.54	3/10	27.9	4.3	12/4	56	5/27	122	137	101	8
Duluth, Minn.	1428	91	7/6	-31	1/7	32.05	2.90	10/9-10	41.9	4.0	1/3	43	10/13	71	189	133	17
Fairbanks, Alaska	436	84	7/25	-51	1/16	9.12	0.76	8/10-11	55.1	7.7	11/10-11	23	8/20+	65	225	87	18
Fresno, Calif.	328	108	6/28+	24	1/7+	12.68	1.11	2/11	T	T	3/3	36	4/1	192	113	62	0
Galveston, Texas	7	90	8/22+	28	1/12	60.47	8.10	3/23-24	4.1	2.5	1/11	46	9/4	NA	NA	118	2
Grand Rapids, Mich.	784	95	8/26	-19	12/31	34.43	1.69	9/17	54.2	8.5	3/16-17	44	1/4+	52	226	140	19
Helena, Montana	3828	102	7/10	-24	1/10+	6.26	0.69	5/24-25	39.8	7.2	10/31	44	6/18	76	204	68	10
Honolulu, Hawaii	7	91	10/5+	55	1/1	14.24	1.84	11/28-29	0.0	0.0	...	33	3/9+	66	102	110	0
Houston, Texas	96	98	7/30	19	1/12	70.16	6.61	6/11-12	4.8	2.0	1/10-11	45	6/5	100	149	130	3
Huron, S.D.	1281	103	8/26	-23	12/31	17.38	1.25	10/9	33.7	6.4	10/20-21	46	7/1	92	157	83	8
Indianapolis, Ind.	792	93	7/3	-5	12/22	42.31	4.18	7/20-21	32.8	11.5	12/19-20	44	3/11	71	194	138	6
Jackson, Miss.	310	98	8/11	13	1/13	55.05	4.98	4/15-16	0.3	0.3	12/20	42	11/4	116	141	117	0
Jacksonville, Fla.	26	96	7/17+	25	12/22	70.57	8.25	4/3-4	T	T	...	48	4/25	88	131	122	0
Juneau, Alaska	12	73	8/20	-8	1/15	45.86	1.51	8/11-12	129.1	17.2	1/12-13	36	12/6+	40	291	232	33
Kansas City, Missouri	742	97	8/25	-8	12/31+	35.26	4.92	10/10-11	20.5	5.0	12/30-31	70	7/2	114	167	114	7
Lander, Wyo.	5563	98	7/11	-26	1/5	19.30	2.21	9/1-2	199.9	20.3	3/13-14	45	7/6+	108	146	89	39
Little Rock, Ark.	257	99	8/20	15	1/12	74.39	4.30	4/22-23	2.6	2.6	1/7	58	4/24	108	155	125	1
Los Angeles, Calif.	97	106	6/20	37	1/5	17.45	2.74	1/16	0.0	0.0	...	33	4/1	NA	NA	32	0
Louisville, Ky.	477	94	9/4+	8	2/17	53.97	5.37	7/21-22	8.8	1.8	12/14-15	45	12/26	82	187	143	3
Marquette, Mich.	677	98	8/27+	-3	1/10	31.66	2.39	5/1-2	68.9	7.8	12/4-5	37	4/15	56	221	156	23
Memphis, Tenn.	258	97	6/25+	15	1/12	64.18	2.84	4/19-20	1.6	1.4	1/7	40	3/10	112	156	115	1
Miami, Fla.	7	91	5/10	39	12/22	53.24	2.73	8/30-31	0.0	0.0	...	40	9/6	62	132	141	0
Milford, Utah	5028	102	7/5	-23	1/7	10.49	1.06	4/17-18	75.1	11.2	4/17-18	56	11/12	136	120	81	19
Milwaukee, Wisc.	672	99	8/27	-4	1/6+	33.75	3.04	4/20-21	47.3	11.6	4/9	56	6/16	78	197	142	17
Minneapolis, Minn.	834	98	6/10	-24	12/31	21.13	1.69	11/19-20	43.3	6.9	1/3	44	4/9	83	185	110	14
Mobile, Alabama	211	97	7/17+	22	1/13	70.82	3.82	4/25-26	3.6	3.6	2/9	35	1/21	99	167	131	1
Moline, Ill.	582	97	6/16	-15	2/17	56.36	5.81	4/20-21	21.8	4.6	2/14-15	57	6/18	87	185	136	8
Nashville, Tenn.	590	96	8/29	8	1/13	59.78	3.74	11/26-27	7.5	4.8	1/7-8	37	12/26	94	169	123	2
New Orleans, La.	4	96	7/17	21	1/13	79.28	5.20	3/23-24	0.7	0.6	2/9	55	5/24	110	151	136	0
New York, N.Y.	132	97	8/28	8	2/17	49.95	3.67	6/21-22	4.1	2.0	12/16-17	40	12/9	87	172	125	1
Nome, Alaska	13	77	6/23	-39	1/21	17.13	0.98	7/24-25	73.4	6.7	1/1-2	44	11/10+	94	208	139	16
Norfolk, Va.	24	95	7/9	12	1/9	45.50	2.28	7/10-11	15.2	9.1	1/8-9	46	7/10+	118	150	121	3
Okla. City, Okla.	1285	100	8/24	-1	1/12	41.77	3.30	9/26-27	9.1	5.3	1/6-7	48	5/27	129	131	103	3
Omaha, Nebraska	977	100	8/26	-13	1/6	38.34	4.62	9/25-26	37.5	5.6	1/3	50	5/9	113	172	119	12
Philadelphia, Pa.	5	99	8/26	8	2/17	46.06	4.62	6/29	4.6	3.8	12/16-17	37	3/17	103	159	122	1
Phoenix, Ariz.	1117	115	7/2+	31	1/21	6.01	1.27	7/11-12	0.0	0.0	...	69	7/12	231	66	35	0
Pittsburgh, Pa.	1137	92	9/1+	-7	2/17	39.74	2.34	5/23-24	21.1	4.5	3/17-18	35	11/1	63	210	158	7
Portland, Me.	43	93	9/3+	-12	1/9	52.29	5.26	4/1-2	26.2	7.9	1/28-29	38	12/9	85	187	140	7
Portland, Oregon	21	99	7/28	22	1/7	41.67	2.62	11/15-16	0.4	0.4	1/5	46	1/9	62	222	151	0
Providence, R.I.	51	95	6/11	2	2/18	48.24	4.23	8/15	6.2	2.0	1/4	33	3/27	78	191	117	2
Raleigh, N.C.	434	95	6/17	6	2/12	46.44	3.42	6/28-29	14.1	5.7	1/8	35	5/28	113	143	108	4
Rapid City, S.D.	3162	110	7/6	-18	12/31	15.12	2.10	3/13-14	40.6	14.9	3/13-14	56	3/14	104	141	84	10
Reno, Nevada	4404	100	7/26+	-4	1/5	9.21	0.91	12/30-31	36.6	7.2	2/10-11	48	5/30	142	118	69	13
Richmond, Va.	164	96	8/12	3	12/18	40.50	2.23	12/8-9	16.0	4.9	12/11	42	7/11	94	156	110	5
Rochester, N.Y.	547	95	9/4+	-2	2/17	29.23	1.57	11/15-16	60.8	7.5	12/16-17	56	6/6	50	216	152	21
St. Louis, Mo.	535	95	8/25+	-6	12/21	39.82	2.11	6/18-19	31.9	12.0	12/19	43	6/18	92	168	134	6
Salt Lake City, Utah	4220	104	7/10+	-13	1/4	20.39	1.51	9/1-2	85.3	8.2	3/13	42	11/12+	112	160	108	26
San Antonio, Tex.	788	97	8/23	17	12/21	52.28	7.28	8/26-27	2.9	2.1	2/8-9	47	3/28	107	141	107	1
San Diego, Calif.	13	93	9/27	38	1/5	7.47	0.71	3/11	0.0	0.0	...	33	2/11	116	136	49	0
San Francisco, Calif.	8	98	9/27	31	1/7	31.38	2.58	12/30-31	T	T	3/21	39	4/17	152	125	78	0
San Juan, P.R.	13	94	6/2+	68	12/14+	44.55	6.37	4/22-23	0.0	0.0	...	47	9/4	82	66	172	0
Sault Ste. Marie, Mich.	721	93	8/28	-16	2/16	36.45	1.70	5/1-2	77.5	8.1	11/8-9	38	10/15+	61	224	163	28
Savannah, Ga.	46	97	7/29	19	2/12	45.40	3.31	6/10-11	3.2	3.2	2/10	40	3/7	95	154	107	1
Seattle, Wash.	400	88	5/14	16	1/8	35.01	1.48	11/8-9	3.7	2.5	1/4	46	12/11	NA	NA	155	2
Sioux City, Iowa	1095	99	8/26	-16	12/31	27.89	2.53	7/9	23.1	4.7	1/21	52	6/18	93	176	99	7
Spokane, Wash.	2356	100	6/22	-7	1/7	17.11	1.12	9/19-20	44.0	9.0	1/1	45	11/12	103	171	106	9
Springfield, Mo.	1268	99	8/24	-5	1/12	59.40	4.49	11/24	18.3	5.1	1/7	39	12/4+	105	159	136	5
Syracuse, N.Y.	410	95	8/9	-11	2/17	52.65	2.20	6/12-13	80.3	13.4	12/17-18	45	10/14	50	220	169	23
Tampa, Fla.	19	95	5/30	30	12/18+	49.71	3.17	3/25	0.0	0.0	...	29	2/10	90	128	107	0
Trenton, N.J.	56	98	8/31+	6	2/17	47.62	3.13	10/28-29	4.8	3.6	12/16-17	48	11/1	99	168	114	2
Washington, D.C.	10	98	8/29	9	2/17	34.98	3.74	8/20-21	11.1	9.5	12/16-17	38	4/10+	92	164	108	2
Williston, N.D.	1899	100	8/16	-28	12/30	12.12	1.77	9/3-4	18.2	2.8	11/18-19	51	12/8	105	169	82	6
Wilmington, Del.	74	100	8/28	10	2/17	47.05	2.21	6/29	7.3	4.2	12/16-17	42	11/1	88	173	121	2

*To get partly cloudy days deduct the total of clear and cloudy days from 365 (1 yr.). T—trace. Date shown is the starting date of the storm (in some cases it lasted more than one day).

Normal Temperatures, Highs, Lows, Precipitation

Source: National Climatic Center, NOAA, Dept. of Commerce

These normals are based on records for the thirty-year period 1941-1970. (See explanation on page 250.) The extreme temperatures (thru 1971) are listed for the stations shown and may not agree with the state's records shown on page 248.

AP indicates airport station; those not so marked are city office stations. The minus (—) sign indicates temperatures below zero. Fahrenheit thermometer registration.

State	Station	Normal temperature January Max.	January Min.	July Max.	July Min.	Extreme temperature Highest	Lowest	Normal annual precipitation (inches)
Alabama	Mobile (AP)	61	41	91	73	102	8	66.98
Alabama	Montgomery (AP)	59	38	92	72	102	5	50.69
Alaska	Juneau (AP)	29	18	64	48	86	—22	54.67
Arizona	Phoenix (AP)	65	38	105	78	116	19	7.05
Arkansas	Little Rock (AP)	50	29	93	70	108	—4	48.52
California	Los Angeles	67	47	83	64	110	28	14.05
California	San Francisco (AP)	55	41	71	54	106	24	19.53
Colorado	Denver (AP)	44	16	87	59	103	—25	15.51
Connecticut	*New Haven (AP)	37	22	81	63	100	—8	46.02
Delaware	Wilmington (AP)	40	24	86	66	102	—4	40.25
Dist. of Col.	Washington (AP)	44	28	88	69	101	3	38.89
Florida	Jacksonville (AP)	65	45	90	72	105	12	54.47
Florida	Key West (AP)	74	65	87	79	95	46	39.99
Florida	Miami (AP)	76	59	89	76	96	34	59.80
Georgia	Atlanta (AP)	51	33	87	69	98	—3	48.34
Hawaii	Honolulu (AP)	79	65	87	73	91	53	22.90
Idaho	Boise (AP)	36	21	91	59	111	—23	11.50
Illinois	Chicago (AP)	32	17	84	65	101	—16	34.44
Indiana	Indianapolis (AP)	36	20	85	65	99	20	38.74
Iowa	Des Moines (AP)	28	11	85	65	100	—24	30.85
Iowa	Dubuque (AP)	27	11	84	62	97	—28	35.71
Kansas	Wichita (AP)	42	22	92	69	113	—12	28.41
Kentucky	Louisville (AP)	42	25	87	66	101	—20	43.11
Louisiana	New Orleans (AP)	62	44	90	73	100	14	56.77
Maine	Portland (AP)	31	12	79	57	100	—39	40.80
Maryland	Baltimore (AP)	42	25	87	66	102	—7	40.46
Massachusetts	Boston (AP)	36	23	81	65	99	—4	42.52
Michigan	Detroit, City (AP)	32	19	83	63	105	—16	30.96
Michigan	Sault Ste. Marie	22	6	75	53	98	—28	31.70
Minnesota	Minn.-St. Paul (AP)	21	3	82	61	99	—34	25.94
Mississippi	**Vicksburg	57	41	90	73	101	2	49.50
Missouri	St. Louis (AP)	40	23	88	69	106	—11	35.89
Montana	Helena (AP)	28	8	84	52	105	—38	11.38
Nebraska	Omaha (AP)	33	12	89	66	107	—17	30.18
Nevada	Winnemucca (AP)	40	15	92	50	106	—24	8.63
New Hampshire	Concord (AP)	31	10	83	57	102	—29	36.17
New Jersey	Atlantic City (AP)	43	27	84	66	106	—8	42.36
New Mexico	Albuquerque (AP)	47	24	92	65	104	—17	7.77
New Mexico	Roswell (AP)	55	21	95	62	110	—8	11.62
New York	Albany (AP)	30	13	84	60	98	—28	33.36
New York	New York	38	26	84	69	107	—2	41.61
No. Carolina	Charlotte (AP)	51	34	89	70	100	2	43.38
No. Carolina	Raleigh (AP)	51	30	88	67	98	0	42.54
No. Dakota	Bismarck (AP)	19	—3	84	57	108	—43	16.16
Ohio	Cincinnati	40	24	87	66	109	—17	40.03
Ohio	Cleveland (AP)	33	20	82	61	98	—19	34.99
Oklahoma	Oklahoma City (AP)	48	26	93	70	108	—1	31.37
Oregon	Portland	44	33	79	55	107	—3	37.61
Pennsylvania	Harrisburg (AP)	39	24	87	65	107	—8	37.65
Pennsylvania	Philadelphia (AP)	40	24	87	67	104	—5	39.93
Rhode Island	Block Island (AP)	38	26	76	63	91	—4	40.45
So. Carolina	Charleston (AP)	60	37	89	71	103	8	52.12
So. Dakota	Huron (AP)	23	2	87	61	112	—39	19.44
So. Dakota	Rapid City (AP)	34	10	86	59	110	—27	17.12
Tennessee	Nashville (AP)	48	29	90	69	103	—6	46.00
Texas	Amarillo (AP)	50	24	94	67	104	—9	19.67
Texas	Galveston	59	48	87	79	101	8	42.20
Texas	Houston (AP)	63	42	94	73	101	19	48.19
Utah	Salt Lake City (AP)	37	18	93	61	107	—18	15.17
Vermont	Burlington (AP)	26	8	81	59	98	—27	32.54
Virginia	Norfolk (AP)	49	32	87	70	103	8	44.68
Virginia	Roanoke (AP)	43	33	75	54	99	6	38.79
Washington	Seattle-Tacoma (AP)	31	20	84	55	108	—25	17.42
Washington	Spokane (AP)	41	24	86	65	106	—27	38.44
West Virginia	Parkersburg	26	9	82	60	98	—30	30.16
Wisconsin	Madison (AP)	26	11	80	59	99	—24	29.07
Wisconsin	Milwaukee (AP)	27	14	85	55	96	—27	15.06
Wyoming	Cheyenne (AP)	37	67	87	74	95	60	64.21
Puerto Rico	San Juan (AP)	81	67	87	74	95	60	64.21

*Closed June 14,1969.   **Closed December 1966.

Mean Annual Snowfall (inches) based on record thru 1972: Boston, Mass. 42.8; Sault Ste. Marie, Mich., 108.2; Albany, N.Y., 67.3; Rochester, N.Y., 86.3; Burlington, Vt., 79; Cheyenne, Wyo., 51.7; Juneau, Alaska, 106.3.

Wettest Spot: Mount Waialeale, Hawaii, on the island of Kauai, is the rainiest place in the world, according to the National Geographic Society, with an average annual rainfall of 460 inches.

Highest Temperature: A temperature of 136° F. observed at Azizia, Tripolitania in Northern Africa on Sept. 13, 1922 is generally accepted as the world's highest temperature recorded under standard conditions.

The record high in the United States was 134° in Death Valley, Calif., July 10, 1913.

Lowest Temperature: A record low temperature of -126.9°F (-88.3°C.) was recorded at the Soviet Antarctic station Vostok on Aug. 24, 1960.

The record low in the United States was —80° at Prospect Creek, Alaska, Jan. 23, 1971.

The lowest official temperature on the North American continent was recorded at 81 degrees below zero in February, 1947, at a lonely airport in the Yukon called Snag.

These are the meteorological champions—the official temperature extremes—but there are plenty of other claimants to thermometer fame. However, sun readings are unofficial records, since meteorological data to qualify officially must be taken on instruments in sheltered and ventilated location.

Low and High Temp. Records of National Weather Service Thru 1972

State	Lowest °F	Highest	Latest Date		Approximate Elevation
Alabama	27		Jan. 30,1966	New Market	725
		112	Sept. 5,1925	Centerville	345
Alaska	-79.8		Jan. 23, 1971	Prospect Creek Camp	1,100
		100	June 27, 1915	Fort Yukon	*419
Arizona	-40		Jan. 7,1971	Hawley Lake	8,180
		127	July 7,1905	Parker	345
Arkansas	-29		Feb. 13,1905	Pond	1,250
		120	Aug. 10,1936	Ozark	396
California	-45		Jan. 20,1937	Boca	5,532
		134	July 10, 1913	Greenland Ranch	-178
Colorado	-60		Feb. 1,1951	Taylor Park	9,206
		118	July 11, 1888	Bennett	5,484
Connecticut	-32		Jan. 22, 1961	Coventry	480
		105	July 22, 1926	Waterbury	409
Delaware	-17		Jan. 17, 1893	Millsboro	535
		110	July 21, 1930	Millsboro	20
Dist. of Col.	-15		Feb. 11, 1899	Washington	112
		106	July 20, 1930	Washington	112
Florida	-2		Feb. 13, 1899	Tallahassee	193
		109	June 29, 1931	Monticello	207
Georgia	-17		Jan. 27, 1940	CCC Camp F-16	1,000
		112	July 24,1952	Louisville	337
Hawaii	18		Feb. 20, 1962	Mauna Loa Slope Obs	11,146
		100	Apr. 27, 1931	Pahala	850
Idaho	-60		Jan. 18, 1943	Island Park Dam	6,285
		118	July 28, 1934	Orofino	1,027
Illinois	-35		Jan. 22, 1930	Mount Carroll	817
		117	July 14, 1954	E. St. Louis	410
Indiana	-35		Feb. 2, 1951	Greensburg	954
		116	July 14, 1936	Collegeville	672
Iowa	-47		Jan. 12, 1912	Washta	1,157
		118	July 20, 1934	Keokuk	614
Kansas	-40		Feb. 13,1905	Lebanon	1,812
		121	July 24, 1936	Alton (near)	1,651
Kentucky	-34		Jan. 24, 1963	Bonnieville (Closed Oct. 1966)	730
	-34		Jan. 28, 1963	Cynthiana	719
		114	July 28, 1930	Greensburg	581
Louisiana	-16		Feb. 13, 1899	Minden	194
		114	Aug. 10, 1936	Plain Dealing	268
Maine	-48		Jan. 19, 1925	Van Buren	510
		105	July 10, 1911	North Bridgton	450
Maryland	-40		Jan. 13,1912	Oakland	2,461
		109	July 10, 1936	Cumberland and Frederick	623-325
Massachusetts	-34		Jan. 18, 1957	Birch Hill Dam	840
		106	July 4, 1911	Lawrence	51
Michigan	-51		Feb. 9, 1934	Vanderbilt	785
		112	July 13, 1936	Mio	963
Minnesota	-59		Feb. 16, 1903	Pokegama Dam	1,280
		114	July 6, 1936	Moorhead	940
Mississippi	-19		Jan. 30, 1966	Corinth	420
		115	July 29, 1930	Holly Springs	600
Missouri	-40		Feb. 13, 1905	Warsaw	700
		118	July 14, 1954	Warsaw	687
Montana	-70		Jan. 20, 1954	Rogers Pass	5,470
		117	July 5, 1937	Medicine Lake	1,950
Nebraska	-47		Feb. 12, 1899	Camp Clarke	3,700
		118	July 24, 1936	Minden	2,169
Nevada	-50		Jan. 8,1937	San Jacinto	5,200
		122	June 23, 1954	Overton	1,240
New Hampshire	-46		Jan. 8, 1968	Mt. Washington	6,262
		106	July 4, 1'11	Nashua	125
New Jersey	-34		Jan. 5, 1904	River Vale	70
		110	July 10, 1936	Runyon	18
New Mexico	-50		Feb. 1, 1951	Gavilan	7,350
		116	July 14, 1934	Orogrande	4,171
New York	-52		Feb. 9, 1934	Stillwater Reservoir	1,670
		108	July 22, 1926	Troy	35
North Carolina	-29		Jan. 30, 1966	Mt. Mitchell	6,525
		109	Sept. 7,1954	Weldon	81
North Dakota	-60		Feb. 15, 1936	Parshall	1,929
		121	July 6, 1936	Steele	1,857
Ohio	-39		Feb. 10, 1899	Millian	800
		113	July 21, 1934	Gallipolis (near)	673
Oklahoma	-27		Jan. 18, 1930	Watts	958
		120	July 26, 1943	Tishmoningo	670
Oregon	-54		Feb. 10, 1933	Seneca	4,700
		119	Aug 10, 1898	Pendleton	1,074
Pennsylvania	-42		Jan. 5, 1904	Smethport	1,469
		111	July 10, 1936	Phoenixville	100
Rhode Island	-23		Jan. 11, 1942	Kingston	100
		102	July 30, 1949	Greenville	420
South Carolina	-13		Jan. 26, 1940	Longcreek (near)	1,631
		111	June 28, 1954	Camden	170
South Dakota	-58		Feb. 17, 1936	McIntosh	2,277
		120	July 5, 1936	Gannvalley	1,750
Tennessee	-32		Dec. 30, 1917	Mountain City	2,471
		113	Aug. 9, 1930	Perryville	377

State	Lowest	°F Highest	Latest Dates	Station	Approximate Elevation
Texas	—23		Feb. 8, 1933	Seminole	3,275
		120	Aug. 12, 1936	Seymour	1,291
Utah	—50		Jan. 5, 1913	Strawberry Tunnel	7,650
		116	June 28, 1892	Saint George	2,880
Vermont	—50		Dec. 30, 1933	Bloomfield	915
		105	July 4, 1911	Vernon	310
Virginia	—29		Feb. 10, 1899	Monterey	3,008
		110	July 15, 1954	Balcony Falls	725
Washington	—48		Dec. 30, 1968	Mazama	2,120
	—48		Dec. 30, 1968	Winthrop	1,755
		118	Aug. 5, 1961	Ice Harbor Dam	475
West Virginia	—37		Dec. 30, 1917	Lewisburg	2,200
		112	July 10, 1936	Martinsburg	435
Wisconsin	—54		Jan. 24, 1922	Danbury	908
		114	July 13, 1936	Wisconsin Dells	900
Wyoming	—63		Feb. 9, 1933	Moran	6,770
		114	July 12, 1900	Basin	3,500

Low and High Temp. Records Thru 1967

Source: Atmospheric Environment Service, Dept. of Environment

Province	Lowest	°F Highest	Latest Dates	Station	Approximate Elevation
Alberta	—78		Jan. 11, 1911	Fort Vermilion	915
		108	July 12, 1886	Medicine Hat	2,365
British Columbia	—74		Jan. 31, 1947	Smith River	2,208
		112	July 17, 1941	Chinook Cove	1324
		112	July 17, 1941	Lillooet	950
		112	July 17, 1941	Lytton	600
Manitoba	—63		Jan. 9, 1899	Norway House	720
		112	July 12, 1936	Emerson	792
		112	July 11, 1936	St. Albans	1,180
Newfoundland	—56		Mar. 7, 1968	Twin Falls	1,499
		107	Aug. 11, 1914	Northwest River	200
New Brunswick	—53		Feb. 1, 1955	Sisson Dam	915
		103	Aug. 18, 1935	Nespisquit Falls	350
		103	Aug. 18, 1935	Woodstock	150
		103	Aug. 19, 1935	Rexton	20
Nova Scotia	—42		Jan. 31, 1920	Upper Stewiacke	75
		101	Aug. 19, 1935	Collegeville	250
Ontario	—73		Jan. 23, 1935	Iroquios Falls	800
		108	Jan. 20, 1919	Biscotasing	1,300
		108	July 11, 1936	Atikokan	1,289
		108	July 13, 1936	Fort Frances	1,160
Prince Edward Island	—35		Jan. 26, 1884	Kilmahumaig	20
		98	Aug. 19, 1935	Charlottetown	74
Quebec	—66		Feb. 5, 1923	Doucet	1,236
		104	July 6, 1921	Barrage Temiscaminigue	595
		104	Aug. 15, 1928	Bark Lake	1,195
Saskatchewan	—70		Feb. 1, 1893	Prince Albert	1,432
		113	July 5, 1937	Midale	1,908
		113	July 5, 1937	Yellow Grass	1,899
North West Territories	—71		Dec. 26, 1917	Fort Smith	665
		103	July 18, 1941	Fort Smith	680
Yukon Territory	—81		Feb. 3, 1947	Snag	1,925
		95	June 18, 1950	Mayo	1,625

Normal Temperatures, Highs, Lows, Precipitation

Source: Atmospheric Environment Service, Dept. of Environment

These normals are based on varying periods of record over the thirty-year period 1941 to 1970 inclusive. Extreme temperatures are based on varying periods of record for each station thru 1970. AP indicates airport station; those not so marked are city office stations. The minus (—) sign indicates temperatures below zero. Fahrenheit thermometer registration.

Province	Station	Normal January Max.	Normal January Min.	Normal July Max.	Normal July Min.	Extreme Highest	Extreme Lowest	Precipitation Normal Annual (inches)
Alberta	Calgary (AP)	23	2	74	49	97	—49	17.21
Alberta	Edmonton (Industrial AP)	14	3	74	53	94	—55	17.58
British Columbia	Prince George (AP)	19	2	72	46	94	—58	24.43
British Columbia	Victoria (AP)	43	32	71	52	97	4	33.72
British Columbia	Vancouver (AP)	41	31	72	55	92	0	42.05
Manitoba	Churchill (AP)	—11	—25	63	45	91	—49	15.61
Manitoba	Winnipeg (AP)	8	—10	79	56	105	—49	21.06
Newfoundland	Gander (AP)	28	14	71	52	96	—17	42.45
Newfoundland	St. John's (AP)	31	19	68	51	87	—10	59.50
New Brunswick	Fredericton (AP)	25	7	78	55	98	—35	41.74
New Brunswick	Moncton (AP)	26	9	76	55	99	—26	43.27
New Brunswick	Saint John (AP)	28	9	72	53	91	—34	55.13
Nova Scotia	Halifax (AP)	29	14	74	55	93	—14	54.94
Nova Scotia	Sidney (AP)	31	17	74	55	95	—13	52.78
Ontario	Ottawa (AP)	21	4	80	59	100	—33	33.50
Ontario	Sudbury (AP)	17	—1	77	55	97	—36	32.87
Ontario	Toronto (AP)	28	13	81	58	101	—24	29.61
Ontario	Windsor (AP)	31	18	82	62	101	—15	32.91
Prince Edward Island	Charlottetown (AP)	27	13	75	58	98	—23	41.69
Quebec	Montreal (AP)	22	6	79	61	96	—36	37.05
Quebec	Quebec City (AP)	19	3	77	56	96	—33	42.85
Quebec	Val-d'Or (AP)	12	— 9	74	52	94	—47	35.52
Saskatchewan	Prince Albert (AP)	5	—17	77	51	100	—58	15.31
Saskatchewan	Regina (AP)	10	— 9	79	53	110	—58	15.66
North West Territories	Alert	—19	—33	44	34	68	—57	6.15
North West Territories	Yellowknife (AP)	—12	—27	69	53	90	—60	9.84
Yukon Territory	Dawson	—13	—26	72	48	95	—73	12.81
Yukon Territory	Whitehorse	6	— 9	68	47	94	—62	10.24

Canadian Monthly Normal Temperature and Precipitation

Source: Atmospheric Environment Service, Dept. of Environment

Normal refers to the mean daily temperature and total monthly precipitation based on varying periods of record over the thirty-year period 1941 to 1970 inclusive. In most cases no adjustment factor was used.

AP indicates airport station; those not so marked are city office stations

T, Temperature in Fahrenheit; P, Precipitation in inches; L, less than .05 inch.

Stations	Jan. T.	Jan. P.	Feb. T.	Feb. P.	Mar. T.	Mar. P.	Apr. T.	Apr. P.	May T.	May P.	June T.	June P.	July T.	July P.	Aug. T.	Aug. P.	Sept. T.	Sept. P.	Oct. T.	Oct. P.	Nov. T.	Nov. P.	Dec. T.	Dec. P.
Calgary, Alta. (AP)	12	0.7	19	0.8	24	0.8	38	1.2	49	2.0	56	3.6	62	2.7	59	2.2	51	1.4	42	0.7	27	0.6	18	0.6
Charlottetown, P.E.I. (AP)	20	3.8	20	3.2	27	3.0	37	2.9	49	3.1	58	3.1	66	2.9	65	3.5	58	3.6	48	3.9	39	4.5	26	3.9
Churchill, Man. (AP)	-17	0.6	-16	0.5	- 5	0.7	12	0.9	28	1.1	43	1.6	54	1.9	53	2.3	42	2.0	30	1.6	10	1.6	- 7	0.8
Dawson, Yukon	-20	0.8	- 9	0.6	7	0.5	29	0.4	46	0.9	57	1.5	60	2.1	55	2.0	44	1.1	26	1.1	2	1.0	-14	1.0
Edmonton, Alta. (Indus. AP)	6	1.0	13	0.8	22	0.7	39	0.9	52	1.4	58	2.9	63	3.2	61	2.8	52	1.4	42	0.7	24	0.7	13	0.8
Fredericton, N.B.(AP)	16	3.7	17	3.6	28	2.7	39	2.9	51	3.2	61	3.1	67	3.4	64	3.4	56	3.2	46	3.4	35	4.3	21	4.4
Frobisher Bay, N.W.T. (AP)	-15	0.9	-13	1.1	-8	0.8	7	0.8	26	0.9	38	1.4	46	2.0	44	2.2	36	1.7	23	1.6	9	1.4	- 5	1.0
Halifax, N.S.(AP)	21	5.3	20	5.0	28	4.0	37	4.2	49	3.8	58	3.1	64	3.1	64	4.2	57	3.7	48	4.6	39	6.4	27	7.0
Hamilton, Ont.	25	2.2	26	2.3	33	2.7	45	2.7	56	3.0	67	2.3	72	2.9	71	2.9	62	2.4	52	2.5	40	2.3	29	2.3
Kitchener, Ont.	20	2.3	21	2.1	30	2.8	44	2.7	54	3.2	65	3.3	69	3.5	68	3.0	60	2.8	49	2.8	37	3.0	25	2.9
London, Ont. (AP)	21	3.0	22	2.5	31	2.8	44	3.0	54	2.9	65	3.1	69	3.2	67	2.8	60	3.1	50	2.9	38	3.2	26	3.4
Moncton, N.B. (AP)	18	4.2	18	3.9	27	3.6	38	3.3	49	3.1	59	3.5	65	3.1	64	3.1	56	2.8	46	3.5	36	4.4	22	4.2
Montreal, Que. (AP)	14	2.9	16	2.7	28	2.7	43	2.9	55	2.6	65	3.2	70	3.3	68	3.4	59	3.1	49	2.9	36	3.4	20	3.4
Ottawa, Ont. (AP)	12	2.3	15	2.2	26	2.4	42	2.6	54	2.7	65	2.8	69	3.2	67	3.2	58	3.1	48	2.6	34	3.0	18	3.0
Quebec City, Que. (AP)	11	3.3	13	3.0	24	2.7	38	2.9	51	3.1	61	4.0	67	4.2	64	4.0	56	4.1	45	3.2	32	3.9	17	3.9
Regina, Sask. (AP)	1	0.7	6	0.6	17	0.7	38	0.9	51	1.6	59	3.2	66	2.2	64	1.9	53	1.4	41	0.7	23	0.7	9	0.6
Saint John, N.B. (AP)	19	5.7	18	5.1	27	4.1	37	4.4	48	4.0	56	3.7	62	3.5	61	3.8	54	4.0	46	4.3	37	6.0	24	6.1
St. John's, Nfld. (AP)	25	5.7	24	6.1	28	5.2	34	4.4	42	3.9	51	3.4	59	3.2	60	4.5	54	4.4	45	5.4	38	6.3	30	6.6
Saskatoon, Sask. (AP)	- 2	0.7	5	0.7	16	0.6	38	0.8	51	1.3	60	2.2	66	2.0	63	1.7	52	1.3	41	0.7	22	0.7	7	0.7
Sault Ste. Marie, Ont. (AP)	13	3.2	11	2.1	23	2.2	38	2.2	48	3.3	58	3.4	64	2.8	62	2.6	56	3.7	47	3.1	34	4.1	20	3.7
Toronto, Ont. (AP)	21	2.1	22	1.9	30	2.3	43	2.5	54	2.8	65	2.4	69	2.9	68	2.8	60	2.4	50	2.3	38	2.4	26	2.2
Vancouver, B.C. (AP)	36	5.8	40	4.5	42	3.6	48	2.4	54	1.8	59	1.7	63	1.1	63	1.4	58	2.4	50	4.8	43	5.5	39	6.5
Victoria, B.C. (AP)	37	5.7	40	3.8	42	2.7	47	1.7	53	1.2	58	1.1	61	0.7	61	0.9	57	1.4	50	3.4	43	5.0	40	5.7
Whitehorse, Yukon (AP)	- 2	0.7	8	0.5	18	0.5	32	0.4	45	0.5	54	1.1	57	1.3	54	1.4	46	1.1	33	0.7	16	0.8	4	0.7
Windsor, Ont. (AP)	24	2.1	26	2.0	34	2.6	47	3.2	57	3.2	68	3.2	72	3.2	70	3.2	63	2.3	53	2.4	40	2.4	28	2.5
Winnipeg, Man. (AP)	- 1	0.9	4	0.7	17	1.0	38	1.4	51	2.2	62	3.1	67	3.1	66	2.9	55	2.0	44	1.3	24	1.0	7	0.9
Yellowknife, N.W.T. (AP)	-19	0.5	-14	0.4	- 1	0.4	18	0.4	39	0.5	54	0.6	61	1.3	57	1.4	44	1.1	30	1.2	6	0.9	-11	0.7

Annual Climatological Data

Source: Atmospheric Environment Service, Dept. of Environment

Station 1973	Elev. ft.	Temperature Highest	Temperature Date D./Mo.	Temperature Lowest	Temperature Date D./Mo.	Precipitation Total (in.)	Precipitation Greatest in 24 hrs.	Precipitation Date D./Mo.	Snow or Sleet (in.)	Snow or Sleet Greatest in 24 hrs.	Snow or Sleet Date D./Mo.	Wind Fastest MPH	Wind Fastest Date D./Mo.	No. of days Prec. .01 in. or more	No. of days Snow, sleet 1 in. or more
Calgary, Alta.	3540	91	10/7	-25	7/1	14.16	0.98	7/8	49.5	4.9	4/2	50	27/7	113	66
Charlottetown, P.E.I.	186	86	9/7	-12	27/2	44.75	1.63	12/7	103.8	11.2	11/2	40	11/2	187	57
Churchill, Man.	115	90	22/7	-39	13/2	16.36	1.30	16/7	60.5	8.9	22/11	48	22/11	108	67
Dawson, Yukon	1062	84	24/7	-62	16/1	12.54	0.62	3/7	60.2	4.4	10/4	25	14/3	137	80
Edmonton, Alta.	2358	89	22/6	-18	7/1	21.91	1.78	24/6	59.0	8.0	13/4	40	2/1	132	69
Fredericton, N.B.	74	90	24/7	-23	10/1	47.71	1.93	28/4	90.6	14.2	29/1	32	22/12	174	49
Frobisher Bay, N.W.T.	68	71	5/8	-50	15/2	16.91	0.94	7/4	101.9	9.7	8/3	37	9/1	149	115
Halifax, N.S.	461	89	9/7	-7	31/1	51.68	2.12	29/4	51.2	15.4	11/2	44	17/6	171	30
Hamilton, Ont.	808	98	28/8	-8	17/2	38.31	2.32	29/10	45.8	7.0	20/12	32	15/3	140	28
Waterloo-Wellington (Kitchener) Ont.	1125	94	28/8	-13	17/2	33.33	1.54	15/11	54.1	8.0	20/12	38	15/3	158	52
London, Ont.	912	93	3/9	-11	17/2	36.98	1.66	15/11	66.5	9.3	17/3	42	17/3	166	59
Moncton, N.B.	248	87	9/7	-18	1/2	47.32	2.26	5/7	86.6	8.2	11/2	35	20/1	174	53
Montreal, Que.	98	90	8/7	-23	31/1	40.64	1.80	27/8	76.3	8.3	20/12	41	14/10	153	52
Ottawa, Ont.	413	94	8/7	-20	31/1	40.96	1.72	8/8	77.1	9.9	20/12	43	17/3	151	53
Quebec City, Que.	245	91	24/7	-22	31/1	62.10	2.24	5/10	128.1	13.1	14/12	31	18/3	191	72
Regina, Sask.	1884	94	1/8	-38	31/12	16.03	1.26	3/6	47.2	4.8	27/3	49	3/6	102	55
Saint John, N.B.	352	90	9/7	-15	1/2	65.37	3.09	28/4	55.2	6.6	29/1	52	3/2	173	42
St. John's, Nfld.	463	82	19/7	1	18/1	53.83	2.64	22/2	89.2	10.4	11/2	50	28/10	206	75
Saskatoon, Sask.	1645	95	13/8	-37	30/12	15.93	1.32	3/6	48.4	4.4	23/12	44	27/4	114	59
Sault Ste. Marie, Ont.	620	92	28/8	-23	6/1	34.04	1.26	2/7	71.4	5.1	29/12	45	15/10	167	66
Thunder Bay, Ont.	644	89	7/7	-30	8/1	34.33	3.43	19/8	38.0	4.6	3/1	30	2/5	121	50
Toronto, Ont.	578	97	28/8	-5	17/2	34.94	1.73	28/8	44.2	8.0	19/12	40	9/4	142	32
Vancouver, B.C.	16	84	5/9	13	9/1	39.32	2.12	15/12	11.6	2.3	2/1	35	18/1	159	11
Victoria, B.C.	67	82	14/5	21	7/1	18.20	1.22	12/10	9.4	5.7	4/1	50	12/12	137	6
Whitehorse, Yukon	2289	77	23/7	-42	17/1	8.46	0.43	23/8	45.5	2.3	23/11	28	20/2	113	72
Windsor, Ont.	637	96	28/8	-4	17/2	37.05	1.56	28/6	43.3	6.8	19/12	51	9/8	124	37
Winnipeg, Man.	786	91	18/8	-38	7/1	23.69	1.80	7/7	30.0	4.7	19/11	45	18/8	111	45
Yellowknife, N.W.T.	682	84	25/6	-44	14/2	12.96	3.26	15/8	64.9	5.8	16/11	40	18/8	112	83

Explanation of Normal Temperatures

Normal temperatures listed in the tables on pages 245 and 247 are based on records of the National Weather Service for the 30-year period from 1941/1970 inclusive.

To obtain the average maximum temperature for any month, the daily maximum temperatures are added; the total is then divided by the number of days in that month. The average minimum temperature for the month is obtained by adding the daily minimum temperatures during that month and dividing by the number of days in that month.

The normal maximum temperature for January, for example, is obtained by adding the average maximums for January, 1941, January, 1942, etc., through January, 1970. The total is then divided by 30. The normal minimum temperature is obtained in a similar manner by adding the average minimums for each January in the 30-year period and dividing by 30. The normal temperature for Januray is one-half of the sum for the normal maximum and minimum temperatures for that month.

The mean temperature for any one day is one-half the total of the maximum and minimum temperatures for that day.

Speed of Winds in Canada

Source: Atmospheric Environment Service, Dept. of Environment

Miles per hour-average in most cases is for the period of record 1955 to 1966. High is based on varying periods of record dependent on the origin of the station thru 1966.

Stations	Avg.	High	Stations	Avg.	High	Stations	Avg.	High
Calgary, Alta.	10.5	65	London, Ont.	10.5	63	Sault Ste. Marie, Ont.	10.0	55
Charlottetown, P.E.I.	12.0	64	Moncton, N.B.	12.5	62	Toronto, Ont.	9.9	67
Churchill, Man.	15.1	78	Montreal, Que.	10.1	50	Vancouver, B.C.	7.6	55
Dawson, Yukon.	4.0	32	Ottawa, Ont.	9.4	54	Victoria, B.C.	7.5	51
Edmonton, Ata.	8.8	54	Quebec City, Que.	11.4	68	Whitehorse, Yukon	9.6	50
Fredericton, N.B.	8.8	43	Regina, Sask.	13.8	60	Windsor, Ont.	10.8	57
Frobisher Bay, N.W.T.	11.3	80	Saint John, N.B.	11.5	60	Winnipeg, Man.	12.4	56
Halifax, N.S.	11.1	53	St. John's, Nfld.	15.4	85	Yellowknife, N.W.T.	10.2	45
Hamilton, Ont.	7.9	41	Saskatoon, Sask.	11.3	65			

Speed of Winds in the United States

Miles per hour — average thru 1973. High thru 1973. Wind velocities in true values.
Source: National Climatic Center, NOAA. Dept. of Commerce

Stations	Avg.	High	Stations	Avg.	High	Stations	Avg.	High
Albany, N.Y.	8.8	71	Helena, Mont.	7.9	73	Pensacola, Fla.	8.2	(b)59
Albuquerque, N.M.	8.9	90	Jacksonville, Fla	8.7	82	Philadelphia, Pa.	9.6	73
Atlanta, Ga.	9.1	70	Key West, Fla.	11.3	122	Pittsburgh, Pa.	9.4	58
Bismarck, N.D.	10.7	72	Knoxville, Tenn.	7.3	73	Portland, Ore.	7.7	88
Boston, Mass.	12.7	65	Little Rock, Ark.	8.2	65	Rochester, N.Y.	9.6	73
Buffalo, N.Y.	12.3	91	Louisville, Ky.	8.4	61	St. Louis, Mo.	9.5	(b)91
Cape Hatteras, N.C.	11.8	(b)110	Memphis, Tenn.	9.2	57	Salt Lake City, Utah.	8.7	71
Chattanooga, Tenn.	6.3	82	Miami, Fla.	9.0	(a)74	San Diego, Calif.	6.7	51
Chicago, Ill.	10.4	60	Minneapolis, Minn.	10.6	92	San Francisco, Calif.	10.5	58
Cincinnati, Ohio	7.1	49	Mobile, Ala.	9.4	(b)63	Savannah, Ga.	8.3	66
Cleveland, Ohio	10.8	74	Montgomery, Ala.	6.8	60	Spokane, Wash.	8.6	59
Denver, Colo.	9.0	56	Nashville, Tenn.	7.9	73	Toledo, Ohio	9.5	72
Detroit, Mich.	10.2	46	New Orleans, La.	8.4	(b)98	Washington, D.C.	9.3	78
Fort Smith, Ark.	7.7	58	New York, N.Y.(c)	9.5	70	Mt. Wash'ton, N.H.	35.2	231
Galveston, Texas	11.0	(d)100	Omaha, Nebr.	10.9	109			

(a) Highest velocity ever recorded in Miami area was 132 mph. at former station in Miami Beach in September, 1926. (b) Previous location. (c) Data for Central Park. Battery Place data through 1960, avg. 14.5, high 113. (d) Recorded before anemometer blew away. Estimated high 120.

Winds, Their Force and Official Designations

Designation	MPH	Designation	MPH	Designation	MPH	Designation	MPH
Calm.	Less than 1	Moderate breeze.	13 to 18	Near gale	32 to 38	Storm.	55 to 63
Light air	1 to 3	Fresh breeze.	19 to 24	Gale	39 to 46	Violent storm.	64 to 73
Light breeze.	4 to 7	Strong breeze.	25 to 31	Strong gale.	47 to 54	Hurricane.	74 and above
Gentle breeze	8 to 12						

Temperature-Humidity Index

The purpose of the temperature-humidity index (THI) is to measure or estimate human discomfort in the summer-time resulting from the combined effects of temperature and humidity. The THI is calculated by adding wet bulb and dry bulb temperature readings, multiplying the sum by 0.4 and adding 15.

At a THI value of 75, a majority of people will be uncomfortable; at an index of 80 or above, almost everyone will be very uncomfortable and many will be miserable. The following table, based on this calculation, lists those combinations of temperature and humidity which correspond to the **(A)** borderline of discomfort and **(B)** borderline of extreme discomfort. For example, a temperature of 85 degrees and a humidity of 33% or more will be uncomfortable for a majority of people; when the humidity at that temperature reaches or exceeds 71%, practically everyone will be acutely uncomfortable. The higher the temperature or humidity values, the greater will be the general discomfort.

Temp. Degrees F.	Relative Humidity in % A	B	Temp. Degrees F.	Relative Humidity in % A	B	Temp. Degrees F.	Relative Humidity in % A	B
75	100		86	29	65	96	Uncomfortable at	20
76	91		87	25	59		any humidity	
77	82		88	20	54	97		16
78	75		89	17	49	98		13
79	68		90	14	43	99		11
80	61		91	10	38	100		8
81	55	100	92	7	34	101		6
82	49	93	93	5	30	102		3
83	43	86	94	3	26	103		1
84	38	78	95	1	23	104	Extremely uncomfortable	
85	33	71					at any humidity	

The Meaning of "One Inch of Rain"

An acre of ground contains 43,560 square feet. Consequently, a rainfall of 1 inch over 1 acre of ground would mean a total of 6,272,640 cubic inches of water. This is equivalent to 3,630 cubic feet.

As a cubic foot of pure water weighs about 62.4 pounds, the exact amount varying with the density, it follows that the weight of a uniform coating of 1 inch of rain over 1 acre of surface would be 226,512 pounds, or 113¼ short tons.

The weight of 1 U.S. gallon of pure water is about 8.345 pounds. Consequently a rainfall of 1 inch over 1 acre of ground would mean 27,154 gallons of water.

United States—Associations and Societies

Source: World Almanac Questionnaire
Arranged according to key words in titles. Last figure indicates membership.

—A—

Aaron Burr Association (1946), Tremont, Inca Rd., Linden, VA 22642; 600.

Abortion, Assn. for the Study of (1964), 120 W. 57th St., N.Y., NY 10021; 23,000.

Accountants, Amer. Institute of Certified Public (1887), 666 5th Ave., N.Y., NY; 100,000.

Accountants, Natl. Assn. of (1919), 919 Third Ave., N.Y., NY10022; 67,000.

Accountants, Natl. Society of Public (1945), 1717 Pennsylvania Ave., NW, Washington, DC 20006; 15,000.

Acoustical Society of America (1929), 335 E. 45 St., New York, NY 10017; 5,000.

Actors' Equity Assn. (1913), 165 W. 46 St., New York, NY 10036; 19,000.

Actors' Fund of America (1882), 1501 Broadway, New York, NY 10036; 2,818.

Actuaries, Society of (1949), 208 S. LaSalle St., Chicago, IL 60604; 4,300.

Adirondack Mountain Club (1922), 172 Ridge St., Glens Falls, NY 12801; 9,000.

Administrative Management Society (1919), Maryland Rd., Willow Grove, PA 19090; 15,500.

Adult Education Assn. of the U.S.A. (1951), Office of Education, 810 18th St., Wash., DC 20006; 6,000.

Advertisers, Assn. of National (1910), 155 East 44th St., New York, NY10017; 412 companies.

Advertising Agencies, American Assn. of (1917), 200 Park Ave., N.Y., NY 10017; 390 agencies.

Aeronautic Assn., Natl. (1922), 806 15th St., NW, Washington, DC 20005; 100,000.

Aeronautics and Astronautics, Amer. Institute of (1963), 1290 Ave. of the Americas, N.Y., NY 10019; 22,217.

Aerospace Industries Assn. of America (1919), 1725 De-Sales St., NW, Wash., DC 20036; 49 companies.

Aerospace Medical Association (1929), Washington National Airport, Wash., DC 20001; 4,552.

Aesthetic Realism, Society for (1946), 39 Grove St., N.Y., NY 10014; 150.

African Violet Society of America (1946), 706 Hamilton Bank Blvd., Knoxville, TN 37901; 14,000.

Afro-American Life and History, Assn. for the Study of (formerly, **Assn. for the Study of Negro Life & History**) (1915), 1407 14th St., Wash., DC 20005; 20,000.

Aging Assn., American (1970), Univ. of Nebr. Medical Cntr., 42nd & Dewey Ave., Omaha, NE 68105; 500.

Agricultural Chemicals Assn., Natl. (1933), 1155 15th St., NW, Washington, DC 20005; 105 companies.

Agricultural Economics Assn. American (1919), Univ. of Kentucky, Lexington, KY 40506; 5,000.

Agricultural Engineers, American Society of (1907), 2950 Niles Rd., St. Joseph, MI 49085; 6,800.

Agricultural History Society (1919), U. S. Dept. of Agriculture, Rm. 144, 500 12th St., SW, Wash., DC 20250; 800.

Agronomy, American Society of (1907), 677 S. Segoe Rd., Madison, WI 53711; 8,000.

Ahepa, Order of (1922), 1422 K St., NW, Washington, DC 20005; 27,500.

Air, Citizens for Clean (1965), 572 Madison Ave., N.Y., NY 10022; 3,000.

Air Force Aid Society (1942), 1117 N. 19th St., Arlington, VA 22209; 23,700.

Air Force Association (1946), 1750 Pennsylvania Ave., NW, Washington, DC 20006; 110,000.

Air Force Sergeants Association (1961), 4235 28th Ave., Marlow Heights, MD 20031; 28,411.

Air Line Employees Assn. (1951), 5600 S. Central Ave., Chicago, IL 60638; 9,500.

Air Line Pilots Assn. (1931), 1625 Massachusetts Ave., Washington, DC 20036; 30,000 pilots.

Air Pollution Control Assn. (1907), 4400 Fifth Ave., Pittsburgh, PA 15213; 6,500.

Air Transport Assn. of America (1936), 1709 New York Ave., NW, Wash. DC 20026; 24 airlines.

Air Transport Assn. Internatl. (1945), 1155 Mansfield St., Montreal 113, Canada; 108 airlines.

Aircraft Owners and Pilots Assn. (1939), 7315 Wisconsin Ave., Bethesda, MD 20014; 181,000.

Alcohol Problems, Amer. Council on (1895), 119 Constitution Ave., NE., Washington, DC 20002.

Alcoholics Anonymous Box 459, N.Y., NY 10017; 650,000.

Alcoholism, Natl. Council on (1944), 2 Park Ave., New York, NY 10016; 160 affiliates.

Allergy, American Academy of (1943), 225 East Michigan St., Milwaukee, WI 53202; 2,300.

Allied Youth (1936), Rosslyn Building, 1901 Ft. Myer Drive, Arlington, VA 22209; 10,000.

Alpine Club, American (1902), 113 East 90th St., New York, NY 10028; 1,200.

Altrusa International (1917), 332 S. Michigan Ave., Chicago, IL 60604; 17,950.

Aluminum Assn. (1935), 750 Third Ave., New York, NY 10017; 70 companies.

Alumni Council, American (1913), One Dupont Circle, Washington DC 20036; 1,600 schools.

American Federation of Labor and Congress of Industrial Organizations (AFL-CIO) (Dec. 5, 1955, by merging **American Federation of Labor** estab. 1881 and **Congress of Industrial Organizations** estab. 1935), 815 16th St., NW, Washington, DC 20006; 13,500,000.

American Field Service (1947), 313 E. 43rd St., New York, NY 10017; 77,000. –

American Indian Affairs, Assn. on (1923), 432 Park Ave., South, N. Y., NY 10016; 75,000.

American Legion, The (1919), 700 N. Pennsylvania St., Indianapolis, IN 46204; 2,700,000.

American Legion Auxiliary (1919), 777 N. Meridian St., Indianapolis, IN 46204; 943,000.

American Veterans of World War II, Korea & Vietnam (AMVETS) (1947), 1710 Rhode Island Ave., NW, Wash., DC 20036; 250,000. **AMVETS Natl. Auxiliary** (1946); Saco Rd., Old Orchard Beach, ME 04064; 26,000.

Americans for Freedom (1960), 1221 Massachusetts Ave., Wash., DC 20005; 70,000.

Amputation Foundation, National, (1919), 12-45 150th St., Whitestone, NY 11357; 2,000.

Animal Protection Institute (1968), 5894 S. Land Park Dr., Sacramento, CA 95822; 66,000.

Animal Welfare Institute (1951), P. O. Box 3650, Washington, DC 20007; 3,511.

Animals, Amer. Society for Prevention of Cruelty to (ASPCA) (1866), 441 E. 92nd St., N.Y., NY 10028; 2,000.

Animals, Friends of (1957), 11 W. 60th St., N.Y., NY 10023; 50,000.

Animals, The Fund for (1967), 140 West 57th St., N.Y., NY 10019; 53,109.

Anthropological Assn., American (1904), 1703 New Hampshire Ave., N.W., Washington, DC 20009; 9,150.

Anti-Vivisection Society, American (1883), 1903 Chestnut St., Philadelphia, PA 19103; 12,000.

Antiquarian Society, American (1812), 185 Salisbury St., Worcester, MA 01609; 256.

Antique Automobile Club of America (1935), 501 West Governor Rd., Hersey, PA 17033; 35,000.

Appalachian Mountain Club (1876), 5 Joy St., Boston, MA 02108; 19,000.

Appalachian Trail Conference (1925), Box 236, Harpers Ferry, WV 25425; 50,000.

Appraisers, Society of (1952), Dulles Airport, P.O. Box 17265, Washington, DC 20041; 4,161.

Arbitration Association, American (1926), 140 W. 51st St., New York, NY 10020; 4,000.

Archaeological Institute of America (1879), 260 W. Broadway , N.Y., NY 10013; 6,500.

Archers Assn., Professional (1961), P. O. Box 7609, Flint, MI 48507; 350.

Archery Assn., Natl. (1879), 1951 Geraldson Dr., Lancaster, PA 17601; 5,168.

Architects, American Institute of (1857), 1735 New York Ave., NW, Wash., DC 20006; 24,000.

Architectural Historians, Society of (1940), 1700 Walnut St., Philadelphia, PA 19103; 4,062.

Archivists, Society of American (1936), Rackham Bldg., Univ. of Michigan, Ann Arbor, MI 48104; 2,500.

Armed Forces Communications and Electronics Assn. (1946), Skyline Center, 5205 Leesburg Pike, Falls Church, VA 22124; 12,000.

Army and Navy Union of U.S.A. (1886), 1391 Main St., Lakemore, OH 44250; 12,000.

Art, Natl. Assn. of Schools of (1944), 1 Dupont Circle, NW, Suite 650, Wash., DC 20036; 65 schools.

Arthritis Foundation (1948), 1212 Ave. of the Americas,

N.Y., NY 10036; 73 chapters.

Artists of America, Allied (1914), 1083 Fifth Ave., New York, NY 10028; 375.

Arts, American Federation of the (1909), 41 E. 65th St., New York, NY 10021; 3,000.

Arts, Natl. Endowment for the (1965), 806 15th St., NW, Washington, DC 20506.

Arts and Letters, American Academy of (1904), 633 West 155th St., New York, NY 10032; 50.

Arts and Letters, Natl. Institute of (1898) as **Amer. Social Science Assn.**, 633 W. 155th St., N.Y., NY 10032; 250

Arts and Sciences, American Academy of (1780), 165 Allandale St., Jamaica Plain, MA 02130; 2,245.

Arts, Associated Councils of the (1955), 1564 Broadway, N.Y., NY 10036; 800.

Assistance League, National (1935), 5627 Fernwood Ave., Hollywood, CA 90028; 11,000.

Associated Press (1848), 50 Rockefeller Plaza, New York, NY 10020.

Astrologers, Amer. Federation of (1938), #6 Library Ct., SE, Wash., DC 20003; 3,000.

Astronautical Society, American (1954), 6060 Duke St., Alexandria, VA 22304; 600.

Astronomical Society, American (1899), Leander-McCormick Observatory, Box 3818, Univ. Station, Charlottesville, VA 22903; 2,943.

Atheist Assn. (formerly, **Amer. Assn. for the Advancement of Atheism)** (1925), Box 2832, San Diego, CA 92112; 200.

Athletic Associations, Natl. Federation of State High School (1920), 400 Leslie St., Elgin, IL 60120; 50 states.

Athletic Conference, Eastern College (1938), Royal Manhattan Hotel, N.Y., NY 10036; 211 schools.

Athletic Union of the U.S., Amateur (1888), 3400 W. 86th St., Indianapolis, IN 46268; 235,000 athletes.

Attorneys General, National Assn. of (1907), Iron Works Pike, Lexington, KY 40511; 56.

Audit Bureau of Circulations (1914), 123 N. Wacker Dr., Chicago, IL 60606; 3,900 companies.

Audubon Society, National (1905), 950 3rd Ave., New York, NY 10022; 291,854.

Authors and Composers, American Guild of (1931), 50 W. 57th St., New York, NY 10019; 2,500.

Authors League of America (1912), 234 W. 44th St., N.Y., NY 10036; 6,000.

Auto License Plate Collectors Assn. (1954), P. O. Box 1017, Chandler, AZ 85224; 1,755.

Automobile Association, American (1902), 8111 Gatehouse Rd., Falls Church, VA 22042; 16,000,000.

Automobile Club, National (1924), 65 Battery St., San Francisco, CA 94111; 335,000.

Automobile Dealers Assn., National (1917), 2000 K St., NW, Washington, DC 20006; 20,728.

Automobile Manufacturers Association (1913), 320 New Center Bldg., Detroit, MI 48202; 10 companies.

Automotive Booster Clubs (1920), 1803 S. Busse Rd., Mt. Prospect, IL 60056; 3,006.

Automotive Engineers, Society of (1909), 2 Pennsylvania Plaza, New York, NY 10001; 26,221.

Automotive Organization Team (formerly, **Automotive Old Timers)** (1939), Box 1742, Midland, MI 48640; 2,600.

Aviation Historical Society, American (1956), P. O. Box 456, Chatsworth, CA 91311; 4,309.

— B —

Badminton Assn., American (1936), 1330 Alexandria Dr., San Diego, CA 92107; 4,000.

Ball Players of America, Assn. of Professional (1924), 530 E. Wardlow Rd., Long Beach, CA 90807; 10,000.

Bankers Assn., American (1875), 1120 Connecticut Ave. NW, Wash., DC 20036; 18,398 banks, branches.

Bankers Assn. of America, Independent (1930), 1168 S. Main St., Sauk Centre, MN 56378; 7,197 banks.

Banker Assn., Internatl. (1968), 422 Washington Bldg., Washington, DC 20005; 1,500.

Bar Association, America (1878), 1155 East 60th St., Chicago, IL 60637; 179,000.

Bar Assn., Federal (1920), 1815 H Street, NW., Wash., DC 20006; 14,000.

Barber Shop Quartet Singing in America, Society for the Preservation and Encouragement of (1937), 6315 Third Ave., Kenosha, WI 53141; 35,092.

Barbers and Beauticians of America, Associated Master (1924), 219 Greenwich Rd., Charlotte, NC 28211; 10,000.

Baseball Congress, American Amateur (1935), 212 Plaza Bldg., 2855 W. Market St., Akron, OH 44313.

Baseball Congress, National (1931), Box 1420, Wichita, KS 67201; 5,000.

Baseball Leagues, Natl. Assn. of Professional (1901), 720 E. Broad St., Columbus, OH 43215; 18 leagues.

Basketball Assn., American (1967), 1700 Broadway, N.Y., NY 10019; 10 teams.

Basketball Assn., Natl. (1946), 2 Penn Plaza, N.Y., NY 10001; 17 teams.

Baton Twirling Assn., Internatl. (1967), Box 234, Waldwick, NJ 07463; 2,000.

Battleship Assn., American (1964), P. O. Box 11247, San Diego, CA 92111; 3,000.

Beta Sigma Phi (1931), 1800 W. 91st Pl., Kansas City, MO 64114; 225,000.

Bible Society, American (1816), 1865 Broadway, N.Y., NY 10023; 588,000.

Biblical Literature, Society of (1880), Harvard Divinity School, 45 Francis Ave., Cambridge, MA 02138; 3,200.

Bibliographical Society of America (1904), P. O. Box 397, Grand Central Station, N.Y., NY 10017; 1,625.

Bicycle Institute of America (1937), 122 East 42nd St., New York, N.Y 10017; 250.

Bide-A-Wee Home Assn. (1903), 410 East 38th St., N.Y., NY 10016; 21,500.

Big Brothers of America (1946), 341 Suburban Station Bldg., Philadelphia, PA 19103; 208 agencies.

Billiard Congress of America (1948), 717 N. Michigan Ave., Chicago, IL 60611; 625.

Biological Chemists, American Society of (1906), 9650 Rockville Pike, Bethesda, MD 20014; 3,600.

Biological Sciences, Amer. Institute of (1947), 3900 Wisconsin Ave., NW, Wash., DC 20016; 14,500.

Blind, American Foundation for the (1921), 15 W. 16th St., New York, NY 10011.

Blind, National Federation of the (1940), 218 Randolph Hotel, Des Moines, IA 50309; 50,000.

Blind and Visually Handicapped, Natl. Accreditation Council for Agencies Serving the (1967), 79 Madison Ave., N.Y., NY 10016; 14 agencies.

Blinded Veterans Assn. (1945), 1735 DeSales St., NW, Wash., DC 20036; 1,800.

Blindness, Natl. Society for the Prevention of (1918), 79 Madison Ave., N.Y., NY 10016. 394.

Blindness, Research to Prevent (1960), 598 Madison Ave., N.Y., NY 10022; 1,200.

Blood Banks, American Assn. of (1947), 1818 L St., NW, Wash., DC 20036; 6,300.

Blueberry Council, North American (1966), P. O. Box 166, Marmora, NJ 08223; 6,000.

Blue Cross Assn. (1948), 840 N. Lake Shore Dr., Chicago, IL 60611.

Blue Shield Plans, Natl. Assn. of (1946), 211 E. Chicago Ave., Chicago, IL 60611; 72 plans.

B'nai B'rith (1843), 1640 Rhode Island Ave., NW, Wash., DC 20036; 500,000. Component units include: **B'nai B'rith Hillel Foundations** (1923); **B'nai B'rith Youth Organization** (1924). Other units: **B'nai B'rith Women, Anti-Defamation League of B'nai B'rith, and B'rith Vocational Service.**

Board of Trade, World (formerly **New York Board of Trade)** (1973), 295 Fifth Ave., New York, NY 10016.

Boat Owners Assn. of the U.S. (1966), 8111 Gatehouse Rd., Falls Church, VA 22042; 20,000.

Book Manufacturers' Institute (1933), Box 368, Ridgefield, CT 06877; 100 companies.

Booksellers Association, American (1900), 800 Second Ave., New York, NY 10017; 4,534.

Botanical Gardens and Arboreta, Amer. Assn. of (1941), Dept. of Horticulture, New Mexico State Univ., Las Cruces, NM 80003; 524.

Botanical Society of America (1893), Botany Dept., Rutgers Univ., New Brunswick, NJ 08903; 4,500.

Bottle Clubs, Federation of Historical (1969), c/o Barbara Robertus, 5001 Queen Ave. N., Minneapolis, MN 55430; 125 clubs.

Bowling Congress, American (1896), 5301 S. 76th St., Greendale, WI 53129; 4,047,596.

Bowling Congress, Women's Internatl (1916), 5301 S. 76th St., Greendale, WI 53129; 3,343,965.

Boy Scouts of America (1910), N. Brunswick, NJ 08902; 6,405,225 scouts and leaders.

Boys' Brigades of America, United (1893), P. O. Box 8406, Baltimore, MD 21234.

Boys' Clubs of America (1860), 771 First Ave., New York, NY 10017; 1,000,000.

Brand Names Foundation (1943), 477 Madison Ave., N.Y., NY 10022; 600.

Brewers Assn., U. S. (1862), 1750 K St., Washington, DC 20006.

Brick Institute of America (formerly, **Structural Clay Products Institute)** (1934), 1750 Old Meadow Rd., McLean, VA 22101; 110 companies.

Brith Sholom (1905), 121 S. Broad St., Philadelphia, PA 19107; 20,000.

Broadcasters, Natl. Assn. of (1922), 1771 N. St., NW,

Washington, DC 20036; 4,395.

Burroughs, Edgar Rice, Bibliophiles (1960), 454 Elaine Dr., Pittsburgh, PA 15236; 910.

Business Bureaus, Council on Better (1970), 845 Third Ave., New York, NY 10022; 137.

Business Clubs, Natl. Assn. of American (1922), P. O. Box 5127, High Point, NC 27262; 5,000.

Business Communication Assn., American (1935), 317b David Kinley Hall, Urbana, IL 61801; 1,000.

Business Education Assn., Natl. (1946), 1906 Association Drive, Reston, VA 22091; 20,695.

Business Law Association, American (1923), c/o Secretary, College of Business, 201 Johnson Hall, Colo. State Univ., Ft. Collins, CO 80521; 700.

Business Press Editors, Amer. Society of (1964), 9 S. Fairview Ave., Park Ridge, IL 60068; 175.

Button Society of America, Natl. (1938), 353 Stockton St., Hightstown, NJ 08520; 2,417.

—C—

Camp Fire Girls (1910), 1740 Broadway, New York, NY 10003; 600,000.

Campers & Hikers Assn., Natl. (1954), 7172 Transit Rd., Buffalo, NY 14221; 67,000 families.

Camping Assn., American (1910), Bradford Woods, Martinsville, IN 46151; 6,500.

Cancer Council, United (1963), 1803 N. Meridian St., Indianapolis, IN 46202; serves 27,500,000 people.

Cancer Society, American (1913), 219 E. 42nd St., New York, NY 10021; 2,300,000 volunteers.

Candy Brokers Assn. of America, P. O. Box 34236, Washington, DC 20034; 200.

Canners Assn. National (1907), 1133 20th St., NW, Washington, DC 20036; 620 companies.

Captive European Nations, Assembly of (1954), 29 West 57th St., New York, NY 10019; 150.

CARE (Cooperative For American Relief Everywhere) (1945), 660 1st Ave., N.Y., NY 10016; 26 agencies.

Carillonneurs in North America, Guild of (1936), 6231 Monero Dr., Palos Verdes, CA 90274; 270.

Carl Schurz Assn., Natl. (1930), 339 Walnut St., Philadelphia, PA 19106; 2,766.

Cartoonists Society, Natl. (1946), 130 W. 44th St. New York, NY 10036; 450.

Casting Assn., American (1906), P. O. Box 51, Nashville, TN 37202; 2,500.

Catch Society (1968), Dept. of English, State Univ. College, Fredonia, NY 14063; 400.

Catholic Bishops, Natl. Conference of - U. S. Catholic Conference (1966), 1312 Massachusetts Ave., NW, Washington, DC 20005; 300.

Catholic Charities, Natl. Conference of (1910), 1346 Connecticut Ave., NW, Wash., DC 20036; 3,000.

Catholic Church Extension Society (1905), 1307 S. Wabash Ave., Chicago, IL 60605; 36,645.

Catholic Daughters of America (1903), 10 West 71st St., New York, NY 10023; 200,000.

Catholic Educational Assn., Natl. (1904), One Dupont Circle, Suite 350, NW, Wash., DC 20036; 16,000.

Catholic Hospital Assn. (1915), 1438 S. Grand Blvd., St. Louis, MO 63104; 879.

Catholic Press Assn. (1911), 432 Park Ave. S., New York, NY 10016; 1,789.

Catholic Rural Life Conference, National (1923), 3801 Grand Ave., Des Moines, IA 50312; 3,582.

Catholic War Veterans of U.S.A. (1935), 2 Massachusetts Ave., NW, Washington, DC 20001; 100,000.

Ceramic Society, American (1899), 65 Ceramic Drive, Columbus, OH 43214; 7,650.

Cerebral Palsy Association, United (1949), 66 East 34th St., New York, NY 10016.

Chamber of Commerce of the U.S. (1912), 1615 H St., NW, Wash., DC 20006; 36,000 business members.

Chartered Life Underwriters, Amer. Society of (1928), 270 Bryn Mawr Ave., Bryn Mawr, PA 19010; 19,000.

Chartered Property and Casualty Underwriters., Society of (1944), P. O. Box 566, Media, PA 19063; 7,500.

Chautauqua Institution (1874), Box 28, Chautauqua, NY 14722.

Chemical Engineers, American Institute of (1908), 345 East 47th St., New York, NY 10017; 38,800.

Chemical Society, American (1876), 1155 16th St., NW, Washington, DC 20036; 105,000.

Chemists, Amer. Institute of (1923), 7315 Wisconsin Ave., Washington, DC 20014; 7,300.

Chemists and Chemical Engineers, Assn. of Consulting (1928), 50 E. 41st St., N.Y., NY 10017; 135.

Chess Federation, US. (1939), 479 Broadway, Newburgh, NY 12550; 61,873.

Chief Warrant and Warrant Officers Assn., USCG (1928), Suite P-203, 955 L'Enfant Plaza N., SW, Wash., DC 20024; 2,917.

Child Study Assn. of America (1885), . 50 Madison Ave., N.Y., NY 10010; 700.

Child Welfare League of America (1920), 67 Irving Place, N.Y., NY 10003; 390 agencies.

Children of the American Revolution, Natl. Society (1895), 1776 D St., NW, Wash., DC 20006; 15,000.

Children's Aid Society (1853), 105 East 22nd St., New York, NY 10010.

Children's Book Council (1945), 175 Fifth Ave., New York, NY 10010; 63.

Chinese Women's Association (1932), , 54-32 152nd St., Flushing, NY 11355; 479.

Chiropractic Association, American (1963), 2200 Grand Ave., Des Moines, IA 50312; 8,755.

Chiropractors Association, International (1926), 741 Brady St., Davenport, IA 52803; 5,029.

Christian Anti-Defamation League (1956), P. O. Box 714, Mt. Vernon, NY 10551; 120,000.

Christian Laymans Counseling Board (1970), 5901 Plainfield Drive, Charlotte, NC 28202; 1,000,000.

Christians and Jews, Natl. Conference of (1928), 43 W. 57th St., N.Y., NY 10019; 200,000.

Cincinnati, Society of the (1783), 2118 Massachusetts Ave., NW, Washington, DC 20008; 2,600.

Circus Fans Assn. of America (1926), P. O. Box 605, Aurora, IL 60507; 2,000.

Circus Historical Society (1939), 2515 Dorset Rd., Columbus, OH 43221; 1,400.

Cities, Natl. League of (1924), 1620 Eye St., NW, Washington, DC 20006; 15,000 municipalities.

City Management Assn., International (1914), 1140 Connecticut Ave., NW, Wash., DC 20036; 4,000.

Civil Engineers, American Society of (1852), 345 East 47th St., New York, NY 10017; 68,000.

Civil Liberties Union, American (1920), 22 E. 40th St., N.Y., NY 10016; 250,000.

Civil Service League, Natl. (1881), 1825 K St., NW, Wash., DC 20006; 1,428.

Civitan International (1920), 115 North 21st St., Birmingham, AL 35203; 53,500.

Classical League, American (1919), Miami Univ., Oxford, OH 45056; 3,600.

Clinical Pathologists, American Society of (1922), 2100 W. Harrison, Chicago, IL 60612; 19,500.

Coal Association, National (1917), 1130 17th St., NW, Wash., DC 20036; 160 companies.

Cocoa Exchange, New York (1925), 127 John St., New York, NY 10038; 183.

Coffee and Sugar Exchange, New York (1882), 79 Pine St., New York, NY 10005; 342.

Collectors Association, American (1939), 4040 W. 70th St., Minneapolis, MN 55435; 2,551 agencies.

College Entrance Examination Board (1900), 888 Seventh Ave., N.Y., NY 10019; 2,000 institutions.

College Physical Education Assn. for Men, Natl. (1897), 108 Cooke Hall, Univ. of Minn., Minneapolis, MN 55455; 1,300.

College Placement Council (1956), 65 E. Elizabeth Ave., Bethlehem, PA 18018; 1,400.

College Public Relations Assn., American (1917), One Dupont Circle, NW, Wash., DC 20036; 1,314.

Colleges, Assn. of American (1915), 1818 R St., NW, Washington, DC 20009; 795 colleges.

Collegiate Athletic Assn., National (1906), Box 1906, Shawnee Mission, KS 66222; 777.

Collegiate Schools of Business, Amer. Assembly of (1916), Suite 50, 760 Office Parkway, St. Louis, MO 63141; 570 schools.

Colonial Dames of America (1890), 421 East 61 St., N.Y., NY 10021; 2,000.

Colonial Dames XVII Century, Natl. Society (1915), 1300 New Hampshire Ave., NW, Wash., DC 20036; 9,000.

Colonial Wars, General Society of (1893), c/o Lawson Whitesides, 840 Woodbine Ave., Glendale, OH 45246; 4,500.

Colored Women's Clubs, Natl. Assn. of (1896), 5808 16th St., NW, Wash., DC 20011; 100,000.

Columbia Assns. in Civil Service, Grand Council of (1938), 299 Broadway, N.Y., NY 10007; 80,000.

Commercial Law League of America (1895), 222 West Adams St., Chicago, IL 60606; 5,000.

Commercial Travelers of America, Order of United (1888), 632 N. Park St., Columbus, OH 43215; 255,000.

Common Cause (1970), 2030 M St., NW, Washington, DC 20036; 300,000.

Composers, Authors and Publishers, American Society of (ASCAP) (1914), One Lincoln Plaza, N.Y., NY 10023; 22,000 writers and publishers.

Composers and Conductors, Natl. Assn. for American

(1933), 133 West 69th St., N.Y., NY 10023; 850.

Computing Machinery, Assn. for (1947), 1133 Ave. of Americas, N.Y., NY 10036; 26,406.

Concrete Institute, American (1905), 22400 W. Seven Mile Rd., Detroit, MI 48219; 15,700.

Conference Board (1916), 845 Third Ave., N.Y., NY 10022; 4,000.

Congress of Racial Equality (1942), 200 West 135th St., New York, NY 10035; 200,000.

Conscientious Objectors, Central Committee for (1948), 2016 Walnut St., Philadelphia, PA 19103; 26,000.

Conservation Engineers, Assn. of (1961), Mo. Dept. of Conservation, P. O. Box 180, Jefferson City, MO 65101; 161.

Conservation Foundation (1948), 1717 Massachusetts Ave., NW, Washington, DC 20036.

Conservation & Trustees of the Universe, Citizens for (1953), 1013 S. Washington Ave., Lansing, MI 48910.

Construction Industry Manufacturers Assn. (1949), 111 E. Wisconsin Ave., Milwaukee, WI 53202; 90 companies.

Consumer Credit Assn., International (1912), 375 Jackson Ave., St. Louis, MO 63130; 51,000.

Consumer Federation of America (1968), 1012 14th St., Wash., DC 20005; 180 organizations.

Consumer Interests, American Council on (1953), 238 Stanley Hall, Univ. of Mo., Columbia, MO 65201; 2,000.

Consumer Protection Council, Natl. Student (1970), Villanova Univ., Villanova, PA 19085; 200.

Consumers League, Natl. (1899), 1785 Massachusetts Ave., NW, Washington, DC 20036; 1,200.

Consumers Union of the U.S. (1936), 256 Washington St., Mount Vernon, NY 10550; 390,000.

Consumers Unions, Internatl. Organization of (1960), 9 Emmastraat, The Hague, Netherlands; 78 members in 35 nations.

Contract Bridge League, American (1937), 2200 Democrat Rd., Memphis, TN 38131; 170,000.

Cooperative League of the U.S.A. (1916), 1828 L St., NW, Wash., DC 20036; 123 organizations.

Corporate Responsibility, Project Center on (1970), 1712 N St., NW, Wash., DC 20036; 5,000.

Correctional Administrators, Assn. of State (1955), 36 W. 44th St., New York, NY 10036; 56.

Correctional Assn., American (1870), 4321 Hartwick Rd., College Park, MD 20740; 10,000.

Cosmopolitan International (1933), 7341 W. 80th St., Overland Park, KS 66204; 4,000.

Cotton Council of America, Natl. (1938), 1918 North Parkway, Memphis, TN 38112; 282.

Council of Churches of City of N.Y. (1815), 475 Riverside Drive, N.Y., NY 10027; 1,700 churches.

Country Music Assn. (1958), 700 16th Ave. South, Nashville, TN 37203; 4,000.

Credit Management, National Assn. of (1896), 475 Park Ave. South, N.Y., NY 10016; 37,500.

Credit Unions, World Council of (formerly, **CUNA International**) (1971), 1617 Sherman Ave., Madison, WI 53701; 55,000 credit unions.

Crime and Delinquency, Natl. Council on (1907), 411 Hackensack Ave., Hackensack, NJ 07601; 60,000.

Criminology, American Assn. of (1953), Box 1115, North Marshfield, MA 02059; 2,500.

Crop Science Society of America (1953), 677 S. Segoe Rd., Madison, WI 53711; 3,200.

Cryptogram Assn., American (1932), 9504 Forest Rd., Bethesda, MD 20014; 800.

Customs Brokers & Forwarders Assn. of America, Natl. (1897), 1 World Trade Center, N.Y., NY 10048; 500.

Cyprus, Sovereign Order of (1192; in U. S. 1964), 853 Seventh Ave., N.Y., NY 10019; 409.

— D —

Dairy Council, Natl. (1915), 111 N. Canal St., Chicago, IL 60606; 700.

Dairy and Food Industries Supply Assn. (1918), 5530 Wisconsin Ave., Wash., DC 20015; 400.

Dairy Goat Assn., Amer. (1906), P. O. Box 186, Spindale, NC 28160; 4,100.

Dairy Science Assn., American (1906), 113 N. Neil St., Champaign, IL 61820 2,600.

Dairylea Cooperative (formerly, **Dairymen's League Coop. Assn.**) (1919), One Blue Hill Plaza, Pearl River, NY 10965 ; 10,-050.

Data Processing Management Assn. (1951), 505 Busse Highway, Park Ridge, IL 60068; 24,500.

Daughters of the American Revolution, Natl. Society (1890), 1776 D St., NW, Wash., DC 20006; 196,681.

Daughters of the Confederacy, United (1894), 328 North Blvd., Richmond, VA 23220; 35,000.

Daughters of the Revolution, Natl. Society (1891), 132

Nassau St., New York, NY 10038; 4,600.

Daughters of the Union Veterans of the War 1861-1865 (1885), 503 S. Walnut St., Springfield, IL 62704; 12,000.

Deaf, Alexander Graham Bell Assn. for the (1890), 3417 Volta Place, NW, Wash., DC 20007; 7,000.

Deaf, Conference of Executives of American Schools for the (1868), 5034 Wisconsin Ave., NW, Wash., DC 20016; 275.

Deaf, Convention of Amer. Instructors of the (1850), 5034 Wisconsin Ave., NW, Wash., DC 20016; 4,000.

Deaf, National Assn. of the (1880), 814 Thayer Ave., Silver Spring, MD 20910; 17,000.

Delta Kappa Gamma Society Internatl. (1929), 416 W. 12th St., Austin, TX 78767; 129,000.

DeMolay, Order of (1919), 201 E. Armour Blvd., Kansas City, MO 64111; 2,800,000.

Dental Association, American (1859), 211 E. Chicago Ave., Chicago, IL 60611; 119,000.

Dental Assn., Natl. (1913), P. O. Box 197, Charlottesville, VA 22902; 2,000.

Descendants of the Colonial Clergy, Society of the (1933), 255 Madison St., Dedham, MA 02026; 800.

Descendants of the Signers of the Declaration of Independence (1907), 1300 Locust St., Philadelphia, PA 19107; 721.

Desert Protective Council (1954), Box 4294, Palm Springs, CA 92262; 618.

Diabetes Assn., American (1940), One West 48th St., New York, NY 10020; 3,147.

Dialect Society, American (1889), 1611 N. Kent St., Arlington , VA 22209; 850.

Dietetic Assn., American (1917), 620 N. Michigan Ave., Chicago, IL 60611; 24,970.

Directors Guild of America (1936), 9750 Sunset Blvd., Los Angeles, CA 90046; 4,200.

Disabled American Veterans (1921), 3725 Alexandria Pike, Cold Spring, KY 41076; 420,000.

Disabled Officers Assn. (1919), 1612 K St., NW, Wash., DC 20006; 6,000.

Divorce Reform, United States (1961), P. O. Box 243, Kenwood, CA 95452; 6,000.

Dowsers, American Society of (1961), 957 Norwood Ave., Schenectady, NY 12303; 1,200.

Drug, Chemical and Allied Trades Assn. (1890), 350 Fifth Ave., Suite 3014, N.Y., NY 10001; 500 firms.

Duckpin Bowling Congress, Natl. (1927), 711 14th St., NW, Washington, DC 20005; 250,000.

Ducks Unlimited (1937), P.O. Box 66300; Chicago, IL 60666; 80,000.

Duodecimal Society of America (1944), 4728 Cielo Dr., Huntington Beach, CA 92649; 120.

Dutch Settlers Soc. of Albany (1924), 1088 Cortland St., Albany, NY 12203; 275.

— E —

Eagles, Fraternal Order of (1898), 2401 W. Wisconsin Ave., Milwaukee, WI 53233; 850,000.

Earth, Friends of the (1969), 529 Commercial St., San Francisco, CA 94111; 20,000.

Easter Seal Society for Crippled Children and Adults, Natl. (1921), 2023 W. Ogden Ave., Chicago, IL 60612.

Eastern Star, Order of the (1876), 1618 New Hampshire Ave., Wash., DC 20009; 2,000,000.

Ecological Society of America (1915), c/o Frank McCormick, Univ. of N. C., Chapel Hill, NC 27514; 5,000.

Economic Assn., American (1885), 1313 21st Ave., S., Nashville, TN 37212; 17,000.

Economic Development, Committee for (1942), 477 Madison Ave., N.Y., NY 10022; 200 trustees.

Edison Electric Institute (1933), 90 Park Ave., New York, NY 10016.

Education, American Council on (1918), One Dupont Circle, NW. Wash., DC 20036; 1,565 schools.

Education, Council for Basic (1956), 725 15th St., NW, Washington, DC 20005; 4,350.

Education Assn., Natl. (1857), 1201 16th St., NW, Wash., DC 20036; 1,400,000.

Education, Society for the Advancement of (1914), 1860 Broadway, N.Y., NY 10023; 1,500.

Education, Natl. Society for the Study of (1902), 5835 Kimbark Ave., Chicago, IL 60637; 4,600.

Education of Young Children, Natl. Assn. for the (1926), 1834 Connecticut Ave., NW, Wash., DC 20009; 20,000.

Education Society, Comparative and International (1956), Graduate School of Education, Univ. of California, Los Angeles, CA 90024; 2,500.

Educational Broadcasters, Natl. Assn. of (1925), 1346 Connecticut Ave., NW, Wash., DC 20036; 3,500.

Educational Exchange, Council on Internatl. (1947), 777 UN Plaza, N.Y., NY 10017; 176 schools.

Educational Research Assn., American (1915), 1126 16th

St., NW, Wash., DC 20036; 10,500.

Educators for World Peace, Internatl. Assn. of (1969), Huntsville, AL 35762; 7,400.

Electric Railroaders Assn. (1934), 145 Greenwich St., New York, NY 10006; 3,669.

Electrical and Electronics Engineers, Institute of (1884), 345 E. 47th St., N.Y., NY 10017; 160,000.

Electrical Manufacturers Assn., Natl. (1926), 155 East 44th St., N.Y., NY 10017; 550 companies.

Electrochemical Society (1902), P. O. Box 2071, Princeton, NJ 08540; 4,000.

Electronic Industries Assn. (1924), 2001 Eye St., NW, Washington, DC 20006; 208 firms.

Electronic Technicians, Internatl. Society of Certified (1971), 1715 Expo Lane, Indianapolis, IN 46224; 800.

Electroplaters' Society, American (1909), 56 Melmore Gardens, E. Orange, NJ 07017; 7,500.

Elks, Benevolent and Protective Order of (1868), 2750 Lakeview Ave., Chicago, IL 60614; 1,541,784.

Elks, Improved Benevolent Protective Order of (1898), 1522 N. 16th St., Philadelphia, PA 19121; 450,000.

Engine and Boat Manufacturers, Natl. Assn. of (1904), 537 Steamboat Rd., Greenwich, CT 06830; 396 firms.

Engineering Education, Amer. Society for (1893), One Dupont Circle NW, Wash., DC 20036; 13,000.

Engineering, Natl. Academy of (1964), 2101 Constitution Ave., NW, Wash., DC 20418; 505.

Engineering Technicians, Amer. Society of Certified (1964), 2029 K St., NW, Washington, DC 20006; 5,000.

Engineering Trustees, United (1904), 345 East 47th St., New York, NY 10017; 5 societies.

Engineers, American Institute of Consulting (1910), 345 East 47th St., New York, NY 10017; 425.

Engineers Joint Council (1941), 345 East 47th St., New York, N Y 10017; 425,000.

Engineers, Natl. Society of Professional (1934), 2029 K St., NW, Wash., DC 20006; 69,000.

English Association, College (1939), Oakland Univ., Rochester, MI 48063; 2,800.

English-Speaking Union of the U.S. (1920), 16 East 69th, New York, NY 10021; 37,000.

Entomological Society of America (1889), 4603 Calvert Rd., College Park, MD 20740; 6,400.

Environmental Defense Fund (1967), 162 Old Town Rd., E. Setauket, NY 11733; 38,000.

Epilepsy Foundation of America (1967 merger of **Epilepsy Foundation** and **Epilepsy Assn. of America),** 1828 L St., NW, Wash., DC 20036; 164 chapters.

Esperanto Assn. of North America (1905), 1837 NE 49th Ave., Portland, OR 97213; 306.

Esperanto League for N. America (1952), P. O. Box 508, Burlingame, CA 94010; 937.

Esperanto Society, American Catholic (1968), 7605 Winona Lane, Sebastopol, CA 95472; 40.

Evangelicals, Natl. Assn. of (1942), 350 S. Main Pl., Wheaton, IL 60187; 3,500,000.

Evangeline Crusades, International (1959), 7970 Woodman Ave., Van Nuys, CA 91402; 25,000.

Exchange Club, National (1911), 3050 Central Ave., Toledo, OH 43606; 50,243.

Executives' Secretaries (1938), 2188 Highland Dr., Salt Lake City, UT 84106; 3,500.

Experiment in International Living (1932), Kipling Rd., Brattleboro, VT 05301; 50,000.

Eye-Bank Assn. of America (1961), 3195 Maplewood Ave., Winston-Salem, NC 27103; 60.

Eye-Bank for Sight Restoration (1944), 210 E. 64th St., N.Y., NY 10021; 20.

— F —

Fairs & Expositions, International Assn. (1885), 500 Ashland Ave., Chicago Heights, IL 60411; 485.

Family Physicians, Amer. Academy of (formerly, **American Academy of General Practice)** (1947), 1740 W. 92nd St., Kansas City, MO 64114; 35,000.

Family Service Assn. of America (1911), 44 East 23rd St., New York, NY 10010; 330 agencies.

Farm Bureau Federation, American (1919), 225 Touhy Ave., Park Ridge, IL 60068; 2,293,680 families.

Farmer Cooperatives, Natl. Council of (1929), 1129 20th St., NW, Washington, DC 20036; 140 firms.

Farmers Educational and Co-Operative Union of America (National Farmers Union) (1902), 12025 E. 45th Ave., Denver, CO 80201; 250,000 families.

Federal Employes, Natl. Federation of (1917), 1737 H St., NW, Wash., DC 20006; 100,000.

Federal Employes Veterans Assn. (1957), 124 Union Ave., Bala Cynwyd, PA 19004; 574.

Feline Society, American (1938), 41 Union Square West,

New York, NY 10003; 665.

Feminists for Life (1972), P.O. Box 5631, Columbus, OH 43221.

Fencers League of America, Amateur (1891), 249 Elton Place, Westfield, NJ 07090; 6,500.

Film Library Assn., Educational (1943), 17 W. 60th St., N.Y., NY 10023; 1,800.

Financial Analysts Federation (1947), 219 E. 42nd St., New York, NY 10017; 14,000.

Financial Executives Institute (1931), 633 Third Ave., N.Y., NY 10017; 8,200.

Fire Chiefs, International Assn. of (1873), Suite 1112, 1725 K St. NW, Wash., DC 20006; 7,300.

Fire Fighters, International Assn. of (1918), 905 16th St., NW, Washington, DC 20006; 155,000.

Fire Marshals Assn. of N. America (1906), 470 Atlantic Ave., Boston, MA 02210; 800.

Fire Protection Assn., Natl. (1896), 470 Atlantic Ave., Boston, MA 02210; 31,000.

Fire Protection Engineers, Society of (1950), 60 Batterymarch St., Boston, MA 02110; 1,650.

Fisheries Society, American (1870), 1319 18th St., NW, Wash., DC 20036; 6,006.

Fishing Institute, Sport (1949), 608 13th St., NW, Washington, DC 20005; 30,000.

Flag Day Assn., American (1888), P. O. Box 1121, Denver, CO 80201.

Flag Foundation, United States (1948), 115 East 86th St., New York, NY 10028; 1,000.

Flat Earth Research Society, International, Box 2533, Lancaster, CA 93534.

Florists, Society of American (1887), 901 N. Washington St., Alexandria, VA 22314; 5,300.

Fluid Power Society (1960), 432 E. Kilbourn Ave., Milwaukee, WI 53202; 3,000.

Folklore Society, American (1888), Center for Folklore & Oral History, Univ. of Texas, Austin, TX 78712; 2,500.

Food Processing Machinery and Supplies Assn. (1885), 7758 Wisconsin Ave., Wash., DC 20014; 325 firms.

Footwear Industries Assn., Amer. (1922), 1611 N. Kent St., Arlington, VA 22209; 400.

Foreign Policy Assn. (1918), 345 E. 46th St., New York, NY 10017.

Foreign Press Assn. (1918), 866 Second Ave., New York, NY 10017; 304.

Foreign Relations, Council on (1921), 58 E. 68th St., N.Y., NY 10021; 1,551.

Foreign Student Affairs, Natl. Assn. for (1948), 1860 19th St., NW, Wash., DC 20009; 2,300.

Foreign Study, Amer. Institute for (1964), 102 Greenwich Ave., Greenwich, CT 06830; 55,000.

Foreign Trade Council, Natl. (1914), 10 Rockefeller Plaza, New York, NY 10020; 600 companies.

Forensic Sciences, American Academy of (1948), 11400 Rockville Pike, Rockville, MD 20852; 1,345.

Forensic League, Natl. (1925), Ripon College, Ripon, WI 54971; 270,000.

Forest Institute, American (1943), 1619 Massachusetts Ave. NW, Wash., DC 20036; 35,000.

Forest Products Assn., Natl. (1902), 1619 Massachusetts Ave., NW, Wash., DC 20036; 30 assns.

Forest Products Research Society (1947), 2801 Marshall Ct., Madison, WI 53705; 4,500.

Foresters, Society of American (1900), 1010 16th St., NW, Washington, DC 20036; 18,000.

Forestry Assn., American (1875), 1319 18th St., NW, Washington, DC 20036; 75,000.

Forty and Eight, The (1920), 777 N. Meridian St., Indianapolis, IN 46204; 70,000.

Foster Parents Plan (1937), P. O. Box 400, Warwick, RI 02886; 36,000.

Founders and Patriots of America, Order of the (1896), Suite 833, 53 State St., Boston, MA 02109; 1,000.

Foundrymen's Society, American (1896), Golf & Wolf Roads, Des Plaines, IL 60016; 14,000.

4-H Clubs (betw. 1901-05), Federal Extension Service, Dept. of Agric., Wash., DC 20250; 5,000,000.

French Institute (1911), 22 East 60th St., New York, NY 10022; 6,000.

French Legion of Honor, American Society of the (1922), 22 East 60th St., N.Y., NY 10022; 440.

Friends Service Committee, American (1917), 160 North 15th St., Philadelphia, PA 19102; 517.

Future Farmers of America (1928), Natl. FFA Center, Box 15160, Alexandria, VA 22309; 447,577.

Future Homemakers of America (1945), 2010 Massachusetts Ave., Wash., DC 20036; 450,000.

— G —

Game Fish Assn., International (1939), 3000 E. LasOlas

Blvd., Ft. Lauderdale, FL 33316; 900 clubs.

Garden Club of America (1913), 598 Madison Ave., New York, NY 10022; 12,750.

Garden Clubs of America, Men's (1932), 5560 Merle Hay Rd., Des Moines, IA 50323; 10,110.

Garden Clubs, Natl. Council of State (1929), 4401 Magnolia Ave., St. Louis, MO 63110; 500,000.

Gas Appliance Manufacturers Assn. (1935), 1901 N. Ft. Myer Drive, Arlington, VA 22209; 400 companies.

Gas Assn., American (1918), 1515 Wilson Blvd., Arlington, VA 22209; 5,000.

Genealogical Society, National (1903), 1921 Sunderland Pl. NW, Wash., DC 20036; 2,900.

Genealogical Society, New England Historic (1845), 101 Newbury St., Boston, MA 02114; 4,000.

General Contractors of America, Associated (1918), 1957 E St., NW, Wash., DC 20006; 9,415.

Genetic Assn., American (1903), 1028 Connecticut Ave., NW, Wash., DC 20036; 1,550.

Geographers, Assn. of American (1904), 1710 16th St., NW, Wash., DC 20009; 6,500.

Geographic Education, Natl. Council for (1914), 115 N. Marion St., Oak Park, IL 60301; 6,000.

Geographic Society, National (1888), 17th & M Sts., NW, Washington, DC 20036; 8,500,000.

Geographical Society, American (1852), Broadway at 156th St., New York, NY 10032; 3,000.

Geological Institute, American (1948), 5205 Leesburg Pike, Falls Church, VA 22041; 18 societies.

Geological Society of America (1888), 3300 Penrose Place, Boulder, CO 80301; 11,093.

Geologists, Assn. of Engineering (1957), 8310 San Fernando Way, Dallas TX 75218; 1,800.

Geophysical Union, American (1919), 1707 L St., NW, Wash., DC 20036; 11,000.

Geophysicists, Society of Exploration (1930), 3707 East 51st St., Tulsa, OK 74135; 8,500.

Geriatrics Society, American (1942), 10 Columbus Circle, N.Y., NY 10019; 8,000.

Gideons International (1899), 2900 Lebanon Rd., Nashville TN 37214; 43,000.

Gifted Children, American Assn. for (1954), 15 Gramercy Park, New York, NY 10003; 100.

Gifted Children, Natl. Assn. for (1954), 8080 Springvalley Dr., Cincinnati, OH 45236; 2,000.

Girl Scouts of the U.S.A. (1912), 830 Third Ave., N.Y., NY 10022; 2,953,000 girls, 585,000 adults.

Girls Clubs of America (1945), 133 East 62nd St., New York, NY 10021; 151,000.

Gladiolus Council, North American (1946), 11345 Moreno Ave., Lakeside CA 92040; 2,000.

Gold Star Mothers, American (1928), 2128 Leroy Pl., NW, Washington, DC 20008; 18,000.

Golf Association, U.S. (1894), Golf House, Far Hills, NJ 07931; 4,230 clubs.

Goose Island Bird & Girl Watching Society (1960), 301 Arthur Ave., Park Ridge, IL 60068; 860.

Gospel Music Assn. (1963), 817 18th Ave., S. Nashville, TN 37203; 2,000.

Governmental Research Assn. (1914), P. O. Box 387, Ocean Gate, NJ 08740; 450.

Graduate Schools in the U.S., Council of (1961), One Dupont Circle NW, Wash., DC 20036; 312.

Grandmother Clubs of America, Natl. Federation of (1938), 203 N. Wabash Ave., Chicago 60601; 18,000.

Grange, National (1867), 1616 H St., NW, Washington, DC 20006; 600,000.

Graphic Artists, Society of American (1920), 1083 Fifth Ave., New York, NY 10028; 232.

Graphic Arts, American Institute of (1914), 1059 Third Ave., N.Y., NY 10021; 1,750.

Grocery Manufacturers of America (1906), 1425 K St. NW, Washington, DC 20005; 150 firms.

Guide Dog Foundation for the Blind (1946), 109-19 72nd Ave., Forest Hills, NY 11375; 25,000.

Guild for Infant Survival, The Internatl. (1964), 6822 Brompton Rd., Baltimore, MD 21207; 700 families.

Gyro International (1912), 1096 Mentor Ave., Painesville, OH 44077; 5,600.

— H —

Hadassah (Women's Zionist Organization of America) (1912), 65 E. 52nd St. N.Y. NY 10022; 325,000.

Handball Assn., U.S. (1951), 4101 Dempster St., Skokie, IL 60076; 14,000.

Handicapped, Federation of the (1935), 211 West 14th St., New York, NY 10011; 1,000.

Handicapped, Natl. Assn. of the Physically (1958), 6473 Grandville, Detroit, MI 48228; 35 chapters.

Hay Fever Relief Assn., Natl. (1923), 401 Broadway, New York, NY 10013; 1,500.

Health Assn., Amer. Social (1912), 1740 Broadway, N.Y., NY 10019; 1,900.

Health Council, Natl. (1920), 1740 Broadway, New York, NY 10019; 75 agencies.

Health Insurance Assn. of America (1965), 1701 K St., NW, Wash., DC 20006; 317 companies.

Health Insurance Institute (1956), 277 Park Ave., New York, NY 10017; 326 companies.

Health, Physical Education & Recreation, Amer. Assn. For (1895), 1201 16th St., NW, Wash., DC 20036; 45,000.

Hearing Aid Society, Natl. (1951), 24261 Grand River, Detroit, MI 48219; 3,700.

Hearing and Speech Agencies, Natl. Assn. of (formerly, American Hearing Society) (1919), 814 Thayer Ave., Silver Spring, MD 20910; 155 agencies.

Heart Association, American (1924), 44 E. 23rd St., New York, NY 10010; 105,000.

Heating, Refrigerating and Air Conditioning Engineers, Amer. Society of (1894), 345 E. 47th St., N.Y., NY 10017; 30,-000.

Helicopter Society, Maerican (1943), 30 East 42nd St., New York, NY 10017; 2,685.

Helicopter Assn. of America (1948), 1156 15th St., NW, Wash., DC 20005; 435.

Hero Fund Commission, Carnegie (1904), 1932 Oliver Bldg., Pittsburgh, PA 15222.

Hias Service, United (1884), 200 Park Ave., South, N.Y., NY 10003; 15,000.

Historians, Organization of American (formerly, Mississippi Valley Historical Assn.) (1907), 112 N. Bryan St., Bloomington IN 47401; 11,800.

Historialsn, The Society of American (1939), 706 Hamilton Hall, Columbia Univ., N.Y., NY 10027; 225.

Historic Preservation, National Trust for (1949), 740 Jackson Place, NW, Wash., DC 20006; 48,700.

Historical Assn., American (1889), 400 A St., SE, Washington, DC 20003; 18,000.

Historical Research Associates, Western (1971), 415 5th Road North, Nampa, ID 83651; 115.

Hockey Assn. of the U.S., Amateur (1937), 7901 Cedar Ave., Bloomington, MN 55420; 250,000, 11,000 teams.

Hockey League, National (1917), 920 Sun Life Bldg., Montreal, Quebec, Canada H3B 2W2; 18 clubs.

Holiday Institute of Yonkers (1969), 82 Borcher Ave., Yonkers, NY 10704.

Holy Cross of Jerusalem, Order of (1965), 853 Seventh Ave., N.Y., NY 10019; 1,032.

Home Builders, Natl. Assn. of (1940), 1625 L St., NW, Washington, DC 20036; 68,140.

Home Economics Assn., American (1909), 2010 Massachusetts Ave., Wash., DC 20036; 50,000.

Home Improvement Council, Natl. (1956), 11 E. 44th St., N.Y., NY 10017; 1,300.

Homoeopathy, American Foundation for (1924), 910 17th St., NW, Wash., DC 20006; 500.

Homoeopathy, American Institute of (1844), 910 17th St., NW, Wash., DC 20006; 105.

Horatio Alger Society (1961), 4907 Allison Dr., Lansing, MI 48910; 213.

Horse Show Assn. of America Limited, Natl. (1883), Empire Hotel, 44 West 63rd St., N.Y., NY 10023; 14.

Horse Shows Assn., American (1917), 527 Madison Ave., N.Y., NY 10022; 17,000.

Horticultural Society, American (1922), Mount Vernon, VA 22121; 20,000.

Hospital Association, American (1898), 840 N. Lake Shore Drive, Chicago, IL 60611; 26,000.

Hospital Public Relations Directors, Amer. Society for (1965), 840 N. Lake Shore Dr., Chicago, IL 60611; 950.

Hot Rod Assn., Natl. (1951), 10639 Riverside Dr., N. Hollywood, CA 91602; 30,000.

Hotel & Motel Assn., American (1925), 888 Seventh Ave., New York, NY 10019; 7,879 hotels & motels.

Humane Assn., American (1877), P. O. Box 1266, Denver, CO 80201, 2,000,000 in 1,050 societies.

Humane Legislation, Committee for (1967), 11 West 60th St., New York, NY 10023; 50,000.

Humane Society of the U.S. (1954), 1604 K St., NW, Washington, DC 20006; 40,000.

Humane Studies, Institute for (1961), 1132 Crane St., Menlo Park, CA 94025.

Humanics Foundation, American (1948), 912 Baltimore Ave., Kansas City, MO 64105; 900.

Humanist Assn., American (1941), 602 Third Ave., San Francisco, CA 94107; 5,500.

Humanities, Natl. Endowment for the (1965), 806 15th St., NW, Washington, DC 20506.

—I—

Iceland Veterans (1946), 2101 Walnut St., Philadelphia, PA 19103; 1,600.

Identification, International Assn. for (1915), P. O. Box 139, Utica, IL 13503; 1,850.

Illuminating Engineering Society (1906), 345 East 47th St., New York, NY 10017; 10,632.

Illustrators, Society of (1901), 128 East 63rd St., N.Y., NY 10021; 575.

Immigration and Nationality Lawyers, Assn. of (1946), 50 Court St., Brooklyn, NY 11201; 650.

Indian Rights Assn. (1882), 1505 Race St., Philadelphia, PA 19102; 3,000.

Indoor Sports Club (1930), 3445 Trumbull St., San Diego, CA 92106; 2,500.

Industrial Advertisers, Assn. of (1922), 41 East 42nd St., N.Y., NY 10017; 3,000.

Industrial Democracy, League for (1905), 112 East 19th St., New York, NY 10003; 2,000.

Industrial Engineers, Amer. Institute of (1948), 25 Technology Park, Norcross, GA 30071; 20,000.

Industrial Health Foundation (1935), 5231 Centre Ave., Pittsburgh, PA 15232; 140 companies.

Industrial Management Society (1935), 570 N.W. Highway, Des Plaines, IL 60018; 750.

Information Industry Assn. (1968), 4720 Montgomery Lane, Bethesda, MD 20014; 65 companies.

Instrument Society of America (1945), 400 Stanwix St., Pittsburgh, PA 15222; 20,136.

Insurance Assn., American (1866), 85 John St., N.Y., NY 10038; 127 companies.

Insured Savings Assocations, Natl. League of (1943), 1200 17th St., NW, Suite 500, Wash., DC 20036; 500 assns.

Intercollegiate Athletics, Natl. Assn. (1940), 1205 Baltimore St., Kansas City, MO 64105; 565 schools.

Intercollegiate (Big Ten) Conference (1896), c/o Sheraton-Chicago Hotel, Chicago IL 60611; 10 univ.

Intercollegiate Lacrosse Assn., U.S. (1883), Hall of Fame, Johns Hopkins Univ., Baltimore, MD 21218; 120 schools.

Interfraternity Conference, Natl. (1909), P. O. Box 40368, Indianapolis, IN 46240; 45 fraternities.

Interior Designers, Amer. Institute of (1931), 730 5th Ave., N.Y., NY 10019; 5,000.

Interior Designers, Natl. Society of (1957), 315 East 62nd St., N.Y., NY 10021; 5,400.

International Education, Institute of (1919), 809 United National Plaza, N.Y., NY 10017.

International Law, Amer. Society of (1906), 2223 Massachusetts Ave., Wash., DC 20008; 5,500.

Investment Clubs, Natl. Assn. of (1951), 1515 E. Eleven Mile Rd., Royal Oak, MI 48067; 158,000.

Iron Founders' Society, Gray and Ductile (1928), 20611 Center Ridge Rd., Rocky River, OH 44116; 200 firms.

Iron and Steel Engineers, Assn. of (1907), Three Gateway Center, Pittsburgh, PA 15222; 12,000.

Iron and Steel Institute, American (1908), 150 East 42nd St., New York, NY 10017; 2,500.

Italian Historical Society of America (1949), 111 Columbia Heights, Brooklyn, NY 11201; 1,870.

Italy-America Chamber of Commerce (1887), 350 Fifth Ave., N.Y., NY 10001; 500.

Izaak Walton League of America (1922), 1800 N. Kent St., Arlington, VA 22209; 60,000.

—J—

Jamestowne Society (1936), P. O. Box 7389, Richmond, VA 23221; 1,739.

Japanese American Citizens League (1930), 22 Peace Plaza, Suite 203, San Francisco, CA 94115; 29,000.

Jaycees, United States (1920), 4 West 21st , Tulsa, OK 74102; 300,000.

Jewish Appeal, United (1939), 1290 Ave. of the Americas, N.Y., NY 10019.

Jewish Center Workers, Assn. of (1918), 15 E. 26th St., N.Y., NY 10010; 900.

Jewish Committee, American (1906), 165 East 56th St., New York, NY 10022; 40,000.

Jewish Congress, American (1918), 15 East 84th St., New York, NY 10028.

Jewish Federations and Welfare Funds, Council of (1932), 315 Park Ave. S., N.Y., NY 10010; 235 agencies.

Jewish Historical Society, American (1892), 2 Thornton Rd., Waltham, MA 02154; 3,000.

Jewish War Veterans of the U.S.A. (1896), 1712 New Hampshire Ave., NW, Wash., DC 20009; 100,000.

Jewish Welfare Board, National (1917), 15 East 26th St., New York, NY 10010; serves 1,000,000.

Jewish Women, National Council of (1893), 1 West 47th St., New York, NY 10036; 100,000.

Job's Daughters, Internatl. Order of (1921), 1820 Douglas, Masonic Temple, Omaha, NE 68102; 90,000.

Jockey Club (1894), 300 Park Ave., N.Y., NY 10022; 73.

John Birch Society (1958), 395 Concord Ave., Belmont, MA 02178; 60,000 to 100,000.

Journalists, Professional Society of, Sigma Delta Chi (1909), 35 E. Wacker Dr., Chicago, IL 60601; 60,000.

Judaism, American Council for (1943), 309 Fifth Ave., N.Y., NY 10016; 15,000.

Judicature Society, American (1913), 1155 East 60th St., Chicago, IL 60637; 46,856.

Junior Achievement (1919), 909 3rd Ave., N.Y., NY 10022; 160,000 children, 23,225 advisers.

Junior College Athletic Assn., Natl., P. O. Box 1586, Hutchinson, KS 67501; 547 colleges.

Junior Colleges, American Assn. of Community and (1920), 1 Dupont Circle, NW, Wash., DC 20036; 905 colleges.

Junior Leagues, Assn. of (1921), 825 Third Ave., N.Y., NY 10022; 110,000.

Jurists, Amer. Justinian Society of (1966), 31 Chambers St., New York, NY 10009; 685.

—K—

Kailtone Adventure Society (1970), P. O. Box 320, Dayton, NV 89403; 106.

Kennel Club, American (1884), 51 Madison Ave., New York, NY 10010; 395 clubs.

Key Club International (1925), 101 E. Erie St., Chicago, IL 60611; 80,000.

Kindergarten Assn., National (1909), 23 East 16th St., New York, NY 10003.

Kiwanis International (1915), 101 East Erie St., Chicago, IL 60611; 273,000.

Knights of Columbus (1882; merged with Supreme Council Catholic Benevolent Legion, 1968), 1 Columbus Plaza, New Haven, CT 06510; 1,168,959.

Knights of Pythias (1864), 47 N. Grant St., Rm. 201 Stockton, CA 95202; 165,865.

Knights Templar of the U.S.A. (1816), 14 East Jackson Blvd., Suite 1700, Chicago, IL 60604; 365,000.

—L—

La Leche League Internatl. (1956), 9616 Minneapolis Ave., Franklin Park, IL 60131; 50,000.

La Societe de Femme (1963), 777 N. Meridian St., Indianapolis, IN 46204; 2,100.

Lambs, The (1874), 128 West 44th St., New York, NY 10036; 1,153.

Landscape Architects, American Society of (1899), 1750 Old Meadow Rd., McLean, VA 22101; 4,300.

Language Teachers Associations, Natl. Federation of Modern (1916), c/o Dept. of French, State Univ. of N.Y., Buffalo, NY 14214.

Law, Ralph Nader Center for Study of Responsive (1968), P. O. Box 19367, Wash., DC 20036.

Law Institute, American (1923), 4025 Chestnut St., Philadelphia, PA 19104; 1,516.

Law and Social Policy, Center for (1969), 1751 N St., NW, Wash., DC 20036.

Law Libraries, American Assn. of (1906), 53 W. Jackson Blvd., Chicago, IL 60604; 1,800.

Lawn Bowls Assn., American (1915), 10337 Cheryl Dr. Sun City, AZ 85351; 10,500.

Lawn Tennis Assn., U. S. (1881), 51 East 42nd St., N.Y., NY 10017; 66,000.

Learned Societies, American Council of (1919), 345 East 46 St., N.Y., NY 10017; 40 societies.

Legal Aid and Defender Assn., National (1911), 1155 East 60th St., Chicago, IL 60637; 3,000.

Legal Secretaries, Natl. Assn. of (1929), 3005 E. Skelly Dr., Suite 120, Tulsa, OK 74105; 18,500.

Legalized Murder, Citizens Against (1966), P. O. Box 24, New York, NY 10024; 6,000.

Legion of Valor of the U.S.A. (1890), 621 S. Taylor St., Arlington, VA 22204; 900.

Leprosy, Leonard Wood Memorial for the Eradication of (American Leprosy Foundation) (1928), 2430 Pennsylvania Ave., NW, Wash., DC 20037; 25,000.

Leprosy Missions, American (1906), 297 Park Ave. So., New York, NY 10010; 50,000.

Letter Carriers, National Assocation of (1889), 100 Indiana Ave., NW, Wash., DC 20001; 212,000.

Leukemia Society of America (1949), 211 E. 43 St., N.Y., NY 10017; 44 chapters.

Liberty Lobby (1955), 300 Independence Ave., SE, Wash., DC 20003; 20,000.

Libraries Association, Special (1909), 235 Park Ave., S., New York, NY 10003; 8,343.

Library Association, American (1876), 50 East Huron St., Chicago, IL 60611; 30,000.

Library Assn., Home and School (1938), 500 Wallace Ave., Covington, KY 41014.

Library Assn., Medical (1898), 919 N. Michigan Ave., Chicago, IL 60611; 3,200

Life Insurance Assn. of America (1973), 1730 Pennsylvania Ave., NW, Wash., DC 20006; 365 companies.

Life Insurance, Institute of (1939), 277 Park Ave., New York, NY 10017; 164 companies.

Life Office Management Assn. (1924), 100 Park Ave., N.Y., NY 10017; 480 companies.

Lifespan (formerly, People Taking Action Against Abortion) (1970), 7152 Michigan Ave., Detroit, MI 48210; 15,000.

Life Underwriters, National Assn. of (1890), 1922 F St., NW, Wash, DC 20006; 115,000.

Lions Clubs, Internatl. Assn. of (1917), York & Cermak Rds., Oak Brook, IL 60521; 1,036,802.

Little League Baseball (1939), P. O. Box 1127, Williamsport, PA 17701; 9,098 chartered leagues, 54,000 teams.

Log Rolling Assn., International (1926), 5855 N. Sheridan Rd., Apt. 5-J, Chicago, IL 60660; 75.

Lone Indian Fellowship (1926), 1010 Huron Ave., Sheboygan, WI 53081; 800.

Lubrication Engineers, Amer. Society of (1945), 838 Busse Highway, Park Ridge, IL 60068; 3,000.

Lung Association, American (formerly, Natl. Tuberculosis & Respiratory Disease Assn.) (1904), 1740 Broadway, N.Y., NY 10019; 6,540.

Lutheran Education Assn. (1942), 7400 Augusta St., River Forest, IL 60305; 2,875.

—M—

Macaroni Manufacturers Assn., Natl. (1904), 19 S. Bothwell, Box 336, Palatine, IL 60067; 130 firms.

Magazine Publishers Assn. (1919), 575 Lexington Ave., N.Y., NY 10022; 130 companies.

Magazine Writers, Society of (1948), c/o Overseas Press Club, 123 W. 43rd., N.Y., NY 10036; 330.

Magicians Guild of America (1946), 20 W. 40th St., N.Y., NY 10018; 80.

Magicians, Society of American (1901), Aqueduct Rd., RD-2, Peekskill, NY 10566; 2,700.

Mail and Marketing Assn., Direct (1917), 6 East 43rd St., New York, NY 10017; 2,739.

Mammalogists, Amer. Society of (1919), c/o Museum, Oklahoma State Univ., Stillwater, OK 74074; 3,500.

Management, American Institute of (1948), 125 East 38th St., New York, NY 10016; 6,000.

Management Assn., American (1923), 135 W. 50th St., N.Y., NY 10020; 50,000.

Management Assn., National (1925), 2210 Arbor Blvd., Dayton, OH 45439; 70,000.

Management Consultants, Institute of (1968), 347 Madison Ave., N.Y., NY 10017; 625.

Management Engineers, Assn. of Consulting (1933), 347 Madison Ave., N.Y., NY 10017; 46 firms.

Management Information Systems, Society for (1968), 221 N. LaSalle St., Chicago, IL 60601; 1,000.

Management, Society for Advancement of (1912), 1472 Broadway, N.Y., NY 10036; 16,000.

Manufacturers' Agents National Assn. (1947), 3130 Wilshire Blvd, Los Angeles, CA 90010; 3,800.

Manufacturers, Natl. Assn. of (1895), 1776 F St., NW, Washington, DC 20006; 12,100.

Manufacturing Chemists Assn. (1872), 1825 Connecticut Ave., NW, Wash., DC 20009; 185 companies.

Manufacturing Engineers, Society of (formerly, Amer. Soc. of Tool and Manufacturing Engineers) (1932), 20501 Ford Rd., Dearborn, MI 48128; 39,296 in 40 countries.

Manuscript Society (1948), 120 Prospect Ave., Princeton, NJ 08540; 1,150.

Marathon Swimming Federation, World Professional (1963), 10295 Windstream Dr., Columbia, MD 21044; 135.

March of Dimes, Natl. Foundation (1938), 1275 Mamaroneck Ave., White Plains, NY 10605; 2,500 chapters.

Marine Corps Combat Correspondents Assn. (1943), 663 5th Ave., N.Y., NY 10022; 1,400.

Marine Corps League (1923), 933 N. Kenmore St., Arlington, VA 22201; 15,000.

Marine Society of the City of N. Y. (1770), 80 Broad St., N.Y., NY 10004; 236.

Marine Surveyors, Natl. Assn. of (1960), Box 55, Peck Slip Station, New York, NY 10038; 315.

Marine Technology Society (1963), 1730 M St., NW, Washington, DC 20036; 5,000.

Marine Underwriters, Amer. Institute of (1898), 99 John St.,

NY 10038; 120.

Marketing Assn., American (1915), 222 S. Riverside Plaza, Chicago, IL 60606; 18,256.

Masonic Service Assn. of the U.S. (1919), 8120 Fenton St., Silver Spring, MD 20910; 44 lodges.

Masons, Ancient Accepted Scottish Rite, Northern Masonic Jurisdiction, Supreme Council 33° (1813), 33 Marrett Rd., Lexington, MA 02173; 511,000.

Masons, Ancient and Accepted Scottish Rite, Southern Jurisdiction, Supreme Council (1801), 1733 16th St., NW, Wash., DC 20009; 620,000.

Masons of the State of N. Y., Grand Lodge of Free & Accepted (1781), 71 W. 23rd St., N.Y.C. 10010; 250,000.

Masons, Royal Arch, General Grand Chapter (1797), Box 5320, Lexington KY 40505; 535,000.

Mathematical Assn. of America (1915), 1225 Connecticut Ave., Wash., DC 20036; 19,000.

Mathematical Society, American (1888), 201 Charles St., Providence, RI 02904; 15,400.

Mathematics, Society for Industrial and Applied (1952), 33 S. 17th St., Phila., PA 19103; 3,948.

Mathematical Statistics, Institute of (1935), c/o Leo Katz, A-426 Wells Hall, M.S.U., E. Lansing, MI 48823; 3,000.

Mattachine Society (1951), 59 Christopher St. N.Y., NY 10014; 500.

Mayflower Descendants, General Society of (1897), 4 Winslow St., Plymouth, MA 02360; 15,800.

Mayors, U. S. Conference of (1933), 1620 Eye St., NW, Washington, DC 20006.

Mechanical Engineers, American Society of (1880), 345 East 47th St., New York, NY 10017; 69,325.

Mechanics, Assn. of Chairmen of Departments of (1969), Dept. of Applied Mechanics, School of Engineering, Stanford Univ., Stanford, CA 94305; 105 institutions.

Mechanics, Junior Order of United American (1853), Lodge Rd., Posquoson, VA 23662.

Mediaeval Academy of America (1925), 1430 Massachusetts Ave., Cambridge, MA 02138; 3,415.

Medical Assn., American (1847), 535 N. Dearborn St., Chicago, IL 60697; 200,000.

Medical Association, National (1895), 2109 E St., NW, Wash., DC 20037; 3,000.

Medical Colleges, Assn. of American (1876), 1 Dupont Circle, NW, Washington, DC 20036; 2,900.

Medical Record Assn., American (1928), 875 N. Michigan Ave., Chicago, IL 60611; 13,688.

Medical Technologists, American (1939), 710 Higgins Rd., Park Ridge, IL 60068; 11,423.

Medical Technologists, Amer. College of (1942), 5608 Lane, Raytown, MO 64133; 368.

Medical Women's Association, American (1915), 1740 Broadway., N.Y., NY 10019; 6,000.

Medicine, New York Academy of (1847), 2 East 103 St., New York, NY 10029; 2,947.

Men Voters of the U. S., League of (1969), 88 Arbol, Oroville, CA 95965.

Mensa (1946), 50 East 42nd St., N.Y., NY 10017; 12,500.

Mental Health, Natl. Assn. for (1909), 1800 N. Kent St., Arlington, VA 22209; 1,000,000.

Mental Health Program Directors, Natl. Assn. of State (1963), 15 E St., NW, Wash., DC 20001; 50.

Merchant Marine Library Assn., American (1921), 1 Bowling Green, N.Y., NY 10004; 4,560.

Metal Finishers, Natl. Assn. of (1955), 248 Lorraine Ave., Upper Montclair, NJ 07043; 886.

Metals, American Society for (1913), Metals Park, OH 44073; 40,000.

Meteorological Society, American (1919), 45 Beacon St., Boston, MA 02108; 9,065.

Metric Assn. (1916), Sugarloaf Star Route, Boulder, CO 80302; 5,500.

Microbiology, American Society for (1899), 1913 Eye St., NW, Washington, DC 20006; 19,000.

Microfilm Assn., Natl. (1943), 8728 Colesville Rd., Silver Spring, MD 20910; 7,000.

Middle East, American Friends of (1952), 1717 Massachusetts Ave., NW, Wash., DC 20036; 300.

Military Chaplains Assn. of the U.S.A. (1925), Suite 401, 7758 Wisconsin Ave., NW, Washington, DC 20014; 2,850.

Military Engineers, Society of American (1920), 800 17th St., NW, Wash., DC 20006; 22,000.

Military Institute, American (1933), Box 568, Benj. Franklin Station, Wash., DC 20044; 975.

Military Order of the Carabao (1900, in Manila), 4829 Fairmont Ave., Bethesda, MD 20014; 1,250.

Military Order of the Loyal Legion of the U. S. A. (1865), 1805 Pine St., Phila., PA 19103; 1,100.

Military Order of the Purple Heart (1782, by Gen. George Washington; reactivated Feb. 22, 1932, by President Herbert Hoover and Chief of Staff Douglas MacArthur), 1444 Rhode Island Ave., NW, Wash., DC 20005; 12,000.

Military Order of the World Wars (1919), 1100 17th St., NW, Washington,DC 20036; 11,500.

Military Surgeons of the U. S., Assn. of (1903), 8502 Connecticut Ave., Chevy Chase, MD 20015; 6,000.

Mining, Metallurgical and Petroleum Engineers, Amer. Institute of (1871), 345 E. 47th St., N.Y.C. 10017; 49,726.

Mining and Metallurgical Society of America (1908), 299 Park Ave., New York, NY 10017; 307.

Ministerial Assn., American (1929), 446 Salem Ave., P. O. Box 1252, York PA 17405; 6,201.

Minute Men of America (1918), P. O. Box 505, Stuart, FL 33494; 16,000.

Model Railroad Assn., Natl. (1935), Box 1328 Station C, Canton, OH 44708; 23,000.

Modern Language Assn of America (1883), 62 Fifth Ave., N.Y., NY 10011; 30,000.

Moose, Loyal Order of (1888), Mooseheart, IL 60539; 1,364,772.

Mothers Committee, American (1935), Waldorf Astoria, N.Y., NY 10022; 3,000.

Motion Picture Arts and Sciences, Academy of (1927), 9038 Melrose Ave., Los Angeles, CA 90060; 3,800.

Motion Picture Assn. of America (1922), 522 Fifth Ave., New York, NY 10036.

Motion Picture and Television Engineers, Society of (1916), 862 Scarsdale Ave., Scarsdale, NY 10583; 10,000.

Motion Pictures, Natl. Board of Review of (1940), 210 E. 68th St., N.Y., NY 10021; 250.

Motor Bus Owners, Natl. Assn. of (1926), 1025 Connecticut Ave., Wash., DC 20036; 450 companies.

Motor Vehicle Administrators, American Assn. of (1933), 1828 St., NW, Wash., DC 20036; 130.

Motorcycle Assn., American (1924), 33 Collegeview Ave., Westerville, OH 43081; 150,000.

Motoress Aid (1970), 28671 Northwestern Highway, Southfield, MI 48025; 5,000.

Multiple Sclerosis Society, National (1946), 257 Park Ave., South, N.Y., NY 10010; 182,000.

Municipal Finance Officers Assn. of the U. S. & Canada (1906), 1313 E. 60th St., Chicago, IL 60637; 5,107.

Municipal League, National (1894), 47 East 68th St., New York, NY 10021; 6,000.

Mural Painters, Natl. Society of (1895), 41 E. 65th St., N.Y., NY 10021; 150.

Muscular Dystrophy Associations of America (1950), 810 7th Ave., N.Y., NY 10019; 76 corporate members.

Museums, American Assn. of (1906), 2233 Wisconsin Ave., NW, Wash., DC 20007; 5,600.

Music Center, American (1939), 2109 Broadway, N.Y., NY 10023; 700.

Music Clubs, Natl. Federation of (1898), Suite 1215, 600 S. Michigan Ave., Chicago, IL 60605; 500,000.

Music Conference, American (1947), 150 E. Huron St., Chicago, IL 60611; 900.

Music Council, National (1940), 2109 Broadway, New York, NY 10023; 60 organizations.

Music Educators National Conference (1906), 8150 Leesburg Pike, Vienna, VA 22180; 60,000.

Music, Natl. Assn. of Schools of (1924), 11250 Roger Bacon Drive, #5, Reston, VA 22090; 410 institutions.

Music Players, Amateur Chamber (1947), Box 66A, Vienna, VA 22180; 7,000.

Music Publishers' Assn., Natl. (1917), 110 E. 59th St., New York, NY 10022; 70.

Music Teachers National Assn. (1876), 408 Carew Tower, Cincinnati, OH 45202; 14,200.

Musicians, American Federation of (1896), 220 Mt. Pleasant Ave., Newark, NJ 07104; 300,000.

Musicological Society, American (1934), 201 S. 34th St., Phila., PA 19104; 2,800.

Mutual Savings Banks, National Assn. of (1920), 200 Park Ave., N.Y., NY 10017; 485 banks.

— N —

NAACP (Natl. Assn. for the Advancement of Colored People) (1909), 1790 Broadway, N.Y., NY 10019; 412,000

NAAFA (Natl. Assn. to Aid Fat Americans) (1969), P. O. Box 475, Westbury, NY 11590; 1,000.

Name Society, American (1951), State University College, Potsdam, NY 13676; 900.

NAPAN (Natl. Assn. for the Prevention of Addiction to Narcotics) (1960), 175 5th Ave., N.Y., NY 10010; 125.

NASCAR (Natl. Assn. for Stock Car Auto Racing) (1948), 1801 Volusia Ave., Daytona Beach, FL 32015; 21,000.

National Guard Assn. (1878), 1 Massachusetts Ave., Washington, DC 20001; 48,500.

Nationalities Service, American Council for (1958), 20 West 40th St., N.Y., NY 10018.

Natural Science for Youth Foundation (1961), 763 Silvermine Rd., New Canaan. CT 06840; 400.

Naturalists, Assn. of Interpretive (1961), 6700 Needwood Rd., Derwood, MD 20855; 1,000.

Nature Conservancy (1950), 1800 N. Kent St., Arlington, VA 22314; 25,000.

Nature and Natural Resources, Internatl. Union for Conservation of (1948), Box 19347, c/o Internatl. Commission on Natl. Parks, Wash., DC 20036; 70 countries, 35 states.

Nature Study Society, American (1908), 5881 Cold Brook Rd., Homer, NY 13077; 900.

Naval Architects and Marine Engineers, Society of (1893), 74 Trinity Pl., N.Y., NY 10006; 10,000.

Naval Cadets of America, Junior (1958), 117 Bridge St., Groton, CT 06340; 2,500.

Naval Engineers, American Society of (1888), 1012 14th St. NW, Wash., DC 20005; 4,000.

Naval Institute, U. S. (1873), U. S. Naval Academy, Annapolis, MD 21402; 63,000.

Naval Order of the U. S. (1890), Box 894, Oakland, CA 94604; 4,000.

Naval Reserve Assn. (1954), 1913 Eye St., NW, Washington, DC 20006; 15,000.

Navigation, Institute of (1945), 815 15th St., NW, Washington, DC 20005; 3,000.

Navy Club of the U. S. A. (1940), 1602 Wells St., Fort Wayne, IN 46801; 4,000. **Navy Club of the U. S. A. Auxiliary, Natl.** (1940), 318 W. Pontiac St., Fort Wayne, IN 46807; 10,000.

Navy League of the U. S. (1902), 818 18th St., NW, Washington, DC 20006; 49,556.

Navy Mothers' Clubs of America (1930), P. O. Drawer E, Fremont, NE 68025; 25,000.

Needlework Guild of America (1885), 1736 Pine St., Philadelphia, PA 19103; 400,000.

Negro Business and Professional Women's Clubs, Natl. Assn. of (1935), 3411 Lynchester Rd., Baltimore, MD 21215; 2,000.

Negro College Fund, United (1944), 55 East 52nd St., N.Y., NY 10022; 41 colleges.

Newspaper Editors, American Society of (1922), 1350 Sullivan Trail, Easton, PA 18042; 800.

Newspaper Promotion Assn., International (1931), 11600 Sunrise Valley Dr., Reston, VA 22090; 1,200.

Newspaper Publishers Assn., American (1887), 11600 Sunrise Valley Dr., Reston, VA 22070; 1,080 firms.

Newspaper Publishers Assn., Natl. (1940), 2400 S. Michigan Ave., Chicago, IL 60616; 80.

Ninety-Nines (1929), P. O. Box 59964; Will Rogers World Airport, Oklahoma City, OK 73159; 4,500.

Non-Commissioned Officers Assn. of the U. S. A. (1960), Box 2268, San Antonio, TX 78298; 168,000.

Norway, Sons of (1895), 1455 West Lake St., Minneapolis, MN 55408; 84,000.

Notaries, American Society of (1965), 810 18th St., NW, Washington, DC 20006; 4,774.

Nuclear Society, American (1954), 244 East Ogden Ave., Hinsdale, IL 60521; 10,225.

Numismatic Assn., American (1891), Box 2366, 818 N. Cascade, Colorado Springs, CO 80901; 28,000.

Numismatic Society, American (1858), Broadway between 155th & 156th Sts., N.Y., NY 10032; 1,696.

Nurse Education and Service, Natl. Assn.for Practical (1941), 122 E. 42nd St., N.Y., NY 10017; 33,000.

Nurses' Assn., American (1896), 2420 Pershing Rd., Kansas City, MO. 64108; 200,000.

Nurses, Assn. of Operating Room (1949), 8085 E. Prentice Ave., Englewood, CO 80110; 17,127.

Nurses, Natl. Federation of Licensed Practical (1949), 250 West 57th St., N.Y., NY 10019; 27,000.

Nursing, Natl. League for (1942), 10 Columbus Circle, New York, NY 10019; 16,000.

Nutrition, American Institute of (1928), 9650 Rockville Pike, Bethesda, MD 20014; 1,500.

— O —

Occupational Therapy Assn., American (1917), 6000 Executive Blvd., Rockville, MD 20852; 14,217.

Odd Fellows, Independent Order of (1819), 16 W. Chase St., Baltimore, MD 21201; 1,200,000.

Old Crows, Assn. of (1964), 2361 S. Jefferson Davis Highway 606, Arlington, VA 22202.

Olympic Committee, U. S. (1894), 57 Park Ave., N.Y., NY 10016.

Optical Society of America (1916), 2100 Pennsylvania Ave., NW, Wash., DC 20037; 6,760.

Optimist International (1919), 4494 Lindell Blvd., St. Louis, MO 63108; 112,000.

Optometric Assn., American (1898), 7000 Chippewa St., St.

Louis, MO 63119; 18,409.

Oral Surgeons, American Society of (1918), 211 E. Chicago Ave., Chicago, IL 60611; 2,774.

Order of the Rainbow for Girls, Supreme Assembly Internatl. (1922), 315 Carl Albert Parkway, McAlester, OK 74501; 1,000,000.

Organists, American Guild of (1896), 630 Fifth Ave., New York, NY 10020; 16,000.

Organization of American States (1890), Pan American Union, 17th & Constitution Ave., NW, Wash., DC 20006; 24 nations.

Oriental Society, American (1842), 329 Sterling Memorial Library, New Haven, CT 06520; 1,728.

Ornithologists' Union, American (1883), c/o Museum of Natural History, Wash., DC 20560; 3,250.

ORT Federation, American (Organization for Rehabilitation through Training) (1972), 817 Broadway, N.Y., NY 10013; 120,-000.

Osteopathic Association, American (1897), 212 E. Ohio St., Chicago, IL 60611; 11,500.

—P—

Paleontological Research Institution (1932), 1259 Trumansburg Rd., Ithaca, NY 14850; 468.

Paper Institute, American (1964), 260 Madison Ave., New York, NY 10016; 200 companies.

Paper Stationery & Tablet Manufacturers Assn. (1934), 444 Madison Ave. N.Y., NY 10022; 30 companies.

Parasitologists, American Society of (1914), 1041 New Hampshire St., Box 368, Lawrence, KS 66044; 1,800.

Parents and Teachers, Natl. Congress of (1897), 700 N. Rush St., Chicago, IL 60611; 7,658,014.

Parents Without Partners (1957), 7910 Woodmont Ave., NW, Wash., DC 20014; 105,000.

Parking Assn., Natl. (1951), 1101 17th St., NW, Washington, DC 20036; 900.

Parkinson's Disease Foundation (1957), 640 W. 168th St., N.Y., NY 10032.

Parks & Conservation Assn., National (1919), 1701 18th St., NW, Washington, DC 20009; 45,000.

Pathologists and Bacteriologists, Amer. Assn. of (1900), 9650 Rockville Pike, Bethesda, MD 20014; 1,086.

Pay Toilets in America, Committee to End (1970), 1326 Amherst Pl., Dayton, OH 45406; 1,600.

Pedestrian Assn., American (formerly, **Pedestrian League of America** (1959), 170 Broadway, New York, NY 10038; 200.

P.E.N. American Center (1922), 156 Fifth Ave., N.Y., NY 10010; 1,600.

Pen Women, Natl. League of American (1897), 1300 17th St., NW, Wash., DC 20036; 6,000.

Pennsylvania Society (1899), Suite 594, Walfdorf-Astoria Hotel, 301 Park Ave., N.Y., NY 10022; 2,500.

P.E.O. Sisterhood (1869), 3700 Grand Ave., Des Moines, IA 50312; 183,030.

Performance Improvement, Amer. Society for (formerly, **Amer. Society for Zero Defects**) (1966), 790 Broad St., Newark, NJ 07102; 300.

Personnel Administration, Amer. Society for, (1948), 19 Church St., Berea, OH 44017; 13,000.

Personnel and Guidance Assn., American (1952), 1607 New Hampshire Ave.. NW, Wash., DC 20009; 34,000.

Personnel Women, Internatl. Assn. (1950), 358 Fifth Ave., New York, NY 10001; 1,000.

Petroleum Geologists, American Assn. of (1917), Box 979, Tulsa, OK 74101; 16,090.

Petroleum Institute, American (1919), 1801 K St., NW, Washington, DC 20006; 7,000.

Petroleum Landmen, Amer. Assn. of (1955), 2404 Continental Life Bldg., Fort Worth, TX 76102; 4,200.

Pharmaceutical Assn., American (1852), 2215 Constitution Ave., NW, Wash., DC 20037; 50,000.

Philatelic Americans, Society of (1894), P. O. Box 42060, Cincinnati, OH 45242; 7,000.

Philatelic Society, American (1886), P. O. Box 800, State College, P A 16801; 31,215.

Philaticans, Society of (1972), P. O. Box 150, Clinton Corners, NY 12514; 200.

Philharmonic Symphony Society of New York (1928 by merger of **Philharmonic Soc. of N. Y.**, estab. 1842, **and Symphony Soc. of N. Y.**, estab. 1887), Philharmonic Hall, Lincoln Center, N.Y., NY 10023; 1,400.

Philological Assn., American (1869), 431-432 N. Burrowes, Penn. State Univ., University Park, PA 61802; 2,800.

Philosophical Assn., American (1969), Hamilton College, Clinton, NY 13323; 5,500.

Philosophical Society, American (1743), 104 S. 5th St., Philadelphia, PA 19106; 500.

Photographers of America, Professional (1880), 1090 Executive Way, Des Plaines. IL 60018; 15,200.

Photographers in Communications, Society of (formerly, **Society of Magazine Photographers**) (1944), 60 East 42nd St., N.Y., NY 10017; 950.

Photographic Society of America (1933), 2005 Walnut St., Philadelphia, PA 19103; 16,000.

Physical Society, American (1899), 345 E. 45th St., N.Y., NY 10017; 28,000.

Physical Therapy Association, American (1921), 1156 15th St., NW, Wash., DC 20005; 21,000.

Physicians, American College of (1915), 4200 Pine St., Philadelphia, PA 19104; 20,000.

Physics, American Institute of (1913), 335 East 45th St., New York, NY 10017; 50,000.

Physiological Society, American, (1887), 9650 Rockville Pike, Bethesda, MD 20014; 4,459.

Pilgrim Society (1820), Pilgrim Hall, 75 Court St., Plymouth, MA 20360; 650.

Pilgrims of the United States (1903), 74 Trinity Pl., New York NY 10006; 1,000.

Pilot Club International (1921), Pilot Bldg., 244 College St., Macon, GA 31208; 17,500.

Pioneer Women (1926), 315 5th Ave., N.Y., NY 10016; 50,-000.

Planned Parenthood Federation of América (1922 as **Amer. Birth Control League;** 1939, **Birth Control Federation of America;** renamed 1942) 810 7th Ave., N.Y., NY 10019; 190 affiliates.

Planners, Amer. Institute of (1917), 1776 Massachusetts Ave., NW, Washington, DC 20036; 9,800.

Planning Assn., Natl. (1934), 1606 New Hampshire Ave., NW, Washington, DC 20009; 3,500.

Planning Officials, Amer. Society of (1934), 1313 E. 60th St., Chicago, IL 60637; 11,000.

Plastics Engineers, Society of (1942), 656 W. Putnam Ave., Greenwich, CT 06830; 17,500.

Plastics Industry, Society of (1937), 250 Park Ave., New York, NY 10017; 1,200 companies.

Platform Assn., Internatl. (1826), 2564 Berkshire Rd., Cleveland Heights, OH 44106; 11,000.

Podiatry Association, American (1912), 20 Chevy Chase Circle, NW, Wash., DC 20015; 6,000.

Poetry Day Committee, Natl. (1965), 1110 N. Venetian Dr., Miami Beach, FL 33139; 12,000.

Poetry Society of America (1910), 15 Gramercy Park, N.Y., NY 10003; 700.

Poets, Academy of America (1934), 1078 Madison Ave., N.Y., NY 10028; 73.

Poland Committee of the U.S.A., Friends of (1940), 55 W. 42nd St., N.Y., NY 10036; 14,791.

Polar Society, American (1934), 98-20 62nd Dr., Apt. 7 H. Rego Park, NY 11374; 2,500.

Police, American Federation of (1966), 1100 NE 125th St., N. Miami, Fl 33161; 33,000.

Police, International Assn. of Chiefs of (1893), Eleven Firstfield Rd., Gaithersburg, MD 20760; 10,300.

Police, Natl. Assn. of Special and Reserve (1965), Box 45, Bay Station, Brooklyn, NY 11235; 1,000.

Police Officers Assn. of America, Natl. (1955), 1890 S. Tamiami Trail, Venice, FL 33593; 23,000.

Policy Placers, Checkers and Raters of America, Natl. Assn. of (1968), 41-43 John St., N.Y., NY 10038; 4,143.

Polish Army Veterans Assn. of America (1921), 17 Irving Pl., N.Y., NY 10003; 9,500.

Polish Legion of American Veterans (1921), 3024 N. Laramie Ave., Chicago, IL 60641; 20,000.

Political Items Collectors, American (1945), 66 Golf St., Newington, CT 06111; 2,000.

Political Science, Academy of (1880), 2852 Broadway, N.Y., NY 10025; 11,000.

Political Science Assn., American (1903), 1527 New Hampshire Ave., NW, Wash., DC 20036; 12,000.

Political and Social Science, Amer. Academy of (1889), 3937 Chestnut St., Philadelphia, PA 19104; 21,500.

Polo Association, U.S. (1890), Suite 706, 1301 W. 22nd St., Oak Brook, IL 60521; 2,000.

Population Assn. of America (1932), Box 14182, Benjamin Franklin Sta., Wash., DC 20044; 2,500.

Portuguese Continental Union of the U.S.A. (1929), 899 Boylston St., Boston, MA 02115; 9,211.

Postal Clerks, United Federation of (1906), 817 14th St., NW, Washington, DC 20005; 285,000.

Postmasters of the U.S., Natl. Assn. of (1898), Suite 4200, 490 L'Enfant Plaza East, SW, Wash., DC 20024; 27,364.

Postmasters of the U.S., National League of (1904), 955 L'Enfant Plaza, SW, Wash., DC 20024; 15,000.

Poultry Science Assn. (1908), c/o Dr. C. B. Ryan, Texas A & M Univ., College Station, TX 77843; 1,750.

Power Boat Assn., American (1903), 22811 Greater Mack, St. Clair Shores, MI 48080; 7,514.

Power Conference, American (1938), Illinois Inst. of Technology, 10 W. 32nd St., Chicago, IL 60616.

Power Engineers, Natl. Assn. of (1882), 176 W. Adams St., Chicago, IL 60603; 12,296.

Power Squadron, U.S. (1914), 50 Craig Rd., Montvale, NJ 07645; 88,000.

Precancel Collectors, Natl. Assn. of (1950), 5121 Park Blvd., Wildwood, NJ 08260; 5,000.

Press Club of America, Overseas (1939), 1271 Ave. of the Americas, N.Y., NY 10020; 2,200.

Press Club, Natl. (1908), 529 14th St., NW, Wash., DC 20004; 4,600.

Press Institute, International (1951), Munstergasse 9 CH-8001 Zurich, Switzerland; 1,800.

Press and Radio Club (1948), P.O. Box 7023, Montgomery, AL 36107; 707.

Press Women, National Federation of (1937), 912 S. Holly St., Medford, OR 97501; 4,000.

Production and Inventory Control Society, American (1957), Suite 504, 2600 Virginia Ave., NW, Wash., DC 20037; 10,000.

Propeller Club of the U.S. (1927), 1730 M St., NW, Wash., DC 20036; 13,000.

Psychical Research, Amer. Society of (1885), 5 W. 73rd St., N.Y., NY 10023; 2,500.

Psychiatric Association, American (1844), 1700 18th St., NW, Wash., DC 20009; 20,227.

Psychoanalytic Assn., American (1911), 1 East 57th St., N.Y., NY 10022; 2,016.

Psychological Assn., American (1892), 1200 17th St., NW, Wash., DC 20036; 35,000.

Psychological Assn. for Psychoanalysis, Natl. (1946), 150 W. 13th St., N.Y., NY 10011; 162.

Psychological Minorities, Society for the Aid of (1968), 42-25 Hampton St., Elmhurst, NY 11373; 500.

Psychotherapy Assn., American Group (1942), 1865 Broadway, N.Y., NY 10023; 2800.

Public Health Assn., American (1872), 1015 18th St., NW, Wash., DC 20036; 50,000.

Public Relations Society of America (1947), 845 Third Ave., New York, NY 10022; 7,200.

Public Welfare Assn., American (1936), 1313 E. 60th St. Chicago, IL 60637; 7,900.

Publishers, Assn. of American (1970), One Park Ave., N.Y., NY 10016; 260.

—Q & R—

Quality Control, Amer. Society for (1946), 161 W. Wisconsin Ave., Milwaukee, WI 53203; 20,000.

Racing Commissioners, National Assn. of State (1935), P.O. Box 4216, Lexington, KY 40504; 285.

Racquetball Assn., Natl. (1973), 4101 Dempster St., Skokie, IL 60067; 3,000.

Radio Free Europe (1949), 2 Park Ave., N.Y., NY 10016.

Radiological Society of North America (1915), 713 E. Genesee St., Syracuse, NY 13210; 6,549.

Radio Liberty (1951), 30 East 42nd St., N.Y., NY 10017.

Radio Relay League, American (1914), 225 Main St., Newington, CT 06111; 105,000.

Radio and Televison Society, International (1939), 420 Lexington Ave., N.Y., NY 10017; 1,200.

Radio Union, International Amateur (1925), 225 Main St., Newington, CT 06111; 86 societies.

Railroad Passengers, Natl. Assn. of (1967), 417 New Jersey Ave., SE, Wash., DC 20003; 6,000.

Railroads, Assn. of American (1934), 1920 L St., Rm. 211, Wash., DC 20036; 171 railroads.

Railway Engineering Assn., American (1899), 59 E. Van Buren St., Chicago, IL 60605; 3,400.

Railway Historical Society, Natl. (1937), 158 Stockbridge Ave., Buffalo, NY 14215; 8,847.

Railway Progress Institute (1908), 801 N. Fairfax St., Alexandria, VA 22314; 175 companies.

Range Management, Society for (1948), 2120 S. Birch St., Denver, CO 80222; 5,000.

Real Estate Investment Funds, Natl. Assn. of (1960), 1101 17th St., NW, Wash., DC 20036; 310.

Realtors, Natl. Assn. of (formerly, **Natl. Assn. of Real Estate Boards)** (1908), 155 E. Superior St., Chicago, IL 60611; 420,000.

Reconcilation, Fellowship of (1915), Box 271, Nyack, NY 10960; 23,467.

Recording Industry Assn. of America (1952), 1 East 57th St., New York, NY 10022; 51 firms.

Records Management Assn., American (1956), Suite 823, 24 N. Wabash Ave., Chicago, IL 60602; 2,400.

Recreation and Park Assn., Natl. (1965), 1601 N. Kent St., Arlington, VA 22209; 14,829.

Red Cross, American National (1881), 17th & D Sts., NW, Wash., DC 20006; 36,464,592.

Red Men, Improved Order of (1765), 1525 West Ave., Box 683, Waco, TX 76707; 60,000.

Regional Plan Assn. (1929), 235 East 45th St., N.Y., NY 10017; 2,100.

Rehabilitation Assn., Natl. (1925), 1522 K St., NW, Wash., DC 20005; 35,000.

Religion, American Academy of (1924), Florida State Univ., Tallahassee, FL 32306; 4,013.

Renaissance Society of America (1954), 1161 Amsterdam Ave., N.Y. NY 10027; 3,289.

Rescue Committee, Internatl. (1933), 386 Park Ave. S., N.Y., NY 10010; 62 directors.

Reserve Officers Assn. of the U.S. (1922), 1 Constitution Ave., NE, Wash., DC 20002; 80,000.

Restaurant Assn., Natl. (1919), Suite 2600, IBM Plaza, Chicago, IL 60611; 125,000.

Retail Druggists, National Assn. of (1898), 1 East Wacker Dr., Chicago, IL 60601; 32,000.

Retail Merchants, Natl. Retail (1911), 100 West 31st St., N.Y., NY 10001; 26,000 stores.

Retarded Children, Natl. Assn. for (1955), 2709 Ave. E East, Arlington, TX 76011; 200,000.

Retired Assn. for the Uniformed Services (1970), Suite 408, 1701 21st Ave. South, Nashville, TN 37212; 24,788.

Retired Federal Employees, Natl. Assn. of (1921), 1533 New Hampshire Ave., NW, Wash., DC 20036; 187,000.

Retired Officers Assn., (1929), 1625 Eye St., NW, Wash., DC 20006; 165,000.

Retired Persons, Amer. Assn. of (1958), 1225 Connecticut Ave., NW, Wash., DC 20036; 5,000,000.

Retired Teachers Assn., Natl. (1947), 1225 Connecticut Ave., NW, Washington DC 20036; 362,555.

Retreads (World War I & World War II) (1947), 40-07 154th St., Flushing, NY 11354; 1,500.

Revolver Assn., U.S. (1900), 59 Alvin St., Springfield, MA 01104; 1,200.

Rhodes Scholars, Assn. of American (1907), 1100 Philadelphia Natl. Bank Bldg., Phila., PA 19107; 1,493.

Rifle Assn. of America, Natl. (1871), 1600 Rhode Island Av., NW, Wash., DC 20036; 1,000,000.

Road Builders' Assn., American (1902), 525 School St., SW Wash., DC 20024; 5,500.

Rocketry, National Assn. of (1956), P.O. 178, McLean, VA 22101; 5,000.

Rodeo Cowboys Assn. (1945), 2929 W. 19th Ave., Denver, CO 80204; 3,500.

Roller Skating Assn., U.S. Amateur (1942), 152 W. 42nd St., N.Y., NY 10036; 11,000.

Roller Skating Confederation of the U.S.A. (1973), 7700 A St., Lincoln, NE 68510; 26,000.

Roller Skating Rink Operators Assn. of America (1937), 7700 A St., Lincoln, NE 68510; 840 rinks.

Rose Society, American (1899), P.O. Box 30,000, Shreveport, LA 71130; 16,000.

Rosicrucian Fraternity (1614 in Germany, 1861 in U.S.), Beverly Hall, Quakertown, PA 18951.

Rosicrucian Order, AMORC (1915), Rosicrucian Park, San Jose, CA 95191; 120,000.

Rosicrucians, Society of (1909), 321 West 101st St., N.Y., NY 10025.

Rotary International (1905), 1600 Ridge Ave., Evanston, IL 60201; 748,500 in 16,000 clubs.

Round Table International (1924), 61 E. Colorado Blvd., Pasadena, CA 91101; 825.

Rowing Assn., Intercollegiate (1895), Hotel Manhattan, 8th Ave. at 44th St., N.Y., NY 10036; 5.

Royal Arcanum, Supreme Council of the (1877), 61 Batterymarch St., Boston, MA 02110; 30,918.

Rubber Manufacturers Assn: (1915), 444 Madison Ave., N.Y., NY 10022; 200 firms.

Ruritan National (1928), Box 487, Dublin, VA 24084; 37,000.

Russian Orthodox Clubs, Federated (1927), 84 East Market St., Wilkes-Barre, PA 18701; 4,500.

—S—

Safety Council, National (1913), 425 N. Michigan Ave., Chicago, IL 60611; 15,400.

Safety Engineers, American Society of (1911), 850 Busse Highway, Park Ridge, IL 60068; 12,000.

St. Paul, National Guilds of (1937), 601 Hill 'N Dale, Lexington, KY 40503; 13,750.

Salt Institute (1934), 206 N. Washington St., Alexandria, VA 22314; 24 companies.

Salvation Army (1865 in England, 1880 in U.S.), 120-130 West 14th St., N.Y., NY 10011; 358,626 in U.S.

Sane World, A Citizen's Organization for a (1957), 318 Massachusetts Ave., NW, Wash., DC 20002; 25,000.

Save-the-Redwoods League (1918), 114 Sansome St., San Francisco, CA 94104; 60,000.

School Administrators, American Assn. of (1865), 1801 N.

Moore St., Arlington, VA 22209; 20,000.

School Boards Assn., Natl. (1940), 800 State Natl. Bank Plaza, Evanston, IL 60201; 77,000.

School Counselor Assn., American (1952), 1607 New Hampshire Ave., NW, Wash., DC 20009; 13,000.

School Principals, Natl. Assn. of Secondary (1916), 1904 Association Dr., Reston, VA 22091; 30,000.

Schools and Colleges, Amer. Council on (1927), 446 Salem Ave., Box 1252, York, PA 17405; 119 schools.

Schweitzer, Albert, Fellowship (1948), 866 United Nations Plaza, N.Y., NY 10017.

Schweitzer, Albert, Friendship House (1967), c/o Erica Anderson, Hurburt Rd., Great Barrington, MA 01230; 67,000.

Science, Amer. Assn. for the Advancement of (1848), 1515 Massachusetts Ave., NW, Wash., DC 20005: 126,686.

Science Service (1921), 1719 N St., NW, Washington, DC 20036.

Science Teachers Assn., Natl. (1944), 1201 16th St., NW, Wash., DC 20036; 20,608.

Science Writers, Natl. Assn. of (1934), Box H. Sea Cliff, NY 11579;950.

Sciences, National Academy of — National Research Council (1863), 2101 Constitution Ave., NW, Wash., DC 20418; 1,000.

Sciences, New York Academy of (1817), 2 East 63rd St., N.Y., NY 10021; 25,000.

Scientific Apparatus Makers Assn. (1918), 1140 Connecticut Ave., NW, Wash., DC 20036; 222 companies.

Scientists, Federation of American (1946), 203 C St., N.E., Washington, DC 20002; 6,000.

Scottish Clans, Order of (1878, merged with **Independent Order of Foresters,** 1971), 111 Washington St., Brookline, MA 02146; 10,000.

Screen Actors Guild (1933), 7750 Sunset Blvd., Ho'lywood, CA 90046; 26,000.

Sculpture Society, Natl. (1893), 75 Rockefeller Plaza, New York, NY 10019; 350.

Seamen's Service, United (1942), 17 Battery Place, N.Y., NY 10004.

Secretaries Assn., Natl. (1942), 616 E. 63 St., Kansas City, MO 64110; 29,000.

Secularists of America, United (1946), 377 Vernon St., Oakland, CA 94610; 960.

Securities Industry Assn. (1972, consolidation of **Investment Banker Assn.** and **Assn. of Stock Exchange Firms**), 20 Broad St., N.Y., NY 10005; 850 firms.

Security Industrial Assn., National (1944), 740 15th St., NW, Wash., DC 20005; 350.

Seeing Eye, The (1929),Morristown, NJ 07960; 26,000.

Semantics, Institute of General (1938), White Hollow Rd., Lime Rock, CT 06039; 1,000.

Separation of Church and State, Americans United for (1948), 8120 Fenton St., Silver Spring, MD 20910; 150,000.

Separationists, Society of (1963), P.O. Box 2117, Austin, TX 78767; 28,000 families.

Sertoma International (1912), 1900 E. Meyer Blvd., Kansas City, MO 64132; 30,104.

Settlements and Neighborhood Centers, Natl. Federation of (1911), 232 Madison Ave., N.Y., NY 10016; 1,350.

Sex Information & Education Council of the U.S. (SIECUS) (1964), 1855 Broadway, N.Y., NY 10023; 50.

Shade Tree Conference, Internatl. (1924), P.O. Box 71, Urbana, IL 61801; 2,500.

Sheriffs' Assn., Natl. (1940), Suite 320, 1250 Connecticut Ave., NW, Wash., DC 20036; 35,000.

Shipbuilders Council of America (1921), Watergate 600, Wash., DC 20037; 37 companies.

Shoe Retailers Assn., Natl. (1912), 200 Madison Ave., New York, NY 10016; 3,200.

Shore & Beach Preservation Assn., Amer. (1926), 10 Rickenbacker Causeway, Miami, FL 33149; 600.

Showmen's League of America (1913), 300 W. Randolph St., Chicago, IL 60606; 1,350.

Shrine, Imperial Council of the A.A. Order of Nobles of the Mystic (1872), 323 N. Michigan Ave., Chicago, IL 60601; 896,-750.

Shut-In Day Society, Natl. (1970), 237 Franklin St., Reading, PA 19602; 6,000.

Sierra Club (1892), 1050 Mills Tower, 220 Bush St., San Francisco, CA 94104; 140,000.

Silurians, Society of the (1924), 103 Park Ave., N.Y., NY 10017; 700.

Spelling Council, Phonemic (merged **Simpler Spelling Assn.**) (1971), Lake Placid, NY 12946; 100.

Skating Union of the U.S., Amateur (1938), 4423 W. Deming Pl., Chicago, IL 60639; 5,200.

Skeet Shooting Assn., Natl. (1946), P.O. Box 28188, San Antonio, TX 78228; 18,000.

Ski Assn., United States (1904), 1726 Champa St., Denver, CO 80202; 120,000.

Small Business, Amer. Federation of (1963), 407 S. Dearborn, Chicago, IL 60605; 5,000.

Small Business Assn., Natl. (1937), 1225 19th St. NW, Washington, DC 20036; 45,000.

Smoking & Health, Natl. Clearinghouse for (1965), 5401 Westbard Ave., Bethesda, MD 20016.

Soaring Society of America (1932), P.O. Box 66071, Los Angeles, CA 90066; 12,729.

Soccer Federation, U.S. (1913), 350 5th Ave., Suite 4010, N.Y., NY 10001; 41 state assns.

Social Biology, Society for the Study of (1926), Psychiatric Institute, 722 W. 168th St., N.Y., NY 10032; 471.

Social Health Assn., American (1912), 1740 Broadway, New York, NY 10019; 1,200.

Social Science Research Council (1923), 605 Third Ave., New York, NY 10016; 30.

Social Sciences, Natl. Institute of (1865), 545 Madison Ave., N.Y., NY 10022; 675.

Social Welfare, Internatl. Council on (1928), 345 E. 46th St., N.Y., NY 10017; 68 natl. committees.

Social Welfare, Natl. Conference on (1873), 22 West Gay St., Columbus, OH 43215; 5,000.

Social Work Education, Council on (1952), 345 East 46th St., New York, NY 10017; 4,600.

Social Workers, National Assn. of (1955), 1425 H St., NW, Wash., DC 20005; 58,000.

Sociological Assn., American (1905), 1722 N St., NW, Wash., DC 20036; 14,050.

Softball Assn., Amateur (1933), 2801 N.E. 50th St., Oklahoma City, OK 73111; 1,250,000 players.

Softball League, Cinderella (1958), 34 E. Market St., Corning, NY 14830; 25,000.

Soft Drink Assn., National (1919), 1101 16th St., NW, Washington, DC 20036; 1,896.

Soil Conservation Society of America (1945), 7515 N.E. Ankeny Rd., Ankeny, IA 50021; 14,500.

Soil Science Society of America (1936), 677 S. Segoe Rd., Madison, WI 53711; 3,400.

Sojourners, National (1921), 4600 Duke St., Alexandria, VA 22304; 8,400.

Soldier's, Sailor's and Airmen's Club (1919), 283 Lexington Ave., N.Y., NY 10016.

Sons of Confederate Veterans (1896), War Memorial Bldg., Jackson, MI 39401; 3,500.

Sons of the American Legion (1932), P.O. Box 1055, Indianapolis, IN 46206; 18,771.

Sons of the American Revolution, Natl. Society (1889), 2412 Massachusetts Ave., Wash., DC 20008; 20,174.

Sons of Italy in America, Order (1905), 1226 S. Broad St., Philadelphia, PA 19146; 250,000.

Sons of Poland, Assn. of the (1903), 655 Newark Ave., Jersey City, NJ 07305; 15,000.

Sons of St. Patrick, Society of the Friendly (1784), 80 Wall St., New York, NY 10005; 1,300.

Sons of the Revolution (1876), Fraunces Tavern, 54 Pearl St., N.Y., NY 10004; 6,000.

Sons of Union Veterans of the Civil War (1881), Box 24, Federal Bldg., Gettysburg, PA 17325; 3,000.

Soroptimist Federation of the Americas (1921), 1616 Walnut St., Philadelphia, PA 19103; 30,000.

Southern Christian Leadership Conference (1957), 334 Auburn Ave., NE, Atlanta, GA 30303; 243 affiliate organizations.

Southern Regional Council (1944), 52 Fairlie St., NW, Atlanta, GA 30303; 110.

Spanish War Veterans, United (1899), P.O. Box 1915, Washington, DC 20013; 600.

Speech Communication Assn. (formerly, **Speech Assn. of America**) (1914), Statler Hilton Hotel, N.Y., NY 10001; 6,730.

Speech and Hearing Assn., American (1925), 9030 Old Georgetown Rd., Wash., DC 20014; 17,500.

Speleological Society of America (1964), 1124 100th Ave. NE, Bellevue, WA 98004; 3,627.

Speleological Society, Natl. (1941), Cave Ave., Huntsville, AL 35810; 4,500.

Sports Car Club of America (1944), 1562 S. Parker Rd., Denver, CO 80231; 22,000.

Sports Fans of America, Professional (1962), 324 Trade Sq.,West, Troy, OH 45373; 109.

Stamp Dealers' Association, American (1914), 595 Madison Ave., New York, NY 10022; 1,000.

Standards Institute, American National (1918), 1430 Broadway, New York, NY 10018; 1,032 organizations.

State & Local History, American Assn. for (1940), 1315 8th Ave., So., Nashville, TN 37203; 4,200.

State Communities Aid Assn. (1872), 105 E. 22nd St., New York, NY 10010; 272.

State Governments, Council of (1933), Iron Works Pike, Lexington, KY 40405.

State High School Assns., Natl. Federation of (1920), 400

Leslie St., Elgin, IL 60120; 50 states, 10 provinces.
State Legislative Leaders, Natl. Conference of (1959), 411 E. Mason St., Milwaukee, WI 53202; 47 states.
State Parks, Natl. Conference on (1921), 1601 N. Kent St., Arlington, VA 22209; 657.
State Universities and Land-Grant Colleges, Natl. Assn. of (1871), One Dupont Circle, NW, Wash., DC 20036.
Statistical Assn., American (1839), 806 15th St., NW, Washington, DC 20005; 10,800.
Steamship Historica Society of America (1935), 414 Pelton Ave., Staten Island, NY 10310; 1,818.
Steel Construction, American Institute of (1921), 101 Park Ave., N.Y., NY 10017; 944.
Steel Founders' Society of America (1902), 20611 Center Ridge Rd., Rocky River, OH 44116; 126 foundries.
Steeplechase and Hunt Assn., Natl. (1895), Box 308, Elmont, NY 11003; 3,000.
Sterilization, Association for Voluntary (1943), 708 Third Ave., New York, NY 10017; 16,000.
Steuben Society of America (1919), 369 Lexington Ave., New York, NY 10017.
Stock Exchange, American (1908), 86 Trinity Pl., New York, NY 10006; 852.
Stock Exchange, New York (1792), 11 Wall St., New York, NY 10005; 1,366.
Stock Exchange, Philadelphia-Baltimore-Washington (1790), 17th St. and Stock Exchange Pl., Phila., PA 19103; 450.
Student Assn., National (1947), 2115 S St., NW, Washington, DC 20008; 700 schools.
Student Councils, Natl. Assn. of (1931), 1904 Association Dr., Reston, VA 22091; 5,000.
Students of German, Natl. Federation of (1967), 339 Walnut St., Philadelphia, PA 19106; 15,000.
Sugar Association (1949), 254 West 31st St., N.Y., NY 10001; 24.
Sugar Brokers Assn., National (1903), 76 Beaver St., N.Y., NY 10005; 301.
Sunbathing Assn., American (1929), 810 N. Mills Ave., Orlando, FL 32803; 20,000.
Sunday League (1933), 279 Highland Ave., Newark, NJ 07104; 25,000.
Sunday School Union, American (1817), 1816 Chestnut St., Phila. PA 19103; 1,586 schools.
Surgeons, American College of (1913), 55 E. Erie St., Chicago, IL 60611; 35,500.
Surgeons, International College of (1935), 1516 N. Lake Shore Dr., Chicago, IL 60610; 12,000.
Surveying and Mapping, American Congress on (1941), Suite 430; Woodward Bldg., 733 15th St., NW, Washington, DC 20005; 6,000.
Symphony Orchestra League, American (1942), P.O. Box 66, Vienna, VA 22180; 2,200.
Systems Management, Assn. for (1947), 24587 Bagley Rd., Cleveland, OH 44138; 11,000.

—T—

Table Tennis Assn., U.S. (1933), Box 815, Orange, CT 06477; 5,000
Tax Accountants, Natl. Assn. of Enrolled Federal (1960), 6108 N. Harding Ave., Chicago, IL 60659; 500.
Tax Administrators, Federation of (1937), 1313 East 60th St., Chicago, IL 60637.
Tax Assn., Natl.-Tax Institute of America (merged 1973), 21 E. State St., Columbus, OH 43215; 2,600.
Tax Foundation (1937), 50 Rockefeller Plaza, N.Y., NY 10020; 1,400 companies.
Tea Assn. of the U.S.A. (1899), 230 Park Ave., N.Y., NY 10017; 250.
Teachers' Agencies, Natl. Assn. of (1915), 1825 K St., NW, Wash., DC 20006; 60.
Teachers, American Federation of (1916), 1012 14th St., NW, Washington, DC 20005; 400,000.
Teachers of English, Natl. Council of (1911), 1111 Kenyon Rd., Urbana, IL 61801; 100,000.
Teachers of French, Amer. Assn. of (1927), 57 E. Armory Ave., Champaign, IL 61820; 11,600.
Teachers of German, Assn. of (1927), 339 Walnut St., Phila., PA 19106; 8,500.
Teachers of Singing, Natl. Assn. of (1944), 250 W. 57th St., New York, NY 10019; 3,000.
Teachers of Spanish and Portuguese, Amer. Assn. of (1917), Wichita State Univ., Wichita, KS 67208; 14,500.
Technical Communication, Society for (formerly, **Society of Technical Writers and Publishers**) (1957), 1010 Vermont Ave., NW, Wash., DC 20005; 3,000.
Television Arts and Sciences, Natl. Academy of (1946), 291 S. La Cienega, Beverly Hills, CA 90211; 7,500.
Television Bureau of Advertising (1955), 1 Rockefeller Plaza, N.Y., NY 10020; 350.

Television and Radio Arts, Amer. Federation of (1937), 1350 Ave. of Americas, N.Y., NY 10019; 29,000.
Telluride Assn. (1911), 217 West Ave., Ithaca, NY 14850; 75.
Tennis League, Youth (1968), 1701 Vandalia, Collinsville, IL 62234; 850.
Testing and Materials, American Society for (1898), 1916 Race St., Phila. PA 19103; 21,000.
Textile Association, Northern (1854), 211 Congress St., Boston, MA 02110; 150 companies.
Textile Manufacturers Institute, American (1949), 1501 Johnston Bldg., Charlotte, NC 28281; 250.
Theatre Assn., American (1936), 1317 F St., NW, Washington, DC 20004; 4,500.
Theatre and Academy, American National (1935), 245 West 52nd St., New York, NY 10019; 800.
Theatre Organ Society, American (1955), Box 1002, Middleburg, VA 22117; 5,000.
Theatre Owners, Natl. Assn. of (1924), 1501 Broadway, N.Y., NY 10036; 8,000.
Theodore Roosevelt Assn. (1921), 28 East 20th St., New York, NY 10003.
Theological Library Assn., American (1947), Lutheran Theological Seminary, 7301 Germantown Ave., Phila., PA 19119; 362 in 133 institutions.
Theological Schools, American Assn. of (1936), P.O. Box 396, Vandalia, OH 45377; 198 schools.
Theosophical Society in America (1886), 1926 North Main St., Wheaton, IL 60187; 5,500.
Thoreau Society (1941), State Univ. College, Geneseo, NY 14454; 1,000.
Thoroughbred Racing Assn. (1942), 5 Dakota Dr., New Hyde Park, NY 11040; 55 race tracks.
Toastmasters International (1924), 2200 N. Grand, Santa Ana, CA 92711; 60,000.
Toastmistress Clubs, Internatl. (1938), 9068 E. Firestone Blvd., Downey, CA 90241; 21,000.
Topical Assn., American (1949), 3306 North 50th St., Milwaukee, WI 53216; 10,000.
Torch Clubs, Internatl. Assn. of (1924), Box 8670, University Station, Knoxville, TN 37916; 5,200.
Toy Manufacturers of America (1916), 200 Fifth Ave., New York, NY 10010; 280.
Trade Relations Council (1885), 1001 Connecticut Ave., NW, Washington, DC 20036; 75.
Traffic and Transportation, Amer. Society of (1946), 547 W. Jackson Blvd., Chicago, IL 60606; 2,650.
Traffic Engineers, Institute of (1930), 1815 N. Ft. Myer Dr., Arlington, VA 22209; 4,246.
Training Corps, American (1961), 107-12 Jamaica Ave., Richmond Hill, NY 11418; 700.
Training & Development, American Society for (1943), P.O. Box 5307, Madison, WI 53705; 10,000.
Transit Assn., American (1882), 465 L'Enfant Plaza, SW, Wash., DC 20024; 500 companies.
Transportation Assn. of America (1935), 1101 17th St., NW, Washington, DC 20036; 850 companies.
Trapshooting Assn., Amateur (1923), 601 W. Natl. Rd., Vandalia, OH 45377; 80,000.
Travel Agents, American Society of (1931), 360 Lexington Ave., N.Y., NY 10017; 12,400.
Travel Organizations, Discover America (1969, merger of **Natl. Assn. of Travel Orgs. & Discover America**) 1100 Connecticut Ave., NW, Wash., DC 20036; 1,000.
Travelers Aid-Internatl. Social Service of America (formerly, **Travelers Aid Assn. of America** merged 1972), 345 E. 46th St., N.Y., NY 10017.
Traveleers International (1943), P.O. Box 1017, Chandler, AZ 85224; 16,688.
Trotting Assn., U.S. (1932), 750 Michigan Ave., Columbus, OH 43215; 35,000.
Trucking Assns., American (1933), 1616 P St., NW, Washington, DC 20036; 51 assns.
True Sisters, United Order (1846), 150 W. 85th St., N.Y., NY 10024; 12,000.
Turners, American (1848), 1550 Clinton Ave., N. Rochester, NY 14621; 14,000.

—U—

UNICEF, U.S. Committee for (1947), 331 East 38th St., N.Y., NY 10016; 3,000,000 volunteers.
Unidentified Flying Objects, Natl. Investigations Committee on (1967), 7970 Woodman Ave., Van Nuys, CA 91402; 3,000.
Uniformed Services, Natl. Assn. for (1968), 956 N. Monroe St., Arlington, VA 22201; 23,000.
United Community Funds and Councils of America (1956), 345 E. 46th St., N.Y., NY 10017; serves 36,000 agencies.
United Nations Assn. of the U.S.A. (1923, as **League of Nations Assn.**; renamed 1945), 345 E. 46th St., N.Y., NY 10017; 60,000.

United Nations, U.S. People for (1967), 777 United Nations Pl., N.Y., NY 10017; 30,000.

United Press International (1907, formerly **United Press Assn.;** renamed 1958 after merger with **International News Service),** 220 East 42nd St., N.Y., NY 10017.

United Service Organizations (1941), 237 East 52nd St., New York, NY 10022; 130,000.

United States Army, Assn. of the (1950), 1529 18th St., NW, Wash., DC 20036; 82,152.

United Way of America (1918), 801 N. Fairfax St., Alexandria, VA 22314; 1,264.

Universities, Assn. of American (1900), One Dupont Circle, NW, Wash., DC 20036; 48 universities.

Universities and Colleges, Assn. of Governing Boards of (1964), One Dupont Circle, NW, Wash., DC 20036; 13,000 trustees.

University Extension Assn., Natl. (1915), One Dupont Circle, NW, Suite 360, Wash., DC 20036; 196 schools.

University Professors, American Assn. of (1915), One Dupont Circle, NW, Wash., DC 20036; 79,000.

University Women, American Assn. of (1882), 2401 Virginia Ave., NW, Wash., DC 20037; 180,000.

Urban Coalition, National (1967), 2100 M St., NW, Wash., DC 20037.

Urban League, National (1910), 55 East 52nd St., New York, NY 10022; 12,000.

Utility Commissioners, Natl. Assn. of Regulatory (1889), 1102 Interstate Commerce Comm. Bldg., Box 684, Wash., DC 20044; 950 agencies.

— V —

Variety Clubs International (1927), 7210 Red Rd., Suite 208, S. Miami, FL 33143; 10,327.

Vegetable Growers Assn. of America (1908), 1616 H. St., NW, Wash., DC 20006; 1,100.

Veteran Motor Car Club of America (1938), 105 Elm St., Andover, MA 01810; 4,075.

Veterans Committee, American (1944), 1333 Connecticut Ave., NW, Wash., DC 20036; 25,000.

Veterans of Foreign Wars of the U.S. and Ladies Auxiliary (1899), V.F.W. Bldg., 34th St., Kansas City, MO 64111; 2,300,-000.

Veterans of World War I of the U.S.A. (1958), 916 Prince St., Alexandria, VA 22314; 171,000.

Veterinary Medical Assn., American (1863), 600 S. Michigan Ave., Chicago, IL 60605; 23,950.

Victorian Society in America (1966), The Athenaeum, E. Washington Sq., Phila., PA 19106; 1,488.

Vocational Assn., American (1925), 1510 H St., NW, Washington, DC 20005; 55,000.

Volleyball Assn.,U.S. (1928), 13 State St., Schenectady, NY 12305; 6,000.

— W —

Walther League (1893), 119 W. Locust St., Chicago, IL 60610; 4,000.

War Dads Auxiliary, American (1945), 1123 Scarritt Arcade Bldg., Kansas City, MO 64111; 2,000.

War Mothers, American (1917), 2615 Woodley Pl. NW, Washington, DC 20008; 14,000.

War of 1812, General Society of (1814), 1307 New Hampshire Ave., NW, Washington, DC 20036; 1,148.

Watch and Clock Collectors, Natl. Assn. of (1943), NAWCC Bldg., 514 Popular St., Columbia, PA 17512; 40,000.

Water Pollution Control Federation (1928), 3900 Wisconsin Ave., NW, Wash., DC 20016; 23,000.

Water Ski Assn., Amer. (1939), 7th St. & Ave. G., SW, Winter Haven, FL 33880; 10,757.

Water Resources Assn., American (1964), Mississippi River at 3rd Ave., Minneapolis, MN 55414; 1,200.

Water Well Assn., Natl. (1948), 88 E. Broad St., Columbus, OH 43215; 3,000.

Water Works Assn., Amer. (1881), 6666 West Quincy Ave., Denver, CO; 23,000.

Welding Society, American (1919), 2501 N.W. 7th St., Miami, FL 33125; 22,995.

Wheelchair Athletic Assn., Natl. (1958), 40-42 62nd St., Woodside, NY 11377; 1,400.

Wilderness Society (1935), 1901 Pennsylvania Ave. NW, Wash., DC 20006; 90,000.

Wildlife, Defenders of (1925), 2000 N. St., NW, Washington, DC 20036; 40,000.

Wildlife Federation, Natl. (1936), 1412 16th St., NW., Washington, DC 20036; 3,500,000.

Wildlife Foundation, N. American (1911), 709 Wire Bldg., Washington, DC 20005; 1,400.

Wildlife Fund, World (1961), 910 17th St., NW, Washington, DC 20006; 48,000.

Wildlife Management Institute (1946), 1000 Vermont Ave.,

NW, Washington, DC 20005.

Wildlife Society (1937), S-176, 3900 Wisconsin Ave., NW Washington, DC 20016; 7,732.

William Penn Assn. (1886), 429 Forbes Ave., Pittsburgh, PA 15219; 68,004.

Wireless Pioneers, Society of (1967), P.O. Box 530, Santa Rosa, CA 95402; 1,712.

Women Geographers, Society of (1925), 1619 New Hampshire Ave., NW, Wash., DC 20009; 450.

Woman's Assn., American, 19 West 44th St., New York, NY 10036.

Woman's Christian Temperance Union, Natl. (1874), 1730 Chicago Ave., Evanston, IL 60201; 250,000.

Women Artists, Natl. Assn. of (1889), 156 5th Ave., N.Y., NY 10010; 700.

Women Engineers, Society of (1949), 345 E. 47th St., New York, NY 10017; 1,803.

Women, Natl. Organization for (NOW) (1966), 5 S. Wabash, Suite 1615, Chicago, IL 60603; 35,000.

Women Strike for Peace (1961), 145 S. 13th St., Room 407, Philadelphia, PA 19107.

Women of the U.S., Natl. Council of (1888), 345 E. 46th St., N.Y., NY 10017; 1,500.

Women Voters of the U.S., League of (1920), 1730 M St., NW, Wash., DC 20036; 155,000.

Women World War Veterans (1919), 237 Madison Ave., New York, NY 10016; 65,000.

Women's Army Corps Veterans Assn. (1946), 6049 Amboy Rd., Dearborn Heights, MI 48127; 1,500.

Women's Clubs, General Federation of (1891), 1734 N St., NW, Wash., DC 20036; 10,000,000.

Women's Clubs, Natl. Federation of Business and Professional (1919), 2012 Massachusetts Ave., NW, Wash., DC 20036; 163,000.

Women's Educational and Industrial Union (1877), 264 Boylston St., Boston, MA 02116; 2,227.

Women's Internatl. League for Peace and Freedom, (1915), 1213 Race St., Phila., PA 19107; 8,000.

Women's Overseas Service League (1921), 5402 Connecticut Ave., NW, Washington, DC 20015; 1,636.

Women's Veterinary Medical Assn. (1948), c/o Dr. Jane Robens, 2 Laurel Pl., Upper Montclair, NJ 07043; 225.

Woodmen of America, Modern (1883), 1710 1st Ave., Rock Island, IL 61201; 474,700.

Woodmen of the World (1890), 1450 Speer Blvd., Denver, CO 80204; 30,968.

Wool Growers Assn., Natl. (1865), 600 Crandall Bldg., Salt Lake City, UT 84101; 22 assns.

Workmen's Circle (1900), 175 East Broadway, New York, NY 10002; 52,000.

World Federalists, World Assn. of (1946), Leliegracht 21, Amsterdam, Netherlands; 40,000.

World Future Society (1966), 4916 St. Elmo Ave., Bethesda, MD 20014; 15,000.

World Health Organization, U.S. Committee for (1953), 777 United Nations Plaza, N.Y., NY 10017; 3,172.

World Ship Society (1946), c/o Dudley Thickens, 3319 Sweet Dr., Lafayette, CA 94549; 3,600.

Wrestling Foundation, U.S. Amateur (1959), 620 N. 48th St., Lincoln, NE 68504; 300.

Writers Assn. of America, Outdoor (1927), 4141 W. Bradley Rd., Milwaukee, WI 53209; 1,400.

— Y & Z —

Yeomen F, National (1926), 11104 Haines Ave. NE, Albuquerque, NM 87112; 1,000.

YMHAs and Jewish Community Centers, World Federation of (1946), 15 E. 26th St., N.Y., NY 10010; 17 nations.

Young Americans for Freedom (1960), 1221 Massachusetts Ave., NW, Wash., DC 20005; 55,000.

YM-YWHAs of Greater New York, Associated (1957), 305 East 45th St., New York, NY 10017; 45,000.

Young Men's Christian Assns., Natl. Council of (1844 in London, 1851 in U.S.), 291 Broadway, N.Y., NY 10007; 7,000,-000.

Young Women's Christian Assn. of the U.S.A. (1855 in England; 1858 in U.S.), 600 Lexington Ave., N.Y., NY 10022; 2,400,000 in the U.S.

Youth Hostels, American (1934), Natl. Campus, Delaplane, VA 22025; 80,000.

Zero Population Growth (1968), 1346 Connecticut Ave., NW, Washington, DC 20036; 12,000.

Zionist Organization of America (1897), 4 East 34th St., New York, NY 10016; 110,000.

Zonta International (1919), 59 E. Van Buren St., Chicago, IL 60605; 23,000.

Zoological Parks & Aquariums, Amer. Assn. of (1924), Oglebay Park, Wheeling, WV 26003; 1,700.

Zoologists, American Society of (1890), Box 2739 Calif. Lutheran College, Thousand Oaks, CA 91360; 4,000.

EDUCATION
American Colleges and Universities

For Canadian Colleges and Universities see Index

Student and Faculty Figures for Spring Term, 1974
Source: World Almanac questionnaires and U.S. Office of Education

All coeducational unless followed by (M) for men only, or (W) for women only. Even though marked (M) or (W) some are coeducational at graduate level and in evening and summer divisions. Asterisk (*) denotes land-grant college.

Governing official is president unless otherwise designated. Year is that of founding. The word college is part of the name listed unless another designation is given.

Affiliation: C-county; D-religious denomination; Di-district; F-federal; Mu-municipal; P-private; S-state; T-territorial govt.; Y-YMCA.

Each institution listed has an enrollment of at least 150 students of college grade. Number of teachers is the total number of individuals on teaching staff. Enrollment and faculty in italics include all branches and campuses.

(A) Designates colleges that have not provided up-to-date information.
(See Index for typical tuition fees)

Education—Senior Colleges

Name	Location	Year	Governing Official and Affiliation	Students	Teachers
Abilene Christian	Abilene, Tex.	1906	John C. Stevens	P	4,105	181
Adams State	Alamosa, Colo.	1925	John A. Marvel	S	2,800	170
Adelphi Univ.	Garden City, N.Y.	1896	Timothy Costello	P	8,000	325
Adrian	Adrian, Mich.	1859	John H. Dawson	P	1,125	92
Agnes Scott (W)	Decatur, Ga.	1889	Wallace M. Alston	P	625	84
Air Force Inst. of Tech.	Dayton, Ohio	1919	Gen. Frank Simokaitis	F	574	120
Akron, Univ. of.	Akron, Ohio	1870	Dominic J. Guzzetta	S	20,839	1,372
Alabama A&M Univ.	Normal, Ala.	1875	Richard D. Morrison	S	3,397	362
Alabama State Univ.	Montgomery, Ala.	1874	Levi Watkins	S	3,879	162
Alabama, Univ. of.	University, Ala.	1831	Forrest David Mathews	S	14,938	732
At Birmingham	Birmingham, Ala.	1966	J. F. Volker	S	9,552	1,074
At Huntsville	Huntsville, Ala.	1951	Benjamin B. Graves	S	3,059	175
Alaska Methodist Univ.	Anchorage, Alaska	1957	John O. Picton	P	1,283	62
Alaska, Univ. of*	Fairbanks, Alaska	1917	Robert W. Hiatt	S	12,000	355
Albany State	Albany, Ga.	1903	Charles L. Hayes	S	1,798	133
Albertus Magnus (W)	New Haven, Conn.	1925	Francis H. Horn	D	472	53
Albion	Albion, Mich.	1835	Bernard Tagg Lomas	P	1,751	126
Albright	Reading, Pa.	1856	Arthur Schultz	P	1,474	108
Albuquerque, Univ. of.	Albuquerque, N.M.	1920	Joseph Zanetti, Jr.	P	2,880	155
Alcorn State Univ.	Lorman, Miss.	1871	Walter Washington	S	2,568	125
Alderson-Broaddus	Philippi, W. Va.	1871	Richard E. Shearer	P	977	89
Alfred Univ.	Alfred, N.Y.	1836	Leland Miles	P	2,450	200
Allegheny	Meadville, Pa.	1815	Lawrence L. Pelletier	P	1,815	120
Allen Univ.	Columbia, S.C.	1870	J. W. Hairston	D	381	43
Allentown	Center Valley, Pa.	1965	Rev. J. Stuart Dooling	D	600	60
Alliance	Cambridge Spgs., Pa.	1912	Herman Szymanski	P	370	44
Alma	Alma, Mich.	1886	Robert D. Swanson	P	1,214	75
Alvernia	Reading, Pa.	1958	Sister Mary Victorine	P	208	33
Alverno (W)	Milwaukee, Wis.	1936	Sister Joel Read	P	1,031	110
American Cons. of Music	Chicago, Ill.	1886	Leo Heim	P	431	55
American International	Springfield, Mass.	1885	Harry J. Courniotes	P	2,546	129
American Univ.	Washington, D.C.	1893	George H. Williams	P	13,000	672
Amherst (M)	Amherst, Mass.	1821	John William Ward	P	1,298	146
Anderson	Anderson, Ind.	1917	Robert H. Reardon	P	1,595	117
Andrews Univ.	Berrien Springs, Mich.	1874	Richard Hammill	D	2,274	199
Angelo State Univ.	San Angelo, Texas	1928	Lloyd Vincent	S	4,267	157
Anna Maria	Paxton, Mass.	1946	Sister Irene Socquet	D	663	68
Annhurst	Woodstock, Conn.	1941	Sister Cecile Comtois	P	385	85
Antioch	Yellow Spgs., Ohio	1852	James P. Dixon	P	4,800	307
Appalachian Bible Inst.	Bradley, W. Va.	1950	Lester E. Pipkin	P	254	16
Aquinas	Grand Rapids, Mich.	1923	Norbert J. Hruby	P	1,536	88
Arizona State Univ.	Temple, Ariz.	1885	John W. Schwada	S	28,724	1,473
Arizona, Univ. of*	Tucson, Arizona	1885	John Paul Schaefer	S	27,458	1,677
Arkansas Baptist	Little Rock, Ark.	1884	James C. Oliver	D	561	43
Arkansas College	Batesville, Ark.	1872	Dan C. West	P	450	42
Arkansas Polytechnic	Russellville, Ark.	1910	Kenneth Kersh	S	2,169	117
Arkansas State Univ.	State Univ., Ark.	1909	Carl R. Reng	S	6,460	325
Arkansas, State Coll. of	Conway, Ark.	1907	Silas D. Snow	S	4,300	275
Arkansas, Univ. of*	Fayetteville, Ark.	1871	David W. Mullins	S	10,784	707
At Little Rock	Little Rock, Ark.	1927	Carey V. Stabler	S	4,171	148
At Pine Bluff	Pine Bluff, Ark.	1873	Lawrence David	S	2,540	167
Armstrong	Berkeley, Calif.	1918	John E. Armstrong	P	450	40
Armstrong State	Savannah, Ga.	1935	Henry L. Ashmore	S	3,000	130
Art Center Coll. of Design	Los Angeles, Calif.	1930	Donald R. Kubly	P	815	135
Asbury	Wilmore, Ky.	1890	Dennis F. Kinlaw	P	1,170	87
Ashland	Ashland, Ohio	1878	Glenn L. Clayton	D	2,201	153
Assumption	Worcester, Mass.	1904	Pasquale DiPasquale	D	1,612	100
Athenaeum of Ohio (M)	Cincinnati, Ohio	1829	Rev. J. Raymond Favret	D	242	51
Athens	Athens, Ala.	1822	Sidney Sandridge	D	802	57
Atlanta College of Art	Atlanta, Ga.	1928	William Voos	P	357	30
Atlantic Christian	Wilson, N.C.	1902	Arthur D. Wenger	D	1,641	110
Atlantic Union	So. Lancaster, Mass.	1882	W.G. Nelson	D	630	70
Auburn Univ.*	Auburn, Ala.	1856	Harry Philpott	S	15,339	897
Augsburg	Minneapolis, Minn.	1869	Oscar A. Anderson	P	1,703	105

Name	Location	Year	Governing Official and Affiliation		Students	Teachers
Augusta	Augusta, Ga.	1925	George A. Christenberry	S	3,904	156
Augustana	Rock Island, Ill.	1860	C. W. Sorensen	D	2,345	164
Augustana	Sioux Falls, S. Dak.	1860	Charles L. Balcer	P	1,936	160
Aurora	Aurora, Ill.	1893	Vacant	P	1,027	103
Austin	Sherman, Tex.	1849	John D. Moseley	D	1,149	91
Austin Peay State Univ.	Clarksville, Tenn.	1929	Joe Morgan	S	4,124	190
Averett	Dansville, Va.	1859	Conwell A. Anderson	P	980	40
Avila	Kansas City, Mo.	1916	Sister Olive Louis	P	1,137	126
Azusa Pacific	Azusa, Calif.	1899	Cornelius Haggard	P	1,144	77
Babson	Babson Park, Mass.	1919	Ralph Sorenson	P	2,217	92
Baker Univ.	Baldwin, Kan.	1858	Neil Malicky, act.	P	744	67
Baldwin-Wallace	Berea, Ohio	1845	Alfred B. Bonds, Jr.	P	2,617	257
Ball State Univ.	Muncie, Ind.	1918	John J. Pruis	S	19,031	800
Baltimore, Univ. of	Baltimore Md.	1925	H. Mebane Turner	S	5,420	215
Baptist Bible College of Pa.	Clarks Summit, Pa.	1932	Ernest Pickering	D	652	35
Baptist Coll. at Charleston	Charleston, S.C.	1965	John Hamrick	P	2,241	106
Barat (W)	Lake Forest, Ill.	1919	Sister Margaret Burke	D	731	79
Barber-Scotia	Concord, N.C.	1867	Jerome Lynwood Gresham	P	477	42
Bard	Annandale, N.Y.	1860	Reamer Kline	P	720	80
Barnard (W)	New York, N.Y.	1889	Martha E. Peterson	P	1,950	200
Barrington	Barrington, R.I.	1900	Charles Hummel	P	574	54
Barry (W)	Miami, Fla.	1940	Sister M. Trinita Flood	D	1,367	126
Bartlesville Wesleyan	Bartlesville, Okla.	1909	Leo G. Cox	D	247	22
Bates	Lewiston, Me.	1864	Thomas H. Reynolds	P	1,223	89
Baylor Univ.	Waco, Tex.	1845	Abner V. McCall	D	8,167	441
Beaver	Glenside, Pa.	1853	Edward D. Gates	P	897	73
Belhaven	Jackson, Miss.	1883	Howard J. Cleland	D	742	43
Belknap	Center Harbor, N.H.	1963	George Schlichte	P	408	40
Bellarmine	Louisville, Ky.	1950	Eugene Petrik	P	1,306	88
Bellevue	Bellevue, Nebr.	1966	Richard Winchell	P	1,137	46
Belmont	Nashville, Tenn.	1951	Herbert C. Gabhart	P	1,033	92
Belmont Abbey	Belmont, N.C.	1876	Rev. John Bradley	D	589	42
Beloit	Beloit, Wis.	1846	Miller Upton	P	1,650	123
Bemidji State	Bemidji, Minn.	1919	Robert Decker	S	4,023	222
Benedict	Columbia, S.C.	1870	Henry Ponder	P	1,220	70
Benedictine	Atchison, Kans.	1971	Rev. Gerard Senecal	P	1,060	88
Benjamin Franklin Univ.	Washington, D.C.	1925	Clephane A. Kennedy	P	1,000	42
Bennett (W)	Greensboro, N.C.	1873	Isaac H. Miller	P	557	61
Bennington	Bennington, Vt.	1925	Gail Thain Parker	P	589	64
Bentley	Waltham, Mass.	1917	Gregory Adamian	P	3,300	128
Berea	Berea, Ky.	1855	W. D. Weatherford	P	1,341	130
Berry	Mount Berry, Ga.	1902	John R. Bertrand	P	1,308	78
Bethany Bible	Santa Cruz, Calif.	1919	C. Morse Ward	D	446	28
Bethany	Lindsborg, Kan.	1881	Alvin Hahn	D	639	51
Bethany	Bethany, W. Va.	1840	Cecil Underwood	P	1,191	79
Bethany Nazarene	Bethany, Okla.	1900	Stephen Nease	D	1,276	69
Bethel	Mishawaka, Ind.	1947	Albert Beutler	P	438	35
Bethel	North Newton, Kan.	1887	Harold Schultz	P	564	50
Bethel	McKenzie, Tenn.	1842	William L. Cottrell, Jr.	D	391	35
Bethel	St. Paul, Minn.	1947	Carl Lundquist	P	1,303	86
Bethune-Cookman	Daytona Beach, Fla.	1872	Richard V. Moore	D,P	1,127	61
Biola	La Mirada, Calif.	1908	J. Richard Chase	P	1,902	119
Birmingham-Southern	Birmingham, Ala.	1856	Ralph M. Tanner	D	872	65
Biscayne	Miami, Fla.	1961	Rev. John McDonnell	P	1,190	83
Bishop	Dallas, Tex.	1881	Milton K. Curry	D	2,085	99
Black Hills State	Spearfish, S. Dak.	1883	M. N. Freeman	S	2,264	103
Blackburn	Carlinville, Ill.	1837	John Alberti	D	572	48
Bloomfield	Bloomfield, N.J.	1868	Merle F. Allshouse	P	1,245	85
Bloomsburg State	Bloomsburg, Pa.	1839	Charles Carson, act.	S	4,972	306
Blue Mountain (W)	Blue Mountain, Miss.	1873	E. Harold Fisher	P	302	35
Bluefield State	Bluefield, W. Va.	1895	Billy Coffindaffer	S	1,170	67
Bluffton	Bluffton, Ohio	1899	Benjamin Sprunger	P	707	52
Bob Jones Univ.	Greenville, S.C.	1927	Bob Jones	P	4,265	287
Boise State	Boise, Idaho	1932	John Barnes	S	10,117	410
Boston	Chestnut Hill, Mass.	1865	Rev. J. Donald Monan	D	12,218	914
Boston State	Boston, Mass.	1852	Kermit C. Morrissey	S	8,800	540
Boston Conserv. of Music	Boston, Mass.	1867	George Brambilla	P	579	100
Boston Univ.	Boston, Mass.	1869	John Silber	P	23,581	1,197
Bowdoin	Brunswick, Me.	1794	Roger Howell, Jr.	P	1,238	100
Bowie State	Bowie, Md.	1865	Samuel L. Myers	S	3,236	188
Bowling Green State Univ.	Bowling Green, Ohio	1910	Hollis A. Moore	S	17,212	1,310
Bradley Univ.	Peoria, Ill.	1897	Martin G. Abegg	P	5,237	335
Brandeis Univ.	Waltham, Mass.	1948	Marver Bernstein	P	2,355	350
Brenau	Gainesville, Ga.	1878	James T. Rogers	P	481	51
Brescia	Owensboro, Ky.	1925	Sister J. Marie Lechner	P	960	81
Briar Cliff	Sioux City, Iowa	1930	Kasper Marking	P	782	56
Briarcliff (W)	Briarcliff Manor, N.Y.	1903	Josiah Bunting	P	375	45
Bridgeport Engineering Inst.	Bridgeport, Conn.	1924	William J. Owens	P	358	65
Bridgeport, Univ. of	Bridgeport, Conn.	1927	Leland Miles	P	8,180	535
Bridgewater	Bridgewater, Va.	1880	Wayne F. Geisert	P	794	74
Bridgewater State	Bridgewater, Mass.	1840	Adrian Rondileau	S	7,000	330
Brigham Young Univ.	Provo. Utah	1875	Dallin H. Oaks	D	26,205	1,136
Brooklyn Law School	Brooklyn, N.Y.	1901	Raymond Lisle, (Dean).	P	1,258	38
Brooks Institute	Santa Barbara, Calif.	1945	Ernest Brooks, 2nd	P	650	20
Brown Univ.	Providence, R.I.	1764	Donald F. Hornig	P	6,524	788
Bryan	Dayton, Tenn.	1930	Theodore Mercer	P	533	34
Bryant	Smithfield, R.I.	1863	Harry Evarts	P	4,600	136
Bryn Mawr (W)	Bryn Mawr, Pa.	1885	Harris L. Wofford, Jr.	P	1,538	184
Bucknell Univ.	Lewisburg, Pa.	1846	C. H. Watts	P	3,189	223
Buena Vista	Storm Lake, Iowa	1891	Lester Williams, act	D	763	50
Butler Univ.	Indianapolis, Ind.	1855	Alexander E. Jones	P	4,443	235
Cabrini	Radnor, Pa.	1957	Sister Mary L. Sullivan	D	523	52

Name	Location	Year	Governing Official and Affiliation		Students	Teachers
Caldwell	Caldwell, N.J.	1939	Sister Ann John	D	896	59
California Baptist	Riverside, Calif.	1950	James R. Staples	D	657	49
Calif. Coll. of Arts and Crafts	Oakland, Calif.	1907	Harry Xavier Ford	P	1,310	125
Calif. College of Podiatric Med.	San Francisco, Calif.	1914	H. D. Bailey	P	275	52
Calif. Inst. of the Arts	Valencia, Calif.	1961	William Lund	P	650	142
Calif. Inst. of Tech.	Pasadena, Calif.	1891	Harold Brown	P	1,544	458
Calif. Lutheran	Thousand Oaks, Calif.	1961	Mark Matthews	P	1,768	64
Calif. Maritime Academy	Vallejo, Calif.	1929	Adm. J. P. Rizza	S	200	23
Calif. State	Bakersfield, Calif.	1966	Jacob Frankel	S	2,700	200
Calif. State	California, Pa.	1852	George Roadman	S	6,000	385
Calif. State	Dominguez Hills, Calif.	1960	Leo Cain	S	5,100	275
Calif. State	Rohnert Park, Calif.	1961	Thomas McGrath	S	5,757	400
Calif. State	San Bernardino, Calif.	1965	John Pfau	S	3,000	180
Calif. State	Turlock, Calif.	1957	Carl Gatlin	S	2,607	177
Calif. State Polytechnic Univ.	San Luis Obispo, Calif.	1901	Robert Kennedy	S	13,115	723
Calif. State Polytechnic Univ.	Pomona, Calif.	1938	Robert C. Kramer	S	10,678	694
Calif. State Univ.	San Diego, Calif.	1897	Brage Golding	S	30,438	1,801
Calif. State Univ.	San Jose, Calif.	1857	John Bunzel	S	27,000	1,300
Calif. State Univ.	Northridge, Calif.	1958	James W. Cleary	S	25,000	1,500
Calif. State Univ.	Chico, Calif.	1887	Stanford Cazier	S	12,201	704
Calif. State Univ.	Fresno, Calif.	1911	Norman Baxter	S	15,323	827
Calif. State Univ.	Fullerton, Calif.	1959	Donald Shields	S	19,000	1,050
Calif. State Univ.	Hayward, Calif.	1957	Ellis McCune	S	11,298	766
Calif. State Univ.	Arcata, Calif.	1913	Alistair McCrone	S	7,459	450
Calif. State Univ.	Long Beach, Calif.	1949	Glen Dumke	S	30,140	1,500
Calif. State Univ.	Los Angeles, Calif.	1947	J.A. Greenlee	S	24,500	1,000
Calif. State Univ.	Sacramento, Calif.	1947	James Bond	S	18,500	800
Calif. State Univ.	San Francisco, Calif.	1899	Paul F. Romberg	S	21,981	1,589
Calif. Univ. of*	Berkeley, Calif.	1868	Charles J. Hitch	S		
Berkeley Campus	Berkeley, Calif.	1873	Albert H. Bowker, Chan.	S	30,000	2,000
Davis Campus	Davis, Calif.	1906	James Meyer, Chan.	S	15,572	906
Irvine Campus	Irvine, Calif.	1960	D.G. Aldrich, Chan.	S	8,517	592
Los Angeles Campus	Los Angeles, Calif.	1919	Charles Young, Chan.	S	29,975	2,150
Riverside Campus	Riverside, Calif.	1954	Ivan Hinderaker, Chan.	S	5,125	600
San Diego Campus	La Jolla, Calif.	1912	William H. McElroy, Chan.	S	7,700	516
San Francisco Campus	San Francisco, Calif.	1864	F.A. Sooy, Chan.	S	2,842	1,370
Santa Barbara Campus	Santa Barbara, Calif.	1891	Vernon Cheadle, Chan.	S	12,100	925
Santa Cruz Campus	Santa Cruz, Calif.	1965	D.E. McHenry, Chan.	S	4,454	357
Calumet	E. Chicago, Ind.	1951	Rev. John Lefko	D	1,496	63
Calvary Bible	Kansas City, Mo.	1932	Ralph Nite	P	311	24
Calvin	Grand Rapids, Mich.	1876	William Spoelhof	P	3,253	184
Cameron	Lawton, Okla.	1968	Don Owens	S	4,511	160
Campbell	Buies Creek, N.C.	1887	Norman A. Wiggins	P	2,056	110
Campbellsville	Campbellsville, Ky.	1906	William R. Davenport	P	693	48
Canisius	Buffalo, N.Y.	1870	V. Rev. James Demske	P	2,793	256
Capital Inst. of Tech.	Kensington, Md.	1932	Edward L. Fleckenstein	P	198	19
Capital Univ.	Columbus, Ohio	1850	Thomas H. Langevin	P	1,982	169
Cardinal Stritch	Milwaukee, Wis.	1937	Sister Mary Aquin Miller	P	740	75
Carleton	Northfield, Minn.	1866	Howard R. Swearer	P	1,600	169
Carlow	Pittsburgh, Pa.	1929	Sister Jane Scully	D	1,019	77
Carnegie-Mellon Univ.	Pittsburgh, Pa.	1900	Richard M. Cyert	P	3,000	500
Carroll	Helena, Mont.	1909	Francis Kerins	D	1,096	77
Carroll	Waukesha, Wis.	1846	Robert V. Cramer	P	1,020	91
Carson-Newman	Jefferson City, Tenn.	1851	John A. Fincher	P	1,696	115
Carthage	Kenosha, Wis.	1847	Harold H. Lentz	P	1,592	113
Case Western Reserve Univ.	Cleveland, Ohio	1967	L. A. Toepfer	P	8,400	1,150
Castleton State	Castleton, Vt.	1787	Harold Abel	S	1,631	136
Catawba	Salisbury, N.C.	1851	M. L. Shotzberger	D	1,155	84
Cathedral	Douglaston, N.Y.	1914	Rev. Thomas Gradilone	P	264	44
Catholic Univ. of America	Washington, D.C.	1887	Clarence C. Walton	D	6,748	525
Cath. Univ. of Puerto Rico	Ponce, Puerto Rico	1948	F. J. Carreras	P	7,071	358
Cedar Crest (W)	Allentown, Pa.	1867	Pauline Tompkins	P	651	79
Cedarville	Cedarville, Ohio	1887	James Jeremiah	P	1,009	60
Centenary	Shreveport, La.	1825	John Horton Allen	D	659	92
Central Bible	Springfield, Mo.	1922	Rev. Philip Crouch	D	984	50
Central	Pella, Iowa	1853	Kenneth J. Weller	P	1,355	87
Central Connecticut State	New Britain, Conn.	1849	F. Don James	S	12,151	727
Central Methodist	Fayette, Mo.	1854	Harold Hamilton	D	676	60
Central Mich Univ.	Mt. Pleasant, Mich.	1892	William Boyd	S	14,270	687
Central Missouri State Univ.	Warrensburg, Mo.	1871	Warren C. Lovinger	S	10,075	586
Central State Univ.	Edmond, Okla.	1890	Garland Godfrey	S	10,309	367
Central State Univ.	Wilberforce, Ohio	1887	Lionel H. Newsom	S	2,207	138
Central Tech. Inst.	Kansas City, Mo.	1931	C. L. Foster	P	396	19
Central Washington State	Ellensburg, Wash.	1890	James E. Brooks	S	6,563	368
Central Wesleyan	Central, S.C.	1906	Claude Rickman	D	307	32
Centre Coll. of Kentucky	Danville, Ky.	1819	Thomas A. Spragens	P	769	81
Chadron State	Chadron, Nebr.	1911	Larry Tangeman	S	1,836	129
Chaminade Col. of Honolulu	Honolulu, Hawaii	1955	Robert Maguire	P	1,408	142
Chapman (A)	Orange, Calif.	1861	John L. Davis	P	3,600	257
Charleston, Coll. of	Charleston, S.C.	1770	Theodore Stern	S	3,323	147
Chatham (W)	Pittsburgh, Pa.	1869	Edward D. Eddy	P	600	60
Chestnut Hill (W)	Philadelphia, Pa.	1924	Sister Mary Xavier Kirby	D	941	102
Cheyney State	Cheyney, Pa.	1837	Wade Wilson	S	2,40	230
Chicago, School of Art Inst.	Chicago, Ill.	1866	Donald Irving, V.P.	P	1,387	100
Chicago Coll. (Osteopathic)	Chicago, Ill.	1913	Thaddeus Kawalek	P	354	175
Chicago Conservatory	Chicago, Ill.	1857	Francois D' Albert	P	180	61
Chicago-Kent Coll. of Law	Chicago, Ill.	1888	John Rettaliatta	P	701	35
Chicago State Univ.	Chicago, Ill.	1869	Benjamin Alexander	S	6,471	300
Chicago Technical (M)	Chicago, Ill.	1904	Leslie Morey	P	754	18
Chicago, Univ. of	Chicago, Ill.	1891	Edward H. Levi	P	9,083	1,125
Christian Brothers	Memphis, Tenn.	1871	Rev. Bernard LoCoco	P	820	68
Cincinnati, Univ. of	Cincinnati, Ohio	1819	Warren G. Bennis	S,Mu	29,506	2,805
Citadel, The (Military) (M)	Charleston, S.C.	1842	Gen. George Seignious	S	2,967	150
Claflin	Orangeburg, S.C.	1869	Hubert V. Manning	P	782	55
Claremont Men's (M)	Claremont, Calif.	1946	Jack Lee Stark	P	806	97
Clarion State	Clarion, Pa.	1867	James Gemmell	S	4,277	309

Name	Location	Year	Governing Official and Affiliation	Stu-dents	Teach-ers
Clark	Atlanta, Ga.	1869	Vivian Henderson P	1,288	101
Clark Univ.	Worcester, Mass.	1887	Glenn W. Ferguson P	2,995	264
Clarke (W)	Dubuque, Iowa	1843	Robert Giroux P	652	70
Clarkson Coll. of Tech.	Potsdam, N.Y.	1896	Robert A. Plane P	2,484	166
Cleary	Ypsilanti, Mich.	1883	Walter Grieg P	510	28
Clemson Univ.	Clemson, S.C.	1889	Robert C. Edwards S	10,112	652
Cleveland Inst. of Art	Cleveland, Ohio	1882	Joseph McCullough P	794	77
Cleveland Inst. of Music	Cleveland, Ohio	1920	Mrs. Martha Joseph P	357	100
Cleveland State Univ.	Cleveland, Ohio	1964	Walter Waetjen S	15,201	668
Coe	Cedar Rapids, Iowa	1853	Leo Nussbaum P	1,162	125
Coker	Hartsville, S.C.	1908	Gus Turbeville P	497	40
Colby	Waterville, Me.	1813	Robert E. L. Strider P	1,542	153
Colgate Univ.	Hamilton, N.Y.	1819	Thomas Bartlett P	2,500	212
Colorado	Colo. Spgs., Colo.	1874	Lloyd E. Worner P	1,824	150
Colorado Sch. of Mines	Golden, Colo.	1874	Guy McBride S	1,708	160
Colorado State Univ.*	Fort Collins, Colo.	1870	A. R. Chamberlain S	18,411	1,129
Colorado, Univ. of.	Boulder, Colo.	1876	Fredrick P. Thieme S	30,428	2,729
Denver Center	Denver, Colo.	1964	Harold Haak, V.P. S	6,621	615
Colorado Springs	Colorado Springs, Colo.	1965	Lawrence Silverman, V.P. S	2,525	97
Colorado Women's (W)	Denver, Colo.	1888	Dumont F. Kenny P	842	77
Columbia Bible	Columbia, S.C.	1923	J. Robertson McQuilkin P	670	32
Columbia	Columbia, S.C.	1854	R. Wright Spears D	940	72
Columbia	Columbia, Mo.	1851	W. Merle Hill P	910	60
Columbia Union	Takoma Park, Md.	1904	George Akers D	934	86
Columbia Univ.	New York, N.Y.	1754	William McGill P	14,475	4,500
Teachers College	New York, N.Y.	1958	John H. Fischer P	5,199	403
Columbus	Columbus, Ga.	1958	Thomas Y. Whitley S	4,412	177
Columbus Business	Columbus, Ohio	1911	Richard Miller (Dir.) P	545	24
Columbus Col. of Art & Design.	Columbus, Ohio	1879	Jospeh Canzani (Dean) P	593	54
Concord	Athens, W. Va.	1872	Billy Coffindaffer S	1,583	96
Concordia	Bronxville, N.Y.	1881	Robert Schnabel P	494	53
Concordia	Moorhead, Minn.	1891	Joseph Knutson D	2,484	173
Concordia	St. Paul, Minn.	1893	Harvey Stegemoeller D	614	55
Concordia Senior	Fort Wayne, Ind.	1957	Herbert Bredemeier D	401	40
Concordia Teachers	River Forest, Ill.	1864	Paul A. Zimmerman D	1,220	109
Concordia Teachers	Seward, Nebr.	1894	W. T. Janzow D	1,347	115
Connecticut	New London, Conn.	1911	Oakes Ames P	2,002	185
Connecticut, Univ. of*	Storrs, Conn.	1881	Edward Gant, act. S	19,972	1,213
Converse (W)	Spartanburg, S.C.	1889	Robert T. Coleman, Jr. P	900	70
Cooper Union	New York, N.Y.	1859	John White P	1,011	177
Coppin State	Baltimore, Md.	1900	Calvin Burnett S	3,027	143
Cornell	Mt. Vernon, Iowa	1853	Charles Cochran, act. P	920	90
Cornell Univ.*	Ithaca, N.Y.	1865	Dale R. Corson P	16,868	1,743
Covenant	Mt. Lookout, Tenn.	1955	Marion Barnes D	480	32
Creighton Univ.	Omaha, Nebr.	1878	Rev. Joseph Labaj D	4,355	756
Culver-Stockton	Canton, Mo.	1853	Harold Doster P	605	48
Cumberland	Williamsburg, Ky.	1889	J. M. Boswell D	1,600	110
Curry	Milton, Mass.	1879	John S. Hafer P	1,114	56
Dakota State	Madison, S.D.	1881	Gordon Foster S	908	64
Dakota Wesleyan Univ.	Mitchell, S.Dak.	1885	Donald E. Messer D	651	50
Dallas, Univ. of.	Irving, Tex.	1956	Donald A. Cowan D	1,561	83
Dana	Blair, Nebr.	1884	Earl Mezoff D	650	50
Daniel Payne	Birmingham, Ala.	1889	Daniel Grant D	300	30
Dartmouth	Hanover, N.H.	1769	John George Kemeny P	3,120	447
David Lipscomb	Nashville, Tenn.	1891	Athens C. Pullias D	2,129	99
Davidson	Davidson, N.C.	1837	Samuel R. Spencer, Jr. P	1,187	103
Davis and Elkins	Elkins, W. Va.	1904	G.E. Hermanson P	860	68
Dayton Art Institute	Dayton, Ohio	1919	Sherwin Silverman (Dir.) P	291	19
Dayton, Univ. of.	Dayton, Ohio	1850	V. Rev. R. A. Roesch D	7,688	388
Defiance	Defiance, Ohio	1850	W. Noell Johnston P	729	50
Delaware State*	Dover, Del.	1891	Luna I. Mishoe S	1,868	113
Delaware, Univ. of*	Newark, Del.	1833	E.A. Trabant S	17,768	1,173
Del. Valley Coll. of S & A.	Doylestown, Pa.	1896	James Work P	1,335	85
Delta State Univ.	Cleveland, Miss.	1924	Aubrey K. Lucas S	3,187	188
Denison Univ.	Granville, Ohio	1831	Joel P. Smith P	2,170	156
Denver, Univ. of.	Denver, Colo.	1864	Maurice B. Mitchell P	8,523	584
DePaul Univ.	Chicago, Ill.	1898	V. Rev. J.R. Cortelyou P	9,567	324
DePauw Univ.	Greencastle, Ind.	1837	William E. Kerstetter P	2,341	174
Detroit Bible	Detroit, Mich.	1945	Wendell Johnston P	285	17
Detroit Coll. of Business	Dearborn, Mich.	1962	Frank Paone, V.P. P	1,150	56
Detroit Coll. of Law	Detroit, Mich.	1891	G. Cameron Buchanan P	955	37
Detroit Inst. of Technology	Detroit, Mich.	1891	Dewey F. Barich P	1,243	94
Detroit, Univ. of.	Detroit, Mich.	1877	V. Rev. M. Carron P	8,806	566
DeVry Inst. of Tech.	Chicago, Ill.	1931	Edward J. Sabol P	2,452	84
Dickinson	Carlisle, Pa.	1773	Howard L. Rubendall P	1,660	120
Dickinson School of Law	Carlisle, Pa.	1834	Dale F. Shughart P	422	24
Dickinson State	Dickinson, N. D.	1920	R.C. Gillund S	1,150	64
Dillard Univ.	New Orleans, La.	1869	Samuel Cook P	1,016	110
District of Col. Teachers	Washington, D.C.	1851	Paul Cooke Mu	2,323	127
Doane	Crete, Nebr.	1872	Philip C. Heckman P	560	52
Dr. Martin Luther	New Ulm, Minn.	1884	Conrad Frey P	661	68
Dominican	Houston, Texas	1945	Sister A. Boykin D	307	41
Dominican Coll. of Blauvelt.	Blauvelt, N.Y.	1952	Sister Natalie Casey D	818	58
Dominican Coll. of S. Rafael	San Rafael, Calif.	1889	Sister M. Samuel Conlon D	677	99
Dordt	Sioux Center, Iowa	1955	B.J. Haan P	895	55
Drake Univ.	Des Moines, Iowa	1881	Wilbur C. Miller P	7,244	377
Drew Univ.	Madison, N.J.	1866	Robert F. Oxnam P	3,127	292
Drexel Univ.	Philadelphia, Pa.	1891	William W. Hagerty P	8,959	600
Drury	Springfield, Mo.	1873	William Everheart P	2,015	171
Dubuque, Univ of	Dubuque, Iowa	1852	Walter F. Peterson P	1,004	66
Duke Univ.	Durham, N.C.	1823	Terry Sanford P	8,698	1,008
Duquesne Univ.	Pittsburgh, Pa.	1878	V. Rev. H. J. McAnulty D	8,359	522
Dyke	Cleveland, Ohio	1848	John Corfias P	995	50
D'Youville	Buffalo, N.Y.	1908	Sister Mary Charlotte P	1,151	90
Earlham	Richmond, Ind.	1847	Landrum Bolling D	1,060	89

Name	Location	Year	Governing Official and Affiliation		Students	Teachers
East Central State	Ada, Okla.	1909	Stanley Wagner	S	3,006	125
East Stroudsburg, State	E. Stroudsburg, Pa.	1891	Darrell Holmes	S	3,695	190
East Tennessee State Univ.	Johnson City, Tenn.	1911	Delos Culp	S	9,530	662
East Texas Baptist	Marshall, Texas	1912	Howard C. Bennett	D	652	42
East Texas State Univ.	Commerce, Texas	1889	F.H. McDowell	S	9,013	400
Eastern	St. Davids, Pa.	1951	Daniel E. Weiss	D	545	55
Eastern Conn. State	Willimantic, Conn.	1889	Charles Richard Webb	S	2,676	114
Eastern Illinois Univ.	Charleston, Ill.	1895	Gilbert C. Fite	S	8,035	635
Eastern Kentucky Univ.	Richmond, Ky.	1906	Robert R. Martin	S	11,488	525
Eastern Mennonite	Harrisonburg, Va.	1917	Myron S. Augsburger	P	917	85
Eastern Michigan Univ.	Ypsilanti, Mich.	1849	Harold E. Sponberg	S	18,392	797
Eastern Montana	Billings, Mont.	1927	Stanley Heywood	S	2,757	140
Eastern Nazarene	Quincy, Mass.	1918	Leslie Parrott	D	876	40
Eastern New Mexico Univ.	Portales, N. Mex.	1934	Charles Meister	S	5,502	180
Eastern Oregon State	La Grande, Ore.	1929	Rodney A. Briggs	S	1,495	108
Eastern Washington State	Cheney, Wash.	1890	Emerson C. Shuck	S	6,415	349
Eckerd	St. Petersburg, Fla.	1958	Billy O. Wireman	P	950	66
Edgecliff	Cincinnati, Ohio	1935	Sister M. A. Molitor	D	755	74
Edgewood	Madison, Wis.	1927	Sister Cecilia Carey	D	582	62
Edinboro State	Edinboro, Pa.	1856	Chester T. McNerney	S	7,002	487
Edward Waters	Jacksonville, Fla.	1866	Samuel J. Tucker	D	552	39
Eisenhower	Seneca Falls, N.Y.	1968	John Rosenkrans	P	732	61
Elizabethtown	Elizabethtown, Pa.	1899	Morley J. Mays	P	1,597	126
Elmhurst	Elmhurst, Ill.	1871	Ivan Frick	P	2,528	150
Elmira	Elmira, N.Y.	1855	J. Ralph Murray	P	3,025	137
Elon	Elon College, N.C.	1889	J. F. Young	P	2,005	93
Embry-Riddle Aero. Univ.	Daytona Beach, Fla.	1926	Jack R. Hunt	P	2,079	156
Emerson	Boston, Mass.	1890	Richard Chapin	P	1,672	154
Emmanuel (W)	Boston, Mass.	1919	Sister Marie Barry	D	1,052	114
Emory & Henry	Emory, Va.	1836	Thomas F. Chilcote	D	858	63
Emory Univ.	Atlanta, Ga.	1915	S. S. Atwood	P	6,267	1,883
Emporia Coll. of	Emporia, Kan.	1882	Robert Prins, act.	D	459	36
Emporia, Kansas State	Emporia, Kansas	1863	John Vissea	S	6,013	273
Erskine	Due West, S.C.	1839	M.S. Bell	D	709	63
Eureka	Eureka, Ill.	1855	Ira W. Langston	D	441	40
Evangel	Springfield, Mo.	1955	Robert Spence	P	1,142	62
Evansville, Univ. of	Evansville, Ind.	1854	Wallace B. Graves	P	4,884	262
Fairfield Univ.	Fairfield, Conn.	1942	Thomas Fitzgerald	P	4,500	278
Fairleigh Dickinson Univ.	Rutherford, N.J.	1942	J. O. Fuller	P	20,000	600
Fairmont State	Fairmont, W. Va.	1867	Eston K. Feaster	S	3,320	180
Faith Baptist Bible	Ankeny, Iowa	1924	David Nettleton	P	578	22
Federal City	Washington, D.C.	1968	Wendell P. Russell	Mu	6,883	764
Ferris State	Big Rapids, Mich.	1884	Robert Ewigleben	S	8,584	445
Finch (W)	New York, N.Y.	1900	Rodney Felder	P	377	43
Findlay	Findlay, Ohio	1882	Glen R. Rasmussen	P	949	85
Fine Arts, School of	Ft. Wayne, Ind.	1922	Russell Oettel	P	251	14
Fisk Univ.	Nashville, Tenn.	1867	J. R. Lawson	P	1,535	124
Fitchburg State	Fitchburg, Mass.	1894	James Hammond	S	3,500	200
Flagler	St. Augustine, Fla.	1968	William L. Proctor	P	489	35
Florence State Univ.	Florence, Ala.	1872	Robert M. Guillot	S	3,642	162
Florida Atlantic Univ.	Boca Raton, Fla.	1961	G. L. Creech	S	5,600	320
Florida A. & M. Univ.*	Tallahassee, Fla.	1887	Benjamin Luther Perry, Jr.	S	5,130	262
Florida Inst. of Tech.	Melbourne, Fla.	1958	Jerome P. Keuper	P	2,437	200
Florida International Univ.	Miami, Fla.	1972	Charles E. Perry	S	4,500	300
Florida Memorial	Miami, Fla.	1879	Royal Puryear	D	681	55
Florida Southern	Lakeland, Fla.	1885	Charles T. Thrift, Jr.	D	1,362	104
Florida State Univ.	Tallahassee, Fla.	1857	Stanley Marshall	S	19,742	1,200
Florida Technological Univ.	Orlando, Fla.	1963	Charles N. Millican	S	7,131	398
Florida, Univ. of*	Gainesville, Fla.	1853	Robert Marston	S	25,641	3,500
Fontbonne (W)	St. Louis, Mo.	1917	Sister Jane Hassett	P	619	58
Fordham Univ.	Bronx, N.Y.	1841	Rev. James C. Finley	P	14,297	808
Ft. Hays Kansas State	Hays, Kan.	1902	John W. Gustad	S	4,603	272
Ft. Lauderdale Coll. of Bus. & Fin.	Ft. Lauderdale, Fla.	1940	Stanley Drake	P	240	23
Ft. Lewis	Durango, Colo.	1962	Rexer Berndt	S	2,523	160
Fort Valley State*	Fort Valley, Ga.	1895	Cleveland W. Pettigrew	S	1,835	148
Ft. Wayne Art Inst.	Fort Wayne, Ind.	1922	Russell Oettel	P	283	10
Fort Wayne Bible	Fort Wayne, Ind.	1904	Timothy Warner	P	605	37
Ft. Wright	Spokane, Wash.	1907	Sister Helen Volkomerer	D	410	62
Framingham State	Framingham, Mass.	1839	D. Justin McCarthy	S	4,937	281
Francis Marion	Florence, S.C.	1970	Walter D. Smith	S	1,757	84
Franconia	Franconia, NH	1961	Leon Botstein	P	467	48
Franklin	Franklin, Ind.	1834	Wesley N. Haines	P	620	59
Franklin and Marshall	Lancaster, Pa.	1787	Keith Spalding	P	2,000	126
Franklin Pierce	Rindge, N.H.	1962	Frank S. DiPietro	P	820	73
Franklin Univ.	Columbus, Ohio	1902	Joseph Frasch	P	3,380	120
Free Will Baptist Bible	Nashville, Tenn.	1942	L. C. Johnson	D	560	28
Friends Univ.	Wichita, Kan.	1898	Harold C. Cope	D	775	53
Frostburg State	Frostburg, Md.	1898	Nelson Guild	S	3,065	161
Furman Univ.	Greenville, S.C.	1826	Gordon W. Blackwell	D	2,160	146
Gallaudet	Washington, D.C.	1864	Edward C. Merrill, Jr.	P	953	162
Gannon	Erie, Pa.	1944	Rev. W. J. Nash	P	3,215	154
Gardner-Webb	Boiling Springs, NC.	1905	Ernest Eugene Poston	D	1,525	93
General Motors Institute	Flint, Mich.	1919	Harold P. Rodes	P	3,150	230
Geneva	Beaver Falls, Pa.	1848	Edwin C. Clarke	D	1,414	90
George Fox	Newberg, Ore.	1891	David La Shana	D	471	48
George Mason Univ.	Fairfax, Va.	1956	V. H. Dykstra	S	4,926	316
George Peabody Coll. for Teachers	Nashville, Tenn.	1785	John Dunworth	P	2,000	150
Geo. Washington Univ.	Washington, D.C.	1821	Lloyd H. Elliott	P	15,160	1,159
George Williams	Downers Grove, Ill.	1890	Richard E. Hamlin	P	1,150	96
Georgetown	Georgetown, Ky.	1829	Robert L. Mills	D	1,068	80
Georgetown Univ.	Washington, D.C.	1789	Rev. R. J. Henle	D	10,359	1,013
Georgia	Milledgeville, Ga.	1889	J. Whitney Bunting	S	3,000	145
Georgia Inst. of Technology	Atlanta, Ga.	1885	Joseph M. Pettit	S	8,000	683
Georgia Southern	Statesboro, Ga.	1906	Pope A. Duncan	S	5,921	329
Georgia Southwestern	Americus, Ga.	1906	William B. King	S	2,375	135

Name	Location	Year	Governing Official and Affiliation		Stu-dents	Teach-ers
Georgia State Univ.	*Atlanta, Ga.	1913	Noah N. Langdale	S	16,380	796
Georgia Univ. of*	Athens, Ga.	1785	Fred C. Davison	S	19,000	2,100
Georgia Court (W)	Lakewood, N.J.	1908	Sis. Mary Stephanie	P	725	82
Gettysburg	Gettysburg, Pa.	1832	Carl Arnold Hanson	P	1,824	160
Glassboro State	Glassboro, N.J.	1923	Mark Chamberlain	S	12,000	437
Glenville State	Glenville, W.Va.	1872	D. Banks Wilburn	S	1,444	82
Goddard	Plainfield, Vt.	1938	Gerald S. Witherspoon	P	1,891	213
Golden Gate Univ.	San Francisco, Calif.	1901	Otto Butz	P	5,700	550
Gonzaga Univ.	Spokane, Wash.	1887	Vacant	P	2,958	199
Gordon	Wenham, Mass.	1889	Harold J. Ockenga	P	897	60
Goshen	Goshen, Ind.	1894	J. Lawrence Burkholder	D	1,242	120
Goucher (W)	Towson, Md.	1885	Rhoda Dorsey, act.	P	1,076	114
Governors State Univ.	Park Forest South, Ill.	1969	William Engbretson	S	2,220	190
Grace	Winona Lake, Ind.	1948	Herman A. Hoyt	D	613	43
Grace Bible Institute	Omaha, Nebr.	1943	Robert Benton	P	497	26
Graceland	Lamoni, Iowa	1895	William Higdon	P	1,295	83
Grambling	Grambling, La.	1901	Ralph W. E. Jones	S	3,627	252
Grand Canyon	Phoenix, Ariz.	1949	William R. Hintze	D	970	41
Grand Valley State	Allendale, Mich.	1960	Arend Lubbers	S	5,920	300
Great Falls, Coll. of	Great Falls, Mont.	1932	Msgr. A. M. Brown	P	1,070	78
Greensboro	Greensboro, N.C.	1838	David G. Mobberley	D	579	55
Greenville	Greenville, Ill.	1892	Orley R. Herron	P	913	66
Grinnell	Grinnell, Ia.	1846	Glenn H. Leggett	P	1,201	113
Grove City	Grove City, Pa.	1876	Charles S. Mackenzie	P	2,100	116
Guilford	Greensboro, N.C.	1837	Grimsley T. Hobbs	D	1,465	111
Gulf-Coast Bible	Houston, Tex.	1953	Max Gaulke	D	258	23
Gustavus Adolphus	St. Peter, Minn.	1862	Frank R. Barth	D	2,043	139
Gwynedd-Mercy	Gwynedd Valley, Pa.	1948	Sister Isabelle Keiss	P	936	90
Hahnemann Medical	Philadelphia, Pa.	1848	Wharton R. Shober	P	685	1,446
Hamilton (M)	Clinton, N.Y.	1812	J.M. Corovano, act.	P	965	96
Hamline Univ.	St. Paul Minn.	1854	Richard Bailey	P	1,297	142
Hampden-Sydney (M)	Hampden-Sydney, Va.	1776	W. Taylor Reveley	D	692	55
Hampshire	Amherst, Mass.	1965	Charles Longsworth	P	1,000	90
Hampton Institute	Hampton, Va.	1868	Roy D. Hudson	P	2,688	205
Hanover	Hanover, Ind.	1827	John E. Horner	P	1,000	
Hardin-Simmons Univ.	Abilene, Tex.	1891	Elwin L. Skiles	D	1,553	101
Harding	Searcy, Ark.	1924	Clinton L. Ganus, Jr.	P	2,319	120
Harris Teachers	St. Louis, Mo.	1857	Richard Stumpe	Mu	1,017	71
Hartford, Univ of	W. Hartford, Conn.	1877	A. M. Woodruff	P	8,707	514
Hartwick	Oneonta, N.Y.	1928	Adolph G. Anderson	P	1,610	115
Harvard Univ.	Cambridge, Mass.	1636	Derek Curtis Bok	P	16,008	4,397
Harvey Mudd	Claremont, Calif.	1957	Joseph B. Platt	P	401	68
Hastings	Hastings, Neb.	1882	Clyde B. Matters	P	681	58
Haverford (M)	Haverford, Pa.	1833	John R. Coleman	P	730	96
Hawaii, The Church Coll. of	Laie, Hawaii	1955	Stephen Brower	P	1,008	75
Hawaii, Univ of*	Honolulu, Hawaii	1907	Wytze Gorter	S	29,194	2,052
Heald Engineering	San Francisco, Calif.	1863	Roy Hurd (Dir.)	P	950	70
Heidelberg	Tiffin, Ohio	1850	Leslie H. Fishel, Jr.	P	1,195	106
Henderson State	Arkadelphia, Ark.	1890	Martin Garrison	S	3,300	152
Hendrix	Conway, Ark.	1884	Roy Shilling	D	1,061	54
High Point	High Point, N.C.	1924	Wendell M. Patton	D	1,020	59
Hillsdale	Hillsdale, Mich.	1844	George C. Roche, 3rd.	P	1,015	65
Hiram	Hiram, Ohio	1850	Elmer Jagow	P	1,304	110
Hobart & William Smith	Geneva, N.Y.	1822	Allan A. Kuusisto	P	1,650	115
Hofstra Univ.	Hempstead, N.Y.	1935	Robert J. Payton	P	12,381	688
Hollins (W)	Hollins, Coll., Va.	1842	John A. Logan, Jr.	P	1,060	93
Holy Corss. Coll. of the	Worcester, Mass.	1843	Rev. John Brooks	D	2,440	205
Holy Family	Philadelphia, Pa.	1954	Sister Mary Lillian	D	865	68
Holy Names	Oakland, Calif.	1868	Sister M. Irene Woodward	P	694	104
Hood	Frederick, Md.	1893	Ross Pritchard	P	826	79
Hope	Holland, Mich.	1866	Gordon Van Wylen	P	2,105	147
Houghton	Houghton, N.Y.	1883	Wilber T. Dayton	P	1,286	98
Houston Baptist Univ.	Houston, Tex.	1963	William Hinton	D	1,006	75
Houston, Univ. of	Houston, Tex.	1927	Philip G. Hoffman	S	26,134	1,587
Howard Payne	Brownwood, Tex.	1889	Roger L. Brooks	D	1,530	92
Howard Univ.	Washington, D.C.	1867	James E. Cheek	P	10,061	1,700
Huntingdon	Montgomery, Ala.	1854	Allen Jackson	D	572	50
Huntington	Huntington, Ind.	1897	E. DeWitt Baker	P	478	42
Huron	Huron, S. Dak.	1883	Richard H. Timmins	P	544	48
Husson	Bangor, Me.	1898	Franklin Peters	P	810	60
Huston-Tillotson	Austin, Tex.	1876	John T. King	D	817	53
Idaho, Coll. of	Caldwell, Idaho	1891	Vacant	P	875	55
Idaho State Univ.	Pocatello, Idaho	1901	William E. Davis	S	8,516	328
Idaho, Univ of*	Moscow, Idaho	1889	Ernest W. Hartung	S	7,110	612
Illinois	Jacksonville, Ill.	1829	Donald Mundinger	P	782	55
Illinois Benedictine	Lisle, Ill.	1887	Rev. Daniel Kucera	D	1,136	73
Illinois Coll. of Optometry	Chicago, Ill.	1892	Alfred Rosenbloom	P	514	49
Illinois Inst. of Technology	Chicago, Ill.	1892	M. P. Venema, act.	P	6,325	665
Illinois State Univ.	Normal, Ill.	1857	Gene Budig	S	17,032	1,038
Illinois, Univ. of*	Urbana; Champaign	1867	John E. Corbally	S		
Chicago Circle	Chicago, Ill.	1965	Warren Cheston, Chan.	S	19,109	1,058
Medical Center	Chicago, Ill.	1896	Joseph Begando, Chan.	S	4,061	696
Urbana — Champaign	Urbana, Ill.	1867	Jack W. Peltason, Chan.	S	34,651	3,245
Illinois Wesleyan Univ.	Bloomington, Ill.	1850	Robert Eckley	P	1,674	140
Immaculata (W)	Immaculata, Pa.	1920	Sister Mary Antione	D	1,039	90
Immaculate Heart	Los Angeles, Calif.	1913	Sister Helen Kelley	P	610	45
Indiana Central	Indianapolis, Ind.	1902	Gene Sease	P	2,250	140
Indiana Inst. of Tech.	Ft. Wayne, Ind.	1932	Charles W. Terrell	P	475	41
Indiana State Univ.	Terre Haute, Ind.	1865	Alan Rankin	S	14,309	830
Indiana Univ.	Bloomington, Ind.	1820	John W. Ryan	S	68,869	3,038
Indiana Univ. of Penn.	Indiana, Pa.	1875	William Hassler	S	10,859	540
Insurance, Coll. of	New York, N.Y.	1962	A. Leslie Leonard	P	1,500	120
Inter American Univ.	San German, P.R.	1912	Sol Luis Descartes	P	9,145	178

Name	Location	Year	Governing Official and Affiliation		Students	Teachers
Iona	New Rochelle, N.Y.	1940	Rev. Bro. John Driscoll	D	4,314	192
Iowa State Univ.*	Ames, Iowa	1858	W. Robert Parks	S	19,629	1,854
Iowa, Univ. of	Iowa City, Iowa	1847	Willard L. Boyd	S	20,528	1,700
Iowa Wesleyan	Mt. Pleasant, Iowa	1842	Louis Haselmayer	P	760	63
Ithaca	Ithaca, N.Y.	1892	Ellis L. Phillips	P	4,403	368
Jackson State Univ.	Jackson, Miss.	1877	John A. Peoples	S	5,205	346
Jacksonville State Univ.	Jacksonville, Ala.	1883	Ernest Stone	S	5,220	260
Jacksonville Univ.	Jacksonville, Fla.	1934	Robert H. Spiro	P	2,216	145
Jamestown	Jamestown, N.D.	1883	Roy Joe Stuckey	P	503	56
Jarvis Christian	Hawkins, Tex.	1912	John Paul Jones	D	625	49
Jersey City State	Jersey City, N.J.	1927	Vacant	S	8,200	471
John Brown Univ.	Siloam Springs, Ark.	1919	John E. Brown Jr.	P	560	58
John Carroll Univ.	Cleveland, Ohio	1886	Rev. Henry Birkenhauer	P	3,700	212
John F. Kennedy Univ.	Martinez, Calif.	1964	Harry L. Morrison	P	453	120
John F. Kennedy	Wahoo, Nebr.	1965	Theodore Dillow	P	300	27
John Marshall Law School	Chicago, Ill.	1899	Noble W. Lee	P	1,688	100
John Wesley	Owosso, Mich.	1909	Kenneth Armstrong	P	356	35
Johns Hopkins Univ.	Baltimore, Md.	1876	Steven Muller	P	9,278	1,502
Johnson C. Smith Univ.	Charlotte, N.C.	1867	Wilbert Greenfield	P	1,184	70
Johnson State	Johnson, Vt.	1867	Vacant	S	1,103	120
Johnson & Wales	Providence, R.I.	1914	Morris J. Gaebe	P	4,966	150
Jones	Jacksonville, Fla.	1918	Jack H. Jones	P	1,618	70
Judson (W)	Marion, Ala.	1838	N.H. McCrummen	D	421	40
Juilliard School, The	New York, N.Y.	1906	Peter Mennin	P	1,233	186
Juniata	Huntingdon, Pa.	1876	John Stauffer	P	1,209	98
Kalamazoo	Kalamazoo, Mich.	1833	George N. Rainsford	D	1,356	74
Kans. City Art Inst.	Kansas City, Mo.	1885	John W. Lottes	P	720	59
Kan. City Coll. of Osteop. Med.	Kansas City, Mo.	1916	Rudolph Bremen	P	456	73
Kansas Newman	Wichita, Kansas	1933	Rev. Roman S. Galiardi	P	600	50
Kansas State	Pittsburg, Kan.	1903	George F. Budd	S	5,017	274
Kansas State Univ.*	Manhattan, Kan.	1863	James A. McCain	S	15,477	1,311
Kansas, Univ. of	Lawrence, Kan.	1864	Archie R. Dykes	S	19,591	1,139
Kansas Wesleyan	Salina, Kan.	1886	Daniel Bratton	P	489	41
Kearney State	Kearney, Nebr.	1905	Brendon McDonald	S	4,921	231
Keene State	Keene, N.H.	1909	Leo Redfern	S	2,293	137
Kent State Univ.	Kent, Ohio	1910	Glenn A. Olds	S	17,816	940
Kentucky State Univ.*	Frankfort, Ky.	1886	Carl M. Hill	S	2,000	130
Kentucky, Univ. of*	Lexington, Ky.	1865	Otis A. Singletary	S	22,663	1,750
Kentucky Wesleyan	Owensboro, Ky.	1783	William James	P	933	71
Kenyon	Gambier, Ohio	1824	William Caples	P	1,404	108
Keuka (W)	Keuka Park, N.Y.	1890	G. Wayne Glick	P	600	59
King	Bristol, Tenn.	1867	Powell A. Fraser	P	339	42
King's	Briarcliff Manor, N.Y.	1938	Robert A. Cook	P	763	56
King's	Wilkes-Barre, Pa.	1946	Rev. Charles Sherrer	P	2,258	145
Kirkland (W)	Clinton, N.Y.	1968	Samuel F. Babbitt	P	625	61
Kirksville Coll. of Osteop. Med.	Kirksville, Mo.	1892	H.C. Moore	P	453	95
Knox	Galesburg, Ill.	1837	E. Inman Fox	P	1,276	108
Knoxville	Knoxville, Tenn.	1875	Edward Brantley	D	752	65
Kutztown State	Kutztown, Pa.	1866	Lawrence M. Stratton	S	4,001	330
Ladycliff	Highland Falls, N.Y.	1933	Rev. Francis J. Breidenbach	P	467	55
Lafayette	Easton, Pa.	1826	K.R. Bergethon	P	2,237	157
LaGrange	LaGrange, Ga.	1834	Waights Henry, Jr.	D	662	45
Lake Erie	Painesville, Ohio	1856	Paul Weaver	P	805	82
Lake Forest	Lake Forest, Ill.	1857	Eugene Hotchkiss	P	1,009	85
Lakeland	Sheboygan, Wis.	1862	John B. Morland	P	451	38
Lake Superior State	Sault Ste. Marie, Mich.	1946	Kenneth Shouldice	S	1,900	101
Lamar Univ.	Beaumont, Tex.	1923	John E. Gray	S	10,236	546
Lambuth	Jackson, Tenn.	1843	James S. Wilder	D	815	67
Lander	Greenwood, S.C.	1872	Larry Jackson	S	1,039	66
Lane	Jackson, Tenn.	1882	Herman Stone	P	715	52
Langston Univ.*	Langston, Okla.	1897	William E. Sims	S	1,139	75
LaRoche	Pittsburgh, Pa.	1963	Sister De la Salle Mahler	D	587	55
La Salle	Philadelphia, Pa.	1863	Bro. Daniel Burke	D	6,046	450
La Verne	La Verne, Calif.	1891	Leland Newcomer	P	1,210	60
Lawrence Inst. Of Tech.	Southfield, Mich.	1932	W.H. Buell	P	4,026	189
Lawrence Univ.	Appleton, Wis.	1847	Thomas S. Smith	P	1,374	124
Lebanon Valley	Annville, Pa.	1866	Frederick Sample	P	1,299	101
Lee	Cleveland, Tenn.	1919	Charles Conn	Mu	1,069	72
Lehigh Univ.	Bethlehem, Pa.	1865	W. Deming Lewis	P	6,050	550
Le Moyne	Syracuse, N.Y.	1946	Rev. William L. Reilly	P	1,671	124
Le Moyne-Owen	Memphis, Tenn.	1870	Odell Horton	P	747	50
Lenoir Rhyne	Hickory, N.C.	1891	Raymond Bost	D	1,287	114
Lesley (W)	Cambridge, Mass.	1909	Don A. Orton	P	1,311	109
LeTourneau	Longview, Tex.	1946	Harry Hardwick	P	713	55
Lewis Univ.	Lockport, Ill.	1930	Lester Carr	D	2,653	145
Lewis & Clark	Portland, Ore.	1867	John R. Howard	D	2,908	174
Limestone	Gaffney, S.C.	1845	Jack Jones Early	D	507	44
Lincoln Christian	Lincoln, Ill.	1944	L.H. Appel	D	852	57
Lincoln Memorial Univ.	Harrogate, Tenn.	1897	Frank W. Welch	P	565	33
Lincoln Univ.	Jefferson City, Mo.	1866	Walter C. Daniel	S	2,345	147
Lincoln Univ.	Lincoln Univ., Pa.	1854	Herman Branson	S	1,054	97
Lincoln Univ.	San Francisco, Calif.	1919	T. Kong Lee	P	1,200	80
Lindenwood	St. Charles, Mo.	1827	John A. Brown	P	797	50
Linfield	McMinnville, Ore.	1849	Gordon Bjork	P	1,090	85
Livingston Univ.	Livingston, Ala.	1835	Asa Green	S	1,170	74
Livingstone	Salisbury, N.C.	1879	F. George Shipman	P	744	74
Lock Haven State	Lock Haven, Pa.	1870	Francis Hamblin	S	2,262	164
Loma Linda Univ	Loma Linda, Calif.	1905	David J. Bieber	D	3,500	500
Lone Mountain	San Francisco, Calif.	1898	Sister Gertrude Patch	D	797	47
Long Island Univ.	Brooklyn, N.Y.	1926	Lester Brookner	P	3,500	300
C.W. Post	Greenvale, N.Y.	1954	Vacant	P	9,700	331
Longwood	Farmville, Va.	1839	Henry I. Willett, Jr.	S	2,125	165
Loras	Dubuque, Iowa	1839	Msgr. Francis P. Friedl	D	1,452	96
Los Angeles Baptist	Newhall, Calif.	1927	John Dunkin	D	245	30
Loretto Heights	Denver, Colo.	1918	Ronald C. Hayes	P	714	95

Name	Location	Year	Governing Official and Affiliation		Students	Teachers
Louisiana	Pineville, La.	1906	G. Earl Guinn	P	898	57
Louisiana Tech. Univ.	Ruston, La.	1894	F. J. Taylor	S	7,280	493
Louisiana St. Univ.*	Baton Rouge, La.	1860	Martin Woodin	S	40,774	4,062
Baton Rouge Campus	Baton Rouge, La.	1860	C. G. Taylor, Chan.	S	22,915	1,293
Medical Center	New Orleans, La.	1931	William H. Stewart, Chan.	S	1,520	1,663
New Orleans Campus	New Orleans, La.	1956	Homer L. Hitt, Chan.	S	12,269	493
Shreveport Campus	Shreveport, La.	1967	Donald Shipp, Chan.	S	2,354	97
Louisville, Univ. of	Louisville, Ky.	1798	James G. Miller	S	12,230	1,567
Lowell State	Lowell, Mass.	1894	D. H. O'Leary	S	2,913	209
Lowell Technological Inst.	Lowell, Mass.	1895	Everett V. Olsen	S	8,000	258
Loyola	Baltimore, Md.	1852	V. Rev. J. A. Sellinger	D	3,588	185
Loyola Univ.	Chicago, Ill.	1872	Rev. R. C. Baumhart	D	14,900	1,764
Loyola Univ.	New Orleans, La.	1912	Vacant.	D	4,600	322
Loyola Marymount Univ.	Los Angeles, Calif.	1911	Rev. D. P. Merrifield	D	5,270	311
Lubbock Christian	Lubbock, Texas	1956	F. W. Mattox	D	1,086	76
Luther	Decorah, Iowa	1861	Elwin D. Farwell	P	1,871	138
Luther Rice	Alexandria, Va.	1967	Chester Bishop	D	225	38
Lycoming	Williamsport, Pa.	1812	Harold Hutson	P	1,490	94
Lynchburg	Lynchburg, Va.	1903	Carey Brewer	P	2,023	107
Lyndon State	Lyndonville, Vt.	1911	H. Franklin Irwin	S	738	56
Macalester	St. Paul, Minn.	1874	James A. Robinson	P	1,703	158
MacMurray	Jacksonville, Ill.	1846	John Wittich	P	814	53
Madison	Harrisonburg, Va.	1908	Ronald Carrier	S	6,288	398
Madison Business	Madison, Wisc.	1856	Otto J. Madland	P	293	19
Madonna	Livonia, Mich.	1947	Sister Mary Danatha	D	1,086	68
Maine Maritime Academy (M)	Castine, Me.	1941	E. A. Rodgers (Supt.)	S	467	47
Maine, Univ. of	Orono, Me.	1865	Winthrop C. Libby	S	8,782	545
at Framington	Farmington, Maine	1864	Einar A. Olsen	S	1,803	89
at Ft. Kent	Ft. Kent, Maine	1878	Richard J. Spath	S	505	28
at Portland-Gorham	Portland, Maine	1970	W. P. Fridinger, act.	S	6,514	225
at Machias	Machias, Maine	1909	Arthur Buswell	S	536	48
at Presque Isle	Presque Isle, Maine	1903	Stanley Salwak	S	1,354	89
Malone	Canton, Ohio	1892	Lon D. Randall	D	832	50
Manchester	N. Manchester, Ind.	1889	Alfred B. Helman	P	1,212	100
Manhattan	Bronx, N.Y.	1853	Brother Gregory Nugent	P	4,285	325
Manhattan Sch. of Music	New York, N.Y.	1917	George Schick	P	968	193
Manhattanville	Purchase, N.Y.	1841	Harold Delaney	P	1,293	146
Mankato State	Mankato, Minn.	1867	Douglas Moore	S	12,500	560
Mansfield State	Mansfield, Pa.	1857	Lawrence Park	S	3,281	218
Marian	Indianapolis, Ind.	1851	Louis C. Gatto	D	959	85
Marian Coll. of Fond du Lac	Fond du Lac, Wis.	1936	James Hanlon	D	465	56
Marietta	Marietta, Ohio	1835	Sherrill Cleland	P	2,035	131
Marion	Marion, Ind.	1920	Woodrow Goodman	P	685	53
Marist	Poughkeepsie, N.Y.	1929	Linus Richard Foy	P	1,700	110
Marlboro	Marlboro, Vt.	1948	Thomas B. Ragle	P	198	36
Marquette Univ.	Milwaukee, Wis.	1881	V. Rev. J.P. Raynor	P	10,929	746
Mars Hill	Mars Hill, N.C.	1856	Fred Blake Bentley	D	1,515	137
Marshall Univ.	Huntington, W. Va.	1837	John G. Barker	S	9,041	370
Mary Baldwin (W)	Staunton, Va.	1842	William Watkins Kelly	D	703	60
Mary Hardin Baylor	Belton, Tex.	1845	Bobby E. Parker	D	1,075	72
Mary Manse	Toledo, Ohio	1922	Sister Anne Marie	D	531	42
Mary Washington	Fredericksburg, Va.	1908	Prince B. Woodward	S	2,100	175
Marycrest	Davenport, Iowa	1939	Sister Cathleen Real	D	914	71
Marygrove	Detroit, Mich.	1925	Raymond Fleck	D	1,128	97
Maryland Inst. of Art	Baltimore, Md.	1826	Eugene W. Leake	P	1,026	93
Maryland, Univ. of*	College Park, Md.	1807	Charles Bishop (Chan.)	S	45,000	6,000
Eastern Shore	Princess Anne, Md.	1886	Archie Buffkins (Chan.)	S	1,041	94
Marylhurst	Marylhurst, Ore.	1893	Sister Marian D. Robinson	D	700	48
Marymount	Salina, Kan.	1922	Emerald Dechant	D	596	52
Marymount (W)	Tarrytown, N.Y.	1919	John Meng	D	1,007	101
Marymount Manhattan (W)	New York, N.Y.	1948	Sis. Colette Mahoney	D	1,572	146
Maryville	Maryville, Tenn.	1819	Joseph J. Copeland	D	750	63
Maryville	St. Louis, Mo.	1872	Sister Harriet Switzer	D	1,040	93
Marywood (W)	Scranton, Pa.	1915	Sister M. Coleman Nee.	D	2,319	183
Massachusetts Coll. of Art.	Boston, Mass.	1873	Jack Nolan	S	1,415	109
Mass. Coll. of Pharmacy	Boston, Mass.	1823	Raymond A. Gosselin	P	972	62
Mass. Institute of Tech*	Cambridge, Mass.	1861	Jerome Wiesner	P	7,376	958
Mass. Maritime Academy (M).	Buzzards Bay, Mass.	1891	Adm. Lee Harrington	S	600	47
Massachusetts, Univ of*	Amherst, Mass.	1863	Robert Wood	S	23,633	1,431
Boston Campus	Boston, Mass.	1964	F.L. Broderick (Chan.)	S	4,235	270
Mayville State	Mayville, N. Dak.	1889	James Schobel	S	560	36
McKendree	Lebanon, Ill.	1828	Eric N. Rackham	D	550	45
McMurry	Abilene, Tex.	1923	Tom K. Kim	D	1,380	92
McNeese State Univ.	Lake Charles, La.	1939	Thomas S. Leary	S	5,837	288
McPherson	McPherson, Kan.	1887	Galen Snell	D	506	37
Medaille	Buffalo, N.Y.	1937	Sister Alice Huber	P	453	34
Medical Coll of Pa.	Philadelphia, Pa.	1850	Robert J. Slater	P	336	423
Meharry Medical	Nashville, Tenn.	1876	Lloyd C. Elam	P	683	435
Memphis Academy of Arts.	Memphis, Tenn.	1936	Edwin C. Rust (Dir.)	P	233	27
Memphis State Univ.	Memphis, Tenn.	1909	Billy Jones	S	21,506	825
Menlo	Menlo Park, Calif.	1927	Richard O'Brien	P	529	46
Mercer Univ.	Macon, Ga.	1833	Rufus C. Harris	P	3,214	160
Mercy	Dobbs Ferry, N.Y.	1950	Donald Grunewald	P	2,050	124
Mercy Coll. of Detroit.	Detroit, Mich.	1941	Sister Agnes Mary Mansour	D	1,914	120
Mercyhurst	Erie, Pa.	1926	Marion Shane	D	1,477	100
Meredith (W)	Raleigh, N.C.	1891	John Edgar Weems	D	1,655	110
Merrimack	No. Andover, Mass.	1947	Rev. John Aherne	D	2,397	194
Messiah	Grantham, Pa.	1909	D. Ray Hostetter	D	945	90
Methodist	Fayetteville, N.C.	1960	Richard Pearce	D	634	45
Metropolitan State	Denver, Colo.	1965	James D. Palmer	S	8,000	344
Miami Univ.	Oxford, Ohio	1809	Phillip R. Shriver	S	16,093	721
Miami, Univ. of	Coral Gables, Fla.	1925	Henry K. Stanford	P	12,909	1,208
Michigan State Univ.*	East Lansing, Mich.	1855	Clifton R. Wharton, Jr.	S	41,649	2,721
Michigan Tech. Univ.	Houghton, Mich.	1885	Raymond L. Smith	S	4,426	300

Name	Location	Year	Governing Official and Affiliation		Students	Teachers
Michigan, Univ. of	Ann Arbor, Mich.	1817	Robben W. Fleming	S	43,160	5,055
at Dearborn	Dearborn, Mich.	1959	Leonard E. Goodall, Chan.	S	2,607	80
Mid-America Nazarene	Olathe, Kansas	1966	R. Curtis Smith	P	804	50
Middle Tenn. State Univ.	Murfreesboro, Tenn.	1911	M. G. Scarlett	S	8,925	553
Middlebury	Middlebury, Vt.	1800	James I. Armstrong	P	1,936	155
Midland Lutheran	Fremont, Nebr.	1883	L. Dale Lund	P	753	53
Midwestern Univ.	Wichita Falls, Tex.	1922	Travis A. White	S	4,004	221
Miles	Birmingham, Ala.	1905	W. Clyde Williams	P	1,100	105
Millersville State	Millersville, Pa.	1855	William Duncan	S	6,147	368
Milligan	Milligan Coll., Tenn.	1881	Jess W. Johnson	P	764	62
Millikin Univ.	Decatur, Ill.	1901	J. Roger Miller	P	1,422	110
Mills (W)	Oakland, Calif.	1852	Robert J. Wert	P	960	100
Mills Coll. of Education (W)	New York, N.Y.	1909	Margaret Devine	P	425	63
Millsaps	Jackson, Miss.	1890	Edward Collins	D	1,026	78
Milton	Milton, Wis.	1844	Edward Sarno	P	500	36
Milwaukee Sch. of Eng.	Milwaukee, Wis.	1903	Karl O. Werwath	P	1,925	135
Minneapolis Coll. of Art & Design	Minneapolis, Minn.	1886	Arnold Herstand	P	744	64
Minnesota, Univ. of*	Minneapolis, Minn.	1851	Malcolm C. Moos	S	64,464	9,561
Duluth Campus	Duluth, Minn.	1947	R. W. Darland (Prov.)	S	6,632	440
Morris Campus	Morris, Minn.	1960	John Imholte (Prov.)	S	1,656	91
Minot State	Minot, N. Dak.	1913	Gordon Olson	S	3,000	175
Misericordia (W)	Dallas, Pa.	1924	Sister Miriam Teresa	P	1,008	85
Mississippi	Clinton, Miss.	1826	Lewis Nobles	D	2,318	101
Mississippi Industrial	Holly Springs, Miss.	1905	E.E. Rankin	D	400	40
Miss. Univ. for Women (W)	Columbus, Miss.	1884	Charles P. Hogarth	S	2,652	170
Mississippi State Univ.*	State Coll., Miss.	1879	William L. Giles	S	9,358	768
Mississippi Univ. of	University, Miss.	1848	P. E. Fortune, Jr. (Chan.)	S	9,000	420
Mississippi Valley State Univ.	Itta Benna, Miss.	1950	E.A. Boykins	S	2,530	148
Missouri Southern State	Joplin, Mo.	1937	Leon Billingsly	S	3,067	120
Missouri, Univ. of*	Columbia, Mo.	1839	C. Brice Ratchford	S	48,681	2,885
at Columbia	Columbia, Mo.	1839	H.W. Schooling, Chan.	S	22,815	1,630
at Kansas City	Kansas City, Mo.	1929	James Olson, Chan.	S	10,087	493
at Rolla	Rolla, Mo.	1870	Vacant	S	4,190	377
at St. Louis	St. Louis, Mo.	1963	Vacant	S	11,589	379
Missouri Valley	Marshall, Mo.	1889	Willis Tompkins	P	601	47
Missouri Western State	St. Joseph, Mo.	1915	Marvin Looney	S	3,161	145
Mobile	Mobile, Ala.	1961	William K. Weaver, Jr.	P	629	40
Molloy	Rockville Ctre, N.Y.	1955	Sister Janet Fitzgerald	D	1,046	117
Monmouth	Monmouth, Ill.	1853	Richard Stine	P	907	78
Monmouth	W. Long Branch, N.J.	1933	Richard J. Stonesifer	P	3,811	240
Montana Coll. of Mineral Science and Technology	Butte, Mont.	1893	Fred W. DeMoney	S	638	49
Montana State Univ.	Bozeman, Mont.	1893	Carl McIntosh	S	8,000	544
Montana, Univ. of	Missoula, Mont.	1893	Robert Pantzer	S	9,072	509
Montclair State	Upper Montclair, N.J.	1908	David W. D. Dickson	S	14,000	619
Monterey Inst. of Foreign Studies	Monterey, Calif.	1955	Fulton Freeman	P	350	55
Montevallo, Univ. of	Montevallo, Ala.	1896	Kermit Johnson	S	3,600	160
Moody Bible Institute	Chicago, Ill.	1886	George Sweeting	P	2,255	157
Moore Coll. of Art (W)	Philadelphia, Pa.	1844	Mayo Bryce	P	633	80
Moorhead State	Moorhead, Minn.	1885	Roland Dille	S	6,309	330
Moravian	Bethlehem, Pa.	1807	Herman E. Collier	D	1,553	125
Morehead State Univ.	Morehead, Ky.	1922	Adron Doran	S	6,500	322
Morehouse (M)	Atlanta, Ga.	1867	Hugh Gloster	P	1,158	100
Morgan State	Baltimore, Md.	1867	King V. Cheek	S	5,986	300
Morningside	Sioux City, Iowa	1894	Thomas S. Thompson	P	1,472	88
Morris Brown	Atlanta, Ga.	1881	John A. Middleton	P	1,417	102
Morris Harvey	Charleston, W. Va.	1888	Marshall Buckalew	P	2,203	145
Mt. Angel	Mt. Angel, Ore.	1887	Rev. Christian Mondor	P	267	40
Mt. Holyoke (W)	So. Hadley, Mass.	1837	David Truman	P	1,931	204
Mt. Marty	Yankton, S.D.	1936	Sister Evangeline Anderson	D	571	74
Mt. Mary (W)	Milwaukee, Wis.	1913	Sister Mary Nora Barber	P	1,179	114
Mt. Mercy	Cedar Rapids, Iowa	1928	Sister Mary Agnes	P	809	71
Mt. St. Joseph-on-the-Ohio (W)	Mt. St. Joseph, Ohio	1920	Robert Wolverton	P	862	101
Mt. St. Mary (W)	Hooksett, N. Hamp.	1934	Sister Amy Hoey	P	202	31
Mt. St. Mary	Newburgh, N.Y.	1959	William O'Hara	P	775	65
Mt. St. Mary's	Los Angeles, Calif.	1925	Sister Cecilia Louise	D	1,280	125
Mt. St. Mary's	Emmitsburg, Md.	1808	John J. Dillon	D	1,157	87
Mt. St. Vincent, Coll. of	Riverdale, N.Y.	1847	Sister Doris Smith	P	1,100	90
Mt. Senario	Ladysmith, Wis.	1962	Robert Lovett	P	200	28
Mt. Union	Alliance, Ohio	1846	Ronald Weber	P	1,146	84
Muhlenberg	Allentown, Pa.	1848	John H. Morey	P	1,885	162
Multnomah Sch. of the Bible	Portland, Ore.	1936	Willard M. Aldrich	P	719	36
Mundelein (W)	Chicago, Ill.	1930	Sister Ann Ida Gannon	P	1,024	89
Murray State Univ.	Murray, Ky.	1922	Harry Sparks	S	6,633	377
Muskingum	New Concord, Ohio	1837	William P. Miller	P	1,160	98
Nasson	Springvale, Me.	1912	John S. Bailey	P	789	60
Nathaniel Hawthorne	Antrim, N.H.	1962	Kenneth McLaughlin	P	800	55
National Coll. of Business	Rapid City, S.D.	1941	John Hauer	P	963	46
National Coll. of Chiropractic	Lombard, Ill.	1906	Joseph Janse	P	600	39
National Coll. of Education	Chicago, Ill.	1886	Calvin Gross	P	6,060	230
Nazareth	Nazareth, Mich.	1924	Sis. Mary L. Bader	P	597	79
Nazareth Coll. of Rochester (W)	Rochester, N.Y.	1924	Alice Foley	P	2,213	114
Nebraska, Univ. of*	Lincoln, Nebr.	1869	Durward Varner	S	34,512	1,850
At Omaha	Omaha, Nebr.	1908	Ronald Roskens, Chan.	S	13,691	600
Nebraska Wesleyan Univ.	Lincoln, Nebr.	1887	Vance D. Rogers	P	1,124	100
Nevada, Univ. of*	Reno, Nev.	1864	Vacant	S	7,120	428
At Las Vegas	Las Vegas, Nev.	1955	Donald Baepler	S	6,500	274
New	Sarasota, Fla.	1964	Arland Christ-Janer	P	586	50
New England	Henniker, N.H.	1946	J. K. Cummiskey	P	1,600	100
New England Cons. of Music	Boston, Mass.	1867	Gunther Schuller	P	679	128
New Hampshire	Manchester, N.H.	1932	Edward Shapiro	P	1,547	77
New Hampshire, Univ. of*	Durham, N.H.	1866	Vacant	S	10,529	734
New Haven, Univ. of*	New Haven, Conn.	1926	Phillip Kaplan	P	5,400	300
New Mexico Highlands Univ.	Las Vegas, N. Mex.	1893	Frank Angel	S	2,346	150
N. Mex. Inst. of Min. & Tech.	Socorro, N. Mex.	1893	Stirling A. Colgate	S	843	93
New Mexico State Univ.*	Las Cruces, N. Mex.	1888	Gerald W. Thomas	S	11,596	426
New Mexico, Univ. Of	Albuquerque, N. Mex.	1889	Ferrel Heady	S	19,470	1,393

Name	Location	Year	Governing Official and Affiliation		Students	Teachers
New Rochelle, Coll. of (W)	New Rochelle, N.Y.	1904	Sister Dorothy Ann Kelly	P	2,925	168
New School for Social Research	New York, N.Y.	1919	John R. Everett	P	15,000	1,000
New York, City Univ. of	New York, N.Y.	1847	Robert J. Kibbee	Mu	155,414	11,727
Bernard M. Baruch	New York, N.Y.	1919	Clyde Wingfield	Mu	15,387	1,154
Brooklyn	Brooklyn, N.Y.	1930	John W. Kneller	Mu	36,967	2,505
City	New York, N.Y.	1847	Robert E. Marshak	Mu	20,366	2,020
Medgar Evers	Brooklyn, N.Y.	1968	Richard D. Trent	Mu	1,997	189
Hunter	New York, N.Y.	1870	Jacqueline G. Wexler	Mu	25,397	1,803
John Jay Coll. of Criminal Just.	New York, N.Y.	1964	D. H. Riddle	Mu	9,839	610
Herbert H. Lehman	Bronx, N.Y.	1931	Leonard Lief	Mu	16,042	1,297
Queens	Flushing, N.Y.	1937	Joseph Murphy	Mu	31,413	2,225
Richmond	Staten Island, N.Y.	1965	Edmond Volpe	Mu	3,871	240
York	Jamaica, N.Y.	1966	Milton G. Bassin	Mu	5,058	397
N.Y. Inst of Technology	Old Westbury, N.Y.	1955	Alexander Schure	P	4,520	200
New York Law School	New York, N.Y.	1891	Sylvester C. Smith, Jr.	P	770	57
New York Medical	New York, N.Y.	1860	Frederick L. Stone	P	613	1,200
New York, State Univ. of	Albany, N.Y.	1948	Ernest L. Boyer, (Chan.)	S	142,751	8,468
State Univ.	Albany, N.Y.	1844	Louis T. Benezet	S	13,571	762
" "	Buffalo, N.Y.	1846	Robert Ketter	S	20,963	949
" "	Binghamton, N.Y.	1946	C. Peter Magrath	S	7,930	418
" "	Stony Brook, N.Y.	1957	John Toll	S	12,058	601
State Univ. Colleges	Brockport, N.Y.	1867	Albert W. Brown	S	9,762	478
" " " "	Buffalo, N.Y.	1867	Elbert K. Fretwell	S	10,660	526
" " " "	Cortland, N.Y.	1866	Richard Jones	S	5,483	297
" " " "	Fredonia, N.Y.	1867	Dallas Beal	S	5,334	287
" " " "	Geneseo, N.Y.	1867	Robert Mac Vittie	S	5,699	291
" " " "	New Paltz, N.Y.	1885	Stanley K. Coffman	S	8,225	383
" " " "	Oneonta, N.Y.	1887	Clifford Craven	S	5,967	368
" " " "	Oswego, N.Y.	1861	Sherwood Dunham, act.	S	8,312	414
" " " "	Old Westbury, N.Y.	1965	John Maguire	S	774	53
" " " "	Plattsburgh, N.Y.	1889	George W. Angell	S	5,885	298
" " " "	Potsdam, N.Y.	1867	Thomas Barrington	S	4,936	266
" " " "	Purchase, N.Y.	1965	Abbott Kaplan	S	1,532	51
" " " "	Utica, N.Y.	1966	William Kunsela	S	613	24
" " Empire State	State Springs, N.Y.	1971	James Hall	S	764	52
Buffalo Health Sciences Ctr	Buffalo, N.Y.	1846	Clyde L. Randall, V.P.	S	2,720	
College of Ceramics	Alfred, N.Y.	1900	W.G. Lawrence, Dean	S	558	42
Env'm'nt'l Sci. & Forestry	Syracuse, N.Y.	1911	Edward Palmer	S	2,095	133
Downstate Medical Center	Brooklyn, N.Y.	1858	Calvin H. Plimpton	S	1,386	565
Health Sciences Center	Stony Brook, N.Y.	1957	Edmund Pellegrino	S	839	
Maritime College (M)	Bronx, N.Y.	1874	Sheldon Kinney	S	782	59
Upstate Medical Center	Syracuse, N.Y.	1834	Lewis Bluemle, Jr.	S	954	486
New York Univ.	New York, N.Y.	1831	James M. Hester	P	35,000	4,900
Newark Coll. of Engineering	Newark, N.J.	1881	William Hazell	S	4,200	291
Newark State	Union, N.J.	1855	Nathan Weiss	S	12,164	712
Newberry	Newberry, S.C.	1856	Fredric Brinker Irvin	D	828	65
Newton Coll. of Sacred Heart (W)	Newton, Mass.	1946	James Whalen	P	974	98
Niagara Univ.	Niagara Un., N.Y.	1856	Rev. K.F. Slattery	D	3,585	197
Nicholls State Univ.	Thibodaux, La.	1948	Vernon Galliano	S	5,285	221
Nichols	Dudley, Mass.	1815	Darcy C. Coyle	P	610	39
Norfolk State	Norfolk, Va.	1935	Lyman Brooks	S	5,782	369
North Adams State	North Adams, Mass.	1897	James Amsler	S	2,500	149
North Carolina, Univ of						
A.&T. State Univ.	Greensboro, N.C.	1891	Lewis Dowdy, Chan.	S	2,500	149
Appalachian State Univ.	Boone, N.C.	1899	Herbert Wey	S	7,545	504
at Asheville	Asheville, N.C.	1969	William Highsmith	S	1,139	71
at Chapel Hill	Chapel Hill, N.C.	1789	N.F. Taylor	S	19,396	1,800
at Charlotte	Charlotte, N.C.	1946	D.W. Colvard, Chan.	S	6,100	310
E. Carolina Univ.	Greenville, N.C.	1907	Leo W. Jenkins	S	10,907	673
Elizabeth City State Univ.	Elizabeth City, N.C.	1891	Marion Dennis Thorpe	S	1,146	101
Fayetteville State Univ.	Fayetteville, N.C.	1877	Charles A. Lyons, Jr.	S	2,891	144
at Greensboro	Greensboro, N.C.	1892	J.S. Ferguson, Chan.	S	7,549	487
North Carolina Central Univ.	Durham, N.C.	1910	Albert N. Whiting	S	4,514	317
North Carolina School of the Arts	Winston-Salem, N.C.	1963	Robert Suderburg	S	570	100
Pembroke State Univ.	Pembroke, N.C.	1887	English E. Jones	S	1,918	107
at Raleigh, State Univ.	Raleigh, N.C.	1887	J.T. Caldwell, Chan.	S	13,445	1,597
Western Carolina Univ.	Cullowhee, N.C.	1889	H.F. Robinson, Chan.	S	6,016	309
Winston-Salem State Univ.	Winston-Salem, N.C.	1892	Kenneth Williams	S	1,578	123
at Wilmington	Wilmington, N.C.	1947	Wm. H. Wagoner, Chan.	S	2,411	1 9
North Carolina Wesleyan	Rocky Mount, N.C.	1956	Thomas A. Collins	D	509	43
North Central Bible	Minneapolis, Minn.	1930	Rev. E.M. Clark	D	557	20
North Central	Naperville, Ill.	1861	Arlo L. Schilling	D	794	55
North Dakota State Univ	Fargo, N. Dak.	1890	L.D. Loftsgard	S	7,000	375
North Dakota, Univ. of	Grand Forks, N. Dak.	1883	Thomas Clifford	S	8,274	532
North Georgia	Dahlonega, Ga.	1873	John H. Owen	S	1,350	75
North Park	Chicago, Ill.	1891	Lloyd Ahlem	P	1,247	110
North Texas State Univ.	Denton, Tex.	1890	C. C. Nolen	S	14,091	654
Northeast Louisiana Univ.	Monroe, La.	1931	George T. Walker	S	9,034	364
Northeast Missouri St. Univ.	Kirksville, Mo.	1867	Charles T. McClain	S	6,323	302
Northeastern Illinois Univ.	Chicago, Ill.	1861	James Mullen	S	8,900	528
Northeastern State	Tahlequah, Okla.	1846	Robert Collier	S	4,758	228
Northeastern Univ.	Boston, Mass.	1898	Asa S. Knowles	P	33,553	1,889
Northern Arizona Univ.	Flagstaff, Ariz.	1899	J. Lawrence Walkup	S	9,300	463
Northern Colorado, Univ. of	Greeley, Colo.	1889	Richard R. Bond	S	10,886	600
Northern Ill. Univ.	DeKalb, Ill.	1895	Richard Nelson	S	22,957	1,164
Northern Iowa, Univ. of	Cedar Falls, Iowa	1876	John Kamerick	S	8,858	528
Northern Kentucky State	Highland Heights, Ky.	1968	Frank Steely	S	4,758	250
Northern Michigan Univ.	Marquette, Mich.	1899	John X. Jamrich	S	8,208	324
Northern Montana	Harve, Mont.	1929	Joseph R. Crowley	S	1,069	70
Northern State	Aberdeen, S. Dak.	1901	Norbert Baumgart	S	2,277	121
Northland	Ashland, Wis.	1892	Malcolm McLean	P	581	50
Northrop Inst. of Tech.	Inglewood, Calif.	1942	B. J. Shell	P	1,335	72
Northwest	Kirkland, Wash.	1934	D. V. Hurst	D	527	30
Northwest Christian	Eugene, Ore.	1895	Barton A. Dowdy	D	558	21
Northwest Missouri State Univ.	Maryville, Mo.	1905	Robert P. Foster	S	5,039	304
Northwest Nazarene	Nampa, Idaho	1913	Kenneth Pearsall	D	1,058	69

Name	Location	Year	Governing Official and Affiliation		Students	Teachers
Northwestern	Watertown, Wisc	1865	Carleton Toppe	D	270	18
Northwestern	Orange City, Iowa	1882	Lars Granberg	P	700	54
Northwestern State Univ	Natchitoches, La	1884	Arnold R. Kilpatrick	S	6.297	335
Northwestern State	Alva, Okla	1897	R. W. Wygle	S	1.842	84
Northwestern Univ	Evanston, Ill	1851	Robert Henry Strotz	P	11.390	2.624
Norwich Univ	Northfield, Vt	1819	Loring Hart	P	1.528	154
Northwood Institute	Midland, Mich	1959	Arthur E. Turner	P	2.000	105
Notre Dame, Coll. of	Belmont, Calif	1868	Sister Catharine Julie	P	1.060	99
Notre Dame (W)	St. Louis, Mo	1954	Sister Barbara Brumleve	D	292	32
Notre Dame (W)	Manchester, N.H	1950	Sister Jeannette Vezeau	P	400	47
Notre Dame (W)	Cleveland, Ohio	1922	Sister Mary Marthe	P	535	69
Notre Dame of Maryland	Baltimore, Md	1895	Sister Kathleen Feeley	D	724	75
Notre Dame, Univ. of (M)	Notre Dame, Ind	1842	Rev. T. M. Hesburgh	D	8.586	725
Nova Univ. of Adv.Technology	Ft. Lauderdale, Fla	1964	Abraham S. Fischler	P	377	39
Nyack	Nyack, N.Y	1882	Harold W. Boon	D	679	58
Oakland Univ	Rochester, Mich	1959	Donald D. O'Dowd	S	9.000	369
Oakland City	Oakland City, Ind	1885	Alton Davis, V.P	D	370	36
Oakwood	Huntsville, Ala	1896	C. B. Rock	D	988	55
Oberlin	Oberlin, Ohio	1833	Vacant	P	2.700	280
Occidental	Los Angeles, Calif	1887	Richard C. Gilman	P	1.708	147
Oglethorpe Univ	Atlanta, Ga	1835	Paul K. Vonk	P	1.000	40
Ohio Dominican	Columbus, Ohio	1911	Sister M. Suzanne Uhrhane	D	1.000	69
Ohio Coll. of Podiatric Med	Cleveland, Ohio	1916	Abe Rubin	P	399	75
Ohio Inst. of Technology	Columbus, Ohio	1952	Richard A. Czesniak	P	1.714	63
Ohio Northern Univ	Ada, Ohio	1871	Samuel L. Meyer	D	2.746	178
Ohio State Univ.*	Columbus, Ohio	1870	Harold L. Enarson	S	51.491	5.368
Ohio Univ	Athens, Ohio	1804	Vacant	S	19.327	1.184
Ohio Wesleyan Univ	Delaware, Ohio	1842	Thomas Wenzlau	P	2.411	150
Oklahoma Baptist Univ	Shawnee, Okla	1910	William G. Tanner	D	1.685	115
Oklahoma Christian	Oklahoma City, Okla	1950	James O. Baird	P	1.139	47
Oklahoma City Univ	Oklahoma City, Okla	1904	Dolphus Whitten, Jr	P	2.590	158
Okla. Coll. of Liberal Arts	Chickasha, Okla	1908	Bruce G. Carter	S	884	75
Oklahoma Panhandle State	Goodwell, Okla	1909	Thomas L. Palmer	S	1.268	65
Oklahoma State Univ.*	Stillwater, Okla	1890	Robert B. Kamm	S	18.877	1.834
Oklahoma, Univ. of	Norman, Okla	1890	Paul F. Sharp	S	23.574	1.219
Old Dominion Univ	Norfolk, Va	1930	James Bugg	S	10.536	485
Olivet	Olivet, Mich	1844	Ray B. Loeschner	P	787	59
Olivet Nazarene	Kankakee, Ill	1909	Harold W. Reed	P	1.786	104
Oral Roberts Univ	Tulsa, Okla	1965	Oral Roberts	P	2.350	110
Oregon College of Education	Monmouth, Ore	1856	Leonard Rice	S	3.274	225
Oregon Inst. of Technology	Klamath Falls, Ore	1947	Robert W. MacVicar	S	14.300	1.520
Oregon State Univ.*	Corvallis, Ore	1868	W. D. Purvine	S	1.596	141
Oregon, Univ. of	Eugene, Ore	1872	Robert Clark	S	16.043	854
Orlando, State Univ. at	Orlando, Fla	1963	Charles N. Millican	S	6.335	404
Osteop. Med. & Surg., Coll. of	Des Moines, Iowa	1898	J. Leonard Azneer	P	430	113
Otis Art Inst. of L.A. County	Los Angeles, Calif	1918	G. E. Woods (Dir.)	C	482	31
Ottawa Univ	Ottawa, Kan	1863	Peter H. Armacost	P	652	64
Otterbein	Westerville, Ohio	1847	Thomas Jefferson Kerr	D	1.377	94
Ouachita Baptist Univ	Arkadelphia, Ark	1885	Daniel R. Grant	D	1.710	95
Our Lady of Angels (W)	Aston, Pa	1965	Sister Madonna Marie	D	407	41
Our Lady of Elms, Col. of (W)	Chicopee, Mass	1928	V. Rev. T. F. Devine	D	430	84
Our Lady of the Lake	San Antonio, Tex	1911	Gerald Burns	D	1.224	152
Ozark Bible	Joplin, Mo	1942	Don E. Boatman	D	717	52
Ozarks, Coll. of the	Clarksville, Ark	1834	Don Davis	P	497	39
Ozarks, School of the	Pt. Lookout, Mo	1906	M. Graham Clark	P	1.068	85
Pace Univ	New York, N.Y	1906	Edward J. Mortola	P	10.349	696
Pacific	Fresno, Calif	1944	Arthur J. Wiebe	D	425	45
Pacific Christian	Long Beach, Calif	1928	Medford Jones	P	354	36
Pacific Lutheran Univ	Tacoma, Wash	1890	Eugene Wiegman	P	3.004	240
Pacific Union	Angwin, Calif	1882	J. W. Cassell	D	2.108	130
Pacific Univ	Forest Grove, Ore	1849	James Miller	P	1.075	111
Pacific, Univ. of the	Stockton, Calif	1851	Stanley McCaffrey	D	5.727	477
Paine	Augusta, Ga	1882	Vacant	D	925	66
Palmer Coll. of Chiropractic	Davenport, Iowa	1895	David Palmer	P	1.370	26
Pan American Univ	Edinburg, Tex	1927	Ralph Schilling	S	7.031	287
Panhandle State	Goodwell, Okla	1909	Thomas L. Palmer	S	1.100	72
Park	Parkville, Mo	1875	Kenneth Beyer	D	1.185	73
Parsons School of Design	New York, N.Y	1896	John R. Everett	P	700	150
Paul Quinn	Waco, Tex	1872	S. E. Rutland	D	470	39
Peabody Cons. of Music	Baltimore, Md	1857	Richard F. Goldman	P	421	85
Pennco Institutes	Wyndmoor, Pa	1962	John A. Hobyak, Jr	P	500	49
Penn. Coll. of Optometry	Philadelphia, Pa	1919	Norman E. Wallis	P	513	67
Penn. State Univ.*	University Park, Pa	1855	John W. Oswald	S	65.476	3.428
Pennsylvania, Univ. of	Philadelphia, Pa	1779	Martin Meyerson	P	19.375	8.688
Pepperdine Univ	Malibu, Calif	1936	William S. Banowsky	P	5.290	350
Peru State	Peru, Nebr	1867	Douglas Pearson	S	758	46
Pfeiffer	Misenheimer, N.C	1885	Douglas Reid Sasser	D	1.037	65
Phila. Coll. of Art	Philadelphia, Pa	1876	George D. Culler	P	1.108	150
Phila. Coll. of Bible	Philadelphia, Pa	1951	D. B. MacCorkle	P	1.267	69
Phila. Coll. of Osteopathic Med	Philadelphia, Pa	1898	Frederick H. Barth	P	709	220
Phila. Coll. of Pharm. & Science	Philadelphia, Pa	1821	Arthur Osol	P	1.056	109
Phila. Coll. of Textiles & Science	Philadelphia, Pa	1884	Lawson A. Pendleton	P	2.069	80
Philander Smith	Little Rock, Ark	1868	Walter Hazzard	D	701	52
Phillips Univ	Enid, Okla	1907	Thomas Broce	D	1.363	87
Piedmont	Demorest, Ga	1897	James E. Walter	D	450	38
Piedmont Bible	Winston-Salem, N.C	1945	Donald Drake	D	409	21
Pikeville	Pikeville, Ky	1889	Robert S. Cope	D	780	47
Pittsburgh, Univ. of	Pittsburgh, Pa	1787	Wesley W. Posvar	S	25.562	1.901
Pitzer	Claremont, Calif	1963	Robert Atwell	P	716	72
Plymouth State	Plymouth, N.H	1871	Harold E. Hyde	S	2.452	122
Point Loma	San Diego, Calif	1906	W. Shelburn Brown	D	1.220	78
Point Park	Pittsburgh, Pa	1962	Vacant	P	1.800	114
Polytechnic Institute	Brooklyn, N.Y	1854	George Bugliarello	P	4.500	280
Pomona	Claremont, Calif	1887	John David Alexander	P	1.300	132

Name	Location	Year	Governing Official and Affiliation		Students	Teachers
Portland State Univ.	Portland, Ore.	1955	Vacant.	S	13,163	590
Portland, Univ. of	Portland, Ore.	1901	Rev. P. E. Waldschmidt.	P	2,024	131
Pratt Institute	Brooklyn, N.Y.	1887	Richardson Pratt, Jr.	P	4,302	473
Prescott.	Prescott, Ariz.	1966	Frank Mertz.	P	421	33
Presbyterian	Clinton, S.C.	1880	Marc C. Weersing.	D	777	60
Princeton Univ.	Princeton, N.J.	1746	William G. Bowen.	P	5,694	730
Principia.	Elsah, Ill.	1910	David K. Andrews.	P	812	65
Providence.	Providence, R.I.	1917	V. Rev. T. R. Peterson.	D	4,616	280
Puerto Rico, Univ. of*.	Rio Piedras, P.R.	1903	Jaime Benitez.	S	42,516	2,785
Puget Sound, Univ. of.	Tacoma, Wash.	1888	Philip M. Phibbs.	P	4,269	283
Purdue Univ.*	Lafayette, Ind.	1869	Arthur G. Hansen.	S	36,857	2,475
Queens (W)	Charlotte, N.C.	1857	John Smylie.	P	633	55
Quincy.	Quincy, Ill.	1859	Rev. Titus Ludes.	D	1,569	92
Quinnipiac.	Hamden, Conn.	1929	Leonard Kent.	P	2,678	279
Racine, College of.	Racine, Wisc.	1947	Thomas Stevens.	P	720	64
Radcliffe (W)	Cambridge, Mass.	1879	Matina Souretia Horner.	P	1,593	(a)
(a) Faculty at Harvard Univ. furnishes instruction.						
Radford.	Radford, Va.	1913	Donald N. Dedmon.	S	3,865	226
Ramapo College of New Jersey.	Mahwah, N.J.	1968	George T. Potter.	S	2,993	146
Randolph-Macon.	Ashland, Va.	1830	Luther W. White.	P	761	72
Randolph-Macon Woman's (W).	Lynchburg, Va.	1891	William F. Quillian, Jr.	P	766	75
Redlands, Univ. of.	Redlands, Calif.	1909	Eugene Dawson.	P	2,687	208
Reed.	Portland, Ore.	1909	Paul Bragdon.	P	1,132	113
Regis.	Denver, Colo.	1877	Rev. David M. Clarke.	D	1,085	100
Regis (W).	Weston, Mass.	1927	Sister M. Jeanne D'Arc.	P	810	80
Rensselaer Poly. Inst.	Troy, N.Y.	1824	Richard Grosh.	P	4,679	392
Rhode Island.	Providence, R.I.	1854	Charles B. Willard.	S	8,650	360
R. I. School of Design.	Providence, R.I.	1877	Talbot Rantoul.	P	1,657	108
Rhode Island, Univ. of.	Kingston, R.I.	1892	Vacant.	S	10,381	900
Rice Univ.	Houston, Tex.	1891	Norman Hackerman.	P	3,344	410
Richard Stockton State	Pomona, N.J.	1969	Richard Biork.	S	2,007	100
Richmond, Univ. of.	Richmond, Va.	1830	E. Bruce Heilman.	P	4,647	274
Ricker.	Houlton, Me.	1848	Charles Heath, V. P.	P	373	36
Rider.	Trenton, N.J.	1865	Frank N. Elliott.	P	5,734	259
Rio Grande.	Rio Grande, Ohio.	1876	Alphus R. Christensen.	P	707	53
Ripon.	Ripon, Wis.	1851	Bernard S. Adams.	P	1,012	84
Rivier.	Nashua, N.H.	1933	Sister Doris Benoit	P	1,003	54
Roanoke.	Salem, Va.	1842	Perry F. Kendig.	D	1,300	77
Robert Morris.	Pittsburgh, Pa.	1921	Charles Sewall.	P	3,500	190
Roberts Wesleyan.	Rochester, N.Y.	1866	Vacant.	P	630	56
Rochester Inst. of Tech.	Rochester, N.Y.	1829	Paul A. Miller.	P	12,031	908
Rochester, Univ. of.	Rochester, N.Y.	1850	Allan Wallis, Chan.	P	8,400	2,319
Rockford.	Rockford, Ill.	1847	John A. Howard.	P	1,105	85
Rockhurst.	Kansas City, Mo.	1910	Rev. M. E. Van Ackeren.	D	2,599	157
Rocky Mountain.	Billings, Mont.	1878	Lawrence F. Small.	P	554	50
Roger Williams.	Bristol, R.I.	1948	Ralph Gauvey.	P	2,800	198
Rollins.	Winter Park, Fla.	1885	Jack Critchfield.	P	3,800	210
Roosevelt Univ.	Chicago, Ill.	1945	Rolf A. Weil.	P	6,532	195
Rosary.	River Forest, Ill.	1901	Sister Candida Lund.	P	1,291	110
Rosary Hill.	Buffalo, N.Y.	1948	Robert S. Marshall.	P	1,195	122
Rose-Hulman Inst. of Tech.	Terre Haute, Ind.	1874	John Logan.	P	960	80
Rosemont.	Rosemont, Pa.	1921	Sister Ann Marie.	D	531	84
Russell Sage.	Troy, N.Y.	1916	Charles Walker.	P	3,810	228
Rust.	Holly Spgs., Miss.	1866	W. A. McMillan.	D	585	38
Rutgers, Univ.*	New Brunswick, N.J.	1766	Edward J. Bloustein.	S	35,229	2,387
Douglass (W).	New Brunswick, N.J.	1918	Margery S. Foster. Dean.	S	2,981	262
Sacred Heart, Coll. of the.	Santurce, P.R.	1935	Pedro Gonzalez Ramos.	D	2,201	147
Sacred Heart Univ.	Bridgeport, Conn.	1963	Robert Kidera.	D	2,253	133
Saginaw Valley.	Univ. Center, Mich.	1963	Samuel Marble.	S	2,073	65
St. Ambrose.	Davenport, Iowa.	1882	William Bakrow.	D	1,236	93
St. Andrews Presbyterian.	Laurinburg, N.C.	1858	Donald J. Hart.	P	716	63
St. Anselm's.	Manchester, N.H.	1889	Joseph J. Gerry.	P	1,517	124
St. Augustine's.	Raleigh, N.C.	1867	Prezell R. Robinson.	P	1,488	76
St. Benedict, Coll. of (W).	St. Joseph, Minn.	1927	Stanley Idzerda.	D	1,425	100
St. Bernard.	St. Bernard, Ala.	1892	Rev. Aloysius Plaisance.	P	469	33
St. Bonaventure Univ.	St. Bonaventure, N.Y.	1856	V. Rev. D. McElrath.	D	2,315	185
St. Catherine, Coll. of (W)	St. Paul, Minn.	1905	Sister Alberta Huber.	P	1,476	132
St. Cloud State.	St. Cloud, Minn.	1869	Charles J. Graham.	S	9,857	408
St. Edward's Univ.	Austin, Tex.	1871	Bro. Stephen Walsh.	D	1,237	79
St. Elizabeth, Coll. of (W).	Convent Station, N.J.	1899	Sister Eliz. Ann Maloney.	D	584	76
St. Francis.	Fort Wayne, Ind.	1890	Sister M. Jo Ellen Scheets.	D	1,604	91
St. Francis.	Biddeford, Maine.	1953	Robert L. Horn.	P	485	42
St. Francis.	Brooklyn, N.Y.	1884	Rev. Donald Sullivan.	P	2,750	132
St. Francis.	Loretto, Pa.	1847	Rev. Sean Sullivan.	D	1,542	88
St. Francis (W).	Joliet, Ill.	1930	Francis Kerins.	D	846	76
St. John Coll. of Cleveland.	Cleveland, Ohio.	1928	Rev. J. T. McManamon.	D	733	76
St. John Fisher.	Rochester, N.Y.	1948	V. Rev. C. J. Lavery.	D	1,505	110
St. John's.	Annapolis, Md.	1784	Richard D. Weigle.	P	369	47
St. John's Univ. (M).	Collegeville, Minn.	1869	Rev. Michael P. Blecker.	D	1,785	127
St. John's Univ.	Jamaica, N.Y.	1870	V. Rev. Joseph T. Cahill.	D	13,155	626
St. Joseph's.	Rensselaer, Ind.	1889	Rev. Charles Banet.	D	1,050	84
St. Joseph's.	North Windham, Me.	1915	Bernard Currier.	P	507	32
St. Joseph's.	Philadelphia, Pa.	1851	Rev. Terrence Toland.	D	6,072	264
St. Lawrence Univ.	Canton, N.Y.	1856	Frank Peter Piskor.	P	2,560	151
St. Leo.	St. Leo, Fla.	1963	Thomas Southard.	P	1,034	74
St. Louis Coll. of Pharmacy.	St. Louis, Mo.	1864	Charles C. Rabe.	P	669	30
St. Louis Univ.	St. Louis, Mo.	1818	V. Rev. Paul Reinert.	P	9,542	1,720
Parks Coll.	Cahokia, Ill.	1927	Leon Z. Seltzer (Dean).	P	505	72
St. Martin's.	Olympia, Wash.	1895	Rev. Matthew Naumes.	D	1,140	83
St. Mary, Coll. of (W).	Omaha, Nebr.	1923	Sister Mary Angelica.	D	568	78
St. Mary (W).	Leavenworth, Kan.	1923	Sister Mary Janet.	D	481	54
St. Mary of the Plains.	Dodge City, Kan.	1952	William V. Tucker.	D	413	40
St. Mary-of-the-Woods (W).	St. Mary-of-Woods, Ind.	1840	Sister Jeanne Knoerle.	D	343	54
St. Mary's (W).	Notre Dame, Ind.	1884	Edward L. Henry.	D	1,464	123

Name	Location	Year	Governing Official and Affiliation		Stu-dents	Teach-ers
St. Mary's	Winona, Minn.	1925	Brother George Pahl	D	1,045	85
St. Mary's Coll. of Calif.	Moraga, Calif.	1863	Bro. Mel Anderson	D	1,074	98
St. Mary's Coll. of Maryland	St. Mary's City, Md.	1839	J. Renwick Jackson	S	949	71
St. Mary's Dominican (W)	New Orleans, La.	1910	Sister Mary Eugene	P	877	68
St. Mary's Univ.	San Antonio, Tex.	1852	Rev. James Young	P	3,700	210
St. Michael's	Winooski, Vt.	1904	Bernard Boutin	D	1,515	101
St. Norbert	De Pere, Wis.	1898	Robert Christin	D	1,422	90
St. Olaf	Northfield, Minn.	1874	Sidney A. Rand	D	2,759	204
St. Paul Bible	St. Paul, Minn.	1916	Francis W. Grubbs	D	342	33
St. Paul's	Lawrenceville, Va.	1888	James Alvin Russell, Jr.	P	533	43
St. Peter's	Jersey City, N.J.	1872	V. Rev. V. R. Yanitelli	D	4,369	301
St. Rose, Coll. of	Albany, N.Y.	1920	Thomas Manion	P	1,615	110
St. Scholastica, Coll. of	Duluth, Minn.	1912	Rev. F. X. Shea	P	1,015	101
St. Theresa, Coll. of	Winona, Minn.	1907	Sister Joyce Rowland	P	1,067	120
St. Thomas Aquinas	Sparkill, N.Y.	1952	Sister Mary Ann Biller	P	666	61
St. Thomas, Coll. of (M)	St. Paul, Minn.	1885	Msgr. Terrence Murphy	D	2,451	140
St. Thomas, Univ. of	Houston, Tex.	1947	Rev. Patrick Braden	P	1,736	121
St. Vincent (M)	Latrobe, Pa.	1846	Rev. Cecil Diethrich	D	965	79
St. Xavier	Chicago, Ill.	1847	Sister M. Irenaeus	D	1,202	115
Salem (W)	Winston-Salem, N.C.	1772	John H. Chandler	P	660	76
Salem	Salem, W. Va.	1888	Dallas Bailey	P	1,229	83
Salem State	Salem, Mass.	1854	Frank Keegan	S	6,500	285
Salisbury State	Salisbury, Md.	1925	Norman Crawford	S	2,332	120
Salve Regina	Newport, R.I.	1947	Sister Lucille McKillop	P	1,266	100
Sam Houston State Univ.	Huntsville, Tex.	1879	E. T. Bowers	S	10,493	370
Samford Univ.	Birmingham, Ala.	1841	Leslie S. Wright	P	3,220	175
San Diego, Univ. of	San Diego, Calif.	1949	A. E. Hughes, Jr.	P	2,600	110
San Francisco Art Inst.	San Francisco, Calif.	1871	Fred Martin (Dir.)	P	680	80
San Francisco, Univ. of	San Francisco, Calif.	1855	Rev. William McInnes	P	5,962	411
Sangamon State Univ.	Springfield, Ill.	1969	Robert Spencer	S	2,475	178
Santa Clara, Univ. of	Santa Clara, Calif.	1851	Rev. Thomas Terry	D	6,185	298
Sante Fe, Coll. of	Sante Fe, N.M.	1947	Bro. Cyprian Luke Roney	P	1,230	80
Sarah Lawrence	Bronxville, N.Y.	1928	Charles DeCarlo	P	923	145
Savannah State (A)	Savannah, Ga.	1776	Howard Jordan, Jr.	S	2,120	105
Scranton, Univ. of	Scranton, Pa.	1888	Rev. Dexter Hanley	P	3,724	156
Scripps (W)	Claremont, Calif.	1926	Mark H. Curtis	P	578	60
Seattle Pacific	Seattle, Wash.	1891	David L. McKenna	P	2,071	171
Seattle Univ.	Seattle, Wash.	1891	Rev. Louis Gaffney	P	3,159	186
Selma Univ.	Selma, Ala.	1878	Marshall C. Cleveland	D	321	23
Seton Hall Univ.	So. Orange, N.J.	1856	Rev. Thomas G. Fahy	D	9,400	704
Seton Hill (W)	Greensburg, Pa.	1883	Sister Mary Schmidt	P	748	69
Shaw Coll. at Detroit	Detroit, Mich.	1936	Romallus O. Murphy	P	932	65
Shaw Univ.	Raleigh, N.C.	1865	J. Archie Hargraves	P	1,514	90
Shenandoah Coll. & Cons. of Music	Winchester, Va.	1875	Robert Parker	D	518	85
Shepherd	Shepherdstown, W. Va.	1871	James Butcher	S	2,156	100
Shimer	Mt. Carroll, Ill.	1853	Esther Weinstein	P	208	25
Shippensburg State	Shippensburg, Pa.	1871	Gilmore B. Seavers	S	5,495	324
Shorter	Rome, Ga.	1873	Randall H. Minor	D	611	47
Siena	Loudonville, N.Y.	1937	Rev. Matthew T. Conlin	P	1,980	120
Siena Heights	Adrian, Mich.	1919	Hugh L. Thompson	D	837	49
Silver Lake	Manitowoc, Wisc.	1939	Sister Anne Kennedy	P	410	49
Simmons (W)	Boston, Mass.	1902	William J. Holmes, Jr.	P	2,513	329
Simpson	Indianola, Iowa	1860	Richard Lancaster	P	908	80
Simpson	San Francisco, Calif.	1921	Mark W. Lee	D	305	22
Sioux Falls	Sioux Falls, S. Dak.	1883	Ronald V. Wells	D	719	57
Skidmore	Saratoga Spgs., N.Y.	1911	Joseph C. Palamountain	P	1,831	185
Slippery Rock State	Slippery Rock, Pa.	1893	Albert A. Watrel	S	5,500	346
Smith (W)	Northampton, Mass.	1871	Thomas C. Mendenhall	P	2,567	243
South Alabama, Univ. of	Mobile, Ala.	1963	Frederick P. Whiddon	S	5,760	259
So. Carolina, Med. Coll. of	Charleston, S.C.	1824	William M. McCord	S	1,918	872
South Carolina St.*	Orangeburg, S.C.	1896	M. M. Nance	S	2,407	189
South Carolina, Univ. of	Columbia, S.C.	1801	Thomas F. Jones	S	24,859	1,200
S. Dak. Sch. of Mines & Tech.	Rapid City, S. Dak.	1885	Harvey R. Fraser	S	1,454	98
South Dakota State Univ.*	Brookings, S. Dak.	1881	H. M. Briggs	S	6,217	569
South Dakota, Univ. of	Vermillion, S. Dak.	1882	Richard L. Bowen	S	5,325	485
At Springfield	Springfield, S.D.	1897	Carrol Drause, Provost	S	1,134	90
South-Eastern Bible	Lakeland, Fla.	1935	Cyril Homer	D	530	25
South Florida, Univ. of	Tampa, Fla.	1956	Cecil Mackey	S	19,514	1,200
South, Univ. of the	Sewanee, Tenn.	1857	James J. Bennett, V. Chan.	D	1,065	106
Southeast Missouri State Univ.	Cape Girardeau, Mo.	1873	Mark Scully	S	7,193	340
Southeastern Louisiana Univ.	Hammond, La.	1925	Clea E. Parker	S	6,129	303
Southeastern Mass. Univ.	No. Dartmouth, Mass.	1960	Donald E. Walker	S	5,912	195
Southeastern Oklahoma State Univ.	Durant, Okla.	1909	Leon Hibbs	S	3,273	126
Southeastern Univ.	Wash., D.C.	1879	Henry J. Duel	P	350	35
Southern California	Costa Mesa, Calif.	1920	Emil Balliet	P	642	45
Southern Calif., Univ. of	Los Angeles, Calif.	1880	John R. Hubbard	P	20,289	2,425
So. Calif. College of Optometry	Fullerton, Calif.	1904	Richard Hopping	P	300	79
Southern Coll. of Optometry	Memphis, Tenn.	1932	Spurgeon B. Eure	P	579	46
Southern Colorado State	Pueblo, Colo.	1961	Harry P. Bowes	S	5,100	284
Southern Conn. State	New Haven, Conn.	1893	Manson Van B. Jennings	S	13,800	550
Southern Illinois Univ.	Carbondale, Ill.	1869	David Derge	S	18,398	2,466
Southern Methodist Univ.	Dallas, Tex.	1915	Paul Hardin	P	9,844	808
Southern Missionary	Collegedale, Tenn.	1892	Frank Knittel	D	1,555	100
Southern Mississippi, U. of	Hattiesburg, Miss.	1912	William D. McCain	S	10,300	600
Southern Oregon	Ashland, Ore.	1869	James K. Sours	S	4,300	253
Southern State	Magnolia, Ark.	1909	Imon E. Bruce	S	1,808	115
Southern Univ.	Baton Rouge, La.	1880	G. Leon Netterville	S	8,376	416
Southern Utah State	Cedar City, Utah	1897	R. C. Braithwaite	S	1,640	104
Southwest Baptist	Bolivar, Mo.	1878	James L. Sells	D	1,027	68
Southwest Minnesota State	Marshall, Minn.	1967	Jay Jones	S	2,000	175
Southwest Missouri St. U.	Springfield, Mo.	1905	Duane Meyer	S	10,200	600
Southwest Texas State Univ.	San Marcos, Tex.	1899	Vacant	S	11,623	532
Southwestern	Winfield, Kan.	1885	Donald Ruthenberg	D	693	50
Southwestern La., Univ. of	Lafayette, La.	1898	Ray Authement	S	11,685	600
Southwestern at Memphis	Memphis, Tenn.	1848	James Daughdrill	P	1,057	100
Southwestern State	Weatherford, Okla.	1901	Al Harris	S	5,053	221

Name	Location	Year	Governing Official and Affiliation		Stu-dents	Teach-ers
Southwestern Union	Keene, Texas	1893	Leroy J. Leiske	D	616	48
Southwestern Univ	Georgetown, Tex	1840	Durwood Fleming	D	900	72
Spalding	Louisville, Ky	1920	Sister Eileen Egan	P	1,022	95
Spelman (W)	Atlanta, Ga	1881	Albert E. Manley	P	1,075	104
Spring Arbor	Spring Arbor, Mich	1873	E. A. Voller	D	622	52
Spring Garden	Philadelphia, Pa	1850	Robert H. Thompson	P	775	55
Spring Hill	Mobile, Ala	1830	Rev. Paul S. Tipton	D	900	96
Springfield	Springfield, Mass	1885	Wilbert Locklin	P	2,645	127
Stanford Univ	Stanford, Calif	1891	Richard W. Lyman	P	11,260	1,322
Stephen F. Austin State U	Nacogdoches, Tex	1923	Ralph W. Steen	S	9,964	425
Stephens (W)	Columbia, Mo	1833	Vacant	P	1,794	175
Sterling	Sterling, Kansas	1887	Robert Baptista	P	413	46
Stetson Univ	De Land, Fla	1883	John E. Johns	P	2,653	138
Steubenville, Coll. of	Steubenville, Ohio	1946	Rev. Kevin Keelan	P	1,118	70
Stevens Inst. of Tech	Hoboken, N.J	1870	Kenneth C. Rogers	P	1,950	220
Stillman	Tuscaloosa, Ala	1876	Harold N. Stinson	D	610	46
Stonehill	No. Easton, Mass	1948	Rev. Ernest Bartell	P	2,105	115
Stratford (W)	Danville, Va	1852	W. Hugh Moomaw	P	467	43
Strayer	Washington, D.C	1904	Murray Donoho	P	1,338	88
Suffolk Univ	Boston, Mass	1906	Thomas Fulham	P	6,077	282
Sul Ross State Univ	Alpine, Tex	1917	Norman L. McNeil	S	2,871	165
Susquehanna Univ	Selinsgrove, Pa	1858	Gustave W. Weber	D	1,535	129
Swarthmore	Swarthmore, Pa	1864	Theodore Friend	P	1,176	154
Sweet Briar (W)	Sweet Briar, Va	1901	Harold B. Whiteman, Jr	P	720	76
Syracuse Univ	Syracuse, N.Y	1870	M. A. Eggers (Chan.)	P	*19,356*	*848*
Tabor	Hillsboro, Kansas	1908	Roy Just	P	451	50
Talladega	Talladega, Ala	1867	Herman H. Long	P	454	57
Tampa, Univ. of	Tampa, Fla	1931	B. D. Owens	P	2,133	125
Tarkio	Tarkio, Mo	1883	Eldon E. Breazier	P	585	40
Taylor Univ	Upland, Ind	1846	Milo Rediger	P	1,445	85
Temple Univ	Philadelphia, Pa	1884	Malvin Wachman	S	*28,459*	*2,900*
Tennessee State Univ	Nashville, Tenn	1912	A. P. Torrence	S	5,256	281
Tennessee Tech. Univ	Cookeville, Tenn	1915	William Everett Derryberry	S	7,062	300
Tennessee Temple	Chattanooga, Tenn	1946	Lee Roberson	P	1,514	70
Tennessee, Univ. of*	Knoxville, Tenn	1794	Edward Boling	S		
At Chattanooga	Chattanooga, Tenn	1886	James Drinnon, Chan	S	4,680	261
At Knoxville	Knoxville, Tenn	1794	Jack Reese, Chan	S	25,426	1,871
At Martin	Martin, Tenn	1900	Larry T. McGhee, Chan	S	4,365	243
Medical Units	Memphis, Tenn	1851	Joseph E. Johnson, Chan	S	1,562	501
Tennessee Wesleyan	Athens, Tenn	1857	Charles Turner	D	509	38
Tex. A & M	College Station, Tex	1876	Jack K. Williams	S	18,520	1,390
Prairie View A. & M. Univ	Prairie View, Tex	1876	Alvin Thomas	S	4,573	250
Tarleton State Univ	Stephenville, Tex	1899	William O. Trogden	S	2,733	150
Texas Christian Univ	Fort Worth, Tex	1873	J. M. Moudy (Chan.)	P	6,405	430
Texas	Tyler, Tex	1894	Allen C. Hancock	P	614	39
Texas A & I Univ	Kingsville, Tex	1925	James C. Jernigan, Chan	S	*8,319*	*406*
Texas Lutheran	Seguin, Tex	1891	Joe Menn	P	1,222	76
Texas Southern Univ	Houston, Tex	1947	Granville Sawyer	S	6,902	325
Texas, Univ. of	Austin, Tex	1883	Charles A. LeMaistre, Chan	S	*72,874*	*6,345*
At Arlington	Arlington, Tex	1895	Wendell Nedderman, act	S	14,866	849
At Austin	Austin, Tex	1883	Stephen Spurr	S	40,611	3,457
At Corpus Christi	Corpus Christi, Tex	1973	D. W. Halliday	S	1,249	68
At Dallas	Dallas, Tex	1969	Bruce Jordan	S	398	77
El Paso	El Paso, Tex	1913	Arleigh Templeton	S	10,980	403
Health Science Center	Houston, Tex	1905	J. V. Olson	S	1,256	354
Medical Branch	Galveston, Tex	1891	Truman G. Blocker, Jr	S	1,056	326
Health Science Center	San Antonio, Tex	1959	Frank Harrison	S	725	265
Health Science Center	Dallas, Tex	1943	C. C. Sprague (Dean)	S	666	432
At Odessa	Odessa, Tex	1969	B. H. Amstead	S	1,112	60
At San Antonio	San Antonio, Tex	1969	Peter Flawn	S	1,113	55
Texas Tech. Univ	Lubbock, Tex	1923	Grover Murray	S	21,510	1,399
Texas Wesleyan	Fort Worth, Tex	1891	William Pearce	D	1,730	104
Texas Woman's Univ. (W)	Denton, Tex	1901	John A. Guinn	S	6,680	350
Thiel	Greenville, Pa	1866	Vacant	D	1,014	76
Thomas	Waterville, Maine	1894	John L. Thomas, Jr	P	500	32
Thomas Jefferson Univ	Philadelphia, Pa	1824	Peter Herbut	P	1,818	1,248
Thomas More	Covington, Ky	1921	Richard A. DeGraff	P	1,455	128
Tiffin Univ	Tiffin, Ohio	1918	Richard Pfeiffer	P	375	15
Tift (W)	Forsyth, Ga	1847	Robert W. Jackson	P	450	36
Toccoa Falls Inst	Toccoa Falls, Ga	1911	Julian Bandy	P	343	30
Toledo, Univ. of	Toledo, Ohio	1872	Glen R. Driscoll	S	14,300	537
Tougaloo	Tougaloo, Miss	1869	George A. Owens	P	747	65
Towson State	Baltimore, Md	1866	James L. Fisher	S	12,420	484
Transylvania Univ	Lexington, Ky	1780	Irvin E. Lunger	P	697	60
Trenton State	Trenton, N.J	1855	C. B. Brower	S	8,000	520
Trevecca Nazarene	Nashville, Tenn	1901	Mark Moore	D	770	42
Trinity	Hartford, Conn	1823	Theodore Lockwood	P	1,741	155
Trinity	Burlington, Vt	1925	Sister Elizabeth Candon	D	495	52
Trinity	Deerfield, Ill	1897	Harry Evans	P	800	61
Trinity	Washington, DC	1897	Sister Margaret Claydon	D	1,010	80
Trinity Univ	San Antonio, Tex	1869	Duncan Wimpress	P	3,234	213
Tri-State	Angola, Ind	1884	Richard Bateman	P	1,431	96
Troy State Univ	Troy, Ala	1887	Ralph W. Adams	P	*6,010*	*211*
Tufts Univ	Medford, Mass	1852	Burton Hallowell	P	*6,200*	*1,824*
Tulane Univ	New Orleans, La	1834	H. E. Longenecker	P	9,656	1,684
Newcomb (W)	New Orleans, La	1886	James F. Davidson (Dean)	P	1,235	120
Tulsa, Univ. of	Tulsa, Okla	1894	J. Paschal Twyman	P	5,955	350
Tusculum	Greenville, Tenn	1794	Thomas Voss, Dean	P	356	35
Tuskegee Institute	Tuskegee Inst., Ala	1881	Luther H. Foster	P	3,171	375
Union	Barbourville, Ky	1879	Mahlon A. Miller	D	927	67
Union	Lincoln, Nebr	1891	Myrl O. Manley	D	815	87
Union	Schenectady, N.Y	1795	Thomas Bonner	D	3,040	179
Union Univ	Jackson, Tenn	1825	Robert E. Craig	D	906	58
U.S. Air Force Academy (M)	Colo. Springs, Colo	1954	Gen. Albert Clark, Supt	F	3,804	600
U.S. Coast Guard Acad. (M)	New London, Conn	1876	Adm. William Jenkins	F	1,000	119

Name	Location	Year	Governing Official and Affiliation		Stu- dents	Teach- ers
U.S. International Univ.	San Diego, Calif.	1952	William Rust	P	5,000	260
U.S. Merch. Marine Acad.	Kings Point, N.Y.	1938	Adm. Arthur Engel, Supt.	F	1,000	90
U.S. Military Academy (M)	West Point, N.Y.	1802	Gen. Sidney Berry, Supt.	F	4,000	400
U.S. Naval Academy (M)	Annapolis, Md.	1845	Adm. William P. Mack, Supt.	F	3,963	549
Upper Iowa	Fayette, Iowa	1857	Aldrich Paul	P	748	58
Upsala	E. Orange, N.J.	1893	Carl J. Fjellman	D	1,611	114
Urbana	Urbana, Ohio	1850	Paul Zehner	P	650	45
Ursinus	Collegeville, Pa.	1869	William Pettit	P	1,661	111
Ursuline	Cleveland, Ohio	1871	Sister M. Kenan Dulzer	D	407	52
Utah State Univ.*	Logan, Utah	1888	Glen L. Taggart	S	9,000	500
Utah, Univ. of	Salt Lake City, Utah	1850	David P. Gardner	S	21,034	3,000
Valdosta State	Valdosta, Ga.	1913	S. Walter Martin	S	4,239	215
Valley City State	Valley City, N.D.	1890	Howard Rose	S	984	57
Valparaiso Univ.	Valparaiso, Ind.	1859	Albert Huegli	P	4,300	291
Vanderbilt Univ.	Nashville, Tenn.	1873	Alexander Heard, Chan.	P	6,552	1,471
Vassar	Poughkeepsie, N.Y.	1861	Alan Simpson	P	2,250	204
Vermont, Univ. of*	Burlington, Vt.	1791	Edward C. Andrews	S	9,974	894
Villa Maria (W)	Erie, Pa.	1925	Sister L. Antoun	P	600	63
Villanova Univ.	Villanova, Pa.	1842	Rev. Edward McCarthy	D	10,000	450
Virgin Islands, Coll. of the	St. Thomas, V.I.	1962	L. C. Wanlass	S	1,693	59
Virginia Commonwealth U.	Richmond, Va.	1968	Warren W. Brandt	S	17,051	1,185
Virginia Intermont	Bristol, Va.	1884	Floyd Turner	D	575	43
Virginia Military Inst. (M)	Lexington, Va.	1839	Gen. Richard Irby, Supt.	S	1,108	124
Virginia Poly. Inst. & Univ.*	Blacksburg, Va.	1872	T. Marshall Hahn, Jr.	S	18,816	1,707
Virginia Union Univ. (A)	Richmond, Va.	1865	A. B. James	D	1,137	81
Virginia State*	Petersburg, Va.	1882	Wendell P. Russell	S	3,222	216
Virginia, Univ. of	Charlottesville, Va.	1819	Edgar F. Shannon, Jr.	S	12,300	1,200
Virginia Wesleyan	Norfolk, Va.	1961	Lambuth M. Clarke	P	626	51
Viterbo	La Crosse, Wis.	1931	Rev. J. Thomas Finucan	P	652	84
Voorhees	Denmark, S.C.	1897	Harry Graham	P	737	48
Wabash (M)	Crawfordsville, Ind.	1832	Thaddeus Seymour	P	794	72
Wagner	Staten Island, N.Y.	1883	Arthur O. Davidson	P	2,813	256
Wake Forest Univ.	Winston-Salem, N.C.	1834	James R. Scales	D	4,116	485
Walla Walla	College Place, Wash.	1892	Robert Reynolds	D	1,607	140
Walsh	Canton, Ohio	1960	Rev. Robert Francoeur	D	903	71
Walsh Coll. of Accounting	Troy, Mich.	1922	Jeffrey Barry	D	543	27
Warner Pacific	Portland, Ore.	1937	E.J. Gilliam	D	380	35
Warren Wilson	Swannanoa, N.C.	1894	Reuben H. Holden	P	388	60
Wartburg	Waverly, Iowa	1852	Vacant.	D	1,290	91
Washburn Univ.	Topeka, Kan.	1865	John W. Henderson	Mu	5,150	190
Washington	Chestertown, Md.	1782	Joseph McLain	P	906	65
Washington and Jefferson	Washington, Pa.	1781	Howard J. Burnett	P	1,181	102
Washington and Lee Univ.	Lexington, Va.	1749	Robert Huntley	P	1,657	157
Washington State Univ.	Pullman, Wash.	1891	Glenn Terrell	S	14,733	893
Washington Univ.	St. Louis, Mo.	1853	W.H. Danforth (Chan.)	P	10,902	2,668
Washington, Univ. of	Seattle, Wash.	1861	John R. Hogness	S	33,200	2,334
Wayland Baptist	Plainview, Tex.	1908	Roy C. McClung	D	965	54
Wayne State	Wayne, Nebr.	1910	Lyle Seymour, act.	S	1,874	108
Wayne State Univ.	Detroit, Mich.	1868	George Cullen	S	32,154	1,400
Waynesburg	Waynesburg, Pa.	1850	B.M. Rich	P	965	67
Weber State.	Ogden, Utah	1889	Joseph Bishop	S	9,140	418
Webster	St. Louis, Mo.	1916	Leigh Gerdine	P	1,665	117
Wellesley (W)	Wellesley, Mass.	1875	Barbara W. Newell	P	1,963	235
Wells	Aurora, N.Y.	1868	John Wilson	P	500	70
Wentworth Coll. of Technology	Boston, Mass.	1970	Edward Kirkpatrick	P	227	15
Wesleyan	Macon, Ga.	1836	W. Earl Strickland	P	490	45
Wesleyan Univ.	Middletown, Conn.	1832	Colin G. Campbell	P	1,833	309
West Chester State	West Chester, Pa.	1812	Vacant.	S	8,500	550
West Coast Univ.	Los Angeles, Calif.	1909	Victor Elconin	P	1,316	127
West Florida, Univ. of	Pensacola, Fla.	1967	Harold Bryan Crosby	S	4,527	216
West Georgia	Carrollton, Ga.	1933	Ward Papport	S	4,999	283
West Liberty State	West Liberty, W. Va.	1837	James L. Chapman	S	2,885	165
West Texas State Univ.	Cayon, Tex.	1910	Lloyd Watkins	S	6,800	300
W. Va. Inst. of Technology	Montgomery, W. Va.	1895	Leonard C. Nelson	S	2,465	145
West Virginia State	Institute, W. Va.	1891	Harold M. McNeill	S	3,677	167
West Virginia Univ.*	Morgantown, W. Va.	1867	James G. Harlow	S	15,203	834
W. Virginia Wesleyan.	Buckhannon, W. Va.	1890	John D. Rockefeller, IV.	P	1,622	113
Western Baptist Bible	Salem, Ore.	1946	F.R. Brock (Chan.)	D	500	30
Western, (The)	Oxford, Ohio	1853	William Spencer	P	345	45
Western Conn. State	Danbury, Conn.	1903	Ruth A. Haas	S	4,561	320
Western Illinois Univ.	Macomb, Ill.	1889	Vacant.	S	14,218	889
Western Kentucky Univ.	Bowling Green, Ky.	1906	Dero Dowling	S	11,749	619
Western Maryland	Westminster, Md.	1867	Ralph C. John	P	2,393	171
Western Mich. Univ.	Kalamazoo, Mich.	1903	John T. Bernhard.	S	21,189	1,245
Western Montana	Dillon, Mont.	1893	James E. Short	S	700	48
Western New England	Springfield, Mass.	1919	Beaumont A. Herman	P	3,387	123
Western New Mexico Univ.	Silver City, N.M.	1893	John Snedeker	S	1,589	75
Western State	Gunnison, Colo.	1901	Harlan Bryant	S	2,665	136
Western Washington State	Bellingham, Wash.	1895	Charles Flora	S	8,126	493
Westfield State.	Westfield, Mass.	1839	Robert L. Randolph	S	4,000	250
Westmar	Le Mars, Iowa	1890	Laurence Smith	P	658	54
Westminster Choir	Princeton, N.J.	1926	Ray E. Robinson	P	449	61
Westminster	Fulton, Mo.	1851	Dale Purcell	P	675	56
Westminster	New Wilmington, Pa.	1852	Earland I. Carlson	P	1,956	117
Westminster	Salt Lake City, Utah	1875	Manford A. Shaw	P	851	59
Westmont	Santa Barbara, Calif.	1940	Lyle C. Hillegas.	P	897	88
Wheaton	Wheaton, Ill.	1860	Hudson T. Armerding.	P	2,150	160
Wheaton (W)	Norton, Mass.	1912	William H. C. Prentice	P	1,191	111
Wheeling	Wheeling, W.Va.	1954	Rev. Charles Currie.	D	557	38
Wheelock	Boston, Mass.	1889	Gordon L. Marshall.	P	791	63
White Plains, College of	White Plains, N.Y.	1923	Katherine Restaino	P	667	45
Whitman	Walla Walla, Wash.	1859	Donald Sheehan.	P	1,140	94
Whittier	Whittier, Calif.	1901	Frederick M. Binder.	P	1,661	104
Whitworth	Spokane, Wash.	1890	Edward B. Lindaman.	P	1,722	119

Name	Location	Year	Governing Official and Affiliation		Stu-dents	Teach-ers
Wichita State Univ.	Witchita, Kan.	1895	Clark Ahlberg	S	14,766	805
Wilberforce Univ.	Wilberforce, Ohio	1856	Rembert E. Stokes	D	1,217	46
Widener .5.	Chester, Pa.	1821	Clarence R. Moll	P	2,762	214
Wiley	Marshall, Texas	1873	T. W. Cole, Sr.	P	468	41
Wilkes	Wilkes-Barre, Pa.	1933	Francis Michelini	P	3,050	225
Willamette Univ.	Salem, Ore.	1842	Robert Lisensky	P	1,611	140
William Carey	Hattiesburg, Miss.	1906	J. Ralph Noonkester	P	1,032	56
William Jewell	Liberty, Mo.	1849	Thomas Field	P	1,246	83
Wm. and Mary, College of	Williamsburg, Va.	1693	Thomas A. Graves	S	5,431	429
Wm. Mitchell Coll. of Law	St. Paul, Minn.	1900	William H. Abbott	P	840	50
Wm. Paterson Coll. of N.J.	Wayne, N.J.	1855	William McKeefery	S	11,000	456
William Penn	Oskaloosa, Iowa	1873	Duane Moon	P	700	53
William Woods (W)	Fulton, Mo.	1870	Randall B. Cutlip	P	1,024	70
Williams	Williamstown, Mass.	1793	John W. Chandler	P	1,875	183
Wilmington	Wilmington, Ohio	1870	Robert E. Hinshaw	D	765	78
Wilmington	New Castle, Del.	1968	Donald E. Ross	P	568	35
Wilson (W)	Chambersburg, Pa.	1869	Charles C. Cole, Jr.	P	465	56
Windham	Putney, Vt.	1951	Harrison Symmes	P	857	65
Winona State	Winona, Minn.	1858	Robt. DuFresne	S	4,289	207
Winthrop	Rock Hill, S.C.	1886	Charles Vail	S	3,769	237
Wisconsin, Medical Coll. of	Milwaukee, Wisc.	1913	G. A. Kerrigan	P	494	278
Wisconsin, Univ. of*	Madison, Wis.	1848	John C. Weaver	S	34,000	3,000
Eau Claire.	Eau Claire, Wisc.	1916	Leonard Haas, Chan.	S	8,888	435
Green Bay.	Green Bay, Wisc.	1969	Edward W. Weidner, Chan.	S	3,661	238
La Crosse	La Crosse, Wisc.	1909	Kenneth Lindner, Chan.	S	6,346	351
Milwaukee.	Milwaukee, Wisc.	1956	Werner A. Baum, Chan.	S	24,000	900
Oshkosh	Oshkosh, Wisc.	1871	Robert Birnbaum, Chan.	S	9,494	483
Parkside.	Kenosha, Wisc.	1968	Irvin Wyllie, Chan.	S	4,856	176
Platteville.	Platteville, Wisc.	1866	Bjarne R. Ullsvik, Chan.	S	3,821	290
River Falls.	River Falls, Wisc.	1874	George Field, Chan.	S	4,084	287
Stevens Point.	Stevens Point, Wisc.	1894	Lee S. Dreyfus, Chan.	S	8,055	560
Stout.	Menomonie, Wisc.	1893	Robert Swanson, Chan.	S	5,227	350
Superior.	Superior, Wisc.	1893	Karl W. Meyer, Chan.	S	2,592	217
Whitewater.	Whitewater, Wisc.	1868	William L. Carter	S	8,144	474
Wittenberg Univ.	Springfield, Ohio	1845	G. Kenneth Andeen	P	2,771	279
Wofford.	Spartanburg, S.C.	1854	J. M. Lesesne, Jr.	P	1,007	76
Woodbury	Los Angeles, Calif.	1884	Dora E. Kirby.	P	1,702	79
Wooster, Coll. of.	Wooster, Ohio.	1866	J. G. Drushal	D	1,830	145
Worcester Polytechnic Inst.	Worcester, Mass.	1865	George W. Hazzard.	P	2,570	214
Worcester State	Worcester, Mass.	1874	Robert Leestamper	S	3,820	181
Wright State Univ.(A).	Dayton, Ohio.	1964	Vacant.	S	9,950	440
Wyoming, Univ. of*	Laramie, Wyo.	1886	William Carlson.	S	8,904	616
Xavier Univ. of Louisiana	New Orleans, La.	1925	Norman C. Francis.	P	1,619	152
Xavier Univ.	Cincinnati, Ohio.	1831	Rev. Robert Mulligan	P	6,139	281
Yale Univ.	New Haven, Conn.	1701	Kingman Brewster, Jr.	P	9,912	2,324
Yankton	Yankton, S. Dak.	1881	Alfred M. Gibbons	P	397	45
Yeshiva Univ.	New York, N.Y.	1886	Samuel Belkin.	P	6,253	2,500
York College of Pa.	York, Pa.	1941	Ray A. Miller.	P	2,901	120
Youngstown State Univ.	Youngstown, Ohio.	1908	John J. Coffelt.	S	13,458	760

Community and Junior Colleges

Enrollment and faculty figures in italics include all branches and campuses

Name	Location	Year	Governing Official and Affiliation		Stu-dents	Teach-ers
Abraham Baldwin Agricultural	Tifton, Ga.	1908	J. Clyde Driggers	S	1,756	86
Adirondacks Community	Glens Falls, N.Y.	1960	Charles R. Eisenhart	S	1,515	58
Aeronautics, Academy of.	Flushing, N.Y.	1932	Walter M. Hartung	P	750	49
Aims.	Greeley, Colo.	1967	Ed Beaty	C	2,952	200
Alabama Christian	Montgomery, Ala.	1942	E. R. Brannan.	P	192	22
Alamance, Tech. Inst. of.	Burlington, NC.	1964	William Taylor.	S	982	100
Albany Junior	Albany, Ga.	1963	B. R. Tilley.	S	1,509	72
Albany, Junior Coll. of	Albany, N.Y.	1957	Charles Walker.	P	700	42
Albemarle, Coll. of the	Elizabeth City, N.C.	1961	S. Bruce Petteway	S	894	67
Alexander City State Junior.	Alexander City, Ala.	1965	W. Byron Causey.	S	1,633	80
Alice Lloyd	Pippa Passes, Ky.	1923	Will Hayes.	P	258	29
Allan Hancock Joint Comm.	Santa Maria, Calif.	1920	Walter E. Conrad.	Di. C	7,597	501
Allegany Community	Cumberland, Md.	1961	W. Ardell Haines	C	1,141	94
Allegheny Co., Comm. College of.	Pittsburgh, Pa.	1966	John B. Hirt.	C	28,000	800
Allen County Comm. Jr.	Iola, Kan.	1923	Bill Spencer.	C	580	27
Alpena Community	Alpena, Mich.	1952	Herbert N. Stoutenburg.	C	1,425	65
Altus Junior.	Altus, Okla.	1926	E. T. Dunlap.	S	642	35
Alvin Junior	Alvin, Tex.	1949	Thomas Jenkins	Di	1,593	93
Amarillo.	Amarillo, Tex.	1929	Albert B. Martin.	S	3,342	140
American Academy of Art.	Chicago, Ill.	1923	Irving Shapiro, Dir.	P	814	22
American River.	Sacramento, Calif.	1955	Kenneth Boettcher.	Di	16,266	407
Anderson	Anderson, S.C.	1911	J. Cordell Maddox	D	1,156	45
Andrew	Cuthbert, Ga.	1854	J.C. Martinson. Jr.	S	300	21
Angelina	Lufkin, Tex.	1968	Jack W. Hudgins, Jr.	S	1,025	70
Anne Arundel Community	Arnold, Md.	1961	Robert P. Ludlum.	C	4,226	215
Anoka-Ramsey Comm.	Coon Rapids, Minn.	1965	H. B. Monroe.	S	300	35
Anson Tech. Inst.	Ansonville, N.C.	1962	Ronald Denison.	S	2000	72
Antelope Valley	Lancaster, Calif.	1929	William Kepley, Jr.	S	3,933	147
Aquinas Junior.	Milton, Mass.	1956	Sister Dorothy Welch.	P	260	31
Aquinas Junior.	Nashville, Tenn.	1961	Sister Mary Suso Fletcher.	D	372	42
Arapahoe Community.	Littleton, Colo.	1965	Joseph K. Bailey.	S	3,842	174
Arizona Western.	Yuma, Ariz.	1963	Robert Garin.	C	3,473	159
Asheville Buncombe Tech. Inst.	Asheville,N.C.	1959	Thomas Simpson.	S	1,384	132

Name	Location	Year	Governing Official and Affiliation	Students	Teachers
Atlantic Comm.	Mays Landing, N.J.	1966	L. R. Winchell. C	3,000	110
Auburn Community	Auburn, N.Y.	1953	Albert T. Skinner. . . . . S	2,856	88
Austin Comm.	Austin, Minn.	1940	Curtis C. Mac Donald. . . . . . S	814	52
Bacone	Bacone, Okla.	1880	Charles D. Holleyman. . . . . . D	496	43
Bakersfield	Bakersfield, Calif.	1913	John J. Collins. C	11,583	402
Baltimore, Com. Col. of.	Baltimore, Md.	1947	Harry Bard. . . . . Mu	7,441	225
Barstow Community	Barstow, Calif.	1960	Mel Huden, act. . . . . S	1,416	34
Barton County Comm. Jr.	Great Bend, Kansas	1965	Paul Hines C	1,082	68
Bay de Noc Comm.	Escanaba, Mich.	1962	Edwin E. Wuehle. C	1,200	54
Bay Path Junior	Longmeadow, Mass.	1897	Randle Elliott. . . . . P	438	27
Beaufort County Tech. Inst.	Washington, N.C.	1968	James P. Blanton . . . . S	462	54
Beaver County, Com. Col. of	Monaca, Pa.	1966	Richard Adams . . . . S	1,537	85
Becker Junior	Worcester, Mass.	1887	Lloyd H. Van Buskirk. . . . . . P	544	34
Beckley	Beckley, W. Va.	1933	John Saunders . . . . P	960	33
Bee County	Beeville, Tex.	1967	Grady C. Hogue. . . . . S	1,481	60
Bell and Howell Schools.	Chicago, Ill.	1969	George Doherty . . . . P	7,200	350
Belleville Area	Belleville, Ill.	1946	Vacant. . . . . S	6,959	225
Bellevue Community	Bellevue, Wash.	1967	Merle Landerholm . . . . S	6,338	334
Belmont Technical.	St. Clairsville, Ohio.	1969	E. Earl Greer. . . . . S	643	48
Bennett	Millbrook, N.Y.	1891	J. William Nystrom . . . . P	304	45
Bergen Community	Paramus, N.J.	1965	Sidney Silverman C	6,692	349
Berkeley-Charleston-Dorch. TEC.	S.C.	1964	Richard E. Waldroup. . . . . . S,C	2,095	60
Berkshire Comm.	Pittsfield, Mass.	1960	T. E. O'Connell. . . . . S	2,350	131
Dig Bend Community	Moses Lake, Wash.	1962	Robert J. Wallenstein. . . . . . S	2,404	50
Bismarck Junior	Bismarck, N.D.	1939	Ralph Werner . . . . Mu	1,900	85
Black Hawk	Moline, Ill.	1946	Alban E. Reid . . . . S	5,889	154
Blackhawk Technical Inst.	Janesville, Wisc.	1968	O. L. Johnson (Dir.). . . . . . Di	1,225	49
Bladen County	Dublin, N.C.	1967	George Resseguie . . . . S	180	15
Blinn	Brenham, Tex.	1883	James H. Atkinson. C	1,845	92
Bliss	Columbus, Ohio.	1899	Gerald J. Wickham . . . . P	769	20
Bluefield	Bluefield, Va.	1922	Charles L. Tyer . . . . D	300	23
Blue Mountain Community	Pendleton, Ore.	1962	Wallace C. McCrae . . . . S	1,790	124
Blue Ridge Comm.	Weyers Cave, Va.	1967	James A. Armstrong . . . . . . S	1,419	43
Brainerd Comm.	Brainerd, Minn.	1938	William Ostey . . . . S	500	30
Brandywine	Wilmington, Del.	1965	Sidney Peters. . . . . P	1,294	48
Brazosport	Lake Jackson, Tex.	1968	J.R. Jackson . . . . S	1,881	84
Brevard	Brevard, N.C.	1853	Robert A. Davis. . . . . P	447	45
Brevard Community	Cocoa, Fla.	1960	Maxwell King. . . . . S	7,600	300
Brewton Parker	Mt. Vernon, Ga.	1904	J. Theodore Phillips . . . . . . D	442	24
Bristol Community	Fall River, Mass.	1965	Jack Hudnall. . . . . S	3,150	125
Bronx Community	Bronx, N.Y.	1957	James A. Colston. . . . . Mu	13,213	4590
Broome Community	Binghamton, N.Y.	1946	Sigmund A. Smith. . . . . S	4,364	165
Broward Community	Ft. Lauderdale, Fla.	1961	Hugh Adams. . . . . S	13,000	273
Brunswick Junior	Brunswick, Ga.	1961	John W. Teel. . . . . S	1,067	66
Bryant & Stratton	Boston, Mass.	1865	L.P.White. . . . . P	520	42
Bucks County Comm.	Newtown, Pa.	1964	Charles Rollins C	5,508	250
Butler County Comm	Butler, Pa.	1965	Thomas Ten Hoeve, Jr. C	2,000	90
Butler County Comm. Jr.	El Dorado, Kansas	1927	Edwin J. Walbourn C	1,499	72
Butte	Durham, Calif.	1968	Albert Schlueter. . . . . S	4,677	208
Cabrillo	Aptos, Calif.	1959	Robert E. Swenson . . . . Di	7,102	241
Caldwell Comm. & TEC	Lenoir, N.C.	1964	H. Edwin Beam . . . . S	750	75
Camden County	Blackwood, N.J.	1967	Otto R. Mauke C	4,800	209
Canada.	Redwood City, Calif.	1968	James W. Duke . . . . Di	6,700	265
Canyons, Coll. of the	Valencia, Calif.	1969	Robert Rockwell. . . . . Di	2,165	87
Cape Cod Comm.	W. Barnstable, Mass.	1961	James F. Hall . . . . S	3,220	161
Cape Fear Tech. Inst.	Wilmington, N.C.	1964	M.J. McLeod . . . . S	664	47
Carl Albert Junior	Poteau, Okla.	1934	Norman McNabb . . . . S	442	17
Carl Sandburg.	Galesburg, Ill.	1967	Eltis Henson . . . . S	2,014	102
Carteret Tech. Inst.	Morehead City, N.C.	1963	Donald Bryant. . . . . S	526	50
Casper.	Casper, Wyo.	1945	Tilghman Aley C	3,024	174
Catawba Valley Tech. Inst.	Hickory, N.C.	1959	Robert E. Paap . . . . S	1,281	125
Catonsville Community	Catonsville, Md.	1957	Robert Barringer C	8,200	409
Cazenovia (W).	Cazenovia, N.Y.	1824	Vincent C. De Baun . . . . . . P	370	40
Cecil Community	No. East, Md.	1968	Robert L. Nash . . . . C,S	976	41
Centenary Coll. for Women (W).	Hackettstown, N.J.	1867	Edward W. Seay. . . . . P	506	43
Central.	McPherson, Kan.	1884	Bruce L. Kline. . . . . Mu	201	19
Central Arizona	Coolidge, Ariz.	1967	Don Pence. C	4,437	76
Central Carolina Tech. Inst.	Sanford, N.C.	1961	James F. Hockaday. . . . . . . S	943	40
Central Florida Community	Ocala, Fla.	1957	Henry E. Goodlett. . . . . S	1,426	92
Central Oregon Community	Bend, Oregon.	1949	Frederick Boyle. . . . . S	2,567	70
Central Piedmont Comm.	Charlotte, N.C.	1963	Richard H. Hagemeyer . . . . . S	15,817	801
Central Tech. Comm.	Hastings, Nebr.	1966	Michael Paradise C	3,339	101
Central Texas.	Killeen, Tex.	1967	L. M. Morton, Jr. . . . . S	3,737	129
Central Virginia Comm.	Lynchburg, Va.	1967	Donald Puyear . . . . S	2,061	91
Central Wyoming	Riverton, Wyo.	1966	William Day . . . . S	612	44
Central YMCA Comm.	Chicago, Ill.	1960	Donald A. Canar . . . . P	4,700	225
Centralia	Centralia, Wash.	1960	Nels W. Hanson. . . . . S	3,928	154
Cerritos Community	Norwalk, Calif.	1956	Wilford Michael. . . . . S	19,002	582
Chabot.	Hayward, Calif.	1961	Reed L. Buffington . . . . Di	12,761	510
Chaffey	Alta Loma, Calif.	1883	T. Stanley Warburton . . . . . S,C	9,600	500
Champlain	Burlington, Vt.	1878	C. Bader Brouilette . . . . P	920	50
Charles Co. Community	La Plata, Md.	1958	J. N. Carsey C	1,300	90
Charles S. Mott Comm.	Flint, Mich.	1923	Charles Pappas . . . . S	19,569	820
Chattanooga St. Tech. Inst.	Chattanooga, Tenn.	1965	Charles W. Branch. . . . . . . S	1,322	70
Chemeketa Comm.	Salem, Oregon.	1955	Paul F. Wilmeth. . . . . Di	7,525	496
Chesapeake	Wye Mills, Md.	1966	George Silver. C	847	47
Chicago, City Colleges of.	Chicago, Ill.	1911	Oscar Shabat. . . . . Mu	35,000	1,200
Loop College.	Chicago, Ill.	1962	David Heller. . . . . Mu	10,965	203
Chipola Junior	Marianna, Fla.	1947	Raymond M. Deming . . . . . . Di	1,267	90
Chowan	Murfreesboro, N.C.	1848	Bruce E. Whitaker . . . . P	1,145	75
Cisco Junior.	Cisco, Tex.	1940	Carroll Scott, act. . . . . S	1,015	60
Citrus Community	Azusa, Calif.	1915	Robert Haugh. . . . . S	8,584	314
Clackamas Comm.	Oregon City, Ore.	1966	John Hakanson . . . . Di	5,038	120
Claremore Junior	Claremore, Okla.	1919	Richard Mosier . . . . S	1,079	46

Name	Location	Year	Governing Official and Affiliation		Students	Teachers
Clarendon Junior	Clarendon, Tex.	1898	Kenneth D. Vaughan	S	400	22
Clark	Vancouver, Wash.	1933	I. S. Hakanson	S	6,100	263
Clark Tech	Springfield, Ohio	1966	Richard Brinkman	S	1,106	66
Clarke	Newton, Miss.	1908	W. L. Compere	P	277	22
Clatsop Community	Astoria, Ore.	1962	Philip Bainer	S	2,850	132
Clayton Junior	Morrow, Ga.	1969	Harry S. Downs	S	2,604	106
Cleveland State Comm.	Cleveland, Tenn.	1967	D. F. Adkisson	S	2,347	118
Clinton Community	Clinton, Iowa	1946	Dean F. Travis	Di	564	44
Clinton Comm.	Plattsburgh, N.Y.	1966	Albert Light	S	740	26
Cloud County Comm	Concordia, Kansas	1965	Arley Bryant	C	581	32
Coahoma Junior	Clarksdale, Miss.	1949	James Earl Miller	S	986	56
Coastal Carolina Community	Jacksonville, NC	1964	James Henderson, Jr.	S	1,404	60
Cochise	Douglas, Ariz.	1962	John R. Edwards.	C	2,269	139
Coffeyville Comm. Junior	Coffeyville, Kan.	1923	Russell Graham	Di	585	40
Colby Comm.	Colby, Kansas	1964	James Tangeman	C	1,038	77
Colby (W)	New London, N.H.	1837	Louis Vaccaro	P	600	52
Colorado Mountain	Glenwood Spgs., Colo.	1967	Elbie L. Gann.	C	600	60
Columbia Basin	Pasco, Wash.	1955	Fred L. Esvelt.	S	4,500	175
Columbia-Greene Comm.	Athens, N.Y.	1966	Edward Owen	S	512	22
Columbia Junior	Columbia, Calif.	1968	Harvey Rhodes	S	2,253	92
Columbia State Comm.	Columbia, Tenn.	1966	Harold S. Pryor	S	1,278	85
Columbus Tech. Inst.	Columbus, Ohio	1967	Harold Nestor, act.	S	2,200	126
Compton Comm.	Compton, Calif.	1927	Abel B. Sykes, Jr.	S	6,039	250
Concordia	Portland, Ore.	1905	Rev. Erhardt P. Weber	D	207	18
Concordia	Milwaukee, Wis.	1881	Walter W. Stuenkel	D	466	38
Concordia	St. Paul, Minn.	1893	Harvey Stegemoeller	D	629	56
Concordia Lutheran	Austin, Tex.	1926	Ray F. Martens	D	262	26
Concordia Lutheran Jr.	Ann Arbor, Mich.	1962	Vacant.	D	500	38
Connors State	Warner, Okla.	1908	Melvin Self	S	950	33
Contra Costa	San Pablo, Calif.	1948	Robert Wynne	Di	7,600	175
Copiah-Lincoln Junior	Wesson, Miss.	1928	Billy Thames	C	1,305	90
Corning Community	Corning, N.Y.	1956	Robert W. Frederick, Jr.	S	2,422	96
Cosumnes River	Sacramento, Calif.	1970	Douglas Burris.	Di	1,953	77
Cowley County Comm.	Arkansas City, Kans.	1922	Gwen Nelson.	C	1,165	42
Craven Comm.	New Bern, N.C.	1965	Thurman E. Brock.	S	672	40
Crowder.	Neosho, Mo.	1964	Dell Reed.	C	707	50
Cuesta.	San Luis Obispo, Calif.	1965	Merlin Eisenbise.	C	4,254	149
Cullman.	Cullman, Ala.	1940	Sr. M. Lourdes Michel	D	250	19
Cumberland Coll. of Tenn.	Lebanon, Tenn.	1842	Ernest L. Stockton.	P	391	24
Cumberland County.	Vineland, N.J.	1963	William J. Sample.	C	1,500	65
Cuyahoga Community.	Cleveland, Ohio	1962	Alfred Livingston, act.	C, S	21,367	853
Cypress.	Cypress, Calif.	1966	Omar Scheidt.	S	9,876	275
Dabney S. Lancaster Comm.	Clifton Forge, Va.	1967	John F. Backels.	S	795	50
Dallas Co. Comm. Col. System.	Dallas, Texas	1965	Bill J. Priest.	C	16,438	412
Dalton Jr.	Dalton, Ga.	1963	Derrell Roberts.	S	1,262	55
Danville Junior.	Danville, Ill.	1946	William Larigas.	S	3,000	100
Davenport Coll. of Business.	Grand Rapids, Mich.	1866	Robert W. Sneden.	P	1,174	45
Davidson County Comm.	Lexington, N.C.	1958	Grady Love.	S	1,500	103
Davis Junior.	Toledo, Ohio	1858	Ruth L. Davis.	P	760	28
Dawson.	Glendive, Mont.	1940	James Hoffman.	C, S	470	33
Daytona Beach Comm.	Daytona Beach, Fla.	1958	Roy F. Bergengren.	S	3,527	144
Dean Junior.	Franklin, Mass.	1865	Richard Crockford.	P	1,091	75
De Anza.	Cupertino, Calif.	1967	A. Robert DeHart.	C	14,000	560
Delaware Tech & Comm.	Georgetown, Del.	1967	Paul K. Weatherly.	S	2,600	125
Delgado Junior.	New Orleans, La.	1921	Marvin E. Thames.	S	6,548	235
Del Mar.	Corpus Christi, Tex.	1935	Jean Richardson.	S	6,548	285
Delaware County Comm.	Media, Pa.	1967	Douglas Libby, Jr.	C	2,300	100
Delta.	University Ctr., Mich.	1958	Donald Carlyon.	C	9,500	320
Des Moines Area Comm.	Ankeny, Iowa	1966	Paul Lowery (Supt.)	S	2,700	100
Desert, Coll. of the.	Palm Desert, Calif.	1958	F. D. Stout.	S	5,951	280
Diablo Valley.	Pleasant Hill, Calif.	1948	William P. Niland.	Di	14,020	280
Dixie Junior.	St. George, Utah.	1911	Ferron C. Losee.	S	1,000	65
Dodge City Community.	Dodge City, Kan.	1935	Charles M. Barnes.	C	915	45
Donnelly.	Kansas City, Kan.	1949	Rev. John Oldfield.	D	426	30
Du Page, Coll. of.	Glen Ellyn, Ill.	1965	Rodney Berg.	C	9,996	513
Durham Tech. Inst.	Durham, N.C.	1965	Harold Collins.	S	992	75
Dutchess Community.	Poughkeepsie, N.Y.	1957	James F. Hall.	S	4,300	138
Dyersburg State Comm.	Dyersburg, Tenn.	1969	Edward Eller.	S	494	55
East Central Junior	Decatur, Miss.	1928	Charles V. Wright.	S	1,144	51
East Los Angeles.	Los Angeles, Calif.	1945	J. M. Duling, act.	Di	14,300	567
East Mississippi Junior.	Scooba, Miss.	1927	William Reeves.	S	987	58
Eastern Arizona.	Thatcher, Ariz.	1888	Dean Curtis.	S, C	2,711	130
Eastern Iowa Comm.	Davenport, Iowa.	1966	Gerald Clemmensen (Supt.)	S	1,926	130
Eastern Oklahoma State	Wilburton, Okla.	1909	James Miller.	S	1,705	65
Eastern Wyoming.	Torrington, Wyo.	1948	Charles Rogers.	S	614	46
Edgecombe Tech. Inst.	Tarboro, N.C.	1968	Charles McIntyre.	S	567	44
Edison Community.	Ft. Myers, Fla.	1962	David G. Robinson.	S	1,813	86
Edmunds Community	Lynnwood, Wash.	1967	James Warren.	S	3,200	157
El Camino.	Torrance, Calif.	1947	Stuart E. Marsee.	Di	24,512	586
El Centro.	Dallas, Tex.	1965	Donald T. Rippey.	S	5,672	309
El Paso Comm.	Colordao Springs, Colo.	1968	Robert O. Hatton.	S	4,054	216
El Paso Community	El Paso, Texas.	1971	Alfredo de los Santos.	S	5,200	250
El Reno.	El Reno, Okla.	1938	A. R. Harrison.	S	481	22
Elgin Community.	Elgin, Ill.	1949	Robert L. Appel, Jr.	Di	2,559	167
Elizabeth Seton.	Yonkers, N.Y.	1960	Eileen Farley.	C	452	42
Ellsworth Comm.	Iowa Falls, Iowa	1890	G. P. Warford (Dean)	Di	822	49
Emmanuel.	Franklin Spgs., Ga.	1919	C. Y. Melton.	D	384	27
Endicott Junior (W)	Beverly, Mass.	1939	Eleanor Tupper.	P	725	52
Erie Community.	Amherst, N.Y.	1946	James Shenton.	S	8,433	249
Essex Community.	Baltimore, Md.	1968	Vernon Wanty.	C	5,104	310
Essex County.	Newark, N.J.	1968	J. Harry Smith.	C	5,528	300
Everett Comm.	Everett, Wash.	1941	Jeanette Poore.	S	6,766	251
Fayetteville Tech. Inst.	Fayetteville, N.C.	1961	Howard Boudreau.	S	946	77
Fashion Inst. Of Technology	New York, N.Y.	1944	Marvin J. Feldman.	S, Mu	5,743	152

Name	Location	Year	Governing Official and Affiliation		Students	Teachers
Feather River	Quincy, Calif.	1968	Dale P. Wren	Di	1,120	36
Fergus Falls Comm.	Fergus Falls, Minn.	1960	W. A. Waage	S	590	38
Ferrum	Ferrum, Va.	1913	Joseph T. Hart	D	1,005	64
Finger Lakes. Comm. Coll. of	Canandaigua, N.Y.	1965	Charles Meder	S	1,557	48
Fisher Junior (W)	Boston, Mass.	1903	Scott Fisher	P	350	30
Flathead Valley Comm.	Kalispell, Mont.	1967	Larry Blake	S	1,298	6
Florence-Darlington TEC	Florence, S.C.	1963	Fred Fore	S	539	35
Florida	Temple Terrace, Fla.	1946	James R. Cope	P	396	26
Florida Jr. Coll. at Jacksonville	Jacksonville, Fla.	1966	Benjamin R. Wygal	S	31,683	1,223
Florida Keys Comm.	Key West, Fla.	1965	John S. Smith	S	1,079	47
Florissant Valley Community	St. Louis, Mo.	1962	Raymond J. Stith	Di	6,869	350
Floyd Junior	Rome, Ga.	1970	David McCorkle	C	1,040	53
Foothill	Los Altos Hills, Calif.	1958	James Fitzgerald	C	11,343	444
Forest Park Community	St. Louis, Mo.	1962	Ralph H. Lee	Di	5,828	367
Forsyth Tech. Inst.	Winston-Salem, N.C.	1964	Harley Affeldt	S	750	75
Fort Scott Comm.	Fort Scott, Kan.	1919	Leon Foster	C	601	42
Ft. Steilacoom Comm.	Tacoma, Wash.	1967	Marion O. Oppelt	S	7,585	259
Fox Valley Tech. Inst.	Appleton, Wisc.	1967	William Sirek (Dir.)	Di	3,000	500
Frank Phillips	Borger, Tex.	1948	James W. Dillard	S	638	46
Franklin Inst. of Boston	Boston, Mass.	1908	L.J. Dunham Jr. (Dir.)	Mu	953	71
Freed-Hardeman	Henderson, Tenn.	1908	E. Claude Gardner	P	823	51
Fresno City	Fresno, Calif.	1910	Clyde McCully	S	14,911	578
Fullerton	Fullerton, Calif.	1913	John Casey	S	17,999	510
Fulton-Montgomery Community	Johnstown, N.Y.	1963	Hadley S. DePuy	S	1,229	53
Gadsden State Junior	Gadsden, Ala.	1965	A. D. Naylor	S	4,802	200
Gainesville Junior	Gainesville, Ga.	1964	Hugh Mills, Jr.	S	1,120	56
Galveston	Galveston, Tex.	1967	Melvin M. Plexco	S	1,700	100
Garden City Community Junior	Garden City, Kan.	1919	Raymond Wamsley	C	1,068	55
Garland, Junior (W)	Boston, Mass.	1872	Alice J. Thurston	P	300	31
Gaston	Dallas, N.C.	1964	W. B. Sugg	S	2,000	100
Gateway Tech. Inst.	Kenosha, Wisc.	1912	Keith Stoehr	C	7,804	174
Gavilan	Gilroy, Calif.	1963	Ralph Schroder	S	1,800	93
Genesee Community	Batavia, N.Y.	1966	Cornelius V. Robbins	S	1,939	97
George C. Wallace State Comm.	Dothan, Ala.	1965	Phillip J. Hamm	S	2,239	96
Germanna Comm.	Locust Grove, Va.	1970	Arnold E. Wirtala	S	900	43
Glen Oaks Comm.	Centreville, Mich.	1967	Justus Sunderman	C	653	56
Glendale	Glendale, Calif.	1927	John Grande	Mu	7,069	275
Gloucester County	Sewell, N.J.	1967	William Apetz	S	2,023	114
Gogebic Community	Ironwood, Mich.	1932	James Perry	C	728	52
Golden West	Huntgtn. Bch., Calif.	1966	R. Dudley Boyce	Mu	16,112	450
Goldey Beacom	Wilmington, Del.	1886	Clarence A. Fulmer	P	477	33
Gordon Junior	Barnesville, Ga.	1852	Jerry M. Williamson	S	750	55
Grahm Junior	Boston, Mass.	1950	Arthur Griffin	P	930	53
Grand Rapids Junior	Grand Rapids, Mich.	1914	Francis McCarthy (Dean)	Mu	5,559	230
Grand View	Des Moines, Iowa	1896	K. F. Langrock	P	1,040	49
Grays Harbor	Aberdeen, Wash.	1930	Joseph Malik	S	3,311	250
Grayson County	Denison, Texas	1964	Truman Webster	S	3,343	130
Greater Hartford Comm.	Hartford, Conn.	1967	Arthur C. Banks, Jr.	S	1,607	65
Greenfield Comm.	Greenfield, Mass.	1962	Lewis O. Turner	S	1,567	83
Green Mountain (W)	Poultney, Vt.	1834	Raymond A. Withey	P	567	44
Green River Comm.	Auburn, Wash.	1965	Melvin Lindbloom	S	5,849	265
Greenville TEC	Greenville, S.C.	1962	Thomas Barton, Jr. (Dir.)	S	1,667	100
Grossmont Community	El Cajon, Calif.	1961	Erv. F. Metzgar	S	13,100	374
Guilford Tech. Inst.	Jamestown, N.C.	1958	Luther R. Medlin	S	2,182	112
Gulf Coast Community	Panama City, Fla.	1957	Richard E. Morley	S	2,400	80
Hagerstown Junior	Hagerstown, Md.	1946	Atlee Kepler	C	1,611	63
Halifax County Tech. Inst.	Weldon, N.C.	1967	Phillip W. Taylor	S	380	45
Harcum Junior	Bryn Mawr, Pa.	1915	Michael A. Duzy	P	600	50
Harford Community	Bel Air, Md.	1957	Kenneth Oosting	S	5,808	662
Harrisburg Area Comm.	Harrisburg, Pa.	1964	Clyde Blocker	Di	4,000	155
Hartford Col. for Wm. (W)	Hartford, Conn.	1939	Laura A. Johnson	P	225	33
Hartford State Tech.	Hartford, Conn.	1946	Thomas Raimondi	S	471	56
Hartnell	Salinas, Calif.	1920	Gibb R. Madsen	S	6,000	250
Haskell Indian Junior	Lawrence, Kans.	1884	Travis Martin (Supt.)	S	1,245	89
Hawkeye Inst. of Technology	Waterloo, Iowa	1966	Wallace Galluzzi	F	915	104
Haywood Tech. Inst.	Clyde, N.C.	1965	M. C. Nix	S	600	50
Henderson County Junior	Athens, Tex.	1946	T. M. Harvey	S.C.	1,316	79
Henry Ford Community	Dearborn, Mich.	1938	Stuart M. Bundy	Mu	13,002	720
Herkimer County Comm.	Herkimer, N.Y.	1966	Robert McLaughlin	S	1,227	46
Hesston	Hesston, Kan.	1907	Laban Peachey	D	470	47
Hibbing Comm.	Hibbing, Minn.	1916	Jennis Bapst	S	633	39
Highland Comm.	Freeport, Ill.	1962	Kenneth E. Borland	Di	1,271	51
Highland Community Junior	Highland, Kan.	1858	T. E. Woodrum	S	435	37
Highland Park Comm.	Highland Park, Mich.	1918	Thomas Lloyd (Dean)	Mu	3,748	94
Highline Comm.	Midway, Wash.	1961	Orville Carnahan	S	5,999	383
Hilbert	Hamburg, N.Y.	1969	Sister Mary Edwina	P	585	45
Hill Junior	Hillsboro, Texas	1962	Oran Bailey	C	600	60
Hillsborough Comm.	Tampa, Fla.	1968	Morton S. Shanberg	S	6,840	350
Hinds Junior	Raymond, Miss.	1917	Robert Mayo	C	5,055	361
Hiwassee	Madisonville, Tenn.	1849	Horace N. Barker	D	600	35
Hocking Technical	Nelsonville, Ohio	1968	John J. Light	S	1,050	95
Holding Tech. Inst.	Raleigh, N.C.	1963	Frank B. Branch	C, S	1,038	55
Holmes Junior	Goodman, Miss.	1925	Bro. John Driscoll	D	260	21
Holy Cross Junior	Notre Dame, Ind.	1966	George E. Frost	S	3,121	208
Holyoke Community	Holyoke, Mass.	1946	G. William Dudley (Dir.)	S	1,500	93
Honolulu Comm.	Honolulu, Hawaii	1920	Candito De Leon	Mu	2,078	150
Horry — Georgetown TEC	Conway, S.C.	1966	Vincent Darnowski	S	2,742	62
Hostos Community	Bronx, N.Y.	1968	Alfred J. Smith, Jr.	C	1,250	40

Name	Location	Year	Governing Official and Affiliation		Stu-dents	Teach-ers
Housatonic Comm.	Bridgeport, Conn.	1966	Thomas Salter	C, S	1,217	55
Houston Comm.	Houston, Tex.	1971	James J. Fitzgibbons	S	6,089	248
Howard Community	Columbia, Md.	1970	John R. Humphreys	P	350	34
Howard	Big Spring, Tex.	1946	A.H. Elland	S	2,136	194
Hudson Valley Community	Troy, N.Y.	1953	Robert LeMay, Jr.	S	1,362	83
Humphreys	Stockton, Calif.	1896	Harlan Cleveland	S	6,000	389
Hutchinson Community Jr.	Hutchinson, Kan.	1928	J. Don Boney	S	14,717	603
Illinois Central	E. Peoria, Ill.	1967	Kenneth L. Edwards	Di	8,800	430
Illinois Valley Comm.	Oglesby, Ill.	1924	R. Earl Trobaugh	Mu	2,545	110
Imperial Valley	Imperial, Calif.	1922	Terrel Spencer	S	2,832	163
Independence Comm. Jr.	Independence, Kan.	1925	Neil Edds	C	574	35
Indian Hills Community	Ottumwa, Iowa	1966	Lyle A. Hellyer	S	1,048	112
Indian River Community	Ft. Pierce, Fla.	1960	Herman Heise	S	1,559	289
Indiana Vocational Tech.	Indianapolis, Ind.	1966	W.A.Gessner	S	1,300	75
Inver Hills State Junior	Inver Hills Hts., Minn.	1970	Donald Skinner (Supt.)	Di	2,012	120
Iowa Area Six Comm.	Marshalltown, Iowa	1966	Edwin Barbour	Di	17,193	522
Iowa Central Comm.	Ft. Dodge, Iowa	1966	Richard Blacker	S	1,050	70
Iowa Lakes Comm.	Esterville, Iowa	1967	Robert Looft (Supt.)	S	1,339	132
Iowa Western Comm.	Clarinde, Iowa	1966	Fred J. Eason	S	565	36
Isothermal Comm.	Spindawe, N.C.	1965	Harold E. Wilson	S	507	28
Itasca Comm.	Grand Rapids, Minn.	1922	Winston O. Benjamin	S	2,676	179
Itawamba Junior	Fulton, Miss.	1948	W. Dwight Renner	Di	1,085	47
Jackson Comm.	Jackson, Mich.	1928	Robert G. Harris	C	4,107	187
Jackson State Comm.	Jackson, Tenn.	1965	Harold V. Sheffer	C	4,043	211
James H. Faulkner State Jr.	Bay Minette, Ala.	1965	F. E. Wright	S	1,423	78
Jamestown Community	Jamestown, N.Y.	1950	Lathem Sibert	S	1,197	45
Jefferson	Hillsboro, Mo.	1963	Roger Seager	S	2,532	88
Jefferson Community	Watertown, N.Y.	1959	B. R. Henry	C	1,038	50
Jefferson Davis State Jr.	Brewton, Ala.	1965	James F. McVean	S	1,452	51
Jefferson State Jr.	Birmingham, Ala.	1965	Woodfin Patterson	S	573	27
John A. Logan	Carterville, Ill.	1968	George Layton	S	6,514	290
John C. Calhoun St. Tech. Jr.	Decatur, Ala.	1965	Thomas Deem	S	1,501	58
John Tyler Comm.	Chester, Va.	1967	Carlton Kelley	S	2,363	119
Johnson County Comm.	Overland Park, Kans.	1968	James R. Walpole	S	909	83
Joliet Junior	Joliet, Ill.	1901	H. D. McAninch	S	4,431	269
Jones County Junior	Ellisville, Miss.	1927	T. Terrell Tisdale	S	2,075	133
Kalamazoo Valley Comm.	Kalamazoo, Mich.	1966	Dale B. Lake	C	4,300	150
Kankakee Comm.	Kankakee, Ill.	1966	John Samlin	S	3,953	270
Kan. City Kan. Comm. Junior	Kansas City, Kan.	1923	Jack M. Flint	C	2,451	125
Kansas Technical Inst.	Salina, Kansas	1965	James O. Thompson, Jr.	S	264	21
Kapiolani Comm.	Honolulu, Hawaii	1964	Frederick Haehnlen, Pro.	S	3,545	154
Kaskaskia	Centralia, Ill.	1940	Ray Searby	Di	2,000	100
Katherine Gibbs School	New York, N.Y.	1911	Fred Stapleford	P	1,750	78
Kauai Community	Lihue, Hawaii	1965	Edward White, Provost.	S	1,030	55
Kellogg Community	Battle Creek, Mich.	1956	Richard F. Whitmore	S	2,233	200
Kendall	Evanston, Ill.	1934	Andrew Cothran	P	984	34
Kennesaw Junior	Marietta, Ga.	1966	Horace W. Sturgis	S	2,031	85
Kettering Coll. of Medical Arts	Kettering, Ohio	1967	Winton Beaven	D	334	48
Keystone Junior	La Plume, Pa.	1868	Harry K. Miller, Jr.	P	839	59
Kilgore Junior	Kilgore, Tex.	1935	Randolph C. Watson	S	2,900	150
King's	Charlotte, N.C.	1901	G. L. Pritchett (Dir.)	P	400	15
Kingsborough Community	Brooklyn, N.Y.	1963	Leon M. Goldstein	Mu	8,996	606
Kirtland Comm.	Roscommon, Mich.	1966	Robert A. Stenger	Di	680	28
Kirkwood Comm.	Cedar Rapids, Iowa	1966	Selby Ballantyne (Supt.)	Di	3,450	200
Kishwaukee Comm.	Malta, Ill.	1967	W. Lamar Fly	Di	1,800	120
Kitrell	Kitrell, N.C.	1886	Haywood Strickland	P	336	24
Labette Community Jr.	Parsons, Kans.	1923	James J. Altendorf	C	545	39
Lackawana Junior	Scranton, Pa.	1894	C. R. Walther Thomas	P	300	25
La Guardia Community	Long Island City, N.Y.	1970	Joseph Shenker	Mu	4,727	303
Lake City Comm.	Lake City, Fla.	1962	Herbert E. Phillips	S	2,052	143
Lake County, Coll. of	Grays Lake, Ill.	1967	Richard Erzen	S	3,142	246
Lake Land	Mattoon, Ill.	1966	Robert Webb	S	2,825	135
Lake Michigan	Benton Harbor, Mich.	1946	James Lehman	S	2,800	60
Lake Region Jr.	Devils Lake, N. Dak.	1941	Merril Berg	Di	750	50
Lake Sumter Comm.	Leesburg, Fla.	1962	Paul P. Williams	Di	1,800	68
Lakeland Comm.	Mentor, Ohio	1967	Wayne L. Rodehorst	C	5,200	225
Lakeshore Tech Inst.	Cleveland, Wisc.	1912	Frederick Nierode (Dir.)	Di.	1,300	80
Lakewood Comm.	White Bear L., Minn.	1967	Carl Gerber	S	2,250	75
Lamar Community	Lamar, Colo.	1937	Carl Westbrook	S	619	35
Lane Community	Eugene, Ore.	1965	Eldon G. Schafer	Di	6,276	343
Laney	Oakland, Calif.	1954	Lawrence A. Davis	C	12,200	450
Lansing Community	Lansing, Mich.	1965	Philip Gannon	C	10,640	450
Laramie County Community	Cheyenne, Wyo.	1968	H. D. Yarbrough	C	1,573	115
Laredo Junior	Laredo, Tex.	1947	Ray A. Laird	S	4,000	125
Lasell Junior (W)	Auburndale, Mass.	1851	Kenneth M. Greene	P	704	71
Lassen	Susanville, Calif.	1925	Robert Theiler	S	2,400	83
LDS Business College	Salt Lake City, Utah	1886	R. F. Kirkham	D	754	29
Lee	Baytown, Tex.	1934	Jim Sturgeon	S	3,619	181
Lees Junior	Jackson, Ky.	1883	Troy R. Eslinger	Mu	321	34
Lees-McRae	Banner Elk, N.C.	1900	H. C. Evans, Jr.	D	721	45
Lehigh County Comm.	Schnecksville, Pa.	1967	John G. Berrier	C	2,146	116
Leicester Jr.	Leicester, Mass.	1784	Henry Borger	P	300	28
Lenoir Comm.	Kinston, N.C.	1960	Jesse L. McDaniel	S	1,455	102
Lewis and Clark Community	Godgrey, Ill.	1971	Wilbur R. L. Trimpe	S	3,100	175
Lima Technical	Lima, Ohio	1971	James S. Biddle (Dir.)	S	650	35
Lincoln Land Comm.	Springfield, Ill.	1967	Robert L. Poorman	Di	4,773	180
Lincoln	Lincoln, Ill.	1865	J. Richard Stoltz	P	567	40
Lincoln Trail	Robinson, Ill.	1969	Joseph Piland	S	850	60
Lindsey Wilson	Columbia, Ky.	1903	L. R. McDonald	D	300	28
Lon Morris	Jacksonville, Tex.	1873	John E. Fellers	D	400	26

Name	Location	Year	Governing Official and Affiliation		Stu-dents	Teach-ers
Long Beach City	Long Beach, Calif.	1927	Wiley Garner	Mu	26,000	1,200
Longview Community	Lee's Summit, Mo.	1969	William D. Hatley	Di	3,370	136
Lorain County Comm.	Elyria, Ohio	1963	Omar Olsen	S, C	4,319	210
Los Angeles City	Los Angeles, Calif.	1929	Louis Kaufman	Mu	17,517	700
Los Angeles Harbor	Wilmington, Calif.	1949	Eugene A. Pimentel	Di	10,050	333
Los Angeles Pierce	Woodland Hills, Calif.	1947	Edward Liston	Mu	17,696	508
Los Angeles Southwest	Los Angeles, Calif.	1967	Herbert Ravetch, act.	S	4,087	149
L.A. Trade Technical	Los Angeles, Calif.	1949	Fred Brinkman	Mu	16,539	893
Los Angeles Valley	Van Nuys, Calif.	1949	Robert Horton	Mu	18,666	400
Louisburg	Louisburg, N.C.	1787	C. W. Robbins	D	748	45
Lower Columbia	Longview, Wash.	1934	David Story	S	3,036	147
Luzerne County Comm.	Wilkes-Barre, Pa.	1967	Byron Rinehimer	C, S	1,430	73
Macomb County Community	Warren, Mich.	1962	J. R. Dimitry	C	19,217	621
MacCormac Junior	Chicago, Ill.	1904	Gordon Borchardt	P	228	14
Macon Junior	Macon, Ga.	1968	William Wright	S	1,938	66
Madison Area Technical	Madison, Wisc.	1912	Norman P. Mitby	Di	5,965	262
Madison Business	Madison, Wisc.	1856	Otto J. Madland	P	221	15
Mainland, Coll. of the	Texas City, Texas	1966	Fred Taylor	Di	1,602	75
Manatee Junior	Bradenton, Fla.	1957	Samuel R. Neel	S	3,500	191
Manchester Comm.	Manchester, Conn.	1963	F. W. Lowe	S	3,150	143
Manhattan Comm.	New York, N.Y.	1963	Edgar Draper	Mu	11,325	604
Manor	Jenkintown, Pa.	1947	Mother M. Olga	P	329	38
Maple Woods Community	Kansas City, Mo.	1969	John M. Gazda	S	1,800	70
Maria	Albany, N.Y.	1958	Sis. Mary B. Mahoney	P	478	48
Maria Regina (W)	Syracuse, N.Y.	1963	Sis. M. Rosalie Brady	P	300	32
Maricopa County Comm.	Phoenix, Ariz.	1963	John F. Prince	C	37,092	1,650
Marin, Coll. of.	Kentfield, Calif.	1926	John A. Grasham	S, C	6,908	371
Marion Institute (M)	Marion, Ala.	1889	Paul B. Robinson	P	374	75
Marshalltown Community	Marshalltown, Iowa	1927	James McKinstry	Di	871	50
Martin	Pulaski, Tenn.	1870	Tom E. Gray	D	400	33
Martin Tech. Inst.	Williamston, N.C.	1968	E. M. Hunt	S	443	25
Mary Holmes	West Point, Miss.	1892	Joseph Gore	P	362	28
Marymount	Boca Raton, Fla.	1963	Donald E. Ross	P	464	33
Massachusetts Bay Comm.	Watertown, Mass.	1961	John McKenzie	S	1,586	106
Massasoit Comm.	Brockton, Mass.	1966	John Musselman	S	3,700	150
Mattatuck Community	Waterbury, Conn.	1967	Charles B. Kinney	S	2,473	100
Maui Community	Kahului, Hawaii	1966	Glen Fishbach	S	1,219	50
McCook	McCook, Nebr.	1926	John N. Harms	S	422	35
McDowell Tech. Inst.	Marion, N.C.	1964	John Price	S	191	11
McHenry County	Crystal Lake, Ill.	1967	James Davis	Di	2,178	134
McLennan Comm.	Waco, Texas	1965	Wilbur Ball	S, C	4,737	220
Memphis, State Tech. Inst. at.	Memphis, Tenn.	1967	Charles Whitehead (Dir)	S	1,729	135
Meramec Community	St. Louis, Mo.	1962	Glynn E. Clark	Di	7,070	378
Merced	Merced, Calif.	1963	Lowell Barker	Di	7,000	300
Mercer County Comm.	Trenton, N.J.	1966	Richard Greenfield	C	6,161	170
Meridian Jr.	Meridian, Miss.	1937	William F. Scaggs	Mu	1,500	90
Merritt	Oakland, Calif.	1953	Donald Godbold	C, S	9,500	250
Mesa	Gd. Junction, Colo.	1925	Theodore E. Albers	S	3,573	125
Mesabi Comm.	Virginia, Minn.	1921	Gilbert Staupe	S	784	38
Metropolitan Comm.	Minneapolis, Minn.	1965	Vacant.	S	2,300	82
Miami-Dade Comm.	Miami, Fla.	1960	Peter Masiko, Jr.	S	30,097	1,376
Miami-Jacobs Jr. Coll. of Bus.	Dayton, Ohio	1860	Charles P. Harbottle	P	710	22
Michael J. Owens Tech.	Perrysburg, Ohio	1967	Jacob S. See	S	1,200	75
Mid Michigan Community	Harrison, Mich.	1965	Eugene W. Gillaspy	S	1,200	55
Middle Georgia	Cochran, Ga.	1885	Louis C. Alderman Jr.	S	1,725	102
Middlesex Comm.	Middletown, Conn.	1966	Philip Wheaton	S	1,864	93
Middlesex County	Edison, N.J.	1965	Frank M. Chambers	C	7,644	367
Midlands TEC	Columbia, S.C.	1962	Robert Grigsby	S	3,500	167
Midway (W)	Midway, Ky.	1847	Albert N. Cox	P	284	23
Miles Comm.	Miles City, Mont.	1939	Vernon R. Kailey	S	543	27
Milwaukee Area Technical	Milwaukee, Wis.	1951	William Ramsey (Dir.)	S	8,978	507
Mineral Area	Flat River, Mo.	1965	Richard Caster	S	980	55
Mira Costa	Oceanside, Calif.	1934	John MacDonald	S	3,643	160
Mississippi Delta Jr.	Moorhead, Miss.	1926	J. T. Hall	S	1,306	93
Mississippi Gulf Coast Jr.	Perkinston, Miss.	1911	J. J. Hayden	S	6,200	331
Mitchell	New London, Conn.	1939	Robert C. Weller	P	817	46
Mitchell Comm.	Statesville, N.C.	1852	Charles Poindexter	S	661	36
Moberly Area Junior	Moberly, Mo.	1927	Henry T. Norris	S	807	57
Modesto Junior	Modesto, Calif.	1921	Kenneth Griffin	Di	12,883	474
Mohawk Valley Community	Utica, N.Y.	1946	W. Stewart Tosh	S	4,603	118
Mohegan Comm.	Norwich, Conn.	1970	Robert N. Rue	S	1,400	50
Monroe Community	Rochester, N.Y.	1961	Moses Kock	S	8,965	287
Monroe County Comm.	Monroe, Mich.	1964	Ronald Campbell	C	1,650	68
Montcalm Comm.	Sidney, Mich.	1965	C. J. Bedore, Jr.	C	928	25
Monterey Peninsula Comm.	Monterey, Calif.	1947	George J. Faul	C	8,740	300
Montgomery Community	Rockville, Md.	1946	William Strasser	C	11,708	621
Montgomery County Comm.	Blue Bell, Pa.	1964	Leroy Brendlinger	C	5,000	250
Montgomery Tech. Inst.	Troy, N.C.	1968	Marvin G. Miles	S	300	30
Montreat-Anderson	Montreat, N.C.	1916	Silas M. Vaughn	D	378	27
Moorpark	Moorpark, Calif.	1967	Robert A. Lombardi	C	9,700	450
Moraine Valley Comm.	Palos Hills, Ill.	1968	Robert E. Turner	S	4,894	238
Morgan Comm.	Ft. Morgan, Colo.	1967	Robert W. Johnson	C	1,262	41
Morris, County College of	Dover, N.J.	1968	Sherman H. Masten	C	5,000	120
Morton	Cicero, Ill.	1924	Vincent A. Guarna	Di	1,757	103
Motlow State Comm.	Tullahoma, Tenn.	1969	Sam H. Ingram	S	1,147	59
Mt. Aloysius Junior	Cresson, Pa.	1939	Sis. Mary Cecilia Meighan	P	476	59
Mt. Hood Comm.	Gresham, Ore.	1965	Earl L. Klapstein	S	9,700	450
Mt. Ida Junior	Newton Ctr., Mass.	1899	F. Roy Carlson	P	600	53
Mt. Olive	Mt. Olive, N.C.	1951	William B. Raper	D	258	24
Mt. St. Clare	Clinton, Iowa	1918	Sister Eileen Smith	D	254	35
Mt. San Antonio Comm.	Walnut, Calif.	1946	Eldon Pearce	S	17,016	545
Mt. San Jacinto	Gilman Hot Spgs., Cal.	1963	Milo P. Johnson	Di	1,585	65
Mt. Vernon Nazarene	Mt. Vernon, Ohio	1966	John A. Knight	D	439	36
Mt. Wachusett Comm.	Gardner, Mass.	1963	Arthur F. Haley	S	1,891	121
Murray State	Tishomingo, Okla.	1908	Clyde Kindell	S	708	36
Muscatine Community	Muscatine, Iowa	1929	Mark L. Hopkins	S	2,186	129

Name	Location	Year	Governing Official and Affiliation	Stu-dents	Teach-ers
Muskegon Business	Muskegon, Mich.	1885	Robert Jewell	P	450	18
Muskegon Community	Muskegon, Mich.	1926	Charles Greene	C	4,361	192
Napa	Napa, Calif.	1942	George Clark	C	4,660	367
Nash Tech. Inst.	Rocky Mount, N.C.	1968	George F. Chambers	S	17,672	568
Nassau Community	Garden City, N.Y.	1959	Kenneth P. Walker	S	966	65
Navarro Junior	Corsicana, Tex.	1946	Ivan R. Simpson	Di	510	32
Nebraska Southern Community	Fairbury, Nebr.	1941	Alex Easton	S	720	60
Nebraska Western	Scottsbluff, Nebr.	1929	J. C. Sanders	S	590	31
Neosho County Comm.	Chanute, Kans.	1936	W. F. Griesemer	P	442	25
New England Aeronautical Inst.	Nashua, N.H.	1965	David Larrabee	S	850	100
New Hampshire Tech. Inst.	Concord, N.H.	1965	George C. Knox (Dir.)	S	636	45
New Hampshire Voc. Tech.	Manchester, N.H.	1945	E. A. McCourt (Dir.)	S	441	28
New Hampshire Voc. Tech.	Portsmouth, N.H.	1945	Jodie C. Smith	C	1,007	60
New Mexico Junior	Hobbs, N.M.	1965	Col. Robert Kemble	S	825	48
New Mexico Military Inst. (M)	Roswell, N.M.	1891	W. Robert Sullins	S	1,728	150
New River Community	Dublin, Va.	1966	Jack Ballard	S	600	88
N.Y. City Community Coll.	Brooklyn, N.Y.	1946	Herbert M. Sussman	Mu	18,379	1,430
New York, State Univ. of Agric. & Tech. Inst.	Alfred, N.Y.	1908	David H. Huntington	S	4,057	232
" " "	Canton, N.Y.	1906	Earl MacArthur	S	2,351	137
" " "	Cobleskill, N.Y.	1911	Walton A. Brown	S	2,594	147
" " "	Delhi, N.Y.	1913	William Kennaugh, act	S	2,490	154
" " "	Farmingdale, N.Y.	1912	Charles W. Laffin	S	12,276	312
" " "	Morrisville, N.Y.	1908	Royson N. Whipple	S	2,966	169
Newton Junior	Newtonville, Mass.	1946	Charles W. Dudley	Mu	541	42
Niagara County Community	Sanborn, N.Y.	1962	Ernest Notar	S	3,495	149
Normandale Comm.	Bloomington, Minn.	1968	Dale Lorenz	S	2,967	99
North Central Michigan	Petoskey, Mich.	1958	A. D. Shankland	S	973	43
North Central Tech. Inst.	Wausau, Wis.	1911	L. B. Hoyt (Dir.)	Di	2,014	116
North Country Comm.	Saranac Lake, N.Y.	1967	George Hodson	S	1,276	42
NDSU-Bottineau	Bottineau, N. Dak.	1907	Robert Johnson (Dean)	S	538	25
N. Dak. St. Sch. of Science	Wahpeton, N. Dak.	1903	Clair I. Blikre	S	3,114	162
North Florida Junior	Madison, Fla.	1958	Stephen McMahon	S	740	51
North Greenville	Tigerville, S.C.	1892	Harold E. Lindsey	D	511	29
North Hennepin Comm.	Minneapolis, Minn.	1966	John F. Helling	S	2,141	100
North Idaho	Coeur d'Alene, Idaho	1939	Barry Schuler	C	1,130	73
North Iowa Area Comm.	Mason City, Iowa	1918	David Randall Pierce	S	1,593	108
North Platte Comm.	North Platte, Nebr.	1965	John Harms	Mu	488	26
North Shore Community	Beverly, Mass.	1965	George Traicoff	S	5,195	275
Northampton County Area Comm.	Bethlehem, Pa.	1966	Richard Richardson, Jr.	C	3,008	215
Northeast Alabama State Jr.	Rainsville, Ala.	1964	E. R. Knox	S	1,034	51
Northeast Iowa Vocational/Tech	Calmar, Iowa	1966	Max Clark	Di	801	53
Northeast Miss. Junior	Booneville, Miss.	1948	Harold T. White	C,S	1,327	62
Northeast Wisconsin Tech. Inst.	Green Bay, Wisc.	1910	K.W. Hanbenschild (Dir.)	Mu	18,122	998
Northeastern Junior	Sterling, Colo.	1941	Ervin S. French	C	2,135	67
Northeastern Okla. A&M.	Miami, Okla.	1919	D. D. Creech	S	2,259	149
Northern Essex Comm.	Haverhill, Mass.	1961	Harold Bentley	S	4,585	204
Northern Oklahoma	Tonkawa, Okla.	1901	Edwin Vineyard	S	1,181	74
Northern Virginia Comm.	No. Springfield, Va.	1965	Richard Ernst	S	17,260	375
Northland Comm.	Thief R. Falls, Minn.	1965	Victor Charles	S	325	22
Northwest Community	Powell, Wyo.	1946	Sinclair Orendorff	C	830	63
Northwest Iowa Vocational	Sheldon, Iowa	1966	D. W. McPherson, Supt.	Di	500	32
Northwest Miss. Junior	Senatobia, Miss.	1927	R. D. McLendon	S	1,461	101
Northwestern Conn. Comm.	Winsted, Conn.	1965	Regina Duffy	S	1,757	67
Northwestern Michigan	Traverse City, Mich.	1951	William J. Yankee	S	2,060	108
Norwalk Community	Norwalk, Conn.	1961	E. I. L. Baker	S	2,656	106
Norwalk State Tech.	Norwalk, Conn.	1962	Frank Juszli	S	1,646	98
Oakland Community	Bloomfield Hills, Mich.	1964	Joseph Hill	C	15,402	502
Oakton Comm.	Morton Grove, Ill.	1969	William Koehnline	S	15,371	671
Ocean County	Toms River, N.J.	1966	Andrew S. Moreland	C	3,200	215
Odessa	Odessa, Tex.	1946	Philip Speegle	C	2,760	172
Ohlone	Fremont, Calif.	1965	Stephen E. Epler	Di	5,477	250
Okaloosa-Walton Jr.	Niceville, Fla.	1963	J. E. McCracken	S	2,253	82
Oklahoma City Southwestern	Oklahoma City, Okla.	1946	W. R. Corvin	P	1,675	104
Oklahoma Sch. of Business, Accountancy, Law & Finance	Tulsa, Okla.	1919	H. Everett Pope	P	652	31
Olney Central	Olney, Ill.	1963	Gail L. Lathrop	Di	2,512	74
Olympic	Bremerton, Wash.	1946	Henry Milander	S	6,000	250
Onondaga Community	Syracuse, N.Y.	1961	Marvin Rapp	S	4,373	150
Orange Coast	Costa Mesa, Calif.	1947	Robert Moore	S	26,064	685
Orange County Community	Middletown, N.Y.	1950	Robert T. Novak	S	3,519	116
Orangeburg Calhoun TEC	Orangeburg, S.C.	1968	M. Rudy Groomes	S	1,800	111
Oscar Rose	Midwest City, Okla.	1970	Joe Leone	S	6,128	189
Otero Junior	La Junta, Colo.	1941	William L. McDivitt	S	900	60
Ottumwa Heights	Ottumwa, Iowa	1925	Jerry Solloway	P	425	33
Owens Technical	Perrysburg, Ohio	1967	Jacob See	S	1,001	60
Paducah Comm.	Paducah, Ky.	1932	Donald J. Clemens	S	1,046	55
Palm Beach Junior	Lake Worth, Fla.	1933	Harold C. Manor	S	7,071	225
Palmer	Charleston, S.C.	1955	Charles E. Palmer	P	598	23
Palomar	San Marcos, Calif.	1946	Frederick R. Huber	C	8,751	355
Palo Verde	Blythe, Calif.	1947	George W. Pennell	C	762	51
Panola Junior	Carthage, Tex.	1947	Charles Hays	C	930	45
Paris Junior	Paris, Tex.	1924	Louis B. Williams	Di	1,530	68
Parkersburg Community	Parkersburg, W.Va.	1971	Robert Stauffer	S	3,065	140
Parkland	Champaign, Ill.	1967	William M. Staerkel	Di	4,911	237
Pasadena City	Pasadena, Calif.	1924	Armen Sarafian	S	17,393	350
Paul D. Camp Comm.	Franklin, Va.	1971	Perry Adams	S	953	48
Paul Smiths	Paul Smiths, N.Y.	1946	Chester L. Buxton	P	1,140	70
Peace (W)	Raleigh, N.C.	1857	S. David Frazier	D	455	32
Pearl River Junior	Poplarville, Miss.	1909	M. R. White	P	1,136	85
Peirce Junior	Philadelphia, Pa.	1865	Thomas M. Peirce	P	1,290	78
Peninsula	Port Angeles, Wash.	1961	E. John Maier	S	2,250	88

Name	Location	Year	Governing Official and Affiliation	Students	Teachers
Penn Valley Community	Kansas City, Mo.	1915	Thomas M. Law	Mu	5,700	210
Pensacola Jr.	Pensacola, Fla.	1948	T. Felton Harrison	S	12,118	470
Permian Jr. Col. System	Odessa, Texas	1946	Jack Rodgers (Chan.)	C	3,549	270
Philadelphia, Comm. Coll. of	Philadelphia, Pa.	1964	Allen T. Bonnell	S	8,200	469
Phillips County Comm.	Helena, Ark.	1966	John Easley	S,C	10,897	350
Phoenix	Phoenix, Ariz.	1920	Ailliam Berry (Dean)	C	10,897	350
Piedmont TEC	Greenwood, S.C.	1966	Lex Walters (Dir.)	S	1,200	90
Piedmont Virginia Comm.	Charlottesville, Va.	1972	Harold McGee	S	1,100	35
Pima Comm.	Tucson, Ariz.	1970	Irwin Spector	P	11,669	631
Pine Manor Junior (W)	Chestnut Hill, Mass.	1911	Donald Gordon	S	493	49
Pitt Tech. Inst.	Greenville, N.C.	1961	W. E. Fulford, Jr.	S	854	72
Platte Tech. Comm.	Columbus, Nebr.	1969	Jerry Lee	S	788	41
Polk Comm.	Winter Haven, Fla.	1964	Frederick T. Lenfestey	S	3,723	150
Porterville	Porterville, Calif.	1927	O. H. Shires	S	2,132	65
Portland Community	Portland, Ore.	1961	Amo De Bernardis	S	25,269	1,351
Post Junior	Waterbury, Conn.	1890	F. Burton Cook	P	719	40
Potomac State	Keyser, W. Va.	1901	A. G. Slonaker (Dean)	S	673	40
Prairie State	Chicago Hts., Ill.	1958	Ashley Johnson	S	3,975	270
Pratt Community Jr.	Pratt, Kan.	1938	Donald Tolbert	C	484	35
Prentiss Institute	Prentiss, Miss.	1931	A. L. Johnson	P	179	16
Presentation	Aberdeen, S.D.	1951	Sister Francis Mary Dunn	P	358	43
Prince George's Community	Largo, Md.	1958	Robert Bickford	C	9,258	494
Queensborough Community	Bayside, N.Y.	1958	Kurt R. Schmeller	Mu	14,705	996
Quincy Junior (A)	Quincy, Mass.	1958	Kenneth P. White	Mu	1,800	135
Quinebaug Valley Comm.	Danielson, Conn.	1971	Robert E. Miller	S	480	30
Quinsigamond Comm.	Worcester, Mass.	1963	Paul Preus	S	4,213	140
R.C.A. Institutes	New York, N.Y.	1909	Robert F. Adams	P	3,100	103
Randolph Tech. Inst.	Asheboro, N.C.	1962	M.H. Branson	S	557	27
Ranger Junior	Ranger, Tex.	1926	Jack Elsom	Di	497	31
Rangely	Rangely, Colo.	1962	James H. Bos	Di	726	35
Redwoods, Coll. of the	Eureka, Calif.	1964	Donald Weichert	C	5,000	220
Reedley	Reedley, Calif.	1926	Clifford M. Boyer	S	2,632	111
Rend Lake	Ina, Ill.	1956	James Snyder	S	1,302	76
Rhode Island Jr.	Warwick, R.I.	1964	William F. Flanagan	S	4,470	286
Richmond Tech. Inst.	Hamlet, N.C.	1965	Joseph Nanney	S	691	38
Ricks	Rexburg, Idaho	1888	Henry B. Eyring	P	4,455	260
Rio Hondo	Whittier, Calif.	1963	Walter Garcia	S	12,283	322
Riverside City	Riverside, Calif.	1916	Kenneth Harper	C	12,300	400
Roanoke-Chowan Tech. Inst.	Ahoskie, N.C.	1967	James W. Young	S	317	40
Robert Morris	Carthage, Ill.	1965	Charles W. Banta	P	187	18
Robeson Tech. Inst.	Lumberton, N.C.	1965	R. Craig Allen	S	650	40
Rochester Comm.	Rochester, Minn.	1915	Charles Hill	S	2,406	140
Rockland Community	Suffern, N.Y.	1957	Seymour Eskow	S	6,331	163
Rock Valley	Rockford, Ill.	1964	Karl Jacobs	S	4,400	163
Rockingham Comm.	Wentworth, N.C.	1966	Gerald B. James	S	1,031	100
Rogue Comm.	Grants Pass, Ore.	1971	Henry O. Pete	C,S	1,800	130
Sacramento City	Sacramento, Calif.	1916	Sam Kipp	Mu	12,350	370
St. Clair County Comm.	Pt. Huron, Mich.	1923	Richard L. Norris	C	3,400	120
St. Gregory's	Shawnee, Okla.	1915	Rev. Michael Roethler	D	457	46
St. John's	Winfield, Kan.	1893	M.J. Stelmachowicz	D	316	30
St. John's River Junior	Palatka, Fla.	1958	Robert L. McLendon	S	1,032	66
St. Mary's Jr.	Minneapolis, Minn.	1964	Sis. Anne Joachim	D	838	78
St. Mary's (W)	Raleigh, N.C.	1842	Rev. Frank W. Pisani	P	505	54
St. Petersburg Junior	St. Petersburg, Fla.	1927	Michael Bennett	S	9,759	306
Sampson Tech. Inst.	Clinton, N.C.	1965	James Vann	S	441	55
San Antonio	San Antonio, Tex.	1925	Jerome Weynand	S	15,664	755
San Bernardino Valley	San Bernardino, Calif.	1926	Arthur Jensen	Di	14,191	464
San Diego City	San Diego, Calif.	1914	Allen Repashy	Mu	5,200	137
San Diego Evening	San Diego, Calif.	1962	Robert S. Hamilton	Mu	13,781	712
San Diego, Mesa	San Diego, Calif.	1963	Ellis Bensen	Di	8,225	220
San Francisco, City Coll. of	San Francisco, Calif.	1935	Harry Buttimer	C	21,374	680
San Jacinto	Pasadena, Texas	1961	Thomas M. Spencer	S	7,559	341
San Joaquin Delta	Stockton, Calif.	1963	Joseph Blanchard	Di	13,510	411
San Jose City	San Jose, Calif.	1921	Theodore Murguia	C	15,407	650
San Mateo, Coll. of	San Mateo, Calif.	1922	David H. Mertes	S	14,000	528
Sandhills Comm.	Southern Pines, N.C.	1963	Raymond A. Stone	S	1,200	160
Sanford D. Bishop Junior	Mobile, Ala.	1965	Sanford D. Bishop	S	1,068	53
Santa Ana	Santa Ana, Calif.	1915	John E. Johnson	S	10,985	344
Santa Barbara City	Santa Barbara, Calif.	1908	Glenn Gooder	Di, S	7,185	250
Santa Fe Community	Gainesville, Fla.	1966	Alan Robertson	C	4,054	187
Santa Monica	Santa Monica, Calif.	1929	Donald Click	Mu	13,365	495
Santa Rosa Junior	Santa Rosa, Calif.	1927	Roy Mikalson	Di	14,305	447
Sauk Valley	Dixon, Ill.	1965	George Cole	S	2,014	119
Sayre Junior	Sayre, Okla.	1938	Harry Patterson	S	260	11
Schenectady County Comm.	Schenectady, N.Y.	1967	Robert Larsson	S	2,513	38
Schoolcraft	Livonia, Mich.	1964	C. Nelson Grote	S	6,178	278
Schreiner	Kerrville, Tex.	1923	Sam Junkin	P	423	28
Seattle Central Community	Seattle, Wash.	1966	Nolen Ellison	S	8,500	250
Selma Univ.	Selma, Ala.	1878	Rev. M. Cleveland, Jr.	D	371	25
Seminole Junior	Sanford, Fla.	1966	E. S. Weldon	S	2,552	240
Sequoias, Coll. of the	Visalia, Calif.	1926	Ivan Crookshanks	S	5,906	216
Shasta	Redding, Calif.	1950	Dale Miller	C	11,134	425
Shawnee	Ullin, Ill.	1968	Loren E. Klaus	S	1,000	66
Shelby State Comm.	Memphis, Tenn.	1970	Jess Parrish	S	2,200	160
Sheldon Jackson	Sitka, Alaska	1878	Robert Uddenberg	P	194	28
Sheridan	Sheridan, Wyo.	1948	Gordon Ward	S	678	33
Shoreline Community	Seattle, Wash.	1964	Richard S. White	S	7,332	306
Sierra	Rocklin, Calif.	1936	William M. Winstead	S	5,098	250
Sinclair Community	Dayton, Ohio	1887	Marvin Knudson	S, C	4,200	188
Siskiyous, Coll. of the	Weed, Calif.	1959	Eugene Schumacher	Di	2,803	101
Skagit Valley	Mt. Vernon, Wash.	1927	Norwood Cole	S	4,333	250
Skyline	San Bruno, Calif.	1969	John C. Petersen	Di	5,164	198
Snead State Jr.	Boaz, Ala.	1935	Virgil McCain	S	1,512	98

Name	Location	Year	Governing Official and Affiliation		Students	Teachers
Snow	Ephraim, Utah	1888	Lee Thompson, act.	S	823	51
Solano Comm.	Suisun City, Calif.	1955	N. Dallas Evans.	C	7,269	220
Somerset County	Somerville, N.J.	1966	Henry Evans.	C	1,241	88
South Central Community	New Haven, Conn.	1968	W. De Homer Waller.	S	1,463	72
South Florida Jr.	Avon Park, Fla.	1965	William A. Stallard.	S	975	45
South Georgia	Douglas, Ga.	1906	Denton Coker.	S	1,212	59
South Oklahoma City Junior	Oklahoma City, Okla.	1972	A. L. Taylor, act.	S	1,620	75
South Plains	Levelland, Tex.	1957	Marvin L. Baker.	S	1,701	105
South Texas Junior	Houston, Tex.	1948	David Royce Reagan.	P	2,609	103
Southeastern Comm.	Burlington, Iowa	1966	C. W. Callison, Supt.	Di	327	28
Southeastern Community	Keokuk, Iowa	1953	W. R. McCarter.	S	1,100	75
Southeastern Community	Whiteville, N.C.	1965	W. H. Abell, act.	Di	696	45
Southeastern Illinois	Harrisburg, Ill.	1960	C. W. Callison (Supt.).	S	1,506	95
Southern Baptist	Walnut Ridge, Ark.	1941	H. E. Williams.	D	307	25
Southern Idaho, Coll. of	Twin Falls, Idaho	1964	James L. Taylor.	C, S	3,004	122
Southern Union State Jr.	Wadley, Ala.	1922	L. Ray Jones.	S	1,028	65
Southwest Mississippi Junior	Summit, Miss.	1918	Horace Holmes.	S	815	45
Southwest Texas Junior	Uvalde, Tex.	1946	Wayne Matthews.	S	1,480	88
Southwest Virginia Comm.	Richlands, Va.	1968	Charles King.	S	1,350	80
Southwestern	Chula Vista, Calif.	1960	C. S. DeVore.	Di	9,532	363
Southwestern Comm.	Creston, Iowa	1966	John A. Smith.	S	609	43
Southwestern Michigan	Dowagiac, Mich.	1966	R. M. Owen.	S	1,300	75
Southwestern Oregon Comm.	Coos Bay, Ore.	1961	Jack E. Brookins.	C	1,956	115
Southwestern Tech. Institute	Sylva, N.C.	1964	Edward E. Bryson.	S	260	26
Spartanburg TEC	Spartanburg, S.C.	1961	Joe Gault (Dir.).	S	800	90
Spartanburg Junior	Spartanburg, S.C.	1911	James S. Barrett.	D	1,008	66
Spokane Comm.	Spokane, Wash.	1963	Hobart Jenkins.	S	3,078	173
Spokane Falls Community	Spokane, Wash.	1963	Max Snyder.	S	3,796	144
Spoon River	Canton, Ill.	1959	Hearl C. Bishop.	Di	1,044	41
Springfield Tech. Comm.	Springfield, Mass.	1967	Edmund Garvey.	S	5,100	310
Springfield Coll. in Illinois	Springfield, Ill.	1929	Sis. M. Patrick O'Brien.	P	577	51
State Fair Comm.	Sedalia, Mo.	1968	Fred E. Davis.	S	1,237	70
State Tech. Inst.	Memphis, Tenn.	1967	Charles Whitehead (Dir.).	S	3,009	101
Staten Island Community	Staten Island, N.Y.	1955	William M. Birenbaum.	Mu	10,145	795
Sue Bennett	London, Ky.	1897	Earl F. Hays.	D	255	21
Suffolk County Community	Selden, N.Y.	1959	Albert M. Ammerman.	S	13,923	418
Sullins	Bristol, Va.	1870	Claude Pritchard Jr.	P	245	30
Sullivan County Community	Loch Sheldrake, N.Y.	1962	Richard F. Grego.	S	1,438	59
Sumter Area TEC	Sumter, S.C.	1963	James Norris, Jr. (Dir.).	S	400	80
Suomi	Hancock, Mich.	1896	Ralph J. Jalkanen.	P	304	21
Surry Community	Dobson, N.C.	1964	Swanson Richards.	S	1,287	92
Sweetwater	Chula Vista, Calif.	1960	Chester De Vore.	Di	4,356	165
Tacoma Comm.	Tacoma, Wash.	1965	Thornton Ford.	S	4,907	243
Taft	Taft, Calif.	1922	Garlyn A. Basham.	Di	959	42
Tallahassee Community	Tallahassee, Fla.	1965	Fred W. Turner.	S	2,611	96
Tarrant County Junior	Ft. Worth, Tex.	1965	Joe B. Rushing.	S	13,500	312
Temple Junior	Temple, Tex.	1926	H. M. Dawson.	S	1,232	64
Texarkana	Texarkana, Tex.	1927	J. W. Cady.	S	2,158	110
Texas Southmost	Brownsville, Tex.	1926	Arnulfo L. Oliveira.	S	2,490	85
Thames Valley St. Tech.	Norwich, Conn.	1963	Donald Welter.	S	1,100	43
Theodore Alfred Lawson St. Jr.	Birmingham, Ala.	1963	Leon Kennedy.	S	1,388	54
Thomas Nelson Comm.	Hampton, Va.	1968	Gerald O. Cannon.	S	3,082	189
Thornton Comm.	So. Holland, Ill.	1927	J. Philip Dalby.	S	8,000	350
Three Rivers Community	Poplar Bluff, Mo.	1966	H. Tudor Westover.	S	945	46
Tidewater Comm.	Portsmouth, Va.	1968	George Pass.	S	4,000	175
Treasure Valley Comm.	Ontario, Ore.	1962	E. J. Skinner.	S	920	57
Tomkins-Courtland Comm.	Groton, N.Y.	1967	Hushang Baher.	S	1,501	34
Tri-County TEC	Pendleton, S.C.	1962	Don Garrison.	S	1,359	125
Trinidad State Junior	Trinidad, Colo.	1925	Thomas Sullivan.	S	1,222	80
Triton	River Grove, Ill.	1964	Herbert Zeitlin.	Di	16,681	732
Truett McConnell	Cleveland, Ga.	1946	Ronald Weitman.	P	433	32
Tulsa Junior	Tulsa, Okla.	1968	Alfred M. Phillips.	S	5,002	225
Tunxis Community	Farmington, Conn.	1970	Benjamin G. Davis.	S	2,046	110
Tyler Junior	Tyler, Tex.	1926	Harry E. Jenkins.	S	3,843	193
Ulster County Community	Stone Ridge, N.Y.	1961	George B. Erbstein.	S	2,160	84
Umpqua Comm.	Roseburg, Ore.	1964	Harry Jacoby.	C	2,500	85
Union	Cranford, N.J.	1933	Albert Meder, act.	P	3,874	298
Utica Junior	Utica, Miss.	1903	J. Louis Stokes.	S	963	60
Valencia Community	Orlando, Fla.	1967	James F. Gollattscheck.	S	5,482	222
Ventura	Ventura, Calif.	1926	Ray C. Loehr.	C	11,616	502
Vermilion Comm.	Ely, Minn.	1922	C. Donald Miller.	S	313	18
Vermont	Montpelier, Vt.	1834	William L. Irvine.	P	389	47
Vermont Technical	Randolph Center, Vt.	1957	Pierre Kieffer.	S	443	45
Victor Valley	Victorville, Calif.	1961	B. W. Wadsworth.	S	2,850	55
Victoria	Victoria, Tex.	1929	J. D. Moore.	C	1,600	63
Villa Julie	Stevenson, Md.	1952	Sister Mary Stephen.	P	362	43
Vincennes Univ.	Vincennes, Ind.	1801	Isaac K. Beckes.	S	3,350	175
Virginia Highlands Comm.	Abingdon, Va.	1969	Emma Schulken.	S	1,028	65
Virginia Western Comm.	Roanoke, Va.	1966	Harold H. Hooper.	S	3,704	159
Wabash Valley	Mt. Carmel, Ill.	1962	John Cox.	S	1,200	36
Waldorf	Forest City, Iowa	1903	Paul Mork.	P	487	32
Walker	Jasper, Ala.	1938	David J. Rowland.	P	721	45
Walla Walla Comm.	Walla Walla, Wash.	1967	Eldon Dietrich.	S	3,454	126
Walters State Community	Morristown, Tenn.	1970	James W. Clark.	S	895	61
Washtenaw Comm.	Ann Arbor, Mich.	1964	David Ponitz.	C	4,401	150
Waterbury State Technical	Waterbury, Conn.	1957	Kenneth Fogg.	S	1,216	52
Wayne Community	Goldsboro, N.C.	1957	Clyde Erwin, Jr.	S	1,743	132
Wayne County Comm.	Detroit, Mich.	1969	Reginald Wilson.	S	12,000	700
Weatherford	Weatherford, Tex.	1869	E. W. Mince.	C	1,082	45
Wenatchee Valley	Wenatchee, Wash.	1939	William Stewart.	S	3,738	111
Wentworth Institue	Boston, Mass.	1904	Edward T. Kirkpatrick.	P	1,474	99
Wesley	Dover, Del.	1873	Robert H. Parker.	P	957	57

Name	Location	Year	Governing Official and Affiliation		Students	Teachers
West Hills	Coalinga, Calif.	1932	Robert A. Annand	S	1,587	105
West Los Angeles	Culver City, Calif.	1969	Morris Heldman	Di	5,700	162
West Shore Comm.	Scottville, Mich.	1967	John Eaton	C	1,200	65
West Valley Comm.	Saratoga, Calif.	1964	James P. Hardy	C	13,749	525
West Virginia North. Comm.	Wheeling, W. Va.	1972	Daniel B. Crowder	S	2,008	80
Westark Comm.	Ft. Smith, Ark.	1928	Shelby Breedlove		4,809	80
Western Wisc. Tech. Inst.	La Crosse Wisc.	1912	Charles Richardson, Dir.	C, S	3,333	150
Westbrook	Portland, Me.	1831	James F. Dickinson	P	502	49
Westchester Community	Valhalla, N.Y.	1946	Joseph N. Hankin	S	6,560	149
Western Iowa Tech. Comm.	Sioux City, Iowa	1966	Robert Kiser	Di	988	73
Western Piedmont Comm.	Morganton, N.C.	1964	Gordon Blank	S	1,281	72
Western Texas	Snyder, Texas	1971	Robert Clinton	C, S	1,002	50
Wharton County Junior	Wharton, Tex.	1946	Theodore Nicksick, Jr.	S	1,672	92
Wilkes Community	Wilkesboro, N.C.	1964	Howard Thompson	S	1,300	60
William Rainey Harper	Palatine, Ill.	1967	Robert E. Lahti	S	13,400	325
Williamsport Area Comm.	Williamsport, Pa.	1965	William Fedderson	S	3,297	206
Willmar Comm.	Willmar, Minn.	1962	John Torgelson	S	714	42
Wilson County Tech. Inst.	Wilson, N.C.	1958	Ernest B. Parry	C	644	51
Wingate	Wingate, N.C.	1896	Thomas Corts	D	1,414	72
Wood Junior	Mathiston, Miss.	1886	Felix A. Sutphin	P	208	24
Worcester Junior	Worcester, Mass.	1905	Ross Dixon	P	800	40
Worthington Comm.	Worthington, Minn.	1936	W. Donald Olsen	S	648	33
Yakima Valley	Yakima, Wash.	1929	William Russell	S	4,505	140
Yavapai	Prescott, Ariz.	1966	Joseph Russo (Act.)	C	1,309	56
York	York, Nebr.	1890	Dale Larsen	P	380	24
York County TEC	Rock Hill, S.C.	1964	Baxter M. Hood	S	293	58
Young Harris	Young Harris, Ga.	1886	Ray Farley	P	529	29
Yuba Comm.	Marysville, Calif.	1927	Daniel G. Walker	Di	10,349	211

Students in Two-Year Colleges Likely To Be Older

Source: Bureau of the Census

There were 6,992,000 students 14 to 34 years old enrolled in the first four years of college in Oct. 1972. About 34% of these students reported they were enrolled in the first two years of 4-year colleges. Students enrolled in two-year colleges comprised 43% of the 4,100,000 students attending the first two years of all colleges. There were 640,000 Negroes enrolled in the first four years of college in Oct. 1972. About 31% of these Negroes were enrolled in two-year colleges. Negro students comprised 9% of all undergraduates in two and four-year colleges in 1972.

Students at two-year colleges were nearly twice as likely to be 20 years old or over, twice as likely to be married, almost 3 times as likely to be attending classes on a part-time basis, and more likely to live in the West. About 18% were children of families in which the head had completed 4 years of college. For 67%, the family head had not completed a single year of college.

Type of College; Sex and Residence of Enrollees

(Numbers in thousands. Civilian non-institutional population.)

	Total enrollment	Type of college			
			4-year colleges (year)		
		2-year colleges	1st and 2nd	3rd and 4th	Not reported
Total, 14 to 34 years	6,992	1,910	2,349	2,506	227
Male	3,982	1,125	1,249	1,494	114
Female	3,010	785	1,100	1,012	113
Metropolitan areas	5,243	1,480	1,720	1,870	173
Inside central cities	2,329	581	782	889	77
Outside central cities	2,915	899	938	981	97
Nonmetropolitan areas	1,748	430	629	635	54
Percent Distribution					
Total, 14 to 34 years	100.0	27.3	33.6	35.8	3.3
Male	100.0	28.3	31.3	37.5	2.9
Female	100.0	26.0	36.5	33.1	4.4
Metropolitan areas	100.0	28.2	32.8	35.7	3.3
Inside central cities	100.0	24.9	33.6	38.2	3.3
Outside central cities	100.0	30.8	32.2	33.7	3.3
Nonmetropolitan areas	100.0	24.6	36.0	36.3	3.1

National Spelling Bee Champions

The National Spelling Bee, conducted by Scripps-Howard Newspapers and other newspapers since 1939, was instituted by the Louisville (Ky.) Courier-Journal in 1925. Children under 16 years of age sponsored by participating newspapers are eligible to compete for the cash prizes and prize trips. Recent winners are:

1972—1. Robin Kral, 14, Lamesa, Texas (Lubbock Avalanche-Journal). 2. Lauren Pringle, 13, Buffalo, N.Y. (Buffalo Evening News). 3. Joseph J. Vissers, 13, Anchorage, Alaska (Anchorage Daily Times).

1973—1. Barrie Trinkle, 13, Fort Worth, Tex. (Fort Worth Press). 2. Stephen Hayes, 14, Oxon Hill, Md. (Washington, D.C., Star-News). 3. Camellia Jane Pratt, 12, Houston, Tex. (Houston Post).

1974—1. Julie Ann Junkin, 12, Gordo, Ala. (Birmingham Post-Herald). 2. Gail Meier, 14, Bartlett, Tenn. (Memphis Press-Scimitar). 3. Tara Farone, 14, Peninsula, Ohio (Akron Beacon Journal).

Degree Granting Canadian Colleges and Universities

All coeducational unless followed by (M) for men only. Governing official is president unless otherwise designated. Year is that of founding. The word college is part of the name listed unless another designation is given. Each institution listed has an enrollment of at least 200 students of college grade. Number of teachers is the total number of individuals on teaching staff. Enrollment and faculty in italics include all branches and campuses.

Name	Location	Year	Governing Official	Students	Teachers
Acadia Univ.	Wolfville, Nova Scotia	1838	James M. R. Beveridge	2,552	180
Alberta, Univ. of	Edmonton, Calgary, Al.	1906	Max Wyman	18,524	1,457
Bathurst, Le College de.	Bathurst, N. B.	1899	Leopold Lanteigne, Rector	645	35
Bishop's Univ.	Lennoxville, Que.	1843	John H. Price	818	70
Brandon Univ.	Brandon, Man.	1899	A. L. Dulmage	2,191	130
British Columbia, Univ. of.	Vancouver, B. C.	1912	Walter Gage	21,358	1,700
Brock Univ.	St. Catharines, Ont.	1964	Alan J. Earp	*4,028*	*198*
Calgary, Univ. of	Calgary, Alberta	1945	A. W. Carrothers	12,284	823
Carleton Univ.	Ottawa, Ont.	1942	Michael Oliver	13,618	778
Dalhousie Univ.	Halifax, Nova Scotia	1818	Henry D. Hicks	*7,700*	*800*
Guelph, Univ. of.	Guelph, Ont.	1964	William C. Winegard	8,902	939
King's Coll, Univ. of.	Halifax, Nova Scotia	1789	J. G. Morgan	284	12
Lakehead Univ.	Thunder Bay, Ont.	1965	Andrew D. Booth	3,700	257
Laurentian Univ.	Sudbury, Ont.	1961	Edward J. Monahan	5,078	200
Laval Universite	Quebec, Que.	1852	Larkin Kerwin	15,667	2,499
Lethbridge, Univ. of.	Lethbridge, Alberta.	1967	William Edwin Beckel	1,500	150
Manitoba, Univ. of.	Winnipeg, Man.	1877	Ernest Sirluck	*18,336*	*1,057*
McGill Univ.	Montreal, Que.	1821	Robert Bell (Prin.)	*18,447*	*1,918*
McMaster Univ.	Hamilton, Ont.	1887	A. N. Bourns	14,601	882
Moncton, Univ. of.	Moncton, N. B.	1963	Clement Cormier, Chan.	*6,170*	*394*
Montreal, Universite de.	Montreal, Que.	1920	Roger Gaudry (Rector)	*23,055*	*2,000*
Mt. Allison Univ.	Sackville, N. B.	1840	Laurence H. Cragg	1,421	130
Mt. St. Vincent Univ.	Halifax, Nova Scotia	1925	Sister Mary Albertus	1,680	100
New Brunswick, Univ. of	Fredericton, N. B.	1785	John Anderson	6,989	500
Newfoundland, Mem. Univ. of.	St. John's, Newfdld.	1925	M. O. Morgan	*9,935*	*722*
Notre Dame Univ.	Nelson, B. C.	1963	Cecil L. Kaller	511	66
Nova Scotia Coll. of Arts & Design	Halifax, Nova Scotia	1887	G. N. Kennedy	400	70
Nova Scotia Technical	Halifax, Nova Scotia	1907	A. E. Steeves	475	65
Ontario Inst. for Studies in Education	Toronto, Ont.	1965	R. W. B. Jackson (Dir.)	377	144
Ottawa, Univ. of	Ottawa, Ont.	1848	V. Rev. R. Guindon (Rect.)	12,225	917
Quebec, Universite de	Montreal, Quebec.	1968	Alphonse Riverin	10,500	410
Queens Univ.	Kingston, Ont.	1841	J. J. Deutsch	10,835	911
Prince Edward Island, Univ. of	Charlottetown, P.E.I.	1969	Ronald J. Baker	2,466	140
Royal Military Coll. of Canada (M).	Kingston, Ont.	1876	J. R. Dacey, Dir.	608	123
Ryerson Polytechnical	Toronto, Ont.	1948	D. L. Mordell	19,200	448
St. Francis Xavier Univ.	Antigonish, N. S.	1853	Rev. Malcolm MacDonell	*2,719*	*236*
St. Louis-Maillet.	Edmundston, N. B.	1948	Marcel Sormany	774	55
St. Mary's Univ.	Halifax, Nova Scotia	1802	D. Owen Carrigan	3,600	200
St. Michael's, Univ. of.	Toronto, Ont.	1851	Rev. John Kelly	2,200	180
St. Paul Univ.	Ottawa, Ont.	1848	Rev. Marcel Patry	528	131
St. Thomas Univ.	Fredericton, N. B.	1910	Rev. Donald Duffie	1,000	70
Saskatchewan, Univ. of	Saskatoon, Sask.	1907	John Diefenbaker	16,483	1,513
Regina Campus.	Regina, Sask.	1964	J. W. T. Spinks	5,400	350
Sherbrooke, Univ. of.	Sherbrooke, Que.	1954	Msgr. Roger Maltais, Rector	*7,363*	*764*
Simon Fraser Univ.	Burnaby, B. C.	1965	Kenneth T. Strand	5,007	356
Sir George Williams Univ.	Montreal, Que.	1948	H. J. Hemens, Chan.	16,099	752
Toronto, Univ. of	Toronto, Ont.	1827	John Robert Evans	*40,131*	*5,141*
Trent Univ.	Peterborough, Ont.	1963	T. E. W. Nind	1,800	155
Trinity.	Toronto, Ont.	1852	George Ignatieff (Provost)	952	51
Victoria Univ.	Toronto, Ont.	1836	G. S. French	2,443	157
Victoria, Univ. of.	Victoria, B. C.	1963	Hugh E. Farquhar	6,288	451
Waterloo, Univ. of	Waterloo, Ont.	1959	B. G. Matthews	13,218	960
Western Ontario, Univ. of.	London, Ont.	1878	D. C. Williams	18,000	1,500
Wilfrid Laurier Univ.	Waterloo, Ont.	1924	Frank C. Peters	6,396	205
Windsor, Univ. of.	Windsor, Ont.	1857	John F. Leddy	11,065	575
Winnipeg, Univ. of.	Winnipeg, Man.	1871	Harry E. Duckworth	4,908	150
York Univ.	Downsview, Ont.	1959	D. W. Slater	*23,316*	*888*

Typical Tuition Fees at Selected Canadian Colleges and Universities

Source: Association of Universities and Colleges of Canada

Institution	Cost Range	Institution	Cost Range
Alberta, The University of.	400-600	McMaster University.	632-702
British Columbia, The University of.	462-698	New Brunswick, University of.	612-642
Calgary, The University of Alberta.	400-800	Ottawa, University of.	586
Carleton University, Ottawa.	659	Queen's University of Kingston.	877.50
Concordia University.	450-475[1]	Quebec, University du.	250*
Dalhousie University.	720-835	Ryerson Polytechnical Institute.	212*
Guelph, University of.	288-353*	Saskatchewan, University of.	460-865
Laval, Universite.	255-280*	Toronto, University of.	566-881
Manitoba, The University of.	425-625	Victoria, University of.	428-600
Montreal, Universite de.	496-546	Waterloo, University of.	680-895
Memorial University of Newfoundland	250-300*	Western Ontario, The University of.	648-833
McGill University.	525	Windsor, University of.	640-725
		York University	660

Universities with enrollment of 5,000 full day-time students or more. Fee is for 1973-74 academic year.
*Per semester. 1. New university (1973) created through the union of Sir George Williams University and Loyola College.

Typical Tuition Fee at Selected Colleges and Universities

Source: World Almanac Questionnaire

The College Entrance Examination Board has estimated that the average cost in a private college in the fall of 1974, including tuition, board, and room will be $4,039, a 9.4% increase over the previous year. The cost at a public college will average $2,400.

Fees for tuition charged per year by colleges and universities for courses, use of libraries, laboratories and other facilities, are a major part of student expenses. Tuition varies considerably, depending on the type of institution, its control and location. The lowest tuition fees are those of state-controlled or other public-controlled institutions for residents of their state, city, etc. Students from other states or areas have to pay more. In the following list, such state or other public institutions are shown with two figures. The lower one is the tuition fee for residents, the higher one the tuition fee for students from other states or areas.

(Tuition does not include room, board or other expenses)

School	Tuition	School	Tuition	School	Tuition
Abilene Christian	$1,320	Georgia, Univ. of	538-1,260	Pfeiffer	2,520
Akron, Univ. of	705-1,605	Gonzaga Univ.	1,865	Portland State Univ.	552-1,734
Alabama, Univ. of	510-1,020	Grambling	405-1,035	Princeton Univ.	3,500
Alaska, Univ. of	512-1,112	Grinnell	3,260	Providence	2,180
Albion	2,300	Hampton Inst.	1,770	Purdue Univ.	740-1,680
Albuquerque, Univ. of	1,200	Harvard Univ.	3,200	Radcliffe	3,200
Amherst	4,359	Hawaii, Univ. of	450-1,800	Redlands, Univ. of	2,625
Anderson	1,860	Houston, Univ. of	294-1,154	Rice Univ.	2,172
Arizona State Univ.	370-890	Idaho, Univ. of	380-1,280	Richmond, Univ. of	2,125
Austin Peay State Univ.	365-1,175	Iowa State Univ.	600-1,320	Rochester, Univ. of	3,275
Belhaven	1,320	Indiana State Univ.	720-1,410	St. Bonaventure Univ.	3,350
Baylor Univ.	1,362	Iowa, Univ. of	620-1,350	San Francisco, Univ. of	2,235
Bemidji State	477-873	Jacksonville Univ.	1,760	Stanford Univ.	3,135
Black Hills State	424-992	John Carroll Univ.	1,950	Santa Clara, Univ. of	2,250
Bob Jones Univ.	783	Kansas State Univ.	526-1,316	Sarah Lawrence	3,900
Boston Univ.	2,690	Kansas, Univ. of	544-1,334	Seattle Univ.	1,860
Bowdoin	3,085	Kentucky, Univ. of	480-1,210	Seton Hall Univ.	1,900
Bradley Univ.	2,200	LaGrange	1,272	Slippery Rock State	750-1,500
Brigham Young Univ. (a)	640	La Salle	2,100	South Carolina, Univ. of	570-1,280
Brown Univ.	3,510	Lehigh Univ.	3,050	South Dakota State Univ.	615-1,355
Bryn Mawr	3,000	Lycoming	2,300	South Dakota, Univ. of	576-1,272
Bucknell Univ.	4,259	Mankato State	400-800	Southern Calif., Univ. of	2,910
Canisius	2,270	Marquette Univ.	2,250	Southern Methodist Univ.	2,200
Carnegie-Mellon Univ.	2,900	Maryland, Univ. of	374-924	Sul Ross State Univ.	250-1,300
Case Western Reserve Univ.	2,875	Mass. Inst. of Tech.	3,350	Swarthmore	4,550
Cedar Crest	2,715	Mass., Univ. of	485-1,085	Syracuse Univ.	3,110
Clemson Univ.	640-1,340	Memphis State Univ.	348-1,158	Texas A & M Univ.	353-553
Coe	2,503	Michigan State Univ.	720-1,620	Texas Tech Univ.	284-1,224
Colgate Univ.	3,330	Minnesota, Univ. of	591-1,521	Tufts Univ.	3,300
Colorado State Univ.	604-1,895	Montana, Univ. of	488-1,388	Tulane Univ.	2,600
Creighton Univ.	2,110	Morgan State	651-1,099	Tulsa, Univ. of	1,325
Dana	2,850	New Mexico State Univ.	466-1,296	Utah State Univ.	450-948
Davidson	3,685	New York Univ.	2,950	Utah, Univ. of	480-1,245
Dayton, Univ. of	1,780	Niagara Univ.	2,000	Valparaiso Univ.	2,354
Delaware, Univ. of	720-1,780	North Carolina, Univ. of	439-1,997	Vanderbilt Univ.	2,800
Denison Univ.	2,980	North Dakota StateUniv.	435-1,164	Vermont, Univ. of	1,088-2,688
Denver, Univ. of	2,850	North Dakota,Univ. of	456-1,184	Villanova Univ.	2,500
DePauw Univ.	2,975	Notre Dame, Univ. of	2,616	Wake Forest Univ.	2,200
Detroit, Univ. of	2,100	Oberlin	3,301	Wash. & Lee Univ.	2,600
Dillard Univ.	1,300	Ohio State Univ.	750-1,800	West Liberty State	280-1,130
Drake Univ.	2,500	Oklahoma State Univ.	464-1,244	Wichita State Univ.	545-1,335
Duke Univ.	2,800	Oral Roberts Univ.	2,535	William & Mary	914-2,212
Duquesne Univ.	2,485	Oregon State Univ.	535-1,717	Winston-Salem State Univ.	517-1,408
		Oregon, Univ. of	540-1,722	Worcester Poly.	3,010
Evansville, Univ. of	1,806	Pan American Univ.	254-1,334	Wyoming, Univ. of	410-1,376
Fairfield Univ.	2,395	Penn State Univ.	900-2,100	Youngstown	570-1,050
Fordham Univ.	2,200	Pennsylvania, Univ. of	3,100	(a) Non-members of Mormon
Georgetown Univ.	2,650	Peru State	285-477	Church $960.

Federal Funds for Education

Source: Office of Education, Dept. of Health, Education and Welfare.
(In thousands of dollars. Includes grants, loans, and directly administered services. Estimated.)

Type of support, level and program	1974	Type of support, level and program	1974
Total grants and loans	$12,868,823	Education Renewal	
Grants, total	12,462,906	Other	27,794
Elementary-secondary education	4,062,779	Higher education	5,937,467
School asst.—federally affected areas	130,910	Basic Research	1,350,000
Economic Opportunity Programs	683,936	Research facilities	218,000
National Defense Education Act	11,764	Training grants	1,010,851
Supporting services	186,020	Fellowships and traineeships	
Asst. for educationally deprived children	455,029	Facilities and equipment	254,260
Teacher Corps	37,565	Other institutional support	350,441
Vocational education	153,536	Other student assistance	2,753,915
Dependents' schools abroad	211,102	Other higher education assistance	
Public lands revenue for schools	98,634	Vocational-tech. and continuing ed.	2,462,660
Assistance in special areas	162,400	Vocational-technical education	1,768,225
Veterans' education	36,378	Veterans' education	555,364
Emergency school asst.	175,012	General continuing education	122,244
Revenue sharing	1,692,699	Training State and local personnel	16,827

(continued)

(continued)

Type of support, level and program	1974	Type of support, level and program	1974
Loans, total	**405,917**	**International education**	**139,098**
Student loan program, Natl. Def. Ed. Act	380,341	Educational exchange program	47,711
College facilities loans	25,576	AID projects	64,889
Other Federal funds, total	**5,037,412**	Action (previously Peace Corps)	18,925
Applied research and development	1,649,000	Other international educ. and training	7,573
School lunch and milk programs	1,273,263	**Other**	**710,280**
Training of Federal personnel	1,115,027	Agricultural extension service	197,198
U. S. Academies	232,340	Educational television facilities	11,000
Professional training, military	867,637	Education in Federal correctional inst.	9,945
Civilian education and training in		Other education and training	109,370
non-Federal facilities	15,050	Value of surplus property transferred:	
Library services	**150,744**	Acquisition cost of personal property	362,767
Grants to public libraries	17,904	Fair value of real property	20,000
National library services	132,840		

Fall Enrollment and Teachers in Full Time Day Schools
Public Elementary and Secondary Day Schools 1972-1973
Source: United States Office of Education

	Pupils Enrolled[1]		Teachers[2]	1972 High School Graduates	
	Elementary	Secondary		Male	Female
United States	31,200,000	14,100,000	2,106,000	1,347,000	1,361,000
Alabama	535,000	240,000	33,870	21,743	23,063
Alaska	62,000	22,000	4,160	1,929	1,831
Arizona	340,000	140,000	20,460	12,028	11,925
Arkansas	318,000	139,000	20,700	13,176	12,716
California	3,052,000	1,405,000	199,330	134,539	135,979
Colorado	392,000	177,000	24,990	16,553	16,901
Connecticut	467,000	191,000	34,220	18,248	19,556
Delaware	91,000	42,000	6,390	3,698	3,968
Dist. of Col.	104,000	34,000	6,590	1,971	2,994
Florida	1,031,000	468,000	66,850	39,176	39,398
Georgia	769,000	310,000	44,730	28,186	30,172
Hawaii	125,000	55,000	8,350	5,579	5,606
Idaho	122,000	61,000	7,700	6,501	6,328
Illinois	1,619,000	707,000	110,990	67,210	69,200
Indiana	836,000	373,000	52,620	36,694	35,807
Iowa	438,000	202,000	32,890	22,623	21,803
Kansas	314,000	157,000	25,470	17,117	17,046
Kentucky	491,000	217,000	31,600	20,214	20,493
Louisiana	593,000	244,000	42,020	21,756	23,807
Maine	175,000	73,000	12,270	7,081	7,275
Maryland	640,000	271,000	41,860	24,052	26,318
Massachusetts	825,000	366,000	60,490	33,609	33,878
Michigan	1,447,000	731,000	90,360	62,829	63,580
Minnesota	606,000	295,000	43,540	31,812	31,323
Mississippi	370,000	150,000	23,430	12,764	13,765
Missouri	705,000	315,000	45,610	30,079	28,797
Montana	119,000	60,000	8,540		
Nebraska	222,000	104,000	17,070	11,070	10,650
Nevada	92,000	39,000	5,430	3,127	3,079
New Hampshire	116,000	50,000	8,600	4,556	4,734
New Jersey	1,048,000	446,000	79,850		
New Mexico	195,000	87,000	12,370	8,481	8,518
New York	2,382,000	1,108,000	180,100	99,470	101,480
North Carolina	796,000	354,000	49,780	34,618	35,624
North Dakota	92,000	48,000	7,490	5,304	5,211
Ohio	1,632,000	767,000	103,930	74,929	74,543
Oklahoma	413,000	188,000	27,520	19,781	18,628
Oregon	312,000	155,000	22,310	16,024	15,858
Pennsylvania	1,568,000	771,000	110,180	80,442	76,420
Rhode Island	132,000	56,000	9,520	5,203	5,706
South Carolina	427,000	190,000	27,070	17,923	19,148
South Dakota	108,000	53,000	8,290	6,072	5,873
Tennessee	622,000	261,000	36,360	25,087	26,535
Texas	1,916,000	794,000	127,780	76,747	76,906
Utah	208,000	95,000	12,140	9,567	9,404
Vermont	73,000	31,000	6,220	2,969	2,916
Virginia	737,000	322,000	49,960	29,727	32,645
Washington	531,000	252,000	32,870	25,773	25,790
West Virginia	281,000	124,000	18,040	11,279	10,880
Wisconsin	653,000	333,000	48,330	34,842	34,975
Wyoming	58,000	27,000	4,760	2,933	2,845
Outlying areas	**594,000**	**175,000**	**27,810**	**12,312**	**14,831**
American Samoa	6,000	2,000	400	204	202
Canal Zone	9,000	4,000	530	404	401
Guam	20,000	6,000	1,190	509	522
Puerto Rico	544,000	157,000	24,660	11,195	13,706
Virgin Islands	15,000	6,000	1,030	NA	NA

[1]Estimates. [2]Full and part-time classroom teachers.

Public School Attendance, Teachers, Expenditures

Source: U.S. Office of Education; Salaries cover supervisors, principals, and teachers

School Year	Pop. 5 to 17 yrs.	Pupils Enrolled	Pupils Av. daily attend.	Teachers' Male	Teachers' Female	Teachers' Total	Teachers' Salary[2]	Total Expend.
1900	21,404,322	15,503,110	10,632,772	126,588	296,474	423,062	$325	$214,964,618
1910	24,239,948	17,813,852	12,827,307	110,481	412,729	523,210	485	426,250,434
1920	27,728,788	21,578,316	16,150,035	95,654	583,648	679,302	871	1,036,151,209
1930	31,571,322	25,678,015	21,264,886	141,771	712,492	854,263	1,420	2,316,790,384
1940	29,805,259	25,433,542	22,042,151	194,725	680,752	875,477	1,441	2,344,048,927
1950	30,788,000	25,111,427	22,283,845	194,968	718,703	913,671	3,010	5,837,643,000
1960	43,881,000	36,086,771	32,477,440	392,700	962,300	1,355,000	5,174	15,613,255,000
1968 (Fall)	52,288,000	44,961,662	41,157,000	617,805	1,324,980	1,942,785	8,200	35,511,170,000
1969 (Fall)	52,799,000	45,618,578	42,283,000	634,358	1,379,478	2,013,836	8,840	40,561,997,000
1970 (Fall)	52,435,000	45,909,088	42,495,346	649,250	1,411,865	2,061,115	9,570	44,423,865,000
1971 (Fall)	52,133,000	46,081,000	42,544,000	668,000	1,395,000	2,063,000	10,100	48,513,986,000
1972 (Fall)	51,637,000	45,744,000	42,408,000	702,000	1,400,000	2,102,000	10,608	51,905,025,000
1973 (P)	51,009,000	45,408,805	42,079,000	718,000	1,407,000	2,125,000	11,185	56,031,041,000

(1.) Prior to 1954 includes other nonsupervisory instructional staff (librarians and guidance and psychological personnel)
(2.) Average annual salary per member of instructional staff. (P) Preliminary.

Cost Per Pupil by State

Source: Office of Education, Dept. HEW
Expenditures per pupil in average daily attendance in public elementary and secondary day schools, by State 1972-73

State	Total	Current	Capital outlay	Interest on school debt	State	Total	Current	Capital outlay	Interest on school debt
United States	$1,182	$1,026	$118	$38	Nebraska	$1,074	953	95	26
					Nevada	1,199	976	165	58
Alabama	680	590	76	14	New Hampshire	1,073	913	129	31
Alaska	1,961	1,473	395	93	New Jersey	1,476	1,294	133	49
Arizona	1,291	1,038	228	25	New Mexico	1,105	994	102	9
Arkansas	731	651	58	22	New York	1,808	1,584	162	62
California	1,129	1,000	92	37	North Carolina	880	802	65	13
Colorado	1,138	955	152	31	North Dakota	956	855	81	20
Connecticut	1,365	1,241	89	35	Ohio	1,038	946	67	25
Delaware	1,575	1,162	349	64	Oklahoma	778	704	64	10
Dist. of Col.	1,626	1,327	299	—	Oregon	1,262	1,155	84	23
Florida	1,030	885	124	21	Pennsylvania	1,427	1,177	160	90
Georgia	895	782	79	34	Rhode Island	1,232	1,113	86	33
Hawaii	1,240	1,055	177	8	South Carolina	847	751	77	19
Idaho	868	772	79	17	South Dakota	900	817	71	12
Illinois	1,394	1,235	118	41	Tennessee	811	730	50	31
Indiana	1,100	855	204	41	Texas	943	778	125	40
Iowa	1,238	1,055	157	26	Utah	843	739	87	17
Kansas	1,025	969	42	14	Vermont	1,360	1,307	20	33
Kentucky	788	707	53	28	Virginia	1,082	920	130	32
Louisiana	1,002	897	79	26	Washington	1,119	953	128	38
Maine	952	840	86	26	West Virginia	826	749	68	9
Maryland	1,473	1,065	365	43	Wisconsin	1,241	1,134	68	39
Massachusetts	1,234	1,090	104	40	Wyoming	1,193	1,059	117	17
Michigan	1,461	1,271	135	55	**Outlying Areas**				
Minnesota	1,387	1,179	154	54	American Samoa	719	653	66	
Mississippi	751	689	53	9	Canal Zone	NA	NA	NA	NA
Missouri	984	861	99	24	Guam	1,047	856	191	—
Montana	NA	NA	NA	NA	Puerto Rico	483	453	30	—

'Estimated.

Fall Enrollment and Teachers in Full-time Day Schools - Canada

Public Elementary and Secondary Day Schools — 1972-73

Source: Statistics Canada

	Pupils Enrolled 5,571,319 Elementary Kdgn. to Gr. 8	Pupils Enrolled 5,571,319 Secondary Grade 9 and up	Full-time teachers 261,637 Elementary Kdgn. to Gr. 8	Full-time teachers 261,637 Secondary Grade 9 and up
Canada	3,887,044	1,684,275	167,029	94,608
Newfoundland	129,648	32,075	4,910	1,983
Prince Edward Island	21,750	7,590	1,120	510
Nova Scotia	157,330	53,932	6,563	3,524
New Brunswick	123,235	50,616	5,130	2,840
Quebec	1,014,887P	511,699P	50,400	26,700
Ontario	1,422,821	605,293	56,720	35,820
Manitoba	170,277	68,584	7,200	4,425
Saskatchewan	165,756	68,396	7,207	3,643
Alberta	297,980	127,271	12,843	7,493
British Columbia	369,702	156,359	14,240	7,494
Yukon	3,676	1,073	182	76
Northwest Territories	9,982	1,387	514	100

E Estimate
P Preliminary

The Principal Languages of the World

Source: Sidney S. Culbert, Assoc. Professor of Psychology, University of Washington

Total number of speakers of languages spoken by at least one million persons (Midyear 1974)
Parenthesized numbers after names of languages refer to notes below table.

	Millions		Millions		Millions
Afrikaans (S. Africa)	5	Ijaw (W. Africa)	1	Pashto (see Pushtu)	
Albanian	3	Ilocano (Philippines)	4	Pedi (see Sotho, Northern)	
Amharic (Ethiopia)	9	Iloko (see Ilocano)		Persian	24
Annamese (see Vietnamese)		Indonesian (see Malay-Indonesian)		Polish	35
Arabic	121	Italian	60	Portuguese	120
Armenian	4	Japanese	109	Provencal (Southern France)	6
Assamese (1) (India)	12	Javanese	44	Punjabi (1) (India; Pakistan)	53
Azerbaijani (USSR; Iran)	8	Kamba (E. Africa)	1	Pushtu (mainly Afghanistan)	14
Bahasa (See Malay-Indonesian)		Kanarese (see Kannada)		Quechua (S. America)	6
Balinese	3	Kannada (1) (India)	28	Rajasthani (India)	20
Baluchi (Pakistan; Iran)	2	Kanuri (W. and Cent. Africa)	2	Romanian	22
Bashkir (USSR)	1	Kashmiri (1)	3	Rundi (S. Central Africa)	3
Batak (Indonesia)	2	Kazakh (USSR)	5	Russian (Great Russian only)	226
Bemba (S. Central Africa)	1	Khalkha (Mongolia)	1	Rwanda (S. Central Africa)	6
Bengali (1) (Bangladesh; India)	120	Kikongo (see Kongo)		Samar-Leyte (Philippines)	1
Berber (2) (N. Africa)		Kikuyu (or Gekoyo) (Kenya)	2	Sango (Central Africa)	1
Bhili (India)	4	Kimbundu (see Mbundu-Kim.)		Santali (India)	4
Bihari (India)	21	Kirghiz (USSR)	2	Sepedi (see Sotho, Northern)	
Bikol (Philippines)	2	Kituba (Congo River)	2	Serbo-Croatian (Yugoslavia)	18
Bisaya (see Cebuano, Panay-		Kongo (Congo River)	1	Shan (Burma)	1
Hiligaynon, and Samar-Leyte)		Konkani (India)	2	Shona (S.E. Africa)	4
Bugi (Indonesia)	2	Korean	51	Siamese (see Thai)	
Bulgarian	9	Kumauni (India)	1	Sindhi (India; Pakistan)	9
Burmese	22	Kurdish (S.W. of Caspian Sea)	6	Sinhalese (Sri Lanka)	10
Byelorussian (mainly USSR)	10	Kurukh (or Oraon) (India)	1	Slovak	4
Cambodian (Cambodia, Asia)	6	Lao (5) (Laos, Asia)	3	Slovene (Yugoslavia)	2
Canarese (see Kannada)		Latvian (or Lettish)	2	Somali (Africa)	4
Cantonese (China)	47	Lingala (see Ngala)		Sotho, Northern (S. Africa)	2
Catalan (Spain; France; Andorra)	5	Lithuanian	3	Sotho, Southern (S. Africa)	2
Cebuano (Philippines)	8	Luba-Lulua (Zaire)	3	Spanish	208
Chinese (3)		Luganda (see Ganda)		Sundanese (Indonesia)	14
Chuang (7) (China)		Luhya (or Luhia) (Kenya)	1	Swahili (E. Africa)	18
Chuvash (USSR)	2	Luo (Kenya)	1	Swedish	10
Czech	11	Macedonian (Yugoslavia)	1	Tagalog (Philippines)	20
Danish	5	Madurese (Indonesia)	7	Tajiki (USSR)	3
Dayak (Borneo)	1	Makua (S.E. Africa)	2	Tamil (1) (India; Sri Lanka)	52
Dutch (see Netherlandish)		Malagasy (Madagascar)	8	Tatar (or Kazan-Turkic) (USSR)	6
Edo (W. Africa)	1	Malay-Indonesian	93	Telugu (1) (India)	53
Efik	2	Malayalam (1) (India)	23	Thai (5)	30
English	352	Malinke-Bambara-Dyula (Africa)	5	Tibetan	7
Esperanto	1	Mandarin (China)	639	Tigrinya (Ethiopia)	4
Estonian	1	Marathi (1) (India)	49	Tiv (E. Central Nigeria)	1
Ewe (W. Africa)	2	Mbundu (Umbundu group)		Tswana (S. Africa)	2
Finnish	5	(S. Angola)	2	Tulu (India)	1
Flemish (see Netherlandish)		Mbundu (Kimbundu group)		Turkish	38
French	87	(Angola)	1	Turkoman (USSR)	2
Fula (W. Africa)	7	Mende (Sierra Leone)	1	Twi-Fante (or Akan) (W. Africa)	4
Galician (Spain)	2	Min (China)	39	Uighur-(Sinkiang, China)	4
Galla (Ethiopia)	7	Moldavian (ind. w/Rumanian)		Ukrainian (mainly USSR)	42
Ganda (or Luganda) (E. Africa)	3	Mongolian (see Khalkha)		Umbundu (see Mbundu-Umbundu)	
Georgian (USSR)	3	Mordvin (USSR)	1	Urdu (1) (Pakistan; India)	57
German	120	More (see Mossi)		Uzbek (USSR)	9
Gondi (India)	2	Mossi (W. Africa)	3	Vietnamese	36
Greek	10	Ndongo (see Mbundu-Kimbundu)		Visayan (see Cebuano, Panay-	
Guarani (mainly Paraguay)	2	Nepali (Nepal; India)	10	Hiligaynon, and Samar-Leyte)	
Gujarati (1) (India)	29	Netherlandish (Dutch and Flem.)	20	White Russian (see Byelorussian)	
Hakka (China)	21	Ngala (or Lingala) (Africa)	2	Wolot (W. Africa)	2
Hausa (W. and Central Africa)	18	Norwegian	4	Wu (China)	42
Hebrew	3	Nyamwezi-Sukuma (S.E. Africa)	1	Xhosa (S. Africa)	4
Hindi (1) (4)	205	Nyanja (S.E. Africa)	2	Yi (China)	3
Hindustani (4)		Oraon (see Kurukh)		Yiddish (6)	
Hungarian (or Magyar)	13	Oriya (1) (India)	23	Yoruba (W. Africa)	12
Ibibio (see Efik)		Panay-Hiligaynon (Philippines)	4	Zhuang (7) (China)	
Ibo (or Igbo) (W. Africa)	9	Panjabi (see Punjabi)		Zulu (S. Africa)	4

(1.) One of the fourteen languages of the Constitution of India. (2.) Here considered a group of dialects. (3.) See Mandarin, Cantonese, Wu, Min, and Hakka. The "national language" (Guoyu) is a standardized form of Mandarin as spoken in the area of Peking. (4.) Hindi and Urdu are essentially the same language, Hindustani. As the official language of India it is written in the Devanagari script and called Hindi. As the official language of Pakistan it is written in a modified Arabic script and called Urdu. (5.) Thai includes Central, Southwestern, Northern and Northeastern Thai. The distinction between Northeastern Thai and Lao is political rather than linguistic. (6.) Yiddish is usually considered a variant of German, though it has its own standard grammar, dictionaries, a highly developed literature, and is written in Hebrew characters. Speakers number about 3,000,000. (7.) A group of Thai-like dialects with about 9 million speakers.

Educational Attainment by Age, Race and Sex

Source: Bureau of the Census   (Number of Persons in thousands)

Age, Race and Sex March 1972	Total Pop.	Elementary 5 years	6 & 7 years	8 years	High School 1 year	2 years	3 years	4 years	College 1 year	2 years	3 years	4 years	5 or more
White													
Total, 14 years and over	134,904	1,600	7,973	16,347	9,187	10,695	8,081	46,213	6,642	7,000	3,002	9,036	5,284
14 and 15 years	7,063	45	1,752	3,256	1,847	102	11	4	-	-	-	-	-
16 and 17 years	6,847	8	115	410	1,598	2,935	1,640	104	4	7	-	-	-
18 and 19 years	6,398	18	50	157	187	398	1,384	3,310	775	59	14	6	-
20 and 21 years	6,006	7	50	128	162	251	249	2,665	846	1,024	507	84	2
22 to 24 years	9,047	33	111	220	272	390	305	3,916	777	745	548	1,362	299
25 years and over	99,543	1,489	5,895	12,177	5,121	6,620	4,483	36,215	4,240	5,165	1,933	7,584	4,983
Male, 14 years and over	64,611	800	4,112	8,057	4,398	4,914	3,759	19,546	3,361	3,620	1,527	4,855	3,704
14 and 15 years	3,602	32	993	1,652	842	47	8	1	-	-	-	-	-
16 and 17 years	3,475	4	72	246	855	1,462	776	41	3	-	-	-	-
18 and 19 years	3,146	6	34	103	92	224	727	1,543	358	21	8	3	-
20 and 21 years	2,843	3	26	69	80	115	113	1,113	474	539	260	30	-
22 to 24 years	4,412	21	57	119	110	148	132	1,690	438	432	341	682	204
25 years and over	47,133	733	2,930	5,868	2,419	2,916	2,002	15,158	2,088	2,628	918	4,139	3,500
25 to 29 years	6,373	25	131	190	234	289	208	2,524	517	498	231	845	630
30 years to 34 years	5,273	25	133	258	235	303	196	2,086	295	380	119	577	584
35 to 44 years	9,814	98	405	720	503	613	439	3,620	467	599	177	1,040	902
45 to 54 years	10,117	119	551	1,170	552	701	547	3,503	422	601	152	817	688
55 to 64 years	8,044	188	719	1,477	471	603	393	2,209	235	367	137	492	411
65 to 74 years	4,893	146	633	1,309	293	292	174	885	117	114	77	261	190
75 years and over	2,618	131	357	744	131	116	44	331	35	69	25	107	95
Female, 14 years and over	70,293	800	3,861	8,291	4,789	5,781	4,313	26,667	3,281	3,380	1,475	4,181	1,580
14 and 15 years	3,461	12	759	1,604	1,005	55	3	3	-	-	-	-	-
16 and 17 years	3,372	4	44	164	743	1,472	865	63	1	7	-	-	-
18 and 19 years	3,252	12	16	54	95	173	657	1,766	417	38	6	3	-
20 and 21 years	3,163	4	24	58	83	136	135	1,551	372	485	247	54	2
22 to 24 years	4,635	12	54	101	163	242	172	2,226	339	313	207	680	95
25 years and over	52,410	756	2,965	6,309	2,701	3,704	2,481	21,057	2,152	2,538	1,015	3,445	1,483
25 to 29 years	6,455	19	128	175	249	328	293	3,134	422	390	190	782	295
30 to 34 years	5,333	16	138	213	239	380	270	2,625	300	279	129	492	195
35 to 44 years	10,137	97	301	616	512	721	602	4,988	440	524	185	677	280
45 to 54 years	10,857	115	485	1,073	532	808	604	4,990	413	554	192	546	299
55 to 64 years	9,052	152	678	1,550	594	752	422	3,054	297	366	160	469	212
65 to 74 years	6,403	206	688	1,509	379	481	183	1,510	195	260	99	328	148
75 years and over	4,173	151	547	1,173	197	233	107	756	86	166	59	151	55
Negro & Other Races													
Total 14 years and over	17,129	561	1,847	1,864	1,627	1,755	1,410	4,312	560	535	220	528	357
14 and 15 years	1,193	23	392	483	252	20	3	3	-	-	-	-	-
16 and 17 years	1,146	7	56	139	306	405	209	17	-	-	-	-	-
18 and 19 years	1,014	3	21	50	60	150	238	403	70	4	1	-	-
20 and 21 years	923	3	25	35	67	70	90	368	102	96	44	6	-
22 to 24 years	1,263	7	27	58	65	112	112	565	86	68	65	68	16
25 years and over	11,590	517	1,326	1,099	876	998	758	2,956	301	368	110	455	341
Male, 14 years and over	7,857	265	903	879	690	774	603	1,848	245	257	98	240	214
14 and 15 years	595	18	226	234	98	5	-	3	-	-	-	-	-
16 and 17 years	569	3	37	82	166	182	90	7	-	-	-	-	-
18 and 19 years	483	3	14	32	28	85	114	163	33	4	1	-	-
20 and 21 years	416	3	14	17	30	33	40	158	52	42	19	-	-
22 and 24 years	576	3	15	24	28	49	44	251	41	35	36	30	9
25 years and over	5,218	234	598	491	341	420	315	1,267	119	177	42	210	205
25 to 29 years	744	4	38	39	40	66	59	298	40	44	12	48	42
30 to 34 years	640	6	36	41	65	62	40	242	13	36	6	44	38
35 to 44 years	1,174	42	114	97	102	121	86	314	37	33	13	57	61
45 to 54 years	1,095	66	157	134	67	107	79	227	20	37	8	39	27
66 to 64 years	804	58	134	102	48	37	40	120	4	11	3	15	27
65 to 74 years	517	38	78	52	15	18	12	55	5	17	-	4	9
75 years and over	244	20	41	27	4	9	-	11	-	-	-	3	1
Female, 14 years and over	9,272	296	944	985	936	980	808	2,464	314	278	122	288	143
14 and 15 years	598	5	166	249	155	15	3	-	-	-	-	-	-
16 and 17 years	577	4	19	57	140	223	119	10	-	-	-	-	-
18 and 19 years	531	-	7	18	33	65	124	241	37	-	-	-	-
20 and 21 years	507	-	11	19	37	37	50	210	50	53	25	6	-
22 to 24 years	687	4	12	34	37	62	67	314	45	34	29	38	7
25 years and over	6,372	283	728	608	535	578	443	1,689	182	191	68	244	137
25 to 29 years	906	7	36	39	59	77	68	393	49	48	23	74	28
30 to 34 years	793	7	37	50	70	87	64	334	36	26	7	31	30
35 to 44 years	1,477	29	129	115	154	171	153	463	49	56	16	65	26
45 to 54 years	1,285	56	161	154	126	143	77	294	31	35	15	36	28
55 to 64 years	932	66	178	123	91	60	57	127	11	19	6	21	14
65 to 74 years	643	68	134	75	26	24	22	56	4	4	-	17	11
75 years and over	336	51	54	51	8	16	2	22	2	3	1	1	-

Income Discrimination: Male and Female, Black and White

Source: Bureau of the Census

Total Money Income (Includes full-and part-time workers, 25 and over, Mar. 1973)	Total	Years of Schooling				
		7 or less	8	9-11	12	13-15	18 or more

Total Money Income (Includes full-and part-time workers, 25 and over, Mar. 1973)	Total	7 or less	8	9-11	12	13-15	18 or more
White Males with Income (1,000)	47,292	5,364	5,539	6,990	15,554	5,909	7,936
Percent	100.0	100.0	100.0	100.0	100.0	100.0	100.0
Loss to $2,999	11.7	33.0	21.5	11.2	6.3	7.3	4.9
$3,000 to $5,999	16.2	30.8	29.8	19.4	11.6	10.0	7.0
$6,000 to $7,999	12.6	13.4	14.9	16.8	13.3	10.6	6.7
$8,000 to $9,999	13.8	9.4	11.9	16.9	17.5	13.8	8.5
$10,000 to $14,999	27.0	10.7	16.2	26.5	34.7	33.6	26.1
$15,000 and over	18.7	2.6	5.6	9.1	16.6	24.6	46.8
Mean Income	$10,537	$5,591	$6,847	$8,763	$10,694	$12,125	$16,531
Black Males with Income (1,000)	4,596	1,382	498	950	1,161	326	278
Percent	100.0	100.0	100.0	100.0	100.0	100.0	100.0
Loss to $2,999	26.1	48.6	22.4	21.3	13.7	12.4	7.4
$3,000 to $5,999	26.9	30.2	36.5	28.3	22.1	20.1	15.8
$6,000 to $7,999	16.3	9.6	14.0	20.2	22.9	19.4	8.3
$8,000 to $9,999	12.9	6.9	13.6	14.1	17.3	17.3	14.3
$10,000 to $14,999	14.3	4.3	12.6	13.9	20.4	24.0	32.0
$15,000 and over	3.5	0.6	0.9	2.1	3.6	6.8	22.1
Mean Income	$6,222	$3,929	$5,759	$6,238	$7,319	$8,284	$11,202
Mean Income, Full-Time Males (66.2% of total)	$12,349	$7,870	$9,113	$9,976	$11,574	$13,678	$17,882
White Females with Income (1,000)	36,087	3,852	4,250	5,704	14,131	4,057	4,093
Percent	100.0	100.0	100.0	100.0	100.0	100.0	100.0
Loss to $2,999	49.2	77.1	68.6	54.5	41.6	40.6	30.1
$3,000 to $5,999	26.6	18.5	23.3	30.3	31.6	26.2	15.9
$6,000 to $7,999	11.5	2.5	5.1	9.4	14.7	15.0	14.5
$8,000 to $9,999	6.1	1.1	1.8	3.2	6.6	9.0	14.6
$10,000 to $14,999	5.2	0.6	0.8	2.1	4.4	7.4	19.1
$15,000 and over	1.4	0.1	0.5	0.4	1.0	1.7	5.8
Mean Income	$4,044	$2,230	$2,662	$3,312	$4,260	$4,728	$6,786
Black Females with Income (1,000)	4,841	1,229	465	1,185	1,263	378	321
Percent	100.0	100.0	100.0	100.0	100.0	100.0	100.0
Loss to $2,999	53.7	84.5	66.3	55.2	35.9	30.2	10.7
$3,000 to $5,999	27.7	13.1	28.0	32.3	38.3	34.4	16.9
$6,000 to $7,999	9.7	2.0	3.8	8.5	14.7	17.7	22.6
$8,000 to $9,999	4.7	1.2	1.8	2.7	7.2	10.1	18.9
$10,000 to $14,999	3.5	—	1.2	1.2	3.1	6.2	26.7
$15,000 and over	0.6				0.2		0.5
Mean Income	$3,543	$1,879	$2,551	$3,126	$4,310	$5,024	$8,011
Mean Income, Full-time Females (33.5% of total)	$6,806	$4,408	$5,098	$5,428	$6,514	$7,323	$9,834

(Percentages may not add to 100.0 due to rounding;—represents zero or rounds to zero.)

Explanation: The tables above demonstrate that while income tends to rise with educational attainment, it rises far less for women and blacks than for white men. For every year of schooling, the black man tends to gain less than his white counterpart. (Black women appear to improve their incomes in comparison with white women, but this is probably because more black women tend to work full-time.)

Looking at the mean incomes for full-time workers, we can see that all women tend to make only a little more than half the earnings of men with the same educational attainments.

---

100 Years of Public Schools

Source: Office of Education, Dept. of Health, Education and Welfare

Pupils and teachers (in thousands)	1869-70	1899-1900	1909-10	1919-20	1929-30	1939-40	1949-50	1959-60	1969-70	1971-72
Total U. S. population	39,818	75,995	90,492	104,512	121,770	130,880	148,665	179,323	203,212	206,217
Population 5-17 years of age	12,055	21,573	24,009	27,556	31,417	30,150	30,168	43,881	52,490	52,297
Percent aged 5-17 years	30.3	28.4	26.5	26.4	25.8	23.0	20.3	24.5	25.8	25.4
Enrollment:										
Elementary and Secondary	6,872	15,503	17,814	21,578	25,678	25,434	25,111	36,087	45,619	46,081
Percent Pop. 5-17 enrolled	17.3	20.4	19.7	20.6	21.1	19.4	16.9	20.1	22.4	NA
Percent in high schools	1.2	3.3	5.1	10.2	17.1	26.0	22.7	23.5	28.5	30.0
High School graduates	....	62	111	231	592	1,143	1,063	1,627	2,589	2,708
Average school term (in days)	132.2	144.3	157.5	161.9	172.7	175.0	177.9	178.0	178.9	179.3
Total instructional staff	....	....	....	678	880	912	962	1,464	2,253	2,322
Teachers, librarians: Men	78	127	110	93	140	195	195	402	691	737
Women	123	296	413	565	703	681	719	985	1,440	1,450
Percent men	38.7	29.9	21.1	14.1	16.6	22.2	21.3	29.0	32.4	33.7
Receipts & Expenditures (in millions)										
Total receipts	....	$219	$433	$970	$2,088	$2,260	$5,437	$14,746	$40,227	$50,004
Total expenditures	$63	214	426	1,036	2,316	2,344	5,837	15,613ᶠ	40,683	48,050
Current, elem. and secondary	....	179	356	861	1,843	1,941	4,687	12,329	34,218	41,818
Capital outlay	....	35	69	153	370	257	1,014	2,661	4,659	4,459
Interest on school debt	....	....	....	18	92	130	100	489	1,171	1,378
Other	....	....	....	3	9	13	35	132	636	395
Salaries and Pupil Cost	Data in unadjusted dollars					Data in adjusted dollars				
Average annual teacher salary[2]	$189	$325	$485	$1,554	$3,133	$3,894	$4,801	$6,651	$8,840	$10,100
Expenditure per capita total pop	1.59	2.83	4.71	17.68	41.98	48.40	62.63	111.93	200.20	233.01
Current expenditure per pupil ADA[3]	....	16.67	27.85	95.15	191.27	238.05	333.06	482.24	815.98	989.68

(1) Because of a modification of the scope, "current expenditures for elementary and secondary schools" data for 1959-60 and later years are not entirely comparable with data for prior years. (2) Includes supervisors, principals, teachers and other non-supervisory instructional staff. (3) "ADA" means average daily attendance in elementary and secondary day schools.

Education Pays—Black or White

(— represents zero or rounds to zero. B means base less than 75,000.)

Race, Age, Income, Occupation (1972)	Total (1,000)	0-8	9-11	12	13-15	16	16+	Median Years
White employed males, age 25-44	19,316	10.3	14.2	38.5	15.3	11.7	10.0	12.7
Under $3,000	933	26.6	16.3	26.7	13.5	10.1	6.8	12.3
$3,000-$5,999.	2,419	23.8	18.3	35.2	11.4	5.9	5.3	12.2
$6,000-$9,999.	6,753	11.7	17.6	44.2	13.8	7.7	4.9	12.5
$10,000-$14,999.	6,115	4.9	12.8	42.7	18.2	11.7	9.7	12.8
$15,000 & over	3,096	2.5	5.8	24.2	16.2	25.2	26.1	16.1
White-collar workers	8,967	2.4	4.9	28.0	21.1	23.0	20.7	15.1
Under $6,000	972	7.9	8.1	25.6	21.4	18.3	18.5	14.2
$6,000 & over.	7,994	1.6	4.5	28.2	21.0	23.5	21.0	15.2
Blue-collar workers	8,660	16.8	23.9	48.0	9.4	1.4	0.4	12.2
Under $6,000	1,715	29.9	25.3	35.0	7.8	1.7	0.3	11.4
$6,000 & over.	6,945	13.6	23.5	51.2	9.8	1.3	0.4	12.2
Service workers	1,107	14.2	14.9	48.3	16.8	3.7	2.1	12.4
Under $6,000	312	32.4	13.1	36.9	11.2	5.4	1.0	12.1
$6,000 & over.	795	6.8	15.6	52.7	19.0	2.9	2.5	12.5
Farm workers	583	28.3	13.0	41.9	9.8	6.0	0.9	12.2
Under $6,000	353	37.2	11.9	38.2	7.4	3.7	0.8	12.0
$6,000 & over.	230	13.5	15.2	47.4	13.5	9.6	1.3	12.4
Black employed males, age 25-44	1,900	22.6	26.0	33.7	9.4	5.1	3.2	12.0
Under $3,000	259	40.8	27.2	21.5	5.9	3.3	1.3	10.0
$3,000-$5,999.	592	33.0	28.4	30.8	5.0	0.8	1.9	10.8
$6,000-$9,999.	727	15.5	28.3	38.7	11.5	5.8	1.3	12.2
$10,000-$14,999.	274	5.5	16.2	40.1	16.3	11.6	10.2	12.7
$15,000 & over	48	(B)	(B)	(B)	(B)	(B)	(B)	(B)
White-collar workers	428	4.4	13.4	31.7	17.1	19.3	14.1	13.1
Under $6,000	116	13.9	20.7	36.2	10.3	6.0	12.1	12.4
$6,000 & over.	312	0.9	10.6	29.8	19.6	24.4	14.4	14.3
Blue-collar workers	1,173	26.5	31.6	34.5	6.7	0.7	—	11.2
Under $6,000	549	37.4	31.5	26.2	4.0	0.7	—	10.2
$6,000 & over.	624	17.2	31.7	41.5	9.1	0.6	—	12.0
Service workers	246	24.9	25.2	36.7	10.9	2.4	—	12.0
Under $6,000	132	31.8	27.3	30.3	8.3	2.3	—	11.0
$6,000 & over.	113	16.0	22.1	43.4	13.3	2.7	—	12.3
Farm workers	53	(B)	(B)	(B)	(B)	(B)	(B)	(B)
Under $6,000	53	(B)	(B)	(B)	(B)	(B)	(B)	(B)
$6,000 & over.	—	(B)	(B)	(B)	(B)	(B)	(B)	(B)
White employed males, age 45-64	15,524	24.1	17.7	32.9	11.1	7.7	6.5	12.2
Under $3,000	847	48.6	17.2	20.2	7.1	3.1	3.7	9.2
$3,000-$5,999.	1,967	46.0	17.6	26.5	5.3	3.0	1.5	9.7
$6,000-$9,999.	5,029	30.2	21.8	34.6	7.7	3.4	2.4	11.7
$10,000-$14,999.	4,518	16.0	19.7	39.1	13.8	7.1	4.4	12.4
$15,000 & over	3,163	5.7	8.6	28.5	17.2	19.9	20.1	14.3
White-collar workers	6,655	7.6	10.4	32.9	18.1	16.1	15.0	13.0
Under $6,000	640	23.0	14.4	31.7	12.2	9.5	9.1	12.4
$6,000 & over.	6,015	5.9	10.0	33.0	18.7	16.8	15.6	13.2
Blue-collar workers	6,974	35.3	24.1	33.6	5.7	1.2	0.2	10.8
Under $6,000	1,281	55.2	19.0	21.6	3.4	0.9	0.1	8.8
$6,000 & over.	5,694	30.9	25.3	36.2	6.2	1.2	0.2	11.3
Service workers	1,043	34.1	23.1	33.5	6.0	2.9	0.4	11.1
Under $6,000	383	48.3	20.4	25.8	2.9	2.1	—	9.2
$6,000 & over.	660	25.8	24.7	37.7	7.7	3.3	0.6	11.9
Farm workers	852	49.0	16.1	26.5	6.5	1.9	—	9.2
Under $6,000	511	55.4	15.5	22.1	6.3	1.2	—	8.8
$6,000 & over.	342	39.8	17.3	33.0	7.0	3.2	—	10.8
Black employed males, age 45-64	1,289	50.1	21.6	18.5	4.7	2.6	2.5	9.0
Under $3,000	187	67.2	19.0	11.0	2.8	—	—	7.3
$3,000-$5,999.	436	63.0	19.7	13.7	2.2	0.9	0.4	8.2
$6,000-$9,999.	435	45.3	24.0	19.6	6.9	2.4	1.8	9.6
$10,000-$14,999.	190	22.6	20.3	34.6	6.3	8.4	7.9	12.2
$15,000 & over	40	(B)	(B)	(B)	(B)	(B)	(B)	(B)
White-collar workers	214	18.1	16.1	31.7	10.3	9.9	13.8	12.5
Under $6,000	51	(B)	(B)	(B)	(B)	(B)	(B)	(B)
$6,000 & over.	163	10.4	17.8	29.4	12.9	12.3	17.2	12.7
Blue-collar workers	774	57.6	23.3	14.0	3.8	1.2	—	8.4
Under $6,000	368	68.5	20.7	7.9	2.2	0.8	—	7.4
$6,000 & over.	406	48.1	25.6	20.0	5.4	1.7	—	9.2
Service workers	240	46.8	22.4	24.6	4.0	1.1	1.2	9.4
Under $6,000	145	53.8	20.7	22.1	4.1	—	—	8.8
$6,000 & over.	95	35.9	24.2	28.4	5.3	3.2	3.2	10.8
Farm workers	61	(B)	(B)	(B)	(B)	(B)	(B)	(B)
Under $6,000	60	(B)	(B)	(B)	(B)	(B)	(B)	(B)
$6,000 & over.	1	(B)	(B)	(B)	(B)	(B)	(B)	(B)

Public Libraries in Selected North American Cities

Source: World Almanac Research

City	No. of Volumes	Circulation	Cost of Operation
Akron, Ohio	759,545	1,920,995	$2,243,847
Albany, N.Y.	242,117	550,570	593,697
*Albuquerque, N.M. (6)	258,000	1,068,000	560,000
Augusta, Ga.	240,519	683,307	531,837
Baltimore, Md.	2,219,965	3,166,894	6,987,763
*Baton Rouge, La. (8)	265,469	825,831	647,318
*Binghamton, N.Y. (5)	246,532	629,524	617,562
Birmingham, Ala.	852,655	3,400,000	1,300,000
Boston, Mass.	3,092,424	49,584	6,470,628
Bridgeport, Conn.	450,000	430,000	902,500
Buffalo, N.Y.	2,628,589	5,799,607	7,102,711
Calgary, Alberta	472,141	2,288,999	1,666,615
Charleston, W. Va.	354,202	1,179,785	660,703
Charlotte, N.C.	533,006	1,365,411	1,290,483
Chattanooga, Tenn.	231,175	514,336	602,256
Chicago, Ill.	4,184,500	9,742,570	14,014,727
Cincinnati, Ohio	3,007,575	5,132,744	5,412,701
Cleveland, Ohio	3,273,948	4,212,844	7,286,899
Columbus, Ohio	1,038,528	2,859,611	2,828,178
Corpus Christi, Tex.	293,943	653,292	441,848
*Dallas, Tex. (16)	1,277,510	3,914,883	4,359,460
Dayton, Ohio	1,194,526	3,785,791	2,362,718
Denver, Colo.	1,281,454	3,117,337	3,505,400
Des Moines, Iowa	337,120	1,076,208	1,006,858
Detroit, Mich.	2,277,000	3,473,000	8,473,000
*El Paso, Tex. (6)	381,318	962,930	727,155
Erie, Pa.	240,000	404,000	410,000
Evansville, Ind.	444,629	1,325,575	818,214
Halifax, Nova Scotia	298,691	1,227,548	801,107
Hamilton, Ont.	625,614	1,910,363	1,800,562
*Hartford, Conn. (8)	453,697	589,409	1,054,000
Houston, Tex.	1,314,680	3,668,813	3,047,051
*Jacksonville, Fla. (10)	735,663	1,457,444	1,309,999
Kansas City, Kan.	243,279	358,920	522,901
Kansas City, Mo.	1,218,135	2,266,362	2,476,578
Kitchener-Waterloo, Ont.	332,812	1,351,276	975,626
Knoxville, Tenn.	445,623	1,293,511	899,411
Little Rock, Ark.	219,121	408,693	311,818
London, Ont.	399,093	1,551,678	2,033,041
Louisville, Ky.	917,000	1,693,827	2,602,215
Memphis, Tenn.	980,008	2,334,287	2,763,546
Miami, Fla.	741,832	2,413,400	3,494,099
Milwaukee, Wis.	2,145,825	3,996,258	5,326,369
*Montreal, Quebec (17)	1,825,268	3,693,060	2,714,255
Nashville, Tenn.	409,320	1,291,540	1,327,573
New Haven, Conn.	468,684	476,677	821,882
New Orleans, La.	657,392	1,320,477	1,645,167
*New York	15,614,850	None	11,623,000
N.Y. branches (84)	5,272,381	11,082,692	18,939,075
Brooklyn (55)	2,951,407	7,986,818	11,967,308
Queens (55)	2,533,218	7,592,572	10,233,529
Norfolk, Va.	426,659	1,045,816	1,085,471
Oklahoma City, Okla.	613,319	1,984,786	1,419,265
Omaha, Neb.	449,412	1,566,409	1,053,047
Orlando, Fla.	362,000	350,000	1,311,600
Ottawa, Ont.	500,000	1,706,801	1,500,000
*Philadelphia, Pa. (44)	2,661,957	6,000,000	10,062,044
Phoenix, Ariz.	704,940	2,371,232	1,928,142
Pittsburgh, Pa.	2,266,112	4,495,283	5,779,537
Portland, Maine	220,043	259,443	393,542
Portland, Ore.	980,679	3,222,002	2,722,993
Providence, R.I.	596,924	822,348	1,496,837
*Regina, Sask. (5)	230,827	1,063,827	945,038
Richmond, Va.	449,225	1,119,021	888,996
Roanoke, Va.	255,854	401,202	458,956
Rochester, N.Y.	829,696	1,752,592	2,714,314
Sacramento, Calif.	750,319	3,276,075	3,236,271
*St. Louis, Mo. (20)	1,426,175	2,772,464	3,234,655
St. Paul, Minn.	780,000	2,000,000	1,600,000
St. Petersburg, Fla.	279,639	1,192,118	602,222
Salt Lake City, Utah	430,045	863,160	912,828
*San Antonio, Tex. (8)	730,137	2,390,294	1,468,850
San Diego, Calif.	1,519,960	6,103,493	4,761,684
San Francisco, Calif.	1,355,966	3,233,782	4,730,390
San Jose, Calif.	1,358,453	5,036,422	3,892,911
*Saskatoon, Sask. (3)	262,828	1,005,827	901,829
Seattle, Wash.	1,449,870	3,859,232	3,834,801
Syracuse, N.Y.	1,081,537	2,135,943	1,801,678
Tallahassee, Fla.	102,844	353,287	244,403
Tampa, Fla.	343,596	1,534,317	1,563,317
Toledo, Ohio	1,270,607	2,762,514	2,687,870
Tucson, Ariz.	392,948	1,750,535	1,696,143
Tulsa, Okla.	577,642	1,647,270	1,496,577
Vancouver, B.C.	624,649	3,734,023	2,000,000
*Washington, D.C. (20)	2,125,000	2,600,000	6,000,000
Wichita, Kan.	314,985	1,157,401	1,068,172
Winnipeg, Manitoba	547,196	2,114,983	1,379,662
Winston-Salem, N.C.	292,500	900,000	860,000

*Figure in parentheses denotes number of branches.

Major American Academic Libraries

Source: Office of Education, Dept. of H.E.W. (1971-72)

Institution	Books Total	Books Added	Microform units	Staff Total	Staff Prof.	Expenditures
Harvard University	8,707,822	387,671	882,471	770	242	$9,222,948
Yale University	5,993,856	219,719	839,737	585	181	7,041,476
University of Illinois	4,992,391	192,896	464,668	429	180	5,715,613
Columbia University	4,448,350	153,308	939,501	451	146	5,958,812
University of Michigan	4,332,518	148,826	761,182	481	161	6,184,074
University of California at Berkeley	4,153,936	156,379	682,048	445	162	6,382,024
Cornell University	3,888,634	130,396	1,048,618	444	126	5,637,360
Stanford University	3,721,343	159,229	608,085	401	140	7,034,657
Indiana University	3,344,141	277,638	612,630	382	158	5,870,200
University of Minnesota	3,245,740	129,638	716,077	320	157	5,084,326
University of Chicago	3,212,296	151,165	276,039	277	78	4,079,694
University of California at Los Angeles	3,164,328	130,618	947,058	407	157	6,331,586
University of Texas	2,734,595	309,853	624,295	272	111	4,737,768
Ohio State University	2,670,984	138,300	792,390	320	106	4,106,832
University of Wisconsin	2,517,796	109,430	844,283	298	93	4,425,897
Northwestern University	2,433,420	65,925	371,631	232	93	3,763,392
Princeton University	2,412,871	99,824	439,753	280	84	3,684,576
University of Pennsylvania	2,410,933	103,879	861,960	292	101	4,189,810
Duke University	2,333,382	110,089	190,460	228	81	3,144,662
New York University	2,175,680	107,815	1,055,156	399	85	4,053,158
Johns Hopkins University	1,993,113	41,039	574,400	155	48	1,840,308
University of Washington	1,938,298	66,148	910,121	335	113	3,692,507
University of North Carolina	1,894,132	83,562	492,269	228	82	3,173,787
Michigan State University	1,867,236	113,768	482,322	195	78	3,169,829
University of Virginia	1,777,936	83,277	1,064,768	225	59	3,383,632
University of Iowa	1,672,927	91,218	619,137	173	71	2,689,190
University of Pittsburgh	1,664,234	126,502	613,418	298	120	3,808,558
University of Missouri	1,639,261	55,050	1,242,848	149	52	1,947,561
University of Kansas	1,639,070	72,377	394,645	169	59	2,487,775
Syracuse University	1,637,442	102,468	1,600,203	182	48	2,168,581
Rutgers University	1,584,259	114,932	583,817	245	94	4,388,480
University of Colorado	1,570,251	71,298	737,986	183	56	2,903,025
University of Florida	1,550,483	63,398	667,760	297	76	2,748,595

Degrees Conferred by Higher Educational Institutions
United States, 1970-71
Source: United States Office of Education

Major sub-classifications do not necessarily add to totals

Major field of study	Bachelor's degree		Master's degree		Doctor's (Ph.D., Ed.D., etc.)	
	Men	Women	Men	Women	Men	Women
Agriculture and natural resources	12,136	536	2,313	144	1,055	31
Agriculture, general	1,445	46	122	1		
Agronomy	812	11	283	10	165	4
Animal Science	2,222	223	318	26	140	5
Agricultural economics	1,165	10	403	14	209	3
Forestry	1,804	22	282	9	92	
Architecture and environmental design	4,906	664	1,469	236	33	3
Architecture	3,284	175	578	47	6	
City, community and regional planning	204	25	658	152	23	
Area studies	1,174	1,318	618	389	120	24
Asian studies	122	118	150	63	15	2
Latin American studies	148	132	78	70	3	
American studies	630	836	106	125	49	18
Biological sciences	25,333	10,410	3,805	1,923	3,050	595
Biology, general	18,253	8,041	1,746	919	405	131
Botany, general	349	197	212	99	195	28
Bacteriology	210	143	47	27	34	8
Zoology, general	4,314	1,066	451	240	346	72
Microbiology	596	526	224	158	264	59
Biochemistry	430	138	152	99	436	81
Business and management	105,060	10,467	25,506	1,038	787	23
General	27,208	2,979	8,316	377	188	2
Accounting	20,036	2,063	994	103	58	3
Banking and finance	5,757	165	1,741	40	23	
Management and administration	26,096	1,932	9,253	318	296	10
Marketing and purchasing	14,696	1,289	1,325	58	25	
Communications	6,989	3,813	1,214	642	126	19
Journalism	2,883	2,261	558	295	13	2
Computer and information sciences	2,064	324	1,424	164	125	3
Education	45,089	131,482	38,899	49,817	5,043	1,355
Elementary education, general	8,090	82,342	3,123	13,947	116	103
Secondary education, general	1,529	2,020	2,937	2,485	170	42
Special education, general	341	1,979	845	2,206	77	37
Pre-elementary education	47	3,358	34	499	2	7
Student personnel	3	4	6,589	6,746	440	116
Educational administration	4	1	6,127	1,575	875	82
Art education	1,598	4,063	334	664	37	16
Music education	3,064	4,200	837	727	95	14
Physical education	15,177	9,555	3,032	1,378	214	69
Business, commerce, and distributive. education	2,627	5,923	777	1,147	56	26
Industrial arts, vocational and technical education	6,965	106	1,988	111	100	6
Home economics education	94	6,355	77	725	1	27
Engineering	49,646	400	16,258	185	3,615	23
Engineering, general	2,829	35	804	9	216	3
Aerospace, aeronautical, astronautical. engineering	2,426	17	711	6	214	3
Chemical engineering	3,516	63	1,074	26	404	2
Civil, construction, and transportation. engineering	6,474	52	2,397	28	443	3
Electrical, electronics, communications engineering	12,122	76	4,252	30	876	3
Mechanical engineering	8,817	41	2,232	5	438	
Industrial and management engineering	3,152	19	1,898	23	136	3
Fine and applied arts	12,256	18,138	3,510	3,165	483	138
Foreign languages	5,075	14,870	1,642	3,113	484	297
French	1,140	6,166	331	1,106	103	89
German	962	1,639	296	394	95	49
Spanish	1,807	5,261	529	927	98	70
Health professions	5,788	19,438	2,567	3,182	389	77
Hospital and health care administration	56	4	436	60	14	
Nursing	253	11,946	31	1,499	1	6
Dental specialties	5		428	22	14	
Medical specialties	11		106	23	29	14
Pharmacy	3,636	913	154	40	93	1
Public health	91	36	772	472	66	19
Speech pathology and audiology	176	1,251	152	671	48	22
Medical laboratory technologies	386	2,711	13	32	3	1
Home economics	301	10,866	88	1,364	48	75
Law	518	27	909	46	20	. . .
Letters	28,546	44,576	5,407	7,303	1,849	567
English, general	17,002	34,560	2,852	4,658	708	300
Literature, English	1,599	2,942	365	520	190	84
Speech, debate and forensic science	2,983	3,987	700	1,015	180	55

	Bachelor's degree Men	Women	Master's degree Men	Women	Doctor's Men	Women
Philosophy	4,620	1,165	449	149	358	36
Religious studies	1,506	855	445	283	152	8
Library science	**81**	**932**	**1,311**	**5,690**	**28**	**11**
Mathematics	**15,369**	**9,432**	**3,673**	**1,518**	**1,106**	**93**
Physical sciences	**18,459**	**2,953**	**5,521**	**846**	**4,144**	**246**
Physics, general	4,708	338	2,027	147	1,407	42
Chemistry, general	9,006	2,031	1,733	464	1,798	154
Astronomy	94	8	88	12	69	7
Atmospheric sciences and meteorology	245	4	149	4	61	
Geology	2,097	262	544	62	279	10
Earth sciences, general	559	108	227	35	24	1
Psychology	21,029	16,851	2,783	1,648	1,355	427
Experimental psychology	44		44	16	57	15
Clinical psychology	16	8	119	72	104	29
Public affairs and services	**4,723**	**4,497**	**4,274**	**3,986**	**135**	**43**
Public administration	372	53	1,255	151	33	3
Parks and recreation management	1,058	563	153	65	1	1
Social work and helping services	1,139	3,469	2,415	3,604	87	39
Law enforcement and corrections	1,856	189	174	20	1	
Social sciences	**98,145**	**57,181**	**11,798**	**4,703**	**3,152**	**507**
Social sciences, general	11,753	9,790	1,522	808	38	12
Economics	13,890	1,868	1,733	262	668	53
History	29,055	15,608	3,470	1,687	871	120
Political science and government	21,966	5,516	1,839	479	615	85
Sociology	13,610	19,653	1,131	677	455	119
Theology	**2,727**	**1,017**	**2,049**	**661**	**305**	**6**
Theological professions, general	1,644	247	1,204	138	246	3
Religious music	64	52	76	30	6	
Religious education	722	643	551	386	31	3
Interdisciplinary studies	**9,824**	**3,943**	**1,106**	**600**	**77**	**14**
Total	**475,594**	**364,136**	**138,146**	**92,363**	**27,530**	**4,577**
Grand Total	**839,730**		**230,509**		**32,107**	

First-professional Degrees Conferred

United States, 1970-71

Control of institution and field of study	First-professional degrees[1] Total	Men	Women
Total, all institutions	**37,946**	**35,544**	**2,402**
Dentistry (D.D.S. or D.M.D.)	3,745	3,703	43
Medicine (M.D.)	8,919	8,110	809
Optometry (O.D.)	531	518	13
Osteopathy (D.O.)	472	461	11
Podiatry (Pod.D. or D.P.) or podiatric medicine (D.P.M.)	240	235	5
Veterinary medicine (D.V.M.)	1,252	1,154	98
Law (L.L.B. or J.D.)	17,421	16,181	1,240
Theology (B.D., M.Div., or Rabbi)	5,055	4,937	118
Other	311	245	66
Total, publicly controlled institutions	**16,139**	**15,111**	**1,028**
Dentistry (D.D.S. or D.M.D.)	2,067	2,045	22
Medicine (M.D.)	5,093	4,682	411
Optometry (O.D.)	182	174	8
Osteopathy (D.O.)			

Control of institution and field of study	First-professional degrees[1] Total	Men	Women
Podiatry (Pod.D. or D.P.) or podiatric medicine (D.P.M.)			
Veterinary medicine (D.V.M.)	1,098	1,016	82
Law (L.L.B. or J.D.)	7,606	7,132	474
Theology (B.D., M.Div., or Rabbi)			
Other	93	62	31
Total, privately controlled institutions	**21,807**	**20,433**	**1,374**
Dentistry (D.D.S. or D.M.D.)	1,678	1,658	20
Medicine (M.D.)	3,826	3,428	398
Optometry (O.D.)	349	344	5
Osteopathy (D.O.)	472	461	11
Podiatry (Pod.D. or D.P.) or podiatric medicine (D.P.M.)	240	235	5
Veterinary medicine (D.V.M.)	154	138	16
Law (L.L.B. or J.D.)	9,815	9,049	766
Theology (B.D., M.Div., or Rabbi)	5,055	4,937	118
Other	218	183	35

[1]Includes degrees which require at least 6 years of college work for completion (including at least 2 years of preprofessional training).

Vocational Education

Source: United States Office of Education

All Federal funds expended for vocational education are matched by State and local funds. This does not include expenditures for buildings, except for construction of area vocational education school facilities allowable since 1965.

Enrollment in Federally Aided Vocational Classes

Fiscal Year	Total Enrollment	Agriculture	Trades and Industry	Home Economics	Distributive Occupations	Health Occupations	Technical Education	Office Occupations	Other Programs
1935	1,178,896	325,685	503,865	349,346					
1940	2,290,741	584,133	758,409	818,766	129,433				
1945	2,612,931	446,953	522,733	890,464	152,781				
1950	3,364,613	764,975	804,602	1,430,366	364,670				
1955	3,314,255	776,138	870,954	1,431,808	235,355				
1960	3,768,149	796,237	938,490	1,588,109	303,784	40,250	101,279		
1965	5,430,611	887,529	1,087,807	2,098,520	333,342	66,772	225,737	730,904	
1969	[1]7,979,366	850,705	1,720,859	2,449,052	563,431	175,101	315,311	1,835,124	
1970	[1]8,793,960	852,983	1,906,133	2,570,410	529,365	198,044	271,730	2,111,160	354,135
1971	10,525,660	845,085	2,075,166	3,129,804	578,075	269,546	313,860	2,226,854	1,087,270
1972	11,710,767	896,460	2,397,968	3,445,698	640,423	336,652	337,069	2,351,878	1,304,619

(1.) Preliminary data.

Forms of Address for Persons of Rank and Public Office

In these examples John Smith is used as a representative American name. The salutation Dear Sir is always permissible when addressing a person not known to the writer.

President of the United States

Address: The President, The White House, Washington, D. C. Also, The President and Mrs. ——.

Salutation: Dear Sir or Mr. President or Dear Mr. President. More intimately: My dear Mr. President. Also: Dear Mr. President and Mrs. ——

The vice president takes the same forms.

Cabinet Officers

Address: Mr. John Smith, Secretary of State, Washington, D.C. or The Hon. John Smith. Similar addresses for other members of the cabinet. Also: Secretary and Mrs. John Smith.

Salutation: Dear Sir, or Dear Mr. Secretary. Also: Dear Mr. and Mrs. Smith.

The Bench

Address: The Hon. John Smith, Chief Justice of the United States. The Hn. John Smith, Associate Justice of the Supreme Court of the United States. The Hon. John Smith, Associate Judge, U. S. District Court.

Salutations: Dear Sir or Dear Mr. Chief Justice. Dear Mr. Justice. Dear Judge Smith.

Members of Congress

Address: The Hon. John Smith, United States Senate, Washington, D. C.or Sen. John Smith, etc. Also The Hon. John Smith, House of Representatives, Washington, D. C. or Rep. John Smith, etc.

Salutation: Dear Mr. Senator or Dear Mr. Smith; for Representative, Dear Mr. Smith.

Officers of Armed Forces

Address: Careful attention should be given to the precise rank, thus: General of the Army John Smith, Fleet Admiral John Smith. The rules for Air Force are same as Army.

Salutation: Dear Sir, or Dear General. All general officers, whatever rank, are entitled to be addressed as generals. Likewise a lieutenant colonel is addressed as colonel and first and second lieutenants are addressed as lieutenant.

Warrant officers and flight officers are addressed as Mister. Chaplains are addressed as Chaplain. A Catholic chaplain may be addressed as Father. Cadets of the United States Military Academy and Air Force Academy are addressed as Cadet. Noncommissioned officers are addressed by their titles. In the U. S. Navy all men from midshipman at Annapolis up to and including lieutenant commander are addressed as Mister.

Ambassador, Governor, Mayor

Address: The Hon. John Smith, followed by his title. He can be addressed either at his embassy, or at the Department of State, Washington, D. C. A foreign ambassador is His Excellency.

Salutation: Dear Mr. Ambassador. A foreign ambassador is Your Excellency.

Governors and mayors are often addressed as The Hon. John Smith, Governor of ——, or The Hon. John Smith, Mayor of ——; also Governor John Smith, State House, Albany, N. Y., or Mayor John Smith, City Hall, Erie, Pa.

The Clergy

Address: His Holiness, the Pope, or His Holiness Pope (name), State of Vatican City, Italy.

Salutation: Your Holiness or Most Holy Father.

Also: His Eminence, John, Cardinal Smith; salutation: Your Eminence. An archbishop or a bishop is addressed The Most Reverend, and the salutation is Your Excellency. A monsignor who is a papal chamberlain is The Very Reverend Monsignor and saluted as Very Reverend Monsignor; a monsignor who is a domestic prelate is The Right Reverend Monsignor and salutation is Right Reverend Monsignor. A priest is addressed Reverend John Smith. A brother of an order is addressed Brother ——. A sister takes the same form.

A bishop of the Protestant Episcopal Church is The Right Reverend John Smith; salutation is Right Reverend Sir, or Dear Bishop Smith. If a clergyman is a doctor of divinity, he is addressed: The Reverend John Smith, D. D., and the salutation is Reverend Sir, or Dear Dr. Smith. When a clergyman does not have the degree the salutation is Dear Mr. Smith.

A bishop of the Methodist Church is addressed Bishop John Smith with titles following.

Royalty and Nobility

An emperor is to be addressed in a letter as Sir, or Your Imperial Majesty.

A king or queen is addressed as His Majesty (Name), King of (Name), or Her Majesty (Name), Queen of (Name). Salutation: Sir, or Madam, or May it please Your Majesty.

Princes and princesses and other persons of royal blood are addressed as His (or Her) Royal Highness, and saluted with May it please Your Royal Highness.

A duke or marquis is My Lord Duke (or Marquis), a duke is His (or Your) Grace.

Famous Fairs and Expositions

Selected U. S. Daily Newspapers' Circulation

Source: Audit Bureau of Circulations' FAS-FAX Report of average paid circulation for 6 months ending Mar. 31, 1974.
(†) Indicates 3 month average.

As of Sept. 30, 1973, there were 1,733 English language daily newspapers in the U. S. (329 morning; 1,365 evening; 17 "all day") with a combined circulation of 62,605,401. Sunday newspapers numbered 618 with a total circulation of 51,088,822. (m) Morning; (e) Evening; *Based on Monday to Friday average. Brackets indicate joint publication.

Newspaper	Daily	Sunday
Albany, N. Y., Times-Union (m)...	{76,810	140,681
Albany, N. Y., Knickerbocker		
News-Union Star (e)........	{65,260	
Akron Beacon Journal (e).......	172,971	211,833
Allentown Call-Chronicle (m&e)...	*126,614	148,802
Atlanta Constitution (m)........	{215,367	
Atlanta Journal (e) & Sunday		
Journal Constitution........	{254,406	577,157
Baltimore News American (e)......	*217,257	296,017
Baltimore Sun (m & e).........	*383,439	355,268
Birmingham News (e).........	{176,671	217,780
Birmingham Post-Herald (m).....	} 72,176	
Boston Globe (m & e)........	*480,381	636,342
Boston Herald American (m) &		
Sunday Advertiser......	346,898	491,000
Buffalo Courier-Express (m)......	129,897	284,737
Buffalo News (e)............	*280,943	
Charlotte News (e)...........	{ 64,242	
Charlotte Observer (m).........	{173,715	220,518
Chicago News (e)............	*434,353	
Chicago Sun-Times (m)........	*568,653	728,977
Chicago Tribune (m)..........	*697,145	1,170,142
Christian Science Monitor (m)....	196,125	
Cincinnati Enquirer (m)........	193,972	302,462
Cincinnati Post & Times-Star (e)...	213,509	
Cleveland Plain Dealer (m).....	412,444	511,679
Cleveland Press (e)..........	376,609	
Columbia, S. C., State (m)......	{107,215	123,828
Columbia, S. C., Record (e).....	{ 32,105	
Columbus, Ga., Enquirer (m) & Sun		
Ledger-Enquirer...........	32,171	59,123
Columbus, Ga., Ledger (e)......	32,096	
Dallas News (m)............	263,175	308,664
Dallas Times Herald (e).......	*245,206	309,043
Dayton Journal Herald (m)......	112,142	
Dayton News (e)............	159,005	229,514
Denver Post (e).............	*242,239	348,744
Denver: Rocky Mt. News (m).....	221,971	246,259
Des Moines Register (m).......	{248,466	481,571
Des Moines Tribune (e)........	{106,573	
Detroit Free Press (m)........	*625,544	730,851
Detroit News (e)............	*693,874	850,989
Ft. Worth Star-Telegram (m & e)..	230,840	228,272
Fort Worth Press (e)..........	44,401	49,008
Fresno Bee (e).............	118,727	141,220
Grand Rapids Press(e)........	130,870	134,930
Hackensack Record (e)........	*156,671	*191,253
Hartford Courant (m).........	177,027	230,840
Hartford Times (e)...........	*103,390	102,284
Honolulu Advertiser (m).......	{ 78,752	
Honolulu Star-Bulletin (e) &		
Sunday S-B & Advertiser.....	{131,516	192,425
Houston Chronicle (e).........	*303,309	373,323
Houston Post (m)...........	*289,119	349,534
Indianapolis News (e).........	*172,219	
Indianapolis Star (m).........	225,435	†372,611
Jacksonville: Florida Journal (e)...	†60,017	
Jacksonville: Fla. Times Union (m)..	{149,540	183,788
Kansas City Star (e).........	{312,579	408,094
Kansas City Times (m).. .~....	{334,922	
Knoxville Journal (m).........	62,953	
Knoxville News-Sentinel (e).....	109,121	163,419
Little Rock: Ark. Democrat (e).....	*64,707	92,229
Little Rock: Ark. Gazette (m).....	*118,641	143,562
Long Beach Independent (m) &		
Sun. Ind. Press-Telegram.....	{*55,521	139,163
Long Beach Press-Telegram (e)....	{*96,782	
Los Angeles Herald Examiner (e)..	*432,050	454,917
Los Angeles Times (m)........	1,036,666	1,226,233
Louisville Courier-Journal (m)....	{231,115	365,134
Louisville Times (e)..........	{175,640	
Memphis Commercial Appeal (m)..	{221,188	290,483
Memphis Press Scimitar (e).....	{123,362	
Miami Herald (m)............	427,685	
Miami News (e)............	*74,376	
Milwaukee Journal (e)........	{356,213	545,859
Milwaukee Sentinel (m).......	{178,219	
Minneapolis Star (e)..........	{257,680	
Minneapolis Tribune (m).......	{231,620	634,195
Nashville Banner (e)..........	104,760	
Nashville Tennessean (m)......	144,510	246,531
New Haven Register (e)........	{*107,888	128,256
New Haven Journal-Courier (m)...	{*32,030	
New Orleans Times-Picayune (m).	{ *205,387	†307,640
New Orleans States-Item (e).....	{†*124,153	
New York: Long Island Press (e)..	†339,558	†326,681
New York: Newsday (e)........	457,755	365,796

Newspaper	Daily	Sunday
New York News (m)............	*2,120,549	2,933,182
New York Post (e)............	650,296	
New York Times (m)...........	*910,185	1,513,389
Newark Star-Ledger (m)........	*361,513	560,692
Norfolk Ledger-Star (e)........	†101,982	
Norfolk Virginian-Pilot (m)......	†130,046	†187,972
Oakland Tribune (e)...........	*186,449	218,338
Oklahoma City Oklahoman (m)...	*184,128	290,384
Oklahoma City Times (e).......	*97,438	
Omaha World-Herald (m & e)....	*248,374	284,837
Orlando Sentinel-Star (m & e)...	*195,645	222,550
Philadelphia Bulletin (e).......	*615,301	687,301
Philadelphia Inquirer (m).......	*454,440	839,238
Philadelphia News (e).........	264,964	
Phoenix Republic (m)..........	†219,864	†327,958
Phoenix Gazette (e)..........	†116,542	
Pittsburgh Post Gazette (m).....	*211,025	
Pittsburgh Press (e)..........	*293,011	711,304
Portland, Me., Press-Herald (m)...	{54,228	
Portland, Me., Express (e) &		
Maine Sun. Telegram.......	{30,168	110,594
Portland: Oregonian (m).......	{241,265	401,391
Portland: Oregon Journal (e).....	{*121,733	
Providence Journal (m)........	{ *66,156	206,067
Providence Bulletin (e)........	{*144,393	
Raleigh News & Observer (m)...	{135,280	†159,774
Raleigh Times (e)...........	{ †34,323	
Richmond News Leader (e)......	{112,390	
Richmond Times-Dispatch (m)...	{133,337	184,991
Rochester Democrat-Chronicle (m)	†37,887	230,713
Rochester Times-Union (e).....	†142,661	
Sacramento Bee (e)..........	*185,850	222,172
Sacramento Union (m)........	*102,898	95,437
St. Louis Globe-Democrat (m)...	*283,411	279,077
St. Louis Post-Dispatch (e).....	*307,098	500,594
St. Paul Dispatch (e).........	{128,008	
St. Paul Pioneer Press (m).....	{110,409	240,778
St. Petersburg Independent (e)...	{ 32,370	
St. Petersburg Times (m).......	{199,871	245,476
Salt Lake City Tribune (m)......	{101,981	173,619
Salt Lake City Deseret News (e)...	{ 75,180	
San Antonio Express (m) & Sun.		
Express-News...........	{*85,692	135,162
San Antonio News (e).........	{*62,909	
San Antonio Light (e).........	*129,283	177,593
San Diego Union (m).........	*175,791	*292,530
San Diego Tribune (e)........	*125,902	
San Francisco Examiner (e)	{*178,647	
San Francisco Chronicle (m) &		
Sun. Examiner Chronicle......	{*475,100	673,194
San Jose Mercury (m) & Sunday		
Mercury-News...........	{135,244	225,405
San Jose News (e)...........	{ 74,212	
Santa Ana Register (m & e).....	200,899	216,741
Seattle Post-Intelligencer (m)....	*205,159	254,066
Seattle Times (e)...........	*243,278	301,369
South Bend Tribune (e)........	117,453	123,712
Spokane Chronicle (e)........	{68,610	
Spokane Spokesman-Review (m)..	{82,619	128,003
Springfield, Ill., State Journal-		
Register (m & e).........	82,603	74,474
Springfield, Mass., Union (m)...	{81,502	
Springfield, Mass., News (e) &		
Sunday Republican........	{90,356	134,599
Syracuse Herald-Journal (e) &		
Sun. Herald-American......	{126,269	240,147
Syracuse Post-Standard (m).....	{*87,092	
Tampa Tribune (m)...........	{174,101	209,288
Tampa Times (e)............	{ 25,142	
Toledo Blade (e)............	{173,115	206,652
Toledo Times (e)............	{*29,260	
Tulsa Tribune (e)...........	{ †79,450	
Tulsa World (m)............	{120,268	†196,492
Wall St. Journal (m) (total)......	1,358,248	
Washington, D. C., Post (m).....	*543,084	720,180
Washington Star & News (e)....	*405,173	351,037
West Palm Beach Post (m) &		
Sunday Post-Times........	{*73,530	107,941
West Palm Beach Times (e).....	{*32,478	
Wichita Eagle (m) & Sunday		
Eagle & Beacon...........	{128,803	187,187
Wichita Beacon (e)..........	{ 57,716	
Winston-Salem Journal (m) & Sun.		
Journal Sentinel..........	{72,856	91,927
Winston-Salem Sentinel (e).....	{42,960	
Youngstown Vindicator (e)......	†103,105	†159,404

Circulation of Leading U.S. Magazines

Source: Audit Bureau of Circulations' FAS-FAX Report

General and farm magazines, exclusive of groups and comics. Based on total average paid circulation during the 6 months prior to Dec. 31, 1973. *Indicates circulation for the 6 months prior to Dec. 31, 1972.

Magazine	Circulation	Magazine	Circulation	Magazine	Circulation
TV Guide	18,702,249	Mechanix & Electronics		New Ingenue	717,215
Reader's Digest	18,198,402	Illustrated	1,545,124	American Girl	701,170
Natl. Geographic	8,276,668	Seventeen	1,519,888	Motor Trend	699,769
Family Circle	8,075,095	Sports Afield	1,432,727	Car & Driver	679,181
Woman's Day	8,002,724	Today's Education	1,418,067	Weight Watchers	670,720
Better Homes &		Sport	1,372,217*	Fortune	669,133
Gardens	7,995,491	Esquire	1,314,602	Saturday Review/World	
McCall's	7,509,143	Scouting	1,295,336		664,022
Ladies' Home Jour.	7,081,855	Ebony	1,289,284	Lion Magazine	659,220
Playboy	6,503,261	Grit	1,242,942	Golf Digest	654,865
Good Housekeeping	5,703,732	Jr. Scholastic Unit.	1,195,487	Popular Photo'y	645,536
Redbook	4,918,624	Sunset	1,182,128	Family Handyman	645,133*
Time	4,672,355	House & Garden	1,145,380	Jet	633,961
Penthouse	3,923,606	True	1,112,862	Forbes	632,081
American Home	3,734,934	Photoplay	1,104,153*	Lady's Circle	630,040
National Enquirer	3,269,468	Southern Living	1,067,231	Saturday Evening Post	625,779
Sr. Scholastic Unit.	3,002,379	Argosy	1,000,252	Sphere Magazine	616,841
Newsweek	2,898,743	Family Health	998,516	Simplicity Fashion	614,111*
American Legion	2,664,484	Co-ed	904,116	Vogue & Vanity Fair	581,713
Sports Illustrated	2,270,731	Nation's Business	891,470	Gourmet	549,784
Boy's Life	2,139,947	House Beautiful	882,548	Scientific American	539,657
Parent's Magazine	2,017,029	Midnight	854,728	Golf & Golfing	524,630
U.S. News & World		Mademoiselle	850,205	Catholic Digest	520,979
Report	2,005,790	Modern Screen	845,132	National Observer	517,319
Outdoor Life	1,886,746	Psychology Today	835,082	Smithsonian	486,390
True Story	1,824,619*	Holiday	824,579*	New Yorker	484,876
Cosmopolitan	1,810,362	Hot Rod	817,172	Modern Photo'y	467,477
Field & Stream	1,806,998	TV Radio Mirror	801,775*	Skiing	464,568
Workbasket	1,803,752*	'Teen	787,808	Capper's Weekly	458,667
Popular Science	1,791,548	National Lampoon	765,997	Rotarian	447,991
Glamour	1,743,127	Simplicity Home Cat.	757,851*	Harper's Bazaar	440,229
V.F.W. Magazine	1,714,873	Modern Romances	752,337	Apartment Life	435,161
Popular Mechanics	1,687,540	Business Week	738,110	True Confessions	428,588*
Oui	1,583,615	Signature	732,524	Motion Picture	427,263*
Elks Magazine	1,561,981	Flower & Garden	724,066*	Vogue Patterns	424,239

Canadian Daily Newspapers of Large Circulation

Source: Audit Bureau of Circulations' FAS-FAX Report of average paid circulation for 6 months ending Mar. 31, 1974. (†)Indicates 3 month circulation average.

As of Sept. 30, 1973, there were 105 English language and 12 French language daily newspapers in Canada (23 morning; 94 evening) with a combined circulation of 4,823,586. Sunday newspapers numbered 10 with a total circulation of 920,285. (m) Morning; (e) Evening. Brackets indicate joint publication.

Newspaper	Daily	Sunday	Newspaper	Daily	Sunday
Calgary Albertan (m)	*30,699		Regina Leader Post (e)	67,310	
Calgary Herald (e)	111,526		St. Catharines Standard (e)	†39,177	
Edmonton Journal (e)	162,560		St. John's Telegram (e)	*30,568	
Halifax Chronicle-Herald (m)	66,376		Saint John Telegraph-Journal (m)	{32,271	
Halifax Mail-Star (e)	49,398		Saint John Times Globe (e)	{28,456	
Hamilton Spectator (e)	†137,493		Saskatoon Star-Phoenix (e)	48,688	
Kitchener-Waterloo Record (e)	†62,860		Sherbrooke: La Tribune (e)	*48,888	
London Free Press (m & e)	128,856		Sudbury Star (e)	37,963	
Moncton Times (m)	{16,876		Toronto Globe and Mail (m)	*265,637	
Moncton Transcript (e)	{21,510		Toronto Star (e)	*506,924	
Montreal Gazette (m)	*129,182		Toronto Sun (m)	*104,503	
Montreal: La Presse (e)	*188,031		Vancouver Sun (e)	253,812	
Montreal: Le Devoir (m)	*41,787		Victoria Colonist (m)'	43,202	48,784
Montreal: Le Journal de Montreal (m)	*152,827		Victoria Times (e)	33,845	
Montreal-Matin (m)	*129,706	105,522	Windsor Star (e)	85,831	
Montreal Star (e)	*178,547		Winnipeg Free Press (e)	135,770	
Ottawa Citizen (e)	*94,453		Winnipeg Tribune (e)²	70,673	
Ottawa Journal (e)	90,038		(1) Excludes Monday; (2) Excludes Friday.		
Quebec: Le Soleil (e)	*133,172				

Circulation of Leading Canadian Magazines

Source: Audit Bureau of Circulations' FAS-FAX Report.

General and farm magazines, exclusive of groups and comics. Statistics based on average paid circulation during the 6 months prior to June 30, 1974. *Indicates circulation for the 6 months prior to June 30, 1973.

Magazine	Circulation	Magazine	Circulation	Magazine	Circulation
Reader's Digest		Maclean's Magazine (English)	741,980	T.W. Hebdo	235,926
(English-French)	1,524,670	Time Canada-The		Miss Chatelaine	161,354
Chatelaine (English-French)	1,264,754	Weekly Newsmagazine	557,713	La Maclean	154,417
Reader's Digest (English)	1,250,347	Legion Magazine	*321,680	Actualite	138,050
Chatelaine (English)	991,326	Selection du Reader's Digest	274,323	Canadian Motorist	113,323
Maclean's Magazine		Chatelaine (French)	273,428		
(English-French)	896,397				

Weights and Measures

Source: National Bureau of Standards, Department of Commerce

U.S. Moving, Inch by 25.4 mm, to Metric System

The U.S. is the only industrial country in the world which is not on the metric system and is not yet involved in an official changeover program. Sen. Claiborne Pell (D.-R.I.) has estimated that the U.S. loses $10 billion to $25 billion a year because U.S. measurements are not compatible with world standards.

On July 2, 1971, following the report of a metric conversion study committee, Commerce Secy. Maurice H. Stans recommended a gradual U.S. changeover during a 10-year period at the end of which the U.S. would be predominantly, but not exclusively, on the metric system. Proposals to that effect are now pending in Congress.

The International System (Metric)

Two systems of weights and measures exist side by side in the United States today, with roughly equal but separate legislative sanction: the U.S. Customary System and the International (Metric) System. Throughout U.S. history, the Customary System (inherited from, but now different from, the British Imperial System) has been, as its name implies, customarily used; a plethora of Federal and State legislation has given it, through implication, standing as our primary weights and measures system. However, the Metric System (incorporated in the scientists' new SI or Systeme International d'Unites is the only system that has ever received specific legislative sanction by Congress. The "Law of 1866" reads:

it shall be lawful throughout the United States of America to employ the weights and measures of the metric system; and no contract or dealing, or pleading in any court, shall be deemed invalid or liable to objection because the weights or measures expressed or referred to therein are weights or measures of the metric system.

Over the last 100 years, the Metric System has seen slow, steadily increasing use in the United States and, today, is of importance nearly equal to the Customary System.

On Feb. 10, 1964, the National Bureau of Standards issued the following bulletin:

Henceforth it shall be the policy of the National Bureau of Standards to use the units of the International System (SI), as adopted by the 11th General Conference on Weights and Measures (October 1960), except when the use of these units would obviously impair communication or reduce the usefulness of a report

What had been the Metric System became the International System (SI), a more complete scientific system.

Seven units have been adopted to serve as the base for the International System as follows: **Length**—meter; **Mass**—kilogram; **Time**—second; **Electric Current**—ampere; **Thermodynamic Temperature**—kelvin; **Amount of Substance**—mole; and **Light Intensity**—candela.

Prefixes

The following prefixes, in combination with the basic unit names, provide the multiples and submultiples in the International System. For example, the unit name "meter," with the prefix "kilo" added, produces "kilometer," meaning "1000 meters."

Prefix	Symbol	Multiples and Submultiples	Equivalent	Prefix	Symbol	Multiples and Submultiples	Equivalent
tera	T	10^{12}	trillionfold	centi	c	10^{-2}	hundredth part
giga	G	10^{9}	billionfold	milli	m	10^{-3}	thousandth part
mega	M	10^{6}	millionfold	micro	u	10^{-6}	millionth part
kilo	k	10^{3}	thousandfold	nano	n	10^{-9}	billionth part
hecto	h	10^{2}	hundredfold	pico	p	10^{-12}	trillionth part
deka	da	10	tenfold	femto	f	10^{-15}	quadrillionth part
deci	d	10^{-1}	tenth part	atto	a	10^{-18}	quintillionth part

Tables of Metric Weights and Measures

Linear Measure

10 millimeters (mm)	= 1 centimeter (cm)
10 centimeters	= 1 decimeter (dm) = 100 millimeters
10 decimeters	= 1 meter (m) = 1,000 millimeters
10 meters	= 1 dekameter (dam)
10 dekameters	= 1 hectometer (hm) = 100 meters
10 hectometers	= 1 kilometer (km) = 1,000 meters

Area Measure

100 square millimeters (mm²)	= 1 square centimeter (cm²)
10,000 square centimeters	= 1 square meter (m²) = 1,000,000 square millimeters
100 square meters	= 1 are (a)
100 ares	= 1 hectare (ha) = 10,000 square meters
100 hectares	= 1 square kilometer (km²) = 1,000,000 square meters

Volume Measure

10 milliliters (ml)	= 1 centiliter (cl)
10 centiliters	= 1 deciliter (dl) = 100 milliliters
10 deciliters	= 1 liter (l) = 1,000 milliliters
10 liters	= 1 dekaliter (dal)
10 dekaliters	= 1 hectoliter (hl) = 100 liters
10 hectoliters	= 1 kiloliter (kl) = 1,000 liters

Cubic Measure

1,000 cubic millimeters (mm³)	= 1 cubic centimeter (cm³)
1,000 cubic centimeters	= 1 cubic decimeter (dm²) = 1,000,000 cubic millimeters
1,000 cubic decimeters	= 1 cubic meter (m³) = 1 stere
1,000,000 cubic centimeters	= 1,000,000,000 cubic millimeters

Weight

10 milligrams (mg)	= 1 centigram (cg)
10 centigrams	= 1 decigram (dg) = 100 milligrams
10 decigrams	= 1 gram (g) = 1,000 milligrams
10 grams	= 1 dekagram (dag)
10 dekagrams	= 1 hectogram (hg) = 100 grams
10 hectograms	= 1 kilogram (kg) = 1,000 grams
1,000 kilograms	= 1 metric ton (t)

Table of United States Customary Weights and Measures

Linear Measure

12 inches (in.)	= 1 foot (ft.)
3 feet	= 1 yard (yd)
5½ yards	= 1 rod (rd), pole, or perch (16½ feet)
40 rods	= 1 furlong (fur) = 220 yards = 660 feet
8 furlongs	= 1 statute mile (mi) = 1,760 yards = 5,280 feet
3 miles	= 1 league = 5,280 yards = 15,840 feet
6076.11549 feet	= 1 International Nautical Mile

Liquid Measure

When necessary to distinguish the liquid pint or quart from the dry pint or quart, the word "liquid" or the abbreviation "liq" should be used in combination with the name or abbreviation of the liquid unit.

4 gills	= 1 pint (pt) = 28,875 cubic inches
2 pints	= 1 quart (qt) = 57.75 cubic inches
4 quarts	= 1 gallon (gal) = 31 cubic inches = 8 pints = 32 gills

Area Measure

Squares and cubes of units are sometimes abbreviated by using "superior" figures. For example, ft² means square foot, and ft³ means cubic foot.

144 square inches	=1 square foot (ft²)
9 square feet	=1 square yard (yd²)=1,296 square inches
30¼ square yards	=1 square rod (rd²)=272¼ square feet
160 square rods	=1 acre=4,840 square yards=43,560 square feet
640 acres	=1 square mile (mi²)
1 mile square	=1 section (of land)
6 miles square	=1 township=36 sections=36 square miles

Cubic Measure

1,728 cubic inches (in³)	=1 cubic foot (ft³)
27 cubic feet	=1 cubic yard (yd³)

Gunter's or Surveyors' Chain Measure

7.92 inches (in.)	=1 link
100 links	=1 chain (ch)=4 rods=66 feet
80 chains	=1 statute mile (mi)=320 rods =5,280 feet.

Troy Weight

24 grains	=1 pennyweight (dwt)
20 pennyweights	=1 ounce troy (oz t)=480 grains
12 ounces troy	=1 pound troy (lb t)=5,760 grains

Dry Measure

When necessary to distinguish the dry pint or quart from the liquid pint or quart, the word "dry" should be used in combination with the name or abbreviation of the dry unit.

2 pints (pt)	=1 quart (qt) =(67.2006 cubic inches)
8 quarts	=1 peck (pk) =(537.605 cubic inches) = 16 pints
4 pecks	=1 bushel (bu)=1,150.42 cubic inches =32 quarts

Avoirdupois Weight

When necessary to distinguish the avoirdupois ounce or pound from the troy ounce or pound, the word "avoirdupois" or the abbreviation "avdp" should be used in combination with the name or abbreviation of the avoirdupois unit.

(The "grain" is the same in avoirdupois and troy weight.)

27 11/32 grains	=1 dram (dr)
16 drams	=1 ounce (oz)=437½ grains
16 ounces	=1 pound (lb)=256 drams =7,000 grains
100 pounds	=1 hundredweight (cwt)°
20 hundredweights	=1 ton=2,000 pounds°

In "gross" or "long" measure, the following values are recognized:

112 pounds	=1 gross or long hundredweight°
20 gross or long hundredweights	=1 gross or long ton=2,240 pounds°

°When the terms "hundredweight" and "ton" are used unmodified, they are commonly understood to mean the 100-pound hundredweight and the 2,000-pound ton, respectively: these units may be designated "net" or "short" when necessary to distinguish them from the corresponding units in gross or long measure.

Tables of Equivalents

When the name of a unit is enclosed in brackets thus, [1 hand], this indicates (1) that the unit is not in general current use in the United States, or (2) that the unit is believed to be based on "custom and usage" rather than on formal definition. *See above about superior figures in Area Measure.*

Equivalents involving decimals are, in most instances, rounded off to the third decimal place except where they are exact, in which cases these exact equivalents are so designated.

Lengths

1 Angstrom (A)	0.1 nanometer (exactly) 0.000 1 micron (exactly) 0.000 000 1 millimeter (exactly) 0.000 000 004 inch
1 cable's length	120 fathoms 720 feet 219.456 meters (exactly)
1 centimeter (cm)	0.3937 inch
1 chain (ch) (Gunter's or surveyors)	66 feet 20.1168 meters (exactly)
1 chain (engineers)	100 feet 30.48 meters (exactly)
1 decimeter (dm)	3.937 inches
1 dekameter (dam)	32.808 feet
1 fathom	6 feet 1.8288 meters (exactly)
1 foot (ft)	0.3048 meters (exactly)
1 furlong (fur)	10 chains (surveyors) 660 feet 220 yards ⅛ statute mile 201.168 meters
[1 hand]	4 inches
1 inch (in.)	2.54 centimeters (exactly)
1 kilometer (km)	0.621 mile 3,280.8 feet
1 league (land)	3 statute miles 4.828 kilometers
1 link (Gunter's or surveyors)	7.92 inches 0.201 meter
1 link (engineers)	1 foot 0.305 meter
1 meter (m)	39.37 inches 1.094 yards
1 micron(μ) [the Greek letter mu]	0.001 millimeter (exactly) 0.000 039 37 inch
1 mil	0.001 inch (exactly) 0.025 4 millimeter (exactly)

1 mile (mi) (statute or land)	5,280 feet 1.609 kilometers
1 International Nautical Mile (INM)	1.852 kilometers (exactly) 1.150779 statute miles 6,076.11549 feet
1 millimeter (mm)	0.039 37 inch
1 nanometer (nm)	0.001 micron (exactly) 0.000 000 039 37 inch (exactly)
1 point (typography)	0.013 837 inch (exactly) 0.351 millimeter
1 rod (rd), pole, or perch	16½ ft. 5½ yards 5.029 meters
1 yard (yd)	0.9144 meter (exactly)

Areas or Surfaces

1 acre	43,560 square feet 4,840 square yards 0.405 hectare
1 are (a)	119.599 square yards 0.025 acre
1 hectare (ha)	2.171 acres
[1 square (building)]	100 square feet
1 square centimeter (cm²)	0.155 square inch
1 square decimeter (dm²)	15.500 square inches
1 square foot (ft²)	929.030 square centimeters
1 square inch (in²)	6.452 square centimeters
1 square kilometer (km2)	247.105 acres 0.386 square miles
1 square meter (m²)	1.196 square yards 10.764 square feet
1 square mile (mi²)	258.999 hectares
1 square millimeter (mm2)	0.002 square inch
1 square rod (rd²), sq. pole, or sq. perch	25.293 square meters
1 square yard (yd²)	0.836 square meters

Capacities or Volumes

1 barrel (bbl), liquid .... 31 to 42 gallons°

°There are a variety of "barrels", established by law or usage. For example: Federal taxes on fermented liquors are based on a barrel of 31 gallons; many State laws fix the "barrel for liquids" as 31½ gallons: one state fixes a 36-gallon barrel for cistern measurement; Federal law recognizes a 40-gallon barrel for "proof spirits"; by custom, 42 gallons conirise a barrel of crude oil or petroleum products for statistical purposes, and this equivalent is recognized "for liquids" by four states.

1 barrel (bbl), standard, for fruits, vegetables, and other dry commodities except cranberries.........	7,056 cubic inches 105 dry quarts 3.281 bushels, struck measure
1 barrel (bbl), standard, cranberry.................	5,826 cubic inches 86⁴⁵/₆₄ dry quarts 2.709 bushels, struck measure
1 bushel (bu) (U.S.) (struck measure)...........	2,150.42 cubic inches (exactly) 35.238 liters
[1 bushel, heaped (U.S.)]....	2,747.715 cubic inches 1.278 bushels, struck measure°

°Frequently recognized as 1¼ bushels, struck measure.

[1 bushel (bu) (British Imperial) (struck measure)].................	1.032 U.S. bushels, struck measure 2,219.36 cubic inches
1 cord (cd) (firewood).....................	128 cubic feet
1 cubic centimeter (cm³)...............	0.061 cubic inch
1 cubic decimeter (dm³)...............	61.024 cubic inches
1 cubic foot (ft³)...........	7.481 gallons 28.317 cubic decimeters
1 cubic inch (in.³)............	0.554 fluid ounce 4.433 fluid drams 16.387 cubic centimeters
1 cubic meter (m³)....................	1.308 cubic yards
1 cubic yard (yd.³)..............	0.765 cubic meter
1 cup, measuring.................	8 fluid ounces ½ liquid pint
[1 dram, fluid (fl dr) (British)]..	0.961 U.S. fluid dram 0.217 cubic inch 3.552 milliliters
1 dekaliter (dal).................	2.642 gallons 1.135 pecks
1 gallon (gal) (U.S.)..........	231 cubic inches 3.785 liters 0.833 British gallon 128 U.S. fluid ounces
[1 gallon (gal) (British) Imperial]....	277.42 cubic inches 1.201 U.S. gallons 4.546 liters 160 British fluid ounces
1 gill.............	7.219 cubic inches 4 fluid ounces 0.118 liter
1 hectoliter (hl).................	26.417 gallons 2.838 bushels
1 liter..............	1.057 liquid quarts 0.908 dry quart 61.024 cubic inches
1 milliliter (ml)............	0.271 fluid dram 16.231 minims 0.061 cubic inch
1 ounce, liquid (U.S.)................	1.805 cubic inches 29.573 milliliters 1.041 British fluid ounces
[1 ounce, fluid (fl oz) (British)]	0.961 U.S. fluid ounce 1.734 cubic inches 28.412 milliliters
1 peck (pk).......................	8.810 liters
1 pint (pt), dry.............	33.600 cubic inches 0.551 liter
1 pint (pt) liquid...........	28.875 cubic inches (exactly) 0.473 liter

1 quart (qt.) dry (U.S.)......	67.201 cubic inches 1.101 liters 0.969 British quart
1 quart (qt.) liquid (U.S.)......	57.75 cubic in. (exactly) 0.946 liter 0.833 British quart
[1 quart (qt) (British)]......	69.354 cubic inches 1.032 U.S. dry quarts 1.201 U.S. liquid quarts
1 tablespoon...................	3 teaspoons° 4 fluid drams ½ fluid ounce
1 teaspoon....................	⅓ tablespoon° 1⅓ fluid drams°

°The equivalent "1 teaspoon — 1½ fluid drams" has been found by the Bureau to correspond more closely with the actual capacities of "measuring" and silver teaspoons than the equivalent "1 teaspoon — 1 fluid dram" which is given by a number of dictionaries.

Weights or Masses

1 assay ton∞ (AT)................29.167 grams	

∞Used in assaying. The assay ton bears the same relation to the milligram that a ton of 2000 pounds avoirdupois bears to the ounce troy; hence the weight in milligrams of precious metal obtained from one assay ton of ore gives directly the number of troy ounces to the net ton.

1 carat (c).......................	200 milligrams 3.086 grains
1 dram avoirdupois (dr avdp).	27¹¹/₃₂ (=27.344) grains 1.772 grams
gamma, see microgram	
1 grain...................	64.799 milligrams
1 gram (g)...............	15.432 grains 0.035 ounce, avoirdupois
1 hundredweight, gross or long∞ (gross cwt).......	112 pounds 50.802 kilograms
1 hundredweight, net or short (cwt. or net cwt.).......	100 pounds 45.359 kilograms
1 kilogram (kg)...............	2.205 pounds
1 microgram (γ [the Greek letter gamma])...............	0.000,001 gram (exactly)
1 milligram (mg.).................	0.015 grain
1 ounce, avoirdupois (oz avdp)...............	437.5 grains (exactly) 0.911 troy ounce 28.350 grams
1 ounce, troy (oz t)........	480 grains 1.097 avoirdupois ounces 31.103 grams
1 pennyweight (dwt).......	1.555 grams
1 pound, avoirdupois (lb avdp)................	7,000 grains 1.215 troy pounds 453.592 37 grams (exactly)
1 pound, troy (lb t)......	5,760 grains 0.823 avoirdupois pound 373.242 grams
1 ton, gross or long ∞ (gross tn).........	2,240 pounds 1.12 net tons (exactly) 1.016 metric tons

∞∞The gross or long ton and hundredweight are used commercially in the United States to only a limited extent, usually in restricted industrial fields. These units are the same as British "ton" and "hundredweight."

1 ton, metric (t)...........	2,204.623 pounds 0.984 gross ton 1.102 net tons
1 ton, net or short (sh ton)...	2,000 pounds 0.893 gross ton 0.907 metric ton

---

Density of Gases and Vapors

Source: National Bureau of Standards (Grams per liter)

Gas	Wt.	Gas	Wt.	Gas	Wt.
Acetylene................	1.171	Ethylene.................	1.260	Methyl fluoride........	1.545
Air....................	1.293	Fluorine.................	1.696	Mono methylamine........	1.38
Ammonia...............	.759	Helium..................	.178	Neon.................	.900
Argon..................	1.784	Hydrogen................	.090	Nitric oxide............	1.341
Arsene.................	3.48	Hydrogen bromide........	3.50	Nitrogen................	1.250
Butane-iso.............	2.60	Hydrogen chloride........	1.639	Nitrosyl chloride........	2.99
Butane-n...............	2.519	Hydrogen iodide.........	5.724	Nitrous oxide...........	1.997
Carbon dioxide.........	1.977	Hydrogen selenide........	3.66	Oxygen................	1.429
Carbon monoxide.......	1.250	Hydrogen sulfide........	1.539	Phosphine.............	1.48
Carbon oxysulfide........	2.72	Krypton.................	3.745	Propane................	2.020
Chlorine................	3.214	Methane................	.717	Silicon tetrafluoride......	4.67
Chlorine monoxide.......	3.89	Methyl chloride.........	2.25	Sulfur dioxide..........	2.927
Ethane.................	1.356	Methyl ether...........	2.091	Xenon..................	5.897

Tables of Interrelation of Units of Measurement

Bold face type indicates exact values

Units of Length

Units	Inches	Links	Feet	Yards	Rods	Chains	Miles	Cm.	Meters
1 inch =	**1**	0.126 263	0.083 333	0.027 778	0.005 051	0.001 263	0.000 016	**2.54**	0.025 4
1 link =	**7.92**	**1**	**0.66**	**0.22**	**0.04**	**0.01**	0.000 125	20.117	0.201 168
1 foot =	**12**	1.515 152	**1**	0.333 333	0.060 606	0.015 152	0.000 189	**30.48**	0.304 8
1 yard =	**36**	4.545 45	**3**	**1**	0.181 818	0.045 455	0.000 568	**91.44**	0.914 4
1 rod =	**198**	**25**	**16.5**	**5.5**	**1**	0.25	0.003 125	502.92	5.029 2
1 chain =	**792**	**100**	**66**	**22**	**4**	**1**	0.012 5	2011.68	20.116 8
1 mile =	**63,360**	**8000**	**5280**	**1760**	**320**	**80**	**1**	160 934.4	1609.344
1 cm =	0.3937	0.049 710	0.032 808	0.010 936	0.001 988	0.000 497	0.000 006	**1**	**0.01**
1 meter =	39.37	4.970 970	3.280 840	1.093 613	0.198 839	0.049 710	0.000 621	**100**	**1**

Units of Area

Units	Sq. inches	Sq. links	Sq. feet	Sq. yards	Sq. rods	Sq. chains
1 sq. inch =	**1**	.015 942 3	0.006 944	0.000 771 605	0.000 025 5	0.000 001 594
1 sq. link =	62.726 4	**1**	0.435 6	0.0484	0.0016	**0.000 1**
1 sq. foot =	**144**	2.295 684	**1**	0.111 111 1	0.003 673 09	0.000 229 568
1 sq. yard =	**1296**	20.661 16	**9**	**1**	0.033 057 85	0.002 066 12
1 sq. rod =	**39 204**	**625**	**272.25**	**30.25**	**1**	**0.062 5**
1 sq. chain =	**627 264**	**10 000**	**4356**	**484**	**16**	**1**
1 acre =	**6 272 640**	**100 000**	**43 560**	**4 840**	**160**	**10**
1 sq. mile =	**4 014 489 600**	**64 000 000**	**27 878 400**	**3 097 600**	**102 400**	**6400**
1 sq. cm =	0.155 000 3	0.002 471 05	0.001 076	0.000 119 599	0.000 003 954	0.000 000 247
1 sq. meter =	1550.003	24.710 54	10.763 91	1.195 990	0.039 536 86	0.002 471 054
1 hectare =	**15 500 031**	**247,105**	107 639.1	11 959.90	395.368 6	24.710 54

Units	Acres	Sq. miles	Sq. cm	Sq. meters	Hectares
1 sq. inch =	0.000 000 159 423	0.000 000 000 249 10	**6.451 6**	**0.000 645 16**	0.000 000 065
1 sq. link =	**0.000 01**	**0.000 000 015 625**	404.685 642 24	0.040 468 56	0.000 004 047
1 sq. foot =	0.000 022 956 84	0.000 000 035 870 06	929.030 4	**0.092 903 04**	0.000 009 290
1 sq. yard =	0.000 206 611 6	0.000 000 322 830 6	8 361.273 6	**0.836 127 36**	0.000 083 613
1 sq. rod =	**0.006 25**	**0.000 009 765 625**	252 928.526 4	25.292 852 64	0.002 529 285
1 sq. chain =	**0.1**	**0.000 156 25**	4 046 856	404.685 642 24	0.040 468 564
1 acre =	**1**	**0.001 562 5**	40 468 564	4046.856 422 4	0.404 685 642
1 sq. mile =	**640**	**1**	25 899 881 103	2 589 988.11	258.998 811 034
1 sq. cm =	0.000 000 024 711	0.000 000 000 038 610	**1**	**0.000 1**	**0.000 000 01**
1 sq. meter =	0.000 247 105 4	0.000 000 000 386 102 2	**10 000**	**1**	**0.0001**
1 hectare =	2.471 054	0.003 861 022	**100 000 000**	**10 000**	**1**

Units of Mass Not Greater Than Pounds and Kilograms

Units	Grains	Pennyweights	Avdp. Drams	Avdp. Ounces
1 grain =	**1**	0.041 666 67	0.036 571 43	0.002 285 71
1 pennyweight =	**24**	**1**	0.877 714 3	0.054 857 14
1 dram avdp. =	27.343 75	1.139 323	**1**	**0.062 5**
1 ounce avdp. =	437.5	18.229 17	**16**	**1**
1 ounce troy =	**480**	**20**	17.554 29	1.097 143
1 pound troy =	**5760**	**240**	210.651 4	13.165 71
1 pound avdp. =	**7000**	291.666 7	**256**	**16**
1 milligram =	0.015 432	0.000 643 015	0.000 564 383	0.000 035 274
1 gram =	15.432 36	0.643 014 9	0.564 383 4	0.035 273 96
1 kilogram =	15 432.36	643.014 9	564.383 4	35.273 96

Units	Troy ounces	Troy pounds	Avdp. pounds	Milligrams	Grams	Kilograms
1 grain =	0.002 083 33	0.000 173 611	0.000 142 857	64.798 91	0.064 798 91	0.000 064 799
1 pennyw't. =	0.05	0.004 166 667	0.003 428 571	1555.173 84	1.555 173 84	0.001 555 174
1 dram avdp. =	0.056 966 15	0.004 747 179	0.003 906 25	1771.845 195	1.771 845 195	0.001 771 845
1 oz. avdp. =	0.911 458 3	0.075 954 86	**0.062 5**	28 349.523 125	28.349 523 125	0.028 349 52
1 oz. troy =	**1**	0.083 333 333	0.068 571 43	31 103.476 8	31.103 476 8	0.031 103 48
1 lb. troy =	**12**	**1**	0.822 857 1	373 241.721 6	373.241 721 6	0.373 241 722
1 lb. avdp. =	14.583 33	1.215 278	**1**	453 592.37	453 592.37	0.453 592 37
1 milligram =	0.000 032 151	0.000 002 679	0.000 002 205	**1**	**0.001**	**0.000 001**
1 gram =	0.032 150 75	0.002 679 229	0.002 204 623	**1000**	**1**	**0.001**
1 kilogram =	32.150 75	2.679 229	2.204 623	**1000 000**	**1000**	**1**

Units of Mass Not Less Than Avoirdupois Ounces

Units	Avdp. oz.	Avdp. lbs.	Short cwt.	Short tons	Long tons	Kilograms	Metric tons
1 oz. av. =	**1**	**0.0625**	**0.000 625**	0.000 031 25	0.000 027 902	0.028 349 523	0.000 028 350
1 lb. av. =	**16**	**1**	**0.01**	**0.000 5**	0.000 446 429	0.453 592 37	0.000 453 592
1 sh. cwt. =	**1 600**	**100**	**1**	**0.05**	0.044 642 86	45.359 237	0.045 359 237
1 sh. ton =	**32 000**	**2000**	**20**	**1**	0.892 857 1	907.184 74	0.907 184 74
1 long ton =	**35 840**	**2240**	**22.4**	**1.12**	**1**	1016.046 908 8	1.016 046 909
1 kg =	35.273 96	2.204 623	0.022 046 23	0.001 102 311	0.000 984 207	**1**	**0.001**
1 metric ton =	35 273.96	2204.623	22.046 23	1.102 311	0.984 206 5	**1000**	**1**

Continued on next page

Continued from previous page

Units of Volume

Units	Cubic inches	Cubic feet	Cubic yards	Cubic cm.	Cubic dm.	Cubic meters
1 cubic inch =	**1**	0.000 578 704	0.000 021 433	**16.387 064**	0.016 387	0.000 016 387
1 cubic foot =	**1728**	**1**	0.037 037 04	**28 316.846 592**	28.316 847	0.028 316 847
1 cubic yard =	**46 656**	**27**	**1**	**764 554.857 984**	764.554 858	0.764 554 858
1 cubic cm =	0.061 023 74	0.000 035 315	0.000 001 308	**1**	**0.001**	**0.000 001**
1 cubic dm =	61.023 74	0.035 314 67	0.001 307 951	**1 000**	**1**	**0.001**
1 cubic meter =	61 023.74	35.314 67	1.307 951	**1 000 000**	**1000**	**1**

Units of Capacity (Liquid Measure)

Units	Minims	Fluid drams	Fluid ounces	Gills	Liquid pt.
1 minim =	**1**	0.016 666 7	0.002 083 33	0.000 520 833	0.000 130 208
1 liquid dram =	**60**	**1**	**0.125**	**0.031 25**	**0.007 812 5**
1 liquid ounce =	**480**	**8**	**1**	**0.25**	**0.062 5**
1 gill =	**1920**	**32**	**4**	**1**	**0.25**
1 liquid pint =	**7680**	**128**	**16**	**4**	**1**
1 liquid quart =	**15 360**	**256**	**32**	**8**	**2**
1 gallon =	**61 440**	**1024**	**128**	**32**	**8**
1 cubic inch =	265.974	4.432 900	0.554 112 6	0.138 528 1	0.034 632 03
1 cubic foot =	459 603.1	7660.052	957.506 5	239.376 6	59.844 16
1 milliliter =	16.230 73	0.270 512 18	0.033 814 02	0.008 453 506	.002 113 376
1 liter =	16 230.73	270.512 18	33.814 02	8.453 506	2.113 376

Units	Liquid quarts	Gallons	Cubic inches	Cubic feet	Liters
1 minim =	0.000 065 104 17	0.000 016 276 04	0.003 759 766	0.000 002 175 790	0.000 061 611 52
1 liq. dram =	**0.003 906 25**	**0.000 976 562 5**	0.225 585 9	0.000 130 547 4	0.003 696 691
1 liquid oz. =	**0.031 25**	**0.007 812 5**	1.804 687 5	0.001 044 379	0.029 573 53
1 gill =	**0.125**	**0.031 25**	**7.218 75**	**0.004 177 517**	**0.118 294 118 25**
1 liquid pt. =	**0.5**	**0.125**	**28.875**	0.016 710 07	**0.473 176 473**
1 liquid qt. =	**1**	**0.25**	**57.75**	0.033 420 14	**0.946 352 946**
1 gallon =	**4**	**1**	**231**	0.133 680 6	**3.785 411 784**
1 cubic in. =	0.017 316 02	0.004 329 004	**1**	0.000 578 703 7	**0.016 387 064**
1 cubic foot =	29.922 08	7.480 519	**1728**	**1**	**28.316 846 592**
1 liter =	1.056 688	0.264 172 05	61.023 74	0.035 314 67	**1**

Units of Capacity (Dry Measure)

Units	Dry pints	Dry quarts	Pecks	Bushels	Cubic in.	Liters
1 dry pint =	**1**	**0.5**	**0.062 5**	**0.015 625**	**33.600 312 5**	0.550 610 47
1 dry quart =	**2**	**1**	**0.125**	**0.031 25**	**67.200 625**	1.101 220 9
1 peck =	**16**	**8**	**1**	**0.25**	**537.605**	8.809 767 5
1 bushel =	**64**	**32**	**4**	**1**	**2150.42**	35.239 07
1 cubic inch =	**0.029 761 6**	0.014 880 8	0.001 860 10	0.000 465 025	**1**	**0.016 387 064**
1 liter =	1.816 166	0.908 083	0.113 510 37	0.028 377 59	61.023 74	**1**

Weight of Water

1	cubic inch	.0360	pound
12	cubic inches	.433	pound
1	cubic foot	62.4	pounds
1	cubic foot	7.48052	U.S gals.
1.8	cubic feet	112.0	pounds
35.96	cubic feet	2240.0	pounds
1	imperial gallon	10.0	pounds
11.2	imperial gallons	112.0	pounds
224	imperial gallons	2240.0	pounds
1	U. S. gallon	8.33	pounds
13.45	U.S. gallons	112.0	pounds
269.0	U. S. gallons	2240.0	pounds

Temperature Conversion Table

The numbers in **bold face type** refer to the temperature either in degrees Celsius or Fahrenheit which are to be converted. If converting from degrees Fahrenheit to Celsius, the equivalent will be found in the column on the left, while if converting from degrees Celsius to Fahrenheit the answer will be found in the column on the right.

For temperatures not shown. To convert Fahrenheit to Celsius subtract 32 degrees and multiply by 5, divide by 9; to convert Celsius to Fahrenheit, multiply by 9, divide by 5 and add 32 degrees.

Celsius		Fahrenheit	Celsius		Fahrenheit	Celsius		Fahrenheit
—273.2	**—459.7**	....	— 17.8	**0**	32	35.0	**95**	203
—184	**—300**	....	— 12.2	**10**	50	36.7	**98**	208.4
—169	**—273**	—459.4	— 6.67	**20**	68	37.8	**100**	212
—157	**—250**	—418	— 1.11	**30**	86	43	**110**	230
—129	**—200**	—328	4.44	**40**	104	49	**120**	248
—101	**—150**	—238	10.0	**50**	122	54	**130**	266
— 73.3	**—100**	—148	15.6	**60**	140	60	**140**	284
— 45.6	**— 50**	— 58	21.1	**70**	158	66	**150**	302
— 40.0	**— 40**	— 40	23.9	**75**	167	93	**200**	392
— 34.4	**— 30**	— 22	26.7	**80**	176	121	**250**	482
— 28.9	**— 20**	— 4	29.4	**85**	185	149	**300**	572
— 23.3	**— 10**	14	32.2	**90**	194			

Water boils at 212° Fahrenheit at sea level. For every 550 feet above-sea level, boiling point of water is lower by about 1° Fahrenheit. Methyl alcohol boils at 148° Fahrenheit. Average human oral temperature, 98.6° Fahrenheit. Water freezes at 32° Fahrenheit. Although "Centigrade" is still frequently used, the International Committee on Weights and Measures and the National Bureau of Standards have recommended since 1948 that this scale be called "Celsius."

Squares, Square Roots, Cubes and Cube Roots of Nos. 1 to 100

No.	Sq.	Cube	Sq. Root	Cube Root	No.	Sq.	Cube	Sq. Root	Cube Root	No.	Sq.	Cube	Sq. Root	Cube Root
1	1.000	1.000	1.000	1.000	35	1225	42875	5.916	3.271	68	4624	314432	8.246	4.081
2	4	8	1.414	1.259	36	1296	46656	6.000	3.301	69	4761	328509	8.306	4.101
3	9	27	1.732	1.442	37	1369	50653	6.082	3.332	70	4900	343000	8.366	4.121
4	16	64	2.000	1.587	38	1444	54872	6.164	3.362	71	5041	357911	8.426	4.140
5	25	125	2.236	1.710	39	1521	59319	6.245	3.391	72	5184	373248	8.485	4.160
6	36	216	2.449	1.817	40	1600	64000	6.324	3.420	73	5329	389017	8.544	4.179
7	49	343	2.645	1.913	41	1681	68921	6.403	3.448	74	5476	405224	8.602	4.198
8	64	512	2.828	2.000	42	1764	74088	6.480	3.476	75	5625	421875	8.660	4.217
9	81	729	3.000	2.080	43	1849	79507	6.557	3.503	76	5776	438976	8.717	4.235
10	100	1000	3.162	2.154	44	1936	85184	6.633	3.530	77	5929	456533	8.775	4.254
11	121	1331	3.316	2.224	45	2025	91125	6.708	3.556	78	6084	474552	8.831	4.272
12	144	1728	3.464	2.289	46	2116	97336	6.782	3.583	79	6241	493039	8.888	4.290
13	169	2197	3.605	2.351	47	2209	103823	6.855	3.608	80	6400	512000	8.944	4.308
14	196	2744	3.741	2.410	48	2304	110592	6.928	3.634	81	6561	531441	9.000	4.326
15	225	3375	3.873	2.466	49	2401	117649	7.000	3.659	82	6724	551368	9.055	4.344
16	256	4096	4.000	2.519	50	2500	125000	7.071	3.684	83	6889	571787	9.110	4.362
17	289	4913	4.123	2.571	51	2601	132651	7.141	3.708	84	7056	592704	9.165	4.379
18	324	5832	4.242	2.620	52	2704	140608	7.211	3.732	85	7225	614125	9.219	4.396
19	361	6859	4.358	2.668	53	2809	148877	7.280	3.756	86	7396	636056	9.273	4.414
20	400	8000	4.472	2.714	54	2916	157464	7.348	3.779	87	7569	658503	9.327	4.431
21	441	9261	4.582	2.758	55	3025	166375	7.416	3.803	88	7744	681472	9.380	4.448
22	484	10648	4.690	2.802	56	3136	175616	7.483	3.825	89	7921	704969	9.434	4.464
23	529	12167	4.795	2.843	57	3249	185193	7.549	3.848	90	8100	729000	9.486	4.481
24	576	13824	4.899	2.884	58	3364	195112	7.615	3.870	91	8281	753571	9.539	4.497
25	625	15625	5.000	2.924	59	3481	205379	7.681	3.893	92	8464	778688	9.591	4.514
26	676	17576	5.099	2.962	60	3600	216000	7.746	3.914	93	8649	804357	9.643	4.530
27	729	19683	5.196	3.000	61	3721	226981	7.810	3.936	94	8836	830584	9.695	4.546
28	784	21952	5.291	3.036	62	3844	238328	7.874	3.957	95	9025	857375	9.746	4.562
29	841	24389	5.385	3.072	63	3969	250047	7.937	3.979	96	9216	884736	9.798	4.578
30	900	27000	5.477	3.107	64	4096	262144	8.000	4.000	97	9409	912673	9.848	4.594
31	961	29791	5.567	3.141	65	4225	274625	8.062	4.020	98	9604	941192	9.899	4.610
32	1024	32768	5.656	3.174	66	4356	287496	8.124	4.041	99	9801	970299	9.949	4.626
33	1089	25937	5.744	3.207	67	4489	300763	8.185	4.061	100	10000	1000000	10.000	4.641
34	1156	39304	5.831	3.239										

Square Roots and Cube Roots, 1000 to 2000

No.	Square Root	Cube Root	No.	Square Root	Cube Root	No.	Square Root	Cube Root	No.	Square Root	Cube Root
1000	31.62	10.00	1255	35.43	10.79	1510	38.86	11.47	1765	42.01	12.09
1005	31.70	10.02	1260	35.50	10.80	1515	38.92	11.49	1770	42.07	12.10
1010	31.78	10.03	1265	35.57	10.82	1520	38.99	11.50	1775	42.13	12.11
1020	31.94	10.07	1275	35.71	10.84	1530	39.12	11.52	1785	42.25	12.13
1025	32.02	10.08	1280	35.78	10.86	1535	39.18	11.54	1790	42.31	12.14
1030	32.09	10.10	1285	35.85	10.87	1540	39.24	11.55	1795	42.37	12.15
1035	32.17	10.12	1290	35.92	10.89	1545	39.31	11.56	1800	42.43	12.16
1045	32.33	10.15	1300	36.06	10.91	1555	39.43	11.59	1810	42.54	12.19
1050	32.40	10.16	1305	36.12	10.93	1560	39.50	11.60	1815	42.60	12.20
1060	32.56	10.20	1315	36.26	10.96	1570	39.62	11.62	1825	42.72	12.22
1065	32.63	10.21	1320	36.33	10.97	1575	39.69	11.63	1830	42.78	12.23
1075	32.79	10.24	1330	36.47	11.00	1585	39.81	11.66	1840	42.90	12.25
1080	32.86	10.26	1335	36.54	11.01	1590	39.87	11.67	1845	42.95	12.26
1085	32.94	10.28	1340	36.61	11.02	1595	39.94	11.68	1850	43.01	12.28
1090	33.02	10.29	1345	36.67	11.04	1600	40.00	11.70	1855	43.07	12.29
1095	33.09	10.31	1350	36.74	11.05	1605	40.06	11.71	1860	43.13	12.30
1100	33.17	10.32	1355	36.81	11.07	1610	40.12	11.72	1865	43.19	12.31
1105	33.24	10.34	1360	36.88	11.08	1615	40.19	11.73	1870	43.24	12.32
1110	33.32	10.35	1365	36.95	11.09	1625	40.31	11.76	1875	43.30	12.33
1115	33.39	10.37	1370	37.01	11.11	1630	40.37	11.77	1880	43.36	12.34
1120	33.47	10.38	1375	37.08	11.12	1635	40.44	11.78	1885	43.42	12.35
1125	33.54	10.40	1380	37.15	11.13	1640	40.50	11.79	1890	43.47	12.36
1130	33.62	10.42	1385	37.22	11.15	1645	40.56	11.80	1895	43.53	12.37
1135	33.69	10.43	1390	37.28	11.16	1650	40.62	11.82	1900	43.59	12.39
1140	33.76	10.45	1395	37.35	11.17	1655	40.68	11.83	1905	43.65	12.40
1145	33.84	10.46	1400	37.42	11.19	1660	40.74	11.84	1910	43.70	12.41
1150	33.91	10.48	1405	37.48	11.20	1665	40.80	11.85	1915	43.76	12.42
1155	33.99	10.49	1410	37.55	11.21	1670	40.87	11.86	1920	43.82	12.43
1160	34.06	10.51	1415	37.62	11.23	1675	40.93	11.88	1925	43.87	12.44
1165	34.13	10.52	1420	37.68	11.24	1680	40.99	11.89	1930	43.93	12.45
1170	34.21	10.54	1425	37.75	11.25	1685	41.05	11.90	1935	43.99	12.46
1175	34.28	10.55	1430	37.82	11.27	1690	41.11	11.91	1940	44.05	12.47
1180	34.35	10.57	1435	37.88	11.28	1695	41.17	11.92	1945	44.10	12.48
1185	34.42	10.58	1440	37.95	11.29	1700	41.23	11.93	1950	44.16	12.49
1190	34.50	10.60	1445	38.01	11.31	1705	41.29	11.95	1955	44.22	12.50
1195	34.57	10.61	1450	38.08	11.32	1710	41.35	11.96	1960	44.27	12.51
1200	34.64	10.63	1455	38.14	11.33	1715	41.41	11.97	1965	44.33	12.53
1205	34.71	10.64	1460	38.21	11.34	1720	41.47	11.98	1970	44.38	12.54
1210	34.79	10.66	1465	32.28	11.36	1725	41.53	11.99	1975	44.44	12.55
1215	34.86	10.67	1470	38.34	11.37	1730	41.59	12.00	1980	44.50	12.56
1220	34.93	10.69	1475	38.41	11.38	1735	41.65	12.02	1985	44.55	12.57
1225	35.00	10.70	1480	38.47	11.40	1745	41.77	12.04	1990	44.61	12.58
1235	35.14	10.73	1490	38.60	11.42	1755	41.89	12.06	1995	44.67	12.59
1245	35.28	10.76	1500	38.73	11.45				2000	44.72	12.60

Electrical Units

The watt is the unit of power (electrical, mechanical, thermal, etc.). Electrical power is given by the product of the voltage and the current.

Energy is sold by the joule, but in common practice the billing of electrical energy is expressed in terms of the kilowatt-hour, which is 3,600,000 joules or 3.6 megajoules.

The horsepower is a non-metric unit sometimes used in mechanics. It is equal to 746 watts.

The ohm is the unit of electrical resistance and represents the physical property of a conductor which offers a resistance to the flow of electricity, permitting just 1-ampere to flow at 1 volt of pressure.

Mathematical Formulas

To find the CIRCUMFERENCE of a:

Circle — Multiply the diameter by 3.14159265 (usually 3.1416).—

To find the AREA of a:

Circle—Multiply the square of the diameter by .785398 (usually .7854).

Rectangle—Multiply the length of the base by the height.

Sphere (surface)—Multiply the square of the radius by 3.1416 and multiply by 4.

Square—Square the length of one side.

Trapezoid—add the two parallel sides, multiply by the height and divide by 2.

Triangle—Multiply the base by the height and divide by 2.

To find the VOLUME of a:

Cone—Multiply the square of the radius of the base by 3.1416, multiply by the height, and divide by 3.

Cube—Cube the length of one edge.

Cylinder—Multiply the square of the radius of the base by 3.1416 and multiply by the height.

Pyramid—Multiply the area of the base by the height and divide by 3.

Rectangular Prism—Multiply the length by the width by the height.

Sphere—Multiply the cube of the radius by 3.1416, multiply by 4 and divide by 3.

Multiplication and Division Table

A number in the top line (19) multiplied by a number in the last column on the left (18) produces the number where the top line and the side line meet (342), and so on throughout the table.

A number in the table (342) divided by the number at the top of that column (19) results in the number (18) at the extreme left; also, a number in the table (342) divided by the number (18) at the extreme left gives the number (19) at the top of the column, and so on throughout the table.

1	2	3	4	5	6	7	8	9	10	11	12	13	14	15	16	17	18	19	20	21	22	23	24	25	
2	4	6	8	10	12	14	16	18	20	22	24	26	28	30	32	34	36	38	40	42	44	46	48	50	2
3	6	9	12	15	18	21	24	27	30	33	36	39	42	45	48	51	54	57	60	63	66	69	72	75	3
4	8	12	16	20	24	28	32	36	40	44	48	52	56	60	64	68	72	76	80	84	88	92	96	100	4
5	10	15	20	25	30	35	40	45	50	55	60	65	70	75	80	85	90	95	100	105	110	115	120	125	5
6	12	18	24	30	36	42	48	54	60	66	72	78	84	90	96	102	108	114	120	126	132	138	144	150	6
7	14	21	28	35	42	49	56	63	70	77	84	91	98	105	112	119	126	133	140	147	154	161	168	175	7
8	16	24	32	40	48	56	64	72	80	88	96	104	112	120	128	136	144	152	160	168	176	184	192	200	8
9	18	27	36	45	54	63	72	81	90	99	108	117	126	135	144	153	162	171	180	189	198	207	216	225	9
10	20	30	40	50	60	70	80	90	100	110	120	130	140	150	160	170	180	190	200	210	220	230	240	250	10
11	22	33	44	55	66	77	88	99	110	121	132	143	154	165	176	187	198	209	220	231	242	253	264	275	11
12	24	36	48	60	72	84	96	108	120	132	144	156	168	180	192	204	216	228	240	252	264	276	288	300	12
13	26	39	52	65	78	91	104	117	130	143	156	169	182	195	208	221	234	247	260	273	286	299	312	325	13
14	28	42	56	70	84	98	112	126	140	154	168	182	196	210	224	238	252	266	280	294	308	322	336	350	14
15	30	45	60	75	90	105	120	135	150	165	180	195	210	225	240	255	270	285	300	315	330	345	360	375	15
16	32	48	64	80	96	112	128	144	160	176	192	208	224	240	256	272	288	304	320	336	352	368	384	400	16
17	34	51	68	85	102	119	136	153	170	187	204	221	238	255	272	289	306	323	340	357	374	391	408	425	17
18	36	54	72	90	108	126	144	162	180	198	216	234	252	270	288	306	324	342	360	378	396	414	432	450	18
19	38	57	76	95	114	133	152	171	190	209	228	247	266	285	304	323	342	361	380	399	418	437	456	475	19
20	40	60	80	100	120	140	160	180	200	220	240	260	280	300	320	340	360	380	400	420	440	460	480	500	20
21	42	63	84	105	126	147	168	189	210	231	252	273	294	315	336	357	378	399	420	441	462	483	504	525	21
22	44	66	88	110	132	154	176	198	220	242	264	286	308	330	352	374	396	418	440	462	484	506	528	550	22
23	46	69	92	115	138	161	184	207	230	253	276	299	322	345	368	391	414	437	460	483	506	529	552	575	23
24	48	72	96	120	144	168	192	216	240	264	288	312	336	360	384	408	432	456	480	504	528	552	576	600	24
25	50	75	100	125	150	175	200	225	250	275	300	325	350	375	400	425	450	475	500	525	550	575	600	625	25
	2	3	4	5	6	7	8	9	10	11	12	13	14	15	16	17	18	19	20	21	22	23	24	25	

Common Fractions Reduced to Decimals

8ths	16ths	32ds	64ths		8ths	16ths	32ds	64ths		8ths	16ths	32ds	64ths	
			1	.015625				23	.359375				45	.703125
		1	2	.03125	3	6	12	24	.375				46	.71875
			3	.046875				25	.390625				47	.734375
	1	2	4	.0625				26	.40625	6	12	24	48	.75
			5	.078125				27	.421875				49	.765625
		3	6	.09375		7	14	28	.4375				50	.78125
			7	.109375				29	.453125			25	51	.796875
1	2	4	8	.125			15	30	.46875				52	.8125
			9	.140625				31	.484375		13	26	53	.828125
		5	10	.15625	4	8	16	32	.5				54	.84375
			11	.171875				33	.515625			27	55	.859375
	3	6	12	.1875			17	34	.53125	7	14	28	56	.875
			13	.203125				35	.546875				57	.890625
		7	14	.21875		9	18	36	.5625			29	58	.90625
			15	.234375				37	.578125				59	.921875
2	4	8	16	.25			19	38	.59375		15	30	60	.9375
			17	.265625				39	.609375				61	.953125
		9	18	.28125	5	10	20	40	.625			31	62	.96875
			19	.296875				41	.640625				63	.984375
	5	10	20	.3125			21	42	.65625	8	16	32	64	1.
			21	.328125				43	.671875					
		11	22	.34375		11	22	44	.6875					

World Weights and Measures

Source: National Bureau of Standards, Department of Commerce

Denominations	Where Used	Amer. Equiv.
Almude	Portugal	4.423 gal
Ardeb	Egypt	5.6189 bu
Arratel (Libra)	Portugal	1.012 lb
Arroba	Argentina	25.32 lb
"	Brazil	32.38 lb
"	Cuba	25.36 lb
"	Paraguay	25.32 lb
"	Venezuela	25.40 lb
" (liquid)	Cuba, Spain and Venezuela	4.263 gal
Arshine	USSR	28 in
" (sq)	"	5.44 sq ft
Artel	Morocco	1.12 lb
Baril	Argentina and	20.077 gal
	Mexico	20.0787 gal
Barile (wine)	Malta	11.2 gal
Berkovets	USSR	361.128 lb
Bongkal	Malaysia	832 grains
Bouw	Sumatra	7,096.5 sq meter
Bu	Japan	0.12 inch
Bushel	British	1.03205 U.S. bu
Caballeria	Cuba	33.162 acres
Caban (cavan)	Philippines	2.13 bu
		19.8 gal
Caffiso	Malta	5.40 gal
Candy	Bombay	560 lb
"	India (Madras)	500 lb
Cantaro	Malta	175 lb
Carat (metric)	World	3.086 grains
Catty	China	1.333¹/₃ lb
" (see Kin)	Japan	
"	Java, Malacca	1.36 lb
"	Thailand	2²/₃ lb
" (stand)	Thailand	1.32 lb
"	Sumatra	2.12 lb
Centaro	Central America	4.2631 gal
Centner	Brunswick	117.5 lb
"	Bremen	127.5 lb
"	Denmark, Norway	110.23 lb
"	Germany	113.44 lb
"	Sweden	93.7 lb
Chetvert	USSR	5.957 bu
Ch'ih	China	12.60 in
" (metric)	China	39.37 in = 1 meter
Cho	Japan	2.451 acres
Coomb	England	4.1282 bu
Coyan	Siam	2,645.5 lb
Cuadra	Argentina	4.2 acres
"	Paraguay	94.71 yd
" (sq)	Paraguay	1.85 acres
"	Uruguay	1.82 acres
Cwt. (hund. weight)	British	112 lb
Dessiatine	USSR	2.6997 acres
Drachma	Greece	49.38 grains
Dunam	Israel	0.22239 acre
Fanega (dry)	Ecuador, Salvador	1.5745 bu
"	Chile	2.75268 bu
" (dry)	Guatemala, Spain	1.57744 bu
"	Mexico	2.57716 bu
" (dry)	Spain	1.57501 bu
" (liquid)	Spain	16 gal
" (dry)	Trinidad & Tobago	110 lb
" (double)	Uruguay	7.776 bu
" (single)	Uruguay	3.888 bu
"	Venezuela	3.334 bu
Feddan	Egypt	1.04 acres
Frail (raisins)	Spain	50 lb
Frasco	Argentina	2.51 liq qt
Frasila	Zanzibar	35 lb
Fuder	Luxembourg	264.18 gal
Funt	USSR	0.9028 lb
Gallon	British	1.20094 U.S. gal
Garniec	Poland	1.0567 gal
Jerib	Iran	2.471 acres
Joch	Austria	1.422 acres
"	Hungary	1.067 acres
Kantar	Egypt	99.05 lb
"	Morocco	112 lb
"	Turkey	124.45 lb
Ken	Japan	5.97 feet
Kin	Japan	1.32 lb

Denominations	Where Used	Amer. Equiv.
Klafter	Austria	2.074 yd
"	Germany	1.90 yd
Koku	Japan	5.119 bu
Kwan	Japan	8.2673 lb
Last	Belgium, Holland	85.134 bu
"	England	82.56 bu
"	Germany	2 metric tons
"	Prussia	112.29 bu
League (land)	Paraguay	4.633 acres
Li	China	1890 ft
"	"	0.01260 in
		= (1/1000 ch'ih)
Libra (lb)	Argentina	1.0128 lb
"	C. America, Chile	1.014 lb
"	Cuba	1.0143 lb
"	Mexico	1.01467 lb
"	Peru, Venezuela	1.0143 lb
"	Uruguay	1.0127 lb
Load, timber	England	50 cu ft
Manzana	Nicaragua	1.742 acres
"	Costa Rica	1.727 acres
"	Salvador	1.727 acres
Marco	Bolivia	0.507 lb
Maund	Bengal	82.²/₇ lb
Mil	Denmark	4.68 miles
Milla	Nicaragua	1.1594 miles
"	Honduras	1.1493 miles
Mina	Greece	0.95 lb
Morgen	Germany	0.63 acre
Oka (Oke)	Greece	2.82 lb
Oke	(Egypt)	2.7514 lb
"	Turkey	2.826 lb
Pic	Egypt	22.83 inches
Picul	Borneo—Celebes	135.64 lb
"	China	133¹/₃ lb
"	Java	136.16 lb
"	Philippines	139.44 lb
Pie	Argentina	0.9471 ft
"	Spain	0.91416 ft
Pik	Turkey	27.9 inches
Pood	Russia	36.113 lb
Pund (lb)	Denmark	1.102 lb
Quart	British	1.20094 liq qt
"	"	1.03205 dry qt
Quarter	"	8.256 bu
Quintal	Argentina	101.3 lb
"	Brazil	129.54 lb
"	Castile, Peru, Chile	101.43 lb
"	Mexico	101.47 lb
Rotl	Israel	6.35 lb
Sagene	USSR	7 feet
Salm	Malta	8.26 bu
Se	Japan	0.02451 acre
Seer	India	2²/35 lb
Shaku	Japan	11.9303 in
Sho	Japan	1.91 liq qt
Skalpund	Sweden	0.937 lb
Stone	British	14 lb
Sun	Japan	1.193 inches
Tael (Kuping)	China	575.64 grs (troy)
Tan	Japan	0.25 acre
To	Japan	2.05 pecks
Tonde (cereal)	Denmark	3.9480 bu
Tonde (land)	Denmark	1.36 acres
Tonne	France	2204.62 lb
Tsubo	Japan	35.58 sq ft
Ts'un	China	1.26 inches
Tunna (wheat)	Sweden	4.16 bu
Tunnland		1.22 acres
Vara	Argentina	34.0944 inches
"	Costa Rica, Salva	32.913 inches
"	Guatemala	32.909 inches
"	Honduras	32.874 inches
"	Nicaragua	33.057 inches
"	Chile and Peru	32.913 inches
"	Cuba	33.386 inches
"	Mexico	32.992 inches
Vedro	USSR	3.249 gal
Verst		0.663 mile
Vloka	Poland	41.50 acres
Wey	Scotland, Ireland	40 bu

The metric carat of 200 milligrams is now very generally in use. The word carat also is used to denote the proportion of alloy in a metal. Thus, pure gold is 24 carats fine.

Chemical Elements, Discoverers, Atomic Weights

Atomic weights, based on the exact number 12 as the assigned atomic mass of the principal isotope of carbon, carbon 12, are provided through the courtesy of the International Union of Pure and Applied Chemistry and Butterworth Scientific Publications.

For the radioactive elements with the exception of uranium and thorium, the mass number of either the isotope of longest half-life (marked with a star) or the better known isotope (marked with two stars) is given.

Chemical element	Symbol	Atomic number	Atomic weight	Year discov.	Discoverer
Actinium	Ac	89	227*	1899	Debierne
Aluminum	Al	13	26.9815	1825	Oersted
Americium	Am	95	243*	1944	Seaborg, et al.
Antimony	Sb	51	121.75	1450	Valentine
Argon	Ar	18	39.948	1894	Rayleigh, Ramsay
Arsenic	As	33	74.9216	13th C.	Magnus
Astatine	At	385	210*	1940	Corson, et al.
Barium	Ba	56	137.34	1808	Davy
Berkelium	Bk	97	247*	1949	Thompson, Ghiorso, Seaborg
Beryllium	Be	4	9.0122	1798	Vanquelin
Bismuth	Bi	83	208.980	15th C.	Valentine
Boron	B	5	10.811a	1808	Davy
Bromine	Br	35	79.904b	1826	Balard
Cadmium	Cd	48	112.40	1817	Stromeyer
Calcium	Ca	20	40.08	1808	Davy
Californium	Cf	98	249**	1950	Thompson, et al.
Carbon	C	6	12.01115a	B.C.	
Cerium	Ce	58	140.12	1803	Klaproth
Cesium	Cs	55	132.905	1861	Bunsen, Kirchoff
Chlorine	Cl	17	35.453b	1774	Scheele
Chromium	Cr	24	51.996b	1797	Vanquelin
Cobalt	Co	27	58.9332	1735	Brandt
Copper	Cu	29	63.546b	B.C.	
Curium	Cm	96	247*	1944	Seaborg, et al.
Dysprosium	Dy	66	162.50	1886	Boisbaudran
Einsteinium	Es	99	254*	1952	Ghiorso, et al.
Erbium	Er	68	167.26	1843	Mosander
Europium	Eu	63	151.96	1901	Demarcay
Fermium	Fm	100	257*	1953	Ghiorso, et al.
Fluorine	F	9	18.9984	1771	Scheele
Francium	Fr	87	223*	1939	Perey
Gadolinium	Gd	64	157.25	1886	Marignac
Gallium	Ga	31	69.72	1875	Boisbaudran
Germanium	Ge	32	72.59	1886	Winkler
Gold	Au	79	196.967	B.C.	
Hafnium	Hf	72	178.49	1923	Coster, Hevesy
Hahnium	Ha	105	262*	1970	Ghiorso, et al.
Helium	He	2	4.0026	1895	Ramsay
Holmium	Ho	67	164.930	1879	Cleve
Hydrogen	H	1	1.00797a	1766	Cavendish
Indium	In	49	114.82	1863	Reich, Richter
Iodine	I	53	126.9044	1811	Courtois
Iridium	Ir	77	192.2	1804	Tennant
Iron	Fe	26	55.847b	B.C.	
Krypton	Kr	36	83.80	1898	Ramsay, Travers
Lanthanium	La	57	138.91	1839	Mosander
Lawrencium	Lr	103	260*	1961	Ghiorso, T. Sikkeland, A.E. Larsh, and R.M. Latimer
Lead	Pb	82	207.19	B.C.	
Lithium	Li	3	6.939	1817	Arfvedson
Lutetium	Lu	71	174.97	1907	Welsbach, Urbain
Magnesium	Mg	12	24.312	1830	Liebig, Bussy
Manganese	Mn	25	54.9380	1774	Gahn
Mendelevium	Md	101	258*	1955	Ghiorso, et al.
Mercury	Hg	80	200.59	B.C.	
Molybdenum	Mo	42	95.94	1782	Hjelm
Neodymium	Nd	60	144.24	1885	Welsbach
Neon	Ne	10	20.183	1898	Ramsay, Travers
Neptunium	Np	93	237*	1940	McMillan, Abelson
Nickel	Ni	28	58.71	1751	Cronstedt
Niobium (Form. Columbium)	Nb	41	92.906	1801	Hatchett
Nitrogen	N	7	14.0067	1772	Rutherford
Nobelium	No	102	259*	1958	Ghiorso, et al.
Osmium	Os	76	190.2	1804	Tennant
Oxygen	O	8	15.9994a	1774	Priestly, Scheele
Palladium	Pd	46	106.4	1803	Wollaston
Phosphorus	P	15	30.9738	1669	Brandt
Platinum	Pt	78	195.09	1735	Ulloa
Plutonium	Pu	94	242**	1940	Seaborg, et al.
Polonium	Po	84	210**	1898	P. and M. Curie
Potassium	K	19	39.102	1807	Davy
Praseodymium	Pr	59	140.907	1885	Welsbach
Promethium	Pm	61	147**	1945	Glendenin, Marinsky
Protactinium	Pa	91	231*	1917	Hahn, Meltner
Radium	Ra	88	226*	1898	P. & M. Curie, Bemont
Radon	Rn	86	222*	1900	Dorn
Rhenium	Re	75	186.2	1925	Noddack, Tacke
Rhodium	Rh	45	102.905	1803	Wollaston
Rubidium	Rb	37	85.47	1861	Bunsen, Kirchoff
Ruthenium	Ru	44	101.07	1845	Claus

Chemical element	Symbol	Number	Weight	Year	Discoverer
Rutherfordium	Rf	104	261*	1969	Ghiorso, et al.
Samarium	Sm	62	150.35	1879	Boisbaudran
Scandium	Sc	21	44.956	1879	Nilson
Seleenium	Se	34	78.96	1817	Berzelius
Silicon	Si	14	28.086a	1823	Berzelius
Silver	Ag	47	107.868b	B.C.	
Sodium	Na	11	22.9898	1807	Davy
Strontium	Sr	38	87.62	1790	Crawford
Sulfur	S	16	32.064a	B.C.	
Tantalum	Ta	73	180.948	1802	Eckeberg
Technetium	Tc	43	99**	1937	Perrier and Segre
Tellurium	Te	52	127.60	1782	Von Reichenstein
Terbium	Tb	65	158.924	1843	Mosander
Thallium	Tl	81	204.37	1861	Crookes
Thorium	Th	90	232.038	1828	Berzelius
Thulium	Tm	69	168.934	1879	Cleve
Tin	Sn	50	118.69	B.C.	
Titanium	Ti	22	47.90	1789	Gregor
Tungsten (Alternate Wolfram)	W	74	183.85	1783	d'Elhujar
Uranium	U	92	238.03	1789	Klaproth
Vanadium	V	23	50.942	1830	Sefstrom
Xenon	Xe	54	131.30	1898	Ramsay, Travers
Ytterbium	Yb	70	173.04	1878	Marignac
Yttrium	Y	39	88.905	1794	Gadolin
Zinc	Zn	30	65.37	B.C.	
Zirconium	Zr	40	91.22	1789	Klaproth

a. Atomic weights so designated are known to be variable because of natural variations in isotopic composition. The observed ranges are: hydrogen$\pm$0.00001; boron$\pm$0.003; carbon$\pm$0.00005; oxygen$\pm$0.0001; silicon$\pm$0.001; sulfur$\pm$0.003.

b. Atomic weights so designated are believed to have the following experimental uncertainties: chlorine$\pm$0.001; chromium$\pm$0.001; iron$\pm$0.003; bromine$\pm$0.001; silver$\pm$0.001; copper$\pm$0.001.

Medical Signs and Abbreviations

Source: American Medical Association

℞ (Lat. Recipe)	take	a.c.	before meals	gr	grain	pulvis	powder
Ʒ	drachm	ad	to, up to	gtt	drops	q. 3 h	every three hours
f Ʒ	fluid drachm	ad libitum	at pleasure	h.s.	at bedtime	q.i.d.	four times daily
℥	ounce	agit	shake	inject	injection	q.s.	as much as is sufficient
f ℥	fluid ounce	aqua	water	lb	pound	sig	sign, write
℥ ss	half an ounce	b.i.d.	twice daily	m	mix	solutio	a solution
℥ i	one ounce	cap	capsule	mg	milligram	ss	one-half
℥ iss	one ounce and a half	cum, or c	with	ml	milliliter	stat	at once
℥ ii	two ounces	e.m.p.	as directed	non. rep. or n.r.		tab	tablet
ℳ	minim, or drop	fiant (ft)	make		do not repeat	t.i.d.	three times daily
o	pint	gargarisma	a gargle	p.c.	after meals	ung	ointment
āā	of each	Gm	gram	p.r.n.	as circumstances may require	ut dict	as directed

Bell Time on Shipboard

Source: Maritime Administration

Time, A.M.		Time, A.M.		Time, A.M.		Time, P.M.		Time, P.M.		Time, P.M.	
1 Bell	12:30	1 Bell	4:30	1 Bell	8:30	1 Bell	12:30	1 Bell	4:30	1 Bell	8:30
2 Bells	1:00	2 Bells	5:00	2 Bells	9:00	2 Bells	1:00	2 Bells	5:00	2 Bells	9:00
3 "	1:30	3 "	5:30	3 "	9:30	3 "	1:30	3 "	5:30	3 "	9:30
4 "	2:00	4 "	6:00	4 "	10:00	4 "	2:00	4 "	6:00	4 "	10:00
5 "	2:30	5 "	6:30	5 "	10:30	5 "	2:30	5 "	6:30	5 "	10:30
6 "	3:00	6 "	7:00	6 "	11:00	6 "	3:00	6 "	7:00	6 "	11:00
7 "	3:30	7 "	7:30	7 "	11:30	7 "	3:30	7 "	7:30	7 "	11:30
8 "	4:00	8 "	8:00	8 "	Noon	8 "	4:00	8 "	8:00	8 "	Midnight

Breaking the Sound Barrier; Speed of Sound

The prefix Mach is used to describe supersonic speed. It derives from Ernst Mach, a Czech-born German physicist, who contributed to the study of sound. When a plane moves at the speed of sound it is Mach 1. When twice the speed of sound it is Mach 2. When it is near but below the speed of sound its speed can be designated at less than Mach 1, for example, Mach .0. Mach is defined as "in jet propulsion, the ratio of the velocity of a rocket or a jet to the velocity of sound in the medium being considered."

When a plane passes the sound barrier—flying faster than sound travels—listeners in the area hear thunderclaps, but pilots do not hear them.

Sound is produced by vibrations of an object and is transmitted by alternate increase and decrease in pressures that radiate outward through a material media of molecules- somewhat like waves spreading out on a pond after a rock has been tossed.

The frequency of sound is determined by the number of times the vibrating waves undulate per second, and is measured in cycles per second. The slower the cycle of waves, the lower the sound. As frequencies increase, the sound is higher.

Sound is audible to human beings only if the frequency falls within a certain range. The human ear is usually not sensitive to frequencies of less than 20 vibrations per second, or more than about 20,000 vibrations per second-although this range varies among individuals. Anything at a pitch higher than the human ear can hear is termed ultrasonic.

Intensity or loudness is the strength of the pressure of these radiating waves, and is measured in decibels. The human ear responds to intensity in a range from zero to 120 decibels. Any sound with pressure over 120 decibels is painful.

The speed of sound is generally placed at 1088 ft. per second at sea level at 32°F. It varies in other temperatures and in different media. Sound travels faster in water than in air, and even faster in iron and steel. If in air it travels a mile in 5 seconds, it does a mile under water in 1 second, and through iron in ¹/₃ of a second. It travels through ice cold vapor at approximately 4,708 ft. per sec., ice-cold water. 4,938; granite, 12,960; hardwood, 12,620; brick, 11,-960; glass, 16,410 to 19,690; silver, 8,658; gold, 5,717.

Great Inventions and Scientific Discoveries

Invention	Date	Inventor	Nation
Adding machine	1642	Pascal	French
Adding machine	1885	Burroughs	U.S.
Addressograph	1892	Duncan	U.S.
Aerosol spray	1941	Goodhue	U.S.
Air brake	1868	Westinghouse	U.S.
Air conditioning	1911	Carrier	U.S.
Air pump	1650	Guericke	German
Airplane, automatic pilot	1929	Green	U.S.
Airplane, experimental	1896	Langley	U.S.
Airplane jet engine	1939	Ohain	German
Airplane with motor	1903	Orville and Wilbur Wright	U.S.
Airplane, hydro	1911	Curtiss	U.S.
Airship	1852	Giffard	French
Airship, rigid dirigible	1900	Zeppelin	German
Arc tube	1923	Alexanderson	U.S.
Autogyro	1920	de la Cierva	Spanish
Automobile, differential gear	1885	Benz	German
Automobile, electric	1892	Morrison	U.S.
Automobile, experim'tal	1875	Marcus	Austrian
Automobile, gasoline	1887	Daimler	German
Automobile, gasoline	1892	Duryea, C. E.	U.S.
Automobile, magneto	1897	Bosch, R.	German
Automobile muffler	...	Maxim, H.P.	U.S.
Automobile self-starter	1911	Kettering	U.S.
Automobile, steam	1889	Roper	U.S.
Babbitt metal	1839	Babbitt	U.S.
Bakelite	1907	Baekeland	Belg. U.S.
Balloon	1783	Montgolfier	French
Barometer	1643	Torricelli	Italian
Bicycle, modern	1884	Starley	English
Bifocal lens	1780	Franklin	U.S.
Block signals, railway	1867	Hall	U.S.
Bomb, depth	1916	Tait	U.S.
Bottle machine	1903	Owens	U.S.
Braille printing	1829	Braille	French
Burner, gas	1855	Bunsen	German
Calculating machine	1823	Babbage	English
Camera, Polaroid Land	1948	Land	U.S.
Car coupler	1873	Janney	U.S.
Carburetor, gasoline	1876	Daimler	German
Card time recorder	1894	Cooper	U.S.
Carding machine	1797	Whittemore	U.S.
Carpet sweeper	1876	Bissell	U.S.
Cash register	1879	Ritty	U.S.
Cathode ray tube	1878	Crookes	English
Cellophane	1911	Brandenberger	Swiss
Celluloid	1870	Hyatt	U.S.
Cement, Portland	1845	Aspdin	English
Chronometer	1735	Harrison	English
Circuit breaker	1925	Hilliard	U.S.
Clock, pendulum	1657	Huygens	Dutch
Coaxial cable system	1929	Affel & Es-pensched	U.S.
Coke oven	1893	Hoffman	Austrian
Compressed air rock drill	1871	Ingersoll	U.S.
Comptometer	1887	Felt	U.S.
Computer, automatic sequence	1939	Aiken, et al	U.S.
Condenser microphone (telephone)	1920	Wente	U.S.
Cotton gin	1793	Whitney	U.S.
Cream separator	1880	DeLaval	Swedish
Cultivator, disc	1878	Mallon	U.S.
Cystoscope	1877	Nitze	German
Dental plate, rubber	1855	Goodyear	U.S.
Diesel engine	1895	Diesel	German
Dynamite	1866	Nobel	Swedish
Dynamo, continuous current	1860	Picinotti	Italian
Dynamo, hydrogen cooled	1915	Schuler	U.S.
Electric battery	1800	Volta	Italian
Electric fan	1882	Wheeler	U.S.
Electrocardiograph	1903	Einthoven	Dutch
Electroencephalograph	1929	Berger	German
Electromagnet	1824	Sturgeon	English
Electron spectrometer	1944	Deutsch, Elliott, Evans	U.S.
Electron tube multigrid	1913	Langmuir	U.S.
Electroplating	1805	Brugnatelli	Italian
Electrostatic generator	1929	Van de Graff	U.S.
Elevator brake	1852	Otis	U.S.
Elevator, push button	1922	Larson	U.S.
Engine, automobile	1879	Benz	German
Engine, gasoline	1872	Brayton, Geo.	U.S.
Engine, gas, compound	1926	Eickemeyer	U.S.
Engine, coal-gas 4-cycle	1877	Otto	German
Engine, compression ignition	1883	Daimler	German
Engine, electric ignition	1880	Benz	German
Engine, gasoline	1886	Daimler	German
Engine, steam, piston	1705	Newcomen	English
Engine, steam, piston	1769	Watt	Scottish
Engraving, half-tone	1893	Ives	U.S.
Filament, tungsten	1915	Langmuir	U.S.
Flanged rail	1831	Stevens	U.S.
Flatiron, electric	1882	Seeley	U.S.
Furnace, (for steel)	1861	Siemens	German
Galvanometer	1820	Sweigger	German
Gas discharge tube	1922	Hull	U.S.
Gas lighting	1792	Murdoch	Scottish
Gas mantle	1885	Welsbach	Austrian
Gasoline (lead ethyl)	1922	Midgely	U.S.
Gasoline, cracked	1913	Burton, W.M.	U.S.
Gasoline, high octane	1930	Ipatieff	Russian
Geiger counter	1913	Geiger	German
Glass, laminated safety	1909	Benedictus	French
Glider	1853	Cayley	English
Gun, breechloader	1811	Thornton	U.S.
Gun, Browning	1916	Browning	U.S.
Gun, magazine	1875	Hotchkiss	U.S.
Gun, silencer	1909	Maxim, H. P.	U.S.
Guncotton	1846	Schoenbein	German
Gyrocompass	1911	Sperry	U.S.
Gyroscope	1852	Foucault	French
Harvester	1836	Moore	U.S.
Harvester-thresher	1888	Matteson	U.S.
Helicopter	1939	Sikorsky	U.S.
Hydrometer	1768	Baume	French
Ice-making machine	1851	Gorrie	U.S.
Iron Lung	1928	Drinker, Slaw	U.S.
Kaleidoscope	1817	Brewster	English
Kinetoscope	1887	Edison	U.S.
Kodak	1888	Eastman-Walker	U.S.
Lacquer, nitrocellulose	1921	Flaherty	U.S.
Lamp, arc	1879	Brush	U.S.
Lamp, incandescent	1879	Edison	U.S.
Lamp, incand., frosted	1924	Pipkin	U.S.
Lamp, incand., gas	1916	Langmuir	U.S.
Lamp, Klieg	1911	Kliegl, A.&J.	U.S.
Lamp, mercury vapor	1912	Hewitt	U.S.
Lamp, miner's safety	1816	Davy	English
Lamp, neon	1915	Claude	French
Lathe, turret	1845	Fitch	U.S.
Launderette	1934	Cantrell	U.S.
Lens, achromatic	1758	Dollond	English
Lens, fused bifocal	1908	Borsch	U.S.
Leydenjar (condenser)	1745	von Kleist	German
Lightning rod	1752	Franklin	U.S.
Linoleum	1860	Walton	English
Linotype	1885	Mergenthaler	U.S.
Lock, cylinder	1865	Yale	U.S.
Locomotive, electric	1851	Vail	U.S.
Locomotive, exper.	1801	Trevithick	English
Locomotive, exper.	1812	Fenton et al.	English
Locomotive, exper.	1813	Hedley	English
Locomotive, exper.	1814	Stephenson	English
Locomotive practical	1829	Stephenson	English
Locomotive, 1st U.S.	1830	Cooper, P.	U.S.
Loom, power	1785	Cartwright	English
Loudspeaker, dynamic	1924	Rice-Kellogg	U.S.
Machine gun	1861	Gatling	U.S.
Machine gun, improved	1872	Hotchkiss	U.S.
Machine gun (Maxim)	1883	Maxim, H.S.	U.S., Eng.
Magnet, electro	1828	Henry	U.S.
Mantle, gas	1885	Welsbach	Austrian
Mason jar	1858	Mason, J.	U.S.
Match, friction	1827	John Walker	English
Mercerized textiles	1843	Mercer, J.	English
Meter, induction	1888	Shallenberger	U.S.

Invention	Date	Inventor	Nation
Meter, parking	1935	Magee	U.S.
Metronome	1816	Malzel	Austrian
Micrometer	1636	Gascoigne	English
Microphone	1877	Berliner	U.S.
Microscope, compound	1590	Janssen	Dutch
Microscope, electronic	1931	Knoll-Ruska	German
Monitor, warship	1861	Ericsson	U.S.
Monotype	1887	Lanston	U.S.
Motor, AC	1892	Tesla	U.S.
Motor, induction	1887	Tesla	U.S.
Motorcycle	1885	Daimler	German
Movie machine	1894	Jenkins	U.S.
Movie, panoramic	1952	Waller	U.S.
Movie, talking	1927	Warner Bros.	U.S.
Mower, lawn	1868	Hills	U.S.
Mowing machine	1831	Manning	U.S.
Neoprene	1930	Carothers	U.S.
Nylon synthetic	1930	Carothers	U.S.
Nylon	1937	Du Pont lab.	U.S.
Oil cracking furnace	1891	Gavrilov	Russian
Oil filled power cable	1921	Emanueli	Italian
Oleomargarine	1868	Mege-Mouries	French
Ophthalmoscope	1851	Helmholtz	German
Paper machine	1809	Dickinson	U.S.
Parachute	1785	Blanchard	French
Pen, ballpoint	1888	Loud	U.S.
Pen, fountain	1884	Waterman	U.S.
Pen, steel	1780	Harrison	English
Pendulum	1581	Galileo	Italian
Percussion cap	1814	Shaw	U.S.
Phonograph	1877	Edison	U.S.
Photo, color	1892	Ives	U.S.
Photo film, celluloid	1887	Goodwin	U.S.
Photo film transparent	1888	Eastman-Goodwin	U.S.
Photoelectric cell	1895	Elster	German
Photographic paper	1898	Baekeland	U.S.
Photography	1835	Fox-Talbot	English
Photography	1837	Daguerre	French
Photography	1839	Niepce, Joseph	French
Photophone	1880	Bell	U.S.
Phototelegraphy	1925	Bell lab	U.S.
Piano	1709	Cristofori	Italian
Piano player	1863	Fourneaux	French
Pin, safety	1849	Hunt	U.S.
Pistol (revolver)	1835	Colt	U.S.
Plow, cast iron	1797	Newbold	U.S.
Plow, disc	1896	Hardy	U.S.
Pneumatic hammer	1890	King	U.S.
Powder, smokeless	1863	Schultze	German
Printing press, rotary	1846	Hoe	U.S.
Printing press, web	1865	Bullock	U.S.
Propeller, screw	1804	Stevens	U.S.
Propeller, screw	1837	Ericsson	Swedish
Punch card accounting	1884	Hollerith	U.S.
Radar	1922	Taylor and Young	U.S.
Radio amplifier	1907	De Forest	U.S.
Radio beacon	1928	Donovan	U.S.
Radio crystal oscillator	1918	Nicolson	U.S.
Radio receiver, cascade tuning	1913	Alexanderson	U.S.
Radio receiver, heterodyne	1913	Fessenden	U.S.
Radio transmitter triode modulation	1914	Alexanderson	U.S.
Radio tube-diode	1905	Fleming	English
Radio tube oscillator	1915	De Forest	U.S.
Radio tube triode	1907	De Forest	U.S.
Radio, signals	1895	Marconi	Italian
Radio, magnetic detector	1902	Marconi	Italian
Radio FM 2-path	1929	Armstrong	U.S.
Rayon	1883	Swan	English
Razor, electric	1931	Schick	U.S.
Razor, safety	1895	Gillette	U.S.
Reaper	1834	McCormick	U.S.
Record, cylinder	1887	Bell-Tainter	U.S.
Record, disc	1887	Berliner	U.S.
Record, long playing	1948	Goldmark	U.S.
Record, wax cylinder	1888	Edison	U.S.
Refrigerants, low-boiling. fluorine compound	1930	Midgely and co-workers	U.S.
Refrigerator car	1868	David	U.S.
Resin, synthetic	1931	Hill	English
Rifle, repeating	1860	Spencer	U.S.
Rocket engine	1929	R. H. Goddard	U.S.
Rubber, vulcanized	1839	Goodyear	U.S.
Saw, band	1808	Newberry	English
Saw, circular	1777	Miller	English
Searchlight, arc	1915	Sperry	U.S.
Sewing machine	1846	Howe	U.S.
Shoe-sewing machine	1860	McKay	U.S.
Shrapnel shell	1784	Shrapnel	English
Shuttle, flying	1733	Kay	English
Sleeping-car	1858	Pullman	U.S.
Slide rule	1620	Oughtred	English
Soap, hardwater	1928	Bertsch	German
Spectroscope	1859	Kirchoff-Bunsen	German
Spectroscope (mass)	1918	Dempster	U.S.
Spinning jenny	1767	Hargreaves	English
Spinning mule	1779	Crompton	English
Steamboat, exp'mtl	1783	Jouffroy	French
Steamboat, exp'mtl	1785	Fitch	U.S.
Steamboat, exp'mtl	1787	Rumsey	U.S.
Steamboat, exp'mtl	1788	Miller	Scottish
Steamboat, exp'mtl	1803	Fulton	U.S.
Steamboat, exp'mtl	1804	Stevens	U.S.
Steamboat, practical	1802	Symington	Scottish
Steamboat, practical	1807	Fulton	U.S.
Steam car	1770	Cugnot	French
Steam turbine	1884	Parsons	English
Steel	1856	Bessemer	English
Steel alloy	1891	Harvey	U.S.
Steel alloy, high-speed	1901	Taylor-White	U.S.
Steel, electric	1900	Heroult	French
Steel, manganese	1884	Hadfield	English
Steel, stainless	1916	Brearley	English
Stereoscope	1838	Wheatstone	English
Stethoscope	1819	Laennec	French
Stethoscope, binaural	1840	Cammann	U.S.
Stock ticker	1870	Edison	U.S.
Storage battery, electric	1812	Ritter	German
Stove, electric	1896	Hadaway	U.S.
Submarine	1891	Holland	U.S.
Submarine, even keel	1894	Lake	U.S.
Submarine, torpedo	1776	Bushnell	U.S.
Tank, military	1914	Swinton	English
Tape recorder, magnetic	1899	Poulsen	Danish
Telegraph, magnetic	1837	Morse	U.S.
Telegraph, quadruplex	1874	Edison	U.S.
Telegraph, wireless, high frequency	1896	Marconi	Italian
Telephone	1876	Bell	U.S., Can.
Telephone amplifier	1912	De Forest	U.S.
Telephone, automatic	1891	Stowger	U.S.
Telephone, radio	1902	Poulsen and Fessenden	U.S.
Telephone, radio	1906	De Forest	U.S.
Telephone, radio, l. d.	1915	Am. T & T.	U.S.
Telephone, recording	1898	Poulson	Danish
Telephone, wireless	1899	Collins	U.S.
Telescope	1608	Lippershey	Neth.
Telescope	1609	Galileo	Italian
Telescope, astronomical	1611	Kepler	German
Teletype	1928	Morkrum-Kleinschmidt	U.S.
Television, iconoscope	1923	V. Zworykin	U.S.
Television, electronic	1927	P. Farnsworth	U.S.
Television, (mech. scanner)	1926	Baird	Scottish
Thermometer	1593	Galileo	Italian
Thermometer	1710	Reaumur	French
Thermometer, mercury	1714	Fahrenheit	German
Time recorder	1890	Bundy	U.S.
Time, self-regulator	1918	Bryce	U.S.
Tire, double-tube	1845	Thompson	English
Tire, pneumatic	1888	Dunlop	Irish
Toaster, automatic	1918	Strite	U.S.
Tool, pneumatic	1865	Law	English
Torpedo, marine	1804	Fulton	U.S.
Tractor, crawler	1900	Holt	U.S.
Transfomer A.C.	1885	Stanley	U.S.

Invention	Date	Inventor	Nation
Transistor.	1947	Shockley, Brattain, Bardeen . . .	U.S.
Trolley car, electric	1884 -87	Van Depoel & Sprague . .	U.S.
Tungsten, ductile.	1912	Coolidge. . . .	U.S.
Turbine, gas	1899	C. G. Curtis. .	U.S.
Turbine, hydraulic.	1849	Francis	U.S.
Turbine, steam.	1896	C. G. Curtis. . .	U.S.
Type, movable.	1450	Gutenberg. . . .	German
Typewriter.	1868	Sholes and Glidden	U.S.

Invention	Date	Inventor	Nation
Vacuum cleaner, electric	1907	Spangler.	U.S.
Washer, electric.	1907	Hurley Co. . . .	U.S.
Welding, atomic hydrogen.	1924	Langmuir-Palmer.	U.S.
Welding, electric.	1877	Thomson.	U.S.
Wind tunnel.	1923	Munk	U.S.
Wire, barbed.	1874	Glidden	U.S.
Wire, barbed.	1875	Haisn	U.S.
X-ray tube.	1916	Coolidge.	U.S.
Zipper.	1891	Judson	U.S.

Discoveries and Innovations: Chemistry, Physics, Biology, Medicine

Product	Date	Discoverer	Nation
Acetylene gas	1892	Wilson	U.S.
ACTH.	1949	Armour & Co.	U.S.
Adrenalin	1901	Takamine	Japan
Aluminum, electrolytic process.	1886	Hall	U.S.
Aluminum, isolated . . .	1825	Oersted	Danish
Analine dye.	1856	Perkin	English
Anesthesia, ether.	1842	Long	U.S.
Anesthesia, local	1885	Koller	Austria
Anesthesia, spinal	1898	Bier	German
Anti-rabies.	1885	Pasteur.	French
Antitoxin, diphtheria. . . .	1891	Von Behring. . . .	German
Antiseptic surgery	1867	Lister	English
Argyrol.		Barnes.	U.S.
Arsphenamine	1910	Ehrlich	German
Aspirin	1889	Dresser.	German
Atomic numbers.	1913	Moseley.	English
Atomic theory.	1803	Dalton.	English
Atomic time clock.	1947	Libby.	U.S.
Atom-smashing theory	1919	Rutherford	English
Atabrine	. . .	Mietzsch, et al.	German
Aureomycin	1948	Duggar.	U.S.
Bacitracin.	1945	Johnson et al . . .	U.S.
Bacteria (described) . .	1676	Leeuwenhoek. . .	Dutch
Barbital.	1903	Fischer	German
Bleaching powder. . . .	1798	Tennnt.	English
Blood, circulation	1628	Harvey.	English
Bordeaux mixture	1885	Millardet.	French
Bromine from sea	1924	Edgar-Kramer	U.S.
Calcium carbide.	1888	Wilson	U.S.
Calculus.	1670	Newton	English
Carbon oxides	1925	Fisher	German
Carbomycin	1952	Tanner.	U.S.
Camphor synthetic. . . .	1896	Haller.	French
Canning (food).	1804	Appert.	French
Chlorine.	1810	Davy.	English
Chloroform.	1831	Guthrie, S.	U.S.
Chloromycetin	1947	Burkholder.	U.S.
Classification of plants and animals. .	1735	Linnaeus.	Swedish
Cocaine	1860	Niermann.	German
Combustion, explained	1777	Lavoisier.	French
Conditioned reflex. . . .	1914	Pavlov.	Russian
Conteben	1950	Belmisch,. . . . . . . Mietzsch, Domagh.	German
Cortisone	1936	Kendall	U.S.
Cortisone, synthesis . .	1946	Sarett.	U.S.
Cosmic rays.	1910	Gockel.	Swiss
Cyanimide	1905	Frank-Caro.	German
Cyclotron	1930	Lawrence.	U.S.
DDT.	1874	Zeidler	German

(Not applied as insecticide until 1939)

Product	Date	Discoverer	Nation
Deuterium (heavy hydrogen)	1932	Urey, Brick-Wedde, Murphy	U.S.
DNA (structure).	1951	Crick. . . . . Watson. . . . . Wilkins.	English U.S. English
Electric resistance (law).	1827	Ohm.	German
Electric waves.	1888	Hertz.	German
Electrolysis	1852	Faraday.	English
Electromagnetism. . . .	1819	Oersted	Danish
Electron	1897	Thomson, J	English
Electron diffraction. . . .	1936	Thomson, G. . . . . Davisson	English U.S.
Electroshock treatment	1938	Cerletti, Bini	Italy
Erythromycin	1952	McGuire.	U.S.

Product	Date	Discoverer	Nation
Evolution, natural selection	1858	Darwin.	English
Falling bodies, law	1590	Galileo	Italian
Gases, law of combining volumes.	1808	Gay-Lussac.	French
Geometry, analytic. . . .	1619	Descartes.	French
Gold (cyanide process for extraction).	1887	MacArthur-Forest.	British
Gravitation, law.	1687	Newton	English
Holograph.	1948	Gabor	British
Human heart transplant	1967	Barnard	S. Africa
Indigo, synthesis of. . . .	1880	Baeyer.	German
Induction, electric.	1830	Henry.	U.S.
Insulin	1922	Banting, Best, MacLeod	Canada
Intelligence testing. . . .	1905	Binet and Simon.	French
Isniazid	1952	Hoffman-La-Roche . . . . . Domagh.	U.S. German
Isotopes, theory	1912	Soddy.	English
Laser (light amplification by stimulated emission of radiation).	1958	Townes, Schawlow .	U.S.
Light, velocity.	1675	Roemer.	Danish
Light, wave theory.	1690	Huygens.	Dutch
Lithography.	1796	Senefelder.	Bohemia
Lobotomy.	1935	Egas Oniz.	Portugal
LSD-25.	1943	Hoffman.	Swiss
Mendelian laws.	1866	Mendel	Austrian
Mercator's projection (map).	1568	Mercator. . . . . . . (Kremer)	Flemish
Methanol.	1925	Patard.	French
Milk condensation. . . .	1853	Borden.	U.S.
Molecular hypothesis. .	1811	Avogadro.	Italian
Motion, laws of.	1687	Newton	English
Neomycin	1949	Waksman & Lechevalier.	U.S.
Neutron.	1932	Chadwick.	English
Nitric acid.	1648	Glauber.	German
Nitric oxide.	1772	Priestley.	English
Nitroglycerin	1846	Sobrero	Italian
Ohm's law.	1827	Ohm, Georg.	German
Oil cracking process . .	1891	Dewar.	U.S.
Oxygen	1774	Priestley.	English
Ozone.	840	Schonbein	German
Paper, from wood pulp, sulfate process	1884	Dahl.	German
Paper, sulfite process .	1867	Tilghman.	U.S.
Penicillin	1929	Alex, Fleming.	English
Practical use	1941	Florey-Chain.	English
Periodic law and table of elements . . .	1869	Mednelejeff.	Russian
Planetary motion, laws.	1609	Kepler.	German
Plutonium fission	1940	Kennedy, J.W.. . . . . Wahl, A. C. . . . . . . Seaborg, G. T. . . . . . Segre, Emilio	U.S. U.S. U.S. U.S.
Polymixin	1947	Ainsworth	English
Positron	1932	Anderson.	U.S.
Proton.	1919	Rutherford	English
Psychoanalysis.	1900	Freud.	Austrian
Quantum theory.	1900	Planck.	German
Quasars.	1963	Matthews & Sandage.	U.S.
Quinine-synthetic	1918	Rabe.	German
Radioactivity.	1896	Becquerel	French
Radium	1898	Curie, Pierre. . . . . Curie, Marie.	French Polish
Relativity theory	1905	Einstein	German

Discovery	Date	Discoverer	Nation	Discovery	Date	Discoverer	Nation
Reserpine	1949	Jal Vakil	India	Uranium fission, atomic reactor	1942	Enrico Fermi	Italian
Salvarsan (606)	1910	Ehrlich	German			Leo Seilard	U.S.
Schick test, diphtheria	1913	Schick	U.S.	Vaccine, measles /	1954	Enders, John Peebles, T.	U.S.
Silicon	1823	Berzelius	Swedish	Vaccine, polio	1955	Sabin, Alb. E.	U.S.
Streptomycin	1945	Waksman	U.S.	Vaccine, polio	1953	Salk, Jonas E.	U.S.
Sulfanilamide theory	1908	Gelmo	German	Vaccine, rabies	1885	Pasteur	French
Sulfanilamide	1934	Domag	German	Vaccine, smallpox	1796	Jenner, Edw.	English
Sulfadiazine	1940	Roblin	U.S.	Vaccine, typhus	1909	Nicolle, J.	French
Sulfapyridine	1938	Ewins Phelps	English	Van Allen belts, radiation	1958	Van Allen	U.S.
Sulfathiazole	...	Fosbinder, Walter	U.S.	Vitamin A	1913	McCollum, Davis	U.S.
Sulfuric acid	1831	Phillips	English	Vitamin B	1916	McCollum	U.S.
Sulfuric acid, lead	1746	Roebuck	English	Vitamin C	1912	Holst, Froelich	Norway
Terramycin	1950	Finlay, et al	U.S.	Vitamin D	1922	McCollum	U.S.
Tuberculin	1890	Koch	German	Wassermann test, syphilis	1906	Wassermann	German
Uranium fission (theory)	1939	Hahn, Strassmann	German	Xerography	1938	Carlson	U.S.
		Borr	Danish	X-ray	1895	Roentgen	German
		Einstein	U.S.				
		Fermi	Italian				
		Pegram	U.S.				
		Wheeler	U.S.				

Colors of the Spectrum

Color, an electromagnetic wave phenomenon, is a sensation produced through the excitation of the retina of the eye by rays of light. The colors of the spectrum may be produced by viewing a light beam refracted by passage through a prism, which breaks the light into its wave lengths.

Customarily, the primary colors of the spectrum are thought of as those six monochromatic colors which occupy relatively large areas of the spectrum: red, orange, yellow, green, blue and violet. However, Sir Isaac Newton named a seventh, indigo, situated between blue and violet on the spectrum. Aubert estimated (1865) the solar spectrum to contain approximately 1,000 distinguishable hues of which according to Rood (1881) 2,000,000 tints and shades can be distinguished; Luckiesh stated (1915) that 55 distinctly different hues have been seen in a single spectrum.

By many physicists only three primary colors are recognized: red, yellow and blue (Mayer, 1775); red, green and violet (Thomas Young, 1801); red, green and blue (Clerk Maxwell, 1860).

The color sensation of black is due to complete lack of stimulation of the retina, that of white to complete stimulation. The infra-red and ultra-violet rays, below the red (long) end of the spectrum and the violet end (short end) respectively, are invisible. Heat is the principal effect of the infra-red rays and chemical action that of the ultra-violet rays.

Playing Cards and Dice Chances

Poker Hands (Four-Suit)

Hand	Number Possible	Odds Against
Royal Flush	4	649,739 to 1
Other Straight Flush	36	72,192 to 1
Four of a kind	624	4,164 to 1
Full House	3,744	693 to 1
Flush	5,108	508 to 1
Straight	10,200	254 to 1
Three of a kind	54,912	46 to 1
Two Pairs	123,552	20 to 1
One Pair	1,098,240	4 to 3 (1.37 to 1)
Nothing	1,302,540	1 to 1
Total	2,598,960	

Dice
Probabilities of Consecutive Winning Plays

No. Consecutive Wins	By 7, 11, or Point	No. Consecutive Wins	By 7, 11, or Point
1	244 in 495	6	1 in 70
2	24 in 100	7	1 in 141
3	3 in 25	8	1 in 287
4	1 in 17	9	1 in 582
5	1 in 34		

Dice
Totals Probabilities on Two Dice

Total	Odds Against (Single toss)	Total	Odds Against (Single toss)
2	35 to 1	8	31 to 5
3	17 to 1	9	8 to 1
4	11 to 1	10	11 to 1
5	8 to 1	11	17 to 1
6	31 to 5	12	35 to 1
7	5 to 1		

Pinochle Auction
Odds Against Finding in "Widow" of Three Cards

Open Places	Odds Against	Open Places	Odds Against
1	5 to 1	4	3 to 2 for
2	2 to 1	5	2 to 1 for
3	Even		

Bridge

The odds—Against suit distribution in a hand of 4-4-3-2 are about 4 to 1, against 5-4-2-2 about 8 to 1, against 6-4-2-1 about 20 to 1, against 7-4-1-1 about 254 to 1, against 8-4-1-0 about 2,211 to 1, and against 13-0-0-0 about 158,753,389,899 to 1.

Simple Interest Table

Time		4%	5%	6%	7%	8%	Time		4%	5%	6%	7%	8%
$1.00	1 month	$.003	$.004	$.005	$.005	$.006	$100.00	4 days	$.045	$.053	$.066	$.077	$.889
..	2 months	.007	.008	.010	.011	.013	..	5	.056	.069	.082	.097	.111
..	3	.010	.013	.015	.017	.020	..	6	.067	.083	.100	.116	.133
..	6	.020	.025	.030	.035	.040	..	1 month	.334	.416	.500	.583	.667
..	12	.040	.050	.060	.070	.080	..	2 months	.667	.832	1.000	1.166	1.332
$100.00	1 day	.011	.013	.016	.019	.022	..	3	1.000	1.250	1.500	1.750	2.000
..	2 days	.022	.027	.032	.038	.044	..	6	2.000	2.500	3.000	3.500	4.000
..	3	.034	.041	.050	.058	.067	..	12	4.000	5.000	6.000	7.000	8.000

Copyright Law of the United States

Source: Copyright Office, Library of Congress

An author, or other owner who derives his rights from the author, may obtain protection for a literary, musical, or artistic work by complying with the provisions of the copyright law (Title 17 of the United States Code). The law gives the copyright owner the exclusive right to print, reprint, publish, copy and sell the copyrighted work; to revise or adapt it; and, with certain limitations, to perform and record it. Applications for registration of claims to copyright are filed with the Copyright Office, Library of Congress, Washington, D.C. 20559. Application forms and information circulars covering various subjects are furnished by the Copyright Office free upon request.

Categories of Works

The copyright law provides that the application for registration of any work shall specify to which of the following classes the work in which copyright is claimed belongs:

(A) Books, including composite and cyclopedic works, directories, gazetteers and other complications; (B) periodicals, including newspapers; (C) lectures, sermons and addresses prepared for oral delivery; (D) dramatic or dramatico-musical compositions; (E) musical compositions; (F) maps; (G) works of art, models or designs for works of art; (H) reproductions of a work of art; (I) drawings or sculptural works of a scientific or technical character; (J) photographs; (K) prints and pictorial illustrations including prints or labels used for articles of merchandise; (L) motion-picture photoplays; (M) motion pictures other than photoplays; and (N) sound recordings.

How Copyright is Secured

Between the time a work is created and the time statutory copyright is secured, it is protected, while unpublished, by the common law against unauthorized copying or other use, without any action being required by the Copyright Office.

Copyright in a published work is secured by publishing the work with the required notice of copyright, and it is important that all copies published bear the notice. The law provides that the notice shall consist of either the word "Copyright," or the abbreviation "Copr.," or the symbol ©, accompanied by the name of the copyright owner. If the work is a printed literary, musical or dramatic work, the notice shall include also the year in which the copyright was secured by publication. For example: © John Doe 1974. In the case, however, of copies of works specified in classes F through K above, the notice may consist of the symbol © accompanied by the initials, monogram, mark, or symbol of the owner, provided that his name appears on some accessible part of the copies.

Promptly after publication, there should be sent to the Copyright Office, Library of Congress, Washington, D.C. 20559, two copies of the best edition of the work, together with an application for registration and a $6 fee.

Manufacturing Requirements

For books and periodicals to be copyrightable, if they are by American authors, or by foreign authors who are domiciled in the U.S. at the time of first publication, the typesetting, printing, and binding of the copies used for first publication must have been done in the U.S. The only general exception to this rule is that a book or periodical in the English language manufactured and first published abroad may secure a 5-year ad interim copyright, provided that registration is made within 6 months of the date of first publication abroad. If ad interim copyright is secured, the importation of 1,500 copies is permitted. Books by American authors manufactured abroad may generally not be imported while they are under U.S. copyright protection, unless an Import Statement issued by the Copyright office at the time of the ad interim registration is presented to U.S. Customs at the port of entry. Further information may be obtained from the Copyright Office.

Copyright for Unpublished Works

Statutory copyright may be had for certain classes of unpublished works by depositing in the Copyright Office one copy of the work, together with an application for registration and the $6 fee. Works for which registration may be made in unpublished form include those in classes C, D, E, G, I, J, L and M, above. There are special provissions concerning what should be deposited in the case of 3-dimensional works of art and motion pictures; information about them is obtainable from the Copyright Office. **NOTE:** Certain kinds of material are not registrable in unpublished form. These include "book material" such as fiction, nonfiction, poetry, directories and catalogs, as well as manuscripts of articles, stories and other works that are to be first published as contributions to periodicals. Such works are, as mentioned above, protected by the common law against unauthorized use while unpublished.

Duration of Copyright

The original term of copyright endures for 28 years, measured from the exact date of first publication of the work; or in the case of works registered in unpublished form, from the date of registration. During the last (the 28th) year of the first term, the copyright may be renewed by filing in the Copyright Office an application for renewal and a fee of $4. It they are not received by the Copyright Office before the original term has expired the work falls into the public domain and the copyright cannot be restored.

Fees

All copyright fees are established by law. Remittances should be in the form of checks or money orders made payable to the Register of Copyrights. The schedule of fees follows:

Registration of copyright claims (including a certificate bearing the Copyright Office seal) all classes of works, $6.

For registration of a claim to renewal, $4.

Each additional certificate, $2.

Other certifications, including certifications of photocopies of Copyright Office records, $3.

For recording each assignment, agreement or other document of 6 pages or fewer, listing no more than one title, $5. For each page over 6 and each title over one, 50c.

Searches: for each hour spent by the Copyright Office staff in searching the official records, $5.

International Protection

The U.S. has copyright relations with some 60 countries, under which works of American authors are protected in those countries, and the works of their authors are protected in the U.S. The basic feature of this protection is "national treatment," under which the alien author is treated by a country in the same manner that it treats its own authors. Relations exist by virtue of bilateral agreements or through the Buenos Aires Convention or the Universal Copyright Convention. Legislation implementing the latter convention, which became effective Sept. 16, 1955, gives the works of foreign authors the benefit of exemptions from the manufacturing requirements of the U.S. copyright law, provided the works are first published abroad with a copyright notice including the symbol ©, the name of the copyright owner and the year date of first publication, and that the work either is by an author who is a citizen of a foreign country which belongs to the Convention or is first published in a foreign member country. Conversely, works of U.S. authors are exempt from certain burdensome requirements in particular foreign member countries.

Trademarks: How to Obtain and Protect Them

U. S. Govt. Bureaus have adopted trademark as a single word compounded from the former trade mark.

A trademark, as defined by Act of Congress, "includes any word, name, symbol, or device, or any combination thereof, adopted and used by a manufacturer or merchant to identify his goods and distinguish them from those manufactured or sold by others." Rights in trademarks are acquired only by use, which must continue if those rights are to be preserved. In order to be eligible for registration a mark must be in use in commerce which may be lawfully regulated by Congress.

Trademarks are registered on the Principal Register and the Supplemental Register of the U.S. Patent Office. "Coined, arbitrary, fanciful or suggestive marks, usually called technical marks, if otherwise qualified," may be registered on the Principal Register. A trademark that is merely descriptive of goods, or their regional origin, or is primarily a surname, is placed on the Supplemental Register.

The Trademark Act of 1946 provides that "For the purposes of registration on the supplemental register, a mark may consist of any trademark, symbol, label package, configuration of goods, name, word, slogan, phrase, surname, geographical name, numeral, or device, or any combination of any of the foregoing, but such mark must be capable of distinguishing the applicant's goods or services."

A trademark cannot be registered if it comprises immoral, deceptive or scandalous matter, or matter that may disparage or falsely suggest a connection with persons living or dead, institutions, beliefs, or national symbols. It cannot use the flag or coat of arms or other insignia of the United States, any state, municipality or foreign nation. It cannot use a portrait, signature or name of a living individual without his consent, or those of a deceased President of the United States without consent of his widow.

An application for registration must be filed in the name of the owner of the mark, who may submit his case or be represented by an attorney at law, or other person authorized to practice in trademark matters. A complete application comprises a written application, a drawing of the mark, five specimens or facsimiles and the required filing fee.

The Patent Office publishes a pamphlet, General Information Concerning Trademarks, which describes the way applications and drawings are to be prepared and gives sample forms for applications. The Patent Office, upon request, will supply forms for the registration of a trademark in the name of (1) an individual, (2) a firm, and (3) a corporation. If facilities permit, the Office will make drawings from the applicant's direction and at his expense. If the application is allowed, the trademark will be published in the Trademark Official Gazette so that anyone who considers that he will be damaged by the new mark may file his opposition in 30 days.

The Trademark Act of 1946 also provides for the registration of service marks, certification marks and collective marks. A service mark is a title, symbol or name used in sale or advertising of services to identify them. A certification mark is used by others than the owner to certify origin or quality, such as work by a union. A collective mark is used by members of a cooperative, an association or other group and indicates membership in a union or other organization. A digest of registered trademarks may be inspected at the Patent Office.

A trademark is registered for 20 years and may be renewed for periods of 20 years if still in use in commerce regulated by Congress, or if nonuse is due to special circumstances which excuse nonuse and is not due to any intention to abandon the mark. The fee for the original application is $35, and for the renewal is $25, with lesser fees for corrections, amendments, abstracts of title and other services.

The pamphlet, General Information Concerning Trademarks, is a general guide. The Trademark Rules of Practice of the Patent Office with Forms and Statutes is also published. The Trademark Official Gazette, issued weekly, contains information concerning trademarks published for opposition, registered, and renewed. For these and other trademark publications inquiries may be addressed to the Supt. of Documents, Government Printing Office, Washington, D.C. 20402.

Patents and How to Apply for Them

A patent for an invention is granted by the United States Patent Office to the inventor of any new and useful process, machine, manufacture, or composition of matter, or any new and useful improvements in these categories. The grant to the patentee is of "the right to exclude others from making, using or selling the invention throughout the United States" for the term of 17 years. A patent is also granted for certain distinct and new varieties of plants, also for 17 years.

Patents for new, original and ornamental designs for articles of manufacture may be obtained for 3½, 7 and 14 years, as requested by the inventor. The filing fee on each design application is $20; the issue fee is $10 for a 3½-yr. term, $20 for 7 years and $30 for 14 years.

Except in special circumstances, an application must be made by the inventor; if two are associated in the invention both must apply; if the inventor is mentally ill or dead, application may be made by the guardian or administrator of the estate. The specification must include a written description of the invention and of the manner and process of making and using it, and is required to be in such full, clear, concise, and exact terms as to enable any person skilled in the art to which the invention pertains, or with which it is most nearly connected, to make and use the same. The claims are full descriptions of the subject matter of the invention. A drawing is required by the statute in all cases which admit of drawings. The filing fee is $65, with $2 additional for each claim in excess of 10, and $10 additional for each claim in independent form in excess of one.

The Patent Office examines the application to determine whether the invention is new and useful and whether the application otherwise complies with the law. If the application is allowed, a notice is sent the applicant and the final fee of $100, plus $10 for each page or portion thereof of specification as printed and $2 for each sheet of drawing, is due within 3 months. The terms "patent applied for" and "patent pending" have no legal significance but falsely using this marking is punishable by a fine.

If the Patent Office rejects an application, the applicant may ask for reconsideration, giving reason; if rejected again he may appeal to the Board of Appeals of the Patent Office, and if rejected there, may go to the Court of Customs and Patent Appeals or file a civil action in the U.S. District Court for the District of Columbia.

Under certain conditions a license must be obtained before an application for a patent can be filed in a foreign country. The Commissioner of Patents may order an invention kept secret if publication would hurt the national safety or defense. Copies of the Patent Laws, the Rules of Practice (37 Code of Federal Regulations) in Patent Cases, and General Information Concerning Patents, can be obtained from the Superintendent of Documents, Government Printing Office, Washington, D.C. 20402.

Delegates from over 40 nations took part in Washington May 25-June 19, 1970, in a diplomatic conference on a Patent Cooperation Treaty. It was unanimously approved and was signed by representatives of 20 governments, including the United States, Great Britain, Germany, Canada and Japan, with many others expected to sign later. The treaty will simplify the filing of patent applications on the same invention in different countries by means of centralized filing procedures and standardized formalities.

RELIGIOUS INFORMATION

Census of Religious Bodies in the United States

Source: THE WORLD ALMANAC Questionnaire and 1974 Yearbook of American Churches

Membership figures in the following table are the latest available. Some denominations submitted carefully compiled data while others approached the task more casually. Some membership figures were obtained by WORLD ALMANAC Questionnaire, others from the 1974 Yearbook of American Churches for 1974. The number of churches is given in parentheses.

Denomination	Members
Adventist Bodies:	**480,708**
Advent Christian Church (400)	30,969
Primitive Advent Christian Ch. (10)	551
Seventh-day Adventists (3,278)	449,188
Amana Church Society (7)	**735**
American Rescue Workers (25)	**2,500**
Anglican Orthodox Church (37)	**2,630**
Apostolic Faith (45)	**4,100**
Armenian Church of America (58)	**372,000**
Assemblies of God (8,920)	**751,818**
Baptist Bodies:	**27,588,478**
American Baptist Assn. (3,361)	1,003,695
American Baptist Convention (6,020)	1,502,759
Baptist General Conference (632)	109,000
Baptist Missionary Assn. of Amer. (1,437)	199,640
Christian Unity Baptist Assn. (5)	345
Conserv. Baptist Assn. of Amer. (1,127)	300,000
Duck River(and Kindred) Assns. of Baptists (86)	8,909
Free Will Baptists, Natl. Assn. of (2,350)	225,000
Gen. Assn. of General Baptists (834)	70,000
Gen. Assn. of Regular Baptist Chs. (1,473)	214,000
General Baptists (773)	66,640
General Six-Principle Baptist (8)	308
Natl. Baptist Conv. of Amer. (11,398)	2,668,799
Natl. Baptist Conv., U.S.A. (26,)	6,487,003
Natl. Primitive Baptist Convention (2,198)	1,645,000
No. Amer. Baptist Gen. Conf. (247)	41,563
Progressive Natl. Baptist Conv. (655)	521,692
Regular Bap. Chs., Gen. Assn. of (1,473)	214,000
Separate Baptists in Christ (84)	7,496
Seventh Day Bapt. Gen. Conf. (68)	5,284
Southern Baptist Convention (34,183)	12,297,346
Berean Fundamental Church (50)	**2,530**
Bethel Ministerial Association (25)	**4,000**
Bible Protestant Church (42)	**2,254**
Bible Way Churches of Our Lord Jesus Christ World Wide (350)	**30,000**
Brethren (German Baptists):	**233,782**
Brethren Ch. (Ashland, Ohio) (119)	16,357
Brethren Churches, Natl. Fellowship of (243)	33,514
Church of the Brethren (1,037)	179,686
Old German Baptist Brethren (54)	4,225
Brethren, Plymouth (740)	**37,500**
Brethren (River):	**10,607**
Brethren in Christ Church (151)	9,730
United Zion Church (16)	877
Buddhist Churches of America (60)	**100,000**
Christadelphians (850)	**15,800**
Christian Catholic Church (6)	**3,000**
Christian Church of N. Amer., Gen. Council (110)	**8,500**
Christian Church (Disciples of Christ) (4,584)	**1,335,458**
Christian & Missionary Alliance (1,145)	**137,710**
Christian Nation Church, U.S.A. (16)	**2,000**
Christian Union (112)	**5,643**
Church of Christ (Holiness) U.S.A. (159)	**9,289**
Church of Christ, Scientist (2,350) (membership not recorded)	
Church of Christ (32)	**2,400**
The Church of God (2,035)	**75,890**
Church of God in Christ (4,500)	**425,000**
Church of Illumination (14)	**9,000**
Church of the Nazarene (4,717)	**417,200**
Church of Revelation (5)	**750**
Churches of Christ (18,000)	**2,400,000**
Chs. of Christ in Christian Union (256)	**8,771**
Churches of God:	**657,531**
Ch. of God (Anderson, Ind.) (2,235)	157,828
Ch. of God (Cleveland, Tenn.) (4,152)	297,103
Church of God of Prophecy (1,711)	59,535
Ch. of God, Seventh Day (7)	2,000

Denomination	Members
Ch. of God, Seventh Day (Denver) (56)	5,500
Churches of God, Gen. Conference (353)	34,675
The Church of God (2,035)	75,890
The (Original) Ch. of God (70)	20,000
The Church of God by Faith (135)	5,000
Churches of the Living God:	**47,670**
Church of the Living God (276)	45,320
House of God, Which is the Church of the Living God, the Pillar and Ground of the Truth (107)	2,350
Church of New Jerusalem, Gen. (33)	**2,143**
Congregational Christian Churches, Natl. Assn. of (346)	**75,000**
Congregational Holiness Ch. (147)	**4,859**
Conservative Cong. Christian Conf. (121)	**20,400**
Eastern Orthodox Churches:	**4,420,005**
Albanian Orthodox Archdio. in Amer. (13)	62,000
Albanian Orthodox Diocese of Amer. (10)	5,150
American Carpatho-Russian Orthodox Greek Catholic Church (70)	108,400
American Catholic Church (Syro-Antiochian) (5)	495
Antiochian Orthodox Archdiocese of Toledo, O. (18)	16,400
Antiochian Orthodox Christian Archdio. (102)	100,000
Armenian Apostolic Ch. of America (29)	125,000
Armenian Church of Amer., Diocese of the (58)	372,000
Bulgarian Eastern Orthodox Ch. (12)	1,500
Church of the East (Assyrians) (12)	5,000
Greek Archdio. of N. and S. America (502)	1,950,000
Holy Orthodox Church in America (Eastern Cath. & Apostolic) (4)	260
Holy Ukrainian Autocephalic Orthodox Ch. in Exile (13)	4,800
Orthodox Church in America (370)	1,000,000
Romanian Orthod. Episc. of Amer. (50)	50,000
Russian Orthodox Church in the U.S.A., Patriarchal Parishes (41)	50,000
Russian Orthodox Church Outside Russia (110)	60,000
Serbian Eastern Orthodox Church (60)	350,000
Syrian Orthodox Church of Antioch (Archdio. of the U.S.A. & Canada) (10)	50,000
Ukrainian Orthodox Ch. of the U.S.A. (95)	79,000
Ukrainian Orthodox Church in Amer. (Ecumenical Patriarchate) (23)	30,000
Ethical Union, American (23)	**4,000**
Evangelical Christian Churches (119)	**21,655**
Evangelical Congregational Ch. (160)	**29,434**
Evangelical Covenant Ch. of America (523)	**68,771**
Evangelical Free Ch. of America (562)	**70,490**
Evangelistic Associations:	**70,956**
Apostolic Christian Chs. of Amer. (78)	9,500
Apostolic Christian Ch. (Nazarean) (54)	3,771
The Christian Congregation (297)	52,585
Pillar of Fire (61)	5,100
Free Christian Zion Ch. of Christ (742)	**22,260**
Friends:	**70,552**
Friends United Meeting (515)	68,717
Religious Society of Friends (Conservative) (61)	1,835
Holiness Church of God (28)	**927**
Independent Fundamental Churches of Amer. (602)	**77,079**
Internatl. Church of the Foursquare Gospel (760)	**109,562**
Jehovah's Witnesses (6,059)	**498,177**

Denomination	Members
Jewish Congregations:	**6,115,000**
Union of Amer. Hebrew Cong. (686)	1,000,000
Union of Orthodox Jewish Cong. of Amer. (3,000)	3,000,000
United Synagogue of Amer. (835)	1,500,000
Latter-Day Saints:	**3,503,758**
Church of Jesus Christ (Bickertonites) (50)	2,439
Church of Jesus Christ of Latter-Day Saints (Mormon) (7,524)	3,321,556
Reorganized Church of Jesus Christ of Latter-Day Saints (1,031)	179,763
Lutheran Bodies:	**8,658,055**
Lutheran Church-Mo. Synod (6,983)	3,055,254
The American Lutheran Church (4,818)	2,464,744
The Lutheran Ch. in America (6,092)	3,138,057
Other Lutheran Churches:	**426,892**
Church of the Lutheran Brethren of America (71)	9,010
Church of the Lutheran Confession (69)	9,490
Evangelical Lutheran Synod (Norwegian Synod) (96)	17,321
Protestant Conference (Lutheran) (7)	2,660
Wisc. Evangelical Lutheran Synod (1,019)	388,411
Mennonite Bodies:	**170,914**
Beachy Amish Mennonite Ch. (62)	4,069
Ch. of God in Christ (Mennonite) (38)	6,204
Evangelical Mennonite Brethren (32)	3,784
Evangelical Mennonite Church (20)	3,136
Gen. Conference Mennonite Ch. (189)	36,129
Hutterian Brethren (29)	3,405
Mennonite Church (1,054)	90,967
Old Order Amish Church (368)	14,720
Old Order (Wisler) Mennonite Ch. (38)	8,000
Reformed Mennonite Church (12)	500
Methodist Bodies:	**13,303,126**
African Meth. Episcopal Ch. (4,500)	1,500,000
African M.E. Zion Church (5,994)	1,024,974
Christian Meth. Episcopal Ch. (2,598)	466,718
Evangelical Methodist Church (141)	10,519
Free Methodist Ch. of N. Amer. (1,058)	65,066
Fundamental Methodist Church (14)	722
The United Methodist Church (39,395)	10,192,265
Primitive Method. Ch. U.S.A. (86)	11,945
Reformed Meth. Union Episc. Ch. (20)	5,000
Reformed Zion Union Apostolic Ch. (50)	16,000
Southern Methodist Church (150)	9,917
Missionary Church, The (273)	20,078
Moravian Bodies:	**62,240**
Moravian Ch. in Amer., North Prov. (99)	33,687
Moravian Ch. in Amer., South Prov. (49)	22,411
Unity of the Brethren (32)	6,142
New Apostolic Church of N. Amer. (276)	**21,023**
Old Catholic Churches:	**67,023**
American Catholic Church, N.Y. Archdio.(4)	200

Denomination	Members
N. Amer. Old R.C. Church (25)	1,290
Old Roman Catholic Ch. (English Rite) (186)	65,128
Open Bible Standard Churches (270)	**25,000**
Pentecostal Assemblies:	**494,518**
Elim Fellowship (70)	5,000
Internatl. Pentecostal Assemblies (55)	10,000
Pentecostal Church of Christ (45)	1,365
Pentecostal Ch. of God of Amer. (975)	115,000
Pentecostal Fire-Baptized Holiness Ch. (41)	545
Pentecostal Free Will Baptist Ch. (150)	13,500
Pentecostal Holiness Church (1,340)	74,108
United Pentecostal Church (2,600)	275,000
Polish Natl. Catholic Ch. of Amer. (162)	**282,411**
Presbyterian Bodies:	**4,015,524**
Associate Reformed Presbyt. Church (General Synod) (148)	28,711
Cumberland Presbyterian Ch. (821)	87,838
Orthodox Presbyterian Ch. (123)	14,871
Presbyterian Ch. in the U.S. (4,284)	951,788
Reformed Presbyterian Ch. Evangelical Synod (129)	17,798
Reformed Presbyterian Church of N. Amer. (68)	5,560
United Presbyt. Ch. in the U.S.A. (8,732)	2,908,958
Protestant Episcopal Church (7,317)	**3,198,212**
Reformed Bodies:	**668,753**
Christian Reformed Church (750)	287,114
Hungarian Reformed Ch. in Am. (27)	11,250
Reformed Church in America (923)	366,381
Reformed Church in the U.S. (24)	4,008
Reformed Episcopal Church (66)	**6,727**
Roman Catholic Church (23,880)	**48,460,427**
Salvation Army (1,121)	**361,571**
The Schwenkfelder Church (5)	**2,250**
Social Brethren (31)	**1,672**
Spiritualists:	
Int. Gen. Assembly of Spiritualists (43)	8,500
Natl. Spiritual Alliance of the U.S.A. (34)	3,230
Natl. Spiritualist Assn. of Chs. (204)	4,962
Triumph the Church and Kingdom of God in Christ (495)	**54,307**
Unitarian Universalist Assn. (1,019)	**210,648**
United Brethren:	**26,809**
United Brethren in Christ (284)	26,409
United Christian Church (12)	400
United Church of Christ (6,617)	**1,867,810**
United Holy Ch. of America (470)	**28,980**
Vedanta Society of New York (13)	**1,000**
Volunteers of America (571)	**30,620**
Wesleyan Church, The (1,864)	**86,854**

Religious Population of the World

Source: The 1974 Encyclopedia Britannica Book of the Year.

Religion	N. America[1]	S. America	Europe[2]	Asia	Africa	Oceania[3]	Total
Total Christian	224,933,250	163,567,000	372,425,700	87,396,500	98,862,000	20,609,000	967,793,450
Roman Catholic	128,995,500	157,831,000	179,684,000	46,456,500	34,587,000	4,395,000	551,949,000
Eastern Orthodox	4,117,000	54,000	67,380,700	2,135,000	17,410,000	484,000	91,580,700
Protestant[4]	91,820,750	5,682,000	125,361,000	38,805,000	46,865,000	15,730,000	324,263,750
Jewish	6,344,475	680,700	3,983,750	3,064,050	297,950	73,000	14,443,925
Muslim	205,000	185,000	4,088,000	414,796,000	93,328,500	572,000	513,174,500
Zorastrian	....	....	....	180,600	450	....	181,050
Shinto	55,000	90,000	....	63,005,000	....	....	63,150,000
Taoist[5]	15,000	12,000	....	31,350,700	....	....	31,367,700
Confucian[5]	92,165	90,000	40,000	275,630,700	500	....	275,898,865
Buddhist	142,000	175,000	200,000	223,136,500	2,000	45,500	223,655,500
Hindu	65,000	470,000	300,000	513,755,500	461,000	529,000	515,580,500
Totals	**231,851,890**	**165,269,700**	**381,037,450**	**1,612,305,550**	**192,952,400**	**21,828,500**	**2,605,245,490**

(1) Includes Central America and the West Indies. (2) Includes the USSR where it is difficult to determine religious affiliation. (3) Includes Australia, New Zealand. (4) Protestant figures include "full members" rather than all baptized persons and are not comparable to those of ethnic religions or churches counting all adherents. (5) Statistics for Confucianism and Taoism are undeterminable in China since the Cultural Revolution.

Headquarters of U.S. Religious Bodies

(Year organized in parentheses)

Advent Christian Church (1854)—Pres., Rev. Joe Tom Tate. Exec. Sec., Rev. J. Howard Shaw, Box 23152, Charlotte, NC 28212.

Adventists, Seventh-day General Conference of (1863)—Pres., Robert H. Pierson, Sec., C.O. Franz, 6840 Eastern Ave., NW, Takoma Park, Wash., DC 20012.

African Methodist Episcopal Zion Church (1796)—Senior Bishop, Herbert Shaw. Sec., Board of Bishops, Bishop Charles H. Foggie, 1200 Windermere Dr., Pittsburgh, PA 15218.

Antiochian Orthodox Archdiocese of Toledo, Ohio (1936)—Archbishop Metropolitan Michael G. Shaheen, 532 Bush St., Toledo, OH 43604.

Antiochian Orthodox Christian Archdiocese (formerly **Syrian Antiochian Orthodox Church**) (1894)—Head of Archdiocese Metropolitan, Archbishop Philip (Saliba), 358 Mountain Rd., Englewood, NJ 07631.

Armenian Church of America, Diocese (1889)—Primate, Most Rev. Archbishop Torkom Manoogian. Sec., Very Rev. Zaven Arzoumanian, 630 Second Ave., N.Y., NY 10016.

Assemblies of God (1914)—Gen. Supt., Thomas F. Zimmerman. Gen. Sec., Bartlett Peterson, 1445 Boonville Ave., Springfield, MO 65802.

Augustana Evangelical Lutheran Church. See The Lutheran Church in America.

Baha'i Faith—About 5,500 communities, groups and isolated centers in the U.S. Sec., Natl. Spiritual Assembly, Glenford E. Mitchell, 536 Sheridan Rd., Wilmette, IL 60091.

Baptist Association, American (1905)—Pres., Albert Garner. Sec., Dr. L. Chester Guinn, 4605 N. State Line, Texarkana, TX 75501.

Baptist Association of America, Conservative (1947)—Pres., Rev. John Berentschot. Corr. Sec., Rev. Charles W. Jewitt. P.O. Box 66, Wheaton, IL 60187.

Baptist Churches in the U.S.A., Amer. (1907)—Pres., Dr. Peter H. Armacost. Gen. Sec., Rev. Dr. Robert Campbell, Valley Forge, PA 19481.

Baptist Convention, Southern (1845)—Pres., Jaroy Weber. Exec. Sec., Dr. Porter Routh, 460 James Robertson Parkway, Nashville, TN 37219.

Baptist Churches, Unified Free Will (1964)—President Bishop, Bishop Caldwell Thomas. Sec., Ernest Leonard, P.O. Box 4255, Newark, NJ.

Baptists, General (1611)—Moderator, Rev. G. Price. Clerk, Vern Whitten, 1629 Stinson Ave., Evansville, IN 47712.

Baptist General Conference (1879)—Gen. Sec., Warren Magnuson, 1233 Central St., Evanston, IL 60201.

Baptist General Conference, North American (1865)—Moderator, Delmar Wesseler. Exec. Sec., Dr. G. K. Zimmerman, 7308 Madison St., Forest Park, IL 60130.

Baptist, Natl. Assn. of Free Will (1727)—Moderator, Dr. J. D. O'Connell. Exec. Sec., Rufus Coffey, P.O. Box 1088, Nashville, TN 37202.

Baptist Missionary Assn. of America (formerly **North American Baptist Assn.**) (1950)—Pres. Rev. Lynn Stephens. Gen. Sec., Craig Branham, 716 Main St., Little Rock, AR 72201.

Buddhist Churches of America (1914)—Bishop Kenryu Takashi Tsuji, 1710 Octavia St., San Francisco, CA 94109.

Bulgarian Eastern Orthodox Church (1909)—Most Rev. Joseph Metropolitan, 312 West 101st St., N.Y., NY 10025.

Calvary Grace Christian Churches of Faith (1898)—Internatl. Gen. Supt., Rev. Dr. Herman Keck Jr., P.O. Box 1674, Ft. Lauderdale, FL 33302.

Calvary Grace Church of Faith (1874)—Rev. A. C. Spern, Internatl. Gen. Supt., P.O. Box 333, Rillton, PA 15678.

Christian Church (Disciples of Christ) (1809)—Gen. Minister and Pres., Dr. Kenneth L. Teegarden. Box 1986, Indianapolis, IN 46205.

Christian Endeavor, International Society of (1881)—Pres., Dr. LaVerne H. Boss. Gen. Sec., Rev. Charles W. Barner, 1221 East Broad St., P.O. Box 1110, Columbus, OH 43216.

Christian and Missionary Alliance (1887)—Pres., Dr. Nathan Bailey. Sec., Dr. R. W. Battles, 350 N. Highland Ave., Nack, NY 10960.

Christian Reformed Church (1857)—Stated Clerk, Rev. William P. Brink, 2850 Kalamazoo Ave., SE, Grand Rapids, MI 49508.

Church of the Brethren (1719) — Gen. Sec., General Board, S. Loren Bowman, 1451 Dundee Ave., Elgin, IL 60120.

Church of Christ, Scientists (1879) — Christian Science Mother Church. The First Church of Christ, Scientist, in Boston, Mass. Pres. Mrs. Georgina Tenant. First Reader, Clem W. Collins. Clerk, George W. Ledbetter. Christian Science Center, Boston, MA 02115.

Church of God (Anderson, Ind.) (1880)—Exec. Sec., W. E. Reed, Box 2420, Anderson, IN 46011.

Church of God, The (1903)—General Overseer, Bishop Voy M. Bullen, 2504 Arrow Wood Dr., SE, Huntsville, AL 35803.

Church of Jesus Christ of Latter Day Saints (Mormon) (1830)—Pres., Spencer W. Kimball. Pres. of the Council of Twelve Apostles, Ezra Taft Benson, 47 E. South Temple St., Salt Lake City, UT 84111.

Church of Jesus Christ of Latter Day Saints, Reorganized (1830)—Pres., W. Wallace Smith. Comm. of Communications, Elroy Hanton, Saints Auditorium, Independence, MO 64051.

Church of the Nazarene (1908)—Gen. Sec., B. Edgar Johnson, 6401 The Paseo, Kansas City, MO 64131.

Churches of Christ—No central organization. B. C. Goodpasture, editor, the Gospel Advocate, 1006 Elm Hill Rd., Nashville, TN 37210.

Churches of God, Gen. Conference (1825)—Pres., Dr. K. E. Boldosser. Sec., Rev. Harry G. Cadamore, 1210 Carlisle St., Natrona Heights, PA 15065.

Congregational Christian Churches, General Council. See United Church of Christ.

Congregational Christian Churches, Natl. Assn. of (1955)—Moderator, Rev. Raymond A. Waser. Sec., Rev. John H. Alexander, P.O. Box 1620, Oak Creek, WI 53154.

Ethical Union, American (Ethical Culture Movement) — Pres., Jack Tourin. Admin., Jean Kotkin, 2 W. 64th St., N.Y., NY 10023. Member of Internatl. Humanist and Ethical Union.

Evangelical Christian Churches (1966)—Pres., Rev. Kenneth T. Giles, P.O. Box 174, Jacksonville, FL 32219.

Evangelical Lutheran Synod (Norwegian Synod) (1918)—Pres., Rev. G. M. Orvick. Sec., Rev. Alf Merseth, 106 13th St., S., Northwood, IA 50459.

Evangelical Methodist Church (1946)—Gen. Supt., Rev. Lloyd H. Garrett. Gen. Sec., Rev. R. D. Driggers, 3036 N. Meridan, Wichita, KS 67204.

Evangelical and Reformed Church. See United Church of Christ.

Finnish Evangelical Lutheran Church (Suomi Synod). See Lutheran Church in America.

Foursquare Gospel, International Church of the (1927)—Pres., Dr. Rolf K. McPherson. Sec., Dr. Leland B. Edwards, 1100 Glendale Blvd., Los Angeles, CA 90026.

Free Methodist Church of North America (1860)—Sec., Board of Bishops. Bishop W. Dale Cryderman, Winona Lake, IN 46590.

Friends, General Conference of the Religious Society of (1900)—Chmn., C. Lloyd Bailey. Gen. Sec., Howard W. Bartram, 1520 Race St., Philadelphia, PA 19102.

Friends United Meeting (formerly **Five Years Meeting of Friends**) (1902)—Presiding Clerk, Thomas R. Bodine. Gen. Sec., Lorton Heusel, 101 Quaker Hill Dr., Richmond, IN 47374.

Greek Orthodox Church of North and South America (1864)—Primate, the Most Rev. Archbishop Iakovos. Chan., Very Rev. George J. Bacopulos, 10 E. 79th St., N.Y., NY 10021.

Harvest Fields Missionary and Evangelistic Assoc. — Pres., Rev. Joseph Morse, 3030 Mayhew Rd., Sacramento, CA 95826.

Union of American Hebrew Congregations —Pres. Rabbi Alexander M. Schindler, 838 Fifth Ave., N.Y., NY 10021.

Independent Fundamental Churches of America (1930)—Pres., Rev. Robert L. Gray. Exec. Dir., Rev. Bryan J. Jones, Box 242, Westchester, IL 60153.

Jehovah's Witnesses (1884)—Pres., Nathan H. Knorr, 124 Columbia Heights, Brooklyn, NY 11201.

Jewish Congregations of America, Union of Orthodox — Pres., Harold M. Jacobs. Natl. Dir., Rabbi David Cohen, 116 East 27th St., N.Y., NY 10016.

Latter-day Saints. See Church of Jesus Christ.

Lutheran Church, The American (1961) — Pres., Dr. David W. Preus. Sec., A. R. Mickelson, 422 S. 5th St., Minneapolis MN 55415.

Lutheran Church in America, The (estab. June 28, 1962 by consolidating Amer. Evangelical Lutheran Ch., Augustana Evangelical Lutheran Ch., Finnish Evangelical Lutheran Ch., and The United Lutheran Ch. in Amer.) — Pres., Rev. Robert J. Marshall. Sec., Rev. George F. Harkins, 231 Madison Ave., N.Y., NY 10016.

Lutheran Church-Missouri Synod (1847)—Pres., Dr. J. A. O. Preus. Sec., Dr. Herbert A. Mueller, 500 N. Broadway, St. Louis, MO 63102.

Lutheran World Federation, U.S.A. National Committee of the (formed Jan. 1, 1967, former **National Lutheran Council**) Sec., Rev. Dr. Carl Mau, 315 Park Ave., N.Y., NY 10010.

Mennonite Church (1863)—Moderator, Newton Gingrich. Sec., Paul N. Kraybill, 528 East Madison St., Lombard, IL 60148.

Methodist Church, The United (1784)—Council of Bishops Pres., Bishop Dwight E. Loder. Sec., Bishop Ralph T. Alton, 1100 W. 42nd St., Indianapolis, IN 46208.

Moravian Church in America (Unitas Fratrum) (1740)—**Northern Province:** Hq., 69 West Church St., Bethlehem, PA 18018; Pres., Provincial Elders' Conf., Dr. J. S. Groenfeldt. **Southern Province:** Hq., 459 S. Church St., Winston-Salem, NC 27101; Pres., Provincial Elders' Conf., Dr. Richard F. Amos.

Open Bible Standard Churches (1919)—Gen. Supt., Raymond E. Smith, Sec.-Treas., O. Ralph Isbill, P.O. Box 1737, Des Moines, IA 50306.

Orthodox Church in America (formerly Russian Orthodox Catholic Ch. of Amer.) (1794)—Primate, Metropolitan Archbishop Ireney. Chancellor, Very Rev. Daniel Hubiak, Rte. 25A, P.O. Box 679, Syosset, NY 11791.

New Jerusalem in the U.S.A., General Convention of the (1782)—Pres., Rev. Ernest O. Martin. Rec. Sec., Mrs. Wilfred G. Rice, 31 Poole St., Brockton, MA 02401.

Pentecostal Church of God of America (1919)—Gen. Supt., Dr. R. D. Heard, 316 Joplin Ave., Joplin, MO 64801.

Pentecostal Church, United (1945)—Gen. Supt. Stanley W. Chambers. Gen. Sec., Cleveland M. Becton, 8655 Dunn Rd., Hazelwood, MO 63042.

Presbyterian Church, Cumberland (1810)—Moderator, David A. Brown. Stated Clerk, H. Shaw Scates, Box 4149, Memphis, TN 38104.

Presbyterian Church in the U.S. (1861)—Moderator, Rev. James E. Andrews. Stated Clerk, Rev. Lawrence W. Bottoms, 341 Ponce de Leon Ave., NE, Atlanta, GA 30308.

Presbyterian Church in the U.S.A., United (formed 1958 through merger of the **Presbyterian Ch. in the U.S.A.** and the **United Presbyt. Ch. of N. America**)—Moderator, Clinton M. Marsh. Stated Clerk, Ruling Elder William P. Thompson, 475 Riverside Dr., N.Y., NY 10027.

Protestant Episcopal Church, The (1789)—Presiding Bishop, Pres. of Exec. Council, Rt. Rev. John M. Allin, 815 Second Ave., N.Y. NY 10017.

Rabbinical Alliance of America—Pres., Rabbi David B. Hollander, 156 5th Ave., N.Y., NY 10010.

Rabbinical Assembly, The—Pres., Rabbi Mordecai Waxman. Exec. V.P., Rabbi W. Kelman, 3080 Broadway, N.Y., NY 10027.

Rabbinical Council of America—Pres., Rabbi Fabian Schonfeld. Exec. V.P., Rabbi Israel Klavan, 220 Park Ave., South, N.Y., NY 10003.

Rabbis, Central Conference of American—Pres. Rabbi Robert I. Kahn. Exec. V.P., Rabbi Joseph B. Glaser, 790 Madison Ave., N.Y., NY 10021.

Reformed Church in America (1628)—Pres., Rev. Raymond H. Rewerts. Gen. Sec., Rev. Marion de Velder, D.D., 475 Riverside Dr., N.Y., NY 10027.

Reformed Episcopal Church (1873)—Pres. and Presiding Bishop, Rev. Howard D. Higgins. Sec., Rev. D. Ellsworth Raudenbush, 560 Fountain St., Havre de Grace, MD 21078.

Reformed Presbyterian Church, Evangelical Synod (Apr. 6, 1965, union of the **Reformed Presbyterian Ch., General Synod** and the **Evangelical Presbyterian Ch.**)—Moderator, Rev. Samuel S. Ward. Stated Clerk, Rev. Paul R. Gilchrist, 107 Hardy Rd., Lookout Mountain, TN 37350.

Regular Baptist Churches, General Assn. of (1932)—Natl. Rep., Dr. Joseph M. Stowell, 1800 Oakton Boulevard, Des Plaines, IL 60018.

Romanian Orthodox Episcopate of America (1929)—Bishop, His Grace Valerian D. Trifa. Sec., Rev. Eugene Lazar, 2522 Grey Tower Rd., Jackson, MI 49201.

Russian Orthodox Church Outside Russia (1920)—Pres., Council of Bishops, Most Rev. Metropolitan Philaret, 75 East 93rd St., N.Y. NY 10028.

Salvation Army, The (1865 in Eng., 1880 in America)—Natl. Cmdr., Commissioner, Paul J. Carlson. Natl. Chief Sec., Col. Ernest W. Holz. Natl. Hq., 120-130 W. 14th St., N.Y., NY 10011.

Seamen's Church Institute of N.Y. (1834)—Dir., Rev. John M. Mulligan. Sec., R. Thornton Wilson Jr., 15 State St., N.Y., NY 10004.

Serbian Eastern Orthodox Church —Diocese for U.S., Canada and Europe. Bishops: Most Rev. Dionisije and Iriney. Sec., Very Rev. Aleksandar Ivanovich, St. Sava Monastery, Libertyville, IL 60048.

Serbian Eastern Orthodox Church in U.S. and Canada—Bishops: Rt. Rev. Firmilian, Midwest Diocese, 5701 N. Redwood Dr., Chicago, IL 60631. Rt. Rev. Gregory, Western Diocese, 2511 W. Garvey, Alhambra, CA 91803. Rt. Rev. Sava, Eastern U.S. and Canadian Diocese, 5095 Broadview Rd., Richfield, OH 44286.

Spiritualists, International General Assembly of (1936)—Pres., Fred Jordan. Sec., Charles Doyle, 1809 E. Bayview Blvd., Norfolk, VA 23503.

Synagogue Council of America—Pres., Rabbi Irwin M. Blank. Exec. V. P. Rabbi Henry Siegman, 432 Park Ave., South, N.Y. NY 10016.

Ukrainian Orthodox Church of the U.S.A. (1919)—Metropolitan Mstyslav S. Skrypnyk, Box 495, South Bound Brook, NJ 08880.

Unitarian Universalist Assn. (formed May 11, 1961 by merger of the **American Unitarian Assn.** and the **Universalist Church of America**)—Pres., Rev. Robert Nelson West. Moderator, Dr. Joseph L. Fisher. Sec., Russel F. Benson, 25 Beacon St., Boston, MA 02108.

United Church of Christ (formed June 25, 1957 through union of the **General Council of the Congregational Christian Churches** with the **Evangelical and Reformed Ch.**)—Pres., Rev. Dr. Robert V. Moss Jr. Sec., Rev. Dr. Joseph H. Evans, 297 Park Ave., South, N.Y. NY 10010.

United Israel World Union—Pres. & Chmn. of the Board, David Horowitz. Natl. Sec., Peter Moyle, 507 Fifth Ave., N.Y., NY 10017.

United Sons & Daughters of True Holiness Assn. (1912)—Gen. Sec., Elder B.W. Shoffner, 109 Daniel St., Greensboro, NC 27401.

United Synagogue of America—Pres., Arthur Levine, V.P., Dr. Bernard Segal, 3080 Broadway, N.Y., NY 10027.

Volunteers of America (1896)—Commander-in-chief, Gen. John F. McMahon. Natl. Field Sec., Col. O.P. Strickland. Hq., 340 West 85th St., N.Y., NY 10024.

Wesleyan Church, The (1968) (organized through the merger of the **Pilgrim Holiness Ch.** and the **Wesleyan Methodist Ch. of America**)—Gen. Superintendents, Dr. Robert W. McIntyre, Dr. M.H. Snyder, Dr. J.D. Abbott, Dr. V.A. Mitchell. Sec., D. Wayne Brown, Box 2000, Marion, IN 46952.

Wesleyan Methodist Church of America, The (1893)—*See Wesleyan Church.*

Wisconsin Evangelical Lutheran Synod (1850)—Pres., Rev. Oscar Naumann. Sec., Prof. Heinrich J. Vogel, 11757 N. Seminary Drive 65W, Mequon, WI 53092.

World Council of Churches, U.S. Conference for the—Chmn., Dr. Robert J. Marshall. Exec. Sec., Rev. Charles H. Long Jr. 475 Riverside Dr., N.Y., NY 10027.

National Council of Churches

The National Council of the Churches of Christ in the U.S.A. is a cooperative federation of 31 Protestant and Orthodox churches which seeks to advance programs and policies of mutual interest to its members. The NCC was formed in 1950 by the merger of 12 inter-denominational agencies. The Council's member churches now have an aggregate membership totaling approximately 42,000,000. The NNC is not a governing body and has no control over the policies or operations of any church belonging to it. The work of the Council is divided into 3 divisions — Church and Society, Education and Ministry, Overseas Ministries, and 15 commissions on Faith and Order, Regional and Local Ecumenism, Broadcasting and Film, Stewardship and Justice, Liberation and Human Fulfillment. The chief administrative officer of the NNC is Dr. Claire Randall, 475 Riverside Drive, N.Y., NY 10027.

Leading Protestant Bodies in the United States

Baptists

The Baptist Church was formed in England in 1609 as part of the separatist movement from the Church of England.

The first Baptist Church in America was founded in 1638 in Providence, R.I., by Roger Williams. National Organization began in 1814, and a Missionary Convention was formed to permit followers to express themselves in terms of missionary activities. Baptist bodies throughout the United States have a membership of 27,588,478.

American Baptist Churches in the U.S.A. (formerly Northern Baptist Convention, renamed American Baptist Convention in 1950, and renamed American Baptist Churches in the U.S.A. in 1973) was organized in 1907. Churches, 6,020, membership, 1,502,759. Headquarters at Valley Forge, Pa., 19481. Agencies operating under this convention of Baptists include the American Baptist Board of International Ministries, American Baptist Board of National Ministries, American Baptist Board of Educational Ministries, and the Ministers and Missionaries Benefit Board, all at Valley Forge, PA 19481.

National Baptist Convention of America, organized 1880. Churches, 11,398, membership, 2,668,799. The General Organization and 11 others. Pres., Dr. James C. Sams, 1724 Jefferson St., Jacksonville, FL 32290.

National Baptist Convention, U.S.A., Inc., founded in 1880, in Montgomery, Ala., is the oldest and parent convention of Negro Baptists. Churches, 27,396; membership, 6,487,003. Pres., Dr. J. H. Jackson; Sec., Rev. T. J. Jemison, 915 Spain St., Baton Rouge, LA 70802.

Southern Baptist Convention. In 1845 Southern Baptists withdrew from the General Missionary Convention over the question of slavery and other matters and formed the Southern Baptist Convention, largest of Baptist bodies. Churches in all 50 states are related to the Convention. 2,534 missionaries serve in 77 countries. Churches, 34,183, membership, 12,297,-346. Executive Committee, 460 James Robertson Parkway, Nashville, TN 37219. Pres., Jaroy Weber, Exec. Sec., Dr. Porter Routh. Boards include Sunday Board, Nashville, Tenn.; Foreign Mission Board, Richmond, Va.; Home Mission Board, Atlanta, Ga.; Annuity Board, Dallas, Tex.

Church of Christ, Scientist

First organized in 1879, under the direction of Mary Baker Eddy, The Christian Science Church took its present form in 1892 as the Mother Church, the First Church of Christ, Scientist, in Boston, Mass. Today there are about 3,200 branches in 54 countries. There are 2,350 Christian Science churches in the United States. Membership figures are not recorded. Christian Science regards the Bible as its ultimate authority and includes spiritual healing as part of its teachings.

The denomination supports radio and television programs, charitable institutions, and a world-wide Board of Lectureship. It also maintains the Christian Science Publishing Society which publishes the Christian Science Monitor and various religious periodicals. The affairs of the denomination are administered by the Christian Science Board of Directors, Christian Science Center, Boston, MA 02115. Pres., Mrs. Georgina Tennant.

Disciples of Christ

The Christian Church (Disciples of Christ) is an American communion arising out of a concern for Christian unity expressed by Barton W. Stone in 1804 and by Thomas Campbell and his son Alexander, in 1809. The first churches were Cane Ridge in Kentucky and Brush Run near Washington, Pa. The "Christians" of Kentucky and the "Disciples" of Pennsylvania and Virginia united in 1832. The first General Convention was held in 1849. The church is thoroughly ecumenical in stance, and is congregational in government. Congregations in the U.S. and Canada number 4,584; membership is 1,335,458. The communion is served by the General Office of the Christian Church (Disciples of Christ), 17 general units, 37 regional bodies and 32 educational institutions. General Minister and Pres., Dr. Kenneth L. Teegarden. Box 1986, Indianapolis, IN 46206.

Evangelical Churches

The Evangelical and Reformed Church. *See United Church of Christ.*

The Evangelical United Brethren Church. *See United Methodist Church.*

Latter-Day Saints

The churches of the Latter-Day Saints do not consider themselves Protestants because they had no part in the 16th century Protestant Reformation and consider themselves to be the "restored" Church of Jesus Christ.

The Church of Jesus Christ of Latter-Day Saints, often called the "Mormon" church, regards the Bible, the Book of Mormon, the Doctrine and Covenants, and the Pearl of Great Price as the word of God. The church was organized Apr. 6, 1830, at Fayette, N.Y., by Joseph Smith, first president. After settling in Kirkland, O., and Independence, Mo., the members located in Nauvoo, Ill., in 1839 to escape persecution. Attacks by a mob led to the fatal shooting of Joseph Smith and his brother Hyrum while they were in the Carthage, Ill., jail for protection from the mob, June 27, 1844. Beginning in 1847 most members, under the leadership of Brigham Young, moved by covered wagons across the Great Plains to Utah.

The church is divided into stakes, wards, branches and missions. Highest authority is the First Presidency, consisting of the president and 2 counselors, assisted by 12 apostles. Spencer W. Kimball is the 12th and current president. Churches 7,524, membership, 3,321,556. Hq. at 47 East South Temple St., Salt Lake City, UT 84111.

The Reorganized Church of Jesus Christ of Latter-Day Saints was founded Apr. 6, 1830, by Joseph Smith and reorganized under the leadership of the founder's son, Joseph Smith, in 1860. The church is established in 25 countries, the U.S. and Canada. Membership is 179,763 in 1,031 churches. Headquarters is at Saints Auditorium, Independence, MO 64051.

Lutherans

The church was started in Europe during the Protestant Reformation by the followers of Martin Luther.

Lutheranism was introduced into the United States by Dutch colonists on Manhattan, later by Swedes on the Delaware, by Palatines in Pennsylvania and New York and by Salzburgers in Georgia.

The American Lutheran Church was organized during a constituting convention at Minneapolis, Minn., in Apr. 1960, merging the American Lutheran Church, and United Evangelical Lutheran Church. The merger brought together Lutherans of Danish, German and Norwegian heritage. A fourth body, The Lutheran Free Church, joined with The American Lutheran Church in Feb. 1963. The American Lutheran Church has 2,465,584 members. Headquarters at 422 S. 5th St., Minneapolis. Dr. David W. Preus is president. The 4,822 congregations are divided territorially into districts in the U.S. The foreign mission program involves 424 missionaries (including wives) on 13 fields in South America, Africa and Asia. The church's Board of Publication operates the Augsburg Publishing House, 422 S. 5th St., Minneapolis MN 55415.

Augustana Evangelical Lutheran Church. *See The Lutheran Church in America.*

The Lutheran Church-Missouri Synod was organized in 1847. It is the leader in the conservative group among the Lutherans with 6,983 churches and a membership of 3,055,254. The Synod is divided into 40 districts (35 in the U.S.; 3 in Canada; 2 in South America). The Synod conducts a world-wide mission program and fosters a system of 16 ministerial and teacher training colleges to staff its congregations and its 1,239 parochial schools. Affiliated are the Lutheran Laymen's League, Lutheran Women's Missionary League, and Walther League (a young people's organization). Valparaiso University, Valparaiso, Ind., is supported and controlled by the Lutheran University Assn. Hq. for the Synod: 500 N. Broadway, St. Louis, MO 63102.

The Lutheran Church in America was organized June 28,1962, by the consolidartion of the American Evangelical Lutheran Church, the Augustana Evangelical Lutheran Church, the Finnish Evangelical Lutheran Church and The United Lutheran Church in America. With 3,138,057 baptized members, the body is the largest of the Lutheran churches in the United States. The Lutheran Church in America has 6,092 congregations, organized in 33 synods in the U.S., Canada, Puerto Rico, and the Virgin Islands. The headquarters of the denomination is at 231 Madison Ave., N.Y., N.Y. 10016, and principal agencies are located at 2900 Queen Lane, Philadelphia, Pa.,327 South LaSalle St., Chicago, Ill., and 608 Second Ave. S., 2nd floor, Minneapolis, Minn.

Wisconsin Evangelical Lutheran Synod was organized in 1850. It has 1,019 congregations, 388,411 members. Formerly the second largest body of the Synodical conference, Wisconsin withdrew from the Conference in Aug. 1963.

Methodists

The name Methodist was originally given to Charles and John Wesley and several other Oxford students, in 1729. It is thought that the term was selected due to the exact and "methodical" manner in which they performed various engagements which a sense of Christian duty induced them to undertake. The Methodist movement was carried to America in 1760, by emigrants from Ireland. Methodist bodies in the United States have a membership of approximately 13,300,000.

The United Methodist Church has 39,395 churches and 10,192,265 members. The present organization of The United Methodist Church was formed Apr. 23, 1968, in Dallas, Tex., by the union of The Methodist Church and The Evangelical United Brethren Church. The two churches shared a common historical and spiritual heritage. The Methodist Church resulted in 1939 from the unification of 3 branches of Methodism — the Methodist Episcopal Church, the Methodist Episcopal Church, South, and the Methodist Protestant Church. The Methodist movement began in 18th Century England under the preaching of John Wesley, but the so-called Christmas Conference of 1784 in Baltimore is regarded as the date on which the organized Methodist Church was founded as an ecclesiastical organization. It was there that Francis Asbury was elected the first bishop in this country. The Evangelical United Brethren Church was formed in 1946 with the merger of the Evangelical Church and the Church of the United Brethren in Christ, both of which had their beginnings in Pennsylvania in the evangelistic movement of the 18th and early 19th centuries. Philip William Otterbein and Jacob Albright were early leaders of this movement among German-speaking settlers of the Middle Colonies.

The supreme policy-making body of The United Methodist Church is the quadrennial General Conference. Principal agencies are in the following cities: New York, N. Y., Evanston, Ill., Nashville, Tenn., Washington, D.C., Dayton, O., and Lake Janaluska, N.C.

African Methodist Episcopal Church, incorporated 1816 under Pennsylvania laws, is second largest of the Methodist bodies. Churches, 4,500, membership, 1,500,000. Pres., Board of Bishops, Bishop Hubert N. Robinson, 951 Old Grove Manor, Jacksonville, FL 32207.

Presbyterians

Presbyterianism is a system of representative church governed by presbyters, or elders. John Calvin (1509-1564) has been regarded as the founder of Presbyterianism. Presbyterians were among the earliest colonists of America. Their first church was established about 1640 and the first presbytery in 1706. Nine Presbyterian bodies in the United States have a membership of 4,015,524.

The United Presbyterian Church in the U.S.A., largest of the Presbyterian bodies, was formed on May 28, 1958, by a merger of the Presbyterian Church in the U.S.A. and the United Presbyterian Church of North America. It has 8,732 churches and 2,908,958 members. Offices of the General Assembly, General Assembly's Mission Council, Support Agency, Program Agency, and Vocations Agency, 475 Riverside Dr., N. Y., NY 10027.

Presbyterian Church in the United States, which established a separate existence in 1861, is sometimes miscalled the Southern Church. Churches, 4,284, membership 951,788. Office of the Gen. Assembly, 341 Ponce de Leon Ave., NE Atlanta, 30308. Moderator, Rev. Lawrence W. Bottoms. GA Stated Clerk, Rev. James E. Andrews.

Protestant Episcopal Church

An American religious denomination directly descended from the Church of England. Brought to America by the Jamestown colonists in 1607. Separated from English church and adopted present name in 1789. Alternate name, "The Episcopal Church" was adopted in 1967. Churches 7,317, membership, 3,198,212. Headquarters of the Exec. Council, 815 Second Ave., N. Y., NY 10017. Presiding Bishop, Rt. Rev. John M. Allin; Interim Exec. Officer of General Convention, Rt. Rev. Scott Field Bailey.

United Church of Christ

Formed in 1957 by a union of the General Council of the Congregational Christian Church and the Evangelical and Reformed Church. It is the first union in the United States of churches with different forms of church government—congregational and modified presbyterian—and different historical backgrounds. Congregationalism was brought to America by both the Pilgrims of the "Mayflower" and the Puritans of the Massachusetts Bay Colony. Eventually it became the dominant form of church organization in New England. The Evangelical and Reformed Church was started in 1934 with the union of the Evangelical Synod of North America and the Reformed Church in the U.S.

A constitution for the United Church of Christ was declared in force in July 1961. The denomination has 1,867,810 members in 6,617 local congregations. The United Church Board of World Ministries has 251 missionaries and other personnel at work in 30 countries. In the United States, the United Church of Christ is active in Christian education, church extension, health and welfare, mass communication, race relations, and social action. Headquarters of United Church of Christ, 297 Park Ave. S., N. Y. NY 10010; Office of Communication, 289 Park Ave. So., N. Y., NY. United Church Board for Homeland Ministries, 287 Park Ave. South. United Church Board for World Ministries, 475 Riverside Dr., New York, NY 10027.

Leading Protestant Denominations in Canada

Source: Corpus Directory and Almanac of Canada 1972, and the Director of Christian Service, Ontario Bible College, Rev. Charles A. Tipp.

Anglicans

The Anglican Church of Canada was established in the early 1700s, and its first bishop Charles Inglis was appointed in 1789. The General Synod, created in 1893, acts to co-ordinate the various activities of the Church, and usually meets biennially. It is made up of the Church's Archbishops and Bishops together with the elected clerical and lay representatives from the 28 dioceses. The Anglican Church has 2,409,068 members.

Baptists

The two largest Baptist churches are the Federation of Canada and the Fellowship of Evangelical Baptist Churches. The Federation has about 410,000 members in 4 subdivisions: the Baptist Convention of Ontario and Quebec; the Baptist Union of Western Canada; the United Baptist Convention of the Atlantic Provinces; and the French Baptist Union. The Fellowship consists of about 110,000 members. Other large Baptist organizations are the Baptist General Conference, the North American Baptist Conference, and the Canadian Southern Baptist Conference. The Baptist faith in Canada has 593,553 adherents.

Lutherans

The first large settlement of Lutherans in Canada was in Halifax in 1749. There are 3 main Lutheran bodies: the Evangelical Lutheran Church of Canada, the Lutheran Church-Canada (Missouri Synod), and the Lutheran Church in America-Canada Section. These bodies cooperate through the Lutheran Council in Canada. The Lutheran churches of Canada have 662,744 members.

Presbyterians

The Presbyterian Church in Canada is connected historically to the Church of Scotland. It is organized into 8 synods and 44 presbyteries, and has 818,558 members.

United Church

The United Church of Canada is the largest Protestant denomination in Canada with 3,664,008 members. It was established in 1925 as a result of a merger among the Methodist Church, the Congregational Churches, and 70% of the Presbyterian Church. The Canada Conference of the Evangelical United Brethren Church joined this union in 1968. The highest policy making body of the United Church of Canada is the General Council which meets biennially.

Headquarters of Religious Bodies in Canada

Source: Corpus Directory and Ontario Bible College.

Anglican Church of Canada (creation of General Synod 1893)—Primate, Most Rev. E.W. Scott, Gen. Sec. of the General Synod, The Ven. E.S. Light, 600 Jarvis St., Toronto, 285, Ontario.

Antiochian Orthodox Christian Church (Syrian)— Rev. Father E. Hanna, 555-575 Jean Talon E., Montreal 328.

Apostolic Church of Pentecost of Canada (Inc.), The — Moderator, Rev. D.W. Breen; Clerk, Mr. F. Assman, 1612 Adelaide St. East, Saskatoon, Sask.

Associated Gospel Church of Canada (Christian Workers Church of Canada 1922) — Pres., Rev. L.K. Redinger, 280 Plains Rd. W., Burlington, Ont.

Baptist Federation of Canada — Gen. Sec.-Treasurer, Rev. R. Fred Bullen, 91 Queen St., Box 1298, Brantford, Ontario.

Brethren in Christ Church, Canada Conference — Box 65, Sherkston, Ontario.

British Israel World Federation — Office Manager and Secretary, Mrs. S. Cunningham, 313 Sherbourne St., Toronto 2, Ontario.

Buddhist Churches of Canada — Bishop, Rev. Neuton Ishiura, 918 Bathurst St., Toronto, Ontario

Byelorussian Autocephalic Orthodox Church Abroad — Rt. Rev. Bishop Mikalay, 524 St. Clarens Ave., Toronto 172, Ontario.

Canadian Council of Churches, The (1938)—Pres., Rev. Dr. A.B.B. Moore, 40 St. Clair Ave. E., Toronto 7.

Canadian Jewish Congress — Exec. Vice-Pres., Saul Hayes, Q.C., 1590 McGregor Ave., Montreal 109, Quebec.

Christian and Missionary Alliance in Canada, The (1889)—District Superintendent for Eastern and Central Canada, Rev. W.J. Newell, 125 Panin Road, Burlington, Ontario; District Superintendent for Canadian Midwest, Rev. A. H. Orthner, 2521 Parliament Avenue, Regina, Sask.; District Superintendent for Western Canada, Rev. Ray McIntyre, 2528 Chicoutimi Drive, N.W., Calgary, Alberta.

Christian Church (Disciples of Christ) (All Canada Committee formed 1922) — Chairman, Mr. R.K. Leland, 130 Merton St., Suite 301, Toronto 7, Ont.

Christian Reformed Churches, The Canadian Council of — Rev. John Van Hormelen, R.R. 8, London, Ont.

Church of Jesus Christ of Latter Day Saints (Mormons), (1830)— Pres., Alberta Stake, Mr. F.N. Spackman, Cardston, Alberta; Pres., Toronto Stake, Mr. W. M. Davies, 139 Richland Cres., Etobicoke, Ont.; Pres., Vancouver Stake, Mr. K. M. Humphreys, 1677 Davenport Pl., N. Vancouver, B. C.

Church of the Nazarene (1902)—Dist. Superintendent of Canada Central District, Rev. N. Hightower, 38 Riverhead Drive, Rexdale, Ont., Chairman of Exec. Board, Dr. Herman L.G. Smith, 2236 Capitol Hill Crescent, N.W., Calgary 44, Alta.

Evangelical Fellowship of Canada — Pres., Dr. R.N. Thompson M.P.; Sec., Rev. C.A. Tipp, 67 Harbord St., Toronto 4, Ontario.

Fellowship of Evangelical Baptist Churches in Canada (merging of **Union of Regular Baptist Churches of Ontario and Quebec**, and **Fellowship of Independent Baptist Churches 1953**) — Gen. Sec., Dr. J.H. Watt, 74 Sheppard Ave. W., Willowdale, Ontario.

Free Methodist Church in Canada (1880) — Pres., Rev. E. S. Bull, 40 Glen Rd., Belleville, Ont. K8P4G1.

Greek Orthodox Church — Ninth Archdiocese District, Canada, Titular Bishop of Ancona, His Grace Theodosios, 27 Teddington Park Ave., Toronto 12.

Independent Holiness Church (merger of former Holiness Movement of Canada with The Free Methodist Church in 1958) — Pres. Rev. Murdo Campbell, R.R. 3, Metcalfe, Ont.

Jehovah's Witnesses (Branch Office established in Winnipeg 1918)—Presiding Minister, Mr. Kenneth A. Little, 150 Bridgeland Ave., Toronto 390, Ontario.

Lutheran Church of Canada, The Evangelical — Pres., Dr. S.T. Jacobson, 212 Wiggins Ave., Saskatoon, Sask.

Lutheran Church-Canada — Pres. Rev. H.A. Merklinger, 7205 Sharon Ave., Niagara Falls, Ontario.

Lutheran Church in America—Canada Section — Pres., Dr. Otto A. Olson Jr., 211-228 Portage Ave., Winnipeg 12, Man.

Lutheran Council in Canada — a joint body of the three main churches, Gen. Sec., Dr. J.M. Zimmerman, 9901-107 St., Edmonton, Alta.

Mennonite Brethren Churches of North America, Canadian Conference—Moderator, Rev. J.H. Quiring, Clearbrook, B.C.

Mennonites in Canada, Conference of — Moderator, Rev. Jacob Tilitzky, 2201 Queen Rd., R.R. #1, Abbotsford, B.C.

Mennonite Church, The (Old) — First Mennonite Church, 117 King St. W., Kitchener, Ont. Mod. Elect., Newton W. Gingrick, Tavistock, Ont.

Missionary Church, The — (an Anabaptist body) — Dist. Supt. (Ontario) Rev. Grant Sloss, Ste. 203, Frederick St. Plaza, Kitchener, Ont.

National Spiritual Assembly of the Baha'is of Canada (incorporated 1949) — Gen. Sec. J.D. Martin, 7290 Leslie St., Thornhill, Ont.

Old German Baptist Brethren in Canada — c/o Elder Amos Baker, Gormley, Ont.

Northern Canada Evangelical Mission — 58 18th St., Prince Albert, Sask.

Overseas Missionary Fellowship (1887) — Gen. Dir., Mr. Michael C. Griffiths, 1058 Avenue Road, Toronto 12, Ontario.

Pentecostal Assemblies of Canada, The (incorporated 1919) — General Superintendent, Rev. Robert W. Tartinger, 10 Overlea Blvd., Toronto 17, Ontario.

Pentecostal Holiness Church in Canada — Gen. Supt., Rev. G.H. Nunn, 4 Hobart Dr. S., Willowdale, Ont.

Presbyterian Church in Canada, The (1875) — 50 Wynford Dr., Don Mills, Ont.; Moderator, Rev. A. H. Johnston, Thunder Bay, Ont.; Deputy Clerk, Rev. D. C. MacDonald; Treasurer, R. R. Merifield, Q. C.

Religious Society of Friends (Quakers), (Canadian Yearly Meeting of the Religious Society of Friends formed 1955) — Presiding Clerk, Burton Hill, Box 33, Rockwood, Ont.; Secretary of Yearly Meeting, Ms. Dorothy Mums, 60 Lowther Ave., Toronto 180, Ont.

Reorganized Church of Jesus Christ of Latter Day Saints, The — Regional Administrator, Mr. Lyle W. Woodstock, 189 Eramosa Road, Guelph, Ontario. Regional Administrator, Harry W. Black, 2035 31st St. Avenue, S.W., Calgary, Alta.

Roman Catholic Church in Canada — Apostolic Pro Nuncio, His Excellency the Most Reverend Guido Del Mestri, Apostolic Nunciature, 724 Manor Ave., Rockcliffe Park, Ottawa 2, Ontario.

Salvation Army, The (1882) — Territorial Commander, Commissioner Clarence D. Wiseman, 20 Albert St., Toronto, Ontario.

Seventh-day Adventist Church in Canada — Pres., Pastor J. W. Bothe, 1148 King St. E., Oshawa, Ontario.

Ukrainian Greek Orthodox Church in Canada — Primate, The Most Rev. Archbishop Michael, 7 St. John's Avenue, Winnipeg, Man., R2W1G8.

Unitarian Church, Canadian (1842) — Pres. Mr. C. Peterson, 175 St. Clair Ave. W., Toronto 7, Ont.

United Church of Canada, The (1925) — Sec. of General Council, Rev. G. Morrison, 85 St. Clair Ave. E., Toronto 7, Ontario.

Protestant Episcopal Calendar and Altar Colors

White — From the First Service (First Vespers) of Christmas Day to the Octave of Epiphany, inclusive (except on the Feasts of Martyrs); on Maundy Thursday (for the celebration); from the First Service of Easter Day to the Vigil of Pentecost (except on Feasts of Martyrs and Rogation Days); on Trinity Sunday, Conversion of St. Paul, Purification, Annunciation, St. John Baptist, St. Michael, All Saints, Saints not Martyrs, and Patron Saints (Transfiguration and Dedication of Church).

Red — From First Vespers of Pentecost to the First Vespers of Trinity Sunday (which includes Ember Days); Holy Innocents, and Feasts of all Martyrs, Apostles and Evangelists.

Violet — From Septuagesima to Maundy Thursday; Easter Even; Advent Sunday to Christmas Eve, Vigils, Ember Days (except in Whitsun Week); and Rogation Days.

An alternate Lenten color scheme: **Violet** — From Septuagesima to the Tuesday before Ash Wednesday; **Lenten White** — From Ash Wednesday to the Saturday after Fourth Lent; and **Crimson** — from Passion Sunday (Fifth Lent) to Easter Even (all inclusive).

Black — Good Friday and at funerals. **Green** — All other days.

Days, Etc.	1973	1974	1975	1976	1977	1978	1979
Golden Number	17	18	0	1	2	3	4
Sunday Letter	G	F	E	DC	B	A	G
Sundays after Epiphany	6	4	2	5	4	2	5
Septuagesima*	Feb. 18	Feb. 10	Jan. 26	Feb. 14	Feb. 6	Jan. 22	Feb. 11
Ash Wednesday	Mar. 7	Feb. 27	Feb. 12	Mar. 3	Feb. 23	Feb. 8	Feb. 28
First Sunday in Lent	Mar. 11	Mar. 3	Feb. 16	Mar. 7	Feb. 27	Feb. 12	Mar. 4
Passion Sunday*	Apr. 8	Mar. 31	Mar. 16	Apr. 4	Mar. 27	Mar. 12	Apr. 1
Palm Sunday	Apr. 15	Apr. 7	Mar. 23	Apr. 11	Apr. 3	Mar. 19	Apr. 8
Good Friday	Apr. 20	Apr. 12	Mar. 28	Apr. 16	Apr. 8	Mar. 24	Apr. 13
Easter Day	Apr. 22	Apr. 14	Mar. 30	Apr. 18	Apr. 10	Mar. 26	Apr. 15
Rogation Sunday*	May 27	May 19	May 4	May 23	May 15	Apr. 30	May 20
Ascension Day	May 31	May 23	May 8	May 27	May 19	May 4	May 24
Whitsunday	June 10	June 2	May 18	June 6	May 29	May 14	June 3
Trinity Sunday	June 17	June 9	May 25	June 13	June 5	May 21	June 10
Sundays after Trinity**	23	24	26	23	24	27	24
First Sunday in Advent	Dec. 2	Dec. 1	Nov. 30	Nov. 28	Nov. 27	Dec. 3	Dec. 2

In the Protestant Episcopal Church the days of fasting are Ash Wednesday and Good Friday. Other days of abstinence are the 40 days of Lent, the Ember Days, and all Fridays of the year except Christmas Day and the Epiphany and any Friday which may fall between them. Ember Days (12 annually at about the beginning of the four seasons) are days of abstinence and prayer for ordinands and the increase of the ministry. They fall on the Wednesday, Friday, and Saturday after the first Sunday in Lent, the Feast of Pentecost (Whitsunday), September 14, and December 13. Rogation Days are the three days from Rogation Sunday (the fifth after Easter) to Ascension Day, and are days of solemn supplication for God's blessing upon the fields and harvests of the world.

The Episcopal Church is studying, and trying out, a revised calendar of the Church Year. If adopted, the following changes in the foregoing list will obtain: *These Sundays will no longer be observed. **This listing will carry the title "Sundays after Pentecost".

Ash Wednesday and Easter Sunday

Year	Ash Wed.	Easter Sunday	Year	Ash Wed.	Easter Sunday	Year	Ash Wed.	Easter Sunday	Year	Ash Wed.	Easter Sunday
1901	Feb. 20	Apr. 7	1951	Feb. 7	Mar. 25	2001	Feb. 28	Apr. 15	2051	Feb. 15	Apr. 2
1902	Feb. 12	Mar. 30	1952	Feb. 27	Apr. 13	2002	Feb. 13	Mar. 31	2052	Mar. 6	Apr. 21
1903	Feb. 25	Apr. 12	1953	Feb. 18	Apr. 5	2003	Mar. 5	Apr. 20	2053	Feb. 19	Apr. 6
1904	Feb. 17	Apr. 3	1954	Mar. 3	Apr. 18	2004	Feb. 25	Apr. 11	2054	Feb. 11	Mar. 29
1905	Mar. 8	Apr. 23	1955	Feb. 23	Apr. 10	2005	Feb. 9	Mar. 27	2055	Mar. 3	Apr. 18
1906	Feb. 28	Apr. 15	1956	Feb. 15	Apr. 1	2006	Mar. 1	Apr. 16	2056	Feb. 16	Apr. 2
1907	Feb. 13	Mar. 31	1957	Mar. 6	Apr. 21	2007	Feb. 21	Apr. 8	2057	Mar. 7	Apr. 22
1908	Mar. 4	Apr. 19	1958	Feb. 19	Apr. 6	2008	Feb. 6	Mar. 23	2058	Feb. 27	Apr. 14
1909	Feb. 24	Apr. 11	1959	Feb. 11	Mar. 29	2009	Feb. 25	Apr. 12	2059	Feb. 12	Mar. 30
1910	Feb. 9	Mar. 27	1960	Mar. 2	Apr. 17	2010	Feb. 17	Apr. 4	2060	Mar. 3	Apr. 18
1911	Mar. 1	Apr. 16	1961	Feb. 15	Apr. 2	2011	Mar. 9	Apr. 24	2061	Feb. 23	Apr. 10
1912	Feb. 21	Apr. 7	1962	Mar. 7	Apr. 22	2012	Feb. 22	Apr. 8	2062	Feb. 8	Mar. 26
1913	Feb. 5	Mar. 23	1963	Feb. 27	Apr. 14	2013	Feb. 13	Mar. 31	2063	Feb. 28	Apr. 15
1914	Feb. 25	Apr. 12	1964	Feb. 12	Mar. 29	2014	Mar. 5	Apr. 20	2064	Feb. 20	Apr. 6
1915	Feb. 17	Apr. 4	1965	Mar. 3	Apr. 18	2015	Feb. 18	Apr. 5	2065	Feb. 11	Mar. 29
1916	Mar. 8	Apr. 23	1966	Feb. 23	Apr. 10	2016	Feb. 10	Mar. 27	2066	Feb. 24	Apr. 11
1917	Feb. 21	Apr. 8	1967	Feb. 8	Mar. 26	2017	Mar. 1	Apr. 16	2067	Feb. 16	Apr. 3
1918	Feb. 13	Mar. 31	1968	Feb. 28	Apr. 14	2018	Feb. 14	Apr. 1	2068	Mar. 7	Apr. 22
1919	Mar. 5	Apr. 20	1969	Feb. 19	Apr. 6	2019	Mar. 6	Apr. 21	2069	Feb. 27	Apr. 14
1920	Feb. 18	Apr. 4	1970	Feb. 11	Mar. 29	2020	Feb. 26	Apr. 12	2070	Feb. 12	Mar. 30
1921	Feb. 9	Mar. 27	1971	Feb. 24	Apr. 11	2021	Feb. 17	Apr. 4	2071	Mar. 4	Apr. 19
1922	Mar. 1	Apr. 16	1972	Feb. 16	Apr. 2	2022	Mar. 2	Apr. 17	2072	Feb. 24	Apr. 10
1923	Feb. 14	Apr. 1	1973	Mar. 7	Apr. 22	2023	Feb. 22	Apr. 9	2073	Feb. 8	Mar. 26
1924	Mar. 5	Apr. 20	1974	Feb. 27	Apr. 14	2024	Feb. 14	Mar. 31	2074	Feb. 28	Apr. 15
1925	Feb. 25	Apr. 12	1975	Feb. 12	Mar. 30	2025	Mar. 5	Apr. 20	2075	Feb. 20	Apr. 7
1926	Feb. 17	Apr. 4	1976	Mar. 3	Apr. 18	2026	Feb. 18	Apr. 5	2076	Mar. 4	Apr. 19
1927	Mar. 2	Apr. 17	1977	Feb. 23	Apr. 10	2027	Feb. 10	Mar. 28	2077	Feb. 24	Apr. 11
1928	Feb. 22	Apr. 8	1978	Feb. 8	Mar. 26	2028	Mar. 1	Apr. 16	2078	Feb. 16	Apr. 3
1929	Feb. 13	Mar. 31	1979	Feb. 28	Apr. 15	2029	Feb. 14	Apr. 1	2079	Mar. 8	Apr. 23
1930	Mar. 5	Apr. 20	1980	Feb. 20	Apr. 6	2030	Mar. 6	Apr. 21	2080	Feb. 21	Apr. 7
1931	Feb. 18	Apr. 5	1981	Mar. 4	Apr. 19	2031	Feb. 26	Apr. 13	2081	Feb. 12	Mar. 30
1932	Feb. 10	Mar. 27	1982	Feb. 24	Apr. 11	2032	Feb. 11	Mar. 28	2082	Mar. 4	Apr. 19
1933	Mar. 1	Apr. 16	1983	Feb. 16	Apr. 3	2033	Mar. 2	Apr. 17	2083	Feb. 17	Apr. 4
1934	Feb. 14	Apr. 1	1984	Mar. 7	Apr. 22	2034	Feb. 22	Apr. 9	2084	Feb. 9	Mar. 26
1935	Mar. 6	Apr. 21	1985	Feb. 20	Apr. 7	2035	Feb. 7	Mar. 25	2085	Feb. 28	Apr. 15
1936	Feb. 26	Apr. 12	1986	Feb. 12	Mar. 30	2036	Feb. 27	Apr. 13	2086	Feb. 13	Mar. 31
1937	Feb. 10	Mar. 28	1987	Mar. 4	Apr. 19	2037	Feb. 18	Apr. 5	2087	Mar. 5	Apr. 20
1938	Mar. 2	Apr. 17	1988	Feb. 17	Apr. 3	2038	Mar. 10	Apr. 25	2088	Feb. 25	Apr. 11
1939	Feb. 22	Apr. 9	1989	Feb. 8	Mar. 26	2039	Feb. 23	Apr. 10	2089	Feb. 16	Apr. 3
1940	Feb. 7	Mar. 24	1990	Feb. 28	Apr. 15	2040	Feb. 15	Apr. 1	2090	Mar. 1	Apr. 16
1941	Feb. 26	Apr. 13	1991	Feb. 13	Mar. 31	2041	Mar. 6	Apr. 21	2091	Feb. 21	Apr. 8
1942	Feb. 18	Apr. 5	1992	Mar. 4	Apr. 19	2042	Feb. 19	Apr. 6	2092	Feb. 13	Mar. 30
1943	Mar. 10	Apr. 25	1993	Feb. 24	Apr. 11	2043	Feb. 11	Mar. 29	2093	Feb. 25	Apr. 12
1944	Feb. 23	Apr. 9	1994	Feb. 16	Apr. 3	2044	Mar. 2	Apr. 17	2094	Feb. 17	Apr. 4
1945	Feb. 14	Apr. 1	1995	Mar. 1	Apr. 16	2045	Feb. 22	Apr. 9	2095	Mar. 9	Apr. 24
1946	Mar. 6	Apr. 21	1996	Feb. 21	Apr. 7	2046	Feb. 7	Mar. 25	2096	Feb. 29	Apr. 15
1947	Feb. 19	Apr. 6	1997	Feb. 12	Mar. 30	2047	Feb. 27	Apr. 14	2097	Feb. 13	Mar. 31
1948	Feb. 11	Mar. 28	1998	Feb. 25	Apr. 12	2048	Feb. 19	Apr. 5	2098	Mar. 5	Apr. 12
1949	Mar. 2	Apr. 17	1999	Feb. 17	Apr. 4	2049	Mar. 3	Apr. 18	2099	Feb. 25	Apr. 12
1950	Feb. 22	Apr. 9	2000	Mar. 8	Apr. 23	2050	Feb. 23	Apr. 10	2100	Feb. 10	Mar. 28

A lengthy dispute over the date for the celebration of Easter was settled by the first Council of the Christian Churches at Nicaea, in Asia Minor, in 325 A.D. The council ruled that Easter would be observed on the first Sunday following the 14th day of the Paschal Moon, referred to as the Paschal Full Moon. The Paschal Moon is the first moon whose 14th day comes on or after March 21. Dates of the Paschal Full Moon, which are not necessarily the same as those of the real or astronomical full moon, are listed in the table below with an explanation of how to compute the date of Easter.

If the Paschal Full Moon falls on a Sunday, then Easter is the following Sunday. The earliest date on which Easter can fall is March 22; it fell on that date in 1761 and 1818 but will not do so in the 20th or 21st century. The latest possible date for Easter is April 25; it fell on that date in 1943 and will again in 2038.

Lent begins on Ash Wednesday, which comes 40 days before Easter Sunday, not counting Sundays.

Originally it was a period of but 40 hours. Later it comprised 30 days of fasting, omitting all the Sundays and also all the Saturdays except one. Pope Gregory added Ash Wednesday to the fast, together with the remainder of that week.

The last seven days of Lent constitute Holy Week, beginning with Palm Sunday. Passion Week precedes Holy Week. The last Thursday—Maundy Thursday—commemorates the institution of the Eucharist. The following day, Good Friday, commemorates the day of the crucifixion.

Easter is the chief festival of the Christian year, commemorating the resurrection of Christ. It occurs about the same time as the ancient Roman celebration of the Vernal Equinox, the arrival of Spring. In the second century, A.D., Easter Day among Christians in Asia Minor was the 14th Nisan, the seventh month of the Jewish calendar. The Christians in Europe observed the nearest Sunday.

Date of Paschal Full Moon, 1900-2199

The Golden Number, used in the table, is greater by unity (one) than the remainder obtained upon dividing the given year by 19. for example, when dividing 1974 by 19, one obtains a remainder of 17. Adding 1 gives 18 as the Golden Number for the year 1974. From the table, then the date of the Paschal Full Moon is Apr. 7, 1974. This being a Sunday, the date of Easter is the following Sunday, Apr. 14.

Golden Number	Date	Golden Number	Date	Golden Number	Date	Golden Number	Date
1	Apr. 14	6	Apr. 18	11	Mar. 25	16	Mar. 30
2	Apr. 3	7	Apr. 8	12	Apr. 13	17	Apr. 17
3	Mar. 23	8	Mar. 28	13	Apr. 2	18	Apr. 7
4	Apr. 11	9	Apr. 16	14	Mar. 22	19	Mar. 27
5	Mar. 31	10	Apr. 5	15	Apr. 10		

Active Bishops of the Protestant Episcopal Church

Source: Rt. Rev. Scott Field Bailey, Sec., House of Bishops, 520 San Jacinto St., Houston, Tex. 77002

Presiding Bishop: Rt. Rev. John M. Allin, 815 Second Ave., N.Y.C. 10017

Executive Council: Edmond L. Browning, Deputy for Jurisdictions; Richard B. Martin, Deputy for Ministries; Milton L. Wood, Deputy for Administration; David E. Richards, Natl. Coordinator for House of Bishops Comm. on Pastoral Development; Clarence C. Hobgood, Suffragan Bishop to Armed Forces. N. Ervine Swift, Bishop of the Convocation of Episcopal Churches in Europe.

(M) Missionary Bishop; (C) Coadjutor; (S) Suffragan

Alabama: Furman C. Stough, Birmingham.
Alaska: David R. Cochran, Fairbanks.
Albany (N.Y.): Wilbur E. Hogg Jr., Charles B. Persell (S).
Arizona: Joseph M. Harte, Phoenix.
Arkansas: Christoph Keller, Little Rock.
Atlanta (Ga.): Bennet J. Sims.
Bethlehem (Pa.): Lloyd E. Gressle.
California: C. K. Myers, G. R. Millard (S), San Fran.
  Northern California: Clarence R. Haden, Jr.
Central Gulf Coast: George M. Murray.
Costa Rica: Jose Antonio Ramos (M), San Jose.
Chicago: J. W. Montgomery, Quinton E. Primo (S).
Colombia, South America: William A. Franklin (M), Bogota.
Colorado: William C. Frey, Denver.
Connecticut: Joseph Warren Hutchens, Morgan Porteus (S).
Dallas (Tex.): A. Donald Davies, Theodore H. McCrea (S).
Delaware:
Dominican Republic: Telesford A. Issac (M), Santo Domingo.
East Carolina: Hunley A. Elebash, Wilmington, N.C.
Easton (Md.): George A. Taylor.
Eau Claire (Wis.): Stanley Atkins.
Ecuador: Adrian D. Caceres (M).
Erie (Pa.): Donald J. Davis.
Florida: Hamilton West, Jacksonville, Frank S. Cerveny (C).
  Central Florida: William H. Folwell, Winter Park.
  Southeast Florida: James L. Duncan, Miami.
  Southwest Florida: William L. Hargrave, St. Petersburg, E. Paul Haynes (C).
Fond du Lac (Wis.): William H. Brady.
Georgia: Geo. Paul Reeves, Savannah.
Guatemala & Honduras: Anselmo Carral (M).
Haiti: Luc Anatole Jacques Garnier (M).
Hawaii: Edwin L. Hanchett.
Idaho: Hanford L. King Jr., Boise.
Indianapolis: John P. Craine.
  Northern Indiana: William C. R. Sheridan.
Iowa: Walter C. Righter, Des Moines.
Kansas: Edward C. Turner, Topeka.
  Western Kansas: William Davidson, Salina.
Kentucky: David B. Reed.
Lexington (Ky.): Addison Hosea.
Liberia: George D. Browne (M), Monrovia.
Long Island: Jonathan G. Sherman, Charles W. MacLean (S).
Los Angeles: Robert C. Rusack.
Louisiana: Iveson B. Noland, New Orleans.
Maine: Frederick B. Wolf, Portland.
Maryland: D. K. Leighton Sr., Baltimore, William J. Cox (S).
  Western Mass.: Alexander Stewart, Springfield.
Massachusetts: Boston, J. M. Burgess, Morris F. Arnold (S).
Mexico: Jose G. Saucedo (M), Mexico City.
  Northern: Leonardo Romero (M), Monterey.
  Western: Melchor Saucedo (M), Guadalajara.
Michigan: H. Coleman McGehee Jr., Detroit.
  Northern Michigan:
  Western Michigan: Charles E. Bennison, Kalamazoo.
Milwaukee: Charles T. Gaskell.
Minnesota: P. F. McNairy, Minn.
Mississippi: Duncan M. Gray Jr.
Missouri: George L. Cadigan, St. Louis.
  West Missouri: Arthur A. Vogel, Kansas City.

Montana: Jackson E. Gilliam, Helena.
Nebraska: Robert P. Varley, Omaha.
Nevada: Wesley Frensdorff, Reno.
New Hampshire: Philip A. Smith, Concord.
New Jersey: A. W. Van Duzer, Trenton.
Rio Grande: Richard M. Trelease Jr., Albuquerque.
New York: Paul Moore, Jr., J. Stuart Wetmore (S), Harold L. Wright (S), N.Y.C.
  Central New York: Ned Cole, Jr., Syracuse.
  Western New York: Harold B. Robinson, Buffalo.
Newark (N.J.): George E. Rath.
Nicaragua: G. Edward Haynsworth (M).
North Carolina: Thomas A. Fraser, Jr., Raleigh, W. Moultrie Moore, Jr. (S).
  Western North Carolina: M. George Henry, Asheville, William G. Weinhauer (C), Black Mountain.
North Dakota: George T. Masuda, Fargo.
Ohio: John H. Burt, Cleveland.
  Southern Ohio: John M. Krumm, Cincinnati.
Oklahoma: Chilton Powell, Frederick W. Putnam Jr. (S), Oklahoma City.
Olympia, Wash.: Ivol I. Curtis, Seattle.
Oregon: Mathew P. Bigliardi, Lake Oswego, Hal R. Gross (S), Portland.
  Eastern Oregon: William B. Spofford, Bend.
Panama Canal Zone: Lemuel B. Shirley (M), Balboa.
Pennsylvania: Lyman C. Ogilby, Philadelphia.
  Central: Dean T. Stevenson, Harrisburg.
Philippines: Central — Benito C. Cabanban (M).
  Northern: Edward G. Longid (M).
  Southern: Constancio B. Manguramas (M).
Pittsburgh: Robert Appleyard.
Puerto Rico: Francisco Reus-Froylan, Saint Just.
Quincy (Ill.): Donald J. Parsons, Peoria.
Rhode Island: Frederick H. Belden, Providence.
Rochester (N.Y.): Robt. R. Spears, Jr.
San Diego (Calif.): Robert M. Wolter Stoff.
San Joaquin (Calif.): Victor M. Rivera, Fresno.
South Carolina: Gray Temple, Charleston.
  Upper South Carolina: George M. Alexander, Columbia.
South Dakota: Walter H. Jones, Harold S. Jones (S).
Spokane (Wash.): John R. Wyatt.
Springfield (Ill.): Albert W. Hillestad.
Taiwan: James T. Pong (M).
Tennessee: John Vander Horst, Nashville; William E. Sanders (C), Knoxville; William F. Gates Jr. (S), Memphis.
Texas: J. Milton Richardson, Houston; Scott F. Bailey (S), Houston.
  Northwest Texas: Willis R. Henton, Lubbock.
  West Texas: H. C. Gosnell, R. Earl Dicus (S), San Antonio.
Utah: Edgar O. Charles, Salt Lake City.
Vermont: Robert S. Kerr, Burlington.
Virgin Islands: Edward M. Turner, St. Thomas.
Virginia: Robert F. Gibson, Jr., Robert B. Hall, John A. Baden (S), Alexandria.
  Southern Virginia: David S. Rose, Petersburg.
  Southwestern Virginia: William H. Marmion, Roanoke.
Washington (D.C.): W. F. Creighton, John T. Walker (S).
West Virginia: Wilburn C. Campbell, Charleston, Robt. P. Atkinson (C).
Wyoming: David R. Thornberry, Laramie.

The three Missionary Districts of Central, Southern and Southwestern Brazil became an independent branch of the Anglican Communion in 1965 fulfilling the action of the General Convention of 1964.

Bishops of the United Methodist Church

Source: United Methodist Communications, 475 Riverside Drive, New York, N. Y. 10027

President: Bishop Dwight E. Loder, Detroit, Mich.; President-designate, Bishop W. Ralph Ward, Rye, N. Y.; Secretary, Bishop Ralph T. Alton, 1100 W. 42nd Street, Indianapolis, Ind. 46208.

Allen, L. Scott, Knoxville, Tennessee
Alton, Ralph T., Indianapolis, Indiana
Armstrong, A. James, Aberdeen, South Dakota
Ault, James M., Philadelphia, Pennsylvania
Blackburn, Robert M., Raleigh, North Carolina
Borgen, Ole E., Stockholm, Sweden
Cannon, William R., Atlanta, Georgia
Carleton, Alsie H., Albuquerque, New Mexico

Carroll, Edward G., Boston, Massachusetts
Choy, Wilbur W., Seattle, Washington
Clymer, Wayne K., Minneapolis, Minnesota
Crutchfield, Finis A., New Orleans, Louisiana
de Carvalho, Emilio, Luanda, Angola
DeWitt, Jesse R., Sun Prairie, Wisconsin
Dixon, Ernest T., Topeka, Kansas
Ensley, F. Gerald, Columbus, Ohio

(continued)

(continued)

Finger, H. Ellis, Jr., Nashville, Tennessee
Frank, Eugene M., Little Rock, Arkansas
Galloway, Paul V., Houston, Texas
Golden, Charles F., Los Angeles, California
Goodrich, Robert E., Jr., St. Louis, Missouri
Goodson, W. Kenneth, Richmond, Virginia
Granadosin, Paul L. A., Baguio City, Philippines
Haertel, Armin, Dresden, Germany
Holter, Don W., Lincoln, Nebraska
Hunt, Earl G., Jr., Charlotte, North Carolina
Joshi, Ram Dutt, Bombay, India
Kearns, Francis E., Canton, Ohio
Lance, Joseph R., Lucknow, India
Loder, Dwight E., Detroit, Michigan
Mathews, James K., Washington, D.C.
McDavid, Joel D., Lakeland, Florida
Milhouse, Paul W., Oklahoma City, Oklahoma
Mitchell, Eric A., Delhi, India
Muzorewa, Abel T., Salisbury, Rhodesia
Nichols, Roy C., Pittsburgh, Pennsylvania
Onema, Fama S., Kananga, Republic of Zaire
Pagura, Frederico, San Jose, Costa Rica

Peter, M. Elia, Hyderabad, India
Robertson, Frank L., Louisville, Kentucky
Sanders, Carl J., Birmingham, Alabama
Schaefer, Franz W., Zurich, Switzerland
Short, Roy H., Nashville, Tennessee
Slater, O. Eugene, San Antonio, Texas
Sommer, C. Ernst, Frankfurt, Germany
Stokes, Mack B., Jackson, Mississippi
Stowe, W. McFerrin, Dallas, Texas
Stuart, R. Marvin, San Francisco, California
Taylor, Prince A., Jr., Princeton, New Jersey
Thomas, James S., Des Moines, Iowa
Tuell, Jack M., Portland, Oregon
Tullis, Edward L., Columbia, South Carolina
Ward, W. Ralph, Rye, New York
Warman, John B., Harrisburg, Pennsylvania
Warner, Bennie D., Monrovia, Liberia
Washburn, Paul A., Chicago, Illinois
Webb, Lance, Springfield, Illinois
Wertz, D. Frederick, Charleston, West Virginia
Wheatley, Melvin E., Denver, Colorado
Yeakel, Joseph H., Syracuse, New York
Zunguze, Escrivao A., Lourenco Marques, Mozambique

Roman Catholic Hierarchy

Source: Apostolic Delegation, Washington, D.C.

Supreme Pontiff

At the head of the Roman Catholic Church is the Supreme Pontiff, Paul VI, Giovanni Battista Montini, born at Concesio, Italy, Sept. 26, 1897, ordained priest May 29, 1920, enthroned archbishop of Milan Jan. 6, 1955, proclaimed cardinal Dec. 15, 1958; elected Pope as successor of John XXIII, June 21, 1963; crowned June 30, 1963.

Cardinals

		Nationality	Born	Chosen
Alfrink: Bernard	Archbishop of Utrecht	Dutch	1900	1960
Antonelli: Ferdinando		Italian	1896	1973
Aponte Martinez: Luis	Archbishop of San Juan in Puerto Rico	American	1922	1973
Arns: Paulo	Archbishop of Sao Paulo	Brazilian	1921	1973
Baggio: Sebastiano	Prefect of the Sacred Congregation for the Bishops	Italian	1913	1969
Barbieri: Antonio Maria	Archbishop of Montevideo	Uruguayan	1892	1958
Bengsch: Alfred	Archbishop-Bishop of Berlin	German	1921	1967
Bertoli: Paolo		Italian	1908	1969
Biayenda: Emile	Archbishop of Brazzaville	Congolese	1927	1973
Brandao Vilela: Avela	Archbishop of Sao Salvador da Bahia	Brazilian	1912	1973
Bueno y Monreal: Jose M.	Archbishop of Seville	Spanish	1904	1958
Caggiano: Antonio	Archbishop of Buenos Aires	Argentinian	1889	1946
Carberry: John	Archbishop of St. Louis	American	1904	1969
Carpino: Francesco		Italian	1905	1967
Casariego: Mario	Archbishop of Guatemala	Guatemalan	1909	1969
Cerejeira: Manuel Goncalves		Portuguese	1888	1929
Cody: John P.	Archbishop of Chicago	American	1907	1967
Colombo: Giovanni	Archbishop of Milan	Italian	1902	1965
Concha: Luis		Colombian	1891	1961
Confalonieri: Carlo		Italian	1893	1958
Conway: William	Archbishop of Armagh	Irish	1913	1965
Cooke: Terence	Archbishop of New York	American	1921	1969
Cooray: Thomas B.	Archbishop of Colombo in Ceylon	Ceylonese	1901	1965
Cordeiro: Joseph	Archbishop of Karachi	Pakistanian	1918	1973
da Costa Nunes: Jose		Portuguese	1880	1962
Darmojuwono: Justin	Archbishop of Semarang	Indonesian	1914	1967
De Araujo Sales: Eugenio	Archbishop of St. Sebastian of Rio de Janeiro	Brazilian	1920	1969
Dearden: John	Archbishop of Detroit	American	1907	1969
de Furstenberg: Maximilian		Belgian	1904	1967
Di Jorio: Alberto		Italian	1884	1958
Dopfner: Julius	Archbishop of Munich	German	1913	1958
Duval: Leon-Etienne	Archbishop of Algiers	Algerian	1903	1965
Enrique y Tarancon: Vincenzo	Archbishop of Madrid	Spanish	1907	1969
Felici: Pericle	President of Pontifical Commission for the Revision of Code of Canon Law	Italian	1911	1967
Feltin: Maurice		French	1883	1953
Flahiff: George	Archbishop of Winnipeg	Canadian	1905	1969
Florit: Ermenegildo	Archbishop of Florence	Italian	1901	1965
Forni: Efrem		Italian	1889	1962
Freeman: James	Archbishop of Sydney	Australian	1907	1973
Frings: Joseph		German	1887	1946
Garrone: Gabriele M.	Prefect of the Sacred Congregation for Catholic Education	French	1901	1967
Gilroy: Norman		Australian	1896	1946
Gonzalez Martin: Marcelo	Archbishop of Toledo	Spanish	1918	1973
Gouyon: Paul	Archbishop of Rennes	French	1910	1969
Gracias: Valerian	Archbishop of Bombay	Indian	1900	1953
Grano: Carlo		Italian	1887	1967
Gray: Gordon	Archbishop of St. Andrews and Edinburgh	Scot	1910	1969

(continued)

(continued)

		Nationality	Born	Chosen
Guerri: Sergio...............	Pro-President of the Pontifical Comm. for Vatican City State...	Italian	1905	1969
Guyot: Louis.................	Archbishop of Toulouse.............................	French........	1905	1973
Heenan: John................	Archbishop of Westminster.........................	English........	1905	1965
Hoffner: Joseph..............	Archbishop of Cologne.............................	German........	1906	1969
Jaeger: Lorenz...............	Archbishop of Paderborn...........................	German........	1892	1965
Journet: Charles.............		Swiss.........	1891	1965
Jubany Arnau: Narciso.......	Archbishop of Barcelona............................	Spanish.......	1913	1973
Kim Sou Hwan: Stephan......	Archbishop of Seoul...............................	Korean........	1922	1969
Knox, James.................	Prefect of the Sacred Congregations of the Sacraments and of Divine Worship.........................	Australian	1914	1973
Koenig: Franz................	Archbishop of Vienna..............................	Austrian.......	1905	1958
Krol: John...................	Archbishop of Philadelphia.........................	American.......	1910	1967
Landazuri Ricketts: Juan.....	Archbishop of Lima................................	Peruvian.......	1913	1962
Leger: Paul..................		Canadian......	1904	1953
Lercaro: Giacomo............		Italian.........	1891	1953
Luciani: Albino..............	Patriarch of Venice................................	Italian.........	1912	1973
Malula: Joseph..............	Archbishop of Kinshasa............................	Congolese.....	1917	1969
Manning: Timothy............	Archbishop of Los Angeles.........................	American......	1909	1973
Marella: Paolo...............		Italian.........	1895	1959
Martin: Joseph...............		French........	1891	1965
Marty: Francis...............	Archbishop of Paris................................	French........	1904	1969
Maurer: Jose.................	Archbishop of Sucre...............................	Bolivian.......	1900	1967
McCann: Owen...............	Archbishop of Cape Town..........................	So. African.....	1907	1965
McGuigan: James...........		Canadian......	1894	1946
McIntyre: James.............		American......	1886	1953
Medeiros: Humberto..........	Archbishop of Boston..............................	American......	1915	1973
Meouchi: Paul...............	Maronite Patriarch of Antioch......................	Lebanese......	1894	1965
Mindszenty: Jozsef...........		Hungarian.....	1892	1946
Miranda y Gomez: Miguel.....	Archbishop of Mexico..............................	Mexican......	1895	1969
Motta: Carlos Carmelo de Vasconcellos............	Archbishop of Aparecida...........................	Brazilian......	1890	1946
Mozzini: Umberto............		Italian.........	1904	1973
Munoz Duque: Anibal.........	Archbishop of Bogota..............................	Colombian.....	1908	1973
Munoz Vega: Paolo...........	Archbishop of Quito...............................	Ecuadorian....	1903	1969
Nasalli Rocca: Mario.........		Italian.........	1903	1969
O'Boyle: Patrick.............		American......	1896	1967
Oddi: Silvio.................		Italian.........	1910	1969
Ottaviani: Alfredo............		Italian.........	1890	1953
Otunga: Maurce..............	Archbishop of Nairobi.............................	Kenyan.......	1923	1973
Palazzini: Pietro.............		Italian.........	1912	1973
Pappalardo: Salvatore........	Archbishop of Palermo.............................	Italian.........	1918	1973
Parecattil: Joseph............	Archbishop of Ernakulam..........................	Indian.........	1912	1969
Parente: Pietro..............		Italian.........	1891	1967
Paupini: Giuseppe............	Grand Penitentiary................................	Italian.........	1907	1969
Pellegrino: Michele..........	Archbishop of Turin...............................	Italian.........	1903	1967
Philippe: Paul...............	Prefect of the Sacred Congregation for the Oriental Churches..	French	1905	1973
Pignedoli: Sergio............	President of the Secretariat for Non-Christians.........	Italian.........	1910	1973
Poletti: Ugo.................	Vicar General of His Holiness for the City of Rome......	Italian.........	1914	1973
Poma: Antonio...............	Archbishop of Bologna.............................	Italian.........	1910	1969
Primatesta: Francisco.........	Archbishop of Cordova.............................	Argentinian....	1919	1973
Quintero: Jose...............	Archbishop of Caracas.............................	Venezuelean...	1902	1961
Raimondi: Luigi..............	Prefect of the Sacred Congregation for Saints' Causes.....	Italian.........	1912	1973
Rakotomalala: Jerome........	Archbishop of Tananarive..........................	Madagascar...	1913	1969
Renard: Alexandre...........	Archbishop of Lyon................................	French........	1906	1967
Ribeiro: Antonio..............	Patriarch of Lisbon................................	Portuguese....	1928	1973
Roberti: Francesco...........		Italian.........	1889	1958
Rosales: Julio...............	Archbishop of Cebu...............................	Filipino........	1906	1969
Rossi Agnelo.................	Prefect of the Sacred Congregation for the Evangelization of Peoples	Brazilian	1913	1965
Roy, Maurice................	Archbishop of Quebec.............................	Canadian......	1905	1965
Rugambwa: Laurean..........	Archbishop of Dar es Salaam.......................	Tanzania......	1912	1960
Salazar: Lopez...............	Archbishop of Guadalajara.........................	Mexican......	1910	1973
Samore: Antonio.............		Italian.........	1905	1967
Scherer: Alfredo.............	Archbishop of Porto Alegre.........................	Brazilian......	1903	1969
Seper: Franjo................	Prefect of Sacred Congregation for the Doctrine of the Faith..	Yugoslav......	1905	1965
Shehan: Lawrence............		American......	1898	1965
Sidarouss: Stephanos........	Coptic Patriarch of Alexandria......................	United Arab Republic......	1904	1965
Silva Henriquez: Raul........	Archbishop of Santiago............................	Chilean........	1907	1962
Siri: Giuseppe...............	Archbishop of Genoa..............................	Italian.........	1906	1953
Slipyi: Josyf.................	Ukrainian Archbishop of Lwow......................	Ukrainian.....	1892	1965
Staffa: Dino.................	Prefect of Supreme Tribunal of Apostolic Signatura.....	Italian.........	1906	1967
Suenens: Leo................	Archbishop of Malines Brussels......................	Belgian........	1904	1962
Tabera Araoz: Arturo.........	Prefect of the Sacred Congregation for Religious and Secular Institutes..................	Spanish	1903	1969
Taguchi: Paul................	Archbishop of Osaka..............................	Japanese......	1902	1973
Taofinu'u: Pio...............	Bishop of Apia...................................	Samoan.......	1923	1973
Tragliac Luigi...............		Italian.........	1895	1960
Ursi: Corrado................	Archbishop of Naples..............................	Italian.........	1908	1967
Vagnozzi: Egidio.............	Pres. of the Prefecture of the Holy See's Economic Affairs..	Italian	1906	1967
Villot: Jean.................	Secretary of State of His Holiness...................	French........	1905	1965
Violardo: Giacomo...........		Italian.........	1898	1969
Volk: Hermann...............	Bishop of Mainz..................................	German.......	1903	1973

(continued)

(continued)

Willebrands: John	President of Secretariat for the Union of Christians	Dutch	1909	1969
Wojtyla: Karol	Archbishop of Krakow	Polish	1920	1967
Wright: John	Prefect of the Sacred Congregation for the Clergy	Amerian	1909	1969
Wyszynski: Stefan	Archbishop of Gniezno-Warsaw	Polish	1901	1953
Yu Pin: Paul	Archbishop of Nanking	Chinese	1901	1969
Zoungrana: Paul	Archbishop of Ouagadougou	Upper Volta	1917	1965

Roman Catholic Hierarchy of the United States

Source: Apostolic Delegation, Washington, D.C.

Archdioceses

See	Archbishop	Cons.	See	Archbishop	Cons.
Anchorage	Joseph T. Ryan	1966	Newark, N. J.	Peter L. Gerety	1966
Atlanta, Ga.	Thomas A. Donnellan	1964		Martin W. Stanton (Aux.)	1957
Baltimore, Md.	William Borders	1968		John J. Dougherty (Aux.)	1962
	Thomas A. Murphy (Aux.)	1962		Joseph A. Costello (Aux.)	1962
	F. Joseph Gossman (Aux.)	1968	New Orleans, La.	Philip M. Hannan	1956
Boston, Mass.	Humberto S. Medeiros	1966		Louis A. Caillouet (Aux.)	1947
	Jeremiah F. Minihan (Aux.)	1954		Harold R. Perry (Aux.)	1965
	Thomas J. Riley (Aux.)	1959	New York, N. Y.	Terence J. Cooke (Card.)	1965
	Lawrence Riley (Aux.)	1972		John J. Maguire (Coad.)	1959
	Joseph Maguire (Aux.)	1972		J. M. Pernicone (Aux.)	1954
Chicago, Ill.	John Cody (Card.)	1947		Edward E. Swanstrom (Aux.)	1960
	Thomas J. Grady (Aux.)	1967		Patrick Ahern (Aux.)	1970
	William McManus (Aux.)	1967		James P. Mahoney (Aux.)	1972
	Michael R. Dempsey (Aux.)	1968		Anthony F. Mestice (Aux.)	1973
	Alfred Abramowicz (Aux.)	1968	Oklahoma, Okla.	John R. Quinn	1967
	Nevin W. Hayes (Aux.)	1965	Omaha, Nebr.	Daniel E. Sheehan	1964
Cincinnati, Ohio	Joseph Bernardin	1966	Philadelphia, Pa.	John J. Krol (Card.)	1953
	Nicholas Elko (Aux.)	1955		Gerald V. McDevitt (Aux.)	1962
Denver, Colo.	James V. Casey	1957		John J. Graham (Aux.)	1964
	George R. Evans (Aux.)	1969		Martin Lohmuller (Aux.)	1970
	Richard Hanifen (Aux.)	1974	Portland, Ore.	Cornelius M. Power	1969
Detroit, Mich.	John F. Dearden	1948	St. Louis, Mo.	John J. Carberry (Card.)	1956
	Walter J. Schoenherr (Aux.)	1968		George Gottwald (Aux.)	1961
	Thomas J. Gumbleton (Aux.)	1968		Joseph A. McNicholas (Aux.)	1969
	Arthur H. Krawczak (Aux.)	1973		Charles R. Koester (Aux.)	1971
	Joseph L. Imesch (Aux.)	1973		Edward O'Meara (Aux.)	1972
Dubuque, Iowa	James J. Byrne	1947	St. Paul, Minn.	Leo Binz	1942
	Francis Dunn (Aux.)	1969		Leo C. Byrne (Card.)	1954
Hartford, Conn.	John F. Whealon	1961		John Roach (Aux.)	1971
	John F. Hackett (Aux.)	1952		Raymond Lucker (Aux.)	1971
	Joseph Donnelly (Aux.)	1965	San Antonio, Tex.	Francis Furey	1960
Indianapolis, Ind.	George J. Biskup	1957		Patrick F. Flores (Aux.)	1970
Kansas City, Kan.	Ignatius J. Strecker	1962	San Francisco, Cal.	Joseph T. McGucken	1941
Los Angeles, Calif.	Timothy Manning	1946		William McDonald (Aux.)	1964
	John J. Ward (Aux.)	1963		Norman F. McFarland (Aux.)	1970
	William R. Johnson (Aux.)	1971	San Juan, P. R.	Luis Aponte Martinez	1960
	Juan Arzurbe (Aux.)	1971		Juan de Dios Lopez de Victoria (Aux.)	1963
Louisville, Ky.	Thomas J. McDonough	1947	Santa Fe, N. Mex.	Robert Sanchez	1974
	Charles G. Maloney (Aux.)	1955	Seattle, Wash.	Thomas A. Connolly	1939
Miami, Fla.	Coleman F. Carroll	1953	Washington, D. C.	William W. Baum	1970
	Rene Gracida	1972		Thomas Lyons	1974
Milwaukee, Wis.	William E. Cousins	1952		Eugene Marino	1974
	Leo Brust (Aux.)	1969			

Canadian Archdioceses

See	Archbishop	Cons.	See	Archbishop	Cons.
Edmonton, Alta.	Joseph Neil MacNeil	1969		Laurent Noel (Aux.)	1963
Grouard-McLennan, Alta.	Henri Legare	1967	Regina, Sask.	C. A. Halpin	1973
Halifax, N. S.	James M. Hayes	1967	Rimouski, Que.	Gilles Ouellet	1968
Keewatin-Le Pas, Man.	Paul Dumouchel	1967	St. Boniface, Man.	Maurice Badoux	1955
Kingston, Ont.	Joseph L. Wilhelm	1966		Antoine Hacualt (Aux.)	1964
Moncton, N. B.	Donat Chiasson	1972	St. John's, Nfld.	Patrick J. Skinner	1951
Montreal, Que.	Paul Gregoire	1968	Sherbrooke, Que.	J. M. Fortier	1968
	Lawrence P. Whelan (Aux.)	1941	Toronto, Ont.	Philip F. Pocock	1971
	Leo Blais (Aux.)	1959		Francis V. Allen (Aux.)	1954
	Valerian Belanger (Aux.)	1956		Thomas Fulton (Aux.)	1969
	Andre Cimichella (Aux.)	1964	Vancouver, B. C.	James F. Carney	1969
	Leonard Crowley (Aux.)	1971	Winnipeg, Man.	George B. Flahiff (Card.)	1961
Ottawa, Ont.	Joseph A. Plourde	1967			
Quebec, Que.	Maurice Roy (Card.)	1947	Ukrainian Byzantine Rite:		
	Lionel Audet (Aux.)	1968	Winnipeg, Man.	Maxim Hermaniuk	1956

Chronological List of Popes

Source: Annuario Pontificio. Table lists year of consecration of each Pope.

The Roman Catholic Church names the Apostle Peter as founder of the Church in Rome. He arrived there C. 42, was martyred there C. 67, and raised to sainthood.

The Pope's temporal title is: Sovereign of the State of Vatican City.

The Pope's spiritual titles are: Bishop of Rome, Vicar of Jesus Christ, Successor of St. Peter, Prince of the Apostles, Supreme Pontiff of the Universal Church, Patriarch of the West, Primate of Italy, Archbishop and Metropolitan of the Roman Province and Sovereign of the Stae of Vatican City.

Anti-Popes are in *Italics*..Anti-Popes were illegitimate claimants of or pretenders to the papal throne.

Year	Name of Pope	Year	Name of Pope	Year	Name of Pope	Year	Name of Pope
See above.	St. Peter	615	St. Deusdedit	974	Benedict VII	1305	Clement V
67	St. Linas		or Adeodatus I	983	John XIV	1316	John XXII
76	St. Anacletus	619	Boniface V	985	John XV	*1328*	*Nicholas V*
	or Cletus	625	Honorius I	996	Gregory V	1334	Benedict XII
88	St. Clement I	640	Severinus	*997*	*John XVI*	1342	Clement VI
97	St. Evaristus	640	John IV	999	Sylvester II	1352	Innocent VI
105	St. Alexander I	642	Theodore I	1003	John XVII	1362	Urban V
115	St. Sixtus I	649	St. Martin I	1004	John XVIII	1370	Gregory XI
125	St. Telesphorus	654	St. Eugene I	1009	Sergius IV	1378	Urban VI
136	St. Hyginus	657	St. Vitalian	1012	Benedict VIII	*1378*	*Clement VII*
140	St. Pius I	672	Adeodatus II	*1012*	*Gregory*	1389	Boniface IX
155	St. Anicetus	676	Donus I	1024	John XIX	*1394*	*Benedict XIII*
166	St. Soterus	678	St. Agatho	1032	Benedict IX	1404	Innocent VII
175	St. Eleutherius	682	St. Leo II	1045	Sylvester III	1406	Gregory XII
189	St. Victor I	684	St. Benedict II	1045	Benedict Ix	*1409*	*Alexander V*
199	St. Zephyrinus	685	John V	1045	Gregory VI	*1410*	*John XXIII*
217	St. Callistus I	686	Conon	1046	Clement II	1417	Martin V
217	*St. Hippolytus*	*687*	*Theodore*	1047	Benedict I X	1431	Eugene IV
222	St. Urban I	*687*	*Paschal*	1048	Damasus II	*1440*	*Felix V*
230	St. Pontian	687	St. Sergius I	1049	St. Leo IX	1447	Nicholas V
235	St. Anterus	701	John VI	1055	Victor II	1455	Callistus III
236	St. Fabian	705	John VII	1057	Stephen IX	1458	Pius II
251	St. Cornelius	708	Sisinnius	*1058*	*Benedict X*	1464	Paul II
251	*Novatian*	708	Constantine	1059	Nicholas II	1471	Sixtus IV
253	St. Lucius I	715	St. Gregory II	1061	Alexander II	1484	Innocent VIII
254	St. Stephen I	731	St. Gregory III	*1061*	*Honorius II*	1492	Alexander VI
257	St. Sixtus II	741	St. Zachary	1073	St. Gregory VII	1503	Pius III
259	St. Dionysius	752	Stephen II	*1080*	*Clement III*	1503	Julius II
269	St. Felix I	757	St. Paul I	1086	Victor III	1513	Leo X
275	St. Eutychian	*767*	*Constantine*	1088	Urban II	1522	Adrian VI
283	St. Caius	*768*	*Philip*	1099	Paschal II	1523	Clement VII
296	St. Marcellinus	768	Stephen III	*1100*	*Theodore*	1534	Paul IIII
308	St. Marcellus I	772	Adrian I	*1102*	*Albert*	1550	Julius III
309	St. Eusebius	795	St. Leo III	*1105*	*Sylvester IV*	1555	Marcellus II
311	St. Melchiades	816	Stephen IV	1118	Gelasius II	1555	Paul IV
314	St. Sylvester I	817	St. Paschal I	*1118*	*Gregory VIII*	1559	Pius IV
336	St. Mark	824	Eugene II	1119	Callistus II	1566	St. Pias V
337	St. Julius I	827	Valentine	1124	Honorius II	1572	Gregory XIII
352	Liberius	827	Gregory IV	*1124*	*Celestine II*	1585	Sixtus V
355	*Felix II*	*843*	*John*	1130	Innocent II	1590	Urban VII
366	St. Damasus I	844	Sergius II	*1130*	*Anacletus II*	1590	Gregory XIV
366	*Ursinus*	847	St. Leo IV	*1138*	*Victor IV*	1591	Innocent IX
384	St. Siricus	855	Benedict III	1143	Celestine II	1592	Clement VIII
399	St. Anastasius I	*855*	*Anastasius*	1144	Lucius II	1605	Leo XI
401	St. Innocent I	858	St. Nicholas I	1145	Eugene III	1605	Paul V
417	St. Zozimus	867	Adrian II	1153	Anastasius IV	1621	Gregory XV
418	St. Boniface I	872	John VIII	1154	Adrian IV	1623	Urban VIII
418	*Eulalius*	882	Marinus I	1159	Alexander III	1644	Innocent X
422	St. Celestine I	884	St. Adrian III	*1159*	*Victor IV*	1655	Alexander VII
432	St. Sixtus III	885	Stephen V	*1164*	*Paschal III*	1667	Clement IX
440	St. Leo I	891	Formosus	*1168*	*Callistus III*	1670	Clement X
461	St. Hilary	896	Boniface VI	*1179*	*Innocent III*	1676	Innocent XI
468	St. Simplicius	896	Stephen VI	1181	Lucius III	1689	Alexander VIII
483	St. Felix III or II	897	Romanus	1185	Urban III	1691	Innocent XII
492	St. Gelasius I	897	Theodore II	1187	Gregory VIII	1700	Clement XI
496	Anastasius II	898	John IX	1187	Clemente III	1721	Innocent XIII
498	St. Symmachus	900	Benedict IV	1191	Celestine III	1724	Bennedict XIII
498	*Lawrence*	903	Leo V	1198	Innocent III	1730	Clement XII
	(501-505)	*903*	*Christopher*	1216	Honorius III	1740	Benedict XIV
514	St. Hormisdas	904	Sergius III	1227	Gregory IX	1758	Clement XIII
523	St. John I	911	Anastasius III	1241	Celestine IV	1769	Clement XIV
526	St. Felix IV or III	913	Landus	1243	Innocent IV	1775	Pius VI
530	Boniface II	914	John X	1254	Alexander IV	1800	Pius VII
530	*Dioscorus*	928	Leo Vi	1261	Urban IV	1823	Leo XII
533	John II	928	Stephen VII	1265	Clement IV	1829	Pius VIII
535	St. Agapitus	931	John XI	1271	Gregory X	1831	Gregory XVI
536	St. Silverius	936	Leo VII	1276	Innocent V	1846	Pius IX
537	Vigilius	939	Stephen VIII	1276	Adrian V	1878	Leo XIII
556	Pelagius I	942	Marinus II	1276	John XXI	1903	St. Pius X
561	John III	946	Agapitus II	1277	Nicholas III	1914	Benedict XV
575	Benedict I	955	John X II	1281	Martin IV	1922	Pius XI
579	Pelagius II	963	Leo VIII	1285	Honorius IV	1939	Pius XII
590	St. Gregory I	964	Benedict V	1288	Nicholas IV	1958	John XXIII
604	Sabinianus	965	John XIII	1294	St. Celestine V	1963	Paul VI
607	Boniface III	973	Benedict VI	1294	Boniface VIII		
608	St. Boniface IV	*974*	*Boniface VII*	1303	Benedict XI		

Roman Catholic Statistics for the United States

Source: Official Catholic Directory, copyright 1974 by P. J. Kenedy & Sons

Archdioceses	Clergy	Parishes	Students	Cath. Pop.
Anchorage	25	16	3,515	24,000
Atlanta	131	41	18,812	61,166
Baltimore	761	145	94,370	455,902
Boston	2,408	408	347,954	1,893,050
Chicago	2,345	456	406,423	2,476,300
Cincinnati	834	262	132,422	517,888
Denver	368	123	55,102	303,969
Detroit	1,099	328	374,247	1,569,104
Dubuque	489	194	72,448	230,763
Hartford	752	218	148,959	827,701
Indianapolis	417	164	40,063	203,530
Kansas City, Kan.	287	97	34,416	138,000
Los Angeles	1,440	319	366,633	1,984,429
Louisville	398	125	44,806	189,650
Miami	470	120	82,099	631,600
Milwaukee	1,173	265	152,774	696,560
Newark	1,361	253	237,905	1,520,163
New Orleans	574	164	128,644	585,546
New York	2,066	407	359,879	1,800,000
Oklahoma City	152	71	14,428	65,715
Omaha	402	136	55,511	203,949
Philadelphia	1,578	311	296,058	1,375,096
Portland, Ore.	333	125	41,435	254,273
St. Louis	1,136	248	117,054	499,405
St. Paul & Minn.	516	218	141,062	532,504
San Antonio	409	158	82,635	538,619
San Francisco	834	150	120,224	827,950
Santa Fe	239	90	47,084	298,604
Seattle	435	126	58,696	343,680
Washington, D.C.	1,165	126	109,512	389,482
Ukr. of Phila.	139	101	7,870	49,813
Byz. of Munhall	92	83	11,545	150,625

Dioceses

Dioceses	Clergy	Parishes	Students	Cath. Pop.
Albany	665	211	89,397	517,716
Alexandria, La.	169	86	18,692	73,500
Allentown	416	151	42,575	260,340
Altoona-Johnstown	235	120	33,943	150,626
Amarillo	94	60	16,940	71,307
Austin	162	80	19,838	138,402
Baker, Ore.	58	31	5,661	23,647
Baton Rouge	154	66	36,241	151,844
Beaumont	85	37	12,830	75,000
Belleville	219	129	25,448	115,100
Belmont Abbey	29	1	625	417
Birmingham	145	58	13,006	42,436
Bismarck	140	79	26,023	73,159
Boise	110	66	12,416	61,272
Bridgeport	370	84	71,394	327,867
Brooklyn	1,302	228	233,333	1,346,220
Brownsville	110	61	34,165	277,124
Buffalo	1,128	297	169,177	925,482
Burlington	247	100	37,366	148,496
Camden	452	122	76,894	331,807
Charleston	142	66	14,602	48,091
Charlotte	78	56	11,496	37,581
Cheyenne	73	39	9,483	45,000
Cleveland	887	237	185,343	904,674
Columbus	304	108	45,949	193,640
Corpus Christi	154	72	30,131	184,122
Covington	210	82	24,698	103,500
Crookston	69	51	12,293	43,681
Dallas	213	55	32,244	110,924
Davenport	222	119	28,430	103,276
Des Moines	137	89	20,432	79,056
Dodge City	71	52	8,877	32,817
Duluth	137	83	22,190	94,426
El Paso	159	72	26,123	226,453
Erie	341	126	59,820	210,748
Evansville	145	75	19,198	87,942
Fairbanks	39	24	2,408	13,312
Fall River	402	113	65,755	320,000
Fargo	175	117	23,533	95,736
Fort Worth	96	49	17,342	72,629
Ft. Wayne-So. Bend	376	82	45,704	159,076
Fresno	173	84	33,882	282,316
Gallup	80	54	11,917	45,662
Galveston-Houston	389	120	71,843	338,774
Gary	240	85	36,671	188,568
Gaylord	77	58	14,297	72,762
Grand Island	83	53	11,822	52,117
Grand Rapids	207	54	33,618	150,429
Great Falls	138	76	16,044	67,681
Green Bay	505	193	83,197	320,015
Greensburg	290	117	41,960	225,079
Harrisburg	243	103	42,819	193,022

Dioceses	Clergy	Parishes	Students	Cath. Pop.
Helena	150	58	13,062	47,722
Honolulu	153	66	30,580	205,000
Jefferson City	152	88	16,969	68,603
Joliet	373	110	74,006	350,086
Juneau	12	9	756	4,800
Kalamazoo	87	45	17,791	83,416
Kan. City-St. Joseph	369	94	34,245	130,020
LaCrosse	367	178	58,609	199,497
Lafayette, Ind.	175	59	17,978	83,587
Lafayette, La.	289	150	81,882	395,368
Lansing	205	80	40,216	205,707
Lincoln	142	91	14,902	60,945
Little Rock	173	80	13,514	55,100
Madison	244	138	46,471	200,948
Manchester	384	126	55,141	264,747
Marquette	156	92	24,702	95,589
Memphis	75	29	12,705	40,183
Mobile	169	71	15,733	48,079
Monterey	124	43	15,149	95,000
Nashville	98	56	15,561	54,963
Natchez-Jackson	210	108	23,169	84,911
New Ulm	125	83	19,764	70,324
Norwich	216	70	45,695	195,450
Oakland	330	84	59,133	346,341
Ogdensburg	239	122	42,295	176,151
Orlando	149	58	27,762	112,260
Owensboro	85	74	12,887	49,365
Paterson	544	102	65,211	310,273
Peoria	371	171	50,748	216,752
Phoenix	210	64	32,832	225,219
Pittsburgh	852	320	173,667	911,928
Portland, Me.	345	142	55,183	262,694
Providence	591	155	88,995	606,840
Pueblo	161	60	16,487	106,150
Raleigh	79	59	11,155	36,421
Rapid City	191	50	13,202	36,000
Reno	92	38	12,783	90,120
Richmond	378	125	67,850	250,000
Rochester	485	160	93,524	358,850
Rockford	279	99	44,060	208,294
Rockville Centre	592	129	233,265	990,151
Sacramento	253	89	33,996	218,227
Saginaw	184	104	39,483	168,551
St. Augustine	126	72	20,210	81,375
St. Cloud	333	146	43,139	145,434
St. Petersburg	206	75	30,824	175,344
Salina	132	98	15,385	58,348
Salt Lake City	93	38	10,857	51,093
San Angelo	73	49	11,253	61,179
San Diego	539	165	52,934	547,000
Santa Rosa	121	36	11,883	71,360
Savannah	107	42	11,777	37,473
Scranton	578	239	79,353	351,539
Sioux City	215	139	32,373	111,618
Sioux Falls	93	122	30,659	100,922
Spokane	190	57	16,522	72,383
Springfield, Ill.	290	143	41,082	180,368
Springfield, Mass.	438	137	81,185	371,092
Spr'gf'd-Cape Gir.	115	59	9,901	38,803
Steubenville	173	73	14,653	57,000
Stockton	90	31	13,951	91,002
Superior	139	87	21,730	85,301
Syracuse	509	170	99,427	389,805
Toledo	395	149	72,984	331,752
Trenton	548	206	149,478	840,863
Tucson	180	55	25,426	182,369
Tulsa	90	53	9,071	42,953
Wheeling	202	101	19,937	95,617
Wichita	186	96	19,525	88,871
Wilmington	200	54	29,147	114,963
Winona	206	128	35,467	116,950
Worcester	526	130	80,882	339,540
Yakima	76	38	8,265	50,946
Youngstown	343	117	56,077	300,961

Eastern Rite:

	Clergy	Parishes	Students	Cath. Pop.
Passaic	98	83	6,923	97,740
Stamford	69	57	3,170	87,650
Parma	56	46	5,363	29,211
St. Nicholas	47	36	2,075	29,857
Melkite	41	25	4	21,676
St. Maron	58	43	162	65,541

	Clergy	Parishes	Students	Cath. Pop.
Totals 1974	56,712	18,433	9,321,474	48,465,438
Totals 1973	56,969	18,384	9,778,361	48,460,427

There were 10 Cardinals (Balt., Boston, Chicago, Detroit, Los Angeles, N.Y., Phila., St. Louis, San Francisco, Wash. D.C.): 38 Archbishops; 249 Bishops; 61 Abbots; 56,712 Priests; 9,233 Brothers; 139,963 Sisters; 18,433 parishes with 17,784 resident pastors, and 649 parishes without resident clergy. Religious order seminaries and novitiates 402 with 19,348 seminarians. Colleges and Universities 258; students 407,081; high schools 1,702; students 911,730; elementary schools 8,647, students 2,717,898; full-time teachers 174,711; protective institutions 138, students 11,679. Orphanage and infant asylums 195 with 15,494 resident children; 688 general hospitals with 158,170 bed capacity; 110 special hospitals; 472 homes for the aged. Converts totaled 74,741; infant baptisms 916,564; 406,908 marriages and 415,412 deaths.

Islamic (Moslem) Calendar 1975-1976

The Islamic calendar, often referred to as Mohammedan, is a lunar reckoning from the year of the hegira, 622 A.D., when Mohammed fled from Mecca. It runs in cycles of 30 years, of which the second, 5th, 7th, 10th, 13th, 16th, 18th, 21st, 24th, 26th and 29th are leap years. Common years have 354 days, leap years 355, the extra day being added to the last month, Zu'lhijjah. Except for this case, the 12 months beginning with Muharram have alternately 30 and 29 days. The month begins at sunset on the day before that given in the tables.

Year	Name of Month	Month Begins	Year	Name of Month	Month Begins
1395	Muharram (New Year)	Jan. 14, 1975	1396	Muharram (New Year)	Jan. 3, 1976
1395	Safar	Feb. 13, 1975	1396	Safar	Feb. 2, 1976
1395	Rabia I	Mar. 14, 1975	1396	Rabia I	Mar. 3, 1976
1395	Rabia II	Apr. 13, 1975	1396	Rabia II	Apr. 2, 1976
1395	Jumada I	May 12, 1975	1396	Jumada I	May 1, 1976
1395	Jumada II	June 11, 1975	1396	Jumada II	May 31, 1976
1395	Rajab	July 10, 1975	1396	Rajab	June 29, 1976
1395	Shaban	Aug. 9, 1975	1396	Shaban	July 29, 1976
1395	Ramadan	Sept. 7, 1975	1396	Ramadan	Aug. 27, 1976
1395	Shawwai	Oct. 7, 1975	1396	Shawwai	Sept. 26, 1976
1395	Zu'lkadah	Nov. 5, 1975	1396	Zu'lkadah	Oct. 25, 1976
1395	Zu'lhijjah	Dec. 5, 1975	1396	Zu'lhijjah	Nov. 24, 1976

Greek Orthodox Church Calendar, 1975

		Holy Days	Date		Holy Days
Jan.	1	The Circumcision of Christ—The Feastday of St. Basil New Year's Day	June	22	Sunday of Pentecost
			June	29	Feastday of Saints Peter and Paul
Jan.	6	The Epiphany, The Baptism of Jesus Christ			
		The Sanctifiction of the Waters	June	30	Feastday of the Twelve Holy Apostles
			Aug.	6	The Transfiguration
Jan.	7	Feastday of St. John the Baptist	Aug.	15	The Dormition of the Virgin Mary
Jan.	30	Feastday of Three Hierarchs: St. Basil, St. Gregory and St. John Chrysostom	Aug.	29	Beheading of St. John The Baptist
			Sept.	1	Beginning of the Church Year
Feb.	2	Presentation of Jesus in the Temple	Sept.	8	Nativity of the Virgin Mary
Mar.	17	Easter Lent begins	Sept.	14	The Elevation of the Holy Cross
Mar.	23	Sunday of Orthodoxy (1st Sun. of Lent)	Oct.	23	The Feast of James (Iakovos)
Mar.	25	The Annunciation of the Virgin Mary	Oct.	26	Feastday of St. Demetrios the Martyr
Apr.	23	Feastday of St. George	Nov.	15	The beginning of the Christmas Lent
Apr.	27	Palm Sunday	Nov.	21	Presentation of Blessed Virgin Mary
Apr. 27-May 4		Holy Week	Nov.	30	The Feast of St. Andrew, Founder Ecumenical Patriarchate of Constantinople
May	2	Good Friday—The Burial of Christ			
May	4	Easter Sunday	Dec.	6	Feastday of St. Nicholas, Bishop of Myra
June	12	The Ascension	Dec.	25	Christmas Day: The Birth of Jesus Christ

The dates above are according to the Gregorian calendar, adopted by the Greek Church in 1923. First Greek Orthodox church in U. S. founded 1864, in New Orleans, La.

Jewish Holidays, Festivals and Fasts

Source: Synagogue Council of America

All Jewish holidays, etc., begin at sunset on the day previous. *Also observed the following day.

Festivals and Fasts	Hebrew Date		1974-1975 (5735)	1975-1976 (5736)	1976-1977 (5737)	1977-1978 (5738)
Rosh Hashana (New Year)*	Tishri	1	Sept. 17 Tu	Sept. 6 Sa.	Sept. 25 Sa	Sept. 13 Tu
Fast of Gedalia	Tishri	3	Sept. 19 Th	Sept. 8 Mo	Sept. 27 Mo	Sept. 15 Th
Fast of Gedalia	Tishri	4	....	....	....	....
Yom Kippur (Day of Atonement)	Tishri	10	Sept. 26 Th	Sept. 15 Mo	Oct. 4 Mo	Sept. 22 Th
Sukkoth (Feast of Tabernacles), 1st Day*	Tishri	15	Oct. 1 Tu	Sept. 20 Sa	Oct. 9 Sa	Sept. 27 Tu
Sukkoth, 8th Day	Tishri	22	Oct. 8 Tu	Sept. 27 Sa	Oct. 16 Sa	Oct. 4 Tu
Simchat Torah (Rejoicing of the Law)	Tishri	23	Oct. 9 We	Sept. 28 Su	Oct. 17 Su	Oct. 5 We
Chanukah (Feast of Lights)	Kislev	25	Dec. 9 Mo	Nov. 29 Sa	Dec. 17 Fr	Dec. 5 Mo
Fast of Tebet	Tebet	10	Dec. 24 Tu	Dec. 14 Su	Dec. 31 Fr	Dec. 20 Tu
Fast of Esther	Adar	13	Feb. 24 Mo	....	Mar. 3 Th	....
Fast of Esther	Adar II	13	....	Mar. 15 Mo	....	Mar. 22 We
Purim (Feast of Lots)	Adar	14	Feb. 25 Tu	....	Mar. 4 Fr	....
Purim	Adar II	14	....	Mar. 16 Tu	....	Mar. 23 Tu
Pesach (Passover), 1st Day*	Nisan	15	Mar. 27 Th	Apr. 15 Th	Apr. 3 Su	Apr. 22 Sa
Pesach, 7th Day	Nisan	21	Apr. 2 We	Apr. 21 We	Apr. 9 Sa	Apr. 28 Fr
Pesach, Last Day	Nisan	22	Apr. 3 Th	Apr. 22 Th	Apr. 10 Su	Apr. 29 Sa
Lag B'Omer	Iyar	18	May 29 Tu	May 18 Tu	May 6 Fr	May 25 Th
Shavuoth (Feast of Weeks)*	Sivan	6	May 16 Fr	June 4 Fr	May 23 Mo	June 11 Su
Fast of Tammuz	Tammuz	17	June 26 Th	July 15 Th	July 3 Su	....
Fast of Tammuz	Tammuz	18	....	....	....	July 23 Su
Tisha B'Av (Fast of Av)	Av	9	July 17 Th	Aug. 5 Th	July 24 Su	....
Tisha B'Av	Av	10	....	....	....	Aug. 13 Su

The months of the Jewish year are: 1 Tishri; 2 Chesvan (also Marchesvan); 3 Kislev; 4 Tebet (also Tebeth); 5 Sebat (also Shebhat); 6 Adar; 6a. added month some years, Adar Sheni (II); 7 Nisan; 8 Iyar; 9 Sivan; 10 Tammuz, 11 Av (also Abh); 12 Elul.

Noted Personalities
American Statesmen of the Past

(Excluding Presidents, Vice Pres's., Sup. Ct. Justices, and most Signers of the Declaration of Independence; listed elsewhere.)

Born	Died	Name	Born	Died	Name	Born	Died	Name
1893	1971	Dean Acheson	1813	1861	Douglas, Stephen A.	1884	1968	Martin, Joseph W.
1807	1886	Adams, Charles Francis	1888	1959	Dulles, John Foster	1863	1941	McAdoo, William G.
1841	1915	Aldrich, Nelson W.	1794	1865	Everett, Edward	1874	1944	McNary, Charles L.
1793	1836	Austin, Stephen	1808	1893	Fish, Hamilton	1891	1967	Morgenthau, Henry, Jr.
1887	1962	Austin, Warren R.	1892	1949	Forrestal, James V.	1752	1816	Morris, Gouverneur
1871	1937	Baker, Newton D.	1706	1790	Franklin, Benjamin	1873	1931	Morrow, Dwight W.
1874	1940	Bankhead, William B.	1813	1890	Fremont, John C.	1861	1944	Norris, George W.
1870	1965	Baruch, Bernard M.	1761	1849	Gallatin, Albert	1757	1824	Pinckney, Charles
1797	1869	Bell, John	1805	1879	Garrison, William Lloyd	1746	1825	Pinckney, Charles C.
1782	1858	Benton, Thomas Hart	1858	1946	Glass, Carter	1753	1813	Randolph, Edmund
1830	1893	Blaine, James G.	1757	1804	Hamilton, Alexander	1773	1833	Randolph, John
1821	1875	Blair, Francis P., Jr.	1737	1793	Hancock, John	1721	1775	Randolph, Peyton
1835	1899	Bland, Richard P.	1838	1905	Hay, John	1880	1973	Rankin, Jeannette
1865	1940	Borah, William E.	1736	1799	Henry, Patrick	1882	1961	Rayburn, Sam
1760	1806	Breckinridge, John	1895	1967	Herter, Christian A.	1872	1937	Robinson, Joseph T.
1860	1925	Bryan, William Jennings	1890	1946	Hopkins, Harry L.	1884	1962	Roosevelt, Eleanor
1891	1967	Bullitt, William C.	1895	1972	Hoover, J. Edgar	1845	1937	Root, Elihu
1904	1971	Bunche, Ralph	1858	1938	House, Edward M.	1829	1906	Schurz, Carl
1887	1966	Byrd, Harry F.	1793	1863	Houston, Samuel	1733	1804	Schuyler, Philip J.
1836	1926	Cannon, Joseph G.	1871	1955	Hull, Cordell	1801	1872	Seward, William H.
1808	1873	Chase, Salmon P.	1874	1952	Ickes, Harold L.	1873	1944	Smith, Alfred E.
1799	1859	Choate, Rufus	1866	1945	Johnson, Hiram W.	1814	1869	Stanton, Edwin M.
1850	1921	Clark, Champ	1874	1956	Jones, Jesse H.	1812	1883	Stephens, Alexander H.
1777	1852	Clay, Henry	1903	1963	Kefauver, Estes	1900	1949	Stettinius, Edward R., Jr.
1769	1828	Clinton, DeWitt	1856	1937	Kellogg, Frank B.	1900	1965	Stevenson, Adlai E.
1829	1888	Conkling, Roscoe	1925	1968	Kennedy, Robert F.	1867	1960	Stimson, Henry L.
1877	1963	Connally, Tom	1755	1827	King, Rufus	1889	1953	Taft, Robert A.
1870	1957	Cox, James M.	1874	1944	Knox, Frank	1884	1968	Thomas, Norman M.
1787	1863	Crittenden, John J.	1855	1925	La Follett, Robert M.	1814	1886	Tilden, Samuel J.
1862	1948	Daniels, Josephus	1882	1947	LaGuardia, Fiorello H.	1890	1961	Tydings, Millard E.
1808	1889	Davis, Jefferson	1807	1870	Lee, Robert E.	1884	1951	Vandenberg, Arthur H.
1873	1955	Davis, John W.	1878	1963	Lehman, Herbert H.	1877	1953	Wagner, Robert F.
1855	1926	Debs, Eugene V.	1850	1924	Lodge, Henry Cabot	1782	1852	Webster, Daniel
1902	1971	Dewey, Thomas E.	1786	1857	Marcy, William L.	1892	1961	Welles, Sumner
1896	1969	Dirksen, Everett M.	1880	1959	Marshall, George C.	1892	1944	Willkie, Wendell L.

American Business Leaders, Philanthropists

Born	Died	Name	Born	Died	Name	Born	Died	Name
1885	1974	Aldrich, Winthrop W.	1837	1904	Hanna, Marcus A.	1875	1970	Neiman, Abraham
1884	1966	Arden, Elizabeth	1874	1940	Harkness, Edward S.	1887	1963	Olds, Irving S.
1832	1901	Armour, Phillip D.	1848	1909	Harriman, Edward	1795	1869	Peabody, George
1764	1848	Astor, John Jacob	1865	1957	Hartford, Geo. L.A.	1887	1973	Post, Marjorie Merriweather
1875	1967	Babson, Roger	1838	1916	Hill, James J.	1839	1937	Rockefeller, John D.
1894	1968	Bache, Harold L.	1795	1873	Hopkins, Johns	1874	1960	Rockefeller, J. D., Jr.
1853	1924	Belmont, August	1821	1900	Huntington, C.P.	1862	1932	Rosenwald, Julius
1786	1844	Biddle, Nicholas	1882	1967	Jergens, Andrew	1740	1785	Salomon, Haym
1835	1919	Carnegie, Andrew	1882	1967	Kaiser, Henry J.	1891	1971	Sarnoff, David
1821	1905	Cooke, Jay	1888	1969	Kennedy, Joseph P.	1847	1920	Schiff, Jacob H.
1791	1883	Cooper, Peter	1876	1958	Kettering, Charles F.	1875	1966	Sloan, Alfred P.
1834	1928	Depew, Chauncey M.	1879	1948	Knudsen, Wm. K.	1845	1912	Straus, Isidor
1806	1893	Drexel, Anthony J.	1867	1966	Kresge, S. S.	1848	1931	Straus, Nathan
1856	1925	Duke, James B.	1863	1955	Kress, Samuel H.	1839	1903	Swift, Gustavus
1739	1817	duPont, Pierre S.	1870	1948	Lamont, Thomas W.	1794	1877	Vanderbilt, Cornelius
1890	1962	Fairless, Benjamin	1880	1952	Lasker, Albert D.	1843	1899	Vanderbilt, Cornelius
1835	1906	Field, Marshall	1891	1969	Lehman, Robert	1849	1920	Vanderbilt, Wm. K.
1860	1937	Filene, Edward A.	1903	1972	Litton, Charles	1835	1900	Villard, Henry
1894	1970	Folsom, Frank M.	1831	1902	Mackay, John W.	1838	1922	Wanamaker, John
1863	1947	Ford, Henry	1855	1937	Mellon, Andrew W.	1896	1969	Warburg, James P.
1846	1927	Gary, Elbert H.	1899	1970	Mellon, Richard K.	1841	1904	Whitney, Wm. C.
1870	1949	Giannini, Amadeo Peter	1884	1968	Mennen, William G.	1886	1972	Wilson, Charles E.
1885	1966	Gimbel, Bernard F.	1825	1910	Mills, Darius	1890	1961	Wilson, Chas. Erwin
1836	1892	Gould, Jay	1837	1913	Morgan, J. Pierpont	1879	1969	Wood, Robert E.
1834	1916	Green, Henrietta (Hetty)	1868	1943	Morgan, J. P., Jr.	1852	1919	Woolworth, Frank
1828	1905	Guggenheim, Meyer	1875	1973	Mott, Charles Stewart			

American Explorers, Naturalists of the Past

Born	Died	Explorers	Born	Died	Name	Born	Died	Name
1884	1960	Andrews, Roy C.	1898	1970	Cruzen, Richard H.	1856	1920	Peary, Robert E.
1778	1838	Ashley, William Henry	1844	1881	De Long, G. W.	1779	1813	Pike, Zebulon M.
1875	1946	Bartlett, Robert A.	1877	1948	Dickey, H.S.	1834	1902	Powell, John W.
1790	1847	Bent, Charles	1880	1951	Ellsworth, Lincoln	1793	1864	Schoolcraft, Henry R.
1875	1956	Bingham, Hiram	1799	1854	Fitzpatrick, Thomas	1849	1892	Schwatka, Frederick
1796	1878	Bonneville, Benjamin	1813	1890	Fremont, John C.	1785	1843	Stuart, Robert
1734	1820	Boone, Daniel	1844	1935	Greely, Adolphus W.	1799	1845	Sublette, William L.
1796	1836	Bowie, James	1821	1871	Hall, Charles F.	1798	1876	Walker, Joseph R.
1804	1881	Bridger, James	1884	1937	Johnson, Martin	1802	1847	Whitman, Marcus
1888	1957	Byrd, Richard E.	1894	1953	Johnson, Osa	1798	1877	Wilkes, Charles
1809	1868	Carson, Kit	1820	1857	Kane, Elisha K.	1787	1849	Williams, W. S. (Old Bill)
1770	1838	Clark, William	1774	1809	Lewis, Meriwether			**Naturalists**
1775	1813	Colter, John	1784	1864	Long, Stephen H.	1864	1926	Akeley, Carl Ethan
1865	1940	Cook, Frederick A.	1874	1970	Macmillan, Donald	1780	1851	Audubon, John J.
			1799	1877	Palmer, Nathaniel	1850	1941	Beard, Daniel C.

Born	Died	Name	Born	Died	Name	Born	Died	Name
1849	1926	Burbank, Luther	1838	1914	Muir, John	1817	1862	Thoreau, Henry D.
1837	1921	Burroughs, John	1887	1969	Osborn, Fairfield	1766	1813	Wilson, Alexander

American Military Leaders of the Past
All Army unless marked (N) Navy; (M) Marine; (AF) Air Force.

Born	Died	Name	Born	Died	Name	Born	Died	Name
1737	1789	Allen, Ethan	1883	1959	Halsey, William F. (N)	1825	1875	Pickett, George E.
1741	1801	Arnold, Benedict	1818	1902	Hampton, Wade	1822	1892	Pope, John
1886	1950	Arnold, Henry F. (Hap) (AF)	1728	1777	Herkimer, Nicholas	1813	1891	Porter, David D. (N)
			1825	1865	Hill, Ambrose P.	1905	1970	Power, Thomas S. (AF)
1816	1894	Banks, Nathaniel	1892	1966	Hobbs, Leland	1809	1867	Price, Stirling
1745	1803	Barry, John (N)	1870	1937	Hobson, Richmond (N)	1896	1973	Radford, Arthur (N)
1818	1893	Beauregard, Pierre	1887	1966	Hodges, Courtney	1890	1973	Rickenbacker, Edward (AF)
1853	1930	Bliss, Tasker H.	1814	1879	Hooker, Joseph	1819	1892	Rodgers, C. R. P. (N)
1878	1967	Bloch, Claude C. (N)	1831	1879	Hood, John B.	1773	1838	Rodgers, John (N)
1817	1876	Bragg, Braxton	1773	1843	Hull, Issac (N)	1819	1898	Rosecrans, William S.
1775	1828	Brown, Jacob J.	1824	1863	Jackson, Thomas (Stonewall)	1736	1818	St. Clair, Arthur
1888	1950	Buchanan, Pat (N)				1840	1903	Sampson, William T. (N)
1823	1914	Buckner, Simon B.	1803	1862	Johnston, Albert S.	1831	1906	Schofield, John
1886	1945	Buckner, Simon, Jr.	1807	1891	Johnston, Joseph	1786	1866	Scott, Winfield
1826	1863	Buford, John	1747	1792	Jones, John Paul (N)	1835	1906	Shafter, William R.
1861	1947	Bullard, Robert L.	1814	1862	Kearny, Philip	1831	1888	Sheridan, Phillip
1824	1881	Burnside, Ambrose	1794	1848	Kearny, Stephen	1896	1951	Sherman, Forrest P. (N)
1818	1893	Butler Benjamin F.	1879	1956	King, Ernest J. (N)	1820	1891	Sherman, William T.
1817	1873	Canby, Edward	1781	1813	Lawrence, James (N)	1858	1936	Sims, William S. (N)
1884	1970	Cates, Clifton B. (M)	1843	1899	Lawton, Henry	1780	1867	Sloat, John D. (N)
1772	1840	Chauncey, Isaac (N)	1875	1959	Leahy, William D. (N)	1882	1967	Smith, Holland M. (M)
1842	1914	Chaffee, Adna R.	1756	1818	Lee, Henry	1895	1961	Smith, W.Bedell
1890	1958	Chennault, Claire (AF)	1807	1870	Lee, Robert E.	1886	1969	Spruance, Raymond (N)
1752	1818	Clark, George Rogers	1821	1904	Longstreet, James	1728	1822	Stark, John
1786	1836	Crockett, David	1818	1861	Lyon, Nathaniel	1883	1946	Stilwell, Joseph W.
1819	1893	Crittenden, Thomas L.	1845	1912	MacArthur, Arthur	1726	1783	Stirling (Alexander)
1828	1890	Crook, George	1880	1964	MacArthur, Douglas	1890	1969	Stratemeyer, George (AF)
1842	1874	Cushing, William B. (N)	1733	1795	Marion, Francis	1833	1864	Stuart, J. E. B.
1839	1876	Custer, George	1806	1873	Maury, Matthew F. (N)	1740	1795	Sullivan, John
1779	1820	Decatur, Stephen (N)	1826	1885	McClellan, George B.	1822	1880	Sykes, George
1837	1917	Dewey, George (N)	1818	1885	McDowell, Irvin	1784	1850	Taylor, Zachary
1857	1927	Dickman, Joseph T.	1828	1864	McPherson, James	1827	1890	Terry, Alfred H.
1879	1951	Drum, Hugh A.	1815	1872	Meade, George	1816	1870	Thomas, George H.
1816	1894	Early, Jubal A.	1839	1925	Miles, Nelson A.	1884	1955	Towers, John H. (N)
1886	1961	Eichelberger, R. L.	1879	1936	Mitchell, Billy	1899	1954	Vanderberg, Hoyt (AF)
1890	1969	Eisenhower, Dwight D.	1887	1947	Mitscher, Marc A. (N)	1883	1953	Wainwright, Jonathan
1846	1912	Evans, Robley D. (N)	1736	1775	Montgomery, Richard	1889	1950	Walker, Walton H.
1817	1872	Ewell, Richard	1736	1802	Morgan, Daniel	1732	1799	Washington, George
1801	1870	Farragut, David G. (N)	1730	1805	Moultrie, William	1745	1796	Wayne, Anthony
1806	1863	Foote, Andrew (N)	1885	1966	Nimitz, Chester (N)	1836	1906	Wheeler, Joseph
1821	1877	Forrest, Nathan B.	1906	1971	O'Donnell, Emmett (Rosy) (AF)	1757	1825	Wilkinson, James
1865	1917	Funston, Frederick				1837	1925	Wilson, James H.
1728	1806	Gates, Horatio	1896	1959	Parks, Floyd L.	1860	1927	Wood, Leonard
1805	1877	Goldsborough, L. M. (N)	1885	1945	Patton, George S.	1818	1897	Worden, John L. (N)
1822	1885	Grant, Ulysses S.	1814	1881	Pemberton, J. C.	1820	1899	Wright, Horatio G.
1742	1786	Greene, Nathaniel	1785	1819	Perry, Oliver H. (N)	1898	1969	Wyman, Willard G.
1896	1970	Groves, Leslie R.	1860	1948	Pershing, John J.	1876	1959	Yarnell, Hy. E. (N)
1815	1872	Halleck, Henry	1739	1817	Pickens, Andrew	1887	1964	York, Alvin C. (Sgt.)

American Scientists, Physicians, Engineers of the Past

Born	Died	Name	Born	Died	Name	Born	Died	Name
1838	1916	Abbe, Cleveland	1903	1973	Gibbon, John H.	1868	1953	Millikan, Robert
1876	1945	Albee, Fred H.	1839	1903	Gibbs, Josiah W.	1866	1945	Morgan, Thomas H.
1807	1873	Agassiz, Louis	1858	1928	Goethals, George W.	1819	1968	Morton, W. T. G.
1823	1887	Baird, Spencer	1874	1929	Goldberger, Joseph	1890	1967	Muller, Hermann J.
1839	1883	Beard, George Miller	1854	1920	Gorgas, William C.	1904	1967	Oppenheimer, J. Robert
1785	1853	Beaumont, William	1863	1914	Hall, Charles M.	1883	1962	Papanicolaou, George N.
1889	1967	Bigelow, Henry B.	1896	1965	Hench, Philip S.	1903	1967	Pincus, Gregory
1899	1964	Blalock, Alfred	1883	1964	Hess, Victor F.	1851	1902	Reed, Walter S.
1773	1838	Bowditch, Nath.	1889	1953	Hubble, Edwin P.	1846	1927	Remsen, Ira
1882	1961	Bridgman, Percy W.	1865	1958	Jackson, Chevalier	1871	1910	Ricketts, Howard T.
1848	1908	Brooks, William K.	1905	1973	Kuiper, Gerard	1806	1869	Roebling, John A.
1868	1939	Cabot, Richard C.	1834	1906	Langley, Samuel P.	1879	1970	Rous, Peyton
1873	1944	Carrel, Alexis	1881	1957	Langmuir, Irving	1745	1813	Rush, Benjamin
1864	1943	Carver, George W.	1884	1964	Lanza, Anthony J.	1877	1967	Schick, Bela
1887	1968	Cobb, Stanley	1901	1958	Lawrence, Ernest O.	1885	1972	Shapley, Harlow
1892	1962	Compton, Arthur H.	1815	1878	Long, Crawford	1813	1883	Sims, James M.
1877	1954	Compton, Karl T.	1885	1916	Lowell, Percival	1859	1934	Smith, Theobald
1901	1974	Condon, Edward	1806	1873	Maury, Matthew F.	1865	1923	Steinmetz, Charles
1869	1939	Cushing, Harvey W.	1865	1939	Mayo, Charles H.	1898	1964	Szilard, Leo
1927	1961	Dooley, Thomas	1898	1968	Mayo, Charles W.	1899	1972	Theiler, Max
1901	1965	Du Mont, Allen	1861	1939	Mayo, William J.	1888	1973	Waksman, Selman
1820	1887	Eads, James P.	1845	1913	McBurney, Charles	1886	1973	White, Paul Dudley
1879	1955	Einstein, Albert	1909	1968	McLean, John Milton	1894	1964	Wiener, Norbert
1706	1790	Franklin, Benjamin	1899	1966	Menninger, William C.	1844	1930	Wiley, Harvey W.
1895	1974	Fremont Smith, Frank	1852	1931	Michelson, Albert A.	1856	1931	Williams, Daniel Hale
1884	1967	Funk, Casimir	1903	1966	Millikan, Clark			

American Sculptors of the Past

Born	Died	Name	Born	Died	Name	Born	Died	Name
1878	1949	Aitken, Robert I.	1819	1911	Ball, Thomas	1865	1925	Bartlett, Paul W.
1887	1964	Archipenko, Alexander	1863	1938	Barnard, George Grey	1867	1915	Bitter, Karl T.

Born	Died	Name	Born	Died	Name	Born	Died	Name
1913	1969	Boehm, Edward M.	1825	1879	Jackson, John Adams	1816	1879	Rimmer, William
1871	1941	Borglum, Gutzon	1868	1925	Jaegers, Albert	1825	1874	Rinehart, William H.
1868	1922	Borglum, Solon H.	1892	1969	Jones, Thomas H.	1829	1904	Rogers, John
1814	1886	Brown, Henry K.	1863	1947	Kitson, Henry Hudson	1825	1892	Rogers, Randolph
1898	1970	Bufano, Benjamino	1871	1932	Kitson, Theo Alice	1879	1922	Rumsey, Charles Cary
1870	1945	Calder, Alexander S.	1882	1935	Lachaise, Gaston	1756	1833	Rush, William
1814	1857	Crawford, Thomas	1877	1954	Laessle, Albert	1848	1907	St. Gaudens, Augustus
1861	1944	Dallin, Cyrus	1877	1963	Lawrie, Lee	1871	1922	Shrady, Henry M.
1884	1952	Davidson, Jo	1871	1935	Lukeman, Henry A.	1839	1913	Simmons, Franklin
1844	1917	Ezekiel, Moses Jacob	1863	1937	MacMonnies, Fred W.	1906	1965	Smith, David
1895	1942	Flannagan, John	1885	1966	Manship, Paul	1819	1895	Story, William W.
1877	1953	Fraser, James E.	1879	1947	McCartan, Edward	1860	1936	Taft, Lorado
1790	1852	Frazee, John	1876	1916	Mears, Helen F.	1830	1910	Ward, J. O. A.
1850	1931	French, Daniel C.	1883	1962	Mestrovic, Ivan	1870	1952	Weinman, Adolph A.
1805	1852	Greenouth, Horatio	1817	1904	Palmer, Erastus Dow	1877	1942	Whitney, Gertrude
1887	1967	Hoffman, Malvina	1905	1973	Powers, Hiram	1877	1957	Young, Mahonri M.
1830	1908	Hosmer, Harriet	1867	1917	Pratt, Bela	1887	1966	Zorach, William
1847	1914	Hoxie, Vinnie Ream	1868	1929	Quinn, Edmond T.			

American Reformers, Social-Economic Leaders of the Past

Born	Died	Name	Born	Died	Name	Born	Died	Name
1860	1935	Addams, Jane	1887	1940	Garvey, Marcus	1842	1933	Parkhurst, Charles H.
1909	1972	Alinsky, Saul O.	1839	1897	George, Henry	1811	1884	Phillips, Wendell
1847	1902	Altgeld, Peter	1837	1927	Gerry, Elbridge T.	1849	1914	Riis, Jacob A.
1820	1906	Anthony, Susan B.	1850	1924	Gompers, Samuel	1816	1906	Sage, Russell
1891	1969	Arnold, Thurman, W.	1873	1952	Green, William	1828	1918	Sage, Margaret Olivia
1867	1961	Balch, Emily G.	1887	1946	Hillman, Sidney	1883	1967	Sanger, Margaret
1821	1912	Barton, Clara H.	1801	1876	Howe, Samuel G.	1747	1825	Shays, Daniel
1818	1895	Bloomer, Amelia J.	1929	1968	King, Martin Luther	1797	1874	Smith, Gerrit
1809	1890	Brisbane, Albert	1855	1925	LaFollette, Robt. M.	1816	1902	Stanton, Eliz. Cady
1800	1959	Brown, John	1880	1969	Lewis, John L.	1818	1893	Stone, Lucy
1859	1947	Catt, Carrie Chapman	1793	1880	Mott, Lucretia	1867	1960	Townsend, Francis E.
1855	1926	Debs, Eugene	1886	1952	Murray, Phillip	1893	1955	White, Walter
1802	1887	Dix, Dorothea	1846	1911	Nation, Carry	1931	1973	Wiley, George
1817	1895	Douglass, Frederick	1811	1886	Noyes, John H.	1839	1898	Willard, Frances E.
1805	1879	Garrison, Wm. L.	1801	1877	Owen, Robt. Dale	1921	1971	Young, Whitney M.

American Painters of the Past

Born	Died	Name	Born	Died	Name	Born	Died	Name
1852	1911	Abbey, Edwin A.	1868	1933	Hart, George O.	1851	1914	Pearce, Charles S.
1779	1843	Allston, Washington	1877	1943	Hartley, Marsden	1884	1970	Peirce, Waldo
1785	1851	Audubon, John James	1859	1935	Hassam, Childe	1912	1956	Pollock, Jackson
1893	1965	Avery, Milton C.	1813	1894	Healy, George P. A.	1823	1879	Powell, William H.
1912	1963	Baziotes, William	1865	1929	Henri, Robert	1861	1924	Prendergast, Maurice, B.
1863	1942	Beaux, Cecelia	1780	1849	Hicks, Edward	1853	1911	Pyle, Howard
1882	1925	Bellows, George W.	1823	1890	Hicks, Thomas	1801	1881	Quidor, John
1830	1902	Bierstadt, Albert	1880	1966	Hofmann, Hans	1861	1909	Remington, Frederic
1811	1879	Bingham, George Caleb	1836	1910	Homer, Winslow	1838	1905	Richards. William T.
1856	1943	Birch, Reginald B.	1882	1967	Hopper, Edward	1903	1970	Rothko, Mark
1848	1936	Blashfield, Edwin H.	1824	1879	Hunt, William M.	1847	1917	Ryder, Albert P.
1847	1927	Bridgman, Frederic A.	1801	1846	Inman, Henry	1856	1925	Sargent, John Singer
1855	1941	Brush, George de Forest	1825	1894	Inness, George	1898	1969	Shahn, Ben
1893	1967	Burchfield, Charles E.	1843	1942	Jackson, William H.	1883	1965	Sheeler, Charles
1845	1926	Cassatt, Mary	1824	1906	Johnson, Eastman	1876	1953	Shinn, Everett
1796	1872	Catlin, George	1838	1911	Keith, William	1871	1951	Sloan, John
1849	1916	Chase, William M.	1818	1872	Kensett, John F.	1883	1962	Speicher, Eugene E.
1826	1900	Church, Frederic	1880	1949	Kuhn, Walt	1880	1946	Stella, Joseph
1801	1848	Cole, Thomas	1835	1910	La Farge, John	1755	1828	Stuart, Gilbert
1737	1815	Copley, John S.	1873	1939	Lawson, Ernest	1783	1872	Sully, Thomas
1856	1919	Cox, Kenyon	1816	1868	Leutze, Emanuel	1861	1930	Symons, Gardner
1843	1909	Currier, J. Frank	1867	1933	Luks, George B.	1849	1921	Thayer, Abbott H.
1897	1946	Curry, John Steuart	1866	1912	MacCameron, Robert L.	1848	1933	Tiffany, Louis C.
1862	1928	Davies, Arthur B.	1872	1953	Marin, John	1756	1843	Trumbull, John
1894	1964	Davis, Stuart	1898	1936	Marsh, Reginald	1849	1925	Tryon, Dwight N.
1883	1935	Demuth, Charles	1836	1897	Martin, Homer	1853	1902	Twachtman, John H.
1884	1958	Du Bois, Guy Pene	1813	1884	Matteson, Tompkins H.	1776	1852	Vanderlyn, John
1796	1886	Durand, Asher Brown	1868	1932	Maurer, Alfred H.	1836	1923	Vedder, Elihu
1848	1919	Duveneck, Frank	1860	1932	Melchiers, Gari	1858	1933	Vonnoh, Robert W.
1844	1916	Eakins, Thomas	1858	1925	Metcalf, Willard L.	1843	1929	Walker, Henry Oliver
1751	1801	Earle, Ralph	1829	1901	Moran, Edward	1881	1961	Weber, Max
1871	1956	Feininger, Lyonel	1837	1926	Moran, Thomas	1841	1926	Weir, John F.
1822	1884	Fuller, George	1860	1961	Moses, Grandma	1852	1919	Weir, Julian Alden
1870	1938	Glackens, William J.	1807	1868	Mount, William S.	1803	1889	Weir, Robert W.
1904	1948	Gorky, Arshile	1867	1940	Myers, Jerome	1738	1820	West, Benjamin
1903	1974	Gottlieb, Adolph	1741	1827	Peale, Charles W.	1834	1903	Whistler, James A. M.
1893	1959	Grosz, George	1749	1831	Peale, James	1820	1910	Whittredge, Worthington
1866	1946	Guerin, Jules	1774	1825	Peale, Raphaelle	1891	1942	Wood, Grant
1792	1866	Harding, Chester	1778	1860	Peale, Rembrandt	1836	1892	Wyant, Alexander H.
1848	1892	Harnett, William M.						

American Inventors of the Past

Born	Died	Name	Born	Died	Name	Born	Died	Name
1891	1954	Armstrong, Edwin	1862	1938	Duryea, Charles E.	1882	1945	Goddard, Robert H.
1847	1922	Bell, Alex. Graham	1870	1967	Duryea, J. Frank	1800	1860	Goodyear, Charles
1890	1970	Bell, Herbert A.	1854	1932	Eastman, George	1803	1855	Gorrie, John
1851	1929	Berliner, Emile	1847	1931	Edison, Thomas A.	1835	1901	Gray, Elisha
1857	1898	Burroughs, William	1803	1889	Ericcson, John	1797	1878	Henry, Joseph
1906	1968	Carlson, Chester F.	1743	1798	Fitch, John	1812	1886	Hoe, Richard M.
1876	1950	Carrier, Willis	1765	1815	Fulton, Robert	1819	1867	Howe, Elias
1874	1961	De Forrest, Lee	1818	1903	Gatling, Richard J.	1866	1945	Lake, Simon

Born	Died	Name
1881	1957	Langmuir, Irving
1826	1886	Loomis, Mahlon
1809	1884	McCormick, Cyrus H.
1854	1899	Mergenthaler, Ottmar
1791	1872	Morse, S. F. B.
1811	1861	Otis, Elisha

Born	Died	Name
1831	1897	Pullman, George M.
1889	1972	Sikorsky, Igor
1894	1970	Spencer, Percy L.
1860	1930	Sperry, Elmer A.
1856	1943	Tesla, Nikola

Born	Died	Name
1853	1937	Thomson, Elihu
1846	1914	Westinghouse, George
1765	1825	Whitney, Eli
1871	1948	Wright, Orville
1867	1912	Wright, Wilbur

American Educators and Religious Leaders

Educators

Born	Died	Name
1897	1967	Allport, Gordon
1829	1916	Angell, James B.
1870	1949	Angell, James R.
1811	1900	Barnard, Henry
1827	1911	Bascom, John
1862	1947	Butler, Nich. Murray
1807	1874	Cornell, Ezra
1862	1948	Cross, Wilbur
1859	1952	Dewey, John
1868	1963	DuBois, William E. B.
1834	1926	Eliot, Charles W.
1863	1940	Finley, John H.
1903	1967	Gassner, John W.
1831	1908	Gilman, Daniel C.
1906	1963	Griswold A. Whitney
1844	1924	Hall, G. Stanley
1856	1906	Harper, William R.
1802	1887	Hopkins, Mark
1842	1910	James, William
1880	1968	Keller, Helen
1797	1849	Lyon, Mary
1800	1873	McGuffey, William H.
1796	1859	Mann, Horace
1872	1964	Meiklejohn, Alexander
1818	1901	Muhlenberg, Fred. A.
1869	1946	Neilson, William A.
1909	1969	Northrop, Eugene P.
1827	1908	Norton, Chas. Eliot
1855	1902	Palmer, Alice Freeman

Born	Died	Name
1804	1894	Peabody, Elizabeth P.
1870	1964	Pound, Roscoe
1855	1916	Royce, Josiah
1885	1963	Seymour, Charles
1779	1864	Silliman, Benjamin
1917	1969	Smith, Courtney C.
1840	1910	Sumner, Wm. Graham
1893	1969	Tannenbaum, Frank
1858	1915	Washington, Booker T.
1832	1918	White, Andrew D.
1787	1870	Willard, Emma

Religious Leaders

Born	Died	Name
1835	1922	Abbott, Lyman
1745	1816	Asbury, Francis
1813	1887	Beecher, Henry Ward
1775	1863	Beecher, Lyman
1835	1893	Brooks, Phillips
1582	1658	Bulkeley, Peter
1802	1867	Bushnell, Horace
1780	1842	Channing, Wm. Ellery
1584	1652	Cotton, John
1895	1970	Cushing, Richard
1752	1817	Dwight, Timothy
1821	1910	Eddy, Mary Baker
1703	1758	Edwards, Jonathan
1900	1968	Fry, Franklin C.
1834	1921	Gibbons, James
1867	1938	Hayes, Patrick J.
1748	1830	Hicks, Elias

Born	Died	Name
1879	1964	Holmes, John Haynes
1590	1643	Hutchinson, Anne
1883	1968	Jones, Bob
1884	1973	Jones, E. Stanley
1843	1926	Kohler, Kaufmann
1866	1949	Manning, William T.
1663	1728	Mather, Cotton
1873	1970	McKay, David O.
1890	1944	McPherson, Aimee Semple
1837	1899	Moody, Dwight L.
1711	1787	Muhlenberg, H. M.
1891	1963	Oxnam, G. Bromley
1810	1860	Parker, Theodore
1913	1969	Pike, James A.
1884	1968	Poling, Daniel A.
1729	1796	Seabury, Samuel
1774	1821	Seton, Elizabeth
1886	1969	Sheil, Bernard J.
1882	1968	Shipler, Guy E.
1881	1968	Silver, Eliezer
1805	1844	Smith, Joseph
1876	1972	Smith, Joseph Fielding
1889	1970	Sockman, Ralph W.
1889	1967	Spellman, Francis
1863	1935	Sunday, Wm. (Billy)
1886	1965	Tillich, Paul
1862	1969	Welch, Herbert
1599	1683	Williams, Roger
1874	1949	Wise, Stephen S.
1801	1877	Young, Brigham

American Writers of the Past

Novelists, Poets, Historians, Journalists, Publishers, Biographers

A

Charles Francis Adams, biographer, diplomat, 1807-1886.

Charles Francis Adams, historian, lawyer, 1835-1915.

Franklin P. Adams, journalist, 1881-1960.

Henry Adams, historian, philosopher 1838-1918.

James Truslow Adams, historian, 1878-1949.

George Ade, humorist, dramatist, 1866-1944.

Conrad Aiken, poet, critic, 1889-1973.

Louisa May Alcott, novelist, 1832-1889. Little Women.

Thomas Bailey Aldrich, author, editor, 1836-1907.

Henry M. Alden, editor, 1836-1919. Harper's Magazine.

Horatio Alger, author of "rags-to-riches" boys' books, 1834-1899.

James Lane Allen, novelist, 1849-1925.

Charlotte Armstrong, mystery writer, 1905-1969.

Hamilton Fish Armstrong, journalist and editor of Foreign Affairs, 1893-1973.

Gertrude Atherton, novelist, 1857-1948. Black Oxen.

Mary Austin, novelist, playwright, 1868-1934.

B

Irving Bacheller, novelist, journalist, 1859-1950. Eben Holden.

Arthur (Bugs) Baer, humorous columnist, 1886-1969.

Ray Stannard Baker, biographer, historian, 1870-1946.

George Bancroft, historian, diplomat, 1800-1891.

Margaret Ayer Barnes, novelist, 1886-1967. Years of Grace.

John Bartlett, publisher, 1820-1905. Familiar Quotations.

Bruce Barton, author, businessman, 1875-1967. The Man Nobody Knows.

Charles A. Beard, historian, 1874-1948.

Mary Ritter Beard, historian, 1876-1958.

Lucius M. Beebe, journalist, author, 1902-1966. N. Y. Herald Tribune.

Edward Bellamy, novelist, 1850-1898. Looking Backward: 2000-1887.

Robert C. Benchley, humorist, journalist, 1889-1945.

Stephen Vincent Benet, poet, novelist, 1898-1943.

William Rose Benet, poet, novelist, 1886-1950.

James Gordon Bennett, journalist, 1795-1872. Founded N. Y. Herald.

James Gordon Bennett, Jr., journalist, 1841-1918. N. Y. Herald. Evening Telegram.

William Benton, publisher, 1900-1973. Encyclopaedia Britannica.

John Berryman, poet, 1914-1972.

Ambrose Bierce, short-story writer, journalist, 1842-1914.

Earl Derr Biggers, novelist, 1884-1933. Created Charlie Chan.

Josh Billings (H. W. Shaw), humorist, 1818-1885.

Louise Bogan, lyric poet, 1897-1970.

Samuel Bowles II, editor, 1826-1878. Springfield Republican.

Gamaliel Bradford, biographer, 1863-1932.

Anne Bradstreet, poet, 1612-1672.

William Cowper Brann (Iconoclast), editor, reformer, 1855-1898.

Arthur Brisbane, journalist, 1864-1936. N. Y. Sun, Evening Sun, World.

Louis Bromfield, novelist, essayist, 1896-1956.

Van Wyck Brooks, historian, critic, 1886-1963.

Heywood Broun, journalist, 1888-1939. N. Y. Tribune, World.

John Mason Brown, drama, literary critic, 1900-1969.

Orestes Brownson, author, editor, clergyman, 1803-1876.

William Cullen Bryant, poet, editor, 1794-1878.

Pearl Buck, author, won the Pulitzer and Nobel Prizes in literature, 1892-1973. The Good Earth.

Henry C. Bunner, journalist, poet, 1855-1896. Editor of Puck.

Ned Buntline, wrote dime novels, 1823-1886. Nicknamed "Buffalo Bill" Cody.

Edgar Rice Burroughs, novelist, 1875-1950. Tarzan of the Apes.

C

George W. Cable, novelist, essayist, 1844-1925.

Henry Seidel Canby, editor, critic, 1878-1961. Saturday Review of Literature.

Jimmy Cannon, sports columnist, 1909-1973.

Will Carleton, poet, journalist, 1845-1912. Over the Hill to the Poorhouse.

Rachel Carson, marine biologist, author, 1907-1964. Silent Spring.

Alice Cary, novelist, 1820-1871.

Phoebe Cary, poet, 1824-1871. One Sweetly Solemn Thought.

Willa Cather, novelist, essayist, 1876-1947. O Pioneers! My Antonia.

Robert W. Chambers, novelist, artist, 1865-1933. The Rogue's Moon.

Raymond Chandler, wrote detective fiction, 1888-1959. Philip Marlowe series.

Winston Churchill, novelist, 1871-1947. The Crisis.

Raymond Clapper, journalist, 1892-1944.

Walter Van Tilburg Clark, novelist, 1909-1972. The Ox-Bow Incident.

Irvin S. Cobb, humorist, journalist, 1876-1944.

James Fenimore Cooper, novelist, 1789-1851. Leather-Stocking Tales.

Royal Cortissoz, journalist, author, 1869-1948. N. Y. Herald Tribune.

Thomas B. Costain, novelist, journalist, 1885-1965. The Black Rose.

Hart Crane, poet, 1899-1932.

Stephen Crane, novelist, 1871-1900. The Red Badge of Courage.

Francis Marion Crawford, novelist, 1854-1909.

Countee Cullen, poet, 1903-1946. The Black Christ.

E. E. Cummings, poet, 1894-1962.

Cyrus H. K. Curtis, magazine, newspaper publisher, 1850-1933.

George William Curtis, journalist, author, 1824-1892.

D

Charles A. Dana, editor, 1819-1897. New York Sun.

Richard H. Dana, author, lawyer, 1815-1882. Two Years Before the Mast.

Josephus Daniels, journalist, statesman, 1862-1948. Raleigh News & Observer.

Elmer Davis, journalist, radio commentator, 1890-1958.

Richard Harding Davis, journalist, novelist, 1864-1916.

Ludwell Denny, journalist, 1894-1970. Scripps-Howard Newspapers.

Bernard De Voto, historian, editor, 1897-1955.

Michael H. De Young, newspaper editor, 1849-1925. San Francisco Chronicle.

Emily Dickinson, poet, 1830-1886.

Thomas Dixon, novelist, clergyman, 1865-1946. The Clansman.

J. Frank Dobie, author, educator, 1888-1964.

Hilda Doolittle (H.D.), poet, 1886-1961.

John Dos Passos, author, 1896-1970. U.S.A., Midcentury.

Joesph Rodman Drake, poet, 1795-1820.

Theodore Dreiser, novelist, 1871-1945. An American Tragedy.

Orvil E. Dryfoos, newspaper publisher, 1912-1963. New York Times.

Paul L. Dunbar, poet, novelist, 1872-1906.

E

Edward Eggleston, novelist, clergyman, 1837-1902.

Ralph Waldo Emerson, poet, essayist, 1803-1882.

John Erskine, novelist, educator, 1879-1951. The Private Life of Helen of Troy.

F

Martha Farquharson, author of juveniles, 1828-1909. Elsie Dinsmore series.

William Faulkner, novelist, 1897-1962. Sanctuary, Light in August.

Edna Ferber, novelist, 1887-1968. Show Boat, Saratoga Trunk, Giant.

Arthur D. Ficke, poet, novelist, 1883-1945.

Eugene Field, poet, journalist, 1850-1895. Little Boy Blue, Wynken, Blynken and Nod.

James T. Fields, editor, author, 1817-1881. Atlantic Monthly.

Louis Fischer, historian, 1896-1970. The Life of Lenin.

Dorothy Canfield Fisher, novelist, writer of juveniles, 1879-1958.

John Fiske, historian, philosopher, 1842-1901.

F. Scott Fitzgerald, novelist, short-story writer, 1896-1940. The Great Gatsby.

John Gould Fletcher, poet, critic, 1886-1950.

Kathryn Forbes, novelist, 1909-1966. Mama's Bank Account.

Paul Leicester Ford, novelist, historian, 1865-1902.

Gene Fowler, journalist, author, 1890-1960. Good Night, Sweet Prince.

John W. Fox, Jr., novelist, 1863-1919. The Little Shepherd of Kingdom Come.

Douglas S. Freeman, historian, editor, 1886-1953. Richmond News Leader.

Mary E. W. Freeman, short-story writer, 1852-1930.

Philip Freneau, poet, journalist, 1752-1832.

Robert Frost, poet, 1874-1963.

G

Zona Gale, novelist, dramatist, 1874-1938.

Frank E. Gannett, newspaper publisher, 1876-1957. Gannett Newspapers.

Erle Stanley Gardner, author, lawyer, 1889-1970. Perry Mason series.

Hamlin Garland, novelist, 1860-1940. Main-Traveled Roads.

Floyd Gibbons, journalist, radio personality, 1887-1939.

Ellen Glasgow, novelist, 1873-1945.

Susan Glaspell, novelist, dramatist, 1882-1948.

Edwin L. Godkin, journalist, 1831-1902. Founded The Nation.

Henry W. Grady, journalist, orator, 1850-1889. Atlanta Constitution.

Horace Greeley, journalist, politician, 1811-1872. N. Y. Tribune.

Abel Green, journalist, editor, 1900-1973. Variety.

Zane Grey, writer of western stories, 1875-1939.

Gilbert H. Grosvenor, editor, geographer, 1875-1966. National Geographic.

Edgar A. Guest, poet, 1881-1959. A Heap of Livin'.

Louis I. Guiney, poet, essayist, 1861-1920.

Arthur Guiterman, poet, 1871-1943.

John Gunther, journalist, author, 1901-1970. Inside U.S.A., Inside Europe.

H

Edward Everett Hale, author, clergyman, 1822-1909. The Man Without a Country.

James Norman Hall, novelist, 1887-1951. Co-author Mutiny on the Bounty.

Dashiell Hammett, writer of detective fiction, 1894-1961. Created Sam Spade.

Norman Hapgood, magazine editor, author, 1868-1937.

Joel Chandler Harris, short-story writer, 1848-1908. Uncle Remus series.

Bret Harte, short-story wirter, poet, 1836-1902. The Luck of Roaring Camp.

George B. M. Harvey, journalist, diplomat, 1864-1928.

Cameron Hawley, novelist, 1905-1969. Executive Suite.

Nathaniel Hawthorne, novelist, 1804-1864. The Scarlet Letter.

John M. Hay, historian, diplomat, 1838-1905. Abraham Lincoln: A History.

Lafcadio Hearn, author, 1850-1904.

Gabriel Heatter, radio commentator, 1890-1972.

William Randolph Hearst, newspaper publisher, 1863-1951.

Ben Hecht, novelist, playwright, journalist, 1894-1964.

Ernest Hemingway, novelist, short-story writer, 1899-1961. A Farewell to Arms.

Burton J. Hendrick, biographer, journalist, 1871-1949.

O. Henry (W. S. Porter), short-story writer, 1862-1910. The Gift of te Magi.

William M. (Bill) Henry, journalist, radio analyst, 1890-1970. Los Angeles Times.

Joseph Hergesheimer, novelist, 1880-1954. Java Head.

Marguerite Higgins, journalist, 1920-1966.

Robert Hillyer, poet, novelist, 1895-1962.

Alice Tisdale Hobart, novelist, 1882-1967. Oil for the Lamps of China.

Samuel Hoffenstein, poet. 1890-1947.

Charles Fenno Hoffman, poet, editor, 1806-1884.

Richard Hofstadter, historian, 1916-1970. The Age of Reform.

Oliver Wendell Holmes, poet, novelist, 1809-1894.

Mark DeWolfe Hopper, historian, 1906-1967.

Roy W. Howard, newspaper publisher, editor, 1883-1964. Scripps-Howard Newspapers.

Ed Howe, journalist, author, 1853-1937.

Julia Ward Howe, poet, reformer, 1819-1910. The Battle Hymn of the Republic.

William Dean Howells, novelist, critic, 1837-1920.

Elbert Hubbard, author, editor, 1856-1915. A Message to Garcia.

Langston Hughes, poet, playwright, 1902-1967.

Rupert Hughes, novelist, playwright, 1872-1956.

Frazier (Spike) Hunt, journalist, war correspondent, 1885-1967.

Chet Huntley, TV newscaster, 1911-1974.

Fannie Hurst, novelist, 1889-1968. Back Street, Lummox.

I

Washington Irving, essayist, author, 1783-1859. Rip Van Winkle.

Wallace Irwin, journalist, humorist, 1876-1959.

Will Irwin, Journalist, author, 1873-1948.

J

Charles Jackson, novelist, 1887-1968. The Lost Weekend.

Henry James, novelist, critic, 1843-1916.

Robinson Jeffers, poet, dramatist, 1887-1962.

Sarah Orne Jewett, novelist, short-story writer, 1849-1909.

James Weldon Johnson, author, poet, 1871-1938.

K

H. V. Kaltenborn, editor, radio commentator, 1878-1965.

Clarence Budington Kelland, novelist, short-story writer, 1881-1964.

Jack Kerouac, author, 1922-1969. On the Road.

Francis Scott Key, poet, 1779-1843. The Star-Spangled Banner.

Frances Parkinson Keyes, author, editor, 1885-1970. Dinner at Antoine's.

Dorothy Kilgallen, journalist, radio-TV personality, 1913-1965.

Bernard Kilgore, journalist, 1908-1967. Wall Street Journal.

Joyce Kilmer, poet, 1886-1918. Trees

Willard M. Kiplinger, journalist, 1891-1967. Changing Times.

Arthur Krock, journalist, 1887-1974. N. Y. Times.

Joseph Wood Krutch, author, naturalist, 1885-1970. The Measure of Man.

L

Oliver La Farge, novelist, 1901-1963. Laughing Boy.

William M. Laffan, publisher, 1848-1900. New York Sun, N. Y. Evening Sun.

Rose Wilder Lane, novelist, 1887-1968. Let the Hurricane Roar.

Sidney Lanier, poet, critic, 1842-1881.

Ring Lardner, short-story writer, journalist, 1885-1933.

David Lawrence, journalist, founder and editor of U. S. News & World Report, 1888-1973.

Emma Lazarus, poet, essayist, 1849-1887. The New Colossus.

Margaret Leech, author, historian, 1893-1974.

Charles Godfrey Leland, author, journalist, 1824-1903.

William Ellery Leonard, poet, 1876-1944.

Fulton Lewis, Jr., radio news commentator, 1903-1966.

Oscar Lewis, author, anthropologist, 1914-1970. La Vida.

Sinclair Lewis, novelist, playwright, 1885-1951. Babbitt, Arrowsmith, Dodsworth.

Ludwig Lewisohn, novelist, critic, 1882-1955.

Willy Ley, science writer, 1906-1969.

Vachel Lindsay, poet, 1879-1931.

Louis Lomax, author, 1922-1970. The Negro Revolt.

Jack London, novelist, journalist, 1876-1916. The Call of the Wild.

Henry Wadsworth Longfellow, poet, 1807-1882. The Wreck of the Hesperus, Evangeline, The Song of Hiawatha.

Benson John Lossing, historian, artist, 1813-1891. Pictorial Field Book of the Revolution.

Elijah P. Lovejoy, journalist, abolitionist, 1802-1837.

Amy Lowell, poet, critic, 1874-1925.

James Russell Lowell, poet, editor, 1819-1891.

Jim Lucas, journalist, 1914-1970. Scripps-Howard Newspapers.

Henry R. Luce, publisher, 1898-1967. Time. Life. Fortune magazines.

M

Edwin Markham, poet, 1852-1940. The Man with the Hoe.

John P. Marquand, novelist, 1893-1960. The Late George Apley.

Don Marquis, humorist, journalist, 1878-1937. The Old Soak.

Edgar Lee Masters, poet, biographer, 1869-1950. Spoon River Anthology.

James McClatchy, publisher, editor, 1824-1883. McClatchy Newspapers.

S. S. McClure, editor, publisher, 1857-1949.

Joseph Medill McCormick, journalist, politician, 1887-1925. Chicago Tribune.

Robert R. McCormick, editor, publisher, 1880-1955. Chicago Tribune.

Carson McCullers, novelist, 1917-1967. The Heart is a Lonely Hunter.

Ralph E. McGill, editor, publisher, Atlanta Constitution. 1898-1969.

John B. McMaster, historian, 1852-1932.

Joseph Medill, journalist, 1823-1899. Chicago Tribune.

Herman Melville, novelist, poet, 1819-1891. Moby Dick.

Henry L. Mencken, editor, author, philologist, 1880-1956. Baltimore Sun, American Mercury.

Thomas Merton, poet, religious writer, 1915-1968. Seven Storey Mountain.

Edna St. Vincent Millay, poet, 1892-1950.

Joaquin Miller, poet, 1839-1913.

Max Miller, novelist, 1889-1967. I Cover the Waterfront.

Margaret Mitchell, novelist, 1900-1949. Gone With the Wind.

William Vaughn Moody, poet, dramatist, 1869-1910.

Clement C. Moore, poet, educator, 1779-1863. A Visit from Saint Nicholas.

Marianne Moore, poet, 1887-1972.

Christopher Morley, journalist, novelist, 1890-1957. Kitty Foyle.

John L. Motley, historian, diplomat, 1814-1877.

Willard Motley, novelist, 1912-1968. Knock at Any Door.

Edward R. Murrow, radio-TV commentator, 1908-1965.

N

Ogden Nash, poet, 1902-1971.

William Rockhill Nelson, journalist, 1841-1915. Kansas City Star.

John G. Nicolay, biographer, 1832-1901. Abraham Lincoln: A History.

Charles B. Nordhoff, novelist, 1887-1947. Co-author Mutiny on the Bounty.

Frank Norris, novelist, journalist, 1870-1902. The Pit.

Kathleen Norris, novelist, 1880-1966.

Frank B. Noyes, newspaper executive, 1863-1948. Associated Press.

O

Edwin G. O'Connor, novelist, 1890-1968. Edge of Sadness, The Last Hurrah.

Adolph S. Ochs, newspaper publisher, 1858-1935. New York Times.

John O'Hara, novelist, 1905-1970. Butterfield 8, Ten North Frederick.

Fremont Older, journalist, 1856-1935. San Francisco Call-Bulletin.

James Oppenheim, poet, novelist, 1882-1932.

P

Thomas (Tom) Paine, author, political theorist, 1737-1809, Common Sense.

Frederick Palmer, war correspondent, 1873-1958.

Dorothy Parker, poet, short-story writer, 1893-1967.

Francis Parkman, historian, 1823-1893.

James K. Pauling, poet, novelist, 1778-1860.

John Howard Payne, poet, dramatist, 1791-1852. Home, Sweet Home.

Alicia Patterson, journalist, 1906-1963. Newsday.

Eleanor Medill Patterson, journalist, 1884-1948. Washington Times-Herald.

Joseph Medill Patterson, publisher, 1879-1946. Founded N. Y. Daily News.

Josephine P. Peabody, poet, dramatist, 1874-1922.

Drew Pearson, newspaper columnist, 1897-1969.

Westbrook Pegler, newspaper columnist, 1894-1969.

David G. Phillips, journalist, novelist, 1867-1911.

Edgar Allan Poe, poet, short-story writer, critic, 1809-1849.

Ernest Poole, journalist, novelist, 1880-1950.

Ezra Pound, poet, 1885-1972.

William H. Prescott, historian, 1796-1859.

Joseph Pulitzer, journalist, 1847-1911. St. Louis Post-Dispatch, N. Y. World.

Joseph Pulitzer, journalist, 1885-1955. St. Louis Post-Dispatch.

Ralph Pulitzer, journalist, 1879-1939. St. Louis Post-Dispatch, N. Y. World.

Ernie Pyle, journalist, war correspondent, 1900-1945.

R

James G. Randall, historian, 1881-1953.

Burton Rascoe, journalist, author, 1892-1957.

Marjorie Kinnan Rawlings, novelist, 1896-1953. The Yearling.

Thomas Buchanan Rad, poet, painter, 1822-1872. Sheridan's Ride.

Lizette Woodworth Reese, poet, 1856-1935.

Ogden M. Reid, journalist, 1882-1947. N. Y. Herald Tribune.

Whitelaw Reid, journalist, diplomat, 1837-1912. N. Y. Tribune.

Erich Maria Remarque, novelist, 1898-1970. All Quiet on the Western Front.

Quentin Reynolds, journalist, author, 1902-1965.

James Ford Rhodes, historian, 1848-1927.

Alice Hegan Rice, novelist, 1870-1952. Mrs. Wiggs of the Cabbage Patch.

Cale Young Rice, poet, novelist, 1872-1943.

Grantland Rice, journalist, 1880-1954.

Conrad M. Richter, novelist, 1890-1968. The Town.

James Whitcomb Riley, poet, 1849-1916.

Mary Roberts Rinehart, mystery writer, 1876-1958. The Circular Staircase, The Bat.

Elizabeth Madox Roberts, poet, novelist. 1886-1941.

Kenneth Roberts, novelist, 1885-1957. Northwest Passage.

Roy A. Roberts, journalist, 1887-1967. Kansas City Star.

Edwin Arlington Robinson, poet, 1869-1935.

Theodore Roethke, poet, 1908-1963.

Robert Ruark, journalist, author, 1915-1965. Something of Value.

Damon Runyon, short-story writer, journalist, 1884-1946. Guys and Dolls.

S

Carl Sandburg, poet, biographer, 1878-1967.

George Santayana, poet, essayist, philosopher, 1863-1952.

Lew Sarett, poet, 1888-1954.

Max L. Schuster, editor, publisher, 1897-1970. Simon & Schuster.

Edward W. Scripps, newspaper publisher, 1854-1926.

Robert P. Scripps, newspaper publisher, 1895-1938. Scripps-Howard Newspapers.

Alan Seeger, poet, 1888-1916. I Have a Rendezvous with Death.

Gilbert Seldes, author, critic, 1893-1970. The 7 Lively Arts, The Great Audience.

Ernest Thompson Seton, author, naturalist, 1860-1946. Wild Animals I Have Known.

Frank Dempster Sherman, poet, educator, 1860-1916.

Lydia H. Sigourney, poet, 1791-1865.

Edward Rowland Sill, poet, educator, 1841-1887.

Upton Sinclair, novelist, 1878-1968. The Jungle, Dragon's Teeth.

Betty Smith, novelist, 1896-1972. A Tree Grows in Brooklyn.

Lillian Smith, novelist, 1897-1966. Strange Fruit.

Merriman Smith, newspaper correspondent, 1913-1970. UPI.

Samuel Francis Smith, poet, clergyman, 1808-1895. America.

Jared Sparks, historian, educator, 1789-1866.

Burt L. Standish (Gilbert Patten), author, 1866-1945. Frank Merriwell series.

Frank L. Stanton, poet, journalist, 1857-1927. Mighty Lak' a Rose.

Lincoln Steffens, editor, author, 1866-1936. The Shame of the Cities.

Edmund C. Stedman, poet, critic, 1883-1908.

Gertrude Stein, author, 1874-1946. Three Lives.

John Steinbeck, novelist, 1902-1968. Of Mice and Men, The Grapes of Wrath.

George Sterling, poet, 1869-1926.

Wallace Stevens, poet, 1879-1955.

Frank R. Stockton, novelist, short-story writer, 1834-1902. The Lady or the Tiger?

Melville E. Stone, journalist, 1848-1929. Associated Press.

Harriet Beecher Stowe, novelist, 1811-1896. Uncle Tom's Cabin.

Edward Stratemeyer, author, 1862-1930. Creator of such series as the Rover Boys, Bobbsey Twins, Tom Swift.

Gene Stratton-Porter, novelist, 1863-1924. A Girl of the Limberlost.

Anna Louise Strong, journalist, 1885-1970.

Mark Sullivan, journalist, author, 1874-1952.
Arthur Hays Sulzberger, publisher, 1891-1968. The New York Times.
Herbert Bayard Swope, journalist, 1882-1958. N. Y. World.

T

John B. Tabb, poet, 1845-1909.
Genevieve Taggard, poet, 1894-1948.
Ida M. Tarbell, editor, author, 1857-1944. The History of the Standard Oil Company.
Booth Tarkington, novelist, 1869-1946. Seventeen, Alice Adams.
Bayard Taylor, poet, novelist, 1825-1878. The Bedouin Love Song.
Edward Taylor, poet, c. 1642-1729.
Sara Teasdale, poet, 1884-1933.
Albert Payson Terhune, novelist, journalist, 1872-1942. Lad: A Dog.
Dorothy Thompson, journalist, author, 1894-1961.
James Thurber, humorist, artist, 1894-1961. The New Yorker.
Eunice Tietjens, poet, novelist, 1884-1944.
Ridgely Torrence, poet, dramatist, 1875-1950.
Charles Hanson Towne, poet, editor, 1877-1949.
George A. Townsend, journalist, war correspondent, 1841-1914.
Frederick J. Turner, historian, educator, 1861-1932.

Mark Twain (Samuel Clemens), novelist, humorist, 1835-1910. The Adventures of Huckleberry Finn, Tom Sawyer.

V

Carl Van Doren, historian, critic, educator, 1885-1950.
Mark Van Doren, poet, author, critic, 1894-1972.
Henry Van Dyke, poet, educator, essayist, 1852-1933.
Hendrik Willem van Loon, historian, journalist, 1882-1944.
Carl Van Vechten, novelist, music critic, 1880-1964.
Oswald G. Villard, editor, author, 1872-1949. The Nation.

W

Lew Wallace, novelist, diplomat, 1827-1905. Ben Hur.
Artemus Ward (Charles F. Browne), humorist, 1834-1867.
Henry Watterson, editor, author, 1840-1921. Louisville Courier-Journal.
Nathanael West, novelist, 1903-1940.
Edith Wharton, novelist, 1862-1937. The Age of Innocence.
Steward Edward White, novelist, 1873-1946.
William Allen White, editor, author, 1868-1944. Emporia (Kan.) Gazette.
Walt Whitman, poet, 1819-1892. Leaves of Grass.
John Greenleaf Whittier, poet, journalist, 1809-1892.

Kate Douglas Wiggin, children's author, educator, 1856-1923. Rebecca of Sunnybrook Farm.
Ella Wheeler Wilcox, poet, 1850-1919.
Ben Ames Williams, novelist, 1889-1953.
William Carlos Williams, poet, physician, 1883-1963.
Nathaniel P. Willis, journalist, author, 1806-1867.
Edmund Wilson, author, literary and social critic, 1895-1972.
Lyle C. Wilson, journalist, 1899-1967. United Press International.
Walter Winchell, Broadway columnist, 1897-1972.
Thomas Wolfe, novelist, 1900-1938. Look Homeward, Angel.
Frederick E. Woltman, journalist, 1907-1970. N. Y. World-Telegram & Sun.
Samuel Woodworth, poet, dramatist, 1784-1842.
Alexander Woollcott, journalist, critic, 1887-1943.
Harold Bell Wright, novelist, 1782-1944 The Shepherd of the Hills.
Richard Wright, novelist, 1908-1960. Native Son.
Elinor Wylie, poet, novelist, 1885-1928.
Philip Wylie, author, 1902-1971. Generation of Vipers.

Z

John Peter Zenger, journalist, printer, 1697-1746. N. Y. Weekly Journal.

Noted American Cartoonists

Addams, Charles, b. 1912. Noted for macabre cartoons.
Peter Arno, 1904-1968. Noted for urban characterizations.
Jim Berry, b. 1932. Berry's World.
Clare Briggs, 1875-1930. Mr. & Mrs.
Milton Caniff, b. 1907. Terry & the Pirates; Steve Canyon.
Al Capp, b. 1909. Li'l Abner.
Roy Crane, b. 1901. Captain Easy; Buzz Sawyer.
Jay N. Darling (Ding), 1876-1962. Political cartoonist won 2 Pulitzer Prizes
Rudolph Dirks 1877-1968. The Katzenjammer Kids.
Bud Fisher, 1885-1954. Mutt & Jeff.
Fontaine Fox, 1884-1964. Toonerville Folks.
Rube Goldberg, 1883-1970. Boob McNutt. Famed for cartoons of mechanical contrivances whose humor is derived from their absurd, unnecessary complexity.
Chester Gould, b. 1900. Dick Tracy.
Harold Gray, 1894-1968. Little Orphan Annie.
John Held, Jr., 1889-1958. His cartoons epitomized the spirit of the "jazz age" of the 20s.
Herb Block, (Herblock), b. 1909; Leading political cartoonist.
George Herriman, 1881-1944. Krazy Kat.
Helen Hokinson, 1900-1949. Known for satirical drawings of plump, bewildered suburban matrons and clubwomen.
Walt Kelly, 1913-1973. Pogo.
Hank Ketcham, b. 1920. Dennis the Menace.

Ted Key, b. 1912. Hazel.
Frank King, 1883-1969. Gasoline Alley.
Rollin Kirby, 1875-1952. Political cartoonist won 3 Pulitzer Prizes.
Bill Mauldin, b. 1921. Depicted the squalid life of the G.I. in WW 2.
Winsor McCay, 1872-1934. Little Nemo.
John T. McCutcheon, 1870-1949. Noted for cartoons of midwestern rural life.
George McManus, 1884-1954. Bringing Up Father (Maggie & Jiggs).
Thomas Nast, 1840-1902. His political cartoons were instrumental in breaking the corrupt Boss Tweed ring in N.Y. Created the Donkey and Elephant to represent the Democratic and Republican parties.
Richard Outcault, 1863-1928. Yellow Kid; Buster Brown.
Frank Burr Opper, 1857-1937. Happy Hooligan.
Art Sansom. The Born Loser.
Charles Schulz, b. 1922. Peanuts.
Elzie C. Segar, 1894-1938. Popeye.
Sydney Smith, 1887-1935. The Gumps.
Mort Walker, b. 1923. Beetle Bailey.
Russ Westover, 1887-1966. Tillie the Toiler.
Art Young, 1866-1943. Political radical and satirist.
Chic Young, 1901-1973. Blondie.

Noted Canadians of the Past

Born	Died	Name	Born	Died	Name	Born	Died	Name
		Statesmen	1804	1873	Howe, Joseph	1850	1931	Beauchemin, Neree
			1874	1950	King, W. Mackenzie	1913	1966	Allen, Ralph
1821	1893	Abbott, John	1841	1919	Laurier, Wilfrid	....	1931	Beck, L. Adams
1878	1943	Aberhart, William	1815	1891	Macdonald, John A.	1861	1924	Blake, W. H.
1804	1858	Baldwin, Robert	1887	1967	Massey, Vincent	1827	1916	Bourassa, Napoleon
1912	1970	Beaudoin, Louis Rene	1795	1861	Mackenzie, Wm. Lyon	1840	1901	Buies, Arthur
1870	1957	Bennett, Richard B.	1822	1905	McDougall, William	1861	1918	Campbell, W. Wilfred
1833	1912	Blake, Edward	1825	1868	McGee, Thomas D'Arcy	1861	1929	Carman, W. Bliss
1854	1937	Borden, Robert	1874	1960	Meighen, Arthur	1831	1904	Casgrain, Henri-R.
1823	1917	Bowell, Mackenzie	1897	1972	Pearson, Lester B.	1858	1946	Chapais, Thomas
1884	1969	Bracken, John	1904	1968	Robertson, Norman A.	1850	1917	Chapman, William
1818	1880	Brown, George	1820	1914	Strathcona (Smith)	1820	1890	Chauveau, Pierre
1875	1940	Buchan, John	1844	1894	Thompson, John	1885	1953	Chopin, Rene
1814	1873	Cartier, Georges	1855	1927	Tupper, Charles H.	1850	1887	Crawford, Isabella
1890	1959	Duplessis, Maurice	1888	1967	Vanier, George P.	1827	1879	Cremazie, Octave
1896	1969	Dupuy, Pierre	1892	1969	Wilgress, Dana	1831	1904	Cosgrain, Abbe R.
1895	1973	Frost, Leslie			**Authors**	1866	1944	Dafoe, John Wesley
1817	1893	Galt, Alexander T.	1748	1784	Alline, Henry	1865	1945	Dantin, Louis
1869	1953	Hepburn, Mitchell F.						

Born	Died	Name
1895	1958	Dawson, R. MacGregor
1848	1917	Dionne, Narcisse
....	1936	Doughty, Arthur G.
1854	1907	Drummond, W. H.
1862	1932	Duncan, Sara J.
1864	1922	Edwards, Robert (Bob)
1799	1870	Faillon, Etienne
1805	1865	Ferland, Jean
1860	1936	Fraser, Alexander
1839	1908	Frechette, Louis H.
1809	1866	Garneau, Francis X.
1786	1871	Gaspe, Philippe de
1824	1882	Gerin-Lajoie, Ant.
1871	1918	Gill, Charles
1860	1937	Gordon, Chas. W. (Ralph Connor)
1878	1967	Groulx, Lionel A.
1871	1948	Grove, Frederick
1842	1910	Hannay, James
1796	1865	Haliburton, Thos. C.
1816	1876	Heavysege, Charles
1880	1913	Hemon, Louis
1766	1844	Heriot, George
1894	1952	Innis, H. A.
1881	1943	Kennedy, W. P. M.
1859	1931	Kingsford, William
1817	1906	Kirby, William
1862	1913	Johnson, Pauline
1871	1960	Laberge, Albert
1861	1899	Lampman, Archibald
1871	1936	Laut, Agnes
1869	1944	Leacock, Stephen
1841	1907	Legendre, Napoleon
1837	1918	Lemay, Pamphile
1857	1954	Lighthall, William
1909	1957	Lowry, Malcolm
1853	1931	Lucas, L. P.
1878	1924	Lozeau, Albert
1874	1942	Macdonald, Lucy M.
1876	1951	Mac Innes, Tom
1862	1933	MacMechan, Archibald
1840	1927	Mair, Charles
1844	1945	Marmette, Joseph
1864	1936	Marquis, Thomas
1882	1958	Martin, Chester
1872	1918	McCrae, John
1820	1907	McMullen, John
1865	1944	Miner, John T. (Jack)
1874	1942	Montgomery, Lucy
1803	1885	Moodie, Susanna
1889	1963	Morin, Paul
1879	1941	Nelligan, Emile
1737	1818	Odell, Jonathan
1895	1960	Panneton, Philippe
1862	1932	Parker, Gilbert
1887	1970	Phelps, Arthur L.
1883	1922	Pickthall, Marj.

Born	Died	Name
1883	1964	Pratt, Edwin J.
1749	1809	Quesnel, Joseph
1796	1852	Richardson, John
1860	1943	Roberts, Chas. G. D.
1885	1961	Roche, Mazo de la
1839	1920	Routhier, Adoph
1870	1943	Roy, Camille
1858	1913	Roy, Joseph E.
1822	1893	Sangster, Charles
1862	1944	Scott, Duncan C.
1874	1958	Service, Robert W.
1859	1931	Short, Adam
1878	1941	Skelton, O. D.
1823	1910	Smith, Goldwin
1841	1923	Sulte, Benjamin
1888	1951	Trotter, R. G.
1856	1926	Weir, R. Stanley
1860	1948	Wrong, George M.

Painters and Sculptors

Born	Died	Name
1863	1936	Ahrens, Carl
1876	1955	Allward, Walter S.
1759	1830	Baillarge, Francois
1740	1794	Beaucort, Francois
1905	1960	Borduas, Paul-Emile
1827	1916	Bourassa, Napoleon
1855	1925	Brymner, William
1871	1945	Carr, Emily
1866	1934	Cullen, Maurice
1769	1819	Field, Robert
1810	1894	Fowler, Daniel
1881	1942	Gagnon, Clarence
1817	1870	Hamel, Theophile
1885	1970	Harris, Lawren Stewart
1849	1919	Harris, Robert
1850	1917	Hebert, Louis P.
1812	1901	Jacobi, Otto
1852	1908	Julien, Henri
1810	1871	Kane, Paul
1815	1872	Krieghoff, Cornelius
1873	1939	Lawson, Ernest
1864	1955	Leduc, Ozias
1795	1855	Legare, Joseph
1887	1968	Loring, Ernest
1847	1939	MacCarthy, Hamilton
1873	1932	MacDonald, J. E. H.
1882	1953	Milne, David
1865	1924	Morrice, James Wilson
1832	1899	O'Brien, Lucius Richard
1860	1892	Peel, Paul
1802	1895	Plamondon, Antoine S.
1739	1819	Ranvoyze, Francois
1816	1853	Ritter, Henry
1869	1937	Suzor-Cote, Aurele de Foy
1877	1918	Thomson, Tom
1798	1849	Valentine, William
1881	1969	Varley, F. H.

Born	Died	Name
1858	1938	Walker, Horatio
1855	1936	Watson, Homer
1903	1966	Wood, Elizabeth Wynn
1881	1968	Wyle, Florence

Science, Industry

Born	Died	Name
1859	1942	Adams, Frank D.
1810	1882	Allan, Hugh
1891	1941	Banting, Fredk. G.
1877	1943	Beatty, Edward W.
1889	1966	Hilton, Hugh G.
1798	1875	Logan, William
1849	1919	Osler, William
1876	1935	Macleod, John J. R.
1863	1892	Stairs, Wm. Grant
1902	1967	Zimmerman, Adam

Anthropologists, Geologists and Naturalists

Born	Died	Name
1876	1961	Anderson, Rudolph M.
1883	1969	Barbeau, Charles M.
1888	1938	Belaney, George Stansfeld (Grey Owl)
1841	1917	Bell, Robert
1820	1876	Billings, Elkanah
1874	1935	Brock, Reginald Walter
1878	1937	Collins, William Henry
1876	1957	Currelly, Charles Trick
1849	1901	Dawson, George Mercer
1846	1925	Dionne, Charles Eusibe
1817	1886	Hale, Horatio
1859	1944	Hill-Tout, Charles
1826	1892	Hunt, Thomas Sterry
1886	1969	Jenness, Diamond
1833	1881	LaRue, Francois A. H.
1875	1947	Laverner, Percy A.
1820	1892	Leon, Provancher
1798	1875	Logan, Sir William E.
1861	1942	Low, Albert Peter
1858	1957	Lyrrell, Joseph Burr
1863	1945	Lyrrell, James Williams
1831	1920	Macoun, John
1862	1920	Macoun, James Melville
1869	1933	Macoun, William Lyrell
1885	1944	Marie-Victorin
1867	1947	Massicotte, Edouard Z.
1857	1942	McConnell, Richard G.
1905	1970	Rousseau, Jacques
1891	1957	Rowan, William
1870	1953	Roy, Pierre Georges
1836	1914	Saunders, William
1867	1937	Saunders, Sir Charles E.
1824	1902	Selwyn, Alfred R. C.
1860	1946	Seton, Ernest Thompson
1872	1940	Smith, Harlan I.
1872	1924	Waugh, Fredrick W.
1881	1964	Wilson, Alice Evelyn
1876	1941	Wintenberg, William J.

Composers of the Western World

Carl Philipp Emanuel Bach, 1714-1788. (G.) Prussian and Wurtembergian Sonatas.

Johann Christian Bach, 1735-1782. (G.) Concertos, sonatas.

Johann Sebastian Bach, 1685-1750. (G.) St. Matthew Passion; The Well-Tempered Clavichord.

Samuel Barber, b. 1910. (U.S.) Adagio for Strings; Vanessa.

Bela Bartok, 1881-1945. (H.) Concerto for Orchestra; The Miraculous Mandarin.

Ludwig Van Beethoven, 1770-1827. (G.) Concertos (Emperor); sonatas (Moonlight, Pastorale, Pathetique); symphonies (Eroica).

Vincenzo Bellini, 1801-1835. (It.) La Sonnambula; Norma; I Puritani.

Alban Berg, 1885-1935. (Aus.) Wozzeck; Lulu.

Hector Berlioz, 1803-1869. (F.) Damnation of Faust; Symphonie Fantastique; Requiem.

Leonard Bernstein, b. 1918. (U.S.) Jeremiah; West Side Story.

Georges Bizet, 1838-1875. (F.) Carmen; Pearl Fishers.

Ernest Bloch, 1880-1959 (Swiss) Schelomo; Voice in the Wilderness; Sacred Service.

Luigi Boccherini, 1743-1805. (It.) Cello Concerto in B Flat; Symphony in C.

Alexander Borodin, 1834-1887. (R.) Prince Igor; In the Steppes of Central Asia.

Johannes Brahms, 1833-1897. (G.) Liebeslieder Waltzes, Rhapsody in E Flat Major, Opus 119 for Piano, Academic Festival Overture; symphonies, quartets.

Benjamin Britten, b. 1913. (Br.) Peter Grimes, Turn of the Screw, Ceremony of Carols.

Anton Bruckner, 1824-1896. (Aus.) Symphonies (Romantic); Intermezzo for String Quintet.

Ferruccio Busoni, 1866-1924. (It.) Doctor Faust, Comedy Overture.

Dietrich Buxtehude, 1637-1707. (G.) Cantatas, Trio sonatas.

William Byrd, 1543-1623 (Br.) Masses, Sacred Songs.

Alexis Emmanuel Chabrier, 1841-1894. (Fr.) Le Roi Malgre Lui, Espana.

Gustave Charpentier, 1860-1956. (F.) Louise.

Frederic Chopin, 1810-1849. (P.) Concertos, Polonaise No. 6 in A Flat Major (Heroic), sonatas.

Aaron Copland, b. 1900. (U.S.) Appalachian Spring.

Claude Achille Debussy, 1862-1918. (F.) Pelleas et Melisande, La Mer, Prelude to the Afternoon of a Faun.

C. P. Leo Delibes, 1836-1891. (F.) Lakme, Coppelia, Sylvia.

Norman Dello Joio, b. 1913. (U.S.) Triumph of St. Joan, Psalm of David.

Gaetano Donizetti, 1797-1848. (It.) Elixir of Love, Lucia di Lammermoor, Daughter of the Regiment.

Paul Dukas, 1865-1935. (Fr.) Sorcerer's Apprentice.

Antonin Dvorak, 1841-1904. (C.) Symphony in E Minor (from the New World).

Edward Elgar, 1857-1934. (Br.) Pomp and Circumstance.
Manuel de Falla, 1876-1946. (Sp.) La Vide Breve, El Amor Brujo.
Gabriel Faure, 1845-1924. (Fr.) Requiem, Ballade.
Friedrich von Flotow, 1812-1883. (G.) Martha.
Cesar Franck, 1822-1890. (Belg.) D Minor Symphony.
George Gershwin, 1898-1937. (U.S.) Rhapsody in Blue, American in Paris, Porgy and Bess.
Umberto Giordano, 1867-1948 (It.) Andrea Chenier.
Alex K. Glazunoff, 1865-1936. (R.) Symphonies, Stenka Razin.
Mikhail Glinka, 1857-1904. (R.) Ruslan & Ludmilla.
Christoph W. Gluck, 1714-1787. (G.) Alceste, Iphigenie en Tauride.
Charles Gounod, 1818-1893. (F.) Faust, Romeo and Juliet.
Edvard Grieg, 1843-1907. (Nor.) Peer Gynt Suite; Concerto in A Minor.
George Frederick Handel, 1685-1759. (G.-Br.) Messiah, Xerxes, Berenice.
Howard Hanson, b. 1896. (U.S.) Symphonies No. 1 (Nordic) and 2 (Romantic).
Roy Harris, b. 1898. (U.S.) Symphonies, Amer. Portraits.
Joseph Haydn, 1732-1809. (Aus.) Symphonies (Clock); oratorios; chamber music.
Paul Hindemith, 1895-1963. (U.S.) Das Marienleben; Mathis Der Maler.
Gustav Holst, 1874-1934. (Br.) The Planets, The Hymn of Jesus.
Arthur Honegger, 1892-1955. (Swiss) Judith, Le Roi David, Pacific 231.
Alan Hovhaness, b. 1911. (U.S.) Symphonies, Magnificat.
Engelbert Humperdinck, 1854-1921. (G.) Hansel and Gretel.
Charles Ives, 1874-1954. (U.S.) Third Symphony.
Aram Khachaturian, b. 1903. (R.) Gayane ballet, symphonies.
Zoltan Kodaly, 1882-1967.(Hung.) Hary Janos, Psalmus Hungaricus.
Fritz Kreisler, 1875-1962. (Aus.) Caprice Viennois, Tambourin Chinois.
Rodolphe Kreutzer, 1766-1831. (F.) 40 etudes for violin.
Edouard V. A. Lalo, 1823-1892. (F.) Fiesque, Symphonie Espagnole.
Ruggiero Leoncavallo, 1858-1919, (It.) I Pagliacci.
Franz Liszt, 1811-1886. (H.) 20 Hungarian Rhapsodies; symphonic poems.
Edward MacDowell, 1861-1908. (U.S.) To a Wild Rose.
Gustav Mahler, 1860-1911. (Aus.) Symphonies, Lied von der Erde.
Pietro Mascagni, 1863-1945. (It.) Cavalleria Rusticana.
Jules Massenet, 1842-1912. (F.) Manon, Le Cid, Thais, Don Quixote.
Mendelssohn-Bartholdy, 1809-1847. (G.) Midsummer Night's Dream, Songs Without Words.
Gian-Carlo Menotti, b. 1911. (It.-U.S.) The Medium, The Consul, Amahl and the Night Visitors.
Claudio Monteverdi, 1567-1643. (It.) Opera, masses, madrigals.
Wolfgang Amadeus Mozart, 1756-1791. (Aus.) Magic Flute, Marriage of Figaro, concertos, symphonies, etc.

Modest Moussorgsky, 1835-1881. (R.) Boris Godunov, Pictures at an Exhibition.
Jacques Offenbach, 1819-1880. (F.) Tales of Hoffman, operetta.
Karl Orff, b. 1895 (G.) Carmina Burana.
Ignace Paderewski, 1860-1941 (P.) Minuet in G.
Giovanni P. da Palestrina, 1524-1594. (It.) Masses, motets, madrigals.
Amilcare Ponchielli, 1834-1886. (It.) La Gioconda.
Francis, Poulenc, 1899-1963. (F.) La voix humaine, Les animaux modeles.
Serge Prokofiev, 1891-1953. (R.) Love for Three Oranges, Lt. Kije, Peter and the Wolf.
Giacomo Puccini, 1858-1924. (It.) La Boheme, Manon Lescaut, Tosca, Madame Butterfly.
Sergei Rachmaninov, 1873-1943. (R.) Prelude in C Sharp Minor.
Maurice Ravel, 1875-1937. (Fr.) Bolero, Daphne et Chloe, Rapsodie Espagnole.
Nikolai Rimsky-Korsakov, 1844-1908. (R.) Golden Cockerel, Cappriccio Espagnol, Scheherazade, Russian Easter overture.
Gioacchino Rossini, 1792-1868. (It.) Barber of Seville, Semiramide, William Tell.
Chas. Camille Saint-Saens, 1835-1921. (F.) Samson and Delilah, Danse Macabre.
Alessandro Scarlatti, 1659-1725. (It.) Cantatas; concertos; operas.
Arnold Schoenberg, 1874-1951. (Aus.) Pelleas and Melisande, Transfigured Night, De Profundis.
Franz Schubert, 1797-1828. (A.) Lieder; symphonies (Unfinished); overtures (Rosamunde).
William Schuman, b. 1910. (U.S.) Credendum, New England Triptych.
Robert Schumann, 1810-1856. (G.) Symphonies (Rhenish); Kinderszenen, songs.
Aleksandr Scriabin, 1872-1915. (R.) Prometheus.
Jean Sibelius, 1865-1957, (Finn.) Finlandia, Karelia.
Dimitri Shostakovich, b. 1906. (R.) Symphonies, Lady Macbeth of Minsk, The Nose.
Bedrich Smetana, 1824-1884. (C.) The Bartered Bride.
Karlheinz Stockhausen, b. 1928. (G.) Kontrapunkte, Kontakte.
Richard Strauss, 1864-1949. (G.) Salome, Elektra, Der Rosenkavalier, Thus Spake Zarathustra.
Igor F. Stravinsky, 1882-1971. (R.-U.S.) Oedipus Rex, Le Sacre du Printemps, Petrushka.
Peter I. Tchaikovsky, 1840-1893. (R.) Nutcracker Suite, Swan Lake, Eugen Onegin.
Ambroise Thomas, 1811-1896. (F.) Mignon.
Ralph Vaughan Williams, 1872-1958, (Br.) Job, London Symphony, Symphony No. 7 (Antarctica).
Giuseppe Verdi, 1813-1901. (It.) Aida, Rigoletto, Don Carlo, Il Trovatore, La Traviata, Falstaff, Macbeth.
Hector Villa Lobos, 1887-1959. (Brazil) Choros.
Antonio Vivaldi, 1669-1741. (It.) operas and cantatas.
Richard Wagner, 1813-1883. (G.) Rienzi, Tannhauser, Lohengrin, Das Rheingold, Die Walkure, Siegfried, Gotterdammerung, Tristan und Isolde, Parsifal.
Karl Maria von Weber, 1786-1826. (G.) Der Freischutz.

Composers of Operettas, Musicals and Popular Music

Leroy Anderson, b. 1908. (U.S.) Syncopated Clock, Typewriter Serenade.
Harold Arlen, b. 1905. (U.S.) Stormy Weather, Over the Rainbow, Blues in the Night, That Old Black Magic.
Burt Bacharach, b. 1928. (U.S.) Raindrops Keep Fallin' on My Head, Blue on Blue, Walk on By, What the World Needs Now is Love.
Ernest Ball, 1887-1912. (U.S.) Mother Machree, When Irish Eyes are Smiling.
Irving Berlin, b. 1888. (U.S.) Ziegfield Follies; Face the Music; As Thousands Cheer; This is the Army; Annie Get Your Gun; Call Me Madam, God Bless America, White Christmas.
Sir Henry Rowley Bishop, 1786-1855. (Br.) Home Sweet Home.
Marc Blitzstein, 1905-1964 (U.S.) The Cradle Will Rock; No for an Answer; Regina; Reuben, Reuben.
Jerry Bock, b. 1928. (U.S.) Mr. Wonderful; Fiorello; Fiddler on the Roof; The Rothschilds.
Carrie Jacobs Bond, 1862-1946. (U.S.) I Love You Truly.
George M. Cohan, 1878-1942. (U.S.) Give My Regards to Broadway, You're A Grand Old Flag, Over There.
Sherman Edwards, b. 1919. (U.S.) See You in September; Wonderful! Wonderful!
Stephen Collins Foster, 1826-1864. (U.S.) My Old Kentucky Home, Old Folks At Home.

Rudolf Friml, 1879-1972. (naturalized U.S.) The Firefly; Rose Marie; Vagabond King; Bird of Paradise.
John Gay, 1685-1732. (Br.) The Beggar's Opera.
Edwin F. Goldman, 1878-1956. (U.S.) Marches.
Percy Grainger, 1882-1961. (Br.) Country Gardens.
Ferde Grofe, 1892-1972. (U.S.) Grand Canyon Suite.
W. C. Handy, 1873-1958. (U.S.) St. Louis Blues.
Victor Herbert, 1859-1924. (Ir.-U.S.) Mlle. Modiste; Babes in Toyland; The Red Mill; Naughty Marietta; Sweethearts; Princess Pat.
Jerry Herman, b. 1932. (U.S.) Milk and Honey, Hello Dolly; Mame, Dear World.
Jerome Kern, 1885-1945. (U.S.) Sally; Sunny; Show Boat; Cat and the Fiddle; Music in the Air; Roberta.
Burton Lane, b. 1912. (U.S.) Three's a Crowd; Finnian's Rainbow; On A Clear Day You Can See Forever.
Franz Lehar, 1870-1948. (Hung.) Merry Widow, Count of Luxembourg.
Mitch Leigh, b. 1928. (U.S.) Man of La Mancha.
Frank Loesser, 1910-1969. (U.S.) Guys and Dolls; Where's Charley?; The Most Happy Fella.
Frederick Loewe, b. 1901. (Aust.-U.S.) The Day Before Spring; Brigadoon, Paint Your Wagon; My Fair Lady; Camelot.
Henry Mancini, b. 1924. (U.S.) Moon River, Days of Wine and Roses, Pink Panther Theme.

Cole Porter, 1893-1964. (U.S.) Anything Goes; Jubilee; Du-Barry Was a Lady; Panama Hattie; Mexican Hayride; Kiss Me Kate; Can Can; Silk Stockings.

Andre Previn, b. 1929. (U.S.) Coco.

Richard Rodgers, b. 1902. (U.S.) Garrick Gaieties; Connecticut Yankee; America's Sweetheart; On Your Toes; Babes in Arms; The Boys from Syracuse; Oklahoma!; Carousel; South Pacific; The King & I; Flower Drum Song; The Sound of Music; Two by Two.

Sigmund Romberg, 1887-1951. (Hung.) Maytime; The Student Prince; Desert Song; Blossom Time.

Harold Rome, b. 1908. (U.S.) Pins and Needles; Call Me Mister; Wish You Were Here; Fanny; Destry Rides Again; I Can Get It for You Wholesale.

Arthur Schwartz, b. 1900. (U.S.) The Band Wagon, Inside U.S.A., A Tree Grows in Brooklyn.

Stephen Sondheim, b. 1930. (U.S.) Follies; A Little Night Music.

John Phillip Sousa, 1854-1932. (U.S.) The Smuggler; Desiree; Queen of Hearts; El Capitan; The Bride-Elect.

Oley Speaks, 1875-1948. (U.S.) Sylvia, The Road to Mandalay.

Oskar Straus, 1870-1954. (Aus.) Waltz Dream, Chocolate Soldier.

Johann Strauss, 1825-1899. (Aus.) Gypsy Baron, Die Fledermaus. Waltzes: Blue Danube, Artist's Life.

Charles Strouse, b. 1928. (U.S.) Bye Bye, Birdie; All American; Golden Boy; Applause.

Jule Styne, b. 1905. (b. London-U.S.) High Button Shoes, Gentlemen Prefer Blondes; Bells Are Ringing; Say Darling; Gypsy: Funny Girl.

Arthur S. Sullivan, 1842-1900. (Br.) H.M.S. Pinafore, Pirates of Penzance, The Mikado (with W. S. Gilbert, 1836-1911, librettist).

Deems Taylor, 1885-1966. (U.S.) The King's Henchmen; Peter Ibbetson.

James Van Heusen, b. 1913. (U.S.) Moonlight Becomes You, Swinging on a Star.

Harry Warren, b. 1893. (U.S.) You're My Everything, We're in the Money, I Only Have Eyes for You, September in the Rain.

Kurt Weill, 1900-1950. (G.-U.S.) Three-Penny Opera; Down in the Valley; Lady in the Dark; Knickerbocker Holiday; One Touch of Venus; Lost in the Stars.

Meredith Willson, b. 1902. (U.S.) The Music Man.

Vincent Youmans, 1898-1946. (U.S.) Two Little Girls in Blue; Wildflower; No, No, Nanette; Hit the Deck; Rainbow; Smiles; Through the Years; Take A Chance.

Noted Black Americans — Past and Present

(Names of black athletes and entertainers are not included here as they are well known and are listed elsewhere in the World Almanac.)

Explorers and Settlers

Pedro Alonzo Nino, navigator of the Nina, one of Christopher Columbus' three ships on his first voyage of discovery to the New World, 1492.

Estevanico (also called Esteban) led the first Spanish explorations into the Arizona and New Mexico area, 1539.

Jean Baptiste Point du Sable, fur trader and first settler of Chicago, 1779.

James P. Beckwourth (1798-c. 1867) western fur-trader, scout, after whom Beckwourth Pass in northern Califnia is named.

Matthew A. Henson (1866-1955), with Robert E. Peary and 4 Eskimos, discovered the North Pole, 1909; Henson planted the U. S. flag at the Pole.

Soldiers, Patriots

Crispus Attucks (c. 1723-1770), leader of a group fired on by British soldiers and one of the 5 slain in the "Boston Massacre," Mar. 5, 1770.

Peter Salem, one of the defenders at the Battle of Bunker Hill, June 17, 1775, shot and killed Maj. John Pitcairn, one of the British commanders.

(About 5,000 blacks served in the Continental Army, mostly in integrated units, some in all-black combat outfits.)

Harriet Tubman, after escaping from slavery made repeated trips to the South and led more than 300 slaves to freedom as an Underground Railroad conductor; served as nurse and spy for Union Army in the Civil War.

(Some 200,000 blacks served in the Union Army during the Civil War; 38,000 gave their lives: 22 won the Medal of Honor, the nation's highest award.)

Isaiah Dorman (19th Century), U.S. Army interpreter, killed with Col. George Custer at Battle of the Little Big Horn (1876).

Henry O. Flipper, first black to graduate from West Point (1877).

Pvt. Henry Johnson of Albany, N.Y., the first American decorated by France in World War I with the Croix de Guerre.

(Of 367,000 blacks in the Armed Forces in World War I, 100,000 served in France.)

Dorie Miller of Waco, Tex., a Navy mess attendant on the battleship Arizona during the Pearl Harbor attack, took over an anti-aircraft gun from a dying white sailor and shot down 4 Japanese bombers, Dec. 7, 1941; awarded the Navy Cross by President Franklin D. Roosevelt.

(More than 1,000,000 blacks served in the U. S. Armed Forces in World War II; all-black fighter and bomber AAF units and infantry divisions gave distinguished service. In 1954 the policy of all-black units was finally abolished.)

Brig. Gen. Benjamin O. Davis Sr., born 1877, first black general (1940) in U. S. Army, rose through ranks to inspector general, retired 1948.

Lt. Gen. Benjamin O. Davis Jr., b. 1912, West Point (1936), first Negro Air Force general (1954), had distinguished service as pilot and commander in World War II, retired 1970.

Admiral Samuel L. Gravely, Jr., first black admiral (1971), served in World War II, Korea and Vietnam.

Scientists, Inventors

Benjamin Banneker (1731-c. 1806), author of annual almanacs (1791-1802), served on commission which surveyed and helped lay out the future city of Washington, D. C.

Henry Blair (19th Century), obtained patent (believed the first issued to a black) for a corn-planter (1834) and for a cotton-planter (1836).

Norbert Rillieux (1806-1894), invented a vacuum pan evaporator which revolutionized the sugar-refining industry (1846).

Lewis H. Latimer (1848-1928), associate of Thomas Edison, wrote textbook on the Edison Co. lighting system in New York City; supervised installation of first electric street lighting in New York.

Jan Matzeliger (1852-1889), invented lasting machine which cut shoe industry costs in half and brought higher wages to shoe workers.

Dr. Daniel Hale Williams (1856-1931), performed one of first two open-heart operations (1893); founded Provident, Chicago's first Negro hospital; first black elected a fellow of the American College of Surgeons.

George Washington Carver (c. 1864-1943), agricultural scientist, philanthropist; brought about an agricultural revolution in the South, finding ways to enrich the soil, adding to its one-crop cotton economy not only emphasis on peanuts, sweet potatoes and soybeans, but discovering some 300 industrial uses for byproducts he synthesized from them.

Dr. William A. Hinton (1883-1959), developed the Hinton and Davies-Hinton tests for detection of syphilis; first black professor at Harvard Medical School (1949).

Dr. Charles Richard Drew (1904-1950, pioneer in development of blood banks; director of American Red Cross blood donor project in World War II.

Writers, Educators

Jupiter Hammon (c. 1720-1800), a Long Island N. Y. poet, the first black American to have his works published.

Phillis Wheatley (c. 1753-1784), poet, second American woman and first black woman to have her works published; b. in Senegal, enslaved, taken to Boston, freed 1773.

John B. Russwurm (1799-1851) with Samuel E. Cornish (1793-1858), founded the nation's first black newspaper, Freedom's Journal (1827) in N. Y. City.

William Wells Brown (1815-1884), b. a slave, first American black to publish a novel (Clotel), as well as a drama, a travel book, 3 histories.

Frederick Douglass (1817-1895), author, editor, orator,

diplomat; a runaway slave (b. Frederick Bailey), edited the abolitionist weekly, The North Star, in Rochester, N. Y., before the Civil War, became U. S. Minister and Consul General to Haiti.

Edward Bouchet (1852-1918), first black to earn a Ph.D. at a U. S. university (Yale, 1876); first to be elected to Phi Beta Kappa.

Booker T. Washington (1856-1915), founder and first president of Tuskegee Institute (1881); author of a dozen books including Up From Slavery; social reformer.

Charles Waddell Chestnutt (1858-1932), novelist; best-known for his short stories including The Conjure Woman.

William Edward Burghardt Du Bois (1868-1963), historian, sociologist, a founder of the NAACP (1909) and founding editor of its magazine The Crisis; author of The Souls of Black Folk (1903) and other books.

James Weldon Johnson (1871-1938), poet, song-lyricist, novelist; first black admitted to Florida bar; a U. S. consul in Venezuela and Nicaragua.

Paul Laurence Dunbar (1872-1906), poet, novelist; won fame with Lyrics of Lowly Life (1896).

Dr. Carter G. Woodson (1875-1950), historian; founded Journal of Negro History and Assn. for Study of Negro Life and History (1915).

Langston Hughes (1902-1967), a major American poet; also author of stories and song lyrics.

Countee Cullen (1903-1946), poet, winner of numerous literary prizes.

Richard Wright (1908-1960), best-selling novels; Native Son (1940), Black Boy (1945), etc.

Willard Motley (1912-1965), novelist; wrote Knock on Any Door (1947).

Ralph Ellison, b. 1914, novelist, winner of 1952 National Book Award for Invisible Man.

Frank Yerby, b. 1916, most successful of American black novelists; some 19 novels with over 20,000,000 copies sold, including The Foxes of Harrow, Vixen.

Gwendolyn Brooks, b. 1917, poet, novelist; first black to win a Pulitzer Prize (1950), for Annie Allen.

Wilson C. Riles, b. 1917, elected California State Superintendent of Public Instruction (1970).

James Baldwin, b. 1924, best-seller author, playwright; Another Country (1962), The Fire Next Time (1963).

Charles Gordone, b. 1925, won 1970 Pulitzer Prize for Drama with play, No Place to Be Somebody.

Lorraine Hansberry (1930-1965), playwright; won N. Y. Drama Critics Circle Award with Raisin in the Sun (1959).

Imamu Amiri Baraka, b. LeRoi Jones, 1934; poet, playwright, community leader in Newark, N. J.

Public Officials

Hiram R. Revels (1822-1901), first black U. S. Senator, elected in Mississippi, served 1870-1871.

Joesph H. Rainey (1832-1887), first black elected to House of Representatives (1869-79) from South Carolina.

Dr. Mary McCleod Bethune (1875-1955), adviser to Presidents Franklin D. Roosevelt and Harry Truman; division administrator in National Youth Administration (1935); founder, president of Bethune-Cookman College.

William L. Dawson (1886-1970), Congressman from Illinois, first black chairman of a major House of Representatives committee.

William H. Hastie, b. 1904, first black Federal Judge (appointed 1937); Governor of Virgin Islands (1946-1949); Judge, U. S. Circuit Court of Appeals (1949).

Dr. Ralph Bunche (1904-1971), first black to win the Nobel Peace Prize (1950); became Undersecretary of the United Nations (1950).

Dr. Robert C. Weaver, b. 1907, first black member of the U. S. Cabinet; Secretary of the Department of Housing & Urban Development (1966).

Adam Clayton Powell (1908-1972), early civil rights leader (1930's), congressman (1945-1969); as head of House Committee on Education and Labor (1960-1967) was responsible for 48 major pieces of social legislation.

Thurgood Marshall, b. 1908, first black U. S. Solicitor General (1965); first black to be made a Justice of the U. S. Supreme Court (1967); as a lawyer led the legal battery which won the historic decision from the Supreme Court declaring segregation of public schools unconstitutional (1954).

Edward W. Brooke, b. 1919; Attorney General of Massachusetts (1962); first black elected to U.S. Senate since 19th Century Reconstruction (1967).

Mrs. Shirley Chisholm b. 1924, first black woman elected to House of Representatives (Brooklyn, N. Y. 1968).

Louis Stokes (Dem., Ohio), chairman of Black Caucus of the 13 black members of the House.

Carl T. Rowan, b. 1925, prize-winning journalist; public official; director of the U. S. Information Agency (1964), making him the first black to sit on the National Security Council; U. S. Ambassador to Finland (1963).

Benjamin Hooks, first black appointed to the Federal Communications Commission (1972).

Andrew F. Brimmer, b. 1926, first black member (1966) of the Federal Reserve Board, the U. S. central banking facility.

Robert C. Henry, elected Mayor of Springfield, Ohio (1965), first black Mayor of a moderate-sized city in the 20th century.

Thomas Bradley, b. 1917, elected mayor of Los Angeles (1973).

Coleman Young, elected mayor of Detroit (1973).

Maynard Jackson, elected mayor of Atlanta (1973).

(As of April, 1974, there were 108 black mayors, including such major cities as Los Angeles, Atlanta, Detroit, Gary, Indiana, Cincinnati, Newark, N.J., Dayton, Ohio, and Raleigh, N. C. There were 1,080 city councilmen, 242 county officers, 40 state senators, 196 state representatives, 1 U. S. senator and 16 U. S. representatives. There are now 2,991 blacks holding elected office in the United States, an increase of 14% over the previous year, and 152% greater than 5 years ago, according to a survey by the Joint Center for Political Studies, Washington, D.C.)

Labor, Civil Rights Leaders

Sojourner Truth (1797-1883), born Isabella Baumfree; preacher, abolitionist; raised funds for Union in Civil War; worked for black educational opportunities.

Nat Turner (1800-1831), leader of the most significant of over 200 slave revolts in U. S. history, in Southhampton, Va.; he and 16 others were hanged.

Marcus Garvey (1887-1940), founded Universal Negro Improvement Assn. (1911), sought to promote a Back to Africa movement.

Willard Townsend (1895-1957), organized (1935) the United Transport Service Employees (redcaps, etc.); Vice President of AFL-CIO.

Elijah Muhammad, b. 1897, founded the Nation of Islam or Black Muslims (1931).

A. Philip Randolph, b. 1889, organized the Brotherhood of Sleeping Car Porters (1925); organizer of 1941 and 1963 March on Washington movements; Vice President of AFL-CIO.

Walter White (1893-1955), Executive Secretary, NAACP, (1931-1955).

Roy Wilkins, b. 1901, became Executive Secretary, NAACP in 1955.

Bayard Rustin, b. 1910, an organizer of the 1963 March on Washington; Executive Director of the A. Philip Randolph Institute.

The Rev. Dr. Ralph David Abernathy, b. 1916, an organizer (1957) of the Southern Christian Leadership Conference; its President (1968).

James Farmer, b. 1920, a founder of the Congress of Racial Equality (1942); Asst. Secretary of H.E.W. (1969).

Whitney M. Young Jr. (1921-1971), Executive Director of the National Urban League (1961); author, lecturer, newspaper columnist.

Floyd McKissick, b. 1922, National Director of CORE (1966).

Malcolm X (1925-1965), founded the Organization of Afro-American Unity (1963), a leading spokesman for black pride.

The Rev. Dr. Martin Luther King Jr. (1929-1968), led 382-day, Montgomery, Ala., boycott which brought 1956 U. S. Supreme Court decision holding segregation on buses unconstitutional; founder and President of the Southern Christian Leadership Conference (1957); leader of rights marches; won Nobel Peace Prize (1964).

Dr. George A. Wiley (1934-1973), Executive Director of National Welfare Rights Organization (founded 1966).

Roy Innis, b. 1934, National Director of CORE (1968).

Eldridge Cleaver, b. 1935, former Black Panther party leader, author of Soul on Ice.

Bobby G. Seale, National Chairman, Black Panther party.

Jesse Jackson, National Director, Operation Bread Basket and major community leader in Chicago.

John Lewis, former chairman of Student Nonviolent Coordinating Committee, leader of Voter Education Project in the South.

Widely Known Americans of the Present

Statesmen, Authors, Military Men and Other Prominent Persons Not Listed in Other Categories.

Name	Birthplace	Birthdate
Abernathy, Ralph (Linden, Ala.)		3/11/26
Abrams, Creighton (Springfield, Mass.)		9/15/14
Abzug, Bella (New York, N.Y.)		7/24/20
Agnew, Spiro (Baltimore, Md.)		11/ 9/18
Albee, Edward (Washington, D.C.)		3/12/28
Albert, Carl (McAlester, Okla.)		5/10/08
Aldrin, Edwin E. (Buzz) (Glen Ridge, N.J.)		1/20/30
Ali, Muhammad (Louisville, Ky.)		1/18/42
Alioto, Joseph (San Francisco, Calif.)		2/12/16
Alsop, Joseph W., Jr. (Avon, Conn.)		10/11/10
Alston, Walter (Butler Co., Ohio)		12/ 1/11
Anderson, Jack (Long Beach, Calif.)		10/19/22
Arcaro, Eddie (Cincinnati, Ohio)		2/19/16
Armstrong, Neil (Wapakoneta, Ohio)		8/ 5/30
Ashe, Arthur (Richmond, Va.)		7/10/43
Askew, Reubin (Muskogee, Okla.)		9/11/28
Bailey, F. Lee (Waltham, Mass.)		1933
Baker, Howard (Huntsville, Tenn.)		11/15/25
Baker, Russell (Loudoun Co., Va.)		8/14/25
Baldwin, Faith (New Rochelle, N.Y.)		10/ 1/93
Baldwin, James, (New York, N.Y.)		8/ 2/24
Ball, George (Des Moines, Iowa)		12/21/09
Barth, John (Cambridge, Md.)		5/27/30
Bayh, Birch (Terre Haute, Ind.)		1/22/28
Beame, Abraham (London, Eng.)		3/20/06
Belli, Melvin (Sonora, Calif.)		7/29/07
Bellow, Saul (Quebec, Canada)		7/10/15
Benton, Thomas Hart (Neosho, Mo.)		4/15/89
Bishop, Jim (Jersey City, N.J.)		11/21/07
Blackmun, Harry (Nashville, Ill.)		11/12/08
Bliss, Ray C. (Akron, Ohio)		12/16/07
Bok, Derek (Ardmore, Pa.)		3/22/30
Bond, Julian (Nashville, Tenn.)		1/14/40
Borman, Frank (Gary, Ind.)		3/14/28
Bowles, Chester (Springfield, Mass.)		4/ 5/01
Bradley, Omar N. (Clark, Mo.)		2/12/93
Bradley, Thomas, (Calvert, Tex.)		12/29/17
Braun, Wernher von (Wirsitz, Germany)		3/23/12
Brennan, William J. (Newark, N.J.)		4/25/06
Breslin, Jimmy (Jamaica, L.I., N.Y.)		10/17/30
Brewster, Kingman (Longmeadow, Mass.)		6/17/19
Brinkley, David (Wilmington, N.C.)		7/10/20
Brooke, Edward (Washington, D.C.)		10/26/19
Buchanan, Patrick (Washington, D.C.)		11/ 2/38
Buchwald, Art (Mt. Vernon, N.Y.)		10/20/25
Buckley, James (New York, N.Y.)		3/ 9/23
Buckley, William F. (New York, N.Y.)		11/24/25
Burns, Arthur F. (Stanislau, Aust.)		4/27/04
Bundy, McGeorge (Boston, Mass.)		3/30/19
Burger, Warren (St. Paul, Minn.)		9/17/07
Bush, George (Milton, Mass.)		6/12/24
Butz, Earl (Albion, Ind.)		7/ 3/09
Byrd, Robert (N. Wilkesboro, N.C.)		1/15/18
Caldwell, Erskine (Coweta Co., Ga.)		12/17/03
Capote, Truman (New Orleans, La.)		9/30/24
Case, Clifford (Franklin Park, N.J.)		4/16/04
Casper, Billy (San Diego, Calif.)		6/24/31
Celler, Emmanuel (Brooklyn, N.Y.)		5/ 6/88
Chamberlain, Wilt (Philadelphia, Pa.)		8/21/36
Chancellor, John (Chicago, Ill.)		7/14/27
Chavez, Cesar (Yuma, Arizona)		3/31/27
Chisholm, Shirley (Brooklyn, N.Y.)		11/30/24
Church, Frank (Boise, Idaho)		7/25/24
Clark, Ramsey (Dallas, Texas)		12/18/27
Clay, Lucius D. (Marietta, Ga.)		4/23/97
Conant, James B. (Dorchester, Mass.)		3/26/93
Connally, John B. (Floresville, Tex.)		2/28/17
Considine, Bob (Washington, D.C.)		11/ 4/06
Cooke, Terence (New York, N.Y.)		3/ 1/21
Cooper, John Sherman (Somerset, Ky.)		8/23/01
Cousins, Norman (Union Hill, N.J.)		6/24/12
Cox, Archibald (Plainfield, N.J.)		5/17/12
Cranston, Alan (Palo Alto, Calif.)		6/19/14
Cronkite, Walter (St. Joseph, Mo.)		11/ 4/16
Daley, Richard (Chicago, Ill.)		5/15/02
Davis, Angela (Birmingham, Ala.)		1/26/44
Dempsey, Jack (Manassa, Colo.)		6/24/95
Dickey, James (Atlanta, Ga.)		2/ 2/23
DiMaggio, Joe (Martinez, Calif.)		11/25/14
Dole, Robert (Russell, Kans.)		7/22/23
Doolittle, James H. (Alameda, Calif.)		12/14/96

Name	Birthplace	Birthdate
Douglas, William O. (Maine, Minn.)		10/16/98
Drury, Allan (Houston, Texas)		9/ 2/18
Dubinsky, David (Brest-Litovsk, Poland)		2/22/92
Durocher, Leo (West Springfield, Mass.)		7/27/06
Eagleton, Thomas (St. Louis, Mo.)		9/ 4/29
Ehrlichman, John (Tacoma, Wash.)		3/20/25
Eisenhower, Mamie (Boone, Iowa)		11/14/96
Eisenhower, Milton S. (Abilene, Kans.)		9/15/99
Ervin, Sam (Morganton, N.C.)		9/27/96
Evers, Charles (Decatur, Miss.)		9/11/22
Farley, James A. (Grassy Point, N.Y.)		5/30/88
Farmer, James (Marshall, Texas)		1/12/20
Finch, Robert (Temple, Ariz.)		10/ 9/25
Fischer, Bobby (Chicago, Ill.)		3/ 9/43
Fong, Hiram (Honolulu, Hawaii)		10/ 1/07
Ford, Gerald R. (Omaha, Nebr.)		7/14/13
Friedman, Milton (Brooklyn, N.Y.)		7/31/12
Fulbright, J. William (Sumner, Mo.)		4/ 9/05
Galbraith, John Kenneth (Ontario, Can.)		10/15/08
Gardner, John (Los Angeles, Calif.)		10/ 8/12
Gavin, James (New York, N.Y.)		3/22/07
Getty, J. Paul (Minneapolis, Minn.)		12/15/92
Glenn, John (Cambridge, Ohio)		7/18/21
Goldberg, Arthur J. (Chicago, Ill.)		8/ 8/08
Goldwater, Barry M. (Phoenix, Ariz.)		1/ 1/09
Graham, Billy (Charlotte, N.C.)		11/ 7/18
Grange, Red (Forksville, Pa.)		6/13/04
Gravel, Mike (Springfield, Mass.)		5/13/30
Griffin, Robert P. (Traverse City, Mich.)		11/ 6/23
Haig, Alexander (Philadelphia, Pa.)		12/ 2/24
Harriman, W. Averell (New York, N.Y.)		11/15/91
Hart, Phillip A. (Bryn Mawr, Pa.)		12/10/12
Hatfield, Mark O. (Dallas, Ore.)		7/12/22
Hayakawa, S. I. (Vancouver, B.C.)		7/18/06
Heller, Walter (Buffalo, N.Y.)		8/27/15
Helms, Richard (St. Davids, Pa.)		3/30/13
Hogan, Ben (Dublin, Tex.)		8/13/12
Hughes, Harold (Ida Grove, Iowa)		2/10/22
Hughes, Howard (Houston, Tex.)		12/24/05
Humphrey, Hubert (Wallace, S.D.)		5/27/11
Inouye, Daniel (Honolulu, Hawaii)		9/ 7/24
Jackson, Henry (Everett, Wash.)		5/31/12
Javits, Jacob K. (New York, N.Y.)		5/18/04
Johnson, Luci Baines (Mrs. Patrick Nugent)		7/ 2/47
Johnson, Lynda Bird (Mrs. Charles Robb)		3/19/44
Johnson, Mrs. Lyndon B. (Karnack, Tex.)		12/22/12
Jones, James (Robinson, Ill.)		11/ 6/21
Kelley, Clarence M. (Kansas City, Mo.)		10/24/11
Kennedy, Edward M. (Brookline, Mass.)		2/22/32
Kennedy, Rose (Mrs. Joseph P.) (Boston)		1890
Kerr, Walter (Evanston, Ill.)		7/ 8/13
Kheel, Theodore (New York, N.Y.)		5/ 9/14
Kissinger, Henry (Fuerth, Germany)		5/27/23
Klein, Herbert (Los Angeles, Calif.)		4/ 1/28
Kleindienst, Richard (Winslow, Ariz.)		8/ 5/23
Koufax, Sandy (Brooklyn, N.Y.)		12/30/35
Kuhn, Bowie (Tacoma Park, Mo.)		10/28/26
Laird, Melvin (Omaha, Nebr.)		9/ 1/22
Landon, Alfred (West Middlesex, Pa.)		9/ 9/87
Lemnitzer, Lyman L. (Honesdale, Pa.)		8/29/99
Lindbergh, Ann Morrow (Englewood, N.J.)		1906
Lindbergh, Charles A. (Detroit, Mich.)		2/ 4/02
Lindsay, John V. (New York, N.Y.)		11/24/21
Lippmann, Walter, (New York, N.Y.)		9/23/89
Lodge, Henry Cabot (Nahant, Mass.)		7/ 5/02
Long, Russell B. (Shreveport, La.)		11/ 3/18
Louis, Joe (Lafayette, Ala.)		5/13/14
Lowell, Robert (Boston, Mass.)		3/ 1/17
Lowenstein, Allard (Newark, N.J.)		1/16/29
Luce, Clare Boothe (New York, N.Y.)		4/10/03
MacGregor, Clark (Minneapolis, Minn.)		7/12/22
MacLeish, Archibald (Glencoe, Ill.)		5/ 7/92
Maddox, Lester (Atlanta, Ga.)		9/30/15
Mailer, Norman (Long Branch, N.J.)		1/31/23
Mansfield, Mike (New York, N.Y.)		3/16/03
Mantle, Mickey (Spavinaw, Okla.)		10/20/31

Name	Birthplace	Birthdate	Name	Birthplace	Birthdate
Marshall, Thurgood (Baltimore, Md.)		7/ 2/08	Salinger, Pierre (San Francisco, Calif.)		6/14/25
Mays, Willie (Fairfield, Ala.)		5/ 6/31	Salk, Jonas (New York, N.Y.)		10/28/14
McCarthy, Eugene (Watkins, Minn.)		3/29/16	Samuels, Howard (Rochester, N.Y.)		12/ 3/19
McCormack, John W. (Boston, Mass.)		12/21/91	Samuelson, Paul A. (Gary, Ind.)		5/15/15
McGinley, Phyllis (Ontario, Ore.)		3/21/05	Scali, John (Canton, Ohio)		4/27/18
McClellan, John J. (Sheridan, Ark.)		2/25/96	Schlesinger, Arthur Jr. (Columbus, Ohio)		10/15/17
McCloskey, Paul (San Bernardino, Calif.)		9/29/27	Schlesinger, James (New York, N.Y.)		2/15/29
McGovern, George (Avon, S.D.)		7/19/22	Scott, Hugh (Fredericksburg, Va.)		11/11/00
McNamara, Robert S. (San Francisco)		6/ 9/16	Scranton, William, W. (Madison, Conn.)		7/19/17
Meany, Goerge (New York, N.Y.)		8/16/94	Seaborg, Glenn T. (Ishpeming, Mich.)		4/19/12
Menotti, Gian-Carlo (Cadegliano, Italy)		7/ 7/11	Sevareid, Eric (Velva, N.D.)		11/26/12
Michener, James A. (New York, N.Y.)		2/ 3/07	Sheen, Fulton J. (El Paso, Ill.)		5/ 8/95
Miller, Arthur (New York, N.Y.)		10/17/15	Shirer, William L. (Chicago, Ill.)		2/23/04
Mills, Wilbur (Kensett, Ark.)		5/24/09	Shoemaker, Willie (Fabens, Texas)		8/19/31
Mitchell, John (Detroit, Mich.)		9/15/13	Shor, Toots (Philadelphia, Pa.)		5/ 6/05
Morton, Rogers (Louisville, Ky.)		9/19/14	Shriver, Sargent (Westminster, Md.)		11/ 9/15
Morton, Thruston (Louisville, Ky.)		8/19/07	Shultz, George (New York, N.Y.)		12/13/20
Moses, Robert (New Haven, Conn.)		12/18/88	Smith, H. Allen (McLeansboro, Ill.)		12/19/06
Moynihan, Daniel P. (Tulsa, Okla.)		3/16/27	Smith, Howard K. (Ferriday, La.)		5/12/14
Musial, Stan (Donora, Pa.)		11/21/20	Smith, Margaret Chase (Skowhegan, Me.)		12/14/97
Muskie, Edmund (Rumford, Maine)		3/28/14	Sorenson, Theodore (Lincoln, Neb.)		5/ 8/28
			Spillane, Mickey (Brooklyn, N.Y.)		3/ 9/18
Nader, Ralph (Winsted, Conn.)		2/27/34	Spock, Benjamin (New Haven, Conn.)		5/ 2/03
Nicklaus, Jack (Columbus, Ohio)		1/21/40	Stassen, Harold (West St. Paul, Minn.)		4/13/07
Nixon, Julie (Mrs. David Eisenhower)			Steinem, Gloria (Toledo, Ohio)		3/25/36
(Wastington, D.C.)		7/ 5/48	Stengel, Casey (Kansas City, Mo.)		7/30/91
Nixon, Mrs. Richard (Ely, Nevada)		3/16/12	Stewart, Potter (Jackson, Mich.)		1/23/15
Nixon, Richard (Yorba Linda, Calif.)		1/ 9/13	Stokes, Carl (Cleveland, Ohio)		6/21/27
Nixon, Tricia (Mrs. Edward Cox) (Calif.)		2/21/46	Stone, Irving (San Francisco, Calif.)		7/14/03
Nizer, Louis (London, England)		2/ 6/02	Symington, Stuart (Amherst, Mass.)		6/26/01
Oates, Joyce Carol (Lockport, N.Y.)		6/16/38	Taft, Robert, Jr. (Cincinnati, Ohio)		2/26/17
O'Brien, Lawrence F. (Springfield, Mass.)		7/ 7/17	Talmadge, Herman (Lovejoy, Ga.)		8/ 9/13
Onassis, Jacqueline (Southampton, N.Y.)		7/28/29	Taylor, Maxwell D. (Keytesville, Mo.)		8/26/01
			Thomas, Lowell (Woodington, Ohio)		4/ 6/92
Paley, William S. (Chicago, Ill.)		9/28/01	Thurmond, J. Strom (Edgefield, S.C.)		12/ 5/02
Palmer, Arnold (Youngstown, Pa.)		9/10/29	Tower, John (Houston, Texae)		9/29/25
Pauling, Linus (Portland, Ore.)		2/28/01	Truman, Mrs. Harry (Independence, Mo.)		2/13/85
Patterson, Floyd (Waco, N. Car.)		1/ 4/35	Truman, Margaret (Mrs. Clifton Daniel)		
Peale, Norman Vincent (Bowersville, Ohio)		5/31/98	(Independence, Mo.)		2/17/24
Percy, Charles H. (Pensacola, Fla.)		9/27/19	Tuchman, Barbara (New York, N.Y.)		1/30/12
Perelman, S. J. (Brooklyn, N.Y.)		2/ 1/04	Tunney, Gene (New York, N.Y.)		5/25/98
Porter, Katherine Ann (Indian Creek, Tex.)		5/15/94	Tunney, John V. (New York, N.Y.)		6/26/34
Powell, Lewis F. (Suffolk, Va.)		9/19/07			
Proxmire, William (Lake Forest, Ill.)		1/11/15	Unitas, John (Pittsburgh, Pa.)		5/ 7/33
Rand, Ayn, (St. Petersburg, Russia)		1905	Vanderbilt, Alfred G. (London, England)		9/22/12
Randolph, A. Philip (Crescent City, Fla.)		4/15/89	Van Buren, Abigail (Sioux City, Iowa)		7/ 4/18
Reagan, Ronald (Tampico, Ill.)		2/ 6/11	Veeck, Bill (Chicago, Ill.)		2/ 9/14
Reasoner, Harry (Dakota City, Iowa)		4/17/23	Vidal, Gore (West Point, N.Y.)		10/ 3/25
Rehnquist, William (Milwaukee, Wisc.)		10/ 1/24	Volpe, John (Wakefield, Mass.)		12/ 8/08
Reston, James (Clydebank, Scotland)		11/ 3/09	Vonnegut, Kurt, Jr. (Indianapolis, Ind.)		11/11/22
Rhodes, John (Council Grove, Kansas)		9/18/16			
Ribicoff, Abe (New Britain, Conn.)		4/ 9/10	Wagner, Robert F. (New York, N.Y.)		4/20/10
Richardson, Elliot L. (Boston, Mass.)		7/20/21	Walcott, Jersey Joe (Merchantville, N.J.)		1/31/14
Rickover, Hyman (Makowa, Poland)		1/27/00	Wallace, George (Clio, Ala.)		8/25/19
Robertson, Oscar (Charlotte, Tenn.)		11/24/38	Warren, Robert Penn (Guthrie, Ky.)		4/24/05
Rockefeller, David (New York, N.Y.)		6/12/15	Weicker, Lowell (Paris, France)		5/16/31
Rockefeller, John D. 3rd (New York, N.Y.)		3/21/06	Weinberger, Casper (San Francisco, Calif.)		8/18/17
Rockefeller, Laurance S. (New York, N.Y.)		5/26/10	Westmoreland, William (Spartanburg, S.C.)		3/26/14
Rockefeller, Nelson A. (Bar Harbor, Me.)		7/ 8/08	White, Byron R. (Ft. Collins, Colo.)		6/ 8/17
Rockwell, Norman (New York, N.Y.)		2/ 3/94	White, Theodore (Boston, Mass.)		5/ 6/15
Rogers, William P. (Norfolk, N.Y.)		6/23/13	Wicker, Tom (Hamlet, N.C.)		6/18/26
Romney, George W. (Chihuahua, Mexico)		7/ 8/07	Wilder, Thornton (Madison, Wisc.)		4/17/97
Roosevelt, Elliot (New York, N.Y.)		9/23/10	Wilkins, Roy (St. Louis, Mo.)		8/30/01
Roosevelt, Franklin D., Jr. (Canada)		8/17/14	Williams, Ted (San Diego, Calif.)		8/30/18
Roth, Philip (Newark, N.J.)		3/19/33	Williams, Tennessee (Columbus, Miss.)		3/26/14
Rozelle, Pete (South Gate, Calif.)		3/ 1/26	Wilson, Malcolm (New York, N.Y.)		2/26/14
Ruckelshaus, William (Indianapolis, Ind.)		7/24/32	Woodcock, Leonard (Providence, R.I.)		2/15/11
Rusk, Dean (Cherokee Co., Ga.)		2/ 9/09	Wouk, Herman (New York, N.Y.)		5/27/15
Ryun, Jim (Wichita, Kansas)		4/29/47			
			Yorty, Sam (Lincoln, Neb.)		10/ 1/09
Safire, William (New York, N.Y.)		12/17/29			
Salinger, J. D. (New York, N.Y.)		1/ 1/19	Ziegler, Ronald (Covington, Ky.)		5/12/39

Modern American Playwrights and Some of Their Plays

George Abbott, b. 1887. Co-author Three Men on a Horse, The Boys from Syracuse, Damn Yankees.

Edward F. Albee, b. 1928. Who's Afraid of Virginia Woolf?, Tiny Alice, A Delicate Balance.

William Alfred, b. 1922. Hogan's Goat.

Maxwell Anderson, 1888-1959. What Price Glory? Winterset, Saturday's Children, High Tor, Key Largo.

Philip Barry, 1886-1949. The Animal Kingdom, Holiday, The Philadelphia Story.

Abe Burrows, b. 1910. Co-author Guys and Dolls, How to Succeed in Business Without Really Trying.

Mary C. Chase, b. 1907. Harvey.

Paddy Chayefsky, b. 1923. Middle of the Night, The Tenth Man, Gideon, The Passions of Josef D.

Marc Connelly, b. 1890. The Green Pastures.

Russell Crouse, 1893-1966. Co-author State of the Union, Life With Father, Call Me Madam, The Sound of Music, Mr. President.

Edna Ferber, 1887-1968. Co-author Dinner at Eight, Stage Door.

Paul Foster, b. 1932. Tom Paine.

Jack Gelber, b. 1932. The Connection, The Cuban Thing.

William Gibson, b. 1914. Two for the Seesaw, The Miracle Worker.

Frank D. Gilroy, b. 1915. The Subject Was Roses, The Only Game in Town.

Charles Gordone, b. 1925. No Place to Be Somebody.

Paul Green, b. 1894. In Abraham's Bosom, Wilderness Road.

William Hanley, b. 1931. Slow Dance on the Killing Ground.

Lorraine Hansberry, 1930-1965. A Raisin in the Sun.

Moss Hart, 1904-1961. Co-author Once in a Lifetime, You Can't Take it With You.

Ben Hecht, 1884-1964. Co-author The Front Page.

Lillian Hellman, b. 1907. The Children's Hour, The Little Foxes, Watch on the Rhine.

Sidney Howard, 1881-1939. The Silver Cord, Yellow Jack, They Knew What They Wanted.

William Inge, 1913-1973. Come Back, Little Sheba; Picnic, Bus Stop, The Dark at the Top of the Stairs, A Loss of Roses.

LeRoi Jones, b. 1934. Dutchman, The Slave.

George S. Kaufman, 1889-1961. Co-author Dinner at Eight, Stage Door, Yooa Can't Take It With You, The Man Who Came to Dinner.

George Kelly, 1887-1947. The Show-off, Craig's Wife.

Jean Kerr, b. 1923. Mary, Mary, Poor Richard; Finishing Touches.

Joseph Kesselring, 1902-1967. Arsenic and Old Lace.

Sidney Kingsley, b. 1906. Men in White, The Patriots, Dead End, Darkness at Noon.

Arthur Kopit, b. 1937. Oh Dad, Poor Dad, Mamma's Hung You in a Closet and I'm Feelin' So Sad.

Howard Lindsay, 1889-1968. Co-author State of the Union, Life With Father, Call Me Madam, The Sound of Music, Mr. President.

Charles MacArthur, 1895-1956. Co-author The Front Page.

Archibald MacLeish, b. 1892. J. B.

Terrence McNally, b. 1939. And Things That Go Bump in the Night, Sweet Eros.

Arthur Miller, b. 1915. All My Sons, Death of a Salesman, Crucible, View from the Bridge, After the Fall, Incident at Vichy, The Price.

Anne Nichols, 1891-1966. Abie's Irish Rose.

Clifford Odets, 1906-1963. Waiting for Lefty, Awake and Sing, Golden Boy, The Country Girl.

Eugene O'Neill, 1888-1953. The Long Voyage Home, The Emperor Jones, Anna Christie, Desire Under the Elms, Strange Interlude, Mourning Becomes Electra; Ah, Wilderness; The Iceman Cometh, Long Day's Journey Into Night.

John Patrick, b. 1905. The Hasty Heart, Teahouse of the August Moon.

Elmer Rice, 1892-1967. The Adding Machine, Street Scene, Counsellor-at-Law, Dream Girl.

Howard Sackler, b. 1930. The Great White Hope.

William Saroyan, b. 1908. My Heart's in the Highlands, The Time of Your Life.

Dore Schary, b. 1905. Sunrise at Campobello.

Murray Schisgal, b. 1926. The Typists and the Tiger, Luv.

Robert Sherwood, 1896-1955. Reunion in Vienna, The Petrified Forest, Idiot's Delight, There Shall Be No Night, Abe Lincoln in Illinois.

Neil Simon, b. 1927. Sweet Charity, Plaza Suite, The Odd Couple, Barefoot in the Park, Last of the Red Hot Lovers, The Gingerbread Lady, The Prisoner of Second Avenue, The Sunshine Boys, The Good Doctor.

Samuel A. Taylor, b. 1912. The Happy Time, The Pleasure of His Company, co-author Sabrina Fair and No Strings.

John Van Druten, 1901-1957. The Voice of the Turtle; I Remember Mama; Bell, Book and Candle, I Am a Camera.

Thornton Wilder, b. 1897. Our Town, The Skin of Our Teeth, The Matchmaker.

Tennessee Williams, b. 1914. The Glass Menagerie. A Streetcar Named Desire, Cat on a Hot Tin Roof, The Night of the Iguana, The Milk Train Doesn't Stop Here Anymore, Camino Real.

American Architects and Some of Their Achievements

Max Abramovitz, b. 1908. Philharmonic Hall at Lincoln Center, N. Y.

Henry Bacon, (1866-1924) Lincoln Memorial.

Pietro Belluschi, b. 1899. Julliard School of Music, Lincoln Center, N.Y.

Marcel Breuer, b. Pecs, Hungary, 1902. Whitney Museum of American Art, N.Y. (with Hamilton Smith).

Charles Bulfinch, (1763-1844) State House, Boston; Capitol, Washington, (part).

Daniel H. Burnham, (1846-1912) Union Station, Washington; Flatiron, New York.

Ralph Adams Cram, (1863-1942) Cathedral of St. John the Divine, New York; U.S. Military Academy (part).

Alexander J. Davis, (1803-1892) Sub-treasury, N.Y.; capitols of Indiana, North Carolina, Illinois, Ohio.

R. Buckminster Fuller, b. 1895. U.S. Pavilion, Expo 67, Montreal (geodesic domes).

William F. Gibbs, (1886-1967) Designed liner United States.

Cass Gilbert, (1859-1934) Custom House, Woolworth Bldg., New York; Capitol, St. Paul.

Bertrand Goldberg, b. 1913. Marina City Towers, Chicago.

Bertram G. Goodhue, (1869-1924) Capitol, Lincoln, Nebr.; St. Thomas, St. Bartholomew, N.Y.

Walter Gropius, (1883-1969) Pan Am Building, N.Y. (with Pietro Belluschi).

Wallace K. Harrison, b. 1895. Metropolitan Opera House at Lincoln Center, N.Y.

Thomas Hastings, (1860-1929) Public Library, Frick Mansion, New York.

James Hoban, (1762-1831) The White House.

Raymond Hood, (1881-1934) Rockefeller Center (part); Daily News, N. Y.; Tribune, Chicago.

Richard M. Hunt, (1828-1896) Metropolitan Museum (part); The Breakers, Newport.

William Le Baron Jenney, (1832-1907) Home Insurance, Chicago (demolished).

Philip C. Johnson, b. 1906. N. Y. State Theater at Lincoln Center, N.Y.

Albert Kahn, (1869-1942) Athletic Club Bldg., General Motors Bldg., New York.

Louis Kahn, (1901-1974). Salk Laboratory, LaJolla, Calif.

Christopher Grant LaFarge, (1862-1938) Chapel, West Point; Cathedral, Seattle.

Benjamin H. Latrobe, (1764-1820) U.S. Capitol (part).

William Lescaze, (1896-1969) Philadelphia Savings Fund Society; Borg-Warner Bldg., Chicago.

Theodore C. Link, (1850-1923) Union Station, St. Louis.

Charles F. McKim, (1847-1909) Public Library, Boston; Columbia Univ. (part).

Charles M. McKim, b. 1920. KUHT-TV Transmitter Building, Houston; Lutheran Church of the Redeemer, Houston.

Medary, Milton B., (1874-1929) Bok Carillon Tower, Mountain Lake, Fla.

Ludwig Mies van der Rohe, (1886-1969). Seagram Building, N. Y. (with Philip C. Johnson); National Gallery, Berlin.

Robert Mills, (1781-1855) Washington Monument.

Richard J. Neutra, (1892-1970). Mathematics Park, Princeton; Orange Co. Courthouse, Santa Ana, Calif.

Frederick L. Olmsted, (1822-1903) Central Park, New York; Fairmount Park, P hiladelphia.

Ieoh Ming Pei, b. Canton, China, 1917. Kips Bay Plaza, N. Y.; Earth Sciences Building (M.I.T.) Cambridge, Mass.; National Center for Atmospheric Research, Boulder, Colo.

John Russell Pope, (1874-1937) National Gallery.

John Portman, b. 1924. Peachtree Center, Atlanta.

James Renwick, Jr., (1818-1895) Grace Church, St. Patrick's Cathedral, N.Y.; Smithsonian, Corcoran Galleries, Wash.

Henry H. Richardson, (1838-1886) Trinity, Boston.

Kevin Roche, b. 1922. Oakland, Calif., Museum; Fine Arts Center, U. of Mass.

James Gamble Rogers, (1867-1947) Columbia-Presbyterian Medical Center, New York; Northwestern Univ., Chicago.

John Weldon Root, b. 1887. Palmolive Building, Chicago; Hotel Statler, Washington; Hotel Tamanaco, Caracas.

Paul Rudolph, b. 1918. Jewitt Art Center, Wellesley College; Art & Architecture Bldg., Yale.

Eero Saarinen, (1910-1961) Gateway to the West arch., St. Louis; Trans World Flight Center, N.Y.

Louis Skidmore, (1897-1962) AEC town site, Oak Ridge, Tenn.; Terrace Plaza Hotel, Cincinnati.

Clarence S. Stein, b. 1882. Temple Emanu-El, New York.

Edward Durell Stone, b. 1902. U.S. Embassy, New Delhi, India; (H. Hartford) Gallery of Modern Art, N.Y.

Louis H. Sullivan, (1856-1924) Auditorium, Chicago.

Richard Upjohn, (1802-1878) Trinity Ch., N. Y.

Ralph T. Walker, (1889-1973). N.Y. Telephone hqrs., New York; IBM Research Lab., Poughkeepsie, N.Y.; General Foods Bldg., White Plains, N.Y.

Roland A. Wank, (1898-1970) Cincinnati Union Terminal; head architect TVA, 1933-44.

Stanford White, (1853-1906) Washington Arch. First Madison Square Garden, New York.

Frank Lloyd Wright, (1869-1959) Imperial Hotel, Tokyo; Guggenheim Museum, New York.

William Wurster, b. 1895. Ghirardelli Sq., San Francisco; Cowell College, U. Cal'f., Berkeley.

Minoru Yamasaki, b. 1912. World Trade Center, New York City.

The Hall of Fame for Great Americans

The Hall of Fame for Great Americans was a gift to the American people by Mrs. Helen Gould Shepard. New York University acts as Trustee for the Shrine for the nation. Busts and tablets are donated. The Americans honored since 1900 are:

1900
John Adams
John James Audubon
Henry Ward Beecher
William Ellery Channing
Henry Clay
Peter Cooper
Jonathan Edwards
Ralph Waldo Emerson
David Glasgow Farragut
Benjamin Franklin
Robert Fulton
Ulysses Simpson Grant
Asa Gray
Nathaniel Hawthorne
Washington Irving
Thomas Jefferson
James Kent
Robert Edward Lee
Abraham Lincoln
Henry Wadsworth Longfellow
Horace Mann
John Marshall
Samuel Finley Breese Morse
George Peabody
Joseph Story
Gilbert Charles Stuart
George Washington
Daniel Webster
Eli Whitney

1905
John Quincy Adams
James Russell Lowell
Mary Lyon

James Madison
Maria Mitchell
William Tecumseh Sherman
John Greenleaf Whittier
Emma Willard

1910
George Bancroft
Phillips Brooks
William Cullen Bryant
James Fenimore Cooper
Oliver Wendell Holmes
Andrew Jackson
John Lothrop Motley
Edgar Allan Poe
Harriet Beecher Stowe
Frances Elizabeth Willard

1915
Louis Agassiz
Daniel Boone
Rufus Choate
Charlotte Saunders Cushman
Alexander Hamilton
Joseph Henry
Mark Hopkins
Elias Howe
Francis Parkman

1920
Samuel Langhorne Clemens
(Mark Twain)

James Buchanan Eads
Patrick Henry
William Thomas Green
Morton
Alice Freeman Palmer
Augustus Saint-Gaudens
Roger Williams

1925
Edwin Booth
John Paul Jones

1930
Matthew Fontaine Maury
James Monroe
James Abbott McNeil
Whistler
Walt Whitman

1935
Grover Cleveland
Simon Newcomb
William Penn

1940
Stephen Collins Foster

1945
Sidney Lanier
Thomas Paine

Walter Reed
Booker T. Washington

1950
Susan B. Anthony
Alexander Graham Bell
Josiah Willard Gibbs
William Crawford Gorgas
Theodore Roosevelt
Woodrow Wilson

1955
Thomas Jonathan Jackson
George Westinghouse
Wilbur Wright

1960
Thomas A. Edison
Edward A. MacDowell
Henry D. Thoreau

1965
Jane Addams
Oliver Wendell Holmes, Jr.
Sylvanus Thayer
Orville Wright

1970
Albert Abraham Michelson
Lillian D. Wald

British
Poets, Dramatists, Essayists, Historians, Novelists

Born	Died	Name	Born	Died	Name	Born	Died	Name
1672	1719	Addison, Joseph	1864	1924	Corelli, Marie	1894	1963	Huxley, Aldous
1805	1882	Ainsworth, W. H.	1731	1800	Cowper, William	1825	1895	Huxley, Thos. H.
1832	1904	Arnold, Edwin	1908	1973	Creasey, John	1709	1784	Johnson, Samuel
1822	1888	Arnold, Matthew	1809	1882	Darwin, Charles	1573	1637	Jonson, Ben
1775	1817	Austen, Jane	1660	1731	Defoe, Daniel	1795	1821	Keats, John
1561	1626	Bacon, Francis	1873	1956	De la Mare, Walter	1896	1967	Kennedy, Margaret
1214	1294	Bacon, Roger	1785	1859	De Quincey, Thomas	1819	1875	Kingsley, Charles
1762	1851	Baillie, Joanna	1812	1870	Dickens, Charles	1865	1936	Kipling, Rudyard
1860	1937	Barrie, James M.	1573	1631	Donne, John	1775	1834	Lamb, Charles
1584	1616	Beaumont, Francis	1868	1952	Douglas, Norman	1332	1400	Langland, William
673	735	Bede, the Venerable	1867	1900	Dowson, Ernest	1885	1930	Lawrence, David H.
1872	1956	Beerbohm, Max	1859	1930	Doyle, Arthur Conan	1838	1903	Lecky, W. E. H.
1870	1953	Belloc, Hilaire	1563	1631	Drayton, Michael	1866	1947	LeGallienne, Richard
1867	1931	Bennett, Arnold	1631	1700	Dryden, John	1894	1957	Lewis, Wyndham
1748	1832	Bentham, Jeremy	1834	1896	Du Maurier, Geo. L.	1895	1970	Liddell Hart, Basil
1662	1742	Bentley, Richard	1819	1880	Eliot, George	1632	1704	Locke, John
1869	1951	Blackwood, Algernon	1888	1965	Eliot, T. S.	1800	1859	Macaulay, Thomas B.
1740	1795	Boswell, James	1620	1706	Evelyn, John	1863	1947	Machen, Arthur
1844	1930	Bridges, Robert	1707	1754	Fielding, Henry	1888	1923	Mansfield, Katherine
1816	1855	Bronte, Charlotte	1809	1883	Fitzgerald, Edward	1564	1593	Marlowe, Christopher
1818	1848	Bronte, Emily	1908	1964	Fleming, Ian	1897	1969	Martin, Kingsley
1806	1861	Browning, Elizabeth B.	1873	1939	Ford, Ford Madox	1878	1967	Masefield, John
1812	1889	Browning, Robert	1889	1966	Forester, C. S.	1583	1640	Massinger, Phillip
1628	1688	Bunyan, John	1879	1970	Forster, E. M.	1874	1965	Maugham, W. Somerset
1729	1797	Burke, Edmund	1908	1967	Frankau, Pamela	1828	1909	Meredith, George
1759	1796	Burns, Robert	1867	1933	Galsworthy, John	1806	1873	Mill, John Stuart
1788	1824	Byron, (Geo. Gordon)	1685	1732	Gay, John	1882	1956	Milne, A. A.
1777	1844	Campbell, Thomas	1737	1794	Gibbon, Edward	1608	1674	Milton, John
1795	1881	Carlyle, Thomas	1857	1903	Gissing, George	1838	1923	Morley, John
1832	1898	Carroll, Lewis	1728	1774	Goldsmith, Oliver	1870	1916	Munro, H. H. (Saki)
1888	1957	Cary, Joyce	1716	1771	Gray, Thomas	1880	1958	Noyes, Alfred
1340	1400	Chaucer, Geoffrey	1840	1928	Hardy, Thomas	1903	1950	Orwell, George
1694	1773	Chesterfield, Earl of	1831	1923	Harrison, Frederic	1839	1894	Pater, Walter
1874	1936	Chesterton, G. K.	1778	1830	Hazlitt, William	1785	1866	Peacock, Thomas L.
1911	1968	Churchill, Randolph	1849	1903	Henley, Wm. Ernest	1632	1703	Pepys, Samuel
1762	1835	Cobbett, William	1591	1674	Herrick, Robert	1688	1744	Pope, Alexander
1772	1834	Coleridge, S. T.	1588	1679	Hobbes, Thomas	1900	1969	Potter, Stephen
1824	1889	Collins, Wilkie	1770	1835	Hogg, James	1664	1721	Prior, Matthew
1670	1729	Congreve, William	1799	1845	Hood, Thomas	1863	1944	Quiller-Couch, Arthur T.
1857	1924	Conrad, Joseph	1859	1936	Housman, Alfred E.	1552	1618	Raleigh, Sir Walter
1878	1957	Coppard, A. E.	1711	1776	Hume, David	1814	1884	Reade, Charles

Born	Died	Name	Born	Died	Name	Born	Died	Name
1882	1957	Richardson, Dorothy	1771	1845	Smith, Sydney	1876	1962	Trevelyan, Geo. M.
1689	1761	Richardson, Samuel	1721	1771	Smollett, Tobias	1815	1882	Trollope, Anthony
1819	1900	Ruskin, John	1774	1843	Southey, Robert	1884	1941	Walpole, Hugh
1872	1970	Russell, Bertrand	1552	1599	Spenser, Edmund	1593	1683	Walton, Izaak
1886	1967	Sassoon, Siegfried	1672	1729	Steele, Richard	1851	1920	Ward, Mrs. Humphry
1771	1832	Scott, Sir Walter	1713	1768	Sterne, Laurence	1674	1748	Watts, Isaac
1564	1616	Shakespeare, William	1850	1894	Stevenson, Robert Louis	1903	1966	Waugh, Evelyn
1856	1950	Shaw, G. Bernard	1880	1932	Strachey, Lytton	1866	1946	Wells, H. G.
1797	1851	Shelley, Mary W.	1667	1745	Swift, Jonathan	1906	1964	White, T. H.
1792	1822	Shelley, Percy Bysshe	1837	1909	Swinburne, Algernon C.	1861	1947	Whitehead, Alfred N.
1751	1816	Sheridan, Richard B.	1809	1892	Tennyson, Alfred	1854	1900	Wilde, Oscar
1554	1586	Sidney, Sir Phillip	1811	1863	Thackeray, W. M.	1770	1850	Wordsworth, William
1887	1964	Sitwell, Edith	1914	1953	Thomas, Dylan	1882	1941	Woolf, Virginia
1892	1969	Sitwell, Osbert	1892	1973	Tolkien, J.R.R.	1640	1715	Wycherly, William

British Painters and Sculptors

Born	Died	Name	Born	Died	Name	Born	Died	Name
1872	1898	Beardsley, Aubrey	1866	1934	Fry, Roger E.	1834	1896	Morris, William
1757	1827	Blake, William	1727	1788	Gainsborough, Thos.	1878	1931	Orpen, William
1833	1898	Burne-Jones, Edward	1648	1721	Gibbons, Grinling	1756	1823	Raeburn, Henry
1896	1967	Charoux, Siegfried	1697	1764	Hogarth, William	1723	1792	Reynolds, Joshua
1776	1837	Constable, John	1758	1810	Hoppner, John	1734	1802	Romney, George
1803	1902	Cooper, Thos. Sidney	1827	1910	Hunt, W. Holman	1828	1882	Rossetti, D. G.
1782	1842	Cotman, John S.	1646	1723	Kneller, Godfrey	1891	1959	Spencer, Stanley
1793	1865	Eastlake, Charles L.	1856	1941	Lavery, John	1775	1851	Turner, J. M. W.
1880	1959	Epstein, Jacob	1769	1830	Lawrence, Thomas	1817	1904	Watts, George
1787	1849	Etty, William	1806	1870	Maclise, Daniel	1785	1841	Wilkie, David
1755	1826	Flaxman, John	1829	1896	Millais, John	1713	1782	Wilson, Richard

Poets Laureate of England

There is no authentic record of the origin of the office of Poet Laureate of England. According to Warton, there was a Versificator Regis, or Kings's Poet, in the reign of Henry III (1216-1272), and he was paid 100 shillings a year. Geoffrey Chaucer (1340-1400) assumed the title of Poet Laureate, and in 1389 got a royal grant of a yearly allowance of wine. In the reign of Edward IV (1461-1483), John Kay held the post. Under Henry VII (1485-1509), Andrew Bernard was the Poet Laureate, and was succeeded under Henry VIII (1509-1547) by John Skelton. Next came Edmund Spenser, who died in 1599; then Samuel Daniel, who died in 1619, and then Ben Jonson (appointed 1619). Sir William D'Avenant was appointed in 1638. He was a godson of William Shakespeare.

Others were John Dryden, 1670-1688; Thomas Shadwell, 1689; Nahum Tate, 1692; Nicholas Rowe, 1715; the Rev. Laurence Eusden, 1718; Colly Cibber, 1730; William Whitehead, 1758, on the refusal of Gray; Rev. Thomas Warton, 1785, on the refusal of Mason; Henry J. Pye, 1790; Robert Southey, 1813, on the refusal of Sir Walter Scott; William Wordsworth, 1843; Alfred Tennyson, 1850; Alfred Austin, 1896; Robert Bridges, 1913 (died 1930); John Masefield, 1930 (died 1967); Cecil Day Lewis (died May 22, 1972); Sir John Betjeman, 1972.

British Army (A), Navy (N), Air Force (F), Explorers (E)

Born	Died	Name	Born	Died	Name	Born	Died	Name
1891	1969	Alexander, Harold R. (A)	1710	1759	Forbes, John (A)	1867	1948	Milne, George (A)
1861	1936	Allenby, Edmund (A)	1786	1847	Franklin, John (E)	1894	1967	Morgan, Frederick (A)
1717	1797	Amherst, Jeffrey (A)	1535	1594	Frobisher, Martin (E)	1782	1853	Napier, Charles J. (A)
1584	1622	Baffin, William (E)	1721	1787	Gage, Thomas (A)	1810	1890	Napier, Robert C. (A)
1871	1936	Beatty, David (N)	1833	1885	Gordon, Chas. G. (A)	1758	1805	Nelson, Horatio (N)
1873	1967	Boyle, Wm. H. D. (N)	1541	1591	Grenville, Richard (N)	1696	1785	Oglethorpe, James (A)
1695	1755	Braddock, Edward (A)	1861	1928	Haig, Douglas (A)	1895	1968	Robb, James (F)
1839	1908	Buller, Redvers (A)	1853	1947	Hamilton, Ian (A)	1832	1914	Roberts, Frederick (A)
1723	1792	Burgoyne, John (A)	1795	1857	Havelock, Henry (A)	1719	1792	Rodney, George (N)
1663	1733	Byng, George (N)	1745	1792	Hearne, Samuel (E)	1800	1862	Ross, James C. (E)
1675	1726	Cadogan, Wm. (A)	1536	1624	Howard, Charles (N)	1893	1969	Scobie, Ronald M. (A)
1593	1676	Cavendish, Wm. (A)	1726	1799	Howe, Richard (N)	1868	1912	Scott, Robert F. (E)
1873	1967	Chatfield, Alfred (N)	1729	1814	Howe, William (A)	1874	1922	Shackleton, Ernest (E)
1738	1795	Clinton, Henry, (A)	1575	1611	Hudson, Henry (E)	1891	1970	Slim, Wm. Joseph (A)
1770	1851	Codrington, Ed. (N)	1883	1966	Humphrey, Noel (E)	1841	1904	Stanley, Henry M. (E)
1727	1779	Cook, James (E)	1880	1959	Ironside, Wm. E. (A)	1869	1951	Swinton, Ernest (A)
1738	1805	Cornwallis, Chas. (A)	1859	1935	Jellicoe, John (N)	1890	1967	Tedder, Arthur W. (F)
1550	1605	Davis, John (E)	1715	1774	Johnson, Wm. (A)	1757	1798	Vancouver, George (E)
1896	1969	Dempsey, Miles (A)	1872	1945	Keyes, Roger (N)	1883	1950	Wavell, Archibald (A)
1883	1970	Dowding, Hugh C. (F)	1850	1916	Kitchener, H. H. (A)	1787	1834	Weddell, James (E)
1540	1596	Drake, Francis (N)	1888	1935	Lawrence, T. E. (A)	1769	1852	Wellington, Duke of (A)
1877	1967	Ellington, Edward (F)	1650	1722	Marlborough, Duke of (A)	1727	1759	Wolfe, James (A)
1841	1920	Fisher, John A. (N)	1871	1951	Maurice, Frederick (A)			

British Statesmen

Born	Died	Name	Born	Died	Name	Born	Died	Name
1852	1928	Asquith, Herbert H.	1863	1937	Chamberlain, Austen	1862	1933	Grey, Edward
1879	1964	Astor, Viscountess	1836	1914	Chamberlain, Joseph	1594	1643	Hampden, John
1883	1967	Atlee, Clement	1869	1940	Chamberlain, Neville	1732	1818	Hastings, Warren
1867	1947	Baldwin, Stanley	1874	1965	Churchill, Winston	1863	1935	Henderson, Arthur
1848	1930	Balfour, Arthur J.	1725	1774	Clive, Robert	1889	1969	Horsbrugh, Florence
1879	1964	Beaverbrook, Lord	1889	1952	Cripps, Stafford	1858	1923	Law, Andrew Bonar
1897	1960	Bevan, Aneurin	1599	1658	Cromwell, Oliver	1863	1945	Lloyd George, David
1881	1951	Bevin, Ernest	1859	1925	Curzon of Kedleston	1866	1937	MacDonald, J. Ramsay
1838	1922	Bryce, James	1804	1881	Disraeli, Benjamin	1854	1925	Milner, Alfred
1884	1968	Cadogan, Alexander	1749	1806	Fox, Charles James	1732	1792	North, Frederick
1770	1827	Canning, George	1906	1963	Gaitskell, Hugh.	1784	1865	Palmerston, Viscount
1769	1822	Castlereagh, Robert	1809	1898	Gladstone, Wm. E.	1788	1850	Peel, Robert
1864	1958	Cecil, Edgar	1764	1845	Grey, Charles	1759	1806	Pitt, William

Born	Died	Name
1708	1778	Pitt, W. (Chatham)
1853	1902	Rhodes, Cecil
1792	1878	Russell, John
1830	1903	Salisbury, Robert
1676	1745	Walpole, Robert

British Scientists, Engineers, Physicians

Born	Died	Name
1813	1898	Bessemer, Henry
1899	1966	Cameron, Roy
1881	1966	Campbell, Donald F.
1731	1810	Cavendish, Henry
1905	1967	Cockcroft, John
1832	1919	Crookes, William
1875	1968	Dale, Henry H.
1766	1844	Dalton, John
1809	1882	Darwin, Charles
1791	1867	Faraday, Michael
1881	1955	Fleming, Alexander
1849	1945	Fleming, Ambrose
1898	1968	Florey, Howard W.
1892	1964	Haldane, J. B. S.
1578	1657	Harvey, William
1792	1871	Herschel, John
1738	1822	Herschel, William
1897	1967	Hinshelwood, Cyril
1861	1947	Hopkins, Frederick
1749	1823	Jenner, Edward
1815	1898	Jenner, William
1827	1912	Lister, Jos.
1831	1879	Maxwell, James Clerk
1642	1727	Newton, Isaac
1903	1969	Powell, Cecil F.
1733	1804	Priestley, Joseph
1857	1932	Ross, Ronald
1871	1937	Rutherford, Ernest
1624	1689	Sydenham, Thomas
1824	1907	Thomson, Wm. (Kelvin)
1823	1913	Wallace, Alf. Russell
1892	1973	Watson-Watt, Robert
1736	1819	Watt, Jemes E.
1802	1875	Wheatstone, Chas.

British Religious Leaders

Born	Died	Name
1117	1170	Becket, Thomas A.
1685	1753	Berkeley, George
1829	1912	Booth, William B.
1566	1644	Brewster, William
1489	1556	Cranmer, Thos.
1624	1691	Fox, George
1554	1600	Hooker, Richard
1860	1954	Inge, William Ralph
1874	1966	Johnson, Hewlett
1505	1572	Knox, John
1491	1555	Latimer, Hugh
1813	1873	Livingston, David
1808	1892	Manning, Henry E.
1801	1890	Newman, John H.
1613	1667	Taylor, Jeremy
1484	1536	Tyndale, William
1703	1791	Wesley, John
1714	1770	Whitefield, Geo.
1802	1865	Wiseman, Nicholas
1475	1530	Wolsey, Thomas
1324	1384	Wycliffe, John

French
French Scientists, Physicians

Born	Died	Name
1775	1836	Ampere, Andre-Marie
1788	1878	Becquerel, A. C.
1852	1908	Becquerel, H. A.
1827	1907	Berthelot, Marcelin
1813	1878	Bernard Claude
1872	1936	Bleriot, Louis
1825	1893	Charcot, Jean M.
1746	1823	Charles, Jacques
1786	1889	Chevreul, Michel
1867	1934	Curie, Marie
1859	1906	Curie, Pierre
1890	1967	Danjon, Andre
1678	1761	Fauchard, Pierre
1842	1925	Flammarion, Camille
1897	1956	Joliot-Curie, Irene
1778	1850	Gay-Lussac, Joseph
1900	1958	Joliot-Curie, Frederic
1781	1826	Laennec, Rene
1736	1813	Lagrange, Joseph
1744	1829	Lamarck, Jean B.
1749	1827	Laplace, Pierre S.
1743	1794	Lavoisier, Antoine
1822	1900	Lenoir, Etienne
1811	1877	LeVerrier, Urbain
1862	1954	Lumiere, Auguste
1864	1948	Lumiere, Louis
1852	1907	Moissan, Henri
1807	1873	Nelaton, Auguste
1863	1933	Painleve, Paul
1647	1714	Papin, Denis
1510	1590	Pare, Ambroise
1822	1895	Pasteur, Louis
1854	1912	Poincare, Henri
1850	1935	Richet, Charles
1875	1965	Schweitzer, Albert

French Military Leaders and Explorers

Born	Died	Name
1769	1821	Bonaparte, Napoleon
1753	1823	Carnot, Lazare
1877	1969	Catroux, Georges
1519	1572	Coligny, Gasp. de
1621	1686	Conde, Prince de
1881	1942	Darlan, Jean F.
1722	1788	DeGrasse, Francois
1739	1823	Dumouriez, Chas. F.
1851	1929	Foch, Ferdinand
1849	1916	Gallieni, Jos. S.
1879	1949	Giraud, Henri H.
1852	1931	Joffre, Jos.
1753	1800	Kleber, Jean-Bapt.
1757	1834	La Fayette, Marquis de
1902	1947	Leclerc, Jacques P.
1854	1934	Lyautey, Louis H.
1756	1817	Massena, Andre
1712	1759	Montcalm, Louis de
1763	1813	Moreau, Jean V.
1767	1815	Murat, Goachim
1769	1815	Ney, Michel
1856	1951	Petain, Henri Philippe
1725	1807	Rochambeau, Jean-Bapt.
1579	1638	Rohan, Henri
1696	1750	Saxe, Maurice de
1769	1851	Soult, Nicolas J.
1611	1675	Turenne, Vicomte de

Explorers

Born	Died	Name
1658	1730	Cadillac, Antoine
1491	1557	Cartier, Jacques
1567	1635	Champlain, Sam'l de
1867	1936	Charcot, Jean B.
1868	1969	David-Neel, Alexandra
1640	1701	Hennepin, Louis
1645	1700	Jolliet, Louis
1643	1687	LaSalle, Robt. de
1637	1675	Marquette, Jacques

French Authors, Dramatists, Historians, Religionists

Born	Died	Name
1079	1142	Abelard, Pierre
1717	1783	Alembert, Jean d'
1885	1969	Allain, Marcel
1880	1918	Apollinaire, Guillaume
1820	1889	Augier, (Emile)
1902	1967	Ayme, Marcel
1799	1850	Balzac, Honore de
1823	1891	Banville, Theodore de
1873	1935	Barbusse, Henri
1862	1923	Barres, Maurice
1821	1867	Baudelaire, Charles
1732	1799	Beaumarchais, Pierre
1837	1899	Becque, Henry
1780	1857	Beranger, Pierre
1859	1941	Bergson, Henri
1888	1948	Bernanos, Georges
1866	1947	Bernard, Tristan
1876	1953	Bernstein, Henri
1876	1967	Birot, Pierre A.
1636	1711	Boileau, Nicolas
1627	1704	Bossuet, Bernard B.
1852	1935	Bourget, Paul
1858	1932	Brieux, Eugene
1707	1788	Buffon, Georges
1509	1564	Calvin, John
1913	1960	Camus, Albert
1541	1603	Charron, Pierre
1768	1848	Chateaubriand, Francois
1762	1794	Chenier, Andre
1895	1969	Chevallier, Gabriel
1889	1963	Cocteau, Jean
1873	1954	Colette, Sidonie
1445	1509	Comines, Philippe de
1798	1857	Comte, Auguste
1743	1794	Condorcet, Marquis de
1767	1830	Constant, Benjamin
1842	1908	Coppee, Francois
1845	1875	Corbiere, Tristan
1606	1684	Corneille, Pierre
1854	1928	Curel, Francois de
1840	1897	Daudet, Alphonse
1596	1650	Descartes, Rene
1902	1969	De Vilmorin, Louise
1713	1784	Diderot, Denis
1881	1958	Du Gard, Roger M.
1802	1870	Dumas, Alexandre
1824	1895	Dumas, Alexandre fils
1926	1967	Fall, Bernard B.
1651	1715	Fenelon, Francois de
1821	1880	Flaubert, Gustave
1886	1914	Fournier, Alain
1844	1924	France, Anatole
1333	1400	Froissart, Jean
1811	1872	Gautier, Theophile
1869	1951	Gide, Andre
1882	1944	Giraudoux, Jean
1816	1882	Gobineau, Comte de
1822	1896	Goncourt, Edmond de
1830	1870	Goncourt, Jules de
1787	1874	Guizot, Francois
1842	1905	Heredia, Jose-Maria de
1857	1915	Hervieu, Paul
1802	1885	Hugo, Victor
1848	1907	Huysmans, Joris-Karl
1876	1944	Jacob, Max
1868	1938	Jammes, Francis
1412	1431	Joan of Arc
1815	1888	Labiche, Eugene
1645	1696	La Bruyere, Jean de
1621	1695	La Fontaine, Jean de
1860	1887	Laforgue, Jules
1790	1869	Lamartine, Alphonse de
1846	1870	Lautreamont, Comte de
1818	1894	Leconte de Lisle
1853	1914	Lemaitre, Jules
1668	1747	Lesage, Alain-Rene
1850	1923	Loti, Pierre (J. Viaud)
1889	1973	Marcel, Gabriel
1842	1898	Mallarme, Stephane
1882	1973	Maritain, Jacques
1688	1763	Marivaux, Pierre

Born	Died	Name	Born	Died	Name	Born	Died	Name
1850	1893	Maupassant, Guy de	1823	1892	Renan, Ernest	1875	1959	Siegfried, Andre
1885	1967	Maurois, Andre	1854	1891	Rimbaud, Arthur	1766	1817	Stael, (Mme. de)
1803	1870	Merimee, Prosper	1866	1944	Rolland, Romain	1783	1842	Stendhal, (Beyle)
1798	1874	Michelet, Jules	1524	1585	Ronsard, Pierre de	1839	1907	Sully-Prudhomme, Rene
1622	1673	Moliere, Jean-Baptiste	1868	1918	Rostand, Edmond	1828	1893	Taine, Hippolyte
1533	1592	Montaigne, Michel de	1712	1778	Rousseau, Jean-Jacques	1795	1856	Thierry, Augustin
1689	1755	Montesquieu, Charles de	1610	1703	Saint-Evremond, de	1805	1859	Tocqueville, A. C. de
1810	1857	Musset, Alfred de	1900	1944	Saint-Exupery, Ant, de	1871	1945	Valery, Paul
1394	1465	Orleans, Charles d'	1675	1755	Saint-Simon, Duc de	1844	1896	Verlaine, Paul
1623	1662	Pascal, Blaise	1804	1869	Sainte-Beuve, Charles A.	1828	1905	Verne, Jules
1873	1914	Peguy, Charles	1567	1622	Sales (Saint Francois de)	1797	1863	Vigny, Alfred de
1697	1763	Prevost (L'Abbe)	1804	1876	Sand, George (Lucile Dupin)	1838	1889	Villiers de l'Isle-Adam
1871	1922	Proust, Marcel				1431	1484	Villon, Francois
1495	1553	Rabelais, Francois	1831	1908	Sardou, Victorien	1694	1778	Voltaire, (Arouet)
1639	1699	Racine, Jean	1791	1861	Scribe, Eugene	1840	1902	Zola, Emile
1864	1936	Regnier, Henri de	1626	1696	Sevigne, (Mme. de)			

French Painters and Sculptors

Born	Died	Name	Born	Died	Name	Born	Died	Name
1834	1904	Bartholdi, Frederic	1880	1954	Derain, Andre	1884	1920	Modigliani, Amadeo
1848	1884	Bastien-Lepage, Jules	1807	1876	Diaz de la Pana, N. V.	1840	1926	Monet, Claude
1822	1899	Bonheur, Rosa	1877	1953	Dufy, Raoul	1824	1898	Moreau, Gustave
1867	1947	Bonnard, Pierre	1811	1889	Dupre, Jules	1830	1903	Pissarro, Camille
1703	1770	Boucher, Francois	1732	1806	Fragonard, Jean	1594	1665	Poussin, Nicolas
1825	1905	Bouguereau, W.	1820	1876	Fromentin, Eugene	1758	1823	Prudhon, Pierre
1876	1957	Brancusi, Constantin	1848	1903	Gauguin, Paul	1824	1898	Puvis de Chavanne
1882	1963	Braque, Georges	1770	1837	Gerard, Francois	1840	1916	Redon, Odilon
1851	1933	Carrier-Belleuse, P.	1791	1824	Gericault, J. L. A. T.	1841	1919	Renoir, Pierre
1839	1906	Cezanne, Paul	1628	1715	Girardon, Fr.	1840	1917	Rodin, Auguste
1699	1779	Chardin, Jean-Bapt.	1725	1805	Greuze, J. B.	1871	1958	Rouault, Georges
1600	1682	Claude Lorrain	1741	1828	Houdon, J. A.	1812	1867	Rousseau, P. E. T.
1796	1875	Corot, J. B. C.	1780	1867	Ingres, J. A. D.	1859	1891	Seurat, Georges
1819	1877	Courbet, Gustave	1887	1965	Le Corbusier	1863	1935	Signac, Paul
1817	1878	Daubigny, C. F.	1891	1973	Lipchitz, Jacques	1839	1899	Sisley, Alfred
1808	1879	Daumier, Honore	1600	1682	Lorrain, Claude	1900	1955	Tanguy, Yves
1748	1825	David, Louis J.	1861	1944	Maillol, Aristide	1864	1901	Toulouse-Lautrec
1783	1856	David d'Angers, P. J.	1832	1883	Manet, Edouard	1883	1955	Utrillo, Maurice
1834	1917	Degas, H. G. E.	1869	1954	Matisse, Henri	1876	1958	Vlaminck, Maurice
1799	1863	Delacroix, Eugene	1815	1891	Meissonier, J. L. E.	1868	1940	Vuillard, Edouard
1797	1856	Delaroche, Paul	1815	1875	Millet, J. F.	1684	1721	Watteau, Antoine

French Political Leaders

Born	Died	Name	Born	Died	Name	Born	Died	Name
1884	1966	Auriol, Vincent	1620	1698	Frontenac, Louis de	1860	1934	Poincare, Raymond
1872	1950	Blum, Leon	1838	1882	Gambetta, Leon	1911	1974	Pompidou, Georges
1862	1932	Briand, Aristide	1872	1957	Herriot, Edouard	1884	1970	Queuille, Henri
1841	1929	Clemenceau, Georges	1883	1945	Laval, Pierre	1878	1966	Reynaud, Paul
1619	1683	Colbert, Jean-Bapt.	1871	1950	Lebrun, Albert	1585	1642	Richelieu, Cardinal de
1884	1970	Daladier, Edouard	1744	1793	Marat, Jean-Paul	1758	1794	Robespierre, Max.
1759	1794	Danton, Georges	1602	1661	Mazarin, Jules	1208	1265	Simon de Montfort
1890	1970	DeGaulle, Charles	1749	1791	Mirabeau, Honore	1754	1838	Talleyrand, Chas. de
1760	1794	Desmoulins, Camille						

Germans

German Artists: Painters, Sculptors, Architects

Born	Died	Name	Born	Died	Name	Born	Died	Name
1480	1538	Altdorfer, Albrecht	1829	1880	Feuerbach, Anselm	1880	1916	Marc, Franz
1476	1545	Baldung, Hans	1774	1840	Friedrich, Caspar	1837	1887	Marees, Hans v.
1870	1938	Barlach, Ernst	1480	1528	Grunewald, Mathias	1815	1905	Menzel, Adolf v.
1884	1950	Beckmann, Max	1847	1921	Hildebrand, Adolf v.	1803	1884	Richter, Ludwig
1726	1801	Chodowiecki, Dan'l	1460	1524	Holbein, Hans (Sr.)	1764	1850	Schadow, Johann
1858	1925	Corinth, Lovis	1497	1543	Holbein, Hans (Jr.)	1781	1841	Schinkel, Karl
1783	1867	Cornelius, Peter	1877	1947	Kolbe, Georg	1839	1924	Thoma, Hans
1472	1553	Cranach, Lucas	1867	1945	Kollwitz, Kaethe	1455	1529	Vischer, Peter
1471	1528	Durer, Albrecht	1847	1935	Liebermann, Max			

German Engineers, Naturalists, Scientists, Industrialists

Born	Died	Name	Born	Died	Name	Born	Died	Name
1840	1905	Abbe, Ernst	1882	1964	Franck, James	1848	1896	Lilienthal, Otto
1902	1958	Adler, Kurt	1400	1468	Gutenberg, Johannes	1734	1815	Mesmer, Franz
1193	1280	Albertus, Magnus	1834	1919	Haeckel, Ernst	1899	1968	Nordhoff, Heinrich
1844	1929	Benz, Carl	1879	1968	Hahn, Otto	1787	1854	Ohm, Geo. S.
1882	1970	Born, Max	1755	1843	Hahnemann, Samuel	1853	1932	Ostwald, Wilhelm
1874	1940	Bosch, Karl	1821	1894	Helmholz, Hermann v.	1858	1947	Planck, Max
1811	1899	Bunsen, Robert	1857	1894	Hertz, Heinrich	1632	1694	Pufendorf, Samuel
1834	1900	Daimler, Gottlieb	1769	1859	Humboldt, Alex. v.	1845	1923	Roentgen, Wilhelm
1858	1913	Diesel, Rudolf	1859	1935	Junkers, Hugo	1822	1890	Schliemann, Heinrich
1895	1964	Domagk, Gerhard	1571	1630	Kepler, Johannes	1816	1892	Siemens, Ernst Werner v.
1884	1969	Dornier, Claude	1843	1910	Koch, Robert	1842	1926	Thyssen, Aug.
1861	1935	Duisberg, Carl	1812	1887	Krupp, Alfred	1821	1902	Virchow, Rudolf
1868	1954	Eckener, Hugo	1907	1967	Krupp, Alfried	1866	1925	Wassermann, Aug. v.
1854	1915	Ehrlich, Paul	1900	1967	Kuhn, Richard	1838	1917	Zeppelin, Ferd. v.
1686	1736	Fahrenheit, Gabriel	1646	1716	Leibnitz, Gottfried v.	1883	1970	Warburg, Otto
1852	1919	Fischer, Emil	1803	1873	Liebig, Justus v.			

German Political and Military Leaders; Economists

Born	Died	Name	Born	Died	Name	Born	Died	Name
1876	1967	Adenauer, Konrad	1815	1898	Bismarck, Otto v.	1885	1970	Bruning, Heinrich
1856	1921	Bethmann-Hollweg, T. v.	1742	1819	Bluecher, Gebhart v.	1849	1929	Buelow, Bernard v.

Born	Died	Name	Born	Died	Name	Born	Died	Name
1780	1831	Clausewitz, Karl v.	1886	1966	Luckner, Felix v.	1867	1922	Rathenau, Walter
1875	1921	Erzberger, Matthias	1865	1937	Ludendorff, Erich	1891	1944	Rommel, Erwin
1760	1831	Gneisenau, August	1880	1919	Luxemburg, Rosa	1876	1953	Rundstedt, Karl v.
1893	1946	Goering, Hermann	1849	1945	Machensen, August v.	1877	1970	Schacht, Hjalmar
1847	1934	Hindenburg, Paul v.	1818	1883	Marx, Karl	1865	1939	Scheidemann, Philipp
1863	1932	Hipper, Franz v.	1800	1891	Moltke, Helmuth von	1833	1913	Schlieffen, Alfred v.
1889	1945	Hitler, Adolf	1848	1916	Moltke, Helmuth von	1878	1929	Stresemann, Gustav
1887	1960	Kesselring, Albert	1879	1969	Papen, Franz v.	1849	1930	Tirpitz, Alf. v.
1871	1919	Liebknecht, Karl	1876	1960	Raeder, Erich	1893	1973	Ulbricht, Walter

German Authors, Dramatists, Essayists, Religionists

Born	Died	Name	Born	Died	Name	Born	Died	Name
1769	1860	Arndt, Ernest Moritz	1813	1863	Hebbel, Friedrich	1796	1835	Platen, August v.
1886	1956	Benn, Gottfried	1770	1831	Hegel, Georg W. F.	1795	1886	Ranke, Leopold, v.
1898	1956	Brecht, Bertolt	1797	1856	Heine, Heinrich	1810	1874	Reuter, Fritz
1778	1842	Brentano, Clemens	1744	1803	Herder, Johann v.	1763	1825	Richter, (Jean Paul)
1491	1551	Bucer, Martin	1877	1962	Hesse, Hermann	1875	1926	Rilke, Rainer Maria
1740	1815	Claudius, Matthias	1878	1945	Kaiser, Georg	1899	1966	Ropke, Wilhelm
1863	1920	Dehmel, Richard	1724	1804	Kant, Immanuel	1788	1866	Rueckert, Friedrich
1788	1857	Eichendorff, Josef v.	1896	1966	Kasack, Hermann	1494	1576	Sachs, Hans
1820	1895	Engels, Friedrich	1777	1811	Kleist, Heinrich v.	1775	1854	Schelling, Friedrich v.
1886	1933	Ernst, Paul	1724	1803	Klopstock, Friedr	1759	1805	Schiller, Friedrich
1170	1220	Eschenbach, Wolfram v.	1875	1967	Kolb, Annette	1767	1845	Schlegel, Aug. W.
1884	1958	Feuchtwanger, Lion	1646	1716	Leibnitz, Gottfried	1772	1829	Schlegel, Friedrich v.
1762	1814	Fichte, Johann G.	1729	1781	Lessing, Gotthold	1768	1834	Schleiermacher, Friedrich
1869	1966	Foerster, Friedrich	1844	1909	Liliencron, Detlev v.	1788	1860	Schopenhauer, Arthur
1819	1898	Fontane, Theodor	1881	1948	Ludwig, Emil	1817	1888	Storm, Theodor
1816	1895	Freytag, Gustav	1483	1546	Luther, Martin	1857	1928	Sudermann, Hermann
1868	1933	George, Stefan	1871	1950	Mann, Heinrich	1893	1939	Toller, Ernst
1749	1832	Goethe, Johann W. v.	1875	1955	Mann, Thomas	1834	1896	Treitschke, Heinrich v.
1785	1863	Grimm, Jakob	1804	1875	Moerike, Eduard	1787	1862	Uhland, Ludwig
1786	1859	Grimm, Wilhelm	1817	1903	Mommsen, Theodor	1873	1934	Wassermann, Jakob
1890	1941	Hasenclever, Walter	1844	1900	Nietzsche, Friedrich	1733	1813	Wieland, Chris. M.
1862	1946	Hauptmann, Gerhart						

Russians

Authors—Poets

Born	Died	Name
1888	1966	Akhmatova, Anna A.
1791	1859	Aksakov, Sergei
1878	1927	Artsibashev, Mikhail
1894	1941	Babel, Issac
1811	1948	Belinsky, Vissarion
1880	1921	Blok, Aleksandr
1891	1940	Bulgakov, Mikhail
1870	1953	Bunin, Ivan
1860	1904	Chekhov, Anton
1821	1881	Dostoyevsky, Fyodor
1891	1967	Ehrenburg, Ilya G.
1809	1852	Gogol, Nicholas V.
1812	1891	Goncharov, Ivan A.
1868	1936	Gorky, Maxim
1886	1921	Gumilev, Nikolai
1812	1870	Herzen, Aleksandr
1853	1921	Korolenko, Vladimir
1768	1844	Krylov, Ivan
1870	1938	Kuprin, Aleksandr
1814	1841	Lermontov, Mikhail
1831	1895	Leskov, Nikolai
1891	1938	Mandelstam, Osip
1893	1930	Mayakovsky, Vladimir
1821	1877	Nekrasov, Nikolai
1823	1886	Ostrovsky, Aleksandr
1890	1960	Pasternak, Boris
1799	1837	Pushkin, Aleksandr
1856	1919	Rozanov, Vasili
1820	1879	Soloviev, Sergei
1883	1945	Tolstoy, Alexei

Born	Died	Name
1828	1910	Tolstoy, Lev
1892	1941	Tsvetaeva, Marina
1818	1883	Turgenev, Ivan
1895	1925	Yesenin, Sergei

Artists

Born	Died	Name
1866	1924	Bakst, Leon S.
1866	1944	Kandinsky, Vasili
1783	1836	Kiprensky, Orest
1878	1927	Kostodiev, Boris
1861	1900	Levitan, Isaak
1844	1918	Repin, Ilya
1865	1911	Serov, Valentin
1842	1904	Vereshchagin, Vasili
1865	1918	Vrubel, Mikhail
1890	1967	Zadkine, Ossip

Political Leaders

Born	Died	Name
1899	1953	Beria, Lavrenti
1814	1876	Bakunin, Mikhail
1888	1938	Bukharin, Nikolai
1875	1946	Kalinin, Mikhail
1883	1936	Kamenev, Lev
1881	1970	Kerensky, Aleksandr
1842	1921	Kropotkin, Pyotr
1870	1924	Lenin, Vladimir
1877	1952	Litvinov, Maxim
1857	1918	Plekhanov, Georgi
1739	1791	Potemkin, Grigori
1772	1839	Speransky, Mikhail
1879	1953	Stalin, Josef

Born	Died	Name
1863	1911	Stolypin, Pyotr
1879	1940	Trotsky, Leon
1849	1915	Witte, Sergei
1883	1936	Zinoviev, Grigori

Military Leaders

Born	Died	Name
1883	1973	Budenny, Semyon
1872	1947	Denikin, Anton
1874	1920	Kolchak, Aleksandr
1897	1973	Konev, Ivan
1870	1918	Kornilov, Lavr
1745	1813	Kutnzov, Mikhail
1859	1914	Samsonov, Aleksandr
1729	1800	Suvorov, Aleksandr
1895	1970	Timoshenko, Semyon
1881	1969	Voroshilov, Klimenti Y.

Scientists

Born	Died	Name
1877	1968	Arbuzov, Aleksandr
1898	1967	Balandin, Aleksei
1857	1927	Bekhterev, Vladimir
1908	1968	Landau, Lev D.
1711	1765	Lomonosov, Mikhail
1909	1967	Maltsev, Anatoli
1834	1907	Mendeleyev, Dmitri
1845	1916	Metchnikov, Elie
1905	1970	Mikoyan, Artem I.
1849	1936	Pavlov, Ivan
1859	1905	Popov, Aleksandr
1907	1966	Sisakian, Norayr M.
1891	1969	Stechkin, Boris S.

Additional Foreign Personalities of the Past

S. Y. Agnon, Israeli novelist, 1888-1970.
Emilio Aguinaldo, Filipino revolutionary, 1869-1964.
Roald Amundsen, Norwegian explorer, 1872-1928.
Hans Christian Andersen, Danish writer, 1805-1875.
Julius Andrassy, Hungarian statesman, 1823-1890.
Pedro Aramburu, Argentine statesman, 1903-1970.
Sholem Asch, Polish-born Yiddish writer, 1880-1957.
Kemal Ataturk, Turkish statesman, 1881-1938.

Vasco Nunez de Balboa, Spanish explorer, 1475-1519.
Karl Barth, Swiss theologian, 1889-1966.
Brendan Behan, Irish playwright, 1923-1964.

Bjarni Benediktson, Icelandic statesman, 1908-1970.
Eduard Benes, Czech. statesman, 1884-1948.
David Ben-Gurion, first Israeli premier, 1886-1973.
Vitus J. Bering, Danish explorer, 1681-1741.
Folke Bernadotte, Swedish statesman, 1895-1948.
Vicente Blasco-Ibanez, Spanish novelist, 1867-1928.
Arnold Boecklin, Swiss painter, 1827-1901.
Niels Bohr, Danish physicist, 1885-1962.
Simon Bolivar, South American revolutionary, 1783-1830.
Jose Bonifacio, Brazilian statesman, 1763-1838.
Louis Botha, South African statesman, 1862-1919.

Emil Brunner, Swiss theologian, 1889-1966.
Martin Buber, Austrian-born Jewish philosopher, 1878-1965.

Plutarco Calles, Mexican statesman, 1877-1945.
Constantine Canaris, Greek statesman, 1790-1877.
Karel Capek, Czech. writer, 1890-1938.
Lazaro Cardenas, Mexican statesman, 1895-1970.
Venustiano Carranza, Mexican political leader, 1859-1920.
Roger Casement, Irish revolutionary, 1864-1916.
Humberto Castelo Branco, Brazilian political leader, 1900-1967.
Miguel de Cervantes Saavedra, Spanish novelist, 1547-1616.
Henri Christophe, Haitian revolutionary, 1767-1820.
Nicholas Copernicus, Polish astronomer, 1473-1543.
Hernando Cortez, Spanish conqueror of Mexico, 1485-1547.
Marie Sklodowska Curie, Polish chemist, 1867-1934.

Hernando De Soto, Spanish explorer, 1500-1543.
Jean J. Dessalines, Haitian emperor, 1758-1806.
Porfirio Diaz, Mexican statesman, 1830-1915.
Ngo Dinh Diem, South Vietnamese president, 1901-1963.
Isak Dinesen, Danish author, 1885-1962.
Engelbert Dollfuss, Austrian statesman, 1892-1934.
Christian Doppler, Austrian physicist, 1803-1853.

Robert Emmet, Irish patriot, 1778-1803.
Enver Pasha, Turkish political leader, 1881-1922.
Erasmus, Desiderius, Dutch author, 1466-1536.
Levi Eshkol, Israeli statesman, 1895-1969.

Manuel de Falla, Spanish composer, 1876-1946.
Ragnar Frisch, Norwegian economist, 1895-1973.

Vasco da Gama, Portuguese explorer, 1469-1524.
Mohandas K. Gandhi, Indian political leader, 1869-1948.
Alberto Giacometti, Swiss sculptor, 1901-1966.
Vincent van Gogh, Dutch painter, 1853-1890.
Francisco Goya y Lucientes, Spanish painter, 1746-1828.
El Greco, Greek painter in Spain, 1541-1614.
Lady Augusta Gregory, Irish dramatist, 1859-1932.
Edvard Grieg, Norwegian composer, 1843-1907.

Franz Hals, Dutch painter, 1584-1666.
Dag Hammarskjold, Swedish statesman, 1905-1961.
Theodor Herzi, Hungarian founder of modern Zionism, 1860-1904.
Ho Chi Minh, North Vietnamese president, 1890-1969.
Yukio Mishima, Japanese author, 1925-1970.
Andreas Hofer, Austrian patriot, 1767-1810.
Nicholas Horthy, Hungarian statesman, 1868-1957.
Mikhailo Hrushevsky, Ukrainian statesman, 1866-1934.
Jan Huss, Czech. religionist, 1369-1415.

Henrik Ibsen, Norwegian playwright, 1828-1906.

James Joyce, Irish author, 1882-1941.
Benito Juarez, Mexican statesman, 1806-1872.
Franz Kafka, Czech.-born Austrian author, 1883-1924.
Joseph Kasavubu, Congolese political leader, 1910-1969.
Abdul Karim Kassem, Iraqi politician, 1914-1963.
Yasunari Kawabata, Japanese novelist, 1899-1972.
Elizabeth (Sister) Kenny, Austrian nurse, 1886-1952.
Paul Klee, Swiss painter, 1879-1940.
Thaddeus Kosciusko, Polish general, 1746-1817.
Paul Kruger, South African statesman, 1825-1904.
Mikola Kulish, Ukrainian dramatist, 1892-1934.
Frank Kupka, Czech. painter, 1871-1957.

Selma Lagerlof, Swedish writer, 1858-1940.
Wanda Landowska, Polish harpsichordist, 1879-1959.
Francisco Largo Caballero, Spanish statesman, 1869-1946.
Trygve Lie, Norwegian statesman, 1896-1968.
Patrice E. Lumumba, Congolese political leader, 1925-1961.
Albert J. Luthuli, South African political leader, 1899-1967.

Francisco I. Madera, Mexican statesman, 1873-1913.
Maurice Maeterlinck, Belgian dramatist, 1862-1949.
Ferdinand Magellan, Portuguese explorer, 1480-1521.
Carl Gustav Mannerheim, Finnish statesman, 1867-1951.
Jose Marti, Cuban patriot, 1853-1895.
Jan Masaryk, Czech. statesman, 1886-1948.
Thomas Masaryk, Czech. statesman, 1850-1937.
Tom Mboya, Kenyan political leader, 1930-1969.
Lise Meitner, Austrian mathematician, 1878-1968.
Gregor J. Mendel, Austrian botanist, 1822-1884.
John Metaxas, Greek statesman, 1871-1941.

Clemens W. N. L. Metternich, Austrian statesman, 1773-1859.
Draja Mikhailovich, Yugoslav soldier, 1893-1946.
Carl Milles, Swedish sculptor, 1875-1955.
Vilhelm Moberg, Swedish novelist, 1898-1973.
Ferenc Molnar, Hungarian dramatist, 1878-1952.
George Moore, Irish novelist, 1852-1933.
Thomas Moore, Irish poet, 1779-1852.
Jose M. Morelos y Pavon, Mexican revolutionary leader, 1765-1815.
Mohammed Mossadegh, Iranian statesman, 1880-1967.
Bartolome E. Murillo, Spanish painter, 1618-1682.

Imre Nagy, Hungarian statesman, 1895-1958.
Fridtjof Nansen, Norwegian explorer, 1861-1930.
Juan Negrin, Spanish statesman, 1891-1956.
Jawaharlal Nehru, Indian statesman, 1889-1964.
Florence Nightingale, English nurse, 1820-1910.
Alfred Nobel, Swedish philantropist, 1833-1898.

Alvaro Obregon, Mexican statesman, 1880-1928.
Sean O'Casey, Irish dramatist, 1884-1964.
Daniel O'Connell, Irish political leader, 1775-1847.
Frank O'Connor, Irish writer, 1903-1966.
Thomas P. O'Connor, Irish journalist, 1848-1929.
Bernado O'Higgins, Chilean revolutionary, 1776-1842.

George Papandreou, Greek statesman, 1888-1968.
Charles Stewart Parnell, Irish nationalist, 1846-1891.
Pablo Picasso, Spanish artist & sculptor, 1881-1973.
Joseph Pilsudski, Polish statesman, 1867-1935.
Miguel Primo de Rivera, Spanish dictator, 1870-1930.
Casimir Pulaski, Polish statesman, 1748-1779.

Manuel L. Quezon, Philippine statesman, 1878-1944.

Adam Rapacki, Polish statesman, 1910-1970.
Fritz Reiner, Austrian orchestra conductor, 1888-1963.
Rembrandt van Rijn, Dutch painter, 1605-1669.
Syngman Rhee, South Korean president, 1875-1965.
Jose Rizal, Filipino patriot, 1861-1896.
Peter Paul Rubens, Flemish painter, 1577-1640.

Antonio de O. Salazar, Portuguese statesman, 1899-1970.
Jose de San Martin, South American revolutionary, 1778-1850.
Antonio L. de Santa Anna, Mexican general, 1794-1876.
Francisco de Paula Santander, Colombian politician, 1792-1840.
Arthur Schnitzler, Austrian dramatist, 1862-1931.
Dudley Senanayake, Ceylon statesman, 1911-1973.
David Alfaro Siqueiros, Mexican artist, 1898-1974.
Moshe Sharett, Israeli statesman, 1894-1965.
Richard B. Sheridan, Irish author, 1751-1816.
Taras Shevchenko, Ukrainian poet, 1814-1861.
Frans E. Sillanpaa, Finnist novelist, 1888-1964.
Jan C. Smuts, South African statesman, 1870-1950.
Paul Henri Spaak, Belgian statesman, 1899-1972.
Baruch Spinoza, Dutch philosopher, 1632-1677.
Antonio Stradivari, Italian violin-maker, 1644-1737.
August Strindberg, Swedish writer, 1849-1912.
Sun Yat-Sen, Chinese statesman, 1866-1925.
Otto Sverdrup, Norwegian explorer, 1854-1930.
Emanuel Swedenborg, Swedish scientist, scholar, 1688-1772.
John M. Synge, Irish author, 1871-1909.

Rabindranath Tagore, Indian poet, 1861-1941.
Vaino A. Tanner, Finnish statesman, 1881-1966.
Hideki Tojo, Japanese political & military leader, 1884-1948.
Rafael L. Trujillo Molina, Dominican dictator, 1891-1961.
Moise K. Tshombe, Congolese leader, 1919-1969.

Lesia Ukrainka, Ukrainian writer, 1871-1913.
Sigrid Undset, Norwegian author, 1882-1949.

Anthony Van Dyck, Flemish painter, 1599-1641.
Getulio D. Vargas, Brazilian statesman, 1883-1954.
Diego Velazquez, Spanish painter, 1599-1660.
Eleutherios Venizelos, Greek statesman, 1864-1936.
Jan Vermeer, Dutch painter, 1632-1675.
Hendrik F. Verwoerd, South African prime minister, 1901-1966.
Vladimir Vinnichenko, Ukrainian novelist, 1880-1951.
Artturi Virtanen, Finnish chemist, 1895-1973.

Franz Werfel, Austrian author, 1890-1945.
Chaim Weizmann, first Israeli president, 1874-1952.

William Butler Yeats, Irish poet, 1865-1939.

Emiliano Zapata, Mexican revolutionary, 1879-1919.
Stefan Zweig, Austrian author, 1881-1942.

Rulers of England and Great Britain

Name	England	Began	Died	Age	Rgd
	Saxons and Danes				
Egbert.............	King of Wessex, won allegiance of all English.................	827	839	—	12
Ethelwulf.........	Son, King of Wessex, Sussex, Kent, Essex.................	839	858	—	19
Ethelbald.........	Son of Ethelwulf, displaced father in Wessex.................	858	860	—	2
Ethelbert.........	2nd son of Ethelwulf, united Kent and Wessex.................	858	866	—	8
Ethelred..........	3rd son, King of Wessex, defeated Danes.................	866	871	—	5
Alfred............	The Great, 4th son, fought Danes, fortified London.................	871	901	52	30
Edward...........	The Elder, Alfred's son, united English, claimed Scotland.................	901	925	55	24
Athelstan.........	The Glorious, Edward's son, King of Mercia, Wessex.................	925	940	45	15
Edmund...........	3rd son of Edward, King of Wessex, Mercia.................	940	946	25	6
Edred............	4th son of Edward.................	946	955	32	9
Edwy.............	The Fair, eldest son of Edmund, King of Wessex.................	955	959	18	3
Edgar............	The Peaceful, son of Edmund, ruled all English.................	959	975	32	17
Edward...........	The Martyr, son of Edgar, murdered by stepmother.................	975	978	17	4
Etheired II........	The Unready, son of Edgar, married Emma of Normandy.................	978	1016	48	37
Edmund...........	Ironside, son of Ethelred II, King of London.................	1016	1016	27	0
Canute...........	The Dane, gave Wessex to Edmund, married Emma.................	1017	1035	40	18
Harold I..........	Harefoot, natural son of Canute.................	1035	1040	—	5
Hardicanute.......	Son of Canute by Emma; Danish King.................	1040	1042	24	2
Edward...........	The Confessor, son of Ethelred II (Canonized 1161).................	1042	1066	62	24
Harold II..........	Edward's brother-in-law, last Saxon King.................	1066	1066	44	0
	House of Normandy				
William I..........	The Conqueror, defeated Harold at Hastings.................	1066	1087	60	21
William II.........	Rufus, 3rd son of William I, killed by arrow.................	1087	1100	43	13
Henry I...........	Beauclerc, youngest son of William I.................	1100	1135	67	35
	House of Blois				
Stephen..........	Son of Adela, 4th dau. of William I, and Count of Blois.............	1135	1154	50	19
	House of Plantagenet				
Henry II..........	Son of Goeffrey Plantagenet (Angevin) by Matilda, Dau. of Henry I.	1154	1189	56	35
Richard I.........	Coeur de Lion, son of Henry II, crusader.................	1189	1199	42	10
John.............	Lackland, son of Henry II, signed Magna Carta, 1215.................	1199	1216	50	17
Henry III.........	Son of John, acceded at 9, under regency till 1227.................	1216	1272	65	56
Edward I.........	Longshanks, son of Henry III.................	1272	1307	68	35
Edward II.........	Son of Edward I, deposed by Parliament, 1327.................	1307	1327	43	20
Edward III........	Of Windsor, son of Edward II.................	1327	1377	65	50
Richard II........	Grandson of Edw. III, minor until 1389, deposed 1399.................	1377	1400	34	22
	House of Lancaster				
Henry IV.........	Son of John of Gaunt, Duke of Lancaster, son of Edw. III.............	1399	1413	47	13
Henry V..........	Son of Henry IV, victor of Agincourt.................	1413	1422	34	9
Henry VI.........	Son of Henry V deposed 1461, died in Tower.................	1422	1471	49	39
	House of York				
Edward IV........	Great-grandson of Edward III, son of Duke of York.............	1461	1483	41	22
Edward V........	Son of Edward IV, murdered in Tower of London.................	1483	1483	13	0
Richard III........	Crookback, bro. of Edward IV, fell at Bosworth Field.................	1483	1485	35	2
	House of Tudor				
Henry VII.........	Son of Edmund Tudor, Earl of Richmond, whose father had married the widow of Henry V; descended from Edward III through his mother, Margaret Beaufort via John of Gaunt. By marriage with dau. of Edward IV he united Lancaster and York.	1485	1509	53	24
Henry VIII........	Son of Henry VII. *See memorable dates*	1509	1547	56	38
Edward VI........	Son of Henry VIII, by Jane Seymour, his 3rd queen, Ruled under regents. Was forced to name Lady Jane Grey his successor. Council of State proclaimed her queen July 10, 1553. Mary Tudor won Council, was proclaimed queen July 19, 1553. Mary had Lady Jane Grey beheaded for treason, Feb., 1554.	1547	1553	16	6
Mary I...........	Daughter of Henry VIII, by Catharine of Aragon.................	1553	1558	43	5
Elizabeth.........	Daughter of Henry VIII, by Anne Boleyn. *Designated Elizabeth I in 1952.*	1558	1603	69	44
	Great Britain				
	House of Stuart				
James I..........	James VI of Scotland, son of Mary, Queen of Scots. *First to call himself King of Great Britain. This became official with the Act of Union, 1707.*	1603	1625	59	22
Charles I.........	Only surviving son of James I: beheaded Jan. 30, 1649.............	1625	1649	48	24
	Commonwealth, 1649-1660				
	Council of State, 1649: Protectorate, 1653				
The Crom-	Oliver Cromwell, Lord Protector.................	1653	1658	59	—
wells...........	Richard Cromwell, Lord Protector, resigned May 25, 1659...........	1658	1712	86	—
	House of Stuart (Restored)				
Charles II.........	Eldest son of Charles I, died without issue.................	1660	1685	55	25
James II..........	Second son of Charles I. Deposed 1688. Interregnum Dec. 11, 1688, to Feb. 13, 1689.	1685	1701	68	3
William III........	Son of William, Prince of Orange, by Mary, dau. of Charles I....... }		1702	51	13
and Mary II	Eldest daughter of James II and wife of William III................. }	1689	1694	33	6
Anne............	Second daughter of James.................	1702	1714	49	12
	House of Hanover				
George I..........	Son of Elector of Hanover, by Sophia, grand-dau. of James I.............	1714	1727	67	13
George II.........	Only son of George I, married Caroline of Brandenburg.............	1727	1760	77	33
George III........	Grandson of George II, married Charlotte of Mecklenburg.............	1760	1820	81	59
George IV........	Eldest son of George III, Prince Regent, from Feb., 1811.............	1820	1830	67	10
William IV........	Third son of George III, married Adelaide of Saxe-Meiningen.......	1830	1837	71	7

Victoria . . . . Dau. of Edward, 4th son of George III; married (1840) Prince Albert of Saxe-Coburg and Gotha, who became Prince Consort	1837	1901	81	63

House of Saxe-Coburg and Gotha

Edward VII . . . . Eldest son of Victoria, married Alexandria, Princess of Denmark	1901	1910	68	9

House of Windsor
Name Adopted July 17, 1917

George V . . . . Second son of Edward VII, married Princess Mary of Teck	1910	1936	70	25
Edward VIII . . . . Eldest son of George V; acceded Jan. 20, 1936, abdicated Dec. 11 . . .	1936	1972	77	1
George VI . . . . Second son of Geroge V; married Lady Elizabeth Bowes-Lyon	1936	1952	56	15
Elizabeth II . . . . Elder daughter of George VI, acceded Feb. 6, 1952.	1952	—	—	—

Rulers of France: Kings, Queens, Presidents

Caesar to Charlemagne

Julius Caesar subdued the Gauls, native tribes of Gaul (France) 57 to 52 B. C. The Romans ruled 500 years. The Franks, a Teutonic tribe, reached the Somme from the East C. 250 A. D. By the 5th Century the Merovingian Franks ousted the Romans. In 451 A. D., with the help of Visigoths, Burgundians and others, they defeated Attila and the Huns at Chalonssur-Marne.

Childeric I became leader of the Merovingians 458 A. D. His son Clovis I (Chlodwig, Ludwig, Louis) crowned 481, founded the dynasty. After defeating the Alemanni (Germans) 496, he was baptized a Christian and made Paris his capital. His line ruled until Childeric III was deposed, 742.

The West Merovingians were called Neustrians, the eastern Austrasians. Pepin of Herstal (687-714) major domus, or head of the palace, of Austrasia, took over Neustria as dux (leader) of the Franks. Pepin's son, Charles, called Martel (the Hammer) defeated the Saracens at Tours-Poitiers, 732; was succeeded by his son, Pepin the Short, 741, who deposed Childeric III and ruled as king until 768.

His son, Charlemagne, or Charles the Great, (742-814), became king of the Franks, 768, with his brother Carioman, who died 771. He ruled France, Germany, parts of Italy, Spain, Austria, enforced Christianity. Crowned Emperor of the Romans by Pope Leo III in St. Peter's, Rome, Dec. 25, 800 A. D. Succeeded by son. Louis, the Pious, 814. At death, 840, Louis left empire to sons, Lothair (Roman emperor); Pepin I (king of Aquitaine); Louis II (of Germany); Charles the Bald (France). They quarreled and by the peace of Verdun, 843, divided the empire.

A.D.   Name and Year of Accession

The Carolingians

840   Charles I, the Bald, Roman Emperor, 875
877   Louis II, the Stammerer, son
879   Louis III (died 882) and Carloman (bro.)
884   Charles II, the Fat; Roman Emperor, 881
888   Eudes (Odo) elected by nobles. Ceded land to
898   Charles III, the Simple, son of Louis II, defeated by
922   Robert, brother of Eudes, killed in war
923   Rodolph (Raoul) Duke of Burgundy
936   Louis IV, son of Charles III
954   Lothair, son, aged 13, defeated by Capet
986   Louis V. the Sluggard, left no heirs

The Capets

987   Hugh Capet, son of Hugh the Great
996   Robert (the Wise), his son
1031   Henry I, his son, last Norman
1060   Phillip I (the Fair), son, king at 14
1108   Louis VI (the Fat), son
1137   Louis VII (the Younger), son
1180   Phillip II (Augusts), son, crowned at Reims
1223   Louis VIII (the Lion), son
1226   Louis IX, son, crusader; Louis IX (1214-1270) reigned 44 years, arbitrated disputes with English King Henry III; led crusades, 1248 (captured in Egypt 1250) and 1270, when he died of plague in Tunis. Canonized 1297 as St. Louis.
1270   Philip III (the Hardy), son
1285   Philip IV (the Fair), son, king at 17
1314   Louis X (the Headstrong), son. His posthumous son, John I, lived only 7 days
1316   Phillip V (the Tall), brother of Louis X
1322   Charles IV (the Fair), brother of Louis X

House of Valois

1328   Phillip VI (of Valois), grandson of Phillip III
1350   John II (the Good), his son, retired to England
1364   Charles V (the Wise), son
1380   Charles VI (the Beloved), son
1422   Charles VII (the Victorious), son. In 1429 Joan of Arc (Jeanne d'Arc) promised Charles to oust the English, who occupied northern France. Joan won at Orleans and Patay and had Charles crowned at Reims July 17, 1429. Joan was captured May 24, 1430, and executed May 30, 1431, at Rouen for heresy. Charles ordered her rehabilitation, effected 1455. Agnes,

Sorel was Charles' mistress
1461   Louis XI (the Cruel), son, civil reformer
1483   Charles VIII (the Affable), son
1498   Louis XII, great grandson of Charles V
1515   Francis I, of Angouleme, nephew, son-in-law. Francis I (1494-1547) reigned 32 years, fought 4 big wars, was patron of the arts, aided Cellini, del Sarto, Leonardo da Vinci, Rabelais. Embellished Fontainebleau
1547   Henry II, son, killed at a joust in a tournament. He was the husband of Catherine de Medici (1519-1589) and the lover of Diane de Poitiers (1499-1566). Catherine was born in Florence. daughter of Lorenzo de Medici. By her marriage to Henry II she became the mother of Francis II, Charles IX, Henry III and Queen Margaret (Reine Margot) wife of Henry IV. She persuaded Charles IX to order the massacre of Huguenots on St. Bartholomew, Aug. 24, 1572, the day her daughter was married to Henry of Navarre.
1559   Francis II, son of Henry II. In 1548, Mary, Queen of Scots since infancy, was betrothed when 6 to Francis, aged 4. They were married 1558. Francis died 1560, aged 16; Mary ruled Scotland, abdicated 1567.
1560   Charles IX, brother of Francis II
1574   Henry III, brother, assassinated

House of Bourbon

1589   Henry IV, of Navarre, assassinated. Henry IV made enemies when he gave tolerance to Protestants by Edict of Nantes, 1598. He was grandson of Queen Margaret of Navarre, literary patron. He married Margaret of Valois, Catherine de Medici's daughter; was divorced: in 1600 married Marie de Medicis, Regent of France, 1610-17 for son, Louis XIII, and was exiled by Richelieu
1610   Louis XIII (the Just), son. Louis XIII (1610-1643) married Anne of Austria. His ministers were Cardinals Richelieu and Mazarin
1643   Louis XIV (The Grand Monarch), son. Louis XIV, was king 72 years. He exhausted a prosperous nation in wars for thrones and territory. By revoking the Edict of Nantes (1685) he caused the emigration of the Huguenots. He said: "I am the state." His mistresses were Louise de la Valliere, Madame de Montespan and Madame de Maintenon
1715   Louis XV, great grandson. Louis XV (1710-1774) married a Polish princess. Lost Canada to the English. His favorites, Mme. Pompadour and Mme. DBarry influenced policies. Noted for saying: Apres moi, le deluge. (After me, the deluge)
1774   Louis XVI, grandson; married Marie Antoinette, dau. of Empress Maria Therese of Austria. King and queen beheaded by Revolution, 1793. Their son, called Louis XVII, died in prison, never ruled.

First Republic

1792   National Convention of the French Revolution
1795   Directory, under Barras and others
1799   Consulate, Napoleon Bonaparte, First Consul. In 1802 elected Consul for life

First Empire

1804   Napoleon I, Emperor. Josephine (de Beauharnais) Empress, 1804-09; Marie Louise, Empress, 1810-1814. Her son, Francois (1811-1832) titular King of Rome, later Duke de Reichstadt and "Napoleon II," never ruled. Napoleon abdicated 1814, died 1821.

Bourbons Restored

1814   Louis XVIII king; brother of Louis XVI.
1824   Charles X, brother: reactionary, deposed by the July Revolution, 1830.

House of Orleans

1830   Louis Philippe, the Citizen King

Second Republic

1848   Louis Napoleon. President, nephew of Napoleon I.   He became:

Second Empire

1852   Napoleon III, Emperor. Eugenie (de Montijo) Empress. Lost

Lost Franco-Prussian war, deposed 1870. Son, Prince Imperial (1856-79), died in Zulu War. Eugenie died 1920.

Third Republic—Presidents

1871 Thiers, Louis Adolphe (1797-1877), historian
1873 MacMahon Marshal Patrice M. (1808-1893)
1879 Grevy, Paul J. (1807-1891), resigned
1887 Sadi-Carnot, M. (1837-1894), assassinated
1894 Casimir-Pernier, Jean P. P. (1847-1907), resigned
1895 Faure, Francois Felix (1841-1899)
1899 Loubet, Emile (1838-1929)
1906 Fallieres, Armand (1841-1931)
1913 Poincare, Raymond (1860-1934)
1920 Deschanel, Paul (1856-1922), resigned
1920 Millerand, Alexandre (1859-1943), resigned
1924 Doumergue, Gaston (1863-1937)

1931 Doumer, Paul (1857-1932), assassinated
1932 Lebrun, Albert (1871-1950), resigned 1940
Vichy govt. under German armistice: Henry Philippe Petain (1856-1951) Chief of State, 1940-1944.
Provisional govt. after liberation: Chas. de Gaulle (1890-1970) Oct., 1944-Jan. 21, 1946; Felix Gouin (1884-   ) Jan. 23, 1946; Georges Bidault (1899-   ) June 24, 1946.

Fourth Republic—Presidents

1947 Auriol, Vincent (1884-1966)
1954 Coty, Rene (1882-1962)

Fifth Republic—Presidents

1958 De Gaulle, Charles Andre M. J. (1890-1970)
1969 Pompidou, Georges J. R. (1911-1974)
1974 Giscard d'Estaing, Valery (1926-

Rulers of Middle Europe; Rise and Fall of Dynasties

Carolingian Dynasty

Charles the Great, or Charlemagne, ruled France, Italy and Middle Europe; established Ostmark (later Austria); crowned Roman emperor by pope in Rome, 800 A. D. Died 814.

Louis I (Ludwig) the Pious, son; crowned by Charlemagne 813, d. 840.

Louis the German, son, succeeded to East Francia (Germany) 843-876.

Charles the Fat, son, inherited East Francia and West Francia (France) 876, reunited empire, crowned emperor by pope, 881, deposed 887.

Arnulf, nephew, 887-899. Partition of empire.

Louis the Child, 900-911, last direct descendant of Charlemagne.

Conrad I, duke of Franconia, first elected German king, 911-918, founded House of Franconia.

Saxon Dynasty; First Reich

Henry I, the Fowler, duke of Saxony, 919-936.

Otto I, the Great, 936-973, son; crowned Holy Roman Emperor by pope; 962.

Otto II, 973-983, son; failed to oust Greeks and Arabs from Sicily.

Otto III, 983-1002, son. Crowned emperor at 16.

Henry II, duke of Bavaria, 1002-1024, great grandson of Henry the Fowler.

House of Franconia

Conrad II, 1024-1039, son-in-law of Otto I.

Henry III, 1039-1056, son; deposed 3 popes; annexed Burgundy.

Henry IV, 1056-1106, son; regency by his mother, Agnes of Poitou. Banned by Pope Gregory VII, he did penance at Canossa.

Henry V, 1106-1125, son; last of Salic House.

Lothair, duke of Saxony, 1125-1137. Crowned emperor in Rome, 1134.

House of Hohenstaufen

Conrad III, duke of Suabia, 1138-1152. In 2nd Crusade.

Frederick I, Barbarossa, 1152-1190; son of Conrad's brother; in 3rd Crusade.

Henry VI, 1190-1196, took Lower Italy from Normans. Son became king of Sicily.

Philipp of Suabia, 1198-1208, son of Frederick I.

Otto IV, of House of Welf, 1198-1215; deposed.

Frederick II, 1215-1250, son of Henry VI; king of Sicily; crowned king of Jerusalem; in 5th Crusade.

Conrad IV, 1250-1254, son, lost Lower Italy to Charles of Anjou.

Conradin, son, king of Jerusalem and Sicily, was beheaded. Interregnum, 1250-1273, rise of the Electors.

Transition

Rudolph of Hapsburg, 1273-1291, defeated King Ottocar II of Bohemia. Bequeathed duchy of Austria to eldest son, Albert.

Adolphus, count of Nassau, 1291-1298, killed in war with Albert of Austria.

Albert I, German king, 1298-1308.

Henry VII, of Luxemburg, 1308-1313, crowned emperor in Rome. Seized Bohemia, 1310.

Louis IV of Bavaria (Wittelsbach), 1314-1347. Also elected was Frederick of Austria, 1314-1330 (Hapsburg).

Charles IV, of Luxemburg, 1347-1378, grandson of Henry VII, German emperor and king of Bohemia, Lombardy, Burgundy; took Mark of Brandenburg.

Wenceslaus, 1378-1400, deposed.

Rupert, Duke of Palatine, 1400-1410.

Hungary

Stephen I, house of Arpad, 907-1038. Crowned king by Pope Silvester II, 1001 A. D., converted Magyars. After

several centuries of feuds Charles Robert of Anjou became Charles I, 1308-1342.

Louis I, the Great, son, 1342-1382, joint ruler of Poland with Casimir III, 1370. Defeated Turks.

Mary, daughter, 1385-1395, ruled with husband. Sigismund of Luxemburg, 1387-1437, also king of Bohemia. As bro. of Wenceslaus he succeeded Rupert as Holy Roman Emperor, 1410.

Albert II, 1438-1439, son-in-law of Sigismund; also Roman emperor. See under Hapsburg.

Ulaszlo I of Poland, died in battle, 1444.

Ladislaus V, child. John Hunyadi (Hunyadi Janos) guardian, fought Turks, Czechs; died 1456.

Matthias I (Corvinus) son of Hunyadi, 1458-1490. Shared rule of Bohemia, captured Vienna, 1485, annexed Austria, Styria, Carinthia.

Ulaszlo II (King of Bohemia) 1490-1516.

Louis II, son, aged 10. 1516-1526. Wars with Suleiman, Turk. In 1527 Hungary was split between Ferdinand I, Archduke of Austria, bro.-in-law of Louis II, and John Zapolya, of Transylvania. After Turkish invasion, 1547, Hungary was split between Ferdinand, Prince John Sigismund (Transylvania) and the Turks.

House of Hapsburg

Albert V of Austria, Hapsburg, crowned king of Hungary, Jan. 1438, Roman emperor, March, 1438, as Albert II; died 1439.

Frederick III, cousin, 1430-1493. Fought Turks.

Maximilian I, son, 1493-1519. Assumed title of Holy Roman emperor (German), 1493.

Charles V, grandson, 1519-1556. King of Spain with mother co-regent; crowned Roman emperor at Aix 1520. Confronted Luther at Worms; attempted church reform and religious conciliation. Abdicated 1556.

Ferdinand I, king of Bohemia, 1526, of Hungary, 1527; disputed German king, 1531. Crowned Roman emperor on abdication of Charles V, 1556.

Maximilian II, son, 1564-1576; Rudolph II, son, 1576-1612.

Matthias, brother, 1612-1619, king of Bohemia and Hungary.

Ferdinand II, of Styria, king of Bohemia, 1617, of Hungary, 1618, Roman emperor, 1619. Bohemian Protestants deposed him, elected Frederick V of Palatine, starting Thirty Years War.

Ferdinand III, son, king of Hungary, 1625, Bohemia, 1627, Roman emperor, 1637. Peace of Westphalia, 1648, ended war. Leopold I, 1658-1705; Joseph I, 1705-1711; Charles VI, 1711-1740.

Maria Theresa, daughter, 1740-1780, Archduchess of Austria, queen of Hungary; ousted pretender, Charles VII, crowned 1742; in 1745 obtained election of her husband Francis I as Roman emperor and co-regent (d. 1765). Fought Seven Years' War with Frederick II (the Great) of Prussia. Mother of Marie Antoinette, Queen of France.

Joseph II, son 1765-1790, Roman emperor; reformer; powers restricted by Empress Maria Theresa until her death, 1780. Leopold II, 1790-1792.

Francis II, 1792-1835. Fought Napoleon. Proclaimed first hereditary emperor of Austria, 1806. Forced to abdicate as Roman emperor, 1806, last use of title. Ferdinand I, son, 1835-1848, abdicated during revolution.

Austro-Hungarian Monarchy

Francis Joseph I, nephew, 1848-1916, emperor of Austria, king of Hungary. Dual monarchy of Austria-Hungary formed, 1867. After assassination of heir, Archduke Francis Ferdinand, June 28, 1914. Austrian diplomacy precipitated World War I.

Charles I, grandnephew, 1916-1918, last emperor of Austria and king of Hungary. Abdicated Nov. 11-13, 1918, died 1922.

Rulers of Prussia

Nucleus of Prussia was the Mark of Brandenburg. First margrave was Albert the Bear (Albrecht), 1134-1170. First Hohenzollern margrave was Frederick, burggrave of Nuremberg, 1415-1440.

Frederick William, 1640-1688, the Great Elector, Son, Frederick III, 1688-1713, was crowned king Frederick of Prussia, 1761.

Frederick II, the Great, 1740-1786, annexed Silesia part of Austria.

Frederick William II, nephew, 1786-1797.

Frederick William III, 1797-1840. Napoleonic wars. Queen Louise.

Frederick William IV, 1840-1861. Uprising of 1848 and first parliament and constitution.

Second and Third Reich

William I, 1861-1888, brother. Annexation of Schleswig and Hanover; Franco-Prussian war, 1870-71, proclamation of German Reich, Jan. 18, 1871, at Versailles; William, German emperor (Deutscher Kaiser), Bismarck, chancellor.

Frederick III, son, 1888.

William II, son 1888-1918. Led Germany in World War I, abdicated as German emperor and king of Prussia, Nov. 9, 1918. Died in exile in Netherlands June 4, 1941. Minor rulers of Bavaria, Saxony, Wurttemberg also abdicated.

Germany proclaimed a republic at Weimar, July 1, 1919. Presidents: Frederick Ebert, 1919-1925, Paul von Hindenburg-Beneckendorff, 1925, reelected 1932, d. Aug. 2, 1934. Adolf Hitler, chancellor, chosen successor as Leader-Chancellor (Fuehrer & Reichskanzler) of Third Reich. Annexed Austria, March, 1938. Precipitated World War II, 1939-1945. Committed suicide April 30, 1945.

Rulers of Scotland

The Romans gave the name of Caledonia to present-day Scotland and called the people Caledonians. The Scots, a Celtic race that spoke Gaelic, came from Ireland, then called Scotia.

Kenneth I (S. C. MacAlpin) was the first Scot to rule both Scots and Picts, 843 A. D.

Duncan I was the first general ruler, 1034. Macbeth seized the kingdom 1040, was slain by Duncan's son, Malcolm Canmore (Malcolm III). 1058.

Malcolm married Margaret, English princess who had fled from the Normans. Queen Margaret introduced English language and English monastic customs. She was canonized. Her son Edgar, 1097, moved the court to Edinburgh. His brothers Alexander I and David I succeeded. Malcolm IV, grandson of David I, 1153, was followed by his brother, William the Lion, 1165, whose son was Alexander II, 1214. The latter's son, Alexander III, defeated the Norse and regained the Hebrides. When he died, 1286, his granddaughter, Margaret, child of Eric of Norway and grandniece of Edward I of England, known as the Maid of Norway, was chosen ruler, but died on the way, 1290.

John Baliol, 1292-1296. (Interregnum, 10 years).

Robert Bruce (The Bruce), 1306-1329, victor at Bannockburn, 1314.

David II only son of Robert Bruce ruled 1329-1371.

Robert II, 1371-1390, grandson of Robert Bruce, son of Walter, the Steward of Scotland, was called The Steward, first of the so-called Stuart line.

Robert III, son of Robert II, 1390-1406.

James I, son of Robert III, 1406-1437.

James II, son of James I, 1437-1460.

James III, 1460-1488, eldest son of James II.

James IV, 1488-1513, eldest son of James III.

James V, 1513-1542, eldest son of James IV.

Mary, daughter, born 1542, became queen when 1 week old; was crowned 1543. Married, 1558, Francis, son of Henry II of France, who became king 1559, died 1560. Mary ruled Scots 1561 until abdication, 1567. She also married (2) Henry Stewart, Lord Darnley, and (3) James, Earl of Bothwell. Imprisoned by Elizabeth I; beheaded 1587.

James VI, 1567-1625, son of Mary and Lord Darnley, became King of England on death of Elizabeth in 1603. Although the thrones were thus united, the legislative union of Scotland and England was not effected until the act of Union, May 1, 1707.

Rulers of Denmark, Sweden, Norway

Denmark

Earliest rulers invaded Britain; King Canute, who ruled in London 1017-1035, was most famous. The Valdemars furnished kings until the 15th century. In 1282 the Danes won the first national assembly, Danehof, from King Erik.

Most redoubtable medieval character was Margaret, daughter of Valdemar IV, born 1353, married at 10 to King Haakon VI of Norway. In 1375 she had her first infant son Olaf made king of Denmark. After his death, 1387, she was regent of Denmark and Norway. In 1388 Sweden accepted her as sovereign. In 1389 she made her grand-newphew, Duke Erik of Pomerania, titular king of Denmark, Sweden and Norway, with herself as regent. In 1397 she effected the Union of Kalmar of the three kingdoms and had Erik crowned. In 1439 the three kingdoms deposed him and elected Christopher of Bavaria king (Christopher III). On his death, 1448, the union broke up.

Succeeding rulers were unable to enforce their claims as rulers of Sweden until 1520, when Christian II conquered Sweden. He was thrown out 1522, and in 1523 Gustavus Vasa united Sweden. Denmark continued to dominate Norway until the Napoleonic wars, when Frederick VI joined the Napoleonic cause after Britain had destroyed the Danish fleet (1807). In 1814 he was forced to cede Norway to Sweden and Helgoland to Britain, receiving Lauenburg. Successors: 1839—Christian VIII; 1848—Frederick VII; 1863-Christian IX; 1906—Frederick VIII; 1912—Christian X; 1947—Frederick IX; 1972—Queen Margrethe.

Sweden

Early kings ruled at Uppsala, but did not dominate the country. Sverker (1134-1156) united the Swedes and Goths. In 1435 Sweden obtained the Riksdag, or parliament. After the Union of Kalmar, 1379, the Danes either ruled or harried the country until Christian II of Denmark conquered it anew, 1520. This led to a rising under Gustavus Vasa, who ruled Sweden 1523-1560, and established an independent kingdom. Charles IX (1594-1611, crowned 1607), conquered Moscow. Gustavus II Adolphus (1611-1633) was called the Great. Later rulers, 1633—Christina; 1654—Charles X; 1660—Charles XI; 1697—Charles XII (invader of Russia and Poland, defeated at Poltava, June 28, 1709); 1718—His sister, Unrika Eleanora, elected queen; 1720—Her husband, Frederick I (of Hesse); 1751—Adolphus Frederick; 1771—Gustavus III; 1792—Gustavus IV; 1809—Charles XIII. (Union with Norway began, 1814). 1818—Charles XIV. He was Jean Bernadotte, Napoleon's Prince of Ponte Corvo, elected 1810 to succeed Charles XIII. He founded the present dynasty. 1844—Oscar I; 1859—Charles XV; 1872—Oscar II; 1907—Gustavus V; 1950—Gustav VI Adolf; 1973—Carl XVI Gustaf.

Norway

Overcoming many rivals, Harald Haarfager (872-930) conquered Norway, Orkneys and Shetlands. Olaf, great-grandson (995-1000) brought Christianity into Norway, Iceland, Greenland. In 1035 Magnus the Good also became king of Denmark. Haakon V (1299-1319) had married his daughter to Erik of Sweden. Their son, Magnus, became ruler of Norway and Sweden at 6. His son, Haakon VI, married Margaret of Denmark; their son Olaf became king of Norway and Denmark, followed by Margaret's regency and the Union of Kalmar, 1397.

In 1450 Norway became subservient to Denmark. Christian IV (1588-1648) founded Christiania, now Oslo. After Napoleonic wars, when Denmark ceded Norway to Sweden, a strong nationalist movement forced recognition of Norway as an independent kingdom united with Sweden under the Swedish kings, 1814-1905. In 1905 the union was dissolved and Prince Carl of Denmark became Haakon VII. He died Sept. 21, 1957, aged 85; succeeded by son, Olav V. b. July 2, 1903.

Rulers of the Netherlands and Belgium

The Netherlands (Holland)

William Frederick, Prince of Orange, led a revolt against French rule, 1813, and was crowned King of the Netherlands, 1815. Belgium seceded Oct. 4, 1830, after a revolt, and formed a separate government. The change was ratified by the two kingdoms by treaty Apr. 19, 1839.

(1840) William II; (1849) William III; (1890) Wilhelmina (daughter of William III and his second wife Princess

Emma of Waldeck); Wilhelmina abdicated Sept. 4, 1948, in favor of daughter Juliana, 39.

Belgium

A national congress elected Prince Leopold of Saxe-Coburg King; he took the throne July 21, 1831, as Leopold I. (1865) Leopold II; (1909) Albert I, nephew of Leopold II;

(1934) Leopold III, son of Albert; (1944) Prince Charles, Regent, Leopold returned, 1950, yielded powers to son Baudouin, Prince Royal, Aug. 6, 1950, abdicated July 16, 1951. Baudouin I took throne July 17, 1951.

For pollitical history prior to 1830 see articles on the Netherlands and Belgium.

Rulers of Modern Spain

From 8th to 11th centuries Spain was dominated by the Moors (Arabs and Berbers). The Christian reconquest established small competing kingdoms of the Asturias, Aragon, Castile, Catalonia, Leon, Navarre and Valencia. In 1474 Isabella (Isabel) B. 1451, became Queen of Castile & Leon. Her husband, Ferdinand, b. 1452, inherited Aragon 1474, with Catalonia, Valencia and the Balearic Islands, became Ferdinand V of Castile. By Isabella's request Pope Sixtus IV established the Inquisition, 1478. Last Moorish kingdom, Granada, fell 1492. Columbus opened New World of colonies, 1492. Isabella died 1504, succeeded by her daughter, Juana "the Mad," but Ferdinand ruled until his death 1516.

Charles I, b. 1500, son of Juana and grandson of Ferdinand and Isabella and of Maximilian I of Hapsburg; succeeded latter as Holy Roman Emperor, Charles V, 1520. Abdicated 1556. Philip II, son, 1556-1598, inherited only Spanish throne; conquered Portugal, fought Turks, persecuted non-Catholics, sent Armada vs. England. Was briefly married to Mary I of England, 1554-1558. Succession: Philip III, 1598-1621; Philip IV, 1621-1665; Charles II, 1665-1700, left Spain to Philip of Anjou, grandson of Louis XIV, who as Philip V, 1700-1746, founded Bourbon dynasty. Ferdinand IV, 1746-1759; Charles III, 1759-1788; Charles IV, 1788-1808, abdicated.

Napoleon now dominated politics and made his brother Joseph King of Spain but the Spanish ousted him finally in 1813. Ferdinand VII, 1814-1833, lost American colonies; succeeded by daughter Isabella II, aged 3, with wife Maria Christina of Naples regent until 1843. Isabella deposed by revolution 1868. Prince Amadeo of

Savoy, 1870-1873. First republic, 1873-1874. Alphonso XII 1875-1885. His posthumous son was Alphonso XIII, with his mother, Queen Maria Christina regent; Spanish-American war, Spain lost Cuba, gave up Puerto Rico, Philippines, Sulu Isl., Marianas, Alphonso took throne 1902, aged 16, married British Princess Victoria Eugenia of Battenberg. The dictatorship of Primo de Rivera, 1923-30, precipitated the revolution of 1931. Alphonso agreed to leave without formal abdication. The monarchy was abolished and the second republic established, with strong socialist backing. Presidents were Niceto Alcala Zamora, to 1936, when Manuel Anzana was chosen.

In July, 1936, the army in Morocco revolted against the government and General Francisco Franco led the troops into Spain. The revolution succeeded by February, 1939, when Anzana resigned. Franco became chief of state, with provisions that if he is incapacitated the Regency Council by two-thirds vote may propose a king to the Cortes, which must have a two-thirds majority to elect him.

Alphonso XIII, died in Rome Feb. 28, 1941, aged 54. His property and citizenship had been restored.

A succession law theoretically restoring the monarchy was approved in a 1947 referendum. A new Constitution, approved by referendum Dec. 14, 1966, affirmed Spain's status as a monarchy under a king or a regent. Prince Juan Carlos was designated by Franco and the Cortes in 1969 as the future king and chief of state. Juan Carlos is the son of the pretender to the throne, Don Juan of Bourbon.

Leaders in the South American Wars of Liberation

Simon Bolivar (1783-1830), Jose Francisco de San Martin (1783-1850) and Francisco Antonio Gabriel Miranda (1750-1816) are among the heroes of the early 19th century struggles of South American nations to free themselves from Spain. All three, and their contemporaries, operated in periods of intense factional strife, during which soldiers and civilians suffered.

Miranda, a Venezuelan, who had served with the French in the American Revolution and commanded parts of the French Revolutionary armies in the Netherlands, attempted to start a revolt in Venezuela in 1806 and failed. In 1810, with British and American backing, he returned and was briefly a dictator, until the British withdrew their support. In 1812 he was overcome by the royalists in Venezuela and taken prisoner, dying in a Spanish prison in 1816.

San Martin was born in Argentina and during 1789-1811 served in campaigns of the Spanish armies in Europe and Africa. He first joined the independence movement in Argentina in 1812 and then in 1817 invaded Chile with 4,000 men over the high mountain passes. Here he and General Bernardo O'Higgins (1778-1842) defeated the Spaniards at Chacabuco, 1817, and O'Higgins was named Chilean dictator and became first dictator of Chile, 1817-1823. In 1821 San Martin occupied Lima and Callao, Peru, and became Protector of Peru.

Bolivar, the greatest leader of South American liberation from Spain, was born in Venezuela, the son of an aristocratic family. His organizing and administrative abilities were superior and he foresaw many of the political difficulties of the future. He first served

under Miranda in 1812 and in 1813 captured Caracas, where he was named Liberator. Forced out next year by civil strife, he led a campaign that captured Bogota in 1814. In 1817 he was again in control of Venezuela and was named dictator. He organized Nueva Granada with the help of General Francisco de Paula Santander (1792-1840). By joining Nueva Granada, Venezuela and the present terrain of Panama and Ecuador, the republic of Colombia was formed with Bolivar president. After numerous setbacks he decisively defeated the Spaniards in the second battle of Carabobo, Venezuela, June 24, 1821.

In May, 1822, Gen. Antonio Jose de Sucre, Bolivar's trusted lieutenant, took Quito, Bolivar went to Guayaquil to confer with San Martin, who resigned as Protector of Peru and withdrew from politics. With a new army of Colombians and Peruvians Bolivar defeated the Spaniards in a saber battle at Juin in 1824 and cleared Peru.

De Sucre organized Charcas (Upper Peru) as Republica Bolivar (now Bolivia) and acted as president in place of Bolivar, who wrote its constitution. Sucre defeated the Spanish faction of Peru at Ayacucho, Dec. 19, 1824.

Continued civil strife finally caused the Colombian federation to break apart. Santander turned against Bolivar, but the latter defeated him and banished him. In 1828 Bolivar gave up the presidency he had held precariously for 14 years. He became ill from tuberculosis and died Dec. 17, 1830. He was honored as the great liberator and is buried in the national pantheon in Caracas.

Roman Rulers

From Romulus to the end of the Empire in the West. Rulers of the Roman Empire in the East sat in Constantinople and for a brief period in Nicaea, until the capture of Constantinople by the Turks in 1453, when it was succeeded by the Ottoman Empire.

B.C.	Name	B.C.	Name	B.C.	Name
	The Kingdom		**The Republic**	366	Praetorship established
753	Romulus (Quirinus)	509	Consulate established	366	Curule Aedileship created
716	Numa Pompilius	509	Quaestorship instituted	362	Military Tribunate elective
673	Tullus Hostillus	498	Dictatorship introduced	326	Proconsulate introduced
640	Ancus Marcius	494	Plebeian Tribunate created	311	Naval Duumvirate elective
616	L. Tarquinius Priscus	494	Plebeian Aedileship created	217	Dictatorship of Fabius Maximus
578	Servius Tullius	444	Consular Tribunate organized	133	Tribunate of Tiberius Gracchus
534	L. Tarquinius Superbus	43	Censorship instituted	123	Tribunate of Gaius Gracchus

B.C.	Name	A.D.	Name	A.D.	Name
82	Dictatorship of Sulla	238	Gordianus I and Gordianus II;		**West (Rome) and East**
60	First Triumvirate formed		Pupienus and Balbinus		**(Constantinople)**
	(Caesar, Pompeius, Crassus)	238	Gordianus III	364	Valentinianus I (West) and Valens
46	Dictatorship of Caesar	244	Philippus (the Arabian)		(East)
43	Second Triumvirate	249	Decius	367	Valentinianus I with Gratianus
	formed	251	Gallus and Volusianus		(West) and Valens (East)
	(Octavianus, Antonius, Lepidus)	253	Aemilianus	375	Gratianus with Valentinianus
	The Empire	253	Valerianus and Gallienus		II (West) and Valens (East)
27	Augustus (Gaius Julius Caesar	258	Gallienus (alone)	378	Gratianus with Valentinianus II
	Octavianus)	268	Claudius II (the Goth)		(W.) Theodosius I (E.)
A.D.		270	Quintillus	383	Valentinianus II (West) and
14	Tiberius I	270	Aurelianus		Theodosius I (East)
37	Gaius (Caligula)	275	Tacitus	394	Theodosius I (the Great)
41	Claudius I	276	Florianus	395	Honorius (West) and Arcadius (East)
54	Nero	276	Probus	408	Honorius (West) and Theodosius
68	Galba	282	Carus		II (East)
69	Galba; Otho; Vitellius	283	Carinus and Numerianus	423	Valentinianus III (West) and
69	Vespasianus	284	Diocletianus		Theodosius II (East) and
79	Titus	286	Diocletianus and Maximianus	450	Valentinianus III (West) and
81	Domitianus	305	Galerius and Constantius I		Marcianus (East)
96	Nerva	306	Galerius, Maximinus II, Severus I	455	Maximus (West); Avitus
93	Trajanus	307	Galerius, Maximinus II, Constantinus		(West); Marcianus (East)
117	Hadrianus		I, Licinius, Maxentius	456	Avitus (W.) Marcianus (E.)
138	Antoninus Pius	311	Maximinus II, Constantinus	457	Majorianus (W.), Leo I (E.)
161	Marcus Aurelius and Lucius Verus		I, Licinius, Maxentius	461	Severus II (W.), Leo I (E.)
169	Marcus Aurelius (alone)	312	Maximinus II, Constantinus	467	Anthemius (W.), Leo I (E.)
180	Commodus		I, Licinius	472	Olybrius (W.), Leo I (E.)
193	Pertinax; Julianus I	314	Constantinus I and Licinius	473	Glycerius (W.), Leo I (E.)
193	Septimius Severus	324	Constantinus I (the Great)	474	Julius Nepos (W.), Leo II (E.)
211	Caracalla and Geta	337	Contantinus II, Constans I,	475	Romulus Augustulus (West) and Zeno
212	Caracalla (alone)		Constantius III		(East)
217	Macrinus	340	Constantius II and Constans I	476	End of Empire in West; Odovacar,
218	Elagabalus (Heliogabalus)	350	Constantius II		King, drops title of Emperor; mur-
222	Alexander Severus	360	Julianus II (the Apostate)		dered by King Theodoric of Ostro-
235	Maximinusi (the Thracian)	363	Jovianus		goths 493 A. D.

Ancient Greeks and Latins

B. C. years are in black type; A. D. years in light. Herodotus believed Homer lived C. 850 B. C.

Greeks

Born	Died	Name	Subj.	Born	Died	Name	Subj.	Born	Died	Name	Subj.
389	314	Aeschines	Orat.	450	...	Empedocles	Philos.	582	500	Pythagoras	Philos.
525	456	Aeschylus	Dram.	55	135	Epictetus	Philos.	600	...	Sappho	Poet
...	550	Aesop	Tales	342	270	Epicurus	Philos.	556	469	Simonides	Poet
563	478	Anacreon	Poet	480	406	Euipides	Dram.	469	399	Socrates	Philos.
500	428	Anaxagoras	Philos.	576	480	Heraclitus	Philos.	495	405	Sophocles	Dram.
287	212	Archimedes	Physt.	484	424	Herodotus	Hist.	63	24	Strabo	Geog.
448	380	Aristophanes	Dram.	...	735	Hesiod	Poet	600	540	Thales	Philos.
384	322	Aristotle	Philos.	460	377	Hippocrates	Medic.	530	460	Themistocles	Philos.
...	194	Athenaeus	Antiq.	...	...	Homer	Poet	...	255	Theocritus	Poet
460	370	Democritus	Philos.	342	292	Menander	Dram.	382	287	Theophrastus	Philos.
310	240	Callimachus	Poet	522	443	Pindar	Poet	471	401	Thucydides	Hist.
382	322	Demosthenes	Orat.	429	347	Plato	Philos.	280	...	Timon	Philos.
50	13	Diodorus	Hist.	49	120	Plutarch	Biog.	490	...	Zeno	Philos.
...	7	Dionysius	Hist	207	122	Polybius	Hist.	430	357	Xenophon	Hist.

Latins

Born	Died	Name	Subj.	Born	Died	Name	Subj.	Born	Died	Name	Subj.
330	390	Ammianus	Hist.	59	17	Livy	Hist.	35	95	Quintilian	Critic
125	200	Apuleius	Satir.	38	65	Lucan	Poet	86	34	Sallust	Hist.
130	175	Aulus Gellius	Satir.	180	103	Lucilius	Satir.	5	65	Seneca	Moral.
475	524	Boethius	Philos.	96	52	Lucretius	Philos.	25	100	Silius	Poet
100	44	Caesar, Julius	States.	43	104	Martial	Poet	61	96	Statius	Poet
234	149	Cato (Elder)	Orat.	100	30	Nepos	Hist.	70	150	Suetonius	Biog.
87	54	Catullus	Poet	43	18	Ovid	Poet	55	117	Tacitus	Hist.
107	43	Cicero	Orat.	34	62	Persius	Satir.	185	159	Terence	Dram.
365	408	Claudian	Poet	254	184	Plautus	Dram.	54	18	Tibullus	Poet
65	8	Horace	Poet	23	79	Pliny	Natur.	70	19	Virgil	Poet
60	140	Juvenal	Satir.	62	113	Pliny (Younger)	Letters	70	16	Vitruvius	Arch.

Rulers of Russia; Premiers of the USSR

First ruler to consolidate Slav tribes was Rurik, leader of the Russ who established himself at Novgorod A. D. 862. He and his immediate successors had Scandinavian affiliations. They moved to Kiev after 972 A. D. and ruled as Dukes of Kiev. In 988 Vladimir was converted and adopted the Byzantine Greek service, later modified by Slav influences. Important as organizer and lawgiver was Yaroslav, 1018-1054, whose daughters married kings of Norway, Hungary and France. His grandson, Vladimir II (Monomachos) 1113-1125, was progenitor of several rulers, but in 1169 Andrew Bogolubski overthrew Kiev and began the line known as Grand Dukes of Vladimir.

Of the Grand Dukes of Vladimir Alexander Nevsky, 1245-1263, had a son, Daniel, first to be called Duke of Muscovy (Moscow) who ruled 1294-1303. His successors became Grand Dukes of Muscovy. After Demetrius III, Donskol, in 1380 defeated the Tartars, they also became Grand Dukes of all Russia. Independence of the Tartars and considerable territorial expansion was achieved under Ivan III, 1462-1505.

Czars of Muscovy—Ivan III was referred to in church ritual as Czar. He married Sofia, niece of the last Byzantine emperor. His successor, Basil, died in 1533 when Basil's son Ivan, was only 3. He became Ivan IV, "the Terrible," crowned 1547 as Czar of all the Russias, ruled till 1584. Under the weak rule of his son, Theodore, Boris Godunov had control. The dynasty died, and after years of tribal strife and invervention by Polish and Swedish armies, the Russians, united under 17-year-old Michael Romanov, distantly related to the first wife of Ivan IV. He ruled 1613-1645 and established the Romanov line. Fourth ruler after Michael was Peter I.

Czars, or Emperors of Russia (Romanovs)—Peter I, 1682-1725, known as Peter the Great, took title of Emperor in 1721. His successors and dates of accession were: Catherine, his widow, 1725, Peter II, his grandson, 1727, d. 1730; Anne, Duchess of Courtland, 1730, daughter of Peter the Great's brother, Czar Ivan; Ivan VI, 1740-1741, great grandson of Ivan V, child, kept in prison and murdered 1764; Elizabeth, daughter of Peter I, 1741; Peter III, grandson of Peter I, 1761, deposed 1762 for his consort, Catherine II, former princess of Anhalt Zerbst (German) who is known as Catherine the Great, 1762-1796; Paul I, her son, 1796, killed 1801. Alexander I, son of Paul, 1801-1825, defeated Napoleon; Nicholas I, his brother, 1825; Alexander II, son of Nicholas 1855, assassinated 1881 by terrorists; Alexander III, son, 1881-1894.

Nicholas II, son, 1894-1917, last Czar of Russia, was forced to abdicate by the Revolution that followed defeat by Germany. The Czar, the Czarina, the Czarevitch (Crown Prince) and the Czar's 4 daughters were murdered by the Bolshevists in Ekaterinburg, July 17, 1918.

Provisional Government—Prince Georgi Lvov and Alexander Kerensky, premiers, 1917.

Union of Soviet Socialist Republics

Bolshevist Revolution, Nov. 7, 1917, displaced Kerensky; Council of People's Commissars formed, Nicolai Lenin, premier. Lenin died Jan. 21, 1924. Alexei Rykov (executed 1938) and V. M. Molotov held the office, but actual ruler was Joseph Stalin (Joseph Vissarionovich Djugashvili), general secretary of the Central Committee of the Communist Party. Stalin became president of the Council of Ministers (premier) May 7, 1941, died Mar. 5, 1953. Succeeded by Georgi M. Malenkov, as head of the Council and premier and Nikita S. Khrushchev, first secretary of the Central Committee. Malenkov resigned Feb. 8, 1955, became deputy premier, was dropped July 3, 1957. Marshal Nikolai A. Bulganin became premier. Marshal Georgi K. Zhukov became minister of defense, was dropped Nov. 1, 1957. Bulganin was demoted and Khrushchev became premier Mar. 27, 1958, Krushchev was ousted Oct. 14-15, 1964, replaced by Leonid I. Brezhnev as first secretary of the party and by Aleksei N. Kosygin as premier.

Rulers of Modern Italy

After the fall of Napoleon in 1814 the Congress of Vienna, 1815, restored Italy as a political patchwork, comprising the Kingdom of Naples and Sicily, the Papal States, and smaller units. Piedmont and Genoa were awarded to Sardinia, ruled by King Victor Emmanuel I of Savoy.

United Italy emerged under the leadership of Camillo, Count of Cavour (1810-1861), Sardinian prime minister. Agitation was led by Giuseppe Mazzini (1805-1872) and Giuseppe Garibaldi (1807-1882), soldier. Victor Emmanuel I abdicated 1821. After a brief regency for a brother, Charles Albert was King 1831-1849, abdicating when defeated by the Austrians at Novara. Succeeded by Victor Emmanuel II (1820-1878).

In 1859 France forced Austria to cede Lombardy to Sardinia, which gave rights to Savoy and Nice to France. In 1860 Garibaldi led 1,000 volunteers in a spectacular campaign, took Sicily and expelled the King of Naples. In 1860 the House of Savoy annexed Tuscany, Parma, Moderna, Romagna, the Two Sicilies, the Marches and Umbria. Victor Emmanuel assumed the title of King of Italy at Turin

Mar. 17, 1861. In 1866 he joined Prussia and Austria in the Triple Alliance and received Venetia from Austria. On Sept. 20, 1870, his troops under Gen. Raffaele Cardorna entered Rome and took over the Papal States, ending the temporal power of the Roman Catholic Church.

Succession. Humbert I, 1878, assassinated 1900; Victor Emmanuel III, 1900, abdicated 1946, died 1947; Humbert II, 1946, ruled a month. In 1921 Benito Mussolini (1883-1945) formed the Fascist party and became prime minister Oct. 31, 1922. He made the King Emperor of Ethiopia, 1937; entered World War II as ally of Hitler. He was deposed July 25, 1943.

At a plebiscite June 2, 1946, Italy voted for a republic. Premier Alcide de Gasperi became Chief of State June 13, 1946. On June 28, 1946, the Constituent Assembly elected Enrico de Nicola, Liberal, Provisional President of the Republic of Italy. Luigi Einaudi was elected President May 11, 1948. Giovanni Gronchi was elected Apr. 29, 1955, inaugurated May 11, 1955. Antonio Segni elected May 6, 1962, Giuseppe Saragat Dec. 28, 1964; Giovanni Leone Dec. 29, 1971.

Italians
Authors, Dramatists, Poets, Philosophers, Historians

Born	Died	Name	Born	Died	Name	Born	Died	Name
1749	1803	Alfieri, Vittorio	1265	1321	Dante, Alighieri	1785	1873	Manzoni, Alessandro
1846	1908	Amicis, Edmond de	1875	1936	Deledda, Grazia	1805	1872	Mazzini, Giuseppe
1227	1274	Aquinas, Thomas	1817	1883	De Sanctis, Francesco	1698	1782	Metastasio (P. Trapassi)
1492	1556	Aretino, Pietro	1909	1967	Emanuelli, Enrico	1672	1750	Muratori, Ludovico
1474	1533	Ariosto, Ludovico	1842	1911	Fogazzaro, Antonio	1848	1923	Pareto, Vilfredo
1829	1907	Ascoli, Graziadio	1778	1827	Foscolo, Ugo	1855	1912	Pascoli, Giovanni
1791	1863	Belli, Giuseppe	1875	1944	Gentile, Giovanni	1788	1854	Pellico, Silvio
1313	1375	Boccaccio, Giovanni	1809	1850	Giusti, Giuseppe	1304	1374	Petrarca, Francesco
1441	1494	Boiardo, Matteo Maria	1707	1793	Goldoni, Carlo	1867	1936	Pirandello, Luigi
1548	1599	Bruno, Giordano	1713	1786	Gozzi, Gaspare	1432	1484	Pulci, Luigi
1568	1639	Campanella, Tommaso	1483	1540	Guicciardini, Francesco	1901	1968	Quasimodo, Salvatore
1835	1907	Carducci, Giosue	1798	1837	Leopardi, Giacomo	1626	1698	Redi, Francesco
1725	1798	Casanova, Giacomo	1836	1909	Lombroso, Cedare	1544	1595	Tasso, Torquato
1478	1529	Castiglione, Baldassarre	1469	1527	Machiavelli, Niccolo	1888	1970	Ungaretti, Giuseppe
1884	1966	Cecchi, Emilio	1898	1957	Malaparte, Curzio	1840	1922	Verga, Giovanni
1866	1952	Croce, Benedetto	1449	1515	Manuzio, Aldo (Aldus)	1668	1744	Vico, Giambattista
1863	1938	D'Annunzio, Gabriele						

Italian Explorers, Scientists, Political Leaders

Born	Died	Name	Born	Died	Name	Born	Died	Name
1776	1856	Avogadro, Amaedo	1564	1642	Galileo (G. Galilei)	1859	1953	Nitti; Francesco
1738	1794	Beccaria, Cesare	1737	1798	Galvani, Luigi	1254	1324	Polo, Marco
1835	1900	Beltrami, Eugenio	1807	1882	Garibaldi, Giuseppe	1626	1698	Redi, Francesco
1476	1507	Borgia, Cesare	1882	1955	Graziani, Rodolfo	1878	1970	Ruini, Meuccio
16th	Cen	Cabot, John (Caboto)	1483	1540	Guicciardini, Francesco	1835	1910	Schiaparelli, Giovanni
1826	1910	Cannizzaro, Stanislao	1628	1694	Malpighi, Marcello	1818	1878	Secchi, Angelo
1810	1861	Cavour, Camillo Benso	1874	1937	Marconi, Guglielmo	1872	1952	Sforza, Carlo
1451	1506	Columbus, Christopher	1389	1464	Medici, Cosimo de' (1)	1729	1799	Spallanzani, Lazzaro
1830	1903	Cremona, Luigi	1519	1574	Medici, Cosimo de' (2)	1608	1647	Torricelli, Evangelista
1881	1954	De Gasperi, Alcide	1449	1492	Medici, Lorenzo de'	1485	1533	Verrazano, Giovanni
1901	1954	Fermi, Enrico	1846	1910	Mosso, Angelo	1454	1512	Vespucci, Amerigo
1847	1897	Ferraris, Galileo	1883	1945	Mussolini, Benito	1745	1827	Volta, Alessandro

Italian Painters, Sculptors and Architects

Born	Died	Name	Born	Died	Name	Born	Died	Name
1404	1472	Alberti, Leon Battista	1387	1455	Angelico, Fra	1426	1507	Bellini, Gentile
1512	1572	Alessi, Galeazzo	1591	1666	Barbieri, Giovanni	1428	1516	Bellini, Giovanni
1447	1522	Amadeo, Giovanni	1475	1517	Bartolomeo, Fra	1400	1470	Bellini, Jacopo

Born	Died	Name	Born	Died	Name	Born	Died	Name
1467	1516	Beltraffio, Giovanni	1378	1455	Ghiberti, Lorenzo	1483	1520	Raphael (Raffaello)
1598	1680	Bernini, Gian Lor.	1449	1494	Ghirlandaio, Domenico	1575	1642	Reni, Guido
1598	1680	Bernini, Lorenzo	1477	1510	Giorgione	1400	1482	Robbia, Luca della
1445	1510	Botticelli, Sandro	1260	1336	Giotto di Bondone	1615	1673	Rosa, Salvator
1444	1514	Bramante, Donato	1420	1497	Gozzoli, Benozzo	1460	1529	Sansovino, Andrea
1377	1446	Brunelleschi, Filippo	1406	1469	Lippi, Fra Filippo	1486	1570	Sansovino, Jacopo
1697	1768	Canaletto (Canale)	1459	1504	Lippi, Filippino	1858	1899	Segantini, Giovanni
1757	1822	Canova, Antonio	1431	1506	Mantegna, Andrea	1883	1966	Severini, Gino
1570	1610	Caravaggio, Merisi	1401	1428	Masaccio, Tommaso	1696	1770	Tiepolo, Giambattista
1450	1522	Carpaccio, Vittore	1827	1887	Mengoni, Giuseppe	1518	1594	Tintoretto, Jacopo
1881	1966	Carra, Carlo	1475	1564	Michelangelo Buonarroti	1477	1576	Titian (Tiziano)
1500	1571	Cellini, Benvenuto	1826	1901	Morelli, Domenico	1397	1475	Uccello, Paolo
1240	1302	Cimabue, Giovanni	1518	1580	Palladio, Andrea	1511	1574	Vasari, Giorgio
1489	1534	Correggio, Antonio da	1480	1528	Palma, Jacopo	1528	1588	Veronese, Paolo
1462	1521	Cosimo, Piero di	1445	1523	Perugino, Pietro	1435	1488	Verrocchio, Andrea
1486	1531	Del Sarto, Andrea	1720	1778	Piranesi, Giovanni	1452	1519	Vinci, Leonardo da
1386	1466	Donatello, Donato	1454	1513	Pinturicchio			

Concert Violinists of the Past

Born	Died	Name	Born	Died	Name	Born	Died	Name
1856	1943	Adamowski, T......Pol.	1889	1934	Kichanski, Paul.... Pol.	1815	1894	Sivori, Ern........ Ital.
1845	1930	Auer, Leopold.... Hung.	1875	1962	Kreisler, Fritz..... Aus.	1888	1953	Spalding, Albert. . . U.S.
1795	1876	Boehm, Jos....... Czech.	1880	1940	Kubelik, Jan...... Boh.	1784	1859	Spohr, Ludwig..... Ger.
1810	1880	Bull, Ole......... Nor.	1790	1861	Lipinski, Karl..... Pol.	1892	1973	Szigeti, Joseph.... Hung.
1653	1713	Corelli, Arcang.... Ital.	1840	1927	Lotto, Isidor....... Pol.	1692	1770	Tartini, Gius....... Ital.
1891	1967	Elman, Mischa..... U.S.	1722	1793	Nardini, Pietro..... Ital.	1880	1953	Thibaud, Jacq..... Fr.
1881	1955	Enesco, Georges.. Rum.	1782	1840	Paganini, Nicolo ... Ital.	1820	1881	Vieuxtemps, H..... Belg.
1667	1762	Geminiani, F....... Ital.	1868	1920	Powell, Maud..... U.S.	1753	1824	Viotti, Giovanni ... Ital.
1716	1796	Giardini, F. di ..... Ital.	1830	1898	Remenyi, Edw..... Hung.	1675	1741	Vivaldi, Antonio. ... Ital.
1858	1937	Hubay, Jeno...... Hung.	1892	1936	Rigo, Jancsi...... Hung.	1835	1880	Wieniawski, H...... Pol.
1882	1947	Huberman, B...... Pol.	1774	1830	Rode, Jacques .... Fr.	1845	1908	Wilhelmj, Aug...... Ger.
1831	1907	Joachim, Joseph ... Hung.	1863	1946	Rose, Arnold...... Aus.	1858	1931	Ysaye, Eugene.... Belg.
			1844	1908	Sarasate, P.M......Span.			

The Dynasties of China

(Until 221 B.C. and frequently thereafter, China was not a unified state. Where dynastic dates overlap, the rulers or events referred to appeared in different areas of China.)

Hsia..	c.2000B.C.-	c.1500B.C.
Shang..	c.1500B.C.-	c.1000B.C.
Western Chou...	c.1000	- 771
Eastern Chou...	770	- 256
Warring States..	403	- 222
Ch'in (first unified empire)..	221	- 206
Han..	202B.C.-	220A.D.
Western Han (expanded Chinese state beyond the Yellow and Yangtze River valleys)	202B.C.-	9A.D.
Hsin (Wang Mang, usurper)...	9A.D.-	23A.D.
Eastern Han (expanded Chinese state into Indo-China and Turkestan).....	25A.D.-	220A.D.
Three Kingdoms (Wei, Shu, Wu)......................................	220	- 264
Chin (western)..	265	- 317
(eastern)...	317	- 420
Northern Dynasties (followed several short-lived governments by Turks, Mongols, etc.).	386	- 581
Southern Dynasties (capital: Nanking)................................	420	- 589
Sui (reunified China)..	581	- 618
T'ang (a golden age of Chinese culture; capital: Sian).................	618	- 907
Five Dynasties (Yellow River basin)..................................	907	- 959
Ten Kingdoms (southern China)......................................	907	- 979
Liao (Khitan Mongols; capital: Peking)................................	947	- 1125
Sung...	960	- 1279
Northern Sung (reunified central and southern China).................	960	- 1127
Western Hsai (non-Chinese rulers in northwest)......................	990	- 1227
Chin (Tartars; drove Sung out of central China)......................	1114	- 1234
Southern Sung (capital: Hangchow).................................	1127	- 1379
Yuan (Mongols; Kublai Khan made Peking his capital in 1267)..........	1271	- 1368
Ming (China reunified under Chinese rule; capital: Nanking, then Peking in 1420).	1368	- 1644
Ch'ing (Manchus, descendents of Tartars)............................	1644	- 1912
Republic (disunity: provincial rulers, warlords).......................	1912	- 1949

Entertainment Personalities of the Past

Born	Died	Name	Born	Died	Name	Born	Died	Name
		A	1886	1954	Anderson, John Murray			**B**
1896	1974	Abbott, Bud	1859	1940	Anderson, Mary	1864	1922	Bacon, Frank
1872	1953	Adams, Maude	1915	1967	Andrews, Laverne	1903	1951	Bailey, Mildred
1931	1968	Adams, Nick	1933	1971	Angeli, Pier	1893	1968	Bainter, Fay
1855	1926	Adler, Jacob P.	1876	1958	Anglin, Margaret	1895	1957	Baker, Belle
1858	1953	Adler, Sarah Levitzka	1887	1933	Arbuckle, Fatty (Roscoe)	1898	1963	Baker, Phil
1898	1933	Adoree, Renee	1868	1946	Arliss, George	1882	1956	Bancroft, George
1909	1964	Albertson, Frank	1900	1971	Armstrong, Louis	1903	1968	Bankhead, Tallulah
1885	1952	Alda, Frances	1890	1956	Arnold, Edward	1890	1952	Banks, Leslie
1894	1956	Allen, Fred	1885	1946	Atwill, Lionel	1897	1950	Banks, Monty
1906	1964	Allen, Gracie	1845	1930	Auer, Leopold	1890	1955	Bara, Theda
1883	1950	Allgood, Sara	1905	1967	Auer, Mischa	1810	1891	Barnum, Phineas T.
1882	1971	Anderson, Gilbert	1900	1972	Austin, Gene	1879	1959	Barrymore, Ethel
		(Bronco Billy)	1898	1940	Ayres, Agnes	1882	1942	Barrymore, John

Born	Died	Name
1878	1954	Barrymore, Lionel
1848	1905	Barrymore, Maurice
1897	1963	Barthelmess, Richard
1891	1962	Barton, James
1873	1951	Bauer, Harold
1893	1951	Baxter, Warner
1880	1928	Bayes, Nora
1904	1965	Beatty, Clyde
1904	1962	Beavers, Louise
1887	1955	Beecher, Janet
1884	1946	Beery, Noah
1889	1949	Beery, Wallace
1901	1970	Begley, Ed.
1903	1931	Beiderbecke, Bix
1854	1931	Belasco, David
1906	1968	Benaderet, Bea
1906	1964	Bendix, William
1905	1965	Bennett, Constance
1924	1970	Benzell, Mimi
1873	1944	Bennett, Richard
1867	1944	Beresford, Harry
1899	1966	Berg, Gertrude
1863	1927	Bernard, Sam
1844	1923	Bernhardt, Sarah
1893	1943	Bernie, Ben
1889	1967	Bickford, Charles
1911	1960	Bjoerling, Jussi
1898	1973	Blackmer, Sidney
1882	1951	Blaney, Charles E.
1900	1943	Bledsoe, Jules
1928	1972	Blocker, Dan
1888	1959	Blore, Eric
1899	1957	Bogart, Humphrey
1885	1965	Boland, Mary
1897	1969	Boles, John
1903	1960	Bond, Ward
1833	1893	Booth, Edwin
1796	1852	Booth, Junius Brutus
1894	1953	Bordoni, Irene
1888	1960	Bori, Lucrezia
1867	1943	Bosworth, Hobart
1905	1965	Bow, Clara
1874	1946	Bowes, Maj. Edward
1893	1939	Brady, Alice
1871	1936	Breese, Edmund
1898	1964	Brendel, El
1901	1948	Breneman, Tom
1875	1948	Brian, Donald
1891	1951	Brice, Fanny
1891	1959	Broderick, Helen
1898	1965	Brokenshire, Norman
1904	1951	Bromberg, J. Edward
1892	1973	Brown, Joe E.
1926	1966	Bruce, Lenny
1895	1953	Bruce, Nigel
1891	1957	Buchanan, Jack
1886	1957	Buck, Gene
1904	1965	Bunce, Alan
1863	1915	Bunny, John
1886	1970	Burke, Billie
1912	1967	Burnette, Smiley
1896	1956	Burns, Bob
1902	1971	Burns, David
1882	1941	Burr, Henry
1883	1966	Bushman, Francis X.
1896	1946	Butterworth, Charles
1893	1971	Byington, Spring
		C
1905	1972	Cabot, Bruce
1895	1956	Calhern, Louis
1858	1942	Calve, Emma
1865	1940	Campbell, Mrs. Patrick
1892	1964	Cantor, Eddie
1878	1947	Carey, Harry
1876	1941	Carle, Richard
1897	1954	Carney, "Uncle Don"
1880	1961	Carrillo, Leo
1892	1972	Carroll, Leo G.
1905	1965	Carroll, Nancy
1910	1963	Carson, Jack
1862	1937	Carter, Mrs. Leslie
1873	1921	Caruso, Enrico
1876	1973	Casals, Pablo
1894	1969	Castle, Irene
1887	1918	Castle, Vernon
1889	1960	Catlett, Walter
1874	1944	Cavalieri, Lina
1887	1950	Cavanaugh, Hobart
1873	1938	Chaliapin, Feodor

Born	Died	Name
1919	1961	Chandler, Jeff
1883	1930	Chaney, Lon
1906	1973	Chaney, Jr., Lon
1893	1940	Chase, Charlie
1893	1961	Chatterton, Ruth
1888	1971	Chevalier, Maurice
1888	1960	Clark, Bobby
1914	1968	Clark, Fred
1887	1950	Clayton, Lou
1920	1966	Clift, Montgomery
1900	1937	Clive, Colin
1932	1963	Cline, Patsy
1892	1967	Clyde, Andy
1877	1961	Coburn, Charles
1887	1934	Cody, Lew
1878	1942	Cohan, George M.
1876	1916	Cohan, Josephine
1919	1965	Cole, Nat (King)
1878	1955	Collier, Constance
1866	1944	Collier, William, Sr.
1891	1958	Colman, Ronald
1908	1934	Columbo, Russ
1907	1944	Compton, Betty
1887	1940	Connolly, Walter
1855	1909	Conried, Henrich
1890	1964	Conroy, Frank
1904	1967	Conway, Tom
1901	1961	Cook, Donald
1890	1959	Cook, Joe
1893	1958	Cook, Phil
1901	1961	Cooper, Gary
1891	1971	Cooper, Gladys
1896	1973	Cooper, Melville
1914	1968	Corey, Wendell
1893	1974	Cornell, Katherine
1890	1972	Correll, Charles
1876	1951	Cossart, Ernest
1904	1957	Costello, Helene
1906	1969	Costello, Lou
1877	1950	Costello, Maurice
1899	1973	Coward, Noel
1890	1950	Cowl, Jane
1924	1973	Cox, Wally
1847	1924	Crabtree, Lotta
1875	1945	Craven, Frank
1916	1944	Cregar, Laird
1880	1942	Crews, Laura Hope
1880	1974	Crisp, Donald
1943	1973	Croce, Jim
1910	1960	Cromwell, Richard
1893	1966	Crouse, Russell
1878	1968	Currie, Finlay
1909	1953	Curtis, Alan
		D
1924	1965	Dandridge, Dorothy
1869	1941	Danforth, William
1894	1963	Daniel, Henry
1901	1971	Daniels, Bebe
1860	1935	Daniels, Frank
1936	1973	Darin, Bobby
1921	1965	Darnell, Linda
1894	1967	Darwell, Jane
1866	1949	Davenport, Harry
1900	1961	Davies, Marion
1908	1961	Davis, Joan
1931	1955	Dean, James
1881	1950	DeCordoba, Pedro
1905	1968	Dekker, Albert
1898	1965	Demarco, Tony
1881	1959	DeMille, Cecil B.
1891	1967	Denny, Reginald
1878	1949	Desmond, William
1878	1930	Destinn, Emmy
1942	1972	De Wilde, Brandon
1916	1974	De Wolfe, Billy
1865	1950	De Wolfe, Elsie
1879	1947	Digges, Dudley
1890	1944	Dinehart, Alan
1901	1966	Disney, Walt
1895	1949	Dix, Richard
1856	1924	Dockstader, Lew
1892	1941	Dolly, Jennie
1892	1970	Dolly, Rosie
1905	1958	Donat, Robert
1903	1972	Donlevy, Brian
1904	1957	Dorsey, Jimmy
1905	1956	Dorsey, Tommy
1907	1959	Douglas, Paul
1889	1956	Draper, Ruth

Born	Died	Name
1881	1965	Dresser, Louise
1869	1934	Dressler, Marie
1820	1897	Drew, Mrs. John
1853	1927	Drew John (son)
1879	1920	Drew, Sydney
1909	1951	Duchin, Eddy
1940	1971	Duel, Peter
1900	1964	Dumke, Ralph
1890	1965	Dumont, Margaret
1877	1927	Duncan, Isadora
1905	1967	Dunn, James
1873	1947	Dupree, Minnie
1907	1968	Duryea, Dan
1859	1924	Duse, Eleanora
		E
1894	1929	Eagles, Jeanne
1896	1930	Eames, Clare
1865	1952	Eames, Emma
1901	1967	Eddy, Nelson
1894	1971	Edwards, Cliff
1879	1945	Edwards, Gus
1899	1974	Ellington, Duke
1941	1974	Elliot, Cass
1871	1940	Elliott, Maxine
1891	1967	Elman, Mischa
1883	1941	Eltinge, Julian
1881	1951	Errol, Leon
1903	1967	Erwin, Stuart
1913	1967	Evelyn, Judith
		F
1883	1939	Fairbanks, Douglas
1915	1970	Farmer, Frances
1870	1929	Farnum, Dustin
1876	1953	Farnum, William
1882	1967	Farrar, Geraldine
1904	1971	Farrell, Glenda
1868	1940	Faversham, William
1861	1939	Fawcett, George
1897	1960	Fay, Frank
1895	1962	Fazenda, Louise
1903	1971	Fernandel
1905	1950	Field, Sidney
1867	1941	Fields, Lew
1879	1946	Fields, W. C.
1865	1932	Fiske, Minnie Maddern
1888	1961	Fitzgerald, Barry
1874	1941	Fitzgerald, Cissy
1895	1962	Flagstad, Kirsten
1900	1971	Flippen, Jay C.
1909	1959	Flynn, Errol
1925	1974	Flynn, Joe
1880	1942	Fokine, Michel
1910	1968	Foley, Red
1905	1951	Forbes, Ralph
1853	1937	Forbes-Robertson
1887	1970	Ford, Ed (Senator)
1895	1973	Ford, John
1899	1965	Ford, Wallace
1806	1872	Forrest, Edwin
1904	1970	Foster, Preston
1854	1928	Foy, Eddie
1905	1968	Francis, Kay
1893	1966	Frawley, William
1885	1938	Frederick, Pauline
1870	1955	Friganza, Trixie
1890	1958	Frisco, Joe
1860	1915	Frohman, Charles
1851	1940	Frohman, Daniel
1885	1947	Fyffe, Will
		G
1901	1960	Gable, Clark
1889	1963	Galli-Curci, Amelita
1877	1967	Garden, Mary
1913	1952	Garfield, John
1922	1969	Garland, Judy
1893	1963	Gaxton, Wm.
1904	1954	George, Gladys
1879	1961	George, Grace
1892	1962	Gibson, Hoot
1890	1957	Gigli, Beniamino
1894	1971	Gilbert, Billy
1897	1936	Gilbert, John
1855	1937	Gillette, William
1867	1943	Gillmore, Frank
1879	1939	Gilpin, Charles
1898	1968	Gish, Dorothy

Born	Died	Name
1886	1959	Gleason, James
1882	1974	Goldwyn, Samuel
1917	1969	Gorcey, Leo
1887	1948	Gordon, Vera
1829	1869	Gottschalk, Louis
1916	1973	Grable, Betty
1901	1959	Gray, Gilda
1879	1954	Greenstreet, Sydney
1874	1948	Griffith, David Wark
1885	1957	Guitry, Sacha
1912	1967	Guthrie, Woody
1875	1959	Gwenn, Edmund

H

Born	Died	Name
1888	1942	Hackett, Charles
1902	1958	Hackett, Raymond
1870	1943	Haines, Robert T.
1892	1950	Hale, Alan
1847	1919	Hammerstein, Oscar
1895	1960	Hammerstein, Oscar, 2nd
1879	1955	Hampden, Walter
1873	1958	Handy, W. C.
1924	1964	Haney, Carol
1893	1964	Hardwicke, Sir Cedric
1892	1957	Hardy, Oliver
1883	1939	Hare, T. E. (Ernie)
1911	1937	Harlow, Jean
1872	1946	Harned, Virginia
1895	1943	Hart, Lorenz
1870	1946	Hart, William S.
1907	1955	Hartman, Grace
1928	1973	Harvey, Laurence
1890	1973	Hayakawa, Sessue
1902	1971	Hayward, Leland
1876	1945	Harwood, John
1910	1973	Hawkins, Jack
1885	1969	Hayes, Gabby
1896	1937	Healy, Ted
1910	1971	Heflin, Van
1879	1936	Heggie, O. P.
1873	1918	Held, Anna
1903	1947	Hellinger, Mark
1885	1955	Hempel, Frieda
1943	1970	Hendrix, Jimi
1913	1969	Henie, Sonja
1879	1942	Herbert, Henry
1887	1951	Herbert, Hugh
1886	1956	Hersholt, Jean
1895	1942	Hibbard, Edna
1857	1927	Hillard, Robert C.
1865	1929	Hitchcock, Raymond
1914	1955	Hodiak, John
1876	1957	Hofmann, Josef
1894	1973	Holden, Fay
1919	1959	Holliday, Billie
1923	1965	Holliday, Judy
1888	1951	Holt, Jack
1871	1947	Homer, Louise
1858	1935	Hopper, DeWolf
1874	1959	Hopper, Edna Wallace
1890	1966	Hopper, Hedda
1916	1970	Hopper, William
1888	1970	Horton, Edward Everett
1874	1926	Houdini, Harry
1881	1965	Howard, Eugene
1867	1961	Howard, Joe
1893	1943	Howard, Leslie
1886	1955	Howard, Tom
1886	1949	Howard, Willie
1914	1972	Hudson, Rochelle
1886	1957	Hull, Josephine
1907	1967	Hume, Benita
1895	1958	Humphrey, Doris
1895	1945	Hunter, Glenn
1925	1969	Hunter, Jeffrey
1901	1962	Husing, Ted
1884	1950	Huston, Walter

I

Born	Died	Name
1892	1950	Ingram, Rex
1895	1969	Ingram, Rex
1838	1905	Irving,I Heny
1871	1944	Irving, Isabel
1872	1914	Irving, Laurence
1862	1938	Irwin, May

J

Born	Died	Name
1875	1942	Jackson, Joe
1911	1972	Jackson, Mahalia
1889	1956	Janis, Elsie

Born	Died	Name
1886	1950	Jannings, Emil
1829	1905	Jefferson, Joseph
1859	1923	Jefferson, Thoma
1900	1974	Jenkins, Allen
1862	1930	Jewett, Henry
1892	1962	Johnson, Chic
1878	1952	Johnson, Edward
1888	1950	Jolson, Al
1899	1940	Jones Billy
1889	1942	Jones, Buck
1911	1965	Jones, Spike
1943	1970	Joplin, Janis
1897	1961	Jordan, Marian (Molly McGee)
1890	1955	Joyce, Alice

K

Born	Died	Name
1878	1965	Kaltenborn, Hans V.
1910	1966	Kane, Helen
1887	1969	Karloff, Boris
1893	1970	Karns, Roscoe
1811	1868	Kean, Charles
1806	1880	Kean, Mrs. Charles
1787	1833	Kean, Edmund
1895	1966	Keaton, Buster
1858	1929	Keenan, Frank
1830	1873	Keene, Laura
1841	1898	Keene, Thomas W.
1899	1960	Keith, Ian
1894	1973	Kellaway, Cecil
1899	1956	Kelly, Paul
1873	1939	Kelly, Walter C.
1909	1968	Kelton, Pert
1823	1895	Kemble, Agnes
1775	1854	Kemble, Charles
1809	1893	Kemble, Fannie
1848	1935	Kendal, Dame Madge
1843	1917	Kendal, Wm. H.
1926	1959	Kendall, Kay
1890	1948	Kennedy, Edgar
1885	1965	Kennedy, Tom
1886	1945	Kent, William
1880	1947	Kerrigan, J. Warren
1886	1956	Kibbee, Guy
1902	1966	Kiepura, Jan
1888	1964	Kilbride, Percy
1913	1965	Kilgallen, Dorothy
1863	1933	Kilgour, Joseph
1899	1965	King, Alexander
1894	1944	King, Charles
1897	1971	King, Dennis
1889	1938	Kohler, Fred
1897	1957	Korngold, Erich W.
1919	1962	Kovacs, Ernie
1909	1973	Krupa, Gene

L

Born	Died	Name
1913	1964	Ladd, Alan
1895	1967	Lahr, Bert
1919	1973	Lake, Veronica
1904	1948	Landi, Elissa
1919	1948	Landis, Carole
1904	1972	Landis, Jessie Royce
1884	1944	Langdon, Harry
1856	1929	Langtry, Lillian
1921	1959	Lanza, Mario
1881	1958	Lasky, Jesse L.
1870	1950	Lauder, Harry
1899	1962	Laughton, Charles
1890	1965	Laurel, Stan
1892	1954	Laurie, Joe, Jr.
1898	1952	Lawrence, Gertrude
1890	1929	Lawrence, Margaret
1907	1952	Lee, Canada
194	1970	Lee, Gypsy Rose
1848	1929	Lehmann, Lilli
1896	1950	Lehr, Lew
1913	1967	Leigh, Vivienn
1852	1908	Leighton, Margaet
1894	1931	Leitzel, Lillian
1831	1905	Lemoyne, W. J.
1870	1941	Leonard, Eddie
1911	1973	Lonard, Jack E.
1906	1972	Levant, Oscar
1881	1955	Levey, Ethel
1902	1971	Lewis, Joe E.
1891	1971	Lewis, Ted
1874	1944	Lhevinne, Josef
1889	1952	Lincoln, Elmo

Born	Died	Name
1820	1887	Lind, Jenny
1889	1968	Lindsay, Howard
1869	1952	Lipman, Clara
1889	1971	Lloyd, Harold
1876	1922	Lloyd, Marie
1891	1957	Lockhart, Gene
1913	1969	Logan, Ella
1876	1943	Loftus, Cissie (Marie)
1909	1942	Lombard, Carole
1890	1950	Lord, Pauline
1888	1968	Lorne, Marion
1904	1964	Lorre, Peter
1917	1970	Louise, Anita
1914	1962	Lovejoy, Frank
1892	1971	Lowe, Edmund
1892	1947	Lubitsch, Ernst
1885	1956	Lugosi, Bela
1895	1971	Lukas, Paul
1902	1947	Lunceford, Jimmy
1853	1932	Lupino, George
1893	1942	Lupino, Stanley
1897	1957	Lyman, Abe
1926	1971	Lynn, Diana
1885	1954	Lytell, Bert
1867	1936	Lytton, Henry

M

Born	Died	Name
1907	1965	MacDonald, Jeanette
1902	1969	MacLane, Barton
1909	1973	Macready, George
1861	1946	Macy, George Carleton
1896	1967	Mahoney, Will
1908	1973	Magnani, Anna
1933	1967	Mansfield, Jayne
1857	1907	Mansfield, Richard
1920	1970	March, Hal
1865	1950	Marlowe, Julia
1890	1966	Marshall, Herbert
1864	1943	Marshall, Tully
1885	1969	Martinelli, Giovanni
1887	1961	Marx, Leonard (Chico)
1888	1964	Marx, Arthur (Harpo)
1862	1951	Maude, Cyril
1922	1972	Maxwell, Marilyn
1879	1948	May, Edna
1885	1957	Mayer, Louis B.
1895	1973	Maynard, Ken
1839	1896	Mayo, Frank
1884	1951	Mayo, Margaret
1884	1945	McCormack, John
1907	1962	McCormick, Myron
1888	1931	McCoy, Bessie
1883	1936	McCullough, Paul
1895	1952	McDaniel, Hattie
1924	1965	McDonald, Marie
1879	1949	McIntyre, Frank J.
1857	1937	McIntyre, James
1879	1937	McKinley, Mabel
1886	1959	McLaglen, Victor
1907	1971	McMahon, Horace
1880	1946	Meed, Donald
1879	1936	Meighan, Thomas
1861	1931	Melba, Nellie
1890	1973	Melchior, Lauritz
1904	1961	Melton, James
1890	1963	Menjou, Adolphe
1902	1966	Menken, Helen
1882	1939	Mercer, Beryl
1880	1946	Merivale, Phillip
1904	1944	Miller, Glenn
1860	1926	Miller, Henry
1898	1936	Miller, Marilyn
1895	1927	Mills, Florence
1903	1955	Minnevitch, Borrah
1917	1955	Miranda, Carmen
1875	1957	Mitchell, Grant
1892	1962	Mitchell, Thomas
1880	1940	Mix, Tom
1845	1909	Modjeska, Helena
1926	1962	Monroe, Marilyn
1912	1973	Monroe, Vaughn
1875	1964	Monteux, Pierre
1824	1861	Montez, Lola
1919	1951	Montez, Maria
1903	1947	Moore, Grace
1885	1955	Moore, Tom
1876	1962	Moore, Victor
1906	1974	Moorehead, Agnes

Born	Died	Name
1882	1949	Moran, George
1884	1952	Moran, Polly
1890	1949	Morgan, Frank
1900	1941	Morgan, Helen
1888	1956	Morgan, Ralph
1901	1970	Morris, Chester
1849	1925	Morris, Clara
1914	1959	Morris, Wayne
1944	1971	Morrison, Jim
1885	1941	Morton, Jelly Roll
1897	1969	Mowbray, Alan
1897	1967	Muni, Paul
1894	1953	Munn, Frank
1906	1955	Munson, Ona
1924	1971	Murphy, Audie
1885	1965	Murray, Mae

N

Born	Died	Name
1897	1970	Nagel, Conrad
1900	1973	Naish, J. Carrol
1902	1961	Naldi, Nita
1888	1950	Nash, Florence
1865	1945	Nash, George
1879	1945	Nazimova, Alla
1846	1905	Neilson, Ada
1848	1880	Neilson, Adelaide
1885	1967	Nesbit, Evelyn
1868	1957	Neilson-Terry, Julia
1870	1951	Nethersole, Olga
1874	1948	Niblo, Fred
1890	1950	Nijinsky, Vaslav
1893	1974	Nilsson, Anna Q.
1898	1930	Normand, Mabel
1879	1959	Norworth, Jack
1905	1968	Novarro, Ramon
1893	1951	Novello, Ivor

O

Born	Died	Name
1898	1943	O'Connell, Hugh
1881	1959	O'Connor, Una
1878	1945	O'Hara, Fiske
1908	1968	O'Keefe, Dennis
1880	1938	Oland, Warner
1860	1932	Olcott, Chauncey
1885	1942	Oliver, Edna May
1892	1963	Olsen, Ole
1847	1920	O'Neill, James
1887	1949	Ouspenskaya, Maria
1887	1972	Owen, Reginald

P

Born	Died	Name
1860	1941	Paderewski, Ignace
1889	1954	Pallette, Eugene
1881	1972	Parsons, Louella
1881	1940	Pasternack, Josef A.
1843	1919	Patti, Adelina
1840	1889	Patti, Carlotta
1885	1931	Pavlova, Anna
1899	1973	Paxinou, Katina
1868	1934	Payton, Corse
1917	1966	Pearce, Alice
1885	1950	Pemberton, Brock
1899	1967	Pendleton, Nat
1904	1941	Penner, Joe
1888	1957	Percy, Esme
1892	1937	Perkins, Osgood
1893	1956	Peters, Brandon
1915	1963	Piaf, Edith
1893	1957	Pinza, Ezio
1900	1963	Pitts, Zasu
1903	1969	Portman, Eric
1904	1963	Powell, Dick
1869	1931	Power, F. Tyrone
1914	1958	Power, Tyrone E.
1872	1935	Powers, Eugene
1900	1964	Price, George E.
1856	1919	Primrose, George
1879	1956	Prouty, Jed
1871	1942	Pryor, Arthur
1908	1944	Purcell, Dick
1925	1970	Pyne, Joe

R

Born	Died	Name
1906	1946	Ragland, John (Rags)

Born	Died	Name
1890	1967	Rains, Claude
1889	1970	Rambeau, Marjorie
1900	1947	Rankin, Arthur
1892	1967	Rathbone, Basil
1897	1960	Ratoff, Gregory
1883	1953	Rawlinson, Herbert
1891	1943	Ray, Charles
1860	1916	Rehan, Ada
1893	1923	Reid, Wallace
1873	1943	Reinhardt, Max
1909	1971	Rennie, Michael
1870	1940	Richman, Charles
1895	1972	Richman, Harry
1872	1961	Ring, Blanche
1888	1958	Risdon, Elizabeth
1907	1974	Ritter, Tex
1905	1969	Ritter, Thelma
1903	1960	Ritz, Al
1878	1949	Robinson, Bill
1893	1973	Robinson, Edward G.
1865	1942	Robson, May
1897	1933	Rodgers, Jimmy
1894	1958	Rodzinsky, Artur
1879	1935	Rogers, Will
1897	1937	Roland, Ruth
1880	1962	Rooney, Pat
1899	1966	Rose, Billy
1882	1936	Rothafel, S. L. (Roxy)
1878	1953	Ruffo, Titta
1892	1970	Ruggles, Charles
1903	1972	Rushing, Jimmy
1864	1936	Russell, Annie
1861	1922	Russell, Lillian
1892	1972	Rutherford, Margaret
1902	1973	Ryan, Irene
1909	1973	Ryan, Robert

S

Born	Died	Name
1877	1968	St. Denis, Ruth
1884	1955	Sakall, S.K.
1885	1936	Sale (Chic), Charles
1906	1972	Sanders, George
1934	1973	Sands, Diana
1896	1960	Savo, Jimmy
1879	1954	Scheff, Fritzi
1892	1930	Schenck, Joe
1895	1964	Schildkraut, Joseph
1865	1930	Schildkraut, Rudolph
1889	1965	Schipa, Tito
1882	1951	Schnabel, Artur
1910	1949	Schumann, Henrietta
1861	1936	Schumann-Heink, E.
1866	1945	Scott, Cyril
1914	1965	Scott, Zachary
1843	1896	Scott-Siddons, Mrs.
1892	1974	Seely, Blossom
1902	1965	Selznick, David O.
1858	1935	Sembrich, Marcella
1884	1960	Sennett, Mack
1881	1951	Shattuck, Arthur
1860	1929	Shaw, Mary
1868	1949	Shean, Al
1915	1967	Sheridan, Ann
1924	1973	Sherman, Allan
1885	1934	Sherman, Lowell
1918	1970	Shriner, Herb
1883	1953	Shubert, Lee
1755	1831	Siddons, Mrs. Sarah
1882	1930	Sills, Milton
1914	1970	Silvera, Frank
1878	1946	Sis Hopkins (Melville)
1891	1934	Skelly, Hal
1858	1942	Skinner, Otis
1870	1952	Skipworth, Alison
1892	1970	Skulnik, Menasha
1894	1937	Smith, Bessie
1863	1948	Smith, C. Aubrey
1826	1881	Sothern, Edward A.
1859	1933	Sothern, Edward H.
1884	1957	Sothern, Harry
1854	1932	Sousa, John Philip
1884	1957	Sparks, Ned
1876	1948	Speaks, Oley
1890	1970	Spitalny, Phil
1873	1937	Standing, Guy
1871	1956	Stephenson, Henry
1900	1941	Stephenson, James
1883	1939	Sterling, Ford

Born	Died	Name
1882	1928	Stevens, Emily A.
1934	1970	Stevens, Inger
1896	1961	Stewart, Anita
1873	1959	Stone, Fred
1879	1953	Stone, Lewis
1871	1954	Straus, Oskar
1911	1960	Sullavan, Margaret
1903	1956	Sullivan, Francis L.
1904	1969	Swarthout, Gladys

T

Born	Died	Name
1897	1957	Talmadge, Norma
1917	1968	Talman, William
1878	1947	Tanguay, Eva
1899	1934	Tashman, Lilyan
1910	1956	Tatum, Art
1885	1966	Taylor, Deems
1899	1958	Taylor, Estelle
1887	1946	Taylor, Laurette
1911	1969	Taylor, Robert
1878	1938	Tearle, Conway
1884	1953	Tearle, Godfrey
1892	1937	Tell, Alma
1881	1934	Tellegen, Lou
1864	1942	Tempest, Marie
1910	1963	Templeton, Alec
1848	1928	Terry, Ellen
1874	1940	Tetrazzini, Luisa
1899	1936	Thalberg, Irving
1857	1914	Thomas, Brandon
1892	1960	Thomas, John Charles
1869	1936	Thurston, Howard
1896	1960	Tibbett, Lawrence
1887	1940	Tinney, Frank
1909	1958	Todd, Michael
1906	1935	Todd, Thelma
1874	1947	Toler, Sidney
1905	1968	Tone, Franchot
1878	1933	Torrence, Ernest
1867	1957	Toscanini, Arturo
1898	1968	Tracy, Lee
1800	1967	Tracy, Spencer
1903	1972	Traubel, Helen
1853	1917	Tree, Herbert Beerbohm
1890	1973	Truex, Ernest
1883	1942	Tucker, Richard
1884	1966	Tucker, Sophie
1911	1970	Tufts, Sonny
1874	1940	Turpin, Ben
1908	1959	Twelvetrees, Helen

U

Born	Died	Name
1894	1970	Ulric, Lenore

V

Born	Died	Name
1895	1926	Valentino, Rudolph
1870	1950	Van, Billy B.
1894	1943	Veidt, Conrad
1886	1957	Von Stroheim, Erich

W

Born	Died	Name
1874	1946	Waldron, Charles D.
1904	1966	Walker, June
1919	1951	Walker, Robert
1904	1943	Waller, Thomas (Fats)
1876	1962	Walter, Bruno
1878	1936	Walthall, Henry B.
1872	1952	Ward, Fannie
1866	1951	Warfield, David
1876	1958	Warner, H. B.
1878	1964	Warwick, Robert
1924	1963	Washington, Dinah
1867	1945	Watson, Billy
1879	1962	Watson, Lucille
1890	1965	Watson, Minor
1896	1966	Webb, Clifton
1867	1942	Weber, Joe
1905	1973	Webster, Margaret
1900	1950	Weill, Kurt
1876	1926	Welch, Ben
1873	1918	Welch, Joe
1883	1953	Werrenrath, Reinald
1879	1942	Westley, Helen
1895	1968	Wheeler, Bert
1889	1938	White, Pearl
1890	1967	Whiteman, Paul
1882	1943	Whiting, George

Born	Died	Name	Born	Died	Name	Born	Died	Name
1865	1948	Whitty, Dame May	1904	1959	Withers, Grant			**Y**
1906	1966	Whorf, Richard	1881	1931	Wolheim, Louis	1891	1960	Young, Clara Kimball
1895	1948	William, Warren	1907	1961	Wong, Anna May	1887	1953	Young, Roland
1877	1922	Williams, Bert	1888	1963	Woolley, Monty	1900	1956	Young, Victor
1867	1918	Williams, Evan	1889	1938	Woolsey, Robert			
1923	1953	Williams, Hank	1881	1956	Wycherly, Margaret			**Z**
1917	1972	Wilson, Marie	1886	1966	Wynn, Ed	1869	1932	Ziegfeld, Florenz
1884	1969	Winninger, Charles	1906	1964	Wynyard, Diana			

Entertainment Personalities — Where and When Born

Actors, Actresses, Composers, Dancers, Musicians, Producers, Radio-TV Performers, Singers

Name	Birthplace	Born	Name	Birthplace	Born
A			Arthur Beatrice	New York, N.Y.	—
Abbott, George	Forestville, N.Y.	1887	Arthur, Jean	New York, N.Y.	1908
Abel, Walter	St. Paul, Minn.	1898	Ashley, Elizabeth	Ocala, Fla.	1940
Abner (Norris Goff)	Cove, Ark.	1906	Asner, Edward	Kansas City, Kansas.	—
Ackermann, Bettye	Cottageville, S.Car.	1928	Astaire, Fred	Omaha, Nebr.	1899
Acuff, Roy	Maynardsville, Tenn.	1903	Astin, John	Baltimore, Md.	1930
Adams, Don	New York, N.Y.	1927	Astor, Mary	Quincy, Ill.	1906
Adams, Edie	Kingston, Pa.	1929	Attenborough, Richard	Cambridge, Eng.	1923
Adams, Joey	New York, N.Y.	1911	Aumont, Jean-Pierre	Paris, France	1913
Adams, Julie	Waterloo, Iowa.	1926	Autry, Gene	Tioga, Texas.	1907
Addams, Dawn	Suffolk, England.	1930	Avalon, Frankie	Philadelphia, Pa.	1940
Adderley, Cannonball	Tampa, Fla.	1928	Ayres, Lew	Minneapolis, Minn.	1908
Adler, Kurt H.	Vienna, Austria	1905	Aznavour, Charles	Paris, France.	1924
Adler, Larry	Baltimore, Md.	1914			
Adler, Luther	New York, N.Y.	1903	**B**		
Agar, John	Chicago, Ill.	1921	Bacall, Lauren	New York, N.Y.	1924
Aherne, Brian	Worcestershire, Eng.	1902	Bacharach, Burt	Kansas City, Mo.	1928
Aimee, Anouk	Paris, France	1932	Backus, Jim	Cleveland, Ohio.	1913
Albanese, Licia	Bari, Italy.	1913	Baclanova, Olga	Moscow, Russia.	1899
Alberghetti, Anna	Pesaro, Italy.	1936	Baer, Max Jr.	Oakland, Calif.	1937
Albert, Eddie	Rock Island, Ill.	1908	Baez, Joan	Staten Island, N.Y.	1941
Albertson, Jack	Malden, Mass.	—	Bailey, Pearl	Newport News, Va.	1918
Albright, Lola	Akron, Ohio.	1925	Bailey, Raymond	San Francisco, Calif.	1905
Alda, Alan	New York, N.Y.	1936	Bain, Barbara	Chicago, Ill.	1934
Alda, Robert	New York, N.Y.	1914	Baird, William B.	Grand Island, Nebr.	1904
Alexander, Jane	Boston, Mass.	1939	Baker, Carroll	Johnstown, Pa.	1935
Alexander, Katherine	Arkansas.	1901	Baker, Diane	Hollywood, Calif.	1938
Allan, Elizabeth	England	1910	Baker, Josephine	St. Louis, Mo.	1906
Allbritton, Louise	Oklahoma City, Okla.	1920	Baker, Kenny	Monrovia, Calif.	1912
Allen, Mel	Birmingham, Ala.	1913	Baker, Stanley	Glamorgan, Wales.	1928
Allen, Steve	New York, N.Y.	1921	Bakewell, William	Hollywood, Calif.	1908
Allen, Woody	Brooklyn, N.Y.	1935	Balanchine, George	St. Petersburg, Russia.	1904
Allison, Fran	LaPorte City, Iowa.	—	Ball, Lucille	Jamestown, N.Y.	1911
Allyson, June	Lucerne, N.Y.	1923	Ballard, Kay	West Cleveland, Ohio.	1926
Alpert, Herb	Los Angeles, Calif.	1935	Balsam, Martin	New York, N.Y.	1919
Ameche, Don	Kenosha, Wis.	1908	Bampton, Rose	Cleveland, Ohio.	1909
Ames, Ed	Boston, Mass.	1929	Bancroft, Anne	New York, N.Y.	1931
Ames, Leon	Portland, Ind.	1903	Bannon, Ian	Airdrie, Scotland.	1928
Ames, Nancy	Washington, D.C.	1937	Barber, Red	Columbus, Miss.	1908
Amos (F. F. Gosden)	Richmond, Va.	1904	Bardot, Brigitte	Paris, France.	1934
Amsterdam, Morey	Chicago, Ill.	1912	Bari, Lynn	Roanoke, Va.	1917
Anderson, Judith	Adelaide, Australia.	1898	Barnett, Vincent	Pittsburgh, Pa.	1902
Anderson, Lynn	Grand Forkes, N.D.	1947	Barrault, Jean-Louise	Le Vesinet, France.	1919
Anderson, Marian	Philadelphia, Pa.	1902	Barrett, Sheila	Washington, D.C.	1909
Anderson, Mary	Birmingham, Ala.	1922	Barrie, Mona	London, Eng.	1909
Anderson, Michael, Jr.	London, England.	1943	Barrie, Wendy	Hong Kong, China.	1913
Anderson, Warner	Brooklyn, N.Y.	1911	Barry, Gene	New York, N.Y.	1922
Andersson, Bibi	Stockholm, Sweden.	1935	Barry, Jack	Lindenhurst, N.Y.	1918
Andress, Ursula	Switzerland.	1938	Barrymore, John, Jr.	Beverly Hills, Calif.	1932
Andrews, Dana	Collins, Miss.	1909	Bartholomew, Freddie	London, England.	1924
Andrews, Edward	Griffin, Ga.	1915	Bartok, Eva	Budapest, Hungary.	1929
Andrews, Julie	Walton, England.	1935	Basehart, Richard	Zanesville, Ohio.	1914
Andrews, Maxene	Minneapolis, Minn.	1918	Basie, Count (Wm.)	Red Bank, N.J.	1904
Andrews, Patty	Minneapolis, Minn.	1920	Bassey, Shirley	Cardiff, Wales.	1937
Angel, Heather	Oxford, England.	1909	Bates, Alan	Allestree, Eng.	1934
Anka, Paul	Ottawa, Canada.	1941	Baum, Kurt	Cologne, Germany.	1908
Ann-Margret	Stockholm, Sweden.	1941	Bavier, Frances	New York, N.Y.	1905
Annabella	Paris, France	1912	Baxter, Anne	Michigan City, Ind.	1923
Ansara, Michael	Lowell, Mass.	1922	Beal, John	Joplin, Mo.	1909
Archer, John	Osceola, Nebr.	1915	Bean, Orson	Cambridge, Mass.	1928
Arden, Eve	Mill Valley, Calif.	1912	Beatty, Robert	Hamilton, Ont.	1909
Arkin, Alan	New York, N.Y.	1934	Beatty, Warren	Richmond, Va.	1938
Arlen, Harold	Buffalo, N.Y.	1905	Becker, Sandy	New York, N.Y.	1922
Arlen, Richard	Charlottesville, Va.	1900	Bedelia, Bonnie	New York, N.Y.	1948
Arnaz, Desi	Santiago, Cuba.	1917	Beery, Noah, Jr.	New York, N.Y.	1916
Arnaz, Desi, Jr.	Los Angeles, Calif.	1953	Belafonte, Harry	New York, N.Y.	1927
Arnaz, Lucie	Hollywood, Calif.	1951	Bel Geddes, Barbara	New York, N.Y.	1922
Arness, James	Minneapolis, Minn.	1923	Bellamy, Ralph	Chicago, Ill.	1904
Arnold, Eddy	Henderson, Tenn.	1918	Belmondo, Jean-Paul	Neuilly-sur-Seine, Fr.	1933
Arquette, Cliff.	Toledo, Ohio.	1905	Benjamin, Dick	New York, N.Y.	1939
Arrau, Claudio	Chillau, Chile.	1903	Bennett, Joan	Palisades, N.J.	1910
Arroyo, Martina	New York, N.Y.	1937	Bennett, Tony	Astoria, N.Y.	1926

Name	Birthplace	Born	Name	Birthplace	Born
Benny, Jack	Waukegan, Ill.	1894	Bruce, Virginia	Minneapolis, Minn.	1910
Bentley, John	Warwickshire, Eng.	1916	Bryant, Anita	Barnsdale, Okla.	1940
Bergen, Candice	Beverly Hills, Calif.	1946	Brynner, Yul	Sakhalin, Japan	1920
Bergen, Edgar	Chicago, Ill.	1903	Bubbles, John	Louisville, Ky.	1903
Bergen, Polly	Knoxville, Tenn.	1930	Buchanan, Edgar	Humansville, Mo.	1903
Berger, Senta	Vienna, Austria	1941	Bucholz, Horst	Berlin, Germany	1933
Bergerac, Jacques	France	1927	Bujold, Genevieve	Canada	1942
Bergman, Ingmar	Uppsala, Sweden	1918	Burke, Paul	New Orleans, La.	1926
Bergman, Ingrid	Stockholm, Sweden	1917	Burnett, Carol	San Antonio, Texas	1935
Bergner, Elisabeth	Vienna, Austria	1900	Burns, George	New York, N.Y.	1896
Berkeley, Busby	Los Angeles, Calif.	1895	Burr, Raymond	New Westminister, B.C.	1917
Berle, Milton	New York, N.Y.	1908	Burrows, Abe	New York, N.Y.	1910
Berlinger, Warren	Brooklyn, N.Y.	1937	Burstyn, Ellen	Detroit, Mich.	1932
Berman, Shelley	Chicago, Ill.	1926	Burton, Richard	South Wales	1925
Bernardi, Hershel	New York, N.Y.	1923	Bushell, Anthony	Kent, England	1904
Bernstein, Elmer	New York, N.Y.	1922	Buttons, Red	New York, N.Y.	1919
Bernstein, Leonard	Lawrence, Mass.	1918	Buzzell, Eddie	Brooklyn, N.Y.	1897
Berry, Ken	Moline, Ill.	—	Buzzi, Ruth	Westerly, R.I.	1936
Bessell, Ted	Flushing, N.Y.	1936			
Best, Edna	Hove, England	1900			
Bethune, Zina	New York, N.Y.	1945	**C**		
Bikel, Theodore	Vienna, Austria	1924	Caan, James	New York, N.Y.	1939
Bing, Rudolf	Vienna, Austria	1902	Cabot, Sebastian	London, England	1918
Birney, David	Washington, D.C.	—	Caesar, Irving	New York, N.Y.	1895
Bishop, Joey	Bronx, N.Y.	1918	Caesar, Sid	Yonkers, N.Y.	1922
Bisset, Jacqueline	Weybridge, Eng.	1944	Cagney, James	New York, N.Y.	1904
Bixby, Bill	San Francisco, Calif.	—	Caine, Michael	London, England	1933
Black, Karen	Park Ridge, Ill.	1942	Caldwell, Zoe	Melbourne, Australia	1933
Blaine, Vivian	Newark, N.J.	1924	Calhoun, Rory	Los Angeles, Calif.	1922
Blair, Janet	Altoona, Pa.	1921	Callahan, James	Grand Rapids, Mich.	1930
Blair, June	San Francisco, Calif.	1937	Callan, Michael	Philadelphia, Pa.	1940
Blake, Robert	Nutley, N.J.	1938	Callas, Maria	New York, N.Y.	1923
Blanc, Mel	San Francisco, Calif.	1908	Calloway, Cab	Rochester, N.Y.	1907
Bloch, Ray	Alsace-Lorraine	1902	Calvert, Phyllis	London, England	1917
Blondell, Joan	New York, N.Y.	1909	Calvet, Corinne	Paris, France	1926
Bloom, Claire	London, Eng.	1931	Cambridge, Godfrey	New York, N.Y.	1933
Blue, Ben	Montreal, Canada	1901	Cameron, Rod	Calgary, Canada	1912
Blyden, Larry	Houston, Tex.	1925	Campbell, Glen	Billstown, Ark.	1938
Blyth, Ann	Mt. Kisco, N.Y.	1928	Canary, David	Elwood, Ind.	1938
Boehm, Karl	Graz, Austria	1894	Cannon, Dyan	Tacoma, Wash.	1937
Bogarde, Dirk	London, Eng.	1921	Canova, Judy	Jacksonville, Fla.	1916
Bolger, Ray	Boston, Mass.	1904	Cantinflas	Mexico City, Mex.	1917
Bonaduce, Danny	Philadelphia, Pa.	1959	Capp, Al	New Haven, Conn.	1909
Bond, Sheila	New York, N.Y.	1928	Capra, Frank	Palermo, Italy	1897
Bondi, Beulah	Chicago, Ill.	1892	Cardinale, Claudia	Tunisia	1939
Bono, Cher	El Centro, Calif.	1946	Carey, Macdonald	Sioux City, Iowa	1913
Bono, Sonny	Detroit, Mich.	1940	Carey, Phil	Hackensack, N.J.	1925
Boone, Pat	Jacksonville, Fla.	1934	Carle, Frankie	Providence, R.I.	1903
Boone, Richard	Los Angeles, Calif.	1917	Carlisle, Kitty	New Orleans, La.	1915
Booth, Shirley	New York, N.Y.	1909	Carlson, Richard	Alberta Lea, Minn.	1914
Borge, Victor	Copenhagen, Denmark	1909	Carmichael, Hoagy	Bloomington, Ind.	1899
Borgnine, Ernest	Hamden, Conn.	1917	Carmichael, Ian	Hull, England	1920
Bosley, Tom	Chicago, Ill.	1927	Carne, Judy	Northampton, Eng.	1939
Boswell, Connee	New Orleans, La.	—	Carney, Art	Mt. Vernon, N.Y.	1918
Bowman, Lee	Cincinnati, Ohio	1914	Carnovsky, Morris	St. Louis, Mo.	1897
Boyd, Stephen	Belfast, Ireland	1928	Caron, Leslie	Boulogne, France	1931
Boyer, Charles	Figeac, France	1899	Carpenter, Karen	New Haven, Conn.	1950
Bracken, Eddie	Astoria, N.Y.	1920	Carpenter, Richard	New Haven, Conn.	1946
Brand, Neville	Kewanee, Ill.	1921	Carr, Vicki	El Paso, Texas	1942
Brando, Marlon	Omaha, Nebr.	1924	Carradine, David	Hollywood, Calif.	1945
Brasselle, Keefe	Elyria, Ohio	1923	Carradine, John	New York, N.Y.	1906
Brazzi, Rossano	Bologna, Italy	1916	Carroll, Diahann	Bronx, N.Y.	1935
Brennan, Eileen	Los Angeles, Calif.	1937	Carroll, Madeleine	W. Bromwich, Eng.	1906
Brennan, Walter	Lynn, Mass.	1894	Carroll, Pat	Shreveport, La.	1927
Brent, Evelyn	Tampa, Fla.	1899	Carter, Jack	New York, N.Y.	1923
Brent, George	Dublin, Ireland	1904	Carson, Jeannie	Yorkshire, Eng.	1929
Brewer, Teresa	Toledo, Ohio	1931	Carson, Johnny	Corning, Iowa	1925
Brian, David	New York, N.Y.	1914	Carson, Mindy	New York, N.Y.	1927
Bridges, Beau	Hollywood, Calif.	—	Casadesus, Gaby	Marseilles, France	1902
Bridges, Lloyd	San Leandro, Calif.	1913	Cash, Johnny	Kingsland, Ark.	1932
Britt, May	Sweden	1936	Cass, Peggy	Boston, Mass.	1926
Britton, Barbara	Long Beach, Calif.	1923	Cassavetes, John	New York, N.Y.	1929
Brolin, James	Los Angeles, Calif.	1942	Cassidy, David	New York, N.Y.	1950
Bronson, Charles	Scooptown, Pa.	1920	Cassidy, Jack	New York, N.Y.	1927
Brook, Clive	London, England	1891	Cassidy, Ted	Pittsburgh, Pa.	1932
Brooks, Louise	Cherryvale, Kansas	1906	Caulfield, Joan	West Orange, N.J.	1922
Brooks, Mel	New York, N.Y.	1926	Cavallaro, Carmen	New York, N.Y.	1913
Brooks, Phyllis	Boise, Idaho	1914	Cavett, Dick	Kearny, Nebr.	1937
Brooks, Stephen	Columbus, Ohio	1942	Chamberlain, Richard	Beverly Hills, Calif.	1935
Brothers, Joyce	New York, N.Y.	1928	Champion, Gower	Geneva, Ill.	1921
Brown, James	Augusta, Ga.	1934	Champion, Marge	Los Angeles, Calif.	1926
Brown, Jimmy	St. Simons Island, Ga.	1936	Channing, Carol	Seattle, Wash.	1923
Brown, Johnny Mack	Dothan, Ala.	1904	Chaplin, Charles	London, England	1889
Brown, Les	Reinerton, Pa.	1912	Chaplin, Geraldine	Santa Monica, Calif.	1944
Brown, Tom	New York, N.Y.	1913	Chaplin, Sydney	Beverly Hills, Calif.	1926
Brown, Vanessa	Vienna, Austria	1928	Charisse, Cyd	Amarillo, Texas	1923
Brubeck, Dave	Concord, Calif.	1920	Charles, Ray	Albany, Ga.	1930
Bruce, Carol	Great Neck, N.Y.	1919	Chase, Ilka	New York, N.Y.	1905

Name	Birthplace	Born
Checker, Chubby	So. Phil. Pa.	1941
Christian, Linda.	Tampico, Mexico.	1924
Christie, Audrey.	Chicago, Ill.	1912
Christie, Julie.	Chukur, India.	1940
Christopher, Jordon.	Youngstown, Ohio.	1941
Christy, June.	Springfield, Ill.	1925
Churchill, Sarah.	London, England.	1916
Cilento, Diane.	Queensland, Aust.	1933
Claire, Ina.	Washington, D.C.	1892
Clark, Dane.	New York, N.Y.	1913
Clark, Dick.	Mt. Vernon, N.Y.	1929
Clark, Petula.	Ewell, Surrey, Eng.	1934
Clark, Roy.	Meherrin, Va.	1933
Clayton, Jan.	Tularosa, N. Mex.	1925
Cliburn, Van.	Shreveport, La.	1934
Clooney, Rosemary.	Maysville, Ky.	1928
Cobb, Lee J.	New York, N.Y.	1911
Coburn, James.	Laurel, Nebr.	1928
Coca, Imogene.	Philadelphia, Pa.	1920
Coco, James.	New York, N.Y.	1929
Cohen, Myron.	Grodno, Poland.	1902
Colbert, Claudette.	Paris, France.	1907
Cole, Dennis.	Detroit, Mich.	1943
Cole, Michael.	Madison, Wis.	1945
Cole, Tina.	Hollywood, Calif.	1943
Collins, Dorothy.	Windsor, Ontario.	1926
Collins, Joan.	London, England.	1933
Collins, Judy.	Seattle, Wash.	1939
Colonna, Jerry.	Boston, Mass.	1903
Como, Perry.	Canonsburg, Pa.	1912
Conklin, Peggy.	Dobbs Ferry, N.Y.	1912
Conley, Eugene.	Lynn, Mass.	1908
Connelly, Marc.	McKeesport, Pa.	1890
Conner, Nadine.	Compton, Calif.	1913
Conniff, Ray.	Attleboro, Mass.	1916
Connors, Michael.	Fresno, Calif.	1925
Connery, Sean.	Edinburgh, Scotland	1930
Connors, Chuck.	Brooklyn, N.Y.	1921
Conrad, Robert.	Chicago, Ill.	1935
Conrad, William.	Louisville, Ky.	1919
Conried, Hans.	Baltimore, Md.	1917
Considine, Tim.	Los Angeles, Calif.	1940
Conte, Richard.	Jersey City, N.J.	1916
Converse, Frank.	St. Louis, Mo.	1938
Conway, Gary.	Boston, Mass.	1938
Conway, Shirl.	Franklinville, N.Y.	1916
Conway, Tim.	Chagrin Falls, Ohio.	1933
Coogan, Jackie.	Los Angeles, Calif.	1914
Cook, Barbara	Atlanta, Ga.	1927
Cooke, Alistair.	England.	1908
Cooper, Jackie.	Los Angeles, Calif.	1922
Corey, Jeff.	New York, N.Y.	1914
Cornell, Don.	New York, N.Y.	1921
Cortez, Ricardo.	Vienna, Austria.	1899
Cosby, Bill.	Philadelphia, Pa.	1937
Cosell, Howard.	Winston-Salem, N.C.	1920
Costello, Dolores.	Pittsburgh, Pa.	1905
Cotsworth, Staats.	Oak Park, Ill.	1908
Cotten, Joseph.	Petersburg, Va.	1905
Courtenay, Tom.	Hull, England.	1937
Crabbe, Buster.	Oakland, Calif.	1909
Crain, Jeanne.	Barstow, Calif.	1925
Crane, Bob.	Waterbury, Conn.	1928
Crane Les.	New York, N.Y.	1934
Crawford, Broderick.	Philadelphia, Pa.	1911
Crawford, Joan.	San Antonio, Tex.	1908
Crawford, Michael.	Salisbury, England.	1942
Crenna, Richard.	Los Angeles, Calif.	1927
Cristal, Linda.	Argentina.	—
Cronyn, Hume.	London, Ont.	1911
Crosby, Bing (Harry).	Tacoma, Wash.	1904
Crosby, Bob.	Spokane, Wash.	1913
Cross, Milton.	New York, N.Y.	1897
Crowley, Pat.	Scranton, Pa.	1929
Cruz, Brandon.	Bakersfield, Calif.	1962
Cugat, Xavier.	Barcelona, Spain.	1900
Cullen, Bill.	Pittsburgh, Pa.	1920
Culp, Robert.	Berkeley, Calif.	1930
Cummings, Constance.	Seattle, Wash.	1910
Cummings, Robert.	Joplin, Mo.	1910
Cummings, Peggy.	Prestatyn, N. Wales	1925
Curtin, Phyllis.	Clarksburg, W. Va.	1930
Curtis, Ken.	Lamar, Colo.	1916
Curtis, Tony.	New York, N.Y.	1925
Cusack, Cyril.	Durban, So. Africa.	1910
Cushing, Peter.	Surrey, Eng.	1913

D

Name	Birthplace	Born
Dagmar (Egnor).	Huntington, W.Va.	1926
Dahl, Arlene.	Minneapolis, Minn.	1927
Dailey, Dan.	New York, N.Y.	1917
Dalrymple, Jean.	Morristown, N.J.	1910
Dalton, Abby.	Las Vegas, Nev.	1935
Daly, James.	Wisconsin Rapids, Wis.	1918
Daly, John.	Johannesburg, S. Afr.	1914
Damita, Lili.	Paris, France.	1907
Damone, Vic.	Brooklyn, N.Y.	1928
Dana, Bill.	Quincy, Mass.	1924
Dangerfield, Rodney.	Babylon, L.I., N.Y.	1921
Daniels, William.	Brooklyn, N.Y.	1927
Danilova, Alexandra.	Peterhof, Russia.	1907
Danton, Ray.	New York, N.Y.	1931
Darby, Kim.	Hollywood, Calif.	1948
Darcel, Denise.	Paris, France.	1925
Darren, James.	Philadelphia, Pa.	1936
Darrieux, Danielle.	Bordeaux, France.	1917
Darrow, Henry.	New York, N.Y.	1933
Da Silva, Howard.	Cleveland, Ohio.	1909
Dassin, Jules.	Middletown, Conn.	1911
Dauphin, Claude.	Corbeil, France.	1905
Davidson, John.	Pittsburgh, Pa.	1941
Davis, Ann B.	Schenectady, N.Y.	1926
Davis, Bette.	Lowell, Mass.	1908
Davis, Miles.	Alton, Ill.	1927
Davis, Sammy, Jr.	New York, N.Y.	1925
Davis, Ossie.	Cogdell, Ga.	1917
Dawn, Hazel.	Ogden, Utah.	1898
Day, Dennis.	New York, N.Y.	1917
Day, Doris.	Cincinnati, Ohio.	1924
Day, Laraine.	Roosevelt, Utah.	1920
Dean, Jimmy.	Plainview, Texas.	1928
De Camp, Rosemary.	Prescott, Ariz.	1913
De Carlo, Yvonne.	Vancouver, B. C.	1924
Dee, Frances.	Los Angeles, Calif.	1907
Dee, Joey.	Passaic, N.J.	1940
Dee, Ruby.	Cleveland, Ohio.	1924
Dee, Sandra.	Bayonne, N.J.	1942
DeFore, Don.	Cedar Rapids, Iowa.	1917
DeHaven, Gloria.	Los Angeles, Calif.	1925
deHavilland, Olivia.	Tokyo, Japan.	1916
Dell, Gabriel.	Brooklyn, N.Y.	1921
Della Chiesa, Vivienna.	Chicago, Ill.	1920
Delon, Alain.	France.	1935
DeLuise, Dom.	Brooklyn, N.Y.	1933
Del Rio, Dolores.	Durango, Mexico.	1905
Demarest, William.	St. Paul, Minn.	1892
De Mille, Agnes.	New York, N.Y.	1905
Dempster, Carol.	Duluth, Minn.	1901
Deneuve, Catherine.	Paris, France.	1943
Denning, Richard.	Poughkeepsie, N.Y.	1914
Dennis, Sandy.	Hastings, Nebr.	1937
Denver, Bob.	New Rochelle, N.Y.	1935
Derek, John.	Hollywood, Calif.	1926
De Sica, Vittorio.	Sora, Italy.	1902
Desmond, Johnny.	Detroit, Mich.	1921
Devine, Andy.	Flagstaff, Ariz.	1905
Dewhurst, Colleen.	Montreal, Canada.	1926
Diamond, Neil.	Brooklyn, N.Y.	1941
Dickinson, Angie.	Kulm, N. Dak.	1936
Dietrich, Marlene.	Berlin, Germany.	1901
Diller, Phyllis.	Lima, Ohio.	1917
Dillman, Bradford.	San Francisco, Calif.	1930
Dixon, Ivan.	New York, N.Y.	1931
Dixon, Jeane.	Waterbury, Conn.	1905
Domino, Fats.	New Orleans, La.	1928
Donahue, Troy.	New York, N.Y.	1936
Donald, James.	Aberdeen, Scotland.	1917
Donald, Peter.	Bristol, England.	1918
Donnelly, Ruth.	Trenton, N.J.	1896
Donovan.	Glasgow, Scotland.	1946
Dors, Diana.	Swindon, England.	1931
d'Orsay, Fifi.	Montreal, Canada.	1908
Douglas, Donna.	Baywood, La.	1939
Douglas, Kirk.	Amsterdam, N.Y.	1918
Douglas, Melvyn.	Macon, Ga.	1901
Douglas, Mike.	Chicago, Ill.	1925
Downey, Morton.	Wallingford, Conn.	1902
Downs, Hugh.	Akron, Ohio.	1921
Dragonette, Jessica.	Calcutta, India.	—
Drake, Alfred.	Bronx, N.Y.	1914
Drake, Betsy.	Paris, France.	1923
Draper, Paul.	Florence, Italy.	1911
Drew, Ellen.	Kansas City, Mo.	1915
Dru, Joanne.	Logan, W.Va.	1923
Drury, James.	New York, N.Y.	1934

Name	Birthplace	Born
Duchin, Peter	New York, N.Y.	1937
Duff, Howard	Bremerton, Wash.	1917
Duke, Patty	New York, N.Y.	1946
Dullea, Keir	Cleveland, Ohio	1936
Dunaway, Faye	Tallahassee, Fla.	1941
Duncan, Sandy	Henderson, Texas	1946
Duncan, Todd	Danville, Ky.	1900
Duncan, Vivian	Los Angeles, Calif.	1902
Dunham, Katherine	Chicago, Ill.	1910
Dunne, Irene	Louisville, Ky.	1904
Dunninger, Joseph	New York, N.Y.	1898
Dunnock, Mildred	Baltimore, Md.	1906
Durante, Jimmy	New York, N.Y.	1893
Durbin, Deanna	Winnipeg, Canada	1922
Duvall, Robert	San Diego, Calif.	1931
Dvorak, Ann	New York, N.Y.	1912
Dylan, Bob	Duluth, Minn.	1941

E

Name	Birthplace	Born
Eastwood, Clint	San Francisco, Calif.	1930
Eaton, Shirley	London, England.	1937
Ebsen, Buddy	Belleville, Ill.	1908
Eckstine, Billy	Pittsburgh, Pa.	1914
Edelman, Herb	Brooklyn, N.Y.	1933
Eden, Barbara	Tucson, Ariz.	1934
Edwards, Douglas	Ada, Okla.	1917
Edwards, Joan	New York, N.Y.	1920
Edwards, Ralph	Merino, Colo.	1913
Edwards, Vincent	Brooklyn, N.Y.	1928
Egan, Richard	San Francisco, Calif.	1923
Eggar, Samantha	London, England.	1939
Eggerth, Marta	Budapest, Hungary	1916
Ekberg, Anita	Malmo, Sweden	1931
Ekland, Britt	Stockholm, Sweden	1942
Eldridge, Florence	Brooklyn, N.Y.	1901
Elgart, Larry	New London, Conn.	1922
Elgart, Les	New Haven, Conn.	1918
Elliott, Bob	Boston, Mass.	1923
Emerson, Faye	Elizabeth, La.	1917
Erickson, Leif	Alameda, Calif.	1911
Esmond, Jill	London, England.	1908
Etting, Ruth	David City, Neb.	1896
Evans, Dale	Uvalde, Texas.	1912
Evans, Dame Edith	London, England.	1888
Evans, Maurice	Dorchester, England.	1901
Everett, Chad	South Bend, Ind.	1937
Evers, Jason	New York, N.Y.	1927
Ewell, Tom	Owensboro, Ky.	1909

F

Name	Birthplace	Born
Fabares, Shelley	Santa Monica, Calif.	1944
Fabian (Forte)	Philadelphia, Pa.	1943
Fabray, Nanette	San Diego, Calif.	1920
Fadiman, Clifton	Brooklyn, N.Y.	1904
Fairbanks, Doug, Jr.	New York, N.Y.	1909
Faith, Percy	Toronto, Ont.	1908
Falk, Peter	New York, N.Y.	1927
Falkenburg, Jinx	Barcelona, Spain	1919
Farber, Barry	Baltimore, Md.	1930
Farentino, James	Brooklyn, N.Y.	1938
Fargo, Donna	Mt. Airy, N.C.	1945
Farr, Felicia	Westchester, N.Y.	1932
Farrell, Charles	Onset Bay, Mass.	1901
Farrell, Eileen	Willimantic, Conn.	1920
Farrow, Mia	Los Angeles, Calif.	1946
Faye, Alice	New York, N.Y.	1915
Feld, Fritz	Berlin, Germany	1900
Feldon, Barbara	Pittsburgh, Pa.	1941
Feliciano, Jose	Puerto Rico	1945
Fellini, Federico	Rimini, Italy	1920
Fellows, Edith	Boston, Mass.	1923
Fenney, Joe	Grand Island, Nebr.	1931
Fenton, Leslie	England	1903
Ferrer, Jose	Santurce, P.R.	1912
Ferrer, Mel	Elberon, N.J.	1917
Ferris, Barbara	London, England.	1942
Fetchit, Stepin	Key West, Fla.	1902
Fiedler, Arthur	Boston, Mass.	1894
Field, Sally	Pasadena, Calif.	1946
Fields, Gracie	Rochdale, England	1898
Fields, Totie	Hartford, Conn.	1931
Finch, Peter	London, England.	1916
Finney, Albert	Salford, England	1936
Firkusny, Napajedla Rudolf	Czechoslovakia	1912
Fisher, Eddie	Philadelphia, Pa.	1928
Fisher, Gail	Orange, N.J.	—
Fitzgerald, Ella	Newport News, Va.	1918
Fitzgerald, Geraldine	Dublin, Ireland.	1914

Name	Birthplace	Born
Fitzgerald, Pegeen	Norcatur, Kansas	1910
Fix, Paul	Dobbs Ferry, N.Y.	1902
Flack, Roberta	Black Mountain, N.C.	1940
Flatt, Lester	Overton County, Tenn.	1914
Fleming, Rhonda	Hollywood, Calif.	1923
Flynn, Joe	Youngstown, Ohio	1926
Foch, Nina	Leyden, Neth.	1924
Fonda, Henry	Grand Island, Nebr.	1905
Fonda, Jane	New York, N.Y.	1937
Fonda, Peter	New York, N.Y.	1939
Fontaine, Frank	Cambridge, Mass.	1920
Fontaine, Joan	Tokyo, Japan	1917
Fontanne, Lynn	London, England.	1887
Fonteyn, Margot	Reigate, England	1919
Foran, Dick	Flemington, N.J.	1910
Forbes, Bryan	London, England.	1926
Ford (Tenn.), Ernie	Bristol, Tenn.	1919
Ford, Glenn	Quebec, Canada.	1916
Ford, Paul	Baltimore, Md.	1901
Ford, Ruth	Hazelhurst, Miss.	1915
Forrest, Sally	San Diego, Calif.	1928
Forrest, Steve	Huntsville, Texas	1925
Forster, Robert	Rochester, N.Y.	1942
Forsythe, John	Penns Grove, N.J.	1918
Fosse, Bob	Chicago, Ill.	1927
Foster, Norman	Richmond, Ind.	1900
Foster, Phil	Brooklyn, N.Y.	1914
Fountain, Pete	New Orleans, La.	1930
Fox, James	London, England.	1939
Foxx, Redd	St. Louis, Mo.	1922
Foy, Eddie, Jr.	New Rochelle, N.Y.	1905
Francescatti, Zino	Marseilles, France	1904
Franciosa, Anthony	New York, N.Y.	1928
Francis, Arlene	Boston, Mass.	1908
Francis, Connie	Newark, N.J.	1938
Franciscus, James	Clayton, Mo.	1934
Frankenheimer, John	Malba, L.I., N.Y.	1930
Franklin, Aretha	Memphis, Tenn.	1942
Franklin, Joe	New York, N.Y.	1926
Franz, Arthur	Perth Amboy, N.J.	1920
Freberg, Stan	Pasadena, Calif.	1926
Freed, Bert	New York, N.Y.	1919
Freeman, Mona	Baltimore, Md.	1926
Frizzel, Lefty	Corsicana, Texas	1928
Froman, Jane	St. Louis, Mo.	1911
Frost, David	Tenterden, England	1939
Frye, David	Brooklyn, N.Y.	1934
Funicello, Annette	Utica, N.Y.	1942
Funt, Allen	New York, N.Y.	1914
Furness, Betty	New York, N.Y.	1916

G

Name	Birthplace	Born
Gabel, Martin	Philadelphia, Pa.	1912
Gabin, Jean	Villette, Paris, France.	1904
Gabor, Eva	Hungary	1924
Gabor, Zsa Zsa	Hungary	1923
Gahagan, Helen	Boonton, N.J.	1900
Galloway, Don	Brooksville, Ky.	1937
Gam, Rita	Pittsburgh, Pa.	1929
Gambling, John A.	New York, N.Y.	1930
Gambling, John B.	Norwich, England	1897
Garagiola, Joe	St. Louis, Mo.	1926
Garbo, Greta	Stockholm, Sweden	1905
Gardiner, Reginald	Wimbledon, England.	1903
Gardner, Ava	Smithfield, N.C.	1922
Gardner, Hy	New York, N.Y.	1908
Gargan, William	Brooklyn, N.Y.	1905
Garfunkel, Art	New York, N.Y.	1941
Garland, Beverly	Santa Cruz, Calif.	1930
Garner, Erroll	Pittsburgh, Pa.	1923
Garner, James	Norman, Okla.	1928
Garner, Peggy Ann	Canton, Ohio.	1932
Garroway, Dave	Schenectady, N.Y.	1913
Garrett, Betty	St. Joseph, Mo.	1919
Garson, Greer	Co. Down, N. Ireland.	1908
Garver, Kathy	Long Beach, Calif.	1948
Gary, John	Watertown, N.Y.	1932
Gavin, John	Los Angeles, Calif.	1932
Gaynor, Janet	Philadelphia, Pa.	1906
Gaynor, Mitzi	Chicago, Ill.	1931
Gazzara, Ben	New York, N.Y.	1930
Gedda, Nicolai	Sweden.	1925
Geer, Will	Frankfort, Ind.	1902
Geeson, Judy	Sussex, England.	1948
Genevieve (G. Auger).	Paris, France	1930
Genn, Leo	London, England.	1905
Gennaro, Peter	Metairie, La.	1924
Gentry, Bobby	Chickasaw Co., Miss.	1944

Name	Birthplace	Born	Name	Birthplace	Born
Gershwin, Ira	New York, N.Y.	1896	Hanson, Howard	Wahoo, Nebr.	1896
Getz, Stan	Philadelphia, Pa.	1927	Harding, Ann	Ft. Sam Houston, Tex.	1904
Ghostley, Alice	Eve, Mo.	1926	Harper, Ron	Turtle Creek, Pa.	1935
Gibson, Henry	Germantown, Pa.	1935	Harper, Valarie	Suffern, N.Y.	—
Gielgud, John	London, England	1904	Harrington, Pat, Jr.	New York, N.Y.	1929
Gifford, Frank	Santa Monica, Calif.	1930	Harris, Barbara	Evanston, Ill.	1935
Gillespie, Dizzy	Cheraw, N.C.	1917	Harris, Julie	Grosse Pte. Park, Mich.	1925
Gillette, Anita	Baltimore, Md.	1936	Harris, Phil	Linton, Ind.	1906
Gingold, Hermione	London, England	1897	Harris, Richard	Co. Limerick, Ire.	1933
Gish, Lillian	Springfield, Ohio	1896	Harris, Rosemary	Ashby, England	1930
Givot, George	Omaha, Nebr.	1903	Harrison, George	Liverpool, England	1943
Gleason, Jackie	Brooklyn, N.Y.	1916	Harrison, Noel	London, England	1933
Gobel, George	Chicago, Ill.	1919	Harrison, Rex	Huyton, England	1908
Godard, Jean Luc	Paris, France	1930	Hartman, David	Pawtucket, R.I.	1935
Goddard, Mark	Lowell, Mass.	1936	Hartman, Elizabeth	Boardman, Ohio	1943
Goddard, Paulette	Great Neck, N.Y.	1911	Hartman, Paul	San Francisco, Calif.	1904
Godfrey, Arthur	New York, N.Y.	1903	Hasso, Signe	Stockholm, Sweden	1915
Goldsboro, Bobby	Marianne, Fla.	1941	Haver, June	Rock Island, Ill.	1926
Goodman, Benny	Chicago, Ill.	1909	Havoc, June	Vancouver, Canada	1916
Gordon, Gale	New York, N.Y.	1906	Hawn, Goldie	Washington, D.C.	1945
Gordon, Max	New York, N.Y.	1892	Haworth, Jill	Sussex, England	1945
Gordon, Ruth	Wollaston, Mass.	1896	Hayden, Melissa	Toronto, Canada	1928
Gore, Lesley	Tenafly, N.J.	1946	Hayden, Russell	Chico, Calif.	1912
Gorin, Igor	Ukraine, Russia	1909	Hayden, Sterling	Montclair, N.J.	1916
Gorme, Eydie	Bronx, N.Y.	1932	Haydon, Julie	Oak Park, Ill.	1910
Gorshin, Frank	Pittsburgh, Pa.	1935	Hayes, Helen	Washington, D.C.	1900
Gould, Elliot	Brooklyn, N.Y.	1938	Hayes, Issac	Covington, Tenn.	1942
Gould, Morton	Richmond Hill, N.Y.	1913	Hayes, Peter Lind	San Francisco, Calif.	1915
Goulding, Ray	Lowell, Mass.	1922	Hayes, Roland	Curryville, Ga.	1887
Goulet, Robert	Lawrence, Mass.	1933	Haymes, Dick	Buenos Aires, Arg'tina	1918
Gowdy, Curt	Green River, Wyo.	1919	Haynes, Lloyd	South Bend, Ind.	1934
Grady, Don	San Diego, Calif.	1944	Hayward, Louis	Johannesburg, S. Afr.	1909
Graham, Martha	Pittsburgh, Pa.	1902	Hayward, Susan	Brooklyn, N.Y.	1919
Graham, Virginia	Chicago, Ill.	1913	Hayworth, Rita	New York, N.Y.	1918
Grahame, Gloria	Los Angeles, Calif.	1929	Healy, Mary	New Orleans, La.	1918
Grahame, Margot	Canterbury, England	1911	Heatherton, Joey	Rockville Centre, N.Y.	1944
Granger, Farley	San Jose, Calif.	1925	Heckart, Eileen	Columbus, Ohio	1919
Granger, Stewart	London, England	1913	Hefner, Hugh	Chicago, Ill.	1926
Granville, Bonita	New York, N.Y.	1923	Heifetz, Jascha	Vilna, Russia	1901
Grant, Cary	Bristol, England	1904	Helmore, Tom	London, England	1912
Grant, Kathryn	Houston, Texas	1933	Helpmann, Robert	Mt. Gambier, Aust.	1909
Grant, Lee	New York, N.Y.	1927	Henderson, Florence	Dale, Ind.	1934
Grauer, Ben	New York, N.Y.	1908	Henderson, Marcia	Andover, Mass.	1932
Graves, Peter	Minneapolis, Minn.	1926	Henderson, Skitch	Halstad, Minn.	1918
Gray, Coleen	Staplehurst, Nebr.	1922	Henning, David	Guildford, England	1941
Gray, Dolores	Chicago, Ill.	1924	Henning, Linda Kaye	Toluca Lake, Calif.	1944
Grayson, Kathryn	Winston-Salem, N.C.	1923	Henreid, Paul	Trieste, Italy	1908
Graziano, Rocky	New York, N.Y.	1922	Hepburn, Audrey	Brussels, Belgium	1929
Greco, Buddy	Philadelphia, Pa.	1926	Hepburn, Katharine	Hartford, Conn.	1909
Greco, Jose	Abruzzi, Italy	1918	Herbert, Evelyn	Philadelphia, Pa.	1898
Greco, Juilette	Paris, France	—	Herlie, Eileen	Glasgow, Scotland	1920
Green, Eddie	Baltimore, Md.	1901	Herman, Woody	Milwaukee, Wis.	1913
Green, Martyn	London, England	1899	Hershfield, Harry	Cedar Rapids, Iowa	1885
Greene, Lorne	Ottawa, Canada	1915	Heston, Charlton	Evanston, Ill.	1923
Greenwood, Charlotte	Philadelphia, Pa.	1893	Heywood, Anne	Birmingham, England	1937
Greenwood, Joan	London, England	1921	Hildegrade	Adell, Wis.	1906
Greer, Jane	Washington, D.C.	1924	Hill, Arthur	Melfort, Sask., Canada	1922
Gregory, Dick	St. Louis, Mo.	1933	Hiller, Wendy	Stockport, England	1912
Grey, Joel	Cleveland, Ohio	1932	Hines, Earl (Fatha)	Duquesne, Pa.	1905
Griffin, Merv	San Mateo, Calif.	1925	Hines, Jerome	Hollywood, Calif.	1921
Griffith, Andy	Mount Airy, N.C.	1926	Hines, Mimi	Vancouver, B.C.	1933
Griffith, Hugh	Wales	1912	Hingle, Pat	Denver, Colo.	1924
Grimes, Tammy	Lynn, Mass.	1936	Hirt, Al	New Orleans, La.	1922
Grizzard, George	Roanoke Rapids, N.C.	1928	Hitchcock, Alfred	London, England	1899
Guardino, Harry	New York, N.Y.	1925	Ho, Don	Kakaako, Oahu, Hawaii	1930
Guinness, Alec	London, England	1914	Hobart, Rose	New York, N.Y.	1906
Gunn, Moses	St. Louis, Mo.	1929	Hodges, Eddie	Hattiesburg, Miss.	1947
Guthrie, Arlo	New York, N.Y.	1947	Hoffman, Dustin	Los Angeles, Calif.	1937
H			Holbrook, Hal	Cleveland, Ohio	1925
Hackett, Buddy	Brooklyn, N.Y.	1924	Holden, William	O'Fallon, Ill.	1918
Hackett, Joan	New York, N.Y.	1933	Holder, Geoffrey	Trinidad	1930
Hackman, Gene	San Bernardino, Calif.	1931	Holloway, Stanley	London, England	1890
Hagen, Uta	Gottingen, Germany	1919	Holloway, Sterling	Cedartown, Ga.	—
Haggard, Merle	Bakersfield, Calif.	1937	Holm, Celeste	New York, N.Y.	1919
Hagman, Larry	Ft. Worth, Texas	1931	Holtz, Lou	San Francisco, Calif.	1898
Hale, Barbara	DeKalb, Ill.	1922	Homeier, Skip	Chicago, Ill.	1930
Haley, Jack	Boston, Mass.	1899	Homolka, Oscar	Vienna, Austria	1903
Hall, Huntz	New York, N.Y.	—	Hooks, Robert	Washington, D.C.	1937
Hall, Monty	Winnipeg, Canada	1923	Hope, Bob	London, England	1903
Hall, Tom T.	Olive Hill, Ky.	1936	Hopkin, Mary	Wales	1950
Hamilton, George	Memphis, Tenn.	1939	Hopper, Dennis	Dodge City, Kansas	1936
Hamilton, Margaret	Cleveland, Ohio	1902	Horne, Lena	Brooklyn, N.Y.	1917
Hamilton, Neil	Lynn, Mass.	1899	Horowitz, Vladimir	Kiev, Russia	1904
Hampshire, Susan	London, England	1941	Horton, Robert	Los Angeles, Calif.	1924
Hampton, Lionel	Birmingham, Ala.	1914	Howard, Clint	Burbank, Calif.	1959
Hampton, Ruth	Throop, Pa.	1932	Howard, Ronnie	Duncan, Okla.	1954
Hanley, Bridget	Minneapolis, Minn.	1943	Howard, Trevor	Kent, England	1916
			Howes, Sally Ann	London, England	1934

Name	Birthplace	Born	Name	Birthplace	Born
Hudson, Rock	Winnetka, Ill.	1925	Keeler, Ruby	Halifax, N.S., Canada	1910
Hull, Henry	Louisville, Ky.	1890	Keeshan, Bob	Lynbrook, N.Y.	1927
Hull, Warren	Gasport, N.Y.	1903	Keith, Brian	Bayonne, N.J.	1921
Humperdinck, Engelbert	Madras, India	1937	Kellerman, Sally	Long Beach, Calif.	1936
Hunnicutt, Arthur	Gravelly, Ark.	1911	Kelley, DeForrest	Atlanta, Ga.	1920
Hunt, Lois	York, Pa.	1925	Kelly, Emmett	Sedan, Kansas	1898
Hunt, Marsha	Chicago, Ill.	1917	Kelly, Gene	Pittsburgh, Pa.	1912
Hunter, Ian	Cape Town, S. Africa	1900	Kelly, Grace	Philadelphia, Pa.	1929
Hunter, Kim	Detroit, Mich.	1922	Kelly, Jack	Astoria, N.Y.	1927
Hunter, Tab	New York, N.Y.	1931	Kelly, Nancy	Lowell, Mass.	1921
Hussey, Olivia	Buenos Aires, Arg.	1952	Kelly, Patsy	Brooklyn, N.Y.	1910
Hussey, Ruth	Providence, R.I.	1917	Kennedy, Arthur	Worcester, Mass.	1914
Huston, John	Nevada, Mo.	1906	Kennedy, George	New York, N.Y.	1926
Hutchins, Will	Los Angeles, Calif.	1932	Kennedy, Madge	Chicago, Ill.	—
Hutchinson, Josephine	Seattle, Wash.	1916	Kent, Allegra	Los Angeles, Calif.	1937
Hutton, Betty	Battle Creek, Mich.	1921	Kenton, Stan	Wichita, Kansas	1912
Hutton, Ina Ray	Chicago, Ill.	1918	Kenyon, Doris	Syracuse, N.Y.	1897
Hutton, Lauren	Charleston, S.C.	1944	Kerr, Deborah	Helensburgh, Scotland	1921
Hyde-White, Wilfrid	England	1903	Kerr, John	New York, N.Y.	1931
Hyer, Martha	Fort Worth, Texas	1929	Kert, Larry	Los Angeles, Calif.	1930
Hyland, Diana	Cleveland Hts., Ohio	1937	Keyes, Evelyn	Port Arthur, Tex.	1925
Hyman, Earle	Rocky Mt., N.C.	1926	Kiley, Richard	Chicago, Ill.	1922
			Kilian, Victor	Jersey City, N.J.	1898
I			King, Alan	Brooklyn, N.Y.	1927
Inescort, Frieda	Edinburgh, Scotland	1901	King, B. B.	Itta Bena, Miss.	1925
Ingels, Marty	Brooklyn, N.Y.	1936	King, Carole	Brooklyn, N.Y.	1943
Ireland, John	Vancouver, B.C.	1915	King, Henry	Christianburg, Va.	1896
Iturbi, Jose	Valencia, Spain	1895	King, Peggy	Greensburg, Pa.	1931
Ives, Burl	Hunt, Ill.	1909	King, Walter Woolf	San Francisco, Calif.	1899
			King, Wayne	Savannah, Ill.	1901
J			King, Zalman	Trenton, N.J.	1942
Jackson, Anne	Allegheny, Pa.	1926	Kirby, Durward	Covington, Ky.	1912
Jackson, Glenda	England	1938	Kirby, Michael	Canada	1925
Jacobi, Lou	Toronto, Ont., Canada	1912	Kirk, Lisa	Brownsville, Pa.	1925
Jaeckel, Richard	Long Beach, Calif.	1926	Kirk, Phyllis	Syracuse, N.Y.	1930
Jaffe, Sam	New York, N.Y.	1891	Kirsten, Dorothy	Montclair, N.J.	1919
Jagger, Dean	Columbus Grove, Ohio	1905	Kitt, Eartha	North, S.C.	1928
Jagger, Mick	Dartford, England	1944	Klemperer, Werner	Cologne, Germany	1930
James, Dennis	Jersey City, N.J.	1917	Klugman, Jack	Philadelphia, Pa.	1922
James, Harry	Albany, Ga.	1916	Knight, Ted	Terryville, Conn.	—
Janney, Leon	Ogden, Utah	1917	Knotts, Don	Morgantown, W.Va.	1924
Janney, William	New York, N.Y.	1908	Knowles, Patric	Horsforth, England	1911
Janssen, David	Naponee, Nebr.	1930	Knox, Alexander	Strathroy, Canada	1907
Jason, Rick	New York, N.Y.	1926	Korjus, Miliza	Warsaw, Poland	1912
Jeanmaire, Renee	Paris, France	1925	Korman, Harvey	Chicago, Ill.	1927
Jeffreys, Anne	Goldsboro, N.C.	1923	Kostelanetz, Andre	St. Petersburg, Russia	1910
Jeffries, Fran	San Jose, Calif.	1939	Kramer, Stanley	New York, N.Y.	1913
Jeffries, Lionel	England	1926	Kristofferson, Kris	Brownsville, Tex.	1937
Jennings, Waylon	Littlefield, Tex.	1937	Kruger, Hardy	Berlin, Germany	1928
Jepson, Helen	Titusville, Pa.	1907	Kruger, Otto	Toledo, Ohio	1885
Jeritza, Maria	Brunn, Austria	1887	Kubelik, Rafael	Bychori, Czechoslovakia	1914
Jessel, George	New York, N.Y.	1898	Kubrick, Stanley	Bronx, N.Y.	1927
John, Elton	Middlesex, England	1947	Kullman, Chas.	New Haven, Conn.	1902
Johns, Glynis	Durban, So. Africa	1923	Kulp, Nancy	Harrisburg, Pa.	1921
Johnson, Ben	Pawhuska, Okla.	—	Kwan, Nancy	Hong Kong	1939
Johnson, Richard	Essex, England	1927	Kyser, Kay	Rocky Mount, N.C.	1905
Johnson, Van	Newport, R.I.	1916			
Johnston, Johnny	St. Louis, Mo.	1916	**L**		
Jones, Allan	Scranton, Pa.	1907	Laine, Frankie	Chicago, Ill.	1913
Jones, Anissa	W. Lafayette, Ind.	1958	Lamarr, Hedy	Vienna, Austria	1915
Jones, Carolyn	Amarillo, Texas	1932	Lamas, Fernando	Buenos Aires, Arg.	1915
Jones, Chris	Jackson, Tenn.	1941	Lamb, Gil	Minneapolis, Minn.	1906
Jones, Dean	Morgan Co., Ala.	1936	Lamour, Dorothy	New Orleans, La.	1914
Jones, Grandpa	Niagra, Ky.	1913	Lancaster, Burt	New York, N.Y.	1913
Jones, Henry	Philadelphia, Pa.	1912	Lanchester, Elsa	London, England	1902
Jones, Jack	Hollywood, Calif.	1938	Landers, Harry	New York, N.Y.	1921
Jones, James Earl	Tate Co., Miss.	1931	Landon, Michael	Forest Hills, N.Y.	1936
Jones, Jennifer	Tulsa, Okla.	1919	Lane, Abbe	Brooklyn, N.Y.	1932
Jones, Quincy	Chicago, Ill.	1933	Lane, Lola	Macy, Ind.	—
Jones, Shirley	Smithtown, Pa.	1934	Lane, Priscilla	Indianola, Iowa.	—
Jones, Tom	Pontypridd, Wales.	1940	Lane, Rosemary	Indianola, Iowa.	1916
Jory, Victor	Dawson, Yukon, Can.	1902	Lane, Sara	New York, N.Y.	1949
Joselyn, Allyn	Milford, Pa.	1905	Lang, Harold	Daly City, Calif.	1924
Jourdan, Louis	Marseilles, France	1922	Lang, June	Minneapolis, Minn.	1915
Jurado, Katy	Guadalajara, Mexico	1927	Lange, Hope	Redding Ridge, Conn.	1933
			Langella, Frank	Bayonne, N.J.	1940
K			Langford, Frances	Lakeland, Fla.	1913
Kamen, Milt	Harleyville, N.Y.	1924	Lansbury, Angela	London, England	1925
Kaminska, Ida	Odessa, Russia	1899	Lansing, Robert	San Diego, Calif.	1929
Kashi, Aliza	Tel-Aviv, Israel	1940	Lanson, Snooky (Roy)	Memphis, Tenn.	1919
Kasznar, Kurt	Vienna, Austria	1913	LaPlante, Laura	St. Louis, Mo.	1904
Kaye, Danny	Brooklyn, N.Y.	1913	La Rosa, Julius	Brooklyn, N.Y.	1930
Kaye, Sammy	Lakewood, Ohio.	1913	La Rue, Jack	New York, N.Y.	—
Kazan, Elia	Constantinople, Turkey	1909	Laurie, Piper	Detroit, Mich.	1932
Kazan, Lainie	New York, N.Y.	1940	Law, John Philip	Hollywood, Calif.	1937
Keach, Stacy	Savannah, Ga.	1941	Lawford, Peter	London, England.	1923
Keaton, Diane	Santa Ana, Calif.	1946	Lawrence, Barbara	Carnegie, Okla.	1930
Keel, Howard	Gillespie, Ill.	1917	Lawrence, Carol	Melrose Park, Ill.	1934

Name	Birthplace	Born
Lawrence, Marjorie	Victoria, Australia	1909
Lawrence, Steve	Brooklyn, N.Y.	1935
Lawrence, Vicki	Inglewood, Calif.	1949
Leachman, Cloris	Des Moines, Iowa	—
Lean, David	Croydon, England	1908
Lederer, Francis	Prague, Czech.	1906
Lee, Brenda	Atlanta, Ga.	1944
Lee, Christopher	London, England	1922
Lee, Lila	New York, N.Y.	1905
Lee, Michele	Los Angeles, Calif.	1942
Lee, Peggy	Jamestown, N.D.	1920
Lee, Pinky	St. Paul, Minn.	—
Le Gallienne, Eva	London, England	1899
Legrand, Michel	Paris, France	1932
Lehmann, Lotte	Perleberg, Germany	1888
Leigh, Janet	Merced, Calif.	1927
Leighton, Margaret	Worcestershire, Eng.	1922
Leinsdorf, Erich	Vienna, Austria	1912
Lembeck, Harvey	New York, N.Y.	1923
Lemmon, Jack	Boston, Mass.	1925
Lennon, Dianne	Los Angeles, Calif.	1939
Lennon, Janet	Culver City, Calif.	1946
Lennon, John	Liverpool, England	1940
Lennon, Kathy	Santa Monica, Calif.	1934
Lennon, Peggy	Los Angeles, Calif.	1941
Leonard, Sheldon	New York, N.Y.	1907
Leontovich, Eugenie	Moscow, Russia	1894
LeRoy, Mervyn	San Francisco, Calif.	1900
Leslie, Joan	Detroit, Mich.	1925
Lester, Jerry	Chicago, Ill.	1911
Lester, Mark	Richmond, England	1958
Lester, Tom	Jackson, Miss.	1938
Levene, Sam	Russia	1905
Levenson, Sam	New York, N.Y.	1911
Lewis, Jerry	Newark, N.J.	1926
Lewis, Jerry Lee	Ferriday, La.	1935
Lewis, Monica	Chicago, Ill.	1925
Lewis, Ramsey	Chicago, Ill.	1935
Lewis, Robert Q.	New York, N.Y.	1924
Lewis, Shari	New York, N.Y.	1934
Liberace	West Allis, Wis.	1919
Lillie, Beatrice	Toronto, Canada	1898
Lincoln, Abbey	Chicago, Ill.	1930
Lindfors, Viveca	Uppsala, Sweden	1920
Lindsay, Margaret	Dubuque, Iowa	1910
Lindsey, Mort	Newark, N.J.	1923
Linkletter, Art	Saskatchewan, Can.	1912
Linn, Bambi	Brooklyn, N.Y.	1926
Lipton, Peggy	Lawrence, N.Y.	1948
Lisi, Virna	Italy	1937
Little, Cleavon	Chickasha, Okla.	1939
Little, Rich	Ottawa, Canada	1938
Livingston, Barry	Los Angeles, Calif.	1953
Livingston, Stanley	Los Angeles, Calif.	1950
Livingstone, Mary	Seattle, Wash.	1909
Lockhart, June	New York, N.Y.	1925
Lockwood, Margaret	Karachi, India	1916
Loden, Barbara	Marion, N.C.	1937
Loder, John	London, England	1898
Logan, Joshua	Texarkana, Texas	1908
Lollobrigida, Gina	Subiaco, Italy	1929
Lom, Herbert	Prague, Czech.	1917
Lombardo, Guy	London, Ont., Can.	1902
London, George	Montreal, Que., Can.	1920
London, Julie	Santa Rosa, Calif.	1926
Long, Richard	Chicago, Ill.	1927
Longet, Claudine	France	1942
Lopez, Perry	New York, N.Y.	1931
Lopez, Trini	Dallas, Texas	1937
Lopez, Vincent	Brooklyn, N.Y.	1895
Lord, Jack	New York, N.Y.	1930
Loren, Sophia	Rome, Italy	1934
Loring, Gloria	New York, N.Y.	1946
Loring, Lynn	New York, N.Y.	1944
Losch, Tilly	Vienna, Austria	1902
Loudon, Dorothy	Boston, Mass.	1932
Louise, Tina	New York, N.Y.	1934
Love, Bessie	Midland, Texas	1898
Loy, Myrna	Helena, Mont.	1905
Ludwig, Christa	Berlin, Germany	1928
Luke, Keye	Canton, China.	1904
Lulu	Glasgow, Scotland	1948
Lum (Chester Lauck)	Allene, Ark.	1902
Lumet, Sidney	Philadelphia, Pa.	1924
Lund, John	Rochester, N.Y.	1913
Lundigan, William	Syracuse, N.Y.	1914
Lunt, Alfred	Milwaukee, Wis.	1892
Lupino, Ida	London, England	1918

Name	Birthplace	Born
Lynde, Paul	Mt. Vernon, Ohio	1926
Lynley, Carol	New York, N.Y.	1942
Lynn, Jeffrey	Auburn, Mass.	1909
Lynn, Loretta	Butcher Hollow, Ky.	—
Lyon, Ben	Atlanta, Ga.	1901
Lyon, Sue	Davenport, Iowa	1946

M

Name	Birthplace	Born
MacArthur, James	Los Angeles, Calif.	1937
MacGrath, Leueen	England	1914
MacGraw, Ali	Pound Ridge, N.Y.	1939
Mack, Ted	Greeley, Colo.	1904
MacKenzie, Gisele	Winnipeg, Man., Can.	1927
MacKay, Jim	Philadelphia, Pa.	1921
MacLaine, Shirley	Richmond, Va.	1934
MacMurray, Fred	Kankakee, Ill.	1908
MacRae, Gordon	East Orange, N.J.	1921
MacRae, Meredith	Houston, Texas	1945
MacRae, Sheila	London, England	1924
Macy, Bill	Revere, Mass.	1922
Madison, Guy	Bakersfield, Calif.	1922
Main, Marjorie	Acton, Ind.	1890
Malbin, Elaine	New York, N.Y.	1932
Malden, Karl	Gary, Ind.	1914
Malone, Dorothy	Chicago, Ill.	1925
Malone, Nancy	New York, N.Y.	1935
Mancini, Henry	Cleveland, Ohio	1924
Mann, Herbie	New York, N.Y.	1930
Mantovani, Annunzio	Venice, Italy	1905
Marceau, Marcel	France	1923
March, Fredric	Racine, Wis.	1897
Margo	Mexico City, Mexico	1918
Margolin, Janet	New York, N.Y.	1943
Markova, Alicia	London, England	1910
Marlowe, Hugh	Philadelphia, Pa.	1914
Marsh, Joan	Porterville, Calif.	1915
Marshall, Brenda	Philippines	1915
Marshall, E. G.	Awatonna, Minn.	1919
Marshall, Everett	Lawrence, Mass.	1901
Marshall, Sarah	London, England	1933
Marshall, William	Chicago, Ill.	1917
Martin, Dean	Steubenville, Ohio	1917
Martin, Dick	Detroit, Mich.	1926
Martin, Mary	Weatherford, Texas	1913
Martin, Ross	Poland	1920
Martin, Tony	San Francisco, Calif.	1913
Martini, Nino	Verona, Italy	1905
Marvin, Lee	New York, N.Y.	1924
Marx, Herbert (Zeppo)	New York, N.Y.	1901
Marx, Julius (Groucho)	New York, N.Y.	1890
Mason, Jackie	Sheboygan, Wisc.	1931
Mason, James	Huddersfield, England	1909
Mason, Pamela	Westgate, England	1918
Massey, Curt	Midland, Texas	—
Massey, Raymond	Toronto, Canada	1896
Massine, Leonide	Moscow, Russia	1896
Mastroianni, Marcello	Italy	1924
Mathis, Johnny	San Francisco, Calif.	1935
Matthau, Walter	New York, N.Y.	1920
Matthews, Jessie	London, England	1907
Mature, Victor	Louisville, Ky.	1916
May, Billy	Pittsburgh, Pa.	1916
May, Elaine	Philadelphia, Pa.	1932
Mayehoff, Eddie	Baltimore, Md.	1914
Mayo, Virginia	St. Louis, Mo.	1920
Mazurki, Mike	Austria	1909
McBride, Mary Marg.	Paris, Mo.	1899
McCaffery, J. K. M.	Moscow, Idaho	1913
McCallum, David	Glasgow, Scotland	1933
McCambridge, Mercedes	Joliet, Ill.	1918
McCarthy, Kevin	Seattle, Wash.	1915
McCartney, Paul	Liverpool, England	1942
McClure, Doug	Glendale, Calif.	1935
McCord, Kent	Los Angeles, Calif.	1942
McCoy, Tim	Saginaw, Mich.	1891
McCrary, Tex (John)	Calvert, Texas	1910
McCrea, Joel	Los Angeles, Calif.	1905
McDowall, Roddy	London, England	1928
McDowell, Malcolm	Leeds, England	1943
McFarland, George	Dallas, Texas	1928
McGavin, Darren	San Joaquin, Calif.	1922
McGee, Fibber, Jordan	Peoria, Ill.	1896
McGiver, John	New York, N.Y.	1913
McGoohan, Patrick	Astoria, N.Y.	1928
McGuire, Sisters:		
Christine	Middletown, Ohio	1928
Dorothy	Middletown, Ohio	1930
Phyllis	Middletown, Ohio	1931

Name	Birthplace	Born	Name	Birthplace	Born
McGuire, Dorothy	Omaha, Nebr.	1919	Mulhall, Jack	Wappingers Falls, N.Y.	1894
McHugh, Frank	Homestead, Pa.	1899	Mulhare, Edward	Ireland.	1923
McIntyre, John	Spokane, Wash.	1907	Mundy, Meg.	London, England.	—
McKay, Scott	Pleasantville, Iowa	1915	Munsel, Patrice.	Spokane, Wash.	1925
McKenna, Siobhan	Belfast, Ireland.	1923	Murray, Arthur.	New York, N.Y.	1895
McKuen, Rod	San Francisco, Calif.	1933	Murray, Don.	Hollywood, Calif.	1929
McLean, Don	New Rochelle, N.Y.	1945	Murray, Jan.	New York	1917
McLerie, Allyn	Grand Mere, Que., Can.	1926	Murray, Kathryn	Jersey City, N.J.	1906
McMahon, Ed	Detroit, Mich.	1923	Murray, Ken	New York, N.Y.	1903
McNair, Barbara	Chicago, Ill.	1939	Myerson, Bess	Bronx, N.Y.	1924
McQueen, Butterfly	Tampa, Fla.	1911			
McQueen, Steve	Indianapolis, Ind.	1930	**N**		
Meadows, Audrey	Wu Chang, China.	1929	Nabors, Jim	Sylacauga, Ala.	1933
Meadows, Jayne	Wu Chang, China.	1926	Namath, Joe	Beaver Falls, Pa.	1943
Meara, Ann	New York, N.Y.	1929	Nardini, Tom	Los Angeles, Calif.	1945
Medford, Kay	New York, N.Y.	1920	Natwick, Mildred	Baltimore, Md.	1908
Meeker, Ralph	Minneapolis, Minn.	1920	Neal, Patricia	Packard, Ky.	1926
Melton, Sid.	Brooklyn, N.Y.	1920	Neff, Hildegarde.	Ulm, Germany.	1925
Menuhin, Yehudi	New York N.Y.	1916	Negri, Pola.	Lipno, Poland.	1899
Mercer, Johnny	Savannah, Ga.	1909	Nelson, Barry	Oakland, Calif.	1920
Mercouri, Melina	Athens, Greece	1929	Nelson, David	New York, N.Y.	1936
Meredith, Burgess	Cleveland, Ohio	1909	Nelson, Ed	New Orleans, La.	1928
Merkel, Una	Covington, Ky.	1903	Nelson, Gene.	Seattle, Wash.	1920
Merman, Ethel	Astoria, N.Y.	1909	Nelson, Harriet.	Des Moines.	—
Merrick, David	Hong Kong.	1911	Nelson, Lori	Santa Fe, N.M.	1933
Merrill, Dina	New York, N.Y.	1925	Nelson, Ozzie	Jersey City, N.J.	1907
Merrill, Gary	Hartford, Conn.	1915	Nelson, Ricky.	Teaneck, N.J.	1940
Merrill, Robert	Brooklyn, N.Y.	1919	Nero, Peter.	New York, N.Y.	1934
Michell, Keith	Adelaide, Australia.	1928	Nesbit, Cathleen	Cheshire, England.	1889
Middleton, Guy	Hove, England.	1907	Nevins, Natalie	Philadelphia, Pa.	1943
Middleton, Ray.	Chicago, Ill.	1907	Newhart, Bob.	Oak Park, Ill.	1929
Midler, Bette	Honolulu, Hawaii.	—	Newley, Anthony.	Hackney, England.	1931
Mielziner, Jo	Paris, France	1901	Newman, Paul	Cleveland, Ohio.	1925
Milanov, Zinka	Zagreb, Yugoslavia.	1908	Newman, Phyllis	Jersey City, N.J.	1935
Miles, Sarah.	Ingatestone, England.	1941	Newmar, Julie.	California	1935
Miles, Vera.	near Boise City, Okla.	1930	Newton, Wayne	Roanoke, Va.	1942
Milland, Ray.	Neath, Wales.	1908	Nicholas, Denise	Detroit, Mich.	—
Miller, Ann.	Houston, Tex.	1923	Nichols, Mike	Berlin, Ger.	1931
Miller, Cheryl	Sherman Oaks, Calif.	1943	Nicholson, Jack	Neptune, N.J.	1936
Miller, Mitch	Rochester, N.Y.	1911	Nielson, Leslie	Regina, Canada.	1926
Miller, Roger	Erick, Okla.	1936	Niesen, Gertrude	At sea.	1913
Mills, Hayley	London, Eng.	1946	Nilsson, Birgit.	W. Karop, Sweden.	1918
Mills, John.	Suffolk, Eng.	1908	Nimoy, Leonard	Boston, Mass.	1931
Mills, Juliet.	London, Eng.	1941	Niven, David	Kirriemuir, Scotland.	1910
Milner, Martin.	Detroit, Mich.	1937	Noble, Ray.	Sussex, England.	1908
Milstein, Nathan.	Odessa, Russia.	1904	Nolan, Doris.	New York, N.Y.	1916
Mimieux, Yvette	Hollywood, Calif.	1942	Nolan, Jeannette	Los Angeles, Calif.	1911
Minnelli, Liza.	Los Angeles, Calif.	1946	Nolan, Kathy.	St. Louis, Mo.	1934
Mineo, Sal.	New York, N.Y.	1939	Nolan, Lloyd.	San Francisco, Calif.	1902
Mitchell, Cameron.	Dallastown, Pa.	1918	North, Jay.	Hollywood, Calif.	1953
Mitchell, Guy.	Detroit, Mich.	1925	North, John Ringling	Baraboo, Wis.	1903
Mitchell, Joni.	Alberta, Canada.	1943	North, Sheree.	Los Angeles, Calif.	1933
Mitchum, Robert.	Bridgeport, Conn.	1917	Norton, Judy.	Santa Monica, Calif.	1958
Moffo, Anna.	Wayne, Pa.	—	Novak, Kim	Chicago, Ill.	1933
Montalban, Ricardo	Mexico City, Mex.	1920	Nugent, Edward	New York, N.Y.	1904
Montand, Yves.	Monsummano, Italy.	1921	Nugent, Elliott	Dover, Ohio.	1899
Montgomery, Eliz.	Hollywood, Calif.	1933	Nureyev, Rudolf.	Russia.	1938
Montgomery, George.	Brady, Mont.	1916	Nuyen, France.	Marseilles, France	1939
Montgomery, Robt.	Beacon, N.Y.	1904			
Moore, Colleen	Port Huron, Mich.	1902	**O**		
Moore, Constance	Sioux City, Iowa	1922	Oakie, Jack.	Sedalia, Mo.	1903
Moore, Dickie.	Los Angeles, Calif.	1925	Oberon, Merle.	Tasmania, Australia.	1914
Moore, Garry	Baltimore, Md.	1915	O'Brian, Hugh.	Rochester, N.Y.	1930
Moore, Mary Tyler.	Brooklyn, N.Y.	1937	O'Brien, Edmond	New York, N.Y.	1915
Moore, Melba.	New York, N.Y.	1945	O'Brien, George.	San Francisco, Calif.	1900
Moore, Roger.	London, Eng.	1928	O'Brien, Margaret	San Diego, Calif.	1937
Moore, Terry.	Los Angeles, Calif.	1932	O'Brien, Pat.	Milwaukee, Wis.	1899
Moorehead, Agnes	Clinton, Mass.	1906	Ochs, Phil.	El Paso, Tex.	1940
Moran, Lois.	Pittsburgh, Pa.	1907	O'Connell, Arthur.	New York, N.Y.	1908
Moreau, Jeanne.	Paris, France.	1929	O'Connor, Carroll.	New York, N.Y.	1925
Moreno, Rita.	Humacao, P.R.	1931	O'Connor, Donald.	Chicago, Ill.	1925
Morgan, Claudia	Brooklyn, N.Y.	1912	Odetta.	Birmingham, Ala.	1930
Morgan, Dennis	Prentice, Wis.	1910	O'Driscoll, Martha.	Tulsa, Okla.	1922
Morgan, Harry.	Detroit, Mich.	1915	O'Hara, Jill.	Warren, Pa.	1947
Morgan, Henry.	New York, N.Y.	1915	O'Hara, Maureen.	Dublin, Ireland.	1920
Morgan, Jane.	Boston, Mass.	1920	O'Herlihy, Dan.	Wexford, Ireland.	1919
Morgana, Nina.	Buffalo, N.Y.	1895	O'Keefe, Walter.	Hartford, Conn.	1907
Morini, Erika.	Vienna, Austria.	1910	Olivier, Laurence.	Dorking, England.	1907
Morison, Patricia.	New York, N.Y.	1915	O'Malley, J. Pat.	Bur nley, Eng.	1901
Morley, Robert.	Wiltshire, England.	1908	O'Neal, Patrick.	Ocala, Fla.	1927
Morris, Greg.	Cleveland, Ohio.	1934	O'Neal, Ryan.	Los Angeles, Calif.	1941
Morris, Howard.	New York, N.Y.	1919	O'Neill, Jennifer.	Brazil.	1948
Morrow, Vic.	Bronx, N.Y.	1932	Opatoshu, David.	New York, N.Y.	1918
Morse, Robert.	Newton, Mass.	1931	Orbach, Jerry.	New York, N.Y.	1935
Moss, Arnold.	Brooklyn, N.Y.	1910	Ormandy, Eugene.	Budapest, Hungary.	1899
Mostel, Zero (Sam).	Brooklyn, N.Y.	1915	O'Sullivan, Maureen.	Boyle, Ireland.	1911
Muir, Gavin.	Chicago, Ill.	1909	O'Toole, Peter.	Connemara, Ireland.	1934
Muir, Jean.	New York, N.Y.	1911	Owens, Buck.	Sherman, Texas.	1929

Name	Birthplace	Born
P		
Paar, Jack	Canton, Ohio	1918
Page, Geraldine	Kirksville, Mo.	1924
Page, Patti	Claremore, Okla.	1927
Paige, Janis	Tacoma, Wash.	1923
Paige, Robert	Indianapolis, Ind.	1910
Palance, Jack	Lattimer, Pa.	1920
Palmer, Betsy	East Chicago, Ind.	1929
Palmer, Gregg	San Francisco, Calif.	1927
Palmer, Lilli	Posen, Germany	1914
Papas, Irene	Greece	1926
Parker, Eleanor	Cedarville, Ohio	1922
Parker, Fess	Ft. Worth, Tex.	1925
Parker, Frank	New York, N.Y.	1906
Parker, Jean	Deer Lodge, Mont.	1916
Parker, Suzy	New York City	1934
Parkins, Barbara	Vancouver, Canada	1942
Parks, Bert	Atlanta, Ga.	1914
Parks, Larry	Olathe, Kans.	1914
Parsons, Estelle	Lynn, Mass.	1927
Parton, Dolly	Sevier County, Tenn.	1946
Pasternak, Joseph	Hungary	1901
Paterson, Pat	Bradford, England	1911
Patterson, Melody	Los Angeles, Calif.	1947
Patterson, Neva	Nevada, Iowa	1922
Paulsen, Pat	South Bend, Wash.	—
Pavan, Marisa	Cagliari, Sardinia	1932
Payne, John	Roanoke, Va.	1912
Pearl, Jack	New York, N.Y.	1895
Pearl, Minnie	Centerville, Tenn.	1912
Peck, Gregory	La Jolla, Calif.	1916
Peerce, Jan	New York, N.Y.	1904
Pelletier, Wilfred	Montreal, Canada	1896
Penn, Arthur	Philadelphia, Pa.	1922
Peppard, George	Detroit, Mich.	1933
Perkins, Anthony	New York, N.Y.	1932
Perry, Margaret	Denver, Colo.	1913
Persoff, Nehemiah	Jerusalem	1920
Peters, Bernadette	Queens, N.Y.	1944
Peters, Brock	New York, N.Y.	1927
Peters, Jean	Canton, Ohio	1926
Peters, Roberta	New York, N.Y.	1930
Peterson, Dorothy	Hector, Minn.	1901
Petit, Pascale	France	1937
Pettet, Joanna	London, Eng.	1944
Phillips, Margaret	Wales	1923
Piatigorsky, Gregor	Russia	1903
Piazza, Ben	Little Rock, Ark.	1934
Piazza, Marguerite	New Orleans, La.	1926
Pickens, Jane	Macon, Ga.	—
Pickens, Slim	Kingsberg, Calif.	1919
Pickford, Mary	Toronto, Canada	1894
Picon, Molly	New York, N.Y.	1898
Pidgeon, Walter	E. St. John, N.B.	1898
Piston, Walter	Rockland, Me.	1894
Pleasence, Donald	Worksop, England	1919
Pleshette, Suzanne	New York City	1937
Plimpton, George	New York, N.Y.	1927
Plowright, Joan	Brigg, England	1929
Plummer, Christopher	Toronto, Canada	1929
Poitier, Sydney	Miami, Fla.	1927
Pollard, Michael	Passaic, N.J.	1939
Pons, Lily	Cannes, France	1904
Ponselle, Carmela	Schenectady, N.Y.	1892
Ponselle, Rosa	Meriden, Conn.	1897
Ponti, Carlo	Milan, Italy	1913
Poston, Tom	Columbus, Ohio	1927
Powell, Eleanor	Springfield, Mass.	1912
Powell, Jane	Portland, Ore.	1929
Powell, William	Pittsburgh, Pa.	1892
Powers, Mala	San Francisco, Calif.	1931
Powers, Stefanie	Hollywood, Calif.	1942
Preminger, Otto	Vienna, Austria	1906
Prentiss, Paula	San Antonio, Texas	1939
Presley, Elvis	Tupelo, Miss.	1935
Preston, Robert	Newton, Mass.	1918
Previn, Andre	Berlin, Germany	1929
Price, Leontyne	Laurel, Miss.	1927
Price, Ray	Perryville, Tex.	1926
Price, Roger	Charleston, W. Va.	1920
Price, Vincent	St. Louis, Mo.	1911
Pride, Charlie	Sledge, Miss.	1938
Prima, Louis	New Orleans, La.	1912
Prince, William	Nichols, N.Y.	1913
Provine, Dorothy	Deadwood, S. D.	1937
Prowse, Juliet	Bombay, India	1937
Puckett, Gary	Hibbing, Minn.	—
Pyle, Denver	Bethune, Colo.	1920

Name	Birthplace	Born
Q.		
Qualen, John	Vancouver, B.C.	1899
Quayle, Anthony	Lancashire, England	1913
Quillan, Eddie	Philadelphia, Pa.	1907
Quinn, Anthony	Chihuahua, Mexico	1916
R.		
Raft, George	New York, N.Y.	1895
Rainer, Luise	Vienna, Austria	1912
Raines, Ella	Snoqualmie Falls, Wash.	1921
Raitt, John	Santa Ana, Calif.	1917
Ralston, Esther	Bar Harbor, Maine	1902
Ralston, Vera	Prague, Czechoslovakia	1921
Rambo, Dack	Delano, Calif.	1941
Randall, Tony	Tulsa, Okla.	1920
Rawls, Lou	Chicago, Ill.	1935
Ray, Aldo	Pen Argyl, Pa.	1926
Ray, Johnnie	Dallas, Ore.	1927
Rayburn, Gene	Christopher, Ill.	1917
Raye, Martha	Butte, Mont.	1916
Raymond, Gene	New York, N.Y.	1908
Reddy, Helen	Melbourne, Aust.	1942
Redford, Robert	Santa Monica, Calif.	1937
Redgrave, Lynn	London, England	1943
Redgrave, Michael	Bristol, England	1908
Redgrave, Vanessa	London, England	1937
Redman, Joyce	Co. Mayo, Ireland	1918
Reed, Donna	Denison, Iowa	1921
Reed, Jerry	Atlanta, Ga.	1937
Reed, Robert	Highland, Park, Ill.	1932
Reese, Della	Detroit, Mich.	1932
Regan, Phil	Brooklyn, N.Y.	1906
Reilly, Charles Nelson	New York, N.Y.	—
Reiner, Bob	Bronx, N.Y.	1946
Reiner, Carl	Bronx, N.Y.	1922
Remick, Lee	Boston, Mass.	1937
Renaldo, Duncan	Camden, N.J.	1904
Resnik, Regina	New York, N.Y.	1923
Reynolds, Burt	Georgia	1935
Reynolds, Debbie	El Paso, Texas	1932
Reynolds, Joyce	San Antonio, Texas	1924
Reynolds, Marjorie	Buhl, Idaho	1921
Reynolds, William	Los Angeles, Calif.	1931
Rhodes, Hari	Cincinnati, Ohio	1932
Rich, Buddy	New York, N.Y.	1917
Rich, Charlie	Forest City, Ark.	1932
Rich, Irene	Buffalo, N.Y.	1897
Richardson, Ralph	Cheltenham, England	1902
Richardson, Tony	Shipley, England	1929
Rickles, Don	New York, N.Y.	1926
Riddle, Nelson	Hackensack, N.J.	1921
Rigg, Diana	England	1938
Ritchard, Cyril	Sydney, Australia	1898
Ritz, Harry	Newark, N.J.	1908
Ritz, Jimmy	Newark, N.J.	1905
Rivers, Joan	Brooklyn, N.Y.	1935
Robards, Jason, Jr.	Chicago, Ill.	1922
Robbins, Jerome	New York, N.Y.	1918
Robbins, Marty	Glendale, Ariz.	1925
Robertson, Cliff	La Jolla, Calif.	1925
Robertson, Dale	Oklahoma City, Okla.	1923
Robeson, Paul	Princeton, N.J.	1898
Robinson, Jay	New York, N.Y.	1930
Robson, Flora	South Shields, England	1902
Rochester (E. Anderson)	Oakland, Calif.	1905
Rockwell, Geo. (Doc.)	Providence, R.I.	1889
Rodgers, Richard	New York, N.Y.	1902
Rodgers, Jimmie	Camas, Wash.	1933
Rodriquez, Johnny	Sabinal, Tex.	1951
Rogers, Chas. (Buddy)	Olathe, Kans.	1904
Rogers, Ginger	Independence, Mo.	1911
Rogers, Roy	Cincinnati, Ohio	1912
Roland, Gilbert	Juarez, Mexico	1905
Roman, Ruth	Boston, Mass.	1924
Romero, Cesar	New York, N.Y.	1907
Rooney, Mickey	Brooklyn, N.Y.	1922
Rose Marie	New York, N.Y.	—
Rosenbloom, Maxie	New York, N.Y.	1906
Ross, David	St. Paul, Minn.	1924
Ross, Diana	Detroit, Mich.	1944
Ross, Katharine	Hollywood, Calif.	1943
Ross, Lanny	Seattle, Wash.	1906
Ross, Shirley	Omaha, Nebr.	—
Roth, Lillian	Boston, Mass.	1910
Roundtree, Richard	New Rochelle, N.Y.	1942
Rowan, Dan	Beggs, Okla.	1922
Rowlands, Gena	Cambria, Wisc.	1936

Name	Birthplace	Born	Name	Birthplace	Born
Rubin, Benny	New York, N.Y.	1899	Singleton, Penny	Philadelphia, Pa.	1912
Rubinoff, David	Grodno, Russia	1897	Skelton, Red (Richard)	Vincennes, Ind.	1913
Rubinstein, Artur	Lodz, Poland	1889	Skinner, Cornelia Otis	Chicago, Ill.	1903
Rudolf, Max	Frankfurt, Germany	1902	Slezak, Walter	Vienna, Austria	1902
Rule, Janice	Norwood, Ohio	1931	Slick, Grace	Chicago, Ill.	1939
Rush, Barbara	Denver, Colo.	1930	Smith, Alexis	Penticton, Canada	1921
Russell, Jane	Bemidji, Minn.	1921	Smith, Bob	Buffalo, N.Y.	1917
Russell, Rosalind	Waterbury, Conn.	1911	Smith, Connie	Elkhart, Ind.	1941
Rutherford, Ann	Toronto, Canada	1924	Smith, Ethel	Pittsburgh, Pa.	1921
Rydell, Bobby	Philadelphia, Pa.	1942	Smith, Kate	Greenville, Va.	1909
			Smith, Keely	Norfolk, Va.	1935
			Smith, Lois	Topeka, Kan.	1931
S.			Smith, Loring	Stratford, Conn.	1900
Sahl, Mort	Montreal, Que.	1927	Smith, Maggie	Ilford, Eng.	1934
Saint, Eva Marie	E. Orange, N.J.	1924	Smith, Muriel	New York, N.Y.	1933
Sainte-Marie, Buffy	Craven, Sask.	1941	Smith, Roger	South Gate, Calif.	1934
St. James, Susan	Los Angeles, Calif.	1946	Smothers, Dick	New York, N.Y.	1939
St. John, Jill	Los Angeles, Calif.	1940	Smothers, Tom	New York, N.Y.	1937
Sales, Soupy	Franklinton, No. Car.	1926	Snodgress, Carrie	Park Ridge, Ill.	1945
Sanders, Lugene	Oklahoma City, Okla.	1934	Snow, Hank	Nova Scotia	1914
Sands, Tommy	Chicago, Ill.	1937	Somes, Michael	nr. Stroud, England	1917
Sargent, Dick	Carmel, Calif.	1933	Sommer, Elke	Berlin, Ger.	1941
Sarnoff, Dorothy	New York, N.Y.	1919	Sorvino, Paul	Brooklyn, N.Y.	1939
Sarrazin, Michael	Quebec City, Quebec	1940	Sothern, Ann	Valley City, N. Dak.	1912
Saunders, Lori	Kansas City, Mo.	1941	Specht, Bobby	Superior, Wis.	1921
Savalas, Telly	Garden City, N.Y.	1924	Spewack, Bella	Hungary	1899
Saxon, John	Brooklyn, N.Y.	1935	Spivak, Lawrence	Brooklyn, N.Y.	1900
Sayao, Bidu	Rio de Janeiro, Brazil	1908	Stack, Robert	Los Angeles, Calif.	1919
Schallert, William	Los Angeles, Calif.	1925	Stafford, Jo	Coalinga, Calif.	1918
Schary, Dore	Newark, N.J.	1905	Stamp, Terence	London, England	1940
Schell, Maria	Vienna, Austria	1926	Stang, Arnold	Chelsea, Mass.	1925
Schell, Maximilian	Vienna, Austria	1930	Stanley, Kim	Tularosa, N.M.	1925
Schenkel, Chris	Bippus, Ind.	1924	Stanley, Pat	Cincinnati, Ohio	1931
Scherman, Thomas	New York, N.Y.	1917	Stanwyck, Barbara	Brooklyn, N.Y.	1907
Schippers, Thomas	Kalamazoo, Mich.	1930	Stapleton, Jean	New York, N.Y.	1923
Schneider, Alexander	Vilna, Poland	1908	Stapleton, Maureen	Troy, N.Y.	1925
Schneider, Romy	Austria	1938	Starr, Kay	Dougherty, Okla.	1924
Schuman, William	New York, N.Y.	1910	Starr, Ringo	Liverpool, Eng.	1940
Schwartz, Arthur	Brooklyn, N.Y.	1900	Steber, Eleanor	Wheeling, W. Va.	1916
Schwarzkopf, Elisabeth	Jarotschin, Poland	1915	Steele, Bob	Pendleton, Ore.	1907
Schofield, Paul	Hurst, Pierpont, England	1922	Steele, Karen	Hawaii	1934
Scott, George C.	Wise, Va.	1927	Steele, Ted	Hartford, Conn.	1917
Scott, Gordon	Portland, Ore.	1927	Steele, Tommy	London, England	1937
Scott, Hazel	Trinidad	1920	Steiger, Rod	W. Hampton, N.Y.	1925
Scott, Lizabeth	Scranton, Pa.	1923	Steinberg, David	Winnipeg, Canada	1942
Scott, Martha	Jamesport, Mo.	1916	Sterling, Jan	New York, N.Y.	1923
Scott, Randolph	Orange Co., Va.	1903	Sterling, Robert	New Castle, Pa.	1917
Scourby, Alexander	New York, N.Y.	1913	Stern, Isaac	Kreminisey, Russia	1920
Seal, Elizabeth	England	1935	Stevens, Cat	London, Eng.	1948
Sebastian, John	New York, N.Y.	1944	Stevens, Connie	Brooklyn, N.Y.	1938
Seberg, Jean	Marshalltown, Iowa	1938	Stevens, Kaye	Pittsburgh, Pa.	1935
Seeger, Pete	New York, N.Y.	1919	Stevens, Mark	Cleveland, Ohio	1902
Segal, George	Great Neck, L.I., N.Y.	1934	Stevens, Onslow	Los Angeles, Calif.	1902
Segal, Vivienne	Philadelphia, Pa.	1897	Stevens, Rise	New York, N.Y.	1913
Sellers, Peter	Southsea, England	1925	Stevens, Stella	Yazoo City, Miss.	1938
Serkin, Rudolf	Eger, Austria	1903	Stewart, Elaine	Montclair, N.J.	1929
Serling, Rod	Syracuse, N.Y.	1924	Stewart, James	Indiana, Pa.	1908
Severinsen, Doc	Arlington, Ore.	1927	Stewart, Rod	London, Eng.	1944
Shankar, Ravi	India	1920	Stickney, Dorothy	Dickinson, N. Dak.	1903
Sharif, Omar	Alexandria, Egypt	1932	Stockwell, Dean	Hollywood, Calif.	—
Shatner, William	Montreal, Canada	1931	Stokowski, Leopold	London, England	1887
Shaw, Artie	New York, N.Y.	1910	Stone, Carol	New York, N.Y.	1916
Shaw, Rita	So. Paris, Maine	1912	Stone, Dorothy	Bensonhurst, N.Y.	1905
Shaw, Robert	Red Bluff, Calif.	1916	Stone, Ezra	New Bedford, Mass.	1917
Shaw, Robert	West Houghton, Eng.	1927	Stone, Milburn	Burton, Kans.	1904
Shaw, Victoria	Sydney, N.S.W.	1935	Stone, Paula	New York, N.Y.	1916
Shaw, Winfred	San Francisco, Calif.	1899	Storch, Larry	New York, N.Y.	1925
Shearer, Moira	Scotland	1926	Storm, Gale	Bloomington, Tex.	1922
Shearer, Norma	Montreal, Canada	1904	Storrs, Suzanne	Salt Lake City, Utah	1934
Shearing, George	London, Eng.	1920	Straight, Beatrice	Old Westbury, N.Y.	1918
Shepherd, Jean	Chicago, Ill.	1929	Strasberg, Susan	New York, N.Y.	1938
Sherman, Bobby	Santa Monica, Calif.	1945	Strauss, Robert	New York, N.Y.	1913
Sherwood, Roberta	St. Louis, Mo.	1913	Streisand, Barbra	Brooklyn, N.Y.	1942
Shirley, Ann	New York, N.Y.	1918	Stritch, Elaine	Detroit, Mich.	1925
Shore, Dinah	Winchester, Tenn.	1920	Strode, Woody	Los Angeles, Calif.	1914
Sidney, Sylvia	New York, N.Y.	1910	Struthers, Sally	Portland, Ore.	1948
Siepi, Cesare	Milan, Italy	1923	Stuart, Gloria	Santa Monica, Calif.	1911
Signoret, Simone	Wiesbaden, Germany	1921	Sullivan, Barry	New York, N.Y.	1912
Sills, Beverly	Brooklyn, N.Y.	1929	Sullivan, Ed.	New York, N.Y.	1902
Silvers, Phil	Brooklyn, N.Y.	1912	Sumac, Yma	Ichocan, Peru.	1928
Sim, Alastair	Edinburgh, Scotland	1900	Susskind, David	New York, N.Y.	1920
Simmons, Jean	London, England	1929	Sutherland, Donald	New Brunswick, Canada	1934
Simone, Nina	Tyron, N.C.	1933	Sutherland, Joan	Sydney, Australia	1926
Simon, Paul	New York, N.Y.	1940	Suzuki, Pat	Cressey, Calif.	1931
Simon, Simone	Marseilles, France	1914	Swanson, Gloria	Chicago, Ill.	1899
Sinatra, Frank	Hoboken, N.J.	1915	Swayze, John Cameron	Wichita, Kan.	1906
Sinatra, Jr., Frank	Jersey City, N.J.	1944	Sweet, Blanche	Chicago, Ill.	1896
Sinatra, Nancy	Jersey City, N.J.	1940	Swenson, Inga	Omaha, Nebr.	1934

Name	Birthplace	Born
T		
Talbot, Lyle	Pittsburgh, Pa.	1902
Talbot, Nita	New York, N.Y.	1930
Tallchief, Maria	Fairfax, Okla.	1925
Tamblyn, Russ.	Los Angeles, Calif.	1935
Tandy, Jessica.	London, England.	1909
Taylor, Billy	Greenville, N.C.	1921
Taylor, Elizabeth.	London, England.	1932
Taylor, James	Boston, Mass.	1948
Taylor, Kent	Nashua, Iowa.	1907
Taylor, Rod	Sydney, Australia.	1930
Tebaldi, Renata	Pesaro, Italy.	1922
Temple, Shirley.	Santa Monica, Calif.	1928
Terris, Norma.	Columbus, Kans.	1904
Terry-Thomas.	London, Eng.	1911
Teyte, Maggie	Wolverhampton, Eng.	1889
Thaxter, Phillis.	Portland, Me.	1921
Thebom, Blanche	Monessen, Pa.	1919
Thibault, Conrad.	Northbridge, Mass.	1898
Thinnes, Roy	Chicago, Ill.	1938
Thomas B. J.	Houston, Tex.	1942
Thomas, Danny	Deerfield, Mich.	1914
Thomas, Lowell	Woodrington, Ohio.	1892
Thomas, Marlo.	Detroit, Mich.	1938
Thomas, Richard	New York, N.Y.	1951
Thompson, Marshall.	Peoria, Ill.	1926
Thompson, Sada	Des Moines, Iowa	1929
Thorndike, Sybil.	Gainsborough, Eng.	1882
Thulin, Ingrid.	Sweden.	1929
Tierney, Gene.	Brooklyn, N.Y.	1920
Tierney, Lawrence	Brooklyn, N.Y.	1919
Tiffin, Pamela.	Oklahoma City, Okla.	1942
Tillstrom, Burr.	Chicago, Ill.	1917
Tiny Tim.	New York, N.Y.	—
Tobias, George.	New York, N.Y.	—
Todd, Richard.	Dublin, Ireland.	1919
Toomey, Regis	Pittsburgh, Pa.	1902
Tomkins, Angel.	Albany, Calif.	1943
Tomlin, Lili	Detroit, Mich.	1940
Tomlinson, David.	Scotland	1917
Torme, Mel	Chicago, Ill.	1925
Torn, Rip.	Temple, Tex.	1931
Totter, Audrey.	Joliet, Ill.	1923
Tracy, Arthur.	Philadelphia, Pa.	1903
Travers, Mary	Louisville, Ky.	1936
Treacher, Arthur	Brighton, England.	1894
Trevor, Claire.	New York, N.Y.	1909
Truffaut, Francois.	Paris, France.	1932
Tryon, Tom	Hartford, Conn.	1926
Tucker, Forrest.	Plainfield, Ind.	1919
Tucker, Orrin.	St. Louis, Mo.	1911
Tucker, Richard.	Brooklyn, N.Y.	1915
Tucker, Tanya.	Seminole, Tex.	1959
Tucker, Tommy.	Souris, N.D.	1907
Turner, Lana.	Wallace, Idaho.	1921
Tushingham, Rita	Liverpool, Eng.	1942
Twiggy (Leslie Hornby).	London, Eng.	1949
Tyrell, Susan.	New Canaan, Conn.	1946
U		
Uggams, Leslie.	New York, City.	1943
Umeki, Miyoshi.	Hokkaido, Japan.	1929
Ure, Mary.	Glasgow, Scotland.	1933
Ustinov, Peter.	London, England.	1921
V		
Vaccaro, Brenda.	Brooklyn, N.Y.	1939
Vale, Jerry.	New York, N.Y.	1931
Valentine, Karen.	Santa Rosa, California.	1947
Vallee, Rudy.	Island Pond, Vt.	1901
Valli, Alida.	Pola, Italy.	1921
Vance, Vivian.	Cherryvale, Kans.	1912
Van Cleef, Lee.	Somerville, N.J.	1925
Van Doren, Mamie.	Rowena, S.D.	1933
Van Dyke, Dick.	West Plains, Mo.	1925
Van Dyke, Jerry.	Danville, Ill.	1932
Van Fleet, Jo.	Oakland, Calif.	1922
Vandervere, Trish.	Tenafly, N.J.	1945
Varnay, Astrid.	Stockholm, Sweden.	1918
Varsi, Diane.	San Francisco, Calif.	1938
Vaughn, Robert.	New York, N.Y.	1932
Vaughn, Sarah.	Newark, N.J.	1924
Venuta, Benay.	San Francisco, Calif.	1911
Vera-Ellen.	Cincinnati, Ohio.	1926
Verdon, Gwen.	Los Angeles, Calif.	1926
Vernon, Jackie.	New York, N.Y.	1929
Vidor, King Louis.	Galveston, Tex.	1895
Vinson, Helen.	Beaumont, Tex.	1907

Name	Birthplace	Born
Vinton, Bobby	Canonsburg, Pa.	1935
Vogel, Mitch.	Alhambra, Calif.	1956
Voight, Jon.	Yonkers, N.Y.	1938
Von Furstenberg, Betsy.	Westphalia, Germany	1931
Von Sydow, Max.	Lund, Sweden.	1929
Von Zell, Harry R.	Indianapolis, Ind.	1906
Voorhees, Donald.	Allentown, Pa.	1903
W		
Waggoner, Lyle.	Kansas City, Kansas.	1935
Wagner, Robert.	Detroit, Mich.	1930
Wain, Bea.	Bronx, N.Y.	1917
Waite, Ralph.	White Plains, N.Y.	1928
Walker, Clint.	Hartford, Ill.	1927
Walker, Nancy.	Philadelphia, Pa.	1922
Walker, Robert, Jr.	Long Island	1941
Wallace, Mike.	Brookline, Mass.	1918
Wallach, Eli.	Brooklyn, N.Y.	1915
Wallenstein, Alfred.	Chicago, Ill.	1898
Wallis, Hal.	Chicago, Ill.	1899
Walston, Ray.	New Orleans, La.	1918
Walters, Barbara.	Boston, Mass.	1931
Ward, Burt.	Los Angeles, Calif.	1946
Warden, Jack.	Newark, N.J.	1920
Warfield, William.	Helena, Ark.	1920
Warhol, Andy.	Cleveland, Ohio.	1931
Waring, Fred.	Tyrone, Pa.	1900
Warner, David.	Manchester, Eng.	1941
Warwicke, Dionne.	E. Orange, N.J.	1941
Waters, Ethel.	Chester, Pa.	1900
Watson, Debbie.	Culver City, Calif.	1940
Watts, Andre.	Germany.	1946
Wayne, David.	Traverse City, Mich.	1914
Wayne, John.	Winterset, Iowa.	1907
Weaver, Charley (Cliff Arquette).	Toledo, Ohio.	1905
Weaver, Dennis.	Joplin, Mo.	1924
Weaver, Fritz.	Pittsburgh, Pa.	1926
Webb, Alan.	York, England.	1906
Webb, Jack.	Santa Monica, Calif.	1920
Weissmuller, Johnny.	Windber, Pa.	1904
Welch, Raquel.	La Jolla, Calif.	1942
Weld, Tuesday.	New York, N.Y.	1943
Welk, Lawrence.	near Strasburg, N.Dak.	1903
Welles, Orson.	Kenosha, Wis.	1915
Wells, Kitty.	Nashville, Tenn.	1919
Werner, Oskar.	Vienna, Austria.	1922
West, Adam.	Walla Walla, Wash.	1929
West, Mae.	Brooklyn, N.Y.	1892
Whitaker, Johnny.	Van Nuys, Calif.	1959
White, Jesse.	Buffalo, N.Y.	1919
Whiting, Margaret.	Detroit, Mich.	1924
Whitman, Stuart.	San Francisco, Calif.	1926
Whitmore, James.	White Plains, N.Y.	1921
Widmark, Richard.	Sunrise, Minn.	1914
Wilcoxon, Henry	British West Indies.	1905
Wilde, Cornel.	New York, N.Y.	1918
Wilder, Billy.	Vienna, Austria.	1906
Wilder, Gene.	Milwaukee, Wisc.	1934
Wilding, Michael.	Essex, England.	1912
Williams, Andy.	Wall Lake, Iowa.	1930
Williams, Barry.	Santa Monica, Calif.	1954
Williams, Clarence.	New York, N.Y.	1946
Williams, Emlyn.	Mostyn, Wales.	1905
Williams, Esther.	Los Angeles, Calif.	1923
Williams, Joe.	Cordele, Ga.	1918
Williams, Mason.	Abilene, Tex.	1938
Williams, Roger.	Omaha, Nebr.	1926
Williamson, Fred.	Gary, Indiana.	1937
Williamson, Nicol.	Hamilton, Scotland.	1936
Wills, Chill.	Seagoville, Tex.	1903
Wilson, Meredith.	Mason City, Iowa.	1902
Wilson, Demond.	Valdosta, Ga.	—
Wilson, Dolores.	Philadelphia, Pa.	1929
Wilson, Don.	Lincoln, Nebr.	1900
Wilson, Flip.	Jersey City, N.J.	1933
Wilson, Julie.	Omaha, Nebr.	1924
Wilson, Nancy.	Chillicothe, Ohio.	1937
Winchell, Paul.	New York, N.Y.	1922
Windom, William.	New York, N.Y.	1923
Winters, Jonathan.	Dayton, Ohio.	1925
Winters, Shelley.	St. Louis, Mo.	1922
Winwood, Estelle.	Lee, England.	1884
Wiseman, Joseph.	Montreal, Canada.	1918
Withers, Jane.	Atlanta, Ga.	1927
Wood, Helen.	Clarksville, Tenn.	1937
Wood, Natalie.	San Francisco, Calif.	1938
Wood, Peggy.	Brooklyn, N.Y.	1892

Name	Birthplace	Born	Name	Birthplace	Born
Woodward, Joanne.....	Thomasville, Ga..........	1930	York, Dick............	Ft. Wayne, Ind...........	1928
Wonder, Stevie.......	Detroit, Mich............	1951	York, Michael........	Fulmer, England........	1942
Worley, Jo Anne......	Lowell, Ind.............	1937	York, Susannah.......	London, England........	1942
Wray, Fay..........	Alberta, Canada.........	1907	Young, Alan...........	Northumberl'd, Eng.......	1919
Wright, Martha........	Seattle, Wash..........	1926	Young, Gig...........	St. Cloud, Minn..........	1917
Wright, Teresa........	New York, N.Y..........	1919	Young, Loretta........	Salt Lake City, Utah......	1913
Wrightson, Earl.......	Baltimore, Md..........	1916	Young, Robert........	Chicago, Ill.............	1907
Wyatt, Jane..........	Campgaw, N.J..........	1912	Young, Stephen.......	Toronto, Canada........	1939
Wyler, William........	Mulhouse, France.......	1902	Youngman, Henny......	Liverpool, England......	1906
Wyman, Jane.........	St. Joseph, Mo...........	1914	Yurka, Blanche........	St. Paul, Minn...........	1887
Wynette, Tammy......	Red Bay, Ala...........	1942			
Wynn, Keenan........	New York, N.Y..........	1916	**Z**		
Wynter, Dana.........	London, England.......	1930	Zanuck, Darryl F.......	Wahoo,Nebr.............	1902
			Zimbalist, Efrem.......	Rostov, Russia..........	1889
			Zimbalist, Efrem, Jr....	New York, N.Y...........	1923
Y			Zimmer, Norma........	Larsen, Idaho...........	—
Yarborough, Glenn.....	Milwaukee, Wisc........	1930	Zorina, Vera..........	Berlin, Germany.........	1917
Yarrow, Peter.........	New York, N.Y..........	1938	Zukor, Adolph........	Ricse, Hungary........	1873

Legal or Public Holidays in the United States in 1975

Technically there are no national holidays in the United States; each state has jurisdiction over its holidays, which are designated by legislative enactment or executive proclamation. In practice, however, most states observe the Federal legal public holidays, even though the President and Congress can legally designate holidays only for the District of Columbia and for Federal employees.

Federal legal public holidays are New Year's, Washington's Birthday, Memorial Day, Independence Day, Labor Day, Columbus Day, Veterans Day, Thanksgiving and Christmas.

1975

Chief Legal or Public Holidays

When a holiday falls on a Sunday it is usually observed on the following Monday.

Jan. 1 (Wednesday) — New Year's Day. All the states.

Feb. 12 (Wednesday)— Lincoln's Birthday. All the states except Ala., Ark., Fla., Ga., Idaho, Ky., La., Me., Mass., Miss., Nev., N.H., N.C., N.D., Okla., R.I., S.C., Tenn., Tex., Va. (In Del., Ill., Minn., Ore., the first Monday in Feb.).

Feb. 17 (Third Monday in Feb.) — Washington's Birthday. All the states. In Hawaii and S.D. known as President's Day. In Ohio, Wisc., and Wyo. as Lincoln-Washington Day.

Mar. 28 — Good Friday. Observed in all the states. A legal holiday in Conn., Del., Fla., Hawaii, Ind., La., Md., N.J., N.D., Penn., Tenn. Partial holiday in Calif., N.M., and Wisc.

May 26 (Last Monday in May) — Memorial Day. All the states except Ala., Miss., S.C., (Confederate Memorial Day in Virginia). Observed on May 30 in La.

July 4 (Friday) — Independence Day. All the states.

Sept. 1 — Labor Day. (First Monday in Sept.). All the states.

Oct. 13 (Second Monday in Oct.) — Columbus Day. All the states except Ark., Iowa, Miss., Nev., N.C., N.D., Okla., Ore., S.C., S.D. (Discover's Day in Hawaii; Discovery Day in Indiana and No. Dakota; Landing Day in Wisc.).

Oct. 27 (Fourth Monday in Oct.) — Veterans or Armistice Day. All the states. In Alaska, Ark., Calif., Conn., Fla., Ga., Idaho, Ill., Iowa, Kansas, Ky., La., Maine, Miss., Mo., Mont., Nebr., N.H., Okla., Ore., S.C., S.D., Vt., Wash., W. Va., Wisc. and Wyo. on Nov. 11. (Additional states have bills pending that would return Veterans Day to Nov. 11.).

Nov. 4 — General Election Day (First Tuesday after the first Monday in Nov.). All the states with the following exceptions — Ala., Alaska, Ark., Conn., Ga., Hawaii, Idaho, Iowa, Kan., Maine, Mass., Minn., Miss., Nebr., Nev., N.C., N.M., Ohio, Okla., Ore., R.I., S.D., Texas, Utah, Vt. (Observed usually only when presidential or general elections are held. Primary election days are observed in some states; see list of Days Usually Observed.)

Nov. 27 — Thanksgiving Day. (Always the fourth Thursday in Nov.). All the states. Florida and Oklahoma observe day after Thanksgiving.)

Dec. 25 (Thursday) — Christmas Day. All the states.

So. Carolina observes day after Christmas.

Other Legal or Public Holidays

Jan. 8 — Battle of New Orleans. In Louisiana.

Jan. 19 — Robert E. Lee's Birthday. Ark., Fla., Ga., La., S. C. In Ala. and Miss. the third Monday in Jan.

Jan. 19 — Confederate Heroes Day. In Texas.

Jan. 20 — Inauguration Day. The District of Columbia observed every fourth year.

Jan. 20 — Lee-Jackson Day. In Virginia (third Monday in Jan.).

Jan. 30 — Franklin D. Roosevelt Day. In Kentucky.

Feb. 11 — Mardi Gras (Shrove Tuesday). Ala., La.

Feb. 14 — Admission Day. In Arizona.

March 2 — Texas Independence Day. In that state.

March 4 — Town Meeting Day. In Vermont (first Tuesday in March).

March 17 — Evacuation Day. In Boston and Suffolk County, Mass.

March 25 — Maryland Day. In that state.

March 26 — Kuhio Day. In Hawaii.

March 31 — Seward's Day. In Alaska (always last Monday in March).

April 13 — Thomas Jefferson's Birthday. In Alabama.

April 21 — Patriot's Day. Maine and Mass. (always third Monday in April).

April 21 — San Jacinto Day. In Texas.

April 22 — Arbor Day. In Nebraska.

April 25 — Arbor Day. In Utah (always last Friday in April).

April 26 — Confederate Memorial Day. In Ga.

April 28 — Fast Day. In New Hampshire (always fourth Monday in April).

April 28 — Confederate Memorial Day. Alabama and Miss. (always last Monday in April).

May 4 — Rhode Island Independence Day. In that state.

May 10 — Confederate Memorial Day. In South Carolina.

June 3 — Birthday of Jefferson Davis or *Confederate Memorial Day. In Ala., Fla., Ga., Ky. *La., Miss., and S. C. In Ala. and Miss. observed on the first Monday in June.

June 11 — Kamehameha Day. In Hawaii.

June 14 — Flag Day. In Penn.

June 20 — West Virginia Day. In that state.

July 24 — Pioneer Day. In Utah.

Aug. 4 — Colorado Day. In that state (always first Monday in August).

Aug. 11 — VJ Day. In Rhode Island (second Monday in August).
Aug. 15 — Admission Day. In Hawaii (third Friday in August).
Aug. 16 — Bennington Battle Day. In Vermont.
Aug. 27 — Lyndon Johnson's Birthday. In Texas.
Aug. 30 — Huey B. Long's Birthday. In Louisiana.
Sept. 9 — Admission Day. In California.
Sept. 12 — Defenders Day. In Maryland.
Oct. 13 — Pioneers Day — In So. Dakota (second Monday in Oct.).
Oct. 31 — Nevada Day. In that state.
Nov. 1 — All Saints' Day. In Louisiana.
Dec. 10 — Wyoming Day. In that state.

Days Usually Observed

Not legal or public holidays:

American Indian Day (Sept. 26 in 1975). Always fourth Friday in September.
Arbor Day. Tree-planting day. First observed April 10, 1872, in Nebraska. Now observed in every state in the Union except Alaska (often on the last Friday in April). A legal holiday in Utah (always last Friday in April), and in Nebraska (April 22).
Armed Forces Day (May 17 in 1975). Always third Saturday in that month, by presidential proclamation. Replaced Army, Navy and Air Force Days.
Bill of Rights Day, Dec. 15. By Act of Congress. Bill of Rights took effect Dec. 15, 1791.
Bird Day. Often observed with Arbor Day.
Child Health Day (Oct. 6 in 1975). Always first Monday in October, by presidential proclamation.
Citizenship Day, Sept. 17. President Truman, Feb. 29, 1952, signed bill designating Sept. 17 as annual Citizenship Day. It replaced I Am An American Day, formerly 3rd Sunday in May and Constitution Day, formerly Sept. 17.
Easter Sunday (March 30 in 1975).
Elizabeth Cady Stanton Day, Nov. 12. Birthday of pioneer leader for equal rights for women.
Father's Day (June 15, in 1975). Always third Sunday in that month.
Flag Day, June 14. By presidential proclamation. It is a legal holiday in Pennsylvania.
Forefathers' Day, Dec. 21. Landing on Plymouth Rock, in 1620. Is celebrated with dinners by New England societies, especially "Down East."
Frances Willard Day, Sept. 28. Observed in Minnesota.
Nathan Bedford Forrest's Birthday, July 13. In Tennessee.
Four Chaplains Memorial Day, February 3.
Gen. Douglas MacArthur Day, Jan. 26. A memorial day in Arkansas.
Gen. Pulaski Memorial Day, Oct. 11. Native of Poland and Revolutionary War hero; died (Oct. 11, 1779) from wounds received at the siege of Savannah, Ga.
Gen. von Steuben Memorial Day, Sept. 17. By presidential proclamation.
Georgia Day, Feb. 12 —In that state.
Groundhog Day, Feb. 2. A popular belief is that if the groundhog sees his shadow this day he returns to his burrow and winter continues 6 weeks longer.
Halloween, Oct. 31. The evening before All Saints or All-Hallows Day. Informally observed in the United States with masquerading and pumpkin-decorations. Traditionally an occasion for children to play harmless pranks.
Andrew Jackson's Birthday, Mar. 15 —in Tennessee.
Leif Ericson Day, Oct. 9. Observed in Minnesota.
Loyalty Day, May 1. By act of Congress.
Martin Luther King's Birthday, Jan. 15 —Observed by many schools and black groups.
May Day. Popularly given to May 1st.
Minnesota Day, May 11. In that state.
Mother's Day (May 11 in 1975). Always second Sunday in that month.

National Aviation Day, Aug. 19. By presidential proclamation.
National Day of Prayer. By presidential proclamation each year on a day other than a Sunday.
National Freedom Day, February 1. To commemorate the signing of a document abolishing slavery, Feb. 1, 1865. By presidential proclamation.
National Maritime Day, May 22. First proclaimed 1935 in commemoration of the departure of the SS Savannah, from Savannah, Ga., on May 22, 1819, on the first successful transatlantic voyage under steam propulsion. By presidential proclamation.
Pan American Day, April 14. In 1890 the First International Conference of American States, meeting in Washington, was held on that date. A resolution was adopted which resulted in the creation of the organization known today as the Pan American Union. By presidential proclamation.
Poetry Day, Oct. 15.
Primary Election Day. Observed usually only when presidential or general elections are held.
Reformation Day, Oct. 31. Observed by Protestant groups.
Sadie Hawkins Day, first Saturday after November 11.
St. Patrick's Day, March 17. Observed by Irish Societies and with parades.
St. Valentine's Day, Feb. 14. Festival of a martyr beheaded at Rome under Emperor Claudius. Association of this day with lovers has no connection with the saint and probably had its origin in an old belief that on this day birds begin to choose their mates.
Susan B. Anthony Day, Feb. 15. Birthday of a pioneer crusader for equal rights for women.
United Nations Day, Oct. 24. By presidential proclamation, to commemorate founding of United Nations.
Verrazano Day, April 17. Observed by New York State, to commemorate the probable discovery of New York harbor by Giovanni da Verrazano in April, 1524.
Will Rogers Day, Nov. 4. In Oklahoma.
Wright Brothers Day, Dec. 17. By presidential designation, to commemorate first successful flight by Orville and Wilbur Wright, Dec. 17, 1903.
Youth Honor Day, Oct. 31. Iowa day of observance.

Weeks and Months

The following list contains special weeks and months designed to call to the attention of the public an event of importance. The dates usually change each year at the discretion of the sponsoring organization. Among the Weeks observed each year are American Art Week, American Education Week, American Heart Month, American Red Cross Fund Drive, Boy Scout Week, Brotherhood Week, Camp Fire Girls Birthday Week, Cancer Control Month, Christmas Seal Sale (sponsored by National Tuberculosis Association), Constitution Week, Earth Week, Fire Prevention Week, Girl Scout Week, Human Rights Week, Jewish Youth Week, March of Dimes (sponsored by National Foundation), National Allergy Month, National Bible Week, National Boys' Club Week (sponsored by Boys Clubs of America), National Crime Prevention Week, National Drum Corps Week, National Employ the Physically Handicapped Week, National Heart Month, National Farm Safety Week, National 4-H Club Week, National Garden Week, National Highway Week, National Hospital Week, National Library Week, National Safe Boating Week, National Salvation Army Week, National Stamp Collecting Week, National Transportation Week, National Wildlife Week (sponsored by National Wildlife Federation), Poppy Week (sponsored by Veterans of Foreign Wars of the U. S.), Red Cross Month, Save Your Vision Week, United Nations Week, United States-Canada Good Will Week (sponsored by the Kiwanis International), World Trade Week, and Youth Week (sponsored by United Christian Youth Movement).

Awards — Medals — Prizes
The Alfred B. Nobel Prize Winners

Alfred B. Nobel, inventor of dynamite, bequeathed $9,000,000, the interest to be distributed yearly to those who had most benefited mankind in the fields of physics, chemistry, medi ine-physiology, literature and peace. The first Nobel Prize in Economics was awarded in 1969. No awards given for years omitted.

Physics

1973 Ivar Giaever, American
Leo Esaki, American
Brian D. Josephson, British
1972 John Bardeen, American
Leon N. Cooper, American
John R. Schrieffer, American
1971 Dennis Gabor, British
1970 Louis Neel, France
Hannes Alfven, Sweden
1969 Murray Gell-Mann, American
1968 Luis W. Alvarez, American
1967 Hans A. Bethe, American
1966 Alfred Kastler, French
1965 Richard P. Feynman, American
Julian S. Schwinger, American
Shinichiro Tomanaga, Japan
1964 Nikolai G. Basov, Russian
Aleksander M. Prochorov, Russ.
Charles H. Townes, American
1963 Maria Goeppert-Mayer, Am.
J. Hans D. Jensen, German
Eugene P. Wigner, American
1962 Lev. D. Landau, Russian
1961 Robert Hofstadter, American
Rudolf L. Mossbauer, German
1960 Donald A. Glaser, American
1959 Owen Chamberlain, American
Emillo G. Segre, American
1958 Paval Cerenkov, Ilya Frank,
Igor J. Tamm, All Russian
1957 Tsung-Dao Lee,
Chen Ning Yang, Both Am.
1956 John Bardeen, American
Walter H. Brattain, American

1955 Polykarp Kusch, American
Willis E. Lamb, American
1954 Max Born, British
Walter Bothe, German
1953 Frits Zernike, Dutch
1952 Felix Bloch, American
Edward M. Purcell, American
1951 Sir John D. Cockroft, British
Ernest T. S. Walton, Irish
1950 Cecil F. Powell, British
1949 Hideki Yukawa, Japanese
1948 Patrick M. S. Blackett, British
1947 Sir Edward V. Appleton, British
1946 Percy Williams Bridgman, Am.
1945 Wolfgang Pauli, American
1944 Isidor Isaac Rabi, American
1943 Otto Sern, American
1939 Ernest O. Lawrence, American
1938 Enrico Fermi, American
1937 Clinton J. Davisson, American
George P. Thomson, British
1936 Carl D. Anderson, American
Victor F. Hess, Austrian
1935 James Chadwick, British
1933 Paul A. M. Dirac, British
Erwin Schrodinger, Austrian
1932 Werner Heisenberg, German
1930 Sir Chandrasekhara V. Raman, Indian
1929 Prince Louis-Victor de Broglie, French
1928 Owen W. Richardson, British
1927 Arthur H. Compton, American

Charles T. R. Wilson, British
1926 Jean B. Perrin, French
1925 James Franck,
Gustav Hertz, Both German
1924 Karl M. G. Siegbahn, Swedish
1923 Robert A. Millikan, American
1922 Niels Bohr, Danish
1921 Albert Einstein, American
1920 Charles E. Guillaume, French
1919 Johannes Stark, German
1918 Max K. E. L. Planck, German
1917 Charles G. Barkla, British
1915 Sir William H. Bragg, British
William L. Bragg, British
1914 Max von Laue, German
1913 Heike Kamerlingh-Onnes, Dutch
1912 Nils G. Dalen, Swedish
1911 Wilhelm Wein, German
1910 Johannes D. van der Waals, Dutch
1909 Carl F. Braun, German
Guglielmo Marconi, Italian
1908 Gabriel Lippmann, French
1907 Albert A. Michelson, American
1906 Sir Joseph J. Thomson, British
1905 Philipp E. A. von Lenard, Ger.
1904 Rayleigh, Lord (John W. Strutt), British
1903 Antoine Henri Becquerel, Fr.
Marie Curie, French
Pierre Curie, French
1902 Hendrik A. Lorentz,
Pieter Zeeman, Both Dutch
1901 Wilhelm C. Rontgen, German

Chemistry

1973 Ernst Otto Fischer, W. German
Geoffrey Wilkinson, British
1972 Christian B. Anfinsen, Am.
Stanford Moore, American
William H. Stein, American
1971 Gerhard Herzberg, Canada
1970 Luis A. Leloir, Arg.
1969 Derek H. R. Barton, British
Odd Hassel, Norway
1968 Lars Onsanger, American
1967 Manfred Eigen, German
Ronald G. W. Norrish, British
George Porter, British
1966 Robert S. Mulliken, American
1965 Robert B. Woodward, American
1964 Dorothy C. Hodgkin, British
1963 Giulio Natta, Italian
Karl Ziegler, German
1962 John C. Kendrew, British
Max F. Perutz, British
1961 Melvin Calvin, American
1960 Willard F. Libby, American
1959 Jaroslav Heyrovsky, Czech
1958 Frederick Sanger, British
1957 Sir Alexander R. Todd, British
1956 Sir Cyril N. Hinshelwood, British
Nikolai N. Semenov, Russian
1955 Vincent du Vigneaud, American
1954 Linus C. Pauling, American

1953 Hermann Staudinger, German
1952 Archer J. P. Martin, British
Richard L. M. Synge, British
1951 Edwin M. McMillan, American
Glenn T. Seaborg, American
1950 Kurt Alder, German
Otto P. H. Diels, German
1949 William F. Glauque, American
1948 Arne W. K. Tiselius, Swedish
1947 Sir Robert Robinson, British
1946 James B. Sumner,
John H. Northrop,
Wendell M. Stanley, All Am.
1945 Artturi I. Virtanen, Finnish
1944 Otto Hahn, German
1943 Georg de Hevesy, Hungarian
1939 Adolf F. J. Butenandt, German
Leopold Ruzicka, Swiss
1938 Richard Kuhn, German
1937 Walter N. Haworth, British
Paul Karrer, Swiss
1936 Peter J. W. Debye, Dutch
1935 Frederic Joliot-Curie, French
Irene Joliot-Curie, French
1934 Harold C. Urey, American
1932 Irving Langmuir, American
1931 Friedrich Bergius, German
Carl Bosch, German

1930 Hans Fischer, German
1929 Arthur Harden, British
Hans von Euler-Chelpin, Swed.
1928 Adolf O. R. Windaus, German
1927 Heinrich O. Wieland, German
1926 Theodor Svedberg, Swedish
1925 Richard A. Zsigmondy, German
1923 Fritz Pergl, Austrian
1922 Francis W. Aston, British
1921 Frederick Soddy, British
1920 Walther H. Nernst, German
1918 Fritz Haber, German
1915 Richard M. Willstatter, German
1914 Theodore W. Richards, Am.
1913 Alfred Werner, Swiss
1912 Victor Grignard, French
Paul Sabatier, French
1911 Marie Curie, French
1910 Otto Wallach, German
1909 Wilhelm Ostwald, German
1908 Ernest Rutherford, British
1907 Eduard Buchner, German
1906 Henri Moissan, French
1905 Adolf von Baeyer, German
1904 Sir William Ramsay, British
1903 Svante A. Arrhenius, Swedish
1902 Emil Fischer, German
1901 Jacobus H. van't Hoff, Dutch

Physiology or Medicine

1973 Karl von Frisch, Konrad Lorenz, both German; Nikolaas Tinbergen, British
1972 Gerald M. Edelman, Am.
Rodney R. Porter, British
1971 Earl W. Sutherland Jr., American
1970 Julius Axelrod, American
Sir Bernard Katz, British
Ulf von Euler, Swedish
1969 Max Delbruck,
Alfred D. Hershey,
Salvador Luria, All American
1968 Robert W. Holley,

H. Gobind Khorana,
Marshall W. Nirenberg, All Am.
1967 Ragnar Granit, Swedish
Haldan Keffer Hartline, Am.
George Wald, American
1966 Charles B. Huggins,
Francis Peyton Rous, Both Am.
1965 Francois Jacob, French
Andre Lwoff, French
Jacquest Monod, French
1964 Konrad E. Bloch, American
Feodor Lynen, German
1963 Sir John C. Eccles, Australian
Alan L. Hodgkin, British

Andrew F. Huxley, British
1962 Francis H. C. Crick, British
James D. Watson, American
Maurice H. F. Wilkins, British
1961 Georg von Bekesy, American
1960 Sir F. MacFarlane Burnet, Australian
Peter B. Medawar, British
1959 Arthur Kornberg, American
Severo Ochoa, American
1958 George W. Beadle, American
Edward L. Tatum, American
Joshua Lederberg, American
1957 Daniel Bovet, Italian

1956 Andre F. Cournand, American
     Werner Forssmann, German
     Dickinson W. Richards, Jr., Am.
1955 Alex H. T. Theorell, Swedish
1954 John F. Enders,
     Frederick C. Robbins,
     Thomas H. Weller, All American
1953 Hans A. Krebs, British
     Fritz A. Lipmann, American
1952 Selman A. Waksman, American
1951 Max Theiler, American
1950 Philip S. Hench,
     Edward C. Kendall, Both Am.
     Tadeus Reichstein, Swiss
1949 Walter R. Hess, Swiss
     Antonio Moniz, Portuguese
1948 Paul H. Muller, Swiss
1947 Carl F. Cori,
     Gerty T. Cori, Both American
     Bernardo A. Houssay, Arg.
1946 Hermann J. Muller, American
1945 Ernst B. Chain, British
     Sir Alexander Fleming, British

     Sir Howard W. Florey, British
1944 Joseph Erlanger, American
     Herbert S. Gasser, American
1943 Henrik C. P. Dam, Danish
     Edward A. Doisy, American
1939 Gerhard Domagk, German
1938 Corneille J. F. Heymans, Belg.
1937 Albert Szent-Gyorgyi, American
1936 Sir Henry H. Dale, British
     Otto Loewi, American
1935 Hans Spemann, German
1934 George R. Minot, Wm. P. Murphy,
     G. H. Whipple, All Am.
1933 Thomas H. Morgan, American
1932 Edgard D. Adrian. British
     Sir Charles S. Sherrington, Brit.
1931 Otto H. Warburg, German
1930 Karl Landsteiner, American
1929 Christiaan Eijkman, Dutch
     Sir Frederick G. Hopkins, British
1928 Charles J. H. Nicolle, French
1927 Julius Wagner-Jauregg, Aus.
1926 Johannes A. G. Fibiger, Danish

1924 Willem Einthoven, Dutch
1923 Frederick G. Banting, Canada
     John J. R. Macleod, Canada
1922 Archibald V. Hill, British
     Otto F. Meyerhof, German
1920 Schack A. S. Krogh, Danish
1919 Jules Bordet, Belgian
1914 Robert Barany, Hungarian
1913 Charles R. Richet, French
1912 Alexis Carrel, American
1911 Allvar Gullstrand, Swedish
1910 Albrecht Kossel, German
1909 Emil T. Kocher, Swiss
1908 Paul Ehrlich, German
     Elie Metchnikoff, French
1907 Charles L. A. Laveran, French
1906 Camillo Golgi, Italian
     Santiago Roman y Cajal, Sp.
1905 Robert Koch, German
1904 Ivan P. Pavlov, Russian
1903 Niels R. Finsen, Danish
1902 Sir Ronald Ross, British
1901 Emil A. von Behring, German

Literature

1973 Patrick White, Australian
1972 Heinrich Boll, W. German
1971 Pablo Neruda, Chile
1970 Aleksandr I. Solzhenitsyn, Russ.
1969 Samuel Beckett, Irish
1968 Yasunari Kawabata, Japan
1967 Miguel Angel Asturias, Guate.
1966 Samuel Joseph Agnon, Israeli
     Nelly Sachs, German
1965 Mikhail Sholokhov, Russian
1964 Jean Paul Sartre, French
     (Prize declined)
1963 Giorgos Seferis, Greek
1962 John Steinbeck, American
1961 Ivo Andric, Yugoslavian
1960 Saint-John Perse, French
1959 Salvatore Quasimodo, Italian
1958 Boris L. Pasternak, Russian
     (Prize declined)
1957 Albert Camus, French
1956 Juan Ramon Jimenez,
     Puerto Rican
1955 Halldor K. Laxness, Icelandic
1954 Ernest Hemingway, American
1953 Sir Winston Churchill, British

1952 Francois Mauriac, French
1951 Par F. Lagerkvist, Swedish
1950 Bertrand Russell, British
1949 William Faulkner, American
1948 T. S. Eliot, British
1947 Andre Gide, French
1946 Hermann Hesse, Swiss
1945 Gabriela Mistral, Chilean
1944 Johannes V. Jensen, Danish
1939 Frans. E. Sillanpaa, Finnish
1938 Pearl S. Buck, American
1937 Roger Martin du Gard, French
1936 Eugene O'Neill, American
1934 Luigi Pirandello, Italian
1933 Ivan A. Bunin, French
1932 John Galsworthy, British
1931 Erik A. Karlfeldt, Swedish
1930 Sinclair Lewis, American
1929 Thomas Mann, German
1928 Sigrid Undset, Norwegian
1927 Henri Bergson, French
1926 Grazia Deledda, Italian
1925 George Bernard Shaw, British
1924 Wladyslaw S. Reymont, Polish
1923 William Butler Yeats, Irish

1922 Jacinto Benavente, Spanish
1921 Anatole France, French
1920 Knut Hamsun, Norwegian
1919 Carl F. G. Spitteler, Swiss
1917 Karl A. Gjellerup, Danish
     Henrik Pontoppidan, Danish
1916 Verner von Heidenstam, Swed.
1915 Romain Rolland, French
1913 Rabindranath Tagore, Indian
1912 Gerhart Hauptmann, German
1911 Count Maurice Maeterlinck,
     Belgian
1910 Paul J. L. Heyse, German
1909 Selma Lagerlof, Swedish
1908 Rudolf C. Eucken, German
1907 Rudyard Kipling, British
1906 Giosue Carducci, Italian
1905 Henryk Sienkiewicz, Polish
1904 Frederic Mistral, French
     Jose Echegaray, Spanish
1903 Bjornsterne Bjornson, Norw.
1902 Theodor Mommsen, German
1901 Rene F. A. Sully Prudhomme,
     French

Peace

1973 Henry Kissinger, American
     Le Duc Tho, No. Vietnamese
1971 Willy Brandt, W. German
1970 Norman E. Borlaug, American
1969 Intl. Labor Organization
1968 Rene Cassin, French
1965 The United Nations Children's
     Fund (UNICEF)
1964 Martin Luther King, Jr., Am.
1963 International Red Cross
     League of Red Cross Societies
1962 Linus C. Pauling, American
1961 Dag Hammarskjold, Swedish
1960 Albert J. Luthuli, South African
1959 Philip J. Noel-Baker, British
1958 Georges Pire, Belgian
1957 Lester B. Pearson, Canadian
1954 Office of the UN High
     Commissioner for Refugees
1953 George C. Marshall, American
1952 Albert Schweitzer, French
1951 Leon Jouhaux, French
1950 Ralph J. Bunche, American
1949 Lord John Boyd Orr of Brechin,
     British
1947 Friends Service Council,

     British American Friends
     Service Committee, American
1946 Emily G. Balch,
     John R. Mott, Both American
1945 Cordell Hull, American
1944 International Red Cross
1938 Nansen International Office
     for Refugees
1937 Viscount Cecil of Chelwood
     (Lord Edgar A. R. G. Cecil), Brit.
1936 Carlos de Saavedra Lamas, Arg.
1935 Carl von Ossietzky, German
1934 Arthur Henderson, British
1933 Sir Norman Angell, British
1931 Jane Addams, American
     Nicholas Murray Butler, Amer.
1930 Nathan Soderblom, Swedish
1929 Frank B. Kellogg, American
1927 Ferdinand E. Buisson, French
     Ludwig Quidde, German
1926 Aristide Briand, French
     Gustav Stresemann, German
1925 Sir J. Austen Camberlain, Brit.
     Charles G. Dawes, American
1922 Fridtjof Nansen, Norwegian
1921 Karl H. Branting, Swedish

     Christian L. Lange, Norwegian
1920 Leon V. A. Bourgeois, French
1919 Woodrow Wilson, American
1917 International Red Cross
1913 Henri La Fontaine, Belgian
1912 Elihu Root, American
1911 Tobias M. C. Asser, Dutch
     Alfred H. Fried, Austrian
1910 Permanent International Peace
     Bureau
1909 Auguste M. F. Beernaert, Belg.
     Paul H. B. B. d'Estournelles de
     Constant, French
1908 Klas P. Arnoldson, Swedish
     Fredrik Bajer, Danish
1907 Ernesto T. Moneta, Italian
     Louis Renault, French
1906 Theodore Roosevelt, American
1905 Baroness Bertha von Suttner,
     Austrian
1904 Institute of International Law
1903 Sir William R. Cremer, British
1902 Elie Ducommun,
     Charles A. Gobat, Both Swiss
1901 Jean H. Dunant, Swiss
     Frederic Passy, French

Economics

1971 Simon Kuznets, American
1970 Paul A. Samuelson, American

1973 Wassily Leontief, American
1972 Kenneth J. Arrow, American
     John R. Hicks, British

1969 Ragnar Frisch, Norway;
     Jan Tinbergen, Netherlands

The Molson Prize

The Molson Prizes of the Canada Council are made in recognition of outstanding contributions to the arts, social sciences or humanities or to national unity. The value of the prize is $15,000 and 3 prizes are awarded each year. Winners were:

1963	Donald Creighton, Alain Grandbois	1966	Rev. Georges-Henri Levesque; H. McLennan
1965	Jean Gascon; Frank Scott	1967	Arthur Erickson; Anne Hebert; Marshall McLuhan

1968	Glen Gould; Jean Le Moyne	1972	John Deutsch; Alfred Pellan; George Woodcock
1970	Jean-Paul Audet; Morley Callaghan; Arnold Spohr	1973	W.A.C.H. Dobson; Celia Franca; Jean-Paul Lemieux
1971	Maureen Forrester; Rina Lasnier; Norman McLaren		

Pulitzer Prizes in Journalism, Letters and Music

The Pulitzer Prizes were endowed by Joseph Pulitzer (1847-1911), publisher of The World, New York, N. Y., in a bequest to Columbia University, New York, N. Y., and are awarded annually by the trustees of the university on recommendation of the Advisory Board on Pulitzer Prizes for work done during the preceding year. Secretary of the Advisory Board is John Hohenberg of Columbia Univ. All prizes are $1,000 (originally $500) in each category, except Meritorious Public Service for which a gold medal is given. No awards given for years omitted.

Pulitzer Prizes in Journalism
Meritorious Public Service

For disinterested and meritorious public service by a United States newspaper.

1918—New York Times. Also special award to Minna Lewinson and Henry Beetle Hough.
1919—Milwaukee Journal.
1921—Boston Post.
1922—New York World.
1923—Memphis (Tenn.) Commercial Appeal.
1924—New York World.
1926—Enquirer-Sun, Columbus, Ga.
1927—Canton (O.) Daily News.
1928—Indianapolis Times.
1929—Evening World, New York.
1931—Atlanta (Ga.) Constitution.
1932—Indianapolis (Ind.) News.
1933—New York World-Telegram.
1934—Medford (Ore.) Mail-Tribune.
1935—Sacramento (Calif.) Bee.
1936—Cedar Rapids (Iowa) Gazette.
1937—St. Louis Post-Dispatch.
1938—Bismarck (N. D.) Tribune.
1939—Miami (Fla.) Daily News.
1940—Waterbury (Conn.) Republican and American.
1941—St. Louis Post-Dispatch.
1942—Los Angeles Times.
1943—Omaha World Herald.
1944—New York Times.
1945—Detroit Free Press.
1946—Scranton (Pa.) Times.
1947—Baltimore Sun.
1948—St. Louis Post-Dispatch.
1949—Nebraska State Journal.
1950—Chicago Daily News; St. Louis Post-Dispatch.
1951—Miami (Fla.) Herald and Brooklyn Eagle.
1952—St. Louis Post-Dispatch.
1953—Whiteville (N. C.) News Reporter; Tabor City (N. C.) Tribune.
1954—Newsday (Long Island, N.Y.).
1955—Columbus (Ga.) Ledger and Sunday Ledger-Enquirer.
1956—Watsonville (Calif.) Register-Pajaronian.
1957—Chicago Daily News.
1958—Arkansas Gazette, Little Rock.
1959—Utica (N. Y.) Observer-Dispatch and Utica Daily Press.
1960—Los Angeles Times.
1961—Amarillo (Tex.) Globe-Times.
1962—Panama City (Fla.) News-Herald.
1963—Chicago Daily News.
1964—St. Petersburg (Fla.) Times.
1965—Hutchinson (Kans.) News.
1966—Boston Globe.
1967—The Louisville Courier-Journal and The Milwaukee Journal.
1968—Riverside (Calif.) Press-Enterprise.
1969—Los Angeles Times.
1970—Newsday (Long Island, N.Y.)
1971—Winston Salem (N.C.) Journal & Sentinel.
1972—New York Times.
1973—Washington Post.
1974—Newsday (Long Island, N.Y.).

Reporting

This category originally embraced all fields, local, national, and international. Later separate categories were created for the different fields of reporting.

1917—Herbert Bayard Swope, New York World.
1918—Harold A. Littledale, New York Evening Post.
1920—John J. Leary, Jr., New York World.
1921—Louis Seibold, New York World.
1922—Kirke L. Simpson, Associated Press.
1923—Alva Johnston, New York Times.
1924—Magner White, San Diego Sun.

1925—James W. Mulroy and Alvin H. Goldstein, Chi. Daily News.
1926—William Burke Miller, Louisville Courier-Journal.
1927—John T. Rogers, St. Louis Post-Dispatch.
1929—Paul Y. Anderson, St. Louis Post-Dispatch.
1930—Russell D. Owens, New York Times. Also $500 to W. O. Dapping, Auburn (N. Y.) Citizen.
1931—A. B. MacDonald, Kansas City (Mo.) Star.
1932—W. C. Richards, D. D. Martin, J. S. Pooler, F. D. Webb, J. N. W. Sloan, Detroit Free Press.
1933—Francis A. Jamieson, Associated Press.
1934—Royce Brier, San Francisco Chronicle.
1935—William H. Taylor, New York Herald Tribune.
1936—Lauren D. Lyman, New York Times.
1937—John J. O'Neill, N. Y. Herald Tribune; William L. Laurence, N. Y. Times; Howard W. Blakeslee, A. P.; Gobind Behari Lal, University Service and David Dietz, Scripps-Howard Newspapers.
1938—Raymond Sprigle, Pittsburgh Post-Gazette.
1939—Thomas L. Stokes, Scripps-Howard Newspaper Alliance.
1940—S. Burton Heath, New York World-Telegram.
1941—Westbrook Pegler, New York World-Telegram.
1942—Stanton Delaplane, San Francisco Chronicle.
1943—George Weller, Chicago Daily News.
1944—Paul Schoenstein, N. Y. Journal-American.
1945—Jack S. McDowell, San Francisco Call-Bulletin.
1946—William L. Laurence, New York Times.
1947—Frederick Woltman, N. Y. World-Telegram.
1948—George E. Goodwin, Atlanta Journal.
1949—Malcom Johnson, New York Sun.
1950—Meyer Berger, New York Times.
1951—Edward S. Montgomery, San Francisco Examiner.
1952—Geo. de Carvalho, San Francisco Chronicle.

(1) to meet a deadline; (2) free of deadline.

1953—(1) Providence (R.I.) Journal and Evening Bulletin; (2) Edward J. Mowery, N. Y. World-Telegram & Sun.
1954—(1) Vicksburg (Miss.) Sunday Post-Herald; (2) Alvin Scott McCoy, Kansas City (Mo.) Star.
1955—(1) Mrs. Caro Brown, Alice (Tex.) Daily Echo; (2) Roland K. Towery, Cuero (Tex.) Record.
1956—(1) Lee Hills, Detroit Free Press; (2) Arthur Daley, New York Times.
1957—(1) Salt Lake Tribune, Salt Lake City, Utah, (2) Wallace Turner and William Lambert, Portland Oregonian.
1958—(1) Fargo (N. D.) Forum; (2) George Beveridge, Evening Star, Washington, D. C.
1959—(1) Mary Lou Werner, Washington Evening Star; (2) John Harold Brislin, Scranton (Pa.) Tribune, and The Scrantonian.
1960—(1) Jack Nelson, Atlanta Constitution; (2) Miriam Ottenberg, Washington Evening Star.
1961—(1) Sanche de Gramont, N. Y. Herald Tribune; (2) Edgar May, Buffalo Evening News.
1962—(1) Robert D. Mullins, Deseret News, Salt Lake City; (2) George Bliss, Chicago Tribune.
1963—(1) Shared by Sylvan Fox, William Longgood, and Anthony Shannon, N. Y. World-Telegram & Sun; (2) Oscar Griffin, Jr., Pecos (Tex.) Independent and Enterprise.

(1) General Reporting; (2) Special Reporting.

1964—(1) Norman C. Miller, Wall Street Journal; (2) Shared by James V. Magee, Albert V. Gaudiosi, and Frederick A. Meyer, Philadelphia Bulletin.
1965—(1) Melvin H. Ruder, Hungry Horse News (Columbia Falls, Mont.); (2) Gene Goltz, Houston, Post.
1966—(1) Los Angeles Times Staff; (2) John A. Frasca, Tampa (Fla.) Tribune.
1967—(1) Robert V. Cox, Chambersburg (Pa.) Public Opinion; (2) Gene Miller, Miami Herald.
1968—Detroit Free Press Staff; (2) J. Anthony Lukas, N. Y. Times.
1969—(1) John Fetterman, Louisville Courier-Journal and Times; (2) Albert L. Delugach, St. Louis Globe Democrat, and Denny Walsh, Life.

1970—(1) Thomas Fitzpatrick, Chicago Sun-Times; (2) Harold Eugene Martin, Montgomery Advertiser & Alabama Journal.
1971—(1) Akron Beacon Journal Staff. (2) William Hugh Jones, Chicago Tribune.
1972—(1) Richard Cooper and John Machacek, Rochester (N.Y.) Times-Union; (2) Timothy Leland, Gerard M. O'-Neill, Stephen A. Kurkjian and Anne De Santis, Boston Globe.
1973—(1) Chicago Tribune; (2) Sun Newspapers of Omaha.
1974—(1) Hugh F. Hough, Arthur M. Petacque, Chicago Sun-Times; (2) William Sherman, N.Y. Daily News.

Criticism or Commentary
(1) Criticism; (2) Commentary
1970—(1) Ada Louise Huxtable, N. Y. Times; (2) Marquis W. Childs, St. Louis Post-Dispatch.
1971—(1) Harold C. Schonberg, N. Y. Times; (2) William A. Caldwell, The Record, Hackensack, N.J.
1972—(1) Frank Peters Jr., St. Louis Post-Dispatch; (2) Mike Royko, Chicago Daily News.
1973—(1) Ronald Powers, Chicago Sun-Times; (2) David S. Broder, Washington Post.
1974—(1) Emily Genauer, Newsday (N.Y.). (2) Edwin A. Roberts Jr., National Observer.

National Reporting
1942—Louis Stark, New York Times.
1944—Dewey L. Fleming, Baltimore Sun.
1945—James B. Reston, New York Times.
1946—Edward A. Harris, St. Louis Post-Dispatch.
1947—Edward T. Folliard, Washington Post.
1948—Bert Andrews, New York Herald Tribune; Nat S. Finney, Minneapolis Tribune.
1949—Charles P. Trussell, New York Times.
1950—Edwin O. Guthman, Seattle Times.
1952—Anthony Leviero, New York Times.
1953—Don Whitehead, Associated Press.
1954—Richard Wilson, Cowles Newspapers.
1955—Anthony Lewis, Washington Daily News.
1956—Charles L. Bartlett, Chattanooga Times.
1957—James Reston, New York Times.
1958—Relman Morin, AP; Clark Mollenhoff, Des Moines Register & Tribune.
1959—Howard Van Smith, Miami (Fla.) News.
1960—Vance Trimble, Scripps-Howard, Washington, D. C.
1961—Edward R. Cony, Wall Street Journal.
1962—Nathan G. Caldwell and Gene S. Graham, Nashville Tennessean.
1963—Anthony Lewis, New York Times.
1964—Merriman Smith, UPI
1965—Louis M. Kohlmeier, Wall Street Journal.
1966—Haynes Johnson, Washington Evening Star.
1967—Monroe Karmin and Stanley Penn, Wall Street Journal.
1968—Howard James, Christian Science Monitor; Nathan K. Kotz, Des Moines Register.
1969—Robert Cahn, Christian Science Monitor.
1970—William J. Eaton, Chicago Daily News.
1971—Lucinda Franks & Thomas Powers, UPI.
1972—Jack Anderson, United Features.
1973—Robert Boyd and Clark Hoyt, Knight Newspapers.
1974—James R. Polk, Washington Star-News; Jack White, Providence Journal-Bulletin.

International Reporting
1942—Laurence Edmund Allen, Associated Press.
1943—Ira Wolfert, No. Am. Newspaper Alliance.
1944—Daniel DeLuce, Associated Press.
1945—Mark S. Watson, Baltimore Sun.
1946—Homer W. Bigart, New York Herald Tribune.
1947—Eddy Gilmore, Associated Press.
1948—Paul W. Ward, Baltimore Sun.
1949—Price Day, Baltimore Sun.
1950—Edmund Stevens, Christian Science Monitor.
1951—Keyes Beech and Fred Sparks, Chicago Daily News; Homer Bigart and Marguerite Higgins, N.Y. Herald Tribune; Relman Morin and Don Whitehead, AP.
1952—John M. Hightower, Associated Press.
1953—Austin C. Wehrwein, Milwaukee Journal.
1954—Jim G. Lucas, Scripps-Howard Newspapers.
1955—Harrison Salisbury, New York Times.
1956—William Randolph Hearst, Jr., Frank Conniff, Hearst Newspapers; Kingsbury Smith, INS.
1957—Russell Jones, United Press.
1958—New York Times.
1959—Joseph Martin and Philip Santora, N. Y. News.

1960—A. M. Rosenthal, New York Times.
1961—Lynn Heinzerling, Associated Press.
1962—Walter Lippmann, N. Y. Herald Tribune Synd.
1963—Hal Hendrix, Miami (Fla.) News.
1964—Malcolm W. Browne, AP; David Halberstam, N. Y. Times.
1965—J. A. Livingston, Philadelphia Bulletin.
1966—Peter Arnett, AP.
1967—R. John Hughes, Christian Science Monitor.
1968—Alfred Friendly, Washington Post.
1969—William Tuohy, L. A. Times.
1970—Seymour M. Hersh, Dispatch News Service.
1971—Jimmie Lee Hoagland, Washington Post.
1972—Peter R. Kann, Wall Street Journal.
1973—Max Frankel, N.Y. Times.
1974—Hedrick Smith, N.Y. Times.

Correspondence
For Washington or foreign correspondence. Category was merged with those in national and international reporting in 1948.
1929—Paul Scott Mowrer, Chicago Daily News.
1930—Leland Stowe, New York Herald Tribune.
1931—H. R. Knickerbocker, Philadelphia Public Ledger and New York Evening Post.
1932—Walter Duranty, New York Times, and Charles G. Ross, St. Louis Post-Dispatch.
1933—Edgar Ansel Mowrer, Chicago Daily News.
1934—Frederick T. Birchall, New York Times.
1935—Arthur Krock, New York Times.
1936—Wilfred C. Barber, Chicago Tribune.
1937—Anne O'Hare McCormick, New York Times.
1938—Arthur Krock, New York Times.
1939—Louis P. Lochner, Associated Press.
1940—Otto D. Tolischus, New York Times.
1941—Bronze plaque to commemorate work of American correspondents on war fronts.
1942—Carlos P. Romulo, Philippines Herald.
1943—Hanson W. Baldwin, New York Times.
1944—Ernest Taylor Pyle, Scripps-Howard Newspaper Alliance.
1945—Harold V. (Hal) Boyle, Associated Press.
1946—Arnaldo Cortesi, New York Times.
1947—Brooks Atkinson, New York Times.

Editorial Writing
The test of excellence is clearness of style, moral purpose, sound reasoning and power to influence public opinion.
1917—New York Tribune.
1918—Louisville (Ky.) Courier-Journal.
1920—Harvey E. Newbranch, Omaha Evening World-Herald.
1922—Frank M. O'Brien, New York Herald.
1923—William Allen White, Emporia Gazette.
1924—Frank Buxton, Boston Herald, Special Prize. Frank I. Cobb, New York World.
1925—Charleston (S. C.) News and Courier.
1926—Edward M. Kingsbury, N. Y. Times.
1927—F. Lauriston Bullard, Boston Herald.
1928—Grover C. Hall, Montgomery Advertiser.
1929—Louis Isaac Jaffe, Norfolk Virginian-Pilot.
1931—Chas. Ryckman, Fremont (Nebr.) Tribune.
1933—Kansas City (Mo.) Star.
1934—E. P. Chase, Atlantic (Ia.) News Telegraph.
1936—Felix Morley, Washington Post. George B. Parker, Scripps-Howard Newspapers.
1937—John W. Owens, Baltimore Sun.
1938—W. W. Waymack, Des Moines (Ia.) Register and Tribune.
1939—Ronald G. Callvert, Portland Oregonian.
1940—Bart Howard, St. Louis Post-Dispatch.
1941—Reuben Maury, Daily News, N. Y.
1942—Geoffrey Parsons, New York Herald Tribune.
1943—Forrest W. Seymour, Des Moines (Ia.) Register and Tribune.
1944—Henry J. Haskell, Kansas City (Mo.) Star.
1945—George W. Potter, Providence (R. I.) Journal-Bulletin.
1946—Hodding Carter, Greenville (Miss.) Delta Democrat-Times.
1947—William H. Grimes, Wall Street Journal.
1948—Virginius Dabney, Richmond (Va.) Times-Dispatch.
1949—John H. Crider, Boston (Mass.) Herald, Herbert Elliston, Washington Post.
1950—Carl M. Saunders, Jackson (Mich.) Citizen-Patriot.
1951—William H. Fitzpatrick, New Orleans States.
1952—Louis LaCoss, St. Louis Globe Democrat.
1953—Vermont C. Royster, Wall Street Journal.
1954—Don Murray, Boston Herald.
1955—Royce Howes, Detroit Free Press.

1956—Lauren K. Soth, Des Moines (Ia.) Register and Tribune.
1957—Buford Boone, Tuscaloosa (Ala.) News.
1958—Harry S. Ashmore, Arkansas Gazette.
1959—Ralph McGill, Atlanta Constitution.
1960—Lenoir Chambers, Norfolk Virginian-Pilot.
1961—William J. Dorvillier, San Juan (Puerto Rico) Star.
1962—Thomas M. Storke, Santa Barbara (Calif.) News-Press.
1963—Ira B. Harkey, Jr., Pascagoula (Miss.) Chronicle.
1964—Hazel Brannon Smith, Lexington (Miss.) Advertiser.
1965—John R. Harrison, The Gainesville (Fla.) Sun.
1966—Robert Lasch, St. Louis Post-Dispatch.
1967—Eugene C. Patterson, Atlanta Constitution.
1968—John S. Knight, Knight Newspapers.
1969—Paul Greenberg, Pine Bluff (Ark.) Commercial.
1970—Philip L. Geyelin, Washington Post.
1971—Horance G. Davis, Jr., Gainesville (Fla.) Sun.
1972—John Strohmeyer, Bethlehem (Pa.) Globe-Times.
1973—Roger B. Linscott, Berkshire Eagle, Pittsfield, Mass.
1974—F. Gilbert Spencer, Trenton (N.J.) Trentonian.

Cartoon

1922—Rollin Kirby, New York World.
1924—Jay N. Darling, New York Herald Tribune.
1925—Rollin Kirby, New York World.
1926—D. R. Fitzpatrick, St. Louis Post-Dispatch.
1927—Nelson Harding, Brooklyn Eagle.
1928—Nelson Harding, Brooklyn Eagle.
1929—Rollin Kirby, New York World
1930—Charles Macauley, Brooklyn Eagle.
1931—Edmund Duffy, Baltimore Sun.
1932—John T. McCutcheon, Chicago Tribune.
1933—H. M. Talburt, Washington Daily News.
1934—Edmund Duffy, Baltimore Sun.
1935—Ross A. Lewis, Milwaukee Journal.
1937—C. D. Batchelor, New York Daily News.
1938—Vaughn Shoemaker, Chicago Daily News.
1939—Charles G. Werner, Daily Oklahoman.
1940—Edmund Duffy, Baltimore Sun.
1941—Jacob Burck, Chicago Times.
1942—Herbert L. Block, Newspaper Enterprise Assn.
1943—Jay N. Darling, New York Herald Tribune.
1944—Clifford K. Berryman, Washington Star.
1945—Bill Mauldin, United Feature Syndicate.
1946—Bruce Alexander Russell, Los Angeles Times.
1947—Vaughn Shoemaker, Chicago Daily News.
1948—Reuben L. (Rube) Goldberg, N. Y. Sun.
1949—Lute Pease, Newark (N. J.) Evening News.
1950—James T. Berryman, Washington Star.
1951—Reginald W. Manning, Arizona Republic.
1952—Fred L. Packer, New York Mirror.
1953—Edward D. Kuekes, Cleveland Plain Dealer.
1954—Herbert L. Block, Washington Post & Times-Herald.
1955—Daniel R. Fitzpatrick, St. Louis Post-Dispatch.
1956—Robert York, Louisville (Ky.) Times.
1957—Tom Little, Nashville Tennessean.
1958—Bruce M. Shanks, Buffalo Evening News.
1959—Bill Mauldin, St. Louis Post-Dispatch.
1961—Carey Orr, Chicago Tribune.
1962—Edmund S. Valtman, Hartford Times.
1963—Frank Miller, Des Moines Register.
1964—Paul Conrad, Denver Post.
1966—Don Wright, Miami News.
1967—Patrick B. Oliphant, Denver Post.
1968—Eugene Gray Payne, Charlotte Observer.
1969—John Fischetti, Chicago Daily News.
1970—Thomas F. Darcy, Newsday.
1971—Paul Conrad, L. A. Times.
1972—Jeffrey K. MacNelly, Richmond News-Leader.
1974—Paul Szep, Boston Globe.

Spot News Photography

1942—Milton Brooks, Detroit News.
1943—Frank Noel, Associated Press.
1944—Frank Filan, AP; Earle L. Bunker, Omaha World-Herald.
1945—Joe Rosenthal, Associated Press, for photograph of planting American flag on Iwo Jima.
1947—Arnold Hardy, amateur, Atlanta, Ga.
1948—Frank Cushing, Boston Traveler.
1949—Nathaniel Fein, New York Herald Tribune.
1950—Bill Crouch, Oakland (Calif) Tribune.
1951—Max Desfor, Associated Press.
1952—John Robinson and Don Ultang, Des Moines Register and Tribune.
1953—William M. Gallagher, Flint (Mich.) Journal.

1954—Mrs. Walter M. Schau, amateur.
1955—John L. Gaunt, Jr., Los Angeles Times.
1956—New York Daily News.
1957—Harry A. Trask, Boston Traveler.
1958—William C. Beall, Washington Daily News.
1959—William Seaman, Minneapolis Star.
1960—Andrew Lopez, UPI.
1961—Yasushi Nagao, Mainichi Newspapers, Tokyo.
1962—Paul Vathis, Associated Press.
1963—Hector Rondon, La Republica, Caracas, Venezuela.
1964—Robert H. Jackson, Dallas Times-Herald.
1965—Horst Faas, Associated Press.
1966—Kyoichi Sawada, UPI.
1967—Jack R. Thornell, Associated Press.
1968—Rocco Morabito, Jacksonville Journal.
1969—Edward Adams, AP
1970—Steve Starr, AP
1971—John Paul Filo, Valley Daily News & Daily Dispatch of Tarentum & New Kensington, Pa.
1972—Horst Faas and Michel Laurent, AP.
1973—Huynh Cong Ut, AP.
1974—Anthony K. Roberts, AP.

Feature Photography

1968—Toshio Sakai, UPI.
1969—Moneta Sleet, Jr., Ebony.
1970—Dallas Kinney, Palm Beach Post.
1971—Jack Dykinga, Chicago Sun-Times.
1972—Dave Kennerly, UPI.
1973—Brian Lanker, Topeka Capitol-Journal.
1974—Slava Veder, AP.

Special Citation

1938—Edmonton (Alberta) Journal, bronze plaque.
1941—New York Times.
1944—Byron Price and Mrs. William Allen White. Also to Richard Rodgers and Oscar Hammerstein, 2nd, for musical, Oklahoma!
1945—Press cartographers for war maps.
1947—(Pulitzer centennial year) Columbia Univ. and the Graduate School of Journalism, and St. Louis Post-Dispatch.
1948—Dr. Frank Diehl Fackenthal.
1951—Cyrus L. Sulzberger, New York Times.
1952—Max Kase, New York Journal-American.
1953—The New York Times; Lester Markel.
1957—Kenneth Roberts, for his historical novels.
1958—Walter Lippmann, New York Herald Tribune.
1960—Garrett Mattingly, for The Armada.
1961—American Heritage Picture History of the Civil War.
1964—The Gannett Newspapers.
1973—James T. Flexner, for "George Washington," a four-volume biography.

Pulitzer Prizes in Letters
Fiction

For fiction in book form by an American author, preferably dealing with American life.
1918—Ernest Poole, His Family.
1919—Booth Tarkington, The Magnificent Ambersons.
1921—Edith Wharton, The Age of Innocence.
1922—Booth Tarkington, Alice Adams.
1923—Willa Cather, One of Ours.
1924—Margaret Wilson, The Able McLaughlins.
1925—Edna Ferber, So Big.
1926—Sinclair Lewis, Arrowsmith. (Refused prize.)
1927—Louis Bromfield, Early Autumn.
1928—Thornton Wilder, Bridge of San Luis Rey.
1929—Julia M. Peterkin, Scarlet Sister Mary.
1930—Oliver LaFarge, Laughing Boy.
1931—Margaret Ayer Barnes, Years of Grace.
1932—Pearl S. Buck, The Good Earth.
1933—T. S. Stribling, The Store.
1934—Caroline Miller, Lamb in His Bosom.
1935—Josephine W. Johnson, Now in November.
1936—Harold L. Davis, Honey in the Horn.
1937—Margaret Mitchell, Gone With the Wind.
1938—John P. Marquand, The Late George Apley.
1939—Marjorie Kinnan Rawlings, The Yearling.
1940—John Steinbeck, The Grapes of Wrath.
1942—Ellen Glasgow, In This Our Life.
1943—Upton Sinclair, Dragon's Teeth.
1944—Martin Flavin, Journey in the Dark.
1945—John Hersey, A Bell for Adano.
1947—Robert Penn Warren, All the King's Men.
1948—James A. Michener, Tales of the South Pacific.
1949—James Gould Cozzens, Guard of Honor.

1950—A. B. Guthrie, Jr., The Way West.
1951—Conrad Richter, The Town.
1952—Herman Wouk, The Caine Mutiny.
1953—Ernest Hemingway, The Old Man and the Sea.
1955—William Faulkner, A Fable.
1956—MacKinlay Kantor, Andersonville.
1958—James Agee, A Death in the Family.
1959—Robert Lewis Taylor, The Travels of Jaimie McPheeters.
1960—Allen Drury, Advise and Consent.
1961—Harper Lee, To Kill a Mockingbird.
1962—Edwin O'Connor, The Edge of Sadness.
1963—William Faulkner, The Reivers.
1965—Shirley Ann Grau, The Keepers of the House.
1966—Katherine Anne Porter, Collected Stories of Katherine Anne Porter.
1967—Bernard Malamud, The Fixer.
1968—William Styron, The Confessions of Nat Turner.
1969—N. Scott Momaday, House Made of Dawn.
1970—Jean Stafford, Collected Stories.
1972—Wallace Stegner, Angle of Repose.
1973—Eudora Welty, The Optimist's Daughter.

Drama

For an American play, preferably original and dealing with American life.

1918—Jesse Lynch Williams, Why Marry?
1920—Eugene O'Neill, Beyond the Horizon.
1921—Zona Gale, Miss Lulu Bett.
1922—Eugene O'Neill, Anna Christie.
1923—Owen Davis, Icebound.
1924—Hatcher Hughes, Hell-Bent for Heaven.
1925—Sidney Howard, They Knew What They Wanted.
1926—George Kelly, Craig's Wife.
1927—Paul Green, In Abraham's Bosom.
1928—Eugene O'Neill, Strange Interlude.
1929—Elmer Rice, Street Scene.
1930—Marc Connelly, The Green Pastures.
1931—Susan Glaspell, Alison's House.
1932—George S. Kaufman, Morrie Ryskind and Ira Gershwin, Of Thee I Sing.
1933—Maxwell Anderson, Both Your Houses.
1934—Sidney Kingsley, Men in White.
1935—Zoe Akins, The Old Maid.
1936—Robert E. Sherwood, Idiot's Delight.
1937—George S. Kaufman and Moss Hart, You Can't Take It With You.
1938—Thornton Wilder, Our Town.
1939—Robert E. Sherwood, Abe Lincoln in Illinois.
1940—William Saroyan, The Time of Your Life.
1941—Robert E. Sherwood, There Shall Be No Night.
1943—Thornton Wilder, The Skin of Our Teeth.
1945—Mary Chase, Harvey.
1946—Russel Crouse and Howard Lindsay, State of the Union.
1948—Tennessee Williams, A Streetcar Named Desire.
1949—Arthur Miller, Death of a Salesman.
1950—Richard Rodgers, Oscar Hammerstein II, and Joshua Logan, South Pacific.
1952—Joseph Kramm, The Shrike.
1953—William Inge, Picnic.
1954—John Patrick, Teahouse of the August Moon.
1955—Tennessee Williams, Cat on a Hot Tin Roof.
1956—Frances Goodrich and Albert Hackett, The Diary of Anne Frank.
1957—Eugene O'Neill, Long Day's Journey Into Night.
1958—Ketti Frings, Look Homeward, Angel.
1959—Archibald MacLeish, J. B.
1960—George Abbott, Jerome Weidman, Sheldon Harnick and Jerry Bock, Fiorello.
1961—Tad Mosel, All the Way Home.
1962—Frank Loesser and Abe Burrows, How To Succeed In Business Without Really Trying.
1965—Frank D. Gilroy, The Subject Was Roses.
1967—Edward Albee, A Delicate Balance.
1969—Howard Sackler, The Great White Hope.
1970—Charles Gordone, No Place to Be Somebody.
1971—Paul Zindel, The Effect of Gamma Rays on Man-in-the-Moon Marigolds.
1973—Jason Miller, That Championship Season.

History

1917—J. J. Jusserand, With Americans of Past and Present Days.
1918—James Ford Rhodes, History of the Civil War.
1920—Justin H. Smith, The War with Mexico.
1921—William Sowden Sims, The Victory at Sea.
1922—James Truslow Adams, The Founding of New England.

1923—Charles Warren, The Supreme Court in United States History.
1924—Charles Howard McIlwain, The American Revolution: A Constitutional Interpretation.
1925—Frederick L. Paxton, A History of the American Frontier.
1926—Edward Channing, The History of the U. S.
1927—Samuel Flagg Bemis, Pinckney's Treaty.
1928—Vernon Louis Parrington, Main Currents in American Thought.
1929—Fred A. Shannon, The Organization and Administration of the Union Army, 1861-65.
1930—Claude H. Van Tyne, The War of Independence.
1931—Bernadotte E. Schmitt, The Coming of the War, 1914.
1932—Gen. John J. Pershing, My Experiences in the World War.
1933—Frederick J. Turner, The Significance of Sections in American History.
1934—Herbert Agar, The People's Choice.
1935—Charles McLean Andrews, The Colonial Period of American History.
1936—Andrew C. McLaughlin, The Constitutional History of the United States.
1937—Van Wyck Brooks, The Flowering of New England.
1938—Paul Herman Buck, The Road to Reunion, 1865-1900.
1939—Frank Luther Mott, A History of American Magazines.
1940—Carl Sandburg, Abraham Lincoln: The War Years.
1941—Marcus Lee Hansen, The Atlantic Migration, 1607-1860.
1942—Margaret Leech, Reveille in Washington.
1943—Esther Forbes, Paul Revere and the World He Lived In.
1944—Merle Curti, The Growth of American Thought.
1945—Stephen Bonsal, Unfinished Business.
1946—Arthur M. Schlesinger, Jr., The Age of Jackson.
1947—James Phinney Baxter 3d, Scientists Against Time.
1948—Bernard De Voto, Across the Wide Missouri.
1949—Roy F. Nichols, The Disruption of American Democracy.
1950—O. W. Larkin, Art and Life in America.
1951—R. Carlyle Buley, The Old Northwest, Pioneer Period 1815-1840.
1952—Oscar Handlin, The Uprooted.
1953—George Dangerfield, The Era of Good Feelings.
1954—Bruce Catton—A Stillness at Appomattox.
1955—Paul Horgan, Great River: The Rio Grande in North American History.
1956—Richard Hofstader, The Age of Reform.
1957—George F. Kennan, Russia Leaves the War.
1958—Bray Hammond, Banks and Politics in America—From the Revolution to the Civil War.
1959—Leonard D. White and Jean Schneider, The Republican Era; 1869-1901.
1960—Margaret Leech, In the Days of McKinley.
1961—Herbert Feis, Between War and Peace: The Potsdam Conference.
1962—Lawrence H. Gibson, The Triumphant Empire: Thunderclouds Gather in the West.
1963—Constance McLaughlin Green, Washington, Village and Capital, 1800-1878.
1964—Sumner Chilton Powell, Puritan Village: The Formation of A New England Town.
1965—Irwin Unger, The Greenback Era.
1966—Perry Miller, Life of the Mind in America.
1967—William H. Goetzmann, Exploration and Empire: the Explorer and Scientist in the Winning of the American West.
1968—Bernard Bailyn, The Ideological Origins of the American Revolution.
1969—Leonard W. Levy, Origin of the Fifth Amendment.
1970—Dean Acheson, Present at the Creation: My Years in the State Department.
1971—James McGregor Burns, Roosevelt: The Soldier of Freedom.
1972—Carl N. Degler, Neither Black Nor White.
1973—Michael Kammen, People of Paradox: An inquiry Concerning the Origins of American Civilization.
1974—Daniel J. Boorstin, the Americans: The Democratic Experience.

Biography or Autobiography

For a distinguished biography or autobiography by an American author, preferably on an American subject.

1917—Laura E. Richards and Maude Howe Elliott, assisted

by Florence Howe Hall, Julia Ward Howe.
1918—William Cabell Bruce, Benjamin Franklin, Self-Revealed.
1919—Henry Adams, The Education of Henry Adams.
1920—Albert J. Beveridge, The Life of John Marshall.
1921—Edward Bok, The Americanization of Edward Bok.
1922—Hamlin Garland, A Daughter of the Middle Border.
1923—Burton J. Hendrick, The Life and Letters of Walter H. Page.
1924—Michael Pupin, From Immigrant to Inventor.
1925—M. A. DeWolfe Howe, Barrett Wendell and His Letters.
1926—Harvey Cushing, Life of Sir William Osler.
1927—Emory Holloway, Whitman, An Interpretation in Narrative.
1928—Charles Edward Russell, The American Orchestra and Theodore Thomas.
1929—Burton J. Hendrick, The Training of an American; The Earlier Life and Letters of Walter H . Page.
1930—Marquis James, The Raven (Sam Houston).
1931—Henry James, Charles W. Eliot.
1932—Henry F. Pringle, Theodore Roosevelt.
1933—Allan Nevins, Grover Cleveland.
1934—Tyler Dennett, John Hay.
1935—Douglas Southall Freeman, R. E. Lee.
1936—Ralph Barton Perry, The Thought and Character of·William James.
1937—Allan Nevins, Hamilton Fish, the Inner History of the Grant Administration.
1938—Divided between Odell Shepard, Pedlar's Progress; Marquis James, Andrew Jackson.
1939—Carl Van Doren, Benjamin Franklin.
1940—Ray Stannard Baker, Woodrow Wilson, Life and Letters.
1941—Ola Elizabeth Winslow, Jonathan Edwards.
1942—Forrest Wilson, Crusader in Crinoline.
1943—Samuel Eliot Morison, Admiral of the Ocean Sea (Columbus).
1944—Carleton Mabee, The American Leonardo: The Life of Samuel F. B. Morse.
1945—Russel Blaine Nye, George Bancroft: Brahmin Rebel.
1946—Linny Marsh Wolfe, Son of the Wilderness.
1947—William Allen White, The Autobiography of William Allen White.
1948—Margaret Clapp, Forgotten First Citizen, John Bigelow.
1949—Robert E. Sherwood, Roosevelt and Hopkins.
1950—Samuel Flag Bemis, John Quincy Adams and the Foundations of American Foreign Policy.
1951—Margaret Louise Colt, John C. Calhoun; American Portrait.
1952—Merlo J. Pusey, Charles Evans Hughes.
1953—David J. Mays, Edmund Pendleton, 1721-1803.
1954—Charles A. Lindbergh, The Spirit of St. Louis.
1955—William S. White, The Taft Story.
1956—Talbot F. Hamlin, Benjamin Henry Latrobe.
1957—John F. Kennedy, Profiles in Courage.
1958—Douglas Southall Freeman (decd. 1953), George Washington, vols. I-VI; John Alexander Carroll and Mary Wells Ashworth, vol. VII.
1959—Arthur Walworth, Woodrow Wilson, American Prophet.
1960—Samuel Eliot Morison, John Paul Jones.
1961—David Donald, Charles Sumner and The Coming of the Civil War.
1963—Leon Edel, Henry James: Vol. II, The Conquest of London, 1870-1881; Vol. III, The Middle Years, 1881-1895.
1964—Walter Jackson Bate, John Keats.
1965—Ernest Samuels, Henry Adams.
1966—Arthur M. Schlesinger, Jr., A Thousand Days.
1967—Justin Kaplan, Mr. Clemens and Mark Twain.
1968—George F. Kennan, Memoirs (1925-1950).
1969—B. L. Reid, The Man from New York; John Quinn and his Friends.
1970—T. Harry Williams, Huey Long.
1971—Lawrance Thompson, Robert Frost: The Years of Triumph, 1915-1938.
1972—Joseph P. Lash, Eleanor and Franklin.
1973—W. A. Swanberg, Luce and His Empire.
1974—Louis Shaeffer, O'Neill, Son and Artist.

American Poetry

Before this prize was established in 1922, the following awards were made from gifts provided by the Poetry Society. **1918**—Love Songs, by Sara Teasdale. **1919**—Old Road to Paradise, by Margaret Widdemer; Corn Huskers, by Carl Sandburg.

1922—Edwin Arlington Robinson, Collected Poems.
1923—Edna St. Vincent Millay, The Ballad of the Harp-Weaver; A Few Figs from Thistles; Eight Sonnets in American Poetry, 1922; A Miscellany.
1924—Robert Frost, New Hampshire: A Poem with Notes and Grace Notes.
1925—Edwin Arlington Robinson, The Man Who Died Twice.
1926—Amy Lowell, What's O'Clock.
1927—Leonora Speyer, Fiddler's Farewell.
1928—Edwin Arlington Robinson, Tristram.
1929—Stephen Vincent Benet, John Brown's Body.
1930—Conrad Aiken, Selected Poems.
1931—Robert Frost, Collected Poems.
1932—George Dillon, The Flowering Stone.
1933—Archibald MacLeish, Conquistador.
1934—Robert Hillyer, Collected Verse.
1935—Audrey Wurdemann, Bright Ambush.
1936—Robert P. Tristram Coffin, Strange Holiness.
1937—Robert Frost, A Further Range.
1938—Marya Zaturenska, Cold Morning Sky.
1939—John Gould Fletcher, Selected Poems.
1940—Mark Van Doren, Collected Poems.
1941—Leonard Bacon, Sunderland Capture.
1942—William Rose Benet, The Dust Which Is God.
1943—Robert Frost, A Witness Tree.
1944—Stephen Vincent Benet, Western Star.
1945—Karl Shapiro, V-Letter and Other Poems.
1947—Robert Lowell, Lord Weary's Castle.
1948—W. H. Auden, The Age of Anxiety.
1949—Peter Viereck, Terror and Decorum.
1950—Gwendolyn Brooks, Annie Allen.
1951—Carl Sandburg, Complete Poems.
1952—Marianne Moore, Collected Poems.
1953—Archibald MacLeish, Collected Poems.
1954—Theodore Roethke, The Waking.
1955—Wallace Stevens, Collected Poems.
1956—Elizabeth Bishop, Poems, North and South.
1957—Richard Wilbur, Things of This World.
1958—Robert Penn Warren, Promises: Poems 1954-1956.
1959—Stanley Kunitz, Selected Poems 1928-1958.
1960—W. D. Snodgrass, Heart's Needle.
1961—Phyllis McGinley, Times Three: Selected Verse from Three Decades.
1962—Alan Dugan, Poems.
1963—William Carlos Williams, Pictures From Breughel.
1964—Louis Simpson, At the End of the Open Road.
1965—John Berryman, 77 Dream Songs.
1966—Richard Eberhart, Selected Poems.
1968—Anne Sexton, Live or Die.
1968—Anthony Hecht, The Hard Hours.
1969—George Oppen, Of Being Numerous.
1970—Richard Howard, Untitled Subjects.
1971—William S. Merwin, The Carrier of Ladders.
1972—James Wright, Collected Poems.
1973—Maxine Winokur Kumin, Up Country.
1974—Robert Lowell, The Dolphin.

General Non-Fiction

For best book by an American, not eligible in any other category.

1962—Theodore H. White, The Making of the President 1960.
1963—Barbara W. Tuchman, The Guns of August.
1964—Richard Hofstadter, Anti-Intellectualism in American Life.
1965—Howard Mumford Jones, O Strange New World.
1966—Edwin Way Teale, Wandering Through Winter.
1967—David Brion Davis, The Problem of Slavery in Western Culture.
1968—Will and Ariel Durant, Rousseau and Revolution.
1969—Norman Mailer, The Armies of the Night; and Rene Jules Dubos, So Human an Animal; How We Are Shaped by Surroundings and Events.
1970—Eric H. Erikson, Gandhi's Truth.
1971—John Toland, The Rising Sun.
1972—Barbara W. Tuchman, Stilwell and the American Experience in China, 1911-1945.
1973—Frances FitzGerald, Fire in the Lake: The Vietnamese and the Americans in Vietnam; and Robert Coles, Children of Crisis, Volumes 2 and 3.
1974—Ernest Becker, The Denial of Death.

Pulitzer Prize in Music

For composition in the larger forms of chamber, orchestral or choral music or for an operatic work including ballet, performed or published by a composer resident in the

United States.

1943—William Schuman, Secular Canatata No. 2, A Free Song.
1944—Howard Hanson, Symphony No. 4, Op. 34.
1945—Aaron Copland, Appalachian Spring.
1946—Leo Sowerby, The Canticle of the Sun.
1947—Charles E. Ives, Symphony No. 3.
1948—Walter Piston, Symphony No. 3.
1949—Virgil Thomson, Louisiana Story.
1950—Gian-Carlo Menotti, The Consul.
1951—Douglas Moore, Giants in the Earth.
1952—Gail Kubil, Symphony Concertante.
1954—Quincy Porter, Concerto for Two Pianos and Orchestra.
1955—Gian-Carlo Menotti, The Saint of Bleecker Street.
1956—Ernest Toch, Symphony No. 3.
1957—Norman Dello Joio, Meditations on Ecclesiastes.

1958—Samuel Barber, Vanessa.
1959—John La-Montaine, Concerto for Piano and Orchestra.
1960—Elliott Carter, Second String Quartet.
1961—Walter Piston, Symphony No. 7.
1962—Robert Ward, The Crucible.
1963—Samuel Barber, Piano Concerto No. 1.
1966—Leslie Bassett, Variations for Orchestra.
1967—Leon Kirchner, Quartet No. 3.
1968—George Crumb, Echoes of Time and the River.
1969—Karel Husa, String Quartet No. 3.
1970—Charles W. Wuorinen, Time's Encomium.
1971—Mario Davidovsky, Synchronisms No. 6.
1972—Jacob Druckman, Windows.
1973—Elliott Carter, String Quartet No. 3.
1974—Donald Martino, Notturno. (Special citation) Roger Sessions.

Special Awards
Awarded in 1974 unless otherwise designated
Books, Allied Arts

American Revolution Round Table Awards, for best book on the American Revolution: Catherine S. Crary for *The Price of Loyalty*.

Anisfield-Wolf Awards, by the Cleveland foundation,for a book on race relations, $1,500: Albie Sachs for *Justice in South Africa*.

Bancroft Prizes, chosen by Columbia Univ. for books in American history, diplomacy and international relations, $4,000 each: Ray Allen Billington for *Frederick Jackson Turner: Historian, Scholar, Teacher*; Stephan Thernstrom for *The Other Bostonians: Poverty and Progress in the American Metropolis, 1880-1970*; Townsend Hoopes for *The Devil and John Foster Dulles*.

Stuart L. Bernath Prize, by the Society of Historians of American Foreign Relations, $500: John Lewis Gaddis for *The United States and the Origins of the Cold War, 1941-1947*.

Copernicus Award, for lifetime achievement in poetry, $10,000: Robert Lowell. **Edgar Allan Poe Award**, for an American poet under 45, $5,000: Mark Strand.

Dexter Prize, by the society for the History of Technology for book on the history of technology, $1,000: D.S.L. Cardwell for *From Watt to Clausius: The Rise of Thermodynamics in the Early Industrial Age*.

Edgar Awards, by the Mystery Writers of America, novel: Tony Hillerman for *The Dance Hall of the Dead*; first novel: Paul E. Erdman for *The Billion Dollar Sure Thing*; fact crime book: Barbara Levy for *Legacy of Death*; juvenile: Jay Bennett for *The Long Black Coat*; paperback mystery: Will Perry for *Death of an Informer*. **Grand Master Award:** Ross MacDonald. **Herbert Brean Memorial Award:** Joseph Wambaugh for *The Onion Field*.

Friends of American Writers Award, First Prize, $1,000: Robert Boston for *A Thorn for the Flesh*. **Other Awards:** Robert O'Neil Bristow for *A Faraway Drummer*; Paul Wilkes for *Fitzgo — The Wild Dog of Central Park*; Betty Biesterveld for *Six Days from Sunday*; Elizabeth Foster and Slim Williams for *The Long Hungry Night*; and Dr. Michael Fox for *The Wolf*.

Horace Gregory Award, to distinguished emeritus faculty members who have combined careers as classroom teachers with achievement in the field of letters, $2,000: William York Tindall.

David D. Lloyd Prize, by the Truman Library Institute for best book on the period of Truman's presidency, $1,000: Alonzo L. Hamby for *Beyond the New Deal: Harry S. Truman and American Liberalism*.

James Russell Lowell Prize, by the Modern Language Assn. of America, $1,000: Leslie A. Marchand for *Byron's Letters and Journals*.

Melcher Award, by the Unitarian Universalist Assn. for best book on religious liberalism, $1,000: Robert Jewett for *The Captain America Complex: The Dilemma of Zealous Nationalism*.

Thomas More Medal, for contribution to Catholic literature: Graham Greene for *The Honorary Consul*.

National Book Awards, for distinguished books by American authors, $1,000 for each award: Fiction (tie): Thomas Pynchon for *Gravity's Rainbow* and Isaac Bashevis Singer for *A Crown of Feathers and Other Stories*; Poetry: Allen Ginsberg for *The Fall of America: Poems of These States, 1965-1971* and Adrienne Rich for *Diving Into the Wreck, 1971-1972*; History: John Clive for *Macaulay: The Shaping of the Historian*; Children's Books: Eleanor Cameron for *The Court of the Stone Children*; Philosophy and Religion: Maurice Natanson for *Edmund Husserl: Philosopher of Infinite Tasks*; Science: S. E. Luria for *Life: the Unfinished Experiment*; Contemporary Affairs: Murray Kempton for *The Briar Patch: The People of the State of New York v. Lumumba Shakur Et Al*; Translation (tie): Karen Brazell for *The Confessions of Lady Nijo*, Helen R. Lane for *Alternating Current* and Jackson Mathews for *Monsieur Teste*; Arts and Letters: Pauline Kael for *Deeper into Movies*.

National Institute of Arts and Letters, Richard and Hinda Rosenthal Foundation Award, $2,000: Alice Walker for *In Love & Trouble: Stories of Black Women*. **E. M. Forster Award**, $5,000: Paul Bailey. **Loines Poetry Award**, $2,500: Philip Larkin. **Award of Merit Medal**, $1,000: Nelson Algren. **Zabel Award**, $2,500: John Logan. **Other Awards in Literature**, $3,000 each: Ann Cornelisen, Stanley Elkin, Elizabeth Hardwick, Josephine Johnson, Donald Justice, David Rabe, Donald Rosen, Sam Shepard, James Tate, Henry Van Dyke, Lanford Wilson.

National Jewish Book Awards, by the Jewish Book Council, $500 each. **Bernard H. Marks Award**, for book on Jewish history: Dr. Bernard D. Weinryb for *The Jews of Poland: A Social and Economic History of the Jewish Community in Poland from 1100 to 1800*. **William and Janice Epstein Award**, for Jewish fiction: Francine Prose for *Judah the Pious*. **Harry and Florence Kovner Memorial Award**, for poetry: Harold Schimmel for translation of Yehuda Amichai's *Songs of Jerusalem and Myself*. **Frank and Ethel S. Cohen Award**, for Jewish thought: Dr. Eugene Borowitz for *The Masks Jews Wear: The Self-Deception of American Jewry*. **Charles and Bertie G. Schwartz Juvenile Award:** Yuri Suhl for *Uncle Misha's Partisans*. **Morris J. Kaplan Memorial Award**, for book on Israel: Dr. Isaiah Friedman for *The Question of Palestine: 1914-1918: British-Jewish-Arab Relations*.

Nebula Awards, by the Science Fiction Writers of America, best novel: Arthur C. Clarke for *Rendezvous with Rama*; novella: Gene Wolfe for *The Death of Dr. Island*; novelette: Vonda McIntyre for *Of Mist, and Grass, and Sand*; short story: James Tiptree Jr. for *Love is the Plan, the Plan is Death*; **Special Award:** Stanley R. Greenberg.

Neustadt International Prize, for literature, $10,-000: Francis Ponge, poet.

P.E.N. Translation Award, by the Book-of-the-Month Club, $1,000: Hardie St. Martin and Leonard Mades for translation of *The Obscene Bird of Night* by Jose Donoso.

Poetry Society of America Awards, Alice Fay di Castagnola Award, $3,000: Charles Edward Eaton for *The Man in the Green Chair.* **Percy Bysshe Shelley Award,** $1,300: W. S. Merwin. **John Masefield Memorial Award,** $500: Penelope Schhott Starkey for *The Orangetrees: For a French Grandmother.* **Melville Cane Award,** $500: William Stafford for *Someday, Maybe.* **Christopher Morley Memorial Award,** $500: Gary Miranda for *The Owl and the Ostrich* and Milton Kaplan for *The Doge's Palace, Venice.* **Gustav Davidson Memorial Award,** $500: Sarah Singer for *In Sickness and in Health.* **Lucille Medwick Memorial Award,** $500: Joan LeBombard for *For the Child of a*

Mixed Marriage.

Academy of American Poets Award, for poetic achievement, $10,000: W. S. Merwin.

Political Book Awards, by the Washington Monthly: John Newhouse for *Cold Dawn: The Story of SALT;* and Ward Just for *The Congressman Who Loved Flaubert and Other Washington Stories.*

St. Lawrence Award, for fiction by Fiction International Magazine, $1,000: Mark Costello for *The Murphy Sisters.*

Delmore Schwartz Memorial Poetry Award, by New York Univ. College of Arts and Science for a first book of poetry, $1,000: Stanley Plumly for *In the Outer Dark.*

Writers Guild of America, Laurel Award: Paddy Chayefsky. **Valentine Davies Awards,** for bringing honor and dignity to writers everywhere: Ray Bradbury and Philip Dunne.

Journalism Awards

Meyer Berger Award, by Columbia Univ. for distinguished local reporting in a New York daily,' $750 each: Penelope McMillan, News, and N. R. (Sonny) Kleinfield, Wall Street Journal.

Heywood Broun Award, by The Newspaper Guild, $1,000: Donald L. Barlett and James B. Steele, Philadelphia Inquirer.

Sevellon Brown Memorial Award, by the New England Associated Press News Executives Assn., for public service: The Boston Globe.

National Cartoonist Society, Reuben Award: Dik Browne for Hagar The Horrible. **Other Awards:** Advertising & Illustration, Allen Jaffee; Editorial Cartoons, Pat Oliphant, Denver Post; Special Features, Frank Fogarty, Illuminated Scrolls; Sports Cartoon, Bill Gallo, N.Y. News; Story Strips, Dick Moores, Gasoline Alley; Syndicated Panels, George Lichty, Grin & Bear It; Animation, John Hart, B.C.

Raymond Clapper Memorial Award, by the White House Correspondents Assn.: James R. Polk, Washington Star-News.

Roy W. Howard Public Service Award, by the Scripps-Howard Foundation (cash prizes as indicated): William Blundell, Wall Street Journal ($2,500); KGW/TV, Portland, Ore. ($2,500); KOOL/TV, Phoenix, Ariz. ($1,000); Seymour Hersh, N.Y. Times ($1,000); Joseph Daughen, Joseph F. Lowry and Charles F. Thomson, Philadelphia Bulletin ($500 each); KAKE/TV, Wichita, Kansas ($500); KDKA/radio, Pittsburgh, Pa. ($500).

National Magazine Awards, by Columbia Univ. Graduate School of Journalism: Scientific American, public service; Sports Illustrated, service to the individual; Texas Monthly, specialized journalism; The New Yorker, fiction, and reporting excellence; Newsweek, visual excellence.

Edward J. Meeman Awards, by The Scripps-Howard Foundation for work in the field of conservation (cash prizes as indicated): George F. Neavoll, Fort Wayne Journal-Gazette ($2,500); John Miller, Detroit Free Press ($1,500); Tom D'Arcy, Newsday ($1,000); Sam C. Rawl, Palm Beach Post ($1,000); and Robert Poole, Twin-City Sentinel, Winston-Salem, N.C. ($1,000); Gordon Bishop, Newark Star-Ledger ($600); Hellen Ochs, Columbus (Ind.) Republic ($600); Roger Latham, Pittsburgh Press ($600); Charles Osolin, Winston-Salem Journal & Sentinel ($600); and Stanley E. Silvernail, Amsterdam (N.Y.) Recorder ($600).

New York Press Club, Schaefer Gold Typewriter Award, for public service: William Sherman, News. **Byline Award:** Robert D. McFadden, Times. **Feature Award:** Roberta Brandes, Post.

Overseas Press Club of America Awards, for distin-

guished service in foreign journalism: Leon Dash, Washington Post; Al Burt, Miami Herald; Sydney H. Schanberg, N.Y. Times; Dan Rather, Marvin Kalb and Bob Schieffer, CBS News; John Laurance, CBS News; Harry Reasoner, ABC News; Anthony Bailey, The New Yorker; Edward Sheehan, N.Y. Times; C. L. Sulzberger, N.Y. Times; Warren King, N.Y. News; Ronald Koven and David Ottaway, Washington Post; Everett G. Martin, Wall Street Journal; Donald Kirk, Chicago Tribune; Robert Northshield and Vo Huynh, NBC.

Page One Awards, by the New York Newspaper Guild. National Reporting, Seymour M. Hersh, Times; Foreign Reporting, Arnaud de Borchgrave, Newsweek; Crusading Journalism, William Sherman, News; Sports Reporting, William H. Rudy, Post; News Features, Michael Pousner, News; Life Style Features, Jacquin Sanders, News; News Photography, Anthony Casale, News; Feature Photography, Neal Boenzi, News; Sports Photography, Bill Stahl, News; Editorial Cartoons, John Pierotti, Post; Feature Cartoons, Joseph Papin, News; Sports Cartoons, Bill Gallo, News.

George Polk Memorial Awards, by Long Island Univ. for achievement in journalism: Foreign Reporting, Henry S. Bradsher, Washington Star-News; National Reporting, Andrew H. Malcolm, N.Y. Times; Metropolitan Reporting, James Savage and Mike Baxter, Miami Herald; Local Reporting, Carol Talley and Joan Hayde, Daily Advance, Dover, N.J.; Community Service: William Sherman, N.Y. News; Investigative Reporting, Seymour Hersh, N.Y. Times; Magazine Reporting, John Osborne, New Republic; News Photography, George Brich, AP; Special Award, Donald L. Barlett and James B. Steele, Philadelphia Inquirer.

Ernie Pyle Memorial Award, by the Scripps-Howard Foundation to the newspaperman most nearly exemplifying the style and craftsmanship of Ernie Pyle, $1,000: James Wooten, Philadelphia Inquirer.

Silurian Awards, by the Silurians, a society of present and former New York newspapermen: Public Service, Nicholas Gage, Times; Spot News, Ann Crawford, The Record, Bergen, N.J.; Feature-Story, Michael Pousner, News; Spot News Photo, Ron Frehm, AP; Feature Photo, Barton Silverman, Times; Editorial Cartoon, Tom Darcy, Newsday; Editorial Cartoon, Bill Andrews, Daily World; story by reporter in profession less than 5 years, Judy Yablonky, AP.

Walker Stone Award, by the Scripps-Howard Foundation for editorial writing, $1,000: Michael Pakenham, Philadelphia Inquirer. **Second Prize,** $500: Don O. Noel, Jr., Hartford Times.

Television and Theater Awards

Emmy Awards, by the Academy of Television Arts and Sciences. **Actors Awards:** comedy series, Alan Alda, M.A.S.H.; dramatic series, Telly Savalas, Kojak; limited series, William Holden, Blue Knight; special,

Hal Holbrook, Pueblo; supporting actor in comedy, Bob Reiner, All in the Family; supporting actor in drama, Michael Moriarty, The Glass Menagerie; supporting actor in comedy-variety series, Harvey Korman, Carol Burnett Show; daytime series, Macdonald Carey, Days of Our Lives; daytime special, Pat O'Brien, The Other Woman. **Actress Awards:** comedy series, Mary Tyler Moore; drama series, Michael Learned, The Waltons; limited series, Mildred Natwick, The Snoop Sisters; special, Cicely Tyson, The Autobiography of Miss Jane Pittman; supporting actress in comedy, Cloris Leachman, Mary Tyler Moore Show; supporting actress in drama, Joanna Miles, The Glass Menagarie; supporting actress in comedy-variety, Brenda Vaccaro, The Shape of Things; daytime series, Elizabeth Hubbard, The Doctors; **Other Awards:** music-variety series, Carol Burnett Show; music special, Lily Tomlin; limited series, Columbo; dramatic series, Upstairs, Downstairs; children's special, Marlo Thomas and Friends in Free to Be . . . You and Me; series writing, Treva Silverman, Mary Tyler Moore Show; special writing, Fay Kanin, Tell Me Where it Hurts; sports, Wide World of Sports; game show host, Peter Marshall, Hollywood Squares; daytime variety hostess, Dinah Shore.

Margo Jones Award, for significant contribution to the theater, $500; Douglas Turner Ward, co-founder of the Negro Ensemble Company.

Antoinette Perry Awards (Tonys), by the league of New York Theaters, 1973-74 season. **Musical:** actor, Christopher Plummer, Cyrano; actress, Virginia Capers, Raisin; supporting actor, Tommy Tune, Seesaw; supporting actress, Janie Sell, Over There; best musical, Raisin; director, Harold Prince, Candide; scenic design, Franne and Eugene Lee, Candide; book, Hugh Wheeler, Candide; costume design, Franne Lee, Candide; choreography, Michael Bennett, Seesaw; score, Frederick Loewe & Alan Lerner, Gigi. **Drama:** actor, Michael Moriarty, Find Your Way Home; actress, Colleen Dewhurst, A Moon for the Misbegotten; supporting actor, Ed Flanders, A Moon for the Misbegotten; supporting actress, Frances Sternhagen, The Good Doctor; best play, The River Niger; director, Jose Quintero, A Moon for the Misbegotten. **Special Awards:** Revival of an American play, A Moon for the Misbegotten. Artistic development of the musical theater, Candide. Contribution to the theater of comedy, Peter Cook and Dudley Moore. Concert Entertainment, Liza Minnelli and Bette Midler.

Miscellaneous Awards

American Film Institute Life Achievement Award: James Cagney.

The Canadian Governor General's Literary Awards, to Canadian writers of outstanding literary merit: $2,500: Michael Bell for Painters in a New Land; Rejean Ducharme for L'hiver de force; Albert Faucher for Quebec en Amerique au XIXe siecle.

G. B. Dealey Awards, for young artists: Piotr Janowski, violinist.

Albert Einstein Commemorative Awards, by Yeshiva Univ. for contributions in a given field: Walter Cronkite, newscaster; Dr. Gerald M. Edelman, immunology and related fields; Sen. Jacob Javits; Neil Simon, playwright; Edward Durell Stone, architect.

First Amendment Freedoms Award, by the Anti-Defamation League: John Troan, and Scripps-Howard Newspapers.

Freedoms Foundation Awards, given annually by the Freedoms Foundation at Valley Forge for contribution toward a better understanding and greater appreciation of the American way of life. **George Washington Award:** John Wayne. **Other Awards:** William A. Smith, Pineville, Pa.; Gordon Sinclair, Toronto; Earl Hamner, Jr., Burbank, Calif.; George Foreman, Hayward, Calif.; Joe Eilers, Granada Hills, Calif. **Defender of Freedom Award**, $1,000: Maj. Robert E. Miller.

Goddard Memorial Trophy, by the National Space Club: Rep. Olin E. Teague.

Sidney Hillman Awards, by the Sidney Hillman Foundation for achievement in mass communications, $500 each: Arthur M. Schlesinger, Jr., Jervis Anderson, Richard Strout, Donald L. Barlett, James B. Steele, Paul Brodeur, and Paul Altmeyer.

Interfaith Movement Humanitarian Service Award: Charles J. Urstadt.

Lyndon Baines Johnson Foundation Award, $25,000: Ivan Allen, Jr., and Franklin A. Thomas.

Metropolitan Opera National Council Awards, Mrs. Frederick K. Weyerhaeuser Award, $5,000: Alma Jean Smith, Bloomington, Ind. **Gramma Fisher Foundation Award**, $4,000: Katherine Ciesinski, Philadelphia. **Mrs. Ogden Phipps Award**, $3,000: Janice Felty.

National Conference of Christians and Jews, Man of the 20th Century Award: Charles H. Silver.

National Institute of Arts and Letters Awards: Art, $3,000 each: Perle Fine, Richard Fleischner, Marilynn Gelfman-Pereira, George Griffin, Nancy Grossman, Ibram Lassaw, and Charlotte Park. **Music**, $3,000 each: Richard Felciano, Raoul Pleskow, Philip Rhodes, and Olly Wilson. **Arnold W. Brunner Memorial Prize in Architecture**, $1,000: Hugh Hardy, Malcolm Holzman and Norman Pfeiffer. **Richard and Hinda Rosenthal Foundation Award**, $2,000: Julie Curtis Reed, painter. **Marjorie Peabody Waite Award**, $1,500: Ray Prohaska, artist. **Gold Medal for Graphic Art:** Saul Steinberg.

Templeton Foundation Prize, for progress in religion, $82,000: Brother Roger, France.

World Meteorological Organization Award, for outstanding work in meteorology and international collaboration: Prof. Joseph Smagorinsky.

Westinghouse Science Talent Search (cash prizes as indicated): Eric Steven Lander, Brooklyn, N.Y. ($10,000), Frank Thomson Leighton, Arlington, Va. ($8,000); Linda Bockenstedt, Dayton, Ohio ($8,000); Emmett Evanoff, Cheyenne Wyo. ($6,000); Richard Alan Dargan, Palm Bay, Fla. ($6,000); John Conlin MacGuire, Casper, Wyo. ($6,000); Edward Frank, Great Neck, N.Y. ($4,000); Carl Taswell, Rochester, Minn. ($4,000); Jordin Kare, Narberth, Pa. ($4,000); and Linda Carol Rabinowitz, Bronx, N.Y. ($4,000).

Motion Picture Academy Awards (Oscars)

1927-28
Actor: Emil Jannings, Way of All Flesh.
Actress: Janet Gaynor, Seventh Heaven.
Picture: Wings, Paramount.
1928-29
Actor: Warner Baxter, In Old Arizona.
Actress: Mary Pickford, Coquette.
Picture: Broadway Melody, MGM.
1929-30
Actor: George Arliss, Disraeli.
Actress: Norma Shearer, The Divorcee.
Picture: All Quiet on the Western Front, Univ.
1930-31
Actor: Lionel Barrymore, Free Soul.
Actress: Marie Dressler, Min and Bill.
Picture: Cimarron, RKO.
1931-32
Actor: Fredric March, Dr. Jekyll and Mr. Hyde.
Actress: Helen Hayes, Sin of Madelon Claudet.

Picture: Grand Hotel, MGM.
Special: Walt Disney, Mickey Mouse.
1932-33
Actor: Charles Laughton, Private Life of Henry VIII.
Actress: Katharine Hepburn, Morning Glory.
Picture: Cavalcade, Fox.
1934
Actor: Clark Gable, It Happened One Night.
Actress: Claudette Colbert, same.
Picture: It Happened One Night, Columbia.
1935
Actor: Victor McLaglen, The Informer.
Actress: Bette Davis, Dangerous.
Picture: Mutiny on the Bounty, MGM.
1936
Actor: Paul Muni, Story of Louis Pasteur.
Actress: Luise Rainer, The Great Ziegfeld.
Picture: The Great Ziegfeld, MGM.

1937
Actor: Spencer Tracy, Captains Courageous.
Actress: Luise Rainer, The Good Earth.
Picture: Life of Emile Zola, Warner.
1938
Actor: Spencer Tracy, Boys Town.
Actress: Bette Davis, Jezebel.
Picture: You Can't Take It With You, Columbia.
1939
Actor: Robert Donat, Goodbye Mr. Chips.
Actress: Vivien Leigh, Gone With the Wind.
Picture: Gone With the Wind, Selznick International.
1940
Actor: James Stewart, The Philadelphia Story.
Actress: Ginger Rogers, Kitty Foyle.
Picture: Rebecca, Selznick International.
1941
Actor: Gary Cooper, Sergeant York.
Actress: Joan Fontaine, Suspicion.
Picture: How Green Was My Valley, 20th Cent.-Fox.
1942
Actor: James Cagney, Yankee Doodle Dandy.
Actress: Greer Garson, Mrs. Miniver.
Picture: Mrs. Miniver, MGM.
1943
Actor: Paul Lukas, Watch on the Rhine.
Actress: Jennifer Jones, The Song of Bernadette.
Picture: Casablanca, Warner.
1944
Actor: Bing Crosby, Going My Way.
Actress: Ingrid Bergman, Gaslight.
Picture: Going My Way, Paramount.
1945
Actor: Ray Milland, The Lost Weekend.
Actress: Joan Crawford, Mildred Pierce.
Picture: The Lost Weekend, Paramount.
1946
Actor: Fredric March, Best Years of Our Lives.
Actress: Olivia de Havilland, To Each His Own.
Picture: The Best Years of Our Lives, Goldwyn, RKO.
1947
Actor: Ronald Colman, A Double Life.
Actress: Loretta Young, The Farmer's Daughter.
Picture: Gentleman's Agreement, 20th Cent.-Fox.
1948
Actor: Laurence Olivier, Hamlet.
Actress: Jane Wyman, Johnny Belinda.
Picture: Hamlet, Two Cities Film, Universal International.
1949
Actor: Broderick Crawford, All the King's Men.
Actress: Olivia de Havilland, The Heiress.
Picture: All the King's Men, Columbia.
1950
Actor: Jose Ferrer, Cyrano de Bergerac.
Actress: Judy Holliday, Born Yesterday.
Picture: All About Eve, 20th Century-Fox.
1951
Actor: Humphrey Bogart, The African Queen.
Actress: Vivien Leigh, A Streetcar Named Desire.
Picture: An American in Paris, MGM.
1952
Actor: Gary Cooper, High Noon.
Actress: Shirley Booth, Come Back, Little Sheba.
Picture: Greatest Show on Earth, Cecil B. DeMille, Paramount.
1953
Actor: William Holden, Stalag 17.
Actress: Audrey Hepburn, Roman Holiday.
Picture: From Here to Eternity, Columbia.
1954
Actor: Marlon Brando, On the Waterfront.
Actress: Grace Kelly, The Country Girl.
Picture: On the Waterfront, Horizon-American Corp., Columbia.
1955
Actor: Ernest Borgnine, Marty.
Actress: Anna Magnani, The Rose Tattoo.
Picture: Marty, Hecht and Lancaster's Steven Productions, U.A.
1956
Actor: Yul Brynner, The King and I.
Actress: Ingrid Bergman, Anastasia.
Picture: Around the World in 80 Days, Michael Todd Co., U.A.
1957
Actor: Alec Guinness, The Bridge on the River Kwai.
Actress: Joanne Woodward, The Three Faces of Eve.
Picture: The Bridge on the River Kwai, Columbia.

1958
Actor: David Niven, Separate Tables.
Actress: Susan Hayward, I Want to Live.
Picture: Gigi, Arthur Freed Production, MGM.
1959
Actor: Charlton Heston, Ben-Hur.
Actress: Simone Signoret, Room at the Top.
Picture: Ben-Hur, MGM.
1960
Actor: Burt Lancaster, Elmer Gantry.
Actress: Elizabeth Taylor, Butterfield 8.
Picture: The Apartment, Mirisch Co., U.A.
1961
Actor: Maximilian Schell, Judgment at Nuremberg.
Actress: Sophia Loren, Two Women.
Picture: West Side Story, United Artists.
1962
Actor: Gregory Peck, To Kill a Mockingbird.
Actress: Anne Bancroft, The Miracle Worker.
Picture: Lawrence of Arabia, Columbia.
1963
Actor: Sidney Poitier, Lilies of the Field.
Actress: Patricia Neal, Hud.
Picture: Tom Jones, Woodfall Prod., UA-Lopert Pictures.
1964
Actor: Rex Harrison, My Fair Lady.
Actress: Julie Andrews, Mary Poppins.
Picture: My Fair Lady, Warner Bros.
1965
Actor: Lee Marvin, Cat Ballou.
Actress: Julie Christie, Darling.
Picture: The Sound of Music, 20th Century-Fox.
1966
Actor: Paul Scofield, A Man for All Seasons.
Actress: Elizabeth Taylor, Who's Afraid of Virginia Woolf?
Picture: A Man for All Seasons, Columbia.
1967
Actor: Rod Steiger, In the Heat of the Night.
Actress: Katharine Hepburn, Guess Who's Coming to Dinner.
Picture: In the Heat of the Night.
1968
Actor: Cliff Robertson, Charly.
Actress: Katharine Hepburn, The Lion in Winter, Barbra Streisand, Funny Girl (tie).
Picture: Oliver.
1969
Actor: John Wayne, True Grit.
Actress: Maggie Smith, The Prime of Miss Jean Brodie.
Picture: Midnight Cowboy.
1970
Actor: George C. Scott, Patton (refused).
Actress: Glenda Jackson, Women in Love.
Picture: Patton.
1971
Actor: Gene Hackman, The French Connection.
Actress: Jane Fonda, Klute.
Picture: The French Connection.
1972
Actor: Marlon Brando, The Godfather (refused).
Actress: Liza Minnelli, Cabaret.
Picture: The Godfather.
1973
Actor: Jack Lemmon, Save the Tiger.
Supporting Actor: John Houseman, The Paper Chase.
Actress: Glenda Jackson, A Touch of Class.
Supporting Actress: Tatum O'Neal, Paper Moon.
Picture: The Sting.
Director: George Roy Hill, The Sting.
Foreign Language Film: Day for Night.
Documentary: (feature) Keith Merrill, The Great American Cowboy; (short subject) Julian Krainin and DeWitt L. Sage, Princeton: A Search for Answers.
Short Subject: (animated) Frank Mouris, Frank Film; (live action) Allan Miller and William Fertik, The Bolero.
Sound: Robert Knudson and Chris Newman, The Exorcist.
Editing: William Reynolds, The Sting.
Costume Design: Edith Head, The Sting.
Cinematography: Sven Nykvist, Cries and Whispers.
Art Direction: Henry Rumstead, The Sting.
Set Decoration: James Payne, The Sting.
Writing: (adapted) William Peter Blatty, The Exorcist; (original) David S. Ward, The Sting.
Music: (score) Marvin Hamlisch, The Sting; (song) Marvin Hamlisch, Alan & Marilyn Bergman, The Way We Were.
Irving Thalberg Award: Lawrence Weingarten.
Jean Hersholt Humanitarian Award: Lew Wasserman.
Special Award: The Marx Brothers.

Canadian Film Awards

Source: Canadian Film Institute

1969
Actor: Chris Wiggins, The Best Damn Fiddler from Calabogie to Kaladar.
Actress: Jackie Burroughs, Dulcima
Picture: The Best Damn Fiddler from Calabogie to Kaladar

1970
Actor: Doug McGrath and Paul Bradley (tied), Goin' Down the Road
Actress: Genevieve Bujold, The Act of Heart
Picture: Psychocratie

1971
Actor: Jean Duceppe, Mon oncle Antoine
Actress: Ann Knox, The Only Thing You Know
Picture: Mon oncle Antoine

1972
Actor: Gordon Pinsent, The Rowdyman

Actress: Micheline Lanctot, Vrai nature de Bernadette
Picture: Wedding in White

1973
Actor: Jacques Godin, O.K. Laliberte
Supporting Actor: Willie Lamothe, La Mort d'un Bucheron
Actress: Genevieve Bujold, Kamouraska
Supporting Actress: Camille Bernard, Kamouraska
Picture: Slipstream
Director: David Acomba, Slipstream
Writer: Jacques Benoit, Denys Arcand, Rejeanne Padovani
Cinematography: Don Wilder, Paperback Hero
Music (score): Willie Lamothe, Tristan Hansinger, Chick Peabody, Peter Van Ginkel, La Mort d'un Bucheron
Direction (Non-Feature): Doug Jackson, The Sloane Affair
Grierson Award: Robert Forget
Wendy Michener Award: Gilles Carle

National Teacher of the Year Award

Awarded by the Ladies' Home Journal magazine for distinguished service in elementary and secondary schools.

1952—Geraldine Jomes, first grade, Hope Public School, Santa Barbara, Calif.
1953—Dorothy Hamilton, social studies, Milford H.S., Milford, Conn.
1954—Willard Widerberg, seventh grade, DeKalb Junior H.S., DeKalb, Ill.
1955—Margaret Perry Teufel, fourth grade, Monmouth Elementary, Monmouth, Ore.
1956—Richard Nelson, science, Flathead County H.S., Kalispell, Montana.
1957—(tie) Eugene Guy Bizzell, speech, English & debate, A.N. McCallum H.S., Austin, Texas; and Mary Field Schwarz, third grade, Bristol Elementary, Kansas City, Mo.
1958—Jean Listebarger Humphrey, second grade, Edwards Elementary, Ames, Iowa.
1959—Edna Donley, mathematics and speech, Alva H.S., Alva, Okla.
1960—Hazel Bragg Davenport, first grade, Central Elementary, Beckley, W. Va.
1961—Helen Adams, kindergarten, Cumberland Public School, Cumberland, Wisc.
1962—Marjorie French, mathematics, Topeka H.S., Topeka, Kansas.
1963—Elmon Ousley, speech, American government & world problems, Bellevue Senior H.S., Bellevue, Wash.
1964—Lawana Trout, English, Charles Page H.S., Sand Springs, Okla.
1965—Richard E. Klinck, sixth grade, Reed Street Elementary, Wheat Ridge, Colo.
1966—Mona Dayton, first grade, Walter Douglas Elementary, Tucson, Ariz.
1967—Roger Tenney, music, Owatonna Junior-Senior H.S., Owatonna, Mich.
1968—David E. Graf, vocational education & industrial arts, Sandwich Comm. H.S., Sandwich, Ill.
1969—Barbara Goleman, language arts, Miami Elementary, Miami, Fla.
1970—Johnnie T. Dennis, physics, math analysis, Walla Walla H.S., Walla Walla, Wash.
1971—Martha Marion Stringfellow, first grade, Lewisville Elementary, Chester Co., S.C.
1972—James Marshall Rogers, American history & Black studies, Durham H.S., Raleigh, N.C.
1973—John A. Ensworth, sixth grade, Kenwood school, Bend, Ore.
1974—Vivian Tom, social studies, Lincoln High, Yonkers, N.Y.

The Spingarn Medal

The Spingarn Medal has been awarded annually since 1914 by the National Association for the Advancement of Colored People for the highest achievement by an American Negro.

1945—Thurgood Marshall
1946—Dr. Percy L. Julian
1947—Channing H. Tobias
1948—Ralph J. Bunche
1949—Charles Hamilton Houston
1950—Mabel Keaton Staupers
1951—Harry T. Moore
1952—Paul R. Williams
1953—Theodore K. Lawless
1954—Carl Murphy

1955—Jack Roosevelt Robinson
1956—Martin Luther King, Jr.
1957—Mrs. Daisy Bates and the Little Rock Nine
1958—Edward Kennedy (Duke) Ellington
1959—Langston Hughes
1960—Kenneth B. Clark
1961—Robert C. Weaver
1962—Medgar Wiley Evers

1963—Roy Wilkins
1964—Leontyne Price
1965—John H. Johnson
1966—Edward W. Brooke
1967—Sammy Davis, Jr.
1968—Clarence M. Mitchell, Jr.
1969—Jacob Lawrence
1970—Leon Howard Sullivan
1971—Gordon Parks
1972—Wilson C. Riles
1973—Damon Keith

Presidential Medal of Freedom

The Presidential Medal of Freedom is the nation's highest civilian award. It was instituted by President Kennedy and first awarded on July 4, 1963, to honor those "who contribute significantly to the quality of American life."

1969 Awards (By President Nixon)
Col. Edwin E. Aldrin, Jr. (astronaut)
Neil A. Armstrong (astronaut)
Lt. Col. Michael Collins (astronaut)
Duke Ellington (musician)

1970 Awards (By President Nixon)
Apollo 13 Mission Operations Team
Earl Charles Behrens (journalist)
Edward T. Folliard (journalist)
Fred Wallace Haise, Jr. (astronaut)
William M. Henry (journalist)*
Arthur Krock (journalist)
David Lawrence (journalist)
George Gould Lincoln (journalist)
James A. Lovell, Jr. (astronaut)

Raymond Moley (journalist)
Eugene Ormandy (conductor)
Adela Rogers St. Johns (journalist)
John Leonard Swigert, Jr. (astronaut)

1971 Awards (By President Nixon)
Sam Goldwyn (film producer)
Manlio Brosio (NATO secretary general)
William J. Hopkins (White House executive clerk)

1972 Awards (By President Nixon)
Lila and DeWitt Wallace (founders of Readers' Digest)
John Paul Vann (adviser in Vietnam war)

1973 Awards (By President Nixon)
John Ford (movie director)
*Awarded posthumously.

WORLD FACTS

The Earth Sciences

Source: U.S. Geological Survey

Outer Continental Shelf: The importance of the submerged lands adjacent to the continents is unquestioned in supplying a significant part of the world's present and future energy needs and increasingly significant parts of future mineral needs. These submerged lands consist of a continental shelf, slope, and rise, which together form the continental margin.

The Outer Continental Shelf (OCS) is the popular term used to describe the area that lies between mean low tide at the shore-line and water depths of 200 meters (656 feet). In U.S. Government publications, Outer Continental Shelf means the submerged lands between the outer limits of states' jurisdiction (generally 3 miles) and a water depth of 200 meters (m).

The continental shelf of the United States measures about 875,000 square miles or about 560,000 acres and is relatively undeveloped. Of this area, 290,000 square miles or about 186,000,000 acres lie in the Gulf of Mexico, off the Atlantic Coast and off the coast of California, Oregon, and Washington.

The continental margins contain many deep sediment-filled basins or troughs that may hold large accumulations of petroleum and other mineral resources. The management of mineral resource development on federal OCS lands is the responsibility of the U.S. Department of the Interior. The Geological Survey, an Interior bureau, assumes the role of insuring orderly development, receipt of fair market value for OCS leases, and development of the mineral resources within acceptable environmental constraints.

At the end of 1973, three percent of the OCS, or 5,600,000 acres were under lease for mineral development and production, including 726 producing and 540 non-producing Federal leases for oil, gas, salt, and sulfur, supervised by the USGS. Total OCS revenue in 1973 from bonuses, royalties, rentals, and shut-in gas payments was $12,577,602,478. In 1973 OCS production of crude oil and condensate was 394,730,000 barrels (11.76 percent of U. S. production) and 3,211,588 million cubic feet of gas (14.02 percent of U.S. production).

By 1972, 276 offshore oil fields and 202 offshore gas fields had been discovered off the United States, mainly offshore from Louisiana in the northern Gulf of Mexico.

No exploratory drilling has been conducted on the Atlantic OCS. The Department of the Interior awarded contract studies to collect economic and environmental data on the north and mid-Atlantic areas. During Federal Fiscal Year 1974 an environmental assessment team on the mid-Atlantic will establish liaison with State and local officials and gather baseline environmental data.

During the last decade, worldwide concern has risen about multi-purpose uses of the seas. The Third United Nations Conference on the Law of the Sea (LOS-3) was convened in Caracas, Venezuela, in June 1974, with representatives from 150 nations of the world attending. The purpose of LOS-3 is the preparation of a "constitution for the oceans." Many significant issues are to be discussed, including (1) extent of territory; (2) transit through and over international straits; (3) coastal states' jurisdiction; (4) protection of marine environment; (5) exploration and development of seabeds; and (6) settlement of disputes.

New Water Demands: The Nation's expanding energy development will demand larger quantities of water than ever before, particularly for generating electrical power. Although cooling of thermal-electric powerplants will continue to be the greatest withdrawal use of water (more than 170 billion gallons per day at the present time), new energy-producing processes, such as coal gasification and liquefaction oil shale production, nuclear fuel processing, and water flooding methods of oil retrieval, will also require large amounts of water.

Recent findings by the U. S. Geological Survey indicate that in the East, South, Midwest, and along the seacoasts, water supplies are generally adequate for energy industries. West of about the 100th meridian, however, runoff is generally less than potential diversions, and energy-producing industries must compete with other users for the limited water supplies.

U. S. Water Use: Three thousand one hundred seventy billion gallons of water — about eight times the average daily flow of the Mississippi River — is funneled daily through the Nation's water pipes, turbines, and irrigation systems. Fortunately, most of the water withdrawn is returned to the water resources system for possible reuse. However, the large and growing demand for a limited supply of water imposes a serious strain on the water resources in some regions of the country, particularly in the Southwest.

The demand for water will continue to grow as more water is used in more ways by more people every day. After subtracting the 2,800 billion gallons per day used to turn the turbines of the hydroelectric industry, USGS hydrologists calculate that for each person in the United States in 1970, about 1,800 gallons of water per day were used for domestic, industrial, rural, and irrigation activities. This means that some 370 billion gallons of water were pumped, piped, or diverted each day — about 19 percent more than in 1965. Daily use will probably rise to 450 billion gallons in 1980 and may exceed 800 billion gallons in the year 2000.

Mapping the Nation: One of the Geological Survey's major responsibilities is the preparation and updating of topographic maps which show the natural, as well as man-made features of the nation's land surface. These maps, produced by the agency's Topographic Division, provide a starting point for many high priority national activities including location and development of the nation's natural resources and land-use planning.

The topographic mapping activity of the Geological Survey, conducted in part in cooperation with state and local government agencies produces the series of standard quandrangle maps which primarily constitute the National Mapping Program. These maps cover most of the area of the 50 States, Puerto Rico, American Samoa, the Virgin Islands, the Trust Territory of the Pacific Islands, and limited parts of Antarctica.

The USGS continues to emphasize completing coverage of the United States at standard quadrangle 1:24,000-scale mapping (1:63,360 scale in Alaska). As of June 30, 1974, published mapping was complete for 64 percent of the nearly 54,000 7.5-minute by 7.5-minute quadrangles required to cover the contermiinous United States at this scale.

The National Cartographic Information Center (NCIC) was established in 1974 to provide one-stop service for users of cartographic and geodetic data. While copies of data will not generally be maintained at NCIC, the customer will be able to determine the availability of information and to place orders. The NCIC supplants the Map Information Office. Information on the availability of published maps for the

United States and outlying areas may be obtained from the National Cartographic Information Center, U. S. Geological Survey, Reston, Virginia 22092.

Flood-prone Area Mapping: The U. S. Geological Survey has prepared more than 12,000 flood maps that outline areas subject to flooding. These maps, called "Flood-Prone Area Maps," show the approximate areas inundated by a 100-year flood (the flood discharge that, on the average, would be equaled or exceeded once in 100 years).

The objective of the flood-prone-area mapping program is to quickly inform individuals and communities of the possible extent of flooding. Emphasis is placed on defining flood areas in populated places where flooding is a major problem.

The program recently was accelerated by financial assistance from the Department of Housing and Urban Development, which requires flood-plain information for management of the Federal flood insurance program.

Delineation of the approximate flood boundary is done on U.S. Geological Survey topographic maps at scale 1:24,000, or 1 inch equals 2,000 feet. Each map covers a 7½ minute quandrangle, roughly 6½ miles east and west by 8½ miles north and south.

Underground Waste Storage: The practice of storing more than 1,000,000,000 gallons of oil-field brine and industrial waste daily beneath the surface of the U.S. is not a foolproof solution to pollution problems, according to USGS scientists. The problems associated with underground waste storage multiply as the volume of waste injected into underground reservoirs increases. The scientists cautioned that serious pollution problems could result if the practices and effects of injecting waste into rocks underground are not studied and understood thoroughly.

Earthquake Research Consolidated: Seismological and geomagnetic programs of the National Oceanic and Atmospheric Administration (NOAA), Department of Commerce were transferred to the U.S. Geological Survey, Department of the Interior, in September 1973. This completed the consolidation of seismological and geomagnetic programs in the USGS providing a central focus in the Federal government for solid earth geophysical research and services. The programs that were transferred involved about 175 scientists, engineers, and technicians. There was a significant exclusion — NOAA retained its observatories in Adak and Palmer, Alaska; and in Honolulu to meet its requirements for the Tsunami Warning Service.

The NOAA groups that became a part of the Geological Survey are:

Albuquerque Seismological Center, Albuquerque, New Mexico, which maintains the Worldwide Network of Standardized Seismographs and carries out research on seismographic instrumentation.

National Earthquake Information Service, Golden, Colorado, which determines earthquake epicenters on a worldwide basis, makes earthquake data available to scientific workers and to the general public.

Observatories Group, which operates 12 geophysical observatories — in Barrow, Collete, and Sitka, Alaska; Castle Rock, California; Baker, Oregon; Newport, Washington; Tucson, Arizona; Dallas, Texas; McMinnville, Tennessee; Boulder, Colorado; Puerto Rico, and in Guam.

World Earthquake Map: The United states Geological Survey has published recently a large (114 cm by 76 cm) **World Seismicity Map** that portrays zones of global earthquake activity. According to the theories of plate tectonics, these earthquake zones delineate the boundaries of lithospheric plates and hence, the places of major plate interaction and plate creation. Dots show the epicenters of 22,895 earthquakes that occurred from July 1, 1963 through December 31, 1972. Three colors distinguish depth-of-focus classes (0-70 km, 71-300 km, 301-700 km), of earthquakes. Open circles represent the 121 great

earthquakes (magnitude 8.0 or greater) that have occurred since 1897.

Dissolved Solids Discharge: Rivers in the conterminous (48) United States discharge an average of nearly 264 million tons of dissolved solids — mainly dissolved salts and minerals — into the oceans annually, according to USGS hydrologists.

About 70 percent of the dissolved solids or 183 million tons per year, is dumped into the Gulf of Mexico. The Mississippi River alone discharges an average of about 157 million tons of dissolved solids yearly, more than all other rivers combined. By comparison, the Atlantic Ocean receives about 37.5 million tons annually and the Pacific Ocean, 43.4 million tons.

Best Space Images of U.S.: Seleted "best" space images of all parts of the conterminous U.S. are among the more than 400,000 images taken by NASA's Earth Resources Technology Satellite-1 (ERTS) and now available from the EROS Data Center, Sioux Falls, South Dakota 57198. ERTS images each cover 115 by 115 miles of the Earth's surface, are taken from an altitude of about 560 miles, and can provide repeat coverage every 18 days.

The images are of interest to the general public because of the new perspective they give to familiar landscapes, and are of interest to specialists because they vividly portray on a regional scale large geologic structures, urban and rural land use, surface waters and their sediment patterns, and vegetation cover and vigor, among other features.

Administered by the U. S. Geological Survey, the E-ROS Data Center was established to provide public access to ERTS data and was formally located in its new building near Sioux Falls, South Dakota in August 1973.

"Work Horse" Satellite Aids Resource Studies: Launched by NASA on July 23, 1972, and designed to operate only one year, the first Earth Resources Technology Satellite (ERTS-1) was still sending images back to Earth more than two years later.

In addition to continuing use of the satellite imagery in the search for new energy and mineral resources, mapping changes in land use, and monitoring floods, recent applications include: the repetitive coverage of ERTS-1 has aided identification of the areal extent, duration, and general types of ephemeral range vegetation in the Southwest United States. Seismic event counts and tiltmeter data from 15 volcanoes in North America telemetered via ERTS have successfully operated as a prototype regional volcano surveillance system. Need for automatic manipulation of ERTS data lead to the experiment in which computer compatible tapes of eight ERTS scenes were digitally processed to produce a color composite mosiac of part of Wyoming, with excellent image quality, high geometric accuracy, and improved resolution.

Geothermal Leasing: The Geothermal Steam Act of 1970 provides for the development of federally-owned geothermal resources by private industry through competitive and non-competitive leasing arrangements.

Geothermal resources are known or geologically inferred to exist locally in the 700 million acres of Federal lands in the Western States and Alaska. Excluded from geothermal leasing are those lands which have been set aside for certain specific purposes, such as National Parks and wildlife refuges.

Over 1.83 million acres of land, about 55 percent federally-owned, have been classified by the USGS as being within Known Geothermal Resource Areas (KGRAs). An additional 99 million acres, about 55 percent federally-owned, have been designated as prospectively valuable for geothermal steam.

Geothermal development was approved by Interior Secretary Morton on December 18, 1973, and the first lease sale was held on January 22, 1974. Through mid-August 1974, six competitive lease sales were held in the following areas: Geysers, Mono Lake-Long Valley, and East Mesa, California; Vale, Oregon; and Roosevelt Hot Springs, Utah.

Oceanography—1974

Major international efforts in oceanographic research marked 1974, with numerous cooperative efforts planned, several major projects carried out, and a few formerly national projects becoming enlarged to include scientists of other nations.

Weather Study

The largest and most complex international scientific experiment ever undertaken was carried out from June 15 to September 23 in a 20-million-square-mile area of tropical land and sea extending from the eastern Pacific Ocean across Latin America, the Atlantic Ocean, and Africa, to the western Indian Ocean. Instruments on 38 ships, more than 60 buoys, 13 aircraft, six types of satellites, and nearly one thousand land stations observed and recorded ocean-weather phenomena from the top of the atmosphere to about 5000 feet below the sea surface. Called GATE — for Global Atmospheric Research Program-Atlantic Tropical Experiment — the project gathered information needed to understand the behavior of the tropical atmosphere and oceans and their effects on the weather.

Simultaneously, in another part of the Atlantic Ocean, a much smaller international experiment was being carried on, using tiny submersibles to probe the Mid-Atlantic Ridge and rift valley that splits the bottom of the ocean and separates the great tectonic plates of Europe and North America. Called FAMOUS—for French-American Mid-Ocean Undersea Study—the project, based in the Azores, used the U.S. Navy's **Alvin**, operated by the Woods Hole Oceanographic Institution, and the French deep-diving submersibles **Cyana** and **Archimede** in a three-month long series of probes. The study sought scientific clues to the origin of the earth's crust, conditions under which metallic ores are found, and the nature of mid-ocean earthquakes. Operating at depths that would crush ordinary submarines, the scientists observed newly formed lava formations and recent manganese deposits along the "split" in the ocean bottom, where new material from deep within the earth is upwelling.

Playing TAG

The United States and the Soviet Union also made significant progress in establishing their cooperative oceanographic studies during 1974. In March the U.S.-U.S.S.R. Joint Committee for Cooperative Studies of the World Ocean signed an agreement covering several areas of joint effort, notably including the Trans-Atlantic Geotraverse (TAG).

Work on the TAG project during 1974 confirmed the existence of what appear to be widespread metallic mineral deposits over some 40 square miles of the median valley of the Mid-Atlantic Ridge. The investigation established that manganese-rich samples dredged from the same Ridge location in 1972 were not unusual, but were part of a larger mineral-concentrating process that is still active. They were also the first hydrothermal mineral deposits discovered in the median valley of a mid-oceanic ridge.

It would have been thought that this undersea mountain chain, which is 47,000 miles long and continuous through all the major ocean basins, would be the site of metallic mineral concentration, as the new material would well up from the earth's interior. In fact, that is what TAG and FAMOUS investigations have shown to be the case.

The manganese deposits found in the TAG hydrothermal field are very poor in iron, nickel, cobalt, copper, and chromium, unlike the "manganese nodules" found in many areas of the ocean.

Another major project that during 1974 took on increasingly international aspects was the National Science Foundation's Deep Sea Drilling Project. Scripps Institution of Oceanography manages DSDP under contract with NSF. During 1974 the drill ship

Glomar Challenger drilled to new depths beneath the Atlantic Ocean floor, reaching more than 1,900 feet into valcanic rocks under 6,000 feet of water at one location. That depth exceeded by seven times the previous record penetration into the hard rocks of the deep ocean floor. Examination of the rock cores obtained during the expedition, which took place in June and July, showed that the upper part of the volcanic oceanic layer is made up of submarine basalt flows sandwiched with layers of deep-sea sediments. This volcanic-sedimentary sequence probably formed on the floor of what was the median valley of the mid-Atlantic ridge some 3.5 million years ago. The accumulation occurred over a period of 100,000 to 200,000 years.

A surprising find beneath only 260 feet of volcanic rock was a complex sequence of rocks of high iron and magnesium content normally associated with the deepest parts of the earth's crust. Uplift along faults may explain the presence of these "plutonic" rocks so close to the sea floor (this particular hole was drilled near such an uplifted area) except that the sequence contains zones of breccias (fragments of plutonic rocks mixed with sediments containing fossils).

The deep penetrations on this expedition were made possible by use of unique remote control equipment which permitted the drilling crew to reinsert the drilling bit into a hole in the ocean floor after replacing worn out drill bits with new ones. Three such reentries were carried out on the deepest hole and one on a shallower penetration.

Medical Benefits

Several Sea Grant projects contributed greatly to knowledge of the oceans and marine animals during 1974. Scientists at the University of Washington have found that a substance called aequorin, which gives certain Pacific jellyfish a mysterious glow, can also be used to measure minuscule changes in calcium concentrations in a person's body fluids or cells. Such changes are frequently early signals of cellular destruction in the body, and point to the onset of diseases such as metastatic carcinoma, bone dysplasia, cardiac dysrhythmias, and others.

The Sea Grant scientists are developing two methods for using aequorin to measure the amount of calcium in such bilogical fluids as blood, saliva, urine, and cerebral spinal fluid. Changes in the amount of glow, or luminescence, is a measure of changes in the amount of calcium in the fluid being measured.

The scientists can obtain from about 600 jellyfish enough aequorin for about 500 calcium measurements. Physiological uses for aequorin are expected to be far-reaching, since before its discovery there was no way to test the calcium theory of cell function.

Seaweed Seeding

Another Sea Grant project at the California Institute of Technology has had continuing success in efforts to develop advanced techniques for establishing and re-establishing valuable Pacific kelp beds. Work has progressed to the point where relatively large numbers of plants can be seeded at a fairly low cost through the dispersion of kelp embryos through the sea.

Two biological oceanographers working under a National Science Foundation grant have concluded that life proceeds at a much slower pace at great depths in the oceans. After measuring the metabolism of deep water animals, they obtained results that may cause proponents of proposals to dump garbage and other wastes on the deep ocean floor to have second thoughts. While the wastes may readily be consumed by the more active shallow water organisms, on the deep ocean floor they may simply accumulate because of the slower pace of life, and dumping wastes in the deep ocean may be equivalent to placing them in cold storage.

Early Explorers of the Western Hemisphere

The first men to discover the New World or Western Hemisphere are believed to have walked across a "land bridge" from Siberia to Alaska, an isthmus since broken by Bering Strait. From Alaska, these ancestors of the Indians spread through North, Central and South America. Anthropologists have placed these crossings at between 18,000 and 14,000 B.C.; but evidence found in 1967 near Puebla, Mex., indicates mankind reached there as early as 35,000-40,-000 years ago.

At first, these people were hunters using flint weapons and tools. In Mexico, about 7000-6000 B.C., they founded farming cultures, developing corn, squash, etc. Eventually, they created complex civilizations — Olmec, Toltec, Aztec and Maya and, in South America, Inca. Carbon-14 tests show men lived about 8000 B.C. near what are now Front Royal, Va., Kanawha, W. Va., and Dutchess Quarry, N.Y. The Hopewell Culture, based on farming, flourished about 1000 B.C.; remains of it are seen today in large mounds in Ohio and other states.

Norsemen (Norwegian Vikings sailing out of Iceland and Greenland) are credited by most scholars with being the first Europeans to discover America, with at least five voyages around 1000 A.D. to areas they called Helluland, Markland and Vinland — possibly Labrador, Nova Scotia or Newfoundland, and New England.

The remains of a settlement at L'Anse-aux-Meadows, near the northern tip of Newfoundland, were uncovered by Dr. and Mrs. Helge Ingstad, Norwegian archeologists, 1960-63, with the aid of a grant from the National Geographic Society. They identified the settlement as Norse. Carbon-14 tests from hearths and the remains of a smithy indicated the site was occupied about 900 A.D. and during several hundred years before and after.

Christopher Columbus, most famous of the discoverers, was born at Genoa, Italy, but made his discoveries sailing for the Spanish rulers Ferdinand and Isabella. Dates of his voyages, places he discovered and other information follow:

1492—First voyage. Left Palos, Spain, Aug. 3 with 88 men (est.). Discovered San Salvador (Guanahani or Watling Isl., Bahamas) Oct. 12. Also Cuba, Hispaniola (Haiti-Dominican Republic); built Fort La Navidad on latter.

1493—Second voyage, first part, Sept. 25, with 17 ships, 1,500 men. Dominica (Lesser Antilles) Nov. 3; Guadaloupe, Montserrat, Antigua, San Martin, Santa Cruz, Puerto Rico, Virgin Islands. Settled Isabela on Hispaniola. **Second part** (Columbus having remained in Western Hemisphere), Jamaica, Isle of Pines, La Mona Isl.

1498—Third voyage. Left Spain May 30, 1498, 6 ships. Discovered Trinidad. Saw South American continent Aug. 1, 1498, but called it Isla Sancta (Holy Island). Entered Gulf of Paria and landed, first time on continental soil. At mouth of Orinoco Aug. 14 he decided this was mainland.

1502—Fourth voyage, 4 caravels, 150 men. St. Lucia, Guanaja off Honduras; Cape Gracias a Dios, Honduras; San Juan River, Costa Rica; Almirante, Portobelo and Laguna de Chiriqui, Panama.

A.D.	Explorer	Nationality and Employer	Discovery or Exploration
1497	John Cabot	Italian-English	Newfoundland or Nova Scotia
1498	John and Sebastian Cabot	Italian-English	Labrador to Hatteras
1499	Alonso de Ojeda	Spanish	South American coast, Venezuela
1500, Feb.	Vicente y Pinzon	Spanish	South American coast, Amazon River
1500, Apr.	Pedro Alvarez Cabral	Portuguese	Brazil (for Portugal)
1500-02	Gaspar Corte-Real	Portuguese	Labrador
1501	Rodrigo de Bastidas	Spanish	Central America
1513	Vasco Nunez de Balboa	Spanish	Pacific Ocean
1513	Juan Ponce de Leon	Spanish	Florida
1515	Juan de Solis	Spanish	Rio de la Plata
1519	Alonso de Pineda	Spanish	Mouth of Mississippi River
1519	Hernando Cortes	Spanish	Mexico
1520	Fernando Magellan	Portuguese-Spanish	Straits of Magellan, Tierra del Fuego
1524	Giovanni da Verrazano	Italian-French	Atlantic Coast-New York harbor
1526-27	Sebastian Cabot	Italian-Spanish	Rio de la Plata (river)
1527	Panfilo de Narvaez	Spanish	Florida
1531	Alfonso de Souza	Portuguese	Rio de Janeiro (river)
1532	Francisco Pizarro	Spanish	Peru
1534	Jacques Cartier	French	Canada, Gulf of St. Lawrence
1536	Pedro de Mendoza	Spanish	Buenos Aires (river)
1536	A. N. Cabeza de Vaca	Spanish	Texas coast and interior
1539	Francisco de Ulloa	Spanish	California coast
1539-41	Hernando de Soto	Spanish	Mississippi River near Memphis
1539	Marcos de Niza	Italian-Spanish	Southwest (now U.S.)
1540	Francisco V. de Coronado	Spanish	Southwest (now U.S.)
1540	Hernando Alarcon	Spanish	Colorado River
1540	Garcia de L. Cardenas	Spanish	Grand Canyon of the Colorado
1541	Francisco de Orellana	Spanish	Amazon River
1541-43	A. N. Cabeza de Vaca	Spanish	Brazil, Paraguay River
1542	Juan Rodriquez Cabrillo	Portuguese-Spanish	San Diego harbor
1565	Pedro Menendez	Spanish	St. Augustine
1573	Pedro Marquez	Spanish	Chesapeake Bay
1576	Martin Frobisher	English	Frobisher's Bay, Canada
1577-80	Francis Drake	English	California coast
1582	Antonio de Espejo	Spanish	Southwest (named New Mexico)
1584	Amadas & Barlow (for Raleigh)	English	Virginia
1585-87	Sir Walter Raleigh's men	English	Roanoke Isl., N.C.
1595	Sir Walter Raleigh	English	Orinoco River
1602	Bartholomew Gosnold	English	Martha's Vineyard and Massachusetts
1603-09	Samuel de Champlain	French	Canadian interior, Lake Champlain
1604	Samuel de Champlain	French	Mt. Desert Island
1607	Capt. John Smith	English	Atlantic coast
1609-10	Henry Hudson	English-Dutch	Hudson River, Hudson Bay
1634	Jean Nicolet	French	Lake Michigan; Wisconsin

Arctic Exploration

Early Explorers

1587 — John Davis (England). Davis Strait to Sanderson's Hope, 72° 12′ N.

1596 — Willem Barents and Jacob van Heemskerck (Holland). Discovered Bear Island, touched northwest tip of Spitsbergen, 79°49′ N., rounded Novaya Zemlya, wintered at Ice Haven.

1607 — Henry Hudson (England). North along Greenland's east coast to Cape Hold-with-Hope, 73° 30′, then north of Spitsbergen to 80° 23′. Returning he discovered Hudson's Touches (Jan Mayen).

1616 — William Baffin and Robert Bylot (England). Baffin Bay to Smith Sound.

1728 — Vitus Bering (Russia). Proved Asia and America were separate by sailing through strait.

1733-40 — Great Northern Expedition (Russia). Surveyed Siberian Arctic coast.

1741 — Vitus Bering (Russia). Sighted Alaska from sea, named Mount St. Elias. His lieutenant, Chirikof, discovered coast.

1771 — Samuel Hearne (Hudson's Bay Co.). Overland from Prince of Wales Fort (Churchill) on Hudson Bay to mouth of Coppermine River.

1778 — James Cook (Britain). Through Bering Strait to Icy Cape, Alaska, and North Cape, Siberia.

1789 — Alexander Mackenzie (North West Co., Britain). Montreal to mouth of Mackenzie River.

1806 — William Scoresby (Britain). North of Spitsbergen to 81° 30′.

1820-3 — Ferdinand von Wrangel (Russia). Completed a survey of Siberian Arctic coast. His exploration joined that of James Cook at North Cape, confirming separation of the continents.

1845 — Sir John Franklin (Britain) was one of many to seek the Northwest Passage — an ocean route connecting the Atlantic and Pacific via the Arctic. His two ships (the Erebus and Terror) were last seen entering Lancaster Sound July 26.

1888 — Fridtjof Nansen (Norway) crossed Greenland's icecap, 1893-96 — Nansen in Fram drifted from New Siberian Isls. to Spitsbergen; tried Polar dash in 1895, reached Franz Josef Land.

1896 — Salomon A. Andree (Sweden) and companion, in June, made first attempt to reach North Pole by balloon; failed and returned in August. On July 11, 1897, Andree and 2 others started in balloon from Danes Isl., Spitsbergen, to drift across Pole to America, and disappeared. Over 33 years later, Aug. 6, 1930, Dr. Gunnar Horn (Norway) found their frozen bodies on White Isl., 82° 56′ N. 29° 52′ E.

1903-06 — Roald Amundsen (Norway) first sailed Northwest Passage.

Discovery of North Pole

Robert E. Peary began exploring in 1886 on Greenland, when he was 30. With his hq. at McCormick Bay he explored Greenland's coast 1891-92, tried for North Pole 1893, returned with large meteorites. In 1900 he reached northern limit of Greenland and 83° 50′N.; in 1902 he reached 84° 06′N; in 1906 he went from Ellesmere Isl. to 87° 06′N. He sailed in the Roosevelt, July, 1908, to winter off Cape Sheridan, Grant Land. The dash for the North Pole began Mar. 1 from Cape Columbia, Ellesmere Land. Peary reached the Pole, 90°N, April 6, 1909.

Peary had several supporting groups carrying supplies until the last group, under Capt. Robt. A. Bartlett, turned back at 87° 47′N. Peary, Matthew Henson and 4 Eskimos proceeded with dog teams and sleds. They crossed Pole several times, finally built an igloo at 90°, remained 36 hours. Started south Apr. 7 at 4 p.m. for Cape Columbia. Eskimos were Coqueeh, Ootah, Eginwah and Seegloo. Adm. Peary died Feb. 20, 1920. Henson, a Negro, born Aug. 8, 1866, died in New York, N.Y., May 9, 1955, aged 88. Ootah, last survivor, died near Thule, Greenland, May, 1955, aged 80.

1914 — Donald Macmillan (U.S.). Northwest, 200 miles, from Axel Hieberg Island to seek Peary's Crocker Land.

1915-17 — Vihjalmur Stefansson (Canada) discovered Borden, Brock, Meighen and Lougheed Islands.

1918-20 — Amundsen sailed Northeast Passage.

1926 — Richard E. Byrd and Floyd Bennett (U.S.) reached 87° 44′N. in attempt to fly to North Pole from Spitsbergen.

1926 — Richard E. Byrd and Floyd Bennett (U.S.) first over North Pole by air, May 9.

1926 — Amundsen, Ellsworth, and Umberto Nobile (Italy) flew from Spitsbergen over North Pole May 12, to Teller, Alaska, in dirigible Norge.

1928 — Nobile crossed North Pole in airship Italia May 24, crashed May 25. Amundsen lost while trying to effect rescue by plane.

1928 — Sir Hubert Wilkins and Eielson flew from Point Barrow to Spitsbergen, 84°N.

Submarine Records

On Aug. 3, 1958, the Nautilus, under Comdr. William R. Anderson, became the first ship to cross the North Pole beneath the Arctic ice.

On Aug. 12, 1958, the nuclear submarine Skate, Comdr. James F. Calvert, became the second ship to make an underwater crossing of the North Pole.

In March, 1959, the Skate returned to the Arctic and, on its third attempt, broke through at the North Pole, the first time any ship had been on the surface at 90° N.

The nuclear-powered U. S. submarine Seadragon, Comdr. George P. Steele II, made the first east-west underwater transit through the Northwest Passage during August, 1960. It sailed from Portsmouth, N. H., headed between Greenland and Labrador through Baffin Bay, then west through Lancaster Sound and McClure Strait to the Beaufort Sea. Traveling submerged for the most part, the submarine made 850 miles from Baffin Bay to the Beaufort Sea in six days. The vessel made a 300-foot dive to sail under an iceberg in Baffin Bay.

In February, 1960, the nuclear submarine Sargo traveled under the Arctic ice pack to and around the North Pole. The Sargo departed from and returned to Honolulu, and spent 31 days and 4 hours under the ice. The submarine successfully smashed its way through ice three feet thick.

Antarctic Exploration

Early History

Antarctica has been approached since 1773-75, when Capt. Jas. Cook (Britain) reached 71° 10′S. Many sea and landmarks bear names of early explorers. Bellingshausen (Russia) discovered Peter I and Alexander I Islands, 1819-21. Nathaniel Palmer (U.S.) discovered Palmer Peninsula, 60° W., 1820, without realizing that this was a continent. Jas. Weddell (Britain) found Weddell Sea, 74°15′S., 1823.

First to announce existence of the continent of Antarctic was Charles Wilkes (U.S.), who followed the coast for 1,500 mi., 1840. Adelie Coast, 140° E., was found by Dumont d'Urville (France), 1840. Ross Ice Shelf was found by Jas. Clark Ross (Britain), 1841-42.

1895 — Leonard Kristensen, Norwegian whaling captain, landed a party on the coast of Victoria Land in Jan. 1895. They were the first ashore on the main continental mass. C. E. Borchgrevink, a member of that party, returned in 1899 with a British expedition, first to winter on Antarctica.

1902-04 — Robert F. Scott (Britain) discovered Edward VII Peninsula. In 1902 he reached 82°17′S., 146°33′E. from McMurdo Sound.

1908-09 — Ernest Shackleton in 1908 introduced the use of Manchurian ponies in Antarctic sledging. In 1909 he reached 88°23′S., discovering a route on to the plateau by way of the Beardmore Glacier and pioneering the way to the Pole.

Discovery of South Pole

1911 — Roald Amundsen (Norway) with four men and dog teams reached the Pole Dec. 14, 1911.

1912 — Capt. Scott reached the Pole from Ross Island Jan. 18, 1912, with four companions (Dr. E. A. Wilson, Lt. Bowers, Capt. Oates, and Petty Officer Edgar Evans), where they found Amundsen's tent. Of Scott's party, Oates and Evans died first; Scott, Wilson and Bowers died in a tent around March 29. They were found Nov. 12, 1912.

1928 — First man to use an airplane over Antarctica was Hubert Wilkins (Britain).

1929 — Richard E. Byrd (U.S.) established Little America on Bay of Whales. On 1600-mi. airplane flight begun Nov. 28 he crossed South Pole Nov. 29 with pilot Bernt Balchen, a radio operator and a photographer. Dropped U. S. flag over Pole, temp. 16° below zero.

1934-35 — Richard E. Byrd (U.S.) led second expedition to Little America, which explored 450,000 sq. mi. Byrd wintered alone at an advance weather station in 80°08′S.

1934-37 — John Rymill led British Graham Land expedition of 1934-37; discovered that Palmer Peninsula is part of Antarctic mainland.

1935 — Lincoln Ellsworth (U.S.) flew south along Palmer Peninsula's east coast, then crossed continent to Little America, making four landings on unprepared terrain in bad weather, a new feat.

1939-41 — U. S. Antarctic Service built West Base on Ross Ice Shelf under Paul Siple and East Base on Palmer Peninsula under Richard Black. U. S. Navy plane flights discovered about 150,000 sq. miles of new land.

1940 — Richard E. Byrd (U.S.) charted most of coast between Ross Sea and Palmer Peninsula.

1946-47 — U. S. Navy undertook Operation Highjump under Rear Admiral Byrd. Ships were commanded by Rear Admiral Richard H. Cruzen. Expedition included 13 ships and 4,000 men, 29 landbased flights from Little America and 35 by seaplanes from tenders, photomapped coastline and penetrated beyond Pole.

1946-48 — Ronne Antarctic Research Expedition, Comdr. Finn Ronne, USNR, determined the Antarctic to be only one continent with no strait between Weddell Sea and Ross Sea; discovered 250,000 sq. miles of land by flights to 79°S. Lat., and made 14,000 aerial photographs over 450,000 sq. miles of land. Mrs. Ronne and Mrs. H. Darlington, who accompanied their husbands, were the first women to winter on Antarctica.

1955-57 — U. S. Navy's Operation Deep Freeze led by Adm. Richard E. Byrd. Supporting U. S. scientific efforts for the International Geophysical Year, the operation was commanded by Rear Adm. George Dufek. It established five coastal stations fronting the Indian, Pacific, and Atlantic Oceans and also three interior stations; explored more than 1,000,000 sq. miles in Wilkes Land. Seven Navy men under Adm. Dufek landed by plane at the Pole Oct. 31, 1956, and landed radar reflectors.

1957-58 — During the International Geophysical year, July, 1957 through Dec., 1958, scientists from 12 countries conducted ambitious programs of Antarctic research. A network of some 60 stations on the continent and sub-Arctic islands studied oceanography, glaciology, metorology, seismology, geomagnetism, the ionosphere, cosmic rays, aurora and airglow. A party from Ellsworth IGY station (US) south of Weddell Sea under the direction of Captain Finn Ronne explored beyond 1947 flight and delineated Berkner Island imbedded in the Filchner Ice Shelf. Pensacola Mountains, first sighted by Argentines in Oct., 1955, and seen by U. S. Navy in Jan., 1956, were accurately located. New mountain ranges about 11,609 ft. high were discovered in Edith Ronne Land.

Dr. V. E. Fuchs led a 12-man Trans-Antarctic Expedition on the first land crossing of Antarctica. Starting from the Weddell Sea, they reached Scott Station Mar. 2, 1958, after traveling 2,158 miles in 98 days.

1958 — A group of 5 U. S. scientists led by Edward C. Thiel, seismologist, moving by tractor from Ellsworth Station on Weddell Sea, identified a huge mountain range, 5,000 ft. above the ice sheet and 9,000 ft. above sea level. The range, originally seen by a Navy plane, was named the Dufek Massif, for Rear Adm. George Dufek.

1959 — Twelve nations — Argentina, Australia, Belgium, Chile, France, Japan, New Zealand, Norway, South Africa, the Soviet Union, the United Kingdom, and the U. S. — signed a treaty suspending any territorial claims for 30 years and reserving the continent for research.

1960-61 — Scientists at Cape Adare found wooden building erected in 1899 by the first men (led by C. E. Borchgrevink) to winter on the continent.

1961-62 — Scientists discovered a trough, the Bentley Trench, running from Ross Ice Shelf, Pacific, into Marie Byrd Land, around the end of the Ellsworth Mtns., toward the Weddell Sea, which may be the long-suspected link between the Atlantic and Pacific Oceans.

1962 — First nuclear power plant began operation at McMurdo Sound.

1963 — On Feb. 22 a U. S. plane made the longest nonstop flight ever made in the S. Pole area, covering 3,600 miles in 10 hours. The flight was from McMurdo Station south past the geographical S. Pole to Shackleton Mtns., southeast to the "Area of Inaccessibility" and back to McMurdo Station.

1963 — Three turbine-powered helicopters made the first copter landings on the S. Pole.

1964 — A British survey team was landed by helicopter on Cook Island, the first recorded visit since its discovery in 1775.

1964 — New Zealanders completed one of the last and most important surveys when they mapped the mountain area from Cape Adare west some 400 miles to Pennell Glacier.

1966-67 — Fifteen Antarctic areas set aside as Specially Protected Areas for the conservation of flora and fauna.

Archeological Events of 1974

World's Oldest Song Deciphered

To the western ear, the tune sounded like a gentle folk song, a lullaby or a child's halting experiment on the piano, hardly extraordinary. But the singing of the song, written in Hurrian, at the University of California last March was an extraordinary event. It was the first time the song had been performed since about 1800 B. C.

The reconstruction of the song, a process which began some 70 years ago, "has revolutionized the whole concept of the origin of western music," said Richard L. Crocker, professor of music history at Berkeley. The Hurrian song has pushed back the origin of western music, previously set in Greece, 1,400 years to an ancient Near Eastern civilization of at least the second millennium B.C.

The reconstruction process entailed the compilation of a series of clay tablets unearthed over the past 70 years. Anne D. Kilmer, professor of Assyriology at Berkeley, made the breakthrough in 1972 when she deciphered the spikey cuneiform writing on thick clay tablets discovered in the fifties by French archeologists at Ras Shamra, the seat of the ancient culture of Ugarit which flourished from about 2,000 to 600 B.C. At that point she discovered that the song had the same heptatonic scale used in Greek and western music of the first millenium B.C.

Since knowledge of Hurrian vocabulary is limited, the song's meaning is cloudy. Prof. Kilmer believes that it is a love song of sorts, an ode to a pantheon of gods and goddesses.

Despite support from Assyriologists and musicologists here and abroad, Prof. Kilmer cautioned that her reconstruction could not be confirmed until another tablet with another song was unearthed.

Geologists vs. Archeologists

Geologists threw a monkey wrench at existing theory on the migration of man to the Western Hemisphere at the annual Geological Society meeting in Albany last November. Dr. Roald Fryxwell of Washington State University, along with Dr. Harold E. Malde and Virginia Steen-McIntyre, both of the U.S. Geological Survey in Denver, presented evidence consisting of sophisticated tools discovered in an ancient Mexican stream bed which suggest man lived in North America 250,000 years ago. The tools, dated by several techniques, were found at Hueyatlaco, a few miles south of Puebla, Mex.

Existing theory, based on archeological data, hypothesizes that man migrated to North America some 12,000 to 20,000 years ago over a then existing land bridge between Siberia and Alaska.

"We're confronted with a dilemma in which we have apparently sound geological data that leads to a head-on confrontation with apparently sound archeological data." The 3 scientists agree that their finds seem archeologically unreasonable.

Beyond the dilemma of contradicting evidence, the tools create another problem: they are considerably more advanced than tools used in Europe and Asia 250,000 years ago. They are, in fact, comparable to Old World tools of 35,000 to 40,000 years ago.

New Test Age North American Man

Using "racemization," a new technique for dating artifacts by studying the light-rotating properties of amino acids, University of California researchers have also challenged archeological theory on man's arrival in North America. New tests on bones discovered between 1920 and 1935 along the southern California coast suggest human beings lived in North America more than 48,000 years ago.

Dr. Jeffrey L. Bada, assistant professor of oceanography at the University of California at San Diego, Roy Schroeder, a graduate student at U. of C. at San Diego, and Dr. George Carter, a geography professor at Texas A. & M., have dated a skull discovered at Del Mar, Calif., at 48,000 years old and a skull fragment found near La Jolla at 44,000 years. Their evidence, if reliable, leads to conjecture that human nomads may have come to America during a previous Ice Age 70,-000 or even 140,000 years ago.

The "racemization" process holds potentially major significance for archeological research because carbon dating is reliable for only some 40,000 years into the past.

"Pittsburgh" Man Unearthed

Unearthing of the "Pittsburgh" man by a University of Pittsburgh archeological team indicates that Ice Age man may have roamed further east in the Western Hemisphere than previously believed. The evidence of human habitation, found under a rock shelter near Arella, Pa., dates to 12,300 to 13,000 years B.C.

The excavation has also unearthed shells, ceramics, blade tools, domesticated seeds, and bark baskets which are some of the oldest artifacts, dating to 2,000 B.C., ever found in the eastern U.S.

Ethiopia Yields Data on Early Man

After only 10 weeks of digging in the rich fossil fields of Ethiopia's Hadar River basin, a young American paleontologist, Dr. C. Donald Johanson of Case Western Reserve University, unearthed rocks containing 4 arm bones.

If his suspicions are confirmed by K/A testing (determining deterioration of a radioactive carbon into argon dates the sample), the bones may place the date man first walked at least 400,000 years earlier than previously known. Johanson feels the find's "biostratographic picture suggests a date in excess of 3 million years."

Richard Leakey's "1470" skull, discovered in Kenya 2 years ago, pushed the date for upright man to 2,500,000 years ago.

Stokesosauraus Clevelandi — A New Dinosaur

The dinosaur ranks have increased by one, the Stokesosauraus clevelandi. It's the first new genus and species discovered in 75 years.

The 2 hip bones and jawbone found by James H. Madsen of the University of Utah at the Cleveland-Lloyd quarry in central Utah show features not found on similar specimens from the quarry. Madsen believes the characteristics indicate a more advanced form of predator with a shorter snout, probably most closely related to the flesh-eating tyrannosaur.

Roaming the Utah region some 140 million years ago, the creature, fully grown at 13 feet in length and 5 feet in height, fed on small reptiles and tiny mammals.

New Data on Pterosaurs

Fossil footprints, perhaps the oldest evidence to date of Pterosaurs, ancient flying reptiles, have been discovered in Utah by Lin Ottinger, a backcountry guide and rock shop owner.

William Lee Stokes, a University of Utah geologist and paleontologist, estimates the age of the tracks at between 150 to 200 million years and feels their "highly irregular" nature should provide valuable information on the actions of reptiles on the ground.

The Pterosaurs, which ranged from the size of sparrows to giants with 30-foot wingspans, ate insects and fish. The creatures had leathery wings believed to have been used for gliding.

Chinese Report New Findings

Two years ago, Chinese scientists performed an autopsy on the incredibly well-preserved body of a noblewoman who died more than 2,000 years ago. A documentary film on the autopsy is circulating in China.

The still moist body was found encased in a series of 6 airtight coffins at Mawantui on the eastern outskirts of Changsa, the capital of Hunan. The body was well-preserved because of the airtight coffins and the use of an embalming fluid containing organic acids and mercurial compounds. The coffins had also been packed in about 10,000 pounds of charcoal to keep out moisture.

A study of the brain, heart, lungs and other internal organs showed the woman to be about 50 years old with type A blood. Study of the burial accessories, including silk fabrics, lacquerware, bamboo and wooden utensils, identified the woman as the wife of the early Western Han Dynasty Marquis of Tao who lived 2,100 years ago.

Further excavation at the site, announced in August, produced a hoard of historical manuscripts, philosophical treatises and medical texts. Included were a 4,000-word essay on how to judge horses, a treatise on the movement of the stars and a book advising rulers to combine punishment with virtue. Medical scripts thought to be connected with "The Yellow Emperor's Classic of External Medicine," a lost work, were also found.

The recent excavations, however, also unearthed a major disappointment. The coffin of the husband of the well-preserved woman discovered 2 years ago was excavated and found to be rotten, as were the objects contained in it. The seals on the coffin did, however, confirm the couple's identity — he was the

Marquis of Tao, a minor nobleman who died in 186 B.C.

The tomb of the couple's son did yield material of historical interest. Buried with him were writing — more than 120,000 words — from books and tracts lost over 2,000 years ago. Included were 2 copies of the philosophical teachings of Lao Tzu, the legendary founder of Taoism. These copies vary from other known texts.

In August, the Chinese also announced a major find at the site of Chenghow, the earliest Chinese city found to date. Unearthed were the foundations of a Shang Dynasty community built some 3,500 years ago. Artifacts discovered included pottery fragments, bone and stone objects, as well as nearly 100 human skulls, presumably the remains of slaves.

Inca History Linked to Calendar

Scholars have widely assumed that the Incas were not greatly concerned with time reckoning. Recently, however, through a study of early Spanish chronicles and the layout of the Incan capital of Cuzco, Gary S. Vescelius, a specialist in Andean archeology, concluded that the shrines around the city, the design of the central temple and the yearly "spring run" were all closely linked to the Inca calendar.

On the basis of his study, Vescelius has proposed radical revisions in the chronology of Incan history prior to the arrival of the Spanish conquistadors. Because the Incas had no written language, scholars had previously been dependent chiefly on Spanish chronicles for a reconstruction of Incan history.

Vescelius has speculated that the distribution of 328 shrines around Cuzco stemmed from the Incan calendar which divided the year into 12 months of 3 weeks of varied length ranging from 9 to 11 days. He suggests that each shrine represents one day with a sabbath for each week plus one special festive day. The total comes to 365 days. He links the calendar to an inscription of the famous Sun Gate at Tiahuanaco which dates to 500 A.D. The inscription, he believes, provides evidence that the calendar originated some 1,000 years prior to the heyday of the Inca empire.

In the yearly "spring run," runners set out along 4 roads radiating from the central temple shouting to banish evil spirits from the city. Vescelius speculates they were assigned to the 328 shrines around the city at which point they relayed shouts to other runners who, in turn, carried them far out into the empire.

Wyoming's Medicine Wheel

An American "Stonehenge," a collection of rocks in the rough shape of a bicycle wheel in the Big Horn Mountains of Wyoming, has long mystified scholars. Now, Colorado astronomer John A. Eddy suggests that the Medicine Wheel, as it is known, once served as a primitive astronomical observatory.

The wheel, believed to have been built by the Plains Indians around 1700, is located on a 9,600-foot exposed ridge. Twenty-eight uneven spokes radiate in the shape of a distorted circle approximately 25 yards in diameter. A cairn, several feet in height, stands in the center and 6 smaller ones are positioned around the rim.

From the approximate symmetry of the cairns in relation to due north, Eddy speculates medicine men used the wheel to pinpoint the summer solstice. The arrival of that day, according to Indian legend, was a sign for certain Plains tribes to perform their sacred sun dance.

Old Merchant Ship Recovered

Some 2,200 years ago, a merchant ship enroute through the eastern Mediterranean sank in stormy waters off the port of Kyrenia on the north coast of Cyprus. The ship was recovered 7 years ago and is now ready to go on display. The 45-foot-long ship will rest on iron scaffolding in the former barracks room of a crusader's castle which has guarded the harbor since 1200 A.D.

According to Michael L. Kataev, the director of the excavation, the ship or "time capsule," as he calls it, is the oldest ship ever recovered under water.

The skeleton of the ship which bears the mark of a skilled and dedicated craftsman had to be cut into sections before it could be surfaced. The recovered wood pieces were bathed in a solution of polyethylene glycol which penetrated the wood to rebuild its lost substance.

Since some pieces were missing, the excavation crew made several models hypothesizing the exact shape and angle of the hull. The existing pieces were then painstakingly knit together with stainless steel wire.

Ancient Suburbia Unearthed

Oplonti, once an ancient suburban community, has been unearthed about 10 miles north of the site of Pompeii. Highlighted by an almost perfectly preserved Roman villa, the site may be as significant as Pompeii and Herculaneum.

Located under the modern town of Torre Annunziata, Oplonti was probably strictly a residential community without market places or forums. The residents were most likely wealthy Pompeiian commuters and rich Roman patricians on vacation. The community is believed to have been covered by eruptions from Vesuvius in 19 A.D. Study of the wall structure of the villa suggests construction was begun in the first century B.C., with successive building in the ages of Augustus and Nero.

The villa which is surrounded by a majestic portico is distinguished by the outstanding quality of its architecture and colorful interior wall paintings, all very well preserved. Most of the paintings are in the Pompeiian Style II which is characterized by scenes of colossal architecture and dramatic fake perspectives. Others, in the Pompeiian Style III, depict mythological themes, including a magnificent one of Hercules in the garden of the Hesperides.

Burial Site Yields Treasures

The remains of a "Latin princess," adorned with rich gold and silver ornaments, small pearls and large amber beads, have been dug up at a burial site near Castel di Decima, 10 miles south of Rome. In total, more than 100 tombs dating from the 8th to the end of the 7th century B.C. have been unearthed.

The princess's tomb was equipped with funeral chariots, a sign of noble rank. Allessandro Bedini, the excavation supervisor, described her gold and silver ornaments as "among the finest found in all Italy." The burial items all point to the existence of a sophisticated civilization in the Rome area almost 27 centuries ago.

Prof. Fausto Zevi, a government expert, believes that the burial area may mark the site of the lost Latin city of Politorium. The city was conquered and razed by the 4th Roman king, Ancus Marcius, who ruled from 640 to 616 B.C. He is believed to have been a chief of the Sabines who rivaled the Latins and Etruscans for supremacy in the area between the Apennine Mountains and the Tyrrhenian Sea.

Possible Key to Lycian Language Found

Archeologists may have found the key to yet another heretofore undecipherable early written language. Lycian was the language of a seafaring kingdom of about 300 to 400 B.C. located in the rugged, mountainous Mediterranean coastal region of what is today southern Turkey.

A team of archeologists headed by Henri Metzger of Lyon University recently discovered, in southern Turkey, a 4-foot-high stone slab inscribed in 3 languages — Lycian, Aramaic and Greek. Metzger has dated the stone to 358 B.C., the beginning of Artaxerxes' reign over the Persian empire.

Metzger believes the slab deals with the establishment of new gods by Pixodaros, a local governor. It is his hope that a comparison of the 3 accounts on the well-preserved stone will broaden knowledge of the Lycian language. But problems abound. It has not yet been determined that the 3 inscriptions are identical. One may be a full account, and the others only paraphrases.

Volcanoes of the World

Source: National Geographic Society, Washington, D.C.

(E) Eruption year in parentheses (R) Rumbling (St.) Steaming (D) Dormant

Mt. Vesuvius, dominating the Bay of Naples, is the most famous of volcanoes. In August, 79 A.D., it buried Pompeii (c. 20,000 pop.) under hot ash and Herculaneum and Stabiae under mud flows. Three-fifths of Pompeii has been excavated; also part of Herculaneum, most of which lies under Resina. Stabiae lies under Castellammare. There was a big eruption in 1139, and a major one in December, 1631, when 5 towns were destroyed and 4,000 people killed. Minor eruptions have occurred in 1779, 1793, 1872, 1906 and 1944.

Krakatau on an island in the Sunda Strait between Sumatra and Java exploded Aug. 27,1883, creating a depth of 1,000 ft. in the ocean. The explosion was heard 2,500 mi. away, and tidal waves killed 35,000. In 1927 Krakatau formed the island of Anak Krakatau, which exploded, 1929, depositing an island in the hole caused in 1883.

Mont Pelee, Martinique, destroyed St. Pierre and more than 30,000 people May 8, 1902. Eruptions slightly less powerful occurred May 20 and Aug. 30, 1902. A major eruption began Sept. 16, 1929, and lasted 3 years.

Mt. Agung, 10,308 ft., on the island of Bali, erupted in January, March and May, 1963; the last two eruptions claimed a total of more than 1,500 lives and a third of Bali's farm land, and left 85,000 homeless. Bali's **Mt. Batur,** 5,636 ft., erupted in September, 1963, forcing 1,200 persons to leave their homes at its base; rumblings and explosions could be heard for 50 miles.

In Alaska's Valley of 10,000 Smokes, the lowest of **Mt. Trident's** 3 peaks erupted Apr. 1, 1963; the cloud of smoke and dust was visible 100 miles away.

Name	Location	Ht. Ft.	Name	Location	Ht. Ft.
Africa			Galunggung (E-1920)	Java	7,113
Kilimanjaro (D)	Tanzania	19,340	Amburombu (E-1924)	Indonesia	7,051
Cameroon Mt. (E-1959)	Cameroon	13,350	Sorikmarapi (E-1917)	Sumatra	7,037
Nyiragongo (E-1972)	Zaire	11,385	Petarangan (E-1939)	Java	7,005
Nyamlagira (E-1971)	Zaire	10,028	Sibajak (St.)	Sumatra	6,870
Fogo (E-1951)	Cape Verde Is	9,281	Tokachi (E-1962)	Japan	6,813
Tristan da Cunha (E-1961)	Atlantic Ocean	6,760	Tangkubanperahu (R)	Java	6,637
San Juan (D)	Canary Is.	2,612	Bagana (E-1966)	Solomons	6,560
Erta Ale (E-1973)	Ethiopia	1,660	Tongariro (E-1950)	5 New Zealand	6,458
Antarctica			Zheltovskaya (E-1972)	U.S.S.R.	6,407
Erebus (St.)		12,450	Sangeang (E-1953)	Indonesia	6,394
Melbourne (St.)		8,500	Kaba (E-1941)	Sumatra	6,358
Deception Island (E-1970)		1,890	Awu (E-1966)	Indonesia	6,102
Asia—Oceania			Tiatia (E-1973)	Kuril Islands	6,013
Klyuchevskaya (E-1962)	U.S.S.R.	15,584	Manam (E-1966)	Bismarck Arch.	6,000
Kerintji (St.)	Sumatra	12,467	Soputan (E-1947)	Celebes	5,994
Fuji (D)	Japan	12,388	Piton de la Fournaise		
Rindjani (E-1964)	Indonesia	12,224	(E-1973)	Reunion Is.	5,981
Tolbachik (E-1941)	U.S.S.R.	12,080	Siau (E-1974)	Indonesia	5,853
Semeru (E-1963)	Java	12,060	Kelud (E-1966)	Java	5,679
Ichinskaya	U.S.S.R.	11,880	Batur (E-1963)	Bali	5,636
Kronotskaya (D)	U.S.S.R.	11,575	Belerang (St.)	Sumatra	5,636
Koryakskaya (E-1957)	U.S.S.R.	11,339	Ternate (E-1938)	Indonesia	5,627
Slamet (E-1953)	Java	11,247	Hibok Hibok (E-1960)	Philippines	5,619
Raung (St.)	Java	10,932	Lewotobi Perampuan		
Shiveluch (E-1964)	U.S.S.R.	10,771	(E-1935)	Indonesia	5,591
Dempo (St.)	Sumatra	10,364	Kirishima (St.)	Japan	5,577
Welirang (D)	Java	10,354	Karymskaya (E-1970)	U.S.S.R.	5,560
Agung (E-1964)	Bali	10,308	Mutu (D)	Indonesia	5,545
Sundoro (D)	Java	10,285	Lamongna (St.)	Java	5,482
Tjareme (E-1938)	Java	10,098	Boleng (E-1950)	Indonesia	5,443
Ontake (E-1970)	Japan	10,049	Gamkonora (E-1949)	Indonesia	5,364
Gede (E-1949)	Java	9,705	Aso (E-1970)	Japan	5,223
Merapi (E-1969)	Java	9,551	Lewotobi Lakilaki (E-1940)	Indonesia	5,217
Bezymyannaya (E-1961)	U.S.S.R.	9,514	Lokon (E-1970)	Celebes	5,184
Marapi (D)	Sumatra	9,485	Bulusan (E-1966)	Philippines	5,115
Apo (D)	Philippines	9,369	Sarycheva (E-1960)	Kuril Is.	4,960
Tambora (D)	Indonesia	9,353	Meakan (E-1959)	Japan	4,931
Ruapehu (E-1971)	New Zealand	9,175	Ibu (D)	Indonesia	4,921
Peuetsagoe (D)	Sumatra	9,121	Lewotolo (D)	Indonesia	4,757
Bromo (St.)	Java	9,088	Lopevi (E-1960)	New Hebrides	4,755
Avachinskaya (St.)	U.S.S.R.	9,026	Ambrim (E-1951)	New Hebrides	4,376
Big Ben (E-1950)	Heard Island	9,007	Mahawu (D)	Celebes	4,367
Balbi (D)	Solomons	9,000	Long Island (E-1953)	Bismarck Arch.	4,278
Papandajan (St.)	Java	8,602	Mt. Langila (!-1973)	New Britain	3,924
Guereudong (E-1924)	Sumatra	8,497	Tongkoko (D)	Celebes	3,770
Asama (E-1973)	Japan	8,340	Komaga Dake (E-1971)	Japan	3,740
Sumbing (E-1926)	Sumatra	8,225	Werung (E-1948)	Indonesia	3,678
Tandikat (E-1924)	Sumatra	8,166	Sakurajima (E-1974)	Japan	3,668
Mayon (E-1968)	Philippines	8,077	Langla (E-1965)	New Britain	3,586
Yake Dake (E-1963)	Japan	8,064	Dukono (E-1950)	Indonesia	3,566
Sinabung (St)	Sumatra	8,041	Lamington (E-1951)	New Guinea	3,500
Idjen (D)	Java	7,828	Minami (E-1971)	Japan	3,478
Alaid (E-1972)	Kuril Is.	7,662	Yasur (R)	New Hebrides	3,420
Ulawan (E-1973)	New Britain	7,532	Lolobau (D)	Bismarck Arch.	3,058
Ngauruhoe (E-1974)	New Zealand	7,515	Asuncion (St.)	Marianas	2,923
Guntur (D)	Java	7,379	Paloe (E-1973)	Indonesia	2,871
Bamus (D)	New Britain	7,338	Sirung (E-1947)	Indonesia	2,828

Name	Location	Ht. Ft.
O Yama (E-1962)	Japan	2,674
Krakatau (E-1953)	Indonesia	2,667
Bam Island (D)	Bismarck Arch.	2,625
Nila (E-1932)	Indonesia	2,562
Batu Tara (St.)	Indonesia	2,454
Alamagan (E-1945)	Marianas	2,441
Ruang (E-1949)	Indonesia	2,379
Bango (D)	New Britain.	2,375
Tinakula (E-1971)	Santa Cruz Is.	2,200
Ija (E-1969)	Indonesia	2,162
Banda (D)	Indonesia	2,152
Teun (D)	Indonesia	2,149
Serua (D)	Indonesia	2,103
Mihara (E-1964)	Japan	2,028
Pagan (D)	Marianas	1,870
Tofua (D)	Tonga Islands.	1,660
Unauna (E-1960)	Indonesia	1,640
Farallon de Pajaros (E-1952)	Marianas	1,096
White Island (E-1971)	New Zealand	1,075
Taal (E-1971)	Philippines	984
Didicas (E-1952)	Philippines	900
Niuafo'ou (E-1946)	Tonga.	853
Tavurvur (E-1941)	New Britain.	741
Fonualei (E-1939).	Tonga.	600
Anak Krakatau (E-1960)	Indonesia	510

Central America—Caribbean

Name	Location	Ht. Ft.
Tajumulco (R)	Guatemala	13,845
Tacana (R).	Guatemala	13,428
Acatenango (R)	Guatemala	12,992
Fuego (E-1973)	Guatemala	12,582
Santa Maria (E-1973)	Guatemala	12,362
Atitlan (R).	Guatemala	11,565
Irazu (E-1964)	Costa Rica.	11,260
San Pedro (R)	Guatemala	9,921
Poas (St.)	Costa Rica.	8,930
Pacaya (E-1972)	Guatemala	8,346
San Miguel (E-1970).	El Salvador.	6,988
Rincon de la Viej (E-1970).	Costa Rica.	6,234
Izalco (E-1967)	El Salvador.	6,184
El Viejo (E-1971)	Nicaragua.	5,840
Ometepe (Concepcion) (E-1957)	Nicaragua.	5,106
Arenal (E-1970)	Costa Rica.	5,092
Pelee (D)	Martinique	4,583
Momotombo (E-1952)	Nicaragua.	4,199
Conchagua (E-1947)	El Salvador.	4,100
Soufriere (E-1972)	St. Vincent.	4,048
Telica (E-1971)	Nicaragua.	3,409
Negro (E-1971).	Nicaragua.	3,204
Santiago (St.).	Nicaragua.	1,969

South America

Name	Location	Ht. Ft.
Guallatiri E-1959)	Chile	19,882
Lascar (E-1951).	Chile	19,652
Cotopaxi (St.).	Ecuador.	19,347
Misti (D).	Peru.	19,098
Cayambe (D)	Ecuador.	18,996
Tupungatito (E-1959)	Chile.	18,504
Sangay (E-1946)	Ecuador.	17,159
Tungurahua (R)	Ecuador.	16,512
Cotacachi (E-1955)	Ecuador.	16,204
Pichincha (D)	Ecuador.	15,696
Purace (E-1950).	Colombia.	15,604
Lautaro (St.).	Chile.	11,090
Llaima (E-1955).	Chile.	10,239
Villarrica (E-1972).	Chile.	9,318
Hudson (E-1973).	Chile.	8,580

Name	Location	Ht. Ft.
Shoshuenco (E-1960)	Chile.	7,743
Ventisquero (E-1971)	Chile.	7,546
Puyehue (E-1972)	Chile.	7,349
Calbuco (E-1961)	Chile.	6,611
Casablanca (E-1960)	Chile.	6,529
Cauye (E-1960)	Chile.	4,692
Alcedo (E-1970)	Galapagos Is.	3,599

Mid-Pacific

Name	Location	Ht. Ft.
Mauna Kea (D)	Hawaii	13,796
Mauna Loa (E-1950)	Hawaii	13,680
Kilauea (E-1973)	Hawaii	4,077

Europe

Name	Location	Ht. Ft.
Etna (E-1974).	Sicily, Italy	10,902
Beeren Berg (E-1971)	Norway.	7,470
Askja (E-1961).	Iceland	4,954
Hekla (E-1970)	Iceland	4,892
Vesuvius (St.)	Italy	4,190
Katla (E-1918)	Iceland	3,182
Stromboli (E-1971)	Italy	3,038
Thera (E-1956)	Greece	1,824
Vulcano (D).	Italy	1,637
Kirkjufell (E-1973).	Iceland	725
Surtsey (E-1965)	Iceland	568
Ilha Nova (E-1958)	Azores.	200

North America

Name	Location	Ht. Ft.
Citlaltepec (D)	Mexico.	18,700
Popocatepetl (St.).	Mexico.	17,887
Wrangell (St.).	Alaska.	14,163
Colima (St.).	Mexico.	14,003
Torbert (E-1953).	Alaska.	11,413
Spurr (E-1953).	Alaska.	11,069
Lassen (D)	California.	10,457
Redoubt (E-1966)	Alaska.	10,197
Iliamna (St.)	Alaska.	10,016
Shishaldin (St.)	Aleutians	9,387
Pavlof (E-1973)	Alaska.	8,261
Veniaminof (D)	Alaska.	8,225
Griggs (St.)	Alaska.	7,600
Paricutin (D).	Mexico.	7,451
Mageik (St.)	Alaska.	7,250
Douglas (St.).	Alaska.	7,064
Chiginagak (D).	Alaska.	6,900
Katmai (E-1962)	Alaska.	6,715
Kukak (St.)	Alaska.	6,700
Makushin (D)	Aleutians	6,680
Pogromni (E-1964)	Aleutians	6,568
Martin (E-1960)	Alaska.	6,050
Trident (E-1963)	Alaska.	6,010
Tanaga (D)	Aleutians	5,925
Great Sitkin (St.)	Aleutians	5,710
Cleveland (E-1944)	Aleutians	5,675
Gareloi (D)	Aleutians	5,334
Korovin (D)	Aleutians	4,852
Kanaga (D)	Aleutians	4,416
Aniakchak (D)	Alaska.	4,400
Akutan (E-1974)	Aleutians	4,275
Kiska (1962)	Aleutians	4,004
Augustine (E-1935)	Alaska.	3,927
Little Sitkin (St.)	Aleutians	3,897
Okmok (E-1958)	Aleutians	3,519
Seguam (D)	Aleutians	3,458
Yunaska (D).	Aleutians	3,133
Kagamil (D).	Aleutians	2,930
Novarupta (St.)	Alaska.	2,760
Cerberus (D).	Alaska.	2,541
Boqueron (E-1955)	Revillagigedo Is. (Mexico)	1,280

Eruptions 1973—1974

Guatemala's Santiaguito, a cone on Santa Maria, 12,362 ft., erupted in September 1973, stripping and burning surrounding vegetation.

New Britain's Ulawan, 7,532 ft., erupted in October 1973 with lava flowing throughout the period of activity.

Indonesia's Api Siau, 5,853 ft., in January began eruptive activity accompanied by earthquakes which caused landslides and the collapse of homes and buildings in the area.

New Zealand's Ngauruhoe, 7,515 ft., following a year of minor activity, erupted in January.

Japan's Tyokai, 7,359 ft., inactive for 153 years, erupted in early March and continued to smoke through April.

Japan's Mt. Yakemaya, 7,920 ft., dormant for 25 years, erupted in late July, spreading ashes on the surrounding area and damaging local vegetation.

Highest and Lowest Continental Altitudes

Source: National Geographic Society, Washington, D.C.

(In feet)

Continent	Highest Point	Elevation	Lowest Point	Below Sea Level
Asia	Mount Everest, Nepal-Tibet	29,028	Dead Sea, Israel-Jordan	1,299
South America	Mount Aconcagua, Argentina	22,834	Peninsula Valdes, Argentina	131
North America	Mount McKinley, Alaska	20,320	Death Valley, California	282
Africa	Kibo (Kilimanjaro), Tanzania	19,340	Lake Assal, Afars & Issas Terr.	512
Europe	Mount El'brus USSR Caucasus Mts.	18,510	Caspian Sea, USSR	92
Antarctica	Vinson Massif	16,860	Unknown	...
Australia	Mount Kosciusko, New South Wales	7,310	Lake Eyre, South Australia	52

Height of Mount Everest

Mt. Everest was considered to be 29,002 ft. tall when Edmund Hillary and Tenzing Norkay scaled it in 1953. This triangulation figure had been accepted since 1850. In 1954 the Surveyor General of the Republic of India set the height at 29,028 ft., plus or minus 10 ft. because of snow. The National Geographic Society accepts the new figure, but many mountaineering groups still use 29,002 ft.

High Peaks in United States, Canada, Mexico

Name	Place	Feet	Name	Place	Feet	Name	Place	Feet
McKinley	Alaska	20,320	Crestone	Colo	14,294	Columbia	Colo	14,073
Logan	Can	19,850	Lincoln	Colo	14,286	Augusta	Alas.Can.	14,070
Citlaltepec (Orizaba)	Mexico	18,700	Grays	Colo	14,270	Culebra	Colo	14,069
St. Elias	Alas-Can.	18,008	Antero	Colo	14,269	Missouri	Colo	14,067
Popocatepetl	Mexico	17,887	Torreys	Colo	14,267	Humboldt	Colo	14,064
Foraker	Alaska	17,400	Castle	Colo	14,265	Bierstadt	Colo	14,060
Iztaccihuatl	Mexico	17,343	Quandary	Colo	14,265	Sunlight	Colo	14,059
Lucania	Can	17,147	Evans	Colo	14,264	Split	Calif	14,058
King	Can	16,971	Longs	Colo	14,255	Nauhcampatepetl		
Steele	Can	16,644	McArthur	Can	14,253	(Cofre de Perote)	Mexico	14,049
Bona	Alaska	16,421	Mt. Wilson	Colo	14,246	Handies	Colo	14,048
Blackburn	Alaska	16,390	White	Calif	14,246	Culebra	Colo	14,047
Kennedy	Alaska	16,286	North Palisade	Calif	14,242	Lindsey	Colo	14,042
Sanford	Alaska	16,237	Shavano	Colo	14,229	Middle Palisade	Calif	14,040
South Buttress	Alaska	15,885	Belford	Colo	14,197	Little Bear	Colo	14,037
Wood	Can	15,885	Princeton	Colo	14,197	Sherman	Colo	14,036
Vancouver	Alas-Can.	15,700	Crestone	Colo	14,197	Redcloud	Colo	14,034
Churchill	Alaska	15,638	Yale	Colo	14,196	Langley	Calif	14,028
Fairweather	Alas-Can.	15,300	Bross	Colo	14,172	Conundrum	Colo	14,022
Zinantecatl (Toluca)	Mexico	15,016	Kit Carson	Colo	14,165	Tyndall	Calif	14,018
Hubbard	Alas-Can.	15,015	Wrangell	Alaska	14,163	Pyramid	Colo	14,018
Bear	Alaska	14,831	Shasta	Calif	14,162	Wilson Peak	Colo	14,017
Walsh	Can	14,780	Sill	Calif	14,162	Muir	Calif	14,015
East Buttress	Alaska	14,730	El Diente	Colo	14,159	Wetterhorn	Colo	14,015
Matlalcueyetl	Mexico	14,636	Maroon	Colo	14,156	North Maroon	Colo	14,014
Hunter	Alaska	14,573	Tabeguache	Colo	14,155	San Luis	Colo	14,014
Alverstone	Alas-Can.	14,565	Oxford	Colo	14,153	Huron	Colo	14,005
Browne Tower	Alaska	14,530	Sneffels	Colo	14,150	Holy Cross	Colo	14,005
Whitney	Calif	14,494	Point Success	Wash	14,150	Colima	Mexico	14,003
Elbert	Colo	14,433	Democrat	Colo	14,148	Sunshine	Colo	14,001
Massive	Colo	14,421	Liberty Cap	Wash	14,133	Grizzly	Colo	14,000
Harvard	Colo	14,420	Capitol	Colo	14,130	Barnard	Calif	13,990
Rainier	Wash	14,410	Lindsey	Colo	14,125	Stewart	Colo	13,980
Williamson	Calif	14,375	Pikes Peak	Colo	14,110	Keith	Calif	13,977
Blanca	Colo	14,345	Snowmass	Colo	14,092	Le Conte	Calif	13,960
La Plata	Colo	14,336	Windom	Colo	14,087	Meeker	Colo	13,911
Uncompahgre	Colo	14,309	Russell	Calif	14,086	Kennedy	Can	13,905
			Eolus	Colo	14,084			

South America

Peak	Country	Feet	Peak	Country	Feet	Peak	Country	Feet
Aconcagua, Argentina		22,834	Laudo, Argentina		20,997	Solo, Argentina		20,492
Bonete, Argentina		22,546	Ancohuma, Bolivia		20,958	Polleras, Argentina		20,456
Ojos del Salado, Arg.-Chile		22,539	Ausangate, Peru		20,945	Pular, Chile		20,423
Tupungato, Argentina-Chile		22,310	Toro, Argentina-Chile		20,932	Chani, Argentina		20,341
Pissis, Argentina		22,241	Illampu, Bolivia		20,873	Aucanquilcha, Chile		20,295
Mercedario, Argentina		22,211	Tres Cruces, Argentina-Chile		20,853	Juncal, Argentina		20,276
Huascaran, Peru		22,205	Huandoy, Peru		20,852	Negro, Argentina		20,184
Llullaillaco, Argentina-Chile		22,057	Parinacota, Bolivia-Chile		20,768	Quela, Argentina		20,128
El Libertador, Argentina		22,047	Tortolas, Argentina-Chile		20,745	Condoriri, Bolivia		20,095
Cachi, Argentina		22,047	Ampato, Peru		20,702	Palermo, Argentina		20,079
Yerupaja, Peru		21,765	Condor, Argentina		20,669	Solimana, Peru		20,068
Galan, Argentina		21,654	Salcantay, Peru		20,574	San Juan, Argentina-Chile		20,049
El Muerto, Argentina-Chile		21,457	Chimborazo, Ecuador		20,561	Sierra Nevada, Arg.-Chile		20,023
Sajama, Bolivia		21,391	Huancarhuas, Peru		20,531	Antofalla, Argentina		20,013
Nacimiento, Argentina		21,302	Cen. Manuel Belgrano, Arg		20,505	Marmolejo, Argentina-Chile		20,013
Illimani, Bolivia		21,201	Pumasillo, Peru		20,492	Licancabur, Argentina-Chile		19,425
Coropuna, Peru		21,079						

The highest point in the West Indies is in the Dominican Republic, Pico Duarte (10,417 ft.).

Africa, Australia and Oceania

Mountain and Country	Feet	Mountain and Country	Feet	Mountain and Country	Feet
Kibo (Kilimanjaro), Tanzania.	19,340	Mandala, New Guinea.	15,420	Toubkal, Morocco.	13,665
Kenya, Kenya.	17,058	Ras Dashan, Ethiopia.	15,158	Kinabalu, Malaysia.	13,455
Margherita Pk.,		Meru, Tanzania.	14,979	Lesatima, Kenya.	13,104
Uganda-Zaire.	16,763	Wilhelm, New Guinea.	14,793	Kerintji, Sumatra.	12,467
Djaja, New Guinea.	16,500	Karisimbi, Zaire-Rwanda.	14,787	Cook, New Zealand.	12,349
Pilimsit, New Guinea.	15,748	Elgon, Kenya-Uganda.	14,178	Teide, Canary Islands.	12,198
Trikora, New Guinea.	15,585	Batu, Ethiopia.	14,131	Kosciusko, Australia.	7,310
		Gughe, Ethiopia.	13,780		

Europe

Peak	Feet	Peak	Feet	Peak	Feet	Peak	Feet
Alps						**Pyrenees**	
		Hohberghorn.	13,842	Fiescherhorn.	13,283		
Mont Blanc.	15,771	Alphubel.	13,799	Grunhorn.	13,266	Aneto.	11,168
Monte Rose (high-		Rimpfischhorn.	13,776	Lauteraarhorn.	13,261	Posets.	11,073
est peak of group).	15,203	Aletschorn.	13,763	Durrenhorn.	13,238	Perdido.	11,007
Dom.	14,911	Strahlhorn.	13,747	Allalinhorn.	13,213	Maladeta.	10,866
Liskamm.	14,852	Dent d'Herens.	13,686	Weissmies.	13,199	Vignemale.	10,820
Weisshorn.	14,780	Breithorn.	13,665	Lagginhorn.	13,156	Long.	10,479
Taschhorn.	14,733	Bishorn.	13,645	Fletschhorn.	13,110	Estats.	10,304
Matterhorn.	14,690	Jungfrau.	13,642	Zupo.	13,109	Montcalm.	10,105
Dent Blanche.	14,293	Ecrins.	13,461	Adlerhorn.	13,081	**Caucasus (Europe-Asia)**	
Nadelhorn.	14,196	Monch.	13,448	Gletscherhorn.	13,068	El'brus.	18,510
Grand Combin.	14,154	Pollux.	13,422	Schalihorn.	13,040	Shkara.	17,064
Lenzspitze.	14,088	Schreckhorn.	13,379	Scerscen.	13,028	Dykh Tau.	17,054
Finsteraarhorn.	14,022	Ober Gabelhorn.	13,330	Eiger.	13,025	Kashtan Tau.	16,877
Castor.	13,865	Gran Paradiso.	13,323	Jagerhorn.	13,024	Kazbek.	16,558
Zinalrothorn.	13,849	Bernina.	13,284	Rottalhorn.	13,022	Dzhangi Tau.	16,565

Asia

Peak	Country	Feet	Peak	Country	Feet
Everest.	Nepal-Tibet.	29,028	Istoro Nal.	Pakistan.	24,240
K2 (Godwin Austen).	Kashmir.	28,250	Tent Peak.	Nepal-Sikkim.	24,088
Kanchenjunga.	Nepal-Sikkim.	28,208	Chamlang.	Nepal.	24,012
Lhotse I (Everest).	Nepal-Tibet.	27,923	Kabru.	Nepal-Sikkim.	24,002
Makalu I.	Nepal-Tibet.	27,824	Alung Gangri.	Tibet.	24,000
Lhotse II (Everest).	Nepal-Tibet.	27,560	Chomo Lhari.	Tibet-Bhutan.	23,997
Dhaulagiri.	Nepal.	26,810	Baltoro Kangri.	Kashmir.	23,990
Manaslu I.	Nepal.	26,760	Mussu Shan.	Sinkiang.	23,890
Cho Oyu.	Nepal-Tibet.	26,750	Mana.	India.	23,860
Nanga Parbat.	Kashmir.	26,660	Baruntse.	Nepal.	23,688
Annapurna.	Nepal.	26,504	Amne Machin.	China.	23,490
Gasherbrum.	Kashmir.	26,470	Nepal Peak.	Nepal-Sikkim.	23,458
Broad.	Kashmir.	26,400	Pumori.	Nepal-Tibet.	23,442
Gosainthan.	Tibet.	26,287	Gauri Sankar.	Nepal-Tibet.	23,440
Annapurna II.	Nepal.	26,041	Badrinath.	India.	23,420
Gyachung Kang.	Nepal-Tibet.	25,910	Nunkun.	Kashmir.	23,410
Disteghil Sar.	Kashmir.	25,868	Lenina Peak.	USSR.	23,405
Himalchuli.	Nepal.	25,801	Api.	Nepal.	23,399
Nuptse (Everest).	Nepal-Tibet.	25,726	Trisul.	India.	23,360
Masherbrum.	Kashmir.	25,660	Kangto.	India-Tibet.	23,260
Nanda Devi.	India.	25,645	Nyenchhen Thangiha.	Tibet.	23,255
Chomo Lonzo.	Nepal-Tibet.	25,640	Tirsuli.	India.	23,210
Rakaposhi.	Kashmir.	25,550	Dunagiri.	India.	23,184
Kamet.	India-Tibet.	25,447	Pauhunri.	Sikkim-Tibet.	23,180
Namcha Barwa.	Tibet.	25,445	Lombo Kangra.	Tibet.	23,165
Gurla Mandhata.	Tibet.	25,355	Saipal.	Nepal.	23,100
Ulugh Muz Tagh.	Tibet-Sinkiang.	25,340	Macha Pucchare.	Nepal.	22,958
Kungur.	Sinkiang.	25,325	Numbar.	Nepal.	22,817
Tirich Mir.	Pakistan.	25,230	Kanjiroba.	Nepal.	22,580
Makalu II.	Nepal-Tibet.	25,130	Ama Dablam.	Nepal.	22,494
Minya Konka.	China.	24,900	Pyramid.	Nepal-Sikkim.	22,430
Kula Gangri.	Tibet-Bhutan.	24,784	Cho Polu.	Nepal.	22,093
Changtse (Everest).	Nepal-Tibet.	24,780	Lingtren.	Nepal-Tibet.	21,972
Muz Tagh Ata.	Sinkiang.	24,757	Khumbutse.	Nepal-Tibet.	21,785
Skyang Kangri.	Kashmir.	24,750	Hlako Gangri.	Tibet.	21,266
Communism Peak.	USSR.	24,590	Mt. Grosvenor.	China.	21,190
Jongsong Peak.	Nepal-Sikkim.	24,472	Thagchhab Gangri.	Tibet.	20,970
Pobedy Peak.	Sinkiang-USSR.	24,406	Damavand.	Iran.	18,934
Sia Kangri.	Kashmir.	24,350	Ararat.	Turkey.	16,946
Haramosh Peak.	Pakistan.	24,272			

Antarctica

Peak	Feet	Peak	Feet	Peak	Feet
Vinson Massif.	16,860	Miller.	13,650	Falla.	12,549
Tyree.	16,290	Long Gables.	13,620	Rucker.	12,520
Shinn.	15,750	Dickerson.	13,517	Goldthwait.	12,510
Gardner.	15,375	Giovinetto.	13,412	Morris.	12,500
Epperly.	15,100	Wade.	13,400	Erebus.	12,450
Kirkpatrick.	14,855	Fisher.	13,386	Campbell.	12,434
Elizabeth.	14,698	Fridtjof Nansen.	13,350	Don Pedro Christophersen.	12,355
Markham.	14,290	Wexler.	13,202	Lysaght.	12,326
Bell.	14,117	Lister.	13,200	Huggins.	12,247
Mackellar.	14,098	Shear.	13,100	Sabine.	12,200
Anderson.	13,957	Odishaw.	13,008	Astor.	12,175
Bentley.	13,934	Donaldson.	12,894	Mohl.	12,172
Kaplan.	13,878	Ray.	12,808	Frakes.	12,064
Andrew Jackson.	13,750	Sellery.	12,779	Jones.	12,040
Sidley.	13,720	Waterman.	12,730	Gjelsvik.	12,008
Ostenso.	13,710	Anne.	12,703	Coman.	12,000
Minto.	13,668	Press.	12,566		

How Deep Is the Ocean?

Principal Ocean Depths. **Source:** Defense Mapping agency Hydrographic Center

Name of Area	Location		Depth Meters	Depth Fathoms	Feet	Ship and/or Country	Year

Pacific Ocean

Name of Area	Location		Meters	Fathoms	Feet	Ship and/or Country	Year
Mariana Trench	11°21′N,	142°12′E	11,034	6,033	36,198	Vityaz (USSR)	1957
	11°19′N,	142°15′E	10,863	5,939	35,631	HMS Challenger	1951
	11°20′N	142°16′E	10,815	5,910	35,460	″ ″ (UK)	1951
	11°18.5′S,	142°15.5′E	10,910	5,967	35,800	Bathyscaph Trieste	1960
Tonga Trench	23°15.3′S,	174°44.7′W	10,882	5,950	34,702	Vityaz (USSR)	1957
	24°00′S,	175°00′W	10,850	5,933	35,598	Nat'l Geographic	1965
	23°16′S,	174°46′W	10,633	5,814	34,884	US Horizon	1953
Kuril Trench	44°15.2′N,	150°34.2′E	10,542	5,764	34,587	Vityaz (USSR)	1954
	44°18′N,	150°30′E	10,382	5,677	34,062	Vityaz (USSR)	1953
Philippine Trench	10°24′N,	126°40′E	10,539	5,763	34,578	Galathea (Danish)	1951
(Mindanao)	10°27′N,	126°39.5′E	10,497	5,740	34,440	USS Cape Johnson	1945
Izu Trench	30°32′N,	142°31′E	10,374	5,673	34,038	USS Ramapo	1932
	30°30′N,	142°30′E	9,985	5,459	32,751	Bathymetric Map (USSR)	1964
	31°54′N,	142°00′E	9,915	5,420	32,521	Bathymetric Map (USSR)	1964
	30°49′N,	142°18′E	9,441	5,159	30,954	Mansyu (Japan)	1924
Kermadec Trench	31°52.8′S,	177°20.6′W	10,047	5,494	32,964	Vityaz(USSR)	1957
	31°51′S,	177°02′W	9,994	5,465	32,790	Galathea (Danish)	1952
Bonin Trench	24°30′N,	143°24′E	9,156	5,005	30,032	Vityaz (USSR)	1964
	24°17′N,	143°23′E	9,150	5,002	30,012	USS Salt Lake City	1945
New Britian Trench	06°34′S,	153°55′E	9,140	4,998	29,988	Planet(German)	1910
	06°18′S,	153°48′E	9,103	4,976	29,858	Bathmetric Map (USSR)	1964
	06°18′S,	153°43′E	8,936	4,886	29,316	USS Blackfin	1959
Yap Trench	08°33′N,	138°02′E	8,527	4,662	27,976	Vityaz (USSR)	1958
	08°08′N,	137°49′E	8,028	4,390	26,340	USCGC Kukui	1965
	07°55′N,	137°39′E	8,028	4,390	26,340	USS Greenfish	1965
Japan Trench	36°08′N,	142°43′E	8,412	4,597	27,591	Bathemetric Map (USSR)	1964
Palau Trench	07°40′N,	135°04′E	8,138	4,449	26,693	Stefan (Germany)	1905
	07°31′N,	134°56′E	7,324	4,005	24,030	USCGC Ironwood	1966
Aleutian Trench	50°53′N,	176°23′E	8,100	4,429	26,574	USCGC Bering Strait	
	51°13′N,	174°48′E	7,882	4,276	25,656	USCGC Chelan	1936
	50°51′N,	172°16′E	7,679	4,199	25,194	Coast & Geodetic	1936
	50°41′N,	177°11′E	7,666	4,192	25,152	Coast & Geodetic	1966
Peru Chile Trench	23°18′S,	71°41′W	8,064	4,409	26,454	USSpencerF.Baird	1957
(Atacama Trench)	23°27′S,	71°21′W	8,064	4,409	26,454	IGY	
	21°00′S,	71°15′W	7,920	4,330	25,980	US Atlantis	1955
New Hebrides Trench	20°36′S,	168°37′E	7,570	4,138	24,830	Planet(Germany)	1910
Ryukyu Trench	25°15′N,	128°32′E	7,507	4,105	24,629	Mansyu (Japan)	1925
	24°00′N,	126°48′E	7,181	3,926	23,554	Bathymetric Map (USSR)	1964
Mid. America Trench	14°02′N,	93°39′W	6,669	3,642	21,852	USS Epce	1965

Atlantic Ocean

Name of Area	Location		Meters	Fathoms	Feet	Ship and/or Country	Year
Puerto Rico Trench	19°35′N,	68°17′W	8,648	4,729	28,374	US Archerfish	1961
	19°45′N,	67°49′W	8,528	4,663	27,978	US Rehoboth	1955
	19°44′N,	67°22′W	8,497	4,646	27,876	San Pablo, Rehoboth	1955
	19°53′N,	66°55′W	8,476	4,635	27,810	US San Pablo	1955
	19°41′N,	67°17′W	8,416	4,602	27,612	US San Pablo	1955
	19°45.5′N,	67°09.7′W	8,604	4,589	27,534	USNS Wyman	1972
	19°42′N,	67°05′W	8,381	4,583	27,498	US Vema	1954
Cayman Trench	19°12′N,	80°00′W	7,535	4,120	24,720	US Vema	1960
	18°59′N,	80°12′W	7,211	3,943	23,658	(British Admiralty)	1955
	18°59′N,	80°23′W	7,191	3,932	23,592	″ ″	1955
	19°03′N,	80°22′W	7,491	4,096	24,576	(Germany)	1937
So. Sandwich Trench	55°14′S,	26°29′W	8,252	4,512	27,072	USS Eltanin	1963
	55°08′S,	26°04′W	8,246	4,509	27,054	USS Eltanin	1963
	55°08′S,	26°05′W	8,219	4,494	26,964	USS Eltanin	1963
	55°07′S,	26°46′W	8,264	4,518	27,113	Meteor (Germany)	1926
Romanche Gap	00°16′S,	18°35′W	7,864	4,300	25,800	US Vema	1957
	00°13′S,	18°26′W	7,729	4,226	25,356	USS Albatross	1948
Brazil Basin	09°10′S,	23°02′W	5,119	3,346	20,076	US Vema	1956

Indian Ocean

Name of Area	Location		Meters	Fathoms	Feet	Ship and/or Country	Year
Java Trench	10°15′S,	109°E′(approx.)	7,725	4,224	25,344	Nat'l Geographic	1967
	10°20′S,	110°10′E	7,450	4,073	24,442	(British Admiralty)	1928
	10°19′S,	108°50′E	7,457	3,977	23,862	Australian Navy Hydrographer	1962
Ob Trench	(no position)		6,874	3,759	22,553	Nat'l Geographic	1967
Vema Trench	(no position)		6,402	3,501	21,004	Nat'l Geographic	1967
Agulhas Basin	(no position)		6,195	3,388	20,325	Nat'l Geographic	1967
Diamantina Trench	35°00′S,	105°35′E	6,062	3,315	19,890	Nat'l Geographic	1967

Arctic Ocean

Name of Area	Location		Meters	Fathoms	Feet	Ship and/or Country	Year
Eurasia Basin	82°23′N,	19°31′E	5,450	2,980	17,880	Fidor Lithke (USSR)	1955

Mediterranean Sea

Name of Area	Location		Meters	Fathoms	Feet	Ship and/or Country	Year
Ionion Basin	36°32′N,	21°06′E	5,150	2,816	16,896	USS Taner	1955
	35°51′N,	22°18′E	5,005	2,737	16,420	Calypso (French)	1955

Ocean Area and Average Depth

Four major bodies of water are recognized by geographers and mapmakers. They are: the Pacific, Atlantic, Indian and Arctic Oceans. The Atlantic and Pacific Oceans are considered divided at the equator into the No. and So. Atlantic; the No. and So. Pacific. The Arctic Ocean is the name for waters north of the continental land masses in the region of the Arctic Circle.

	Sq. Miles	Avg. Depth		Sq. Miles	Avg. Depth
Pacific Ocean	64,186,300	13,739	Hudson Bay	281,900	305
Atlantic Ocean	33,420,000	12,257	East China Sea	256,600	620
Indian Ocean	28,350,500	12,704	Andaman Sea	218,100	3,667
Arctic Ocean	3,662,200	4,362	Black Sea	196,100	3,906
South China Sea	1,148,500	4,802	Red Sea	174,900	1,764
Caribbean Sea	971,400	8,448	North Sea	164,900	308
Mediterranean Sea	969,100	4,926	Baltic Sea	147,500	180
Bering Sea	873,000	4,893	Yellow Sea	113,500	121
Gulf of Mexico	582,100	5,297	Gulf of California	59,100	2,375
Sea of Okhotsk	537,500	3,192	Persian Gulf	88,800	328
Sea of Japan	391,100	5,468			

The Malayan Sea is not considered a geographical entity but a term used for convenience for waters between the South Pacific and the Indian Ocean.

Principal World Rivers

Source: National Geographic Society, Washington, D.C. (Length in miles)

River	Outflow	Lgth	River	Outflow	Lgth	River	Outflow	Lgth
Albany	James Bay	610	Japura	Amazoon River	1,750	Rhone	Gulf of Lion	505
Amazon	Atlantic Ocean	4,000	Jordan	Dead Sea	200	Rio de la Plata	Atlantic Ocean	150
Amu	Aral Sea	1,578	Kootenay	Columbia Riv	407	Rio Grande	Gulf of Mexico	1,885
Amur	Tatar Strait	2,705	Leena	Laptev Sea	2,653	Rio Roosevelt	Aripuana	400
Angara	Yenisey River	1,151	Loire	Bay of Biscay	634	Saguenay	St. Lawrence R.	105
Arkansas	Mississippi	1,450	Mackenzie	Arctic Ocean	2,635	St. John	Bay of Fundy	418
Back	Arctic Ocean	605	Madeira	Amazon River	2,013	St. Lawrence	Gulf of St. Law.	760
Brahmaputra	Bay of Bengal	1,800	Magdalena	Caribbean Sea	956	St. Maurice	St. Lawrence R.	325
Bug, Southern	Dnieper River	532	Marne	Seine River	326	Salween	Andaman Sea	1,500
Bug, Western	Wisla River	481	Mekong	S. China Sea	2,600	Sao Francisco	Atlantic Ocean	1,988
Canadian	Arkansas River	906	Meuse	North Sea	580	Saskatchewan	Lake Winnipeg	1,615
Churchill, Man.	Hudson Bay	1,000	Mississippi	Gulf of Mexico	2,348	Seine	English Chan.	482
Churchill, Que.	Atlantic Ocean	408	Missouri	Mississippi	2,466	Shannon	Atlantic Ocean	230
Colorado	Gulf of Calif.	1,450	Murray-Darling	Indian Ocean	2,310	Snake	Columbia Riv.	1,038
Columbia	Pacific Ocean	1,214	Negro	Amazon	1,400	Sungari	Amur River	1,150
Congo	Atlantic Ocean	2,716	Nelson	Hudson Bay	400	Syr	Aral Sea	1,370
Danube	Black Sea	1,776	Niger	Gulf of Guinea	2,600	Tajo, Tagus	Atlantic Ocean	626
Dnieper	Black Sea	1,420	Nile	Mediterranean	4,187	Tennessee	Ohio River	652
Dniester	Black Sea	877	Ob-Irtysh	Gulf of Ob	3,460	Thames	North Sea	215
Don	Sea of Azov	1,224	Oder	Baltic Sea	567	Tiber	Tyrrhenian Sea.	252
Drava	Danube River	447	Ohio	Mississippi	975	Tigris	Euphrates	1,180
Dvina, North	White Sea	466	Orange	Atlantic Ocean	1,300	Tisza	Danube River	600
Dvina, West.	Gulf of Riga	634	Orinoco	Atlantic Ocean	1,281	Tocantins	Para River	1,677
Ebro	Mediterranean	565	Ottawa	St. Lawrence R.	696	Ural	Caspian Sea	1,575
Elbe	North Sea	724	Paraguay	Parana River	1,584	Uruguay	Rio de la Plata	1,000
Euphrates	Persian Gulf	2,235	Parana	Rio de la Plata	1,827	Usumacinta	Gulf of Mexico	270
Fraser	Str. of Georgia	850	Peace	Slave River	1,195	Volga	Caspian Sea	2,293
Gambia	Atlantic Ocean	700	Pilcomayo	Paraguay River	1,000	Weser	North Sea	400
Ganges	Bay of Bengal	1,557	Po	Adriatic Sea	405	Wisla	Bay of Danzig	675
Garonne	Bay of Biscay	357	Purus	Amazon River	2,100	Yangtze	E. China Sea	3,434
Hsi	S. China Sea	1,200	Red	Mississippi	1,018	Yellow (See Huang)		
Huang	Yellow Sea	3,000	Red River of N.	Lake Winnipeg	355	Yenisey	Kara Sea	2,566
Iindus	Arabian Sea	1,800	Rhine	North Sea	820	Yukon	Bering Sea	1,979
Irrawaddy	Bay of Bengal	1,300				Zambezi	Indian Ocean	1,700

Continental Statistics

Source: National Geographic Society, Washington, D.C.

Continents	Area (sq. mi.)	% of Earth	Highest Point (In feet)	Lowest Point	Population (est.)	% World Total
Asia	16,988,000	29.5	1 Everest, 29,028	1 Dead Sea, —1,299	2,265,000,000	58
Africa	11,506,000	20.0	2 Kilimanjaro, 19,340	2 Lake Assal, —512	374,000,000	9.7
North America	9,390,000	16.3	3 McKinley, 20,320	3 Death Valley, —282	335,000,000	8.6
South America	6,795,000	11.8	4 Aconcagua, 22,834	4 Valdes Penin., 131	206,000,000	5.3
Europe	3,745,000	6.5	5 El'brus, 18,510	5 Caspian Sea, —92	659,000,000	17
Australia	2,968,000	5.2	6 Kosciusko, 7,310	6 Lake Eyre, —52	13,300,000	0.3
Antarctica	5,500,000	9.6	7 Vinson Massif, 16,860	Not Known		

Important Islands and Their Areas

Source: National Geographic Society, Washington, D.C.

Figure in parentheses shows rank among the world's ten largest islands. Some islands have not been surveyed accurately; in such cases estimated areas are shown. °See footnotes.

Location-Ownership
Area in Square Miles

Arctic Ocean
Canadian Islands

Axel Heiberg	15,779
Baffin (5)	183,810
Banks	23,230
Bathurst	7,609
Devon	20,861
Ellesmere (9)	82,119
Melville	16,369
Prince of Wales	12,830
Somerset	9,370
Southampton	15,700
Victoria (10)	81,930

USSR Islands

Franz Josef Land	6,400
Novaya Zemlya (two ls.)	31,900
Wrangel	2,800

Norwegian Islands

Svalbard	24,100
Nordaust Landet	5,792
Spitsbergen	15,251

Atlantic Ocean

Anticosti, Canada	3,043
Ascension, UK	34
Azores, Portugal	888
Faial	66.2
Sao Miguel	299
Bahama Is.	5,380
Bermuda Is., UK	20.59
Block, Rhode Island	10.8
Canary Is., Spain	2,808
Fuerteventura	670
Gran Canaria	634
Tenerife	919
Cape Breton, Canada	3,970
Cape Verde, Portugal	1,557
Faeroe Is., Denmark	540
Falkland Is., UK	4,618
Fernando de Noronha (Archipelago), Brazil	10
Fernando Poo, Equatorial Guinea	785

British Isles

Great Britain, mainland (8)	84,186
Channel Islands	75
Guernsey	30
Jersey	45
Sark	1.99
Hebrides	2,662
Ireland	32,598
Irish Republic	27,136
Northern Ireland	5,462
Man	227
Orkney Is.	375
Scilly	6.3
Shetland Is.	549
Skye	670
Wight	147
Greenland, Denmark (1)	840,000
Iceland	39,768
Long Island, N. Y.	1,723
Madeira Is., Portugal	308
Marajo, Brazil	1,553
Martha's Vineyard, Mass.	108.7
Mount Desert, Me.	105.4
Nantucket, Mass.	57
Newfoundland, Canada	43,359
Prince Edward, Canada	2,184
St. Helena, UK	47

Location-Ownership
Area in Square Miles

South Georgia, UK	1,450
Tierra del Fuego, Chile and Argentina	18,800
Tristan da Cunha, UK	40

Baltic Sea

Aland, Finland	572
Bornholm, Denmark	217
Gotland, Sweden	1,212

Caribbean Sea

Antigua, UK	170
Aruba, Netherlands	74
Barbados	166
Cuba	44,217
Isle of Pines	1,180
Curacao, Netherlands	182
Dominica, UK	290
Guadeloupe, France	687
Hispaniola, (Haiti and Dominican Republic)	29,530
Jamaica	4,232
Martinique, France	425
Puerto Rico, U. S.	3,435
Tobago	116
Trinidad	1,864
Virgin Is., U.S.	133

Indian Ocean

Andamans, India	2,500
Ceylon	25,332
Madagascar (Malagasy Republic) (4)	226,657
Mauritius	720
Pemba, Tanzania	380
Reunion, France	969
Seychelles, UK	145
Zanzibar, Tanzania	950

Persian Gulf

Bahrain	231

Mediterranean Sea

Balearic Is., Spain	1,936
Corfu, Greece	246
Corsica, France	3,367
Crete, Greece	3,207
Cyprus	3,572
Elba, Italy	87.4
Malta	122
Rhodes, Greece	545
Sardinia, Italy	9,194
Sicily, Italy	9,817
Euboea, Greece	1,508

Pacific Ocean

Aleutian Is., U. S.	6,821
Adak	289
Amchitka	114
Attu	318
Kanaga	135
Kiska	110
Tanaga	185
Umnak	675
Unalaska	1,064
Unimak	1,600
Canton, U. S., UK*	
Caroline Is., U. S. trust terr.	
Christmas, U. S. UK*	52
Diomede, Big, USSR	11.3
Diomede, Little, U.S.	2.4

Location-Ownership
Area in Square Miles

Easter, Chile	63.9
Formosa (Taiwan)	13,885
Funafuti, U. K., U. S.*	17
Galapagos Is., Ecuador	3,028
Guadalcanal, UK	1,130
Hainan, China	13,000
Hawaiian, U. S.	6,450
Hawaii	4,037
Oahu	596
Hong Kong, UK	29
Japan	142,811
Hokkaido	30,077
Honshu (7)	89,008
Iwo Jima	7.8
Kyushu	13,768
Okinawa	454
Shikoku	6,857
Kodiak, U.S.	3,670
Mariana Is., U.S. trust terr. excluding Guam	184
Guam, U. S.	212
Marquesas Is., France	492
Marshall Is., U. S. trust terr.	69.8
Bikini*	
Nauru	8.2
New Caledonia, France	7,336
New Guinea (2)	305,577
New Hebrides, UK-Fr.	5,700
New Zealand	103,739
Chatham	372
North	44,281
South	58,093
Stewart	670
Philippines	115,830
Leyte	3,090
Luzon	41,845
Mindanao	36,381
Mindoro	3,995
Negros	5,278
Palawan	5,751
Panay	4,749
Samar	5,184
Quemoy, Formosa	50
Sakhalin, USSR	29,498
Samoa Islands	1,173
American Samoa	76
Tutuila	53
Western Samoa	1,097
Savaii	662
Upolu	430
Santa Catalina, U. S.	74
Tahiti, France	402
Tasmania, Australia	26,383
Tonga Is.	270
Vancouver, Canada	12,408
Vanua Levi (Fiji)	2,137
Viti Levu (Fiji)	4,010

East Indies

Bali, Indonesia	2,269
Borneo, Indonesia- Malaysia, UK (3)	280,107
Celebes, Indonesia	72,987
Java, Indonesia	48,763
Madura, Indonesia	2,113
Moluccas, Indonesia	28,767
New Britain, Aust.	14,600
New Ireland, Aust.	3,340
Sumatra, Indonesia (6)	182,860
Timor	13,071
Indonesian Timor	5,800
Portuguese Timor	5,763

Australia, often called an island, is a continent. Its mainland area is 2,968,000 sq mi.

Islands in minor waters: Manhattan (31 sq. mi.) Staten (64 sq. Mi.) and Governors (173 acres), all in New York Harbor, U.S.; Isle Royale (209.9 sq. mi.), Lake Superior, U.S.; Manitoulin (1,068 sq. mi.), Lake Huron, Canada; Penang (110 sq. mi.), Strait of Malacca, Malaysia; Singapore (224 sq. mi.), Singapore Strait, Singapore.

Atolls: Bikini (lagoon area, 280 sq. mi., land area 2.87 sq. mi.), U.S. Trust Territory of the Pacific Islands; Canton (lagoon 20 sq. mi., land 4.3 sq. mi.), U.S. and UK; Christmas (lagoon 89 sq. mi., land 52 sq. mi.), U.S. and UK; Funafuti (lagoon 84 sq. mi., land 17 sq. mi.) U.S. and UK.

Major Rivers in North America
Source: U.S. Geological Survey

River	Source or Upper Limit of Length	Outflow	Miles
Alabama	Gilmer County, Ga.	Mobile River	735
Albany	Lake St. Joseph	James Bay	320
Allegheny	Potter County, Pa.	Ohio River	325
Altamaha-Ocmulgee	Junction of Yellow and South Rivers, Newton County, Ga.	Atlantic Ocean	392
Apalachicola-Chattahoochee	Towns County, Ga.	Gulf of Mexico, Fla.	524
Assiniboine	Eastern Saskatchewan	Red River	450
Arkansas	Lake County, Colo.	Mississippi River, Ark.	1,459
Atchafalaya	Red River, La.	Grand Lake, La.	135
Attawapiskat	Attawapiskat	James Bay	465
Black (N.W.T)	Contwoyto Lake	Chantrey Inlet	600
Big Black (Miss.)	Webster County, Miss.	Mississippi River	330
Big Horn	Junction of Wind and Popo Agie Rivers, Fremont County, Wyo.	Yellowstone River, Mont.	336
Black (Mo.-Ark.)	Junction Middle and West Forks, Reynolds County, Mo.	White River	280
Bow	Rocky Mountains	South Saskatchewan River	315
Brazos	Junction of Salt and Double Mountain Forks, Stonewall County, Tex.	Gulf of Mexico	870
Canadian	Las Animas County, Colo.	Arkansas River, Okla.	906
Cape Fear	Junction of Haw and Deep Rivers, Chatham County, N.C.	Alantic Ocean	202
Cedar (Iowa)	Dodge County, Minn.	Iowa River, Iowa	329
Cheyenne	Junction of Antelope Creek and Dry Fork, Converse County, Wyo.	Missouri River	290
Churchill	Methy Lake	Hudson Bay	1,000
Cimarron	Colfax County, N. Mex.	Arkansas River, Okla.	600
Clark Fork-Pend Oreille	Silver Bow County, Mont.	Columbia River, B.C.	505
Colorado (Ariz.)	Rocky Mountain National Park, Colo. (90 miles in Mexico)	Gulf of Calif., Mexico	1,450
Colorado (Texas)	West Texas	Matagorda Bay	840
Columbia	Columbia Lake, British Columbia	Pacific Ocean, bet. Ore. and Wash.	1,243
Columbia, Upper	Columbia Lake, British Columbia	To mouth of Snake River	890
Colville	Brooks Range	Beaufort Sea	350
Connecticut	Third Connecticut Lake, N.H.	L.I. Sound, Conn.	407
Coosa	Junction of Etowah and Oostanaula River, Floyd County, Ga.	Alabama River	286
Copper	Alaska Range	Gulf of Alaska	280
Coppermine (N.W.T.)	Lac de Gras	Coronation Gulf (Atlantic Ocean)	525
Cumberland	Letcher County, Ky.	Ohio River	720
Delaware	Schoharie County, N.Y.	Liston Point, Delaware Bay	390
Deschutes	Lava Lake, Deschutes County, Ore.	Columbia River	250
Des Moines	Junction of East and West Forks, Humboldt County, Iowa	Mississippi River	327
Dolores	Dolores County, Colo.	Colorado River	230
Flint	Hapeville, Fulton County, Ga.	Apalachicola River	265
Fraser	Near Mount Robson (on Continental Divide)	Strait of Georgia	850
French Broad	Junction of North and West Forks, Transylvania County, N.C.	Tennessee River	210
Gila	Catron County, N. Mex.	Colorado River, Ariz.	630
Grand (Mich.)	Jackson County, Mich.	Lake Michigan	260
Great Whale (Que.)	Lake Bienville	Hudson Bay	230
Green (Ky.)	Lincoln County, Ky.	Ohio River, Ky.	360
Green (Utah-Wyo.)	Junction of Wells and Trail Creeks, Sublette County, Wyo.	Colorado River, Utah	730
Hamilton (Lab.)	Lake Ashuanipi	Atlantic Ocean	600
Hudson	Henderson Lake, Essex County, N.Y.	Upper N.Y. Bay, N.Y.-N.J.	306
Humboldt	Wells, Nev.	Humboldt Lake	390
Illinois	St. Joseph County, Ind.	Mississippi River	420
Iowa	Hancock County, Iowa	Mississippi River	291
James (N. Dak.-S. Dak.)	Wells County, N.Dak.	Missouri River, S. Dak.	710
James (Va.)	Junction of Jackson and Cowpasture Rivers, Botetourt County, Va.	Hampton Roads	340
Jefferson-Beaverhead-Red Rock	Source of Red Rock River in Beaverhead County, Mont.	Missouri River	217
John Day	Blue Mountains, Grant County, Ore.	Columbia River	281
Kanawha-New	Junction of North and South Forks of New River, N.C.	Ohio River	352
Kentucky	Junction of North and Middle Forks, Lee County	Ohio River	259
Klamath	Lake Ewauna, Klamath Falls, Ore.	Pacific Ocean	250
Koyukuk	Endicott Mountains, Alaska	Yukon River	470
Kuskokwim	Alaska Range	Kuskokwim Bay	680
Liard	Southern Yukon	Mackenzie River	570
Licking	Magoffi County, Ky.	Ohio River	350
Little Colorado	Latitude 34°, Apache County, Ariz.	Colorado River	300
Little Missouri	Crook County, Wyo.	Missouri River	560
Mackenzie	Great Slave Lake	Arctic Ocean	900
Milk	Junction of North and South Forks, Alberta Province	Missouri River, Mont.	625
Minnesota	Big Stone Lake, Minn.	Mississippi River, St. Paul, Minn.	332
Mississippi	Lake Itasca, Minn.	Mouth of Southwest Pass	2,348

River	Source or Upper Limit of Length	Outflow	Miles
Mississippi, Upper	Lake Itasca, Minn.	To mouth of Missouri R.	1,171
Mississippi-Missouri-Red Rock	Source of Red Rock River, Mont.	Mouth of Southwest Pass	3,710
Missouri	Junction of Jefferson, Madison, and Gallatin Rivers, Madison County, Mont.	Mississippi River	2,315
Missouri-Red Rock	Source of Red Rock River, Mont.	Mississippi River	2,533
Mobile-Alabama-Coosa	Gilmer County, Ga.	Mobile Bay	780
Neches	Van Zandt County, Tex.	Sabine Lake	280
Nelson (Manitoba)	Lake Winnipeg	Hudson Bay	410
Neosho	Morris County, Kans.	Arkansas River, Okla.	460
Neuse	Junction of Eno, Little, and Flat Rivers, Durham County, N.C.	Pamlico Sound	260
New	Junction of North and South Forks, Ashe County, N.C.	Kanawha River	255
Niobrara	Niobrara County, Wyo.	Missouri River, Nebr.	431
Noatak	Brooks Range, Alaska	Kotzebue Sound	350
North Canadian	Union County, N.Mex.	Canadian River, Okla.	760
North Platte	Junction of Grizzly and Little Grizzly Creeks, Jackson County, Colo.	Platte River, Nebr.	618
Nueces	Edwards County, Tex.	Nueces Bay	338
Ohio	Junction of Allegheny and Monongahela Rivers, Pittsburgh, Pa.	Mississippi River, Ill.-Ky.	981
Ohio-Allegheny	Potter County, Pa.	Mississippi River	1,306
Osage	East-central Kansas	Missouri River, Mo.	500
Ottawa	Lake Capimitchigama	St. Lawrence	696
Ouachita	Polk County, Ark.	Red River, La.	605
Owyhee	Elko County, Nev.	Snake River	250
Pearl	Neshoba County, Miss.	Gulf of Mexico, Miss.-La.	411
Peace	Stikine Mountains	Slave River	1,054
Pecos	Mora County, N. Mex.	Rio Grande, Texas	735
Pee Dee	Junction of Yadkin and Uwharrie Rivers, Montgomery County, N.C.	Winyah Bay	233
Pee Dee-Yadkin	Watauga County, N.C.	Winyah Bay, S.C.	435
Pend Oreille	Near Butte, Mont.	Columbia River	490
Platte	Junction of North and South Platte Rivers, Nebr.	Missouri River, Nebr.	310
Porcupine	Ogilvie Mountains, Alaska	Yukon River, Alaska	460
Potomac	Garrett County, Maryland	Chesapeake Bay	383
Powder	Junction of South and Middle Forks, Wyo.	Yellowstone River, Mont.	375
Red (Okla.-Tex.-La.)	Curry County, N. Mex.	Mississippi River	1,270
Red River of the North	Junction of Otter Tail and Bois de Sioux Rivers, Wilkin County, Minn.	Lake Winnipeg, Manitoba	545
Republican	Junction of North Fork and Arikaree River, Nebr.	Kansas River, Kans.	445
Rio Grande	San Juan County, Colo.	Gulf of Mexico	1,885
Roanoke	Junction of North and South Forks, Montgomery County, Va.	Albemarle Sound, N.C.	380
Rock (Ill.-Wis.)	Dodge County, Wis.	Mississippi River, Ill.	300
Sabine	Junction of South and Caddo Forks, Hunt County, Tex.	Sabine Lake, Tex.-La.	380
Sacramento	Siskiyou County, Calif.	Suisun Bay	377
St. Francis	Iron County, Mo.	Mississippi River, Ark.	425
St. Johns (Fla.)	Lake Washington, Brevard County, Fla.	Atlantic Ocean	276
St. Joseph	Hillsdale County, Mich.	Lake Michigan	210
St. Lawrence	Lake Ontario	Gulf of St. Lawrence (Atlantic Ocean)	800
Salmon (Idaho)	Custer County, Idaho	Snake River, Idaho	420
San Joaquin	Junction of South and Middle Forks, Madera County, Calif.	Suisun Bay	350
San Juan	Silver Lake, Archuleta County, Colo.	Colorado River, Utah	360
Santee-Wateree-Catawba	McDowell County, N.C.	Atlantic Ocean, S.C.	538
Saskatchewan, North	Rocky Mountains	Lake Winnipeg	1,100
Saskatchewan, South	Rocky Mountains	Lake Winnipeg	1,205
Savannah	Junction of Seneca and Tugaloo Rivers, Anderson County, S.C.	Atlantic Ocean, Ga.-S.C.	314
Scioto	Auglaize County, Ohio	Ohio River	237
Severn (Ontario)	Sandy Lake	Hudson Bay	610
Skeena (B.C.)	Skeena Mountains	Pacific Ocean	360
Smoky Hill	Cheyenne County, Colo.	Kansas River, Kans.	540
Snake	Teton County, Wyo.	Columbia River, Wash.	1,038
South Platte	Junction of South and Middle Forks, Park County, Colo.	Platte River, Nebr.	424
Stikine	Stikine Range, B.C.	Pacific Ocean	310
Susitna	Alaska Range	Cook Inlet	300
Susquehanna	Otsego Lake, Otsego County, N.Y.	Chesapeake Bay, Md.	444
Tallahatchie	Tippah County, Miss.	Yazoo River, Miss.	301
Tallapoosa	Near Embry in Paulding County, Ga.	Alabama River	268
Tanana	Wrangell Mountains	Yukon River, Alaska	620
Tar-Pamlico	Person County, N.C.	Pamlico Bay	215
Tennessee	Junction of French Broad and Holston Rivers	Ohio River, Ky.	652
Tennessee-French Broad	Bland County, Va.	Ohio River	900
Tombigbee	Prentiss County, Miss.	Mobile River, Ala.	525
Tongue	Junction of North and South Forks, Sheridan County, Wyo.	Yellowstone River	246
Trinity	North of Dallas, Tex.	Galveston Bay, Tex.	360
Wabash	Darke County, Ohio	Ohio River, Ill.-Ind.	529
Washita	Hemphill County, Tex.	Red River, Okla.	500
White (Ark.-Mo.)	Madison County, Ark.	Mississippi River	720
Willamette	Douglas County, Ore.	Columbia River	270
Wisconsin	LeVieux Desert, Vilas County, Wis.	Mississippi River	430
Yellowstone	Park County, Wyo.	Missouri River, N. Dak.	671
Yukon	Junction of Lewes and Pelly Rivers, Yukon	Bering Sea, Alaska	1,770

Flows of Largest Rivers in the United States

(Ranked according to average discharge in cubic feet per second (cfs) at mouth)
Source: U.S. Geological Survey (Average discharges for the period 1941-70)

Rank	River	Average Discharge	Length[a] (miles)	Drainage Area	Most Distant Source	Maximum Discharge at Gaging Station Farthest Downstream	(date)
1	Mississippi	[b]640,000	[c]3,710	[d]1,247,300	Beaverhead Co., Mont.	2,080,000	2-17-37
2	Columbia	262,000	1,243	258,000	Columbia Lake, B.C.	1,240,000	June 1894
3	Ohio	258,000	1,306	203,900	Potter Co., Pa.	1,850,000	2-1-37
4	St. Lawrence	[e]243,000	—	[e]302,000		[f]314,000	May 1870
5	Yukon	[g]240,000	1,770	327,600	Coast Mountains, B.C.	1,030,000	6-22-64
6	[h]Atchafalaya	183,000	135	95,105	Curry Co., N. Mex.		
7	Missouri	76,300	2,533	529,400	Beaverhead Co., Mont.	892,000	June 1844
8	Tennessee	64,000	900	40,910	Bland Co., Va.	500,000	2-17-48
9	Red	[i]62,300	1,270	93,244	Curry Co., N. Mex.	233,000	4-17-45
10	Kuskokwim	62,000	680	49,000	Alaska Range, Alaska	392,000	6-5-64
11	Mobile	61,400	780	43,800	Gilmer, Co., Ga.		
12	Snake	50,000	1,038	109,000	Teton Co., Wyo.	409,000	June 1894
13	Arkansas	45,100	1,459	160,600	Lake Co., Colo.	536,000	5-27-43
14	Copper	[j]43,000	280	24,000	Alaska Range, Alaska	[k]280,000	7-15-71
15	Tanana	[l]41,000	620	44,000	Wrangell Mtn., Alaska	186,000	8-18-67
16	Susitna	[m]40,000	300	20,000	Alaska Range, Alaska	90,700	6-7-64
17	Susquehanna	37,190	444	27,570	Otsego Co., N.Y.	1,080,000	6-23-72
18	Willamette	35,660	270	11,200	Douglas Co., Oreg.	500,000	12-4-1861
19	Alabama	32,400	735	22,600	Gilmer Co., Ga.	267,000	3-7-61
20	White	32,100	720	28,000	Madison Co., Ark.	343,000	4-17-45
21	Wabash	30,400	529	33,150	Darke Co., Ohio	428,000	3-30-13
22	Pend Oreille	29,900	490	25,820	Near Butte, Mont.	171,300	6-13-48
23	Tombigbee	27,300	525	20,100	Prentiss Co., Miss.	280,000	1874 and 1900
24	Cumberland	[n]26,900	720	18,080	Letcher Co., Ky.	201,000	2-18-50
25	Stikine	[o]26,000	310	20,000	Stikine Range, B.C.	120,000	6-26-55
26	Sacramento	—	377	27,100	Siskiyou Co., Calif.	[p]332,000	12-25-64
27	Apalachicola	24,700	524	19,600	Towns Co., Ga.	293,000	3-20-29
28	Illinois	22,800	420	27,900	St. Joseph Co., Ind.	123,000	May 1943
29	Koyukuk	[q]22,000	470	32,400	Endicott Mtns., Alaska	266,000	6-6-64
30	Porcupine	[r]20,000	460	45,000	Ogilvie Mtns., Alaska	289,000	5-25-71
31	Hudson	19,500	306	13,370	Essex Co., N.Y.	215,000	3-19-36
32	Allegheny	19,290	325	11,700	Potter Co., Pa.	365,000	3-18-36
33	Delaware	[s]17,200	390	11,440	Schoharie Co., N.Y.	329,000	8-20-55

(a)-Because river lengths and methods of measurement may change from time to time, the length figures given are subject to revision; (b)-about 25 percent of flow occurs in the Atchafalaya River; (c)-the length from mouth to source of the Mississippi River in Minnesota is 2,348 miles; (d)-at Baptiste Collette Bayou, Louisiana; (e)-at international boundary lat. 45°; (f)-maximum monthly discharge; (g)-period 1957-70; (h)-continuation of Red River; (i)-flow of Ouachita River added; (j)-period 1956-69; (k)-provisional; (l)-period 1962-69; (m)-based on records of Chulitna, Talkeetna, and Yetna Rivers; (n)-period 1931-60; (o)-period 1954-63, summer records only; (p)-discharge of American River not included; (q)-period 1960-69; (r)-period 1964-69; (s)-at Liston Point on Delaware Bay.

Large Rivers in Canada

Source: "Facts from Canadian Maps" Published by Canada Department of Energy Mines and Resources
(Ranked according to mean discharge in cubic feet per second (cfs))

Rank	River	Mean Discharge	Length (miles)	Drainage Area (sq. mi.)
1	St. Lawrence River	348,000	1,900	396,000[1]
2	Mackenzie (to head of Finlay)	343,000	2,635	697,000
3	Fraser	125,000	850	84,800
4	Columbia (International Boundary to head of Columbia Lake)	98,700	498	59,700[2]
5	Nelson (to head of Bow)	83,600	1,600	414,000[3]
6	Yukon (International Boundary to head of Nisutlin)	82,000	714	114,800[4]
7	Ottawa	69,000	790	56,500
8	Churchill (to head of Ashuanipi)	55,700	532	30,800
9	Churchill (to head of Churchill Lake)	42,400	1,000	108,600
10	Saskatchewan (to head of Bow)	24,800	1,205	130,000

(1) Including 195,000 sq. mi. in U.S.A. (2) Including 20,000 sq. mi. in U.S.A. (3) Including 69,500 sq. mi. in U.S.A. (4) Including 9,000 sq. mi. in U.S.A.

The Largest Lake in Each Province of Canada

Source: Standard Encyclopedia of the World's Rivers and Lakes. 1965 & The Canada Yearbook. 1970-1971

Province	Largest within:	Largest partly in:	Shared with	Origin	Area sq. miles	Ft. above sea level
Alta	Claire			Natural	545	699
		Athabasca	Sask.	Natural	940	699
B.C.	Kootenay			Natural	168	1,745
Man.	Winnipeg			Natural	9,465	713
Nfld.	Melville			Natural	1,133	S.L.
N.B.	Grand			Natural	65	Tidal
N.W.T.	Great Bear			Natural	12,275	511
N.S.	Bras d'Or			Natural	360	Tidal
Ont.	Nipigon			Natural	1,870	855
P.E.I.		Huron	U.S.A.	Natural	15,353	580
Que.	Mistassini			Natural	840	1,220
Sask.	Wollaston			Natural	796	1,300
		Athabasca	Alta.	Natural	2,180	699

The Largest Lake in Each State of the United States

Source: National Geographic Society, Washington, D.C.

*indicates reservoir

State	Largest entirely within state	Largest partly in another state	Shared with	Origin	Total Area in square miles	Feet above sea level	Maximum depth feet	Shoreline length miles
Ala.	Wheeler			Man-made	104.8	556	58	1,063
		Guntersville	Tenn.	Man-made	108	595	60	962
Alaska.	Iliamna			Natural	1,010	44	980	297
Ariz.	Painted Rock*			Man-made	83	661	181	—
		Powell	Utah	Man-made	252	3,700	580	1,800
Ark.	Ouachita			Man-made	57	571	190	640
		Bull Shoals	Mo.	Man-made	71	654	203	740
Calif.	Salton Sea			Natural	360	-235	48	—
		Tahoe	Nev.	Natural	192	6,229	1,644	71
Colo.	Blue Mesa*			Man-made	14.3	7,519	333	96
		Navajo*	N. Mex.	Man-made	24.3	6,102	382	157
Conn.	Candlewood			Man-made	8.5	429	85	65
Del.	Lum's Pond			Man-made	.31	50	10	6
Fla.	Okeechobee			Natural	700	14	20	117
Ga.	Sidney Lanier			Man-made	59.4	1,070	156	540
		Clark Hill	S.C.	Man-made	109.4	330	150	1,200
Hawaii.	Waita*			Man-made	.66	233	23	3
Idaho.	Pend Oreille			Natural	146.9	2,064	1,400	120
Ill.	Carlyle			Man-made	40	445	40	83
		Michigan	Wis., Ind., Mich.	Natural	22,300	579	923	1,660
Ind.	Monroe			Man-made	16.8	538	45	142
		Michigan	Wis., Ill., Mich.	Natural	22,300	579	923	1,660
Iowa.	Rathbun*			Man-made	32.8	926	71	180
Kan.	Milford*			Man-made	25.3	1,144	78	163
Ky.	Cumberland			Man-made	78.5	723	183	1,085
		Kentucky	Tenn.	Man-made	247.3	359	60	2,025
La.	Pontchartrain			Natural	621	Sea Lev.	15	117
Me.	Moosehead			Natural	117	1,058	246	—
Md.	Deep Creek			Man-made	7.0	2,462	60	55
		Conowingo*	Penna.	Man-made	13.4	109	110	38
Mass.	Quabbin*			Man-made	39.4	524	150	104
Mich.	Houghton			Natural	30.6	1,138	20	32
		Superior	Wis., Mich., Ont.	Natural	31,700	600	1,333	2,980
Minn.	Red			Natural	751.2	1,175	35	127
		Superior	Wis., Mich., Ont.	Natural	31,700	600	1,333	2,980
Miss.	Ross Barnett*			Man-made	51.5	297	50	150
Mo.	Lake of the Ozarks			Man-made	91.5	660	120	1,150
Mont.	Fort Peck			Man-made	385.9	2,234	220	1,520
Nebr.	McConaughty			Man-made	54.7	3,270	142	105
Nev.	Pyramid			Natural	168.7	3,789	330	66
		Mead	Ariz.	Man-made	247	1,221	432	550
N.H.	Winnipesaukee			Natural	69.6	504	169	240
N.J.	Hopatcong			Natural	4.2	915	60	22
N.M.	Elephant Butte*			Man-made	58.9	4,450	193	250
N.Y.	Oneida			Natural	80	369	55	55
		Erie	Mich., Pa., Ont., Ohio	Natural	9,910	570	210	856
N.C.	Norman			Man-made	50.8	760	100	520
		John H. Kerr*	Va.	Man-made	76.4	320	120	800
N.D.	Sakakawea			Man-made	609	1,850	180	1,605
		Oahe*	S.D.	Man-made	579.7	1,620	200	2,250
Ohio.	Grand			Man-made	20	869	10	60
		Erie	Mich., Pa., N.Y., Ont.	Natural	9,910	570	210	856
Okla.	Eufaula			Man-made	160.1	585	87	600
Ore.	Klamath			Natural	145.3	4,143	45	165
		Goose Lake	Calif.	Natural	193.7	4,716	24	90
Pa.	Wallenpaupack			Man-made	9	1,182	50	45
		Erie	Mich., N.Y., Ohio, Ont.	Natural	9,910	570	210	856
R.I.	Scituate*			Man-made	5.68	284	80	38
S.C.	Marion			Man-made	157	75	35	299
S.D.	Francis Case			Man-made	159.4	1,375	140	540
		Oahe*	N.D.	Man-made	579.7	1,620	200	2,250
Tenn.	Watts Bar*			Man-made	60.3	741	105	783
		Kentucky	Ky.	Man-made	250.5	359	88	2,380
Texas.	Sam Rayburn			Man-made	178.9	173	84	560
		Toledo Bend*	La.	Man-made	308.8	175	—	1,200
Utah.	Great Salt Lake			Natural	1,650	4,200	30	—
Vt.	Bomoseen			Natural	3.7	411	55	19
		Champlain	N.Y., Que.	Natural	490	95	399	—
Va.	Smith Mountain			Man-made	32.2	795	217	500
		John H. Kerr*	N.C.	Man-made	76.4	320	120	800
Wash.	F.D. Roosevelt			Man-made	123.4	1,288	375	660
W. Va.	Tygart			Man-made	5.44	1,010	—	106
Wis.	Winnebago			Natural	215.26	747	21.6	91.96
		Superior	Minn., Mich., Ontario	Natural	31,700	600	1,333	2,980
Wyo.	Yellowstone			Natural	139	7,733	309	110
		Flaming Gorge*	Utah	Man-made	65.7	6,040	437	400

Famous Waterfalls

Source: National Geographic Society, Washington, D. C.

Height=total drop in one or more leaps. †=falls of more than one leap; °=falls that diminish greatly seasonally; ∞=falls that reduce to a trickle or are dry for part of each year. If river names not shown, they are same as the falls. R.=river; L.=lake; (C)=cascade-type. See notes following list.

Name and Location	Ft.
Africa	
Angola	
Duque de Braganca,	
Lucala R.	344
Ruacana, Cunene R.	406
Ethiopia	
Baratieri, Ganale	
Dorya R.	459
Dal Verme, Ganale	
Dorya R.	98
Fincha	508
*Tesissat, Blue Nile R.	140
Lesotho	
Maletsunyane	630
Rhodesia-Zambia	
*Victoria, Zambezi R.	355
South Africa	
*Aughrabies, Orange R.	400
Howick, Umgeni R.	311
† Tugela (5 falls)	3,110
Highest fall	1,350
Tanzania-Zambia	
*Kalambo	726
Uganda	
Kabalega (Murchison) Victoria	
Nile R.	140
Zambia	
Chirombo, Ieisa R.	880

Asia

Name and Location	Ft.
India—**Cauvery	330
† **Gersoppa (Jog),	
Sharavati R.	830
Japan	
**Kegon, L. Chuzenji.	330
Yudaki, L. Yuno	335

Australasia

Name and Location	Ft.
Australia	
New South Wales	
† Wentworth	518
Highest fall	360
Wollomombi	1,100
Queensland	
Coomera	210
Tully	450
New Zealand	
*Bowen (from Glaciers)	540
Helena	890
Stirling	505
† Sutherland, Arthur R.	1,904

Europe

Name and Location	Ft.
Austria—Upper Gastein	207
Lower Gastein	280
(Both on Ache R.)	
† Golling, Schwarzbach R.	200
Krimml (Krimmler)	1,250
France—† Gavarnie (C)	1,385
Great Britain—**Wales**	
Pistyll Cain, Afon Gain R.	150
Pistyll Rhaiadr	240
Scotland	
Glomach	370
Iceland—Detti, Jokul R.	144
Gull, Hvita R.	101

Name and Location	Ft.
Italy—Toce (C)	470
Norway—	
† Eastern Mardalsfoss	1,696
Highest fall	974
Western Mardalsfoss	1,535
(Both on L. Eikesdal)	
Skjeggedal	525
Skykkje, Skykkjua R.	820
Vettis, Morkedola R.	1,214
Highest Fall	889
Voring, Bjoreia R.	597
Sweden	
† Handol, Handol Cr.	345
† *Stora Sjofallet, Lule R.	130
Tannforsen, Are R.	120
Switzerland	
† Gietroz (Glacier) (C)	1,640
† Diesbach	394
† Giessbach	1,312
Handegg, Aare R.	151
Iffigen	394
Pissevache, La Salanfe R.	213
† Reichenbach	656
Rhine	65
† Simmen, Simme R.	459
Stauber	590
Staubbach	984
† Trummelbach	1,312

North America

Name and Location	Ft.
Canada	
British Columbia	
†Takakkaw (Daly Glacier)	1,650
Highest fall	1,200
Della Falls	1,443
Panther, Nigel Cr.	600
Labrador	
Churchill Falls, Churchill R.	245
Mackenzie District	
Virginia, S. Nahanni R.	315
Quebec	
Montmorency	274
Canada—United States	
Niagara: American	193
Horseshoe	186
United States	
California	
Feather, Fall R.	640
Yosemite National Park	
Bridalveil	620
Illilouette	370
Nevada	594
**Ribbon	1,612
Silver Strand	1,170
Vernal	317
†Yosemite	2,425
*Yosemite (upper)	1,430
*Yosemite (lower)	320
*Yosemite (middle)	675
Colorado	
Seven	266
Georgia	
† Tallulah	251
Hawaii	
Akaka	442

Name and Location	Ft.
Idaho	
Henry's Fork (upper)	96
Henry's Fork (lower)	70
**Shoshone, Snake R	195
**Twin, Snake R.	125
Kentucky	
Cumberland	68
Maryland	
Great, Potomac R. (C).	90
Minnesota	
**Minnehaha	54
Montana	
Missouri	75
New Jersey	
**Passaic	70
New York	
Taughannock	215
Oregon	
† Multnomah	620
Highest fall	542
Tennessee	
Fall Creek	256
Rock House Creek	125
Washington	
Fairy Falls	700
Mt. Rainier Nat. Pk.	
Narada, Paradise R.	168
Sluiskin, Paradise R.	300
Palouse	198
Snoqualmie	270
Wisconsin	
Manitou, Black R.	165
Wyoming	
Yellowstone Pk. Tower.	132
Yellowstone (upper)	109
Yellowstone (lower)	308
Mexico—El Salto	218
**Juanacatlan Santiago R.	66

South America

Name and Location	Ft.
Argentina—Brazil	
† Iguazu	237
Brazil—Glass	1,325
Herval	400
Paulo Afonso, Sao Francisco R.	275
Patos-Maribondo, Rio Grande.	115
Urubupunga, Alto Parana R.	40
Brazil–Paraguay	
Sete Quedas, or Guaira	
Alto Parana R.	130
Colombia—Tequendama,	
Bogota R.	427
Catarata de Candelas,	
Cusiana R.	984
Ecuador	
Agoyan, Pastaza R.	200
Guyana	
Kaieteur, Potaro R.	741
King George VI, Utshi R.	1,600
† Marina, Ipobe R.	500
Highest Fall	300
Peru	
Sewerd, Cutibirene R.	877
Venezuela— † Angel	3,212
Highest Fall	2,648
Cuquenan	2,000

The earth has thousands of waterfalls, some of considerable magnitude. Their importance is determined not only by height but volume of flow, steadiness of flow, crest width, whether the water drops sheerly or over a sloping surface, and one leap or a succession of leaps. A series of low falls flowing over a considerable distance is known as a cascade.

Sete Quedas or Guaira is the world's greatest waterfall when its mean annual flow (estimated at 470,000 cusecs, cubic feet per second) is combined with height. A greater volume of water passes over Stanley Falls, though not one of its seven cataracts, spread over nearly 60 miles of the Congo River, exceeds 10 feet.

Estimated mean annual flow, in cusecs, of other major waterfalls are: Niagara, 212,200; Paulo Afonso, 100,000; Urubupunga, 97,000; Iguazu, 61,600; Patos-Maribondo, 53,000; Victoria, 38,400; Churchill, Labrador, 40,000; and Kaieteur, 23,400.

Notable Bridges in North America

Source: State Highway Engineers; Canadian Civil Engineering — ASCE

Asterisk (*) designates Railroad Bridge. Span of a bridge is distance (in feet) between its supports.

Suspension

Year	Bridge	Location	Longest Span
1964	Verrazano-Narrows	New York, N.Y.	4,260
1937	Golden Gate	San. Fran. Bay.	4,200
1957	Mackinac	Sts. of Mackinac	3,800
1931	Geo. Washington	Hudson River	3,500
1952	Tacoma	Washington	2,800
1936	Transbay	San Fran. Bay	2,310
1939	Bronx-Whitestone	East R., N.Y.C.	2,300
1970	Quebec Road	Quebec	2,190
1951	Del. Memorial	Wilmington, Del.	2,150
1968	Del. Mem. (new)	Wilmington, Del.	2,150
1957	Walt Whitman	Phila., Pa.	2,000
1929	Ambassador	Detroit-Canada	1,850
1961	Throgs Neck	Long Is. Sound	1,800
1926	Benjamin Franklin	Philadelphia	1,750
1924	Bear Mt., N.Y.	Hudson River	1,632
1952	²Wm. Preston Lane Mem.	Sandy Point, Md.	1,600
1903	Williamsburg	East R., N.Y.C.	1,600
1969	Newport	Narragansett Bay, R.I.	1,600
1883	Brooklyn	East R., N.Y.C.	1,595
1930	Mid-Hudson, N.Y.	Poughkeepsie	1,500
1954	Vincent Thomas	Los Angeles Har.	1,500
1909	Manhattan	East R., N.Y.C.	1,470
1936	Triborough	East R., N.Y.C.	1,380
1931	St. Johns	Portland, Ore.	1,207
1929	Mount Hope	Rhode Island	1,200
1939	Deer Isle	Maine	1,080
1931	Maysville (Ky.)	Ohio River	1,060
1867	Cincinnati	Ohio River	1,057
1900	Miampimi	Mexico	1,030
1849	Wheeling, W. Va.	Ohio River	1,010
1929	Royal Gorge	Colorado	880
1938	Thousand Islands	St. Lawrence R.	800
1933	Anthony Wayne	Ohio	782
1915	Belpre, O.-W. Va.	Ohio River	775
1904	E. Liv'p'l, O.-W. Va.	Ohio River	750
1933	South 10th St.	Pittsburgh, Pa.	750
1932	Waldo-Hancock	Maine	750
1935	Memorial Twin (Ill.)	Mississippi R.	710

Cantilever

Year	Bridge	Location	Longest Span
1917	*Quebec (Railway)	Quebec	1,800
1970	Chester, Pa.	Delaware River	1,644
1958	New Orleans, La.	Mississippi River	1,575
1936	Transbay	San. Fran. Bay	1,400
1968	Baton Rouge, La.	Mississippi River	1,235
1955	Nyack-Tarrytown	Hudson River	1,212
1930	Longview	Columbia River	1,200
1909	Queensboro	East R., N.Y.C.	1,182
1892	Muscatine, Iowa	Mississippi River	1,164
1932	Savanna-Sabvia, Ill.	Mississippi River	1,160
1927	Carquinez Strait	California	1,100
1958	Parallel Span		1,100
1968	Isaiah D. Hare	Jacksonville, Fla.	1,088
1957	³Richmond	San Fran. Bay	1,070
1929	Grace Memorial	Charleston, S.C.	1,050
1918	MacArthur, Ill.Mo.	Mississippi River	1,000
1963	Newburgh-Beacon	Hudson R., N.Y.	1,000
UC(1975)	Caruthersville, Mo.	Mississippi R.	920
1969	Ohio River	Pt. Pleasant, W.Va.	900
1940	Natchez	Mississippi R.	875
1938	Blue Water	Pt. Huron, Mich.	871
1972	Vicksburg	Mississippi River	870
1954	St. Petersburgh, Fla.	Tampa Bay	864
1940	*Baton Rouge	Mississippi R.	848
1899	*Cornwall	St. Lawrence R.	843
1940	Greenville	Mississippi R.	840
1961	Helena, Ark.	Mississippi R.	840
1963	Brent Spence	Covington, Ky.	831
1963	Cincinnati, O.	Ohio River	830
1956	Earl C. Clements	Ohio R., Ill.-Ky.	825ª
1930	*Vicksburg	Mississippi R.	825
1929	Louisville	Ohio River	820
1943	Jeff'rson Barr'ks., Mo.	Mississippi R.	804
1950	Maurice J. Tobin	Boston, Mass.	800
1935	Rip Van Winkle	Catskill, N.Y.	800
1938	Cairo, Ill.	Ohio River	800
1940	Ludlow Ferry	Potomac R.	800
1932	Washington Mem.	Seattle, Wash.	800

Suspension (continued)

Year	Bridge	Location	Longest Span
1930	Cairo, Ill.	Mississippi R.	800
1936	North Bend, Oreg.	Coos Bay	793
1936	McCullough	Coos Bay, Ore.	793
1935	*Huey P. Long	New Orleans.	790
1916	*Memphis (Harahan)	Mississippi R.	790
1892	*Memphis	Mississippi R.	790
1949	Memphis-Arkansas	Mississippi R.	790
1904	*Mingo Jct., W. Va.	Ohio River	769
1910	*Beaver, Pa.	Ohio River	767
1966	*S.N. Pearman	Charleston, S.C.	760
1940	Owensboro	Ohio River	750
1911	Sewickley, Pa.	Ohio River	750
1928	Outerbridge, N.Y.-N.J.	Arthur Kill.	750
1964	Sunshine, Don'ville	Mississippi, La.	750
1964	Ohio River	Henderson, Ky.	720
1956	Talmadge Memorial	Savannah, Ga.	710
1940	Bridge of the Gods	Oregon	705
1927	Bellaire, O.	Ohio River	700
1955	Belpre, O.-W. Va.	Ohio River	700
1927	Rim to Rim	Twin Falls, Ida	700
1928	Goethals, N.Y.-N.J.	Arthur Kill.	672
1905	*Thebes, Ill.	Mississippi R.	671
1942	Chester, Ill.	Mississippi R.	670
1957	Rappahannock	White Stone, Va.	648
1959	Corpus Christi	Nueces Co., Texas	620
1968	Reedy Point	Ches. & Del. Can.	600
1960	Summit	Ches. & Del. Can.	600
1959	Castleton	Hudson R., N.Y.	600
1943	Gold Star	New London, Conn.	540
1934	Gastineau Channel	Juneau, Alaska.	516
1960	West Piver	Brattleboro, Vt.	440
1953	Luck Peak Reservoir	nr Boise, Idaho	432
1965	Jeremiah Morrow	Warren Co., Ohio.	427
1952	Mormon Pioneer	Omaha	420
1930	Plattsmouth, Nebr.	Missouri River.	403

Simple Truss

Year	Bridge	Location	Longest Span
1917	*Metropolis	Ohio River	720
1929	Paducah, Ky.	Ohio River	716
1922	*Tanana River	Nenana, Alaska.	700
1911	MacArthur	St. Louis	668
1933	*Henderson	Ohio River	665
1967	IR 77, Ohio River.	Marietta, Ohio.	650
1919	Louisville	Ohio River	644
1933	Atchafalaya	Morgan City, La.	608
1924	*Castleton	Hudson River.	598
1906	Elizabethtown	Great Miami R., O.	586
1929	*Louisville	Ohio River	546
1889	*Cincinnati	Ohio River	542
1951	Allegheny River	Allegheny Co., Pa.	533
1914	Pittsburgh	Allegheny R.	531
1930	*Martinez	California	528
1967	Tanana River	Alaska	500
1963	216 Nenana River	Rex, Alaska.	406

Steel Truss

Year	Bridge	Location	Longest Span
1940	Gov. Nice Mem.	Potomac River, Md.	800
1937	US-60, Ky.	Ohio River	800
1938	US-62, Ky.	Green River	700
1952	US-62, Ky.	Cumberland River	700
1940	Jamestown	Jamestown, R.I.	640
1940	Greenville	Mississippi R., Ark.	640
1949	Memphis	Mississippi R., Ark.	621
1938	US-421	Ohio River, Ky.	600
1960	Summit	Chespeak-Del. Canal.	600
1938	US-22	Delaware River, N.J.	540
1972	Mississippi River	Muscatine, Iowa	512
1896	Newport	Ohio River, Ky.	511
1897	Missouri River	Sioux City, Neb.-la.	504
1931	US-60	Cumberland R., Ky.	500
1958	Lake Oahe	Mobridge, S.D.	500
1958	Lake Oahe	Gettysburg, S.D.	500
1910	McKinley, St. Louis	Mississippi River.	500
1963	Millard E. Tydings	Susquehanna R., Md.	490
1930	Lake Champlain	Lake Champlain, N.Y.	434
1952	Bellevue (GAR)	Missouri R., Nebr.	420
1947	Mayo	Blountstown, Fla.	420
1929	Clarendon	White River, Ark.	400
1931	US-60	Tennessee R., Ky.	400
1965	Moyie Springs	Moyie River, Idaho.	378
1944	US-68	Tennessee R., Ky.	368

Year	Name	Location	Length
1929	Augusta	White River, Ark.	360
1932	US-62	Kentucky River	360
1951	SR-80	Fishing Creek, Ky.	360
1953	Lake Francis Case	Chamberlain, S.D.	336
1876	High Bridge, Ky.	Kentucky River	332
1963	US-68	Cumberland R., Ky.	321
1939	US-431	Green & Rough R., Ky.	320
1940	Deep Creek Lake	Deep Creek Lake, Md.	300
1953	Montague Twp.	Delaware River, N.J.	300
1958	Little Colorado	Cameron, Ariz.	296
1950	Somerset	Cumberland R., Ky.	280
1927	US-27	Kentucky River, Ky.	275
1951	Comm. Isaac Hull	Housatonic R., Conn.	254

Continuous Truss

Year	Name	Location	Length
1959	Rocheport, Mo. (9)	Missouri River	2,500
1939	Lyons-Fulton	Mississippi R., Ill.	1,340
1966	Astoria, Ore.	Columbia R.	1,232
1966	Marquam	Willamette R., Ore.	1.044
UC	(1975) Miss. R.	Dyersburg, Tenn.	900
1969	Irondequoit Bay	Rochester, N.Y.	891
1943	Dubuque, Ia.	Mississippi R.	845
1953	John E. Mathews	Jacksonville, Fla.	810
1957	Kingston-Rhinecliff	Hudson R., N.Y.	800
1961	Sherman Minton	New Albany, Ind.	800
1918	*Sciotoville	Ohio River	775
1929	Madison-Milton	Ohio River	727
1973	1275, Boone Co., Ky.	Ohio River	720
1964	John F. Kennedy	Louisville, Ky	700
1966	Matthew E. Welsh	Mauckport, Ind.	707*
1929	Chain of Rocks	Mississippi R.	699
1966	Braga	Taunton R., Mass	682
1938	Port Arthur-Orange	Texas	680
1929	*Cincinnati	Ohio River	675
1932	Mt. Carmel, Ill.	Wabash River	675
1928	Cape Girardeau, Mo.	Mississippi R.	672
1946	Chester, Ill.	Mississippi R.	670
1930	Quincy, Ill.	Mississippi R.	628
1934	Bourne	Cape Cod Canal	616
1935	Sagamore	Cape Cod Canal	616
1965	Clarion River	Clarion Co., Pa.	612
1965	Rio Grande Gorge	Taos, N.M.	600
1941	Columbia River	Kettle Falls, Wash.	600
1962	W. Br. Feather River	Oroville, Cal.	576
1936	Meredosia	Illinois River	567
1936	Mark Twain Mem.	Hannibal, Mo.	562
1937	Homestead	Pittsburgh	553
1961	Ship Canal	Seattle, Wash.	552
1932	Pulaski Skyway	Passaic R., N.J.	550
1927	Ross Island	Portland, Ore.	535
1936	South Omaha	Mo. R., Neb.-Iowa	525
1962	Columbia River	Beebe, Wash.	520
1970	Snake River	Central Ferry, Wash.	520
1954	Columbia River	Pasco, Wash.	520
1962	Columbia River	Vantage, Wash.	520
1958	Stevenson, Ala.	Tennessee River	500
1922	Memorial	Missouri River, N.D.	475
1962	Martinez, Calif.	Carquinex Strait	475
1967	Mississippi River	Minneapolis, Minn.	456
1963	175 Ky. (Twin)	Kentucky R.	448
1956	Decatur, Neb.	Missouri R.	420
1939	Florence, Ala.	Tennessee R.	420

Continuous Box and Plate Girder

Year	Name	Location	Length
1953	Neches River	Orange County, Tex.	850
1967	San Mateo- Hayward No. 2	San Fran. Bay, Cal.	750
1969	San Diego-Coronado	San Diego Bay, Cal.	660'
1972	Ship Channel	Houston, Tex.	630
1967	Poplar St.	St. Louis, Mo.	600
1971	Lake Koocanusa	Lincoln Co., Mont.	500
1967	LaCrosse	Mississippi R., Wisc.	450
1967	Mississippi R.	LaCrescent, Minn.	450
1972	Sitka Harbor	Sitka, Alaska.	450
1974	I-430	Arkansas R.	430
1972	Kansas City	Missouri R., Kan-Mo.	425
1967	Chattanooga	Tennessee R., Tenn.	420
1941	Susquehanna	Susquehanna R., Md.	400
1963	Lake Charles B'Pass.	Louisiana.	399
1971	St. Croix River	Hudson, Minn.	390
1957	Conn. Turnpike	Quinnipiac R.	387
1960	Route 34	New Haven, Conn.	379
1971	S.H. No. 1	Pendleton, Ark.	377
1960	Tennessee River	Chattanooga, Tenn.	375
1966	LeClaire	LeClaire, Iowa	370
1971	Sacramento R.	Bryte, Cal.	370
1966	Benton-Humphrey	Tennessee R., Tenn.	366
1967	San Mateo Creek	Hillsborough, Cal.	360
....	Gunnison River	Gunnison, Colo.	360

Year	Name	Location	Length
1950	US-62	Tennessee R., Ky.	350
1961	Whiskey Creek.	Trinity Co., Cal.	350
1972	Franklin Falls	Snoq'lmie Pass, Wash.	350
1971	Don Pedro Reserv.	Tuolumne Co., Cal.	350
1970	Columbia River	Brewster, Wash.	343
1968	Darmouth.	Minneapolis.	340
1967	Lexington Ave.	St. Paul.	340
1971	Cumberland River.	Nashville, Tenn.	330
1969	Buffalo Creek.	Armstrong Co., Pa.	325
1963	Western Ky. Pkwy.	Green River, Ky.	320
1965	Blue Grass Pkwy.	Kentucky River, Ky.	320
1964	Cumberland River.	Nashville, Tenn.	320
1967	Carroll County.	Kentucky R., Ky.	320
1936	Kentucky River.	Frankfort, Ky.	315
1966	Washington Ave.	Minneapolis.	315
1959	William H. Putnam	Conn. River, Conn.	311
1971	Copper River.	Chitina, Alaska.	310
1973	Main Street	Little Rock, Ark.	303
1967	Rouge River.	Detroit, Mich.	300
1972	Mission Valley	San Diego, Calif.	300
1953	Carrollton	Kentucky R., Ky.	300
1950	Guthrie	Guthrie, Ariz.	300
1942	Charter Oak	Hartford, Conn.	300
1970	Sacramento River	Eikhorn, Calif.	285
1964	West Camas Slough	Camas, Wash.	284
1950	US-231	Green River, Ky.	276
1964	Duwamish R. (Twins)	Seattle.	275
1940	Lakefront.	Cleveland, Ohio.	271
1951	SR-61	Green River, Ky.	260
1954	Wenatchee River	Wenatchee, Wash.	260
1971	Lake Bomoseen.	Castleton, Vt.	260
1973	East 148 St.	Seattle, Wash.	258
1966	Hansen.	Hansen, Idaho.	258
1965	Susitna River	Alaska.	250
1940	Thomas A. Edison.	Raritan River	250
1965	Barren River.	165, Kentucky.	250
1962	Snohomish River	Monroe, Wash.	255
1954	Garden State Pkwy	Raritan River, N.J.	250
1958	P't Wash'gt'n Narr.	Bremerton, Wash.	250
1966	Lake Francis Case	Platte, S.D.	250
1973	Swinomish Slough	Mt. Vernon, Wash.	246
1972	Arkansas River	Pine Bluff, Ark.	243
1948	Baldwin.	Connecticut R.	240
1968	Sharon.	Sharon, Vt.	239
1962	Lake Sharpe	Pierre, S.D.	235
1959	Mulholland Dr.	Los Angeles, Cal.	235
1968	11th (Twins)	Anacostia R., Wash., D.C.	234
1967	White River.	Hartford, Vt.	233
1968	Royalton	Royalton, Vt.	225
1964	Theodore Roosevelt	Potomac R., Wash., D.C.	222
1961	W'r'w Wilson Mem.	Potomac River.	222
1969	Snohomish R.	Monroe, Wash.	222
1973	Chattahoochee R.	Ft. Gaines, Ga.	220
1940	Tallulah River.	Tallulah Gorge, Ga.	220
1970	Chulitna River.	Alaska.	220

Continuous Plate

Year	Name	Location	Length
1965	New Chain of Rocks.	Mississippi R., Ill (9).	2,755
1973	Great Congress Gty.	Shenectady, N.Y.	1,870
1971	Congress St.	Troy, N.Y.	1,420
1965	Rock Island.	Mississippi R., Ill.	1,136
1955	Four Bears.	Missouri R., N.D.	475
1966	I-480.	Missouri R., Iowa-Neb.	425
1972	I-80.	Missouri R., Iowa-Neb.	425
1970	Green River	Hendersonville, N.C.	350
1969	Fort Smith	Arkansas River	340
1957	Snake River	Alpine Jct., Wyo.	264
1973	Lewis & Clark	Williston, N.D.	235
1971	Washburn	Missouri R., N.D.	235
1965	Grant-Marsh	Missouri R., N.D.	235
1964	Galveston Bay	Galveston Co., Tex.	215

I-Beam Girder

Year	Name	Location	Length
1941	US-31E	Rolling Fork R., Ky.	340
1948	US-27	Licking River, Ky.	316
1947	US-31E.	Green River, Ky.	316
1941	US-62	Rolling Fork, Ky.	240
1942	Licking River.	Owingsville, Ky.	240
1954	Fuller Warren	Jacksonville, Fla.	224
1957	Freeway	Arkansas River.	210

Steel Arch

Year	Name	Location	Length
1931	Bayonne, N.J.	Kill Van Kull	1,652
1972	Fremont.	Portland, Ore.	1,255

Year	Name	Location	Length
1964	Port Mann	British Columbia	1,200
1959	Glen Canyon	Colorado River	1,028
1967	Trois-Rivieres	St. Lawrence R., P.Q.	1,100
1962	Lewiston-Queenston	Niagara River, Ont.	1,000
1917	*Hell Gate	East R., N.Y.C.	977
1941	Rainbow	Niagara Falls	950
1970	Lake Quinsigamond	Worcester, Mass.	849
1966	Charles Braga	Somerset, Mass.	840
1967	Lincoln Trail	Ohio R., Ind.-Ky.	825
1966	Lincoln Trail	Cannelton, Ind.	806
1961	Sherman Minton	Louisville, Ky.	800
1936	Henry Hudson	Harlem River	800
1936	French King	Conn. R. (Rt. 2, Mass.)	782
1931	West End	Pittsburgh	778
1972	Piscataqua R.	I-95, N.H.-Me.	756
1963	Cold Spring Canyon	Santa Barbara, Calif.	700
1964	John Kennedy	Ohio River, Ind.-Ky.	700
1973	I-24, Paducah, Ky.	Ohio River	700
1955	Pa.-N.J. Turnpike	Delaware River	682
1964	Burro Creek	(Wikieup) Ariz.	680
1954	Newark-Bayonne	Newark Bay, N.J.	670
1924	*Michigan Central	Niagara Falls	640
1955	Missouri River	Jefferson City, Mo.	640
1929	Navajo	Colorado River, Ariz.	616
1961	Duluth Harbor	Lake Superior	600
1961	St. Louis Bay	Superior, Wis.	600
1938	Middletown	Connecticut	600
1936	Yaquina Bay	Oregon	600
1954	Gt. So. Bay	West Islip, N.Y.	600
1963	Fire Isl. Inlet	Fire Isl., N.Y.	600
1916	Colorado River	Ariz.-Calif.	592
1917	Cuyahoga River	Cleveland, Ohio	591
1929	Palmyra Boro.	Delaware R., N.J.	550
1949	Chesapeake City	Ches. & Del. Can.	540
1941	St. Georges	Ches. & Del. Can.	540
1940	Centennial	Miss. R., Ill.-Iowa	539
1967	Gerald Desmond	Long Bea. H'b'r, Cal.	527
1874	Eads, St. Louis	Mississippi R.	520
1951	Hastings, Minn.	Mississippi R.	514
1888	Washington, N.Y.C.	Harlem River	509
1962	Alex'der Hamilton	Harlem R., N.Y.	505
1848	High Bridge, N.Y.C.	Harlem River	496
1956	Wabash Memorial	Wabash River, Ind.	441

Concrete Arch

Year	Name	Location	Length
1934	New River	Ripplemead, Va. (9)	1,321
1932	Clark Memorial	Wabash River (9)	1,033
1971	Selah Creek (twin)	Selah, Wash.	549
1968	Cowlitz River	Mossyrock, Wash.	520
1931	Westinghouse	Pittsburgh	425
1923	Cappelen	Minneapolis	400
1930	Jack's Run	Pittsburgh	400
1973	Elwha River	Port Angeles, Wash.	380
1931	Bixby Creek	Monterey Coast, Calif.	330
1953	Arroyo Seco	Pasadena, Calif.	320
1927	Mendota	Ft. Snelling, Minn.	304
1915	Rocky River	Cleveland, Ohio	280
1929	10th Ave.	Minneapolis	266
1918	Third Ave.	Minneapolis	211
1929	Chisholm Pk.	Rumford, Me.	210
1934	Waldport	Alsea Bay, Ore.	210
1925	Key	Potomac R.,Wash.D.C.	208
1930	Cornwall, Conn.	Housatonic R.	184

Twin Concrete Trestle

Year	Name	Location	Length
1963	Slidell, La.	L. Pontchartrain	28,547(9)

Concrete Slab Dam

Year	Name	Location	Length
1927	Conowingo Dam	Maryland	4,611
1952	John H. Kerr Dam	Roanoke River, Va.	2,785
1936	Hoover Dam	Boulder City, Nev.	1,324

Drawbridges

Vertical Lift

Year	Name	Location	Length
1959	*Arthur Kill	N.Y.-N.J.	558
1935	*Cape Cod Canal	Massachusetts	544
1960	*Delair, N.J.	Delaware River	542
1937	Marine Parkway	New York City	540
1931	Burlington, N.J.	Delaware R.	534
1912	*A-S-B Fratt	Kansas City	428
1945	*Harry S. Truman	Kansas City	427
1932	*M-K-T R.R.	Missouri R.	414
1969	Wilm'gton Mem.	Wilmington, N.C.	408
1930	Duluth	Minnesota	386
1941	St. Johns River	Jack'ville, Fla.	386
1941	Doremus	Passaic River, N.J.	366
1922	*Cincinnati	Ohio River	365
1967	Benj. Harrison Mem	James River, Va.	363
1961	Corpus Christi, Tex.	Port Aransas-RR.-Highway Corpus Christi	344
1933	Troy-Mendands	Hudson River	341
1962	Sand Island Aess.	Oahu, Hawaii	340
1929	Carlton	Bath-Woolwich, Me.	328
1930	*Martinez	California	328
1960	West Bay	Panama City, Fla.	327
1929	*Penn-Lehigh	Newark Bay	322
1920	*Chattanooga	Tennessee R.	310
1936	Triboro, N.Y.C.	Illinois River	310
1936	Hardin	Illinois River	309
1960	Sacramento River	Rio Vista, Calif.	306
1957	Claiborne Ave.	New Orleans	305
1927	Cochrane	Mobile, Ala.	300
1928	James River	Newport News	300
1929	San Mateo	California	300
1926	*Missouri Pacific	Kragen, Ark.	300
1956	Sidney Lanier	Brunswick, Ga.	295
1960	Interstate	Columbia River, Ore.-Wash.	279
1928	Jordan	Norfolk, Va.	277
1959	Houghton-Hancock	Michigan	268
1955	Hackensack, N.J.	Hackensack River	222
1949	Newark, N.J.	Passaic River	222

Bascule

Year	Name	Location	Length
1926	*At &SFRR (Iowa-Ill.)	Mississippi R.	525
1969	Pearl River	Slidell, La.	482
1916	*Keokuk Municipal	Mississippi R., Iowa	377
1940	Lorain, Ohio	Black River	295
1969	Elizabeth River	Chesapeake, Va.	281
1957	Craig Memorial	IR-280, Toledo, Ohio	271
1952	Downtown	Norfolk, Va.	230

Swing Bridges

Year	Name	Location	Length
1950	Douglass Memorial	Anac'tia R., Wash. D.C.	386
1945	Lord Delaware	Mattaponi River, Va.	252
1957	Eltham	Pamunkey River, Va.	237
1939	Chickahominy River	Route 5, Va.	222
1930	Nansemond River	Route 125, Va.	200

Swing Span

Year	Name	Location	Length
1927	*Fort Madison	Mississippi R.	525
1908	*Willamette R.	Portland, Ore.	521
1903	*East Omaha	Missouri R.	519
1952	Yorktown	York River, Va.	500
1897	*Duluth, Minn.	St. Louis Bay	486
1899	*C.M.&N.R.R.	Chicago	474
1895	Sioux City, Ia.	Missouri R.	470
1914	*Coos Bay	Oregon	458

Floating Pontoon

Year	Name	Location	Length
1963	Evergreen Pt.	Seattle, Wash.	7,518
1940	Lacey V. Murrow	Seattle	6,561
1961	Hood Canal	Pt. Gamble, Wash.	6,471

(1) The Transbay Bridge has 2 spans of 2,310 ft. each. (2) A second bridge in parallel will be completed. (3) The Richmond Bridge has twin spans 1,070 ft. each. (4) Railroad and vehicular bridge. (5) Two spans each 760 ft. (6) Two spans each 707 ft. (7) Two spans each 660 ft. (8) Two spans each 825 ft. (9) Total length of bridge. (10) Dumbarton has 7 spans each 225 ft. long.

Construction Details of Large and Unusual Bridges

Verrazano-Narrows Bridge, between Staten Island and Brooklyn, N.Y., has a suspension span of 4,260 ft., longest in the world and exceeding the Golden Gate Bridge, San Francisco, by 60 ft. One level in use November, 1964, second opened June 28, 1969. The name is a compromise; it spans the Narrows and commemorates a visit to New York Harbor in April, 1524, deduced from certain notes left by Giovanni da Verrazano, Italian navigator sailing for Francis I of France.

Allegheny River Bridge (Interstate 80) near Emlenton, Pa., 270 ft. above the water, tallest in eastern U.S., a continuous truss, 688 ft. long, 1968.

Angostura, suspension type, span 2,336 feet, 1967, at Ciudad Bolivar, Venezuela. Total length, 5,507.

Charles Braga Bridge over Taunton River between Fall River and Somerset, Mass. It is 5,780 feet long.

Bendorf Bridge on the Rhine River, 5 mi. n. of Coblenz, completed 1965, is a 3-span cement girder bridge, 3,378 ft. overall length, 101 ft. wide, with the main span 682 ft.

Burro Creek Bridge with 4 spans over Burro Creek on highway 93 near Kingman, Ariz. Main span steel truss 680 ft. Others plate girder, 110 and 2 of 85 ft. 1966.

Champlain Bridge at Montreal crossing the St. Lawrence River was opened 1962. It is 4 mil long. Three others connect Montreal with the South Bank, the Jacques Cartier, Victoria and Mercier bridges.

Corpus Christi, Texas, has a high level port entrance bridge. It is a cantilever truss with anchor spans 310 ft. and main span 620 ft., total length approx. 5,862 ft.

Cross Bay Parkway Bridge (N.Y.) 3,000 feet long with 6 traffic lanes, 11 eight foot wide precast, prestressed concrete T girders to support spans 130 feet long each with main span 275 feet.

Delaware Memorial Bridge over Delaware River near Wilmington. A twin suspension bridge paralleling the original 250 ft. upstream has a 2,150-ft. main span suspended from 440-ft. towers

Eads Bridge across the Mississippi R. between St. Louis and E. St. Louis, built in 1874 has 4 main spans 1,520 ft., 2,502 ft. and 1,118 ft. crossing Miss R., a railroad and a road.

Evergreen Point Bridge in Wash., consists of 33 floating concrete pontoons weighting 4,700 tons each, held in place by 77 ton crete anchors. Pontoon structure is 6,561 ft. long, with approaches bridge is 12,596 ft. long.

Fremont Bridge part of Stadium Freeway, Portland, Ore., crossing Williamette R. 1,255 ft. steel arch span with two 452 ft. flanking steel arch spans. 1971.

Frontenac Bridge, Quebec, suspension, span 2,190 ft., open 1970.

Gladesville Bridge at Sydney, Australia, has the longest concrete arch in the world (1,000 ft. span).

George Washington Bridge, New York City, 4th longest suspension bridge in the world, spans the Hudson River between W. 178th St., Manhattan, and Ft. Lee, N. J.; 4,760 ft. between anchorages, two levels, 14 traffic lanes. Triborough Bridge connects Manhattan, the Bronx and Queens; project comprises a suspension bridge, a vertical lift bridge, and a fixed bridge, all connected by long viaducts. The famous Brooklyn Bridge over the East River, connecting Manhattan and Brooklyn, was completed in 1883, breaking all previous records by spanning 1,595 ft.

Golden Gate Bridge, crossing San Francisco Bay, has the second longest single span, 4,200 ft.

Hampton Roads Bridge-Tunnel, Va. A crossing completed in 1957 consisting of two man-made islands, two concrete trestle bridges, and one tunnel, under Hampton Roads with a length of 7,479 ft. A parallel facility is under construction with estimated completion date in 1974.

Hood Canal Floating Bridge, Wash., 23 floating concrete pontoons 4,980 tons ea. Roadway is supported on crete T-beam sections mounted on pontoons 20 feet above canal. Floating section is 6,471 ft. long, overall 7,866 ft.

International Bridge, a series of 8 arch and truss bridges crossing St. Mary's and the Soo Locks between Mich. and Ontario. 2-mile toll completed 1962.

Lacey V. Murrow Floating Bridge, Wash., 25 floating pontoons of 4,558 tons ea. Bridge with approaches is 8,583 ft.

Lake Pontchartrain Twin Causeway, a twin-span crete trestle bride and 24-mile link within metropolitan New Orleans that connects the north and south shore. First span opened 1956, second 1969.

Lavaca Bay Causeway, Texas. 2.2 miles long, consisting of one 260 ft. continuous plate girder unit and 194 precast, prestressed concrete spans of 60 ft. length. 1961.

Newport Bridge between Newport and Jamestown, R. I. Total length 11,248 ft., a main suspension span of 1,600 feet, two side spans each 688 feet long. It has U.S.A.'s first prefabricated wire strands.

New York City bridges, see Verrazano-Narrows Bridge and George Washington Bridge above.

Ogdensburg-Prescott Internat'l Bridge across the St. Lawrence River from Ogdensburg, N. Y., to Johnston, Ont., opened 1960, is 13,510 ft. long with approaches and 7,260 ft. between abutments.

Oland Island Bridge under construction in Sweden will be completed in 1972. It will be 19,882 feet long when completed and will be Europe's longest.

Oosterscheldebrug, opened Dec. 15, 1965, is a 3.125-mile causeway for automobiles over a sea arm in Zeeland, the Netherlands. It completes a direct connection between Flushing and Rotterdam.

Poplar St. Bridge over the Mississippi at St. Louis. a 5-span continuous orthotropic deck plate girder bridge, longest span 600 ft. 8 lane 2, 165 ft. long.

Quebec Road, suspension, span 2,190 feet, 1969, Quebec, Canada.

Robert Opie Norris Bridge, Rappahannock R. between Greys Pt. and White Stone, Va. 9,989 ft. long. Main spans are two 144 foot cantilever truss spans with a 360 foot truss span suspended between them.

Rockville Bridge, world's longest 4-track stone arch bridge, 3,810 ft., with 48 arches. Part of the Penn-Central RR system west of Harrisburg, Pa. It contains 440,000,000 lbs. of stone, 100,000 cubic yds. of masonry and crosses the Susquehanna River to Rockville, Pa.

Rio-Niteroi, Guanabara Bay, Brazil, under construction, will be world's longest continuous box and plate girder bridge, 8 miles, 3,363 feet long, with a center span of 984 feet and a span on each side of 656 feet.

Royal Gorge Bridge, 1,053 ft. above the Arkansas River in Colorado, is the highest bridge above water. Opened Dec. 8, 1929, it is 1,260 ft. long with a main span of 880 ft., width 18 ft.

San Mateo-Hayward Bridge across San Francisco Bay is first major orthotropic bridge in U.S. It is 6.7 miles long, 4.9 mile low-level concrete trestle and 1.8 miles high-level steel bridge.

Seven Mile Bridge is the longest of an expanse of bridges connecting the Florida Keys. It was built by the Florida East Coast Railway between 1904 and 1916, now a state highway.

Shenandoah River Bridges, one spans the south fork, 1,924 ft. long, the other the north fork 1,090 ft. long, Warren County Va.

Straits of Mackinac Bridge, completed in 1957, is the longest suspension bridge between anchorages and with approaches extends nearly 5 mi. between Mackinaw City and St. Ignace, Mich.

Sunshine Skyway, a 15-mile-long bridge-causeway with twin roadbeds that crosses Tampa Bay at St. Petersburg, Fla., a system of twin bridges 864 feet long and 4 smaller bridges with 6 causeways.

Tagus River Bridge near Lisbon, Portugal, longest suspension bridge outside the United States, has a 3,323-ft. main span. Opened Aug. 6, 1966, it was named Salazar Bridge for the former premier.

Thomas A. Edison Memorial Bridge (causeway) across Sandusky Bay between Martin Point and Danbury, Ohio, is 2.67 miles long. The main bridge is 2,044 feet long.

Thousand Island Bridge, St. Lawrence River. American span 800 ft.; Canadian 750 ft.

Union St. Bridge in Woodstock, Vt., a Timber Lattice Truss with a span of 122 feet built in 1969 using old time procedure of hand drilled holes and wooden pegs.

Vancouver Bridge, Canada's longest railway lift span conecting Vancouver and North Vancouver over Burrard Inlet. It is in 3 sections the longest 493 ft. Spans are part of a project that includes a 2-mile tunnel under Vancouver Hgts.

Woodrow Wilson Memorial Bridge across the Potomac River at Alexandria, Va. is over a mile long.

Zoo Bridge across the Rhine at Cologne, with steel box girders,has a main span of 850 ft.

The Interstate Highway 610 crossing of the Houston Ship Channel in Texas is 6,300 feet in length and consists of various lengths of prestressed concrete beam and slab approach spans and a 1,233 foot main unit of two 471'6" plate girder units and one 290 ft. simple span.

Underwater Vehicular Tunnels in North America
Over 3,000 feet in length

Name	Location	Waterway	Lgth. Ft.
Bart Trans-Bay Tube (Rapid Transit)....	San Francisco..........	S.F. Bay..............	3.6 Miles
Brooklyn-Battery................	New York, N.Y.....	East River...........	9,117
Holland Tunnel..................	New York, N.Y.....	Hudson River.........	8,557
Lincoln Tunnel.................	New York, N.Y.....	Hudson River.........	8,216
Baltimore Harbor Tunnel..........	Baltimore, Md......	Patapsco River........	7,650
Hampton Roads................	Norfolk, Va........	Hampton Roads.......	7,479
Queens Midtown...............	New York, N.Y.....	East River...........	6,414
Thimble Shoal Channel...........	Cape Henry, Va.....	Chesapeake Bay.......	5,738
Sumner Tunnel.................	Boston, Mass.......	Boston Harbor........	5,650
Louis-Hippolyte Lafontaine Tunnel.....	Montreal, Que......	St. Lawrence River.....	5,280
Detroit-Windsor.................	Detroit, Mich.......	Detroit River.........	5,135
Chesapeake Channel..............	Cape Charles, Va....	Chesapeake Bay.......	5,450
Callahan Tunnel.................	Boston, Mass.......	Boston Harbor........	5,046
Midtown Tunnel.................	Norfolk, Va........	Elizabeth River.......	4,194
Baytown Tunnel.................	Baytown, Tex.......	Houston Ship Channel...	4,111
Posey Tube....................	Oakland, Calif......	Oakland Estuary.......	3,500
Downtown Tunnel................	Norfolk, Va........	Elizabeth River.......	3,350
Webster St....................	Alameda, Calif......	Oakland Estuary.......	3,350
Bankhead Tunnel................	Mobile, Ala........	Mobile River.........	3,109
I-10 Twin Tunnel................	Mobile, Ala........	Mobile River.........	3,000

Land Vehicular Tunnels in United States (Over 1 000 feet long)

Name	Location	Lgth. Ft.	Name	Location	Lgth. Ft.
Eisenhower Memorial ..	Route 70, Colorado.....	8,941	Battery Park..........	New York City.........	2,300
Copperfield...........	Copperfield, Utah......	6,989	Battery St............	Seattle, Wash.........	2,140
Allegheny (Twin)......	Penna. Turnpike......	6,070	Big Oak Flat..........	Yosemite Natl. Pk.....	2,083
Liberty Tubes........	Pittsburgh, Pa.........	5,920	Prudential............	Boston, Mass.........	1,980
Zion Natl. Park.......	Rte. 1, Utah..........	5,766	Internatl. Underpass.....	Los Angeles, Calif.....	1,910
East River Mt. (Twin)...	Interstate 77, W.Va.-Va..	5,661	Street-Car............	Providence, R.I........	1,793
Tuscarora (Twin)......	Penna. Turnpike......	5,326	Broadway............	San Francisco, Calif....	1,616
Kittatinny (Twin)......	Penna. Turnpike......	4,727	9th Street Expy........	Washington, D.C.......	1,610
Lehigh..............	Penna. Turnpike......	4,379	F.D. Roosevelt Dr......	42-48 Sts. NYC.......	1,600
Blue Mountain (Twin)..	Penna. Turnpike......	4,339	Lowry Hill...........	Minneapolis..........	1,496
Wawona.............	Yosemite Natl. Pk.....	4,233	Wheeling............	Interstate 70, W. Va.....	1,490
Squirrel Hill.........	Pittsburgh, Pa........	4,225	Mt. Baker Ridge (3).....	Seattle, Wash.........	1,466
Big Walker Mt........	Route I-77, Va........	4,200	Knowls Creek.........	Lane County, Ore......	1,430
Fort Pitt............	Pittsburgh, Pa........	3,560	Mule Pass............	Near Bisbee, Ariz......	1,400
Mall Tunnel..........	Dist. of Columbia.....	3,400	Arch Cape............	Oregon Coast Hwy. 9....	1,228
Caldecott............	Oakland, Calif........	3,371	Queen Creek..........	Superior, Ariz........	1,200
Kalihi..............	Honolulu, Hawaii.....	2,780	West Rock............	New Haven, Conn......	1,200
Memorial...........	W. Va. Tpke. (I-77).....	2,669	Green River..........	Route I-80, Wyo.......	1,135
Cross-Town..........	178 St. N.Y.C........	2,414	Nouanu Pali..........	Koolau Mt. Oahu, Hawaii	1,080
F.D. Roosevelt Dr......	81-89 Sts. NYC........	2,400	Elk Creek............	Umpqua Hwy 45, Ore...	1,080
Dewey Sq...........	Boston, Mass........	2,400	Golden..............	Clear Cr'k Cany'n, Colo..	1,068

World's Longest Railway Tunnels
Source: 1969-1970 Railway Directory & Year Book. Tunnels over 4 miles in length.

Tunnel	Date	Miles	Yds	Operating Railway	Country
Simplon No. I and II..............	1922	12	559	Swiss Fed. & Italian St...........	Switz.-Italy
Apennine...................	1934	11	892	Italian State................	Italy
Cotthard...................	1882	9	562	Swiss Federal...............	Switzerland
Lotschberg.................	1913	9	140	Bern-Lotschberg-Simplon.........	Switzerland
Hokuriku...................	1962	8	1,089	Japanese National..........	Japan
Mont Cenis (Frejus)...........	1871	8	855	Italian State................	France-Italy
Cascade....................	1929	7	1,397	Great Northern...............	United States
Flathead Tunnel, Mont........	1970	6	1,758	Great Northern...............	United States
Arlberg....................	1884	6	650	Austrian Federal.............	Austria
Moffat.....................	1928	6	373	Denver & Rio Grande..........	United States
Shimizu....................	1931	6	50	Japanese National...........	Japan
Kvineshei..................	1943	5	1,112	Norwegian State.............	Norway
Rimutaka..................	1955	5	821	New Zealand Gov............	New Zealand
Ricken....................	1910	5	608	Swiss Federal...............	Switzerland
Grenchenberg...............	1915	5	581	Swiss Federal...............	Switzerland
Otira......................	1923	5	564	New Zealand Gov............	New Zealand
Tauern....................	1909	5	551	Austrian Federal.............	Austria
Haegebostad...............	1943	5	467	Norwegian State.............	Norway
Ronco....................	1889	5	277	Italian State................	Italy
Hauenstein (Lower)...........	1916	5	95	Swiss Federal...............	Switzerland
Connaught.................	1916	5	39	Canadian Pacific.............	Canada
Karawanken................	1906	4	1,683	Austrian Federal.............	Austria-Yugo.
New Tanna.................	1964	4	1,663	Japanese National............	Japan
Somport...................	1928	4	1,572	French National..............	France-Spain
Tanna.....................	1934	4	1,493	Japanese National............	Japan
Ulrikken...................	1964	4	1,338	Norwegian State.............	Norway
Hoosac...................	1875	4	1,230	Boston & Maine..............	United States
Monte Orso................	1927	4	1,230	Italian State................	Italy
Lupacino..................	1958	4	1,178	Italian State................	Italy
Vivola....................	1927	4	1,004	Italian State................	Italy
Monte Adone...............	1934	4	760	Italian State................	Italy
Jungfrau..................	1912	4	750	Jungfrau...................	Switzerland
Borgallo..................	1884	4	700	Italian State................	Italy
Severn....................	1886	4	628	Western Region..............	Great Britain
Lusse (Vosges).............	1937	4	474	French National..............	France

Dams and Reservoirs; Water Conservation

Source: Bureau of Reclamation

The Bureau of Reclamation, an agency of the Department of the Interior, administers a multiple-purpose water resources program that develops projects for municipal, industrial and irrigation water supply, hydroelectric power generation, flood control, water quality improvement, fish and wildlife enhancement, outdoor recreation, and maintenance of a satisfactory natural environment. To these ends it builds dams, reservoirs, hydropower plants, canals, and tunnels in the 17 contiguous western states, and conducts a many-faceted water resources research program to develop new sources of water supply and also water and land conservation techniques.

Alaska Power Administration, located in Juneau, Alaska, is the agency of the Department of the Interior given charge of promoting development and use of the water, power and related resources of Alaska. The hydro power resources of Alaska are practically untouched. Of the 32 million kilowatts of hydroelectric power potential, the 30,000-kilowatt Eklutna Project is the only major operating project. When completed, the Snettisham Project will add 70,000 kilowatts of capacity to the APA system.

Colorado River Storage Project. Construction began in 1973 on the Crystal Dam and Powerplant on the Gunnison River in Colorado. A principal feature of the Curecanti Unit of the 5-state Colorado River Storage Project, authorized in 1956, the concrete, thin-arch Crystal Dam near Montrose, Colorado, will be 620 feet long at the crest and 340 feet high. It will be the thinnest dam of its type in the world. The dam and powerplant will be the third in a series of structures comprising the Curecanti Unit on the Gunnison River, the other two dams being Morrow Point and Blue Mesa. Three other storage units of CRSP are fully in operation: Glen Canyon Dam, reservoir and power plant on the Colorado R. in Utah and Ariz. Flaming Gorge Dam, reservoir and power plant on the Green in Utah and Wyo.; and Navajo Dam and reservoir on the San Juan in N.M. and Colo.

High up on the eastern slope of the Rocky Mountains in N.M. construction has been completed on Heron Dam, a feature of the San Juan-Chama participating project. Water from the tributary streams of the Colorado R. west of the Rocky Mountains is brought under the Continental Divide by the Azotea Tunnel to be impounded by Heron Dam then released to flow down the Rio Chama and Rio Grande for municipal and industrial use and for irrigation of farmlands.

Central Valley Project, California. Construction work is underway on the Bureau of Reclamation's $311,000,000 Auburn Dam, chief feature of the Auburn-Folsom South Unit of the Central Valley Project. On the North Fork of the American R., this structure will be Reclamation's longest and highest double curvature concrete dam, spanning 3,500 ft. at its crest 680 ft. above bedrock. Its reservoir, with 2,300,000 acre-feet storage capacity, will provide a full irrigation water supply for 29,340 acres and a supplemental supply for 300,000 acres, and will also supply municipal and industrial water for communities in the area, as well as to furnish recreational and fish and wildlife benefits. A power plant having an initial capacity of 300,000 kilowatts will be constructed at the toe of the dam.

Third Powerplant at Grand Coulee Dam. A $57.8 million contract was awarded in 1973 for manufacture and installation of three giant turbines and generators at the Bureau's Third Powerplant at Grand Coulee Dam on the Columbia River. These 700,000 kilowatt generators and huge turbines, possibly the largest ever constructed, are the second group of three to be installed at the Third Powerplant. Work is also progressing on the Forebay Dam and on the powerplant which will house the big turbines and generators.

Fryingpan-Arkansas Project. Sugar Loaf and Ruedi Dams, major earth-fill impoundment structures were completed in 1969. The former, east of the Continental Divide, will result in the enlargement of Turquoise Lake from 17,000 to 130,000 acre-feet.

Ruedi Dam on the western slope will create a 101,000 acre-foot impoundment on the Fryingpan R., compensating water users in western Colorado for the supply diverted at higher elevations through the Divide by the Charles H. Boustead Tunnel into Turquoise Lake for use in the Akansas basin. The 5.4 mile-long tunnel under the Continental Divide is complete and construction work has commenced on **Pueblo Dam** and reservoir on the eastern slope. Pueblo Reservoir will impound 357,000 acre-feet of water.

Pick-Sloan Missouri Basin Program. Construction is underway on the Snake Creek pumping plant, and the McClusky canal, key features of the Garrison Diversion Unit, which will provide irrigation for 250,000 acres of land in N.D.

Yellowtail Dam on the Bighorn River in southern Mont. was dedicated in 1968. The 525-foot high dam, its 71-mile long reservoir, and its 250,000-kilowatt power plant comprise the Yellowtail unit of the P-SMBP.

Southern Nevada Water Project. A 4-mile tunnel has been bored through the River Mountains, which lie between the Las Vegas Valley and Lake Mead behind **Hoover Dam** on the Colorado R. Several pumping plants to lift water from Lake Mead to the tunnel, which will convey it to the valley to meet the municipal and industrial needs of the area have been completed and project put in operation.

Work got underway in 1972 on the **Teton Dam and Power and Pumping Plant,** located on the Teton River in southeastern Idaho. The first phase of this development, estimated to cost $65 million, will provide a supplemental water supply to 112,210 acres and a power supply of 20,000 kilowatts in 1976. The project will also provide recreation and flood control.

Southeastern Power Administration (Dept. of the Interior) with headquarters at Elberton, Ga., markets power produced at projects controlled by the Corps of Engineers in Va., W. Va., N.C., S.C., Ga., Fla., Ky., Ala., Miss., and Tenn.

Southwestern Power Administration, with hq. in Tulsa, Okla., is the agency of the Dept. of the Interior designated to market surplus hydroelectric power and energy generated at Federal multiple purpose reservoirs in a 6 state area of the southwest. Of 23 hydro-electric plants 19 are in commercial operation, and 4 are under construction.

Tennessee Valley Authority

TVA is a corporate agency of the Federal government, established by Congress in 1933 to develop the Tennessee River system and to aid in the development of other resources of the Tennessee Valley region. This includes resource development work in flood control, navigation, electric power, recreation, agriculture, forestry, and water quality.

TVA has built or acquired 27 major dams on the Tennessee and its tributary rivers, and by agreement with Alcoa controls water releases at 6 of its major dams. These structures make the main stream of the Tennessee navigable over its 650-mile length from Knoxville to the Ohio River, regulate flood waters, and generate hydroelectric power.

TVA is a wholesale power supplier to 160 local electric systems serving 2 million customers in parts of 7 states, and sells power directly to several large atomic, military, and industrial installations

The TVA Power System is financially self-supporting and self-liquidating.

Major World Dams

Source: Bureau of Reclamation. Dept. of the Interior. Revised May 1973. *Replaces existing dam.

Volume in cubic yards. Capacity (Gross) in acre feet. Year of completion. **U.C.** under construction.
Type: A—Arch. **B**—Buttress. **E**—Earthfill. **G**—Gravity. **R**—Rockfill. **MA**—Multi-arch.

Name of Dam	Type	Year	River and Basin	Country	Height Feet	Crest Length Feet	Volume (1,000 C.Y.)	Res. Cap. (1,000 A.F.)
Akosombo-Main	R	1965	Volta	Ghana	463	2,100	10,400	120,000
Almendra	A	UC	Tormes-Douro	Spain	649	13,438	3,267	2,025
Alpe Gera	G	1965	Comor-Adda-Po	Italy	584	1,710	2,265	53
Amir Kabir*	A	1962	Karadj-Caspian Sea	Iran	591	1,280	821	166
Auburn	MA	UC	N. F. American-Sacramento	U.S.A.	695	4,000	6,000	2,300
Balimela	E	UC	Sileru	India	230	15,200	29,600	3,100
Beas	E	UC	Beas-Indus	India	436	6,401	42,261	6,600
W.A.C. Bennett*	E	1967	Peace-Mackenzie	Canada	600	6,700	57,203	57,006
Bhakra	A	1963	Sutlent-Indus	India	742	1,700	5,400	8,000
Bhumiphol (Yanhee)	GA	1964	Ping-Chao Phraya	Thailand	505	1,594	1,307	9,891
Bratsk	GE	1964	Angara	USSR	410	17,105	22,219	137,214
Bukhtarma	G	1960	Irtish	USSR	295	1,247	1,530	42,970
Cabora Basa	A	UC	Zambezi	Mozambique	550	994	589	129,389
Canelles	A	1960	Noguera Ribagorzana-Ebro	Spain	492	689	436	549
Castaic	E	1971	Castaic Cr.-Santa Clara	U.S.A.	340	5,200	44,000	350
Charvak	E	1970	Chirchik-Sir Darya	USSR	551	2,499	24,975	1,620
Chirkey	A	UC	Sulak-Caspian Sea	USSR	764	1,109	1,602	2,252
Cochiti	E	UC	Rio Grande	U.S.A.	251	28,200	41,100	602
Contra	A	1965	Verzasca-Ticino-Po	Switz	754	1,246	863	70
Curnera	A	1967	Rein de Curnera-Rhine	Switz	499	1,115	735	32.4
Dneprodzerzhinsk	GE	1964	Dnieper	USSR	115	119,038	35,857	1,985
Don Pedro*	ER	1970	Tuoume-San Joaquin	U.S.A.	585	1,900	16,760	2,030
Dworshak	G	UC	N. F. Clearwater Columbia	U.S.A.	717	3,287	6,500	3,453
Elephant Butte	G	1916	Rio Grande	U.S.A.	301	1,674	630	2,201
Emosson	A	UC	Barberine	Switz	590	1,736	1,400	182
Esmeralda	E	1964	Bota	Colombia	754	919	14,126	661
Flaming Gorge	GA	1964	Green-Colorado	U.S.A.	502	1,285	987	3,789
Fort Peck	E	1940	Missouri	U.S.A.	250	21,026	125,600	19,400
Fort Randall	E	1956	Missouri	U.S.A.	165	10,700	50,200	6,100
Gardiner*	E	1968	South Saskatchewan	Canada	223	16,700	85,739	8,000
Garrison	E	1956	Missouri	U.S.A.	210	11,300	66,500	24,500
Gatum	E	1912	Chagres	Panama	115	7,700	22,958	4,413
Gepatsch	E	1964	Faggenbach-Inn	Austria	500	2,070	9,250	114
Glen Canyon	A	1964	Colorado	U.S.A.	710	1,560	4,901	27,000
Gokcekaya	A	UC	Sakarya	Turkey	518	1,529	850	737
Gorky	EG	1955	Volga-Caspian S.	USSR	105	42,340	57,969	7,055
Goschernalp	G	1960	Goschenerreuss-Rhine	Switz	508	1,771	12,230	61
Grand Coulee	G	1942	Columbia	U.S.A.	550	4,173	10,585	9,724
Grande Dixence	G	1962	Dixence-Rhone	Switz	932	2,296	7,792	324
Gran Suarna	MA	UC	Navia	Spain	499	1,150	882	567
Guri	GER	1968	Caroni-Orinoco	Venezuela	348	2,264	4,917	14,349
High Aswan (Saad-El-Aali)	ER	1971	Nile	U.A.R.	364	12,565	55,747	133,000
Hirakud	GE	1956	Mahanadi	India	202	15,748	25,100	6,600
Hoover	A	1936	Colorado	U.S.A.	726	1,244	4,400	29,755
Hungry Horse	AG	1953	S.F. Flathead-Columbia	U.S.A.	564	2,115	3,086	3,468
Idikki	MA	UC	Periyar	India	561	1,201	609	1,182
Ihla Solteria	EG	UC	Parana Rio de la Plata	Brazil	291	20,300	35,741	17,172
Inguri	A	UC	Inguri	USSR	892	2,513	4,967	891
Irkutsk	GE	1956	Angara	USSR	144	8,989	16,220	37,290
Iroquois	G	1958	St. Lawrence	Canada	76	2,665		24,288
Ivankovo	EG	1937	Volga-Caspian S.	USSR	98	31,398	20,207	908
Jari	E	1967	Jari	Pakistan	234	5,700	42,400	400
Jaya Kwadi	E	UC	Godavari	India	120	32,493	15,409	2,110
Daniel Johnson*	MA	1968	Manicougan-St. Lawrence	Canada	703	4,311	2,950	115,000
Kakhovka	EG	1955	Dnieper	USSR	121	5,380	46,617	14,755
Kanev	E	UC	Dnieper	USSR	82	52,950	49,520	2,125
Kapchagay	E	1970	Ili	USSR	164	1,542	5,078	22,813
Kariba	A	1959	Zambesi	Rhodesia-Zambia	420	2,025	1,350	130,000
Keban	RG	UC	First (Euphrates)	Turkey	679	3,598	19,600	25,110
Kiev	E	1964	Dnieper	USSR	72	177,448	57,552	3,021
King Paul (Kremasta)	ER	1965	Acheloos	Greece	541	1,510	10,686	3,850
Krasnoyarsk	G	UC	Yenisei	USSR	407	3,493	5,685	59,425
Krememchug	EG	1961	Dnieper	USSR	98	35,727	36,282	10,945
Kurobegawa No. 4	A	1964	Kurobe	Japan	610	1,603	1,782	162
Las Portas	A	UC	Camba	Spain	498	1,587	977	609
Luzzone	A	1963	Brenno di Luzzone-Ticino	Switz	682	1,738	1,776	70
Mangla	E	1967	Jhelum	Pakistan	380	11,000	85,872	5,150
Marimbondo	E	UC	Grande	Brazil	295	11,970	24,328	5,184
Mauvoisin	A	1958	Drance de Bagnes-Rhone	Switz	777	1,706	2,655	146
Mica	R	UC	Columbia	Canada	794	2,600	42,000	20,000
Mohamed Re Chah Pahlavi	A	1963	Dez-Karun	Iran	66	696	608	2,717
Mingechaur	E	1953	Kura	USSR	262	5,085	20,400	12,970
Monteynard	A	1962	Drac-Isere-Rhone	France	509	705	595	195
Mossyrock	MA	1968	Cowlitz-Columbia	U.S.A.	605	1,750	1,240	1,300
Mratinje	A	UC	Piva-Drina-Danube	Yugo.	722	853	1,019	749
Nagwado	A	UC	Azua-Shinano	Japan	508	1,200	865	100
New Bullards Bar	A	1968	North Yuba-Sacramento	U.S.A.	635	2,200	2,700	930
New Melones	R	UC	Stanislaus-San Joaquin	U.S.A.	625	1,600	15,970	2,400
Nurek	E	1972	Vakhsh	USSR	1,040	2,390	75,864	8,424
Oahe	E	1963	Missouri	U.S.A.	245	9,300	92,000	23,600
Okutadami	G	1961	Tadami	Japan	515	1,575	2,145	487
Oroville	E	1968	Feather-Sacramento	U.S.A.	770	6,920	78,008	3,538
Owen Falls	G	1954	Lake Victoria-Nile	Uganda	100	2,725		166,000
Place Moulin	AG	1965	Buthier-Dora Baltea	Italy	502	2,181	1,962	81

(Continued)

(continued)

Name of Dam	Type	Year	River and Basin	Country	Ht.	Lgth.	Vol.	Cap.
Reza Shah Kabir	A	UC	Karoun	Iran	656	1,247	1,570	2,351
Roselend	AB	1961	Doronde Beaufort-Rhone	France	492	2,644	1,236	152
Ross	A	1949	Skagit	U.S.A.	540	1,300	909	1,405
Rybinsk	GE	1941	Volga-Caspian S.	USSR	98	2,060	3,329	20,590
Sakuma	G	1956	Tenryu	Japan	510	963	1,465	265
Sanmen Hsia	G	1962	Hwang Ho-Yellow	China	351	2,752		52,700
San Luis	E	1967	San Luis-San Joaquin	U.S.A.	382	18,600	77,670	2,110
Santa Giustina	A	1950	Noce-Adige	Italy	500	407	146	148
Saratov	E	UC	Volga-Caspian S.	USSR	131	4,130	34,531	10,458
Sayansk	A	UC	Yenisei	USSR	774	3,503	11,916	25,353
Shasta	G	1945	Sacramento	U.S.A.	602	3,460	8,711	4,500
Speccheri	A	1957	Leno Di Vallarsa-Adige	Italy	514	631	153	8
Swift	E	1958	Lewis-Columbia	U.S.A.	512	2,100	15,431	756
Tachien	A	UC	Tachia	Taiwan	656	853	940	235
Talbingo	R	1971	Tumut	Australia	530	2,300	18,500	747
Tankiangkow	G	1962	Tan & Han	China	427			41,833
Tarbela	ER	UC	Indus	Pakistan	470	9,000	186,000	11,100
Tignes	A	1952	Isere-Rhone	France	592	1,411	830	186
Toktogul	A	UC	Naryn-Syr Darya	USSR	705	1,352	3,480	15,800
Trinity	E	1962	Trinity-Klamath	U.S.A.	537	2,600	29,251	2,500
Tsimlyansk	EG	1952	Don	USSR	128	43,411	44,323	17,715
Tuttle Creek	ER	1962	Big Blue-Missouri	U.S.A.	157	7,500	21,000	2,367
Twin Buttes	E	1963	Concho-Colorado Texas	U.S.A.	134	42,460	21,442	641
Ust-Ilim	GE	UC	Angara	USSR	344	11,695	11,382	48,100
Vajont	MA	1961	Vajont-Piave	Italy	858	624	460	137
Verkhne-Svirskaya	EG	1952	Svir	USSR	105	1,775	1,988	14,190
Vidraru	A	1965	Arges-Danube	Rumania	544	1,000	653	377
Volga-22nd congress U.S.S.	ERG	1958	Volga-Caspian S.	USSR	144	13,038	33,020	27,160
Volga-V. I. Lenin	EG	1955	Volga-Caspian S.	USSR	148	12,405	44,298	47,020
Yellowtail	A	1966	Bighorn-Missouri	U.S.A.	525	1,480	1,456	1,375
Zervreila	A	1957	Valserrhein-Rhine	Switz.	495	1,653	819	81
Zeuzier	A	1957	Lienne-Rhone	Switz.	512	918	392	41
Zeya	G	UC	Zeya	USSR	371	2,312	10,456	55,080

Major Public and Private Dams and Reservoirs in U.S.

Source: Bureau of Reclamation, Dept. of the Interior; Corps of Engineers, U.S. Army and Tennessee Valley Authority
Heights over 250 feet, volume over 1,000,000 cubic yards.
Where reservoir name is different it is shown in italics

Height—Difference in elevation in feet, between lowest point in foundation and top of dam, exclusive of parapet or other projections.
Length—Overall length of barrier in feet; main dam and its integral features as located between natural abutments.
Volume—Total volume in cubic yards of all material in main dam and its appurtenant works.
Year—Date structure was originally completed for use. (1) Under construction subject to revision.
River—Mainstream.
Purpose—Irr or I—Irrigation; FC—Flood Control; P—Power Production; N—Navigation; WS—Water Supply; RR—River Regulation; DC—Debris Control.
Parentheses after name indicate type of dam as follows: (C)—Concrete; (E) Earth; (G)—Gravity; (M)—Masonry; (R)—Rock Fill.
*Replacing existing dam.

Name of dam	State	River	Ht.	Lgth.	Vol. (1,000)	Purpose	Yr.
Oroville (E)	Calif.	Feather	770	6,920	80,300	Irr-WS-P-FC	1968
Hoover (C) *Mead*	Ariz.-Nev.	Colorado	726	1,244	4,400	FC-I-P-RR-N-WS	1936
Dworshak (G)	Idaho	N. Fork Clearwater	717	3,287	6,500	FC-P-N	(1)
Glen Canyon (C) *Powell*	Ariz.	Colorado	710	1,560	4,901	P-RR	1964
Auburn (C)	Calif.	N. F. American	680	3,500	6,000	I-WS-FC-P	(1)
New Bullards Bar (C)	Calif.	North Yuba	635	2,200	2,700	FC-WS-P	1968
Melones (E)	Calif.	Stanislaus	625	1,600	15,970	I-P	(1)
Mossy Rock (C)	Wash.	Cowlitz	605	1,750	1,240	P	1968
Shasta (C)	Calif.	Sacramento	602	3,460	8,711	FC-I-P-RR-N	1945
Don Pedro (E.R.)	Calif.	Tuolumne	585	1,900	16,760	I-FC-P-WS	1970
Hungry Horse (C)	Mont.	South Fork Flathead	564	2,115	3,086	Irr-P-FC-N	1953
Grand Coulee (C) F. D. Roosevelt	Wash.	Columbia	550	4,173	10,585	I-P-RR-FC-N	1942
Ross	Wash.	Skagit	540	1,300	909	FC-P	1949
Trinity (E)	Calif.	Trinity	537	2,600	29,251	I-P	1962
Yellowtail (C)	Mont.	Bighorn	525	1,480	1,460	I-P-FC	1966
Swift (E)	Wash.	Lewis	512	2,100	15,431	P	1958
Flaming Gorge	Utah	Green	502	1,285	987		1964
Fontana (C)	N.C.	Little Tennessee	480	2,365	3,576	FC-P-RR	1944
New Exchequer (R)	Calif.	Merced	490	1,240	5,300	I-P-FC	1966
Morrow Point	Colo.	Gunnison	468	741	365	WS-D	1968
Anderson Ranch (E)	Idaho	South Fork, Boise	456	1,350	9,653	FC-Irr-P	1950
Detroit (C)	Oreg.	North Santiam	454	1,528	1,357	FC-N-P-Irr-WS-RR	1953
Carters (R, E)	Georgia	Coosawattee	454	2,053	14,272	FC-P-RR	(1)
Cougar Reservoir (E)	Oreg.	So. Fork McKenzie	445	1,730	12,572	FC-P-N-I-WS	1964
Libby (G)	Mont.	Kootenia	445	2,955	3,800	FC-P	(1)
Pine Flat (C)	Calif.	Kings	430	1,840	2,200	FC-Irr-RR-P	1954
Mud Mt. (Stevens) (E)	Wash.	White	425	700	2,300	FC	1948
Union Valley (E)	Calif.	Silver Creek	428	1,950	10,000	P	1963
Mammoth Pool (E,R)	Calif.	San Joaquin	411	820	5,151	P	1960
Lower Hell Hole (R)	Calif.	Rubicon	410	1,550	8,315	P-I-WS	1966
Navajo (E)	N. Mex.	San Juan	402	3,648	26,841	I-FC	1963
Summersville (R)	W. Va.	Gauley	398	2,280	11,494	FC	1966
Brownlee (R)	Idaho	Snake	395	1,700	6,700	P-FC	1959
Blue Mesa (E)	Colo.	Gunnison	390	785	3,080	Irr-P-FC	1966
Jocassee (ER)	S. Carolina	Kaowee	390	1,787	9,962	WS	(1)
San Luis (E)	Calif.	San Luis Cr.	382	18,600	77,670	I-P	1967
Folsom (C)	Calif.	American	375	10,200	9,010	FC-Irr-P	1955
Green Peter (G)	Oreg.	Mid. Santiam	365	1,380	942	I-P-FC-N	1967

(continued)

Continued

Name of Dam	State	River	Ht.	Lgth.	Vol.	Purpose	Yr.
Boundary (C)	Wash.	Pend Oreille	360	740	150	P	1967
Grasshopper Hollow (E)	W. Va.	Potomac (branch)	350	1,610	2,500	DC	(1)
Neversink (E)	N. Y.	Neversink	275	2,820	10,500	WS-P-FC-RR	1952
Lucky Peak (E)	Idaho	Boise	316	1,700	6,300	FC-Irr	1955
Castaic (E)	Calif.	Castaic Cr.	340	5,200	44,000	WS-I-P	(1)
Hills Creek Dam (E, G, R)	Oreg.	Mid. Fk. Willamette	338	2,170	11,789	FC-P-WS-N-Irr	1962
Casitas (E)	Calif.	Coyote Creek	334	2,000	9,310	I-WS	1959
Hell's Canyon (E)	Ore.	Snake	330	910	640	P	1968
Cherry Valley (E) *L. Lloyd*	Calif.	Cherry Creek	330	2,800	7,000	I-WS-P-FC	1955
Salt Springs (R)	Calif.	No. Fk., Mokelumne	328	1,300	3,000	P	1931
Abiquiu (E)	N. M.	Rio Chama	325	1,540	11,701	FC	1962
Yale (E)	Wash.	Lewis	323	1,550	4,201	P	1953
Beardsley (E)	Calif.	Stanislaus	320	960	3,250	IP	1957
Friant (C&G) *Millerton*	Calif.	San Joaquin	319	3,488	2,135	Irr-FC	1942
Blue River (GER)	Oregon.	Blue	319	1,420	5,180	FC-IN	(1)
Watauga (ER)	Tenn.	Watauga	318	900	3,578	FC-P-RR	1948
San Gabriel #1 (E, R)	Calif.	San Gabriel	377	1,500	11,823	FC	1939
Courtright (R)	Calif.	Helms Creek	310	850	1,450	P	1958
Sultan No. 1 (G)	Wash.	Sultan	310				1952
Green Mountain (E)	Colo.	Blue	309	1,150	4,360	Irr-P	1943
Kensico (G)	N. Y.	Bronx	307	1,843	2,975	WS	1915
Hiwassee (C)	N. C.	Hiwassee	307	1,376	801	FC-P-RR	1940
Lewis Smith (R)	Ala.	Black Warrior	305	2,200	5,140	P	1961
Downsville (E)	N. Y.	East branch, Delaware	254	2,450	9,900	FC-RR-WS-P	1955
Upper Baker (G)	Wash.	Baker	308	1,200	628	P	1959
Elephant Butte	N. M.	Rio Grande	301	1,674	630	IH	1916
Gorge (C)	Wash.	Skagit	300	656	280	P	1960
The Dalles (C & E)	Ore-Wash.	Columbia	300	8,875	5,061	N-P-I-R	1957
Granby (E)	Colo.	Colorado	298	861	2,974	Irr-P	1950
New Croton (G) *Croton*	N. Y.	Croton	297	2,168	1,450	WS	1905
Winsor (E) *Quabbin*	Mass.	Swift	295	2,640	4,000	PWS	1940
Blue River (E)	Oreg.	Blue	319	1,420	5,180	I-FC-N	(1)
Wishon (R)	Calif.	N. F., Kings	290	1,109	179	P	1958
Sly Creek (E)	Calif.	Lost Creek	289	1,490	4,345	I-P	1961
South Holston (ER)	Tenn.	South Fork, Holston	285	1,600	5,995	FC-P-RR	1950
Amistad (EC)	Texas-Mex.	Rio Grande	285	32,022	16,955	WS-FC	1969
Ruedi (E, R)	Colo.	Fryingpan	322	1,060	3,823		1968
Lemon (E)	Colo.	Florida	284	1,360	3,042	I	1963
Alamo (E)	Ariz.	Bill Williams	283	975	3,045	FC-WS	1968
Laurel River (R)	Ky.	Laurel	282	1,420	3,200	P	(1)
Whiskeytown (E)	Calif.	Clear Creek	282	4,070	4,535	I-P	1963
Cogswell (R)	Calif.	West Fork, San Gabriel	280	585	1,045	FC-I	1934
Diablo (E)	Wash.	Skagit	389	1,180	350	I-P-FC	1929
Cachuma (E)	Calif.	Santa Ynez	279	3,350	6,695	Irr-FC-WS	1953
Marshall Ford (C & E) *Travis*	Texas	Colorado (Texas)	278	5,093	2,714	P-FC-RR-N-I	1942
Santa Felicia (E) *Piru*	Calif.	Piru Creek	275	1,260	3,900	I-FC	1955
Dix River (RR)	Ky.	Dix	275	1,032	1,747	P	1924
Palisades (E)	Idaho	South Fork, Snake	270	2,100	13,571	Irr-P-FC	1957
El Capitan (ER)	Calif.	San Diego	270	1,200	2,680	WS	1934
Nacimiento (E)	Calif.	Nacimiento	270	1,470	3,412	I-FC	1957
Briones (E)	Calif.	Bear Creek	268	2,100	14,200	WS-I	1964
DeValle (E)	Calif.	Arroyo Valle	268	880	4,200	WS-I	1968
Northfield	Colo.	W. Monument	267	4,600	3,883	WS	(1)
Ball Mountain Res. (E, R)	Vt.	West	275	1,150	2,319	FC-WS	1961
Heron (E, R)	N. Mexico	Willow Cr.	265	1,250	3,227	FC-WS-I	1969
Alcova (E)	Wyo.	North Platte	265	763	1,635	Irr-P	1938
Norris (C)	Tenn.	Clinch	265	1,860	1,184	FC-P-RR	1936
Mathews (E)	Calif.	Cajalco Creek	264	2,584	3,600	WS	1938
Quabbin Dike (E)	Mass.	Swift	264	2,140	2,500	WS	1937
Wyman (GE)	Me.	Upper Kennebec	263	2,650	2,610	P	1930
Table Rock (G)	Mo.	White	261	6,423	4,550	FC-P	1959
Leroy Anderson (ER)	Calif.	Coyote Creek	260	1,385	3,320	FC	1950
Muddy Run (E)	Pa.	Offstream	265	4,800	5,600	P	1967
Lookout Point (E, R, G)	Oregon.	Middle Fork, Willamette	258	3,381	8,593	Irr-P-N-FC-WS-RR	1955
Bull Shoals (E)	Ark.	White	258	2,256	2,036	FC-P	1951
Wolf Creek (E, G)	Ky.	Cumberland	258	5,736	11,569	FC-P	1952
Gathright (R)	Va.	Jackson	257	1,172	2,330	FC-RR-WS	(1)
John W. Flannagan (R)	Va.	Pound	260	916	2,386	FC	1966
Ashokan (Olive Bridge) (G)	N.Y.	Esopus Creek	252	4,650	2,472	WS-P	1912
Cochiti (E)	N. Mexico	Rio Grande	251	28,200	41,100	FC-WS	(1)
Fort Peck (E)	Mont.	Missouri	250	21,026	125,600	FC-P-N-Irr	1940
Tygart River (G)	W. Va.	Tygart	250	1,921	1,380	FC-RR-N	1938
Terminus (E)	Calif.	Kaweah	255	2,375	6,450	FC-Irr	1962

World's Largest Dams

Source: Bureau of Reclamation, Dept. of the Interior

Based on total volume of structure. All dams listed are predominantly earthfill or rockfill and may contain concrete sections. UC—Under Construction.

Name of Dam	Cubic Yards	Completed	Name of Dam	Cubic Yards	Completed
Tarbela, Pakistan	186,000,000	U.C.	W. A. C. Bennett, Canada[2]	57,203,000	1968
Fort Peck, U.S.A.	125,612,000	1940	High Aswan (Saad-El-Aili), Egypt	55,747,000	1970
Oahe, U.S.A.	92,008,000	1963	Fort Randall, U.S.A.	50,205,000	1956
Mangla, Pakistan	85,872,000	1967	Kanev, USSR	49,520,000	U.C.
Gardiner, Canada	85,743,000	1968	Kakhovka, USSR	46,617,000	1955
Oroville, U.S.A.	78,008,000	1968	Tsimlyanska, USSR	44,323,000	1952
San Luis, U.S.A.	77,666,000	1967	Volga, V. I. Lenin, USSR	44,298,000	1955
Nurek, USSR	75,864,000	U.C.	Castaic, U.S.A.	44,000,000	1971
Nagarjuna Sagar, India	73,575,000	U.C.	Jari, Pakistan	42,400,000	1967
Garrison, U.S.A.	66,506,000	1956	Beas, India	42,261,000	U.C.
Cochiti, U.S.A.	61,005,000	U.C.	Mica, Canada	42,001,000	U.C.
Gorky, USSR	57,967,000	1955	Kremenchug, USSR	41,192,000	1961
Kiev, USSR	57,552,000	1964	[1]Formerly South Saskatchewan [2]Formerly Portage Mt.		

Hispanic Americans and the Labor Force

Source: Bureau of Labor Statistics

In April, 1974, the Bureau of Labor Statistics published the first quarterly report in a new series that will provide ongoing information on the status of Americans of Spanish origin in the labor force. The initial report compares the conditions of Hispanic Americans to blacks and whites with regard to their employment circumstances. The following are among the most interesting and relevant of the survey's findings about the Spanish-origin worker.

Hispanic teenagers in the work force represent a much higher percentage of their total group than do their white counterparts.

In relation to blacks, the Hispanic labor force has a greater percentage of adult men and a lower percentage of adult women.

Adult Spanish men engage in the labor force at a rate somewhat higher than whites and considerably higher than blacks. Adult Spanish women, however, participate at a rate slightly lower than white women and much lower than black females.

Employment Status, 1973 Averages

(Numbers in thousands.)

	Spanish	White	Black
Males, 20 years old and over			
Civilian noninstitutional population.	2,425	54,503	5,662
Civilian labor force	2,084	44,490	4,430
Percent of population.	85.9	81.6	78.2
Employed	1,973	43,183	4,170
Agriculture	167	2,269	193
Non-agriculture.	1,806	40,915	3,977
Unemployed	111	1,307	260
Rate.	5.3	2.9	5.9
Females, 20 years old and over			
Civilian noninstitutional population.	2,718	61,319	7,050
Civilian labor force	1,118	26,647	3,635
Percent of population.	41.1	43.5	51.6
Employed	1,038	25,494	3,325
Agriculture	28	506	37
Non-agriculture.	1,010	24,988	3,288
Unemployed	81	1,153	310
Rate.	7.2	4.3	8.5
Both sexes, 16 to 19 years old			
Civilian noninstitutional population.	855	13,481	2,076
Civilian labor force	401	7,552	824
Percent of population.	46.9	56.0	39.7
Employed	321	6,602	566
Agriculture	27	370	28
Non-agriculture.	294	6,232	537
Unemployed	79	950	259
Rate.	19.8	12.6	31.4
Total, 16 years and over			
Civilian noninstituuional population	5,997	129,302	14,788
Civilian labor force	3,603	78,689	8,890
Percent of population.	60.1	60.9	60.1
Employed	3,333	75,278	8,061
Agriculture	222	3,144	258
Non-agriculture.	3,111	72,134	7,803
Unemployed	280	3,411	829
Rate.	7.5	4.3	9.3

Note: Since persons of Spanish origin are also counted as white or black, the 3 groups shown will not sum to total.

Approximately two-thirds of Hispanic workers hold blue-collar or service positions and less than one-third are employed in white-collar jobs; almost half of the white work force has white-collar positions.

The unemployment rate for Spanish-origin workers, though lower than that for blacks, is considerably higher than that of whites, and women and teenagers are particularly hard hit by unemployment.

In the prime working years of 25 to 54, the percentage of unemployed Hispanic men is twice that of white men.

Type of Employment, Experienced Workers

	Employment (Numbers in thousands)			Unemployment rate (Percent of labor force)		
Occupation	Spanish	White	Black	Spanish	White	Black
Total exp'd.	3,333	75,278	8,061	6.6	3.7	7.8
Percent distri-						
bution.	100.0	100.0	100.0	...	...	...
White-collar.	28.9	49.8	28.6	4.3	2.7	6.7
Prof. & tech. . .	6.5	14.4	8.5	3.3	2.0	4.5
Mgrs. & admin. .						
non farm	5.5	10.0	3.5	1.4	1.4	2.2
Sales.	3.7	6.9	2.1	5.9	3.4	11.5
Clerical	13.2	17.5	14.5	5.5	3.8	8.2
Blue-collar	49.8	34.7	42.3	7.7	5.0	8.0
Crafts, etc.	13.0	13.9	8.8	6.4	3.6	5.3
Operative, ...						
exc. trans. . .	24.3	12.5	17.5	8.3	5.6	9.4
Transport	4.5	3.7	5.8	4.4	3.9	5.1
Nonfarm	8.0	4.6	10.2	9.5	8.1	9.5
Service	15.8	11.7	26.4	6.2	5.0	8.7
Priv. home. . . .	1.8	1.1	6.3	3.2	2.9	6.8
Other	14.0	10.6	20.1	6.6	5.2	9.2
Farm.	5.6	3.7	2.7	8.7	2.2	6.0

Some of the conditions pointed out here and shown in the tables can be explained by the unequal age distribution of the three groups, particularly the

Unemployment Ratios, 1973 Averages

	Unemployment rate			Ratio	
Age and Sex	Spanish	White	Black	Spanish-White	Black-White
Total, 16 years and over	7.5	4.3	9.3	1.7:1	2.2:1
Both sexes, 16 to 19 years . . .	19.8	12.6	33.4	1.6:1	2.5:1
Males, 20 years- and over	5.3	2.9	5.9	1.8:1	2.0:1
20 to 24 years	8.2	6.5	12.8	1.3:1	2.0:1
25 to 54 years.	4.6	2.3	4.6	2.0:1	1.0:1
55 years and over	5.2	2.5	3.2	2.1:1	1.3:1
Females, 20 years and over	7.2	4.3	8.5	1.7:1	2.0:1
20 to 24 years.	9.0	7.0	18.3	1.3:1	2.6:1
25 to 54 years.	7.0	4.0	7.0	1.8:1	1.8:1
55 years and over	4.5	2.7	3.4	1.7:1	1.3:1

Note: A ratio of 1.7:1 means that, relative to the size of their respective labor forces, for every 10 unemployed whites there were 17 unemployed Hispanic Americans.

disproportionate representation of teenagers and young adults in the Spanish-origin labor force. But this disproportion also reflects the fact that fewer Spanish-origin young men, aged 16 to 19, are attending school.

This educational disparity, in turn, results in a concentration of blue-collar workers of Spanish origin far out of proportion to other groups and occupations.

The information provided in this government report presents a rather bleak picture. Hispanic men are better situated in the labor force than black men and Hispanic women are less favorably situated than black women, but the white work force, male and female, holds a far better position than both.

Note: Spanish origin in this survey was established by self-identification with one of seven catagories: Mexican-American, Chicano, Mexican, Puerto Rican, Cuban, Central or South American, and "Other Spanish."

American Indians, by Tribe, for the U. S. and Selected States

Source: U.S. Bureau of Census

Tribe	1970	Historic[1]	Alas.	Ariz.	Calif.	Ill.	Mich.	Minn.	Mont.	N.Mex.
Total, all Indians	763,594		16,080	94,310	88,263	10,304	16,012	22,322	26,385	71,582
Apache	22,993	6,000	4,245	10,515	2,089	155	42	6	41	2,963
Blackfeet	9,921	15,000	5	47	910	82	76	32	5,415	58
Cherokee	66,150	22,000	113	519	9,491	922	858	182	82	456
Cheyenne	6,872	3,500	—	41	473	16	—	15	2,383	56
Chickasaw	5,616	8,000	5	72	625	27	7	—	—	30
Chippewa	41,946	35,000	58	121	1,621	994	4,191	15,502	2,680	43
Choctaw and Houma	23,562	20,000	7	145	2,747	228	61	19	13	175
Comanche	4,250	7,000	—	40	506	28	—	15	—	40
Creek	17,004	22,500	5	184	1,630	188	71	—	35	19
Iroquois: Mohawk	6,105		8	8	301	60	505	29	38	29
Oneida	5,673		5	5	192	375	247	48	—	31
Seneca	4,644	16,000	7	15	218	16	11	—	5	6
Onondaga, etc.	5,051		—	15	306	27	209	39	6	20
Kaw, Omaha, Osage, etc.	6,849		—	83	581	14	13	54	5	66
Kiowa	4,337	2,000	—	168	224	19	—	—	—	120
Lumbee	27,520	16,000	11	—	78	22	92	—	4	—
Menominee	4,307	3,000	—	6	64	296	37	52	—	—
Navajo	96,743	8,000	70	44,306	4,770	318	58	23	23	37,450
Papago and Pima	16,690	10,000	—	14,964	1,357	18	—	—	—	52
Potawatomi	4,626	4,000	—	39	335	114	965	—	5	12
Hopi	7,236	3,000	—	5,823	582	31	—	—	—	294
Keresan	10,087	5,000	—	429	515	29	—	5	39	8,636
Tanoan	6,342	7,500	6	207	342	13	5	—	—	5,293
Zuni	7,306	2,500	3	179	899	36	51	—	5	5,425
Seminole	5,055	2,000	19	—	340	41	14	6	16	75
Shoshone, Piaute, Chemehuevi	14,248	14,500	9	555	4,085	23	37	11	40	52
Sioux (Dakota)	47,825	25,000	144	294	3,455	358	296	1,731	2,786	154
Ute	3,815	5,000	—	65	252	—	—	7	4	53
Yakima	3,856		10	32	106	—	—	—	7	16
Yuman	7,635		4	2,746	4,432	20	—	5	—	31
All other tribes	92,962		2,193	855	19,965	843	3,317	494	10,204	464
Tribe not reported	161,543		2,131	10,090	23,506	4,853	4,702	4,004	2,534	9,453

Tribe	N.Y.	N.C.	N.D.	Okla.	Ore.	S.D.	Tex.	Utah	Wash.	Wisc.
Total, all Indians	25,560	44,195	13,565	96,803	13,210	31,043	16,921	10,551	30,824	18,776
Apache	203	33	9	746	120	4	278	54	209	64
Blackfeet	506	37	7	89	306	50	151	13	994	65
Cherokee	1,613	6,075	50	27,197	848	50	2,663	81	868	266
Cheyenne	—	20	—	2,914	11	134	135	32	214	5
Chickasaw	21	—	5	3,772	26	11	595	—	52	8
Chippewa	267	186	6,721	65	598	498	133	26	1,372	4,940
Choctaw and Houma	53	30	—	12,859	144	12	1,868	51	100	48
Comanche	23	15	—	2,743	7	—	378	16	28	—
Creek	81	32	18	10,960	68	—	863	47	68	20
Iroquois: Mohawk	3,873	22	—	56	5	—	11	9	16	6
Oneida	557	42	35	10	15	—	10	5	18	3,587
Seneca	3,340	43	—	464	43	—	37	—	26	—
Onondaga, etc.	3,543	5	5	169	21	8	62	—	57	37
Kaw, Omaha, Osage, etc.	26	5	33	3,153	58	52	125	—	41	8
Kiowa	5	—	—	3,051	38	—	394	13	5	5
Lumbee	18	26,059	33	25	—	—	19	—	30	—
Menominee	17	5	—	4	24	59	18	—	10	3,592
Navajo	22	69	—	306	221	14	676	4,903	172	35
Papago and Pima	10	—	—	66	27	11	23	15	20	—
Potawatomi	4	—	—	1,006	47	44	147	—	102	518
Hopi	48	4	—	39	38	—	59	84	27	—
Keresan	61	—	7	17	—	—	85	9	—	4
Tanoan	4	6	—	20	4	14	164	26	10	—
Zuni	4	—	—	65	27	—	113	74	36	5
Seminole	208	18	—	2,821	9	—	160	—	17	11
Shoshone, Piaute, Chemehuevi	48	4	11	100	440	79	29	505	237	18
Sioux (Dakota)	282	144	3,655	348	471	26,090	420	148	1,071	208
Ute	—	3	5	40	30	—	11	1,972	—	6
Yakima	—	—	5	211	330	—	25	—	3,053	4
Yuman	35	34	—	20	16	—	11	17	70	—
All other tribes	1,556	599	1,602	9,617	5,970	455	1,187	265	14,090	2,401
Tribe not reported	8,812	10,964	1,359	13,835	3,115	3,458	5,510	2,157	6,167	2,863

([1]) Population estimates are made from notes of explorers and other early whites in the area. The figures have been gathered from a variety of sources which vary considerably. In general, these are minimum estimates; other sources have estimated early Indian populations at 10% to 30% greater, with the larger increases going to the smaller tribes.

AGRICULTURE
Total Net Income Per Farm by States, 1965-72[1]
Source: U.S. Department of Agriculture, Economic Research Service

State	1965	1966	1967	1968	1969	1970	1971	1972
Alabama	$ 2,893	$ 2,878	$2,681	$ 3,070	$ 3,070	$ 3,663	$ 3,716	$ 4,523
Alaska	1,346	1,803	382	2,609	1,397	2,222	2,635	2,594
Arizona	23,954	19,020	23,417	30,073	31,350	27,516	31,614	32,672
Arkansas	4,099	5,775	5,146	5,539	5,681	7,061	6,432	8,725
California	11,999	13,917	13,769	17,295	16,758	15,445	16,492	21,104
Colorado	5,723	5,377	4,190	5,709	6,326	7,793	8,177	8,998
Connecticut	6,952	8,605	6,543	8,455	9,194	9,962	8,723	7,438
Delaware	8,040	7,670	9,573	8,990	15,943	9,940	10,953	14,373
Florida	10,275	10,432	11,482	13,119	14,729	13,061	17,299	21,064
Georgia	4,499	5,186	5,214	4,810	6,331	5,981	6,450	7,020
Hawaii	16,348	18,399	17,953	19,321	17,356	17,232	19,084	19,348
Idaho	6,642	5,129	6,422	5,579	8,824	8,372	8,352	10,033
Illinois	6,404	6,822	6,875	5,431	6,451	5,403	6,971	10,344
Indiana	5,063	4,635	4,355	4,125	5,800	3,946	5,924	5,968
Iowa	7,537	8,102	6,682	7,029	8,717	8,781	7,216	11,626
Kansas	4,996	5,550	4,819	4,798	6,056	7,744	8,741	11,052
Kentucky	2,740	2,857	2,915	2,972	3,563	3,265	3,446	4,243
Louisiana	3,107	4,160	5,471	5,750	4,973	6,057	6,828	8,817
Maine	8,387	7,998	3,952	5,031	7,882	7,857	7,062	8,399
Maryland	4,516	4,202	5,130	5,032	7,455	6,694	4,835	6,620
Massachusetts	5,163	6,487	4,580	5,789	6,893	5,958	5,500	4,621
Michigan	2,674	3,509	2,937	2,873	3,294	3,331	2,636	4,202
Minnesota	4,277	4,962	4,598	4,615	5,225	6,923	5,811	6,886
Mississippi	3,375	3,691	4,267	4,448	4,589	4,903	5,142	6,402
Missouri	3,833	3,295	3,272	3,872	3,696	4,141	4,245	5,798
Montana	6,258	7,834	6,162	6,106	8,453	10,714	8,430	13,438
Nebraska	6,408	8,084	7,047	6,190	9,144	7,892	8,083	11,456
Nevada	2,896	5,843	3,772	4,117	11,474	12,173	13,421	18,099
New Hampshire	2,117	2,917	1,561	2,201	2,866	3,037	3,512	5,370
New Jersey	7,512	7,896	7,265	6,724	7,116	4,910	3,762	2,460
New Mexico	6,536	8,367	7,860	8,961	10,190	11,928	10,859	11,137
New York	4,398	5,688	5,242	5,320	6,284	5,667	5,238	3,916
North Carolina	2,967	3,762	3,840	3,516	4,480	4,518	4,332	5,387
North Dakota	6,492	6,017	5,362	4,610	7,102	5,039	8,272	8,450
Ohio	2,944	4,180	2,948	3,465	3,389	3,905	3,221	4,786
Oklahoma	3,210	3,171	3,145	2,515	3,359	4,207	3,378	4,466
Oregon	3,173	3,817	3,840	3,020	4,739	4,123	3,955	5,625
Pennsylvania	3,173	3,166	4,229	3,603	4,537	4,468	3,597	2,602
Rhode Island	3,190	4,062	1,246	2,349	4,753	4,864	3,669	2,030
South Carolina	2,682	3,117	3,392	2,735	3,365	3,403	3,621	4,556
South Dakota	5,879	7,297	6,612	7,363	7,879	7,138	7,996	11,044
Tennessee	1,967	2,062	1,861	1,803	2,091	2,139	2,129	2,580
Texas	4,573	5,206	4,246	5,117	5,308	6,513	5,165	6,645
Utah	2,388	2,571	3,443	3,375	4,099	4,570	4,643	5,748
Vermont	3,666	5,278	4,158	5,324	6,301	7,399	7,866	8,465
Virginia	2,406	2,036	2,592	2,203	2,614	2,465	2,162	2,945
Washington	4,719	6,813	6,828	6,466	8,238	5,842	6,048	9,898
West Virginia	749	544	928	599	841	515	395	709
Wisconsin	4,011	4,990	4,260	4,875	4,789	6,350	5,414	5,279
Wyoming	4,306	5,749	6,719	4,751	5,937	10,975	7,487	12,601
Total U.S.	4,465	4,990	4,707	4,828	5,620	5,725	5,817	7,089

(1.) Includes changes in inventories and represents income of farm operators.

Farm Income—Cash Receipts from Marketings (in $1,000)

1972 State	Crops	Live-stock	Gov't. Pay.	Total	1972 State	Crops	Live-stock	Gov't. Pay.	Total
Ala.	303,369	616,394	68,091	987,854	Neb.	765,031	1,915,112	233,324	2,913,467
Alaska.	1,729	2,841	197	4,767	Nev.	16,207	94,313	2,619	113,139
Ariz.	342,253	479,986	49,013	871,252	N.H.	15,203	42,829	461	58,493
Ark.	730,139	673,596	81,624	1,485,359	N.J.	135,840	90,194	3,676	229,710
Calif.	3,268,272	2,205,784	122,443	5,596,499	N.M.	105,704	471,737	42,503	619,944
Colo.	303,291	1,396,479	70,906	1,770,676	N.Y.	270,757	830,801	19,939	1,121,497
Conn.	62,600	101,255	509	164,364	N.C.	1,016,828	642,372	57,529	1,716,729
Dela.	51,447	103,186	1,975	156,608	N.D.	534,445	365,261	208,122	1,107,838
Florida.	1,198,524	464,033	18,183	1,680,740	Ohio.	781,205	875,527	89,578	1,746,310
Georgia	634,392	786,774	81,064	1,502,230	Okla.	297,951	1,081,723	119,400	1,499,074
Hawaii.	177,198	46,238	11,108	234,544	Ore.	355,433	288,767	24,558	668,758
Idaho.	410,289	397,734	51,067	859,090	Pa.	249,047	840,966	22,892	1,112,905
Illinois	1,933,153	1,463,589	243,879	3,640,621	R.I.	8,204	8,946	57	17,207
Ind.	860,394	967,171	133,101	1,960,666	S.C.	345,150	214,337	49,285	608,772
Iowa.	1,436,140	3,260,692	318,511	5,015,343	S.D.	238,269	969,470	111,519	1,319,258
Kansas.	921,044	1,899,276	246,409	3,066,729	Tenn.	335,287	514,789	57,753	907,829
Ky.	492,067	593,327	36,837	1,122,231	Texas.	1,368,752	2,564,846	528,567	4,462,165
La.	506,944	323,639	50,953	881,536	Utah.	44,545	201,636	13,861	260,042
Maine.	89,425	155,248	1,295	245,968	Vt.	18,349	160,981	828	180,158
Md.	134,834	278,085	9,572	422,491	Va.	273,833	385,752	19,563	679,148
Mass.	70,067	83,768	478	154,313	Wash.	692,160	332,331	56,411	1,080,902
Mich.	466,083	564,735	61,203	1,102,021	W.V.	26,928	90,209	3,324	120,461
Minn.	799,371	1,563,993	179,974	2,543,338	Wis.	251,644	1,598,147	57,106	1,906,897
Miss.	535,054	549,527	125,875	1,210,456	Wyo.	51,535	293,786	20,595	365,916
Mo.	701,799	1,237,845	150,203	2,089,847	**Total**				
Mont.	266,536	495,517	103,169	865,222	U.S.	[1]25,075,158	35,595,544	3,961,109	[1]64,631,811

[1]Preliminary United States totals for crops and all cash receipts include an additional $180,427 not distributed to States.

Average Prices Received by U.S. Farmers

Source: Economic Research Service; Department of Agriculture

The figures represent dollars per 100 lbs. for hogs, beef cattle, veal calves, sheep, lamb and milk (wholesale); dollars per head for milk cows; cents per lb. for milk fat (in cream), chickens, broilers, turkeys and wool; cents for eggs per dozen. *Revised.

Year[1]	Hogs	Cattle (beef)	Calves (veal)	Sheep	Lambs	Cows (milk)	Milk (wholesale)	Milk fat (in cream)	Chickens (excl. broilers)	Broilers	Turkeys	Eggs	Wool
1930..	8.84	7.71	9.68	4.74	7.76	74.20	2.21	34.5	...	...	20.2	23.7	19.5
1940..	5.39	7.56	8.83	3.95	8.10	61.00	1.82	28.0	13.0	17.3	15.2	18.0	28.4
1950..	18.00	23.30	26.30	11.60	25.10	198.00	3.89	62.0	22.0	27.4	32.9	36.3	62.1
1960..	15.30	20.40	22.90	5.61	17.90	223.00	4.21	60.5	12.2	16.9	25.4	36.1	42.0
1965*	19.60	19.90	22.00	6.34	22.80	212.00	4.23	61.1	8.9	15.0	22.2	33.7	47.1
1968*	18.50	23.40	27.60	6.58	24.40	274.00	5.24	68.4	8.2	14.2	20.5	34.0	40.5
1969*	22.20	26.20	31.50	8.10	27.20	300.00	5.49	68.9	9.7	15.2	22.4	40.0	41.9
1970.	22.70	27.10	34.50	7.51	26.40	332.00	5.71	70.0	9.1	13.6	22.6	39.1	35.5
1971.	17.50	29.00	36.40	6.59	25.90	358.00	5.87	69.1	7.7	13.7	22.1	31.4	19.4
1972.	25.10	33.50	44.70	7.28	29.10	397.00	6.07	67.5	8.9	14.1	22.2	30.9	35.0
1973.	38.40	42.80	56.60	12.70	35.10	496.00	7.13	67.8	15.0	24.0	38.2	52.5	82.7

The figures represent cents per bushel for oats; cents per lb. for cotton, apples and peanuts; dollars per bushel for wheat, corn, barley and soybeans; dollars per 100 lbs. for rice, sorghum and potatoes; dollars per ton for cottonseed and baled hay.

Crop Year	Corn	Wheat	Cotton	Oats	Barley	Rice	Soy- beans	Sor- ghum	Peanuts	Cotton- seed	Hay	Potatoes	Apples
1930.	.663	.550	9.46	31.1	.420	1.74	1.34	1.02	3.46	22.00	11.00	1.47	...
1940.	.674	.601	9.83	29.8	.393	1.80	.892	.873	3.33	21.70	9.78	.850	...
1950.	2.00	1.52	39.90	78.8	1.19	5.09	2.47	1.88	10.9	86.60	21.10	1.50	...
1960.	1.74	.997	30.08	59.8	.838	4.55	2.13	1.49	10.0	42.50	21.70	2.00	4.79
1965.	1.35	1.16	29.26	62.2	1.02	4.93	2.54	1.76	11.4	46.70	23.20	2.53	4.32
1968.	1.24	1.08	22.98	59.8	.921	5.00	2.43	1.69	11.9	50.50	23.60	2.23	6.11
1969*	1.25	1.16	21.86	58.4	.885	4.95	2.35	1.91	12.3	41.10	24.70	2.24	4.06
1970.	1.33	1.33	22.81	62.3	.973	5.17	2.85	2.03	12.8	56.50	26.10	2.21	4.54
1971.	1.34	1.08	28.07	60.5	.993	5.34	3.03	1.88	13.6	56.80	28.10	1.90	4.92
1972.	1.76	1.57	27.20	72.5	1.21	6.73	4.37	2.45	14.4	49.50	31.30	3.01	6.43
1973.	4.00	2.38	44.60	116.0	2.13	13.80	5.57	3.80	16.2	100.00	41.60	4.05	8.80

(1) Weighted calendar year prices for livestock and livestock products other than wool. 1943 through 1963, wool prices are weighted on marketing year basis. The marketing year has been changed (1964) from a calendar year to a Dec.-Nov. basis for hogs, chickens, broilers and eggs. (2) Weighted crop year prices. Crop years are as follows: apples, June-May; wheat, oats, barley, hay and potatoes, July-June; cotton, rice peanuts and cottonseed, August-July; soybeans, September-August; and corn and sorghum grain, October-September. (3) Beginning 1964, 480 lb. net weight bales.

Index Numbers of Prices Received by Farmers

Source: Economic Research Service; Department of Agriculture index (1910-14 = 100 per cent)

Year	All Farm Products	All Crops	Livestock[1]	Food Grains	Feed Grains and Hay	Feed Grains	Cotton	Tobacco	Oil-bearing Crops	Fruit	Commercial Vegetables[2]	Potatoes Sweetpot[3]	Meat Animals	Dairy Products	Poultry and Eggs	Wool
1910.	104	105	102	109	96	97	118	84	120	100	...	83	101	100	104	117
1920.	211	235	190	249	202	209	262	233	208	188	...	294	171	202	222	214
1930.	125	115	134	93	106	109	104	140	111	149	128	162	133	142	128	119
1940.	100	90	109	84	85	86	83	134	103	81	122	89	108	120	09	160
1950.	258	233	280	224	193	198	282	402	276	194	211	166	340	249	186	341
1960.	239	222	253	203	152	151	254	500	214	244	230	203	296	259	160	235
1965.	248	233	261	164	174	173	245	513	265	246	261	295	319	261	145	261
1970.	280	226	326	163	177	176	183	604	266	233	294	222	405	345	151	194
1972.	320	260	371	192	183	176	245	685	320	273	328	233	494	366	137	202
1973.	438	370	496	378	283	280	274	718	574	332	379	397	666	428	232	449

(1.) Livestock and livestock products. (2.) For fresh market and processing beg. 1952. (3.) Including dry edible beans.

Average Farm Wages

Calendar year	Per month — With house	Per month — With board & room	Per week — With board & room	Per week — Without board or room	Per day — With house	Per day — With board & room	Per day — Without board or room	Per hour — With house	Per hour — Without board or room
1950.	$121.00	$99.00	$23.50	$31.00	$3.50	$4.45	$4.50	$.62	$.69
1955.	154.00	123.00	29.75	38.00	4.20	5.40	5.30	.74	.82
1960.	192.00	149.00	35.50	45.75	5.30	6.50	6.60	.88	.97
1965.	223.00	171.00	40.25	51.50	6.20	7.40	7.60	1.03	1.14
1969.	307.00	234.00	56.75	73.00	9.00	10.10	10.90	1.42	1.58
1970.	328.00	251.00	60.75	78.00	9.80	10.70	11.70	1.50	1.64
1971.	340.00	263.00	64.50	81.00	10.30	11.20	12.20	1.56	1.73
1972.	361.00	280.00	67.80	85.50	11.20	12.00	13.20	1.65	1.84
1973.	393.00	309.00	74.00	94.75	12.30	13.10	14.50	1.81	2.00

Government Payments by Programs, by States

Source: Economic Research Service: Department of Agriculture (in $1,000)

1972 State	Conser-vation[1]	Sugar Act	Wool Act	Feed Grain Program	Wheat Program	Cotton	Cropland Adjust-ment	Other[2]	Total
Alabama	5,054	.....	8	14,402	383	45,663	2,372	209	68,091
Alaska	90	.....	107	.....	.....	.....	.....	.....	68,091
Arizona	1,455	365	1,898	4,343	835	39,172	122	823	49,013
Arkansas	4,216	.....	22	2,252	1,128	73,540	255	211	81,624
California	4,653	15,270	7,912	11,802	4,862	76,765	128	1,051	122,443
Colorado	3,346	5,266	6,409	23,644	29,896	.....	887	1,458	70,906
Connecticut	299	.....	23	114	1	.....	69	3	509
Delaware	217	.....	3	1,395	316	.....	44	.....	1,975
Florida	3,164	6,086	10	6,627	118	1,048	975	155	18,183
Georgia	6,110	.....	13	34,483	1,299	35,228	3,748	183	81,064
Hawaii	137	10,971	.....	.....	.....	.....	.....	.....	11,108
Idaho	2,023	7,415	5,714	4,798	30,757	.....	57	303	51,067
Illinois	6,125	.....	1,425	211,251	23,964	112	988	14	243,879
Indiana	4,361	.....	1,266	109,108	17,255	.....	1,101	10	133,101
Iowa	7,829	50	3,318	304,948	1,173	.....	1,166	27	318,511
Kansas	6,216	1,353	1,226	98,480	137,240Rz	.....	1,096	798	246,409
Kentucky	6,253	.....	363	26,213	2,213	385	1,408	2	36,837
Louisiana	3,756	8,624	46	2,138	262	35,832	101	194	50,953
Maine	1,071	.....	97	68	3	.....	33R112	12	1,295
Maryland	1,107	.....	99	6,524	1,749	.....	90	3	9,572
Massachusetts	353	.....	37	27	.....	.....	40	21	478
Michigan	3,760	3,106	1,130	34,496	16,009	.....	2,596	106	61,203
Minnesota	5,104	3,984	2,401	147,890	17,762	.....	2,675	158	179,974
Mississippi	5,951	.....	21	9,207	593	108,985	571	547	125,875
Missouri	7,315	.....	1,172	98,121	20,800	2,532	.....	24	150,203
Montana	4,602	2,063	5,853	16,540	73,216	.....	215	680	103,169
Nebraska	4,982	3,378	1,319	166,119	54,004	.....	2,256	1,266	233,324
Nevada	493	.....	1,383	71	424	245	.....	3	2,619
New Hampshire	405	.....	28	26	.....	.....	2	.....	461
New Jersey	631	.....	36	2,233	635	.....	136	5	3,676
New Mexico	1,983	25	3,436	13,038	7,922	12,542	2,904	653	42,503
New York	4,613	.....	524	8,998	4,911	.....	882	11	19,939
North Carolina	6,245	.....	67	30,520	4,802	14,637	1,236	22	57,929
North Dakota	5,763	2,761	2,048	53,587	141,244	.....	1,929	790	208,122
Ohio	4,711	1,476	3,384	58,597	19,731	.....	1,655	24	89,578
Oklahoma	6,032	.....	437	19,259	70,637	20,937	872	1,226	119,400
Oregon	2,828	995	3,271	3,399	13,880	.....	46	139	24,558
Pennsylvania	4,719	.....	753	11,691	4,721	.....	1,007	1	22,892
Rhode Island	48	.....	6	2	.....	.....	.....	1	57
South Carolina	3,043	.....	4	12,535	2,126	29,642	1,927	8	49,285
South Dakota	3,923	.....	6,638	57,714	40,720	.....	1,677	847	111,519
Tennessee	5,085	.....	149	18,366	1,542	31,246	1,353	12	57,753
Texas	18,943	882	25,948	153,621	54,157	265,553	6,400	3,063	528,567
Utah	1,379	1,099	6,073	1,198	3,965	.....	51	96	13,861
Vermont	668	.....	30	101	.....	.....	20	9	828
Virginia	4,588	.....	1,076	9,895	3,176	309	508	11	19,563
Washington	3,050	3,950	886	5,823	41,542	.....	61	1,099	5,641
West Virginia	1,564	.....	889	662	169	.....	40	.....	3,324
Wisconsin	4,672	.....	689	47,704	575	.....	3,206	260	57,106
Wyoming	2,052	2,712	10,150	1,354	3,689	.....	61	577	20,595
Total U.S.	186,987	81,831	109,797	1,845,384	855,845	812,641	51,509	17,115	3,961,109

(1) Includes amounts paid under other similar programs not listed separately.
(2) Includes Milk Indemnity, Great Plains Conservation.

Cooperative Farm Credit System

Loans outstanding to farmers and farmer's cooperatives from banks and associations supervised by the Farm Credit Admin.

Year ended Dec. 31	Farm mort-gage loans Federal land banks	Farm produc-tion loans Production Credit ass'ns	Loans to co-operatives by banks for cooperatives	FICB loans and discounts other than interagency	Total
1950	946,469,000	455,472,000	344,979,000	70,220,000	1,816,940,000
1955	1,497,165,000	653,478,000	370,683,000	70,785,000	2,592,111,000
1960	2,563,772,000	1,490,138,000	648,859,000	91,951,000	4,794,720,000
1965	4,280,675,000	2,598,460,000	1,055,163,000	146,091,000	8,080,389,000
1970	7,187,139,000	5,334,495,000	2,029,864,000	222,098,000	14,773,598,000
1971	7,918,185,000	6,115,524,000	2,013,491,000	238,931,000	16,286,131,000
1972	9,104,930,000	6,636,075,000	2,297,805,000	252,681,000	18,291,429,000
1973	11,073,276,000	7,859,554,000	2,576,748,000	333,207,000	21,842,785,000

Farm Employment—Annual Averages

Source: Economic Research Service; Department of Agriculture

Yr.	Total Aver. No. (1,000)	Index %	Family Aver. No. (1,000)	Index %	Hired Aver. No. (1,000)	Index %	Yr.	Total Aver. No. (1,000)	Index %	Family Aver. No. (1,000)	Index %	Hired Aver. No. (1,000)	Index %
1920	13,432	99	10,041	99	3,391	100	1960	7,057	52	5,172	52	1,885	55
1930	12,497	92	9,307	92	3,190	94	1970	4,523	34	3,348	33	1,175	35
1940	10,979	81	8,300	82	2,679	79	1972	4,373	32	3,228	32	1,145	34
1950	9,926	73	7,597	75	2,329	69	1973	4,337	32	3,169	31	1,168	34

Index (1910-14-100 per cent)

Farm-Mortgage Debt Outstanding by Lender Groups

Source: National Economic Analysis Division, U.S. Department of Agriculture

Year (Jan. 1)	Total farm-Mortgage Debt[1]	Amounts held by principal lender groups				
		Federal land Banks[2]	Farmers Home Adminis-tration[33]	Life In-surance Com-panies[4]	Commer-cial & Savings Banks[5]	Indi-viduals and Others[6]
	$1,000	$1,000	$1,000	$1,000	$1,000	$1,000
1961	12,812,210	2,538,425	481,610	2,974,609	1,686,139	5,131,427
1963	15,159,843	3,023,149	585,263	3,391,183	2,053,369	6,106,879
1964	16,792,450	3,280,842	601,397	3,778,537	2,356,130	6,775,544
1965	18,880,151	3,685,501	615,463	4,284,921	2,662,479	7,631,787
1966	21,168,703	4,234,021	627,109	4,798,970	2,933,814	8,574,789
1967	23,283,052	4,908,094	581,589	5,210,915	3,164,223	9,418,231
1968	25,465,138	5,552,844	532,702	5,537,000	3,537,172	10,305,420
1969	27,117,924	6,070,619	490,264	5,761,200	3,851,297	10,944,544
1970	28,387,125	6,660,275	452,412	5,731,700	4,109,158	11,433,580
1971	29,506,876	7,128,323	343,967	5,608,300	4,440,766	11,985,520
1972	31,334,044	7,861,624	310,382	5,562,400	4,214,206	13,385,432
1973	34,470,812	9,050,067	272,406	5,643,300	4,792,185	14,712,854
1974[7]	39,419,744	10,949,800	174,000	5,991,754	5,458,280	16,845,910

(1.) Excludes Alaska, Hawaii, Territories and possessions.

(2.) Includes regular mortgages, purchase-money mortgages, and sales contracts.

(3.) Direct farm loans only. Includes farm-purchase, farm-enlargement, farm-development and loans primarily for refinancing purposes, project-liquidation, rural-housing (excludes nonfarm), and soil and water loans to individuals, and loans for these purposes from State Corporation trust funds. Farmers Home Administration also insures farm mortgage loans. They are held by miscellaneous lenders and are reported in the "Individuals and others" column, except for banks in years 1961-70.

(4.) Estimates based on direct reports from life insurance companies and official reports submitted to state insurance commissioners. Includes legal reserve companies only and regular mortgages, purchase-money mortgages, and unpaid principal sales contracts. Beginning 1965, excludes sales contracts.

(5.) All operating banks from 1961-71 includes bank holdings of soil and water loans and farm-ownership loans insured by the Farmers Home Administration. In 1971, a change in bank reporting procedures required banks to report F.H.A. insured loans they held as government securities rather than as farm loans as had been the case previously.

(6.) The amounts shown are residuals or differences between the amounts reported by institutional lenders and the estimates of total farm-mortgage debt. They may be taken as debt held by individuals and other nonreporting lenders.

(7.) Preliminary.

Canadian Farm Cash Receipts[1]

Source: Statistics Canada

(in millions of dollars)

Crops

Year and quarter	Total cash receipts	Total crops	Wheat[2]	Oats[2]	Barley[2]	CWB Advance pay-ments[3]	Other grains[4]	Sugar beets	Pota-toes	Fruits	Vege-tables	Tobacco	Other crops[5]
1971	4,529.76	1,713.13	721.18	33.70	208.88	—84.57	290.29	18.58	63.90	84.40	99.73	135.36	131.71
1972	5,307.43	2,081.89	948.20	31.85	221.41	—27.46	312.59	20.89	86.58	84.61	115.04	150.03	138.12
1973 1	1,419.51	511.81	179.10	7.01	33.63	—4.31	119.28	3.07	41.24	5.95	13.03	84.75	29.06
2	1,408.74	400.34	181.27	4.17	39.78	—2.41	107.42	1.32	33.70	6.60	9.34	—	19.16
3	1,899.58	794.99	362.73	11.14	88.17	5.66	132.12	2.42	36.89	58.52	62.99	—	34.35

Livestock and Products

Year & Quarter	Total	Cattle	Hogs	Sheep	Dairy Products	Poultry	Eggs	Other	Total forest and maple products	Dairy sup-plementary payments	Deficiency payments
1971	2,697.74	1,079.97	443.55	7.90	705.70	262.58	151.72	46.34	17.31	100.35	1.24
1972	3,076.56	1,195.84	575.71	9.06	778.82	295.85	163.77	57.31	24.46	101.41	23.10
1973 1	887.29	389.45	194.86	2.46	160.89	69.99	51.74	17.90	2.44	17.91	0.06
2	968.35	394.42	192.78	2.18	228.32	84.83	56.42	9.40	17.93	22.06	0.06
3	1,064.37	391.85	213.31	2.59	235.81	144.37	62.52	13.92	0.66	39.57	—

[1]Cash receipts from farming operations excluding supplementary payments. Excludes Newfoundland. [2]Including participation payments made by the Canadian Wheat Board direct to producers on crops delivered in previous years. [3]Net cash. [4]Includes rye, flaxseed, rapeseed, soybeans, and corn. [5]Includes clover and grass seed, hay, clover, greenhouse products, mustard seed, sunflower seed, hops, dry beans and dry peas and miscellaneous products.

Canada-Farm Cash Receipts from Farming Operations

Source: Statistics Canada

Province	1969	1970	1971	1972	1973
Prince Edward Island	37,870	44,533	39,111	44,017	73,520
Nova Scotia	63,380	65,855	64,383	70,147	93,281
New Brunswick	51,281	57,526	51,633	64,151	94,916
Quebec	672,495	654,285	686,044	776,678	951,583
Ontario	1,378,868	1,393,263	1,387,619	1,581,364	1,920,608
Manitoba	350,409	340,364	378,415	484,370	629,307
Saskatchewan	718,329	725,200	915,457	1,200,782	1,435,077
Alberta	729,598	715,344	803,673	921,794	1,219,505
British Columbia	197,589	212,004	221,668	243,447	323,477
Total	**4,199,819**	**4,208,374**	**4,548,003**	**5,386,750**	**6,741,274**

Production of Chief United States Crops

Source: Economic Research Service: Department of Agriculture

Year	Corn grain 1,000 bushels	Oats 1,000 bushels	Barley 1,000 bushels	Sorghums for grain 1,000 bushels	All Wheat 1,000 bushels	Rye 1,000 bushels	Flax- seed 1,000 bushels	Cotton Lint 1,000 bales	Cotton Seed 1,000 tons
1965...	4,102,867	929,554	393,055	672,698	1,315,603	33,307	35,402	14,938	6,237
1968...	4,449,542	950,689	426,151	731,277	1,556,635	22,971	26,983	10,926	4,640
1969...	4,687,057	965,863	427,055	729,919	1,442,679	30,204	34,929	9,990	4,068
1970...	4,151,938	917,159	416,139	683,571	1,351,558	36,840	29,548	10,192	4,068
1971...	5,641,112	881,227	463,601	875,752	1,617,789	49,288	18,198	10,477	4,244
1972...	5,573,320	691,973	423,461	809,264	1,544,936	29,183	13,909	13,702	5,440
1973...	5,643,320	663,860	424,483	936,587	1,711,400	26,398	16,437	12,961	5,216

Year	Tobacco 1,000 lbs.	All Hay 1,000 tons	Beans dry edible 1,000 cwt.	Peas dry field 1,000 cwt.	Peanuts 1,000 cwt.	Soy- beans 1,000 bushels	Pota- toes 1,000 cwt.	Sweet Pota- toes 1,000 cwt.	Five seed crops* 1,000 lbs.
1965...	1,854,568	125,610	16,457	3,031	2,389,596	845,608	291,109	15,469	302,592
1968...	1,710,348	124,244	17,435	2,727	2,546,591	1,106,958	295,401	13,378	219,015
1969...	1,803,272	126,026	18,913	3,736	2,535,394	1,133,120	312,418	14,370	229,455
1970...	1,906,453	126,971	17,399	3,315	2,979,465	1,127,100	325,752	13,409	254,429
1971...	1,704,884	129,119	15,917	3,930	3,005,118	1,175,989	319,354	11,718	220,059
1972...	1,749,280	128,614	18,118	2,103	3,274,761	1,270,630	295,955	12,453	165,876*
1973...	1,768,063	134,608	16,803	1,665	3,447,892	1,566,518	297,352	12,375	171,097

*Five seed crops include alfalfa, red clover, sweet clover, lespedeza, and timothy. Beginning 1972 sweet clover was discontinued.

Year	Sugar and seed* 1,000 tons	Syrup 1,000 gallons	Sugar 1,000 tons	Pecans 1,000 tons	Al- monds 1,000 tons	Wal- nuts 1,000 tons	Fil- berts 1,000 tons	Oranges and tan- gerines 1,000 boxes	Grape- fruit 1,000 boxes
1965...............	23,663	2,923	20,918,100	125.6	72.9	80.3	7.7	139,650	46,695
1968...............	24,825	2,661	25,363,300	96.2	74.5	95.6	7.6	188,090	54,170
1969...............	22,615	Disc.	27,736,300	113.0	122.0	105.5	7.4	189,640	53,910
1970...............	23,996	...	26,387,000	77.6	124.0	111.8	9.3	194,790	60,560
1971...............	24,172	...	27,096,000	123.6	134.0	136.4	11.4	196,400	64,140
1972...............	28,332	...	28,410,000	-91.6	125.0	116.8	10.2	229,390	65,640
1973...............	27,542	...	24,540,000	130.0	133.0	168.9	12.0	219,300	63,700

Agricultural Products, Production and Exports

Source: Foreign Agricultural Service, Dept. of Agriculture

Commodity[1]	Unit	Production U.S.	Production World	Production %U.S.	Exports U.S.	Exports World	Exports %U.S.
Wheat, grain only	Mil. M.T.	42.0	334.5	12.6	30.7	67.3	45.6
Oats	Mil. M.T.	10.0	51.3	19.5	0.1	1.6	6.3
Corn	Mil. M.T.	141.6	286.7	49.4	29.6	43.4	68.2
Barley	Mil. M.T.	9.2	138.7	6.6	3.9	11.8	33.1
Soybeans	Mil. M.T.	42.6	57.8	73.7	[3]13.2	[2] [3]15.0	88.0
Rice	Mil. M.T.	4.2	308.8	1.4	[4] [3]1.2	[4] [3]6.5	18.5
Lard[2]	Mil. Lbs.	1,252.2	8,139.6	15.4	113.3	997.0	11.4
Tallow & Grease[2]	Mil. Lbs.	5,317.9	9,728.7	54.7	2,235.6	3,086.0	72.4
Tobacco, Unmftd	Mil. Lbs.	1,788.0	10,429.0	17.1	613.0	2,337.0	26.2
Edible Veg. Oils	Mil. M.T.	[5]15.7	[6]47.5	33.1	[6] [5]1.6	[6] [8]13.5	11.9
Cotton	1,000 Bales[9]	13,792.0	59,392.0	23.2	5,311.0	20,629.0	25.7

[1]Crop 1972-73 as follows: wheat, oats and barley year beginning July 1; corn, October 1; soybeans, September 1; rice and cotton, August 1; other commodities on calendar year 1973 and partially estimated. Excludes Alaska, Hawaii and Puerto Rico except for exports. [2]Calendar year. [3]Excludes estimates for Peoples Republic of China. [4]Milled rice. [5]U.S. oil production figures include oil equivalent of exported oilseeds. [6]Excludes the palm oils. [7]Excludes re-exports and exports of oil produced from imported oilseeds. [8]Exports from producing countries. [9]Bales of 480 pounds net weight.

Canadian Harvested Acreage

Source: Statistics Canada

Principal Crops[1] (in thousands of acres)

Province	1970	1971	1972	Province	1970	1971	1972
Prince Edward Island.........	389	394	315	Manitoba.................	7,624	9,304	8,923
Nova Scotia	253	254	189	Saskatchewan.............	19,423	27,584	25,147
New Brunswick	378	373	282	Alberta.................	15,729	18,406	17,302
Quebec.................	4,732	4,728	3,889	British Columbia...........	826	871	933
Ontario.................	7,538	7,618	7,798	Total[2].................	56,891	69,532	85,803

[1]Crops included are winter wheat, spring wheat, oats, barley, fall rye, spring rye, flaxseed, mixed grains, corn for grain, buckwheat, peas, dry beans, soybeans, rapeseed, potatoes, mustard seed, sunflower seed, tame hay, fodder corn, field roots and sugar beets.
[2]Excluding Newfoundland.

Farms in United States by State — Number, Acreage and Value

Source: Bureau of the Census (Census of 1970)

State	Farms No.	Average Acreage	$ Value per Acre	2,000 Acres or more	10-49 Acres	Total Acreage
Alabama	72,491	188.3	$199.60	629	21,439	13,654,215
Alaska	322	4,831.9	12.73	35	32	1,604,211
Arizona	5,890	6,486.0	69.72	897	1,229	38,202,667
Arkansas	60,433	259.7	260.03	625	10,935	15,694,527
California	77,875	458.7	474.65	2,926	28,915	35,722,348
Colorado	27,950	1,312.9	94.58	4,166	3,048	36,697,132
Connecticut	4,490	120.5	921.19	6	1,245	541,372
Delaware	3,710	181.6	498.96	14	872	673,895
Florida	35,586	394.3	354.58	1,062	12,413	14,031,998
Georgia	67,431	234.4	234.00	693	13,737	15,805,892
Hawaii	3,896	528.2	296.82	70	1,281	2,058,087
Idaho	25,475	565.9	176.55	1,218	4,382	14,416,521
Illinois	123,565	242.0	489.52	145	13,487	29,913,190
Indiana	101,479	173.1	406.05	65	19,522	17,572,865
Iowa	140,354	239.1	391.73	84	9,586	33,569,629
Kansas	86,057	573.9	158.78	3,341	5,231	49,390,369
Kentucky	125,069	127.6	253.05	114	26,761	15,968,243
Louisiana	42,269	231.5	321.33	536	13,610	9,788,662
Maine	7,971	220.7	160.79	25	948	1,759,700
Maryland	17,181	163.1	639.63	41	3,733	2,803,442
Massachusetts	5,703	122.8	564.63	7	1,622	700,578
Michigan	77,946	152.7	326.31	43	14,334	11,900,689
Minnesota	110,747	260.4	225.76	305	6,459	28,845,240
Mississippi	72,577	221.0	233.53	894	17,060	16,039,665
Missouri	137,067	236.5	224.22	396	16,823	32,420,284
Montana	24,951	2,521.6	59.57	7,596	1,485	62,918,247
Nebraska	72,257	677.4	154.38	3,509	3,113	48,949,376
Nevada	2,112	5,070.2	53.35	333	305	10,708,346
New Hampshire	2,902	211.1	238.78	6	443	612,750
New Jersey	8,493	121.9	1,092.31	13	2,471	1,035,678
New Mexico	11,641	4,019.6	41.87	2,660	1,704	46,792,302
New York	51,909	195.5	273.13	50	6,589	10,148,359
North Carolina	119,386	106.6	333.31	205	42,911	12,733,751
North Dakota	46,381	929.6	93.82	3,157	721	43,117,831
Ohio	111,332	153.6	398.51	53	19,729	17,111,459
Oklahoma	83,037	433.6	172.58	2,024	7,655	36,007,719
Oregon	29,063	619.9	150.22	1,739	9,000	18,017,850
Pennsylvania	62,824	141.6	372.88	38	10,428	8,900,767
Rhode Island	700	98.1	733.75	....	235	68,720
South Carolina	39,559	176.7	261.23	286	12,129	6,991,718
South Dakota	45,726	996.9	83.69	4,148	1,402	45,584,164
Tennessee	121,406	124.0	267.50	212	35,117	15,056,907
Texas	213,550	667.6	148.49	9,941	27,315	142,566,826
Utah	13,045	867.2	91.90	849	3,159	11,312,951
Vermont	6,874	278.6	223.73	17	465	1,915,520
Virginia	64,572	164.9	286.13	206	15,169	10,649,862
Washington	34,033	515.9	225.83	1,693	10,817	17,559,187
West Virginia	23,142	187.5	135.69	67	3,808	4,340,554
Wisconsin	98,973	182.9	231.98	81	8,118	18,109,273
Wyoming	8,838	4,014.0	40.73	2,689	473	35,476,374
Total	**2,730,242**	**390.5**	**—**	**59,909**	**473,465**	**1,066,218,650**

Egg Production in Canada

Source: Statistics Canada
(thousand dozens)

Province	1971	1972	1973	Province	1971	1972	1973
Newfoundland	8,736	8,481	6,835	Ontario	192,618	191,091	190,728
Prince Edward Island	2,490	2,350	2,377	Manitoba	55,540	52,068	53,622
Nova Scotia	20,471	17,373	18,443	Saskatchewan	26,187	23,931	21,914
New Brunswick	9,590	9,932	10,139	Alberta	42,143	41,315	41,437
Quebec	73,547	64,490	58,897	British Columbia	58,341	57,324	56,873
				Total	**489,663**	**468,355**	**461,265**

Gross income from farm eggs (1971) $161,416,000; (1972) $173,882,000; (1973) $255,303,000. Average price of eggs sold for consumption taking the month of February (1971) $.295; (1972) $.304; (1973) $.450. Gross income from farm chickens (1971) $178,942,000; (1972) $211,851,000; (1973) $311,425,000. Fowl produced (1971) 25,368,000, $10,539,000; (1972) 21,191,-000, $8,631,000; (1973) 23,965,000, $13,567,000. Gross income from eggs and chickens (includes fowls) (1971) $343,863,000; (1972) $386,617,000; (1973) $570,662,000.

Canada — Production of Sawn Lumber [1]

Source: Canadian Statistical Review (July, 1974)
(million feet, board measure)

Year	Canada	N.S.	N.B.	Que.	Ont.	Sask.	Alta.	B.C.
1971	12,723.0	157.9	298.8	1,808.6	960.7	111.0	470.0	8,916.0
1972	13,887.5	179.2	313.6	2,146.9	1,082.9	135.6	580.0	9,446.9
1973	15,089.7	195.2	336.6	2,274.0	1,167.8	181.6	657.0	10,277.5
1974 Jan.	1,289.8	11.6	23.6	187.9	100.7	14.2	14.0	811.8

(1) Excludes Newfoundland, P.E.I., Manitoba, the Yukon and the Northwest Territories which, together, account for less than 1% of the total.

Production of Principal Field Crops in Canada

Source: Statistic Canada

1973	Wheats 1,000 bushels	Oats 1,000 bushels	Barley 1,000 bushels	Ryes 1,000 bushels	Flaxseed 1,000 bushels
Canada[1]	628,738	326,880	474,570	14,282	19,400
Prince Edward Island	284	2,107	518	—	—
Nova Scotia	95	617	187	—	—
New Brunswick	96	1,748	355	—	—
Quebec	1,091	19,912	1,255	41	—
Ontario	15,172	25,596	17,255	1,320	—
Manitoba	80,000	63,000	83,000	2,145	7,600
Saskatchewan	395,000	99,000	164,000	4,920	8,900
Alberta	134,000	111,000	202,000	5,800	2,900
British Columbia	3,000	3,900	6,000	56	—

	Mixed Grains 1,000 bushels	Corn Grain 1,000 bushels	Soybeans 1,000 bushels	Rapeseed 1,000 bushels	Potatoes 1,000 c.w.t.
Canada[1]	97,013	108,941	14,570	53,200	46,803
Prince Edward Island	3,402	—	—	—	8,610
Nova Scotia	221	—	—	—	557
New Brunswick	231	—	—	—	9,964
Quebec	3,384	7,011	—	—	7,275
Ontario	49,350	101,050	14,570	—	7,717
Manitoba	12,500	880	—	7,700	4,400
Saskatchewan	8,800	—	—	24,000	580
Alberta	18,800	—	—	21,500	4,500
British Columbia	325	—	—	—	3,200

	Mustard seed 1,000 pounds	Sunflower seed 1,000 pounds	Tame hay 1,000 tons	Fodder corn 1,000 tons	Sugar beets 1,000 tons
Canada[1]	262,000	90,900	26,448	11,276	993
Prince Edward Island	—	—	258	—	—
Nova Scotia	—	—	284	—	—
New Brunswick	—	—	333	—	—
Quebec	—	—	5,377	1,991	106
Ontario	—	—	7,296	8,820	—
Manitoba	32,000	87,500	2,200	165	307
Saskatchewan	180,000	2,000	2,900	—	—
Alberta	50,000	1,400	6,400	—	580
British Columbia	—	—	1,400	400	—

(1) Excluding Newfoundland

Grain Receipts at Western Grain Centers

Source: Canadian Grain Commission (In thousands of bushels)

Crop Year 1972-73

Province	Wheat	Oats	Barley	Rye	Flaxseed	Rapeseed	Total
Western Canada	633,258	32,484	236,816	9,252	18,346	62,949	993,105
Manitoba	64,992	14,152	51,297	1,359	4,823	8,426	145,049
Saskatchewan	445,744	8,661	99,642	4,612	10,695	32,086	601,440
Alberta	122,523	9,670	85,876	3,281	2,829	22,437	246,616

Farmers' Marketing, Farm Supply, Related Service Cooperatives

Source: Farmer Cooperative Service, U.S. Dept. of Agriculture (Marketing Season 1969-70[1])

A marketing season includes the period during which the farm products of a specified year are moved into the channels of trade. Marketing seasons overlap.

State	Cooperatives No.	Memberships	Net business[2] ($1,000)	State	Cooperatives No.	Memberships	Net business[2] ($1,000)
Alabama	67	70,740	169,201	Montana	163	64,365	139,005
Alaska	2	420	2,820	Nebraska	346	261,555	557,435
Arizona	17	84,085	157,579	Nevada	3	675	6,498
Arkansas	106	99,455	318,259	New Hampshire	6	2,885	32,119
California	321	86,970	2,113,428	New Jersey	48	21,490	132,249
Colorado	94	49,905	298,184	New Mexico	25	7,835	40,624
Connecticut	19	5,685	80,144	New York	302	135,235	955,507
Delaware	8	12,995	18,931	North Carolina	38	155,680	314,919
Florida	96	50,720	433,694	North Dakota	495	229,645	418,466
Georgia	76	132,525	384,000	Ohio	214	246,255	717,700
Hawaii	21	1,750	17,251	Oklahoma	158	139,030	282,259
Idaho	73	56,770	189,148	Oregon	78	66,620	329,706
Illinois	361	388,910	1,049,542	Pennsylvania	126	82,000	516,522
Indiana	117	419,800	624,338	Rhode Island	1	790	12,267
Iowa	478	418,775	1,259,908	South Carolina	20	31,955	89,997
Kansas	283	209,000	555,587	South Dakota	282	172,700	274,700
Kentucky	85	200,370	255,398	Tennessee	127	153,330	207,440
Louisiana	93	19,155	130,251	Texas	501	169,905	717,801
Maine	14	10,495	69,179	Utah	50	17,975	140,936
Maryland	42	51,215	154,211	Vermont	15	8,630	128,176
Massachusetts	18	8,990	96,874	Virginia	120	180,445	273,585
Michigan	160	132,080	522,604	Washington	164	114,205	480,114
Minnesota	984	562,815	1,270,271	West Virginia	66	48,680	60,006
Mississippi	125	139,635	312,088	Wisconsin	565	419,845	1,166,704
Missouri	186	399,395	567,529	Wyoming	31	10,425	28,787

(1) Preliminary. (2). The volume of a Hawaiian sugar coop based in Calif. is included in the dollar volume of Calif.

Grain, Hay, Potato, Cotton, Tobacco Production

Source: Economic Research Service: Department of Agriculture (preliminary)

1973 State	Barley 1,000 bushels	Corn; grain 1,000 bushels	Cotton¹ lint 1,000 bales	All Hay 1,000 tons	Oats 1,000 bushels	Potatoes 1,000 cwt.	Rye 1,000 bushels	Tobacco 1,000 pounds	All Wheat 1,000 bushels
Alabama	...	28,060	450	977	740	2,298	...	869	2,024
Alaska	...	...	...	...	...	...	...	...	...
Arizona	9000	288	653	1,518	...	2,079	...	...	15,120
Arkansas	(2)	735	1,035	1,546	3,685	(2)	...	...	6,076
California	47,940	24,675	1,750	7,865	4,620	21,208	...	...	30,880
Colorado	12,361	44,676	...	3,044	1,763	9,665	209	...	59,568
Connecticut	...	...	...	189	...	572	...	7,048	...
Delaware	946	15,810	...	54	...	1,326	198	...	910
Florida	...	14,620	12	367	418	5,510	...	23,999	660
Georgia	560	80,160	395	1,165	3,500	...	1,610	98,210	3,240
Hawaii	...	...	...	...	...	...	...	...	...
Idaho	43,460	2,492	...	4,130	3,000	77,530	(2)	...	48,395
Illinois	490	996,010	...	3,251	19,780	279	462	...	37,800
Indiana	462	534,480	...	2,121	12,528	1,407	299	12,900	24,605
Iowa	(2)	1,204,200	...	7,324	63,600	455	104	...	837
Kansas	3,280	154,000	...	5,796	4,000	(2)	840	...	384,800
Kentucky	1,925	85,850	...	3,081	504	(2)	46	340,714	5,412
Louisiana	...	2,730	525	745	344	191	...	150	396
Maine	...	...	...	376	1,564	28,700	...	...	...
Maryland	4,128	42,500	...	604	1,352	320	276	26,400	3,944
Massachusetts	...	...	...	252	...	592	...	2,079	...
Michigan	897	133,510	...	3,394	16,500	8,640	825	...	19,880
Minnesota	40,230	513,360	...	8,007	142,800	14,970	3,150	...	78,152
Mississippi	...	5,772	1,800	1,208	800	170	...	...	2,700
Missouri	429	228,800	185	5,948	1,394	(2)	252	3,990	25,500
Montana	60,000	803	...	4,100	10,260	1,462	(2)	...	96,714
Nebraska	1,188	544,050	...	7,619	22,080	1,352	1,780	...	93,800
Nevada	750	...	2	891	86	...	...	...	800
New Hampshire	...	...	...	172	...	90	...	...	...
New Jersey	833	5,925	...	304	258	1,721	192	...	1,368
New Mexico	1,380	1,470	145	1,001	...	880	...	...	8,526
New York	480	27,720	...	5,204	17,875	12,170	480	...	5,040
North Carolina	2,852	114,800	165	533	3,750	1,984	266	813,235	5,600
North Dakota	103,230	10,080	...	4,109	73,800	19,140	3,157	...	252,476
Ohio	468	240,160	...	3,386	25,920	2,220	208	18,060	23,040
Oklahoma	7,755	7,830	430	3,892	7,954	...	1,333	...	157,800
Oregon	10,920	810	...	2,266	5,940	15,915	216	...	35,276
Pennsylvania	6,820	81,120	...	4,380	17,625	6,000	405	23,100	7,392
Rhode Island	...	...	...	18	...	796	...	...	...
South Carolina	936	23,650	295	461	2,856	...	612	132,660	2,525
South Dakota	22,085	142,020	...	5,505	100,580	770	7,956	...	58,270
Tennessee	420	33,528	440	1,850	1,160	336	38	103,204	4,464
Texas	3,510	60,800	4,676	5,808	26,650	3,778	648	...	98,600
Utah	7,695	1,430	...	1,660	756	1,100	...	...	6,331
Vermont	...	...	...	907	...	150	...	...	...
Virginia	4,606	46,200	3	1,823	1,932	3,255	360	138,590	6,475
Washington	15,000	7,208	...	2,215	2,200	35,260	120	...	89,200
West Virginia	430	5,229	...	1,034	828	256	...	3,230	372
Wisconsin	777	173,470	...	10,622	56,170	11,515	176	19,625	890
Wyoming	6,240	2,225	...	1,886	2,288	1,220	180	...	5,542
Total U.S.	**424,483**	**5,643,256**	**12,961**	**134,608**	**663,860**	**297,352**	**26,398**	**1,768,063**	**1,711,400**

¹Equiv. 480 lbs. ²Estimates discontinued after 1972.

Production and Consumption of Meat and Lard

Source: Economic Research Service: Department of Agriculture (in million lbs.)

Year	Beef Production	Beef Consumption	Veal Production	Veal Consumption	Lamb and Mutton Production	Lamb and Mutton Consumption	Pork (exclud. Lard) Production	Pork (exclud. Lard) Consumption	All Meats Production	All Meats Consumption	Lard Production	Lard Consumption
1940	7,175	7,257	981	981	876	873	10,044	9,701	19,076	18,812	2,288	1,901
1950	9,534	9,529	1,230	1,206	597	596	10,714	10,390	22,075	21,721	2,631	1,891
1960	14,753	15,147	1,109	1,093	768	852	11,607	11,566	28,237	28,658	2,562	1,358
1965	18,727	19,060	1,020	992	651	716	11,141	11,235	31,539	32,003	2,045	1,225
1969	21,158	22,065	673	654	550	687	12,953	12,938	35,334	36,334	1,904	1,011
1970	21,685	22,926	588	581	551	657	13,436	13,391	36,260	37,555	1,913	939
1971	21,902	23,084	546	545	555	645	14,792	14,904	37,795	39,178	1,960	880
1972	22,419	23,962	459	465	543	684	13,640	13,921	37,061	39,032	1,559	796
1973	21,277	22,812	357	376	514	557	12,751	12,820	34,899	36,565	1,254	714

Harvested Acreage of Principal Crops

Source: Economic Research Service: Department of Agriculture. In thousands of acres

State	1971	1972	1973	State	1971	1972	1973
Alabama	2,920	2,914	3,054	Nebraska	16,271	15,415	17,452
Alaska	—	—	—	Nevada	505	471	497
Arizona	1,052	1,043	1,097	New Hampshire	112	111	108
Arkansas	7,253	7,193	7,541	New Jersey	380	360	390
California	5,781	5,628	5,912	New Mexico	1,063	1,024	1,193
Colorado	5,583	5,418	5,765	New York	3,866	3,730	3,872
Connecticut	149	142	146	North Carolina	4,371	4,116	4,556
Delaware	461	444	465	North Dakota	19,025	17,286	19,286
Florida	1,140	1,186	1,247	Ohio	9,548	9,262	9,744
Georgia	4,283	4,073	4,544	Oklahoma	8,111	7,979	9,510
Hawaii	122	115	116	Oregon	2,407	2,393	2,545
Idaho	3,890	3,865	4,079	Pennsylvania	4,394	4,247	4,330
Illinois	20,461	19,946	22,221	Rhode Island	18	18	17
Indiana	11,110	10,697	11,640	South Carolina	2,561	2,438	2,600
Iowa	21,820	20,916	23,583	South Dakota	15,110	13,755	14,918
Kansas	19,686	18,809	20,731	Tennessee	4,081	3,991	4,221
Kentucky	4,076	4,047	4,262	Texas	17,623	17,671	21,946
Louisiana	3,660	3,716	3,741	Utah	1,061	1,070	1,114
Maine	447	430	423	Vermont	584	574	566
Maryland	1,355	1,332	1,407	Virginia	2,724	2,661	2,699
Massachusetts	152	146	151	Washington	4,212	4,189	4,423
Michigan	5,757	5,533	5,815	West Virginia	751	735	765
Minnesota	18,580	17,090	19,746	Wisconsin	8,972	8,526	8,843
Mississippi	5,246	5,194	5,223	Wyoming	1,761	1,740	1,755
Missouri	12,085	11,486	12,309				
Montana	8,739	8,333	8,935	Total U. S.	295,319	283,458	311,503

Crop acreages included are corn, sorghum, oats, barley, wheat, rice, rye, soybeans, flaxseed, peanuts, popcorn, cotton, all hay, dry beans, dry peas, potatoes, sweet potatoes, tobacco, sugarcane and sugar beets.

Livestock on Farms in the United States

Source: Economic Research Service: Dept. of Agriculture (in 1,000)

Year On Jan. 1	All Cattle	Milk Cows	All Sheep	Hogs	Horses* and Mules	Year On Jan. 1	All Cattle	Milk Cows	All Sheep	Hogs
1890	60,014	15,000	44,518	48,130	18,054	1965	109,000	²15,380	25,127	50,792
1900	59,739	16,544	48,105	51,055	21,004	1966†	108,862	14,490	24,734	³50,519
1910	58,993	19,450	50,239	48,072	24,211	1967†	108,783	13,725	23,953	³57,125
1920	70,400	21,455	40,743	60,159	25,742	1968†	109,371	13,115	22,223	³58,818
1925	63,373	22,575	38,543	55,770	22,569	1969†	110,015	12,550	21,350	³60,829
1930	61,003	23,032	51,565	55,705	19,124	1970†	112,369	12,091	20,423	³57,046
1935	68,846	26,082	51,808	39,066	16,683	1971†	114,578	11,909	19,686	³67,433
1940	68,039	24,940	52,107	61,165	14,478	1972†	117,862	11,778	18,710	³62,507
1945	85,573	27,770	46,520	59,373	11,950	1973†	121,534	11,599	17,724	³59,180
1950	77,963	23,853	29,826	58,937	7,781	1974¹	127,540	11,259	16,545	³61,022
1955	96,592	23,462	31,582	50,474	4,309					
1960	96,236	19,527	33,170	59,026	3,089					

*Discontinued in 1960. †Revised. (1) Total estimated value on farms as of January 1, 1974 was as follows (avg. value per head in parenthesis): cattle and calves $40,905,700 ($321); sheep and lambs $540,651 ($32.70); hogs $3,685,700 ($60.40); chickens $669,120,000 ($1.62); turkeys $34,529,000 ($9.58). (2) New series, milk cows and heifers that have calved beginning 1965. (3) December 1, preceding year.

Egg Production in the U. S.

Source: Economic Research Service, Department of Agriculture (in millions of eggs)

State	1971	1972	1973	State	1971	1972	1973	State	1971	1972	1973	State	1971	1972	1973
Ala.	2,861	2,852	2,853	Ind.	2,993	3,036	2,770	Neb.	862	813	775	S. C.	1,341	1,381	1,319
Alaska	6	7	7	Iowa	2,406	2,295	2,122	Nev.	3	3	4	S. D.	901	814	785
Ariz.	195	164	154	Kansas	754	718	673	N. H.	312	313	320	Tenn.	1,012	1,113	1,088
Ark.	3,641	3,795	3,695	Ky.	566	537	515	N. J.	804	746	756	Texas.	2,607	2,685	2,496
Calif.	9,012	8,652	7,680	La.	757	744	665	N. M.	219	234	208	Utah	287	295	306
Colo.	305	297	317	Me.	1,368	1,443	1,549	N. Y.	2,316	2,271	2,052	Vt.	96	128	150
Conn.	830	924	932	Md.	326	334	327	N. C.	3,377	3,433	3,213	Va.	858	825	789
Del.	131	130	128	Mass.	513	535	522	N. D.	168	153	153	Wash.	1,022	1,035	1,063
Fla.	2,802	2,840	2,806	Mich.	1,505	1,523	1,539	Ohio	2,338	2,324	2,060	W. Va.	271	261	242
Ga.	5,600	5,465	5,534	Minn.	2,493	2,584	2,465	Okla.	528	502	446	Wisc.	1,344	1,313	1,267
Hawaii	211	204	208	Miss.	2,317	2,281	1,981	Ore.	514	554	535	Wyo.	33	32	31
Idaho	186	167	197	Mo.	1,460	1,473	1,347	Pa.	3,541	3,599	3,576				
Ill.	1,799	1,778	1,664	Mont.	221	217	215	R. I.	70	57	52	Total U. S.			
													70,882	69,879	66,551

Gross income in farm eggs 1971, $1,833,187,000; 1972, $1,799,874,000; 1973, $2,911,435,000. Prices received by farmers per dozen 1971, 31.4 cents; 1972, 30.9 cents; 1973, 52.5 cents. Gross income from farm chickens 1971, $95,722,000; 1972, $106,046,000; 1973, $173,754,000. Commercial broilers produced 1971, 2,945,374,000 ($1,487,091,000); 1972, 3,074,921,000 ($1,622,638,000); 1973, 3,008,110 ($2,689,563,000). Gross income from eggs and chickens 1971, $3,416,000,000; 1972, $3,528,558,000; 1973, $5,774,752,000.

Civilian Consumption of Major Food Commodities per Person

Source: Economic Research Service: Department of Agriculture

Commodity[1]	Avg. (lbs.) 1957-59	1972	1973	Commodity[1]	Avg. (lbs.) 1957-59	1972	1973
Meats (carcass wt.)	156.6	188.9	175.5	Other (exc. melons)	40.5	32.4	34.3
Beef	82.1	116.0	109.5	Processed:			
Veal	7.1	2.2	1.8	Canned fruit	22.4	21.5	19.7
Lamb and mutton	4.4	3.3	2.6	Canned juice	13.5	15.7	16.5
Pork (excl. lard)	63.0	67.4	61.6	Frozen (Inc. Juices)	8.6	10.1	11.1
Fish (edible wt.)	10.5	12.3	12.6	Dried	3.3	2.0	2.4
Poultry products				**Vegetables**			
Eggs (farm Basis)				Fresh[2]	104.1	95.9	97.5
Number	356	307	294	Canned, excl. potatoes			
Chicken (ready to cook)	27.5	43.0	41:4	and sweet pot.	43.3	52.2	54.1
Turkey (ready to cook)	6.0	9.1	8.7	Frozen, excl. pot.	6.6	10.0	10.7
Dairy products				**Potatoes,** fresh equiv.	106.9	118.0	115.7
Cheese	7.9	13.2	13.5	**Sweet potatoes,** fresh			
Condensed and				equivalent	8.3	5.1	5.3
evap. milk	14.8	6.4	6.0	**Grains**			
Fluid milk and cream				Cornmeal and flour	7.4	7.4	7.5
(milk equiv.)	337	258	252	Corn syrup	9.4	18.7	21.7
Ice Cream (prod. wt.)	18.4	17.5	17.7	Corn sugar	3.6	4.8	5.2
Fats and Oils-Total,				Wheat flour[3]	120	109	109
fat content	45.3	53.3	53.5	Wheat cereals	2.8	2.9	2.9
Butter (actual wt.)	8.2	4.9	4.8	Rice, milled	5.4	7.0	7.0
Margarine (act. wt.)	8.9	11.3	11.3	**Other**			
Lard	9.3	3.8	3.4	Coffee (green beans)	15.7	13.9	13.6
Shortening	11.4	16.7	16.4	Tea	.58	.77	.79
Other edible fats and oils	10.8	19.6	20.7	Cocoa Beans	3.5	4.4	4.2
Fruits				Peanuts (shelled)	4.6	6.2	6.6
Fresh	95.5	76.9	76.3	Dry edible beans	7.7	6.4	6.7
Citrus	34.0	27.3	27.5	Melons	25.1	21.8	21.5
Apples (com.)	21.0	17.2	14.5	Sugar (refined)	96.1	103.0	102.5

[1]Quantity in pounds except for eggs. Data on calendar year basis except for dried fruits, which are on pack-year basis, fresh citrus fruits and peanuts on a crop-year basis, and rice on August 1 year. Fresh citrus year begins in previous October and rice year begins in previous August. [2]Commercial production for sale as fresh produce. [3]Includes white, whole wheat, and semolina flour.

Federal Food Program Costs, 1971-1974 (Calendar Years)

Source: U.S. Department of Agriculture, Food and Nutrition Service (millions of Dollars)

Year	Food Stamps		Food Distribution[2]				Child Nutrition				Total
	Total Issued	Bonus Stamps[1]	Needy Families	Supp. Food	Schools	Institu-tions	School Lunch	School Bkfst.	Special Food	Special Milk	
1971	3,105	1,699	318	13	296	26	647	22	34	92	3,147
1972	3,614	1,981	271	13	282	27	807	28	43	90	3,541
1973[3]	4,048	2,211	224	14	338	27	941	41	52	64	3,912
1974											
1st Qt.	1,314	792	47	3	131	6	361	19	8	22	1,389
2nd Qt.	1,355	799	38	4	60	4	287	16	16	18	1,242

[1]Includes Food Certificate Program. [2]Cost of food delivered to state distribution centers. [3]Includes estimates for third and fourth quarters.

Recommended Daily Dietary Allowances

The Recommended Daily Dietary Allowances are amounts of nutrients recommended by the Food and Nutrition Board of the National Research council as adequate for maintenance of good nutrition in healthy persons in the U.S. The minimum daily requirements for the adult man are: Vitamin A, 4,000 I.U.; thiamin 1 milligram; riboflavin 1.2 mg.; niacin 10 mg.; ascorbic acid 30 mg.; Calcium 750 mg.; iron 10 mg.

	Years From-up to	Wgt. (lbs.)	Hgt. (in.)	Calories	Protein (grams)	Calcium (grams)	Iron (mg.)	Vit. A (IU)	Thia-min (mg.)	Ribo-flavin (mg.)	Niacin (mg.)	Ascorbic acid (mg.)
Infants	0-1/6	9	22	lb. × 54.5	lb. × 1.0	0.4	6	1,500	0.2	0.4	5	35
	1/6-1/2	15	25	lb. × 50.0	lb. × .9	0.5	10	1,500	0.4	0.5	7	35
	1/2-1	20	28	lb. × 45.5	lb. × .8	0.6	15	1,500	0.5	0.6	8	35
Children	1-2	26	32	1,100	25	0.7	15	2,000	0.6	0.6	8	40
	2-3	31	36	1,250	25	0.8	15	2,000	0.6	0.7	8	40
	3-4	35	39	1,400	30	0.8	10	2,500	0.7	0.8	9	40
	4-6	42	43	1,600	30	0.8	10	2,500	0.8	0.9	11	40
	6-8	51	48	2,000	35	0.9	10	3,500	1.0	1.1	13	40
	8-10	62	52	2,200	40	1.0	10	3,500	1:1	1.2	15	40
Boys	10-12	77	55	2,500	45	1.2	10	4,500	1.3	1.3	17	40
	12-14	95	59	2,700	50	1.4	18	5,000	1.4	1.4	18	45
	14-18	130	67	3,000	60	1.4	18	5,000	1.5	1.5	20	55
Men	18-22	147	69	2,800	60	0.8	10	5,000	1.4	1.6	18	60
	22-35	154	69	2,800	65	0.8	10	5,000	1.4	1.7	18	60
	35-55	154	68	2,600	65	0.8	10	5,000	1.3	1.7	17	60
	55-75×	154	67	2,400	65	0.8	10	5,000	1.2	1.7	14	60
Girls	10-12	77	57	2,250	50	1.2	18	4,500	1.1	1.3	15	40
	12-14	97	61	2,300	50	1.3	18	5,000	1.2	1.4	15	45
	14-16	114	62	2,400	55	1.3	18	5,000	1.2	1.4	16	50
	16-18	119	63	2,300	55	1.3	18	5,000	1.2	1.5	15	50
Women	18-22	128	64	2,000	55	0.8	18	5,000	1.0	1.5	13	44
	22-35	128	64	2,000	55	0.8	18	5,000	1.0	1.5	13	55
	35-55	128	63	1,850	55	0.8	18	5,000	1.0	1.5	13	55
	55-75×	128	62	1,700	55	0.8	10	5,000	1.0	1.5	13	55
Pregnant				×200	65	×0.4	18	6,000	×0.1	1.8	15	60
Lactating				×1,000	75	×0.5	18	8,000	×0.5	2.0	20	60

Nutritive Value of Foods (Calories, Proteins, etc.)

Source: Home and Garden Bulletin No. 72, U. S. Department of Agriculture

Available for 75c from Supt. of Documents, U. S. Government Printing Office, Washington, D. C. 20402

Food	Measure	Water %	Food Energy (Calories)	Protein (grams)	Fat (grams)	Carbohydrate (grams)	Calcium (mg)	Iron (mg)	Vit. A (I.U.)	Thiamin (mg)	Riboflavin (mg)	Niacin (mg)	Ascorbic acid (mg)
Milk, Cream, Cheese													
Milk, fluid, whole, 3.5% fat	1 cup	87	160	9	9	12	288	0.1	350	0.07	0.41	0.2	2
Milk, fluid nonfat (skim)	1 cup	90	90	9	T	12	296	.1	10	.09	.44	.2	2
Buttermilk, fluid, cultured, made from skim milk	1 cup	90	90	9	T	12	296	.1	10	.10	.44	.2	2
Cheese, Roquefort type	1 oz.	40	105	6	9	1	89	.1	350	.01	.17	.3	0
Cheese, Cottage, creamed	12 oz.	78	360	46	14	10	320	1.0	580	.10	.85	.3	0
Cream, half-and-half	1 cup	80	325	8	28	11	261	.1	1,160	.07	.39	.1	2
Cream, heavy	1 cup	57	840	5	90	7	179	.1	3,670	.05	.26	.1	2
Custard, baked	1 cup	77	305	14	15	29	297	1.1	930	.11	.50	.3	1
Yoghurt, whole milk	1 cup	88	150	7	8	12	272	.1	340	.07	.39	.2	2
Eggs (large)													
Raw	1 egg	74	80	6	6	T	27	1.1	590	.05	.15	T	0
Scrambled (milk and fat)	1 egg	72	110	7	8	1	51	1.1	690	.05	.18	T	0
Meat, Poultry													
Bacon	2 sli.	8	90	5	8	1	2	.5	0	.08	.05	.8	...
Beef, lean and fat	3 oz.	53	245	23	16	0	10	2.9	30	.04	.18	3.5	...
Hamburger, regular	3 oz.	54	245	21	17	0	9	2.7	30	.07	.18	4.6	...
Steak, broiled, lean and fat	3 oz.	44	330	20	27	0	9	2.5	50	.05	.16	4.0	...
Corned beef	3 oz.	59	185	22	10	0	17	3.7	20	.01	.20	2.9	...
Chicken, cooked:													
Flesh only, broiled	3 oz.	71	115	20	3	0	8	1.4	80	.05	.16	7.4	...
With bone, ½ breast, fried	3.3 oz.	58	155	25	5	1	9	1.3	70	.04	.17	11.2	...
Chicken, potpie, baked	8 oz.	57	535	23	31	42	68	3.0	3,020	.25	.26	4.1	5
Lamb chop, thick with bone	4.8 oz.	47	400	25	33	0	10	1.5	...	.14	.25	5.6	...
Lamb, lean and fat	3 oz.	54	235	22	16	0	9	1.4	...	.13	.23	4.7	...
Liver, beef, fried	2 oz.	57	130	15	6	3	6	5.0	30,280	.15	2.37	9.4	15
Ham, light cure, lean	3 oz.	54	245	18	19	0	8	2.2	0	.40	.16	3.1	...
Boiled ham, sliced	2 oz.	59	135	11	10	0	6	1.6	0	.25	.09	1.5	...
Pork roast, lean and fat	3 koz.	46	310	21	24	0	9	2.7	0	.78	.22	4.7	...
Frankfurter, heated	2 oz.	57	170	7	15	1	3	.8	...	.08	.11	1.4	...
Veal cutlet	3 oz.	60	185	23	9	...	9	2.7	...	.06	.21	4.6	...
Veal roast	3 oz.	55	230	23	14	0	10	2.9	...	.11	.26	6.6	...
Fish													
Bluefish, baked with fat	3 oz.	68	135	22	4	0	25	.6	40	.09	.08	1.6	...
Clams, raw, meat only	3 oz.	82	65	11	1	2	59	5.2	90	.08	.15	1.1	8
Crabmeat, canned	3 oz.	77	85	15	2	1	38	.7	...	.07	.07	1.6	...
Oyster, raw, meat	1 cup	85	160	20	4	8	226	13.2	740	.33	.43	6.0	...
Salmon, pink, canned	3 oz.	71	120	17	5	0	167	.7	60	.03	.16	6.8	...
Shrimp, canned, meat	3 oz.	70	100	21	1	1	98	2.6	50	.01	.03	1.5	...
Swordfish, broiled with butter	3 oz.	65	150	24	5	0	23	1.1	1,750	.03	.04	9.3	...
Tuna, canned in oil	3 oz.	61	170	24	7	0	7	1.6	70	.04	.10	10.1	...
Nuts													
Almonds, shelled, whole	1 cup	5	850	26	77	28	332	6.7	0	.34	1.31	5.0	T
Cashew nuts, roasted	1 cup	5	785	24	64	41	53	5.3	140	.60	.35	2.5	...
Peanuts, roasted	1 cup	2	840	37	72	27	107	3.0	...	.46	.19	24.7	0
Pecans, halves	1 cup	3	740	10	77	16	79	2.6	140	.93	.14	1.0	2
Walnuts, black or native, chopped	1 cup	3	790	26	75	19	T	7.6	380	.28	.14	.9	...
Vegetables & Products													
Asparagus, cooked, spears	4 sp.	94	10	1	T	2	13	.4	540	.10	.11	.8	16
Asparagus, canned	1 cup	94	45	5	1	7	44	4.1	1,240	.15	.22	2.0	37
Beans, lima, immature, cooked	1 cup	71	190	13	1	34	80	4.3	480	.31	.17	2.2	29
Beans, snap, green, cooked	1 cup	92	30	2	T	7	63	.8	680	.09	.11	.6	15
Beans, snap, canned, green	1 cup	94	45	2	T	10	81	2.9	690	.07	.10	.7	10
Beans, snap, yellow or wax	1 cup	93	30	2	T	6	63	0.8	290	.09	.11	.6	16
Beans, sprouted mung, cooked	1 cup	91	35	4	T	7	21	1.1	30	.11	.13	.9	8
Beets, cooked	2 beets	91	30	1	T	7	14	.5	20	.03	.04	.3	6
Broccoli, cooked	1 stalk	91	45	6	1	8	158	1.4	4,500	.16	.36	1.4	162
Brussels sprouts, cooked	1 cup	88	55	7	1	10	50	1.7	810	.12	.22	1.2	135
Cabbage, raw, shredded	1 cup	92	15	1	T	4	34	.3	90	.04	.04	.2	33
Cabbage, cooked	1 cup	94	30	2	T	6	64	.4	190	.06	.06	.4	48
Carrots, raw 5½ by 1 in.	One	88	20	1	T	5	18	.4	5,500	.03	.03	.3	4
Carrots, cooked, diced	1 cup	91	45	1	T	10	48	.9	15,220	.08	.07	.7	9
Cauliflower, cooked, flower buds	1 cup	93	25	3	T	5	25	.8	70	.11	.10	.7	66
Celery, raw, stalk, large	1 stalk	94	5	T	T	2	16	.1	100	.01	.01	.1	4
Corn, cooked ear 5 x 1¾ in.	1 ear	74	70	3	1	16	2	.5	310	.09	.08	1.0	7
Corn, canned	1 cup	81	170	5	2	40	10	1.0	690	.07	.12	2.3	13
Cucumbers, raw, pared	10 oz.	96	30	1	T	7	35	.6	T	.07	.09	.4	23
Lettuce, Boston type	1 head	95	30	3	1	6	77	4.4	2,130	.14	.13	.6	18
Mushrooms, canned	1 cup	93	40	5	T	6	15	1.2	T	.04	.60	4.8	4
Onions, mature, raw, 2½ in.	One	89	40	2	T	10	30	.6	40	.04	.04	.2	11
Peas, green, cooked	1 cup	82	115	9	1	19	37	2.9	860	.44	.17	3.7	33
Peas, green, canned	1 cup	83	165	9	1	31	50	4.2	1,120	.23	.13	2.2	22
Potatoes, medium, baked	One	75	90	3	T	21	9	.7	T	.10	.04	1.7	20
Potatoes, medium, boiled in skin	One	80	105	3	T	23	10	.8	T	.13	.05	2.0	22
Potatoes, mashed, milk added	1 cup	83	125	4	1	25	47	.8	50	.16	.10	2.0	19
Potato chips, medium	10 chips	2	115	1	8	10	8	.4	T	.04	.01	1.0	3
Sauerkraut, canned	1 cup	93	45	2	T	9	85	1.2	120	.07	.09	.4	33
Spinach, cooked	1 cup	92	40	5	1	6	167	4.0	14,580	.13	.25	1.0	50
Squash, summer, diced, cooked	1 cup	96	30	2	T	7	52	.8	820	.10	.16	1.6	21
Squash, winter, baked, mashed	1 cup	81	130	4	1	32	57	1.6	8,610	.10	.27	1.4	27
Sweet potatoes, baked	1	64	155	2	1	36	44	1.0	8,910	.10	.07	.7	24

Food	Measure	Water %	Food Energy (Calories)	Protein (grams)	Fat (grams)	Carbohydrate (grams)	Calcium (mg)	Iron (mg)	Vit A (I.U.)	Thiamin (mg)	Riboflavin (mg)	Niacin (mg)	Ascorbic acid (mg)
Sweet potatoes, candied 3½ by 2¼ in.	1	60	295	2	6	60	65	1.6	11,030	.10	.08	.8	17
Tomatoes, raw, medium	1	94	40	2	T	9	24	.9	1,640	.11	.07	1.3	42
Tomato catsup, tablespoon	1 tbsp.	69	15	T	T	4	3	.1	210	.01	.01	.2	2
Tomato juice, canned	1 cup	94	45	2	T	10	17	2.2	1,940	.12	.07	1.9	39
Fruits and Fruit Products													
Apples, medium, raw	One	85	70	T	T	18	8	.4	50	.04	.02	.1	3
Apple juice, bottled or canned	1 cup	88	120	T	T	30	15	1.5		.02	.05	.2	2
Applesauce, canned, sweetened	1 cup	76	230	1	T	61	10	1.3	100	.05	.03	.1	3
Bananas, raw 6 by 1½ in.	1	76	100	1	T	26	10	.8	230	.06	.07	.8	12
Blueberries, raw	1 cup	83	85	1	1	21	21	1.4	140	.04	.08	.6	20
Cantaloups, raw, medium	½ melon	91	60	1	T	14	27	.8	6,540	.08	.06	1.2	63
Cranberry sauce, sweetened, canned	1 cup	62	405	T	T	104	17	.6	60	.03	.03	.1	6
Grapefruit, raw, medium, white	½	89	45	1	T	12	19	.5	10	.05	.02	.2	44
Grapefruit juice, canned, unsweetened	1 cup	89	100	1	T	24	20	1.0	20	.07	.04	.4	84
Grapes, raw, American type	1 cup	82	65	1	1	15	15	.4	100	.05	.03	.2	3
Grapejuice, canned	1 cup	83	165	1	T	42	28	.8		.10	.05	.5	T
Lemons, raw, medium	One	90	20	1	T	6	19	.4	10	.03	.01	.1	39
Lemon juice, raw	1 cup	91	60	1	T	20	17	.5	50	.07	.02	.2	112
Lime juice, fresh	1 cup	90	65	1	T	22	22	.5	20	.05	.02	.2	79
Oranges, raw, 2⅝ in. diam.	One	86	65	1	T	16	54	.5	260	.13	.05	.5	66
Orange juice, frozen, undiluted	6 oz. can	55	360	5	T	87	75	.9	1,620	.68	.11	2.8	360
Peaches, raw, whole, medium	One	89	35	1	T	10	9	.5	1,320	.02	.05	1.0	7
Peaches, canned, halves or sliced	1 cup	79	200	1	T	52	10	.8	1,100	.02	.06	1.4	7
Pears, raw, 3 by 2½ in.	One	83	100	1	1	25	13	.5	30	.04	.07	.2	7
Pineapple, canned, sliced	Large sli.	80	90	T	T	24	13	.4	50	.09	.03	.2	8
Plums, raw, 2 in. diam.	1 plum	87	25	T	T	7	7	.3	140	.02	.02	.3	3
Prune juice, canned	1 cup	80	200	1	T	49	36	10.5		.03	.03	1.0	5
Raisins, seedless, pkged. ½ oz.	1 pkg.	18	40	T	T	11	9	.5	T	.02	.01	.1	T
Strawberries, raw, capped	1 cup	90	55	1	1	13	31	1.5	90	.04	.10	1.0	88
Watermelon, raw, wedge	1 wedge	93	115	2	1	27	30	2.1	2,510	.13	.13	.7	30
Grain Products													
Bagel, 3 in. diam. egg.	One	32	165	6	2	28	9	1.2	30	.14	.10	1.2	0
Biscuits, baking powder	One	27	105	2	5	13	34	.4	T	.06	.06	.1	T
Bran flakes (40% bran)	1 cup	3	105	4	1	28	25	12.3	0	.14	.06	2.2	0
Bread, cracked wheat	1 loaf	35	1,190	40	10	236	399	5.0	T	.53	.41	5.9	T
Bread, enriched, French	1 loaf	31	1,315	41	14	251	195	10.0	T	1.27	1.00	11.3	T
Bread, enriched, Italian	1 loaf	32	1,250	41	4	256	77	10.0	0	1.32	.91	11.8	0
Bread, raisin, loaf	1 loaf	35	1,190	30	13	243	322	5.9	T	.23	.41	3.2	T
Bread, American, rye	1 loaf	36	1,100	41	5	236	340	7.3	0	.82	.32	6.4	0
Bread, white, enriched	1 loaf	36	1,225	39	15	229	381	11.3	T	1.13	.95	10.9	T
Cakes, Angelfood	1 cake	34	1,645	36	1	377	603	1.9	0	.03	.70	.6	0
Cupcakes, small, choc, icing.	1 cake	22	130	2	5	21	47	.3	60	.01	.04	.1	T
Cakes, Boston cream pie	1 pce.	35	210	4	6	34	46	.3	140	.02	.08	.1	T
Cake pound	1 loaf	17	2,430	29	152	242	108	4.1	1,440	.15	.46	1.0	0
Saltines	4	4	50	1	1	8	2	.1	0	T	T	.1	0
Danish Pastry, round piece.	1 pastry	22	275	5	15	30	33	.6	200	.05	.10	.5	T
Doughnuts, cake type	One	24	125	1	6	16	13	.4	30	.05	.05	.4	T
Macaroni, enriched, cooked.	1 cup	64	190	6	1	39	14	1.4	0	.23	.14	1.8	0
Noodles, enriched.	1 cup	70	200	7	2	37	16	1.4	110	.22	.13	1.9	0
Oatmeal, or rolled oats, cooked	1 cup	87	130	5	2	23	22	1.4	0	.19	.05	.2	0
Pie, apple ⅐ of 9 in.	1 sector	48	350	3	15	51	11	.4	40	.03	.03	.5	1
Pie, custard ⅐ of 9 in. pie.	1 sector	58	285	8	14	30	125	.8	300	.07	.21	.4	0
Pie, lemon meringue ⅐ of 9 in. pie.	1 sector	47	305	4	12	45	17	.6	200	.04	.10	.2	4
Pie, mince ⅐ of 9 in. pie.	1 sector	43	365	3	16	56	38	1.4	T	.09	.05	.5	1
Pie, pumpkin ⅐ of 9 in. pie.	1 sector	59	275	5	15	32	66	.7	3,210	.04	.13	.7	T
Pizza (cheese) ⅛ of 14 in. diam.	1 sector	45	185	7	6	27	107	.7	290	.04	.12	.7	4
Popcorn, plain.	1 cup	4	25	1	T	5	1	.2			.01	.1	0
Rolls, home recipe	1 roll	26	120	3	3	20	16	.7	30	.09	.09	.8	T
Spaghetti, enriched, cooked.	1 cup	72	155	5	1	32	11	1.3	0	.20	.11	1.5	0
Fats, Oils													
Butter, regular.	½ cup	16	810	1	92	1	23	0	3,750				0
Lard	1 cup	0	1,850	0	205	0	0	0	0	0	0	0	0
Vegetable fats.	1 cup	0	1,770	0	200	0	0	0		0	0	0	0
Margarine	½ cup	16	815	1	92	1	23	0	3,750				0
Salad dressing, French, regular.	1 tbsp.	39	65	T	6	3	2	.1					
Salad dressing, mayonnaise.	1 tbsp.	15	100	T	11	T	3	.1	40	T	.01	T	
Salad dressing, 1,000 island.	1 tbsp.	32	80	T	8	3	2	.1	50	T	T	T	T
Sugars, Sweets													
Candy: milk chocolate, sweetened.	1 oz.	1	145	2	9	16	65	.3	80	.02	.10	.1	T
Candy, plain fudge.	1 oz.	8	115	1	4	21	22	.3	T	.01	.03	.1	T
Chocolate syrup, fudge type	1 oz.	25	125	2	5	20	48	.5	60	.02	.08	.2	T
Honey, strained or extracted.	1 tbsp.	17	65	T	0	17	1	.1	0	T	.01	.1	T
Jellies.	1 tbsp.	29	50	T	T	13	4	.3	T	T	.01	T	1
Sugars, brown.	1 cup	2	*280	0	0	212	187	7.5	0	.02	.07	.4	0
Sugars, granulated	1 cup	T	770	0	0	199	0	.2	0	0	0	0	0
Miscellaneous													
Barbecue sauce.	1 cup	81	230	4	17	20	53	2.0	900	.03	.03	.8	13
Beer.	12 oz.	92	150	1	0	14	18	T		.01	.11	2.2	
Alcoholic beverage, 86-proof.	1½ fl. oz.	64	105			T							
Cola type beverage.	12 fl. oz.	90	145	0	0	37			0	0	0	0	0
Ginger ale	12 fl. oz.	92	115	0	0	29			0	0	0	0	0
Soup, cream of chicken.	1 cup	85	180	7	10	15	172	.5	610	.05	.27	.7	2
Soup, Tomato.	1 cup	84	175	7	7	23	168	.8	1,200	.10	.25	1.3	15
Bean with pork.	1 cup	84	170	8	6	22	63	2.3	650	.13	.08	1.0	3
Clam chowder.	1 cup	92	80	2	3	12	34	1.0	880	.02	.02	1.0	

T indicates a trace.

Giant Trees of the United States

Source: The American Forestry Association

There are 865 species of trees native to the continental U.S. including a few imports that have become naturalized to the extent of reproducing themselves in the wild state.

The oldest living trees in the world are reputed to be the bristlecone pines, the majority of which are found growing on the arid crags of California's White Mts. Some of them are estimated to be more than 4,600 years old. The largest known bristlecone pine is the "Patriarch," believed to be 1,500 years old. The oldest known redwoods are about 3,500 years old.

Recognition as the National Champion of each species is determined by total mass of each tree, based on this formula: the circumference in inches as measured at a point 4½ feet above the ground plus the total height of the tree, plus ¼ of the average crown spread in feet. In case of a tie the Champion is determined on the basis of circumference. It is not possible, due to lack of space, to list all the 865 trees registered with the American Forestry Assn.

(Figure in parentheses is year tree was reported)

Species	Height (Ft.)	Location
Acacia, Koa (1969)	140	Kau, Hawaii
Ailanthus,		
Tree-of Heaven (1955)	80	Head of Harbor, L.I., N.Y.
Alder, European (1969)	87	Berks County, Pa.
Apple,		
Southern Crab (1968)	40	Columbia, S.C.
Ash, Blue (1970)	86	Danville, Ky.
Aspen, Bigtooth (1963)	93	Walker, N.Y.
Bald cypress,		
Common (1950)	122	nr. Sharon, Tenn.
Basswood,		
American (1971)	115	Grand Traverse Cty., Mich.
Bayberry, Pacific (1961)	38	Siuslaw Natl. Forest, Ore.
Beech, American (1970)	108	Ashtabula, Ohio
Birch, River (1968)	85	Germantown, Pa.
Blackbead, Catlaw (1972)	81	Ft. Myers, Fla.
Blackhaw, Rusty (1961)	25	Nr. Washington, Ark.
Bladdernut,		
American (1966)	36	nr. Utica, Mich.
Boxelder (1972)	95	Washtenaw Co., Mich.
Buckeye, Painted (1970)	144	Union County, Ga.
Buckthorn, Cascara (1945)	60	nr. Rockport, Wash.
Buckwheat tree (1967)	30	nr. Crooked Creek, Fla.
Buffaloberry, Silver (1970)	20.5	Inyo Natl. Forest, Calif.
Bumelia, Gum (1964)	52	nr. Fairfield, Texas
Butternut (1968)	100	Portland, Ore.
Buttonbush,		
Common (1966)	29	nr. Clinton, Mich.
Button-Mangrove (1971)	49	Black Is. Lee City, Fla.
Cajeput (1968)	60	Miami, Fla.
Camphor-tree (1971)	65	nr. Zephyhills, Fla.
Casuarina,		
Horsetail (1965)	81	No. Miami Beach, Fla.
Catalpa, Northern (1962)	94	Lansing, Mich.
Cedar, Port-Orford (1968)	219	Siskiyou Natl. Forest, Ore.
Cercocarpus,		
Birchleaf (1972)	34	Central Point, Ore.
Cherry, Black (1959)	114	Lawrence, Mich.
Chestnut,		
American (1964)	91	Oregon City, Ore.
Chinaberry (1970)	78	nr. Luverne, Alabama
Chinkapin, Golden (1954)	127	nr. Annapolis, Calif.
Coconut (1969)	63	Clewiston, Fla.
Coffeetree,		
Kentucky (1966)	101	Bryn Mawr, Pa.
(1973)	82	Lake County, Ohio
Chokecherry,		
Common (1967)	66	Ada, Mich.
Cottonwood, Black (1969)	147	Unionvalle, Ore.
Cypress, Monterey (1968)	63	Pt. Lobos St. Pk., Calif.
Dahoon (1971)	35	Berkeley Cty., S.C.
Desertwillow (1971)	40	Gila Nat'l. Forest, N.M.
Devil's-walkingstick (1949)	30	Great Smoky Nat'l. Pk., Tenn.
Devilwood (1967)	37	Mayo, Fla.
Dogwood, Pacific (1972)	60	Keizer, Ore.
Douglas Fir, Coast (1945)	221	Olympic Natl. Pk., Wash.
Doveplum (1965)	45	Miami, Fla.
Ebony, Mountain (1967)	46	Ellenton, Fla.
Elder, Blackbead (1954)	30	nr. Prescott, Ore.
Elm, American (1971)	130	Dundee, Kentucky
False-Mastic (1955)	56	nr. Miami, Fla.
Fig, Florida Strangler (1965)	51	Miami, Fla.
Fir, Noble (1964)	278	Gifford Pinchot Natl. Forest, Wash.
Franklinia (1968)	25	Wyndmoor, Pa.
Grapefruit (1967)	38	Ellenton, Fla.
Gumbo-limbo (1972)	60	Ft. Myers, Fla.
Hackberry,		
Common (1972)	118	Wayland, Mich.
Hawthorn (1967)	50	Glenview, Ill.
Hemlock, Western (1954)	163	Olympic Natl. Pk., Wash.
Hercules-club (1961)	38	Little Rock, Ark.
Hickory, Pignut (1970)	125	nr. Brunswick, Ga.
Holly, Tawnyberry (1968)	55	Homestead, Fla.
Honeylocust,		
Thornless (1970)	128	Mt. Erie, Ill.
Hophornbeam,		
Eastern (1945)	78	nr. Winthrop, Me.
Hoptree, Common (1972)	31	Ada, Michigan
Hornbeam, American		
(1966)	42	Canton, Ohio
Joshua-tree (1967)	32	San Bernardino Natl. Forest, Calif.
Juniper, Western (1945)	87	Stanislaus Natl. Forest, Calif.
Larch, Western (1945)	177	nr. Kootenai Natl. Forest, Mont.
Laurelcherry,		
Carolina (1970)	44	Dellwood, Fla.
Lebbek (1970)	58	Princeton, Fla.
Loblolly-Bay (1963)	84	Hugh's Island, Fla.
Locust, Black (1972)	74	Albany, N.Y.
Lysiloma, Bahama (1955)	48	Key Largo, Fla.
Madrone, Pacific (1955)	80	Humboldt Cty., Calif.
Magnolia, Cucumber tree		
(1969)	97	Chester, Pa.
Mangrove, Red (1973)	60	North Miami, Fla.
Maple, Red (1964)	125	nr. Armada, Mich.
Mesquite, Velvet (1949)	55	Coronado Natl. Forest, Ariz.
Mountain-Ash,		
Showy (1968)	58	nr. Gould City, Mich.
Mountain-Laurel (1970)	20	Chattahoochee Natl. Forest, Ga.
Mulberry, White (1970)	77	St. Joseph Co., Mich.
(1973)	68	Logan Co., Ill.
Oak, California		
white (1967)	120	Nr. Gridley, Calif.
Oleander, Common (1963)	22	Phoenix, Ariz.
Osage-Orange (1969)	51	Charlotte Cty., Va.
Palmetto, Cabbage (1965)	90	Highlands Hammock State Pk., Fla.
Paloverde, Blue (1967)	52	Ajo, Ariz.
Paulownia, Royal (1969)	105	Philadelphia Cty., Pa.
Pawpaw, Blue (1971)	41	nr. Smith Mills, Ky.
Pear (1966)	51	Clawson, Oakland Co., Mich.
(1972)	74	Leslie Co., Ky.
Pecan (1973)	128	Hopewell, Va.
Peppertree (1969)	47	San Juan Capistrano, Cal.
Pinckneya (1968)	21	nr. Mt. Pleasant, Fla.
Pine, ponderosa (1969)	161	nr. Lapine, Oregon
Planetree (1967)	77	nr. Chattahoochee, Fla.
Plum, American (1972)	35	Oakland Co., Mich.
Poison Sumac (1972)	20	Robin's island, N.Y.
Pondcypress (1969)	135	nr. Newton, Ga.
Poplar, Balsam (1969)	98	So. Egremont, Mass.
Posumhaw (1970)	25	Richland Cty., S.C.
Redbay (1971)	58	Randolph Cty., Ga.
Redwood, Coast (1966)	362	Humboldt Redwoods State Park, Calif.
Royalpalm, Florida (1972)	78	Collier Seminole Pk., Fla.
Sassafras (1954)	100	Owensboro, Ky.

Species	Height (Ft.)	Location
Seagrape (1972)	57	Miami, Fla.
Sequoia, Giant (1945)	272	Sequoia Natl. Pk., Calif.
Serviceberry, Downy (1966)	48	nr. Standish, Mich.
Silk-oak (1972)	78	nr. La Belle, Fla.
Silktree (1971)	41	Gilmer, Texas
Silverbell, Two-wing (1971)	55	Tallahassee, Fla.
Smoketree, American (1963)	33	Dawes Arboretum, Ohio
Soapberry, Western (1969)	67	Newton County, Tex.
Sourwood (1968)	118	nr. Robbinsville, N.C.
Sparkleberry tree (1970)	29	Keltys, Texas
Spruce, Sitka (1967)	248	"The Helen Clapp Spruce", Forks, Wash.
Sugarberry (1970)	148	Richland Cty., S.C.
Sumac, Shining (1967)	47	nr. Chattahoochee, Fla.
Sweetleak, Common (1967)	55	Tallahassee, Fla.
Sycamore, Calif. (1945)	116	nr. Santa Barbara, Calif.
Tallowtree (1967)	42	Polk County, Texas
Tamarack (1966)	95	Jay, Me.

Species	Height (Ft.)	Location
Tamarisk, Five-Stamen (1967)	37	Alburquerque, N.M.
Tanoak (1969)	100	Kneeland, Calif.
Tesota (1972)	31.6	nr. Quartzsite, Ariz.
Torreya, California (1945)	141	nr. Mendocino, Calif.
Trifoliate-Orange (1968)	26	Harrisburg, Pa.
Tupelo, Black (1969)	117	Harrison Co., Texas
(1971)	139	Nr. Easterly, Texas
Wahoo, Eastern (1971)	14	Carrollton, Mo.
Walnut, California (1973)	116	Santa Rosa, Calif.
Willow, Crack (1964)	112	nr. Utica, Mich.
Winterberry, Common (1971)	40	Wildwood, Fla.
Witch-Hazel, Common (1967)	44	Franklin, Mich.
Yaupon (1964)	45	nr. Devers, Texas
Yellow-Poplar (1972)	124	Bedford, Va.
Yellowwood (1964)	58	Morrisville, Pa.
Yew, Pacific (1959)	60	nr. Mineral, Wash.
Yucca, Aloe (1967)	15	Lakeland, Fla.

Grain Storage Capacity at Principal Grain Centers in U.S. and Canada

Source: Chicago Board of Trade

United States

Cities	Capacity Bushels	Cities	Capacity Bushels
Amarillo	27,883,534	Milwaukee	5,600,000
Buffalo	31,260,000	Minneapolis-St. Paul	120,341,100
California ports	16,473,000	New Orleans area	36,698,000
Chicago	60,658,000	Omaha-Council Bluffs	35,338,262
Des Moines	10,640,000	Peoria	6,820,000
Duluth-Superior	72,779,000	Portland-Columbia R.	31,499,535
Enid	66,102,000	Puget Sound	6,700,000
Fort Worth	57,565,398	Sioux City	13,406,000
Galveston-Houston	31,200,000	St. Joseph	20,584,000
Hutchinson	41,733,000	St. Louis	19,815,000
Kansas City	90,786,554	Toledo	32,200,000
Lincoln	42,812,584	Wichita	82,295,000
Lubbock	29,219,000		

Canada

Cities	Capacity	Cities	Capacity
Baie Comeau	13,778,000	Prescott, Ont.	5,500,000
Churchill, Man.	5,000,000	Prince Rupert, B.C.	2,250,000
Collingwood, Ont.	2,000,000	Quebec, Que.	8,000,000
Goderich, Ont.	4,600,000	Saint John, N.B.	500,000
Halifax, N.S.	5,152,500	Sarnia, Ont.	5,400,000
Kingston, Ont.	2,350,000	Sorel, Que.	5,230,000
Midland, Ont.	11,550,000	Three Rivers, Que.	5,880,000
Montreal, Que.	22,262,000	Thunder Bay	101,097,210
N. Vancouver, B.C.	6,972,000	Toronto, Ont.	4,000,000
Owen Sound, Ont.	4,000,000	Vancouver, B.C.	18,056,500
Port Cartier	10,462,000	Victoria, B.C.	1,040,000
Port Colborne, Ont.	5,250,000	West St. John, N.B.	2,576,800
Port McNicoll, Ont.	6,500,000		

Grain Receipts at Western Grain Centers

Source: Chicago Board of Trade (in thousands bushels)

1972	Wheat	Corn	Oats	Rye	Barley	Soybeans	Total
Chicago	17,024	92,285	2,221	9	860	32,257	144,656
Duluth	113,670	19,372	11,805	4,262	52,874	1,993	203,976
Enid	82,310	71	.....	.....	11	.....	82,392
Hutchinson	68,374	70	.....	.....	.....	.....	68,444
Kansas City	100,446	59,138	1,820	62	740	18,741	180,947
Milwaukee	143	26,700	111	.....	27,268	1,316	55,538
Minneapolis	136,826	26,906	64,448	8,123	82,382	5,058	323,743
Omaha	21,194	37,430	354	143	11	6,218	65,350
Peoria	72	28,238	298	206	.....	414	29,228
Sioux City	5,299	20,030	7,378	198	114	11,458	44,477
St. Joseph	1,538	5,748	1,674	.....	.....	2,582	11,542
St. Louis	25,585	15,337	12,646	.....	.....	6,643	60,211
Toledo	22,943	54,597	1,827	30	3	40,419	119,819
Wichita	17,375	900	12	.....	34	4,030	22,351
Total	**612,799**	**386,822**	**104,594**	**13,033**	**164,297**	**131,129**	**1,412,674**

The 1972-1973 Wildfire Season

Source: Forest Service, U. S. Dept. of Agriculture

Federal, State and Private Protected Area

Drought again plagued southwestern United States in 1972. Precipitation was the lowest on record for January into May. During this critical period a careless person started the "Battle" fire on the Prescott National Forest, Arizona, an area which had been closed due to extreme fire danger. It spread out of control for seven days, threatening the town of Prescott and destroying 28,000 acres of watershed and timberland.

However, 96 percent of all fires were controlled at 10 acres or less in size on the 210 million acres of Forest Service protected lands. Less than one percent were large fires burning over 300 acres. These accounted for approximately 75 percent of burned acreage. Forest fires burned 0.6 acres for each 1,000 acres protected.

Late summer two fires in California severely endangered human lives and homes, besides damaging watershed and other valuable resources. Sadly, six firefighters lost their lives in a helicopter accident on one of these conflagrations, the "Bear" fire, Los Padres National Forest, California. All told, only three fires accounted for 42 percent of all acres burned in 1972.

Man-caused fires increased 15 percent over previous years. However 14,154 fires burned only 116,703 acres. Aggressive prevention measures followed by hard-hitting attack forces reduced the potential for major conflagrations on National Forests.

Success of this effort is borne out by the record. Only 4 percent of the fires escaped initial attack. An example of payoff from readiness and mobility occurred during a 5-day period in Southwest Idaho, when lightning ignited 250 fires in hazardous fuels. Only one of the fires reached large size. The rest were contained at less than ten acres.

On all Federal, State, and private forest and non-forested watershed lands during 1973, a total of 117,957 fires were reported; a decrease of 6,597 fires below the 124,554 reported during 1972. However, acreage burned on all lands totaled 1,915,273, a decrease of 725,893 acres below the 2,641,166 acres burned during 1972.

Through carelessness or incendiarism, man is blamed for the largest portion of wildfires. During 1973 some 81,493 or 89% of the 91,683 reported as having burned on protected land were man-caused. Lightning-started fires amounted to 10,190 or 11 percent of the protected area fires. Causes of the 26,274 fires which occurred on unprotected lands are not known.

More than 626,523,000 acres of state and private forest and nonforested watershed lands are protected under the federal-state cooperative Forest Fire Control Program. Since the area qualifying for protection under the program is 690,482,000 acres, the goal of the program is to bring protection to the more than 63,959,000 acres not now receiving protection. All states participate in the cooperative forest fire protection effort. The record on state and private protected lands for 1973 follows:

Group	Number of Fires	Acres Burned
Rocky Mountain	6,199	183,119
Pacific	10,942	190,788
North Central	6,821	186,788
Southern	42,645	494,692
Eastern	12,270	30,845
Total	78,877	1,086,222

The record on state and private unprotected lands is:

Rocky Mountain	788	7,650
North Central	425	15,800
Southern	2,061	129,699
Eastern	23,000	(no data)
Total	26,274	153,149

Total Fires and Acres Burned—National Forest Protection

Calendar Year	Lightning	Man Caused	Total	Acres Burned	Calendar Year	Lightning	Man Caused	Total	Acres Burned
1967	6,790	4,981	11,771	204,106	1972	8,406	5,748	14,154	116,703
1969	4,726	5,308	10,034	92,126	Average				
1970	7,804	7,172	14,976	519,978	1967-72	6,324	5,903	12,227	222,619
1971	5,876	6,363	12,239	171,867	1973	6,376	6,048	12,424	168,692

National Forest System

Administered by the Forest Service, U. S. Dept. of Agriculture, the National Forest System is made up of 155 National Forests, 19 National Grasslands, and other minor acreages which total 187,101,120 acres in 44 states, Puerto Rico, and the Virgin Islands. All lands within the National Forest System are managed under two guiding principles; multiple use — the management of lands to make each area yield the combination of uses best suited to public needs; and sustained yield — maintenance of a continuous supply of all forest resources through wise use, management, and protection.

National Forest lands which supply water for agriculture, industry, recreation, and domestic use, for example, also are managed to prevent erosion and help control floods, yet there also may be camping, skiing, and timber harvesting on the same land.

The scenic beauty and recreation opportunities available on National Forests yearly draw millions of Americans to these lands to hunt, fish, camp, picnic, boat, recreational play, swim, hike, ski, and to make pack trips into the wilderness. Use reached 183,958,300 visitor days during calendar year 1972.

National Forest Areas

Source: Forest Service, Dept. of Agriculture. (In Acres) Data as of June 30, 1973

States	Area	States	Area	States	Area	States	Area
Alabama	634,741	Iowa	360	N.Hampshire	683,203	Tennessee	613,780
Alaska	20,723,028	Kansas	107,914	N. Mexico	9,196,495	Texas	776,480
Arizona	11,422,784	Kentucky	616,757	New York	13,779	Utah	8,042,711
Arkansas	2,457,685	Louisiana	594,849	N. Carolina	1,135,448	Vermont	243,383
California	20,070,067	Maine	50,103	N. Dakota	1,105,234	Virgin Islands	147
Colorado	14,361,432	Michigan	2,687,578	Ohio	154,173	Virginia	1,538,438
Connecticut	10	Minnesota	2,796,564	Oklahoma	290,672	Washington	9,067,260
Florida	1,081,459	Mississippi	1,136,313	Oregon	15,480,408	W. Virginia	950,055
Georgia	851,410	Missouri	1,441,016	Pennsylvania	495,882	Wisconsin	1,489,590
Idaho	20,351,894	Montana	16,704,075	Puerto Rico	27,998	Wyoming	9,246,849
Illinois	247,572	Nebraska	350,567	S. Carolina	598,276	Total	
Indiana	168,238	Nevada	5,108,731	S. Dakota	1,985,702	Acreage	187,101,120

Giant Trees of Canada

Source: Native Trees of Canada by R. C. Hosie
(Canadian Forestry Service. Dept. of Fisheries & Forestry)

There are nearly 140 species of trees native to Canada on which information is easily available. A "Native" tree is defined as a single-stemmed perennial woody plant growing to a height of more than ten feet, and which is indigenous to Canada. Most of the 'giant' trees in Canada are to be found in the Forest Regions. These regions reflect differences caused by terrain, soil, and climate. The nine Forest Regions are: The Grassland, Boreal, Great Lakes-St. Lawrence, Columbia, Deciduous, Coast, Subalpine, Acadian and Montane.

It is difficult to obtain precise records of single trees of outstanding heights. Given below are several common species of trees native to Canada showing the usual or normal height of the species. But many exceptions have been noted. For example the Douglas Fir whose average range in height is given at 150 to 200 ft. with diameters of up to 9 ft., occasionally may attain heights above 300 ft. and diameters of 15 ft. or more. The Sitka Spruce is also known to have reached heights of at least 280 ft., and the Western White Pine is recorded as having attained 200 ft.

Species	Height (Ft.)	Forest Region
Alpine Fir	65-100	Subalpine; N.W. Boreal
Amabilis Fir	80-125	Coast & Coastal parts of Subalpine
Balsam Poplar	60-80	Boreal, Great Lakes-St. Lawrence & Acadian
Black Cottonwood	80-125	Throughout B.C. and Western Alberta
Black Maple	80-90	Ontario to Montreal Is.
Douglas-Fir	150-200	Coast
Eastern Cottonwood	75-100	Gt. Lakes-St. Lawrence
Eastern White Pine	100-175	Through east Canada
Engelmann Spruce	100-120	Southern Subalpine
Grand Fir	100-125	S. Coast & Columbia
Mockernut Hickory	75-90	Deciduous
Silver Maple	80-90	S.E. Parts of G. Lakes-St. Lawrence

Species	Height (Ft.)	Forest Region
Sitka Spruce	125-175	Coast
Sugar Maple	80-90	Gt. Lakes-St. Lawrence
Sycamore	Up to 150	Deciduous
Western Hemlock	120-160	Coast & Columbia
Western Larch	100-180	Southern part of Columbia & Montane, B.C.
Western Red Cedar	150-200	Coast & Columbia
Western White Pine	90-110	S. Coast & Columbia
White Birch	Med.-80	Throughout Canada
White Elm	60-80	G. Lakes-St. Lawrence & Acadian
White Oak	Med.-100	Southern Ontario
White Spruce	80-120	Boreal
Yellow Cypress	60-80	Coast & in coastal parts of Subalpine

The 1972 Forest Fire Season in Canada

The 1972 fire season got off to an early start with an unprecedented 3,030 forest fires or 37 per cent of the annual total, reported in the single month of May. During that period, forest fire control organizations in eastern Canada were kept under almost constant alert, particularly in Quebec and Ontario, as both provinces reported an all time record number of fire starts. A second but more localized fire situation developed in early July as a rash of lightning fires spread through northwestern Ontario, severely taxing the local fire suppression forces on several occasions.

Despite the early season onslaught, fire occurence in 1972 dropped for the first time in the last three years.

A total of 8,263 forest fires were reported in Canada compared with 9,205 in 1971 and 9,313 the previous year. Without question, strong prevention measures and aggressive initial-attack action paid off in that 85 per cent of the fires were brought under

control at 10 acres or less in size. Less than 3 per cent of the fires were over 500 acres in size.

Forest fire control officers have further reason to be gratified with the current fire season. The total acreage burned on all federal and provincial forest lands dropped from 4,148,911 acres in 1971 to 1,927,-932 in 1972, a decrease of 2,220,979. It is interesting to note that during that same period, areas burned as a result of lightning strikes also dropped by a similar amount, with 1,211,000 acres in 1972 compared to 3,448,933 the previous year — a decrease of 2,237,933 acres.

Human negligence and incendiarism continued to be responsible for the greatest proportion of forest fires. In 1972, a total of 5,739 or seven out of every ten fires reported in Canada were man caused.

The total area afforded some form of organized protection in 1972 reached 1,692,453 sq. mi., an increase of some 111,703 sq. mi. over the previous year.

Forest Fires on Provincial and Federal Protected Lands, 1972

Provincial Lands	Number of Fires	Acres Burned		Number of Fires	Acres Burned
Newfoundland	247	106,950	Alberta	737	121,799
Nova Scotia	568	5,882	British Columbia	1,905	64,413
Prince Edward Island	36	488	**Federal Lands**		
New Brunswick	488	11,209	Yukon	142	163,495
Quebec	1,100	260,281	Northwest Territories	327	555,886
Ontario	1,604	79,145	National Parks	83	1,052
Manitoba	539	46,112	Other Federal Lands	27	162
Saskatchewan	460	511,058	Total all lands	8,263	1,927,932

Total Fires and Acreage Burned by Causes

	Man-caused		Lightning			Man Caused		Lightning	
Year	Number of Fires	Acres Burned	Number of Fires	Acres Burned	Year	Number of Fires	Acres Burned	Number of Fires	Acres Burned
1967	6,429	586,583	2,221	1,625,371	1971	6,287	699,978	2,918	3,448,933
1968	5,917	1,904,476	1,384	307,129	Average				
1969	5,003	809,063	1,658	1,522,641	'67-'71	5,930	880,109	2,296	1,824,353
1970	6,014	400,447	3,299	2,217,690	1972	5,739	716,932	2,524	1,211,000

THEATER — RECORDINGS — FILMS
Broadway's Principal Events of 1973-74
*still running July 1, 1974; (M) designates musical; performers are original cast.

Play	Performers	Opened	Run
	1973		
Raisin (M) — Virginia Capers, Joe Morton		Oct. 18	293*
Children of the Wind — James Callahan, Ann Thomas, Sarah Hardy		Oct. 24	6
Veronica's Room — Eileen Heckart, Arthur Kennedy, Regina Baff		Oct. 25	75
Molly (M) — Kay Ballard, Lee Wallace, Eli Mintz		Nov. 1	68
Full Circle — Bibi Andersson, Leonard Nimoy		Nov. 7	21
Gigi (M) — Alfred Drake, Agnes Moorehead, Karen Wolfe		Nov. 13	103
Good Evening — Peter Cook, Dudley Moore		Nov. 14	263*
The Good Doctor — Christopher Plummer, Marsha Mason, Frances Sternhagen		Nov. 27	208
The Pajama Game (M) — Barbara McNair, Hal Linden, Cab Calloway		Dec. 9	49
	1974		
Find Your Way Home —Michael Moriarty, Lee Richardson, Jane Alexander		Jan. 2	134
Lorelei (M)—Carol Channing		Jan. 27	177*
The Freedom of the City—Kate Reid, Lenny Baker, Allan Carlsen		Feb. 17	9
Noel Coward in Two Keys—Anne Baxter, Hume Cronyn, Jessica Tandy		Feb. 28	141
Over Here! (M)—Patty Andrews, Maxene Andrews, Janie Sell		Mar. 6	135*
Ulysses in Nighttown—Zero Mostel, Fionnuala Flanagan		Mar. 10	69
Clarence Darrow—Henry Fonda		Mar. 26	29
My Fat Friend—Lynn Redgrave, George Rose, John Lithgow		Mar. 31	104*
Thieves—Marlo Thomas, Richard Mulligan, Irwin Corey		Apr. 7	96*
An American Millionaire—Paul Sorvino, Austin Pendleton, Bob Dishy		Apr. 20	76
Jumpers—Remak Ramsay, Jill Clayburgh, Brian Bedford		Apr. 22	48
Bad Habits—Cynthia Harris, Paul Benedict, Doris Roberts		May 5	160
Will Rogers, U.S.A.—James Whitmore		May 6	8
Scapino—Gavin Reed, Jim Dale		May 18	67*
The Magic Show—Doug Henning, David Ogden Stiers		May 28	39*

Record Long Run Broadway Plays *Still Running July 1, 1974

Fiddler on the Roof	3,242	How to Succeed in		Butterflies Are Free	1,128
Life With Father	3,213	Business Without Really		Pins and Needles	1,108
Tobacco Road	3,182	Trying	1,416	Plaza Suite	1,098
Hello Dolly	2,844	Hellzapoppin	1,404		
My Fair Lady	2,717	The Music Man	1,376		
Man of La Mancha	2,328	Funny Girl	1,348	**Off-Broadway**	
Abie's Irish Rose	2,327	Oh! Calcutta!	1,314	*The Fantasticks	5,894
Oklahoma!	2,246	Angel Street	1,295	The Threepenny Opera	2,611
South Pacific	1,925	Lightnin'	1,291	You're A Good Man Charlie	
Harvey	1,775	Promises, Promises	1,281	Brown	1,597
Hair	1,750	The King and I	1,246	Jacques Brel is Alive and Well	
Born Yesterday	1,643	Cactus Flower	1,234	and Living in Paris	1,847
Mary, Mary	1,572	Sleuth	1,222	This Was Burlesque	1,509
Voice of the Turtle	1,558	"1776"	1,217	The Premise	1,490
Barefoot in the Park	1,532	Guys and Dolls	1,200	The Blacks	1,408
Mame	1,508	Cabaret	1,166	*Godspell	1,293
Arsenic and Old Lace	1,444	Mister Roberts	1,157	Little Mary Sunshine	1,143
The Sound of Music	1,442	Annie Get Your Gun	1,147	The Boys in the Band	1,001

Plays in London *Still running Aug. 31, 1974

*The Mousetrap	9,041	Fiddler on the Roof	2,030	The Beggars Opera	1,463
Black and White Minstrels	4,354	Blithe Spirit	1,997	Simple Spymen	1,404
Oliver	2,811	*Sleuth	1,905	Our Boys	1,362
There's a Girl in my Soup	2,547	Worms Eye View	1,745	Knights of Madness	1,361
Sound of Music	2,385	*Oh! Calcutta!	1,675	*No Sex, Please, We're British	1,353
Salad Days	2,283	Me and My Girl	1,646	Maid of the Mountains	1,352
My Fair Lady	2,281	Reluctant Heroes	1,610	Arsenic and Old Lace	1,337
Chu Chin Chow	2,238	Together Again	1,566	The Farmer's Wife	1,329
The Man Most Likely To	2,213	Seagulls Over Sorrento	1,551	Annie Get Your Gun	1,304
Charlie Girl	2,201	Oklahoma	1,543	The Little Hut	1,261
The Boy Friend	2,084	Irma La Douce	1,512	A Little Bit of Fluff	1,241
Canterbury Tales	2,082	Dry Rot	1,475	Sailor Beware	1,231
*Hair	2,076	Charley's Aunt	1,466	One for the Pot	1,221
Boeing Boeing	2,036	The Secretary Bird	1,463	Beyond the Fringe	1,184

Symphony Orchestras of the United States and Canada
(As of Sept. 10, 1974)
Source: American Symphony Orchestra League, Inc.
Classifications are based on annual budgets of orchestras.

Major Symphony Orchestras

		Conductors
Atlanta Symphony	1280 Peachtree St., N.E., Atlanta, GA. 30309	Robert Shaw
Baltimore Symphony	120 West Mount Royal Ave., Baltimore, MD. 21201	Sergiu Comissiona
Boston Symphony	Symphony Hall, Boston, MA. 02115	Seiji Ozawa
Buffalo Philharmonic	26 Richmond Ave., Buffalo, N.Y. 14122	Michael Thomas
Chicago Symphony	220 S. Michigan Ave. Chicago, IL. 60604	George Solti
Cincinnati Symphony	1241 Elm St., Cincinnati, OH. 45210	Thomas Schippers
Cleveland Orchestra	11001 Euclid Ave., Cleveland, OH. 44106	Lorin Maazel
Dallas Symphony	P.O. Box 26207, Dallas, TX 75226	Max Rudolf
Denver Symphony	1615 California St., Denver, CO. 80202	Brian Priestman

(Continued)

		Conductors
Detroit Symphony	20 Auditorium Dr., Detroit, MI. 48226	Aldo Ceccato
Houston Symphony	615 Louisiana, Houston, TX. 77002	Lawrence Foster
Indianapolis Symphony	4600 Sunset Ave., Indianapolis, IN. 46208	Izler Solomon
Kansas City Philharmonic	210 W. 10th St. Kansas City, MO. 64105	Jorge Mester
Los Angeles Philharmonic	135 North Grand, Los Angeles, CA. 90012	Zubin Mehta
Milwaukee Symphony	929 N. Water St., Milwaukee, WI. 53202	Ken Schermerhorn
Minnesota Orchestra	807 Hennepin Ave., Minneapolis, MN 55403	S. Skrowaczewski
Montreal Symphony	Place des Arts, Montreal, Que., Can., H2X 1Y1	Rafael Fruhbeck De Burgos
National Symphony	JFK Center for the Performing Arts, Wash., DC 20566	Antal Dorati
New Jersey Symphony	150 Halsey St., Newark, NJ 07102	Henry Lewis
New Orleans Philharmonic	203 Carondelet St. New Orleans, LA 70130	W. Torkanowsky
New York Philharmonic	Broadway at 65th St., New York, NY 10023	Pierre Boulez
Philadelphia Orchestra	230 S. 15th St., Philadelphia, PA 19102	Eugene Ormandy
Pittsburgh Symphony	600 Penn Ave., Pittsburgh, PA 15222	William Steinberg
Rochester Philharmonic	60 Gibbs St., Rochester, NY 14604	David Zinman
St. Louis Symphony	718 N. Grand Blvd., St. Louis, MO 63103	Walter Susskind
San Antonio Symphony	600 HemisFair Plaza Way, San Antonio, TX78205	Victor Alessandro
San Francisco Symphony	War Memorial Veterans' Bldg., San Fran., CA 94102	Seiji Ozawa
Seattle Symphony	305 Harrison St., Seattle, WA 98109	Milton Katims
Toronto Symphony	215 Victoria St., Toronto, Ontario, Can. M5B 1V1	Victor Feldbrill
Utah Symphony	55 W. 1st So. St., Salt Lake City, UT 84101	Maurice Abravanel

Metropolitan Orchestras

		Conductors
Akron Symphony	Thomas Hall, Hill & Center Sts., Akron, OH 44303	Louis Lane
Albany Symphony	19 Clinton Ave., Albany, NY 12207	Julius Hegyi
Albuquerque Symphony	120 Madeira N.E., Albuquerque, NM 87108	Yoshimi Takeda
Amarillo Symphony	P.O. Box 2552, Amarillo, TX 79105	Thomas Hohstadt
Austin Symphony	701 West 15th St., Austin, TX 78701	Walter Ducloux
Birmingham Symphony	City Hall, Birmingham, AL 35203	Amerigo Marino
Brooklyn Philharmonia	30 Lafayette Ave., Brooklyn, NY 11217	Lukas Foss
Calgary Philharmonic	830 Ninth Ave., S.W., Calgary, Alberta, Can. T2P 1L7	Maurice Handford
Cedar Rapids Symphony	200 Guaranty Bldg., Cedar Rapids, IA 52401	Richard D. Williams
Charlotte Symphony	511 E. Morehead St., Charlotte, NC 28202	Jacques Brourman
Chattanooga Symphony	730 Cherry St., Chattanooga, TN 37402	Richard Cormier
Chautauqua Symphony	Chatauqua Institution, Chautauqua, NY 14722	Guest Conductors
Clarion Music Society	415 Lexington Ave., New York, NY 10017	Newell Jenkins
Colorado Springs Symphony	P.O. Box 1692, Colorado Springs, CO 80901	Charles Ansbacher
Columbus Symphony	200 East Town St., Columbus, OH 43215	Evan Whallon
Corpus Christi Symphony	P.O. Box 495, Corpus Christi, TX 78403	Maurice Peress
Dayton Philharmonic	15 East First St., Dayton, OH 45402	Paul Katz
Duluth Symphony	401 Lonsdale Bldg., Duluth, MN 55802	Joseph Hawthorne
Eastern Music Festival	712 Summit Ave., Greensboro, NC 27405	Sheldon Morgenstern
Edmonton Symphony	P.O. Box 4232, Edmonton, Alberta, Can. T6E 4T2	Pierre Hetu
El Paso Philharmonic	P.O. Box 180, El Paso, TX 79942	Guest Conductors
Erie Philharmonic	720 G. Daniel Baldwin Bldg., Erie, PA 16501	Harold Bauer
Evansville Philharmonic	P.O. Box 84, Evansville, IN 44701	Minas Christian
Flint Symphony	1025 E. Kearsley St., Flint, MI 48502	Guest Conductors
Florida Gulf Coast Symphony	P.O. Box 569, St. Petersburg, FL 33731	Irwin Hoffman
Florida Symphony	P.O. Box 782, Orlando, FL 32802	Pavle Despalj
Florida West Coast Symphony	P.O. Box 1107, Sarasota, FL 33578	Paul C. Wolfe
Fort Lauderdale Symphony	450 E. Las Olas Blvd., Fort Lauderdale, FL 33301	Emerson Buckley
Fort Wayne Philharmonic	927 S. Harrison, Fort Wayne, IN 46802	Thomas Briccetti
Fort Worth Symphony	3505 W. Lancaster, Ft. Worth, TX 76107	John Giordano
Fresno Philharmonic	1362 N. Fresno St., Fresno, CA 93703	Guy Taylor
Glendale Symphony	121 W. Lexington Dr., Glendale, CA 91203	Carmen Dragon
Grand Rapids Symphony	Exhibitors Bldg., Grand Rapids, MI 49502	Theo Alcantara
Hamilton Philharmonic	50 Main St. W. Hamilton, Ont. Can. L8N 3H8	Boris Brott
Hartford Symphony	15 Lewis St., Hartford, CT 06103	Arthur Winograd
Honolulu Symphony	1000 Bishop St., Honolulu, HA 96813	Robt. LaMarchina
Hudson Valley Philharmonic	P.O. Box 191, Poughkeepsie, NY 12602	Claude Monteux
Jackson Symphony	P.O. Box 4584 Jackson, MS 39216	Lewis Dalvit
Jacksonville Symphony	46 W. Duval St., Jacksonville, FL 32202	Willis Page
Kalamazoo Symphony	426 S. Park St., Kalamazoo, MI 49007	Yoshimi Takeda
Knoxville Symphony	618 Gay St., Knoxville, TN 37902	Arpod Joo
Louisville Orchestra	333 W. Broadway, Louisville, KY 40202	Jorge Mester
Madison Symphony	211 N. Carroll St., Madison, WI 53703	Roland Johnson
Memphis Symphony	1503 Monroe, Memphis, TN 38104	Vincent DeFrank
Miami Beach Symphony	420 Lincoln Rd. Mall, Miami Beach, FL 33139	Barnett Breeskin
Miami Philharmonic	174 Flagler St., Miami, FL 33131	Alain Lombard
Midland Odessa Sym. & Chorale	P.O. 6266, Air Terminal Sta., Midland, TX 79701	Thomas Hohstadt
Monterey County Symphony	P.O. Box 3965, Carmel, CA 93921	Haymo Taeuber
Nashville Symphony	1805 West End Ave., Nashville, TN 37203	Thor Johnson
New Haven Symphony	33 Whitney Ave., New Haven, CT 06511	Erich Kunzel
New World, Symphony of the	2504 W. 57th St., New York NY 10019	Everett Lee
Norfolk Symphony	P.O. Box 26, Norfolk, VA 23501	Russell Stanger
North Carolina Symphony	P.O. Box 2508 UNC, Chapel Hill, NC 27514	John Gosling
Northeastern Penna., Philharmonic Soc. of	P.O. Box 71, Avoca, PA 18641	Thomas Michalak
Oakland Symphony	2025 Broadway, Oakland, CA 94612	Harold Farberman
Oklahoma City Symphony	Civic Center Music Hall, Oklahoma City, OK 73102	Ainslee Cox
Omaha Symphony	P.O. Box 897, Omaha, NE 68101	Yuri Krasnapolsky
Orchestra Da Camera	200 Emory Rd., Mineola, NY 11501	Herbert Grossman
Oregon Symphony	1119 S.W. Park, Portland, OR 97205	Lawrence Smith
Pasadena Symphony	300 E. Green St., Pasadena, CA 91101	Daniel Lewis
Peoria Symphony	1508 W. Moss Ave., Peoria, IL 61606	Robert Kreis
Phoenix Symphony	6328 N. 7th St., Phoenix, AZ 85014	Eduardo Mata
Portland Symphony	30 Myrtle St., Portland, ME 04111	Paul Vermel
Quebec Symphony	1115 Rue Claire Fontaine, Que., Can. G1R 3B2	Pierre Dervaux

(continued)

Rhode Island Philharmonic	The Arcade, Providence, RI 02903	Francis Madeira
Richmond Symphony	112 E. Franklin St., Richmond, VA 23219	Jacques Houtmann
Sacramento Symphony	451 Parkfair Dr., Sacramento, CA 95825	Harry Newstone
San Diego Symphony	P.O. Box 3175, San Diego, CA 92103	Peter Eros
San Jose Symphony	St. Claire Hotel, San Jose, CA 95113	George Cleve
Santa Barbara Symphony	210 E. Figueroa, Santa Barbara, CA 93101	Ronald Ondrejka
Savannah Symphony	P.O. Box 9505, Savannah, GA 31402	Michael Charry
Shreveport Symphony	P.O. Box 4057, Shreveport, LA 71104	John Shenaut
Spokane Symphony	West 905 Riverside, Spokane, WA 99201	Donald Thulean
Springfield Symphony	49 Chestnut St., Springfield, MA 01103	Robert Gutter
Syracuse Symphony	113 E. Onondaga St., Syracuse, NY 13202	Frederik Prausnitz
Toledo Orchestra	One Stranahan Sq., Toledo, OH 43604	Serge Fournier
Tri-City Symphony	P.O. Box 67, Davenport, IA 52801	James Dixon
Tucson Symphony	8 Paseo Redondo, Tucson, AZ 85705	Gregory Millar
Tulsa Philharmonic	2210 S. Main, Tulsa, OK 74114	Thomas Lewis
Utica Symphony	255 Genesee St., Utica, NY 13501	Fritz Maraffi
Vancouver Symphony	566 Hornby St., Vancouver, B.C., Can.	Kazuyoshi Akiyama
Vermont Symphony	P.O. Box 548, Middlebury, VT 05753	Alan Carter
Victoria Symphony	748 Johnson St., Victoria, B.C., Can. V8W 1N1	Lazlo Gati
Wichita Symphony	225 W. Douglas, Wichita, KS 67202	Francois Huybrechts
Winnipeg Symphony	555 Main St. Winnipeg, Manitoba, Can. R3B 1C3	Piero Gamba
Winston-Salem Symphony	610 Coliseum Dr., Winston-Salem, NC 27106	John Iuele
Youngstown Symphony	260 West Federal St., Youngstown, OH 44503	Franz Bibo

Chamber Orchestras

Los Angeles Chamber Orch.	1017 N. LaCienega Blvd., Los Angeles, CA 90069	Neville Marriner
St. Paul Chamber Orch.	75 W. 5th St., St. Paul, MN 55102	Dennis Davies

Recordings
Disc and Tape Sales Surpass $2 Billion a Year

U.S. recording industry sales, including both phonograph records and pre-recorded tapes, exceeded the $2 billion mark in 1974. Total sales in 1973 were $2.017 billion, up 4.8% from $1.924 billion in 1972, as reported by the Recording Industry Association of America (RIAA).

Long-play albums went up only 3.6% to $1.246 billion; singles rose 5.6% to $190 million; 8-track cartridges were up 15.1% to $489 million; pre-recorded cassettes dropped 25% to $76 million; reel-to-reel tapes declined by 50% to $4 million; sales of quadrasonic tapes doubled to $12 million.

From Jan. 1, 1974, through Sept. 20, 1974, the RIAA issued 132 Gold Recording Awards. These are made in 2 categories: for single discs which RIAA certifies as having sold one million copies, and for long-play albums and tape equivalents it certifies as having $1 million in sales at the manufacturer's level. The awards for 12 months follow:

Artists and Recording Titles
(A) Album. (S) Single.

September 1973
Charlie Rich: Behind Closed Doors. (S).
Original Movie Soundtrack: Jesus Christ Superstar.(A).
Carly Simon: Anticipation. (A).
War: Deliver the Word. (A).
Sly & the Family Stone: If You Want Me to Stay. (S).
J. Geils Band: Bloodshot. (A).
Donny Osmond: Twelfth of Never. (S).
Donny Osmond: My Best To You. (A)
Carlos Santana & Mahavishnu John McLaughlin: Love Devotion Surrender. (A)
Gilbert O'Sullivan: Get Down. (A).
Helen Reddy: Long Hard Climb. (A)
Allman Bros. Band: Beginnings. (A)
Rolling Stones: Goats Head Soup. (A)
Focus: Focus 3. (A)

October 1973
Isley Brothers: That Lady. (S).
Cheech & Chong: Los Cochinos. (A).
Grand Funk Railroad: We're an American Band. (S)
Paul Simon: Loves Me Like a Rock. (S)
Dawn: Say, Has Anybody Seen My Sweet Gypsy Rose. (S)
Cher: Half-Breed. (S)
Elton John: Goodbye Yellow Brick Road. (A)
Three Dog Night: Cyan. (A)
Rod Stewart: Sing It Again Rod. (A)
Uriah Heep: Uriah Heep Live. (A)
Gladys Knight & the Pips: Midnight Train to Georgia. (S)
Johnny Taylor: I Believe in You (You Believe in Me). (S)
Arthur Garfunkel: Angel Clare. (A)
The Who: Quadrophenia. (A)
Pink Floyd: Meddle. (A)
Neil Diamond/Original Movie Soundtrack: Jonathan Livingston Seagull. (A)

November 1973
Sha Na Na: The Golden Age of Rock 'N' Roll. (A).

Jim Croce: Life and Times. (A)
Joe Walsh: The Smoker You Drink, The Player You Get. (A)
Gladys Knight & the Pips: Imagination. (A)
Barry White: I've Got So Much to Give. (A)
The DeFranco Family featuring Tony DeFranco: Heart Beat — It's a Lovebeat. (S)
Earth, Wind & Fire: Head to the Sky. (A)
Kris Kristofferson: Why Me. (S)
Ringo Starr: Ringo. (A)
Kris Kristofferson: The Silver Tongued Devil and I.
Isley Brothers: 3 + 3. (A)
Rolling Stones: Angie. (S)
Jim Croce: You Don't Mess Around with Jim. (A)
Charlie Rich: Behind Closed Doors. (A)
Isaac Hayes: Joy. (A)
Santana: Welcome. (A)
Kris Kristofferson: Jesus Was a Capricorn. (A)
John Lennon: Mind Games. (A).

December 1973
Jim Croce: I Got a Name. (A)
Steve Miller Band: The Joker. (A)
Marie Osmond: Paper Roses. (S)
Alice Cooper: Muscle of Love. (A)
Loggins & Messina: Full Sail. (A)
Neil Young: Time Fades Away. (A)
Paul McCartney & Wings: Band on the Run. (A)
Charlie Rich: The Most Beautiful Girl. (S)
John Denver: John Denver's Greatest Hits. (A)
The Carpenters: The Singles 1969-1973. (A)
The Carpenters: Top of the World. (S)
Emerson, Lake & Palmer: Brain Salad Surgery. (A)
Bette Midler: Bette Midler. (A)
Al Wilson: Show and Tell. (S)
Billy Preston: Space Race. (S)
Staple Singers: If You're Ready. (S)
Anne Murray: Snowbird. (A)
Dylan: Dylan. (A)
Movie Soundtrack: American Graffiti. (A)
Harold Melvin & the Blue Notes: The Love I Lost. (S)
Ringo Starr: Photograph. (S)

January 1974

Chicago: Just You and Me. (S)
Jim Croce: Time in a Bottle. (S)
Elton John: Goodbye Yellow Brick Road. (S)
Byron MacGregor: Americans. (S)
Helen Reddy: Leave Me Alone (Ruby Red Dress). (S)
The Beatles: The Early Beatles. (A)
Steve Miller: The Joker. (S)
Brownsville Station: Smokin' in the Boy's Room. (S)
Jim Nabors: The Lord's Prayer. (A)
The O'Jays: Ship Ahoy. (A)
Al Green: Livin' for You. (A)
Eagles: Eagles. (A)
Judy Collins: Colors of the Day. (A)
Carly Simon: Hot Cakes. (A)
Bob Dylan: Planet Waves. (A)
Johnny Winter: Johnny Winter Live. (A)
Gladys Knight & the Pips: I Have Got to Use My Imagination. (A)
Ringo Starr: You're Sixteen. (S)

February 1974

Barbra Streisand: The Way We Were. (S)
Pointer Sisters: The Pointer Sisters. (A)
Dave Mason: Alone Together. (A)
Barry White: Never, Never, Gonna Give Ya Up. (S)
Love Unlimited Orchestra: Love's Theme. (S)
Love Unlimited: Under the Influence of Love Unlimited. (A)
Barry White: Stone Gon'. (A)
J. Geils Band: Live — Full House. (A)
Yes: Tales from Topographic Oceans. (A)
Olivia Newton-John: Let Me Be There. (S)
Terry Jacks: Seasons in the Sun. (S)
Aretha Franklin: Until You Come Back to Me. (S)
Kool and the Gang: Jungle Boogie. (S)
Barbra Streisand: The Way We Were. (A)
Joni Mitchell: Court and Spark. (A)
Pink Floyd: Ummagumma. (A)

March 1974

Cher: Half Breed. (A)
Uriah Heep: Sweet Freedom. (A)
Greg Allman: Laid Back. (A)
Jim Stafford: Spiders and Snakes. (S)
Seals & Crofts: Unborn Child. (A)
War: War Live. (A)
James Brown: The Payback. (A)
Chicago: Chicago VII. (A)
Deep Purple: Burn. (A)
Black Sabbath: Sabbath, Bloody Sabbath. (A)
Cher: Dark Lady. (S)
David Essex: Rock On. (S)
Mike Oldfield: Tubular Bells. (A)
Blue Swede: Hooked on a Feeling. (S)
John Denver: Sunshine on My Shoulder. (S)
Grand Funk Railroad: Shinin' On. (A)

April 1974

MFSB: TSOP. (S)
The Doobie Brothers: What Were once Vices are Now Habits. (A)
Sister Janet Mead: The Lord's Prayer. (S)
Bobby Womack: Lookin' for a Love. (S)
Cat Stevens: Buddah and the Chocolate Box. (A)
Elton John: Bennie and the Jets. (S)
Gladys Knight & the Pips: The Best Thing That Ever Happened to Me. (S)
MFSB: Love Is the Message. (A)
Three Dog Night: Hard Labor. (A)
James Brown: The Payback. (S)
Original Motion Picture Soundtrack: The Sting. (A)
Charlie Rich: Very Special Love Songs. (S)
Redbone: Come and Get Your Love. (S)
Herbie Hancock: Head Hunters. (A)
Ray Stevens: The Streak. (S)
Grand Funk Railroad: The Loco-Motion. (S)
Love Unlimited Orchestra: Rhapsody in White. (A)
Merle Haggard: The Best of the Best of Merle Haggard. (A)

May 1974

Bachman-Turner-Overdrive: Bachman-Turner Overdrive II. (A)

The Main Ingredient: Just Don't Want to Be Lonely. (S)
Kool & the Gang: Wild and Peaceful. (A)
Maria Muldaur: Maria Muldaur. (A)
Carly Simon & James Taylor: Mockingbird. (S)
Earth, Wind & Fire: Open Our Eyes. (A)
Steely Dan: Pretzel Logic. (A)
Three Dog Night: The Show Must Go On. (S)
Original Soundtrack Recording: The Way We Were. (A)

Spinners: Mighty Love. (A)
The Stylistics: You Make Me Feel Brand New. (S)
Z. Z. Top: Tres Hombres. (A)
William DeVaughn: Be Thankful for What You Got. (S)
Gordon Lightfoot: Sundown. (A)
The New Birth: It's Been a Long Time. (A)

June 1974

Paul McCartney & Wings: Band on the Run. (S)
Eagles: On the Border. (A)
Helen Reddy: Love Song for Jeffrey. (A)
Bo Donaldson & the Heywood: Billy Don't Be a Hero. (S)
Gladys Knight & the Pips: Claudine. (A)
Original Motion Picture Soundtrack: The Entertainer. (S)
Paul Simon: Live Rhymin'. (A)
David Bowie: Ziggy Stardust. (A)
The O'Jays: For the Love of Money. (S)
Loggins & Messina: On Stage. (A)
Gordon Lightfoot: Sundown. (S)
Kool & the Gang: Hollywood Swinging. (S)
John Denver: Back Home Again. (A)
The Hues Corporation: Rock the Boat. (S)
Ohio Players: Skin Tight. (A)

July 1974

Original Soundtrack: Original Soundtrack Recording from the Paramount Picture the Great Gatsby. (A)
Elton John: Caribou. (A)
Bob Dylan/The Band: Before the Flood. (A)
The Grateful Dead: Workingman's Dead. (A)
The Greatful Dead: American Beauty. (A)
Gladys Knight & the Pips: On & On. (S)
The Edgar Winter Group: Shock Treatment. (A)
Pointer Sisters: That's a Plenty. (A)
John Denver: Annie's Song. (S)
Bowie: Diamond Dogs. (A)
Olivia Newton-John: If You Love Me (Let Me Know). (S)

August 1974

Roberta Flack: Feel Like Makin' Love. (S)
Eric Clapton: 461 Ocean Boulevard. (A)
Rufus: Tell Me Something Good. (S)
Paper Lace: The Night Chicago Died. (S)
The Stylistics: Let's Put It All Together. (A)
Paul Anka: (You're) Having My Baby. (S)
Beach Boys: Endless Summer. (A)
Blue Magic: Sideshow. (S)
The Hollies: The Air That I Breathe. (S)
Bachman-Turner Overdrive: Not Fragile. (A)

September 1974

Rick Wakeman: Journey to the Centre of the Earth. (A)
Rufus: Rags to Rufus. (A)
Elton John: Don't Let the Sun Go Down On Me. (S)
Olivia Newton-John: If You Love Me, (Let Me Know.) (A)
Neil Diamond: His 12 Greatest Hits. (A)
Robin Trower: Bridge of Sighs. (A)
Barry White: Can't Get Enough of Your Love, Babe. (S)
Barry White: Can't Get Enough. (A)
Crosby, Stills, Nash & Young: So Far. (A)
Eric Clapton: I Shot the Sheriff. (S)
Emerson, Lake & Palmer: Welcome Back, My Friends, to the Show That Never Ends—Ladies & Gentlemen. (A)
Bad Company: Bad Company. (A)
Donny & Marie Osmond: I'm Leaving It (All) Up to You. (S)

Grammy Awards

The Grammy Awards for what were judged the best efforts of the recording industry in 1973 were announced March 2, 1974, by the National Academy of Recording Arts and Sciences. The Grammys are golden statuettes of early gramophones. Also announced were the first group of 5 early records named to the NARAS Hall of Fame. The categories and winners were:

Record of the Year, Song of the Year and Best Female Pop Vocal Performance: Killing Me Softly with His Song, Roberta Flack. Producer: Joel Dorn. Songwriters: Norman Gimbel, Charles Fox.

Album of the Year and Best Engineered Recording: Innervisions, Stevie Wonder. Producer: Stevie Wonder. Engineers: Robert Margouleff, Malcolm Cecil.

Best New Artist of the Year: Bette Midler.

Best Instrumental Arrangement: Summer in the City, Quincy Jones. Arranger: Quincy Jones.

Best Arrangement Acccompanying Vocalists: Live and Let Die, Paul McCartney & Wings. Arranger: George Martin.

Best Album Package: Tommy, London Symphony and Chambre Choir. Art Director: Wilkes & Braun Inc.

Best Jazz Performance by a Soloist and Best Album Notes: God Is In the House, Art Tatum. Annotator: Dan Morgenstern.

Best Jazz Performance by a Group: Supersax Plays Bird, Supersax.

Best Jazz Performance by a Big Band: Giant Steps, Woody Herman.

Best Pop Vocal Performance, Male: You Are the Sunshine of My Life, Stevie Wonder.

Best Pop Vocal Performance by a Group: Neither One of Us, Gladys Knight & the Pips.

Best Pop Instrumental Performance: Also Sprach Zarathustra, Eumir Deodato.

Best Rhythm & Blues Vocal Performance, Female: Master of Eyes, Aretha Franklin.

Best Rhythm & Blues Song and Best R. & B. Vocal Performance, Male: Superstition, Stevie Wonder. Songwriter: Stevie Wonder.

Best R. & B. Vocal Performance by a Group: Midnight Train to Georgia, Gladys Knight & the Pips.

Best R. & B. Instrumental Performance: Hang on Sloopy, Ramsey Lewis.

Best Soul Gospel Performance: Loves Me Like a Rock, Dixie Hummingbirds.

Best Country Vocal Performance, Female: Let Me Be There, Olivia Newton.

Best Country Vocal Performance, Male: Behind Closed Doors, Charlie Rich.

Best Country Vocal Performance by a Group: From the Bottle to the Bottom, Kris Kristofferson, Rita Coolidge.

Best Country Instrumental Performance: Dueling Banjos, Eric Weissberg, Steve Mandell.

Best Country Song: Behind Closed Doors. Songwriter: Kenny O'Dell.

Best Inspirational Performance: Let's Just Praise the Lord, Bill Gaither Trio.

Best Gospel (other than soul) Performance: Release Me, Blackwood Brothers.

Best Ethnic or Traditional Performance: Then and Now, Doc Watson.

Best Recording for Children: Sesame Street Live, Sesame Street Cast. Producer: Joe Raposo.

Best Comedy Recording: Los Cochinos, Cheech & Chong.

Best Spoken Word Recording: Jonathan Livingston Seagull, Richard Harris.

Best Instrumental Composition: Last Tango in Paris. Composer: Gato Barbieri.

Best Original Score Album: Jonathan Livingston Seagull. Composer: Neil Diamond.

Best Score from Original Cast Album: A Little Night Music. Composer: Stephen Sondheim. Producer: Goddard Lieberson.

Album of the Year, Classical; Best Orchestra Performance and Best Engineered Recording, Classical: Bartok's Concerto for Orchestra, Pierre Boulez conducting N. Y. Philharmonic. Producer: Thomas Z. Shepard. Engineers: Edward T. Graham, Raymond Moore.

Best Opera Recording: Bizet's Carmen, Leonard Bernstein conducting Metropolitan Opera Orchestra and Manhattan Opera Chorus. Producer: Thomas W. Mowrey.

Best Choral Performance, Classical: Walton's Belshazzar's Feast, Andre Previn conducting London Symphony Orchestra and Chorus. Choral Director: Arthur Oldham.

Best Chamber Music Performance: Joplin's The Red Back Book, Gunther Schuller & New England Ragtime Ensemble.

Best Classical Instrumental Soloist: Vladimir Ashkenazy with Georg Solti conducting Chicago Symphony.

Best Classical Vocal Soloist: Puccini's Heroines, Leontyne Price with Edward Downes conducting New Philharmonia.

Best Classical Instrumental Soloist (without orchestra): Horowitz Plays Scriabin, Vladimir Horowitz.

Best Album Notes, Classical: Hindemith's Sonatas for Piano, Glenn Gould. Annotator: Glenn Gould.

NARAS Hall of Fame

The first group of 5 early records was named to the NARAS Hall of Fame in 1974. Chosen were : Body & Soul, Coleman Hawkins (1939); Christmas Song, Nat King Cole (1954); Rhapsody in Blue, Paul Whiteman with George Gershwin (1927); West End Blues, Louis Armstrong (1928); White Christmas, Bing Crosby (1942).

Miss America Winners

For the winners of 1921 through 1958 see the 1972 issue of the World Almanac

		Height	Bust	Waist	Hips	Wgt.	Age	Hair	Eyes
1959	Mary Ann Mobley, Brandon, Miss.	5-5	34½	22	35	114	21	Brown	Brown
1960	Lynda Lee Mead, Natchez, Miss.	5-7	36	24	36	120	20	Brown	Green
1961	Nancy Fleming, Montague, Michigan.	5-6	35	22	35	116	18	Brown	Green
1962	Maria Fletcher, Asheville, N.C.	5-5½	35	24	35	118	19	Brown	Hazel
1963	Jacquelyn Mayer, Sandusky, Ohio.	5-5	36	22	36	115	20	Brown	Hazel
1964	Donna Axum, El Dorado, Arkansas.	5-6½	35	23	35	124	21	Brown	Brown
1965	Vonda Kay Van Dyke, Phoenix, Ariz.	5-6	36	24	36	124	21	Brown	Brown
1966	Deborah Irene Bryant, Overland Park, Kansas.	5-7	36	23	36	115	19	Brown	Blue
1967	Jane Anne Jayroe, Laverne, Oklahoma.	5-6	36	24	35	116	19	Brown	Green
1968	Debra Dene Barnes, Moran, Kansas.	5-9	36½	24	36½	135	20	Brown	Blue
1969	Judith Anne Ford, Belvidere, Ill.	5-7	36	24½	36	125	18	Blond	Blue
1970	Pamela Anne Eldred, Birmingham, Mich.	5-5½	34	21½	34	110	21	Blond	Green
1971	Phyllis Ann George, Denton, Texas.	5-8	36	23	36	121	21	Brown	Brown
1972	Laurie Lea Schaefer, Columbus, Ohio.	5-7	36	24	34	118	22	Auburn	Green
1973	Terry Anne Meeuwsen, DePere, Wisconsin.	5-8	36	25	36	120	23	Brown	Brown
1974	Rebecca Ann King, Denver, Colorado.	5-9	36	24	36	125	23	Blond	Blue
1975	Shirley Cothran, Fort Worth, Texas.	5-8	36	23	36	119	21	Brown	Hazel

Network TV Program Ratings
Average Audience Estimates of Households and Persons
Source: A. C. Nielsen, February '74 NAD Report

Program Type	U.S. TV House-Holds	Women Total	Women 18-34	Women 25-49	Men Total	Men 18-34	Men 25-49	Teens 12-17	Children 2-11
Prime Evening:									
Situation Comedy	21.2%	16.5%	14.3	14.8	13.2%	10.3	12.1	10.9%	14.2%
Variety	21.1	15.8	13.7	14.3	12.7	9.1	11.4	11.6	13.8
Suspense/Mys. Drama	20.4	15.4	14.3	14.8	14.0	11.9	13.9	10.3	10.2
Western Drama	20.2	14.6	12.9	12.7	13.4	12.4	12.6	11.7	14.2
General Drama	19.9	15.6	14.7	14.8	11.6	9.6	11.1	11.4	12.4
Feature Films	19.9	14.8	15.7	16.4	13.5	13.5	14.8	12.9	10.1
All 7:30-11 PM	20.2	15.3	14.7	15.2	13.3	11.8	13.4	11.5	11.6
Early Evening:									
Informational 6-7:30 PM	13.0	9.3	6.0	6.9	8.6	5.6	6.5	4.0	3.9
Weekday Daytime									
Drama	8.2	6.9	7.0	6.9	1.6	1.2	1.2	2.0	1.8
Quiz & Aud. Partic.	7.8	5.7	4.4	4.3	2.3	1.5	1.3	1.9	2.7
Children's Weekend	6.0	1.4	2.0	1.5	1.1	1.4	1.3	3.4	12.4
Total TV Base (millions)	66.2	71.3	26.6	31.5	63.7	25.2	29.8	24.5	36.5

U.S. Television Sets[1]
(in millions)
Source: A.C. Nielsen, Co.

Total TV Households 68,500	No. of TV Sets	Type of TV Sets	With CATV 7,640
	One: 40,140	Color: 46,850	
	Two: 28,360	B & W: 21,650	

1. Estimated: May, 1974

Best Selling Books of 1973-1974
Listed according to frequency of citation in best-seller reports between Sept. 16, 1973 and Sept. 15, 1974.

Fiction

1. *Burr, Gore Vidal
2. Jaws, Peter Benchley
3. The Hollow Hills, Mary Stewart
4. Watership Down, Richard Adams
5. *The Honorary Consul, Graham Greene
6. Come Nineveh, Come Tyre, Allen Drury
7. The Snare of the Hunter, Helen MacInnes
8. The Fan Club, Irving Wallace
9. Theophilus North, Thornton Wilder
10. Tinker, Tailor, Soldier, Spy, John le Carre
11. *The Billion Dollar Sure Thing, Paul Erdman
12. The First Deadly Sin, Lawrence Sanders
13. Cashelmara, Susan Howatch
14. The Salamander, Morris West
15. *Breakfast of Champions, Kurt Vonnegut Jr.
16. The Dogs of War, Frederick Forsyth
17. Postern of Fate, Agatha Christie
18. The Partners, Louis Auchincloss
19. World Without End, Amen, Jimmy Breslin
20. *Once is Not Enough, Jacqueline Susann
21. I Heard the Owl Call My Name, Margaret Craven
22. Harvest Home, Thomas Tryon
23. Nickel Mountain, John Gardner
24. Facing the Lions, Tom Wicker
25. The House of a Thousand Lanterns, Victoria Holt

General

1. *How to be Your Own Best Friend, Mildred Newman and Bernard Berkowitz with Jean Owen
2. *The Joy of Sex, Alex Comfort
3. You Can Profit from a Monetary Crisis, Harry Browne
4. *Alistair Cooke's America, Alistair Cooke
5. Plain Speaking, Merle Miller
6. Times to Remember, Rose Fitzgerald Kennedy
7. In One Era and Out the Other, Sam Levenson
8. Alive: The Story of the Andes Survivors, Piers Paul Read
9. All the President's Men, Carl Bernstein and Bob Woodward
10. Upstairs at the White House, J. B. West
11. The Gulag Archipelago, Aleksandr Solzhenitsyn
12. Pentimento, Lillian Hellman
13. Management, Peter F. Drucker
14. Cosell, Howard Cosell
15. The Memory Book, Harry Lorayne and Jerry Lucas
16. Portrait of a Marriage, Nigel Nicolson
17. Working, Studs Terkel
18. The Making of the President 1972, Theodore H. White
19. The Onion Field, Joseph Wambaugh
20. Thomas Jefferson, Fawn Brodie
21. The Best of Life, David E. Scherman
22. *Dr. Atkin's Diet Revolution, Robert C. Atkins
23. *Sybil, Flora R. Schreiber
24. *Weight Watchers Program Cookbook, Jean Nidetch
25. The Secret Life of Plants, Peter Tompkins

*One of 10 best-sellers in calendar year 1973 according to Publishers' Weekly.

Advertising Expenditures in the United States

Source: Advertising Age; prepared by
Robert J. Coen of McCann-Erickson, Inc.

MEDIUM	1971 Dollars-millions	1971 Per cent of total	1972 Dollars-millions	1972 Per cent of total	1973 Dollars-millions	1973 Per cent of total	% Change '73 vs. '72
Newspapers							
Total	6,198	29.9	7,008	30.1	7,595	30.2	+8.4
National	991	4.8	1,103	4.7	1,111	4.4	+0.7
Local	5,207	25.1	5,905	25.4	6,484	25.8	+9.8
Magazines							
Total	1,370	6.6	1,440	6.2	1,448	5.8	+0.6
Weeklies	626	3.0	610	2.6	583	2.3	−4.5
Women's	340	1.6	368	1.6	362	1.5	−1.6
Monthlies	404	2.0	462	2.0	503	2.0	+8.9
Farm Publications	57	0.3	59	0.3	65	0.3	+11.0
Television							
Total	3,534	17.0	4,091	17.6	4,493	17.9	+9.8
Network	1,593	7.7	1,804	7.7	1,968	7.8	+9.1
Spot	1,145	5.5	1,318	5.7	1,450	5.8	+10.0
Local	796	3.8	969	4.2	1,075	4.3	+11.0
Radio							
Total	1,445	7.0	1,612	6.9	1,690	6.7	+5.0
Network	63	0.3	74	0.3	70	0.3	−5.0
Spot	395	1.9	402	1.7	380	1.5	−5.0
Local	987	4.8	1,136	4.9	1,240	4.9	+9.0
Direct Mail	3,067	14.8	3,420	14.7	3,698	14.7	+8.1
Business Papers	720	3.5	781	3.3	865	3.4	+10.8
Outdoor							
Total	261	1.2	292	1.2	308	1.2	+5.5
National	172	0.8	192	0.8	200	0.8	+4.0
Local	89	0.4	100	0.4	108	0.4	+8.0
Miscellaneous							
Total	4,088	19.7	4,597	19.7	4,958	19.7	+7.9
National	2,202	10.6	2,437	10.4	2,590	10.3	+6.3
Local	1,886	9.1	2,160	9.3	2,368	9.4	+9.6
Total							
National	11,775	56.8	13,030	55.9	13,845	55.1	+6.3
Local	8,965	43.2	10,270	44.1	11,275	44.9	+9.8
Grand Total	20,740	100.0	23,300	100.0	25,120	100.0	+7.8
Inflation Adjustment (1967 Dollars)	17,098	——	18,595	——	18,730	——	+0.7

Commercial Broadcast Stations on the Air

Source: Federal Communications Commission (January 1, 1973)

State	Total	AM	FM	TV	State	Total	AM	FM	TV
Total	7,357	4,343	2,307	707	Nebraska	79	48	17	14
United States	7,263	4,295	2,278	694	Nevada	39	21	11	7
Alabama	208	136	56	16	New Hampshire	44	27	14	3
Alaska	27	17	3	7	New Jersey	67	36	27	4
Arizona	88	59	18	11	New Mexico	84	58	19	7
Arkansas	137	85	44	8	New York	288	160	100	28
California	441	231	161	49	North Carolina	295	202	75	18
Colorado	107	66	30	11	North Dakota	49	27	10	12
Connecticut	64	38	21	5	Ohio	258	119	113	26
Delaware	15	10	5	—	Oklahoma	113	66	37	10
Dist. of Columbia	19	6	7	6	Oregon	111	78	20	13
Florida	318	195	97	26	Pennsylvania	313	170	119	24
Georgia	259	172	71	16	Rhode Island	24	15	7	2
Hawaii	38	24	4	10	South Carolina	156	102	43	11
Idaho	56	43	7	6	South Dakota	50	30	10	10
Illinois	255	122	110	23	Tennessee	235	150	68	17
Indiana	182	86	79	17	Texas	476	287	134	55
Iowa	129	73	43	13	Utah	45	32	10	3
Kansas	101	58	31	12	Vermont	25	17	6	2
Kentucky	187	108	67	12	Virginia	201	127	62	12
Louisiana	156	92	48	16	Washington	154	97	42	15
Maine	58	36	15	7	West Virginia	96	60	27	9
Maryland	95	53	35	7	Wisconsin	196	99	79	18
Massachusetts	115	64	40	11	Wyoming	33	29	1	3
Michigan	234	128	84	22					
Minnesota	144	87	45	12	Other areas	93	51	29	13
Mississippi	153	101	42	10	Puerto Rico	83	47	26	10
Missouri	183	109	50	24	Guam	3	1	1	1
Montana	62	41	10	11	Virgin Islands	7	3	2	2

Movies of the Year (Oct. 1, 1973 to Oct. 1, 1974)

Selected and Rated by the New York Daily News Film Critics

Listed below alphabetically, are films rated by the New York Daily News star system; ★★★★ is for excellent, ★★★½ very good, ★★★ good, ★★½ fair, ★★ mediocre, ★½ poor, ★ very poor, 0★ not worth rating.

Kathleen Carroll, N. Y. Daily News Movie Editor and Critic

Movie	Star Rating	Stars	Director
Alfredo, Alfredo	★★★	Dustin Hoffman, Stephania Sandrelli	Pietro Germi
All-American Boy, The	★★★	Jon Voight, Carol Androsky	Charles Eastman
Apprencticeship of Duddy Kravitz, The	★★½	Richard Dreyfuss, Micheline Lanctot	Ted Kotcheff
Ash Wednesday	★★½	Elizabeth Taylor, Henry Fonda	Larry Peerce
Badlands	★★★½	Martin Sheen, Sissy Spacek	Terence Malick
Bank Shot	★★½	George C. Scott, Joanna Cassidy	Gower Champion
Black Belt Jones	★	Jim Kelly, Gloria Hondry	Robert Clouse
Black Windmill, The	★★★	Michael Caine, Donald Pleasence	Don Siegel
Blazing Saddles	★★★½	Cleavon Little, Gene Wilder	Mel Brooks
Bring Me the Head of Alfredo Garcia	★★½	Warren Oates, Isela Vega	Sam Peckinpah
Buster and Billie	★★★	Jan-Michael Vincent, Joan Goodfellow	Daniel Petrie
California Split	★★★	George Segal, Elliott Gould	Robert Altman
Charley Varrick	★★½	Walter Matthau, Joe Don Baker	Don Siegel
Cinderella Liberty	★★½	James Caan, Marsha Mason	Mark Rydell
Chinatown	★★★★	Jack Nicholson, Faye Dunaway	Roman Polanski
Claudine	★★★½	Diahann Carroll, James Earl Jones	John Berry
Conrack	★★★½	John Voight, Paul Winfield	Martin Ritt
Conversation, The	★★★½	Gene Hackman, John Cazale	Francis Ford Coppola
Daisy Miller	★★½	Cybill Shepherd, Cloris Leachman	Peter Bogdanovich
Day for Night	★★★★	Jacqueline Bisset, Valentina Cortese	Francois Truffaut
Day of the Dolphin, The	★★★	George C. Scott, Trish Van Devere	Mike Nichols
Death Wish	★★★	Charles Bronson, Hope Lange	Michael Winner
Exorcist, The	★★★★	Ellen Burstyn, Max von Sydow	William Friedkin
Fantastic Planet	★★½	animated cartoon	Rene Laloux
Five on the Black Hand Side	★★★	Clarice Taylor, Leonard Jackson	Oscar Williams
Frankenstein, Andy Warhol's	0★	Joe Dallesandro, Monique van Vooren	Paul Morrissey
Free Woman, A	★★★★	Margarethe von Trotta, Friedhelm Ptok	Volker Schlondorff
Girl From Petrovka, The	★★½	Goldie Hawn, Hal Holbrook	Robert E. Miller
Going Places	★★★½	Gerard Depardieu, Patrick Dewaere	Bertrand Blier
Great Gatsby, The	★★★	Robert Redford, Mia Farrow	Jack Clayton
Happy New Year	★★★½	Lino Ventura, Francoise Fabian	Claude Lelouch
Harry and Tonto	★★★	Art Carney, Ellen Burstyn	Paul Mazursky
Hell Up in Harlem	★	Fred Williamson, Julius W. Harris	Larry Cohen
Huckleberry Finn	★	Jeff East, Paul Winfield	J. Lee Thompson
Jonathan Livingston Seagull	★★½		Hal Bartlett
Juggernaut	★★½	Richard Harris, Omar Sharif	Richard Lester
Last Detail, The	★★★½	Jack Nicholson, Otis Young	Hal Ashby
Longest Yard, The	★★½	Burt Reynolds, Eddie Albert	Robert Aldrich
Lords of Flatbush, The	★★½	Perry King, Sylvester Stallone	Verona and Martin Davidson
Long Goodbye, The	★★★½	Elliott Gould, Nina van Pallandt	Robert Altman
Love and Anarchy	★★★★	G. Gianinni, Mariangela Melato	Lina Wertmuller
Mad Adventures of Rabbi Jacob, The	★★★½	Louis de Funes, Suzy Delair	Gerard Oury
Magnum Force	★★½	Clint Eastwood, Hal Holbrook	John Milius
Mame	★★★	Lucille Ball, Beatrice Arthur	Gene Saks
Man on a Swing	★★★	Cliff Robertson, Joel Grey	Frank Perry
McQ	★★½	John Wayne, Colleen Dewhurst	John Sturgis
Mean Streets	★★½	Robert De Niro, Harvey Keitel	Martin Scorsese
Mother and the Whore, The	★★★	Bernadette Lafont, Jean-Pierre Leaud	Jean Eustache
New Land, The	★★★½	Max von Sydow, Liv Ullmann	Jan Troell
Nine Lives of Fritz the Cat, The	★½	animated cartoon	Robert Taylor
Optimists, The	★★½	Peter Sellers, Donna Mullane	Anthony Simmons
Paper Chase, The	★★★½	Timothy Bottoms, Lindsay Wagner	James Bridges
Papillon	★★½	Steve McQueen, Dustin Hoffman	Franklin J. Schaffner
Parallax View, The	★★½	Warren Beatty, Paula Prentiss	Alan J. Pakula
Pedestrian, The	★★★½	Maximilian Schell, Rudolf Sellner	Maximilian Schell
Ra Expeditions, The	★★★	Thor Heyerdahl	Thor Heyerdahl
Robin Hood	★★★★	animated cartoon	Wolfgang Reitherman
Scalawag	★½	Kirk Douglas	Kirk Douglas
Serpico	★★★★	Al Pacino, Tony Roberts	Sidney Lumet
Seven-Ups, The	★★★	Roy Scheider, Tony Lo Bianco	Philip D'Antoni
Sleeper	★★★½	Woody Allen, Diane Keaton	Woody Allen
Sting, The	★★★½	Robert Redford, Paul Newman	George Roy Hill
Sugarland Express, The	★★★½	Goldie Hawn, Ben Johnson	Steven Spielberg
Super Cops, The	★★★½	Ron Leibman, David Selby	Gordon Parks
Summer Wishes, Winter Dreams	★★★½	Joanne Woodward, Martin Balsam	Gilbert Gates
Tamarind Seed, The	★★★	Julie Andrews, Omar Sharif	Blake Edwards
Terminal Man, The	★★½	George Segal, Joan Hackett	Mike Hodges
That's Entertainment	★★★★	Fred Astaire, Gene Kelly	Jack Haley, Jr.
Thieves Like Us	★★★	Keith Carradine, Shelley Duvall	Robert Altman
Thomasine and Bushrod	★★½	Vonetta McGee, George Murdock	Gordon Parks, Jr.
Three Musketeers, The	★★½	Oliver Reed, Raquel Welch	Richard Lester
Uptown Saturday Night	★★★½	Bill Cosby, Harry Belafonte	Sidney Poitier
Walking Tall	★★★	Joe Don Baker, Elizabeth Hartman	Phil Karlson
Way We Were, The	★★★½	Barbra Streisand, Robert Redford	Sydney Pollack
Westworld	★★★½	Yul Brynner, Richard Benjamin	Michael Crichton
Zardoz	★★★½	Sean Connery, Charlotte Rampling	John Boorman

Famous Paintings and Where You Can See Them

These paintings are listed because of their fame, not necessarily their artistic merit, and because they are in public collections. They are listed chronologically.

Giotto: **Pieta**, 1305; Arena Chapel, Padua.
Fra Filippo Lippi: **Adoration of the Child**, c. 1435; Staatliches Museum, Berlin.
Piero Della Francesca: **Duke of Urbino**, 1465; Uffizi Gallery, Florence.
Giovanni Bellini: **Pieta**, c. 1466; Brera, Milan.
Botticelli: **The Birth of Venus**, c. 1480; Uffizi.
Hieronymus Bosch: **Christ Crowned with Thorns**, c. 1500; National Gallery, London.
Leonardo da Vinci: **Mona Lisa (La Gioconda)**, c. 1505; Louvre, Paris.
Michelangelo: **Creation of Adam**, 1508-12; Sistine Chapel, Vatican, Rome.
Giorgione: **Sleeping Venus**, c. 1508; Gemaldegalerie, Dresden.
Raphael: **The Sistine Madonna**, 1515-19; Gemaldegallerie.
Titain: **The Tribute Money**, 1516; Gemaldegalerie.
Durer: **The Four Apostles**, 1523-26; Alte Pinakothek, Munich.
Holbein: **Henry VIII**, 1540; National Gallery, Rome.
Pieter Brueghel the Elder: **Massacre of the Innocents**, 1566; Kunsthistorisches Museum, Vienna.
El Greco: **The Burial of Count Orgaz**, 1586; Santo Tome, Toledo, Spain.
Rubens: **Venus and Adonis**, c. 1620; Met., N. Y.
Frans Hals: **Laughing Cavalier**, 1624; Wallace Collection, London.
Van Dyck: **Charles I of England**, c. 1635; Louvre.
Ribera: **The Martyrdom of St. Bartholomew**, 1630-39; Prado, Madrid.
Rembrandt: **The Night Watch**, 1642; Rijksmuseum, Amsterdam.
Velasquez: **Maids of Honor**, 1656; Prado, Madrid.
Vermeer: **Young Woman with a Water Jug**, c. 1658-64; Met., N.Y.
Ruisdael: **View of Haarlem**, c. 1670; Rijksmuseum.
Murillo: **Virgin and Child**, c. 1672; Met., N. Y.
Watteau: **The Embarkation for Cythera**, c. 1712; Louvre.
Hogarth: **The Orgy (Rake's Progress)**, 1734; Soane's Museum, London.
Fragonard: **The Love Letter**, c. 1769; Met., N. Y.
Gainsborough: **The Blue Boy**, c. 1770; Huntington Gallery, San Marino, Cal.
John Singleton Copley: **Watson and the Shark**, 1778; Museum of Fine Arts, Boston.
Joshua Reynolds: **Mrs. Siddons as the Tragic Muse**, 1784; Huntington Gallery, San Marino, Cal.
John Trumbull: **The Declaration of Independence**, 1786-94; Capitol, Washington, D. C.
Gilbert Stuart: **George Washington**, c. 1795; Museum of Fine Arts, Boston. (Others in Met., N. Y., etc.
David: **The Rape of the Sabines**, 1799; Louvre.
Goya: **The Naked Maja**, 1799; Prado, Madrid.
Ingres: **Odalisque**, 1814; Louvre.
John Constable: **The Hay Wain**, 1821; National Gallery, London.
Thomas Lawrence: **Calmady Children**, 1823; Met.
John James Audubon: **Birds of America** (433 of the original 435 paintings), early 19th Century; New York Historical Society.
Joseph M. W. Turner: **The Grand Canal**, Venice, early 19th Century; Met., N. Y.
George Caleb Bingham: **Fur Traders Descending the Missouri**, 1845; Met., N. Y.
Emanuel Leutze: **Washington Crossing the Delaware**, 1851; Washington Crossing State Park, Pa.
Rosa Bonheur: **The Horse Fair**, 1855; Met., N.Y.
Jean-Baptiste Corot: **Le Lac de Terni**, 1861; Corcoran Gallery, Washington.
Honore Daumier: **The Third-Class Carriage**, c. 1862; Met., N. Y.
Jean-Francois Millet: **Man with the Hoe**, 1863; San Francisco Museum.

James McNeil Whistler: **Arrangement in Grey and Black—The Artist's Mother**, c. 1872; Louvre.
Thomas Eakins: **The Gross Clinic**, 1875; Jefferson Medical College, Philadelphia.
A. M. Willard: **Spirit of '76**, 1876; (3 versions): Cleveland City Hall; Western Reserve Historical Society, Cleveland; Abbot Hall, Marblehead, Mass.
Edgar Degas: **La Danseuse au Bouquet**, 1878; Rhode Island School of Design, Providence.
Edouard Manet: **In a Boat**, 1879; Met., N. Y.
Pierre Auguste Renoir: **Luncheon of the Boating Party** 1881; Phillips Collection, Washington.
Georges Seurat: **Sunday Afternoon on the Grande Jatte** 1884-86; Art Institute of Chicago.
Paul Cezanne: **Mont Sainte-Victoire** 1885-87; Met., N.Y.
Vincent Van Gogh: **Wheat Field and Cypress Trees**, 1889; National Gallery, London.
Albert Pinkham Ryder: **Toilers of the Sea**, c. 1890; Addison Gallery, Andover, Mass.
Paul Gauguin: **Ia Orana Marie (Hail Mary)**, 1891; Met., N. Y.
Henri De Toulouse-Lautrec: **At the Moulin Rouge**, 1892; Art Institute of Chicago.
Claude Monet: **Rouen Cathedral**, 1894; Met., N. Y.
Winslow Homer: **Gulf Stream**, 1899; Art Institute of Chicago.
John Singer Sargent: **Wyndham Sister**, 1900; Met.
Frederic Remington: **Cavalry Charge on the Southern Plains**, 1907; Met., N. Y.
Georges Braque: **Head of a Woman**, 1909; Musee d'Art Moderne, Paris.
Henri Rousseau: **The Dream**, 1910; Modern Art, N. Y.
Marc Chagall: **I and the Village**, 1911; Modern Art, N. Y.
Marcel Duchamp: **Nude Descending a Staircase**, 1912; Philadelphia Museum of Art.
Paul Chabas: **September Morn**, 1912; Met., N. Y.
Amadeo Modigliani: **Portrait of Madame Zborosкi** 1917-18; Rhode Island School of Design, Providence.
Piet Mondrian: **Composition**, 1921; Kunstmuseum, Basel, Switzerland.
Paul Klee: **Twittering Machine**, 1922; Modern Art, N. Y.
George Bellows: **The Dempsey-Firpo Fight**, 1924; Whitney Museum of American Art, N. Y.
Vasily Kandinsky: **Several Circles**, 1926; Guggenheim Museum, N. Y.
Henri Matisse: **Odalisque**, 1928; Musee d'Art Moderne, Paris.
Grant Wood: **American Gothic**, 1930; Art Institute of Chicago.
Joan Miro: **Man, Woman and Child**, 1931; Philadelphia Museum of Art.
Jose Clemente Orozco: **Zapatistas**, 1931; Modern Art, N. Y.
Maurice Utrillo: **Sacred-Heart and Montmartre Square**, 1932; Musee d'Art et d'Histoire, Geneva.
William Gropper: **The Senate**, 1935; Modern Art, N. Y.
Pablo Picasso: **Guernica**, 1937; Modern Art, N. Y.
Georges Rouault: **The Old King**, 1937; Carnegie Institute Museum, Pittsburgh.
Thomas Hart Benton: **Threshing Wheat**, 1939; Swope Gallery, Terre Haute, Ind.
John Steuart Curry: **John Brown**, 1939; Met., N. Y.
Anna (Grandma) Moses: **The Thanksgiving Turkey**, 1943; Met., N. Y.
Andrew Wyeth: **Christina's World**, 1948; Modern Art, N. Y.
Jackson Pollock: **Autumn Rhythm**, 1950; Met., N. Y.
Salvador Dali: **Crucifixion**, 1954; Met., N. Y.
Raphael Soyer: **Hugo Kastor**, 1957; Met., N. Y.

Famous Sculptures and Where You Can See Them

The statues, monuments and other sculptures in the following list have been chosen because of the fame they have won, independent of their artistic merit, and because they are on public view. They are listed chronologically, except for the group titled Non-Western. Some of the works are representative of a famed artist, many of whose works are equally well-known. The creators of some of the earliest works are unknown.

Ancient Egypt
The Great Sphinx, c. 2900 B.C., limestone and masonry; Giza, United Arab Republic.
Queen Nofretete, c. 1365 B.C., painted limestone; State Museum, West Berlin.
Colossi of Ramses II, c. 1230 B.C., sandstone; Abu Simbel, United Arab Republic.

Ancient Greece
Charioteer of Delphi, c. 470 B.C., bronze; Delphi, Greece, Museum.
Myron: Discobolus (Discus Thrower), marble Roman copy of Myron's bronze original of c. 450 B.C.; Terme Museum, Rome.
Phidias: Parthenon Sculptures, c. 438 B.C., marble (by or under direction of Phidias); British Museum, London.
Polyclitus: Doryphorus (Spear Bearer), marble Roman copy of Polyclitus original of late 5th Century B.C.; National Museum, Naples.
Praxiteles: Hermes with the Infant Dionysus, c. 350 B.C., Museum, Olympia; **Aphrodite of Cnidus**, marble Roman copy of Praxiteles' original of 330 B.C.; Vatican, Rome.
Scopas: Head from the Temple at Tegea, c. 350 B.C.; National Museum, Athens.
Lysippus: Apoxyomenos (athlete cleansing himself with a scraper), marble Roman copy of Lysippus' bronze original of 330 B.C.; Vatican, Rome.
Nike of Samothrace (Winged Victory), c. 300 B.C., marble; Louvre, Paris.
Aphrodite of Melos (Venus de Milo), 2d Century B.C., marble; Louvre, Paris.
Laocoon, 2d Century B.C., marble, by Agesander, Athenodorus and Polydorus of Rhodes; Vatican, Rome.

Ancient Rome
Augustus, c. 20 B.C., marble; Vatican, Rome.
Caracalla, 211-217 A.D., marble; National Museum, Naples.

Gothic
Virgin of Paris, early 14th Century, stone; Notre Dame Cathedral, Paris.
Claus Sluter: Moses, c. 1400, stone; Champmol Monastery, near Dijon.
Tomb of Philippe Pot, c. 1480, painted stone; Louvre, Paris.

Renaissance
Donatello: St. George, c. 1415, marble, National Museum, Florence; **Gattamelata**, 1445-50, bronze, Piazza del Santo, Padua.
Andrea del Verrocchio: Colleoni, c. 1485; bronze; Campo SS. Giovani e Paolo, Venice.
Michelangelo Buonarroti: David 1501-04, marble; Academy, Florence; **Pieta**, 1498-99, marble; St. Peter's Rome.
Benvenuto Cellini: Perseus with the Head of Medusa, 16th Century, marble; Loggia dei Lanzi, Florence.
Gianlorenzo Bernini: Ecstasy of St. Theresa, 1645-52, marble; Santa Maria della Vittoria Church, Rome.

Non-Western
Buddha Vairocana, 8th Century A.D., bronze; Nara, Japan.
Thaloc (Toltec Rain God), 900 A.D. or earlier, stone; Anthropology Museum, Mexico City.
Amida Buddha, 1252, bronze; Kamakura, Japan.
Aztec Calendar Stone, 1427-29, painted volcanic rock; Anthropology Museum, Mexico City.

Stone Heads, 17th Century or earlier, Easter Island.
Mark with Horns, 19th Century, wood, from southeast Congo (Baluba); Royal Museum of Central Africa, Tervuren, Belgium.
Buddha, 1960, concrete; Changhua, Taiwan.

18th-19th Centuries
Jean Antoine Houdon: George Washington, 1788-92, marble; State Capitol, Richmond, Va.
Thomas Crawford: Statue of Freedom, bronze, 1863; atop the Capitol dome, Washington, D. C.
Frederic Auguste Bartholdi: Liberty Enlightening the World, 1886, copper on steel frame; Liberty Is., N. Y.
Auguste Rodin: The Thinker, 1879-89, bronze; Metropolitan Museum of Art, N. Y.
Augustus St. Gaudens: Abraham Lincoln, 1887, bronze; Lincoln Park, Chicago.
John Quincy Adams Ward: Henry Ward Beecher, bronze, 1891; Cadman Plaza, Brooklyn, N. Y.

20th Century
Aristide Maillol: The Mediterranean, 1902-05, bronze; Museum of Modern Art, N. Y.
Mateo Alonso: Christ of the Andes, 1904, bronze; Uspallata Pass, Chile-Argentina border.
Ivan Mestrovic: My Mother, 1908, marble; State Museum, Belgrade.
Constantin Brancusi: The Kiss, 1908, stone; Philadelphia Museum of Art; **Bird in Space**, 1927, bronze; Museum of Modern Art, N. Y.
Wilhelm Lehmbruck: Kneeling Woman, 1911, cast stone; Museum of Modern Art, N. Y.
Edvard Erichsen: The Little Mermaid, 1913, bronze, Copenhagen harbor.
Daniel Chester French: Abraham Lincoln, 1922, marble; Lincoln Memorial, Washington, D. C.
William Zorach: Child with Cat, 1926, marble; Museum of Modern Art, N. Y.
Gaston Lachaise: Standing Woman, 1912-27, bronze; Albright Art Gallery, Buffalo.
Ernst Barlach: Hovering Angel, 1927, bronze; Antoniter Church, Cologne.
Jacob Epstein: Madonna and Child, 1927, bronze; Riverside Church, N. Y.
Heitor da Silva Costa and Paul Landowski: Christ the Redeemer, 1931, reinforced concrete; Corcavado Mtn., Rio de Janeiro.
Vernon March: Canadian War Memorial, 1926-32, (dedicated 1939), bronze; Confederation Sq., Ottawa.
Paul Manship: Prometheus, 1934, bronze and goldleaf; Rockefeller Center, N. Y.
Alexander Calder: Lobster Trap and Fish Tail, 1939, steel wire, aluminum; Museum of Modern Art, N. Y.
Carl Milles: Meeting of the Waters Fountain, 1940; Aloe Plaza, St. Louis; **Millesgarden Sculptures**, Stockholm.
Gutzon Borglum: Mt. Rushmore Natl. Memorial, 1927-41, granite; near Keystone, S.D.
Gustav Vigeland: Sculpture Park, 1906-43, stone and bronze, Oslo.
Pablo Picasso: She-Goat, bronze, 1950; Museum of Modern Art, N.Y.
Felix de Weldon: Marine Corps War Memorial (Iwo Jima Flag-Raising), 1954, bronze; near Arlington National Cemetery, Va.
Jose de Creeft: Alice in Wonderland, 1959, bronze; Conservatory Lake, Central Park, N. Y.
Henry Moore: Reclining Figure, 1963-65, bronze; Lincoln Center, N. Y.

Memorable Manned Space Flights

Sources: National Aeronautics and Space Administration and The World Almanac.

Crew, Date	Mission Name	Orbits	Duration	Remarks
Yuri A. Gagarin (4/12/61)	Vostok 1	1	1h 48m	First manned orbital flight.
Alan Z. Shepard Jr. (5/5/61)	Mercury-Redstone 3	(2)	15m 22s	First American in space.
Virgil I. Grissom (7/21/61)	Mercury-Redstone 4	(2)	15m 37s	Spacecraft sank, Grissom rescued.
Gherman S. Titov (8/6-7/61)	Vostok 2	16	25h 18m	First space flight of more than 24 hrs.
John H. Glenn Jr. (2/20/62)	Mercury-Atlas 6	3	4h 55m 23s	First American in orbit.
M. Scott Carpenter (5/24/62)	Mercury-Atlas 7	3	4h 56m 05s	Manual retrofire error caused 250 mi. landing overshoot.
Andrian G. Nikolayev (8/11-15/62)	Vostok 3	64	94h 22m	Vostok 3 and 4 made first group flight.
Pavel R. Popovich (8/12-15/62)	Vostok 4	48	70h 57m	On first orbit it came within 3 miles of Vostok 3.
Walter M. Schirra, Jr. (10/3/62)	Mercury-Atlas 8	6	9h 13m 11s	Closest splashdown to target to date (4.5 mi.).
L. Gordon Cooper (5/15-16/63)	Mercury-Atlas 9	22	34h 19m 49s	First U.S. evaluation of effects on man of one day in space.
Valery F. Bykovsky (6/14-6/19/63)	Vostok 5	81	119h 06m	Vostok 5 and 6 made 2d group flight.
Valentina V. Tereshkova (6/16-19/63)	Vostok 6	48	70h 50m	First woman in space.
Vladimir M. Komarov, Konstantin P. Feoktistov, Boris B. Yegorov (10/12/64)	Voskhod 1	16	24h 17m	First 3-man orbital flight; first without space suits.
Pavel I. Belyayev, Aleksei A. Leonov (3/18/65)	Voskhod 2	17	26h 02m	Leonov made first "space walk" (10 min.).
Virgil I. Grissom, John W. Young (3/23/65)	Gemini-Titan 3	3	4h 53m 00s	First manned spacecraft to change its orbital path.
James A. McDivitt, Edward H. White 2d, (6/3-7/65)	Gemini-Titan 4	62	97h 56m 11s	White was first American to "walk in space" (20 min.).
L. Gordon Cooper Jr., Charles Conrad Jr. (8/21-29/65)	Gemini-Titan 5	120	190h 55m 14s	First use of fuel cells for electric power; evaluated guidance and navigation system.
Frank Borman, James A. Lovell Jr. (12/4-18/65)	Gemini-Titan 7	206	330h 35m 31s	Longest duration Gemini flight.
Walter M. Schirra Jr., Thomas P. Stafford (12/15-16/65)	Gemini-Titan 6-A	16	25h 51m 24s	Completed world's first space rendezvous with Gemini 7.
Neil A. Armstrong, David R. Scott (3/16-17/66)	Gemini-Titan 8	6.5	10h 41m 26s	First docking of one space vehicle with another; mission aborted, control malfunction.
Thomas P. Stafford, Eugene A. Cernan (6/3-6/66)	Gemini-Titan 9-A	44	72h 21m 00s	Made rendezvous, but didn't dock due to malfunction; landed 0.38 mi. from target.
John W. Young, Michael Collins (7/18-21/66)	Gemini-Titan 10	43	70h 46m 39s	First use of Agena target vehicle's propulsion systems; rendezvoused with Gemini 8.
Charles Conrad Jr., Richard F. Gordon Jr. (9/12-15/66)	Gemini-Titan 11	44	71h 17m 08s	Docked, made 2 revolutions of earth tethered; set Gemini altitude record (739.2 mi.).
James A. Lovell Jr., Edwin E. Aldrin Jr. (11/11-15/66)	Gemini-Titan 12	59	94h 34m 31s	Final Gemini mission; record 5$\frac{1}{2}$ hrs. of extravehicular activity.
Vladimir M. Komarov (4/23/67)	Soyuz 1	17	26h 40m	Crashed after re-entry killing Komarov.
Walter M. Schirra Jr., Donn F. Eisele, R. Walter Cunningham (10/11-22/68)	Apollo-Saturn 7	163	260h 09m 03s	First manned flight of Apollo spacecraft command-service module only.
Georgi T. Beregovoi (10/26-30/68)	Soyuz 3	64	94h 51m	Made rendezvous with unmanned Soyuz 2.
Frank Borman, James A. Lovell Jr., William A. Anders (12/21-27/68)	Apollo-Saturn 8	10^9	147h 00m 42s	First flight to moon (command-service module only); views of lunar surface televised to earth.
Vladimir A. Shatalov (1/14-17/69)	Soyuz 4	45	71h 14m	Docked with Soyuz 5.

Crew	Spacecraft	Rev.	Flight Time	Remarks
Boris V. Volyanov, Aleksei S. Yeliseyev, Yevgeny V. Khrunov (1/15-18/69).........	Soyuz 5	46	72h 46m	Docked with Soyuz 4; Yeliseyev and Khrunov transferred to Soyuz 4.
James A. McDivitt, David R. Scott, Russell L. Schweick- art (3/3-13/69).......	Apollo-Saturn 9	151	241h 00m 54s	First manned flight of lunar module.
Thomas P. Stafford, Eugene A. Cernan, John W. Young (5/18-26/69).........	Apollo-Saturn 10	31[4]	192h 03m 23s	First lunar module orbit of moon.
Neil A. Armstrong, Edwin E. Aldrin Jr., Michael Collins (7/16-24/69).........	Apollo-Saturn 11	30[3]	195h 18m 35s	First lunar landing made by Armstrong and Aldrin; collected 48.5 lbs. of soil, rock samples; lunar stay time 21 h, 36 m, 21 s.
Georgi S. Shonin, Valery N. Kubasov (10/11-16/69).......	Soyuz 6	79	118h 42m	First welding of metals in space.
Anatoly V. Filip- chenko, Vladislav N. Volkov, Viktor V. Gorbatko (10/12-17/69).......	Soyuz 7	79	118h 41m	Space lab construction tests made; Soyuz 6, 7, 8-first time 3 spacecraft 7 crew orbited earth at once.
Vladimir A. Shatalov, Aleksei S. Yeliseyev (10/13-18/69).......	Soyuz 8	79	118h 41m	Orbiting space laboratory construction tests were made.
Charles Conrad Jr., Richard F. Gordon, Alan L. Bean (11/14-24/69).......	Apollo-Saturn 12	45[3]	244h 36m 25s	Conrad and Bean made 2d moon landing; collected 74.7 lbs. of samples; lunar stay time 31 h, 31 m.
James A. Lovell Jr., Fred W. Haise Jr., John L. Swigart Jr. (4/11-17/70).........	Apollo-Saturn 13	. .	142h 54m 41s	Aborted after service module oxygen tank ruptured; crew returned safely using lunar module oxygen and power.
Adrian G. Nikolayev, Vitaly I. Sevastyanov (6/17/70)...........	Soyuz 9	287	424h 59m	Studied man's physical reactions to long periods of weightlessness during space travel.
Alan B. Shepard Jr., Stuart A. Roosa, Edgar D. Mitchell (1/31-2/9/71).......	Apollo-Saturn 14	34[3]	216h 01m 57s	Shepard and Mitchell made 3d moon landing, collected 96 lbs. of lunar samples; lunar stay 33 h, 31 m.
Vladimir A. Shatalov, Aleksei S. Yeliseyev, Nikolai Rukavishnikov (4/22-24/71).......	Soyuz 10	32	47h 46m	Docked with prototype Salyut orbiting space station for 5½ hrs, then mission was aborted.
Georgi T. Dobrovolsky, Vladislav N. Volkov, Viktor I. Patsayev (6/6-30/71)..........	Soyuz 11	360	569h 40m	Docked with Salyut space station; and orbited in Salyut for 23 days; crew died during re-entry from loss of pressurization.
David R. Scott, Alfred M. Worden, James B. Irwin (7/26-8/7/71).......	Apollo-Saturn 15	74[3]	295h 11m 53s	Scott and Irwin made 4th moon landing; first lunar rover use; first deep space walk; 170 lbs. of samples; 66 h, 55 m, stay.
Charles M. Duke Jr., Thomas K. Mattingly, John W. Young (4/16-27/72)........	Apollo-Saturn 16	64[3]	265h 51m 05s	Young and Duke made 5th moon landing; collected 213 lbs. of lunar samples; lunar stay time 71 h, 2 m.
Eugene A. Cernan, Ronald E. Evans, Harrison H. Schmitt (12/7-19/72)........	Apollo-Saturn 17	75[3]	301h 51m 59s	Cernan and Schmitt made 6th manned lunar landing; collected 243 lbs. of samples; record lunar stay of 75 h.
Charles Conrad Jr., Joseph P. Kerwin, Paul J. Weitz (5/25-6/22/73).......	Skylab 2	. .	672h 49m 49s	First American manned orbiting space station; made long-flight tests, crew repaired damage caused during boost.
Alan L. Bean, Jack R. Lousma, Owen K. Garriott (7/28-9/25/73).......	Skylab 3	. .	1,427h 09m 04s	Crew systems and operational tests, exceeded pre-mission plans for scientific activities; space walk total 13 h, 44 m.
Gerald P. Carr, Edward G. Gibson, William Pogue (11/16/73-2/8/74)....	Skylab 4	. .	2,017h 16m 30s	Final Skylab mission; record space walk of 7 h, 1 m., record space walks total for a mission 22 h, 21 m.

(1) The Americans measure orbital flights in revolutions while the Soviets use "orbits." (2) Suborbital. (3) Moon orbits in command module. (4) Moon orbits.

Fire aboard spacecraft Apollo I on the ground at Cape Kennedy, Fla. killed Virgil I. Grissom, Edward H. White and Roger B. Chaffee on Jan. 27, 1967. They were the only U.S. astronauts killed in space tests.

Notable Ocean and Intercontinental Flights

Pilot, Plane	From	To	Miles	Time	Date
		Dirigible Balloons			
British R-34 (1)	East Fortune, Scot.	Mineola, N.Y.		108 hrs.	July 2-6, 1919
	Mineola, N.Y.	Pulham, Eng.		75 hrs.	July 9-13, 1919
Amundsen-Ellsworth-Nobile expedition	Spitsbergen	Teller, Alaska		80 hrs.	May 11-14, 1926
Graf Zeppelin	Friedrichshafen	Lakehurst, N. J.	6,630	4d 15h 46m	Oct. 11-15, 1928
Hindenburg Zeppelin	Germany	Lakehurst, N. J.		51h 17m	June 30-July 2, 1936
	Lakehurst, N. J.	Frankfort, Ger.		42h 53m	Aug. 9-11, 1936
USN ZPG-2 Blimp	S. Weymouth, Mass.	Africa			
	Africa	Key West, Fla	7,000	275h	Mar. 4-16, 1957
		Airplanes			
USN NC-4	Rockaway, L. I.	Lisbon, Port.			May 8-27, 1919
John Alcock-A. W. Brown (2)	St. John's, Nfld.	Clifden, Ireland	1,960	16h 12m	June 14-15, 1919
Richard E. Byrd (3)	Spitsbergen	North Pole	1,545	15h 30m	May 9, 1926
Chas. A. Lindbergh (4)	Mineola, N. Y.	Paris	3,610	33h 29m 30s	May 20-21, 1927
Chars. A. Levine-Clarence D. Chamberlin (5)	Roosevelt Field, Mineola, N. Y.	Eisleben, Germany	3,911	42h 31m	June 4-6, 1927
Baron G. von Huenefeld, crew (6)	Dublin	Greenly Isl., Lab.		37 hrs.	Apr. 12-13, 1922
Sir Hubert Wilkins (9)	Point Barrow, Alaska	Spitsbergen			April 16, 1928
Sir Chas. Kingsford-Smith, crew (7)	Oakland, Calif.	Brisbane, Aust.			May 31-June 8, 1928
Amelia Earhart Putnam, W. Stultz, L. Gordon	Trepassy, Nfld.	Burry Port, Wales		20h 40m	June 17-18, 1928
Richard E. Byrd (8)	Bay of Wales	South Pole			Nov. 28-29, 1929
Capt. D. Coste-M. Bellonte	Paris	Valley Stream, N.Y.	4,100	37h 18m 30s	Sept. 1-2, 1930
Lt. L. Challe-Lt. T. L. Borres	Seville, Spain	Natal, Brazil	3,600		Dec. 15-17, 1930
Wiley Post-Harold Gatty	Harbor Grace, Nfld.	England	2,200	16h 17m	June 23-24, 1931
Clyde Pangborn-Hugh Herndon Jr. (10)	Tokyo	Wenatchee, Wash.	4,458	41h 34m	Oct. 3-5, 1931
Amelia Earhart Putnam (11)	Harbor Grace, Nfld.	Ireland	2,026½	14h 56m	May 20-21, 1932
James A. Mollison (12)	Portmarnock, Ire.	Pennfleid, N.B.			Aug. 18, 1932
Amelia Earhart Putnam (11)	Honolulu	Oakland, Cal.	2,408	18h 16m	Jan. 11-12, 1935
China Clipper (Pan Am. Airways) (13)	San Francisco	Manila, P. I.			Nov. 22-28, 1935
	Manila, P.I.	San Francisco			Dec. 1-6, 1935
Gromoff, Yumasheff, Danilin (USSR)	Moscow, USSR	San Jacinto, Cal.	6,262	62h 02m	July 12-14, 1937
Douglas C. Corrigan	Floyd Bennett Field	Dublin, Ire.		28h 13m	July 17-18, 1938
B-29 (Lt. Col. C. J. Miller)	Honolulu	Washington, D.C.	4,640	17h 21m	Sept. 1, 1945
C-54 (Maj. G.E. Cain)	Tokyo	Washington D.C.		31h 25m	Sept. 3, 1945
William P. Odom	Honolulu	Teterboro, N. J.	5,300	36 hrs.	Mar. 8, 1949
USN Caroline Mars	Honolulu	San Diego, Cal.		14h 17m	June 17-18, 1950
Col. David C. Schilling, USAF (14)	England	Limestone, Me.	3,300	10h 01m	Sept. 22, 1950
Chas. F. Blair Jr.	New York	London	3,500	7h 48m	Jan. 31, 1951
Chas. F. Blair Jr. (15)	Bardufoss, Norway	Fairbanks, Alaska	3,300	10h 29m	May 29, 1951
Chas. F. Blair, Jr.	Fairbanks, Alaska	New York	3,450	9h 31m	May 30, 1950
Canberra Bomber	England	Australia		20h 20m	Mar. 16, 1952
Two U. S. S-55 Helicopters (16)	Westover AFB, Mass.	Prestwick, Scotland	3,410	42h 30m	July 15-31, 1952
British Comet	London-Tokyo	Tokyo-London	20,400	74h 52m	April 3-7, 1953
British Comet	London	Rio de Janeiro	6,000	12h 30m	Sept. 13-14, 1953
Max Conrad (solo)	New York	Paris		22h 23m	Nov. 7, 1954
Canberra Bomber (17)	Aldergrove, No. Ire.	Gander, Nfld.	2,073	4h 34m	Aug. 26, 1952
	Gander, Nfld.	Aldergrove, No. Ire.	2,073	3h 25m	Aug. 26, 1952
Canberra Bomber	London (round trip)	New York	6,920	14h 21m 45.4s	Aug. 23, 1955
Capt. William F. Judd	New York	Paris		24h 11m	Jan. 29-30, 1956
Three USAF F-100Cs	London	Los Angeles, Cal.	6,710	14h 5m	May 13, 1957
Spirit of St. Louis II (USAF F-100F jet)	McGuire AFB, N. J.	Le Bourget, Paris		6h 38m	May 21, 1957
USAF KC-135	Tokyo	Lajes AFB, Azores	10,230	18h 48m	Apr. 7-8, 1958
Max Conrad (solo)	New York	Palermo, Sicily	4,440	32h 55m	June 22-23, 1958
Capt. Marion Boling	Manila, P. I.	Pendleton, Ore.	6,979	45h 42m	July 31-Aug. 1/58
USAF KC-135	Yokota AB, Japan	Washington, D. C.	7,100	12h 28m	Sept. 12, 1958
Max Conrad (solo)	Chicago	Rome	5,000	34h 3m	Mar. 5-6, 1959
Max Conrad (solo)	Casablanca, Africa	Los Angeles	7,700	58h 36m	June 2-4, 1959
USSR TU-114 (18)	Moscow	New York	5,092	11h 6m	June 28, 1959
Boeing 707 airliner	San Francisco	Sydney, Australia	7,630	16h 10m	July 2, 1959
Boeing 707-320	New York	Moscow	c.5,090	8h 54m	July 23, 1959
Max Conrad (solo)	Casablanca, Mor.	El Paso, Tex.	6,911	56h 26m	Nov. 22-26, 1959
Col. J. B. Swindal	Washington, D.C.	Moscow	5,004	8h 39m 02.2s	May 19, 1963
Mrs. Jerrie Mock (19)	Columbus, Ohio	Columbus, Ohio	23,206	29d 11h 59m	Mar. 19-Ap. 18/64
Joan Merriam (20)	Oakland, Cal.	Oakland, Cal.	27,750	56d	Mar. 17-May 12/64
Sheila Scott (solo)	London	London	28,633	33d 03m	May 18-June 20/67
Elgen Long (solo) (21)	San Francisco	San Francisco	38,896	28d 00h 43m	Nov. 5-Dec. 3/71

Notable first flights: 1, Atlantic aerial round trip. 2, Non-stop transatlantic flight. 3, Polar flight. 4, Solo transatlantic flight in the Ryan monoplane the "Spirit of St. Louis." 5, Transatlantic passenger flight. 6, East-West transatlantic crossing. 7, U.S. to Australia flight. 8, South Pole flight. 9, Trans-Arctic flight. 10, Non-stop Pacific flight. 11, Woman's transoceanic solo flight. 12, Westbound transatlantic solo flight. 13, Pacific airmail and U. S. to Philippines crossing. 14, Non-stop jet transatlantic flight. 15, Solo across North Pole. 16, Transatlantic helicopter flight. 17, Transatlantic round trip on same day. 18, Non-stop between Moscow and New York. 19, First woman pilot to circle globe; first woman to fly both North Atlantic and Pacific. 20, Followed route Amelia Earhart partly completed in 1937. 21, Speed record around the world over both the earth's poles.

International Aeronautical Records

Source: The National Aeronautic Association, 806 15th St., N.W., Washington, D.C. 20005, representative in the United States of the Federation Aeronautique Internationale, certifying agency for world aviation and space records. The International Aeronautical Federation was formed in 1905 by representatives from Belgium, France, Germany, Great Britain, Spain, Italy, Switzerland and the United States, with headquarters in Paris. Regulations for the control of official records were signed Oct. 14, 1905. World records are defined as maximum performance, regardless of class or type of aircraft used. Records to Aug. 1, 1973.

World Air Records—Maximum Performance in any Class

Speed over a straight course—3,331,507 kmph. (2,070.101 mph)—Col. R. L. Stephens, USAF, United States; Lockheed YF-12A; Edwards Air Force Base, Calif., May 1, 1965.

Speed over a closed circuit—2,981.5 kmph. (1,850.61 mph)—Mikhail Komarov, USSR; E-266 jet; Oct. 5, 1967.

Distance in a straight line—20,168.75 kms (12,532.28 mi.)—Maj. Clyde P. Evely, USAF, United States; Boeing B52-H; Kadena, Okinawa, to Madrid, Spain, Jan. 11, 1962.

Distance over a closed circuit—18,245.5 kms (11,336.92 mi.)—Capt. William Stevenson, USAF, United States; Boeing B52-H; Seymour-Johnson, N.C., June 6-7, 1962.

Altitude — 95,935.99 meters (314,750 feet)—Maj. Robert M. White, USAF, United States; North American X-15-1; Edwards AFB, Calif., July 17, 1962.

Altitude in horizontal flight—24,462,596 meters (80,257.86 ft.)—Col. R. L. Stephens, USAF, United States; Lockheed YF12A; Edwards Air Force Base, Calif., May 1, 1965.

Manned Space Craft

Duration — 84 days 1 hr. 15 min. 32 sec.—Gerald P. Carr, Edward G. Gibson, William R. Pogue, U.S.; Skylab 3; Nov. 16, 1973-Feb. 8, 1974.

Altitude—377,668.9 kms (234,672.5 mi.)—Frank Borman, James A. Lovell Jr., William Anders, United States; Spacecraft Apolo 8; Dec. 21-27, 1968.

Greatest mass lifted—127,980 kgs. (282,197 lbs.)—Frank Borman, James A. Lovell Jr., William Anders, United States; Spacecraft Apollo 8; Dec. 21-27,1968.

Distance — 55,560,000 kms. (34,523,000 mi.)—Gerald P. Carr, Edward G. Gibson, William R. Pogue, U.S.; Skylab 3; Nov. 16, 1973-Feb. 8, 1974.

World "Class" Records

All other records, international in scope, are termed World "Class" records and are divided into classes: airships, free balloons, airplanes, seaplanes, amphibians, gliders, and rotorplanes. Airplanes (Class C) are sub-divided into four groups: Group I—piston engine aircraft, Group II—turbo-prop aircraft, Group III—jet aircraft, Group IV—rocket powered aircraft. A partial listing of world records follows:

Airplanes (Class C, Group 1—Piston Engine)

Distance, closed circuit—14,441.26 kms (8,974 mi.)—James R. Bede, United States; BD-2, 1 Continental IO 360-C engine, Columbus, Ohio to Kansas City course, Nov. 7-9, 1969.

Distance, airline (international)—18,081.990 kms. (11,235.6 miles)—Cmdr. Thomas D. Davies, USN; Cmdr. Eugene P. Rankin, US; Cmdr. Walter S. Reid, USN, and Lt. Cmdr. Ray A. Tabeling, USN; United States; Lockheed P2V-1; from Pearce Field, Perth, Australia, to Port Columbus, Ohio, Sept. 29-Oct. 1, 1946 (United States)—same.

Maximum speed over 3-kilometer measured course (international)—776.449 kmph. (482.462 mph)—Darryl Greenamyer, United States, Grumman F8F Bearcat, Edwards AFB, Calif., Aug. 16, 1969. (United States)—663.054 kmph. (412.002 mph.)—Jacqueline Cochran, United States; North American F-51, Thermal, Calif., Dec. 17, 1947.

Speed for 100 kilometers (62.137 miles) without payload (international) — 755.668 kmph (469.549 mph.)2—Jacqueline Cochran, United States; North American P-51; Coachella Valley, Calif., Dec. 10, 1947, **(United States)-same.**

Speed for 1,000 kilometers (621.369 miles) without payload — 693.78 kmph. (431.09 mph.)—Jacqueline Cochran, United States; North American P-51; Santa Rosasummit, Calif. — Flagstaff, Arizona course, May 24, 1948.

Speed for 5,000 kilometers (3,106.849) without payload — 544.59 kmph. (338.39 mph.)—Capt. James Bauer, USAF, United States; Boeing B-29; Dayton, Ohio, June 28, 1946.

Speed around the world — 318.28 kmph. (197.77 mph.)—Trevor K. Brougham, Australia; Beechcraft Baron C-55, 2 Rolls-Royce Continental 10-470-L engines; Darwin, Australia, Aug. 5-10, 1971. Time: 5 days 5 hrs. 57 min.

Light Airplanes—Class C-1.d

Distance airline (international) — 12,341.26 kms. (7,668.48 miles)—Max Conrad, United States; Piper Comanche 250, Lycoming 0540-A1A5 250 hp.; Casablanca, Morocco to Los Angeles, June 2-4, 1959.

Speed for 100 kilometers — (62.137 miles) in a closed circuit (international) — 519.480 kmph. (322.789 mph.)—Miss R. M. Sharpe, Great Britain; Vickers Supermarine Spitfire 5-B; Wolverhampton, June 17, 1950.

Gliders (Class D—Single-place)

Distance, straight line — 1,460.8 kms. (907.7 miles)—Hans Werner Grosse, West Germany; ASK12 sailplane; Luebeck to Biarritz, Apr. 25, 1972.

Altitude above sea level - 14,102 meters (46,267 feet) — Paul F. Bikle, United States; Sailplane Schweizer SGS 123E; Mojave, Lancaster, Calif., Feb. 25, 1961.

Helicopters (Class E-1)

Distance in a straight line—3,561.55 kms. (2,213.04 miles)—Robert G. Ferry, United States; Hughes YOH-6A helicopter; Culver City, Calif., to Daytona, Fla., Apr. 6-7, 1966.

Speed over 3-km. course — 348.971 kmph. (216.839 mph.)—Byron Graham, United States; Sikorsky S-67 helicopter; Windsor Locks, Conn., Dec. 14, 1970.

Airplanes (Class C, Group II—Turbo-prop)

Distance in a straight line — 14,052.95 kms. (8,732.09 miles) — Lt. Col. Edgar L. Allison Jr., U. S. Lockheed HC-130 Hercules aircraft; Feb. 20, 1972.

Speed over a 15-25 km. course —Cmdr. D. H. Lilienthal, USN, United States; Lockheed P3C Orion aircraft; 806 kmph. (501 mph.): Jan. 27, 1971.

Altitude —15,549 meters (51,014 ft.) — Donald R. Wilson, Greenville, Tex., LTV L450F aircraft; Mar. 27, 1972.

Speed for 1,000 kilometers (621.369 miles) without payload (international)—871.38 kmph (541.449 mph)—Ivan Soukhomline, Boris Timochok and crew, USSR; TU-114 swept wing monoplane, 4 turbo-prop TV-12 engines; Sternberg Course. Mar. 24, 1960.

Speed for 5,000 kilometers (3,106,849 miles) without payload (international)—877.212 kmph (545.072 mph) — Ivan Soukhomline, K. Sapielkine and crew, USSR; TU-114 swept wing monoplane, 4 turbo-prop TB-12 engines; Sternberg-Svierdlovsk-Sebastopol-Sernberg, Apr. 9, 1960.

Airplanes (Class C, Group III—Jet-powered)

Distance in a straight line — 20,168.78 kms. (12,532.28 mi.) — Maj. Clyde P. Evely, USAF, United States; Boeing B52-H, 8 Pratt & Whitney TF-33P-3 engines; Kadena, Okinawa, to Madrid, Spain, Jan. 10-11, 1962.

Distance in a closed circuit — 18,245.05 kms. (11,336.92 miles) — Capt. William Stevenson, USAF, United States; Boeing B52-H, 8 Pratt & Whitney TF-33P-3 engines; terminal: Seymour-Johnson, N. C., June 6-7, 1962.

Altitude — 34,714 meters (113,890.848 feet) — Gueorgui Mossolov, USSR; E-66A jet monoplane, triangular wing, T.R.D. and G.R.D. engines; Podmoskovnoe, USSR, Apr. 28, 1961.

Speed over a 3-kilometer course — 1,452.777 km.p.h. (902,769 m.p.h.) — Lt. Hunt Hardisty, USN, United States; McDonnell F4H Phantom, 2 GE J-79 jet engines; White Sands, N. M., Aug. 29, 1961.

Speed for 100 kilometers — 2,600 kmph (1,615 mph) — Alexander Fedotov, USSR; E-266 airplane, 2 RD jet engines, Apr. 8, 1973.

Speed for 500 kilometers in a closed circuit—2,981.5 kmph (1,852.61 mph) — Mikhail Komarov, USSR; E-266 airplane. 2 RD jet engines, Oct. 5, 1967.

Speed for 1,000 kilometers in a closed circuit — 2,920.67 kmph (1,814.81 mph) — Pyotr Ostapenko, USSR; E-266 airplane, 2 RD jet engines, Oct. 27, 1967.

Speed for 2,000 kilometers in closed circuit — 1,708.817 kmph (1,061.808 mph) — Maj. H. J. Deutchendorf Jr., USAF, United States; Convair B58 Hustler Bomber; Desert, Stoval, Boundary, Morris, Desert, Edwards AFB, Calif. course, Jan. 12, 1961.

Sustained altitude — 24,462.596 meters (80,257.86 feet) — Col. R. L. Stephens, USAF; Lockheed YF-12A, 2 Pratt & Whitney J58 engines; Edwards AFB, Calif., May 1, 1965.

Free Balloons (Tenth category, 4001 cu. meters or more)

Altitude — 34,668 meters (113,739.9 feet) — Cmdr. Malcolm D. Ross, USNR, United States; Lee Lewis Memorial Winzen Research Balloon; Gulf of Mexico, May 4, 1961.

F.A.I. Course Records

Los Angeles to New York — 1,954.79 kmph (1,214.65 mph)—Capt. Robert G. Sowers, USAF, United States; Convair B58 Hustler, 4 GE-J-79-5B engines; Elapsed time: 2 hrs. 58.71 sec., Mar. 5, 1962.

New York to Los Angeles — 1,741 kmph (1,081.80 mph)—Capt. Robert G. Sowers, USAF, United States; Convair B58 Hustler; Elapsed time: 2 hrs. 15 min. 50.08 sec., Mar. 5, 1962.

Los Angeles-New York-Los Angeles — 1,681.71 kmph (1,044.46 mph)—Capt. Robert G. Sowers, USAF, United States; Convair B58 Hustler; Elapsed time: 4 hrs. 41 min. 14.98 sec., Mar. 5, 1962.

New York to Paris — 1,753.068 kmph (1,089.36 mph)—Maj. W. R. Payne, United States; Convair B58 Hustler; Elapsed time: 3 hrs. 10 min. 58 sec., May 26, 1961.

London to New York (international) — 945.423 kmph (587.457 mph)—Maj. Burl B. Davenport, Lt. James J. Jones, and crew USAF, United States; Boeing KC-135 Stratotanker; London International Airport to Idlewild International Airport, Long Island, June 27, 1958. Elapsed time: 5 hours 29 minutes 14.64 seconds.

Baltimore to Moscow, USSR — 906.64 kmph (563.36 mph)—Col. James B. Swindal, USAF, United States; Boeing VC-137 (707), May 19, 1963. Elapsed time: 8 hours 33 minutes 45.4 seconds.

Moscow to Washington, D. C. — 788.67 kmph (490.06 mph)—Col. James B. Swindal, USAF, United States, Boeing VC-137 (707). Elapsed time: 9 hrs. 54 min. 48.5 sec, May 20-21, 1963.

Belfast to Gander, Newfoundland (international) — 774.255 kmph (481.099 mph)—Wing commander R. P. Beamont and crew, Great Britain; Canberra bomber, two Rolls-Royce turbo-jet engines, Aug. 31, 1951. Elapsed time: 4 hours 18 min., 24.4 sec.

New York to London (international) — 2,914.3 kmph (1,810.9 mph)—Maj. James V. Sullivan, USAF, United States; Lockheed SR-71; Elapsed time 1 hr. 55 min. 32 sec., Sept. 1, 1974.

London to Los Angeles (international) —2,394.39 kmph (1,487.81 mph)—Capt. Harold B. Adams, USAF, United States; Lockheed SR-71; Elapsed time: 3 hrs. 47 min. 39 sec., Sept. 13, 1974.

The Busiest Airports, 1973
(Total take-offs and landings)

United States		Canada	
Source: Dept. of Transportation		Source: Dept. of Transport	
O'Hare (Chicago)	695,303(1)	St. Hubert (Montreal)	290,574
Santa Ana, Calif.	632,657	Pitt Meadows, B.C.	250,050(2)
Van Nuys, Calif.	581,341	Edmonton	231,351
Long Beach, Calif.	551,615	Toronto	227,498(1)
Atlanta	516,685(2)	Buttonville, Ont.	185,065
Los Angeles	491,121(3)	Montreal	183,996(2)
Dallas	446,158	Vancouver	182,764(3)
Torrance, Calif.	427,655	Ottawa	181,259
San Jose, Calif.	416,320	Hamilton, Ont.	171,707
Opalocka, Fla.	405,913	Springbank, Alberta	168,040
J F Kennedy (New York)	. . . .(4)	Calgary	. . . .(4)
San Francisco	. . . .(5)	Winnipeg	. . . .(5)

Numbers in parentheses indicate top 5 in air carrier operations only.

Fastest Trips Around the World

Fast circuits of the earth have been a subject of wide interest since Jules Verne, French novelist, described an imaginary trip by Phileas Fogg in Around the World in 80 Days, assertedly occurring Oct. 2 to Dec. 20, 1872. Notable actual such events follow:

Craft, pilot	Terminal	Miles	Time	Date
Nellie Bly	New York, N.Y.		72d 06h 11m	1889
George Francis Train	New York, N.Y.		67d 12h 03m	1890
Charles Fitzmorris	Chicago		60d 13h 29m	1901
J. W. Willis Sayre	Seattle		54d 09h 42m	1903
Henry Frederick			54d 07h 02m	1903
Col. Burnlay-Campbell			40d 19h 30m	1907
Andre Jaeger-Schmidt			39d 19h 42m 38s	1911
John Henry Mears			35d 21h 36m	1913
Two U.S. Army airplanes	Seattle (57 hops, 21 countries)	26,103	35d 1h 11m	1924
Edward S. Evans and Linton Wells (New York World) (1)	New York	18,400	28d 14h 36m 05s	June 16-July 14, 1926
John H. Mears and Capt. C. B. D. Collyer	New York		23d 15h 21m 03s	June 29-July 22, 1928
Graf Zeppelin	Friedrichshafen, Ger. via Tokyo, Los Angeles, Lakehurst, N.J.	21,700	20d 04h	Aug. 14-Sept. 4, 1929
Wiley Post and Harold Gatty (Monoplane Winnie Mae)	Roosevelt Field, via Arctic Circle	15,474	08d 15h 51m	June 23-July 1, 1931
Wiley Post (Monoplane Winnie Mae) (2)	Floyd Bennett Field, via Arctic Circle	15,596	115h 36m 30s	July 15-22, 1933
H. R. Ekins (Scripps-Howard Newspapers in race) (Zeppelin Hindenburg to Germany, airplanes from Frankfurt)	Lakehurst, N.J., via Frankfurt, Germany	25,654	18d 11h 14m 33s	Sept. 30-Oct. 19, 1936
Howard Hughes and 4 assistants	New York, Paris, Moscow, Siberia, Fairbanks, Alaska	14,824	03d 19h 08m 10s	July 10-13, 1938
Mrs. Clara Adams (Pan American Clipper)	Port Washington, N.Y., return Newark, N.J.		16d 19h 04m	June 28-July 15, 1939
Globester, U.S. Air Transport Command	Washington, D.C.	23,279	149h 44m	Sept. 28-Oct. 4, 1945
Capt. William P. Odom (A-26 Reynolds Bombshell)	New York, via Paris, Cairo, Tokyo, Alaska	20,000	78h 55m 12s	Apr. 12-16, 1947
America, Pan American 4-engine Lockheed Constellation (3)	New York, eastward	22,219	101h 32m	June 17-30, 1947
Col. Edward P. F. Eagan	New York	20,559	147h 15m	Dec. 13, 1948
USAF B-50 Lucky Lady II (Capt. James Gallagher) (4)	Fort Worth, Texas	23,452	94h 01m	Feb. 26-Mar. 2, 1949
Thos. G. Lapphier Jr.	New York	22,180	119h 47m	Dec. 2-7, 1949
Jean-Marie Audibert	Paris		04d 19h 38m	Dec. 11-15, 1952
Horace C. Boren	Idlewild Airport, New York		99h 16m	June 21-25, 1953
Pamela Martin	Midway Airport, Chicago		90h 59m	Dec. 5-8, 1953
Three USAF B-52 Stratofort resses (5)	Castle AFB, Merced, Cal., via Nfld., Morocco, Saudi Arabia, India, Ceylon, P. I., Guam, Riverside, Cal.	24,325	45h 19m	Jan. 15-18, 1957
Joseph Cavoli	Cleveland, Ohio		89h 13m 37s	Jan. 31-Feb. 4, 1958
Miss K. Kanetake Tokyo,	via Bangkok, Karachi. Rome, Anchorage	18,580	73h 09m	July 28-31, 1958
Peter Gluckmann (solo)	San Francisco	22,800	29d	Aug. 22-Sept. 20, 1959
Milton Reynolds	San Francisco		51h 45m 22s	Jan. 12-14, 1960
Sue Snyder	Chicago	21,219	62h 59m	June 22-24, 1960
Max Conrad (solo)	Miami, Fla.	25,946	08d 18h 35m 57s	Feb. 28-Mar. 8, 1961
Sam Miller & Louis Fodor	New York		46h 28m	Aug. 3-4, 1963
Jack Martin, Fred Austin, Harrison Finch, Robert Buck, James Gannett	Honolulu	26,230	62h 27m 35s	Nov. 15-17, 1965
Henry G. Beaird	Wichita, Kan.	22,992	65h 38m 49s	May 23-26, 1966
Robert & Joan Wallick (6)	Manila, Philippines	23,129	05d 6h 17m 10s	June 2-7, 1966
Arthur Godfrey, Richard Merrill Fred Austin, Karl Keller	New York	23,333	86h 9m 1s	June 4-7, 1966
Trevor K. Brougham	Darwin, Australia	24,800	05d 05h 57m	Aug. 5-10, 1972

1. Mileage in train and auto, 4,100; by plane, 6,300; by steamship, 8,000. 2. First to fly solo around northern circumference of the world, also first to fly twice around the world. 3. Inception of regular commercial global air service. 4. First non-stop round-the-world flight, refueled 4 times in flight. 5. First non-stop global flight by jet planes; refueled in flight by KC-97 aerial tankers; average speed, approx. 525 mph. 6. Official world record for light planes.

Consolidated Airline Traffic

Source: Civil Aeronautics Board Air Carrier Traffic Statistics, Calendar year, 1973.

	1971	1972	1973
Passenger Traffic			
Revenue passengers enplaned	173,667,000	195,305,000	202,208,000
Revenue passenger miles	135,651,780,000	164,015,261,000	161,957,307,000
Available seat miles	279,869,172,000	297,966,766,000	310,597,107,000
Cargo Traffic (ton miles)	**5,108,616,000**	**6,388,595,000**	**6,481,206,000**
Freight	3,712,257,000	5,110,974,000	5,182,735,000
Express	82,998,000	87,424,000	100,497,000
Priority U.S. Mail	595,666,000	608,493,000	602,709,000
Overall Traffic and Service			
Nonscheduled traffic-total	375,000	2,058,659,000	1,685,764,000
Total revenue ton miles	20,905,505,000	22,805,047,000	22,241,875,000
Total available ton miles	47,223,830,000	48,682,429,000	49,019,300,000

Air Line Distances Between Selected Cities of the World

Source: Defense Mapping Agency Aerospace Center (Statute Miles)
Point-to-point measurements are usually from City Hall

	Bangkok	Berlin	Cairo	Capetown	Caracas	Chicago	Hong Kong	Honolulu	Lima	London
Bangkok.....	....	5,352	4,523	6,300	10,555	8,570	1,077	6,609	12,244	5,933
Berlin........	5,352	....	1,797	5,961	5,238	4,414	5,443	7,320	6,896	583
Cairo........	4,523	1,797	....	4,480	6,342	6,141	5,066	8,848	7,726	2,185
Capetown.....	6,300	5,961	4,480	....	6,366	8,491	7,376	11,535	6,072	5,989
Caracas......	10,555	5,238	6,342	6,366	....	2,495	10,165	6,021	1,707	4,655
Chicago......	8,570	4,414	6,141	8,491	2,495	....	7,797	4,256	3,775	3,958
Hong Kong....	1,077	5,443	5,066	7,376	10,165	7,797	....	5,556	11,418	5,990
Honolulu......	6,609	7,320	8,848	11,535	6,021	4,256	5,556	....	5,947	7,240
London.......	5,933	583	2,185	5,989	4,655	3,958	5,990	7,240	6,316	....
Madrid........	6,337	1,165	2,087	5,308	4,346	4,189	6,558	7,872	5,907	785
Melbourne.....	4,568	9,918	8,675	6,425	9,717	9,673	4,595	5,505	8,059	10,500
Mexico City....	9,793	6,056	7,700	8,519	2,234	1,690	8,788	3,789	2,639	5,558
Montreal......	8,338	3,740	5,427	7,922	2,438	745	7,736	4,918	3,970	3,254
Moscow......	4,389	1,006	1,803	6,279	6,177	4,987	4,437	7,047	7,862	1,564
New Delhi.....	1,813	3,598	2,758	5,769	8,833	7,486	2,339	7,412	10,432	4,181
New York.....	8,669	3,979	5,619	7,803	2,120	714	8,060	4,969	3,639	3,469
Paris.........	5,877	548	1,998	5,786	4,732	4,143	5,990	7,449	6,370	214
Peking........	2,046	4,584	4,698	8,044	8,950	6,604	1,217	5,077	10,349	5,074
Rio de Janeiro..	9,994	6,209	6,143	3,781	2,804	5,282	11,009	8,288	2,342	5,750
Rome........	5,494	737	1,326	5,231	5,195	4,824	5,774	8,040	6,750	895
San Francisco..	7,931	5,672	7,466	10,248	3,902	1,859	6,905	2,398	4,518	5,367
Singapore.....	883	6,164	5,137	6,008	11,402	9,372	1,605	6,726	11,689	6,747
Stockholm.....	5,089	528	2,096	6,423	5,471	4,331	5,063	6,875	7,166	942
Tokyo........	2,865	5,557	5958	9,154	8,808	6,314	1,791	3,859	9,631	5,959
Warsaw.......	5,033	322	1,619	5,935	5,559	4,679	5,147	7,366	7,215	905
Washington. .·.	8,807	4,181	5,822	7,895	2,047	596	8,155	4,838	3,509	3,674

	Madrid	Melbourne	Mexico City	Montreal	Moscow	Nairobi	New Delhi	New York	Paris	Peking
Bangkok......	6,337	4,568	9,793	8,338	4,389	4,483	1,813	8,669	5,877	2,046
Berlin........	1,165	9,918	6,056	3,740	1,006	3,949	3,598	3,979	548	4,584
Cairo.........	2,087	8,675	7,700	5,427	1,803	2,186	2,758	5,619	1,998	4,698
Capetown.....	5,308	6,425	8,519	7,922	6,279	2,542	5,769	7,803	5,786	8,044
Caracas......	4,346	9,717	2,234	2,438	6,177	7,178	8,833	2,120	4,732	8,950
Chicago......	4,189	9,673	1,690	745	4,987	8,011	7,486	714	4,143	6,604
Hong Kong....	6,558	4,595	8,788	7,736	4,437	5,449	2,339	8,060	5,990	1,217
Honolulu......	7,872	5,505	3,789	4,918	7,047	10,741	7,412	4,969	7,449	5,077
London.......	785	10,500	5,558	3,254	1,564	4,231	4,181	3,469	214	5,074
Madrid.......	....	10,758	5,643	3,448	2,147	3,841	4,530	3,593	655	5,745
Melbourne.....	10,758	....	8,426	10,395	8,950	7,153	6,329	10,359	10,430	5,643
Mexico City....	5,643	8,426	....	2,317	6,676	9,219	9,120	2,090	5,725	7,753
Montreal......	3,448	10,395	2,317	....	4,401	7,267	7,012	331	3,432	6,519
Moscow......	2,147	8,950	6,676	4,401	....	3,930	2,698	4,683	1,554	3,607
New Delhi.....	4,530	6,329	9,120	7,012	2,698	3,374	....	7,318	4,102	2,353
New York.....	3,593	10,359	2,090	331	4,683	7,364	7,318	....	3,636	6,844
Paris.........	655	10,430	5,725	3,432	1,554	4,022	4,102	3,636	....	5,120
Peking........	5,745	5,643	7,753	6,519	3,607	5,727	2,353	6,844	5,120	....
Rio de Janeiro..	5,045	8,226	4,764	5,078	7,170	5,560	8,753	4,801	5,684	10,768
Rome........	851	9,929	6,377	4,104	1,483	3,339	3,684	4,293	690	5,063
San Francisco..	5,803	7,856	1,887	2,543	5,885	9,597	7,691	2,572	5,577	5,918
Singapore.....	7,080	3,759	10,327	9,203	5,228	4,638	2,571	9,534	6,673	2,771
Stockholm.....	1,653	9,630	6,012	3,714	716	4,281	3,414	3,986	1,003	4,133
Tokyo........	6,706	5,062	7,035	6,471	4,660	6,999	3,638	6,757	6,053	1,307
Warsaw.......	1,427	9,598	6,337	4,022	721	3,801	3,277	4,270	852	4,325
Washington....	3,792	10,180	1,885	489	4,876	7,551	7,500	205	3,840	6,942

	Rio de Janiero	Rome	San Francisco	Singapore	Stockholm	Teheran	Tokyo	Vienna	Warsaw	Wash. D.C.
Bangkok......	9,994	5,494	7,931	883	5,089	3,391	2,865	5,252	5,033	8,807
Berlin........	6,209	737	5,672	6,164	528	2,185	5,557	326	322	4,181
Cairo.........	6,143	1,326	7,466	5,137	2,096	1,234	5,958	1,481	1,619	5,822
Capetown.....	3,781	5,231	10,248	6,008	6,423	5,241	9,154	5,656	5,935	7,895
Caracas......	2,804	5,195	3,902	11,402	5,471	7,320	8,808	5,372	5,559	2,047
Chicago......	5,282	4,824	1,859	9,372	4,331	6,502	6,314	4,698	4,679	596
Hong Kong....	11,009	5,774	6,905	1,605	5,063	3,843	1,791	5,431	5,147	8,155
Honolulu......	8,288	8,040	2,398	6,726	6875	8,070	3,859	7,632	7,366	4,838
London.......	5,750	895	5,367	6,747	942	2,743	5,959	771	905	3,674
Madrid.......	5,045	851	5,803	7,080	1,653	2,978	6,706	1,128	1,427	3,792
Melbourne.....	8,226	9,929	7,856	3,759	9,630	7,826	5,062	9,790	9,598	10,180
Mexico City....	4,764	6,377	1,887	10,327	6,012	8,184	7,035	6,320	6,337	1,885
Montreal......	5,078	4,104	2,543	9,203	3,714	5,880	6,471	4,009	4,022	489
Moscow......	7,170	1,483	5,885	5,228	716	1,532	4,660	1,043	721	4,876
New Delhi.....	8,753	3,684	7,691	2,571	3,414	1,583	3,638	3,465	3,277	7,500
New York.....	4,801	4,293	2,572	9,534	3,986	6,141	6,757	4,234	4,270	205
Paris.........	5,684	690	5,577	6,673	1,003	2,625	6,053	645	852	3,840
Peking........	10,768	5,063	5,918	2,771	4,133	3,490	1,307	4,648	4,325	6,942
Rio de Janeiro..	....	5,707	6,613	9,785	6,683	7,374	11,532	6,127	6,455	4,779
Rome........	5,707	....	6,259	6,229	1,245	2,127	6,142	477	820	4,497
San Francisco..	6,613	6,259	....	8,448	5,399	7,362	5,150	5,994	5,854	2,441
Singapore.....	9,785	6,229	8,448	....	5,936	4,103	3,300	6,035	5,843	9,662
Stockholm.....	6,683	1,245	5,399	5,936	....	2,173	5,053	780	494	4,183
Tokyo........	11,532	6,142	5,150	3,300	5,053	4,775	....	5,689	5,347	6,791
Warsaw.......	6,455	820	5,854	5,843	494	1,879	5,689	347	....	4,472
Washington....	4,779	4,497	2,441	9,662	4,183	6,341	6,791	4,438	4,472	....

Pollution Costs Billions

Source: President's Council on Environmental Quality, 4th Annual Report, September, 1973

The costs of pollution are divided into 4 types. Damage costs are those that result from the harm done by pollution — illness and property damage being the largest costs of air pollution, for example. These costs can be roughly estimated.

Estimated Air Pollution Damage Costs With No Controls
(in billions of dollars)

Damage to —	1968[1]	1977[2]
Health[3]	$ 6.1	$ 9.3
Residential Property	5.2	8.0
Materials, vegetation[4]	4.9	7.6
Total	**$16.2**	**$24.9**

(1) In 1968 dollars. (2) In 1970 dollars. (3) Includes treatment and prevention of illnesses plus income lost by disability and early death. (4) Includes damage to approx. 50 materials most susceptible to air pollution damage, and direct visible damage affecting yield, quality and marketability of crops and forests.

Avoidance costs are those that people incur when they attempt to avoid or reduce damage costs. These costs are very difficult to determine. They include the costs of driving to a more distant beach, because the one nearby is polluted. Also included may be part of the cost of some clothes dryers; in some areas, the air is too dirty to hang clothes out to dry.

Transaction costs refer to expenditures for research and development, planning monitoring the environment and specific polluters, the setting and enforcement of standards, etc. A large portion of federal anti-pollution funds are spent on transaction costs.

Monitoring is one of the major transaction costs. It is estimated that there are 70,000 to 100,000 major air pollution sources, each emitting over 25 tons of any one pollutant each year. A single measurement and anaylsis of emissions from one smoke stack can cost up to $5,000.

Abatement costs are those involved in attempting to reduce pollution at its source and decrease the damage it does to the environment. Abatement costs include the expense of buying, and paying interest on loans for, such items as "scrubbers" to clean smokestack emissions. They should also properly include such industrial costs as changes in production methods, lowered by-product revenues, etc. but these costs are hard to estimate.

The Environmental ProtectionAgency estimates that by 1981, the total annual cost of pollution abatement will more than triple to reach $39.5 billion dollars. (Their estimate is figured in 1972 dollars to take account of the effect of future inflation.)

Federal, state and local government expenditures will cover only about 35% of abatement costs between 1971 and 1981. The rest will be paid for out of private funds in the form of higher retail prices or lower stock dividends.

Given the costs of preventing further damage to the environment, is pollution control worth the price? If the costs of air pollution and prevention are any indication, the answer is a firm Yes.

While the table below shows an estimated savings of less than $2 billion, it should be noted that health damage costs from some auto emission pollutants are not included. Savings in direct health costs and indirectly through decreases in auto accident and insurance costs could be considerable.

Total Pollution Control Costs, 1971
(estimated, in billions of 1972 dollars)

	O&M[1]	Capital[2]	Total
Air pollution			
Public	0.2	—	0.2
Private			
Mobile[3]	1.1	—	1.2
Stationary	.4	.3	.7
Total	**1.7**	**.4**	**2.1**
Water pollution			
Public			
Federal	.2	na	na
State, local	1.2	3.8	5.0
Private			
Mfg.	.4	.3	.7
Utilities	.2	.1	.3
Total	**2.0**	**4.2**	**6.0**
Solid wastes			
Public	1.0	.2	1.2
Private	2.0	—	2.0
Total	**3.0**	**.2**	**3.2**
Grand Total	**6.7**	**4.8**	**11.3[4]**

(—) less than $50 million.
(1) Operating and maintaining pollution control devices. (2) Interest and depreciation. (3) Excluding heavy-duty vehicles. (4) Nothing was spent on control of water pollution from feedlots; no data are available on costs for noise and radiation control or for land reclamation after surface mining.

Air Pollution Damage and Control Costs, 1977
(estimated in billions of 1970 dollars)

Pollution Source	Damages Without Controls	Damages With Controls	Control Costs
Mobile	2.2	1.2	8.4
Solid Waste	.6	.2	.2
Stationary fuel use	12.8	3.4	2.5
Industry processes	7.0	3.7	1.2
Miscellaneous	2.3	2.3	0
Total	**24.9**	**10.8**	**12.3**

1972 Federal Transaction Costs
(in millions of dollars)

	Air	Water	Land	Other	Multi-media[1]	Total
Research and Development	136.5	70.2	26.3	82.3	32.8	348.1
Planning	2.2	19.8	.2	3.5	1.2	26.9
Monitoring	29.0	30.8	4.4	18.4	2.0	84.6
Administration, enforcement	82.2	72.8	0	16.6	27.4	199.0
Other	15.0	92.5	7.5	83.4	4.5	202.9
Total	**264.9**	**286.1**	**38.4**	**204.2**	**67.9**	**861.5**

[1]Two or more environmental factors: air and water, land and water, etc.

Environmental Quality Index

Source: National Wildlife Federation.

Adapted from the 1974 February/March issue of NATIONAL WILDLIFE Magazine.

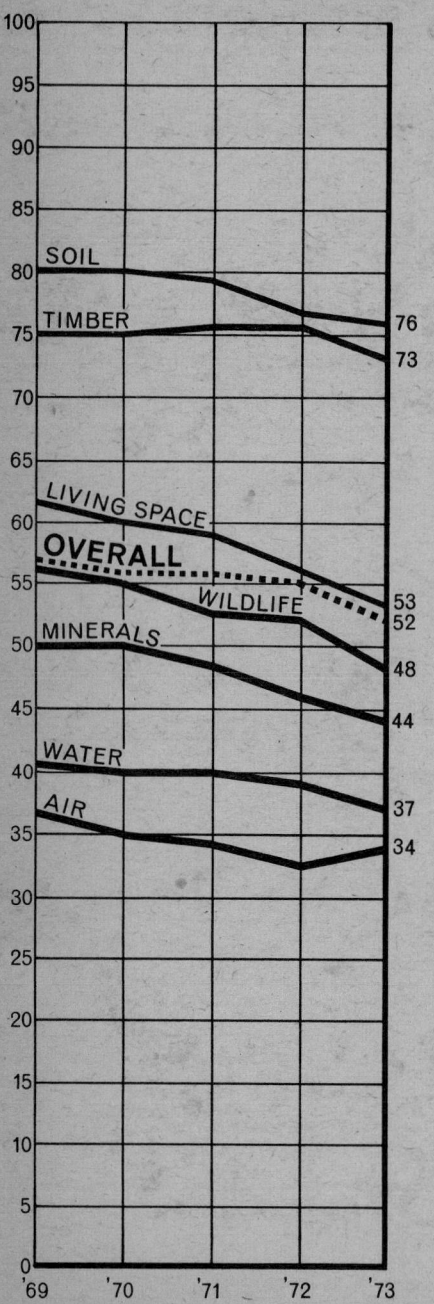

In 1969, the National Wildlife Federation began to record an index of environmental quality which measures progress or decline in 7 environmental areas. The index represents the rough judgement of environmental protection experts and advocates influenced by very high standards of environmental quality. While their judgement is, in part, subjective and open to dispute, it does provide a relative indication of success and failure in achieving one set of goals.

Soil: erosion removes 3.5 billion tons of topsoil per year; paved areas equal all of New England (except Maine) plus Delaware; tax rate on farms pricing many out of agricultural use; land use planning needed if U.S. is to meet food demands of growing population.

Timber: forest product demand projected to double in 30 years, production only in 50 years; per capita paper consumption is about 1.5 pounds daily; recycling presently provides only 20% of raw material for paper; efficient management of timber areas and lumber production can increase production dramatically.

Living space: about 75% of Americans live on 2% of the land; cities overcrowded, dirty; decay and abandonment of buildings spreading from central cities to suburbs; inefficiencies caused by noise cost $4 billion a year; many cities and states are turning away from unrestricted development.

Wildlife: increasing habitat destruction; 1 million acres for wildlife is buried under concrete or new reservoirs each year; over 150,000 birds die each year in oil field sumps alone; endangered species list up from 101 in 1972 to 109 in 1973; all-terrain vehicles add new threat; over 250,000 acres added to National Wildlife Refuge System during 1972 and 1973.

Minerals: known reserves (i.e. minable with present technology at present prices) will last 72 years for iron, 38 for copper, 28 for zinc, 27 for lead; recycling now common in copper (60%), aluminum (48%), lead (42%), nickel (40%), steel (26%) and zinc (14%); coal, the fuel in greatest supply, is dirtiest; natural gas, the cleanest, is in shortest supply; strip mining for coal is cheaper economically but damages land; only 17% of strip-mined land has been reclaimed.

Water: new research shows increasing contamination of drinking water with toxic synthetics, poisons and viruses; many water treatment plants inadequate to deal with modern pollutants; only 25% of industrial waste goes through treatment plants; the rest goes directly into lakes, rivers, oceans; according to Environmental Protection Agency, the Ohio River system and lower Great Lakes are most polluted waters in the nation; strip mining, shale oil development and nuclear plant cooling threaten further pollution, particularly in the Mountain states where pollution is presently slight; increasing acidity of rain and snow, especially in Northeast, endangers plant life, fish and corrodes buildings.

Air: a slight improvement in air quality due to the 1970 Clean Air Act; air pollution in most areas of the nation exceeds official air quality standards for at least one pollutant; no standards created yet for combinations of pollutants, such as particulate matter and sulfur dioxide which are more dangerous in combination; urban areas are hardest hit by combinations of pollutants, threatening more people; air pollution presently costs about $16 billion per year in damage to crops, landscape, property and health.

Medical News 1974

By David Hendin
Science Editor, Newspaper Enterprise Assn.

One of the biggest stories in the field of medicine in 1974 was a scandal.

In April Dr. William T. Summerlin, a physician-scientist at the Memorial Sloan-Kettering Cancer Center in New York, was permanently relieved of his position and given a year's pay with the proviso that he receive psychiatric counseling.

It was charged that Summerlin falsified potentially important research findings. Controversy swirled in the scientific community for months in what was widely referred to as "a medical Watergate."

A year or more before, Summerlin had reported that he could transplant tissue between different animals without using dangerous drugs to suppress the body's natural reaction — rejection and death of the tissue. If true, that observation held spectacular implications for transplantation of tissues and organs as well as cancer research.

But Summerlin was charged with falsifying his research data and painting black patches on white mice to make them look as if they had accepted skin grafts from black mice.

Summerlin admitted to darkening the skin of the mice, but denied any other falsification of data. He attributed the episode to "extreme pressure placed on me by the institute director."

That director is Dr. Robert A. Good, who had been heavily touting Summerlin's work ever since it was first announced, and had used its spectacular nature to improve fund raising for his institution.

Dr. Good concluded that it was an unfortunate episode, and noted that "In science, it is completely senseless (to falsify). The nature of research is to test and retest until something stands up. A scientist cannot get away with falsifying results."

Disease Deaths Decline

In May the National Center for Health Statistics made the report that death rates from heart disease, cancer, stroke and six other diseases has declined over the past 20 years, but nobody can say why.

"Mysterious and energizing," said Dr. Harold Margulies of the Department of Health, Education and Welfare, who called the trends surprising and called for research to explain them. Data was gathered from every one of the 33,637,548 death certificates recorded in the United States in the 1950s and 1960s. It showed declines in 9 of the 15 leading causes of death among Americans and increases in 6 others. Accidents, suicides, homicides and cirrhosis of the liver were all on the rise.

Heading up the American Cancer Society's Environmental Cancer Research Project, Drs. E. Cuyler Hammond and Irving Selikoff began in 1974 to answer questions about how environmental changes affect people. They are looking for data to confirm the World Health Organization estimate that some 85 percent of all cancer is derived from environmental sources.

In January it was revealed that 7 workers (of fewer than 300) working at the B.F. Goodrich plastics plant in Louisville, Ky. died of a rare tumor, angiosarcoma of the liver. Within weeks after the disclosure, other cases were discovered in New York, Texas, West Virginia and elsewhere.

The medical detectives have traced this alarmingly high incidence of the rare liver cancer to the fact that affected workers have been heavily exposed to the chemicals polyvinyl chloride (PVC) and vinyl chloride. They are widely used in the production of plastics, some of which are actually called vinyls.

The federal government has put a limit on the amount of vinyl chloride factory workers can be exposed to, but there was controversy among industry, consumer and government scientists as to just how much — if any — vinyl chloride might cause cancer.

It will be a long time before this is known, for environmental carcinogens carry with them something known as the 20-year rule, which means that it usually takes a human being 20 to 30 years to develop cancer after being exposed to an environmental carcinogen. All of the plastics workers who came down with the rare liver cancer had been exposed to the chemical for at least 20 years.

Acupuncture Dangers

In mid-year hundreds of newspapers ran stories exposing how hundreds of doctors are taking 3-day quickie courses in acupuncture and then going out and trying it on patients. Such courses are little more than diploma mills.

Acupuncture clinics across the country continued to do a booming business, and more were in operation than ever before. But Dr. John Bonica, chairman of the Ad Hoc Committee on Acupuncture of the National Institutes of Health and the American Society of Anesthesiologists, made important conclusions after intensive study of acupuncture here and in China. "The misuse of therapeutic acupuncture is an important health problem and the widespread clinical use of acupuncture is unwarranted at the present time," Dr. Bonica said.

Articles in medical journals detailed various complications of acupuncture therapy ranging from damaged nerves and arteries to puncture of the lung and at least one death caused by a blood leak in the heart after needling in the area.

Dr. Samuel Rosen, New York ear specialist, did a six-month research study to determine whether acupuncture could relieve nerve deafness, as many proponents had claimed. Results were negative. "We see no basis for recommending acupuncture as a treatment modality for children with profound neuro-sensory deafness. I do not do this myself, nor do I recommend it to my colleagues," said Dr. Rosen.

Doctors Review Doctors

The controversial Professional Standards Review Organizations (PSROs) got underway in 1974. The first contract for peer review of physicians went to the Utah PSRO, which served as a model for the peer review legislation. The program provides for peer review of medical work performed on patients whose bills are paid in any way by the federal government.

In July Prof. Douglas Bevis, a British gynecologist at Leeds University, announced that three babies that had been conceived in test tubes had been born normally. But controversy over the development upset Bevis, who later announced that he was giving up his research in this area altogether.

The federal government reported in 1974 that more evidence has been compiled to show that cigarette smoking is the major cause of lung cancer, which killed 72,000 Americans in 1973. The U.S. Department of HEW also said that cigarette smoking is the primary cause of chronic bronchitis and emphysema and is a contributing factor leading to heart disease.

Zoo News, 1974

by Edward Ricciuti

While the nation's oldest zoo, in Philadelphia, celebrated its centennial during 1974, a zoo building boom took place across the nation, with new zoos opening their gates and established animal gardens unveiling new exhibits.

The Philadelphia Zoo marked its 100th anniversary July 1 with appropriate ceremonies and a proclamation by the city's mayor that July was "Philadelphia Zoo Month." Featured in the ceremonies was the First Troop Philadelphia City Cavalry, the unit with which the zoo's founder, Dr. William Camac, served during the Civil War.

The Philadelphia Zoo began as the only institution of its kind in the New World and, while it covers only 42 acres, has an enviable record. It was the first zoo in the land to breed cheetahs, orang-utans, chimpanzees, trumpeter swans, and other rare forms of wildlife.

Earlier in the year the Philadelphia Zoo opened the first phase of a major new complex, the African Plains Exhibit, where zebras, giraffes, antelopes, ostriches, cranes and waterfowl mingle freely as they do in the wild. Hidden moats separate animals from visitors to the exhibit, which cost nearly a million dollars.

Electrically heated animal shelters in the exhibit are concealed by artificial kopjes designed to resemble the rock formations of the African savannahs. The exhibit also features a 40-foot-high baobab tree made of fiberglass. The artificial tree has a built-in door so that ostriches and other birds can use it for shelter. In nature, the baobab may reach 60 feet in height and 1000 years in age. It has one of the thickest trunks of any tree, with a maximum diameter of 30 feet.

Drive-In Zoos

For the past few years the so-called "drive-through zoo," where animals roam large compounds traversed by visitors in automobiles or other vehicles, has set a new trend in American zoological parks. Most of the new zoos are commercial ventures, and as such particularly sensitive to economic pressures. Despite gasoline shortages and inflation, however, the drive-through zoo trend seems to be continuing, as four large new parks opened to the public during 1974.

Two are operated by Lion Country Safari, the California-based organization that pioneered the drive-through zoo concept in the United States, in association with the Taft Broadcasting Company of Cincinnati, Ohio. Both new Lion Country Safaris are linked to amusement parks, one at Kings Island, Ohio, and the other at Kings Dominion, Virginia. The Ohio park, near Cincinnati, carts its visitors through the animal compounds on a monorail train. It covers 100 acres and features about 600 animals, mostly African species such as white rhinoceros, lion, and antelope.

The Kings Dominion park, 20 miles north of Richmond, is the first phase of a larger entertainment center. Visitors now tour the zoo's 120 acres by automobile, but a monorail is expected to go into operation in 1975. As with other Lion Country Safaris, the Kings Dominion park is African in theme. Visitors drive slowly through compounds where an illusion of driving through the wild is created by animals such as lions and elephants roaming free.

Most drive-through zoos have an entertainment area, restaurants, shops and similar facilities, and Kings Dominion is no exception. The park also features performances by Hanna-Barbera television cartoon characters, such as Yogi Bear, Scooby Doo and the Flintstones.

Another drive-through zoo built in association with a large theme park is Great Adventure, which opened this past summer in Jackson, New Jersey. The complex is a subsidiary of the Hardwicke Companies, Inc. which operate hotels, restaurants and similar establishments.

Great Adventure features 2,000 wild animals, including a herd of 30 young elephants, cheetahs, tigers, lions, and a large variety of antelopes.

A special feature of Great Adventure is a group of leopards, the only large grouping of this species found in a drive-through zoo, and the Siberian as well as Bengal race of tiger.

The Wildlife Preserve, which opened in Upper Marlboro, Maryland, is the American Broadcasting Companies, Inc., entry in the drive-through zoo field. A dozen miles from downtown Washington, the Wildlife Preserve has developed North American, South American and African compounds on its 400 acres, half of which are yet undevelped. This park features a bird of prey show, a reptile institute, and a theater in which multi-media wildlife presentations are given for visitors.

Among the 500 animals exhibited at the Wildlife Preserve are lions, giraffes, baboons, wolves, and antelope.

New Exhibits

Several older zoos either opened new exhibits or began construction of new facilities. The Beardsley Zoological Gardens, formerly Beardsley Park Zoo, in Bridgeport, Conn. opened exhibits for mountain lions, giant anteaters and South American cacomistles, tropical relatives of the raccoon. The Beardsley Zoo has on exhibit the only breeding pair of this species in the nation. During the fall, construction began at the Beardsley Zoo on a new Children's Zoo and Farmyard complex, which with the other new exhibits is part of the zoo's long-range redevelopment plan.

The San Diego Wild Animal Park, where visitors view free-roaming animals from a monorail train, has offered an alternative way to tour its grounds. The park, operated by the San Diego Zoological Society, opened a hiking trail that takes visitors near compounds where tigers, lions, giraffes and other creatures roam. The hikers are separated from the animals by concealed fencing and moats along the trail, which crosses a 70-foot suspension bridge over a deep ravine.

Early in the year the Jacksonville (Florida) Zoo opened its Joseph Hixon Bird of Prey Flight Cage to the public. A huge structure, 140 feet long, 80 feet wide and 32 feet high, it houses about two dozen large birds of prey. Visitors tour the cage along a wood-chip walkway.

Water Zoos

The Scripps Aquarium in La Jolla, California, began construction on a tidepool exhibit that features a rising and falling tide with surface waves. The wave mechanism was designed by scientists at the Scripps Hydraulic Facility.

Mystic Marinelife Aquarium, Mystic, Conn., which opened last year, began developing plans for a new seal and sea lion complex on the aquarium's grounds. The complex, in the open air, will house seals and sea lions of several species in settings representing their natural habitats.

Most aquariums have amphitheaters in which dolphins and whales perform for the benefit of visitors, but the New England Aquarium, Boston, has one with a brand new twist. The amphitheater at the Boston institution is a ship. 180 feet long and 54 feet wide, fully Coast Guard approved.

Named "Discovery", the floating dolphin theater sailed into Boston Harbor in August to the accompaniment of fire boats with spurting hoses. Seating 1,000 people in a stadium around a 250,000-gallon pool, the amphitheater was built in Sturgeon Bay, Wisconsin, at a cost of $2 million. The Discovery was towed from Sturgeon Bay 2,880 miles through the St. Lawrence Seaway to the sea. It made the trip to the aquarium on the harbor in 18 days.

The Discovery is a three-story structure that now houses sea lions and dolphins. Both creatures are used in demonstrations of their learning and physical capabilities for aquarium visitors.

Saving Rare Animals

With wild populations of many animals declining, and tough new federal laws regulating the importation of wild animals, zoos in the United States are finding it more and more necessary to breed animals for their own collections. Although it has been a long-term goal of many zoos to breed rare species, the nuts and bolts problem of stocking exhibits has accelerated zoo breeding plans. In June, the federal government took a major step to promote captive breeding of wild animals with the opening of a 3,300-acre Research and Conservation Center for the National Zoo, Washington, D.C., part of the Smithsonian Institution.

Not only will the center promote captive breeding of rare species for zoos but it is large enough for scientists to study the behavior of wild animals housed there under relatively natural conditions. It is hoped that knowledge gained in this way will help management of the animals in the wild.

The site of the unique new center is the former Beef Cattle Research Station of the United States Department of Agriculture at Front Royal, Virginia. The center will be developed gradually. It includes both pastures and wooded land, and a large assortment of buildings for personnel, research and servicing the facility.

The Oryx Mix

The first animals on the site arrived on June 8. They were a male and two female scimitar-horned oryx antelope, which were released in a 25-acre pasture with knee-high grass. The scimitar-horned oryx lives in the arid grasslands along the southern fringes of the Sahara Desert. from Mali to the central Sudan. Although herds of up to 60 of the animals have been seen, the species generally roams in bands of from two to a dozen individuals. It is listed by the International Union for the Conservation of Nature and Natural Resources as a species that is highly vulnerable to extinction.

The wild populations of scimitar-horned oryx are threatened by hunting and destruction of habitat by the cattle of various nomadic tribes. Moreover, the severe drought that has gripped the Sahel section of Africa has further threatened the species.

In past years the species also inhabited the Middle East and in 1972 the National Zoo donated a pair of animals to Israel's Hai Bar Reserve, where conservationists are trying to re-establish animals once native to that area.

Father David's Deer

The second species to be located at the center was the Pere David deer, a species that has been preserved purely through captive breeding. Approximately 4,000 years ago the deer existed as a wild animal in marshes of northern China. Its wide, spreading hooves enabled it to gallop over the soggy ground with little difficulty. A very large deer, the Pere David deer became extinct in the wild long before the present era, as its marshland habitat was converted to farmland.

Chinese emperors, however, preserved the animal in hunting parks. The species was made known to western scientists little more than a century ago when a French missionary, Pere Armand David, bribed guards to let him look into the walled imperial hunting park near Peking.

A half-century after Pere David reported on the deer, however, natural disasters and war eliminated the game park herd. The only deer surviving were those that had been sent by the Chinese to European zoos and their descendants.

A noted deer fancier, the British Duke of Bedford, gathered together many of Europe's Pere David deer on his estate near London, Woburn Abbey. There he bred the animals. Today, the Woburn herd numbers almost 300 animals and is the largest in the world. All living Pere David deer, including those sent to China a few years ago by the London Zoological Society, are descended from the Woburn herd.

Wombats, Bongos and Dogs

The National Zoo also is beginning a three-year breeding and research program on various wild dogs at the center. The species involved are all New World animals — the bush dog, maned wolf, and crab-eating fox, which hail from South America.

Each species has different habits and lives in a different type of environment. The bush dog is a pack hunter of the forest. The crab-eating fox, also hunts in packs, but lives in the marshy llanos and gallery forrest, while the long-legged maned wolf is a solitary rover of the pampas.

Scientists hope to learn how each species social system method of communication relate to the conditions under which it lives.

Several other major research programs are planned at the center during the next three years. Work is beginning on wombats, the lesser panda and Grant's zebra. Next year will see the start of research on creatures such as the golden marmoset, a very rare South American monkey, and on the giant anteater and Burmese brown-antlered deer. After that, researchers will study several other species of monkeys, the two toed sloth, bactrian camel, and the brocket deer.

Meanwhile, work is underway to move several large species into the center. Among them is the Masai giraffe, the cape buffalo, greater kudu — an antelope with spiral horns — and the bongo, a rare and lyre-horned animal from the forests of the Congo region.

Some Endangered Species in North America

Source: U.S. Fish and Wildlife Service

Common Name	Scientific Name	Range
Mammals		
Wood Bison	Bison bison athabascae	Alberta, Canada
Black-Footed Ferret	Mustela nigripes	U.S., Canada
Northern Kit Fox	Vulpus velox hebes	Canada
West Indian (Florida) Manatee	Trichechus inunguis	Caribbean (once U.S.)
Sonoran Pronghorn	Antilocapra americana sonoriensis	U.S., Mexico
Eastern Timber Wolf	Canis lupus lycaon	(endangered in U.S. only)
Northern Rocky Mountain Wolf	Canis lupus irremotus	U.S., Canada
Red Wolf	Canis rufus	U.S.
Eastern Cougar	Felis concolor cougar	U.S., Canada
Birds		
Bald Eagle	Haliaetus leucocephalus	U.S., Canada
Masked Bobwhite	Colinus virginianus ridgwayi	U.S., Mexico
California Condor	Gymnogyps californianus	Southern California
Whooping Crane	Grus americana	Canada, U.S.
Eskimo Curlew	Numenius borealis	Canada to Argentina
American Peregrine Falcon	Falco peregrinus anatum	Canada to Mexico
Arctic Peregrine Falcon	Falco peregrinus tundrius	Canada to Mexico
Aleutian Canada Goose	Branta canadensis leucopareia	U.S. to Japan
Brown Pelican	Pelecanus occidentalis	Canada to Panama
Attwater's Greater Prairie Chicken	Tympanuchus cupido attwateri	U.S.
Bachman's Warbler	Vermivora bachmani	Southeast U.S., Cuba
Kirtland's Warbler	Dendroica kirtlandi	Michigan, Bahamas
Ivory-Billed Woodpecker	Campephilus principalis	Southeast U.S., Cuba

Some Other Endangered Species in the World

Source: U.S. Fish and Wildlife Service

Common Name	Scientific Name	Range
Mammals		
Asiatic Wild Ass	Equus hemionus	Iran to Mongolia
Dugong	Dugong dugon	East Africa to Okinawa
Slender-Horned Gazelle	Gazella leptoceros	North Africa, Arabia
Mountain Gorilla	Gorilla gorilla beringei	Central Africa
Orang Utan	Pongo pygmaeus	Indonesia, Malaysia
Great Indian Rhinoceros	Rhinoceros unicornus	India, Nepal
Javan Rhinoceros	Rhinoceros sondaicus	Indonesia
Sumatran Rhinoceros	Didermocerus sumatrensis	Bangladesh to Vietnam, Indonesia
Northern White Rhinoceros	Ceratotherium simum cottoni	Sudan, Zaire, Uganda
Blue Whale	Balaenoptera musculus musculus	Oceanic
Humpback Whale	Megaptera novaeangliae	Oceanic
Birds		
Great Indian Bustard (largest land bird)	Choriotis nigriceps	India, Pakistan
Japanese Crane	Grus japonicus	Japan (once all north Asia)
Chinese Egret	Egretta eulophotes	China (once all east Asia)
Japanese Crested Ibis	Nipponia nippon	Japan (once all north Asia)

Young of Animals have Special Names

The young of many animals, birds and fish have come to be called by special names. A young eel, for example, is an elver. Many young animals, of course, are often referred to simply as infants or babies. Some of the more distinctive names, and the animals, fish or birds of which these young are the offspring, follow.

bunny: rabbit.
calf: cattle, elephant, antelope, rhino, hippo, whale, etc.
cheeper: grouse, partridge, quail.
chick, chicken: fowl.
cockerel: rooster.
codling, sprag: codfish.
colt: horse (male).
cub: lion, bear, shark, fox, etc.
cygnet: swan.
duckling: duck.
eaglet: eagle.

elver: eel.
eyas: hawk, others.
fawn: deer.
filly: horse (female).
fingerling: fish generally.
flapper: wild fowl.
fledgling: birds generally.
foal: horse, zebra, others.
fry: fish generally.
gosling: goose.
heifer: cow.
joey: kangaroo, others.
kid: goat.

kit: fox, beaver, rabbit, cat.
kitten, kitty, catling: cats, other fur-bearers.
lamb, lambkin, cosset, hog: sheep.
leveret: hare.
nestling: birds generally.
owlet: owl.
parr, smolt, grilse: salmon.
piglet, shoat, farrow, suckling: pig.
polliwog, tadpole: frog.
poult: turkey.
pullet: hen.

(continued)

pup: dog, seal, sea lion, fox.
puss, pussy: cat.
spike, blinker, tinker: mackerel.

squab: pigeon.
squeaker: pigeon, others.
whelp: dog, tiger, beasts of prey.

yearling: cattle, sheep, horse, etc.
younglet, youngling: animals generally.

Speeds of Animals

Source: *Natural History* Magazine, March 1974.
Copyright © The American Museum of Natural History, 1974.

Animals	Speeds in mph	Animals	Speeds in mph	Animals	Speeds in mph
Cheetah	70	Mongolian wild ass	40	Cat (domestic)	30
Pronghorn antelope	61	Greyhound	39.35	Man	27.89
Wildebeest	50	Whippet	35.50	Elephant	25
Lion	50	Rabbit (domestic)	35	Black mamba snake	20
Thomson's gazelle	50	Mule Deer	35	Six-lined race runner	18
Quarter horse	47.5	Jackal	35	Squirrel	12
Elk	45	Reindeer	32	Pig (domestic)	11
Cape hunting dog	45	Giraffe	32	Chicken	9
Coyote	43	White-tailed deer	30	Spider (Tegenaria atrica)	1.17
Gray fox	42	Wart hog	30	Giant tortoise	0.17
Hyena	40	Grizzly bear	30	Three-toed sloth	0.15
Zebra	40			Garden snail	0.03

Most of these measurements are for maximum speeds over approximate quarter-mile distances. Exceptions — which are included to give a wide range of animals — are the lion and elephant, whose speeds were clocked in the act of charging; the whippet, which was timed over a 200-yard course; the cheetah over a 100-yard distance; man for a 15-yard segment of a 100-yard run (of 13.6 seconds); and the black mamba, six-lined race runner, spider, giant tortoise, three-toed sloth, and garden snail, which were measured over various small distances.

Gestation, Longevity and Incubation

Note: The figures on gestation, incubation and longevity given below are averages based on estimates by leading authorities. The potential life span of mammals is rarely attained in nature. The longevity figures for wild animals listed below were based on experience with such animals in zoos.

Animal	Gestation (Days)	Longevity (Years)	Animal	Gestation (Days)	Longevity (Years)	Animal	Gestation (Days)	Longevity (Years)
Ass	365	24	Dog	61	16	Pig	112	14
Baboon	187	27	Elephant	645	47	Puma	90	11
Badger	60	15	Elk	250	22	Rabbit	37	5
Bat		6	Fox	52	8	Rhinoceros	450	27
Bear			Giraffe	425	10	Sea Lion	350	19
Black	219	19	Goat (dom.)	151		Sheep	154	13
Grizzly	225	31	Goat (mtn.)	184	9	Squirrel	44	8
Polar	240	31	Gorilla	257	25	Tiger	105	19
Beaver	122	13	Guinea Pig	68	4	Whale	365	37
Buffalo	278	20	Horse	330	27	Wolf	63	12
Camel	406	20	Kangaroo	42	19	Zebra	365	20
Cat (domestic)	63	15	Leopard	98	17			
Chimpanzee	231	30	Lion	100	15-29	**Incubation Time**		
Chipmunk	31	7	Monkey	164	7	Chicken	21	
Cow	284	18	Moose	240	8	Duck	30	
Deer	201	17	Mouse			Goose	30	
			(meadow)	21	4	Pigeon	18	
			Opossum	14-17	4	Turkey	26	

A Collection of Animal Collectives

The English language boasts an abundance of nouns used to describe groups of things, particularly pairs or aggregations of animals. Some of these words have fallen into comparative disuse, but many of them are still in service, helping to enrich the vocabularies of those who like their language to be precise, who tire of hearing a group referred to as "a bunch of," or who enjoy the sound of words that aren't overworked.

Here is a lexicon of some of these "collectives":

band of gorillas
bed of clams, oysters
bevy of quail, swans
brace of ducks
brood of chicks
cast of hawks
cete of badgers
charm of goldfinches
chattering of choughs

cloud of gnats
clowder of cats
clutch of chicks
clutter of cats
colony of ants
congregation of plovers
covert of coots
covey of quail, partridge
cry of hounds

down of hares
draught of fish
drift of swine
drove of cattle, sheep
exaltation of larks
flight of birds
flock of sheep, geese
gaggle of geese
gam of whales

gang of elks
grist of bees
herd of curlews, elephants
hive of bees
horde of gnats
husk of hares
kindle or **kendle** of kittens
knot of toads

(continued)

leap of leopards	nest, nide of pheasants	skein of geese	tribe of goats
leash of greyhounds, foxes	pack of hounds, wolves	skulk of foxes	trip of goats
litter of pigs	pair of horses	sleuth of bears	troop of kangaroos, mon-
murder of crows	pod of whales, seals	sounder of boars, swine	keys
muster of peacocks	pride of lions	span of mules	volery of birds
mute of hounds	school of fish	spring of teals	watch of nightingales
nest of vipers	sedge or siege of cranes	swarm of bees	wing of plovers
	shoal of fish, pilchards	team of ducks, horses	yoke of oxen

Timber Wolf Transplant

One hundred years ago the eastern timber wolf ranged across the northeastern U.S. from Minnesota to New England and south to Ohio. While packs still roam Canada, the wolf population of the U.S. is now limited to 500 to 1,000 in northern Minnesota and 40 or less in Michigan.

Released in Michigan

Recently the Department of Interior Fish and Wildlife Service and Northern Michigan University attempted to resettle the timber wolf in a wilderness area of upper Michigan. In January, 1974, 4 wolves were caught near International Falls, Minnesota. During 2 months in captivity, the wolves were inoculated against disease and dosed with vitamins and penicillin. On March 12, the animals were released in the Huron Mountains of upper Michigan.

Two adults, male and female mates, joined a second adult male in a slow drift westward. The fourth wolf, an 11-month-old female, remained in the release area. Each wolf wore a radio transmitter on a collar, which allowed the experimenters to track them.

The research team expected the 3 wolves to settle down when the female, believed to be pregnant, started "denning". In early April, the group did stabilize within an area of about 200 square miles.

In early summer, the radio transmission of the male of the mating pair showed no sign of movement. A search by the experimenters found the wolf's body by the side of a road in Iron County. An examination indicated it had been hit by a car.

The second male was found dead in Dickinson County in early July. It had been shot 3 times with a small caliber gun. The Fish and Wildlife Service is investigating this death; the shooting of endangered animals is a punishable offense.

A Partial Success

The older female is still active in the "territory" of the group. There is no certain evidence that she did whelp, and the research team is awaiting winter, when tracks in the snow should indicate the size and health of her litter, if any.

A spokesman for the Department of Interior said the death of the 2 males was "a serious setback" for the experiment. However, the experiment did show that wolves can be successfully established in new areas and plans are being made to release more wolves in the areas around the 2 females.

A Look At The Future

Source: *The Futurist*, World Future Society, Feb. 1974

The following timetable of future developments in environmental protection and management was put together by Dr. Vaclav Smil, assistant professor of geography at the University of Manitoba in Winnipeg. Dr. Smil arrived at the estimated dates by using the Delphi method, a newly developed technique for peering into the future.

Under the Delphi method, experts are interviewed separately so that they do not influence each other directly. Successive rounds of interviews, with feedback to the experts of information and opinion distilled from previous interviews, results in a relatively clear-cut and useful consensus of expert opinion.

Dr. Smil polled 40 energy and environmental experts, asking them to list major scientific, technological and management breakthroughs which they regarded as urgently needed and feasible in the next 50 years. After collating the lists, Dr. Smil asked the experts to estimate the year in which there would be a 50-50 chance of each development having occured. The dates below are the ones which fall in the middle of the range of estimates.

1978 Environmentally motivated higher price for energy.

1978 Acceptance of the idea that all consumers share responsibility for pollution and its cost.

1980 Safe, large-scale disposal of radio-active wastes.

1980 Abolition of "growth for growth's sake" concept.

1980 Effective, harmless control of accidental oil spills.

1983 Development of waste heat utilization (desalting, heating, sewage treatment, etc.)

1983 Control of thermal pollution in water.

1983 Control of nitrogen oxides.

1985 New car (batteries, fuel cells, steam, etc.)

1985 Offshore siting of large power plants.

1986 Removal of noxious matter from fossil fuels before combustion.

1988 Establishment of worldwide environmental quality standards (air and water).

1990 Taxes to alleviate pollution problems (effluent taxes, tax incentives for dispersal of people from large cities).

1990 Establishment of worldwide environmental surveillance and warning agency.

1990 Supression of sound along highways and airways.

1992 New fast and safe mass transit systems.

1995 Coordinated international planning of energy consumption.

2000 Planned decrease of per capita energy demand and consumption.

2000 Effective population control.

2005 Conservation of fossil fuels for other future needs.

2010 Man will largely destroy his ability to survive in great numbers and in great cities.

2020 Utilization of heat sinks other than atmosphere and surface waters.

After 2020: Polar siting of large power plants.

After 2020: Elimination of all generators using fossil fuel.

Never: No private cars allowed.

NATIONAL DEFENSE

Data as of Aug., 1974

Chairman, Joint Chiefs of Staff
George S. Brown (USAF)

Army
General of the Army

	Date of Rank
Bradley, Omar N.	Sept. 20, 1950

Generals

Bennett, Donald V.	Sept.	1, 1972
Davison, Michael S.	May	26, 1971
DePuy, William E.	July	1, 1973
Goodpaster, Andrew J.	July	3, 1968
Kerwin, Walter T., Jr.	Feb.	1, 1973
Miley, Henry A., Jr.	Nov.	1, 1970
Palmer, Bruce, Jr.	Aug.	1, 1968
Rosson, William B.	May	15, 1969
Stilwell, Richard G.	July	31, 1973
Weyand, Frederick C.	Oct.	31, 1970
Zais, Melvin	Aug.	1, 1973

Air Force
Chief of Staff—David C. Jones
Generals

Carlton, Paul K.	Oct.	9, 1972
Clay, Lucius D., Jr.	Sept.	1, 1970
Dixon, Robert J.	Oct.	1, 1973
Dougherty, Russell E.	May	5, 1972
Eade, George J.	Apr.	18, 1973
Ellis, Richard H.	Sept.	30, 1973
Phillips, Samuel C.	Aug.	1, 1973

Seith, Louis T.	Aug.	1, 1974
Vogt, John W., Jr.	Apr.	7, 1972
Wilson, Louis L., Jr.	July	1, 1974

Navy
Chief of Naval Operations
Admiral James L. Holloway III

Admirals

Bagley, Worth J.	Sept.	1, 1973
Cousins, Ralph W. (Aviation)	Oct.	30, 1970
Gayler, Noel A.M. (Aviation)	Sept.	1, 1972
Johnson, Means, Jr.	Nov.	25, 1973
Kidd, Isaac C., Jr.	Dec.	1, 1971
Weisner, Maurice F. (Aviation)	Sept.	1, 1972

Marine
Corps Commandant, with rank of General

Cushman, Robert E., Jr.	Jan.	1, 1972

Asst. Commandant with rank of General

Anderson, Earl E.	Apr.	1, 1972

Coast Guard
Commandant, with rank of Admiral

Bender, Chester R.	June	1, 1970

Vice Commandant, with rank of Vice Admiral

Sargent, Thomas R., 3rd	July	1, 1970

United States Unified and Specified Commands

Alaskan Command — Lt. Gen. James C. Sherrill, USAF.

Atlantic Command — Adm. Ralph Cousins, USN.

North American Air Defense Command & Continental Air Defense Command — Gen. Lucius D. Clay Jr., USAF.

European Command — Gen. Andrew J. Goodpaster, USA.
Pacific Command — Adm. Noel A. M. Gayler, USN.
Southern Command — Gen. William B. Rosson, USA.
Strat. Air Command — Gen. Russell E. Dougherty, USAF
U.S. Readiness Command — Gen. Bruce Palmer, Jr., USA.

North Atlantic Treaty Organization International Commands

Supr. Allied Commander, Europe (SACEUR) — Gen. Andrew J. Goodpaster, USA.
Deputy SACEUR — Gen. Sir John Mogg (UK).
C-in-C, Allied Forces, Northern Europe — Gen. Sir John Sharp (UK).
C-in-C, Allied Forces, Central Europe — Gen. Ernst Ferber (Germany).
C-in-C, Allied Forces, Southern Europe — Adm. Means Johnston, USN.

Cmdr. Naval Forces, Southern Europe — Adm. G. Ciccolo (Italy).
Supr. Allied Cmdr. Atlantic (SACLANT) — Adm. Ralph Cousins, USN.
Deputy SACLANT — V. Adm. Sir Jerard Mansfield, KBE (Britain).
Cmdr. Striking Fleet Atlantic — V. Adm. John G. Finneran, USN.
Allied Cmdr. in Chief, Channel — Adm. Sir Edward Ashmore (Britain).

Primary U.S. Military Training Centers
Army

Name, P.O. Address	Zip	Nearest City	Name, P.O. Address	Zip	Nearest City
Aberdeen Proving Ground, MD.	21005	Aberdeen	Fort Jackson, SC.	29207	Columbia
Carlisle Barracks, PA.	17013	Carlisle	Fort Knox, KY.	40121	Louisville
Fort Belvoir, VA.	22060	Alexandria	Fort Leavenworth, KS.	66027	Leavenworth
Fort Benning, GA.	31905	Columbus	Fort Lee, VA.	23801	Petersburg
Fort Bliss, TX.	79906	El Paso	Fort McClellan, AL.	36201	Anniston
Fort Bragg, NC.	28307	Fayetteville	Fort Monmouth, NJ.	07703	Red Bank
Fort Devens, MA.	01433	Ayer	Fort Ord, CA.	93941	Seaside
Fort Dix, NJ.	08640	Trenton	Fort Polk, LA.	71459	Leesville
Fort Eustis, VA.	23604	Newport News	Fort Rucker, AL.	36362	Dothan
			Fort Sill, OK.	73503	Lawton
Fort Gordon, GA.	30905	Augusta	Fort Leonard Wood, MO.	65473	Rolla
Fort Hamilton, NY.	11252	Brooklyn	Redstone Arsenal, AL.	35809	Huntsville
Fort Benjamin Harrison, IN.	46216	Indianapolis	Rock Island Arsenal, IL.	61202	Rock Island
Fort Sam Houston, TX.	78234	San Antonio	The Judge Advocate		Charlottes-
Fort Huachuca, AZ.	85613	Sierra Vista	General School, VA.	22901	ville

Navy

Great Lakes, IL.	60088	Waukegan	Orlando, FL.	32813	Orlando
San Diego, CA.	92133	San Diego			

465

Marine Corps

Name, P.O. Address	Zip	Nearest City	Name, P.O. Address	Zip	Nearest City
Camp Lejeune, N.C.	28542	Jacksonville, N.C.	Marine Corps Development		
Marine Corps Air Station, N.C.	28533	Cherry Point, N.C.	& Educ. Command, Va.	22134	Quantico
Marine Corps Air Station, SC.	29902	Beaufort	Parris Island, S.C.	29905	Beaufort
Marine Corps Air Station, CA.	92630	El Torro	Camp Pendleton, Calif.	92055	Oceanside
Marine Corps Air Station, AZ.	85364	Yuma	San Diego, Calif.	92140	San Diego

Air Force

Name, P.O. Address	Zip	Nearest City	Name, P.O. Address	Zip	Nearest City
Chanute AFB, Ill.	61866	Rantoul	Maxwell AFB, Ala.	36112	Montgomery
Columbus AFB, Miss.	39701	Columbus	Moody AFB, Ga.	31601	Valdosta
Craig AFB, Ala.	36701	Selma	Nellis AFB, Nev.	89110	Las Vegas
Fairchild AFB, Wash.	99011	Spokane	Randolph AFB, Texas	78148	San Antonio
Keesler AFB, Miss.	39534	Biloxi	Reese AFB, Tex.	79489	Lubbock
Lackland AFB, Texas	78236	San Antonio	Sheppard AFB, Tex.	76311	Wichita Falls
Laughlin AFB, Tex.	78840	Del Rio	Vance AFB, Okla.	73701	Enid
Lowry AFB, Colo.	80230	Denver	Webb AFB, Texas.	79720	Big Spring
Mather AFB, Calif.	95655	Sacramento	Williams AFB, Ariz.	85224	Chandler

Personal Salutes and Honors

The United States national salute, 21 guns, is also the salute to a national flag. The independence of the United States is commemorated by the salute to the Union—one gun for each state—fired at noon on July at all military posts provided with suitable artillery.

A 21-gun salute on arrival and departure, with 4 ruffles and flourishes, is rendered to the President of the United States, to an ex-President and to a President-elect. The national anthem or *Hail to the Chief*, as appropriate, is played for the President, and the national anthem for the others. A 21-gun salute on arrival and departure, with 4 ruffles and flourishes, also is rendered to the sovereign or chief of state of a foreign country or a member of a reigning royal family; the national anthem of his or her country is played. The music is considered an inseparable part of the salute and will immediately follow the ruffles and flourishes without pause.

Rank	Salute—guns Arrive—Leave		Ruffles flour- ishes	Music
Vice President of United States	19		4	Hail Columbia
Speaker of House	19		4	March
American or foreign ambassador	19		4	Nat. anthem of official
Premier or prime minister	19		4	Nat. anthem of official
Secretary of Defense, Army, Navy or Air Force	19	19	4	March
Other Cabinet members, Senate President pro tempore, Governor, or Chief Justice of U.S.	19		4	March
Chairman, Joint Chiefs of Staff	19	19	4	
Army Chief of Staff, Chief of Naval Operations, Air Force Chief of Staff, Marine Commandant	19	19	4	General's or
General of the Army; General of the Air Force; Fleet Admiral.	19	19	4	Admiral's March
Generals, Admirals	17	17	4	
Assistant Secretaries of Defense, Army, Navy or Air Force	17	17	4	March
Chairman of a Committee of Congress	17		4	March

Other salutes (on arrival only) include 15 guns for American envoys or ministers and foreign envoys or ministers accredited to the United States; 15 guns for a lieutenant general or vice admiral; 13 guns for a major general or rear admiral (upper half); 13 guns for American ministers resident and ministers resident accredited to the U.S.; 11 guns for a brigadier general or rear admiral (lower half); 11 guns for American charges d'affaires and like officials accredited to U.S.; and 11 guns for consuls general accredited to U.S.

Military Units, U.S. Army and Air Force

Army units. Squad. In infantry usually ten men under a staff sergeant. **Platoon.** In infantry 4 squads under a lieutenant. **Company.** Headquarters section and 4 platoons under a captain. (Company in the artillery is a battery; in the cavalry, a troop.) **Battalion.** Hdqts. and 4 or more companies under a lieutenant colonel. (Battalion size unit in the cavalry is a squadron.) **Brigade.** Hdqts. and 3 or more battalions under a colonel. **Division.** Hdqts. and 3 brigades with artillery, combat support and combat service support units under a major general. **Army Corps.** Two or more divisions with corps troops under a lieutenant general. **Field Army.** Hdqts. and two or more corps with field Army troops under a general.

Air Force Units. Flight. Small components of a squadron organized for special purpose such as medical evacuation flights. **Squadron.** The basic organized unit of the Air Force, used by operational as well as support forces but not limited by numbers of personnel assigned; two to three tactical squadrons are assigned to a tactical wing. **Group.** Terminology used for special tactical forces and for many support elements. They do not necessarily have subordinate units assigned. **Wing.** Used for tactical and support forces. A tactical wing usually has two to three operational squadrons assigned. **Division.** An organizational component of operational numbered Air Forces consisting of two to three wings, also used to designate numerous support and research components. **Air Force.** An intermediate echelon of command directly under the headquarters of a large operational command, usually with four to seven subordinate divisions. **Major command.** A major subdivision of the Air Force that is assigned a major segment of the USAF mission, usually two or four subordinate Air Force elements.

Armed Services Senior Enlisted Adviser

The U.S. Army, Navy and Air Force in 1966-67 each created a new position of senior enlisted adviser whose primary job is to represent the point of view of his services' enlisted men and women on matters of welfare, morale and any problem concerning enlisted personnel. The senior adviser will have direct access to the military chief of his branch of service and policy-making bodies.

The senior enlisted adviser for each Dept. is:

Army-Sgt. Major of the Army Silas I. Copeland.

Navy-Master Chief Petty Officer of the Navy John D. Whittet.

Air Force-Chief Master Sgt. of the Air Force Thomas N. Barnes.

Marines-Sgt. Major of the Marine Corps Clinton A. Puckett.

U. S. Army Insignia and Chevrons

Source: Department of the Army

Grade	Insignia

General of the Armies
(General John J. Pershing, the only person to have held this rank, was authorized to prescribe his own insignia, but never wore in excess of four stars. The rank originally was established by Congress for George Washington in 1799, but no record has been found to show that the appointment was made.)

General of the Army . . . Five silver stars fastened together in a circle and the coat of arms of the United States in gold color metal with shield and crest enameled.

General . . . . Four silver stars
Lieutenant General . . . . .Three silver stars
Major General . . . . .Two silver stars
Brigadier General . . . . .One silver star
Colonel . . . . .Silver eagle
Lieutenant Colonel . . . . .Silver oak leaf
Major . . . . .Gold oak leaf
Captain . . . . .Two silver bars
First Lieutenant . . . . One silver bar
Second Lieutenant . . . . One gold bar

Warrant officers

Grade Four—Silver bar with 4 enamel black bands.
Grade Three—Silver bar with 3 enamel black bands.
Grade Two—Silver bar with 2 enamel black bands.
Grade One—Silver bar with 1 enamel black band.

Non-Commissioned officers

Sergeant Major of the Army (E-9). Same as Command Sergeant Major (below). Also wears distinctive red and white shield on lapel.

Command Sergeant Major (E-9). Three chevrons above three arcs with a 5-pointed star with a wreath around the star between the chevrons and arcs.

Sergeant Major (E-9). Three chevrons above three arcs with a five-pointed star between the chevrons and arcs.

First Sergeant (E-8). Three chevrons above three arcs with a lozenge between the chevrons and arcs.

Master Sergeant (E-8). Three chevrons above three arcs.

Platoon Sergeant or Sergeant First Class (E-7). Three chevrons above two arcs.

Staff Sergeant (E-6). Three chevrons above one arc.

Sergeant (E-5). Three chevrons.

Corporal (E-4). Two chevrons.

Specialists

Specialist Seven (E-7). Three arcs above the eagle device.
Specialist Six (E-6). Two arcs above the eagle device.
Specialist Five (E-5). One arc above the eagle device.
Specialist Four (E-4). Eagle device only.

Other Enlisted

Private First Class (E-3). One chevron above one arc.
Private (E-2). One chevron.
Private (E-1). None.

United States Army

Source: Department of the Army

Army Military Personnel on Active Duty (a)

June 30 (b)	Total strength	Commissioned officers			Warrant officers		Enlisted personnel		
		Total	Male	Female (c)	Male (d)	Female	Total	Male	Female
1940	267,767	17,563	16,624	939	763	—	249,441	249,441	. . . .
1942	3,074,184	203,137	190,662	12,475	3,285	—	2,867,762	2,867,762	. . . .
1943	6,993,102	557,657	521,435	36,222	21,919	0	6,413,526	6,358,200	55,325
1944	7,992,868	740,077	692,351	47,726	36,893	10	7,215,888	7,144,601	71,287
1945	8,266,373	835,403	772,511	62,892	56,216	44	7,374,710	7,283,930	90,780
1946	1,889,690	257,300	240,643	16,657	9,826	18	1,622,546	1,605,847	16,699
1950	591,487	67,784	63,375	4,409	4,760	22	518,921	512,370	6,551
1955	1,107,606	111,347	106,173	5,174	10,552	48	985,659	977,943	7,716
1960	871,348	91,056	86,832	4,224	10,141	39	770,112	761,833	8,279
1961	856,853	90,066	85,853	4,213	9,817	38	756,932	748,372	8,560
1962	1,064,522	105,225	100,920	4,305	10,777	48	948,597	939,876	8,721
1963	974,070	98,622	94,810	3,812	9,640	40	865,768	857,476	8,292
1964	971,384	100,640	96,905	3,735	10,193	37	860,514	852,556	7,958
1965	967,049	101,812	98,029	3,783	10,285	23	854,929	846,409	8,520
1966	1,197,468	106,468	102,347	4,121	11,296	22	1,079,682	1,070,503	9,179
1967	1,440,120	127,393	122,685	4,708	16,090	34	1,296,603	1,286,862	9,741
1968	1,567,900	145,988	140,919	5,069	20,158	27	1,401,727	1,391,016	10,711
1969	1,509,637	148,836	143,699	5,137	23,734	20	1,337,047	1,316,326	10,721
1970	1,319,735	143,704	138,469	5,235	23,005	13	1,153,013	1,141,537	11,476
1971	1,120,822	130,261	125,240	5,021	18,670	19	971,872	960,047	11,825
1972	807,985	105,364	100,961	4,403	15,907	19	686,695	674,346	12,349
1973	798,177	101,194	96,936	4,258	14,990	21	681,972	665,515	16,457
1974	780,464	91,873	87,504	4,369	14,106	19	674,466	648,138	26,328

(a)Represents strength of the active Army, including Philippine Scouts, retired Regular Army personnel on extended active duty, and National Guard and Reserve personnel on extended active duty; excludes U. S. Military Academy cadets, contract surgeons, and National Guard and Reserve personnel not on extended active duty.

(b)Data for 1940 to 1947 include personnel in the Army Air Forces and its predecessors (Air Service and Air Corps).

(c)Includes: Women Doctors, Dentists and Medical Service Corps Officers for 1946 and subsequent years, women in the Army Nurse Corps for all years, and the Women's Army Corps and Women's Medical Specialists Corps (dieticians, physical therapists and occupational specialists) for 1943 and subsequent years.

(d)Act of Congress approved April 27, 1926, directed the appointment as warrant officers, of field clerks still in active service. Includes Flight Officers as follows: 1943, 5,700; 1944, 13,615; 1945, 31,117; 1946, 2,580.

Army Expenditures for Military Functions (1)

(in millions of dollars)

Fiscal Year	Amount	Fiscal Year	Amount	Fiscal Year	Amount	Fiscal Year	Amount
1942	14,805	1953	16,337	1961	10,131	1968	25,223
1943	42,573	1954	12,910	1962	11,427	1969	25,035
1944	49,289	1955	8,899	1963	11,499	1970	24,749
1945	49,750	1957	9,063	1964	12,050	1971	23,077
1946	27,176	1958	9,051	1965	11,600	1972	22,596
1947	8,027	1959	9,468	1966	11,832	1973	20,576
1950	3,985	1960	9,392	1967	21,010	1974	21,649

(1)Excludes expenditures for all civil functions as defined in "The Budget of the United States Government." Data for fiscal years to 1947 include all Army Air Force expenditures.

U.S. Navy Insignia

Navy
Stripes and corps device are of gold embroidery.

Stripes
Fleet Admiral . . . . .1 two inch with 4 one-half inch.
Admiral . . . . .1 two inch with 3 one-half inch.
Vice Admiral . . . . 1 two inch with 2 one-half inch.
Rear Admiral . . . . 1 two inch with 1 one-half inch.
Commodore
(war time only) . . . . . 1 two inch.
Captain . . . . 4 one-half inch.
Commander . . . . 3 one-half inch.
Lieut. Commander . . . .2 one-half inch, with 1 one quarter
inch between.
Lieutenant . . . . .2 one-half inch.
Lieutenant (j.g.) . . . . . . 1 one-half inch with 1 one quarter
inch above.
Ensign . . . . 1 one-half inch.
Warrant Officers—One ½" (½" for warrant officer W-1)
broken with ½" intervals of blue as follows:
Chief Warrant Officer W-4—1 break
Chief Warrant Officer W-3—2 breaks, 2" apart

Chief Warrant Officer W-2—3 breaks, 2" apart
The breaks are symmetrically centered on outer face of
sleeve.

Enlisted personnel (non-commissioned petty officers) . . . A
rating badge worn on the upper left arm, consisting of a
spread eagle, appropriate number of chevrons and centered specialty mark.

Marine Corps
Marine Corps and Army officer insignia are similar. Marine Corps and Army enlisted insignia, although basically
similar, differ in color, design, and fewer Marine Corps
subdivisions. The Marine Corps' distinctive cap and collar
ornament is a combination of the American eagle, globe
and anchor.

Coast Guard
Coast Guard insignia follow Navy custom, with certain
minor changes such as the officer cap insignia. The Coast
Guard shield is worn on both sleeves of officers and on the
right sleeve of all enlisted men.

United States Naval Budget Outlays
Source: Department of the Navy.

Fiscal year	Total amount expended	Shipbuilding conversion and modernizations	Aircraft and missile procurement	Military construction	All other expenditures
1940.	$885,769,794	$328,819,394	$24,011,998	$72,503,151	$460,435,251
1945.	29,380,421,832	7,228,192,871	3,541,009,589	1,576,096,922	17,035,122,450
1950.	4,065,484,778	281,328,056	452,723,233	86,054,932	3,245,378,557
1955.	9,637,637,835	903,303,717	1,834,511,038	238,631,005	6,661,192,075
1960.	11,848,690,002	1,380,031,231	2,027,098,025	284,928,383	8,228,632,362
1967.	19,291,496,288	1,398,414,838	3,006,902,022	522,638,470	14,363,540,958
1968.	22,106,320,837	1,355,850,877	3,642,007,920	92,966,944	17,015,495,096
1969.	22,507,495,249	1,948,757,741	3,315,166,323	424,837,766	16,818,733,419
1970.	2,501,628,282	2,065,660,211	3,183,464,921	333,271,852	16,919,231,298
1971.	22,046,000,000	2,592,000,000	3,273,000,000	327,000,000	15,854,000,000
1972.	24,100,000,000	3,010,000,000	3,983,000,000	353,000,000	16,754,000,000
1973.	25,425,000,000	2,962,000,000	3,673,000,000	486,000,000	18,122,000,000
1974 (Plan)	27,500,000,000	3,493,000,000	3,743,200,000	704,000,000	23,350,000,000

United States Navy Personnel on Active Duty
Source: DOD Comptroller (*Excludes Nurses)

June 30	Officers*	Nurses	Enlisted	Off. Cand.	Total
1940.	13,162	442	144,824	2,569	160,997
1945.	320,293	11,086	2,988,207	61,231	3,380,817
1950.	42,687	1,954	331,860	5,037	381,538
1955.	72,423	2,104	579,864	6,304	660,695
1960.	67,456	2,103	544,040	4,385	617,984
1965.	75,996	1,870	587,183	6,399	671,448
1969.	82,875	2,324	684,145	6,525	775,869
1970.	78,488	2,273	605,899	6,000	692,660
1971.	72,825	1,957	542,298	6,168	623,248
1972.	71,041	2,114	510,669	4,219	588,043
1973.	68,432	2,134	490,009	3,959	564,534

Marine Corps Personnel On Active Duty
Source: DOD Comptroller

Yr.	Officers	Enl.	Total	Yr.	Officers	Enl.	Total	Yr.	Officers	Enl.	Total
1955.	18,417	186,753	205,170	1965 . . .	17,258	172,955	190,213	1972	19,843	178,395	198,238
1960.	16,203	154,408	170,621	1970 . . .	24,941	234,796	259,737	1973 . . .	19,282	176,816	196,098

The Federal Service Academies

U.S. Military Academy, West Point, N.Y. Founded
1802. Awards B.S. degree and Army commission
for a 5-year service obligation. For admissions
information, write Admissions Office, USMA, West
Point, N.Y. 10996.
U.S. Naval Academy, Annapolis, Md. Founded 1845.
Awards B.S. degree and Navy or Marine Corps
commission for a 5-year service obligation. For
admissions information, write Dean of Admissions,
Naval Academy, Annapolis, Md. 21402.
U.S. Air Force Academy, Colorado Springs, Colo.
Founded 1954. Awards B.S. degree and Air Force
commission for a 5-year service obligation. For
admissions information, write Registrar, U.S. Air
Force Academy, Colo. 80840.

U.S. Coast Guard Academy, New London, Conn.
Founded 1876. Awards B.S. degree and Coast
Guard commission for a 5-year service obligation.
For admissions information, write Admissions Of-
fice, Coast Guard Academy, New London, Conn.
06320.

U.S. Merchant Marine Academy, Kings Point, N.Y.
Founded 1943. Awards B.S. degree, a license as a
deck or engineer officer, and a U.S. Naval Reserve
commission. Service obligations vary according to
options taken by the graduating ensign. For admissions information, write Admission Office, U.S.
Merchant Marine Academy, Kings Point, N.Y.
11024.

The Medal of Honor

The Medal of Honor is the highest military award for bravery that can be given to any individual in the United States. The first Army Medals were awarded on March 25, 1863, and the first Navy Medals went to sailors and Marines on April 3, 1863.

The Medal of Honor, established by Joint Resolution of Congress, 12 July 1862 (amended by Act of 9 July 1918 and Act of 25 July 1963) is awarded in the name of Congress to a person who, while a member of the Armed Forces, distinguishes himself conspicuously by gallantry and intrepidity at the risk of his life above and beyond the call of duty while engaged in an action against any enemy of the United States; while engaged in military operations involving conflict with an opposing foreign force; or while serving with friendly foreign forces engaged in an armed conflict against an opposing armed force in which the United States is not a belligerent party. The deed performed must have been one of personal bravery or self-sacrifice so conspicuous as to clearly distinguish the individual above his comrades and must have involved risk of life. Incontestable proof of the performance of service is exacted and each recommendation for award of this decoration is considered on the standard of extraordinary merit.

Prior to World War I, the 2,625 Army Medal of Honor awards up to that time were reviewed to determine which past awards met new stringent criteria. The Army removed 911 names from the list, most of them former members of a volunteer infantry group during the Civil War who had been induced to extend their enlistments when they were promised the Medal.

Since that review Medals of Honor have been awarded in the following numbers:

World War I	124	Korean War	131
World War II	431	Vietnam (to date)	206

(For names of Vietnam winners of the Medal of Honor, see the 1972 and 1973 editions of the World Almanac.)

American Military Action, 1900-1973

1900—Occupation of Puerto Rico (ceded to U.S., 1899).
1900—500 Marines, 1,500 Army troops help relieve Peking in Boxer Rebellion.
1900-1902—Occupation of Cuba.
1900-1902—Guerrilla war in Philippines.
1903—Sailors and Marines from U.S.S. Nashville stop Colombian Army at Panama.
1904—Brief intervention in Dominican Republic.
1906-1909—Intervention in Cuba.
1909—Brief intervention in Honduras.
1910, 1912-1913—Intervention in Nicaragua.
1911—Intervention (to collect customs) in Honduras, Nicaragua, Dominican Republic.
1912-1917—Intervention in Cuba.
1914—Intervention in Dominican Republic.
1914—April 21 to Nov. 23. Marines in Vera Cruz; also Atlantic fleet and Brig. Gen. Fredk. Funston.
1914—Navy and Marines enter Haiti, stay until 1934.
1916—Gen. John J. Pershing and 10,000 into Northern Mexico to stop raids by Villa, Mar. 15-Nov. 24.
1916-1924—Marines in Dominican Republic.
1917—Apr. 6 to Nov. 11, 1918. War with Germany, Austria-Hungary.
1918-1920—Expeditions into North Russia, Siberia.
1918-1923—Occupation of Germany.
1922-24—Marines in Nicaragua.
1926-33—Marines in Nicaragua.
1927—1,000 U.S. Marines in China.

1941-1945—War with Japan, Germany, Italy and allies. Army units posted in Japan and West Germany.
1950-1953—U.S. and other UN countries aid the Republic of Korea to repel North Korean invaders; U.S. Navy protects Taiwan.
1956—U.S. Fleet evacuates U.S. nationals during Suez crisis.
1957—U.S. Fleet to Near East during Jordan crisis.
1958—Navy, Marines and Army units support Lebanon.
1960—Navy patrol in Caribbean to protect Guatemala and Nicaragua.
1961—Army units to Vietnam.
1962—Units of U.S. Navy on Cuban quarantine duty. Marines in Thailand.
1962-65—U.S. Military Assistance Command, Vietnam; units of U.S. Army, Navy, Air Force, Marine Corps, Coast Guard.
1965—Navy, Marines, U.S. Army units to Dominican Republic.
1965—American commanders in Vietnam authorized to send U.S. Armed Force into combat.
1969—President Nixon announces, June 8, first phase of withdrawal of U.S. troops from Vietnam.
1970—Army units participate in Cambodian sanctuary operations, Apr. 29-June 30.
1973—Last U.S. troops leave Vietnam, U.S. Military Assistance Command deactivated, March 29.
1973—End of all U.S. bombing operations over Indochina, Aug. 15.

Adjutant General's Figures of Civil War Deaths

Figures reported from the Adjutant General's Office previous to the above revision, and accepted for many years, are as follows:

Union Army, according to records in the office of the Adjutant General of the War Department in Washington — killed or died of wounds, 110,070 (6,365 officers, 103,705 men); died of disease, 224,586 (2,795 officers, 221,791 men); other deaths, 24,872 (424 officers, 24,448 men). Totals, 359,528 (9,584 officers, 349,944 men).

Confederate Army, estimated, no official records in the office of the Adjutant General of the War Department in Washington — killed in battle, 52,954 (2,086 officers, 50,868 men); died of wounds, 21,570 (1,246 officers, 20,324 men); died of disease, 59,297 (1,294 officers, 58,003 men). **Total, 133,821 (4,626 officers, 129,195 men).**

World War II Merchant Marine Casualties

Source: U.S. Coast Guard

Died from direct causes while serving on American flag ships, 845; died in prisoner-of-war camps, 37; listed as missing, 4,780.

There were 572 released prisoners of war, and one prisoner unaccounted for. Another 500 men died while serving on foreign flag ships under U.S. control.

The number of U.S. flag ships lost was 605 of 6,000,000 deadweight tons.

How the Military Hand Salute Originated

Hand-raising as a formal greeting originated with the cavemen, who wanted to prove to one another that they carried no weapons, according to the National Geographic Society. Later an armored knight raised his right arm to lift his helmet visor and to show friendship by keeping his sword hand away from the weapon. Before the 19th Century, British soldiers saluted by tipping their hats. In the modern U.S. military salute the right hand is raised smartly so the forefinger touches the forehead just above and to the right of the right eye, thumb and fingers extended, forearm and wrist at a 45-degree angle. This salute, with variations, is common among military forces around the world.

United States Air Force

Source: Department of the Air Force

The Army Air forces were started Aug. 1, 1907, as the Aeronautical Division of the Signal Corps, U.S. Army. The division consisted of one officer and two enlisted men, and it was more than a year before it carried out its first mission in an airplane of its own. When the U.S. entered World War I (April 6, 1917), the Aviation Service, as it was called then, had 55 planes and 65 officers, only 35 of whom were fliers. On the day the Japanese struck at Pearl Harbor

(Dec. 7, 1941), the Army Air Forces, as they had been renamed six months previously, had 10,329 planes, of which only 2,846 were suited for combat service. But when the Army's air arm reached its peak during World War II (in July, 1944), it had 79,908 of all types of aircraft and (in May, 1945) 43,248 combat aircraft and (in March, 1944) 2,411,294 officers and enlisted men. The Air Force was established under the Armed Services Unification Act of July 26, 1947.

USAF Personnel at Home and Overseas — Officers and Enlisted Men

June 30	Continental U. S.	Overseas	Total	June 30	Continental U. S.	Overseas	Total
1940	40,229	10,936	51,165	1967	617,632	279,862	897,494
1945	1,153,373	1,128,886	2,282,259	1968	616,163	285,035	901,198
1950	317,816	93,461	411,277	1969	566,475	291,936	858,411
1955	689,635	270,311	959,946	1970	531,386	255,819	787,205
1957*	651,674	268,161	919,835	1971	528,493	222,586	751,079
1960[1]	607,383	207,369	814,752	1972	529,672	191,776	721,449
1965	635,430	189,232	824,662	1973	515,439	171,399	686,838

*Since 1957 continental U.S. includes Air Force Academy Cadets as follows: (1957) 504; (1960) 1,949; (1963) 2,660; (1964) 2,838; (1965) 2,907; (1966) 3,152; (1967) 3,361; (1968) 3,652; (1969) 3,941; (1970) 4,144; (1971) 2,997; (1972) 2,885; (1973) 4,356.
(1.) Since 1960 Overseas includes Alaska and Hawaii. All figures include Mobilized Personnel. Officers 292, airmen 1,323.

USAF Military Personnel

June 30	Officers & Airmen	USAF (Reg.) & RA	USAFR & ORC	ANG & NG	AFUS & AUS	Total Warrant Officers
		Male Commissioned Officers				
1950	411,277	19,735	33,585	14	55	2,085
1955	959,946	23,463	105,587	984	2	3,961
1960	814,752	49,584	72,115	248	3	4,069
1965	824,662	62,076	62,537	280	54	2,532
1970	787,205	63,678	65,852	168	105	639
1971	624,980	63,903	61,817	154	45	398
1972	721,448	61,045	54,549	146	30	238
1973	686,838	60,456	49,568	146	37	114

Female Commissioned Officers, and Enlisted Personnel

June 30	Total	WAF	Nurses	WMSC	Female WO	Total	Male	Female
	Female commissioned officers					Enlisted personnel		
1950	1,525	303	1,143	79	7	354,271	350,489	3,782
1960	3,858	679	3,020	159	5	685,063	679,412	5,651
1965	4,099	708	3,185	206	1	690,177	685,436	4,741
1970	4,667	1,072	3,407	188	....	657,402	648,415	8,987
1971	4,718	1,157	3,383	178	....	625,160	615,028	10,132
1972	4,766	1,214	3,391	161	....	599,774	588,049	11,725
1973	4,727	1,241	3,304	182	....	571,790	556,767	15,023

Those Who Served in United States' Wars

Source: Veterans Administration

Revolution (1775-1784)
Participants 290,000
Deaths in Service 4,000
Last Veteran Died April 5, 1869 ...... Age 109
War of 1812 (1812-1815)
Participants 287,000
Deaths in Service 2,000
Last Veteran Died May 13, 1905 .... Age 105
Mexican War (1846-1848)
Participants 79,000
Deaths in Service 13,000
Last Veteran Died September 3, 1929 . Age 98
Civil War (1861-1865) (Union Forces Only)
Participants 2,213,000
Deaths in Service 364,000
Last Veteran Died August 2, 1956 ...... Age 109
Indian Wars (Approx. 1817-1898)
Participants 106,000
Deaths in Service 1,000
Last veteran died June 18, 1973 .... Age 101
Spanish-American War (1898-1902)
Participants 392,000
Deaths in Service 11,000
Living Veterans 1,372
World War I (1917-1918)
Participants 4,744,000
Deaths in Service 116,000
Living Veterans 1,075,000

World War II (1940-1947)
Participants .... [1]16,535,000
Deaths in Service 406,000
Living Veterans 13,759,000
Korean Conflict (June 27, 1950-Jan. 31, 1955)
Participants .... [2]6,807,000
Deaths in Service 55,000
Living Veterans 5,925,000
Service Between Korean Conflict and Vietnam Era (Jan. 31, 1955 — Aug. 5, 1964)
Participants 3,195,000
Deaths in Service 20,000
Living Veterans 3,099,000
Vietnam Era (Active duty service after Aug. 4, 1964)
Participants .... [2]9,408,000
On Active Duty 2,150,000
America's Wars
Total through December 31, 1973
Participants* 44,056,000
Deaths in Service 1,091,000
Living Veterans 29,265,000
*Persons who served in more than one war period are counted as participants in each.
1. Includes 1,476,000 who served in both World War II and the Korean Conflict.
2. Includes 1,255,000 who served in both the Vietnam Era and the Korean Conflict.

Veterans Administration Expands Services As Rolls Grow

Source: Veterans Administration, Richard L. Roudebush, Administrator, Washington, D. C.

New and expanded programs, both in the educational and medical fields were inaugurated by the Veterans Administration in 1974 as returning Vietnam era veterans swelled the living veteran population of the U.S. over the twenty-nine and one-quarter million mark (29,265,000 as of June 1974.)

The G.I. Bill educational benefits were expanded as more than 2.5 million Vietnam era veterans had taken advantage of the training programs as of August, 1974. This was a higher participation rate (53.2%) than for veterans of World War II (50.2) or the Korean Conflict (42.6.)

To cut down on the paperwork and to make sure student-veterans get allowance checks on time, VA set up a system of having a VA man — a "Vet Rep" stationed on all college campuses to help on a person-to-person basis. More than 1,300 such "Vet Reps" were on duty in early fall of the 1974-75 school year.

Expanding its "Outreach" program VA continued to contact returning servicemen, personally and by mail, to tell them of their entitlements. The VA Mobile Vans continued to roll through sparsely-settled areas and store offices were opened in economically distressed areas to tell educationally disadvantaged veterans that they could finish high school and not have it count against their G.I. Bill college time.

VA medical experts toured the system's 171 hospitals to return with suggestions on how to make hospital life easier for the younger veteran. Nearly 150 narcotic treatment centers were set up, but it was found that the "dope scare" was just that — highly overrated. There were fewer dope users among returning veterans than there were among men their own age who were not veterans. VA increased its activity in opening more alcoholic treatment centers as more medical experts realized that alcoholism was among the nation's top killers, after heart disease.

VA's research in medicine and surgery continued with some amazing results. In the same hospital (Buffalo, N. Y.) where 10 years ago the first Pacemaker was implanted to regulate the beat of the heart, the same team of VA doctors in 1974 implanted the first battery powered regulator. That Buffalo research, headed by a VA team that implanted the first successful Pacemaker, is now responsible for saving the lives of untold thousands — for today cardiac Pacemakers are almost common. New techniques in organ transplants and open heart surgery were recorded and— as in all VA research — the results and techniques were shared with all the world. One VA physician, who had experimented for years with high blood pressure, found it wasn't anything to be dismissed lightly—as it had been by many—but is a serious illness: one that could successfully be treated by a combination of drugs. For this remarkable discovery he won the plaudits of fellow physicians and the famed Lasker Award. In all, there are more than 5,000 different research projects under way as 32 multi-hospital studies. These studies range from comparative study of the aging process to cancer. Medical journals have called VA's research and achievements in treating spinal cord injured veterans (paraplegics and quadriplegics) "miraculous." With about 50 per cent of all persons hospitalized in this country being treated for mental diseases, VA has concentrated on that problem in a group hospital project. Thousands of hospitals now use VA's guideline books for treatment of mental illnesses.

In fiscal 1975, VA will send $4.5 billion in disability and death payments to 2.6 million service-disabled veterans and survivors of deceased veterans. The maximum payment is $1,454 a month— for a total disabled veteran needing constant care and attendance.

In 1974, VA took over administration of the National Cemetery system that had been under the jurisdiction of the Army. The Army maintains control of the Arlington National Cemetery as a national shrine. The National Cemetery system included 103 burial places. VA has recommended that because most of them are closed to further burials, the system be expanded.

The G.I. Home Loan program continued strong despite a 1974 marked by limited financing. In 1974, a total of 306,200 loans were made—only 16 per cent below last year. The loans closed in 1974 had a face value of $7.7 billion. Since the G.I. Home Loan program started near the end of World War II, 8.8 million loans worth $106.3 billion have been closed. Less than 3 per cent of the G.I. Mortgage had to be foreclosed—and that's lower than the rate for conventional mortgages.

In budget and personnel, VA is the third largest U.S. government agency. VA employs 200,000 persons and has a budget of more than $14 billion.

Veteran Population, July 1974

1.	Veterans in civil life, end of month — Total	29,284,000
2.	War Veterans — Total	26,185,000
3.	Vietnam Era — Total(a)	7,133,000
4.	And service in Korean Conflict	464,000
5.	No service in Korean Conflict	6,669,000
6.	Korean Conflict — Total (includes line 4)	(b)5,960,000
7.	And service in WW II	1,254,000
8.	No service in WW II	4,706,000
9.	World War II (includes line 7)	13,743,000
10.	World War I	1,066,000
11.	Spanish-American War	1,000
12.	Service between Korean Conflict (January 31, 1955) and Vietnam (August 5, 1964) Only(c)	3,099,000

(a) Service after Aug. 4, 1964; (b) includes 2,385,000 veterans who also served after the end of the Korean Conflict (Jan. 31, 1955); (c) excludes men who served on active duty for training only.

Pension Cases and Compensation Payments

Fiscal year	Living veteran cases No.	Deceased veteran cases No.	Total cases No.	Total disbursement Dollars	Fiscal year	Living veteran cases No.	Deceased veteran cases No.	Total cases No.	Total disbursement Dollars
1890	415,654	122,290	537,944	106,093,850	1965	3,204,275	1,277,009	4,481,284	3,901,598,010
1900	752,510	241,019	993,529	138,462,130	1966	3,200,871	1,339,209	4,540,080	4,305,367,751
1910	602,622	318,461	921,083	159,974,056	1967	3,130,390	1,334,634	4,465,024	4,284,265,036
1920	419,627	349,916	769,543	316,418,029	1968	3,112,038	1,389,379	4,501,417	4,406,319,385
1930	542,610	298,223	840,833	418,432,808	1969	3,107,162	1,443,367	4,550,529	4,722,489,826
1940	610,122	239,176	849,298	429,138,465	1970	3,127,338	1,487,176	4,614,514	5,113,649,490
1950	2,368,238	658,123	3,026,361	2,009,462,298	1971	3,222,394	1,584,167	4,806,561	5,726,485,000
1955	2,668,786	808,303	3,477,089	2,634,292,537	1972	3,268,826	1,641,370	4,910,196	6,045,214,000
1960	3,008,935	950,802	3,959,737	3,314,761,383	1973	3,256,746	1,654,287	4,911,033	6,426,647,000

The Nuclear Debate

The Jargon

Since the dawn of the nuclear era, the basic policy of defense has been **deterrence** — discouraging the opponents' use of nuclear weapons by maintaining sufficient nuclear forces to cause unacceptable, massive damage to the opponent's population and economy even if he should strike first. This policy led to the **mutual assured destruction** (MAD) policy of both the USSR and the U.S.

Deterrence works only if each side's forces have **credibility**: each side must be convinced that the opponent is ready and willing to use nuclear weapons in certain circumstances and that those weapons are secure from attack and will be devastatingly effective.

The effectiveness of nuclear forces is based on the power and accuracy of missiles, the explosive power of warheads, and the number of warheads and missiles. The security of these forces is based on **redundancy**: a land-based missile force protected in concrete underground silos (**hard sites**) is duplicated by missiles on submarines which are virtually impossible to find and destroy and by nuclear bombs and missiles carried by long range aircraft which are already airborne or on constant alert.

In recent years, two factors have thrown some doubt on the security and effectiveness of the U.S. nuclear force. The threat to security comes from the greater power (**throw-weight**) of Soviet missiles. When Soviet missiles achieve the same accuracy as U.S. missiles, that advantage in throw-weight will enable the Soviet Union to launch many more warheads with more explosive power and precision.

The effectiveness of both Soviet and U.S. missile forces has been questioned because of the newly-raised **fratricide** problem — that is, the atmospheric havoc created by the first explosion of a nuclear warhead may deflect, damage or destroy a second warhead aimed into the same area.

Nuclear warheads can be aimed at industrial and civilian targets (**countervalue targeting**) or at military command centers, bases and missile sites (**counterforce targeting**). Counterforce targeting can range from an ability to destroy some bases and a small percentage of the opponent's missiles up to an ability to destroy most of an opponent's missiles and, therefore, his ability to retaliate effectively. In the latter case, counterforce targeting — from the opponent's point of view — looks exactly like a **first-strike capability** — the ability to attack first with little fear of an effective response. One response to an opponent's first-strike capability would be to adopt a **launch-on-warning** system that would immediately (and perhaps automatically) launch retaliatory missiles at the first sign that the other side had fired first.

Since the mid-1960s, U.S. policy has favored targeting against industrial and population centers as the best deterrent. However, in January 1974, Defense Secretary Schlesinger announced the flexible re-targeting of some missiles so they could strike at military installations as well as cities. The wisdom of this change is still under debate.

The Issues

1. Should the U.S. work toward achieving maximum targeting flexibility?

YES — The president should not be limited to a choice between surrender and slaughter.

— Because there is uncertainty about how a nuclear war might start, a wide range of possible responses should be available.

— A properly limited response to a small scale nuclear attack would not only not invite escalation, but would provide incentives against it.

NO — If nuclear war becomes more manageable, it will also become more likely.

— In a crisis, a variety of military options might cause leaders to overlook some diplomatic possibilities.

2. Is there a difference between a counterforce capability and a disarming first-strike capability?

YES — A disarming first-strike is not possible because of redundancy of missile forces.

— Destroying hard-sited missiles is more difficult than supposed because of the fratricide problem.

NO — As technology improves, counterforce targeting will inevitably result in first strike capability.

— In spite of one side's good intentions, the other side might launch a preemptive attack to destroy first-strike missiles.

— Fear of a first-strike could lead to a launch-on-warning doctrine, increasing the possibility that a nuclear war might begin by accident or miscalculation.

3. Can improvement of counterforce capability be kept from provoking an uncontrollable arms race?

YES — Even if an arms race does develop, that is better than falling behind the other side.

— Technology and bureaucracy influence weapons development more than do the actions of the other side.

— If only minor improvements are made, an arms race can be avoided.

NO — It happened once in the early 60s when McNamara chose to pursue a counterforce capability.

— Increase in types and numbers of weapons would increase problems of negotiations to limit weapons and make verification more difficult.

4. Is limited nuclear warfare possible?

YES — There is nothing inevitable about escalation or mass destruction of population.

— The kinds of weapons available and the way they are used can limit deaths and forestall escalation.

— Small, accurate, clean weapons directed against military targets can limit civilian casualties.

— Targeting can concentrate on military sites far removed from large populations.

NO — Many important military targets are in or near large population centers.

— The number of casualties resulting from even a small attack would be so large that retaliation against urban industrial targets would be almost inevitable.

5. Would an American lack of targeting flexibility and limited war options lead our allies to doubt that we would come to their defense?

YES — The idea that the U.S. would risk a major nuclear exchange to defend West Germany, for example, is not really believable. No one believes that U.S. decision makers are prepared to sacrifice Houston to save Munich.

NO — Rough equality of nuclear forces is important, but diplomacy and economics, not nuclear strength, are the real bonds between the U.S. and its allies.

— Maintainance of U.S. forces in Europe and Asia and U.S. preparedness to involve and defend those forces are guarantees enough.

— U.S. allies are relatively unaware of and unmoved by details of U.S. strategic planning.

6. Does the U.S have to follow suit if the Soviet Union develops great targeting flexibility and counterforce capability?

YES — Deterrence works only if the U.S. is genuinely the equal of the Soviet Union in capability.

If the U.S. does not have similar options, the deterrent against limited nuclear attacks in a political crisis would be weakened.

NO — U.S. aims differ from those of the Soviet Union, so U.S. strategy need not ape the Soviets.

— Improving counterforce capability is expensive, probably ineffective, and would lead to an arms race.

Strategic Nuclear Armaments: United States and Soviet Union

Source: International Institute for Strategic Services, London

United States

Type		Range[2] (statute miles)	Estimated warhead yield[3]	Deployed (July 1973)
Land-based Missiles[1]				
ICBM	Titan 2	7,250	5-10 MT	54
	Minuteman 1	7,500	1 MT	140
	Minuteman 2	8,000	1-2 MT	510
	Minuteman 3	8,000	3x200 KT	350
IRBM		—	—	—
MRBM		—	—	—
Sea-based Missiles				
SLBM	UGM-27B	—	—	—
(nuclear subs)	Polaris A2	1,750	800 KT	
	UGM-27C Polaris A3[6]	2,880	{ 1 MT or 3x200 KT }	336
	UGM-73A Poseidon	2,880	10x50 KT	320
SLBM (diesel subs)				

Type		Range[8] (statute Miles)	Weapons load (lb)	Deployed (July 1973)
Aircraft[7]				
Long-range	B-52D-F	11,500	60,000	442[9]
	B-52G/H	12,500	75,000	
Medium-range	FB-111A	3,800	37,500	74
Strike aircraft;	F-105D	2,100	16,500	
land-based	F-4	2,300	16,000	1,300[10]
	F-11A/E	3,800	25,000	
	A-7D	3,400	15,000	
Strike aircraft	A-4	2,055	10,000	
carrier-	A-6A	3,225	18,000	1,300[10]
based	RA-5C	3,000	13,500	
	A-74/B/E	3,400	15,000	

Soviet Union

Type		Range[2] (statute miles)	Estimated warhead yield[3]	Deployed (July 1973)
Land-based Missiles[1]				
ICBM	SS-7 Saddler	6,900	5 MT	209
	SS-8 Sasin	6,900	5 MT	
	SS-9 Scarp	7,500	20-25 MT[4]	288
	SS-11	6,500	1-2MT[5]	970
	SS-13 Savage	5,000	1 MT	60
IRBM	SS-5 Skean	2,300	1 MT	100
MRBM	SS-4 Sandal	1,200	1 MT	500
Sea-based Missiles				
SLBM	SS-N-5 Serb	750	MT range	30
(nuclear subs)	SS-N-6	1,750	MT range	496
	SS-N-8	4,000	MT range	36
SLBM (diesel subs)	SS-N-5 Serb	750	MT range	30

Type		Range (statute miles)	Weapons load (lb)	Deployed (July 1973)
Aircraft[7]				
	Tu-95 Bear	7,800	40,000	100
	Mya-4 Bison	6,050	20,000	40
	Tu-16 Badger	4,000	20,000	800
	Il-28 Beagle	2,500	4,850	
	Tu-22 Blinder	1,400	12,000	
	Yak-28 Brewer	1,750	4,400	1,300[10]
	MiG-21 Fishbed J	1,150	2,000	
	MiG-? Flogger	1,800	n.a.	

(1) ICBM = intercontinental ballistic missile. IRBM = intermediate-range ballistic missile. MRBM = medium-range missile. SLBM = submarine-launched ballistic missile. (2) Operation range depends upon the payload carried; use of maximum payload may reduce missile range by up to 25%. (3) MT = megaton = 1,000,000 tons of TNT equivalent (MT range = 1 MT or over); KT = kiloton = 1,000 tons of TNT equivalent (KT range = less than 1 MT). (4) SS-9 missiles have also been tested with 3 warheads of 4-5 MT each. (5) SS-11 missiles have also been tested with 3 smaller warheads. (6) Most of all Polaris A3 missiles have been modified to carry 3 warheads. (7) All aircraft listed are dual-capable and many, especially in the categories of strike aircraft, would be more likely to carry conventional than nuclear weapons. (8) Theoretical maximum range, with internal fuel only, at optimum altitude and speed. Ranges for strike aircraft assume no weapons load. Especially in the case of strike aircraft, therefore, range falls sharply for flights at lower altitude, at higher speed or with full weapons load. (9) Including approximately 22 B-52 D-F and 43 G-H aircraft in active storage. (10) These aircraft are nuclear capable but may not have a nuclear role.

Women In The Armed Forces

Women are now eligible for 81% of all military job classifications and enlistments are coming in at a rate that strains the capacity of the armed forces to handle them. The services had planned on having 88,000 women in uniform by 1977. With enlistments coming in at 100% of the goals the services set themselves, there are plans to increase barracks space and other facilities to accommodate 110,000 by that date — double the present number.

Women's Army Corps — Brig. Gen. Mildred C. Bailey, WAC Director, Dept. of Army, Pentagon, Washington, D.C.; 1,109 officers, 16,455 enlisted women; wide variety of assignments, world-wide; subsidizes some college training.

Army Nurse Corps — Brig. Gen. Lillian Dunlap, Chief, Office of the Surgeon General, Dept. of Army, Washington, D.C. 20314; 2,818 officers; nursing and supervision assignments, world-wide; subsidizes some training; includes men.

Navy — Fully integrated, no commander; for information: Commander, Naval Recruiting, Dept. of Navy, Washington, D.C. 20370; 1,320 officers, 8,800 enlisted women; variety of assignments.

Navy Nurse Corps — Rear Adm. Alene B. Duerk, Director, Navy Nurse Corps, Bureau of Medicine and Surgery, Navy Dept. Washington, D.C.; 2,134 officers; nursing and supervision assignments at U.S. and foreign bases, and shipboard; subsidizes some training.

Air Force — Colonel Billie M. Bobbitt, Director, WAF, Hq. USAF, Pentagon, Washington, D.C. 20330; 1,400 officers, 16,500 enlisted women; variety of assignments, world-wide.

Air Force Nurse Corps — Brig. Gen. Ethel A. Hoefly, Chief, Office of the Surgeon General, USAF, Washington, D.C. 20333; 3,295 officers; nursing and supervision assignments, world-wide; subsidizes some training; includes men.

Women Marines — Col. Margaret A. Brewer, Director, Headquarters, Marine Corps, Washington, D.C. 20380; 300 officers, 2,000 enlisted women.

Coast Guard Spars — Capt. Eleanor L'Ecuyer, Commandant G-RA/82, U.S. Coast Guard, Washington, D.C. 20590; 9 officers, 385 enlisted women.

Monthly Pay Scale of the Army,

Commissioned Officers

Pay grade	Rank or pay grade Army or Air Force rank	Navy rank	Under 2	Over 2	Over 3	Over 4	Over 6	Over 8
O-10[1]	Chief of Staff		$3,000.00	$3,000.00	$3,000.00	$3,000.00	$3,000.00	$3,000.00
O-10	General*	Admiral.	2,415.00	2,500.20	2,500.20	2,500.20	2,500.20	2,595.90
O-9	Lieutenant General .	Vice Admiral.	2,140.50	2,196.90	2,243.70	2,243.70	2,243.70	2,300.40
O-8	Major General	Rear Admiral (up. half).	1,938.60	1,996.80	2,044.50	2,044.50	2,044.50	2,196.90
O-7	Brigadier General. .	Rear Admiral (low. half).	1,610.70	1,720.80	1,720.80	1,720.80	1,797.30	1,797.30
O-6	Colonel.	Captain	1,194.00	1,312.20	1,397.70	1,397.70	1,397.70	1,397.70
O-5	Lieutenant Colonel.	Commander.	954.90	1,121.70	1,198.80	1,198.80	1,198.80	1,198.80
O-4	Major.	Lieutenant Comdr.	805.20	979.80	1,046.10	1,046.10	1,064.70	1,112.10
O-3	Captain	Lieutenant	748.20	836.40	893.70	989.40	1,036.50	1,073.70
O-2	First Lieutenant . . .	Lieutenant (J.G.)	652.20	712.50	855.90	884.40	903.00	903.00
O-1	Second Lieutenant	Ensign.	566.10	589.50	712.50	712.50	712.50	712.50

Commissioned officers with over 4 years service as enlisted members

Pay grade	Rank or pay grade Army or Air Force rank	Navy rank	Under 2	Over 2	Over 3	Over 4	Over 6	Over 8
O-3	Captain	Lieutenant				989.40	1,036.50	1,073.70
O-2	First Lieutenant	Lieutenant (J.G.)				884.40	903.00	931.50
O-1	Second Lieutenant .	Ensign.				712.50	760.80	789.30

Warrant Officers

Pay grade	Army or Air Force rank	Navy rank	Under 2	Over 2	Over 3	Over 4	Over 6	Over 8
W-4	Chief Warrant.	Comm. Warrant.	762.00	817.50	817.50	836.40	874.50	912.90
W-3	Chief Warrant.	Comm. Warrant.	693.00	751.50	751.50	760.80	770.10	826.50
W-2	Chief Warrant.	Comm. Warrant.	606.60	656.10	656.10	675.30	712.50	751.50
W-1	Warrant Officer.	Warrant Officer.	505.50	579.90	579.90	627.90	656.10	684.60

Enlisted Personnel[2]

Pay grade	Army or Air Force rank	Navy rank	Under 2	Over 2	Over 3	Over 4	Over 6	Over 8
E-9[3]	Sergeant Major**	Master C. P. O.						726.60
E-8[3]	Master Sergeant	Senior C. P. O.						
E-7	Sgt. 1st Class	Chief Petty Officer.	507.30	547.20	567.60	587.40	607.80	627.00
E-6	Staff Sergeant	Petty Officer 1st Class. .	438.00	477.90	497.70	518.10	537.90	557.70
E-5	Sergeant	Petty Officer 2nd Cl. . .	384.60	418.80	438.90	458.10	488.10	507.90
E-4	Corporal.	Petty Officer 3rd Cl. . . .	369.90	390.60	413.10	445.50	463.20	463.20
E-3	Private 1st Class	Seaman	355.80	375.30	390.30	405.60	405.60	405.60
E-2	Private.	Seaman Apprentice . . .	342.30	342.30	342.30	342.30	342.30	342.30
E-1	Private.	Seaman Recruit	307.20	307.20	307.20	307.20	307.20	307.20

The pay scale also applies to: Coast Guard and Marine Corps, Coast and Geodetic Survey, Public Health Service, National Guard, and the Organized Reserves.

*Four star General or Admiral—personal money allowances of $2,200 per annum, or $4,000 if Chief of Staff or Chief of Naval Operations. Three star General or Admiral—personal money allowance of $500 per annum.

**A new title of Chief Master Sergeant created in 1965 rates E-9 classification.

(1) While serving as Chairman of Joint Chiefs of Staff, Chief of Staff of the Army, Chief of Naval Operations, Chief of Staff of the Air Forces, or Commandant of the Marine Corps, basic pay for this grade is $3,000 regardless of years of service.

(2) Air Force enlisted personnel pay grades, E-9, Chief Master Sergeant; E-8, Sr. Master Sergeant; E-7, Master Sergeant; E-6, Technical Sergeant; E-5, Staff Sergeant; E-4, Sergeant; E-3, Airman 1st Class; E-2, Airman; E-1, Basic Airman.

Marine Corps enlisted ranks are as follows: E-9, Sergeant Major and Master Gunnery Sergeant; E-8, First Sergeant and Master Sergeant; E-7, Gunnery Sergeant; E-6, Staff Sergeant; E-5, Sergeant; E-4, Corporal; E-3, Lance Corporal; E-2, Private First Class Marine; E-1, Private.

Marine Corps officer ranks are same as Army and AF.

(3) While serving as Sergeant Major of the Army, Master Chief Petty Officer of the Navy, Chief Master Sergeant of the Air Force, or Sergeant Major of the Marine Corps, basic pay for this grade is $1,355.40 regardless of years of service.

Hazardous Duty

Flying Duty (crew member) and Submarine Duty Additional Monthly Pay

	Under 2 yrs.	Over 2 yrs.	Maximum Over—Amt.	
O-10	$165	$165	$165	
O-9	165	165	165	
O-8	155	155	165	
O-7	150	150	160	
O-6	200	200	18 yrs.	—245
O-5	190	190	18 "	—245
O-4	170	170	18 "	—240
O-3	145	145	14 "	—205
O-2	115	125	14 "	—185
O-1	100	105	14 "	—170
W-4	115	*	18 "	—165
W-3	110	115	14 "	—140
W-2	105	110	14 "	—135
W-1	100	105	12 "	—130
E-9	105	105		105
E-8	105	105		105
E-7	80	85	12 yrs.	—105
E-6	70	75	14 "	—100
E-5	60	70	12 "	— 95
E-4	55	65	8 "	— 80
E-3	55	60	2 "	— 60
E-2	50	60	2 "	— 60
E-1	50	55	2 "	— 55

Aviation Cadet under 2 years $50.
*W-4 Under 6 years receives $115.

Incentive Pay

Officers and Warrant Officers.	$110.00
Enlisted men.	55.00

Types of duties for which these flat rates are payable are as follows—(1) Frequent and regular aerial flights not as a crew member. (2) Parachute jumping as an essential part of military duty. (3) Duty involving intimate contact with leprosy. (4) Duty involving demolition of explosives. (5, 6) Special pay is authorized for diving duty. Pay varies with rank and type of duty. (7) Human acceleration or deceleration duty. (8) High-or-low pressure chamber duty. (9) Thermal stress duty. (10) Training for assignment to submarines of advanced design or for positions of increased responsibility aboard a submarine. Rates payable for this category are the same as those paid flying crew members listed under Hazardous Duty. (11) Flight Deck Duty.

Sea and Foreign Duty
Defense Secretary designates places where special duty pay may be awarded.

E-9.	$22.50	E-4.	13.00
E-8.	22.50	E-3.	9.00
E-7.	22.50	E-2.	8.00
E-6.	20.00	E-1.	8.00
E-5.	16.00	. . . .	

Navy and Air Force (1974)

Commissioned Officers

Over 10	Over 12	Over 14	Over 16	Over 18	Over 20	Over 22	Over 26	Basic allowances for quarters Without Dependents $	With Dependents $
$3,000.00	$3,000.00	$3,000.00	$3,000.00	$3,000.00	$3,000.00	$3,000.00	$3,000.00		
2,595.90	2,794.80	2,794.80	2,994.90	2,994.90	3,195.00*	3,195.00*	3,394.20	230.40	288.00
2,300.40	2,395.80	2,395.80	2,595.90	2,595.90	2,794.80	2,794.80	2,994.90	230.40	288.00
2,196.90	2,300.40	2,300.40	2,395.80	2,500.20	2,595.90	2,700.30	2,700.30	230.40	288.00
1,902.00	1,902.00	1,996.80	2,196.90	2,347.80	2,347.80	2,347.80	2,347.80	230.40	288.00
1,397.70	1,397.70	1,445.10	1,673.70	1,759.20	1,797.30	1,902.00	2,062.50	211.80	258.30
1,235.70	1,301.40	1,388.40	1,492.50	1,578.30	1,625.70	1,683.00	1,683.00	198.30	238.80
1,187.70	1,254.90	1,312.20	1,369.20	1,407.30	1,407.30	1,407.30	1,407.30	178.80	215.40
1,131.30	1,187.70	1,216.80	1,216.80	1,216.80	1,216.80	1,216.80	1,216.80	158.40	195.60
903.00	903.00	903.30	903.30	903.30	903.30	903.30	903.30	138.60	175.80
712.50	712.50	712.50	712.50	712.50	712.50	712.50	712.50	108.90	141.60
1,131.30	1,187.70	1,235.70	1,235.70	1,235.70	1,235.70	1,235.70	1,235.70	158.40	195.60
979.80	1,017.90	1,046.10	1,046.10	1,046.10	1,046.10	1,046.10	1,046.10	138.60	175.80
817.50	846.30	884.40	884.40	884.40	884.40	884.40	884.40	108.90	141.60

Warrant Officers

Over 10	Over 12	Over 14	Over 16	Over 18	Over 20	Over 22	Over 26	Without Dependents	With Dependents
950.70	1,017.90	1,064.70	1,102.50	1,131.30	1,169.10	1,207.80	1,301.40	172.50	207.90
874.50	903.00	931.50	959.70	989.40	1,027.20	1,064.70	1,102.50	155.40	191.70
780.00	808.20	836.40	865.50	893.70	922.20	959.70	959.70	137.10	173.70
712.50	741.60	770.10	798.60	826.50	855.90	855.90	855.90	123.90	160.80

Enlisted Personnel

Over 10	Over 12	Over 14	Over 16	Over 18	Over 20	Over 22	Over 26	Without Dependents	With Dependents
865.80	885.60	905.70	926.40	946.80	965.40	1,016.40	1,115.10	130.80	184.20
746.70	766.50	786.60	807.00	826.20	846.60	896.10	996.00	122.10	172.20
646.80	667.20	697.50	717.00	736.80	746.70	796.80	896.10	104.70	161.40
577.80	607.80	627.00	646.80	657.00	657.00	657.00	657.00	95.70	150.00
528.00	547.20	557.70	557.70	557.70	557.70	557.70	557.70	92.70	138.60
463.20	463.20	463.20	463.20	463.20	463.20	463.20	463.20	81.60	121.50
405.60	405.60	405.60	405.60	405.60	405.60	405.60	405.60	72.30	105.00
342.30	342.30	342.30	342.30	342.30	342.30	342.30	342.30	63.90	105.00
307.20	307.20	307.20	307.20	307.20	307.20	307.20	307.20	60.00	105.00

*Limited under existing law to $3,000

Basic Allowances for Subsistence

This allowance, the quarters allowance, and any other allowance are not subject to income tax.
Officers — Subsistence (food) is paid to all officers regardless of rank.................................$47.88 per month
Enlisted members: When rations in kind are not available..$2.57 per day
When permission is granted to mess off the base.....................................$1.65 per day
When assigned to duty under emergency conditions where
no government messing facilities are available.....................$3.42 per day (maximum rate)

Family Separation Allowance

Under certain conditions of family separation of more than 30 days, members in Pay Grades E-4 (with over 4 years' service) and above will be allowed $30 a month in addition to any other allowances to which he is entitled. When separated from family and required to maintain a home for his family and one for himself, the member is entitled to an additional monthly basic allowance for quarters at the "without dependents" rate for his grade.

Uniform Allowance

Enlisted personnel receive an initial uniform allowance valued at $164 to $285, with variations between services. After 6 months and up to the 36th month maintenance allowance of $4.50 is paid. After 36 months the monthly allowance is $6.60. An officer is entitled to an initial allowance of not more than $300.00.

Enlistment Bonus

DOD currently authorizes a bonus of $2,500 for a four-year enlistment in certain combat arms skills.

Reenlistment Bonuses

Reenlistment Bonuses are paid to enlisted members who reenlist within a specified period of time following their discharge from active service. The Regular Reenlistment Bonus is paid to all reenlistees at each reenlistment point prior to completion of 20 years of service. It is paid in fractions of monthly basic pay multiplied by the number of years in the reenlistment contract. Maximum total amount for any one individual during a 20 year career is $2,000.

Members serving in critical military specialties may, as a special incentive, receive an additional bonus, the Variable Reenlistment Bonus. This retention incentive is paid at the first reenlistment point to individuals designated as having a critical military specialty. It is paid in multiples (not to exceed 4) of the Regular Reenlistment Bonus. Maximum allowable Variable Reenlistment Bonus is $8,000 which provides for a maximum combined total of $10,000 for both the Regular and Variable Reenlistment Bonuses.

Special Pay

Members of the uniformed services entitled to receive basic pay shall, in addition thereto, be entitled to receive incentive pay for the performance of hazardous duty required by competent orders. The President, may in time of war, suspend the payment of hazardous duty incentive pay. Officers receive no additional pay for overseas or sea duty.

Duty Subject to Hostile Fire

Except in time of war declared by the Congress, a special pay of $65 a month is authorized for any member of the Uniformed Services during any month in which he was subject to hostile fire.

Medical and Dental Corps

Commissioned officers in the Medical and Dental Corps of the Army, Navy and Air Force and commissioned medical, dental, and veterinary officers of the Regular Corps of the Public Health Service receive special pay based on cumulative years of service (0-2 years, $100; 2 to 6 years, $150; 6 to 10 years, $250; over 10 years, $350). In addition to basic pay and allowance, Optometrists and Veterinary Corps Officers receive $100 per month extra.

Casualties in Principal Wars of the United States

Data prior to World War I are based upon incomplete records in many cases. Casualty data are confined to dead and wounded personnel and therefore exclude personnel captured or missing in action who were subsequently returned to military control. Dash (—) indicates information is not available.

Wars	Branch of service	Number serving	Battle deaths	Other deaths	Wounds not mortal[3]	Total
Revolutionary War	**Total**	—	**4,435**	—	**6,188**	**10,623**
1775-1783	Army	184,000	4,044	—	6,004	10,048
	Navy	to .	342	—	114	456
	Marines	250,000	49	—	70	119
War of 1812	**Total**	[9]**286,730**	**2,260**	—	**4,505**	**6,765**
1812-1815	Army	—	1,950	—	4,000	5,950
	Navy	—	265	—	439	704
	Marines	—	45	—	66	111
Mexican War	**Total**	[9]**78,718**	**1,733**	**11,550**	**4,152**	**17,435**
1846-1848	Army	—	1,721	11,550	4,102	17,373
	Navy	—	1	—	3	4
	Marines	—	11	—	47	58
Civil War	**Total**	[9]**2,213,363**	**140,414**	**224,097**	**281,881**	**646,392**
(Union forces only)	Army	2,128,948	138,154	221,374	280,040	639,568
1861-1865	Navy		2,112	2,411	1,710	6,233
	Marines	84,415	148	312	131	591
Confederate forces	**Total**	—	**74,524**	**59,297**	—	**133,821**
(estimate)[1]	Army	600,000	—	—	—	—
1863-1866	Navy	to	—	—	—	—
	Marines	1,500,000	—	—	—	—
Spanish-American	**Total**	**306,760**	**385**	**2,061**	**1,662**	**4,108**
War	Army[4]	280,564	369	2,061	1,594	4,024
1898	Navy	22,875	10	0	47	57
	Marines	3,321	6	0	21	27
World War I	**Total**	**4,743,826**	**53,513**	**63,195**	**204,002**	**320,710**
April 6, 1917-	Army[5]	4,057,101	50,510	55,868	193,663	300,041
Nov. 11, 1918	Navy	599,051	431	6,856	819	8,106
	Marines	78,839	2,461	390	9,520	12,371
	Coast Gd.	8,835	111	81	—	192
World War II	**Total**	**16,353,659**	**292,131**	**115,185**	**670,846**	**1,078,162**
Dec. 7, 1941-	Army[6]	11,260,000	234,874	83,400	565,861	884,135
Dec. 31, 1946[2]	Navy[7]	4,183,466	36,950	25,664	37,778	100,392
	Marines	669,100	19,733	4,778	67,207	91,718
	Coast Gd.	241,093	574	1,343	—	1,917
Korean War	**Total**	**5,764,143**	**33,629**	**20,617**	**103,284**	**157,530**
June 25, 1950-	Army	2,834,000	27,704	9,429	77,596	114,729
July 27, 1953[3]	Navy	1,177,000	458	4,043	1,576	6,077
	Marines	424,000	4,267	1,261	23,744	29,272
	Air Force	1,285,000	1,200	5,884	368	7,452
	Coast Gd.	44,143	—	—	—	—
Vietnam (preliminary)	**Total**	—	**45,937**	**10,300**	**303,622**	**359,859**
Jan. 1, 1961-	Army	—	30,591	7,146	201,518	239,255
Jan. 25, 1973	Navy	—	1,426	875	10,075	12,376
	Marines	—	12,936	1,680	88,593	103,209
	Air Force	—	984	599	3,436	5,019

[1]Authoritative statistics for the Confederate Forces are not available. An estimated 26,000-31,000 Confederate personnel died in Union prisons.

[2]Data are for the period Dec. 1, 1941 through Dec. 31, 1946 when hostilities were officially terminated by Presidential Proclamation, but few battle deaths or wounds not mortal were incurred after the Japanese acceptance of Allied peace terms on Aug. 14, 1945. Numbers serving from Dec. 1, 1941-Aug. 31, 1945 were: Total—14,903,213; Army—10,420,-000; Navy—3,883,520; and Marine Corps—599,693.

[3]Tentative final data based upon information available as of Sept. 30, 1954, at which time 24 persons were still carried as missing in action.

[4]Number serving covers the period April 21-Aug. 13, 1898, while dead and wounded data are for the period May 1-Aug. 31, 1898. Active hostilities ceased on Aug. 13, 1898, but ratifications of the treaty of peace were not exchanged between the United States and Spain until April 11, 1899.

[5]Includes Air Service. Battle deaths and wounds not mortal include casualties suffered by American forces in Northern Russia to Aug. 25, 1919 and in Siberia to April 1, 1920. Other deaths cover the period April 1, 1917-Dec. 31, 1918.

[6]Includes Army Air Forces.

[7]Battle deaths and wounds not mortal include casualties incurred in Oct. 1941 due to hostile action.

[8]Marine Corps data for World War II, the Spanish-American War and prior wars represent the number of individuals wounded, whereas all other data in this column represent the total number (incidence) of wounds.

[9]As reported by the Commissioner of Pensions in his Annual Report for Fiscal Year 1903.

American Military Cemeteries and Memorials on Foreign Soil

Administered by the American Battle Monuments Commission, Washington, D.C. 20315
(Numbers of graves, and numbers of commemorated missing in parentheses)

World War I Cemeteries

Aisne-Marne, near Belleau (Aisne) France (2,288-1,060)
Brookwood (Surrey) England (468-563)
Flanders Field, Waregem, Belgium (368-43)
Meuse-Argonne, Romagne (Meuse), France (14,246-954)
Oise-Aisne, Seringes (Aisne), near Fere-en-Tardenois (Aisne), France (6,012-241)
St. Mihiel, Thiaucourt (M. et M.), France (4,153-284)
Somme, Bony (Aisne), France (1,837-333)
Suresnes (Seine), France (1,541-974). In this cemetery rest also 24 of our unknown dead of World War II. The World War I chapel was, by the addition of two loggias, converted into a shrine to commemorate our dead of both wars. Senior representatives of the American and French governments assemble here on ceremonial occasions to pay homage to our military dead of these wars.

World War I Monuments

Audenarde, Belgium.
Bellicourt (Aisne), France.
Brest (Finistere), France.
Cantigny (Somme), France.
Chateau-Thierry (Aisne), Fr.
Gibraltar.
Kemmel, near Ypres, Belgium.
Montfaucon (Meuse), France.
Montsec (Meuse), France.
Sommepy (Marne), France.
Tours (Indre et Loire), France.

World War II Cemetery Memorials

Ardennes, near Neuville-en-Condroz, Belgium (5,310-462)
Brittany, near St. James (Manche), France (4,410-498)
Cambridge, near Cambridge, England, (3,811-5,125)
Epinal, near Epinal (Vosges), France (5,255-424)
Florence, near Florence (Tuscany), Italy (4,402-1,409)
Henri-Chapelle, near Henri-Chapelle, Belgium (7,989-450)

Lorraine, St. Avold (Moselle), France (10,489-444)
Manila, near Manila, Rep. of the Philippines (17,206-36,279)
Netherlands, Margraten, Holland (8,301-1,722)
Normandy, near St. Laurent (Calvados), Fr. (9,386-1,557)
North Africa, Carthage, Tunisia (2,840-3,724)
Rhone, Draguignan (Var), France (861-293)
Sicily-Rome, Nettuno, Italy (7,862-3,094)

World War II Memorials

To commemorate those who met their deaths in the American coastal waters of the Atlantic and Pacific Oceans the commission has erected a memorial in Battery Park, New York City, on which are inscribed 4,596 names, and at the Presidio of San Francisco, California, which carries 412 names. At the Honolulu Cemetery a memorial was erected which records the names of 18,093 missing of World War II and 8,191 missing resulting from the Korean operations.

The commission also maintains a cemetery in Mexico City where the remains of 750 Americans who gave their lives in the Mexican War (1846-1848) are buried.

Services

The commission provides the following services: exact location and other information concerning place of interment or memorialization; best routes and modes of travel in-country to the cemeteries and memorials; escort service within the cemetery memorials for next-of-kin and members of their immediate families; letters authorizing "non-fee" passports for members of the immediate families; color lithographs of World War I and II cemeteries together with black-and-white photographs of the appropriate gravesite or section of the Tablets of the Missing; and arrangements for floral decorations of gravesites or the Tablets of the Missing.

National Cemeteries (with ZIP Code)

On June 18, 1973, Pres. Nixon signed the National Cemeteries Act. (Public Law 93-43) transferring 82 Dept. of the Army National Cemeteries to the Veterans Admin., effective Sept. 1, 1973. The two remaining with the Army are marked*.

Alabama
Mobile Natl. Cemetery
Mobile 36604
Alaska
Sitka Natl. Cemetery
Sitka 99501
Arkansas
Fayetteville Natl. Cemetery
Fayetteville 72701
Fort Smith Natl. Cemetery
Fort Smith 72901
Little Rock Natl. Cemetery
Little Rock 72206
California
Fort Rosecrans Natl. Cemetery
San Diego 92106
Golden Gate Natl. Cemetery
San Bruno 94067
San Francisco Natl. Cemetery
94129
Colorado
Fort Logan Natl. Cemetery
Denver 80235
Dist. of Columbia
*Soldiers' Home Natl. Cemetery Washington, D.C. 20011
Florida
Barrancas Natl. Cemetery
Pensacola 32508
St. Augustine Natl. Cemetery
St. Augustine 32084
Georgia
Marietta Natl. Cemetery
Marietta 30060
Hawaii
Natl. Memorial Cemetery of the Pacific
Honolulu 96813
Illinois
Alton Natl. Cemetery
Alton 62004
Camp Butler Natl. Cemetery
Springfield 62707

Mound City Natl. Cemetery
Mound City 62963
Quincy Natl. Cemetery
Quincy 62301
Rock Island Natl. Cemetery
Rock Island 61201
Indiana
Crown Hill Natl. Cemetery
Indianapolis 46208
New Albany Natl. Cemetery
New Albany 47150
Iowa
Keokuk Natl. Cemetery
Keokuk 52632
Kansas
Fort Leavenworth Natl. Cemetery
Fort Leavenworth 66027
Fort Scott Natl. Cemetery
Fort Scott 66701
Kentucky
Camp Nelson Natl. Cemetery
Nicholasville 40356
Cave Hill Natl. Cemetery
Louisville 40204
Danville Natl. Cemetery
Danville 40422
Lebanon Natl. Cemetery
Lebanon 40033
Lexington Natl. Cemetery
Lexington 40508
Mill Springs Natl. Cemetery Nancy 42544
Perryville Natl. Cemetery
Perryville 40468
Zachary Taylor Natl. Cemetery
Louisville 40207
Louisiana
Alexandria Natl. Cemetery
Pineville 71360
Baton Rouge Natl. Cemetery
Baton Rouge 70806
Port Hudson Natl. Cemetery
Zachary 70791
Maryland
Annapolis Natl. Cemetery

Annapolis 21401
Baltimore Natl. Cemetery-
Baltimore 21228
Loudon Park Natl. Cemetery
Baltimore 21229
Minnesota
Fort Snelling Natl. Cemetery
St. Paul 55111
Mississippi
Corinth Natl. Cemetery
Corinth 38834
Natchez Natl. Cemetery
Natchez 39120
Missouri
Jefferson Barracks Natl. Cemetery
St. Louis 63125
Jefferson City Natl. Cemetery
Jefferson City 65101
Springfield Natl. Cemetery
Springfield 65804
Nebraska
Fort McPherson Natl. Cemetery
Maxwell 69151
New Jersey
Beverly Natl. Cemetery
Beverly 08010
Finn's Point Natl. Cemetery
Salem 08079
New Mexico
Santa Fe Natl. Cemetery
Santa Fe 87501
New York
Cypress Hills Natl. Cemetery
Brooklyn 11208
Long Island Natl. Cemetery
Farmingdale 11735
Woodlawn Natl. Cemetery
Elmira 14901
North Carolina
New Bern Natl. Cemetery
New Bern 28560
Raleigh Natl. Cemetery
Raleigh 27602

Salisbury Natl. Cemetery
Salisbury 28144
Wilmington Natl. Cemetery
Wilmington 28403
Oklahoma
Fort Gibson Natl. Cemetery
Fort Gibson 74434
Oregon
Willamette Natl. Cemetery
Portland 97266
Pennsylvania
Philadelphia Natl. Cemetery
Philadelphia 19138
Puerto Rico
Puerto Rico Natl. Cemetery
Bayamon 00620
South Carolina
Beaufort Natl. Cemetery
Beaufort 29904
Florence Natl. Cemetery
Florence 29501
South Dakota
Black Hills Natl. Cemetery
Sturgis 57785
Tennessee
Chattanooga Natl. Cemetery
Chattanooga 37401
Knoxville Natl. Cemetery
Knoxville 37917
Memphis Natl. Cemetery
Memphis 38122
Nashville Natl. Cemetery
Madison 37115
Texas
Fort Bliss Natl. Cemetery
Fort Bliss 79906
Fort Sam Houston Natl. Cemetery
San Antonio 78209
San Antonio Natl. Cemetery
San Antonio 78202
Virginia
Alexandria Natl. Cemetery
Alexandria 22314
*Arlington Natl. Cemetery
Arlington 22211
Contains Tomb of the Unknown Soldier.
(continued)

Balls Bluff Natl. Cemetery
  Leesburg 22075
City Point Natl. Cemetery
  Hopewell 23800
Cold Harbor Natl. Cemetery
  Mechanicsville 23111

Culpeper Natl. Cemetery
  Culpeper 22701
Danville Natl. Cemetery
  Danville 24541
Fort Harrison Natl.
  Cemetery
  Richmond 23231

Glendale Natl. Cemetery
  Richmond 23231
Hampton Natl. Cemetery
  Hampton 23369
Richmond Natl. Cemetery
  Richmond 23231
Seven Pines Natl. Cemetery
  Sandston 23150

Staunton Natl. Cemetery
  Staunton 24401
Winchester Natl. Cemetery
  Winchester 22601
West Virginia
Grafton Natl. Cemetery
  Grafton 26354

Debt Owed U.S. Arising from World War I

Source: Treasury Department (June 30, 1973)

Country	Original Indebtedness	Interest thru June 30, 1972	Cumulative Payments		Unmatured Principal	Principal and Interest due and unpaid
			Principal	Interest		
Armenia.....	$11,959,917.49	$32,175,040.29	$32.49	$	$	$44,134,925.29
Austria¹.....	26,843,148.66	44,058.93	862,668.00	....	....	26,024,539.50
Belgium.....	419,837,630.37	368,780,720.47	19,157,630.37	33,033,642.87	156,780,000.00	579,647,077.60
Cuba.......	10,000,000.00	2,286,751.58	10,000,000.00	2,286,751.58	....	....
Czechoslov...	185,071,023.07	138,585,089.09	19,829,914.17	304,178.09	67,740,000.00	235,781,938.90
Estonia.....	16,466,012.87	25,304,960.01	10.66	1,248,432.07	6,600,000.00	33,922,530.15
Finland......	8,999,999.97	12,337,320.96	5,550,099.97²	12,337,320.96²	3,449,000.00	....
France......	4,089,689,588.18	4,046,328,302.14	226,039,588.18	260,036,302.82	1,435,303,603.57	6,214,638,395.75
Great Britain..	4,802,181,641.56	7,891,531,958.11	434,181,641.56	1,590,672,656.18	1,789,000,000.00	8,879,859,301.93
Greece......	34,319,843.67	5,045,224.32	1,398,868.34³	4,701,575.79	19,565,975.33³	13,698,648.53
Hungary⁴.....	1,982,555.50	3,173,639.66	73,995.50	482,924.26	822,590.00	3,776,635.40
Italy........	2,042,364,319.28	444,456,220.22	37,464,319.28	63,365,560.88	945,900,000.00	1,440,090,659.34
Latvia.......	6,888,664.20	10,685,968.91	9,200.00	752,349.07	2,790,200.00	14,022,884.04
Liberia......	26,000.00	10,471.56	26,000.00	10,471.56	....	....
Lithuania....	6,432,465.00	9,905,518.12	234,783.00	1,003,173.58	2,777,467.00	12,322,559.54
Nicaragua⁵....	141,950.36	26,625.48	141,950.36	26,625.48	....	....
Poland......	207,344,297.37	322,437,184.38	1,287,297.37⁶	21,359,000.18	87,784,000.00	419,351,184.20
Romania.....	68,359,192.45	62,152,382.42	4,498,632.02⁷	292,375.20⁷	25,870,000.00	99,850,567.65
Russia.......	192,601,297.37	533,870,068.67	....	8,750,311.88⁸	....	717,721,054.16
Yugoslavia....	63,577,712.55	38,766,527.92	1,952,712.55	636,059.14	28,679,000.00	710,764,668.78
Totals....	**12,195,087,259.92**	**13,947,903,952.24**	**762,710,244.32**	**2,001,299,711.59**	**4,573,061,835.90**	**18,805,919,420.85**

(1.) The Federal Republic of Germany has recognized liability for securities falling due between March 12, 1938 and May 8, 1945.
(2.) $8,480,090.26 has been made available for educational exchange programs with Finland pursuant to 22 U.S.C. 2455 (e).
(3.) Includes $13,155,921.00 refunded by the agreement of May 28, 1964. The agreement was ratified by Congress November 5, 1966.
(4.) Interest payments from December 15, 1932 to June 15, 1937 were paid in pengo equivalent.
(5.) The indebtedness of Nicaragua was canceled pursuant to the agreement of April 14, 1938.
(6.) Excludes claim allowance of $1,813,428.69 dated December 15, 1969.
(7.) Excludes payment of $100,000.00 on June 14, 1940 as a token of good faith.
(8.) Principally proceeds from liquidation of Russian assets in the United States.
(9.) Includes $12,813,601.32 on agreement of May 28, 1964.

Peak Strength of Armed Forces: Battle Deaths in World War II

Allies and Associated Powers

Country	Strength	Deaths	Country	Strength	Deaths
Australia...............	680,000	23,365	New Zealand...........	157,000	10,033
Belgium...............	650,000	7,760	Norway...............	45,000	1,000
Canada...............	780,000	37,476	Poland...............	1,000,000	320,000
China.................	5,000,000	¹2,200,000	So. Africa, Union of.......	140,000	6,840
Denmark..............	25,000	3,006	United Kingdom.........	5,120,000	244,723
France................	5,000,000	210,671	United States...........	12,300,000	291,557
Greece................	414,000	²73,700	USSR.................	12,500,000	7,500,000
India.................	2,150,000	24,338	Yugoslavia.............	500,000	410,000
Netherlands...........	410,000	6,238			

(1.) 1937-1945 against Japan. (2.) Includes 50,000 killed in guerrilla warfare.

Other Powers that Declared War on Axis

Country	Strength	Country	Strength	Country	Strength	Country	Strength
Albania.......	25,000	Czechoslovakia.	150,000	Honduras......	3,500	Paraguay......	10,000
Argentina......	160,000	Dom. Republic..	5,000	Iran...........	120,000	Peru..........	40,000
Bolivia........	10,000	Ecuador.......	9,000	Iraq...........	47,000	Philippines....	200,000
Brazil.........	200,000	Egypt.........	54,000	Liberia........	1,000	Turkey........	850,000
Chile.........	60,000	El Salvador.....	3,500	Luxembourg....	1,000	Uruguay.......	11,000
Colombia......	19,000	Ethiopia.......	38,000	Mexico........	70,000	Venezuela.....	15,000
Costa Rica.....	500	Guatemala.....	6,000	Nicaragua.....	3,500		
Cuba.........	20,000	Haiti.........	4,000	Forces engaged and losses, if any, not available.			

Axis

Country	Strength	Deaths	Country	Strength	Deaths
Bulgaria..............	450,000	10,000	Italy.................	3,750,000	*77,494
Finland...............	250,000	82,000	Japan................	6,095,000	1,219,000
Germany (inc. Austria)....	10,200,000	3,500,000	Romania..............	600,000	300,000
Hungary..............	350,000	140,000	*Includes 17,494 on Allied side.		

The Flag of the United States—The Stars and Stripes

The 50-star flag of the United States was raised for the first time officially at 12:01 a.m. on July 4, 1960, at Fort McHenry National Monument in Baltimore, Md. The 50th star had been added for Hawaii; a year earlier the 49th, for Alaska. Before that, no star had been added since 1912, when N. M. and Ariz. were admitted to the Union.

History of the Flag

The true history of the Stars and Stripes has become so cluttered by a volume of myth and tradition that the facts are difficult, and in some cases impossible, to establish. For example, it is not certain who designed the Stars and Stripes, who made the first such flag, or even whether it ever flew in any sea fight or land battle of the American Revolution.

One thing all agree on is that the Stars and Stripes originated as the result of a resolution offered by the Marine Committee of the Second Continental Congress at Philadelphia and adopted June 14, 1777. It read:

Resolved: that the flag of the United States be thirteen stripes, alternate red and white; that the union be thirteen stars, white in a blue field, representing a new constellation.

Congress gave no hint as to the designer of the flag, no instructions as to the arrangement of the stars, and no information on its appropriate uses. Historians have been unable to find the original flag law.

The resolution establishing the flag was not even published until Sept. 2, 1777, more than 11 weeks after its passage. Despite repeated requests by the American commander, Gen. George Washington, for the "Standard of the United States" for his army, he did not get the flags until 1783, after the Revolutionary War was over. And there is no certainty that they were the Stars and Stripes.

Early Flags

Although it was never officially adopted by the Continental Congress, many historians consider the first flag of the United States to have been the Grand Union (sometimes called Great Union) flag. This was a modification of the British Meteor flag, which had the red cross of St. George and the white cross of St. Andrew combined in the blue canton. For the Grand Union flag, 6 horizontal stripes were imposed on the red field, dividing it into 13 alternate red and white stripes. On Jan. 1, 1776, when the Continental Army came into formal existence, this flag was unfurled on Prospect Hill, Somerville, Mass. Washington wrote that "we hoisted the Union Flag in compliment to the United Colonies."

One of several flags about which controversy has raged for years is at Easton, Pa. Containing the devices of the national flag in reversed order, this has been in the public library at Easton for over 150 years. Supporters of the movement contend that this flag was actually the first Stars and Stripes, and that it was first displayed on July 8, 1776, on the occasion of the public reading of the Declaration of Independence at the court house in Easton. This flag has 13 red and white stripes in the canton, 13 white stars centered in a blue field.

A flag was hastily improvised from garments by the defenders of Fort Schuyler at Rome, N.Y., Aug. 3-22, 1777, and this has led to the assumption that it was the Stars and Stripes. Historians believe it was the Grand Union Flag.

The Sons of Liberty had a flag of 9 red and white stripes, to signify 9 colonies, when they met in New York in 1765 to oppose the Stamp Tax. By 1775 the flag had grown to 13 red and white stripes, with a rattlesnake on it.

At Concord, Apr. 19, 1775, the minute men from Bedford, Mass., are said to have carried a flag having a silver arm with sword on a red field.

At Cambridge, Mass., the Sons of Liberty used a plain red flag with a green pine tree on it.

In June, 1775, Washington went from Philadelphia to Boston to take command of the army, escorted to New York by the Philadelphia Light Horse Troop. It carried a yellow flag which had an elaborate coat of arms — the shield charged with 13 knots, the motto "For These We Strive" — and a canton of 13 blue and silver stripes.

In February, 1776, Col. Cristopher Gadsden, member of the Continental Congress, gave the South Carolina Provincial Congress a flag "such as is to be used by the commander-in-chief of the American Navy." It had a yellow field, with a rattlesnake about to strike and the words Don't Tread on Me. Benjamin Franklin's paper, the Pennsylvania Gazette, had suggested sending rattlesnakes to London to retaliate for British injustice.

At the battle of Bennington, Aug. 16, 1777, patriots used a flag of 7 white and 6 red stripes with a blue canton extending down 9 stripes and showing an arch of 11 white stars over the figure 76 and a star in each of the upper corners. The stars are seven-pointed. This flag is preserved in the Historical Museum at Bennington, Vt.

At the Battle of Cowpens, Jan. 17, 1781, the 3rd Maryland Regt. is said to have carried a flag of 13 red and white stripes, with a blue canton containing 12 stars in a circle around one star.

Legends about the Flag

Who Designed the Flag? No one knows for a certainty. Francis Hopkinson, a signer of the Declaration of Independence and designer of seals for the State Department, the Treasury Board and of a naval flag, declared he also had designed the flag and in 1781 asked Congress to reimburse him for his services. Congress did not do so. Dumas Malone of Columbia Univ. wrote: "This talented man . . . designed the American flag."

Who Called the Flag Old Glory? — The flag is said to have been named Old Glory by William Driver, a sea captain of Salem, Mass. One legend has it that when he raised the flag on his brig, the Charles Doggett, in 1824, he said: "I name thee Old Glory." But his daughter, who presented the flag to the Smithsonian Institution, said he named it at his 21st birthday celebration Mar. 17, 1824, when his mother presented the homemade flag to him.

Washington Coat-of-Arms Legend — The idea that the flag was suggested by Washington's coat of arms was publicized by Martin F. Tupper, an English writer, in a play in the 1870s. It rests on a coincidence and has no validity.

Washington's Invocation Legend — Circulation has been given to this speech attributed to General Washington: "We take the stars from heaven, the red from our mother country, separating it by white stripes, thus showing that we have separated from her, and the white stripes shall go down to posterity representing liberty." There is no proof that Washington ever said this.

The Betsy Ross Legend — The widely publicized legend that Mrs. Betsy Ross made the first Stars and Stripes in June, 1776, at the request of a committee composed of George Washington, Robert Morris and George Ross, an uncle, was first made public in 1870 by a grandson of Mrs. Ross. Historians have been unable to find a historical record of such a meeting or committee. Dr. Milo Milton Quaife wrote: "No record has ever been found of the creation by Mrs. Ross of the first Stars and Stripes." The New Century Cyclopedia of Names (1954) says: "There is documentary evidence that she was paid in May, 1777, for 'making ships colours, etc.' but no direct documentary evidence has been found to link her with the flag adopted by the Continental Congress on June, 14, 1777, as the national emblem, and most historians now doubt if she made it."

Adding New Stars

The flag of 1777 was used until 1795. Then, on the admission of Vermont and Kentucky to the Union, Congress passed and President Washington signed an act that after May 1, 1795, the flag should have 15 stripes, alternate red and white, and 15 white stars on a blue field in the union.

When new states were admitted it became evident that the flag would become burdened with stripes. Congress thereupon ordered that after July 4, 1818, the flag should have 13 stripes, symbolizing the 13 original states; that the union have 20 stars, and that whenever a new state was admitted a new star should be added on the July 4 following its admission. No law designates the permanent arrangement of the stars. However, since 1912 when a new state has been admitted, the new design has been announced by executive order. No star is specifically identified with any state.

Code of Etiquette for Display and Use of the U.S. Flag

Although the Stars and Stripes originated in 1777, it was not until 146 years later that there was a serious attempt to establish a uniform code of etiquette for the United States flag. The War Department issued Feb. 15, 1923, a circular on the rules of flag usage. These were adopted almost in their entirety June 14, 1923, by a conference of 68 patriotic organizations in Washington. Finally, on June 22, 1942, a joint resolution of Congress codified "existing rules and customs pertaining to the flag for civilians."

When to Display the Flag—The flag should be displayed on all days when the weather permits, especially on legal holidays and other special occasions, on official buildings when in use, in or near polling places on election days, and in or near schools when in session. A citizen may fly the flag at any time he wishes. It is customary to display the flag only from sunrise to sunset on buildings and on stationary flagstaffs in the open. However, it may be displayed at night on special occasions, preferably lighted. In Washington, the flag now flies over the White House both day and night. It flies over the Senate wing of the Capitol when the Senate is in session and over the House wing when that body is in session. It flies day and night over the east and west fronts of the Capitol, without floodlights at night but receiving light from the illuminated Capitol Dome. It flies 24 hours a day at several other places, including the Fort McHenry Nat'l Monument in Baltimore, where it inspired Francis Scott Key to write The Star Spangled Banner.

How to Fly the Flag—The flag should be hoisted briskly and lowered ceremoniously, and should never be allowed to touch the ground or the floor. When hung over a sidewalk from a rope extending from a building to a pole, the union should be away from the building. When hung over the center of a street it should have the union to the north in an east-west street and to the east in a north-south street. No other flag may be flown above or, if on the same level, to the right of the United States flag, except that at the United Nations Headquarters the UN flag may be placed above flags of all member nations and other national flags may be flown with equal prominence or honor with the flag of the United States. At services by Navy chaplains at sea, the church pennant may be flown above the flag.

When two flags are placed against a wall with crossed staffs, the U.S. flag should be at right—its own right, and its staff should be in front of the staff of the other flag; when a number of flags are grouped and displayed from staffs, it should be at the center and highest point of the group.

Church and Platform Use—In an auditorium, the flag may be displayed flat, above and behind the speaker. If on a staff in a church chancel or on a speaker's platform, it should be in the position of honor at the clergyman's or speaker's right as he faces the congregation or audience. Any other flag in the chancel or on the platform should be displayed at the clergyman's or speaker's left. If elsewhere than in chancel or on platform, the flag should be displayed at the right of the congregation or audience as they face the speaker.

When the flag is displayed horizontally or vertically against a wall, the stars should be at the observer's left.

When to Salute the Flag—All persons present should face the flag, stand at attention and salute on the following occasions: (1) When the flag is passing in a parade or in a review, (2) During the ceremony of hoisting or lowering, (3) When the National Anthem is played and the flag is dis-

played, and (4) During the pledge of allegiance. Those present in uniform should render the military salute. When not in uniform men should remove the hat with the right hand holding it at the left shoulder, the hand being over the heart. Men without hats should salute in the same manner. Aliens should stand at attention. Women should salute by placing the right hand over the heart.

On Memorial Day, May 30, the flag should fly at half-staff until noon, then be raised to the peak.

As provided by Presidential proclamation the flag should fly at half-staff for 30 days from the day of a death of a President or former President; for 10 days from the day of death of a Vice President, Chief Justice or retired Chief Justice of the U.S., or Speaker of the House of Representatives; from day of death until burial of an Associate Justice of the Supreme Court, Cabinet member, former Vice President, or Senate President pro tempore, Majority or Minority Senate Leader, or Majority or Minority House Leader; for a U.S. Senator, Representative, Territorial Delegate, or the Resident Commissioner of Puerto Rico, on day of death and the following day within the metropolitan area of the District of Columbia and from day of death until burial within the decedent's state, Congressional district, territory or commonwealth; and for the death of the governor of a state, territory or possession of the U.S., from day of death until burial within that state, territory or possession.

When used to cover a casket, the flag should be placed so that the union is at the head and over the left shoulder. It should not be lowered into the grave nor touch the ground.

Prohibited Uses of the Flag—The flag should not be dipped to any person or thing. It should never be displayed with the union down save as a distress signal. It should never be carried flat or horizontally, but always aloft and free.

It should not be displayed on a float, motor car or boat except from a staff.

It should never be used as a covering for a ceiling, nor have placed upon it any word, design, or drawing. It should never be used as a receptacle for carrying anything. It should not be used to cover a statue or a monument.

The flag should never be used for advertising purposes, nor be embroidered on such articles as cushions or handkerchiefs, printed or otherwise impressed on boxes or used as a costume or athletic uniform. Advertising signs should not be fastened to its staff or halyard.

The flag should never be used as drapery of any sort, never festooned, drawn back, nor up, in folds, but always allowed to fall free. Bunting of blue, white and red always arranged with the blue above and the white in the middle, should be used for covering a speaker's desk, draping the front of a platform, and for decoration in general.

An Act of Congress approved Feb. 8, 1917 provided certain penalties for the desecration, mutilation or improper use of the flag within the District of Columbia. A 1968 Federal law provided penalties of up to a year's imprisonment or a $1,000 fine or both, for publicly burning or otherwise desecrating any flag of the United States. In addition, many states have laws against flag desecration.

How to Dispose of Worn Flags—The flag, when it is in such condition that it is no longer a fitting emblem for display, should be destroyed in a dignified way, preferably by burning in private.

Pledge of Allegiance to the Flag

I pledge allegiance to the flag of the United States of America and to the republic for which it stands, one nation under God, indivisible, with liberty and justice for all.

This, the current official version of the Pledge of Allegiance, has developed from the original pledge, which was first published in the Sept. 8, 1892, issue of the Youth's Companion, a weekly magazine then published in Boston. The original pledge contained the phrase "my flag," which was changed more than 30 years later to "flag of the United States of America." An act of Congress in 1954 added the words "under God."

The authorship of the pledge has been in dispute for

many years. The Youths Companion stated in 1917 that the original draft was written by James B. Upham, an executive of the magazine who died in 1910. A leaflet circulated by the magazine later named Upham as the originator of the draft "afterwards condensed and perfected by him and his associates of the Companion force."

Francis Bellamy, a former member of the Youth's Companion editorial staff, publicly claimed authorship of the pledge in 1923. The United States Flag Assn., acting on the advice of a committee named to study the controversy, upheld in 1939 the claim of Bellamy, who had died 8 years earlier. The Library of Congress issued in 1957 a report attributing the authorship to Bellamy.

AFGHANISTAN

ALBANIA

ALGERIA

ANDORRA

ARGENTINA

AUSTRALIA

AUSTRIA

BAHAMAS

BAHRAIN

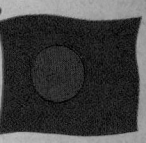

BANGLADESH

BARBADOS

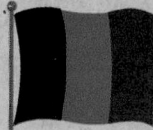

BELGIUM

BHUTAN

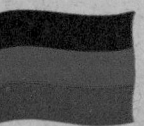

BOLIVIA

BOTSWANA

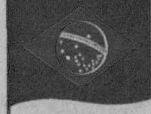

BRAZIL

BULGARIA

BURMA

BURUNDI

CAMBODIA

CAMEROON

CANADA

CENTRAL AFRICAN
REPUBLIC

CHAD

CHILE

CHINA (MAINLAND)

CHINA (TAIWAN)

COLOMBIA

CONGO

COSTA RICA

CUBA

CYPRUS

CZECHOSLOVAKIA

DAHOMEY

DENMARK

DOMINICAN REPUBLIC

ECUADOR

EGYPT

EL SALVADOR

EQUATORIAL GUINEA

482

Flags shown are *national* flags in common use and vary slightly from official *state* flags, most particularly by omitting coats of arms in some cases.

ETHIOPIA	FIJI	FINLAND	FRANCE	GABON
GAMBIA	GERMAN DEM. REP.	GERMANY, FED. REP. OF	GHANA	GREECE
GRENADA	GUATEMALA	GUINEA	GUYANA	HAITI
HONDURAS	HUNGARY	ICELAND	INDIA	INDONESIA
IRAN	IRAQ	IRELAND	ISRAEL	ITALY
IVORY COAST	JAMAICA	JAPAN	JORDAN	KENYA
KOREA, NORTH	KOREA, SOUTH	KUWAIT	LAOS	LEBANON

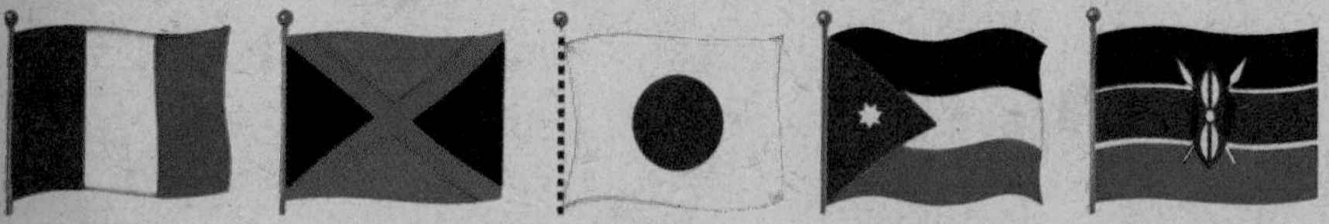

LESOTHO

LIBERIA

LIBYA

LIECHTENSTEIN

483

LUXEMBOURG MADAGASCAR MALAWI MALAYSIA MALDIVES

MALI MALTA MAURITANIA MAURITIUS MEXICO

MONACO MONGOLIA MOROCCO NAURU NEPAL

NETHERLANDS NEW ZEALAND NICARAGUA NIGER NIGERIA

NORWAY OMAN PAKISTAN PANAMA PARAGUAY

PERU PHILIPPINES POLAND PORTUGAL QATAR

RHODESIA ROMANIA RWANDA SAN MARINO SAUDI ARABIA

SENEGAL SIERRA LEONE SINGAPORE SOMALIA

484

SOUTH AFRICA	SPAIN	SRI LANKA	SUDAN
SWAZILAND	SWEDEN	SWITZERLAND	SYRIA
TANZANIA	THAILAND	TOGO	TONGA
TRINIDAD & TOBAGO	TUNISIA	TURKEY	UGANDA
U.S.S.R.	UNITED ARAB EMIRATES	UNITED KINGDOM	UNITED STATES
UPPER VOLTA	URUGUAY	VATICAN CITY	VENEZUELA
VIETNAM, NORTH	VIETNAM, SOUTH	WESTERN SAMOA	YEMEN
YEMEN, P.D.R. OF	YUGOSLAVIA	ZAIRE	ZAMBIA

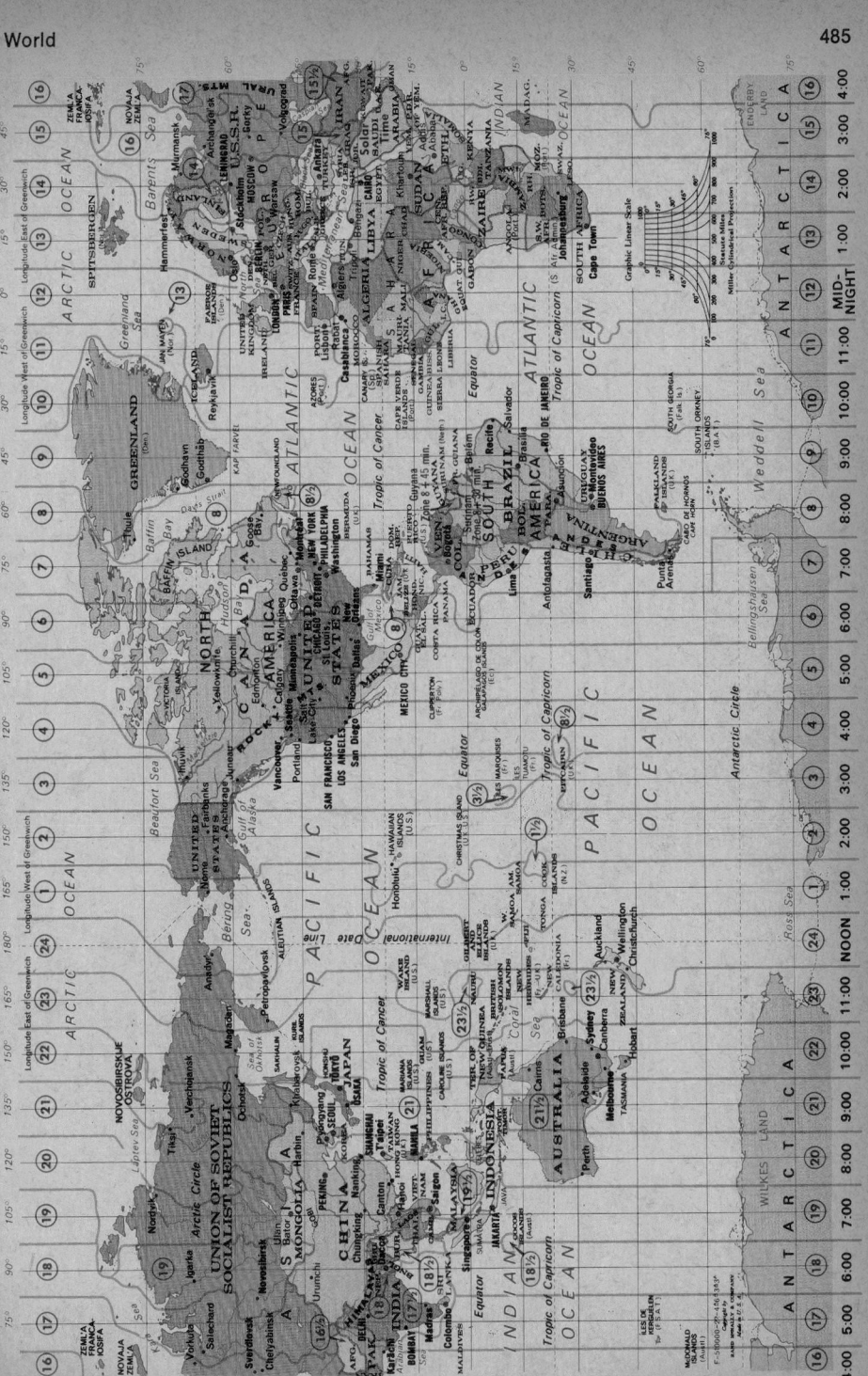

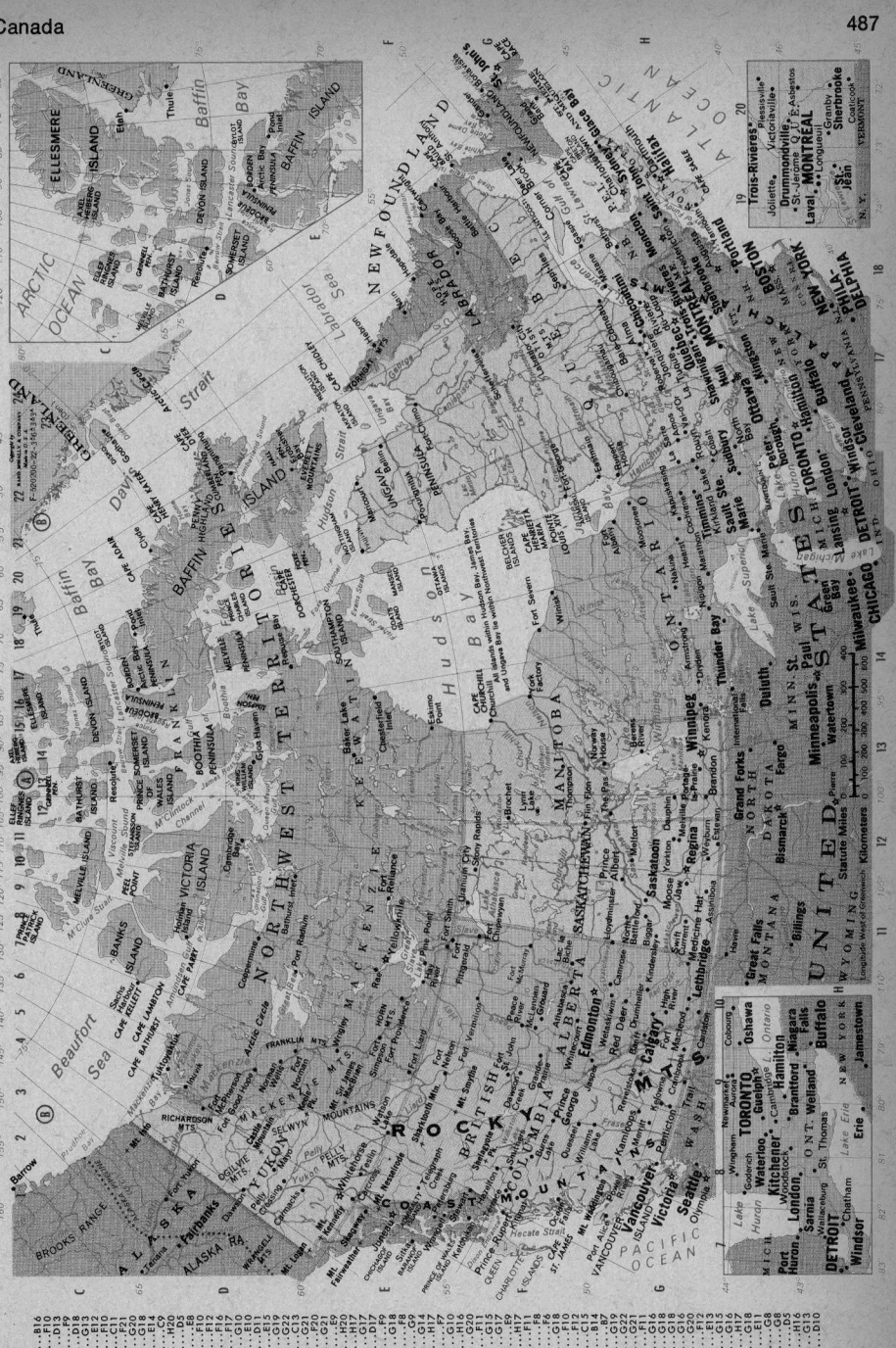

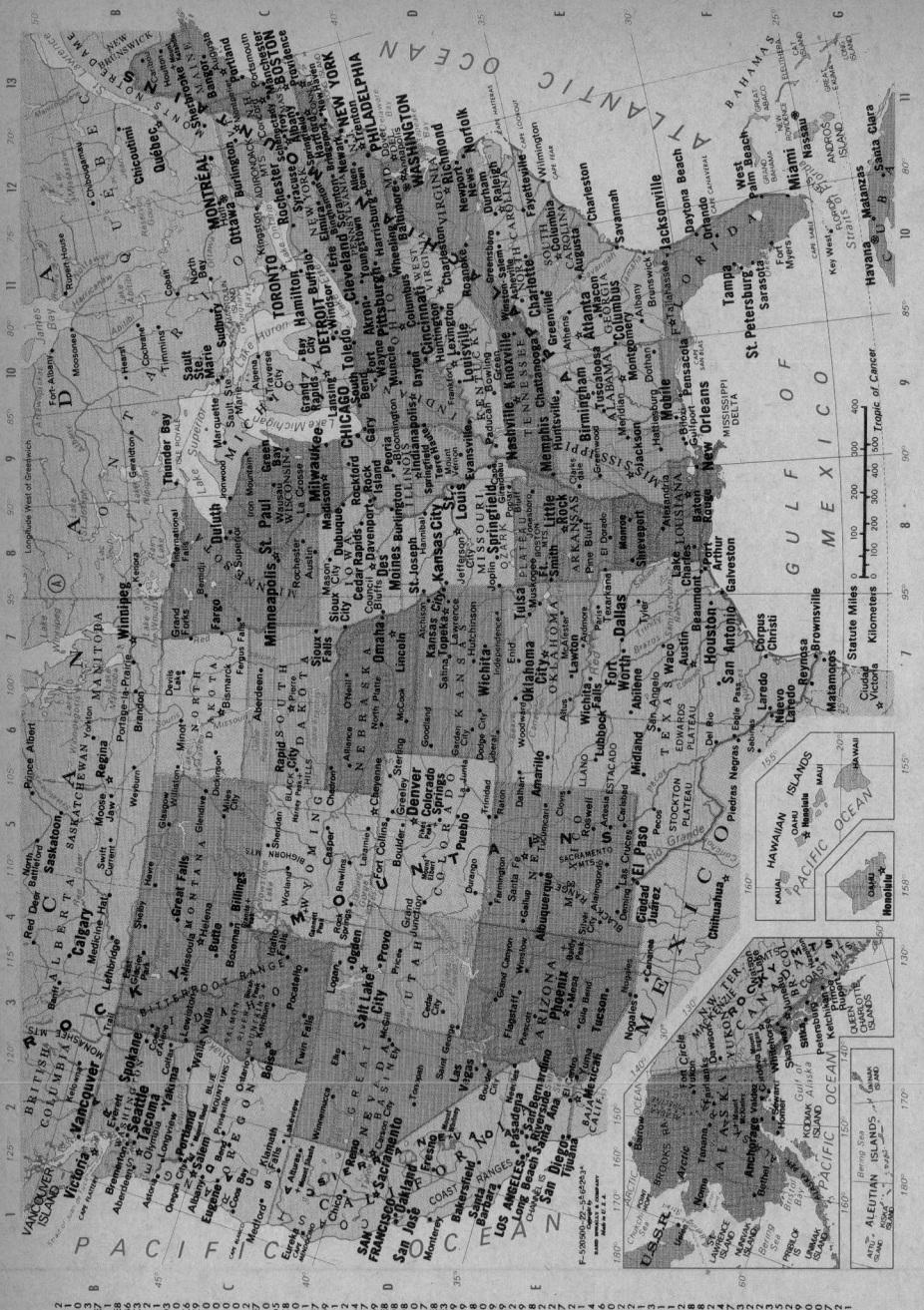

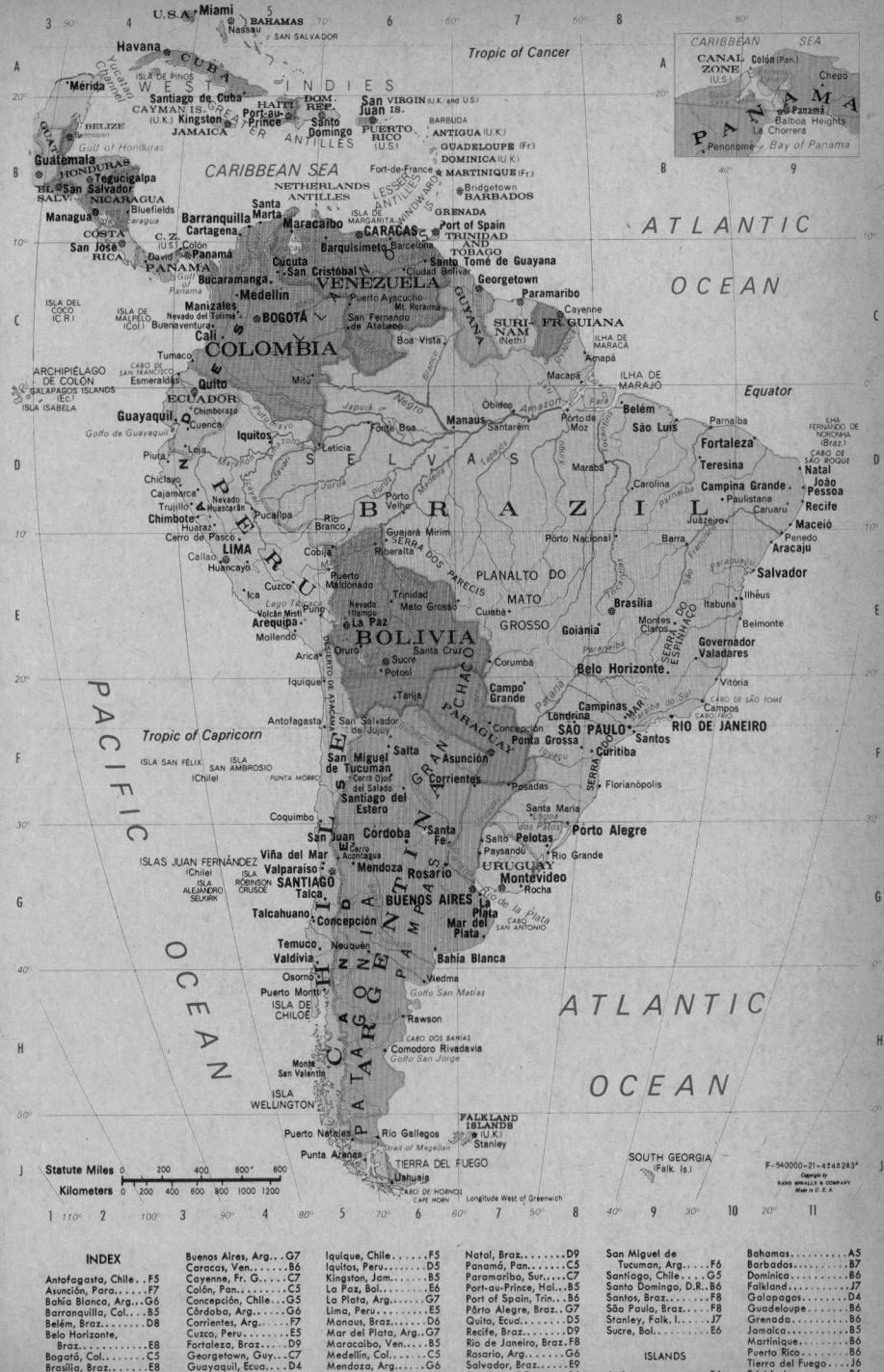

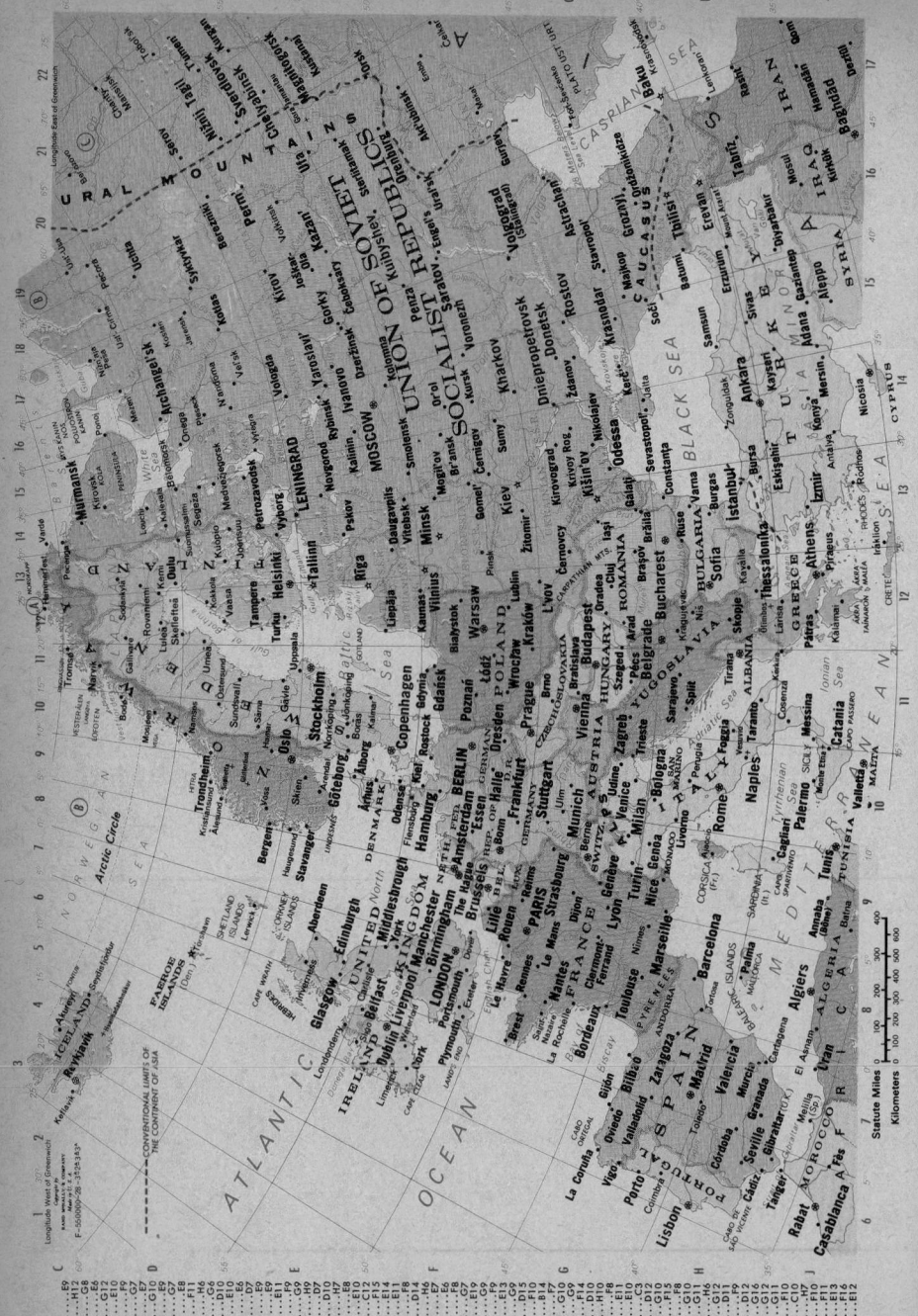

Statute Miles 0 300 600 900 1200
Kilometers 0 300 600 900 1200 1500 1800

Longitude West of Greenwich   Longitude East of Greenwich

F-560000-21-9586383²

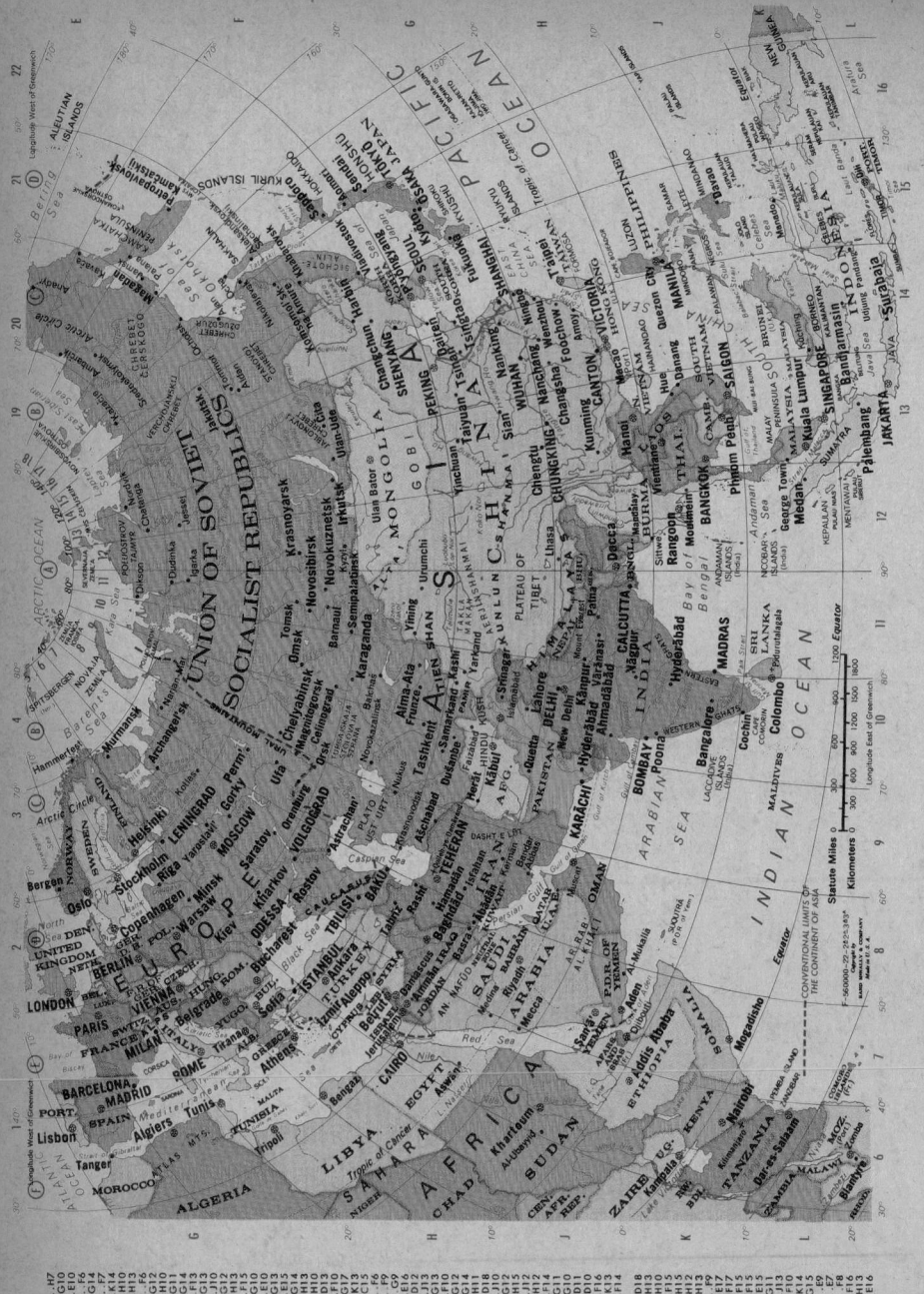

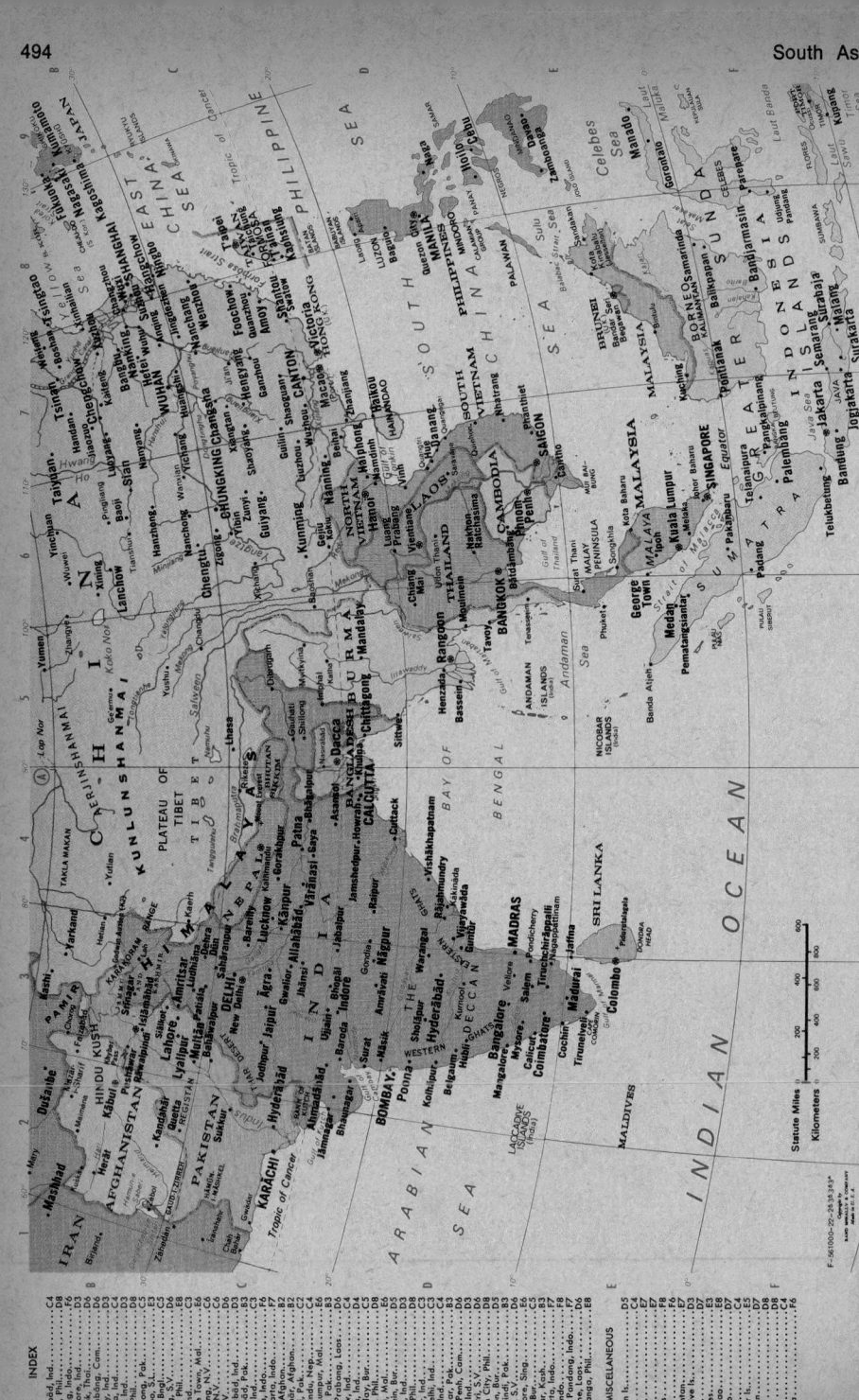

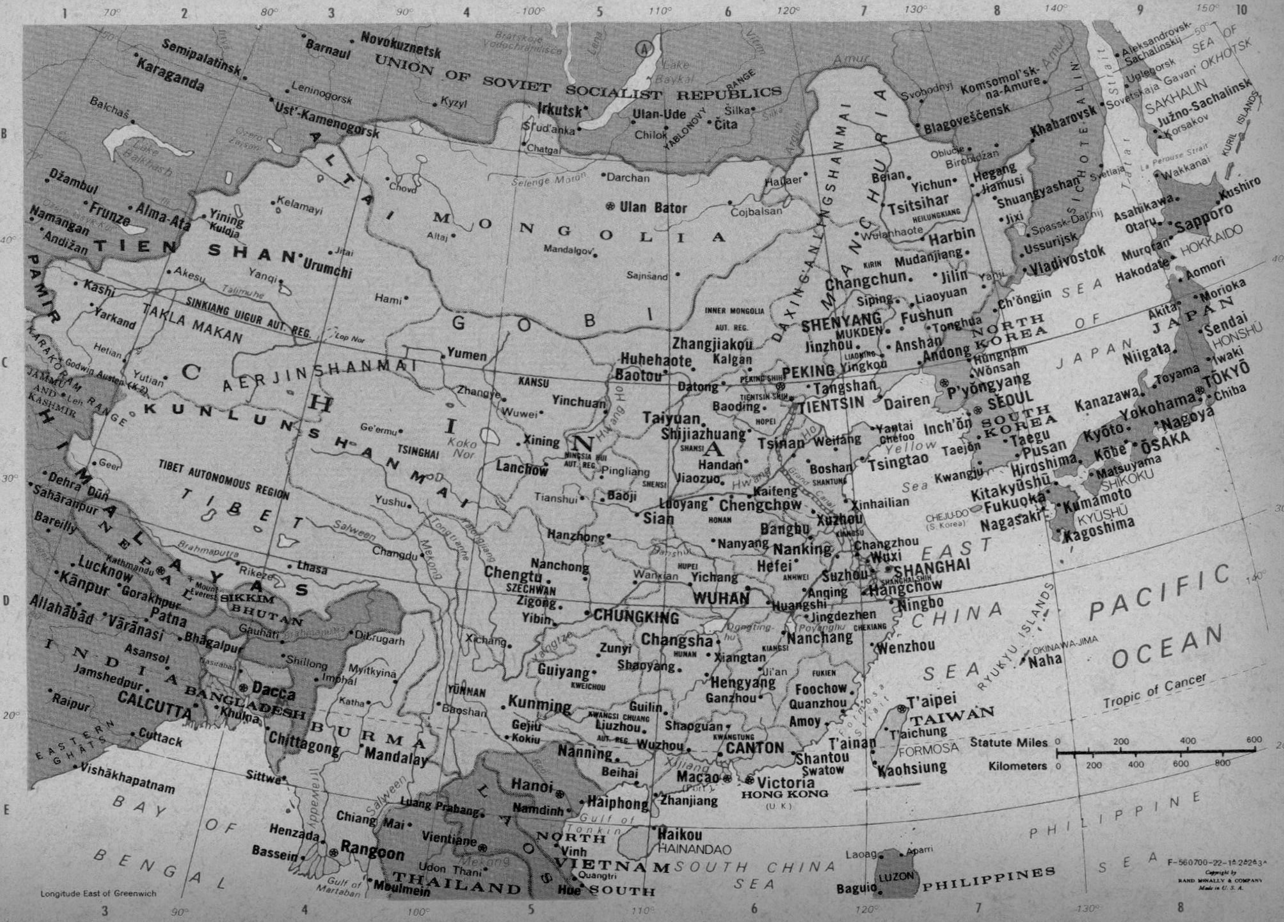

INDEX

PROVINCES OF CHINA

CANADA

See Index for Calgary, Edmonton, Halifax, Hamilton, Kitchener-Waterloo, Lethbridge, London, Montreal, Ottawa, Quebec, Regina, Saskatoon, Toronto, Vancouver, Windsor, Winnipeg.

Capital: Ottawa. Area, 3,851,809 sq. mi. Population (Govt. est., April, 1973) 22,047,000. Monetary unit: Canadian dollar.

Liberals Regain Majority

Prime Minister Pierre Trudeau's Liberals, who almost lost the 1972 election and formed a minority government during the 29th Parliament, galloped to a majority victory in the July 8, 1974, election, capturing 141 of the 264 seats with 43% of the popular vote. The Liberals' surprising win was based on massive support from the 2 largest provinces, Ontario and Quebec. The Liberals won 55 out of 88 seats in Ontario, a gain of 19, and 60 out of 74 in Quebec, an increase of 4. Liberal representation increased slightly in some other provinces. The government gained 1 seat in each of Newfoundland, Nova Scotia, and New Brunswick, 2 in Saskatchewan, and 4 in British Columbia. The opposition Conservatives won 95, the NDP 16, Creditistes 11, with 1 Independent. Few experts predicted such a big Liberal sweep, most pundits forcasting another minority government which could be Conservative.

During the previous Liberal minority government, the New Democratic Party (NDP), Canada's oldest and largest third party, helped keep the Liberals in power for 16 months, but they joined the opposition Progressive Conservatives to defeat the government on its budget, complaining that it did not solve the problem of inflation.

Inflation was the biggest issue in the election. Conservative Leader Robert Stanfield campaigned chiefly on his proposal for a temporary income and price freeze, followed by perhaps as much as 2 years of price and wage controls, the controls to be negotiated with the provinces, labor and business. Conservative ranks were divided on the policy and the Liberals capitalized on the split in the party.

The NDP also attacked the Conservative proposal for dealing with inflation, urging instead a powerful National Prices Control Board with the power to investigate and to stop or roll back unjustified price increases. NDP Leader, David Lewis, was also a strong advocate of a two-price system that would set the domestic price lower than the export price as is currently the situation with Canadian oil.

The Liberals rejected the opposition's measures for curbing inflation, and from the election results, so did the voters. Conservative losses have been attributed to the firm stand Mr. Stanfield took on the wage-price freeze and control issue. The NDP lost nearly half its seats in Parliament, including that of its leader. The Creditistes also lost heavily. Voters elected 9 women to the 30th Parliament.

The Economy

In 1974 Canada's economy registered the fastest real growth rate of any major industrial country. The expected growth rate (excluding inflation) for the Canadian gross national product was between 4.5 and 5 per cent, a slowdown from the extremely rapid 6.8% rate in 1973. Growth during the first quarter of 1974 compared favorably with growth in the same period in the preceding year. In the first quarter the Canadian economy performed well on almost all national economic indicators. Current dollar gross national product grew at an annual rate of 17.3% in Canada, compared with 8.8% in the United States.

Real GNP grew by 7.6% in Canada, compared with 0.1% in the United States. Price inflation was 9.7% in Canada and 8.7% in the United States. The Canadian economy outdistanced the U.S. economy in various sectors, including industrial production, retail trade and housing starts.

However, while the Canadian economy remained buoyant in the first quarter, it was expected to register a slump in the second quarter. Economic growth was predicted to be on an erratic course in 1974. Factors contributing to the economic decline in the second quarter were fewer housing starts due to record high mortgage rates and lack of mortgage funds. But the heaviest setback to the economy was the declining trade balance. Exports were not rising as fast as imports. Canada exports one-quarter of its production and is highly vulnerable to an economic slump in foreign countries.

Higher rates of unemployment were one ill effect of the drop in economic activity during the second quarter. The unemployment rate at the end of the first quarter was 5.4%, although this compared favorably with the figure for the same period in 1973.

Corporate profits showed a healthy increase of about 38.7% but growth was slower than the preceding year.

Inflation offset the benefits gained by increased incomes. Average weekly wages and salaries of individual wage earners increased to $170.65 by March 1974, up from $157.09 for the same period in 1973. But the gain was wiped out by the rising prices of consumer goods. The consumer price index recorded its highest 12-month gain in 23 years in June 1974, having increased by 11.4%. The largest increase was in food prices.

Foreign Relations

Canada's foreign relations have been altered significantly since the Trudeau government came to power first in 1968. The prime minister has put less stock in the traditional links with Western Europe and the U. S. and fostered closer relations with Far Eastern countries such as Japan and China. In mid-summer, 1973, the prime minister announced he would visit China in the autumn.

Mr. Trudeau has also reduced Canada's NATO commitments, trimmed the size of the armed forces, and insisted on establishing Canadian sovereignty in the Arctic. The government's reservations about peacekeeping were supported by the Canadian people when, after reluctantly providing troops for the international truce force in Vietnam, the Canadian government found its experience frustrating and pulled its troops out.

Since the U. S. is the country most involved in Canadian affairs, Canadian nationalism often smacks of anti-Americanism. There have been growing demands for limits on American ownership of Canadian industries and resources, for curbs on American investment, which now amounts to more than $24 billion, and for restraints on the importation of American culture.

The Land

Canada is the world's second largest country in land size, extending south from the North Pole to the U.S. border and including all the islands of the Arctic from near Greenland to near the Alaskan border. Its seacoast, one of the longest in the world, includes 17,-860 miles of mainland and 41,810 miles of islands.

A great sweep of the nation, stretching across the northern territories and prairies through northern Ontario and Quebec down to the Atlantic provinces, is known as the Canadian Shield, where past ice ages scraped most soil and vegetation off the land. This is the world's oldest surface rock, and it is here that most Canadian mineral discoveries have been made.

Canada's continental climate, while generally temperate, can run to freezing cold and blistering heat. The range is well beyond 100 degrees Fahrenheit.

History
French explorer Jacques Cartier is generally regarded as the founder of Canada. But his 1534 exploration of the Gulf of St. Lawrence followed by 37 years the sighting of Newfoundland in 1497 by English seaman John Cabot. Centuries prior to that, increasing evidence shows, Vikings had reached Newfoundland and Canada's Atlantic coast.

France pioneered Canadian settlement and the French have multiplied to become about 27% of the Canadian population today. Quebec was settled as early as 1608, Montreal in 1642; New France was declared a colony in 1663.

Britain and France clashed in Canada as a result of European rivalries and British expansion in America. Britain acquired Acadia (later Nova Scotia) in 1713, and captured Quebec in 1759, obtaining control of the rest of New France in 1763. The Quebec Act in 1774 gave the French rights to their own language, religion, and civil law. This was one reason why the French-Canadian settlers did not join American colonists in the War of Independence.

During the American Revolution, many former colonials moved north to settle in Canada, proudly calling themselves United Empire Loyalists.

The fur trade and exploration opened up the western plains and led Canadians across the continent to the Pacific. Alexander Mackenzie scrawled on a rock by the Pacific "From Canada, by land, 1793".

In Upper and Lower Canada (later called Ontario and Quebec) and in the Maritimes, legislative assemblies appeared in the 18th century and reformers called for responsible government. But the War of 1812 with the U.S. intervened. The war ended in a stalemate that was symbolic of the end to armed conflict between Canada and the U.S.

In 1837 political agitation for more democratic government culminated in rebellions in Upper and Lower Canada. The British sent Lord Durham to investigate and, in a famous report, he recommended union of the two parts into one colony called Canada. The union lasted until Confederation brought two additional colonies, Nova Scotia and New Brunswick, to join the new country in 1867. During the period 1840 to 1867, the Canadian colonies won the right to internal self-government.

The Dominion of Canada was launched on July 1, 1867, by the proclamation of the British North America Act, which became the country's written constitution, establishing a federal system of government on the model of a British parliament and cabinet structure under the crown. Canada was proclaimed a self-governing Dominion within the British Empire in 1931. Empire has now given way to Commonwealth, and Canada remains an independent member.

World War I had much to do with the development of Canadian nationhood. The pride it engendered and the industrial base it created in Canada led to the demand for full sovereignty.

But the achievement of nationhood was dulled by the blight of the Great Depression in the 1930s. It took World War II and Canada's accomplishments in it to revive the country's pride and sense of direction. It also fired the furnaces of industry, converting the country into an urban, industrial state.

Industrial Boom
On the Pacific coast a chain of rivers and lakes was reversed to flow backwards through the mountains to power electric generators for the huge aluminum smelters at Kitimat. The Columbia and Kootenay Rivers and Arrow Lakes were dammed to provide electricity. Oil wells and mineral strikes led to an El Dorado. Immense iron ore resources were discovered and developed in the wilds of Labrador. Uranium was unearthed in Northern Ontario and turned into nuclear power.

Canada joined with the U.S. to build the St. Lawrence River Seaway, and Ottawa shared costs with the provinces to complete the Trans-Canada Highway, the longest in the world. Two million immigrants arrived in Canada in the 2 decades after World War II and the country imported a billion dollars a year of foreign capital to finance a new industrial boom.

Economic System
The Canadian economy is a blend of private and public ownership. Despite a long historical tradition of state aid which has been necessary because of Canada's harsh climate and sparse population, private enterprise has flourished. But like Sweden, with which it vies for the second highest standard of living in the world, Canada accepts the idea of state capitalism and collectivism.

Most hydroelectric and many transportation and communication facilities are owned by either federal, provincial, or municipal governments. Air Canada, one of the largest airlines in the world, is a federal crown corporation, while the competing Canadian Pacific airline is privately owned. Canadian National Railways is another crown corporation. Its chief rival is the Canadian Pacific company. The Canadian Broadcasting Corp. is publicly owned, although independently managed. There are also private radio chains and private television networks.

Social Security
Under the British North America Act (1867), the provinces are responsible for welfare programs to benefit their citizens. The federal government helps the provinces bear the cost of welfare programs. Federal payments reimburse up to 50% of the cost of welfare assistance provided by the provinces. Ottawa has also used its fiscal strength to launch the social security system and help bring about a certain uniformity in the existing programs, ensuring a high level of equity in programs among the provinces.

In the mid-1960s the federal government conceived of a universal and compulsory medicare and hospitalization system. Strenuous provincial opposition to the proposals delayed implementation of a revised plan until 1968.

Some changes have been made recently in existing programs. One major change was the increase in the family allowance payments to $20 per child (under 18 years). This replaced the former sliding scale of payments based on age. Another major advance was an increase in the basic old age pension for a single person to $105.30 a month from $100 with a cost of living increase 4 times a year based on the Statistic Canada price index 2 months earlier.

Election Results by Province and Party, July 8, 1974

Province	Total Valid Votes[1]	Liberal	Conservative	New Dem.	Soc. Cred.	Other
Alberta	682,424	168,850	417,320	63,305	22,953	2,848
British Columbia	1,008,797	336,420	423,857	230,587	12,426	5,385
Manitoba	447,248	122,506	213,333	104,981	4,736	1,430
New Brunswick	287,113	135,554	94,894	24,852	8,396	23,417
Newfoundland	173,922	81,318	75,780	16,439	143	242
Nova Scotia	387,254	157,962	183,948	43,432	1,455	457
Ontario	3,565,011	1,609,029	1,252,438	679,976	6,583	13,296
Pr. Edward Isl.	58,253	26,932	28,578	2,666	—	—
Quebec	2,459,045	1,330,280	520,534	162,288	420,099	19,250
Saskatchewan	413,868	127,285	150,856	130,315	4,536	876
N. W. Territories	12,854	3,173	4,271	5,410	—	—
Yukon	8,315	2,784	3,913	1,618	—	—
TOTAL	9,504,104	4,102,093	3,369,722	1,465,869	481,327	67,201
Percent	100.00	43.16	35.46	15.42	5.06	0.71
Seats	264	141	95	16	11	1

[1]Includes 17,892 valid ballots with no vote for a parliamentary candidate.

The Political Parties

Canadian parties, from whatever point in the political spectrum they begin, tend to move to the middle of the road where most of the votes lie. They all take much of the same kind of moderate line.

Conservatives—The oldest party, they have adopted the prefix "Progressive" and moved to the left, advocating farm support programs and endorsing an extension of social welfare. Their support comes from older voters, Protestants, and English-speaking rural residents.

Liberals—Originally the Canadian equivalent of the American Jacksonian Democrats, favoring strict representation by population and the rural pioneer against the urban elite, they now get most of their electoral support from the middle and upper classes in cities, from ethnic voters, and among French-speaking Canadians. Liberals are cautious about extending the welfare state.

New Democratic Party—Successor to the Cooperative Commonwealth Federation, which combined the agrarian protest movement in western Canada with a democratic socialism of the British Labor party variety, the N.D.P. was founded in 1961. It now attempts to attract the vote of middle-class Canadians and fuse it with the party's labor support.

Social Credit — Adopting the unorthodox monetary theories of its English founder, Major C. H. Douglas, Social Credit has appealed to the have-nots, especially now in rural Quebec.

Provinces of Canada

Alberta

With about 8% of the country's population, amounting to an estimated 1,714,000 people in June, 1974, Alberta ranks 4th in population and area (255,285 sq. mi.).

The province figured prominently in the news during 1974 because of its dispute with the federal government over energy policy. Having long suffered subservience to wealthier Ontario and British Columbia, Alberta is now struggling to assert equality.

The key to Alberta's success story is its rich energy resources — oil, natural gas, and petroleum. In 1973 fossil fuel production was worth $2.67 billion, a gain of 39.8% in one year. Oil production reached a record high of 1.65 million barrels a day, a gain of more than 10% from 1972; marketable gas production was estimated to be in the order of 2.1 trillion cubic feet, up by about 15% from the previous year. Petroleum revenues pour into the provincial treasury at the rate of more than $3 million every working day.

Alberta also enjoyed large-scale industrial development. The Interprovincial Steel and Pipe Corp. Ltd. of Regina (Ipsco) started a $40 million expansion of its facilities. Agriculture, traditionally the primary industry, had a good year in 1973 with a 37% increase over 1972. The rate of seasonally adjusted unemployment was only 2.7% in mid-1974.

Edmonton is the provincial capital. A Conservative government headed by Premier Peter Lougheed was elected in 1971. Its victory brought the demise of the Social Credits government that had controlled Alberta for 36 years.

British Columbia

Situated on the Pacific Coast, British Columbia is the 3d largest province in Canada, both in size (366,-255 sq. mi.) and population (est. 2,395,000, June 1974, slightly over 10% of Canada's total). Close to 55.3% of the population lives in Vancouver and Victoria. Population growth at 3.5% annual increase, is more than 2.5 times the national average.

The 1974 increase in the gross provincial product will be lower than in 1973, when it grew 16% to $13.8 billion. Activity in the forest industry should account for 60% of all exports from British Columbia.

Critics of the government allege that the New Democratic Party (NDP) administration under Premier Dave Barret, elected in 1972 when the incumbent Social Credit Party was defeated, has failed to generate confidence in his administration among the industrialists and big business men.

The provincial budget should win applause from voters in the province. There were no tax increases for individual citizens. Another tax concession to the individual was a $30 annual grant to persons renting accommodation. The aged (65 and over) will get a $30 increase in similar grants which will rise to $80 a year.

British Columbia records the highest average weekly income in Canada. In May 1974 the average weekly salary was $192.93. The unemployment rate in the province as of July 1974 (seasonally adjusted) was 6.1%, 1% higher than the national average. British Columbia suffers a critical labor shortage.

Manitoba

Occupying a strategic position between eastern and western Canada, Manitoba is 6th largest in area (251,000 sq. mi.) and 5th in population (est. 1,011,000, June, 1974; about 4.5% of Canada's total population). Metropolitan Winnipeg has close to 55% of Manitoba's population.

Manitoba's gross provincial product reached $5.1 billion in 1973. Forecasts for real growth in 1974 are 8.5%, compared with the 6.7% national rate. Average weekly wages and salaries rank 5th nationally. The seasonally adjusted unemployment rate was only 1.1%, the lowest in Canada.

The province's push to build a stronger industrial base is paying off. After slumping badly, mineral performance in the two basic industries — mining and the pulp and paper — explains Manitoba's economic recovery. Nickel, copper, and zinc, the most important minerals produced in Manitoba, accounted for about 84% of the value of mining industry output in 1973. A major problem facing the province is a shortage of skilled labor, especially in the aerospace and heavy construction industries.

Agriculture continues to be the leading industry. Farm cash receipts took off to a flying start in the first 5 months of 1974, reaching $388.1 million, more than double the revenues for the same period in 1973.

Headed by Premier Ed. Schreyer, Manitoba's New Democratic government is more conservative than socialist in ecomomic policy. A heavy mining tax related to both the prices of metals and the volume of production, was withdrawn and replaced by a simple increase in royalty rate. Winnipeg is the provincial capital.

New Brunswick

New Brunswick presented the gloomiest economic outlook at the start of the year. Inflation threatened to wipe out moderate gains made in 1973. But by mid-1974 a record capital outlay had gone a long way to improve the economic outlook. A number of major projects are expected to brighten the economic prospects of the province. The latest project calls for a $900-million nuclear power plant at Point Lepreau, 24 miles west of Saint John, with the first $500 million phase financed 50-50 by a federal loan and by the New Brunswick Power Commission through the bond market.

New Brunswick's unemployment rate is among the highest in Canada. In July 1974 it was 9.1%. Average weekly income has traditionally been among the lowest in Canada. As of May 1974 the average weekly wage was $147.72.

The 2 principal crops are potatoes of which New Brunswick is the leading producer, and oats. Farm cash receipts from potatoes has gone a long way in improving the province's economic outlook.

The province is governed by a Progressive Conservative government under the leadership of Premier Richard Hatfield. Seat of government is Fredericton.

Newfoundland

Newfoundland has the largest area of any Atlantic province, but ranks 7th for Canada as a whole. In June 1974 its estimated population was 542,000, or 2.4% of Canada's total.

The economy of the province varied. Total value of fish landings up to May 1974 dropped disastrously to $11.4 million from the corresponding 1973 period total of $14.2 million. But the value of shipments of all manufactured goods increased to $154.6 million from $137.3 million. Retail trade also increased by 17.5% over the preceding year. New housing starts rose to 122,200 from 111,936.

Unemployment is the highest in Canada, climbing to a staggering 16.9% seasonally adjusted at the end of July. Despite the high unemployment rate, jobs went begging in the timber industry. The average weekly wage for the province was $161.29 in July 1974, which is 6th for Canada as a whole.

The gross provincial product in 1973 is projected at $1.7 billion, an advance of 13% over 1972, of which 6% was real growth and the rest inflation. Estimated gross revenues for the province in 1974 are $537.6 million, of which $153.6 million come from the federal government in the form of equalization payments.

The Progressive Conservative party under Premier Frank Moores has governed the province since 1972. St. John's is the province's capital.

Nova Scotia

Although Nova Scotia's population amounts to only 3.6% of Canada's total, the province has more residents than any of its Atlantic neighbors, 813,000 (est. June, 1974), 27% of which live in the metropolitan area of Halifax, the capital. Nova Scotia is the 2d smallest in area (21,425 sq. mi.).

While stronger economically than any other Atlantic province, it lags behind the central and western provinces; about 22% of the province's predicted $701.6-million gross revenues will come from federal government equalization grants.

Unemployment in Nova Scotia for July 1974 was 6.1% (seasonally adjusted), but there was a shortage of skilled labor. The average weekly wage was the second lowest in Canada, $144.44 in May.

For the period ending May 1974 fish landings had declined some $5 million from the previous year figure of $28.2 million. Estimated value of shipments in all manufacturing goods was expected to increase to $566.5 million. Retail trade gained by 15.3%, increasing to $104.2 million. Total farm cash receipts indicates rapid strides in this sector.

The Liberal party, headed by Premier Gerald Regan, was re-elected in 1974.

Ontario

Ontario is the 2d largest province in Canada (412,382 sq. mi.), with the largest population of any province (est. 8,094,000 June 1974).

Situated in the country's heartland, Ontario stretches from the St. Lawrence River and the Great Lakes to Hudson and James Bays in the north. This area of the Canadian Shield produces 40% of Canada's mineral output. The District of Sudbury is the source of most of the world's nickel. About 80% of the nation's steel industry is located in Ontario, which also produces about one-third of the country's paper and paper-board products.

By far the wealthiest province, Ontario in 1973 had a per capita income of $3,770. The estimated provincial product in 1974, including a 6.5% rate of inflation, was about $53.3 billion, up from $47.8 billion in 1973. In 1974 new capital investment was expected to increase by anywhere from 14 to 21% over the $11.7 billion figure for the previous year. The rate of seasonally adjusted unemployment was 4% in July 1974. There was a marked shortage of skilled personnel in certain trades, though the province continues to attract the largest number of new immigrants coming to Canada.

Although the province was prosperous, a decrease of about 2% was predicted in the rate of economic growth in 1974.The slowdown from 6.7% to 5% resulted from weakness in the export and residential housing sectors.

Toronto is the provincial capital. The Progressive Conservative party, headed by Premier William Davis, is now entering its 31st consecutive year of government. One event of historical interest for 1974 was the government's appointment of the first woman Lieutenant Governor of any Canadian province, the Hon. Pauline E. McGibbon.

Prince Edward Island

Prince Edward Island is the smallest province in area and population. Its 117,000 residents (est. June, 1974) occupy 2,184 sq. mi.

A boom was predicted in 1974 for most of the island's economy, which is based on agriculture and tourism. Agriculture still takes the lead with potatoes being the chief crop. In the first 5 months of 1974, farm cash receipts totalled $50.1 million and potatoes accounted for more than $32 million.

Tourism increased by 3.9% in 1973 during the centennial celebration of the province's entry into Confederation. The island attracts 28% of its visitors from Ontario and 25% from the United States.

Other sectors of industry reported more modest gains. By May 1974 retail trade had increased by 16.7% to $16.9 million. Estimated value of fish landings dropped by almost 50% to $1.4 million.

Charlottetown is the provincial capital. The Liberal party led by Premier Alex Campbell continues to govern the province.

Quebec

Quebec's 594,860 sq. mi. make it the largest province, but its population (est. 6,134,000 June 1974) ranks 2d, giving the province slightly over 27.8% of Canada's total. Rocky and barren except for lakes and coniferous trees, the Canadian Shield spreads over the largest part of the province north of the St. Lawrence River. South of the river, the Appalachian Mountains run to the east and south to the U.S.A. A fertile agricultural band called the St. Lawrence Lowlands surrounds the western end of the river.

Headed by Premier Robert Bourassa and acting on its strong majority (95%) of seats in the House, the Liberal government in 1974 gave French legal priority over English in Quebec in order to encourage greater use of French, particularly in the business and industrial sectors. The act provoked criticism on the ground that it infringed language rights guaranteed in the British North America Act, and contradicted the federal government's bilingual policies.

The new official Language Act is unlikely to satisfy nationalist and separatist sentiments. Quebec's independence party, the Parti-Quebecois launched a new daily "Le Jour" to give voice to those supporting Quebec's separation. Some sources estimate that the separatists number 900,000.

The government has suffered from charges that Premier Bourassa's family has interests in companies which have been doing substantial business with the provincial government and that key ministers have been corrupted by underworld figures.

The province is likely to continue to be a hotbed of controversy as the provincial Government seeks to assume jurisdiction over cable television, and to embark on the renegotiation of an immigration agreement with the federal government, which has left Quebec with almost no say when it comes to deciding who is to be allowed to immigrate to Quebec.

Labor unrest is a feature of the province although other provinces experienced problems in this area as well. Montreal's public transit system has been virtually paralyzed by wildcat strikes.

Predicted real growth for Quebec's gross provincial product in 1974 is put at 5.5% at best. Unemployment continued to decline in 1974. The seasonally adjusted figure in July 1974 was 6.7%, still above the national average. Retail trade up to May increased 12.9%.

Saskatchewan

Saskatchewan's population (4.2% of Canada's total) has shown a steady decline, reaching a new low of 907,000 (est. June, 1974). The decline is attributable to the province's lack of economic diversification.

Saskatchewan has a farm economy that relies heavily on crops, especially wheat. Strong world demand and grain prices combined to produce an excellent economic outlook for the province in 1974. Wheat planting is estimated to be up by 7% and the province expects to grow about 65% of the Canadian crop. In the first 5 months of 1974, farm cash receipts rose by 151.7% to $1 billion. However, gains in farm prices are being eliminated by skyrocketing farm costs. Nature, too, has taken its toll with spring flooding, drought in some areas, and a grasshopper menace.

The seasonally adjusted unemployment rate at the end of July stood at 2.2%, the 2d lowest in Canada. A perennial problem is lack of farm labor. Wages in the province continue to be among the lowest in Canada with weekly income averaging $154.34 in May 1974.

Saskatchewan had the first democratic socialist government in North America. After being in power from 1944 to 1964, the New Democratic socialist party regained office from the Liberals in 1971 and Allan Blakeney, now 47, became premier.

Superlative Canadian Statistics

Area	Total: Land 3,560,238 sq. mi.; Water 291,571 sq. mi.	3,851,809 sq. mi.
Largest city in area	Whitehorse	162 sq. mi.
Smallest city in area (east)	Thetford Mines, Que.	7 sq. mi.
Smallest city in area (west)	Prince George, B.C.	17 sq. mi.
Northernmost point	Cape Columbia, N.W.T.	83°07′ N.
Northernmost town	Inuvik, N.W.T.	68°21′ N.
Southernmost point	Middle Island (Lake Erie), Ont.	42°41′ N.
Southernmost town	Kingsville, Ont.	42°02′ N.
Westernmost point	Mount St. Elias, Yukon	141° W.
Westernmost town	Dawson, Yukon	139°25′ W.
Easternmost point	Cape Spear, Nfld.	52°37′ W.
Easternmost town	St. John's, Nfld.	52°43′ W.
Highest city	Rossland, B.C. at R.R. Stn. (49°05′ 117°47′)	3,465 ft.
Highest town	Lake Louise, Alta.	5,051 ft.
Highest waterfall	Takakkaw Falls, B.C. (51°30′ 116°29′)	1,248 ft.
Longest river	Mackenzie (from head of Finlay R.)	2,635 mi.
Highest mountain	Mt. Logan	19,850 ft.
Rainiest spot	Henderson Lake, Vancouver Is. yrly avg. rainfall	262.0 inches
Highest lake	Chilco Lake (51°20′ 124°05′) 75.1 sq. mi.	3,842 ft.

The Government of Canada

Canada is a constitutional monarchy with a parliamentary system of government. It is also a federal state. The head of state is Queen Elizabeth, represented in Canada, a self-governing member of the Commonwealth of Nations, by a resident Governor-General, appointed by Her Majesty on the advice of the federal cabinet.

The cabinet is drawn from members of the party holding the largest number of seats in the House of Commons. Its members are appointed by the Governor-General on the advice of the prime minister, the leader of the party. The prime minister is the head of the executive branch of government which is composed of the cabinet and the Governor-General, the formal title of the body being "the governor-in-council", also known constitutionally as the Privy Council.

Canada has a bicameral Parliament. The House of Commons, the more important chamber, is composed of 264 members elected at least every 5 years. The prime minister chooses the date within this period.

The upper house is the senate, comprised of 102 Senators who now are appointed to serve until 75. Prime ministers are free to choose appointees, the tradition being that they are party patronage nominations. The British North America Act requires that 30 members come from the Atlantic provinces, 24 from Quebec, 24 from Ontario, and 24 from the 4 western provinces.

Legislation becomes law by receiving 3 "readings" in the Commons, passing in the Senate and obtaining assent from the Governor-General. Financial bills can be introduced only in the Commons.

Each province has a modified version of the Ottawa pattern. Each province has a unicameral legislature. The executive head in the province is referred to usually as the Premier.

Head of State

Queen Elizabeth, succeeded to the throne in 1952, is represented by Governor-General Rt. Hon. Jules Leger, appointed 1974.

The Cabinet

(listed according to precedence) (August 1974)

Prime Minister — Pierre Elliott Trudeau
Leader of the Government in the Senate — Ray Perrault
Secretary of State for External Affairs — Allan Joseph MacEachen
President of the Privy Council — Mitchell Sharp
President of the Treasury Board — Jean Chretien
Transport (Minister) — Jean Marchand
Finance (Minister) — John N. Turner
Indian Affairs and Northern Development — J. Dudd Buchanan
Energy, Mines and Resources (Minister) — Donald Stovel Macdonald
Labour (Minister) — John Carr Munro
Communications (Minister) — Gerard Pelletier
Environment (Minister) — Jeanne Sauve
Public Works (Minister) — Charles Mills Drury
Minister of State for Urban Affairs — Barnett Jerome Danson
Regional Economic Expansion (Minister) — Donald Campbell Jamieson

Manpower and Immigration — Robert Knight Andras
National Defence (Minister) — James A. Richardson
Minister of Justice and Attorney General — Otto E. Lang
Consumer and Corporate Affairs (Minister) — Andre Ouellet
National Revenue (Minister) — Stanley Robert Basford
Supply and Services (Minister) — Jeane-Pierre Goyer
Industry, Trade and Commerce (Minister) — Alastair William Gillespie
Fisheries (Minister of State) — Romeo LeBlanc
Agriculture (Minister) — Eugene F. Whelan
Solicitor General of Canada — W. Warren Allmand
Secretary of State — James Hugh Faulkner
Postmaster General — Bryce Stuart Mackasey
Veterans Affairs (Minister) — Daniel MacDonald
National Health and Welfare (Minister) — Marc Lalonde
Minister of State for Science and Technology — Charles Mills Drury

Governors-General of Canada Since Confederation, 1867

Name	Term
The Viscount Monck of Ballytrammon ...	1867-1868
The Baron Lisgar of Lisgar and Bailieborough ...	1869-1872
The Earl of Dufferin ...	1872-1878
The Marquis of Lorne ...	1878-1883
The Marquis of Lansdowne ...	1883-1888
The Baron Stanley of Preston ...	1888-1893
The Earl of Aberdeen ...	1893-1898
The Earl of Minto ...	1898-1904
The Earl Grey ...	1904-1911
Field Marshal H.R.H. The Duke of Connaught ...	1911-1916
The Duke of Devonshire ...	1916-1921

Name	Term
General The Baron Byng of Vimy ...	1921-1926
The Viscount Willingdon of Ratton ...	1926-1931
The Earl of Bessborough ...	1931-1935
The Baron Tweedsmuir of Elsfield ...	1935-1940
Major General The Earl of Athlone ...	1940-1946
Field Marshal The Viscount Alexander of Tunis ...	1946-1952
The Right Hon. Vincent Massey ...	1952-1959
General The Right Hon. Georges P. Vanier ...	1959-1967
The Right Hon. Roland Michener ...	1967-1974
The Right Hon. Jules Leger ...	1974-

Recent Prime Ministers

Name	Party	Term
Sir John A. Macdonald ...	Conservative	1867-1873
		1878-1891
Alexander Mackenzie ...	Liberal	1873-1878
Sir John J. C. Abbott ...	Conservative	1891-1892
Sir John S. D. Thompson ...	Conservative	1892-1894
Sir Mackenzie Bowell ...	Conservative	1894-1896
Sir Charles Tupper ...	Conservative	1896
Sir Wilfrid Laurier ...	Liberal	1896-1911
Sir Robert L. Borden ...	Conservative	1911-1920
	Unionist	

Name	Party	Term
Arthur Meighen ...	Conservative	1920-1921
	Unionist	1926
W. L. M. King ...	Liberal	1921-1926
		1926-1930
		1935-1948
R. B. Bennett ...	Conservative	1930-1935
Louis St. Laurent ...	Liberal	1948-1957
John G. Diefenbaker ...	Prog. Cons.	1957-1963
Lester B. Pearson ...	Liberal	1963-1968
Pierre Elliott Trudeau ...	Liberal	1968-

Canadian Armed Forces

In February, 1968, Canada carried out the unification of its traditionally separate services: the Royal Canadian Navy, the Canadian Army and the Royal Canadian Air Force. The first step towards a unified force was taken in 1964 when the 3 services were brought together under one control with common logistics and supply and training systems, but retaining their separate legal entities. The positions of Chairman of the Chiefs of Staff and Chiefs of the Navy, Army and Air Force were abolished and replaced by the Chief of the Defence Staff. On February 1, 1968, the 3 services ceased to exist. They were unified into the Canadian Armed Forces in which all officers, men and women are managed within a single body, with a common uniform.

Chief of the Defence Staff: General J. A. Dextraze

Vice Chief of the Defence Staff: Vice Admiral R. H. Falls

Air Defence Command — Maj. Gen. W. M. Garton	**Canadian Forces Europe** — Maj. Gen. J. W. Quinn	
Air Transport Command — Maj. Gen. K. E. Lewis	**Maritime Command** — Rear Admiral D. S. Boyle	
Communication Command — Col. L. H. Wylie	**Mobile Command** — Lieut. Gen. S. C. Waters	
Training Command — Rear Admiral R. S. Stephens		

Regular Forces Strength

March 31	Navy	Army	Air Force	Total	March 31	Navy	Army	Air Force	Total
1940	6,135	76,678	9,483	92,296	1968	17,439	40,192	44,045	101,676
1945	92,529	494,258	174,254	761,041	1969	.....	.....	.....	98,340
1950	9,259	20,652	17,274	47,185	1971	.....	.....	.....	89,563
1955	19,207	49,409	49,461	118,077	1972	.....	.....	.....	84,933
1960	20,675	47,185	51,737	119,597	1973	.....	.....	.....	82,402
1965	19,756	46,264	48,144	114,164	1974	.....	.....	.....	81,243

Canadian Military Participation in Major Conflicts

Northwest Rebellion (1885)[1]
Participants—3,323
Killed—38
Last veteran died at the age of 104 in 1971.
South African War (1899-1902)
Participants—7,368[2]
Killed—89
Living Veterans—less than 50
First World War (1914-1918)
Participants—626,636[3]

Killed—61,332[4]
Living Veterans—96,900
Second World War (1939-1945)
Participants—1,086,343 (inc. 45,423 women)
Killed—37,714 (inc. 8 women)
Living Veterans—801,000
Korean War (1950-1953)
Participants—25,583
Killed—314
Living Veterans—25,000

[1]First battle in history to be fought entirely by Canadian troops. [2]Includes Canadians in the South African constabulary and 8 nursing sisters. [3]Includes 2,854 nursing sisters. [4]Includes 21 nursing sisters and 1,563 airmen serving with the British air forces.

Canadian Peacekeeping Operations

Canada has provided either policing or observer troops for every peacekeeping operation since World War II.

Nearly 900 Canadian soldiers served in the Gaza Strip following the Israeli-Egyptian crisis of 1956 until the force was disbanded in 1967.

In the Congo, a 300-man signals unit provided communications for the UN Force from 1960 to 1964.

Canadian participation in the International Commission for Control and Supervision in Vietnam and Laos began in 1954 and at the high point of participation in 1973, following the US military withdrawal from Vietnam, there were 245 Canadian Forces personnel involved in the supervision of the ceasefire. The Canadian Vietnam supervisory contingent was withdrawn in July 1973 and the Laos mission was withdrawn in the Spring of 1974.

Canada's largest peacekeeping commitment at the present time (mid 1974) is in the Middle East where approximately 1,100 Canadian Forces personnel are serving with the United Nations Emergency Force.

The UN Force in Cyprus is another of Canada's large military commitments. Since 1964 Canadian participation included provision of a reduced Infantry Battalion and a Canadian element in the UN Headquarters — a total of approximately 580 officers and men. However, in July 1974, following the troubles in Cyprus, Canada, at the request of the UN, augmented the Cyprus contingent by an additional force of approximately 480 officers and men and some additional military equipment.

Other Canadian peacekeeping operations in 1974 were as follows:

— 17 Canadian Forces personnel with the UN Military Observer Group, India-Pakistan

— 20 Canadian officers with the UN Truce Supervisory Organization, Palestine

— 2 Canadian Forces personnel in Korea with the UN Military Armistice Commission.

Canadian Winners of the Victoria Cross

The Victoria Cross is Britain's highest military honor. It has been accorded to 94 Canadians since its inception in 1856. The cross was originally cast from metal of a Russian cannon captured during the Crimean War. Canadian winners in World War II:

Name	Unit	Theater of War & Date
Sgt. Mjr. J. R. Osborn	Winnipeg Grenadiers	Hong Kong, Dec. 19, 1941
Lt. Col. C. E. Merritt	S. Sask. Regiment	Dieppe, Aug. 19, 1942
Capt. J. W. Foote	Royal Hamilton Light Infantry	Dieppe, Aug. 19, 1942
Capt. F. T. Peters	Royal Navy	Oran, North Africa, Nov. 8, 1942
Capt. Paul Triquet	Royal 22nd Regiment	Casa Berardi, Dec. 14, 1943
Maj. C. F. Hoey	Lincolnshire Regiment	Burma, Feb. 16, 1944
Maj. John K. Mahoney	Westminster Regiment	Melfa River, May 24, 1944
P.O.A.C. Mynarksi	RCAF	Camria, France, June 12, 1944
Flt. Lieut. D. E. Hornell	RCAF	"Northern waters", June 25, 1944
Sqd. Ldr. Ian Bazalgette	RAF	Trossy St. Maximin, Aug. 4, 1944
Maj. D. V. Currie	South Alberta Regiment	Normandy, Aug. 20, 1944
Pvt. E. A. Smith	Seaforth Highlanders	Savio River, Italy, Oct. 22, 1944
Sgt. Aubrey Cosens	Queen's Own Rifles	Holland, Feb. 26, 1945
Maj. F. A. Tilston	Essex Scottish	Hochwald Forest, March 1, 1945
Cpl. F. G. Topham	1st Canadian Parachute Battalion	Germany, March 24, 1945
Lt. R. H. Gray	Royal Canadian Navy	Pacific, Aug. 9, 1945

Canadian Time Zones

There are seven time zones in Canada. In terms of the number of hours behind the Universal Time established on the zero meridian at Greenwich these are, from East to West:

Newfoundland Standard Time	3½	hours	Mountain Standard Time	7	hours
Atlantic Standard Time	4	hours	Pacific Standard Time	8	hours
Eastern Standard Time	5	hours	Yukon Standard Time	9	hours
Central Standard Time	6	hours			

The location of the time zone boundaries in Canada, together with other regulations governing time, is a matter of provincial jurisdiction. The adoption or rejection of Daylight Saving Time, therefore, is decided by provincial legislation except in those cases where the province leaves the decision to the municipalities.

Canadian Shipping Traffic

Source: Canadian Statistical Review, July 1974 (thousand short tons)

Year and Month	Halifax	Saint John	Quebec	Montreal	Toronto	Vancouver	All Ports	Coastwise
1970	11,072	6,401	8,552	22,376	5,163	26,923	290,708	126,318
1971	10,999	7,438	10,811	21,690	4,710	30,813	286,606	122,536
1972	11,355	10,263	14,901	20,431	4,534	29,894	298,076	122,403
Jan.	936	695	725	383	—	2,111	10,765	3,531
Apr.	986	1,048	1,256	1,391	335	3,497	22,682	8,315
July	901	1,068	1,264	2,223	501	2,931	30,835	13,795
Oct.	937	1,133	1,475	2,278	807	3,573	35,116	13,923

Canadian Postal Code

The Canadian Postal Code consists of 6 alphanumeric characters with 2 components separated by a single space. The Area Code is a combination of letter-number-letter. The Local Code is a combination of number-letter-number.

The Postal Code precisely describes the location of the point of delivery for each item of mail. The Area Code makes it possible to sort mail into geographic areas, or forward sortation areas. The Local Code makes it possible to sort mail for Post Offices in rural areas, for letter carrier routes, large volume points of delivery, or forms of delivery service in urban areas.

As a matter of interest, only 18 letters are used in the first position, whereas 20 letters are used in 3rd and 5th position. There are a total of 7,200,000 possible codes, i.e., (18 x 10 x 20) (10 x 20 x 10) but only about 10% will be used initially.

Personal Expenditure on Consumer Goods and Services in Current Dollars

(millions of dollars)
Source: Statistics Canada

	1965	1966	1967	1968	1969	1970	1971	1972
Food, Beverages and Tobacco	8,097	8,671	9,240	9,739	10,411	11,235	12,021	13,462
Clothing and Footwear	2,855	3,067	3,354	3,617	3,908	4,034	4,381	4,871
Gross Rent, Fuel and Power	6,064	6,573	7,247	7,960	8,742	9,623	10,351	11,273
Furniture, Furnishings, Household Equipment and Operation	3,426	3,743	4,024	4,322	4,658	4,785	5,227	5,974
Medical Care and Health Services	1,516	1,652	1,789	1,902	1,912	1,758	1,571	1,715
Transportation and Communication	5,114	5,479	5,940	6,458	6,863	6,945	7,733	8,671
Recreation, Entertainment, Education and Cultural Services	2,400	2,787	3,334	3,682	4,104	4,467	5,023	5,775
Personal Goods and Services	4,460	4,898	5,497	6,034	6,683	7,106	7,582	8,410
Net Expenditure Abroad	15	20	-463	-10	151	133	100	126
Total	33,947	36,890	39,972	43,704	47,492	50,084	53,989	60,277
Durable Goods	5,085	5,490	5,915	6,494	6,975	6,798	7,776	9,030
Semi-Durable Goods	4,671	5,054	5,539	5,953	6,426	6,645	7,224	8,113
Non-Durable Goods	11,526	12,364	13,219	14,019	15,073	16,205	17,376	19,414
Services	12,665	13,982	15,299	17,238	19,018	20,438	21,613	23,720

Canadian Government Budget

(in millions of dollars)
Source: Canadian Statistical Review, July, 1974

Expenditures

Fiscal year or month	National Defence	Health and Welfare	Agriculture	Post Office	Public Works	Transport	Veterans Affairs	Payments to Provinces	Total Expenditures
1970-71...	1,817.9	2,338.0	277.0	368.6	330.7	429.7	410.0	1,229.0	13,182.2
1971-72...	1,895.2	2,706.1	286.1	413.3	336.8	512.4	423.3	1,425.5	14,840.9
1972-73...	1,932.9	2,916.0	322.5	497.3	374.3	599.3	452.5	1,501.4	16,120.7
Apr......	88.1	145.9	8.5	21.9	9.9	38.9	32.2	95.0	953.6
July.....	170.8	227.7	15.8	36.3	25.6	62.1	42.2	135.3	1,352.0
Dec......	177.0	234.9	38.5	43.1	29.5	57.5	37.8	99.9	1,358.8
1973									
Apr......	117.3	151.8	9.2	27.4	10.7	46.6	35.8	112.4	1,931.7
July.....	184.9	258.2	17.9	44.4	35.7	79.0	44.1	115.0	1,469.1
Dec.....	205.9	286.0	48.5	48.4	30.1	73.9	44.8	127.2	1,470.1

Revenues [1]

Fiscal Year or Month	Personal Income Tax	Corporation Income Tax	Sales Tax	Other Excise Tax	Excise Duties	Customs Duties	Estate Taxes	Post Office	Total Budgetary Revenues
1970-71...	3,778.5	2,218.5	1,707.5	403.2	561.0	814.5	120.2	337.6	12,803.1
1971-72...	5,582.0	2,183.1	1,984.7	388.4	606.6	988.6	132.4	403.8	14,226.6
1972-73...	7,172.8	2,653.5	2,288.7	400.4	638.0	1,181.8	61.4	470.1	16,601.6
Apr......	402.7	492.1	124.2	22.1	42.2	76.2	7.3	27.4	1,306.7
July	625.7	236.2	217.3	31.1	45.5	92.4	5.3	38.8	1,404.0
Dec.....	599.1	189.4	200.7	16.7	49.3	91.8	3.0	54.5	1,436.2
1973-74									
Apr......	506.9	510.7	154.1	21.9	44.0	91.2	1.2	34.0	1,475.0
July	741.5	317.0	232.9	38.6	50.2	114.6	0.7	36.4	1,694.7
Dec....	740.8	217.4	230.6	37.2	57.9	96.8	0.7	50.1	1,727.7

(1) This statement includes only receipts relating to budgetary revenue. Excluded are non-budgetary revenues such as Old Age Security Fund taxes, Prairie Farm Assistance Act levies, employer and employee contributions to government-held funds (Unemployment Insurance, Superannuation etc.), interest on government-held funds, and taxes collected on behalf of and transferred to other governments.

Canadian Consumer Price Index

Source: Canadian Statistical Review, July 1974 (1961:100)

	All Items	Food	Shelter	Clothing	Trans- portation	Health, Personal	Recreation, Education	Tobacco, Alcohol	Total Services
1972......	139.8	141.4	157.9	132.0	133.3	149.2	139.4	132.1	157.9
1973......	150.4	162.0	168.7	138.6	136.8	156.4	145.2	136.3	167.6
Jan...	144.5	150.0	163.9	134.7	133.3	151.9	141.5	135.3	162.8
Mar..	145.7	152.2	165.7	134.5	133.9	152.8	142.5	135.8	164.4
May..	148.4	157.4	167.7	137.5	134.9	156.3	143.8	136.2	166.2
1974									
Jan...	157.6	174.0	173.8	144.8	143.5	161.8	149.0	136.9	173.4
Mar..	160.8	180.5	176.0	148.1	144.2	163.5	150.6	139.3	175.5
May..	164.6	186.1	178.1	150.5	148.4	168.3	154.6	142.8	178.2

Assets and Deposits of Chartered Banks

Source: Supplement to the Canada Gazette (July 6, 1974).

Bank	Assets	Deposits
Royal Bank of Canada...	20,782,101,000	18,691,666
Canadian Imperial Bank of Commerce.........................	17,864,444,000	16,475,100
Bank of Montreal..	16,842,587,000	15,514,079
Bank of Nova Scotia...	11,939,413,000	10,720,499
Toronto-Dominion Bank......................................	11,231,019,000	10,231,232
Banque Canadienne Nationale................................	3,769,160,000	3,522,851
Banque Provinciale du Canada...............................	2,369,216,000	2,252,792
Mercantile Bank of Canada..................................	673,543,000	595,707
Bank of British Columbia...................................	413,102,000	385,707
Unity Bank of Canada.......................................	129,624,000	103,254

Canadian Foreign Trade

Source: Canadian Statistical Review (July, 1974)
(in millions of dollars)

Year and Month	Exports including re-exports				Imports			
	All Countries	U.S.	U.K.	All other countries	All countries	U.S.	U.K.	All other countries
1969...............	14,931	10,614	1,113	3,204	14,130	10,243	791	3,096
1970...............	16,820	10,917	1,485	4,404	13,951	9,917	738	3,296
1971...............	17,744	12,006	1,361	4,377	15,607	10,941	837	3,827
1972...............	20,140	13,932	1,358	4,780	18,678	12,878	950	4,844
1973...............	25,325	17,070	1,598	6,632	23,302	16,483	1,005	5,813
1974								
Jan................	2,294.9	1,492.6	135.7	666.6	2,172.2	1,527.7	79.9	564.7
Mar...............	2,439.6	1,675.9	146.3	617.5	2,429.2	1,712.8	80.6	635.8
May	3,050.9	1,929.1	202.4	919.4	2,933.6	1,985.7	97.5	850.4

Population and Area of Canada by Provinces
Source: Statistics Canada

Province, territory	Capital	Area in square miles Land	Fresh Water	Total	1966 Census	Population 1971 Census	April 1974 Estimate
Newfoundland	St. John's	143,045	13,140	156,185	493,396	522,105	541,000
Prince Edward Island	Charlo tetown	2,184	. . .	2,184	108,645	111,645	116,000
Nova Scotia	Halifax	20,402	1,023	21,425	756,039	788,960	811,000
New Brunswick	Fredericton	27,385	519	28,354	616,788	634,555	660,000
Quebec	Quebec	523,860	71,000	594,860	5,780,845	6,027,765	6,124,000
Ontario	Toronto	344,092	68,490	412,582	6,960,870	7,703,110	8,067,000
Manitoba	Winnipeg	211,775	39,225	251,000	963,066	988,245	1,008,000
Saskatchewan	Regina	220,182	31,518	251,700	955,344	926,245	907,000
Alberta	Edmonton	248,800	6,485	255,285	1,463,203	1,627,870	1,709,000
British Columbia	Victoria	359,279	6,976	366,255	1,873,674	2,184,620	2,384,000
Northwest Territories	Yellowknife	1,253,438	51,465	1,304,903	28,738	34,805	38,000
Yukon Territory	Whitehorse	205,345	1,730	207,076	1,382	18,390	19,000
Total		3,560,238	291,571	3,851,809	20,014,880	21,568,315	22,384,000

Population by Mother Tongue, for Canada and Provinces, 1971
Source: Statistics Canada

Province	English	French	German	Indian, Eskimo	Italian	Dutch	Polish	Ukrainian	Other
Newfoundland	514,520	3,635	515	1,620	175	120	45	50	1,430
Prince Edward Island	103,105	7,360	140	145	35	280	40	30	510
Nova Scotia	733,560	39,330	2,000	2,710	1,495	1,850	555	435	7,020
New Brunswick	410,400	215,730	1,110	2,725	755	665	155	110	2,905
Quebec	789,185	4,867,250	31,025	21,050	135,455	4,660	15,480	11,385	152,265
Ontario	5,971,570	482,045	184,880	28,590	344,285	77,475	73,985	80,230	460,050
Manitoba	662,720	60,550	82,720	31,665	7,265	10,385	15,900	72,925	44,130
Saskatchewan	685,920	31,605	75,885	26,020	2,045	4,695	7,675	53,385	39,025
Alberta	1,263,935	46,500	92,800	29,920	15,570	20,670	13,730	70,895	73,855
British Columbia	1,807,250	38,035	89,020	18,550	31,030	23,955	7,100	20,055	149,620
Yukon	15,345	450	565	1,030	75	100	55	150	620
Northwest Territories	16,305	1,160	425	15,800	175	80	60	205	595
Total	12,973,810	5,793,650	561,085	179,825	538,360	144,920	134,780	309,855	932,020

Canadian Cities with Metropolitan Populations Over 100,000
Source: Statistics Canada

	Metro Area*	City		Metro Area*	City
Montreal, Que.	2,743,208	1,214,352	Kitchener, Ont.	226,846	111,804
Toronto, Ont.	2,628,043	712,786	Halifax, N.S.	222,637	122,035
Vancouver, B.C.	1,082,352	426,256	Victoria, B.C.	195,800	61,761
Ottawa, Ont.	602,510	302,341	Sudbury, Ont.	155,424	90,535
Winnipeg, Man.	540,262	246,246	Regina, Sask.	140,734	139,469
Hamilton, Ont.	498,523	309,173	Chicoutimi, Que.	133,703	33,893
Edmonton, Alta.	495,702	438,152	St. John's, Nfld.	131,814	88,102
Quebec, Que.	480,502	186,088	Saskatoon, Sask.	126,449	126,449
Calgary, Alta.	403,319	403,319	Oshawa, Ont.	120,318	91,587
St. Catharines, Ont.	303,429	109,722	Thunder Bay, Ont.	112,093	108,411
London, Ont.	286,011	223,222	Saint John, N.B.	106,744	89,039
Windsor, Ont.	258,643	203,300			

*1971 Census Metropolitan Area

Immigration to Canada, by Province of Intended Destination
Source: Canadian Statistical Review (June, 1974)

Year	Canada	Nfld.	P.E.I.	N.S.	N.B.	Que.	Ont.	Man.	Sask.	Alta.	B.C.	Yukon N.W.T.
1971	121,900	819	172	1,817	1,038	19,222	64,357	5,301	1,426	8,653	18,907	183
1972	122,006	686	175	1,872	1,301	18,592	63,805	5,262	1,511	8,390	20,107	305
1973	184,200	984	273	2,548	1,729	26,871	103,187	6,621	1,866	11,904	27,949	268

Immigration to Canada, by Country of Last Permanent Residence
Source: Canadian Statistical Review, June 1973

Year	Total	U.K. and Ireland	France	Germany	Netherlands	Greece	Italy
1971	121,900	16,281	2,966	2,275	1,301	4,769	5,790
1972	122,006	18,317	2,742	2,025	1,471	4,016	4,608
1973	184,102	28,100	3,586	2,564	1,898	5,833	5,468

Year	Portugal	Other Europe	Asia	Australasia	United States	West Indies	All Other
1971	9,157	9,294	22,369	2,906	24,366	10,843	9,583
1972	8,737	8,871	23,831	2,148	22,618	8,214	14,408
1973	13,483	10,949	43,193	2,671	25,242	19,180	22,031

Births and Deaths in Canada by Province

Source: Statistics Canada

Province	Births 1971	Births 1972	Deaths 1971	Deaths 1972	Province	Births 1971	Births 1972	Deaths 1971	Deaths 1972
Nfld.	12,767	12,898	3,199	3,349	Sask.	16,054	15,473	7,413	7,590
P.E.I.	2,103	2,010	1,007	1,052	Alberta	30,545	29,282	10,525	10,699
Nova Scotia	14,250	13,536	6,682	6,904	B.C.	34,852	34,563	17,783	18,021
N.B.	12,187	11,806	4,943	4,982	Yukon	506	451	104	103
Quebec	89,210	83,603	40,738	42,311	N.W. Terr.	1,287	1,239	230	272
Ontario	130,395	125,060	56,623	58,905	Total	362,187	347,319	157,272	162,413
Manitoba	18,031	17,398	8,025	8,225					

Suicide Deaths — Canada

Source: Statistics Canada

Province	Number	Rate*	Province	Number	Rate*
Total	2,657	12.2			
Newfoundland	15	2.8	Manitoba	120	12.1
Prince Edward Island	5	4.4	Saskatchewan	144	15.7
Nova Scotia	93	11.7	Alberta	214	12.9
New Brunswick	49	7.6	British Columbia	356	15.8
Quebec	602	9.9	Yukon	5	26.5
Ontario	1,045	13.4	Northwest Terr.	9	25.00

*Rate per 100,000 population

Marriages and Divorces by Province, 1972

Source: Statistics Canada

Province	Marriages	Divorces*	Province	Marriages	Divorces*
Newfoundland	5,106	177	Saskatchewan	7,877	826
Prince Edward Island	1,013	65	Alberta	16,345	3,767
Nova Scotia	7,291	927	British Columbia	20,659	5,036
New Brunswick	6,455	466	Northwest Territories	254	36
Quebec	53,830	6,421	Yukon	181	47
Ontario	72,278	13,183	Total	200,470	32,364
Manitoba	9,181	1,413	*Preliminary		

Marriages, Divorces and Rates in Canada

(Rates per 1,000 population)

Year	Marriages No.	Marriages Rate	Divorces No.	Divorces Rate	Year	Marriages No.	Marriages Rate	Divorces No.	Divorces Rate
1936	82,941	7.4	1,570	0.14	1966	155,596	7.8	10,239	0.51
1940	125,799	10.8	2,416	0.21	1967	165,879	8.1	11,165	0.54
1945	111,376	9.0	5,101	0.42	1968	171,766	8.3	11,343	0.54
1950	125,083	9.1	5,386	0.39	1969	182,183	8.7	26,079	1.23
1955	128,029	8.2	6,053	0.38	1970	188,428	8.8	29,775	1.37
1960	130,338	7.3	6,980	0.39	1971	191,324	8.9	29,626	1.39
1965	145,519	7.4	8,974	0.45	1972	200,470	9.2	32,364*	1.48

*Preliminary

Divorces and Rates; Canada and Provinces, 1960-1972

	Canada	Nfld.	P.E.I.	N.S.	N.B.	Que.	Ont.	Man.	Sask.	Alta.	B.C.	Yukon	N.W.T.
1960	6,980	6	10	221	178	481	2,965	361	213	951	1,592	—	2
1961	6,563	6	8	245	194	348	2,739	312	251	1,039	1,397	24	—
1962	6,768	—	5	229	181	—	3,140	339	281	1,084	1,490	14	5
1963	7,686	8	8	271	172	491	3,237	369	331	1,268	1,516	13	2
1964	8,623	7	5	315	210	834	3,508	418	315	1,389	1,596	24	2
1965	8,974	3	16	323	237	226	4,087	443	312	1,348	1,961	12	6
1966	10,239	11	18	406	155	988	4,101	524	321	1,567	2,124	21	3
1967	11,165	11	18	394	292	727	4,350	477	399	1,736	2,734	21	6
1968	11,343	15	20	497	143	606	5,036	465	384	1,916	2,220	30	11
1969*	26,093	103	102	791	347	2,947	11,845	1,334	882	3,446	4,224	42	30
1970*	29,775	140	65	823	386	4,865	12,451	1,234	871	3,771	5,111	41	17
1971*	29,626	150	59	721	483	5,195	12,189	1,370	813	3,652	4,942	47	5
1972**	32,364	177	65	927	466	6,421	13,183	1,413	826	3,767	5,036	47	36
					Rate per 100,000 population								
1960	39.1	1.3	9.7	30.4	30.2	9.4	48.5	39.8	23.3	73.7	99.4	—	9.1
1961	36.0	1.3	7.6	33.2	32.4	6.6	43.9	33.9	27.1	78.0	85.8	164.1	—
1962	36.4	—	4.7	30.7	29.9	—	49.4	36.2	30.2	79.2	89.8	93.3	20.0
1963	40.6	1.7	7.4	36.1	28.2	9.0	49.9	38.9	35.5	90.4	89.2	86.7	7.7
1964	44.7	1.4	4.6	41.7	34.4	14.9	52.9	43.6	33.4	97.1	91.5	160.0	7.4
1965	45.7	0.6	14.7	42.7	38.5	4.0	60.2	45.9	32.8	93.0	109.1	85.7	22.2
1966	51.2	2.2	16.6	53.7	25.1	17.1	58.9	54.4	33.6	107.1	113.4	146.0	10.4
1967	54.8	2.2	16.5	51.8	47.1	12.4	61.0	49.5	41.7	116.5	140.6	140.0	20.7
1968*	54.8	3.0	18.2	64.8	22.9	10.2	69.3	47.9	40.0	125.7	110.8	200.0	36.7
1969*	124.2	20.0	91.9	102.1	55.3	49.2	160.4	136.3	92.1	221.0	205.0	262.5	96.8
1970*	139.8	27.1	59.1	105.2	61.6	80.9	164.9	125.5	92.6	236.4	240.2	241.2	51.5
1971*	137.4	28.7	52.8	91.4	76.1	86.2	158.2	138.6	87.8	224.3	226.2	255.6	14.4
1972**	148.3	33.3	57.5	116.7	72.5	106.1	168.5	142.5	90.1	227.8	224.1	248.7	100.0

*These include divorces granted under old as well as new legislation of July 2, 1968; hence these totals differ from the subsequent tables in which only those divorces filed under new legislation are considered.
**Preliminary.

Number of Canadian Households with Television Sets[1]
Source: Statistic Canada (April, 1973)

Province	Number Households	Black & White			Color		
		One Set	Two Sets or More	No sets	One Set	Two Sets or More	No Sets
Newfoundland	113	88	10	15	17	*	95
Prince Edward Island	28	22	*	5	5	*	23
Nova Scotia	214	156	21	36	53	*	159
New Brunswick	161	113	21	27	40	*	121
Quebec	1,652	1,103	299	250	462	18	1,173
Ontario	2,372	1,567	295	511	818	34	1,520
Manitoba	292	198	32	62	86	*	204
Saskatchewan	263	169	26	68	92	*	170
Alberta	481	304	47	131	190	4	287
British Columbia	690	437	55	197	248	8	435
Total	**6,266**	**4,158**	**807**	**1,301**	**2,011**	**70**	**4,186**

(1) Estimates in thousands * Less than 4,000

Value of Canadian Fishery Products and By-products[1]
Source: Statistics Canada ($1,000)

Province	1969	1970	1971	1972
Total[3]	408,802	450,631	463,013	545,587
Newfoundland	72,302	85,104	94,943	100,599
Prince Edward Island	12,701	18,375	16,143	19,964
Nova Scotia	123,492	105,939	127,215	142,102
New Brunswick	64,820	67,404	68,629	86,380
Quebec	19,026	24,130	26,022	25,938
Ontario	14,778	13,070	13,896	16,238
Manitoba	6,700			
Saskatchewan	4,587	13,276	12,674	15,449
Alberta	1,563			
Northwest Territories	946			
British Columbia[2]	87,852	123,333	120,167	159,132
Yukon	35	—	42	46

(1) Final sales for the provinces by fish processors, handlers and fishermen.
(2) Includes halibut landed in United States ports.
(3) The sum of the provincial totals differ from the Canada total as duplications (intershipments between provinces) have been removed from the Atlantic Coast totals.

Canadian Sea Fish Catch and Exports[1]
(in millions of pounds)
Source: Canadian Statistical Review-July, 1974

Year and month	Total[2] Value ($1,000)	Total Quantity	Landings of Sea Fish						Exports to[3]			Exports By Type	
			Nfld	P.E.I.	N.S.	N.B.	Que.	B.C.	Total	United States	Other	Salmon	Lobster
1971	192,993	2,466.1	871.6	97.5	658.1	370.1	240.2	228.7	607.6	438.3	169.3	58.5	22.5
1972	219,829	2,215.1	649.3	59.9	654.0	394.5	182.1	336.7	642.0	443.6	169.3	77.6	19.8
1973	279,618	2,050.2	531.9	63.0	624.9	289.7	158.8	382.0	752.6	491.6	211.1	93.1	20.1
1974-Jan	5,532	63.8	16.9	0.7	37.1	5.5	0.6	2.9	39.6	26.0	13.6	5.2	2.6
Feb	5,333	55.9	14.7	0.3	33.1	1.9	0.6	5.3	40.8	26.5	14.3	5.3	1.0
Mar	14,265	122.5	27.7	0.1	15.8	1.6	0.5	76.8	42.9	31.4	11.5	5.8	1.3
Apr	10,930	75.2	29.9	0.0	24.7	5.2	2.8	12.6	29.2	19.6	9.7	3.6	1.1

[1] Monthly totals for current years are not equivalent to annual data due to receipt of additional statistics which cannot be allocated by months.
[2] Includes also seaweeds and other species such as whales, worms, etc.
[3] Exports include sea and freshwater fish and shellfish products but exclude bait, meal, oils, offal, livers, fish roe, n.e.s. and fishery foods and feeds n.e.s.

Approximate Land and Freshwater Areas
Source: Canada Year Book

Province or Territory	Land sq. miles	Freshwater sq. miles	Total sq. miles	Percentage of Total Area
Newfoundland	143,045	13,140	156,185	4.1
Island of Newfoundland	41,164	2,195	43,359	1.1
Labrador	101,881	10,945	112,826	3.0
Prince Edward Island	2,184	—	2,184	0.1
Nova Scotia	20,402	1,023	21,425	0.6
New Brunswick	27,835	519	28,354	0.7
Quebec	523,860	71,000	594,860	15.4
Ontario	344,092	68,490	412,582	10.7
Manitoba	211,775	39,225	251,000	6.5
Saskatchewan	220,182	31,518	251,700	6.5
Alberta	248,800	6,485	255,285	6.6
British Columbia	359,279	6,976	366,255	9.5
Yukon Territory	205,346	1,730	207,076	5.4
Northwest Territories	1,253,438	51,465	1,304,903	33.9
Franklin	541,753	7,500	549,253	14.3
Keewatin	218,460	9,700	228,160	5.9
Mackenzie	493,225	34,265	527,490	13.7
Canada	**3,560,238**	**291,571**	**3,851,809**	**100.0**

NATIONS OF THE WORLD

The nations of the world are listed in alphabetical order, except for Canada and the United States (see Index for listings). Initials in the following articles include UN (United Nations), OAS (Organization of American States), NATO (North Atlantic Treaty Org.), EEC (European Economic Community or Common Market), OAU (Org. of African Unity), CENTO (Central Treaty Org. of the Middle East), SEATO (Southeast Asia Treaty Org.).

See special color section for maps and flags of all nations.

Afghanistan

Capital: Kabul. Area: 253,861 sq. mi. Population (UN est. 1973): 18,290,000. Monetary unit: Afghani.

Afghanistan is a landlocked republic occupying a mountainous area much of which is 4,000 ft. and more above sea level. It is slightly smaller than Texas. Its neighbors are Iran, Pakistan and the USSR. The northeast tip of the country just touches China's Sinkiang Province; both India and Pakistan claim Kashmir, which borders on Afghanistan.

The Hindu Kush mountains tower 16,000 ft. above the capital of Kabul and reach a height of more than 25,000 ft. some 200 miles to the E. Trade with Pakistan flows through the 35-mile long Khyber Pass from Kabul to Peshawar. The climate is dry, with extreme temperatures.

About 90% of the country's exports are agricultural products. Chief items are natural gas, cotton, wool, karakul pelts, hides, oilseeds and fruit. Hand-woven carpets, cotton, wool, fruits and nuts and sheepskin coats are exported. Some 4 million head of broadtail karakul sheep are raised, as well as goats and camels. The sheep provide the principal meat item in the Afghan's diet and the tightly curled, glossy black coats of the newborn lambs are a valuable fur. Minerals include copper, lead, gas, coal, zinc, iron, silver, asbestos and oil. The country has received considerable economic aid from the U.S., USSR and mainland China. The USSR is Afghanistan's largest trading partner.

Textile mills, cement factories, highways and irrigation projects are among recent developments.

Famine, following a drought, brought death to thousands in 1972. The U.S. led other nations in gifts of relief wheat.

History and Government. Afghanistan was so named in about the middle of the 18th Century. In ancient times it was known as Aryana, in the Middle Ages as Khorasan. Pukhtuns (Pushtuns) comprise 53.5% of the population; Tajiks 36.7%; Uzbeks 6%; Hazaras 3%.

In 1964 a Grand Assembly approved a new constitution providing for an elected Lower House, partly-elected Upper House, an independent judiciary, a prime minister chosen by the king. The last king was Mohammed Zahir Shah, who ascended the throne Nov. 8, 1933, on the assassination of his father, Mohammed Nadir Shah. In a July 17, 1973, coup, Gen. Mohammad Daud Khan, the king's brother-in-law, proclaimed Afghanistan a republic with himself as president and premier.

Bordering on both Russia and China, Afghanistan has been traditionally neutral. Armed forces: over 80,000.

Education and Religion. Education is free and, where facilities are available, compulsory. The University of Kabul was established in 1932. Principal languages are Pushtu and Persian. English is taught. Islam is the predominant religion.

Albania

Capital: Tirana, Area: 11,100 sq. mi. Population (1973 est.): 2,350,000. Monetary unit: Lek.

Albania, a Balkan communist republic, is a narrow mountainous land, slightly larger than Maryland, extending for 225 mi. along the E coast of the Adriatic, Yugoslavia and Greece are its neighbors. Mt. Korab, 9,066 ft. is the tallest peak.

Resources and Industries. Still a preponderantly agricultural nation, Albania in the 1960s and 1970s pressed programs of industrialization and agricultural modernization with the aid of communist China.

New industrial installations included chemical fertilizer, textile, electric cable and electric power plants.

Principal exports include petroleum, bitumen, chrome, iron and copper; cotton textiles, wood products and tobacco. More than half of Albania's foreign trade is with communist China.

History and Government. Albania has been overrun by warring armies for over 2,000 years. It declared its independence from the Turks in 1912; this was backed by a conference of European powers which placed Prince William of Wied on the throne in 1914. He fled within months because of uprisings. During World War I armies of several nations occupied the land by turns. In 1920, a republic was set up. In 1925, Ahmed Zogu seized the presidency; in 1928 he proclaimed himself king, assuming the title Zog I.

King Zog fled in 1939 when Italy invaded and annexed Albania. When Italy surrendered to the Allies in 1943, German troops took over; they left in 1944 and communist partisans seized power. Gen. Enver Hoxha was named provisional president; a communist front won a 1945 election; in 1946 a new constitution, modeled on that of the USSR, was adopted under Hoxha's leadership.

The U.S. and Britain voted against Albanian admission to the UN in 1946; it finally won admission in 1955 with Britain voting "yes" and the U. S. abstaining. In 1955 it was admitted to the Warsaw Pact. Its policies have been strongly pro-Stalinist, anti-Khrushchev, pro-communist China and hostile to Tito's Yugoslav regime. The USSR broke relations with Albania in Dec. 1961 and in 1962 barred it from Warsaw Pact meetings. Albania withdrew from the pact in 1968.

In 1970 communist China and Albania signed a new treaty providing for expanded trade and additional Chinese financial credits for Albania. In 1971, after years of mistrust, Albania resumed diplomatic relations with Yugoslavia and Greece.

Education and Religion. Historically, the largest segment of the population was Moslem, followed by Orthodox Christians and Roman Catholics. Primary education nominally is compulsory and free under the constitution. In 1969 there were 14,000 university and college students.

Racially the Albanians are mainly Ghegs in the north and Tosks in the south.

Defense. Military strength totals 38,000.

Algeria

Capital: Algiers. Area: 919,951 sq. mi. Population (UN est. 1973): 15,770,000. Monetary unit: Dinar.

Algeria, an independent republic more than 3 times the size of Texas, is located in northern Africa extending for 640 mi. along the Mediterranean Sea between Tunisia and Morocco. The southern Saharan Departments extend into the Sahara Desert and border on Niger, Mali and Mauritania. The Tell, located on the coast, comprises fertile plains from 50 to 100 mi. wide. Several chains of the Atlas Mtns., running roughly E-W and reaching altitudes of 7,000 ft., separate the coast regions from inland plateaus and the Sahara. Algiers, the capital, is the largest city.

Resources and Industries. Agricultural products include wheat, barley, oats, corn, potatoes, artichokes, flax and tobacco. Wine and olive oil are produced. Dates, pomegranates and figs grow abundantly. Cattle raising is important. There are large deposits of oil, iron, zinc, lead, mercury, coal, copper.

Exports consist chiefly of wines, fruits, iron and zinc ores, phosphate rock, cork, tobacco products, vegetables, liquefied natural gas and petroleum. Algeria is the world's 12th largest oil-producing nation. Trade is mainly with France.

Exploitation of the Sahara's vast oil and gas deposits and its tourist potentiality is being pressed.

In 1967-68 foreign oil distribution companies were nationalized; in 1970-71 several foreign oil producing companies were nationalized.

In 1972, the government pressed its industrialization program with an oil refinery, natural gas liquefication and iron and steel plants, and fertilizer and textile factories.

History and Government. The fertile Tell plains have attracted a succession of conquerors to Algeria from before the time of Christ. Once ruled by Carthage, the country after 146 B.C. came under control of the Romans. But it was the Arabs, who arrived in the 7th Century, who were to have the most lasting influence on the country. In 1518 Algiers and the coastal area came under Turkish domination. France took control in 1830, annexed it in 1842 and began to develop the land.

From 1954-62 growing Arab nationalism led to warfare between the French and the Algerians. The political impasse was not broken until French president Charles de Gaulle negotiated with the Front de Liberatione Nationale (FLN). Algeria in a referendum July, 1962, voted overwhelmingly for independence; de Gaulle proclaimed it independent July 3.

Internal strife continued, however, between opposing Algerian factions, and Ahmed Ben Bella, with Army support, assumed control in Aug. 1962.

A constitution was approved Sept. 8, 1963, and Premier Ben Bella, sole candidate, was elected president for a 5-year term Sept. 15. Nationalization of lands and industries proceeded rapidly. Algeria received a $100 million long-term industrial loan from the USSR in 1963, French aid continued.

Ben Bella was arrested and deposed June 19, 1965, in a bloodless, army-backed coup d'etat led by Col. Houari Boumediene (born Mohammed Boukharouba), defense minister. Col. Boumediene, on July 11, announced a new cabinet with himself as president.

Algeria is a member of the UN, OAU and Arab League.

Education and Religion. The population before independence included approx. 1 million Europeans, 80% of them Algerian-born, since reduced to about 80,000. Most Algerians are Arabs and Berbers, of Moslem faith. There are 3 universities and 21 technical institutes.

Defense. Armed forces, modernized with USSR aid, total 63,000.

Andorra

Capital: Andorra la Vella. Area: 179 sq. mi. Population (1973 Census): 25,000. Monetary units: Franc, Peseta.

Andorra is a tiny principality of valleys and mountains set high in the Pyrenees on the border of France and Spain. It has two co-princes, the president of France and the Spanish Catholic bishop of Urgel, whose representatives are charged with the administration of justice, but the country has enjoyed practical sovereignty since 1278. It pays an annual tribute of 960 francs to France and 460 pesetas to the bishop of Urgel.

Actual government is in the hands of a Council-

General of 24 members elected by universal suffrage, who enact laws and elect a syndic general, the top administrator. Women won voting rights in 1970.

The main industry is tourism (215 hotels), followed by sheep-raising. Andorra has considerable iron, lead, alum, stone and timber. Skiing, trout fishing and chamois hunting are among tourist attractions.

The official language is Catalan; Spanish and French are spoken; principal religion is Roman Catholicism.

Argentina

Capital: Buenos Aires. Area: 1,072,067 sq. mi. Population (UN est. 1972): 23,920,000. Monetary unit: Peso.

Argentina, 4 times the size of Texas, extends from Bolivia 2,300 miles to Tierra del Fuego and from the Andes to the South Atlantic, and is the 2d largest and 2d most populous country in South America, next to Brazil.

The mountains are grouped into 4 isolated systems: the Andean, Central, Misiones and Southern. Aconcagua is the highest peak in the Western Hemisphere, altitude 22,834 ft.

East of the Andes are great plains, heavily wooded and called the Gran Chaco in the north, and the fertile, treeless Pampas, given over to wheat and cattle raising, in the central region. Patagonia, in the south, is bleak and arid; petroleum and sheep are its main products.

Rio de la Plata is the estuary of one of the world's great drainage systems. It is a wide gulf of mostly fresh water, 170 mi. long, 140 mi. wide at its mouth. On its banks are 3 important cities, Buenos Aires and La Plata in Argentina and Montevideo in Uruguay. Emptying into it are the Parana River, 2,500 mi. long, and the Uruguay, 1,000, both starting far to the north in Brazil. Further south, other large rivers flow from the Andes, in the west, to the Atlantic, including the Colorado and Negro.

Resources and Industries. The mountains of Argentina contain deposits of coal, lead, zinc, iron, sulphur, silver, copper and gold. Petroleum is important.

Cotton, wheat, barley, rye, linseed, oats, alfalfa are important. Sugar, wine, cotton, fruit, corn, sorghum, tobacco and peanuts are produced. Sheep, cattle, horses, goats and pigs form the chief wealth of the ranches. In 1974 there were 56 million cattle and 43 million sheep, both high in world rankings. Meat processing is the chief industry. Flour milling is 2d. Argentina is the world's 4th largest meat exporter.

Railroads are state-owned.

Also important in the country's growing industrialization are chemicals, textiles, sugar-refining and machinery. In June 1973 price controls, moderate wage increases and a no-strike-for-two-years pledge by major unions were announced.

Foreign trade in thousands of U. S. dollars:

	Imports	Exports
1971	$1,869,000	$1,740,000
1972	$1,865,000	$1,885,000

History and Government. Discovered 1515-16 by Spanish explorers headed by Juan Diaz de Solis, Argentina remained under Spanish domination until the provinces, in a successful revolt, established an independent republic, May 25, 1810. In 1853 a liberal constitution was adopted.

The present constitution, proclaimed May 1, 1956, is essentially that of 1853.

There are 22 provinces which elect their own governors and legislatures, and a Federal District, Buenos Aires (area 72 sq. mi.), whose mayor is appointed by the president.

The president and vice president must be Roman Catholic and Argentine by birth. They are elected for 4-year terms by direct popular vote. Congress consists of a Senate of 69 and a House of Deputies. Voting is compulsory for both men and women.

Beginning in 1944, and after the election of Juan D. Peron, an army officer, as president in 1946, Argentine democracy was replaced by dictatorship. By concessions to labor Peron built a following; he then suppressed freedom of speech and press and religious schools and ran the country deeply into debt. Civilians, clericals and part of the armed forces unseated Peron Sept. 16, 1955, and he went into exile. A provisional government was replaced November, 1955, by a military junta, which chose Maj. Gen. Pedro Aramburu provisional president. He restored civil liberties, dissolved the Peronist party and returned expropriated property.

In the first free elections in 12 years, Feb. 22, 1958, Dr. Arturo Frondizi was elected president. Dissension among military leaders, democratic parties and the Peronist unions which had supported Dr. Frondizi resulted in a bloodless military coup Mar. 29, 1962. Another election and another military coup followed. In March 1971, Lt. Gen. Alejandro A. Lanusse took over as president; he ordered a return to civilian government.

In March 1973 elections, Hector J. Campora, a follower of Peron, was elected president. On July 13, 1973, Campora resigned and Peron, 77, returned after nearly 18 years in exile and was elected president Sept. 23, taking office Oct. 12. His 3d wife, Maria Estela, was elected vice president.

Peron died July 1, 1974, and Mrs. Peron, 43, succeeded, becoming the first woman president in the Western Hemisphere.

Guerrilla violence increased in the 1970s with political slayings and lucrative kidnapings; an American Exxon official was ransomed for $14.2 million in Mar. 1974.

Argentina is a member of the UN and OAS.

Education and Religion. The population is about 90% Roman Catholic, the constitutional religion since 1810. Primary education is free, secular, and compulsory. There are national universities in Cordoba (founded in 1613), Buenos Aires and 9 other cities, and numerous private universities. The language is Spanish. The people are of Spanish and Italian descent, with Basques, Swiss, Germans and British represented.

Defense. The 3 services total over 135,000 plus several hundred thousand reserves.

Australia

Capital: Canberra. Area: 2,967,909 sq. mi. (7,678,-700 sq. km.). Population (Govt. est. 1974): 13,268,000. Monetary unit: Australian dollar.

The continent of Australia, a huge island almost the size of the 48 conterminous U.S. states, is SE of Asia and below the islands of Indonesia. The Indian Ocean is W and S, the Pacific E and their waters meet N of Australia in the Timor and Arafura Seas. The Great Barrier Reef extends along the NE coast. About 150 mi. S of the state of Victoria lies the island state, Tasmania. Branches of the Pacific are the Coral Sea, NE, and the Tasman Sea, SE.

The Tropic of Capricorn bisects Australia. The Great Dividing Range along the E coast has Mt. Kosciusko, 7,316 ft., in New South Wales. The W plateau rises to 2,000 ft., with arid areas in the Great Sandy and Great Victoria Deserts. The NW part of Western Australia and Northern Territory are arid and torrid; Arnhem Land, in the latter, is a rugged wooded area reserved for aborigines. The NE has heavy rainfall and Cape York Peninsula has jungles. The Murray River rises in New South Wales, flows 1,600 mi. into the Indian Ocean and supplies hydro-electric plants.

States and territories of Australia with their areas in sq. mi. and 1972 est. populations were:

	Area	Population
New South Wales	309,433	4,680,700
Victoria	87,884	3,562,000
Queensland	667,000	1,883,900
South Australia	380,070	1,190,900
Western Australia	975,920	1,059,000
Tasmania	26,383	393,000
Northern Territory	520,280	94,800
Australian Capital Terr.	939	162,000
Totals	2,967,909	13,026,300

The capitals are: New South Wales, Sydney; Victoria, Melbourne; Queensland, Brisbane; South Australia, Adelaide; Western Australia, Perth; Tasmania, Hobart; Northern Terr., Darwin; Capital Territory, Canberra.

Home of the kangaroo, Australia also is the habitat of other strange flora and fauna: the koala, or living teddy bear; the platypus, wombat, dingo, Tasmanian devil, a blind mole, and barking and frilled lizards.

By 1973, Australia had added almost 3 million population from immigration since World War II. About one-half was British. Australia's aborigines in the tribal state are primitive and nomadic, but most now are detribalized. Programs are directed toward their ultimate assimilation.

The Melbourne Cup horse race is the biggest annual sports event; cricket, tennis and football are played extensively. Excellent beaches are numerous.

Resources and Industries. Almost from earliest days of settlement a primary producing country, Australia has become highly industrialized. More than 25% of the total labor force of approx. 5,550,000 work in factories; about 15% are engaged in rural occupations.

Wool and meat are important products. With an annual clip of more than 1.9 billion lbs., Australia produces 30% of the world's wool, 50% of its merino wool and is the largest exporter of both beef and lamb. It is also one of the largest wheat producers, with over 385 million bu. annually. Over one-half is exported. Other important products are sugar, wine, fruit, vegetables, meat, grains, minerals, including uranium, gold, coal, copper, iron, silver, lead, bauxite, rutile and petroleum products.

Discovery of vast iron ore deposits in Western Australia brought a mining boom to desolate areas in the northwest in 1965. New oil and gas fields were discovered 1965-1968, nickel in 1969, uranium in 1972.

Principal manufactures include iron and steel, textiles, electrical and radio equipment, drugs, chemicals, paints, machinery, metal work, clothing, motor cars and engines, aircraft and ships. Unemployment in 1973 was est. at 1.5% of the work force. Gross domestic product in 1972-73 was $40,763 million (US $60.6 billion).

In recent years exports of mineral and industrial products have increased considerably.

Australia changed its currency from pounds-shillings-pence to dollars and cents Feb. 14, 1966, with its dollar worth half the old Australian pound. It will complete adoption of metric weights and measures by 1980.

Foreign trade, in thousands of U.S. dollars:

	Imports	Exports
1972	$4,556,000	$6,329,000
1973	$6,802,000	$9,389,000

Tourism is a rapidly expanding industry. In 1972 Australia had 426,400 overseas visitors, more than double the number 5 years earlier.

History and Government. Australia has been settled since 1788. The Commonwealth, proclaimed Jan. 1, 1901, is a self-governing federation of 6 states and 2 territories. Parliament consists of the Crown (represented by the governor-general), the Senate and House of Representatives. In Dec. 1972 elections, the Labor party ended 23 years of rule by the Liberal and Country parties coalition.

In May 1974 elections, Labor won 66 seats in the House; the Liberal and Country parties won 61. Each group won 29 seats in the Senate.

Gough Whitlam, Labor prime minister, ended

restrictions on non-white immigrants, ended the draft and military aid to South Vietnam and recognized China and North Vietnam.

Pension acts provide for payments of war, old age and invalid pensions; also cover the blind, the unemployed, victims of tuberculosis and, in some cases, dependents of former soldiers. The National Health Scheme provides free drugs and subsidizes hospital and medical expenses.

A maternity act provides for the payment of a maternity allowance for every child born in Australia. Social security for children includes child endowment payments for children under 16.

Education and Religion. Education is free and compulsory. There are 15 universities and 3 university colleges. The Church of England claims 37.7% of the population, the remainder being Roman Catholic, 23.3%; Presbyterian, 9.7%; Methodist, 10.8%.

Defense. Armed forces total 73,300.

Australian Territories

The jointly administered **Territory of Papua New Guinea**, originally 2 separate territories, is governed by a 1949 Act placing New Guinea under the UN Trusteeship system, but retaining the status of Papua as a Crown territory. Combined pop. of the 2 was est. in 1973 at 2,610,000.

New Guinea, once German New Guinea, later a League of Nations mandate and UN Trust Territory of Australia, occupies the NE quarter of the island of New Guinea, N. of Australia, and includes nearby island groups: **New Britain, New Ireland** and the **Admiralty Islands** of the Bismarck Archipelago; **Bougainville**, 3,880 sq. mi.; **Buka**, 220 sq. mi., and smaller islands of the Solomons. Total area of the territory is about 93,000 sq. mi., with a population est. in 1972 at 1,840,000.

Papua is the southeastern part of the island. Area, 90,540 sq. mi.; population est. 1972, 740,000.

Papua New Guinea is governed by an administrator, a cabinet and a legislative House of Assembly, with 96 of its 100 members elected by popular vote in 1972, an increase over the previous number. Australia granted it self-government except for defense, foreign affairs and internal security Dec. 1, 1973. Full independence was planned for Dec. 1974 or 1975.

Principal products are timber, copra, cocoa, rubber and coffee. Gold and copper are mined.

Norfolk Island was taken over by Australia, 1914. It has an area of 13.5 sq. mi. and a population (est. 1973) of 1,380. The soil is very fertile and is suitable for the cultivation of citrus fruits, bananas and coffee. Many of the inhabitants are descendants of the Bounty mutineers; some descendants moved to Norfolk in 1856 from Pitcairn Is.; some stayed, some returned to Pitcairn.

Territory of Ashmore and Cartier Islands, area 2 sq. mi., in the Indian Ocean came under the authority of Australia May 1934 and are administered as part of Northern Territory. **Heard** and **McDonald Islands** are governed by Capital Territory.

Cocos-Keeling Islands, 27 small coral islands in the Indian Ocean 1,300 miles NW of Australia. Pop. (est. 1972): 618; area: 5 sq. mi.

Christmas Island, 52 sq. mi., pop. 3,361 (est. 1970), 230 mi. S. of Java, was taken over from Singapore in 1958. It has phosphate deposits.

Australian Antarctic Territory was claimed by Australia in 1933, including 2,472,000 sq. mi. of territory S of 60th parallel S. Lat. and between 160th-45th meridans E. Long.

Austria

Capital: Vienna. Area: 32,374 sq. mi. Population (UN est. 1973): 7,520,000. Monetary unit: Schilling.

Austria is a republic in the mountainous region of central Europe, 360 mi. long, 160 mi. wide — slightly smaller than Maine. Mountain passes cross frontiers; the Brenner, below the Stubai Alps, has been a major route to Italy since ancient times.

Principal river, the Danube, flows from Bavaria in NW to Czechoslovakia, E. Others are the Enns, Inn, Drau, Ill, Mur and Salzach, some furnishing hydroelectric power. There are numerous lakes and popular spas, such as Bad Gastein and Bad Ischl.

Resources and Industries. Austria produces iron ore, oil, timber, magnesite, aluminum, coal, lignite, cement and copper. It is an important source of high-grade graphite. Hydroelectric power has been widely developed. Manufactures include steel, machinery, vehicles, electrical and optical instruments, glassware, sporting goods, paper, yarns, textiles, fertilizers, chemicals and artistic leather goods.

Although farmland is limited, Austria produces about 85% of its foodstuffs. It grows wheat, rye, barley, oats, corn, potatoes, sugar beets. Vineyards flourish in Lower Austria and in Burgenland.

Over 11 million tourists visit annually. The Salzburg Festival, the Vienna State Opera, skiing and spas are among attractions.

Principal exports are iron, steel, paper, textiles, machinery, chemicals, metal products, vehicles, aluminum, electric power. Trade is heavy with West Germany, Italy and the U.S.

Foreign trade in thousands of U.S. dollars:

	Imports	Exports
1972	$5,216,000	$3,883,000
1973	$7,120,000	$5,289,000

History and Government. Austria, the East Mark (Ost Mark) of Charlemagne (788 A.D.) came under the Hapsburgs in 1278. Tyrol was added 1363, Bohemia (Czech) and Hungary, 1526. The Turks were twice turned back at Vienna, 1529 and 1683. Austrian dominance of German lands was challenged in the 18th Century and Empress Maria Theresa (ruled 1740-1780) lost Silesia to Frederick II (the Great) of Prussia. Austria took slices of Poland in the partitions of 1772, 1793 and 1795. Austria was the scene of major Napoleonic battles and helped defeat him. The Congress of Vienna, 1815, awarded it Istria, Illyria, and the Italian provinces of Lombardy and Venetia. Austria lost Lombardy to Italy 1859 and Venetia 1866, after Prussia defeated Austria in the Seven Weeks' War.

Under the Dual Monarchy of Austria-Hungary, established 1867 to recognize the aspirations of the Magyars, Francis Joseph was Emperor of Austria and King of Hungary. The nation had an area of 261,259 sq. mi., population c. 51 million. It contained Austria, Hungary, Bohemia, Transylvania, Polish Galicia, Trentino, Slavonia, Croatia, Bosnia, Herzegovina, Banat. After Archduke Francis Ferdinand, heir to the Austrian throne, and his consort were assassinated in Sarajevo, Bosnia, June 28, 1914, Austria declared war on Serbia, which helped precipitate World War I. It was dismembered after that war; became a republic comprised of 9 small states in 1918.

Between the 2 world wars Austria had a turbulent political history. Socialists introduced some socio-economic changes. These were checked by Chancellor Engelbert Dollfuss, 1934. Dollfuss was murdered by Nazi conspirators July 25, 1934. Germany, under Hitler, occupied Austria Mar. 13, 1938, and proclaimed its union with Germany. It was reestablished as a republic in 1945, consisting of the states of Burgenland, Lower Austria, Upper Austria, Salzburg, Styria, Carinthia, Tyrol, Vorarlberg, and the city of Vienna.

Dr. Karl Renner was elected president of the provisional government after liberation by the Allies, 1945. After 17 years of occupation, delayed by tactics of the Soviet Union, a treaty of March 15, 1955 restored the frontiers of Jan. 1, 1938, prohibited economic or political union with Germany, required support of democratic institutions. With ratification July 27, 1955, Austria formally regained sovereignty. It declared its perpetual neutrality.

The president is elected by secret ballot for a 6-

year term. He appoints the chancellor; Parliamentary elections Oct. 10, 1971, gave the Socialist party a majority of seats; a Socialist was elected president in June 1974.

Austria is a member of the UN and EFTA. In 1972 Austria and 5 other EFTA members joined with EEC (Common Market) members in agreements for mutual abolition of tariffs on industrial goods.

Education and Religion. The predominant religion is Roman Catholicism. Elementary education is free and compulsory between the ages of 6 and 15. There are universities in Vienna, Graz, Innsbruck and Salzburg. The language is almost entirely German.

Defense. Armed forces total 52,000.

The Bahamas

Capital: Nassau. Area: 4,404 sq. mi. Population (UN est. 1973): 190,000. Monetary unit: Bahamian dollar.

The Commonwealth of the Bahamas achieved full independence from Great Britain on July 10, 1973. The Bahamas comprise nearly 700 islands (30 inhabited) and over 2,000 islets in the western Atlantic. They extend 760 mi. NW to SE from a point 50 mi. off Florida to about 70 mi. from Haiti.

Christopher Columbus first set foot in the New World on the island of San Salvador (also called Watling Is.) on the eastern fringe of the Bahamas in 1492. British settlement started in 1647; the islands became a British colony in 1783. Internal self-government was granted by Britain in 1964. Elections to the Assembly in 1967 resulted in the selection of the islands' first black prime minister, Lynden O. Pindling.

The prime minister leads the majority part of the 38-member, elected Assembly. The 16-member Senate is appointed by the governor-general (nominally representing the British queen) on the advice of the prime minister and the opposition leader. The Bahamas joined the UN and Commonwealth.

Tourism is the main industry; second is international banking and investment management. Fruit and vegetables are grown mostly for local use. There are cement and pharmaceutical plants. Exports include salt, rock lobster, tomatoes, cucumbers, handicraft objects.

English is the official language; Anglican is the predominant religion. Elementary schools are free and compulsory except on a few of the "Out Islands." Over 80% of the population is of African descent.

Bahrain

Capital: Manama. Area: 231 sq. mi. Population: (est. 1973); 230,000. Monetary unit: Dinar.

Bahrain, long a British Protected State, declared its complete independence Aug. 14, 1971. It includes the main island, Bahrain, and several smaller islands midway along the Persian (also called Arabian) Gulf, about 20 mi. off the Arabian Peninsula's NE coast.

Pearls, shrimp, fruit and vegetables were the mainstays of the economy until oil, discovered in 1932, gradually became most important. By the 1970s, oil reserves showed signs of depletion. Important contributions were made to the economy by a large refinery handling oil pumped by undersea pipeline from Saudi Arabia as well as the local product, by a large aluminum smelter using local natural gas, and by increased use of Bahrain as a trade trans-shipment center. Bahrain took part in the 1973-74 Arab oil embargo against the U. S. and other nations.

Long ruled by the Khalifa family, Bahrain signed a treaty in 1861 giving Great Britain responsibility for Bahrain's defense and foreign relations. When Britain announced it would remove its military forces from the Persian Gulf area by the end of 1971, Bahrain sought to form a federation with the 7 Trucial Sheikhdoms (now the United Arab Emirates) and Qatar, which were also British Protected States. The attempt failed and Bahrain declared itself an independent nation. It is ruled by an Emir, a Prime Minister and a Council of Ministers (cabinet). In 1973 a constitution created the first Bahrain parliament, the National Assembly; 30 members are elected by male citizens 18 or over; 14 Cabinet members also sit in the Assembly.

Most of the Bahrainis are of northern Arabian descent, half of the Sunni branch of Islam, half of the Shi'ite branch. Arabic is the official language; Persian and English are also spoken. Education and health services are free.

In Oct. 1973 Bahrain canceled an agreement allowing U. S. Navy ships to use facilities in the former British naval base.

Bangladesh

Capital: Dacca. Area: 55,126 sq. mi. Population (1974 census): 71,316,517. Monetary unit: Taka.

East Pakistan, the smaller but more populous of the 2 sections of Pakistan, achieved independence as Bangladesh (Bengal Nation) during the Dec. 3-16, 1971, India-Pakistan war. Separated from West Pakistan by 1,000 mi. of India, it is mostly a low plain cut by the Ganges and Brahmaputra Rivers and is bounded by India, Burma and the Bay of Bengal. It is subject to heavy monsoon rains. A Nov. 13, 1970, cyclone killed at least 300,000 persons in coastal areas.

Resources and Industries. Bangladesh is primarily agricultural, with small, fertile farms. The area normally produces most of the world's jute, used in twine and sacks, and has large rice crops. Resources include rivers for irrigation and hydroelectric power, and natural gas. Small industries, many destroyed in 1971 fighting, were reestablished in 1972. Food shipments and other economic aid were provided by India, the U. S., USSR and others after the war. In Mar. 1972 Bangladesh announced nationalization of banks and some industries.

History and Government. British rule over the vast Indian sub-continent, dating from the 18th Century, ended in Aug. 1947 when India and Pakistan became independent nations. Pakistan's government power was centered in West Pakistan, while East Pakistan, with about 56% of the population, demanded greater economic benefits and political reforms. There were riots in 1968-69.

In Dec. 1970 elections, the Awami League, which demanded greater autonomy for East Pakistan, won a majority of seats in the National Assembly, which was to draft a new Pakistan constitution. But Pakistan Pres. A. M. Yahya Khan postponed the Assembly sessions. A general strike and riots swept East Pakistan and on Mar. 25, 1971, West Pakistani troops launched attacks on rebellious Bengalis. Awami League leaders declared independence the next day. Months of fighting followed in which it was estimated a million or more died as, it was charged, West Pakistan troops conducted repressive attacks on the populace and guerrilla forces. Some 10 million Bengalis fled to India, which was supporting their cause.

Following border skirmishes, India and Pakistan each declared on Dec. 3, 1971, that the other had launched war. Pakistani troops surrendered Dec. 15 in the East; the Pakistan government accepted India's offer of a cease-fire on both East and West Pakistan fronts Dec. 16. India had recognized Bangladesh as independent Dec. 6. The U.S., which had earlier indicated sympathy with Pakistan, recognized Bangladesh Apr. 4, 1972.

Sheik Mujibur Rahman, Awami League leader arrested in Mar. 1971, was freed by Pakistan and became Bangladesh prime minister Jan. 12, 1972.

Bangladesh joined the Commonwealth but UN membership was vetoed by Communist China, 1972.

A constitution providing for a parliamentary government took effect Dec. 16, 1972. In elections Mar. 7, 1973, Sheik Mujib's Awami League party won 305 of 313 seats.

In Aug. 1973 an India-Pakistan agreement on return of 1971 war prisoners paved the way for future recognition of Bangladesh by Pakistan and release of

Bangladesh and Pakistani nationals stranded in each other's country. By 1974 most war prisoners were returned to Pakistan which, in turn, accepted more than 100,000 of the non-Bengali Biharis, 500,000 of whom sought to leave Bangladesh.

Most of the Bangladesh people are Moslem Bengalis. The official language is Bengali.

Barbados

Capital: Bridgetown. Area: 166 sq. mi. Population (UN est. 1973): 240,000. Monetary unit: East Caribbean dollar.

Barbados achieved full independence from Great Britain Nov. 30, 1966. Furthest east of the West Indies, the island is about 2½ times the size of the District of Columbia; it lies alone in the Atlantic almost completely surrounded by coral reefs. Its highest point is Mt. Hillaby, 1,115 ft. The name Barbados (bearded) was believed given it by Portuguese or Spanish sailors, referring to bearded fig trees.

An English ship visited the island in 1605; English settlers arrived in 1627. Slaves were imported, but freed in 1834. Most of the islanders are Negroes, the language is English and the religion of most is Anglican.

A charter of 1652 provided for a governor-general, council and assembly. Self-rule was achieved gradually; universal suffrage was granted in 1950, cabinet government in 1958, full internal self-government in 1961. It has a parliament and prime minister and, as a member of the Commonwealth, a governor-general.

Sugar, molasses, rum, cotton and building lime are the main products; there is a lively flying fish industry and, thanks mainly to the attractions of excellent beaches, the tourist business has boomed. But unemployment is high. In 1973 Barbados joined other West Indies states in the Caribbean Common Market.

With over 1,400 persons per sq. mi., the population density is one of the world's highest. Barbados also has one of the world's lowest illiteracy rates.

Belgium

Capital: Brussels. Area: 11,779 sq. mi. Population (est. 1973): 9,711,000. Monetary unit: Franc.

Belgium's seacoast of 40 mi. borders on the North Sea at the Strait of Dover. Slightly larger than Maryland, the country shares borders with the Netherlands, Germany, Luxembourg and France. The Meuse (Maas) River crosses the country from France to the Netherlands. The Scheldt (Escaut Schelde) makes Antwerp an ocean port via the Netherlands.

Brussels, Bruges, Ghent and Antwerp are noted for art and architecture; Liege and Charleroi are important industrially. Antwerp is the world's 3d largest port.

Resources and Industries. Coal is the nation's only important mineral. Although Belgium is essentially a manufacturing country, agriculture and forestry are profitable industries. The principal crops are oats, rye, wheat, potatoes, barley and sugar beets.

Important industries are mining, steel manufacture, glassware, diamond cutting, food and beverages, fishing, textiles and chemicals. Beurs voor Diamant in Antwerp is the world's largest diamond trading center.

Belgium lives by its foreign trade; about 40% of its entire production is sold abroad (75% of steel and glass). The Belgium-Luxembourg Economic Union is one of the world's foremost exporters of steel.

The gross national product rose from $35.9 billion in 1970 to $41.6 billion in 1973.

Foreign trade in thousands of U.S. dollars:

	Imports	Exports
1972	$17,055,800	$17,603,375
1973	$21,925,000	$22,301,000

History and Government. Belgium, land of the Belgae conquered by Julius Caesar, has a 2,000-year history during which it was ruled by the Romans,

Merovingian Franks, Burgundy, Spain, Austria and France. After the fall of Napoleon, 1815, Belgium was made a part of the Netherlands. Its citizens demanded separation from the Dutch in 1830. Belgium became an independent constitutional monarchy in 1830 and chose Prince Leopold of Saxe-Coburg king, as Leopold I.

By the treaty of London, Apr. 19, 1839, Austria, France, Great Britain, Netherlands, Prussia and Russia guaranteed the inviolability of Belgium; this was the "scrap of paper" repudiated by Germany when its troops entered Belgium, Aug. 2, 1914. After World War I Belgium was awarded 382 sq. mi. of territory formerly held by Germany, including Malmedy.

During World War II, Leopold III surrendered to Germany, May 28, 1940, to avoid further bloodshed. His cabinet maintained a government-in-exile in London. Nevertheless, Belgium suffered heavily. Ancient churches, houses and records were ruined at Nivelles, Mons, Tournai, Liege, Louvain; the University Library at Louvain, burned in 1914, restored with American aid, was again burned with 900,000 vols. About 50,000 Belgians died, some in Nazi prison camps.

In 1950 Belgians voted 57% in favor of recalling Leopold III (who had been in Switzerland since being freed from German internment), but Socialist opposition-was so vehement that the king abdicated and his son became King Baudouin I July 17, 1951. Born Sept. 7, 1930, he was the son of Leopold's first wife, Princess Astrid of Sweden. Baudouin married (Dec. 15, 1960) Dona Fabiola de Mora y Aragon of Spain.

Universal suffrage is in force and those who fail to vote are fined. Women have voted since 1949.

Parliament consists of a Senate with members elected for 4 years, partly directly and partly indirectly; the number elected directly is equal to half the number of members of the House of Representatives. The representatives are directly elected, for 4 years, by proportional representation (one for every 40,000 population).

The Flemings of northern Belgium speak Dutch while French is the language of the Walloons in the south. The language difference has been a perennial source of controversy, particularly as it affects education, with Flemish parents unwilling to have their children taught in French.

Disagreement between the 2 groups became embittered in 1968 elections in which minority extremist parties increased their strength. In 1971 Belgium sought to solve the problem through creation of decentralized administrative and cultural communities.

Belgium is a member of the UN, NATO, EEC and the Benelux economic union.

Education and Religion. Roman Catholicism is the religion of the great majority. Part of the income of the ministers of the Catholic, Jewish, Church of England and Protestant Evangelical religions is paid by the government. There are universities in Ghent, Liege, Brussels, Mons, Antwerp and Louvain and agricultural, technical, art and music schools.

Defense: Armed forces total 89,000.

Bhutan

Capital: Thimphu. Area: 19,305 sq. mi. Population (est. 1973): 1,150,000. Monetary unit: Indian rupee.

The tiny kingdom of Bhutan or Druk-Yul (Dragon-Nation) is a constitutional monarchy in the eastern Himalayas, adjoining Tibet, Sikkim and the Indian provinces of West Bengal and Assam. It is 190 mi. long from east to west and 90 mi. across, with high mountains and jungles. Most of the people are Bhotias of Tibetan origin and are Buddhists; a minority are of Nepalese descent.

Agriculture is the chief industry. The principal products are rice, corn, yak butter, lac, wax, cloth, elephants, ponies and timber.

The ruler of the kingdom is the "Dragon King,"

Jigme Singye Wangchuk (born 1955), who inherited the throne July 24, 1972, and was crowned June 2, 1974. The 150-member Tsongdu (Assembly) may remove the king by a two-thirds vote; he would be succeeded by his heir. Bhutan is guided by India in its foreign affairs. It joined the UN in 1971.

Modernization has begun, including the country's first road network usable by automobiles, linking central Bhutan and India. There is also airline service from India. Dzongs (castles), monasteries and a game sanctuary are among attractions.

Bolivia

Capital: Sucre. Seat of gov't: La Paz. Area: 424,162 sq. mi. Population (UN est. 1973): 5,330,000. Monetary unit: Peso.

Bolivia is a landlocked nation, over 8 times the size of N.Y. State. It lies across the Andes, and its chief topographical feature is the great central plateau at an altitude of 12,000 ft., over 500 mi. long, lying between two great cordilleras having 3 of the highest peaks in South America. More than 65% of the population are Indians; 10% are white, and 25% are mixed (cholo).

Lake Titicaca, on the Peruvian-Bolivian border, is the highest lake in the world on which steamboats ply (12,506 ft.), and is the 2d largest lake in South America (est. 3,200 sq. mi.).

The legal capital is Sucre, but La Paz, a city more accessible, is the actual seat of government. La Paz lies in the heart of a gigantic canyon about 3 mi. wide, 10 mi. long and 1,500 ft. deep, at an altitude of about 11,800 ft., and framed with high Andean peaks. Its huge cathedral seating 12,000, begun 1835, was dedicated 1933.

Resources and Industries. Agriculture claims 50% of the work force. Products include potatoes, sugar, coffee, barley, cocoa, highland rice, corn, bananas, citrus, rubber and cinchona bark.

The most important industry is mining. There are large deposits of tin, silver, copper, lead, zinc, petroleum, antimony, bismuth, wolfram, gold, iron, cadmium, borate of lime and natural gas. More than 12% of the world's output of tin is produced in Bolivia, running to 28,000 tons or more annually. The 3 largest tin producers were nationalized in 1952. The oilfields and plants of a U.S. company were nationalized in Oct. 1969. A U.S. company's lead and zinc mine concession was canceled in April 1971.

Bolivian tin-miners' attempts to negotiate better working conditions with the government-owned Bolivian Mining Corp. were led during 1967-68 by a group of Roman Catholic priests. An agreement was reached in March 1968 in which the corporation agreed to permit union activities and provide better working conditions and more housing and hospitals.

Bolivia receives economic aid from the U.S. and the Inter-American Development Bank, the World Bank and the International Monetary Fund. It is a member of the UN and OAS.

In May 1969 Bolivia joined Chile, Colombia, Ecuador and Peru in an Andean Common Market.

History and Government. Once part of the ancient Inca empire, Bolivia was under Spanish domination for centuries before it gained independence Aug. 6, 1825, naming itself after Simon Bolivar, famed liberator.

Bolivia's 16th constitution, adopted in 1967, provides for strong executive power, nationalization of mines, and agrarian reform. The Congress it provided for was dissolved in Sept. 1969.

Dr. Victor Paz Estenssoro, elected to a 3d term as President May 31, 1964, was ousted Nov. 4 and the government was taken over in one of a series of military coups. Military and civilian anti-Communist forces under Col. Hugo Banzer Suarez took over the government in a brief conflict, Aug. 19-22, 1971. In 1973 the government pressed school-building and oil-exploration programs. In 1974 Brazil contracted to build steel, cement and petrochemical plants in

Bolivia and a pipeline to carry Bolivian natural gas 1,000 mi. to Sao Paulo, Brazil.

Unrest continued as peasants and miners staged protests; in July 1974 Banzer dismissed civilian members of his cabinet but promised constitutional rule in 1975.

Education and Religion. Primary education is free and compulsory. Adult illiteracy, estimated at 58%, is being lowered. There are 7 universities. Roman Catholicism is the predominant religion. Spanish is the official language.

Defense. Bolivia's armed forces total over 21,000.

Botswana

Capital: Gaborone. Area: 219,815 sq. mi. Population (UN est. 1973): 650,000. Monetary unit: South African rand.

The former British Protectorate of Bechuanaland received full independence Sept. 30, 1966 and joined the UN Oct. 17, 1966.

In the center of Southern Africa and populated predominantly by blacks, Botswana shares borders with the Republic of South Africa, South-West Africa (Namibia) and Rhodesia. It also claims to border on Zambia, its nearest black-ruled neighbor. It is slightly larger than Texas.

The Kalahari Desert, supporting only nomadic Bushmen and a few wild animals, spreads over the southwestern areas of Botswana; there are swamplands and farming areas in the north, and rolling plains in the east where livestock are grazed.

Cattle raising is the largest industry. Large copper and nickel deposits were discovered in 1967 and diamonds in 1969. Corn, sorghum, beans and peanuts are raised in the north. Tourism is flourishing; black-maned lions and swamp antelopes are hunted by safaris.

Many of the Botswana work as migrant labor in South Africa and much of the country's chief export, meat, goes to that country.

In 1885, Bechuanaland was made a British protectorate after local chiefs appealed to Great Britain for aid to halt encroachment on their territories by Boers of South Africa's Transvaal.

It is a republic with a president, a House of Chiefs (which handles questions of tradition) and a National Assembly.

Brazil

Capital: Brasilia. Area: 3,286,470 sq. mi. Population (Govt. est. 1974): 105,137,000. Monetary unit: Cruzeiro.

Brazil is the largest nation in South America in area and population. Larger in area than the 48 states in conterminous U.S., it is smaller than the 50 states. It has a coastline on the Atlantic Ocean of 4,603 mi., and extends approximately 2,689 from N to S and 2,684 from E to W. The northern part is the great, heavily-wooded basin of the Amazon (1,465,637 sq. mi. in Brazil) which rises in the Peruvian Andes and empties into the Atlantic.

The Amazon basin has a network of rivers which are navigable for 15,814 mi. The Amazon River by itself flows 2,093 mi. through Brazil, and is navigable for 2,300 mi., to the Peruvian riverport of Iquitos.

The majestic falls of the Iguazu, 230 ft. high but extremely wide, are on the Brazil-Argentina border; Glass Falls, in Bahia west of Salvador, are 1,325 ft. high. Tallest mountain is Pico da Neblina, 10,046 ft., on the Venezuela border.

The south central region, favored by climate, resources and communications, has 45% of the population and produces 75% of agricultural goods and 80% of industrial output.

Brasilia, the capital city, was inaugurated Apr. 21, 1960, superseding Rio de Janeiro. Fast-growing Sao Paulo is the largest city in South America.

Resources and Industries: Brazil has vast mineral wealth and exploitation is being spurred. It leads the world in output of quartz crystal and beryl; is 2d in sheet mica; 3d in manganese, columbium and tantalum; 7th in iron ore. It has large deposits of iron (one-third of the world's reserves) and monazite, a source of thorium, alternate to uranium as a supplier of fissionable material. Gold output is about 142,000 troy oz. annually. Also important are oil, nickel, chrome, diamonds, coal, tungsten, tin, bauxite, various gem stones.

Cotton weaving is among important manufacturing industries, occupying 25% of workers. Brazil produces more than 5 million tons of steel annually, about 40% in the Volta Redonda national mills. Automotive, aluminum, petrochemical, cement, pharmaceutical, plastics, food and beverage, electrical appliances, shipbuilding, ceramics, shoe, tire, paper, glass and heavy machinery industries are growing.

Brazil, world's greatest coffee grower, supplies about 30% of the coffee consumed in the U.S. Cotton, soybeans, sugar, cocoa and iron ore are also important exports. There are large crops of bananas, manioc, oranges, pineapples, rice and corn. Also exported are castor oil and tobacco.

Brahman (zebu) cattle of India thrive in Brazil, which is 5th among world leaders with 90 million cattle. It also has 35 million hogs and 26 million sheep.

Brazil's economy boomed in the 1970s; the gross national product was up 11.4% in 1973. Exports also showed strong gains. But inflation, though slowed, remained a problem. Brazil celebrated the 150th anniversary of its independence with Export 72, a world trade fair, in Sao Paulo. In 1974 Brazil completed its 3,150-mi. Trans-Amazon Highway, stretching from the Atlantic coast to the Peruvian border, and a 9-mi. bridge across Rio de Janeiro harbor.

Foreign trade in thousands of U.S. dollars:

	Imports	Exports
1972	$4,723,000	$3,990,000
1973	$7,210,000	$6,199,000

History and Government. Pedro Alvares Cabral, a Portuguese navigator, is generally credited as the first European to reach Brazil, 1500.

Brazil was developed as a colony of Portugal until the royal house of Braganca, fleeing from Lisbon before Napoleon's army in 1807, transferred the seat of government to Rio de Janeiro, March, 1808. Brazil thereupon became a kingdom under Dom Joao VI. After his return to Portugal, his son Pedro I, proclaimed the independence of the country, Sept. 7, 1822, and was acclaimed emperor, Oct. 12, 1822. The second emperor, Dom Pedro II, was driven from the throne Nov. 15, 1889, by a revolution which established a republic, the United States of Brazil, which was the nation's official name until Jan. 1967 when a new constitution changed it to Federative Republic of Brazil.

There are 22 states, with limited autonomy, a federal district and 4 territories: Roraima, Rondonia, Amapa and Fernando de Noronha Is.

Brazil took part in World Wars I and II on the Allied side. It is a member of both the UN and OAS.

A military junta took control in 1930. Getulio Vargas became provisional president until 1933, when he was elected president under a new constitution. Out in 1945, he was reelected in 1950, but in 1954 the army forced him to retire.

In 1964, after a succession of presidents, economic and social problems brought the ouster of Pres. Joao Goulart, in a part-military, part-civilian coup. Gen. Humberto Castelo Branco was named president. A new constitution, adopted in 1967, strengthened the powers of the presidency, reducing those of Congress. Both Pres. Castelo Branco and his successor, Pres. Arthur da Costa e Silva, an army marshal elected by Congress in 1966, at times ruled by decree.

Pres. Costa e Silva suffered a stroke and died in 1969. Military leaders named Gen. Emilio G. Medici to succeed him and he was confirmed by Congress. He said certain curbs on civil liberties would be continued. He named Gen. Ernesto Geisel to succeed

him, and on Jan. 15, 1974, an electoral college consisting of representatives of Congress and of the state legislatures, elected Geisel president.

Education and Religion. Roman Catholicism is the predominant religion.

There are 65 universities in Brazil as well as other institutions of higher education. Primary, 5-year schools number more than 165,000 and there are more than 22,000 median level schools. Primary and secondary schools are free. The language is Portuguese.

Armed forces total over 200,000.

Bulgaria

Capital: Sofia. Area: 42,829 sq. mi. Population (UN est. 1973): 8,620,000. Monetary unit: Lev.

The People's Republic of Bulgaria, fronting on the Black Sea, is about the size of Ohio. It is bounded by Romania, Turkey, Greece and Yugoslavia. The Balkan Mtns. stretch across the center of the country with the Danubian Plain in the north and the Rhodope Mts. and Thracian Plain in the south.

Resources and Industries. Under communism after World War II, farms were collectivized, resources nationalized and foreign trade made a government monopoly. The principal crops are wheat, fruit, rye, barley, oats, corn, potatoes and tobacco. Agriculture claimed a large percentage of the population, but the country has been industrialized under a nationalized planned economy which emphasizes electric power, chemicals, coal, machinery, metals, textiles, building materials, fur, leather goods and oil. About 62% of the work force is non-agricultural.

In 1971 productive enterprises were centralized into some 60 state economic amalgamations. The index of industrial production (1963=100) reached 285 in 1973. Tourism is promoted and over 2 million tourists visit Bulgaria annually.

About 80% of trade is with nations of the communist bloc. Exports include maize, wheat, vegetables, chemicals, silver, textiles, hides, tobacco, rose attar, lead, zinc, cement, machinery, industrial vehicles (fork-lifts), wine.

Foreign trade in thousands of U.S. dollars:

	Imports	Exports
1972	$2,548,000	$2,603,000
1973	$3,266,000	$3,301,000

History and Government. The Bulgars and Slavs settled Bulgaria in the 7th Century and became Christians in 865 A.D. The Turks conquered Bulgaria in 1396. It revolted in 1876, and in 1878 was made a principality. In 1908 it became an independent kingdom and Ferdinand of Saxe-Coburg-Gotha became Czar Ferdinand I of Bulgaria. It expanded after the first Balkan war but lost its Aegean coastline in World War I, when it sided with Germany.

Under the influence of King Boris III, Bulgaria joined the Axis in World War II, occupying considerable Balkan territory. King Boris died 1943 and a regency ruled for Simeon II, born 1937. In 1944 Bulgaria withdrew from the war, but the USSR refused to recognize its neutrality, declared war Sept. 5. Bulgaria asked for an armistice and declared war on Germany Sept. 7. In a plebiscite Sept. 8, 1946, the monarchy was abolished and a republic voted, which was established one week later. Georgi Dimitrov, Communist party leader, became the first premier.

A new constitution, adopted in May 1971, provides that the National Assembly, elected for 5 years, is technically the supreme organ of government. The Assembly chooses a premier and a State Council whose president is the head of state.

Bulgaria was admitted to the UN in 1955 and is a member of the Warsaw Pact.

Education and Religion. Bulgarian is a Slavonic language. Elementary education is obligatory from 7 to 14 years of age. There are more than a score of universities and colleges, including the University of Sofia. The main religion is Eastern Orthodox. There are over 750,000 Moslems. Religious observance is

discouraged.
Defense. Armed forces total over 150,000.

Burma

Capital: Rangoon. Area: 261,789 sq. mi. Population (est. 1973): 29,560,000. Monetary unit: Kyat.

The Union of Burma, slightly smaller than Texas, is a republic in the western part of the former Indochinese peninsula. It is bounded by China, Laos, Thailand, India, Bangladesh and the Bay of Bengal. Rivers flowing from the rugged mountains in the north provide habitable valleys down the peninsula. The largest is the Irrawaddy which is navigable for 900 mi.

The **Burma Road**, extending from Lashio to Kunming in Yunnan province, China, was the principal military supply line from Burma into China 1938-1942. It winds for 700 mi. over an airline distance of 260 mi. It was completed by American help and protected by Gen. Claire Chennault's Flying Tigers. The **Ledo Road** was used when the Japanese closed the Burma Road.

Rangoon, on the Gulf of Martaban, is the chief port. Mingaladon airport, near Rangoon, handles international traffic.

Resources and Industries. Mineral wealth is great; included are petroleum, lead, silver, tin, tungsten, zinc, rubies, sapphires and jade. Principal products are rice, cotton, maize, teakwood, tobacco, tin, silver and petroleum. In value of exports, rice accounts for 50%.

However, production in some industries declined in the 1960s. Exports, especially rice, fell off in 1970 but rose slightly in 1971 only to fall again in 1972 and 1973.

History and Government. Burma was a Buddhist monarchy in the Middle Ages. Britain, through 3 wars, gained control of Lower Burma in 1824 and of Upper Burma in 1884 and administered them as part of India until 1937, when Burma became a self-governing unit of the British Commonwealth. It was overrun by the Japanese in World War II. Burma became an independent nation outside the Commonwealth by treaty effective Jan. 4, 1948, and a member of the UN in 1948.

The constitution which went into effect in 1948 created a parliamentary democracy and provided for nationalization of certain industries. In a 1958 political crisis, Gen. Ne Win took over the government from Premier U Nu. Elections were held in 1960 and the Union party, headed by U Nu, won a large majority; he again became premier in April, 1960.

Political and economic problems continued and the government was again taken over by Gen. Ne Win, Mar. 2, 1962; he set up a Revolutionary Council with himself as chief of state, dissolving Parliament and setting aside the constitution. In 1972 he became premier.

The Ne Win government pursued a socialist program and nationalized many industries. It continued a neutralist foreign policy, and isolated the nation from most foreign contacts. On Jan. 4, 1974, a new constitution, aimed at making Burma a "socialist republic" under one-party rule, was adopted. Ne Win continued as premier.

Recurrent problems facing the government have been the need to stimulate production, rebellions staged by Chinese-backed Communist forces and pressures from extremist groups seeking greater autonomy for local ethnic groups.

Education and Religion. The Burmans are the main ethnic group; others are Karens, Shans, Kachins, Chins, etc. Burmese or one of its variants is spoken by nearly three-fourths of the population. Higher education is provided at the Universities of Rangoon, Mandalay and 5 smaller cities. A state-controlled system of schools was introduced after 1948.

The chief religion is Buddhism (about 90%).
Defense. Armed forces total about 150,000.

Burundi

Capital: Bujumbura. Area: 10,739 sq. mi. Population (est. 1973): 3,600,000. Monetary unit: Franc.

Burundi, a country the size of Maryland in east central Africa, became independent July 1, 1962. Formerly part of the Belgian UN Trusteeship of Ruanda-Urundi, it is bordered by Rwanda, Tanzania, lake Tanganyika and Zaire. Much of the country is grasslands and mountains.

For 3 centuries in the present Burundi and Rwanda area, the Tutsi, a minority tribe, were overlords and political masters of the Hutu. (The Tutsi are an extremely tall race; the Hutu, the vast majority, are of average height; a 3d tribe, the Twa, are pygmies.) Under German control in the late 19th Century, the area was taken over by Belgium in World War I; the League of Nations in 1923 gave the king of Belgium a mandate over the combined Ruanda-Urundi territory; Belgium received a UN Trusteeship in 1946.

Burundi became an independent constitutional monarchy in 1962 with Mwami Mwambutsa IV as king; there were a premier and cabinet, an Assembly elected by universal suffrage and a Senate. The government was mainly supported by the Uprena party, a coalition of moderate Tutsi and Hutu. Two premiers were slain by extremists and in Oct. 1965 a 3d, Leopold Biha, was severely wounded. Hutu extremists opposed the power of the minority Tutsi in the government; Tutsi extremists, accused of receiving Communist China aid, opposed the government as too moderate.

In July 1966 the king's son, Prince Charles, 19, deposed him, appointing Michael Micombero premier. Extremist Tutsi returned to power; on Sept. 1 Prince Charles was proclaimed King Mwami Ntare V. But in a coup d'etat Nov. 28, he was overthrown by Micombero, who declared himself president and Burundi a republic. Ntare was killed in April 1972, supposedly during an attempt to seize power.

A Hutu revolt, starting Apr. 29, 1972, was put down; it was estimated 10,000 Tutsi were slain by rebels and 100,000 Hutu by government troops. In 1973, renewed fighting was reported and thousands of Hutus fled to Tanzania and Zaire.

The economy is agricultural, with 90% of the people farmers or livestock raisers. Coffee is the main crop and export. Much of the land is over-grazed and eroded. The nation receives aid from Belgium and the UN. It is a member of the UN and OAU.

Cotton production has become increasingly important. With outside technical aid, tea plantations have been established.

Over half the population is Christian, mostly Roman Catholic. Many others believe in a supreme deity, Imana, called the Principle of Good. Kirundi, a Bantu tongue, and French are the official languages; Swahili is also widely used. *(See also Rwanda.)*

Cambodia

Capital: Phnom Penh. Area: 69,898 sq. mi. Population (Est. 1974): 7,640,000. Monetary unit: Riel.

Cambodia, the Khmer Republic, is in southeast Asia and, with Vietnam and Laos, comprised the former associated states of French Indochina. It is slightly larger than Utah. It is bordered by Laos, Thailand, the Gulf of Siam and South Vietnam. Three-fourths is forested; the central part is level, forming a basin for the Mekong River. The climate is tropical.

Resources and Industries. The country is largely undeveloped; 50% of the land is virgin forest. Main industries are forestry, fishing, and agriculture, rice occupying about 80% of the land usage. Other products are rubber, maize, pepper, kapok, palm-sugar, tobacco, cotton, silk, oil seeds, beans. Cattle flourish; the forests have valuable hardwoods. Some iron, copper, manganese and gold exist. Industry includes textiles, paper, plywood. An oil refinery opened in 1968.

Continuing warfare has created a rice shortage; until 1970 Cambodia was an exporter of rice.

History and Government. Early kingdoms dating from that of Founan in the 1st Century A.D. culminated in the great Khmer civilization which flourished from the 9th Century to the 13th. The Khmer "God-Kings" built a series of monumental cities, distinguished for their temple tower architecture and striking wall sculptures. Most famous temple is that of Angkor Wat.

Cambodia came under French protection in 1863. A national constitution promulgated May 6, 1947, replaced the former absolutism. It became an associated state within the French Union by a treaty of Nov. 8, 1949, but declared its independence from France, Nov. 9, 1953. It is a UN member.

Prince Norodom Sihanouk was king, 1941-55; he abdicated in favor of his father, Norodom Suramarit, who died Apr. 3, 1960. On June 13, 1960, Sihanouk, refusing to become king again, was named chief of state.

Sihanouk broke off diplomatic relations with the U.S. in 1965 after an attack by South Vietnamese planes on Vietcong forces fleeing into Cambodia. In 1968 Sihanouk said Vietnamese communists were arming Cambodian insurgents. In July 1969 diplomatic relations between the U.S. and Cambodia were restored. In 1969-70 the U.S. bombed North Vietnamese forces in Cambodia but did not announce that action until 1973.

In Mar. 1970, while Sihanouk was in Europe, the Cambodian government demanded, without result, that North Vietnam and the Vietcong withdraw their troops, estimated at 40,000, from Cambodia. On Mar. 18, 1970, Sihanouk's premier, Lt. Gen. Lon Nol, seized control of the government. Sihanouk later announced in Peking formation of a government-in-exile.

The Lon Nol government charged increasing attacks on its troops by the communist forces and appealed for arms from other nations.

On Apr. 30, 1970, U.S. President Nixon announced that U.S. troops were moving into Cambodia to drive communist forces from border area sanctuaries used for attacks on South Vietnam. More than 30,000 U.S. troops and over 40,000 South Vietnamese took part in the operations. On June 30 Nixon announced the end of the U.S. incursion, reported huge enemy losses of supplies and manpower and said the operation had insured continued withdrawal of U.S. troops from Vietnam.

Despite the Jan. 1973 cease-fire in Vietnam, fighting continued in Cambodia. From Mar. 1970 to Sept. 1974 over 33,000 government troops had been killed and over 42,000 of the insurgents (the Khmer Rouge) and their North Vietnamese and Vietcong allies. Wounded and civilian casualties numbered in the hundreds of thousands. The rebels controlled about 75% of the territory and nearly half the population had become refugees.

On Oct. 9, 1970, by action of the legislature, the monarchy was abolished and Cambodia's name was officially changed to the Khmer Republic. In Apr. 1972 a new constitution, providing for a president and 2-house legislature, was approved by referendum. On June 4 Lon Nol was elected president; in Sept. a National Assembly and Senate were elected.

Education and Religion. The national language is Cambodian, or Khmer; French is widely spoken and English is taught. In 1965 there were over 4,000 schools and 37 faculties of higher learning. Buddhism is the state religion.

Cameroon

Capital: Yaounde. Area: 183,568 sq. mi. Population (est. 1973): 6,170,000. Monetary unit: CFA franc.

Cameroon, which became a republic in 1960, lies on the western coast of Africa, bounded N and NW by Nigeria, NE by Chad, E by Central African Republic, S by People's Republic of Congo, Gabon and Equatorial Guinea, W by Gulf of Guinea. It is larger than California.

Cameroon is comprised of 2 states: East Cameroon, formerly the Republic of Cameroon, previously a French mandate and trusteeship; and West Cameroon, formerly British Southern Cameroons. Douala has the principal seaport and one of 9 airports.

The population comprises some 200 tribes, including Bantus, Semitic and Sudanese peoples, Kirdis, Foulbes and Bamilekes. There are about 600,000 Christians and 600,000 Moslems; others are animists.

Resources and Industries. Mainly agricultural, Cameroon exports cocoa, coffee, palm products, leather, timber, rubber, peanut oil, tea, bananas, cotton.

Aluminum processing is the most important manufacturing industry. Trade is heavy with France and United Kingdom. Import and export totals are each over $300 million annually. New railroad and power dam construction and agricultural modernization were pressed in 1973.

History and Government. Cameroon embraces the larger part of the former German protectorate of Kamerun which was occupied by France and Britain in 1916, and placed under trusteeship, 1919. France passed a statute Dec. 31, 1958, conferring internal autonomy on the French trusteeship as a step toward complete independence which took effect Jan. 1, 1960.

Following a referendum by the UN in former British Cameroons, the southern section joined the republic to form the Federal Republic of Cameroon, Oct. 1, 1961. The republic, composed of 2 federated states, is a member of the UN. (The northern section of British Cameroons voted to become part of Nigeria.)

The president and the 120-member National Assembly are elected for 5-year terms by direct universal suffrage.

Canada

See Index and special article preceding this section.

Central African Republic

Capital: Bangui. Area: 241,313 sq. mi. Population (UN est. 1973): 1,720,000. Monetary unit: CFA franc.

The former French Overseas Territory of Ubangi-Shari in Equatorial Africa is 350 mi. NE of the Gulf of Guinea and is bounded by Chad, Sudan, Congo, Zaire and Cameroon. Slightly N of the equator, it is mostly rolling plateau, average alt. about 2,000 ft. with rivers draining S to the Congo and N to Lake Chad. Landlocked, it is slightly smaller than Texas.

It achieved partial self-government in 1958. Complete independence was proclaimed Aug. 13, 1960, and the republic became a UN member Sept. 20.

A few months after his election in 1960, Pres. David Dacko dissolved all political parties. He was re-elected Jan. 1965, running as the sole candidate. The country became a center for Communist Chinese activities.

On Jan. 1, 1966, Col. Jean Bedel Bokassa deposed Pres. Dacko; a few days later Pres. Bokassa broke off diplomatic relations with Peking. He was named president-for-life, Mar. 8, 1972.

French is the official language; Sangho is a lingua franca of the 4 ethnic groups: Banda, M'Baka, Zande, Mandjia-Baya.

Diamonds are the main export, accounting for about half the nation's total export earnings, which amount to about $30 million annually. Uranium has been found. Cotton, coffee and peanuts are the chief cash crops and production was increased in the late 1960s. There are large herds of cattle and sheep; lumber exports have increased. About 90% of the population makes its living from farming.

Small factories for textiles, food processing, soap and beer and for assembling motorbikes and radios have been given impetus.

Republic of Chad

Capital: N'Djamena. Area: 495,752 sq. mi. Population (UN est. 1973): 3,870,000. Monetary unit: CFA franc.

A former French Overseas Territory in Equatorial Africa, 500 mi. NE of the Gulf of Guinea, 550 mi. S of the Mediterranean, Chad is bounded N by Libya, E by Sudan, S by Central African Republic, W by Cameroon, Nigeria, Niger. It is four-fifths the size of Alaska.

Moslem groups predominate in the north, and black animists and Christians in the south. Chad has a southern wooded savannah, a steppe and a desert region, part of the Sahara, in the north. On the west is Lake Chad.

Chad proclaimed complete independence Aug. 11, 1960, and joined the UN Sept. 20. There is a president and a National Assembly elected by universal adult suffrage. Chad is a member of the OAU and UN. French is the official language. But in 1973 the nation began replacing French names with African ones. The capital, Fort-Lamy, became N'Djamena.

Cotton is the main export; others are refrigerated meat, leather, dried fish and sodium carbonate.

In 1969-71, with the aid of French troops, government forces fought many skirmishes with rebellious Arab nomads in the northeast. French troops began leaving in 1972. Chad had accused Libya of aiding the rebels. In 1973 Chad broke off diplomatic relations with Israel, and Libya reportedly responded by halting aid to the rebels.

Years of drought which began in 1969 afflicted Chad and 5 other nations in the Sahel, the sub-Sahara region of West Africa. U.S. gifts of food were increased in 1972 and other Western nations aided in 1973; the U.S. provided over 40% of food shipments, over twice as much as any other nation. Although the Sahel is predominantly Moslem, oil-rich Arab nations provided little or no aid.

Chile

Capital: Santiago. Area: 286,396 sq. mi. Population (UN est. 1973): 10,230,000. Monetary unit: Escudo.

The Republic of Chile lies along the southern half of the west coast of South America, a narrow strip of land 2,620 mi. long between the towering Andes and the South Pacific. In area it is slightly larger than Texas.

Most of Chile lies in the temperate zone, but the Atacama Desert in the north is one of the world's driest regions, with little or no rainfall. The Christ of the Andes, a heroic-size statue in Uspallata Pass, symbolizes peace between Chile and Argentina.

Tierra del Fuego is the largest (18,800 sq. mi.) island in the archipelago of the same name at the southern tip of South America, an area of majestic mountains, tortuous channels and high winds. It was discovered 1520 by Magellan, who sailed through the strait (named after him) which separates the main island from the mainland; he named the island Land of Fire because of its many Indian bonfires. Part of the island is in Chile, part in Argentina. Punta Arenas, on a mainland peninsula in Chile, is a center of sheepraising and the world's southernmost city (pop. over 64,000); Puerto Williams, pop. 949, at a Chilean naval base on Navarino Is., is the southernmost settlement. Beagle Channel, between Navarino and the main island, and Mt. Darwin were named for Charles Darwin's visit to the area aboard the ship Beagle. The area's tallest peak is Sarmiento, 7,546 ft. Cape Horn, about 1,400 ft., is a tiny island, named Hoorn by Dutch explorers after a town in the Netherlands.

Possessions in Pacific: Sala y Gomez and **Easter Is. (Rapa Nui)**, with its huge stone statues, both over 2,000 mi. to the W; **San Ambrosio** and **San Felix**, 600 mi. W, and **Juan Fernandez Islands** (2 large, 1 small), 450 mi. W. and the place where Alexander Selkirk, whose life reputedly was the inspiration for Defoe's Robinson Crusoe, lived for 4 years.

Resources and Industries. The arid deserts of northern Chile contain incalculable mineral wealth. Mining industries account for more than 70% of Chile's exports. Nitrate production is about 100,000 metric tons a month. About 47% of the world's supply of iodine is a by-product of Chilean nitrate works. Chile produces about 12% of world copper output.

The provinces of Atacama and Coquimbo have enormous iron deposits estimated at a billion tons. Coal reserves are estimated at 2 billion tons. Oil wells, mostly in Tierra del Fuego, partly supply Chile's needs and natural gas offers an export potential. Other minerals are gold, silver, molybdenum, cobalt, zinc, manganese, borate, mica, mercury, iodine, salt, sulphur, marble, onyx. Chile has abundant waterpower. Patagonia, the sparsely-populated southern third of the nation, is undergoing extensive industrial development.

Agriculture is an important industry. There are many large dairy farms. Wheat, rice, barley, oats, beans, lentils, apples, melons, peaches, plums, nectarines, peas and potatoes are grown in abundance. Sugar beet, automotive and textile industries are being developed. Vineyards cover 250,000 acres and much wine is exported. Forests have large reserves of hard and soft woods. Coastal waters have shellfish, lobster, tuna, swordfish, sardines. Chile ranks 10th in weight of its fish catch.

Manufacturing industries have developed greatly.

Besides minerals the exports are mainly fishmeal, barley, oats, wine, onions, garlic, leather, lentils, fruits, fish, sea-food, cellulose, newsprint, wood.

Chile is served by 15 international airlines. The Pan American Highway runs 2,000 mi. from Arica in the N to Puerto Montt.

In the late 1960s the government pressed a wide program of social and economic reforms.

In 1970 Dr. Salvador Allende Gossens, a Marxist, was elected president and in July 1971 a constitutional amendment provided for full nationalization of copper mines owned by 3 U.S. companies, with compensation to be negotiated. A policy of nationalizing large industries and banks and expropriating large farms was launched. In 1972 middle class groups staged street demonstrations protesting food shortages and socialist policies. Strikes and riots increased in 1973. Food shortages and inflation continued.

A U.S. Senate Foreign Relations subcommittee in 1973 accused the International Telephone & Telegraph Corp. and the U.S. Central Intelligence Agency of discussing, but not carrying out, plans to prevent Allende's election in 1970. The Allende government nationalized ITT phone systems in Chile, without compensation.

In an attack on the Presidential Palace, Sept. 11, 1973, a military junta seized power and said Allende killed himself. The junta named Gen. Augusto Pinochet Ugarte president, swore in a mostly-military cabinet and broke off diplomatic relations with Cuba, which Allende had resumed. Pinochet announced the junta would "exterminate Marxism."

A year after the coup, some 6,000 Allende sympathizers were reported still in prison camps, at least 80 had been executed, and more than 1,000, mostly foreigners, had been allowed to leave the country. Inflation, which had raged under the Allende administration, reached 100% in the first 5 months of 1974. The Pinochet government agreed to pay U.S. companies for mines expropriated under Allende.

History and Government. Diego de Almagro entered Chile for Pizarro 1536 and Valdivia completed Spanish conquest 1540.

Independence was gained 1810-18, under Jose de San Martin and Bernardo O'Higgins; the latter as supreme director, 1817-1823, sought social and economic reforms until deposed. Chile defeated Peru and Bolivia in 1836-39 and 1879-84, taking Tacna and Arica provinces from Peru, returned Tacna, 1929. Arica (town) and Antofagasta are now free ports for landlocked Bolivia.

Under the constitution the president is elected for

6 years, the 50 senators for 8 and 150 deputies for 4, all by direct popular vote. Voting age was lowered from 21 to 18 in 1970. Chile is a member of the UN and OAS.

About two-thirds of the Chileans are of mixed Spanish and Indian descent; about one-fourth of Spanish only; a small percentage are Indian only; there are some of German and other European descent.

Education and Religion. Education is free and compulsory between 7 and 15. There are 9 universities. The Roman Catholic religion is dominant. The language is Spanish.

China

The ancient land of China is split into two hostile parts, with the Republic of China limited to Taiwan (Formosa), and the mainland controlled by a communist regime named the People's Republic of China.

China, with about one-fourth of the world's population, occupies a territory in the eastern part of Asia about one-third larger than continental United States.

The mainland is of rolling topography, rising to high elevations in the N in the Khinghan Mtns., separating Manchuria and Mongolia; the Tarabagata Mtns. in Sinkiang; the Himalayan and Kunlun Mtns. in the SW in Tibet. Its length from N to S is 1,860 mi. and its breadth from E to W more than 2,000 mi.

The eastern half of China is one of the best-watered lands in the world. Three great river systems, the Yangtze, the Hwang (Yellow) and the Si (Si Kiang) provide water for vast farmlands.

Resources and Industry. Until communism prevailed, China was chiefly agricultural. Wheat, barley, corn, koaliang, and millet and other cereals, peas and soy beans are produced in the north; rice, sugar and indigo in the south. Rice is the staple food of the Chinese and mainland China is the world's largest producer. Fiber crops include abutilon, hemp, jute, ramie and flax. Cotton is produced mostly in the Yangtze and Yellow River valleys. Tea is cultivated principally in the west and south. One of the most important industries is silk production which has flourished for 4,000 years. Livestock is raised in large numbers. Before World War II, flour and rice milling, tanning, cement and glass making were the main manufactures.

China is the world's 3d largest coal producer. Other minerals are iron ore, tin, antimony, petroleum, tungsten, molybdenum, salt.

Education and Religion. Buddhism had the largest following. Confucianism, which reveres God but stresses ethical and philosophical principles rather than divine revelation, had wide acceptance. Taoism (after Lao Tze, b. 604 B.C.) is more metaphysical and looks to immortality. Islam, at one time, had 50 million followers; there were 3,280,000 Roman Catholics and 700,000 Protestants. On the mainland foreign missionaries and church schools are no longer tolerated.

Republic of China

Provisional Capital: Taipei, Taiwan. Area under control, 13592 sq. mi. Population (Govt. est. 1974): 15,736,835. Monetary unit: Taiwan dollar.

History and Government. One of the oldest of monarchies, with a history reaching back to 2205 B.C., China became a republic Jan. 1, 1912, following the Wuchang Uprising inspired by Dr. Sun Yat-sen, begun Oct. 10, 1911.

For a period of 50 years after the Sino-Japanese War, 1894-95, China was involved in conflicts with Japan. On Sept. 18, 1931, Japan seized the Northeastern Provinces (Manchuria) and set up a puppet state called Manchukuo. The border province of Jehol was cut off as a buffer state in 1933. Japan invaded China in the vicinity of Peiping (now Peking), July 7, 1937,

precipitating war. After its defeat in World War II Japan returned all seized land.

After the war with Japan ended, Aug. 5, 1945, internal disturbances arose involving the Kuomintang, Communists and other factions. Manchuria was lost by the Nationalist regime in 1948, and China proper came under domination of Chinese Communist armies during 1949-1950. The Nationalist government moved to Taipei, Taiwan (Formosa), 90 mi. off the mainland, Dec. 8, 1949.

China had concluded a treaty of friendship and alliance with the USSR, Aug. 14, 1945. After the Chinese Communists overran the mainland in 1949, the Soviet Union repudiated the treaty, withdrew its recognition of the Nationalist government, and signed a new treaty with the communist regime, Feb. 15, 1950.

A new constitution became effective Dec. 25, 1947. The National Assembly is the supreme organ of the people. Members are elected on the basis of territorial and professional representation. They serve for a 6-year term, subject to recall. The Assembly elects the president and vice president, who likewise serve 6-year terms; it also has the power to amend the constitution. A Yuan (Council), elected on the basis of regional and vocational representation, serves as the legislature. The cabinet, appointed by the president, is responsible to the Yuan.

Generalissimo Chiang Kai-shek, except for a period of semi-retirement, has been virtual ruler since 1927. He was elected president for a 6-year term in Apr., 1948; re-elected in 1954, 1960, 1966 and 1972. The Nationalist government was a founding member of the UN. On Oct. 25, 1971, the UN General Assembly expelled Nationalist China from the UN and admitted Communist China in its place. By 1973, only 37 nations, including the U.S., still recognized the nationalist regime.

Although agriculture remains a vital and growing part of the economy, industrial production has grown much more rapidly. Important industries include textiles, clothing, electrical and electronic equipment, TV sets, processed foods, chemicals, glass, metals and machinery.

Foreign trade, with 1973 imports at $3.8 billion and exports at $4.4 billion, has also shown strong and steady growth. Gross national product was up 10% in 1973.

U.S. economic aid, begun in 1951 and totaling $1.5 billion, terminated June 30, 1965 (with exception of some funds previously committed through 1967). Military aid, which totaled $2.5 billion, continued, but at a reduced scale. Textile products are the most important export. The republic has extended technical assistance to some 30 countries in Asia, Africa and Latin America.

Defense. Armed forces total 500,000. The Nationalist government signed a mutual defense treaty with the U.S., in force Mar. 3, 1955. It provides for consultation on threats of attack and promises that if Taiwan is subject to unprovoked attack the U.S. will act according to its constitutional procedures. About 5,000 U.S. troops are stationed on Taiwan.

Taiwan (Formosa)

Taiwan is an island 110 mi. E of the mainland, but the term Taiwan is used by the Nationalist government to include 14 other islands nearby and 64 others comprising the Penghu group.

Taiwan was ceded by China to Japan in 1895, after the Sino-Japanese War and was returned to China as a province, 1945, after Japan's defeat in World War II. Japan renounced all claims to Taiwan and the Penghus in a general treaty of peace, Sept. 8, 1951. China did not take part in the treaty, signing a separate treaty with Japan Apr. 27, 1952.

A range of mountains forms the backbone of the island. The eastern half is exceedingly steep and craggy but the western slope is flat, fertile and well cultivated, yielding 2 rice crops a year. The principal crops, besides rice, are tea, sugar, sweet potatoes, ramie, jute, turmeric and camphor. Minerals include gold, silver, copper and coal.

The **Penghus** (Pescadores), 50 sq. mi., pop. (1964) 108,800, lie between Taiwan and the cost of China, by which they were ceded to Japan in 1895. The islands remained under Japanese rule until restored to China, 1945.

The islands of **Quemoy** and **Matsu** are within a few miles of the mainland.

People's Republic of China

Capital: Peking. **Area under control; 3,691,502 sq. mi. Population (Chinese Govt. est. 1974): "Almost 800 million." Monetary unit: Yuan.**

The People's Republic of China was proclaimed in Peking (Peiping) Sept. 21, 1949, by the Chinese People's Political Consultative Conference under Mao Tse-tung, communist leader. Chou En-lai was named premier and foreign minister Oct. 1, 1949. With defeat of the Nationalist armies, the Chinese mainland, the islands of Hainan and Chusan and the principal cities fell to the communists.

Under the communist regime, China comprises 22 provinces, including Taiwan, which it claims; 5 autonomous regions (Inner Mongolia, Sinkiang-Uighur, Kwangsi-Chuang, Ningsia-Hui, Tibet-Chamdo) and 2 municipalities — Peking and Shanghai. The government pressed birth control programs; without them experts said, China's population would reach 1 billion by 1980.

The communist regime and the USSR signed a 30-year treaty of "friendship, alliance and mutual assistance." Feb. 15, 1950, repudiating the 1945 treaty between the Soviet Union and nationalist China authorized by the Yalta Agreement. Great Britain recognized the People's Republic in 1950 and France did so in 1964. By 1973, over 60 nations had recognized the regime.

United States Policies. The U.S. refused recognition, and after its consular officers met with abuse, withdrew them. On Nov. 26, 1950, when U.S. military forces and those of certain other UN members had the North Korean communists virtually defeated, the People's Republic sent armies of "volunteers" into Korea and, with the help of limitations on U.S. offensive action, forced a stalemate.

In April 1971, after the U.S. relaxed restrictions on visits by its citizens, a U.S. table tennis team was invited to the People's Republic.

On Oct. 25, 1971, the UN General Assembly ousted nationalist China from the UN and seated communist China in its place. The U.S. had supported the mainland's admission but opposed Taiwan's expulsion.

U.S. President Nixon visited China Feb. 21-28, 1972, on invitation from Premier Chou En-lai, ending years of antipathy between the 2 nations. They agreed to continue progress toward normalization of relations. In April, U.S. businessmen made purchases at the Canton export fair.

China and the U.S. moved close to formal diplomatic relations by opening liaison offices in each other's capitals, May-June 1973.

In 1973, because of food shortages, China ordered 6 million tons of grain from the U.S., Australia and other countries. In 1974 trade with the U.S. was greater than Soviet-U.S. trade, mainly because of Chinese purchases of food.

Peking Foreign and Domestic Policies. On Feb. 27, 1957, Mao Tse-tung, then chief of state, condemned the Stalinist terror but admitted an est. 800,000 anticommunist Chinese were executed 1949-54. Leniency for political criticism, proposed by Mao Tse-tung, led to anti-communist disturbances among students and a quick return to repressive measures. In 1958 the regime announced all "rightists" in government service had been removed. It endorsed the Soviet attack on Hungary, condemned Yugoslavia's independence, it pursued a more rigid communist ideology than the

USSR and, with Albania, maintained a continuous propaganda campaign against the USSR.

Early in 1966 a long, widespread purge of "anti-party intellectuals" was launched; it was viewed as a possible symptom of a struggle for power and the succession to the aging Mao. Premier Chou En-lai called the purge a "cultural revolution." Ousted from office and denounced were the chief of the Army's General Staff, minister of culture, the party propaganda chief, 3 university presidents, newspaper editors and writers, opera producers, youth officials, economists, Peking's mayor, etc.

By late 1968-69 the long disruption had tapered off; much power was taken from the students and given to Revolutionary Committees and the military. In 1974 a new ideological campaign was launched; it was aimed at the teachings of the ancient sage, Confucius, but its purpose was obscure.

In August, 1966 Defense Minister Lin Piao emerged as top deputy and heir apparent to Mao. But in 1972 China said Lin died in a 1971 plane crash trying to flee to the USSR after attempting a coup.

On Mar. 2, 1969, Chinese and Russian soldiers fought one of a series of border clashes on an island in the Ussuri River on the border between the two nations in the Far East, north of Vladivostok. The island, called Chenpao by Chinese and Damansky by Russians, was claimed by both nations. Both sides reported dead and wounded. There were later clashes on the island and reports of skirmishes far to the west on the Sinkiang-USSR border. In 1970, ambassadors were exchanged for the first time since 1966. In 1974 China seized a Soviet helicopter, charging it had been spying.

On Oct. 16, 1964, communist China exploded a low-yield atomic bomb in Sinkiang Province, becoming the 5th nation to possess such power. An explosion of a hydrogen bomb was announced June 17, 1967. The nation's first orbiting space satellite was launched Apr. 24, 1970.

Internationally, communist China has sought to promote revolutionary movements in Africa, Asia and South America. The program suffered serious setbacks, 1965-66. By the 1970s, China was again reported sending military and economic aid to several nations.

Application of radical theories to industry and agriculture resulted in erratic economic development. Serious food shortages existed beginning in 1959 after more than 148 million acres of farm land were damaged by floods, drought and failure of the "Great Leap Forward" 5-year plan. The regime was forced to obtain grain from Argentina, Mexico, Canada and Australia. Light industries dependent on agriculture for their raw materials also were affected — cotton textiles, knitted goods, vegetable oils, sugar and cigarets. The "people's commune" system of agriculture in effect since 1958 was drastically modified in 1960-61 to increase individual incentives to stimulate production, but the collectivization drive was renewed in 1963-64. Many thousands fled to overcrowded Hong Kong.

In 1969-1972, after the "cultural revolution" eased off, both industry and agriculture showed production gains.

China leads all nations in number of hogs, is 3d in sheep, 4th in cattle. Its fish catch is 2d in value to Japan's.

Institutes of higher education include 15 universities, 48 engineering colleges and 31 agricultural colleges. English and Russian are required in high schools.

Defense. Regular forces total 2,900,000. There is a growing stockpile of nuclear weapons and intermediate range missiles.

Manchuria, 404,428 sq. mi., is administered as part of communist China. Seized by Japan in 1931, and renamed Manchukuo, a puppet "independent" nation, Mar. 1, 1932. In 1945 it was returned to China.

Kuantung is the southern part of the Liaotung peninsula, the southernmost portion of Manchuria.

Russia in 1898 forced China to lease it Kuantung and constructed the strongly fortified city of Port Arthur (Lushun) and the nearby commercial ice-free port of Dairen (Luta).

Japan seized Port Arthur in 1905, and at the close of the Russo-Japanese War took over the lease in the Treaty of Portsmouth. It was restored to the USSR by the Yalta Agreement, Feb. 11, 1945, which also internationalized Dairen. Following the 1950 Soviet-Chinese treaty the USSR returned the Changchun railroad, Port Arthur and Dairen to Communist China.

Inner Mongolia was organized by the People's Republic as an Autonomous Region on May 12, 1947. Its boundaries have undergone frequent changes. In 1950 it comprised northern Chahar and parts of former Manchuria. Suiyan province was incorporated June 1954, and parts of Jehol in Aug. 1955. Population is about 6,200,000 of which less than 20% are Mongol. Capital: Huhehot (Kweisui).

Outer Mongolia: *For People's Republic of Mongolia, see Mongolia in Index.*

Sinkiang Uigur Autonomous Region, in Central Asia, comprising Chinese Turkestan, Kulia and Kashgaria, is 633,802 sq. mi.; pop. (est. 1958) is 6 million, of whom 75% are Uigurs, a Turkic Moslem group, with a heavy Chinese increase in recent years. Urumchi is the capital. It is considered China's richest region in strategic materials, including tungsten, wolfram, molybdenum, copper, zinc, coal, uranium and oil.

Tibet, 470,000 sq. mi., is a thinly populated region of high plateaus and massive mountains, almost twice the size of Texas. The Himalayas ring it on the S, the Kunluns on the N. Lofty passes link it with India and Nepal to the S; roads lead into China proper. The capital is Lhasa. The average altitude is 15,000 ft. Jiachan, 15,870 ft., is believed to be the highest inhabited town on earth. Agricultural methods are primitive. Cereals are the main crops. The religion is Lamaism, a form of Buddhism. Pop. (1964 est.) 1,300,000.

With only token resistance, Tibet accepted suzerainty of Communist China under a pact signed May 23, 1951. A communist Tibetan Autonomous Government was announced Dec. 20, 1953, revising the quasi-religious administration of the Dalai and Panchen Lamas.

A revolt against the communists occurred in 1959, when the latter attempted to arrest the Dalai Lama. The Tibetan cabinet denounced the 1951 treaty. The communists crushed the revolt and placed the Panchen Lama on the Tibetan throne. The Dalai Lama fled to India. The Panchen Lama was demoted Dec. 1964. A new ruler was sponsored by Peking Sept. 9, 1965, when it announced election of Ngapo Ngawang Jigme as chairman of the newly-established Tibet Autonomous Region. Revolts continued in 1965 and 1966.

A reform program, including land redistribution and abolition of serfdom (assertedly practiced in some monasteries) was announced July 3, 1959.

The International Commission of Jurists at Geneva in 1961 charged the Communist regime with genocide in Tibet. About 20,000 Tibetans have fled to India since the Chinese takeover.

Colombia

Capital: Bogota. Area: 455,335 sq. mi. Population (UN est. 1973): 23,210,000. Monetary unit: Peso.

The Republic of Colombia, in the extreme northwest of South America, extends up the Isthmus of Panama to the Republic of Panama. It has a coastline of 913 mi. on the Pacific Ocean, and 1,094 mi. on the Caribbean Sea. It has as neighbors Venezuela and Brazil on the E, and Ecuador and Peru on the S. Its area is greater than those of Texas and California combined.

Three great ranges of the Andes, the Western, Cen-

tral and Eastern Cordilleras, run through the country from N to S. The eastern range consists mostly of high table lands, cool and healthful, and densely populated. The Magdalena River, in the NE, rises in the high Andes and flows N into the Caribbean Sea near Barranquilla. It is navigable for over 800 mi. The Magdalena Valley is a plain of rich alluvial land.

Snow-crested mountains standing almost directly over the Equator are one of many examples of scenic splendor in Colombia. Tourists are also attracted by the famous Tequendama Falls near Bogota, 427 ft. high. The Salt Cathedral of Zipaquira, 32 mi. N of Bogota, is an actual church carved with Gothic arches 1,300 ft. underground in a salt mine. It can accommodate 10,000 worshipers.

Bogota, the capital, founded in 1538, is in the Andes, 8,660 ft. above sea level.

Resources and Industries. Colombia is second to Brazil in exports of coffee, accounting for 50% of its export trade. Rice, tobacco and cotton are cultivated, besides cocoa, sugar, tagua, wheat and bananas. Dyewoods, rubber, balsam and copaiba trees are important.

The country is rich in minerals. It has become a heavy producer of petroleum. Seventy-five miles from Bogota are the Muzo emerald mines which have been in operation for 4 centuries. Colombia produces 95% of the world's gem emeralds. Other minerals are gold, silver, copper, lead, mercury, cinnabar, manganese, platinum, coal, iron, nickel, salt. Colombia is accelerating expansion of its hydro-electric power which has est. potential of 85 million kw. Food processing is the leading manufacturing industry; other products are textiles, rubber goods, steel, and chemicals. Textiles have become an important export.

Loans from international agencies have helped expand industry and modernize agriculture. An oil pipeline from the Orito field in the SE, crosses the Andes to the Pacific port of Tumaco; it was finished in 1969.

The government has sought to reduce vast land holdings and increase the size of small farms. From 1961 to 1970 the Institute for Land Reform acquired or developed 9,800,000 acres; more than 95,000 families were given title to farm plots.

History and Government. The country, conquered and ruled for 300 years by Spain, won its freedom in the revolt of the Spanish-American colonies 1810-1824. The liberator, Simon Bolivar, established the Republic of Greater Colombia in 1819; Venezuela and Ecuador withdrew in 1829-1830. From the remainder of the confederation evolved New Granada, Confederation Granadina, and finally the Republic of Colombia under a constitution dated Aug. 5, 1886. Panama withdrew Nov. 3, 1903, becoming a separate republic. Colombia is a member of the UN and OAS.

The Congress consists of a Senate of 118 members and a House of Representatives with 210 members, elected directly by the people for 4-year terms. The president is elected by direct vote for 4 years and is ineligible for the following term.

Education and Religion. Most of the people are of mixed Indian and white descent; the next largest group is white; the smallest groups are Indians and Negroes. Education is free but not compulsory. The National Univ., founded 1572, is in Bogota. Roman Catholicism is the prevailing religion. Spanish is the language.

Defense. Armed forces total 63,000.

People's Republic of Congo

Capital: Brazzaville. Area: 132,046 sq. mi. Population (UN est. 1973): 1,001,000. Monetary unit: CFA franc.

Formerly the French Middle Congo Overseas Territory, the People's Republic of the Congo straddles the Equator. It is bounded on the E and S by Zaire; on the W by Portuguese Cabinda, the Atlantic and Gabon; on the N by Cameroon and Central African Republic. It is twice the size of Missouri.

Complete independence was proclaimed Aug. 15, 1960, and the republic joined the UN Sept. 20. Fulbert Youlou was elected president Nov. 21, 1959, and resigned in Aug. 1963 in a coup sparked by trade unions. Under his successor, President Alphonse Massamba-Debat, the country came under Communist China's influence and announced a "scientific Socialist state" with one-party control.

In Aug. 1965 the U. S. withdrew its embassy staff, a step short of breaking off relations, charging harassment of American officials. Massamba-Debat was ousted in a military coup, Sept. 4, 1968. Maj. Marien Ngouabi became president Jan. 1, 1969.

In Jan. 1970, the earlier name, Republic of the Congo-Brazzaville, was changed to People's Republic of the Congo. The government advocates socialism.

The nation has received aid from both France and Communist China.

Forests are a prime resource, covering 54 million acres, and wood products form a major export. Chief commercial agricultural products are palm oil and kernels, cocoa, bananas, and peanuts. Industrialization has progressed and its output now accounts for 11% of the total national product. Potash reserves are extensive.

Costa Rica

Capital: San Jose. Area: 19,653 sq. mi. Population (Est. 1973): 1,890,000. Monetary unit: Colon.

Costa Rica, in Central America, has Nicaragua for its neighbor on the N and Panama on the S. The lowlands by the Caribbean have a tropical climate. The interior plateau, with an altitude of about 4,000 ft., is temperate.

San Jose, the capital, situated inland (103 mi. by rail from Puerto Limon on the Atlantic, 93 by rail from Puntarenas on the Pacific) is the country's industrial and cultural center. Limon and Puntarenas are the principal ports. The crater atop Poas Volcano is the largest in the world. Puerto Limon occupies one of the sites where Columbus landed on his fourth and last visit to America.

Resources and industries. A 1962 law giving new industries a tax holiday of up to 10 years brought in a wide variety of factories. The Irazu volcano near San Jose erupted from March 1963 to Dec. 1964, dropping millions of tons of ash which severely damaged coffee, vegetable and dairy crops. Coffee of a high quality is the chief crop and export, followed by bananas, sugar, cocoa, beef, cotton, fish and hemp.

Despite growing, small-scale industrialization, agriculture remains the mainstay of the economy, employing half the work force. New industries include fiberglass products, aluminum processing, textiles, fertilizer, roofing and cement. Gross national product rose 4.8% in 1973.

The forests are extensive, and the lumber industry is important. Gold and silver are mined on the Pacific slope. Other minerals are quartz, alabaster, granite, oil, alum, slate, onyx, mercury, sulphur, copper.

Chief imports are flour, industrial machinery, gasoline, leather, hardware and tools. Nearly half of the foreign trade is with the U. S.

The nation has a comparatively high standard of living and of social services.

History and Government. Once a part of the Confederation of Central America, 1824-1829, Costa Rica has been independent since 1821.

An unusual constitution was adopted Nov. 8, 1949. It abolishes the Army as a permanent institution. The legislative power is vested in a Chamber of Deputies, 57 in number, with 4-year terms, under universal suffrage. The president, elected for 4 years, appoints a Cabinet of 12. Deputies may not serve successive terms but may be reelected after an intervening 4 years. A president may not be reelected. There is a fine for not voting.

In Feb. 1974 a liberal, Daniel Oduber Quiros, was elected president.

Religion and Education. Primary education is compulsory. Higher education is free. There are universities in Cartago, Heredia, San Jose and Turrialba. The language is Spanish; English is taught in the public schools. Roman Catholicism is the predominant religion.

Defense. Order within the country is kept by a Civil Guard and police forces. Costa Rica is a member of the UN and OAS.

Cuba

Capital: Havana. Area: 44,218 sq. mi. Population (UN est. 1973): 8,870,000. Monetary unit: Peso.

Cuba, "Pearl of the Antilles," is both an island, the largest in the West Indies, and a nation which is about the area of Pennsylvania. The Straits of Florida lie to the N, the Gulf of Mexico to the W, the Caribbean to the S.

Key West, Fla., is about 90 mi. N. The Windward Passage, 50 mi. wide, separates Cuba from Haiti to the E, and Jamaica lies 90 mi. to the S. Cuba's length is 730 mi.; its breadth averages 50 mi. The coastline, including the larger keys, is about 2,500 mi. It has numerous harbors, notably that of Havana, one of the finest in the world.

The Isle of Pines, off the SW coast, is 1,180 sq. mi. in area. Mountains rise in Pinar del Rio Province in the W, and in Oriente in the E where they reach about 3,000 ft., with Pico Turquino, 6,467 ft., the highest.

Havana, pop. over 1,500,000, is the busiest port. Santiago de Cuba, on the SE coast, is the next largest port.

Resources and Industries. Chief barometer of the nation's economy is the sugar industry which represents about 80% of exports. American-owned sugar mills, seized by the revolutionary regime in 1960, represented an investment of about $275 million, producing about 40% of Cuba's output.

Raising tobacco and manufacturing cigars and cigarettes rank second. Other products are molasses, coffee, pineapples, bananas, citrus fruit and coconuts. Textiles, cabinet woods (mahogany and cedar), dyewoods, fibers, gums, resins and oils are important. Iron, copper, manganese, nickel and salt are some of the minerals. Industries include rayon, cement, chemicals.

Poor sugar crops and food shortages resulted in collectivization of farms and stringent labor controls under the revolutionary government. Rationing of food, shoes, clothing, gasoline, was ordered. Some rationing and economic difficulties continued in the 1970s, despite massive aid from the USSR and assistance from other Communist countries.

History—Cuba was discovered by Christopher Columbus in Oct. 1492. Its name derives from the Indian Cubanacan. Except for British occupation of Havana, 1762-63, Cuba remained Spanish until 1898.

Under Spanish governors Cubans were denied citizenship, slavery was retained until 1886, and patriots who revolted were executed. On Oct. 10, 1868, Carlos Manuel de Cespedes led Cubans in a proclamation of independence. Their 10-years' war ended in 1878 with guarantees of rights by Spain, which Spain failed to carry out. A full-scale movement began Feb. 24, 1895, under Jose Marti, with the military under the command of Maximo Gomez, Antonio Maceo and Calixto Garcia. By 1897 over half the island was in Cuban hands. The Spanish governor, Valeriano Weyler, destroyed sugar plantations, banned export of tobacco and held patriots in "reconcentration camps." A U. S. offer to mediate was rejected by Spain.

The movement to help Cuba gain its independence was speeded by the sinking of the U.S.S. Maine in Havana harbor. The U. S. declared war on Spain Apr. 25, 1898, and defeated it in the short Spanish-American War. In the Treaty of Paris, Dec. 10, 1898, Spain gave up all claims to Cuba. The U. S. formally withdrew May 20, 1902, when Tomas Estrada Palma was inaugurated first president of the republic.

Under 1903 and 1934 agreements, the U. S. leases a site for its naval base at Guantanamo Bay, on the SE coast.

In 1952 Fulgencio Batista seized control of the government and imposed a dictatorship. Opposition to the corrupt Batista regime became vigorous in 1956 under leadership of Fidel Castro, born 1927, lawyer and former leader of student opposition. Known as the 26th of July Movement, the revolutionists in 1958 carried on intensified guerrilla warfare. Batista resigned Jan. 1, 1959. He died in Spain Aug. 6, 1973.

Castro proclaimed Dr. Manuel Urrutia Lleo provisional president and Urrutia dissolved the Cuban Congress, Jan. 6, 1959. Castro became premier Feb. 16.

Pres. Urrutia resigned after accusing communists of plotting treason. The government, quickly dominated by left-wing extremists, began a program of sweeping economic and social changes, led by an agrarian reform law in May 1959. It executed hundreds of dissidents, and ousted moderates.

The National Institute of Agrarian Reform nationalized cattle and tobacco lands and instituted a system of cooperatives. All private enterprise was brought under control by a Central Planning Board created Feb. 20, 1969. By the end of 1960 all Cuban banks and industrial companies had been nationalized, including an est. $1 billion worth of U. S.-owned properties.

Soviet, Communist Chinese and Czechoslovakian economic penetration was extended by trade and credit agreements, including sugar purchases and USSR credits for construction of factories, etc.

Citing the open hostility of the regime, the U. S. cut back Cuba's remaining 1960 sugar quota by 700,000 tons. On Oct. 19 the U. S. imposed an extensive embargo on exports to Cuba and, Feb. 4, 1962, President Kennedy ordered a total embargo.

The OAS nations voted July 26, 1964, 15-4, a resolution for mandatory sanctions against Cuba and for strengthening defenses against Cuban subversion efforts. But by 1974 Latin American nations having diplomatic relations with Cuba included Mexico, Argentina, Peru, Panama, Trinidad-Tobago, Jamaica, Guyana, Barbados.

In 1974 U.S. President Ford said relations with Cuba could be improved, depending on Cuba's actions, adding that the U. S. would act in concert with the other OAS nations.

Bay of Pigs Raid. In April, 1961, Jose Miro Cardona, Head of the Cuban National Revolutionary Council, called on Cubans to unite to overthrow the Castro regime. On Apr. 17 about 1400 Cuban patriots, who had trained in the U.S. and Guatemala, landed at the Bahia de Cochinos (Bay of Pigs) on Cuba's southern coast. They were over-whelmed by Castro forces and killed or imprisoned. The attempt created severe criticism in Congress of activities of the U.S. Central Intelligence Agency. President Kennedy previously had declared there would be no intervention by the U. S. On Dec. 21, 1962, Castro agreed with James B. Donovan, representing welfare agencies, to release 1,113 prioners in exchange for medical supplies worth a reputed $53 million. American drug concerns and religious groups raised the supply.

Kennedy vs. Soviet Missiles. In the fall, 1962, the U.S. ascertained that the Soviet Union was delivering nuclear missiles and other weapons to Cuba and building bases. On Oct 22 President Kennedy warned that any missile launched from Cuba would be regarded as an attack by the Soviet Union and would call for full retaliation. He asked Premier Khrushchev to halt this "clandestine, reckless and provocative threat to world peace." Khrushchev removed the missiles.

Cuba complained of numerous raids by infiltrators, 1964-70.

In Feb. 1973 Cuba and the U.S. signed an agreement providing for extradition or punishment of hijackers of planes or vessels, and for each nation to bar activity from its territory against the other.

More than 500,000 Cubans have gone into exile since the Castro takeover, most of them to the U.S., including 260,000 via an airlift paid for by the U.S. which started Dec. 1965 and ended April 1973. In late 1973-74, the U.S. began admitting more thousands of Cuban refugees who had flown to Spain.

Cuba is a member of the UN and Comecon.

Education and Religion. Education is compulsory between the ages of 6 and 14. Among the institutions of higher learning is the University of Havana, founded in 1721. The Roman Catholic religion is dominant. The language is Spanish with English widely understood.

Education was nationalized June 7, 1961, and many Catholic schools were seized. Many Catholic priests of Spanish origin were ordered deported.

Defense. Armed forces total 108,000.

Cyprus

Capital: Nicosia. **Area:** 3,572 sq. mi. **Population (Govt. est. 1973):** 660,000. **Monetary unit:** Pound.

Cyprus, former British Crown Colony, became a republic Aug. 16, 1960, and joined the Commonwealth, UN and Council of Europe. It is the third largest island in the Mediterranean Sea, 40 mi. S. of Turkey, 60 mi. W of Syria, and 350 mi. E of Crete. Two mountain ranges run E-W, separated by a wide, fertile plain. It is smaller than Connecticut.

Four-fifths of the inhabitants are Greek Orthodox Christians, nearly all the rest are Turkish Moslems. Greek and Turkish are official languages; English is widely spoken.

Resources and Industries. Cyprus is mainly agricultural, with cereals, grapes, wine, carobs, citrus fruits, potatoes and olives as principal crops. Agricultural products account for about 60% of the island's exports. Minerals are important but declining — copper, iron pyrites, asbestos, gypsum, chrome and umber. Manufacturing is limited mainly to light industries. Exports include shoes and clothing. Cement and oil refining industries are under development.

The nation suffers an unfavorable balance of trade, offset by tourism, etc.

History and Government. Cyprus was inhabited as early as the New Stone Age in the 4th millennium B.C. Achaeans from Greece traded with the early Cypriots from 1600 B.C., set up colonies after the end of the Trojan War (c. 1184 B.C.). From the middle of the 8th Century B.C., Cyprus was dominated successively by Phoenicians, Assyrians, Egyptians, Persians, Alexander and the Ptolemies, Romans, Byzantines, Moslems, Crusaders, Venetians and Turks. Great Britain took over administration in 1878 under an agreement with Turkey, annexed the island in 1914, made it a Crown Colony in 1925.

Agitation for enosis (union) with Greece resulted in the British abolishing the legislative council in 1931. Demands for enosis were renewed after World War II; the Turkish minority was opposed. Widespread violence in 1955-56, led by EOKA, an underground organization, brought harsh disciplinary measures, including the temporary exiling of Archbishop Makarios III, head of the Independent Orthodox Church in Cyprus and leader of the enosis movement.

In 1959, conflict was brought to a temporary halt by an agreement signed by British, Greek, Turkish and Cypriot leaders, under which Cyprus would become a republic, with a president elected from and by the ethnic Greek community, and a vice president from and by the corresponding Turkish community. A 70-30% proportion of the Greek and Turkish communities was to be represented in the House of Representatives. Separate Greek and Turkish Communal Chambers dealt with religious, educational and other communal affairs. Britain retained 2 military enclaves, Akrotiri and Dhekelia.

Archbishop Makarios was elected president for a 5-

year term and Dr. Fazil Kutchuk, a Turkish Cypriot, vice president, Dec. 14, 1959. The constitution was approved April 6, 1960; independence became final Aug. 16, 1960, and Pres. Makarios took office.

Communal strife again broke out in December, 1963, following proposals by Makarios to make changes in the constitution which the Turkish minority felt would reduce their rights.

The UN Security Council approved Mar. 4, 1964, a resolution providing for an international peace-keeping force and UN troops took stations Mar. 27.

Tension worsened after Turkey charged that Turkish Cypriots had been massacred in a Greek push against the northwest coast and bombed and strafed Greek areas Aug. 7-10, 1964. Both sides accepted a cease-fire.

War between Greece and Turkey over Cyprus appeared imminent in Nov. 1967 but was averted mainly because of mediation work by Cyrus R. Vance, special envoy of U.S. President Johnson.

Archbishop Makarios, whose term as president had been twice extended by Parliament, was re-elected Feb. 25, 1968, by an overwhelming popular vote, and again on Feb. 8, 1973.

The Cypriot National Guard, led by officers from the Army of Greece, seized the government July 15, 1974, and named Nikos Sampson, an advocate of union with Greece, president. Makarios fled the country. On July 20, Turkey invaded the island; Greece mobilized its forces but did not intervene. A cease-fire was arranged July 22. On the 23d, Sampson turned over the presidency to Glafkos Clerides (on the same day, Greece's military junta resigned). A peace conference collapsed Aug. 14; fighting resumed. Greek Cypriots and Turks charged each other with massacres and atrocities. By Aug. 16 Turkish forces had occupied the NE third of the island; Turkey declared a new cease-fire and indicated it sought to make the area a separate žone for Turkish Cypriots. On Aug. 19 the U.S. ambassador to Cyprus was slain by a bullet during a riot in Nicosia.

Czechoslovakia

Capital: Prague (Praha). Area: 49,371 sq. mi. Population (UN est. 1973): 14,580,000. Monetary unit: Koruna.

Czechoslovakia is a central European socialist republic about 600 mi. long and 50 to 100 mi. wide — about the area of New York State. It is bounded by West Germany (Bavaria), East Germany (Saxony), Poland, the Soviet Union, Austria and Hungary.

The Vltava (Moldau) and Labe (Elbe) flow from Bohemia to Germany; the Danube separates Slovakia from Hungary. The Carpathian Mtns. are in the E and NE; tallest are the Tatras, with Gerlachovka peak 8,737 ft.

Resources and Industries. Czechoslovakia has considerable natural resources, developed by farming, mining and industry. The nation is highly industrialized but agriculture remains important; chief crops are wheat, sugar beets, potatoes, rye, hops.

Coal and iron are mined; oil, imported mainly from the USSR, is refined at Bratislava. Jachymov has Europe's richest deposits of pitchblende (for radium) and uranium. Czechoslovakia is a major exporter of arms and machinery. Ostrava and Kosice are important steel centers. There is a large glass and china industry; other products include chemicals, beer, aircraft, wood pulp, textiles, shoes.

Imports for 1973 were valued at $6.4 billion, exports at $6.5 billion.

History and Government. In Feb. 1948 Czechoslovakia became a unitary socialist republic composed of 2 Slav nations—the Czechs and the Slovaks—with a socialist constitution, nationalized industry and one-state elections. The Czechs make up 65% of the population and Slovaks about 30%. In addition, there are some 450,000 Hungarians, 200,000 Germans, 200,000 gypsies, 100,000 Ruthenian-Ukrainians and 100,000

Poles. Large numbers of Hungarians were moved out of Slovakia and many Slovaks were moved from Hungary to Slovakia in 1945-46. An estimated 3 million Sudeten Germans were transferred to Germany under the Potsdam Agreement.

Bohemia, Moravia and Slovakia were part of the Great Moravian Empire when overrun by the Magyars 906 A.D. Bohemia and Moravia later became part of the Holy Roman Enpire. Under the kings of Bohemia, Prague in the 14th Century was the cultural center of Central Europe. In 1526 Ferdinand, brother of Holy Roman Emperor Charles V, became king of Bohemia and Hungary. Later the lands became part of Austria-Hungary.

In 1914-1918 Thomas G. Masaryk and Eduard Benes formed a provisional government with the support of Slovak leaders, of whom Milan Stefanik organized freedom fighters in foreign countries. When Austria fell, Oct. 28, 1918, they proclaimed the Republic of Czechoslovakia Oct. 30. Masaryk became president, Benes foreign minister and Stefanik minister of war. Benes succeeded Masaryk in 1935.

By 1938 Adolf Hitler of Nazi Germany had worked up disaffection among German-speaking citizens in Sudetenland and demanded its cession. To avoid war, Prime Minister Neville Chamberlain of Great Britain, with the acquiescence of France, signed an agreement with Hitler at Munich, Sept. 30, 1938, agreeing to the cession, with a guaranty of peace by Hitler and Mussolini. Nazi Germany occupied Sudentenland Oct. 1-2. President Benes resigned Oct. 5.

Hitler on Mar. 15, 1939, dissolved Czechoslovakia, made protectorates of Bohemia and Moravia, and supported the autonomy of Slovakia, which was proclaimed independent Mar. 14, 1939, with Jozef Tiso president.

Soviet troops with some Czechoslovak contingents entered eastern Czechoslovakia in 1944 and reached Prague in May 1945; Benes returned as president. In May 1946 elections, the Communist Party won 38% of the votes, largest for a single party, and Benes accepted Klement Gottwald, a communist, as prime minister. Tiso was executed in 1947.

In Feb. 1948 a crisis resulted in the resignation of 12 anti-Communist ministers and Benes accepted a new Gottwald Cabinet Feb. 25. Jan Masaryk, son of Thomas Masaryk, had not resigned as foreign minister. He was found dead March 10, apparently a suicide, but there was widespread speculation he was murdered.

In May 1948 a new constitution was approved by the constituent assembly; Benes refused to sign it. On May 30 the voters were offered a one-slate ballot and the communists won full control. Benes resigned June 7, Gottwald became president and Benes died Sept. 3.

In Jan. 1968 a liberalization movement spread explosively through Czechoslovakia. Antonin Novotny, long the communist boss of the nation, was deposed as party leader and succeeded by Alexander Dubcek, a Slovak, who declared he intended to make communism democratic. On Mar. 22 Novotny resigned as president and was succeeded by Gen. Ludvik Svoboda. On Apr. 6, Premier Joseph Lenart resigned and was succeeded by Oldrich Cernik, whose new cabinet was pledged to carry out democratization and economic reforms.

In July 1968 the USSR and 4 hard-core Warsaw Pact nations demanded an end to liberalization. On Aug. 20, Russian, Polish, East German, Hungarian and Bulgarian military forces invaded Czechoslovakia.

Some Soviet troops remained and Soviet pressure brought agreements from officials that the liberal policies would be "normalized." Despite demonstrations and riots by students and workers, press censorship was imposed, many liberal leaders were ousted from office and promises of loyalty to Soviet policies were made by some old-line Communist party leaders.

On Apr. 17, 1969, Dubcek resigned as leader of the

Communist party and was succeeded by Gustav Husak. In Jan. 1970, Premier Cernik was ousted. In 1972, more than 40 liberals were jailed on subversion charges. In 1973, amnesty was offered to some of the 40,000 who fled the country after the 1968 invasion.

On Jan. 2, 1969, Czechoslovakia became a federal state. In addition to a federal president, premier and Assembly for the Czechoslovak Socialist Republic, there were separate governments, a Czech Socialist Republic and a Slovak Socialist Republic, each with a National Council, a premier and Cabinet. The central government retained control over foreign affairs, defense and finance. In the Federal Assembly, a House of People was chosen by electoral districts; a House of Nations had 75 Czech and 75 Slovak members.

West Germany and Czechoslovakia resumed diplomatic relations in 1973 and declared the 1938 Munich pact void.

Education and Religion. An estimated 75% of the population is Roman Catholic, the rest are Protestant (Hussite), Greek Orthodox, etc.

Institutions of higher learning are Charles University in Prague, founded in 1348; the Universities of Brno, Bratislava, Kosice, Hradec Kralove, Plzen; also technical universities. Czech and Slovak are official languages.

Defense. Military forces total 190,000.

Dahomey

Capitals: Porto-Novo, Cotonou. Area: 43,483 sq. mi. Population (UN est. 1973): 2,910,000. Monetary unit: CFA franc.

The Republic of Dahomey, former Overseas Territory in French West Africa, is a narrow strip 415 mi. long and 77 mi. wide, bounded by the Republics of the Niger and Upper Volta, Nigeria, Gulf of Guinea and the Republic of Togo. It is about as large as Tennessee.

In accordance with the 1958 French constitution, Dahomey became fully independent Aug. 1, 1960, and became a member of the UN Sept. 20. Dahomey signed agreements Apr. 24, 1961, providing for close ties with France.

Under the constitution the president and National Assembly are elected for 5-year terms. Pres. Hubert Maga, elected Dec. 11, 1960, was deposed Oct. 28, 1963, and replaced by a provisional government headed by Gen. Christophe Soglo. The constitution of the second republic was adopted Dec. 19, 1963; Sourou Migan Apithy was elected president Jan. 24, 1964; several coups followed. In Oct. 1972 Maj. Mathieu Kerekou became president in a military coup.

Principal products: palm oil, kernels and nuts; peanuts, cotton, kapok, coffee, tobacco.

Small industries were constructed in the late 1960s, including a bicycle plant, cotton mill and peanut-oil plant. Oil was discovered offshore in 1969. France gives the nation an annual subsidy.

French is the official language. About 65% of the people are animists; 15%, in the S, are Christians; 13%, in the N, are Moslems.

Denmark

Capital: Copenhagen. Area: 16,615 sq. mi. Population including Faeroe Islands and Greenland (Govt. est. 1974): 5,130,000. Monetary unit: Krone.

Denmark occupies the peninsula of Jutland, thrusting out to the N from Germany, which is its only land neighbor, between the North Sea and the Baltic Sea, and adjacent islands. The Skagerrak separates it from Norway; the Kattegat and Oresund from Sweden. The country consists of low undulating plains. It is about the size of New Hampshire and Massachusetts combined.

The **Faeroe Islands** in the North Atlantic, about 300 mi. NE of the Shetlands, and 850 mi. from Denmark proper, 18 inhabited, have an area of 540 sq. mi. and

pop. (est. 1974) of 40,000. They are part of the nation as is **Greenland,** described below.

Resources and Industries. About 10% of the population lives by agriculture on more than 70% of the usable land. Denmark exports much butter, cheese, poultry, eggs, bacon and beef. Its fishing industry ranks 11th in the world. Tourist trade accounts for 10% of foreign exchange. Denmark exports machinery, ships, textiles, furniture, iron and steel goods. Most raw materials and fuels have to be imported, but manufactures have increased; industrial exports surpass agricultural.

Denmark is the world's largest exporter of pork and 4th largest of meat in general.

The first cooperative consumers' society was established 1866; the system currently has about 1,650 affiliated societies and includes 863,000 households, about 51%.

More than a million tourists visit Denmark annually. Many leave their children in Danish camps while visiting other countries.

Foreign trade in thousands of U.S. dollars:

	Imports	Exports
1972	$5,054,000	$4,410,000
1973	$7,791	$6,242

History and Government. The origin of Copenhagen dates back to ancient times, when the fishing and trading place named Havn (port) grew up on a cluster of islets, but Bishop Absalon (1128-1201) is regarded as the actual founder of the city. On one of the islets he built a stronghold against the pirating Wends and the remnants of this still exist underground in front of Christiansborg. Elsinore (Helsingor) contains the reputed grave of Hamlet, the Danish prince immortalized by Shakespeare.

Denmark is a constitutional monarchy with a Queen. A new constitution, signed June 5, 1953, substituted a unicameral parliament, the Folketing, of 179 members for the former two-chamber Rigsdag. A cabinet of ministers, which must have the support of a majority in the Folketing, conducts the government.

The Queen of Denmark is Margrethe II (born Apr. 16, 1940) who succeeded to the throne Jan. 14, 1972, after the death of her father, King Frederik IX. She was married June 10, 1967, to Count Henri Marie Andre Laborde de Monpezat of France who became Prince Henrik of Denmark. They had 2 sons: Prince Frederik (born May 26, 1968), heir to the throne, and Prince Joachim (born June 7, 1969). Queen Margrethe had 2 sisters: Princess Benedikte (born Apr. 29, 1944), married to German Prince Richard Casimir of Sayn-Wittgenstein, and Princess Anne-Marie (born Aug. 30, 1946) who married King Constantine of Greece and became Queen of Greece.

Denmark has public assistance, health insurance, disability and old-age pensions, workmen's compensation and unemployment insurance. Pensions are paid to men aged 67, widows and single women aged 62.

Denmark is a member of the UN and NATO, and joined the EEC Jan. 1, 1973.

Education and Religion. Evangelical Lutheran is the established religion, but there is complete religious freedom. Education is compulsory and includes vocational courses. The University of Copenhagen was founded in 1479.

Defense. Military forces total 45,500.

Greenland

Greenland, a huge island between the North Atlantic and the Polar Sea, is separated from the North American continent by Davis Strait and Baffin Bay. Its total area is 840,000 sq. mi., 705,234 of which are ice-capped. Most of the island is a lofty plateau 9,000 to 10,000 ft. in altitude. The average thickness of the ice cap is 1,000 ft. The population (est. 1974) is 50,000. The capital is Godthaab. Under the 1953 Danish constitution the colony became an integral part of the realm with representatives in the Folketing. Fish and fur are exported.

Dominican Republic

Capital: Santo Domingo. Area: 18,704 sq. mi. Population (UN est. 1973): 4,430,000. Monetary unit: Peso.

The Dominican Republic occupies the eastern two-thirds of the Island of Hispaniola (discovered by Columbus in 1492), second largest of the Greater Antilles, lying between Cuba on the W and Puerto Rico on the E. The boundary between it and the Republic of Haiti, which occupies the western part of the island, is 241 mi. long. It has a coastline of 979 mi. It is twice the size of New Hampshire. Climate is generally sub-tropical.

The city of Santo Domingo, founded 1496, is the oldest settlement by Europeans in the hemisphere and has the supposed ashes of Columbus in an elaborate tomb in its ancient cathedral.

Resources and Industries. The land is fertile. Chief products are sugar, cocoa, coffee, tobacco, corn, peanuts, bananas and livestock products.

The country has nickel, gold, copper, iron, salt, chalk, bauxite, marble, amber, kaolin.

Chief manufactures are sugar, molasses, rum, alcohol, cement, peanut oil, chocolate, tobacco products, cordage, textiles, apparel, lumber, furniture. The U. S. buys more than 50% of its exports, mostly sugar, cocoa and coffee, and supplies about 50% of imports.

Agricultural products, including sugar, showed strong gains in the early 1970's. A large nickel refining plant opened in 1972.

History and Government. Spain ceded Santo Domingo to France, 1795. Toussaint L'Ouverture, Haitian leader, seized it, 1801. Spain returned intermittently 1803-1821, and several native republics came and went. From 1822 to 1844 Haiti governed it. The republic was formed 1844. Spain occupied it 1861-63.

The country was occupied by U.S. Marines from 1916 until 1924, when a constitutionally elected government was installed.

In 1930, Gen. Rafael Leonidas Trujillo Molina was elected president. Trujillo remained in power, ruling the nation with an iron hand (though turning the presidency over to his brother, Hector, in 1952 and to Joaquin Balaguer in 1960) until his assassination May 30, 1961.

Balaguer resigned under pressure Jan. 17, 1962. Pending general elections, the country was governed by a 7-member Council of State headed by Rafael F. Bonnelly who was named president Jan. 18, 1962. He was succeeded by Juan Bosch, elected president Dec. 20, 1962, in first free elections in 38 years. Bosch was overthrown Sept. 25, 1963, and his regime replaced by an army-backed civilian triumvirate led by Donald Reid Cabral.

On April 24, 1965, a revolt was launched by followers of Bosch and others, including communists, and led by Col. Francisco Caamano Deno. The Reid Cabral government was ousted, but the rebel regime was replaced Apr. 28 by a 3-man counter-revolutionary junta led by Gen. Elias Wessin y Wessin; on May 7 it was succeeded by a 5-man regime headed by Gen. Antonio Imbert Barreras, another anti-Bosch leader; fighting continued in Santo Domingo.

A force of 405 U. S. Marines landed by helicopter April 28, primarily, according to U. S. President Johnson, to save American and other lives; U. S. forces were expanded to a high of 24,000 as the U. S. sought to restore order and prevent a communist take-over.

At U. S. urging, the Organization of American States sent an Inter-American Peace Force to Santo Domingo starting May 23, under a Brazilian commander with the head of the U. S. forces as deputy commander. Some U. S. forces were withdrawn and the Inter-American Force consisted of 11,200 men, including 9,400 U.S. troops, 1,100 Brazilians, and units from Honduras, Nicaragua, Paraguay and Costa Rica.

On Sept. 3, Hector Garcia-Godoy became provisional president under sponsorship of the OAS with agreement by all major local groups.

An election was held June 1, 1966; former president Balaguer defeated former president Bosch, 754,409 votes to 517,783. The Balaguer Reformist party won control of both houses of Congress. The new president was inaugurated July 1. The Inter-American Peace Force began moving troops out and completed their departure Sept. 20. President Balaguer was reelected, 1970 and 1974.

Education and Religion. The population is mostly mixed white and Negro, plus about 15% whites and a slightly larger percentage of blacks. Roman Catholicism is the state religion. Education is free and compulsory. The language is Spanish, but English is widely spoken. The University of Santo Domingo was established 1538 by Dominican fathers.

Defense. Armed forces total over 15,000. The nation is a member of the UN and OAS.

Ecuador

Capital: Quito. Area: 105,685 sq. mi. Population (est. 1973): 6,730,000. Monetary unit: Sucre.

On the NW coast of South America, Ecuador (Sp. for Equator) straddles the world's midsection, extending 100 mi. into the Northern Hemisphere, 400 into the Southern. It is bounded by Colombia, Peru and the Pacific. Two ranges of the Andes run N and S, splitting the country into 3 zones: hot, humid lowlands on the coast; temperate highlands between the ranges, and rainy, tropical lowlands to the E. There are 22 peaks over 14,000 ft.; highest is Chimborazo, 20,561 ft.; many are snowcapped; some volcanoes have erupted in recent years. Ecuador is larger than Arizona.

The **Galapagos Islands,** 600 mi. to the W, are the home of huge tortoises and other unusual animals. Charles Darwin visited the islands aboard the Beagle in 1835; his studies of wildlife there provided most of the facts for his theory of evolution.

Ecuador has sought revision of its Amazon valley boundary with Peru. It claims jurisdiction over Pacific waters 200 mi. out from its coast. It has seized and fined U.S. fishing boats within that limit. In Jan. 1971 the U.S. in reply temporarily suspended military sales to Ecuador. But other U.S. aid continued.

Guayaquil, Ecuador's largest city, is the chief seaport and, together with Quito, is served by major airlines. Rail lines link Quito with Guayaquil and San Lorenzo on the coast. Quito is famed for its 17th Century churches.

Resources and Industries. The country is rich in undeveloped minerals. Large deposits of copper, iron, lead, coal and sulphur are known to exist. In Aug. 1972 Ecuador began exporting oil, brought by pipeline from eastern Ecuador to a Pacifc coast terminal. Modern farm methods have speeded agricultural growth and made Ecuador the world's largest exporter of bananas. Other agricultural products are rice, cereals, potatoes, fruits, cocoa, coffee, kapok, rubber, mangrove bark.

Industry now contributes 20% to the national income, with large production increases in cement, edible oils, textiles, sugar, chemicals. Ecuador is the chief source of light but strong balsa wood. Ecuador was the original home of the Cinchona tree, source of quinine.

History and Government. Spain conquered the region, which was the northern Inca empire, in the 16th Century. Liberation forces defeated the Spanish May 24, 1822, near Quito. Ecuador became part of the Republic of Colombia but seceded, May 13, 1830, and became a republic. It has had a history of numerous coups.

In June 1968 elections, Dr. Jose Maria Velasco Ibarra, who had been elected president 4 times but had been ousted 3 times by coups, was again chosen by the voters. In June 1970, he assumed dictatorial powers. On Feb. 15, 1972, he was ousted by a military junta which named Gen. Guillermo Rodriguez Lara president.

Education and Religion. Roman Catholicism is the chief religion. Primary education is compulsory. The language is Spanish. The population is over one-third Indian and one-third mixed; whites, mostly of Spanish descent, and Negroes are minority groups.

Defense. Armed forces total about 22,000.

Egypt

Capital: Cairo. Area (1966): 386,872 sq. mi. Population (Govt. est. 1973): 35,620,000. Monetary unit: Egyptian pound.

The Arab Republic of Egypt occupies the NE corner of Africa on the Mediterranean. On the E lie Israel and the Red Sea which separates Egypt from Saudi Arabia. Libya is to the W and Sudan to the S. The Gulf of Suez and the Suez Canal (linking the gulf to the Mediterranean) separate Egypt's main area in Africa from its Sinai Peninsula, in Asia.

Alexandria, founded 332 B.C., is the chief port. Cairo, largest city, is rich in archeological treasures, cafes, bazaars. Tourist attractions include the pyramids, Sphinx, temple ruins at Karnak and Luxor, and other ancient monuments.

Resources and Industries. Productive acreage lies in the Valley of the Nile and in its delta, or Lower Egypt, north of Cairo. The Nile flows through 960 mi. in Egypt, and covers 2,850 sq. mi. with waters and marshes. Irrigated lands produce cotton, cereals, vegetables and sugar cane. Fruit is plentiful and includes grapes, dates, figs, pomegranates, peaches, apricots, oranges, lemons, bananas and olives. Egypt is the world's 7th largest producer of cotton.

The billion-dollar Aswan High Dam project, begun 1960, completed 1971, provided irrigation for more than a million acres of additional land and 10 billion kwh of electricity per year. Artesian wells, drilled in the Western Desert, reclaimed 43,000 acres for cultivation, 1960-66.

A variety of minerals is found in Egypt; petroleum is most important, with fields in the Red Sea and the Western Desert. Other minerals are phosphate rock, salt, iron, manganese, cement, gold, gypsum, kaolin, titanium.

A series of decrees in July, 1961, nationalized about 90% of industry and reduced land holdings to 52 acres per family.

Egypt has textile plants, chemical, steel, cement and fertilizer factories, and a film industry supplying the Middle East, Africa and Asia. Principal exports are cotton, rice, petroleum, textiles, refrigerators, tires, cement, electrical instruments.

History and Government. Archeological records of ancient empires in Egypt go back to 4000 B.C. A high civilization of rulers and priests dominated the lowly serfs. Assyrians, Persians, Greeks (Alexander of Macedon), Romans, Saracens, Turks, French (Napoleon) and British invaded Egypt. Under Turkish sultans the khedive as hereditary viceroy had wide authority but repeated insolvency led to regulation by European powers. Britain, which supervised the administration after 1882, made Egypt a protectorate 1914-1922. Britain then recognized Egypt as a sovereign state but reserved defense, security of British communications, and the Sudan.

The sultan became King Fouad I in 1922 and a constitution was adopted in 1923. King Fouad I died in 1936 and was succeeded by his son, Farouk, who abdicated in 1952 and left the country. His son was named nominal ruler under a regency council, Aug. 5, 1952, but the crown was abolished when Egypt was declared a republic, June 18, 1953.

In 1936 an Anglo-Egyptian treaty of alliance revised the conditions of association. Britain agreed to a condominium over the Sudan, with British and Egyptian troops cooperating, and agreed to retain 10,000 soldiers and 400 airmen to defend the Suez Canal for 20 years until Egypt would take over,

and also held naval bases in Alexandria and Port Said.

Egypt became a charter member of the UN and in 1944 led in organizing the Arab League. In 1947 Egypt brought before the UN Security Council a demand for unification of Egypt and Sudan and evacuation of all British troops from the Suez. In Oct. 1951 Egypt abrogated its 1936 treaty with Britain. The Sudan, with UN support, became independent in 1956.

Delays in reforms, corruption in public office and royal extravagance led to an uprising July 23, 1952, led by the Society of Free Officers which named Maj. Gen. Mohammed Naguib commander in chief and forced Farouk to abdicate. Naguib became premier Sept. 7, 1952. When the republic was proclaimed June 18, 1953, Naguib became its first president and premier. Lt. Col. Gamal Abdel Nasser, the principal influence behind the revolt, removed Naguib and succeeded him as premier on Apr. 18, 1954. On June 23, 1956, voters elected Nasser president.

A new constitution, guaranteeing individual rights, was approved by the voters Sept. 11, 1971. At the same time, Egypt joined Libya and Syria in a loose Federation of Arab Republics and Egypt adopted the name Arab Republic of Egypt, dropping the name United Arab Republic, which it had used since its brief union with Syria, 1958-1961. Egypt has a president, premier and a National Assembly all of whose 350 members must be members of the only legal party, the Arab Socialist Union.

In July, 1956, the United States, Great Britain and the International Bank withdrew support for loans to start the Aswan High Dam. President Nasser nationalized the Suez Canal and seized control of the assets of the canal company. Later he obtained credits and technicians from the USSR to build the dam.

When the state of Israel was proclaimed in 1948, Egypt joined other Arab nations invading Israel and was defeated. No peace treaties were made and Egypt later denied Israeli shipping the use of the Suez Canal.

Border hostilities with Israel heightened and on Oct. 29, 1956, Israeli forces invaded Egypt's Sinai Peninsula. Egypt rejected a cease-fire demand by Britain and France; on Oct. 31 the 2 nations dropped bombs and on Nov. 5-6 landed forces. Egypt and Israel accepted a UN cease-fire, followed by Britain and France; fighting ended Nov. 7.

A UN Emergency Force guarded the 117-mile long border between Egypt and Israel until May 19, 1967, when it was withdrawn at Nasser's demand. Egyptian troops took over the Gaza Strip and the heights at Sharm el Sheikh and 3 days later closed the Strait of Tiran leading into the Gulf of Aqaba to all Israeli shipping. Full-scale war broke out June 5 and before it ended under a UN cease-fire June 10, Israel had captured Gaza and the Sinai Peninsula, controlled the east bank of the Suez Canal and reopened the gulf.

Sporadic fighting with Israel broke out late in 1968. In 1969-70 there were almost daily artillery duels across the Suez Canal, ground forays and air raids in which Israeli planes penetrated deep into Egypt. Military and economic aid was received from the USSR and it was est. in 1971 there were 19,000 or more Soviet military personnel in Egypt. Israel and Egypt agreed, Aug. 7, 1970, to a cease-fire and peace negotiations proposed by the U.S. Negotiations, pressed by the UN and U.S., failed to achieve results, but the cease-fire continued into 1973.

Nasser died Sept. 28, 1970. Anwar el-Sadat was elected president Oct. 14 by a 90% vote.

In July 1972 Sadat ordered most of the 20,000 Soviet military advisers and personnel to leave Egypt. They complied, leaving behind bases and equipment they had installed for the Egyptians.

In a surprise attack Oct. 6, 1973 (Yom Kippur, most sacred day on the Jewish calendar), Egyptian forces crossed the Suez Canal into the Sinai, attacked Israeli forces and established 2 long but narrow bridgeheads along the E side of the canal. (At the same time, Syrian forces attacked Israelis on the Golan Heights, also achieving temporary gains.) Egypt was supplied by a USSR military airlift; the U.S. responded with an airlift to Israel. Israel counter-attacked, crossed the canal between the Egyptian bridgeheads, surrounded Suez City and trapped the Egyptian 3d Army in its Sinai bridgehead. A UN cease-fire took effect Oct. 24; a UN peace-keeping force went to the area.

A disengagement agreement was signed Jan. 18, 1974, mainly through the efforts of U.S. Secretary of State Henry Kissinger. Under it, Israeli forces withdrew from the canal's W bank; limited numbers of Egyptian forces occupied a strip, 6 to 7.5 mi. wide, along the E bank from the Mediterranean to the Gulf of Suez; UN forces took over a buffer zone, 3.5 to 5 mi. wide, E of the Egyptians; Israelis, further E, could have only limited forces adjoining the UN zone. Withdrawals to the new lines were completed Mar. 4.

The U.S. and Egypt resumed, in Feb. 1974, diplomatic relations, severed by Egypt after the 1967 war. In June, U.S. President Nixon announced he would provide Egypt nuclear technology for peaceful purposes.

Sadat charged in Aug. that Libyan leader Muammar el-Qaddafi had backed a plot to overthrow the Egyptian government.

Education and Religion. There are 3 ethnic elements: the Fellahin, basic Egyptian group; the Bedouin, nomadic Arabs; Nubians, a mixed group. Moslems form 92% of the population and Coptic Christians about 7%.

Education is compulsory for all children beginning at age 7 and free through high school. There is a famous seat of Moslem learning in the University of Al-Azhar in Cairo, founded about 968 A.D. Four modern universities are Cairo, Alexandria, Ein-Shams and Assiut. Arabic is the official language.

Defense. Military forces, equipped by USSR, total 300,000 with reserves of over 500,000.

The Suez Canal

The Suez Canal, 103 mi. long, links the Mediterranean and the Red Sea. It was begun April 25, 1859, by a French corporation under Ferdinand de Lesseps and opened Nov. 17 1869. Benjamin Disraeli, British prime minister, obtained control for Britain Nov. 24, 1875, by buying 176,752 shares from the Khedive Ismail of Egypt for about $20 million.

The British ended a 74-year military occupation of the canal area June 13, 1956, withdrawing all troops. On July 26, Egypt proclaimed nationalization of the canal, seizing it from its French and British stockholders. It barred Israeli ships and cargoes destined for Israel.

A final agreement between Egypt and the Universal Suez Canal Co., signed July 13, 1958, called for payments to stockholders of $64,400,000. Final payments were made Jan. 1, 1963.

After nationalization, Egypt widened and deepened the canal, improving its capacity. The canal was closed to all shipping by Cairo at the height of the Israeli-Arab War in June 1967. Subsidies to replace lost canal revenues were paid the UAR by Saudi Arabia, Kuwait and Libya. In 1974, operations to clear the canal of war debris began, with aid from the U.S. and others, to be completed in April 1975.

El Salvador

Capital: San Salvador. Area: 8,260 sq. mi. Population (UN est 1973): 3,860,000. Monetary unit: Colon.

El Salvador, smallest of the 6 Central American or Middle American republics and the only one without an Atlantic seacoast, is bounded by Guatemala, Honduras and a Pacific coastline of about 160 mi. A country of mountains, including many volcanoes, and upland plains, it is entirely within the tropics, but tropic heat is modified by the elevation. It is about the size of Massachusetts.

The 3 racial types are white, 5%; mixed white and Indian descent, 85%; Indian, 10%.

Resources and Industries. Mountain slope plantations make El Salvador the world's 8th largest producer and a large exporter of coffee. Cotton production has made large strides; coffee represents 44% of the value of exports, cotton 8%. Primarily agricultural, the country is becoming industrialized; it produces cement, refined sugar and textiles.

Economic development has been helped by U.S. aid.

History and Government. El Salvador became independent of Spain in 1821; member of the Central American Federation until 1839. The constitution provides for a unicameral legislative system, the National Assembly of Deputies, elected by popular vote. Voting is compulsory for all over 18 years of age. Executive power is vested in the president who is elected for a 5-year term by direct, popular vote and is ineligible for immediate reelection.

In July 1969, a dispute over the presence of 300,000 Salvadorean workers and settlers in Honduras broke into open warfare between the two nations. After 5 days, the OAS arranged a truce. In 1970, after new clashes, a demilitarized zone was agreed on. Clashes continued in 1974.

Education and Religion. Education is free but illiteracy rate is 50%. The language is Spanish. The dominant religion is Roman Catholicism.

Defense. Military forces number about 5,500. El Salvador is a member of the UN and OAS.

Equatorial Guinea

Capital: Santa Isabel. Area: 10,832 sq. mi. Population (Est. 1973): 300,000. Monetary unit: Pereta.

The Republic of Equatorial Guinea, which received its independence from Spain on Oct. 12, 1968, consists of the Province of Fernando Po, including Fernando Po Is., in the Gulf of Guinea off the W. coast of Africa, and Annobon Is., 370 mi. SW., and the Province of Rio Muni, on the mainland facing the gulf. Santa Isabel, the capital, is on Fernando Po Is. which has an area of 780 sq. mi. and population (est. 1972) of 90,000.

Self-government and independence were achieved in steps, with local elections in 1960 and increased autonomy in 1964. The 1968 independence constitution provided for a president, a 35-member Assembly and two Provincial Councils, all elected by universal adult suffrage, and an advisory Council of the Republic chosen by the president. Francisco Macias Nguema was elected the first president. In 1971 he assumed complete control of the government and in 1972 was named president for life.

Important exports are cocoa and timber for plywood. Other exports are coffee, bananas and palm oil.

More than half the population is Roman Catholic. Spanish is the official language; numerous African languages are also spoken. Fernando Po natives were mostly Bubis; by the late 1960s Nigerian workers and settlers numbered almost half the island population. In Rio Muni, the Fangs were the largest group. Before a 1969 confrontation, there were about 7,000 Europeans, mostly Spanish, but many left during the dispute.

The nation is a member of the UN and OAU.

Ethiopia

Capital: Addis Ababa. Area: 457,142 sq. mi. Population (Est. 1973): 26,080,000. Monetary unit: Ethiopian dollar.

Ethiopia is a ruggedly mountainous, independent empire in NE Africa. It faces on the Red Sea, but its main rivers are important tributaries of the Nile: the Abbai or Blue Nile, one of the 2 main branches of that mighty river, has its source in Ethiopia's Lake Tana. The country is as large as Texas, Oklahoma and New Mexico combined.

Resources and Industries. Economy is some 70%

agricultural but industrial resources are potentially great, including vast hydroelectric power. Industries include food processing, cement, shoes, textiles.

Fertile soil and abundant rainfall produce 2 crops annually. Coffee, wheat, barley, millet, tobacco, and sugar are principal crops. Coffee of extremely high quality from Kaffa, in SW Ethiopia, reputed birthplace of the coffee plant, accounts for half of the country's foreign exchange. Over 185,000 tons are exported annually. Value of exports in 1973 rose to $237 million; imports totaled $213 million.

Cattle, sheep, mules and goats are raised. Hides and skins, oilseeds and vegetables also are exported. Mineral resources include platinum, gold, silver, manganese, tin, copper, asbestos, potash, sulphur, mica, cement and salt. There are known deposits of coal and iron.

Ethiopia has used large credits from the World Bank and other agencies for road building (there are over 4,000 mi. of all-weather roads). Aid and investment funds are received from the U. S. and other western nations and from communist countries. Ethiopia is a member of the UN and Addis Ababa is hq. for the Organization of African Unity.

History and Government. Ethiopia is a constitutional monarchy derived from a number of earlier kingdoms, descendants of ancient Hamite and Semite tribes. Italy invaded the country in 1880 and acquired a sphere of influence and later organized its colony of Eritrea. In 1936 Italy invaded Ethiopia without declaring war. The League of Nations applied sanctions against Italy, which proved ineffective. Mussolini added Ethiopia to Italy. British forces freed Ethiopia in 1941.

The present emperor, Haile Selassie I, 225th consecutive Solomonic ruler, was born July 23, 1892, crowned Nov. 2, 1930. He voluntarily established a parliament and judiciary system, 1931, and promulgated a new constitution 1955, incorporating a bill of rights and granting the franchise to all over 21. The Senate of 125 is appointed for 6-year terms; Chamber of Deputies, approx. 250, is elected for 4 years. In 1966, the emperor made further moves toward democracy, including empowering the premier to appoint his own cabinet.

In 1974 parts of the nation suffered famine and unrest; a military committee deposed the Emperor in a peaceful coup Sept. 12, 1974 after months of gradually reducing his powers.

Education and Religion. Ethiopian culture has been influenced by Greece and Egypt. Christianity is the predominant religion, embraced in 330 A.D.; the Coptic, Monophysite branch is practiced. Until 1952 the Egyptian Coptic patriarch was the head of the church, but the emperor now appoints the Ethiopian archbishop. The population is largely composed of a mixture of Hamites, Semites and Negroes. The largest number are Coptic Christians; next are Moslems; others practice tribal religions.

There are 2 universities and a number of colleges. The official language is Amharic; English is widely taught.

Eritrea, which had been an Italian colony since 1890, was administered after World War II by Great Britain; the UN General Assembly voted to return it to Ethiopia and the action became effective Sept. 11, 1952. In 1970-72 secessionist guerrillas were active in Eritrea.

Fiji

Capital: Suva. Area: 7,055 sq. mi. Population (UN est. 1973): 550,000. Monetary unit: Fiji dollar.

The Fiji Islands lie in the South Pacific, E of Australia and N of New Zealand. There are about 840 islands (106 inhabited), many of them mountainous, with tropical forests and large fertile areas. The capital, Suva, is on Viti Levu, the largest island (4,011 sq. mi.).

Descendants of the native Fijians (Melanesians and Polynesians) form about 43% of the population but have been protected by law in ownership of 83% of the land. Descendants of Indian contract laborers, brought to the islands in the late-19th Century, make up slightly over 51%. Most of the others are of Chinese or European descent. English is the official language. Most of the Fijians are Christians; the Indians are about 80% Hindu, 15% Moslem. Literacy is about 85%.

A British colony since 1874, Fiji received gradual measures of self-government in the 1960s. On Oct. 10, 1970, Fiji became a fully independent parliamentary democracy, with a Senate, a House of Representatives, a prime minister and, as a member of the Commonwealth, a governor-general representing the British Queen. It is a member of the UN.

Sugar is the main export, along with molasses, cement, coconut products, timber, ginger and gold. Tourism is important. A cement factory, shipyards and small manufacturing plants have been built.

Finland

Capital: Helsinki. Area: 130,119 sq. mi. Population (UN est. 1973): 4,660,000. Monetary unit: Markka.

Finland is a republic in northern Europe, with Sweden, Norway and the USSR for neighbors. South and central Finland are mostly flat areas with low hills; there are mountainous areas, 3,000-4,000 ft., in the N. It is half the size of Texas.

About 70% of the land is forested. Lakes and canal waterways are navigable for 3,000 mi. Rail and air transport is well developed.

Aland Islands, constituting an autonomous department, is a group of small islands, 572 sq. mi., in the Gulf of Bothnia, 25 mi. from Sweden, 15 mi. from Finland. They are demilitarized. Mariehamn is the principal port.

Resources and Industries. Rapid industrialization has taken place. Forest products (paper, etc.) account for 55% of exports, metal products 25%, foods 5%. Principal crops are oats, barley, wheat, rye, potatoes, hay. There are ship building, textiles, leather and chemicals industries.

In 1972, 2 million tourists visited Finland.

Foreign trade (in thousands of U.S. dollars):

	Imports	Exports
1972	$3,198,000	$2,947,000
1973	$4,311,000	$3,794,000

History and Government. The early Finns probably migrated from the Ural area at about the beginning of the Christian era. Swedish settlers brought the country into the kingdom of Sweden, 1154 to 1809, when Finland became an autonomous grand duchy of the Russian Empire. Russian exactions created a strong national spirit; on Dec. 6, 1917, Finland declared its independence and on July 17, 1919, became a republic. On Nov. 30, 1939, the Soviet Union invaded Finland, and although the Finns took heavy toll, in March, 1940, were forced to cede 16,173 sq. mi., including the Karelian Isthmus, Viipuri, and an area on Lake Ladoga. When Germany attacked the USSR June 22, 1941, Finland again was involved. An armistice was signed Sept. 19, 1944, and the USSR exacted the former cessions, plus Petsamo in the N. and a lease for 50 years on Porkkala, near Helsinki, for a military base. The treaty of Feb. 10, 1947, also exacted $300 million in goods in term payments. In April, 1948, Finland signed a treaty of mutual assistance and friendship with the USSR; in Jan. 1956 Russia returned Porkkala.

The president is chosen for a term of six years by an electoral college of 300 named by direct vote; he appoints the cabinet.

There is a single legislative chamber, the Eduskunta, numbering 200, elected to 4-year terms. Voting is by proportional representation.

The prime minister and cabinet normally represent a coalition of parties in the Eduskunta.

Education and Religion. The Evangelical Lutheran Church is the leading religion, and both Finnish and

Swedish are official languages. The nation is considered completely free from illiteracy. There are 6 major universities (the oldest founded 1640) and 6 colleges of university level.

Defense. Military strength for 1972-73 was 39,500, including 34,000 in the Army, 3,000 in the Air Force and 2,500 in the Navy.

Finland is a member of the UN, Nordic Council and EFTA and has a trade agreement with the EEC.

France

Capital: Paris. Area: 212,973 sq. mi. Population (Govt. est. 1974): 52,350,000. Monetary unit: Franc.

France has coastlines on the Atlantic and Mediterranean and is about four-fifths the size of Texas. It shares borders with Belgium, Luxembourg, Germany, Switzerland, Italy, Andorra and Spain. It is separated from England by the English Channel and the Strait of Dover. The Rhine River is on the German boundary, the Jura Mts. form the Swiss boundary and the Pyrenees Mtns. rise along the borders of Andorra and Spain.

Mont Blanc, on the Franco-Italian border, is the tallest W of the Caucasus, 15,771 ft. A highway tunnel, 7.25 mi., under Mont Blanc, was opened in 1965, linking France and Italy.

There are 4 important rivers, the Seine, the Loire, the Garonne and the Rhone. There are some 5,005 mi. of navigable rivers and canals.

The island of Corsica, in the Mediterranean W of Italy and N of Sardinia, is an integral part of France. It has an area of 3,369 sq. mi. and a population of 269,-831 (1968 census). The capital is Ajaccio, birthplace of Napoleon.

Resources and Industries. Agriculturally, France is a country of small diversified farms involving 45,800,000 acres and 15% of the employed, making France the biggest food producer in Western Europe. Agricultural exports are valued at more than $1.7 billion annually. Leading crops are wheat, barley, corn, oats, rice, and a wide variety of fruits and vegetables. Cattle, poultry, forestry and fishing are large-scale. France is the world's 4th ranking producer of beef and of pork. Approx. 1,500,000 farmers belong to cooperative unions.

The country is rich in minerals, and the basins of Pas de Calais and Lorraine are noted for their huge coal deposits, iron ore, bauxite, pyrites, mineral oils, auriferous ore, asphalt, rock salt and potash salts. The iron ore deposits in eastern France and the bauxite deposits in central France are among the richest in the world. Power stations produced about 174 million kwh in 1973.

France tested atomic bombs in the Sahara beginning in 1960 and, beginning in 1966 exploded nuclear devices at Mururoa, an atoll 750 mi. SE of Tahiti, continuing the tests through 1974. (France was not a signer of the 1963 treaty banning such tests.) Australia and New Zealand protested the tests and in 1973 the International Court of Justice asked France to suspend the tests.

Manufacturing includes chemicals, silk and cotton textiles, perfumes, automobiles, aircraft, ships, instruments, plastics, electronic equipment. Index of industrial production (1963=100) was 187 in 1973.

France leads the world in wine-making, producing over 1.5 billion gallons a year.

Foreign trade in thousands of U.S. dollars

	Imports	Exports
1972	$26,754,000	$26,052,000
1973	$36,987,000	$35,565,000

History and Government. The monarchial system was overthrown by the French Revolution (1789-1793) and succeeded by the First Republic; thereafter successively followed by the First Empire under Napoleon (1804—1814), a monarchy (1814-1848), the Second Republic (1848-1852), the Second Empire (1852-1870), the Third Republic (1871-1946), the Fourth Republic (1946-1958), Fifth Republic (1958).

France suffered severe losses in manpower and

wealth in the first World War, 1914-1918, when it was invaded by Germany. By the Treaty of Versailles, France exacted return of Alsace and Lorraine, French provinces seized by Germany in 1871. Germany invaded France again in May, 1940, occupied Paris June 14; 1940, and signed an armistice with a government that made its hq. in Vichy. Marshal Philippe Petain became chief of state. After France was liberated by the Allies Sept., 1944, Gen. Charles De Gaulle became premier of the provisional government, serving from Nov. 1944 to Jan. 1946.

De Gaulle again became premier June 1, 1958. His proposed constitution for the Fifth Republic and new French Community was approved by the voters by an overwhelming margin. De Gaulle was elected first president of the Fifth Republic Dec. 21, 1958; inaugurated Jan. 8, 1959. De Gaulle ran for reelection Dec. 5, 1965; he failed to win a majority of the votes, getting about 44% compared to 32% for Francois Mitterand, left-wing candidate. In a runoff election Dec. 19, De Gaulle won with about 55%.

The constitution provides for a strong executive branch headed by the president, a legislature composed of a National Assembly and a Senate.

A constitutional amendment adopted by referendum Oct. 28, 1962, provided that future presidents be elected by popular vote rather than by an electoral college. The president, elected for 7 years, appoints the premier (formerly invested by the Assembly), and may dissolve the Assembly and call for new elections; he may call for referendums on specific issues and may assume full powers in a national emergency.

Women, who had less than equal rights under provisions of the 1804 Code Napoleon, won the right to take jobs, open checking accounts and own their own businesses by a 1966 law.

In May 1968 rebellious students at the Sorbonne and elsewhere rioted, battled police and were joined by some 10 million workers who launched nationwide strikes and took over many factories. The nation was almost completely paralyzed. The government awarded pay increases to the strikers May 26; on May 30 De Gaulle dissolved the Assembly. A threat of civil war was eased as Army tank units, loyal to the government, maneuvered in Paris outskirts. By early June, normalcy was returned. In elections to the Assembly in late June 1968, De Gaulle's backers won a landslide victory.

In Nov. 1968 De Gaulle weathered an economic storm, refusing to devalue the franc. But on Apr. 28, 1969, he resigned from office after losing a nationwide referendum on his proposals for constitutional reform. He had asked approval as a personal vote of confidence but over 52% of the votes were against his proposals.

A nationwide election for a successor, June 1, resulted in a runoff election June 15 in which the winner was Georges Pompidou, who had been De Gaulle's premier from 1962 until July 1968. In the runoff, he took over 57% of the vote, defeating Poher. Pompidou died Apr. 2, 1974. Valery Giscard d'Estaing, a conservative, was elected president, May 19, 1974, ending 16 years of Gaullist party rule.

Education and Religion. Primary, secondary and higher education are free and instruction is compulsory between the ages of 6 and 16.

The country is predominantly Roman Catholic, only about 800,000 being Protestants. The state recognizes no religion and tolerates all.

Both employers and employees contribute to the old-age pension fund. There is provision for family allowances and compulsory social insurance for illness, maternity, disability and death. A profit-sharing agreement was signed Jan. 7, 1959.

Defense. Military forces total over 500,000; reserves number over 600,000.

France is a member of the UN, SEATO and EEC but announced in 1973 it would stop paying dues to SEATO after 1974.

Pres. De Gaulle announced Mar. 9, 1966, France withdrew all its troops from the integrated military command of NATO and that NATO hq. and bases would have to be removed from France. But France maintained its membership in the political meetings of NATO.

Afars and Issas Territory

The French Territory of the Afars and the Issas, formerly French Somaliland, lies between Ethiopia and Somalia and is separated by the Straits of Bab-el-Mandeb from Yemen.

The area is 8,996 sq. mi. and population (est. 1974), 150,000; the capital is Djibouti. France took control of the area in gradual steps, beginning in 1862.

The territory has few industries, except fishing and livestock. Salt is its most valuable product. Half of Ethiopia's foreign commerce passes along the rail line from Addis Ababa and through the port of Djibouti.

In a referendum Mar. 19, 1967, the territory elected to remain French. It sends a deputy and a senator to the French Parliament.

Comoro Islands

Comoro Islands, an Overseas Territory, is an archipelago of small islands off SE Africa in Mozambique Channel NW of Madagascar. Chief islands are Grande Comore, Anjouan, Mayotte, Moheli. Total area, about 902 sq. mi.; population (est. 1974), 286,762. Capital; Moroni. Chief products are vanilla, coconuts and essential oils. It elects 2 deputies, one senator to the French Parliament. France has offered the territory independence "about 1978."

Reunion

Reunion, Overseas Department, is an island in the Indian Ocean, about 420 miles east of Madagascar, and has belonged to France since 1665. The area is 969 sq. mi.; the population (est. 1972) 470,000, is 30% of French extraction. Capital: Saint-Denis. The chief products are sugar, rum, corn, perfume essences, vanilla and spices. It elects 3 deputies, 2 senators to the French Parliament.

Guadeloupe

Guadeloupe, Overseas Department in the West Indies' Leeward Islands, consists of 2 large islands, Basse-Terre and Grande-Terre, separated by the Salt River, plus Marie Galante and the Saintes group to the S and, to the N, Desirade, St. Barthelemy, and over half of St. Martin (the Netherlands portion is St. Maarten). A French possession since 1635, the department is represented in the French Parliament by 2 senators and 3 deputies; administration consists of a prefect (governor) and an elected General Council.

Area of the islands is 687 sq. mi.; population (est. 1972) 340,000, mainly descendants of slaves; capital is Basse-Terre on Basse-Terre Is. The land is fertile; sugar, rum and bananas are exported; tourism is an important industry.

Martinique

Martinique, one of the Windward Islands, in the West Indies, has been a possession since 1635, and a Department since March, 1946. It is represented in the French Parliament by 2 senators and 3 deputies. Martinique's famous volcano, Mt. Pelee, erupted May 8, 1902, destroying the city of St. Pierre with more than 30,000 inhabitants. The island was the birthplace of Napoleon's Empress Josephine.

Martinique has an area of 431 sq. mi. and population (est. 1972) 340,000 mostly descendants of slaves. The capital is Fort-de-France. It is a popular tourist stop.

The chief exports are sugar, rum, bananas, pineapples and cocoa. Trade is mainly with France and the U.S.

St. Pierre and Miquelon

St. Pierre and Miquelon, an Overseas Territory, are 2 groups of rocky barren islands close to the SW coast of Newfoundland, inhabited by fishermen. A governor, assisted by a Council, rules the islands. The exports are chiefly cod, dried and fresh, and other fish products.

The St. Pierre group has an area of 10 sq mi.; Miquelon, 83 sq. mi. Total population (est. 1974), 5,450. The capital is St. Pierre. A deputy and a senator are elected to the French Parliament.

French Guiana

French Guiana, an Overseas Department, is on the NE coast of South America with Surinam (Netherlands Guiana) on the W and Brazil on the E and S. Its area is 35,135 sq. mi.; population (est. 1972), 60,000. Guiana sends one senator and one deputy to the French Parliament. Guiana has a prefect and a Council General of 15 elected members; capital is Cayenne.

In 1944 France closed the famous penal colony, Devil's Island, and repatriated 2,800 inmates.

Immense forests of rich timber cover 90% of the land. Very little of the land is cultivated. The principal crops are rice, corn, manioc, cacao, bananas, and sugar cane. Placer gold mining is the most important industry. Exports comprise cocoa, bananas, various woods, gold, fish glue, rum, rosewood essence, shrimp and hides.

French Polynesia

French Polynesia, Overseas Territory, comprises 130 islands widely scattered among 5 archipelagos in the South Pacific; administered by a governor, Territorial Assembly and a Council with headquarters at Papeete, Tahiti, one of the Society Islands. A deputy and a senator are elected to the French Parliament.

Other groups are the Marquesas Islands, the Tuamotu Archipelago, the Gambier Islands, and the Austral Islands.

Total area of the islands administered from Tahiti is 1,544 sq. mi.; pop. (est. 1974), 130,000, more than half on Tahiti. Tahiti is picturesque and mountainous with a productive coastline bearing coconut, bananas and orange trees, sugar cane and vanilla.

Tahiti was visited by Capt. James Cook in 1769 and by Capt. Bligh in the Bounty, 1788-89. The beauty of its women and the landscape impressed Herman Melville, Paul Gauguin, Charles Darwin and Robert Louis Stevenson who called Tahitians "God's sweetest works."

New Caledonia

New Caledonia and its dependencies, an Overseas Territory, are a group of islands in the Pacific Ocean about 1,115 mi. E of Australia and approx. the same distance NW of New Zealand. Dependencies are the Loyalty Islands, the Isle of Pines, Huon Islands and the Chesterfield Islands.

New Caledonia, the largest, has 6,530 sq. mi. Total area of the territory is 8,548 sq. mi.; population (est. 1974) 130,000. The group was acquired by France in 1853.

The territory is administered by a governor and government council. There is a popularly elected Territorial Assembly. A deputy and a senator are elected to the French Parliament. Capital: Noumea.

Mining is the chief industry. New Caledonia has large deposits of nickel. Other minerals found are chrome, cobalt, manganese, antimony, mercury, cinnebar, silver, gold, lead and copper. Agricultural products include coffee, copra, cotton, manioc (cassava), corn, tobacco, bananas and pineapples.

Wallis and Futuna Islands, 2 archipelagos raised to status of Overseas Territory July 29, 1961, are in the SW Pacific S of the Equator between Fiji and Samoa. The islands have a total area of 106 sq. mi. and population (est. 1972) of 7,500. Alofi, attached to Futuna, is uninhabited. Capital: Mata-Utu. Chief products are copra, yams, taro roots, bananas. A senator and a deputy are elected to the French Parliament.

French Antarctica

French Southern and Antarctic Lands, Overseas Territory, comprises **Adelie Land,** on Antarctica, and 4 island groups in the Indian Ocean. Adelie, discov. 1840, has 2 research bases, a coastline of 185 mi. and tapers 1,240 mi. inland to the South Pole. Heights rise to 8,200 ft. There are 2 huge glaciers, Ninnis, 22 mi wide, 99 mi. long, and Mentz, 11 mi. wide, 140 mi. long. Climate varies from -36° F. to 40° F. The Indian Ocean groups are:

Kerguelen Archipelago, discovered 1772, has 300 islands. The chief is 87 mi. long, 74 mi. wide, and has Mt. Ross, 6,429 ft. tall. Principal research station is Port-aux-Francais. Seals often weigh 2 tons; there are blue whales, coal, peat, semi-precious stones. **Crozet Archipelago** (discov. 1772), covers 195 sq. mi. Eastern Island rises to 6,560 ft. **Saint Paul,** in southern Indian Ocean, has warm springs and tropical climate, with earth at places heating to 120° to 390° F. **New Amsterdam,** nearby, has temperate climate, produces cod and rock lobster.

New Hebrides

New Hebrides, a condominium administered since 1906 by France and Great Britain, is a group of 11 main islands and about 69 islets 250 mi. NE of New Caledonia and 500 mi. W of Fiji. It has an est. 5,700 sq. mi. and population (est. 1974) of 90,000, mostly Melanesian. It has 2 administrations—French and British. Chief products are copra, frozen fish, cocoa and coffee.

Gabon Republic

Capital: Libreville. Area: 102,317 sq. mi. Population (est. 1973): 520,000. Monetary unit: CFA franc.

A former French Overseas Territory, Gabon is on the west coast of Equatorial Africa, straddling the Equator and bounded by Cameroon, Equatorial Guinea, People's Republic of Congo and the Atlantic. Heavily forested, the country consists of coastal lowlands, plateaus in N, E and S, mountains in N, SE and center. It is about the size of Colorado.

Gabon's economy is thriving, with exports far exceeding imports in value. Valuable timber, plywood and veneers were the main export until the late 1960s when manganese, crude oil and uranium topped them in value. There are also large iron ore deposits.

Agriculture, roads, port facilities and hydroelectric power are being extensively developed. Main crops are cocoa, coffee, rice, peanuts, palm products, cassava, bananas.

Gabon proclaimed independence Aug. 17, 1960; it became a UN member Sept. 20. It is a republic, with an elected president and unicameral National Assembly. The first president, Leon M'ba, died in 1967; he was succeeded Dec. 1 by vice president Albert Bongo who declared a one-party state.

Dr. Albert Schweitzer, Nobel Peace Prize winner, physician, philosopher, musicologist and theologian, founded a hospital for lepers and others in 1913 at Lambarene. He died Sept. 4, 1965, at the age of 90 and was buried at the hospital.

The Gambia

Capital: Banjul. Area: 4,003 sq. mi. Population (Govt. est. 1973): 490,000. Monetary unit: Dalasi.

Gambia, Africa's smallest country in area, is a former British Colony and protectorate in western Africa. It includes the island of Banjul at the mouth of the Gambia River and a 10-mile wide strip of territory on each side of the river. Except for its Atlantic coastline, Gambia is surrounded by Senegal.

Gambia attained internal self-government Oct. 4, 1963. Its legislature comprises a speaker and 32 elected members. Britain granted complete independence to the colony Feb. 18, 1965.

In April 1970, after a referendum, Gambia became a republic within the Commonwealth. Former Prime Minister Dawda K. Jawara became the first president.

Peanuts are the main export. Rice and other foods are also grown. Tourism has become important. Britain provides development aid.

English is the official language. Islam and animism are the main religions.

Germany

Area: 136,461 sq. mi. Population (UN est. 1973): 78,950,000. Now comprises 2 nations: Federal Republic of Germany (West Germany), German Democratic Republic (East Germany).

Germany, prior to World War II, was a central European nation composed of numerous states which had a common language and traditions and which had been united in one country since 1871; since World War II it has been split in 2 parts, West and East (see below).

The climate and terrain are varied, with fertile lowlands in the N, rolling farmlands and forests in the center, and mountainous areas in the S.

Resources and Industries. Some of more important crops are wheat, rye, barley, oats, potatoes, sugar beets and hay. Other commercial products are fruit, tobacco, hops, nuts.

Principal minerals are coal, lignite, iron, zinc, lead, copper, salt, potash and petroleum. Bulk of mining is in North Rhine-Westphalia, Central Germany, the Harz, and Westerwald. Oil comes chiefly from Emsland near the Netherlands border, and Lower Saxony. Iron and steel production is greatest in the Ruhr and Saar.

History and Government. Germanic tribes were defeated by Julius Caesar, 55 and 53 B. C. but Roman expansion N of the Rhine was stopped with the wiping out of 3 legions under Varus in 9 A.D. Charlemagne, ruler of the Franks, consolidated Saxon, Bavarian, Rhenish, Frankish and other lands; after him the eastern part became the German Empire. The Thirty Years' War, 1618-1648, split Germany into small principalities and kingdoms. After Napoleon, Austria contended with Prussia for dominance, but lost the Seven Weeks' War to Prussia, 1866. Otto von Bismarck, Prussian chancellor, formed the North German Confederation, 1867.

In 1870 Bismarck maneuvered Napoleon III into declaring war. After the quick defeat of France Bismarck formed the **German Empire** and on Jan. 18, 1871, in Versailles, proclaimed King Wilhelm I of Prussia German emperor (Deutscher kaiser).

The German Empire reached its peak before World War I in 1914. At that time the homeland comprised 208,780 sq. mi., plus a colonial empire. After that war Germany ceded Alsace-Lorraine to France; Eupen and Malmedy to Belgium; parts of Silesia to Poland and Czechoslovakia; part of Schleswig to Denmark; lost all of its colonies as well as the ports of Memel and Danzig.

Republic of Germany, 1919-1933, adopted the Weimar constitution, met reparation payments and elected Fredrich Ebert and Gen. Paul von Hindenburg presidents.

Third Reich, 1933-1945. Adolf Hitler, born in Braunau, Austria, 1889, led the National Socialist German Workers' (Nazi) party after World War I. In 1923 with the help of Gen. Erich Ludendorff he attempted to unseat the Bavarian government in the "Beer Hall putsch," and was imprisoned. He wrote Mein Kampf while in prison. President von Hindenburg named Hitler chancellor Jan. 30, 1933; on Aug. 3, 1934, the day after Hindenburg's death, the cabinet joined the offices of president and chancellor and made Hitler fuehrer (leader). Hitler abolished freedom of speech and assembly, and began a long series of persecutions climaxed by the mass extermination of Jews and opponents.

Hitler repudiated the Versailles treaty and reparations agreements. He remilitarized the Rhineland 1936 and annexed Austria (Anschluss, 1938). At Munich he made an agreement with Neville Chamberlain, British prime minister, enabling him to annex Czechoslovakia's Sudetenland. He signed a non-aggression treaty with the Soviet Union, 1939. He declared war on Poland Sept. 1, 1939, precipitating World War II.

With total defeat near, Hitler committed suicide in Berlin Apr. 30, 1945. The victorious Allies voided all acts and annexations of Hitler's Reich.

Postwar changes — The zones of occupation administered by the Allied Powers and later relinquished gave the Soviet Union Saxony, Saxony-Anhalt, Thuringia, and Mecklenburg, and the former Prussian provinces of Saxony and Brandenburg. The U.S. administered territory bounded on the E by the Russian zone and Czechoslovakia, on the N by the British zone, on the W by the French zone, and on the S by Austria, including Bavaria (except Lindau district), Wurttemberg (northern), Baden (northern), most of Hesse and Hesse-Nassau, and the city state of Bremen.

The territory E of the Oder-Neisse line within 1937 boundaries comprising the provinces of Silesia, Pomerania, West Prussia and the southern part of East Prussia, totaling about 41,220 sq. mi., population (1939) 9,600,000,was put under Polish administration; northern East Prussia was put under Soviet domination.

The Western Allies ended the state of war with Germany in 1951. The USSR did so in 1955.

There was also created the area of Greater Berlin, within but not part of the Soviet zone, administered by the 4 occupying powers under the Allied Command. In 1948 the Soviet Union withdrew and established its single command in East Berlin. The Communists cut off supplies, whereupon the Allies utilized a gigantic airlift to bring food to West Berlin during 1948-1949. In Aug. 1961 the East Germans built a wall dividing Berlin.

West Germany

Capital: Bonn. Area (including West Berlin): 95,815 sq. mi. Population (UN est. 1973): 61,970,000. Monetary unit: Deutsche mark.

The Federal Republic of Germany was proclaimed May 23, 1949, in Bonn, after a constitution had been drawn up by a consultative assembly formed by representatives of the 11 Laender (states) in the French, British and American zones. Later reorganized into 9 units, the Laender number 10 with the addition of the Saar Jan. 1, 1957: Schleswig-Holstein, Hamburg, Lower Saxony, Bremen, North Rhine-Westphalia, Hesse, Rhineland-Palatinate, Baden-Wuerttemberg, Bavaria, Saarland. Berlin also was granted Land (state) status, but the 1945 occupation agreements placed restrictions on it.

The occupying powers, the U.S., Britain and France, restored the civil status, Sept. 21, 1949. The U. S. resumed diplomatic relations July 2, 1951. The powers lifted controls and the republic became fully independent May 5, 1955.

Parliament has 2 chambers, serving 4-year terms. The Bundestag, lower house, is elected. It has 496 voting members from the republic and 22 nonvoting observers from West Berlin. The Bundesrat, upper house, represents the states; it has 41 delegates from the Laender and 4 non-voting members from West Berlin. The Bundesrat president serves one year and acts as deputy to the federal president.

The Federal president is elected for a 5-yr. term by the Federal Assembly, convened for this purpose only and made up of deputies of the Bundestag and an equal number of delegates from the Land parliaments. Re-election is possible only once. The president concludes treaties with foreign states, and signs laws, which must be countersigned by the chancellor and the minister in charge. The chancellor is elected by majority vote of the Bundestag.

Dr. Konrad Adenauer, Christian Democrat, was made chancellor Sept. 15, 1949, reelected 1953, 1957, 1961. Dr. Ludwig Erhard, Christian Democrat, was elected 1963, 1965. Kurt Georg Kiesinger was elected chancellor Dec. 1, 1966, heading a coalition government of Christian Democrats and Social Democrats. Willy Brandt, heading a coalition of Social Democrats and Free Democrats, became chancellor Oct. 21, 1969.

In 1970 Brandt signed friendship treaties with the USSR and Poland. In 1971, the U.S., Britain, France and the USSR signed an agreement on Western access to West Berlin. In 1972 the Bundestag approved the USSR and Polish treaties and East and West Germany signed their first formal treaty, implementing the agreement easing access to West Berlin. In 1973 a West Germany-Czechoslovakia pact normalized relations and nullified the 1938 "Munich Agreement".

In May 1974 Brandt resigned, saying he took full responsibility for "negligence" for allowing an East German spy to become a member of his staff. Helmut Schmidt, Brandt's finance minister, succeeded him.

West Germany is a member of NATO, EEC, European Coal and Steel Community and Council of Europe. Both West and East Germany gained full membership in the UN in Sept. 1973.

Resources and Industries. West Germany has experienced tremendous economic growth since 1950. It is one of the world's top industrial nations. The index of industrial production (1963=100) was 174 for 1973.

West Germany leads Western Europe as a steel producer. Shipyards annually produce more than 1 million gross registered tons of shipping, more than half of it for export. The oil industry has a refining capacity of more than 133 million tons annually.

Germany lost most of its merchant marine during World War II. However, the merchant fleet recovered rapidly and on Jan. 1, 1974, comprised 702 vessels over 1,000 gross tons each.

Frankfurt Rhine-Main airport, 3d largest in Europe, handles annually about 5 million passengers and is 2nd largest in freight shipments.

Foreign trade (in thousands of U.S. dollars):

	Imports	Exports
1972	$39,776,000	$46,202,000
1973	$54,503,000	$67,468,000

Education and Religion. The Federal Republic and West Berlin have 31 universities, 9 technical universities and over 100 musical, theological and other institutions of higher education. School attendance is compulsory, ages 6 to 15.

Complete religious freedom is guaranteed by the constitution. The country is 49% Protestant, 44.6% Roman Catholic. The Evangelical Church in Germany (EKD) was formed by the Lutheran, United and Reformed churches after World War II, supplanting an earlier group.

Defense. Armed Forces, 1974, total 467,000.

Helgoland, an island of 130 acres in the North Sea, was taken from Denmark by a British Naval Force in 1807 and later ceded to Germany to become a part of Schleswig-Holstein province in return for rights in East Africa. The heavily fortified island was surrendered to Great Britain, May 23, 1945, demilitarized in 1947 and returned to West Germany, Mar. 1, 1952. It is a free port.

The Saar (Fr. Sarre), 10th land (state) of the Federal Republic, is an industrial and mining area N of Lorraine, originally 738 sq. mi., now extended to about 991 and population (1973) of 1.1 million. Capital: Sarrbrucken. After World War II it had semi-autonomy and economic links to France until it became a German state again Jan. 1, 1957.

East Germany

Capital: East Berlin. Area: 40,646 sq. mi. Population (UN est. 1973): 16,980,000. Monetary unit: DDR Mark.

The German Democratic Republic was proclaimed in the Soviet sector of Berlin Oct. 7, 1949. Wilhelm Pieck was named president, reelected 1953, and 1957 (died Sept. 7, 1960); Willi Stoph, prime minister; Walter Ulbricht, Communist party secretary. The unicameral legislature is called the Volkskammer or People's Chamber. A ministry of state security, the SSD, and a militarized People's Police were organized.

The Soviet Union proclaimed East Germany a sovereign republic Mar. 25, 1954, but kept Soviet troops there on grounds of security and the 4-power Potsdam agreement.

The Volkskammer approved a constitutional amendment Sept. 12, 1960, that abolished the presidency, replacing it with a new Council of State designated as East Germany's highest governing body, with Walter Ulbricht as chairman.

Ulbricht negotiated a treaty with Poland placing Poland's boundary at the line formed by the Oder and Neisse Rivers. The U.S. registered its disapproval, declaring that it violated the Potsdam agreement and that no boundaries could be settled "unilaterally or bilaterally" outside a peace treaty. The Republic also ratified an agreement with Czechoslovakia, accepting the expulsion of over 2 million Germans from Sudetenland as "permanent and just." Its industry was integrated with other communist nations.

The Volkskammer abolished, 1952, the 5 traditional provinces of East Germany as administrative units in favor of 14 districts of 217 counties. Brandenburg, Mecklenburg, Saxony and Thuringia were divided into 3 districts each, Saxony-Anhalt into 2.

Coincident with the entrance of West Germany into the European Defense Community, May 27, 1952, the East German government decreed a prohibited zone 3 mi. deep along its 600-mile border with West Germany and cut Berlin's telephone system into 2 sections. Berlin was further divided by erection of a fortified wall, 1961, but the exodus of refugees from East Germany into Western sectors continued though on a much smaller scale. By 1974, 34,000 had crossed the wall.

The regime signed a 20-year treaty of friendship and co-operation with the USSR June 12, 1964.

East Germany suffered severe economic problems until the mid-1960s. A "new economic system" was introduced, easing the former central planning controls and allowing factories to make "profits" provided they were reinvested in operations or distributed to workers as bonuses. By the early 1970s, the economy was highly industrialized. In May 1972 the few remaining private firms were ordered sold to the government. The nation was credited with the highest standard of living among communist countries.

On Apr. 8, 1968, a new constitution, announced as approved by 94.49% of voters, went into effect. It reaffirmed Communist party control and close ties with the USSR and declared German reunification could "take place only on the basis of socialism."

In May 1971 Ulbricht resigned as leader of the Communist party and was replaced by Erich Honecker, but retained his post as chairman of the Council of State. Ulbricht died Aug. 1, 1973.

Travel restrictions between the 2 Germanies were eased slightly in the first formal treaty signed by the 2, in May 1972. East and West Germany gained admission to the UN in Sept. 1973.

The U.S. and East Germany established diplomatic relations Sept. 4, 1974. East Germany agreed to negotiate claims of U.S. citizens for properties seized under the Nazis.

Regular armed forces total 130,000. An est. 20 USSR divisions are stationed in East Germany.

Ghana

Capital: Accra. Area: 92,100 sq. mi. Population (UN est. 1973): 9,360,000. Monetary unit: Cedi.

The Republic of Ghana, a member of the UN and the Commonwealth, is composed of the former British Gold Coast colony including Ashanti and Northern Territories, and British Togoland, former UN trusteeship. Slightly smaller than Oregon, it faces the Gulf of Guinea in Western Africa, bounded N by Upper Volta, E by Togo and W by the Ivory Coast.

Resources and Industries. Ghana is rich in mineral wealth. It ranks among world leaders in production of diamonds (mostly industrial type), manganese and bauxite.

Ghana is the world's leading cocoa producer; it exports over 350,000 tons annually, about 30% of world output. Timber is 2d in value, including mahogany and rare woods.

The huge Akosombo hydroelectric project on the Volta River, partly financed by U.S., was completed in 1965 and began serving Ghana's 1st giant industry, an aluminum reduction plant near the port of Tema, built and owned by U.S. companies. In 1972-73 the government pressed a program of both small and large farms, "Operation Feed-Yourself," to cut costly food imports.

History and Government. Named after an earlier African state along the Niger River, 800-1076 A.D., Ghana has long been settled by the Adansi, Akwamu, Ga and other tribes, and was ruled by Great Britain for 113 years. Its independence was gained by rapid steps after 1951 when Britain granted the colony a new constitution and its chief spokesman, Kwame Nkrumah, was elected prime minister. The UN General Assembly on Dec. 13, 1956, approved termination of the British Togoland trusteeship and merger of the territory with the new state following a 1956 plebiscite.

Full independence within the Commonwealth, with a British governor-general, was effective Mar. 6, 1957. It became a republic July 1, 1960, but remained within the Commonwealth. Kwame Nkrumah became president.

In 1962 Parliament made Nkrumah president for life. In 1964 a referendum gave him dictatorial powers and made Ghana a one-party Socialist state.

Nkrumah built hospitals and schools, raised the literacy rate, created a state-owned airline and ship line, but ran the country into debt, jailed hundreds of political dissenters and was accused of corruption.

On Feb. 24, 1966, a National Liberation Council of Army and police officers took over the government. The Council expelled Communist Chinese and East German teachers and technicians. It promised a "balanced neutrality" and slashed expenditures.

Elections were held in Aug. 1969 and Ghana returned to civilian rule, with an elected National Assembly, a prime minister and a president.

On Jan. 13, 1972, a National Redemption Council, headed by Army Col. Ignatius K. Acheampong, took over the government in a bloodless coup. His government has sought national self-reliance.

Greece

Capital: Athens. Area: 50,547 sq. mi. Population (est. 1973): 9,030,000. Monetary unit: Drachma.

Greece occupies the southern part of the Balkan peninsula, reaching into the Mediterranean Sea with the Ionian Sea on the W and the Aegean Sea on the E. Its neighbors are Albania, Yugoslavia, Bulgaria and Turkey. The Pindus Mtns. run through the country N to S. Total length of the heavily indented coastline is 9,385 mi. Hundreds of islands account for 8,918 sq. mi. of the total land area, which is approx. that of Alabama; 166 islands are inhabited; among them Crete, Rhodes, Milos, Kerkira (Corfu), Chios, Lesbos, Samos. Principal seaport is Piraeus, near Athens.

Resources and Industries. Greece is still largely

agricultural. Only one-fourth of the total area is arable: 13,350,000 of the total of 16,074,000 acres are covered by mountains, lakes and rivers. Four-fifths of the forests are state-owned. Chief agricultural products are wheat, rye, barley, oats, corn, rice, cotton, tobacco, olives, citrus fruits, raisins and figs. Sheep are the most important livestock.

Heavily damaged in World War II, Greece's industrial and agricultural output has far surpassed prewar levels thanks to economic development programs helped in part by U.S. aid. Hydroelectric development is remedying the lack of coal. Principal industries are textiles, food-processing, wine, cement, chemicals, aluminum.

Greek-owned merchant marine tonnage is among world leaders, but most of it is registered under other flags.

Exports are mainly agricultural — tobacco, cotton, citrus fruits, raisins, vegetables. Ores, esp. bauxite, are also important. Aiding the economy is the tourist industry, which produces over $300 million annually.

Foreign trade, in thousands of U.S. dollars:

	Imports	Exports
1972	$2,145,000	$871,000
1973	$3,473,000	$1,454,000

History and Government. The achievements of Ancient Greece in art, architecture, science, mathematics, philosophy, drama, literature and democracy became legacies for succeeding ages. Greece reached the height of its glory and power, particularly in the Athenian city-state, in the 5th Century B.C.

Greece fell under Roman domination in the 2d and 1st Centuries B.C. In the 4th Century A.D. it became part of the Eastern Byzantine Empire and, after the fall of Constantinople to the Turks in 1453, part of the Ottoman Empire.

Greece won its war of independence from Turkey 1821-1829, and became a kingdom under guarantee of Britain, France and Russia, 1830. A republic was established 1925; the monarchy was restored, 1935, and George II, King of the Hellenes, resumed the throne. In Oct., 1940, Greece rejected an ultimatum from Italy and, when attacked, Greece drove the Italians back into Albania. Nazi support resulted in the defeat and occupation of Greece by Germans, Italians and Bulgarians. By the end of 1944 the invaders withdrew. Armed communists attempted to seize the country but were thwarted by British liberation troops.

A plebiscite recalled King George II. He died Apr. 1, 1947, and was succeeded by his brother, Paul I. King Paul died Mar. 6, 1964, succeeded by his son, Crown Prince Constantine, born June 2, 1940. The king married Princess Ann-Marie of Denmark Sept. 18, 1964.

Communists waged guerrilla war 1947-49 against the government but were defeated with the aid of the U.S. (acting under the Truman Doctrine).

In Feb. 16, 1964, elections the coalition Center Union led by George Papandreou won 174 of 300 seats in the Chamber of Deputies. A prolonged government crisis was precipitated July 15, 1965, when Premier Papandreou resigned; at issue was a Papandreou plan to purge the Army of right-wing officers. King Constantine opposed the purge saying it would expose the armed forces to communist influence. Leftists and backers of Papandreou staged riots in Athens as the king sought a new premier who could win a Parliamentary majority over the opposition of the Papandreou bloc and the extreme leftists. He finally won with Stephanos Stephanopoulos, who was sworn in Sept. 17, 1965.

Continuing political crises ended in a pre-election coup d'etat Apr. 21, 1967, by rightist Army officers under Col. George Papadopoulos. They jailed hundreds of monarchists, communists and political leaders. Constantine on Dec. 13 sought to oust the junta but failed to rally military support and flew with his family to exile in Rome, Dec. 14. Papadopoulos was named premier and a general was appointed "viceroy." In 1968 the Papadopoulos government freed some political prisoners but tightened its hold, replacing many officials including judges.

A new constitution, approved in a referendum, went into effect Nov. 10, 1968. It strengthened the powers of the premier, weakened those of the king and Parliament. Certain provisions on civil rights were kept in abeyance.

Papadopoulos abolished the monarchy and proclaimed Greece a republic with himself as president, June 1, 1973. A July 29 referendum, it was announced, approved the actions by a 78.4% vote. Papadopoulos promised parliamentary elections and freed hundreds; on Nov. 25 he was ousted and replaced by Gen. Phaedon Gizikis.

Greek Army officers, serving in the National Guard of Cyprus, seized control of that nation's government July 15, 1974, in a move to unite Cyprus with Greece. Turkey invaded the island July 22, seizing control of its NE third. On July 24, the Greek military junta turned the Greek government over to former Premier Constantine Karamanlis, hurriedly called back from exile. As premier again, ending 7 years of military rule, Karamanlis named a civilian cabinet, including conservatives and leftists, freed all political prisoners, restored the 1952 constitution and sought to settle the Cyprus crisis.

Education and Religion. Greek Orthodox is the official church. Nine years of education is compulsory. There are 6 schools of university rank in Athens, and others in Thessaloniki, Patras and Ioannina.

Defense. Military strength totalled 160,000. In 1972 Athens became a home port for U.S. Navy ships.

Greece is a member of the UN and an associate member of EEC. It withdrew its forces from NATO during the 1974 crisis with Turkey over Cyprus.

Dodecanese and Crete

The **Dodecanese** are a group of 13 islands in the southeastern Aegean Sea. They were occupied by Italy during the Balkan War of 1912 with Turkey and though claimed by Greece were retained by Italy. Rhodes is the capital.

After World War II the islands were ceded to Greece at the Paris Conference of Foreign Ministers, June 27, 1946, and annexed Mar. 7, 1948.

Crete, largest Greek island and 5th largest in Mediterranean, original site of Minoan civilization, lies south of the Peloponnesos peninsula and is 160 mi. long, 35 mi. wide, with area of 3,207 sq. mi. Principal towns: Heraklion (Candia) and Khania (Canea).

Grenada

Capital: St. George's. Area: 133 sq. mi. Population: (UN est. 1973): 100,000. Monetary unit: East Caribbean dollar.

Southernmost in the long arc of the Windward Islands, Grenada (pronounced gren-ay-dah) lies in the SE Caribbean, 90 mi. N of the Venezuelan coast. The main island is mountainous and roughly 21 mi. by 12; the nation's territory includes one of the Grenadine islets, Carriacou, just to the N, about 7 mi. by 3.

Formerly a British Associated State with limited self-government, Grenada became fully independent Feb. 7, 1974, the smallest independent nation in the Western Hemisphere. It is a member of the Commonwealth group of nations.

First European visitor was Christopher Columbus, 1498. First European settlers were French, 1650. The island was held alternately by France and England until final British occupation, 1784. Beginning in 1925, increasing amounts of self-government were granted.

Over 50% of the population is of African descent; over 40% of mixed descent, including descendants of indentured laborers from India; there are a few Carib Indians, descendants of the original inhabitants, and a few whites. About 60% are Roman Catholics; others include Anglicans and Methodists. The language is English; a French-African patois is also spoken.

The economy is agricultural; main products are nutmegs, bananas, cocoa, sugar and rum.

Guatemala

Capital: Guatemala City. Area: 42,042 sq. mi. Population (UN est. 1973): 5,540,000. Monetary unit: Quetzal.

Guatemala is the most northerly country of Central America and about the size of Ohio. It faces on both the Caribbean and the Pacific. There are numerous volcanoes in the south, more than a half dozen over 11,000 ft. About 50% of the population is pure Indian and most of the remainder is of mixed Spanish and Indian descent.

There are famous Mayan ruins in Uaxatcun, Tikal and other sites in northern Guatemala. Other Mayan ruins of temples and monoliths are at Zaculeu in the west and at Quirigua, about 140 mi. from Guatemala City.

Santo Tomas and Puerto Barrios, main ports on the Atlantic, are connected by railroad and highway with Guatemala City in the highlands and ports on the Pacific.

Resources and Industries. Agriculture is the most important industry, the Guatemalan soil being exceedingly fertile. Coffee accounts for a third of the exports. Other important export crops are sugar, meat, bananas, cotton, chicle gum. Rare woods and cattle are important. Silver, gold, copper, iron, lead, zinc, and nickel are found. A search for oil is being pressed in the north, where natural gas has been found. Shoes and textiles are manufactured.

History and Government. The old Mayan Indian empire flourished in what is today Guatemala for over 1,000 years before the Spanish conquest.

Guatemala was a Spanish colony 1524-1821; briefly a part of Mexico and then of the U.S. of Central America; the republic was established in 1839.

Since 1945 when a liberal government was elected to replace the long-term dictatorship of Jorge Ubico, the country has seen a swing toward socialism, an armed revolt, renewed attempts at social reform and a military coup. Communist-led guerrillas have terrorized parts of the nation and kidnaped officials. Guerrillas killed a U.S. ambassador in 1968 and a West German ambassador in 1970.

In Mar. 1974 Gen. Kjell Laugerud Garcia was elected president.

Education and Religion. Roman Catholicism is the dominant religion. Education is compulsory. There are 5 universities in Guatemala City, with divisions in Quezaltenango. The language is Spanish.

Guatemala is a member of the UN and OAS.

Guinea

Capital: Conakry. Area 94,925 sq. mi. Population (UN est. 1973): 4,210,000. Monetary unit: Syli.

Guinea, a former French Overseas Territory, is in western Africa with the Atlantic on the W; Guinea-Bissau, Senegal and Mali on the N, Ivory Coast on the E and Liberia and Sierra Leone on the S. Chief tribes are the Fullah, Malinke, and Soussou. Guinea is about the size of Oregon.

Guinea has a variety of climates, from the humid coastal tropics (Conakry, the capital has an average annual rainfall of 169") to cooler plateaus and uplands. Wildlife is varied and abundant, including elephant, hippopotamus, buffalo, antelope, lion, leopard, chimpanzee.

Resources and Industries. Although Guinea is still primarily an agricultural country, the importance of minerals to its economy is growing. Bauxite, iron and diamonds (both gem and industrial) are the principal minerals. First bauxite exports, mined by an international consortium, were shipped in 1973. A large Soviet-owned mine opened in 1974.

Economic progress has been aided by large grants from both communist and non-communist countries. Acceleration of agricultural output is a government goal. Chief agricultural exports are bananas and pineapples. Production of rice, the staple food of the population, has been expanded. Other crops include corn, palm nuts, coffee and honey.

History and Government. With France's acquiescence, Guinea proclaimed itself an independent republic Oct. 2, 1958. Premier Sekou Toure became first president. The nation's first constitution was adopted Nov. 12, 1958. It provided for rule by a president with a term of 7 years and a National Assembly elected by universal suffrage. The Political Bureau of the single legal party, the Parti Democratique de Guinee, exercises great power in making governmental decisions. Guinea is a member of the UN. French is the official language.

It has agreements with Czechoslovakia, East Germany, Poland, USSR and Communist China, and criticized U. S. "colonial" attitudes in Africa, but continues to avow a neutral course.

Guinea-Bissau

Capital: Bissau. Area: 13,948 sq. mi. Population (UN est. 1973): 510,000.

Portuguese Guinea, a colonial possession described by Portugal as an overseas province, achieved independence as Guinea-Bissau, a republic, Sept. 10, 1974. Almost twice the size of New Jersey, it is in the West African bulge, facing the Atlantic to the W, with Senegal to the N and Guinea to the E and S. The land is mostly level and low, with forests, swamps and numerous offshore islands.

Portuguese mariners explored the area in the mid-15th Century; the slave trade flourished in the 17th and 18th Centuries, but in the 19th normal colonization began. In the early 20th Century, Portuguese troops put down uprisings in the interior.

Beginning in the 1960s, the African Party for the Independence of Guinea-Bissau and the Cape Verde Islands conducted guerrilla warfare against Portuguese troops and formed a government in the interior with an elected National Assembly. The party's founder, Dr. Amilcar Cabral was slain in nearby Guinea in 1973 and his brother Luiz became Guinea-Bissau's first president.

The Cape Verde Islands, once linked with Portuguese Guinea, lie in the Atlantic some 300 mi. NW of Bissau. Portugal said a future referendum would decide the disposition of the islands.

Most of the Guinea-Bissau population is black with about 2,200 white and 10,000 of mixed descent. Most follow tribal religions; a large minority are Moslems.

There is little industry. Chief products are peanuts, palm oil and hides. In 1972 a large deposit of bauxite and traces of oil were discovered.

Guyana

Capital: Georgetown. Area: 83,000 sq. mi. Population (UN est. 1973): 760,000. Monetary unit: Guyana dollar.

British Guiana, a British colony for 152 years, became the independent nation of Guyana on May 26, 1966. It was the first South American nation to become independent since Venezuela in 1830.

Fronting on the Atlantic in northern South America, Guyana borders on Venezuela, Brazil and Surinam. It is about the size of Kansas. The population is about 50% of East Indian (from India) descent, 31.5% of African descent, 12% of mixed descent, 4.6% American Indian descent, and small numbers of Chinese or European descent.

Dense tropical forests cover much of the land, although a flat coastal area about 50 mi. wide, where 90% of the population lives, provides space for agriculture.

Sugar and rice are the main cash crops and account for almost half the total exports. Other products are coconuts, coffee, cocoa, citrus fruits, timber and livestock.

The main industry is the mining of bauxite ore; Guyana is the 5th largest producer of the mineral, supplying over 6% of the world's needs. Also exported are gold and diamonds. Deposits of a wide range of other minerals have been found but not yet exploited.

Manufacturing has shown an average 5% annual growth; products include cigarettes, rum, clothing, furniture, drugs and insecticides.

Guyana was discovered in 1499 by Spanish sailors. The country became a British possession in 1814. African slaves and indentured servants from India were brought in to work on plantations. The Indians soon outnumbered the Negro population and still do. Venezuela has claimed ownership of the western half of Guyana. In 1970 an agreement suspended the claim for 12 years.

A parliamentary democracy with a British governor-general after becoming independent in 1966, Guyana became a republic, with a president, prime minister and National Assembly on Feb. 23, 1970. It is a UN and Commonwealth member.

Haiti

Capital: Port-Au-Prince. Area: 10,714 sq. mi. Population (UN est. 1973): 5,200,000. Monetary unit: Gourde.

Haiti, only French-speaking republic in the Americas, occupies the western third of the island known as Hispaniola, the second largest of the Greater Antilles, lying between Cuba on the W and Puerto Rico on the E. The boundary which separates Haiti from the Dominican Republic to the E is 241 mi. long. Haiti is a little larger in area than Maryland.

Blacks form over 90% of the population, the remainder being of mixed descent from former slaves and French settlers.

Resources and Industries. Major mineral exports are bauxite and copper. Other minerals are gold, silver and cement.

Coffee is the chief product, along with sisal, cotton, sugar, bananas, cocoa, tobacco and rice. Molasses and rum are produced; valuable woods are exported.

Haiti encourages tourism and is served by several major airlines, with an international jet airport at Port-au-Prince. However, tourist spending and private foreign investment in Haiti dwindled under the regime of President Francois Duvalier. They revived in 1971 after his death. Economic improvement was reported, 1972-74.

History and Government. Haiti, discovered by Columbus, 1492, and a French colony from 1677, attained its independence, 1804, following the rebellion begun by Toussaint L'Ouverture. There were Republican constitutions in 1806 and 1816. In 1811 Henri Christophe proclaimed himself King Henri 1, in the north; the southern part of Haiti continued to be a republic, with a president. Henri died in 1820 and President Jean Pierre Boyer reunited the nation. Following a period of political violence, 1910-1915, the U. S. occupied the country and restored order. The occupation terminated Aug. 14, 1934.

Five regimes failed between 1950-1957. In Sept., 1957, Dr. Duvalier was elected president for a 6-year term.

In June 1964 a new constitution made Dr. Duvalier president-for-life. There were unsuccessful outbreaks against his rule in 1963 and 1970. He died Apr. 21, 1971, and was succeeded by his son, Jean-Claude Duvalier, 19, as president-for-life.

Haiti is a member of the UN and OAS.

Education and Religion. Roman Catholicism is the main religion. Education is compulsory, but illiteracy rate is est. at 90%. French is the official language of the country, but French Creole, a dialect, is spoken by the majority. The teaching of English and Spanish in the schools is obligatory.

Honduras

Capital: Tegucigalpa. Area (govt. est.): 43,277 sq. mi. Population (est. 1974): 2,780,000. Monetary unit: Lempira.

Honduras is a republic in Central or Middle America, bounded on the N by the Caribbean; E and S by Nicaragua; S by Pacific Ocean and El Salvador; W by Guatamala. It is about the size of Pennsylvania.

The coastline on the Caribbean is 500 mi. long. On the Pacific side it has a coastline of 40 mi. on the Gulf of Fonseca. There are ports on both coasts. The country is mountainous, very fertile, with rich forests. The inhabitants are mostly of Spanish and Indian extraction.

At Copan, near the western border, are the imposing remains of a large Mayan city which flourished from the 4th Century A.D.; it had declined by the time Spaniards arrived in 1576.

Resources and Industries. Mineral resources are abundant but undeveloped and include gold, silver, copper, lead, zinc, iron, antimony and coal. The chief export is bananas, grown in the Caribbean coast. Coffee, timber, cotton, sugar, tobacco and cattle raising are important. Hurricane Fifi, Sept. 18-19, 1974, killed at least 7,000 persons, made 50,000 homeless.

Manufacturing industries are small but growing; they include clothing, textiles, cement, chemicals, food products. In 1974 the government said it would nationalize the lumber industry.

History and Government. Honduras became independent after freeing itself from Spain, Sept. 15, 1821, and from the Federation of Central America, 1838.

Pres. Roman Villeda Morales, elected Nov. 15, 1957, was overthrown in a military coup Oct. 3, 1963, and replaced by a military regime headed by Oswaldo Lopez Arellano. The country returned to constitutional government and Lopez was inaugurated president June 6, 1965.

The 1965 constitution provided for a president, popularly elected for 6 years, and a unicameral Congress, also elected for 6 years. In free elections, Mar. 28, 1971, Ramon Ernesto Cruz was chosen president. In Dec. 1972 Lopez seized the presidency again.

Honduras and El Salvador fought a 5-day war in July 1969 over the presence in Honduras of 300,000 Salvadorean workers and settlers. After new clashes in 1970, a demilitarized zone was agreed on.

Honduras is a member of the UN and OAS.

Education and Religion. Education is secular and free. The literacy rate is about 50%. Roman Catholicism is the prevailing religion. The language is Spanish.

Hungary

Capital: Budapest. Area: 35,919 sq. mi. Population (UN est. 1972): 10,410,000. Monetary unit: Forint.

The Hungarian People's Republic, in central Europe, is bounded by Czechoslovakia, the USSR, Romania, Yugoslavia and Austria. It is about the size of Indiana.

The Danube forms the Czech border in the NW, then swings S to bisect the country. The eastern half of Hungary is mainly a great fertile plain, the Alfold; the west and north are hilly.

Resources and Industries. Before World War II, Hungary was primarily agricultural, but industry has surpassed it in value. The index of industrial production (1963 = 100) was 164 for 1972, 175 for 1973. Most means of production have been socialized.

Major economic reforms were launched early in 1968, switching from a central planning system to one where market forces and a profit principle control much of production. Productivity was reportedly increased.

About 70% of foreign trade is with Eastern bloc countries. Value of imports rose from $2.99 billion in

1971 to $3.8 billion in 1973; exports rose from $2.5 billion to $4.47 billion.

In addition to a wide range of grains and vegetable crops, fruit production has expanded. Near Tokay, in the northeast, the best-known Hungarian wines are vinted.

Industries include iron and steel, machines, machine tools, chemicals, vehicles, railways and communications equipment, milling and distilling. Hungary has become an important supplier of industrial products to communist bloc countries. Hungary produces large amounts of bauxite. Also important is natural gas.

History and Government. Earliest settlers, chiefly Slav and Germanic, were overrun by Huns and Magyars from the east. Stephen I (997-1038) was made king by Pope Silvester II in 1001 A.D. The country suffered repeated Turkish invasions in the 15th-17th Centuries. After the defeats of the Turks, 1686-1697, Austria dominated, but Hungary obtained concessions until it regained internal independence in 1867, with the emperor of Austria as king of Hungary in a dual monarchy with a single diplomatic service. Defeated with the Central Powers in 1918, Hungary lost Transylavania to Romania, Croatia and Bacska to Yugoslavia, Slovakia and Carpatho-Ruthenia to Czechoslovakia. A republic under Michael Karoly and a bolshevist revolt under Bela Kun were followed by a vote for a monarchy in 1920 with Admiral Nicholas Horthy as regent.

Hungary joined Germany in World War II; Horthy was removed and Nazi supporters put in power, 1944. Russian troops captured most of the country, 1945. By terms of an armistice with the Allied powers Hungary agreed to give up territory acquired by the 1938 dismemberment of Czechoslovakia and to return to its borders of 1937.

Hungary declared for a republic Feb. 1, 1946, and elected Zoltan Tildy president. In 1947 the communists forced Tildy out. A Soviet-type constitution was adopted Aug. 18, 1949, which vests power in a Presidential Council and a National Assembly of 349 members elected for 4-year-terms. Hungary is a member of the UN and Warsaw Pact.

Premier Imre Nagy, in office since mid-1953, was ousted for his moderate policy of favoring agriculture and consumer production, April 18, 1955.

In 1956, popular demands for the ousting of Erno Gero, Hungarian Communist party secretary, and for formation of a new government by Nagy, resulted in the latter's appointment Oct. 23, but demonstrations against communist rule in Budapest developed into open revolt when security police fired on demonstrators. Gero called in Soviet armed forces to crush the rioting. The insurrection appeared halted by Oct. 18 when Premier Nagy announced the Soviet Union had agreed to withdraw its troops from Hungary. However, by Nov. 1 Soviet forces again surrounded Budapest and launched a massive surprise attack against the city Nov. 4 with an estimated 200,000 troops, 2,500 tanks and armored cars.

The bid for free government was crushed. Estimates varied from 6,500 to 32,000 dead. Many rebels were reported executed and thousands deported. Between 170,000 and 196,000 persons fled the country. The U.S. received 38,248 under a refugee emergency program. In the spring of 1963 the regime freed many anti-communists and captives from the revolution in a sweeping amnesty.

Nagy was executed by the Russians. Janos Kadar, sponsored by the USSR, became first secretary of the Hungarian Workers (Communist) party.

In 1973 Hungary agreed to pay the U.S. $18,900,000 for nationalized U.S. properties in Hungary.

Education and Religion. There is no state religion, and all are tolerated. About two-thirds of the population were Roman Catholics; most of the remainder, Calvinists.

Public school education is compulsory and free for 8 years. Most church schools were nationalized in 1948. There are 91 insititutes of higher learning. The language is Hungarian (Magyar).

Jozsef Cardinal Mindszenty, Roman Catholic primate of Hungary, was jailed for life in 1949. He was freed by the 1956 insurgents and was granted refuge in the Budapest U.S. Embassy. In 1971, under an agreement between Hungary and the Vatican, he went into exile in Vienna.

Defense. Military forces totaled 103,000. About 40,-000 USSR troops are stationed in Hungary.

Iceland

Capital: Reykjavik. Area: 39,702 sq. mi. Population (UN est. 1973): 210,000. Monetary unit: Krona.

The Republic of Iceland is an island of volcanic origin, close to the Arctic Circle in the North Atlantic. There are geysers and hot springs and the climate is modified by the Gulf Stream. Iceland is about the size of Virginia.

Natural hot water from volcanic springs is piped into towns and provides heat for office buildings, homes and hot houses. In Jan. 1973 a volcanic eruption on Heimaey forced evacuation of 5,500 residents of the small island off the SE coast of Iceland.

Resources and Industries. Agriculture engages about 13% of the population; industry and services 70%; fisheries 14%. About six-sevenths of the land is unproductive and only about 65,000 acres are under cultivation, producing potatoes, turnips and hay. The fishing industry is most important. It includes herring, cod and haddock. Fish products, in salted, smoked, canned or frozen form, account for 78% of exports.

Iceland's largest industrial plants include an ammonium nitrate factory, an aluminum smelter, a cement factory and a diatomite plant and hydroelectric power is being developed.

History and Government. Iceland was an independent republic, 930-1262; then it joined with Norway. The two came under Danish rule in 1380. Denmark acknowledged Iceland as a sovereign state, 1918, united with Denmark only in that the Danish King Christian X, was also king of Iceland. In 1941 the Althing (Parliament) voted to dissolve all ties with Denmark, and adopt the constitution of a republic. The republic, with a president and prime minister, was proclaimed June 17, 1944.

Iceland celebrated the 1,000th anniversary of the Althing, the oldest parliamentary assembly in the world, in 1930. The prime minister and his cabinet are responsible to the Althing. There is universal suffrage for men and women at age 20.

In 1972 Iceland barred foreign ships from fishing within 50 mi. of its coast. British trawlers defied the ban and in 1973 were fired on by Icelandic gunboats. British frigates were sent to the disputed waters; the confrontation won the name "cod war." In Nov. 1973 the dispute was settled; Britain agreed to limit its catch.

A conservative coalition won power in June 1974 elections and stopped plans to oust 3,300 U.S. NATO Air Force and Navy personnel stationed by treaty on the island.

Education and Religion. The Icelandic language has maintained its purity, as in Eddas and Sagas, for 1,000 years. Danish and English also are taught. Eight years of elementary education is compulsory. There is no illiteracy. There are 5 colleges and a university. The national church is Evangelical Lutheran, but there is complete religious freedom.

Defense. Iceland has no Army, Navy, Air Force or forts. It is a charter member of NATO. It is also a member of the UN, Council of Europe and Nordic Council.

India

Capital: New Delhi. Area: 1,229,919 sq. mi. Population (UN est. 1973): 574,220,000. Monetary unit: Rupee.

An independent republic since 1950 and a member of the Commonwealth, India occupies most of the subcontinent of India. It is a third the size of the U.S.

India's climate varies from tropical heat in the south to the nearly Arctic cold of the Himalayas. Approximately 22.3% of the area is forested.

The population is 80% rural, 20% urban. The annual increase rate, 2½%, poses food and housing shortages.

In 1967 the government supplemented its birth control programs with monetary inducements to men to volunteer for sterilization. In 1973 the government reported 13 million persons had undergone operations.

Sikkim, bordered by Tibet, Bhutan, Nepal and India, formerly British protected, became a protectorate of India in 1950. Area, 2,818 sq. mi.; population 1973, 210,000; capital, Gangtok. The ruler is Chogyal (Maharaja) Palden Thondup Namgyal; in 1963, while crown prince, he married Hope Cooke, a New York debutante. In Apr. 1973 the chogyal asked Indian troops to help suppress demonstrations against his rule. In May he and India signed an agreement providing for a legislative assembly. In Sept. 1974 India's Parliament voted to make Sikkim an associate Indian state, absorbing it into India.

Kashmir, a predominantly Moslem region in the northwest, has been in dispute between India and Pakistan since 1947 when British rule was ending and Indian and Pakistani troops entered the area. A cease-fire was negotiated by the UN, Jan. 1, 1949; it gave Pakistan control of one-third of the area, in the west and northwest, and India the remaining two-thirds, the Indian state of Jammu and Kashmir. In late Aug. 1965, clashes broke out along the line and soon involved the armed forces of the 2 nations in a spreading war.

On Sept. 20, 1965, the UN Security Council demanded a cease-fire and both sides agreed Sept. 22, to stop the fighting. USSR Premier Aleksei N. Kosygin invited India Prime Minister Lal Bahadur Shastri and Pakistan Pres. Ayub Khan to a conference at Tashkent, USSR, and on Jan. 10, 1966, the 2 signed the "Tashkent Declaration," pledging to withdraw their forces to behind the old cease-fire line by Feb. 28.

A new truce line, slightly altering the old cease-fire line, was agreed on in Dec. 1972, accommodating changes made during the Dec. 1971 war.

There were also clashes in April 1965 along the Assam-East Pakistan border and in the **Rann** (swamp) **of Cutch** area along the West Pakistan-Gujarat border near the Arabian Sea.

An international arbitration commission on Feb. 19, 1968, awarded 90% of the Rann to India, 10% to Pakistan.

France, 1952-54, peacefully yielded to India its 5 colonies on the Bay of Bengal, former **French India,** comprising Pondicherry, Kirkal, Mahe, Yanaon and Chandernagor, totalling 196 sq. mi. and 346,000 pop.

Goa, 1,426 sq. mi., pop., 1962, 626,978, which had been administered by Portugal since 1505 A.D., first as a colony and later as a province, was taken by India by military action Dec. 18, 1961, together with 2 other Portuguese enclaves, Damao and Diu, located about 250 mi. S. of Bombay.

India is a union of 21 states and 9 centrally administered union territories.

Resources and Industries. Agriculture occupies 70% of the workers. Principal food products are rice, corn, millet, wheat, barley, coffee, sugar cane, spices, tea, cashew nuts. Other important products include cotton, copra, coir, jute, linseed, rubber, lumber.

Severe droughts in northern areas have repeatedly threatened mass starvation and brought large shipments of grain from the U.S. In July 1967 plentiful rains broke the drought; there were bumper crops, 1968-72; the drought and food shortages returned in 1972-73 and 1974.

Indian agriculture has made progress with high-yield seeds, with fertilizers, irrigation and limited mechanization.

For many years India has had large textile industries with a wide variety of cotton, woolen and silk products. In the 1960s, other industries, including steel, processed foods, cement, machinery, chemicals and fertilizers came into prominence, along with many finished products such as sewing machines, typewriters, bicycles, telephones and transportation equipment.

India's 1st nuclear power plant, built with U.S. help, was dedicated in 1970 near Bombay; Canada helped India build 2 reactors. In May 1974 India exploded a nuclear device, underground. Canada halted shipments of nuclear equipment and material to India and the U.S. announced a halt in its shipments.

The 1972 index of industrial production (1963 - 100) was 154; the 1973 index rose only to 155. Industrial production, distribution and prices are regulated by law. Railroads, airlines, banks, insurance and coal industries are state owned.

India is a leading producer of coal, mica and manganese; also important are salt, iron ore, bauxite and gypsum. Exports include tea, sugar, raw and processed jute, cotton fabrics and other textiles, tanned hides and skins, manganese ore, pepper, tobacco. Largest trade is with the U.S.

Foreign trade, in thousands of U.S. dollars:

	Imports	Exports
1972	$2,228,000	$2,439,000
1973	$3,066,000	$2,940,000

History and Government. India has one of the oldest civilizations in the world. Excavations trace the Indus Valley civilization back for at least 5,000 years. Paintings in the mountain caves of Ajanta in South India, richly carved temples, the Taj Mahal in Agra and the Kutab Minar in Delhi are among relics of the past.

Vasco da Gama established Portuguese trading posts 1498-99, 1502-03. The Dutch followed. The British East India Co. sent Capt. William Hawkins, 1609, to get concessions from the Mogul emperor for spices and textiles. Operating as the East India Co. the British gained control of most of India. Warren Hastings, first governor-general (1774-1785), set up civil government. The British parliament assumed political direction; under Lord Bentinck, 1828-35, misrule by rajahs was curbed, infanticide stopped, suttee (suicide of a widow on her husband's funeral pyre) made illegal.

Liberal policies were set back when the Sepoy troops mutinied, 1857-58. Thereafter the British supported the native rulers.

Nationalism grew rapidly after World War I. The National Congress and the Moslem League demanded constitutional reform. A leader emerged in Mohandas K. Gandhi (called Mahatma, or Great Soul), born Oct. 2, 1869, assassinated Jan 30, 1948. A Hindu, trained in law in England, he began advocating self-rule, non-violence, pursuit of native handicrafts, removal of untouchability (which forced millions of poor to remain menials by heredity) in 1919. In 1930 he launched "civil disobedience," including boycott of British goods and rejection of taxes without representation.

In 1935 Britain gave India a constitution providing a bicameral federal congress, with a council of states and an assembly. Suffrage was granted about 30 million. The Moslems protested Hindu dominance. Mohammed Ali Jinnah, head of the Moslem League, sought creation of a Moslem nation, Pakistan.

Following more than 40 years' active struggle for freedom by both Hindus and Moslems, the British government announced Feb. 20, 1947, its intention to partition India into 2 dominions and set June, 1948, for British withdrawal from India. Aug. 15, 1947, was designated Indian Independence Day. India became a self-governing member of the Commonwealth and a member of the UN. The dominion became a democratic republic, Jan. 26, 1950. *(See Pakistan.)*

It was estimated that more than 11 million refugees (Hindus and Moslems) crossed the India-Pakistan borders in a mass transferral of some of the two peoples during 1947.

The constitution provides for a president, elected for a 5-year term by an electoral college consisting of members of both houses of Parliament (Council of States and House of the People), and elected members of the lower houses of the federating states. A Council of Ministers (cabinet) is headed by a prime minister who is the practical head of the government. The federating states have governors, appointed by the president, at the head of state organizations similar to the federal system.

Prime Minister Mrs. Indira Gandhi, named Jan. 19, 1966, succeeded Lal Bahadur Shastri, who on June 2, 1964, succeeded India's first prime minister, Jawaharlal Nehru. Mrs. Gandhi, Nehru's daughter, was no relation to Mahatma Gandhi. Nehru, prime minister from the beginning of India's independence in 1947, died May 24, 1964.

Long the dominant power in India's politics, the Congress party lost some of its near monopoly by 1967. The party split into New and Old Congress parties in 1969. Mrs. Gandhi's New Congress party won control of the House.

After Pakistan troops began attacks on Bengali separatists in East Pakistan, Mar. 25, 1971, some 10 million refugees fled into India. Border skirmishes between India and Pakistan increased. On Aug. 9, India and the USSR signed a 20-year friendship pact while U.S.-India relations soured. India and Pakistan went to war Dec. 3, 1971, on both the East and West fronts. Pakistan troops in the East surrendered Dec. 16; Pakistan agreed to a cease-fire offer in the West Dec. 17. India recognized Bangladesh (East Pakistan) as a separate nation Dec. 6.

India and Pakistan signed a pact agreeing to withdraw troops from their borders and seek peaceful solutions to all problems, including Kashmir, July 3, 1972. In Aug. 1973 India agreed to release 93,000 Pakistanis, soldiers and civilians, held prisoner since 1971; the return was completed in Apr. 1974.

Education and Religion. The constitution provides for free, compulsory education through age 14. There are now 90 universities, 1,946 colleges, and 27 research institutes.

There are 14 language groups, 12 originating from Sanskrit, and over 1,600 "mother tongues." Hindi is spoken by nearly 50%, with Urdu, the principal Moslem language, spoken by 10%. Hindi became the official language in Jan. 1965 with English the associate official language. Much official government work and instruction at universities continues to be done in English.

The religion of 83% of the people is Hinduism. The constitution guarantees freedom of worship. Moslems are the largest minority, 61,417,934 in the 1971 Census; there were 14,223,382 Christians, 10,378,797 Sikhs, 3,812,325 Buddhists, 2,604,646 Jains. Hindus totaled 453,292,086.

Defense. Military forces total 322,000.

Indonesia

Capital: Jakarta (Djakarta). Area: 735,268 sq. mi. Population (1973 est.): 124,600,000. Monetary unit: Rupiah.

Indonesia, world's largest archipelago, formerly the Netherlands East Indies, lies along the Equator SE of Asia, N and NW of Australia. Indonesia comprises about 13,000 islands, the largest being Java (one of the most densely populated areas in the world with 1,500 persons to the sq. mi.), Sumatra, Kalimantan (most of Borneo), Sulawesi (Celebes) and West Irian (Irian Jaya, the west half of New Guinea). Among others are Bangka, Billiton, Madura, Bali,

Lombok, Sumbawa, part of Timor. The land area is 6 times that of New Mexico.

Many races are included, the principal ones being Achinese, Bataks, Menangkabaus, Javanese, Sundanese, Madurese, Balinese, Sasaks, Menadonese, Buginese, Dayaks and Papuans.

The capital, called Batavia by the Dutch, is Jakarta, on the island of Java.

Resources and Industries. Indonesia is one of the richest countries in natural resources. There are vast supplies of tin, oil and coal, and sizable deposits of bauxite, manganese, copper, nickel, gold and silver.

Agriculture occupies 80% of the population. Products include rice, maize, casava, peanuts, soybeans, tobacco, coffee, rubber, cinchona, pepper, kapok, coconuts, palm oil, tea, sugar and indigo.

Inflation spiraled during the 1960's, but by 1969 comparative stability was achieved and a 5-year development plan was undertaken. Oil accounts for 35% of export income, followed by rubber and timber. Indonesia is the world's 11th largest oil producer. There are food processing, textile and other small factories.

History and Government. Until March, 1942, Indonesia was a Netherlands overseas territory. Following Japanese military occupation, 1942-1945, nationalists, led by Dr. Sukarno and Dr. Hatta, proclaimed a republic Aug. 17, 1945. Four years of intermittent warfare between Netherlands and Indonesian forces ended with agreements signed Nov. 2, 1949, transferring sovereignty over all Indonesia, except Netherlands New Guinea (West Irian) to a new interim government effective Dec. 27, 1949. Dr. Sukarno was elected president, Dec. 16, 1949. On July 20, 1950, the member states agreed to form a strongly centralized government; a unitarian state with an amended constitution was proclaimed Aug. 15 and its name formally changed to Republic of Indonesia. It joined the UN 1950.

After the Dutch in Nov. 1957 rejected proposals for new negotiations over West Irian, Indonesia's government stepped up the seizure of Dutch property. A U.S. mediator's plan was adopted in 1962, providing that West Irian be turned over temporarily to the UN, then to Indonesia. Under the agreement Indonesia pledged to hold a plebiscite allowing the people of West Irian the choice of staying with Indonesia or separating from it. The UN turned the area over to Indonesia May 1, 1963. In 1969, voting by tribal chiefs and other representatives favored staying with Indonesia.

President Sukarno suspended the original elected 257-member Parliament Mar. 5, 1960, and announced a new 261-member appointed group, Mar. 27, and swept aside anti-leftist criticism. He was named president-for-life May 18, 1963.

The USSR announced in 1964 plans to step up its contributions of modern arms to Indonesia to aid in attempting to "crush" the new nation, Malaysia, formation of which Indonesia opposed. In 1964 and 1965 Indonesia staged numerous guerrilla raids into Malaysia.

Indonesia withdrew from the UN in Jan. 1965. Many anti-American demonstrations were staged at U.S. consulates, including stonings, during the year.

Indonesia's large, pro-Peking Communist party tried to seize complete control Sept. 30, 1965, taking strategic points and murdering 6 high generals. The army smashed the coup and later intimated that Sukarno had played a role in it. In Central and East Java, Reds seized control of several distr cts and fighting continued. It was later reported that many thousands of communists were executed.

Gen. Suharto was named head of the Army; on Mar. 11,1966, Sukarno turned over all government powers to him but continued as president, apparently in name only. Gen. Suharto was officially named president for a 5-year term by the Consultative Assembly Mar. 27, 1968. He was reelected in Mar. 1973.

On Aug. 11, 1966, Indonesia and Malaysia signed an agreement ending the Sukarno policy of hostility to

Malaysia. On Sept. 28 Indonesia resumed membership in the UN. The U. S. resumed economic aid.

In July 1971, in the first popular vote in 16 years, a coalition party backing the Suharto government won a strong majority in the House of Representatives.

Education and Religion. 90% of the inhabitants are Moslems, the remainder Christians, Hindus and Buddhists. There is compulsory primary education for children 6 to 12, plus optional secondary training and higher education. There are 7 institutions of higher education. Many languages are spoken; the official one is Bahasa Indonesia, derived from Malay.

Iran

Capital: Tehran. Area: 636,363 sq. mi. Population (est. 1973); 32,001,000. Monetary unit: Rial.

A constitutional monarchy, Iran is a mountainous land, much of it a high plateau region, in SW Asia. Slightly larger than Alaska, it has coastlines on the Caspian Sea, Persian Gulf and Gulf of Oman. For neighbors it has the USSR, Afghanistan, Pakistan, Iraq and Turkey. Large salt deserts comprise 25% of the land but there are many beautiful oases.

Tehran, Isfahan, Shiraz and Abadan have jet airports. Shiraz is noted for ancient ruins of Persepolis.

Resources and Industries. Iran is the world's 4th largest oil producer and 2d largest exporter; petroleum provides most of its foreign exchange and government income. Iran refused to join the 1973-74 Arab oil embargo, but did join in raising oil prices.

In 1974 Iran invested some of its oil wealth in purchase of 5 nuclear reactors from France, a 25% interest in West Germany's Krupp enterprises, military planes from the U.S. and a $1.2 billion loan to Britain.

Other mineral wealth includes chromite, copper, iron, lead, manganese, zinc, barite, sulphur and coal. Also mined are emeralds and turquoise.

The first Iranian steel mill, near Isfahan, was built by the Soviet Union and paid for by natural gas piped to the USSR. Iran has contracted with the French for development of a petrochemical industry. There are cement, vehicle assembly and sugar refining plants.

Agriculture is a prime industry; wheat, barley, corn, rice, fruits, gums, wool, tobacco, raw silk, sugar beets and cotton are the chief products. Some wines are famous, as are Persian carpets. Sturgeon fishing in Caspian Sea is important, especially for caviar. Major dams built in the 1960s provide hydroelectric power and aid irrigation.

Under Shah Mohammed Reza Pahlavi's leadership, Iran has undergone an economic and social revolution to become a vigorous modern state. His improvements included major land reform, introduction of industry to towns, the spread of literacy and wide gains in women's rights.

History and Government. Iran, derived from Aryan, is the proper name to the country long referred to as Persia. The Iranians, who came from the E during the 2d millenium B. C., were Aryans, an Indo-European people related to the Aryans of India, and included Medes, Persians and other groups. Use of the name Iran became widespread in the 1920s and 1930s.

In 549 B.C. Cyrus the Great united the Medes and Persians in the Persian Empire, conquered Babylonia, 538 B.C. Darius I began the invasion of Greece; crossed the Hellespont, fought Spartans at Thermopylae, was defeated at Salamis, 480 B.C. and Plataea, 479 B.C. Alexander the Great of Macedon invaded Persia, defeated Darius III at Issus, 333 B.C.

Subsequently Persia was ruled by the Seleucids; the Parthians, beginning c. 250 B. C.; the Sassanians, c. 226 A.D. Arabs brought Islam to Persia in the 7th Century and for many years the religious-political Caliphate ruled the land. Omar Khayyam (c. 1050-c. 1123) wrote his famous Rubaiyat and created a calendar renowned for its accuracy.

Mongols invaded the country in 1250 and again

under Tamerlane c. 1370. After the downfall of the Mongols in 1502 Persia became a monarchy under a shah.

In 1906 a constitution was enacted. It provided for an executive with power vested in a cabinet and government officials who act in the name of the shah. The legislature has a national assembly (Majlis) elected for 4 years and a senate of 60, 30 elected and 30 nominated by the shah. Women voted and were elected to the legislature for the first time in 1963.

The shah is Mohammed Reza Pahlavi (born Oct. 26, 1919), ascended in 1941. He married Princess Fawzia, eldest sister of Farouk I of Egypt, March 15, 1939; divorced Nov. 19, 1948. The shah married his 2d wife, Soraya Esfandiary, Feb. 12, 1951, divorced Mar. 14, 1958. Both wives had failed to produce a male heir. The shah married Farah Diba Dec. 21, 1959; Crown Prince Reza Pahlavi was born Oct. 31, 1960.

British and Russian forces entered Iran Aug. 25, 1941, withdrawing later. Britain and the USSR signed an agreement Jan. 29, 1942, to respect Iran integrity and give economic aid. In 1946 a Soviet attempt to take over the Azerbaijan region in the NW was defeated when a puppet regime was ousted by force.

In 1951 the Majlis voted nationalization of the oil industry, the Anglo-Iranian Oil Co. closed its refinery and the industry was at a standstill until the shah in 1954 signed an agreement with a consortium of British, U.S., Dutch and French companies. It gave the consortium the rights to Iran's oil, with much of the earnings going to Iran. In 1973 a new agreement gave the National Iranian Oil Co. greater control over all operations.

In 1969-74 Iran and Iraq were involved in a dispute over Iran's claimed right to use the Shatt al Arab, a border river estuary, for shipping. Border clashes, reflecting rivalry for power in the Persian Gulf area, continued in 1974; a UN-sponsored agreement to negotiate the dispute May 1974, was followed by repeated Iraqi attacks, Iran charged. In late 1971, Iran occupied 3 islands at the mouth of the gulf, claimed by states of the United Arab Emirates. To protect oil shipments, Iran in the 1970s modernized its military forces, aided by sales of new equipment from the U.S.

Education and Religion. The Shiah branch of Islam predominates. Education is nominally compulsory. Higher education is available at 7 universities. A Literacy Corps is composed of high school and college graduates who teach in rural areas in lieu of military service. A Health Corps of graduate doctors and other graduates is patterned after the Literacy Corps. The language is Farsi (Persian), written in Arabic script.

Defense. Military strength totals over 210,000.

Iran is a member of the UN and CENTO.

Iraq

Capital: Baghdad. Area: 167,567 sq. mi. Population (UN est. 1973): 10,410,000. Monetary unit: Dinar.

Iraq is the modern name for Mesopotamia, the area around the Euphrates and Tigris Rivers, about twice the size of Utah. It is bounded by Turkey, Iran, the Persian (also called Arabian) Gulf, Kuwait, Saudi Arabia, Jordan and Syria.

The country is mostly alluvial plain. The temperature varies widely: 120°F in the shade is common, contrasted with severe frosts in the winter.

Resources and Industries. Wheat, barley, rice, dates, millet and cotton are the chief crops, with tobacco in the Kurdish hills. Large flocks of sheep are raised in the north and wool and skins are exported.

Iraq is the world's 8th largest oil producer. About 70% of its national income is from oil. European and U.S. companies controlled the Iraq Petroleum Co. New fields were developed with USSR aid, 1970-72, and in June 1972 Iraq nationalized the Western-controlled company and nationalized other U.S. oil interests in Oct. 1973.

History and Government. The Tigris-Euphrates valley was the site of the ancient cities of Eridu, Ur,

Nineveh and Babylon. The Sumerian culture of 3000 B. C. influenced Crete, Egypt and Greece.

Iraq, then known as Mesopotamia, was taken from Turkey in World War. I. The League of Nations gave a mandate to Britain, which ended 1932 when Iraq was recognized as a sovereign state.

Emir Faisal, then king of the Hejaz, was chosen ruler by a referendum in 1921 and a constitutional monarchy was created in 1924. On his death, Sept. 1933, he was succeeded by his son, Ghazi Ibn Faisal. King Ghazi was killed in an automobile accident April 4, 1939; succeeded by his son, King Faisal II (born May, 2, 1935).

King Faisal was assassinated July 14, 1958, when the Free Officers, led by Brig. Gen. Abdul Karim Kassem revolted and proclaimed Iraq "part of the Arab nation." Gen. Kassem became premier of a republic. Iraq received Soviet arms aid. It withdrew from the Baghdad pact and 3 U. S. arms agreements.

On June 7, 1967, Iraq broke diplomatic relations with the U. S. following Egyptian charges that America was aiding Israel in the 6-day, 1967 war.

After several coups, the government was taken over by a group headed by Gen. Ahmed Hassan al-Bakr, a member of the right wing of the international Baath Socialist party, July 17, 1968.

In 1969, in a series of trials, Iraq condemned and executed more than a score as spies for Israel, Iran and the U. S. It has had border clashes for several years with Iran in a dispute over navigation rights on the Shatt al Arab, a border river estuary. Iraq reportedly maintained 12,000 troops in Jordan as part of the general Arab confrontation with Israel. It withdrew them in 1971. In 1972 there were new border skirmishes with Iran. In April 1972 Iraq and the USSR signed a friendship pact. Soviet military aid was increased. In Mar. 1973 Kuwait charged Iraqi troops entered its territory in a border dispute. In the 1973 "Yom Kippur" war, Iraq sent forces to aid Syria.

Years of battling with the Kurds, a minority in the northeast area, ended in 1970 with recognition by the government of partial Kurdish autonomy and Kurdish representation in a legislature to be created in a new constitution. After a coup attempt failed in 1973, Gen. Bakr announced the legislature, an appointive body, would be created before the end of the year.

Education and Religion. Elementary and secondary education is free and compulsory. Arabic is the language of the majority. The people are preponderantly Moslems, divided between the Sunni and Shiah sects. Christians number 150,000.

Defense. Military strength for 1972-73 was 101,800.

Ireland

Capital: Dublin. Area 26,600 sq. mi. Population (UN est. 1973): 3,030,000. Monetary unit: Irish pound.

Ireland, or Eire, an island in the Atlantic near the European mainland, is a sovereign democratic republic about the size of. W. Va. It is separated from Great Britain on the E by the Irish Sea and the North Channel and on the SE by St. George's Channel.

Ireland consists mainly of a central plateau surrounded by isolated groups of hills and mountains. Ireland's coastline is much indented by the sea, affording many inlets and coves. The mean annual temperature ranges from 48°F, in the N to 52°F, in the S. There are numerous lakes (called loughs); the best known are those of Killarney. The most important river is the Shannon, about 250 mi. long. Tallest mountains are in SW; Carrantuohill, 3,414 ft. in Kerry; Brandon Hill on the coast, 3,127 ft.

Tourist attractions include the scenery, historic houses, cultural and folk festivals and medieval banquets. The famous Blarney stone is in an old castle in the village of Blarney, 4 mi. NW of Cork. A legend says it confers oratorical powers on those who kiss it.

Emigration had been high and for years the population remained static. Since 1961, however, it has annually increased and emigration has recently decreased.

Resources and Industries. About 28% of the work force is employed in agriculture, forestry and fishing. The nearness of the Gulf Stream causes considerable rainfall; lush pastures of the "Emerald Isle" support an extensive cattle and dairy industry. Important crops are potatoes, wheat, oats, barley, sugar beets, fruits and vegetables. Food and animals comprise 43% of the exports.

Industrialization increased, 1962-74, with over 750 new factories, many with foreign participation.

Major industries are tobacco, food processing, vehicle assembly, metals, textiles, chemicals and brewing. Marked gains have been recorded in electrical and non-electrical machinery, fertilizers and computers.

A mining boom, following discovery of zinc, lead and silver deposits, brought new strength to the economy. The index numbers of industrial production (1963100) showed that the mining index jumped from 105 in 1965 to 265 in 1973. The index for general industrial production rose to 184 in 1973. Natural gas was discovered off the SE coast in May 1974.

Tourism normally provides Ireland with earnings of over $250 million annually.

Foreign trade, in thousands of U. S. dollars:

	Imports	Exports
1972	$2,102,000	$1,611,000
1973	$2,776,000	$2,131,000

A switch to decimal currency was made in 1971.

History and Government. Celtic tribes invaded the islands about the 4th Century B. C.; their Gaelic culture and literature flourished and spread to Scotland and elsewhere in the 5th Century A. D., the same century in which St. Patrick converted the Irish to Christianity. Invasions by Norsemen began in the 8th Century, but were ended with defeat of the Danes by the Irish King Brian Boru in 1014. English invasions started in the 12th Century; for over 700 years the Anglo-Irish struggle continued with bitter rebellions and savage repressions.

The Easter Monday Rebellion (1916) failed but was followed by guerrilla warfare and harsh reprisals by British troops, the "Black and Tans." The Dail Eireann, or Irish parliament in Dublin, reaffirmed independence in Jan. 1919. The British offered dominion status to Ulster (6 counties) and southern Ireland (26 counties) Dec. 1921. The constitution of the Irish Free State, a British dominion, was adopted Dec. 11, 1922. By treaty with Great Britain Northern Ireland could vote itself out, which it did, Dec. 12, 1922.

A new constitution adopted by plebiscite came into operation Dec. 29, 1937. It declared the name of the state Eire in the Irish language and Ireland in the English and declared it a sovereign democratic state.

On Dec. 21, 1948, an Irish law declared the country a republic rather than a dominion and withdrew it from the Commonwealth. In 1949 the British Parliament recognized both actions, but re-asserted its claim to incorporate the 6 northeastern counties (Antrim, Armagh, Derry, Down, Fermanagh and Tyrone) in the United Kingdom. This claim has not been recognized by Ireland. *See United Kingdom — Northern Ireland.*

First president was William T. Cosgrove, 1922-32. Eamon de Valera, hero of the rebellion, was president 1932-38, 1959-66, 1966-73. He was prime minister 1937-48, 1951-54, 1957-59. Erskine Childers, a Protestant, was elected president in 1973.

Following Feb. 28, 1973, elections the Fianna Fail party was ousted from power after 16 years, although it won 69 seats, by a coalition of Fine Gael, 54 seats, and Labor, 19. Independents won 2. Liam Cosgrave became president.

The parliament is composed of a house, Dail Eireann, of 144 elected members, and a senate, Seanad Eireann, of 60, 11 of them nominated by the prime minister, 6 by the universities and the rest elected from 5 panels of candidates representing public interests.

Irish governments have maintained that solution of Northern Ireland troubles can be reached only by peaceful unification of all Ireland. In 1974 Ireland and Britain agreed to create a Council of Ireland, a body with limited functions of which both the Republic and Northern Ireland would be represented.

Education and Religion. Roman Catholicism is the prevailing religion, claiming more than 90% of the population. In a 1972 referendum voters repealed a Constitutional provision giving the Roman Catholic Church a "special position."

Elementary education is free and compulsory, and the Irish language is a required study in all national schools.

Defense. Armed forces total 10,500.

Ireland is a member of the UN, Council of Europe and the EEC.

Israel

Capital: Jerusalem. Area: (pre-1967) 8,017 sq. mi.; (post 1967) 34,493 sq. mi. Population (est. 1973, pre 1967 territory): 3,228,000. Monetary unit: Israeli pound.

The nation of Israel was re-established, as a republic, in 1948. It occupies part of the ancient land first called Canaan, then Israel, then Palestine. About the size of New Jersey, it faces the Mediterranean to the W, Lebanon to the N, Syria and Jordan to the E, and Egypt to the SW.

The coastal plain on the W is 120 mi. long, 15 wide, fertile and well watered. In the center is the plateau of Judea. A triangular-shaped semi-desert region, the Negev, extends from south of Beersheba to an apex at the head of the Gulf of Aqaba. The eastern border drops sharply into the depressed valley of the River Jordan and the Dead Sea which is 46 mi. long, with an average width of 8 mi., 1,296 ft. below sea level, lowest point on the earth's surface.

Israel's area, as defined by armistices with the Arab nations, includes all the land assigned to it under the 1947 partition resolution of the UN General Assembly, as well as Western Galilee and a corridor to Jerusalem. By the terms of the armistice with Syria, July 20, 1949, last of the Arab states to end military action after the creation of modern Israel, demilitarized zones were set up on the eastern edge of Lake Huleh and the southeastern shore of the Sea of Galilee, site of Israel's Ein Gev settlement.

After the Israel-Arab war of June 1967 in which Israel occupied the Sinai Peninsula, the west bank of the Jordan and a small area of Syria, Israel indicated it would not consider returning these areas unless the Arab states negotiated peace treaties directly with Israel and unless Egypt agreed Israel would have the same shipping rights as other nations in the Suez Canal.

Non-Jewish population (1972): Moslem, 358,600; Christian, 79,600; Druse, 38,700.

The chief ports are Haifa, Elath and Ashdod.

Resources and Industries. Citrus fruit is the most valuable agricultural product. Other principal crops include wheat, barley, durra, olives, melons, grapes, figs, tomatoes, bananas, cotton. Since 1955 total cultivated area has been increased from 412,500 to more than 1,058,000 acres, of which 448,000 acres are under irrigation. Wine making is an extensive industry.

Israel has deposits of some minerals including limestone, sandstone, gypsum, copper, iron, phosphates, magnesium, manganese, ceramic clays. The valley of Jordan and the Dead Sea yield rock salt, sulphur and potash.

Israel's over-all economy and industrialization have both grown rapidly. The economy has been aided by German reparations payments, U. S. aid, international loans and contributions. West Germany completed payment of $860 million in reparations (cash and goods) in 1965. The 2 countries also set up full diplomatic relations.

The index of industrial production (1963 = 100) reached 223 in 1971, 249 in 1972.

The Negev region in the south is Israel's primary development area, receiving nearly half of the immigrants. It has large phosphate deposits, copper, oil, natural gas and potash.

A 150-mi. pipeline, major link in Israel's national water plan, was completed in June 1964 and began carrying water from Lake Kinneret (Sea of Galilee) to the Negev. Several desalination plants have been built.

In 1970 Israel completed construction of a 160-mi., 42-inch, oil pipeline from Elath on the Gulf of Aqaba to Ashkelon on the Mediterranean.

Israel's first atomic reactor at Nahal Rubin began operations in July, 1960. The nation launched its first successful solid-fuel rocket 50 mi. into the atmosphere July 5, 1961, for meteorological study.

Israel's main exports are citrus fruits, polished diamonds, chemicals, textiles and fashion goods, machinery, plastics, tires and pharmaceutical products.

Tourism is second only to citrus products in earnings, over $150 million annually.

Foreign trade in thousands of U. S. dollars:

	Imports	Exports
1972	$1,922,200	$1,101,300
1973	$2,944,000	$1,382,000

History and Government. The Jewish people lived in Israel from about 1200 B.C.; many were driven from the land by some of its various conquerors. The Judaic moral and ethical code and the Bible originated here. The modern Zionist movement for a homeland in Palestine, led by Dr. Chaim Weizmann (born in Motele, Russia, Nov. 27, 1874) caused the cabinet of Great Britain to give its support in the Balfour Declaration, Nov. 2, 1917. Under the Palestine Mandate, about four-fifths of Palestine was detached in 1922 to form Trans-Jordan, now the Kingdom of Jordan. When the Nazi persecutions began in Germany great numbers of Jews set out for Palestine. The UN General Assembly voted Nov. 29, 1947, to partition Palestine into two independent states by Oct. 1, 1948. A separate enclave of Jerusalem, area 289 sq. mi., was to be administered by a governor appointed by the UN. Great Britain gave up its mandate May 15, 1948.

A new Zionist state, the Republic of Israel, was proclaimed May 14, 1948. A few hours after Israel proclaimed its independence, the armies of Egypt, Jordan, Syria, Lebanon and Iraq, with Saudi Arabian contingents, crossed its frontiers at several points. They were defeated.

Separate armistices with the Arab nations were signed in 1949, but no general peace settlement was obtained. The Arab nations continued policies of economic boycott, blockade in the Suez Canal, political warfare and local incitement.

Saying an Arab attack was imminent, Israel invaded Egypt's Sinai, Oct. 29, 1956, aided briefly by British and French forces. A UN ceasefire was arranged Nov. 6.

An uneasy truce between Israel and the Arab countries, supervised by a UN Emergency Force, prevailed until May 19, 1967, when the UN force withdrew at the demand of Egypt's President Gamal Abdel Nasser. Egyptian forces rapidly reoccupied the Gaza Strip and closed the Gulf of Aqaba to Israeli shipping. In a full-scale 6-day war that started June 5, the Israelis took the Gaza strip, occupied the Sinai Peninsula to the Suez Canal, and captured Old Jerusalem, Syria's Golan Heights and Jordan's West Bank. The fighting was halted June 10 by UN-arranged cease-fire agreements.

By 1969-70 there were almost daily Egyptian-Israeli artillery duels across the Suez Canal as well as ground forays and air raids with Israeli planes penetrating deep into Egypt. Palestinian guerrilla raids and Israeli reprisals continued across the Jordanian, Syrian, and Lebanese frontiers; there were also encounters with Syrian and Jordanian forces.

It was est. in 1970 there were 10,000 or more Soviet military men in Egypt, and increasing supplies of planes and anti-aircraft missiles, some of which Israel charged were manned by Russians. In July 1972 the Russians, then est. at 20,000, were sent home by Egypt.

In June 1970 the U.S. proposed a 3-month, standstill cease-fire and peace negotiations. Israel, Egypt and Jordan agreed; the cease-fire began Aug. 7; negotiations under UN auspices began Aug. 25. Palestinian guerrilla groups said they would continue attacks on Israel.

The cease-fire was formally ended by Egypt Mar. 7, 1971, but continued unofficially in effect as the U.S. and UN continued to seek peace agreements. Guerrilla terrorist attacks continued in 1972-73 and Israel made reprisal raids against guerrilla groups in Lebanon and Syria.

Egypt and Syria launched a surprise war on Israel, Oct. 6, 1973 (Yom Kippur, most solemn day on the Jewish calendar). Large Egyptian forces crossed the Suez Canal into the Sinai and established 2 long but narrow bridgeheads along the E side of the canal. Syrian forces drove into the Israeli-held Golan Heights. Egypt and Syria were supplied by massive USSR military airlifts; the U.S. responded with an airlift to Israel. Israel counter-attacked, first driving the Syrians back, but halting 20 mi. short of Damascus. Then the Israelis crossed the Suez Canal between the Egyptian bridgeheads, surrounded Suez City and trapped the Egyptian 3d Army in its Sinai salient.

Israel and Egypt agreed to a UN cease-fire which took effect Oct. 24; a UN peace-keeping force went to the area. A disengagement agreement was signed Jan. 18, 1974, following negotiations by U.S. Secretary of State Henry Kissinger. Israel withdrew from the canal's W bank; limited numbers of Egyptians occupied a strip, 5 to 7.5 mi. wide along the canal's E bank; UN forces took over a buffer zone between them and an Israeli limited-forces zone futher E. The withdrawals were completed Mar. 4.

Israel and Syria did not agree to disengagement until June 1; Israel completed withdrawing from its salient (and a small part of the land taken in the 1967 war) June 25.

In the wake of the war, Golda Meir, long Israel's premier resigned; severe inflation gripped the nation. Palestinian guerillas staged 2 massacres, killing 18 Israelis at Qiryat Shemona Apr. 11, and 24, mostly schoolchildren, at Maalot May 15. Israel conducted punitive attacks on guerrilla areas in Lebanon. By mid-1974 the USSR had replenished arms and equipment lost by Syria in the October war.

Israel is a parliamentary democracy. The first constituent assembly (Knesset), was formed Feb. 14, 1949, with 120 members, including 8 Arabs, The assembly elected Dr. Chaim Weizmann, who had been provisional president from the start, first president of Israel Feb. 17, 1949. He died Nov. 9, 1952. Israel's first premier was David Ben-Gurion.

The Knesset (Parliament) members are elected by universal suffrage for 4-year terms by all citizens over 18, under proportional representation.

Israel maintained formal diplomatic relations with 100 nations. About 400 specialists in many fields share their knowledge with those in less developed nations in Africa and elsewhere. But many African nations broke off relations with Israel in 1972-73, reportedly at the urging of Libya.

Education. Israel has compulsory education from 5 years of age to 16. Total enrollment in 6,118 state schools in 1972 was 918,702. Of these, 133,347 were enrolled in Arab schools run by the state and 28,000 in non-state Arab schools. Total students in all educational institutions was 918,702 in 1972, compared to 130,000 in 1948.

Over 53,000 students attend 7 universities and other specialized institutes.

Defense. Military service is compulsory for men and, between ages 18-26, unmarried women. Military forces total 125,000 which can be raised to 300,000 by mobilization of reservists.

Israel became a member of the UN in 1949.

Italy

Capital: Rome. Area: 116,303 sq. mi. Population (Govt. est. 1973): 55,262,000. Monetary unt: Lira.

The Republic of Italy occupies a long peninsula shaped like a boot, extending SE from the Alps into the Mediterranean, with the island of Sicily separated from the mainland by the 2-mi. Strait of Messina at the toe of the boot. The country is about 700 mi. long and not over 220 mi. wide. Its area is about the same as Arizona's. Lying directly W of mid-Italy is the major island of Sardinia, slightly smaller than Sicily.

Sicily, 9,927 sq. mi., pop. (1971) 2,985,678, is a triangular island 180 by 120 mi., seat of a region that embraces the island of **Pantelleria,** 32 sq. mi., and the **Lipari** group, 44 sq. mi., pop. 14,000, including 2 with active volcanoes: **Vulcano,** 1,637 ft. and **Stromboli,** 3,038 ft. From prehistoric times Sicily has been settled by Mediterranean peoples; a strong Greek state had its capital at Syracuse. Rome took Sicily from Carthage 215 B.C. **Mt. Etna,** 10,705 ft. active volcano, is tallest peak. Sicily leads in citrus fruits, also produces wheat, grapes, wine, sulphur, salt, olives. Cattle and sheep are raised.

Sardinia, 9,283 sq. mi., pop. (1971), 1,106,345, lies in the Mediterranean, 115 mi. W of Italy and 7½ mi. S of Corsica. Like Sicily, it is under a regional administration. It is 160 mi. long, 68 mi. wide, mountainous, with mining of coal, zinc, lead, copper; it raises grapes, olives, tobacco, also cattle and sheep. In 1720 Sardinia was added to the possessions of the Dukes of Savoy in Piedmont and Savoy to form the Kingdom of Sardinia. Giuseppe Garibaldi is buried on the nearby isle of Caprera. Capital: Cagliari.

Elba, 87 sq. mi., pop. 30,000 6 mi. west of Tuscany. Industries include fishing, iron mining, wine making. Napoleon I lived in exile on Elba 1814-1815.

Capri, 4 sq. mi., pop. c. 9,000, 20 mi. SW of Naples, is famous for its beauty and equable climate.

The allure of historical monuments, great museums of painting and sculpture, imposing churches, as well as good living attracts about 28 million tourists a year. Florence, with its galleries; Rome with its religious associations and ancient relics, Venice, and the Riviera are the principal objectives.

The 3.4-mi. Great St. Bernard tunnel, between Italy and Switzerland, first auto tunnel in the Alps, was opened Mar. 19, 1964. The Mont Blanc tunnel, 7.25 mi. linking Italy and France, was opened July 16, 1965.

Resources and Industries. Italy has enjoyed an extraordinary industrial growth since World War II. But in 1973-74, a fourfold increase in international oil prices helped disrupt the economy. Taxes were boosted in July 1974; in Aug. West Germany gave Italy a $2 billion loan to ease the financial crisis.

Grapes, olives, citrus fruits, vegetables, wheat, rice and cattle are the major agricultural products. The wines of Italy have great variety. Chianti from Tuscany is popular, as are Asti Spumante, Orvieto, Capri.

White marble is quarried at Carrara, Volterra and Pisa; colored marble at Verona, Siena and Vicenza. Alabaster comes chiefly from Volterra.

Natural gas is found in the valley of the Po, the Marches, Abruzzi, Apulia, Basilicata and Sicily.

In 1973 electric plants produced about 140 billion kwh. There were nuclear power plants. The electrical industry was nationalized in 1962.

Steel production was 21 million metric tons in 1973. Italy is a heavy producer of industrial and electrical machinery, automobiles, steel products, typewriters, shoes, textiles, synthetic fabrics, machine tools. Its chemical industry has expanded rapidly.

The index of industrial production (1963=100) was 171 for 1973.

Italy's merchant marine ranks high. It has over 635 ships of more than 1,000 gross tons.

Tourism brings in $1.5 billion a year.

Foreign trade, in thousands of U.S. dollars:

	Imports	Exports
1972	$19,282,000	$18,548,000
1973	$27,797,000	$22,224,000

History and Government. Divided and dismembered since the fall of the Roman Empire, Italy began to reunite after the war of 1859 when Lombardy came under the crown of King Victor Emmanuel II of Sardinia of the house of Savoy. By plebiscite in 1860, Parma, Modena, Romagna and Tuscany joined, followed by Sicily and Naples, and by the Marches and Umbria. The first Italian parliament declared Victor Emmanuel king of Italy Mar. 17, 1861. Mantua and Venetia were added in 1866 as an outcome of the Austro-Prussian war. The Papal States were taken by Italian troops, Sept. 20, 1870, on the withdrawal of the French garrison. The states were annexed to the kingdom by plebiscite. Italy recognized the State of Vatican City as independent Feb. 11, 1929.

Fascism appeared in Italy Mar. 23, 1919 when the original Fascisti organized an association against communism and socialism under the guidance of Benito Mussolini. They took over the government at the invitation of the king Oct. 28, 1922. Mussolini acquired dictatorial powers and was called duce (leader). He made war on Ethiopia and proclaimed Victor Emmanuel III emperor, defied the sanctions of the League of Nations, joined the Berlin-Tokyo axis, sent troops to fight for Franco against the Republic of Spain and joined Germany in World War II.

After Fascism was overthrown in 1943, Italy declared war on Germany and Japan and contributed to the Allied victory. It surrendered conquered lands and lost its colonies. Part of Venezia Giulia went to Yugoslavia, and Trieste was made a free territory. Mussolini was put to death by a firing squad of partisans near the village of Dongo on Lake Como, Apr. 28, 1945.

Victor Emmanuel III abdicated May 9, 1946; his son Humbert II, was king until June 10, when Italy became a republic after a referendum, June 2-3.

The Senate has 315 members, elected for 5-year terms, plus 5 whom the president may appoint for life. Ex-presidents are eligible for life membership. The Chamber of Deputies has 630 members elected for 5 years. Titles of nobility are no longer recognized. Reorganization of the Fascist party is forbidden. The prime minister and Cabinet normally represent a coalition of the Christian Democrats, largest of Italy's many parties, and one or 2 other parties.

There are 20 regional governments performing some functions previously belonging to the central and local governments.

Trieste. Following prolonged negotiations an agreement was signed Oct. 5, 1954, by Italy and Yugoslavia which gave Italy provisional administration over the northern section and the seaport of Trieste, with 90 sq. mi. and about 300,000 pop., and Yugoslavia the part of Istrian peninsula it had occupied, 200 sq. mi. and 73,500 pop., and provision for emergency access to the port. The 2 areas are treated as parts of Italy and Yugoslavia.

Italy is a member of NATO, EEC and Council of Europe; admitted to the UN Dec. 14, 1955.

Education and Religion. Roman Catholicism is the state religion. In 1974 Italians voted by a 3-to-2 margin to retain a 3-year-old law permitting divorce which was opposed by the church.

Italy has 34 state universities, including Bologna (founded 1088). There are 24 other institutes of higher education. Education is compulsory between 6 and 14.

Defense. Military forces total over 425,000. A large proportion are committed to NATO.

Ivory Coast

Capital: Abidjan. Area: 124,503 sq. mi. Population (UN est. 1973): 4,640,000. Monetary unit: CFA franc.

The Republic of Ivory Coast, a former French Overseas Territory in West Africa, is on the coast of the Gulf of Guinea. Roughly square in shape and about the area of New Mexico, it is bounded by Liberia, Guinea, Mali, Upper Volta and Ghana and has 340 mi.

of coastline on the Atlantic. Abidjan, the capital, is the chief port. A new port, San Pedro, opened in 1971.

Under the 1958 constitution of France, Ivory Coast became fully independent Aug. 7, 1960. Its present constitution was adopted Oct. 31, 1960. It signed an agreement, 1961, retaining close ties with France. Ivory Coast is a member of the West African economic community, formed in 1972, with Dahomey, Mali, Mauritania, Niger, Senegal and Upper Volta.

Agriculture, forestry, stock raising and fishing occupy 90% of the population. Chief export crops are coffee, cocoa, tropical woods and bananas; cotton, rice, oil palms also are raised. Electric power, lumbering and industrialization are being expanded.

The Ivory Coast has been the most prosperous of West African nations. It has a favorable balance of trade. Exports grew and continued to exceed imports in 1973. The number of small factories also increased.

About 18% of the people are Catholics or Protestants; 20% are Moslems and the rest animists. French is the official language.

Jamaica

Capital: Kingston. Area: 4,411 sq. mi. Population (UN est. 1973): 1,980,000. Monetary unit: Jamaican dollar.

Jamaica is a mountainous island in the Caribbean Sea, 90 mi. south of Cuba. Its area is 12% less than that of Connecticut.

Temperatures range from 80 to 86 on the coast and down to 40 in the Blue Mtns. Montego Bay and Ocho Rios are among popular resort areas; most of about 493,000 annual tourists are American.

Jamaica was discovered by Columbus, 1494, and ruled by Spanish (under whom native Arawak Indians died out) until seized by the English, 1655. The island figures largely in the history of the buccaneers of the West Indies before and during the time of Sir Henry Morgan, once its governor. Port Royal, old haunt of the pirate, at the entrance to Kingston harbor, was largely destroyed by earthquake, 1692.

Jamaica won independence from Britain Aug. 6, 1962. There is a governor-general representing the British crown, an elected House of Representatives and an appointed Senate; executive power lies with a prime minister and cabinet.

Principal exports are bauxite (world's largest production) and alumina. Other products include sugar cane, coffee, bananas, rum, coconuts, ginger, cocoa, pimento, citrus fruits and cigars.

Value of imports exceeds that of exports but earnings from tourism help offset this. Manufacturing plants have grown in number, aided by government-sponsored incentives. In 1974 Jamaica sought a large increase in taxes paid by U.S. and Canadian companies which mine bauxite on the island.

Japan

The World Almanac is sponsored in Japan by the Mainichi Newspapers, 1-1 Hitotsubashi, Chiyoda-ku, Tokyo 100; phone 03-212-0321. Mainichi founded 1876, Osaka, Japan; circulation 5,070,620 (m), 2,958,-995 (e), (Mainichi Daily News, English language 41,-500); president Mitsuharu Yamamoto, vice president, executive editor Toshio Sumimoto.

Capital: Tokyo. Area: 143,574 sq. mi. Population (Govt. est. 1973): 108,710,000. Monetary unit: Yen.

Japan consists of 4 main islands: Honshu ("mainland"), 88,952 sq. mi.; Hokkaido, 30,304; Kyushu, 16,-191; and Shikoku, 7,240. Total area is about twice that of Missouri. The islands lie in the North Pacific separated from the Soviet Union and Korea by the Sea of Japan and from China by the East China Sea.

By the terms ending World War II, Japan was forced to surrender captured lands, including Manchuria (Manchukuo), the southern half of Sakhalin Is., the Kuriles, Korea, Taiwan, and the mandated islands in the Pacific; the Marshalls, the Carolines and the

Marianas. *(See Index for these.)*

The Japanese coast is deeply indented, measuring 16,654 mi. The northern islands are a continuation of the Sakhalin mountain chain running through Hokkaido and the main island. The continuation of the Kunlun mountain range of China appears in the southern islands, the ranges meeting in the Japanese Alps. In the vast transverse fissure crossing the main island from the Sea of Japan to the Pacific rises a group of volcanoes, mostly extinct or dormant, with Fuji-San (Fujiyama), 60 mi. SW of Tokyo, lifting its white cone 12,388 ft.

Most important ports are Yokohama, Kobe, Nagoya, and Osaka. **Tokyo**, the capital, is one of the 3 largest cities of the world. It has a modern business section centering about the Ginza, a major avenue. The Imperial Palace, surrounded by a moat on a 250-acre site and the white-marble Diet building, erected in 1936, are also in Tokyo. Its International Airport is Asia's busiest. Tokyo Tower is a 1,089-ft. steel structure built for radio-TV broadcasting and sightseeing.

At Kamakura, 30 mi. SW of Tokyo is the Great Buddha or Daibutsu, a bronze figure 42 ft. 6 in. tall with base, cast in 1252. The Hakone hot spring area is noted for the reflection in Lake Ashino of Fuji-San. Also famous is the Toshogu Shrine at Nikko, where a national park of 347,000 acres preserves the natural beauty of Japanese flora. Kyoto, for 1,000 years a capital city, with massive temples and colorful shrines, is a cultural center.

The 2.34-mi. Kanmon undersea highway tunnel connecting Honshu and Kyushu, is the world's first double-deck tunnel, with one level for vehicles and one for pedestrians.

Resources and Industries. More than half the arable land is used for growing rice, the chief food. Wheat, barley, potatoes, tobacco, tea, beans, peaches, pears, apples, grapes, persimmons and mandarins are also produced. Minerals include gold, silver, copper, lead, zinc, chromite, white arsenic, coal, sulphur, salt and petroleum.

The principal industries are iron and steel products, transportation equipment, machinery, electronics, shipbuilding, precision instruments, chemicals, fertilizers, textiles (cotton, wool, silks, synthetics), ceramics, wood products, fisheries. The 1971 fish catch, valued at $3.3 billion, led all nations.

Japan is 2d to the U.S. in motor vehicle production; exports in 1972 totaled 1,965,490 autos, trucks and buses. It is also 2d to the US. in number of telephones in use. The index of industrial production (1963=100) zoomed to 270 for 1971, 318 for 1973.

Japan's shipyards lead the world, especially in construction of super tankers and bulk carriers of over 300,000 tons. Japan's own merchant fleet included 2,145 ships of 1,000 or more gross tons in 1974, 3d among nations.

Electric power production was about 384 billion kwh in 1972, about half from hydroelectric plants. An atomic power station at Tokai, near Tokyo, began commercial distribution of electricity in 1966.

Mayor exports are steel and related products, clothing, chemicals, motor vehicles, optical goods, ships, radio and TV sets, toys.

Tourism is an increasingly important source of foreign exchange; in 1972, 723,744 visitors spent over $210 million.

The U.S. is Japan's biggest customer, taking about one-third of all its exports. In 1973, value of imports topped that of exports for the first time in many years.

Foreign trade in thousands of U.S. dollars:

	Imports	Exports
1972	$23,481,000	$28,655,000
1973	$38,321,000	$36,971,000

History and Government. According to Japanese legend, the empire was founded by Emperor Jimmu, 660 B.C. Political power was held by successive families of shoguns (military dictators), 1192-1867, until recovered by the Emperor Meiji in 1868. The Por-

tuguese and Dutch had minor trade with Japan in the 16th and 17th Centuries. Commodore Matthew C. Perry, USN, opened it to U.S. trade in a treaty ratified 1854. Japan fought China, 1894-95, gaining Taiwan. In war with Russia, 1904-05, Russia's fleet was wiped out at Tsushima; Russia ceded S half of Sakhalin and gave concessions in China. Japan annexed Korea, 1910. In World War I Japan ousted Germany from Shantung, took over German Pacific islands as mandates from the League of Nations. Japan took Manchuria, 1931, started war with China 1932, taking Peking and Shanghai. Frustrated in efforts to have a free hand in the East, Japan launched war against the U.S. by attack on Pearl Harbor, Dec. 7, 1941. Japan surrendered Aug. 14, 1945, and Gen. Douglas MacArthur headed occupation of Japan as supreme commander for the Allied Powers.

In a new constitution adopted May 3, 1947, Japan renounced the right to wage war; the emperor was acknowledged as hereditary symbol of the nation, but gave up claims to divinity; the Diet became the sole law-making authority. The House of Councilors has 252 members elected for 6 yr. terms and the House of Representatives 491 members, elected for 4 yrs., both by popular vote. The constitution separates church and state. Japan has granted suffrage to women and lowered the voting age to 20.

The emperor is Hirohito, the 124th of his line, born April 29, 1901, succeeded to the throne Dec. 25, 1926. The crown prince is Akihito Tsugu No Miya, born Dec. 23, 1933.

The U.S. and 48 other non-Communist nations signed a peace treaty and the U.S. a bilateral defense agreement with Japan, in San Francisco, Sept. 8, 1951, restoring Japan's sovereignty as of April 28, 1952. Under the treaty, Japan was reduced territorially to the 4 main islands, but it was to have an opportunity eventually to regain the Ryukyu and Bonin Islands. Japan signed separate treaties with Nationalist China, 1952; India, 1952; a declaration with USSR ending a technical state of war, 1956. In Dec. 1965 Japan and South Korea agreed to resume diplomatic relations.

On June 26,1968, the U.S. returned to Japanese control the Bonin Islands, the Volcano Islands (including Iwo Jima) and Marcus Island. On May 15, 1972, Okinawa and the other Ryukyu Islands and the Daito Islands were returned to Japan by the U.S., but it was agreed the U.S. would continue to maintain large military bases on Okinawa.

On Sept. 29, 1972, Japan and mainland China agreed to resume diplomatic relations; Japan and Taiwan severed relations.

Education and Religion. The principal forms of religion are Buddhism, with 12 sects, and Shintoism with 13. There are over 100,000 Shinto shrines, 106,634 Buddhist temples and several thousand Christian churches.

Nine years of education is compulsory, consisting of 6 years of elementary and 3 years of lower secondary education. There were 382 colleges and universities, including 75 national universities, and 479 junior colleges in 1970. English is required study in lower secondary schools.

Defense. Legislation effective July 1, 1954, established new Self-Defense Forces. Military strength is over 265,000.

During 1969, the U.S. began turning over 50 military installation sites, a third of its facilities in Japan, to the Japanese. The U.S. reduced its forces in Japan in 1971.

Jordan

Capital: Amman. Area: 37,297 sq. mi. Population (UN est. 1973): 2,560,000. Monetary unit: Dinar.

Jordan is a constitutional monarchy in SW Asia, formerly under the Palestine Mandate. The country's former name, Transjordan, was dropped Apr. 26, 1949, after it occupied the West Bank lands, west of the Jordan River, in favor of the constitutional name,

Hashemite Kingdom of Jordan.

About 12% of the land is fertile; the rest is arid. In the extreme south is its only port, Aqaba, on the Gulf of Aqaba. It shares the Dead Sea (1,296 ft. below sea level) with Israel. Jordan is slightly larger than Indiana.

Resources and Industries. The fertile western portions have a high agricultural potential. Principal crops are tomatoes, vegetables, wheat, barley, olives, grapes, citrus fruits and bananas.

Industries include tobacco, flour milling, distilling, building materials, olive oil, soap, mother-of-pearl, textiles, plastics, cement, steel, batteries, leather.

Potash from the Dead Sea and phosphate rock are the main minerals. Phosphate is 30% of value of exports.

History and Government. The area was part of the Ottoman Empire from the 16th Century until World War I. It was set up within the Palestine Mandate Sept. 1, 1922, and gained its independence as Transjor in 1946. Abdullah Ibn Al Husein, born 1882, was proclaimed king, May 25, 1946; he was assassinated by an Arab extremist, 1951. His eldest son was proclaimed King Talal I.

Parliament removed King Talal on medical advice, installing his son King Hussein I (born Nov. 14, 1935), May 11, 1952. His first marriage to Sherifa Deena (a daughter, Princess Alya, was born 1956) was dissolved 1958. He married (May 25, 1961) Antoinette Avril Gardiner, of England, entitled Princess Muna. They had 2 sons and 2 daughters. But in 1965 King Hussein designated one of his younger brothers, Hassan, to be crown prince and heir to the throne. In Dec. 1972 Hussein divorced Muna and married Alia Toukan, an Arab from the West Bank.

Legislature comprises a Senate of 30 nominated by the king and a lower house of 60 elected by manhood suffrage. Jordan is a member of the UN and Arab League.

After creation of the state of Israel, May 14, 1948, Jordan joined in the Arab attack on the new nation. An armistice was reached in 1949; Jordan seized areas of central Palestine including the West Bank and the old city of Jerusalem. Several hundred thousand Palestinian refugees fled into Jordan.

In the 6-day Israeli-Arab war in June 1967 Israel took control of the old city of Jerusalem and the West Bank.

In 1968-70, Palestinian guerrillas based in Jordan continued raids on Israel, including artillery attacks. Israel staged reprisal raids against commando bases inside Jordan.

Fighting between Jordanian troops and Palestinian commandos in 1970 included a 10-day civil war in Sept. In renewed fighting in July 1971 Jordanian troops dispersed thousands of commandos from their bases. Syria, Algeria and Libya suspended relations with Jordan, and Iraq closed its border. Syria reopened its border in 1972.

In the Oct. 1973 Arab war on Israel, Jordan sent troops to aid Syria, but the Israel-Jordan border remained peaceful.

Education and Religion. The population is chiefly Arab, of whom the majority are Arab Moslems; 250,-000 Arab Christians, and 10,000 Moslem Circassians. The language is Arabic. Public school education is growing, with English and Arabic taught. The Jordanian Univ. was established in 1962.

Defense. Military forces total over 72,000. The U.S. has provided military aid.

Kenya

Capital: Nairobi. Area: 224,960 sq. mi. Population (UN est 1973): 12,480,000. Monetary unit: Kenya shilling.

Kenya, former British Colony and Protectorate which became independent in 1963, extends from its Indian Ocean coast NE to Somali, N to Ethiopia, W to Uganda, and S to Tanzania. It has twice the area of New Mexico.

The northern three-fifths is arid. Most economic production is centered in the south, a low coastal area and a plateau varying from 3,000 to 10,000 ft. The main products are coffee, tea, cereals, cotton, sisal, dairy products, hides, bark extract, timber and minerals. Kenya is the largest producer of tea in Africa.

In 1953 Kenya became the scene of terroristic activities of the Mau Mau, an oath-bound unit of some of the Kikuyu, Meru, Embu and other tribes which killed Africans and whites during an 8-year rebellion.

Kenya won independence Dec. 12, 1963. Jomo Kenyatta, once imprisoned as a Mau Mau leader, became its first prime minister. It became a republic within the Commonwealth Dec. 12, 1964, and Kenyatta became its first president. The National Assembly is a unicameral legislature.

Since independence, Kenya's economy has continued to grow, including both agriculture and manufacturing. Tourism has boomed. Schools and health centers have increased. Drought caused setbacks in 1971 but eased off in 1972.

In Jan. 1968 Kenya and Somalia resumed diplomatic relations as efforts were made to end 4 years of skirmishes caused by "invasions" of nomadic Somali herders seeking grass and water.

From 1968 through 1973, thousands of Asians holding old British passports were ordered evicted from Kenya. In 1973 it was announced Swahili would become the national language, with English still used for international communications.

Republic of Korea

Capital: Seoul. Area: 38,031 sq. mi. Population (Govt. est. 1974): 33,333,333. Monetary unit: Won.

Korea, Land of the Morning Calm, occupies a mountainous peninsula in NE Asia separating the Yellow Sea from the Sea of Japan. South Korea is about the size of Indiana.

Resources and Industries. Once chiefly an agricultural country, South Korea has a cultivated area of about 5,095,655 acres. Main crops are rice, barley, wheat, tobacco and beans, but the mountainous terrain, poor soil and cold winters limit yields.

Division of Korea in 1945 left the South with only light industry and about 10% of the power generating capacity. Large infusions of foreign aid have since helped to build an industrial base especially in mining of tungsten (supplies 6% of world's needs), coal, iron ore, bismuth, fluorspar, graphite and cement. The fishing timber, rubber, glass, shipbuilding, electronics and silk industries have expanded rapidly; chemical and fertilizer plants and oil refineries have been built. Growth was at record highs, 1971-73.

U.S. support in South Korea has been military, financial, technical and educational. Since 1954 it has totaled more than $2.2 billion. Index of industrial production (1963-100) was 416 for 1972, 565 for 1973.

Foreign trade in thousands of U.S. dollars:

	Imports	Exports
1972	$2,522,000	$1,633,000
1973	$4,218,000	$3,221,000

History and Government. Korea, once called the Hermit Kingdom, has a recorded history since the 1st Century B.C. and was united in a kingdom under the Silla Dynasty, 668 A.D. It was at times associated with the Chinese empire and the treaty that concluded the Sino-Japanese war of 1894-95 recognized Korea's complete independence. In 1910 Japan forcibly annexed Korea as Chosun.

At the Cairo conference, Nov. 1943, it was agreed that Korea should be "free and independent." At the Potsdam conference, July, 1945, the 38th parallel was designated as the line dividing the Soviet and the American occupation. Russian troops entered Korea Aug. 10, 1945, U.S. troops entered Sept. 8, 1945. The Soviet military organized socialists and communists and blocked efforts to let the Korens unite their country. Although the Soviet Union, at a foreign ministers' conference in Moscow, Dec., 1945, agreed to a joint trusteeship for Korea, it thwarted efforts to put this into effect. A commission appointed by the UN to supervise elections in Korea in 1948 was denied admission to North Korea. *(See Index Korean War.)*

The South Koreans formed the **Republic of Korea** in May, 1948, with Seoul as the capital. Dr. Syngman Rhee was chosen president July 20 and the republic was formally proclaimed Aug. 15, 1948. President Rhee was reelected to a 4th term, Mar. 15, 1960, when 85 years old. A movement spearheaded by college students forced his resignation, Apr. 26, amid charges of corruption and election fraud.

A constitutional amendment passed June 15, 1960, replaced an autocratic presidential system with a cabinet system.

In an army coup, May 16, 1961, Gen. Park Chung Hee became chairman of the ruling junta. He was formally elected president Oct. 15, 1963; a referendum, Nov. 22, 1972, provided more presidential powers and allowed him to be reelected for 6-year terms unlimited times. In 1974 scores of political dissidents were jailed in a long series of trials. An assassin, firing at Park, fatally wounded Mrs. Park.

North Korean raids across the border tapered off in 1971, but 2 South Korean soldiers were killed in 1973; in 1974, 2 South Korean boats were sunk and North Koreans fired on a U.S. helicopter south of the neutral zone. In July, 1972, South and North Korea agreed on a common goal of reunifying the 2 nations by peaceful means. Red Cross delegates from both nations met to find ways to aid divided families.

Education and Religion. Christianity, Confucianism, Buddhism and Chondogyo are the principal religions.

Primary education is compulsory. In 1970 there were 5961 primary schools, 1608 junior high schools, 889 high schools, 207 universities and colleges.

Defense. Military strength is over 630,000. By Mar. 1973, South Korea withdrew the last of 50,000 troops that had been aiding the Allies in South Vietnam.

During 1970-71 U.S. forces authorized in South Korea were reduced; in 1974 there were 38,000. South Korean troops replaced U.S. forces on the armistice border.

North Korea

Capital: Pyongyang. Area: 46,768 sq. mi. Population (UN est. 1973): 15,090,000. Monetary unit: Won.

The Democratic People's Republic of Korea was formed May 1, 1948. The U.S. did not recognize it.

North Korea has good mineral resources that are fairly well developed. The country ranks among the first 5 in the world in the output of tungsten, graphite and magnesite. Other products of significance include lead, zinc, pyrite, cement, iron ore, copper, gold, phosphate, salt and fluorspar. A well-developed hydroelectric system and sizeable reserves of coal provide power needs for industry. Agriculture is collectivized and industry nationalized.

North Korea is slightly larger than N. Y. State.

The import and export trade is largely with Communist countries, particularly China and Russia.

The USSR signed a military aid treaty with North Korea July 6, 1961, pledging defense protection and financial help. A similar treaty was signed with Communist China. *(See Index for Korean War.)*

Soviet prestige declined in the early 1960s as North Korea sided with the Chinese in the Sino-Soviet dispute. By 1974 North Korea apparently had good relations with both Communist super-powers.

North Korean patrol boats seized the U.S. Navy intelligence ship Pueblo on Jan. 23, 1968, charged it had entered North Korean territorial waters and held its crew captive. The 82 surviving crew members were freed Dec. 23 (Korean time).

North Korean planes shot down a U S. Navy intelligence plane over the Sea of Japan Apr. 15, 1969 (Korean time). No survivors were found.

In July 1972 North and South Korea agreed they would seek reunification of the two nations by peaceful means.

North Korea's armed forces totaled over 450,000, including a large Air Force. *(See also preceeding article, South Korea.)*

Kuwait

Capital: Kuwait City. Area: 7,780 sq. mi. Population (UN est. 1973): 880,000. Monetary unit: Kuwaiti dinar.

Kuwait, a small Arab state formerly under British protection, became fully independent June 19, 1961. It extends along the NW coast of Persian (also called Arabian) Gulf, bordered by Iraq and Saudi Arabia. Kuwait City is a principal Gulf port. In area, Kuwait is slightly larger than Connecticut.

Resources and Industries. Oil, discovered in 1938 and first exported in 1946, is Kuwait's economic mainstay and the tiny nation has become the world's 6th largest producer. Reserves are estimated at 10 billion tons, about 15% of the world's total.

Crude oil production in 1973 was over one billion barrels. Annual payments to the Kuwait government in royalties and taxes exceed 1974 est.) $8 billion. Per capita income was estimated at more than $10,000 in 1974.

Revenues from oil from a former Kuwait-Saudi neutral zone are split 50-50 with Saudi Arabia.

History and Government. Kuwait traditionally is governed by members of the Al-Sabah dynasty founded in 1756. Under a treaty of 1899 Great Britain administered its foreign relations and guaranteed its territorial integrity until it became fully independent, 1961, by mutual agreement. It joined the Arab League, 1961, the UN 1963. The nation's first constitution was proclaimed in Jan. 1963, and the first general elections for a 50-member National Assembly were held.

The Emir Sabah Al-Salim Al-Sabah became ruler Nov. 27, 1965, after the death of his older brother, the Emir Abdullah Al-Salim Al-Sabah.

Iraqi troops crossed the Kuwait border in Mar. 1973 but soon withdrew; Iraq demanded possession of 2 islands claimed by Kuwait.

Education and Religion. The government has utilized its enormous national income from petroleum to create a welfare state that guarantees free medical care, education and social security for all. A $600 million fund aids other Arab nations. There are no taxes except customs duties. Educational facilities are being rapidly expanded. There were, in 1973, 225 schools of all types, with 150,000 students and over 9,000 teachers. The University of Kuwait was opened in Oct. 1966. Islam is the official religion.

Laos

Capital: Vientiane, Luang Prabang. Area: 91,428 sq. mi. Population (UN est. 1973): 3,180,000. Monetary unit: Kip.

Laos is a constitutional monarchy in SE Asia, one of the 3 former French Indo-Chinese states. It is bounded by Communist China, North and South Vietnam, Cambodia, Thailand and Burma. It is landlocked, smaller than Oregon, largely jungle and mountains.

Laos became a French protectorate in 1893 and a member of the Indo-Chinese Union in 1899. As in Vietnam and Cambodia, nationalist aims grew in the 1940s, and the king promulgated a constitution May 11, 1947, providing for a constitutional monarchy under the Luang Prabang dynasty, and a parliamentary government.

Laos became an independent sovereign state by a treaty with France, July 19, 1949.

The king is Sri Savang Vatthana, acceded Oct. 30, 1959, on the death of his father, King Sisavang Vong. The National Assembly is elected for 5 years.

Conflicts among neutralist, communist and conservative factions created a chaotic political situation despite 1954 agreements. Although Laos was intended to be neutral, rivalry between the communist

Pathet Lao movement in the northern third of the country, led by Prince Souphanouvong. and right-wing and neutralist factions prevented integration of the Pathet Lao into the royalist army. Armed conflict increased after 1960 with the arrival of Russian arms and North Vietnamese troops.

The 3 factions formed a coalition government in June 1962, with neutralist Prince Souvanna Phouma as premier. A 14-nation conference in Geneva signed agreements July 23, 1962, guaranteeing neutrality and independence of Laos.

By 1964, the Pathet Lao had withdrawn from the coalition government and, with aid from North Vietnamese troops, renewed sporadic attacks on government positions. Both Laos and U. S. planes bombed the Ho Chi Min trail, supply line from North Vietnam to communist forces in northern Laos and South Vietnam.

In 1970 communist forces seized more territory in central and southeast Laos. On March 6, U.S. President Nixon urged the USSR and Britain to seek restoration of the 1962 accords; he confirmed that the U.S. had stepped up air support and military aid to Laos government forces. There were an est. 67,000 North Vietnamese troops in Laos, and some 15,000 Thai "irregulars" financed by the U.S.

On Feb. 8, 1971, South Vietnamese ground forces, with U.S. air and artillery support, launched a 44-day attack on the Ho Chi Minh trail in Laos, South Vietnam claimed heavy communist losses and disruption of the North Vietnamese supply line. Laotian and North Vietnamese forces continued fighting in 1972.

Following a Feb. 21, 1973, ceasefire, the neutralists and Pathet Lao signed an agreement, Sept. 14, for a coalition government and withdrawal of foreign troops. The coalition, with Souvanna Phouma as premier and Souphanouvong as president of a National Political Council, took office in Apr. 1974.

Chief products are tin, rice, maize, tobacco, cotton, opium, citrus fruits, benzoin, shellac, teakwood and coffee. The population comprises peoples ot Thai, Indonesian and Chinese origin. Lao and French are the most important languages. Buddhism is the state religion.

Lebanon

Capital: Beirut. Area: 4,015 sq. mi. Population (UN est. 1973): 3,213,000. Monetary unit: Lebanese pound.

The Republic of Lebanon, in SW Asia, occupies a strip along the Mediterranean coast about 120 mil. long and 30 to 35 mi. wide, extending from the Israeli frontier on the S to Syria on the E and N. It is smaller than Connecticut. There is a narrow coastal strip and 2 main mountain ranges running N and S with fertile land between. Beirut, with one-third of the country's population, is the chief sea and air port.

Resources and Industries. Trade provides two-thirds of national income. Agriculture employs half the workers; chief crops are apples, citrus fruit, olives, tobacco, grapes, vegetables, cereals. Manufacturing is growing rapidly; important are food products, textiles, leather goods, cement, oil refining. Tripoli and Sidon are terminals of oil pipelines from Iraq and Saudi Arabia. Large hydroelectric and irrigation projects are being developed. Beirut is an Arab publishing center.

Lebanon has a free enterprise economy and banking secrecy laws. Private capital from other Arab states has poured into the country. Tourism is also important.

History and Government. Lebanon was formed from 5 former Turkish Empire districts and became, with Syria, an independent state Sept. 1, 1920, administered under French Mandate 1920-1941. In 1944 France yielded its powers to the Syrian and Lebanese governments. French troops were withdrawn in 1946.

Attempts by several factions to undermine the pro-western administration of Lebanon led to an open revolt in May 1958. Lebanon became the center of inter-national controversy when the U. S. sent Marines in reply to a government call for help. The revolt dwindled and American forces were withdrawn in Oct. 1958.

On Dec. 28, 1968, an Israeli helicopter raid on Beirut Airport destroyed 13 Lebanese airliners; Israel had accused Lebanon of aiding Arab terrorists who attacked an Israeli airliner at Athens, Dec. 26, killing an Israeli.

Lebanon's efforts to restrict Palestinian commandos caused armed clashes in 1969. Continued commando raids, 1970-74, brought Israeli reprisal raids against guerrilla camps and offices, especially after raids in which 18 Israelis were massacred, Apr. 11, 1974, and 24 killed, May 15.

The republic's constitution instituted a democratic parliamentary regime. There is a unicameral legislature (Chamber of Deputies) of 99, elected every 4 years.

The president is elected for a 6-year term. Traditionally he is a Christian, the premier a Moslem. Lebanon is a member of the UN and Arab League.

Education and Religion. Christians (mostly Maronites) number about half the population, Moslems most of the remainder. There are 8 universities and institutions of higher learning in Beirut: American, French, Lebanese, and the private Academy of Arts. Arabic is the official language; French and English are widely spoken.

Lesotho

Capital: Maseru. Area: 11,716 sq. mi. Population (Govt. est. 1973): 1,200,000. Monetary unit: Rand.

The former British dependency, Basutoland, became independent as the Kingdom of Lesotho Oct. 4, 1966. An African state without white settlers or landowners, it is about the size of Maryland and completely surrounded by the Republic of South Africa.

The land is mountainous, altitudes ranging from 5,000 to 11,000 ft. There are air, rail and road links with South Africa. Agriculture has been advanced with U.S. and UN technical aid. Maize, sorghum, barley, beans and peas are grown. The main industry is livestock raising which produces wool and mohair, the chief exports. There are small industries including diamond polishing. About 40% of the men work in South Africa, many in the mines, earning about $2,800,000 a year. Tourism is being promoted.

In 1868, Lesotho became a British protectorate upon the request of Moshesh, the paramount chieftain, who sought protection against the Boers of South Africa. The British granted a constitution for the area in 1959 providing for a universally elected Legislative Council. The government consists of a king, an elected National Assembly of 60, a Senate, Cabinet and prime minister. In 1970, elections were suspended by Prime Minister Leabua Jonathan. A new constitution was planned in 1973.

Liberia

Capital: Monrovia. Area: 43,000 sq. mi. Population (est. 1973): 1,660,000. Monetary unit: U.S. dollar, also Liberian silver and copper coinage.

The independent Republic of Liberia lies on the southern side of the West African bulge adjacent to Sierra Leone, Guinea and the Ivory Coast and has an Atlantic coastline of about 350 mi. Much of the country is forest with valuable timber and mineral resources. It is slightly larger than Ohio.

Liberia has no natural harbors. The Free Port of Monrovia, built 1945-48 with U. S. funds, was turned over to the Liberian government in 1964, with payments to be concluded by 1999. The country is served by several international airlines.

Resources and Industries. Iron ore and rubber are the main products. Loans from the U. S. and other Western nations helped increase iron ore and rubber production in the 1960s. In 1970 a U. S. company began developing the nation's timer resources.

Diamonds and gold are also mined; other products are fibers, palm kernels, rice, cassava, coffee, cocoa and sugar. U. S. aid is promoting schools, hospitals, and food production.

History and Government. The population is entirely of African descent. Liberia was founded in 1822 when a settlement was made at Monrovia by black freedmen from the U. S. with the assistance of American colonization societies. It was declared a republic July 26, 1847. Its constitution is modeled on that of the U. S. Only persons of African descent may acquire citizenship and only citizens may own real estate.

There is a president elected for one 8-year term (thereafter for 4-year terms); a Senate of 18 elected for 6 years and a House of Representatives of 52, elected for 4 years. William V. S. Tubman, president since 1943, died July 23, 1971, and was succeeded by the vice president, William R. Tolbert.

Education and Religion. Christianity predominates. There are nearly 4,000 schools, one university and two colleges. English is the official language.

Libya

Capital: Tripoli. Area: 679,536 sq. mi. Population (1973 census): 2,257,037. Monetary unit: Libyan Dinar.

Libya is an Arab republic comprising 10 provinces in the former states of Tripolitania, Cyrenaica and Fezzan. Larger than Alaska, it is on the North African coast, bounded by the Mediterranean, Egypt, Sudan, Chad, Niger, Algeria and Tunisia.

Resources and Industries. Discovery of major oil fields in the northern part of the country beginning in 1957 brought prosperity and an improved standard of living to the country.

By 1973, government revenues from taxes on oil companies were about $6 billion a year and the nation was the world's 6th largest petroleum producer. In 1973 it expropriated 51% of several U.S. oil firms' assets. In 1974 it took over complete ownership. It joined the 1973-74 Arab oil embargo against Western nations.

In the 1960s-70s, several hundred schools were built, boosting enrollment from 40,000 to over 365,-000. Homes, hospitals, roads and power stations were constructed. Per capita gross national product rose from $145 in 1959 to $2,036 in 1971. Education and health services are provided free.

Libya had been basically agricultural, producing dates, olives, lemons, almonds, figs, grapes and tobacco. Carpets, leather goods and embroidered fabrics are also produced. Food processing and other factories have been built.

In 1973 "people's committees" took over many factories, firms, radio and TV stations, hospitals and farms, with government approval.

History and Government. Libya's strategic position has caused it to come under the domination successively of Carthage, Rome, the Vandals, the Ottoman Empire and Italy. After World War II Tripoli and Cyrenaica were placed under British administration, the Fezzan under French.

Emir Mohammed Idris El Senussi (born 1890), ruler of the Senussi tribesmen, was recognized by Great Britain as emir of Cyrenaica, June, 1949. He promulgated a constitution and set up an interim government over internal affairs, Sept. 18, 1949. Libya, as a sovereign state, was approved by the UN, 1949, effective Jan. 2, 1952. A pre-independence constituent assembly chose the constitutional monarchy form of government and named the emir as king of Libya, Dec. 3, 1950. A hereditary monarachy was proclaimed by King Idris I, Dec. 24, 1951.

On Sept. 1, 1969, a Revolutionary Command Council headed by Col. Muammar el-Qaddafi overthrew the government and announced formation of the Arab Republic of Libya.

On Sept. 1, 1971, Libya joined Egypt and Syria in a Federation of Arab Republics. Each nation retained its national sovereignty. In Aug. 1972 Libya and Egypt agreed to prepare unification of the 2 nations by Sept. 1, 1973. But Egypt put off the union and in Aug. 1974 charged that Qaddafi conspired in the bombing of an Egyptian presidential palace. Qaddafi and Tunisia's president, Habib Bourguiba, announced in Jan. 1974 their nations would unite, but Bourguiba soon dropped the plan.

Education and Religion. Libya's population is mostly Arab Moslems and Islam is the state religion. Schools were taken over by the "people's committees" in 1973. There are 2 universities.

Defense. In 1970, Libya arranged to buy jet planes from France and received tanks and other arms from the USSR; the U.S. turned over its Wheelus Air Force Base to Libya. Armed forces total 25,000.

Liechtenstein

Capital: Vaduz. Area: 62 sq. mi. Population (Govt. est. 1972): 22,800. Monetary unit: Swiss franc.

Liechtenstein is a principality on the Upper Rhine between Austria and Switzerland. It is slightly smaller than the District of Columbia. It received independence in 1866 when the German Confederation dissolved and was in an economic union with Austria from 1852 to 1918. By treaty with Switzerland (1920-23) that country administers its posts and telegraphs, customs and foreign interests. There is no army, only a police force of 33 with 31 auxiliaries.

Resources and Industries. The country is highly industrialized. Chief industries are machines and tools, cotton spinning and weaving, precision instruments, false teeth, pharmaceuticals, ceramics and canned food. Finely engraved postage stamps are sold to philatelists around the world. Exports from 1973 were valued at $166 million. Thousands of foreign workers are employed in Liechtenstein and constitute about 34% of the resident population.

History and Government. Liechtenstein is a hereditary, constitutional monarchy. Under the constitution, granted in 1921, legislative powers rest in a Diet of 15 members, elected for four years by direct vote, on a basis of male suffrage and proportional representation. The reigning prince is Franz Joseph II. He succeeded his uncle, Prince Franz I, on the latter's abdication March 30, 1938. Taxes are very low and consequently many international corporations have made their headquarters there.

Education and Religion. The country is predominantly Catholic. German is the language.

Luxembourg

Capital: Luxembourg. Area: 999 sq. mi. Population (UN est. 1973): 350,000. Monetary unit: Luxembourg franc.

Luxembourg is a European Grand Duchy, bounded by Germany, Belgium and France. It measures only 55 mi. long by 34 mi. wide, smaller than Rhode Island.

Resources and Industries. About 9,500 farmers cultivate 336,000 acres. The principal crops are oats, wheat, rye, barley and potatoes.

Luxembourg's iron ore deposits, in the south, are the basis for an important steel industry. It employs nearly half the labor force, and accounts for 45% of total industrial production, and most of the value of exports. The country also produces chemicals, beer, tires, tobacco and metal products, cement, roses and dairy products.

History and Government. Luxembourg, founded about 963, passed under the domination of Burgundy, Spain, Austria and France from 1443 to 1815; regained autonomy under the Treaty of Vienna, 1815. It left the Germanic Confederation in 1866, its integrity and neutrality guaranteed by the Treaty of London, 1867. Overrun by Germany in 2 World Wars, Luxembourg abolished its unarmed neutrality in 1948. Customs union with Netherlands and Belgium was adopted 1948, expanded to the Benelux Economic Union, 1958. Luxembourg is a member of the UN, NATO, OECD, Council of Europe, European Coal & Steel Community, Western European Union and the EEC.

As a Grand Duchy, Luxembourg is a constitutional monarchy, governed under the constitution of 1868, with modifications. Legislative power rests with a Council of State of 21, chosen for life, and a 59-member Chamber of Deputies elected by universal suffrage with executive power delegated to a minister of state and a Cabinet. The country is headed by Grand Duke Jean (b. Jan. 5, 1921) who became chief of state Nov. 12, 1964, when his mother, Grand Duchess Charlotte, abdicated in his favor after a 45-year reign.

The population is almost entirely Roman Catholic. Education is compulsory. Official languages are French and German; national language is Luxembourgeois.

Madagascar

Capital: Tananarive. Area: 203,035 sq. mi. Population (Govt. est. 1973): 7,655,134. Monetary unit: Ariary.

Formerly a French Overseas Territory, Madagascar is a large island off the SE coast of Africa, from which it is separated by the 240-mi. wide Mozambique Channel. It is about 980 mi. long and 360 mi. wide at its greatest breadth. It is a little smaller than Texas. There is a humid coastal strip on the E, fertile valleys in the mountainous center plateau region, and a wider coastal strip on the W.

The name of the nation and the island is Madagascar; the government is officially the Malagasy Republic.

The people, called the Malagsy, consist of many ethnic groups from succeeding waves of immigration, including those of SE Asian, Arab and African descent. They speak Malagasy, a language of Malayan origin. Over 3 million are animists; 3 million are Christians, about equally divided between Catholics and Protestants.

Madagascar became a French protectorate, 1885, and was declared a French colony in 1896. It proclaimed itself an autonomous republic Oct. 14, 1958. Full sovereignty became effective June 26, 1960.

Discontent with inflation and French domination of the university led to student demonstrations, followed by a coup in May 1972. President Philibert Tsiranana was ousted. In Oct. a referendum approved a new government with Gen. Gabriel Ramanantsoa as head of government, a Superior Council and a National Popular Council.

Most of the population is engaged in agriculture. Chief crops are coffee, cloves, vanilla (producing 80% of the world's supply), rice, livestock, sugar, sisal, tobacco, peanuts, etc. Small factories have been established.

Malawi

Capital: Zomba. Area: 45,747 sq. mi. Population (UN est. 1973): 4,790,000. Monetary unit: Kwacha.

Malawi stretches more than 500 mi. north and south along the western and southern shores of Lake Nyasa (Lake Malawi) in SE Africa. High mountains, dense forests and broad plains make it a scenic though landlocked country. It is about the size of N.Y. State.

Visited by Dr. David Livingstone in 1859, it became a British protectorate, Nyasaland, in 1891. From 1953 to 1963 it was a member of the Federation of Rhodesia and Nyasaland. On Feb. 1, 1963, it became internally self-governing and, on July 6, 1964, achieved full independence from Britain, taking the name Malawi. It became a republic July 6, 1966.

Malawi is almost entirely an agricultural country with only a few light industries. Four crops—tea, tobacco, peanuts and cotton— account for 90% of the

exports. Other important products are sugar, rubber, soybeans and coffee.

In 1967-68, factories were built for textiles, shoes, sugar, farm implements, and other products formerly imported.

Main trading partners are the United Kingdom, South Africa and the U.S. Malawi is dependent on Portuguese Mozambique for her rail trade routes to the sea. Construction continued in 1974 on a new capital at Lilongwe.

The Univ. of Malawi, which has 5 colleges, was built partly with U.S. aid; the first class graduated in July 1969. Population is mostly African; there are about 12,000 Indians and 8,000 of European descent.

Malaysia

Capital: Kuala Lumpur. Area: 128,328 sq. mi. Population (UN est. 1972): 10,920,000. Monetary unit: Malaysian dollar.

Occupying the southern part of the Malay Peninsula in SE Asia and the northern part of the island of Borneo, Malaysia is the world's largest producer of rubber and tin. Total area is larger than Arizona.

Malaysia was created Sept. 16, 1963. It included the old Federation of Malaya (11 Malayan states which had become an independent constitutional monarchy and member of the Commonwealth Aug. 31, 1957), plus the formerly-British Singapore (an island and city off the southern tip of the Malay Peninsula), Sabah (former British North Borneo) and Sarawak (former British Colony in NW Borneo.).

Indonesia harassed the new nation with guerrilla action 1963-65. After Indonesian President Sukarno lost power, Malaysia and Indonesia agreed Aug. 11, 1966, to restore normal relations; full relations were restored Aug. 31, 1967.

On Aug. 9, 1965, the separation of Singapore from Malaysia was announced under an agreement by Malaysia and Singapore officials that this was the best way to end tensions between the ethnic Chinese, largest group in Singapore, and the Malays, who were in control of the Malaysia government. *(See Index for Singapore.)*

With Singapore's departure, the Malays numbered 44% of the population and ethnic Chinese 36%.

The 11 Malay states, which form West Malaysia, and their capitals are: Jahore (Johore Bahru), Kedah (Alor Star), Kelantan (Kota Bharu), Malacca (Malacca), Negri Sembilan (Seremban), Pahang (Kuantan), Penang (George Town), Perak (Ipoh), Perlis (Kangar), Selangor (Kuala Lumpur), Trengganu (Kuala Trengganu). Largest in area is Pahang, 13,820 sq. mi.

Forming East Malaysia are Sabah (former British North Borneo; capital, Kota Kinabalu) and Sarawak (capital, Kuching). They lie on the N Coast of the island of Borneo and have a total pop. of 1,730,000 (1972) an area of 77,638 sq. mi.

A constitutional monarch, known as the yang dipertuan agong (supreme head of Malaysia) is elected by a council of hereditary rulers of the Malayan states every 5 years. There is a Senate, an elected House of Representatives, prime minister and Cabinet.

In May 1969 at least 180 persons died in riots between ethnic Chinese and Malays in Kuala Lumpur. Communist guerrillas renewed activities in 1971-72.

Resources and Industries: Rubber, tin, timber, iron ore, palm oil and copra are the main products. Rubber, much of it produced by new high-yield trees, accounts for 41% of exports; tin, of which Malaysia produces 33% of the world output, amounts to 13% of her exports.

Other agricultural products are rice, coconuts, tapioca, sugar, pepper, camphor. Rubber trees were originally introduced from Brazil. Small-scale industry includes rubber goods, pottery, cement, pewterware, furniture, bricks, tiles, soap, fertilizers, processing plants.

Religion and Language. The Malays and some others are Moslems; other religions are Buddhist,

Christian and Hindu. Malay is the national language and official in W. Malaysia; Malay and English are official in E. Malaysia.

Defense. In 1971 Malaysia increased its armed forces to 50,000 to compensate for reduction of British Southeast Asia forces. Britain, Australia and New Zealand maintain small forces in Malaysia to aid its defense.

Republic of Maldives

Capital: Male. Area: 115 sq. mi. Population (Govt. census 1973): 122,673. Monetary unit: Rupee.

The Maldive Islands are a group of 19 atolls containing 1,087 islands, 210 of which are inhabited. Totaling about twice the area of the District of Columbia, they are in the Indian Ocean 300 mi. SW of the southern tip of India. The country obtained full independence from Great Britain on July 26, 1965, in an agreement under which Britain retained its RAF base on Gan Is. in Addu Atoll in the southern Maldives. The Maldives became a member of the UN, 1965.

The island had been a British-protected state since 1887, with Britain responsible for their defense and foreign relations until the 1965 agreement. Long a sultanate, the islands became briefly a republic in 1953 and a sultanate again in 1954. After a referendum, the country became a republic once more, Nov. 11, 1968, with a popularly elected president and legislature (Majlis).

The people are Moslems and seafarers. Coconuts, fruit and millet are grown; the chief occupation is fishing. Production of processed fish, to be marketed in Ceylon, is the main industry. Also exported is coir, a coconut fiber, copra and cowries and other shells.

Mali

Capital: Bamako. Area: 464,873 sq. mi. Population (UN est. 1973): 5,380,000. Monetary unit: Mali franc.

The Republic of Mali, formerly the Sudanese Republic (1959-60) and a one-time French Overseas Territory in West Africa, is a landlocked nation which is larger than Texas but smaller than Alaska. It is mostly a vast plain in the uppper basins of the Senegal and Niger Rivers, extending N into the Sahara.

From the 11th to 15th Centuries the area was part of the great Mali Empire which stretched from the western Sudan to the Atlantic; Timbuktu was a renowned center of Islamic learning.

Under provisions of the 1958 French constitution French Sudan became the Sudanese Republic, an autonomous republic, and formed with neighboring Senegal Jan. 17, 1959, the Mali Federation. Complete independence was proclaimed June 20, 1960. Senegal withdrew from the federation Aug. 20, 1960, and Sudan took the name Republic of Mali Sept. 22. It signed economic and cultural agreements with France. On June 8, 1963, Mali and Senegal reached customs, trade and railway traffic agreements, with use of Senegalese harbors by Mali.

On Nov. 19, 1968, a coup ended the socialist regime of President Modibo Keita; Lt. Moussa Traore became president Dec. 6, 1968.

The country is mainly agricultural and pastoral. Millet, rice and peanuts are the chief crops. Cotton, rubber and river fishing are also important. Livestock raising is a major prop of the economy. Famine, following a long drought, struck Mali and other sub-Saharan nations in 1973-74. Aid was sent by many nations, 40% of it from the U.S.

The people are mostly Moslem, with a minority of Christians. French is the official language.

Malta

Capital: Valletta. Area: 122 sq. mi. Population (Govt. est. 1973): 318,530. Monetary unit: Pound.

Malta lies in the Mediterranean 58 mi. S of Sicily and 180 mi. from Africa. The island of Malta itself is 95 sq. mi.; the other islands in the group are Gozo, 26 sq. mi., and Comino, one sq. mi.

For 35 centuries Malta was under successive rule by Phoenicians, Carthaginians, Romans, Arabs, Normans, the Knights of Malta, France and Britain (which annexed Malta in 1814). It achieved limited self-government in 1887; home rule, 1961. On Sept. 21, 1964, it became independent, with the British monarch as head of state, represented by a governor-general, and agreed to permit British forces to maintain a base for 10 years. It is a member of the Commonwealth, Council of Europe and UN. A House of Representatives with 55 members is elected by universal suffrage; the prime minister and Cabinet are chosen from the House.

Once a vital British stronghold, it withstood Axis air attacks for 3 years during World War II. Population density in 1972 was 2,643 per sq. mi.; there is continuous migration, much of it to Australia, the United Kingdom and Canada.

A Labor party victory in June 1971 elections brought a Maltese demand that NATO remove its naval hq. from Malta. NATO moved the hq. to Naples in Aug. In 1972 Malta agreed to Britain's use of its military bases for 7 more years in return for greatly increased payments; USSR forces would be barred.

Leading industries are ship repairing, food and beverages, textiles and tourism. Visiting tourists rose from 23,000 in 1962 to 212,000 in 1973. Historic sites, a casino and village fetes are among the attractions.

Mauritania

Capital: Nouakchott. Area: 419,229 sq. mi. Population (UN est. 1973): 1,260,000. Monetary unit: Ouguiya.

The Islamic Republic of Mauritania, former French Overseas Territory in West Africa, is bounded by the Atlantic Ocean, Spanish Sahara, Algeria, Mali and Senegal. Population is largely Moorish. Mauritania is about four-fifths the size of Alaska.

The economy has been agricultural and pastoral. Products include dates, grain, meat, fish. There are large herds of cattle, camels, sheep and goats and large deposits of iron and copper.

A large new iron mine was opened in 1968 to add to the nation's annual production of 12 million tons of iron ore; fishing, which produced 270,000 tons of fish in 1970, was being expanded; a copper mine began production in 1971; a new cattle slaughterhouse and freezing plant was opened. It has received aid from France and Communist China. Drought and famine struck in 1973-74; aid was sent by several nations, most of it from the U.S.

Mauritania became fully independent Nov. 28, 1960. Prime Minister Mokhtar Ould Daddah, appointed June 26, 1959, became president by popular vote in Aug. 1962.

Mauritius

Capital: Port Louis. Area: 787 sq. mi. Population (Gov't. est. 1974): 870,000. Monetary unit: Rupee.

Mauritius, an island in the Indian Ocean 550 mi. E of Malagasy (Madagascar), became an independent nation within the Commonwealth on Mar. 12, 1968, after 158 years of British rule. It has a parliamentary government.

Mauritius has one of the world's most complex racial, religious and political mixtures as well as one of the world's highest population densities. There are 4 main groups: over 408,000 Hindus; 224,000 of mixed European and African descent and whites; 130,000 Moslems and 25,000 Chinese. Although the official language is English, French is spoken by many persons, and Creole, a French patois, is the lingua franca. Chinese and Indian languages are also spoken.

The country had a nearly one-crop economy, sugar.

However, a flourishing tea industry has been developed and tourism is growing. Commonwealth subsidies support sugar prices and aid the economy. Unemployment was about 20% in 1971; the literacy rate is very high.

Mauritius was uninhabited until 1638 when the Dutch settled there, introduce sugar cane and gave the island its present name in honor of Prince Maurice of Nassau. The French took over in 1721 and imported African slaves. The British, who seized the island in 1810, brought Hindus and Moslems from India to work the sugar plantations.

Mexico

Capital: Mexico City. Area: 761,601 sq. mi. Population (UN est. 1973): 54,300,000. Monetary unit: Peso.

Second most populous nation in Latin America and 3d largest in area, Mexico compiled an enviable record for progress, social improvement and fiscal responsibility in the middle decades of the 20th Century.

With housing, health, farm and industrial programs, the nation lifted itself and its people into the mainstream of the modern world; life expectancy, for example, was raised from 39 years in 1940 to 67 years in 1968.

Ever-growing streams of foreign visitors (958,000 in 1962; 2,234,682 in 1972) find spectacular scenery, striking art and architecture, cosmopolitan and colonial cities and luxurious resorts. The mountainous topography provides a variety of climates, from temperate to tropical.

The Sierra Madre Occidental Mtns. run NW-SE near the west coast. The Sierra Madre Oriental Mtns., a continuation of the Rockies, run near the Gulf of Mexico coast nearly as far S as Veracruz.

Between the 2 ranges lies the central plateau of Mexico, altitude from 5,000 to 8,000 ft. with a pleasant climate and with the vegetation and products of the temperate zone. The lowlands along the coast are tropical, rising to subtropical in the foothills, with a heavy rainfall on the Gulf side. Along the Pacific slope and in the interior irrigation is needed. Mexico is nearly 3 times the size of Texas.

Tampico and Veracruz, on the Gulf, are the busiest of Mexico's 49 ocean ports.

Mexico's population is composed of descendants of the Toltecs, Aztecs, Mayas and the Spaniards who conquered and colonized the country. Archeological remains of the early Indian civilizations are important tourist attractions.

Resources and Industries. Mexico is rich in minerals and timber. It is one of the top 2 producers of silver; also important are gold, copper, lead, zinc, antimony, mercury, arsenic, amorphous graphite, molybdenum, sulphur, coal and opal. Mexico is the world's 15th largest petroleum producer and is self-sufficient in oil. The industry is nationalized. Natural gas is sold to the U.S. Electric power generated in 1972 rose to 33.6 billion kwh.

Farming, stock raising and fishing are important. The land is rich, but the rugged topography and lack of sufficient rainfall are major obstacles. Crops and farm prices are controlled, as are export and import. Large estates have been expropriated; since 1915 the government has distributed about 160 million acres to small farmers through landholding communities (ejidos). Major irrigation projects in Sonora and Sinaloa have increased production of cotton and wheat.

Principal export crops are cotton, coffee, cane sugar, tomatoes, cattle, fruit, fresh and frozen meats.

Mexico is the 5th largest coffee producer; other major crops are corn, rice, tobacco garbanzos, cocoa, sisal, bananas. About 50% of the world supply of sisal comes from Yucatan, in southern Mexico.

Mexican industry is producing products formerly imported, especially in iron and steel, chemicals, electric goods. Other products are cotton, wool and synthetic textiles, flour, beverages, soap, cigarettes and cigars, rubber, paper, rubber products, cement, shoes, glass, furniture and tiles. Mexico is famous for industrial and native handicraft in silver, pottery, leather, wood, fibers and textiles. The U.S. buys a large portion of Mexico's exports.

Index of industrial production (1963=100) was 227 in 1973. The estimated gross national product (in U.S. dollars) was $26.7 billion for 1968, $44 billion for 1973.

Foreign trade, in thousands of U.S. dollars:

	Imports	Exports
1972	$2,936,000	$1,809,000
1973	$4,146,000	$2,452,000

History and Government. Mexico was the site of advanced Indian civilizations before the Spanish conquest. The Mayas, an agricultural people, moved up from Yucatan and built immense stone pyramids and invented a calendar. The Toltecs were overcome by the Aztecs, who founded Tenochtitlan 1325 A.D., now Mexico City. Hernando Cortes, Spanish conquistador, destroyed the Aztec empire, 1519-1521.

After 3 centuries of misrule the people rose, under Fr. Miguel Hidalgo y Costilla (a priest), 1810, Fr. Morelos y Pavon (another priest), 1812, and Gen. Agustin Iturbide, who made independence effectual Sept. 27, 1821, but made himself emperor as Agustin I. A republic was chosen in 1823.

Mexican territory extended into the present American Southwest and California until Texas revolted and established a republic in 1836; the Mexican legislature refused recognition but was unable to enforce its authority there. After numerous clashes, the U.S.-Mexican War, 1846-48, resulted in the loss by Mexico of the lands north of the Rio Grande, about half its total area.

French arms supported an Austrian archduke on the throne of Mexico as Maximilian I, 1864-67, but pressure from the U.S. forced France to withdraw troops, and led to his defeat by Mexican patriots under Benito Juarez, and subsequent execution. A dictatorial rule by Porfirio Diaz, president 1877-80, 1884-1911, led to fighting by rival forces until the new constitution of Feb. 5, 1917, provided social reform. Since then Mexico has developed large-scale programs of social security, labor protection and school improvement. A constitutional provision requires management to share profits with labor.

Mexico is a federal democratic republic of 29 states, with president, legislature and judiciary elected by universal suffrage; 2 territories (Baja California Sur and Quintana Roo) with governors appointed by the president, and a federal district (Distrito Federal) containing Mexico City. The president is elected for 6 years and thereafter ineligible; 60 senators for 6 years and deputies for 3 years, ineligible for reelection until one term has intervened.

The Institutional Revolutionary party has been dominant in politics since 1929. In 1970 the legal voting age was lowered from 21 to 18.

Education and Religion. Education is secular, with primary education free and compulsory up to 15 years of age. Vocational instruction particularly in agriculture is promoted and there are many technical schools. The National University of Mexico continues an educational foundation of 1551 A.D. Spanish is the language.

Most of the people are Roman Catholics. All church real estate is vested in the nation, but care of church buildings is the responsibility of the clergy.

Defense. The armed forces total 71,000 regulars, 250,000 part-time. Mexico is a member of the UN and OAS.

(See also Index for Mexico City.)

Monaco

Capital: Monaco. Area: 453 acres. Population (est. 1973): 30,000. Monetary unit: French franc.

Monaco is a small principality on the Mediterranean surrounded on all but the sea side by France. It is noted for its mild climate and magnificent scenery.

There is a local police force of 200.

Resources and Industries. Monaco's fame as a tourist resort and international conference city is widespread. Its revenues derive from indirect taxation, a tobacco monopoly, postage and the gambling tables of the Monte Carlo Casino.

About a dozen subsidiaries of large drug manufacturers were established in Monaco and their drugs entered France free of duty. In October, 1962, when the customs union with France expired, France put up customs barriers pending imposition of taxes and ended domestic mail rates. By a 1963 agreement the barriers were eliminated in April and domestic mail rates restored. French citizens living in Monaco less than 5 years must pay income taxes to France.

Monaco endeavored to cover possible revenue losses by enacting a profits tax on Monaco companies that do 25% of their business outside Monaco. The company tax rate is now 35%.

History and Government. An independent principality for over 300 years, Monaco has belonged to the House of Grimaldi except during the French Revolution. It was placed under the protectorate of Sardinia in 1815 (Treaty of Vienna), and under that of France, 1861. The Prince of Monaco was an absolute ruler until a constitution was promulgated in 1911.

A new constitution, proclaimed Dec. 17, 1962, provided for female suffrage and abolition of capital punishment, and established a court to guarantee fundamental liberties. The legislature (National Council) consists of 18 members elected for 5 years.

The ruler of Monaco is Prince Rainier III who succeeded his grandfather, Prince Louis II, who died May 9, 1949. He married Grace Kelly, American motion picture actress, Apr. 18, 1956. A daughter, Princess Caroline Louise Marguerite, was born Jan. 23, 1957. The heir apparent, Prince Albert Alexander Louis Pierre, was born Mar. 14, 1958. Princess Stephanie Marie Elizabeth was born Feb. 1, 1965.

In 1967 the government purchased for $8 million the holdings of Aristotle Onassis in the Societe des Bains de Mer, owner of the Casino and other interests. The prince launched a program of reclaiming land from the sea and developing new tourist facilities.

Mongolia

Capital: Ulan Bator. Area: 604,247 sq. mi. Population (UN est. 1973): 1,360,000. Monetary unit: Tughrik.

The Mongolian People's Republic comprises Outer Mongolia in northeastern Asia. It is bounded on the N by the Siberian provinces of USSR, and on 3 other sides by Mainland China. It is larger than Alaska. Much of Mongolia is a high plateau with vast grasslands; arid lands in the south are part of the Gobi Desert.

Resources and Industries. In the early 1970s Mongolia was changing from a nomadic culture to one of settled agriculture and growing industries with aid from the USSR and East European nations. Irrigation and scientific farming methods were pressed to increase grain crops and fodder for the large livestock herds which long were the mainstay of the economy. Food processing, textile, chemical, brick and cement factories were established in growing cities in the north. Electric power plants were built, running on coal; Mongolia has large coal deposits as well as tungsten, copper, gold, tin.

History and Government. One of the world's oldest countries, Mongolia reached the zenith of its power in the 13th Century when Genghis Khan and his successors conquered all of China and extended their influence as far W as Hungary and Poland. In later centuries, the empire dissolved and Mongolia came under the suzerainty of China.

With the advent of the 1911 Chinese revolution,

Mongolia, with Russian backing, declared its independence. The Mongolian People's Republic was proclaimed July 11, 1921. China, however, continued to claim the country until 1945 when recognition of independence was given.

The constitution vests power in the elected Great People's Khural from which is drawn a 7-member Presidium and a Council of Ministers. Actual power is in the hands of the Communist party and its 9-man Politburo.

Mongolia has sided with the Russians in the Sino-Soviet dispute. A Mongolian-Soviet mutual assistance pact was signed Jan. 15, 1966. Mongolia is a UN member.

Education and Religion. There are primary, secondary and technical schools, and 7 higher educational institutes. Buddhist Lamaism is the leading religion. Khalka Mongol is the main language.

Morocco

Capital: Rabat. Area: 171,953 sq. mi. Population (UN est. 1973): 16,310. Monetary unit: Dirham.

The monarchy of Morocco lies on the NW tip of Africa separated from Europe by the 8-mile-wide Strait of Gibraltar. It is bounded by Algeria, Spanish Sahara, the Mediterranean and the Atlantic. Until 1956 it was a protectorate of France and Spain.

It consists of 5 natural regions: A series of mountain ranges (Riff, facing Gibraltar; Middle Atlas, extending NW of Marrakesh; Upper Atlas, and Anti-Atlas); a series of rich plains in the W; the alluvial plains of Haouz in the SW; the "mesata," a well-cultivated series of plateaus in the center; a pre-Saharan zone extending from S to E.

The inhabitants largely are a mixture of Arabs and the original Berbers.

Resources and Industries. Morocco is primarily agricultural and pastoral. Cereals rank first among agricultural products, including barley, wheat and corn. Fruit and vineyards are abundant and dates a staple crop. Carpets, leather goods, clothing and textiles are among the manufactures.

Morocco ranks 3d in world production of phosphate rock and is first in phosphate exports. It produces 4% of the world's cobalt. Other minerals are antimony, manganese, zinc, lead, oil and anthracite.

In the late 1960s, a number of dams were constructed for irrigation, including a large project built with U.S. aid. Foreign-owned agricultural lands were nationalized in 1973.

Tourism attracts 600,000 visitors annually to see Morocco's casbahs. Roman ruins, fortresses, oases.

History and Government. Morocco is a remnant of an early empire founded by the Arabs at the close of the 7th Century which encompassed all NW Africa and most of the Iberian Peninsula.

Part of Morocco came under Spanish rule in the 19th Century; in the early 20th France took control of the rest of it. A general uprising of tribes in 1910 culminated in the dispatch of a French expeditionary force that occupied Fez in 1911. Uprisings continued for 2 decades until the exile of Abd-el-Krim in 1926 and the surrender of Sidi Ali Hociene in 1933.

Morocco became independent Mar. 2, 1956, after agreement by France to end its protectorate. Spain signed similar agreements.

Tangier, a seaport which had been internationalized, was turned over to Moroccan control in 1956. Ifni, a small Spanish enclave on the Atlantic coast, was turned over to Morocco June 30, 1969.

Mohammed V, Sultan since 1927 (with the title of king since 1957), died Feb. 26, 1961. His eldest son became King Hassan II.

Under a constitution approved by referendum Dec. 7, 1962, Morocco became a constitutional monarchy. The first Parliament was elected May 17, 1963.

The king suspended Parliament in June 1965. A new constitution was approved by voters in July 1970, providing for a unicameral, elected Chamber of

Deputies. An attempted army revolt failed in July 1971. Air force pilots tried unsuccessfully to assassinate the king in Aug. 1972.

Morocco accepted U.S. and USSR military and economic aid on a basis of non-interference in its internal affairs. It has agreements with France on economic, technical and cultural cooperation. It is a member of the UN, OAU and Arab League.

Education and Religion. Trade schools and agricultural training centers have been developed, in addition to regular schools. The main university is in Rabat. Arabic is the official language. The population is Sunni Moslem.

Defense. Armed forces total 56,000.

Nauru

Capital: Uaboe District. Area: 8 sq. mi. Population (est. 1973): 6,500. Monetary unit: Australian dollar.

Nauru, one of the world's smallest nations, became independent Jan. 31, 1968, after 80 years of foreign rule. In the southwest Pacific about 30 mi. S of the Equator and 1,300 mi. NE of Australia, Nauru is comfortably affluent because of its high-grade phosphate deposits.

Phosphate exports provide per capita revenue equal to over $6,000 a year for each of the 4,000 native Nauruans (about 1,300 foreigners work in the phosphate industry; there are about 1,200 other foreigners on the island). The deposits are expected to be depleted by 1990.

The island was discovered in 1798 by the British but was formally annexed to the German Empire in 1888. After World War I, Nauru became a League of Nations mandate administered by Australia. During World War II the Japanese occupied the island and shipped 1,200 Nauruans to the fortress island of Truk as slave laborers.

In 1947 Nauru was made a UN trust territory, administered by Australia on behalf of the 3 trust powers: Australia, Great Britain and New Zealand. Because of its small size Nauru has not sought UN membership.

There is an elected Parliament. Hammer De Roburt was elected first president.

Nepal

Capital: Katmandu. Area: 54,362 sq. mi. Population (est. 1973): 12,020,000. Monetary unit: Nepalese rupee.

Nepal is a monarchy in the Himalayas, bounded on the N by China (Tibet) and E, S and W by India. It is about the size of Arkansas.

There are many fertile valleys lying in the slopes of the lofty mountains, including Mt. Everest, on the Tibet border. The capital is in the valley of Katmandu, 15 mi. long and 20 wide, which is noted for its many lavishly decorated shrines.

Virtually closed to the outside world for centuries, Nepal is now linked to India and Pakistan by modern roads and air service and to Tibet by road.

Nepal has established a 500 sq. mi. game preserve for elephants, tigers, rhinoceroses, leopards, boars, crocodiles and over 500 species of birds.

Resources and Industries. Nepal has rich forests and quartz deposits. The country exports jute, rice, grain, cattle, hides, wheat and drugs. Trade is 90% with India. Tourism provides vital funds.

U.S technical aid has made possible settlement of the fertile but once inaccessible Rapti Valley with a 53-mi. $500,000 highway. Nepal also receives financial aid from India, China and others. Its 4th 5-year plan stresses hydroelectric power and roads.

History and Government. Nepal was originally a group of petty principalities, the inhabitants of one of which, the Gurkhas, became dominant about 1769. In 1951 King Tribhubana Bir Bikram, member of the Shah family, ended the system of rule by hereditary premiers of the Ranas family, who had kept the kings

virtual prisoners. He established a cabinet system of government Feb. 18, 1951.

King Tribhubana died Mar. 13, 1955, and was succeeded by his son, Mahendra Bir Bikram Shah Dev, who died Jan. 31, 1972, and was succeeded by his son, Birendra Bir Bikram Shah Dev. King Mahendra promulgated a new constitution Dec. 16, 1962, providing for a three-tier system of indirectly elected councils topped by a National Assembly or National Panchayat.

Education and Religion. There are more than 2,400 English schools in addition to Sanskrit and Nepali schools and other institutions of learning. Buddha was born at Lumbini in South-Central Nepal. Hinduism and Buddhism are the main relgions. Polygamy, child marriage and the caste system were abolished in 1963.

The Netherlands

Capital: Amsterdam. Area (land): 14,192 sq. mi. Population (est. 1974): 13,500,000. Monetary unit: Guilder.

The Kingdom of the Netherlands, a constitutional monarchy in NW Europe, is bounded by Germany, Belgium, and the North Sea. Its surface is flat, with an average height above sea level of 37 ft., with much land below sea level, reclaimed and protected by dikes, of which there are 1,500 mi. The country is about twice the area of New Jersey.

Since 1927 the government has been draining the IJsselmeer, formerly the Zuider Zee, and converting the reclaimed land into farms. The total will add over 550,000 acres. By 1972, 410,000 acres had been reclaimed.

The Hague is the seat of government, but Amsterdam is the sole capital of the kingdom and the inaugurations of sovereigns are held there.

Rotterdam, located along the principal mouth of the Rhine, handles the most cargo of any ocean port in the world.

Resources and Industries. About 46% of the land is given to pasture, farming takes 26%, heath, dunes and forest 7%, horticulture 5%. Of the arable land 80% is in holdings of fewer than 50 acres and about 25% of fewer than 10 acres. Cereals, potatoes, sugar beets, vegetables and fruits are raised. Agriculture and fishing engage about 6% of the workers. Dairy products are an important industry. In pork exports the nation ranks 2d to Denmark. Flowers, bulbs, seeds and trees are grown commercially.

The most important industries are shipbuilding, the manufacture of machinery,, textiles (including rayon), chemical products, oil refining, brewing, distilling and flour milling. Amsterdam is famous for diamond cutting; Delft for pottery. Eindhoven has electrical and radio factories. Natural gas reserves are large. Index of industrial production (1963=100) was 203 for 1972, 218 for 1973.

Canals, of which there are 3,478 mi., are important in transportation. The Rhine, Meuse and Schelde reach the sea through the Netherlands and carry enormous traffic.

The 1973-74 Arab oil embargo against Western nations was not lifted from the Netherlands until July 1974; the Dutch had refused Arab demands to condemn Israel.

Foreign trade in thousands of U.S. dollars:

	Imports	Exports
1972	$16,985,000	$16,826,000
1973	$23,835,000	$23,910,000

History and Government. After the empire of Charlemagne (d. 814) fell apart, the Netherlands (Holland, Belgium, Flanders), split among counts, dukes and bishops, passed to Burgundy and thence to charles V of Spain. His son, Philip II, sent the Duke of Alva as governor to check the Dutch drive toward political freedom and Protestantism (1568-1573). William the Silent, prince of Orange, led a confederation of the northern provinces, called Estates, in the Union of Utrecht, 1579. The Estates retained individual sovereignty, but were represented jointly in the States-General, a body that had control of foreign affairs and defense. In 1581 they repudiated allegiance to Spain. The rise of the Dutch republic to naval, economic and artistic eminence came in the 17th Century.

The United Dutch Republic ended 1795 when the French formed the Batavian Republic. Napoleon made his brother Louis king of Holland, 1806; Louis abdicated 1810 when Napoleon annexed Holland. In 1813 the French were expelled. In 1815 the Congress of Vienna formed a kingdom of the Netherlands, including Belgium, under William I. In 1830, the Belgians seceded and formed a separate kingdom.

The constitution, promulgated 1814, and subsequently revised, assures a hereditary constitutional monarchy. Executive power rests in the crown (the queen and ministers). Legislative powers are exercised jointly by the crown and Parliament (States-General) of 2 chambers: First Chamber, 75 members, elected for 6 years (one half every 3d year) by the provincial legislatures, and the Second Chamber, 150 deputies, elected for 4 years directly. Universal suffrage for all citizens over 18 and proportional representation are in force. The sovereign exercises the executive authority through a Council of Ministers, the president thereof corresponding to a prime minister. There is a State Council named by the sovereign, of which she is president, to be consulted on all legislative and some executive matters.

The reigning sovereign is Queen Juliana Louise Emma Marie Wilhelmina, born April 30, 1909, only daughter of former Queen Wilhelmina. She succeeded to the throne, Sept. 6, 1948, on the abdication of her mother. Queen Juliana on Jan. 7, 1937, married Prince Bernard of Lippe-Biesterfeld, born June 29, 1911, known as the Prince of the Netherlands since the accession of Juliana. They have 4 daughters, Princess Beatrix Wilhelmina Armgard, born Jan. 31, 1938, heir presumptive, married Claus von Amsberg, West German diplomat, Mar. 10, 1966. On Apr. 27, 1967, Princess Beatrix gave birth to a son, Willem-Alexander, Prince of Orange, first male heir to the throne in 3 generations.

Education and Religion. There is complete liberty of worship. The royal family belongs to the Netherlands Reformed Church. The population is 39.5% Roman Catholic; 30% Protestant; others 8%; non-church members 22.5%. Education is obligatory from ages 6 through 15. Instruction is free in both public and denominational schools and teachers are paid by the state. There are 13 universities.

Defense. Military forces total 110,000.

The Netherlands is a member of the UN, NATO, EEC, Council of Europe and Benelux.

Surinam and Netherlands Antilles

A revision of the Netherlands charter, promulgated Dec. 15, 1954, raised Surinam and the Netherlands Antilles to equality with the Netherlands homeland in the Kingdom of the Netherlands, with complete internal autonomy and a voice in government of the kingdom. The kingdom is represented in each by the governor who also is head of the local government. Local governments comprise the governor, council, ministers, and representative bodies (Staten), the latter elected by universal suffrage.

Surinam, also known as Dutch Guiana, is on the N coast of South America, between French Guiana on the E and Guyana on the W; forests and savannahs on the S stretch to the Tumuc Humac Mtns. The area is 63,251 sq. mi. The population (1973 est.) was 430,000. Capital: Paramaribo.

The country is rich in minerals, and hydroelectric power is being developed on a large scale. Oil was discovered, 1966. Exports include bauxite, alumina,

lumber, sugar, rice, citrus, coffee, bananas and shrimp.

The Dutch by the Treaty of Breda, 1667, ceded New Netherland (New York) to England in exchange for Surinam.

The **Netherlands Antilles** consist of 2 groups of islands in the West Indies. **Curacao, Aruba** and **Bonaire** are near the South American coast; **St. Eustatius, Saba** and the southern part of **St. Maarten** are SE of Puerto Rico. Northern two-thirds of St. Maarten belong to French Guadeloupe; the French call the island St. Martin. Total area of the 2 groups is 395 sq. mi., including: Aruba 70, Bonaire 112, Curacao 180, St. Eustatius 12, Saba 5, St. Maarten (Dutch part) 16.

The Netherlands Antilles population (est. 1973) was 230,000. Willemstad is the capital. Chief products are corn, pulse, salt and phosphate; principal industry is the refining of oil. On Curacao and on Aruba there are large oil refineries, processing crude oil from Venezuela. Tourism is an important industry.

New Zealand

Capital: Wellington. Area: 103,736 sq. mi. (268,676 sq. km). Population (est. 1973): 2,961,869. Monetary unit: New Zealand dollar.

The main islands of New Zealand lie in the South Pacific about 1,300 mi. E of Australia; total area is about that of Colorado. Including remote islands to the N and the Ross Dependency to the S, the reach of New Zealand is from the tropics to Antarctica.

Snow-topped mountains, smoking volcanoes, deep fjords, boiling geysers, golden beaches and the glow-worm caves of Waitomo are among attractions.

New Zealand comprises **North Island,** 44,281 sq. mi.; **South Island,** 58,093 sq. mi.; **Stewart Island,** 670 sq. mi.; **Chatham Islands,** 372 sq. mi. Both the North and South Islands slightly exceed 500 mi. in length. Cook Strait, separating the two, is only 16 mi. wide at its narrowest.

In 1965, the **Cook Islands** (pop. 1972, 21,217; area 93 sq. mi.) became self-governing although New Zealand retains responsibility for defense and foreign affairs.

Wellington and Auckland, on North Is., are the chief ports. South Is. has the picturesque Southern Alps and Tasman, Fox and Franz Josef Glaciers. There are 15 named peaks over 10,000 ft., the highest being Mt. Cook, 12,349 ft. Christchurch and Dunedin are the main cities of South Is.

Resources and Industries. New Zealand is largely dependent on agricultural products for export income; wool, meat and dairy products account for 80% of the total value. Next to Australia, New Zealand is the world's largest exporter of meat (mostly lamb).

Imports totaled $2.19 billion (in U.S. dollars) in 1973; $1.5 billion in 1972. Exports were $2.57 billion in 1973; $1.8 billion in 1972.

Agriculture engages 13% of the population, manufacturing industries 27%. Private enterprise is basic in the economy, but state ownership or regulation affects many industries. Railroads are largely state-owned.

Food processing is the largest industry with value added amounting to about $180 million; forest products account for more than $126 million.

The pulp and paper industry on North Is. is partly powered by natural steam from volcanic areas. The first iron and steel plant commenced production in 1968. Natural gas was discovered at Kapuni, North Is., 1967, and is piped to several towns. A large hydroelectric plant at Lake Manapouri, South Is., began providing power for an aluminum smelter in 1971.

About 200,000 tourists visit New Zealand annually, over 50,000 of them from the U.S.

History and Government. New Zealand was discovered in 1642 by Abel Janszoon Tasman, a Dutch navigator, and its coasts were explored by British Capt. James Cook, 1769-1770. British sovereignty was proclaimed in 1840, with organized settlement commencing in the same year. Representative institutions were granted in 1853. The Colony became a Dominion in 1907 and an independent member of the Commonwealth in 1947.

The native Maoris are Polynesians. Early in the 19th Century they numbered an est. 200,000; violence and European diseases cut them to 40,000 by the end of the century. Recently they have increased at 3% annually and totaled 239,136 in 1973.

Government consists of a governor-general, representing the British Crown; a House of Representatives whose members are elected by universal suffrage for a 3-year term; a prime minister and Cabinet who are members of the House and accountable to it. In Nov. 1972 elections the Labor party returned to power after 12 years of National (conservative) party rule.

In July 1973, to protest France's testing of nuclear devices above Mururoa Atoll, a New Zealand Navy frigate cruised just outside the French South Pacific island's 12-mi. limit but within the test area.

New Zealand is a member of the UN, Commonwealth, SEATO and ANZUS.

New Zealand's tax rates reach a maximum of 50 cents per dollar at the $12,000 income level. "Cradle-to-grave" social security includes maternity, school, medical, hospital, medicine, pension and other benefits.

Education and Religion. Education is free and compulsory between the ages of 6 and 15. There are 6 universities. The Anglican and Presbyterian Churches have the largest followings.

Defense. Military forces total 12,700. New Zealand had a force of 265 in Vietnam in 1971; it was withdrawn at the end of that year.

Ross Dependency, administered by New Zealand since 1923, comprises 160,000 sq. mi. of Antarctic territory.

Nicaragua

Capital: Managua. Area: 57,143 sq. mi. Population (UN est. 1973): 2,010,000. Monetary unit: Cordoba.

Nicaragua, largest of the Central or Middle American States, lies between the Caribbean and the Pacific with more than 200 mi. of coastline on each. The country is bordered by Honduras on the N and Costa Rica on the S. The Cordillera range of mountains, including many volcanic peaks, runs NW-SE through the middle of the country. Between this range and a range of t`\e volcanic peaks to the W lie Lake Managua, 38 mi. by 15, and Lake Nicaragua, 100 mi. by 45, of great importance to the transport system. The government-owned Pacific Railroad, Corinto to Leon and Managua to Granada, 171 mi., is the principal rail line.

Resources and Industries. The nation has valuable forests, some gold is mined. It is essentially an agricultural country, but industrialization, including oil refining, is growing. On the broad tropical plains of the east coast, bananas, cotton, fruit and yucca are cultivated. Products of the western half include coffee, sugar, corn, beans, cocoa, rice, tobacco and wheat.

Cotton, coffee and sugar account for 70% of the value of exports.

A severe earthquake, Dec. 23, 1972, destroyed much of Managua; about 10,000 died and 200,000 were left homeless. The nation was also hit by severe drought, lasting into 1973.

History and Government. After gaining independence from Spain, 1821, Nicaragua was united for a short period with Mexico then with the United Provinces of Central America, finally becoming an independent republic, 1838.

The constitution, revised in 1960, provided for a Congress of 2 chambers, a House of Deputies of 45 members and a Senate of 18 members, all elected by popular vote. Ex-presidents also serve in the Senate and are appointed for life. The president is elected for 5 years and may not succeed himself.

Gen. Anastasio Somoza Debayle was elected presi-

dent 1967. He resigned 1972 and was succeeded by a 3-man National Junta. He was elected president again Sept. 1, 1974.

Education and Religion. Roman Catholicism is the prevailing religion. There are 3 universities. Spanish is the official language Nicaragua is a UN and OAS member.

Niger

Capital: Niamey. Area: 489,206 sq. mi. Population (UN est. 1973): 4,300,000. Monetary unit: CFA franc.

The Republic of the Niger, a former French Overseas Territory in the heart of West Africa, is bounded by Libya, Algeria, Chad, Upper Volta, Dahomey, Nigeria and Mali. Chief access to the country, a vast plateau almost twice the size of Texas, is by air. The Niger River flows through the western corner.

Niger became fully independent Aug. 3, 1960. It signed a bilateral agreement Apr. 24, 1961, retaining close ties with France. The republic has a president and National Assembly, elected for 5-year terms. Hamani Diori, president since independence, was overthrown in a military coup, Apr. 15, 1974.

Niger is an agricultural and pastoral land. Peanuts are the principal cash crop; livestock (cattle, sheep, camels donkeys, goats) are second in importance. Cotton is being promoted. Drought and famine struck in 1973-74; aid was sent by several nations, 40% of it by the U.S.

Uranium mines began production in 1971.

The people are predominantly Moslems. French is the official language.

Nigeria

The World Almanac is sponsored in Nigeria by the Daily and Sunday Times, 3 Kakawa St., Lagos, Nigeria; founded 1925; circulation 114,434 daily, 141,695 Sunday; published by The Daily Times of Nigeria, Ltd.

Capital: Lagos. Area: 356,669 sq. mi. Population (1973 census): 79,758,969. Monetary unit: Naira.

The Federal Republic of Nigeria, Africa's most populous country, became independent of Britain in 1960. Larger than Texas and Oklahoma combined, it lies on the southern side of the West African bulge, between Dahomey and Cameroon, with Niger to the N and Chad NE. It comprises nearly 250 tribal and linguistic groups, including the Hausas in the N, Ibos in the E, Yorubas in the W.

Nigeria's rich natural resources include oil, coal, iron, limestone and natural gas. It produces much of the world's columbium ore (for steel alloys).

By 1973, Nigeria became the world's 7th largest petroleum producer; oil accounted for 80% of export value with cocoa 2d. Other exports are tobacco, tin, palm oil, palm kernels, cotton lint, hides and skins lumber, rubber and peanuts. Under an "indigenization" program, 55% of businesses were to be run by blacks only by 1974.

Nigeria became a sovereign country Oct. 1, 1960, and a republic Oct. 1, 1963. It is a member of the UN and Commonwealth. Its first constitution provided for 4 regions with local autonomy, and a federal Parliament and prime minister.

In 1966 there were 2 military coups and periods of interracial strife ending a long period of coalition governments of the majority Northern Region and other regions. On Jan. 15, junior Army officers seized control; Gen. Johnson Aguyi-Ironsi, an easterner, made himself head of state; Prime Minister Abubakar Tafawa Balewa was assassinated. On Aug. 1, Col. Yakubu Gowon, a northerner, became head of state; Gen. Ironsi was assassinated.

On May 27,1967, the military government created 12 new states, replacing the 4 regions. On May 30, the Eastern Region seceded, proclaiming itself the Republic of Biafra. The move plunged the country into civil war.

Casualties in the war were estimated at over 1 million, including many "Biafrans" (mostly Ibos) who died of starvation despite international efforts to provide relief. The secessionists, after steadily losing ground, capitulated Jan. 12, 1970; Gen Odumegwu Ojukwu, rebel leader, fled to the Ivory Coast. Gen. Gowon announed a general amnesty.

The northern parts of the nation are predominantly Moslem; there are many animists, Christians and Moslems in the south.

Norway

Capital: Oslo. Area: 125,181 sq. mi. Population (UN est. 1973): 3,960,000. Monetary unit: Krone.

Norway occupies the W part of the Scandinavian Penisula in NW Europe. It shares borders with Sweden, Finland and the USSR. The rocky W cost is deeply cut by fjords of scenic grandeur. Norway's area is about that of New Mexico.

The country's greatest length is 1,100 mi.; its width varies from 270 to only 4 mi. at the narrowest point. The coastine, including the fjords and largest of the 150,000 islands, is 17,000 mi. long. The climate is mild and moist on the W coast, but fairly cold and dry in the E.

The midnight sun is a phenomenon of the northern area where the sun does not set from the middle of May until the end of July, and does not rise above the horizon from approximately Nov. 20 to Jan. 24.

Resources and Industries. Only 3% of the land, 4,300 sq. mi., is cultivated; rivers and lakes occupy 5,000; forests 29,455.

Forests supply a sizable wood and paper industry. Large quantities of cod, herring, mackerel and salmon are caught. Norway has the world's 5th largest fish catch. Mines yield copper, pyrites, nickel, iron, zinc, lead. North Sea oil production began in 1971. Norway has harnessed its waterfalls to provide power. Important industries by rank, are engineering (including shipbuilding), metallurgical; food, beverages and tobacco; chemical, paper and pulp, mining. Farm products include oats, rye, potatoes, dairy products and fruits.

Norway's merchant marine fleet is the world's 4th largest. It earnings help offset the unfavorable balance of trade. Foreign trade in thousands of U.S. dollars:

	Imports	Exports
1972	$4,369,000	$3,280,000
1973	$6,233,000	$4,688,000

History and Government. The first supreme ruler of Norway was Harald the Fairhaired who came to power in 872 A.D. Between 800 and 1000, Norway's Vikings raided and occupied parts of Europe. Christianity was introduced 1030.

The country was united with Denmark 1381-1814, and with Sweden 1814-1905. When the Swedish union was dissolved, a Danish prince was named King Haakon VII of Norway. Nazi Germany attacked Norway Apr. 9, 1940, and held it until liberation May 8, 1945.

Norway is a constitutional monarchy . The king is Olav V (born July 2, 1903), son of Haakon VII; he became king Sept. 21, 1957. The heir to the throne, Crown Prince Harald, was born Feb. 21, 1937.

Legislative power is vested in the Storting, whose 150 members are elected for 4 years. Executive power is held by a prime minister and his cabinet.

Social security includes health and unemployment insurance and pensions.

Education and Religion. The Evangelical Lutheran religion is endowed by the state. All religions enjoy complete freedom of worship. Education is free at all levels and compulsory from ages 7 to 16. Universities are subsidized by the state.

Defense. Armed forces total 41,000.

Norway is a member of UN, NATO, EFTA, Nordic Council and Council of Europe. A trade agreement was reached with the EEC in 1973.

Spitsbergen (Svalbard)

Spitsbergen is a group of mountainous islands in the Arctic Ocean, c. 23,957 sq. mi., pop. varying seasonally from 1,500 to 3,000, incorporated in Norway as Svalbard. The largest, West Spitsbergen, c. 15,000 sq. mi., seat of governor, is about 370 mi. N of Norway. Named Svalbard by Norse who discovered it in 1194, it was visited by Barents 1596 and became locale of whaling until 19th Century. By a treaty signed in Paris, 1920, major European powers recognized the sovereignty of Norway, which incorporated it 1925. Sealing, fishing are followed; there are rich coal deposits. Mt. Newton (West Spitsbergen) is 5,633 ft. tall.

Oman

Capital: Muscat. Area: 82,000 sq. mi. Population (UN est. 1973): 720,000. Monetary unit: Riyal Omani.

The Sultanate of Oman (formerly Muscat and Oman) is an independent monarchy occupying the E corner of the Arabian Peninsula and including the tip of a nearby peninsula, Ruus-al-Jebal, to the N. The Sultanate has a coastline of 1,000 mi. along the Gulf of Oman to the NE and the Arabian Sea to the SE. Climate is generally hot and dry.

There is a narrow coastal plain up to 10 mi. wide, a range of barren mountains with Jebal Akhdar, the highest, reaching c. 9,900 ft., and a wide, stony, mostly waterless plateau averaging 1,000 ft. in altitude. The Sultanate is the size of Utah.

Exports are mainly oil, dates and some dried fish, limes and pomegranates. Cultivated areas also produce bananas, grapes, wheat, vegetables, coconuts and frankincense. Goats and sheep are raised.

Oil was discovered in 1964 and production began in 1967. By 1972 Oman was the world's 16th largest producer.

The people are predominantly Arab, but there are also Indians, Baluchi, Negroes and others. The language is Arabic, but Hindi, Urdu, Baluchi and others are also spoken. The religion is mainly Islam of the Ibadhi sect.

A long history of rule by other lands ended with ouster of the Persians in 1744. On July 23, 1970, Sultan Said bin Taimur was overthrown by his son, who became Sultan Qabus bin Said. The new sultan changed the nation s name to Sultanate of Oman. He launched a domestic development program and battled leftist rebels in the southern Dhofar area. The government received arms aid from Iran; the guerrillas reportedly got arms from Iraq and the Peoples Democratic Republic of Yemen.

Pakistan

Capital: Islamabad. Area: 342,750 sq. mi. Population (UN est. 1973): 66,750,000. Monetary unit: Rupee.

Pakistan became a sovereign nation Aug. 14, 1947, when what had been the British Empire of India achieved independence and was partitioned into 2 countries, Pakistan and India. At first a dominion, Pakistan declared itself a republic on Mar. 23, 1956.

Pakistan was divided into 2 sections, West Pakistan and East Pakistan. The 2 areas were nearly 1,000 mi. apart on opposite sides of India.

East Pakistan became the separate, independent nation of Bangladesh as a result of its 1971 rebellion and the Dec. 3-17, 1971, Pakistan-India war.

Pakistan (the former West Pakistan) adjoins Iran, Afghanistan, India and the Arabian Sea. In the NE is Kashmir, ownership long disputed with India.

Pakistan is a land of rugged mountains and river valleys, where irrigation aids agriculture, the occupation of 80% of the people. The Indus flows for c.1.-

000 mi. from the base of the Himalayas to the Arabian Sea and with its tributaries supplies reservoirs, canals and hydroelectric plants. In the W are the Hindu Kush Mts., with Tirich Mir 25,230 ft. In the N is Mt. K2 (Godwin Austen), 28,250 ft., 2d highest in the world. The climate is mostly dry with little rainfall and summer temperatures up to 120°F.

Resources and Industries. Rice, wheat, cotton, oilseeds, tobacco, sugar, flour, wool and fish are important products. Minerals include sulphur, gypsum, salt, chromite, cement, petroleum, gas, coal, asbestos, antimony, magnesite and silica.

Pakistan manufactures cotton textiles (its largest industry), wool, silk, rayon, cement, card and paper board, sugar, chemicals, dyes, synthetic fertilizers.

Foreign trade in thousands of U.S. dollars:

	Imports	Exports
1972	$681,000	$697,000
1973	$981,000	$958,000

History and Government. The land now called Pakistan shares the 5,000-year history of the India-Pakistan sub-continent. At the present day sites of Harappa and Mohenjo Daro, the Indus Valley Civilization, with large cities and elaborate irrigation systems, flourished c. 4000-2500 B.C.

A lasting influence on Pakistan was the arrival of Islam with the first Arab invasion of 711 A.D.

After World War I the Moslems of British India began agitation for minority rights in elections.

Mohammad Ali Jinnah (1876-1948) was the principal architect of the Pakistan state. A lawyer who studied in England, he was a leader of the Moslem League from 1916, and worked for constitutional reform and dominion status for India. Convinced Moslem-Hindu relations in government were irreconcilable, he advocated a separate Moslem state in 1940.

When the British withdrew Aug. 14, 1947, the Islamic majority areas of India acquired self-government as Pakistan, with dominion status in the Commonwealth. Jinnah became the first governor-general (1947-1948). He died in 1948.

Pakistan became a republic in 1956. In Oct. 1958, Gen. Mohammad Ayub Khan took power in a coup. He was elected president in 1960 and reelected in 1965. Pakistan had a National Assembly (legislature) with equal membership from East and West Pakistan, and 2 Provincial Assemblies.

Ayub resigned Mar. 25, 1969, after several months of violent rioting and unrest, most of it in East Pakistan. There were demands for a parliamentary form of government, for direct elections and economic reforms. In East Pakistan, which had about 56% of the population, there were demands for greater political power or autonomy.

The government was turned over to Gen. Agha Mohammad Yahya Khan and martial law was declared; Yahya assumed the presidency.

The Awami League, which sought regional autonomy for East Pakistan, won a majority in Dec. 1970 elections to a National Assembly which was to write a new constitution. In March 1971 Yahya postponed the Assembly. Rioting and strikes broke out in the East.

On Mar. 25, 1971, government troops launched attacks in the East, allegedly to forestall an Awami League rebellion. The Easterners proclaimed the independent nation of Bangladesh. In months of widespread fighting estimates of those killed ran as high as a million. Some 10 million Easterners fled into India. Pakistan charged India with aiding the rebels; India said Pakistan troops fired across the border.

Pakistan and India went to war Dec. 3, 1971, on both the East and West fronts. Pakistan troops in the East surrendered Dec. 16; Pakistan agreed to a cease-fire in the West Dec. 17. India recognized Bangladesh as a separate nation Dec. 6.

Yahya resigned as president Dec. 20 and Zulfikar Ali Bhutto, leader of the Pakistan People's party, which had won the most West Pakistan votes in the Dec. 1970 elections, became presidnet. In 1972 he announced new land reforms and said the government would control management of major industries.

On July 3, 1972, Pakistan and India signed a pact agreeing to withdraw troops from their borders and seek peaceful solutions to all problems.

In Aug. 1973 India agreed to release 93,000 Pakistani prisoners held since 1971. The return was completed in April 1974. Pakistan agreed to release 175,000 Bengali nationals stranded in Pakistan, and agreed to accept Biharis (non-Bengalis) unwanted in Bangladesh.

A new constitution adopted Apr. 10, 1973, made Pakistan a federal Islamic republic, with a 2-chamber Parliament and a president, but with executive power given to the prime minister. Bhutto became prime minister Aug. 15.

(See article on India for disputes over Kashmir, Rann of Cutch, etc.).

Education and Religion. Most of the population is Moslem. Free and compulsory education is a prime goal. Urdu is the national language.

Defense. Armed forces total 400,000.

Pakistan is a member of the UN and CENTO. Following border warfare between India and Communist China in 1962, Pakistan made commercial and aid agreements with Communist China. U.S. aid to both Pakistan and India was suspended during the 1966 war over Kashmir but both economic aid and "nonlethal" military aid were resumed in 1966. Military aid was suspended again in 1971. The U.S. agreed in 1973 to sell "non-lethal" military equipment to both Pakistan and India.

Panama

Capital: Panama. Area: 28,753 sq. mi. Population (UN est. 1973): 1,570,000. Monetary unit: Balboa.

The Republic of Panama occupies the isthmus of Panama, connecting Central and South America. Smaller than South Carolina, it has a shoreline of 477 mi. on the Caribbean and 767 mi. on the Pacific. Its width varies from about 37 to 110 mi. It is bounded by Colombia and Costa Rica, and is bisected by the 10-mi. wide U.S. Canal Zone.

Resources and Industries. Panama has extensive forests, and exports mahogany. Only about half of the rich arable land is cultivated. Sufficient cement, clay and salt are produced for domestic needs. Bananas are the main export, rivaled by products of a large petroleum refinery (which imports crude oil). Also exported are pineapples, cocoa, coconuts, sugar, shrimp.

Due to easy Panama ship regulations and strictures in the U.S., merchant tonnage registered in Panama since World War II ranks high in size. Registered number of ships more than 1,000 gross tons each is over 1,100.

History and Government. The coast of Panama was discovered by Rodrigo de Bastidas, sailing with Columbus for Spain in 1501, and was visited by Columbus in 1502. Vasco Nunez de Balboa crossed the isthmus and "discovered" the Pacific Ocean Sept. 13, 1513. Spanish colonies were ravaged by Francis Drake, 1572-95, and Henry Morgan, 1668-71. Morgan destroyed the old city of Panama which had been founded in 1519. Freed from Spain, Panama joined Colombia in 1821. Separatist forces in Panama sought to gain independence from Colombia several times.

Panama declared its independence from Colombia Nov. 3, 1903, with U.S. recognition. U.S. Naval forces discouraged action by Colombia. On Nov. 18, 1903, Panama granted use, occupation and control of the Canal Zone to the U.S. by treaty, ratified Feb. 26, 1904. *(See also Canal Zone and Panama Canal.)*

Rioting began Jan. 9, 1964, in a dispute over the flying of the U.S. and Panamanian flags and terms of the 1903 treaty. At least 21 Panamanians and 3 U.S. soldiers died in the rioting.

In 1967 new treaties were proposed, but in 1970 Panama said the proposed treaties were unacceptable. New negotiations started in 1971. In Feb. 1974 the U.S. and Panama agreed to negotiate a new treaty which would give the U.S. the right to operate and protect the canal for a certain period, with Panama sharing in the revenues, and would also set a date for final transfer of jurisdiction to Panama.

In a bitter election, May 12, 1968, Dr. Arnulfo Arias was elected president. Inaugurated Oct. 1, Dr. Arias was ousted Oct. 11 by a military junta.

Panama adopted its 4th constitution in 1972, providing for a president, Legislative Council and an elected Assembly. The Assembly gave Gen. Omar Torrijos powers as head of government.

Education and Religion. Most Panamanians are Roman Catholics. Education is compulsory, ages 7-15. Two universities are in Panama Ciy. Spanish is the official language; English is widely spoken.

Paraguay

Capital: Asuncion. Area: 157,047 sq. mi. Population (UN est. 1973): 2,670,000. Monetary unit: Guarani.

The Republic of Paraguay, one of the 2 landlocked countries of South America, is bounded by Bolivia (also landlocked), Brazil and Argentina. Extensive plains are excellent for pastures and farms, and the mountain slopes are covered with luxuriant forests. Paraguay is about the size of California. The Paraguay River, the most important waterway, is 1,800 mi. long.

Resources and Industries. Timber resources are large. Most of the population is agricultural and pastoral, with cattle breeding the principal industry. Most important agricultural crops are corn, wheat, cotton, beans, peanuts, tobacco and citrus fruits.

Chief exports are beef and other food products: cotton, wood products, hides, tobacco, yerba mate (tea), vegetable oils.

The first stages of a large hydroelectric project were completed in 1968-70; a highway to Brazil to aid trade shipments for the landlocked nation was completed.

In 1974 Paraguay and Brazil announced partnership plans to build a 10-million-kilowatt hydroelectric plant, largest in the world, at Itaipu on the Parana River, the border between the 2 nations.

History and Government. Visited by Sebastian Cabot in 1527 and settled as a Spanish possession in 1535, Paraguay gained its independence from Spain in 1811. After fighting Brazil, Argentina and Uruguay (War of the Triple Alliance 1865-1870) it adopted in 1870 a democratic constitution.

A new constitution, adopted in Aug. 1967, provided for a president, a Senate of 30 members and a House of representatives of 60.

In elections held Feb. 11, 1973, Gen. Alfredo Stroessner, who had ruled Paraguay since 1954, was reelected president for a 5-year term.

Education and Religion. Roman Catholicism is the established religion but others are guaranteed freedom. Primary education is compulsory, ages 7-14. Spanish is the official language; but Spanish and Guarani, an Indian tongue, are designated national languages.

Peru

Capital: Lima. Area: 496,222 sq. mi. Population (UN est. 1973): 14,910,000. Monetary unit: Sol.

Peru, on the Pacific coast of South America, is bounded by Ecuador, Colombia, Brazil, Bolivia, Chile and the Pacific. It has a Pacific coastline of 1,410 mi. and an extreme width, from western coast to eastern jungle, of about 800 mi. It is about the size of Arizona, New Mexico and Texas combined.

The Andes reach 22,205 ft. (Mt. Huascaran); 7 peaks tower above 19,000 ft. The uplands of western slopes of the Andes are well watered as are the eastern slopes and lowlands reaching the Amazon basin, where the port of Iquitos loads ocean-going vessels

for a 2,300-mi. trip down the Amazon through Peru and Brazil.

The coastal area on the west is almost rainless, but the soil is fertile, and irrigation, using rivers pouring down from the Andes, has made the area highly productive.

Lima, the capital, is in the coastal region and is also the nation's commercial center. Callao, the chief seaport, is 7 mi. west of Lima.

Inca and earlier Chimu ruins make Peru a mecca for archeologists, notably at Cuzco, Chan Chan and the Andean city of Machu Picchu.

A severe earthquake hit northern Peru May 31, 1970, destroying many towns and killing an est. 50,000.

Resources and Industries. Agriculture and stock raising occupy half the population.

The leading agricultural product is cotton. Wool, hides, skins, sugar, coffee, rice, potatoes, beans, barley and tobacco also are produced. Corn, native to Peru, is a staple food.

Peru is normally the world's top fishing nation; it takes about a sixth of total world tonnage, mostly anchovies from the plankton-rich waters of the coastal Peru current. Most of the take is ground into fish meal for poultry and livestock feed. But in 1972 the industry was crippled by a disappearance of anchovies from offshore waters. In 1973 the government nationalized the industry. In 1974, a shift in the ocean currents brought the anchovies back.

The mountains are rich in minerals. The Toquepala copper mine in the southern Andes is one of the world's largest. The steel industry has expanded. The first petroleum shipments, from rich eastern fields, went down the Amazon in 1974.

Fishmeal is the leading export with copper 2d. Other exports are cotton, sugar, iron ore, lead.

In 1968-71, the military government converted large farmlands into cooperatives, expropriated a large U.S. oil company, forced foreign mining companies to expand investments and ordered local industries to turn over 50% of ownership to their workers.

In 1974, the government nationalized the U.S.-owned Cerro mines, several W. R. Grace industries and other American companies, but agreed to pay compensation.

History and Government. The powerful Inca empire had its seat at Cuzco in the Andes (alt. 11,000 ft.) when Francisco Pizarro, Spanish conquistador, began raiding Peru for its wealth, 1532. In 1533 he had the ruling Inca, Atahualpa, fill a room with gold, then executed him and enslaved the natives.

Lima was the seat of Spanish viceroys until the Argentine liberator, Jose de San Martin, captured it in 1821; Spain was defeated by Simon Bolivar and Antonio J. de Sucre and recognized Peruvian independence, 1824. Chile defeated Peru and Bolivia, 1879-84, and took Tarapaca, Tacna and Arica; returned Tacna, 1929.

The constitution provided for a president and a bicameral legislature, all elected for 6-year terms. On Oct. 3, 1968, a military coup ousted Pres. Fernando Belaunde Terry and Gen. Juan Velasco Alvarado assumed the presidency.

Education and Religion. Religious liberty prevails; Roman Catholicism is the state religion.

About 47% of the population is Indian; most of the remainder are of Spanish descent, or mestizos (mixed), with small percentages of Negroes, Chinese and Japanese.

Education is free and compulsory, ages 7-14. There are 33 universities. Spanish is the official language, but many Indians speak Quechua or Aymara. Peru is a member of the UN and OAS.

Philippines

Capital: Quezon City. Area: 115,707 sq. mi. Population (UN est. 1973): 40,220,000. Monetary unit: Piso.

The Republic of the Philippines occupies an archipelago in the western Pacific, 500 mi. from the SE coast of Asia, 7,000 mi. from San Francisco. About 7,100 islands extend 1,150 mi. N to S, 682 E to W.

Eleven of the islands comprise the bulk of the area. The country is about the size of Arizona.

The archipelago has a coastline of 10,850 mi. Manila Bay, with an area of 770 sq. mi., and a circumference of 120 mi., is the finest harbor in the Far East.

Resources and Industries. Agriculture, manufacturing, mining, lumbering and fishing are the main activities. Forests, which cover 42% of the area, provide a variety of products from lumber and resins to medicinal plants. In 1972 the nation had the world's 5th most valuable fish catch.

The islands are rich in mineral resources. Gold, silver, lead, zinc, nickel, copper, iron, coal, chromite, asbestos and manganese are mined.

Chief agricultural products are manila hemp, copra, sugar, rice, canned pineapple and tobacco.

In the late 1960s, self-sufficiency in rice production was achieved after introduction of "miracle" high-yield varieties.

In 1972 and 1974, severe floods destroyed crops in central Luzon. In 1974, the first in a series of flood-control dams, built with U.S. aid, was dedicated.

Manufacturing showed steady gains, mostly in processing or assembly of food, clothing, pharmaceuticals, paper products, appliances. Tourists number over 100,000 annually, providing further income.

History and Government. The archipelago was visited by Magellan 1521. The Spanish founded Manila 1571. The islands, named for King Philip II of Spain, were ceded by Spain to the U.S. in the Treaty of Paris, Dec. 10, 1898, following the Spanish-American War. The U.S. paid Spain $20 million for the territory.

Japan attacked the Philippines Dec. 8, 1941 (Far Eastern time). Gen. Douglas MacArthur was put in command of the U.S.-Filipino forces (15,000 Americans, 40,000 in Filipino Army, 100,000 Filipino reservists). Japan conquered the islands in May, 1942. It was ousted by Sept. 1945.

On July 4, 1946, independence was proclaimed in accordance with an act passed by the U.S. Congress in 1934, providing for Philippine independence in 1946. A republic, with a president, Senate and House, was established.

All natural resources of the Philippines belong to the state and their exploitation is limited to citizens of the Philippines or corporations and associations of which 60% of the capital is owned by citizens. In 1946 the right to develop natural resources and to own and operate public utilities until 1974 was extended to U.S. citizens.

President Ferdinand E. Marcos visited the U.S. Sept. 1966; concluded pact reducing U.S. base leases from 99 to 25 years. There were riots by radical youth groups and terrorism by leftist guerrillas and outlaws, increasing from 1970. On Sept. 23, 1972, Marcos declared martial law to combat leftist terrorists. Ruling by decree, he ordered land reform, cut crime and stabilized prices.

On Jan. 17, 1973, he proclaimed a new constitution, establishing a parliamentary government with wide powers to himself as president and premier and extending his term of office.

Government troops battled Moslem secessionists in 1973-74 in southern Mindanao.

Education and Religion. Primary and secondary education is free, instruction is in English. There are several universities.

The official national language is Pilipino, based on Tagalog. English and Spanish, also official, are commonly used in government and commerce.

About 83% of the inhabitants are Roman Catholics and about 10% belong to the Philippine Independent Church, organized by a Filipino priest, Fr. Gregorio Aglipay. Other Christians, Moselms, Buddhists are among minorities.

Defense. The Philippines and U.S. have treaties for U.S. military and naval bases and a 1951 Mutual Defense Treaty, pledging joint action against external attack. Military forces total 42,000. The republic is a member of the UN and SEATO. A batallion of 2,200 construction troops served with the U.S. in Vietnam, 1966-69.

Poland

Capital: Warsaw. Area: 120,359 sq. mi. Population (UN est. 1973): 33,360,000. Monetary unit: Zloty.

The Polish People's Republic, in Central Europe, is bounded by the Baltic Sea, USSR, Czechoslovakia and East Germany. It is about the size of New Mexico.

Its terrain consists largely of lowlands. Gdynia, Gdansk (once Danzig), Szczecin, Swinoujscie and Kolobrzeg are the principal ports.

Resources and Industries. About 22% of the population was still engaged in agriculture in the early 1970s. Chief crops are rye, wheat, barley, oats, potatoes, sugar beets, tobacco, flax. Coal mining, shipbuilding, textiles, chemicals, woodworking and metal industries are important. Products include automobiles, tractors, heavy machinery, aircraft. Key industries are nationalized and operate under a planned economy. About 85% of the farms and some businesses are privately operated. The index of industrial production (1963 = 100) was 212 for 1972.

Poland produces 6% of world coal output and much zinc. Other minerals are sulphur, cement, salt, cadmium, iron, copper. Imported raw materials supply aluminum plants and oil refineries.

History and Government. Poland, whose history dates from 966, was a great power from the 14th to the 17th Centuries. In 3 partitions (1772, 1793, 1795) it was apportioned among Prussia, Russia and Austria, and in 1939 between Germany and the USSR. Overrun by the Austro-German armies in World War I, its independence, self-declared on Nov. 11, 1918, was recognized by the Treaty of Versialles, June 28, 1919.

Nazi Germany and the Soviet Union invaded Poland Sept. 1-27, 1939, and divided the country. With Germany's defeat, a Polish government-in-exile in London was recognized by the U. S., but the Soviet Union pressed the claims of a Lublin group, the Polish Committee of National Liberation, to which a few members of the London committee were admitted. The U. S. and Britain opposed it but compromised with Stalin when he agreed to free elections in Poland. However, he rejected international supervision and the election of 1947 was completely dominated by the communists.

Before World War II, Poland's population was 34,775,698 and its area 150,470 sq. mi. In compensation for 69,860 sq. mi. ceded to the USSR, 1945, Poland received approx. 40,000 sq. mi. of German territory east of the Oder-Neisse line comprising Silesia, Pomerania, West Prussia and part of East Prussia.

The 1952 constitution describes Poland as a people's republic with a Sejm (parliament) elected for a 4-year term by direct ballot. The Sejm elects a Council of State and a Council of Ministers (cabinet). Policy is decreed by the Communist party Politburo.

During 12 years of rule by Stalinist extremists large estates were abolished, industry was nationalized, schools secularized and some Roman Catholic prelates jailed. Farm production fell off. Harsh working conditions caused a riot by workmen in Poznan June 28-29, 1956.

A new Politburo, committed to development of a more independent Polish Communism, was named Oct. 1956, with Wladyslaw Gomulka as first secretary of the Communist party. Collectivization of farms was ended and many collectives were abolished.

In 1970, Poland and West Germany signed a treaty to normalize relations.

In Dec. 1970 workers in port cities rioted because of price rises and new incentive wage rules. On Dec. 20 Gomulka resigned as party leader; he was succeeded by Edward Gierek; the incentive rules were dropped, price rises were revoked. In June 1971 a new 5-year plan was announced, placing more stress on housing and consumer goods production.

Parliamentary elections in March 1972 endorsed Gierek's policies. U. S. President Nixon visited Poland in May; later, a U. S. trade information office was opened in Warsaw and the U. S. said it would make loans available to Poland.

Education and Religion. Education is free and compulsory. There are 75 institutions of higher learning.

Roman Catholicism is the religion of over 90%. A law promulgated Feb. 13, 1953, required government consent to high church appointments. In October, 1956, Gomulka released Stefan Cardinal Wyszynski from prison and agreed to permit religious liberty in public institutions and religious publications, provided the church kept out of politics. But in 1961 religious studies in public schools were halted.

The government barred a Vatican visit by Cardinal Wyszynski in 1966 but permitted it in 1968. In 1974 the church charged the government with seeking to eliminate it from the field of education.

Defense. Military forces total 280,000. Poland is a UN and Warsaw Pact member.

Portugal

Capital: Lisbon. Area: 35,340 sq. mi. Population (UN est. 1973): 8,560,000. Monetary unit: Escudo.

Portugal occupies the SW part of the Iberian Peninsula and is bordered by Spain and the Atlantic. It is about the size of Indiana. The Azores Islands, in the Atlantic, 740 mi. W. of Portugal, have an area of 904 sq. mi. and population (1970) of 291,028. The Madeira Islands, 360 mi. off the NW coast of Africa, have an area of 307 sq. mi. and a population (1970) of 253,220. Other overseas areas in Africa, Asia and Oceania (see below) are provinces, similar to provinces of "metropolitan" Portugal. In 1974 Portugal began freeing its African possessions.

Portugal is mountainous, but about two-thirds of the land is cultivated.

Resources and Industries. Wheat, corn, oats, barley, rye and rice are important crops. Wines, olive oil, sardines, anchovies, resins and fruits are major industries. Forests of pine, oak and chestnut cover 19% of the country, and the nation leads the world in cork production. Among main industries are textiles, pottery, shipbuilding, petrochemical products, paper and glassware. Tourism is important. A trade agreement was signed with the EEC in 1973.

History and Government. Portugal, an independent state since the 12th Century, was a kingdom until a revolution in 1910 drove out King Manoel II and a republic was proclaimed.

From 1932 a strong, repressive government was headed by Premier Antonio de Oliveira Salazar. Illness forced his retirement in Sept. 1968; he was succeeded by Marcello Caetano.

Portugal was the last European nation to hold an extensive empire in Africa, maintaining over 140,000 troops there to battle various independence movements while seeking to improve social and economic conditions.

On Apr. 25, 1974, the government was seized by a military junta. Gen. Antonio de Spinola, who had led Portuguese troops in Africa and had authored a book saying Portugal could not win the fighting there, was named president May 15 and installed a left-leaning government dedicated to establishing democracy in Portugal and in Africa.

The new government reached agreements with the former Portuguese Guinea and Mozambique liberation movements, granting independence to the former (Guinea-Bissau) and partial independence to the latter. General Spinola resigned Sept. 30, 1974, in face of increasing leftist pressure. General Francisco Costa da Gomes was named the new president.

Education and Religion. The dominant religion is Roman Catholicism; there is freedom of worship. Primary education is compulsory. There are 9 universities, 3 university schools, 4 colleges of music, 43 lyceums, a number of technical and art schools. Portugal went on year-long daylight saving time in 1966.

Defense. Military forces total 200,000. A 1951 agreement gave the U.S. rights to use defense facilities in the Azores. During the Oct. 1973 Middle East war Portugal allowed U.S. airlift-to-Israel planes to refuel there. Portugal is a member of NATO and the UN.

Portuguese Overseas Provinces

Portuguese Guinea was given its freedom Sept. 10, 1974. (See Guinea-Bissau.) Referendums were promised for all overseas territories to allow the populations to decide their own future.

Angola, Portuguese West Africa, has a 1,000 mi. coastline stretching S from the mouth of the Congo. It is governed by a Governor General and an elected Legislative Council. The Portuguese have owned it since 1575. Its area is 481,351 sq. mi., population est. (1972) 5,810,000, including about 340,000 Europeans. The capital is Luanda.

Large oil deposits discovered in Angola's northern coastal area, Cabinda, began production in 1969.

Chief products are coffee, fishmeal, corn, sisal, fish, sugar, cotton, coconuts, oilseeds, ivory, cattle, iron ore, diamonds. There are deposits of copper, manganese, sulphur, phosphates, gold. Manufacturing of alcohol, cotton goods, fish products, paper, footwear, soap, sugar, tobacco is growing. Metropolitan Portugal supplies nearly 25% of the imports.

Mozambique, Portuguese East Africa, faces the Indian Ocean and Mozambique Channel in SE Africa.

Mozambique has 303,373 sq. mi., and a population est. at 8,820,000. The capital is Lourenco Marques. Chief products are cement, flour, sugar, coconuts, cotton, copra, sisal, and cashews. Minerals include tantalum, coal, copper, gold, asbestos.

On Sept. 20, 1974 an interim government, dominated by black liberationists, was installed pending full independence, promised for June 25, 1975.

The Cape Verde Islands in the North Atlantic 280 mi. W of Dakar, Africa, are 15 in number. The total area is 1,557 sq. mi. and the population (1973) 280,000. Chief products are coffee, medicinal products, hides fruits and grain.

The Islands of Sao Tome and **Principe** are about 125 mi. off the W coast of Africa on the Gulf of Guinea. The islands have an area of 372 sq. mi.; population about 80,000. Chief products are cocoa, coffee, coconut, copra, palm oil and cinchona.

Macao, with an area of 6 sq. mi., is an enclave, a peninsula and 2 small islands, at the mouth of the Canton River in China. Population est. (1973): 280,000.

Portuguese Timor occupies the E part of the island of Timor N of Australia in the Timor Sea. Indonesia owns the W part. The area is 7,332 sq. mi. and the population (1973) 640,000. Exports are coffee, sandlewood, sandal root, copra and wax. Capital, Dili.

Qatar

Capital: Doha (Al Dawhah). Area: 4,000 sq. mi. Population: (est. 1972): 115,000. Monetary unit: Riyal.

Qatar, formerly a British Protected State, declared its complete independence Sept. 1, 1971. it occupies the Qatar Peninsula, extending into the Persian (also called Arabian) Gulf from the coast of Arabia.

A mainly arid land, slightly larger than Connecticut, Qatar is the world's 14th largest petroleum producer. Production started in 1949 and provides an income of several hundred million dollars. Doha has become a modern city with seawater desalting plants. Commercial fishing, government-aided agriculture and herds of camels, sheep and goats are also important.

Qatar was under Turkish control from 1872 to 1915. In a treaty signed in 1916 Qatar gave Great Britain responsibility for its defense and foreign relations. After Britain announced it would remove its military forces from the Persian Gulf area by the end of 1971, Qatar sought a federation with other British Protected States in the area; this failed and Qatar declared itself independent. It is a mo 1archy, ruled by an emir aided by a prime minister, Council of Ministers and Advisory Council. Its first ruler under independence, Emir Ahmed bin Ali al-Thani, was replaced by his cousin, Khalifa bin Hamad al-Thani, Feb. 22, 1972, in a bloodless coup. Qatar is a member of the UN and Arab League.

Most Qataris are Arabs of the Sunni branch of Islam. Arabic is the official language. Education is free and compulsory, ages 6-16.

Rhodesia

Capital: Salisbury. Area: 150,333 sq. mi. Population (UN est. 1972): 5,690,000. Monetary unit: Rhodesian dollar.

Rhodesia, which declared itself independent of Great Britain in 1965, is mostly high plateau country, bordered by the Zambezi River and Zambia to the N, Mozambique to the E, the Republic of South Africa to the S and Botswana to the W. It is almost the size of California.

Victoria Falls on the Zambezi, partly in Zambia, are 355 ft. high, 5,580 ft. wide. They were discovered by Dr. David Livingstone in 1855.

The vast majority of the people are Africans (mostly Bantus); there are about 270,000 whites and small minorities of Asians and mixed descent. English is the official language but most Africans speak Bantu.

Rich farmlands and mineral deposits are the mainstays of the economy. Tobacco is normally the leading export, followed by asbestos, meat, sugar, copper, clothing, iron, chemical products, cotton, coal and chrome.

Britain took over the area as Southern Rhodesia in 1923 from the British South Africa Co. and granted internal self-government. Under a 1961 constitution, there was a governor representing the British Crown, a prime minister and Legislative Assembly with voting restricted to maintain whites in power. On Nov. 11, 1965, Prime Minister Ian D. Smith announced his country's unilateral declaration of independence. Britain termed the act illegal, and demanded Rhodesia broaden voting rights to provide for eventual rule by the majority Africans.

The British government imposed sanctions, including embargoes on oil shipments to Rhodesia, which were backed by most nations including the U.S. Some oil and gasoline reached Rhodesia, however, from South Africa and Mozambique. Some African nations denounced Britain for refusing to use force against the Rhodesian government. In May 1968, the UN Security Council ordered a trade embargo against Rhodesia.

Rhodesia claimed the sanctions were ineffective. A new constitution came into effect Mar. 2, 1970, providing for a republic with a president and prime minister; a Senate of 23 members, and a House of Assembly elected by separate white and black voter rolls, eventually to have 50 representatives each (but effectively delaying full black representation through income tax requirements).

A proposed British-Rhodesian settlement was dropped in May 1972 when a British commission reported most Rhodesian blacks opposed it. In 1973-74 there were small clashes between black nationalist guerrillas and Rhodesian security forces.

In 1974 U.S. President Ford sought repeal of a U.S. law allowing U.S. import of Rhodesian chrome.

Romania

Capital: Bucharest. Area: 91,699 sq. mi. Population (UN est. 1973): 20,830,000. Monetary unit: Leu.

The Socialist Republic of Romania, a Balkan state in SE Europe is almost the size of Oregon. It is bounded by the USSR, the Black Sea, Bulgaria, Yugoslavia and Hungary. The Danube flows along the southern border and through eastern Romania into the Black Sea. The Carpathian Mtns. enclose the north-central Transylvanian plateau. There are wide plains S and E of the mountains.

Resources and Industries. Romania has become heavily industrialized, industry accounting for more than half the total national product by the late 1960s. Industrial growth rate for 1972 was 11%. But 47% of labor was still agricultural.

Main industries are iron-steel, other metallurgy, machinery, oil and chemicals, building materials, timber, textiles, footwear, food processing.

There is considerable mineral wealth: oil, natural gas, coal, salt, bauxite, manganese, lead, zinc, gold, silver. In 1973 over 106 million barrels of oil were produced; in 1974 over 8 million tons of steel were scheduled; both figures were increases over previous years.

Farms and forests contribute 29% of the national product. State farms and cooperatives own 96.4% of arable land. Romania is the world's 6th largest corn producer; also important are wheat, sugar beets, grapes and fruits.

In 1974, Romania had over 14 million sheep, 8 million hogs, 5 millign cattle.

Imports in 1973 were valued at $3.44 billion, exports at $3.67 billion.

History and Government. Romania's earliest known people were merged with invading Proto-Thracians, preceding by centuries the Dacians. The Dacian kingdom was occupied by Rome 101 A.D.-271 A.D.; the people and language were Romanized. The principalities of Wallachia and Moldavia, dominated by Turkey, were united in 1859; became Romania in 1861. In 1866 the house of Hohenzollern-Sigmaringen placed a prince in control. In 1877 Romania proclaimed independence from Turkey, became an independent state by the Treaty of Berlin, 1870, and kingdom, 1881, under Carol I. In 1886 Romania became a constitutional monarchy with a bicameral legislature.

Romania's location on the border of warring states made it a frequent victim of strife. It helped Russia against Turkey, 1877-78. It was defeated by Germany and Austria-Hungary in World War I, 1914-15; later rejoined the Allies and won Bessarabia, Bukovina, Transylvania and Banat. In 1940 it ceded Bessarabia and Northern Bukovina to the USSR and part of Southern Dobrudja to Bulgaria.

King Carol II made himself dictator in 1938, abdicated 1940 (died 1953). Michael I (born Oct. 25, 1921) became king 1940.

Marshal Ion Antonescu, leader of a militarist movement, came to power and forced Romania to join Germany against the USSR in World War II in 1941. In 1944 Antonescu was overthrown by King Michael with Soviet help and Romania joined the Allies.

With occupation by Soviet troops the National Democratic Front, headed by the Communist party, displaced the National Peasant party. A People's Republic was proclaimed, Dec. 30, 1947, and Michael was forced to abdicate. Land owners were dispossessed and most banks, factories and transportation units were nationalized. A new constitution on the Soviet model was voted Sept. 24, 1952. A modification, March 1961, replaced the Presidium with the State Council, elected by the Grand National Assembly from its own membership. A Council of Ministers is the administrative body. The Assembly has 465 deputies, elected for 5-year terms.

On Aug. 22, 1965, a new constitution proclaimed Romania a Socialist, rather than People's Republic. Since 1966, Romania has adopted an increasingly independent attitude toward the USSR, a stand pointed up by the visit of U.S. President Nixon in Aug. 1969. Romanian President Nicolae Ceausescu visited the U.S. in 1970 and 1973. Since 1959, USSR troops have not been permitted to enter Romania. In 1974, Ceausescu declared Russia was Romania's top ally.

Education and Religion. Education is compulsory for 10 years, all education is free. There are universities in Bucharest, Jassy, Cluj, Craiova, Timisoara, Brason. The language has a Latin base, with traces of French, Greek, Slav and Turkish influences.

Romanian Orthodox clergy are paid by the state, other clergy receive subsidies but church and state are called separated. Roman Catholic orders·have been abolished and the Greek Catholic Church has been absorbed by the Romanian Orthodox.

Defense. Military forces total 170,000. Romania is a member of the UN and Warsaw Pact.

Rwanda

Capital: Kigali. Area: 10,169 sq. mi. Population (UN est. 1973): 3,980,000. Monetary unit: Rwanda franc.

The Republic of Rwanda, which became independent July 1, 1962, had been part of the former Belgian UN Trusteeship of Ruanda-Urundi. Rwanda lies in East Central Africa, bounded N by Uganda, E by Tanzania, W by Zaire and S by Burundi.

The source of the Nile River, long sought by explorers and geographers, has been located in the headwaters of the Kagera River, SW of Kigali; from there it is 4,145 mi. to where the Nile empties into the Mediterranean.

About the size of Maryland, Rwanda is one of the most densely populated nations in Africa. The population includes the Hutu (90% of population), the Tutsi (Watusi, 8%) and the Twa (2%). For centuries the Tutsi (an extremely tall race) subjugated the Hutu (average height) and the Twa (pygmies). A civil war broke out in 1960 and Tutsi power was ended. *(See Index for Burundi.)*

The majority of Rwandans are Christians. French and Kinyarwanda are the official languages.

A Legislative Council, organized in Oct. 1960, declared Rwanda a republic Jan. 28, 1961, and a referendum, Sept. 25, abolished the monarchic system. The new government was dominated by the Hutu. A president and National Assembly are elected for 4-year terms. Rwanda is a member of the UN and OAU.

Coffee is the principal crop; cotton, tea, pyrethrum, tobacco, cattle and hides also are produced. Minerals include tin, gold, wolframite.

Kagera National Park, in the northeast, covers a tenth of the country; here the flora and fauna of East Central Africa are preserved intact. Lake Kivu, on the nation's western border with Zaire, is 4,788 ft. above sea level and considered one of Africa's most beautiful.

San Marino

Capital: San Marino. Area: 23.5 sq. mi. Population (est. 1973): 20,000. Monetary unit: Italian lira.

San Marino, one of the world's smallest nations, lies on the slopes of Mt. Titano in the Apennines near the Adriatic, in north central Italy. It is one-third the size of the District of Columbia.

Principal industries are printing postage stamps, tourism, woolen goods, paper, cement, industrial ceramics. There is no unemployment. Cradle-to-grave social security is provided. A ceremonial army of 180 men is maintained.

History and Government. The republic claims to be the oldest state in Europe and to have been founded in the 4th Century. It has had a treaty of friendship with Italy since 1862. It is a member of the International Court of Justice.

San Marino is governed by a Grand Council of 60 members elected by popular vote, 2 of whom are chosen to exercise executive power for a term of 6 months. Women were allowed to vote for the first time Sept. 13, 1964. A Sept. 1973 law gave them the right to hold public office and make legal contracts.

Saudi Arabia

Capital: Riyadh. Area: 873,000 sq. mi. Population (est. 1973): 8,100,000. Monetary unit: Riyal.

Saudi Arabia occupies four-fifths of the Arabian Peninsula, with the Red Sea on most of its W coast and the Persian Gulf (also called Arabian Gulf) on the E. The highlands of the W, up to 9,000 ft., slope as an arid, barren desert to the Persian Gulf. Its neighbors are Jordan, Iraq, Kuwait, Bahrain, Qatar, United Arab Emirates, Oman and the 2 Yemens. It is more than 3 times the size of Texas.

Saudi Arabia comprises 4 provinces: the former sultanate of Nejd, the old kingdom of Hejaz, Asir and El hasa (now known as the Eastern Province).

The Hejaz contains the holy cities of Islam — Medina where the Mosque of the Prophet enshrines the tomb of Mohammed, who died in the city June 7, 632, and Mecca, his birthplace, containing a great mosque sheltering the sacred shrine, the Kaaba, which holds the black stone given by Gabriel to Abraham. More than 400,000 Moslems from 60 nations pilgrimage to Mecca annually.

Two major airports, Dhahran and Jidda, handle the bulk of international traffic. Jidda, on the Red Sea, is the main seaport.

Resources and Industries. Saudi Arabia possesses the world's largest oil reserves and is the 3d largest producer (after the U.S. and USSR), accounting for 9.9% of world total. Production centers along the Persian gulf. Refineries and piers for tankers are at Ras Tanura, and a pipeline runs from Abqaiq to Saida on the Lebanese Mediterranean coast. Operations are mostly in the hands of the Arabian American Oil Co. (Aramco), owned by several American companies. Most of the oil is shipped to Western Europe. Government income from oil, 1974, was $25 billion. In 1973, the Saudi government acquired 25% ownership of Aramco and in 1974 increased that to 60%.

Income from oil royalties defrays many expenses of the state, the cost of internal improvements and free medical care for its citizens.

An agricultural country except for oil and recently discovered gold, silver and rich iron ore, Saudi Arabia's products are dates, wheat, barley, fruit, hides, wool. Camels, horses, donkeys and sheep are raised. Some hides, wool and gum are exported. It receives UN technical assistance. A steel mill and fertilizer plant have been built.

History·and Government: Nejd, long an independent state and center of the Wahhabi sect, fell under Turkish rule in the 18th Century, but in 1913 Ibn Saud, founder of the Saudi dynasty, overthrew the Turks and captured the Turkish province of Hasa; took the Hejaz in 1925 and by 1926 most of Asir.

The form of government is a hereditary monarchy. On Nov. 2, 1964, Crown Prince Faisal took the throne from his ailing half-brother Saud at the royal family's behest. There is no constitution and no parliament. The king exercises authority in conjunction with a Council of Ministers.

Education and Religion. Elementary, secondary and higher education are free, but not compulsory.

Development of education is extensive, taking more than 10% of the government budget. But illiteracy was still high in 1973. Population is almost entirely Moslem.

Defense. Military forces total 42,000. Saudi Arabia is a member of the UN and Arab League. Arms purchases have been from Britain and the U. S.

Saudi Arabia and Egypt opposed each other during the 1960s civil war in Yemen, Egyptian troops aiding the republicans and Faisal providing military supplies to the royalists, who lost. But, beginning with the 1967 Arab-Israeli war, he provided large annual financial gifts to Egypt. He also gave financial aid to Jordan and Palestinian guerrilla groups.

Faisal played a leading role in the 1973-74 Arab oil embargo against the U. S. and other nations and continued it against the Netherlands and Denmark in an attempt to force them to adopt an anti-Israel policy.

Senegal

Capital: Dakar. Area: 76,124 sq. mi. Population (UN est. 1973): 4,230,000. Monetary unit: CFA franc.

A former French Overseas Territory on the Atlantic coast of western Africa, Senegal has for neighbors Mauritania, Mali, Guinea and Guinea-Bissau and it almost surrounds tiny Gambia on 3 sides. It is about as large as South Dakota.

Senegal became an autonomous state in 1958 and with the Sudanese Republic formed the Mali Federation, Jan. 17, 1959. The federation became completely independent June 20, 1960, but after political conflict arose Senegal withdrew from the federation Aug. 20, 1960. The Sudanese Republic assumed the name Mali. The president and National Assembly are elected by adult suffrage.

About 70% of the population is engaged in agriculture and stock raising; peanuts are the mainstay of the economy. Dakar is an important seaport, handling 4,000 ships annually. Phosphates are an important export, along with peanut oil. Developing industries include food processing, chemicals, cement. A long drought brought famine in 1973-74. Food supplies were sent to Senegal and its neighbors; 40% was from the U. S.

French is the official language, but the majority speak various tribal languages. About 80% of the population is Moslem.

Sierra Leone

Capital: Freetown. Area: 27,925 sq. mi. Population (UN est. 1973): 2,860,000. Monetary unit: Leone.

Sierra Leone, former British Colony and Protectorate, became an independent state within the Commonwealth Apr. 27, 1961. It is in the SW corner of the West African bulge. The coastline on the Atlantic is about 210 mi.; the country extends inland about 180 mi., between Guinea and Liberia. It is a bit smaller than South Carolina. Its name, meaning Mountain of the Lion, was applied by an early Portuguese mariner because of thunderstorms around its coastal peaks.

Freetown, the capital, was founded in 1787 by the British government as a home for destitute freed slaves. Their descendants, known as Creoles, number more than 50,000.

Principal exports are industrial diamonds, iron ore, bauxite, cocoa, coffee, palm kernels, kola nuts, ginger, piassava (palm fiber). More than 80% are employed in agriculture.

Successive steps toward independence followed introduction of the first constitution in 1951. The Sierra Leone People's party was dominant until a military coup d'etat Mar. 23, 1967. The coup followed general elections in which the vote was almost equally divided between the People's party and the All People's Congress.

Col. A. T. Juxon-Smith, who headed the coup, was himself ousted in another coup, Apr. 8, 1968, led by non-commissioned officers. The nation was returned to civilian rule with swearing-in of Siaka Stevens as prime minister, Apr. 26. Sierra Leone became a republic Apr. 19, 1971, and Stevens was named president.

English is the official language but the majority speaks Krio or tribal languages. Most of the people are animists; there are over 700,000 Moslems and over 100,000 Christians.

Singapore

Capital: Singapore. Area: 226 sq. mi. Population (UN est. 1973): 2,190,000. Monetary unit: Singapore dollar.

Singapore is an independent island republic 27 mi. long and 14 mi. wide at the southern tip of the Malay Peninsula in SE Asia. About 3 times the size of the District of Columbia, the main island is linked to the mainland by a three-quarter mile long causeway. The narrow Straits of Singapore separate it from its isles to the south.

Singapore, the capital, is the world's 4th largest port and the largest in SE Asia.

Founded in 1819 by Sir Thomas Stamford Raffles, Singapore was a British colony until 1959 when it became an internally autonomous state within the Commonwealth. On Sept. 16, 1963, it joined with Malaya, Sarawak and Sabah to form the Federation of Malaysia.

Tensions between Malayans, dominant in the federation, and ethnic Chinese, dominant in Singapore, led to an agreement under which Singapore became a separate nation, Aug. 9, 1965. It has a one-house Parliament, elected by compulsory suffrage; a president elected by Parliament, and a prime minister.

Singapore's population is 76% Chinese, 15% Malay and 9% Indians, Pakistanis, Ceylonese, Eurasians, etc. Industries include shipbuilding, oil refining, textiles, and food, rubber, copra and lumber processing. Port activities are the basis of the economy but manufacturing has boomed.

Tourism is an important source of income; there were over a million visitors in 1973. Attractions include festivals, foods, Tiger Balm Gardens, some 500 Chinese temples, the harbor with its junks and sampans and Malay sea villages.

Primary education for 6 years is free but not compulsory. There are 2 universities and 2 technical colleges.

Armed forces total 20,000. Singapore is a member of the Commonwealth and UN.

Somalia

Capital: Mogadishu. Area: 246,155 sq. mi. Population (est. 1973): 3,100,000. Monetary unit: Somali shilling.

The Somali Democratic Republic is comprised of the former protectorate of British Somaliland and the former Italian UN trusteeship of Somalia in eastern Africa. It is bordered by the Gulf of Aden, Indian Ocean, Kenya, Ethiopia and the French Territory of Afars and Issas. It is about the size of Texas. The population is predominantly Moslem.

Resources and Industries. Somalia has a weak economy and long depended on outside aid, part of it from the U.S., Italy, Great Britain and the USSR. Principal occupations are livestock raising and agriculture. Products include incense, sugar, bananas, sorghum, corn, gum, hides, kapok.

Its mineral resources, largely undeveloped, include iron, tin, gypsum, sandstone, bauxite, meerschaum, titanium and others. In 1968 the government announced discovery of large uranium deposits.

History and Government. Many of the Somali peoples are nomadic and include large numbers in Kenya and Ethiopia. The Italian Protectorate of Somalia, 194,000 sq. mi., extended along the Indian Ocean from the Gulf of Aden to the Juba River. It was proclaimed a protectorate by Italy, 1889. The UN General Assembly in 1949 approved eventual creation of Somalia as a sovereign state and on April 1, 1950, Italy took over the trusteeship held by Great Britain since World War II.

British Somaliland, formed in the 19th Century in the northwest, had 68,000 sq. mi. Britain gave it independence June 26, 1960, and on July 1 it joined with the former Italian part to create the independent Somali Republic.

On Oct. 21, 1969, a Supreme Revolutionary Council seized power in a bloodless army and police coup, named a mainly civilian cabinet to aid it, and abolished the Assembly. It made Somali the official language. In May 1970 several foreign companies were nationalized.

Republic of South Africa

Capitals: Pretoria and Cape Town. Area: 471,819 sq. mi. Population (UN est. 1973): 23,720,000. Monetary unit: Rand.

The Republic of South Africa occupies the southern portion of the continent and includes the former colonies of the **Cape of Good Hope, Natal,** the **Transvaal** and the **Orange Free State,** which became provinces. It is about the size of Texas, Oklahoma and New Mexico.

Cape Town, seat of Parliament, is the legislative capital and Pretoria the administrative capital. Largest cities are Johannesburg, Cape Town and Durban.

Population growth of government-designated racial groups in terms of 1960 and 1970 censuses, was: Bantu, 10,907,789, 15,057,952; white, 3,088,492, 3,751,328; Colored (mixed) 1,509,258, 2,018,453; Asians, 477,125, 620,436.

Kruger National Park, an 8,000-sq. mi. wild game preserve; Cape Peninsula, and the Drakensberg Mtns. are among numerous tourist attractions.

Resources and Industries. Corn, wool, wheat, tobacco, sugar, fruit, peanuts, wine, karacul, butter and cheese are major agricultural products. Industry products include steel, tires, electric motors, textiles, furniture, plastics.

With vast mineral resources, South Africa leads the world in production of gold, gem diamonds and antimony; it is among top producers of platinum, chrome, copper, uranium, vanadium, vermiculite, manganese and asbestos. Coal and iron resources are large. Annual production of more than 50 minerals is est. at over $2 billion.

South Africa has enjoyed an industrial boom. Index numbers of industrial production (1963=100) were 182 in 1973 for manufacturing and 132 for mining.

Foreign trade (in thousands of U.S. dollars), excluding gold:

	Imports	Exports
1972	$3,647,000	$2,602,000
1973	$5,020,000	$3,435,000

History and Government. The Cape of Good Hope area was settled by Dutch, beginning in the 17th Century. Britain seized the Cape in 1806. Many Dutch trekked north and founded 2 republics, the Transvaal and the Orange Free State. Diamonds were discovered, 1870, and gold, 1886. The Dutch (Boers) resented encroachments by the British and others; the Anglo-Boer War followed, 1899-1902. Britain won and, effective May 31, 1910, created the Union of South Africa, incorporating the British colonies of the Cape and Natal, the Transvaal and the Orange Free State.

It was a dominion within the British Commonwealth until it became, after a referendum, the Republic of South Africa, May 31, 1961, and withdrew from the Commonwealth.

With the election victory of Daniel Malan's National party in 1948, the policy of separate development of the races, or apartheid, already existing unofficially, became official. This called for separate development, separate residential areas and ultimate political independence for the whites, Bantus, Asians and Coloreds.

In 1959 the government passed acts providing the eventual creation of 9 Bantu nations or Bantustans. In 1963, the Transkei, an area in the SE, became the first of these partially self-governing territories or "Homelands." By 1974 there were 8: Transkei, Ciskei, Lebowa, Bophuthatswana, KawZulu, Basotho-Qwaqwa, Gazankulu and Venda.

The white-operated government includes a president chosen for a 7-year term by the Senate and Assembly, and a prime minister who holds the actual executive power and who represents the party in power in the Assembly. Members of the partly appointed, partly indirectly-elected Senate, and of the elected Assembly, are chosen for 5-year terms; all members must be white. There is a separate, advisory Indian Council, partly elected, partly appointed, to represent those of Asian Indian descent. In 1969, a Colored People's Representative Council was created. There is an elected Provincial Council in each of the 4 provinces.

Education and Religion. There are 16 universities, 11 of them for white students; enrollment exceeds 88,000. Primary education is free to all citizens.

Dutch Protestant churches predominate, with Anglicans and Methodists next among whites. English and Afrikaans are official languages.

Defense. Military forces total 110,000.

South-West Africa or Namibia

South-West Africa, a sparsely populated land twice the size of California, became the object of international dispute in 1966. Made a German protectorate in 1884, it was surrendered to South Africa in 1915 and was administered by that country under an old League of Nations mandate. South Africa refused to accept UN authority under the trusteeship system.

Other African nations charged South Africa imposed apartheid, built military bases and exploited S-W Africa; 36 African states called on the UN to take over the mandate. The UN General Assembly in May 1968 created an 11-nation council to take over administration of S-W Africa and lead it to independence. In April 1968 the council charged that South Africa had blocked its effort to visit S-W Africa.

In 1968 the UN General Assembly gave the area the name Namibia. In Jan. 1970 the UN Security Council condemned South Africa for "illegal" control of the area. In an advisory opinion in June 1971 the International Court of Justice declared South Africa was occupying the area illegally. In 1973, a South Africa-style "homeland," Ovamboland, in the northern area, was given limited self-government.

Most of S-W Africa is a plateau, 3,600 ft. high, with plains in the N, Kalahari Desert to the E, Orange River on the S, the Atlantic on the W. Area is 318,261 sq. mi.; population (UN est. 1973) 670,000 including over 96,000 whites; capital, Windhoek. There is a South African administrator; voters choose 18 members of a Legislative Assembly and send 6 members to the South African Assembly; 4 are appointed to the South Africa Senate.

Products include cattle, sheep, diamonds, lead, zinc, vanadium, fish. People include Namas (Hottentots), Ovambos (Bantus), Bushmen and others.

Spain

Capital: Madrid. Area: 194,883 sq. mi. Population (UN est. 1973): 34,860,000. Monetary unit: Peseta.

Spain, a nominal monarchy, occupies the entire Iberian peninsula in Western Europe, except for Portugal. It is separated from France by the Pyrenees.

The interior is a high arid plateau traversed E and W by mountain ranges. Spain is twice the size of Wyoming.

The **Balearic Islands** in the western Mediterranean, 1,935 sq. mi., are a province of Spain; they include **Majorca** (Mallorca), with the capital, Palma; **Minorca, Cabrera, Ibiza** and **Formentera.** The **Canary Islands,** 2,807 sq. mi., in the Atlantic W of Morocco, form 2 provinces, including the islands of **Tenerife, Palma, Gomera, Hierro, Grand Canary, Fuerteventura** and **Lanzarote** with Las Palmas and Santa Cruz thriving ports. **Ceuta** and **Melilla,** small enclaves on Morocco's Mediterranean coast, are part of Metropolitan Spain.

Spanish Sahara is an overseas province on the W coast of Africa, S of Morocco; area 102,703 sq. mi., population (1970 census) 76,425.

Spain has sought return of Gibraltar, in British control since 1704. (See Index.)

Resources and Industries. Only about 40% of the land is cultivable, the remainder is arid or mountainous. Farm mechanization and irrigation are increasing.

Principal agricultural products are wheat, barley, oats, rye, olives, grapes, lemons, oranges and other fruit, onions, almonds, esparto, flax, hemp, pulse and cork. Tobacco, cotton, and rice are also grown. Wine making is a large and ancient industry. Spain possesses an abundance of minerals, including lead, iron, copper, zinc, coal, cobalt, mercury, silver, sulphur and phosphates.

Between 1960 and 1974 Spain changed from an agricultural nation into one of the world's top industrial powers. Manufacturing includes cotton and woolen goods, shoes, paper, automobiles, cork and cement. Spain's commercial fish catch is the world's 4th largest, by value. Coal production is more than 10 million metric tons annually.

The index of general industrial production showed a large rise from 100 in 1963 to 287 for 1973. A trade pact with the USSR was signed in 1972. Spain recognized Communist China in 1973. More than 18 million tourists spend $1.3 billion a year in Spain.

History and Government. Spain was settled by Iberians. Basques and Celts, partly overrun by Carthaginian armies, conquered by Rome under Scipio Africanus c. 200 B.C. The Germanic Visigoths, in power by the 5th Century A.D., adopted Christianity but by 711 A.D. lost to the Islamic invasion from Africa. The Christian reconquest from the N led to a Spanish nationalist movement. In 1469 the kingdoms of Aragon and Castile were united by the marriage of Ferdinand II and Isabella I, and the last Moorish power broken by the fall of the kingdom of Granada, 1492. Spain became a bulwark of Roman Catholicism, and the Inquisition, under which non-believers were slain, converted or exiled, came into power.

Spain obtained a great colonial empire with the discovery of America by Columbus, 1492, the conquest of Mexico by Cortes and Peru by Pizarro. It also controlled the Netherlands and parts of Italy and Germany. Spain lost Mexico, Peru and other American colonies in the 1820s. It lost Cuba, the Philippines and Puerto Rico during the Spanish-American War, 1898.

Primo de Rivera became dictator in 1923. King Alfonso XII revoked the dictatorship, 1930, but was forced to leave the country Apr. 14, 1931. A republic was proclaimed which disestablished the church, curtailed its privileges and secularized education. A conservative reaction to these measures occurred 1933 but was followed by a Popular Front (1936-1939) composed of socialists, communists, republicans, and anarchists.

Army officers headed a revolt against the government, 1936, under Francisco Franco (b. Dec. 14, 1892). In a destructive 3-yr. war, in which one million were said to have died, Franco received help from Italy and Germany, while the Soviet Union, France and Mexico were active on behalf of the republic. About 600 Americans served in the Abraham Lincoln brigade for the republic. War ended when Madrid fell to Franco Mar. 28, 1939.

Franco was named caudillo, or leader of the nation. The Cortes (Parliament) was reestablished July 1942, with elected, appointed and ex officio members.

Spain was neutral in World War II but its relations with facist countries and support for repressive measures caused its exclusion from the UN in 1946. It was admitted in 1955.

Dec. 14, 1966, a new constitution, called the "Organic Law," was approved by the people in a plebiscite. The new law implied a liberalization of government policy in the areas of religion, the press, trade unions and other social and political aspects of Spainish life.

In July 1969, Franco and the Cortes designated Prince Juan Carlos, then 31, as the future king and chief of state, to assume office in the event of the death or incapacitation of Gen. Franco, who was then 76. Juan Carlos was the son of the pretender to the throne, Don Juan of Bourbon. In 1973, Franco, then 80, named Adm. Luis Carrero Blanco premier but kept the title of chief of state. Carrero Blanco was assassinated Dec. 20, 1973.

Education and Religion. Franco reestablished Catholicism as the state religion. The clergy are paid by the state. Primary education is compulsory and free. There are 13 universities. More than two-thirds speak Castilian; Basque is spoken in the N; Galician in the NW, and Catalan in the NE.

Defense. Military forces total 293,000. Under an agreement with the U.S. signed in 1953, renewed in 1970, Spain received military aid and the U.S. was granted use of military bases in Spain.

Sri Lanka

Capital: Colombo. Area: 25,332 sq. mi. Population (UN est. 1973): 13,250,000. Monetary unit: Rupee.

Sri Lanka, formerly Ceylon, is an independent republic, an island in the Indian Ocean 20 mi. off the southern tip of India at its closest point. Its greatest length from N to S is 270 mi., and its greatest width, 140 mi. The coastal area of the island is flat, but the central part is mountainous with the highest peak, Pidurutalagala, 8,281 ft. The climate is hot, with high relative humidity. There are many mountain streams, navigable only by small river craft. Colombo is served by world airlines.

Resources and Industries. Minerals and metals include graphite, limestone, iron, precious and semiprecious stones, ilmenite, monazite, zircon, quartz. Manufactures include plywood, paper, glassware, ceramics, cement, chemicals, textiles, fertilizers and vegetable oil products.

Principal agricultural products are tea, rubber, coconuts, rice, cocoa, cinnamon, citronella, tobacco. Accounting for 90% of exports are tea, rubber and coconuts.

A major source of precious stones, the island produces about 20 varieties including sapphires, rubies, alexandrites, topaz, tourmalines and cat's-eyes. Most are mined at pits in Ratnapura.

History and Government. The island was known to the ancient world as Taprobane (Greek for copper-colored) and later as Serendip (from Arabic). It was first settled by colonists from the valley of the Ganges in India who immigrated about 543 B.C. and whose descendants, the Sinhalese, still form most of the population. Descendants of Tamil immigrants from southern India account for one-fifth of the population. Parts of the maritime areas were occupied in turn by the Portuguese in 1505 and by the Dutch in 1658. The British seized the island in 1796 and it became a Crown colony in 1802. Universal suffrage was granted in 1931 and a new constitution on the British model in 1946.

As Ceylon it became an independent member of the Commonwealth in 1948. It is a member of the UN.

Prime Minister W. R. D. Bandaranaike, appointed Apr. 12, 1956, was assassinated Sept. 25, 1959. New elections were held in which the Freedom party was victorious. Its leader, Mrs. Sirimavo Bandaranaike, widow of the former prime minister, was sworn in to the office.

Her regime pledged itself to a neutralist policy and nationalized a number of industries. In April, 1962, the government expropriated service and terminal facilities of one British and 2 U.S. oil companies. In March 1965 elections, the conservative, pro-Western United National party won the largest number of seats and its leader, Dudley Senanayake, became prime minister.

In Dec. 1965, the new government agreed to pay compensation for the seized oil companies. The U.S. in Feb. 1966, agreed to resume economic aid, which had been cut off when the oil companies were expropriated.

In May 1970 elections, a leftist coalition led by the Freedom party won control of the House of Representatives and Mrs. Bandaranaike became prime minister again. In 1971 the nation suffered economic problems and terrorist activities by ultra-leftists. Unemployment anl food shortages plagued the nation in 1973.

On May 22, 1972, Ceylon became the Republic of Sri Lanka with a president, prime minister and a unicameral National Assembly.

Education and Religion. All education is free in government schools from kindergarten to university. The majority of the population, Sinhalese, belongs to the Buddhist faith. The Tamils, mostly Hindu, are est. at about 2 million. Sinhalese became the official language in 1961, but laws must also be written in Tamil.

Defense. Armed forces total 12,000.

Sudan

Capital: Khartoum. Area: 967,491 sq. mi. Population (UN est. 1973): 16,900,000. Monetary unit: Pound.

Sudan, a former Anglo-Egyptian condominium in Africa, proclaimed itself a republic Jan. 1, 1956. It is bounded by Egypt, the Red Sea, Ethiopia, Uganda, Kenya, Zaire, the Central African Republic, Chad and Libya. It is about the size of Texas, Alaska and New Mexico combined.

The northern zone consists of the Libyan Desert, in the W, and the mountainous Nubian Desert, extending to the Red Sea on the E, separated by the narrow valley of the Nile; the central zone contains large fertile areas, including the rainlands of Kassala and Tokar, the Gezira Plain and the pastures and gum forests of Kordofan; in the southern equatorial belt the soil is richest and watered by tropical rains.

The White Nile flows N through the center of the country; the Blue Nile, flowing from the mountains of Ethiopia, joins the White at Khartoum; the combined river flows N in a huge S curve to enter Egypt N of Wadi Halfa.

Resources and Industries. The Sudan is the world's principal source of gum arabic. Chief grain crop is durra (sorghum), the country's staple food. Cotton is the principal export; American and extra-long staple cottons are grown in the fertile Gezira, between the White and Blue Niles. Other important products are sesame, peanuts, rice, coffee, sugarcane, tobacco, dates, hides, mahogany, chrome. Live camels and sheep are exported to Egypt. There are textile and food processing factories.

History and Government. In the 1820s Egypt took over the Sudan, defeating the last of earlier empires, including the Fung. In the 1880s a revolution was led by Mohammed Ahmed who called himself the Mahdi (leader of the faithful) and his followers, the dervishes. British Gen. Charles Gordon (called Chinese Gordon for his exploits in China), who had earlier put down the slave trade in the Sudan, was sent by Egypt to evacuate its troops; he was besieged and finally slain at Khartoum, 1885.

In 1898 Horatio Kitchener (later titled Lord Kitchener of Khartoum) led an Anglo-Egyptian force which crushed the successors of the Mahdi at Omdurman.

In Oct. 1951 the Egyptian Parliament abrogated its 1899 and 1936 treaties with Great Britain, and amended the constitution, Oct. 16, to provide for a separate Sudanese constitution.

Sudan voted for complete independence effective Jan. 1, 1956. A 5-member Supreme Commission (Council of State) and a Cabinet were sworn in.

A parliamentary government was set up but in 1958 Gen. Ibrahim Abboud took power; he resigned under pressure in 1964; a Constituent Assembly was elected in 1965 which approved a coalition government.

In May 1969, in a second military coup, a Revolutionary Council took power but a civilian premier and cabinet were appointed and the new government announced it would create a socialist state. It also announced plans to negotiate an end to guerrilla warfare which had beset the southern third of the nation for years. The northern 5 provinces are predominantly Arab-Moslem and have been dominant in the central government. The 3 southern provinces, in which there was a strong separatist movement, are Negro and predominantly pagan, with small Christian and Moslem minorities. A peace agreement, giving the South regional autonomy, was reached in 1972.

The government nationalized a number of businesses in May 1970. An attempted communist coup in July 1971 failed.

Diplomatic relations with the U.S., broken by Sudan during the 1967 Arab-Israeli war, were restored in 1972.

On Mar. 2, 1973, the U. S. ambassador and the charge d'affaires and a Belgian diplomat were tortured and slain in Khartoum by 8 Black September Palestinian terrorists. The 8 were convicted of murder by a Sudanese court in June 1974 but were promptly freed by President Gaafar al-Nimeiry and turned over to a Palestinian liberation group in Egypt. The U. S. recalled its current ambassador.

Education and Religion. Sudanese inhabitants are Arabs, Negroes, and Nubians of mixed Arab and Negro blood; the Arabs and Nubians are Mohammedans. Higher education is available at Khartoum Univ. (formerly Gordon College). Arabic is the national language.

Swaziland

Capital: Mbabane. Area: 6,705 sq. mi. Population (UN est. 1973): 460,000. Monetary unit: Lilangeni.

The Kingdom of Swaziland is in SE Africa, almost completely surrounded by the Republic of South Africa except for part of the E Border which adjoins Mozambique. The Swazis came under British protection in 1903.

The example of neighboring former British territories Bechuanaland and Basutoland, which became the independent nations of Botswana and Lesotho in 1966, encouraged the drive for Swazi independence; Swaziland was economically the most healthy of the 3. On Apr. 25, 1967, it achieved full internal self-government under a constitution and on Sept. 6, 1968, it became completely independent and a member of the Commonwealth.

The constitution provided for a partly elected, partly appointed Assembly and Senate, and a prime minister; the former paramount chief, Sobhuza II, became King Sobhuza, a constitutional head of state. The royal house of Swaziland traces back 400 years, and remains one of Africa's last ruling dynasties. In April 1973 the king repealed the constitution and assumed full powers.

Polygamy has been the common marital status but women have the right to vote.

About 97% of the residents are Swazi, a Bantu group. South African whites constitute a small minority. English is the official language but Swazi is spoken by the vast majority.

The country is rich in mineral resources, including one of the world's largest asbestos mines, the Havelock Mine, and iron ore resources estimated at some 47 million tons. In addition, there are gold, tin, coal, mica and other minerals.

In recent years Swaziland developed a multi-million-dollar timber and pulp industry, a railway link out of the landlocked country to ports in Mozambique, hydro-electric power and tarred roads. The major export items are asbestos, iron ore, wood pulp, citrus fruits and sugar. The land is fertile and has abundant water, producing such other crops as corn, cotton, rice, pineapples and cattle. About 8,000 Swazis hold jobs in South Africa.

Sweden

Capital: Stockholm. Area: 173,665 sq. mi. Population (Govt. est. 1974): 8,144,428. Monetary unit: Krona.

Sweden occupies the eastern and larger part of the Scandinavian peninsula in NW Europe. Its greatest N-S length is 977 mi.; greatest width 311 mi. The country is larger than California, but smaller than Texas. Sweden is separated from Norway on the W by the Kjolen Mtns., and from Finland on the E by the Baltic Sea except in the N where the 2 meet along the Tornea River.

Stockholm and Goteborg are the largest ports.

Resources and Industries. Although half of the country is forested, Sweden contains much productive land on which the Swedes have attained high efficiency in agriculture. Of the total land area, 9.9% is cultivated, 2.5% pasture, and 50% forests. About one-third is unreclaimable. Chief Agricultural products are beef, pork, grains, potatoes, sugar beets, vegetable oils and dairy products.

Main natural resources are forests, iron ore and water power. Coal and oil have to be imported; oil constitutes 11.4% of all imports. Industry employs 38% of the work-population, agriculture 8%. Swedish steel is of especial value for toolmaking. Other metals produced are; lead, copper, zinc, gold and silver. In 1973, 77.2 billion kwh were produced; the Stornorrforsen hydroelectric plant on the Ume River is the largest in Western Europe.

Although over 95% of the economy is in private hands, the government holds a large interest in water power production and the railroads are operated by a public agency.

Consumer cooperatives are in extensive operation, with 1,700,000 member households served by about 2,650 stores. Cooperatives also are important in agriculture and housing.

Shipping is privately operated. The merchant fleet included (1974) 322 ships of over 1,000 gross tons.

Sweden is one of the leading exporters of iron ore and cellulose. About one-fourth of the exports come from pulp, lumber, paper and other forestry products. Other important products are machinery, instruments, autos, iron and steel, ships.

Foreign trade in thousands of U. S. dollars:

	Imports	Exports
1972	$8,062,000	$8,749,000
1973	$10,625,000	$12,171,000

History and Government. Sweden is a parliamentary democracy with a king as head of state and a prime minister as political chief executive. The Riksdag (Parliament) has, since 1970, a single chamber with 350 members elected for 3 years. All over 20 are entitled to vote. As of Autumn 1975, the Riksdag will have 349 members and all citizens 18 and over will be able to vote.

King Gustaf VI Adolf died at the age of 90, Sept. 15, 1973, after a 23-year reign and was succeeded by his grandson, Carl XVI Gustaf, 27. Under a constitutional change effective Jan. 1, 1975, only symbolic powers are left to the king.

In parliamentary elections, Sept. 16, 1973, the Social Democrats, in power 41 years, and the non-Socialist parties each won 175 of the 350 seats.

About 20% of the national income is redistributed through the social welfare system which includes compulsory health insurance, pensions, unemployment and industrial injuries insurance, family and educational allowances. Unemployment during 1973 averaged 1.9%.

Sweden was critical of U.S. participation in the Vietnam War and provided haven to about 450 U.S. deserters and draft resisters. After the war's end, the U.S. and Sweden, in 1974, ended a 15-month diplomatic "freeze" and exchanged ambassadors again.

Sweden is a member of the Nordic Council, UN, EFTA, and Council of Europe and has a free-trade agreement with EEC.

Education and Religion. The population is homogeneous, being of the Scadinavian branch of the Germanic family, except for foreign workers. About 95% of the people are Lutheran, which is the state religion. Education is compulsory and illiteracy is nonexistent. There are 6 state universities.

Defense. Full mobilizable strength is 750,000.

Switzerland

Capital: Bern.   Area: 15,941 sq. mi. Population (UN est. 1973): 6,440,000. Monetary unit: Franc.

Switzerland, a federal republic in Central Europe, is bounded by France, Germany, Austria, Liechtenstein and Italy. It is twice the size of New Jersey.

Switzerland is the most mountainous of all European countries. The Alps cover 60% of land area, the Jura 10%; running between them, NE to SW are the midlands, about 30%. Highest peak is Dufour, 15,203 ft.; more than 70 are over 10,000 ft. Swiss lakes are famous for their beauty. The Rhine, Rhone and feeders of the Danube and Po originate in Switzerland.

Resources and Industries. Switzerland's abundant streams power 431 major hydroelectric plants. Salt is the principal mineral. Watches (50% of the world's watch trade), machinery, and precision instruments are important manufactures; also textiles, iron, steel and electrical products; industrial chemicals, clothing, perfumes, and pharmaceuticals. Dairy products, especially cheese, are the leading farm activity. Machine making employs 26% of all factory workers and accounts for 34% of exports. Included are textile machinery, machine tools, dynamo-electric plants, transformers and diesels.

Switzerland is one of the world's greatest banking centers. Stability of its currency brings funds there from many quarters. Tourism is a vital part of the economy. Nearly 7 million tourists visit annually.

History and Government. Switzerland, the Helvetia of ancient times, is a federation of 22 cantons (19 full cantons and 6 half cantons), 3 of which in 1291 created a defensive league and later were joined by other districts. In 1648 the Swiss Confederation obtained its independence from the Holy Roman Empire. The cantons were joined under a Federal Constitution in 1848, with large powers of local control retained by each canton. Legislative authority vests in a parliament of 2 chambers, a Standerat or State Council to which each canton sends 2 members; and a lower house, Nationalrat or National Council, with 200 members.

Executive power is vested in the Bundesrat (Federal Council) of 7 members. The president is selected from membership of the Federal Council, serves for one year and customarily is succeeded by the vice president. Women won the right to vote in federal elections in 1971 and some were elected to parliament.

Switzerland enters into no military alliance and is not a member of UN or NATO. It is however a member of various international agencies of the UN, such as the International Labor Org., World Health Org., UNESCO, FAO and others. In 1972 it signed an agreement with the EEC for gradual abolition of tariffs on industrial goods.

Geneva is the seat of a number of UN organizations, International Committee of the Red Cross, League of Red Cross Societies and Int'l. Union for Telecommunications. The Universal Postal Union is in Bern.

Education and Religion. Primary education has been free and compulsory since 1874. There are 9 universities. Swiss German dialects are spoken by a majority of the people in 16 of the cantons; other languages are French, Italian, and Romansch.

There is complete freedom of worship; 47.8% of the people are Protestants, 49.4% Roman Catholics.

Defense. Service in the national militia is compulsory. Its easily mobilized divisions comprise more than 600,000 men. The Air Force has about 300 combat craft.

Syria

Capital: Damascus. Area: 71,498 sq. mi. Population (UN est. 1973): 6,895,000. Monetary unit: Syrian pound.

A land of Middle East contrasts, the Syrian Arab Republic has a short coastline on the Mediterranean, then stretches E and S with fertile valleys and plains alternating with mountainous and desert areas. Main rivers are the Euphrates and Orontes. Chief seaport is Latakia. The nation is about the size of South Dakota.

Resources and Industries. Syria is primarily an agricultural and stock-raising nation. Cotton, barley, wheat, fruits, vegetables, meat, textiles and wool are the main exports. Growing industries include flour milling, oil refining, textiles, cement, tobacco, glassware, sugar and brassware. In 1965 the Socialist regime nationalized most industries. Oil production is small. Royalties are collected from Iraqi and Saudi Arabian pipelines crossing the nation to Mediterranean ports. In 1973 a $300 million power and irrigation dam was completed on the upper Euphrates.

History and Government. One of the world's ancient inhabited lands, the state of Syria was formed from former Turkish Empire Sanjaks (districts). Syria was made a separate entity by the Treaty of Sevres, 1920 and divided into the states of Syria and Greater Lebanon. Both were administered under a French League of Nations mandate 1920-1941.

Syria was proclaimed a republic by the occupying French Sept. 16, 1941, and exercised full independence effective Jan. 1, 1944. French troops left in 1946.

Syria joined with Egypt in Feb. 1958 in the United Arab Republic but seceded Sept. 30, 1961. The Socialist Baath party and military leaders seized power in March 1963. The Baath, an international Arab organization, became the only legal party. In Mar. 1973 voters approved, by 97%, a new constitution providing for a 186-member People's Council but giving most powers to the president.

In the Israeli-Arab war of June 1967, Israel seized and occupied the Golan Heights area inside Syria, from which Israeli settlements had for years been shelled by Syria. Syria broke off relations with the U.S. They were renewed in June 1974.

Syria aided Palestinian guerrillas fighting Jordanian forces in Sept. 1970, and, after a renewal of that fighting in July 1971, broke off relations with Jordan.

Syria joined Egypt and Libya, Sept. 1, 1971, in a new Federation of Arab Republics.

Syria received large shipments of arms from the USSR in 1972-73 and on Oct. 6, 1973, Syria joined Egypt in a surprise war on Israel. (For details, see article on Israel.)

It is a member of the UN. Military supplies used or lost in the 1973 war were replaced by the USSR in 1974.

Education and Religion. The population is composed mainly of Sunni Moslems but there are many Christians. Arabic is the official language. Syria has universities in Damascus, Aleppo and Latakia.

Tanzania

Capital: Dar es Salaam. Area 363,708 sq. mi. Population (est. 1973): 14 million. Monetary unit: Tanzanian shilling.

The Republic of Tanganyika in E. Africa and the Republic of Zanzibar, a large island in the Indian Ocean off the coast of Tanganyika, joined in a single nation, the United Republic of Tanzania, Apr. 26, 1964. The new central government at Dar es Salaam (Haven of Peace), an important port and capital of Tanganyika, was given jurisdiction over defense, foreign affairs and public services.

Julius K. Nyerere, Tanganyika's president, became president of the new nation; Zanzibar's president became 1st vice president.

In 1967 the government nationalized all banks, including some in which U.S. banks held a part interest, and many industries; some of the latter were taken over completely, in others the government took a part interest. The government also ordered that Swahili, not English, be used in all official business.

Tanzania is a member of the UN and Commonwealth. In 1974, a road to Zambia was completed with U.S. aid and a railroad to Zambia was finished with aid from the People's Republic of China.

Tanganyika

Tanganyika stretches from the Indian Ocean on the E to 3 of Africa's Great Lakes; Victoria, Tanganyika and Nyasa (now also called Malawi). Its area is 362,-688 sq. mi., larger than Texas and Oklahoma combined; pop. (Govt. est. 1967): 13 million. Most of the people are Bantus and speak Swahili.

Snow-capped Mt. Kilimanjaro, tallest in Africa, rises 19,340 ft. in the N. Nearby are the famed Serengeti Plains, teeming with vast herds of wild animals, protected in one of Tanzania's several large national park game preserves. Safaris, sport fishing and mountain climbing are among attractions.

Principal products are sisal, cotton, coffee, tea, tobacco and hides. Both gem and industrial diamonds are mined as are gold, salt, tin and mica. Diamonds account for 77% of the mineral income, gold for 12%.

Factories include food processing, clothing.

Arab colonization began in the 8th Century A.D.; Portuguese sailors explored the coast by about 1500. Other Europeans followed and it was under a mango tree at Ujiji on Lake Tanganyika that Henry M. Stanley found David Livingstone Nov. 10, 1871.

In 1885 Germany established German East Africa of which Tanganyika formed the bulk. After World War I it was taken by Britain as a League of Nations mandate and after 1946 as a UN trust territory.

Constitutional changes gave it internal autonomy in Sept. 1960. It became fully independent Dec. 9, 1961, and was proclaimed a republic within the Commonwealth a year later.

Zanzibar

Zanzibar, the Isle of Cloves, lies 23 mi. off the coast of Tanganyika; its area is 640 sq. mi. The island of Pemba, 25 mi. to the NE, area 380 sq. mi., is included in the administration. The population is mainly Africans and Arabs. The total area of the 2 islands is about that of Rhode Island; population (Govt. est. 1967): 354,360.

Chief industry is the production of cloves and clove oil of which Zanzibar and Pemba produce the bulk of the world's supply. Coconuts and copra also are exported. Pottery, coir fiber, rope, soap, oil, jewelry and mats are manufactured.

Portugal ruled Zanzibar for 2 centuries until ousted by Arabs around 1700. Zanzibar became an independent Sultanate in 1856 and a British Protectorate in 1890.

Independence within the Commonwealth was attained Dec. 10, 1963. Revolutionary forces overthrew Sultan Seyyid Jamshid bin Abdullah bin Khalifa Jan. 12, 1964. The new government ousted American and British diplomats and newsmen and nationalized farms. Union with Tanganyika followed, 1964.

Thailand

Capital: Bangkok. Area: 198,455 sq. mi. Population (Govt. fig. 1974): 39,950,306. Monetary unit: Baht.

Thailand is a constitutional monarchy in SE Asia bordered by Burma, Laos, Cambodia, the Gulf of Thialand (or Siam) and Malaysia. It is about twice the size of Colorado with large areas under irrigation.

Bangkok, the capital, is a modern city. Its Don Muang airfield is one of the largest and most modern in SE Asia, served by 24 international airlines. It is also an important port. There is an extensive inland waterway system and network of roads.

Resources and Industries. There are large forests, teakwood being an important article of export. Agriculture occupies 80% of the population.

Thailand is the world's 4th largest producer of tin ore; other minerals are iron, manganese, tungsten, antimony. Offshore natural gas was discovered, 1974.

The chief crop is rice, the staple food of the people and heavily exported, accounting for about 17% of foreign exchange earnings. Other important exports are tin, rubber, corn, teak and tungsten. Coconuts, tobacco, pepper, tapioca flour, peanuts, beans and cotton are produced.

Foreign investment in industry is encouraged — auto assembly plants, pharmaceuticals, textiles, electrical goods. Tourism is important.

History and Government. Thailand, an ancient monarchy, noted for picturesque architecture and pageantry, is the only country in SE Asia never taken over by a colonial power, thanks to King Mongkut and his son King Chulalongkorn who ruled from 1851 to 1910, modernized the country and signed trade treaties with both Britain and France.

Thailand underwent a bloodless revolution in 1932. King Prajadhipok, a liberal, signed a new constitution, establishing a limited monarchy, but he refused to sign a measure abdicating the royal power of life and death and resigned. He was succeeded by his nephew, Prince Ananda, who was found dead of a bullet wound, June 9, 1946, and the legislature named his brother, Prince Phumiphol Aduldet (Bhumibol Adulyadej) (born 1927), to succeed him. The new king formally took the throne May 5, 1950, as Rama IX.

A military-civilian junta, headed by Gen. Thanom Kittikachorn, took over the government in Nov. 1971. Civilians, led by students, overwhelmed police, Oct. 1973, and forced Thanom to resign as premier. A civilian cabinet was named.

There was sporadic communist terrorism in the NE and far S, 1965-74.

Education and Religion. Education is compulsory between 7 and 14. There are 9 universities, 31 training colleges and many vocational schools. The language is Thai, derived from Pali and Sanskrit. English is widely used. About 94% of the people are Buddhists; others are Moslems, Christians, etc.

Defense. Military strength for 1972-73 was 160,000. Thailand is a member of the UN and SEATO.

U.S. forces in Thailand, mostly airmen, totaled 45,-000 in 1973; during the year, U.S. Southeast Asia military hq. was moved from Saigon to Nakhon Phanom in Thailand. The U.S. withdrew most of its forces from Thailand during 1973 and 1974.

The last of 11,000 Thai troops were withdrawn from South Vietnam in 1972. About 15,000 Thai "irregular" forces, financed by the U.S., returned from Laos in 1974.

Togo

Capital: Lome. Area, 21,853 sq. mi. Population (UN est. 1973): 2,120,000. Monetary unit: CFA franc.

The republic of Togo is comprised of part of the one-time German colony of Togoland, surrendered in 1914, and administered by France as a UN trusteeship, 1946-1960.

Togo is a thin sliver of land on the southern edge of the West African bulge. It is bounded by Upper Volta, Dahomey, the Atlantic and Ghana.

In 1958 France received UN approval to end its trusteeship and the republic was proclaimed Apr. 27, 1960. Official language is French.

A draft constitution on the U.S. model was published Mar. 20, 1961. It provided for a president and a 46-member unicameral parliament. First president, Sylvanus Olympio, elected Apr. 9, 1961, was assassinated by a military junta, Jan. 13, 1963. His successor was Nicolas Grunitzky, elected May 5, 1963. Grunitzky resigned Jan. 13, 1967, and was replaced by

Gnassingbe Eyadema, head of the armed forces.

Togo has received aid from France, the U.S. and West Germany. Tourism is a growing industry.

Principal products: phosphates, coffee, cocoa, palm kernels, copra, cotton, kapok and peanuts. There are textile and shoe factories.

Tonga

Capital: Nukualofa. Area: 269 sq. mi. Population (UN est. 1973): 90,000. Monetary unit: Pa'anga.

The Kingdom of Tonga, a constitutional monarchy, comprises 150 volcanic and coral islands (45 inhabited) in the South Pacific, NE of New Zealand and S of Samoa. The capital, Nukualofa, is on the main island, Tongatapu.

The islands were first visited by the Dutch in the early 17th Century. A series of civil wars ended in 1845 with establishment of the Tupou dynasty. In 1900 Tonga became a British protectorate. On June 4, 1970, Tonga became completely independent and a member of the Commonwealth.

Government consists of a king, a prime minister and a partly elected Legislative Assembly.

Agriculture and fishing are the mainstays of the economy. Chief exports are coconut products and bananas. Tourism is being encouraged.

The Tongans are Polynesians; languages are Tongan and English. Education is free and compulsory, ages 6-14; medical care is free.

Trinidad and Tobago

Capital: Port of Spain. Area: 1,979 sq. mi. Population (UN est. 1973): 1,060,000. Monetary unit: Trinidad and Tobago Dollar.

Trinidad, area 1,864 sq. mi., is the most southerly of the West Indies, lying off the NE coast of South America approx. 7 mi. from Venezuela. It was discovered by Columbus in 1498. Tobago, 116 sq. mi. lies 20 mi. to the NE of Trinidad.

Second largest of the old British West Indies and a British possession since 1802, Trinidad and Tobago won independence Aug. 31, 1962. A governor-general represents the British crown. A prime minister is the actual executive. Parliament consists of a 24-member Senate, appointed by the prime minister and the opposition, and a 36-member House of Representatives, elected by universal suffrage. The country is a member of the UN, Commonwealth and OAS.

Import trade is heaviest with England, export trade with the U. S. Exports are mostly petroleum, sugar, asphalt, rum, cocoa, coffee, citrus, bananas, cement, bitters.

The nation is one of the most prosperous in the West Indies, but unemployment averages 13%.

Trinidad claims to have originated the steel band, calypso songs and the limbo dance. Tourism is an important source of revenue.

The population is mixed: Black 43%, East Indian (descended from immigrants from India) 36%; Lebanese, Syrians, Europeans and Chinese comprise the rest. Religions include Roman Catholic 36%, Protestant 34%, Hindu 23%, Moslem 6%.

Public primary and secondary education is free to age 18. Some units of the Univ. of West Indies are in Trinidad, some in Jamaica. There are 2 technical institutes.

Tunisia

Capital: Tunis. Area: 63,378 sq. mi. Population (UN est. 1973): 5,510,000. Monetary unit: Dinar.

Tunisia is a former French protectorate which became independent Mar. 20, 1956. It is on the Mediterranean coast of Africa wedged between Algeria and Libya. It is about the size of Florida. The people are mostly Arabs and Berbers.

Resources and Industries. The chief industry is agriculture and the fertile soil produces an abundance of grains, dates, olives, citrus fruits, almonds, figs, vegetables, alfa grass. Livestock is extensively raised. Phosphates, iron, oil, lead and zinc are leading minerals.

Industries include food processing, textiles, clothing, leather, oil refining, contruction materials. Principal exports are olive oil, wine, iron ore, lead, phosphates, fruits, oil and grains. A 10-year economic development program was begun in 1962. A farm collectivization program was dropped in 1970.

Tourism is growing and attractions include numerous well-preserved Roman ruins, excellent beaches, and resorts on Djerba Is., reputed home of the Lotus Eaters of the Odyssey.

The tourist industry earns over $100 million a year. New industries include steel and auto-assembly plants, a paper mill and sugar refinery.

History and Government. A former Barbary state under the suzeranity of Turkey, Tunisia became a protectorate of France under a treaty signed May 12, 1881, after France sent a military force to combat the raiding Khroumer tribes. After receiving increasing measures of self-government since 1947, a constituent assembly, elected Mar. 25, 1956, chose a government headed by Habib Bourguiba, named premier Apr. 10. The basic law, adopted by the assembly, Apr. 13, vested sovereignty in the people, ignoring the titular ruler, Mohammed el Amim, bey of Tunis. The assembly unanimously voted, July 25, 1957, to end the monarchy. It deposed the bey and proclaimed a republic; Premier Bourguiba became president.

Under a U.S.-style constitution adopted June 1, 1959, the president is elected for 5 years, limited to 3 consecutive terms. The National Assembly also is elected for 5-year terms. A prime minister was added in 1969.

Although Tunisia is a member of the Arab League, Bourguiba in the 1960s urged negotiations to end Arab-Israeli disputes and was denounced by other members. In 1966 he broke relations with Egypt but resumed them after the 1967 Israeli-Arab war. He again urged negotiations with Israel in June 1973.

Tunisia and Libya announced in Jan. 1974 that the 2 nations would merge, but Bourguiba soon dropped the plan.

Education and Religion. The majority of the population is Moslem. Europeans number fewer than 100,-000. Arabic is the national and official language. From 1956-1968 Tunisia raised the number of primary school student from 200,000 to 826,069, secondary from 15,500 to 124,607 and higher education from 1,350 to 11,224.

Defense. The armed forces total over 24,000.

Turkey

Capital: Ankara. Area: 301,380 sq. mi. Population (UN est. 1973): 37,930,000. Monetary unit: Lira.

About 90% of Turkey's population live in the Asian portion of the country on the Anotolian Peninsula — and area of 292,184 sq. mi. The remainder live in the European part which is bordered by Bulgaria and Greece. A republic since 1923, Turkey is a little larger than Texas and has extensive coastlines on the Black Sea, the Mediterranean and the Aegean. Its Asian neighbors are the USSR, Iran, Iraq and Syria.

Central Turkey has wide plateaus, with hot dry summers and cold winters with snow remaining until May. High mountains ring the interior on all but the W side. More than 20 peaks top 10,000 ft.

The world's 4th longest suspension bridge, linking Europe and Asia across the Bosporus, opened in 1973.

Resources and Industries. About 60% of the labor force is engaged in agriculture, the products including tobacco (it is the world's 5th largest producer), cereals, cotton, olive oil, wool, mohair, silk, figs, nuts, fruits, sugar, opium for medicinal purposes, and gums. About 45 million acres are in forests.

In June 1971 Turkey agreed to stop all opium poppy production, to end smuggling, in return for $37.5 million in economic aid from the U.S. In 1974 it announced it would resume opium production.

In 1973 Turkey sentenced 3 young Americans, convicted of smuggling hashish from Syria, to life imprisonment.

There are large deposits of antimony, borate, copper and chrome (of which Turkey is one of the world's largest producers). Other minerals include manganese, lead, zinc, coal, iron, oil, silver, mercury, sulphur, molybdenum, magnesite and asbestos.

Turkey manufactures silk, cotton and woolen yarn and cloth, steel, foundry products, sugar, footwear, office furniture, cement, paper, glassware and appliances. About 12% of trade is with the U.S.

Foreign trade, in thousands of U.S. dollars:

	Imports	Exports
1972	$1,508,000	$885,000
1973	$2,049,000	$1,317,000

History and Government. Up to World War I, Turkey, or the Ottoman Empire, included European Turkey, Anatolia, Syria, Lebanon, Iraq, Jordan, Palestine, Arabia, Yemen and islands in the Aegean Sea.

Turkey joined Germany and Austria in World War I and its defeat resulted in loss of much territory and fall of the sultanate. A republic was declared Oct. 29, 1923, with Mustafa Kemal Ataturk first president. The Caliphate (spiritual leadership of Islam) was renounced 1924. Turkey was permitted (1936) to refortify the Dardanelles and Bosporus, to close them if threatened, but to permit free passage of merchant vessels in peace or war. The USSR proposed joint control of the straits but Turkey refused.

In 1968 Turkey and the USSR agreed on a $200 million loan from the Soviet Union to build factories in Turkey which would be paid for in Turkish products.

The present constitution, adopted July 9, 1961, provides for a bicameral legislature composed of a Senate of 150 and a National Assembly of 450 deputies. The president is elected by Parliament to a 7-year term and is ineligible for reelection. A premier is chosen from the leading party.

Turkey is a member of the UN, CENTO, NATO, Council of Europe and an associate in EEC. Communism is outlawed, and many leftist terrorists have been jailed. Martial law, imposed in 1971, was ended in 1973.

Long embroiled with Greece over Cyprus, off Turkey's south coast, Turkey invaded the island July 20, 1974, after Greek officers seized the Cypriot government as a step toward unification with Greece. Turkey sought a new government for Cyprus, with Greek Cypriot and Turkish Cypriot zones. (See Cyprus for details.)

Education and Religion. About 98% of the population is Moslem. Public elementary education is free and compulsory; higher public education, through the university level, is free but optional.

Defense. Armed forces total 455,000. Most of the forces were assigned to NATO.

Uganda

Capital: Kampala. Area: 91,134 sq. mi. Population (UN est. 1973): 10,810,000. Monetary unit: Uganda shilling.

The Republic of Uganda, a former British protectorate, is in east-central Africa with Kenya to the E, Lake Victoria and Tanzania to the S, Lakes Albert and Edward (also called Lakes Sese Seko and Idi Amin) and Zaire to the W, Sudan to the N. It is about the size of Oregon. On the border with Zaire, the Ruwenzori Range, identified with the legendary "Mountains of the Moon," rises 16,000 ft. In the SW there are several volcanoes over 11,000 ft. high.

Uganda is the world's 6th largest coffee producer. Cotton, tea, maize, peanuts, sisal, oil seeds, tobacco, sugar, are also produced. Copper and tin are important mineral exports. Textile, steel and chemical plants have been built.

Uganda became independent Oct. 9, 1962, a republic Oct. 9, 1963. It is a member of the UN, OAU and Commonwealth.

A long-standing political feud erupted Feb. 22, 1966, when Milton Obote, then prime minister, seized full power and on Mar. 2 ousted President Edward Mutesa (who earlier had been king).

A 1967 constitution provided for a president and National Assembly, both popularly elected. Gen. Idi Amin seized government control Jan. 25, 1971, and was named president.

In 1972 Amin expelled all Asians holding British passports (Indians and Pakistanis). There were reportedly over 25,000, many of them business and professional men. Britain, the U.S. and some other nations accepted the deportees. In 1973 the U.S., Canada and Norway ended economic aid programs; Amin seized all British firms.

Nearly half the population is Christian (mostly Roman Catholics). English, Luganda, and Luo are the main languages.

At Owen Falls on the Victoria Nile, outlet of Lake Victoria, a major dam and hydroelectric project has been constructed.

Union of Soviet Socialist Republics

Capital: Moscow. Area: 8,647,250 sq. mi. Population (Govt. est. 1974): 250,900,000. Monetary unit: Ruble.

The Union of Soviet Socialist Republics—in area the largest country in the world—stretches across 2 continents from the North Pacific to the Baltic Sea. It occupies the northern part of Asia and the eastern half of Europe. Its western borders brush against Norway, Finland, the Baltic, Poland, Czechoslovakia, Hungary and Romania. To the S are Romania, the Black Sea, Turkey, Iran, Afghanistan, China, Mongolian Peoples Republic and North Korea. In the far NE, Bering Strait separates it from Alaska.

The vast territory of the USSR, one-sixth of the earth's land surface, contains every phase of climate, except the distinctly tropical, and a varied topography. The European portion is a vast low plain with the Ural Mtns. on its eastern edge, the Caucasus Mtns. and others on the S. The Urals, separating the European from the Asiatic portions of the country, stretch N-S for 2,500 mi. The Asiatic portion also consists largely of an immense plain, with mountain ranges on the S and in the E.

There are some 150,000 rivers and 250,000 lakes. The larger European rivers include the Dnieper, flowing into the Black Sea, the Volga and the Ural into the Caspian Sea, the Don into the Sea of Azov, the Western Dvina into the Baltic and the Northern Dvina into the White Sea. The Asiatic section is drained by the Ob, the Yenisei and the Lena, each over 2,000 mi. long, flowing into the Arctic Ocean, and the Amur, flowing into the Pacific.

The Caspian Sea, with its S end in Iran, is the world's largest lake in surface area (143,550 sq. mi.). Other lakes are the Aral Sea (25,300 sq. mi.), Lake Baykal (11,780 sq. mi.), Lake Balkhash (6,720 sq. mi.), Lake Ladoga (6,835 sq. mi.).

In Moscow, the Kremlin, ancient citadel of the Czars, forms the nerve center of the federated republics. Leningrad (formerly St. Petersburg and Petrograd), in the delta of the Neva River, is the 2d largest city. Kiev, the 1,000-year-old capital of the Ukrainian SSR, is the industrial center of the south. The Crimea and the eastern shore of the Black Sea, beneath the towering Caucasus Mtns., are a modern vacationland.

Beginning in 1939 the USSR by means of military action and negotiation overran contiguous territory and independent republics. Transfer of part of East Germany was approved at the Potsdam Conference. The Yalta Agreement conceded Soviet claims to Japanese territory in the Kurile islands and southern half of Sakhalin.

Political Organization

The USSR is a federation consisting of 15 union republics, within certain of which are further subdivisions. Four of the union republics contain 20 autonomous soviet socialist republics and 8 autonomous regions; the largest union republic, the Russian Soviet Federal Socialist Republic, has also 10 national districts. The Union Republics are:

Republic	Area, sq. miles	Pop. (Census 1970)
Russian SFSR	6,593,391	130,090,000
Ukrainian SSR	232,046	47,136,000
Kazakh SSR	1,064,092	12,850,000
Uzbek SSR	158,069	11,963,000
Byelorussian SSR	80,154	9,003,000
Azerbaijan SSR	33,436	5,111,000
Georgian SSR	26,911	4,688,000
Moldavian SSR	13,012	3,572,000
Lithuanian SSR	26,173	3,129,000
Kirghiz SSR	76,642	2,933,000
Tadzhik SSR	54,019	2,900,000
Armenian SSR	11,306	2,493,000
Latvian SSR	24,695	2,365,000
Turkmen SSR	188,417	2,158,000
Estonian SSR	17,413	1,357,000

The Russian Soviet Federal Socialist Republic, contains over 50% of the population of the Soviet Union and includes 76% of its territory. Its territories stretch from the old Estonian, Latvian and Finnish borders and the Byelorussian and Ukrainian lines on the W, to the shores of the Pacific, and from the Arctic on the N to the Black and Caspian Seas and the borders of Kazakh SSR, Mongolia and Manchuria on the S. Siberia, divided into a number of administrative units, encompasses a large part of the RSFSR area. Capital: Moscow.

Eastern and Western Siberia have been transformed by steel mills, huge dams, oil and gas industries, electric railroads and new highways.

Ukrainian SSR is the most densely populated of the constituent republics. It borders on the Black Sea, with Poland, Czechoslovakia, Hungary and Romania on the W and SW. The population is 80% Ukrainian. Capital: Kiev. Northern Bukovina was added to the Ukrainian SSR from Romania in 1940.

The Ukraine contains the arable black soil belt, the chief wheat-producing section of the Soviet Union. Sugar beets, potatoes and livestock are important.

The Donets Basin has large deposits of coal, iron and other metals. Here are produced 34% of the coal mined in the country, 50% of the pig iron, 40% of the steel and 35% of the manganese. There are chemical and dye industries and salt mines.

Byelorussian SSR (White Russia), bordering on Poland, suffered greatly under the Czars from periodical pogroms and from inter-racial struggles. In the World Wars it was a field for military operations. Capital: Minsk. Chief industries include machinery, tools, appliances, tractors, clocks, cameras, steel, cement, textiles, paper, leather, glass. Main crops are grain, flax, potatoes.

Azerbaijan SSR boasts near Baku, the capital, important oil fields. Its natural wealth includes deposits of iron ore, cobalt, etc. Irrigation has boosted cotton production. A high-yield winter wheat also is grown. It produces iron, steel, cement, fertilizers, synthetic rubber, electrical and chemical equipment. It borders on Iran and Turkey.

Georgian SSR, which lies in the western part of Transcaucasia, contains the largest manganese mines in the world. There are rich timber resources and coal mines. Basic industries are food, textiles, iron, steel. Grain, tea, tobacco, fruits, grapes are grown. Capital: Tbilisi (Tiflis).

Armenian SSR is mountainous, sub-tropical, extensively irrigated with a wide range of crops. Copper, iron, marble are mined. Instrument making is important. Capital: Erevan.

Uzbek SSR, most important economically of the Central Asia republics, produces 68% of USSR cotton,

33% of silk, 34% of astrakhan, 85% of hemp. Industries include iron, steel, cars, tractors, TV and radio sets, textiles, food. Mineral wealth includes coal, sulphur, copper and oil. Capital: Tashkent.

Turkmen SSR in Central Asia, produces cotton, grain, carpets, chemicals. Mineral wealth: oil, coal, sulphur, barite, lime, gypsum. The Kara Kum desert occupies four-fifths of the area. Capital: Ashkhabad.

Tadzhik SSR (Tadzhikistan), formed from the former regions of Bokhara and Turkestan, was admitted as a constituent republic Dec. 5, 1929. Over half the population are Tadzhiks, mostly Moslems, speaking an Iranian dialect. Chief occupations are farming and cattle breeding. Cotton, grain, rice and a variety of fruits are grown. Heavy industry, based on rich mineral deposits, coal and hydroelectric power, has replaced handicrafts. Capital: Dushanbe.

Kazakh SSR extends from the lower reaches of the Volga in Europe to the Altai Mtns. on the Chinese border. It has vast deposits of coal, oil, iron, tin, copper, etc. Fish for its canning industry are caught in Lake Balkhash and the Caspian and Aral Seas. Manufacturing, grains and cattle are important. The capital is Alma-Ata.

Kirghiz SSR is in the eastern part of Soviet Central Asia, on the frontier of Sinkiang (western China). The people, once nomadic, breed cattle and horses and grow tobacco, cotton, rice, sugar beets. New industries include machine and instrument making, chemicals. Capital: Frunze.

Moldavian SSR in the SW part of the USSR, is a fertile black earth plain bordering Romania, and includes Bessarabia. It is an agricultural region that grows grains, fruits, vegetables and tobacco. Textiles, wine, food and electrical equipment industries have been developed. Capital: Kishinev.

Lithuanian SSR, on the Baltic, produces cattle, hogs, electric motors and appliances. The capital is Vilnius (Vilna). **The Latvian SSR** on the Baltic and the Gulf of Riga, has timber and peat resources estimated at 3 billion tons. In addition to agricultural products it produces rubber goods, dyes, fertilizers, glassware, telephone apparatus, TV and radio sets, railroad cars. The capital is Riga. **The Estonian SSR** also on the Baltic, has textiles, shipbuilding, road-making and mining equipment industries and a shale oil refining industry. Tallinn is the capital. The 3 Baltic states were provinces of imperial Russia before World War I, were independent nations between World Wars I and II, and became SSRs, within the USSR, in 1940. They were occupied by Germany 1941-44. The U.S. has never formally recognized the incorporation of Lithuania, Latvia and Estonia into the USSR.

Economics and Production

The economic foundation of the USSR is the socialist ownership of the instruments and means of production. Socialist property exists in 2 forms: (1) State property; (2) Cooperative and collective farm property. State property includes the land, minerals, waters, forests, mills, factories, mines, rail, water and air transport, banks, communications, large agricultural enterprises and the bulk of dwellings.

The common enterprises of collective farms and cooperative organizations, their output and common buildings constitute their socialized property. Members may use small plots of land attached to their dwellings.

"Backyard" farms, from which farmers may sell produce and keep the profit, swelled in size and number in the 1960s.

Cultivated land in 1968 was est. at 515,249,900 acres. There were 36,800 collective farms and 12,783 state farms. In 1974 there were 106 million cattle (topped by India and the U.S.), 69 million hogs (2d to China) and 142 million sheep (2d to Australia). The fish catch is 2d only to Japan's.

In poor crop years, the USSR has been forced to make huge purchases of grain from Canada and other countries. In 1972 it reached agreement to make large purchases of U.S. grains, at least $175 million over 3 years, but actually bought $1.1 billion worth in 1972 alone and ordered additional large amounts for 1973 and 1974.

The USSR is incalculably rich in natural resources. It claims to possess 57% of the world's coal deposits, 11.2% of its oil, 41% of iron ore, 88% of manganese, 54% of potassium salts, 30% of phosphates, and 25% of all timber land.

The USSR produces 26% of world iron ore output, 19.5% of steel, 19% of coal, 14% of gold. Oil production in 1973 was 2d to the U.S.; steel production led the world. The index of industrial production (1963-100) was 216 for 1973.

In 1966 many major factories were put on an incentive profit-sharing system. In mid-1966 a system of bonuses to farms and farm workers (called "Socialist competition") was introduced to spur food production. In 1973 steps were taken to group factories into "production associations" partly resembling large U.S. corporations.

In 1971 a proposed new 5-year plan set goals of a 37-40% rise in national income. Premier Kosygin stressed growth in consumer goods. But figures for 1972 showed food and consumer production actually fell while heavy industry showed gains. National income growth rate for 1972 was 4%, lowest in 10 years; it was 6.7% in early 1974.

Foreign Trade

Exports include petroleum and its products, iron and steel, rolled non-ferrous metals, industrial plant equipment, arms, lumber, cotton, asbestos, gold, manganese and others. Most of its trade is with Socialist nations, but trade with others is increasing. Foreign trade, in thousands of U.S. dollars:

	Imports	Exports
1972	$16,047,000	$15,361,000
1973	$21,108,000	$21,463,000

Early History

The first Russian state centered on Kiev in the 9th Century. In the 13th Century the Mongols overran the country. It recovered under the grand dukes and princes of Muscovy, or Moscow, and by 1480 freed itself from the Mongols. Ivan the Terrible was the first to be formally proclaimed Czar (1547). Peter the Great (1682-1725), extended the domain and in 1721 founded the Russian Empire.

Revolution of 1917

The abortive Revolution of 1905 demonstrated the insecurity of the czarist regime and led to mild concessions. The 1917 Revolution began in March with a series of sporadic strikes for higher wages by factory workers. A provisional democratic government under Prince Georgi Lvov was established but was quickly followed in May by the second provisional government, led by Alexander Kerensky. The Kerensky government was overthrown in a communist coup led by Vladimir Ilyich Lenin Nov. 7.

Lenin's death Jan. 21, 1924, resulted in an internal power struggle from which Joseph Stalin eventually emerged the absolute ruler of Russia. Stalin secured his position at first by exiling opponents such as Leon Trotsky. But in the 1930s he resorted to a series of "purge" trials and mass executions. In 1974 it was estimated there still were 10,000 political prisoners, mostly in labor camps.

Khrushchev, Brezhnev

After Stalin died, Mar. 5, 1953, Nikita Khrushchev was elected first secretary of the Central Committee. In 1956 he condemned Stalin and his tyrannical methods before the Soviet Communist Party Congress in Moscow, said Stalin cultivated a "cult of personality" and subverted communist aims. Khrushchev lifted some restrictions, extended barter and trade policies. The names of Stalin, Molotov, Malenkov and other supporters of Stalin were eliminated from regions, cities and other sites in 1961-62 after Stalin's body was removed from the Lenin-Stalin tomb in Moscow.

Khrushchev was elected premier by the Supreme Soviet, Mar. 27, 1958, succeeding Marshal Bulganin.

Under Khrushchev the open antagonism of Poles and Hungarians toward domination by Moscow was brutally suppressed in 1956. He advocated peaceful co-existence with the capitalist countries, but continued arming the USSR with nuclear weapons, promised aid to all "suppressed peoples" and to so-called wars of liberation. He aided the Cuban revolution under Fidel Castro but withdrew Soviet missiles from Cuba during confrontation by U.S. President Kennedy, Sept.-Oct. 1962.

The USSR, the U. S. and Great Britain initialed a joint treaty July 25, 1963, banning above-ground nuclear tests.

The co-existence policy alienated the leaders of Albania and Communist China. The latter continued to preach world revolution and denounced the Khrushchev methods as deviating from true Communism.

Khrushchev was suddenly deposed, Oct. 14-15, 1964, and replaced as party first secretary by Leonid I. Brezhnev, 57, and as premier by Aleksei N. Kosygin, 60. Brezhnev's title was changed in 1966 to general secretary, and Khrushchev's de-Stalinization policy was relaxed.

Communist China's Premier Chou En-lai visited the new USSR chiefs in Nov. 1964 but the visit failed to heal the growing rift between the 2 communist powers.

In 1968, the U. S. and USSR joined 59 other nations in signing a treaty to bar spread of nuclear weapons.

In Aug. 1968 Russian, Polish, East German, Hungarian and Bulgarian military forces invaded Czechoslovakia to put a curb on liberalization policies of the Czech government. The USSR declared it had a duty to intervene in nations where socialism was "imperiled," the "Brezhnev Doctrine." Although the invasion succeeded in "normalizing" Czech policies, the action brought strong criticism from Communist parties in some nations.

In March 1969 troops of the USSR and Communist China fought the first of a series of clashes on a disputed island in the Ussuri River on the border between the 2 nations in the Far East, north of Vladivostok. In 1970 ambassadors were exchanged, after a lapse; but both nations increased their border forces. The USSR signed a treaty with West Germany in 1970 recognizing current European boundaries. In 1971 the USSR signed friendship pacts with Egypt, Canada and India, and joined in a Big 4 agreement on West Berlin.

The USSR in 1971 continued heavy arms shipments to Egypt. In July 1972 Egypt ordered most of the 20,-000 Soviet military personnel in that country to leave. The USSR then increased arms shipments to Syria. A large Soviet fleet was maintained in the Mediterranean, about 55 ships in 1973, plus fleets in other seas.

When Egypt and Syria attacked Israel in Oct. 1973, the USSR launched huge arms airlifts to the 2 Arab nations. In 1974, the Soviet replenished the arms used or lost by the Syrians in the 1973 war.

'Detente'

During the May 1972 visit of U.S. President Nixon, the U.S. and USSR reached agreements to freeze intercontinental missiles at their current levels, to limit defensive missiles to 200 each, to cooperate on health and environment problems, to stage a joint space flight and to set up commissions for trade and scientific cooperation.

In the June 1973 visit of Brezhnev to the U.S., agreements were signed to seek ways to promote trade, peace and cultural and scientific exchanges. Meanwhile, under Brezhnev, dissident intellectuals were repressed and purge-type trials resumed. An-

drei Sakharov, creator of the USSR hydrogen bomb, warned Western nations that aid given Russia would be used against them.

Government

The first Soviet constitution was adopted in 1918 for the RSFSR. The USSR was formed in Dec. 1922 and the first Union constitution adopted 1923. The current constitution, adopted 1936, provides for universal direct suffrage with secret ballot. Voting age is 18; candidates for election must have reached 23. Each Union republic is organized similarly to the central government.

The mainly nominal legislative authority is the Supreme Soviet consisting of 2 chambers, the Soviet of the Union and the Soviet of Nationalities. The first house is elected on the basis of one deputy for every 300,000 population; the second on the basis of 25 deputies from each Union republic, 11 from each autonomous republic, 5 from each autonomous region, and one from each national district. The Supreme Soviet normally meets briefly twice a year, serves for a 4-year term. It elects a 37-member Presidium which serves between sessions.

Titular chief of state, chairman of the Presidium (president) of the Supreme Soviet, Nikolai V. Podgorny, was chosen Dec.9, 1965.

Elections for the Supreme Soviet are by universal suffrage but from single slates of candidates approved by the party; voters are offered a choice only of striking out names.

The highest judicial organ is the Supreme Court, whose members are elected by the Supreme Soviet for 5-year terms. Other courts are elected within the constituent republics.

The highest executive and administrative organ of state power is the Council of Ministers (premier and deputies) appointed by and theoretically responsible to the Supreme Soviet.

The Communist party of the USSR is the only legal party. Its highest organ is the Party Congress of about 1,500 elected representatives which normally meets once every 4 years. It elects a Central Committee, the party's directive body, and other committees. The Central Committee elects from its number a Politburo which makes party policy between Central Committee meetings; and a Secretariat, the party's chief executive body. The Politburo normally consists of 15 full members and 6 candidate members.

Membership in the Communist party in 1971 was reported at about 14,500,000.

Education

Education is free. It is compulsory from ages 7 to 16. In 1968 there were 41,444,000 students in 8-year primary-polytechnical schools; 14,500,000 in secondary, evening and vocational schools and junior colleges; 4,300,000 in institutes of higher learning. Illiteracy was reduced to 1.5%.

Social Benefits

All workers are entitled to free public health services, paid vacations, sickness insurance, pensions for men at 60 and women at 55. There are lower pension requirements for those in hazardous or difficult occupations. State payments are made to mothers on the birth of the 3d and successive children. In 1968 there were 35 million receiving pensions.

Religion

Separation of church and state was effected in 1918. Nine branches of Christianity are represented, led by the Orthodox Church, which in 1956 had 22,-000 congregations. Islam has the second largest following. Jewish and Buddhist faiths are also present.

In 1970-72 many Jews sought to leave the USSR. In 1970 about 1,000 were permitted to leave; in 1971, 13,500; in 1972, 30,000; in 1973, 35,000. In 1974 it was reported Russia had agreed to permit 60,000 Jews and others to emigrate yearly. The increases were credited to U.S. pressure and world opinion.

Defense

Armed forces on active duty are est. to total 3,425,-000. The Army had about 2 million men, organized in 164 divisions. There were 31 divisions stationed in satellite nations (20 of them in East Germany); 60 divisions in European Russia; 23 in the Caucasus and central Asia; 45 in the Far East. The Army was equipped with tactical missiles, including nuclear warheads.

Navy personnel totaled 475,000. The main power of the Soviet fleet was its 350 submarines, some 90 of which were nuclear-powered. Some were equipped with ballistic nuclear missiles. The Russian fleet in 1974 had over 1,000 ships.

Air Force personnel totaled 550,000; there was a total of about 9,000 combat aircraft including intercontinental bombers.

In 1972 when Russia and the U.S. agreed on a temporary freeze on numbers of intercontinental nuclear missiles, the USSR reportedly had 1,618 in place, the U.S. 1,054. The USSR reportedly had 710 submarine-borne missiles, the U.S. 656. But the U.S. had some missiles with multiple warheads (MIRVs). The USSR developed MIRVs in 1973.

The USSR is a member of the UN and Warsaw Pact.

United Arab Emirates

Capital: Abu Dhabi. Area: 32,278 sq. mi. Population (UN est. 1973): 210,000. Monetary unit: Dirham.

The United Arab Emirates, formerly known as the Trucial States or Trucial Sheikdoms, were British Protected States until they became an independent nation Dec. 2, 1971. It stretches 400 mi. along the Persian (also called Arabian) Gulf and the Gulf of Oman, from Qatar to Oman. Inland, it borders on Saudi Arabia.

The 7 sheikdoms signed treaties with Great Britain in the 19th Century giving Britain responsibility for defense and foreign relations. When Britain announced it would let the treaties lapse by the end of 1971, the 7 sought to form a federation with Bahrain and Qatar, also British Protected States. The attempt failed. The UAE was formed by 6 of the 7, Abu Dhabi, Dubai, Sharja, Ajman, Fujaira and Umm al Quaiwan. The 7th, Ras al Khaima, joined shortly. The city of Abu Dhabi became the capital and the Abu Dhabi ruler became president. There is a prime minister, a Supreme Council of Rulers and a National Council or legislature.

Abu Dhabi, Dubai and Sharja have large and increasing oil production, totaling the 10th largest in the world. Fujaira and Ras al Khaima have substantial food production. In Sept. 1974 Abu Dhabi acquired a 60% interest in the Abu Dhabi Petroleum Co. which had been owned by a group of western nation oil companies.

A 1968 census gave Dubai 59,000 inhabitants; Abu Dhabi, 49,000; Sharja, 31,500; Ras al Khaima, 24,500; Fujaira, 9,700; Ajman, 4,200; Umm al Quaiwan, 3,700. They are predominantly Arab, plus some Iranians, Indians and Baluchis.

United Kingdom of Great Britain And Northern Ireland

Capital: London. Area: 94,209 sq. mi. Population (UN est. 1973): 55,930,000. Monetary Unit: Pound.

The United Kingdom of Great Britain and Northern Ireland comprises England, Wales, Scotland and Northern Ireland.

The British Isles lie off the W. coast of Europe, with the North Atlantic on the N and W. Separating Britain from the mainland are the North Sea on the E, the Strait of Dover on the SE and the English Channel on the S. The Thames, 210 mi. from its source to the

North Sea, is England's longest river.

England has an area of 50,331 sq. mi. and Wales has 8,016 sq. mi.; combined population (est. 1972), 49,029,000; Scotland, 30,411 sq. mi., 5,210,000; Northern Ireland, 5,451 sq. mi., 1,549,000.

The climate of the British Isles is mild and somewhat warmer than that of the continent because of the Gulf Stream modifying the temperature, which has a mean of 48°. Rainfall averages 41 inches annually, and fogs are frequent.

Queen and Royal Family. The ruling sovereign is Elizabeth II of the House of Windsor, the former Princess Elizabeth Alexandra Mary, born Apr. 21, 1926, eldest daughter of King George VI and Queen Elizabeth. She succeeded to the throne Feb. 6, 1952, and was crowned June 2, 1953. As Princess Elizabeth, she was married Nov. 20, 1947 to Lt. Philip Mountbatten, born June 10, 1921, former Prince of Greece. He was created Duke of Edinburgh Nov. 19, 1947, H.R.H. Prince Philip Nov. 20, 1947, and given the title Prince of the United Kingdom Feb. 22, 1957.

They have 4 children. Prince Charles Philip Arthur George, born Nov. 14, 1948, is the prince of Wales and heir apparent to the throne.

Parliament is the legislative governing body for the United Kingdom, with certain powers over dependent units but none over the independent states. It consists of 2 Houses. The **House of Lords** includes hereditary and life peers and peeresses, legal advisers, archbishops and bishops. Total membership is over 1,000 but actual attendance is approximately 200. Women became eligible to sit in the House of Lords for the first time in 1958. Previously, women had been eligible to sit only in Commons.

The House of Commons has 630 members, who are elected by direct ballot and divided as follows: England, 511; Wales and Monmouth, 36; Scotland 71; Northern Ireland, 12.

Clergymen of the Church of England, ministers of the Church in Scotland and Roman Catholic clergymen are disqualified from sitting as members, also certain government officers, and sheriffs. Women have had the right to vote since 1918.

Resources and Industries. Great Britain's major occupations are manufacturing and trade. Metals and metal-using industries contribute more than 50% of the exports. Agriculture provides wheat, barley, oats, sugar beets, rye, livestock products and garden truck. Of about 60 million acres of land in England, Wales and Scotland, 49 million are farmed, of which 18 million are arable, the rest pastures.

Large oil and gas fields have been found in the North Sea. There are large deposits of coal, the annual output is over 125 million tons. Limestone, igneous rock and iron ore are valuable products. Other important minerals are salt, clay, chalk, gypsum, lead ore, tin ore and silica.

There are approximately 140 airports for civil use in Great Britain. The railroad lines, nationalized since 1948, have been reduced in total length, with a basic network of 11,000 mi. designated for modernization and development.

Telephone service is part of the postal system. There are about 15 million telephones. Broadcast receiving licenses in 1973 totaled 12,308,000 for black-and-white TV, 5,007,000 for color.

The government in 1967 took ownership of 14 steel companies which comprised 90% of the nation's steel-making industry, paying shareholders in the companies more than $1.4 billion in government securities. The new British Steel Corp. became Britain's largest industrial enterprise.

The Labor government raised taxes several times, 1966-69; it devalued the pound from a value of $2.80 to $2.40 in 1967 and took various measures to improve exports and cut imports. The Conservative government put a freeze on prices, wages and rents in 1972 to combat inflation. In 1973 it substituted "restraints" for the freeze.

On Feb. 15, 1971, Britain completed a changeover to a system of decimal currency, continuing the same pound but, dividing it into 100 new pence. By 1975 it plans to complete conversion to the metric system of measures.

Tourism ranks high in earnings. Visitors from abroad totaled more than 9,492,000 in 1973, of whom 1,572,000 were from the U.S.

Index of industrial production (1963=100) was 135 in 1973.

The merchant marine totaled 29,161,000 gross registered tons in Jan. 1974, comprising over 10% of active world shipping. British shipyards have an estimated annual capacity of 1,259,000 tons.

The world's first power station using atomic energy to create electricity for civilian use began operation Oct. 17, 1956, at Calder Hall in Cumberland.

Britain's aid to less developed countries has more than doubled since 1956, totaling over $3 billion and amounting to $592,800,000 in 1971.

The United Kingdom is a member of the UN, Commonwealth, NATO, SEATO, CENTO, Council of Europe and, since Jan. 1, 1973, EEC.

Britain imports all of its cotton, rubber, sulphur, four-fifths of its wool, half of its food and iron ore, also certain amounts of paper, tobacco, chemicals. Manufactured goods made from these basic materials have been exported since the industrial age began.

Gross national product for 1973 was $159.9 billion.

Main exports are machinery, chemicals, woolen and synthetic textiles, autos and trucks, iron and steel, locomotives, jet aircraft, farm machinery, drugs, radio, TV, radar and navigation equipment, arms, whisky.

Foreign trade in thousands of U.S. dollars:

	Imports	Exports
1972	$27,860,000	$24,344,000
1973	$38,920,000	$30,549,000

Religion and Churches. The Church of England is Protestant Episcopal. The queen is supreme governor, with rights of appointment to. archbishoprics, bishoprics and other offices. There are 2 provinces, Canterbury and York, each headed by an archbishop.

The Church of England has an est. 27,600,000 members. In 1970 there were some 14,300 parishes. Most famous church is Westminster Abbey (1050-1760), site of coronations; tombs of Elizabeth I, Mary of Scots, kings, poets and of the Unknown Warrior.

The Roman Catholic Church — Membership in the United Kingdom was approximately 5,500,000 in 1974.

The Methodist Church — This is headed by a conference governing body which has a president; there were about 14,000 churches and 601,000 full members in 1974.

Others: There are an est. 410,000 Jews in Great Britain; 80% of them are Orthodox and more than half live in the London area. There are 198,000 Baptists and about 167,000 Congregationalists. The Calvinistic Methodist (Presbyterian) Church of Wales has 104,000 communicants. The Unitarians have 330 chapels. The Presbyterian Church of England has 318 congregations, 59,000 members. The Society of Friends has over 440 meeting houses, nearly 21,000 members. There are 100,000 Mormons. The Church of Christ Scientist has 330 branches in Great Britain and Ireland. The Presbyterian Church in Ireland has a membership in Northern Ireland of about 139,000. The number of Moslems in Britain has been growing steadily.

The Church of Scotland is Presbyterian. It is presided over by a moderator, chosen annually. Churches numbered 2,070, members 1,110,000 in 1974.

Education. Primary and secondary education is free and compulsory from 5 to 16.

The most celebrated of British universities are Oxford and Cambridge, each with colleges founded in the 13th Century. There are 40 other universities in England, Scotland, Wales and Northern Ireland.

Social Welfare. Under the Dept. of Health and Social Security, National Insurance provides for virtually universal compulsory insurance covering sickness, maternity, unemployment and industrial accidents, and death benefits and pensions for widows, orphans and the aged. The National Health Service provides free medical and nursing care, small dental fees and minimum charges for certain appliances and prescriptions. Under the Family Allowance Act the government pays 90 pence a week for each child of compulsory school age, after the first, and one pound each for the third or more.

Supplementary benefits provide for those not fully protected by National Insurance. Contributions are made by purchase of National Insurance stamps, the amounts varying according to sex and classification (employed, self-employed, non-employed). In the case of employed, the employer pays slightly over one-half.

Defense: Armed forces total 349,269 (1974). Britain exploded its 1st atomic bomb in 1952 and has a stockpile of these weapons.

Wales

The Principality of Wales and Monmouthshire in western Britain has an area of 7,969 sq. mi. and a population (est. 1971) of 2,723,596.

England and Wales are administered as a unit and Wales does not have a separate local government act, as has Scotland. More than one-fourth the population speak both English and Welsh; under 50,000 speak Welsh solely. Welsh nationalism is advocated by a small segment.

Early Anglo-Saxon invaders drove certain Celtic peoples into the mountains of Wales, terming them Waelise (Welsh, or foreign). There they developed a distinct nationality and culture. Members of the ruling house of Gwynedd in the 13th Century fought England but were crushed, 1282-1283. Edward of Caernarvon, son of Edward I of England, was created Prince of Wales, 1301.

Scotland

Scotland, a kingdom now united with England and Wales in Great Britain, occupies the northern 37% of the main British island, and the Hebrides, Orkney, Shetland and smaller islands. The Atlantic lies N and W; the North Sea, E. Length, 275 mi., breadth approx. 150 mi., area, 30,411 sq. mi., population (est. 1972) 5,210,000. Principal rivers are the Clyde, 106 mi.; the Tay, 117 mi., and the Tweed, 96 mi.

The Lowlands, a belt of land approximately 60 miles wide from the Firth of Clyde to the Firth of Forth, divide the farming region of the Southern Uplands from the granite Highlands of the north. Only one-tenth of the land area, the Lowlands contain three-quarters of the population and most of the industry. The Highlands, famous for hunting and fishing, have been opened to industry by many hydroelectric power stations.

Edinburgh, pop. (1972) 449,632 is the capital. It lies on the Firth of Forth in Midlothian County and has notable memorials of its royal and cultural history.

Glasgow, pop. (1971) 893,790, is the largest city, 3d largest in Britain, and Britain's greatest industrial center. It is a shipbuilding complex on the Clyde and an ocean port.

Aberdeen, pop. (1971) 178,441, 95 mi. NE of Edinburgh, is a major North Sea port, center of granite industry and fish processing.

Dundee, pop. (1971) 182,930, 40 mi. NE of Edinburgh, is an industrial and fish processing center on the Firth of Tay.

History. Scotland was called Caledonia by the Romans who battled early Picts and Celtic tribes and occupied southern areas from the 1st to the 4th Centuries. The Romans supposedly called one group Picti because they painted their bodies. The Scots were an Irish tribe from Scotia (an early name for Ireland). Missionaries from Britain introduced Christianity in the 4th Century; St. Columba, an Irish monk, converted most of Scotland to Christianity in the 6th Century.

The Kingdom of Scotland was established in the 11th Century. William Wallace, patriot leader, defeated an invading English army at Stirling Bridge, 1297, and Robert Bruce defeated another at Bannockburn, 1314.

In 1603 James VI of Scotland, son of Mary, Queen of Scots, succeeded Queen Elizabeth I on the throne of England as James I, and effected the Union of the Crowns. In 1707 Scotland received representation in the British Parliament, resulting from the union of former separate Parliaments. Its executive in the British cabinet is the Secretary of State for Scotland. John Knox led the Scottish church Reformation in the 16th Century. There is a small Scottish Nationalist party which urges independence for Scotland.

There are 8 universities. Education receives some support from trusts founded by Andrew Carnegie. St. Andrews is the birthplace of golf.

Historic sites and literary associations, where memorials of Robert Burns, Sir Walter Scott, John Knox, Mary, Queen of Scots, are preserved, draw many tourists, as do the beauties of the Trossachs, Loch Katrine, Loch Lomond and abbey ruins that are now state property.

Industries. Engineering products are the most important industry, with growing emphasis on lighter products such as office machinery, autos, electronics and other consumer goods and less dependence on locomotives, ships, boilers, pumps, valves and other industrial machinery. Oil has been discovered offshore in the North Sea.

Scotland produces fine woolens, worsteds, tweeds; silk textiles at Paisley and Glasgow; fine linens and jute. It is known for its special breeds of cattle and sheep, Shetland ponies and Clydesdale draft horses. Fisheries have large hauls of herring, cod, whiting. Whisky is the biggest export product.

Atomic projects to produce plutonium and electrical energy are at Dounreay, Chapelcross, Hunterston.

The Hebrides are a group of c. 500 islands, 100 inhabited, off the W coast. The Inner Hebrides include **Skye, Mull** and **Iona**, the last famous for the arrival of St. Columba, 563 AD. The Outer Hebrides include **St. Kilda** and **Harris.** Industries include sheep raising and weaving.

The Orkney Islands, c. 90, are separated from Scotland by the Pentland Firth. The capital is Kirkwall, on Pomona Is. Fish curing, sheep raising and weaving are occupations. NE of the Orkneys are the 200 **Shetland Islands,** 24 inhabited, home of Shetland pony.

Northern Ireland

Six of the 9 counties of Ulster, the NE corner of Ireland, constitute Northern Ireland, with the parliamentary boroughs of Belfast and Londonderry; they are Antrim, Armagh, Down, Londonderry, Fermanagh and Tyrone. The country has an area of 5,451 sq. mi. and a population (1971 census prelim.) 1,528,-000. Belfast is the capital and chief industrial center.

Industries. Shipbuilding, including large tankers, has long been an important industry, centered in Belfast, the largest port. Linen manufacture has also long been important, along with apparel and rope and twine. Growing diversification has added engineering products, synthetic fibers and electronics.

Agriculture is also important. There are large numbers of cattle, hogs and sheep; potatoes, poultry and dairy foods are also among the products. There is an agricultural surplus, most of which is shipped to England.

Government. An act of the British Parliament, 1920, divided Northern from Southern Ireland, each with a parliament and government. When Ireland became a dominion, 1921, and later a republic, Northern Ireland chose to remain a part of the United Kingdom. It elects 12 members to the British House of Commons.

During 1968-69, large demonstrations were con-

ducted by groups of Roman Catholics who charged they were discriminated against in voting rights, housing and employment. The Catholics, a minority comprising about a third of the population of Northern Ireland, demanded abolition of property qualifications for voting in local elections and demanded institution of "one man, one vote." Violence and terrorism intensified, involving branches of the Irish Republican Army (outlawed in the Irish Republic), Protestant groups, police and large British Army units. In 1974, over 15,000 British troops were on duty.

A succession of Northern Ireland prime ministers pressed reform programs but failed to satisfy extremists on both sides. By July 1974 over 1,046 civilians and British soldiers (over 200 soldiers) had been killed in 5 years of bombings and shootings. Britain suspended the Northern Ireland parliament Mar. 30, 1972, and imposed direct British rule under a Secretary of State.

In 1973 Britain's Parliament created a single-chamber Assembly to replace the old 2-chamber, Protestant-dominated Stormont Parliament in Northern Ireland. It was designed to insure Catholics a share of political power.

In June 28 elections, moderate parties, pledged to make the system work, won nearly two-thirds of the 78 Assembly seats.

A 14-day general strike, led by Protestant extremists, brought an end in May 1974 to a coalition Protestant-Catholic government which had lasted 5 months. Direct British rule was resumed.

Education and Religion. Northern Ireland is preponderantly Protestant. Elementary education is compulsory to age 15. There are 2 Universities.

Northern Ireland has similar social service programs.

Channel Islands

The Channel Islands, area 75 sq. mi., est. pop. 1972 120,000, off the NW coast of France, the only parts of the one-time Dukedom of Normandy belonging to England, are **Jersey, Guernsey** and the dependencies of Guernsey — **Alderney, Brechou, Great Sark, Little Sark, Herm, Jethou and Lihou.** Jersey has a separate legal existence and a lieutenant governor named by the Crown. The islands were the only British soil occupied by German troops in World War II.

Isle of Man

The Isle of Man, area 227 sq. mi., est. 1972 pop. 60,-000, is in the Irish Sea, 20 mi. from Scotland, 30 mi. from Cumberland. It is rich in lead and iron. The island has its own laws and a lt. gov. who has wide constitutional powers, appointed by the Crown. The Tynwald (legislature) consists of the Legislative Council, partly elected, the House of Keys, elected. Capital: Douglas.

Farming, tourism and fishing are chief occupations. The mild climate is popular with tourists. Ronaldsway Airport handles 250,000 passengers a year. Herring (kippers) and scallops top fishing trade. Man is famous for the Manx tailless cat.

Gibraltar

Gibraltar, a colony southeast of Spain, guards the entrance to the Mediterranean. The width of the strait dividing Europe from Africa varies from 7.75 mi. at the narrowest part to 23.75 at the widest. The Rock has been in British possession since 1704. There is a large harbor and as a naval base its position is of great strategic importance. The Rock is 2.75 mi. long, ¾ of a mi. wide and 1,396 ft. in height; a narrow isthmus connects it with the mainland. Est. pop. 1973 was 30,000.

In 1966 Spain called on Britain to give "substantial sovereignty" of Gibraltar to Spain and imposed a partial blockade of the isthmus. In 1967, in a referendum sponsored by Britain, the residents voted 12,138 for remaining under British rule against 44 for returning to Spain.

A new constitution, May 30, 1969, gave an elected House of Assembly more control in domestic affairs. A UN General Assembly resolution requested Britain to end Gibraltar's colonial status by Oct. 1, 1969. Britain did not do so.

British West Indies

Swinging in a vast arc from the coast of Venezuela NE, then N and NW toward Puerto Rico are the Windward and Leeward Islands, forming a coral and volcanic barrier sheltering the Caribbean from the open Atlantic. Most of the islands are British possessions which have internal self-government. Universal suffrage was instituted 1951-4; ministerial systems of government were set up 1956-1960.

Moving northward from the southern end of the arc lie the **Windward Islands,** starting with **Grenada** (which won independence in 1974 — see separate article), **St. Vincent,** (1973 pop. 100,000, area 150 sq. mi., capital Kingstown), **St. Lucia** (1973 pop. 110,000, area 238 sq. mi., capital Castries) and **Dominica** (1973 pop. 70,000, area 290 sq. mi., capital Roseau).

Further north, in the **Leeward Islands,** are **Montserrat** (1970 pop. 12,300, area 33 sq. mi., capital Plymouth), **Antigua** (1973 pop. 70,000, area 171 sq. mi., capital St. John's) and **St. Christopher-Nevis-Anguilla,** three islands also referred to as **St. Kitts** (1973 pop. 70,000, area 138 sq. mi., capital Basseterre on St. Christopher). Nearby are the small **British Virgin Islands.**

Britain granted self-government to 5 of these islands and island groups in 1967; each became an Associated State, with Britain retaining responsibility for the foreign affairs and defense of each. These 5 were Antigua, Dominica, Grenada, St. Lucia and the St. Christopher-Nevis-Anguilla Federation. Similar status was received by St. Vincent in 1969.

Anguilla declared its independence June 16, 1967, but accepted appointment of a British administrator. Controversy continued and in March 1969 British paratroops were landed. They left in Sept. A commission was set up to administer the island. Anguilla's area is 35 sq. mi., its pop. 5,000. The main exports are lobsters and salt.

Sugar is the major crop of Antigua and St. Kitts; bananas are the main product of the Windwards; Dominica produces cocoa; Antigua, Montserrat, St. Kitts and St. Vincent have Sea Island cotton; St. Vincent has arrowroot; Dominica grows citrus fruits. Many of these products are exported; imports include other foods, clothing, machinery. Tourism is of mounting importance.

The three **Cayman Islands,** a colony, lie S of Cuba, NW of Jamaica. Population is 10,423 (1970), most of it on Grand Cayman, about 1,300 on Cayman Brac, about 16 on Little Cayman. It is a free port; in the 1970s Grand Cayman became a tax-free refuge for foreign funds and branches of many Western World banks were opened there in the 1970s to house such funds. Fishing, banking and tourism are the main industries. Total area: 93 sq. mi. Capital: Georgetown.

The **Turks and Caicos Islands,** at the SE end of the Bahama Islands, are a separate British possession. There are about 30 islands, only 6 inhabited, pop. est. 6,000, area 166 sq. mi., capital Grand Turk. Salt, crayfish and conch shells are the main exports.

Bermuda

Bermuda is a British dependency governed by a royal governor and a representative legislature, the oldest legislative body among British dependencies. Capital is Hamilton.

It is a group of 360 small islands of coral formation, 20 inhabited, comprising 21 sq. mi. in the western Atlantic, 677 mi. SE of New York, 580 mi. E of North Carolina. Population, 1973, was 60,000 (about 63% are of African descent). Density is high, about 2,850 per sq. mi.

Bermuda's Parliament dates from 1620. In general elections May 22, 1968, the first on the basis of full universal adult suffrage without property qualifications, the predominantly white United Bermuda party won 30 of the 40 Assembly seats, the predominantly Black Progressive Labor party the other 10. Both sides ran white and black candidates; 16 of the 40 elected were blacks. A black member of the United Bermuda Party, Sir Edward Richards, became prime minister in 1971.

The British-appointed governor controls foreign and defense affairs and internal security. The Assembly, its members elected for 5-year terms, controls all local affairs. Bermuda adopted a dollar-decimal currency in 1970.

Gov. Richard Sharples and an aide-de-camp were slain by gunmen Mar. 10, 1973. The police commissioner was shot to death in 1972.

The U.S. maintains air and naval bases in the Bermudas, under long-term lease, and a NASA tracking station.

Bermuda boasts many modern resort hotels. Planes and cruise ships bring in upwards of 280,000 visitors a year, most of them from the U.S.

The government raises most of its revenue from import duties. There are also a real estate rental value tax, excise and other taxes, but none on income or inheritances.

Bermuda exports Easter lilies, drugs, essences, beauty preparations.

Belize

Belize (formerly called British Honduras) is in Central America facing the Caribbean to the E, with Mexico on the N and Guatemala on the W. Population (UN est. 1973) 130,000, area 8,866 sq. mi., capital Belmopan.

Internal self-government was granted by Britain in 1964.

The area has long been claimed by Guatemala, but also was promised independence by Britain. In Apr. 1968, a mediator proposed that British Honduras be made independent but have close association with Guatemala, consulting with it on foreign affairs of mutual concern. The proposal was rejected by Belize.

Main export is sugar, along with citrus fruits, mahogany and other hardwoods, chicle, lobsters and fish.

South Atlantic Dependencies

Falkland Islands and Dependencies, a British Colony, lies 300 mi. E of the Strait of Magellan at the southern end of South America.

The Falklands or Islas Malvinas include about 200 islands with an area of 4,618 sq. mi. and pop. (1970) of 2,045. Sheep-grazing is the main industry; wool is the principal export. The islands are also claimed by Argentina. **South Georgia,** area 1,450 sq. mi., and pop. 439, and the uninhabited **South Sandwich Islands** are dependencies of the Falklands.

British Antarctic Territory, south of 60° S lat., was made a separate colony in 1962 and comprises mainly the **South Shetland Islands,** the **South Orkneys** and **Graham's Land.** A chain of meteorological stations is maintained.

St. Helena, an island 1,200 mi. off the W. coast of Africa and 1,800 E of South America, has 47 sq. mi. and est. pop., 1970 of 4,952. Flax, lace and rope making are the chief industries. After Napoleon Bonaparte was defeated at Waterloo the British exiled him to St. Helena, where he lived from Oct. 16, 1815, to his death, May 5, 1821. He was buried there until 1840, when his remains were transferred to Paris. Capital is Jamestown.

Tristan da Cunha is the principal of a group of islands of volcanic origin, total area 40 sq. mi., half way between the Cape of Good Hope and South America, which form one of the loneliest places on the globe. The other islands are Inaccessible, Gough (or Diego Alvarez) and the 3 Nightingale Islands. An ancient volcanic peak 6,760 ft. high erupted in Oct. 1961, and ruined the settlement. The 262 inhabitants were removed to England for resettlement, but most returned in 1963. The islands are administered as dependencies of St. Helena.

Ascension is an island of volcanic origin, 34 sq. mi. in area, 700 mi. NW of St. Helena, through which it is administered. It lies midway between Africa and South America and is an important communications relay center for Britain and has a U.S. satellite tracking center. Est. pop., 1971, was 1,232, about half of them communications workers. The island is noted for its sea turtles.

Brunei

Brunei has been since 1888 a protected sultanate on the N side of the Island of Borneo, between the Malaysian states of Sarawak and Sabah. Its area is 2,226 sq. mi., the size of Delaware, with population (1973 UN est), 150,000, two-thirds Malay and indigenous races, one-third of Chinese descent.

A 1959 constitution was amended, 1965, to provide for general elections to the Legislative Council, some members of which are appointed. There is a sultan and a British high commissioner. A 1971 agreement gave Brunei full internal self-government.

Brunei's rich Seria oilfield provides tax revenues well in excess of government expenditures. Rubber is also exported. Some of the surplus has been spent on a growing program of school building and social services.

Hong Kong

Hong Kong is a Crown Colony at the mouth of the Canton River in China, 90 mi. south of Canton. Its nucleus is Hong Kong Island, 35½ sq. mi., acquired from China 1841, on which is located Victoria, the colonial capital. Opposite is Kowloon Peninsula, 3 sq. mi. and Stonecutters Island, ¼ sq. mi., added to the colony, 1860. An additional 355 sq. mi. known as the New Territories, comprised of an adjacent mainland area and numerous islands, were leased from China, 1898, for 99 years. Total area of the colony is 391 sq. mi., with a population, 1973 UN est., of 4,160,000 including many refugees from Communist China and fewer than 20,000 British. From 1949 to 1962 Hong Kong absorbed more than a million refugees from the mainland. The flow of refugees continued, on a lesser scale, into the 1970s.

Hong Kong harbor, one of the finest in the East, was long an important British naval station and one of the world's great trans-shipment ports. It is served by many international airlines.

Principal industries are shipbuilding and textiles; also iron and steel, apparel, fishing, cement, and small manufactures. American tourists spend an est. $29 million yearly.

Since 1945 Hong Kong industry has zoomed from a few hundred factories to over 5,000. Its spinning mills, among the best in the world, and low wages compete with textiles elsewhere and have resulted in protective measures in some countries. It also has a booming electronics industry. The U.S. is the largest market for Hong Kong products.

During 1967 Communist China launched a campaign against British authority in Hong Kong, including demonstrations, strikes, riots, bombings, border incidents and slowdowns in supplying food from the mainland, accompanied by charges the British were mistreating Chinese residents.

Indian Ocean Dependencies

The **Seychelles** are a group of islands N of Madagascar, area 91 sq. mi., pop. 1973 UN est., 60,000. The capital is Victoria, on Mahe, a port with a coaling station. Coconuts are the chief product, followed by cinamon, patchouli, mangrove bark, vanilla and tortoise shell. Copra is the chief export.

British Indian Ocean Territory was formed Nov. 1965, embracing islands formerly dependencies of Mauritius or Seychelles: the Chagos Archipelago (including Diego Garcia), Aldabra, Farquhar and Des Roches. Population, 558. In 1973 the U.S. Navy established a communications station on Diego Garcia and in 1974 planned to establish a naval base. The USSR and some other nations opposed the step.

Pitcairn Island

Pitcairn Island is in the Pacific, halfway between South America and Australia. The island was discovered in 1767 by Carteret but was not inhabited until 23 years later when the mutineers of the Bounty landed there. The area is 18 sq. mi. and population, 1974, was 78. It is a British colony and is administered by a British Representative in New Zealand and a local Council. The uninhabited islands of **Henderson, Ducie** and **Oeno** are in the Pitcairn group.

Principal island groups administered by the British High Commissioner for the Western Pacific Islands, head office at Honiara, Guadalcanal, include the British Solomon Islands and the Gilbert and Ellice Islands:

British Solomon Islands

The **British Solomon Islands,** a protectorate, number 10 large islands and 4 groups of small islands with a total area of 11,500 sq. mi. and population, est. 1973, of 180,000, mostly Melanesians. The Solomons lie E of New Guinea. The chief islands in the group are **Guadalcanal, Malaita, San Cristobal, New Georgia, Santa Ysabel, Choiseul, Shortland, Mono** or **Treasury, Vella Lavella, Ganongga, Gizo, Rendova, Russell, Florida** and **Rennel.** Among the groups of islands are the **Lord Howe, Santa Cruz, Tucopia, Mitre, Duff** or **Wilson,** and **Reef.** Some of the Solomons, including Bougainville, are an Australian UN Trusteeship.

Exports: copra, timber, nuts, and trochus shell.

Gilbert and Ellice Islands

The **Gilbert and Ellice Islands** were proclaimed a protectorate in 1892 and were annexed as a colony. The colony includes the **Gilbert Islands** (16), **Ellice Islands** (9), **Phoenix Islands, Ocean Island, Line Islands,** composed of **Fanning, Washington** and **Christmas Islands,** the last the largest atoll in the Pacific (also claimed by the U.S.). The total area is 369 sq. mi. and the population, 1973 est., 60,000. Exports: chiefly copra and phosphates.

New Hebrides

New Hebrides, a condominium jointly administered since 1906 by Great Britain and France, is a group of 11 main islands and about 69 islets lying 500 mi. W of Fiji, with an aggregate area of about 5,700 sq. mi. Population, 1973 UN est. 90,000, mostly Melanesian. Chief products are copra, cotton, cocoa, fish and coffee.

British and French resident commissioners are joint heads of the administration.

Banks (309 sq. mi.) and **Torres** (40 sq. mi.) **Islands,** with pop. of 2,640, are attached to the New Hebrides for administration.

United States

(See Index for listings)

Upper Volta

Capital: Ouagadougou. Area: 105,869 sq. mi. Population (UN est. 1973): 5,740,000. Monetary unit: CFA franc.

The Republic of Upper Volta, one-time French Overseas Territory, is an inland plateau region in west Africa, bounded by Mali, Niger, the Ivory Coast, Ghana, Togo and Dahomey. It is the size of Colorado.

More than 90% of the people are subsistence farmers. Greatest wealth is in livestock, mostly cattle and sheep, accounting for 55% of exports. Principal market crops are cotton, rice, peanuts and karite. Climate is extremely dry but irrigation efforts, using water from the Black Volta, White Volta and pumped from underground, have been started with aid from the UN Special Fund. There are rich manganese deposits. A long drought brought famine in 1973-74; the U. S. provided 40% of the aid sent to the area.

Upper Volta became an autonomous state in 1958. It became fully independent Aug. 5, 1960 and a member of the UN. It signed a bilateral agreement, 1961, maintaining close ties with France.

A constitution, adopted 1960, provided for a presidential form of government and a unicameral National Assembly. In 1966 the army chief of staff, Gen. Sangoule Lamizana, took over the presidency during demonstrations against austerity measures. A new constitution, providing for a premier, was adopted 1970. In Feb. 1974 Lamizana, who was both president and premier, dissolved the Assembly and named a mostly military cabinet.

Uruguay

Capital: Montevideo. Area: 68,548 sq. mi. Population (UN est. 1973): 2,990,000. Monetary unit: Peso.

Uruguay is one of the smallest republics in South America. Slightly larger than Missouri, it is a country of rich, rolling, grassy plains on the South Atlantic coast. Brazil and Argentina are its neighbors, with the Uruguay River forming the boundary line with Argentina.

Resources and Industries. Some 85% of Uruguay's area is devoted to stock raising; 9.6% to agriculture; 3.5% woods and forest; 1.8% is unproductive. The chief products are meat, wool, hides, corn, wheat, citrus fruits, rice, oats and linseed. Meat-packing, metallurgical, textile and wine-making industries are large.

More than a third of the population lives in one city, Montevideo. More than a third of the workers are employed by the government. The state owns the power, telephone, railroad, cement, oil-refining and other industries.

Uruguay's standard of living was one of the highest in South America. Inflation, plus floods, drought and a cold wave in 1967 and a general strike in 1968 brought attempts by the government to strengthen the economy through a series of devaluations of the peso and wage and price controls. But inflation continued. The cost of living rising 94% in 1972. In 1973 beef sales were banned for 3 months to promote meat exports.

History and Government. Once a part of the Spanish Viceroyalty of Rio de la Plata and later a province of Brazil, Uruguay declared its independence, Aug. 25, 1825. The constitution provides for a president, a Chamber of Deputies and a Senate elected for 5-year terms. Suffrage is universal.

Uruguay has one of the world's most extensive social welfare programs with old age pensions, child welfare.

Leftist guerrillas, called Tupamaros, increased terrorist actions in 1970; a U. S. police adviser was slain in Aug. In 1971 the guerrillas kidnaped and, after 8 months, freed the British ambassador. Violence continued and in Feb. 1973 President Juan Maria Bordaberry agreed to military control of his administration. In June he abolished Congress and set up a Council of State in its place. By 1974 the military had apparently defeated the Tupamaros, but the economic decline continued.

Education and Religion. Church and state are separate and there is complete religious tolerance. Preponderant religion is Roman Catholic. Education, including college is free; primary education is compulsory. The language is Spanish.

Defense. Armed forces total 21,000, all paid volunteers. Uruguay is a member of the UN and OAS.

State of Vatican City

Area: 108.7 acres. Population: about 700.

The popes for many centuries, with brief interruptions, held temporal sovereignty over mid-Italy (the so-called Papal States), comprising an area of some 16,000 sq. mi., with a population in the 19th Century of more than 3 million. This territory was incorporated in the new Kingdom of Italy, the sovereignty of the pope being confined to the palaces of the Vatican and the Lateran in Rome and the villa of Castel Gandolfo, by an Italian law, May 13, 1871. This law also guaranteed to the pope and his successors a yearly indemnity of over $620,000. This allowance, however, remained unclaimed.

A Treaty of Conciliation, a Concordat and a financial convention were signed in the Lateran Palace, Feb. 11, 1929, by Cardinal Gasparri and Premier Mussolini. The Treaty and Concordat established the independent state of Vatican City, and gave the Catholic religion special status in Italy. The treaty (Lateran Agreement) was made an integral part of the Constitution of Italy (Article 7) in 1947.

Vatican City includes St. Peter's, the Vatican Palace and Museum covering more than 13 acres, the Vatican gardens, and neighboring buildings between Viale Vaticano and the Church. Thirteen buildings in Rome, although outside the boundaries, enjoy extraterritorial rights; these include buildings housing the congregations or officers necessary for the administration of the Holy See.

The legal system is based on the code of canon law, the apostolic constitutions and the laws especially promulgated for the Vatican City by the pope. In cases not covered the Italian law of Rome applies. The Secretariat of State represents the Holy See in its diplomatic relations. By the Treaty of Conciliation the pope is pledged to a perpetual neutrality unless his mediation is specifically requested by both parties in political disputes. This, however, does not prevent the defense of the Church whenever it is persecuted. A total of 70 nations maintain diplomatic representatives in Vatican City. The U.S. does not have an official ambassador, but in June 1970 President Nixon named Henry Cabot Lodge to be his personal envoy.

The present sovereign of the State of Vatican City is the Supreme Pontiff Paul VI, Giovanni Battista Montini, born in Concesio, Italy, Sept. 26, 1897, elected June 21, 1963, in succession to Angelo Giuseppe Roncali, John XXIII, who died June 3, 1963.

Venezuela

Capital: Caracas. Area: 352,143 sq. mi. Population (Gov. est. 1973): 11,519,582. Monetary unit: Bolivar.

Venezuela, a land of wide plains and lofty mountains, lies within the torrid zone in northern South America, with a 1,750-mi. coastline on the Caribbean and the Atlantic. Its neighbors are Guyana, Brazil and Colombia. It includes 72 islands totaling 14,650 sq. mi., the largest being Margarita, 40 mi. by 20, which is one of Venezuela's 20 states and an important pearl center. Venezuela is more than twice the size of California.

The Orinoco River with its tributaries drains about four-fifths of the country. About 1,700 mi. in length and 13.5 mi. across at its widest point, it is the 2d largest river system in South America, and is navigable for about 700 mi.

Caracas, the capital, is 12 mi. inland from its port, La Guaira. It has an international airport and airlines reach cities in the interior. It is noted for its modern architecture and luxury hotels. In its Pantheon are enshrined the ashes of Simon Bolivar, South American liberator (1783-1830.).

Resources and Industries. Mining, agriculture, fishing and manufacturing are the chief industries. Venezuela in 1973 was the world's 5th largest oil producer. Lake Maracaibo is the largest oil field in

South America. Concessions are held by U.S. and other foreign companies, under state control, with 80% of the income going to the government. In 1974 the government announced plans to nationalize the oil industry "within a year."

Other minerals are iron, gold, copper, coal, salt, nickel, manganese, asbestos, diamonds and mica. Iron ore production is more than 20 million tons annually and is the 2d most important export, next to oil.

Coffee is the major agricultural product. Exports also include cocoa, canned fish, fruit, sugar, steel products, rice. Industries include steel, petrochemicals, textiles, containers, tobacco products, paper, tires, shoes.

Tourists increased from 95,000 in 1965 to 175,000 in 1972. Attractions include resorts on Margarita Is.; Merida in the Andes with its cable car to snowcapped Mirror Peak, 15,000 ft.; beaches near Caracas.

Construction is booming, including skyscrapers in Caracas; a new $3.8 billion city, Ciudad Guyana, 300 mi. SE of Caracas; and a 4,175-ft. suspension bridge across the Orinoco which was opened in 1967.

Oil profits help finance the extensive industrial development. The gross national product rose from $8.9 billion in 1966 to $14.3 billion in 1973.

History and Government. Columbus first set foot on the South American continent on the peninsula of Paria, Aug. 1498; on the same voyage he found the mouth of the Orinoco. Alonso de Ojeda, 1499, found Lake Maracaibo, called the land Venezuela, or Little Venice, because natives had houses on stilts. Venezuela was under Spanish domination until 1821. The republic was formed after secession from the Colombian Federation in 1830.

The 1961 constitution provided for a strong central government; a president, Senate and Chamber of Deputies elected for 5 years by direct universal vote, and a Supreme Court appointed by the Congress. Member: UN, OAS.

Education and Religion. The language is Spanish and Roman Catholic is the religion of the majority, but religious freedom is guaranteed. All education, including college, is free. Primary education is compulsory.

Defense. Armed forces total 37,000.

Vietnam

Total area: 126,436 sq. mi. Total population (UN est. 1973): 41,850,000. Vietnam is split between 2 hostile governments, the Republic of Vietnam, which controls the southern half, and the Communist regime of North Vietnam.

Vietnam, one of 3 former French Indo-Chinese Associated States, is in SE Asia, bounded on the N. by China, on the E and S by the South China Sea, and on the W by Cambodia and Laos. It consists of the former French protectorates of Tonkin and Annam, and former colony of Cochin China. Principal cities are Saigon, Hanoi, Haiphong, Hue and Danang.

Resources and Industries. Chief products are rice, principal food staple; rubber; and coal. Peacetime exports included rubber, rice, fish, coal, lumber, pepper, cattle and hides, corn, zinc and tin. Tea, coffee, and quinine are grown in the South. Rice and coal are chief products of the North; also coffee, tea, maize, sweet potatoes, tobacco, sugar cane and shellac.

History and Government. Vietnam's recorded history began in Tonkin before the Christian era; settled by the Viets who emigrated from central China. It was held by China, 111 B.C.-939 A.D., and was a vassal state during many subsequent periods. Vietnam defeated the armies of Kublai Khan at Bach Dang Giang, 1288. Piecemeal conquest by France began in 1858 and ended in 1884 with acceptance of a French protectorate.

In 1940 Vietnam was occupied by Japan; during the occupation nationalist aims gathered force. A number of groups formed the Vietminh (Independence)

League, headed by Ho Chi Minh, communist guerrilla leader. In Aug. 1945 the Vietminh forced out Bao Dai, former emperor on Annam, head of a short-lived regime sponsored by Japan. France, seeking to reestablish colonial control, battled communist and nationalist forces, 1946-1954, incurring huge losses and was finally defeated at Dienbienphu, May 8, 1954. Meanwhile, on July 1, 1949, Bao Dai had formed a State of Vietnam, with its capital at Saigon and himself as chief of state, with French approval. Communist China backed Ho Chi Minh.

A cease-fire accord signed in Geneva July 21, 1954, divided Vietnam along the Ben Hai River. It provided for a buffer zone, withdrawal of French troops from northern Vietnam and elections to determine the country's future. Under the agreement the communists gained control of the territory north of the 17th parallel, 22 provinces with approx. area of 62,000 sq. mi. and 13 million pop., with its capital at Hanoi and Ho Chi Minh as president. South Vietnam was to comprise the 39 southern provinces with approx. area of 65,000 sq. mi. and pop. of 12 million. Some 800,000 North Vietnamese fled to South Vietnam. Neither South Vietnam nor the U. S. signed the agreement.

Republic of Vietnam

Capital: Saigon. Area: 66,280 sq. mi. Population (UN est. 1973): 19,370,000. Monetary unit: Piastre.

On Oct. 26, 1955, Ngo Dinh Diem, premier of the interim government of South Vietnam, proclaimed the southern zone the Republic of Vietnam and became its first president under a provisional constitution act, following a referendum Oct. 23 which ousted Bao Dai as chief of state.

Fighting persisted from 1956, with the communist Vietcong, aided by North Vietnam, pressing a spreading war in the south and South Vietnam receiving increasing U.S. aid and, by June 1965, active U.S. combat participation.

A serious political conflict arose in 1963 when Buddhist groups charged the government with authoritarianism and brutality. This and government delays in reforms paved the way for a military coup Nov. 1-2, 1963, which overthrew the Diem regime and resulted in the deaths of Diem and 2 brothers.

Several military coups followed. Air Force Commander Nguyen Cao Ky became premier, on June 19, 1965, of the 9th regime since the fall of Diem. In Sept. 1966 South Vietnamese voters chose members of an assembly which drafted a new constitution for a civilian government early in 1967.

In elections Sept. 3, 1967, Chief of State Nguyen Van Thieu was chosen president and Ky, vice president. A 60-member Senate was also elected Sept. 3 and 137-member House on Oct. 22. Thieu was reelected in a one-candidate election, Oct. 3, 1971.

Following attacks on 2 U.S. destroyers by North Vietnamese PT boats in the Gulf of Tonkin Aug. 2-4, 1964, the U.S. retaliated with heavy air strikes against North Vietnam. Beginning in 1965, the raids were stepped up and U.S. troops became combatants.

U.S. troop strength in Vietnam, which reached a high of 543,400 in Apr. 1969, was ordered reduced by U.S. President Nixon in a series of withdrawals, beginning in June 1969.

A ceasefire agreement which President Nixon said would bring "peace with honor" was signed in Paris Jan. 27, 1973 (EST), by the U.S., North and South Vietnam and the Vietcong, to take effect the same day (Jan. 28 in Vietnam). It provided for withdrawal of U.S. troops (about 23,000 were still in Vietnam) and return of U.S. prisoners (590), both within 90 days, an International Commission to supervise the ceasefire, and for the U.S. and North Vietnam to respect the South Vietnamese people's right to self-determination.

The war's toll included — Combat deaths: U.S. 46,-079; South Vietnam 184,089; other free world forces

5,225. Displaced war refugees in South Vietnam totaled over 6,500,000. Fighting between South Vietnamese and communist forces continued, in South Vietnam, in 1974.

(See also Vietnam in Index).

Most Vietnamese practice parts of several religions or mixtures of Confucianism, Taoism, Buddhism, ancestor worship and animism. About 20% practice Buddhism and about 12% Roman Catholicism. New indigenous religions include Cao Dai (1919) and Hoa Hao (1939). There are 7 universities.

Democratic Republic of Vietnam

Capital: Hanoi. Area: 60,156 sq. mi. Population (UN est. 1973): 22,480,000. Monetary unit: Dong.

The Democratic Republic of Vietnam adopted a constitution Dec. 31, 1959, based on communist principles and calling for reunification of all Vietnam. It provides for a president elected by Parliament and a prime minister appointed by the president. President Ho Chi Minh, reelected July 15, 1960, by unanimous vote of the National Assembly, had held office since 1945. He died Sept. 3, 1969 and was succeeded as president by Ton Duc Thang.

North Vietnam sought to take over South Vietnam beginning in 1954. Aid to Vietcong guerrillas was intensified in 1959 and with large-scale troop infiltration in 1964. In that year U.S. response increased with bombing of military targets in North Vietnam; the bombings were ended in 1968 but renewed in 1972. North Vietnam had large forces in Laos and Cambodia, and, at the time of the Vietnam ceasefire, Jan. 27, 1973 (EST), 145,000 troops in South Vietnam.

(See also Republic of Vietnam, above.)

Western Samoa

Capital: Apia. Area: 1,133 sq. mi. Population (UN est. 1973): 150,000. Monetary unit: Tala.

Western Samoa, which became an independent nation Jan. 1, 1962, comprises 4 inhabited islands of a group in the South Pacific lying about 2,613 mi. SW of Hawaii. Largest of the islands are **Savaii** and **Upolu.** Eastern Samoa, the smaller portion of the group with its capital at Pago Pago, is a dependency of the U.S.

Western Samoa was a German colony, 1899 to 1914, when New Zealand landed troops and took over. It became a New Zealand mandate under the League of Nations and, in 1945, a New Zealand UN Trusteeship.

An elected local government took office in Oct. 1959 and the country became fully independent in 1962. New Zealand has continued economic aid and educational assistance. Western Samoa changed from pounds to decimal currency July 10, 1967.

The population is composed almost solely of Polynesians. The islands are fertile and life is leisurely. Chief products are tropical hardwoods, fish, cocoa, coconuts, bananas, taro, coffee, bark cloth (tapa), mats.

Robert Louis Stevenson's grave is on a hill near Apia.

Yemen Arab Republic

Capital: Sana. Area: 75,289 sq. mi. Population (Govt. est. 1973): 7 million. Monetary unit: Rial.

Yemen is an ancient, mountainous country, near the southern tip of the Arabian Peninsula on the Red Sea. Its neighbors are the People's Democratic Republic of Yemen (formerly Southern Yemen) and Saudi Arabia. It is about the size of Nebraska.

Hodeida, Mocha and Loheiya are major ports. Marib and Sana are archeological sites.

Resources and Industries. On the plateau of El Jebel, the most fertile section of Arabia, coffee, barley and grain are grown. Mocha coffee, hides, dates, cotton, sesame, herbs, fruits and precious stones are exported. Oil was discovered in 1972.

History and Government. Yemen's territory once was part of the ancient kingdom of Sheba, or Saba, a prosperous link in trade between Africa and India. A Biblical reference speaks of its gold, spices and precious stones as gifts borne by the Queen of Sheba to King Solomon.

Yemen was described as a democratic Islamic monarchy during the regime of the Imam Ahmed, who had ruled 1948-1962. The king was reported assassinated Sept. 26, 1962, and a revolutionary group headed by Brig. Gen. Abdullah al-Salal declared the country to be the Yemen Arab Republic. He became president.

The Imam Ahmed's heir, the Imam Mohamad al-Badr, fled to the mountains where tribesmen joined royalist forces; internal warfare between them and the republican forces continued. Egyptian president Nasser sent 70,000 troops to aid the republicans; Saudi Arabia supported the royalists with military aid.

After Egypt's defeat in the June 1967 Israeli-Arab war, Egypt announced it would withdraw its troops from Yemen; the last of them left Nov. 29, 1967, and Saudi Arabia said it would stop aiding the royalists.

This was accompanied by a bloodless coup in which Salal was overthrown, Nov. 5, 1967. Leadership was taken over by a Presidential Council headed by Abdul Rahman al-Iryani, who later became president.

Fighting continued between the republican and royalist forces. Saudi Arabia announced in Feb. 1968 it was renewing its aid to the royalists, charging that both Soviet Russia and Syria, as well as Southern Yemen, were aiding the republicans.

In April 1970 hostilities ended with an agreement between Yemen and Saudi Arabia and appointment of several royalists to the Yemen government.

There were border skirmishes with forces of the People's Democratic Republic of Yemen in 1972-73. The U.S. and Yemen in 1972 resumed diplomatic relations, broken by Yemen after the 1967 Arab-Israeli war.

On June 13, 1974, an Army group, led by Col. Ibrahim al-Hamidi, seized the government.

Yemen is a member of the UN and Arab League.

People's Democratic Republic of Yemen

Capitals: Aden and Medina as-Shaab. Area: 111,000 sq. mi. Population (Gov. est. 1974): 1,600,000. Monetary unit: Dinar.

This nation became independent as the People's Republic of Southern Yemen Nov. 30, 1967, after 129 years of British rule. It changed its name to People's Democratic Republic of Yemen on Nov. 30, 1970. It consists of the port city of Aden, 17 states of the former South Arabian Federation, 3 small sheikdoms, 3 larger sultanates, Quaiti, Kathiri and Mahri, which made up the Eastern Aden Protectorate, and Socotra, the largest island in the Arabian Sea.

One of the cities mentioned in the Bible, Aden has been a port for trade in incense, spices and silk between the East and West for 2,000 years. British rule began in 1839 when the British East India Co. seized control to put an end to the piracy threatening trade with India. Aden provided Britain with a controlling position at the southern entrance to the Red Sea.

With only 1% of the land fertile and few mineral deposits, the Port of Aden has been the area's most valuable natural resource. The port is 10 mi. across, well-sheltered and deep. In 1966 more than 6,000 ships put in at Aden for refueling, servicing and transshipment of goods, bringing over 227,000 visitors.

But, with the closing of the Suez Canal because of the Israeli-Arab War in June 1967, the port lost much of its business. Local products exported include cotton, fish, coffee, hides.

The struggle for independence began in earnest in Oct. 1963, when 2 nationalist groups, the National Liberation Front (NLF) and the Egypt-supported Front for the Liberation of Occupied South Yemen, waged a guerrilla war against the British and local dynastic rulers. The 2 groups vied with each other for political control. The NLF succeeded in naming the first president, Qahtan al-Shaabi. In a June 1969 coup the left wing of the NLF seized power.

The new government broke off relations with the U.S. and nationalized some foreign firms. Aid has been furnished by the USSR and Communist China.

In 1972-73 there were border skirmishes with forces of the Yemen Arab Republic.

Yugoslavia

Capital: Belgrade. Area: 98,766 sq. mi. Population (Gov. est. 1974): 21,126,000. Monetary unit: Dinar.

The Socialist Federal Republic of Yugoslavia is a rugged mountainous land, densely forested, which rises from the eastern shore of the Adriatic Sea. Its neighbors are Italy, Austria, Hungary, Romania, Bulgaria, Greece and Albania. It is about the size of Wyoming.

The federation comprises 6 republics: Serbia, Croatia, Slovenia, Montenegro, Bosnia-Herzegovina and Macedonia, and 2 autonomous provinces: Kosovo and Voyvodina.

Resources and Industries. Chief crops are cereals, maize, wheat, barley, rye, tobacco, oats, hops and fruits. Principal minerals are coal, iron, copper, chrome, antimony, manganese, lead, mercury, salt and bauxite.

Most industry is socialized and private enterprise is restricted to small-scale production. Since 1952 workers are guaranteed a basic wage and a share in cooperative profits.

Management of industrial enterprises is handled by workers' councils. Farmland is 85% privately owned but farms are restricted to 25 acres.

Yugoslavia has conducted several large-scale programs to improve its economy. Beginning in the late 1950s, successful efforts were made to strengthen agriculture by improving fertilizers, grain varieties and livestock.

Tourism was promoted, particularly along the country's colorful Adriatic coast. Large numbers of visitors from nations of the West provided an important source of foreign income.

Beginning in 1965, reforms designed to decentralize the administration of economic development and to force industries to produce more efficiently in competition with foreign producers were introduced.

Yugoslavia has developed considerable trade with Western Europe as well as with the USSR and Eastern European countries and elsewhere. While its import-export balance has continued to show deficits, money earned by Yugoslavs working temporarily in Western Europe, and money brought in by tourists come close to making these up. In 1970 a trade treaty was signed with the EEC.

The index for industrial production (1963=100) was 213 for 1973.

Foreign trade in thousands of U.S. dollars:

	Imports	Exports
1972	$3,233,000	$2,237,000
1973	$4,511,000	$2,853,000

History and Government. Serbia, which had since the Battle of Kosovo (1389) been a vassal principality of Turkey, was established as an independent kingdom by the Treaty of Berlin, 1878. After the Balkan wars its boundaries were enlarged by the annexation of Old Serbia and Macedonia, 1913. When the Austrian Archduke Francis Ferdinand and wife were assassinated at Sarajevo June 28, 1914, the Austrian government forced war on Serbia, the onset of World War I, 1914-1918.

When the Austro-Hungarian empire collapsed, the Kingdom of the Serbs, Croats and Slovenes was formed from the former provinces of Croatia, Dalmatia, Bosnia, Herzegovina, Slovenia, Voyvodina and the independent state of Montenegro, with Peter I of Serbia as king. The name was later changed to Yugoslavia. Peter (d. 1921) was succeeded by his son Alexander I (assassinated at Marseille Oct. 9, 1934), after which Prince Paul became regent. He was overthrown in Mar. 1941 and Crown Prince Peter, born Sept. 6, 1923, was proclaimed king. Germany invaded April, 1941, and King Peter II fled to London.

But many Yugoslav troops continued to fight the Nazis from their mountain strongholds. Among these guerrilla forces were the Chetniks led by Draja Mikhailovich, who became involved in open warfare with other partisan forces led by Josip Broz, known as Marshal Tito, for control of the resistance movement. Tito, backed by the USSR and Great Britain, won and, by the time the Germans had been driven from Yugoslavia in 1944, was in control. Mikhailovich was captured and executed in Belgrade July 17, 1946, by the Tito regime.

A constituent assembly proclaimed Yugoslavia a republic Nov. 29, 1945. It became a federated republic Jan. 31, 1946, and Marshal Tito, a communist, became head of the government. By terms of a treaty with Italy the greater part of Venezia-Giulia, Zara, Pelagosa and adjacent islands were ceded to Yugoslavia.

The Stalin policy of dictating the communist line to all communist nations was rejected by Marshal Tito. He accepted economic aid and military equipment from the U. S. and received aid in foreign trade also from France and Great Britain.

Yugoslavia is governed by the president, as chairman of a 22-man collective presidency (created in 1971), a premier, and a parliament (Federal Assembly), from which cabinet members are drawn.

A new constitution was approved by the Assembly in Feb. 1974, providing that representatives in the Assembly be chosen for it through a system of subordinate assemblies whose members consist of delegates from labor organizations. Tito was elected president-for-life in Feb. 1974.

Tito supported the liberalization government of Czechoslovakia in 1968 before its fall under Russian pressure, but he paid a friendship visit to Moscow in 1972.

A separatist movement among Croatians, 2d to the Serbs in numbers, brought arrests and a change of government leaders in the Croatian Republic in Jan. 1972.

Education and Religion. All education is free; elementary training is compulsory to age 14. There are 9 universities. Principal languages are Slovene, Macedonian, Serbo-Croat. All religions are recognized and enjoy equal rights. Serbo-Orthodox comprises 42%, Roman Catholic 32%, Moslem 12%.

Complete social security is in force, including unemployment, medical, maternity benefits.

Defense. Military forces total 240,000.

Zaire

Capital: Kinshasa. Area: 905,063 sq. mi. Population (UN est. 1973): 23,560,000. Monetary unit: Zaire.

The Democratic Republic of Congo changed its name to Republic of Zaire on Oct. 27, 1971; the Congo River was changed to Zaire and in 1972 Zairians with Christian names were ordered to change them to African names.

Until June 30, 1960, the Congo was a colony of Belgium in Equatorial Africa, entirely inland except for 25 mi. on the Atlantic Ocean, N of the mouth of the Congo (Zaire) River. It is larger than Texas and Alaska combined.

Along the eastern border lie several of Africa's Great Lakes, North of the Equator on the Uganda border, stand the Ruwenzori Mtns., believed to the "Mountains of the Moon" of ancient legend. Mt.

Margherita is 16,763 ft.

The Zaire River, one of the world's longest, rises near the Zambian border in the SE and flows 2,718 mi. N, then W and finally SW, emptying into the South Atlantic.

Wildlife is abundant and includes most of the species Africa is famous for: elephant, lion, gorilla, hippopotamus, crocodile, python, etc.

Resources and Industry. There are extensive mineral deposits in the Katanga, Ituri and Kivu highlands. Zaire normally produces 6% of the world's copper, and over 60% of its cobalt and 40% of its industrial diamonds. Also produced are cadmium, gold, silver, tin, germanium, zinc, iron, tungsten, manganese, uranium and radium.

Tropical rain forests cover much of the land; trees often are 150 to 200 ft. tall. They include mahogany, ebony, teak, copal, palms, cedars and gum and resin trees. Bananas, coffee, rubber, mangoes, plantain, coconuts are grown. Chief agricultural exports are fats and oil, timber, coffee, cotton, rubber, tea, cocoa, bananas.

History and Government. Leopold II, king of the Belgians, formed an international group to exploit the Congo in 1876. In 1877 Henry M. Stanley explored the Congo and in 1878 the king's group sent him back to organize the region and win over the native chiefs. Claims having been advanced by Portugal and others, the Conference of Berlin, 1884-85, organized the Congo Free State with Leopold as king and chief owner. Exploitation of native laborers on the rubber plantations caused international criticism and led to granting of a colonial charter, 1908, whereby the state became a Belgian colony.

Belgian and Congolese leaders agreed Jan. 27, 1960, that the Congo would become independent June 30. In the first general elections, May 31, the National Congolese movement of Patrice Lumumba won 35 of 137 seats in the National Assembly, lower House of Parliament. He was appointed premier June 21, and formed a coalition cabinet. Belgium's King Baudouin formally proclaimed the territory's independence at Leopoldville (now Kinshasa) June 30, 1960.

Widespread violence in which mutinous Congolese troops took part caused Europeans and others to flee the country. Pres. Moise Tshombe of Katanga seceded from the republic July 11, but ended the secession in 1963. Katanga was the seat of the copper-mining operations of the Union Miniere. The UN Security Council Aug. 9, 1960, called on Belgium to withdraw its troops and sent a UN contingent to guard against civil war. President Kasavubu removed Lumumba as premier and Lumumba fought for control with the backing of Ghana, Guinea and India. On Feb. 12, 1961, Lumumba was murdered in Katanga.

The last UN troops left the Congo June 30, 1964, and Cyrille Adoulla, premier since Aug. 1, 1961, resigned, succeeded by Tshombe.

On Sept. 7, 1964, leftist rebels set up a "People's Republic" in Stanleyville with Christopher Gbenye as president. Premier Tshombe hired foreign mercenaries and sought to rebuild the Congolese Army. In Nov. and Dec. 1964 rebels slew scores of white hostages and thousands of Congolese; Belgian paratroops, dropped from U. S. transport planes, rescued hundreds. By July 1965 the rebels, though supplied with smuggled arms, had lost their effectiveness.

Growing rivalry between President Kasavubu and Premier Tshombe ended when the former ousted the latter from office Oct. 13, 1965. Evariste Kimba became premier but both he and Kasavubu were ousted

Nov. 25 by Gen. Joseph D. Mobutu who was named president. He later changed his name to Mobutu Sese Seko.

In March 1966 Mobutu took over from Parliament all of its legislative powers. On July 1 he renamed Leopoldville Kinshasa; Stanleyville, Kisangani; and Elisabethville, Lubumbashi.

In 1969-74, political stability under President Mobutu was reflected in improved economic conditions. In 1970, he was elected to a 7-year term as president. In 1974 most foreign-owned businesses were ordered sold to Zaire citizens.

Education and Religion. The population is principally Bantu. More than 200 tribes are represented. Swahili, Lingala, Tshiluba and Kikongo are widely spoken; French is the official language. There are an estimated 9 million African Christians, predominantly Roman Catholic. There are 3 universities.

Zambia

Capital: Lusaka. Area: 290,724 sq. mi. Population (UN est. 1973): 4,640,000. Monetary unit: Kwacha.

The Republic of Zambia is the former British Protectorate of Northern Rhodesia. It is a land-locked country located in South Central Africa. Bordering it are Zaire, Tanzania, Malawi, Mozambique, Rhodesia, Botswana, South-West Africa (Namibia) and Angola. It is slightly larger than Texas.

The terrain is mostly high plateau covered with thick forest and suitable for both farming and grazing. The country is rich in minerals, including copper, zinc, cobalt, gold, vanadium, manganese, and coal. Zambia's wealth is mainly its copper; it is one of the world's largest copper producers.

Victoria Falls on the Zambezi River, the border with Rhodesia, is 3 times the width and more than twice the height of Niagara.

As Northern Rhodesia, the country was under the administration of the South Africa Company, 1889 until 1924 when the office of governor was established, and, subsequently, a legislature.

A new constitution, announced in 1963, granted internal self-government with a prime minister and cabinet, effective Jan. 22, 1964. The United National Independence party won the first elections Jan. 21 and its leader, Kenneth D. Kaunda, became the country's first prime minister. He was elected president and, on Oct. 24, 1964, Zambia became an independent republic within the Commonwealth. It has a National Assembly of 125 elected members and 10 nominated by the president. In 1973 a new constitution provided for a one-party system.

After the white government of Rhodesia declared its independence from Britain Nov. 17, 1965, relations between Zambia and Rhodesia became strained and use of their jointly owned railroad was disputed. Britain gave Zambia an extra $12 million aid in 1966 after imposing an oil embargo on Rhodesia, and Zambia set up a temporary airlift to carry copper out from its mines and gasoline in. In Aug. 1968 a 1,958-mi. pipeline was completed, bringing oil from Tanzania. In 1973 a truck road to carry copper to Tanzania's port of Dar es Salaam was completed with U. S. aid; A railroad, built with Chinese aid across Tanzania, reached the Zambian border in 1974.

As part of a program of government participation in major industries, a government corporation in 1970 took over 51% of the ownership of 2 foreign-owned copper mining companies, paying with bonds.

National Population Density, Growth Rate, Life Expectancy

Source: United Nations Demographic Yearbook 1972

Country	Den- sity[1]	Growth Rate[2]	Life Ex- pectancy[3]	Country	Den- sity[1]	Growth Rate[2]	Life Ex- pectancy[3]
Algeria	6	3.5	50.7*†	Korea, South	330	2.1	59.74
Argentina	9	1.5	64.06*	Kuwait	51	9.8	64.4*†
Australia	2	1.9	68.46	Liberia	14		50.8*

Country	Density[1]	Growth Rate[2]	Life Expectancy[3]	Country	Density[1]	Growth Rate[2]	Life Expectancy[3]
Belgium	318	0.5	67.73	Mali	4	2.0	37.2*
Bolivia	5	2.6	49.71	Mexico	27	3.5	61.03*
Brazil	12	2.9	60.7*†	Morocco	35		50.5*†
Bulgaria	77	0.7	68.81	Netherlands	326	1.2	71.0
Canada	2	1.6	68.75	Nigeria	63	2.5	37.2
Ceylon	199	2.3	61.9	Norway	12	0.8	71.03
Chad	3	2.0	29.0	Peru	11	3.1	52.59*
China	83	1.8	50.0*†	Philippines	130	3.0	48.81
Colombia	20	3.2	44.18	Poland	106	0.8	66.85
Cuba	76	2.0	66.8*†	Portugal	96		65.30
Czechoslovakia	113	0.5	66.21	Puerto Rico	316	1.3	68.96
Egypt	35	2.5	51.6	Rhodesia	14	3.4	51.4*†
Ethiopia	21	1.9	38.5*†	Romania	87	1.1	65.50
Finland	14	0.2	65.4	Saudi Arabia	4	2.8	42.3*†
France	95	0.9	68.6	Senegal	21	2.4	41.0*†
Germany, East	157	0.1	69.16	Singapore	3,695	2.0	68.2*†
Germany, West	248	0.8	67.55	Spain	68	1.1	67.32
Ghana	38	2.9	46.0	Sudan	7	2.7	47.6*†
Greece	68		67.46	Sweden	18	0.7	71.69
Guatemala	50	2.9	48.29	Switzerland	156	1.2	69.21
Guinea	17	2.3	26.0	Syria	36	3.3	52.8*†
Haiti	183	2.1	44.5	Tanzania	14	2.6	41.0*†
Hong Kong	3,924	2.0	66.74	Turkey	45	2.5	53.7*†
Iceland	2	1.3	70.8	USSR	11	1.1	65.0*
India	172	2.2	41.89	United Kingdom	229	0.4	67.81
Indonesia	81	2.1	47.5*	United States	22	1.1	71.1*†
Iran	19	3.0	50.0*†	Uruguay	17	1.2	65.51
Ireland	43	0.6	68.58	Venezuela	12	3.4	63.8
Israel	149	2.9	70.08	Vietnam, North	139	2.3	50.0*†
Italy	180	0.7	67.87	Vietnam, South			50.0*†
Jamaica	175	1.4	62.15	Yugoslavia	81	1.0	64.79
Japan	287	1.1	69.05	Zaire	10	3.9	37.6
Kenya	21	3.1	51.2	Zambia	6	2.6	43.5*†

(1) persons per sq. kilometer; 2 percent annual rate of increase, 1963-71; (3) for males at age one, except (*) at birth and (†) both sexes. Life expectancy figures are arrived at from statistics and estimates from a variety of years since 1950.

Gross National Product Estimates
For Calendar Year 1972 in current Market Prices—U.S. $
Compiled by Agency for International Development

Nation	GNP Total $ Millions	GNP Per Capita	Nation	GNP Total $ Millions	GNP Per Capita	Nation	GNP Total $ Millions	GNP Per Capita
Algeria	6,950	469	India	58,250	98	Philippines	8,245	202
Argentina	27,200	1,095	Indonesia	10,620	84	Portugal	8,700	1,021
Australia	50,460	3,924	Iran	17,400	542	Rhodesia	2,233	376
Austria	22,730	3.033	Ireland	5,535	1,839	Saudi Arabia	5,250	920
Belgium	39,260	4,043	Israel	6,895	2,199	Singapore	3,110	1,430
Brazil	49,570	495	Italy	122,090	3,215	South Africa	21,060	891
Canada	102,610	4,696	Japan	335,170	3,165	Spain	50,930	1,476
Cyprus	647	1,328	Korea, So.	9,720	294	Sweden	43,600	5,369
Denmark	23,150	4,557	Kuwait	4,225	5,280	Switzerland	37,000	5,763
Ecuador	2,014	309	Lebanon	2,312	730	Syria	2,244	336
Egypt	8,270	243	Libya	4,583	2,262	Tanzania	1,583	113
Ethiopia	2,265	230	Mexico	40,670	753	Thailand	7,684	194
Finland	13,980	3,019	Netherlands	50,520	3,790	Turkey	16,990	459
France	217,810	4,213	Nigeria	8,650	150	United Kingdom	151,450	2,714
Germany, W.	285,690	4,693	Norway	16,000	4,071	Venezuela	13,410	1,166
Greece	12,592	1,400	Panama	1,277	840	Zaire	2,262	122
Iceland	672	3,215	Peru	7,490	525	Zambia	1,800	384

United Nations
History, Membership, Organization and Purpose

The 29th regular session of the United Nations General Assembly opened Sept. 17, 1974. *See Chronology for developments at UN sessions during 1974.*

Foundations of the United Nations were laid at the Dumbarton Oaks Conference in Washington between the United States, the United Kingdom and the Soviet Union, Aug. 21-Sept. 28, 1944, and between the United States, the United Kingdom and the Republic of China (Nationalist) Sept. 29-Oct. 7, 1944. Proposals to establish an organization of nations for maintenance of world peace led to the United Nations Conference on International Organization at San Francisco, Apr. 25-June 26, 1945, where the charter of the United Nations was drawn up. It was signed June 26 by 50 nations, and by Poland, one of the original 51, on Oct. 15 1945. The charter came into effect Oct. 25, 1945, when the requisite ratification by the 5 permanent members of the Security Council, China,

France, Soviet Union, United Kingdom and United States, and a majority of other signatories had been completed.

United Nations headquarters are located in New York, N. Y., between First Ave. and Roosevelt Drive and E. 42nd St. and E. 48th St. The General Assembly Bldg. (opened 1952), Secretariat, Conference and Library bldgs. are interconnected. The Dag Hammarskjold Library, built by a $6,200,000 grant from the Ford Foundation, was dedicated Nov. 16, 1961. It has room for 400,000 vols. To build the headquarters the U. S. Government advanced an interest-free loan of $65 000,000, payable in annual installments until 1982. John D. Rockefeller, Jr., contributed $8,000,000 for land and the City of New York contributed an est. $26,500,000 for adapting the site. United Nations has a post office originating its own stamps. *See Postal Information.*

Roster of the United Nations
(As of Sept. 17, 1974)

The 138 Members of the United Nations, with the dates on which they become Members.

Member	Date	Member	Date	Member	Date
Afghanistan.....	Nov. 19, 1946	Greece.........	Oct. 25,1945	Pakistan.........	Sept. 30, 1947
Albania.........	Dec. 14, 1955	Grenada........	Sept. 17, 1974	Panama.........	Nov. 13,1945
Algeria.........	Oct. 8, 1962	Guatemala.....	Nov. 21, 1945	Paraguay.......	Oct. 24, 1945
Argentina.......	Oct. 24, 1945	Guinea........	Dec. 12, 1958	Peru...........	Oct. 31, 1945
Australia........	Nov. 1, 1945	Guinea-Bissau..	Sept. 17, 1974	Philippines......	Oct. 24, 1945
Austria.........	Dec. 14, 1955	Guyana.........	Sept. 20, 1966	Poland..........	Oct. 24, 1945
Bahamas........	Sept. 18, 1973	Haiti...........	Oct. 24, 1945	Portugal........	Dec. 14, 1955
Bahrain.........	Sept. 21, 1971	Honduras.......	Dec. 17, 1945	Qatar..........	Sept. 21, 1971
Bangladesh......	Sept. 17, 1974	Hungary........	Dec. 14, 1955	Romania........	Dec. 14, 1955
Barbados......	Dec. 9, 1966	Iceland.........	Nov. 19, 1946	Rwanda........	Sept. 18, 1962
Belgium........	Dec. 27, 1945	India..........	Oct. 30, 1945	Saudi Arabia....	Oct. 24, 1945
Bhutan.........	Sept. 21, 1971	Indonesia......	Sept. 28, 1950	Senegal........	Sept. 28, 1960
Bolivia.........	Nov. 14, 1945	Iran...........	Oct. 24, 1945	Sierra Leone....	Sept. 27, 1961
Botswana.......	Oct. 17, 1966	Iraq...........	Dec. 21, 1945	Singapore.......	Sept. 21, 1965
Brazil..........	Oct. 24, 1945	Ireland........	Dec. 14, 1955	Somalia........	Sept. 20, 1960
Bulgaria........	Dec. 14, 1955	Israel..........	May 11,1949	South Africa.....	Nov. 7, 1945
Burma.........	Apr. 19, 1948	Italy..........	Dec. 14, 1955	Spain..........	Dec. 14, 1955
Burundi........	Sept. 18, 1962	Ivory Coast.....	Sept. 20, 1960	Sri Lanka.......	Dec. 14, 1955
Byelorussian SSR.	Oct. 24, 1945	Jamaica........	Sept. 18, 1962	Sudan..........	Nov. 24, 1956
Cambodia......	Dec. 14, 1955	Japan..........	Dec. 18, 1956	Swaziland......	Sept. 24, 1968
Cameroon.......	Sept. 20, 1960	Jordan.........	Dec. 14, 1955	Sweden........	Nov. 19, 1946
Canada........	Nov. 9, 1945	Kenya.........	Dec. 16, 1963	Syria[2].........	Oct. 24, 1945
Central African R.	Sept. 20, 1960	Kuwait.........	May 14, 1963	Thailand.......	Dec. 16, 1946
Chad..........	Sept. 20, 1960	Laos..........	Dec. 14, 1955	Togo..........	Sept. 20, 1960
Chile..........	Oct. 24, 1945	Lebanon.......	Oct. 24, 1945	Trinidad &......	
China[4]........	Oct. 24, 1945	Lesotho.......	Oct. 17, 1966	Tobago........	Sept. 18, 1962
Colombia.......	Nov. 5, 1945	Liberia........	Nov. 2, 1945	Tunisia........	Nov. 12, 1956
Congo.........	Sept. 20, 1960	Libya.........	Dec. 14, 1955	Turkey.........	Oct. 24, 1945
Costa Rica......	Nov. 2, 1945	Luxembourg....	Oct. 24, 1945	Uganda........	Oct. 25, 1962
Cuba..........	Oct. 24, 1945	Malagasy Rep...	Sept. 20, 1960	Ukrainian Soviet	
Cyprus.........	Sept. 20, 1960	Malawi........	Dec. 1, 1964	Socialist Repub.	Oct. 24, 1945
Czechoslovakia..	Oct. 24, 1945	Malaysia[1]......	Sept. 17, 1957	Union of Soviet	
Dahomey.......	Sept. 20, 1960	Maldives......	Sept. 21, 1965	Soc. Repub's...	Oct. 24, 1945
Denmark.......	Oct. 24, 1945	Mali..........	Sept. 28, 1960	United Arab	
Dominican Rep...	Oct. 24, 1945	Malta.........	Dec. 1, 1964	Emirates.....	Dec. 9, 1971
Ecuador........	Dec. 21, 1945	Mauritania.....	Oct. 27, 1961	United Kingdom .	Oct. 24, 1945
Egypt[2]........	Oct. 24, 1945	Mauritius......	Apr. 24, 1968	United States	Oct. 24, 1945
El Salvador......	Oct. 24, 1945	Mexico........	Nov. 7, 1945	United Rep. of ..	
Equatorial Guinea	Nov. 12, 1968	Mongolia......	Oct. 27, 1961	Tanzania[3].....	Dec. 14, 1961
Ethiopia........	Nov. 13, 1945	Morocco.......	Nov. 12, 1956	Upper Volta.....	Sept. 20, 1960
Fiji.............	Oct. 13, 1970	Nepal.........	Dec. 14, 1955	Uruguay........	Dec. 18, 1945
Finland........	Dec. 14, 1955	Netherlands.....	Dec. 10, 1945	Venezuela......	Nov. 15, 1945
France.........	Oct. 24, 1945	New Zealand	Oct. 24, 1945	Yemen Arab Rep.	Sept. 30, 1947
Gabon.........	Sept. 20, 1960	Nicaragua......	Oct. 24, 1945	Yemen, Peoples ..	
Gambia........	Sept. 21, 1965	Niger.........	Sept. 20, 1960	Dem. Rep. of ...	Dec. 14, 1967
Germany, East ...	Sept. 18, 1973	Nigeria........	Oct. 7, 1960	Yugoslavia......	Oct. 24, 1945
Germany, West ..	Sept. 18, 1973	Norway........	Nov. 27, 1945	Zaire..........	Sept. 20, 1960
Ghana.........	Mar. 8, 1957	Oman.........	Oct. 7, 1971	Zambia........	Dec. 1, 1964

(1.) The Federation of Malaya joined the UN on Sept. 17, 1957. On Sept. 16, 1963, its name changed to Malaysia, following the admission to the new federation of Singapore, Sabah (North Borneo) and Sarawak. Singapore became an independent State Aug. 9, 1965 and a Member of the UN Sept. 21.

(2.) Egypt and Syria were original members of the United Nations from Oct. 24, 1945. Following a plebiscite held on Feb. 21, 1958, the United Arab Republic was established by a union of Egypt and Syria and continued as a single Member of the United Nations. On Oct. 13, 1961, Syria resumed its separate membership.

(3.) Tanganyika was a member of the United Nations from Dec. 14, 1961 and Zanzibar was a Member from Dec. 16, 1963. Following the ratification, on Apr. 26, 1964, of Articles of Union between Tanganyika and Zanzibar, the United Republic of Tanganyika and Zanzibar continued as a single Member of the United Nations, later changing its name to United Republic of Tanzania.

(4.) The General Assembly voted Oct. 25, 1971 to expel the Chinese National government of Taiwan and admit the Peking government in its place.

Operations of the United Nations Under Its Charter

The following article describes both the powers of the United Nations and its present organization. It is based on the provisions of the charter of the United Nations, and on an official report furnished by the Secretariat. The text of the Charter may be obtained from the Office of Public Information, United Nations, N. Y.

General Assembly

Pres. of 29th Session — Abdelaziz Bouteflika, Algeria.

The General Assembly is composed of representatives of all the member nations. Each nation may send not more than five representatives to each session. Each nation is entitled to one vote.

The General Assembly meets in regular annual sessions and in special session when necessary. Special sessions are convoked by the Secretary General at the request of the Security Council or of a majority of the members of the UN.

Any matter within the scope of the charter may be brought before the General Assembly, which may make recommendations on all except issues on the agenda of the Security Council. However, the General Assembly in November, 1950, decided that if the Security Council, because of lack of unanimity of the permanent members, fails to exercise its primary responsibility for the maintenance of international peace and security, in any case where there appears to be a threat to the peace, breach of the peace or act of aggression, the Assembly may consider it and recommend collective measures including, in the case of a breach of peace or act of aggression, the use of armed forces to maintain or restore peace. In such cases, the General Assembly may be convened within 24 hours in an emergency special session.

On important questions a two-thirds majority of members present and voting is required; on other questions a simple majority is sufficient. Questions that require a two-thirds majority include: recommendations on maintenance of international peace and security, election of non-permanent members of the Security Council, election of members of the Economic and Social Council, election of members of the UN that are to designate the members of the Trusteeship Council, admission of members to the UN, suspension and expulsion of members, trusteeship questions and budgetary matters.

The General Assembly must approve the budget and apportion expenses among members. A member in arrears will have no vote if the amount of arrears equals or exceeds the amount of the contributions due for the preceding two full years. The General Assembly may permit such a member to vote if it is satisfied that the failure is due to conditions beyond control.

A general or steering committee co-ordinates the proceedings of the Assembly and is composed of 26 members—the president of the Assembly, the 18 vice-presidents, and the chairmen of the seven main committees.

Security Council

The Security Council consists of 15 members, 5 with permanent seats. The remaining 10 are elected for 2-year terms by the General Assembly; they are not eligible for immediate re-election.

Permanent members of the Council: China, France, USSR, United Kingdom, United States.

Non-permanent members are Australia, Austria, Guinea, India, Indonesia, Kenya, Panama, Peru, Sudan, Yugoslavia.

The Presidency of the Council is held monthly in turn by the member states in English alphabetical order.

The Security Council has the primary responsibility for maintaining international peace and security and members agree to carry out its decisions. The Council may investigate any dispute that threatens international peace and security. When the Security Council is handling a dispute or situation the General Assembly makes no recommendation unless the Council requests it.

The Security Council functions continuously, each member being represented at all times. It may change its place of meeting. Any member of UN at UN headquarters may participate in its discussions and a nation not a member of UN may appear if it is a party to a dispute.

Decisions on procedural questions are made by an affirmative vote of 9 members. On all other matters the affirmative vote of 9 members must include the concurring votes of all permanent members; it is this clause which gives rise to the so-called "veto." A party to a dispute must refrain from voting.

The Security Council may decide to enforce its decisions without the use of arms. Such measures include interruption of economic relations, break in transportation and communications, and severance of diplomatic relations. If such measures fail the Council may call on UN members to furnish armed forces, assistance and facilities, based on agreements made by the Council with the states and subject to ratification by the members of the UN "in accordance with their constitutional processes."

The right of individual or collective self-defense is not prohibited by membership in the UN, and if a member nation is attacked it may do what is necessary, reporting this to the Security Council, which may take independent action. However, the Council encourages regional arrangements or agencies by means of which local disputes can be settled without getting as far as the Council, after the Council has approved this method.

In the event of a conflict between the obligations of members to the UN and to other international bodies of which they may be members, then obligations to the UN are paramount.

Economic and Social Council

The Economic and Social Council consists of 54 members elected by the General Assembly for 3-year terms of office. The council is responsible under the General Assembly for carrying out the functions of the United Nations with regard to international economic, social, cultural, educational, health and related matters. The council meets usually twice a year.

The Economic and Social Council had the following commissions in 1973:

Functional Commissions

Statistical; Population; Social Development; Narcotic Drugs; Human Rights (and its Sub-Commission on the Prevention of Discrimination and the Protection of Minorities); Status of Women.

Regional Economic Commissions

Economic Commission for Europe.
Economic Commission for Asia and the Far East.
Economic Commission for Latin America.
Economic Commission for Africa.
Economic Commission for Western Asia.

Trusteeship Council

The administration of Trust territories is subject to the supervision of the United Nations. Administering authorities are required to render an account of their stewardship to the Trusteeship Council. The Council may entertain petitions from private persons or organizations regarding conditions in the Trust territories and may dispatch missions to study conditions there.

The membership of the Council is made up of (1) countries which administer trust territories (Australia and the United States); (2) countries which are permanent members of the Security Council but which do not administer trust territories (China, France, the United Kingdom, USSR); and (3) as many other countries as may be necessary to ensure equal representation in the Council between administering and non-administering members. Those in the last named category are elected by the General Asembly for 3-year terms and are eligible for immediate reelection.

The Council usually meets once a year, in the spring.

The trust territories and the members administering them are: New Guinea (Australia), Pacific Islands (United States).

Non-Self-Governing Territories

Members of the United Nations responsible for the admisinistration of non-self-governing territories not under trusteeships recognize the principle that the interests of the inhabitants are paramount and promote their welfare. They are bound by the charter to transmit to the Secretary-General technical information concerning economic, social and educational conditions in the territories. This information is summarized, analyzed and classified by the Secretariat. Since 1961 a committee has been studying the implementation of the 1960 General Assembly declaration on the granting of independence to colonial countries and peoples. This committee also receives the reports on non self-governing territories.

International Court of Justice

The International Court of Justice is the principal judicial organ of the United Nations. All members are *ipso facto* parties to the statute of the Court. Other states may become parties to the Court's statute on conditions determined in each case by the General Assembly on the recommendation of the Security Council.

The jurisdiction of the Court comprises cases which the parties submit to it and matters especially provided for in the charter or in treaties. The Court gives advisory opinions and renders judgments. Its decisions, which are final, are only binding between the parties concerned and in respect to a particular dispute. If any party to a case fails to heed a judgment of the Court, the other party may have recourse to the Security Council, which may decide what is to be done.

The Court consists of 15 judges elected for 9-year terms by the General Assembly and the Security Council voting independently. No two of the judges may be nationals of the same state. Retiring judges are eligible for re-election. The Court remains permanently in session, except during the judicial vacations. A quorum of 9 judges suffices to constitute the Court. All questions are decided by majority. In the event of a tie, the President of the Court or the judge who acts in his place casts the deciding vote.

Judges
Nine-year term in office ending 1982:
Issaac Forster, Senegal.
Andre Gros, France.
Jose Maria Ruda, Argentina.
Nagendra Singh, India.
Sir Humphrey Waldock, Britain.
Nine-year term in office ending 1979:
Hardy C. Dillard, U.S.
Louis Ignacio-Pinto, Dahomey.
Federico de Castro, Spain.
Platon D. Morozov, USSR.
Eduardo Jimenez de Arechago, Uruguay.
Nine-year term in office ending 1976:
Sture Petran, Sweden
Cesar Bengzon, Philippines
Fouad Ammoun, Lebanon
Manfred Lachs, Poland
Charles D. Onyeama, Nigeria

The president until 1976 is Manfred Lachs, Poland, and the vice president is Fouad Ammoun, Lebanon.

Agencies Related to the United Nations

Working in partnership with the United Nations in various economic, social, scientific and technical fields is a group of intergovernmental organizations related to the United Nations by special agreements. Among these agencies (with their headquarters) are:

International Atomic Energy Agency (IAEA) aims to promote the peaceful uses of atomic energy. (Vienna)

International Labor Org. (ILO) aims to promote social justice; improve labor conditions and living standards; and promote economic stability. (Geneva)

Food & Agriculture Org. (FAO) aims to increase production from farms, forests and fisheries; improve distribution, marketing and nutrition. (Rome)

United Nations Educational, Scientific & Cultural Org. (UNESCO) aims to promote collaboration among nations through education, science and culture in order to further human rights and freedoms without distinction of race, sex, language or religion. (Paris)

World Health Org. (WHO) aims to aid the attainment of the highest possible level of health. (Geneva)

International Bank for Reconstruction & Development (World Bank) aims to help in the economic development of members by facilitating investment of capital; promote foreign investment and supplement private investment by providing loans for productive purposes out of its capital funds raised by it and its other resources; and to promote growth of international trade and equilibrium in balance of payments. (Washington, D. C.)

International Development Assn. (IDA) aims to further economic development of members by financing on terms bearing less heavily on balance of payments than those of conventional loans. (Washington, D. C.)

International Finance Corp. (IFC) aims to further economic developement in member countries by encouraging private enterprise, particularly in less developed areas. It is empowered to invest in private enterprises in association with private investors, and without government guarantee of repayment in cases where sufficient private capital is not available on reasonable terms; and to bring together private capital and management. (Washington, D. C.)

International Monetary Fund (Fund) aims to promote international monetary co-operation and currency stabilization. Sells currency to help members meet temporary foreign payments difficulties. (Washington, D. C.)

International Civil Aviation Org. (ICAO) promotes international civil aviation standards and regulations. (Montreal)

Universal Postal Union (UPU) aims to perfect postal services and promote international colaboration. To this end, members agree to handle other members mail by the best means used for its own mail. (Berne)

International Telecommunication Union (ITU) sets up international regulations of radio, telegraph, telephone and space radio-communications. Allocates radio frequencies. (Geneva)

World Meteorological Org. (WMO) aims to co-ordinate, standardize and improve world meteorological work. (Geneva)

Intergovernmental Maritime Consultative Org. (IMCO) aims to promote co-operation on technical matters affecting international shipping. (London)

General Agreement on Tariffs and Trade (GATT) was drafted in 1946. It establishes and administers code for orderly conduct of international trade. Provides export promotional assistance for developing countries. (Geneva)

United Nation's Children's Fund (UNICEF) helps requesting countries meet the urgent needs of their children. Supported entirely by voluntary contributions from governments and individuals. (New York)

Secretariat

The Secretariat is composed of a Secretary-General appointed by the General Assembly upon the recommendation of the Security Council and such staff as the organization may require.

The Secretary General is the chief administrative officer of the UN. He may bring to the attention of the Security Council any matter that threatens international peace. He reports to the General Assembly.

Kurt Waldheim (Austria), Secretary General.

He was chosen to succeed U Thant by the UN Security Council and General Assembly for a 5-year term begining. Jan. 1, 1972.

United Nations Budget

The General Assembly voted a gross budget of $540,473,000 for 1974-75. It also approved estimates of income totalling $92,646,000 for 1974-75 bringing the net budget for 1974-75 to $447,827,000.

Sources of Information

Public Inquiries Unit, Office of Public Information, United Nations, N. Y. Provides pamphlets, study guides, speakers, films; arranges group visits. Telephones-Information on UN activities: 754-1234.

UN Publications: UN Bookshop, United Nations, N.Y.

United Nations Assn. of th' United States of American Inc., 345 E. 46th St., New York, N.Y. Publications Center, 78 Fifth Ave., New York, N.Y.

Heads of States and Prime Ministers
Data to Sept. 1, 1974

Country	Head of State, Title	Born	Acceded or Elected	Premier or Prime Minister
Afghanistan	Mohammed Daud, pres		July 19, 1973	Mohammed Daud
Albania	Maj.-Gen. Haxhi Lleshi, pres	1913	July 1953	Maj. Gen. Mehmet Shehu
Algeria	Houari Boumediene, pres	1925	June 19, 1965	
Andorra	Pres. of France & Spanish bishop of Urgel			
Argentina	Maria Estela M. de Peron, pres	Feb. 6, 1931	July 1, 1974	
Australia (C)	Sir John R. Kerr, gov.-gen.(*)	Sept. 24, 1914	July 11, 1974	Edward Gough Whitlam
Austria	Rudolf Kirchslager, pres	Mar. 20, 1915	June 23, 1974	Dr. Bruno Kreisky
Bahamas(C)	Milo Butler, gov.-gen.(*)	Aug. 11, 1906	Aug. 1, 1973	Lynden Pindling
Bahrain	Isa bin Sulman al-Khalifa	July 3, 1933	Dec. 16, 1961	Isa bin Sulman al-Khalifa
Bangladesh(C)	Mohammadullah	Nov. 21, 1921	Dec. 24, 1973	Sheikh Mujibur Rahman
Barbados(C)	Sir A. W. Scott, gov.-gen.(*)	Mar. 17, 1900	May 18, 1967	E. W. Barrow
Belgium	Baudouin I, king	Sept. 7, 1930	July 17, 1951	Leo Tindemans
Bhutan	Jigme Singhi Wangchuk, king	Nov. 11, 1955	July 24, 1972	
Bolivia	Gen. Hugo Banzer Suarez, pres	May 10, 1926	Aug. 21, 1971	
Botswana(C)	Sir Seretse Khama, pres	July 1, 1921	Sept. 10, 1966	
Brazil	Gen. Ernesto Geisel, pres	Aug. 3, 1907	Jan. 15, 1974	
Bulgaria	Todor Zhivkov, pres	1911	July 7, 1971	Stanko Todorov
Burma	Ne Win	1911	Mar. 2, 1962	Ne Win
Burundi	Michel Micombero, pres	1939	Nov. 28, 1966	
Cambodia (Khmer Rep.)	Lon Nol, pres	1914	June 4, 1972	Long Boret
Cameroon	Ahmadou Ahidjo, pres	Aug. 24, 1924	Jan. 1, 1960	
Canada(C)	Jules Leger, gov.-gen.(*)	Apr. 4, 1913	Jan. 14, 1974	Pierre E. Trudeau
Central African Rep	Gen. Jean-Bedel Bokassa, pres	Feb. 22, 1920	Jan. 1, 1966	
Chad Rep	N'Garta Tombalbaye, pres	1918	Aug. 11, 1960	
Chile	Augusto Pinochet Ugarte, pres	Nov. 25, 1915	June 27, 1974	
China, People's Republic				Chou En-lai
China (Taiwan)	Chiang Kai-shek, pres	Oct. 31, 1887	Apr. 1948	Chiang Ching-kuo
Colombia	Alfonso Lopez Michelsen, pres	June 30, 1913	Aug. 7, 1974	
Congo, People's Rep	Maj. Marien Ngouabi, pres	1937	Jan. 1, 1969	
Costa Rica	Daniel Oduber Quiros, pres	Aug. 25, 1921	May 8, 1974	
Cuba	Osvaldo Dorticos Torrado, pres	1919	July 17, 1959	Fidel Castro
Cyprus(C)	Glafkos Clerides, pres	Apr. 24, 1919	Aug. 23, 1974	
Czechoslovakia	Ludvik Svoboda, pres	Nov. 25, 1895	Mar. 30, 1968	Lubomir Strougal
Dahomey Rep	Maj. Mathieu Kerekou, pres		Oct. 28, 1972	
Denmark	Margrethe II, queen	Apr. 16, 1940	Jan. 14, 1972	Poul Hartling
Dominican Rep	Dr. Joaquin Balaguer, pres	1908	July 1, 1966	
Ecuador	Guillermo Rodriguez Lara, pres	Nov. 4, 1923	Feb. 15, 1972	
Egypt	Anwar el-Sadat, pres	Dec. 25, 1918	Oct. 15, 1970	
El Salvador	Arturo Armando Molina, pres	Aug. 6, 1927	July 1, 1972	
Equatorial Guinea	Francisco Macias Nguema, pres	Jan. 1, 1924	Oct. 12, 1968	
Ethiopia	Haile Selassie I, emperor	July 23, 1892	Nov. 2, 1930	Michael Imru
Fiji(C)	Ratu Sir George Cakobau, gov.-gen.(*)	Nov. 6, 1912	Jan. 13, 1973	Sir Kamisese Mara
Finland	Dr. Urho Kekkonen, pres	Sept. 3, 1900	Feb. 15, 1956	Kalevi Sorsa
France	Giscard d'Estaing, pres	Feb. 2, 1926	May 27, 1974	Jacques Chirac
Gabon Rep	Albert Bernard Bongo, pres	Dec. 30, 1935	Dec. 1, 1967	
Gambia(C)	Sir Dawda Kairaba Jawara, pres	May 16, 1924	Apr. 24, 1970	
Germany, Fed. Rep	Walter Scheel, pres	July 8, 1919	May 15, 1974	Helmut Schmidt
Germany, East	Willi Stoph, chmn. council of state	July 9, 1914	Aug. 1973	Horst Sindermann
Ghana(C)	Col. Ignatius K. Acheampong	Sept. 23, 1931	Jan. 13, 1972	Kofi A. Busia
Greece	Faidon Ghizikis, pres	1917	Nov. 25, 1973	Constantine Caramanlis
Guatemala	Gen. Kjell Laugerud-Garcia, pres	Jan. 24, 1930	July 1, 1974	
Guinea, Rep	Sekou Toure, pres	Jan. 19, 1922	Oct. 2, 1958	Lansana Beavogui
Guyana (C)	Arthur Chung, pres	Jan. 19, 1918	Feb. 23, 1970	Forbes Burnham
Haiti	Jean-Claude Duvalier, pres	July 3, 1951	Apr. 21, 1971	
Honduras	Gen. Oswaldo Lopez Arellano, pres	1922	Dec. 4, 1972	
Hungary	Pal Losonczi, pres	1919	Apr. 14, 1967	Jeno Fock
Iceland	Kristjan Eldjarn, pres	Dec. 16, 1916	June 30, 1968	Geir Hallgrimsson
India (C)	Fakhruddin Ali Ahmed, pres	May 13, 1905	Aug. 24, 1974	Indira Nehru Gandhi
Indonesia	Suharto, pres	Feb. 28, 1921	Mar. 11, 1967	
Iran	Mohammed Reza Pahlavi, shah	Oct. 26, 1919	Sept. 18, 1941	Amir Abbas Hoveyda
Iraq	Ahmed Hassan al-Bakr, pres	1912	July 17, 1968	
Ireland	Erskine Childers, pres	Dec. 11, 1905	May 30, 1973	Liam Cosgrave
Israel	Ephraim Katzir, pres	May 16, 1916	Apr. 10, 1973	Yitzhak Rabin
Italy	Giovanni Leone, pres	Nov. 3, 1908	Dec. 24, 1971	Mariano Rumor
Ivory Coast	Felix Houphouet-Boigny, pres	Oct. 18, 1905	Nov. 27, 1960	
Jamaica (C)	Florizel Glasspole, gov.-Gen.(*)	Sept. 25, 1909	June 27, 1973	Michael Maniey
Japan	Hirohito, emperor	Apr. 29, 1901	Dec. 25, 1926	Kakuei Tanaka
Jordan	Hussein I, king	Nov. 14, 1935	May 2, 1952	Zaid al-Rifai
Kenya (C)	Jomo Kenyatta, pres	1890	Dec. 12, 1964	
Korea, Republic	Park Chung Hee, pres	Sept. 30, 1917	Nov. 26, 1963	Kim Jong Pii
Korea, People's Dem Rep	Choi Yung Kun, presidium chmn	1903		Marshal Kim Il-Sung
Kuwait	Sabah al-Salim al-Sabah, emir	1915	Nov. 27, 1965	Jaber al-Ahmed al-Jaber
Laos	Sri Savang Vatthana, king	Nov. 13, 1907	Oct. 30, 1959	Souvanna Phouma
Lebanon	Suleiman Franjieh, pres	1910	Aug. 17, 1970	Takieddin Solh
Lesotho (C)	Motlotlehi Moshoeshoe II, king	1898	Oct. 4, 1969	Chief Leabua Jonathan
Liberia	William R. Tolbert, Jr. pres	May 13, 1913	July 23, 1971	
Libya	Muammar el-Qaddafi	1942	Sept. 1, 1969	Abdel Salam Jailoud

(continued)

Country	Head of State, Title	Born	Acceded or Elected	Priemier or Prime Minister
Liechtenstein	Prince Franz Jo-seph II, ruler	Aug. 16, 1906	July 26, 1938	Dr. Walter Kieber
Luxembourg	Grand Duke Jean	Jan. 5, 1921	Nov. 12, 1964	Gaston Thorn
Madagascar	Gen. Gariel Ramanantsoa	1916	Oct. 9, 1972	
Malawi (C)	Dr. H. Kamuzu Banda, pres.	1906	July 6, 1966	
Malaysia (C)	Abdul Halim Muazam, paramount ruler	1928	Sept. 21, 1970	Abdul Razak
Maldives, Rep. of	Ibrahim Nasir, pres.	Sept. 2, 1926	Nov. 11, 1968	Ahmed Zaki
Mali	Moussa Traore, pres.	Sept. 25, 1936	Nov. 19, 1968	
Malta (C)	Sir Anthony Mamo, gov.-gen.(*)	Jan. 9, 1909	July 3, 1971	Dom Mintoff
Mauritania	Moktar O. Daddah, pres.	Apr. 25, 1925	Nov., 1958	Moktar Daddah
Mauritius (C)	Sir Abdool Raman Osman, gov.-Gen.(*)	Aug., 1902	Dec. 27, 1972	Sir Seewoosagur Ramgoolan
Mexico	Luis Echeverria Alvarez	Jan. 17, 1922	July 5, 1970	
Monaco	Rainier III, prince	May 31, 1923	May 9, 1949	
Mongolia	Y. Tsendenbal, presidium chmn.	Sept. 17, 1916	June 11, 1974	Jambyn Batmunkh
Morocco	Hassan II, king	July 11, 1929	Mar. 3, 1961	Ahmed Osman
Nauru (C)	Hammer De Roburt, pres.	Sept. 25, 1922	Jan. 31, 1968	
Nepal	Birendra Bir Bikram, shah	Dec. 28, 1945	Jan. 31, 1972	Nagendra Prashah Rijal
Netherlands	Juliana, queen	Apr. 30, 1909	Sept. 6, 1948	Joop M. den Uyl
New Zealand (C)	Sir Denis Blundell, gov.-gen.(*)	May 29, 1907	Sept. 27, 1972	Vacant
Nicaragua	3-man natl. governing council			
Niger	Hamani Diori, pres.	June 16, 1916	Nov. 9, 1960	
Nigeria (C)	Gen. Yakubu Gowon, head of mil. govt.	Oct. 19, 1934	Aug. 1, 1966	
Norway	Olav V, king	July 2, 1903	Sept. 21, 1957	Trygve M. Bratteli
Oman	Sultan Qabus bin Said	Nov. 18, 1940	July 23, 1970	
Pakistan	Chaudhri Fazal Elahi, pres.	1904	Aug. 14, 1973	Zulfikar Ali Bhutto
Panama	Demetrio B. Lakas, pres. prov. govt.	Aug. 29, 1925	Mar., 1972	
Paraguay	Gen. Alfredo Stroessner, pres.	Nov. 3, 1912	Aug. 15, 1954	
Peru	Gen. Juan Velasco Alvarado, pres.	1910	Oct. 3, 1968	Gen. Edgardo Mercado
Philippines	Ferdinand Marcos, pres.	Sept. 11, 1917	Dec. 30, 1965	
Poland	Edward Gierek, chmn. council of state	Jan. 6, 1913	Mar. 28, 1972	Piotr Jaroszewicz
Portugal	Gen. Antonio de Spinola, pres.	Apr. 11, 1910	May 15, 1974	Col. Vasco de Goncalves
Qatar	Khalifa bin Hamad Al-Thani	1936	Feb. 22, 1972	
Rhodesia	C. W. Dupont, pres.	Dec. 6, 1905	Mar. 2, 1970	Ian Smith
Romania	Nicolae Ceausescu, state council pres.	Jan. 26, 1918	Dec. 7, 1967	Manea Manescu
Rwanda	Maj. Gen. Habyalimana Juvenal, pres.			
San Marino	Co-regents			
Saudi Arabia	Faisal Abdel Aziz al Saud, king	1906	Nov. 2, 1964	
Senegal Rep.	Leopold S. Senghor, pres.	1907	Sept., 1960	Abdou Diouf
Sierra Leone (C)	Siaka Stevens, pres.	1906	Apr. 28, 1971	S. I. Korma
Singapore (C)	Benjamin H. Sheares, pres.	Aug. 12, 1907	Jan. 2, 1971	Lee Kuan Yew
Somali, Dem. Rep.	Mohamed Siad Barre, council pres.		Oct. 15, 1969	
South Africa	Jacobus J. Fouche, pres.	June 6, 1898	June 10, 1968	B. John Vorster
Spain	Gen. Francisco Franco Bahamonde, chief of state	Dec. 4, 1892	Aug. 9, 1969	Carlos Arias Navarro
Sri Lanka (Ceylon) (C)	William Gopallawa, pres.	Sept. 16, 1897	May 22, 1972	Mrs. Sirimavo Bandaranaike
Sudan	Gaafar al-Nimeiry, pres.	1929	May 25, 1969	Ba Bakr Awadallah
Swaziland (C)	Sobhuza II, king	July 22, 1899	Apr. 25, 1967	Prince Makhosini
Sweden	Carl XVI Gustaf, king	Apr. 30, 1946	Sept. 15, 1973	Olof Palme
Switzerland (1)	Ernest Brugger, pres.	Mar. 10, 1914	Jan. 1, 1974	Pierre Graber, vice pres.
Syria	Hafez al-Assad, chief of state	Mar., 1930	Mar. 14, 1971	Mahmoud Al-Ayoubi
Tanzania (C)	Julius K. Nyerere, pres.	1922	Apr. 26, 1964	R. M. Kawawa
Thailand	Phumiphol Aduldet, king	Dec. 5, 1927	June 9, 1946	Sanya Dharmasakti
Togo	Gen. Gnassingbe Eyadema, pres.	1932	Jan. 13, 1967	
Tonga	Taufa'ahau Tupou IV, king	July 4, 1918	July 5, 1967	Prince Tu'pelehake
Trinidad-Tobago (C)	Sir Ellis E. I. Clarke, gov.-gen.(*)	Dec. 28, 1917	Feb., 1973	Eric Williams
Tunisia	Habib Bourguiba, pres.	Aug. 3, 1903	July 25, 1957	Hedi Nouira
Turkey	Fahri Koruturk, pres.	1903	Apr. 6, 1973	Bulent Ecevit
Uganda (C)	Maj. Gen. Idi Amin, pres.	1925	Jan. 25, 1971	
USSR	Nikolai V. Podgorny, presidium pres.	Feb. 18, 1903	Dec. 9, 1965	Aleksei N. Kosygin
United Arab Emirates	Sheikh Zayed bin Sultan al-Nahayan, pres.	1923	Dec. 2, 1972	
United Kingdom (C)	Elizabeth II, queen	Apr. 21, 1926	Feb. 6, 1952	Harold Wilson
United States	Gerald R. Ford, pres.	July 14, 1913	Aug. 9, 1974	
Upper Volta	Gen. Sangoule Lamizana, pres.	1921	Jan. 3, 1966	Gerard Kango Ouedraogo
Uruguay	Juan M. Bordaberry, pres.	1928	Mar. 1, 1972	
Vatican City	Giovanni Battista Montini, Pope Paul VI	Sept. 26, 1897	June 21, 1963	
Venezuela	Carlos Andres Perez, pres.	Oct. 27, 1922	Mar. 12, 1974	
Vietnam, Dem. Republic of	Ton Duc Thang	1888	Sept. 23, 1969	Pham Van Dong
Vietnam, Rep. of	Nguyen Van Thieu, pres.	Apr. 5, 1923	June 12, 1965	Tran Thein Khiem
Western Samoa (C)	Malietoa Tanumafili II, head of state	Jan. 4, 1913	Jan. 1, 1962	Fiame Mata'afa Faumuina Mulinuu II
Yemen, People's Dem. Rep. of	Salem Robaye Ali, council pres.	1934	June 23, 1969	Ali Nasser Hassani
Yemen Arab Rep.	Lt. Col. Ibrahim Al-Hamdy, pres.	1944	June 13, 1974	Mohsin Al-Aini
Yugoslavia	Josip Broz Tito, pres.	May 25, 1892	Jan. 31, 1946	Dzemal Bijedic
Zaire	Mobutu Sese Seko, pres.	Oct. 30, 1939	Nov. 25, 1965	
Zambia (C)	Kenneth Kaunda, pres.	Apr. 28, 1924	Oct. 24, 1964	

(1) President serves one-year term, the vice president customarily succeeds him.
(C) Member of the Commonwealth of Nations.
(*) Gov.-Gen. Acts as representative of the British monarch, who is recognized as head of state.

Ambassadors and Envoys
As of September 1, 1974

The address of foreign embassies to the United States is Washington, D.C.
*Embassy was closed and personnel withdrawn. Limited staffs remain but no ambassadors in Algeria and Iraq are assigned. Names followed by (nom.) have been nominated but not confirmed by U.S. Senate.

Countries	Envoys from United States	Envoys to United States
Afghanistan	Theodore L. Eliot Jr., Amb.	Abdullah Malikyar, Amb.
*Algeria	Vacant	Vacant
Argentina	Robert C. Hill, Amb.	Alejandro Orfila, Amb.
Australia	Marshall Green, Amb.	Sir Patrick Shaw, Amb.
Austria	John P. Humes, Amb.	Arno Halusa, Amb.
Bahamas	Seymour Weiss, Amb.	Livingston B. Johnson, Amb.
Bahrain	Joseph W. Twinam Amb.	M. Hossain Ali, Amb.
Bangladesh	Davis E. Boster, Amb.	
Barbados	Eileen R. Donovan, Amb.	Cecil B. Williams, Amb.
Belgium	Leonard K. Firestone, Amb.	Herman Dehennin, Charge d'Affaires
Bolivia	William P. Stedman Jr., Amb.	Edmundo Valencia-Ibanez, Amb.
Botswana	David B. Bolen, Amb.	Amos M. Dambe, Amb.
Brazil	John Hugh Crimmins, Amb.	Joao Augusto Araujo Castro, Amb.
Bulgaria	Martin F. Herz, Amb.	Lubomir D. Popov, Amb.
Burma	David L. Osborn, Amb.	U Lwin, Amb.
Burundi	David E. Mark, Amb.	Joseph Ndabaniwe, Amb.
Cameroon	C. Robert Moore, Amb.	Francois-Xavier Tchoungui, Amb.
Cambodia(Khmer Rep.)	John Gunther Dean, Amb.	Um Sim, Amb.
Canada	William J. Porter, Amb.	Marcel Cadieux, Amb.
Centr. African Rep.	William N. Dale, Amb.	Gaston Banda-Bafiot, Amb.
Chad	Vacant	Bawoyeu Alingue, Amb.
Chile	David H. Popper, Amb.	Walter Heitmann, Amb.
China (Taiwan)	Leonard Unger, Amb.	James C. H. Shen, Amb.
China, People's Rep.[1]	David K.E. Bruce[1]	Huang Chen[1]
Colombia	Viron P. Vaky, Amb.	Dr. Douglas Botero-Boshell, Amb.
Congo (Kinshasa)	(See Zaire).	
Costa Rica	Stanton D. Anderson (nom.), Amb.	Rodolfo Silva Vargas, Amb.
Cyprus	William R. Crawford Jr. Amb.	Nicos G. Dimitriou, Amb.
Czechoslovakia	Albert W. Sherer Jr., Amb.	Dr. Dusan Spacil, Amb.
Dahomey	James B. Engle (nom.), Amb.	Tiamiou Adjibade, Amb.
Denmark	Philip K. Crowe, Amb.	Eyvind Bartels, Amb.
Dominican Republic	Robert A. Hurwitch, Amb.	S. Salvador Ortiz, Amb.
Ecuador	Robert C. Brewster, Amb.	Alberto Quevedo-Toro, Amb.
Egypt	Hermann F. Eilts, Amb.	Ashraf A. Ghorbal, Amb.
El Salvador	James F. Campbell, Amb.	Francisco Bertrand Galindo, Amb.
Equatorial Guinea	C. Robert Moore, Amb.	Ernst Jaakson, Consul General
Estonia	*	
Ethiopia	Vacant	Kifle Wodajo, Amb.
Fiji	Armistead I. Selden Jr., Amb.	S. K. Sikivou, Amb.
Finland	V. John Krehbiel, Amb.	Leo Tuominen, Amb.
France	John N. Irwin II, Amb.	Jacques Kosciusko-Morizet, Amb.
Gabon	John A. McKesson 3d, Amb.	Vincent Mavourgou, Amb.
Gambia, Rep. of	O. Rudolph Aggrey, Amb.	Vacant
Germany	Martin J. Hillenbrand, Amb.	Berndt von Staden, Amb.
Ghana	Shirley Temple Black (nom.), Amb.	Harry R. Amonoo, Amb.
Great Britain	Walter H. Annenberg, Amb.	Sir Peter Ramsbotham, Amb.
Greece	Jack B. Kubisch, Amb.	Constantine P. Panayotacos, Amb.
Guatemala	Francis E. Meloy Jr., Amb.	Julio Asensio-Wunderlich, Amb.
Guinea	Terence A. Todman, Amb.	Hibib Bah, Amb.
Guyana	Max V. Krebs, Amb.	Frederick Hillborn Talbot, Amb.
Haiti	Heyward Isham, Amb.	Gerard S. Bouchette, Amb.
Honduras	Phillip V. Sanchez, Amb.	Roberto Alonzo Cleaves, Charge d'Affaires
Hungary	Richard F. Pedersen, Amb.	Dr. Karoly Szabo, Amb.
Iceland	Frederick Irving, Amb.	Haraldur Kroyer, Amb.
India	Daniel P. Moynihan, Amb.	Triloki Nath Kaul, Amb.
Indonesia	David D. Newsom, Amb.	Abdul Habir, Charge d'Affaires
Iran	Richard Helms, Amb.	Ardeshir Zahedi, Amb.
Iraq	*Vacant	Vacant
Ireland	John D. J. Moore, Amb.	John G. Molloy, Amb.
Israel	Kenneth B. Keating, Amb.	Simcha Dinitz, Amb.
Italy	John A. Volpe, Amb.	Edgido Ortona, Amb.
Ivory Coast	Robert S. Smith, Amb.	Timothee N'Guetta Ahoua, Amb.
Jamaica	Sumner Gerard, Amb.	Douglas V. Fletcher, Amb.
Japan	James D. Hodgson, Amb.	Takeshi Yasukawa, Amb.
Jordan	Thomas R. Pickering, Amb.	Abdallah Salah, Amb.
Kenya	Anthony D. Marshall, Amb.	Leonard Oliver Kibinge, Amb.
Korea	Richard L. Sneider, Amb.	Pyong-choon Hahm, Amb.
Kuwait	William A. Stoltzfus Jr., Amb.	Salem S. Al-Sabah, Amb.
Laos	Charles S. Whitehouse, Amb.	Phagna Pheng Norindr, Amb.
Latvia		Dr. Anatole Dinbergs, Charge d'Affaires
Lebanon	G. McMurtrie Godley, Amb.	Najati Kabbani, Amb.

Lesotho	David B. Bolen, Amb........	Ephraim Tsepa Manare, Amb.
Liberia	Melvin L. Manfull, Amb......	S. Edward Peal, Amb.
Libya	*Vacant*	Hussein Zagaar, Charge d'Affaires
Lithuania		Joseph Kajeckas, Charge d'Affaires
Luxembourg	Dr. Ruth Lewis Farkas, Amb..	Jean Wagner, Amb.
Malagasy Rep.	Joseph A. Mendenhall, Amb..	Henri Raharijaona, Amb.
Malawi	Robert A. Stevenson, Amb...	Robert B. Mbaya, Amb.
Malaysia	Francis T. Underhill Jr., Amb.	Mohamed Khir Johari, Amb.
Maldives, Rep.	Christopher Van Hollen, Amb....................	*Vacant*
Mali	Ralph J. McGuire, Amb......	Seydou Traore, Amb.
Malta	Robert P. Smith, Amb.......	Joseph Attard-Kingswell, Amb.
Mauritania	Richard W. Murphy, Amb....	Ahmedou Ould Abdallah, Amb.
Mauritius	Philip W. Manhard, Amb.....	Pierre Guy Girald Balancy, Amb.
Mexico	Joseph J. Jova, Amb.........	Dr. Jose Juan de Olloqui, Amb.
Morocco	Robert G. Neumann, Amb....	Badreddine Senoussi, Amb.
Nepal	William I. Cargo, Amb.......	Yadu Nath Khanal, Amb.
Netherlands	Kingdon Gould Jr., Amb.....	Baron Rijnhard Van Lyden, Amb.
New Zealand	Armistead I. Selden Jr., Amb.	Lloyd White, Amb.
Nicaragua	Turner B. Shelton, Amb.....	Dr. Guillermo Sevilla-Sacasa, Amb.
Niger	L. Douglas Heck, Amb.......	Abdoulaye Diallo, Amb.
Nigeria	John E. Reinhardt, Amb.....	John M. Garba, Amb.
Norway	Thomas R. Byrne, Amb......	Soren Christian Sommerfelt, Amb.
Oman	William D. Wolle, Amb......	Ahmed Macki, Amb.
Pakistan	Henry A. Byroade, Amb.....	Sahabzada Yaqub-Khan, Amb.
Panama	William J. Jorden, Amb......	Nicolas Gonzalez Revilla, Amb.
Paraguay	George W. Landau, Amb.....	Miguel Solano Lopez, Amb.
Peru	Robert W. Dean, Amb.......	Fernando Berckemeyer, Amb.
Philippines	William H. Sullivan, Amb....	Eduardo Z. Romualdez, Amb.
Poland	Richard T. Davies, Amb.....	Witold Trampczynski, Amb.
Portugal	Stuart Nash Scott, Amb.....	Joao Hall Themido, Amb.
Qatar	Robert P. Paganelli, Amb....	Abdullah S. Al-Mania, Amb.
Romania	Harry G. Barnes Jr., Amb....	Corneliu Bogdan, Amb.
Rwanda	Robert E. Fritts, Amb.......	Joseph Nizeyimana, Amb.
Saudi Arabia	James E. Akins, Amb........	Ibrahim Al-Sowayel, Amb.
Senegal	O. Rudolph Aggrey, Amb.....	Andre Coulbary, Amb.
Sierra Leone	Clinton L. Olson, Amb.......	Philip J. Palmer, Amb.
Singapore	Edwin M. Cronk, Amb.......	Dr. Ernest S. Monteiro, Amb.
Somali, Democratic Rep.	Roger Kirk, Amb...........	Dr. Adbullahi Ahmed Addou, Amb.
South Africa	John G. Hurd, Amb.........	Johan S. F. Botha, Amb.
Spain	Adm. Horacio Rivero, Amb...	Joaquin Cervino, Charge d'Affaires
Sri Lanka (Ceylon)	Christopher Van Hollen, Amb....................	Neville Kanakaratne, Amb.
Sudan	William D. Brewer, Amb.....	Abdel Aziz Harnza, Charge d'Affaires
Swaziland	David B. Bolen, Amb........	J.L.F. Simelane, Amb.
Sweden	Robert Strausz-Hupe, Amb...	Count Wilhelm Wachtmeister, Amb.
Switzerland	Shelby Davis, Amb..........	Felix Schnyder, Amb.
Syrian Arab Rep.	Richard W. Murphy, Amb....	Sabah Kabbani, Charge d'Affaires
Tanzania	W. Beverly Carter Jr., Amb..	Paul Bomani, Amb.
Thailand	William R. Kintner, Amb.....	Anand Panyarachun, Amb.
Togo	Nancy V. Rawls, Amb.......	Michel Messanvi Kekeh, Amb.
Trinidad and Tobago	Lloyd I. Miller, Amb........	Victor McIntyre, Amb.
Tunisia	Talcott W. Seelye, Amb.....	Ali Hedda, Amb.
Turkey	William B. Macomber Jr., Amb....................	Melih Esenbel, Amb.
Uganda	Thomas Patrick Melady, Amb.	S.M. Nsubuga, Charge d'Affaires
USSR	Walter J. Stoessel Jr., Amb...	Anatoliy F. Dobrynin, Amb.
United Arab Emirates	Michael Sterner, Amb.......	Hamad Abdul Rahman Al Madfa, Charge d'Affaires
Upper Volta	Pierre R. Graham, Amb......	Telesphore Yaguibou, Amb.
Uruguay	Ernest V. Siracusa, Amb.....	Dr. Hector Luisi, Amb.
Venezuela	Robert McClintock, Amb.....	Andres Aguilar, Amb.
Vietnam	Graham A. Martin, Amb.....	Tran Kim Phuong, Amb.
Western Samoa	*Vacant*	*Vacant*
Yemen Arab Rep.	*Vacant*	Yahya Geghman, Amb.
Yugoslavia	Malcolm Toon, Amb........	Toma Granfil, Amb.
Zaire	Deane R. Hinton, Amb......	Mbeka Makosso, Amb.
Zambia	Jean M. Wilkowski, Amb.....	Siteke Gibson Mwale, Amb.

1.No formal diplomatic relations; Huang and Bruce are heads of missions.

Special Missions

U.S. Mission to North Atlantic Treaty Organization, Brussels—Donald Rumsfeld.
U.S. Mission to the European Communities, Brussels—Joseph A. Greenwald.
U.S. Mission to the International Atomic Energy Agency, Vienna—Gerald F. Tape.
U.S. Mission to the United Nations, New York—John A. Scali.
U.S. Mission to the European Office of the UN & Other Internatl. Organizations, Geneva—Francis L. Dale.
U.S. Mission to the Organization for Economic Cooperation and Development, Paris—William C. Turner.
U.S. Mission to the International Civil Aviation Organization, Montreal—Mrs. Betty Crites Dillon.

U.S. Aid to Foreign Countries

Source: Bureau of Economic Analysis, U.S. Department of Commerce

Data shown by country includes the military supplies and services furnished under the Foreign Assistance Act and direct Defense Department appropriations. This aid is principally to the Southeast Asia countries. Data shown include credits which have been extended to private entities in the country specified.

Grants are largely outright gifts for which no payment is expected or which at most involve an obligation on the part of the receiver to extend aid to the United States or other countries to achieve a common objective.

Net grants and credits take into account all known returns to the U.S. government, including reverse grants, returns of grants and payments of principal. A minus sign indicates that the total of these returns to the U.S. is greater than the total of grants or credits.

Other assistance represents the transfer of U.S. farm products in exchange for foreign currencies, less the government's disbursements of the currencies as grants, credits, or for purchases. The net acquisitions of currencies represents net transfers of resources to foreign currencies in addition to those classified as grants or credits.

Amounts do not include investments in international financial institutions in 1973 as follows: Asian Development Bank (ADB) $11,746,000; Inter-American Development Bank (IDB) $196,750,000; International Bank for Reconstruction and Development $12,019,000; International Development Association (IDA) $152,105,000.

In millions of dollars or equivalent (*Less than $500,000)

Calendar Year 1973	Total	Net grants	Net credits	Net other	Calendar Year 1973	Total	Net grants	Net credits	Net other
TOTAL..................	6,392	4,751	1,688	-47	Papua New Guinea......	3	—	3	—
Military grants...........	2,818	2,818	—	—	Philippines.............	70	36	34	*
Other grants, credits, ass't..	3,574	1,933	1,688	-47	Thailand................	21	19	1	—
Western Europe..........	-20	-102	85	-3	Trust Terr. Pacific......	63	63	—	—
Austria.................	-2	—	-2	—	Vietnam................	438	444	-1	-6
Belgium-Luxembourg	3	—	3	—	Other & unspecified......	35	1	34	—
Denmark................	24	—	24	—	**Africa..................**	**296**	**153**	**149**	**-7**
Finland................	-6	—	-6	*	Algeria................	50	*	50	—
France.................	12	—	12	—	Cameroon.............	3	1	2	—
Germany, West.........	8	—	8	*	Chad.................	1	1	—	—
Iceland................	-3	—	-3	—	Dahomey.............	*	*	*	—
Ireland................	-10	—	-10	—	Ethiopia..............	17	10	8	—
Italy..................	11	*	11	—	Ghana................	6	6	*	*
Netherlands............	52	—	52	—	Guinea...............	8	*	12	-4
Norway................	38	—	38	—	Ivory Coast...........	22	1	21	—
Portugal	11	—	11	—	Kenya................	5	4	1	—
Spain.................	106	3	103	*	Lesotho..............	3	3	—	—
Sweden................	4	—	4	—	Liberia...............	-3	6	-10	—
United Kingdom........	-132	—	-132	*	Libya................	*	*	*	—
Yugoslavia.............	-44	—	-42	-2	Madagascar...........	*	*	*	—
European Payments					Malawi...............	1	*	*	—
Union...............	-118	-118	—	—	Mali.................	8	7	1	—
Atomic EEC............	-1	—	-1	—	Morocco..............	13	12	5	-4
Coal-Steel EEC.........	-5	—	-5	—	Niger................	10	10	*	—
Other & unspecified......	32	13	20	-1	Nigeria...............	24	9	15	—
					Senegal..............	8	8	*	*
Eastern Europe..........	**369**	**1**	**385**	**17**	Sierra Leone..........	2	2	*	—
Hungary...............	1	—	1	1	Somalia..............	1	*	1	—
Poland................	11	1	27	-17	Sudan................	16	3	14	-1
Romania...............	-1	*	-1	—	Tanzania.............	8	5	3	—
Soviet Union...........	359	—	359	—	Togo.................	2	2	—	—
					Tunisia..............	12	12	-2	2
Near East & South Asia....	**1,026**	**516**	**520**	**-9**	Uganda..............	2	2	*	—
Afghanistan............	30	13	17	*	Upper Volta..........	7	7	—	—
Bangladesh............	137	122	15	—	Zaire................	10	4	7	*
Cyprus................	-1	1	-1	—	Zambia..............	8	*	8	—
Egypt.................	-20	4	-21	-4	Other & unspecified......	51	38	13	*
Greece................	43	*	43	*	**Western Hemisphere......**	**521**	**172**	**352**	**4**
India.................	67	108	-38	-3	Argentina............	-11	*	-11	*
Iran..................	221	1	220	*	Bermuda.............	11	—	11	—
Iraq..................	-2	*	-2	—	Bolivia...............	10	6	4	*
Israel.................	237	115	123	*	Brazil................	80	22	59	*
Jordan................	65	54	11	*	Canada..............	65	—	65	—
Kuwait................	-10	—	-10	—	Chile................	28	5	23	*
Lebanon...............	4	3	1	—	Colombia.............	94	13	81	*
Nepal.................	11	11	*	*	Costa Rica...........	9	5	5	—
Pakistan...............	134	31	105	-2	Dominican Republic....	19	7	13	—
Saudi Arabia...........	-17	*	-17	—	Ecuador.............	10	9	1	*
Sri Lanka (Ceylon)	24	2	22	*	El Salvador...........	8	4	5	—
Syria.................	*	*	*	—	Guatemala...........	14	6	8	—
Turkey................	65	13	52	*	Guyana..............	4	1	2	—
Yemen (Sana)	2	2	—	—	Haiti................	4	4	-1	—
Other & Unspecified......	36	36	—	—	Honduras............	9	6	3	—
East Asia & Pacific........	**943**	**748**	**203**	**-10**	Jamaica..............	18	2	15	—
Australia...............	-59	—	-59	—	Mexico..............	-5	*	-6	—
Brunei................	4	—	4	—	Nicaragua...........	20	8	12	—
Burma................	1	*	*	*	Panama.............	38	7	31	—
Cambodia.............	128	99	31	-1	Paraguay............	5	7	1	-3
China-Taiwan..........	39	4	36	-2	Peru................	42	12	31	*
Hong Kong............	*	*	—	—	Trinidad-Tobago......	1	*	1	—
Indonesia.............	160	14	147	*	Uruguay.............	5	2	3	*
Japan.................	-230	-2	-227	*	Venezuela............	-17	2	-19	—
Korea.................	214	13	201	-1	Other & unspecified......	62	45	18	*
Laos..................	54	54	—	—	**International organizations**				*
Malaysia..............	-6	3	-9	—	**& unspecified areas.....**	**439**	**444**	**-5**	**—**
New Zealand..........	8	—	8	—					

Population of Important World Cities

Source: Latest census reports and latest official estimates; *(asterisk) denotes capital;
Gr. denotes Greater, or metropolitan area
See index for U.S. and Canadian cities

Afghanistan
*Kabul 318,094
Kandahar 133,799

Albania
*Tirana 169,300

Algeria
*Algiers 903,530
Constantine 243,558
Oran 327,493

Andorra
*Andorra La Vella . . 8,062

Angola
Luanda, Gr 224,540

Argentina
*Buenos Aires . . 2,972,453
Cordoba, Gr 798,663
La Plata, Gr 506,287
Mendoza, Gr 470,896
Rosario, Gr 810,840
Santa Fe, Gr 244,579
Tucuman, Gr 365,757

Australia
Adelaide, Gr 842,693
Brisbane, Gr 867,784
*Canberra 141,795
Melbourne, Gr . . 2,503,450
Newcastle, Gr . . . 249,962
Perth, Gr 703,199
Sydney, Gr 2,807,828

Austria
Graz 249,211
Linz 204,627
Salzburg 128,845
*Vienna 1,614,841

Bahamas
*Nassau, Gr 101,503

Bahrain
*Manama 88,785

Bangladesh
Chittagong 416,733
*Dacca 1,310,976
Khulna 436,000

Barbados
*Bridgetown 8,789

Belgium
 1,195,000
*Brussels, Gr . . . 1,540,000
Charleroi, Gr 217,349
Ghent, Gr 224,728
Liege, Gr 880,000

Belize (Br. Honduras)
*Belize, Gr 48,421

Bermuda
*Hamilton 3,000

Bolivia
*La Paz 700,000
Santa Cruz 200,000
*Sucre 53,000

Botswana
*Gaborone 17,718

Brazil
Belem 762,000
Belo Horizonte . 1,542,000
*Brasilia 600,000
Curitiba 760,000
Fortaleza 1,059,000
Niteroi 324,367
Porto Alegre . . . 1,105,000
Recife 1,352,000
Rio de Janeiro . . 4,658,000
Salvador 1,311,000
Santos 262,048
Sao Paulo 7,693,000

Bulgaria
Plovdiv 249,982
*Sofia 876,943

Burma
 195,348
Moulmein 108,020
*Rangoon 1,717,649

Burundi
*Bujumbura, Gr . . . 78,810

Cambodia (Khmer Rep.)
*Phnom-Penh 393,995

Cameroon
Douala, Gr 250,000
*Yoaunde 165,810

Central African Rep.
*Bangui, Gr 187,000

Chad
*N'Djamena, Gr . . 179,000

Chile
Concepcion 196,317
*Santiago, Gr . . 2,661,920
Valparaiso 292,847

China
Amoy 224,300
Arshan 805,000
Canton 1,840,000
Changchun 975,000
Changsha 703,000
Chengchow 766,000
Chengtu 1,107,000
Chungking 2,121,000
Foochow 616,000
Fushun 985,000
Hangchow 784,000
Harbin 1,552,000
Lanchow 699,000
Nanking 1,419,000
*Peking 7,570,000
Port Arthur,
Dairen 1,508,000
Shanghai 10,820,000
Shenyang 2,411,000
Sian 1,310,000
Taiyuan 1,020,000
Tientsin 4,280,000
Tsinan 862,000
Tsingtao 1,121,000
Tsitsihar 668,000
Wuhan 2,146,000

China (Taiwan)
Kaohsiung 950,729
Keelung 338,519
Taichung 513,293
Tainan 505,758
*Taipei 1,972,571

Colombia
Barranquilla . . . 816,706
*Bogota 2,680,100
Bucaramanga . . 324,400
Cali 1,100,000
Cartagena 315,200
Medellin 1,091,600

Congo, People's Rep.
*Brazzaville, Gr . . 136,200

Congo, Democratic Rep.
See Zaire

Costa Rica
*San Jose 205,650

Cuba
Camaguey 178,600
*Havana, Gr . . . 1,565,700
Santa Clara 137,700
Santiago de Cuba 259,000

Cyprus
*Nicosia, Gr 115,000

Czechoslovakia
Bratislava 293,333
Brno 338,985
Ostrava 282,312
Plzen (Pilsen) . . . 147,650
*Prague 1,101,257

Dahomey
Cotonou 111,100
*Porto Novo 74,500

Denmark
Arhus 233,162
*Copenhagen, Gr.
 1,383,073
Odense 164,166

Dominican Republic
*Santo Domingo . . 671,402

Ecuador
Guayaquil 860,600
*Quito 564,900

Egypt
Alexandria 4,961,000
*Cairo 2,032,000
Giza 711,900
Port Said 313,000
Suez 315,000

El Salvador
*San Salvador 337,171

Ethiopia
*Addis Ababa 881,400
Asmara 240,700

Fiji
*Suva 60,000

Finland
*Helsinki 532,182
Tampere 156,375
Turku 153,347

France
Bordeaux 270,996
Le Havre 200,940
Lille 194,948
Lyon 535,000
Marseille 893,771
Nantes 265,009
Nice 325,400
*Paris 2,607,625
*Paris, Gr 9,250,647
St. Etienne 216,020
Strasbourg 254,038
Toulouse 380,340

Gabon
*Libreville, Gr 57,000

Gambia
*Banjul 31,800

Germany
Aachen 177,600
Augsburg 214,400
Berlin (West) . . 2,134,300
Bielefeld 169,300
Bochum 346,900
*Bonn 299,400
Bremen 607,200
Brunswick 225,200
Cologne 866,300
Darmstadt 141,100
Dortmund 648,900
Duesseldorf 680,000
Duisburg 457,900
Essen 704,800
Frankfurt 660,400
Gelsenkirchen . . 348,600
Hamburg 1,817,100
Hannover 517,800
Heidelberg 121,900
Karlsruhe 257,100
Kassel 213,500
Kiel 276,600
Krefeld 228,700
Luebeck 242,200
Ludwigshafen . . 174,700
Mannheim 330,900
Muelheim (Ruhr) 191,100
Munich 1,326,300
Nuremberg 477,100
Oberhausen 249,000
Stuttgart 628,400
Wiesbaden 260,600
Wuppertal 414,700

Germany (East)
*Berlin (East) . . . 1,086,374
Dresden 502,432
Halle 257,261
Karl Marx Stadt
(Chemnitz) 299,411
Leipzig 583,885
Magdeburg 272,237

Ghana
*Accra 615,800

Greece
*Athens-Piraeus 2,540,000
Thessaloniki
(Salonika) 345,799

Guatemala
*Guatemala City . . 730,991

Guinea
*Conakry, Gr 197,267

Guyana
*Georgetown 66,070

Haiti
*Port-au-Prince . . 386,250

Honduras
*Tegucigalpa 350,000

Hungary
*Budapest 2,027,300
Debrecen 168,300
Miskolc 186,600

Iceland
*Reykjavik 82,392

India
Agra 594,858
Ahmedabad . . . 1,588,378
Allahabad 491,702
Amritsar 432,663
Bangalore 1,540,741
Bombay 5,968,546
Calcutta 3,141,180
Calcutta (Met.) . 7,005,362
Delhi-
*New Delhi 4,065,698
Howrah 737,877
Hyderabad . . . 1,612,276
Kanpur 1,154,388
Lucknow 750,512
Madras 2,469,449
Madurai 549,114
Nagpur 866,144
Patna 474,349
Poona 856,105
Varanasi (Benares)583,856

Indonesia
Bandung 1,201,730
*Jakarta 4,576,009
Jogjakarta 342,267
Makassar 434,766
Malang 422,428
Medan 635,562
Palembang 532,961
Semarang 646,590
Surabaja 1,556,255
Surakarta 414,285

Iran
Abadan 300,000
Isfahan 546,200
Mashhad 530,500
Shiraz 335,700
Tabriz 475,600
*Tehran 3,800,000

Iraq
*Baghdad 1,499,759
Basra 310,950
Mosul 264,146

Ireland
Cork 122,146
*Dublin 568,772

Israel
Haifa 217,100
*Jerusalem 304,500
Ramat Gan 120,100
Tel Aviv-Jaffa . . 362,200

Italy		**Mexico**		**Portuguese Guinea**		Khabarovsk.....	462,000
Bari...........	356,733	Chihuahua, Gr...	363,850	*Bissau, Gr........	18,309	Kharkov......	1,280,000
Bologna........	491,873	Guadalajara, Gr.	1,196,218	**Qatar**		Kiev..........	1,764,000
Catania........	413,670	Juarez, Gr.......	436,054	*Doha...........	45,000	Krasnodar.....	491,000
Florence.......	461,602	Mexicali, Gr....	390,411	**Rhodesia**		Krasnoyarsk....	698,000
Genoa.........	841,978	*Mexico........	7,005,855	*Salisbury, Gr....	477,000	Krivoy Rog.....	600,000
Messina........	273,526	*Mexico, D.F...	8,541,070	**Romania**		Kuibyshev.....	1,094,000
Milan.........	1,724,173	Monterrey, Gr..	1,177,361	*Bucharest.....	1,488,328	Leningrad.....	3,620,000
Naples........	1,277,438	Puebla, Gr......	521,885	Ploesti........	165,721	Lvov..........	579,000
Palermo.......	661,477	Tijuana, Gr.....	335,125	Timisoara......	195,470	Makeyevka.....	396,000
*Rome........	2,799,836	Torreon, Gr.....	257,045	**Saudi Arabia**		Minsk.........	996,000
Trieste........	277,752	Veracruz, Gr...	242,351	Jidda..........	194,000	*Moscow......	7,151,000
Turin.........	1,183,864	**Mongolian Rep.**		Mecca.........	185,000	Moscow, Gr...	7,300,000
Venice.........	90,000	*Ulan Bator....	267,400	*Riyadh.......	225,000	Novokuznetsk...	508,000
Ivory Coast		**Morocco**		**Senegal**		Novosibirsk....	1,199,000
*Abidjan, Gr....	282,000	Casablanca....	1,506,373	*Dakar, Gr......	581,000	Odessa........	941,000
Jamaica		Fez............	325,327	**Sierra Leone**		Omsk.........	876,000
*Kingston.......	117,400	Marrakech.....	332,741	*Freetown......	178,600	Perm.........	881,000
Japan		Meknes........	248,369	**Somalia**		Riga..........	755,000
Amagasaki.....	553,696	*Rabat—Sale	530,366	*Mogadishu......	230,000	Rostov........	823,000
Fukuoka.......	853,270	Tangier........	187,994	**South Africa**		Saratov........	790,000
Hiroshima.....	541,998	**Mozambique**		*Cape Town, Gr.	1,096,597	Sverdlovsk.....	1,073,000
Kawasaki......	973,486	*Lourenco		Durban, Gr.....	721,265	Tashkent.....	1,461,000
Kitakyushu....	1,042,321	Marques, Gr....	178,655	Johannesburg, Gr.		Tbilisi........	927,000
Kobe..........	1,288,937	**Namibia**		....	1,432,643	Ufa...........	821,000
Kyoto.........	1,419,165	*Windhoek......	36,051	*Pretoria........	561,703	Vladivostok.....	472,000
Nagasaki......	421,114	**Nepal**		**Spain**		Volgograd.....	852,000
Nagoya.......	2,036,053	*Katmandu.....	121,019	Barcelona.....	1,745,142	Voronezh.....	693,000
Osaka........	2,980,487	**Netherlands**		Bilbao.........	410,490	Yaroslavl......	538,000
Sapporo......	1,010,023	*Amsterdam....	826,520	Cordoba.......	235,632	Zaporozh'ye....	697,000
Sendai........	545,065	Eindhoven.....	189,411	*Madrid.......	3,146,071		
*Tokyo, Gr...	11,454,000	Groningen.....	172,347	Malaga........	374,452	**United Kingdom**	
Yokohama....	2,238,264	The Hague.....	531,506	Murcia........	243,759	**England**	
Jordan		Haarlem.......	172,347	Seville.........	548,072	Birmingham....	1,013,366
*Amman........	520,700	Rotterdam.....	674,546	Valencia.......	653,690	Bristol........	426,170
Kenya		Utrecht........	278,498	Zaragoza......	479,843	Coventry.......	334,839
Mombasa, Gr....	255,400	**New Zealand**		**Sri Lanka (Ceylon)**		Leeds.........	501,080
*Nairobi, Gr....	535,200	Auckland......	151,900	*Colombo......	562,160	Leicester.......	283,549
Korea, Dem. People's		Christchurch...	166,800	**Sudan**		Liverpool......	606,834
Rep. of		*Wellington.....	136,400	*Khartoum.....	261,840	*London, Gr....	8,104,050
*Pyong Yang....	653,100	**Nicaragua**		Omdurman.....	258,532	Manchester.....	542,430
Korea, Republic of		*Managua......	398,514	**Surinam**		Newcastle.....	222,153
Inchon........	646,013	**Niger**		*Paramaribo.....	110,867	Nottingham.....	299,758
Pusan........	1,880,710	*Niamey........	78,991	**Sweden**		Sheffield.......	519,703
*Seoul........	5,536,377	**Nigeria**		Goteborg......	451,806	**Wales**	
Taegu........	1,082,750	Ibadan.........	758,332	Malmo........	265,505	*Cardiff........	278,221
Kuwait		Kano..........	357,098	*Stockholm.....	740,486	Swansea.......	172,566
*Kuwait........	80,405	*Lagos.........	900,969	*Stockholm, Gr..	1,352,359	**Scotland**	
Laos		Ogbomosho.....	386,650	Uppsala........	130,097	Aberdeen......	186,006
*Luang Prabang..	60,000	Port Harcourt..	217,043	**Switzerland**		Dundee.......	182,084
*Vientiane......	132,253	**Norway**		Basel..........	204,791	*Edinburgh.....	453,422
Lebanon		Bergen.........	214,000	*Berne.........	157,016	Glasgow......	896,958
*Beirut........	474,870	*Oslo..........	480,000	Geneva........	168,530	**Northern Ireland**	
Tripoli........	127,611	Trondheim.....	132,000	Zurich........	410,892	*Belfast.......	360,150
Lesotho		**Oman**		**Syria**		Londonderry....	53,744
*Maseru.........	17,000	*Muscat........	5,080	Aleppo........	639,361	**Upper Volta**	
Liberia		**Pakistan**		*Damascus.....	836,668	*Ouaggadougou...	77,500
*Monrovia......	96,226	Hyderabad, Gr...	834,000	**Tanzania**		**Uruguay**	
Libya		*Islamabad.....	50,000	*Dar es Salaam...	343,911	*Montevideo...	1,159,085
*Bengazi.......	137,295	Karachi, Gr....	3,650,000	**Thailand**		**Venezuela**	
*Tripoli........	213,506	Lahore, Gr.....	2,073,000	*Bangkok, Gr...	1,608,305	*Caracas, Gr...	2,175,000
Liechtenstein		Lyalpur, Gr....	1,109,000	Thonburi, Gr...	459,555	Maracaibo......	690,400
*Vaduz.........	4,280	Rawalpindi, Gr...	508,000	**Togo Rep.**		Valencia.......	224,800
Luxembourg		**Panama**		*Lome.........	192,745	**Vietnam, Dem. Republic**	
*Luxembourg......	78,032	*Panama.......	418,013	**Trinidad and Tobago**		Haiphong......	182,490
Macau		**Papua**		*Port of Spain...	73,900	*Hanoi.........	414,620
*Macau........	241,413	*Port Moresby...	41,848	**Tunisia**		**Vietnam, Republic of**	
Madagascar		**Paraguay**		*Tunis.........	468,997	Danang.......	437,668
*Tananarive, Gr..	347,466	*Asuncion......	288,882	**Turkey**		Hue..........	199,893
Malawi		**Peru**		*Ankara.......	1,208,791	*Saigon........	1,804,880
Blantyre-Limbe, Gr.		Callao.........	335,400	Istanbul.......	2,247,630	**Western Samoa**	
....	109,461	Cuzco.........	108,900	Izmir.........	520,686	*Apia, Gr.......	25,480
*Zomba, Gr.....	19,666	*Lima, Gr......	2,541,300	**Uganda**		**Yemen**	
Malaysia		**Philippines**		*Kampala......	331,889	*Sana.........	120,000
*Kuala Lumpur...	451,728	Cebu..........	372,146	**USSR**			
George Town....	270,019	Davao.........	438,769	Alma-Ata.......	776,000	**Peoples Dem. Rep. of**	
Maldives, Rep. of		Manila........	1,399,583	Baku..........	884,000	**Yemen**	
*Male.........	15,740	*Quezon City....	848,788	Barnaul........	459,000	Aden..........	150,000
Mali		**Poland**		Chelyabinsk....	910,000	**Yugoslavia**	
Bamako, Gr....	196,800	Gdansk (Danzig).	370,800	Dniepropetrovsk	903,000	Belgrade.......	746,000
Malta		Krakow.......	595,100	Donetsk........	905,000	Sarajevo.......	244,000
*Valletta........	15,401	Lodz..........	765,400	Erevan........	818,000	Skopje........	313,000
Mauritania		Poznan.......	476,300	Frunze........	452,000	Zagreb.......	566,000
*Nouakchott......	15,000	*Warsaw.......	1,326,200	Gorky.........	1,213,000	**Zambia**	
Mauritius		Wroclaw (Breslau)		Irkutsk........	473,000	*Lusaka, Gr.....	381,000
*Port Louis, Gr..	141,100	....	531,100	Ivanovo.......	434,000	**Zaire**	
		Portugal		Karaganda.....	541,000	Lubumbashi....	357,369
		*Lisbon........	782,266	Kazan.........	904,000	*Kinshasa, Gr...	1,623,760
		Porto.........	310,437				

Cost of Living in Various Cities of the World

This comparison of the cost of living in various cities was drawn up in 1974 by the UN Statistical Office, based on prices for goods, services and housing for international officials stationed in these cities. Figures show relative costs, based on about 120 items. New York City was assigned the index figure 100. Thus, while expenditure for certain items might be $1,000 in New York, it would be $1,112 for them in Paris and $780 in Rio de Janeiro. Figures with an asterisk (*) omit cost of housing (rent, utilities and domestic service) in cities where they are furnished at nominal cost by governments.

Index	City	Index	City	Index	City
*116	Abidjan, Ivory Coast	111	The Hague, Netherlands	103	Ouagadougou, Upper Volta
*96	Accra, Ghana	87	Havana, Cuba	86	Panama City, Panama
99	Addis Ababa, Ethiopa	70	Islamabad, Pakistan	112	Paris, France
87	Aden, Yemen (Dem.)	98	Jakarta, Indonesia	86	Port-au-Prince, Haiti
*105	Algiers, Algeria	90	Kabul, Afghanistan	78	Port-of-Spain, Trinidad
84	Amman, Jordan	*102	Kampala, Uganda	83	Quito, Ecuador
71	Ankara, Turkey	83	Katmandu, Nepal	95	Rabat, Morocco
*102	Apia, Western Samoa	*105	Kigali, Rwanda	84	Rangoon, Burma
71	Asuncion, Paraguay	87	Kingston, Jamaica	88	Rio de Janeiro, Brazil
88	Athens, Greece	98	Kinshasa, Zaire	90	Rome, Iraly
83	Baghdad, Iraq	93	Kuala Lumpur, Malaysia	*102	Saigon, Vietnam
114	Bamako, Mali	100	Kuwait, Kuwait	88	Sana, Yemen (Rep.)
86	Bangkok, Thailand	*109	Lagos, Nigeria	79	San Jose, Costa Rica
*143	Bangui, Cen. African Rep.	73	LaPaz, Bolivia	84	San Salvador, El Salvador
91	Beirut, Lebanon	*113	Libreville, Gabon	36	Santiago, Chile
88	Belgrade, Yugoslavia	82	Lima, Peru	93	Seoul, South Korea
64	Bogota, Colombia	83	London, United Kingdom	95	Singapore, Singapore
116	Bonn, West Germany	*111	Lusaka, Zambia	77	Suva, Fiji
*94	Brazzaville, Congo	88	Managua, Nicaragua	105	Sydney, Australia
84	Bridgetown, Barbados	76	Manila, Philippines	101	Tananarive, Malagasy
78	Buenos Aires, Argentina	81	Mbabane, Swaziland	91	Tehran, Iran
77	Cairo, Egypt	89	Mexico City, Mexico	121	Tokyo, Japan
90	Caracas, Venezuela	88	Mogadishu, Somalia	*122	Tripoli, Libya
69	Colombo, Sri Lanka	*94	Monrovia, Liberia	102	Tunis, Tunisia
126	Conakry, Guinea	70	Montevideo, Uruguay	*106	Ulan Bator, Mongolia
111	Copenhagen, Denmark	84	Montreal, Canada	67	Valetta, Malta
96	Cotonou, Dahomey	80	Nairobi, Kenya	102	Vienna, Austria
71	Damascus, Syria	80	New Delhi, India	91	Vientiane, Laos
104	N'Djamena, Chad	100	New York, U.S.	92	Washington, D.C., U.S.
*107	Freetown, Sierra Leone	*110	Niamey, Niger	103	Yaounde, Cameroon
111	Geneva, Switzerland	77	Nicosia, Cyprus	*72	Zomba, Malawi
65	Georgetown, Guyana				

Population of World's Largest Urban Areas

City populations often cannot be used to compare urban areas because city limits may fall short of or exceed the built-up or urban area. The problem of comparison is compounded by the difficulty in obtaining reliable population data for a common year. The ranking of urban areas below represents one attempt at comparing the world's largest urban areas, taking into account, where necessary and within the limits of available data, urban development extending outward from the principal city named in the table. Thus, the Tokyo area included Tokyo plus neighboring smaller cities, towns and villages. (Some computations include Yokohama as part of Tokyo's urban population.) New York's urban area in 1970 included part or all the population of 10 New Jersey and 5 New York counties in addition to the 5 boroughs of New York City. However, the urban population figures reported for Bombay, Budapest, Canton, Hamburg, Istanbul, Jakarta, Kiev, Peking, Rio de Janeiro, Rome, Saigon, Seoul, Singapore, Shanghai, Teheran and Tientsin did not run beyond the city proper.

*New York, N.Y. (census 1970)	16,206,841	Bogota, Colombia (est. 1972)	2,818,300
Tokyo, Japan (census 1973)	11,324,417	Rome, Italy (census 1973)	2,799,836
Shanghai, China (est. 1970)	10,820,000	Montreal, Canada (census 1971)	2,743,210
Paris, France (est. 1970)	9,250,647	Sydney, Australia (census 1971)	2,725,064
Mexico City, Mexico (census 1970)	8,589,630	Santiago, Chile (census 1970)	2,661,920
Buenos Aires, Argentina (census 1970)	8,352,900	Boston, Mass. (census 1970)	2,652,575
Los Angeles-Long Beach (census 1970)	8,351,266	Toronto, Canada (census 1971)	2,628,043
Osaka, Japan (census 1973)	7,638,722	Lima, Peru (est. 1970)	2,541,300
Sao Paulo, Brazil (est. 1973)	7,693,000	Athens, Greece (census 1971)	2,540,000
Peking, China (est. 1970)	7,570,000	Washington, D.C.-Md.-Va. (census 1970)	2,481,489
London, England (est. 1971)	7,418,020	Shenyang (Mukden) China (est. 1958)	2,423,000
Moscow, USSR (est. 1972)	7,300,000	Melbourne, Australia (census 1971)	2,342,000
Calcutta, India (census 1971)	7,031,382	Manchester, England (census 1971)	2,386,774
Chicago, Ill. (census 1970)	6,714,578	Birmingham, England (census 1971)	2,369,205
Bombay, India (census 1971)	5,970,575	Yokohama, Japan (est. 1971)	2,342,000
Seoul, Rep. of Korea (census 1970)	5,536,377	Istanbul, Turkey (census 1970)	2,247,630
Cairo, Egypt (est. 1970)	4,961,000	Wuhan, China (est. 1958)	2,226,000
Rio de Janeiro, Brazil (est. 1973)	4,658,000	Caracas, Venezuela (est. 1970)	2,175,400
Jakarta, Indonesia (census 1971)	4,576,009	Chungking, China (est. 1958)	2,165,000
Tientsin, China (est. 1970)	4,280,000	Singapore (census 1970)	2,074,507
Essen (Ruhr-Gebiet), W. Germany (est. 1966)	4,259,230	Lahore, Pakistan (est. 1972)	2,073,000
Victoria-Hong Kong (est. 1970)	4,127,800	Baltimore, Md. (census 1970)	2,070,670
Leningrad, USSR (est. 1972)	4,066,000	Nagoya, Japan (est. 1971)	2,052,000
Delhi-New Delhi, India (census 1971)	4,065,698	Alexandria, Egypt (est. 1970)	2,032,000
Philadelphia, Pa.-N.J. (census 1970)	4,021,066	Budapest, Hungary (est. 1971)	2,027,300
Detroit, Mich. (census 1970)	3,970,584	Cleveland, Ohio (census 1970)	1,959,880
Teheran, Iran (est. 1973)	3,800,000	St. Louis, Mo.-Ill. (census 1970)	1,882,944
Karachi, Pakistan (est. 1972)	3,650,000	Pusan, Rep. of Korea (census 1970)	1,880,710
Berlin, E. & W. Germany (est. 1970)	3,218,028	Canton, China (est. 1958)	1,867,000
Madras, India (census 1971)	3,169,930	Vienna, Austria (census 1971)	1,858,700
Madrid, Spain (census 1970)	3,146,071	Pittsburgh, Pa. (census 1970)	1,846,042
Bangkok, Thailand (census 1970)	3,051,000	Hamburg, W. Germany (est. 1970)	1,818,600
Manila, Philippines (census 1973)	3,000,000	Saigon, Rep. of Vietnam (est. 1971)	1,804,880
San Francisco-Oakland, Calif. (census 1970)	2,987,850	Hyderabad, India (census 1971)	1,796,339

*New York-Northeastern New Jersey urbanized area, including the 5 boroughs of New York City plus all or part of the counties of Nassau, Putnam, Rockland, Suffolk and Westchester in New York State and all or part of the counties of Bergen, Essex, Hudson, Middlesex, Morris, Passaic, Somerset, Union, Monmouth and Ocean in New Jersey.

NORTH AMERICAN CITIES

Their History, Business and Industry, Educational Facilities, Cultural Advantages, Tourist Attractions and Transportation

Akron, Ohio

The World Almanac is sponsored in the Akron area by the Akron Beacon Journal, 44 E. Exchange St., Akron, O. 44328; (216) 375-8111; founded 1809; circulation 172,971 daily, 211,833 Sunday; John S. Knight, president and editorial chairman; Ben Maidenburg, publisher; Mark Ethridge, vice president and editor; Robert Giles, exec. editor; William Ott, vice president and general manager.

Population: 276,450 (city); 714,960 (metro) 5th in state; total employed 303,050; 1973 average metro household income, $13,853.

Area: 56 sq. mi. (city); 413 sq. mi. (metro) on Ohio Canal 30 mi. south of Lake Erie; founded 1825.

Industry: $1.9 billion value added by Akron area mfg. industry in 1973; home plants of Firestone, Goodyear, Goodrich & General employ 40,000, using 40% of entire world rubber supply; other products include auto bodies, salt, clay, matches, rubber toys, road building equipment, missile components.

Transportation: Akron-Canton Airport served by 3 major carriers; Akron Muni Airport; 9 rail and trunk lines; 93 home-based truck carriers; Metro Transit System; bisected east-west & north-south by Interstate highways; Greyhound bus terminal.

Communications: 3 TV, one Cablevision and 5 radio stations.

New construction: Downtown Superblock including $17 million Federal Office bldg., $16 million new Ohio Edison Co. Headquarters and $80 million new Innerbelt Freeway system.

Medical facilities: 7 major hospitals including specialized children's treatment center; Ohio State Fallsview Mental Health Center.

Education: University of Akron, Kent State University, Firestone Conservatory of Music.

Sports: New $17 million coliseum, home of the NBA Cleveland Cavaliers, WHA Crusaders and WTT Nets; Firestone Country Club, home of the World Series of Golf; Derby Downs, home of the All-American Soap Box Derby; 35,000-seat Akron Rubber Bowl.

Cultural attractions: E. J. Thomas Performing Arts Center; Blossom Music Center, summer home of the Cleveland Orchestra; Stan Hywet mansion; Akron Art Institute; Akron Symphony Orchestra.

Other attractions: Children's Zoo; Simon Perkins Mansion; John Brown home; Railway Museum.

Accommodations: Nearly 2,000 rooms in 13 downtown hotels and motels.

Further information: Akron Area Chamber of Commerce, Delaware Bldg., Akron, O. 44308; or Akron Convention Bureau, Inc., 2600 First National Tower, Akron, O. 44308.

Albany, New York

The World Almanac is sponsored in the Albany-Schenectady-Troy area by The Times-Union and Knickerbocker News-Union Star, 645 Albany-Shaker Road, Albany, N.Y. 12201; (518) 453-5454; Times-Union founded 1856; Knickerbocker News 1843; Union-Star 1855; circulation Times-Union (morn) 80,048, Sunday Times-Union 145,- 691, Knickerbocker News-Union Star (aft) 69,251, publisher Robert J. Danzig.

Population: 115,781 (city), 286,742 (county); total employed 99,047.

Area: 19.6 sq. mi. on west bank of Hudson River, 150 miles north of New York City.

Industry: chief products are felts, woolen goods, meat products, paper products, iron and brass castings, drugs and medicines; 295 manufacturing firms.

Commerce: 5 savings banks, 9 commercial banks.

Transportation: 2 major freight lines; 4 airlines at Albany County Airport; New York State Thruway, Adirondack Northway; Port of Albany.

Communications: 4 TV and 11 radio stations.

Medical facilities: 5 major hospital complexes including a Veteran's Administration installation.

Cultural facilities: Albany Symphony Orchestra, art museum, 90 church buildings, city libraries.

Educational facilities: Albany Law School, Albany College of Pharmacy, Albany Medical College, the State University of New York at Albany, Siena College, Saint Rose College, Albany Junior College and Maria College; 24 elementary schools, 2 senior high schools, 25 private and parochial schools.

New construction: Albany is in the midst of a major revamping of its downtown area. The $1-billion South Mall includes a 44-story state office tower, 4 large state agency buildings, as well as cultural buildings.

Recreational facilities: municipal golf course, private clubs, 2 large city parks with tennis, baseball, swimming facilities.

Other attractions: Dudley Observatory, Fort Crailo in Rensselaer; Joseph Henry Memorial Building, Ten Broeck Mansion, First Church in Albany (Reformed); Schuyler Mansion, the State Capitol and the new South Mall; 65 hotels and motels with over 6,000 rooms.

Sports: Bleecker Stadium (seating 7,000) is employed for professional and amateur baseball.

Government: 2nd only to Washington, Albany is the most important governmental city in the U.S.; home city of the governor, state officials and 30,000 state employes.

History: founded 1609 when Henry Hudson terminated his voyage in the Half Moon at the location where Albany was later settled by the Dutch.

Albuquerque, New Mexico

The World Almanac is sponsored in the Albuquerque area by the Albuquerque Tribune, 701 Silver Ave. SW, Albuquerque, N.M. 87103; (505) 842-2300; founded June 22, 1922, by Carl Magee; a Scripps-Howard Newspaper since Sept. 24, 1923; circulation 38,000; editor Ralph Looney; sponsors Tribune Annual Spelling Bee, Charming Miss Charm Workshop.

Population: 293,550 (city), 356,380 (metro area). First in state, 58th in nation; total employed, 152,900.

Area: 81 sq. mi. on Rio Grande and U.S. 66. Bernalillo County seat.

Industry: electronics with Singer, GTE-Lenkurt, Gulton, Sparton; clothing with Levi Strauss, Pioneer Wear; movie production center.

Commerce: retail sales $1.052 billion; per capita income $4,087; bank resources $1.288 billion in 9 banks.

Transportation: Santa Fe Railway, Amtrak, Continental Trailways and Greyhound bus lines; Albuquerque Intl. Airport, hub for 4 airlines, average 583 air movements daily.

Communications: 4 TV and 15 radio stations.

Federal facilities: Kirtland AF Base, Bureau of Indian Affairs, Forest Service, Social Security.

Medical facilities: 7 major hospitals.

Cultural facilities: symphony orchestra, 26 art galleries, 4 museums, 7 library branches.

Educational facilities: Univ. of N.M., Univ. of Albuquerque, 117 public schools.

Recreational facilities: Sandia Peak Ski Area with longest tramway in North America; 80 city parks, one state park, Cibola National Forest; 8 golf courses, 83 tennis courts and 8 public swimming pools; Rio Grande Zoo.

Convention facilities: $9.2 million convention center, 104 motels and hotels.

Sports attractions: Dukes baseball.

History: founded Feb. 7, 1706; named for Duke of Albuquerque, viceroy of New Spain.

Further information: Chamber of Commerce, 401 Second NW.

Allentown, Pennsylvania

The World Almanac is sponsored in the Allentown-Bethlehem-Easton area by Call-Chronicle Newspapers, 101 N. 6th St., Allentown, 18105; (215) 433-4241; Call founded 1883, daily circulation 103,000, Sunday 149,000; Chronicle founded 1870, circulation 23,000; publisher Donald P. Miller, executive editor Edward D. Miller; sponsors Park & Shop, housing development, newspaper-in-the-classroom, newsprint recycling.

Population: Allentown 109,871; Bethlehem 72,686; Easton 30,256; metro area 543,620, 3d in state; total employed 229,934.

Area: 5,000 sq. mi. (metro) in eastern Pa. at Lehigh and Delaware rivers; Allentown is Lehigh Co. seat.

Industry: Bethlehem Steel Corp., 2d largest in U.S.; home offices for Mack Truck Inc., Air Products & Chemicals, New Jersey Zinc Co., Allen Products (ALPO); area leads in textile production; transistor developed in Western Electric here.

Commerce: retail center for east-central Pa.; retail sales (1972) $970 million; average family buying power $11,647.

Transportation: 3 major rail, 5 bus lines; 9 federal and state highways intersect area; jet airport averages 335 movements per day on 6 airlines.

Communications: 3 TV and 12 radio stations.

Medical facilities: 6 major hospitals.

Cultural facilities: Allentown Art Museum (including Kress Renaissance and Baroque collection), Bethlehem Bach Choir, Allentown Symphony, 7 theater groups (plus 4 summer); Allentown Band is oldest continuing concert band in U.S.; 10 colleges including Lehigh Univ., Muhlenberg, Cedar Crest and Lafayette serve 12,000 students.

Other attractions: center of "Pennsylvania Dutch" area, covered bridges; 1,400-acre park system; 1,170-acre game preserve, pre-Cambrian mountain range, access to Appalachian Trail, many historic houses, Allentown Fair, folk festivals, Liberty Bell Shrine.

Sports: fishing, small game hunting, auto racing at Pocono Raceway, Allentown Jets basketball.

History: settled in 1600s by Germans seeking religious freedom; Allentown founded 1762; hiding place for Liberty Bell during Revolutionary War; GAR founded Flag Day here 1906; Allentown one of 5 First Defender Companies in Civil War.

Further information: Chambers of Commerce in Allentown: 462 Walnut St. (18105); Bethlehem: 11 W. Market St. (18018); Easton: 157 S. 4th St. (18042).

Amarillo, Texas

The World Almanac is sponsored in the Amarillo area by the Amarillo Globe-News, 900 S. Harrison, Amarillo, Tex., 79166, (806) 376-4488; a division of Southwestern Newspapers Corp., and publisher of Daily News, Globe-Times and Sunday News-Globe; daily circulation 78,789, Sunday 73,568; James L. Whyte, vice president and general manager; Jerry Huff, executive editor.

Population: 138,860 city; 157,745 metro area; 11th in state; total employed 67,510.

Area: 68.98 sq. mi. in central Texas Panhandle at junction of Interstates 40 and 27 in Potter and Randall Counties. Potter County seat.

Industry: 3-state hub of $8 billion agribusiness market including wheat, beef and produce, value $17.3 million; American Smelting & Refining zinc plant and $100 million copper refinery; Bell Helicopter, Levi Strauss, natural gas, petroleum, $25 million Iowa Beef facility.

Commerce: wholesale-retail center for 3-state area; retail sales $337,302,000; bank resources, $495 million in 9 banks, 5 savings and loan associations; 104th in wholesale sales ($475 million) among 230 metro areas.

Transportation: air terminal served by 5 airlines with 182,774 passengers in 1973; 3 railroads with 8 mainline routes; 4 bus lines; 22 truck lines; 2 interstate, 4 federal and one state highways intersect Amarillo.

Communications: 4 TV and 6 radio stations.

Medical: 5 hospitals including VA facility, paramedical training; mental health centers.

Culture, recreation: Amarillo Symphony; College arts complex; Civic Center complex, summer musical "Texas"; area historical museum; 46 parks, 3 institutions higher learning.

Sports: Giants baseball, college and high school football, basketball, drag racing.

History: settled 1887 as railroad crew camp, incorporated 1892. Named for yellow lake clay.

Anchorage, Alaska

The World Almanac is sponsored in the Anchorage area by the Anchorage Daily Times, 820 W. 4th Avenue, Anchorage, Alaska, 99510; (907) 279-5622; founded 1915; circulation 45,000; editor-publisher Robert B. Atwood; sponsors Spelling Bee, Airline Ski Races.

Population: 76,610 (1974), largest in state; 154,610 in Greater Anchorage, nearly half of Alaska's population.

Area: 927 sq. mi. (census district), at head of Cook Inlet on south central coast.

Industry and commerce: business center for most of Alaska; aviation, oil companies, railroading, shipping and national defense activities are largest elements in area's economy; headquarters for construction of $4.5 billion trans-Alaska oil pipeline.

Transportation: Anchorage International Airport is major refueling stop on transpolar flights; thousands of small planes make city one of country's busiest air traffic centers with 5 airports and 25% of world's seaplanes in area; headquarters of Alaska Railroad; $10 million port.

Communications: 3 TV and 7 radio stations; 2 daily newspapers.

Medical facilities: 5 hospitals.

Cultural facilities: Annual Festival of Music; 4 theatre groups; fine arts museum; community concert organization.

Educational facilities: 56 elementary and secondary schools enroll 35,600; Univ. of Alaska, Alaska Methodist Univ.

Recreation: 2 major ski areas; cross-country skiing and bicycling; annual Fur Rendezvous with dogsled races; Iditarod dogsled race to Nome; Chugach National Forest.

Convention facilities: 5 major hotels and motels offer facilities for over 1,000 persons.

History: founded 1915 as construction camp for Alaska Railroad; twice winner of All America city award, for coping with rapid growth and for swift recovery from catastrophic 1964 earthquake.

Further information: Chamber of Commerce, 612 F St. (99501).

Atlanta, Georgia

Population: 479,900 (city), 1,732,500 (metro), first in state, 18th in nation; total employed 745,800 (metro).

Area: 136 sq. mi. in north central Georgia, on Piedmont plateau of Blue Ridge foothills, 1,050 ft. above sea level; 4,326 sq. mi. in 15-county metro area.

Industry: over 2,000 manufacturers produce more than 3,500 commodities; 442 of Fortune 500 firms operate in Atlanta; Ford assembly plant, 2 GM assembly plants, Lockheed-Ga. Co.; home base for Coca-Cola, Fuqua Ind., Delta Air Lines, Retail Credit, Scripto, Genuine Parts.

Commerce: financial, retail, wholesale center of Southeast; annual metro retail sales over $5 billion (1973); massive Merchandise Mart; 6th Federal Reserve District hdqtrs.; 81 banks, 263 branches with resources of $5.64 billion (metro); bank clearings of $6.56 billion (Dec., 1973); 22 savings and loan associations with assets of $3.1 billion.

Transportation: founded as railroad center, now served by 6 systems; Greyhound and Trailways bus terminals used by 5 companies carrying over 14,000 passengers; 9 passenger airlines, one commuter carrier, one freight-only carrier; more than 1,000 scheduled flights daily; non-stop service to 97 cities from Hartsfield Internat'l Airport, 2d busiest in U.S., handling 23,352,739 passengers (1973). Approved rapid transit system to have 50 mi. of high speed rail, 14 mi. of busways coordinated with street bus operations; 6 legs of 3 interstate highways intersect 100-

acre downtown interchange; $7 million, 63 mi. highway encircles city.

Communications: 5 commercial, 2 educational TV stations; 42 commercial, one educational radio stations; Protestant Radio and TV Center; largest Bell system toll-free dialing area; one of nation's 5 TV and radio network control centers; 9 daily newspapers; 10th in the nation in U.S. postal receipts.

New construction: boom in luxury hotels, office towers and parks, condominiums; total value 1973 city building permits $236,170,283; metro private construction, $847,100,000.

Medical facilities: 40 hospitals, VA hospital; National Center for Disease Control.

Federal facilities: 27,600 federal employees; Ft. McPherson, hdqtrs. U.S. Army Forces Command; Ft. Gillem; Dobbins A.F. Base; NAS Atlanta; GSA Warehouse.

Cultural facilities: Memorial Arts Center with Museum, Symphony Orchestra, Ballet, School of Art; Civic Center with auditorium-theater-exhibition hall, site of annual Met performances; 24 degree-granting schools including Ga. Institute of Technology, Ga. State Univ., Emory Univ., Atlanta Univ.

Sports: NBA Hawks; NFL Falcons; NL Braves; NHL Flames; Stadium seats 52,000, Omni arena, 16,500.

Convention facilities: 538,000 delegates attended 602 conventions in 1973.

History: named 1845, chartered 1847; burned by Gen. Wm. Sherman 1864.

Augusta, Georgia

The World Almanac is sponsored in the Augusta area by The Chronicle-Herald, 725 Broad St., 30903; (404) 724-0851; Chronicle established in 1785, circulation 50,000; Herald 20,000; Sunday, 72,000. William S. Morris III publisher, E.B. Skinner general manager, L.C. Harris editor, David L. Playford managing editor Herald.

Population: 56,800 (city), 275,787 (metro area); Total employed, 110,100 (metro).

Area: 1,713 sq. mi. (metro: Richmond, Columbia counties, Ga.; Aiken County, S.C.) straddling Savannah River.

Industry: diversified; Continental Can, Du Pont, Procter & Gamble, Lily-Tulip, Olin, Dymo, Monsanto.

Commerce: wholesale, retail center of 17 counties in 2 states; 1972 retail sales, $546,492,000; per capita income, $3,231; per family income, $11,015; effective buying income, $912,053,000; 4 banks, 3 savings-loan assns.; distribution center.

Transportation: 5 railroads, 26 truck lines, 3 airlines at modern airport and in-city field for executive planes; Interstate 20, other federal highways; river shipping.

Communications: 3 TV and 10 radio stations.

Medical facilities: 5 major hospitals, including Eisenhower Memorial at Ft. Gordon, Medical College of Georgia.

Federal facilities: Ft. Gordon and Savannah River (AEC) Plant.

Cultural facilities: Augusta College, Paine College; museum, art gallery, arts council with 25 affiliates.

Recreational facilities: hunting, fishing, boating, camping; 7 golf courses; home of Masters Golf Tournament.

History: founded as fort 1717; named for wife of Prince of Wales 1735; capital of Georgia, 1778.

Austin, Texas

The World Almanac is sponsored in the Austin area by The Austin American-Statesman, 308 Guadalupe St., Austin, Texas, 78701; (512) 476-2661; Statesman founded 1871; American 1914; combined 1924; published by Newspapers, Inc.; circulation, American (morn.) 68,518, Statesman (aft.) 34,740, American-Statesman (Sunday) 107,275; Harlon M. Fentress chairman, Pat Taggart president, Richard F. Brown vice-president and publisher, Sam Wood editor, Bill Meroney, general manager.

Population: 283,700 (city), 334,000 (metro area), 6th in state, 56th in nation; total employed 158,500.

Area: 91 sq. mi. in mid-Texas on Colorado River.

Industry: electronics — Texas Instruments, IBM, Motorola, Tracor; Glastron (Conroy) boats, John Roberts jewelry, gas turbines by Westinghouse Electric; county has 360 manufacturing firms.

Commerce: wholesale, retail center for 10 counties (750,000 pop.) in triangle of Dallas-Fort Worth, San Antonio, Houston; retail sales (1972) $616,000,000; bank assets $1.3 billion in 13 banks; 7 savings associations with assets $442 million; 33 insurance home offices.

Transportation: 3 airlines; 3 railroads, Amtrak; 4 bus lines; 13 motor freight carriers; U.S. Interstate 35, State 71, 79, 183, 290.

Communications: 4 TV and cable, 12 radio stations.

Medical facilities: 7 hospitals, 1,032 beds; 389 physicians; 174 dentists.

Federal facilities: Bergstrom AF Base; Internal Revenue Service center with 3,300 employees.

Cultural facilities: University of Texas System & UT at Austin with 40,000 students, 12,500 staff; Southwest conference football champions. Lyndon Baines Johnson Library dedicated 1971 with 1,700,000 visitors in 2 years; other libraries; Texas Memorial & Art Museums; 85,000-seat stadium; law and other graduate schools; 4 small colleges. O Henry Home, Laguna Gloria, Elizabet Ney & French Legation museums; 4 local theater companies, Austin Symphony, 2 ballet companies. City library, branches and mobile service. Austin public school district, 76 schools, 55,000 students.

State facilities: Capitol and office building complex; 5 special schools for handicapped and psychiatric hospital; 36,578 employes.

Convention facilities: $4 million city center seats 5,000.

Recreational facilities: 2 lakes; 7,000 acres of parks, pools, 6 golf courses, tennis courts; 3 annual fiestas; Aqua (motor boat racing), Laguna Gloria, and Highland Lakes arts and crafts.

Further information: Chamber of Commerce, 901 W. Riverside Dr., Austin, Texas 78701

Baltimore, Maryland

The World Almanac is sponsored in the Baltimore area by the Baltimore News American, 301 E. Lombard St., Baltimore, Md. 21203; (301)752-1212; founded 1773 as Maryland Journal and General Advertiser; Baltimore News founded 1872; adopted present name 1964; daily circulation 217,257, Sunday 296,017; publisher Mark F. Collins, executive editor Thomas J. White, general manager Roy W. Anderson; American Medical Association Award and Albert Lasker Award; sponsors I Am an American Day Parade.

Population: 881,640 (city), 2,107,000 (metro), 1st in state, 7th in U.S.; total employment, 380,855 (city), 846,400 (metro).

Area: 91 sq. mi. (city), 2,225 sq. mi. (metro); on Patapsco River, a tributary of Chesapeake Bay.

Industry: highly diversified; none dominating; most important are steel fabricating, shipbuilding and repairing, manufacture of electrical equipment and food containers, food processing, sugar, petroleum, chemicals, copper; added value of manufacturing in 1973 was $3.2 billion.

Commerce: metro area consists of city and 5 adjacent counties; estimated buying income $4,018 per capita; retail sales topped $4 billion in 1973; area has 208 shopping centers with 3,530 stores; home ownership 57%.

Transportation: 3 railroads including Amtrak;

Baltimore-Washington International Airport, used by 13 lines, served over 3 million passengers in 1973; over 150 certified truck lines; tunnel carries motor traffic through city under river; buses operated by state authority carry 100,000 passengers daily.

Port facilities: 120 steamship lines use port, the nation's fourth largest and farthest inland on the Atlantic coast; in 1973, a record 4,310 ships moved 37.6 million tons of cargo; world's leading receiver of imported cars; other leading cargoes are petroleum products, ores, grain, coal, bananas.

Communications: 3 daily newspapers in city, 2 more in metro area; 3 VHF TV stations and UHF public broadcast station; 25 radio stations.

Cultural facilities: Enoch Pratt Free Library, 30 branches, 2.2 million volumes; metro county libraries have 26 branches; Symphony Orchestra, Civic Opera Company, Art Museum, Walters Gallery, Peale Museum, Md. Academy of Sciences, Davis Planetarium, Morris A. Mechanic Theater, and Center State.

Educational facilities: 30 colleges and 9 junior colleges, including Johns Hopkins Univ. and medical institutions, Univ. of Maryland, and Goucher, Loyola, Morgan State and Towson State colleges; Peabody Inst. of Music, Maryland Inst. College of Art, Ner Israel Rabbinical College, St. Mary's Seminary.

Medical facilities: 26 general hospitals, with 7,231 beds in metro area, including renowned Johns Hopkins, Univ. of Maryland and its Institute for Emergency Medicine, and Greater Baltimore Medical Center.

Sports: Memorial Stadium, seating 62,000, is home of football Colts and baseball Orioles; horse racing, including annual Preakness at Pimlico in city and International Race at Laurel; Bowie and Timonium tracks nearby. Chesapeake Bay's 1,700 sq. mi. of open water is noted for fishing, boating and wildfowl hunting; 18 ski resorts within 3 hours driving distance.

Convention facilities: Civic Center, 45 meeting rooms, 87,160 sq. ft. of exhibition space; 7 hotels downtown and 109 motels in or near city; 44,349 visitors attended 104 conventions and spent $7.5 million in 1973.

Other attractions: Fort McHenry Historic Shrine where Francis Scott Key wrote "The Star Spangled Banner"; U.S. frigate Constellation; Baltimore and Ohio railroad museum; Edgar Allan Poe's home and grave; Babe Ruth home; annual Preakness Festival Week. Most of central business district rebuilt in past 15 years; Inner Harbor project will provide World Trade Center, Science Building, marine, hotels. U.S. Naval Academy and new city of Columbia are in metro area.

History: founded 1729 by act of the Provincial Assembly of the Maryland Colony which was established by members of the Calvert family, Barons of Baltimore; early economy based on shipment of tobacco, grain and flour and on shipbuilding; privateering in War of 1812 tempted British to try to capture the American "nest of pirates." When Baltimore's economic growth was threatened by completion of the Erie Canal, the city's business leaders countered by building the nation's first railroad, the Baltimore and Ohio.

Further information: Chamber of Commerce Metro Baltimore, 22 Light St.; Baltimore Promotion Council, 102 St. Paul St., Baltimore 21202.

Baton Rouge, Louisiana

The World Almanac is sponsored in the Baton Rouge area by the Morning Advocate and State-Times, 525 Lafayette St., B.R., La. 70821; (504) 383-1111; founded 1842; combined daily circ., 106,660; Sunday, 100,713; pres., Charles P. Manship Jr.; publisher, Douglas L. Manship; production dir. Richard Palmer; bus. mgr., Charles Garvey; MEs, Edwin Price Jr. (MA); Jim Hughes (ST).

Population: 165,963 (city); 392,400 (metro); total 1973 city-parish employment, 168,475.

Area: city, 42.83 sq. mi.; parish, 407.01 sq. mi.; on east bank of Mississippi River, 80 mi. northeast of New Orleans; state capitol, East Baton Rouge Parish seat.

Industry: northern anchor of 100-mi. long petrochemical complex along Miss. River; largest oil refinery in nation.

Commerce: marketing center for major trade area of 400,000; bank resources, $1.3 billion; 6 banks, 7 savings and loan associations.

Transportation: major transfer point on southern federal interstate system; 2 airports with 4 air lines; two buslines; 4 railroad trunklines; Port of Baton Rouge handled over 55 million tons in 1973.

Communications: 4 TV and 9 radio stations.

Cultural facilities: 6 museums, 4 theaters, symphony, planetarium, 5 art galleries.

Educational facilities: Louisiana State Univ., founded 1860, center of 8-campus system, city enrollment, 23,-000; Southern Univ., largest Negro land-grant college in U.S., center of 3-college system, city enrollment, 8,500.

Sports: LSU Tigers and Southern Jaguars home stadia, football, basketball, track.

Other attractions: state capitol building; city-parish zoo and arboretum, 67 parks; major recreational lakes. Bi-centennial attractions.

History: First noted by French explorer Iberville in 1699, Baton Rouge (French: red stick) was already occupied by the Istrouma (also translates red stick) Indians. Louisiana's capitol since 1836. Government structure is a city-parish combination with a mayor-president and city-parish council.

Further information: Chamber of Commerce, P.O. Box 1868, Baton Rouge, La. 70821; Louisiana Tourist Commission, P.O. Box 44291, Capitol Station, Baton Rouge, La. 70804.

Billings, Montana

The World Almanac is sponsored in the Billings area by the Billings Gazette, 401 N. Broadway, Billings, Mont., 59101; telephone (406) 245-3071; founded 1885; member of Lee Enterprises Inc., since 1960; circulation daily 56,598, Sunday 58,129; publisher J. S. Hilleboe, editor D. W. Bowler.

Population: 65,331 (city), 79,406 (metro area), 1st in state; total employed 34,996.

Area: south central Montana on Yellowstone River; 125 mi. from Yellowstone Park.

Industry: 3 oil refineries, beet sugar refinery, 2 packing plants; 3rd largest livestock auction yards in U.S., 500,000 head annually; new center for Rocky Mountain coal industry.

Commerce: wholesale-retail center for eastern Montana and northern Wyoming; retail sales (1971) $221 million; bank debits (1973) $3.7 billion; 6 banks, 2 savings and loan associations; 200 wholesale firms with $300 million volume; 800 retail firms with $265.6 million volume; per capita income $3,545.

Transportation: 3 air lines; one railroad; 2 bus lines. 98 motor carriers, Interstates 90 and 94.

Communications: 2 TV and 5 radio stations; one weekly, one daily newspaper.

Medical facilities: 2 hospitals. 400 beds; 11 clinics; 116 doctors, 40 dentists.

Cultural facilities: 3 art galleries, symphony orchestra. 2 western museums, studio theater; 4-year liberal arts college. business college. private (church-related) college.

Other attractions: big game hunting, fishing, boating, skiing, within hour's drive; 21 city parks; 3,000 hotel-motel rooms and facilities for conventions up to 5,000.

History: founded 1882 with arrival of railroad; named after Frederic Billings, then Northern Pacific president.

Binghamton, New York

The World Almanac is sponsored in the Binghamton area by The Evening Press and The Sunday Press, Vestal Parkway East, Binghamton, N.Y. 13902; (607)798-1234; founded 1904; circulation daily 76,637, Sunday 82,040; president and publisher Robert R. Eckert, editor Laurence S. Hale, managing editor George R. Venizelos.

Population: 61,100 (city), 296,000 (metro area), 12th in state; total employed 123,800.

Area: 10.98 sq. mi. at junction of Chenango and Susquehanna Rivers. Broome County seat.

Industry: GAF, second largest producer of film in country; computers, IBM; electronics & simulators, Singer Co.; shoes, Endicott Johnson Corp.; a major railroad center.

Commerce: wholesale, retail center of area producing $475 million a year; 5 banks; national headquarters of Security Mutual Life Insurance Co.

Transportation: 3 airlines, major being Allegheny, out of Broome County Airport; intersection Interstates 81 & 88 and Route 17; Erie-Lackawanna and Delaware and Hudson freight rail carriers.

Communications: 3 TV and 4 radio stations.

Medical facilities: 2 major hospitals.

Cultural facilities: Roberson Center Arts & Sciences; State Univ. at Binghamton; Broome County College; Tri-Cities Opera Co.; symphony orchestra; public library; Civic Theater.

Other attractions: municipal parks zoo; major state park on outskirts; new Veterans Memorial Arena.

Sports: Dusters pro-hockey team.

History: Settled 1800, on main river route of General Washington's border fight against Indians in early 1700's; became rail center by 1848, with roads replacing old Chenango Canal that fed Erie Canal; named for Philadelphia patriot and multi-millionaire William Bingham.

Birmingham, Alabama

The World Almanac is sponsored in the Birmingham area by The Birmingham Post-Herald, 2200 Fourth Ave., N, Birmingham, Ala. 35202; telephone (205) 325-2222; Post founded 1921 by Scripps-Howard Newspaper; Herald founded 1887; circulation, 75,630; editor Duard LeGrand, vice president W. H. Metz, managing editor George Cook; major public service projects include Goodfellow Christmas Fund, Alabama Favorite Teacher selection.

Population: 308,600 (city, 1972 est.), 778,500 (metro area), employment 323,500 (metro).

Area: 82 sq. mi. in north central Alabama.

Industry: heavy manufacturing in metals; U.S. Steel is area's largest employer; U.S. Pipe and Foundry and American Cast Iron Pipe Co. are in top 10 employers; South Central Bell's 5-state headquarters located in city.

Commerce: wholesale-retail center for Alabama; retail sales (1973) $1.884 billion; bank deposits (1973) $2.056 billion; 12 banks (county), 6 bank holding companies; 7 savings and loan associations.

Transportation: 5 major rail freight lines, Amtrak; Greyhound and Continental Trailways bus lines; Eastern, Delta, United and Southern air lines with modern airport terminal completed in 1973; 75 truck line terminals; 3 interstate highways, I-65, I-59 and I-20 all under construction.

Communications: 3 commercial TV stations, 1 PBS TV outlet and 15 radio stations.

Medical facilities: Univ. of Alabama in Birmingham Medical Center covers 60 sq. blocks; heart surgery team brings patients from all over the world; Veterans Administration hospital, in same complex, is the base of organ transplant program; Baptist Medical Centers have 2 major hospitals; 13 other hospitals.

Cultural facilities: symphony orchestra, Oscar Wells Museum of Art with more than $4 million in assets; Civic Opera; 4 resident civic theaters; 2 resident ballet companies.

Education: Samford Univ. Birmingham-Southern, Miles, and Daniel Payne Colleges; Jefferson State and Lawson State Junior College.

Convention facilities: new $50 million civic center with exhibition hall, theater and music hall; coliseum under construction; several new convention motels in civic center area.

Sports attractions: Birmingham Americans (WFL); nicknamed "Football Capital of the South" for Univ. of Alabama and Auburn Univ. games played at municipal stadium, Legion Field; Birmingham A's, farm club of Oakland A's, play at Richwood Field, municipally owned.

Other attractions: World's second largest cast iron statue, Vulcun, mythical god of the forge, overlooks Birmingham from Red Mountain as a symbol of the steel industry; Arlington Shrine, antebellum home that housed federal troops during Civil War; Botanical Gardens complex with Japanese Garden; Jimmie Morgan Zoo; extensive city park system.

History: chartered 1871; soon became known as the "Magic City" because of its rapid growth brought on by the presence of the 3 ingredients in steelmaking — coal, iron ore and lime; mining died out in recent years and most iron ore is now imported by ship and barge to Birmingport on Warrior River from South America; Coal mining, in decline since the 1940s, is on the upswing.

Bismarck, North Dakota

The World Almanac is sponsored in western North Dakota by The Bismarck Tribune, 222 Fourth St., Bismarck, N.D., 58501; (701) 223-2500; founded 1873 as weekly, became daily 1881; circ. 24,100; publisher A.G. Sorlie, editor John O. Hjelle, advertising director J. Joe Miller; major awards include Pulitzer Prize Gold Medal, 1937.

Population: 39,500, 3d in state; total employed 16,120.
Area: 11 sq. mi. on Missouri River. State capital and Burleigh County seat.
Industry: Agriculture, printing, trucking, farm machinery, state government, electric power, manufacturing, concrete products, railroad, insurance, livestock sales rings.
Commerce: retail trade area radius 100 miles, serving 150,000 people; retail sales (1973) $110,643,000; bank deposits (1973) $339,022,138; 4 banks, 4 building and loan associations.
Transportation: 2 railroad trunk lines, 1 transcontinental; 1,124-acre airport, hub for 3 airlines; 13 truck lines; 4 bus lines; U.S. Highways #10, #83 and I-94.
Communications: 2 daily newspapers; 3 AM, 2 FM radio stations; 2 TV stations.

New construction: 1973 building permits: $37,056,-625.
Medical facilities: 2 hospitals, 500-bed capacity, served by 70 M.D.s.
Cultural facilities: Bismarck Junior College; 4-year Mary College; 8,000-seat Civic Center; 67,000-volume public library; state library.
Recreation: 20 parks with over 1,250 acres; indoor artificial ice arena; YMCA; excellent duck and goose hunting and fishing in area.
Other attractions: Dakota Zoo; Garrison Dam.
History: founded 1872 as Edwinton, a rail town; name changed to Bismarck to bring in German investment capital.
Further information: Chamber of Commerce, 412 Sixth St., Bismarck, 58501.

Bloomington, Illinois

The World Almanac is sponsored in Bloomington-Normal and Central Illinois by The Daily Pantagraph, 301 W. Washington St., Bloomington, Ill. 61701; (309) 829-9411; founded 1837 by Jesse W. Fell; circulation 51,907; president and publisher Davis U. Merwin; editor Harold Liston; general manager William Diesel; managing editor Gene F. Smedley.

Population: 77,367 Bloomington-Normal, 107,800 (metro area) McLean County; mid-way between Chicago and St. Louis in central Illinois.
Industry: over 50 industries in county, ranks 9th in insurance cities in U.S., home offices of State Farm, Country Companies, Union Auto; uniform diversity of non-agricultural employment in all major work force areas; leads nation in corn and soybean production with 2,316 farms in county.
Commerce: metro retail sales $277.8 million; per household income $13,044; per household retail sales, 15th in nation, $8,293.
Transportation: new terminal at B-N Airport, 3 bus lines, 6 federal and state highways, 4 railroads, Amtrak, 35 interstate and 23 intrastate motor carriers, Ozark Airlines.

Communications: 6 radio stations.
Medical Facilities: 3 hospitals; Watson-Gailey Foundation Eye Bank.
Cultural Facilities: Illinois Wesleyan Univ., 1,800 in Bloomington; Illinois State Univ., 18,000, in Normal; 49 churches; home of American Passion Play; B-N Symphony, Community Players, Amateur Musical.
History: incorporated 1850. Site of A. Lincoln's "Lost Speech" and David Davis mansion, state historical shrine; city's Stevenson family has produced 3 generations of leadership; vice president Adlai E.; governor, presidential candidate and UN Ambassador, Adlai E. II; and U.S. Senator Adlai E. III.
Further Information: Association of Commerce and Industry of McLean County, 210 S. East St., Bloomington, Ill. 61701.

Boise, Idaho

The World Almanac is sponsored in the Boise area by the Idaho Statesman, 1200 N. Curtis Road, Boise, Idaho 83704; (208) 376-2121; founded 1864 as Tri-Weekly; daily circulation 60,822; Sunday 69,724; publisher Robert B. Miller Jr., general manager C. Ralph Guilieri, managing editor Richard P. Hronek; a Gannett newspaper.

Population: 86,800 (city), 120,200 (metro area), 1st in state, 224th in nation; total employed 76,848.
Area: 1,054 sq. mi. on Boise River at foot of Salmon River Mountains.
Industry: mobile home and recreational trailers produced $150 million in 1973; world headquarters Boise Cascade Corp., Morrison-Knudsen Co. and Albertson Food Stores.
Commerce: wholesale and retail center for southwest Idaho; retail sales $285.4 million (1973); bank resources $6,980 million in 16 banks with 16

branches; 4 saving and loan associations and 7 insurance company offices.
Transportation: 2 major airlines, 2 feeder airlines, 1 rail freight line, 4 bus lines and 17 common carrier truck lines.
Communications: 4 TV and 9 radio stations.
Medical facilities: 3 major hospital complexes including a Veteran's Administration facility.
Cultural facilities: Boise Philharmonic Orchestra, art gallery, state museum, Boise Little Theatre, new $1.4 million public library and Boise State University.
Other attractions: 33 parks, Southwestern Idaho

Fairgrounds, 2 major recreational lakes, scenic mountain areas.
History: founded 1863; name derived from "les bois" (the trees), a description for area used by French fur

trappers in 1811.
Further Information: Boise Chamber of Commerce, P.O. Box 2368, 83701, or Department of Commerce & Development, Idaho Statehouse, 83701.

Boston, Massachusetts

The World Almanac is sponsored in the Boston area by The Boston Globe, a wholly-owned subsidiary of Affiliated Publications, Inc., 135 Mossissey Blvd., Boston, Mass. 02107; (617) 929-2000; established 1872; combined daily circulation 480,381; Sunday 636,342. Chairman of the board and publisher Wm. Davis Taylor, president John I. Taylor, general manager William D. Taylor, editor Thomas L. Winship. Three Pulitzer prizes; Sigma Delta Chi and AP Managing Editors meritorious public service awards; UPI, University of Missouri and Sevellon Brown memorial (1969 and 1974) awards; sponsors Mass. Drama Festival, High School Art Competition, Science Fair, Newspaper in the Classroom program and Boston Globe Book Festival.

Population: 641,071 (city); 2,899,401 (metro area of 92 cities and towns around Boston); 8th largest metro area in nation; total employed, 266,505.
Area: 50 sq. mi. on Massachusetts Bay; state capital and Suffolk County seat.
Commerce: northeast center for finance and insurance; home for 50 insurance companies and regional hqs. for most U.S. and foreign companies; banking center for New England with total deposits of $12.264 billion (1972); birthplace of mutual fund, accounts for 35% of the nation's mutual fund holdings; retail center for northern New England; 1973 retail sales of $1.8 million, median family income $9,133 (city); $11,449 (metro); major electronics industry and publishing center.
Transportation: terminating point for 2 railroads, Penn Central and Boston & Maine; Logan International Airport, operated by Mass. Port Authority, terminal for 38 scheduled airlines, including 10 commuter lines, 8th busiest in world, served 10,750,000 passengers in 1973; Volpe International terminal opened 1974; 5 interstate highways.
Communications: 2 Boston newspapers; 7 TV and 31 radio stations.
New Construction: Now under construction: John Hancock Tower, Blue Cross-Blue Shield, Mass. Hqs.; Stone & Webster Engineering Hqs.; Federal Reserve Tower; major addition to Sheraton-Boston Hotel; Faneuil Hall Market Area; National Shawmut Bank; West End Residential-Office Complex, Atlantic Ave. waterfront.
Medical Facilities: In terms of dollars invested, health care is Boston's largest industry. Major institutions: Mass. General, Children's & New England Medical Centers, Boston City, Beth Israel, Deaconess Hospitals; Harvard, Boston Univ. & Tufts Medical Schools; Lahey Clinic. Proposed: Affiliated Hospital Center, merger of Peter Bent & Robert B. Brigham Hospitals and Boston Hospital for Women.
Federal facilities: 50 federal agencies employ 45,700 (military facilities not included.)

Cultural facilities: the "Athens of America"; Boston Public Library, new addition (1973) includes capacity for 500,000 books on open shelf, plus large lecture hall; Boston Symphony Orchestra; Boston Pops led by Arthur Fiedler; Opera Company headed by Sarah Caldwell; Boston Ballet; Museums of Fine Art of Science and Hayden Planetarium; New England Aquarium.
Educational facilities: 16 degree-granting institutions in the city and 47 in the metro area, including Harvard, Boston College and Boston Univ., Tufts, M.I.T., Brandeis, Univ. of Mass., Suffolk, Emanuel, Simmons and Wentworth Inst.
Recreation: 2,327 acres of city recreation area, includes historic Boston Common and Public Garden; Metropolitan District Commission provides extensive facilities, including beaches and harbor islands.
Convention facilities: 49 hotels equipped to handle conventions; exhibition halls include Commonwealth Pier Exhibition Hall with 168,000 sq. ft. and John B. Hynes Veterans Auditorium in Prudential Center with 154,000 sq. ft. and auditorium seating 5,800.
Sports: Pro teams include Red Sox (baseball), Celtics (basketball), New England Patriots (football), Bruins (hockey), Astros and Minutemen (soccer) and Lobsters (tennis.)
Other attractions: "The Freedom Trail," a 1½ mile walk through historic Boston; Beacon Hill and Back Bay historical districts; U. S. S. Constitution, "Old Ironsides," oldest commissioned ship in U. S. Navy; reconstruction of Boston Tea Party ship the Beaver, plus other Bicentennial events and attractions.
Nicknames: The Hub (of the Universe), Bean Town.
History: capital city of Commonwealth, founded 1630; from 1770, Boston was scene of many events leading to American Revolution, including Boston Tea Party on Dec. 16, 1773; incorporated Feb. 23, 1822.
Further information: Boston 200 Corp., P. O. Box 1773, Boston 02114, and Boston Chamber of Commerce, 125 High Street, Boston.

Bridgeport, Connecticut

The World Almanac is sponsored in the Bridgeport area by The Bridgeport Post (evening), The Bridgeport Telegram (morning) and The Bridgeport Sunday Post, published by The Post Publishing Co., 410 State Street, Bridgeport, Conn. 06602; (203) 333-0161; circulation Post, 81,073, Telegram, 12,074, Sunday Post, 89,239; John E. Pfriem president and general manager, Leonard E. Gilbert managing editor.

Population: 155,500 (State Health Dept. estimate 1973), first in state; planning region, 315,900; 8-town district labor force, 175,000.
Area: 17.5 sq. mi. on north shore of Long Island Sound at mouth of the Pequonnock River.
Industry: "Industrial Capital of Connecticut"; prod-

ucts include tools, metallic cartridges, wiring devices, brass goods, valves, corsets, electrical apparatus and appliances; nearby are Sikorsky Aircraft and Avco Lycoming; General Electric has new corporate headquarters in Fairfield, one mile from city line.

Commerce: retail sales, $324,671,000 (1973); downtown renewal includes completed complex with Gimbels and Sears stores, mall, 2,000-car parking garage, U.S. courthouse; also, 2 new bank buildings, major addition to another; new state courthouse opened 1974; construction started on downtown residential project.

Transportation: new $3 million railroad station under construction, to be connected with planned $7 million multi-transportation center with bus terminal, 1,500-car parking garage. City served by Conn. Turnpike (Interstate 95), historic U.S. 1 (Boston Post Road); 3 airlines at municipal Sikorsky Memorial Airport; Penn Central RR; 2 national bus lines; summer ferry to Port Jefferson, L.I.

Medical facilities: 3 general hospitals, state mental health center; work begun on new $5.5 million municipal convalescent hospital, only one of kind in state.

Cultural facilities: Univ. of Bridgeport, Fairfield Univ., Sacred Heart Univ., Housatonic Community College; Museum of Art, Science, Industry; P. T. Barnum museum; symphony orchestra; American Shakespeare theater in adjoining town of Stratford.

Recreational facilities: "The Park City" has 1,200 acres of parks, including Seaside with 2-mile shoreline; zoo; municipal indoor ice-skating rink.

Other attractions: Barnum Festival honoring former mayor and founder of circus, an annual 2-week celebration with largest July 4 weekend parade in the nation.

Buffalo, New York

The World Almanac is sponsored in the Buffalo area by the Courier-Express, 785 Main St., Buffalo, N.Y. 14240; (716) 847-5353; founded 1926, as merger of Courier and Express by William J. Conners Sr.; circulation mornings 127,861, Sunday 289,728; publisher William J. Conners III, asst. to publisher Howard W. Clother; gen. mgr. R. C. Lyons, sponsors hole-in-one tournament, learn to swim program, ski school, Goodfellows.

Population: 1,349,211 (metro area), 462,768 (city) 2d in state; metro area 24th in U.S.; employment about 500,000 (metro); hub of broad 8 county area with population of 1,758,000.

Area: 49.6 sq. mi. city, 1,567 sq. mi. metro; at western end of N.Y. State on Lake Erie, Niagara River, and U.S.-Can. boundary. Metro area includes cities of Niagara Falls, Lockport, Tonawanda, N. Tonawanda, Lackawanna.

Industry: 1,602 manufacturing establishments, highly diversified; headquarters for National Gypsum, Carborundum, Buffalo Forge, Trico Products, Fisher-Price Toys; large plants for Bethlehem Steel, Chevrolet, Ford, Westinghouse, Union Carbide.

Commerce: wholesale and financial center for western New York area; distribution center for northeastern U.S. and Canada; $6.5 billion in trade between U.S. and Canada handled each year; 9 commercial banks, 3 savings banks, 17 savings and loans.

Transportation: Greater Buffalo Int. Airport served by 4 scheduled airlines with 2.6 million passengers, 150,119 scheduled and non-scheduled flights in 1973; 6 major railroads, 10 freight terminals, 25,000 trains scheduled annually; about 150 motor carriers; excellent highway system includes New York State Thruway. Direct highway and rail service to all parts of Canada; direct water service to entire Great Lakes-St. Lawrence Seaways system, overseas, and Atlantic seaboard.

Communications: 2 newspapers, 3 additional dailies and one Sunday in surrounding cities; 5 TV and 20 AM and FM radio stations; 5 cable systems.

Cultural facilities: Buffalo Philharmonic in Kleinhans Music Hall; Albright-Knox Art Gallery; Studio Arena theater; Museum of Science; Historical Museum; Zoological Gardens (23 acres); Shaw Festival at Niagara-on-the-Lake, Ontario; Performing Arts Center in Lewiston.

Educational facilities: State Univ. at Buffalo (now building $650 million new campus), State College at Buffalo, Niagara University and Canisius College; 5 other colleges; several 2-year institutions.

Convention facilities: newly rebuilt Memorial Auditorium seats up to 17,000; new Niagara Falls Convention Center seats up to 12,000; additional facilities available at several hotels and motels.

Sports attractions: Buffalo Bills football (AFL), Sabres hockey (NHL), Braves (NBA); new 80,000 seat stadium completed in 1973.

Recreation: abundant facilities for water and winter sports and activities; near to both U.S. and Canada vacationlands.

Other attractions: Niagara Falls and river areas from Buffalo to Lake Ontario; Robert Moses and Adam Beck hydro stations, St. Lawrence Seaway, Welland Canal Locks, Ceramics Center (Niag. Falls), Aquarium (Niag. Falls), Our Lady of Victory Basilica (Lackawanna); Old Fort Niagara; Letchworth and Allegany State Parks.

Further information: Chamber of Commerce, 238 Main, Buffalo 14202

Calgary, Alberta, Canada

The World Amanac is sponsored in the Calgary and southern Alberta area by the Calgary Albertan, 830 Tenth Ave., S.W., Calgary, Alberta, T2R 0B1; (403) 263-7730; Founded 1902; circulation 33,824; publisher Bruce L. Rudd; managing editor Les Buhasz; business manager Al Vogt.

Population: 440,389.

Area: 157 sq. mi., one of Canada's highest cities (elevation 3,440 feet); in foothills of Rocky Mountains, 150 miles north of the Montana-Alberta border.

Industry: over 400 firms directly connected with the oil industry have headquarters in Calgary; also chemical, fertilizer and supply industries and older agricultural industries; assistance in locating industrial information is provided by Ken Ford, Director, Industrial Development, City Hall, Calgary, Alberta.

Transportation: 2 railways; Greyhound Bus Lines; International Airport served by 6 airlines.

Communications: 2 TV and 6 radio stations; 2 cable TV channels.

Medical facilities: 6 major hospital complexes.

New construction: building permits in 1973 totaled

$241,953,797; new convention center for 2,500 opened Sept. 1, 1974.

Cultural facilities: 2,700-seat auditorium, Glenbow Museum; Allied Arts Centre; centennial planetarium; symphony orchestra and live theatre; University of Calgary enrolls over 12,290.

Other attraction: Calgary Exhibition and Stampede in July; Heritage Park reconstructs life in early days; Horseman's Hall of fame recalls western historical events; Calgary Zoo and Natural History Park show life-size dinosaurs; 626 ft. rotating Calgary Tower gives panoramic view of city, seats 200 for dining and 300 in observation area.

Sports: every active sport; facilities for hockey, football and curling; Stampeders of Canadian Football League play in McMahon Stadium.

History: began as Mounted Police Outpost; as early as 1885, when the railway arrived, had a population of 1,800; discovery of oil in 1914 at Turner Valley contributed to Calgary's present prominence.

Further information: Chamber of Commerce, 300 Canada Permanent Building, 315 Eighth Ave., S.W.; Calgary Tourist and Convention Bureau, Mewata Park, 1300 Sixth Ave., S.W.

Charleston, West Virginia

The World Almanac is sponsored in the Charleston area by The Charleston Gazette, 1001 Virginia St., E., Charleston, W. Va. 25330; (304) 348-5140; founded 1873 as the Kanawha Chronicle, became The Charleston Gazette 1898; W. E. Chilton III publisher; Harry G. Hoffmann editor; Dallas C. Higbee executive editor.

Population: 71,505 (city), 230,600 (Kanawha County), most populous county in state; county labor force, 85,800.

Area: 29.3 sq. mi. at meeting place of Elk and Kanawha rivers; state capital.

Industry: diversified industrial complex, with coal and chemicals dominating; center for production of limestone, lumber, salt brines, vitreous clays and natural gas; also glass, petroleum products, alloys.

Commerce: wholesale, retail center for central and southern West Virginia; county retail sales, $648,459,000; average family income, $11,570.

Transportation: 2 rail freight lines, Amtrak, bus lines, state's busiest airport; barge lines, 3 interstate highways.

New construction: $25,622,426 in 1974.

Communications: 3 TV and 7 radio stations.

Medical facilities: 6 hospitals, 2 of them major complexes.

Cultural facilities: modern civic center and auditorium, Sunrise Cultural and Art Center, symphony orchestra, Community Music Assn., Light Opera Guild, Kanawha Players, State Museum, Morris Harvey College, W. Va. Univ. Graduate Center.

Other attractions: Coonskin Park, Kanawha State Forest, 6 golf courses, public tennis, International League baseball.

History: First settlement, Fort Lee, 1788; Virginia Assembly established Charles Town 1794; named Charleston 1818.

Further information: Chamber of Commerce, 818 Virginia St., East, Charleston, 25301.

Charlotte, North Carolina

The World Almanac is sponsored in the Charlotte area by The Charlotte Observer, 600 S. Tryon St., Charlotte, N.C. 28233; (704) 374-7070; founded 1886 as Charlotte Chronicle, changed to Charlotte Daily Observer March, 1892; sold to Knight Newspapers Inc. 1955; circulation 175,416 daily, 218,721 Sunday; president and publisher James L. Knight; vice-president and general manager Erwin R. Potts; editor C. A. McKnight; executive editor James K. Batten.

Population: 302,500 (city), 388,500 (Mecklenburg County), 602,500 (metro), 2d in state, 66th in nation; labor force 285,000.

Area: 530 sq. mi. in Piedmont section of N.C., a plateau extending from the Appalachians to the Coastal Plains.

Industry: electronic data processing, industrial chemicals, textiles, food products, machinery, printing & publishing; over 600 manufacturing companies.

Commerce: major distribution center; 1,400 wholesale firms with $6 billion sales; retail sales (SMSA 1973) $2.3 billion; E. B. I. per household $13,167; 16 banks, 11 mortgage banks, 6 building and loan associations.

Transportation: 3 major railway lines; 4 buslines; 5 airlines with 150 air movements per day; 111 trucking firms.

Communications: 5 TV and 12 radio stations.

Medical facilities: outstanding center in southeast, 7 hospitals including 3 large general.

Cultural facilities: Opera Assoc.; Symphony Orchestra; Oratorio Society; Mint Museum (art); Coliseum Auditorum, Civic Center; Johnson C. Smith Univ.; Univ. of N.C. — Charlotte; Davidson College; Queens College; Central Piedmont Community College.

Sports attractions: Charlotte Checkers (Eastern Hockey League); Charlotte Motor Speedway (NASCAR) with World 600 and National 500 races; Kemper Open golf tournament.

Other attractions: 2 major recreational lakes; nature museum; CAROWINDS, a family entertainment park.

History: Incorporated 1768; named for Queen Charlotte of England; played major part in American Revolution; county was the gold mining capital of the country before 1849; U.S. Mint was built in Charlotte in 1836 to serve the gold mining industry.

Further information: Chamber of Commerce, P.O. Box 1867, Charlotte, N.C. 28233.

Chattanooga, Tennessee

The World Almanac is sponsored in the Chattanooga area by the Chattanooga News-Free Press, 400 E. 11th St., Chattanooga, Tenn., 37401; (615) 266-0171, circulation 63,000 daily and Sunday; publisher Roy McDonald, president Frank McDonald, senior vice president Everett Allen, vice president and editor Lee Anderson, secretary J. W. Hoback, treasurer Clifford Welch.

Population: 119,923 (city), 370,857 (metro area); 4th in state, 89th in nation; 168,400 employed.

Area: 2,109.8 sq. mi. at juncture of Tennessee River and North Georgia boundary line.

Industry: over 600 manufacturers employ 55,000; receipts added by manufacture in 1973, $754 million; agriculture grossed $19 million in 1973.

Commerce: wholesale and retail center; wholesale sales (1973), $721 million; bank assets, $1.15 billion; 8 banks, 2 mortgage banks, 4 savings and loan assns., 3 major life insurance companies.

Transportation: 2 major freight lines, 2 bus lines, 10 federal and state highways; modern municipal airport serves 4 airlines.

New construction: development underway on Twin Tower Complex to feature two 21-story towers.

Communications: 5 TV and 20 radio stations.

Medical facilities: speech and hearing rehabilitation center; children and adults rehabilitation and education center; 11 major hospital complexes including psychiatric hospital.

Cultural facilities: Univ. of Tenn. at Chattanooga; 3 liberal arts colleges, 1 state tech community college, 1 state vocational-tech school; symphony orchestra, opera assoc., civic chorus.

Other attractions: multi-million-dollar vacation complex; Chattanooga Choo-Choo, in one of the world's largest restaurants, in restored railroad terminal; recreational lakes, mountains, museums.

History: explored by DeSoto 1540, settled 1828 at Ross' landing, incorporated 1839.

Further information: Chattanooga Convention and Visitors Bureau, Memorial Auditorium.

Chicago, Illinois

The World Almanac is sponsored in the Chicago area by the Chicago Tribune, 435 N. Michigan Ave., Chicago, Ill., 60611; (312) 222-3232; founded 1847 by Joseph Medill; cirrculation daily 697,145; Sunday 1,170,142; publisher Stanton R. Cook; editor Clayton Kirkpatrick; major awards include 6 Pulitzer prizes won by staff members; sponsors college-pro All Star football game, academic honors dinner, Nutcracker Ballet, Golden gloves, Silver Skates Derby and Chicago Tribune swimming meet.

Population: 3,334,500 (city). 2d largest in nation; 7,749,700 (8-county metro area in Illinois and Indiana): 1,177,600 households in city and 2,511,700 in metro area; total employed 3,273,900.
Area: 227 sq. mi. on s.w. shore of Lake Michigan.
Industry: metro area is leading producer of steel, telephone equipment, radios, TV sets, confectionery products, household products, diesel engines, and frozen and canned foods. Largest industry is primary metals worth $7.9 billion; food and related products follow at $7.0 billion; then come electrical equipment, metal products, non-electrical machinery, chemicals, printing and publishing, petroleum, and transportation equipment. Chicago accounts for 5.1% of the gross national product.

Commerce: 18,600 manufacturers have sales of $48.2 billion in metro area; 54,000 retailers do a $20.6 billion business; wholesale sales are estimated at $53.6 billion. Average spendable family income $14,311. Midwest Stock Exchange markets stocks and bonds; 7th Federal Reserve District Bank; world's leading grain futures market; Chicago Board of Trade; Mercantile Exchange.

Transportation: 3 major airports with 27 commercial airlines handled 34,300,000 passengers in 1973. O'Hare is world's largest and busiest commercial airport. Lake, ocean and river shipping makes city link between Mississippi River and St. Lawrence Seaway; Chicago handles one-third of Seaway cargo; 1973 overseas tonnage totaled 4,105,000 tons. Amtrak rail system headquarters. Over 12 major highways, expressways, tollways.

New Construction: total industrial construction, development and investment for 1973, $1,173 million; total commercial construction for 1973, $860 million, of which total shopping center construction accounted for $361 million.

Convention facilities: 1,000 trade shows and conventions in 1973 attended by over 2,700,000 people.
Educational facilities: 95 institutions of higher learning, include University of Chicago, Illinois Institute of Technology, Northwestern University; 6 medical schools; 3 dental colleges and one college of pharmacy and osteopathy.
Medical facilities: over 150 hospitals.
Recreation: 529 parks with an area of 6,465 acres; 72 swimming pools, baseball diamonds, golf courses, bicycle paths (30), handball courts, etc.
Cultural facilities: Art Institute; Museum of Science and Industry; Field Museum of Natural History; Shedd Aquarium is largest in world; Adler Planetarium; Lincoln Park and Brookfield Zoos; museums of Academy of Science and Historical Society.
Sports: National Football League Bears, World Football League Chicago Fire, American (baseball) League White Sox, National (baseball) League Cubs, National Hockey League Black Hawks, World Hockey Assoc. Cougars, National Basketball Assoc. Bulls.
History: Indians named area Checagou after area's strong-smelling wild onions; incorporated 1837 with population of 4,170.

Further information: Visitors Bureau and information Center, Association of Commerce and Industry, 130 South Michigan Avenue, Chicago, Il. 60603.

Cincinnati, Ohio

The World Almanac is sponsored in the Cincinnati area by The Post, a Scripps-Howard Newspaper, 800 Broadway, Cincinnati, Ohio 45202; (513) 721-1111; founded 1881 by Alfred and Walter Wellman; evening circulation 213,509; began special Saturday morning delivery of Weekender Jan. 1; editor Walter Friedenberg; business manager Joe Williams.

Population: 444,803 (city), 1,425,280 (metro area), 3rd   in state, 21st in nation; total employed 542,000.

Area; 2,150 sq. mi. (metro) in s.w. Ohio, s.e. Indiana and 3 north central counties in Ky.

Industry: home of Procter and Gamble, Federated Department Stores, Kroger Foods, Armco Steel, U.S. Shoe, Western-Southern Life Insurance, Baldwin Piano and Organ, Cincinnati Milacron; also the home of GM, Ford and GE plants; production of jet engines, playing cards, cosmetics, chemicals, machine tools, printing and publishing.

Commerce: retail sales (1973 est.) $3.084 billion; bank assets and deposits, $3.555 billion (metro area), with 44 banks with 153 branches; 161 savings and loan associations with 72 branches.

Transportation: 6 rail lines, Amtrak; 106 truck lines; Greater Cincinnati Airport with 300 incoming-outgoing flights daily serving 7 airlines; Lunken Airport (municipal) with 200 private planes; Port of Cincinnati with 4 Ohio River barge lines making up 8% of total river traffic of 130 million tons; 2 major transcontinental bus lines; city-owned local bus lines; metro freeway; construction moving to completion on interstate highway I-71.

Communications: 5 TV, 12 AM, 22 FM radio stations; 2 daily newspapers.

New construction: Greater Cincinnati Airport completed $46 million expansion program; Over-the Rhine, Findlay Market $2.6 million renewal completed; Riverfront Sports Arena under construction; $37 million Cincinnati Bell expansion; $20 million Environmental Protection Agency Research Center.

Medical facilities: 28 hospitals with over 9,500 beds; 120.7 physicians per 1,000 population; UC Medical Center where Sabin oral vaccine was discovered; Burn Institute and VA hospital.

Cultural facilities: Art Museum, Historical Society, symphony orchestra, Krohn Conservatory, Lloyd Library, May Festival, Taft Museum, Summer Opera, Museum of Natural History, Shubert Theater, Contemporary Arts Center, UC Observatory.

Educational facilities: Cincinnati and Xavier Univs.; Edgecliff, Mt. St. Joseph, Hebrew Union, Thomas More, Bible Seminary colleges; 8 technical and 2 year colleges; 47 technical vocational schools.

Convention facilities: numerous hotels and Cincinnati Convention and Exposition Center; Cincinnati Gardens; Emery Auditorium and Music Hall.

Other attractions: zoo, Cincinnati Reds baseball, Bengals football, Cincinnati Swords (1973 Calder Cup winner), Fountain Square Plaza, River Downs Race Track, Kings Island Amusement Park.

Further information: Chamber of Commerce, 120 W. Fifth Street, Cincinnati, Ohio 45202.

Cleveland, Ohio

The World Almanac is sponsored in the Cleveland area by The Cleveland Press, 901 Lakeside Ave., Cleveland, Ohio 44114; (216) 623-1111; founded 1878 by E. W. Scripps; circulation 376,609; editor Thomas L. Boardman; managing editor Richard R. Campbell; business manager Robert H. Hartmann; major awards include Pulitzer Prize, Lasker Award.

Population: 708,968 (city), 2,111,100 (metro area), first in state, 10th in nation; total employed 838,200 (nonagricultural).

Area: 3,617 sq. mi. along southern shore of Lake Erie, east and west of Cuyahoga River.

Industry: city has been described as "an industrial powerhouse"; bills itself "The Best Location in the Nation." Within 500 miles are: more than 50% of populations of the U.S. and Canada, more than 55% of U.S. manufacturing plants, more than 50% of retail sales in the U.S. and more than 60% of U.S. product value. City has more corporate headquarters than any U.S. city of its size. No single industry dominates economy — steel and metal products are mainstays; manufacturing complex occupied essentially with primary metals, fabricated metal products, machinery, tools, automotive products. Important industries include making of electric motors, products of petroleum, rubber, plastic, stone, clay and glass, chemicals, paints, wearing apparel, measuring instruments, electronic components, food products, and publishing-printing. Value of products is $15 billion a year. Retail sales are almost $5 billion with average family spending about $6,000 on retail merchandise. More than 50% of families earn more than $10,000 a year.

Transportation: Hopkins Airport with more than 5 million passengers each year; Burke Lakefront Airport, 5 minutes from Public Square and capable of handling intermediate jets; Port of Cleveland visited by more than 50 overseas steamship lines and Great Lakes fleet; largest city on Lake Erie and 3rd largest on Great Lakes. Cleveland is only U.S. city with airport-to-downtown rail service. Ride takes 20 minutes and costs about $10 less than a cab ride.

Communications: Cleveland Press, evening daily; Cleveland Plain Dealer, morning daily plus Sunday; numerous foreign language newspapers; 6 TV stations; 12 AM and 14 FM radio stations.

New construction: downtown rebuilding plan has seen completion of more than 30 facilities. Under construction are 2 hotels, a parking garage, a $61 million justice center, and others. Projects on the drawing boards include a 32-acre complex of offices, stores and apartments, and a Gateway and Jetport on Lake Erie.

Cultural facilities: Cleveland Orchestra; Play House, nation's oldest and largest resident professional theater; Museum of Art; Karamu House for interracial arts; Western Reserve Historical Society; Health Museum; Natural Science Museum; Cultural Gardens; zoo; Blossom Music Center; Salvador Dali Museum; Garden Center; Sea World; aquarium.

Educational facilities: Case Western Reserve Univ., Baldwin-Wallace College, Cleveland State Univ., Cuyahoga Community College, John Carroll Univ., and Notre Dame, St. John and Ursuline Colleges.

Sports attractions: NFL Browns, American League Indians, WHA Crusaders, NBA Cavaliers, and World Team Tennis Nets; also golfing, horse and car racing, boating.

Other attractions: downtown Convention Center is largest city-owned convention facility in U.S.; public library is 2d in size of book collection only to New York. Public Square, hub of city, marked by 52-story Terminal Tower. "The Forest City" is encircled by "Emerald Necklace," 18,000 acres of metropolitan parks. Cleveland Clinic, known for medical research, attracts patients from throughout the world.

History: settlement established in summer, 1796 by Gen. Moses Cleaveland, was capital of the Western Reserve, became a city in 1836.

Further information: Greater Cleveland Growth Assn., 690 Union Commerce Bldg., Cleveland 44115.

Columbia, South Carolina

The World Almanac is sponsored in the Columbia area by Columbia Newspapers, Inc., P.O. Box 1333, Columbia, S.C. 29202; phone (803) 765-2111; circulation, The State (morn.), 108,298; The Columbia Record (eve.), 32,298; The State (Sunday), 124,246; Ambrose G. Hampton, publisher; William E. Rone, editorial page editor (State); Thomas N. McLean, editor (Record); James R. Holton Jr., advertising director.

Population: 113,542 (1970); 2-county metro area, 341,700; 153,100 employed.

Area: 105 sq. mi. (Richland County); 1,525 sq. mi. (metro); center of state, at confluence of Broad and Saluda Rivers.

Government: state capital with about 100 state agencies; 19 federal agencies; 25,000-man Ft. Jackson within city limits.

Industry: 150 large firms; more than $600 million spent in new capital investments 1961-1971, led by Bendix, Westinghouse, Kodak, Litton, General Electric, Allied Chemical and Rockwell; recreational equipment, heavy equipment, nuclear, fibers, electronics and fertilizer.

Commerce: retail sales, $733 million (1973); median household income, $11,828; consumer spendable income, $1.1 billion.

Transportation: Metropolitan Airport with 4 major airlines and freight service; 3 rail freight lines, Amtrak; 44 motor freight companies; 3 interstate, 6 federal, and 5 state highways.

Communications: 4 TV and 8 radio stations.

Medical facilities: 6 general hospitals, including modern Richland Memorial; William S. Hall Psychiatric Institute; 2 state mental hospitals.

Cultural facilities: Town Theatre, the oldest continuous community theater in nation; 3 other theaters; Museum of Art and Sciences; Gibbes Planetarium; Township Auditorium, home of Artist Series; Dreher Auditorium with Philharmonic Orchestra, City Ballet, Lyric Theatre and Choral Society; Fraser Hall.

Recreation facilities: 13 golf courses; city park system; 2 municipal pools; wide range of hunting activities; Riverbanks Zoological Park, part of 135-acre complex; Lake Murray, water sports.

Sports: 54,564-seat Williams-Brice Stadium, home of Univ. of South Carolina Fighting Gamecock football team; 13,000-seat Carolina Coliseum for basketball, conventions.

Educational facilities: 20,000-student Univ. of South Carolina; 4 private colleges; Technical Education Center; Lutheran Seminary.

History: established 1786 as state capital; burned in 1865 by Union General Sherman.

Further information: Chamber of Commerce, 1308 Laurel St., Columbia, S.C. 29202.

Columbus, Georgia

The World Almanac is sponsored in the Columbus area by The Columbus Enquirer and The Columbus Ledger, 17 W. 12th St., Columbus, Ga. 31902; phone (404) 322-8831; combined daily circulation 65,010; Sunday 59,132. Enquirer founded 1828, awarded Pulitzer Prize, 1955. Published by the R. W. Page Corporation; acquired by Knight Newspapers, Inc., 1973. M. R. Ashworth, president; Glenn Vaughn, general manager; Carrol Dadisman, executive editor.

Population: 167,377 (city); 227,000 (metro); 84.4 thousand employed (metro).

Area: 220 sq. miles on Chattahoochee River, Georgia's western border.

Industry: major textile production center: Swift, Fieldcrest, Jordan, Columbus Mills, Bibb Mfg., Reeves Bros., West Point Pepperell; Int'l. hqs. Royal Crown Cola, Tom's Foods, Ltd., Burnham Van Lines; lumber products, beverages, concrete, bakery goods.

Commerce: hub of west Georgia finance, agriculture, textiles, hydroelectric power; retail sales $479 million; spendable family income, $10,356; 5 banks, 4 savings and loan associations.

Federal facilities: Ft. Benning, world's largest infantry school; $270 million annual disbursements.

Transportation: 2 rail lines, 2 bus lines; Delta, Eastern, Southern airlines; 33 truck lines; Chattahoochee is navigable river.

Communications: 3 TV and 10 radio stations.

New construction: Peachtree Mall, 70 retail stores; Columbus East Industrial Park, 402 acres.

Medical facilities: 4 hospitals, 1 under construction.

Cultural facilities: Springer Opera House, state theater of Ga.; Three Arts Theater; Museum of Arts and Crafts; Bradley Memorial Library; Columbus College.

Sports: Astros, Southern baseball league.

History: Founded 1828. Gained early prominence as shipping center for cotton, fish; birthplace Coca Cola (formula originated here).

Further information: contact Columbus Chamber of Commerce, P.O. Box 1200, Columbus, Ga. 31902.

Columbus, Ohio

The World Almanac is sponsored in the Columbus area by the Columbus Citizen-Journal, 34 S. Third St., Columbus, Ohio, 43216; (614) 461-5000; Citizen founded 1899, Journal 1811; circ. 119,500 a.m. daily except Sun.; owned by E. W. Scripps Co.; editor Charles Egger, business manager Gregory A. Demski, managing editor Jack Keller.

Population: 576,100 (city), 1,088,400 (metro area), 1974 ests; 2d in state, 33rd in nation, total employed 489,200.

Area: 158 sq. mi., central Ohio, state capital, Franklin County seat.

Industry: diversified; 1053 manufacturers including General Motors, Rockwell International, Western Electric, Westinghouse, Borden (natl. hqs.); planes, missiles, refrigerators, mining machinery, telephones, glass products, auto parts; 1973 industrial payroll $768 million; home office of Battelle Memorial Institute with world-wide research laboratories.

Commerce: wholesale, retail center for central, southern Ohio, parts of W. Va., Ky. Retail sales:

$1,681,480; bank assets: $8.5 billion, 7 banks; 20 savings & loan assocs.; 39 insurance co. home offices, assets $3.2 billion. Per capita income: $4,383. Defense Construction Supply Center, world's largest; 21% of business is government.

Transportation: 87 truck lines, 6 intercity bus lines, 4 railroads, 8 airlines using Port Columbus International with 750 air movements daily; 11 major highways.

Communications: 4 TV stations, 15 radio stations.

Medical facilities: 19 hospitals, medical centers; Children's Hospital leads nation in children admitted; Ohio State Univ. School of Medicine.

Cultural: Ohio Theatre; symphony orchestra, public library with 21 branches; art museums, Center of Science and Industry, Ohio Historical Center with re-created early 19th Century village.

Other attractions: 104 parks, Park of Roses world's largest; Ohio Railway Museum, zoo, boating.

Educational facilities: Ohio State, Capital, Franklin Univ., Ohio Dominican College, Columbus College of Art & Design, Columbus Technical Institute.

Sports: 83,080 seats in Ohio Stadium; Owls (hockey), Beulah Park (thoroughbreds), Scioto Downs (harness).

History: founded 1812 as state capital, named for Christopher Columbus.

Further information: Chamber of Commerce, P. O. Box 1527, Columbus, Ohio 32164.

Corpus Christi, Texas

The World Almanac is sponsored in the Corpus Christi area by The Caller-Times, 820 Lower N. Broadway, Corpus Christi, Tex. 78401; Caller (a.m.) founded 1883; Times (p.m.) founded 1911; merged 1929. Caller circ. 66,003; Times 34,895; Sunday 88,079; editor & publisher Edward H. Harte; pres. & gen. mgr. Allan P. Johnson III; exec. ed. John L. Stallings, managing ed. John B. Anderson.

Population: 215,000 (est.), 204,590 (metro, 1970).

Area: 328 sq. mi. (226 water), 210 miles SW of Houston on Corpus Christi Bay.

Industry: oil refineries and chemical, petrochemical, synthetics, aluminum and zinc plants.

Commerce: Port of Corpus Christi handled 30.03 million tons in 1973; 72-foot-deep superport proposed for 1977; economic hub of South Texas; farming, ranching, oil and gas production, commercial fishing, tourist trade; 13 banks have deposited in excess of $551 million; payrolls total more than $453 million.

Federal facilities: Corpus Christi Naval Air Station is headquarters for Naval Air Training Command; Corpus Christi Army Depot is Army's only complete helicopter overhaul plant; combined payroll $90 million.

Cultural facilities: museum, symphony, little theatre, Art Museum of South Texas, Del Mar College (junior), Texas A&I University at Corpus Christi (upper level).

Recreation: Free public beaches and fishing piers on Corpus Christi Bay and along Gulf of Mexico on Mustang Island and in 88-mile-long Padre Island National Seashore; surf and charter boat fishing, sailing, municipal marina with public launching ramps, large public tennis center, 3 private tennis clubs; 2 public and 3 private golf courses.

Further information: Corpus Christi Chamber of Commerce, P. O. Box 640, Corpus Christi, Texas 78403.

Dallas, Texas

The World Almanac is sponsored in Dallas by The Dallas Morning News, Communications Center, Dallas, Tex. 75222; (214) 245-8222; published by the oldest business in Texas, The News was founded in 1842 by Samuel Bangs; circulation, 308,664 Sunday, 263,175 daily. President Joe M. Dealey, managing editor Tom J. Simmons. Winner of numerous national awards including Freedoms Foundation and National Headliner; Sponsors Teen-age Citizenship Tribute, Fly-the-Flag program, Spelling Bee, Sports Show, etc.

Population: city, 867,300 (8th in nation); county, 1,393,400; Dallas-Fort Worth metro area, 2,503,700 (10th in nation); Total employed, 1,144,000 with 2.9% unemployment.

Area: 900 sq. mi. astride Trinity River in North Texas, about 75 miles south of Oklahoma border; elevation 450 to 750 feet.

Industry: banking and insurance capital of the Southwest, Dallas ranks 4th among U.S. cities in the number of million-dollar-net-worth companies with 629 such firms. Manufacturing accounts for one-fourth of employment, about evenly divided between durable (including electronics, aviation, aerospace and machinery) and non-durable (including food products, apparel and printing-publishing).

Commerce: a $2.5 billion wholesale market ($5 billion retail), Dallas ranks first nationally in giftware, home furnishing and floor covering wholesaling, 2d in apparel. Metro retail sales totaled $6.8 billion in 1973, while estimated buying income reached $11.6 billion and bank deposits $12.7 billion.

Transportation: Dallas-Fort Worth Airport, completed in 1974, is the world's largest; Dallas Love Field is nation's fourth busiest in itinerant operations, 6,668,398 passengers enplaned there (1973). City served by 10 airlines, 8 railroads, 2 trans-continental bus lines, 84 motor freight lines, 2 taxicab companies with 553 cabs; Dallas Transit System serves 125,000 people daily on 97 lines, 481 route miles.

Communications: 2 metropolitan daily newspapers, numerous suburban dailies, 4 commercial VHF TV stations, public television, 1 UHF station, 17 AM and 18 FM radio stations, 2 city magazines.

New construction: $692 million in building permits issued in 1973 ($362 million nonresidential); projects announced include 300-acre, $300 million Park Central office park.

Medical facilities: Dallas has 57 hospitals with 9,000 beds, 500 bassinets; Baylor University Medical Center was recently chosen No. 4 among the country's top 13 "super hospitals."

Culture: symphony orchestra, opera, summer musicals, ballet, Sunday Concert Series; drama at Dallas Theater Center, Theater Three, National Children's Theater, Repertory Theater and 3 dinner theaters; 7 museums; SMU's Owens Fine Arts Center with a collection of paintings and sculpture; numerous art galleries.

Education: 114,727 students attend 28 colleges and universities within 50 miles of Dallas; Southern Methodist Univ., the Univ. of Texas at Dallas, Univ. of Dallas, North Texas State, Univ. of Texas at Arlington, Baylor Univ. College of Dentistry, Southwestern Medical School; and the Dallas Community College System with 32,500 students on 4 campuses, 3 more planned.

Convention Facilities: 3 major convention centers, including expanded Dallas Convention Center with more combined meeting-exhibit space (611,000 sq. ft.) than any other in U.S.; nearly 24,000 air-conditioned hotel rooms. Dallas consistently ranks in top 5 convention cities. In 1973, 1,082,000 people attended 706 conventions in Dallas.

Sports attractions: professional sports include football, baseball, tennis, golf, hockey, soccer and rodeo;

Cotton Bowl is site of annual New Year's Day football game and SMU home games.

Other attractions: Six Flags Over Texas, Dallas Zoo, Seven Seas, Lion Country Safari; State Fair of Texas 16 days each October; museums of fine arts, health and science, natural history; Hall of State; Garden Center and Music Hall; excellent lakes, golf courses, parks.

History: First settler was Tennessee frontiersman John Neely Bryan who established a trading post and plotted the townsite in 1844; incorporated 1856; named for Vice-President George Millifin Dallas. Since 1931, the city has had council-manager form of government. Spectacular population growth began after World War II, when aircraft manufacturing augmented an economy that had been built first on cotton, then on oil, banking and insurance. Diversified economic expansion fed the growth of the 1960s.

Further information: Dallas Chamber of Commerce, Fidelity Union Tower, Dallas, Texas 75201.

Dayton, Ohio

The World Almanac is sponsored in the Dayton area by The Journal Herald, 37 South Ludlow St., Dayton, Ohio 45401; (513) 223-1111; founded 1808 as Dayton Repertory; circulation, 112,142; Editor and publisher Charles T. Alexander, managing editor Ralph Langer, editorial page editor Alvin P. Sanoff, Modern Living department editor Virginia Hunt.

Population: 241,900 (city), 862,700 (metro), 4th in state, 41st in nation; total employed 354,500.
Area: 41.72 sq. mi. at junction of Miami, Mad and Stillwater rivers.
Industry: NCR Corp., McCall Printing Co., General Motors Corp. (Delco Moraine, Delco Products, Inland Mfg. and Frigidaire); more than 800 other manufacturing facilities.
Commerce: retail sales (1972), 1.872 billion; average spendable household income, $12,640.
Transportation: 2 airports, 6 airlines, 4 trunk rail systems, 6 bus lines and Dayton Regional Transit Authority.
Communications: 4 TV and 10 radio stations.
Medical facilities: 10 hospitals, including a veteran's administration facility.
Federal facilities: Wright Patterson AFB, headquarters for the Air Force Logistics Command and Aeronautical Systems Division; Defense Electronics Supply Center.
Convention facilities: new downtown convention and exhibition center.

New construction: downtown transportation center, Winters, First National Bank Towers completed; new federal building and hi-rise senior citizen apartments.
Educational facilities: Univ. of Dayton, Wright State Univ.; 2 junior colleges — Sinclair (new downtown campus) and Miami Jacobs (jr. college of business); Dayton Art Institute; United Theological Seminary.
Cultural facilities: Philharmonic Orchestra, opera, ballet, 4 amateur theatrical groups, 2 professional companies; Diehl Memorial band shell and Deed's Carillon.
Sports attractions: Dayton Gems (IHL); Amateur Trapshoot Hdqtrs; college sports.
Other attractions: Air Force Museum, Carillon Park (Dayton historical exhibits), Paul Lawrence Dunbar homestead, Wright Bros. Memorial, Aviation Hall of Fame; new Court House Plaza at Old Courthouse Museum.
Further information: Dayton Area Chamber of Commerce, 111 West First St., Dayton 45402.

Denver, Colorado

The World Almanac is sponsored in the Denver area by the Rocky Mountain News, 400 W. Colfax Ave., Denver, Colo. 80201; (303) 892-5000; founded 1859 by William N. Byers; circulation daily 221,971, Sunday 246,259; editor Vincent M. Dwyer, business manager William W. Fletcher; sponsors Colorado-Wyoming spelling bee, Golden Wedding party, Huck Finn Day, Ski School.

Population: 507,700 (city), 1,306,100 (metro area), first in state, 26th in nation; total employed 666,300.
Area: 116.69 sq. mi. on So. Platte River at edge of Great Plains near Rocky Mountains.
Industry: Gates Rubber Co. is world's largest maker of v-belts and hose, 6th largest U.S. rubber company; Samsonite Corp. is world's largest luggage manufacturer, also makes furniture and toys; Adolph Coors Co. is nation's 4th largest brewer of beer. Center for smokeless industry with 1,550 manufacturing firms.
Commerce: largest distribution center in region embracing one-third of U.S. geographical area; retail sales, $7 billion (1973). Bank deposits $3.895 billion,

79 banks, 13 savings and loan associations and 45 insurance company home offices. Per capita income, $4,675.
Transportation: 6 major rail freight lines, Amtrak; Continental and Greyhound bus lines; 3 Interstate highways intersect city. Stapleton International Airport is nation's 11th largest, with 600 daily flights, hub for 6 trunk airlines; Frontier Air Lines based here, as is United Air Lines Flight Training Center.
Communications: 5 TV and 28 radio stations.
Medical facilities: largest medical center between Kansas City and San Francisco; one of 16 regional cancer information centers with operations to begin

in 1975; facilities include Univ. of Colorado Medical Center, National Jewish Hospital, Children's Asthma Research Institute and Hospital (CARIH); 22 major hospitals.

Federal facilities: largest complex of federal offices outside Washington, D.C., with 28,000 federal employes; site of Atomic Energy Commission's Rocky Flats plant, U.S. Mint, Lowry Air Force Base, Air Force Accounting and Finance Center, Army's Fitzsimons Medical Center, Army's Rocky Mountain Arsenal.

Cultural facilities: symphony orchestra, 3 nonprofessional orchestras, 2 choral groups, Denver Art Museum, 3 theater companies; 3-sq.-block convention center; 12,000-seat Red Rocks open-air theater.

Educational facilities: Univ. of Denver, Colorado

School of Mines; Colorado Women's Metropolitan State Loretto Heights and Regis Colleges; Univ. of Colorado School of Medicine, Iliff School of Theology.

Recreational facilities: 150 named parks, 13,400 acres of mountain parks, 34 golf courses in metro area, City Park Zoo, 2 amusement parks; more than a dozen ski areas.

Sports: pro teams include NFL Broncos, Bears (baseball, AAA, American Association), Rockets (basketball, ABA), Dynamos (soccer, NASL), Racquets (tennis, WTT,) and Spurs (hockey, CHL; NHL in 1976).

Other attractions: Museum of Natural History, Botanic Gardens, State Historical Museum.

History: founded 1858 with discovery of gold, fast became supply center for mountain mining camps; named for territorial governor.

Des Moines, Iowa

The World Almanac is sponsored in Iowa by the Des Moines Register and Tribune, 715 Locust St., Des Moines, Ia. 50304; (515) 284-8000; founded 1849; circulation evening Tribune 109,384, morning Register 253,557, Sunday Register 489,657; president and publisher David Kruidenier, editor Kenneth MacDonald, business manager Louis Norris; sales director J. Robert Hudson.

Population: 201,404 (city, 1970), 324,500 (est. 1973 metro); 1st in Iowa, 64th in nation.

Area: 66 sq. mi., at juncture of Racoon and Des Moines rivers, south central Iowa.

Industry: considered to be 2nd largest insurance center in nation (52 home companies) and 2nd largest tire center with Firestone, Armstrong plants; publishing center — Meredith Co., Better Homes and Gardens, Wallace-Homestead, others; Farm implements — North American headquarters and plant of Massey-Ferguson, John Deere; lawn and garden equipment, sporting goods, food products, cosmetics, dental equipment, automotive accessories, concrete forms, nozzles, tools, 700 wholesale and jobbing firms.

Commerce: retail sales in metro area, $831,088,000 (1972); per capital income, $4,451 (1972); bank deposits, $700,000,000.

Transportation: newly enlarged in-city airport, 3 major air lines; 4 bus lines; 5 railroads; 69 truck lines, Interstate Highways 80 and 35.

New construction: 36-story bank-office building (tall-

est in Iowa); 25-story financial center; bulk mail center; Standard Oil credit card center; 2 major hospital additions; Farm Bureau building.

Medical facilities: 11 hospitals with 2,500 beds.

Cultural facilities: Art Center, Center of Science and Industry, Community Playhouse, Drama Workshop, Drake University, symphony orchestra; Grand View Junior, Area Community, and 2 Bible Colleges; College of Osteopathic Medicine and Surgery, Technical High School.

Recreation: 1,400 acres of parks, 9 public golf courses, 11 public pools, tennis, new YMCA and YWCA buildings, two huge reservoirs.

Other attractions: AAA baseball, pro hockey, Drake Relays, Missouri Valley and Big Eight (Iowa State U.) conferences; 15,000-seat auditorium; boys and girls state basketball tournaments, State Fair, Living History Farm.

History: founded 1843 as a fort to protect the rights of the Indians; incorporated 1853, became Iowa capital in 1857.

Detroit, Michigan

The World Almanac is sponsored in the Detroit area by The Detroit News, 615 W. Lafayette, Detroit, Mich. 48231; (313) 222-2000; founded 1873 by James E. Scripps; circulation (D) 693,874 (S) 850,989; president and publisher Peter B. Clark Sr., v.p. R.M. Spitzley, v.p. and gen. mgr. J. T. Dorris, v.p. and editor Martin S. Hayden; major awards won include Pulitzer Prize, Nat'l Headliners; 66 community projects include NCAA Indoor Track Championships, Policeman and Fire Fighter of the Month, Science Fair, Scholastic Writing and Art Awards, Spelling Bee.

Population: 1,500,000 (city), 4,250,000 (metro area), (1972); first in state, 5th in U.S.

Area: 139.6 sq. mi. on the Detroit River, a Great Lakes connecting link and the world's busiest inland waterway.

Industry: "The Motor City"; area plants produce 25% of the nation's cars and trucks, employing more than 200,000. Nonautomotive manufacturing and nonmanufacturing firms employ more than 1,400,000. Other products are machine tools, iron products, metal stampings, hardware, industrial chemicals, drugs, paint, wire products.

Commerce: total metro personal income per household was $14,111 (1971); area retail sales were $8.6 billion.

Transportation: served by 5 railroads, over 200 inter-

city truck lines, 19 airlines, and 31 scheduled steamship lines serving more than 40 countries; air passengers 7,073,191 (1971).

Communications: 9 TV and 18 radio stations.

New construction: $500 million riverfront development, Renaissance Center, will be built on eastside waterfront area, incorporating living units, business offices and hotels; other projects include 660-acre $284 million downtown residential developments, and a 235-acre, $500 million mid-town medical center.

Cultural Facilities: symphony orchestra, International Institute, Meadow Brook music and drama programs, Institute of Arts, concert band, and the annual Freedom Festival, celebrating Canada's

Dominion Day, July 1, and U.S. Independence Day, July 4.

Educational facilities: 11 colleges and universities are located in the metro area, including Wayne State Univ., Univ. of Detroit, and branches of the Univ. of Michigan and Michigan State Univ.

Convention facilities: 75-acre, $100 million Civic Center, including Cobo Hall and Convention Arena with 400,000 sq. ft. of exhibit space; more than 24,000 rooms in 250 hotels and motels.

Sports attractions: Tigers baseball (American League), NFL Lions, NHL Red Wings, NBA Pistons, WHA Stags, WFL Wheels, Loves (World Team Tennis); 6 winter skiing areas within short driving distance.

Other attractions: Chrysler, Ford and General Motors auto plants, Henry Ford Museum and Greenfield Village historical displays, Cranbrook Institute (science museum and arts), Belle Isle (1,000-acre park), zoo, public library, Historical Museum and Fort Wayne Military Museum.

History: founded 1701 by the Frenchman Cadillac as a strategic frontier fort and trading post, ceded to the British in 1763 and turned over to the U.S. in 1796 as a village of 2,500; reoccupied by the British for a year in the War of 1812. Completion of the Erie Canal in 1825 opened a cheap water transport route from New York to the Northwest and made Detroit an important commercial center. R. E. Olds built Detroit's first auto factory in 1899; and Henry Ford, who hand-built his first car in 1896, formed his first company in 1899, and the present Ford Motor Co. in 1903. The area's industries made it the "Arsenal of Democracy" in World War II.

Further information: Greater Detroit Chamber of Commerce, 150 Michigan Ave., Detroit 48226; Cities Reporting and Information Dept., City-County Bldg., Detroit, 48226; Detroit Convention Bureau, 1400 Book Bldg., Detroit, 48226.

Edmonton, Alberta, Canada

The World Almanac is sponsored in central and northern Alberta by the Edmonton Journal, 10006 - 101 St., Edmonton, Alberta, T5J 2S6; telephone (403) 425-9120; founded Nov. 11, 1903; a division of Southam Press Ltd.; circulation 165,000; publisher Ross Munro; editor Andrew Snaddon; sponsor Learn to Ski, Curl, Play Golf, Tennis, and Fitness Finders programs; Literary Awards.

Population: 438,425 (city), 518,000 (est. metro), capital of Alberta, largest Alberta city, 4th in Canada; total employed 206,080.
Area: 121 sq. mi. on North Saskachewan River.
Industry: 2d largest refining center in Canada, 7,000 producing wells; petrochemical industries include plastics, fertilizers, steel tube mills; 2d largest meat processing center in Canada; prosperous mixed farming.
Commerce: major supply center for Northwest Territories, Yukon and Canadian Arctic; originating terminus of 5 oil and natural gas pipelines to the east from Alberta, Alaska and the Canadian north; retail sales (1973) over $1 billion; trading area population, 990,000.
Transportation: Alaska and Mackenzie Highways; Canadian National, Canadian Pacific, Pacific Northern, Great Slave and Alberta Resources railroads; 4 airports, 6 airlines, 156,870 itinerant movements, 5th busiest in Canada.
Communications: 3 TV, 3 cable TV and 8 radio stations.
Medical facilities: 5 general and 5 auxiliary hospitals,

2 rehabilitation centers, 9 nursing homes.
Cultural facilities: Symphony Orchestra, Art Gallery, Centennial Library, Provincial Museum and Archives; Univ. of Alberta, Northern Alberta Institute of Technology, Grant McEwan Community College, 2 ballet companies, professional theater, opera, Northern Alberta Jubilee Auditorium, Queen Elizabeth Planetarium.
Other attractions: Klondike Days, celebration of 1898 Yukon gold rush, mid-July; Storyland Valley Zoo, Fort Edmonton, Mayfair Park, Alberta Game Farm, Elk Island Park.
Sports: C.F.L. Eskimos, W.H.A. Oilers, Western Major Fastball League Monarchs; new 16,000-seat Coliseum was to be completed in 1974, new 40,000-seat sport complex being built for the 1978 Commonwealth Games; Speedway, one of top auto race tracks on continent; Kinsmen Field House indoor track seats 4,000.
History: Fort Edmonton built 1795, named for town now a borough of London, England; oil discovered at Leduc (20 miles south) in 1947.

El Paso, Texas

The World Almanac is sponsored in the El Paso area by the El Paso Herald-Post, 401 Mills Ave., El Paso, Tex. 79999; (915) 532-1661; Herald founded 1881, Post 1922, merged (under Scripps-Howard) 1931; circulation 47,370. Robert W. Lee, editor; Robert McBrinn, managing editor.

Population: 358,938 (city); with twin city, Juarez, Mexico, 836,328; 5th in state, 45th in nation; total employed, 146,572.

Area: 158.8 sq. mi., western tip of Texas where Rio Grande cuts boundaries of Texas, New Mexico, and Mexico; includes Franklin Mtns.

Industry: manufacturing payroll, $158 million (1973), manufacturing employment, 32,303; clothing largest employer including Farah and Mann. Juarez-El Paso border in-bond industries at 94 and 18,447 employed since 1967, many in electronics including RCA, GE and Sylvania; home of El Paso Natural Gas, American

Smelting & Refining, Phelps Dodge, Standard and Texaco refineries; also leather goods, dairies, processed Mexican foods, meat packing, nut processing, cattle, agriculture.

Commerce: wholesale-retail center for West Texas, New Mexico, northern Mexico; retail sales 1972, $720 million; bank deposits (1973) $926 million; bank clearings, $6 billion; 16 banks, 6 savings and loans associations.

Transportation: 4 major rail lines, Amtrak; 8 buslines, 29 truck lines, 5 major highways, gateway to Mexico; international airport, 4 airlines with 184,095

(1973), flights and 1,073,467 passengers, freight 11,-000 tons.

Communications: 4 TV and 14 radio stations.

New construction: 1973 building permits totaled $170,522,288.

Medical facilities: 13 hospitals with 1,732 beds; area cancer treatment center; El Paso School of Nursing.

Federal facilities: Ft. Bliss (U.S. Army Air Defense Center, Allied Students Missile Center, Sgts. Major Academy) and William Beaumont Medical Center;

near McGregor and White Sands Missile Range, N.M.

Cultural facilities: University of Texas at El Paso (10,-980), El Paso Community College (5,937); El Paso Symphony, Museum of Art, university ballet, opera companies, theater groups; $20 million civic-convention center; public libraries.

Other attractions: Annual Sun Carnival-Sun Bowl, Chamizal Park, Tigua Indian community, historic missions, horse and dog races, Cavalry Museum, zoo, and visit to foreign country in Juarez, Mexico.

Erie, Pennsylvania

The World Almanac is sponsored in the Erie area by the Erie Daily Times, 205 W. 12th Street, Erie, Pa., 16501; (814) 456-8531; founded in 1888; circulation 74,000 daily, 92,000 Sunday; president Edward M. Mead, executive editor Joseph Meagher, managing editor Len Kholos.

Population: 129,231 (city), 186,652 (metro area), 3rd in state; total employed, 51,175.

Area: 19.53 sq. mi. at tip of northwestern Pa.

Commerce: Erie County, pop. 220,000, produces $133 million in exports, highest per capita export in U.S.; tourism — 5 miles of beaches, good fishing, boating, winter sports; seaport — 60 or more oceangoing vessels each year; over 506 industrial plants producing machinery and parts, iron and steel forgings, hardware, meters, plastics, paper (Hammermill), furniture, and toys; General Electric producing Amtrak passenger trains.

New construction: main street transformed into pedestrian walkway; 8-story 200-room Hilton Hotel with convention-tourist facilities under construction;

General Telephone computer center; $4.5 million St. Vincent Hospital office-apartment building complex.

Special Awards: All America City through 1974; one of 16 showcase planned cities.

Transportation: 4 railroads, Boston-Chicago Amtrak line; airport; 35 trucking companies, 4 bus lines.

Cultural facilites: Penn State Univ. extension, Gannon, Mercyhurst, and Villa Maria Colleges; Philharmonic Society, Council of the Arts, theatre groups; new Field House for plays, entertainment, sports.

History: Named after Eriez Indians; site of building of ship Niagara with which Oliver Hazard Perry defeated British in 1813.

Further information: Chamber of Commerce, 1006 State, 16501.

Evansville, Indiana

The World Almanac is sponsored in Southwestern Indiana, Western Kentucky and Southeastern Illinois by The Evansville Press, 201 N.W. Second Street, Evansville, Ind. 47701; (812) 424-7711; founded July 2, 1906 by E.W. Scripps and J.C. Harper; circulation, 47,000; editor Michael Grehl managing editor, William R. Burleigh.

Population: 138,764 (city), 287,600 (metro area), 4th in state.

Area: 47 sq. mi. at bend of Ohio River in southwest corner of state; Vanderburgh County seat.

Industry: Whirlpool Corp. plants (refrigeration and air conditioning); Mead Johnson & Co. (pharmaceutical division of Bristol-Myers Co.); Alcoa Warrick Operations (aluminum) just east of city; 19 plastics firms, 303 manufacturing firms.

Commerce: retail sales, $758,099,000 (1973); effective buying income per household, $10,436 (1973); home offices of Credit Thrift of America, Inc.: 5 banks, 7 savings and loan associations.

Transportation: world headquarters of Atlas Van Lines; 4 railroads; 5 commercial barge lines; 4 inter-

state bus lines; Allegheny, Delta and Eastern air lines.

Communications: 2 daily newspapers; 3 TV and 6 radio stations.

Medical facilities: 5 general and mental hospitals; branch of Indiana University Medical School.

Cultural facilities: Philharmonic Orchestra, Museum of Arts and Science, Mesker Zoo, Univ. of Evansville, Indiana State Univ. Evansville; national headquarters of Phi Mu Alpha music fraternity. Abraham Lincoln boyhood home nearby.

Sports: Evansville Triplets, American Association baseball (AAA); site of NCAA college division basketball tournament.

Further information: Chamber of Commerce, Southern Securities Building, Evansville, Ind. 47708.

Fort Wayne, Indiana

The World Almanac is sponsored in the Fort Wayne area by The Journal-Gazette, 600 W. Main St., Fort Wayne, Ind., 46802; (219) 423-3311; established June 14, 1899 by consolidation of The Journal and The Daily Gazette; circulation daily 66,531, Sundays 108,014; president-publisher Richard G. Inskeep; secretary-treasurer Naomi Erb; editor Larry W. Allen; managing editor James P. Lovette.

Population: 182,000 (city); 377,900 (metro area); total employed 165,500.
Area: 50.4 sq. mi. at confluence of St. Joseph, St. Mary's and Maumee rivers. Allen County seat.

Industry: General Electric and International Harvester largest employers; Magnavox, Essex International and Central Soya home offices; several firms manufacture about 85% of world's diamond wire dies.

Commerce: wholesale and retail center for northeastern Indiana, southeastern Michigan, northwestern Ohio; retail sales (metro) over $1 billion; bank deposits $1.156 billion; 5 banks, 4 savings-and-loan; 6 life insurance companies, including Lincoln National Life, based here.

Transportation: 2 major rail freight lines; Amtrak; 56 motor freight lines including home-based North American Van, Elway Express, Scott and Transport Motor; I-69 connects city with Indianapolis and Indiana Toll Road; U.S. 30 dual lane to Chicago; municipal airport (Delta, United and Skystreams); hq. for

122nd Tactical Fighter Wing, Indiana Air National Guard.

Communications: 9 radio, 3 TV stations.

Medical facilities: 4 hospitals including Vet. Admn.

Cultural facilities: Philharmonic orchestra; Fine Arts and Performing Arts complex; 9 universities and colleges; 4 museums.

Sports: Komet Hockey Team (IHL) plays at Allen Co. War Memorial Coliseum.

Other attractions: children's zoo; 61 parks and playgrounds; 11 golf courses; 36 shopping centers.

History: first white settlement in Indiana (circa 1692).

Further information: Chamber of commerce, 826 Ewing St.

Fort Worth, Texas

The World Almanac is sponsored in the Fort Worth area by the Fort Worth Press, Fifth and Jones Sts., Fort Worth, Texas 76101; (817) 336-2626; founded 1921 by Scripps-Howard Newspapers; editor Delbert Willis, business manager Leslie E. Yates, managing editor Jack Moseley.

Population: 401,800 (city, 1973 est.); county 758,350 (1973); 4th largest Texas city. 3.1 per cent unemployment; work force of 356,400.

Area: 233 sq. mi. on the Trinity River in North Central Texas.

Commerce: all types of manufacturing; wholesale and retail center for large area including West Texas; retail sales (estimated 1972) $1,641 billion; family buying income $8,411. Bank deposits $2,169 billion; over 50 banks in the county, over 60 mortgage institutions, insurance companies and savings and loans associations.

Transportation: Dallas-Fort Worth Regional Airport, largest in the world, opened January 1974, 17 miles from downtown; Meacham Field, general aviation airport, many smaller airports; 9 railroads, Amtrak, 38 motor carriers, and 5 bus companies.

Communications: 2 TV and 18 area radio stations; 2 daily newspapers, several weekly and monthly publications.

Medical facilities: over 20 hospitals.

Federal facilities: 14 federal agencies and Carswell Air Force Base; reserve training centers.

Cultural: Casa Manana, America's first permanent musical arena theater; symphony, opera, Van Cli-

burn Piano Competition; museums include Kimball Art Museum, Amon Carter Museum of Western Art, and others.

Educational facilities: 2 campuses of Tarrant County Junior College, a third planned; Texas Christian Univ., Univ. of Texas at Arlington, Texas Wesleyan College, Southwestern Baptist Seminary; Texas Woman's Univ.; medical school planned to open about 1975, and other technical and vocational schools.

Recreation: 6 Flags over Texas in Arlington, Seven Seas, Forest Park and Fort Worth Zoological Park; several other parks.

Convention facilities: Tarrant County Convention Center, Will Rogers Memorial Center.

Sports attractions: Texas Rangers Baseball, Fort Worth Wings in hockey, Colonial National Golf Tournament; other semi-pro and college leagues.

Other attractions: Fat Stock Show and Rodeo; Miss Texas Pageant.

History: founded 1849 as a frontier Army post on the Chisholm Trail; became major railhead.

Further Information: Chamber of Commerce, 700 Throckmorton St., Fort Worth, Texas 76102.

Fresno, California

The World Almanac is sponsored in the Fresno area by The Fresno Bee, Van Ness and Calaveras, Fresno, CA. 93721; phone (209) 268-5221; founded 1922; circulation daily 118,727, Sunday 141,220; president Eleanor McClatchy, editor Walter Jones, managing editor George Gruner.

Population: 174,100 (city), 438,700 (county) total employed 196,900.

Area: one of largest counties in the state, 3,819,456 acres. Fresno is located in geographical center of the state midway between San Francisco and Los Angeles.

Agriculture: leading county in United States in annual value of agricultural production; state's leading county in production of grapes, barley, figs, turkeys, irrigated pasture, nectarines, cantaloupes, safflower, raisins and alfalfa; peaches, plums, melons and cotton are also major crops.

Industry: 475 diversified manufacturing establishments; food processing is major industry; 2d in importance is production of beverages, primarily wine, brandy and spirits.

Transportation: 2 airports, regularly scheduled daily service by 5 airlines; freeways connect to all major metropolitan areas in California; served by 29 com-

mon truck carriers, 2 interstate bus lines and 2 mainline railroads with complete freight handling facilities.

Communications: 6 TV and 16 radio stations.

Medical facilities: 4 general hospitals, including a Veteran's Administration installation.

Cultural facilities: $10,000,000 Community and Convention Center opened in 1967; community philharmonic, opera, ballet and theater; California State Univ.-Fresno, Pacific College and 3 community colleges.

Recreation: 3 national parks: Yosemite, Sequoia and Kings Canyon with groves of giant Sequoia trees plus complete facilities for boating, sailing, hunting, fishing, skiing, hiking, pack trips and camping.

Other attractions: City Zoo, nationally famous rodeo, county fair, underground gardens, Kearney museum and downtown malls with one of the best outdoor art displays in the West.

History: area explored by the Spaniards in the early

1800s and visited by fur trappers before 1840; settlement began when gold miners came in the 1850s;

county created Apr. 19, 1856 from parts of Mariposa, Merced and Tulare counties.

Halifax, Nova Scotia, Canada

The World Almanac is sponsored in Nova Scotia by The Chronicle-Herald and The Mail-Star, 1650 Argyle Street, Halifax; phone (902) 426-2811; circulation Chronicle (morning) 66,376, Mail-Star (aft.) 49,398; publisher and president Graham W. Dennis, chairman of the board Ira B. MacCallum, general-manager Fred G. Mounce, managing editor Alvin M. Savage, secretary-treasurer W. D. Coleman.

Population: 122,035 (1971); labor force 57,305; employed 53,170.
Area: 24.19 sq. mi. of land, on the southeast coast of the province.
Industry: leading industrial area in Atlantic provinces; establishments include oil refineries, electronic equipment manufacturers, ship yards, car assembly plant, plastic fabricators, metal works, breweries and fish processing; 3rd largest and one of Canada's most diversified scientific research centers.
Commerce: financial center of region, regional head offices for all major banks and investment houses; retail sales over $300 million annually; average income $8,396 (1971); all three levels of government constitute employment for 12,000; armed forces have over 14,000 stationed in city.
Transportation: 2 major passenger-freight rail lines, 6 container lines call regularly at eastern most commercial port on mainland North America; only Cana-

dian container port with 3 sea-shore cranes; handled 130,000, 20-foot equivalent containers (1973), over 300,000 tons break bulk general cargo; new cargo movement records set each year in last 3 years; international airport.
Communication: 5 radio and 2 TV stations.
New construction: building permits issued for $47.9 million worth of construction last year.
Education: 6 degree-granting universities, 74 common and 3 private schools, one technical institute.
Medical facilities: 9 hospitals (3 teaching).
Cultural facilities: Atlantic Symphony Orchestra, 2 professional live theatres and one amateur, 2 public libraries.
Parks: 3 major parks (403 acres).
Sports: home of Halifax Voyageurs of the AHL.
History: founded in 1749; meeting place of first legislative assembly in Canada (1758).

Hamilton, Ontario, Canada

The World Almanac is sponsored in Hamilton and the Niagara Peninsula by The Spectator (a division of Southam Press Ltd.), 115 King Street East, Hamilton, Ontario; phone (416) 522-8642; founded in 1846; circulation 138,000; publisher John D. Muir, business manager James S. Thomson, executive editor Gordon Bullock, managing editor Paul Warnick.

Population: 309,173 (city), 513,000 (metro area); 3d in province, 6th in Canada; total work force, 227,200 (1973 metro).
Area: 54 sq. mi. at the westerly extremity of Lake Ontario.
Industry: 60% of all of Canada's steel is produced at the Steel Company of Canada and Dominion Foundries and Steel Limited; city ranks 3d in Canada in industrial production; about 750 plants in the metropolitan area, manufacturing iron and steel products, electrical apparatus, agricultural equipment, tires, food products, wire, heavy machinery, chemicals and textiles.
Commerce: retail sales (1973) $952,000,000; average annual wage (1973) $8,984; 7th in Canada in total retail sales, 6th in annual wage.
Transportation: Canadian National and Canadian Pacific railways, as well as the Toronto, Hamilton and Buffalo line; provincial highways through Toronto to Windsor and Buffalo pass metropolitan area; city airport 9 miles south at Mount Hope, with commercial movements to Montreal, Ottawa, Windsor and Pittsburgh.
Communications: one TV and 4 radio stations.

New construction: St. Peter's Geriatric Centre, to take up a city block; plans call for construction of 15,000 seat professional hockey arena.
Medical facilities: new $73,000,000 medical center at McMaster Univ. with latest in teaching facilities; 4 other major hospitals in metropolitan area.
Educational facilities: McMaster Univ. one of Canada's largest post-secondary schools; Mohawk College of Applied Arts and Technology, Hamilton Campus of the Ontario Teachers College.
Cultural facilities: Hamilton Place, the new theatre-auditorium; Hamilton Art Gallery; year-round Philharmonic Orchestra, plus variety of theatrical groups.
Sports attractions: Hamilton Tiger-Cats of the Canadian Football League, also 2 municipal golf courses; Chedoke and King's Forest.
Other attractions: Dundurn Castle, restored mansion of the 1850 period; Whitehearn, restored Victorian home; Royal Botanical Gardens; Canadian Football League Hall of Fame; one of the largest park systems per capita in Canada.
History: explorer Sieur de La Salle discovered Hamilton area in 1669.

Hartford, Connecticut

The World Almanac is sponsored in the Hartford area by The Hartford Times, 10 Prospect St., Hartford, Conn. 06101; phone (203) 249-8211; founded 1817 by Frederick D. Bolles and John M. Niles; circulation 102,000 afternoons and Sundays; publisher Lionel S. Jackson, editor Don Noel Jr., Pulitzer citation as a newspaper, Pulitzer Prize to staff member; sponsor of Times Farm Camp for less priviledged children, Learn-to-swim, Little League.

Population: 155,300 (city), 822,800 (county); total employed (county) 348,320.

Area: 17.2 sq. miles.

Industry: "Insurance City", headquarters for 33 insurance firms employing 39,200; East Hartford is home office of United Aircraft, one of the world's largest aircaft firms, manufacturers of Pratt & Whitney jet engines.

Commerce: total retail sales (county, 1973) $2.12 billion; per household consumer spendable income (1973) $14,628.

Transportation: intersection of highways 84 and 91; Amtrak, Penn Central Railroad; Bradley International Airport with 8 scheduled airlines, several providing cargo service.

New construction: to be completed by January 1975 — Hartford Civic Center complex, including $18 million Aetna Life & Casualty shopping arcade, 20-story Sheraton Hotel, 10,000 seat coliseum, 70,000 sq. ft. exhibition hall and 17,000 sq. ft. assembly hall.

Communications: 6 radio and 4 TV stations.

Educational facilities: Trinity College, Univ. of Hartford, Graduate Center of Rensselaer Polytechnic Institute, St. Joseph College, Hartford Seminary Foundation, Univ. of Connecticut Law School, Greater Hartford Community College.

Cultural facilities: Wadsworth Atheneum, the oldest public art museum in America; Mark Twain House; symphony orchestra; Connecticut Opera Association; Stage Company; Mark Twain Masques; Ballet Company.

Sports: Greater Hartford Open (golf), Aetna World Cup (tennis); Connecticut Wildcats (soccer); New England Whalers (hockey).

History: founded 1636 by Thomas Hooker and company of settlers from Newtown (Cambridge), Mass.; became Connecticut's capital city 1665.

Further information: Chamber of Commerce, 250 Constitution Plaza, Hartford, Conn. 06103.

Honolulu, Hawaii

The World Almanac is sponsored in Hawaii by The Honolulu Advertiser, P.O. Box 3110, Honolulu, Hi., 96802; (808) 537-2977; founded July 2, 1856, as Pacific Commercial Advertiser by Henry M. Whitney; circulation 78,752 mornings, 192,425 Sunday; president and publisher Thurston Twigg-Smith, editor-in-chief George Chaplin, executive editor Buck Buchwach, managing editor Mike Middlesworth; awards from American Political Science Assn., American Assn. for the Advancement of Science, others.

Population: 680,000 (metro); 1st in state; total employed, 265,300.

Area: 595 sq. mi., encompassing Oahu Island.

Commerce: major destination for U.S., Japanese tourists; persons staying a night or more, 2.6 million in 1972, up from 430,000 a decade earlier; tourist spending $890 million in 1973, up from $186 million 10 years earlier; visitor dollars top military spending, which totaled $840.9 million in 1973; sugarcane and pineapple major agriculture export crops; retail sales (statewide) $2.6 billion, per capita income $5,309, family $12,437, total income $4.4 billion; Pacific Basin business and financial center.

Transportation: dependent on ships, planes for most goods; passengers arrive mostly by air; ocean liners seldom call; 21 airlines serve airport: 8 domestic trunk carriers, 11 foreign, 2 inter-island; airport 13th busiest in nation.

Communications: 5 TV, 32 radio stations.

Medical facilities: 18 hospitals, including U.S. Army Tripler Hospital; Univ. of Hawaii School of Medicine, research labs, specialize in tropical diseases, run projects in Micronesia.

Cultural facilities: 9-campus University of Hawaii with 40,000 students; main campus at Manoa in Honolulu, 22,272 students; university stresses oceanography, geophysics, tropical agriculture; U.S. State Department co-sponsors East-West Center at Manoa, attracts international student body; Bernice Pauahi Bishop Museum is center for archeological study of Pacific cultures, houses artifacts, maintains floating square-rigger Falls of Clyde, plus branch museum in Waikiki.

Other attractions: Waikiki Beach, extinct volcano Diamond Head, balmy weather, tradewinds, multiracial population, racial tolerance, Polynesian heritage.

History: Honolulu ("sheltered bay" in Hawaiian) was a small village when first Westerners called aboard 2 British ships in 1786, 8 years after Capt. James Cook discovered Hawaiian Islands.

Houston, Texas

The World Almanac is sponsored in the Southwest by The Houston Post, 4747 Southwest Freeway, Houston, Tex. 77001. Tel.: (713) 621-7000; founded 1836; Oveta Culp Hobby chairman of the board and editor; William P. Hobby Jr., president. Circulation: daily 298,119; Saturday 329,536; Sunday 349,534. Awards include Pulitzer Prize, Grand Prix, Editor & Publisher. Community events sponsored include Science Fair, Spring Art Festival, travel fairs, charity football, others.

Population: 1,386,000 (city) 6th in nation; 2,210,000 (metro); total employed 967,600 (1973); total wages-salaries (metro 1973) $9.8 billion.

Area: 506.52 sq. mi. (city) on upper center Gulf Coast prairies, 41 ft. above sea level; Harris County seat; connected to Gulf of Mexico by 50-mile inland waterway, the Ship Channel.

Industry: world's petroleum refining capital, with 2.9 million barrels refined products per day in 1973; nation's leading mfgr.-distributor petroleum equipment, pipeline transmissions; nation's greatest concentration of chemical/petrochemical industries; 2,846 manufacturing firms (metro), 40% of all basic petrochemical products in U.S. come from Houston.

Commerce: metro area retail sales, $4.6 billion (1973), largest in South; metro wholesale sales exceed $7 billion (1973); 164 banks in metro area with 1973 resources of $12.4 billion, deposits of $10 billion.

Transportation: Port of Houston (3rd largest in nation) moved 86 million tons in 1973; 100 steamship lines; inland-waterway 1972 tonnage exceeded 28 million short tons; 9 common carrier lines; 20 contract and specialized operators; 2 airports, 7 major airlines, one intrastate airline; 2 all-cargo carriers; 6

major rail systems moved 23 million short tons (1973); 391 miles of freeways; 400-bus local passenger service; 4 intercity bus lines.

Communications: 2 daily newspapers; 29 radio stations; 5 commercial, one educational TV stations.

New construction: non-residential contract awards $963 million; residential units completed value $747 million, in 1973.

Medical facilities: Texas Medical Center, with 28 institutions on 200-acre site; 54 hospitals (metro) have 11,963 beds, including VA hospital; 1,500 additional beds scheduled for 1974.

Federal facilities: Lyndon B. Johnson Space Center, a $202 million complex on 1,640-acre site 22 mi. from downtown Houston, conceives, designs, develops, operates manned spacecraft, controls flights and trains astronauts.

Cultural facilities: Symphony Orchestra; Grand Opera Assoc.; Houston Chorale; Alley Theatre in its 28th season; Miller Outdoor Theatre; 25 major art institutes; Natural Science Museum & Planetarium; 27-branch library system; Fine Arts Museum; Contemporary Arts Museum.

Educational facilities: 6th largest school district in nation, nearly 500,000 public school students (metro); 25 colleges and universities in area, including Univ. of Houston and Rice Univ.

Recreational facilities: 258 parks and playgrounds; 4 municipal golf courses; Astroworld 60-acre amusement park; botanical garden, arboretum; Hermann Park & Zoo; 50 community recreation centers; 28

Harris County parks; 70 miles of Gulf beaches in one hour's driving distance.

Convention facilities: world's largest single-level facility Astrohall, 795,000 sq. ft., next to famous Astrodome; addition to Astrohall, Abercrombie Arena, completion Feb. 1975, 196,000 sq. ft., 8,000 seating capacity around indoor, air-conditioned arena, plus stall facilities for horse shows; downtown facilities include Albert Thomas Convention Center (300,000 sq. ft.); Coliseum (50,000 sq. ft.); adjoining Music Hall auditorium seats 3,036; Exposition Hall (83,000 sq. ft.).

Sports attractions: pro teams Astros baseball; Oilers football; Texans football; Aeros hockey; Rockets basketball; Easy Riders tennis; world-famous Astrodome, capacity 45,000 to 66,000; Summit, capacity 18,000, to be completed Sept. 1975.

Climate: temperatures moderated by winds from the Gulf of Mexico; rainfall abundant, with 70.16 in. in 1973; avg. yearly temperatures 68° with highs in 90's, lows in 40's; avg. humidity 76%.

History: founded 1836 by Allen brothers; named for Gen. Sam Houston, first president of Republic of Texas; was early capital of Republic; Battle of San Jacinto (1836) fought nearby, winning Texas independence from Mexico; oil discovered (1901) at Spindletop; port opened in 1915.

Further information: Houston Convention & Travel Bureau, 4089 Westheimer, Houston, Tex., 77027; Houston Convention & Visitors Council, 1006 Main, Houston, Tex. 77002.

Huntington, West Virginia

The World Almanac is sponsored in the Huntington area by The Herald-Dispatch (morn), and The Huntington Advertiser (aft), Huntington Publishing Company, 946 Fifth Avenue, Huntington, West Virginia 25720, member of the Gannett Group; circulation 69,038, Sunday 58,360. Publisher and president N. S. Hayden, business manager James D. Hoffman, executive editor John H. McMillan; managing editors, C. Donald Hatfield (Advertiser), and Donald G. Mayne (Herald-Dispatch).

Population: 74,315 (city), 286,935 (5-county metro area); largest city in the state.

Area: 15.86 sq. mi., on Ohio River near where West Virginia, Ohio and Kentucky meet.

Industry: home of Alloys Products division of the International Nickel Company, Inc.; center for handcrafted glass; coal transport center; headquarters for several railroad operations.

Commerce: largest port for inland vessels in U.S. handles nearly 23,000,000 tons of materials per year, moved by 7 freight companies; 1972 total retail sales in metro area $747,288,000.

Transportation: Tri-State Airport, now being ex-

panded, is served by 2 airlines, 500 air movements a month; 18 truck lines; urban bus transport system; 2 interstate bus lines.

Communications: 4 TV and 11 radio stations.

Cultural facilities: Marshall University with nearly 9,000 students; The Huntington Galleries of art.

Medical facilities: 5 general hospitals with 1,076 total beds; 3 specialty hospitals included a VA hospital.

New construction: $32,000,000 renewal program calls for large shopping mall, riverfront marina, civic auditorium and additional convention facilities.

Further information: Chamber of Commerce, 522 Ninth Street, Huntington, W. Va. 25701.

Indianapolis, Indiana

The World Almanac is sponsored in the Indianapolis area by the Indianapolis Star, The Indianapolis News, 307 N. Pennsylvania St., Indianapolis, Ind. 46206; (317) 633-1240; News founded 1869, Star 1903; circ. Star 225,435; News 172,219, Sunday 372,611; president-publisher Eugene C. Pulliam, asst. publ. Eugene S. Pulliam, Star editor Frank Crane, News editor Dr. Harvey Jacobs; Pulitzer Prize-News; Nat'l Headliners first prize-Star.

Population: 745,739 (1970) Consolidated City, nation's 11th largest; 1,111,173 (metro 1970); total employed 514,800.

Area: 379.4 sq. mi., geographic center of state; State Capital and Marion County seat.

Industry: over 1,400 diversified manufacturers including plane and auto engines and parts, electronics, pharmaceuticals, machinery; 1973 manufacturing payroll over $1.3 billion.

Commerce: commercial center for Indiana; retail

sales $2.9 billion; per capita personal income $5,300; 6 banks with resources over $5.2 billion; home offices of over 60 insurance companies.

Transportation: 9 airlines; 5 rail freight lines, Amtrak; 2 interstate buslines, over 100 truck lines, 7 interstate freeway routes.

New construction: projects totalling over $488 million under const. 1974.

Communications: 6 TV and 18 radio stations.

Medical facilities: 16 hospitals, over 7,700 beds.

Federal facilities: Fort Harrison incl. Army Finance and Acctng. Center, U.S.A. Admin. Center.

Cultural facilities: Museum of Art and Oldfields Museum of Decorative Arts; Indiana State Museum; Children's Zoo; Conner Prairie Pioneer Settlement and Museum of Indian Heritage; Clowes Hall, home of Symphony Orch; Civic Theatre, oldest U.S. amateur theatrical group; Repertory Theatre.

Education facilities: Butler Univ., Indiana Central and Marian Colleges, Christian Theological and St. Mauer's seminaries, and Indiana Univ., Purdue Univ.

at Indianapolis, with nation's largest medical school.

Recreational facilities: 9,000 park acres, 15 major swimming pools, 9 municipal golf courses; pro basketball and hockey in 18,000-seat domed sports arena, home of ABA 1973 champion "Pacers"; Minor league baseball, football.

Other attractions: Indianapolis 500, Yankee 300 and annual National Drag Racing championships.

History: sesquicentennial in 1971; important before Civil War, with nation's first union railway station (1853); home of James Whitcomb Riley, Booth Tarkington and President Benjamin Harrison.

Jacksonville, Florida

The World Almanac is sponsored in the Jacksonville area by The Florida Times-Union and the Jacksonville Journal, One Riverside Ave. 32202; phone (904) 791-4111; circulation, Times-Union 149,540, Journal 60,017, combined Sunday 183,788; president Robert R. Feagin, vice president John A. Tucker, executive editor John S. Walters; Journal won Pulitzer Prize for photography in 1967.

Population: 528,865 (1970); total employment, 235,600 at end of 1973.

Area: 827 sq. mi., including nearly all of Duval Co. in Northeast Fla.; largest incorporated developed area in Western Hemisphere.

Industry: 500 industries, added value total of $290 million annually; Offshore Power Systems investing $250 million in floating nuclear power plant production facility to employ 10,000 when completed.

Commerce: emphasis on finance, distribution; home or regional headquarters for 34 insurance companies; 1972 retail sales, $1.365 billion; effective buying income per household in 1972, $10,387.

Transportation: 3 major railroads and Amtrak; 16 major truck lines; 6 airlines averaging 140 air movements daily; 2 interstate bus lines; port handled 14.9 million tons in 1972.

Communications: 4 TV and 14 radio stations.

New Construction: $280.6 million in building permits issued in 1973; 37-story Independent Life building tallest in Florida.

Medical facilities: 10 general hospitals and one naval

hospital with total of 3,158 beds.

Federal facilities: 2 naval air stations, one naval station add $233 million yearly to economy.

Cultural facilities: Cummer Art Gallery, Jacksonville Art Museum, Children's Museum; Jacksonville Symphony, Ballet Guild, 4 community theaters.

Education: Univ. of North Florida, Jacksonville Univ., Edward Waters College, Florida Jr. College.

Sports: Gator Bowl, 70,000-seat stadium; Greater Jacksonville Open, $150,000 PGA tournament; World Football League "Sharks."

Other attractions: Civic Auditorium, Coliseum, Jacksonville Zoo, Fort Caroline, Kingsley Plantation; 8 miles of public beaches.

History: founded in 1822 by Isaiah Hart, named for Andrew Jackson; fire in 1901 destroyed 2,368 buildings, left 10,000 homeless; city and county governments merged in 1968 after referendum.

Further information: Chamber of Commerce, 604 Hogan St., or Convention & Visitors Bureau, Hemming Park, Jacksonville, Fla. 32202.

Kalamazoo, Michigan

The World Almanac is sponsored in the Kalamazoo area by The Kalamazoo Gazette, 401 S. Burdick, Kalamazoo, Mich. 49003; telephone (616) 345-3511, founded 1833; circulation daily 58,085, Sunday 61,593; owned and operated by Booth Newspapers Inc.; president Gordon H. Craig, editor Daniel M. Ryan, general manager Ralph H. Bastien Jr.

Population: 85,800 (city), 206,600 (county); total employed in county, 86,700.

Area: located equidistant to the 3rd and 5th largest metro areas in nation — Chicago and Detroit, 140 miles away.

Industry: paper-making is the traditional industry, with 5 large plants here. Checker Motors Corp. manufacturers of cars; large Fisher Body Division body stamping plant; Upjohn Company, pharmaceuticals.

Commerce: shopping center for large part of Southwestern Michigan. In 1959, city became first in country to close downtown streets and create a pedestrian mall; now known as "Mall City." Retail sales in (1973) $609 million; 4 banks had combined assets in 1973 of $737,000,000, 3 savings and loan associations have assets of over $200,000,000.

Transportation: 2 railroads provide freight service. Amtrak passenger service; 33 general carriers provide trucking services; airport with freight and passenger service; 3 buslines.

Cultural facilities: 4 auditoriums offering music and theatrical performances, 6 live arts theaters, an art center, symphony orchestra, Kalamazoo Civic Players.

Educational facilities: 3 colleges and one university with combined student enrollment over 27,000.

Other attractions: Kalamazoo Nature Center, 83 lakes (county), National Junior Tennis Championships, 2 major hospitals.

Further information: Kalamazoo County Chamber of Commerce, 500 W. Crosstown, Kalamazoo, Michigan 49008, telephone (616) 381-4000.

Kansas City, Missouri

The World Almanac is sponsored in the Kansas City area by The Kansas City Star, 1729 Grand Ave., Kansas City, Mo. 64108; telephone (816) 421-1200; founded by William Rockhill Nelson; circulation morning 335,361, evening 315,560, Sunday 404,519; president Paul V. Miner, executive assistant to the president William T. Shields, general manager Frank S. McKinney, editor W. W. Baker, executive editor Cruise Palmer, advertising director W. W. Meyer.

Population: 511,600 (city); 1,324,000 (metro area), 27th in nation; total employed 592,200.

Area: 316.3 sq. mi., at confluence of Missouri and Kansas rivers.

Industry: 2d in nation in automotive assembly; 1st in production of vending machines, greeting cards, underground freezer space and winter wheat trading. Top employers: U.S. government, General Motors, TWA, Bendix, Western Electric, Ford. Presently Kansas City is a leading hard wheat center, stocker and feeder market, and is among the top 5 cities in flour production and grain elevator capacity.

Commerce: Total retail sales in 1972 $3.226 billion; the center of a 7-county metro area: Jackson, Clay, Platte, Cass and Ray counties in Missouri; Johnson and Wyandotte counties in Kansas.

Transportation: 8 airlines and 150 daily flights out of the new Kansas City International Airport; 169 truck lines and 4 barge companies. The city is one of the nation's major rail centers.

New construction: $250,000,000 Crown Center business and apartment complex covers 25 square blocks; new medical center of University of Missouri; American Royal Arena; Mercantile Bank Building; United Missouri Bank headquarters; 30-story office and retail building downtown. Worlds of Fun recreation center. More than 6 large hotels and several hospital additions.

Cultural facilities: Starlight Theater, nation's 2d largest outdoor theater; William Rockhill Nelson Gallery of Art, among the 10 top American museums with the 3d largest Oriental collection outside China; Performing Arts Foundation formed in 1965 to present festival events; University of Missouri at Kansas City; Rockhurst College; Kansas City Art Institute; University of Kansas Medical Center. Within commuting distance are University of Kansas, Park College, William Jewell College. Truman Library in Independence. Linda Hall Library of Science and Technology is one of the largest privately endowed technical reference libraries in the nation.

Recreational facilities: More than 100 parks cover 5,345 acres, including Swope Park, 2d largest in nation, with fine zoo.

Sports: The American Royal Livestock and Horse Show each fall attracts entries from throughout the country, Home of the Chiefs of the National Football League, Royals of American Baseball League, the Kings National Basketball Association team, and a National Hockey team.

History: Kansas City's beginnings can be traced to a trading post of French fur trappers about 1826. It became an important trade and transportation center as the overland routes of the Oregon and Santa Fe Trails spread westward. As agricultural production boomed, it became an important market and distribution center for crops from throughout the Middle West.

Further information: Chamber of Commerce of Greater Kansas City, 920 Main, Kansas City, Missouri.

Kitchener-Waterloo, Ontario, Canada

The World Almanac is sponsored in the Kitchener-Waterloo area by the Kitchener-Waterloo Record, 225 Fairway Road, Kitchener, Ont.; phone (519) 579-2231; founded 1878, circulation 62,439, president and publisher John E. Motz, executive vice-president K. A. Baird, editor in chief Carl B. Schmidt.

Population: 122,481 (Kitchener) and 41,998 (Waterloo), 265,683 (metro area); total employed 93,100.

Area: 48.85 sq. mi. (Kitchener) and 25.47 sq. mi. (Waterloo), 65 miles west of Toronto.

Industry: highly diversified industry (509 companies), rubber, plastics, electronics, metal fabrication, brewing, distilling, meat packing, footwear, furniture, food processing, automotive components; Budd Automotive Co., largest autoframe manufacturer in Canada, capable of 1.4 million frames a year.

Agricultural: beef and dairy area; Waterloo County's 1,976 farms accounted for $56 million production in 1973.

Commerce: wholesale and retail center for area; metro retail sales (1973) $455.5 million; 6 banks, 56 branches; 6 trust companies, 16 branches; 34 life insurance offices, 21 other insurance offices; Waterloo, "The Hartford of Canada," head office for 6 insurance companies.

Transportation: 2 major rail lines, 34 truck lines, on Ontario's key highway 401; Waterloo-Wellington Airport with scheduled air service; 45 mi. from Toronto International.

Communications: one TV and 4 radio stations.

Medical facilities: 2 major hospitals.

Cultural facilities: Symphony Orchestra, Kitchener-Waterloo Art Gallery, Doon School of Fine Arts, Doon Pioneer Village; 28 mi. from famed Stratford Festival Theatre.

Educational facilities: Univ. of Waterloo (13,250 students), Wilfrid Laurier Univ. (2,500 students), Conestoga College (2,000 students).

Other attractions: nationally-known farmers market; Canada's largest annual Oktoberfest celebration; Woodside, national historic park, boyhood of W. L. Mackenzie King, Canadian prime minister 22 years.

History: founded 1807 by German settlers; retains strong Germanic flavor.

Further information: Kitchener Chamber of Commerce, 68 King East; Waterloo Chamber of Commerce, Waterloo Square.

Knoxville, Tennessee

The World Almanac is sponsored in the Knoxville area by The Knoxville News-Sentinel, 204 West Church Ave., Knoxville, TN., 37901. Sentinel founded in 1886; News in 1921 by Scripps-Howard Newspapers; Sentinel purchased by Scripps-Howard in 1926 and combined with News. Circulation 109,121 daily; 163,419 Sunday; editor Ralph L. Millett Jr., managing editor Harold E. Harlow.

Population: 178,493 (city), 431,961 (metro area); 3rd in state; total employed metro area 174,600; unemployment rate 3.1%.

Area: 77.6 sq. mi. located almost in exact center of that portion of United States lying east of the Mississippi River and south of Great Lakes.

Industry: major manufacturing industry is clothing. Nearly 1,000 plants representing 51 diversified major industries (coal and zinc mining, marble quarrying, meat packing, steel fabrication, industrial controls eqpt.) with Aluminum Co. of America, Union Carbide Corp. Nuclear Div. at Oak Ridge, included in Knoxville market.

Commerce: trade center of a 42-county area in East Tennessee, Virginia, Kentucky, N. Carolina; city retail sales (1972), $551 million; average family income $6,855.00; Metro retail sales (1973), $1.043 billion; spendable family income, $11,283.00. Ranked 11th in nation (1973) in department store sales gain (14.5%).

Transportation: 2 rail lines, 5 airlines, 2 inter-state bus lines, 25 motor freight carriers serve Knoxville; interstate Highways I-40 and I-75 intersect in heart of city.

New construction: U.S. News and World Report (1974) survey ranked Knoxville top city in nation in construction gain (32%) over early part of 1973; downtown redevelopment involving $170 million, in public and private funds, now under way.

Cultural facilities: Univ. of Tennessee, Knoxville College, Knoxville Symphony Orchestra, 2 museums, art gallery, auditorium-coliseum, City-County library (487,960 book volume), Zoological Park; University-community theater, Choral Society.

Sports: Neyland Stadium, seating 70,650; home of Tennessee Vols football team; Knoxville Sox, baseball farm club of Chicago White Sox.

Other attractions: Great Smoky Mountains National Park, 39 miles from Knoxville, offers year-round scenic beauty, skiing in season; within 30 miles of Knoxville, 6 TVA lakes offer 2,320 miles of shoreline providing fishing, boating, swimming.

Further information: Chamber of Commerce, 705 Gay St. or Tourist Bureau, 811 Henley St., Knoxville, TN 37902.

Las Vegas, Nevada

The World Almanac is sponsored in the Las Vegas area by the Las Vegas Review-Journal, 1111 W. Bonanza, Las Vegas 89101; phone (702)385-4241; founded as a weekly 1909; purchased 1956 by Donald W. Reynolds, present publisher; member Donrey Media Group; circulation 61,410 weekdays, 64,647 Sundays; general manager Wm. Wright; editor Don Digilio.

Population: 330,000 greater Las Vegas (1972); 1973 total employment 131,500.
Area: southern Nevada, 283 miles NW of Phoenix, 289 miles NE of Los Angeles.
Industry: 24-hour tourism; hotel/gaming/recreation payroll $305.6 million; 1973 tourist volume 8.5 million; convention and tourist revenue $1.2 billion, gaming revenue $586 million.
Commerce: 6 banks, total resources over $1 billion; 4 savings and loans, resources $458 million; retail sales $885 million; average spendable family income $9,660.
Transportation: McCarran Int'l. Airport, total 1973 passengers 5.4 million; 7 major airlines plus foreign carriers; U.S. Customs Port of Entry; 3 bus lines; daily auto traffic entering area 11,000.
Communications: 5 TV and 10 radio stations.
Medical facilities: 9 hospitals, 1,579 rooms; 7 convalescent homes, one under construction.
Federal facilities: Nellis Air Force Base, 7,075 military, 1,054 civilian personnel; annual federal payroll, $44.2 million.

Cultural facilities: UNLV art, music, ballet, drama; community societies of art, dance, theater, history; 2,200-seat concert hall approved for construction; 3 libraries (7 locations).
Education: enrollment (public, private) 80,997; Univ. of Nevada Las Vegas, 6,600 students; Clark County Community College, 3,450 students.
Recreation: Lake Mead Recreation area, 5.5 million visitors; Hoover Dam; Mt. Charleston, Lee and Kyle Canyons, skiing; Valley of Fire; Lost City Museum; one-day drive ghost towns, Death Valley.
Convention facilities: Las Vegas Convention Center, 45 acres, 500,000 sq. ft. under roof, 330,000 sq. ft. exhibit area; $2.7 million project under construction, 7,300 seat rotunda; 8 hotels with convention facilities; 305 conventions in city (1973).
Sports: 13 golf courses; 100 tennis courts; 16,000-seat Las Vegas Stadium; Casinos, pro football; Gamblers, hockey; UNLV basketball, football, baseball.
Further information: Las Vegas Chamber of Commerce, 2301 East Sahara, Las Vegas, Nevada 89105.

Lethbridge, Alberta

The World Almanac is sponsored in the Lethbridge area by The Lethbridge Herald, 504 7th St. S., Lethbridge, Alberta; phone (403) 328-4411; founded as weekly in 1905; became daily in 1907; circulation, weekdays, 23,775, Saturdays, 25,273; editor and publisher Cleo W. Mowers, general manager Donald Doram, managing editor Donald H. Pilling.

Population: 43,612, 3rd in province.
Area: 22 square miles; located on Oldman River 60 miles north of Montana border, 125 miles south of

Calgary.
Industry: heavily dependent on agriculture; federally-inspected packing plants slaughtered 30.9%

of cattle slaughtered in Alberta in 1973; large dry-land grain growing, ranching area and extensive irrigation district; brewery, distillery, flour mill, foundry, oil seed processing.

Commerce: 1973 retail sales of $138.7 million (compared with $120 million in 1972); 5 banks; 3 trust companies, 12 finance companies.

Transportation: CP Rail; 2 bus lines; depots for 50 trucking firms; regional airline flies out of Lethbridge Airport.

New construction: Building permits valued at $28.4 million in 1973, compared with $16.5 in 1972.

Communications: 2 radio, 2 TV stations.

Medical facilities: 2 general hospitals, one long-term care hospital, 4 nursing homes for aged.

Cultural facilities: Canada agriculture research station, Univ. of Lethbridge, Lethbridge Community College, Alexander Galt Museum, Nikka Yuko Centennial Japanese Garden, symphony orchestra and chorus, local theatre groups.

Other attractions: 2 major parks, 4 artificial ice arenas, Stewart Game Farm.

Sports: Lethbridge chosen to host the 1975 Canada Winter Games in February; home of Lakers of Montreal Expos farm system and Broncos of Western Canada Hockey League.

History: early coal-mining town, named Lethbridge Oct. 16, 1885 after a coal executive.

Little Rock, Arkansas

The World Almanac is sponsored in Arkansas by the Arkansas Gazette, 112 West Third Street, Little Rock 72203, phone (501) 376-6161; founded 1819 at Arkansas Post, A. T., by Wm. E. Woodruff, moved to Little Rock 1821; circulation 118,641 daily, 143,562 Sunday; Hugh B. Patterson Jr., publisher and president; J. O. Powell, editorial director; Robert R. Douglas, managing editor; J. R. Williamson, vice president-general manager.

Population: 169,398 (city), 344,600 (metro); 152,500 employed.

Area: 110 sq. mi. at point where Ozarks-Ouachita highlands meet central coastal plain at geographical center of state.

Industry: 378 manufacturing plants, employing 31,500 persons and including Allis-Chalmers, Armstrong Rubber Co., Timex, AMF Cycle Division, Remington Arms, Jacuzzi Bros., Teletype and Westinghouse among others.

Commerce: Retail sales (1972 estimated), $702,858,000; bank resources, $1.243 billion; building permits (1973), $131 million; 11 banks, 6 building & loan associations, 4 old-line insurance companies.

Transportation: 3 trunkline railroads, 5 federally certified airlines, 8 bus lines, 14 common carrier barge lines.

Communications: 3 commercial TV, 1 ETV 12 radio stations.

Medical facilities: 9 hospitals including UA Medical Center, 2 VA hospitals and Ark. State Hospital for Nervous Diseases.

Cultural facilities: Univ. of Arkansas at Little Rock with Schools of Law, Medicine, Nursing and Pharmacy, UA School of Graduate Technology; Philander Smith, Shorter, and Arkansas Baptist colleges; Arkansas State Symphony, Arkansas Arts Center, 3 major public libraries, convention center-auditorium-hotel.

History: French explorer Bernard de la Harpe noted "le petit roche" on his map of the Arkansas River Valley in 1722.

Further information: Chamber of Commerce, Continental Bldg., Markham & Main Streets; Arkansas Parks & Tourist Dept., State Capitol — both Little Rock 72201.

London, Ontario, Canada

The World Almanac is sponsored in London and Southwestern Ontario by The London Free Press, 369 York St., London N6A 4G1, Ontario; (519) 679-1111; founded 1849; combined morning-evening circulation, 124,000; publisher Walter J. Blackburn, advertising director C. G. Fenn, editor W. C. Heine, production manager C. R. Turnbull, planning and development manager P. G. White.

Population: 230,000, 10th largest city in Canada; within an 80-mile radius population is 800,000.

Area: 43,929.6 acres, hub of prosperous industrial-agricultural area, 130 miles east of Detroit, 124 miles west of Toronto.

Industry: Diversified; 12 new industries added total investment of $3.4 million in 1973; 39 existing industries expanded adding investment of $6.3 million; recruitable labor force is estimated at 11,000; prime farm land around city supports major beef and dairy industry, tobacco, fruit and vegetables; nearby is highly industrial area of Sarnia, St. Thomas, Woodstock and Chatham.

Commerce: wholesale and retail center of the region, London is 10th largest in retail sales in Canada; 5th in automobile sales, 6th in per capita income; shoppers pour $5 million annually into economy.

Transportation: 2 major railways, 3 major bus lines and 2 airlines; direct air and rail connection with the U. S. and all parts of Canada; St. Lawrence Seaway ports serve the region.

Communications: one TV and 4 radio stations.

Medical facilities: 4 major hospitals.

Federal facilities: headquarters for one of Canada's major military units — Royal Canadian Regiment; historically the city has been a garrison town, the military plays a major role in community life.

Cultural facilities: Stratford Shakespearian Festival, professional theatre; symphony orchestra, art museum and public library; Univ. of Western Ontario with 15,000 students.

Recreational facilities: extensive green belt, parks and recreational facilities; Fanshawe Park with 200 acres of parkland and 640 acres of water; miles of sandy beaches and parkland are located on Lake Erie and Lake Huron.

Other attractions: Storybook Gardens, a major tourist attraction featues storybook characters and items for family entertainment.

History: incorporated in 1855; was once considered as site for the capital of Upper Canada.

Further information: Development Commissioner, City Hall; London Tourist and Convention Bureau, 272 Dundas St.

Los Angeles, California

Population: 2,817,323 (1973, city), 7,095,163 (county); 9.7 million (metro); 1st in state, 3rd in nation; total employed 3,417,200 (county).

Area: 463.7 sq. mi. on Pacific, 418 mi. south of San Francisco, 145 mi. north of Mexico; Los Angeles county seat, one of 77 cities in county.

Industry: Leading aerospace industry with 17 of top 100 defense contractors in nation located in Southern California; center of entertainment industry with over 600 firms in movie work; women's clothing, sports wear, electronics, rubber, tires, printing, furniture, paper, autos, auto parts, chemicals; manufacturing work force 783,300; trade 664,100; services 563,700; government 437,500. Among nation's leaders in agriculture; farm income $120.7 million (1972); cattle slaughter 1.5 million (1972).

Commerce: total taxable sales by retail stores $5.7 billion (city, 1973); $14.3 billion (county); median family income $10,970; average per capita income $5,426 (county); personal income $37.8 billion (county, 1972); approximately 90 commerical banks, 80 savings and loans; commercial bank deposits over $5 billion (city, 1973); S&L savings over $17.6 billion (county); international trade through Los Angeles customs district $6.2 billion — imports $4.3 billion, exports $1.9 billion (1972).

Transportation: Santa Fe, Union Pacific, Southern Pacific railroads, Amtrak; 6 major bus lines; largest concentration of trucks in western United States, 58,-000 est.); more than 3.7 million private cars, 143.7 miles of freeway in city, 463.2 miles in county; 36 domestic and international airlines serving Los Angeles International Airport, world's second busiest, handling 491,121 landings and takeoffs, 23,501,697 passengers, 1.3 billion pounds cargo (1973); more than 46 miles of commercial waterfront in Los Angeles-Long Beach Harbor which served 5,678 ships, handled 55,838,591 tons of cargo (1973).

Communications: 11 TV stations, more than 60 radio stations; over 25 daily publications in English and for-eign languages in county.

New construction: Building permits $2.3 billion (county, 1972), including $1.1 billion residential, 53,-100 new housing units.

Medical facilities: 168 hospitals, estimated 27,000 beds (county).

Educational facilities: 436 elementary schools, 75 junior high schools, 54 high schools, more than 150 private schools; 150 libraries; Univ. of California at Los Angeles (approx. 29,000 students), Univ. of Southern California (approx. 13,300 students), Calif. Institute of Technology, Loyola Univ., Claremont College, Whittier College, Pepperdine Univ., regional campuses of State University and Colleges at Los Angeles, Northridge, Long Beach, Dominguez.

Cultural facilities: 1,600 churches; Huntington Art Gallery and Library; Hollywood Bowl; Greek Theater; Griffith Park Planetarium; Mt. Wilson and Mt. Palomar Observatories; Los Angeles Museum; Music Center, County Art Museum; UCLA Botanical Gardens; Southwest Museum.

Recreational facilities: 206 parks and playgrounds; 6 public golf courses; 15 public beaches within 35 miles of downtown; within two hours driving, mountains, lakes, skiing, deserts, Disneyland, Marineland, Knott's Berry Farm.

Convention facilities: Large convention center; more than 50,000 rooms.

Sports: Professional teams in baseball (Dodgers), football (Rams), basketball (Lakers), Hockey (Kings); Santa Anita and Hollywood Park thoroughbred racing; collegiate basketball and football, including Rose Bowl.

History: Discovered in 1542 by Portuguese navigator Juan Rodriguez Cabrillo; Mission San Gabriel founded Sept. 8, 1771; city formally founded on Sept. 4, 1781, by Spanish colonial governor as El Pueblo de Nuestra Senora la Reina de los Angeles de Porciuncula; incorporated Apr. 4, 1850.

Further information: Chamber of Commerce, P.O. Box 3696, Terminal Annex, Los Angeles, Calif. 90051.

Louisville, Kentucky

The World Almanac is sponsored in Kentucky and Southern Indiana by The Courier-Journal and The Louisville Times, 525 West Broadway, Louisville, Kentucky 40202; Courier-Journal founded 1868; Times 1884; Courier circulation 232,939; Times, 175,344; Sunday 364,400; chairman of the board Barry Bingham Sr., editor and publisher Barry Bingham Jr.; major awards include 5 Pulitzer Prizes, 11 National Headliner Awards, and, since 1963, 36 national photo awards.

Population: 347,300 (city), 899,600 (metro area); 1st in state; total employed 369,600.

Area: 65.2 sq. mi. (city), 908 sq. mi. (metro); on southern bank of Ohio River.

Industry and commerce: one of top 20 industrial markets; famous for baseball bats, cigarettes, railroad repair shops, electrical appliances, farm machinery, motor vehicles, plumbing fixtures and whiskey; 900 manufacturing firms in area; estimated retail sales, Jefferson County (1972), $1.553 billion.

Transportation: 6 trunk-line railroads, 2 terminal railroads; 87 inter-city truck lines; 5 barge lines; 5 bus lines; 7 airlines, and 2 municipal airports.

Communications: 14 radio and 4 TV stations, one educational.

Medical facilities: 21 hospitals, 5,811 total beds.

Cultural facilities: 10 colleges and universities in area; Louisville Orchestra, Kentucky Opera Association, Art Center Association, J. B. Speed Art Museum, 20 private art galleries, Macauley Theatre, Actors Theatre, The Children's Theatre, Louisville Civic Ballet, Louisville-Jefferson County Youth Orchestra; 678 churches, 46 denominations.

Recreation: 147 public parks, covering 6,646 acres.

Convention facilities: Kentucky Fair & Exposition Center, largest multi-purpose exposition building in U.S., with 22 acres under one roof, 20,000-plus seating, parking for 27,000 cars; Convention Center, downtown, handles up to 7,000; new 400,000 sq. ft. exhibition hall and convention center in downtown Louisville under construction.

Sports attractions: Kentucky Derby, held annually at Churchill Downs since 1875, attended annually by over 125,000; Kentucky Colonels, American Basketball Association franchise.

Other: Belle of Louisville excursion steamboat; Churchill Downs Museum; Louisville Zoo; American Printing House for the Blind.

History: founded by explorer George Rogers Clark, in 1778; named after King Louis XVI of France.

Lubbock, Texas

The World Almanac is sponsored in the Lubbock area by the Lubbock Avalanche-Journal, 8th St. and Ave. J., Lubbock, Texas, 79408; (806) 762-8844; founded 1900 as Leader, became Avalanche 1908, daily 1921; Plains Journal weekly founded 1923; consolidated 1926; circulation, (morn) 63,321, (eve) 19,025, (Sat) 73,131, (Sun) 82,-009; member Southwestern Newspaper Corp.; general manager Robert R. Norris; editor Jay Harris.

Population: 159,350 (city), 189,000 (metro area), 8th in state; total employed 87,400.

Area: 82.2 sq. mi.; center of South Plains territory of northwest Texas.

Industry: vegetable oils, cotton, cotton seed flour grain sorghum, livestock, petroleum, sand and gravel; 228 manufacturing companies.

Commerce: wholesale and retail center for west Texas and eastern New Mexico; retail sales $324 million; bank resources: $679 million; 8 banks and 4 savings and loan associations.

Transportation: 12 motor freight carriers; 2 major railroads, and 3 bus lines; Lubbock Regional Airport, 3 major airlines, averaging 60 air movements per day; 6 major federal and state highways.

Communications: 4 TV and 9 radio stations.

Medical facilities: 8 hospitals, Lubbock State School for Mentally Retarded; medical school being constructed on Texas Tech campus.

Federal facilities: Reese Air Force Base, Federal Building, Federal Aviation Admin. and National Weather Service.

Cultural facilities: symphony orchestra, Theatre Centre; Museum of Texas Tech Univ., Moody Planetarium; Ranch Headquarters (authentic ranch houses dating to 1835); Christian College: Memorial Convention Center under contruction; Texas Tech Univ.

Recreational facilities: 39 city parks, 1,750 acres; Mackenzie State Park, state's largest, with Prairie Dog Town, Buffalo Lakes; Municipal Auditorium, 3,200 seats; Municipal Coliseum, 10,000 capacity; annual Panhandle South Plains Fair.

Sports: Texas Tech and Christian College sports schedules; Tech Jones Stadium, site of annual Coaches All-American football game.

Further information: Chamber of Commerce, 902 Texas Avenue, Lubbock, Tex.

Macon, Georgia

The World Almanac is sponsored in the Macon area by The Macon Telegraph & News, 120 Broadway, Macon, Ga. 31208; phone (912) 743-2621; acquired by Knight Newspapers Inc., 1969; circulation, Telegraph (morn) 54,-131, News (eve) 23,294, Sat. 71,132, Sun. 79,376; general manager Bert Struby, executive editor Don Carter, News editor Joseph Parham.

Population: 122,423 (city), 226,782 (metro), 3d in state; labor force, 94,700.

Area: 52 sq. mi., 6 miles northeast of geographic center of Georgia; Bibb County seat.

Industry: textiles, Bibb Company, longtime industry leader, headquartered with plants in area; 2 textile-related plants — YKK Zipper Co. of Japan and Texprint, Inc. — opened 1974; forestry, Armstrong Cork Co. acoustical tile plant is area's largest; pulpwood also is used to manufacture cardboard, packaging; tobacco, Brown & Williamson Tobacco Corp. began construction of $150 million cigarette plant in 1974; Kaolin (clay) deposits are mined in area and processed in numerous ways; Government Employees Insurance Co. opened regional office in 1974 to employ 2,500.

Federal Facilities: Warner Robins Air Logistics Center and Robins Air Force Base, 16 miles from Macon, are area's largest employers.

Educational facilities: Wesleyan College, nation's oldest college for women, and Mercer Univ. with law school, are among state's principal private institutions; state-supported Macon Jr. College opened in 1968.

Other attractions: Ocmulgee National Monument displays archeological remains of 3 prehistoric Indian civilizations; $4.5 million coliseum seats 10,000.

History: settled when U. S. established Fort Hawkins in 1806; chartered in 1823, named for Nathaniel Macon of North Carolina.

Further information: Chamber of Commerce, 640 First St., Macon, Ga. 31201.

Madison, Wisconsin

The World Almanac is sponsored in Madison by Madison Newspapers, Inc., publisher of The Capital Times and Wisconsin State Journal, 115 S. Carroll St., Madison, Wis., 53701; (608) 256-5511; circulation, State Journal (morn) 75,500, Capital Times (eve) 46,031, Sunday Journal 121,446.

Population: 177,000 (city), 299,200 (metro), 2d in state; metro work force 152,000.

Area: 50.4 sq. mi. (city), 1,197 sq. mi. (metro); in south-central Wisconsin, state capital and Dane County seat.

Commerce: home office of 29 insurance firms; 316 industrial firms; 18 banks, 5 savings and loans; retail sales (1973), $514,923,000 (city), $772,325,000 (metro); average spendable family income, $11,014.

Transportation: Dane County airport, 3 airlines; 3 railroads, Amtrak, major Interstate highway system;

3 bus lines; 10 truck lines; city owned bus system.

Communications: 4 TV, 6 AM and 7 FM stations.

Medical facilities: 9 hospitals, including U.W. hospital and V.A.; 22 clinics, 500 physicians.

Federal facilities: Forest Products Laboratory.

Cultural facilities: Dane County Coliseum (seats 10,134); 2 art centers, ballet company, 5 drama groups, 7 music organizations; 14 Catholic, 120 Protestant, one Greek Orthodox churches, 2 synagogues.

Education: Univ. of Wis. and 3 colleges; 34 elementary, 10 middle, 4 high schools; 17 parochial, one vocational-technical, 48 specialized; 6 city and 32 university libraries.

Recreation: 5 lakes with total of 18,000 acres of water surface; 2,382 acres of parks.

Convention facilities: Dane County Coliseum; 8 hotels with large convention facilities.

Sports: Madison Mustangs Central States football; Madison Blues, professional hockey; Univ. of Wis. in all Big Ten sports.

Further information: Greater Madison Chamber of Commerce, 615 E. Washington Ave. 53701.

Memphis, Tennessee

The World Almanac is sponsored in the Memphis area by the Memphis Press-Scimitar, 495 Union Ave., Memphis, Tenn., 38101; phone (901) 526-2141; Scimitar founded 1880 by G. P. M. Turner; Press 1906 by Scripps-McRae League, predecessor of Scripps-Howard Newspapers; circulation 123,362; editor Charles H. Schneider, managing editor Ed Ray.

Population: 623,530 (city), 830,304 (metro area); first in state, 17th in nation; 324,100 employed.

Area; 267 sq. mi., Shelby County seat, on east bank Mississippi River.

Industry: world's largest hardwood lumber center; manufacture of furniture and flooring; extensive cotton marketing-warehousing and processing of cotton seed into vegetable oil products; headquarters of Holiday Inns Inc., Cook Industries (cotton and grain), and Conwood Corp. (tobacco and food products). Other large industries include Schering-Plough (drugs), International Harvester (cotton pickers, hay balers), and Firestone (tires).

Commerce: wholesale-retail center for large parts of Tennessee, Arkansas and Mississippi; retail sales (1972) $1.8 billion; bank deposits $2.2 billion; 17 banks, 7 savings-loan assns. Per capita personal income $3,688 (1971).

Transportation: 10 airlines, 150 arrivals a day; 7 trunk line railroads, 82 motor freight lines, 6 barge lines; river port handled 10.6 million tons of freight in 1972.

Communications: 4 TV and 17 radio stations.

Medical facilities: Univ. of Tennessee medical units and a Veterans Administration hospital in complex with public hospital; 3 private general hospitals and St. Jude Hospital, research center for childhood illnesses, particularly leukemia.

Federal facilities: Naval Air Station, Naval Air Technical Training Center, Defense Depot Memphis and Air Forces's 164th Air Transport Group.

Cultural facilities: symphony orchestra, Opera Theater, Little Theater, Brooks Art Gallery, Museum; annual performances of Metropolitan Opera.

Educational facilities: Memphis State Univ., Southwestern College, LeMoyne-Owen College, Christian Brothers College, Univ. of Tennessee medical units, Shelby State Community College, State Technical Institute, Southern College of Optometry, Mid-South Bible College.

Recreational facilities: Meeman-Shelby Forest state park, 12,500 acres; also 137 other parks.

Convention facilities: $27 million Cook Convention Center, 1.3 million sq. ft., seating 16,500.

Sports: Memorial Stadium, seating 50,000, home of Southmen of World Football League and Memphis State University football team; Mid-South Coliseum, seating 12,000, home of MSU's basketball team and Memphis Tams of American Basketball Assn.; also Memphis Blues, in International Baseball League (AAA), and Danny Thomas Memphis Classic golf tournament.

Other attractions: Cotton Carnival each May; Mid-South Fair each September; Beale Street, home of the blues, where composer W. C. Handy lived.

History: DeSoto, exploring Mississippi River, stopped here in 1541; Ft. Adams established in 1797; Memphis incorporated in 1826. Yellow fever in 1878 nearly depopulated city, but its population grew back to 64,-589 in 1890.

Further information: Memphis Area Chamber of Commerce, 42 S. 2nd St., Memphis, 38103.

Mexico City (Ciudad de Mexico), Mexico

Population: 2,902,969 (1970).

Area: About 53 sq. mi. within the 573 sq. mi. Federal District (Distrito Federal; population, 8,541,070); in central Mexico at an altitude of 7,349 ft.

Industry and commerce: capital of Mexico; the political and economic hub of the nation; manufactures include steel, automobiles, appliances, textiles, rubber goods, furniture and electrical equipment; marketing center of Mexico.

Transportation: center of modern highway and rail system; 25-mi. subway system; served by most international air lines, Mexico City is 4 hrs. by jet from New York and 3 hrs. from Los Angeles.

Communications: major media center for Mexico and parts of Latin America; major film center.

Cultural facilities: Palace of Fine Arts and Ballet Folklorico; National Palace (Diego Rivera murals); National University with over 90,000 students; National Museum of Anthropology; city itself is an architectural exhibit of Aztec ruins, baroque cathedrals, and ultra-modern buildings.

Other attractions: Xochimilco with the "floating gardens" and gondolas; Chapultepec Castle, palace of the French-supported Emperor and Empress of Mexico, Maximilian and Carlota; 22-ton Aztec Calendar Stone; 2 volcanoes, Popocatepetl (17,887 ft.) and Iztaccihuatl (17,343 ft.); sports centers.

History: traditionally founded 1321 by Aztecs, city was called Tenochtitlan; captured by Spanish under Cortez in 1519 and again in 1521; occupied by the U. S. in 1847 and by the French from 1863 to 1867; Distrito Federal established 1824.

Further information: Mexican National Tourist Council, Mariano Escobedo 726, Mexico, D.F., or 677 5th Ave., New York 10022; or 9445 Wilshire Blvd., Beverly Hills 90212.

Miami, Florida

The World Almanac is sponsored in the Miami area by The Miami Herald, 1 Herald Plaza, Miami, Fla. 33101; phone (305) 350-2111; founded Dec. 1, 1910 by Frank B. Shutts; circulation 484,846 daily, 507,777 Sunday; editorial chairman John S. Knight, editor Don Shoemaker, executive editor Larry Jinks, managing editor Ron Martin; newspaper or staff writers have won or shared in 4 Pulitzer prizes, the latest in 1973, and numerous other honors.

Population: 350,000 (city), 1,350,000 (metro); 1st in state, 24th in nation; total enployed in metro area, 683,500.

Area: 53.8 sq. mi., land and water, on Biscayne Bay at mouth of Miami River; Dade County seat.

Industry: 4,900 light manufacturing plants; tourism and aviation are mainstays of economy; 1,000 hotels and motels employ 50,000 and handle 12 million visitors a year; aviation accounts for 80,000 jobs; Eastern (largest industrial employer), National and Pan American operate bases; winter agriculture center.

Commerce: center of Pan-American finance and commerce, with 76 banks, 15 savings and loan associations, Federal Reserve Bank branch; retail sales (1973), nearly $4 billion; Port of Miami busy in waterborne commerce as well as Caribbean cruise center, with 20 cruise sailings weekly.

Transportation: Miami International, served by 105 air carriers, handled 12.8 million travelers in 1973; Seaboard Coast Line (Amtrak) and all-freight Fla. East Coast Railroads operate in Miami, as do Greyhound and Trailways buses; 40 truck lines.

Communications: 5 commercial and 5 educational or closed-circuit TV stations, 36 radio stations.

New construction: major new office buildings downtown, topped by 40-story One Biscayne Tower, in a $500 million building surge; ground broken at $150 million Inter-American Center exposition site.

Medical facilities: 38 hospitals, 9,296 beds; over 13,000 beds at 54 nursing and convalescent homes in metro area; 2,800 members of Dade County Medical Association; Jackson Memorial Hospital one of area's leading research facilities.

Federal facilities: Homestead Air Force Base south of Miami manned by 8,900 men and women; Federal Aviation Administration; Coast Guard bases; 2 federal hospitals; oceanographic center; 12,400 U.S. employees.

Cultural facilities: Philharmonic, Opera Guild and other musical groups perform regularly; 18 auditoriums, including new downtown Gusman Hall; resident and touring theatrical productions; 4 major art museums; 7 playhouses and 55 night clubs and theater restaurants, some in major hotels.

Educational facilities: 8 colleges and universities, plus 3 campuses of Miami-Dade Community College, total enrollment of 62,000; Univ. of Miami is largest independent institution of higher learning in southeast; Florida International Univ. opened in 1972; public school system with 297,000 students is nation's 6th largest.

Recreational facilities: 14 miles of public beach on ocean and bay; 297 parks and playgrounds, 11 stadiums and grandstands; resort-oriented, Miami offers 42 golf courses and 57 marinas for boaters, with 36,000 pleasure craft registered; 72 movie houses.

Convention facilities: newly expanded Miami Beach Convention Hall can handle largest conventions; about 700 conventions brought 365,000 delegates to Miami Beach in 1973; 226 brought 96,185 delegates to Miami proper.

Sports attractions: pro football champion Miami Dolphins and U. of Miami play in Orange Bowl, which seats 80,050 after 1973 expansion; stadium also hosts Orange Bowl game, Orange Blossom classic, North-South All-Star Shrine Game; parimutuel wagering at 5 horse and greyhound tracks, jai-alai fronton.

Other attractions: balmy subtropical climate, with mean annual temperature of 75.3 degrees; 530 Protestant, 49 Catholic and 41 Jewish synagogues and churches; city is bilingual with 400,000 Latin American residents; one of nation's largest Jewish communities; marine stadium features powerboat and regatta racing and twilight concerts; Everglades National Park, 40 miles south of Miami, is virgin wilderness.

History: America's newest big city, Miami had only 3 houses in 1895 in a community called Fort Dallas. Julia Tuttle persuaded Henry M. Flagler to extend his railroad from West Palm Beach south to stimulate Miami development. City was incorporated in 1896, when railroad arrived.

Further information: Miami-Metro Department of Publicity and Tourism, 499 Biscayne Blvd., Miami, Fla., 33132.

Milwaukee, Wisconsin

The World Almanac is sponsored in the Milwaukee area by The Milwaukee Journal, Journal Square, Milwaukee, Wis. 53201; telephone (414) 224-2000; founded 1882 by Lucius W. Nieman; circulation 350,005 daily, 543,992 Sunday; chairman of the board Irwin Maier, publisher Donald B. Abert, president of The Journal Co. Donald D. Abert, editor Richard H. Leonard; major awards include 2 Pulitzer Prizes to the newspaper and 2 to staff members.

Population: 718,030 (city) 1,427,200 (metro area); city 12th and metro area 19th in U.S.; total employment 666,200 (metro area).

Area: 95.8 sq. mi. on shore of Lake Michigan, Milwaukee County seat.

Industry: largest U.S. producer of diesel and gasoline engines, outboard motors, motorcycles, tractors, padlocks, beer; 4th largest U.S. automaking center; graphic arts and food processing are largest nondurable goods employers; location for 10 "Fortune 500" industries.

Commerce: wholesale and retail trade center for Wisconsin, Upper Michigan; total retail sales $2.9 billion; wholesale trade $4 billion. Average household spendable income $12,601; 79 banks with $4.1 billion deposits; 53 savings and loan associations with $2.7 billion deposits.

Transportation: 4 major rail lines; Amtrak; 5 major airlines provide direct service to East and West Coasts, south, southeast and Florida for 2,000,000 users of Gen. Mitchell field; 30 U.S. and foreign-flag ship lines use Milwaukee's St. Lawrence seaway port, handling over 6,000,000 tons annually including 1,000,000 tons overseas cargo; port of Milwaukee gateway for 400 cities in 29 states and overseas ports, producing $240 million in exports 14th in total U.S.

exports; 4 inter-city bus lines, 68 motor freight carriers; I-94, 5 federal and 14 state highways intersect Milwaukee.
Communications: morning, evening and Sunday metropolitan newspaper; 4 commercial, 2 educational TV stations; 28 AM and FM radio stations.
Medical facilities: 21 major hospitals and medical centers, including new Veterans Administration hospital.
Cultural facilities: Milwaukee Symphony, Repertory Theater, 2 opera and one operetta companies; Mid-America Ballet; Milwaukee Art Center; Milwaukee museum; University of Wisconsin - Milwaukee, Marquette University, Medical College of Wisconsin, 8 other colleges and vocational schools enroll 45,000 annually; new $13,000,000 Performing Arts Center;

$15,900,000 addition to convention-arena-auditorium complex; Mitchell Park Conservatory and Milwaukee County Zoo are parts of 13,000-acre county park system.
Sports attractions: baseball, Milwaukee Brewers (Amer. League); basketball, Marquette Univ. Warriors; Univ. Wisconsin-Milwaukee Panthers; Milwaukee Bucks (NBA); football, Green Bay Packers (NFL) play 5 of 11 home games in Milwaukee.
History: Founded by Solomon Juneau, one of many French trappers in area in early 1800s; incorporated as town 1837; as city 1846.
Further information: Metropolitan Milwaukee Association of Commerce, 828 N. Broadway, Milwaukee, Wisc. 53202.

Minneapolis, Minnesota

Population: 428,000 (city) 2.1 million (metro); 1st in state, 17th in nation; total employed: 853,000 (metro area).
Area: 59 sq. mi. (city), 4,000 sq. mi. (10-county metro area) around St. Anthony Falls near junction of Minnesota and Mississippi Rivers.
Industry: diverse; major electronics-computer manufacturing center, including Honeywell, Control Data, Medtronics; headquarters for nation's 4 largest grain millers, including General Mills, Pillsbury and International Multifoods.
Commerce: metro area 14th in nation in per household retail sales (1972) and 7th in median household income ($10,300); total retail sales metro area (1973) $4.1 billion; 24 commercial banks, 6 savings and loan associations; headquarters for Ninth Federal Reserve District; world trade center, 12th among U.S. metro areas in exports.
Transportation: Amtrak regional terminal, 5 trunk railroads; 150 trucking firms; 5 major barge lines headquartered in city; Mples.-St. Paul International Airport, 650 flights daily.

Communications: 6 TV and 30 radio stations.
New construction: General Hospital (completion 1975); Hennepin County Government Center; Minnesota Orchestra Hall.
Medical facilities: 21 hospitals, including a leading heart hospital at Univ. of Minn.
Cultural facilities: Minnesota Orchestra, 7 art galleries-museums, Tyrone Guthrie Theatre, Walker Art Center, Univ. of Minnesota.
Sports attractions: Minnesota Twins (American League) Minnesota Vikings (NFL) Minnesota North Stars (NHL) Minnesota Buckskins (World Team Tennis).
Other attractions: 153 parks, 22 lakes; 57-story IDS Tower; Mpls. Aquatennial celebration in July; average yearly snowfall: 41 inches.
History: first visited in 1680s by Fr. Louis Hennepin who discovered and named St. Anthony Falls on the Mississippi River; French fur traders used the area in 18th century; incorporated 1871. Falls became power source for lumber and milling operations in 19th century.

Mobile, Alabama

The World Almanac is sponsored in the Mobile area by The Mobile Press Register, 304 Government St., 36630; phone (205) 433-1551; circulation, Register (morn) 44,660, Press (eve) 59,117, combined (Sat., Sun.) 94,912; Register founded 1813, Press 1928; William J. Hearin publisher and president, Fallon Trotter executive editor, John Fay associate executive editor.

Population: 190,026 (city), 376,690 (metro), 2d city in state, 68th in nation; total employed (metro), 125,000.
Area: 142 sq. mi., at head of Mobile Bay.
Industry: home of Alabama State Docks, a $200 million complex where 33 ocean-going ships can be docked at one time; over $835 million is invested in diversified industry, including paper and paper products, forest products, shipbuilding, chemicals, roofing, paints, alumina, oil, aircraft engines and metals.
Commerce: wholesale-retail center for large portion of southwest Alabama and southeast Mississippi; Mobile County retail sales (1973), $602,115,000.
Transportation: served by 4 major railroads, one of the great river systems, 3 major airlines, 55 truck lines and about 100 steamship lines.

Communications: 2 TV and 12 radio stations.
Medical facilities: Univ. of South Alabama Medical College and 4 modern hospitals.
Cultural facilities: $12 million Municipal Auditorium-Theater complex seats 16,000; art gallery, museum, amateur dramatic theater, public library and branches; Univ. of South Alabama, Spring Hill and Mobile Colleges, and Bishop State Junior College.
Annual attractions: America's Junior Miss Pageant, Senior Bowl Football Game, and Mardi Gras.
History: founded in 1702 by Jean Baptiste Le Moyne; 6 flags have flown over the city since then.
Further information: Chamber of Commerce, Commercial Guaranty Bank Bldg.

Montgomery, Alabama

The World Almanac is sponsored in the Montgomery area by the Advertiser-Journal, 200 Washington Street, Montgomery, Alabama 36102; phone: (205) 262-1611; Advertiser founded 1828, Journal 1881; one ownership since 1940; circulation Advertiser (morn) 54,884, Journal (eve) 26,523; combined Sunday 77,579; publisher Harold Martin, managing editor Ben R. Davis.

Population: 141,000 (city), 238,900 (metro); 147th in nation; total employed 98,656.
Area: 50.34 sq. mi. (city), 442 sq. mi. (county).
Industry: machinery manufacture, glass products, textiles, refrigeration equipment, axles, furniture, food products, paper, and fertilizers; over 250 industries.
Commerce: wholesale-retail center for 13 counties in central Alabama; retail trade area sales (1973), $871,848,000; 7 banks, 3 savings & loans associations, 6 insurance company home offices; state capital.
Transportation: 5 railroads, 3 airlines, 2 national bus lines; Interstate 65 and 85 intersect in the city; Alabama River navigable to the Gulf of Mexico.

Medical facilities: 7 general hospitals and a VA hospital; over 2,000 beds.
Military: Home of Maxwell Air Force Base, The Air University and Gunter Field.
Cultural Facilities: Art Guild, Civic Ballet, Little Theater, and a Community Concert Series; Museum of Fine Arts; 5 major colleges and universities.
Sports: Rebels, farm team of Detroit, play at Patterson Field; Blue-Gray Football Classic, played in Cramton Bowl; Southeastern Championship Rodeo.
History: incorporated 1819; Jefferson Davis inaugurated president of the Confederate States of America, Feb. 18, 1861, in Montgomery.

Montreal, Quebec, Canada

The World Almanac is sponsored in the Montreal area by The Gazette, a Southam newspaper, 1000 St. Antoine Street, Montreal H3C 3R7, Quebec, Canada; phone (514) 861-1111; founded 1778 by Fleury Mesplet; circulation 138,194 daily; publisher Mark Farrell; general manager J. Peter Kohl; editorial page editor Tim Creery; managing editor R. Lindsay Crysler; sponsors Christmas fund; 5 National Newspaper Awards in last 2 years.

Population: 1,214,300 (city), 2,761,000 (metro); after Paris, the 2d largest French-speaking city in the world, 67% French origin, 12% Anglo-Saxon, 21% other origins; Canada's largest urban center.
Area: some 68 sq. mi. on an island of 190 sq. mi. in the St. Lawrence River where the Ottawa and Richelieu Rivers flow into it at the head of the St. Lawrence Seaway. The metropolitan area extends more than 1,000 sq. mi. Except for the 769 ft. Mount Royal mountain, the island is flat and averages 100 ft. above sea level.
Industry: Canada's industrial hub; ($6.9 billion, value of shipments of goods of own manufacture), petroleum refining, women's and men's clothing, slaughtering and meat packing, tobacco products, brewing, foods, and primary metal industries.
Commerce: headquarters of many of the largest financial institutions in Canada, and home of the Montreal and Canadian Stock Exchanges; about 75% of countries having official representation in Canada have a consulate or representative in Montreal; $4.1 billion total retail sales.
Transportation: St. Lawrence Seaway, a $1-billion Canadian-U.S. waterway and power project which runs 1,300 miles to the Great Lakes in the heart of North America, has helped Montreal, 1,000 miles from the sea, become the world's 2d greatest inland port, after Rotterdam; harbor extends 42 miles. Air capital of the world, headquarters of the International

al Civil Aviation Organization and the International Air Transport Association; some 30 airlines serve Dorval International airport. A new $500 million airport, Mirabel, is under construction north of Montreal Island. Canadian National and Canadian Pacific Railways maintain head offices and terminals in Montreal. The Metro, Montreal's $225,000,000 16-mile subway system, the 8th largest in the world, opened in 1966; system is being extended in all directions to be completed before Montreal hosts the 1976 Summer Olympic Games.
Cultural facilities: a major cultural center; Place des Arts, a 3,000-seat concert hall and 2 theaters, home of the Symphony Orchestra, attracts the finest in drama, opera, ballet, and music; Museum of Fine Arts, the Musée de l'Art Contemporain. Some of the continent's most beautiful churches, including the Roman Catholic Mary Queen of the World Basilica, a half-size replica of St. Peter's in Rome; 2 famous universities, McGill and l'Universite de Montreal.
Sports: NHL Canadiens, the Canadian Football League Alouettes, and the Expos of baseball's National League.
History: first visited by Jacques Cartier in 1535; founded under the name of Ville Marie in 1642. Old Montreal, some 1,000 acres in all, is the largest such area undergoing restoration in North America and retains the general atmosphere of the 18th century.

Nashville, Tennessee

The World Almanac is sponsored in Nashville by The Tennessean, 1100 Broadway, 37202; phone (615) 255-1221; founded as The Tennessean in 1907 but incorporated publications date to 1812; circulation daily 141,809, Sunday 241,-431; president Amon Carter Evans, publisher John Seigenthaler; 3 Pulitzer prizes, 8 Headliner awards, 2 Sigma Delta Chi Awards.

Population: 470,000 (in unified Metro government), 2d in state; labor force 238,400.

Area: 532 sq. mi., straddling Cumberland River, in north central part of state.

Industry: recording, 25% of singles and 20% of albums sold in U.S. are recorded in Nashville's 35 studio complexes, grossing $250 million annually; clothing, headquarters of Genesco, world's largest and most diversified clothing and footwear manufacturer; insurance, 2 of largest U.S. companies located here; world's largest auto glass plant; chemicals, printing (especially religious materials), aerostructures, tires, heating equipment.

Commerce: retail center for Middle Tennessee, South Kentucky; retail sales (1973) $1,186 million; per capita income (1972), $4,508; Bank resources, over $3 billion in 8 banks, 90 branches.

Transportation: 9 U.S. highways and 6 branches of the interstate system radiate from Nashville; 9 commercial airlines with 157 daily flights; 2 railroads, Amtrak; bus service, 73 motor freight lines.

Communications: 5 TV stations (one public), and 22 AM and FM radio stations.

Medical facilities: 15 hospitals, 2 with medical schools, VA hospital, speech-hearing center.

Cultural: symphony orchestra; replica of Parthenon

with art gallery; public and state libraries; botanic garden and art center, 2 community theaters; new $26 million performing arts center under construction.
Educational facilities: 14 colleges and universities; 137 public schools, 37 private schools.
Convention facilities: 10,000-seat auditorium; Opryland convention center under construction.
Other attractions: Grand ole Opry, Opryland ($28 million theme park featuring music); Country Music

Hall of Fame; Hermitage (home of Andrew Jackson); Belle Meade antebellum mansion.
Recreation facilities: water sports, outdoor activity on Old Hickory and Percy Priest lakes.
History: settled in 1780 as a fort in then western North Carolina; incorporated, 1784, with first written charter west of Alleghenies.
Further information: Chamber of Commerce, 161 4th Ave. N., Nashville, Tn., 37203.

New Haven, Connecticut

The World Almanac is sponsored in the greater New Haven area by the New Haven Register (founded 1812) and the New Haven Journal-Courier (founded 1755); circulation Register (eve.) 107,907, Sunday 125,916; Journal-Courier (morn) 32,756; president and publisher Lionel S. Jackson, vp and general manager Donald A. Spargo, vp and treasurer George S. Stearns Jr., vp and editor Robert J. Leeney.

Population: 135,500 (city), 360,400 (metro); 3d in state.
Area: 21.1 sq. mi. southern coast of Conn. on north shore of Long Island Sound; county seat.
Industry: 1,000 firms in immediate area; principal products are guns, hardware, rubber goods, paper products, machinery and tools.
Commerce: wholesale-retail center for southern Conn.; retail city sales (1973), $369,485,000, highest in Conn.; serves 850,000, people within a radius of 25 miles; busy harbor, particularly with cargo ships delivering oil.
Transportation: Penn Central, Amtrak Cosmopolitan turbotrain; 25 major truck lines; 14 federal and state highways; Tweed-New Haven Airport served by 3 airlines; limo service to N. Y. airports, 2 bus lines.
Communications: one TV and 6 radio stations.
Medical facilities: Yale Medical Center; Yale-New Haven Hospital; Hospital of St. Raphael.
Cultural facilities: Yale Univ. Library with over 6,000,000 books one of the world's largest collections;

Yale's Peabody Museum of Natural History, Art Gallery and Beinecke Rare Book Library; the New Haven Historical Society; Cultural Center; 2 legitimate theatres, and The New Haven Symphony.
Educational facilities: Yale Univ. and graduate schools; Albertus Magnus, Southern Conn. State, South Central Community, Quinnipiac Colleges; Univ. of New Haven.
Recreational facilities: Yale Bowl, Woolsey Hall, Ingalls Rink, the Coliseum, 15 parks, including Frederick Brewster's estate, East and West Rock scenic drives, 50 playgrounds, West Rock Nature Center; 7 golf courses, 30 tennis courts, 5 skating rinks.
Convention facilities: Coliseum-convention center with a 19-story hotel nearby.
Sports attractions: AHL Nighthawks; NFL New York Giants use Yale Bowl for home games.
History: founded 1638 by Puritans; named after Newhaven in England; incorporated 1638, became a part of Conn. 1662; first mayor was Roger Sherman, signer of Declaration of Independence.

New Orleans, Louisiana

The World Almanac is sponsored in the New Orleans area by The States-Item, 3800 Howard Ave., New Orleans, La. 70140; phone (504) 521-7011; founded Jan. 3, 1880, by Maj. Henry J. Hearsey, circulation 130,188 daily, 117,-130 Saturday; editor Walter G. Cowan, associate editor Charles A. Ferguson, city editor William U. Madden; sponsors Women Against Crime Crusade and Football Fund for Underprivileged.

Population: 593,471 (city), 1,034,316 (metro area); first in state; total employed, 434,200.
Area: 363.5 sq. mi. of which 199.4 are land.
Industry: Port of New Orleans, second largest in nation, handled 31.6 million tons of cargo valued at $5.6 billion in 1973.
Commerce: trade center for lower Mississippi valley. Bank resources $4.6 billion.
Transportation: rail hub for north, east and westbound commerce. Amtrak passenger service to Chicago, New York, Los Angeles. New Orleans International Airport serves major airlines; Lakefront Airport private aviation.
New construction: hotel building booming in expectation of Dome opening and popularity of annual Mardi Gras festival; tallest building in South, 51-story One Shell Square, opened at cost of $45,000,000.
Communications: 4 commercial TV stations and educational channel.
Medical facilities: major medical center with Charity Hospital, 2 schools of medicine and one of dentistry; Oschner Clinic, Touro Infirmary.
Cultural facilities: new Center for the Performing Arts seats 2,317 for operas, concerts. Museums in-

clude Louisiana State Museum, Isaac Delgado Museum of Art, the Middle American Research Institute of Tulane University and many small galleries.
Educational facilities: Tulane University, Louisiana State University in New Orleans, Loyola, Dillard, Southern University in New Orleans, Xavier, St. Mary's Dominican.
Other attractions: Louisiana Superdome scheduled for completion in 1975 at a cost of more than $150,000,000; will seat 80,000 for major events; French Quarter remains major historic tourist attraction.
Sports: New Orleans Saints (NFL), now play in Tulane Stadium, will move to dome by 1975. Dome will also be home for New Orleans Jazz of the NBA. Sugar Bowl is major college attraction.
History: named after the Duke of Orleans, founded on the edge of a swamp within crescent of the Mississippi River 100 miles upstream from the Gulf of Mexico by Jean Baptiste Le Moyne, Sieur de Bienville; became capital of Louisiana Territory in 1722, when Adrien de Pauger laid out what is now the French Quarter; became part of U. S. with signing of Louisiana Purchase in 1803.

New York City, New York

The World Almanac is sponsored in the Greater New York City metropolitan area by the Daily News and Sunday News, 220 E. 42d St., New York, N.Y. 10017, phone (212) MU 2-1234; New York News Inc., founded June 26, 1919 by Joseph Medill Patterson; circulation daily 2,120,549; Sunday 2,933,182; chairman of the board F.M. Flynn, president and publisher W. H. James, executive editor Floyd Barger, managing editor Michael J. O'Neill, treasurer R. J. Rohrbach, general manager Bruce G. McCauley; Pulitzer Prizes for news photography, cartoon, editorial writing and international and local investigative reporting; sponsors Golden Gloves, Harvest Moon Ball, numerous school events.

Population: 7,895,563 (city), 16,133,500 (consolidated area); 1st in state and nation; total employed 3,518,-000; per capita personal income $5,292.

Area: 300 sq. mi. at mouth of Hudson River; embraces 5 boroughs—Manhattan, Bronx, Brooklyn, Queens and Richmond (Staten Island)—and is host to United Nations.

Industry: nation's leader in manufacturing and service industries; produces 25.3% of America's apparel, 18.2% of printing and publishing, 10% of leather and leather products, 7% of jewelry, toys, notions and miscellaneous products; 4.6% of fabricated metal products and electrical machinery; 4.3% of textile mill products; 3.2% of food products; 23,207 manufacturing establishments (Sept., 1973).

Commerce: nation's richest port, handling annual 196,842,857 tons of maritime cargo; Wall Street, world's largest financial center, with New York and American Stock exchanges; wholesale-retail center for New York, New Jersey and southwestern Connecticut; retail sales $14.7 billion (1972); 47 commercial banks, resources $187.8 billion; 43 savings banks, resources $44.7 billion; World Trade Center, twin 110-story towers, cost $850 million.

Transportation: Kennedy International Airport handles 42% of nation's overseas air travel and 51% of export-import air tonnage, served by 52 scheduled air carriers; LaGuardia Airport served by 15 domestic airlines; 4 heliports. Penn Central Railroad, Amtrak; 2 major rail terminals, Pennsylvania and Grand Central stations; 42 interstate bus lines; subway network covers every borough except Richmond; ferry and the 4,260-ft. Verrazano-Narrows Bridge (world's longest suspension span) link Richmond to Manhattan and Brooklyn; 18 bridges connect Manhattan with other boroughs, George Washington Bridge over the Hudson connects New Jersey; 5 tunnels under the Hudson and East Rivers.

Communications: 11 TV stations (6 commercial, 2 educational, 1 municipal, 2 CATV); 36 AM and FM radio stations; WPIX-TV and WPIX-FM are broadcast affiliates of The News.

Medical facilities: 123 hospitals, (19 municipal, 34 private, 70 voluntary non-profit); 5 major medical research centers specialize in cancer, heart diseases, sickle cell anemia and other research; Sloan-Kettering Institute for Cancer Research; 4 VA hospitals.

Educational facilities: 6 universities, 23 colleges, including 5 medical colleges, 4 law schools, 3 colleges of pharmacy, 2 colleges of dentistry, 2 institutes of art and architecture; 926 schools in the public school system; more than 1,000 private schools; public libraries total 194.

Cultural facilities: Lincoln Center for the Performing Arts (Philharmonic, Ballet Company, Metropolitan Opera and other theatrical arts), Carnegie Hall, Brooklyn Academy of Music. Broadway and Off-Broadway alliance for varied theatrical productions; Shakespeare Festival at Delacorte Theatre. Museum total of 42 includes the American Museum of Natural History, Metropolitan Museum of Art, Museum of the Performing Arts, Museum of Modern Art, Whitney Museum, and South Street Seaport Museum.

Other attractions: Botanic gardens in the Bronx and Brooklyn; Central Park and Prospect Park; 5 zoos; 15 municipal golf courses, 527 tennis courts, 28 outdoor swimming pools.

Sports: NBA Knicks, NHL Rangers and WHA Golden Blades; NL Mets and NFL Jets play in Shea Stadium; AL Yankees will play in Shea during Yankee Stadium renovations. For 1974-1975, NFL Giants play in Yale Bowl in New Haven, Conn.; WFL Stars; tennis WTT Sets; soccer NASL Cosmos.

History: discovered by Giovanni da Verrazano in 1524; in 1626 Peter Minuit bought the island from the Manhattan Indians for about $24 in goods and trinkets; settlement named New Amsterdam. In 1664, British troops occupied city without resistance and named it New York in honor of the Duke of York, brother of the King. On Jan. 1, 1898, Manhattan and large areas to the NE, E and S were consolidated into one City of New York.

Newark, New Jersey

Population: 382,417; first in state, doubles on weekdays with non-residents employed and working in the city; 1,856,554 (metro area) including Essex, Morris and Union Counties; 137,134 employed (city, non agricultural).

Area: 24.4 sq. mi. (city), 16 miles west of New York City.

Industry: wide diversity of manufacturers, fine craftsmanship; more than 10,000 businesses, major banking and insurance center. Headquarters for several national firms.

Transportation: Newly opened international airport; 2 major ports; 4 railroads; world's largest privately owned bus transportation system; world's largest truck terminal.

Communication: New Jersey's largest newspaper; one radio station.

Medical facilities: 8 major hospitals with new home of the College of Medicine and Dentistry under construction; Beth Israel Medical Center known worldwide for heart surgery.

Federal facilities: new federal building; old federal courthouse.

Cultural facilities: Museum and Public Library are largest in state; New Jersey Historical Society; home of New Jersey Symphony Orchestra and Symphony Hall.

Educational facilities: New Jersey College of Medicine and Dentistry; Rutgers Univ.; Seton Hall Univ. Law School; Newark College of Engineering; Essex County College; Muhammad's University of Islam. Drake's College of Business.

Recreational facilities: parks in Newark cover 783.97 acres; 7 swimming pools, 74 playgrounds and an ice skating rink.

Convention facilities: one large hotel and two large

motor inns, with others under construction, attract conventioners.
Other attractions: 7 famous works of sculpture, including 'John F. Kennedy' by Jacques Lipchitz.

History: founded in 1666, incorporated 1836; British troops ravaged the town during the Revolution; scene of tragic riots in 1967 in which at least 26 persons were killed.

Norfolk, Virginia

The World Almanac is sponsored in the Norfolk Metropolitan Area by the Virginian-Pilot and Ledger-Star, 150 W. Brambleton Ave., Norfolk, Va. 23501; phone (804) 446-2000; Virginia founded 1865, Ledger, 1876; circulation : LS (even) 104,715; VP (morn) 131,542, VP (Sun) 188,459; Frank Batten publisher, Derek Dunn-Rankin president & general manager, Perry Morgan exec. editor, Robert H. Mason VP editor, George J. Hebert LS editor.

Population: 297,200 (city), 715,700 (metro); 1st in state; civilian employed, 241,600; military pop., 80,-000.
Area: 915 sq. mi. in southeastern Virginia.
Industry: General Electric, Ford Motor Co., Norfolk Shipbuilding & Drydock Corp, Smith-Douglas.
Commerce: retail sales (1972) $1.2 billion; median household income, $8,966.
Transportation: Port of Hampton Roads, world's finest natural harbor; ranks first in export tonnage (47,698,244 tons handled 1973) among Atlantic ports; biggest coal port in world; $26 million. Regional Airport, 4 major airlines; Chesapeake Bay Bridge-Tunnel supplies direct north highway route; 8 trunk line railroads, 50 major common carrier trucking companies, 2 bus companies.
Communications: 5 TV, 13 AM, 9 FM stations.
Medical facilities: 11 hospitals including oldest and 2d largest naval hospital in U.S.
Federal facilities: greatest concentration of naval installations in world; 38 major commands include Atlantic Fleet, Second Fleet, NATO Supreme Allied Command Atlantic (SACLANT), Armed Forces Staff

College and Commandant 5th Naval Dist.
Cultural facilities: symphony orchestra, Feldman Chamber Quartet, repertory theater, dinner and little theaters, civic and univ. ballet. Chrysler Museum collection covers all cultures from Egyptian to pop art; yearly Festival of the Arts.
Educational facilities: Old Dominion Univ., Norfolk State, Virginia Wesleyan and Tidewater Community Colleges; Eastern Va. Medical School.
Recreational facilities: General Douglas MacArthur Memorial, Adam Thoroughgood House (1636), Gardens-by-the-sea; Dismal Swamp located in Chesapeake and resort city of Virginia Beach offers 38 mi. of swimming, fishing and surfing; camping facilities at Seashore State Park.
Convention facilities: Scope-$30 million cultural and convention center.
Sports: Va. Squires (ABA), Va. Red Wings (AHL), Tidewater Tides (International League).
Climate: Average summer temp.: 78° to 41°.
Further information: Chamber of Commerce/Convention & Visitor Bureau, 475 St. Paul Blvd., Norf., Va. 23501.

Oakland, California

Population: 342,400.
Area: 53.4 sq. mi.; seat of Alameda County.
Industry: food processing, fabricated metal products, transportation equipment, chemicals and paint; Port of Oakland is 2d in containerized cargo; home base for Kaiser Industries.
Commerce: 8,120 retail outlets with taxable sales (1973) of 1.1 billion; median family income, $8,237 per annum.
Transportation: western terminus for Southern Pacific, Santa Fe and Western Pacific Railroads; International Airport is major airfreight terminal and center for supplemental air carriers; headquarters for Bay Area Rapid Transit, underground, underwater 75-mile subway connecting 15 communities.
Medical facilities: 9 hospitals include Children's Hospital Medical Center, Kaiser Foundation and the Veteran's Administration.
New construction: major downtown redevelopment with $100 million invested in construction.
Cultural facilities: Museum, half garden, half gallery design, has divisions of Natural Science, History and

Art; symphony, Chinese Community Cultural Center.
Educational facilities: Univ. of California at Berkeley, Mills College, College of Holy Names, Cal State, Hayward, Chabot, California College of Arts and Crafts, Peralta Community College.
Recreational facilities: 26,000 acre Regional Park System serving the East Bay; zoo in 100-acre Knowland State Park has large collection of gibbons and aerial tram; Lake Merritt Park includes botanical garden, wildfowl refuge, natural science center and Children's Fairyland.
Sports attractions: Raiders (football), Athletics (baseball), Seals (hockey) and Golden State Warriors (basketball).
Other attractions: Oakland Coliseum, over 50,000 capacity, for theatrical entertainment, exhibits, conventions and circus; Jack London Square.
History: area explored in 1772, settled in 1850; incorporated as town in 1852, as city in 1854.
Further information: Chamber of Commerce, 1320 Webster St., Oakland, California 94612.

Oklahoma City, Oklahoma

The World Almanac is sponsored in the Oklahoma City area by The Daily Oklahoman and Oklahoma City Times, Oklahoma City, Okla. 73125; phone (405) 232-3311; The Oklahoman founded in 1894; Times in 1888; Oklahoma Publishing Co. acquired The Oklahoman 1903 and the Times 1916; circulation Oklahoman 176,545; Times 100,-105; Sunday, 296,675; editor and publisher E. L. Gaylord, executive editor Charles L. Bennett.

Population: 368,856 (city), 669,092 (metro); largest in state; labor force 346,700.

Area: city area, among nation's largest, is 647.5 sq. mi.; metro area, 3,491 sq. mi.; located in state's center on Canadian River.

Industry: oil, with about 1,800 producing wells in metro area, employs about 30,000 residents; Tinker Air Force Base, one of world's largest air depots, employs 22,000 civilians and 2,500 military on $100 million installation; FAA and other aviation employ some 37,000 residents, with total annual payroll of $300 million; agricultural and ranching area; manufactured goods include aircraft, telephone equipment, oil field machinery, oil and greases, building materials, feed, flour, meat and tires.

Commerce: regional, national and international marketing center; effective buying income, $10,839 per household, consumer sales near $1.8 billion.

Transportation; 5 passenger airlines; 4 primary federal and 3 major state highways, with I-40 and I-35 intersecting the city; fully planned urban expressway system, major bus, truck and rail lines.

Medical Facilities: Oklahoma Univ. Health Sciences Center and 25 hospitals and clinics.

Cultural Facilities: symphony and junior symphony; Oklahoma Art Center; Lyric Theater at Oklahoma City Univ. Warehouse Theater; Oklahoma Theater Center; Southwest Repertory Theater, Univ. of Oklahoma.

Education: Univ. of Oklahoma, Oklahoma City Univ., Central State Univ.

Convention Facilities: $23 million Myriad Convention Center, seating 15,000 in the center of a downtown redevelopment project costing nearly $300 million, hosts 350 conventions yearly with more than 150,000 delegates.

Other attractions: National Cowboy Hall of Fame; 130 municipal parks; major college sports; pro sports: Oklahoma City 89ers, American Assn. baseball; International Softball headquarters.

History: founded by land run, Apr. 22, 1889.

Further information: Chamber of Commerce, 1 Santa Fe Plaza, Oklahoma City, 73102.

Omaha, Nebraska

The World Almanac is sponsored in Nebraska by The Omaha World-Herald, World-Herald Square, Omaha, Nebraska 68102; phone (402) 444-1000; Evening World, founded 1885 by G. M. Hitchcock, acquired Daily Herald, founded 1865; adopted present name 1889; circulation 251,792 daily, 290,064 Sunday; president Harold W. Andersen, vice-president and executive editor Louis G. Gerdes; 3 Pulitzer Prizes; sponsors Midwest Spelling Bee, Newspapers in the Classroom, summer recreation, Good Fellows Charities, college scholarships.

Population: 368,050 (city), 568,950 (metro).
Area: 83 sq. mi. of rolling hills.

Industry: manufacturing accounts for $2.1 billion a year; 600 plants employ 40,000 people; Western Electric, 7,000 employees, is Nebraska's largest employer; 2d in the nation in frozen food production and world leader in salable receipts or livestock market.

Commerce: 19 banks; 4th largest insurance center in nation with 36 insurance company home offices, including Mutual of Omaha, the largest provider of individual health insurance in the world, and Woodmen of the World Life Insurance Society, largest fraternal life company; effective buying income per household, $14,316; retail sales over $1 billion.

Transportation: 4th largest rail center; Union Pacific and Burlington Northern main offices; transcontinental passenger trains and 75 freight trains daily; nearly 2,000,000 tons carried on Missouri River annually; 6 major airlines.

Medical facilities: 16 hospitals with 4,680 beds; 2 medical schools—Univ. of Nebraska Medical School

and Creighton School of Medicine; $2.5 million Eppley Institute for Research in Cancer is one of best in world; $100 million in medical construction planned or underway.

Federal facilities: Strategic Air Command's global headquarters at Offutt Air Base; Missouri River Division of the U.S. Army Corps of Engineers.

Cultural facilities: symphony orchestra, opera company, Ballet Society; 100 amateur and professional live theatre groups, 7 art galleries, 5 museums including $4,000,000 Joslyn Art Museum.

Educational facilities: 250 metro area schools, 6 colleges in the area teach 21,000 students; Voc-Tec program, College of Nursing.

Recreation: 1,200 acre Fontenelle Forest Preserve and Nature Center, new $3 million Henry Doorly Zoo; Civic Auditorium; pro basketball, baseball, hockey; 55-day Ak-Sar-Ben pari-mutuel horseracing season; NCAA College World Series.

Further information: Chamber of Commerce, 1620 Dodge St., Omaha, Nebraska 68102.

Orange County, California

The World Almanac is sponsored in Orange County by The Register, 625 N. Grand, Santa Ana, CA, 92711; telephone (714) 835-1234; circulation combined daily 200,899, Sunday 216,741; purchased in 1935 by late R. C. Hoiles, president-founder Freedom Newspapers Inc., now headed by son, Clarence H. Hoiles, also publisher of The Register. General manager David Threshie, executive editor Jim Dean, managing editor Mike Maloney, research and promotion dir. Jim Lyons Sr.

Population: Estimated 1,667,500, up 17.3 percent since 1970 in shift from fastest growing U.S. metropolitan area by rate to fastest numerically. Compares with 212,364 in 1950; 2.5 million projected 1985.

Area: 500,000 acres stretching 25 mi. inland, 42 miles along Pacific Ocean from Long Beach past Huntington Beach surfing, Newport Beach yacht harbor, Laguna Beach art colony to Camp Pendleton.

Industry and commerce: Bank deposits 3.23 billion; spendable income topped $7.7 billion as new business facilities opened at average of more than one per day. Housing construction reached 35,100 units or near 700 daily. Retail sales hit $4.533 billion as median family income was $14,990. Employment rose 6.2% to 554,400, with 134,100 in manufacturing, 116,300 in trade 26,500 insurance, finance, real estate, 86,500 in services, 10,700 in $100-million agricultural output and 79,900 in government. Biggest manufacturing employer Rockwell Intl's. Autonetics, Minuteman missiles and electronic calculators, sewing and reading machines firm. IR's Space Division built Apollo moon rocket second stage; McDonnell Douglas Astronautics, Apollo third stage and current Skylab. Other major employers include corporate or major unit headquarters for international firms such as Hughes, developer of NATO radar defense umbrella; Philco-Ford Aeronutronics, Beckman Instruments, AMF-Voit, Hunt-Wesson Foods, Santa Fe International, Westinghouse, ITT, Textron, Uniroyal, Cypress Mines, TRW and scores of others. County is center for such industries as sailboat construction, fiberglass products, glass containers, food processing, computers, construction both nationally and locally and even agriculture. One-fifth of U.S. strawberries produced here, cauliflower, oranges, and 90 percent of U.S. paprika. Tourism brought over 20 million people to county in 1973, conventions several million more.

Transportation: 4 major freeways in county which is center of what apparently will be San Diego-to-Santa Barbara megalopolis. Nation's 4th busiest airport.

Communications: 7 major TV stations, half a dozen minor ones, and more than 40 radio stations.

Convention facilities: Anaheim Convention Center, Disneyland Hotel convention center and Newporter Inn building expanded facilities.

Other attractions: Disneyland, 11 million in 1973 attendance; Knott's Berry Farm, 4.5 million, Movieland Wax Museum and Cars of Stars; Japanese Village; Lion Country Safari; air and car museums.

Cultural facilities: 2 major tax-supported universities, 4 private liberal arts colleges, multiple trade and special interest schools, 6 community colleges of more than 5,000 enrollment, and more than 50 high schools, symphony orchestra, 2 master chorales, light opera, one pro and 5 amateur ballet companies, 32 community theater groups, 6 performing art support groups, 4 major art museums, art associations.

Sports attractions: AL Angels, WFL California Sun and other pro teams in training, and heavy college, high school, amateur schedules.

Orlando, Florida

The World Almanac is sponsored in the Orlando area by the Sentinel Star, 633 N. Orange Ave., Orlando, Fla. 32802; phone (305) 423-4411; Sentinel and Evening Star founded as dailies in 1913; merged 1931; acquired by Tribune Co. of Chicago in 1965; combined to create "all-day" newspaper in 1973; circulation, 195,458 weekdays, 187,893 Saturday, 222,360 Sunday: editor-publisher William G. Conomos.

Population: 117,500 (city), 615,000 (metro); 271,800 employed (metro).

Area: 30.1 sq. mi. in East Central Florida; 52 lakes inside city limits; average temperature 72.1

Industry: center of citrus belt; insurance headquarters for Southeastern U.S., 7 home and 10 regional insurance company offices; Martin Marietta Co., aerospace division; 2 General Electric plants; Westinghouse Electric Co., minicomputer division; 12 industrial parks; 3d largest naval training center in U.S. and only one training women recruits, 5,338 personnel, over 30,000 recruits trained annually.

Commerce: 50 commercial banks; total deposits, $1.7 billion; 9 savings and loan assocs.; 23 major shopping centers; retail sales, $1.9 billion.

Transportation: 6 airlines serving jetport at McCoy, about 80 scheduled flights daily; Seaboard Coastline Railroad, Amtrak; 9 intercity bus lines, 195 common carrier truck lines and 7 freight forwarding services; every major Florida market less than 4 hours by highway.

Communications: 20 radio and 6 TV stations.

Medical facilities: 15 hospitals in metro area.

Cultural facilities: Florida Symphony Orchestra; Loch Haven Art Center, John Young Museum and Planetarium, Central Florida Civic Theater; 4 colleges and one junior college including Rollins and Florida Technological Univ.

Other attractions: Walt Disney World, 18 miles from downtown Orlando; Sea World, $17 million marine park on 125 acres; Circus World Preview Center; Church Street Station, $5 million renovated area in downtown Orlando.

Convention facilities: 26,299 rooms, 2,631 rooms under construction; 553 conventions in 1973 attended by 100,000 people; $500,000 tourist information center.

Sports: Tinker Field, site of spring training for Minnesota Twins; Tangerine Bowl Sports Week; Florida Blazers (WFL); 3 pro golf tournaments: $150,000 Florida Citrus Invitational in March, $150,000 Walt Disney World Tournament in Dec., $30,000 Lady Errol Classic in Nov.; Ben White Raceways, training ground for trotters; Seminole Turf Club, harness racing; Sanford-Orlando Kennel Club; Jai-Alai Fronton.

Ottawa, Ontario, Canada

Population: 303,000 (city), 602,510 (metro region including greater Ottawa and Hull, Que.); Canada's 5th largest city, linked with neighboring city of Hull (pop. 130,000) by bridge.

Area: 30,481 acres (city), 1,100 sq. mi. (region) on Ontario-Quebec border at the Chaudiere Falls on the Ottawa River.

Industry: major employer is the federal government; E.B. Eddy Co., producer of paper products, is the largest private employer.

Commerce: capital city of Canada with a large tourist business and developing convention capacity; some 57 hotels and motels offer more than 5,180 rooms for tourists and conventioneers.

Transportation: 45 miles of parkways and bicycle paths in and around the city; linked with the city of Hull in Quebec by 5 bridges; Canadian Pacific and Canadian National Railways; International Airport, nation's 5th busiest, more than 85 scheduled flights daily by 5 airlines and major operations by Canadian Armed Forces aircraft.

Cultural facilities: $45 million National Arts Centre with 2,300-seat opera house-concert hall, a theatre and an experimental studio; Ottawa Little Theatre.

National museums: National Gallery of Canada, Museum of Man, Museum of Natural Sciences, Museum of Science and Technology, Canadian War Museum, National Aeronautical Collection.

Other attractions: Gothic-style Parliament buildings, housing Canada's House of Commons and Senate; Peace Tower, memorial to Canada's war dead; Central Canada Exhibition, a 10-day summer fair at

Lansdowne Park; Winter Fair; more than 80 camping and trailer parks, 7 city beaches and mountain and lake recreation facilities.
Sports: Canadian Football League Ottawa Rough Riders and the Ottawa 67's, a junior hockey team, play in the new $9-million Civic Centre arena-stadium at Lansdowne Park.
History: founded 1827 as Bytown, incorporated as

Ottawa 1855; named after Outaouac (or Outaouais Indian tribe); became capital of Canada 1857; governed by regional chairman Denis Coolican and city mayor Pierre Benoit.
Further information: Canada's Capital Visitors and Convention Bureau, 251 Laurier Ave. West, Ottawa, Ont., K1P-5J6

Pensacola, Florida

The World Almanac is sponsored in the Pensacola area by the Pensacola News-Journal, 101 E. Romana St., Pensacola, Fla. 32501; (904) 433-0041; predecessor The Floridian founded 1821, first daily News 1899, Journal 1898; merged 1924; combined circulation daily 86,204, Sunday 71,612; member Gannett Group; publisher James H. Jesse, editor J. Earle Bowden.

Population: 60,700 (city), 284,395 (county), 450,000 (primary trade area).
Area: southern end of 759 sq. mi. Escambia County at westernmost edge of Florida Panhandle.
Industry: U.S. Navy employs 15,200 military, 5,000 civilian personnel; major manufacturers are Monsanto, St. Regis Paper, Armstrong Cork, Tenneco, Westinghouse, Air Products and Chemical, American Cyanamid, Vanity Fair; major industries are food and kindred products, lumber, printing and stone, clay, glass and concrete.
Commerce: wholesale, retail center for 4 counties in west Florida, one in Alabama; effective buying income $1.132 billion; retail sales (1971) $666.241 million; 16 banks, 3 savings and loan banks, 26 mortgage firms; tourist industry $60 million, and farm and forest income $18.33 million annually.

Transportation: 2 railways, 2 airlines, 2 bus lines, 16 truck lines; 3 U.S. highways, Interstate 10.
Communications: one TV, 8 radio stations.
Medical facilities: 4 hospitals in addition to the U.S. Naval Aviation Medical Center.
Cultural facilities: public library; 5 museums: Historical Museum, T. T. Wentworth Museum, Hispanic Museum, Transportation Museum, Museum of Naval Aviation; Little Theater; symphony orchestra; Art Association; Arts Council, Inc.; Oratorio Society.
Other attractions: historic forts, Pensacola Beach, Gulf Islands National Seashore, Seville Quarter.
Sports: Monsanto Open PGA tournament, Falstaff Classic Amateur Golf Classic, intercollegiate basketball.
History: colonized in 1559, failed; city founded in 1698, existing under 5 flags until ceded by Spain to U.S. in 1813.

Philadelphia, Pennsylvania

The World Almanac is sponsored in the Philadelphia area by The Philadelphia Inquirer, 400 N. Broad St., Philadelphia, Pa. 19101; phone (215) 854-2000; established 1829, lineage traced to Pennsylvania Packet, founded 1771; circulation 452,524 daily, 826,302 Sunday; published by Philadelphia Newspapers Inc.; president Frederick Chait; vice president and general manager Sam S. McKeel; executive editor Eugene L. Roberts Jr.; editor Creed C. Black; managing editors Gene Forman (news) and Will Jarrett (special projects); sponsors Delaware Valley Science Fair, Old Newsboys' Day, Book & Author Luncheons. PNI also publishes the Philadelphia Daily News, an afternoon tabloid, at same address; founded 1925; circulation 256,568; editor Rolfe Neill; managing editor David Lawrence; senior vice president Natt Getlin; sponsors annual Circus Party for disadvantaged children, Secret Witness rewards.

Population: 1,916,000 (4th in U.S.); 4,877,500 (metro: 5 counties in Pa., 3 in N.J.); employment 1,957,400 (metro).
Area: 130 sq. mi. (city); 3,575 sq. mi. (metro area); city located in southeastern Pa. on Delaware and Schuylkill rivers; 90 mi. from N.Y.C., 136 mi. from Wash., D.C., 60 mi. from Atlantic City.
Industry: diversified, with over 90% of all U.S. basic industries represented; major center for textiles and apparel, food processing, electrical machinery, petroleum (largest oil refining region on East Coast), instruments, transportation equipment, chemicals and pharmaceuticals; large companies headquartered in metro area include Campbell Soup, Leeds & Northrup, Scott Paper, SmithKline, Rohm & Haas, Sun Oil, Crown Cork & Seal, Pennwalt.
Commerce: retail sales (1973, metro), $11.3 billion; 15 commercial banks, over $4 billion total deposits; 4 savings banks, over $5 billion.
Transportation: largest fresh-water port in world (50 mi. of waterfront); scheduled sailings to over 200 ports in 100 countries; facilities for bulk and general cargo; 2 new marine terminals for containerized cargo; Penn Central, Reading and B & O provide RR freight service (first 2 and Amtrak also provide passenger service); over 200 truck lines, vast highway

network, 5 bridges in metro area for motor traffic between Pa. and N.J.; International Airport's $450 million passenger terminal expansion under way (7.8 million passengers in 1973); Cargo City, $50 million air freight facility, will be completed in 1975; area transit (operated by SEPTA) conveyed 277.5 million passengers on subway, el, bus and streetcar lines in 1973.
Communications: 3 major daily newspapers: Inquirer, Bulletin and News; 23 AM, 23 FM, 6 commercial TV stations; cable TV.
New construction: Market Street East, $500 million reconstruction of major retailing area; Franklin Town, privately financed $400 million redevelopment of 50-acre midcity site (will provide 4,000 residential units, employment for 20,000); 1818 Market Street, $50 million, 40-story office bldg.
Medical facilities: 117 hospitals, over 36,500 beds (metro area).
Federal facilities: Defense Industrial Supply Center; Defense Personnel Support Center; U.S. Naval Publications and Forms Center; naval base; U.S. Mint; Frankford Arsenal.
Cultural facilities: orchestra, Pa. Ballet, Lyric Opera Co., Grand Opera Co.; Acad. of Music; Museum of Art; Franklin Institute; Pa. Acad. of the Fine Arts;

Rodin Museum; Acad. of Natural Sciences; Barnes Fdtn.; Robin Hood Dell; Walnut Street Theater (oldest in America); Shubert, Forrest and New Locust theaters; many community and summer theaters.
Educational facilities: 54 colleges and universities within 25 mi. of City Hall; 6 medical schools in city; University City Science Center.
Recreational facilities: 4,100-acre Fairmount Park; smaller parks and playgrounds; swimming pools, golf courses, tennis courts and ice-skating rinks (public and private); easy access to mountains and seashore.
Convention facilities: Civic Center with 321,000 sq. ft. of air-conditioned exhibit space, 57 meeting rooms, including 12,500-seat Convention Hall, can accommodate 24,000 people.
Sports attractions: NL Phillies, NFL Eagles and Atoms soccer team at Veterans Stadium; NHL

Flyers, NBA 76ers, Freedoms tennis and Wings lacrosse teams at Spectrum; WFL Bell team at J. F. Kennedy Stadium (site of Army-Navy game); Penn Relays at Franklin Field.
Other attractions: City Hall; restored Society Hill area: Elfreth's Alley; zoo (nation's first); Longwood Gardens; Mummers Parade (Jan. 1); Freedom Week (June 27-July 4).
History: Wm. Penn founded his "Greene Countrie Towne" as Quaker colony in 1682; gave it name that means "City of Brotherly Love"; national capital 1790-1800; historical shrines include Independence Hall, Liberty Bell, Carpenters' Hall, Betsy Ross House, Gloria Dei Church, Christ Church, USS Olympia, Fort Mifflin.
Further information: City Representative, 1660 Municipal Services Bldg., Phila., Pa. 19107.

Phoenix, Arizona

The World Almanac is sponsored in the Phoenix area by The Phoenix Gazette, 120 East Van Buren Street, Phoenix, Arizona 85004; phone (602) 271-8000; founded Oct. 28, 1880 as Arizona Gazette by Charles H. McNeil; circulation 112,003; publisher Eugene C. Pulliam, managing editor Alan D. Moyer; sponsors Christmas Fund Drive, Music Memory Programs, Science Fair, Phoenix Suns Christmas Day Basketball Game, Family Symphony Concerts and other events.

Population: 743,000 (city), 1,256,000 (metro), capital and largest city in state, 32d in nation; total employed 483,200.
Area: 269.3 sq. mi. (city), 9,155 sq. mi. (metro), in south central Arizona.
Industry: electronic equipment manufacturers, Honeywell Information Systems and Motorola, Inc. each employ more than 2,500; aircraft and parts manufacturers, AiResearch, a division of The Garrett Corp., and Sperry Flight Systems each employ more than 2,500; other major employers are E. L. Gruber (apparel), Goodyear Aerospace, General Electric, Western Electric Cable, Reynolds Metals, Marathon Steel, Arizona Public Service, Salt River Project, Mountain Bell, Amerco, Greyhound, American Express, and Phoenix newspapers.
Commerce: wholesale-retail center for state; retail sales (1973) $3.6 billion; effective household buying income, $12,578; bank and S&L assets $8.7 billion; 11 banks with 196 area offices, 5 S&Ls with 60 offices in metro area.
Transportation: transportation center of the Southwest; Sky Harbor International Airport served by 10 airlines, 3,776,725 passengers (1973); 2 railroads; 2 transcontinental buslines; 10 transcontinental truck lines; 4 transcontinental heavy equipment haulers; 30 interstate and 39 intrastate truck lines.
Communications: 6 TV and 32 radio stations.
New construction: in 1973, 31,771 new residential building units were permitted; total value all types of

building permits: $814 million.
Medical facilities: Barrow Neurological Institute, one of nation's finest such facilities; 20 general care hospitals, Veterans' Hospital; other special service facilities.
Cultural facilities: art museum, public library, symphony orchestra, Indian museums, zoo, botanical gardens, community and professional theaters; Civic Plaza convention center; Grady Gammage Auditorium.
Educational facilities: Arizona State Univ. American Graduate School of International Management; 4 community colleges; Maricopa Technical College (vocational); 53 public and parochial high schools.
Sports attractions: 50 golf courses and $150,000 Phoenix Open; inland surfing beach; ice skating rinks; amusement park; pro hockey, basketball, baseball teams; auto racing, greyhound and horse racing; annual Fiesta Bowl (holiday football game).
Other attractions: Frank Lloyd Wright's Taliesin West; Paolo Soleri's Cosanti Foundation; Firebird Festival of the Arts; Dons' Club guided tours of Arizona; full calendar of events including state and county fairs and rodeos, horse shows, regattas, polo tournaments.
History: founded 1870, on site of ancient Indian settlement; the Hohokam tribe, which flourished ca. 500-1200 A.D., developed an intricate system of irrigations canals which form the base of the canal system in use today.

Pittsburgh, Pennsylvania

The World Almanac is sponsored in the Pittsburgh area by The Pittsburgh Press, 34 Blvd. of the Allies, Pittsburgh, Pa. 15222; phone (412) 263-1100; founded June 23, 1884, as Evening Penny Press by Thomas J. Keehan; circulation 293,011 daily, 711,304 Sunday; editor John Troan, business manager Barney G. Cameron, executive editor Leo Koeberlein, managing editor Ralph Brem; sponsors Press Old Newsboys Fund for Children's Hospital which raised $415,200 in 1973.

Population: 520,117 (city), 2,401,245 (4-county metro area), 2d in state and 24th in nation; metro area labor force of 997,300 is 6th in nation.
Area: 55.5 sq. mi. at juncture of Allegheny and Monongahela rivers which form Ohio River; Allegheny County seat; altitude, 702 feet.
Industry: one-fifth of nation's steelmaking capacity concentrated in metro area; Western Pennsylvania

mines produce 44 million tons of bituminous coal annually; 6,000 different products made in area; home of world's first full-scale nuclear power plant, world's largest manufacturers of aluminum, steel rolls, rolling mill machinery, air brakes, plate and window glass and safety equipment; 3d largest headquarters city in nation.
Commerce: retail sales (1972), $4.79 billion; exports

abroad totaled over $370 million (1973) while river tonnage totaled 66.8 million tons, more than any other inland area; average household effective buying income $12,666.

Transportation: 7 scheduled airlines handled 7,376,-449 passengers on 109,516 flights at International Airport (1973) where $250 million expansion is underway; 19 railroads; Continental Trailways and Greyhound Bus lines; over 400 common carriers; Port Authority Transit vehicles carried 91,753,819 passengers (1973) over 172 bus routes and 5 rail routes; 9 major highways serve city; rapid and mass transit plan under development.

Communications: 2 daily newspapers; 5 TV (including country's first educational station) and 27 radio stations.

Medical facilities: 21 hospitals include Univ. of Pittsburgh Health and Medical complex where Dr. Jonas Salk developed polio vaccine; Veterans Administration installation.

Federal facilities: Federal Building contains scores of U.S. government offices (information center: 412-644-3456); U.S. Army base at Oakdale; U.S. Air Force base.

Cultural facilities: Heinz Hall is home of the Opera Co., ballet, Civic Light Opera, Youth Symphony and symphony orchestra; 3 community and 2 legitimate theaters; Frick Art Museum; Carnegie Museum and Art Gallery, home of the triennial Carnegie International; American Wind Symphony.

Educational facilities: Univ. of Pittsburgh, Duquesne Univ.; Point Park, Chatham, Carlow, Robert Morris and La Roche Colleges, Carnegie-Mellon Univ., Community College of Allegheny County; 18 Carnegie public libraries, 3 bookmobiles, dozens of community libraries.

Sports: NL Pirates, NFL Steelers, NHL Penguins; World Team Tennis Triangles.

Other attractions: Highland Park Zoo, children's zoo, Twilight Zoo, aquarium, aviary, Buhl Planetarium, Allegheny Observatory, Phipps Conservatory, Fort Pitt Museum; 4 amusement parks; 2 operating passenger inclines; folk festival; Three Rivers Arts Festival every June; harness racing; river cruises; Civic Arena with retractable roof, 50,000-seat Three Rivers Stadium across river from Golden Triangle.

History: first hunters and trappers came through here in 1714; city itself dates from Nov. 25, 1758, when English forces under Brig. Gen. John Forbes occupied the ruins of Fort Duquesne, which French soldiers had buried and abandoned, and built a new and bigger fortress called Fort Pitt. By the time it was incorporated in 1816, it already had a reputation as a "Smoky City" from factories and coal-burning homes. Massive "Renaissance Plan" has cleared the skies and rebuilt the heart of the city during the past 25 years.

Further information: Chamber of Commerce, 411 Seventh Ave.; Convention and Visitors Bureau, 3001 Jenkins Arcade; both Pittsburgh, Pa. 15222.

Portland, Maine

The World Almanac is sponsored in the Portland area by the Maine Sunday Telegram, 390 Congress, Portland, Me., 04104; phone (207) 775-5811; published by Guy Gannett Publishing Co., founded 1921; circulation 111,703; president Jean Gannett Hawley; editor Ernest Chard; also publishes morning Press Herald, circulation 54,106, and Evening Express, 29,928.

Population: 66,500 (city), 163,488 (metro area), 1st in state; total employed, 26,959 (1970).

Area: 21.6 sq. mi.; peninsula on Casco Bay.

Industry: Atlantic Coast's 2d busiest oil shipping center, east terminus Montreal pipeline; fishing fleet base, seafood shipping center; landbased products: printed materials, clothing, metal, processed food, electronic parts, wooden goods.

Commerce: Tourist center, regional retail-wholesale hub, large shopping complex, 1,000 retail, 350 wholesale, 600 service enterprises; retail sales (1972), $247,156,000; median family income (1970), $8,456.

Transportation: municipal jetport, Delta airline; 3 rail freight lines, integrated bus system, Greyhound and Continental bus terminals, 25 truck lines; Maine Turnpike, Interstate 95 and 295 highways connect to all New England; deep water anchorage, auto cruise

ferries year round to Yarmouth, Nova Scotia.

Communications: 3 TV, 5 AM, 4 FM stations.

New construction: 2 hotels, 1 bank, housing.

Medical facilities: Medical center, 2 hospitals.

Cultural: symphony orch., Kotzschmar organ, one of world's largest; public, historical libraries; Victorian, art museums; Henry Longfellow home (1785); branch Univ. of Maine, Westbrook College, art, vocational and business schools; Portland Headlight, oldest lighthouse in country.

Recreation: 18-hole municipal golf course, 9 others in area; scenic cruises; swimming, tennis, fishing within easy travel, scenic parks.

Convention facilities: 2 large assembly halls, meeting rooms in modern hotels and motels. Tourist Bureau: 142 Free St.

Portland, Oregon

The World Almanac is sponsored in the Portland area by The Oregon Journal, 1320 SW Broadway, Portland, Ore. 97201; phone (503) 221-8275; founded Mar. 1902; circulation 129,913; editor Donald J. Sterling Jr.; managing editor Edward F. O'Meara.

Population: 385,600 (city), 1,059,300 (metro) in 1973; 1st in state; 30th in nation; total employed, 490,000.

Area: 80 sq. mi., at juncture of Columbia and Willamette rivers.

Industry: electrical and electronic industries along with lumber and wood products, food and paper; ranks first in manufacture of logging, lumbering equipment; home of Georgia-Pacific, Louisiana-Pacific (forest products), Tektronix (oscilloscopes), Omark (saw cutting chain), Hyster (lifts, hoists, lumber handling), White Stag, Pendleton, Jantzen (clothing).

Commerce: wholesale-retail center for large part of Oregon, SW Washington; retail sales metro area (1973), $2.78 billion. There are 16 banks, 11 savings and loan associations.

Transportation: 4 major rail freight lines, Amtrak, Greyhound, Trailways buses; 10th largest freshwater port in U.S., with 27-mile frontage, 29 marine berths; 11 million tons of cargo pass over docks annually; more than 1,000 ships visit annually, most active harbor in U.S.; hub for 9 airlines, flights to all parts of world.

Communications: 5 TV and 19 radio stations.

Medical facilities: 17 major hospitals, Univ. of Oregon Medical School, VA Hospital.

Cultural facilities: Art Museum, Oregon Symphony Orchestra, Opera Association, Oregon Historical Society, Portland State Univ., Univ. of Portland, and Lewis & Clark, Reed and Concordia Colleges.

Other attractions: annual Rose Festival, Rose Show; park system includes Washington Park, Hoyt Arboretum International Rose Test Garden, Portland Zoo.

Oregon Museum of Science and Industry; Forest Park is largest forest area in a U.S. city's limits; sports events and other attractions are presented in Memorial Coliseum.

History: chartered 1851 with population of 821; named after Portland, Me., rather than Boston, Mass., on flip of coin by 2 early citizens.

Further information: Chamber of Commerce, 824 SW 5th, Portland, Oregon 97204.

Providence, Rhode Island

The World Almanac is sponsored in the Providence area by The Providence Journal-Bulletin, 75 Fountain St., Providence, R.I. 02902; phone (401) 277-7000; Journal founded 1829, Bulletin 1863, Sunday Journal 1883; circulation, Journal (morn) 67,165, Bulletin (eve) 147,143, Sunday Journal 204,425; publisher John C. A. Watkins, president Michael P. Metcalf, v.p. and asst. publ. Edwin P. Young, v.p.-admin. Charles P. O'Donnell, v.p. and exec. editor Charles McC. Hauser.

Population: 173,300 (city), 877,600 (metro); total employed 115,866.

Area: 18.91 sq. mi., at the head of Narragansett Bay. Bay.

Industry: jewelry, silverware, plated ware, costume jewelry are largest industries; Textron is based in Providence; 1,245 manufacturing companies in the city.

Commerce: wholesale-retail center for entire state; retail sales $3.4 billion (metro); consumer spendable income per household $11,549 (metro); Allendale Insurance, world's largest mutual insurer of industrial firms, is based outside of city in Johnston; home of Narragansett Capital, largest small business investment company in nation; 2 savings and loan assns., 2 mutual savings banks, one cooperative bank, 6 commercial banks.

Transportation: Penn Central Railroad, fast "Turbo-Liner" passenger service between Boston, Providence and N.Y.; 5 bus lines; 45 locally-based common carriers and contract truckers; 9 major highways link Providence to every corner of R.I.; 6 major airgines out of T.F. Green Airport in Warwick (15 min. away); port is 3d largest in New England with 27 wharves and docks, 10.5 miles of commercial waterfront on the bay.

Communications: 3 TV and 8 radio stations.

Medical facilities: 7 hospitals; one VA hospital.

Cultural facilities: Trinity Square Repertory Co., R. I. Philharmonic, R. I. School of Design Museum.

Education: Brown University, founded 1764, is 7th oldest college in nation; 7-year M.D. program inaugurated 1973; Providence and R. I. Colleges and R.I. School of Design.

Recreational: one of America's most attractive recreational areas centers around Providence: 69 salt water beaches, 25 fresh water beaches, 49 golf and country clubs, 4 ski areas, 26 yacht clubs, 23 parks, all within 45 minutes of city.

Convention facilities: R.I. Civic Center (seats 12,000).

Sports: America's Cup races held since 1930; Newport-Bermuda race starts at Newport every other year; home of R. I. Reds (hockey) and R. I. Oceaneers (soccer).

Other attractions: largest collection of original early American homes of any city; located along Benefit St., they have been preserved by the Providence Preservation Society.

History: founded 1636 by Roger Williams; incorporated 1832; official state name is "Rhode Island and Providence Plantations."

Further information: Chamber of Commerce, 10 Dorrance St. or R. I. Tourist/Travel Assn., Turks Head Bldg.; both Providence, R. I. 02903.

Quebec City, Quebec, Canada

Population: 186,088 (city), 480,500 (metro); oldest city in Canada (1608) and the capital city of the Province of Quebec.

Area: 30 sq. mi.; natural citadel on north shore of St. Lawrence River at confluence with St. Charles River; 400 miles from Gulf of St. Lawrence; 167 miles east of Montreal; older part is built on a cliff 360 ft. above the St. Lawrence.

Industry: some 300 industrial firms, ranging from primary industry products to a variety of consumer products, employ over 16,000 people; food and beverage, leather footwear and leather products, textiles, apparel, wood products, pulp and paper, printing and publishing, iron and steel products, non-ferrous metal and chemical products.

Commerce: Quebec harbor, one of the busiest seaports of Canada, accommodates the largest oceangoing vessels with year-round facilities, an important container terminal on the North Atlantic coast; Provincial Government, with more than 15,000 employees, is the largest single employer and consumer in the city.

Transportation: Canadian Pacific and Canadian National Railroads; Air Canada, Quebecair, Nordair;

major bus center.

Communications: 3 TV stations (2 French, 1 bilingual); 5 radio stations (4 French, 1 English).

Medical facilities: 5 large general hospitals, many smaller ones.

Cultural facilities: historic character, cultural appeal and natural beauty make tourism important area of economic activity; annual "Carnaval" in Feb. is internationally known; annual summer Festival (July) changes the city into an open theater for numerous artistic events; Expo-Quebec, an annual provincial exhibition (industrial, commercial and agricultural), draws over 500,000 people a year.

Educational facilities: Laval University, the first in North America; Quebec University; 3 colleges for general and vocational training, numerous private schools.

Other attractions: only walled city in North America with fortifications standing today as they were 125 years ago; the Citadel, built from 1823-1832, contains within its walls 25 buildings, including the summer residence of Governor-General of Canada, Parliament buildings (1886), Quebec Museum, Battlefield Park, Ursulines Museum, Seminary (1663), Talon cellars, Notre Dame des Victoires Church and Tresor Street.

History: founded 1608 by French explorer Samuel de Champlain; cradle of French civilization in America; once the key to the interior of the North American Continent.

Raleigh, North Carolina

The World Almanac is sponsored in eastern North Carolina by The News & Observer and The Raleigh Times, 215 S. McDowell St., Raleigh, NC 27601, (919) 832-4411; circulation N&O (morn) 135,954, Times (eve) 32,955, N&O Sunday 160,231; publisher Frank Daniels Jr., editorial director Claude Sitton, editor Times A. C. Snow, managing editor N&O Bob Brooks, Times Mike Yopp.

Population: 143,000 (city), 275,000 (county), 500,000 (metro area); 4th in state; 200,000 employed (metro area).

Area: 45 sq. mi. in geographical center of state where piedmont joins coastal plain; alt. 363 ft.; state capital and Wake Co. seat.

Industry: major industry is government, employing 25% of workforce; also electrical machinery, foods and textiles.

Commerce: financial, retail center of eastern N.C.; retail sales (1973) $928.7 million; 12 banks with $29.4 billion debits; income average per household $15,000, per capita (1972) $4,354.

Education: 6 colleges; N.C. State Univ. largest, with Univ. of N.C. (Chapel Hill) and Duke Univ. (Durham) within 30 mi. form Research Triangle; 5,000 acre Triangle Park employs 10,000 in drug, fiber, biomedical and engineering research.

Transportation: 3 rail and 3 bus lines; airport has 4 airlines and 46 flights daily.

Communications: 4 TV and 13 radio stations.

New construction: $85,219,763 (1972).

Medical facilities: 3 hospitals, 818 beds; major mental hospital, 2,765 beds; 350 doctors.

Convention facilities: 30 motels, 4,000 rooms.

Cultural facilities: 3 museums, state fairgrounds; Dorton Arena seats 9,111, Memorial Auditorium 3,000 and Reynolds Coliseum 12,000.

Recreation: 4,200-acre Umstead Park; Carter Stadium seats 43,000; 100 city parks.

Sports: one pro golf meet; college sports popular.

History: founded 1792; Andrew Johnson birthplace.

Further information: Chamber of Commerce, 411 S. Salisbury St., Raleigh, NC 27601.

Regina, Saskatchewan, Canada

The World Almanac is sponsored in southern Saskatchewan by The Leader-Post, 1964 Park St., Regina, Sask., phone (306) 527-8511; founded 1885 by Nicholas Flood Davin; circulation 67,210; president Michael Sifton, Toronto; executive vice-president Max Macdonald; editor W. Ivor Williams; managing editor C.E.W. Bell; business manager William Duffus; advertising manager George Crawford; MacLaren Trophy for editorial page reproduction excellence.

Population: 145,600, first in province, 17th in nation; labor force, 57,600.

Area: 30.98 sq. mi., 100 miles north of Canada-U.S. border; provincial capital.

Industry: over 250 manufacturing industries; gross production value (1973) $221,155,000, 36% of Saskatchewan total.

Commerce: service center for oil, potash, grain production area; retail sales (1973) $629,785,000, 23.01% of province.

Transportation: 2 rail lines, 2 airlines, 3 bus lines and 80 trucking companies; main Trans-Canada highway bisects; city-run transit system, including Telebus, hybrid system with demand response taxi service and multiple request of mass transit, provides to-and-from service to user's home.

Communications: 2 TV and 5 radio stations.

Medical facilities: 3 major hospitals, 1,483 beds.

Cultural facilities: Saskatchewan Centre of Arts, multi-purpose theater-convention center with: Jubilee theater (seats 450) stage, ballroom, reception hall and dining room; Centennial theater (seats 2,029); Hanbidge Hall convention area, 12,200 square feet, 9 meeting rooms, seats 1,600, serves 1,200. Regina Symphony; Globe Repertory; Museum Natural History; Norman Mackenzie Art Gallery; RCMP Museum.

Educational facilities: Regina Campus, University of Saskatchewan; 13 collegiates; 76 elementary; Saskatchewan Institute of Applied Arts and Science.

Recreation facilities: Saskatchewan Roughriders (Canadian pro football); 96 parks and playgrounds; 9 golf courses; 5 swimming pools; indoor ice rinks.

Other attractions: Wascana Centre, 2,000-acre development, with man-made lake, public buildings, parks, recreation in heart of city.

History: founded 1882, and since that time headquarters for RCMP training depot.

Further information: Regina Chamber of Commerce 2145 Albert Street, Regina, Saskatchewan.

Reno, Nevada

The World Almanac is sponsored in the northern Nevada area by the Nevada State Journal and the Reno Evening Gazette, 401 West 2nd St., Reno, Nev. 89504; phone (702) 786-8989; Journal founded 1870; Gazette 1876; combined daily circulation 48,984, Sunday 38,873; publisher Richard J. Schuster, executive editor Warren L. Lerude.

Population: 72,863 (city), 121,064 (county) in 1970; annual growth rate estimated at 10% for 1973 pop. of 95,880 (city), 134,300 (county); 2d largest in state; 1973 labor force, 74,200.

Area: 36.07 sq. mi. (including Stead annexation), in northwestern part of state at the eastern foot of the Sierra Nevada; Washoe County seat.

Industry: gross gaming revenue for county, $141.4 million (1973) netted state taxes of $11.8 million; 94,-456 delegates attended 337 conventions, staying in 11,000 rooms, paying $1.8 million in room taxes; Warehousing continues to grow because of Nevada's

liberal free port law; marriages (34,788) outnumbered divorces (3,211).
Commerce: taxable sales in metro area (including Sparks) for Jan.-Oct., 1973, $535.6 million; assessed valuation (city) $381 million; median household income $9,492; bank resources, $1.6 billion.
Transportation: 12 motor freight lines, 3 freight railroads, Amtrak, and 3 commercial airlines; airport handled 910,00 passengers as international port of entry; U.S. 395 and Interstate 80.
New construction: 1,769 building permits (1973) valued at $79 million.
Communications: 3 TV, 10 radio stations; one CTV.
Medical facilities: 3 hospitals, including VA.
Educational facilities: Univ. of Nevada, Reno, 8,321 enrollment; Community college; public school enrollment, 30,700, parochial, 1,209.
Sports: semi-pro Aces hockey, Silver Sox baseball.
Cultural facilities: 1,428 seat Pioneer Theater Auditorium and 8,000 seat Centennial Coliseum. Fleischman Atmospherium Planetarium and 180,000-volume library; national annual air races and rodeo and parade; little theater.
Recreation: 21 ski resorts within a 2-hour drive;Lake Tahoe and Pyramid Lake offer fishing, boating and sun-bathing; medium game hunting.
History: established 1868 with public auction of land by Central Pacific RR; named after Civil War hero Gen. Jesse L. Reno.
Further information: Chamber of Commerce, P.O. Box 3499, Reno, Nev., 89505.

Richmond, Virginia

The World Almanac is sponsored in the Richmond area by the Richmond Times-Dispatch and News Leader, 333 E. Grace St., Richmond, Va. 23213; (804) 649-6000; Times-Dispatch founded 1950 by James A. Cowardin, circulation 132,010 daily, 192,632 Sunday; News Leader founded 1896 by Joseph Bryan, circulation 112,881; publisher D. Tennant Bryan; president Alan S. Donnahoe, executive editor John E. Leard, Times-Dispatch managing editor Alf Goodykoontz, News leader managing editor J. A. Finch.

Population: 249,621 (city), 518,319 (metro area), total employed (non-agricultural) 263,500.
Area: 62.5 sq. mi. (city), located at fall line of James River, 90 miles from Atlantic Ocean.
Industry: tobacco, with 10,900 workers, and 9,200 in chemicals are leaders in employment; Philip Morris cigarette plant nearing completion will be world's largest; printing, publishing, manufacture of paper and allied products and food.
Commerce: wholesale-retail center for central Virginia; retail sales $1.6 billion, per capita income $4,684, family $10,777, total income $2.54 bilion.
Transportation: 4 major railroads, 5 intercity bus lines, 3 commercial air lines, one commuter air line, 50 motor truck lines; 3 interstate, 6 U. S. and 9 state highways; deepwater terminal accessible to ocean-going ships.
Communications: 4 TV, 16 radio stations.
Medical facilities: Medical College of Virginia known worldwide for heart and kidney transplants, medical research; 21 other hospitals, including McGuire VA Hospital.
Federal facilities: Defense General Supply Center, Fifth Federal Reserve Bank, U. S. Fourth Circuit Court, Ft. Lee (Quartermaster Corps).
Cultural Facilities: Va. Museum and Theater with professional artists make city a center for dramatic, other performing arts; variety of other drama group; symphony orchestra.
Educational facilities: Virginia Commonwealth Univ. has state's largest enrollment; Univ. of Richmond, Virginia Union Univ., Union Theological Seminary (Presbyterian), Randolph-Macon College.
Recreational facilities: 12,000-seat Coliseum for athletic, entertainment events; city-owned Mosque auditorium, Parker Field, City Stadium, numerous parks.
Convention facilities: large downtown hotels near Mosque and Coliseum.
Sports attractions: Braves (IL baseball), Robins (hockey), national ranked track and tennis events; Russian-American indoor track meets 1972, 1973 and scheduled for 1975.
Other attractions: St. John's Church, scene of Patrick Henry's "Liberty or Death" speech; Virginia Capitol, designed by Thomas Jefferson; White House of the Confederacy; Civil War battlefields.
History: exploration here in 1607 by Capt. John Smith, first settlement 1609, incorporated as town 1742, made Va. capital 1780, Confederate Capital 1861-65; burned 1781 by Benedict Arnold, and 1865 when cotton, tobacco stockpiles fire set by fleeing Confederates spread to city; damaged by floods 1771, 1969, 1972.
Further information: Chamber of Commerce, 201 E. Franklin St., Richmond, Va. 23219.

Roanoke, Virginia

The World Almanac is sponsored in the Roanoke area by The Roanoke Times and The World-News, 201-203 Campbell Avenue, Roanoke, Va. 24010, telephone (703) 981-3000; Times founded 1886, World-News founded 1889; Lee C. Kitchin, president; Barton W. Morris Jr., publisher; circulation combined daily, 119,427; Sunday 113,452.

Population: 92,115 (city), 212,300 (metro area), 4th largest metro area in Virginia; over 97,000 employed.
Area: located at mouth of Shenandoah Valley.
Industry: center of furniture industry; distribution center for 2 grocery chains; General Electric, Eaton Corp., ITT, Johnson-Carper Division of Singer Co., and regional headquarters for All-State and Atlantic life insurance.
Commerce: retail center for 20 counties and parts of W. Virginia and North Carolina: retail sales per household tops U.S. southeastern region.
Transportation: 2 airlines, Piedmont and Eastern; Trailways and Greyhound bus companies; 12 major trucking firms; connected to I-81 by spur I-581; Norfolk & Western home.
Communications: 3 TV and 14 radio stations.
Medical facilities: 5 major hospitals and large VA facility; new psychiatric hospital construction started in 1973.
Cultural facilities: symphony orchestra, children's zoo and Transportation Museum; Roanoke Virginia Western and National Business and Hollins colleges. Barn Theatre and Theatre-in-the-Round; Civic Center and Auditorium.

Other attractions: Smith Mountain Lake and Claytor Lake State Park; Peaks of Otter; Blue Ridge Parkway.
Sports: Professional hockey and baseball.
History: first known as Big Lick, became Roanoke (Indian word for shell money) in 1882 with building of Shenandoah Valley Railroad to link with Norfolk & Western Railway.
Further information: Chamber of Commerce, 14 Kirk Ave., W., Roanoke, Va. 24010.

Rochester, New York

The World Almanac is sponsored in the Rochester area by Gannett Rochester Newspapers, 55 Exchange St., Rochester, N. Y. 14614; phone (716) 232-7100; circulation, Democrat and Chronicle (morn) 137,887; Times-Union (eve), 142,661; Democrat and Chronicle, (Sun.) 230,713; publisher Eugene C. Dorsey; executive editor Stuart Dunham; director of advertising Cortland Peterson; 2 Times-Union reporters awarded a 1972 Pulitzer Prize.

Population: 295,011 (1970 adj.); 5-county metro area 990,400 (1973 est.); 420,900 employed; unemployment 3.8%.
Area: 675 sq. mi. (Monroe County) straddling Genesee River, on Lake Ontario; 2,966 sq. mi. (metro).
Industry: World leader in production of photographic, optical and scientific instruments, with Eastman Kodak (46,000 employees), Xerox (15,000) and Bausch & Lomb (5,100), all founded in Rochester, the most prominent; other fields include machinery, food products, apparel, printing and publishing; industrial wage increase, 41% since 1969.
Commerce: retail sales (1973 est.) over $2 billion; 19 commercial and savings banks, with assets of $5.8 billion; 1973 median household income (Monroe County) $12,423, (metro area), $10,242, 16th in nation.
Transportation: Monroe County Airport, with 3 major airlines and several freight companies; rail freight service by 4 lines, Amtrak; port of Rochester; over 75 motor freight firms.
Communications: 4 TV and 15 radio stations.
Medical facilities: one of the nation's most advanced health care centers: 8 general hospitals, including Strong Memorial Hospital.
Cultural facilities: Eastman Theater, part of Univ. of Eastman School of Music, and home of the Philharmonic Orchestra: Memorial Art Gallery; Museum and Science Center, including Strasenburgh Planetarium; George Eastman House of Photography; 3 resident theatre companies.
Educational facilities: 8 private and 2 public 4-year colleges; 3 community colleges.
Recreational facilities: Finger Lakes area, with 13 parks, summer and winter sports, golf, tennis, bowling; 16-park Monroe County system, including Seneca Park Zoo and Highland Park, with Lilac Festival (May).
Sports: International League Red Wings, top Baltimore Orioles farm team; AHL Amerks, North American Soccer League Lancers, National Lacrosse League Griffins; thoroughbred racing and Finger Lakes Race Track. (Canandaigua).
Further information: Chamber of Commerce, 55 St. Paul St., Rochester, N. Y. 14604; or Convention and Publicity Bureau, 100 Exchange St., Rochester, N. Y. 14614.

Sacramento, California

The World Almanac is sponsored in the Sacramento area by The Sacramento Bee, 21st & Q, Sacramento, CA. 95816; telephone (916) 442-5011; founded 1857; circulation daily 185,850, Sunday 222,172; president Eleanor McClatchy, editor Walter Jones, managing editor Martin Smith.

Population: 263,800 (city), 682,100 (county) 875,100 (metro); total employed, (metro) 335,100.
Area: 94 sq. mi. (city), 997 sq. mi. (county) in Sacramento Valley, 85 mi. northeast of San Francisco.
Industry: 475 manufacturing plants including Campbell Soup, Procter and Gamble, Libby McNeil and Libby, California Almond Growers Exchange, Del Monte, Teichert Construction and Aerojet-General.
Commerce: state capital; wholesale-retail center for large area of Sacramento Valley; retail sales, (1973) $1.8 billion; bank debits, $7.1 billion (city).
Transportation: new metropolitan airport; $55-million Port of Sacramento gives access to the Pacific; 2 mainline transcontinental rail carriers; junction 4 major highways.
Communications: 5 TV and 17 radio stations.
New construction: downtown Mall in final stages of redevelopment; Old Sacramento being restored as state and federal historical project; Rancho Seco Atomic Power Plant; regional sewage treatment plant; 2 new major hotels.
Medical facilities: 11 major hospitals, Univ. of California Medical School in nearby Davis.
Federal Facilities: 2 large Air Force bases, Army depot, many regional federal offices.
Cultural facilities: $20 million Convention Center complex opened June 1974; symphony orchestra, ballet; Civic Theater; Crocker Art Gallery; California State Univ., Sacramento; McGeorge College of Law; Lincoln Univ. Law School and 3 community colleges.
Other attractions: zoo, many public parks and play grounds, 14 public and 4 private golf courses, Sutter's Fort, State Capitol, Stanford Home, Pony Express Terminal, Fairytale Town and Governor's Mansion; fishing, hunting, boating, camping, hiking and skiing in nearby high Sierras; annual State Fair at Cal Expo.
History: founded by John Augustus Sutter in 1839; James Marshall discovered gold at Sutter's Mill, in 1848. 35 miles northeast, gateway to Mother Lode Country; Pony Express and Central Pacific Railroad which crossed the Sierra Nevada were part of early history.

St. Louis, Missouri

The World Almanac is sponsored in the St. Louis area by the Post-Dispatch, 900 N. 12th Blvd., 63101; phone (314) 621-1111; founded Dec. 12, 1878, by Joseph Pulitzer; circulation, 307,098 daily, 500,594 Sunday; editor and publisher Joseph Pulitzer Jr., managing editor Evarts A. Graham Jr., general manager Alex T. Primm, director of promotion and public affairs William J. Isam; major awards include 5 Pulitzer Prizes to the newspaper and 11 to staff members.

Population: 581,000 (city), 991,000 (county), 2,454,000 (metro), 10th in nation payroll employment 981,500.
Area: 4,935 sq. mi. (metro) just south of confluence of Missouri and Mississippi rivers.
Industry: 2d to Detroit in auto assembly with Ford, GM and Chrysler plants; McDonnell Douglas headquarters, air and spacecraft manufacturer; other headquarters include nation's largest shoemaker, Interco; Anheuser-Busch, world's largest brewer; Monsanto, General Dynamics, Ralston-Purina, Pet Inc., Emerson Electric, Granite City Steel, and Peabody Coal; grain market with 48.5 million bushel annual yield; 3,200 manufacturing concerns employing 250,700 persons.
Commerce: $5.3 billion retail sales (est. 1974, metro); $12,055 median family income; 165 banking institutions, total deposits $6.67 billion.
Transportation: 10 major airlines with 5.8 million passenger movements (1973); 2d largest railroad center in the nation, 17 railroads; largest inland Mississippi River port; 8 major highways; 14 motorbus lines; 350 freight lines.
Communications: 6 TV and 18 radio stations.
New construction: industrial and commercial contracts totaled $341.5 million (1973); residential, $366.7 million; work begun on Mercantile Center, a $150 million office, store and hotel complex.
Medical facilities: 57 hospitals with 16,652 beds; Washington Univ. and St. Louis Univ. medical schools and affiliated hospitals provide specialized treatment in many areas.
Federal facilities: Military Personnel Records Center, Defense Mapping Agency Aerospace Center, Granite City Army base, Scott Air Force Base.
Cultural facilities: Art Museum; Museum of Science and Natural History; restored historic homes; symphony orchestra; Mississippi River Festival near Edwardsville in summer; Municipal Theatre (Muny Opera) offers Broadway shows in one of nation's largest outdoor theaters in Forest Park.
Educational facilities: 4 major universities: Washington, St. Louis, Univ. of Missouri at St. Louis and Southern Illinois Univ. at Edwardsville; private colleges; 3-branch junior college system; numerous preparatory, vocational and theological schools.
Recreational facilities: Jefferson National Expansion Memorial with 630-foot Gateway Arch on the riverfront; 1,326-acre Forest Park with 3 golf courses, ball fields, floral displays, the McDonnell Planetarium and Zoo; National Museum of Transportation; Six Flags Over Mid-America; Grant's Farm with President Grant's cabin and animal displays; Missouri Botanical Gardens with advanced research-display greenhouse, the Climatron.
Convention facilities: 12,000 hotel rooms; largest exhibit space is 90,000 sq. ft. in Kiel Auditorium which seats 10,500; work begun on $25 million convention center for city.
Sports attractions: 54,000-seat Busch Stadium home of St. Louis Cardinals baseball and football teams and Soccer Stars; St. Louis Blues (NHL) play in the arena.
Other attractions: climate has 4 distinct seasons; spring and autumn warm, winters mild, summers hot with 90-degree temperatures on 40 days; average temperature is 54.1 degrees; average precipitation 36.6 inches. Downtown area contains significant architecture such as Eads Bridge, Old Post Office, Old Courthouse, Old Cathedral, Spanish Pavilion and Louis Sullivan's Wainwright Building.
History: named for French King Louis IX by fur trapper Pierre Laclede whose trading post became major fur market and gateway to the West; starting point of Lewis and Clark's expedition and other explorations.
Further information: Convention and Tourist Board, 911 Locust St., or Commerce and Growth Assoc., 10 South Broadway.

St. Paul, Minnesota

The World Almanac is sponsored in the St. Paul area by the St. Paul Dispatch and Pioneer Press, 55 E. 4th St., St. Paul Minn. 55101; phone (612) 222-5011; founded 1849 as Minnesota Pioneer by James Goodhue; circulation, Pioneer Press (morn) 108,481, Dispatch (eve) 127,882, Sunday Pioneer Press 241, 868; Bernard H. Ridder, Sr., chairman of the board emeritus, and Bernard H. Ridder Jr., president, Ridder Pub. Inc.; publisher Thomas L. Carlin, executive editor John R. Finnegan, editor William G. Sumner.

Population: 310,600 (city); 1,999,200 (metro), 2d in state, 46th in nation; total employed (city) 200,468.
Area: 55 sq. mi. in eastern Minnesota on banks of Mississippi River close to Minnesota and Wisconsin vacation lands.
Industry: 4th in printing and publishing, 5th in cosmetics, 4th in electronics; Union Stock Yards is 2d largest livestock center in nation, 3,561,626 head.
Commerce: retail sales (1972) $4.199 billion (metro); median household income, $10,153; 25 banks and 6 savings and loan associations.
Transportation: 5 major and 2 regional rail lines, Amtrak; 21 intercity truck firms, 37 terminals; 3 interstate bus lines; 730-mile public transit system; metropolitan airport, hub of 8 commercial airlines, headquarters for Northwest and North Central airlines, averages 824 air movements per day; Downtown Airport; 60 firms operate barges on Mississippi River, using a 9-foot channel downtown.
Communications: 4 commercial TV and 2 educational stations; 29 radio stations.
Medical facilities: 12 private hospitals; a 611 bed community hospital and research center: Ramsey Hospital.
Cultural facilities: Minnesota Symphony Orchestra; Univ. of Minnesota Institute of Agriculture, Hamline Univ., Colleges of St. Thomas and St. Catherine, and Bethel, Concordia, and Macalester Colleges and William Mitchell College of Law; $66 million city school system with 74 public schools and 61 private schools.
New construction: building permits of $100,000 and over totalled $85,126,935 in 8-month period.
Recreation facilities: more than 900 lakes in metro area, 438 tennis courts, 148 swimming beaches, 513 parks, 50 golf courses, 27 ski centers; 52 neighborhood recreation centers, 35 miles of parkways, 100 miles of hiking and biking trails.
Convention facilities: Civic Center complex with 101,000 sq. ft. exhibit space, total seating for 35,000 in 4 main buildings, 15 meeting halls; 50 hotels and motels, 2,500 rooms.
Other attractions: Winter Carnival, Minnesota State Fair, Como Park Zoo and Conservatory; onyx statue of Indian God of Peace in City Hall, State Capitol, Minnesota Historical Society Museums, Arts & Science Center, Fort Snelling State Park.
History: once called "Pig's Eye" for first settler, Pierre "Pig's Eye" Parrant; changed to St. Paul when Father Lucien Galtier built St. Paul's Chapel 1841; became town 1847, city 1854.

St. Petersburg, Florida

The World Almanac is sponsored in Florida Suncoast area by The St. Petersburg Times and Evening Independent, 490 1st Ave. S., St. Petersburg, Fla., 33701; phone (813) 893-8111; Times founded 1884, Independent 1906; circulation, Times (morn) 186,155; Independent 30,904; Sunday Times 227,690; chairman of the board Nelson Poynter, editor and president Eugene Patterson, Independent editor Robert Stiff, Times managing editor Robert Haiman, publisher John B. Lake.

Population: 267,000 (city), 641,400 (Pinellas County), 1,318,800 (metro); Pinellas County 1974 employment 234,200; unemployment 2.8%.

Area: 58 sq. mi., midway on Florida's West Coast between Tampa Bay and Gulf of Mexico; over 100 mi. of shoreline.

Industry and commerce: tourism, over 3½ million visited county in 1973, spending over $1 billion; industries include General Electric, Honeywell, Sperry, Milton Roy Co., Jim Walter Research, Allstate Insurance Fla. regional office, U.S. Homes hq.; county retail sales (1973) over $2 billion.

Transportation: U.S. 19, 41 and 98 link city to rest of Gulf Coast Florida; Interstates 275, 75 and 4 link St. Petersburg with Tampa, Orlando and east coast; $100-million Tampa International Airport 25 minutes from downtown St. Petersburg; other airports are St. Petersburg-Clearwater International and Albert Whitted; Amtrak, Seaboard Coast Line railroads; Greyhound and Trailways.

Communications: 6 TV and 46 radio stations.

Convention facilities: Over 52,000 units can house 160,000 visitors; Bayfront Center seats 9,400 in arena, 2,200 in auditorium.

New construction: St. Petersburg-Tampa metro area 3d in U.S. housing starts (1973).

Medical facilities: 7 major hospitals; Bay Pines complex; All Children's Hospital.

Cultural facilities: Museum of Fine Arts, Gulf Coast Symphony, Historical Museum, amateur theatres, Eckerd College Free Institutions Forums, varied musical, dancing and theatrical events at Bayfront Center Complex.

Educational facilities: University of South Florida Bay Campus, Stetson College of Law, Eckerd College, St. Petersburg Jr. College.

Recreational facilities: 76 parks on 1,800 acres of land, many with recreation centers, pools, tennis courts, boating facilities and picnic grounds; municipal marina; deep sea fishing, golf courses, baseball fields.

Sports attractions: Cardinals and Mets spring training; spectator sports include greyhound racing, baseball, jai alai, horse racing, basketball, NFL football, pro tennis, boat racing.

Salt Lake City, Utah

The World Almanac is sponsored in the Salt Lake City area by the Salt Lake Tribune, 143 S. Main St., Salt Lake City, Utah 84110; phone (801) 524-4545; founded Apr. 15, 1871; cir. 108,619 daily, 182,657 Sunday; publisher, John W. Gallivan; executive editor, Arthur C. Deck; 1957 Pulitzer Prize; civic projects: statewide civic beautification awards, Sub for Santa program, Community Christmas Tree, Intermountain Organ Bank, Organ Donor program.

Population: (1973 est.) 175,885 (city); 490,000 (county); 758,000 (metro); 1st in state, 50th in nation; 52% of state pop. lives within 30 miles; state capital and Salt Lake County seat.

Area: nestled in a vast valley (elev. 4,327 ft.) surrounded by Wasatch and Oquirrh Mountains.

Industry: labor force, 217,270; effective buying income, $2.6 billion (1973), per family income, $11,662; 55% of state construction in county; total construction value, $202 million (1973, record high); major employers are Hill Air Force Base (30 miles north), local defense industries, and Kennecott Copper; metro area becoming major center for electronics, apparel manufacturing; mining, smelting, refining, distribution, warehousing center of West.

Commerce: trade center of Mountain West; retail sales $1,595,623 (1973).

Transportation: 6 air lines, customs office, International Airport; geographic center of 11 Western states; hub of central transcontinental highway system; 3 railroads, all major western truck, bus lines.

Communications: 2 daily newspapers; 3 commercial and 2 public TV, 18 radio stations.

New construction: Downtown ZCMI Mall, $38 million, 70 shops, 27-story office bldg., completion 1975; $40 million Fashion Place Mall.

Medical facilities: 10 hospitals, including Univ. of Utah Medical Center, major research in transplant surgery.

Cultural facilities: Utah Symphony Orchestra among 12 best in U.S.; Mormon Tabernacle Choir, Ballet West, Repertory Dance Theatre.

Other Attractions: Temple Square, home of 3,500,000-member Church of Jesus Christ of Latter Day Saints; 14,000-seat Salt Palace Civic Auditorium; 700 acres in 22 parks, 25 playgrounds, 10 golf courses, 75 tennis courts; near Great Salt Lake (7 times more salty than ocean); Pioneer Village, Hogle Zoological Gardens, Kennecott Copper's Bingham Mine.

Sports: 9 major ski resorts; Utah Stars (ABA), Golden Eagles (Western Hockey League), Salt Lake Angels (AAA baseball); Bonneville Salt Flats.

History: founded July 24, 1847, by Brigham Young and contingent of pioneers.

Education: Univ. of Utah, Westminster College.

Other: 4 well-defined seasons, mean annual temperature is 50.9°F.

Further Information: Chamber of Commerce, 19 E. 2nd So.; Utah Travel Council, Council Hall, Salt Lake City, Utah.

San Antonio, Texas

The World Almanac is sponsored in the San Antonio area by the S. A. Express (morning) and S. A. News (evening), P. O. Box 2171, San Antonio, Tex., 78297; tel (512) 225-7411; circulation daily, Express 84,301, News 63,569, Sunday Express-News 142,345; chairman K. Rupert Murdoch, publisher and editor Charles O. Kilpatrick; Express-News Corp. is a division of News America, Inc.

Population: 763,720 city; 937,000 metro area. Total employed, 335,800.
Area: Bexar County, 1,247 sq. mi., 2½ hours from Gulf Coast and Mexican border.
Industry: 5 military bases include Kelly AFB, largest employer; fast-growing medical industry; diverse manufacturing, tourism, construction, trade and service industries.
Commerce: center for 50-county retail trade area, truck crops, livestock production; retail sales (1973), $2.3 billion.
Federal facilities: Kelly AFB, hq. AF Air Security Service; Randolph AFB, hq. AF Air Training Command & AF Personnel Center; Brooks AFB, hq. AF Aerospace Medical Division; Lackland AFB with Wilford Hall USAF Medical Center; Fort Sam Houston, hq. Fifth Army & Army Health Services Command, Brooke Army Medical Center.
Medical facilities: University of Texas Medical, Dental, Nursing Schools; Audie Murphy VA Hospital; Southwest Research Institute; Southwest Foundation of Research and Education.
Transportation: International Airport, 9 major airlines; 3 rail freight, 2 Amtrak lines.
Education facilities: University of Texas at San Antonio; Trinity & St. Mary's Universities; Our Lady of the Lake and Incarnate Word Colleges; 2 jr. colleges, San Antonio College & St. Philip's College; permanent extension of National University of Mexico.
Convention facilities: Convention Center with large arena, theater, exhibit, meeting space.
Cultural facilities: symphony orchestra; Institute of Texan Cultures, Mexican Cultural Institute, Witte Museums, McNay Art Institute.
Other attractions: historic Alamo, old Spanish missions of San Jose, Concepcion, Capistrano, Espada; Hemis Fair Plaza with 622-foot observation tower-restaurant; downtown River Walk; zoo; annual events: Fiesta San Antonio, Livestock Show & Rodeo, Folklife Festival; professional sports: San Antonio Spurs of ABA plus minor league football (Toros) and baseball (Brewers).

San Bernardino, California

The World Almanac is sponsored in the San Bernardino area by the Sun-Telegram, 399 North D St., San Bernardino, Cal. 92401, phone (714) 889-9666; Telegram founded 1873, Sun 1894; daily circulation 84,080, Sunday 87,-208; member Gannett chain; editor-publisher James Geehan, vice president-operations Paul Balosso, managing editor Ted Warmbold.

Population: 114,863 (city), 1,199,000 (2-county metro area); 43rd in state, 145th in nation; total employed 38,374.
Area: 47.22 sq. mi. at base of Cajon Pass, 58 miles east of Los Angeles; county seat.
Industry: 165 business and industrial firms including Culligan, Edginton Oil, Fleetwood Enterprises, Hanford Foundry, Knudsen Dairy, Mode O'Day, Pepsi Cola and Seven-Up bottling plants, Santa Fe Railway, TRW Systems.
Commerce: trading center for 20,189 sq. mi. San Bernardino County, largest in the nation; retail sales (1973) $498,866,000; 7 banks, 23 branches; 8 savings and loans associations; 2 major shopping center complexes, each parking over 5,000 cars.
Transportation: Santa Fe, Southern Pacific and Union Pacific rail lines, Amtrak; Greyhound and Continental bus lines; major interstate highways leading from Mexico to Canada and West to East Coast; municipal airport and nearby Ontario International Airport, over 1,170,000 passengers (1973).
Communications: 15 radio and one VHF educational TV stations, access to 5 Los Angeles channels.
Medical facilities: 3 major hospitals with 995 beds; major research and training center for heart surgery and hip and knee replacement surgery.
Federal facilities: Norton Air Force Base, annual payroll $168,395,704 to 10,211 employees.
Cultural facilities: symphony orchestra, Civic Light Opera, nearby Redlands Bowl (summer concerts); National Orange Show with year-round activities and orange festival every spring; Convention Center-Exhibit Hall complex.
Educational facilities: California State College, junior college, 3 major universities nearby.
History: founded 1852 by Mormons who purchased land from Spanish grant holders.
Further information: Chamber of Commerce, 546 West 6th St., San Bernardino, Calif. 92401.

San Diego, California

The World Almanac is sponsored in San Diego by The San Diego Union and Evening Tribune (Copley Newspapers), P.O. Box 191, San Diego 92112; (714) 299-3131; Union founded 1869 (pioneer daily of Southwest); circulation, Union (morn) 175,791, Tribune (eve) 125,902, Sunday Union 292,530; publisher Helen K. Copley, general manager Al De Bakcsy, director of editorial and news policy Victor Krulak, Union editor Gene Gregston, Tribune editor Fred Kinne.

Population: 755,900 (1973, city); 1,482,200 (county); 11th in U.S. (official state estimate); total civilian employment, 461,500.
Area: (county) 4,255 sq. mi.; 70 mi. Pacific Coast, San Clemente to Mexican border.
Industry: Tourism, manufacturing, military, and agriculture; manufactured products earn $2.3 billion a year; non-military payroll $3.3 billion, military $741,756,000; tourist spending $333,362,230; corporations with bases or divisions include Bendix, Burroughs, Control Data, Cubic, General Dynamics, Gulf, Honeywell, International Harvester's Solar division, NCR Corp., Pacific Southwest Airlines, Rohr, Sea World, Teledyne Ryan, TraveLodge, Wickes; aerospace, rapid transit design and manufacture; oceanography; nuclear energy, medicine important; also shipbuilding, tuna fishing, clothing, ocean shipping; among top 20 counties in farm products (avocados, cut flowers, eggs); Marine Corps Recruit Depot, Naval Training Center, North Island and Miramar Naval Air Stations, Naval Electronics Lab and Undersea Center, Marine Corps base at Camp Pendleton.
Transportation: freeway system state's 2d largest; urban transit service, 25-cent fare, Mexican border to 35 miles north; Amtrak, 9 airlines, bus lines; primary airport Lindbergh Field.

Communications: Some 30 TV and radio stations.
Medical facilities: Salk Institute for Biological Studies, Scripps Clinic & Research Foundation; Naval Hospital; many hospitals.
Educational and cultural facilities: San Diego State Univ., U.S. International Univ., Univ. of San Diego; Univ. of California, San Diego (3 colleges and Scripps Institution of Oceanography), Point Loma College; symphony; Old Globe Theatre (functioning reproduction of Shakespeare's Globe Theatre); opera; ballet; Fine Arts and Timken Galleries; La Jolla Museum of Contemporary Art.
Other attractions: world famous zoo and Wild Animal Park; Balboa Park, central 1,400 acres containing museums, Zoo, Fleet Space Theatre (computerized planetarium), many other attractions; Mission Bay Park includes Sea World; "Old San Diego" State Historical Park; "Star of India" ship-museum; visits to neighboring Mexico (Tijuana); 70 miles of beaches.
Sports: NFL Chargers, NL Padres, ABA Conquistadors, WHA team slated; racing at Del Mar and Caliente.
History: area discovered 1542 by Cabrillo, founded in 1769 by Father Serra.
Other attractions: climate sunny; summer and winter resort; average temp. 68 in summer, 57 in winter, rainfall mainly December to March; famous "place names" include La Jolla (part of city of San Diego); 70 golf courses, including Torrey Pines; large convention facilities; off-shore "whale watching."

San Francisco, California

The World Almanac is sponsored in the San Francisco-Oakland area by the San Francisco Examiner, P. O. Box 3100, Rincon Annex, S.F., CA. 94103 (415) 781-2424; founded June 12, 1865; circulation daily Examiner, 179,522; Sunday Examiner & Chronicle, 664, 744; publisher Charles Gould, editor R. A. Hearst, asst. to editor W. R. Hearst, III, executive editor Thomas Eastham; major awards: Pulitzer Prize, Freedoms Foundation; Examiner sponsors Examiner Games, Golden Gloves, Bay to Breakers Race.

Population: 675,600, 3rd in state, 13th in nation; total employed: 727,500
Area: 44.6 sq. mi. on the northern tip of a peninsula. San Francisco County seat.
Industry: food products, printing, publishing, fabricated metal products; West's financial capital and administrative center for many of the nation's leading corporations; West Coast operation headquarters for a majority of the Federal agencies; finance, insurance and real estate; chief port of the Pacific Coast.
Commerce: wholesale-retail trade employment (1973) 283,800; services 250,000; manufacturing 193,- 700; total retail outlets (1973) 20,228; taxable sales 2.6 billion; 40 banks with 157 branches; 25 savings and loans with 39 branches; Pacific Coast Stock Exchange, 2nd largest after N.Y., traded shares worth 6.3 billion in 1973.
Transportation: 23 major airlines serve the San Francisco Bay Area; International Airport processed 16,590,703 passengers, 729,168,038 lbs. of freight and 187,026,176 lbs. of mail (1973); Municipal Railway (intra-city); AC-Transit and Bay Area Rapid Transit System (BART) to East Bay cities; Greyhound Bus and Southern Pacific Railroad to Peninsula areas; Golden Gate Bridge District Bus and Ferry service to Marin County; Port of San Francisco services available: LASH, BULK, general cargo, containerization and barge service.
Communications: 2 major newspapers; 118 others serving the Bay Area; 45 radio stations, 7 TV channels received directly, 1 TV cable system.
Medical facilities: 21 general hospitals with over 6,516 total bed cpacity and 5 specialty hospitals with over 1,935 total bed capacity; 3,033 physicians/surgeons and 772 dentists; One of the largest medical complexes in the world, Univ. of California Medical Center, 42 buildings a general teaching and research institute, is the largest kidney transplant center in the world, and its facilities include a neuro-psychiatric clinic, metabolic, immunization and pathology units, psychological testing and counseling and cancer, hormone and cardio-vascular research. The school has a total enrollment of 2,500 students.
Cultural facilities: San Francisco Opera, Spring Opera, Western Opera Theater, symphony, ballet, Civic Light Opera, American Conservatory Theater, Japanese Cultural Center, Chinese Cultural Center, International Film Festival, 3 museums, 29 libraries and 540 churches.
Educational facilities: 100 public elementary schools with a total enrollment of 37,500 and 19 junior high and 11 high schools with a combined enrollment of 38,000 students; Univ. of California, San Francisco; California State Univ., Univ. of San Francisco, Lone Mountain College and City College of San Francisco.
Recreational facilities: 120 parks and many miniparks, 78 playgrounds, 6 golf courses, numerous tennis courts, 10 swimming pools, 5½ miles of ocean beach, 1 lake, 1 fishing pier, Marina small craft harbor and 3 yacht clubs.
Convention facilites: 124 hotels and motels with over 20,000 rooms.
Sports attractions: Candlestick Park, home of the NL Giants and the NFL 49ers; also NBA Golden State Warriors.
Other attractions: zoo and 1,013-acre Golden Gate Park containing the California Academy of Sciences, De Young Museum, Japanese Tea Garden and Arboretum; cable cars, Fisherman's Wharf, Chinatown; the Ferry Building, Coit Tower, the Palace of Fine Arts and Grace Cathedral.
History: San Francisco Bay discovered 1769 by Sgt. Jose Ortega; pueblo of Yerba Buena established 1834, renamed San Francisco on January 3, 1847; incorporated April 15, 1850.

San Jose, California

The World Almanac is sponsored in the San Jose area by the Mercury and News, 750 Ridder Pk. Dr., San Jose, Cal. 95190; (408) 289-5000; Mercury founded June 20, 1851; News July 23, 1883; combined daily circulation, 209,- 456; Sunday Mercury-News; 225,405; publisher Joseph B. Ridder; general manager A. F. Peterson; business manager P. A. Ridder; executive editor Paul Conroy.

Population: 524,000 (city), 1,159,500 (metro area co-extensive with Santa Clara County); total employed 505,000 (metro).
Area: broad alluvial 832,256-acre valley at south end of San Francisco Bay.
Industry: largest county in northern California for manufacturing employment and total wages; called "Silicone Valley" due to high technology semi-conductor and other electronics firms: I.B.M., Fairchild-Semi-conductor, Hewlett-Packard, Varien Associ-

ates, Intel Corp., National Semi-conductor; diversity shown by Ford Motor Co., Lockheed Missiles & Space, FMC Corp., Syntex Laboratories; county a major producer of cut flowers.

Commerce: leading retail trade center of northern California, $2.65 billion in sales; 126 shopping centers; 3rd nationally in median household income, 59% of households earn $10,000 & over annually, 28% over $15,000 (metro).

Transportation: Municipal Airport served by 9 airlines; highway system interconnected with interstate in north/south, east/west directions; Southern Pacific and Western Pacific railroads.

Education: San Jose State, Santa Clara, and Stanford universities, plus community colleges have total enrollments of 94,700; 37% of adult pop. is college educated (metro).

Cultural facilities: Symphony, First State Capital Museum, Rosicrucian Egyptian Temple, Science Museum and Planetarium, De Saisset Gallery & Museum, Villa Montalvo estate and arboretum, City Gallery, Triton Museum of Art, New Almaden Museum.

Sports: Earthquakes (soccer); Bees, farm club for KC Royals; 8 reservoirs with boat ramps, 2 with camping; outlet to S.F. Bay for ocean sports.

Other attractions: Japanese Tea Gardens, Lick Observatory, Winchester Mystery House (St. Monument).

History: founded 1777, first civil settlement in California; county is one of the original 27 in California; first public school in California, San Jose Granary, 1795; first California State Capitol Dec. 15, 1849.

San Juan, Puerto Rico

The World Almanac is sponsored in Puerto Rico by the San Juan Star, GPO Box 4187, San Juan, Puerto Rico 00936; telephone (809) 782-4200; founded Nov. 2, 1959; circulation 44,000 daily, 45,000 Sunday; president and general manager John A. Zerbe, Jr.; vice president and editor Andrew T. Viglucci; major awards include 1961 Pulitzer Prize for editorial writing; APME citations 1960, 1965; staff awards include 1970 LAPA Mergenthaler Award, 1972 Overseas Press Club Award; National Spelling Bee sponsor.

Population: 463,244 (city), 851,247 (metro area), 1st in commonwealth.

Area: 47 sq. mi. in Caribbean.

Industry: San Juan is seat of Puerto Rico's tourism industry with more than 24 luxury hotels and several dozen high rise condominiums. City is also the commercial and shipping hub of the island and is a major stop for cruise ships plying the Caribbean. Major industries are apparels, pharmaceuticals and an expanding petrochemical industry serviced by three major refineries. Petrochemical industry represents $1.5 billion in investments. San Juan is center of island's rum industry with the Bacardi distillery on San Juan Bay, the largest in the world. More than 75 per cent of all rum sold in U.S. is now Puerto Rican rum with vast percentage of those sales Bacardi. Electronics industry ranks fifth in terms of income.

Transportation: San Juan International Airport handles more than 500,000 passengers monthly with four major U.S. airlines and ten foreign lines. Isla Grande Airport handles most of the small aircraft traffic on the other side of the city.

Education: Seat of the Rio Piedras campus of the University of Puerto Rico, the public university system with 26,000 enrolled in San Juan. Also located in San Juan are InterAmerican University, College of the Sacred Heart, UPR Medical Sciences campus and UPR Law School, World University and several junior and regional colleges.

Cultural Facilities and Events: The Casals Festival, guided for 15 years by the late Maestro Casals, is an annual June event bringing together some of the world's finest musicians; The Puerto Rico Institute of Culture is housed in a restored Dominican convent; El Morro, the Spanish-built fortress that guards the entrance to San Juan Harbor; numerous art museums in Old San Juan; the Puerto Rico Symphony Orchestra in concerts spread over the year; the Capitol building and Governor's Mansion.

New construction: Old City restoration program administered by the Institute of Culture; new banking district located in Hato Rey and the start of the New Center for San Juan, the new downtown of the modern San Juan.

Sports: Hiram Bithorn Stadium, winter baseball, track, and outdoor events; Roberto Clemente Coliseum, basketball, boxing and indoor events; soccer, cockfighting arenas (legal).

History: Discovered by Columbus on his second voyage to the New World in 1493, colonized by Juan Ponce de Leon, Puerto Rico's first Spanish governor; since 1952 a commonwealth freely associated with the United States. Free market with U.S. and same currency, common citizenship.

Santa Ana, California
See Orange County, California

Saskatoon, Saskatchewan, Canada

The World Almanac is sponsored in northern Saskatchewan by the Saskatoon Star-Phoenix, 204 Fifth Ave. North, Saskatoon, Sask., S7K 2P1; (306) 652-9200; Daily Star and Phoenix, founded in 1906 and 1902 respectively, merged in 1928 into the Star-Phoenix; circulation daily, 50,491; publisher Michael C. Sifton, executive vice president James K. Struthers.

Population: 132,596, 2d in prov., 19th in nation.

Area: 38.5 sq. mi. land, 1.5 sq. mi. water, on S. Sask. River, center of agricultural province.

Commerce: retail, wholesale, service, distribution hub for 400,000 in 100-mi. radius trading area; world's richest, largest potash reserves; meat packing, grain milling dominant; garment and electronics newest; base for northern mineral explorations; retail sales (1973) $270 million.

Transportation: 2 railways, 2 airlines, 2 buslines, new air and bus terminals being built; on Yellowhead Highway, easiest access through Rockies from prairies to West Coast ports.

Communications: One daily, 2 TV, 5 radio stations, one farm weekly, one community weekly.

Medical facilities: 3 major hospitals, 6 nursing homes; Univ. hospital known for kidney transplants, open-heart surgery; $26 million expansion planned.

Cultural facilities: $7 million, 2,000-seat Centennial Auditorium, convention facilities for over 1,800;

Mendel Art Gallery/Civic Conservatory; Western Development Museum houses N. America's largest display of antique cars, farm implements and 1910 Pioneer Village; theme pavillion for summer fair.
Education: Univ. of Sask. (10,300 students), famed for agriculture, space, Arctic, physics, medicine, veterinary college; Kelsey Institute for Applied Arts and Science (1,610 students); School for Deaf.

Recreation: 1,456 acres parkland; wild animal farm; man-made ski mountain; camping, fishing.

History: founded 1883 as temperance colony; incorporated 1906; battle sites of 1885 Riel Rebellion nearby.

Further information: Board of Trade, Bessborough Hotel, Saskatoon, Sask. S7K 3GB.

Savannah, Georgia

The World Almanac is sponsored in the Savannah area by the Savannah News-Press, 111 W. Bay St., Savannah, Ga. 31401, phone (912) 236-9511, publisher of the Savannah Morning News and Savannah Evening Press; combined daily circulation 77,593; Sunday 69,773. Donald E. Harwood, general manager; Wallace M. Davis Jr., executive editor.

Population: 119,100 (city), 368,200 (metro).
Area: 37 sq. mi. on Savannah River 18 miles from Atlantic Ocean.
Industry: world's largest pulpwood-to-paper container plant owned by Union Camp Corp; Savannah Sugar Refining Corp., nation's 3d largest seller; jet aircraft manufacture (Grumman American Aviation), tea packaging (Tetley), fertilizer materials, ship repair, titanium dioxide production (American Cyanamid).
Commerce: hub of "Coastal Empire," economic center of 8 Georgia and 3 South Carolina counties; Southeast's leading foreign trade port, 75 steamship lines, 33 deep water terminals; retail sales (1973) $588.1 million; 6 commercial banks, resources (1973) $5.7 billion; 2 savings and loan associations.

Transportation: 2 rail freight lines, Amtrak; Greyhound, Trailways bus lines; 70 truck lines; Delta, National Air Lines.
Communications: 4 TV and 14 radio stations.
Medical facilities: 7 hospitals.
Cultural facilities: symphony orchestra, ballet guild, dance theater, little theater, Telfair Academy of Arts and Sciences; maritime museum, science museum, military museum; $10.4 million Civic Center; Savannah State, Armstrong State Colleges.
Sports: Savannah Braves, Southern League.
History: founded 1733 by Gen. James Oglethorpe, first planned U.S. city; much of old city is national Historic Landmark, largest in country.
Further information: Chamber of Commerce, P.O. Box 530, Savannah, Georgia 31402.

Schenectady, New York

Population: 77,958; total employed, 38,000.
Area: 11.3 sq. mi., 13 miles northwest of Albany.
Industry: General Electric, employing about 27,000, is largest employer. Other firms manufacture industrial chemicals, pollution control and measuring devices, and military vehicles.
Commerce: there are 2,100 retail establishments with net sales of over $200,000,000; 9 banks, with

total deposits over $500 million.
Cultural facilities: Union College, 66 homes and buildings built between 1700-1850; the Schenectady Museum and County Historical Society.
Other attractions: 5 hospitals, 87-acre Industrial Park; 65 schools; 175 churches; 25 parks, 5 golf courses, 30 tennis courts, 18 playgrounds; Schenectady Community College.

Seattle, Washington

The World Almanac is sponsored in the Seattle area by The Seattle Times, Fairview Ave. N. & John St., P.O. Box 70, Seattle, Wash. 98111; phone (206) MA 2-0300; founded 1896 by Alden J. Blethen; circulation 243,278 daily, 301,369 Sunday; publisher John A. Blethen; president W.J. Pennington; vice president and general manager Harold G. Fuhrman.

Population: 515,000 (city), 1,143,800 (metro): first in state, 17th in nation; total employed (metro) 603,100.
Area: 91.6 sq. mi. between Puget Sound and Lake Washington; King County seat.
Industry: headquarters for Boeing, 53,000 employes, world's largest manufacturer of commercial jet aircraft; Port of Seattle has $370 million in facilities, nation's 4th largest containerized-shipping seaport; area has 1,630 manufacturers; major industries are transportation products, retail trade, shipbuilding, wood products and food products.
Commerce: business center for Western Wash. and Alaska; major import-export center for Far East; principal supply point for construction of Trans-Alaska oil pipeline; total retail sales (1973) $1.23 billion; per capita income (1971) $4,484; 29 commercial banks.
Transportation: 3 transcontinental railroads, Amtrak; International Airport served by 12 scheduled airlines, 6 commuter airlines, handled 5.2 million passengers (1973); ferries serve Puget Sound, Canada and Alaska.
Communications: 3 daily newspapers in metro area;

6 TV, 18 AM and 15 FM stations.
Medical facilities: 26 hospitals, including Univ. of Wash. Health Sciences Center and Fred Hutchinson Cancer Research Center, which is under construction.
Educational facilities: Three 4-year colleges: Univ. of Wash., Seattle Univ. and Seattle Pacific College; 7 community colleges.
Cultural facilities: Symphony Orchestra, Opera Association, Art museum and 10 other museums, 2 professional theater companies.
Recreation: major boating center; several nearby ski areas; Mt. Rainier and Olympic National Parks within 2-hour drive.
Sports: NBA SuperSonics, Sounders, North American Soccer League; Totems, Central Hockey League; Rainiers, Northwest League (baseball); National Football League and National Hockey League teams to begin play in 1976. 65,000-seat King County domed stadium to open in 1975.
Other attractions: $50 million Seattle Center, site of 1962 world's fair, has 14,000-seat Coliseum, Opera House, Playhouse, Arena, Space Needle and Pacific

Science Center.
History: settled 1851, named for an Indian chief who befriended the settlers; virtually destroyed by fire in 1889, quickly rebuilt; Alaska Gold Rush of 1897 spurred economic and population growth and propelled

Seattle toward its status as the Northwest's principal city.
Other information: Chamber of Commerce, 215 Columbia St., or Convention and Visitors Bureau, 1815 7th Ave.

Shreveport, Louisiana

The World Almanac is sponsored in the Shreveport area by the Shreveport Journal (eves. except Sunday), 222 Lake St., Shreveport, La. 71130; phone (318) 424-0373; founded 1895 as The Judge, given present name in 1897; circulation 50,000; president Douglas F. Attaway, vice-president D. Wesley Attaway, managing editor Jack F. Clark.

Population: 193,745 (special 1974 census); total employed approximately 120,000.
Area: 80.286 sq. mi., on Red River in Caddo Parish, northwest Louisiana.
Industry: oil, gas, timber, agriculture, largest manufacturer of telephones in the world, steel products, glassware, car batteries; Barksdale Air Force Base across Red River in Bossier Parish.
Commerce: wholesale-retail center for Ark-La-Tex area; retail sales (1973) over $500 million; total bank deposits $937 million; 7 banks, 2 savings and loan companies.
Transportation: 6 railroads, 4 airlines, 1 busline, 14 motor-freight lines; Interstate Hwy. 20; north-south toll road and Red River barge traffic proposed for 1980s.

Communications: 3 TV and 8 radio stations.
Cultural facilities: State Exhibit Museum and Planetarium, 2 major art galleries, symphony orchestra, 5 colleges.
Other attractions: Shreve Square, restoration project downtown on riverfront; Louisiana State Fair; Holiday-in-Dixie spring festival; 12 hospitals, including VA.
Sports: Major college basketball (Centenary College); Shreveport Captains Texas League baseball.
History: founded 1836 as Shreve Town, named for riverboat Capt. Henry M. Shreve who cleared massive logjam on river; starting point for the Texas Trail during westward expansion; Louisiana capital for 2 years during Civil War.

Sioux Falls, South Dakota

The World Almanac is sponsored in the Sioux Falls area by the Sioux Falls Argus-Leader, 200 S. Minnesota Ave., 57102, tel. (605) 336-1130; a Speidel newspaper; founded 1885; circulation: 51,408 daily, 57,062 Sunday; publisher William H. Leopard, executive editor Anson Yeager.

Population: 72,444 (city), 95,209 (metro area) according to 1970 census; largest in state.
Area: 26 square miles in southeastern South Dakota at junction of interstates 29 and 90; Minnehaha County seat.
Federal facilities: Earth Resources Observation Systems Data Center of the U.S. Department of Interior is located near Sioux Falls.
Industry and commerce: located in the nation's breadbasket, Sioux Falls Stockyards is the 4th largest public market in the U.S. John Morrell & Co. is the largest of 170 manufacturers. There are 18 banks with clearings in excess of $1.3 billion and 3 savings and loan associations. Wholesale and retail center for South Dakota, parts of Minnesota and Iowa, Sioux Falls has yearly retail sales over $300 million, whole-

sale over $500 million.
Transportation: served by 4 major rail lines, 4 bus lines, 5 major highways. Joe Foss Field with new modern terminal is within 2 miles of business district, has 3 major airlines offering 34 daily flights.
Medical facilities: 4 hospitals including Royal C. Johnson Veterans Hospital and Crippled Children's Hospital and School.
Communications: 3 TV and 8 radio stations.
Culture & Education: Public library, Convention Center, Civic Fine Arts Center, Sioux Falls Symphony, Community Playhouse. Augustana College and Sioux Falls College, North American Baptist Seminary, the South Dakota School For the Deaf, a vocational school, business college, 2 nurses training schools and 3 high schools.

Springfield, Illinois

The World Almanac is sponsored in the Springfield area by The State Journal-Register (morn and eve), oldest newspaper in Illinois, 313 S. 6th St., Springfield, Ill. 62701; (217) 544-5711; Circulation, 82,603; John P. Clarke, publisher; Edward H. Armstrong, editor; DeVan L. Shumway, associate editor; Patrick Coburn, managing editor.

Population: 93,360 (city), 176,700 (metro), 4th in state; total employed, 80,975.
Area: 39.79 sq. mi. on Sangamon River in center of state; state capital and Sangamon County seat.
Commerce: state and federal offices; 10 banks; 6 savings and loan associations; 8 insurance company home offices; 113 state organizations; 5 national orgs.; 27 civic orgs.; 36 social service orgs.; 167 women's orgs.; annual retail sales of $500 million.
Transportation: 6 railroads; 39 truck carriers; one airport; nearby barge facilities.
Communications: one TV and 6 radio stations.
Medical facilities: 2 hospitals with 1,281 beds and one 200-bed hospital under construction; 509 doctors; 15

clinics; 21 nursing homes.
Cultural facilities: municipal band, opera, symphony, chorus; Theatre Guild; State Capitol, Museum; Lincoln Historical Sites; New Salem State Park; Old State Capitol; art assns.
Education: Sangamon State Univ.; Lincoln Land Community College; Springfield College; Southern Illinois School of Medicine; Concordia Theological Seminary.
Recreation: 23 District parks; swimming, boating, skiing at 6 parks on Lake Springfield; public golf, tennis.
Special events: Ill. State Fair; Old Capitol Art Fair; NCAA College Division World Series; International

Carillon Festival; Midwest Horse Show.
History: settled 1818-1819; became county seat 1823;

incorporated as town 1832, chartered as city 1840; selected as state capital 1837.

Springfield, Massachusetts

The World Almanac is sponsored in the Springfield area by The Springfield Union, Sunday Republican, and Daily News, 1860 Main St., Springfield, Mass. 01101; phone (413) 787-2411; Union founded 1864; Republican 1824; Daily News 1880; circulation, Union, 81,502; Republican, 134,599; Daily News, 90,356; publisher Sidney R. Cook; Union-Republican editor Joseph W. Mooney; Daily News, Richard C. Garvey.

Population: 160,027 (city); 529,922 (metro); 2d in state (metro area), 4th in New England; total employed in city, 63,400.
Area: 33.1 sq. mi. in south central Massachusetts.
Industry and commerce: 288 manufacturing firms; Eastfield Mall, 75 retail outlets; retail area population, 550,000; annual sales, $1.6 billion; 6 commercial banks, 5 savings banks, one cooperative bank, 2 savings and loan associations, 2 major insurance companies; total bank resources, $4.2 billion; Baystate West, a combined shopping mall, office building and hotel; new home of the sponsoring Springfield newspapers and new federal building, civic center and bulk mail facility.
Transportation: major bus lines; Amtrak, 2 rail lines — Penn Central and Boston and Maine; Bradley

International Airport (18 miles away); Mass. Turnpike and I-91 give access to New York and New England points.
Communications: 3 TV and 9 radio stations.
Medical facilities: 8 major hospital complexes.
Cultural facilities: American International, Springfield, Western New England and Springfield Technical Community Colleges; symphony orchestra; Basketball Hall of Fame; museums, 143 churches and 7 synagogues; Tangelwood festival in the Berkshires Mountains.
Other attractions: 155 parks; Kings hockey team.
History: founded 1636 by William Pynchon; first U.S. musket developed at city's armory 1795; in 1903, Springfield rifle developed and produced here as was the M-1.

Syracuse, New York

The World Almanac is sponsored in the Syracuse area by the Herald-Journal, Clinton Square, Syracuse, N.Y. 13201; telephone (315) 473-7700; founded Jan. 15, 1877, by Arthur Jenkins; circulation 125,292 daily, 241,507 Sunday Herald-American Post-Standard; publisher, Stephen Rogers; editor, William D. Cotter; sponsors college scholarship fund for police.

Population: 197,297 (city), 636,507 (metro), 5th in state, 66th in nation; 267,500 employed.
Area: 25.82 sq. mi. near center of state; Interstate Routes 90 and 81 intersect at Syracuse.
Industry: some 500 manufacturing plants produce electrical and non-electrical machinery, primary metals, food, transportation equipment, chemicals, pharmaceuticals, paper, candles, china; new $100 million Schlitz brewery, world's largest ever built at one time, under construction in suburban Lysander; major Miller brewery planned just north of city; major employers: General Electric, Carrier Corp., Crucible Steel, Crouse-Hinds, Allied Chemical.
Commerce: retail sales (1973 est.) $1.4 billion; average household spendable income (1973 est.) $13,585.
Transportation: 2 rail freight lines, Amtrak; 3 bus

lines, 140 truck lines; 3 airlines.
Communications: 4 TV, 14 radio stations.
Medical facilities: 4 major hospital complexes.
Cultural facilities: Syracuse Univ., State Univ. College of Environmental Science and Forestry, and Le Moyne, Maria Regina, and Onondaga Community Colleges; Everson Museum of Art; symphony; $22 million county office-cultural center ready in 1976.
Sports: Syracuse Univ. football; Syracuse Chiefs of International League (baseball).
History: first explored 1615 by French; salt deposits led to area development, known as "Salt City"; "crossroads" since Indian days; became city 1847.
Further information: Chamber of Commerce, One MONY Plaza, Syracuse, N.Y. 13202.

Tallahassee, Florida

The World Almanac is sponsored in the north Florida-south Georgia panhandle area by The Tallahassee Democrat, 277 N. Magnolia Drive, Tallahassee, Florida 32302; (904) 877-6181; founded 1905; circulation 39,995 (eve), 42,216 Sunday; member Knight Newspapers Inc., Alvah H. Chapman, president; W. H. Harwell Jr., v.p. and general manger; Malcolm B. Johnson, v.p. and editor.

Population: 82,041 (city) 117,920 (metro); total employment 58,500.
Area: 26.14 sq. mi. between Gulf of Mexico and Georgia line; state capital and Leon County seat.
Commerce: 44% of economic base is state government; small manufacturers; agriculture only 1.1% of economic base; retrail-wholesale center serving 17-county area; 2 shopping malls and 7 shopping centers containing 186 outlets; retail sales (1972) $297,320,-000, 3d highest in state; effective buying income per household is $11,970, 2d highest in state; 10 commercial banks (resources, $319,880,000) and 3 savings & loans.
Transportation: 3 major airlines, 2 commuter flight services, one railroad and 5 motor carriers.

Communications: 8 radio, 9 TV stations by cable.
Medical facilities: One major hospital, a retardation hospital and a university hospital.
Recreational facilities: 5 recreation centers, 10 playgrounds, 45 ball fields, 21 tennis courts; salt water fishing, bass fishing in Lake Jackson; deer, dove, quail, duck, geese hunting; 4 golf courses, PGA Tallahassee Open Invitational.
Other Attractions: college athletic events at Florida State Univ. and Florida A&M; symphony, ballet, repertory theater, opera, touring plays and art exhibits; 1845 historic capitol and other historic sites; Apalachicola National Forest; Junior Museum; Wakulla Springs, Maclay Gardens State Park, LeMoyne Art Gallery, Natural Bridge State Historic

Memorial and Florida State Univ. "Flying High" Circus.
History: established as state capital 1823; Tallahassee means "old town" or "deserted fields" in Creek; area

prospered with large plantations and antebellum mansions, many still standing.
Further information: Chamber of Commerce, P. O. Box 1639, (904) 224-8116, Tallahassee, Florida 32302.

Tampa, Florida

The World Almanac is sponsored in the Tampa Bay area by The Tampa Tribune and The Tampa Times, 507 E. Kennedy Blvd., Tampa, Fla., 33602; (813) 224-7711; Times founded 1893, Tribune 1895; comb. cir. 195,921; A.S. Donnahoe, pres.; J. Clendinen, chmn. of ed. bd.; R.F. Pittman, Jr. v.p./gen. mgr.; J.S. Bryan, III, exec. v.p.; J. Urbanski, bus. mgr.; R. Hudson, exec. ed.; P. Hogan, Tribune mgr. ed.; D. Harvill, Times mgr. ed.

Population: 299,600 (city), 548,700 (co.); 3d in state, 48th in nation; total employed 224,600 (co.).
Area: 84.45 sq. mi., halfway between the northern edge of Florida and southern tip; Hillsborough County seat.
Industry: port ranks 8th in the nation; principal export cargo, phosphate; Ybor City section well-known for cigar manufacturing.
Commerce: retail sales (1973) $1.403 billion; 25 banks, resources $1.675 billion, 8 savings & loan assns.
Transportation: 22 freight lines, Amtrak; 5 bus lines; city-owned bus system; 48 truck lines; junction of I-75 & I-4; Intl. Airport, 10 major airlines.
Communications: 5 TV and 15 radio stations.
New construction: Univ. Square; Tampa Cultural Center; Univ. of So. Fla. Graduate Research Library and College of Med.; Hillsborough Community College; Tampa Medical Center; Tribune Co. Blvd.; Dale Mabry Office Blvd.; East Lake Square Mall; expansion of Busch Gardens, General Telephone, and Univ.

Community Hosp.
Medical facilities: 6 major hospital complexes; W.T. Edwards Tuberculosis Hospital.
Federal facilities: MacDil AFB, U.S. Federal Bldg.
Cultural facilities: Fla. Gulf Coast Symphony; 2 museums; Univ. of So. Fla., Univ. of Tampa, Fla. College, and Hillsborough Community College; Curtis Hixon Convention Center; a $2.4 million library; Tampa Community Theatre.
Other attractions: Lowry Park Zoo; Busch Gardens; sightseeing cruises aboard the Tom Sawyer; Ybor City (Latin Quarter); 26 parks, 11 picnic areas; annual Gasparilla Pirate Invasion & Parade.
Sports: Tarpons, Cincinnati Reds farm team; Cincinnati Reds spring training; dog track; Jai-Alai Fronton; 50,000 seat stadium; National Football League franchise.
History: Fort Brooke est. 1824 on site of present Tampa; incorporated 1885.
Further information: Chamber of Commerce, 801 E. Kennedy Blvd., Tampa, Fla., 33602.

Toledo, Ohio

The World Almanac is sponsored in the Toledo area by The Blade, 541 Superior St., Toledo, Ohio 43660; phone (419) 259-6000; founded 1835; circulation, 173,111 daily, 206,652 Sunday; publishers Paul Block Jr. and William Block; associate publisher John D. Willey; editor Bernard Judy; executive editor Joseph O'Conor; managing editor William Rosenberg.

Population: 390,000 (city), 774,200 (metro), 5th in state, 45th in nation; total employed, 298,000.
Area: 85.3 sq. mi. at juncture of Maumee River and Lake Erie, in northwestern Ohio.
Industry: glass, headquarters for Owens-Illinois, Owens Corning & Libbey-Owens-Ford; automotive parts, largest producer in nation, home of American Motors Jeep, Toledo Scale and Haughton Elevator; largest petroleum refining center between Chicago and the East Coast.
Commerce: growing port on Great Lakes, annual overseas cargo runs to 500,000 tons; 2d in international tonnage, 3d in total tonnage, 11th among all ports, only inland foreign trade zone in the nation; total retail sales $1.68 billion; spendable income per household: $12,466.
Transportation: 9 railroads, 4 major airlines, 120 motor freight lines, 2 interstate bus lines; 13 major highways converge here, permitting the rapid flow of goods to almost 60% of the nation's consumers.

Communications: 3 TV, 15 radio stations and one cablevision company.
Medical facilities: 12 major hospital complexes, including the Medical College of Ohio Hospital.
Cultural facilities: Museum of Art with largest display of antique glass in the world and Peristyle used for the performing arts; symphony, Opera Society.
Education: Univ. of Toledo and its Community and Technical College; Michael J. Owens Technical College; Mary Manse College; and Bowling Green State Univ.
Other Attractions: Municipal Zoo among top 10 in the nation; modern 2,500 seat Masonic Auditorium with a Great Hall annex.
Sports: Mud Hens, farm club of the Philadelphia Phillies at the Lucas County Recreation Center.
History: founded in 1835; took its name from sister city, Toledo, Spain.

Toronto, Ontario, Canada

The World Almanac is sponsored in the Metropolitan Toronto area by The Toronto Star, One Yonge St., Toronto, Ontario, M5E 1E6. (416) 367-2000; established 1892, Joseph E. Atkinson, publisher, 1899-1948; circulation daily, 526,700; Saturday, 752,000: president and publisher, Beland H. Honderick; senior vice-president, Burnett M. Thall; editor-in-chief, Martin Goodman. Canada's largest newspaper in circulation, display and classified advertising linage; winner of 29 national newspaper awards and sponsor of the Santa Claus Fund and Fresh Air Fund.

Population: 712,786 (city), 2,086,703 (metro); 2d largest city in Canada, 15th in North America; total labor

force: 800,000.
Area: 241 sq. mi., on northwest shore of Lake Ontar-

io; provincial capital.

Industry: Canada's leading commercial and industrial center; 5,800 manufacturing establishments; value of 1973 factory shipments: $12.2 billion; principal industries: slaughtering and meat packing, clothing, printing and publishing, machinery, electrical goods, furniture, food products, rubber goods, sheet metal products.

Commerce: Retail sales (1973 est.) $5.5 billion; headquarters for Eaton's and Simpson's, Canada's largest department store and mail order firms; head offices of 10 trust companies and 4 of 10 federally chartered banks; value of cheques cashed (1972) $460.5 billion; Toronto Stock Exchange, 4th in North America, traded shares worth $6.7 billion in 1973; per capita disposable income $4,030.

Transportation: 10 railway lines carry 275 freight and passenger trains daily; 7,000 trucks use 12 major highways to every province; Transit Commission carries 329 million passengers annually on 670 miles of routes, including 26.5 miles of subways; 3.3 million tons of cargo unloaded (1973) at this major Great Lakes port; 17 airlines handle 8.3 million passengers annually at International Airport.

Communications: 6 TV stations including educational and French-language channels; 10 AM and 4 FM radio stations; 3 daily newspapers; 42 foreign language newspapers.

New construction: Value of building permits (1973) $1.9 billion; work in progress on Metro Centre, $1.5 billion 190-acre commercial-residential project will employ 50,000 office workers and provide 20,000 housing units.

Medical facilities: 27 active-treatment hospitals including renowned Hospital for Sick Children; special treatment centers: Clarke Institute for Psychiatry, Addiction Research Centre, Ontario Crippled Children's Cenre.

Cultural facilities: 20 local groups offer experimental, repertory and revue theatre; National Ballet of Canada and Canadian Opera Company perform in 3,200-seat O'Keefe Centre; symphony orchestra and Mendelssohn Choir at Massey Hall; original and touring productions at Royal Alexandra Theatre; 65 public libraries, Art Gallery of Ontario, Royal Ontario Museum.

Educational facilities: 2 universities: York and Toronto, Canada's largest (1973-74 enrollment: 44,211); Ryerson Polytechnical Institute, 4 colleges of applied arts and technology, 2 teachers' colleges, Royal Conservatory of Music, Ontario College of Art, Osgoode Hall Law School.

Recreational facilities: Canadian National Exhibition, world's biggest annual fair; Ontario Place, 100 acres of offshore islands with restaurants, marina and 1,000-seat Cinesphere for film showings; Toronto Islands have 3 yacht clubs, 560 acres of beaches and picnic grounds; harbor-front, 86-acre entertainment park, opened 1974.

Convention facilities: Canada's top convention center; 246,460 visitors attended 409 conventions in 1973, spent $40 million; total rooms, 17,680.

Sports attractions: 9 public golf courses; thoroughbred and harness racing, lacrosse and hockey in 16,435-seat Maple Leaf Gardens, home of NHL Maple Leafs and WHA Toros; Argonauts play Canadian Football League games at Exhibition Park Stadium, World Team Tennis in Coliseum.

Other attractions: Ontario Science Centre, designed for participation and involvement; Black Creek Pioneer Village, living displays of Upper Canada; McMichael Conservation Collection of works by Canada's famed Group of Seven painters; zoo, opened 1974, will have 5,000 species roaming on 700 acres.

History: town of York founded 1793 on site of French fort as capital of British colony of Upper Canada; incorporated as city 1834 and named Toronto from Indian word for meeting place.

Further information: Convention and Tourist Bureau, 85 Richmond St. West, Suite 300, Toronto, Ontario M5H 1H9.

Troy, New York

Population: 62,918.
Area: 9.8 sq. mi., 8 miles northeast of Albany.
Industry: known for manufacture of collars and shirts; military equipment, precision machines, automobile parts, abrasive materials, metals.
Commerce: 7 banks.
Cultural facilities: Rensselaer Polytechnic Institute Fieldhouse (seating 7,500); Troy Music Hall, Junior Museum, Historical Society.
Other attractions: 21 playgrounds, 3 hospitals, Russell Sage College, Hudson Valley Community College, Emma Willard School for Girls, 31 public and parochial schools.

Tucson, Arizona

The World Almanac is sponsored in the Tucson area by The Arizona Daily Star, 4850 S. Park Ave., Tucson, Arizona, 85726: (602) 294-4433; founded 1877 as a weekly. Michael E. Pulitzer, editor and publisher; Frank E. Johnson, managing editor; Abe Chanin, editorial section director; Frank Delehanty, business manager; Arnold A. Lewin, promotion director; sponsors Sportsmen's Fund.

Population: 262,933 within city limits, 360,000 in Pima County (US Census, 1970).
Industry: Hughes Aircraft, Hamilton Aircraft; center of the Copper Circle: hundreds of millions of development dollars have been spent by Anaconda, Duval, American Smelting and Refining, Pima Mining, Kennecott and other companies.
Transportation: International Airport northern terminus of Aero Mexico, served by most major airlines; 3 smaller airports; 2 bus lines and Southern Pacific Railroad; numerous motor freight lines.
Communications: 2 newspapers; 5 TV and 17 radio stations.
Medical facilities: 10 hospitals including University Medical Center, a teaching hospital.

Climate: mild, dry; rare freezing temperatures in winter; summer brings some rain, mostly after July 1, and temperatures to about 100°F.

Culture: symphony orchestra, several theatre groups, and programs by the Univ. of Arizona.

Sports: Toros of Pacific Coast League, farm club of Oakland Athletics; spring training for Cleveland Indians; Dean Martin Open Golf Tournament.

History: original site on Santa Cruz river near Mission of San Xavier del Bac. Rev. Eusebio Francisco Kino, S. J., 17th century missionary to Northern Mexico and what is now Southern Arizona, generally credited with being founder.

Tulsa, Oklahoma

The World Almanac is sponsored in the Tulsa area by The Tulsa Tribune, 315 So. Boulder, Tulsa, Oklahoma, 74102; phone (918) 582-1101; founded 1904 as The Tulsa Democrat, renamed The Tulsa Tribune in 1920; circulation, 86,868; editor Jenkin Lloyd Jones; managing editor Jenkin Lloyd Jones Jr.; executive editor Harmon Phillips.

Population: 338,690 (city), 485,900 (metro); 224,700 employed.
Area: 175 sq. mi., on Arkansas River at 96th meridian.
Industry: petroleum, 30,000 employed by 825 oil and oil-related firms with $185 million annual payroll, Sun Oil and Texaco refineries; aviation, 15,000 in aviation and aerospace industries, including Rockwell International, McDonnell Douglas and American Airlines; world's largest manufacturer of industrial heaters and winches; 1,200 diversified manufacturing plants.
Commerce: retail sales (1973): $1.240 billion; 17 banks (resources $1.721 billion), 10 savings and loan assns.; per capita income, $3,977.
Transportation: Tulsa Port of Catoosa, nation's most inland port, head of Arkansas-Verdigris navigation channel, total 1973 barge tonnage, 326,588; 4 rail freight lines; 3 bus lines; 32 truck lines; 6 airlines with 1,213,624 passenger movements (1973).

Communications: 2 daily newspapers, 3 TV and 15 radio stations.
New construction: building permits valued at $210.9 million (1973), including Ford glass plant, regional hq. for Metropolitan Life Insurance.
Medical facilities: 5 hospitals, 2,000 beds, Osteopathic College, Univ. of Oklahoma medical school branch.
Federal facilities: District Corps of Engineers, 1,200 employees; hq. Southwestern Power Administration.
Cultural facilities: Univ. of Tulsa, Oral Roberts Univ., American Christian and Tulsa Junior Colleges, Philharmonic, Opera, Civic Ballet, 2 art museums, including Thomas Gilcrease Institute of American History and Art.
Convention facilities: Assembly Center seats 10,000; 367 conventions with 139,191 attendance (1973).
Sports: Tulsa Oilers, St. Louis Cardinals farm team; pro hockey in Central Hockey League; intercollegiate athletics; 4 public and 7 country club golf courses.

Vancouver, British Columbia, Canada

The World Almanac is published in the Vancouver area by The Vancouver Sun, 2250 Granville Street, Vancouver, B. C.; phone (604) 732-2111; founded 1886; circulation 253,812; publisher Stu Keate; editorial director Bruce Hutchison; managing editor Bill Galt; sponsors world's largest free Salmon Derby; free swim classes (annual enrollment 10,000); Sun Tournament of Soccer Champions and many other community services.

Population: 440,139 (city), 1,158,081 (metro area), 1st in province, 3rd in Canada.
Area: 44 sq. miles on the Pacific coast at the mouth of the north arm of the Fraser River; scenic beauty of the city accented by the towering, snowcapped Rocky Mountains to the north and rich greenery of agricultural land to the east and south.
Industry: 98 miles of waterfront, stretching up Burrard Inlet, the largest cargo port on the Pacific and Canada's 2d busiest, with 42,019,000 tons handled in 1973; major cargos: grain, lumber, coal, mineral ore, chemicals and manufactured goods; tourism a major industry, with an estimated 6,500,000 visitors bringing in $354,000,000 in 1973.
Commerce: retail sales: $3.32 billion in 1973; value of shares traded on the Vancouver stock exchange $438,500,000 in 1973.
Transportation: western terminus of Canada's 2 national railways; Canadian National Railway and Canadian Pacific; headquarters of provincially-operated British Columbia Railway (formerly the Pacific Great Eastern), and is linked to the U. S. by Amtrak along the Burlington Northern Railway right-of-way; 3 major long-distance bus carriers; Provincial Stage Lines, Trailways and Greyhound; International Airport served by 7 major airlines handled more than

3.9 million passengers in 1973.
Communications: 12 radio and 2 local TV stations; also 4 U.S. network TV outlets.
Medical facilities: General and St. Paul's are largest hospitals; Royal Columbian in New Westminster, Burnaby General, Lion's Gate in North Vancouver and Riverview Psychiatric Hospital are also major facilities.
Cultural facilities: symphony orchestra, opera association, several professional theatre groups, Centennial and Maritime Museums, and Art Gallery; Queen Elizabeth Theatre is the major arts facility.
Other attractions: Pacific National Exhibition, Gastown, Chinatown, the H.R. MacMillan Planetarium, Bloedel Conservatory, Public Aquarium, 1,000-acre Stanley Park, zoo, 18 golf courses, Grouse Mountain and Mount Seymour ski areas, Univ. of British Columbia, Simon Fraser Univ. and 18 public beaches.
Sports: B.C. Lions (professional football); Canucks and Vancouver Blazers (hockey), Whitecaps (soccer); Exhibit-Racetrack (thoroughbreds); and several amateur teams and sports activities.
History: discovered by Spaniards; first mapped 1791; taken possession of by Capt. George Vancouver for British 1792; Hudson's Bay Company post established early 1800s, city incorporated 1886.

Washington, District of Columbia

The World Almanac is sponsored in the Washington, D. C., area by the Washington Star-News, 225 Virginia Ave., S.E., Washington, D.C., 20003; phone (202) 484-5000; founded Dec. 16, 1852; pres. John H. Kauffmann, editor Newbold Noyes, managing editor Charles Seib; awards received by newspaper and staff include 7 Pulitzer Prizes.

Population: 745,000 (city) 3,200,000 (metro, includes   D.C. and parts of Maryland and Virginia.).

Area: 62 sq. mi. (city), 2,855 sq. mi. (metro) on the Potomac River.

Industry: U. S. Capital, federal government employs 332,000, about ¼ of labor force, with annual payroll over $5 billion; government related activity, law, journalism, professional and trade associations (about 2,000), unions, lobbying groups and scientists, provide another large portion of employment base; tourism a major industry; manufacturing minor.

Commerce: metro area 3d in per capita income $5,862 (1972); bank clearings over $12 billion a year.

Transportation: circumferential highway; 98-mile rapid rail-transit system to be completed 1980, with downtown subway to open mid-1975; Metro-liner to New York, long distance rail and bus service; National and Dulles International airports.

Communicaions: several national magazines; news bureaus of major newspapers, wire services and TV networks; 19 FM, 25 AM radio stations; 4 daily, over 30 weekly newspapers.

Educational facilities: American, Catholic, George Washington and Howard Universities, and Gaulladet College; nearby Univ. of Maryland and George Mason Univ.

Medical facilities: major medical research center; National Institutes of Health, Walter Reed Hospital, Bethesda Naval Medical Center; about 40 general hospitals and 3 teaching hospitals.

Cultural facilities: Kennedy Center with 3 performance halls and Wolf Trap Farm Park in nearby Vienna, Va. present major concerts, ballet, opera; Arena Stage, Ford's Theater, National Theater, many community theater groups; Smithsonian Institution, including major art collections; Corcoran Gallery of Art, Library of Congress; D.C. Public Library with 19 branches.

Sports: Pro sports include football (Redskins), basketball (Capital Bullets) hockey (Capitals).

History: named for George Washington and Christopher Columbus; created as seat of federal government by Act of Congress 1790; governed by elected mayor and city council with budget controlled by Congress.

Further information: Convention and Visitors Bureau, 1129 20th St. N.W., Washington, D.C. 20036.

West Palm Beach, Florida

The World Almanac is sponsored in Palm Beach County, Florida by Palm Beach Newspapers, Inc., 2751 S. Dixie Highway, West Palm Beach, Florida 33405, phone (305) 833-7411; publisher of The Palm Beach Post and The Palm Beach Times; combined daily circulation 100,000, Sunday, The Palm Beach Post-Times 115,000.

Population: 61,663 (city), 427,983 (metro).

Area: 41.75 sq. mi. (city), 2,230 sq. mi. (metro), largest county (same as metro area) in total area east of the Mississippi; Palm Beach County seat.

Industry: on the top of the "Gold Coast," Pratt and Whitney Aircraft, research and development; IBM, computer manufacturer; RCA, electrical equipment; ITT, electronic circuitry; Rel-Reeves, manufacturer of radar equipment.

Commerce: 38 general service banks, 9 savings and loan facilities, total assets $3.172 billion; retail sales (1972) $1.27 billion.

Transportation: 2 rail freight lines, Amtrak; Greyhound, Trailways bus lines; 15 truck lines; Delta, Eastern, National, United, Mackey and Shawnee air lines; deepwater port, 6 shipping lines.

Communications: 2 TV, 12 radio stations.

Medical facilities: 9 hospitals with 1,790 licensed beds.

Cultural facilities: Society of the Four Arts, Flagler Museum, Science Museum, Norton Gallery of Art. 6 community theaters, 3 legitimate theaters; 15 movie, 6 drive-in theaters; Florida Atlantic Univ., Palm Beach Atlantic College, Palm Beach Jr. College.

Sports: Class A baseball, West Palm Beach Expos, greyhound racing, jai-alai, 60 golf courses.

History: founded late 1800s by workers and business people associated with the construction of the famed Royal Poinciana Hotel by Henry Morrison Flagler who set aside 48 homesites on the western shore of Lake Worth; incorporated 1894.

Further information: Chamber of Commerce, 501 N. Flagler Dr.

Wichita, Kansas

The World Almanac is sponsored in the Wichita area by the Wichita Eagle and Beacon Publishing Co. Inc., 825 E. Douglas, Wichita, Kan. 67202; phone (316) 268-6000; founded 1872 as weeklies; became dailies 1884, consolidated 1961; circulation, Eagle (morn) 128,803, Beacon (eve) 57,716, Sunday Eagle and Beacon 187,187; publisher Britt Brown, general manager Darrow Tully, editor Don Boyett, managing editors Keith Ashley and Lynne Holt.

Population: (city) 261,846, first in state, 51st in nation; (metro) 373,475, first in state, 75th in nation; 171,250 employed.

Area: 90.74 sq. mi. (Sedgwick County), at juncture of Big and Little Arkansas Rivers.

Industry: 60% of all U.S. general aviation aircraft manufactured in Wichita by Beech Aircraft (6,600 employes), Cessna Aircraft (9,200), Gates Learjet (1,700) and Boeing (9,000); other fields: meat processing, flour mills, grain storage, petroleum, natural gas, chemicals; largest non-aero manufacturer, Coleman Co.

Commerce: wholesale-retail center for large part of Kansas and northern Oklahoma; metro retail sales (1973) $1.13 billion; bank resources, $1.24 billion; median household income $8,750.

Transportation: 4 major rail freight lines, Amtrak;

Continental bus lines, 51 truck lines; 8 major highways; Mid-Continent Airport, 5 airlines, averages 750 air movements per day; National Flying Farmers headquarters.

Communications: 4 TV and 10 radio stations.

Medical facilities: World's largest speech and hearing rehabilitation center (Institute of Logopedics); 5 major hospital complexes, including a VA installation.

Federal facility: McDonnell Air Force Base.

Education facilities: Wichita State Univ., Friends Univ. and Kansas Newman College.

Cultural facilities: symphony orchestra, 2 art museums, Century II auditorium and convention center, Community Theater, $2.5-million city library and 440 churches.

Other attractions: $3-million city-county zoo, recreational lakes, 52 parks, Cow Town (restoration of 1872 Wichita), Historical Museum; averages 65% possible sunshine.

Sports: Aeros, top Chicago Cubs farm team; National Baseball Congress tournament.

History: founded 1870, became railhead on the Chisholm Trail; named after Wichita Indians.

Further information: Chamber of Commerce, 350 W. Douglas 67202.

Windsor, Ontario, Canada

The World Almanac is sponsored in Windsor and a large part of Southwestern Ontario including Essex, Kent and Lambton Counties, by The Windsor Star (circ. 82,727) 167 Ferry St., Windsor 12, Ontario; a division of Southam Press Ltd.; published daily since 1890 (present name since 1957); publisher J. Patrick O'Callaghan, general manager A. H. Fast, editor R. M. Pearson.

Population: 203,300 (city); 258,645 (metro); 506,007 (tri-county); 10th in nation; total employed 117,086.

Area: 50 sq. mi. one-half mile across Detroit River from Detroit, Mich.; largest Canadian city on U.S.-Canada border.

Industry: autos and feeder plants, more than 25% national production (Chrysler, Ford, GM); tool and die shops; alcoholic beverages (home office Hiram Walker and Sons); food processing (H. J. Heinz, Green Giant); salt mining; zinc and plastic die-casting; pharmaceuticals; agriculture (rich producer early vegetables) tomatoes, corn, soybeans, peaches, tobacco; tourism (largest port of entry in nation for U.S. visitors).

Commerce: retail sales $487.7 million (6% above national average); personal disposable income $993.2 million (1.4% Canadian total); average weekly income $183.33 (22% above national average); 6 banks, 7 loan companies, 65 branches.

Transportation: 7 rail lines; 2 airlines; linked to Detroit by suspension bridge and underwater tunnel; western terminus Highway 401; major harbor terminal; private marinas; yacht club; municipal busline.

Communications: 6 radio, 1 TV outlets; access to Detroit's 50 radio and 6 TV outlets; 1 monthly magazine.

Medical facilities: 5 major hospitals including large hospital complex for chronically ill and burn unit.

Cultural facilities: Univ. of Windsor; St. Clair Community College; symphony orchestra; Light Opera Association; Art Gallery; Hiram Walker Museum; new public library; Cleary Auditorium and convention centre.

Other attractions: 60 parks and playgrounds, sunken gardens; close access to Great Lakes resort areas; site of International Freedom Festival.

Winnipeg, Manitoba, Canada

The World Almanac is sponsored in the Winnipeg area by the Winnipeg Free Press, 300 Carlton St., Winnipeg, Man., Canada; phone (204) 943-9331; founded 1872; daily circulation 135,770; publisher Richard C. Malone; president R. H. Shelford; editor Peter McLintock; managing editor Albert Boothe; the newspaper and its staff have received numerous awards for outstanding journalism.

Population: 563,700, 1st in province; capital of Manitoba.

Area: 161 sq. mi., junction Red and Assiniboine rivers, near center of North America.

Industry: manufacturing is single largest source of jobs; 1,045 establishments, 42,600 employees; value of factory shipments, $1,271,349,000.

Commerce: retail sales over $1 billion; Winnipeg Commodity Exchange is only gold futures market in Canada; headquarters Canada Grains Council, Canadian Grain Commission, Canadian International Grains Institute, Canadian Wheat Board.

Transportation: International Airport Canada's 4th busiest, served by 4 airlines; 2 national rail lines and freight link to U. S.; 5 national and regional bus lines; major trucking hub.

Communications: 3 TV and 5 radio stations.

New construction: valued at $173 million (1973) compared with record $190 million (1972); $25 million convention center to be completed end of 1974 and $16 million Royal Canadian Mint.

Medical facilities: one of Canada's largest medical teaching centers; research in immunology, transplant-tissue rejection problems; of Manitoba's 85 active treatment hospitals, 13 are in Winnipeg, including 2 major teaching centers.

Cultural facilities: Art Gallery, Royal Winnipeg Ballet, Contemporary Dancers, Symphony Orchestra, Manitoba Theatre Centre, Manitoba Opera Association plus over 20 amateur theater groups.

Educational facilities: Univ. of Manitoba with 4 affiliated colleges, Univ. of Winnipeg and Red River Community College.

Sports attractions: Blue Bombers (Canadian Football League), Jets (World Hockey Assn.).

Other attractions: major zoo; Red River Exhibition and multi-cultural Folklorama festival in summer;

French Canadian festival in winter; museums and planetarium.

History: first colony, Lord Selkirk Settlers, 1812; incorporated Nov. 8, 1873; on Jan. 1, 1972, amalgamated city government replaced 7 cities, 4 urban municipalities, one town and a metropolitan government.

Additional information: Chamber of Commerce, 177 Lombard Ave.; Tourist Information: 101 Legislative Bldg.

Winston-Salem, North Carolina

The World Almanac is sponsored in the Piedmont Triad area by the Winston-Salem Journal and the Twin City Sentinel, 416-20 Marshall St., Winston-Salem, N.C. 27102; phone (919) 725-2311; Sentinel founded 1856, Journal 1897; brought under one ownership in 1927; now an affiliate of Media General; Charles W. Crowder, publisher-general manager.

Population: 140,728 (city), 225,668 (Forsyth County); 1974 estimates.

Area: 58.57 square miles (city), 419 square miles (county) in north central North Carolina.

Industry: R. J. Reynolds Industries, with diversified interests in tobacco, food, shipping, oil, packaging; Western Electric; Jos. Schlitz Brewery; Westinghouse; Hanes Corp.; Hanes Dye and Finishing; Duplan; Brenner Industries; Bahnson; Graveley Corp.; Dennis Inc.; Wachovia Corp.

Commerce: total retail sales (city 1973) nearly $800 million; part of Piedmont Triad which, with Greensboro and High Point, comprise a rapidly-growing industrial and business area.

Transportation: headquarters for Piedmont Airlines at Smith Reynolds Airport; city also served by regional airport with 4 airlines; 2 bus lines; 54 motor-freight carriers.

Communication: 4 TV and 9 radio stations.

Medical facilities: Bowman Gray School of Medicine of Wake Forest Univ.; Baptist, Forsyth Memorial, Medical Park, and Reynolds hospitals.

Cultural facilities: one of the nation's first arts councils, formed in 1949; N. C. School of the Arts; Wake Forest Univ., Salem College, and Winston-Salem State Univ.; Old Salem, restoration of colonial town.

Convention facilities: $10 million Hyatt House hotel complex completed 1974 sits across from the $5 million Benton Convention Center; hotels and motels offer 2,500 rooms.

Recreation: more than 50 public parks, 10 community centers, 10 swimming centers, fishing and boating on Winston and Salem lakes; 11 public and 5 private golf courses, including Tanglewood, site of the 1974 PGA.

Sports: Polar Twins, member of the Southern Hockey League, Red Sox, farm club of Boston Red Sox, member of the Carolina League; stock car racing; Wake Forest teams play football at Groves Stadium, basketball at Memorial Coliseum.

History: Salem founded 1766 by members of the Moravian Church; Winston founded 1849; merged in 1913.

Youngstown, Ohio

The World Almanac is sponsored in the Youngstown area by The Vindicator, Vindicator Sq., Youngstown, O., 44501; phone (216) 747-1471; founded 1863 by J. H. Odell; Wm. F. Maag began daily Sept. 25, 1889; daily circulation 103,094, Sunday 160,004; president, publisher, general manager William J. Brown; advertising manager William Mittler; managing editor Irving L. Mansell.

Population: 140,909 (city) Ohio's 7th largest; 536,836 (metro) 63d largest in U. S.; Mahoning County seat.

Area: 35 sq. mi. in northeastern Ohio at juncture of Ohio Turnpike, I-80, Ohio Rt. 11.

Industry: historically a strong iron and steel center, still important producer with Youngstown Sheet & Tube, Republic Steel and U. S. Steel; local steel supplied to big nearby plants of General Motors-Packard Electric Div. in Warren and GMAD plant in Lordstown, where Chevrolet Vegas and trucks are made; GF Business Equipment sells offfice furnishings worldwide; Commercial Shearing does worldwide tunnel frame and hydraulics business; other fabricators use local steel, rubber.

Commerce: wholesale-retail center for large area of northeast Ohio and western Penn.; retail sales for metro area (est.) over $1 billion; estimated value added by mfg. $1.7 billion.

Transportation: rail and truck transport center with 7 railroads and 92 motor freight terminals; airport served by 2 major airlines, headquarters for Beckett Aviation, largest fleet of executive aircraft in U. S.

Communications: 3 TV, 5 radio stations.

New construction: building permits (1973) totaled $68,828,718.

Medical facilities: 6 large hospitals in area.

Federal facilities: Air Force reserve base at municipal airport; Ravenna Arsenal nearby; Army, Navy reserve units in city, with own buildings.

Cultural facilities: symphony orchestra with downtown bldg.; ballet guild; Youngtown Playhouse in own modern bldg.; Butler Institute of American Art with renowned collection.

Educational facilities: Youngstown State Univ. with over 15,500 students and graduate program; 55 public and parochial schools; branches of Kent State Univ. in nearby Warren and Salem; YSU medical college being established.

Recreational facilities: 10 parks, 44 playgrounds, golf course, 6 swim pools; Mill Creek Park, 2,383 acres, 36-hole golf course.

Washington, Capital of the United States

The Capitol

The Capitol (building) since 1961 has presented an entirely new east central front, the central portion having been reconstructed and extended. It was moved forward 32½ ft. The former facade of Virginia sandstone was reproduced in Georgia marble, the original wall becoming an interior wall. The new section added 78 offices and other important facilities. The cost of the extension project was $11,400,000; improved illumination and other work brought the total to $24,000,000.

The original plan for the Capitol was drawn by Dr. William Thornton, of Tortola, West Indies, and accepted April 5, 1793. It had a central section, nearly square, a low dome and rectangular buildings north and south, 126 by 120 ft. The southeast cornerstone of the north section was laid by President Washington with Masonic ceremonies Sept. 18, 1793. Sandstone from Aquia Creek, Va., was used. The northern wing was completed first. The Congress occupied it in Nov. 1800. The Supreme Court met there in Feb. 1801, and other local courts also used the Capitol. In charge of early construction were architects Stephen H. Hallet, Geo. Hadfield, and James Hoban who was architect of the White House. Benjamin H. Latrobe was architect of the South or House wing which was occupied in 1807, but not completed until 1811. All the interiors were burned by the British in 1814. Latrobe had charge of the rebuilding until 1818 when Charles Bulfinch became the architect for 11 years. Congress reoccupied the Capitol in 1819 and the central rotunda area was finished in 1829.

The present Senate and House wings were designed and constructed under the architect Thomas U. Walter in 1851-1863. The wing extensions are white marble from Lee, Mass., and the columns are from Maryland. Daniel Webster spoke at the laying of the cornerstone.

The House moved in Dec. 16, 1857; the Senate Jan. 4, 1859. In 1860 the Supreme Court moved into the former Senate Chamber, and in 1864 the old Hall of the House was designated Statuary Hall. The court moved into its own building in 1935.

The original dome of the Capitol, wood covered with copper, was replaced, 1856, by the present dome of cast iron, completed 1865. Its greatest exterior diameter is 135 ft. 5 in. The rotunda is 96 ft. diameter, height from floor to base of lantern, 180 ft. 3 in. In the "eye" of the dome is a fresco by Constantino Brumidi, the "Apotheosis of Washington." Below the dome runs a 300-ft. frieze in fresco, portraying American history from Columbus, 1492, to Kitty Hawk, 1903. Brumidi painted part of it by 1880. Costaggini added panels by 1888. Allyn Cox completed the frieze in 1953 and it was dedicated in 1954.

The Statue of Freedom on the dome, 19½ ft. tall, is of bronze and weighs 14,985 pounds. At its base are the words "E Pluribus Unum" (Out of Many One). It was modeled in plaster by Thomas Crawford in Rome and cast in bronze. It cost $23,796, exclusive of erection.

Inaugurations of presidents and vice presidents are usually held on a platform erected over the great steps on the east front. The oath of office of the president is usually given by the chief justice of the United States.

Prayer Room
A nondenominational room for meditation and prayer is located off the rotunda. Decorated in blue, it has a white oak altar with an open Bible, and candelabra, 10 seats and 2 kneeling benches.

National Statuary Hall
Statuary Hall was created in 1864 to occupy the former Hall of the House of Representatives. States were invited to contribute not more than two statues of distinguished persons judged worthy of national commemoration by the States. In 1933 the number of statues in Statuary Hall was limited to one statue from each state, others to be placed in other parts of the Capitol. To date 91 statues have been contributed by 50 states. The statues in Statuary Hall:

Alabama—Gen. Jos. Wheeler, U.S.A., C.S.A.
Arizona—John C. Greenway, U.S.A.
Arkansas—Uriah M. Rose, jurist.
California—Junipero Serra, mission founder.
Colorado—Dr. Florence Rena Sabin, scientist.
Connecticut—Roger Sherman, statesman.
Delaware—Caesar Rodney, statesman.
Florida—Dr. John Gorrie, inventor.
Georgia—Alex H. Stephens, statesman.
Hawaii—King Kamehameha I, (united islands)
Idaho—Geo. L. Shoup, first governor.
Illinois—Francis E. Willard, WCTU head.
Indiana—Lew Wallace, U.S.A., author.
Iowa—Saml. J. Kirkwood, governor.
Kansas—John J. Ingalls, senator.
Kentucky—Henry Clay, statesman.
Louisiana—Huey P. Long, senator.
Maine—Hannibal Hamlin, vice president.
Maryland—Charles Carroll, signer, D. of I.
Massachusetts—Samuel Adams, statesman.
Michigan—Lewis Cass, statesman.
Minnesota—Henry M. Rice, senator.
Mississippi—Jefferson Davis, statesman.
Missouri—Thos. H. Benton, senator.
Montana—Charles Marion Russell, artist.
Nebraska—Wm. Jennings Bryan, statesman.
Nevada—Patrick A. McCarran, senator.
New Hampshire—Daniel Webster, statesman.
New Jersey—Richard Stockton, statesman.
New York—Robt. R. Livingston, statesman.
North Carolina—Zebulon B. Vance, governor.
North Dakota—John Burke, U.S. treasurer.
Ohio—William Allen, senator, governor.
Oklahoma—Sequoyah, Cherokee leader.
Oregon—Rev. Jason Lee, pioneer.
Pennsylvania—Robert Fulton, inventor.
Rhode Island—Roger Williams, founder.
South Carolina—John C. Calhoun, statesman.
South Dakota—Gen. W.H.H. Beadle, educator.
Tennessee—John Sevier, first governor.
Texas—Sam Houston, pioneer leader.
Utah—Brigham Young, Mormon leader.
Vermont—Ethan Allen, Revolutionary leader.
Virginia—Robt. E. Lee, U.S.A., C.S.A.
Washington—Dr. Marcus Whitman, pioneer.
West Virginia—Francis H. Pierpont, statesman.
Wisconsin—Robt. M. La Follette Sr., statesman.
Wyoming—Esther Hobart Morris, suffragette.

Located Elsewhere
Alaska—E. L. "Bob" Bartlett, senator.
New Mexico—Dennis Chavez, senator.

Under the dome in the **Great Rotunda** are statues and busts of Washington (Va.), Lincoln, Jefferson, Hamilton, Jackson (Tenn.), Lafayette, Grant, Garfield (Ohio) and Edward Dickinson Baker.

Adjoining it, the **South Small Rotunda** has statues of George Clinton (N.Y.), Stephen F. Austin (Tex.) and John Peter Muhlenberg (Pa.). The corridor leading from Statuary Hall to the House has statues of Jonathan Trumbull (Conn.), Wm. King (Me.), Father Jacques Marquette (Wis.), Wade Hampton (S.C.), Will Rogers (Okla.), E. L. "Bob" Bartlett (Alaska), and Dr. John McLoughlin (Ore.).

In the foyer of the former Senate and Supreme Court Chamber are statues of John Stark (N.H.), Dennis l Greene (R.I.). In the corridor leading to the Senate wing are statues of Dr. Ephraim McDowell (Ky.) and Dr. Crawford W. Long (Ga.), first to use ether as anaesthetic; John Hanson (Md.), 9th president of the Continental Congress, and John M. Clayton (Del.), secy. of state; Wm. E. Borah (Idaho), Edward D. White (La.) and Maria L. Sanford (Minn.).

In the **Hall of Columns** on the first floor, House wing are statues of E. Kirby Smith (Fla.), Zachariah Chandler (Mich.), Jas. Harlan (Ia.), Francis P. Bair, Jr. (Mo.), Gen. Philip Kearny (N.J.), Gen. Jas. Shields (Ill.), John Winthrop (Mass.), Oliver P. Morton (Ind.), J. Sterling Morton (Neb.), Rev. Thos. Starr King (Calif.), J. L. McCurry (Ala.), J. P. Clarke (Ark.), Geo. W. Glick (Kan.), Jas. Z. George (Miss.), Chas B. Aycock (N.C.), Jacob Collamer (Vt.), John E. Kenna (W. Va.), Joseph Ward (S.D.), Eusebio F. Kino, S. J. (Ariz.), and Father Damien (Hawaii).

Office Buildings for Members

Members of Congress meet constituents and transact other business in five office buildings on Capitol Hill, two for the Senate and three for the House.

The original Senate building, now named the Richard Brevard Russell Office Building, was completed in 1909, enlarged in 1933; the second Senate building, now named the Everett McKinley Dirksen Office Building, was constructed in 1958. A subway connects both with the Capitol.

The original House building (1908) was named for former Speaker Joseph G. Cannon (R.Ill), the second (1933) for former Speaker Nicholas Longworth (R.Ohio) and the third (1964) for former Speaker Sam Rayburn (D.Tex.). The Rayburn Building has underground transportation to the Capitol.

Also on Capitol Hill is the bell tower and statue memorial to Sen. Robert A. Taft of Ohio (1889-1953). It was erected by popular subscription and dedicated Apr. 14, 1959 by President Eisenhower.

Hours for Visiting

The Capitol is normally open from 9 a.m. to 4:30 p.m. daily. The Capitol is closed Christmas, New Year's Day and Thanksgiving Day. Should either the House or the Senate remain in session beyond closing time, the wing of the Capitol in use stays open until the session closes.

Tours, through the Capitol, including the House and Senate Galleries, are conducted from 9 a.m. to 4 p.m. without charge. It is not necessary to take a tour to see the Capitol. Visitors desiring to hear debate in either chamber for a longer period than the tour allows must obtain a visitor's card from their Senator or Representative.

The White House

The White House, the president's residence, stands on 18 acres on the south side of Pennsylvania Avenue, between the Treasury and the Executive Office Building. The main building, 170 by 85 ft., has 6 floors, with the East Terrace, 135 by 35 ft., leading to the East Wing, a 3-story building, 139 by 82 ft., used for offices and as an entrance for official functions. The West Terrace, 174 by 35 ft., contains offices and new press facilities above the boarded over swimming pool, and leads to the Executive Office, 3 stories high, 148 by 98 ft., erected in 1902 and enlarged several times since.

The White House was designed by James Hoban, an Irish-born architect, in a competition that paid $500. The main facade resembles the Duke of Leinster's house in Dublin. President Washington chose the site, which was included on the plan of the Federal City prepared by the French engineer, Major Pierre L'Enfant. The cornerstone was laid Oct. 13, 1792. President Washington never lived in the house. President John Adams entered in November 1800, and Mrs. Adams hung her washing in the uncompleted East Room.

The walls are of sandstone, quarried at Aquia Creek, Va. The exterior walls were painted during the course of construction, causing the building to be termed the "White House." For many years, however, it was generally referred to as the "President's House" or the "President's Palace." Thos. Jefferson developed the east and west terraces and built one-story offices, woodsheds and a wine cellar. On Aug. 24, 1814, during Madison's administration, the house was burned by the British. James Hoban completed rebuilding by Dec. 1817, and President Monroe moved in.

The south portico was added in 1824 and the north colonnade and porch in 1829 by Benjamin Latrobe, Surveyor of Public Buildings, based on sketches by Hoban, approved by Jefferson. In 1948 President Truman had a second-floor balcony built into the south portico. In 1948 he had Congress authorize complete rebuilding because the White House was unsafe. During its reconstruction he lived in Blair House, 1651 Pennsylvania Ave.

Reconstruction cost $5,761,000. The interior was completely removed, new underpinning 24 ft. deep was placed under the outside walls and a steel frame was built to support the interior. All original trim and metal work were preserved.

The Green Room, used for informal receptions, is in American Sheraton style, with green silk moire on the walls, a white marble fireplace and white enamel wainscoting and door trim. On the west wall hangs a portrait of Benjamin Franklin, painted in 1767. Most of the furniture now in the room was made in New York City about 1815-1825 by Duncan Phyfe or his contemporaries.

The Blue Room, an oval drawing room, is the main reception room. The parquet floor is exposed; the walls are covered with wallpaper reproduced from a French document of 1800. Portraits of Washington, Adams, Jefferson, Jackson, Monroe, Taylor and Tyler, as well as two seascapes by Fitz Hugh Lane of Boston harbor and Baltimore harbor decorate the walls. Seven chairs and a French clock

from Monroe's original 1817 furnishings remain in the room.

The Red Room, used as a parlor, is furnished in the Empire period, hung in red twill satin with gold scroll borders. There are a Savonnerie carpet of the period and a marble-topped gueridon labeled by Charles Honore Lannuier. There are portraits of Pierce, Polk, T. Roosevelt, Abigail Adams, Dolley Madison, Angelica Van Buren, Audubon, and Alexander Hamilton in the room. Also there is a marble bust of Martin Van Buren by Hiram Powers.

The State Dining Room has a large chief table. Other tables are brought in for large dinners but do not remain there. Centerpiece of the main table is a French bronze-dore plateau purchased by Monroe in 1817. China in use was ordered during the Lyndon B. Johnson Administration. Chairs are in Queen Anne style. The room is paneled in oak with Corinthian pilasters, painted white.

The Family Dining Room, used for breakfasts and luncheons, has a portrait of Mrs. Theodore Roosevelt by Theobold Chartran.

The President's Dining Room is on the second floor. It has scenic wallpaper and is furnished with American Federal furniture, an 18th Century chandelier and blue silk window hangings. There is a mahogany sideboard once owned by Daniel Webster.

The Diplomatic Reception Room, an oval room on the ground floor, is used as the entrance to the mansion at state functions. It has scenic wallpaper based on 1820 engravings and a new Aubusson style rug with seals of the 50 states, installed in June 1971.

The Library, on the ground floor, has the painted decor of an early American room. In August 1963, 2,780 titles were selected to be placed in the library. All but a few are by American authors. They were chosen by a committee headed by the late James T. Babb, librarian emeritus of Yale University.

The Lincoln Bedroom which contains an ornately carved bed and furniture of his period, is at the east end of the second floor. It served as Lincoln's cabinet room and in it he signed the Emancipation Proclamation of Jan. 1, 1863. A portrait of Jackson, admired by Lincoln, hangs there today. Seven pieces of furniture have Lincoln associations. The bed was used in the State Bedroom during the Lincoln administration. In the room is a copy of the Gettysburg Address, written out by Lincoln and donated to the White House by the will of Oscar B. Cintas, one-time Cuban ambassador, who died in 1957.

The Treaty Room, one door removed from Lincoln's cabinet room was used by Andrew Johnson as his cabinet room, and so used until 1902, when it became a sitting room. Here in 1899 was signed the peace protocol, a forerunner to the final treaty of peace with Spain. It is now a waiting or meeting room for the President and contains some of the original Victorian furniture. There are portraits of Presidents A. Johnson, Grant and Taylor and paintings of McKinley observing the signing of the treaty and of Lincoln and Grant in conference.

The Queen's Bedroom is assigned to distinguished women guests, and has sheltered five queens — Queen Mother Elizabeth, and Queen Elizabeth II of Britain, Wilhelmina and Juliana of the Netherlands, Queen Mother Frederika of Greece. The English overmantel mirror was presented by Princess Elizabeth in 1951.

The Yellow Oval Room, directly above the Blue Room is used as a private sitting room by the President and First Lady.

The Map Room, on the ground floor, a top-secret war room during World War II, was redecorated in 1970 at the request of President and Mrs. Nixon. Furnished in American Chippendale style, it contains 4 American landscape paintings and a portrait of Benjamin Franklin which was taken from Franklin's Philadelphia home by a British officer quartered there during the American Revolution.

The President's Office, oval in form, is in the West Wing and looks out on the rose garden. The office was added in 1909 to the West Wing, which had been built 7 years earlier by Theodore Roosevelt. The West Wing also contains the Roosevelt Room and the Cabinet Room.

Visiting Hours

The White House is open from 10 a.m. to 12 noon, Tuesday through Friday, except on holidays. Also Saturdays, 10 a.m. to 2 p.m. June 1 through Labor Day, and 10 a.m. to noon Labor Day through May 31. Only the public rooms in the basement and the first floor rooms, may be visited. No permit is required.

President's Guest House

Blair House, the President's Guest House, fronts on Pennsylvania Ave., nw of the White House grounds. It is supervised by the Dept. of State and is the official residence of heads of state who visit Washington. Built 1824, it was the home of Francis Preston Blair (1791-1876), political leader and Lincoln advisor. President Truman lived there 1948-1952 during rebuilding of the White house, and two Puerto Rican fanatics tried to shoot their way in Nov. 1, 1950, killing one guard and wounding two others.

Restoration and refurnishing began in 1963 and the house was reopened Jan. 14, 1964, on the occasion of the visit of President Antonio Segni of the Italian Republic. The Blair House Fine Arts Committee continues to provide for the house.

Other Centers of Interest

Arlington National Cemetery

Arlington National Cemetery, on the former Custis-Lee estate in Virginia, is the site of the **Tomb of the Unknown Soldier** and the final resting place of John Fitzgerald Kennedy, president of the United States, who was buried there Nov. 25, 1963. A torch burns day and night over his grave. The remains of his brother Sen. Robert F. Kennedy (N.Y.) were interred on June 8, 1968 in an area adjacent. Many other famous Americans also are buried at Arlington, as well as American soldiers from every major war.

Arlington National Cemetery, administered by the Department of the Army, was established June 15, 1864, on land originally the estate of George Washington Parke Custis. The land was part of the District of Columbia from 1791 until 1847, when Arlington County was returned to Virginia.

The Unknown Soldier of World War I was entombed on the east front of the Arlington Memorial Amphitheater Nov. 11, 1921, in the presence of President Warren G. Harding. The tomb is inscribed: *Here rests in honored glory an American soldier known but to God.* The body had been chosen at Chalons-sur-Marne from unidentified dead in Europe. On Memorial Day, May 30, 1958, two unidentified servicemen, one of whom died in World War II and one in the Korean War, were placed in crypts beside the first, in ceremonies led by President Eisenhower and Vice President Nixon. The president placed the Medal of Honor on each of the two coffins.

As of Mar. 31, 1974, a total of 162,669 interments had been made in Arlington National Cemetery. Among the unknown dead are 2,111 who died on the battlefields of Virginia in the Civil War and 167 who lost their lives when the battleship Maine was blown up in Havana Harbor Feb. 15, 1898. The total of unknown dead interred in Arlington National Cemetery is 4,724.

Arlington House

On a hilltop above the cemetery, stands Arlington House, the Robert E. Lee Memorial, which from 1955 to 1972 was officially called the Custis-Lee Mansion. The house has a portico 60 ft. wide, with 8 Doric columns and faces the Potomac. With its two wings the house extends 140 ft. It was built by George Washington Parke Custis, grandson of Martha Washington and father of Mary Ann Randolph Custis, who married Lee in this house in 1831. Here Lee wrote his resignation from the U.S. Army, Apr. 20, 1861. The house became a military hq. and was confiscated by the government. The U.S. Supreme Court restored it to the legal heir, George Washington Custis Lee, grandson of the builder, who sold the entire estate (including the mansion)

to the government in 1883 for $150,000.

The mansion and grounds are administered by the National Park Service of the Dept. of the Interior.

U.S. Marine Corps War Memorial

North of the National Cemetery, approximately 350 yards, stands the bronze statue of the raising of the United States flag on Iwo Jima, executed by Felix de Weldon from the photograph by Joe Rosenthal, and presented to the nation by members and friends of the U.S. Marine Corps; at a cost of $850,000. It was dedicated Nov. 10, 1954, and is under the administration of the Dept. of the Interior, National Park Service.

Folger Shakespeare Library

The Folger Shakespeare Library on Capitol Hill, Washington, D. C., is a research institution devoted to the advancement of learning in the background of Anglo-American civilization in the 16th and 17th centuries and in most aspects of the continental Renaissance. It has the largest collection of Shakespeareana in the world with 79 copies of the First Folio. Its collection of English books printed before 1640 is the largest in the Western Hemisphere. It also has extensive source materials for the history of theatre and drama from the Middle Ages to the end of the 19th century, both English and American. The library owns approximately 250,000 books and manuscripts, about half of them rare.

The library was founded and endowed by Henry Clay Folger, a former president of the Standard Oil Co. of New York, and his wife, Emily Jordan Folger. He left its administration to the trustees of his alma mater, Amherst College. The exhibition gallery and replica Elizabethan Theatre are open free every day except federal holidays and Sundays from Labor Day to April 15.

Library of Congress

Established by and for Congress in 1800, the Library of Congress has extended its services over the years to other Government agencies and other libraries, to scholars, and to the general public, and it now serves as the national library. Two buildings, an ornate Italian Renaissance structure (1897) and a modern annex (1939), cover 6 acres of the 15⅜-acre library site and contain 35 acres of floor space. In addition the library occupies 10 other buildings dispersed throughout the Metropolitan area. In October 1965, Congress passed a law authorizing construction of a third library building, the James Madison Memorial Building; completion is expected in 1977.

L. Quincy Mumford, the 11th Librarian of Congress, took office September 1, 1954.

The library had over 3,000 volumes when it was destroyed in the burning of the Capitol, August 24-25, 1814. In January 1815, Congress bought Thomas Jefferson's library of some 6,000 volumes. In 1851 fire destroyed about half the collections. In 1866 the science library of the Smithsonian Institution was transferred to the library, and in 1870 the library became the repository for materials deposited for copyright. Today the library's collections contain over 72,000,000 items, including more than 16,000,000 volumes and pamphlets.

In addition to providing a variety of reference and bibliographic services to other government agencies, the Library of Congress serves as a cataloging and bibliographic center for libraries throughout the country. Its cataloging data is available on printed cards (a service offered since 1901), on magnetic tapes for libraries using computers, and in book catalogs. A recent program called Cataloging in Publication makes cataloging information available in books themselves so that they can be processed and put into circulation almost immediately after their delivery to libraries.

The library's exhibit halls are open to the public. Guided tours are given on the hour from 9 to 4 Monday through Friday; arrangements for groups should be made in advance with the Tour Coordinator. Many of the library's treasures are on exhibit — the Gutenberg Bible, the first and second drafts of the Gettysburg Address, Jefferson's so-called "rough draft" of the Declaration of Independence, and many items from the Presidential Papers collection. Changing exhibits feature interesting selections from the library's collection of photographs, rare books, music, maps, and manuscripts. These are sometimes seen outside Washington as well, as traveling exhibits circulated by the Library of Congress to libraries and museums elsewhere in the country. The library's resources are also made available to the public through publications of guides, bibliographies, catalogs, and facsimiles. An annual list of **Publications in Print** is available free of charge from the Central Services Division, Library of Congress, Washington, D.C. 20540. A monthly **Calendar of Events** listing exhibits currently on view, literary programs, chamber music and concerts scheduled is also available from the same address. Information about the Library of Congress, publications, posters, and greeting and postal cards are available at the Information Counter, in the west entrance ground floor lobby of the Main Building.

Thomas Jefferson Memorial

The **Thomas Jefferson Memorial** stands on the south shore of the Tidal Basin in West Potomac park. It is a circular stone structure, with Vermont marble on the exterior and Georgia white marble inside and combines architectural elements of the dome of the Pantheon in Rome and the rotunda designed by Jefferson for the University of Virginia. The central circular chamber, 86¼ ft. in diameter, is dominated by a 19-ft. tall full-length figure of Thomas Jefferson by the American sculptor Rudulph Evans. The architects were John Russell Pope and his associates Otto R. Eggers and Daniel P. Higgins. The Memorial was dedicated by President F. D. Roosevelt Apr. 13, 1943, the 200th anniversary of Jefferson's birth.

On the pediment over the portico is a sculptured group by Adolph A. Weinman showing Jefferson standing before the committee appointed by the Continental Congress to draft the Declaration of Independence. On the interior walls are four panels with inscriptions from Jefferson's writings. On the frieze of the main entablature are Jefferson's lines: "I have sworn upon the altar of God eternal hostility against every form of tyranny over the mind of man."

The memorial is open daily from 8 a.m. to midnight, except Christmas Day.

John F. Kennedy Center

John F. Kennedy Center for the Performing Arts, designated by Congress as the National Cultural Center and the official memorial in Washington to President Kennedy, was opened September 8, 1971. The marble building, designed by Edward Durell Stone, houses a 2,300-seat Opera House, a 2,750-seat Concert Hall, the 1,150-seat Eisenhower Theater, the 224-seat American Film Institute Theater, an unfinished 500-seat studio theater and 3 restaurants. All facilities are in full operation throughout the year. Tours are available daily, free of charge, between 10:00 a.m. and 1:00 p.m.

Lincoln Memorial

The **Lincoln Memorial** in West Potomac Park, on the axis of the Capitol and the Washington Monument, consists of a large marble hall enclosing a heroic statue of Abraham Lincoln in meditation sitting on a large armchair. It was dedicated on Memorial Day, May 30, 1922. The Memorial was designed by Henry Bacon. The statue was made by Daniel Chester French. Murals and ornamentation on the bronze ceiling beams are by Jules Guerin.

The memorial built on bedrock, is of white Colorado-Yule marble. There are 2 Doric columns at the entrance and 36 others in the colonnade. The frieze above the 36 columns bears the names of the 36 states existing at the time of Lincoln's death. On the attic parapet are recorded names of the 48 states existing in 1922.

Inside are 3 memorials to Lincoln. The seated figure of Lincoln is 19 ft. from head to foot and the classic armchair is 12½ ft. tall. Over the back of the chair a flag is draped in marble. The statue was fashioned out of 28 blocks of Georgia white marble. On the north wall is inscribed the Second Inaugural Address. On the south wall is the Gettysburg Address.

The walls of the interior are Indiana limestone. The panels between the overhead girders are of Alabama marble saturated with melted beeswax to produce translucency. The interior floor and the wall base are of pink Tennessee marble. The cost of the Memorial was $2,957,000 and of the statue $88,400.

The memorial is open 24 hours daily, except Christmas Day.

Mount Vernon

Mount Vernon on the south bank of the Potomac, 16 miles below Washington, D. C., is part of a large tract of land in Northern Virginia which was originally included in a royal grant made to Lord Culpepper, who in 1674 granted 5,000 acres to Nicholas Spencer and John Washington. The division between Spencer and Washington put John Washington's son Lawrence in possession of the Washington half in 1690. Later it became the property of Lawrence Washington's son Augustine, the father of George Washington.

The present house is an enlargement of one apparently built on the site of an earlier one by Augustine Washington, who lived there 1735-1738. His son Lawrence came there in 1743, when he renamed the plantation Mount Vernon in honor of Admiral Vernon under whom he had served in the West Indies. Lawrence Washington died in 1752 and was succeeded as proprietor of Mount Vernon by his half-brother, George Washington.

To Mount Vernon in 1759 Washington brought his wife, Martha Dandridge Custis, having previously enlarged the house from 1½ to 2½ stories. Just before the Revolution he planned additions, and when he was called away to war his kinsman Lund Washington supervised the work, which was completed after Washington returned in 1783. During the Revolution Washington visited Mount Vernon only twice, on the way to and from Yorktown in 1781. In 1789 he left to become president and lived in New York and Philadelphia, with brief visits to the plantation. He came back in 1797 and died in Mount Vernon Dec. 14, 1799. He was buried in the old family vault. He had made plans for a new burial vault and this was built in 1831. Both his remains and those of Martha, who died in 1802, were transferred there.

Mount Vernon was left to Washington's nephew, U.S. Supreme Court Justice Bushrod Washington, and by him to his nephew, John Augustine Washington, whose son, John A. Washington, Jr., was the last private owner. In 1853 when the place was run down, Miss Ann Pamela Cunningham of South Carolina organized the Mount

Vernon Ladies' Assn., which bought the mansion and 200 acres, since extended to just under 500 acres. The Association reassembled original Washington furniture and repaired the buildings. It restored the kitchen garden, flower garden and experimental botanical garden, reconstructed the greenhouse, and built a museum. Several trees planted by Washington still exist, and the boxwood dates from 1798.

The Association preserves house and tomb with the visitor's fee. The regent of the Mount Vernon Ladies' Association is Mrs. Thomas Turner Cooke. About 31 states are represented by vice regents. The Resident Director is Chas. C. Wall; the assistant director is Walter C. Densmore.

National Arboretum

The National Arboretum, established in 1927 for the study of trees and plants, has become one of Washington's great show places. Occupying 415 acres of rolling land along the Anacostia River in the northeastern section of the city, it is administered by the secretary of agriculture through the Plant Science Research Division of the Agricultural Research Service.

The Arboretum is open every day of the year except Christmas. The visiting hours are as follows: April through October-8 a.m. to 7 p.m. Monday through Friday; 10 a.m. to 7 p.m. Saturdays and Sundays, November through March-8 a.m. to 5 p.m. Monday through Friday; 10 a.m. to 5 p.m. Saturdays and Sundays.

National Archives

The Declaration of Independence, the Constitution of the United States and the Bill of Rights are now enshrined in the National Archives Exhibition Hall. They are sealed in glass-and-bronze cases filled with inert helium gas. They can be lowered at a moment's notice into a large shockproof and fireproof safe.

The National Archives holds all the permanently valuable federal records of the United States government, 1774 to the present. As a research institution, it is designed to preserve these records and make them available to scholars, students, writers, and the general public.

The National Archives and Records Service is a part of the General Services Administration. Through the Presidential Libraries Office it administers the Franklin D. Roosevelt Library at Hyde Park, N. Y., the Harry S. Truman Library at Independence, Mo., the Dwight D. Eisenhower Library at Abilene, Kan., the Herbert Hoover Library at West Branch, Iowa, the Lyndon Baines Johnson Library at Austin, Tex., and the John Fitzgerald Kennedy Library, temporarily at Waltham, Mass., later to be in Cambridge, Mass.

The National Archives and Records Service is headed by Dr. James B. Rhoads, archivist of the United States, Pennsylvania Ave. and 8th St. N.W. For research information, call 202-963-6411. For visitor information, call 202-962-2000.

National Gallery of Art

The National Gallery of Art, situated in an area bounded by Constitution Avenue and the Mall, between Third and Seventh Streets, was established by Joint Resolution of Congress Mar. 24, 1937, and opened Mar. 17, 1941. Although technically a bureau of the Smithsonian Institution, the gallery is an autonomous organization governed by its own board of trustees. The chairman of the board is the Chief Justice of the United States. Other members are the Secretaries of State and of the Treasury, the Secretary of the Smithsonian Institution, and five distinguished private citizens.

The collections comprise gifts of over 150 donors (none of the works were acquired with Government funds) and cover more than a dozen schools in the history of western art from the 13th century to the present.

The building was erected with funds given by Andrew W. Mellon, who also gave his collection, consisting of 126 paintings and 26 pieces of sculpture, the latter largely from the Dreyfus Collection. The paintings cover the various European schools from the 13th century to the 19th, and include such masterpieces as Raphael's Alba Madonna, the Niccolini-Cowper Madonna, and St. George and the Dragon; van Eyck's Annunciation; Botticelli's Adoration of the Magi; and 9 Rembrandts. Twenty-one paintings came from the Hermitage in Leningrad. Also in this collection are the Vaughan Portrait of George Washington, by Gilbert Stuart, and The Washington Family, by Edward Savage.

The Samuel H. Kress Collection includes the great tondo of the Adoration of the Magi by Fra Angelico and Fra Filippo Lippi, the Laocoon by El Greco, and fine examples by Giorgione, Titian, Grunewald, Durer, Emling, Bosch Juan de Flandes, Francois Clouet, Poussin, Watteau, Chardin, Boucher, Fragonard, David and Ingres. Also included are a number of masterpieces of sculpture, especially of the Italian and French schools.

The Widener Collection of over 100 paintings includes 14 Rembrandts, 8 Van Dycks, 2 Vermeers and examples of Italian, Spanish, English and French painting; also Renaissance and French sculpture and examples of the decorative arts.

The Chester Dale Collection includes masterpieces by Manet, Cezanne, Renoir. Toulouse-Lautrec. Monet, Modiliani, Pissarro, Degas, van Gogh, Gauguin, Matisse, Picasso, Braque, and a group of American paintings.

Major works of art by some of the most important artists of the last hundred years, including Picasso, Cezanne, Gauguin, and the American painter, Walt Kuhn, have been given to the gallery by the W. Averell Harriman Foundation in memory of Marie N. Harriman.

Pictures to round out the collection have been bought with funds provided by the late Ailsa Mellon Bruce, daughter of Andrew W. Mellon. Preeminent among them is the portrait of Ginevra de' Benci, the only generally acknowledged painting by Leonardo da Vinci outside Europe, and Pablo Picasso's Femme Nue, the key work of the artist's analytical cubist period. Among others are: Rubens' Daniel in the Lions' Den; Claude Lorrain's Judgment of Paris; Saint George and the Dragon attributed to van der Weyden; and a number of American paintings, including Cole's second set of The Voyage of Life.

Cezanne's great early portrait of his father and 351 paintings by George Catlin, mostly of North and South American Indians, are among recent acquisitions given by Paul Mellon, president of the gallery and son of Andrew Mellon. A fine collection of French Impressionist pictures are on loan to the gallery from Mr. and Mrs. Mellon.

The National Gallery's rapidly expanding graphic arts holdings, in great part given by Lessing J. Rosenwald, numbers about 30,000 items and dates from the 12th century to the present. Mr. Rosenwald's gift, one of the world's great collections of prints and drawings, forms the nucleus of the gallery's holdings in this field.

The Index of American Design contains over 17,000 watercolor renderings and 5000 photographs of American crafts and folk arts.

The gallery's Education Department gives daily talks on the collections in the galleries. The Extension Service lends audio-visual materials, films, slide lectures and exhibits to schools, colleges and civic groups in some 4000 communities in the United States and Canada. Nearly all of the gallery's services are available to the public free of charge.

Construction is in progress for the expansion of the National Gallery in the block immediately east of the present building. Funds for this project have come from the Mellon family. The architect is I. M. Pei. Expected to be finished in 1976, the East Building will provide space for temporary exhibitions, for the National Gallery's growing collection of 20th century paintings and sculpture, for a Center for Advanced Study in the Visual Arts, and for a greatly expanded library and photographic archive.

Open daily except Christmas and New Year's. Hours 10 a.m. to 5 p.m. weekdays, noon to 9 p.m. Sundays. From April to Labor Day open weekdays 10 a.m. to 9 p.m., noon to 9 p.m. Sundays.

National Geographic Society

The National Geographic Society, founded in 1888 "for the increase and diffusion of geographic knowledge," is the world's largest nonprofit scientific and educational institution. The Society produces the illustrated monthly *National Geographic*, books, maps, globes, atlases, other educational materials, and television programs. Its activities are supported by the dues of 9,000,000 members.

The society's 10-story headquarters building in Washington, D. C., was dedicated by President Lyndon B. Johnson in 1964. It attracts many thousands of visitors, including members of the society from all over the world. Explorers Hall offers exhibits, artifacts, and mementos depicting the organization's research and exploration activities.

In 1968 the society occupied its new Membership Center Building on a 100-acre tract near Gaithersburg, Md. The building accommodates 1,200 employes charged with handling membership files, correspondence, changes of address, and other clerical operations.

Executive officers are: Melville Bell Grosvenor, editor-in-chief and chairman of the board of trustees; Thomas W. McKnew, advisory chairman of the board; Melvin M. Payne, president and editor; Robert E. Doyle, vice president and secretary; Thomas M. Beers, vice president and associate secretary; Hilleary F. Hoskinson, treasurer.

The Pentagon

The Pentagon, headquarters of the Department of Defense, is the world's largest office building, twice as large as the Merchandise Mart in Chicago and with 3 times the floor space of the Empire State Building in New York. Situated on the Virginia side of the Potomac River, it houses 26,000 employees in offices that occupy 3,707,745 square feet.

The Pentagon was completed Jan. 15, 1943, at a cost of about $83,000,000. It covers 34 acres and has 204 acres of lawns and terraces. It is 5 stories high and consists of 5 rings of buildings connected by 10 corridors, with a 5-acre pentagonal court in the center. Each of the outer-most sides of the building is 921 ft. long and the perimeter is seven-eighths of a mile. Total length of corridors is 17½ miles. There is a partial mezzanine below the first floor and a partial basement below that.

Smithsonian Institution

The Smithsonian Institution is one of the world's great historical, scientific, educational, and cultural establishments. It comprises numerous facilities, mostly in the metropolitan Wash. D. C. area. It was founded by an Act of Congress in 1846, pursuant to a bequest of James Smithson, a British scholar-scientist, to the United States to found at Washington "an establishment for the increase and diffusion of knowledge among men." The Smithsonian, ever since its founding, has been a center for basic scientific research; it engages in programs of education and it is also the largest museum-gallery complex in the world. More than 21,000,000 persons visit its halls annually. S. Dillon Ripley became the 8th secretary of the Smithsonian Feb. 1, 1964.

The Anacostia Neighborhood Museum opened in 1967 as a satellite museum located in a low-income urban setting. The first of its kind in the nation, it provides an environment for open, nondirected learning through actual contact with real things, for adults and children who rarely, if ever, use existing museums and other cultural resources. Its programs include exhibits drawn from Smithsonian collections in art, history, and science; workshops, clubs, and classes related to the exhibits; and exhibits assembled or made by the residents of the neighborhood. a mobile unit brings small portable exhibitions to the schools and street corners of the Anacostia community.

The Freer Gallery of Art, the gift of Detroit industrialist Charles Lang Freer, is an outstanding museum and research center in art of the Far and Near East. The gallery also houses the Whistler Peacock Room and his etchings and paintings.

The Joseph H. Hirshhorn Museum and Sculpture Garden, opened in 1974, houses works in the Hirshhorn collection which were donated in 1966 to the people of the United States. Primary emphasis is on art of the 20th century although the sculpture section ranges from antiquity to works of the most significant European and American contemporaries.

The National Museum of History and Technology has exhibits illustrating American culture, civil and military history and the history of science and technology. The museum consists of 3 floors of exhibitions, and food facilities for its visitors. In the rotunda the visitor will find the original Star-Spangled Banner and a Foucault pendulum demonstrating the earth's rotation. Other major exhibits feature gowns of the First Ladies, the Petroleum Hall, the history of transporation, American political and military history, numismatics, philately, ceramics and glass, musical instruments, timekeeping, phsycial and medical sciences, graphic arts, electricity, photography, and news reporting. National treasures on display include the desk on which Thomas Jefferson drafted the Declaration of Independence and Samuel Morse's first telegraph. A popular attraction is an authentic 19th century country store-post office where mail is hand-stamped with a "Smithsonian Station" postmark.

The National Museum of Natural History serves as a national and international center for the natural sciences: It maintains the largest reference collection in the nation and conducts a broad program of basic research on man, plants, animals, fossil organisms, rocks, minerals, and materials from outer space. Exhibits show aspects of life and cultures in Asia, Africa, and the Pacific. Other exhibits include fossil plants and invertebrate animals, fishes, amphibians, dinosaurs, primitive reptiles and archaeology of the Americans, osteology, physical anthropology, geology, the World of Mammals, the Hall of Birds, the Fenykovi Elephant, and the Hall of Gems and Minerals, including the 44½ carat blue Hope diamond and the largest gem emerald on public exhibit, the 858 carat Gachala emerald.

The National Air and Space Museum. Pending new construction, the Arts and Industries building and the temporary Air and Space building house the historic Wright Brothers' airplanes, Charles A. Lindbergh's "Spirit of St. Louis," spacecrafts of John Glenn and Alan Shepard, the Apollo 11 command module which carried Armstrong, Collins and Aldrin to the moon and back, and other significant air and space artifacts.

The National Collection of Fine Arts, opened its doors in 1968 in the renovated Old Patent Office Building, noted for its classical Greek architecture. In addition to its Two-Century Survey of American Art, there are special and loan exhibits of American sculpture, painting, and graphics. The National Portrait Gallery, also located in the Old Patent Office Bldg., exhibits the likenesses of persons who have made significant contributions to the history, development, and culture of the people of the United States.

The Renwick Gallery, a division of the National Collection of Fine Arts, is a new national showcase for creativity in design, crafts, and the decorative arts. Two permanent public rooms, restored and furnished in styles of the post-Civil War period, and special temporary exhibitions can be seen in the renovated building.

The National Zoological Park is noted for its outstanding collections including two giant pandas from China. Its research includes investigation in animal behavior, ecology, nutrition and reproduction physiology, pathology, and clinical medicine. Conservation-oriented studies cover maintenance of wild population and long-term captive breeding and care of endangered species.

The Smithsonian Associates was founded to stimulate interest and active participation in the Smithsonian's work. Its membership programs for adults and young people include seminars, lectures, workshops, demonstrations, concerts, theater, exhibition previews, dramas, films, tours, and field and camping trips. *Smithsonian*, a monthly magazine of the arts, sciences, and history is available to members of the Associates.

The **Smithsonian Institution Traveling Exhibition Service** (SITES) organizes and circulates exhibitions for art and science museums, colleges, and other educational institutions around the United States and Canada. More than one hundred twenty-five exhibitions are on continuous tour, with fifty or sixty openings of these shows occurring monthly across the country.

Washington National Monument

The **Washington National Monument** is a tapering shaft or obelisk of white marble, 555 ft., 5⅛ inches in height and 55 ft., 1½ inches square at base. Eight small windows, 2 on each side, are located at the 500-ft. level, where Washington points of interest are indicated.

The capstone weighs 3,300 lbs. and was placed Dec. 6, 1884. The monument was dedicated Feb. 21, 1885, and opened Oct. 9, 1888. It weighs 81,120 tons. It is dressed with white Maryland marble in 2-ft. courses. The first 150 ft. are backed by rubble masonry. From that point to 452 ft. Maine granite was used as backing, and above 452 ft. marble was used. The face of the monument is primarily marble from Maryland. Set into the interior wall are 190 memorial stones from states, foreign countries and organizations. An iron stairway has 50 landings and 898 steps. A modern elevator takes sightseers to the 500-ft. level in one minute, compared with 12 "precarious minutes" in 1888.

The erection of the monument by the Washington National Monument society with funds obtained by popular subscription was authorized by Congress in 1848. The cornerstone was laid July 4 of the same year. Work progressed slowly until 1854 when $300,000 had been subscribed and 152 ft. of the shaft erected. In that year the enterprise became controversial and contributions ceased. Work was resumed in 1880 at government expense by the Corps of Engineers.

The Monument is open 7 days a week, 9 a.m. to 5 p.m. Extended summer hours are 8 a.m. to 12 midnight. It is closed Christmas Day.

Famous Churches

The **National Shrine of the Immaculate Conception**, at Fourth St. and Michigan Ave., NE, Washington, D. C. is the largest Catholic church in the United States and one of the largest in the world. Built by all the bishops and Catholics of the U. S. it honors the Blessed Virgin Mary as Patroness of the United States. The Shrine is impressive not only in size but also in beauty, its blue and gold dome and soaring bell-tower having become Washington landmarks. Open daily from 7 a.m. to 8 p.m., Sunday masses, 7, 8, 9, 10, 11 a.m. and noon, 1:15 and 4:30 p.m. Free guided tours 9 a.m. to 5 p.m. daily; Sunday tours 2 p.m. to 4 p.m. Carillon concerts on Sundays and preceding organ and choral concerts. Organ recitals every Sun. at 7:00 p.m. (June through August) and 4th Friday organ recitals (Sept. through May).

Washington Cathedral, Massachusetts and Wisconsin Aves., NW, is atop Mt. Saint Alban, the highest point in Washington, D.C. It is the seat of the Presiding Bishop of the Episcopal Church and of the Bishop of Washington. Started in 1907, it is only three-quarters complete, and when finished in 1985 is expected to be the 6th largest church in the world. Notables buried in the Cathedral include Woodrow Wilson, Adm. George Dewey, Cordell Hull, and Frank B. Kellogg. The Cathedral is considered one of the finest examples of Gothic architecture in the country.

Several Protestant churches commemorate the association of presidents with their congregations. **St. John's Episcopal Church**, across Lafayette Sq. from the White House, designed by Benj. Latrobe in 1815, was regularly attended by Madison and F. D. Roosevelt and at times by other Presidents. **New York Ave. Presbyterian Church**, 1313 New York Ave., NW, preserves the pew in which Lincoln sat, also an original manuscript of the first draft of his first proposal to abolish slavery. The church was rebuilt on same site in 1950-51.

The **new National Presbyterian Church**, on a 13-acre tract, at Nebraska Ave. and Van Ness St., NW, was dedicated on May 10, 1970. The Church traces its origin to a group of stonemasons who met in a carpenter's shop in the grounds of the White House in 1795, later becoming the First Presbyterian Church in the District of Columbia. The Church of the Covenant, founded in 1883, united with the original Presbyterian body in 1930 to become the congregation of the National Presbyterian Church. President Eisenhower was baptized by the pastor, Dr. Edward L. R. Elson, and became a member of the Church on Feb. 1, 1953. He laid the cornerstone of the new Church on his 77th birthday, Oct. 14, 1967, and the Chapel of the Presidents is dedicated to him. The Chapel of the Presidents contains the Eisenhower pew, and pews representing 16 additional presidents who worshipped with the congregation. The oldest president's pew, occupied by Jackson, Polk, Pierce, Buchanan and Cleveland is on view together with much historic memorabilia.

The **Islamic Center**, 2551 Massachusetts Ave, NW, a magnificent monument of Islamic culture and outstanding landmark for visitors, a mosque for worship, and an institute for study of Islamic culture.

Cherry Blossom Time

Cherry blossom time in Washington is looked upon as the opening of spring. The famous cherry trees encircle the Tidal Basin in West Potomac Park and for 2 miles line the roadside in East Potomac Park. A gift by the Mayor of Tokyo to the city of Washington, the original 3,000 trees were propagated from the trees on the Arawaka River in a suburb of Tokyo. The first trees were planted by Mrs. William Howard Taft, wife of the president, and by Viscountess Chinda, wife of the Japanese Ambassador, Mar. 27, 1912. Today many of the 650 trees around the Tidal Basin have white blossoms, while some have pink; deep pink blossoms are in East Potomac Park. The trees usually are in full blossom the first week in April, but no precise date can be given earlier than 10 days prior to full blossom, which lasts about one week.

Other Points of Interest

Pan American Union Building, 17th St. and Constitution Ave., NW, houses the General Secretariat of the Organization of American States, the oldest major international organization in the world, representing 24 countries of the western hemisphere. Of traditional Spanish architecture with a tropical garden courtyard, the building is one of the more gracious sights in Washington. It contains the Hall of the Americas assembly room, permanent and temporary exhibits of Latin American art, the Columbus Memorial Library, and behind the building, the Aztec Gardens.

National Society, Daughters of the American Revolution on a block bounded by 17th and 18th Sts., and C and D Sts. NW.

American National Red Cross, 17th and D Sts. NW, occupies three white marble buildings of neoclassic design, embellished with a Corinthian portico, colonnades and bronze doors. The Red Cross Museum is in the east building.

Federal Reserve Building, Constitution Ave., between 20th and 21st Sts. NW, is a 4-story white marble building of Georgian design, with formal gardens and fountains and tasteful but relatively simple interiors, built 1937. An annex, the William McChesney Martin Building, will be occupied in 1974.

The Corcoran Gallery of Art, 17th St. between New York Ave., and E. St. NW, Washington, was donated by William Wilson Corcoran in 1859. Other donors, including Sen. W. A. Clark, have augmented its collection. The Gallery is open 11 a.m. to 5 p.m., Tuesday through Sunday; closed Mondays, and on Jan. 1, July 4, Thanksgiving, and Dec. 24, 25 and 31. Admission is $1.00; free on Tues. and Weds. and at all times to senior citizens, children under 12 accompanied by an adult, and clergy; 50 cents to students with I.D. and military, EA rank and below..

New York City Museums, Libraries, Centers of Interest

See Index for Statue of Liberty

The New York Aquarium, in Coney Island, exhibits marine life from all climes, with over 3,000 live specimens including whales, sharks, seals, sea lions, fish, penguins; whale and dolphin training sessions.

The New York Botanical Garden occupies 230 acres in the Bronx. An 11-greenhouse Main Conservatory features seasonal shows and permanent exhibits of palms, tropical and temperate plants, ferns, orchids. There are specialized gardens, a museum of plant evolution and uses and a botanical library.

The New York Cultural Center, Columbus Circle, features exhibitions of painting, sculpture, photography and documentary work, changed periodically. The building was designed by Edward Durrell Stone.

The Frick Collection, 1 E. 70th St., was founded by Henry Clay Frick (1849-1919). The principal part of the collection consists of 14th-19th Century paintings as well as sculpture.

The Solomon R. Guggenheim Museum, 5th Ave. and 89th St.; permanent collection contains over 3,000 paintings, drawings, sculptures and graphic works by 19th and 20th Century artists. The museum's unique spiral building was designed by Frank Lloyd Wright.

The Hayden Planetarium, facing 81st St. near Central Park W., presents dramatic representations of the skies inside a large hemispheric dome with a Zeiss planetarium projector and other instruments; about 9,000 stars are shown. Also: astronomy, space, weather, time exhibits; Guggenheim Space Theater.

The Hispanic Society of America is a free public museum and reference library devoted to the art and literature of Spain and Portugal. It is on Audubon Terrace, between 155th and 156th Sts., west of Broadway. Collections run from ancient to modern.

The Jewish Museum, 5th Ave. at 92d St., offers exhibitions of Jewish art and ceremonial objects and exhibits of Jewish interest. The permanent collection of Judaica is considered the most comprehensive in the world. There are lectures and a book and print shop.

The Metropolitan Museum of Art, 5th Ave. at 82d St. With over 1,000,000 works of art, the museum's collection is the largest of its kind in the Western Hemisphere. Great masters of all the ages of art are included in the collections: Egyptian, Green, Roman, Ancient Near Eastern, Islamic, Far Eastern, Medieval, Arms and Armor, European, Pre-Columbian, American, Contemporary Arts, Musical Instruments, Costume Institute and Junior Museum. A new American Bicentennial Wing is to be completed in 1976.

The Cloisters, in Manhattan's Fort Tryon Park, is a branch of the Metropolitan devoted to Medieval art and architecture in 5 cloisters and other early European structures.

The Museum of the American Indian, Heye Foundation, Broadway at 155th St., maintains the world's largest collection of American Indian materials, extensive archeological and ethnological displays from North, Central and South America, as well as study and photographic facilities.

The Museum of Modern Art, 11 W. 53d St., est. 1929, presents 20th Century painting, sculpture, drawings, prints, architectural and industrial design, photography and film. A library contains about 30,000 vols. and a reference collection of more than 100,000 photographs. The film department has more than 12,000,000 ft. of film. Bookstore, restaurant and gift shop.

The American Museum of Natural History occupies a group of buildings at Central Park West between 77th and 81st Sts. There are large exhibits of man and beast from the most primitive times to the present, with extensive reconstruction of fossilized remains, dioramas of men and animals in their natural settings, dinosaurs, birds, Indians, Eskimos and glass models of protozoa, rotifers and coelenerates. The

collections of gems and ocean life are famous. Visitors may handle artifacts in the People Center.

The Museum of the City of New York on 5th Ave. at 104th St., illustrates the history and life of the city. Its collections include dioramas, paintings, prints, maps, photographs, portraits, miniatures, vehicles, ship models, costumes, silver, furniture, theatrical and musical memorabilia, toys and rare books.

The New York Historical Society, founded 1804, is at 170 Central Park W. between 76th and 77th Sts. The Society maintains a museum devoted to Americana; A large gallery of American portrait, landscape and genre paintings; a reference library of American and especially New York history; manuscripts from all periods of the nation's past; maps, prints, broadsides and photographs. Of special interest are the original water color drawings by John James Audubon for his *Birds of America.* Also, fire engine, carriage, toy collections.

The American Numismatic Society, founded 1858, maintains a museum of coins and other currency, ancient and modern medals and decorations at Broadway and 156th St.

The New York Public Library: In 1974, its resources were placed at more than 34,500,000 items of which over 9,000,000 were books, over 10,000,000 manuscripts, over 6,000,000 pictures, 3,500,000 posters, photographs and broadsides, 6,000,000 pamphlets, scrapbooks and clippings. Of this total, 4,000,000 books and the pictures are in the collections of the Branch Libraries which are maintained by the City of New York and which operate 83 branch libraries in Manhattan, the Bronx and Staten Island and 6 bookmobiles. The Research Libraries, based at 5th Ave. and 42d St., include the Performing Arts Research Center, in Lincoln Center, and the Schomburg Center for Research in Black Culture, 103 W. 135th St.

Seamen's Church Institute, facing Manhattan's Battery Park, has dining room, cafeteria, collections of ships' bells and models, marine paintings, gym, sauna and showers, all open to public.

South St. Seaport Museum, on the East River waterfront in Lower Manhattan, is a growing restoration of earlier eras of New York's port. At piers on South St. at Fulton, the museum has 10 ships, including an iron-hulled windjammer, a Hudson River sidewheeler and the original Ambrose Lightship. Ashore on Fulton St. are museum galleries and a bookshop. Special features include puppet and craft shows, songfests, plays for children and adults, and seminars on nautical subjects. Restorations will include 100 early buildings with art shops, retail stores, apartments, offices and restaurants.

The Staten Island Institute of Arts and Sciences, founded 1881, has a museum of art, natural science, conservation and Indian life at 75 Stuyvesant Pl., St. George, S.I., and library at 51 Stuyvesant Pl. It offers lectures and classes for children and adults.

Whitney Museum of American Art, Madison Ave. at 75th St., holds exhibitions of group and individual artists, historical and contemporary. Comprehensive permanent collection of American art.

Zoos. One of the world's largest zoos is the N.Y. Zoological Park (the Bronx Zoo), Pelham Parkway and Southern Blvd., the Bronx. About 3,000 mammals, birds, reptiles are displayed in its 252 acres, including African Plains exhibit, World of Birds and Children's Zoo. The city's Parks Administration runs the Central Park Zoo and the adjoining Children's Zoo at 5th Ave. and 64th St. in Manhattan, the Prospect Park Zoo and Children's Farmyard in Brooklyn, and the Queens Zoo and Children's Farm in Flushing Meadows-Corona Park, Queens. The Staten Island

Brooklyn Centers

Brooklyn Academy of Music, 30 Lafayette Ave., is the Brooklyn Center for the Performing Arts. It presents music, dance, theater, lectures and special membership events.

Brooklyn Botanic Garden, Eastern Parkway, Washington and Flatbush Aves., has 50 acres of gardens, including rose, herb, wild flower and Japanese, and a fragrance garden for the blind.

The Brooklyn Museum, Eastern Parkway and Washington Ave., estab. 1897, has comprehensive exhibitions in all major fields of art. An Outdoor Sculpture Garden contains ornaments from razed N. Y. area buildings.

The Brooklyn Public Library occupies the Ingersoll Building, Grand Army Plaza, and 55 branches. It operates two bookmobiles. The Ingersoll Building has 5 major-subject divisions and Periodicals Division, Audio-Visual section, children's room and telephone reference service.

Churches

John St. United Methodist Church, 44 John St., erected 1841, on site of Wesley Chapel of 1768, "first Methodist preaching-house in America," houses oldest Methodist Society, formed 1766. Has noontime services for office workers. It also has a museum.

Little Church Around the Corner is the name by which the Church of the Transfiguration (Episcopal), 1 E. 29th St., has become famous. It was so called in 1870 by a rector of another church, who, unwilling to read the burial service for an actor, advised Joseph Jefferson to apply there. It became the actors' church. It is a National Historic Landmark.

Marble Collegiate Church (Collegiate Reformed Protestant Dutch), 5th Ave. and W. 29th St., erected 1854, is notable for the preaching by Dr. Norman Vincent Peale.

Plymouth Church of the Pilgrims (Congregational), Orange St., Brooklyn, is a National Historic Site, built 1847, present structure 1849. Has windows illustrating Puritan influence on America and pew where Lincoln sat to hear Henry Ward Beecher, the first minister. In 1860 Beecher raised funds at an auction here to purchase the freedom of a slave girl, Pinky.

Riverside Church (Interdenominational-American Baptist and United Church of Christ), Riverside Drive and W. 122d St. The chief donor was John D. Rockefeller, Jr. The tower, reminiscent of Chartres, is 100 ft. square, rises 392 ft.

Russian Orthodox Cathedral of the Transfiguration (Orthodox Church in America), 228 N. 12th St., Brooklyn, is of a design similar to Moscow's Cathedral of the Assumption, with 5 onion-shaped domes. A screen of icons includes one from the 13th Century.

Cathedral of St. John the Divine on Morningside Heights, Amsterdam Ave. and W. 112th St. (Protestant Episcopal), was begun 1892 as a Romanesque building; the design was changed to Gothic. The church is 601 ft. long, 146 wide at nave and will be 330 ft. wide at transept. Two front towers will rise to over 250 ft.

St. Bartholomew's (Protestant Episcopal), Park Ave., and E. 51st St., exemplifies Byzantine-Romanesque design, with a French Romanesque portico in colored marble and mosaic and the main structure in amber-colored brick and stone.

St. Mark's-in-the-Bowery (Protestant Episcopal), 2d Ave. and E. 10th St., originally a chapel built on the farm of Director General Peter Stuyvesant in 1660, rebuilt in 1799. A statue of Stuyvesant in the churchyard was presented by Queen Wilhelmina of the Netherlands in 1915. The church has a modern theater and poetry center.

St. Patrick's Cathedral (Roman Catholic) occupies a block facing 5th Ave., between E. 50th and E. 51st

Sts., opposite Rockefeller Center. It was begun in 1858 in granite and marble in a Gothic revival style designed by James Renwick. It was opened in part in 1877 and dedicated May 25, 1879. It has two spires, 330 ft. tall, and a 26-ft. rose window. St. Patrick's is the cathedral church of the Archdiocese of N. Y.

St. Paul's Chapel of Trinity Parish (Protestant Episcopal), Broadway and Vesey St., is the oldest colonial church edifice in Manhattan. It was opened Oct. 30, 1766. Much of the interior decoration was by L'Enfant, who laid the plans for Washington, D.C. There is a unique collection of 14 Waterford Irish cut glass chandeliers.

St. Peter's Church (Roman Catholic), Barclay and Church Sts., has the form of a Greek temple with large porch, wide steps, granite pillars, erected 1836-38 to replace the original church of 1785 of the first Catholic parish of New York.

St. Vartan Armenian Cathedral (Armenian Church of America), 2d Ave. and 35th St. Steel arches support a gilded, conic dome.

Temple Emanu-El, 5th Ave. and 65th St., was erected 1929 by Congregation Emanu-El (Reform), which dates from 1845. It was built of limestone in early Romanesque style, its auditorium 77 ft. wide by 150 ft. long and 103 ft. high, one of the largest temples in the world. Noteworthy are the high arch at the entrance, the rose window, mosaics and 3 bronze doors.

Trinity Church (Protestant Episcopal) faces Broadway at the head of Wall St. It was built 1841-46 of brown sandstone in perpendicular Gothic, designed by Richard Upjohn, is 78 ft. wide by 202 ft. long. The first church was opened in 1698. In the churchyard are buried Alexander Hamilton, Robert Fulton, Capt. James Lawrence and Revolutionary soldiers who died in British prisons.

Historic Sites

Edgar Allan Poe Cottage, Grand Concourse and Kingsbridge Rd., Bronx, is a restored cottage, built 1812, in which Poe lived 1846-49, and in which his wife, Virginia Clem, died, 1847.

Federal Hall National Memorial, Wall and Nassau Sts., is a Greek Revival structure of 1842, originally the Custom House, later the U. S. Sub-Treasury. On the site stood the Colonial City Hall and later Federal Hall, where the Stamp Act, Continental and U. S. Congresses met and George Washington took the oath of office as President.

Fraunces Tavern, Broad and Pearl Sts., was erected 1719 as the DeLancey mansion, acquired 1762 by Samuel Fraunces and operated as the Queen's Head Tavern. The Long Room was the scene of Washington's farewell to his officers, Dec. 4, 1783. It was restored by the Sons of the Revolution in the State of New York and is their headquarters. It contains a Revolutionary War museum and art gallery, free to the public.

General Grant National Memorial (Grant's Tomb), Riverside Dr. and W. 122d St., is a formal Roman-style mausoleum in which Gen. U. S. Grant, 18th President, and Mrs. Grant are buried. The tomb is 165 ft. tall.

The Jumel Mansion, W. 160th St. and Edgecombe Ave., is a 3-story colonial mansion with 4-pillared portico built in 1765 by Col. Roger Morris of the British Army. From Sept. 15-Oct. 19, 1776, it was the headquarters of Gen. George Washington. In 1810 Stephen Jumel bought 63 acres of the property. In 1833, the widowed Mrs. Jumel married Aaron Burr. He lived there briefly.

Washington Square, at the foot of 5th Ave., is the best known landmark of Greenwich Village, a colorful community and tourist attraction. Facing the lower end of 5th Ave. is the marble **Washington Arch,** designed by Stanford White to commemorate the centenary of the first inauguration and completed in 1895. To the east and south are buildings of **New York University,** which also owns many of the old redbrick houses of Federal design on the north side.

Important Buildings

Battery Park City. On a mile-long, 100-acre site reclaimed from the Hudson River, running north from Battery Park in lower Manhattan, buildings will provide 16,000 housing units, 6 million sq. ft. of office space, a hotel, and entertainment, cultural, shopping and recreational facilities. Occupancy to begin in 1976.

City Hall, headquarters of the Mayor, the City Council and the Board of Estimate of the City of New York, is in City Hall Park (the original Common), bounded by Broadway, Park Row and Chambers St. Erected 1803-1812, it is an adaptation of French Renaissance with clock cupola surmounted by a figure of Justice.

The Coliseum, facing Columbus Circle between W. 58th and W. 60th Sts., is New York's principal center for national and international exhibitions. Opened Apr. 28, 1956, it cost about $35,000,000. The Coliseum has over 320,000 sq. ft. of exhibition space.

Empire State Building, 5th Ave., between W. 33d and 34th Sts., is one of the world's tallest buildings (see also World Trade Center, below), 1,250 ft. high plus a 222-ft. television and FM radio transmitting tower. The building was completed May 1, 1931. More than 1,500,000 persons annually visit the 86th and 102d floor observatories. On a clear day viewers can see a distance of 80 mi.

Lincoln Center for the Performing Arts was opened Sept. 23, 1962, with a concert in Philharmonic (later renamed Avery Fisher) Hall. The center is located between W. 62d and 66th Sts., Amsterdam and Columbus Aves. It is a private, nonprofit tax-exempt corporation of 8 constituent organizations. The New York State Theater opened in 1964; the Vivian Beaumont Theater, for repertory, and the Library-Museum of the Performing Arts, 1965; the Metropolitan Opera House, 1966; the Juilliard School of music, including Alice Tully Hall, 1969.

Madison Square Garden Center, Pennsylvania Plaza (7th-8th Aves., 31st-33d Sts.), opened in the 1967-68 season. The huge development, above the modernized underground Pennsylvania RR station, includes a 29-story office building and the Sports and Entertainment Center which has the Garden Arena seating over 20,000, the 5,000-seat Felt Forum, 48 bowling lanes, the National Art Museum of Sport, an Exposition Rotunda for trade and walk-around shows, and a 500-seat Cinema.

Pan Am Building, north of Grand Central Station, is one of the world's largest commercial office buildings. It has 59 floors rising 808 ft., with provision for a rooftop heliport, and was erected over the tracks of Grand Central Terminal. It covers a ground area of 3½ acres. Estimated office population is 17,000.

Rockefeller Center, the largest privately owned business and entertainment center in America was started Sept., 1931. Its area includes the three blocks from 48th to 51st Sts. between 5th Ave. and the Ave. of the Americas, a large portion of the 51st-52d St. block and 4 blockfronts on the west side of the Ave. of the Americas between 47th and 51st Sts. There are 21 buildings. It has 175,000 daily visitors; over 66,000 work there.

The surface area of Rockefeller Center covers 24 acres; almost one half are leased for a long period from Columbia University. Rockefeller Center pays Columbia an annual rental of nearly $4 million. The lease with options for renewal runs until 2069.

The part of Rockefeller Center comprising theaters and radio and television studios is often referred to as Radio City. Studios of the National Broadcasting Co. are located in the 70-story RCA building (850 ft. tall). There is an observation roof on the 70th Floor.

Radio City Music Hall, Ave. of the Americas and W. 50th St., largest indoor theater in the world, seats 6,000 people. Its stage, 144 ft. wide by 67 ft. deep, has a proscenium arch 60 ft. high and 100 ft. wide. Has first-run films and stage spectacles with the Rockettes, Symphony Orchestra and guest artists, plus concerts and other special events.

New York Stock Exchange, visitors' entrance 20 Broad St., has visitors' gallery, films, guided tours, Mon. through Fri., 10 a.m. to market closing.

American Stock Exchange, visitors' entrance 78 Trinity Pl., has visitors' gallery, guides, films and other exhibits, Mon. through Fri. during trading hours.

United Nations Headquarters occupies over 16 acres between 1st Ave. and F.D.R. (East River) Drive, E. 42d and E. 48th Sts. Most unusual is the Secretariat Bldg., 505 ft. high at front entrance, 286 ft. long and only 72 ft. wide. The 2 sides have 5,400 windows; the end walls are of 2,000 tons of Vermont marble. General Assembly Bldg. has a hall 165 ft. long, 115 ft. wide. Conference Bldg. houses 3 Council chambers, etc. There are guided tours daily.

World Trade Center, dedicated Apr. 4, 1973, on Manhattan's lower West Side, has twin towers of 110 stories, 1,350 ft. each (2d in height to Chicago's Sears Tower) and 4 other buildings. In 1974, over 21,000 of an eventual 50,000 persons worked in trade firms in the North and South Towers. Construction of this office complex for international trade, a Port Authority of N.Y. and N.J. facility, is to be completed in 1976.

A Guide to Avenue Addresses in New York City

To find the location of a number on the following avenues of Manhattan, cancel the last figure of the number, divide the remainder by 2 and add the given key number. Thus: Where is 596 7th Ave.? Divide 59 by 2 equals 30, plus 12 equals 42d St.

Ave. A............add	4	Up to 600.......add	18	Above 1800...add	20	Ft. Wash. Ave..... add	158
Ave. B............add	3	Up to 775.....add	20	8th Ave.......... add	9	Lenox Ave........add	110
Ave. C............add	3	From 775 to 1286		9th Ave.......... add	13	Lexington Ave.... add	22
Ave. D............add	3	see exception below:		10th Ave......... add	13	Madison Ave......add	27
1st Ave...........add	4	Up to 1500....... add	45	11th Ave......... add	15	Manhattan Ave...add	100
2d Ave...........add	3	Up to 2000 Morris Pk.		Amsterdam Ave...add	59	Park Ave.........add	34
3d Ave........... add	10	Above........ add	24	Audubon Ave..... add	165	Pleasant Ave.....add	101
4th Ave..........add	8	Ave. of Americas (6th)		Columbus Ave.... add	60	St. Nicholas Ave.. add	110
5th Ave. to 200 .. add	13	subtract 12 or 13		Convent Ave......add	127	Wadsworth Ave... add	175
Up to 400.....add	16	7th Ave.......... add	12	Edgecomb Ave.... add	134	West End Ave.....add	59

Exceptions

Broadway: Up to 754 below East 8th st.
Above 754, apply above rule but deduct following key numbers:
From 754 to 858 deduct 29.
From 857 to 958 deduct 25.
Above 1000 deduct 31.

Riverside Drive: Below 567, drop last figure, add 75, do not divide by two.
Above 577, drop last figure, add 78.
Central Park West: Drop last figure, add 60.
5th Ave.: From 775 to 1286, drop last figure and deduct 18 from remainder.

Note: From Washington Square north most crosstown streets have 100 numbers to the block. Numbering of these streets starts east and west from 5th Ave.

Notable Tall Buildings in North American Cities

Height from sidewalk to roof, including penthouse and tower if enclosed as integral part of structure: actual number of stories beginning at street level. Asterisks (*) denote buildings still under construction Jan. 1975.

City	Hgt. ft	Stories
New York City, Manhattan		
World Trade Center (2 towers)	1,350	110
Empire State, 34th St., 5th Ave.	1,250	102
TV tower, 222 ft., makes total	1,472	...
Chrysler, Lexington Ave. & 43d St.	1,046	77
60 Wall Tower, 70 Pine St.	950	67
40 Wall Tower	900	71
RCA, Rockefeller Center	850	70
Chase Manhattan Bldg.	813	60
Pan Am Bldg., 200 Park Ave.	808	59
Woolworth, 233 Broadway	792	60
1 Penn Plaza	764	57
U.S. Steel, 165 Broadway	743	50
20 Exchange Place	741	57
Esso, 1251 Ave. of the Americas	735	54
One Astor Plaza	730	54
9 W. 57th St.	725	50
Union Carbide Bldg., 270 Park Ave.	707	52
General Motors Bldg.	705	50
Metropolitan Life, 1 Madison Ave.	700	50
500 Fifth Avenue	697	60
Chem. Bank N.Y. Trust Bldg.	687	50
Marine Midland Bldg., 140 Bway.	677	52
McGraw Hill, 1221 Ave. of the Am.	674	51
Chanin, Lexington Ave. and 42d St.	680	56
55 Water St.	680	53
Lincoln 60 E. 52d Street	673	53
Gulf & Western Bldg., 15 Columbus Circle	679	44
1633 Broadway	670	50
American Tobacco, 245 Park Ave.	648	47
Irving Trust, 1 Wall Street	640	50
345 Park Ave.	634	44
Monsanto Bldg., 1114 Ave. of the Am.	630	50
1 New York Plaza	630*	50
Home Insurance Co. Bldg.	630	44
Waldorf-Astoria, 301 Park Ave.	625	47
Burlington House, 1345 Ave. of the Americas	625	50
Olympic Tower, 643 5th Ave.	620	50
10 East 40th Street	620	48
General Electric, Lexington Ave.	616	50
New York Life, 51 Madison Ave.	615	40
Penney Bldg., 1301 6th Ave.	609	46
Celanese Bldg., 1211 Ave. of the Am.	592	45
U.S. Court House, 505 Pearl St.	590	37
Federal Bldg., Foley Square	587	41
Time & Life, 1271 Ave. of the Am.	587	47
Cooper Bregstein Bldg., 1250 Bway.	580	40
1185 Ave. of the Americas	580	42
Municipal, Park Row & Centre St.	580	34
Westvaco Bldg., 299 Park Ave.	574	42
Socony Mobil Bldg., East 42nd St.	572	45
Sperry Rand Bldg., 1290 Ave. of Am.	570	43
600 3rd Ave.	570	42
1 Madison Square Plaza	568	42
N.Y. General, 230 Park Ave.	565	35
30 Broad Street	562	48
Sherry-Netherland, 5th Ave., 59th St.	560	40
Continental Can, 633 Third Ave.	557	39
Sperry & Hutchinson, 330 Madison.	555	39
Interchem Bldg., 1133 Ave. of the Americas	552	44
919 3rd Ave.	550	47
Burroughs Bldg., 605 3rd Ave.	550	44
Bankers Trust, 33 E. 48 St.	547	41
Transportation Bldg., 225 Bway.	546	45
Equitable Life, 1285 Ave. of the Am.	540	42
Ritz Tower, Park Ave. & 57th St.	540	41
Bankers Trust, 6 Wall Street	540	39
Equitable, 120 Broadway	538	42
1700 Broadway	533	41
Downtown Athletic Club, 19 West St.	530	45
Nelson Towers, 7th Ave. & 34th St.	525	45
Hotel Pierre, Fifth Ave & 61st St.	525	44
House of Seagram, 375 Park Ave.	525	38
Random House, 825 3rd Ave.	522	40
Du Mont Bldg., 515 Madison Ave.	520	42
26 Broadway	520	31
Newsweek Bldg., 444 Madison Ave.	518	43
Sterling Drug Bldg., 90 Park Ave.	515	41
First National City Bank	515	41
Bank of New York, 48 Wall Street	513	32

City	Hgt. ft	Stories
Navarre, 512 Seventh Avenue	513	43
Williamsburg Savings Bank, Bklyn.	512	42
ITT—American, 437 Madison Ave.	512	40
International, Rockefeller Center.	512	41
1407 Broadway Realty Corp.	512	44
United Nations, 405 E. 42 St.	505	39
2 New York Plaza	504	40
22 East 40th Street	503	43
60 Broad St.	503	39
Americana Hotel	501	51
World Apparel Center, 1411 Bway.	501	42
Akron, Ohio		
First National Tower Bldg.	330	28
Cascade, 10 W. Bowery	316	24
Albany, N.Y.		
Office Tower, So. Mall	589	44
University Towers	480	40
State Office Building	388	34
Agency (four bldgs.), So. Mall.	310	23
Capitol Hill Twin Towers	260	20
Atlanta, Ga.		
Peachtree Center Plaza Hotel	721	71
First National Bank, 2 Peachtree St.	556	44
Equitable Building, 100 Peachtree St.	453	34
101 Marietta Tower, 101 Marietta St.	446	36
National Bank of Georgia, 34 Peachtree	439	32
*Peachtree Summit #1	406	31
*Atlanta Hilton Hotel, 255 Courtland St.	404	30
*Tower Place, 3361 Piedmont Road	401	29
*Peachtree Center Harris Bldg.	382	31
Southern Bell Telephone.	380	...
Trust Company of Georgia, 26 Pryor St.	377	28
Coastal States Insurance, 260 Peachtree	377	27
Peachtree Center Cain Building.	376	30
Peachtree Center Building, 230 Peachtree	374	31
Life of Georgia Building	371	29
Peachtree Center South, 225 Peachtree	332	27
Gas Light Tower, 235 Peachtree Street	331	27
Hyatt Regency Hotel, 265 Peachtree.	330	23
100 Colony Square, 1175 Peachtree St.	328	25
*Atlanta Plaza Hotel, 170 Carnegie Way	320	31
Georgia Power Building, 270 Peachtree.	318	22
Fairmont Hotel, 180 Fourteenth St.	310	28
400 Colony Square, 1195 Peachtree St.	308	23
260 Piedmont Building, 260 Piedmont Ave.	301	23
Merchandise Mart, 240 Peachtree St.	300	22
Austin, Tex.		
*City Bank Bldg.	331	15
American Bank	313	21
State Capitol	309	...
Univ. of Texas Admin. Bldg.	307	29
J. Frank Dobie Univ. Center	299	29
Westgate Bldg.	261	24
Baltimore, Md.		
U.S. Fidelity & Guaranty Company	529	40
Maryland National Bank Bldg.	509	34
Blaustein Bldg.	354	30
Arlington Federal Bldg.	338	28
2 Charles Center South	336	30
Tower Bldg.	330	16
222 Saint Paul	328	37
Emerson Tower	319	15
First National Bank	305	21
2 Charles Center North	301	27
British American Bldg.	300	21
Lord Baltimore Hotel	287	19
1 Charles Center	284	24
Baltimore Gas and Electric Company	283	22

City	Hgt. ft.	Stories
Baton Rouge, La.		
State Capitol	460	34
American Bank Bldg.	310	25
Hilton Hotel	290	28
La. Natl. Bank Bldg.	277	21
Birmingham, Ala.		
First Natl. Southern Natural Bldg.	390	30
City Federal Bldg.	325	27
Thomas Jefferson Hotel	287	21
Daniel Bldg.	283	20
Bank for Savings Bldg.	264	19
Boston, Mass.		
John Hancock Tower	790	60
Prudential Tower	750	52
Boston Co. Bldg., Court St.	601	41
First National Bank of Boston	591	37
Employers Commercial Union Co's.	507	40
New England Merch. Bank Bldg.	500	40
U.S. Custom House	496	32
John Hancock Bldg.	495	26
State St. Bank Bldg.	477	34
Keystone Custodian Funds	400	32
State Office Bldg.	350	22
Federal Bldg. & Post Office	345	22
Suffolk County Courthouse	330	19
Sheraton-Boston Hotel	310	29
State Service Center	300	23
Buffalo, N.Y.		
Marine Midland, Main St.	529	40
City Hall	378	32
Rand Bldg., not incl. 40-ft. beacon	351	29
Erie County Savings Bank, Main St.	350	26
Manuf. & Trades Trust Co.	317	21
Liberty Bank	305	23
Electric Tower	294	18
10 Lafayette Square	263	23
Calgary, Alta.		
Husky Tower (Calgary Tower)	626	
Sun Oil Bldg.	397	32
Capitol Plaza	389	40
Western Centre	385	40
Two Bow Valley Square	378	39
Mobil Tower	362	32
One Palliser Square	350	28
Place Concorde	339	37
Mount Royal House	330	32
International Hotel	321	36
Standard Life Bldg.	316	27
Penthouse Towers	312	34
Two Calgary Place	300	28
Charlotte, N.C.		
NCNB Plaza, 101 S. Tryon	503	40
Jefferson First Union Tower	433	32
Wachovia Center, 400 S. Tryon	420	32
NCNB Bank, 200 S. Tryon	299	18
Bank of NC Bldg., 112 S. Tryon	280	20
Chicago, Ill.		
Sears Bldg.	1,454	110
Standard Oil (Indiana)	1,136	80
John Hancock Center	1,127	100
*Water Tower Plaza	871	74
Water Tower Plaza	850	74
First Natl. Bank	850	60
IBM Bldg.	695	52
Civic Center (City Hall)	662	31
Lake Point Tower	645	70
Board of Trade, incl. 81 ft. statue	605	44
Prudential Bldg., 130 E. Randolph	601	41
Antenna tower, 311 ft., makes total	912	
1000 Lake Shore Plaza Apts.	590	55
Marina City Apts., 2 buildings	588	61
Mid Continental Plaza	580	50
Pittsfield, 55 E. Washington St.	557	38
Kemper Insurance Bldg.	555	45
Newberry Plaza, State & Oak	553	56
*Harbor Point	550	54
LaSalle Natl. Bank, 135 S. LaSalle St.	535	44
One LaSalle Street	530	49
111 E. Chestnut St.	529	56
Pure Oil, 35 E. Wacker Drive	523	40
United Ins. Bldg., 1 E. Wacker Dr.	522	41
Lincoln Tower, 75 E. Wacker Dr.	519	42

City	Hgt. ft.	Stories
Carbide & Carbon, 230 N. Mich.	503	37
Walton Colonnade	500	44
Edgewater Beach Apts., 5445 Sheridan	499	39
LaSalle-Wacker, 221 N. LaSalle St.	491	41
Amer. Nat'l. Bank, 33 N. LaSalle St.	479	40
Bankers, 105 W. Adams St.	476	41
Brunswick Bldg.	475	37
Continental Companies	475	45
American Furniture Mart	474	24
Sheraton Hotel, 505 N. Mich. Ave.	471	42
Playboy Bldg., 919 N. Mich. Ave.	468	37
188 Randolph Tower	465	45
Tribune Tower, 435 N. Mich. Ave.	462	36
Equitable Life, 401 N. Michigan	457	35
Roanoke, 11 S. LaSalle St.	452	37
Cincinnati, Ohio		
Carew Tower	574	48
Central Trust Tower	495	34
Dubois Tower, 5th & Walnut	423	32
Kroger Bldg.	345	25
U. of Cinn., Sander Hall	297	27
Terrace Hilton Hotel	273	19
Cincinnati Gas & Electric Co.	268	18
Provident Tower	267	20
Cleveland, Ohio		
Terminal Tower	708	52
Erieview Plaza Tower	529	40
Federal Bldg.	419	32
Cleveland Trust Tower No. 1	383	29
Ohio-Bell Telephone	365	22
Park Centre	320	26
Central Natl. Bank Bldg.	305	23
Diamond Shamrock Bldg.	300	23
CEI Bldg.	300	22
Union Commerce Bldg.	289	21
Standard Bldg.	282	21
Crystal Tower	280	26
East Ohio Bldg.	275	21
Bond Court, 1300 E. 9th	270	20
B. F. Keith Bldg.	267	21
Cleveland State Univ.	265	21
Superior Bldg., 815 Superior Ave.	265	21
Winton Place	264	30
Columbus, Ohio		
Thirty East Broad Street	620	41
LeVeque-Lincoln Tower, 50 W. Broad	555	47
Borden Building, 180 E. Broad	438	34
Columbus Center, 100 E. Broad	357	26
Ohio Bell Building, 75 N. 4th St.	348	26
*Ohio National Plaza, E. Broad	317	25
Motorists Building, 471 E. Broad	297	21
Midland Building, 250 E. Broad	278	21
Corpus Christi, Tex.		
Wilson Tower	263	21
Dallas, Tex.		
First International Bldg.	710	56
First National Bank	625	52
Republic Bank Tower	598	50
Southland Life Tower	550	42
2001 Bryan St.	512	40
Republic Bank Bldg., not incl. 150-ft. ornamental tower	452	36
One Main Place	445	34
Ling-Tempco-Vought Tower	434	31
Mercantile Natl. Bank Bldg., not incl. 115-ft. weather beacon	430	31
Mobil Bldg.	430	31
Fidelity Union Tower	400	33
Southwestern Bell Toll Bldg.	372	22
Court House & Fed. Office Bldg.	362	16
Mercantile Dallas Bldg.	360	22
Sheraton Hotel	352	38
Elm Place, 1005-09 Elm St.	341	22
Main Tower	336	26
Adolphus Tower	327	27
Bell Telephone Bldg.	326	23
Davis Bldg.	323	21
Manor House, Bank of Service & Trust.	319	26
Preston Tower	316	29
Tower Petroleum Bldg.	315	23
Adolphus Hotel	312	25
Fairmont Hotel	308	24
Baptist Annuity Center	303	17
Life Bldg.	302	22
Santa Fe Bldg. (1st unit)	300	20

City	Hgt. ft.	Stories	City	Hgt. ft.	Stories
Dayton, Ohio			**Hartford, Conn.**		
Winters Bank Bldg.	404	30	Travelers Ins. Co. Bldg.	527	34
Hulman Bldg.	295	23	Hartford Plaza.	420	22
Knott Bldg.	297	21	Hartford Natl. Bank & Trust.	360	26
Grant-Deneau Bldg.	290	22	One Financial Plaza, 755 Main	335	26
1 First National Plaza	265	21	Bushnell Plaza	263	27
Denver, Colo.			**Honolulu, Hawaii**		
Brooks Towers, 1020 15th St.	420	42	Ala Moana Hotel.	390	38
*First of Denver Plaza	415	32	Pacific Trade Center.	360	30
Colorado Nat'l. Bank, 17th & Curtis.	389	26	*Hemmeter Center.	350	39
First National Bank	385	28	Regency Tower, 2525 Date St.	350	42
Security Life Bldg.	384	33	Yacht Harbor Towers.	350	40
Lincoln Center.	366	30	*Chateau Waikiki.	349	39
Western Fed. Savings Bldg.	354	27	Rainbow Plaza	348	37
Colorado State Bank.	352	27	Waipuna.	343	38
Brooks Tower Annex.	350	30	*The Villa on Eaton Square.	335	37
D&F Tower.	330	20	The Skyrise.	333	38
Prudential Tower Plaza.	322	26	*Diamond Head Vista.	322	35
Denver Club Building.	277	23	Reed & Martin Apt. Bldg.	321	36
			1350 Ala Moana	309	33
Des Moines, Iowa			Ala Moana Bldg.	300	23
*Ruan Center.	457	36	**Houston, Tex.**		
Financial Center, 7th & Walnut.	345	25	One Shell Plaza.	714	50
Equitable Bldg.	318	19	1100 Milam Bldg.	651	47
State Capitol.	275	4	Exxon Bldg.	606	44
			2 Houston Center	570	40
Detroit, Mich.			Dresser Tower.	550	40
*Detroit Plaza Hotel.	748	70	Pennzoil, 700 Milam.	523	36
City Natl. Bank Bldg., 637 Griswold.	557	47	United Gas Bldg.	518	35
Guardian, 500 Griswold.	485	40	Tenneco Bldg.	502	33
*Renaissance Center (4 bldgs.)	479	39	Conoco Bldg.	465	32
Book Tower, 1227 Wash. Blvd.	472	35	One Allen Center.	452	34
Cadillac Tower, 51 Cadillac Sq.	437	40	Gulf Bldg.	428	37
David Stott, 1150 Griswold.	436	38	First City Natl. Bank.	410	32
Mich. Cons. Gas Co. Bldg.	430	32	Houston Lighting & Power.	410	27
Fisher, W. Grand Blvd. & 2d St.	420	28	Neils Esperson Bldg.	409	31
*J. L. Hudson Bldg.	397	28	Regency Hyatt Hotel.	401	34
Detroit Bank & Trust Bldg.	370	28	Houston Natural Gas Bldg.	386	28
Walker Cisler	365	25	Bank of the Southwest.	369	24
David Broderick Tower.	358	34	Sheraton-Lincoln Hotel.	352	28
Buhl, 535 Griswold.	350	26	Two Shell Plaza.	341	26
Michigan Bell Telephone.	340	19	American General Life.	337	25
1st Federal Savings & Loan Assn.	338	23	Transco.	333	25
Pontchartrain Motor Hotel.	336	23	609 Fannin Bldg.	325	22
Michigan Bell Telephone.	327	17	Holiday Inn.	325	30
Commonwealth Bldg.	325	25	Capitol Natl. Bank.	320	21
1300 Lafayette East.	325	30	*Post Oak Central.	318	25
McNamara Federal Office Bldg.	320	28	St. Luke's Hospital.	316	26
First National Bldg.	319	25	500 Jefferson Bldg.	316	21
City-County Bldg.	317	20	Marathon Manufacturing Co. Bldg.	313	21
The Executive Plaza, 1200 6th Ave.	313	21	Sterling Bldg.	312	22
Sheraton Cadillac Hotel.	310	28	Melrose Bldg.	308	21
Mich. Blue Cross/Blue Shield.	307	22	Chamber of Commerce Bldg.	306	22
The Jeffersonian.	305	29	Control Data Center.	303	22
			First National Life Bldg.	302	22
Edmonton, Alta.			Prudential Bldg.	300	21
Telephone Bldg.	490	33	Kellogg Bldg.	300	22
AGT Tower, 10020-100 St.	441	34	**Indianapolis, Ind.**		
Edmonton House.	402	45	Indiana Natl. Bank Tower	504	37
Canadian National	376	25	City-County Bldg.	377	26
CN Tower, 1004-104 Ave.	365	26	Indiana Bell Telephone	320	20
Edmonton Centre, Tower One.	325	25	Riley Towers (2 bldgs.).	294	30
Imperial Oil, 10025 Jasper Ave.	272	24	Monument Circle	284	..
Centennial Bldg., 10015-103 Ave.	262	20	Market Square Office Bldg.	283	20
MacDonald Place, 9925 Jasper Ave.	261	26			
			Jacksonville, Fla.		
Fort Wayne, Ind.			Independent Life & Accident Ins. Co.	535	37
Ft. Wayne Natl. Bank.	339	26	Gulf Life Ins. Co. Bldg.	432	28
Lincoln Natl. Bank	312	23	Prudential Ins. Co. of America	295	22
			Blue Cross-Blue Shield.	287	20
Fort Worth, Tex.			Atlantic National Bank.	278	19
Ft. Worth Natl. Bank.	454	37	Universal Marion Bldg.	268	20
Continental Natl. Bank Bldg.	380	30			
Continental Life Ins. Bldg.	282	23	**Jersey City, N.J.**		
Ft. Worth Natl. Bank, 800 Main St.	275	20	Medical Center, Tuberculosis.	320	24
Texas Electric, 7th & Lamar.	275	18	Medical Center, 4 other bldgs.	294	22
First Natl. Bank.	272	22			
W. T. Waggoner Bldg.	270	22	**Kansas City, Mo.**		
Service Life Center.	270	19	Kansas City Light and Power Bldg.	476	32
			City Hall.	443	29
Halifax, N.S.			Federal Office Bldg.	413	35
Fenwick Towers.	300	31	Commerce Tower.	402	32
			Southwest Bell Telephone Bldg.	394	27
Harrisburg, Pa.			Continental Bldg.	365	30
State Capitol.	272	6	A. T. & T. Long Line Bldg.	331	20
Presbyterian Apts., 322 N. 2nd Ave.	260	23			

City	Hgt. ft.	Stories
Bryant Bldg.	319	26
Federal Reserve Bldg.	311	21
Holiday Inn	300	28

Las Vegas, Nev.

City	Hgt. ft.	Stories
International Hotel	346	30
Landmark Tower	308	27
Mint Hotel	268	26
MGM Grand Hotel	263	26

Little Rock, Ark.

City	Hgt. ft.	Stories
First National Bank	454	30
Worthern Bank & Trust	375	24
Union National Bank	330	21
Tower Bldg.	300	18

Los Angeles, Cal.

City	Hgt. ft.	Stories
United Cal. Bank	858	62
Security Pacific Natl. Bank	738	55
Atlantic Richfield Plaza (2 bldgs.)	699	52
Crocker-Citizen Plaza	620	42
Theme Towers	571	44
Union Bank Square	516	41
City Hall	454	28
Equitable Life Bldg.	454	34
Occidental Life Bldg.	452	32
Mutual Benefit Life Ins. Bldg.	435	31
Broadway Plaza	414	33
1900 Ave. of Stars	398	27
1 Wilshire Bldg.	395	28
Calif. Fed. Savings & Loan Bldg.	363	28
Century City Office Bldg.	363	24
Bunker Hill Towers	349	32
International Industries Plaza	347	24
City Natl. Bank Bldg.	344	24
Wilshire West Plaza	327	24
Luxury Towers	316	27
Getty Realty Bldg.	312	22
Water & Power Bldg.	310	20
6312 Wilshire Office Bldg.	307	21
Los Angeles Fed. Savings Bldg.	306	22
Barrington Plaza Bldg.	300	25

Louisville, Ky.

City	Hgt. ft.	Stories
First Natl. Bank	512	40
Citizen's Plaza	420	30
Galt House	325	25
Louisville Trust Bldg.	312	24
800 Apartments Bldg.	290	29
Lincoln Income Life Ins. Bldg.	289	16
Blanton House	260	20

Memphis, Tenn.

City	Hgt. ft.	Stories
100 N. Main Bldg.	430	37
Commerce Square	396	31
Sterick Bldg.	365	31
Clark, 5100 Poplar	365	32
First Natl. Bank Bldg.	332	25
Lowenstein's Towers	296	25
Lincoln American Life Tower	290	22
White Station Tower	280	24
Exchange Bldg.	264	22

Miami, Fla.

City	Hgt. ft.	Stories
One Biscayne Corp.	456	40
First Federal Savings & Loan	375	32
Dade County Court House	357	28
Ferre Bldg.	340	30
*Flagler Center Bldg.	318	25
Brickell Bay Club	286	29
Palm Bay Club	279	24
*Wimbledon Racquet Club	275	24

Milwaukee, Wis.

City	Hgt. ft.	Stories
First Wisc. Center & Office Tower	625	42
City Hall	350	9
Wisconsin Telephone Co.	313	19
Marine Plaza Bldg.	288	22
Allen-Bradley Co.	280	17
Marshall & Ilsley Bank	277	21
Regency House Apts.	274	27
Prospect Towers Apts.	268	23
Juneau Village Apts.	265	28
Schroeder Hotel	265	24
Carl Sandburg Dorm. (U. of Wisc.)	264	26
Locust Court Apts.	262	24

Minneapolis, Minn.

City	Hgt. ft.	Stories
IDS Center	772	57
Foshay Tower, not including 163-ft. antenna tower	447	32
Hennepin County Civic Center	403	24
First Natl. Bank Bldg.	366	28
Municipal Building	355	14
North Western Bell Telephone	350	26
Cedar-Riverside	337	39
Dane Tower	311	26
Midwest Federal Savings & Loan	276	20
Batzli Apts.	266	23
River Towers Apts.	260	27

Montreal, P.Q.

City	Hgt. ft.	Stories
Place Victoria	624	47
Place Ville Marie	616	49
Canadian Imperial Bank of Commerce	580	45
Chateau Champlain	480	38
CIL House	429	32
Royal Bank	397	22
Sun Life	390	26
Banque Canadienne National	390	32
Place du Canada	372	33
Alexis Nihon Plaza	331	33
Bell Telephone	324	22
Le Cartier Apts.	320	32

Nashville, Tenn.

City	Hgt. ft.	Stories
Natl. Life & Acc. Ins. Co.	452	31
Nashville Life & Casualty Tower	409	30
First American Natl. Bank	354	28
Hyatt Regency	300	28
Third Natl. Bank Bldg.	292	20
Andrew Jackson State Office Bldg.	286	17
Parkway Towers	261	21

Newark, N. J.

City	Hgt. ft.	Stories
National Newark & Essex Bank	465	36
Raymond-Commerce	448	36
Prudential Corporate Bldg.	369	27
Western Electric Bldg.	359	31
Gateway 1, tower	355	30
Prudential Insurance Company	353	21
American Insurance Company	326	21
N. J. Bell Telephone Co.	275	21
Gateway 2, Western Electric	272	20
Mutual Benefit Life Ins. Co.	271	18

New Haven, Conn.

City	Hgt. ft.	Stories
Knights of Columbus Hqs.	320	24

New Orleans, La.

City	Hgt. ft.	Stories
One Shell Square	697	51
Plaza Tower	531	45
Marriott Hotel	450	42
Bank of New Orleans	438	31
Int'l. Trade Mart Bldg.	407	33
225 Baronne St.	362	28
Hibernia Bank Bldg.	355	23
American Bank Bldg.	330	23
Canal LaSalle Bldg.	288	24
Charity Hospital of Louisiana	279	19
Lykes Center, 300 Poydras	276	22

Oakland, Cal.

City	Hgt. ft.	Stories
Ordway Bldg., 2150 Valdez St.	404	28
Kaiser Bldg.	390	28
City Hall	319	15
Tribune Tower	305	21
United Calif. Bank Bldg.	297	18
Blue Cross Bldg.	296	21
Telephone Bldg.	289	15
565 Bellevue Apts.	270	25
St. Paul Towers	267	22

Oklahoma City, Okla.

City	Hgt. ft.	Stories
Liberty Tower	500	36
First National Bank	493	33
City National Bank Tower	440	32
Kerr-McGee Center	393	30
Fidelity Plaza	310	15
Southwestern Bell Telephone	303	15
Hotel Oklahoma	298	24
The Regency Tower	288	25

City	Hgt. ft.	Stories
Southwestern Bell Telephone........	265	16
Citizen's Tower Bldg..............	265	20
United Founders Life Bldg........	264	20
Omaha, Neb.		
Woodmen Tower.................	469	30
Northwestern Bell Telephone Hdqrs..	334	16
Masonic Manor.................	320	22
First Natl. Bank................	295	22
Mutual of Omaha...............	269	13
Ottawa, Ont.		
Place de Ville, Tower C...........	368	29
Place Bell Canada..................	318	26
DBS Tower......................	308	26
Holiday Inn......................	308	28
Peace Tower.....................	301	. . .
Parliment Bldgs., Peace Tower........	291	. . .
Skyline Hotel.....................	286	25
Dept. of National Defense...........	261	22
Philadelphia, Pa.		
City Hall Tower, incl. 37-ft. statue of Wm. Penn..............	548	7
Fidelity Mutual Life Ins. Bldg.........	490	38
Phila. Saving Fund Society...........	490	39
Central Penn Natl. Bank..............	490	36
Industrial Valley Bank Bldg...........	482	32
Philadelphia National Bank...........	475	25
2000 Market St. Bldg................	435	29
Fidelity Bank Bldg..................	410	30
Two Girard Plaza...................	404	30
2000 Market St....................	399	29
Lewis Tower, 15th & Locust..........	397	33
Fifteen Hundred Locust..............	390	44
Philadelphia Electric Co.............	384	27
Penn Mutual Life...................	375	20
The Drake, 15th & Spruce............	375	33
Medical Tower, 255 So. 17th.........	364	33
State Bldg., 1400 Spring Garden......	351	18
Packard, 15th & Chestnut...........	340	25
Inquirer Building..................	340	18
Dorchester Aprt...................	339	32
Transportation Centre...............	336	18
Land Title, Broad & Chestnut.........	331	22
Suburban Benefit Bldg...............	330	. . .
Edison, 9th & Sansom...............	325	23
Penn Towers......................	320	31
1 East Penn Square.................	319	24
Architects, 17th & Sansom...........	316	24
1500 Walnut Street.................	313	23
Rittenhous Towers..................	312	28
Society Hill Towers.................	309	32
1616 Walnut Street.................	309	25
Sheraton Hotel, Inc. Tower...........	307	21
Kennedy House....................	306	29
Mutual Benefit Bldg................	304	20
Hopkinson House..................	301	35
1528 Walnut St....................	300	21
Phoenix, Ariz.		
Valley National Bank................	483	40
*Arizona Bank....................	407	31
First National Bank.................	372	27
First Federal Savings Bldg...........	341	26
Mayer Central Plaza................	315	25
Regency Apts......................	297	21
Rosenzweig Center No. 2.............	280	22
Rosenzweig Center No. 1.............	271	17
Pittsburgh, Pa.		
U.S. Steel Bldg....................	841	64
Gulf, 7th Ave. and Grant St..........	582	44
University of Pittsburgh.............	535	42
Mellon Bank Bldg..................	520	41
1 Oliver Plaza.....................	511	39
Grant, Grant St. at 3rd Ave..........	485	40
Koppers, 7th Ave. and Grant.........	475	34
Pittsburgh National Bldg............	424	30
Alcoa Bldg., 425 Sixth Ave...........	410	30
Westinghouse Bldg.................	355	23
Oliver, 535 Smithfield St.............	347	25
Gateway Bldg. No. 3................	344	24
Smithfield Plaza...................	341	26
Federal Bldg., 1000 Liberty Ave.......	340	23
Bell Telephone, 416 7th Ave..........	339	21
Hilton Hotel......................	333	22
Frick, 437 Grant St.................	330	20

City	Hgt. ft.	Stories
301 Fifth Ave.....................	322	24
Washington Plaza Apts..............	300	23
Commonwealth, 316 Fourth Ave......	300	21
Portland, Ore.		
First Natl. Bank of Oregon...........	538	41
Georgia Pacific Bldg................	367	27
Providence, R.I.		
Industrial National Bank............	420	26
Rhode Island Hospital Trust Tower...	408	30
First Hartford Realty Corp...........	301	23
Richmond, Va.		
First & Merchants Natl. Bank........	313	26
City Hall.........................	310	18
Central National Bank Bldg...........	282	24
First National Bank Bldg.............	262	19
Fidelity Bankers Life................	261	23
Rochester, N.Y.		
Xerox Tower......................	443	30
Lincoln First Tower.................	390	26
Eastman Kodak Bldg................	360	19
*First Federal Bank Bldg., 28 E. Main St.	305	22
Marine Midland Bank Bldg...........	280	22
Alliance Bldg......................	261	15
St. Louis, Mo.		
Gateway Arch.....................	630	. . .
Laclede Gas. Bldg., 8th & Olive.......	400	34
S. W. Bell Telephone Bldg............	398	31
Civil Courts......................	387	13
Mercantile Trust Bldg...............	380	35
Queeny Tower.....................	321	19
Counsel House Plaza................	320	27
Park Plaza Hotel...................	310	30
Pierre Laclede Tower...............	309	24
Riverfront Inn, 3rd St...............	301	30
Mansion House....................	285	28
500 Broadway.....................	282	22
Continental Bldg...................	277	23
Railroad Exchange Bldg..............	277	21
University Club Bldg................	276	23
77 Bonhomme Bldg.................	275	25
Boatman's Bank Tower..............	275	22
Equitable Bldg....................	275	21
Lennox Hotel.....................	275	25
Park Tower Apts...................	264	24
Missouri Pacific Bldg...............	264	23
Chromallay Bldg...................	263	22
Gateway Towers, 1 Mem. Drive.......	261	20
City Towers Apt...................	260	22
St. Paul, Minn.		
First Natl. Bank Bldg., incl. 100-ft. sign......................	517	32
Osborn Bldg......................	368	20
Kellogg Square Apts................	366	32
Northwestern Bell Telephone Bldg....	340	15
American National Bank Bldg.........	335	25
St. Paul Cathedral..................	307	. . .
U.S. Post Office Bldg................	274	12
St. Paul Hilton Hotel...............	273	24
City Hall & Court House.............	261	18
Salt Lake City, Utah		
L.D.S. Church Office Bldg............	420	30
34 South State....................	351	27
City & County Bldg.................	290	. . .
State Capitol......................	285	. . .
Univ. Club Bldg....................	277	24
Kennecott Bldg....................	267	18
Walker Bank Bldg..................	262	18
San Antonio, Tex.		
Tower of the Americas..............	622	. . .
Tower Life........................	404	30
Nix Professional Bldg...............	375	23
Natl. Bank of Commerce.............	310	24
First Natl. Bank Tower..............	302	20
Alamo National Bldg................	288	23
Milam Bldg.......................	280	20
Southwestern Bell Telephone Co......	260	16
San Diego, Cal.		
So. Calif. First Natl. Bank Bldg........	388	25

City	Hgt. ft.	Stories
U.S. Natl. Bank Bldg.	340	25
Financial Square, 6th & B Sts.	339	24
Union Bank.	320	22
San Diego Gas & Electric Bldg.	293	21
Charter Oil Bldg.	281	23
Security Pacific Natl. Bank Bldg.	278	18
Home Tower.	278	18

San Francisco, Cal.

City	Hgt. ft.	Stories
Transamerica Pyramid.	853	48
Bank of America.	778	52
Security Pacific Bank.	569	45
*Southern Pacific.	565	43
Wells Fargo Bldg.	561	43
Standard Oil, 575 Market St.	551	39
Aetna Life.	529	38
First & Market Bldg.	529	38
Metropolitan Life.	524	38
Hilton Hotel.	493	46
Pacific Gas & Electric.	492	34
Union Bank.	487	37
Pacific Insurance.	476	34
Hartford Bldg.	465	33
Mutual Benefit Life.	438	32
Russ Bldg.	435	31
Telephone Bldg.	435	26
Levi Strauss.	412	31
Calif. State Automobile Assn.	399	29
Alcoa Bldg.	398	27
St. Francis Hotel.	395	32
Shell Bldg.	386	29
*Southern Pacific.	378	28
Great Western Savings.	359	26
Union Square Hyatt House Hotel.	355	35
Equitable Life Bldg.	355	25
Fox Plaza.	354	29
International Bldg.	350	22
450 Sutter Street.	343	26
Cathedral Apartments.	340	21
Royal Towers.	330	24
Fairmont Hotel.	330	29
Bechtel Bldg.	327	23
Standard Oil Bldg.	327	22

Seattle, Wash.

City	Hgt. ft.	Stories
Seattle-1st Natl. Bank Bldg.	609	50
Space Needle.	607	
Bank of Calif. 900 4th Ave.	548	42
*Commerce House, 4th & Univ.	536	40
L. C. Smith Bldg.	522	42
Federal Office Bldg.	487	37
Financial Center.	414	30
Washington Plaza Hotel.	397	40
*Safeco Ins. Co. America.	325	22

Syracuse, N.Y.

City	Hgt. ft.	Stories
State Tower.	315	22
Mony Office Bldg.	268	19
Carrier Tower.	268	19

Tampa, Fla.

City	Hgt. ft.	Stories
First Financial Tower.	458	36
Exchange Natl. Bldg.	280	22

Toledo, Ohio

City	Hgt. ft.	Stories
Owens-Corning Fiberglas Tower.	400	30
Owens Illinois Bldg.	368	27
Toledo Trust Bldg.	288	21

Toronto, Ont.

City	Hgt. ft.	Stories
*CN Tower, Metro Centre.	1,805	
*Bank of Montreal Centre.	930	72
Commerce Court.	784	57
Toronto-Dominion Bank Tower.	740	56
Royal Trust Tower.	600	46
Manulife Centre Apts.	540	52
*Royal Bank Plaza.	520	41
Bank of Commerce Bldg.	476	34
Simpson Tower.	473	33
Two Bloor Street West.	450	34
Four Seasons Sheraton Hotel.	443	44
*Two Bloor East.	440	34
*Lake Shore City Apts.	425	60
*Castle Harbour Hotel.	420	40
Commercial Union Tower, (T-D Centre).	420	32
*Upper Canada Place Apts.	420	42
The Fairbanks.	405	42
Royal York Hotel.	397	26
390 Bay St.	394	32
*Richmond-Adelaide Center #2.	380	30
*Castle Harbour Hotel, West.	380	36
*Yonge-Eglinton Centre.	380	30
Leaside Park Apts.	376	42
*100 Bloor West.	370	29
York Center.	360	28
*Hotel Toronto Plaza.	350	28
Bloor-Islington Square.	350	23
Hyatt Regency Hotel.	365	31
Summerhill Square.	354	37
MacDonald Block.	349	24
Richmond-Adelaide.	340	26

Tulsa, Okla.

City	Hgt. ft.	Stories
*National Bank of Tulsa.	667	50
1st National Tower.	516	41
4th Natl. Bank of Tulsa.	412	32
National Bank of Tulsa.	400	24
Cities Service Bldg.	388	28
Univ. Club Tower.	377	32
Philtower.	343	23

Vancouver, B.C.

City	Hgt. ft.	Stories
Vancouver Square.	586	32
Royal Bank Centre.	468	37
Scotiabank Bldg.	462	36
T-D Bank Tower.	410	31
Granville Square.	403	30
Sheraton-Landmark Hotel.	394	41
Bank of Montreal Tower.	386	28
Regency-Hyatt House Hotel.	357	36
Hotel Vancouver.	352	22
*Board of Trade Tower.	342	26
MacMillan-Bloedel Bldg.	340	28
Guinness Tower.	328	23
Marine Bldg.	321	21
Martello Tower.	300	31

Wilmington, Del.

City	Hgt. ft.	Stories
Hercules Tower.	287	23
American Life Ins. Co. Bldg.	282	21

Winnipeg, Man.

City	Hgt. ft.	Stories
Richardson Bldg., 1 Lombard Place.	439	34
55 Nassau St.	354	39
North Star Inn.	300	30
1 Evergreen Place.	294	32

Winston-Salem, N.C.

City	Hgt. ft.	Stories
Wachovia Bldg.	410	30
Reynolds Bldg.	315	21

Tall Buildings in Other Cities

Figures denote number of stories. Height in feet is in parentheses.

Cape Canaveral, Fla., Vehicle Assembly Bldg., 40 (552); Albuquerque, N.M., National Bldg., 18 (272); Allentown, Pa., Power & Light Bldg., 23 (320); Amarillo, Texas, American Natl. Bank, 33 (374); Bethlehem, Pa., Martin Tower, 21 (332); Charleston, W. Va., Kanawha Valley Bldg., 20 (384); Cuyahoga Falls, Ohio, Cathedral Tower Restaurant, 60 (554); Frankfort, Ky., Capital Plaza Office Tower, 28 (338); Galveston, Tex., American National Ins., 20 (358); Greenville, S.C., Daniel Bldg., 22 (305); Lansing, Mich., Michigan Natl. Tower, 25 (300, not including antenna tower); Lincoln, Neb., State Capital (432); Long Beach, Calif. International Tower, 27 (277); Mobile, Ala., First Natl. Bank, 33 (420); Niagara Falls, Ont., Skylon, (520); Norfolk, Va., Va. Natl. Bank, 23 (304); Reading, Pa., Berks County Courthouse (280); So. Bend, Indiana, American National Bank Bldg., 25 (312); Springfield, Mass., Valley Bank Tower, (370); Tacoma, Wash., Washington Plaza, 23 (290).

NOTE: The World Almanac is compiling a list of persons interested in tall buildings. Our purpose is to allow readers interested in this subject to be put in touch with those who share their interest. Readers who wish to have their name included and to receive a copy of the list should write to: The World Almanac, 230 Park Ave., New York, N.Y., 10017.

STATES AND OTHER AREAS OF THE U.S.

Their Resources, Histories, Industries, Agriculture, Mineral Products, Tourist Attractions, Nicknames, State Symbols

Areas of the states are total land and water areas reported by the Geography Division, Bureau of the Census; populations are July 1, 1973, estimates by the Bureau of the Census, including armed forces personnel in each state but excluding such personnel stationed overseas; agricultural figures are based on reports of the Dept. of Agriculture and state agencies; mineral statistics are those reported by the Bureau of Mines; manufacturing statistics are from the Bureau of the Census.

For maps and for descriptive articles on cities, see Index.

Alabama

Heart of Dixie, Cotton State

CAPITAL: Montgomery. AREA: 51,609 sq. mi., rank 29th. POPULATION: 3,539,000 (est. 1973). MOTTO: We Dare Defend Our Rights. FLOWER: Camellia. BIRD: Yellowhammer. TREE: Southern pine. SONG: Alabama. ADMISSION: 22d.

Alabama lies in the cotton belt of the Old South but introduction of new and diversified industries has given the state a more balanced economy. Natural wealth includes coal, which underlies about 7,000 sq. mi. in the northern Appalachian region; iron, bauxite and timber.

Cheaha Mtn., 2,407 ft., is the state's highest point.

Abundant water for hydroelectric power and river shipping has contributed to the growth of Alabama's economy. Three Tennessee Valley Authority dams and a large nuclear power plant are in the northern part of the state. Historic sites, fishing and hunting are among its attractions.

With two-thirds of the state's land area in timber, Alabama has important and expanding pulp, paper and paperboard production. It is a leader in production of southern pine plywood and pulpwood.

Iron and steel production is the most important of Alabama's manufacturing industries; there is also a large segment of manufacturing devoted to primary metal products of wide diversity, particularly structural steel. Other important industry groupings include chemicals and fertilizers, textile mill products and apparel, processing of foods, stone-clay-glass products, transportation equipment, electrical and other machinery. Value added by manufacture is over $4.5 billion a year.

Industrial growth in 1973 saw over $1.6 million invested in 1,005 new or expanded plants, providing 42,998 new jobs. Per capita personal income was $3,724 in 1973 (U.S. average was $4,918).

Birmingham, center of the steel industry, has long been known as "the Pittsburgh of the South."

At Huntsville is the George C. Marshall Space Flight Center of NASA and a space and rocket museum.

Agriculture remains a vital part of the economy. Cotton has long been king among Alabama's crops but is rivaled by corn, soybeans, pecans and peanuts. Among the states, Alabama ranked 3d in production of pecans in 1973, 4th in peanuts. Also important are potatoes, watermelons, tobacco and peaches.

Livestock, especially poultry, has grown in importance. Alabama was 4th among the states in number of chickens in 1974. Farm receipts for livestock and livestock products in 1973 totaled $896 million; for crops, the total was $386 million. Forest product sales totaled $157 million in 1973.

Alabama ranks 2d behind Arkansas in production of bauxite and is the 2d largest producer of asphalt and mica. But bituminous coal accounts for over 50% of the value of its total mineral production, which in 1973 reached a total estimated at $403 million. Also important are cement, stone and petroleum.

There are 56 institutions of higher education. But per pupil expenditure in public schools in 1973-74 ($716) was the lowest in the 50 states.

Alabama, first explored by De Narvaez, Spanish, 1528, is rich in historical markers and sites. Andrew Jackson defeated the Creek Indians at Talledega and Horseshoe Bend. The Confederate States were organized at Montgomery, Feb. 4, 1861, and Jefferson Davis took the oath as president at State Capital there Feb. 18. Davis' "first White House" now is a state shrine; others include the house in Tuscumbia where Helen Keller was born June 27, 1880; Statue of Vulcan near Birmingham.

The area was organized as Alabama Territory Mar. 3, 1817, and became a state Dec. 14, 1819.

Tourists spent an estimated $655 million in Alabama in 1973.

At Russell Cave National Monument, near Bridgeport, may be seen a detailed record of occupancy by humans from about 7000 B.C. to 1650 A.D., including tools, weapons and pottery. The exhibit is free.

The George Washington Carver Museum at Tuskegee Institute, Tuskegee, contains records of the famous black scientist's contributions to agronomy and dioramas of achievements by blacks.

The University of Alabama Museum of Natural History, in Tuscaloosa, displays Alabama fossils, shells and aboriginal materials and collections. Mound State Monument, Moundville, an adjunct of the museum, shows aboriginal burials.

(See also Index for Birmingham, Mobile, Montgomery.)

Alaska

No official nickname

CAPITAL: Juneau. AREA: 586,412 sq. mi., rank 1st. POPULATION: 330,000 (est. 1973). FLOWER: Forget-me-not. BIRD: Willow ptarmigan. TREE: Sitka spruce. SONG: Alaska's Flag. FISH: King salmon. MOTTO: North to the Future. ADMISSION: 49th.

Alaska became the 49th state Jan. 3, 1959. Largest political division of the U.S., it is two and one-fifth times the size of Texas. Alaska occupies the NW part of North America, separated from the rest of the continental U.S. by Canada's British Columbia. Alaska's general coastline runs 6,640 mi.; including all its islands, 33,904 mi. It has mountain ranges, volcanoes, fjords and glaciers.

About one-fifth of the population are Eskimos and Indians.

Pt. Barrow in Arctic Alaska is the northernmost spot in the state. The Yukon River flows E to W 1,200 mi. through Central Alaska, from the Canadian border to the Bering Sea. In South Central Alaska stands Mt. McKinley, 20,320 ft., highest point in North America.

In West Central Alaska, off the tip of the Seward Peninsula, lies Little Diomede Is., only 2.4 mi. from the Big Diomede Is., owned by the USSR. The Alaska Peninsula and the Aleutian Islands into which it tapers, extends SW and W for 1,200 mi., with numerous volcanoes; at the base of the peninsula is Katmai National Monument, containing the Valley of 10,000 Smokes, scene of a 1912 eruption.

Alaska's Panhandle stretches SE; it is a narrow strip of mainland and islands, with fjords and Glacier Bay National Monument (containing the Muir Glacier, 2 mi. wide and 250 ft. high), facing the Pacific W of British Columbia.

History. Vitus Bering, a Dane employed by Russia, discovered Bering Strait, separating Asia and North

673

America, in 1728, but may not have found Alaska until his second voyage, in 1741, when he explored Alaska's coast. Other early visits were made by Spanish explorers (1775, 1788); by the British Cook (1776), Vancouver (1791-94) and Mackenzie (1793); by the French LaPerouse (1786); and by the U.S. Capts. Robert Gray and John Kendrick (1788). Alexander Baranov, first Russian governor of Alaska, set up headquarters at New Archangel, near present Sitka, 1799.

William H. Seward, as secretary of state under President Andrew Johnson, bought Alaska from Czarist Russia for $7,200,000, a transaction some labeled at the time "Seward's Folly." The treaty was signed Mar. 30, 1867, the transfer of territory took place Oct. 18, 1867. Alaska was a District until Aug. 24, 1912, and an Organized Territory until becoming a state in 1959.

The "Gold Rush" began when gold was discovered near the Klondike River in Canada, Aug. 16, 1896. Of 100,000 prospectors, 1897-1899, many died of exposure, others took up trading and farming. On the south coast of Seward Peninsula lies Nome, where gold-bearing sands were worked by placer mining.

Resources and Industries. The Good Friday, Mar. 27, 1964, earthquake, the most powerful ever recorded in North America, caused a temporary setback to the economic development of South Central Alaska, but reconstruction was speedily completed. Anchorage, Seward, Valdez and Kodiak benefited with new facilities.

Principal income is from fisheries, minerals (esp. oil), wood products, tourism and furs. Salmon, halibut, herring, cod and shellfish are frozen or canned; Alaska is the leading state in value of its commercial catch, about $162 million in 1973.

Processing of fish and other foods is the largest manufacturing industry, followed by forest products.

Spruce, yellow cedar and hemlock are plentiful; there also are red cedar and birch. Commercial timberland of Alaska's vast forest totals 28,000,000 acres. The forest products industry in SE is expanding as pulp mills increase. Timber products value is over $118,000,000 yearly.

Furs produced are those of the seal, sable, ermine, wolverine, land otter, muskrat, beaver, mink, red fox, blue fox, lynx, marten. Wildlife includes the gray wolf, moose, caribou and 5 kinds of bear: black, grizzly, polar, Kodiak and glacier. There are plenty of sea fowl, but whales, walrus, sea lion and sea otter have diminished.

The seal herd on the Pribilof Islands is owned by the federal government and seal harvesting is managed by the U.S. Commerce Dept. Reindeer herds are multiplying and their meat is marketed.

Oil production, mainly from offshore fields in Cook Inlet, had an est. value of $246 million in 1973. Total mineral production value was est. at $303 million.

Sale of leases for the vast North Slope oil discovery area at Prudhoe Bay brought the state $900 million in 1969. After long delay caused by ecological controversy, Congress in Nov. 1973 authorized construction of a $4-billion, 796-mi., trans-Alaska pipeline to carry oil from Prudhoe Bay to the south Alaska port of Valdez. Oil was to start flowing by mid-1977.

The value of gold production in 1973 was $625,000. Alaska also has natural gas, tin, bituminous coal and mercury.

Principal ports are in the Panhandle where Juneau, the capital, is on the mainland shore; N of it is Skagway, historic entry to Klondike gold fields via Chilkoot Pass and White Pass. Sitka, Wrangell and Ketchikan (center of salmon industry), are on islands of the Alexander group.

At the head of Cook Inlet, in S Central Alaska, is the state's largest city, Anchorage. Seward, S of Anchorage, is government-terminus for the government-owned Alaska Railroad, which runs N to Fairbanks. Nine domestic airlines serve Alaska. International lines flying via Arctic routes make stops. Ships transport 90% of the goods and foods to

and from Alaska, linking some 50 Alaskan ports with Seattle, etc.

More than 125,000 tourists visit Alaska annually, spending some $45,000,000.

There are 2 motor routes to Alaska. The newer is by way of Marine Highway, a 450-mile ferry route from Prince Rupert, B.C., to Skagway, Alaska. Motorists leaving the ferry at Haines may drive to Fairbanks, Anchorage, etc., with part of the route passing through Canada. The older route is the Alaska Highway, from British Columbia. Fairbanks, largest city in Central Alaska, has the northernmost international airport on the continent. Nearby is Eielson AFB.

There are 9 institutions of higher education.

Pay of public school teachers, $16,053 in 1974, is the highest in the 50 states. Average per capita income was $5,613 in 1973.

The Alaska State Museum in Juneau features Eskimo and Indian exhibits, mounted wildlife specimens, rocks and minerals and historical exhibits.

The University of Alaska Museum, in College, near Fairbanks, maintains cultural and natural history collections for research and for the public.

(See also Index for Anchorage.)

Arizona
Grand Canyon State

CAPITAL: Phoenix. AREA: 113,809 sq. mi., rank, 6th. POPULATION: 2,058,000 (est.1973). MOTTO: Ditat Deus, God Enriches. FLOWER: Giant cactus or saguaro. BIRD: Cactus wren. TREE: Paloverde. SONG: Arizona. ADMISSION: 48th.

Arizona leads the nation in copper production with half of the total U.S. output, but its rapidly-growing manufacturing industries, such as machinery, aerospace and electronics, form the largest source of income. Agriculture and tourism are also important.

Loads of sunshine and a wealth of scenic attractions give Arizona a mounting tourist business; 12 million out-of-staters spent an est. $650 million in 1973.

The climate is dry in southern regions and the northern plateau, but high mountains and forests in central areas have heavy snows in winter. Highest point is Humphreys Peak, 12,633 ft. Over 44% of the land is U.S. owned.

The only point in the U.S. at which 4 states meet is the juncture of Arizona, Utah, Colorado and New Mexico.

Arizona is noted for the Grand Canyon of the Colorado, an immense, vari-colored fissure 217 mi. long, 4 to 13 mi. wide at the brim, 4,000 to 5,500 ft. deep. Hoover Dam (formerly Boulder), in Black Canyon of the Colorado, is 726 ft. high, 60 ft. wide at base, 1,244 ft. long at top, creating Lake Mead.

Nature has given Arizona the Painted Desert, extending for 30 mi. along U.S. 66; the Petrified Forest; Canyon Diablo, 225 ft. deep and 500 ft. wide; and Meteor Crater, 4,150 ft. across, 570 ft. deep, made by a prehistoric meteor. The state has 17 national monuments, 2 national parks. Rodeos and historic sites of Indian and Spanish eras are other attractions.

Copper is king among Arizona's many minerals and the state normally produces a half or more of the nation's copper output. The 1973 est. value of the state's copper production was $1.1 million. Arizona also ranks high among the states in pumice, silver, molybdenum and gold. Total value of mineral production in 1973 was est. at $1.2 billion.

Cotton is a major crop; Arizona's harvest ranked 5th among the states in 1973. Cash receipts for all crops in 1973 were $407 million; receipts from livestock and livestock products, $580 million. The state ranks 12th in number of sheep. Fruit production is important; Arizona ranks high in lemons, oranges, grapefruit and grapes. Lettuce, melons and alfalfa are valuable crops.

Manufacturing has made large strides in recent years. Value added by manufacture is over $1.9 billion a year. Electrical machinery, including electronic components, accounts for over $335 million of this total; other machinery is also highly important.

Federal spending on defense contracts, construction projects, air bases, etc., is an important factor in Arizona's economy. Per capita personal income was $4,504 in 1973.

Schools include the Univ. of Arizona at Tucson, Arizona State Univ. at Tempe and Northern Arizona Univ. at Flagstaff. The new observatory of the National Science Foundation is located on Kitt Peak near Tucson. Taliesin West is the Frank Lloyd Wright architectural school near Phoenix.

Originally part of the Territory of New Mexico, which was ceded in 1848 by Mexico with the Gadsden Purchase added in 1853, Arizona became a Territory itself in 1863 and a state Feb. 14, 1912.

Museums include Arizona State Museum, Tucson, which stresses the archeology and ethnology of the Southwest. The Museum of Northern Arizona, 3 mi. N of Flagstaff, has exhibits illustrating the geology and paleontology of the area.

The Southwestern Arboretum, on U.S. 60 and 70 near Superior, has over 6,000 plants and trees from arid regions of the world, from lowly cactus to lofty boojum tree. The Phoenix Zoo is one of the nation's largest. The Arizona-Sonora Desert Museum, near Tucson, displays animals and plants of the desert.

(See also Index for Phoenix and Tucson.)

Arkansas
Land of Opportunity

CAPITAL: Little Rock. AREA: 53,104 sq. mi., rank, 27th. POPULATION: 2,037,000 (est. 1973). MOTTO: Regnat Populus. Let the People Rule. FLOWER: Apple Blossom. BIRD: Mockingbird. TREE: Pine. SONG: Arkansas. ADMISSION: 25th.

Arkansas is an important agricultural state with growing industries, has valuable mineral production and thermal springs and is popular with sportsmen. Highest point is Magazine Mtn., 2,753 ft.

Arkansas became a state June 15, 1836; it seceded in 1861 and was readmitted to the Union in 1868.

Manufacturing is growing in importance with a 64% increase in employees in a 10-year period. Per capita income was $3,680 in 1973. Lumber, petroleum, bauxite and cotton are major products.

The $1.2 billion Arkansas River program, involving navigation, flood control and power developments and construction of 17 dams and locks in Arkansas and Oklahoma, was completed to Catoosa, near Tulsa, Okla., in 1971 and provided an important boost to the area's economy.

The state has 18,500,000 acres of oak, hickory, gum, cypress and pine, and forest industries have a $500,000,000 annual payroll. Cotton accounts for 48% of farm income and Arkansas ranked 4th in cotton production in the U.S. in 1973 with more than a million bales. It was 1st in rice. It was 3d in number of chickens, 5th in turkeys.

Arkansas accounts for by far the greatest amount of bauxite (aluminum ore) produced in the U.S. It has the only diamond field in the U.S., ranks 1st in bromine and vanadium.

But petroleum is the state's main mineral product; 1973 output was valued at $61 million; that of bauxite was $22 million. Natural gas and stone were also important. Total value of mineral production was est. at $264 million.

Arkansas has 24 institutions of higher learning.

Fresh-water fishing, duck-hunting in southeast lowlands, and recreation areas in 21 state parks and 3 national forests attract visitors. There are several reservoir-recreation areas, as at Norfork, Bull Shoals, Nimrod and Dardanelle, and others are being created. There are 47 hot springs in government-operated Hot Springs National Park, which entirely surrounds the city of Hot Springs, about 50 mi. SW of Little Rock. Spring water ranges from 95° to 147°F. and is piped in insulated conduits for baths and drinking. The state has 93 airports.

Out-of-state visitors spent more than $623 million in Arkansas in 1973.

Historic attractions in Little Rock include the Territorial Capital Restoration, a block of 13 original frame and brick buildings, furnished as in 1820-36, including the governor's home and an early print shop of the Arkansas Gazette, oldest newspaper west of the Mississippi. The Old State House in Little Rock was the state capitol 1836-1912; it houses many historical exhibits.

The Little Rock Museum of Science and Natural History occupies the building where Gen. Douglas MacArthur was born; also in MacArthur Park is the Arkansas Museum of Fine Arts.

(See also Index for Little Rock.)

California
Golden State

CAPITAL: Sacramento. AREA: 158,693 sq. mi., rank, 3d. POPULATION: 20,601,000 (est. 1973). MOTTO: Eureka. I Have Found It. FLOWER: California poppy. BIRD: Valley quail. TREE: Redwood. SONG: I Love You, California. ADMISSION: 31st.

California is the leading agricultural state and is 2d only to New York in manufacturing.

Third largest in area, California also has, within only 85 mi. of each other, the highest and lowest points in the conterminous 48 states; Mt. Whitney, 14,494 ft., and Death Valley, 282 ft. below sea level.

The U.S. Bureau of the Census estimated California's population as of July 1, 1964, at 18,084,000 and New York's at 17,915,000, giving California 1st place; New York had been in 1st place from 1820 through the census of 1960. In the 1970 census, New York had 18,241,266; California, 19,953,134. California also has the most dogs and cats — an est. 50,000,000.

Among scenic regions are the Yosemite Valley, Lassen and Sequoia-Kings Canyon national parks, Lake Tahoe, the Mojave and Colorado deserts, San Francisco Bay and Monterey Peninsula. National forests cover one-fifth of the state.

Oldest living trees on earth are believed to be a stand of Bristlecone pine in the Inyo National Forest, est. to be 4,600 years old.

The world's tallest tree, the Howard Libbey redwood, 368 ft. with a girth of 44 ft., stands on Redwood Creek, Humboldt County.

California's huge fruit and vegetable production is fed by large irrigation systems. Receipts from crops in 1973 totaled $4.09 billion (tops in U.S.); from livestock, $2.7 billion (3d in U.S.); total receipts were $6.8 billion (most in U.S.).

The state ranked 1st in numbers of chickens, 2d in turkeys, 4th in sheep, 7th in cattle, as of Jan. 1, 1974.

California produces the most apricots, avocados, grapes and raisins, peaches, persimmons, pomegranates, plums, prunes, lemons, nectarines, olives, dates, almonds, walnuts and sugarbeets. Its total vegetable crop is the largest; it ranks 2d to Florida in oranges and has large cotton, potato and rice crops.

It was 2d to Alaska in commercial fishing in 1973 with a catch valued at $102 million.

The state's giant aerospace industries employ a third of all its manufacturing employees. Value added by manufacture is over $27 billion annually; transportation equipment, especially aircraft and missiles, led; food products, particularly frozen and canned foods, were 2d; electrical machinery, including electronic components, was 3d followed by ordnance, other machinery, metal products. Per capita income was $5,438 in 1973, 9th highest among the states.

Gold, discovered at Sutter's sawmill Jan. 24, 1848, set off the historic Gold Rush and gave initial impetus to California's development, but petroleum is the leading mineral product today.

Oil output in 1973 was valued at an est. $945 million, over half the state's total mineral production value, $1.92 billion (3d highest in the U.S. after Texas and Louisiana). Ranking 3d in oil production, California is a leader in output of asbestos, cement, boron, gypsum and tungsten.

The Oroville Dam, main unit in the world's largest water project — the $2.8 billion Feather River Project -- was dedicated May 4, 1968, N of Sacramento; electric power and water for irrigation were flowing even before completion.

Tourists spend about $4.8 billion a year in California.

There are some 200 institutions of higher learning. Three of the world's largest observatories are located on Palomar Mtn., Mt. Hamilton and Mt. Wilson.

The Tournament of Roses and the Rose Bowl football game at Pasadena are held annually, Jan. 1. Winter sports are featured in many mountain areas.

Vandenberg AFB, 170 mi. NW of Los Angeles, is center of an interservice missile range.

California, named by Spanish explorers, was Alta (Upper) California under Spain. Mexico took over, 1822, ceded it 1848. California Republic at Sonoma, June 14, 1846, was led by Gen. William B. Ide. Commander John D. Sloat raised U.S. flag at Monterey July 7, 1846. The state was admitted to the Union Sept. 9, 1850.

Among museums the Pasadena Art Museum has collections of modern German painting, American painting, Oriental art and prints. The Santa Barbara Museum of Art has exhibits of Greek and Roman sculpture, Oriental art, old master and modern paintings, primitive arts, American paintings and old and modern European drawings. The Santa Barbara Historical Society Museum displays and interprets objects of state and local history and operates the Gledhill Library for historical research. In Sacramento, the Crocker Art Gallery has collections of paintings, drawings, prints, sculpture and crafts representing all European schools, American glass, and pottery from 5th Century B.C. to contemporary American.

The J. Paul Getty Museum in Malibu opened in 1974 with collections of Greek and Roman antiquities, 18th Century French furniture and Western European paintings.

Spanish Missions. Twenty-one churches built by Franciscans of the Roman Catholic Church, 1769-1823, have been restored, rebuilt or are in ruins. They are located on or near El Camino Real, the Royal Highway, U.S. 101. Father Junipero Serra led a missionary expedition from Mexico City and founded 9 churches between 1769 and his death, 1784. The missions converted Indians and raised livestock and grain. Mexico secularized and sold the missions in the 1830s. After the Mexican War the U.S. returned the missions to the church. The buildings suffered from fire, earthquake, military and secular use; some have been entirely rebuilt.

(See also Index for Fresno, Los Angeles, Oakland, Orange County, Sacramento, San Diego, San Francisco, San Jose.)

Colorado
Centennial State

CAPITAL: Denver. AREA: 104,247 sq. mi., rank, 8th. POPULATION: 2,437,000 (est. 1973). MOTTO: Nil Sine Numine. Nothing Without Deity. FLOWER: Columbine. BIRD: Lark bunting. TREE: Colorado blue spruce. ANIMAL: Big horn sheep. SONG: Where the Columbines Grow. ADMISSION: 38th.

Once primarily a mining and grazing state, Colorado now draws the largest segment of its income from manufacturing, followed by agriculture, tourism and mining. Its snow-capped .peaks, ski centers, ghost towns and health spas make it a popular vacation-recreation area.

Colorado was organized as a Territory Feb. 28, 1861, and was admitted to the Union Aug. 1, 1876, 100 years after the Declaration of Independence; hence its nickname, the Centennial State.

The total of value added by Colorado's varied

manufacturing industries is over $2.6 billion yearly. Important industry groups are processing of meat, dairy and other food products, as well as machinery, electronics, metals and stone-clay-glass products. Research and aerospace industries are growing. Per capita income was $5,046 in 1973.

Farm receipts in 1973 totaled $2.19 billion, about 80% from livestock and livestock products. Colorado ranked 3d among the states in the number of sheep in 1974, 11th in cattle. Its sugar beet crop is the 5th largest in the U.S. Other important crops are wheat, corn, barley, alfalfa, potatoes, apples, peaches, pears.

Gold was discovered on the Platte in 1858 and at Leadville in 1860.

Climax, near Leadville, now produces most of the world's molybdenum. Colorado produces a rich variety of minerals and is a leader among the states in output of tin, vanadium, tungsten, carbon dioxide, uranium, lead, zinc and pyrites. Total 1973 mineral production was valued at $467 million; petroleum accounted for $136 million of the total.

With Utah and Wyoming, Colorado shares the world's richest oil shale deposits, still to be developed.

Colorado is the highest state in the Union, with an average altitude of 6,800 ft. It has 54 of the nation's highest mountains and 1,500 peaks over 10,000 ft. Pikes Peak, 14,110 ft., was found by Lt. Zebulon M. Pike, 1806. Highest is Mt. Elbert, 14,433 ft. Frozen Lake, altitude 12,940 ft., is the highest lake in the 48 conterminous states.

The Continental Divide, which forms the crest of the continent and separates watersheds of the Pacific Ocean and the Gulf of Mexico, runs through the west-central part in a general N-S direction.

Six major rivers—the Colorado, Rio Grande, Arkansas, North Platte, South Platte and Republican—rise in Colorado, supply water to 19 states. The western rivers have cut great canyons; the Black Canyon of the Gunnison and the Royal Gorge of the Arkansas, 1,000 to 1,500 ft. deep. One of the world's highest bridges crosses the Arkansas 1,053 ft. above the river at Royal Gorge.

The Federal Government owns 36.4% of the land, including 2 National Parks, 6 monuments, 2 Recreation Areas, 12 forests, 2 Indian reservations, 7 major military reservations.

Colorado has 29 institutions of higher education.

Colorado was the 1st of several states which in 1966 liberalized their abortion laws.

Attractions for an annual 8 million tourists include Rocky Mountain National Park, Garden of the Gods, Great Sand Dunes and Dinosaur National Monuments, Pikes Peak and Mt. Evans Highways, Mesa Verde National Park (pre-historic cliff dwellings). The Grand Mesa tableland comprises Grand Mesa Forest, 659,584 acres, with 200 lakes stocked with trout. Other attractions include the U.S. Air Force Academy near Colorado Springs, Denver Western Stock Show, Colorado State Fair, horse, dog and auto races, rodeos and pioneer celebrations. Thirty-one major ski areas operate from November to May.

The old mining towns of Aspen and Central City have become cultural centers.

Big game include deer, bear, elk, mountain lion, gray wolf, coyote. There are thousands of miles of trout streams and 2,000 fishing lakes.

Museums include the Colorado Springs Fine Arts Center which has paintings, prints and drawings by contemporary artists, exhibits of the cultural history of the SW and Latin America, and the John F. Huckel collection of 112 Navajo sand painting reproductions. The University of Colorado Museum, in Boulder, has more than a million objects in its exhibits of rocks, plants and early peoples as well as an art gallery.

(See also Index for Denver.)

Connecticut
Constitution State

CAPITAL: Hartford. AREA: 5,009 sq. mi., rank,

48th. POPULATION: 3,076,000 (est. 1973). MOTTO: Qui Transtulit, Sustinet. He Who Transplanted, Sustains. FLOWER: Mountain laurel. BIRD: American robin. TREE: White oak. Fifth of the original 13 states to ratify Constitution.

Connecticut's heavily industrialized cities are in sharp contrast to its picturesque New England villages and scenic countryside. Despite its small size, the state has large and diverse manufacturing industries, mainly of high-value specialty products. Per capita income was $5,889 in 1973, highest of all states.

It is a leading maker of jet engines, helicopters, nuclear subs, pins and needles, silverware, hardware, cutlery, and ball bearings. Ranking 48th in area, it is 16th in value added by manufacturing, a total of over $6.05 billion annually. Its factories employ over 34% of the working force. Hartford is headquarters for many of the nation's largest insurance companies.

Poultry and dairy products account for the largest part of farm receipts, which totaled $188 million in 1973. Much of the soil is stony, but tobacco, potatoes, fruits and vegetables and nursery products are grown.

The vacation-recreation industry is important. Attractions include historic sites, charming villages, the American Shakespeare Festival in Stratford, Mystic Seaport and Marine Museum, trolley museums, skiing, boating on Long Island Sound. Greenhouse, nursery and forest products are valued at over $21 million annually.

There are 85 state parks, recreation areas, and historic sites, covering 30,337 acres.

Tourism brings Connecticut about $400 million a year from out-of-state vacationers.

Mineral production is mostly of sand, stone and gravel for construction of roads and buildings. Total value for 1973 was $35.4 million.

Adriaen Block, Dutch, explored the Connecticut River, 1614. English from Massachusetts settled in 1630s. First practical constitution was the Fundamental Orders, adopted 1639. The royal charter of 1662 was exceptionally liberal; when Gov. Edmund Andros tried to seize it, 1687, it was hidden in the Hartford Oak, commemorated in Charter Oak Place.

Free public schools were established in New Haven, 1642, Hartford, 1643. Compulsory education in elementary and Latin grammar schools was established in 1650.

There are 49 institutions of higher education.

Museums include the P. T. Barnum Museum, Bridgeport; American Clock and Watch Museum, Bristol; trolley museums, East Haven and Warehouse Point; Hill-Stead Museum, a country house with paintings by famous impressionists, Farmington; Museum of American Art, New Britain; Old Lighthouse, Stonington; Lyman Allyn Museum, New London; Bruce Museum, Greenwich; Wadsworth Atheneum, Hartford.

In New Haven museums include the Winchester Gun Museum, with 5,000 items from the 15th Century to present. The Yale University Art Gallery's collections range from ancient to modern. The Peabody Museum at Yale has collections in paleontology, mineralogy, zoology and archeology.

Mystic Seaport, Mystic, is a recreated 19th Century village, including smithy, chapel and schoolhouse. At the docks lie the wooden whaleship Charles W. Morgan, the squarerigger Joseph Conrad; the Gloucester fishing schooner L. A. Dunton.

(See also Index for Bridgeport, Hartford, New Haven.)

Delaware

First State, Diamond State

CAPITAL: Dover. AREA: 2,057 sq. mi., rank, 49th. POPULATION: 576,000 (est. 1973). MOTTO: Liberty and Independence. FLOWER: Peach blossom. BIRD: Blue hen chicken. TREE: American holly. SONG: Our Delaware. First of original 13 states to ratify Constitution.

Delaware occupies part of the Delmarva Peninsula, so-called because Delaware and parts of Maryland and Virginia share the peninsula separating Delaware and Chesapeake Bays. Delaware is 96 mi. long and from 9 to 35 mi. wide. The land slopes from rolling hills (442 ft. highest elevation) in the N to a near sea-level plain.

Second smallest of the states in area, Delaware has a high per capita income $5,540 in 1973, with large chemical and other industries, the hqs. of many large corporations, prosperous farms and important shellfish production.

Important in Delaware's total of value added by manufacture are canned and frozen foods, leather and metal products, textiles and machinery. Total value added by manufacture is over $1.28 billion.

Broiler chickens are the largest item of farm income. Farm receipts for 1973 were $245 million.

Mineral production is mainly sand, gravel and stone used for construction. Total value in 1973 was est. at $3 million. There is also a sizable commercial fishing catch, valued at over $1.9 million.

Delaware's major tourist attractions include several famed beaches, racetracks and historic sites and museums. Annual value of tourism is about $300 million.

Delaware Bay was reported in 1609 by Henry Hudson, under Dutch commission, and in 1610 by Samuel Argall, in Virginia service. The latter called the estuary after his governor, Thomas West, Lord de la Warr, a name soon extended to the river and its lower western shore, and later adopted by the state.

An attempted Dutch settlement at Zwaanendael (Lewes) in 1631, failed. Swedish colonization began at Fort Christina (Wilmington) in 1638. New Sweden fell to Dutch forces in 1655. England conquered the area in 1664 under the Duke of York, who in 1682 transferred the Counties on Delaware to William Penn. Though in his proprietorship to 1776, they were separately governed from 1704 and fought during the Revolution as a state. On Dec. 7, 1787, Delaware became the first state to ratify the federal Constitution.

Fort Christina Monument marks the site of founding of New Sweden in 1638. Holy Trinity (Old Swedes) Church erected 1698 is the oldest Protestant church in the U.S. still in use. Center New Castle comprises a unique survival of a colonial capital nearly in its late 18th Century form. The home of John Dickinson, "Penman of the Revolution," and drafter of the Articles of Confederation, has been restored near Dover.

Museums include the Delaware Art Center in Wilmington which has collections of Pre-Raphaelite English paintings, American paintings and manuscripts and drawings. The Henry Francis du Pont Winterthur Museum, at Winterthur near Wilmington, has 100 American period rooms from 17th to early 19th Centuries (reservations are required to visit some of them). The Hagley Museum at Wilmington includes many of the old du Pont powder mills and other exhibits illustrating the development of American industry. The Delaware Museum of Natural History is in Greenville.

The Delaware State Museum, Dover, has varied exhibits on Delaware history and life and collection on the development of the Victor Talking Machine and related sound recording.

Delaware has 7 institutions of higher education.

Wilmington

Wilmington had a population of 80,386 (1970 Census). Laid out near Fort Christina, 1730-1736, by Thomas Willing and others, it was chartered in 1739 as Wilmington. Early a milling, shipping and manufacturing center, its business has remained varied. Current industries include the largest braided hose plant and the largest single cotton dyeing and finishing works. It is a world chemical center, with the home office and central laboratories of the I.C.I., du Pont and Hercules companies.

Du Pont maintains its executive department and a number of research laboratories in Wilmington. In 1802, Eleuthere Irenee du Pont established a powder works on the Brandywine, the forerunner of the present corporation. Its original nylon plant is at Seaford, Del.

Florida
Sunshine State
CAPITAL: Tallahassee. AREA: 58,560 sq. mi., rank, 22d. POPULATION: 7,678,000 (est. 1973). MOTTO: In God We Trust. FLOWER: Orange blossom. BIRD: Mockingbird. TREE: Sabal palm. SONG: Old Folks at Home. ADMISSION: 27th.

Florida's many miles of beaches and other resort areas offer fun in the sun to millions of vacationers. The state also has a tremendous agricultural output, producing 80% of the nation's citrus fruits and ranking 2d only to California in production of vegetables. Its growing and diversified manufacturing industries provide even more income than its agriculture. Per capita income was $4,647 in 1973.

The Florida peninsula juts southward 500 mi. between the Atlantic and the Gulf of Mexico; Cuba is only 90 mi. from its southern tip. It has some 30,000 lakes; Okeechobee, covering 700 sq. mi., is the 4th largest natural lake inside the U.S. Highest elevation in the state is 345 ft., in the NW.

Florida was discovered by Ponce de Leon 1513; acquired from Spain 1819 by treaty ratified 1821. It was organized as a Territory Mar. 30, 1822, and admitted to the Union Mar. 3, 1845. It seceded 1861 and was readmitted 1868.

Tourism is a major industry; about 23,150,000 visitors spend some $3.6 billion annually in Florida. It offers a wide variety of tourist attractions in addition to climate, resorts and water sports.

Many tourists have become permanent residents.

Major tourist objectives are metropolitan Miami, with the nation's greatest concentration of luxury hotels at Miami Beach; Palm Beach; St. Augustine, founded 1565 and oldest city in U.S.; Daytona Beach, Fort Lauderdale, all on the E coast; Sarasota, Tampa, Key West, St. Petersburg on the W; Walt Disney World, an entertainment and vacation development near Orlando.

Everglades National Park, 3d largest of U.S. national parks, preserves the beauty of the vast Everglades swamp. Castillo de San Marcos (St. Augustine), Fort Matanzas, Fort Jefferson (Dry Tortugas), De Soto National Memorial (Bradenton), and Fort Caroline (Jacksonville) are national monuments.

The John F. Kennedy Space Center is another big tourist attraction. From it the nation's first earth satellite was launched Jan. 31, 1958; first U.S. manned space flight, May 5, 1961; first manned orbital flight, Feb. 20, 1962 (Col. John H. Glenn), as well as the first man-on-the-moon launch, July 16, 1969.

Key West became the 1st U.S. city to get its fresh water from the sea when a desalting plant, capable of producing 3.5 million gallons a day, was opened in 1967.

Florida produces most of the nation's oranges and grapefruit; 1973 output was an est. 7.6 million tons of oranges and 1.9 million tons of grapefruit, both several times the amount produced by California. It also produces vegetables, avocados, watermelons, limes, tangerines, sugarcane, peanuts, cotton, tobacco, strawberries and honey. Florida also ranks high in number of chickens.

The cattle industry has grown in importance. Crop and livestock receipts for 1973 were $1.86 billion.

Manufacturing has made great gains and provides payrolls totaling $2.28 billion. Leading industries, in terms of value added by manufacturing, are food processing, chemicals, electrical equipment, transportation equipment, metal products, paper products.

Florida leads the U.S. in production of phosphate rock and is 2d to New York in titanium. Total mineral production value in 1973 was est. at $575 million, up 35% from 1972.

The commercial catch of fish and shellfish is worth over $64 million a year, ranking high among the states.

Florida has 17 airports with scheduled service, 62 scheduled airlines and 5 major railroads. There are 14 deepwater ports which handle domestic and foreign trade valued at $1.8 billion a year.

Florida has 66 institutions of higher learning.

Florida has no state income tax. Its excise taxes (beverage, tobacco, parimutuel), sales and other taxes account for 69% of total state revenue.

Museums include the Florida State Museum in Gainesville, with exhibits in archeology, ethnology, paleontology, ornithology, history and industry. Castillo de San Marcos in St. Augustine is a Spanish fort built 1672-1696 which is now a national monument. Marineland of Florida, 18 mi. S of St. Augustine, has some 2,500 marine specimens ranging from sharks and porpoises to tiny tropical fish; trained porpoises and pilot whales perform in shows. Miami's Seaquarium has similar shows.

At Pensacola is the Naval Aviation Museum with exhibits tracing flight development into the space age; Fort Pickens, built 1829, where Geronimo was imprisoned; the T. T. Wentworth Museum, with exhibits of local historical interest; the Pensacola Historical Museum and Spanish Village Museum.

In Sarasota, the John and Mable Ringling Museum of Art, willed to the state, contains works by Rembrandt, Rubens, Hals, Tiepolo, Velasquez, Murillo, Gainsborough, Reynolds and other masters. The Ringling Museum of the Circus includes elaborately decorated wagons, costumes and printed bills showing performers at fairs and circuses from the 16th to 20th Centuries; the Asolo Theater presents plays and operas.

Also in Sarasota, the Circus Hall of Fame gives circus acts and puppet shows, displays mementos such as a coach given Tom Thumb by Queen Victoria, a sleigh P. T. Barnum gave Jenny Lind, costumes, rigging and circus equipment.

(See also Index for Jacksonville, Miami, Orlando, Pensacola, St. Petersburg, Tallahassee, Tampa, West Palm Beach.)

Georgia
Empire State of the South, Peach State
CAPITAL: Atlanta. AREA: 58,876 sq. mi., rank, 21st. POPULATION: 4,786,000 (est. 1973). MOTTO: Wisdom, Jusice, Moderation. FLOWER: Cherokee rose. BIRD: Brown thrasher. TREE: Live oak. SONG: Georgia. Fourth of the original 13 states to ratify Constitution.

Largest in area of the states east of the Mississippi, Georgia is rich in a number of natural resources and in its growing, diversified industries.

There are large deposits of marble in the mountainous N, along with fertile plains and industry centers in the NW. The central Georgia Piedmont plateau boasts rich farmlands and a flourishing textile industry. The SE coastal plain produces pecans and peanuts and its forests yield a wealth of pulpwood and turpentine. Off its 100-mi. Atlantic coast lie its famed Golden Isles. The state also has large deposits of clay, limestone and talc.

Okefenokee in the SE is one of the largest swamps in the U.S., a wetland wilderness and peat bog covering 660 sq. mi. A large part of it is a National Wildlife Refuge, a home for wild birds, alligators, bear, deer, otter, etc.

Highest point in the state is Brasstown Bald in the NE, 4,784 ft., Stone Mtn., near Atlanta, is 1,686 ft.

Manufacturing production has increased many times over since World War II, but the textile industry remains the largest, both in terms of number of workers and value added by manufacture. Also of great importance are paper products, transportation equipment, apparel, food products and chemicals.

Value added by manufacture totals over $6.5 billion a year. Per capita income was $4,243 in 1973.

Georgia ranks high among the states in forest products, particularly in its output of pulpwood and turpentine.

Georgia is by far the nation's largest producer of peanuts, harvesting 1.3 million tons in 1973, more than twice that of any other state. It is among the leading growers of pecans, peaches and rye.

It ranked 2d among the states in numbers of chickens, about 41 million in 1973, and also had a large hog production. Farm receipts totaled over $1.9 billion in 1973, more than half from livestock and livestock products.

Georgia is also a leader in production of marble, zirconium, bauxite and kyanite. Total value of mineral production in 1973 was an est. $283 million.

There are 83 institutions of higher education.

Savannah and Brunswick are the main ports. The state is served by 6 major railroads and 10 airlines.

Notable among attractions are the Little White House in Warm Springs where President Franklin D. Roosevelt died Apr. 12, 1945, the 2,500-acre Callaway Gardens, Jekyll Island State Park, the restored 1850s farming community of Westville; Dahlonega, site of America's first gold rush; Helen, a mountain village with Alpine motif, Stone Mountain and Six Flags over Georgia.

Georgia has also become a sports center, with professional baseball, basketball, football and hockey teams.

Andersonville Prison Park and National Cemetery are on the site of the Confederate prison camp in which a total of 50,000 Union soldiers were confined, Feb. 1864 to Apr. 1865.

There are 62 institutions of higher learning.

Georgia was visited by DeSoto, 1540. It was a part of land granted to the lords proprietors of Carolina, 1663 and 1685; became an independent colony by charter of 1732 with first permanent settlement under James Oglethorpe, 1733. Georgia ratified the Confederate constitution, Mar. 1861, was readmitted to the Union, July, 1870.

(See also Index for Atlanta, Augusta, Columbus, Macon, Savannah.)

Hawaii
The Aloha State
CAPITAL: Honolulu. AREA: 6,450 sq. mi., rank, 47th. POPULATION: 832,000 (est 1973). MOTTO: The Life of the Land is Perpetuated in Righteousness. FLOWER: Hibiscus. BIRD: Nene (Hawaiian goose). TREE: Kukui (candlenut). OFFICIAL SONG: Hawaii Ponoi. ADMISSION: 50th.

Hawaii, prosperous paradise of the Pacific, became the 50th state Aug. 21, 1959, and the 50-star U. S. flag became official the following July 4.

The Hawaiian Islands lie in the North Pacific, 2,397 mi. from San Francisco (5 hrs. by commercial jet). They consist of 8 major islands (7 inhabited) and 124 minor islands.

The principal islands are Hawaii, the largest; Oahu, on which are Honolulu and Pearl Harbor; Lanai, Maui, Molokai, Kauai, Niihau and Kahoolawe (uninhabited).

The islands are volcanic. Highest point is Mauna Kea, on Hawaii, an extinct volcano 13,796 ft. above sea level. Its twin is Mauna Loa, about 100 ft. lower but an active volcano. Average annual rainfall is 22 inches at Honolulu Airport, 136.6 inches in Hilo, and 486 inches atop Waialeale, a mountain on Kauai. Honolulu is subtropical (all-time range, 57° to 88°) but Mauna Kea is often snowcapped.

Lake Waiau, at 13,020 ft. near the summit Mauna Kea, is the highest lake in the U. S.

Ka Lae, or South Cape, on the island of Hawaii, is the southernmost point in the 50 states.

The islands were settled by Polynesians, probably about 700-750 A. D. These Polynesians are believed to have sailed to Hawaii from other islands, settled earlier, more than 2,000 mi. to the south, using large double canoes.

Hawaii was visited 1778 by British Capt. James Cook who called the group the Sandwich Islands. It was a kingdom until Jan. 17, 1893, when Queen Liluokalani was deposed and annexation to the United States asked. President Cleveland blocked this on the ground of collusion by Americans. Hawaii organized a republic, 1894, with Sanford B. Dole as president. Congress voted annexation July 7, 1898, under President McKinley. The Territory was established June 14, 1900.

Hawaii, among the states, has a very heterogeneous population with Americans of Polynesian, Asian, European and African extraction.

Many of the Polynesians intermarried with the other racial groups, which arrived mainly in the 19th Century.

The 1970 Census gave as racial origins: Japanese, 28.3%; Caucasian, 38.8%; the remainder, Hawaiian, Chinese, Filipino, Korean, etc., with many of mixed racial descent.

Major sources of income are defense expenditures, tourism, sugar and pineapple production, in that order. Visitors totaled 2.6 million in 1973, with an average 59,100 present daily.

Value added by manufacturing, led by food processing, was $435,000,000 in 1972. There were 4,300 farms, with a total of 2,340,000 acres; farm receipts for 1973 were $223 million.

Mineral production, mostly cement and stone for construction, was valued at $32.9 million in 1973.

Per capita income was $5,309 in 1973.

More than 1,800 ships put into Honolulu each year. Honolulu International Airport has an average of over 300,000 arrivals and departures annually.

A marine exposition is scheduled for 1978, bicentennial of Capt. Cook's arrival in the islands.

There are 13 institutions of higher education.

(See also Index for Honolulu.)

Idaho
Gem State
CAPITAL: Boise. AREA: 83,557 sq. mi., rank, 13th. POPULATION: 770,000 (est. 1973). MOTTO: Esto Perpetua, Let It Be Forever. FLOWER: Lewis mock orange (syringa). BIRD: Mountain bluebird. TREE: Western white pine. SONG: Here We Have Idaho. GEM: Star garnet. ADMISSION: 43d.

A land of rugged grandeur, Idaho nevertheless ranks high in agricultural production.

Exploration of Idaho began with the visits of the Lewis and Clark Expedition, 1805-6. Fur traders and missionaries followed and the area became part of Oregon Territory, 1848; Idaho Territory, Mar. 3, 1863, and a state July 3, 1890.

Idaho was chiefly a farming, grazing, timber and mineral state for many years, but manufacturing has recently become second in importance to agriculture. There are rugged mountains, beautiful valleys, plateau regions, and extensive lava fields. Mt. Borah, in the Sawtooth Mts., is the highest peak, 12,662 ft.

The Snake River runs through Hells Canyon, which averages 5,510 ft. in depth for 40 mi., at one point 7,900 ft., exceeding Grand Canyon, and is 10 mi. from rim to rim at widest point. The Snake has several noted waterfalls, among them Shoshone, Twin and American.

Idaho is the nation's leading potato producer, growing about 77.5 million cwt. annually, worth more than $205 million. It ranks 2d in sugar beets and 4th in barley and has large crops of wheat, hops and apples.

It ranks high in wool production and was 9th among the states in number of sheep in 1973 with 665,000. Farm marketing receipts in 1973 totaled $1.1 million, more than half from crops, the rest from livestock.

Manufacturing's gains were mainly in processing of

potatoes and other foods, phosphates, paper, etc. Total value added by manufacturing was est. at over $775 million. Per capita income was $4,323 in 1973.

Discovery of silver in 1884 at Coeur d'Alene caused a stampede; Idaho still leads the nation in production of that metal. It also ranks high among the states in antimony, lead, cobalt, garnet, phosphate rock, vanadium, zinc and mercury. Total mineral production in 1973 was estimated at $138 million.

With 39% of its area in forests, Idaho produces much lumber, with the world's largest white pine lumber mill at Lewiston. Yellow pine, Douglas fir, white spruce, larch, hemlock abound; the DeVoto Grove has cedars 1,000 years old. Total value of forest products is more than $153 million a year.

Hells Canyon, Brownlee and Oxbow Dams are 3 recent hydro-electric projects on the Snake River. The National Reactor Testing Station of the AEC on Upper Snake River Plains has more than a score of reactors in operation.

Tourism brings in an est. $200 million or more annually, making it one of the state's important industries.

The state offers excellent hunting and fishing and Lake Pend Oreille, which has a 111-mile shoreline, is home of the world's largest trout, Kamloop rainbow.

Craters of the Moon National Monument, 18 mi. W of Arco, is a jagged landscape; lava covers the land and subterranean explosions have created many caves.

The Nez Perce National Historic Park, in northern Idaho, includes many sites visited by the Lewis and Clark Expedition. The State Historical Museum in Boise has displays of early Idaho Indian life, the fur trade, mining, farm and houshold gear of the pioneers.

There are 9 institutions of higher education.
(See also Index for Boise.)

Illinois
The Inland Empire
CAPITAL: Springfield. AREA: 56,400 sq. mi., rank, 24th. POPULATION: 11,236,000 (est. 1973). MOTTO: State Sovereignty, National Union. FLOWER: Native violet. BIRD: Cardinal. TREE: White oak. SONG: Illinois. SLOGAN: Land of Lincoln. ADMISSION: 21st.

Illinois ranks high among the states as both an agricultural and industrial empire It is rich in coal and oil reserves and boasts highly developed rail, water and air transportation facilities.

The soil is rich and level, with the high point, Charles Mound near the Wisconsin line, only 1,235 ft.

Illinois ranks 4th highest among the states in terms of value added by manufacture with a total of close to $22.8 billion. Manufacturing payrolls total $11.7 billion.

Major manufacturing lines are machinery (particularly construction and farm), processing of food products (especially grain, beverages and bakery), electrical machinery (communications, electronic components and appliances), primary metals (mainly iron and steel), transportation equipment (for railroads, aircraft and cars) and chemicals. Rockford is one of the nation's largest machine-tool centers; Peoria is a distilling center. Per capita income was $5,753 in 1973, 3d highest among the states.

In 1973 Illinois ranked 2d to California in receipts from farm crops, $3.16 billion. It stood 8th in receipts for livestock and livestock products and was 4th among the states in total cash farm receipts, $5.07 billion.

Illinois and Iowa vie closely with each other for the largest corn crop. Illinois produces the most soybeans; in 1974 it ranked 2d to Iowa in number of hogs and stood high in cattle and milk cows.

The state has large coal and oil reserves. It ranks high among the states in annual bituminous coal production, est. at $412 million in 1973. Petroleum production, 2d in value to coal, was est. to be worth

$118 million. The state is a leader in output of fluorspar, tripoli, stone and peat. Total 1973 minerals were valued at $802 million.

A major research and development installation of the Atomic Energy Commission is the Argonne National Laboratory, Lemont, Ill., directed by the Univ. of Chicago, which also operates the Argonne Cancer Research Hospital in Chicago. At Batavia, W of Chicago, the AEC completed the nation's largest atom-smasher in 1971.

Illinois has 138 institutions of higher education.

The Illinois State Fair is held annually in August in Springfield. More than 37,000 entries compete for more than $270,000 in cash awards. Attendance is over 667,000.

State forests, parks and conservation areas cover 251,819 acres. Some are associated with the history of the Middle West, including Lincoln's home and tomb in Springfield; the restored Fort de Chartres, seat of French 18th Century authority; old settlements such as Kaskaskia. Part of the territory taken from the British by George Rogers Clark, Illinois became a state in 1818.

The Illinois State Museum in Springfield has large collections of local art and archeology; art and architecture of the ancient Near East, and antique furnishings.

Located in Springfield is a state memorial including Abraham Lincoln's tomb and the Lincoln home which the family occupied for 17 years beginning in 1844. The Old State Capitol Building has been restored.

New Salem State Park, 20 mi. NW of Springfield, contains the restored pioneer village of New Salem where Lincoln lived as storekeeper, surveyor and postmaster, 1831-37. Annual performances are staged of Robert Sherwood's Abe Lincoln in Illinois.
(See also Index for Chicago, Springfield.)

Indiana
Hoosier State
CAPITAL: Indianapolis. AREA: 36,291 sq. mi., rank, 38th. POPULATION: 5,316,000 (est. 1973). MOTTO: Cross-roads of America. FLOWER: Peony. BIRD: Cardinal. TREE: Tulip (yellow poplar). SONG: On the Banks of the Wabash. ADMISSION: 19th.

Indiana is heavily industrialized, yet is also important among the states for its agricultural output. It ranks among the top states in production of both steel and corn; it quarries much of the building limestone used in the U.S. and is a large producer of coal.

It was explored by LaSalle, 1679; French trading posts grew during the 18th Century. Vincennes, the 1st permanent settlement, was taken over by the British, 1763, and its capture by George Rogers Clark in 1779 led to the opening of the old Northwest Territory to the U.S. Indiana became a Territory July 4, 1800, and a state Dec. 11, 1816.

There are sand dunes and lakes in the N, a level plain through most of the central area, and hills in the S. Highest point is 1,257 ft. in Wayne Co., in the east central area.

The Calumet region in the state's NW corner, including Gary, Hammond, East Chicago and Whiting, has one of the world's greatest concentrations of heavy industry, especially steel, cement and oil-refining plants. Gary was a sand dune in 1906 when U.S. Steel began constructing mills there ; in 1970 it had a pop. of 175,415. Inland Steel and Youngstown have large plants in East Chicago.

Per capita income was $4,908 in 1973.

Another vast steel complex has been developed further E along Lake Michigan, including a deep-water port at Burns Harbor in the famed Dunes area, a large plant of the Midwest Steel Div. of the National Steel Corp., and a large group of facilities of the Bethlehem Steel Corp.

While steel and other metal industries are

responsible for $1.8 billion of the $12 billion in value added annually by manufacture, electrical machinery, including television sets and household appliances, is a close 2d with $1.9 billion. Auto parts, aircraft and other transportation equipment is next, with $1.6 billion, followed by industrial farm and other machinery, 4th; chemicals, 5th; processing of food products, 6th.

Indiana is a leader in production of pre-fabricated wood products, mobile homes and band instruments. More than 40 cities are involved in the manufacture of furniture.

Corn is the principal crop and much of it goes to fatten the hogs. Among the states, Indiana ranks 3d in hogs and soybeans, 4th in corn, 8th in chickens. Farm marketing receipts for 1973 totaled $2.8 billion, 8th highest among the states.

Coal accounts for over a third of the value of mineral production which in 1973 totaled $340 million. Portland cement, petroleum, limestone, clay and gypsum are also important.

Indiana limestone, from vast quarries in the southern part of the state, sheathes tens of thousands of buildings, including the Empire State, Rockefeller Center, the United Nations, the Pentagon, the National Cathedral, many federal buildings and many state capitols.

Spending by out-of-state tourists is est. at $500 million a year.

Indiana has 22 state parks and recreation areas, including Dunes State Park on Lake Michigan; prehistoric Indian mounds; over 1,000 lakes; French Lick and other mineral spas; Wyandotte Cave, 3d largest in the U.S.; the Indianapolis 500-mile auto race, and the famous post office, Santa Claus.

Lincoln's boyhood home in Spencer County and the grave of his mother, Nancy Hanks Lincoln, are part of the Lincoln Boyhood National Memorial. State memorials commemorate the capture of Vincennes by George Rogers Clark in the Revolution, the defeat of Indian forces at Tippecanoe, and the Rappite and Robert Owen communities at New Harmony.

Spring Mill Village, 3 mi. E of Mitchell, is a restored pioneer settlement. The restored Whitewater Canal is in Brookville.

There are 45 institutions of higher education.
(See also Index for Bloomington, Evansville, Fort Wayne, Indianapolis.)

Iowa
Hawkeye State

CAPITAL: Des Moines. AREA: 56,290 sq. mi., rank, 25th. POPULATION: 2,904,000 (est. 1973). MOTTO: Our Liberties We Prize and Our Rights We will Maintain. FLOWER: Wild rose. BIRD: Eastern goldfinch. TREE: Oak. SONG: Iowa. ADMISSION: 29th.

Iowa, the heart of the rich Midwest farm belt, is one of the nation's wealthiest agricultural states, but its industrial buildup has been so great that the value of its manufacturing output is far greater than that of its farms.

Many industries process farm products or produce farm implements. However, the fast-growing industrial economy includes a wide variety of manufacturing plants, with electronics items, home appliances, tires, railway equipment, furnaces, automobile accessories, chemicals and fertilizers, vending machines, office furniture, and gypsum wallboard among the diversified products. Value added by manufacture is over $3.9 billion a year. Per capita income was $4,869 in 1973.

Iowa's broad plains contain much of the finest soil in the world. Its huge harvests support the nation's richest livestock industry. Iowa had by far the most hogs, 14.7 million in 1974, twice as many as Illinois, the next largest raiser. In cattle, with 7.6 million, Iowa was 2d only to Texas. It also had large numbers of chickens, turkeys and sheep.

In field crops, Iowa ranked first in corn, 2d in soybeans and 4th in alfalfa.

Receipts for livestock and livestock products totaled $4.2 billion in 1973, over $1 billion more than Texas, the next ranking state. In receipts for crops, Iowa stood 3d. Its total farm receipts were $6.7 billion, 2d only to California.

Iowa's forests produce hardwood lumber, particularly walnut.

Mineral production was valued at $150 million in 1973. Products, in order of value, were cement, limestone, sand and gravel, gypsum and coal.

Visitors from other states add more than $400 million to Iowa's economy annually.

Tourist attractions include the Herbert Hoover birthplace and library near West Branch, tulip festivals at Pella and Orange City in May, Iowa State Fair at Des Moines in August, several rodeos, the National Antique Airplane "Fly-In" and National Hot Air Balloon Races. The Little Brown Church in the Vale, near Nashua, inspired a well-known hymn and draws about 100,000 visitors annually. There are 91 state parks and other recreation areas. Effigy Mounds National Monument at Marquette is a prehistoric Indian burial site.

The Davenport Municipal Art Gallery has a collection of paintings and memorabilia of the Iowa painter Grant Wood, as well as other American, Mexican, Haitian and European paintings. The Davenport Public Museum displays the history of the area; archeology and ethnology of Egypt, Europe, South America and Asia; extensive collections of birds, mammals, insects, fossils, minerals and a herbarium of 20,000 plants.

In Decorah, the Norwegian-American Museum preserves homes, household utensils, etc., of pioneers who came from Norway.

Waterloo's Museum of History and Science has exhibits on Iowa history, pioneer life, Indian lore and earth sciences and a planetarium.

Iowa has 55 institutions of higher education.

The first Europeans to visit the Iowa area were the French explorers, Father Jacques Marquette and Louis Jolliet, in 1673. It formed part of the Louisiana Purchase in 1803 and became a state Dec. 28, 1846.
(See also Index for Des Moines.)

Kansas
Sunflower State

CAPITAL: Topeka. AREA: 82,264 sq. mi., rank, 14th. POPULATION: 2,279,000 (est. 1973). MOTTO: Ad Astra per Aspera. To the Stars through Difficulties. FLOWER: Sunflower. BIRD: Western meadowlark. TREE: Cottonwood. SONG: Home on the Range. ADMISSION: 34th.

Rolling fields of wheat, clusters of oil well derricks, great herds of cattle and towering grain storage elevators feature the landscape of Kansas, the geographical center of the 48 conterminous states. The land rises from broad plains in the E, 680 ft. above sea level, to slightly over 4,000 ft. in the W.

Manufacturing, farming and mining (especially petroleum and natural gas) are major factors in the Kansas economy. Large industry fields include transportation equipment, food processing, machinery and chemicals. Value added by manufacture is $2.5 billion a year. Per capita income was $5,057 in 1973.

Most of the land of Kansas is devoted to agriculture, and much of that to growing wheat. Kansas ranked first among the states in its wheat crop in 1973, 2d in sorghum, 4th in cattle. Total farm receipts for 1973 were $4.1 billion, 5th highest in the U. S. Forest products, particularly walnut lumber are valued at about $14 million a year.

Wichita is one of the nation's largest aircraft manufacturing centers, ranking first in production of private aircraft.

Kansas stands high in petroleum production and has large reserves of natural gas and helium. It ranks first among the states in helium production.

Petroleum production in 1973 was valued at an est.

$269 million, almost half the total mineral production value, $614 million. Also important are natural gas and salt.

Coronado in 1541 headed a Spanish troop in a vain search for wealth in the area. France claimed all territory drained by the Mississippi through LaSalle's explorations, 1682. France ceded the vast area to Spain, 1763, and received it back in 1800. In 1803 the U.S. obtained the land through the Louisiana Purchase. The Kansas part of it became a Territory May 30, 1854; a state Jan. 29, 1861.

During the fight over statehood Kansas was rent between free-state and pro-slavery forces. Frontier posts were at Forts Leavenworth, Riley, Scott, Larned, Hays, and other sites.

In Abilene, the boyhood home of the late President Dwight D. Eisenhower, is the Eisenhower Center, with the Eisenhower Home, Museum and Library. Near them, in a chapel named "Place of Meditation," the 34th president was buried Apr. 2, 1969.

The Agricultural Hall of Fame and National Center, 14 mi. W of Kansas City, Kan., displays farm equipment of the past such as a wooden-wheeled corn planter, anvils, wheat drills, etc. In Dodge City are extensive reproductions of the original Front Street, saloons and Boot Hill cemetery.

The Wichita Art Museum has works by Bellows, Eakins, Copley, Sargent, Cassatt, Hopper, Ryder, Grosz, Marin, Andrew Wyeth, Stuart Davis, Lachaise, De Creeft, Zorach. The Kansas State Historical Society in Topeka has displays and period rooms of Midwest history and a library with newspaper and manuscript collections.

In Lawrence, the Univ. of Kansas has a Museum of Natural History which presents a panorama of North American mammals from the Arctic to the tropics; a Museum of Art, with European and American painting and sculpture and European and Oriental decorative arts; and the Snow Entomological Museum, with over 2,000,000 insects.

It is estimated that tourists spend over $527 million a year in the state.

Kansas has 53 institutions of higher learning.

Kansas has developed an extensive recreation system around its federal reservoirs, lakes and roadside parks.

(See also Index for Wichita.)

Kentucky
Blue Grass State

CAPITAL: Frankfort. AREA: 40,395 sq. mi., rank, 37th. POPULATION: 3,342,000 (est. 1973). MOTTO: United We Stand, Divided We Fall. FLOWER: Goldenrod. BIRD: Cardinal. SONG: My Old Kentucky Home. TREE: Tulip tree. ADMISSION: 15th.

Kentucky was the first area W of the Allegheny Mtns. settled by American pioneers, and one of the first of them to arrive was Daniel Boone, 1769. The first permanent settlement was that of James Harrod at Harrodsburg in 1774; the following year Boone blazed the Wilderness Trail and founded Boonesboro. Originally part of Fincastle Co., Va., the area became Kentucky Co., Va., in 1776, and an independent state in 1792.

Kentucky rises from an elevation of less than 260 ft., at the Mississippi, to over 4,000 ft. in the Cumberland and Pine mountains. Over 42% of the state is forested, and lumbering, particularly of hardwoods, is an important industry. Forest products are valued at over $50 million a year.

Manufacturing has shown important gains but agriculture and mining remain vital parts of Kentucky's economy. Per capita income was $3,967 in 1973.

Tobacco is the principal crop, 2d only to that of North Carolina. Corn, soybeans, wheat, fruit, hogs and cattle, especially milk cows, are also important. Farm receipts in 1973 totaled $746 million from livestock, $606 million from crops.

In 1973 Kentucky produced more tons of coal than West Virginia but was 2d in terms of its value. Kentucky also produces important amounts of petroleum, natural gas, fluorspar, clay and stone. But coal accounts for 90% of the total mineral value, est. at $1.03 billion for 1973.

In 1966 Kentucky enacted a law requiring surface and strip miners of coal to restore and regrade earth removed by their operations, but problems have remained.

Manufacturing has shown needed growth and diversity. Leading fields are food processing and beverages (including liquor), tobacco products, machinery, chemicals, transportation equipment and apparel. Value added by manufacture is over $5.16 billion a year. Per capita income was $3,967 in 1973.

Tourists bring in an est. $425 million a year. There are 48 state and national parks and shrines.

Two of the largest man-made lakes in the world, Kentucky Lake and Lake Barkley, parallel each other in Western Kentucky, creating a 170,000-acre isthmus called the Land Between the Lakes National Recreation Area. Two major vacation resort parks, Kentucky Dam Village and Kenlake, are on the west shore of Kentucky Lake.

Lexington, heart of the Bluegrass country, has the University of Kentucky and Transylvania, oldest college west of the Alleghenies (1780), and a large tobacco market and holds annual trotting and running races and a horse show. Near Lexington are farms famous for blooded horses, including the Calumet, Castleton, Spendthrift, Walnut Hall, Greentree.

Fort Knox, repository of the nation's gold reserve, also contains the George S. Patton Jr. Military Museum of World War II equipment.

Mammoth Cave, 40 mi. from Bowling Green, is in a national park. Discovered 1799, it has 150 mi. of passageways, rooms with 200-ft ceilings, blind fish and an Echo River 360 ft. below ground.

Old Fort Harrod State Park, Harrodsburg, contains the reconstructed fort with stockade, blockhouses and cabins; the log cabin in which Thomas Lincoln and Nancy Hanks, Abraham Lincoln's parents, were married, and a museum with relics of Shakertown, Ky.

Abraham Lincoln Birthplace National Historic Site, 3 mi. from Hodgenville, contains the original Thomas Lincoln farm and the traditional Lincoln birthplace cabin.

My Old Kentucky Home, 1 mi. E of Bardstown, was the home of John Rowan, senator and state chief justice. Stephen Foster, a relative, visited the Rowan family in 1852 and is said to have written My Old Kentucky Home on a desk preserved in the house.

Kentucky has 36 institutions of higher learning.
(See also Index for Louisville.)

Louisiana
Pelican State

CAPITAL: Baton Rouge. AREA: 48,523 sq. mi., rank, 31st. POPULATION: 3,764,000 (est. 1973). MOTTO: Union, Justice, Confidence. FLOWER: Southern magnolia. BIRD: Eastern brown pelican. SONG: Give Me Louisiana. TREE: Bald cypress. ADMISSION: 18th.

Louisiana blends a wealth of historic charm, rich natural resources and giant modern industries. Fertile soil, huge mineral deposits and over 7,000 mi. of navigable waterways linking the nation's heart with deepsea ports are factors basic to the state's wealth.

Mardi Gras and other festivals, the beat of Dixieland jazz in the land of its origin, and the nostalgic relics of the days of French and Spanish rule and the prosperous pre-Civil War era are among the attractions which bring Louisiana an est. $776 million a year in tourist revenues.

In total value of its 1973 mineral output, $5.6 billion, Louisiana was 2d only to Texas among the 50 states. It was first in value of its natural gas and salt production, 2d in petroleum and sulphur. Much of the oil and sulphur comes from offshore deposits.

The lush Louisiana land produces one of the nation's largest crops of sweet potatoes. It is also a leader in rice and sugarcane. Also important are pecans, soybeans, cotton and corn.

Farm receipts in 1973 included $753 million from crops, $412 million from livestock.

Total value added by manufacture is over $3.5 billion annually. Per capita income was $3,825 in 1973.

Leading manufacturing industries include chemicals, food processing, petroleum and coal products (especially oil refining), paper (particularly paperboard), lumber and wood products, transportation equipment, stone clay-glass products, apparel.

With 7,409 sq. mi. under water, Louisiana marshes supply most of the nation's muskrat fur; there are also opossum, raccoon, mink, otter and large numbers of game birds. The annual catch of fresh and salt water fish, shrimp and oyster is valued at about $98 million. Lake Pontchartrain covers 630 sq. mi., is the 5th largest natural lake wholly within the U.S.

Much of the land is a rich alluvial plain; there are also rolling hills, bluffs on the Mississippi and coastal marshes. The elevation ranges from 5 ft. below sea level, protected by vast levees, to 535 above.

Louisiana is rich in historical relics and traditions, with Spanish-French backgrounds, pirate lore, fashionable French society in the 18th Century, picturesque customs today. Early explorers were Pineda, 1519, de Vaca, 1528, De Soto, 1541, La Salle, 1682. New Orleans was founded 1718. Louisiana became a French crown colony under Louis XV, 1731; was ceded to Spain, 1763, returned to France, 1801; sold by Napoleon to U.S. Dec. 20, 1803, (with large territory to N and NW). It became a U.S. Territory Mar. 26, 1804, effective Oct. 1. State was admitted to the Union, Apr. 30, 1812; seceded Jan. 26, 1861, and joined Confederacy; readmitted June 25, 1868.

Louisiana has 25 institutions of higher education.

Louisiana Creoles are descendants of early French and/or Spanish settlers. About 4,000 Acadians, French settlers in Nova Scotia, Canada, were forcibly transported by the British to Louisiana in 1755 (an event commemorated in Longfellow's Evangeline) and settled near Bayou Teche; their descendants became known as Cajuns. Another group, the Islenos, were descendants of Canary Islanders brought to Louisiana by a Spanish governor in 1770. Traces of Spanish and French survive in local dialects.

(See also Index for Baton Rouge, New Orleans, Shreveport.)

Maine
Pine Tree State

CAPITAL: Augusta. AREA: 33,215 sq. mi., rank, 39th. POPULATION: 1,028,000 (est. 1973). MOTTO: Dirigo. I Direct. FLOWER: Pine cone and tassel. BIRD: Chickadee. TREE: Eastern white pine. SONG: State of Main Song. ADMISSION: 23d.

Maine is noted for its scenic and vacation attractions, lobsters, potatoes, poultry and forest products, fishing and hunting.

Largest of the 6 New England states, it is the farthest NE and borders on only one other state, New Hampshire. Its rugged coast, because of deep indentations, measures 3,478 mi. Tides are often high; in Passamaquoddy Bay they average 20 ft.

Mt. Cadillac, on Mt. Desert Is., 1,532 ft., is the highest Atlantic seacoast point N of Brazil; West Quoddy Head, Long 66° 57′ W, is the farthest east point on the U.S. Atlantic coast. Lubec is the most easterly town on the U.S. mainland.

John Cabot and his son, Sebastian, are believed to have visited the Maine coast in 1498. Long governed as a part of Massachusetts, Maine became a state in 1820.

Maine's coastal waters produce an annual 20,000,-000 lbs. of lobsters, 75% of the nation's total, and 50% of its soft-shelled clams. The state packs over 150,000,000 cans of sardines a year, tops among the states. The fish and shellfish catch is worth $40 million annually to the fisherman.

Maine grows about 12% of the nation's potatoes, 2d to Idaho, and is the leading supplier of seed potatoes. It produces 90% of the nation's low bush blueberries. Also grown are apples, sweet corn, peas, beans. Farm income totaled $422 million in 1973, with poultry and eggs the largest item.

With more than 80% of its area forested, Maine turns out wood products from boats to toothpicks, paper, lumber and Christmas trees. Over 98% of the forest land is privately owned. Forest products are valued at over $700 million a year. Spruce, white pine and birch are the most important woods. Also vital to Maine's economy are processed foods, shoes and textiles. Boatyards build fishing and sailing craft.

Per capita income was $3,944 in 1973.

Granite, cement and feldspar account for much of the 1973 value of mineral products, est. at $31.5 million.

Maine's scenic seacoast, beaches, lakes, mountains and resorts make it a popular vacationland; tourism is a $500 million-a-year industry. There are 26 state parks, including Baxter, where Mt. Katahdin, tallest of the state's 10 mountains over 4,000 ft., rises 5,268 ft. Maine has over 2,500 lakes, 1,300 wooded islands and 5,000 streams. Moosehead Lake is 40 mi. long and 2 to 10 mi. wide. Deer, grouse, black bear abound; game fish include salmon, tuna, trout, bass. There are over 45 public skiing facilities. Acadia National Park and the famed resort of Bar Harbor are on Mt. Desert Island.

Museums include the Bowdoin College Museum of Fine Arts, Brunswick, which has portraits by Gilbert Stuart, Smibert, Feke, Blackburn, Copley, Winslow Homer, Cassatt, etc.; also Assyrian, Greek and Roman sculpture.

The Colby College Art Museum, Waterville, has paintings by classic and contemporary Europeans and by Americans—Hassam, Homer, Denn, Inness, Moran, Poor, Sterne, Andrew Wyeth.

The Farnsworth Library and Museum, Rockland, has 19th and 20th Century American paintings, drawings, prints and sculpture.

The Portland Museum of Art comprises the Sweat Museum of American art and the Sweat Mansion, a Federal-style house built in 1800. Other historic homes in Portland are the Tate House, 1755, and the Victoria Mansion, 1859.

There are 18 institutions of higher learning.

(See also Index for Portland.)

Maryland
Old Line State, Free State

CAPITAL: Annapolis. AREA: 10,577 sq. mi., rank, 42d. POPULATION: 4,070,000 (est. 1973). MOTTO: Fatti Maschi. Parole Femine. Manly Deeds. Womanly Words. FLOWER: Black-eyed Susan. BIRD: Baltimore oriole. TREE: White oak. SONG: Maryland, My Maryland. Seventh of the original 13 states to ratify Constitution.

Maryland stretches from the Atlantic Ocean to the Allegheny Mountains with 2 major interruptions, Chesapeake Bay and the District of Columbia. Both contribute importantly to the state's economy.

The bay cuts off the low coastal plain of the Eastern Shore from the rest of the state, provides both commercial and sports fishing and leads to the port of Baltimore, which handles some $3 billion in imports and exports a year. The 7.11-mi. Chesapeake Bay Highway Bridge spans the bay near Annapolis, S of Baltimore.

The national Capital area provides a market for much of Maryland's produce as well as adding to the crowds which enjoy the state's many recreational facilities.

Backbone Mtn. in the far W part of the state is its highest point, 3,360 ft.

Settlers, led by Leonard Calvert, brother of Cecilius Calvert, Lord Baltimore, arrived at St. Clements Island on March 25, 1634. They shortly moved to the mainland and established the colony at St. Marys.

Maryland has a diversified economy. Leading industries in number of workers are wholesale and retail trade, 326,400; government, 324,100; services, 254,100; manufacturing 250,400. Value added by manufacture totals over $4.28 billion annually. Important manufacturing industries are food products, primary metals, electrical equipment, printing and publishing, apparel, machinery. Per capita income was $5,331 in 1973.

Almost half of the land area is covered with forests. About 40% of timber cut is softwood. Stone and cement are leading mineral products; there is some coal mining. Mineral output was valued $122 million in 1973.

Seafood is an important industry. In a typical year, the fish and shellfish catch has a value of about $20 million. Striped bass is the principal contributor to the fin fish revenues, while oysters account for about 60% of the shellfish, followed by soft-shelled clams; Maryland is a leader in its catch of all 3.

Much of Maryland's farms are fertile though not extensive. The state's largest cash crops are tobacco, corn, soybeans, apples and tomatoes. Commercial broilers and dairy products are important.

The first U.S. steam locomotive, Peter Cooper's Tom Thumb, was built in Baltimore and made its first run on the tracks of the Baltimore & Ohio R.R., 1830.

There are 47 institutions of higher education.

Famous racing events include the Preakness, at Pimlico track, Baltimore; the International at Laurel Race Course, and John B. Campbell Handicap at Bowie. Annapolis is a center for yacht races. Ocean City is a popular summer resort.

Famous historic sites include Fort McHenry, Baltimore, restored, where in 1814 waved the flag that inspired Francis Scott Key to write the Star-Spangled Banner; Antietam Battlefield near Hagerstown (1862); South Mountain Battlefield (1862); Edgar Allan Poe house, Baltimore. The State House, Annapolis (1772), is the oldest in the U.S.

The U.S. Frigate Constellation, which was launched at Baltimore in 1797, has been made a National Historic Landmark and is a tourist attraction in Baltimore.

The Chesapeake Bay Maritime Museum in St. Michael's exhibits typical bay boats, including the last surviving oyster sloop, a cottage-type lighthouse and models of Baltimore clippers, log canoes, bugeyes and skipjacks.

The tourist industry is valued at over $300 million a year.

(See also Index for Baltimore, Washington, D. C.)

Massachusetts

Bay State, Old Colony

CAPITAL: Boston. AREA: 8,257 sq. mi., rank 45th. POPULATION: 5,818,00 (est. 1973). MOTTO: Ense Petit Placidam Sub Libertate Quietem. By the Sword We Seek Peace, but Peace Only Under Liberty. FLOWER: Mayflower. BIRD: Chickadee. TREE: American elm. SONG: All Hail to Massachusetts. Sixth of the original 13 states to ratify Constitution.

Massachusetts has played important roles in the political, intellectual and economic development of the U.S. Here the Pilgrims, seeking religious freedom, founded Plymouth Colony in 1620.

As Massachusetts grew, it became a leader in resisting British oppression. Its citizens staged the Boston Tea Party in 1773 to protest unjust taxation. The Minutemen battled British troops at Lexington and Concord, Apr. 19, 1775, launching the American Revolution.

The state became the home of great universities such as Harvard and Massachusetts Insitute of Technology. In the 19th Century its authors were giants among the nation's men of letters. It was also a hotbed of abolitionism.

In Massachusetts ports a great shipping industry, including the famed China trade, developed, along with vast whaling and fishing interests. Abundant waterpower helped create a variety of manufacturing industries.

While the Puritans demanded religous freedom for themselves, their leaders denied it to others; but some among them protested this, and the loudest protesters, Roger Williams, Anne Hutchinson and others were banished and settled Rhode Island in the 1630s as a haven for religious liberty. Meanwhile, in Massachusetts, Quakers and Baptists were persecuted and in Salem the infamous witchcraft trials and hangings were staged in 1692.

Eventually, religious freedom was achieved. In 1867, Mary Baker Eddy founded Christian Science in Lynn. Heavy immigration of Irish, Italians, Poles, Czechs and French Canadians brought many Catholics to the state.

The state had the first tax to support free schools and its first school at Dedham, 1649, and a uniform system in 1840. It has 118 institutions of higher learning.

Commercial fishing, in the rich waters off Massachusetts and the Grand Banks off Newfoundland, was one of the area's earliest industries. Whalers sailed the oceans around the world. Modern trawlers with huge nets help bring in a catch valued at about $57 million a year, ranking high among the states.

Massachusetts was a pioneer in the manufacture of textiles and shoes and in creation of specialized machinery for them. The Bay State remains one of the top producers of shoes. A power loom, perfected by Francis Cabot Lowell in 1822, launched cotton manufacturing in Lowell.

Production of electrical machinery, including electronics and communications equipment, has become the leading manufacturing division, in terms of numbers of employees and value added by manufacture. It is closely followed by other types of machinery. Also important are apparel, metal and food products, and plastics.

Total value added by manufacture is over $9.4 billion a year, placing Massachusetts, despite its relatively small size, 11th among the states. A third of the state's workers are employed in manufacturing. Per capita income was $5,233 in 1973.

Massachusetts' cranberry crop is the nation's largest. Also important are dairy and poultry products, cigar wrapper tobacco, apples, peaches, maple syrup. Farm receipts totaled $170 million in 1973. Mineral production for that year was valued at an est. $56 million, mostly of stone, sand and gravel for construction industries.

Because of the state's numerous recreational areas and historic landmarks, tourism has become an important factor in the economy of the state. It is estimated that 2.5 million out-of-state tourists visit Massachusetts annually, representing a value to the tourist industry of $1.25 billion.

Cape Cod has summer theaters, sports and an artists' colony at Princetown. Tanglewood, in the Berkshires, has the summer concerts of the Boston Symphony Orch.

In New Bedford the Old Dartmouth Historical Society and Whaling Museum has a large and unique collection of whaling implements, scrimshaw and logbooks as well as furniture, costumes, and firearms. In Old Deerfield are Deerfield Memorial Hall (1799), Hall Tavern (1765), Parson Ashley House (1732), etc.

In Pittsfield, the Berkshire Athenaeum has memorabilia of Herman Melville, who lived there while writing Moby Dick; a scrimshaw and whaling collection and a large library. The Berkshire Museum, Pittsfield, has paintings by Rubens, Van Dyck,

Reynolds, Murillo, the Hudson River artists, etc.; mineral and animal rooms; one of the sledges with which Robert E. Peary reached the North Pole.

In Plymouth, Pilgrim Hall contains relics of the Mayflower Pilgrims, including swords of Myles Standish, Bibles of Gov. William Bradford and John Alden, and the cradle of Peregrine White, first child born in the colony.

Old Sturbridge Village, in Sturbridge, is a recreated early New England village of 35 authentic homes and shops, shown functioning.

The Sterling and Francine Clark Art Institute, Williamstown, displays 14th-17th Century European paintings, a large collection of Impressionists, sculpture, silver and drawings.

The Worcester Art Museum presents a survey of art through 50 centuries, stressing early American painting, pre-Columbian and contemporary arts. Also in Worcester, the John W. Higgins Armory displays medieval armor, and the American Antiquarian Society has a collection of early printing, including newspapers and almanacs.

(See also index for Boston, Springfield.)

Michigan
Wolverine State

CAPITAL: Lansing. AREA: 58,216 sq. mi., rank, 23d. POPULATION: 9,044,000 (est. 1973). MOTTO: Si Quaeris Peninsulam Amoenam Circumspice. If You Seek a Pleasant Peninsula, Look About You. FLOWER: Apple blossom. BIRD: Robin. TREE: White pine. SONG: (unofficial) Michigan, My Michigan. ADMISSION: 26th.

Bordering on 4 of the 5 Great Lakes, Michigan is divided into an Upper and Lower Peninsula by the Straits of Mackinac, which link Lakes Michigan and Huron. The two parts of the state are connected by the Mackinac Bridge, which has the 3d largest suspension span in the U. S. To the N, separating Michigan from Canada, is the Sault Ste. Marie (Soo) Ship Canal, one of the world's most heavily used waterways.

Michigan contains the world's greatest concentration of automobile manufacturers; its rich orchards near the shores of Lake Michigan grow large fruit crops; the Upper Peninsula produces important amounts of iron, copper and other minerals, and the state's lakes and forests make it a highly popular vacationland. The highest point is Mt. Curwood, 1,980 ft., in the Upper Peninsula.

While Michigan ranks first among the states in production of motor vehicles and parts, it is also a leader in many other manufacturing and processing lines including prepared cereals, machine tools, hardware, steel springs, public office furniture, padding and upholstering, industrial patterns, nonferrous castings, industrial leather belts, paperboard mills and gray iron foundries.

The state ranked 6th in the U. S. in terms of value added by manufacture, $23.3 billion. Motor vehicles and equipment accounted for $8.3 billion of that and also provided the most jobs, almost 400,000. Other major industry groups were primary metals and metal products, machinery, food and chemicals. Per capita income was $5,439 in 1973, ranking 8th.

Tourist attractions are many and spending by tourists has been est. at over $1.6 billion a year. The state has 36,000 mi. of streams, over 11,000 lakes and the longest freshwater shoreline (facing 4 of the Great Lakes). Water sports, music festivals, skiing, winter carnivals, fishing and hunting are among attractions. Isle Royale in Lake Superior is a national park with 539,339 acres. There are 5 national forests, 78 state parks and recreational areas and numerous canoe trails.

Farm receipts in 1973 totaled $1.4 billion, more than half from livestock products. The state ranked 6th in the U.S. in number of milk cows. It grew the most tart and sweet cherries and ranked high in apples, pears, grapes and sugar beets. Truck farm vegetables were valued at $160 million; forest products at $1.75 billion.

Iron ore is the largest source of Michigan's income from minerals. With continued depletion of high-grade iron ore deposits, production of high-grade pellets from low-grade taconite iron ore has increased, amounting to over 85% of the ore total.

Michigan was 2d only to Minnesota among the states in value of iron ore output, $176 million in 1973. It was also a leading producer of gypsum, peat, iodine, bromine, salt, magnesium compounds, lime, gravel and cement. Other minerals include copper and petroleum. Total output was est. at $765 million.

There are some 88 institutions of higher education.

The state was originally explored by the French and many names (Detroit, Sault Ste. Marie) are of French origin. Etienne Brule (1618), Jean Nicolet (1634), Pere Allouez (1666), Pere Marquette (1668) and Louis Jolliet (1669) were early visitors. France was ousted by Britain, 1763. Under the Ordinance of 1787 Michigan Territory embraced parts of other western states. It was organized as a separate Territory 1805, admitted to the Union Jan. 26, 1837.

(See Index for Detroit and Kalamazoo.)

Minnesota
North Star State, Gopher State

CAPITAL: St. Paul. AREA: 84,068 sq. mi., rank 12th. POPULATION: 3,897,000 (est. 1973). MOTTO: L'Etoile du Nord, Star of the North. FLOWER: Showy lady's-slipper. BIRD: Loon. TREE: Red (Norway) pine. SONG: Hail! Minnesota. ADMISSION: 32d.

Minnesota is a land rich in natural resources. Its fertile prairies support large crops and an important dairy industry, its mines yield most of the iron ore produced in the U.S., its forests produce mountains of pulpwood, its manufacturing is varied and vigorous, its thousands of lakes and other attractions lure millions of sportsmen and vacationers.

The headwaters of 3 great drainage systems lie within Minnesota; the Mississippi, leading to the Gulf of Mexico, with its source at Lake Itasca; the Red River of the North, which flows into Canada's Lake Winnipeg, draining into Hudson Bay; the St. Louis and other rivers draining into Lake Superior and thence through the Great Lakes and the St. Lawrence to the Atlantic.

Known as the "land of 10,000 lakes," Minnesota actually has 15,291 larger than 10 acres each. Two-thirds of the state is rolling prairie. Highest point is Eagle Mt. in the NE, 2,301 ft.

Fishing, hunting, water sports and winter sports are among attractions for more than 5.5 million vacationers who spend some $920 million yearly.

Minnesota produces about 63% of the iron ore mined in the U.S., despite depletion of the high-grade ore in the famed Mesabi and other ranges in the NE part of the state. Lost production from the huge open pit and underground mines is being replaced by high-grade pellets refined from low-grade taconite iron ore. By 1973, shipments of taconite pellets comprised about 72% of the total iron ore value and were increasing.

One taconite company, Reserve Mining, was enjoined in 1974 from polluting Lake Superior drinking waters but won a stay of the court order.

Iron ore production in 1973 was valued at $752 million, the major part of the total mineral production value, $814 million.

Manufacturing has shown both growth and diversity. Largest industries are food processing and machinery. Also important are electrical machinery, chemicals, paper, stone-clay-glass products, apparel, lumber, fabricated metal products. Value added by manufacture is $5.6 billion.

Per capita income was $4,921 in 1973.

Much of the land is richly fertile. With $3.6 billion in farm receipts for 1973, Minnesota ranked 7th among the states. About 55% of that income was from livestock products, the rest from crops. Ranking 2d in number of milk cows in 1973, the state was the leader in butter; also in turkeys.

Minnesota's farms grew the most oats and it ranked among the top states in spring wheat, corn, rye, alfalfa and sugar beets.

Forest products have a yearly estimated value of over $500 million, most of it in pulpwood.

Nationally known is the Mayo Clinic at Rochester, founded by Drs. William J. and Charles H. Mayo.

Minnesota has 57 institutions of higher learning.

The Minnesota Orchestra, the Tyrone Guthrie Theater in Minneapolis and the St. Olaf College Choir in Northfield are well known.

Minnesota has a large system of state parks and recreation areas. Minnehaha Falls in Minneapolis became famous through Longfellow's "The Song of Hiawatha."

Other attractions are the St. Paul Winter Carnival, the Minneapolis Aquatennial and the Minnesota State Fair.

French traders and missionaries were the first European visitors. Father Hennepin, 1680, named St. Anthony Falls, a 50-ft. drop in the Mississippi in present-day Minneapolis. France ceded the land E of the Mississippi to Great Britain, 1763; Britain to U.S., 1783. It became part of the Northwest Territories. The land W of the Mississippi was part of the Louisiana Purchase, 1803. Henry R. Schoolcraft found the source of the Mississippi in Lake Itasca, July 13, 1832. Organized as a Territory in 1849, it became a state May 11, 1858.

(See also Index for Minneapolis, St. Paul.)

Mississippi
Magnolia State

CAPITAL: Jackson. AREA: 47,716 sq. mi., rank, 32d. POPULATION: 2,281,000 (est. 1973). MOTTO: Virtute et Armis, By Valor and Arms. FLOWER: Magnolia. TREE: Magnolia. BIRD: Mockingbird. SONG: Go, Mississippi! ADMISSION: 20th.

Mississippi's economy, long based on one crop, "King Cotton," has become balanced and diversified, thanks to promotion of industry, varied crops, tourism and federal agency installations.

The land slopes from the NE hills, where the high point is Woodall Mt. (806 ft.), to the Delta, a cotton-producing alluvial plain in the W and NW lying between the Yazoo River and the Mississippi, which flows along the state's western border. The land also slopes to the S where the sandy beaches on the Gulf of Mexico have created a popular vacationland.

Indian tribes, including the Chickasaw, Choctaw and Natchez, inhabited the Mississippi area when the first Europeans, under Spain's Hernando de Soto, passed through in 1540. The first permanent settlement by Europeans was by a French group under Pierre le Moyne, Sieur d' Iberville, in 1699, at Fort Maurepas near present-day Biloxi.

Great Britain took over the area in 1763 after the French and Indian War, ceding it to the U.S. in 1783 after the Revolution. Spain also claimed the land and did not relinquish it until 1798.

The population grew steadily and Mississippi became a state Dec. 10, 1817. It was the 2d state to join the Confederacy, 1861, and was readmitted to the Union in 1870.

Soybeans have taken over as Mississippi's largest crop, although the state ranks 2d only to Texas in cotton production. Other important farm products include large crops of pecans and sweet potatoes; other crops include rice and sugarcane syrup. Poultry and eggs are also important. Farm receipts totaled $1.5 billion in 1973.

Biloxi has a large seafood canning industry, operating deep-sea trawlers for shrimp and oysters. Value of the commercial catch is over $16 billion a year.

With more than 50% of the land classified as forest, timber products yielded over $1 billion in 1973.

The state produces the most hardwood pulpwood, much hardwood lumber and slashpine products, including fiberboard, kraft paper, newsprint.

Petroleum production was valued at $189 million for 1973; natural gas output was valued at $30 million; total value of mineral production was est. at $262 million.

Mississippi has achieved considerable industrial expansion. The main fields have been lumber, along with furniture and paper, food processing, apparel, chemicals, transportation equipment, machinery.

Per capita income was $3,448 in 1973, lowest in the nation. Annual pay for public school teachers was $7,854, also the nation's lowest.

A $250 million NASA space installation is used as a center for International Earth Sciences by NOAA and NASA. There are 42 institutions of higher learning.

Mississippi became the last state to abandon prohibition, adopting a local-option liquor law May 21, 1966.

Tourism is of growing economic importance. It is estimated that out-of-state tourists spend over $420 million a year in the state.

Gulfport holds an annual yacht regatta and a fishing rodeo in July, Biloxi has a Mardi Gras, Pass Christian has a tarpon rodeo. Natchez holds a pilgrimage each spring which features visits to many of the city's ante bellum mansions. Also sponsoring such pilgrimages are Columbus, Holly Springs, Oxford, Carrollton, Jackson, Vicksburg, Woodville, Hattiesburg, Raymond, Meridian.

In Vicksburg National Military Park, visitors may see remains of forts, trenches and other works which featured the 1863 siege of the city.

The Old Court House Museum in Vicksburg, built in 1858 by slave labor, has a museum with relics of the siege of Vicksburg, including flags, documents, newspapers printed on the back of wallpaper, guns, swords, etc.

The Lauren Rogers Library and Museum of Art in Laurel contains works of 19th and early 20th Century Americans and Europeans, local artifacts and an unusual basket collection (about half of them Indian).

Missouri
Show Me State

CAPITAL: Jefferson City. AREA: 69,686 sq. mi., rank, 19th. POPULATION: 4,757,000 (est. 1973). MOTTO: Salus Populi Suprema Lex Esto, The Welfare of the People Shall Be the Supreme Law. FLOWER: Hawthorn. BIRD: Eastern bluebird. TREE: Dogwood. SONG: Missouri Waltz. ADMISSION: 24th.

The gateway through which the pioneers passed on their way West, Missouri today is a leading manufacturing state, with aerospace and a wide variety of other industries; it is the nation's largest producer of lead; it ranks high among the states in agricultural products; its areas of scenic and historic interest attract over 24 million vacationers each year.

Gently rolling hills in the N and W produce large crops and support cattle, sheep and hogs. The Ozark highlands in the S are famed for fishing, hunting and rugged scenery, including numerous caves and springs. The "delta" area in the SE produces soybeans, cotton and melons.

The Mississippi forms the state's boundary on the E; the Missouri forms part of the boundary in the W, then flows across the state to join the Mississippi above St. Louis. Highest point in the state is Taum Sauk Mt., 1,772 ft., in the E central area.

Missouri has endeared itself to generations of Americans with its river lore, folk tales and especially the writings of Mark Twain (Samuel L. Clemens). Statues of 2 of his creations, Tom Sawyer and Huckleberry Finn, stand in Hannibal, his boyhood home. His birthplace near Florida, Mo., has been enshrined in Mark Twain State Park.

The farm birthplace of notorious bandit Jesse James (1847-1882), is near Excelsior Springs. A log cabin built by U.S. Grant is near St. Louis. The farm where George Washington Carver, agricultural scientists, was born near Diamond is now a National Monument. The Harry S. Truman Library, near Independence, contains Presidential papers and memorabilia. Mr. Truman, who died Dec. 26, 1972, is buried in the library courtyard.

Manufacturing, paced by the state's large aerospace industries, is the top income producer and employs more persons than any other segment of the economy. Value added by manufacture is over $7.5 billion yearly. Transportation equipment, including space capsules, rocket engines, aircraft and auto assemblies, ranks first, followed by food processing, esp. meat packing, grain milling, beer and other beverages. Also important are chemicals, printing, metal products, machinery, shoes. Corncob pipes and charcoal are well-known products.

Agriculture is also an important income producer. Farm receipts in 1973 totaled $2.6 billion, two-thirds from livestock products. Missouri ranked 4th among the states in hogs, 5th in cattle and 4th in turkeys. It has large soybean, corn and clover crops. Also important are winter wheat, tobacco, apples, peaches, alfalfa, popcorn, rye.

Per capita income was $4,672 for 1973.

Tourism, described as the 3d largest industry, produces $1 billion annually. There is a wide variety of vacation facilities; large resort areas include Lake of the Ozarks, Lake Taneycomo and Table Rock Lake.

Missouri is rich in minerals. Its output of lead, valued at $159 million for 1973, was the largest in the U.S. Total mineral production value was worth $493 million. It was also a leader in barite and lime. Other products include cement, coal, iron ore, copper, zinc, asphalt.

There are 7 institutions of higher learning. The nation's first Journalism School, founded 1908, is at the University of Missouri in Columbia.

DeSoto visited the Missouri area in 1541. French fur traders founded Ste. Genevieve about 1735, St. Louis 1764. It was part of the Louisiana Territory purchased by the U.S. from France in 1803. Missouri was organized as a separate territory, 1812; admitted to the Union, Aug. 10, 1821.

The St. Joseph Museum in St. Joseph stresses the natural history and wildlife of the region and has exhibits on Indian tribes from Alaska to Florida. Also in St. Joseph is the Pony Express Museum.

(See also Index for Kansas City and St. Louis.)

Montana
Treasure State

CAPITAL: Helena. AREA: 147,138 sq. mi., rank, 4th. POPULATION: 721,000 (est. 1973). MOTTO: Oroy Plata, Gold and Silver. FLOWER: Bitterroot. TREE: Ponderosa pine. BIRD: Western meadow lark. SONG: Montana. ADMISSION: 41st.

The Rocky Mountains, with snow-capped peaks, forested slopes, broad valleys and many lakes, cover the western 40% of Montana; the rest is High Plains country devoted to grazing and farming. Montana is rich in minerals, hydroelectric power and impressive scenery. Highest mountain is Granite Peak, 12,799 ft.

Agriculture plays a vital role in Montana's economy, along with manufacturing, mining and tourism/recreation. Per capita income was $4,418 in 1973.

Oceans of grain cover much of Montana's plains; it ranks high among the states in wheat and barley output. Also grown are rye, oats, flaxseed, sugar beets and potatoes. Montana ranks 6th in sheep and 13th in cattle. Farm receipts totaled over $1 billion in 1973, more than half from livestock.

Manufacturing industries have grown, with value added by manufacture over $330 million a year. Processing of forest products and primary metal industries are most important and have the most

employees, followed by food processing, wood products include pulp, plywood and lumber.

The state ships more than 3 million Christmas trees annually.

Total mineral production for 1973 was est. at $362 million, with petroleum accounting for $112 million and copper $154 million. Other products include silver, gold, natural gas. In 1973, 10 million tons of coal were strip-mined.

Out-of-state tourists spend an est. $210 million annually. Tourist attractions include hunting, fishing, skiing, dude ranching. The Big Sky ski and golf resort opened in 1974.

Hunters annually take about 100,000 deer, 11,000 antelope, 10,000 elk, 1,100 black bear, 500 moose, 350 mountain goats.

Glacier National Park, on the Continental Divide, is a scenic and recreational wonderland, with 60 glaciers, 200 lakes and many streams with good trout fishing.

Flathead Lake, in the NW, covers 189 sq. mi. Fort Peck Reservoir, in the NE, covers 382.8 sq. mi.

Important historical site is Custer Battlefield National Cemetery, in Big Horn County (near Hardin), site of Custer's defeat by the Sioux, June 25, 1876. First visited by the French Verendryes, father and sons, 1743; Lewis and Clark, 1805. Montana became a territory, 1864, and a state Nov. 8, 1889.

There are 7 Indian reservations, covering over 5 million acres; tribes are Blackfeet, Crow, Confederated Salish & Kootenai, Assiniboine, Gros Ventre, Sioux, Northern Cheyenne, Chippewa, Cree. Population of the reservations is approximately 25,500.

The Museum of the Plains Indian, on the Blackfeet Reservation near Browning, features exhibits of historic and contemporary arts and crafts of the Northern Plains Indians and an Indian craft shop; the museum is administered by the U.S. Interior Dept.

The Historical Society of Montana, in Helena, has paintings, dioramas and other exhibits of Montana's Indian and buffalo days, mining camps, frontier settlements, cattle roundups. Outstanding is the collection of nearly 100 Charles M. Russell paintings.

There are 12 colleges and universities.

(See also Index for Billings.)

Nebraska
Cornhusker State

CAPITAL: Lincoln. AREA: 77,227 sq. mi., rank, 15th. POPULATION: 1,542,000 (est. 1973). MOTTO: Equality Before The Law. FLOWER: Goldenrod. TREE: Cottonwood. BIRD: Western meadowlark. SONG: Beautiful Nebraska. ADMISSION: 37th.

Fields of corn, wheat and sorghum cover the Nebraska plain, sloping gently toward the Missouri River, the eastern border of the state; vast herds of cattle roam the grassy sandhills which rise to the W, ending in the broken tablelands which mark the foothills of the Rockies. Highest point, 5,426 ft., is in the far SW corner.

With more than 23 million acres under cultivation, Nebraska is an agricultural stronghold, an important grain and livestock producer. Many of its manufacturing industries are agriculture-related.

But manufacturing has also become diversified, broadening the state's economic base. Firms making electronic components, auto accessories, pharmaceuticals and other sophisticated products have joined the older industries.

Processing of meat, grain and dairy products is by far the largest manufacturing field, accounting for more than a third of the total value added by manufacture, which is estimated at almost $1.8 billion, as well as for the largest number of workers.

Other important manufacturing fields are electrical machinery and other machinery, especially farm equipment; chemicals, metal products, transportation equipment, instruments and related products. Per capita income was $4,827 in 1973.

Nebraska ranked 6th among the states in total farm receipts for 1973; $3.7 billion, with the larger part coming from livestock products. Its cattle herds ranked 3d among the states; it had 7.4 million cattle in 1974. It ranked 6th in hogs. Nebraska was also a leader in several crops, ranking high in sorghum, winter wheat, corn and rye. Also important are soybeans, sugar beets and oats.

Mineral production in Nebraska was valued at $70 million for 1973. Oil continued to be the most important product, valued at $26 million. Other products included cement, lime, pumice, sand and gravel.

Nebraska has a unicameral or one-house legislature with 49 members elected on a non-partisan ballot. All electric power facilities are state or municipally owned.

Nebraska has 27 institutions of higher education.

Arbor Lodge State Park at Nebraska City is a memorial to J. Sterling Morton, founder of Arbor Day, which is observed as a legal holiday on his birthday, Apr. 22. Boys Town is 11 mi. W of Omaha.

The Sheldon Memorial Art Gallery at the Univ. of Nebraska, Lincoln, housed in a building designed by Philip Johnson, has works by Bellows, Stuart Davis, Eakins, Gauguin, Homer, Hopper, Miro, O'Keeffe, Picasso, Ryder, Calder, Lachaise, Henry Moore, Rodin, Zorach.

The Joslyn Art Museum, Omaha, has works by Titian, El Greco, Rembrandt, Goya, Renoir, etc.; exhibits of furniture, the early West, fur trade, Indian art.

Pioneer Village, Minden, has some 30,000 items of Americana displayed in a rural schoolhouse, depot, general store, fort, fire house, sod house, Pony Express station, etc., plus old locomotives, tractors, a steam-powered merry-go-round. The Stuhr Museum of the Prairie Pioneer has 57 original 19th Century buildings near Grand Island.

The House of Yesterday, Hastings, has exhibits of pioneer days and natural science and the J. M. McDonald Planetarium. The Strategic Aerospace Museum is in Bellevue.

French fur traders visited the Nebraska area about 1700. It was part of the Louisiana Purchase, 1803, and was visited by Lewis and Clark, 1804-06. The Union Pacific began its transcontinental railroad at Omaha in 1865 (completed 1869). The Territory of Nebraska was created by the Kansas-Nebraska Act, 1854; it became a state Mar. 1, 1867.

(See also Index for Omaha)

Nevada
Sagebrush State, Silver State

CAPITAL: Carson City. AREA: 110,540 sq. mi., rank, 7th. POPULATION: 548,000 (est. 1973). MOTTO: All for Our Country. FLOWER: Sagebrush. BIRD: Mountain bluebird. TREE: Single-leaf pinon. SONG: Home Means Nevada. ADMISSION: 36th.

Nevada lies mostly in the Great Basin, a rugged plateau region broken by mountain chains running N-S. It is enclosed on the E by the Rockies and the Wasatch Range in Utah, and on the W by California's Sierra Nevada and Cascade Ranges which rob the clouds of moisture, making Nevada's climate extremely dry. Boundary Peak, near the SW border with California, is the state's highest point, 13,140 ft.

One of the smallest states in population, Nevada has attracted large numbers of outsiders, starting with the famed rush to the Comstock Lode (discovered 1859) and other fabulous gold and silver mines. Today, the attractions are legalized gambling, highly-developed entertainment and recreation facilities, and lenient divorce laws requiring only 6-weeks residence.

Spending by visitors is the biggest factor in Nevada's economy. More than 12 million from out of state, about 22 times the state's population, visit Nevada annually.

Tourist-connected industries—hotels, casinos, amusement and recreation facilities—make up the largest employment category. Per capita income was $5,560 in 1973.

State collections from gaming were $62,256,051 in 1972-73, up $7,375,939 from the previous fiscal year. This income provides about 43% of the state's revenue. Gross gambling receipts for 1973 were $731,170,284.

There are big resort areas, with nearby skiing as well as sunbathing, near Lake Tahoe, Reno, Las Vegas and elsewhere. Ghost towns, rodeos, trout fishing, water skiing and deer hunting are other attractions.

Large recreation areas include those at Pyramid Lake, wholly within the state; Lake Tahoe, partly in California; Lake Mead, formed by Hoover Dam, and Lake Mohave, formed by Davis Dam, both in Lake Mead National Recreation Area, which is shared with Arizona.

Mineral production value for 1973 was est. at $197 million with copper accounting for $109 million. Nevada is also a leader in gold, mercury, lithium, barite and silver.

Nevada is the largest manufacturer of gaming devices. Also important are electronic devices, chemicals, forest products, suntan lotion, stone-clay-glass products. About $161 million is the est. value added annually by growing manufacturing industries.

Farm receipts totaled $136 million for 1973, more than 80% from livestock products. The dry climate makes much of the state more suitable for grazing than for crops, although large-scale irrigation has expanded the growing areas.

The Nevada Test Site, NW of Las Vegas, is a proving ground for various atomic devices.

Nevada has 6 institutions of higher learning.

Trappers and traders entered the Nevada area in the 1820s, including Jedediah Smith and Peter Skene Ogden. It became U.S. territory at the end of the Mexican War. It became a state Oct. 31, 1864.

The Nevada State Museum, Carson City, occupies a former U.S. Mint, and exhibits coins, habitat groups of mammals and birds of the Great Basin area, Indian baskets, full-scale replicas of underground mining operations and thousands of arrowheads.

(See also Index for Las Vegas, Reno.)

New Hampshire
Granite State

CAPITAL: Concord. Area: 9,304 sq. mi., rank, 44th. POPULATION: 791,000 (est. 1973). MOTTO: Live Free or Die. FLOWER: Purple lilac. BIRD: Purple finch. TREE: Paper (white) birch. SONG: Old New Hampshire. Ninth of the original 13 states to ratify Constitution.

One of the 6 New England states, New Hampshire is a land of impressive mountains, picturesque lakes, swift rivers and, in the north, thick forests. Mountain slopes provide excellent ski trails. Numerous lakes and streams afford fishing for trout, bass, pickerel, perch, whitefish.

Abundant water power early turned New Hampshire into an industrial state, with manufacturing the principal source of income. Soil and climate have curtailed agricultural growth, but scenic and recreation resources have been developed and the tourist-vacation business, over $400 million a year, ranks 2d in its contribution to the state's economy. Per capita income was $4,578 in 1973.

In 1964, to raise funds to support education, the state ran the first legal sweepstakes lottery in the U.S. since 1894 (in that year, a lottery in Louisiana was outlawed). Profits from the state lottery are turned over to local school districts.

Most important industrial products are shoes and boots, electrical and other machinery, wool and other textiles, and paper.

Most factories are concentrated along the Merrimack and Connecticut Rivers and in the seacoast area. Manufacturing employs about 100,000 workers. Value added by manufacture is over $1.09 billion a year.

Farm receipts for 1973 totaled $67 million, about 55% from dairy and poultry products. Crops include apples, peaches, maple sugar and syrup.

Mineral products, mainly sand, gravel and stone for construction, were valued at $10 million for 1973.

Recreation and vacation attractions include Lake Winnipesaukee, largest of 1,300 lakes and ponds; the White Mountains, with skiing and scenic beauty; beaches on the Atlantic Coast and historic sites.

One-third of the state is over 2,000 ft. above sea level. Highest land in Northeast U.S. is the Presidential range of the White Mountains, with Mt. Washington, 6,288 ft. (first cog railway in world opened 1869); Mt. Jefferson, 5,717 ft.; Mt. Adams, 5,789 ft. National forests cover 677,559 acres; 142 state forests and parks, 63,805 acres.

State-owned parks include areas in Crawford and Franconia Notches; the latter includes the Old Man of the Mountains, described by Nathaniel Hawthorne as the Great Stone Face.

Portsmouth is the state's only port. Manchester is the largest city.

New Hampshire was visited by Samuel Champlain in 1605. Under an English land grant, Capt. John Mason in 1623 sent 2 groups to establish a fishing colony at the mouth of the Piscataqua River. One group settled Little Harbor of Pannaway (now town of Rye); the other set up fishing stages at Northam, later named Dover. The colony was called after Hampshire, England, in 1629. It declared its independence Jan. 5, 1776, and contributed to the victories at Bennington and Saratoga, entering the Union June 21, 1788.

New Hampshire shared the educational pioneering of Massachusetts Bay from 1642; it established its first free public library at Dublin, 1822.

There are 25 institutions of higher education. The MacDowell colony at Peterborough, established in 1908 in honor of Edward MacDowell, is a summer haven for writers, composers, artists.

The Currier Gallery of Art, Manchester, exhibits silver by Paul Revere, textiles, hooked rugs, pewter and glass and works by Tintoretto, Ruisdael, Monet, Corot, Constable, Picasso, Roualt, Copley, Stuart, Trumbull, Sargent, Homer, Wyeth, Marin, etc.

The New Hampshire Historical Society, Concord, has a museum displaying New Hampshire furniture, silver, pewter, glass, china, quilts, costumes, weapons, etc.

New Jersey
Garden State

CAPITAL: Trenton. AREA. 7,836 sq. mi., rank, 46th. POPULATION: 7,361,000 (est. 1973). MOTTO: Liberty and Prosperity. FLOWER: Purple violet. BIRD: Eastern goldfinch. TREE: Red oak. Third of the original 13 states to ratify Constitution.

Smallest of the Middle Atlantic states, New Jersey was settled by the Dutch early in the 17th Century and was the scene of much action during the American Revolution. Today it has the heaviest pop. per sq. mi. of the 50 states, ranks near the top in manufacturing, is rich in poultry and vegetable production, and has a flourishing resort industry.

There are vast shipping facilities and New Jersey divides authority over important airports, harbors, tunnels and bridges with the Port Authority of N.Y. and N.J. and the states of Delaware and Pennsylvania.

About 63% of the state's land area is in farms and forests. Highest point is High Point, Sussex County, 1,803 ft.

Small in area, New Jersey has a heavy concentration of factories, highways, railroads and farms, and is a leader in many fields.

It also has the greatest population density among the 50 states, reaching that status in 1965, when it passed Rhode Island. In the 1970 Census, New Jersey had 953.1 persons per sq. mi., Rhode Island had 905.5.

Per capita income was $5,759 in 1973, 2d highest in the U.S. next to Connecticut.

Highly industrialized, New Jersey ranks 7th among the states in value added by manufacture, over $14 billion annually. It ranks 1st among the states in chemical products, having large pharmaceutical, basic chemical and paint industries.

It is also a leader in other manufacturing lines: apparel, food processing, electrical and other machinery, stone-clay-glass products, printing, rubber and plastics, petroleum products, leather products. It has a large concentration of research installations in many lines.

New Jersey also ranks high in the U.S. in gross income per farm acre. Chief crops are tomatoes, corn, asparagus, apples, cranberries, peaches, spinach. Poultry and dairy products are also important. The first dairy cattle artificial insemination project was launched in Hunterdon County; also the first common-carrier shipments of day-old chicks.

Total farm receipts in 1973 were $297 million, more than half from crops.

Mineral production is mostly stone, sand and gravel, mainly for construction work. Zinc, peat and clays were among other products. Total value was $110 million.

Large refineries, which process oil from out of state, have a total crude capacity of more than 500,-000 barrels a day.

The commercial fishing catch is valued at over $18 million a year.

There are 61 institutions of higher learning.

A state lottery, with proceeds to benefit education and other institutions was launched in 1971.

Atlantic City, Ocean City, Cape May, Asbury Park, Ocean Grove, Wildwood are among more than 100 resorts. The resort industry generates over $2.6 billion in business annually. There are 40 state parks with 47,252 acres. The 10 state forests comprise 192,000 acres. There are several historic sites relating to the Revolutionary War period.

In Camden, the Walt Whitman House, home of the poet from 1884 until his death, Mar. 26, 1892, contains books, mementos and furnishings used by Whitman. The U. S. Army Signal Corps Museum, Fort Monmouth, contains communications equipment from the earliest visual methods to modern satellites.

The Montclair Art Museum exhibits art of many periods and lands, emphasizing the American. The Newark Museum is a museum of art, science and industry, including American paintings and sculpture; Chinese, Japanese and Tibetan art; collections of economic botany, birds, insects, minerals, shells, glass, ceramics and jewelry. The New Jersey Historical Society Museum, Newark, has old New Jersey rooms and collections of New Jersey furniture, paintings, china, costumes, etc.

The Garden State Arts Center is an amphitheater for concerts and stage shows at Telegraph Hill Park.

The Johnston Historical Museum, adjacent to the national hq. of the Boy Scouts of America, New Brunswick, depicts Scouting history, has a weather station, ham radio station and 22-acre Outdoor Museum of Nature and Conservation.

The Edison National Historic Site, West Orange, displays in buildings set by Thomas Alva Edison his chemical laboratory, machine shop and library; a reproduction of the "Black Maria," Edison's first movie studio; originals or replicas of his phonograph; incandescent lamp and movie camera. In South Orange, the New Jersey Fire Museum displays 19th Century hand-pumpers, hose carts, helmets, etc.

In Trenton, the New Jersey State Museum displays the state's achievements in the arts, sciences, history, technology and industry, and has a planetarium.

The New Jersey Meadowlands, lying close to the state's northeastern metropolitan centers, are the target of new development plans, including a New Jersey Sports Complex with a baseball-football stadium and race track. The N.Y. Giants plan to play their 1975 football season in the stadium.

The state's network of modern highways gives New Jersey more miles of roads per sq. mi. of area than any other state.

There are 16 airlines and 17 railroads. New Jersey has the most concentrated trackage per sq. mi. in the U.S.

(See also Index for Newark.)

New Mexico
Land of Enchantment
CAPITAL: Santa Fe. AREA: 121,666 sq. mi., rank, 5th. POPULATION: 1,106,000 (est. 1973). MOTTO: Crescit Eundo, It Grows as It Goes. FLOWER: Yucca. BIRD: Roadrunner. TREE: Pinon (nut pine). SONGS: O, Fair New Mexico, Asi Es Nuevo Mejico. ADMISSION: 47th.

New Mexico is a land of contrasts, presenting remnants of old Indian and Spanish cultures along with nuclear and space research centers; mountains over 13,000 ft. and a cavern 829 ft. below ground; ski slopes and desert vistas.

Vast areas are made fertile by irrigation through dams and reservoirs on the Rio Grande, San Juan, Pecos, Canadian, Cimarron, Gila and San Francisco Rivers. Wheeler Peak, 13,161 ft., is highest point.

The climate is dry and invigorating; annual rainfall is 7'' to 16''; mean temperature is 50°, reaching 100° on the plains in summer.

National forests cover 13,281 sq. mi. Douglas fir, Ponderosa pine and spruce are cut for timber. Almost 34% of the land is Federally owned.

Minerals are New Mexico's richest natural resource and the state leads the U.S. in output of uranium and potassium salts.

Mineral production reached a total value of $1.2 billion in 1973. Petroleum accounted for the largest single part of this, $367 million, followed by natural gas, $261 million, and copper, $244 million. Also high in value were potassium salts and uranium. New Mexico ranks high among the states in perlite and carbon dioxide. Its rich variety of minerals also includes gold, silver, zinc, lead, molybdenum.

Farm receipts accounted for $740 million for 1973, more than two-thirds from livestock products. New Mexico ranked 7th among the states in number of sheep. Cotton, pecans and sorghum are the most important field crops. Also grown are corn, peanuts, beans, onions and lettuce.

Manufacturing industries have grown and diversified. Principal lines are food products, chemicals, ordnance and transportation equipment, lumber, electrical machinery, stone-clay-glass products. Value added by manufacture is over $270 million annually.

Federal government activities, especially nuclear and space research and testing, have played a large role in New Mexico's economic growth. Nuclear and space centers are at Los Alamos, White Sands, Holloman, Kirtland and Sandia.

Per capita income was $3,764 in 1973, ranking 48th among the states.

New Mexico's most awe-inspiring natural wonder, Carlsbad Caverns, has more than a half-million visitors annually. A national park, the caverns are on 3 levels and have the largest natural cave "room" in the world, 1,500 by 300 ft., 300 ft. high.

There are 4 large Indian reservations and 19 inhabited pueblos, including Acoma, the "sky city," built atop a 357-ft. mesa. There are pueblo ruins from 1000 A.D. in Chaco Canyon.

Skiing, hunting, fishing, ghost towns and dude ranches help tourism show steady gains. Visitors

spend more than $350 million in the state annually.

Spaniards seeking gold explored New Mexico in the early 16th Century; the area was labeled New Mexico on a 1583 map. It was colonized 1598, with the first church at San Juan pueblo. The land remained under Spain until 1821, then under Mexico till U.S. troops occupied it in 1846.

It was formally ceded by Mexico to the U.S. in 1848, was made a Territory in 1850, was separated in 1863 from the part which was to become Arizona. New Mexico became a state in 1912.

There are 13 institutions of higher education.

Santa Fe (c. 1609) is the 2d oldest city in the U.S. It and Taos have large artist colonies. Albuquerque (1706) is the state's largest city.

The Museum of Navaho Ceremonial Art, Santa Fe, housed in a modernized version of a ceremonial hogan has over 600 sandpaintings, recordings of 2,000 Navaho chants; books, manuscripts, baskets, blankets.

The Museum of New Mexico, Sante Fe, maintains the oldest public building in the U.S., the Palace of the Governors (built 1610), a hall of modern Indian culture, collected works of artists of the SW, folk art exhibits.

The Roswell Museum and Art Center, Roswell, has 19th and 20th Century art collections, archeology and geology exhibits, the Robert H. Goddard rocket collection.

(See also Index for Albuquerque.)

New York
Empire State
CAPITAL: Albany. AREA: 49,576 sq. mi., rank, 30th. POPULATION: 18,265,000 (est. 1973). MOTTO: Excelsior. Ever Upward. FLOWER: Rose. BIRD: Bluebird. TREE: Sugar maple. Eleventh of the original 13 states to ratify Constitution.

New York is the nation's leading manufacturing state and within its borders are the financial capital of the nation, the largest city and port, the headquarters of the United Nations, the head offices of many of the greatest national corporations and insurance companies and a great variety of industries.

New York's manufacturing industries outrank those of all other states in number, employees, payrolls and value added by manufacture (28.86 billion annually).

Value added by manufacture in New York exceeded that of every other state in apparel ($3 billion), printing and publishing ($4.16 billion), instruments ($3.1 billion), paper and paper products ($809 million), and in the miscellaneous group, which includes jewelry, silverware, toys and sporting goods, pens and pencils, etc. ($1.07 billion).

The state produces more than 33% of the nation's instruments, 25% of apparel, 23% of printing and publishing and 19% of the miscellaneous category. It is the largest producer of both leather and paper products.

Average employment for 1973 was 7.8 million. Wages and salaries totaled over $50 billion.

The bi-state Port Authority of New York and New Jersey handled 20% of the nation's foreign trade (by value) in 1973 by U.S. Commerce Dept. figures. The 3 Customs Districts (New York, Buffalo and Ogdensburg) handled 28% of U.S. exports and imports by value in 1973.

Kennedy International Airport in N.Y. City handles about 50% of the nation's overseas air travel and is the nation's largest air cargo center, handling 53% of export-import air tonnage (by value).

The state Barge Canal System is 800 mi. long. There are 33 railroads and 526 landing facilities, including 27 seaplane bases and heliports. The Verrazano-Narrows Bridge has the world's longest suspension span.

The Dewey Thruway runs from N.Y. City to the Pennsylvania border on Lake Erie, 559 mi.; most of the state's 1,347-mi. portion of the Interstate Highway System was completed by 1972.

Tourism and business travel provide $4 billion a year to businesses in the state. Major vacation areas include the Adirondack and Catskill Mtns., Finger Lakes, Great Lakes, Thousand Islands, Long Island, N.Y. City and Niagara Falls.

Rich, rolling farmlands support a large agricultural output. New York usually ranks 1st among the states in production of clover and timothy and ice cream; it is 2d to Washington in apples and 2d to California in grapes (it has large wine and grape juice industries). Usually 1st in maple syrup, it was 2d to Vermont in 1973, led again in 1974.

It is also a leader in milk production, with the 3d largest number of milk cows in the U.S., and in vegetables and melons, sweet and tart cherries, pears and potatoes. Also important are corn, oats, wheat, peaches, peas, beans, beets, cabbages. Poultry and egg production is also high. Farm production supports large canning and freezing industries in the state.

Farm receipts for 1973 were est. at $1.31 billion, with more than two-thirds of the total from livestock and dairy products. Commercial fishing produces $18 million a year.

The state has a rich and varied mineral industry, normally ranking 1st in the U.S. in talc, titanium, emery, abrasive garnet and wollastonite, and among the leaders in salt and zinc. Other products include lead, gypsum, petroleum, clay, stone, iron. Total value for 1973 was $373 million.

Per capita income was $5,663 in 1973, 4th highest among the states.

Highest point in the state is Mt. Marcy in the Adirondacks, 5,344 ft. The 128 state parks are visited annually by over 45 million persons.

In 1967, a state lottery, with proceeds to be used for education, went into operation.

There are 259 institutions of higher education, most in any state. Expenditure per pupil in public schools is highest of any state, $1,809 in 1974.

New York was the nation's most populous state from 1820 through 1964. As of July 1, 1964, the U.S. Census Bureau estimated California's pop. reached 18,084,000. New York's 17,915,000 (including Armed Forces stationed in the 2 states; without them, New York still led 17,870,000 to 17,749,000). By July 1, 1965, the Bureau estimated California led in both categories. In the 1970 census, California had 19,953,-134; New York had 18,241,266.

Giovanni da Verrazano, Italian-born navigator sailing for France, is believed to have seen what is now New York Bay in 1524. Henry Hudson, an Englishman sailing for the Dutch, reached the bay in 1609.

Sunnyside, the home of Washington Irving, "as full of angles and corners as an old cocked hat," is in Tarrytown. The Dutch Church of Sleepy Hollow (1697), North Tarrytown, overlooks a bridge commemorating Irving's story of the "headless horseman"; Irving is buried close by in Sleepy Hollow Cemetery. Also in Tarrytown is Lyndhurst, 19th century mansion of Jay Gould, maintained by the National Trust for Historic Preservation.

The Franklin D. Roosevelt National Historic Site, in Hyde Park, includes the graves of President and Mrs. Roosevelt, the home occupied by the Roosevelt family from 1867, greenhouse, etc. The Roosevelt Library has historic papers, trophies and ship models.

Philipsburg Manor, in North Tarrytown, a trading center of the early 1700s, includes the restored Frederick Philipse home, a dam and grist mill. Van Cortlandt Manor, Croton-on-Hudson, has the restored Van Cortlandt home and ferry house.

In Kingston, the Senate House, seat of the first Senate of the state, exhibits early historical objects; its museum has works by John Vanderlyn, local historical painter. In Newburgh, Washington's Hq., the Jonathan Hasbrouck House has Revolutionary relics.

The Suffolk Museum and Carriage House, Stony Brook, L. I., has early American paintings and furniture, apothecary shop, tavern, Wells Fargo stage, Conestoga and gypsy wagons, etc.

In Cooperstown are the National Baseball Hall of Fame and Museum with a wide collection of mementos of the national game; nearby is Abner Doubleday Field, said to be where baseball originated in 1839. Near Cooperstown are Fenimore House, hq. of the State Historical Society, with collections including James Fenimore Cooper memorabilia and an art gallery; the Farmer's Museum, with craft demonstrations, and the Village Crossroads, with blacksmith shop, country store, etc; the Carriage and Harness Museum preserves the stables and vehicles of the early 20th Century.

The restored Fort Ticonderoga, overlooking the waters connecting Lakes George and Champlain, has a museum of relics of the French and Indian War and the Revolution in which the fort played important roles.

The New York State Museum in Albany has exhibits of natural resources, Indian life, Louis Agassiz Fuertes' paintings of birds, colonial housewares, etc.

The Corning Glass Center, Corning, has a museum and the Steuben factory, where visitors may see crystal glass formed and engraved. Also in the Finger Lakes area are the Curtiss Museum of aviation and the Wine Museum at Hammondsport and several wineries which offer tours to visitors. In Binghamton, the Roberson Center for the Arts and Sciences has art and historical collections.

In Utica, the Munson-Williams-Proctor Institute has a museum of 19th and 20th Century art and Fountain Elms, a restored mid-19th Century home.

The Remington Art Memorial Museum, Ogdensburg, has paintings and bronzes by Frederic Remington (1861-1909), who was born in nearby Canton.

(See also index for Albany, Binghamton, Buffalo, N.Y. City, Rochester, Schenectady, Syracuse, Troy.)

North Carolina
Tar Heel State, Old North State

CAPITAL: Raleigh. AREA: 52,586 sq. mi., rank, 28th. POPULATION: 5,273,000 (est. 1973). MOTTO: Esse Quam Videri, To be, Rather Than To Seem. FLOWER: Dogwood. BIRD: Cardinal. TREE: Pine. SONG: The Old North State. Twelfth of the original 13 states to ratify Constitution.

From a low coastal plain, with Capes Hatteras, Lookout and Fear jutting into the Atlantic, North Carolina rises to a central Piedmont plateau region and, in the W, to the scenic Blue Ridge and Great Smoky Mountains. Mt. Mitchell, 6,684 ft., is the highest peak E of the Mississippi.

Modernization of production methods has brought North Carolina increasing prosperity from its factories in recent years. Per capita personal income was $4,120 in 1973.

The state leads the U.S. in production of textiles, bricks and household furniture, and in both tobacco grown and cigarettes made.

In 1973, 104 new industrial plants opened and 208 expanded their facilities, creating an est. 22,172 new jobs through an investment of $727 million.

About 771,500 are employed in factories. The textile industry is the state's largest, with shipments valued at about $23.8 billion annually.

North Carolina ranks 1st among the states in tobacco production; in 1973 it totaled 406,117 tons. It was also 1st in sweet potatoes, in peanuts. Other large crops are cotton, corn and soybeans. Also 6 grown are wheat, oats, barley, peaches, apples. In crop receipts the state ranked 9th in 1973 with $1.3 million; livestock product receipts totaled $951 million.

There is a large poultry products business. The state ranked 3d in turkeys, 5th in chickens in 1973.

Mineral production value was est. at $129 million for 1973. North Carolina ranked 1st in mica, feldspar and lithium; it was also a leader in talc and asbestos.

Tourism is important; in 1973 travelers spent an est. $955 million in the state. Sports include year-round golfing, skiing at mountain resorts, fishing in both fresh and salt water, hunting for both large and small game.

Among attractions are the Great Smoky Mtns. (half in Tennessee), the Blue Ridge Parkway (partly in Virginia) and the Cape Hatteras and Cape Lookout National Seashores.

Other attractions include the restored Fort Raleigh National Historic Site, Roanoke Is., where Virginia Dare, first child of English parents in the New World, was born Aug. 18, 1587. Wright Brothers National Memorial near Kitty Hawk, has aviation exhibits and a reproduction of the plane in which Wilbur and Orville Wright made their first flights, 1903; Guilford Court House and Moore's Creek parks, sites of Revolutionary battles . The Battleship North Carolina, a war memorial is berthed at Wilmington.

In Asheville is one of the world's largest rayon plants as well as Biltmore Industries, native craft plants set up by Mrs. George W. Vanderbilt in 1901 to continue handweaving traditions of the area. Just S of Asheville is the 19th Century Biltmore mansion of the Vanderbilts, which has a large collection of paintings, antiques and Ming china. Also in Asheville, the Thomas Wolfe Memorial was the home of the author.

Bennett Place, 6 mi. NW of Durham, is the site where Gen. Joseph E. Johnston surrendered the last Confederate army to Gen. William Tecumseh Sherman.

The Mint Museum of Art, Charlotte, has collections of paintings, sculpture, and ceramics. The North Carolina Museum of Art, Raleigh, exhibits American and European paintings, sculpture and decorative art. Tryon Palace, New Bern, is the reconstructed colonial capitol of 1770-1794, furnished with antiques.

Old Salem, in Winston-Salem, includes buildings erected by the Moravians from 1766 on. The R.J. Reynolds Tobacco Co. welcomes visitors at its plant and warehouses.

There are 99 institutions of higher education.

Verrazano, 1524, touched the coast. DeSoto went into the Great Smoky Mts. in 1540. Sir Walter Raleigh sent an expedition to Roanoke Is., 1584; colony was settled 1585, 1587; this, the Lost Colony, disappeared. Bath, oldest town in North Carolina, was settled in 1696. North Carolina seceded from the Union May 20, 1861; revoked secession, 1865; was readmitted 1868.

(See also Index for Charlotte, Raleigh and Winston-Salem.)

North Dakota

Sioux State, Flickertail State

CAPITAL: Bismarck. AREA: 70,665 sq. mi., rank, 17th. POPULATION: 640,000 (est. 1973). MOTTO: Liberty and Union, Now and Forever, One and Inseparable. FLOWER: Wild prairie rose. BIRD: Western meadowlark. TREE: American elm. SONG: North Dakota Hymn. ADMISSION: 39th or 40th with South Dakota.

The easter plains of North Dakota are rich in vast fields of grain and support large numbers of livestock, in sharp contrast to the rough, colorful Badlands in the W which have elements of scenic beauty and include Theodore Roosevelt National Memorial Park. Highest point is White Butte, 3,506 ft., in the SW.

North Dakota's economy is based on agriculture and mining; but manufacturing industries, especially processing of food, have grown in number and size. More than 90% of the usable land is in farms and ranches.

North Dakota led the other states in production of spring and durum wheat, barley and flaxseed in 1973. It was also a leader in rye, oats and potatoes. Farm receipts for 1973 totaled $1.7 million, more than half

from its large grain crops. In 1974 there were 2.6 million cattle in the state.

Mineral production in 1973 was valued at $101 million. The larger part of this was from petroleum. Other products include natural gas, natural gas liquids, coal (lignite), salt, peat.

There are 14 institutions of higher education.

Tourism brings in over $46 million a year.

Per capita income was $4,782 in 1973.

There are 65 state parks and historic sites. The International Peace Garden, on a 2,200-acre tract extending across the border into Manitoba, commemorates the friendly relations between the U.S. and Canada. The state is known for its waterfowl, grouse and deer hunting, bass, trout and northern pike fishing. Lake Sakakawea, formed by the Garrison Dam across the Missouri River, is 609 sq. mi. in area.

A museum with exhibits of pioneer life, the Northern Plains Indians and natural history of the area, is maintained by the State Historical Society on the State Capitol grounds, Bismarck.

Explorations in what is now North Dakota were made as early as 1738-1740 by French Canadians. The Lewis and Clark expedition (1804-1806) passed through the territory and established Fort Mandan. With South Dakota and parts of Montana and Wyoming it comprised Dakota Territory, organized Mar. 2, 1861. It became a separate state Nov. 2, 1889.

Fort Abraham Lincoln, now a state park near Mandan, was the base from which Col. George Custer set out in 1876 on the campaign which ended in the deaths of Custer and 5 companies of the 7th Cavalry at the hands of the Sioux Indians at the Little Big Horn in Montana.

There are 12 institutions of higher learning.

(See also Index for Bismarck.)

Ohio

Buckeye State

CAPITAL: Columbus. AREA: 41,222 sq. mi., rank 35th. POPULATION: 10,731,000 (est. 1973). MOTTO: With God, All Things Are Possible. FLOWER: Scarlet carnation. BIRD: Cardinal. TREE: Ohio buckeye. SONG: Beautiful Ohio. ADMISSION: 17th.

Ohio is the nation's 3d greatest industrial state; it ranks among the wealthier states in livestock and crop receipts, and is a leader in output of lime, coal and coke.

Ohio leads the U.S. in a wide variety of products: tires, machine tools, playing cards, business machines, glassware, cutlery, dishwashers, clay and metal products. Industrial expansion has continued at a rapid pace.

Per capita income was $5,012 in 1973.

Total value added by manufacture was $23.1 billion. Of this, autos, aircraft, boats and parts accounted for $2.9 billion; iron, steel and other metals, $2.9 billion; machinery, especially industrial, $3.4 billion; electrical machinery, especially household appliances, $2.4 billion. Also important are metal products, chemicals, rubber and plastic products, food processing.

Farm receipts for 1973 totaled over $2.2 billion, more than half of it from livestock products. Ohio has a large numbers of milk cows, hogs and sheep; it ranks high in milk production. It is also a large producer of corn, grapes, clover, popcorn, oats, soybeans and other crops.

Mineral production was valued at a total $752 million for 1973, with the largest item being bituminous coal. Ohio was the top state in lime production and one of the leaders in clays, salt, sand and gravel. Other important products include petroleum, cement, gypsum and natural gas.

It was estimated that the value of the tourist industry was more than $3.7 billion for 1973.

There are 62 state parks, over 300 roadside parks, and many historic memorials including Fallen Timbers Battlefield, Prehistoric Indian mounds and the restored first settlement, Schoenbrunn (1772).

The National Rifle and Pistol Matches are held at Camp Perry and the Grand American Trapshoot at Vandalia.

Unusual museums include the Air Force Museum and Paul Lawrence Dunbar House, Dayton; Dental Museum, Bainbridge; Auto-Aviation Museum, Cleveland; Ohio Historical Museum, Columbus.

The state is served by 27 railroads and 21 scheduled airlines. It has busy ports on Lake Erie and the Ohio River. Highest point is Campbell Hill 1,550 ft., in the W. central area.

There are 104 institutions of higher education.

George Rogers Clark defeated the Indians at Piqua, 1780; later Ohio had British-Indian raids and battles; Gen. Anthony Wayne defeated Indians at Fallen Timbers Aug. 20, 1794, imposed Treaty of Greenville, 1795. Oliver Hazard Perry defeated the British on Lake Erie near Put-in-Bay, Sept. 10, 1813. As governor of the Northwest Territories, Gen. Arthur St. Clair sat at Marietta (1789) and Cincinnati (1791). Ohio became a state in 1803. Colunbus became the seat of government in 1816.

In Canton, the Pro Football Hall of Fame has a museum, library and daily movies; the Stark County Historical Society has science, industry and historical museums.

(See also index for Akron, Cincinnati, Cleveland, Columbus, Dayton, Toledo, Youngstown.)

Oklahoma

Sooner State

CAPITAL: Oklahoma City. AREA: 69,919 sq. mi., rank, 18th. POPULATION: 2,663,000 (est. 1973). MOTTO: Labor Omnia Vincit—Labor Conquers All Things. FLOWER: Mistletoe. BIRD: Scissortailed flycatcher. TREE: Redbud. SONG: Oklahoma. ADMISSION: 46th.

Most of Oklahoma is a great, rolling plain sloping S and E with a mean altitude of 1,300 ft. There are 4 mountainous areas; the Ozark Plateau in the NE, the Ouachitas in the SE, the Arbuckles in the S central and the Wichitas in the SW. In the western Panhandle, the land rises toward the Rockies with Black Mesa, 4,973 ft., the highest point.

Oil, wheat and cattle are the basic ingredients of Oklahoma's economy, but manufacturing industries have gained increasing importance. Per capita income was $4,189 in 1973.

The $1.2 billion Arkansas River Navigation System, involving shipping, flood control and power dams, was completed to Catoosa, near Tulsa, in 1971. It made Catoosa a "seaport," with barge shipping to the Mississippi and beyond.

The state's output of petroleum was valued at $753 million for 1973, accounting for much of the total value of mineral production, $1.3 billion. The state is one of the leaders in the U.S. in petroleum production, and in total mineral production.

Natural gas was 2d most important among minerals; production was valued at $371 million. Other minerals include helium, in which the state is a leader, gypsum, zinc, cement, coal, copper, silver.

Oklahoma's rich plains produced the nation's 2d largest winter wheat crop in 1973 as well as large crops of sorghum, other grains and peanuts. Its cattle herd was the 6th largest in the U.S. Total farm receipts were $2.04 billion, more than half from livestock products.

While much of Oklahoma's manufacturing industry is based on processing of the state's own meat, wheat and oil, other lines have become important rivals. Value added by manufacture exceeds $1.7 billion annually. Important lines include food processing, machinery (especially construction and oil equipment), transportation equipment, metal products, petroleum and coal products.

There are 41 institutions of higher education.

Total tourist revenues are estimated at more than $544 million annually. Attractions include 30 state parks, large lakes and reservoirs such as Eufaula (102,500 acres) and Lake Texoma (93,080 acres); Ouachita National Forest (176,000 acres), rodeos, Indian powwows, the National Cowboy Hall of Fame and Western Heritage Center in Oklahoma City, bass fishing and quail hunting.

The Will Rogers Memorial, Claremore, has collections of the great humorist's saddles and ropes, as well as trophies; his tomb is also there. In Anadarko, the Southern Plains Indian Museum and Crafts Center exhibits Indian arts and has a crafts sales shop. The Woolaroc Museum near Bartlesville has 55,000 exhibits in a panorama of New World history, and a collection of paintings of the West.

The restored Fort Gibson Stockade, with many of the original buildings, near Muskogee, was erected 1824 and was the army's largest outpost in the Indian lands.

Near Tahlequah is the Cherokee Cultural Center with a restored 1700 Cherokee village and a spring and summer pageant.

The first permanent white settlement in the area was made in 1796 by Maj. Jean Pierre Chouteau on the site of present-day Salina, Okla.

Part of the Louisiana Purchase, 1803, Oklahoma was known as Indian Territory (but was not given territorial government) after it became the home of the Five Civilized tribes—Cherokee, Choctaw, Chickasaw, Creek and Seminole—1828-1846. The land was also used by Comanche, Osage and other plains Indians. As white settlers pressed west, land was opened for homesteading by runs and lottery, a run being a race for a claim at a specific time. The first run took place Apr. 22, 1889; the most famous was the run to the Cherokee Outlet, 1893. The portion thus opened was organized as a Territory; this and Indian Territory were joined by Congress in the State of Oklahoma, admitted to the Union Nov. 16, 1907. Oklahoma's Indian population (1970 Census) was 97,731, largest in the U.S.

(See also Index for Oklahoma City and Tulsa.)

Oregon

Beaver State

CAPITAL: Salem. AREA: 96,981 sq. mi., rank, 10th. POPULATION: 2,225,000 (est. 1973). MOTTO: The Union. FLOWER: Oregon grape. BIRD: Western meadowlark. COLORS: Navy blue and gold. FISH: Chinook salmon. ANIMAL: Beaver. TREE: Douglas fir. SONG: Oregon, My Oregon. ADMISSION: 33d.

Oregon is rich in timber, fish and wildlife, water power and scenic beauty, with lofty mountain ranges, deep river gorges and broad, fertile valleys.

Half of Oregon, or about 30 million acres, is thickly forested and the state leads the nation in value of forest products, over $1.9 billion a year. Production of lumber, furniture, paper and other forest products provides jobs for about 83,000 workers and is a major factor in the state's economy.

Also important are food processing, transportation equipment, machinery, fabricated metal products. Total value added by manufacture is over $2.8 billion a year.

Per capita income was $4,697 in 1973.

Oregon's agriculture is rich and varied. While farmers grow fair-sized crops of wheat, oats, potatoes and other staples, the state is a leader in production of berries, pears, cherries, filberts, walnuts, vegetables. It also ranks high in number of turkeys and of sheep. Total farm receipts for 1973 were $885 million, more than half from crops, the rest from livestock.

Stone, nickel, cement, lime and pumice are important in mineral production, valued at $83 million for 1973.

Hydroelectric power, from both privately-owned and publicly-owned utilities, is abundant. A federal agency, the Bonneville Power Administration, markets electric power, much of it from a series of great dams across the Columbia River, to many of the utilities and to large industrial plants. Among users are plants for the refining and processing of metals from out of state, including aluminum.

The commercial fish catch, including salmon, tuna, halibut, sole, cod and shellfish, was worth over $28 million in 1973.

Tourism is also an important industry, est. at over $588 million annually. There are 221 state parks and both state and national forests. Crater Lake, a national park is a body of sapphire blue water in a former volcano, 6 mi. in diameter and 1,932 ft. deep—deepest lake in the U.S. Oregon Dunes National Recreation Area was created in 1972.

Fort Clatsop National Memorial includes a replica of the fort in which the Lewis and Clark expedition spent the winter of 1805-06. Oregon Caves National Monument contains stone waterfalls. Skiing and the annual Pendleton Round-Up are other attractions.

A summer Shakespearean Festival is staged annually in Ashland.

Snow-capped Mt. Hood, which rises 11,235 ft., is the highest point in the state; nearby are scenic recreation areas.

The Columbia River brings ocean shipping to Portland, 100 miles inland but one of the Pacific Coast's principal ports, and to other river ports.

The state is served by 5 major railroad systems and 10 airlines.

Oregon has 40 institutions of higher education.

The Univ. of Oregon in Eugene has a Museum of Art with oriental, Pacific Northwest and other art collections. It also has a Museum of Natural History.

Capt. Robert Gray, in the Columbia, discovered the river named after his ship May 11, 1792, and claimed the area for the U.S. President Jefferson sent the Lewis and Clark expedition to the area, 1805-06. John Jacob Astor's fur depot, Astoria, was founded in 1811.

A provisional government was established in Champoeg, May 2, 1843, and U.S. title was established in 1846 in a settlement of U.S. and British claims to the area. Oregon became a state Feb. 14, 1859.

(See also Index for Portland.)

Pennsylvania
Keystone State

CAPITAL: Harrisburg. AREA: 45,333 sq. mi., rank, 33d. POPULATION: 11,902,000 (est. 1973). MOTTO: Virtue, Liberty and Independence. FLOWER: Mountain laurel. BIRD: Ruffed grouse. TREE: Eastern hemlock. Second of original 13 states to ratify Constitution.

Pennsylvania has extensive mineral resources and fertile farmlands, is a leader in manufacturing and boasts a wealth of historic landmarks and scenic attractions.

Roughly rectangular in shape, Pennsylvania has prosperous farmlands in the SE and the W. Through the center, running NE-SW, are parallel mountain ridges with valleys between. Highest point is Mt. Davis in the SW, 3,213 ft.

Many of the nation's largest steel plants are in Pennsylvania, with the greatest concentration in the Pittsburgh area. Pennsylvania ranks 1st among the states in steel wire and structural metal.

Mill and factory products are many and varied; value added by manufacture is over $23.2 billion. Primary metals are the most important, over $3.6 billion. Other large lines were machinery and electrical machinery, food processing, chemicals, metal products, transportation equipment, women's dresses and men's suits.

Per capita income was $4,984 in 1973.

Pennsylvania produces almost all of the nation's anthracite coal; it ranked 3d in 1973 in output of bituminous coal. Also important are cement, stone, petroleum, natural gas, lime, clays, zinc, iron. Total mineral production value for 1973 was $1.3 billion.

Prosperous farms, such as those in the Pennsylvania Dutch country in the SE, brought in total livestock and crop receipts for the state of $1.3 billion in 1973, much of it from dairy and poultry products. The state ranked high in number of milk cows, chickens and turkeys.

The state ranks high in its output of grapes, peaches, apples and cherries. It claims 1st place in scrapple, pretzels, mushrooms and plantation-grown Christmas trees. It also ranks high in ice cream. Forest products are valued at over $3.1 billion annually.

The Commonwealth is rich in historic areas, including Valley Forge and the Gettysburg Battlefield, both national shrines. The Articles of Confederation, the Declaration of Independence and the Constitution were all adopted in Philadelphia.

Pennsylvania is among the leading states in hunting, fishing, golf and winter sports. Tourism, it was estimated, produces direct sales of $5.4 billion annually.

There are more than 100 state and federal parks, recreation areas and historic sites. Scenic attractions include the Delaware Water Gap in the east and the 1,000-ft. deep Pine Creek Gorge in the north. Dutch folk festivals, country fairs, and fall foliage in the Poconos draw many visitors.

Valley Forge Historic Park, 22 mi. NW of Philadelphia, preserves the site of Washington's encampment during the winter of 1777-78; of 11,098 soldiers, close to 3,000, ill-equipped, died during the bitter weather; there is a museum, restored buildings, etc. Washington Crossing State Park, where Continental troops crossed the Delaware to attack Hessian-British forces in Trenton, Christmas Night 1776, has restored buildings and picnic areas.

Longwood Gardens, near Kennett Square, include conservatories and rock, heather, flower and water gardens; arboretum, illuminated fountains, open-air theater; open every day of the year.

Lancaster County and nearby areas in the southeast are known as Pennsylvania Dutch Country. Descendants of early German (Deutsch) and Swiss settlers still maintain many of the early customs and "old world" culture which make their farms, festivals and market places attractive to tourists.

The William Penn Memorial Museum, Harrisburg, has collections of folk art, ironwork, glass, pewter, china, textiles, stage coaches, sleighs; replicas of artisans' shops, period rooms; fine arts exhibits and a planetarium.

There are 146 institutions of higher learning.

First permanent settlement was in 1643 on Tinicum Is., near Chester, as part of New Sweden. In 1655, the Dutch took over; in 1664, the English. In 1681, Charles II granted land to William Penn as payment for debts owed Penn's father and called the land Pennsylvania (Penn's Woods) in honor of the elder Penn.

(See also Index for Allentown, Erie, Philadelphia, Pittsburgh.)

Rhode Island
Little Rhody

CAPITAL: Providence. AREA: 1,214 sq. mi., rank, 50th. POPULATION: 973,000 (est. 1973). MOTTO: Hope. FLOWER: Violet. BIRD: Rhode Island red (hen). TREE: Red maple SONG: Rhode Island. Thirteenth of original 13 states to ratify Constitution.

Rhode Island is the smallest of the 50 states but has the longest official name: State of Rhode Island and Providence Plantations. It is not an island, although its Narragansett Bay, extending from the Atlantic 28 mi. inland, contains many islands, the largest of which is named Rhode Is. Highest point, Jerimoth Hill in Providence County, is 812 ft.

Tiny Rhode Island is densely populated and highly industrialized. For many years, Rhode Island had the greatest density of population per square mile of all the states. By 1965, estimates showed it was 2d to New Jersey in this respect. The 1970 Census showed New Jersey averaging 953.1 persons per sq. mi.; Rhode Island 905.5.

Industries show more than $1.4 billion in value added annually by manufacturing. Until 1940, textile mills, dating back to Samuel Slater's 1790 cotton mill, employed more workers than all other Rhode Island industries put together. Employment in the mills has fallen off sharply in recent years, but jobs in other fields have increased.

The state also pioneered in the manufacture of jewelry and silverware and remains tops in the U. S. Other leading industry groups are primary metal processing, metal products, machinery, rubber and plastics, food processing, chemicals, apparel. The value of the tourist industry is est. at over 100 million annually.

Per capita income was $4,780 in 1973.

Only 1% of the labor force is engaged in farming, and farm receipts in 1973 totaled $18.9 million. Dairy and poultry (notably Rhode Island reds) are the most important lines; potatoes and apples are principal crops. The fish and shellfish catch is valued at over $15 million annually.

There are 13 institutions of higher education.

Rhode Island is distinguished historically for its battle for freedom of conscience and action, begun by Roger Williams, founder of Providence, who was exiled from Massachusetts Bay Colony in 1636. William Coddington, John Clark, and other religious exiles founded Pocasset, now Portsmouth, in 1638 and Newport in 1639. The first Baptist church in the U. S. was founded in Providence in 1638. Rhode Island gave protection to Quakers in 1657 and to Jews from Holland in 1658.

The struggle for individual rights included defiance of British trade restrictions and taxation, and was climaxed in 1772 by the burning of the British revenue vessel Gaspee. Rhode Island declared its independence from Britain on May 4, 1776, before the Declaration of Independence. It ratified th U. S. Constitution May 29, 1790, last of the original 13 states. Rhode Island had prohibition of liquor in the 19th Century, but repealed it in 1889 and refused later to ratify the 18th Amendment.

Providence is a major manufacturing and educational center and a port handling over 15 million tons of cargo per year.

The Rhode Island Historical Society in Providence occupies the historic John Brown House, with rooms containing furniture by 18th Century cabinet makers and other items of local origin. Also in Providence, the Rhode Island School of Design has a museum with collections of classic art, 18th Century American furniture, 19th Century paintings, etc.

Newport became famous as the summer capital of society in the mid-19th Century, when industrial magnates built showy mansions. Easton's Beach and Bailey's Beach are noted resorts and Ocean Drive and Bellevue Avenue are showplaces. Touro Synagogue (1763) is the oldest in the U. S. and is a national historic site.

The Newport Historical Society has a marine museum; extensive exhibits of silver, furniture, china, etc.; a grist mill, several forts, a Seventh Day Baptist meeting house built 1729.

In Pawtucket, the Old Slater Mill Museum is a restored 1793 cotton mill, considered the first to spin yarn successfully in this country; it has demonstrations of hand spinning and weaving.

(See also Index for Providence.)

South Carolina
Palmetto State

CAPITAL: Columbia. AREA: 31,055 sq. mi., rank, 40th, POPULATION: 2,726,000 (est. 1973). MOTTO: Dum Spiro, Spero — While I Breathe, I Hope, and

Animis Opibusque Parati — Prepared in Spirit and Resources. FLOWER: Carolina (yellow) jessamine. BIRD: Carolina wren. SONG: Carolina. TREE: Palmetto. Eighth of the original 13 states to ratify Constitution.

In South Carolina the land slopes from the Blue Ridge Mountains in the NW, through thick pine forests and fertile farmlands with great fields of tobacco and cotton, to semi-tropic beaches and busy ports on the Atlantic. Deep-sea and inland fishing, hunting, the charm of ante bellum houses, public gardens and famed shore resorts are among the state's attractions. Highest point is Sassafras Mtn. in NW, 3,560 ft.

Efforts to diversify industry and expand foreign trade and tourism have been highly successful. Per capita income was $3,817 in 1973.

Manufacturing is by far the major source of income; value added by manufacture is over $4.2 billion annually. The textile industry is still the most important, comprising almost half of the value of all manufactured products and employing the most workers. South Carolina's mills rank high in cotton goods and are also a major producer of synthetic and woolen goods.

Other important manufacturing lines are chemicals, apparel, paper, lumber, food processing, machinery and stone-clay-glass products.

In 1973, new industrial investment was valued at $1.2 billion; it was estimated this would provide 15,662 jobs. Major areas of expansion were in chemical, textile and metal-working fields.

Farms have become fewer but larger in recent years. South Carolina grows more peaches than any other state except California; it ranks 4th in tobacco. Also grown are cotton, peanuts, sweet potatoes, pecans, etc. Poultry and eggs are important revenue producers; the state has large sales of chickens and turkeys.

Total farm receipts for 1973 were $747 million.

The state's mineral production value for 1973 was est. at $85 million. It is i a leader in production of vermiculite, pused in insulation, and of kyanite and skaolin used in ceramics. Also produced lare mica, cement and stone, including Winnsboro blue granite. Lumber for pulp and saw-timber is a major resource, especially the loblolly pine. Pulpwood production is over 2.5 million cords annually.

Income from tourism has risen steadily, travelers spending an est. $443 million in 1973.

Attractions include state parks, famed gardens, historic sites, coastal islands, shore resorts such as Myrtle Beach, fishing and quail hunting.

There are many historic churches and white-pillared houses in Charleston, Columbia and Beaufort. Gardens near Charleston include Middleton Place, Magnolia and Cypress; Brookgreen, south of Myrtle Beach, has 340 outdoor statues; other gardens are Edisto, at Orangeburg, Glencairn, at Rock Hill, Swan Lake, at Sumter.

Fort Sumter National Monument in Charleston harbor is the place where the Civil War began with bombardment of the fort by Confederate batteries, Apr. 12-13, 1861.

Charleston Museum, estab. 1773, has exhibits of interior paneling, furniture, arts, crafts and utensils from early South Carolina days.

South Carolina played an important part in American beginnings. First settled by Spaniards, 1526 and 1566, it was given by England's Charles I to Robert Heath as Carolina, 1629; the first permanent settlement by the English was Charles Town, now Charleston, 1670. Charles Pinckney helped frame the Constitution of the U.S., 1787. The state was first to secede, Dec. 20, 1860; readmitted 1868.

There are 47 institutions of higher education.
(See also Index for Columbia.)

South Dakota

Coyote State, Sunshine State

CAPITAL: Pierre. AREA: 77,047 sq. mi.; rank, 16th. POPULATION: 685,000 (est. 1973). MOTTO: Under God, the People Rule. FLOWER: American pasque. BIRD: Ringnecked pheasant. SONG: Hail South Dakota. TREE: Black Hills spruce. ADMISSION: 39th or 40th with North Dakota.

South Dakota is a rectangle split down the middle by the Missouri and a chain of huge lakes formed behind dams on the river. In the E. are rich farmlands which produce large crops of rye, oats and other grains. In the W. are rolling grasslands which support millions of cattle and sheep, as well as vast acreages of wheat. In the far W. are the Black Hills with Harney Peak, 7,242 ft., the highest point in the nation E. of the Rockies.

With more than 44,000 farms and ranches, occupying most of the land area, agriculture is South Dakota's basic industry. Its livestock and livestock products account for the greater part of farm income. Mining and lumbering are also important natural resource industries. Per capita income was $4,296 in 1973.

The state normally ranks first in the U.S. in size of its rye crop and high in spring wheat, flaxseed, oats, barley. In 1974 South Dakota had 5 million cattle, almost a million sheep and 2 million hogs. Total farm receipts for 1973 were $1.7 billion.

Large areas are reclaimed by irrigation and plans were under way for additional hundreds of thousands of acres to be fed from the Oahe Reservoir.

South Dakota leads the nation in gold production; the Homestake Mine in Lawrence County is the largest in the U.S. Gold accounted for $35 million of the state's total mineral production value which was $80 million for 1973. The state was also a leader in production of beryllium. Other products include silver, petroleum, uranium, cement.

Processing of foods produced by farms and ranches is the largest of South Dakota's manufacturing industries. Also important are lumber and wood products, and machinery, including farm equipment. Total value added by manufacture is over $229 million.

South Dakota has 8,400 sq. mi. of Indian Reservations. The Indians, estimated to number about 32,365, are largely Sioux.

There are 16 institutions of higher education and 12 state parks, 35 recreation areas and 49 roadside parks. Pheasant, duck and geese are abundant. There are large herds of white-tail and mule deer and elk and about 5,000 bison in state and private herds.

Mount Rushmore in the Black Hills has an altitude of 6,200 ft. Sculptured on its granite face are the heads of Washington, Jefferson, Lincoln and Theodore Roosevelt. These busts by Gutzon Borglum are proportionate to men 465 ft. tall. Rushmore is visited by about 2 million persons annually.

Other tourist attractions include Custer State Park, with the world's largest herd of bison, the Black Hills Passion Play, staged from June to Sept. in an amphitheater at Spearfish.

The "Great Lakes of South Dakota" are 4 reservoirs created behind Oahe, Big Bend, Fort Randall and Gavins Point Dams on the Missouri River with total water surface area of 571,000 acres.

Out-of-state tourists, it is estimated, spend more than $250 million a year in South Dakota.

Fort Sisseton State Park, 18 mi. SE of Britton, is a restored army frontier post of 1864. The Sioux Indian Museum in Rapid City features historic and contemporary arts of the Sioux and an Indian craft sales shop.

Discovery of this area dates back to 1743 when the first Europeans, the Verendrye brothers, Frenchmen, came in search of a route to the Pacific. South Dakota was admitted to the Union Nov. 2, 1889, together with its twin state, North Dakota, after 28 years as a part of Dakota Territory. The South Dakota Historical Society asserts both states can be 39th or 40th state, since President Harrison intentionally shuffled the proclamations before signing.

Tennessee

Volunteer State

CAPITAL: Nashville. AREA: 42,244 sq. mi., rank, 34th. POPULATION: 4,126,000 (est. 1973). MOTTO: Agriculture, Commerce. FLOWER: Iris. BIRD: Mockingbird. TREE: Tulip poplar. SONG: Tennessee Waltz. ADMISSION: 16th.

Eastern Tennessee is rugged country with the Great Valley separating the Great Smoky Mtns., on the state's E border, from the Cumberland Mtns.; the Central Basin is a rolling area containing the famed Bluegrass country; from there the state slopes W to the bottomlands on the Mississippi River. Clingman's Dome, in the Great Smokies, is the highest point, 6,643 ft.

Manufacturing has taken the top place in Tennessee's economy; products are many and varied. Among the most important are chemicals (especially plastic fibers), textiles, apparel, electrical machinery. Other important lines are food processing, furniture, lumber, paper, primary metals, metal products, leather.

Value added by manufacture is over $6.7 billion annually. Per capita income was $3,946 in 1973.

There are 24 research centers including Oak Ridge, TVA and Arnold Engineering Development Center for rocket research.

Tennessee ranks among the top states in tobacco production. Farm receipts for 1973 totaled $1.1 billion, more than half of it from livestock, the rest from crops. It has large numbers of hogs and cattle.

Forest products are also important, providing full-time jobs to 40,000 persons and contributing over $500 million annually to the economy. The state is known as the U.S. hardwood flooring center.

Tennessee produces a wide range of minerals and leads the other states in zinc. Other products include silver, cement, copper, coal and phosphate rock. Total mineral production was valued at $269 million for 1973.

Tourism is of increasing importance; tourists spend about $750 million annually in Tennessee. Folk music and the "Nashville sound" have made that city a leading recording center.

With 6 other states, Tennessee shares in federal reservoir developments on the Tennessee and Cumberland River systems. About 41,000 sq. mi. area drawn on by the Tennessee Valley Authority, which built Norris Dam on the Clinch River and operates a number of other dams in the state. Their reservoirs cover 756,321 acres.

Tennessee has a number of natural wonders—Reelfoot Lake, the reservoir basin of the Mississippi River formed by an earthquake (1811); Lookout Mountain, a rock-faced promontory carved by the currents of the Tennessee River and overlooking Moccasin Bend, at Chattanooga; Fall Creek Falls, 256 ft. high; and the west half of Great Smoky Mountains National Park.

The American Museum of Atomic Energy in Oak Ridge has displays, models, lectures. The Hermitage, 13 mi. E of Nashville, home of Andrew Jackson, contains furniture and personal effects of the president. The Ancestral Home of James K. Polk, in Columbia, has portraits, furniture and various articles used by President Polk in the White House. The home, tailor shop and grave of President Andrew Johnson are a national monument at Greeneville. The Parthenon, in Centennial Park, Nashville, is a full-size replica of the Parthenon of Athens. There are 26 state parks.

There are 62 institutions of higher education.

Tennessee is believed to have been reached by De Soto in 1541. La Salle built a fort in 1682. It was part of the Carolina grant of Charles II and home of Cherokee tribes. During 1784-1788 settlers formed the "state" of Franklin. North Carolina ceded it to the federal government in 1790; it was part of the Territory South of the Ohio until it became a state in

1796. It seceded in 1861, was the site of more than 700 Civil War battles and skirmishes and was readmitted in 1866.

(See also Index for Chattanooga, Knoxville, Memphis, Nashville.)

Texas
Lone Star State

CAPITAL: Austin. AREA: 267,338 sq. mi., rank 2d. POPULATION: 11,794,000 (est. 1973). MOTTO: Friendship. (Carrying out meaning of Indian word, Tejas—friends, from which Texas derives name). FLOWER: Bluebonnet. TREE: Pecan. BIRD: Mockingbird. SONG: Texas, Our Texas. ADMISSION: 28th.

Texas leads all other states in many categories, among them oil, cattle, sheep, and cotton. While these are basic to the Texas economy, manufacturing, as measured in terms of value added, makes an even greater contribution than either mineral output or farm receipts.

It is 2d only to Alaska in area.

Texas normally produces a third of the nation's total petroleum output. The state's 1973 petroleum production, 1.303 billion barrels, was valued at $4.9 billion. Texas is also the leading producer of asphalt, graphite, natural gas liquids and magnesium chloride; Louisiana and Texas are the leading producers of natural gas. Texas ranks first among the states in output of sulphur, 2d in salt, helium and bromine, and 3d in cement and clays.

The total value of the state's annual mineral production is by far the greatest of any state, $7.9 billion in 1973.

Texas ranked 4th among the states in 1973 in cash receipts for crops, $2.3 billion; 2d for livestock products, $3.1 billion; 3d in total farm receipts $5.5 billion.

It led all states in number of cattle, 16 million (giving the state more cattle than people), and in sheep, 3.2 million; it ranked 4th in turkeys and 9th in chickens. It grew the largest crops of rice, pecans, sorghum and cotton, and ranked high in peanuts. It also grows large amounts of vegetables and melons; its varied output includes sweet potatoes, oranges, grapefruit, peaches and roses. Irrigation has reclaimed large arid areas in the west. Forest products are worth $115 million yearly.

The largest of its many livestock expositions are held annually in Fort Worth, San Antonio, Houston and El Paso; the largest cattle auction in Amarillo.

Manufacturing industries have shown tremendous growth. Value added by manufacture was over $13.7 billion a year. About 20% of the total value is in chemicals, the largest manufacturing industry. Other important lines are petroleum refining, processing of foods, transportation equipment, machinery, primary metals and metal products. Per capita income was $4,336 in 1973.

Texas ranks high among the states in commercial fishing with the 1973 catch valued at over $91 million.

About 18 million tourists spend over $1.7 billion dollars annually in Texas. There are 70 state parks, recreation areas and historic sites; Big Bend and Guadalupe Mtns. National Parks, Padre Is. National Seashore and Fort Davis National Historic Site. Named for President Lyndon B. Johnson, who died Jan. 22, 1973, are a National Historic Site, a National Park and a State Park, marking his birthplace, boyhood home and ranch, all near Johnson City.

In 1974, Texas listed 376 museums; included were renowned art and historical collections and restored frontier buildings.

Texas has 136 institutions of higher education.

Texas is the only state that was an independent republic, recognized by the U.S., before annexation. Over it have flown the flags of Spain, France, Mexico, the Lone Star Flag of the Republic, the Confederate States and the United States.

The first Europeans to arrive in the area were Spaniards. Alonso de Pineda, in 1519, and Cabeza de Vaca, 1536, explored coastal areas; Francisco de Coronado crossed inland in 1541. Texas became a Spanish province in 1691 and a Mexican state in 1821.

American settlers revolted in 1835; after defeat at the Alamo, Mar. 6, 1836, they defeated the Mexicans at San Jacinto, Apr. 21, 1836. They formed the Republic of Texas and, in 1845, voted for annexation to the U.S. Texas was admitted as a state Dec. 29, 1845. It seceded and joined the Confederacy Feb. 1, 1861. It freed all slaves June 19, 1865, and was readmitted to the Union Mar. 30, 1870.

(See also Index for Amarillo, Austin, Corpus Christi, Dallas, El Paso, Fort Worth, Houston, Lubbock, San Antonio.)

Utah
Beehive State

CAPITAL: Salt Lake City. AREA: 84,916 sq. mi., rank 11th. POPULATION: 1,157,000 (est. 1973). MOTTO: Industry. FLOWER: Sego lily. BIRD: California gull. TREE: Blue spruce. EMBLEM: Beehive. SONG: Utah We Love Thee. ADMISSION: 45th.

Wrested from the wilderness by Mormon settlers in the mid-19th Century, Utah is for the most part a mountainous area, broken by fertile irrigated valleys, several deserts and two large lakes, Great Salt Lake in the N and Lake Powell in the S.

Great Salt Lake is 4,200 ft. above sea level, but has no known outlet. Its salt density varies from 20 to 25%, 2d only to that of the Dead Sea; it covers more than 1,500 sq. mi.; it is crossed by a 13-mi., rock-fill railroad causeway. Lake Powell, created by construction of the Glen Canyon Dam on the Colorado River just over the border in Arizona, is 186 mi. long, most of it in Utah. Highest point in Utah is Kings Peak in the NE, 13,528 ft.

Manufacturing has become the state's major industry, well ahead of mining, agriculture and tourism. Value added by manufacture in 1972 was over $864,200,000. Transportation equipment was the most important line, followed by food products, machinery, metal products, printing-publishing and electrical equipment. Per capita income was $4,005 in 1973.

Utah is an important center for research on and production of intercontinental missiles, rocket engines, solid fuel propellants, supersonic engines, aircraft navigational systems and military computer components. Many of the nation's largest aerospace firms have plants and divisions in Utah.

The state is a leading warehousing area and distribution center for much of the western U.S.

Utah is a rich storehouse of a wide variety of minerals. Among the states, it is a leading producer of copper, gold, silver, ashphalt, molybdenum, lead, vanadium and potassium salts.

Copper has by far the greatest value among Utah's mineral products. In 1973, copper production was valued at $312 million, 2d only to Arizona's, and total mineral production value was $644 million.

The nation's largest open-pit copper mine at Bingham Canyon, normally employs about 7,000 persons and produces about 20% of the newly-mined copper in the U.S. There are large smelters and refineries.

Petroleum has also been a large product; 1973 production was valued at $101 million. With Colorado and Wyoming, Utah shares what have been called the world's richest oil shale deposits. Studies of economical ways to recover this oil were under way.

Utah ranked 8th among the states in number of sheep in 1973 with nearly 800,000. It also raises large flocks of turkeys. It is a leader in apricots and cherries. Other crops include barley, sugar beets, alfalfa, winter wheat, potatoes. Farm receipts for 1973 included $260 million from livestock, $69 million from crops.

There are 13 institutions of higher education.

Over 66% of the land is owned by the Federal government.

Tourists annually spend about $190 million in the state.

Utah is a great recreational area, with 11,000 mi. of fishing streams and 147,000 acres of lakes and reservoirs, numerous winter sports areas and camp grounds. Natural wonders may be seen at Zion, Canyonlands and Bryce Canyon National Parks, and Arches, Capitol Reef, Dinosaur, Rainbow Bridge and Natural Bridges National Monuments. The Lake Powell Recreation Area and Flaming Gorge Dam are other attractions.

Works by Utah artists and archeological, botanical, mineral and fossil collections may be seen at the Brigham Young University Collections in Provo.

The Latter-day Saints number about 72% of the state population. The Mormons reached Utah July 24, 1847.

Utah was organized as a Territory Sept. 9, 1850; admitted to the Union Jan. 4, 1896.

(See also Index for Salt Lake City.)

Vermont
Green Mountain State

CAPITAL: Montpelier. AREA: 9,609 sq. mi., rank, 43d. POPULATION: 464,000 (est. 1973). MOTTO: Freedom and Unity. FLOWER: Red clover. TREE: Sugar maple. BIRD: Hermit thrush. SONG: Hail, Vermont. ADMISSION: 14th.

Vermont, first state to join the Union after the original 13, was the home of the Green Mountain Boys who played heroic roles in several victories of the American Revolution. They took their name from the Green Mountains which form the N-S backbone of the state. There are rich marble quarries in the western part of the state and large granite beds in the E. The Connecticut River runs along the E boundary, Lake Champlain forms much of the W line; among the many lakes is Memphremagog which lies partly in Canada to the N. Seven peaks rise over 4,000 ft. with Mt. Mansfield, 4,393 ft., the highest.

Vermont has long been known for its stoneworking, forest and dairy industries. Manufacturing employs the most persons. Tourism is the 2d industry, attracting 6.3 million annually. Per capita income was $4,011 in 1973.

Principal manufactured goods are machine tools, computer components, stone and clay products, lumber, furniture and paper. Value added by manufacture is over $562 million a year.

Tourism is important; the accent is on recreation, which produces more than $250 million a year. Skiing has accounted for a tremendous growth, with spending by skiers multiplying many times in recent years. There are more than 95 miles of ski lifts in the state and many ski areas, including Stowe, Killington, Mt. Snow, Stratton, Bromley, Jay Peak and Sugarbush.

Vermont has 72 state parks and forests covering over 130,000 acres. The Long Trail is popular for hiking and camping. There is fishing for trout, salmon, bass, muskellunge, and hunting for deer and game birds.

Vermont and New York are the largest producers of maple syrup. Large milk and butter production accounts for most of the total value of farm receipts which was $197 million for 1973. For its small size, Vermont has a large number of milk cows.

The state ranks high in output of marble, granite and limestone; it is also a leader in production of asbestos and talc.

The Shelburne Museum, 7 mi. S of Burlington, preserves 35 early American buildings, including furnished homes, doctor's and dentist's offices, stagecoach inn; covered bridge, side-wheeler, old trains, folk art, etc.; Webb gallery of paintings by Rembrandt, Goya, Corot, Manet, Cassatt.

The Bennington Museum displays early American glass, furniture, pottery and what is said to be the oldest Stars and Stripes flag in existence.

The Vermont area was visited by Samuel de Champlain, 1609, and had its first permanent settlement at Fort Dummer near Brattleboro, 1724.

Jurisdiction over the area was disputed by New Hampshire and New York. During the Revolution, the Green Mountain Boys under Ethan Allen took Fort Ticonderoga and under Seth Warner captured Crown Point; later they helped defeat the British in the Battle of Bennington and at Saratoga.

In 1777 the colonists declared their independence, adopted a constitution, the first giving universal manhood suffrage without property qualifications, and elected a governor. Vermont ratified the U.S. Constitution Jan. 1791, entered the Union Mar. 4, 1791. Vermonters were intense anti-slavery men and supported Lincoln over their native son Stephen Douglas.

Vermont has 20 institutions of higher learning.

Virginia
Old Dominion

CAPITAL: Richmond. AREA: 40,817 sq. mi., rank, 36th. POPULATION: 4,811,000 (est. 1973). MOTTO: Sic Semper Tyrannis. Thus always to Tyrants. FLOWER: American dogwood. BIRD: Cardinal. TREE: American dogwood. SONG: Carry Me Back to Old Virginia. Tenth of the original 13 states to ratify Constitution.

The Commonwealth of Virginia is famed for its colonial heritage, for the statesmen it produced, its historic homes and estates, and great battlefields on which the fate of the nation was decided in both the 18th and 19th Centuries.

It was first settled, 1607, at Jamestown by English colonists and named for Elizabeth I, called the Virgin Queen. It had the New World's first representative legislature, the House of Burgesses, 1619; this assembly was elected by male suffrage. Virginia was active in resistance to the British Stamp Act and it provided much of the leadership that led to American independence and the writing of the Constitution.

Virginia's coastal plain, the Tidewater, consists mostly of 4 peninsulas formed by Chesapeake Bay and the Potomac, Rappahannock, York and James Rivers. The central Piedmont plateau rises, toward the W, to the Blue Ridge Mtns. Beyond the Blue Ridge and between it and the Alleghenies on the W border lies the Shenandoah Valley, a rich farming region. Highest point is Mt. Rogers in the SW, 5,729 ft.

Virginia's manufacturing industries have grown steadily and are diversified. They provide jobs for 380,000, over 5 times the number employed in agriculture. Total value added by manufacture is more than $6 billion, with payrolls totaling $2.8 billion; value of shipments was estimated at $12.5 billion.

Largest lines were chemicals, textiles, food products and clothing. Other important lines were lumber, furniture, paper, electrical machinery, transportation equipment, cigarettes, metal products, stone-clay-glass products.

Largest lines were chemicals, testiles, food products and clothing. Other important lines were lumber, furniture, paper, electrical machinery, transportation equipment, cigarettes, metal products, stone-clay-glass products.

The federal government is a major employer with military installations at Hampton Roads and U.S. agencies near Washinton, D.C.

Per captita income was $4,715 in 1973.

Hampton Roads is the major port, a leader in bulk export tonnage.

Agriculture remains a vital factor in the economy. Virginia ranks among the leaders in the U.S. in its crops of tobacco, peanuts, apples and sweet potatoes. Other important crops are corn, vegetables, barley, peaches. It has large numbers of turkeys; its Smithfield hams are famous. Farm receipts for 1973 totaled $878 million, more than half from livestock, the rest from crops.

Coal is Virginia's leading mineral commodity, in terms of both tonnage and value, and usually accounts for about 70% of the value of total mineral production. Also important are lime, zinc, stone, cement. Total mineral production for 1973 was valued at $544 million.

The commercial fishing catch was worth $39 million in 1973.

With its wealth of historical attractions and recreational facilities such as Shenandoah National Park in the Blue Ridge Mts. and Virginia Beach, the state drew 25 million out-of-state travelers who spent about $662 million in 1973. Tourism is 2d to manufacturing and ahead of agriculture as a source of income.

Virginia was the birthplace of 8 presidents: Washington, Jefferson, Monroe, Madison, Tyler, William H. Harrison, Taylor and Wilson—the last 3 elected from other states. It has many historic shrines, including Washington's birthplace, Wakefield; his home and grave at Mount Vernon; Jefferson's Monticello, near Charlottesville and the Univ. of Virginia he designed; Robert E. Lee's birthplace, Stratford Hall, and grave at Lexington.

Colonial Williamsburg is a restoration of the 18th Century buildings and living conditions in what was the capital of Virginia when Washington, Jefferson, Patrick Henry and George Mason were young men. There are more than 800 buildings, many of them the originals.

At Jamestown, first permanent English settlement, are foundations and ruins of early buildings, relics, statues and monuments and a nearby exhibit of glassblowing.

At Yorktown, where the surrender of British Gen. Cornwallis to American and French forces, Oct. 19, 1781, virtually ended the American Revolution, may be seen colonial buildings, the restored house in which terms of surrender were drawn up, earthworks and Revolutionary cannons.

In Fredericksburg, the James Monroe Law Office and Museum is the original building in which President Monroe practiced law in the 1780s; among other possessions is the desk at which he signed the Monroe Doctrine.

Appomattox Court House National Monument includes the rebuilt Wilmer McLean house in which Gen. Lee surrendered the Confederate Army of Northern Virginia to Lt. Gen.Ulysses S. Grant, Apr. 9, 1865.

Fort Monroe Casement Museum has relics of the imprisonment in the fort of Jefferson Davis and Chief Black Hawk and of the battle between the Monitor and Merrimac. The Quartermaster Museum, Fort Lee, exhibits clothing, saddles, etc., of American soldiers from the Revolution on. The War Memorial Museum of Virginia, in Newport News, displays World War I and II weapons and equipment of many nations.

In Lexington are Washington and Lee University and Virginia Military Institute, both closely linked with leaders and action in the Civil War. Also in Lexington is the George C. Marshall Research Library and Museum with displays of the life of the famed World War II general and statesman.

At Staunton is the Woodrow Wilson birthplace, with memorabilia of his family. The Gen. Douglas MacArthur Memorial in Norfolk contains the general's sarcophagus, flags of 30 units he commanded, documents and murals of important events in his life.

Virginia seceded from the Union Apr. 17, 1861, and Richmond became the capital of the Confederate States. Virginia was readmitted Jan. 26, 1870.

There are 70 institutions of higher education.

(See also Index for Norfolk, Richmond, Roanoke.)

Washington
Evergreen State

CAPITAL: Olympia. AREA: 68,192 sq. mi., rank 20th. POPULATION: 3,429,000 (est. 1973). MOTTO: Al-Ki, By and By. FLOWER: Coast rhododendron. TREE: Western hemlock. BIRD: Willow goldfinch. SONG: Washington, My Home. ADMISSION: 42d.

The state of Washington in the Pacific Northwest is a leader in many ways — in lumber, in fruit and other crops, and in aircraft production; its ports on Puget Sound are gateways to Alaska and the Far East; the great dams on the Columbia River provide power for production of aluminum and irrigation for the rich Columbia Basin.

The lofty Cascade Range splits the state, running N-S. To the W, the Puget Sound lowlands support dairy, poultry and truck-farming; in the extreme W the Olympic Peninsula is studded with the peaks of the Olympic Mtns. and the Coast Ranges. On the E slopes of the Cascades are great fruit orchards; further E, plateau country provides sheep and cattle lands and a rich wheat belt. Highest peak is Mt. Rainier in the Cascades, 14,410 ft.

The Columbia River cuts a zig-zag course across Washington from the NE, then flows W along the Oregon border to the Pacific.

Puget Sound has many deep harbors beside which Seattle, Tacoma, Everett and other great cities have grown. Foreign trade, mainly with Japan and Canada, has increased greatly.

Manufacturing industries employ 223,200 workers with payrolls of $2.3 billion and value added by manufacture over $4.5 billion a year. Transportation equipment, mostly aircraft but including ships and trucks, accounts for $1.12 billion.

Other important manufacturing lines are lumber, food processing, pulp and paper, metals and metal products, chemicals and machinery. The Atomic Energy Commission plant at Hanford produces nuclear fuels and electricity. Per capita income was $4,989 in 1973.

Washington's large production of fruits, berries and other crops places it first among the states in apples, blueberries, hops and red raspberries; it is among the top producers of potatoes, winter wheat, pears, grapes, apricots, filberts, cranberries, cherries, asparagus, strawberries. Farm receipts for 1973 totaled $1.4 billion, over half from crops, rest from livestock products.

The commercial fishing catch is valued at over '$47 million a year. Salmon accounts for half the total, followed by halibut and bottomfish.

Mineral production in 1973 was valued at an est. $117 million. Sand and gravel, silver, cement, zinc and lead were the most important products.

Large aluminum reduction plants, using refined ore from out-of-state and hydro-electric power, have expanded. Aluminum output is 25% of U.S. total.

A series of great dams on the Columbia, including the massive Grand Coulee in the NE and Bonneville on the Oregon border, provide power and irrigation.

More than half the state is in forests; one-sixth of the nation's standing sawtimber is in Washington. Towering Douglas firs and Ponderosa pines, western hemlocks and red cedars are among commercially important trees. Wood products are worth $1.2 billion a year.

There are 43 institutions of higher education.

First visited by explorers in the late 18th Century, Washington was organized as a territory Mar. 2, 1853; admitted to the Union Nov. 11, 1889.

The state has 3 national parks, Mt. Rainier, North Cascades and Olympic National Park. Its state parks and national forests of nearly 10 million acres have large hunting, fishing and recreation areas.

The Washington State Historical Society, Tacoma, has exhibits of the fur trade, Indian and Eskimo arts, and pioneer cabins, schoolhouse and covered wagon.

Tourists it has been estimated, spend about $640 million annually in the state.

(See also Index for Seattle.)

West Virginia
Mountain State

CAPITAL: Charleston, AREA: 24,181 sq. mi., rank, 41st. POPULATION: 1,794,000 (est. 1973). MOTTO: Montani Semper Liberi, Mountaineers Always Free. FLOWER: Rhododendron maximum. BIRD: Cardinal. TREE: Sugar maple. SONGS: The West Virginia Hills, This Is My West Virginia, and West Virginia, My Home, Sweet Home. ADMISSION: 35th.

West Virginia's fortunes have long been based on those of the bituminous coal industry; the state usually is first in coal production with about 20% of the U.S. total. Increased output of coal and natural gas, plus growth in the chemical, steel, glass and tourist industries, have aided the economy.

The terrain is mountainous with the Alleghenies running NE-SW in the eastern half of the state; the western half is a plateau sloping down to the Ohio River which forms most of the boundary on the W. Highest point is Spruce Knob in the NE, 4,863 ft.

West Virginia was part of Virginia until that state seceded in 1861; delegates of 40 western counties adopted a state government at Wheeling, Nov. 27, 1861; West Virginia was admitted to the Union June 20, 1863.

Coal accounts for more than 88% of the total value of mineral production. In 1973 the total mineral production was valued at an est. $1.49 billion. Kentucky had a slight lead in tonnage but West Virginia led in its value.

West Virginia produces and markets more natural gas than any other state east of the Mississippi. Also important are petroleum, salt, stone, cement, lime and clays.

Production of a wide variety of chemicals, based in the state's resources of salt brine, gas, oil and coal, and including synthetic fibers and plastics, dominates the manufacturing field, accounting for about 35% of the $2.38 billion in valued added annually by manufacture. Large plants are in the Ohio and Kanawha valleys, where electric power is abundant. The state is also a major producer of steel and iron, glass and pottery.

Farm receipts totaled $149 million for 1973; the hilly terrain is not conducive to large-scale agriculture. Poultry, dairy products, cattle and sheep accounted for most of the receipts. Apples and peaches are profitable crops. About 79% of the state is in forests.

Per capita income was $3,828 in 1973; the national average was $4,918.

Tourism is being promoted and visitors spend over $700 million annually. More than a million acres have been set aside for recreation in 34 state parks, 9 state forests; Monongahela, George Washington and part of Jefferson National Forests and large reservoir recreation areas.

Attractions include Harpers Ferry National Historical Park, mineral water resorts at White Sulphur and Berkeley Springs, trout fishing, turkey, deer and bear hunting.

Part of the town of Harpers Ferry has been restored to its condition in 1859, when John Brown seized the U.S. Armory. Still standing is the fire-engine house in which Brown and a score of followers were besieged and captured by a force of U.S. Marines under Robert E. Lee, then a U.S. colonel.

The State Museum in Charleston displays local relics and artifacts from prehistoric cultures (as early as 8,000 B.C.), Indians, pioneers, and more recent eras.

The Huntington Galleries, Huntington, has collections of 19th and 20th Century European and American paintings, furniture and decorative arts.

The Oglebay Mansion-Museum displays colonial furniture and 19th Century glassware.

There are 25 institutions of higher education.

(See also Index for Charleston, Huntington.)

Wisconsin
Badger State

CAPITAL: Madison. AREA: 56,154 sq. mi., rank 26th. POPULATION: 4,569,000 (est. 1973). MOTTO: Forward. FLOWER: Butterfly violet. BIRD: Robin. TREE: Sugar maple. ANIMAL: Badger. FISH: Muskellunge. SONG: On, Wisconsin! ADMISSION: 30th.

Known as America's Dairyland. Wisconsin produces more milk and cheese than any other state and agriculture is a vital part of the state's economy. However, manufacturing, including processing of foods, has become the state's largest employer and biggest income producer.

Mining has declined with the near-cessation in 1965 of iron mining, but output of several other minerals has increased. Reforestation has kept the paper and wood product industries important. There are 14 ports on Lakes Michigan and Superior. Per capita income was $4,634 in 1973.

The state has an abundance of recreation resources; water and winter sports, hunting and fishing are among its attractions. Vacationers, it is estimated, spend over $1 billion a year.

Highest point is Timms Hill in the N, 1,952 ft.

Wisconsin's rolling pasturelands and large crops support the nation's largest herd of milk cows, about 1.8 million; 80% of its farms are dairy farms.

The state produces the most milk, cheese, hay and alfalfa in the U.S. It is also a leading producer of butter, oats, corn, cranberries and maple syrup. In addition to cattle, it also has large numbers of hogs and turkeys.

Farm receipts for 1973 totaled $2.26 billion, 11th highest among the states, most of it from livestock products.

About 40% of income produced in Wisconsin comes from manufacturing and, with over 500,000 factory employees, the state ranks among the top 12. Value added by manufacturing is over $10 billion a year.

Most important products, in terms of value added, are: machinery, especially engines, turbines, industrial and construction; food products, including dairy, meat and beer; transportation equipment, especially motor vehicle parts and equipment and mobile homes; iron and steel, metal products, paper and lumber.

Mineral production for 1973 was valued at $97 million. Zinc, lime, cement and stone are important. Iron mining was resumed with production of pelletized low-grade taconite ore late in 1969.

Most of Wisconsin's timber production goes into pulp and paper, but the state is also a leading producer of hardwood plywood and veneer.

Wisconsin has over 8,500 lakes, of which Winnebago is the largest, and fronts on both Lakes Michigan and Superior. Water sports, ice-boating, and fishing for trout, bass and muskellunge are popular as are skiing and hunting for deer, bear and wildfowl. Public parks and forests take up one-seventh of the land area; there are 49 state parks, 9 state forests, 2 national forests.

Other attractions include small towns which preserve Swiss, Scandinavian, German and other European cultures, visits to breweries and cheese factories, Indian festivals and the Dells (scenic gorges) of the Wisconsin River.

The Circus World Museum in Baraboo has over 100 circus wagons and other displays, and presents circus shows daily, early May-early Sept.

There are 59 institutions of higher learning.

The first European to visit the Wisconsin area was Jean Nicolet in 1634; he was followed by French explorers and missionaries and the land became part of

New France. The French surrendered it to the British in 1763; the British ceded it to the U.S. in 1783, but were not completely dislodged until 1815. Wisconsin became a state May 29, 1848.
(See also Index for Madison, Milwaukee.)

Wyoming
Equality State

CAPITAL: Cheyenne. AREA: 97,914 sq. mi., rank, 9th. POPULATION: 353,000 (est. 1973). MOTTO: Equal Rights. FLOWER: Indian paintbrush. BIRD: Western meadowlark. TREE: Plains cottonwood (balsam poplar). SONG: Wyoming State Song. ADMISSION: 44th.

Wyoming's towering mountains and rolling plains provide spectacular scenery, grazing ranges for sheep and cattle, and a wealth of mineral resources.

Ranges of the Rockies cover the western two-thirds of the state; the eastern third is Great Plains country. Highest point is Gannett Peak in the W, 13,804 ft. The spectacular Teton Mtns. lie S of Yellowstone National Park, which is mostly carved out of Wyoming's NW corner.

The most important industry is mining, particularly of oil and natural gas. Agriculture, especially livestock, runs 2d. Of growing importance are both tourism and manufacturing. Per capita income was $4,813 in 1973.

Wyoming has large reserves of coal, oil, gas, oil shale, iron ore and gypsum.

Production of petroleum in 1973 was valued at $474 million; total mineral production value for the year was est. at $842 million. The state ranked first in the U.S. in sodium carbonate production, 2d in uranium. Also important are coal, natural gas, clays and iron ore.

Wyoming is 2d among the states in wool production and in 1974 its sheep numbered 1.5 million, exceeded only by Texas; it also had 1.6 million cattle. Principal crops include wheat, oats, sugar beets, corn, potatoes, barley and alfalfa. Livestock receipts for 1973 totaled $352 million; receipts for crops were $63 million.

Much of Wyoming's manufacturing is based on its mining and agricultural products. Leading lines include petroleum and coal products, processed foods, timber and wood, construction materials, iron and steel, electronic components, equipment for farms and for food preparation. Value added by manufacture is about $119 million annually.

Wyoming is a main source for 3 important river systems, the Missouri, Colorado and Columbia, Both power and irrigation are provided by a growing number of dams and reservoirs. Tourism produces an est. annual $175 million.

Wyoming was organized as a Territory July 25, 1868; admitted to the Union July 10, 1890. Women were given the right to vote, for the first time in the U.S., by the Territorial Legislature in 1869.

Grand Teton National Park, with mountains 13,000 ft. high, comprises 299,326 acres; the National Elk Refuge covers 25,000 acres. Devils Tower, a cluster of rock columns 865 ft. high, became the first National Monument in the U.S. in 1906. Fort Laramie, partly preserved, partly restored, is a National Historic Site. The annual Cheyenne Frontier Days Celebration, last full week in July, is the state's largest rodeo. Hunting, fishing and skiing are other attractions.

The Buffalo Bill Historical Center in Cody has a museum with personal effects of William F. Cody (Buffalo Bill) and the Whitney Gallery of Modern Art with Indian art and paintings by Frederic Remington, Charles M. Russell, George Catlin, etc.

The Bradford Brinton Memorial Ranch, near Big Horn, has collections of western painting and sculpture, antiques, Indian arts, hunting trophies and firearms; open May 15-Sept. 15.

There are 8 institutions of higher education.
(See Index for Yellowstone National Park).

District of Columbia

AREA: 67 sq. mi. POPULATION: 746,000 (est. 1973). MOTTO: Justitia Omnibus, Justice for All. FLOWER: American beauty rose. TREE: Scarlet oak. BIRD: Wood thrush. The city of Washington is coextensive with the District of Columbia.

The District of Columbia is the seat of the federal government of the United States. It lies on the west central edge of Maryland on the Potomac River, opposite Virginia. Its area was originally 100 sq. mi. taken from the sovereignty of Maryland and Virginia. Virginia's portion south of the Potomac was given back to that state in 1846.

The 23d Amendment, ratified in 1961, granted residents of the District the right to vote for president and vice president for the first time and gave it 3 members in the Electoral College. Residents cast the first such votes in Nov. 1964.

Congress governed the District 1878-1967 through 3 commissioners appointed by the president. The Reorganization Plan of 1967 substituted a single commissioner (also called mayor) and assistant and a 9-member City Council, all likewise appointed by the president; budgetary funds were still appropriated by Congress; residents had no vote in local government (except for recently granted right to elect school board members).

In Sept. 1970, Congress approved legislation giving the District one delegate to the House of Representatives. The delegate may vote in committee but not on the House floor. The first delegate was elected Mar. 23, 1971.

In May 1974 voters approved a charter giving them the right to elect their own mayor and a 13-member city council in Nov. 1974, to take office Jan. 1, 1975. The district won the right to levy its own taxes but Congress retained power to rescind any council action.

Proposals for a "federal town" for the deliberations of the Continental Congress were made in 1783, four years before the adoption of the Constitution that gave the Confederation a national government. Rivalry between northern and southern delegates over the site appeared in the First Congress, meeting in New York in 1789. John Adams, presiding officer of the Senate, cast the deciding vote of that body for Germantown, Pa. In 1790 Congress compromised by making Philadelphia the temporary capital for 10 years. The Virginia members of the House wanted a capital on the eastern bank of the Potomac; they were defeated by the Northerners, while the Southerners defeated the Northern attempt to have the nation assume the war debts of the 13 original states, the Assumption Bill fathered by Alexander Hamilton. Hamilton and Jefferson arranged a compromise: the Virginia men voted for the Assumption Bill, and the Northerners conceded the capital to the Potomac. President Washinton chose the site in October 1790 and persuaded landowners to sell their holdings to the government at £25, then about $66, an acre. The capital was named Washington.

Washington appointed Pierre Charles L'Enfant, a French engineer who had come over with Lafayette, to plan the capital on an area not over 10 miles square. The L'Enfant plan was considered grandiose, for streets 100 to 110 feet wide and one avenue 400 feet wide and a mile long on the Potomac pastures seemed foolhardy. But Washington endorsed his plans. When L'Enfant ordered a wealthy landowner to remove his new manor house because it obstructed a vista, and demolished it when the owner refused, Washington had to step in and dismiss L'Enfant. The official map was completed by Andrew Ellicott, surveyor, and Benjamin Banneker, black mathematician.

On Sept. 18, 1793, the cornerstone of the north wing of the Capitol was laid by President Washington. The occasion was expected to drum up sales of city lots, but there were few purchasers. Washington bought several lots. In the next few years Robert Morris and others invested. By 1799 the Senate wing of the Capitol had been roofed, the walls of the Presi-

dent's house were up and the Treasury building was ordered. On June 3, 1800, President John Adams moved to Washington and on June 10, Philadelphia ceased to be the temporary capital. The City of Washington was incorporated in 1802; the District of Columbia was created as a municipal corporation in 1871, embracing Washington, Georgetown and Washington County.

(See also Index for Washington, D. C.)

Outlying U S. Areas

Commonwealth of Puerto Rico

Estado Libre Asociado de Puerto Rico

CAPITAL: San Juan. AREA: 3,435 sq. mi. POPULATION: (est. 1972) 2,794,000. FLAG: Three red, two white horizontal stripes; white star in blue triangle at staff. SONG: La Borinquena.

Puerto Rico is a hilly, tropical island lying between the Atlantic to the N and the Caribbean to the S; it is the easternmost of the West Indies group called the Greater Antilles, of which Cuba, Hispaniola and Jamaica are the larger units. It lies about 1,600 mi. SE of New York, 500 mi. N of Venezuela. It is roughly rectangular, 105 mi. long by 35 wide. Numerous small islands include Vieques, Culebra and Mona.

The soil of the coast plain is fertile and there are many lush valleys, but there are dry areas in the S which need irrigation and an extensive system has been constructed by the government. The climate is mild, with a mean temperature of 76°; the mean maximum is 82° and the mean minimum 73°. Highest point is Cerro de Punta, 4,389 ft., near the island's center.

President Truman, on Aug. 5, 1947, signed an act giving Puerto Rico the right to choose its chief executive by popular vote. An act of 1950, affirmed by special election, June 4, 1951, permitted Puerto Rico to draft its own constitution. One similar to that of the United States was approved in a convention Feb. 4, 1952, and ratified by a popular vote March 3, 1952. President Truman signed, July 3, 1952, a Congressional resolution approving the new constitution, elevating Puerto Rico to the status of a free commonwealth associated with the United States, effective July 25, 1952.

In a July 23, 1967, referendum, Puerto Ricans strongly favored continuation of commonwealth status. The vote was: commonwealth, 425,081; statehood, 273,315; independence, 4,205.

The Legislative Assembly consists of a Senate and House of Representatives, elected by direct vote every 4 years. Eight senatorial districts elect 2 senators each; 40 representative districts one member each; also 11 senators and 11 representatives at large. Its directly elected resident commissioner in the U.S. Congress has only committee voting privileges. Puerto Ricans were granted American citizenship under the Organic Act of 1917. They do not vote for president unless they move to the U.S., where they come under local laws.

Executive power is vested in a governor elected by direct vote. There are 12 executive departments each headed by a secretary: State, Justice, Education, Health, Treasury, Labor, Agriculture, Commerce, Social Services, Housing, Natural Resources and Transportation-Public Works. The judiciary is vested in a Supreme Court and lower courts.

The Commonwealth's "Operation Bootstrap" program for economic development has radically raised the standard of living; per capita income for 1973 was $1,836, up $1,008 from 1964.

Puerto Rico derives its largest income from manufacturing, $1.29 billion in 1973, up $160 million from 1972. Products include textiles and apparel, electrical and electronic equipment, plastics, chemicals,

petrochemicals, petroleum products, processed foods, metal, leather, professional instruments.

Gross capital investment in 1973 reached $1.78 billion; gross product was $6.43 billion.

Mineral production is mainly of construction materials, with cement accounting for a large part of the value; total value for 1973 was $97.6 million.

Agriculture, a large source of income, rose by 5.7% in 1973 to $223 million. Income from dairy and livestock products has surpassed that from sugar. Also important are tobacco, coffee, pineapples, coconuts, fruits, garden truck, rum, molasses.

Off-island trade is chiefly with the United States.

	Imports	Exports
1972	$3,108,000,000	$1,974,000,000
1973	$3,496,000,000	$2,465,000,000

The flow of migrants to mainland U.S. after 1945 was reversed in 1963, reversed again in 1970, and in 1973 there was an excess of 31,001 arrivals over departures. These changes are caused mainly by employment conditions, mainland and Puerto Rican. Unemployment on the island is usually over 11%.

San Juan, with its international airport and resort hotels, is the center of the tourism industry. Visitors totaled 1,322,258 in 1973, up from 1,172,885 in 1972, and their spending rose to $317.3 million, up from $258.9 million.

Spanish is the official language but most persons also speak English. Public school education is free and compulsory at the elementary school level; English is taught as a language and is compulsory in all 8 grades. Chief religion is Roman Catholicism.

Puerto Rico (or Borinquen, after the original Indian name Boriquen) was discovered by Columbus, Nov. 19, 1493. Ponce de Leon conquered it for Spain, 1509, and established the first settlement at Caparra, across the bay from San Juan. Ruled by Spain until 1898, it was occupied by Maj. Gen. Nelson A. Miles in the Spanish-American war and ceded to the U. S. by the Treaty of Paris, Dec. 10, 1898.

(See also Index for San Juan.)

Canal Zone and Panama Canal

For Panama Canal cargo traffic see Index.

The Canal Zone has been, in effect, a U. S. Government reservation. It is a strip of land extending 5 mi. on each side of the axis of the Panama Canal, under jurisdiction of the U.S. by treaty with the Rep. of Panama.

Efforts to change the Zone's status have been made by both nations for several years.

The canal connects the Caribbean with the Bay of Panama on the Pacific. Because of the geographic loop made by the Isthmus of Panama, the Caribbean end of the canal, which could be called the eastern end, is actually further west than the Pacific end.

The Zone has an area of 553 sq. mi. of which 371 are land. Population (1971 est.) was 45,000. About 11,000 U.S. army, air force and navy personnel are normally stationed in the zone.

The Canal Zone government and the Pamana Canal Co. are the two operating agencies, both headed by an individual who acts as governor of the Canal Zone.

and president of the company. The governor is appointed by the president of the U.S. As governor he reports directly to the secretary of the army. As president of the company he reports to its board of directors, appointed by the secretary of the army. The Canal Zone government maintains civil government. The company operates the canal, the Panama Railroad and a ship between New Orleans and the Canal Zone.

A French syndicate under Ferdinand de Lesseps failed to complete a canal, 1880-89, and a second French company failed in 1899. The U. S. bought their rights and offered Colombia compensation for a canal zone, but Colombia failed to ratify the treaty, Oct. 1903. Panama declared itself independent of Colombia Nov. 3, 1903, and was recognized by President Theodore Roosevelt Nov. 6. American naval forces discouraged action by Colombia. On Nov. 18 Panama granted the canal strip to the U.S. by treaty, ratified Feb. 26, 1904, compensation $10 million, with annual payments of $250,000 after 9 years, and a guarantee of Panama independence.

Under terms of the 1903 treaty, Panama granted the U.S. perpetual sovereignty over the Canal Zone "to the entire exclusion of the exercise by the Republic of Panama of any such sovereign rights, power or authority."

The canal was opened to traffic Aug. 15, 1914. In 1922, Colombia accepted $25 million from the U. S. plus special land transportation privileges, and agreed to recognize Panama. The U. S. increased its annual payment to Panama to $430,000 and withdrew its guarantee of independence.

A further treaty regulating relations between the U. S. and Panama was signed Jan. 25, 1955, increasing the annuity paid Panama to $1,930,000. In addition, the U. S. gave Panama $28 million worth of real estate and buildings no longer needed by the Canal Zone administration. U. S. citizen and non-citizen employees were guaranteed equality of pay and opportunity. In addition, the U. S. agreed to build the high level bridge over the Pacific entrance to the canal, opened Oct. 12, 1962, as a link in the Inter-American Highway.

Negotiations for a new treaty began after Panamanian riots protesting the 1903 and 1955 treaties caused the death of 21 Panamanians and 3 U. S. soldiers, Jan. 9, 1964. Preliminary agreement was reached in 1967, but in 1970, after a change of government, Panama declared the proposed new treaty was unacceptable.

In Mar. 1973, the U. S. vetoed a Panama-backed resolution in the UN Security Council which called on the U. S. and Panama to negotiate a new treaty to "guarantee full respect for Panama's effective sovereignty over all its territory." The U. S. said it wished to negotiate with Panama "without outside pressure."

In Feb. 1974, U. S. and Panama representatives agreed on principles for negotiating a new treaty which would set a date for giving Panama jurisdiction over the canal area but give the U. S. the right to operate and protect the canal for a certain period, with Panama sharing in the revenues, until a date set for final transfer to Panama.

Virgin Islands

CAPITAL: Charlotte Amalie, on St. Thomas Is. AREA: 133 sq. mi. POPULATION: (1971 est. 65,000. FLOWER: Yellow cedar.

The Virgin Islands of the United States, an unincorporated territory administered by the Interior Dept., lie to the E of Puerto Rico at the western end of the Lesser Antilles, 1,629 mi. SE of New York. There are about 100 islands in the Virgins, of which more than 50 islands and islets in the western area belong to the U.S.; the remainder are the British Virgin Islands.

The 3 largest and most populous of the U.S. islands are St. Croix, St. Thomas and St. John. Formerly the Danish West Indies, the islands were purchased by the U. S. from Denmark for $25 million (effective Mar. 31, 1917) for defense purposes. The islands were discovered by Columbus in 1493. About 80% of the population is of Negro descent.

Mean winter temperature is 78°; summer, 82°. Virgin Islands National Park occupies about three-fourths of St. John, smallest of the 3 principal islands.

The inhabitants have been citizens of the U.S. since 1927. Legislation originates in a unicameral house of 15 senators, elected for 2 years.

The governor, formerly appointed by the president of the U. S., was elected for a 4-year term in Nov. 1970 and took office Jan. 4, 1971. In 1972 a U. S. law gave the Virgin Islands one delegate to the U. S. House of Representatives; the delegate may vote in committee but not on the House floor.

Tourism is the largest industry, but it was hurt by a series of murders in 1973 and early 1974. Principal exports are watch movements, jewelry, rum, wool textile products, thermometers, bay rum.

Minor Caribbean Islands

Quita Sueno Bank, Roncador Cay, Serrana Bank and Seranilla Bank lie in the Caribbean between Nicaragua and Jamaica. They are uninhabited. They were to be turned over to Colombia under a 1972 agreement, but this still awaited U. S. Senate ratification in mid-1974.

Navassa lies between Jamaica and Haiti, covers about 2 sq. mi., is reserved by the U. S. for a lighthouse and is uninhabited.

American Samoa

CAPITAL: Pago Pago, Island of Tutuila. AREA: 76 sq. mi. POPULATION: (1971 est.) 29,000.

Blessed with spectacular scenery and delightful South Seas climate, American Samoa is the most southerly of all lands under U. S. ownership. It is an unincorporated territory consisting of 6 small islands of the Samoan group: Tutuila (where Pago Pago, the capital, lies by a crescent bay beneath tall mountains), Aunuu, the Manua Islands (Tau, Olosega and Ofu), and Rose. Also administered as part of American Samoa is Swain's Is., 210 mi. to the NW, acquired by the U. S. in 1925. The islands are 2,300 mi. SW of Hawaii.

American Samoa became U. S. territory by a treaty with the United Kingdom and Germany in 1899, confirmed by local chiefs in 1900 and 1904. Pago Pago had been a U. S. navy coaling station under an 1872 commercial treaty.

Western Samoa, comprising the larger islands of the Samoan group, was a New Zealand mandate and UN Trusteeship until it became an independent nation Jan. 1, 1962. (See Index.)

Tutuila has an area of 52 sq. mi. Tau has an area of 17 sq. mi., and the islets of Ofu and Olosega 5 sq. mi., with a population of a few thousand. Swain's Island has nearly 2 sq. mi. and about 100 population. Highest peak is Lata, on Tau Is., 3,056 ft.

About 70% of the land is forest. Chief products and exports are fish products, copra and handicrafts. Taro, bread-fruit, yams, coconuts, pineapples, oranges and bananas are also produced.

Formerly under jurisdiction of the navy, since July 1, 1951, it has been administered by the Interior Dept., which appoints a governor and a lieutenant governor. It has a bicameral legislature.

The American Samoans are of Polynesian origin. They are nationals of the U. S.

Educational television was started in Sept., 1964, and serves an important role in Samoa's public schools.

Wake, Midway, Other Islands

Wake Island, and its sister islands, Wilkes and Peale, lie in the Pacific Ocean on the direct route from Hawaii to Hong Kong, about 2,000 mi. W of Hawaii and 1,290 mi. E of Guam. The group is 4.5 mi. long, 1.5 mi. wide, and totals less than 3 sq. mi. Population (1970 census) was 1,647.

The United States flag was hoisted over Wake Island, July 4, 1898, by Gen. F. V. Greene, commanding 2d Detachment, Philippine Expedition. Formal possession was taken Jan. 17, 1899; Wake has been administered by the U. S. air force since 1972. Wake Island Air Base supports military flights.

The **Midway Islands**, acquired in 1867, are a group of 2, **Sand** and **Eastern**, in the North Pacific 1,150 mi. NW of Hawaii, with area of about 2 sq. mi., administered by the Navy Dept. Population (1970 census) was 2,220.

Johnston Atoll, SW of Hawaii, is under air force control, and **Kingman Reef**, S of Hawaii, is under navy control.

Howland, Jarvis and **Baker Islands** south of the Hawaiian group, uninhabited since World War II, are under the Interior Dept.

Palmyra is an atoll SW of Hawaii, 4 sq. mi. Privately-owned, it has been under the Interior Dept. since 1961.

Guam

The World Almanac is sponsored on Guam by the Pacific Daily News, 90 O'Hara St., Agana, Guam 96910; phone 777-9711; successor in 1970 to Guam Daily News; circulation throughout Micronesia, 20,060; a Gannett newspaper; president and publisher Robert E. Udick, editor Joe Murphy, managing editor George Blake.

CAPITAL: Agana. AREA: 212 sq. mi. POPULATION: (1970 census) 84,996.

Guam, the largest of the Mariana Islands, now an unincorporated territory, was ceded to the U. S. by Spain in the treaty of Paris, Dec. 10, 1898. It is 30 mi. long and 4 to 8½ mi. wide. Distance from Manila, 1,499 mi.; from San Francisco, 5,053 mi. Mean annual temp. is 81°, average annual rainfall, July to September, 70 in. The island is volcanic and mountains rise 700 to 1,329 ft. Highest peak is Mt. Lamlam.

Magellan discovered the group of islands, Mar. 6, 1521, and called them the Ladrones (thieves). They were colonized in 1668 by Spanish missionaries who renamed them the Mariana Islands in honor of Maria Anna, queen of Spain.

When Spain ceded Guam to the U. S., it sold the other Marianas to Germany. Japan obtained a League of Nations mandate over the German islands in 1919; in Dec. 1941 it seized Guam; the island was retaken by the U. S. in July 1944. Guam has navy and air force bases.

Guam is under the jurisdiction of the Dept. of the Interior. It is administered under the Organic Act of 1950, which provides for a governor, a 21-member unicameral legislature, elected biennially by the residents, who are American citizens but do not vote for president.

Beginning in Nov. 1970, Guamanians elected their own governor, previously appointed by the U. S. president. He took office in Jan. 1971. In 1972 a U. S. law gave Guam one delegate to the U. S. House of Representatives; the delegate may vote in committee but not on the House floor.

School attendance is compulsory. The University of Guam provides higher education. English is the official language. Chief religion is Roman Catholicism.

The Guamanians are of primarily Chamorro (Micronesian) stock, with some of mixed Spanish or Filipino descent.

Copra, fish and handicraft products are exported. Tourism has become a major aspect of Guam's economy. Over 125,000 tourists, most from Japan, visit annually.

Islands Under Trusteeship
Carolines, Marianas, Marshalls

The U. S. Trust Territory of the Pacific Islands, also called Micronesia, includes 3 major archipelagoes;

the **Caroline Islands, Marshall Islands,** and **Mariana Islands (except Guam: see above).** There are 2,141 islands, 98 of them inhabited; land area total 717 sq. mi. but the islands are scattered over 3 million sq. mi. of Micronesia in the western Pacific N of the Equator and E of the Philippines. Total pop. (1970 census) was 94,940.

In 1885, many of the islands were claimed by Germany. Others, held by Spain, were sold to Germany at the time of the Spanish-American War, 1898. After the outbreak of World War I, Japan took over the islands and, after the war, League of Nations mandates over them were awarded to Japan.

After World War II, the United Nations assigned them (1947) as a Trust Territory to be administered by the U. S. They were placed under administration of the U. S. Interior Dept. in 1951.

There is a high commissioner, appointed by the U.S. president. Saipan is the headquarters of the administration. The Congress of Micronesia, an elected legislature with limited powers, held it first meeting in 1965. It has a Senate of 12 members and a House of Representatives of 21.

In 1969, a commission of the Congress of Micronesia recommended that Micronesia be given internal self-government in free association with the U. S.

A U. S. offer of commonwealth status, similar to Puerto Rico's, was rejected by Micronesian leaders in 1970.

In 1974 talks, tentative agreement was reached on parts of a U. S. plan for self-government for the Marshalls and Carolines in free association with the U. S. (which would be responsible for foreign affairs and defense). The Marianas were seeking to become a permanent commonwealth of the U. S.

Among the noted islands are: **Saipan** and **Tinian** in the Marianas, scene of bitter fighting when they were taken by the U. S. from Japan in World War II; the former Japanese strongholds of **Palau, Peleliu, Truk** and **Yap** in the Carolines; **Bikini** and **Eniwetok**, where U. S. nuclear tests were staged, and **Kwajalein**, another World War II battle scene, all in the Marshalls.

Many of the islands are volcanic with luxuriant vegetation; others are of coral formation. Only a few are self-sustaining. Principal exports are copra, trochus shells, fish products, handicrafts and vegetables.

Disputed Pacific Islands

In the central Pacific, S and SW of Hawaii, lie 25 islands and atolls claimed by the U. S.; 18 of them are also claimed by the United Kingdom, and 7 by New Zealand. All are S of the Equator except Christmas Island.

Those claimed by the UK are:

The **Line Islands**, S of Hawaii, including Christmas, Flint, Maiden, Starbuck and Vostok Islands and Caroline Atoll; only Christmas is inhabited. All are administered by the UK

Also, the **Phoenix Islands**, SW of Hawaii, including Canton and Enderbury Islands and Birnie, Gardner, Hull, McKean, Sydney and Phoenix Atolls. All are inhabited and administered by the UK except for Canton and Enderbury which are under joint U.S. and UK administration. A U.S. missile tracking station on Canton was discontinued in Dec. 1967.

Also, the **Ellice Islands**, further to the SW, including Funafuti, Nukufetau and Nukulailai Atolls and Nurakita; all inhabited and all administered by the UK.

Those claimed by New Zealand are:

The **Tokelau (Union) Islands**, S of the Phoenix group, including Nukunono, Atafu and Fakaofu Atolls. All are inhabited and administered by New Zealand.

Also, the **Northern Cook Islands**, E of the Tokelaus, including Danger, Manahiki, Rakahanga and Penrhyn (Tongareva) Atolls. All are inhabited and administered by New Zealand.

Confederate States and Secession

The American Civil War, 1861-1865, grew out of sectional disputes over the employment of slavery in the South and the contention of southern legislators that the states retained many sovereign rights, including the right to secede from the Union.

The principal product of the South was cotton, harvested by slave labor. For 50 years Northern leaders had been trying to curtail slavery, but were checkmated in Congress by Southern legislators. Extreme partisans in the North, called Abolitionists, demanded the immediate end of slavery for moral reasons.

The Southern states argued that the U.S. Constitution was a contract between sovereign states, which could withdraw (secede) when state rights were violated. This has led Southern historians to call the Civil War the War Between the States. Actually the war was not fought by state against state but by one federal regime against another, the Confederate government in Richmond assuming control over the economic, political and military life of the South, under protest from Georgia and South Carolina.

Early Slavery Laws

Milestone U.S. laws on the slavery issue included the Missouri Compromise of 1820 which admitted Missouri as a slave state but prohibited slavery in the Louisiana Territory north of Arkansas; the Compromise of 1850, which admitted California as a free state, omitted action on slavery in organizing Utah and New Mexico as territories, ended slave trade in the District of Columbia, amended the Fugitive Slave Act to punish any who aided a fugitive and abolished trial by jury for fugitives; Kansas-Nebraska Act, 1854, which left choice of slavery in Kansas and Nebraska to residents there (squatter sovereignty).

Harriet Beecher Stowe's *Uncle Tom's Cabin*, 1851-52, intensified feeling against slavery.

Tension increased when the Supreme Court ruled Mar. 6, 1857, that Dred Scott, a Negro, did not become free when taken to a free state and did not have rights as a citizen; also that the Missouri Compromise on slavery was unconstitutional.

John Brown's attempt to arm slaves at Harpers Ferry, Oct. 16-18, 1859, inflamed partisans.

Abraham Lincoln's stand for free soil (no slavery) in new states and territories, and his general condemnation of slavery, caused Southern fanatics to threaten secession if he were elected. When Sen. Stephen A. Douglas split the Democratic party by his stand against secession, Lincoln's election was assured. Even before inauguration Lincoln had Sen. William H. Seward (N.Y.) offer a resolution that the Constitution never be altered to interfere with slavery where established, that the Fugitive Slave Law be amended to include trial by jury, that all states repeal laws contrary to the Constitution.

Secession of States

South Carolina voted an ordinance of secession from the Union repealing its 1788 ratification of the U. S. Constitution on Dec. 20, 1860, to take effect Dec. 24. Other states seceded in 1861 and their votes in convention were:

Mississippi, Jan. 9, 1861, by 84 to 15.
Florida, Jan. 10, 1861, by 62 to 7.
Alabama, Jan. 11, 1861, by 61 to 39.

Georgia, Jan. 19, 1861, by 208 to 89.
Louisiana, Jan. 26, 1861, by 113 to 17.
Texas, Feb. 1, 1861, by 166 to 7, ratified by popular vote Feb. 23, 1861 (for 34,794; against 11,325).
Virginia had delayed action, but when President Lincoln called for troops after Fort Sumter fell (Apr. 14, 1861) it voted for secession April 17, 1861, by 88 to 55, ratified by popular vote May 23, 1861 (for secession, 128,884; against, 32,134).
Arkansas, May 6, 1861, by 69 to 1.
North Carolina, May 21, 1861, voted secession but refused by two-thirds vote to submit it to people for ratification.
Tennessee, May 7, 1861, entered a military league with the Confederacy (popular vote, June 8, for secession, 104,019; against 47,238).
Missouri Unionists stopped secession in the convention at Jefferson City Feb. 28 and at the second session in St. Louis Mar. 9. The legislature condemned secession Mar. 7. Under the protection of Confederate troops, secessionist members of the legislature adopted a resolution of secession at Neosho, Oct. 31, 1861. The Confederate Congress seated the secessionists' representatives.

Kentucky did not secede and its government remained Unionist. In a part occupied by Confederate troops Kentuckians approved secession and the Confederate Congress admitted their representatives.

The Maryland legislature voted against secession Apr. 27, 53 to 13. Delaware did not secede. Western Virginia held conventions at Wheeling, named a pro-Union governor June 11, 1861; admitted to Union as West Virginia June 30, 1863; its constitution provided for gradual abolition of slavery.

Confederate Government

Forty-two delegates from South Carolina, Georgia, Alabama, Mississippi, Louisiana and Florida met in convention at Montgomery, Ala., Feb. 4, 1861. The Congress adopted a provisional constitution of the Confederate States of America Feb. 8, 1861, and on the next day elected Jefferson Davis (Miss.), provisional president, and Alexander H. Stephens (Ga.), provisional vice president. Davis was inducted into office at Montgomery, Feb. 18, 1861.

A permanent constitution was adopted Mar. 11, 1861. It provided that the president should be elected for a single term of 6 years; it also abolished the African slave trade. The Congress moved to Richmond, Va., July 20, 1861. Jefferson Davis was elected president, October, 1861; inaugurated Feb. 22, 1862.

Jefferson Davis (1808-1889) was a West Point graduate, 1828; served in Black Hawk and Mexican Wars; senator from Mississippi, 1847-1851; secretary of war, 1853-1857; senator, 1857-1861.

The Congress adopted a flag, consisting of a red field with a white stripe in the middle third, and a blue jack with a circle of white stars, going two-thirds of the way down the flag. This flag was unfurled in Montgomery, Mar. 4, 1861. Later the more popular flag was the red field with blue diagonal cross bars that held 13 white stars, designed by Gen. P. G. T. Beauregard.

(See also Civil War, U. S., in Index.)

Dixie

The name Dixie is popularly associated with the southern states of the U.S. Several possible origins have been suggested.

One is said to be the French word dix (ten) which was printed on $10 bills used in early Louisiana which were called "dixies" by Americans. Louisiana became known as "Dix's Land" or "Land of the Dixie's."

Some sources suggest that the name originated from a kind-hearted Dutch farmer, Dixie (Dixye), who unsuccessfully tried to cultivate tobacco in Harlem, New York City, in the late 1700s. When he sold his slaves to a farmer in Piedmont County, S.C., they are said to have longed to return to Dixie's farm and sang of its joys.

In the South many consider Dixie a derivation from the "Mason-Dixon Line" which divided the free and slave states.

The National Anthem — The Star-Spangled Banner

The Star-Spangled Banner was ordered played by the military and naval services by President Woodrow Wilson in 1916. It was designated the National Anthem by Act of Congress, March 3, 1931. It was written by Francis Scott Key, of Georgetown, D. C., during the bombardment of Fort McHenry, Baltimore, Md., Sept. 13-14, 1814. Key was a lawyer, a graduate of St. John's College, Annapolis, and a volunteer in a light artillery company. When a friend, Dr. Beanes, a physician of Upper Marlborough, Md., was taken aboard Admiral Cockburn's British squadron for interfering with ground troops, Key and J. S. Skinner, carrying a note from President Madison, went to the fleet under a flag of truce on a cartel ship to ask Beanes' release. Admiral Cockburn consented, but as the fleet was about to sail up the Patapsco to bombard Fort McHenry he detained them, first on H. M. S. Surprise, and then on a supply ship.

Key witnessed the bombardment from his own vessel. It began at 7 a.m., Sept. 13, 1814, and lasted, with intermissions, for 25 hours. The British fired over 1,500 shells, each weighing as much as 220 lbs. They were unable to approach closely because the Americans had sunk 22 vessels in the channel. Only four Americans were killed and 24 wounded. A British bomb-ship was disabled.

During the bombardment Key wrote a stanza on the back of an envelope. Next day at Indian Queen Inn, Baltimore, he wrote out the poem and gave it to his brother-in-law, Judge J. H. Nicholson. Nicholson suggested the tune, Anacreon in Heaven, and had the poem printed on broadsides, of which two survive. On Sept. 20 it appeared in the Baltimore American. Later Key made 3 copies; one is in the Library of Congress and one in the Pennsylvania Historical Society.

The copy that Key wrote in his hotel Sept. 14, 1814, remained in the Nicholson family for 93 years. In 1907 it was sold to Henry Walters of Baltimore. In 1934 it was bought at auction in New York from the Walters estate by the Walters Art Gallery, Baltimore, for $26,400. The Walters Gallery in 1953 sold the manuscript to the Maryland Historical Society for the same price.

The flag that Key saw during the bombardment is preserved in Smithsonian Institution, Washington. It is 30 by 42 ft., and has 15 alternate red and white stripes and 15 stars, for the original 13 states plus Kentucky and Vermont. It was made by Mary Young Pickersgill. The Baltimore Flag House, a museum, occupies her premises, which were restored in 1953.

The Star-Spangled Banner

I

Oh, say can you see by the dawn's early light
　What so proudly we hailed at the twilight's last
　　gleaming?
Whose broad stripes and bright stars thru the
　perilous fight,
　O'er the ramparts we watched were so gallantly
　　streaming?
And the rocket's red glare, the bombs bursting in
　air,
　Gave proof through the night that our flag was
　　still there.
Oh, say does that star-spangled banner yet wave
　O'er the land of the free and the home of the
　　brave?

II

On the shore, dimly seen through the mists of the
　deep,
Where the foe's haughty host in dread silence
　reposes,
What is that which the breeze, o'er the towering
　steep,
　As it fitfully blows, half conceals, half discloses?
Now it catches the gleam of the morning's first
　beam,
　In full glory reflected now shines on the stream:
'Tis the star-spangled banner! O long may it wave
　O'er the land of free and the home of the
　　brave!

III

And where is that band who so vauntingly swore
　That the havoc of war and the battle's confusion,
A home and a country should leave us no more!
　Their blood has washed out their foul footsteps'
　　pollution
No refuge could save the hireling and slave
　From the terror of flight, or the gloom of the
　　grave:
And the star-spangled banner in triumph doth
　wave
　O'er the land of the free and the home of the
　　brave!

IV

Oh! thus be it ever, when freemen shall stand
　Between their loved homes and the war's desolation!
Blest with victory and peace, may the heav'n
　rescued land
　Praise the Power that hath made and preserved
　　us a nation.
Then conquer we must, when our cause it is just,
　And this be our motto: "In God is our trust."
　And the star-spangled banner in triumph shall
　　wave
　O'er the land of the free and the home of the
　　brave!

Yankee Doodle

The first known American printing of the popular song "Yankee Doodle" was as part of Benjamin Carr's *Federal Overture* in Baltimore in 1795. The origin of the song is unknown but it is believed to have been composed in the 1750's and used to deride the colonials. It became instead a patriotic American air. Some of the verses are:

Father and I went down to camp
Along with Captain Gooding,
And there we saw the men and boys
As thick as hasty pudding.

　Yankee Doodle keep it up
　Yankee Doodle Dandy,
　Mind the music and the step,
　And with the girls be handy.

There was Captain Washington
Upon a slapping stallion
A-giving orders to his men—
There must have been a million.

　There I saw a wooden keg
　With heads made out of leather;
　They knocked upon it with some sticks
　To call the folks together.

Then they'd fife away like fun
And play on cornstalk fiddles,
And some had ribbons red as blood
All bound around their middles.

　I can't tell you all I saw—
　They kept up such a smother,
　I took my hat off, made a bow,
　And scampered home to mother.

Origin of the Names of U.S. States

Source: State officials, the Smithsonian Institution and the Topographic Division, U.S. Geological Survey.

Alabama—Indian for tribal town, later a tribe (Alabamas or Alibamons), of the Creek confederacy.

Alaska—Russian version of Aleutian (Eskimo) word, alakshak, for "peninsula" or "great lands."

Arizona—Spanish version of Pima Indian word for "little spring place," or Aztec arizuma, meaning "silver-bearing."

Arkansas—French variant of Kansas, a Sioux Indian name for "south wind people."

California—Bestowed by the Spanish conquistadors (possibly by Cortez). It was the name of an imaginary island, an earthly paradise, in "Las Serges de Esplandian," a Spanish romance written by Montalvo in 1510. Baja California (Lower, California, in Mexico) was first visited by Spanish in 1533. The present U.S. state was called Alta (Upper) California.

Colorado—Spanish, red, first applied to Colorado River.

Connecticut—From Mohican and other Algonquin words meaning "long river place."

Delaware—Named for Lord De La Warr, early governor of Virginia; first applied to river, then to Indian tribe (Lenni-Lenape) and the state.

District of Columbia—For Columbus, 1791.

Florida—Named by Ponce de Leon on Pascua Florida, "Flowery Easter," on Easter Sunday, 1513.

Georgia—For King George II of England by James Oglethorpe, colonial administrator, 1732.

Hawaii—Possibly derived from native word for homeland, Hawaiki or Owhyhee.

Idaho—Shoshone derivation. State calls it "light on the mountains."

Illinois—French for Illini or land of Illini, Algonquin word meaning men or warriors.

Indiana—Means "land of the Indians."

Iowa—Indian word variously translated as "one who puts to sleep" or "beautiful land."

Kansas—Sioux word for "south wind people."

Kentucky—Indian word variously translated as "dark and bloody ground," "meadow land" and "land of tomorrow."

Louisiana—Part of territory called Louisiana by LaSalle for French King Louis XIV.

Maine—From Maine, ancient French province.

Maryland—For Queen Henrietta Maria, wife of Charles I of England.

Massachusetts—From Indian tribe named after "large hill place" identified by Capt. John Smith as near Milton, Mass.

Michigan—From Chippewa words mici gama meaning "great water," after the lake of the same name.

Minnesota—From Dakota Sioux word meaning "cloudy water" or "sky-tinted water" of the Minnesota River.

Mississippi—Probably Chippewa: mici zibi, "great river" or "gathering-in of all the waters."

Missouri—Indian tribe named after Missouri River, meaning "muddy water."

Montana—Latin or Spanish for "mountainous."

Nebraska—From Omaha or Otos Indian word meaning "broad water" or "flat river," describing the Platte River.

Nevada—Spanish, meaning snow-clad.

New Hampshire—Named 1629 by Capt. John Mason of Plymouth Council for county in England.

New Jersey—The Duke of York, 1664, gave a patent to John Berkeley and Sir Geo. Carteret to be called Nova Caesaria, or New Jersey, after England's Isle of Jersey.

New Mexico—Spaniards in Mexico applied term to land north and west of Rio Grande in the 16th Century.

New York—For Duke of York and Albany who received patent to New Netherland from his brother Charles II and sent an expedition to capture it, 1664.

North Carolina—In 1619 Charles I gave a large patent to Sir Robt. Heath to be called Province of Carolana, from Carolus, Latin name for Charles. A new patent was granted by Charles II to Earl of Clarendon and others. Divided into North and South Carolina, 1710.

North Dakota—Dakota is Sioux for friend or ally.

Ohio—Iroquois word for "beautiful river."

Oklahoma—Choctaw coined word meaning red man, proposed by Rev. Allen Wright, Choctaw-speaking Indian.

Oregon—From Algonquin word Wauregan, meaning "beautiful water," early name for the Columbia River.

Pennsylvania—William Penn, the Quaker, who was made full proprietor by King Charles II in 1681, suggested Sylvania, or woodland, for his tract. The king's government owed Penn's father, Admiral William Penn, £16,000, and the land being granted in part settlement, the king added the Penn to Sylvania, against the desires of the modest proprietor, in honor of the admiral.

Puerto Rico—Spanish for Rich Port.

Rhode Island—Named Roode Eylandt by Adriaen Block, Dutch explorer, because of its red clay. Name of Roger Williams' settlement was added to give the small state its long, official title: State of Rhode Island and Providence Plantations.

South Carolina—See North Carolina.

South Dakota—See North Dakota.

Tennessee—From 1784 to 1788 this was the State of Franklin, or Frankland. Tanasi was the name of Cherokee villages on the Little Tennessee River.

Texas—Variant of word used by Caddo and other Indians meaning friends or allies, and applied to them by the Spanish in eastern Texas. Also written texias, tejas, teysas.

Utah—From a Navajo word meaning upper, or higher up, as applied to a Shoshone tribe called Ute. Spanish form is Yutta, English Uta or Utah. Proposed name Deseret, "land of honeybees," from Book of Mormon, was rejected by Congress.

Vermont—From French words Vert, green, and Mont, mountain. The Green Mountains were said to have been named by Samuel de Champlain. The Green Mountain Boys were Gen. Stark's men in the Revolution. When the state was formed, 1777, Dr. Thos. Young suggested combining vert and mont into Vermont.

Virginia—Named by Sir Walter Raleigh, who fitted out the expedition of 1584, in honor of Queen Elizabeth, the Virgin Queen of England.

Washington—Named after George Washington. When the bill creating the Territory of Columbia was introduced in the 32nd Congress, the name was changed to Washington because of the existence of the District of Columbia.

West Virginia—So named when western counties of Virginia refused to secede from the United States, 1863.

Wisconsin—An Indian name, spelled Ouisconsin and Misconsing by early chroniclers. Believed to mean "grassy place" in Chippewa. Congress made it Wisconsin.

Wyoming—The word was taken from Wyoming Valley, Pa., which was the site of an Indian massacre and became widely known by Campbell's poem, Gertrude of Wyoming. In Algonquin it means "large prairie place."

Accession of Territory by The United States

Source: Statistical Abstract of the United States

Division	Yr.	Sq. mi.[1]	Division	Yr.	Sq. mi.[1]	Division	Yr.	Sq. mi.[1]
Total (1860)		3,628066	Texas	1845	390,143	American Samoa. . .	1900	76
			Oregon	1846	285,580	Canal Zone[4]	1904	550
United States		3,615,122	Mexican cession. . .	1848	529,017	Corn Islands[5]	1914	4
Terrritory 1790[2]		888,685	Gadsden Purchase. .	1853	29,640	Virgin Islands.	1917	183
Louisiana Purchase.	1803	827,192	Alaska	1867	586,412	Trust Territory of		
By Treaty with Spain			Hawaii	1898	6,450	the Pacific Isl.. . . .	1947	8,489
Florida.	1819	58,560	The Philippines[3]	1898	115,600	All other[6].	. . . .	42
Other areas.	1819	13,443	Puerto Rico.	1899	3,435			
			Guam	1899	212			

(1.)Gross area (land and water). (2.)Includes drainage basin of Red River on the North, south of 49th parallel, sometimes considered a part of the Louisiana Purchase. (3.)Area not included in totals; became Republic of the Philippines July 4 1946. (4.)Under U.S. jurisdiction by treaty with Panama. (5.)Leased from Nicaragua for 99 years but returned April 25 1971. (6.)See index for Outlying Areas; U.S.

Public Lands of the United States

Source: Bureau of Land Management, U.S. Dept. of the Interior

Acquisition of the Public Domain 1781-1867

Acquisition	Area*(in Acres)	Land	Water	Total	Cost[1]
State Cessions (1781-1802)		233,415,680	3,409,920	236,825,600	$6,200,000
Louisiana Purchase (1803)[3]		523,446,400	6,465,280	529,911,680	23,213,568
Red River Basin[4]		29,066,880	535,040	29,601,920	
Cession from Spain (1819)		43,342,720	2,801,920	46,144,640	6,674,057
Oregon Compromise (1846)		180,644,480	2,741,760	183,386,240	
Mexican Cession (1848)		334,479,360	4,201,600	338,680,960	16,295,149
Purchase from Texas (1850)		78,842,880	83,840	78,926,720	15,496,448
Gadsden Purchase (1853)		18,961,920	26,880	18,988,800	10,000,000
Alaska Purchase (1867)		365,481,600	9,814,400	375,296,000	7,200,000
Total		**1,807,681,920**	**30,080,640**	**1,837,762,560**	**$85,079,222**

*All areas except Alaska were computed in 1912, and have not been adjusted for the recomputation of the area of the United States which was made for the 1950 Decennial Census.
(1.)Cost data for all except "State Cessions" obtained from U.S. Geological Survey.
(2.)Paid by Federal Government for Georgia Cession, 1802 (56,689,920 acres).
(3.)Excludes areas eliminated by Treaty of 1819 with Spain.
(4.)Basin of the Red River of the North, south of the 49th parallel.

Disposition of Public Lands 1781 to 1970 (in acres)

Disposition by methods not elsewhere classified[1]		Granted to States for:	
Granted or sold to homesteaders	303,500,000 287,500,000	Support of common schools	77,600,000
Granted to railroad corporations	94,300,000	Reclamation of swampland	64,900,000
Granted to veterans as military bounties	61,000,000	Construction of railroads	37,100,000
Confirmed as private land claims[2]	34,000,000	Support of misc. institutions[6]	21,700,000
Sold under timber and stone law[3]	13,900,000	Purposes not elsewhere classified[7]	117,500,000
Granted or sold under timber culture law[4]	10,900,000	Canals and rivers	6,100,000
Sold under desert land law[5]	10,700,000	Construction of wagon roads	3,400,000
		Total granted to States	**328,300,000**
		Grand Total	**1,144,100,000**

(1.)Chiefly public, private, and preemption sales, but includes mineral entries, script locations, sales of townsites and townlots.
(2.)The Government has confirmed title to lands claimed under valid grants made by foreign governments prior to the acquisition of the public domain by the United States.
(3.)The law provided for the sale of lands valuable for timber or stone and unfit for cultivation.
(4.)The law provided for the granting of public lands to settlers on condition that they plant and cultivate trees on the lands granted.
(5.)The law provided for the sale of arid agricultural public lands to settlers who irrigate them and bring them under cultivation.
(6.)Universities, hospitals, asylums, etc.
(7.)For construction of various public improvements (individual items not specified in the granting act) reclamation of desert lands, construction of water reservoirs, etc.

Land Owned by the Federal Government (in acres)

Agency (June 30, 1971)	Public Domain	Acquired	Total
Bureau of Land Management	471,680,093.0	2,364,892.1	474,044,985.1
U.S. Forest Service	160,176,950.0	26,637,350.4	186,814,300.4
U.S. Fish and Wildlife Service	24,401,982.7	3,505,275.9	27,907,258.6
U.S. Park Service	19,587,492.2	4,883,982.8	24,471,475.0
U.S. Army	7,051,453.0	3,998,858.0	11,050,311.0
Bureau of Reclamation	5,829,133.1	1,749,102.4	7,578,235.5
U.S. Air Force	6,941,946.0	1,383,762.0	8,325,708.0
Corps of Engineers	787,232.7	6,599,510.2	7,386,742.9
Bureau of Indian Affairs	4,204,809.2	781,155.9	4,985,965.1
U.S. Navy	2,155,750.0	1,431,366.7	3,587,116.7
Atomic Energy Commission	1,446,299.6	678,684.5	2,124,984.1
Other Agencies	530,489.5	1,395,991.4	1,926,480.9
Totals	**704,793,631.0**	**55,409,932.3**	**760,203,563.3**

The Homestead Act; Sale of Public Land

The Homestead Act became effective Jan.1, 1863, the same day that President Lincoln issued his Emancipation Proclamation. Its purpose was to open the vacant lands of America's vast public domain to agricultural settlement.

To qualify for a homestead a person had to be a citizen of the United States or express his intention of becoming one, be over 21 years of age or the head of a household, and own less than 160 acres of land.

To acquire title to 160 acres of public land the homesteader had to establish residence on the land and bring a portion under cultivation. After 6 months residence he could purchase the land for $1.25 per acre, or after 5 years residence he could acquire title for a $15 filing fee.

Originally passed by Congress on May 20, 1862, the Homestead Act was later amended to increase acreage limitations under certain conditions. Under the Homestead Act and its several amendments, more than a million families received title to over 248,000,000 acres of public land across the plains, prairies and mountains of western United States. But as subsequent waves of settlers moved onto vacant land the supply of arable land dwindled; by the late 1930s some homesteaders had settled on submarginal lands that would not support a farm family. In 1937 Congress passed the Bankhead-Jones Act authorizing the Government to repurchase bankrupt farms to relieve the plight of such families. Under this program about 2,000,000 acres of homestead land was returned to Federal ownership.

By the time of its 100th anniversary the Homestead Act had accomplished its purpose—the transformation of a wilderness into productive farmland. Now outdated, the Homestead Act will always be a part of the American heritage.

Public Land Sale

From time to time the Bureau of Land Management sells public land to private individuals. Public land is always sold for its fair market value as determined by public auction. The Federal Govt. offers no free land. Persons wishing to purchase public land should contact the Bureau of Land Management, Wash., D. C. 20240, or one of the Bureau's Land Offices in the public land states.

The Bureau stresses that it is the only authoritative source of information on the sale of land under its jurisdiction.

States: Settled, Capitals, Entry into Union, Area, Rank

The Original Thirteen States—The 13 colonies that seceded from Great Britain and fought the War of Independence (American Revolution) became the 13 original states. They were Massachusetts, Rhode Island, Connecticut, New Hampshire, New York, New Jersey, Pennsylvania, Delaware, Maryland, Virginia, North Carolina, South Carolina and Georgia.

State / Area	Set-tled*	Capital	Entered Union Date	Order**	Long	Wide	Land	Inland water	Total	Rank In Area
Ala......	1702...	Montgomery......	Dec. 14, 1819	22	330	200	50,708	901	51,609	29
Alaska....	1784...	Juneau...........	Jan. 3, 1959	49	(a)900	800	566,432	19,980	586,412	1
Ariz......	1848...	Phoenix.......	Feb. 14, 1912	48	390	335	113,417	492	113,909	6
Ark......	1785...	Little Rock....	June 15, 1836	25	275	240	51,945	1,159	53,104	27
Cal......	1769...	Sacramento......	Sept. 9, 1850	31	770	375	156,361	2,332	158,693	3
Colo......	1858...	Denver........	Aug. 1, 1876	38	390	270	103,766	481	104,247	8
Conn......	1635...	Hartford.......	Jan. 9, 1788	5	90	75	4,862	139	5,009	48
Del......	1683...	Dover........	Dec. 7, 1787	1	110	35	1,982	75	2,057	49
Dist. Col...		Washington.......			...	...	61	6	67	51
Fla......	1565...	Tallahassee......	Mar. 3, 1845	27	460	400	54,090	4,470	58,560	22
Ga......	1733...	Atlanta..........	Jan. 2, 1788	4	315	250	58,073	803	58,876	21
Hawaii...		Honolulu......	Aug. 21, 1959	50	...	...	6,425	25	6,450	47
Idaho....	1842...	Boise........	July 3, 1890	43	490	305	82,677	880	83,557	13
Ill......	1720...	Springfield.......	Dec. 3, 1818	21	380	205	55,748	652	56,400	24
Ind......	1733...	Indianapolis......	Dec. 11, 1816	19	265	160	36,097	102	36,291	38
Iowa....	1788...	Des Moines......	Dec. 28, 1846	29	300	210	55,941	349	56,290	25
Kan....	1727...	Topeka.........	Jan. 29, 1861	34	400	200	81,787	477	82,264	14
Ky....	1774...	Frankfort......	June 1, 1792	15	350	175	39,650	745	40,395	37
La....	1699...	Baton Rouge......	Apr. 30, 1812	18	280	275	44,930	3,593	48,523	31
Me....	1624...	Augusta........	Mar. 15, 1820	23	235	205	30,920	2,295	33,215	39
Md....	1634...	Annapolis.......	Apr. 28, 1788	7	200	120	9,891	686	10,577	42
Mass....	1620...	Boston........	Feb. 6, 1788	6	190	110	7,826	431	8,257	45
Mich....	1668...	Lansing........	Jan. 26, 1837	26	400	310	56,817	1,399	58,216	23
Minn.....	1805...	St. Paul........	May 11, 1858	32	400	350	79,289	4,779	84,068	12
Miss....	1699...	Jackson........	Dec. 10, 1817	20	340	180	47,296	420	47,716	32
Mo....	1735...	Jefferson City.....	Aug. 10, 1821	24	300	280	68,995	691	69,686	19
Mont....	1809...	Helena........	Nov. 8, 1889	41	580	315	145,587	1,551	147,138	4
Nebr......	1847...	Lincoln........	Mar. 1, 1867	37	415	205	76,483	744	77,227	15
Nev......	1850...	Carson City.....	Oct. 31, 1864	36	485	315	109,889	651	110,540	7
N.H....	1623...	Concord.......	June 21, 1788	9	185	90	9,027	277	9,304	44
N.J....	1664...	Trenton.......	Dec. 18, 1787	3	160	70	7,521	315	7,836	46
N.M....	1605...	Santa Fe.......	Jan. 6, 1912	47	390	350	121,412	254	121,666	5
N.Y.......	1614...	Albany........	July 26, 1788	11	320	310	47,831	1,745	49,576	30
N.C.......	1650...	Raleigh........	Nov. 21, 1789	12	520	200	48,798	3,788	52,586	28
N.D....	1766...	Bismarck.....	Nov. 2, 1889	39	360	210	69,273	1,392	70,665	17
Ohio....	1788...	Columbus......	Mar. 1, 1803	17	230	205	40,975	247	41,222	35
Okla....	1889...	Oklahoma City.....	Nov. 16, 1907	46	585	210	68,782	1,137	69,919	18
Ore......	1811...	Salem.........	Feb. 14, 1859	33	375	290	96,184	797	96,981	10
Pa......	1682...	Harrisburg......	Dec. 12, 1787	2	300	180	44,966	367	45,333	33
R.I....	1636...	Providence......	May 29, 1790	13	50	35	1,049	165	1,214	50
S.C....	1670...	Columbia......	May 23, 1788	8	285	215	30,225	830	31,055	40
S.D....	1856...	Pierre.........	Nov. 2, 1889	40	380	245	75,955	1,092	77,047	16
Tenn.....	1757...	Nashville........	June 1, 1796	16	430	120	41,328	916	42,244	34
Texas....	1691...	Austin........	Dec. 29, 1845	28	760	620	262,134	5,204	267,338(b)	2
Utah....	1847...	Salt Lake City....	Jan. 4, 1896	45	345	275	82,906	2,820	84,916	11
Vt....	1724...	Montpelier......	Mar. 4, 1791	14	155	90	9,267	342	9,609	43
Va....	1607...	Richmond......	June 26, 1788	10	425	205	39,780	1,037	40,817	36
Wash.....	1811...	Olympia.........	Nov. 11, 1889	42	340	230	66,570	1,622	68,192	20
W. Va....	1727...	Charleston......	June 20, 1863	35	225	200	24,070	111	24,181	41
Wis....	1766...	Madison........	May 29, 1848	30	300	290	54,464	1,690	56,154	26
Wyo......	1834...	Cheyenne.......	July 10, 1890	44	365	275	97,203	711	97,914	9

*First permanent settlement. **The order for the original thirteen states is the order in which they ratified the constitution. (a) Aleutian Islands and Alexander Archipelago are not considered in these lengths. (b) Total area of Texas reduced 1 sq. mile by Chamizal boundary solution between U.S. and Mexico, 1963.

The Continental Divide

Source: U.S. Geological Survey, Department of the Interior

Continental Divide: watershed, created by mountain ranges or table-lands of the Rocky Mountains, from which the drainage is easterly or westerly; the easterly flowing waters reaching the Atlantic Ocean chiefly through the Gulf of Mexico, and the westerly flowing waters reaching the Pacific Ocean through the Columbia River, or through the Colorado River, which flows into the Gulf of California.

The location and route of the Continental Divide across the United States may briefly be described as follows:

Beginning at point of crossing the United States-Mexican boundary, near long. 108°45'W., the Divide, in a northerly direction, crosses New Mexico along the western edge of the Rio Grande drainage basin, entering Colorado near long. 106°41'.

Thence by a very irregular route northerly across Colorado along the western summits of the Rio Grande and of the Arkansas, the South Platte, and the North Platte River basins, and across Rocky Mountain National Park, entering Wyoming near long. 106°52'.

Then in a northwesyerly direction, forming the western rims of the North Platte, Big Horn, and Yellowstone River basins, crossing the southwestern portion of Yellowstone National Park.

Thence in a westerly and then a northerly direction forming the common boundary of Idaho and Montana, to a point on said boundary near long. 114°00'W.

Thence northeasterly and northwesterly through Montana and the Glacier National Park, entering Canada near long. 114°04'W.

Chronological List of Territories

Name of Territory	Date of Organic Act	Organic Act Effective	Admission as State	Yrs. Terr.
Northwest Territory (a)	July 13, 1787	No fixed date		
Territory south of Ohio River	May 26, 1790	No fixed date	June 1, 1796b	6
Mississippi	Apr. 7, 1798	When President acted	Dec. 10, 1817	19
Indiana	May 7, 1800	July 4, 1800	Dec. 11, 1816	16
Territory northwest of Ohio River	May 7, 1800	July 4, 1800	Mar. 1, 1803c	2
Orleans	Mar. 26, 1804	Oct. 1, 1804	Apr. 8, 1812d	7
Michigan	Jan. 11, 1805	June 30, 1805	Jan. 26, 1837	31
Louisiana-Missouri (e)	Mar. 3, 1805	July 4, 1805	Aug. 10, 1821	16
Illinois	Feb. 3, 1809	Mar. 1, 1809	Dec. 3, 1813	9
Alabama	Mar. 3, 1817	When Miss. became a State	Dec. 14, 1819	2
Arkansas	Mar. 2, 1819	July 4, 1819	June 15, 1836	17
Florida	Mar. 30, 1822	No fixed date	Mar. 3, 1845	23
Indian (organized 1834)*				
Wisconsin	Apr. 20, 1836	July 3, 1836	May 29, 1848	12
Iowa	June 12, 1838	July 3, 1838	Dec. 28, 1846	7
Oregon	Aug. 14, 1848	Date of act	Feb. 14, 1859	10
Minnesota	Mar. 3, 1849	Date of act	May 11, 1859	9
New Mexico	Sept. 9, 1850	On president's proclamation	Jan. 6, 1912	61
Utah	Sept. 9, 1850	Date of act	Jan. 4, 1896	44
Washington	Mar. 2, 1853	Date of act	Nov. 11, 1889	36
Nebraska	May 30, 1854	Date of act	Feb. 9, 1867	12
Kansas	May 30, 1854	Date of act	Jan. 29, 1861	6
Colorado	Feb. 28, 1861	Date of act	Aug. 1, 1876	15
Nevada	Mar. 2, 1861	Date of act	Oct. 31, 1864	3
Dakota°	Mar. 2, 1861	Date of act	Nov. 2, 1889	28
Arizona	Feb. 24, 1863	Date of act	Feb. 14, 1912	49
Idaho	Mar. 3, 1863	Date of act	July 3, 1890	27
Montana	May 26, 1864	Date of act	Nov. 8, 1889	25
Wyoming	July 25, 1868	When officers were qualified	July 10, 1890	22
Oklahoma	May 2, 1890	Date of act	Nov. 16, 1907	17
Hawaii	Apr 30, 1900	June 14, 1900	Aug. 21, 1959	59
Alaska	Aug. 24, 1912	Nov. 5, 1912	Jan. 3, 1959	47

(a) Included present Ohio, Indiana, Illinois, Michigan, Wisconsin, Eastern Minnesota; (b) as the State of Tennessee; (c) as the State of Ohio; (d) as the State of Louisiana; (e) organic act for Missouri Territory of June 4, 1812, became effective Dec. 7, 1812.

*Indian Territory was set aside in 1834 for the "5 civilized Indian Tribes"—Cherokee, Chocktaw, Chickasaw, Creek and Seminole. In 1889 part of it was included in the Territory of Oklahoma. In 1906 Indian Territory and the Territory of Oklahoma were merged to form the state of Oklahoma.

Geographic Centers, United States and Each State
Source: U. S. Geological Survey, Department of the Interior

United States, including Alaska and Hawaii — South Dakota; Butte County, 17 miles W of Castle Rock, 14 miles E of junction of borders of South Dakota, Montana and Wyoming. Approx. Lat. 44°58'N, Long. 103°46'W.

Conterminous U. S. (48 States)—Near Lebanon, Smith Co., Kansas. Lat. 39°50'N, Long. 98°35'W.

North American Continent—The geographic center is in Pierce County, North Dakota, 6 miles W of Balta. Latitude 48°10', Longitude 100°10'W.

STATES

State	County	Locality
Alabama—Chilton, 12 miles SW of Clanton.
Alaska—Lat. 63°50'N, Long. 152°00'W. Approx. 60 mi. NW of Mt. McKinley.
Arizona—Yavapai, 55 miles ESE of Prescott.
Arkansas—Pulaski, 12 miles NW of Little Rock.
California—Madera, 38 miles E of Madera.
Colorado—Park, 30 miles NW of Pikes Peak.
Connecticut—Hartford, at East Berlin.
Delaware—Kent, 11 miles S of Dover.
District of Columbia—Near Fourth and "L" Streets, NW.
Florida—Hernando, 12 miles NNW of Brooksville.
Georgia—Twiggs, 18 miles SW of Macon.
Hawaii—Hawaii, 20°15'N,156°20'W, off Maui Island.
Idaho—Custer, at Custer, SW of Challis.
Illinois—Logan, 28 miles NE of Springfield.
Indiana—Boone, 14 miles NNW of Indianapolis.
Iowa—Story, 5 miles NE of Ames.
Kansas—Barton, 15 miles NE of Great Bend.
Kentucky—Marion, 3 miles NNW of Lebanon.
Louisiana—Avoyelles, 3 miles SE of Marksville.
Maine—Piscataquis, 18 miles north of Dover.

Maryland—Prince Georges, 4δ miles NW of Davidsonville.
Massachusetts—Worcester, north part of city.
Michigan—Wexford, 5 miles NNW of Cadillac.
Minnesota—Crow Wing, 10 miles SW of Brainerd.
Mississippi—Leake, 9 miles WNW of Carthage.
Missouri—Miller, 20 miles SW of Jefferson City.
Montana—Fergus, 12 miles west of Lewistown.
Nebraska—Custer, 10 miles NW of Broken Bow.
Nevada—Lander, 26 miles SE of Austin.
New Hampshire—Belknap, 3 miles E of Ashland.
New Jersey—Mercer, 5 miles SE of Trenton.
New Mexico—Torrance, 12 miles SSW of Willard.
New York—Madison, 12 miles S of Oneida and 26 miles SW of Utica.
North Carolina—Chatham, 10 miles NW of Sanford.
North Dakota—Sheridan, 5 miles SW of McClusky.
Ohio—Delaware, 25 miles NNE of Columbus.
Oklahoma—Oklahoma, 8 miles N of Oklahoma City.
Oregon—Crook, 25 miles SSE of Prineville.
Pennsylvania—Centre, 28 miles SW of Bellefonte.
Rhode Island—Kent, 1 mile SSW of Crompton.
South Carolina—Richland, 13 miles SE of Columbia.
South Dakota—Hughes, 8 miles NE of Pierre.
Tennessee—Rutherford, 5 mi. NE of Murfreesboro.
Texas—McCulloch, 15 miles NE of Brady.
Utah—Sanpete, 3 miles N of Manti.
Vermont—Washington, 3 miles E of Roxbury.
Virginia—Buckingham, 5 miles SW of Buckingham.
Washington—Chelan, 10 mi. WSW of Wenatchee.
West Virginia—Braxton, 4 miles E of Sutton.
Wisconsin—Wood, 9 miles SE of Marshfield.
Wyoming—Fremont, 58 miles ENE of Lander.

There is no generally accepted definition of geographic center, and no satisfactory method for determining it. The geographic center of an area may be defined as the center of gravity of the surface, or that point on which the surface of the area would balance if it were a plane of uniform thickness.

No marked or monumented point has been established by any government agency as the geographic center of either the 50 states, the conterminous United States, or the North American continent. A monument was erected in Lebanon, Kan., conterminous U.S. center, by a group of citizens.

Highest and Lowest Altitudes in the United States

Source: U. S. Geological Survey. (Minus sign means below sea level; elevations are in feet.)

State	Highest Point Name	County	Elev.	Lowest Point Name	County	Elev.
Alabama	Cheaha Mountain	Cleburne	2,407	Gulf of Mexico		Sea level
Alaska	Mount McKinley		20,320	Pacific Ocean		Sea level
Arizona	Humphreys Peak	Coconino	12,633	Colorado R.	Yuma	70
Arkansas	Magazine Mountain	Logan	2,753	Ouachita R.	Ashley Union	55
California	Mount Whitney	Inyo-Tulare	14,494	Death Valley	Inyo	—282
Canal Zone	Cerro Galera	Balboa District	1,205	Atlantic Ocean		Sea level
Colorado	Mount Elbert	Lake	14,433	Arkansas R	Prowers	3,350
Connecticut	Mount Frissell	Litchfield	2,380	L. I. Sound		Sea level
Delaware	On Ebright Road	New Castle	442	Atlantic Ocean		Sea level
Dist. of Col.	Tenleytown	N. W. part	410	Potomac R.		1
Florida	West boundary	Walton	345	Atlantic Ocean		Sea level
Georgia	Brasstown Bald	Towns-Union	4,784	Atlantic Ocean		Sea level
Guam	Mount Lamlam	Agat District	1,329	Pacific Ocean		Sea level
Hawaii	Mauna Kea	Hawaii	13,796	Pacific Ocean		Sea level
Idaho	Borah Peak	Custer	12,662	Snake R.	Nez Perce	710
Illinois	Charles Mound	Jo Daviess	1,235	Mississippi R.	Alexander	279
Indiana	Franklin Township	Wayne	1,257	Ohio R.	Posey	320
Iowa	NE of Sibley	Osceola	1,670	Mississippi R.	Lee	480
Kansas	Mount Sunflower	Wallace	4,039	Verdigris R.	Montgomery	680
Kentucky	Black Mountain	Harlan	4,145	Mississippi R.	Fulton	257
Louisiana	Driskill Mountain	Bienville	535	New Orleans	Orleans	—5
Maine	Mount Katahdin	Piscataquis	5,268	Atlantic Ocean		Sea level
Maryland	Backbone Mountain	Garrett	3,360	Atlantic Ocean		Sea level
Massachusetts	Mount Greylock	Berkshire	3,491	Atlantic Ocean		Sea level
Michigan	Mount Curwood	Baraga	1,980	Lake Erie		572
Minnesota	Eagle Mountain	Cook	2,301	Lake Superior		602
Mississippi	Woodall Mountain	Tishomingo	806	Gulf of Mexico		Sea level
Missouri	Taum Sauk Mt.	Iron	1,772	St. Francis R.	Dunklin	230
Montana	Granite Peak	Park	12,799	Kootenai R.	Lincoln	1,800
Nebraska	Johnson Township	Kimball	5,426	S.E. cor. State	Richardson	840
Nevada	Boundary Peak	Esmeralda	13,140	Colorado R.	Clark	470
New Hampshire	Mt. Washington	Coos	6,288	Atlantic Ocean		Sea level
New Jersey	High Point	Sussex	1,803	Atlantic Ocean		Sea level
New Mexico	Wheeler Peak	Taos	13,161	Red Bluff Res.	Eddy	2,817
New York	Mount Marcy	Essex	5,344	Atlantic Ocean		Sea level
North Carolina	Mount Mitchell	Yancey	6,684	Atlantic Ocean		Sea level
North Dakota	White Butte	Slope	3,506	Red River	Pembina	750
Ohio	Campbell Hill	Logan	1,550	Ohio R.	Hamilton	433
Oklahoma	Black Mesa	Cimarron	4,973	Little River	McCurtain	287
Oregon	Mount Hood	Clakamas-Hood, R.	11,235	Pacific Ocean		Sea level
Pennsylvania	Mt. Davis	Somerset	3,213	Delaware R.	Delaware	Sea level
Puerto Rico	Cerro de Punta	Ponce	4,389	Atlantic Ocean		Sea level
Rhode Island	Jerimoth Hill	Providence	812	Atlantic Ocean		Sea level
Samoa	Lata Mtn.	Tau Island	3,160	Pacific Ocean		Sea level
South Carolina	Sassafras Mountain	Pickens	3,560	Atlantic Ocean		Sea level
South Dakota	Harney Peak	Pennington	7,242	Big Stone Lake	Roberts	962
Tennessee	Clingmans Dome	Sevier	6,643	Mississippi R.	Shelby	182
Texas	Guadalupe Peak	Culberson	8,751	Gulf of Mexico		Sea level
Utah	Kings Peak	Duchesne	13,528	Beaverdam Cr.	Washington	2,000
Vermont	Mount Mansfield	Lamoille	4,393	Lake Champlain	Franklin	95
Virginia	Mount Rogers	Grayson-Smyth	5,729	Atlantic Ocean		Sea level
Virgin Islands	Crown Mt.	Is. St. Thomas	1,556	Atlantic Ocean		Sea level
Washington	Mount Rainier	Pierce	14,410	Pacific Ocean		Sea level
West Virginia	Spruce Knob	Pendleton	4,863	Potomac R.	Jefferson	240
Wisconsin	Timms Hill	Price	1,952	Lake Michigan		581
Wyoming	Gannett Peak	Fremont	13,804	B. Fourche R.	Crook	3,100

U. S. Coastline by States*

Source: NOAA, Department of Commerce

State	Coastline[1]	Shoreline[2]	State	Coastline[1]	Shoreline[2]
Atlantic Coast	2,069	28,673	Gulf coast	1,631	17,141
Connecticut	(-)	618	Alabama	53	607
Delaware	28	381	Florida	770	5,095
Florida	580	3,331	Louisiana	397	7,721
Georgia	100	2,344	Mississippi	44	359
Maine	228	3,478	Texas	367	3,359
Maryland	31	3,190	Pacific coast	7,623	40,298
Massachusetts	192	1,519	Alaska	5,580	31,383
New Hampshire	13	131	California	840	3,427
New Jersey	130	1,792	Hawaii	750	1,052
New York	127	1,850	Oregon	296	1,410
North Carolina	301	3,375	Washington	157	3,026
Pennsylvania	(-)	89	Arctic coast, Alaska	1,060	2,521
Rhode Island	40	384			
South Carolina	187	2,876	United States	12,383	88,633
Virginia	112	3,315			

*In statute miles (April 1, 1961). (-). Represents zero.

(1.) Figures are lengths of general outline of seacoast. Measurements were made with a unit measure of 30 minutes of latitude on charts as near the scale of 1:1,200,000 as possible. Coastline of sounds and bays is included to a point where they narrow to width of unit measure, and includes the distance across at such point.

(2.) Figures obtained in 1939-40 with a recording instrument on the largest-scale charts and maps then available. Shoreline of outer coast, offshore islands, sounds, bays, rivers and creeks is included to the head of tidewater or to a point where tidal waters narrow to a width of 100 feet.

International Boundary Lines of the United States

The length of the northern boundary of the conterminous United States the U.S.-Canadian border, excluding Alaska — is 3,987 miles according to the U.S. Geological Survey, Dept. of the Interior. The length of the Alaskan-Canadian border is 1,538 miles. The length of the U.S.-Mexican border, from the Gulf of Mexico to the Pacific Ocean, is approximately 1,933 miles (1963 boundary agreement).

Superlative United States Statistics
Source: National Geographic Society, Washington, D.C.

Area for fifty states	Total	3,615,122 sq. mi.
	Land 3,536,855 sq. mi. — Water 78,267 sq. mi.	
Largest state	Alaska	586,412 sq. mi.
Smallest state	Rhode Island	1,214 sq. mi.
Largest county	San Bernardino County, California	20,119 sq. mi.
Smallest county	New York, N.Y.	23 sq. mi.
Largest city in area	Jacksonville, Florida	827 sq. mi.
Smallest cities in area	Belvedere, Calif.; Bonne Terre, Mo.;	
	Montgomery, W. Va.	each .4 sq. mi.
Smallest independent cities	Clifton Forge, Emporia, Falls Church	
(all in Virginia)	South Boston, Suffolk	Each 2 sq. mi.
Northernmost city	Barrow, Alaska	71° 17′N.
Northernmost point	Point Barrow, Alaska	71° 23′N.
Southernmost city	Hilo, Island of Hawaii	19° 43′N.
Southernmost town	Naalehu, Island of Hawaii	19° 03′N.
Southernmost point	Ka Lae (South Cape), Island of Hawaii	18°56′N. (155° 41′W.)
Easternmost city	Eastport Maine	66° 59.5′W.
Easternmost town	Lubec, Maine	66° 59′W.
Easternmost point	West Quoddy Head, Maine	66° 57′W.
Westernmost city	Lihue, Island of Kauai, Hawaii	159° 22′W.
Westernmost town	Adak, Aleutians, Alaska	176° 45′W.
Westernmost point	Cape Wrangell, Attu Island, Aleutians, Alaska	172° 27′E
Highest city	Leadville, Colo.	10,200 ft.
Lowest town	Calipatria, Calif.	—183 ft.
Highest point on Atlantic coast	Cadillac Mountain, Mount Desert Isl., Maine	1,530 ft.
Largest and oldest national park	Yellowstone National Park (1872), Wyoming	3,472 sq. mi.
	Montana, Idaho	
Largest national monument	Glacier Bay, Alaska	4,381 sq. mi.
Highest waterfall	Yosemite Falls—Total in three sections	2,425 ft.
	Upper Yosemite Fall	1,430 ft.
	Cascades in middle section	675 ft.
	Lower Yosemite Fall	320 ft.
Longest river	Mississippi-Missouri	3,710 mi.
Highest mountain	Mount McKinley, Alaska	20,320 ft.
Lowest point	Death Valley, California	—282 ft.
Deepest lake	Crater Lake, Oregon	1,932 ft.
Highest lake	Lake Waiau, Hawaii	13,020 ft.
Rainiest spot	Mt. Waialeale, Hawaii;	Annual Aver. rainfall 460 inches
Largest gorge	Grand Canyon, Colorado River, Arizona; 217 miles	
	long, 4 to 13 miles wide, 1 mile deep	
Deepest gorge	Hells Canyon, Snake River, Idaho;	7,900 ft.
Strongest surface wind	Mount Washington, New Hampshire recorded 1934	231 mph
Biggest dam	Ft. Peck, Missouri River, Mont.	125,628,000 cu. yds. material used
Tallest building	Sears Tower, Chicago, Ill.	1,454 ft.
Largest building	Boeing 747 Manufacturing Plant, Everett, Wash. 205,600,000	
	cu. ft.; covers 47 acres.	
Tallest structure	TV tower, Blanchard, N. Dakota	2,063 ft.
Longest bridge span	Verrazano-Narrows, New York;	4,260 ft.
Highest bridge	Royal Gorge, Colorado;	1,053 ft. above water
Deepest well	Oil well, Beckham County, Oklahoma	30,050 ft.

The Forty-Nine States, Including Alaska

Area for forty-nine states	Total	3,608,672 sq. mi.
	Land 3,530,430 sq. mi. — Water 78,242 sq. mi.	

The Forty-Eight States

Area for forty-eight states	Total	3,022,260 sq. mi.
	Land 2,963,998 sq. mi. — Water 58,262 sq. mi.	
Largest state	Texas	267,338 sq. mi.
Northernmost cities	Portal, North Dakota	48° 59′N.
	Sumas, Washington	48° 59′N.
Northernmost town	Angle Inlet, Minnesota	49° 22′N.
Northernmost point	Northwest Angle, Minnesota	49° 23′N.
Southernmost city	Key West, Florida	24° 33′N.
Southernmost mainland town	Florida City, Florida	25° 27′N.
Southernmost point	Key West Florida	24° 33′N.
Westernmost city	Gold Beach, Oregon	124° 25′W.
Westernmost town	La Push, Washington	124° 38′W.
Westernmost point	Cape Alava, Washington	124° 44′W.
Highest mountain	Mount Whitney, California	14,494 ft.

Note to users: The distinction between cities and towns varies from state to state. In this table the U.S. Bureau of the Census usage was followed.

Statistical Information About the United States

In the *Statistical Abstract of the United States* the Bureau of the Census of the Social and Economic Statistics Administration, U.S. Dept. of Commerce annually publishes a summary of social, political and economic information. A book of more than 1,000 pages, it presents in 33 sections comprehensive data on population, housing, health, education, employment, income, prices, business, banking, science, defense, trade, government finance, foreign country comparison and other subjects. Special features include comprehensive data for metropolitan areas and a summary of recent trends. The book is prepared under the direction of William Lerner, Data User Services Office, Bureau of the Census. Supplements to the *Statistical Abstract* are *Pocket Data Book USA, 1973. County and City Data Book, 1972; Congressional District Data Book, 93rd Congress; Historical Statistics of the United States, Colonial Times to 1970.* Information concerning these and other publications may be obtained from the Supt. of Documents, Government Printing Office, Wash., D.C. 20402, or from the U.S. Bureau of the Census, Data User Services Office, Wash., D.C. 20233.

Geodetic Datum Point of North America

The geodetic datum point of the United States is the National Ocean Survey's triangulation station Meades Ranch in Osborne County, Kansas, at latitude 39° 13′26″. 686 N and longitude 98° 32′30″. 506 W. (Frequently this is referred to as the geodetic center of the U.S., which has no meaning.) This geodetic datum point is a fundamental point from which all latitude and longitude computations originate for North America and Central America.

National Parks, Other Areas Administered by Nat'l Park Service

National Parks

Acadia, Me. (1916) 41,651. Includes Mount Desert Island, half of Isle au Haut, Schoodic Point on mainland. Highest elevation on Eastern seaboard.

Arches, Utah (1929) 73,389. Contains giant red sandstone arches and other products of erosion.

Big Bend, Texas (1935) 708,118. On Rio Grande River.

Bryce Canyon, Utah (1923) 36,0344. Spectacularly colorful and unusual display of erosion effects in Southwestern Utah.

Canyonlands, Utah (1964) 344,482. At junction of Colorado and Green Rivers, extensive evidence of prehistoric Indians.

Capitol Reef, Utah (1937) 241,866. A 70-mile uplift of sandstone cliffs dissected by high-walled gorges.

Carlsbad Caverns, N.M. (1923) 46,756. Largest known underground caverns, not yet fully explored.

Crater Lake, Ore. (1902) 160,290. Extraordinary blue lake in crater of extinct volcano encircled by lava walls 500 to 2,000 feet high.

Everglades, Fla. (1934) 1,400,533. Largest remaining subtropical wilderness in Continental U.S., abundant wildlife includes rare birds.

Glacier, Mont. (1910) 1,013,277. Superb Rocky Mountain scenery, numerous glaciers and glacial lakes. Part of Waterton-Glacier International Peace Park established by U.S. and Canada in 1932.

Grand Canyon, Ariz. (1908) 673,561. Most spectacular part of Colorado River's greatest canyon.

Grand Teton, Wyo. (1929) 310,463. Most impressive part of the Teton Mountains, winter feeding ground of largest American elk herd.

Great Smoky Mountains, N.C.-Tenn. (1926) 516,860. Largest eastern mountain range, magnificent forests.

Guadalupe Mountains, Texas (1966) 79,972. Extensive and significant Permian limestone fossil reef; tremendous earth fault. INFORMATION OFFICE OPEN: **NO OTHER FACILITIES.**

Haleakala, Hawaii (1960) 27,283. 10,023 foot dormant volcano on Maui.

Hawaii Volcanoes, Hawaii (1916) 229,174. Contains Kilauea and Mauna Loa, active volcanoes on the island of Hawaii.

Hot Springs, Ark. (1832) 5,729. Government supervised bath houses use waters of 45 of the 47 natural hot springs.

Isle Royale, Mich. (1931) 539,498. Largest island in Lake Superior, noted for its wilderness area and wildlife.

Kings Canyon, Calif. (1890) 460,134. Mountains wilderness, dominated by Kings River Canyons and High Sierra, contains giant sequoias.

Lassen Volcanic, Calif. (1907) 106,446. Contains Lassen Peak, most recently active volcano in continental U.S., and other volcanic phenomena.

Mammoth Cave, Ky. (1926) 51,311. 144 miles of surveyed underground passages, beautiful natural formations, river 360 feet below surface.

Mesa Verde, Colo. (1906) 52,036. Most notable and best preserved prehistoric cliff dwellings in the United States,

Mount McKinley, Alaska (1917) 1,939,493. Highest Mountain in North America, large glaciers, and unusual wildlife.

Mount Rainier, Wash. (1899) 235,404. Greatest singlepeak glacial system in the U.S. radiates from this dormant volcano.

North Cascades, Wash. (1968) 505,000. Spectacular mountainous region with many glaciers, lakes, and rugged peaks.

Olympic, Wash. (1909) 897,360. Mountain wilderness containing finest remnant of Pacific Northwest rain forest, active glaciers, Pacific shoreline, rare elk.

Petrified Forest, Ariz. (1906) 94,189. Extensive petrified wood and Indian artifacts. Contains part of Painted Desert.

Platt, Okla. (1906) 912. Numerous natural springs.

Redwood, Calif. (1968) 56,238. Forty miles of Pacific coastline, virgin groves of ancient redwoods.

Rocky Mountain, Colo. (1915) 261,973. Beautiful scenery on the continental divide includes 107 named peaks over 11,000 feet.

Sequoia, Calif. (1890) 386,822. Groves of giant sequoias, largest mountain in conterminous United States — Mount Whitney (14,494 feet).

Shenandoah, Va. (1926) 194,248. Portion of the Blue Ridge Mountains; this park overlooks much of the famous Shenandoah Valley.

Virgin Islands, Virgin Islands (1956) 14,470. Covers ¾ of St. John Island, lush growth, lovely beaches, Indian relics, evidence of colonial Danes.

Voyageurs, Minn. (1971) 219,128. Abundant lakes, for-

ests, wildlife, unusual recreation. LIMITED FACILITIES.

Wind Cave, S.D. (1903) 28,060. Limestone Caverns in Black Hills. Extensive wildlife includes a herd of bison.

Yellowstone, Ida., Mont., Wyo., (1872) 2,219,823. Oldest and largest National Park. World's greatest geyser area has about 3,000 geysers and hot springs; the spectacular falls and impressive canyons of the Yellowstone River are major attractions.

Yosemite, Calif. (1890) 761,155. Yosemite Valley, the nation's highest waterfall, 3 groves of giant sequoias, and mountainous terrain.

Zion, Utah (1909) 146,845. Unusual shapes and landscapes have resulted from the effects of erosion and faulting activity, Zion Canyon, with sheer walls ranging up to 2,500 feet, is readily accessible.

National Historical Parks

Appomattox Court House, Va. (1930) 995. Where Lee surrendered to Grant.

Chalmette, La. (1907) 142. Scene of part of the Battle of New Orleans.

Chesapeake and Ohio Canal, Md.-W. Va.-D of C. (1961) 20,239. 185 mile historic canal; D.C. to Cumberland, Md.

City of Refuge, Hawaii (1955) 181. Until 1819, a sanctuary for Hawaiians vanquished in battle, and those guilty of crimes or breaking taboos.

Colonial, Va. (1930) 9,146. Includes most of Jamestown Island, site of first successful English colony; Yorktown site of Cornwallis' surrender to George Washington; Cape Henry Memorial, approximate site of the first landing of the Jamestown colonists; and the Colonial Parkway.

Cumberland Gap, Ky.-Tenn.-Va. (1940) 20,267. Mountain pass of the Wilderness Road which carried the first great migration of pioneers into America's interior.

George Rogers Clark, Vincennes, Ind. (1966) 23. Commemorates American defeat of British in West during Revoltuion.

Harpers Ferry, Md., W. Va. (1944) 1,530. At the confluence of the Shenandoah and Potomac Rivers, the site of John Brown's 1859 raid on the Army arsenal. Scene of several Civil War Battles.

Independence, Pa., (1948) 18. Contains several properties in Philadelphia associated with the Revolutionary War and the founding of the U.S.

Minute Man, Mass. (1959) 746. Where the colonial Minute Men battled the British, April 19, 1775. Also contains Nathaniel Hawthorne's home.

Morristown, N.J. (1933) 1,377. Sites of important military encampments during the Revolutionary War; Washington's headquarters 1777, 1779-80.

Nez Perce, Ida. (1965) 2,213. Illustrates the history and culture of the Nez Perce Indian country. 22 separate sites.

San Juan Island, Wash. (1966) 1,752. Commemorates the peaceful relations of the U.S., Canada and Great Britain since the 1872 boundary disputes at this site.

Saratoga, N.Y. (1938) 3,337. Scene of a major battle which became a turning point in the War for Independence.

Sitka, Alaska (1910) 108. Scene of last major resistance of the Tlingit Indians to the Russians, 1804.

International Park

Roosevelt-Campobello, New Brunswick, Canada (1964) 2,722. Administered by U.S.-Canadian joint commission. FDR's vacation home.

National Memorial Park

Theodore Roosevelt, N.D. (1947) 70,403. Part of T.R.'s Elkhorn Ranch along the Little Missouri River. Has bison and some original prairie.

National Battlefields

Big Hole, Mont. (1910) 1,383. Site of major battle with Nez Perce Indians.

Cowpens, S.C. (1929) 846. Revolutionary War Battlefield.

Fort Necessity, Pa. (1931) 500. First battle of French and Indian War.

Petersburg, Va. (1926) 2,310. Scene of 10-month Union campaign 1864-65.

Stones River, Tenn. (1927) 331. Civil War battle leading to Sherman's "March to the Sea."

Tupelo, Miss. (1929) 1.5 Crucial battle over Sherman's supply line.

Wilson's Creek, Mo. (1960) 1,728 Civil War battle for control of state of Missouri.

National Battlefield Parks

Kennesaw Mountain, Ga. (1917) 3,683. Two major battles of Atlanta campaign.

Manassas, Va. (1940) 3,283. Two early Civil War battles.

Richmond, Va. (1936) 742. Site of battles defending Confederate capital.

National Battlefield Sites

Antietam, Md. (1890) 1,829. End of first Confederate invasion of North.

Brices Cross Roads, Miss. (1929) 1. Civil War Battlefield.

National Military Parks

Chickamauga and Chattanooga, Ga.—Tenn. (1890) 7,976. Four Civil War Battlefields.

Fort Donelson, Tenn. (1928) 538. Site of first major Union victory.

Fredericksburg and Spotsylvania County, Va. (1927) 4,660. Sites of several major Civil War battles and campaigns.

Gettysburg, Pa. (1895) 3,788. Major Confederate defeat in North.

Guilford Courthouse, N.C. (1917) 220. Revolutionary War battle.

Horseshoe Bend, Ala. (1956) 2,040. On Tallaposa River, place where Gen. Andrew Jackson broke the power of the Creek Indian Confederacy.

Kings Mountain, S.C. (1931) 3,950. Revolutionary War battle.

Moores Creek, N.C. (1926) 50. Pre-Revolutionary War battle.

Pea Ridge, Ark. (1956) 4,279. Civil War battle.

Shiloh, Tenn. (1894) 3,702. Major Civil War battle; site includes some well-preserved Indian burial mounds.

Vicksburg, Miss. (1899) 1,741. Union victory gave North control of the Mississippi and split the Confederacy in two.

Historic Area

Fort Scott, Kan. (1965) 7. Commemorates historic events in Kansas.

National Memorials

Arkansas Post, Ark. (1960) 305. First permanent French settlement in the lower Mississippi River Valley.

Arlington House, The Robert E. Lee Memorial (Custis-Lee Mansion), Va. (1925) 3. 19th century mansion.

Benjamin Franklin, Philadelphia, Pa. (1972) 0.12. Colossal seated statue of inventor-statesman.

Chamizal, El Paso Texas (1966) 55. Commemorates 1963 settlement of 99-year border dispute with Mexico.

Coronado, Ariz.: (1952) 2,834. Commemorates first European exploration of the Southwest under Francisco Vasquez Coronado.

De Soto, Fla. (1948) 30. Commemorates 16th-century Spanish explorations.

Federal Hall, N.Y. (1939) 0.45. First seat of U.S. government.

Fort Caroline, Fla. (1950) 141. On St.Johns River, overlooks site of second attempt by French Huguenots to colonize. N.A.

Fort Clatsop, Ore. (1958) 125. Lewis and Clark encampment 1805-06.

Frederick Douglass Home, D. of C. (1962) 8. 19th-century black leader, ex-slave and Ambassador to Haiti.

General Grant, N.Y. (1958) 76. Tombs of Gen. and wife.

Hamilton Grange, N.Y. (1962) .71. Home of Alexander Hamilton.

Johnstown Flood, Pa. (1964) 108. Commemorates tragic flood.

Lincoln Boyhood, Ind. (1962) 200. Farm Lincoln grew up on.

Lincoln Memorial, D. of C. (1911) 164.

Mount Rushmore, S. D. (1925) 1,278. World famous sculpture of 4 presidents.

Perry's Victory and International Peace Memorial, Ohio (1936) 26. American naval victory, War of 1812.

Thomas Jefferson Memorial, D. of C. (1934) 18.

Washington Monument, D. of C. (1848) 106.

Wright Brothers, N.C. (1927) 431. First powered flight.

National Historic Sites

Abraham Lincoln Birthplace, Hodgenville, Ky. (1916) 117.

Adams, Quincy, Mass. (1946) 8. Home of Presidents John Adams, John Quincy Adams, and celebrated descendants.

Allegheny Portage Railroad, Pa. (1964) 767. Part of the Pennsylvania Canal system.

Andersonville, Andersonville, Ga. (1970) 494. Noted Civil War prison. LIMITED FEDERAL FACILITIES.

Andrew Johnson, Greeneville, Tenn. (1935) 17. Home of the President.

Ansley Wilcox House, Buffalo, N.Y. (1966) (Where President Theodore Roosevelt took the oath of office.

Bent's Old Fort, Colo. (1960) 178. Old West fur-trading post.

Chicago Portage, Chi., Ill. (1952) 91. Part of original trader's link between the Great Lakes and the Mississippi River.

Chimney Rock, Nebr. (1956) 83. Landmark and campsite on Oregon Trail.

Christiansted, St. Croix; Virgin Islands (1952) 27. Commemorates Danish colony.

Dorchester Heights, Boston, Mass. (1951) 5. Memorial tower to colonial batteries, 1776.

Edison, West Orange, N.J. (1955) 20. Home and laboratory.

Ford's Theatre, Washington, D.C. (1866) 0.25. Includes theater, now restored, where Lincoln was assassinated, house where he died, and Lincoln Museum.

Fort Bowie, Ariz. (1964) 970. Focal point of operations against Geronimo and the Apaches. LIMITED FACILITIES.

Fort Davis, Texas (1961) 460. Frontier outpost battled Comanches and Apaches.

Fort Laramie, Wyo. (1938) 563. Military post on Oregon Trail.

Fort Larned, Kan. (1964) 681. Military post on Santa Fe Trail.

Fort Point, San Francisco, Calif. (1970) 96. Largest West Coast fortification.

Fort Raleigh, N.C. (1941) 160. First English settlement.

Fort Smith, Ark. (1961) 19. Active post from 1817 to 1890.

Fort Union Trading Post, Mont., N.D. (1966) 446. Principal fur-trading post on upper Missouri, 1828-1867. LIMITED FACILITIES.

Fort Vancouver, Wash. (1948) 170. Hdqts. for Hudson's Bay Company in 1825. Early military and political seat of Pacific N.W.

Gloria Dei Church, Philadelphia, Pa. (1942) 3. Second oldest Swedish church in U.S., founded 1677, built approx. 1700.

Golden Spike, Utah (1957) 2,172. Commemorates completion of first transcontinental railroad in 1869.

Hampton, Md. (1948) 45. 18th-century Georgian mansion.

Herbert Hoover, West Branch, Iowa (1965) 148. Home of the President.

Home of Franklin D. Roosevelt, Hyde Park, N.Y. (1944) 188. Birthplace, home and "Summer White House".

Hopewell Village, Pa. (1938) 848. 19th-century iron making.

Hubbell Trading Post, Ariz. (1965) 160. Indian trading post.

Jamestown, Va. (1940) 21. First permanent English settlement.

Jefferson National Expansion Memorial, St. Louis, Mo. (1935) 94. Commemorates westward expansion with park and memorial arch.

John Fitzgerald Kennedy, Brookline, Mass. (1967) .09. Birthplace and childhood home of the President.

John Muir, Martinez, Calif. (1964) 9. Early conservationist and writer.

Lincoln Home, Springfield, Ill. (1971) 12. Residence when he was elected President, 1860. NO FEDERAL FACILITIES.

Longfellow, Mass. (1972) 2. Longfellow's home, 1837-82, and Washington's hq. during Boston Siege, 1775-76. NO FEDERAL FACILITIES.

Lyndon B. Johnson, Johnson City, Texas (1969) 8. Birthplace and boyhood home of the 36th President.

McLoughlin House, Oregon City, Ore. (1941) 63. Home of Dr. John McLoughlin, "The father of Oregon."

Pennsylvania Avenue, Wash. D.C. (1965) Area between the White House and the Capitol.

Sagamore Hill, Oyster Bay, N.Y. (1962) 85. Home of President Theodore Roosevelt from 1885 until his death in 1919.

Saint-Gaudens, Cornish. N.H. (1964) 86. Home, studio and gardens of American sculptor Augustus Saint-Gaudens.

Saint Paul's Church, Mount Vernon, N.Y. (1943) 6. Architectural landmark, had important role in Revolutionary War and the establishment of the freedom of the press.

St. Thomas, Charlotte Amalie, V.I. (1960) 2. Contains Fort Christian, oldest (1680) structure in the Virgin Islands, part of Danish settlemnt. NO VISITOR FACILITIES.

Salem Maritime, Mass. (1938) 11. Only port never seized from the Patriots by the British. Major fishing and whaling port.

San Jose Mission, San Antonio, Texas (1941) 4. Spanish mission established in 1720.

San Juan, Puerto Rico (1949) 48. 16th-century Spanish fortifications.

Saugus Iron Works, Mass. (1968) 9. Reconstructed 17th-century colonial ironworks.

Theodore Roosevelt Birthplace, N.Y., N.Y. (1962) 11.

Theodore Roosevelt Inaugural, Buffalo, N.Y. (1966) 1. Wilcox House where he took oath of office, 1901. NO

FEDERAL FACILITIES.

Touro Synagogue, Newport, R.I. (1946) 23. Colonial Syn.

Vanderbilt Mansion, Hyde Park, N.Y. (1940) 212. Mansion of 19th-century financier.

Whitman Mission, Wash. (1936) 98. Site where Dr. and Mrs. Marcus Whitman ministered to the Indians until slain, 1847.

William Howard Taft, Cincinnati, Ohio (1969) 0.78. Birth-place and early home of the 27th President, 1909-13; Chief Justice, 1921-30. **LIMITED FACILITIES.**

National Capital Parks

District of Columbia — Maryland — Virginia (1790) 7,052. Includes 704 reservations.

White House

Washington, D.C. (1961) 18. Presidential residence since November 1800.

National Monuments

Name	State	Year	Acreage
Agate Fossil Beds	Nebr	1965	3,050
Alibates Flint Quarries and Texas Panhandle Pueblo Culture*	Tex	1965	93
Aztec Ruins	N.M.	1923	27
Badlands	S.D.	1929	243,508
Bandelier	N.M.	1916	29,661
Biscayne**	Fla.	1968	95,127
Black Canyon of the Gunnison	Colo.	1933	13,671
Booker T. Washington	Va.	1956	218
Buck Island Reef	Virgin Isls.	1961	850
Cabrillo	Calif.	1913	123
Canyon de Chelly	Ariz.	1931	83,840
Capulin Mountain	N.M.	1916	775
Casa Grande Ruins	Ariz.	1892	473
Castillo de San Marcos	Fla.	1924	20
Castle Clinton	N.Y.	1946	1
Cedar Breaks	Utah	1933	6,155
Chaco Canyon	N.M.	1907	21,510
Channel Islands	Calif.	1938	18,167
Chiricahua	Ariz.	1924	10,648
Colorado	Colo.	1911	17,669
Craters of the Moon	Idaho	1924	53,545
Custer Battlefield	Mont.	1879	765
Death Valley	Calif.-Nev.	1933	1,913,985
Devils Postpile	Calif.	1911	798
Devils Tower	Wyo.	1906	1,347
Dinosaur	Colo.-Utah	1915	207,398
Effigy Mounds	Iowa	1949	1,467
El Morro	N.M.	1906	1,279
Florissant Fossil Beds**	Colo.	1969	5,992
Fort Frederica	Ga.	1936	215
Fort Jefferson	Fla.	1935	47,125
Fort McHenry National Monument & Historic Shrine	Md.	1925	43
Fort Matanzas	Fla.	1924	299
Fort Pulaski	Ga.	1924	5,517
Fort Stanwix*	N.Y.	1935	18
Fort Sumter	S.C.	1948	34
Fort Union	N.M.	1954	721
Fossil Butte*	Wyo.	1972	8,178
G. Washington Birthplace	Va.	1930	456
George Washington Carver	Mo.	1943	210

Name	State	Year	Acreage
Gila Cliff Dwellings	N.M.	1907	533
Glacier Bay	Alaska	1925	2,805,269
Grand Canyon	Ariz.	1932	198,260
Grand Portage	Minn.	1951	710
Gran Quivira	N.M.	1909	611
Great Sand Dunes	Colo.	1932	36,696
Hohokam Pima*	Ariz.	1972	1,555
Homestead Nat'l. Monument of America	Nebr.	1936	195
Hovenweep	Colo-Utah	1923	505
Jewel Cave	S.D.	1908	1,275
Joshua Tree	Calif.	1936	558,234
Katmai	Alaska	1918	2,792,137
Lava Beds	Calif.	1925	46,239
Lehman Caves	Nev.	1922	640
Marble Canyon	Ariz.	1969	26,080
Montezuma Castle	Ariz.	1906	842
Mound City Group	Ohio	1923	68
Muir Woods	Calif.	1908	554
Natural Bridges	Utah	1908	8,011
Navajo	Ariz.	1909	360
Ocmulgee	Ga.	1934	683
Oregon Caves	Ore.	1909	480
Organ Pipe Cactus	Ariz.	1937	330,878
Pecos	N.M.	1965	341
Pinnacles	Calif.	1908	14,498
Pipe Spring	Ariz.	1923	40
Pipestone	Minn.	1937	282
Rainbow Bridge	Utah	1910	160
Russell Cave	Ala.	1961	310
Saguaro	Ariz.	1933	78,986
Saint Croix Island**	Me.	1949	35
Scotts Bluff	Nebr.	1919	3,060
Statue of Liberty	N.J.-N.Y.	1924	58
Sunset Crater	Ariz.	1930	3,040
Timpanogos Cave	Utah	1922	250
Tonto	Ariz.	1907	1,120
Tumacacori	Ariz.	1908	10
Tuzigoot	Ariz.	1939	52
Walnut Canyon	Ariz.	1915	1,879
White Sands	N.M.	1933	144,855
Wupatki	Ariz.	1924	35,253
Yucca House*	Color.	1919	10

National Cemeteries

Antietam	Md.	1870	11
Battleground	D. of C.	1867	1
Fort Donelson	Tenn.	1867	15
Fredericksburg	Va.	1865	12
Gettysburg	Penn.	1870	21
Poplar Grove	Va.	1866	9
Shiloh	Tenn.	1866	10
Stones River	Tenn.	1865	20
Vicksburg	Miss.	1865	118
Yorktown	Va.	1866	3

National Seashores

Assateague Island	Md.-Va.	1965	39,631
Cape Cod	Mass.	1961	44,600
Cape Hatteras	N.C.	1937	28,500
Cape Lookout**	N.C.	1966	24,500
Cumberland Island*	Ga.	1972	39,494
Fire Island	N.Y.	1964	19,311

Gulf Islands, Fla.-Miss. (1971) 124,690. White sand beaches, primitive off-shore islands, historic forts**

Padre Island	Texas	1962	133,918
Point Reyes	Calif.	1962	64,546

National Lakeshores

Apostle Islands, Wis. (1970) 42,826. Picturesque islands and coastal portion of Bayfield Peninsula on south shore of Lake Superior**

Indiana Dunes**	Ind.	1966	8,330
Pictured Rocks**	Mich.	1966	67,000

Sleeping Bear Dunes,Mich.(1970)71,105.Notable for its beaches, massive sand dunes, forests, lakes. **Benzie and D.** H. Day State Parks open to public.**

National River

Buffalo	Ark.	1972	95,840

National Scenic Riverways

Lower Saint Croix**	Minn.-Wis.	1972	7,845
Ozark	Mo.	1964	82,321
Saint Croix**	Minn.-Wis.	1968	67,747
Wolf**	Wis.	1968	5,516

National Recreation Areas

Amistad	Texas	1965	65,000
Arbuckle	Okla.	1965	5,631
Bighorn Canyon	Mont.-Wy.	1964	140,459
Coulee Dam	Wash.	1946	100,059
Curecanti	Colo.	1965	41,572
Delaware Water Gap**	N.J.-Pa.	1965	58,985
Gateway**	N.Y.-N.J.	1972	26,172
Glen Canyon	Ariz.-Utah	1958	1,236,880
Golden Gate**	Calif.	1972	34,202
Lake Chelan	Wash.	1968	62,000
Lake Mead	Ariz.-Nev.	1936	1,936,978
Ross Lake	Wash.	1968	107,000
Lake Meredith	Texas	1965	41,097
Shadow Mountain	Colo.	1952	18,240
Whiskeytown-Shasta-Trinity	Calif.	1962	42,445

National Scenic Trail

Appalachian	Me. to Ga.	1968	50,000

National Scientific Reserve

Ice Age	Wis.	1964	32,500

*Not Open to the Public **Limited or No Federal Facilities

Statue of Liberty National Monument

Since 1886 the Statue of Liberty Enlightening the World has stood as a symbol of freedom in New York harbor. It also commemorates Franco-American friendship for it was given by the people of France, designed by Frederic Auguste Bartholdi (1834-1904). A $2.5 million building housing the American Museum of Immigration was opened by Pres. Nixon Sept. 26, 1972, at the base of the statue. Exhibit halls, a library and study rooms as well as a hall of records will be grouped within the star-shaped Fort Wood which encompasses the statue. The statue is a National Monument, administered by the National Park Service.

Edouard de Laboulaye, French historian and admirer of American political institutions, suggested that the French present a monument to the United States, the latter to provide pedestal and site. Bartholdi visualized a colossal statue at the entrance of New York harbor, welcoming the peoples of the world with the torch of liberty.

The French approved the idea and formed the Franco-American Union to raise funds, which eventually reached $250,000. Bartholdi began work about 1874 in Paris. He made several models and one 36 ft. tall, enabled him to compute the statue in sections. Wooden battens were made and sheets of copper 3/32 of an inch thick were hammered into shape on them by hand. A framework of four steel supports was designed by Gustave Eiffel, creator of the Eiffel Tower.

On Washington's birthday, Feb. 22, 1877, Congress approved the use of a site on Bedloe's island suggested by Bartholdi. This island of 12 acres had been owned in the 17th century by a Walloon named Isaac Bedloe, who came to New Amsterdam in 1639. He died in 1673 and his wife sold the island for £ 80. In later years it was owned by the City of New York and the U.S. Government. It was called Bedloe's until Aug. 3, 1956, when President Eisenhower approved a resolution of Congress changing the name to Liberty Island.

The hand of the statue holding aloft the torch was exhibited at the Centennial Exposition in Philadelphia in 1876 and later in Madison Square.

The head was shown at the Paris exposition of 1878. When framework and base were put in place in Paris the American minister, Levi P. Morton, drove the first rivet on Oct. 24, 1881, in honor of the centennial of the battle of Yorktown, in which the French and Americans were allies.

The statue was finished May 21, 1884, and formally presented to U.S. Minister Morton July 4, 1884, by Ferdinand de Lesseps, head of the Franco-American Union and promoter of the Panama Canal.

On Aug. 5, 1884, the Americans laid the cornerstone for the pedestal. This was to be built on the foundations of Fort Wood, which had been erected by the government in 1811. The American committee had raised $125,000, but when the pedestal was 15 ft. high, this was found to be inadequate. Joseph Pulitzer, owner of the New York World appealed on Mar. 16, 1885, for general donations. By Aug. 11, 1885, he had raised $100,000. The pedestal was made of concrete with granite facing and steel girders were built into it to connect with framework of the statue.

The statue arrived dismantled, in 214 packing cases, in the steamship Isere, which reached New York from Rouen, France, in June, 1885. The last rivet of the statue was driven Oct. 28, 1886, when President Grover Cleveland dedicated the monument. The total cost of statue and pedestal was estimated at $500,000.

Funds for permanently lighting the statue were raised by the World in 1916 and President Wilson turned on the lights Dec. 2, 1916.

At the celebration of the statue's 50th anniversary, in 1936, President Franklin D. Roosevelt said: "The realization that we are all bound together by hope of a common future rather than by reverence for a common past has helped us to build upon this continent a unity unapproached in any similar area or similar-size population in the whole world. For all our millions of people, there is a unity in language and speech, in law and economics, in education and in general purpose which nowhere finds its match.

"It was the hope of those who gave us this statue and the hope of the American people in receiving it that the Goddess of Liberty and the Goddess of Peace were the same."

The statue weighs 450,000 lbs. or 225 tons. The copper sheeting weighs 200,000 lbs. There are 167 steps from the land level to the top of the pedestal, 168 steps inside the statue to the head, and 54 rungs on the ladder leading to the arm that holds the torch. Visitors may enter the head, which holds from 30 to 40 persons, but not the torch. The statue is open daily.

Dimensions of the Statue

	Ft.	In.
Height from base to torch (45.3 meters)	151	1
Foundation of pedestal to torch (91.5 meters)	305	1
Heel to top of head	111	1
Length of hand	16	5
Index finger	8	0
Circumference at second joint	3	6
Size of finger nail . . . . 13x10 in.		
Head from chin to cranium	17	3
Head, thickness from ear to ear	10	0
Distance across the eye	2	6
Length of nose	4	6
Right arm, length	42	0
Right arm, greatest thickness	12	0
Thickness of waist	35	0
Width of mouth	3	0
Tablet, length	23	7
Tablet, width	13	7
Tablet, thickness	2	0

Emma Lazarus' Famous Poem

A poem by Emma Lazarus is graven on a tablet within the pedestal on which the statue stands:

The New Colossus

Not like the brazen giant of Greek fame,
With conquering limbs astride from land to land;
Here at our sea-washed, sunset gates shall stand
A mighty woman with a torch, whose flame
Is the imprisoned lightning, and her name
Mother of Exiles. From her beacon-hand
Glows world-wide welcome; her mild eyes command
The air-bridged harbor that twin cities frame.
"Keep ancient lands, your storied pomp!" cries she
With silent lips. "Give me your tired, your poor,
Your huddled masses yearning to breathe free,
The wretched refuse of your teeming shore.
Send these, the homeless, tempest-tost to me,
I lift my lamp beside the golden door!"

Nearby Ellis Island, abandoned as an immigration center in 1954 after serving as the gateway to America for 16,000,000, was proclaimed by President Johnson in 1965 part of the Statue of Liberty National Monument.

LAWS AND DOCUMENTS

Declaration of Independence

The Declaration of Independence was adopted by the Continental Congress in Philadelphia, on July 4, 1776. John Hancock was president of the Congress and Charles Thomson was secretary. A copy of the Declaration, engrossed on parchment, was signed by members of Congress on and after Aug. 2, 1776. On Jan. 18, 1777, Congress ordered that "authenticated copies, with the names of the members of Congress subscribed the same, be sent to each of the United States, and that they be desired to have same put upon record." Authenticated copies were printed in broadside form in Baltimore, where the Continental Congress was then in session. The following text is that of the original printed by John Dunlap at Philadelphia for the Continental Congress.

IN CONGRESS, July 4, 1776.

A DECLARATION
By the REPRESENTATIVES of the
UNITED STATES OF AMERICA,
In GENERAL CONGRESS assembled

When in the Course of human Events, it becomes necessary for one People to dissolve the Political Bands which have connected them with another, and to assume among the Powers of the Earth, the separate and equal Station to which the Laws of Nature and of Nature's God entitle them, a decent Respect to the Opinions of Mankind requires that they should declare the causes which impel them to the Separation.

We hold these Truths to be self-evident, that all Men are created equal, that they are endowed by their Creator with certain unalienable Rights, that among these are Life, Liberty, and the Pursuit of Happiness—That to secure these Rights, Governments are instituted among Men, deriving their just Powers from the Consent of the Governed, that whenever any Form of government becomes destructive of these Ends, it is the Right of the People to alter or to abolish it, and to institute new Government, laying its Foundation on such Principles, and organizing its Powers in such Form, as to them shall seem most likely to effect their Safety and Happiness. Prudence, indeed, will dictate that Governments long established should not be changed for light and transient Causes; and accordingly all Experience hath shewn, that Mankind are more disposed to suffer, while Evils are sufferable, than to right themselves by abolishing the Forms to which they are accustomed. But when a long Train of Abuses and Usurpations, pursuing invariably the same Object, evinces a Design to reduce them under absolute Despotism, it is their Right, it is their Duty, to throw off such Government, and to provide new Guards for their future Security. Such has been the patient Sufferance of these Colonies; and such is now the Necessity which constrains them to alter their former Systems of Government. The History of the present King of Great-Britain is a History of repeated Injuries and Usurpations, all having in direct Object the Establishment of an absolute Tyranny over these States. To prove this, let Facts be sumitted to a candid World.

He has refused his Assent to Laws, the most wholesome and necessary for the public Good.

He has forbidden his Governors to pass Laws of immediate and pressing Importance, unless suspended in their Operation till his Assent should be obtained; and when so suspended, he has utterly neglected to attend to them.

He has refused to pass other Laws for the Accommodation of large Districts of People, unless those People would relinquish the Right of Representation in the Legislature, a Right inestimable to them, and formidable to Tyrants only.

He has called together Legislative Bodies at Places unusual, uncomfortable, and distant from the Depository of their public Records, for the sole Purpose of fatiguing them into Compliance with his Measures.

He has dissolved Representative Houses repeatedly, for opposing with manly Firmness his Invasions on the Rights of the People.

He has refused for a long Time, after such Dissolutions, to cause others to be elected; whereby the Legislative Powers, incapable of Annihilation, have returned to the People at large for their exercise; the State remaining in the mean time exposed to all the Dangers of Invasion from without, and Convulsions within.

He has endeavoured to prevent the Population of these States; for that Purpose obstructing the Laws for Naturalization of Foreigners; refusing to pass others to encourage their Migrations hither, and raising the Conditions of new Appropriations of Lands.

He has obstructed the Administration of Justice, by refusing his Assent to Laws for establising Judiciary Powers.

He has made Judges dependent on his Will alone, for the Tenure of their Offices, and the Amount and payment of their Salaries.

He has erected a Multitude of new Offices, and sent hither Swarms of Officers to harrass our People, and eat out their Substance.

He has kept among us, in Times of Peace, Standing Armies, without the consent of our Legislatures.

He has affected to render the Military independent of and superior to the Civil Power.

He has combined with others to subject us to a Jurisdiction foreign to our Constitution, and unacknowledged by our Laws; giving his Assent to their Acts of pretended Legislation:

For quartering large Bodies of Armed Troops among us:

For protecting them, by a mock Trial, from Punishment for any Murders which they should commit on the Inhabitants of these States:

For cutting off our Trade with all Parts of the World:

For imposing Taxes on us without our Consent:

For depriving us, in many Cases, of the Benefits of Trial by Jury:

For transporting us beyond Seas to be tried for pretended Offences:

For abolishing the free System of English Laws in a neighbouring Province, establishing therein an arbitrary Government, and enlarging its Boundaries, so as to render it at once an Example and fit Instrument for introducing the same absolute Rule into these Colonies:

For taking away our Charters, abolishing our most valuable Laws, and altering fundamentally the Forms of our Governments:

For suspending our own Legislatures, and declaring themselves invested with Power to legislate for us in all Cases whatsoever.

He has abdicated Government here, by declaring us out of his Protection and waging War against us.

He has plundered our Seas, ravaged our Coasts, burnt our towns, and destroyed the Lives of our People.

He is, at this Time, transporting large Armies of foreign Mercenaries to compleat the works of Death, Desolation, and Tyranny, already begun with circumstances of Cruelty and Perfidy, scarcely paralleled in the most barbarous Ages, and totally unworthy the Head of a civilized Nation.

He has constrained our fellow Citizens taken Captive on the high Seas to bear Arms against their Country, to become the Executioners of their Friends and Brethren, or to fall themselves by their Hands.

He has excited domestic Insurrections amongst us, and has endeavoured to bring on the Inhabitants of our Frontiers, the merciless Indian Savages, whose known Rule of Warfare, is an undistinguished Destruction, of all Ages, Sexes and Conditions.

In every stage of these Oppressions we have Petitioned for Redress in the most humble Terms: Our repeated

Petitions have been answered only by repeated Injury. A Prince, whose Character is thus marked by every act which may define a Tyrant, is unfit to be the Ruler of a free People.

Nor have we been wanting in Attentions to our British Brethren. We have warned them from Time to Time of Attempts by their Legislature to extend an unwarrantable Jurisdiction over us. We have reminded them of the Circumstances of our Emigration and Settlement here. We have appealed to their native Justice and Magnanimity, and we have conjured them by the Ties of our common Kindred to disavow these Usurpations, which, would inevitably interrupt our Connections and Correspondence. They too have been deaf to the Voice of Justice and of Consanguinity. We must, therefore, acquiesce in the Necessity, which denounces our Separation, and hold them, as we hold the rest of Mankind, Enemies in War, in Peace, Friends.

We, therefore, the Representatives of the UNITED STATES OF AMERICA, in General Congress, Assembled, appealing to the Supreme Judge of the World in the Rectitude of our Intentions, do, in the Name, and by Authority of the good People of these Colonies, solemnly Publish and Declare, That these United Colonies are, and of Right ought to be, Free and Independent States; that they are absolved from all Allegiance to the British Crown, and that all political Connection between them and the State of Great-Britain, is and ought to be totally dissolved; and that as Free and Independent States, they have full Power to levy War, conclude Peace, contract Alliances, establish Commerce, and to do all other Acts and Things which Independent States may of right do. And for the support of this declaration, with a firm Reliance on the Protection of divine Providence, we mutually pledge to each other our lives, our Fortunes, and our sacred Honor.

JOHN HANCOCK, President.

Attest.

CHARLES THOMSON, Secretary.

Signers of the Declaration of Independence

Delegate and State	Vocation	Birthplace	Born	Died
Adams, John (Mass.)	Lawyer	Braintree (Quincy), Mass	1735, Oct. 30	1826, July 4
Adams, Samuel (Mass.)	Political Leader	Boston, Mass.	1722, Sept. 27	1803, Oct. 2
Bartlett, Josiah (N. H.)	Physician, Jurist	Amesbury, Mass.	1729, Nov. 21	1795, May 19
Braxton, Carter (Va.)	Farmer	King & Queen C.H. Va.	1736, Sept. 10	1797, Oct. 10
Carroll, Chas. of Carrollton (Md.)	Lawyer	Annapolis, Md.	1737, Sept. 19	1832, Nov. 14
Chase, Samuel (Md.)	Jurist	Princess Anne, Md.	1741, April 17	1811, June 19
Clark, Abraham (N. J.)	Surveyor	Elizabeth, N. J.	1726, Feb. 15	1794, Sept. 15
Clymer, George (Pa.)	Merchant	Philadelphia, Pa.	1739, March 16	1813, Jan. 23
Ellery, William (R. I.)	Jurist	Newport, R. I.	1727, Dec. 22	1820, Feb. 15
Floyd, William (N. Y.)	Soldier	Brookhaven, N. Y.	1734, Dec. 17	1821, Aug. 4
Franklin, Benjamin (Pa.)	Printer, Publisher	Boston, Mass.	1706, Jan. 17	1790, April 17
Gerry, Elbridge (Mass.)	Merchant	Marblehead, Mass.	1744, July 17	1814, Nov. 23
Gwinnett, Button (Ga.)	Merchant	Down Hatherly, Eng.	1732	1777, May 19
Hall, Lyman (Ga.)	Physician	Wallingford, Conn.	1724, April 12	1790, Oct. 19
Hancock, John (Mass.)	Merchant	Braintree (Quincy), Mass.	1737, Jan. 12	1793, Oct. 8
Harrison, Benjamin (Va.)	Farmer	Berkeley, Va.	1726, April 5	1791, April 24
Hart, John (N. J.)	Farmer	Stonington, Conn.	(1707-1711?)	1779, May 11
Hewes, Joseph (N. C.)	Merchant	Kingston, N. J.	1730, Jan. 23	1779, Nov. 10
Heyward, Thos. Jr. (S. C.)	Lawyer, Farmer	St. Luke's Parish, S. C.	1746, July 28	1809, March 6
Hooper, William (N. C.)	Lawyer	Boston, Mass.	1742, June 28	1790, Oct. 14
Hopkins, Stephen (R. I.)	Jurist, Educator	Providence, R. I.	1707, March 7	1785, July 13
Hopkinson, Francis (N. J.)	Jurist, Author	Philadelphia, Pa.	1737, Sept. 21	1791, May 9.
Huntington, Samuel (Conn.)	Jurist	Windham County, Conn.	1731, July 3	1796, Jan. 5
Jefferson, Thomas (Va.)	Lawyer	Old Shadwell, Va.	1743, April 13	1826, July 4
Lee, Richard Henry (Va.)	Farmer	Stratford, Va.	1732, Jan. 20	1794, June 19
Lee, Francis Lightfoot (Va.)	Farmer	Stratford, Va.	1734, Oct. 14	1797, Jan. 11
Lewis, Francis (N. Y.)	Merchant	Landaff, Wales	1713, March	1803, Dec. 30
Livingston, Philip (N. Y.)	Merchant	Albany, N. Y.	1716, Jan. 15	1778, June 12
Lynch, Thomas Jr. (S. C.)	Farmer	Winyah, S. C.	1749, Aug. 5	1779, (at sea)
McKean, Thomas (Del.)	Lawyer	New London, Pa.	1734, March 19	1817, June 24
Middleton, Arthur (S. C.)	Farmer	Charleston, S. C.	1742, June 26	1787, Jan. 1
Morris, Lewis (N. Y.)	Farmer	Morrisania, N. Y. (N.Y.C.)	1726, April 8	1798, Jan. 22
Morris, Robert (Pa.)	Merchant	Liverpool, Eng.	1734, Jan. 20	1806, May 8
Morton, John (Pa.)	Jurist	Ridley, Pa.	1724	1777, April
Nelson, Thos. Jr. (Va.)	Farmer	Yorktown, Va.	1738, Dec. 26	1789, Jan. 4
Paca, William (Md.)	Jurist	Abingdon, Md.	1740, Oct. 31	1799, Oct. 23
Paine, Robert Treat (Mass.)	Jurist	Boston, Mass.	1731, March 11	1814, May 12
Penn, John (N. C.)	Lawyer	Near Port Royal, Va.	1741, May 17	1788, Sept. 14
Read, George (Del.)	Jurist	Near North East, Md.	1733, Sept. 18	1798, Sept. 21
Rodney, Caesar (Del.)	Jurist	Dover, Del.	1728, Oct. 7	1784, June 29
Ross, George (Pa.)	Jurist	New Castle, Del.	1730, May 10	1779, July 14
Rush, Benjamin (Pa.)	Physician	Byberry, Pa. (Philadelphia)	1745, Dec. 24	1813, April 19
Rutledge, Edward (S. C.)	Lawyer	Charleston, S. C.	1749, Nov. 23	1800, Jan. 23
Sherman, Roger (Conn.)	Lawyer	Newton, Mass.	1721 April 19	1793, July 23
Smith, James (Pa.)	Lawyer	Dublin, Ireland.	1713	1806, July 11
Stockton, Richard (N. J.)	Lawyer	Near Princeton, N. J.	1730, Oct. 1	1781, Feb. 28
Stone, Thomas (Md.)	Lawyer	Charles County, Md.	1743	1787, Oct. 5
Taylor, George (Pa.)	Ironmaster	Ireland	1716	1781, Feb. 23
Thornton, Matthew (N. H.)	Physician	Ireland	1714	1803, June 24
Walton, George (Ga.)	Jurist	Prince Edward County, Va.	1741	1804, Feb. 2
Whipple, William (N. H.)	Merchant, Jurist	Kittery, Maine	1730, Jan. 14	1785, Nov. 28
Williams, William (Conn.)	Merchant	Lebanon, Conn	1731, April 23	1811, Aug. 2
Wilson, James (Pa.)	Jurist	Carskerdo, Scotland.	1742, Sept. 14	1798, Aug. 28
Witherspoon, John (N. J.)	Educator	Gifford, Scotland	1723, Feb. 5	1794, Nov. 15
Wolcott, Oliver (Conn.)	Jurist	Windsor, Conn.	1726, Dec. 1	1797, Dec. 1
Wythe, George (Va.)	Lawyer	Elizabeth City, Va.	1726	1806, June 8

How the Declaration of Independence Was Adopted

On June 7, 1776, Richard Henry Lee, who had issued the first call for a congress of the colonies, introduced in the Continental Congress at Philadelphia a resolution declaring "that these United Colonies are, and of right ought to be, free and independent states, that they are absolved from all allegiance to the British Crown, and that all political connection between them and the state of Great Britain is, and ought to be, totally dissolved."

The resolution, seconded by John Adams on behalf of the Massachusetts delegation, came up again June 10 when a committee of 5, headed by Thomas Jefferson, was appointed to express the purpose of the resolution in a declaration of independence. The others on the committee were John Adams, Benjamin Franklin, Robert R. Livingston, and Roger Sherman.

Drafting the Declaration was assigned to Jefferson, who worked on a portable desk of his own construction in a room at Market and 7th Sts. The committee reported the result June 28, 1776. The members of the Congress suggested a number of changes, which Jefferson called "deplorable." They didn't approve Jefferson's arraignment of the British people and King George III for encouraging and fostering the slave trade, which Jefferson called "an execrable commerce." They made 86 changes, eliminating 480 words and leaving 1,337. In the final form capitalization was erratic. Jefferson had written that men were endowed with "inalienable" rights; in the final copy it came out as "unalienable" and has been thus ever since.

The Lee-Adams resolution of independence was adopted by 12 yeas July 2 — the actual date of the act of independence. The Declaration, which explains the act, was adopted July 4, in the evening.

After the Declaration was adopted, July 4, 1776, it was turned over to John Dunlap, printer, to be printed on broadsides. The original copy was lost and one of his broadsides was attached to a page in the journal of the Congress. It was read aloud July 8 in Philadelphia, Easton, Pa., and Trenton, N. J. On July 9 at 6 p.m. it was read by order of Gen. George Washington to the troops assembled on the Common in New York City (City Hall Park).

The Continental Congress on July 19, 1776, adopted the following resolution:

"Resolved, That the Declaration passed on the 4th, be fairly engrossed on parchment with the title and stile of 'The unanimous Declaration of the thirteen united States of America' and that the same, when engrossed, be signed by every member of Congress."

Not all delegates who signed the engrossed Declaration were present on July 4. Robert Morris (Pa.), William Williams (Conn.) and Samual Chase (Md.) signed on Aug. 2. Oliver Wolcott (Conn.), George Wythe (Va.), Richard Henry Lee (Va.) and Elbridge Gerry (Mass.) signed in August and September. Matthew Thornton (N. H.) joined the Congress Nov. 4 and signed later. Thomas McKean (Del.) rejoined Washington's Army before signing and said later that he signed in 1781.

Charles Carroll of Carrollton was appointed a delegate by Maryland on July 4, 1776, presented his credentials July 18, and signed the engrossed Declaration Aug. 2. Born Sept. 19, 1737, he was 95 years old and the last surviving signer when he died Nov. 14, 1832.

Two Pennsylvania delegates who did not support the Declaration on July 4 were replaced.

The 4 New York delegates did not have authority from their state to vote on July 4. On July 9 the New York state convention authorized its delegates to approve the Declaration and the Congress was so notified on July 15, 1776. The 4 signed the Declaration on Aug. 2.

The original engrossed Declaration is preserved in the National Archives Building in Washington.

The Liberty Bell; Its History and Significance

The Liberty Bell, in Independence Hall, Philadelphia, is an object of great reverence to Americans because of its association with the historic events of the War of Independence.

The original Province bell, ordered to commemorate the 50th anniversary of the Commonwealth of Pennsylvania, was cast by Thomas Lister, Whitechapel, London, and reached Philadelphia in August 1752. It bore an inscription from Leviticus XXV, 10: "Proclaim liberty throughout all the land unto all the inhabitants thereof."

The bell was cracked by a stroke of its clapper in September 1752 while it hung on a truss in the State House yard for testing. Pass & Stow, Philadelphia founders, recast the bell, adding 1½ ounces of copper to a pound of the original metal to reduce brittleness. It was found that the bell contained too much copper, injuring its tone, so Pass & Stow recast it again, this time successfully.

In June 1753 the bell was hung in the wooden steeple of the State House, erected on top of the brick tower. In use while the Continental Congress was in session in the State House, it rang out in defiance of British tax and trade restrictions, and proclaimed the Boston Tea Party and the first public reading of the Declaration of Independence.

On Sept. 18, 1777, when the British Army was about to occupy Philadelphia, the bell was moved in a baggage train of the American Army to Allentown, Pa., where it was hidden in the Zion Reformed Church until June 27, 1778. It was moved back to Philadelphia after the British left.

In July 1781 the wooden steeple became insecure and had to be taken down. The bell was lowered into the brick section of the tower. Here it was hanging in July, 1835, when it cracked while tolling for the funeral of John Marshall, chief justice of the United States. Because of its association with the War of Independence it was not recast but remained mute in this location until 1846, the year of the Mexican War, when it was placed on exhibition in the Declaration Chamber of Independence Hall.

In 1876, when many thousands of Americans visited Philadelphia for the Centennial Exposition, it was placed in its old walnut frame in the tower hallway. In 1877 it was hung from the ceiling of the tower by a chain of 13 links. It was returned again to the Declaration Chamber and in 1896 taken back to the tower hall, where it occupied a glass case. In 1915 the case was removed so that the public might touch it. It remains there today.

The measurements of the bell follow: Circumference around the lip, 12 ft.; circumference around the crown, 7 ft. 6 in.; lip to the crown, 3 ft.; height over the crown, 2 ft. 3 in.; thickness at lip, 3 in.; thickness at crown, 1¼ in.; weight, 2080 lbs.; length of clapper, 3 ft. 2 in.; cost, L 60 14s 5d.

Origin of the United States National Motto

In God We Trust, designated as the U. S. National Motto by Congress in 1956, originated during the Civil War as an inscription for U. S. coins, although it was used by Francis Scott Key in a slightly different form when he wrote The Star-Spangled Banner in 1814. On Nov. 13, 1861, when Union morale had been shaken by battlefield defeats, the Rev. M. R. Watkinson, of Ridleyville, Pa., wrote to Secy. of the Treasury Salmon P. Chase, "From my heart I have felt our national shame in disowning God as not the least of our present national disasters," the minister wrote, suggesting "recognition of the Almighty God in some form on our coins." Secy. Chase ordered designs prepared with the inscription *In God We Trust* and backed coinage legislation which authorized use of this slogan. It first appeared on some U. S. coins in 1864, disappeared and reappeared on various coins until 1955, when Congress ordered it placed on all paper money and all coins.

Constitution of the United States

The Original Seven Articles

PREAMBLE

We, the people of the United States, in order to form a more perfect Union, establish justice, insure domestic tranquility, provide for the common defense, promote the general welfare, and secure the blessings of liberty to ourselves and our posterity, do ordain and establish this Constitution for the United States of America.

ARTICLE 1.

Section 1—Legislative powers; in whom vested:

All legislative powers herein granted shall be vested in a Congress of the United States, which shall consist of a Senate and House of Representatives.

Section 2—House of Representatives, how and by whom chosen. Qualifications of a Representative. Representatives and direct taxes, how apportioned. Enumeration. Vacancies to be filled. Power of choosing officers, and of impeachment.

1. The House of Representatives shall be composed of members chosen every second year by the people of the several States, and the electors in each State shall have the qualifications requisite for electors of the most numerous branch of the State Legislature.

2. No person shall be a Representative who shall not have attained to the age of twenty-five years, and been seven years a citizen of the United States, and who shall not, when elected, be an inhabitant of that State in which he shall be chosen.

3. (Representatives and direct taxes shall be apportioned among the several States which may be included within this Union, according to their respective numbers, which shall be determined by adding to the whole number of free persons, including those bound to service for a term of years, and excluding Indians not taxed, three-fifths of all other persons.)(The previous sentence was superseded by Amendment XIV, section 2.) The actual enumeration shall be made within three years after the first meeting of the Congress of the United States, and within every subsequent term of ten years, in such manner as they shall by law direct. The number of Representatives shall not exceed one for every thirty thousand, but each State shall have at least one Representative; and until such enumeration shall be made, the State of New Hampshire shall be entitled to choose three, Massachusetts eight, Rhode Island and Providence Plantations one, Connecticut five, New York six, New Jersey four, Pennsylvania eight, Delaware one, Maryland six, Virginia ten, North Carolina five, South Carolina five, and Georgia three.

4. When vacancies happen in the representation from any State, the Executive Authority thereof shall issue writs of election to fill such vacancies.

5. The House of Representatives shall choose their Speaker and other officers; and shall have the sole power of impeachment.

Section 3—Senators, how and by whom chosen. How classified. Qualifications of a Senator. President of the Senate, his right to vote. President pro tem., and other officers of the Senate, how chosen. Power to try impeachments. When President is tried, Chief Justice to preside. Sentence.

1. The Senate of the United States shall be composed of two Senators from each State, (chosen by the Legislature

(Continued on next page)

Origin of the Constitution

The War of Independence was conducted by delegates from the original 13 states, called the Congress of the United States of America and generally known as the Continental Congress. In 1777 the Congress submitted to the legislatures of the states the Articles of Confederation and Perpetual Union, which were ratified by New Hampshire, Massachusetts, Rhode Island, Connecticut, New York, New Jersey, Pennsylvania, Delaware, Virginia, North Carolina, South Carolina and Georgia, and finally, in 1781, by Maryland.

The first article of the instrument read: "The stile of this confederacy shall be the United States of America." This did not signify a sovereign nation, because the states delegated only those powers they could not handle individually, such as power to wage war, establish a uniform currency, make treaties with foreign nations and contract debts for general expenses, such as paying the army. Taxes for the payment of such debts were levied by the individual states. The president under the Articles signed himself "President of the United States in Congress assembled," but here the United States were considered in the plural, a cooperating group. Canada was invited to join the union on equal terms but did not act.

When the war was won it became evident that a stronger federal union was needed to protect the mutual interests of the states. The Congress left the initiative to the legislatures. Virginia in January 1786 appointed commissioners to meet with representatives of other states, with the result that delegates from Virginia, Delaware, New York, New Jersey and Pennsylvania met at Annapolis. Alexander Hamilton prepared their call asking delegates from all states to meet in Philadelphia in May 1787 "to render the Constitution of the Federal government adequate to the exigencies of the union." Congress endorsed the plan Feb. 21, 1787. Delegates were appointed by all states except Rhode Island.

The convention met May 14, 1787. George Washington was chosen president (presiding officer). The states certified 65 delegates, but 10 did not attend. The work was done by 55, not all of whom were present at all sessions. Of the 55 attending delegates, 16 failed to sign, and 39 actually signed Sept. 17, 1787, some with reservations. Some historians have said 74 delegates were named and 19 failed to attend. These 9 additional persons refused the appointment, were never delegates and never counted as absentees. Washington sent the Constitution to Congress with a covering letter and that body, Sept. 28, 1787, ordered it sent to the legislatures, "in order to be submitted to a convention of delegates chosen in each state by the people thereof."

The Constitution was ratified by votes of state conventions as follows: Delaware, Dec. 7, 1787, unanimous; Pennsylvania, Dec. 12, 1787, 43 to 23; New Jersey, Dec. 18, 1787, unanimous; Georgia, Jan. 2, 1788, unanimous; Connecticut, Jan. 9, 1788, 128 to 40; Massachusetts, Feb. 6, 1788, 187 to 168; Maryland, April 28, 1788, 63 to 11; South Carolina, May 23, 1788, 149 to 73; New Hampshire, June 21, 1788, 57 to 46; Virginia, June 25, 1788, 89 to 79; New York, July 26, 1788, 30 to 27. Nine states were needed to establish the operation of the Constitution "between the states so ratifying the same" and New Hampshire was the 9th state. The government did not declare the Constitution in effect until the first Wednesday in March 1789 which was March 4. After that North Carolina ratified it Nov. 21, 1789, 197 to 77; and Rhode Island May 29, 1790, 34 to 32. Vermont in convention ratified it Jan. 10, 1791, and by act of Congress approved Feb. 19, 1791, was admitted into the Union as the 14th state, Mar. 4, 1791.

thereof,) (The preceding five words were superseded by Amendment XVII, section 1.) for six years; and each Senator shall have one vote.

2. Immediately after they shall be assembled in consequence of the first election, they shall be divided as equally as may be into three classes. The seats of the Senators of the first class shall be vacated at the expiration of the second year, of the second class at the expiration of the fourth year, and of the third class at the expiration of the sixth year, so that one-third may be chosen every second year; *(and if vacancies happen by resignation, or otherwise, during the recess of the Legislature of any State, the Executive thereof may make temporary appointments until the next meeting of the Legislature, which shall then fill such vacancies.) (The words in parenthesis were superseded by Amendment XVII, section 1.)*

3. No person shall be a Senator who shall not have attained to the age of thirty years, and been nine years a citizen of the United States, and who shall not, when elected, be an inhabitant of that State for which he shall be chosen.

4. The Vice-President of the United States shall be President of the Senate, but shall have no vote, unless they be equally divided.

5. The Senate shall choose their other officers, and also a President pro tempore, in the absence of the Vice-President, or when he shall exercise the office of President of the United States.

6. The Senate shall have the sole power to try all impeachments. When sitting for that purpose, they shall be on oath or affirmation. When the President of the United States is tried, the Chief Justice shall preside: and no person shall be convicted without the concurrence of two-thirds of the members present.

7. Judgment in cases of impeachment shall not extend further than to removal from office, and disqualification to hold and enjoy any office of honor, trust or profit under the United States: but the party convicted shall nevertheless be liable and subject to indictment, trial, judgment and punishment, according to law.

Section 4—Times, etc., of holding elections, how prescribed. One session in each year.

1. The times, places and manner of holding elections for Senators and Representatives, shall be prescribed in each State by the Legislature thereof; but the Congress may be any time by law make or alter such regulations, except as to the places of choosing Senators.

2. The Congress shall assemble at least once in every year, and such meeting shall *(be on the first Monday in December.) (The words in parenthesis were superseded by Amendment XX, section 2.)* unless they shall by law appoint a different day.

Section 5—Membership, quorum, adjournments, rules. Power to punish or expel. Journal. Time of adjournments, how limited, etc.

1. Each House shall be the judge of the elections, returns and qualifications of its own members, and a majority of each shall constitute a quorum to do business; but a smaller number may adjourn from day to day, and may be authorized to compel the attendance of absent members, in such manner, and under such penalties as each House may provide.

2. Each House may determine the rules of its proceedings, punish its members for disorderly behavior, and, with the concurrence of two-thirds, expel a member.

3. Each House shall keep a journal of its proceedings, and from time to time publish the same, excepting such parts as may in their judgment require secrecy; and the yeas and nays of the members of either House on any question shall, at the desire of one-fifth of those present, be entered on the journal.

4. Neither House, during the session of Congress, shall, without the consent of the other, adjourn for more than three days, nor to any other place than that in which the two Houses shall be sitting.

Section 6—Compensation, privileges, disqualifications in certain cases.

1. The Senators and Representatives shall receive a compensation for their services, to be ascertained by law, and paid out of the Treasury of the United States. They shall in all cases, except treason, felony and breach of the peace, be privileged from arrest during their attendance at the session of their respective Houses, and in going to and returning from the same; and for any speech or debate in either House, they shall not be questioned in any other place.

2. No Senator or Representative shall, during the time for which he was elected, be appointed to any civil office under the authority of the United States, which shall have been created, or the emoluments whereof shall have been increased during such time; and no person holding any office under the United States, shall be a member of either House during his continuance in office.

Section 7—House to originate all revenue bills. Veto. Bill may be passed by two-thirds of each House, notwithstanding, etc. Bill, not returned in ten days, to become a law. Provisions as to orders, concurrent resolutions, etc.

1. All bills for raising revenue shall originate in the House of Representatives; but the Senate may propose or concur with amendments as on other bills.

2. Every bill which shall have passed the House of Representatives and the Senate, shall, before it become a law, be presented to the President of the United States; if he approve he shall sign it, but if not he shall return it, with his objections to that House in which it shall have originated, who shall enter the objections at large on their journal, and proceed to reconsider it. If after such reconsideration two-thirds of that House shall agree to pass the bill, it shall be sent, together with the objections, to the other House, by which it shall likewise be reconsidered, and if approved by two-thirds of that House, it shall become a law. But in all such cases the votes of both Houses shall be determined by yeas and nays, and the names of the persons voting for and against the bill shall be entered on the journal of each House respectively. If any bill shall not be returned by the President within ten days (Sundays excepted) after it shall have been presented to him, the same shall be a law, in like manner as if he had signed it, unless the Congress by their adjournment prevent its return, in which case it shall not be a law.

3. Every order, resolution, or vote to which the concurrence of the Senate and House of Representatives may be necessary (except on a question of adjournment) shall be presented to the President of the United States; and before the same shall take effect, shall be approved by him, or being disapproved by him, shall be repassed by two-thirds of the Senate and House of Representatives, according to the rules and limitations prescribed in the case of a bill.

Section 8—Powers of Congress.

The Congress shall have power

1. To lay and collect taxes, duties, imposts and excises, to pay the debts and provide for the common defense and general welfare of the United States; but all duties, imposts and excises shall be uniform throughout the United States;

2. To borrow money on the credit of the United States;

3. To regulate commerce with foreign nations, and among the several States, and with the Indian tribes;

4. To establish a uniform rule of naturalization, and uniform laws on the subject of bankruptcies throughout the United States;

5. To coin money, regulate the value therof, and of foreign coin, and fix the standard of weights and measures;

6. To provide for the punishment of counterfeiting the securities and current coin of the United States;

7. To establish post-offices and post-roads;

8. To promote the progress of science and useful arts, by securing for limited times to authors and inventors the exclusive right to their respective writings and discoveries;

9. To constitute tribunals inferior to the Supreme Court;

10. To define and punish piracies and felonies committed on the high seas, and offenses against the law of nations;

11. To declare war, grant letters of marque and reprisal, and make rules concerning captures on land and water;

12. To raise and support armies, but no appropriation of money to that use shall be for a longer term than two years;

13. To provide and maintain a navy;

14. To make rules for the government and regulation of the land and naval forces;

15. To provide for calling forth the militia to execute the laws of the Union, suppress insurrections and repel invasions;

16. To provide for organizing, arming, and disciplining the militia, and for governing such part of them as may be employed in the service of the United States, reserving to the States respectively, the appointment of the officers, and the authority of training the militia according to the discipline prescribed by Congress;

17. To exercise exclusive legislation in all cases whatsoever, over such district (not exceeding ten miles square) as may, by cession of particular States, and the acceptance of Congress, become the seat of the Government of the United States, and to exercise like authority over all places purchased by the consent of the Legislature of the State in which the same shall be, for the erection of forts, magazines, arsenals, dockyards, and all other needful buildings; — And

18. To make all laws which shall be necessary and proper for carrying into execution the foregoing powers, and all other powers vested by this Constitution in the Government of the United States, or in any department or officer thereof.

Section 9—Provision as to migration or importation of certain persons. Habeas corpus, bills of attainder, etc. Taxes, how apportioned. No export duty. No commercial preference. Money, how drawn from Treasury, etc. No titular nobility. Officers not to receive presents, etc.

1. The migration or importation of such persons as any of the States now existing shall think proper to admit, shall not be prohibited by the Congress prior to the year one thousand eight hundred and eight, but a tax or duty may be imposed on such importation, not exceeding ten dollars for each person.

2. The privilege of the writ of habeas corpus shall not be suspended, unless when in cases of rebellion or invasion the public safety may require it.

3. No bill of attainder or ex post facto law shall be passed.

4. No capitation, or other direct, tax shall be laid, unless in proportion to the census or enumeration herein before directed to be taken. *(Modified by Amendment XVI.)*

5. No tax or duty shall be laid on articles exported from any State.

6. No preference shall be given by any regulation of commerce or revenue to the ports of one State over those of another: nor shall vessels bound to, or from, one State, be obliged to enter, clear, or pay duties in another.

7. No money shall be drawn from the Treasury, but in consequence of appropriations made by law; and a regular statement and account of the receipts and expenditures of all public money shall be published from time to time.

8. No title of nobility shall be granted by the United States: and no person holding any office of profit or trust under them, shall, without the consent of the Congress, accept of any present, emolument, office, or title, of any kind whatever, from any king, prince, or foreign state.

Section 10—States prohibited from the exercise of certain powers.

1. No State shall enter into any treaty, alliance, or confederation; grant letters of marque and reprisal; coin money; emit bills of credit; make anything but gold and silver coin a tender in payment of debts; pass any bill of attainder, ex post facto law, or law impairing the obligation of contracts, or grant any title of nobility.

2. No State shall, without the consent of the Congress, lay any imposts or duties on imports or exports, except what may be absolutely necessary for executing its inspection laws: and the net produce of all duties and imposts, laid by any State on imports or exports, shall be for the use of the Treasury of the United States; and all such laws shall be subject to the revision and control of the Congress.

3. No State shall, without the consent of Congress, lay any duty of tonnage, keep troops, or ships of war in time of peace, enter into any agreement or compact with another State, or with a foreign power, or engage in war, unless actually invaded, or in such imminent danger as will not admit of delay.

ARTICLE II.

Section 1—President: his term of office. Electors of President; number and how appointed. Electors to vote on same day. Qualification of President. On whom his duties devolve in case of his removal, death, etc. President's compensation. His oath of office.

1. The Executive power shall be vested in a President of the United States of America. He shall hold his office during the term of four years, and together with the Vice President, chosen for the same term, be elected as follows

2. Each State shall appoint, in such manner as the Legislature thereof may direct, a number of electors, equal to the whole number of Senators and Representatives to which the State may be entitled in the Congress: but no Senator or Representative, or person holding an office of trust or profit under the United States, shall be appointed an elector.

(The electors shall meet in their respective States, and vote by ballot for two persons, of whom one at least shall not be an inhabitant of the same State with themselves. And they shall make a list of all the persons voted for, and of the number of votes for each; which list they shall sign and certify, and transmit sealed to the seat of the Government of the United States, directed to the President of the Senate. The President of the Senate shall, in the presence of the Senate and House of Representatives, open all the certificates, and the votes shall then be counted. The person having the greatest number of votes shall be the President, if such number be a majority of the whole number of electors appointed; and if there be more than one who have such majority, and have an equal number of votes, then the House of Representatives shall immediately choose by ballot one of them for President; and if no person have a majority, then from the five highest on the list the said House shall in like manner choose the President. But in choosing the President, the votes shall be taken by States, the representation from each State having one vote; a quorum for this purpose shall consist of a member or members from two-thirds of the States, and a majority of all the States shall be necessary to a choice. In every case, after the choice of the President, the person having the greatest number of votes of the electors shall be the Vice President. But if there should remain two or more who have equal votes, the Senate shall choose from them by ballot the Vice President.)

(This clause was superseded by Amendment XII.)

3. The Congress may determine the time of choosing the electors, and the day on which they shall give their votes; which day shall be the same throughout the United States.

4. No person except a natural born citizen, or a citizen of the United States, at the time of the adoption of this Constitution, shall be eligible to the office of President; neither shall any person be eligible to that office who shall not have attained to the age of thirty-five years, and been fourteen years a resident within the United States.

(For qualification of the Vice President, see Amendment XII.)

5. In case of the removal of the President from office, or of his death, resignation, or inability to discharge the power and duties of the said office, the same shall devolve on the Vice President, and the Congress may by law provide for the case of removal, death, resignation or inability, both of the President and Vice-President, declaring what officer shall then act as President, and such officer shall act accordingly, until the disability be removed, or a President shall be elected.

(This clause has been modified by Amendment XX, sections 3 and 4).

6. The President shall, at stated times, receive for his services, a compensation, which shall neither be increased nor diminished during the period for which he shall have been elected, and he shall not receive within that period any other emolument from the United States, or any of them.

7. Before he enter on the execution of his office, he shall take the following oath or affirmation:

"I do solemnly swear (or affirm) that I will faithfully execute the office of President of the United States, and will to the best of my ability, preserve, protect and defend the Constitution of the United States."

Section 2—President to be commander-in-chief. He may require opinions of cabinet officers, etc., may pardon. Treaty-making power. Nomination of certain officers. When President may fill vacancies.

1. The President shall be Commander-in-Chief of the Army and Navy of the United States, and of the militia of the several States, when called into the actual service of the United States; he may require the opinion, in writing, of the principal officer in each of the executive departments, upon any subject relating to the duties of their respective offices, and he shall have power to grant reprieves and pardons for offenses against the United States, except in cases of impeachment.

2. He shall have power, by and with the advice and consent of the Senate, to make treaties, provided two-thirds of the Senators present concur; and he shall nominate, and by and with the advice and consent of the Senate, shall appoint ambassadors, other public ministers and consuls, judges of the Supreme Court, and all other officers of the United States, whose appointments are not herein otherwise provided for, and which shall be established by law: but the Congress may by law vest the appointment of such inferior officers, as they think proper, in the President alone, in the courts of law, or in the heads of departments.

3. The President shall have the power to fill up all vacancies that may happen during the recess of the Senate, by granting commissions, which shall expire at the end of their next session.

Section 3—President shall communicate to Congress. He may convene and adjourn Congress, in case of disagreement, etc. Shall receive ambassadors, execute laws, and commission officers.

He shall from time to time give to the Congress information of the state of the Union, and recommend to their consideration such measures as he shall judge necessary and expedient; he may, on extraordinary occasions, convene both Houses, or either of them, and in case of disagreement between them, with respect to the time of adjournment, he may adjourn them to such time as he shall think proper; he shall receive ambassadors and other public ministers; he shall take care that the laws be faithfully executed, and shall commission all the officers of the United States.

Section 4—All civil offices forfeited for certain crimes.

The President, Vice President, and all civil officers of the United States, shall be removed from office on impeachment for, and conviction of, treason, bribery, or other high crimes and misdemeanors.

ARTICLE III.

Section 1—Judicial powers, Tenure. Compensation.

The judicial power of the United States, shall be vested in one Supreme Court, and in such inferior courts as the Congress may from time to time ordain and establish. The judges, both of the Supreme and inferior courts, shall hold their offices during good behavior, and shall at stated times, receive for their services, a compensation, which shall not be diminished during their continuance in office.

Section 2—Judicial power; to what cases it extends. Original jurisdiction of Supreme Court; appellate jurisdiction. Trial by jury, etc. Trial, where.

1. The judicial power shall extend to all cases, in law and equity, arising under this Constitution, the laws of the United States, and treaties made, or which shall be made, under their authority; to all cases affecting ambassadors, other public ministers and consuls; to all cases of admiralty and maritime jurisdiction; to controversies to which the United States shall be a party; to controversies between two or more States; between a State and citizens of another State; between citizens of different States, between citizens of the same State claiming lands under grants of different States, and between a State, or the citizens thereof, and foreign states, citizens, or subjects.
(This section is modified by Amendment XI.)

2. In all cases affecting ambassadors, other public ministers and consuls, and those in which a State shall be a party, the Supreme Court shall have original jurisdiction. In all the other cases before mentioned, the Supreme Court shall have appellate jurisdiction, both as to law and fact, with such exceptions, and under such regulations as the Congress shall make.

3. The trial of all crimes, except in cases of impeachment, shall be by jury; and such trial shall be held in the State where the said crimes shall have been committed; but when not committed within any State, the trial shall be at such place or places as the Congress may by law have directed.

Section 3—Treason Defined. Proof of, Punishment of.

1. Treason against the United States, shall consist only in levying war against them, or in adhering to their enemies, giving them aid and comfort. No person shall be convicted of treason unless on the testimony of two witnesses to the same overt act, or on confession in open court.

2. The Congress shall have power to declare the punishment of treason, but no attainder of treason shall work corruption of blood, or forfeiture except during the life of the person attainted.

ARTICLE IV.

Section 1—Each State to give credit to the public acts etc. of every other State.

Full faith and credit shall be given in each State to the public acts, records, and judicial proceedings of every other State. And the Congress may by general laws prescribe the manner in which such acts, records and proceedings shall be proved, and the effect thereof.

Section 2—Privileges of citizens of each State. Fugitives from justice to be delivered up. Persons held to service having escaped, to be delivered up.

1. The citizens of each State shall be entitled to all privileges and immunities of citizens in the several States.

2. A person charged in any State with treason, felony, or other crime, who shall flee from justice, and be found in another State, shall on demand of the Executive authority of the State from which he fled, be delivered up, to be removed to the State having jurisdiction of the crime.

(3. No person held to service or labor in one State, under the laws thereof, escaping into another, shall in consequence of any law or regulation therein, be discharged from such service or labor, but shall be delivered up on claim of the party to whom such service or labor may be due.) (This clause was superseded by Amendment XIII.)

Section 3—Admission of new States. Power of Congress over territory and other property.

1. New States may be admitted by the Congress into this Union; but no new State shall be formed or erected within the jurisdiction of any other State; nor any State be formed by the junction of two or more States, or parts of States, without the consent of the Legislatures of the States concerned as well as of the Congress.

2. The Congress shall have power to dispose of and make all needful rules and regulations respecting the territory or other property belonging to the United States; and nothing in this Constitution shall be so construed as to prejudice any claims of the United States, or of any particular State.

Section 4—Republican form of government guaranteed. Each State to be protected.

The United States shall guarantee to every State in this Union a Republican form of government, and shall protect each of them against invasion; and on application of the Legislature, or of the Executive (when the Legislature cannot be convened) against domestic violence.

ARTICLE V.

Constitution: how amended; proviso.

The Congress, whenever two-thirds of both Houses shall deem it necessary, shall propose amendments to this constitution, or, on the application of the Legislaures of two-thirds of the several States, shall call a convention for proposing amendments, which, in either case, shall be valid to all intents and purposes, as part of this Constitution, when ratified by the Legislatures of three-fourths of the several states, or by conventions in three-fourths thereof, as the one or the other mode of ratification may be proposed by the Congress; provided that no amendment which may be made prior to the year one thousand eight hundred and eight shall in any manner affect the first and fourth clauses in the Ninth Section of the First Article; and that no State, without its consent, shall be deprived of its equal suffrage in the Senate.

ARTICLE VI.

Certain debts, etc., declared valid. Supremacy of Constitution, treaties, and laws of the United States. Oath to support Constitution, by whom taken. No religious test.

1. All debts contracted and engagements entered into, before the adoption of this Constitution, shall be as valid against the United States under this Constitution, as under the Confederation.

2. This Constitution, and the laws of the United States which shall be made in pursuance thereof; and all treaties made, or which shall be made, under the authority of the United States, shall be the supreme law of the land; and the judges in every State shall be bound thereby, any thing in the Constitution or laws of any State to the contrary notwithstanding.

3. The Senators and Representatives before mentioned, and the members of the several State Legislatures, and all executive and judicial officers, both of the United States and of the several States, shall be bound by oath or affirmation, to support this Constitution; but no religious test shall ever be required as a qualification to any office or public trust under the United States.

ARTICLE VII.

What ratification shall establish Constitution.

The ratification of the Conventions of nine States, shall be sufficient for the establishment of this Constitution between the States so ratifying the same.

Done in convention by the unanimous consent of the States present the Seventeenth day of September in the year of our Lord one thousand seven hundred and eighty seven, and of the independence of the United States of America the Twelfth. In witness whereof we have hereunto subscribed our names.

George Washington, President and deputy from Virginia.
New Hampshire—John Langdon, Nicholas Gilman.
Massachusetts—Nathaniel Gorham, Rufus King.
Connecticut—Wm. Saml. Johnson, Roger Sherman.
New York—Alexander Hamilton.
New Jersey—Wil: Livingston, David Brearley, Wm. Paterson, Jona: Dayton.
Pennsylvania—B. Franklin, Thomas Mifflin, Robt. Morris, Geo. Clymer, Thos. FitzSimons, Jared Ingersoll, James Wilson, Gouv. Morris.
Delaware—Geo: Read, Gunning Bedford Jun., John Dickinson, Richard Bassett, Jaco: Broom.
Maryland—James McHenry, Daniel of Saint Thomas Jenifer, Danl. Carroll.
Virginia—John Blair, James Madison Jr.
North Carolina—Wm. Blount, Rich'd. Dobbs Spaight, Hugh Williamson.
South Carolina—J. Rutledge, Charles Cotesworth Pinckney, Charles Pinckney, Pierce Butler.
Georgia—William Few, Abr. Baldwin.
Attest: William Jackson, Secretary.

Ten Original Amendments—The Bill of Rights

In Force Dec. 15, 1791

(The First Congress, at its first session in the City of New York, Sept. 25, 1789, submitted to the state 12 amendments to clarify certain individual and state rights not named in the Constitution. They are generally called the Bill of Rights.

(Influential in framing these amendments was the Declaration of Rights of Virginia, written by George Mason (1725-1792) in 1776. Mason, a Virginia delegate to the Constitutional Convention, did not sign the Constitution and opposed its ratification on the ground that it did not sufficiently oppose slavery or safeguard individual rights.

(In the preamble to the resolution offering the proposed amendments, Congress said: "The conventions of a number of the States having at the time of their adopting the Constitution, expressed a desire, in order to prevent misconstruction or abuse of its powers, that further declaratory and restrictive clauses should be added, and as extending the ground of public confidence in the government will best insure the beneficent ends of its institution, be it resolved," etc.

(Ten of these amendments now commonly known as one to 10 inclusive, but in reality three to 12 inclusive, were ratified by the states as follows: New Jersey, Nov. 20, 1789; Maryland, December 19, 1789; North Carolina, Dec. 22, 1789; South Carolina, Jan. 19, 1790; New Hampshire, Jan. 25, 1790; Delaware, Jan. 28, 1790; New York, Feb. 24, 1790; Pennsylvania, March 10, 1790; Rhode Island, June 7, 1790; Vermont, Nov. 3, 1791; Virginia, Dec. 15, 1791; Massachusetts, March 2, 1939; Georgia, March 18, 1939; Connecticut, April 19, 1939. These original 10 ratified amendments follow as Amendments I to X inclusive.

(Of the two original proposed amendments which were not ratified by the necessary number of states, the first related to apportionment of Representatives; the second, to compensation of members.)

AMENDMENT I.

Religious establishment prohibited. Freedom of speech, of the press, and right to petition.

Congress shall make no law respecting an establishment of religion, or prohibiting the free exercise thereof; or abridging the freedom of speech, or of the press; or the right of the people peaceably to assemble, and to petition the Government for a redress of grievances.

AMENDMENT II.

Right to keep and bear arms.

A well-regulated militia, being necessary to the security of a free State, the right of the people to keep and bear arms, shall not be infringed.

AMENDMENT III.

Conditions for quarters for soldiers.

No soldier shall, in time of peace be quartered in any house, without the consent of the owner, nor in time of war, but in a manner to be prescribed by law.

AMENDMENT IV.

Right of search and seizure regulated.

The right of the people to be secure in their persons, houses, papers, and effects, against unreasonable searches and seizures, shall not be violated, and no warrants shall issue, but upon probable cause, supported by oath or affirmation, and particularly describing the place to be searched, and the persons or things to be seized.

AMENDMENT V.

Provisions concerning prosecution. Trial and punishment—private property not to be taken for public use without compensation.

No person shall be held to answer for a capital, or otherwise infamous crime, unless on a presentment or indictment of a Grand Jury, except in cases arising in the land or naval forces, or in the militia, when in actual service in time of war or public danger; nor shall any person be subject for the same offense to be twice put in jeopardy of life or limb; nor shall be compelled in any criminal case to be a witness against himself, nor be deprived of life, liberty, or property, without due process of law; nor shall private property be taken for public use without just compensation.

AMENDMENT VI.

Right to speedy trial, witnesses, etc.

In all criminal prosecutions, the accused shall enjoy the right to a speedy and public trial, by an impartial jury of the State and district wherein the crime shall have been committed, which district shall have been previously ascertained by law, and to be informed of the nature and cause of the accusation; to be confronted with the witnesses against him; to have compulsory process for obtaining witnesses in his favor, and to have the assistance of counsel for his defense.

AMENDMENT VII.

Right of trial by jury.

In suits at common law, where the value in controversy shall exceed twenty dollars, the right of trial by jury shall be preserved, and no fact tried by a jury shall be otherwise reexamined in any court of the United States, than according to the rules of the common law.

AMENDMENT VIII.

Excessive bail or fines and cruel punishment prohibited.

Excessive bail shall not be required, nor excessive fines imposed, nor cruel and unusual punishments inflicted.

AMENDMENT IX.

Rule of construction of constitution.

The enumeration in the Constitution, of certain rights, shall not be construed to deny or disparage others retained by the people.

AMENDMENT X.

Rights of States under Constitution.

The powers not delegated to the United States by the Constitution, nor prohibited by it to the States, are reserved to the States respectively, or to the people.

Amendments Since the Bill of Rights

AMENDMENT XI.

Judicial powers construed.

The judicial power of the United States shall not be construed to extend to any suit in law or equity, commenced or prosecuted against one of the United States by citizens of another State, or by citizens or subjects of any foreign state.

(This amendment was proposed to the Legislatures of the several States by the Third Congress on March 4, 1794, and was declared to have been ratified in a message from the President to Congress, dated Jan. 8, 1798.

(It was on Jan. 5, 1798, that Secretary of State Pickering received from 12 of the States authenticated ratifications, and informed President John Adams of that fact.

(As a result of later research in the Department of State, it is now established that Amendment XI became part of the Constitution on Feb. 7, 1795, for on that date it had been ratified by 12 States as follows:

(1. New York, Mar. 27, 1794. 2. Rhode Island, Mar. 31, 1794. 3. Connecticut, May 8, 1794. 4. New Hampshire, June 16, 1794. 5. Massachusetts, June 26, 1794. 6. Vermont, between Oct. 9, 1794, and Nov. 9, 1794. 7. Virginia, Nov. 18, 1794. 8. Georgia, Nov. 29, 1794. 9. Kentucky, Dec. 7, 1794. 10. Maryland, Dec. 26, 1794. 11. Delaware, Jan. 23, 1795. 12. North Carolina, Feb. 7, 1795.

(On June 1, 1796, more than a year after Amendment XI had become a part of the Constitution (but before anyone was officially aware of this), Tennessee had been admitted as a State; but not until Oct. 16, 1797, was a certified copy of the resolution of Congress proposing the amendment sent to the Governor of Tennessee (John Sevier) by Secretary of State Pickering, whose office was then at Trenton, New Jersey, because of the epidemic of yellow fever at Philadelphia; it seems, however, that the Legislature of Tennessee took no action on Amendment XI, owing doubtless to the fact that public announcement of its adoption was made soon thereafter.

(Besides the necessary 12 States, one other, South Carolina, ratified Amendment XI, but this action was not taken until Dec. 4, 1797; the two remaining States, New Jersey and Pennsylvania, failed to ratify.)

AMENDMENT XII.

Manner of choosing President and Vice-President.

(Proposed by Congress Dec. 9, 1803; ratification completed June 15, 1804.)

The Electors shall meet in their respective States and vote by ballot for President and Vice-President, one of whom, at least, shall not be an inhabitant of the same State with themselves; they shall name in their ballots the person voted for as President, and in distinct ballots the person voted for as Vice-President, and they shall make distinct lists of all persons voted for as President, and of all persons voted for as Vice-President, and of the number of votes for each, which lists they shall sign and certify, and transmit sealed to the seat of the Government of the United States, directed to the President of the Senate; the President of the Senate shall, in the presence of the Senate and House of Representatives, open all the certificates and the votes shall then be counted;—The person having the greatest number of votes for President, shall be the President, if such number be a majority of the whole number of Electors appointed; and if no person have such majority, then from the persons having the highest numbers not exceeding three on the list of those voted for as President, the House of Representatives shall choose immediately, by ballot, the President. But in choosing the President, the votes shall be taken by States, the representation from each State having one vote; a quorum for this purpose shall consist of a member or members from two-thirds of the States, and a majority of all the States shall be necessary to a choice. (*And if the House of Representatives shall not choose a President whenever the right of choice shall devolve upon them, before the fourth day of March next following, then the Vice-President shall act as President, as in case of the death or other constitutional disability of the President.*) *(The words in parenthesis were superseded by Amendment XX, section 3.)* The person having the greatest number of votes as Vice-President, shall be the Vice-President, if such number be a majority of the whole number of Electors appointed, and if no person have a majority, then from the two highest numbers on the list, the Senate shall choose the Vice-President; a quorum for the purpose shall consist of two-thirds of the whole number of Senators, and a majority of the whole number shall be necessary to a choice. But no person constitutionally ineligible to the office of President shall be eligible to that of Vice-President of the United States.

THE RECONSTRUCTION AMENDMENTS

(Amendments XIII, XIV and XV are commonly known as the Reconstruction Amendments, inasmuch as they followed the Civil War, and were drafted by Republicans who were bent on imposing their own policy of reconstruction on the South. Post-bellum legislatures there — Mississippi, South Carolina, Georgia, for example — had set up laws which, it was charged, were contrived to perpetuate Negro slavery under other names.)

AMENDMENT XIII.
Slavery abolished.

(Proposed by Congress Jan. 31, 1865; ratification completed Dec. 6, 1865. The amendment, when first proposed by a resolution in Congress, was passed by the Senate, 38 to 6, on April 8, 1864, but was defeated in the House, 95 to 66 on June 15, 1864. On reconsideration by the House, on Jan. 31, 1865, the resolution passed, 119 to 56. It was approved by President Lincoln on Feb. 1, 1865, although the Supreme Court had decided in 1798 that the President has nothing to do with the proposing of amendments to the Constitution, or their adoption.)

1. Neither slavery nor involuntary servitude, except as a punishment for crime whereof the party shall have been duly convicted, shall exist within the United States or any place subject to their jurisdiction.

2. Congress shall have power to enforce this article by appropriate legislation.

AMENDMENT XIV.
Citizenship rights not to be abridged.

(The following amendment was proposed to the Legislatures of the several states by the 39th Congress, June 13, 1866, and was declared to have been ratified in a proclamation by the Secretary of State, July 28, 1868.

(The 14th amendment was adopted only by virtue of ratification subsequent to earlier rejections. Newly constituted legislatures in both North Carolina and South Carolina (respectively July 4 and 9, 1868), ratified the proposed amendment, although earlier legislatures had rejected the proposal. The Secretary of State issued a proclamation, which, though doubtful as to the effect of attempted withdrawals by Ohio and New Jersey, entertained no doubt as to the validity of the ratification by North and South Carolina. The following day (July 21, 1868), Congress passed a resolution which declared the 14th Amendment to be a part of the Constitution and directed the Secretary of State so to promulgate it. The Secretary waited, however, until the newly constituted Legislature of Georgia had ratified the amendment, subsequent to an earlier rejection, before the promulgation of the ratification of the new amendment.)

1. All persons born or naturalized in the United States, and subject to the jurisdiction thereof, are citizens of the United States and of the State wherein they reside. No State shall make or enforce any law which shall abridge the privileges or immunities of citizens of the United States; nor shall any State deprive any person of life, liberty, or property, without due process of law; nor deny to any person within its jurisdiction the equal protection of the laws.

2. Representatives shall be apportioned among the several States according to their respective numbers, counting the whole number of persons in each State, excluding Indians not taxed. But when the right to vote at any election for the choice of Electors for President and Vice-President of the United States, Representatives in Congress, the executive and judicial officers of a State, or the members of the Legislature thereof, is denied to any of the male inhabitants of such State, being twenty-one years of age, and citizens of the United States, or in any way abridged, except for participation in rebellion, or other crime, the basis of representation therein shall be reduced in the proportion which the number of such male citizens shall bear to

the whole number of male citizens twenty-one years of age in such State.

3. No person shall be a Senator or Representative in Congress, or Elector of President and Vice-President, or hold any office, civil or military, under the United States, or under any State, who, having previously taken an oath, as a member of Congress, or as an officer of the United States, or as a member of any State Legislature, or as an executive or judicial officer of any State, to support the Constitution of the United States, shall have engaged in insurrection or rebellion against the same, or given aid or comfort to the enemies thereof. But Congress may by a vote of two-thirds of each House, remove such disability.

4. The validity of the public debt of the United States authorized by law, including debts incurred for payment of pensions and bounties for services in suppressing insurrection or rebellion, shall not be questioned. But neither the United States nor any State shall assume or pay any debt or obligation incurred in aid of insurrection or rebellion against the United States, or any claim for the loss or emancipation of any slave; but all such debts, obligations and claims, shall be held illegal and void.

5. The Congress shall have power to enforce, by appropriate legislation, the provisions of this article.

AMENDMENT XV.
Race no bar to voting rights.

(The following amendment was proposed to the legislatures of the several States by the 40th Congress, Feb. 26, 1869, and was declared to have been ratified in a proclamation by the Secretary of State, March 30, 1870.)

1. The right of citizens of the United States to vote shall not be denied or abridged by the United States or by any State on account of race, color, or previous condition of servitude.

2. The Congress shall have power to enforce this article by appropriate legislation.

AMENDMENT XVI.
Income taxes authorized.

(Proposed by Congress July 12, 1909; ratification completed Feb. 3, 1913.)

The Congress shall have power to lay and collect taxes on incomes, from whatever sources derived, without apportionment among the several States, and without regard to any census or enumeration.

AMENDMENT XVII.
United States Senators to be elected by direct popular vote.

(Proposed by Congress May 13, 1912; ratification completed Apr. 8, 1913.)

1. The Senate of the United States shall be composed of two Senators from each State, elected by the people thereof, for six years; and each Senator shall have one vote. The electors in each State shall have the qualifications requisite for electors of the most numerous branch of the State Legislatures.

2. When vacancies happen in the representation of any State in the Senate, the executive authority of such State shall issue writs of election to fill such vacancies: Provided, That the Legislature of any State may empower the Executive thereof to make temporary appointments until the people fill the vacancies by election as the Legislature may direct.

3. This amendment shall not be so construed as to affect the election or term of any Senator chosen before it becomes valid as part of the Constitution.

AMENDMENT XVIII.
Liquor prohibition amendment.

(Proposed by Congress Dec. 18, 1917; ratification completed Jan. 16, 1919. Repealed by Amendment XXI, effective Dec. 5, 1933.)

(1. After one year from the ratification of this article the manufacture, sale, or transportation of intoxicating liquors within, the importation thereof into, or the exportation thereof from the United States and all territory subject to the jurisdiction thereof for beverage purposes is hereby prohibited.

(2. The Congress and the several States shall have concurrent power to enforce this article by appropriate legislation.

(3. This article shall be inoperative unless it shall have been ratified as an amendment to the Constitution by the Legislatures of the several States, as provided in the Constitution, within seven years from the date of the submission hereof to the States by the Congress.)

(The total vote in the Senates of the various States was 1,310 for, 237 against — 84.6% dry. In the lower houses of the States the vote was 3,782 for, 1,035 against — 78.5% dry.

(The amendment ultimately was adopted by all the States except Connecticut and Rhode Island.)

AMENDMENT XIX.

Giving nation-wide suffrage to women.

(Proposed by Congress June 4, 1919; ratification certified by Secretary of State Aug. 26, 1920.)

1. The right of citizens of the United States to vote shall not be denied or abridged by the United States or by any State on account of sex.

2. Congress shall have power to enforce this Article by appropriate legislation.

AMENDMENT XX.

Terms of President and Vice President to begin on Jan. 20; those of senators, representatives, Jan. 3.

(Proposed by Congress Mar. 2, 1932; ratification completed Jan. 23, 1933.)

1. The terms of the President and Vice President shall end at noon on the 20th day of January, and the terms of Senators and Representatives at noon on the 3rd day of January, of the years in which such terms would have ended if this article had not been ratified; and the terms of their successors shall then begin.

2. The Congress shall assemble at least once in every year, and such meeting shall begin at noon on the 3rd day of January, unless they shall by law appoint a different day.

3. If, at the time fixed for the beginning of the term of the President, the President elect shall have died, the Vice President elect shall become President. If a President shall not have been chosen before the time fixed for the beginning of his term, or if the President elect shall have failed to qualify, then the Vice President elect shall act as President until a President shall have qualified; and the Congress may by law provide for the case wherein neither a President elect nor a Vice President shall have qualified, declaring who shall then act as President, or the manner in which one who is to act shall be selected, and such person shall act accordingly until a President or Vice President shall have qualified.

4. The Congress may by law provide for the case of the death of any of the persons from whom the House of Representatives may choose a President whenever the right of choice shall have devolved upon them, and for the case of the death of any of the persons from whom the Senate may choose a Vice President whenever the right of choice shall have devolved upon them.

5. Sections 1 and 2 shall take effect on the 15th day of October following the ratification of this article (Oct., 1933).

6. This article shall be inoperative unless it shall have been ratified as an amendment to the Constitution by the Legislatures of three-fourths of the several States within seven years from the date of its submission.

AMENDMENT XXI.

Repeal of Amendment XVIII.

(Proposed by Congress Feb. 20, 1933; ratification com-
pleted Dec. 5, 1933.)

1. The eighteenth article of amendment to the Constitution of the United States is hereby repealed.

2. The transportation or importation into any State, Territory, or Possession of the United States for delivery or use therein of intoxicating liquors, in violation of the laws thereof, is hereby prohibited.

3. This article shall be inoperative unless it shall have been ratified as an amendment to the Constitution by conventions in the several States, as provided in the Constitution, within seven years from the date of the submission hereof to the States by the Congress.

AMENDMENT XXII.

Limiting Presidential terms of office.

(Proposed by Congress Mar. 21, 1947; ratification completed Feb. 27, 1951.)

1. No person shall be elected to the office of the President more than twice, and no person who has held the office of President, or acted as President, for more than two years of a term to which some other person was elected President shall be elected to the office of the President more than once. But this Article shall not apply to any person holding the office of President when this Article was proposed by the Congress, and shall not prevent any person who may be holding the office of President, or acting as President, during the term within which this Article becomes operative from holding the office of President or acting as President during the remainder of such term.

2. This article shall be inoperative unless it shall have been ratified as an amendment to the Constitution by the Legislatures of three-fourths of the several States within seven years from the date of its submission to the States by the Congress.

AMENDMENT XXIII.

Presidential vote for District of Columbia.

(Proposed by Congress June 17, 1960; ratification completed Mar. 29, 1961.)

1. The District constituting the seat of Government of the United States shall appoint in such manner as the Congress may direct:

A number of electors of President and Vice President equal to the whole number of Senators and Representatives in Congress to which the District would be entitled if it were a State, but in no event more than the least populous State; they shall be in addition to those appointed by the States, but they shall be considered, for the purposes of the election of President and Vice President, to be electors appointed by a State; and they shall meet in the District and perform such duties as provided by the twelfth article of amendment.

2. The Congress shall have power to enforce this article by appropriate legislation.

AMENDMENT XXIV.

Barring poll tax in federal elections.

(Proposed by Congress Aug. 27, 1962; ratification completed Jan. 23, 1964.)

1. The right of citizens of the United States to vote in any primary or other election for President or Vice President, for electors for President or Vice President, or for Senator or Representative in Congress, shall not be denied or abridged by the United States or any State by reason of failure to pay any poll tax or other tax.

2. The Congress shall have power to enforce this article by appropriate legislation.

AMENDMENT XXV.

Presidential disability and succession.

(Proposed by Congress July 6, 1965; ratification completed Feb. 10, 1967.)

1. In case of the removal of the President from office or of his death or resignation, the Vice President shall become President.

2. Whenever there is a vacancy in the office of the Vice President, the President shall nominate a Vice President

who shall take office upon confirmation by a majority vote of both houses of Congress.

3. Whenever the President transmits to the President pro tempore of the Senate and the Speaker of the House of Representatives his written declaration that he is unable to discharge the powers and duties of his office, and until he transmits to them a written declaration to the contrary, such powers and duties shall be discharged by the Vice President as Acting President.

4. Whenever the Vice President and a majority of either the principal officers of the executive departments or of such other body as Congress may by law provide, transmit to the President pro tempore of the Senate and the Speaker of the House of Representatives their written declaration that the President is unable to discharge the powers and duties of his office, the Vice President shall immediately assume the powers and duties of the office as Acting President.

Thereafter, when the President transmits to the President pro tempore of the Senate and the Speaker of the House of Representatives his written declaration that no inability exists, he shall resume the powers and duties of his office unless the Vice President and a majority of either the principal officers of the executive department or of such other body as Congress may by law provide, transmit within four days to the President pro tempore of the Senate and the Speaker of the House of Representatives their written declaration that the President is unable to discharge the powers and duties of his office. Thereupon Congress shall decide the issue, assembling within forty-eight hours for that purpose if not in session. If the Congress,

within twenty-one days after receipt of the latter written declaration, or, if Congress is not in session, within twenty-one days after Congress is required to assemble, determines by two-thirds vote of both houses that the President is unable to discharge the powers and duties of his office, the Vice President shall continue to discharge the same as Acting President; otherwise, the President shall resume the powers and duties of his office.

AMENDMENT XXVI.

Lowering voting age to 18 years.

(Proposed by Congress Mar. 23, 1971; ratification completed June 30, 1971.)

1. The right of citizens of the United States, who are 18 years of age or older, to vote shall not be denied or abridged by the United States or any state on account of age.

2. The Congress shall have the power to enforce this article by appropriate legislation.

PROPOSED EQUAL RIGHTS AMENDMENT

(Proposed by Congress Mar. 22, 1972; ratification completed, as of Mar. 22, 1974, by 33 states, rejected by 12; needs total of 38 for adoption.)

1. Equality of rights under the law shall not be denied or abridged by the United States or by any State on account of sex.

2. The Congress shall have the power to enforce, by appropriate legislation, the provisions of this article.

3. This amendment shall take effect two years after the date of ratification.

Independence Hall, American Patriotic Shrine

Independence Hall is the central and main building of a group in Philadelphia, located in Independence Square and facing Chestnut St. It is connected by arcades with 2 buildings, the East and West Wings, and 2 separate corner buildings. Of the latter, Congress Hall is at Sixth St., and Old City Hall at Fifth St.

Independence Hall originally was the State House. It was begun in 1732, and completed in 1759. The East and West Wings were intended to house offices. Tower and spire were completed by June 1753.

The Pennsylvania Assembly occupied Assembly Hall in 1735, before the whole structure was completed. In 1775 it gave the use of the room to the Second Continental Congress. Here, on June 16, 1775, George Washington accepted command of the Continental Army. Here the Declaration

of Independence was adopted on July 4, 1776; the Articles of Confederation and Perpetual Union were signed beginning on July 9, 1778, and the Constitution of the United States was framed by the Constitutional Convention in 1787.

Congress Hall, at the west end of the group, was erected in 1787 and was the seat of the United States Congress from 1790 to 1800, when the Congress moved to Washington, D.C. The Court House, or Old City Hall, at the east end, was built in 1790 for the municipal courts, and was the first seat of the United States Supreme Court.

Independence Hall and the other buildings in Independence Square form the nucleus around which has been developed the Independence National Historical Park, established in 1956. Much restoration work has been done.

The Monroe Doctrine; Its Origin and Meaning

President James Monroe, in his annual message to Congress on Dec. 2, 1823, made the statement of policy since known as the Monroe Doctrine. Its major assertion is that the United States would consider as dangerous to its peace and safety any attempt of the European powers to extend their political system to any portion of the western hemisphere.

Balancing this statement in the same message is Monroe's declaration that in regard to Europe it is the policy of the United States "not to interfere in the internal concerns of any of its powers, to consider the government *de facto* as the legitimate (one) for us . . ."

Statesmen besides Monroe associated in the development of the Doctrine were John Quincy Adams, Secretary of State; Richard Rush, American Minister in London, and George Canning, British Secretary for Foreign Affairs. Consulted were Thomas Jefferson, John C. Calhoun, Secretary of War, and William Wirt, Attorney General.

History of Its Origin. The message grew out of 2 complications. The first was the decree of Russia reserving exclusively to Russian subjects the whole of the northwest coast of North America, from the Bering Straits to 51° N. Lat. and from the Aleutians to Siberia, for commerce, whaling, fishery and other industries, and prohibiting any foreign ship from approaching within 100 miles, on penalty of seizure. Secretary Adams rejected this, and after negotiations Russia reversed itself. In the message President

Monroe said the American continents, "by the free and independent condition which they have assumed and maintain, are henceforth not to be considered as subjects for colonization by any European power."

The other part originated in the threat of foreign encroachment on Latin-American states, the independence of which had been recognized by the United States. George Canning, British Foreign Secretary, on Aug. 20, 1823, suggested to Rush, the American Minister, that the British and American governments declare "in the face of the world" their attitude toward the Spanish-American countries. He believed the two governments entertained similar views, and cited that the British conceived the recovery of the colonies by Spain to be hopeless; thought recognition of them as independent states to be a matter "of time and circumstances."

Canning thought such a declaration might forestall any military attempts to coerce Latin America. When the United States did not act by October he addressed a similar statement to the French ambassador in London, Prince de Polignac, and received the assurance that France did not intend to take any of the Spanish colonies in America.

Secretary Adams, writing to Minister Rush Nov. 29, 1823, endorsed Canning's views but urged as indispensable the recognition of the independence of the new governments by Britain. He thought a unilateral statement better, and the joint declaration was never issued.

Lincoln's Address at Gettysburg, 1863

Fourscore and seven years ago our fathers brought forth on this continent a new nation, conceived in liberty and dedicated to the proposition that all men are created equal.

Now we are engaged in a great civil war, testing whether that nation or any nation so conceived and so dedicated can long endure. We are met on a great battle field of that war. We have come to dedicate a portion of that field, as a final resting-place for those who here gave their lives that that nation might live. It is altogether fitting and proper that we should do this.

But, in a larger sense, we can not dedicate — we can not consecrate — we can not hallow — this ground. The brave men, living and dead, who struggled here, have consecrated it, far above our poor power to add or detract. The world will little note, nor long remember, what we say here, but it can never forget what they did here. It is for us the living, rather, to be dedicated here to the unfinished work which they who fought here have thus far so nobly advanced. It is rather for us to be here dedicated to the great task remaining before us — that from these honored dead we take increased devotion to that cause for which they gave the last full measure of devotion — that we here highly resolve that these dead shall not have died in vain — that this nation, under God, shall have a new birth of freedom — and that government of the people, by the people, for the people, shall not perish from the earth.

History of the Address

President Lincoln delivered his address at the dedication of the military cemetery at Gettysburg, Pa., Nov. 19, 1863. The battle had been fought July 1-3, 1863. He was preceded by Edward Everett, former president of Harvard, secretary of state and senator from Massachusetts, then 69 and one of the nation's great orators. Everett gave a full resume of the battle. Lincoln's speech was so short that the photographer did not get his camera adjusted in time. The report that newspapers ignored Lincoln's address is not entirely accurate; Everett's address swamped their columns, but the greatness of Lincoln's speech was immediately recognized. Everett wrote him: "I should be glad if I could flatter myself that I came as near the central idea of the occasion in two hours as you did in two minutes."

Five copies of the Gettysburg address in Lincoln's hand are extant. The first and second draft, prepared in Washington and Gettysburg just before delivery, are in the Library of Congress. The third draft, written at the request of Everett to be sold at a fair in New York for the benefit of soldiers, was given the Illinois State Historical Library by popular subscription.

The fourth copy was written out by Lincoln for George Bancroft, the historian, and remained in custody of the Bancroft family until 1929, when it was acquired by Mrs. Nicholas H. Noyes, of Indianapolis, Ind. In 1949 Mrs. Noyes presented this copy to the Cornell University Library, Ithaca, N.Y. The fifth copy, usually described as the clearest and best, was also written by Lincoln for George Bancroft, for facsimile reproduction in a volume to be sold for the benefit of soldiers and sailors in Baltimore, where Bancroft lived. It is the second Bancroft copy. It passed to Bancroft's stepchildren, named Bliss, and was sold for $54,000 by the estate of Dr. William J. A. Bliss in New York April 27, 1949, to Oscar B. Cintas, former Cuban ambassador to the United States. He died in May, 1957, and willed it to the Lincoln Room of the White House, where it was placed in March, 1959. Lincoln's spelling of battle field and can not as separated words in that version is reproduced above.

Sen. John Sherman Cooper (R.-Ky.) president of the Lincoln Sesquicentennial Commission, on June 17, 1959, presented a Latin translation of Lincoln's Gettysburg Address to the Apostolic Delegation of the Roman Catholic Church, in Washington, D.C. It was engrossed on vellum and was to be sent to Pope John XXIII for deposit in the Vatican Library. The presentation took place in the presence of government officials and members of the diplomatic corps. The translation was made by the Rt. Rev. Edwin Ryan of White Plains, N.Y. The Latin version was ordered printed in the Congressional Record.

Washington's Letter on Bigotry and Persecution

During a tour of various New England states in 1790, then President George Washington was greeted by various leaders in Newport, R.I. Among the clergy was Moses Seixas, the warden of the Hebrew congregation, who greeted Washington and praised the new government for its opposition to bigotry. Washington acknowledged the greeting in a letter to the congregation:

Gentlemen:

While I received with much satisfaction, your address replete with expressions of affection and esteem; I rejoice in the opportunity of assuring you, that I shall always retain a grateful remembrance of the cordial welcome I experienced in my visit to Newport from all classes of Citizens.

The reflection on the days of difficulty and danger which are past is rendered the more sweet, from a consciousness that they are succeeded by days of uncommon prosperity and security. If we have wisdom to make the best use of the advantages with which we are now favored, we cannot fail, under the just administration of a good Government, to become a great and happy people.

The Citizens of the United States of America have a right to applaud themselves for having given to mankind examples of an enlarged and liberal policy; a policy worthy of imitation. All possess alike liberty of conscience and immunities of citizenship. It is now no more that toleration is spoken of, as if it was by the indulgence of one class of people, that another enjoyed the exercise of their inherent natural rights. For happily the Government of the United States, which gives to bigotry no sanction, to persecution no assistance, requires only that they who live under its protection, should demean themselves as good citizens, in giving it on all occasions their effectual support.

It would be inconsistent with the frankness of my character not to avow that I am pleased with your favorable opinion of my administration, and fervent wishes for my felicity. May the Children of the Stock of Abraham, who dwell in this land, continue to merit and enjoy the good will of the other Inhabitants; while everyone shall sit in safety under his own vine and fig tree, and there shall be none to make him afraid. May the father of all mercies scatter light and not darkness in our paths, and make us all in our several vocations useful here, and in his own due time and way everlastingly happy.

Go. Washington

U. S. Passport, Visa and Health Requirements

Source: Passport Office, U.S. Dept. of State and U.S. Public Health Service

Passports are issued by the United States Department of State to citizens and nationals of the United States for the purpose of documenting them for their foreign travel and to identify them as Americans. Some countries require a visa, or stamp of approval, to be affixed to the passport by the consulate of the country to be visited, while others waive this formality. Also some countries, which do not require visas, require tourist cards from visitors making a short stay.

Unless specifically endorsed, passports may not be used for travel into or through Cuba, North Korea or North Vietnam, or for travel into or through other countries or areas as determined to be in the national interest by the Secretary of State.

How to Obtain a Passport

An applicant for a passport who has never been previously issued a passport in his own name, must execute an application in person before (1) a Passport Agent; (2) a clerk of any Federal court; (3) a clerk of any State court of record or a judge or clerk of any probate court; (4) a postal clerk designated by the Postmaster General; or (5) a diplomatic or consular officer of the U.S. abroad. A wife/husband who is to be included in the application must appear with the applicant and execute the application. Passport Agencies are located at Boston (John F. Kennedy Bldg., Government Center), Chicago (Everett M. Dirksen Bldg., 219 S. Dearborn); Honolulu (Fed. Bldg.); Los Angeles (Hawthorne Fed. Bldg., 15000 Aviation Blvd., Rm. 2W16, Lawndale, Calif.); Miami (51 S.W. First Ave.); New Orleans (International Trade Mart, 2 Canal Street); New York (630 Fifth Ave.); Philadelphia (William J. Green, Jr., Federal Bldg., 600 Arch Street); San Francisco (Fed. Bldg., 450 Golden Gate Ave.); Seattle (Logan Bldg., 500 Union St.); Washington D.C. (Passport Office, 1425 K St., N.W.).

A passport previously issued to, or one in which applicant was included, will be accepted as proof of citizenship in lieu of the following documents. A person born in the United States shall present his birth certificate. To be acceptable, the certificate must show the given name and surname, the date and place of birth and that the birth record was filed shortly after birth. The certificate must also be certified with the registrar's signature and the raised, impressed or multi-colored seal of his office. Uncertified copies of birth certificates are not acceptable.

If such primary evidence is not obtainable, a notice from the registrar shall be submitted stating that no birth record exists. The notice shall be accompanied by the best obtainable secondary evidence such as a baptismal certificate, a certificate of circumcision, a hospital birth record, affidavits of persons having personal knowledge of the facts of the birth or other documentary evidence such as early census, school or family bible records, newspaper files and insurance papers. Secondary evidence should be created as close to the time of birth as possible.

A person in the U.S. who has been issued a passport in his own name within the last eight years may obtain a new passport by filling out, signing and mailing a passport by mail application together with his previous passport, two duplicate signed photographs taken within the last 6 months and the established fee to the nearest Passport Agency or to the Passport Office in Wash., D.C. If, however, an applicant is applying for a passport for the first time, if his prior passport was issued before his 18th birthday, if he wishes to include a person other than himself in the passport, or if he is applying for an official, diplomatic, or other no-fee passport, he must execute a passport application in person before a Passport Agent; a clerk of any Federal court, a clerk of any State court

of record or a judge or clerk of any probate court; a postal clerk designated by the Postmaster General; or a diplomatic or consular officer of the U.S. abroad.

A naturalized citizen should present his naturalization certificate. A person born abroad claiming citizenship through either a native-born or naturalized citizen must submit a certificate of citizenship issued by the Immigration and Naturalization Service; or a Consular Report of Birth or Certification of Birth issued by the Dept. of State. If one of the above documents has not been obtained, he must submit evidence of citizenship of the parent through whom citizenship is claimed; document(s) through would establish the parent, and evidence which tionally, if through parent/child relationship. Additional alien through birth to one American and one parent, an affidavit from parent(s) showing periods and places of residence in the United States and abroad, specifying periods spent abroad in the employment of the U.S. Government, including the Armed Forces, or with certain international organizations; if through naturalization of parents, evidence of admission to the United States for permanent residence.

A married woman must submit evidence of citizenship and, under certain conditions, marriage. Special regulations govern women married prior to Sept. 22, 1922; should be discussed with the person executing the application.

The applicant shall establish his identity to the satisfaction of the person executing the application. Proof of identity may be established through a personal knowledge of the applicant by the Clerk or Agent or by an item which contains the signature and either a physical description or photograph of the applicant. The following items of identification are acceptable: previous United States Passport; certificate of naturalization; driver's license (not temporary or learner's license); a governmental (Federal, State, Municipal) identification card or pass.

If the applicant is not able to establish his identity by personal knowledge or by presentation of one of the above acceptable documents, he should be accompanied by an identifying witness who has known him for at least 2 years, and who is a U.S. citizen or a permanent resident alien of the United States. The witness shall be required to establish his own identity to the satisfaction of the person executing the application by one of the above means.

The identifying witness shall sign an affidavit in the presence of the same person who executes the passport application. The affidavit shall show:

The witness resides at a specific address;

The witness knows or has reason to believe that the applicant is a citizen of the United States;

The basis of the witness' knowledge concerning the applicant;

The information set forth in the affidavit is true to the best of his knowledge and belief.

A person included in the passport of another may not use the passport for travel unless he is accompanied by the bearer.

Aliens — An alien leaving the U.S. must request passport facilities from his home government. He must have a permit from his local Collector of Internal Revenue, and if he wishes to return he should request a re-entry permit from the Immigration and Naturalization Service if it is required.

Contract Employees — Persons traveling because of a contract with the Government must submit with their applications letters from their employer stating position, destination and purpose of travel and Armed Forces contract number when pertinent.

Photographs and Fees

Photographs — Duplicate photographs taken within six months, both signed by the applicant and which are a good likeness, must accompany the passport application. A group photograph is preferred if more than one person is included in the passport. Photographs may be in color or in black and white. They must be full face, printed on a thin, nonglossy paper base on a light background and must be no smaller than 2½ x 2½ inches nor larger than 3 x 3 inches in size. They must also be capable of withstanding a mounting temperature of over 200°F.

Fees — The passport fee is $10. A fee of $2 shall be paid to the person executing the application. No execution fee is payable where a passport is applied for by mail. All applicants must pay the passport fee and, where applicable, the execution fee unless specifically exempted by law. If applying in person, service will be expedited by presenting exact fees. An emergency service fee of $10 is charged in addition to all other fees where work must be performed after hours. The only other fees are for special postage. "A passport is valid for five years. Upon expiration, passports may no longer be renewed. New passports must be obtained."

During the calendar year 1973 the Passport Office, Dept. of State, issued 2,729,104 passports to American citizens.

The loss of a valid passport is a serious matter and should be reported in writing immediately to the Passport Office, Dept. of State, Wash., D.C. 20524, or to the nearest consular office of the U.S. when abroad.

Foreign Regulations

A visa is an endorsement or a notation, usually rubber stamped in a passport by a representative of the country to be visited. It certifies that the bearer of the passport is to be permitted to enter that country for a certain purpose and length of time. With the exception of the Iron Curtain countries, no visas are required for brief tourist travel to Western European countries. Authoritative visa information can be obtained by writing directly to foreign consular officials. The locations of foreign consular offices in the U.S. may be obtained by consulting the Congressional Directory available in most libraries. (Check appropriate city telephone directories for complete address.)

Health Information

Smallpox — A Smallpox Vaccination is required for travel to most countries of the world ex-

cept Europe. However, in the event of an outbreak of smallpox in any country in Europe, all countries remaining on the itinerary **following a visit to the infected country** will require a Certificate; the United States will also require a Certificate upon the traveler's return if, in the preceding 14 days, a traveler has visited a country reporting smallpox. The local health department can furnish current information on specific country requirements.

Regardless of the foreign country's requirements, the U.S. Public Health Service recommends that all travelers to Africa, Southeast Asia, and Brazil be vaccinated for their own protection.

A Vaccination Certificate is not required for travel from the U.S. **directly to and from** Europe, Canada, Mexico, Australia, and New Zealand. For travel to more than one island in the Caribbean, a Certificate will probably be required.

Yellow fever — A Yellow Fever Vaccination Certificate may be required for travel in yellow fever-infected countries.

Cholera — A Cholera Vaccination Certificate is required by most countries if a traveler has visited a cholera-infected country in the preceding 6 days. The U.S. has no cholera vaccination requirement.

Plague — Vaccination is not required by any country as a condition of entry. Selective immunization is advisable for travelers to Vietnam, Cambodia, and Laos.

Yellow fever vaccine must be obtained at an officially designated Yellow Fever Vaccination Center, and the Certificate must be stamped by the Center. It remains valid for 10 years. Other vaccinations may be obtained from licensed physicians, and sometimes from local health departments. The Smallpox Certificate, valid for 3 years, and the Cholera Certificate, valid for 6 months, must be stamped by the State or local health department.

Vaccination must be recorded on approved version of PHS-731, International Certificates of Vaccination, which are available from State and local health departments, passport offices, travel agencies, and the Superintendent of Documents, U.S. Printing Office, Wash., D.C. 20402.

United States Immigration Law

The national origins quota system disappeared from United States immigration procedures July 1, 1968, as provided by the Act of Oct. 3, 1965, which amended the Immigration and Nationality Act.

The Immigration and Nationality Act, as amended, provides for numerical limitations on immigration from the Eastern and Western Hemispheres. Not subject to any numerical limitations, however, are immigrants who are spouses or children of U.S. citizens, or parents of citizens who are 21 years of age or older; returning residents; certain former U.S. citizens; ministers of religion; and certain long-term U.S. Government employees.

The Act of Oct. 3, 1965, established new controls to protect the American labor market from an influx of skilled and unskilled foreign labor. The primary responsibility was placed on the would-be immigrant to obtain the Secretary of Labor's clearance, prior to the issuance of a visa, establishing that there are not sufficient workers in the U.S. at the alien's destination who are able, willing and qualified to perform the skilled or unskilled labor; and that the employment of the alien will not adversely affect wages and working conditions of workers in the U.S. similarly employed.

Eastern Hemisphere Immigrants

Persons born in countries of the Eastern Hemisphere and dependent areas thereof are subject to an annual limitation of 170,000. Within this numerical

limitation there is an annual limitation of 20,000 for each country and 200 for each dependent area. Applicants are classified as either preference or nonpreference.

The preference visa categories are based on certain relationships to persons in the U.S.; i.e., unmarried sons and daughters of United States citizens, spouses and unmarried sons and daughters of resident aliens, married sons and daughters of U.S. citizens, and brothers and sisters of U.S. citizens (first, second, fourth, and fifth preference, respectively); Certain professions and skills (third preference); and certain categories of workers which are in short supply in the U.S. (6th preference); refugees (7th preference). Spouses and children of preference applicants are entitled to the same preference if accompanying or following to join such persons.

Except for refugee status, preference status is based upon approved petitions, filed with the Immigration and Naturalization Service, by the appropriate relative or employer (or in the 3rd preference by the alien himself). Visa numbers for qualified preference applicants are made available in the order of the preference classes and, within such classes, in the order of the filing dates of the petitions.

Immigrants not entitled to classification within one of the above-mentioned preference groups are nonpreference applicants and receive only those visa numbers not needed by preference applicants.

A prerequisite for nonpreference classification is a labor certification under Section 212(a) (14) of the Immigration and Nationality Act, or satisfactory evidence that the provisions of that section do not apply to the alien's case. The availability of nonpreference visa numbers is contingent on the level of preference demand and cannot therefore be predicted with real accuracy. However, in some countries and dependent areas the higher preference categories may utilize the entire numerical limitation which will prevent any visa numbers from becoming available for persons from such countries or areas in the nonpreference category.

Western Hemisphere Immigrants

The Act establishes an annual ceiling of 120,000 on immigration by persons born in independent countries of the Western Hemisphere (Canada, Mexico, Central and South America and the Caribbean Area). Within this over-all ceiling there is no numerical limitation set for individual countries, and no preference classes have been established for such applicants. Visas within the 120,000 limitation will be made available to qualified applicants in the chronological order of the priority dates. An applicant's date is the date a labor certification for the applicant is accepted for processing by the Dept. of Labor or the date proof is received by a consular officer that a labor certification is not required.

Excludable Aliens

Aliens who are excludable on medical grounds are those who are mentally retarded, insane, psychopathic, mentally defective, sexual deviates, chronic alcoholics, narcotic addicts, and those who are afflicted with any dangerous contagious disease or who have a physical defect impairing the ability to earn a living. Also excludable are paupers, beggars, illiterates, stowaways, prostitutes, persons engaged in commercial vice, narcotics traffickers, persons convicted of crimes involving moral turpitude, persons who obtain or try to obtain a visa by fraud, or who left the U. S. to avoid military service. Those excludable on security grounds include persons who are anarchists, members or affiliates of certain proscribed organizations, and those who teach or advocate overthrow of the U. S. Government by force or violence.

For more detailed information consult the nearest office of the U. S. Immigration & Naturalization Service, or any U. S. Consul abroad.

Customs Exemptions and Advice to Travelers

United States residents returning after a stay abroad of at least 48 hours are, generally speaking, granted customs exemptions of $100 each. Each returning resident may bring home free of duty articles totaling $100 in fair retail value in the country of acquisition, subject to limitations on liquors and cigars. These articles must accompany the traveler at the time of his return, must be for his personal or household use, must have been acquired as an incident of his trip, and must be properly declared to Customs. Not more than one quart of alcoholic beverages may be included in the $100 exemption.

If a U. S. resident arrives directly or indirectly from American Samoa, Guam, or the Virgin Islands of the United States, his purchase may be valued up to $200 fair retail value, but not more than $100 of the exemption be applied to the value of articles acquired elsewhere than in such insular possessions, and one gallon of alcoholic beverages may be included in his exemption, but not more than 1 quart of such beverages may have been acquired elsewhere than in the designated islands.

The exemption for articles acquired in the Virgin Islands of the United States and in Mexico is not conditional upon the 48-hour absence requirement.

In either case, the exemption for alcoholic beverages is accorded only when the returning resident has attained 21 years of age at the time of his arrival. One hundred cigars may be included (except Cuban products) in either exemption.

The $100 or $200 exemption may be granted only if the exemption, or any part of it, has not been used within the preceding 30-day period.

Bona fide gifts costing no more than $10 fair retail value may be mailed to friends at home duty-free; addressee cannot receive in a single day gifts exceeding the $10 limit.

Air Travel

On a first-class trans-Atlantic flight a passenger may carry 66 lbs. of luggage free; a tourist class passenger, 44 lbs. free. A charge is made for extra weight.

Precautions for Travel

In some cases naturalized United States citizens desiring to visit the countries of their birth, and sometimes their American-born children traveling to those countries, may be subject to military service and other regulations there. The United States Department of State advises such travelers to get specific information from the consulates of the countries concerned before departure.

Service in Foreign Armed Forces

Voluntary service in the armed forces of a foreign state engaged in hostilities against the U. S. is highly persuasive evidence of an intention to relinquish citizenship and will normally result in loss of U. S. citizenship. Voluntary service in the armed forces of a foreign state not engaged in hostilities against the U. S. does not result in loss of U. S. citizenship unless there is persuasive evidence of an intent to transfer or abandon allegiance by reason of such military service.

Naturalization: How to Become an American Citizen ✳

Source: The Federal Statutes

A person who desires to be naturalized as a citizen of the United States may obtain the necessary application form as well as detailed information from the nearest office of the Immigration and Naturalization Service or from the clerk of a court handling naturalization cases.

There are no racial bars to naturalization. Women have the same right as men to become naturalized.

An applicant must be at least 18 years old. He must have been a lawful resident of the United States continuously for 5 years. For husbands and wives of U.S. citizens the period is 3 years in most instances. Special provisions apply to certain veterans of the Armed Forces.

An applicant must have been physically present in this country for at least half of the required 5 years' residence.

Every applicant for naturalization must:

(1) sign the petition in his own handwriting, if physically able to write;

(2) demonstrate an understanding of the English language, including an ability to read, write, and speak words in ordinary usage in the English language (persons physically unable to do so, and persons who were on December 24, 1952 over 50 years of age and had been residing in the United States for 20 years are excepted).

(3) have been a person of good moral character, attached to the principles of the Constitution, and well disposed to the good order and happiness of the

United States for five years just before filing the petition or for whatever other period of residence is required in his case and continue to be such a person until admitted to citizenship; and

(4) demonstrate a knowledge and understanding of the fundamentals of the history, and the principles and form of government, of the U.S.

The petitioner also is obliged to have two credible citizen witnesses. These witnesses must have personal knowledge of the applicant.

A person not of good moral character includes a habitual drunkard, an adulterer, a polygamist, a violator of criminal law, a gambler, one who gave false testimony to obtain a benefit under the immigration law, one in prison for 180 days or more, one convicted of murder.

Naturalization is denied to any person who, within 10 years, has been subversive, including communists and others who favor totalitarian government, and who were members of a proscribed organization, unless the petitioner was under 16 or joined under duress.

A law approved Aug. 20, 1958, provides for the expeditious naturalization of alien spouses and adopted children of U.S. citizens who are missionaries or performing religious duties and are stationed abroad.

When the applicant files his petition he pays the court clerk $25. At the preliminary hearing he may be represented by a lawyer or social service agency. There is a 30-day wait. If action is favorable, there is a final hearing before a judge, who administers the following oath of allegiance:

Oath of Allegiance

I hereby declare, on oath, that I absolutely and entirely renounce and abjure all allegiance and fidelity to any foreign prince, potentate, state or sovereignty, of whom or which I have heretofore been a subject or citizen; that I will support and defend the Constitution and laws of the United States of America against all enemies, foreign and domestic; that I will bear true faith and allegiance to the same; that I will bear arms on behalf of the United States when required by the law; that I will perform noncombatant service in the armed forces of the United States when required by the law; that I will perform work of national importance under civilian direction when required by the law, and that I take this obligation freely without any mental reservation or purpose of evasion; so help me God.

Immigrants Admitted From All Countries

Source: Immigration and Naturalization Service, U.S. Dept. of Justice

Year	Number	Year	Number	Year	Number	Year	Number
1820.......	8,385	1881-1890...	5,246,613	1951-1960...	2,515,479	1968........	454,448
1821-1830...	143,439	1891-1900...	3,687,564	1961........	271,344	1969........	358,579
1831-1840...	599,125	1901-1910...	8,795,386	1962........	283,763	1970........	373,326
1841-1850...	1,713,251	1911-1920...	5,735,811	1963........	306,260	1971........	370,478
1851-1860...	2,598,214	1921-1930...	4,107,209	1964........	292,248	1972........	384,685
1861-1870...	2,314,824	1931-1940...	528,431	1965........	296,697	1973........	400,063
1871-1880...	2,812,191	1941-1950...	1,035,039	1966........	323,040	**1820-1973...**	**46,317,864**

Passports Issued and Renewed

Source: Passport Office, Dept. of State

Passports are actual count; other data based on sample. Projections are subject to error: While size of sample is constant from month to month total volume of passports by month may vary by a factor of four. In addition size of sample has not changed since 1955, but volume of passports has increased by 400%.

Item	1960	1965	1968	1969[6]	1970	1971	1972	1973
New and renewed passports.....	859,087	1,330,290	1,748,416	1,820,192	2,219,159	2,398,968	2,728,021	2,729,104
Object of Travel.[1]								
Government................	115,910	119,140	210,116	167,562	146,169	98,938	136,901	146,494
Nongovernment.............	737,177	1,139,150	1,538,300	1,652,630	2,072,990	2,300,030	2,591,120	2,582,610
Personal reasons[2]...........	321,590	487,470	912,430	1,475,630	1,791,330	2,156,640	2,042,560	1,245,780
Pleasure[3].................	350,897	535,150	442,770	130,670	216,700	109,210	441,010	1,077,240
Business[4].................	24,540	76,201	103,560	25,180	39,940	15,570	68,700	154,820
Education................	31,240	31,120	68,680	15,490	20,230	16,040	33,290	95,240
Religion.................	6,780	6,770	6,970	2,180	3,350	1,380	3,980	7,930
Health..................	1,460	500	1,530	220	640	130	800	1,140
Other...................	670	1,930	2,360	3,260	800	1,060	780	460
First area destination:								
Africa..................	8,440	19,580	21,450	19,760	18,790	14,820	29,750	26,420
Australia and Oceania.........	35,220	50,750	61,380	68,190	51,210	48,350	78,580	80,670
Europe.................	669,662	992,800	1,294,786	1,460,212	1,910,169	2,139,508	2,244,161	2,181,114
Far East................	55,960	111,310	159,750	125,100	116,730	73,250	135,230	139,740
North, Central and South America.	58,935	99,620	128,600	91,850	72,410	68,630	135,720	189,280
Middle-East..............	24,670	55,080	82,430	54,990	48,890	54,380	103,870	111,000
Not Stated[5]..............	200	150	....	....	....	30	710	880
Mode of Travel—departure:[7]								
Ship...................	226,245	39,340	15,498	2,766	....	....	....	....
Air....................	626,842	1,290,950	1,732,918	1,817,426	....	....	....	....
Sex of Passport Recipients:								
Male...................	419,615	700,080	902,840	945,520	1,123,620	1,266,770	1,358,530	1,321,050
Female.................	433,472	630,210	845,576	874,672	1,095,539	1,132,198	1,369,491	1,408,054
Citizenship of Passport Recipients:								
Native.................	710,172	1,236,791	1,603,074	1,702,320	2,072,560	2,270,610	2,553,750	2,511,266
Naturalized...............	142,915	93,493	145,342	117,872	146,599	128,358	174,271	217,838

(1). Data not entirely comparable because of changes in classifications in 1961.
(2). Includes "Personal business," "Join husband," "Accompany husband," "Business and pleasure," "Visit family."
(3). Includes "Sightsee," "Vacation," "Visit," and "Tourist." (4). Includes applicants formerly listed under "Employment" and "Commercial business."
(5). Beginning 1960, includes applicants who listed "World tour."
(6). Legislation effective Aug. 26, 1968 eliminated passport renewals.
(7). Data eliminated. Over 99% of passport recipients indicate departure by air.

Election Statistics

Popular and Electoral Vote for President 1972

Compiled by The World Almanac from official returns of the States.
Blank and void ballots are excluded from all totals.

States	Electoral Vote Nixon	McGovern	Republican Nixon	Democrat McGovern	American Schmitz	Soc. Labor Fisher	Soc. Worker Jenness or Reed	Communist Hall	Others**	Total
Ala.....	9	....	728,701	256,923	11,918	....	....	....	8,551	1,006,093
Alaska...	3	....	55,349	32,967	6,903	....	....	....	....	95,219
Ariz....	6	....	402,812	198,540	21,208	....	30,945 †	....	....	653,505
Ark......	6	....	445,751	198,899	3,016	....	....	....	....	647,666
Calif....	45	....	4,602,096	3,475,847	232,554	197	574	373	56,218	8,367,859
Colo....	7	....	597,189	329,980	17,269	4,361	666	432	3,981	953,878
Conn.	8	....	810,763	555,498	17,239	....	....	....	777	1,384,277
Del.....	3	....	140,357	92,298	2,638	....	....	....	238	235,516
D. of C..	....	3	35,226	127,627	....	....	316	252	....	163,421
Fla.....	17	....	1,857,759	718,117	....	....	....	....	7,407	2,583,283
Ga.....	12	....	881,496	289,529	2,288	3	....	....	1,456	1,174,722
Hawaii..	5	....	168,865	101,409	....	....	....	....	....	270,274
Idaho....	4	....	199,384	80,826	28,869	....	397	....	903	310,379
Ill.......	26	....	2,788,179	1,913,472	2,471	12,344	....	4,541	2,229	4,723,236
Ind......	13	....	1,405,154	708,568	....	1,688	5,575	....	4,544	2,125,529
Iowa....	8	....	706,207	496,206	22,056	195	488	272	520	1,225,944
Kansas..	7	....	619,812	270,287	21,808	....	....	....	4,188	916,095
Ky......	9	....	676,446	371,159	17,627	....	685	464	1,118	1,067,499
La.......	10	....	686,852	298,142	52,099	....	14,398	....	....	1,051,491
Me......	4	....	256,458	160,584	....	....	....	....	229	417,271
Md......	10	....	829,305	505,781	18,726	....	....	....	....	1,353,812
Mass....	....	14	1,112,078	1,332,540	22,877	129	10,600	46	486	2,458,756
Mich....	21	....	1,961,721	1,459,435	63,381	2,437	1,603	1,210	....	3,489,727
Minn....	10	....	898,269	802,346	31,407	4,261	940	662	3,767	1,741,652
Miss.....	7	....	505,125	126,782	11,598	....	2,458	....	....	645,963
Mo......	12	....	1,154,058	698,531	....	....	....	....	....	1,852,589
Mont....	4	....	183,976	120,197	13,430	....	....	....	....	317,603
Nebr....	5	....	406,298	169,991	....	....	....	....	817	577,225
Nev.....	3	....	115,750	66,016	....	....	....	....	....	181,766
N. H....	4	....	213,724	116,435	3,386	....	368	....	142	334,055
N. J.....	17	....	1,845,502	1,102,211	34,378	4,544	2,233	1,263	7,098	2,997,229
N. M....	4	....	235,606	141,084	8,767	....	474	....	....	385,931
N. Y.....	41	....	4,192,778	2,951,084	....	4,530	7,797	5,641	....	7,161,830
N. C.....	13	....	1,054,889	438,705	25,018	....	....	....	....	1,518,612
N. D.....	3	....	174,109	100,384	5,646	....	288	87	....	280,514
Ohio.....	25	....	2,441,827	1,558,889	80,067	7,107	....	6,437	460	4,094,787
Okla.....	8	....	759,025	247,147	23,728	....	....	....	....	1,029,900
Ore......	6	....	486,686	392,760	46,211	....	....	....	2,289	927,946
Pa.......	27	....	2,714,521	1,796,951	70,593	....	4,639	2,686	2,715	4,592,105
R. I......	4	....	218,290	191,981	....	....	729	....	....	411,000
S. C.....	8	....	477,044	186,824	10,075	....	....	....	17	673,960
S. D.....	4	....	166,476	139,945	....	....	994	....	....	307,415
Tenn....	10	....	813,147	357,293	30,373	....	....	....	369	1,201,182
Texas....	26	....	2,298,896	1,154,289	6,039	....	8,664	....	3,393	3,471,281
Utah....	4	....	323,643	126,284	28,549	....	....	....	....	478,476
Vt.......	3	....	117,149	68,174	....	....	296	....	1,328	186,947
Va.*.....	11	....	988,493	438,887	19,721	9,918	....	....	....	1,457,019
Wash....	9	....	837,135	568,334	58,906	1,102	623	566	4,181	1,470,847
W. Va....	6	....	484,964	277,435	....	....	....	....	....	762,399
Wisc.....	11	....	989,430	810,174	47,525	998	506	663	3,594	1,852,890
Wyo.....	3	....	100,464	44,358	748	....	....	....	....	145,570
Total U.S.	**520**	**17**	**47,165,234**	**29,168,110**	**1,101,052**	**53,814**	**97,256**	**25,595**	**123,015**	**77,734,195**

*One elector in Virginia voted for John Hospers and Theodora Nathan.
**Dr. Benjamin Spock, People's Party: Calif. 55,167, Col. 2,403, Idaho 903, Ind. 4,544, Ky. 1,118, Mass. 101, Minn. 2,805, N. J. 5,355, Wash. 2,644, Wis. 2,701. Total 77,741. In Vermont, under label of Liberty Party, 1,010. John Mahalchik, America First: New Jersey 1,743. Earle H. Munn, Prohibition: Alabama 8,551, Calif. 50, Colo. 467, Dela. 238, Kansas 4,188. Total 13,494. John Hospers, Libertarian: Calif. 980, Colo. 1,111, Mass. 43, Wash. 1,537. Total 3,671. Gabriel Green, Universal Party: Calif. 21, Iowa 199. Total 220. Scattered: Conn. 777, Fla. 7,407, Ga. 1,456, Ill. 2,229, Iowa 321, Maine 229, Minn. 962, Nebr. 817, N. H. 142, Ohio 460, Ore. 2,289, Pa. 2,715, S. C. 17, Tenn. 369, Texas 3,393, Vt. 318, Wis. 893. Total 25,136.
†Due to a confused ballot, thousands of Arizonians mistakenly voted for two candidates.

Major Parties' Popular and Electoral Vote for President

(F) Federalist; (D) Democrat; (R) Republican; (DR) Democrat Republican; (NR) National Republican;
(W) Whig; (P) People's; (PR) Progressive; (SR) States' Rights; Asterisk (*)—See notes below.

Year	President Elected	Popular	Elec.	Losing Candidate	Popular	Elec.
1789	George Washington (F)	Unknown	69	No opposition		
1792	George Washington (F)	Unknown	132	No opposition		
1796	John Adams (F)	Unknown	71	Thomas Jefferson DR)	Unknown	68
1800	Thomas Jefferson (DR)	Unknown	73	Aaron Burr (DR)	Unknown	73
	Elected by House of Representatives (due to tie vote)					
1804	Thomas Jefferson (DR)	Unknown	162	Charles Pinckney (F)	Unknown	14
1808	James Madison DR)	Unknown	122	Charles Pinckney (F)	Unknown	47
1812	James Madison (DR)	Unknown	128	DeWitt Clinton (F)	Unknown	89
1816	James Monroe (DR)	Unknown	183	Rufus King (F)	Unknown	34
1820	James Monroe (DR)	Unknown	231	John Quincy Adams (DR)	Unknown	1
1824	John Quincy Adams (NR)	105,321	84	Andrew Jackson (D)	155,872	99
	Elected by House of Representatives (no candidate having polled a majority)			Henry Clay (DR)	46,587	37
				William H. Crawford (DR)	44,282	41
1828	Andrew Jackson (D)	647,231	178	John Quincy Adams (NR)	509,097	83
1832	Andrew Jackson (D)	687,502	219	Henry Clay (DR)	530,189	49
	First national Presidential convention					
1836	Martin Van Buren (D)	762,678	170	William H. Harrison (W)	548,007	73
1840*	William H. Harrison (W)	1,275,017	234	Martin Van Buren (D)	1,128,702	60
1844	James K. Polk (D)	1,337,243	170	Henry Clay (W)	1,299,068	105
1848*	Zachary Taylor (W)	1,360,101	163	Lewis Cass (D)	1,220,544	127
1852	Franklin Pierce (D)	1,601,474	254	Winfield Scott (W)	1,386,578	42
1856	James C. Buchanan (D)	1,927,995	174	John C. Fremont (R)	1,391,555	114
1860	Abraham Lincoln (R)	1,866,352	180	Stephen A. Douglas (D)	1,375,157	12
				John C. Breckinridge (D)	845,763	72
				John Bell (Const. Union)	589,581	39
1864*	Abraham Lincoln (R)	2,216,067	212	George McClellan (D)	1,808,725	21
1868		3,015,071	214	Horatio Seymour	2,709,615	80
1872	Ulysses S. Grant (R)	3,597,070	286	Horace Greeley (D-T)	2,834,079	
1876*	Rutherford B. Hayes (R)	4,033,950	185	Samuel J. Tilden (D)	4,284,757	184
1880*	James A. Garfield (R)	4,449,053	214	Winfield S. Hancock (D)	4,442,030	155
1884	Grover Cleveland (D)	4,911,017	219	James G. Blaine (R)	4,848,334	182
1888*	Benjamin Harrison (R)	5,444,337	233	Grover Cleveland (D)	5,540,050	168
1892	Grover Cleveland (D)	5,554,414	277	Benjamin Harrison (R)	5,190,802	145
				James Weaver (P)	1,027,329	22
1896	William McKinley (R)	7,035,638	271	William J. Bryan (D-P)	6,467,946	176
1900*	William McKinley (R)	7,219,530	292	William J. Bryan (D)	6,358,071	155
1904	Theodore Roosevelt (R)	7,628,834	336	Alton B. Parker (D)	5,084,491	140
1908	William H. Taft (R)	7,679,006	321	William J. Bryan (D)	6,409,106	162
1912	Woodrow Wilson (D)	6,286,214	435	Theodore Roosevelt (PR)	4,216,020	88
				William H. Taft (R)	3,483,922	8
1916	Woodrow Wilson (D)	9,129,606	277	Charles E. Hughes (R)	8,538,221	254
1920*	Warren G. Harding (R)	16,152,200	404	James M. Cox (D)	9,147,353	127
1924	Calvin Coolidge (R)	15,725,016	382	John W. Davis (D)	8,385,586	136
				Robert M. LaFollette (PR)	4,822,856	13
1928	Herbert Hoover (R)	21,392,190	444	Alfred E. Smith (D)	15,016,443	87
1932	Franklin D. Roosevelt (D)	22,821,857	472	Herbert Hoover (R)	15,761,841	59
				Norman Thomas (Socialist)	884,781	
1936	Franklin D. Roosevelt (D)	27,751,597	523	Alfred Landon (R)	16,679,583	8
1940	Franklin D. Roosevelt (D)	27,243,466	449	Wendell Willkie (R)	22,304,755	82
1944*	Franklin D. Roosevelt (D)	25,602,505	432	Thomas E. Dewey (R)	22,006,278	99
1948	Harry S. Truman (D)	24,105,812	303	Thomas E. Dewey (R)	21,970,065	189
				J. Strom Thurmond (SR)	1,169,021	39
				Henry A. Wallace (PR)	1,157,172	
1952	Dwight D. Eisenhower (R)	33,936,252	442	Adlai E. Stevenson (D)	27,314,992	89
1956*	Dwight D. Eisenhower (R)	35,585,316	457	Adlai E. Stevenson (D)	26,031,322	73
1960*	John F. Kennedy (D)	34,227,096	303	Richard M. Nixon (R)	34,108,546	219
1964	Lyndon B. Johnson (D)	43,126,506	486	Barry M. Goldwater (R)	27,176,799	52
1968	Richard M. Nixon (R)	31,785,480	301	Hubert H. Humphrey (D)	31,275,166	191
				George C. Wallace (3rd party)	9,906,473	46
1972	Richard M. Nixon (R)	47,165,234	520	George S. McGovern	29,168,110	17

1872 — Greeley died Nov. 29, 1872. His electoral votes were split among 4 individuals.
1876 — Fla., La., Ore., and S. C. election returns were disputed. Congress in joint session (Mar. 2, 1877) declared Hayes and Wheeler elected President and Vice-President.
1888 — Cleveland had more votes than Harrison but the 233 electoral votes cast for Harrison against the 168 for Cleveland elected Harrison president.
1956 — Democrats elected 74 electors but one from Alabama refused to vote for Stevenson.
1960 — Sen. Harry F. Byrd (D-Va.) received 15 electoral votes.
1972 — John Hospers of Calif. and Theodora Nathan of Ore., received one vote from an elector of Virginia.

Presidential Election Returns by States

Compiled by the World Almanac from official state returns.

Alabama

1932 (Pres.), Roosevelt, Dem., 207,910; Hoover, Rep., 34,675; Foster, Com., 406; Thomas, Soc., 2,030; Upshaw, Proh., 13.

1936 (Pres.), Roosevelt, Dem., 238,195; Landon, Rep., 35,358; Colvin, Proh., 719; Browder, Com., 679; Lemke, Union, 549; Thomas, Soc., 242.

1940 (Pres.), Roosevelt, Dem., 250,726; Willkie, Rep., 42,174; Babson, Proh., 698; Browder, Com., 509; Thomas, Soc., 100.

1944 (Pres.), Roosevelt, Dem., 198,918; Dewey, Rep., 44,540; Watson, Proh., 1,095; Thomas, Soc., 190.

1948 (Pres.), Thurmond, States' Rights, 171,443; Dewey, Rep., 40,930; Wallace, Prog., 1,522; Watson, Proh., 1,085.

1952 (Pres.), Eisenhower, Rep., 149,231; Stevenson, Dem., 275,075; Hamblen, Proh., 1,814.

1956 (Pres.), Stevenson, Dem., 290,844; Eisenhower, Rep., 195,694; Independent electors, 20,323.

1960 (Pres.), Kennedy, Dem., 324,050; Nixon, Rep., 237,981; Faubus, States' Rights, 4,367; Decker, Proh., 2,106; King, Afro-Americans, 1,485; Scattering, 236.

1964 (Pres.), Dem., 209,848 (electors unpledged); Goldwater, Rep., 479,085; Scattering, 105.

1968 (Pres.), Nixon, Rep. 146,923; Humphrey, Dem., 196,579; Wallace, 3rd party 691,425; Munn, Proh., 4,022.

1972 (Pres.), Nixon, Rep., 728,701; McGovern, Dem. 219,108 plus 37,815 Natl. Demo. Party of Alabama; Schmitz, Conservative 11,918; Munn, Proh. 8,551.

Alaska

1960 (Pres.), Kennedy, Dem., 29,809; Nixon, Rep., 30,-953.

1964 (Pres.), Johnson, Dem., 44,329; Goldwater, Rep., 22,930.

1968 (Pres.), Nixon, Rep., 37,600; Humphrey, Dem., 35,411; Wallace, 3rd party, 10,024.

1972 (Pres.), Nixon, Rep., 55,349; McGovern, Dem., 32,967; Schmitz, American, 6,906.

Arizona

1932 (Pres.), Roosevelt, Dem., 79,264; Hoover, Rep., 36,104; Thomas, Soc., 2,030; Foster, Com., 406.

1936 (Pres.), Roosevelt, Dem., 86,722; Landon, Rep., 33,433; Lemke, Union, 3,307; Colvin, Proh., 384; Thomas, Soc., 317.

1940 (Pres.), Roosevelt, Dem., 95,267; Willkie, Rep., 54,030; Babson, Proh., 742.

1944 (Pres.), Roosevelt, Dem., 80,826; Dewey, Rep., 56,287; Watson, Proh. 421.

1948 (Pres.), Truman, Dem., 95,251; Dewey, Rep., 77,-597; Wallace, Prog., 3,310; Watson, Proh., 786; Teichert, Soc. Lab., 121.

1952 (Pres.), Eisenhower, Rep., 152,042; Stevenson, Dem., 108,528.

1956 (Pres.), Eisenhower, Rep., 176,990; Stevenson, Dem., 112,880; Andrews, Ind. 303.

1960 (Pres.), Kennedy, Dem., 176,781; Nixon, Rep., 221,241; Hass, Soc. Lab., 469.

1964 (Pres.), Johnson, Dem., 237,753; Goldwater, Rep., 242,535; Hass, Soc. Labor, 482.

1968 (Pres.), Nixon, Rep., 266,721; Humphrey, Dem., 170,514; Wallace, 3rd party, 46,573; McCarthy, New Party, 2,751; Halstead, Soc. Worker, 85; Cleaver, Peace and Freedom, 217; Blomen, Soc. Labor, 75.

1972 (Pres.), Nixon, Rep., 402,812; McGovern, Dem., 198,540; Schmitz, American, 21,208; Soc. Worker, 30,945. (Due to ballot peculiarities in 3 counties (particularly Pima), thousands of voters cast ballots for the Socialist Workers Party and one of the major candidates. Court ordered both votes counted as official).

Arkansas

1932 (Pres.), Roosevelt, Dem., 189,602; Hoover, Rep., 28,467; Thomas, Soc., 1,269; Harvey, Ind., 1,049; Foster, Com., 175.

1936 (Pres.), Roosevelt, Dem., 146,765; Landon, Rep., 32,039; Thomas, Soc., 446; Browder, Com., 164; Lemke, Union, 4.

1940 (Pres.), Roosevelt, Dem., 158,622; Willkie, Rep.,42,121; Babson, Proh., 793; Thomas, Soc., 305.

1944 (Pres.), Roosevelt, Dem., 148,965; Dewey, Rep., 63,551; Thomas, Soc. 438.

1948 (Pres.), Truman, Dem., 149,659; Dewey, Rep., 50,959; Thurmond, States' Rights, 40,068; Thomas, Soc., 1,037; Wallace, Prog., 751; Watson, Proh., 1.

1952 (Pres.), Eisenhower, Rep., 177,155; Stevenson, Dem., 226,300; Hamblen, Proh., 886; MacArthur, Christian Nationalist, 458; Hass, Soc. Lab. 1.

1956 (Pres.), Stevenson, Dem., 213,277; Eisenhower, Rep., 186,287; Andrews, Ind., 7,008.

1960 (Pres.), Kennedy, Dem., 215,049; Nixon, Rep., 184,508; National States' Rights, 28,952.

1964 (Pres.), Johnson, Dem., 314,197; Goldwater, Rep., 243,264; Kasper, Nat'l. States Rights, 2,965.

1968 (Pres.), Nixon, Rep., 189,062; Humphrey, Dem., 184,901; Wallace, 3rd party, 235,627.

1972 (Pres.), Nixon, Rep. 445,751; McGovern, Dem., 198,899; Schmitz, Amer. Party, 3,016.

California

1932 (Pres.), Roosevelt, Dem., 1,324,157; Hoover, Rep., 847-902; Thomas, Soc., 63,299; Upshaw, Proh., 20,637; Harvey, Liberty, 9,827; Foster, Com., 1,023.

1936 (Pres.), Roosevelt, Dem., 1,766,836; Landon, Rep., 836,431; Colvin, Proh., 12,917; Thomas, Soc., 11,325; Browder, Com., 10,877.

1940 (Pres.), Roosevelt, Dem., 1,877,618; Willkie, Rep., 1,351,419; Thomas, Prog., 16,506; Browder, Com., 13,586; Babson, Proh., 9,400.

1944 (Pres.), Roosevelt, Dem., 1,988,564; Dewey, Rep., 1,512,965; Watson, Proh., 14,770; Thomas, Soc., 3,923; Teichert, Soc. Lab., 327.

1948 (Pres.), Truman, Dem., 1,913,134; Dewey, Rep., 1,895,269; Wallace, Prog., 190,381; Watson, Proh., 16,926; Thomas, Soc., 3,459; Thurmond, States' Rights, 1,228; Teichert, Soc. Lab., 195; Dobbs, Soc. Wkr. 133.

1952 (Pres.), Eisenhower, Rep., 2,897,310; Stevenson, Dem., 2,197,548; Hallinan, Prog., 24,106; Hamblen, Proh., 15,653; MacArthur, (Tenny Ticket), 3,326; (Kellems Ticket) 178; Hass, Soc. Lab., 273; Hoopes, Soc., 206; Scattered, 3,249.

1956 (Pres.), Eisenhower, Rep., 3,027,668; Stevenson, Dem., 2,420,136; Holtwick, Proh., 11,119; Andrews, Constitution, 6,087; Hass, Soc. Lab., 300; Hoopes, Soc., 123; Dobbs, Soc. Workers, 96; Smith, Christian Nat'l., 8.

1960 (Pres.), Kennedy, Dem., 3,224,099; Nixon, Rep., 3,259,722; Decker, Proh., 21,706; Hass, Soc. Lab., 1,051.

1964 (Pres.), Johnson, Dem., 4,171,877; Goldwater, Rep., 2,879,108; Hass, Soc. Labor, 489; DeBerry, Soc. Worker, 378; Munn, Proh., 305; Hensley, Universal, 19.

1968 (Pres.), Nixon, Rep., 3,467,664; Humphrey, Dem., 3,244,318; Wallace, 3rd party, 487,270; Peace and Freedom party, 27,707; McCarthy, Alternative, w0,721; Gregory, write-in, 3,230; Mitchell, Communist, 260; Munn, Prohibition, 59; Blomen, Socialist, 341; Soeters, Defense, 17.

1972 (Pres.), Nixon, Rep., 4,602,086; McGovern, Dem., 3,475,847; Schmitz, Amer., 232,554; Spock, Peace and Freedom, 55,167; Hall, Communist, 373; Hosper, Libertarian, 980; Munn, Prohibition, 53; Fisher, Soc. Labor, 197; Jenness, Soc. Workers, 574; Green, Universal, 21.

Colorado

1932 (Pres.), Roosevelt, Dem., 250,877; Hoover, Rep., 189,617; Thomas, Soc., 14,018; Upshaw, Proh., 1,928.

1936 (Pres.), Roosevelt, Dem., 295,081; Landon, Rep., 18 ,267; Lemke, Union, 9,962; Thomas, Soc., 1,593; Browder, Com., 497; Aiken, Socm Labor, 336.

1940 (Pres.), Roosevelt, Dem., 265,554; Willkie, Rep., 279,576; Thomas, Soc., 1,899; Babson, Proh., 1,597; Browder, Com., 378.

1944 (Pres.), Roosevelt, Dem., 234,331; Dewey, Rep., 268,731; Thomas, Soc., 1,977.

1948 (Pres.), Truman, Dem., 267,288; Dewey, Rep., 239,714; Wallace, Prog., 6,115; Thomas, Soc., 1,678; Dobbs, Soc. Workers, 228; Teichert, Soc. Lab., 214.

1952 (Pres.), Eisenhower, Rep., 379,782; Stevenson, Dem., 245,504; MacArthur, Constitution, 2,181; Hallinan, Prog., 1,919; Hoopes, Soc., 365; Hass, Soc. Lab., 352.

1956 (Pres.), Eisenhower, Rep., 394,479; Stevenson, Dem., 263,997; Hass, Soc. Lab., 3,308; Andrews, Ind., 759; Hoopes, Soc., 531.

1960 (Pres.), Kennedy, Dem., 330,629; Nixon, Rep., 402,242; Hass, Soc. Lab., 2,803; Dobbs, Soc. Workers, 572.

1964 (Pres.), Johnson, Dem., 476,024; Goldwater, Rep., 296,767; Hass, Soc. Labor, 302; DeBerry, Soc. Worker, 2,537; Munn, Proh., 1,356.

1968 (Pres.), Nixon, Rep., 409,345; Humphrey, Dem., 335,174; Wallace, 3rd party, 60,813; Blomen, Soc., 3,016; Gregory, New-party, 1,393; Munn, Proh., 275; Halstead, Soc. Work., 235.

1972 (Pres.), Nixon, Rep., 597,189; McGovern, Dem., 329,980; Fisher, Soc. Labor, 4,361; Hospers, Libertarian, 1,111; Hall, Com., 432; Jenness, Soc. Wrks., 666; Munn, Proh., 467; Schmitz, American, 17,269; Spock, Peoples, 2,403.

Connecticut

1932 (Pres.), Roosevelt, Dem., 281,632; Hoover, Rep., 288,420; Thomas, Soc., 22,767.

1936 (Pres.), Roosevelt, Dem., 382,129; Landon, Rep., 278,685; Lemke, Union, 21,805; Thomas, Soc., 5,683; Browder, Com., 1,193.

1940 (Pres.), Roosevelt, Dem., 417,621; Willkie, Rep., 361,021; Browder, Com., 1,091; Aiken, Soc. Lab., 971; Willkie, Union, 798.

1944 (Pres.), Roosevelt, Dem., 435,146; Dewey, Rep., 390,527; Thomas, Soc., 5,097; Teichert, Soc. Lab., 1,220.

1948 (Pres.), Truman, Dem., 423,297; Dewey, Rep., 437,754; Wallace, Prog., 13,713; Thomas, Soc., 6,964; Teichert, Soc. Lab., 1,184; Dobbs, Soc. Workers, 606.

1952 (Pres.), Eisenhower, Rei., 611,012; Stevenson, Dem., 481,649; Hoopes, Soc., 2,244; Hallinan, Peoples, 1,466; Hass, Soc. Lab., 535; Write-in, 5.

1956 (Pres.), Eisenhower, Rep., 711,837; Stevenson, Dem., 405,079; Scattered, 205.

1960 (Pres.), Kennedy, Dem., 657,055; Nixon, Rep., 565,813.

1964 (Pres.), Johnson, Dem., 826,269; Goldwater, Rep., 390,996; Scattered, 1,313.

1968 (Pres.), Nixon, Rep., 556,721; Humphrey, Dem., 621,561; Wallace, 3rd party, 76,650; scattered, 1,300.

1972 (Pres.), Nixon, Rep., 810,763; McGovern, Dem., 555,498; Schmitz, Amer. Party, 17,239; Scattered 777.

Delaware

1932 (Pres.), Hoover, Rep., 57,074; Roosevelt, Dem., 54,319; Thomas, Soc., 1,376; Foster, Com., 133.

1936 (Pres.), Roosevelt, Dem., 69,702; Landon, Rep., 54,014; Lemke, Union, 442; Thomas, Soc., 179; Browder, Com., 52.

1940 (Pres.), Roosevelt, Dem., 74,599; Willkie, Rep., 61,440; Babson, Proh., 220; Thomas, Soc., 115.

1944 (Pres.), Roosevelt, Dem., 68,166; Dewey, Rep., 56,747; Watson, Proh., 294; Thomas, Soc., 154.

1948 (Pres.), Truman, Dem., 67,813; Dewey, Rep., 69,-688; Wallace, Prog., 1,050; Watson, Proh., 343; Thomas, Soc., 250; Teichert, Soc. Lab., 29.

1952 (Pres.), Eisenhower, Rep., 90,059; Stevenson, Dem., 83,315; Hass, Soc. Lab., 242; Hamblen, Proh., 234; Hallinan, Prog., 155; Hoopes, Soc., 20.

1956 (Pres.), Eisenhower, Rep., 98,057; Stevenson, Dem., 79,421; Holtwick, Proh., 400; Hass, Soc. Lab., 110.

1960 (Pres.), Kennedy, Dem., 99,590; Nixon, Rep., 96,-373; Faubus, States' Rights, 354; Decker, Proh., 284; Hass, Soc. Lab., 82.

1964 (Pres.), Johnson, Dem., 122,704; Goldwater, Rep., 78,078; Hass, Soc. Lab., 113; Munn, Proh., 425.

1968 (Pres.), Nixon, Rep., 96,714; Humphrey, Dem., 89,194; Wallace, 3rd party, 28,459.

1972 (Pres.), Nixon, Rep., 140,357; McGovern, Dem., 92,283; Schmitz, Amer. Party, 2,638; Munn, Proh., 238.

District of Columbia

1964 (Pres.), Johnson, Dem., 169,796; Goldwater, Rep., 28,801.

1968 (Pres.), Nixon, Rep., 31,012; Humphrey, Dem., 139,566.

1972 (Pres.), Nixon, Rep., 35,226; McGovern, Dem., 127,627; Reed, Soc. Worker, 316; Hall, Communist, 252.

Florida

1932 (Pres.), Roosevelt, Dem., 206,307; Hoover, Rep., 69,170; Thomas, Soc., 775.

1936 (Pres.), Roosevelt, Dem., 249,117; Landon, Rep., 78,248; Thomas, Soc., 775.

1940 (Pres.), Roosevelt, Dem., 359,334; Willkie, Rep., 126,158.

1944 (Pres.), Roosevelt, Dem., 339,377; Dewey, Rep., 143,215.

1948 (Pres.), Truman, Dem., 281,988; Dewey, Rep., 194,280; Thurmond, States' Rights, 89,755; Wallace, Prog., 11,620.

1952 (Pres.), Eisenhower, Rep., 544,036; Stevenson, Dem., 444,950; Scattered, 351.

1956 (Pres.), Eisenhower, Rep., 643,849; Stevenson, Dem., 480,371.

1960 (Pres.), Kennedy, Dem., 748,700; Nixon, Rep., 795,476.

1964 (Pres.), Johnson, Dem., 948,540; Goldwater, Rep., 905,941.

1968 (Pres.), Nixon, Rep., 886,804; Humphrey, Dem., 676,794; Wallace, 3rd party, 624,207.

1972 (Pres.), Nixon, Rep., 1,857,759; McGovern, Dem., 718,117; scattered 7,407.

Georgia

1932 (Pres.), Roosevelt, Dem., 234,118; Hoover, Rep., 19,863; Upshaw, Proh., 1,125; Thomas, Soc., 461; Foster, Com., 23.

1936 (Pres.), Roosevelt, Dem., 255,364; Landon, Rep., 36,942; Colvin, Proh., 660; Lemke, Union, 141; Thomas, Soc., 68.

1940 (Pres.), Roosevelt, Dem., 265,194; Willkie, Rep., 23,934; Ind. Dem., 22,428; total. 46,362; Babson, Proh., 983.

1944 (Pres.), Roosevelt, Dem., 268,187; Dewey, Rep., 56,506; Watson, Proh., 36.

1948 (Pres.), Truman, Dem., 254,646; Dewey, Rep., 76,691; Thurmond, States' Rights, 85,055; Wallace, Prog., 1,636; Watson, Proh., 732.

1952 (Pres.), Eisenhower, Rep., 198,979; Stevenson, Dem., 456,823; Libery Party, 1.

1956 (Pres.), Stevenson, Dem., 444,388; Eisenhower, Rep., 222,778; Andrews, Ind., write-in, 1,754.

1960 (Pres.), Kennedy, Dem., 458,638; Nixon, Rep., 274,472; write-in 239.

1964 (Pres.), Johnson, Dem., 522,557; Goldwater, Rep., 616,600.
1968 (Pres.), Nixon, Rep., 380,111; Humphrey, Dem., 334,440; Wallace, 3rd party, 535,550; write-in votes 162.
1972 (Pres.), Nixon, Rep., 881,496; McGovern, Dem., 289,529; Schmitz, Amer. Party, 2,288; scattered 1,459.

Hawaii

1960 (Pres.), Kennedy, Dem., 92,410; Nixon, Rep., 92,-295.
1964 (Pres.), Johnson, Dem., 163,249; Goldwater, Rep., 44,022.
1968 (Pres.), Nixon, Rep., 91,425; Humphrey, Dem., 141,324; Wallace, 3rd party, 3,469.
1972 (Pres.), Nixon, Rep., 168,865; McGovern, Dem., 101,409.

Idaho

1932 (Pres.), Roosevelt, Dem., 109,479; Hoover, Rep., 71,312; Harvey, Lib., 4,712; Thomas, Soc., 526; Foster, Com., 491.
1936 (Pres.), Roosevelt, Dem., 125,683; Landon, Rep., 66,256; Lemke, Union, 7,684.
1940 (Pres.), Roosevelt, Dem., 127,842; Willkie, Rep., 106,553; Thomas, Soc., 497; Browder, Com., 276.
1944 (Pres.), Roosevelt, Dem., 107,399; Dewey, Rep., 100,137; Watson, Proh., 503; Thomas, Soc., 282.
1948 (Pres.), Truman, Dem., 107,370; Dewey, Rep., 101,514; Wallace, Prog., 4,972; Watson, Proh., 628; Thomas, Soc., 332.
1952 (Pres.), Eisenhower, Rep., 180,707; Stevenson, Dem., 95,081; Hallinan, Prog., 443; Write-in, 23.
1956 (Pres.), Eisenhower, Rep., 166,979; Stevenson, Dem., 105,868; Andrews, Ind., 126; Write-in, 16.
1960 (Pres.), Kennedy, Dem., 138,853; Nixon, Rep., 161,597.
1964 (Pres.), Johnson, Dem., 148,920; Goldwater, Rep., 143,557.
1968 (Pres.), Nixon, Rep., 165,369; Humphrey, Dem., 89,273; Wallace, 3rd party, 36,541.
1972 (Pres.), Nixon, Rep., 199,384; McGovern, Dem., 80,826; Schmitz, American, 28,869; Spock, Peoples, 903; Jenness, Soc. Worker, 397.

Illinois

1932 (Pres.), Roosevelt, Dem., 1,882,304; Hoover, Rep., 1,432,756; Thomas, Soc., 67,258; Foster, Com., 15,582; Upshaw, Proh., 6,388; Reynolds, Soc. Lab., 3,638.
1936 (Pres.), Roosevelt, Dem., 2,282,999; Landon, Rep., 1,570,393; Lemke, Union, 89,439; Thomas, Soc., 7,530; Colvin, Proh., 3,439; Aiken, Soc. Lab. 1,921.
1940 (Pres.), Roosevelt, Dem., 2,149,934; Willkie, Rep., 2,047,240; Thomas, Soc., 10,914; Babson, Proh., 9,190.
1944 (Pres.), Roosevelt, Dem., 2,079,479; Dewey, Rep., 1,939,314; Teichert, Soc. Lab., 9,677; Watson, Proh., 7,411; Thomas, Soc., 180.
1948 (Pres.), Truman, Dem., 1,994,715; Dewey, Rep., 1,961,103; Watson, Proh., 11,959; Thomas, Soc., 11,-522; Teichert, Soc. Lab., 3,118.
1952 (Pres.), Eisenhower, Rep., 2,457,327; Stevenson, Dem., 2,013,920; Hass, Soc. Lab., 9,363; Write-in, 448.
1956 (Pres.), Eisenhower, Rep., 2,623,327; Stevenson, Dem., 1,775,682; Hass, Soc. Lab., 8,342; Write-in, 56.
1960 (Pres.), Kennedy, Dem., 2,377,846; Nixon, Rep., 2,368,988; Hass, Soc. Lab., 10,560; Write-in, 15.
1964 (Pres.), Johnson, Dem., 2,796,833; Goldwater, Rep., 1,905,946; Write-in, 62.
1968 (Pres.), Nixon, Rep., 2,174,774; Humphrey, Dem., 2,039,814; Wallace, 3rd party, 390,958; Blomen, Soc. Labor, 13,878; write-ins 325.
1972 (Pres.), Nixon, Rep., 2,788,179; McGovern, Dem., 1,913,472; Fisher, Soc. Labor, 12,344; Schmitz,

Amer., 2,471; Hall, Communist, 4,541; Others 2,229.

Indiana

1932 (Pres.), Roosevelt, Dem., 862,054; Hoover, Rep., 677,184; Thomas, Soc., 21,388; Upshaw, Proh., 10,-399; Foster, Com., 2,187; Reynolds, Soc. Lab., 2,070.
1936 (Pres.), Roosevelt, Dem., 943,974; Landon, Rep., 691,570; Lemke, Union, 19,407; Thomas, Soc., 3,856; Browder, Com., 1,090.
1940 (Pres.), Roosevelt, Dem., 874,063; Willkie, Rep., 899,466; Babson, Proh., 6,437; Thomas, Soc., 2,075; Aiken, Soc. Lab., 706.
1944 (Pres.), Roosevelt, Dem., 781,403; Dewey, Rep., 875,891; Watson, Proh., 12,574; Thomas, Soc., 2,223.
1948 (Pres.), Truman, Dem., 807,833; Dewey, Rep., 821,079; Watson, Proh., 14,711; Wallace, Prog., 9,649; Thomas, Soc., 2,179; Teichert, Soc. Lab., 763.
1952 (Pres.), Eisenhower, Rep., 1,136,259; Stevenson, Dem., 801,530; Hamblen, Proh., 15,335; Hallinan, Prog., 1,222; Hass, Soc. Lab., 979.
1956 (Pres.), Eisenhower, Rep., 1,182,811; Stevenson, Dem., 783,908; Holtwick, Proh., 6,554; Haas, 1,334.
1960 (Pres.), Kennedy, Dem., 952,358; Nixon, Rep., 1,175,120; Decker, Proh., 6,746; Hass, Soc. Lab., 1,136.
1964 (Pres.), Johnson, Dem., 1,170,848; Goldwater, Rep., 911,118; Munn, Proh., 8,266; Hass, Soc. Lab. 1,374.
1968 (Pres.), Nixon, Rep., 1,067,885; Humphrey, Dem., 806,659; Wallace, 3rd party 243,108; Munn, Prohibition, 4,616; Halstead, Soc. Worker, 1,293; Gregory, 36.
1972 (Pres.), Nixon, Rep., 1,405,154; McGovern, Dem., 708,568; Reed, Soc. Worker, 5,575; Fisher, Soc. Labor, 1,688; Spock, Peace & Freedom, 4,544.

Iowa

1932 (Pres.), Roosevelt, Dem., 598,019; Hoover, Rep., 414,433; Thomas, Soc., 20,467; Upshaw, Proh., 2,111; Coxey, Farm-Lab., 1,094; Foster, Com., 559.
1936 (Pres.), Roosevelt, Dem., 621,756; Landon, Rep., 487,977; Lemke, Union, 29,687; Thomas, Soc., 1,373; Colvin, Proh., 1,182; Browder, C., 506; Aiken, S., 252.
1940 (Pres.), Roosevelt, Dem., 578,800; Willkie, Rep., 632,370; Babson, Proh., 2,284; Browder, Com., 1,524; Aiken, Soc. Lab., 452.
1944 (Pres.), Roosevelt, Dem., 499,876; Dewey, Rep., 547,267; Watson, Proh., 3,752; Thomas, Soc., 1,511; Teichert, Soc. Lab., 193.
1948 (Pres.), Truman, Dem., 522,380; Dewey, Rep., 494,018; Wallace, Prog., 12,125; Teichert, Soc. Lab., 4,274; Watson, Proh., 3,382; Thomas, Soc., 1,829; Dobbs, Soc. Workers, 2 6.
1952 (Pres.), Eisenhower, Rep., 808,906; Stevenson, Dem., 451,513; Hallinan, Prog., 5,085; Hamblen, Proh., 2,882; Hoopes, Soc., 219; Haas, Soc. Lab., 139; Scattering 29.
1956 (Pres.), Eisenhower, Rep., 729,187; Stevenson, Dem., 501,858; Andrews (A.C.P of Iowa), 3,202; Hoopes, Soc., 192; Haas, Soc. Lab., 125.
1960 (Pres.), Kennedy, Dem., 550,565; Nixon, Rep., 722,381; Haas, Soc. Lab., 230; Write-in, 634.
1964 (Pres.), Johnson, Dem., 733,030; Goldwater, Rep., 449,148; Haas, S. L., 182; DeBerry, S. W. 159; Munn, P., 1,902.
1968 (Pres.), Nixon, Rep., 619,106; Humphrey, Dem., 476,699; Wallace, 3rd party, 66,422; Munn, Pro. 362; Halstead, Soc. Worker, 3,377; Cleaver, Peace and Freedom, 1332; Dlomen, S. L., 241.
1972 (Pres.), Nixon, Rep., 706,207; McGovern, Dem., 496,206; Schmitz, American, 22,056; Jenness, Soc. Worker, 488; Fisher, Soc. Labor, 195; Hall, Communist, 272; Green, Universal, 199; scattered 321.

Kansas

1932 (Pres.), Roosevelt, Dem., 424,204; Hoover, Rep., 349,498; Thomas, Soc., 18,276.

1936 (Pres.), Roosevelt, Dem., 464,520; Landon, Rep., 397,727; Thomas, Soc., 2,766; Lemke, Union, 494.
1940 (Pres.), Roosevelt, Dem., 464,725; Willkie, Rep., 489,169; Babson, Proh., 4,056; Thomas, Soc., 2,347.
1944 (Pres.), Roosevelt, Dem., 287,458; Dewey, Rep., 442,096; Watson, Proh., 2,609; Thomas, Soc., 1,613.
1948 (Pres.), Truman, Dem., 351,902; Dewey, Rep., 423,039; Watson, Proh., 6,468; Wallace, Prog., 4,603; Thomas, Soc., 2,807.
1952 (Pres.), Eisenhower, Rep., 616,302; Stevenson, Dem., 273,296; Hamblen, Proh., 6,038; Hoopes, Soc., 530.
1956 (Pres.), Eisenhower, Rep., 566,878; Stevenson, Dem., 296,317; Holtwick, Proh., 3,048.
1960 (Pres.), Kennedy, Dem., 363,213; Nixon, Rep., 561,474; Decker, Proh., 4,138.
1964 (Pres.), Johnson, Dem., 464,028; Goldwater, Rep., 386,579; Munn, Proh., 5,393; Haas, Soc. Labor, 1,901.
1968 (Pres.), Nixon, Rep., 478,674; Humphrey, Dem., 302,996; Wallace, 3rd, 88,921; Munn, Proh., 2,192.
1972 (Pres.), Nixon, Rep., 619,812; McGovern, Dem., 270,287; Schmitz, Cons. 21,808; Munn, Proh. 4,188.

Kentucky

1932 (Pres.), Roosevelt, Dem., 580,574; Hoover, Rep., 394,716; Upshaw, Proh., 2,252; Thomas, Soc., 3,853; Reynolds, Soc. Lab., 1,396; Foster, Com., 272.
1936 (Pres.), Roosevelt, Dem., 541,944; Landon, Rep., 369,702; Lemke, Union, 12,501; Colvin, Proh., 929; Thomas, S., 627; Aiken, S. L., 294; Browder, Com., 204.
1940 (Pres.), Roosevelt, Dem., 557,222; Willkie, Rep., 410,384; Babson, Proh., 1,443; Thomas, Soc., 1,014.
1944 (Pres.), Roosevelt, Dem., 472,589; Dewey, Rep., 392,448; Watson, Proh., 2,023; Thomas, Soc., 535; Teichert, Soc. Lab., 326.
1948 (Pres.), Truman, Dem., 466,756; Dewey, Rep., 341,210; Thurmond, States' Rights, 10,411; Wallace, Prog. 1,567; Thomas, Soc., 1,284; Watson, Proh., 1,245; Teichert, Soc. Lab., 185.
1952 (Pres.), Eisenhower, Rep., 495,029; Stevenson, Dem., 495,729; Hemblen, Proh., 1,161; Haas, Soc. Lab., 893; Hallinan, Proh., 336.
1956 (Pres.), Eisenhower, Rep., 572,192; Stevenson, Dem., 476,453; Byrd, States' Rights, 2,657; Holtwick, Proh., 2,145; Haas, Soc. Leb., 358.
1960 (Pres.), Kennedy, Dem., 521,855; Nixon, Rep., 602,607.
1964 (Pres.), Johnson, Dem., 669,659; Goldwater, Rep., 372,977; John Kasper, Nat'l. States Rights, 3,469.
1968 (Pres.), Nixon, Rep., 462,411; Humphrey, Dem., 397,547; Wallace, 3rd p., 193,098; Halstead, S. W., 2,843.
1972 (Pres.), Nixon, Rep., 676,446; McGovern, Dem., 371,159; Schmitz, Amer., 17,627; Jenness, Soc. Worker, 685; Hall, Comm., 464; Spock, Peoples, 1,118.

Louisiana

1932 (Pres.), Roosevelt, D., 249,418; Hoover, R., 18,-863.
1936 (Pres.), Roosevelt, D., 292,894; Landon, R., 36,-791.
1940 (Pres.), Roosevelt, D., 319,751; Willkie, R., 52,446.
1944 (Pres.), Roosevelt, D., 281,564; Dewey, R., 67,-750.
1948 (Pres.), Thurmond, States' Rights, 204,290; Truman, D., 136,344; Dewey, R., 72,657; Wallace, Prog., 3,035.
1952 (Pres.), Eisenhower, R., 306,925; Stevenson, D., 345,027.
1956 (Pres.), Eisenhower, Rep., 329,047; Stevenson, Dem., 243,977; Andrews, States' Rights, 44,520.
1960 (Pres.), Kennedy, Dem., 407,339; Nixon, Rep., 230,890; States' Rights (unpledged) 169,572.
1964 (Pres.), Johnson, D., 387,068; Goldwater, R., 509,225.

1968 (Pres.), Nixon, Rep., 257,535; Humphrey, Dem., 309,615; Wallace, 3rd party, 530,300.
1972 (Pres.), Nixon, Rep., 686,852; McGovern, Dem., 298,142; Schmitz, American, 52,099; Jenness, Soc. Worker, 14,398.

Maine

1932 (Pres.), Roosevelt, Dem., 128,907; Hoover, Rep., 166,631; Thomas, Soc., 2,439; Reynolds, Soc. Lab., 255; Foster, Com., 162.
1936 (Pres.), Landon, Rep., 168,823; Roosevelt, Dem., 126,333; Lemke, Union, 7,581; Thomas, Soc., 783; Colvin, Proh., 334; Browder, Com., 257; Aiken, Soc. Lab., 129.
1940 (Pres.), Roosevelt, Dem., 156,478; Willkie, Rep., 165,951; Browder, Com., 411.
1944 (Pres.), Roosevelt, Dem., 140,631; Dewey, Rep., 155,434; Teichert, Soc. Lab., 335.
1948 (Pres.), Truman, Dem., 111,916; Dewey, Rep., 150,234; Wallace, Prog., 1,884; Thomas, Soc., 547; Teichert, Soc. Lab., 206.
1952 (Pres.), Eisenhower, Rep. 232,353; Stevenson, Dem., 118,806; Hallinan, Prog., 332; Hass, Soc. Lab., 156; Hoopes, Soc., 138; Scattered, 1.
1956 (Pres.), Eisenhower, Rep., 249,238; Stevenson, Dem., 102,468.
1960 (Pres.), Kennedy, Dem., 181,159; Nixon, Rep., 240,608.
1964 (Pres.), Johnson, Dem., 262,264; Goldwater, Rep., 118,701.
1968 (Pres.), Nixon, Rep., 169,254; Humphrey, Dem., 217,312; Wallace, 3rd party, 6,370.
1972 (Pres.), Nixon, Rep., 256,458; McGovern, Dem., 160,584; scattered, 229.

Maryland

1932 (Pres.), Roosevelt, Dem., 314,314; Hoover, Rep., 184,184; Thomas, Soc., 10,489; Reynolds, Soc. Lab., 1,036; Foster, Com., 1,031.
1936 (Pres.), Roosevelt, Dem., 389,612; Landon, Rep., 231,435; Thomas, Soc., 1,629; Aiken, Soc. Lab., 1,305; Browder, Com.,915.
1940 (Pres.), Roosevelt, Dem., 384,546; Willkie, Rep., 269,534; Thomas, Soc., 4,093; Browder, Com., 1,274; Aken, Lab., 657.
1944 (Pres.), Roosevelt, Dem., 315,490; Dewey, Rep., 292,949.
1948 (Pres.), Truman, Dem., 286,521; Dewey, Rep., 294,814; Wallace, Prog., 9,983; Thomas, Soc., 2,941; Thurmond, States' Rights, 2,476; Wright, Write-in 2,294.
1952 (Pres.), Eisenhower, Rep., 499,424; Stevenson, Dem., 395,337; Hallinan, Prog., 7,313.
1956 (Pres.), Eisenhower, Rep., 559,738; Stevenson, Dem., 372,613.
1960 (Pres.), Kennedy, Dem., 565,800; Nixon, Rep., 489,538.
1964 (Pres.), Johnson, Dem., 730,912; Goldwater, Rep., 385,495; Write-in, 50.
1968 (Pres.), Nixon, Rep., 517,995; Humphrey, Dem., 538,310; Wallace, 3rd party, 178,734.
1972 (Pres.), Nixon, Rep., 829,305; McGovern, Dem., 505,781; Schmitz, American Party, 18,726.

Massachusetts

1932 (Pres.), Roosevelt, Dem., 800,148; Hoover, Rep., 736,959; Thomas, Soc. 34,305; Foster, Com., 4,821; Reynolds, Soc. Lab., 2,668; Upshaw, Proh., 1,142.
1936 (Pres.), Roosevelt, Dem., 942,716; Landon, Rep., 768,613; Lemke, Union, 118,639; Thomas, Soc., 5,111; Browder, Com., 2,930; Aiken, Soc. Lab., 1,305; Colvin, Proh. 1,032.
1940 (Pres.), Roosevelt, Dem., 1,076,522; Willkie, Rep., 939,700; Thomas, Soc., 4,091; Browder, Com., 3,806; Aiken, Soc. Lab., 1,492; Babson, Proh., 1,370.
1944 (Pres.), Roosevelt, Dem., 1,035,296; Dewey, Rep., 921,350; Teichert, Soc. Lab., 2,780; Watson, Proh., 973.
1948 (Pres.), Truman, Dem., 1,151,788; Dewey, Rep.,

909,370; Wallace, Prog., 38,157; Teichert, Soc. Lab., 5,535; Watson, Proh., 1,663.

1952 (Pres.), Eisenhower, Rep., 1,292,325; Stevenson, Dem., 1,083,525; Hallinan, Prog., 4,636; Hass, Soc. Lab., 1,957; Hamblen, Proh., 886; Scattered, 69; Blanks, 41,150.

1956 (Pres.), Eisenhower, Rep., 1,393,197; Stevenson, Dem., 948,190; Hass, Soc. Lab., 5,573; Holtwick, Proh., 1,205; Others, 341.

1960 (Pres.), Kennedy, Dem., 1,487,174; Nixon, Rep., 976,750; Hass, Soc. Lab., 3,892; Decker, Proh., 1,633; Others, 31; Blank and void, 26,024.

1964 (Pres.), Johnson, Dem., 1,786,422; Goldwater, Rep., 549,727; Hass, Soc. Lab., 4,755; Munn, Proh., 3,735; scattered 159; Blank 48,104.

1968 (Pres.), Nixon, Rep., 766,844; Humphrey, Dem., 1,469,218; Wallace, 3rd party, 87,088; Blomen, Soc. Labor, 6,180; Munn, Prohibition, 2,369; scattered 53; blanks 25,394.

1972 (Pres.), Nixon, Rep., 1,112,078; McGovern, Dem. 1,332,540; Jenness, Soc. Worker, 10,600; Fisher, Soc. Labor, 129; Schmitz, American, 2,877; Spock, Peoples, 101; Hall, Communist, 46; Hospers, Libertarian, 43; scattered 342.

Michigan

1932 (Pres.), Roosevelt, Dem., 871,700; Hoover, Rep., 739,894; Thomas, Soc., 39,025; Foster, Com., 9,318; Upshaw, Proh., 2,893; Reynolds, Soc. Lab., 1,041; Harvey, Lib., 217.

1936 (Pres.), Roosevelt, Dem., 1,016,794; Landon, Rep., 699,733; Lemke, Union, 75,795; Thomas, Soc., 8,208; Browder, Com., 3,384; Aiken, Soc. Lab., 600; Colvin, Proh., 579.

1940 (Pres.), Roosevelt, Dem., 1,032,991; Willkie, Rep., 1,039,917; Thomas, Soc., 7,593; Browder, Com., 2,834; Babson, Proh., 1,795; Aiken, Soc. Lab., 795.

1944 (Pres.), Roosevelt, Dem., 1,106,899; Dewey, Rep., 1,084,423; Watson, Proh., 6,503; Thomas, Soc., 4,598; Smith, America First, 1,530; Teichert, Soc. Lab., 1,264.

1948 (Pres.), Truman, Dem., 1,003,448; Dewey, Rep., 1,038,595; Wallace, Prog., 46,515; Watson, Proh., 13,052; Thomas, Soc., 6,063; Teichert, Soc. Lab., 1,263; Dobbs, Soc. Workers, 672.

1952 (Pres.), Eisenhower, Rep., 1,551,529; Stevenson, Dem., 1,230,657; Hamblen, Proh., 10,331; Hallinan, Prog., 3,922; Hass, Soc. Lab., 1,495; Dobbs, Soc. Workers, 655; Scattered, 3.

1956 (Pres.), Eisenhower, Rep., 1,713,647; Stevenson, Dem., 1,359,898; Holtwick, Proh., 6,923.

1960 (Pres.), Kennedy, Dem., 1,687,269; Nixon, Rep., 1,620,428; Dobbs, Soc. Workers, 4,347; Decker, Proh., 2,029; Daly, Tax Cut, 1,767; Hass, Soc. Lab., 1,718; Ind. American 539.

1964 (Pres.), Johnson, Dem., 2,136,615; Goldwater, Rep., 1,060,152; DeBerry, Soc. Worker, 3,817; Hass, Soc. Lab., 1,704; Proh. (no candidate listed), 699; Scattering, 145.

1968 (Pres.), Nixon, Rep., 1,370,665; Humphrey, Dem., 1,593,082; Wallace, 3rd party, 331,968; Halstead, Soc. Worker, 4,099; Blomen, Soc. Labor, 1,762; Cleaver, New Politics, 4,585; Munn, Prohib., 60; Scattering 29.

1972 (Pres.), Nixon, Rep., 1,961,721; McGovern, Dem., 1,459,435; Schmitz, Amer., 63,321; Fisher, Soc. Labor, 2,437; Jenness, Soc. Worker, 1,603; Hall, Communist, 1,210.

Minnesota

1932 (Pres.), Roosevelt, Dem., 600,806; Hoover, Rep., 363,959; Thomas, Soc., 25,476; Foster, Com., 6,101; Coxey, Farm.-Lab., 5,731; Reynolds, Ind., 770.

1936 (Pres.), Roosevelt, Dem., 698,811; Landon, Rep., 350,461; Lemke, Union, 74,296; Thomas, Soc., 2,872; Browder, Com., 2,574; Aiken, Soc., 961.

1940 (Pres.), Roosevelt, Dem., 644,196; Willkie, Rep., 596,274; Thomas, Soc., 5,454; Browder, Com., 2,711; Aiken, Ind., 2,553.

1944 (Pres.), Roosevelt, Dem., 589,864; Dewey, Rep., 527,416; Thomas, Soc., 5,073; Teichert, Ind., Gov't., 3,176.

1948 (Pres.), Truman, Dem., 692,966; Dewey, Rep., 483,617; Wallace, Prog., 27,866; Thomas, Soc., 4,646; Teichert, Soc. Lab., 2,525; Dobbs, Soc. Workers, 606.

1952 (Pres.), Eisenhower, Rep., 763,211; Stevenson, Dem., 608,458; Hallinan, Prog., 2,666; Hass, Soc. Lab., 2,383; Hamblen, Proh., 2,147; Dobbs, Soc. Workers, 618.

1956 (Pres.), Eisenhower, Rep., 719,302; Stevenson Dem., 617,525; Hass, Soc. Lab. (Ind. Gov.), 2,080; Dobbs, Soc. Workers, 1,098.

1960 (Pres.), Kennedy, Dem., 779,933; Nixon, Rep., 757,915; Dobbs, Soc. Workers, 3,077; Industrial Gov., 962.

1964 (Pres.), Johnson, Dem., 991,117; Goldwater, Rep., 559,624; DeBerry, Soc. Workers, 1,177; Hass, Industrial Gov., 2,544.

1968 (Pres.), Nixon, Rep., 658,643; Humphrey, Dem., 857,738; Wallace, 3rd party, 68,931; scattered 2,443; Halstead, Soc. Worker, 808; Blomen, Ind. Gov't., 285; Mitchell, Communist, 415; Cleaver, Peace, 935; McCarthy, write-in 585; scattered 170.

1972 (Pres.), Nixon, Rep. 898,269; McGovern, Dem., 802,346; Schmitz, American, 31,407; Spock, Peoples, 2,805; Fisher, Soc. Labor, 4,261; Jenness, Soc. Worker, 940; Hall, Communist, 662; scattered 962.

Mississippi

1932 (Pres.), Roosevelt, Dem., 140,168; Hoover, Rep., 5,180; Thomas, Soc., 686.

1936 (Pres.), Roosevelt, Dem., 157,318; Landon, Rep., Howard faction, 2,760; Rowlands faction, 1,675; total, 4,435; Thomas, Soc., 329.

1940 (Pres.), Roosevelt, Dem., 168,252; Willkie, Ind. Rep., 4,550; Rep., 2,814; total, 7,364; Thomas, Soc., 103.

1944 (Pres.), Roosevelt, Dem., 158,515; Dewey, Rep., 3,742; Reg. Dem., 9,964; Ind. Rep., 7,859.

1948 (Pres.), Thurmond, States' Rights, 167,538; Truman, Dem., 19,384; Dewey, Rep., 5,043; Wallace, Prog., 225.

1952 (Pres.), Eisenhower, Ind. vote pledged to Rep. candidate, 112,966; Stevenson, Dem., 172,566.

1956 (Pres.), Stevenson, Dem., 144,498; Eisenhower, Rep., 56,372; Black and Tan Grand Old Party, 4,313; total, 60,685; Byrd, Independent, 42,966.

1960 (Pres.), Democratic unpledged electors, 116,248; Kennedy, Dem., 108,362; Nixon, Rep., 73,561. Mississippi's victorious slate of 8 unpledged Democratic electors cast their votes for Sen. Harry F. Byrd (D-Va.).

1964 (Pres.), Johnson, Dem., 52,618; Goldwater, Rep., 356,528.

1968 (Pres.), Nixon, Rep., 88,516; Humphrey, Dem., 150,644; Wallace, 3rd party, 415,349.

1972 (Pres.), Nixon, Rep., 505,125; McGovern, Dem., 126,782; Schmitz, American, 11,598; Jenness, Soc. Worker, 2,458.

Missouri

1932 (Pres.), Roosevelt, Dem., 1,025,406; Hoover, Rep., 564,713; Thomas, Soc., 16,374; Upshaw, Proh., 2,429; Foster, Com., 568; Reynolds, Soc. Lab., 404.

1936 (Pres.), Roosevelt, Dem., 1,111,403; Landon, Rep., 697,891; Lemke, Union, 14,630; Thomas, Soc., 3,454; Colvin, Proh., 908; Browder, Com., 417; Aiken, Soc. Lab., 292.

1940 (Pres.), Roosevelt, Dem., 958,476; Willkie, Rep., 871,009; Thomas, Soc., 2,226; Babson, Proh., 1,809; Aiken, Soc. Lab., 209.

1944 (Pres.), Roosevelt, Dem., 807,357; Dewey, Rep., 761,175; Thomas, Soc., 1,750; Watson, Proh., 1,175; Teichert, Soc. Lab., 221.

1948 (Pres.), Truman, Dem., 917,315; Dewey, Rep., 655,039; Wallace, Prog., 3,998; Thomas, Soc., 2,222.

1952 (Pres.), Eisenhower, Rep., 959,429; Stevenson,

Dem., 929,830; Hallinan, Prog., 987; Hamblen, Proh., 885; MacArthur, Christian Nationalist, 302; America First, 233; Hoopes, Soc. 227; Hess, Soc. Lab., 169.
1956 (Pres.), Stevenson, Dem., 918,273; Eisenhower, Rep., 914,299.
1960 (Pres.), Kennedy, Dem., 972,201; Nixon, Rep., 962,221.
1964 (Pres.), Johnson, Dem., 1,164,344; Goldwater, Rep., 653,535.
1968 (Pres.), Nixon, Rep., 811,932; Humphrey, Dem., 791,444; Wallace, 3rd party, 206,126.
1972 (Pres.), Nixon, Rep., 1,154,058; McGovern, Dem., 698,531.

Montana

1924 (Pres.), Coolidge, Rep., 74,138; LaFollette, Prog., 61,105; Davis, Dem., 33,805; Foster, Workers, 357; Johns, Soc., Lab., 247.
1928 (Pres.), Hoover, Rep., 113,300; Smith, Dem., 78,578; Thomas, Soc., 1,667; Foster, Com., 563.
1932 (Pres.), Roosevelt, Dem., 127,286; Hoover, Rep., 78,078; Thomas, Soc., 7,891; Foster, Com., 1,775; Harvey, Lib., 1,449.
1936 (Pres.), Roosevelt, Dem., 159,690; Landon, Rep., 63,598; Lemke, Union, 5,549; Thomas, Soc., 1,066; Browder, Com., 385; Colvin, Proh., 224.
1940 (Pres.), Roosevelt, Dem., 145,698; Willkie, Rep., 99,579; Thomas, Soc., 1,443; Babson, Proh., 664; Browder, Com., 489.
1944 (Pres.), Roosevelt, Dem., 112,556; Dewey, Rep., 93,163; Thomas, Soc., 1,296; Watson, Proh., 340.
1948 (Pres.), Truman, Dem., 119,071; Dewey, Rep., 96,770; Wallace, Prog., 7,313; Thomas, Soc., 695; Watson, Proh., 429.
1952 (Pres.), Eisenhower, Rep., 157,394; Stevenson, Dem., 106,213; Hallinan, Prog., 723; Hamblen, Proh., 548; Hoopes, Soc. 159.
1956 (Pres.), Eisenhower, Rep., 154,933; Stevenson, Dem., 116,238.
1960 (Pres.), Kennedy, Dem., 134,891; Nixon, Rep., 141,841; Decker, Proh., 456; Dobbs, Soc. Workers, 391.
1964 (Pres.), Johnson, Dem., 164,246; Goldwater, Rep., 113,032; Kasper, Nat'l States Rights, 519; Munn, Proh., 499; DeBerry, Soc. Worker, 332.
1968 (Pres.), Nixon, Rep., 138,835; Humphrey, Dem., 114,117; Wallace, 3rd party, 20,015; Halstead, Soc. Worker, 457; Munn, Prohibition 510; Caton, New Reform, 470.
1972 (Pres.), Nixon, Rep., 183,976; McGovern, Dem., 120,197; Schmitz, American, 13,430.

Nebraska

1932 (Pres.), Roosevelt, Dem., 359,082; Hoover, Rep., 201,177; Thomas, Soc., 9,876.
1936 (Pres.), Roosevelt, Dem., 347,454; Landon, Rep., 248,731; Lemke, Union, 12,847.
1940 (Pres.), Roosevelt, Dem., 263,677; Willkie, Rep., 352,201.
1944 (Pres.), Roosevelt, Dem., 233,246; Dewey, Rep., 329,880.
1948 (Pres.), Truman, Dem., 224,165; Dewey, Rep., 264,774.
1952 (Pres.), Eisenhower, Rep., 421,603; Stevenson, Dem., 188,057.
1956 (Pres.), Eisenhower, Rep., 378,108; Stevenson, Dem., 199,029.
1960 (Pres.), Kennedy, Dem., 232,542; Nixon, Rep., 380,553.
1964 (Pres.), Johnson, Dem., 307,307; Goldwater, Rep., 276,847..
1968 (Pres.), Nixon, Rep., 321,163; Humphrey, Dem., 170,784; Wallace, 3rd party, 44,904.
1972 (Pres.), Nixon, Rep., 406,298; McGovern, Dem., 169,991; scattered 817.

Nevada

1932 (Pres.), Roosevelt, Dem., 28,756; Hoover, Rep., 12,674.

1936 (Pres.), Roosevelt, Dem., 31,925; Landon, Rep., 11,923.
1940 (Pres.), Roosevelt, Dem., 31,945; Willkie, Rep., 21,229.
1944 (Pres.), Roosevelt, Dem., 29,623; Dewey, Rep., 24,611.
1948 (Pres.), Truman, Dem., 31,291; Dewey, Rep., 29,357; Wallace, Prog., 1,469.
1952 (Pres.), Eisenhower, Rep., 50,502; Stevenson, Dem., 31,688.
1956 (Pres.), Eisenhower, Rep., 56,049; Stevenson, Dem., 40,640.
1960 (Pres.), Kennedy, Dem., 54,880; Nixon, Rep., 52,387.
1964 (Pres.), Johnson, Dem., 79,339; Goldwater, Rep., 56,094.
1968 (Pres.), Nixon, Rep., 73,188; Humphrey, Dem., 60,598; Wallace, 3rd party, 20,432.
1972 (Pres.), Nixon, Rep., 115,750; McGovern, Dem. 66,016.

New Hampshire

1932 (Pres.), Roosevelt, Dem., 100,680; Hoover, Rep., 103,629; Thomas, Soc., 947; Foster, Com., 264.
1936 (Pres.), Roosevelt, Dem., 108,640; Landon, Rep., 104,642; Lemke, Union, 4,819; Browder, Com., 193.
1940 (Pres.), Roosevelt, Dem., 125,292; Willkie, Rep., 110,127.
1944 (Pres.), Roosevelt, Dem., 119,663; Dewey, Rep., 109,916; Thomas, Soc., 46.
1948 (Pres.), Truman, Dem., 107,995; Dewey, Rep., 121,299; Wallace, Prog., 1,970; Thomas, Soc., 86; Teichert, Soc. Lab., 83; Thurmond, States' Rights, 7.
1952 (Pres.), Eisenhower, R., 166,287; Stevenson, D., 106,663.
1956 (Pres.), Eisenhower, R., 176,519; Stevenson, D., 90,364; Andrews, Const., 111.
1960 (Pres.), Kennedy, D., 137,772; Nixon, R., 157,989.
1964 (Pres.), Johnson, D., 182,065; Goldwater, R., 104,029.
1968 (Pres.), Nixon, Rep., 154,903; Humphrey, Dem., 130,589; Wallace, 3rd party, 11,173; New Party, 421; Halstead, Soc. Worker, 104.
1972 (Pres.), Nixon, Rep., 213,724; McGovern, Dem., 116,435; Schmitz, American, 3,386; Jenness, Soc. Worker, 368; Scattered, 142.

New Jersey

1932 (Pres.), Roosevelt, Dem., 806,630; Hoover, Rep., 775,684; Thomas, Soc., 42,998; Foster, Com., 2,915; Reynolds, Soc. Lab., 1,062; Upshaw, Proh., 774.
1936 (Pres.), Roosevelt, Dem., 1,083,549; Landon Rep., 719,421; Lemke, Union, 9,405; Thomas, Soc., 3,895; Browder, Com., 1,590; Colvin, Proh., 916; Aiken, Soc. Lab., 346.
1940 (Pres.), Roosevelt, Dem., 1,016,404; Willkie, Rep. 944,876; Browder, Com., 8,814; Thomas, Soc., 2,823; Babson, Proh., 851; Aiken, Soc. Lab., 446.
1944 (Pres.), Roosevelt, Dem., 987,874; Dewey, Rep., 961,335; Teichert, Soc. Lab., 6,939; Watson, Nat'l Proh., 4,255; Thomas, Soc., 3,385.
1948 (Pres.), Truman, Dem., 895,455; Dewey, Rep., 981,124; Wallace, Prog., 42,683; Watson, Proh., 10,593; Thomas, Soc., 10,521; Dobbs, Soc. Workers, 5,825; Teichert, Soc. Lab., 3,354.
1952 (Pres.), Eisenhower, Rep., 1,373,613; Stevenson, Dem., 1,015,902; Hoopes, Soc., 8,593; Hass, Soc. Lab., 5,815; Hallinan, Prog., 5,589; Krajewski, Poor Man's, 4,203; Dobbs, Soc. Workers, 3,850; Hamblen, Proh., 989.
1956 (Pres.), Eisenhower, Rep., 1,606,942; Stevenson, Dem., 850,337; Holtwick, Proh., 9,147; Hass, Soc. Lab., 6,736; Andrews, Conservative, 5,317; Dobbs, Soc. Workers, 4,004; Krajewski, American Third Party, 1,829.
1960 (Pres.), Kennedy, Dem., 1,385,415; Nixon, Rep., 1,363,324; Dobbs, Soc. Workers, 11,402; Lee, Conservative, 8,708; Hass, Soc. Lab., 4,262.
1964 (Pres.), Johnson, Dem., 1,867,671; Goldwater,

Rep., 963,843; DeBerry, Soc. Workers, 8,181; Hass, Soc. Labor, 7,075,
1968 (Pres.), Nixon, Rep., 1,325,467; Humphrey, Dem., 1,264,206; Wallace, 3rd party, 262,187; Halstead, Soc. Worker, 8,667; Gregory, Peace Freedom, 8,084; Blomen, Soc. Labor, 6,784.
1972 (Pres.), Nixon, Rep., 1,845,502; McGovern, Dem., 1,102,211; Schmitz, American, 34,378; Spock, Peoples, 5,355; Fisher, Soc. Labor, 4,544; Jenness, Soc. Worker, 2,233; Mahalchik, Amer. First, 1,743; Hall, Communist, 1,263.

New Mexico

1932 (Pres.), Roosevelt, Dem., 95,089; Hoover, Rep., 54,217; Thomas, Soc., 11,776; Harvey, Lib., 389; Foster, Com., 135.
1936 (Pres.), Roosevelt, Dem., 1105,838; Landon, Rep., 961,710; Lemke, Union, 942; Thomas, tSoc., 343; Browder, Com., 43.
1940 (Pres.), Roosevelt, D., 9103,699; Willkie, R., 79,-315.
1944 (Pres.), Roosevelt, Dem., 81,389; Dewey, Rep., 170,688; Watson, Proh., 148.
1948 (Pres.), Truman, Dem., 105,464; Dewey, ,Rep., 80,303; Wallace, Prog., 1,037; Watson, Proh., 127; Thomas, Soc., 83; Teichert, Soc. Lab., 49.
1952 (Pres.), Eisenhower, Rep., .132,170; Stevenson, Dem., .105,661; Hamblen, Proh., 297; Hallinan, Ind. Prog., 225; MacArthur, Christian ; National, 220; Hass, Soc. Lab., 35.
1956 (Pres.), Eisenhower, Rep., 2146,788; Stevenson, Dem., 1106,098; Holtwick, Proh., 607; Andrews, Ind., 364; Hass, Soc. Lab., 69.
1960 (Pres.), Kennedy, Dem., 156,027; Nixon, Rep., 1153,733; Decker, Proh., 777; Hass, Soc. Lab., 570.
1964 (Pres.), Johnson, Dem., 194,017; Goldwater, Rep., 131,838; Hass, Soc. Labor, 1,217; Munn, Proh., 543.
1968 (Pres.), Nixon, Rep., 169,692; Humphrey, Dem., 130,081; Wallace, 3rd party, 25,737; Chavez, 1,519; Halstead, Soc. Worker, 252.
1972 (Pres.), Nixon, Rep., 235,606; McGovern, Dem., 141,084; Schmitz, Amer., 8,767; Jenness, S. W., 474.

New York

1932 (Pres.), Roosevelt, Dem., 2,534,959; Hoover, Rep., 1,937,963; Thomas, Soc., 177,397; Foster, Com., 27,956; Reynolds, Soc. Lab., 10,339.
1936 (Pres.), Roosevelt, Dem., 2,018,298; American Lab., 274,924; total, 3,293,222; Landon, Rep., 2,180,-670; Thomas, Soc., 86,879; Browder, Com., 35,609.
1940 (Pres.), Roosevelt, Dem., 2,834,500; American Lab., 417,418; total 3,251,918; Willkie, Rep., 3,027,-478; Thomas, Soc., 18,950; Babson, Proh., 3,250.
1944 (Pres.), Roosevelt, Dem., 2,478,598; American Lab., 496,405; Liberal, 329,325; total, 3,304,238; Dewey, Rep., 2,987,647; Teichert, Ind. Gov't., 14,-352; Thomas, Soc., 10,553.
1948 (Pres.), Truman, Dem., 2,557,642; Liberal, 222,-562; total, 2,780,204; Dewey, Rep., 2,841,163; Wallace, Amer, Lab., 509,559; Thomas, Soc., 40,879; Teichert, Ind. Gov't., 2,729; Dobbs, Soc. Workers, 2,675.
1952 (Pres.), Eisenhower, Rep., 3,952,815; Stevenson, Dem., 2,687,890, Liberal, 416,711; total, 3,104,601; Hallinan, American Lab., 64,211; Hoopes, Soc., 2,664; Dobbs, Soc. Workers, 2,212; Hass, Ind. Gov't., 1,560; scattering, 178; blank and void, 87,813.
1956 (Pres.), Eisenhower, Rep., 4,340,340; Stevenson, Dem., 2,458,212; Liberal, 292,557; total, 2,750,769. Write-in votes for Andrews, 1,027; Werdel, 492; Haas, 150; Hoopes, 82; others, 476.
1960 (Pres.), Kennedy, Dem., 3,423,909; Liberal, 406,-176; total, 3,830,085. Nixon, Rep., 3,446,419; Dobbs, Soc. Workers, 14,319; scattering, 256; blank and void, 88,896.
1964 (Pres.), Johnson, Dem., 4,913,156; Goldwater, Rep., 2,243,559; Hass, Soc. Labor, 6,085; DeBerry, Soc. Workers, 3,215; scattering, 188; blank and void, 151,383.

1968 (Pres.), Nixon, Rep., 3,007,932; Humphrey, Dem., 3,378,470; Wallace, 3rd party, 358,864; Blomen, Soc. Labor, 8,432; Halstead, Soc. Worker, 11,851; Gregory, Freedom and Peace, 24,517; blank, void and scattering, 171,624.
1972 (Pres.), Nixon, Rep. 3,824,642; Conservative 368,136; McGovern, Dem., 2,767,956; Liberal 183,-128; Reed, Soc. Worker, 7,797; Fisher, Soc. Labor, 4,530; Hall, Communist, 5,641; blank, void or scattered 161,641.

North Carolina

1932 (Pres.), Roosevelt, Dem., 497,566; Hoover, Rep., 208,344; Thomas, Soc., 5,591.
1936 (Pres.), Roosevelt, Dem., 616,141; Landon, Rep., 223,283; Thomas, Soc., 21; Browder, Com., 11; Lemke, Union, 2.
1940 (Pres.), Roosevelt, Dem., 609,015; Willkie, Rep., 213,633.
1944 (Pres.), Roosevelt, Dem., 527,399; Dewey, Rep., 263,155.
1948 (Pres.), Truman, Dem., 459,070; Dewey, Rep., 258,572; Thurmond, States' Rights, 69,652; Wallace, Prog., 3,915.
1952 (Pres.), Eisenhower, Rep., 558,107; Stevenson, Dem., 652,803.
1956 (Pres.), Eisenhower, Rep., 575,062; Stevenson, Dem., 590,530.
1960 (Pres.), Kennedy, Dem., 713,136; Nixon, Rep., 655,420.
1964 (Pres.), Johnson, Dem., 800,139; Goldwater, Rep., 624,844.
1968 (Pres.), Nixon, Rep., 627,192; Humphrey, Dem., 464,113; Wallace, 3rd party, 496,188.
1972 (Pres.), Nixon, Rep., 1,054,889; McGovern, Dem., 438,705; Schmitz, American, 25,018.

North Dakota

1932 (Pres.), Roosevelt, Dem., 178,350; Hoover, Rep., 71,772; Harvey, Lib., 1,817; Thomas, Soc., 3,521; Foster, Com., 830.
1936 (Pres.), Roosevelt, Dem., 163,148; Landon, Rep., 72,751; Lemke, Union, 36,708; Thomas, Soc., 552; Browder, Com., 360; Colvin, Proh., 197.
1940 (Pres.), Roosevelt, Dem., 124,036; Willkie, Rep., 154,590; Thomas, Soc., 1,279; Knuttson, Com., 545; Babson, Proh., 325.
1944 (Pres.), Roosevelt, Dem., 100,144; Dewey, Rep., 118,535; Thomas, Soc., 943; Watson, Proh., 549.
1948 (Pres.), Truman, Dem., 95,812; Dewey, Rep., 115,139; Wallace, Prog., 8,391; Thomas, Soc., 1,000; Thurmond, States' Rights, 374.
1952 (Pres.), Eisenhower, Rep., 191,712; Stevenson, Dem., 76,694; MacArthur, Christian Nationalist, 1,075; Hallinan, Prog., 344; Hamblen, Proh., 302.
1956 (Pres.), Eisenhower, Rep., 156,766; Stevenson, Dem., 96,742; Andrews, American, 483.
1960 (Pres.), Kennedy, Dem., 123,963; Nixon, Rep., 154,310; Dobbs, Soc. Workers, 158.
1964 (Pres.), Johnson, Dem., 149,784; Goldwater, Rep., 108,207; DeBerry, Soc. Worker, 224; Munn, Proh., 174.
1968 (Pres.), Nixon, Rep., 138,669; Humphrey, Dem., 94,769; Wallace, 3rd party, 14,244; Halstead, Soc. Worker, 128; Munn, Prohibition, 38; Troxell, Ind., 34.
1972 (Pres.), Nixon, Rep., 174,109; McGovern, Dem., 100,384; Jenness, Soc. Worker, 288; Hall, Communist, 87; Schmitz, American, 5,646.

Ohio

1932 (Pres.), Roosevelt, Dem., 1,301,695; Hoover, Rep., 1,227,679; Thomas, Soc., 64,094; Upshaw, Proh., 7,421; Foster, Com., 7,221; Reynolds, Soc. Lab., 1,968.
1936 (Pres.), Roosevelt, Dem., 1,747,122; Landon, Rep., 1,127,709; Lemke, Union, 132,212; Browder, Com., 5,251; Thomas, Soc., 117; Aiken, Soc. Lab., 14.

1940 (Pres.), Roosevelt, Dem., 1,733,139; Willkie, Rep., 1,586,773.
1944 (Pres.), Roosevelt, Dem., 1,570,763; Dewey, Rep., 1,582,293.
1948 (Pres.), Truman, Dem., 1,452,791; Dewey, Rep., 1,445,684; Wallace, Prog., 37,596.
1952 (Pres.), Eisenhower, Rep., 2,100,391; Stevenson, Dem., 1,600,367.
1956 (Pres.), Eisenhower, Rep., 2,262,610; Stevenson, Dem., 1,439,655.
1960 (Pres.), Kennedy, Dem., 1,944,248; Nixon, Rep., 2,217,611.
1964 (Pres.), Johnson, Dem., 2,498,331; Goldwater, Rep., 1,470,865.
1968 (Pres.), Nixon, Rep., 1,791,014; Humphrey, Dem., 1,700,586; Wallace, 3rd party, 467,495; Gregory, 372; Munn, Prohibition, 19; Blomen, Soc. Labor, 120; Halstead, Soc. Worker, 69; Mitchell, Communist, 23.
1972 (Pres.), Nixon, Rep., 2,441,827; McGovern, Dem., 1,558,889; Fisher, Soc. Labor, 7,107; Hall, Communist, 6,437; Schmitz, American, 80,067; Wallace, Ind., 460.

Oklahoma

1932 (Pres.), Roosevelt, Dem., 515,468; Hoover, Rep., 188,165.
1936 (Pres.), Roosevelt, Dem., 501,069; Landon, Rep., 245,122; Thomas, Soc., 2,221; Colvin, Proh., e1,328.
1940 (Pres.), Roosevelt, Dem., 474,313; Willkie, Rep., 348,872; Babson, Proh., 3,027.
1944 (Pres.), Roosevelt, Dem., 401,549; Dewey, Rep., 319,424; Watson, Proh., 1,663.
1948 (Pres.), Truman, Dem., 452,782; Dewey, Rep., 268,817.
1952 (Pres.), Eisenhower, Rep., 518,045; Stevenson, Dem., 430,939.
1956 (Pres.), Eisenhower, Rep., 473,769; Stevenson, Dem., 385,581.
1960 (Pres.), Kennedy, Dem., 370,111; Nixon, Rep., 533,039.
1964 (Pres.), Johnson, Dem., 519,834; Goldwater, Rep., 412,665.
1968 (Pres.), Nixon, Rep., 449,697; Humphrey, Dem., 301,658; Wallace, 3rd party, 191,731.
1972 (Pres.), Nixon, Rep., 759,025; McGovern, Dem., 247,147; Schmitz, American, 23,728.

Oregon

1932 (Pres.), Roosevelt, Dem., 213,871; Hoover, Rep., 136,019; Thomas, Soc., 15,450; Reynolds, Soc. Lab., 1,730; Foster, Com., 1,681.
1936 (Pres.), Roosevelt, Dem., 266,733; Landon, Rep., 122,706; Lemke, Union, 21,831; Thomas, Soc., 2,143; Aiken, Soc. Lab., 500; Browder, Com., 104; Colvin, Proh., 4.
1940 (Pres.), Roosevelt, Dem., 258,415; Willkie, Rep., 219,555; Aiken, Soc. Lab., 2,487; Thomas, Soc., 398; Browder, Com., 191; Babson, Proh., 154.
1944 (Pres.), Roosevelt, Dem., 248,635; Dewey, Rep., 225,365; Thomas, Soc., 3,785; Watson, Proh., 2,362.
1948 (Pres.), Truman, Dem., 243,147; Dewey, Rep., 260,904; Wallace, Prog., 14,978; Thomas, Soc., 5,051.
1952 (Pres.), Eisenhower, Rep., 420,815; Stevenson, Dem., 270,579; Hallinan, Ind., 3,665.
1956 (Pres.), Eisenhower, Rep., 406,393; Stevenson, Dem., 329,204.
1960 (Pres.), Kennedy, Dem., 367,402; Nixon, Rep., 408,060.
1964 (Pres.), Johnson, Dem., 501,017; Goldwater, Rep., 282,779; Write-in, 2,509.
1968 (Pres.), Nixon, Rep., 408,433; Humphrey, Dem., 358,866; Wallace, 3rd party, 49,683; Write-ins. McCarthy, 1,496; N. Rockefeller, 69; others, 1,075.
1972 (Pres.), Nixon, Rep., 486,686; McGovern, Dem., 392,760; Schmitz, American, 46,211; Write-in, 2,289.

Pennsylvania

1932 (Pres.), Roosevelt, Dem., 1,295,948; Hoover, Rep., 1,453,540; Thomas, Soc., 91,119; Upshaw, Proh., 11,319; Foster, Com., 5,658; Cox, Jobless, 725; Reynolds, Indust., 659.
1936 (Pres.), Roosevelt, Dem., 2,353,788; Landon, Rep., 1,690,300; Lemke, Royal Oak, 67,467; Thomas, Soc., 14,375; Colvin, Proh., 6,691; Browder, Com., 4,060; Aiken, Ind., Lab., 1,424.
1940 (Pres.), Roosevelt, Dem., 2,171,035; Willkie, Rep., 1,889,848; Thomas, Soc., 10,967; Browder, Com., 4,519; Aiken, Ind. Gov., 1,518.
1944 (Pres.), Roosevelt, Dem., 1,940,479; Dewey, Rep., 1,835,054; Thomas, Soc., 11,721; Watson, Proh., 5,750; Teichert, Ind. Gov., 1,789.
1948 (Pres.), Truman, Dem., 1,752,426; Dewey, Rep., 1,902,197; Wallace, Prog., 55,161; Thomas, Soc., 11,325; Watson, Proh., 10,338; Dobbs, Militant Workers, 2,133; Teichert, Ind. Gov., 1,461.
1952 (Pres.), Eisenhower, Rep., 2,415,789; Stevenson, Dem., 2,146,269; Hamblen, Proh., 8,771; Hallinan, Prog., 4,200; Hoopes, Soc., 2,684; Dobbs, Militant Workers, 1,502; Hass, Ind. Gov., 1,347; Scattered, 155.
1956 (Pres.), Eisenhower, Rep., 2,585,252; Stevenson, Dem., 1,981,769; Hass, Soc. Lab., 7,447; Dobbs, Militant Workers, 2,035.
1960 (Pres.), Kennedy, Dem., 2,556,282; Nixon, Rep., 2,439,956; Hass, Soc. Lab., 7,185; Dobbs, Soc. Workers, 2,678; Scattering, 440.
1964 (Pres.), Johnson, Dem., 3,130,954; Goldwater, Rep., 1,673,657; DeBerry, Soc. Worker, 10,456; Hass, Soc. Labor, 5,092; Scattering, 2,531.
1968 (Pres.), Nixon, Rep., 2,090,017; Humphrey, Dem., 2,259,405; Wallace, 3rd party, 378,582; Blomen, Soc. Labor, 4,977; Halstead, Soc. Worker, 4,862; Gregory, 7,821; others, 2,264.
1972 (Pres.), Nixon, Rep., 2,714,521; McGovern, Dem., 1,796,951; Schmitz, American, 70,593; Jenness, Soc. Worker, 4,639; Hall, Communist, 2,686; Ohers 2,715.

Rhode Island

1932 (Pres.), Roosevelt, Dem., 146,604; Hoover, Rep., 115,266; Thomas, Soc., 3,138; Foster, Com., 546; Reynolds, Soc. Lab., 433; Upshaw, Proh., 183.
1936 (Pres.), Roosevelt, Dem., 165,238; Landon, Rep., 125,031; Lemke, Union, 19,569; Aiken, Soc. Lab., 929; Browder, Com., 411.
1940 (Pres.), Roosevelt, Dem., 182,182; Willkie, Rep., 138,653; Browder, Com., 239; Babson, Proh., 74.
1944 (Pres.), Roosevelt, Dem., 175,356; Dewey, Rep., 123,487; Watson, Proh., 433.
1948 (Pres.), Truman, Dem., 188,736; Dewey, Rep., 135,787; Wallace, Prog., 2,619; Thomas, Soc., 429; Teichert, Soc. Lab., 131.
1952 (Pres.), Eisenhower, Rep., 210,935; Stevenson, Dem., 203,293; Hallinan, Prog., 187; Hass, Soc. Lab., 83.
1956 (Pres.), Eisenhower, Rep., 225,819; Stevenson, Dem., 161,790.
1960 (Pres.), Kennedy, D., 258,032; Nixon, R., 147,502.
1964 (Pres.), Johnson, D., 315,463; Goldwater, R., 74,615.
1968 (Pres.), Nixon, Rep., 122,359; Humphrey, Dem., 246,518; Wallace, 3rd party, 15,678; Halstead, Soc. Worker, 383.
1972 (Pres.), Nixon, Rep., 220,383; McGovern, Dem., 194,645; Jenness, Soc. Worker, 729.

South Carolina

1932 (Pres.), Roosevelt, Dem., 102,347; Hoover, Rep., 1,978; Thomas, Soc., 82.
1936 (Pres.), Roosevelt, Dem., 113,791; Landon, Rep., Tolbert faction (953), Hambright faction (693), total, 1,646.
1940 (Pres.), Roosevelt, Dem., 95,470; Willkie, Rep., 1,727.

1944 (Pres.), Roosevelt, Dem., 90,601; Dewey, Rep., 4,547; Southern Democrats, 7,799; Watson, Proh., 365; Rep. (Tolbert facton), 63.

1948 (Pres.), Thurmond, States' Rights, 102,607; Truman, Dem., 34,423; Dewey, Rep., 5,386; Wallace, Prog., 154; Thomas, Soc., 1.

1952 (Pres.), Eisenhower ran on two tickets. Under State law vote cast for two Eisenhower slates of electors could not be combined. Eisenhower, Ind., 158,189; Rep., 9,793; total 168,082; Stevenson, Dem., 173,004; Hamblen, Proh., 1.

1956 (Pres.), Stevenson, Dem., 136,372; Byrd., Ind., 88,509; Eisenhower, Rep., 75,700; Andrews, Ind., 2.

1960 (Pres.), Kennedy, Dem., 198,129; Nixon, Rep., 188,558; Write-in, 1.

1964 (Pres.), Johnson, Dem., 215,700; Goldwater, Rep., 309,048; Write-ins: Nixon, 1; Wallace, 5; Powell, 1; Thurmond, 1.

1968 (Pres.), Nixon, Rep., 254,062; Humphrey, Dem., 197,486; Wallace, 3rd party, 215,430.

1972 (Pres.), Nixon, Rep., 477,044; McGovern, Dem., 184,559, United Citizens, 2,265; Schmitz, American, 10,075; Write-in 17.

South Dakota

1932 (Pres.), Roosevelt, Dem., 183,515; Hoover, Rep., 99,212; Harvey, Lib., 3,333; Thomas, Soc., 1,551; Upshaw, Proh., 463; Foster, Com., 364.

1936 (Pres.), Roosevelt, Dem., 160,137; Landon, Rep., 125,977; Lemke, Union, 10,338.

1940 (Pres.), Roosevelt, D., 131,862; Willkie, R., 177,065.

1944 (Pres.), Roosevelt, D., 96,711; Dewey, R., 135,365.

1948 (Pres.), Truman, Dem., 117,653; Dewey, Rep., 129,651; Wallace, Prog., 2,801.

1952 (Pres.), Eisenhower, Rep., 203,857; Stevenson, Dem., 90,426.

1956 (Pres.), Eisenhower, Rep., 171,569; Stevenson, Dem., 122,288.

1960 (Pres.), Kennedy, Dem., 128,070; Nixon, Rep., 178,417.

1964 (Pres.), Johnson, Dem., 163,010; Goldwater, Rep., 130,108.

1968 (Pres.), Nixon, Rep., 149,841; Humphrey, Dem., 118,023; Wallace, 3rd party, 13,400.

1972 (Pres.), Nixon, Rep., 166,476; McGovern, Dem., 139,945; Jenness, Soc. Worker, 994.

Tennessee

1932 (Pres.), Roosevelt, Dem., 259,817; Hoover, Rep., 126,806; Upshaw, Proh., 1,995; Thomas, Soc., 1,786; Foster, Com., 234.

1936 (Pres.), Roosevelt, Dem., 327,083; Landon, Rep., 146,516; Thomas, Soc., 685; Colvin, Proh., 632; Browder, Com., 319; Lemke, Union, 296.

1940 (Pres.), Roosevelt, Dem., 351,601; Willkie, Rep., 169,153; Babson, Proh., 1,606; Thomas, Soc., 463.

1944 (Pres.), Roosevelt, Dem., 308,707; Dewey, Rep., 200,311; Watson, Proh., 882; Thomas, Soc., 892.

1948 (Pres.), Truman, Dem., 270,402; Dewey, Rep., 202,914; Thurmond, States' Rights, 73,815; Wallace, Prog., 1,864; Thomas, Soc., 1,288.

1952 (Pres.), Eisenhower, Rep., 446,147; Stevenson, Dem., 443,710; Hamblen, Proh., 1,432; Hallinan, Prog., 885; MacArthur, Christian Nationalist, 379.

1956 (Pres.), Eisenhower, Rep., 462,288; Stevenson, Dem., 456,507; Andrews, Ind., 19,820; Holtwick, Proh., 789.

1960 (Pres.), Kennedy, Dem., 481,453; Nixon, Rep., 556,577; Faubus, States' Rights, 11,304; Decker, Proh., 2,458.

1964 (Pres.), Johnson, Dem., 635,047; Goldwater, Rep., 508,965; Write-in, 34.

1968 (Pres.), Nixon, Rep., 472,592; Humphrey, Dem., 351,233; Wallace, 3rd party, 424,792.

1972 (Pres.), Nixon, Rep., 813,147; McGovern, Dem., 357,293; Schmitz, American, 30,373; Write-in, 369.

Texas

1924 (Pres.), Davis, Dem., 484,605; Coolidge, Rep., 130,023; LaFollette, Prog., 42,881.

1928 (Pres.), Hoover, Rep., 367,036; Smith, Dem., 341,032; Thomas, Soc., 722; Foster, Com., 209.

1932 (Pres.), Roosevelt, Dem., 760,348; Hoover, Rep., 97,959; Thomas, Soc., 4,450; Harvey, Lib., 324; Foster, Com., 207; Jackson Party, 104.

1936 (Pres.), Roosevelt, Dem., 734,485; Landon, Rep., 103,874; Lemke, Union, 3,281; Thomas, Soc., 1,075; Colvin, Proh., 514; Browder, Com., 253.

1940 (Pres.), Roosevelt, Dem., 840,151; Willkie, Rep., 199,152; Babson, Proh., 925; Thomas, Soc., 728; Browder, Com., 212.

1944 (Pres.), Roosevelt, Dem., 821,605; Dewey, Rep., 191,425; Texas Regulars, 135,439; Watson, Proh., 1,017; Thomas, Soc., 594; America First, 250.

1948 (Pres.), Truman, Dem., 750,700; Dewey, Rep., 282,240; Thurmond, States' Rights, 106,909; Wallace, Prog., 3,764; Watson, Proh., 2,758; Thomas, Soc., 874.

1952 (Pres.), Eisenhower, Rep., 1,102,878; Stevenson, Dem., 969,228; Hamblen, Proh., 1,983; MacArthur, Christian Nationalist, 833; MacArthur, Constitution, 730; Hallinan, Prog., 294.

1956 (Pres.), Eisenhower, Rep., 1,080,619; Stevenson, Dem., 859,958; Andrews, Ind., 14,591.

1960 (Pres.), Kennedy, Dem., 1,167,932; Nixon, Rep., 1,121,699; Sullivan, Constitution, 18,169; Decker, Proh., 3,870; Write-in, 15.

1964 (Pres.), Johnson, Dem., 1,663,185; Goldwater, Rep., 958,566; Lightburn, Constitution, 5,060.

1968 (Pres.), Nixon, Rep., 1,227,844; Humphrey, Dem., 1,266,804; Wallace, 3rd party, 584,269; Write-ins, 489.

1972 (Pres.), Nixon, Rep., 2,298,896; McGovern, Dem., 1,154,289; Schmitz, American, 6,039; Jenness, Soc. Worker, 8,664; Others 3,393.

Utah

1924 (Pres.), Coolidge, Rep., 77,327; Davis, Dem., 47,001; LaFollette, Prog., 33,662.

1928 (Pres.), Hoover, Rep., 94,618; Smith, Dem., 80,985; Thomas, Soc., 954; Foster, Com., 47.

1932 (Pres.), Roosevelt, Dem., 116,750; Hoover, Rep., 84,795; Thomas, Soc., 4,087; Foster, Com., 947.

1936 (Pres.), Roosevelt, Dem., 150,246; Landon, Rep., 64,555; Lemke, Union, 1,121; Thomas, Soc., 432; browder, Com., 280; Colvin, Proh., 43.

1940 (Pres.), Roosevelt, Dem., 154,277; Willkie, Rep., 93,151; Thomas, Soc., 200; Browder, Com., 191.

1944 (Pres.), Roosevelt, Dem., 150,088; Dewey, Rep., 97,891; Thomas, Soc., 340.

1948 (Pres.), Truman, Dem., 149,151; Dewey, Rep., 124,402; Wallace, Prog., 2,679; Dobbs, Soc. Workers, 73.

1952 (Pres.), Eisenhower, Rep., 194,190; Stevenson, Dem., 135,364.

1956 (Pres.), Eisenhower, Rep., 215,631; Stevenson, Dem., 118,364.

1960 (Pres.), Kennedy, Dem., 169,248; Nixon, Rep., 205,361; Dobbs, Soc. Workers, 100.

1964 (Pres.), Johnson, Dem., 219,628; Goldwater, Rep., 181,785.

1968 (Pres.), Nixon, Rep., 238,728; Humphrey, Dem., 156,665; Wallace, 3rd party, 26,906; Halstead, Soc. Worker, 89; Peace and Freedom, 180.

1972 (Pres.), Nixon, Rep., 323,643; McGovern, Dem., 126,284; Schmitz, American, 28,549.

Vermont

1932 (Pres.), Roosevelt, Dem., 56,266; Hoover, Rep., 78,984; Thomas, Soc., 1,533; Foster, Com., 195.

1936 (Pres.), Landon, Rep., 81,023; Roosevelt, Dem., 62,124; Browder, Com., 405.

1940 (Pres.), Roosevelt, Dem., 64,269; Willkie, Rep., 78,371; Browder, Com., 411.

1944 (Pres.), Roosevelt, Dem., 53,820; Dewey, Rep., 71,527.

1948 (Pres.), Truman, Dem., 45,557; Dewey, Rep., 75,-926; Wallace, Prog., 1,279; Thomas, Soc. 585.
1952 (Pres.), Eisenhower, Rep., 109,717; Stevenson, Dem., 43,355; Hallinan, Prog., 282; Hoopes, Soc., 185.
1956 (Pres.), Eisenhower, Rep., 110,390; Stevenson, Dem., 42,549; Scattered, 39.
1960 (Pres.), Kennedy, Dem., 69,186; Nixon, Rep., 98,-131.
1964 (Pres.), Johnson, Dem., 107,674; Goldwater, Rep., 54,868.
1968 (Pres.), Nixon, Rep., 85,142; Humphrey, Dem., 70,255; Wallace, 3rd party, 5,104; Halstead, Soc. Worker, 295; Gregory, New Party, 579.
1972 (Pres.), Nixon, Rep., 117,149; McGovern, Dem., 68,174; Spock, Liberty Union, 1,010; Jenness, Soc. Worker, 296; Scattered 318.

Virginia

1932 (Pres.), Roosevelt, Dem., 203,979; Hoover, Rep., 89,637; Thomas, Soc., 2,382; Upshaw, Proh., 1,843; Foster, Com., 86; Coxn Ind., 15.
1936 (Pres.), Roosevelt, Dem., 234,980; Landon, Rep., 98,366; Colvin, Proh., 594; Thomas, Soc., 313; Lemke, Union, 233; Browder, Com., 98.
1940 (Pres.), Roosevelt, Dem., 235,961; Willkie, Rep., 109,363; Babson, Proh., 882; Thomas, Soc., 282; Browder, Com., 71; Aiken, Soc. Lab., 48.
1944 (Pres.), Roosevelt, Dem., 242,276; Dewey, Rep., 145,243; Watson, Proh., 459; Thomas, Soc., 417; Tei-chert, Soc. Lab., 90.
1948 (Pres.), Truman, Dem., 200,786; Dewey, Rep., 172,070; Thurmond, States' Rights, 43,393; Wallace, Prog., 2,047; Thomas, Soc., 726; Teichert, Soc. Lab., 234.
1952 (Pres.), Eisenhower, Rep., 349,037; Stevenson, Dem., 268,677; Hass, Soc. Lab., 1,160; Hoopes, So-cial Dem., 504; Hallinan, Prog., 311.
1956 (Pres.), Eisenhower, Rep., 386,459; Stevenson, Dem., 267,760; Andrews, States' Rights, 42,964; Hoopes Soc. Dem., 444; Hass, Soc. Lab., 351.
1960 (Pres.), Kennedy, Dem., 362,327; Nixon, Rep., 404,521; Coiner, Conservative, 4,204; Hass, Soc. Lab., 397.
1964 (Pres.), Johnson, Dem., 558,038; Goldwater, Rep., 481,334; Hass, Soc. Lab., 2,895.
1968 (Pres.), Nixon, Rep., 590,319; Humphrey, Dem., 442,387; Wallace, 3rd party, *320,272; Blomen, Soc. Labor, 4,671; Munn, Prohibition, 601; Greogry, Peace and Freedom, 1,680.
1972 (Pres.), Nixon, Rep., 988,493; McGovern, Dem., 438,887; Schmitz, American, 19,721; Fisher, Soc. Labor, 9,918.*10,561 votes for Wallace were omit-ted in the count.

Washington

1932 (Pres.), Roosevelt, Dem., 353,260; Hoover, Rep., 208,645; Harvey, Lib., 30,308; Thomas, Soc., 17,080; Foster, Com., 2,972; Upshaw, Proh., 1,540; Rey-nolds, Soc. Lab., 1,009.
1936 (Pres.), Roosevelt, Dem., 459,579; Landon, Rep., 206,892; Lemke, Union, 17,463; Thomas, Soc., 3,496; Browder, Com., 1,907; Pellsy, Christian, 1,598; Colvin, Proh., 1,041; Aiken, Soc. Lab., 362.
1940 (Pres.), Roosevelt, Dem., 462,145; Willkie, Rep., 322,123; Thomas, Soc., 4,586; Browder, Com., 2,626; Babson, Proh., 1,686; Aiken, Soc. Lab., 667.
1944 (Pres.), Roosevelt, Dem., 486,774; Dewey, Rep., 361,689; Thomas, Soc., 3,824; Watson, Proh., 2,396; Teichert, Soc. Lab., 1,645.
1948 (Pres.), Truman, Dem., 476,165; Dewey, Rep., 386,315; Wallace, Prog., 31,692; Watson, Proh., 6,117; Thomas, Soc., 3,534; Teichert, Soc. Lab., 1,133; Dobbs, Soc. Workers, 103.
1952 (Pres.), Eisenhower, Rep., 599,107; Stevenson, Dem., 492,845; MacArthur, Christian Nationalist, 7,290; Hallinan, Prog., 2,460; Hass, Soc. Lab., 633; Hoopes, Soc., 254; Dobbs, Soc. Workers, 119.
1956 (Pres.), Eisenhower, Rep., 620,430; Stevenson, Dem., 523,002; Hass, Soc. Lab., 7,457.

1960 (Pres.), Kennedy, Dem., 599,298; Nixon, Rep., 629,273; Hass, Soc. Lab., 10,895; Curtis, Constitut-uion, 1,401; Dobbs, Soc. Workers, 705.
1964 (Pres.), Johnson, Dem., 779,699; Goldwater, Rep., 470,366; Hass, Soc. Labor, 7,772; DeBerry, Freedom Soc., 537.
1968 (Pres.), Nixon, Rep., 588,510; Humphrey, Dem., 616,037; Wallace, 3rd party, 96,990; Blomen, Soc. Labor, 488; Cleaver, Peace and Freedom, 1,609; Halstead, Soc. Worker, 270; Mitchell, Free Ballot, 377.
1972 (Pres.), Nixon, Rep., 837,135; McGovern, Dem., 568,334; Schmitz, American, 58,906; Spock, Ind., 2,644; Fisher, Soc. Labor, 1,102; Jenness, Soc. Worker, 623; Hall, Communist, 566; Hospers, Libertarian, 1,537.

West Virginia

1932 (Pres.), Roosevelt, Dem., 405,124; Hoover, Rep., 330,731; Thomas, Soc., 5,133; Upshaw, Proh., 2,342; Foster, Com., 444.
1936 (Pres.), Roosevelt, Dem., 502,582; Landon, Rep., 325,358; Colvin, Proh., 1,173; Thomas, Soc., 832.
1940 (Pres.), Roosevelt, Dem., 495,662; Willkie, Rep., 372,414.
1944 (Pres.), Roosevelt, Dem., 392,777; Dewey, Rep., 322,819.
1948 (Pres.), Truman, Dem., 429,188; Dewey, Rep., 316,251; Wallace, Prog., 3,311.
1952 (Pres.), Eisenhower, R., 419,970; Stevenson, D., 453,578.
1956 (Pres.), Eisenhower, R., 449,297; Stevenson, D., 381,534.
1960 (Pres.), Kennedy, D., 441,786; Nixon, R., 395,995.
1964 (Pres.), Johnson, D., 538,087; Goldwater, R., 253,953.
1968 (Pres.), Nixon, Rep., 307,555; Humphrey, Dem., 374,091; Wallace, 3rd party, 72,560.
1972 (Pres.), Nixon, Rep., 484,964; McGovern, Dem., 277,435.

Wisconsin

1932 (Pres.), Roosevelt, Dem., 707,410; Hoover, Rep., 347,741; Thomas, Soc., 53,379; Foster, Com., 3,112; Upshaw, Proh., 2,672; Reynolds, Soc., Lab., 494.
1936 (Pres.), Roosevelt, Dem., 802,984; Landon, Rep., 380,828; Lemke, Union, 60,297; Thomas, Soc., 10,-626; Browder, Com., 2,197; Colvin, Proh., 1,071; Aiken, Soc. Lab., 557.
1940 (Pres.), Roosevelt, Dem., 704,821; Willkie, Rep., 679,260; Thomas, Soc., 15,071; Browder, Com., 2,394; Babson, Proh., 2,148; Aiken, Soc. Lab., 1,882.
1944 (Pres.), Roosevelt, Dem., 650,413; Dewey, Rep., 674,532; Thomas, Soc., 13,205; Teichert, Soc. Lab., 1,002.
1948 (Pres.), Truman, Dem., 647,310; Dewey, Rep., 590,959; Wallace, Prog., 25,282; Thomas, Soc., 12,-547; Teichert, Soc. Lab., 399; Dobbs, Soc. Workers, 303.
1952 (Pres.), Eisenhower, Rep., 979,744; Stevenson, Dem., 622,175; Hallinan, Ind., 2,174; Dobbs, Ind., 1,350; Hoopes, Ind., 1,157; Hass, Ind., 770.
1956 (Pres.), Eisenhower, Rep., 954,844; Stevenson, Dem., 586,768; Andrews, Ind., 6,918; Hoopes, Soc., 754; Hass, Soc. Lab., 710; Dobbs, Soc. Workers, 564.
1960 (Pres.), Kennedy, Dem., 830,805; Nixon, Rep., 895,175; Dobbs, Soc. Workers, 1,792; Hass, Soc. Lab., 1,310.
1964 (Pres.), Johnson, Dem., 1,050,424; Goldwater, Rep., 638,495; DeBerry, Soc. Worker, 1,692; Hass, Soc. Lab., 1,204.
1968 (Pres.), Nixon, Rep., 809,997; Humphrey, Dem., 748,804; Wallace, 3rd party, 127,835; Blomen, Soc. Labor, 1,338; Halstead Soc. Worker, 1,222; scatter-ing, 2,342.
1972 (Pres.), Nixon, Rep., 989,430; McGovern, Dem., 810,174; Schmitz, American, 47,525; Spock, Ind., 2,701; Fisher, Soc. Labor, 998; Hall, Communist, 663; Reed, Ind., 506; scattered, 893.

Wyoming

1932 (Pres.). Roosevelt, Dem., 54,370; Hoover, Rep., 39,583; Thomas, Soc. 2,829; Foster, Com., 180.

1936 (Pres.). Roosevelt, Dem., 62,624; Landon, Rep., 38,739; Lemke, Union, 1,653; Thoms, Soc., 200; Browder, Com., 91; Colvin, Proh., 75.

1940 (Pres.). Roosevelt, Dem., 59,287; Willkie, Rep., 52,633; Babson, Proh., 172; Thomas, Soc., 148.

1944 (Pres.). Roosevelt, Dem., 49,419; Dewey, Rep., 51,921.

1948 (Pres.). Truman, Dem., 52,354; Dewey, Rep., 47,-947; Wallace, Prog., 931; Thomas, Soc., 137; Teichert, Soc. Lab., 56.

1952 (Pres.). Eisenhower, Rep., 81,047; Stevenson, Dem., 47,934; Hamblen, Proh., 194; Hoopes, Soc., 40; Hass, Soc. Lab., 36.

1956 (Pres.). Eisenhower, Rep., 74,573; Stevenson, Dem., 49,554.

1960 (Pres.). Kennedy, Dem., 63,331; Nixon, Rep., 77,-451.

1964 (Pres.). Johnson, Dem., 80,718; Goldwater, Rep., 61,998.

1968 (Pres.). Nixon, Rep., 70,927; Humphrey, Dem., 45,173; Wallace, 3rd party, 11,105.

1972 (Pres.). Nixon, Rep., 100,464; McGovern, Dem., 44,358; Schmitz, American, 748.

Electoral Votes for President, 1956-72

The Constitution, Article 2, Section 1 (consult index), provides for the appointment of electors, the counting of the electoral ballots and the procedure in the event of a tie. (See Electoral College.)

State	1956 R.	1956 D.	1960 R.	1960 D.	1964 R.	1964 D.	1968 R.	1968 D.	1968 3d	1972 R.	1972 D.
Ala.		[1]11		[5]5	10				10	9	
Alaska			3			3	3			3	
Ariz.	4		4		5		5			6	
Ark.		8		8		6			6	6	
Calif.	32		32			40	40			45	
Colo.	6		6		6		6			7	
Conn.	8			8	8			8		8	
Del.	3			3	3		3			3	
D. of C.					[3]3			3			3
Fla.	10		10			14	14			17	
Ga.		12		12	12				12	12	
Hawaii				3	4		4			4	
Idaho	4		4		4		4			4	
Ill.	27			27	26		26			26	
Ind.	13		13		13		13			13	
Iowa	10		10			9	9			8	
Kan.	8		8		7		7			7	
Ky.	10		20			9	9			9	
La.	10			10	10				10	10	
Me.	5		5		4		4			4	
Md.	9			9	10		10			10	
Mass.	16			16	14		14				14
Mich.	20			20	21		21			21	
Minn.	11			11	10		10			10	
Miss.		8		13	(²)	7			7	7	
Mo.		13	13		12		12			12	
Mont.	4		4		4		4			4	
Neb.	6		6		5		5			5	
Nev.	3			3		3	3			3	
N. H.	4		4			4	4			4	
N. J.	16			16	17		17			17	
N. M.	4			4	4		4			4	
N. Y.	45			45	43			43		41	
N. C.		14		14	13		12		[1]1	13	
N. D.	4		4			4	4			3	
Ohio	25		25			26	26			25	
Okla.	8		[7]7		8		8			8	
Oreg.	6		6			6	6			6	
Penn.	32			32	29			29		27	
R. I.	4			4	4		4			4	
S. C.		8		8	8			8		8	
S. D.	4		4		4		4			4	
Tenn.	11		11		11		11			10	
Texas	24			24	25			25		26	
Utah	4		4		4		4			4	
Vt.	3		3		3		3			3	
Va.	12		12			12	12			[1]11	
Wash.	9		9			9		9		9	
W. Va.	8			8	[7]7			7		6	
Wis.	12		12			12	12			11	
Wyo.	3		3		3		3			3	
Totals	457	[1]74	[2]19	303	52	486	301	191	46	520	17
Plurality	383		[2]84		434		110			[1]503	

(1.) In 1956 in Alabama one Democratic elector refused to vote for Stevenson and cast his ballot for Walter B. Jones, making the Democratic total actually 73.

(2.) In 1960 Sen. Harry F. Byrd (D.-Va.) got 15 electoral votes, including those of 8 unpledged Mississippi Democratic electors, 6 unpledged Alabama Democrats and one Oklahoma Republican.

(3.) First Presidential election.

(4.) In 1968 in North Carolina one Republican elector cast his ballot for Wallace.

(5.) In 1972 one Republican elector in Virginia cast his ballot for John Hospers.

Presidents, Vice Presidents, Congresses

President	Service				Vice President	Congress
1 George Washington	Apr.	30,	1789-Mar.	3, 1797	1 John Adams	1, 2, 3, 4
2 John Adams	Mar.	4,	1797-Mar.	3, 1801	2 Thomas Jefferson	5, 6
3 Thomas Jefferson	Mar.	4,	1801-Mar.	3, 1805	3 Aaron Burr	7, 8
do	Mar.	4,	1805-Mar.	3, 1809	4 George Clinton	9, 10
4 James Madison	Mar.	4,	1809-Mar.	3, 1813	do[1]	11, 12
do	Mar.	4,	1813-Mar.	3, 1817	5 Elbridge Gerry[2]	13, 14
5 James Monroe	Mar.	4,	1817-Mar.	3, 1825	6 Daniel D. Tompkins	15, 16, 17, 18
6 John Quincy Adams	Mar.	4,	1825-Mar.	3, 1829	7 John C. Calhoun	19, 20
7 Andrew Jackson	Mar.	4,	1829-Mar.	3, 1833	do[3]	21, 22
do	Mar.	4,	1833-Mar.	3, 1837	8 Martin Van Buren	23, 24
8 Martin Van Buren	Mar.	4,	1837-Mar.	3, 1841	9 Richard M. Johnson	25, 26
9 William Henry Harrison[4]	Mar.	4,	1841-Apr.	4, 1845	10 John Tyler	27
10 John Tyler	Apr.	6,	1841-Mar.	3, 1845		27, 28
11 James K. Polk	Mar.	4,	1845-Mar.	3, 1849	11 George M. Dallas	29, 30
12 Zachary Taylor[4]	Mar.	5,	1849-July	9, 1850[4]	12 Millard Fillmore	31
13 Millard Fillmore	July	10,	1850-Mar.	3, 1853		31, 32
14 Franklin Pierce	Mar.	4,	1853-Mar.	3 1857	13 William R. King[5]	33, 34
15 James Buchanan	Mar.	4,	1857-Mar.	3, 1861	14 John C. Breckinridge	35, 36
16 Abraham Lincoln	Mar.	4,	1861-Mar.	3, 1865	15 Hannibal Hamlin	37, 38
do[4]	Mar.	4,	1865-Apr.	15, 1865	16 Andrew Johnson	39
17 Andrew Johnson	Apr.	15,	1865-Mar.	3, 1869		39, 40
18 Ulysses S. Grant	Mar.	4,	1869-Mar.	3, 1873	17 Schuyler Colfax	41, 42
do	Mar.	4,	1873-Mar.	3, 1877	18 Henry Wilson[6]	43, 44
19 Rutherford B. Hayes	Mar.	4,	1877-Mar.	3, 1881	19 William A. Wheeler	45, 46
20 James A. Garfield[4]	Mar.	4,	1881-Sept.	19, 1881	20 Chester A. Arthur	47
21 Chester A. Arthur	Sept.	20,	1881-Mar.	3, 1885		47, 48
22 Grover Cleveland[7]	Mar.	4,	1885-Mar.	3, 1889	21 Thomas A. Hendricks[8]	49
23 Benjamin Harrison	Mar.	4,	1889-Mar.	3, 1893	22 Levi P. Morton	51, 52
24 Grover Cleveland[7]	Mar.	4,	1893-Mar.	3, 1897	23 Adlai E. Stevenson	53, 54

President	Service	Vice President	Congress
25 William McKinley	Mar. 4, 1897-Mar. 3, 1901	24 Garret A. Hobart[9]	55, 56
do[4]	Mar. 4, 1901-Sept. 14, 1901	25 Theodore Roosevelt	57
26 Theodore Roosevelt	Sept. 14, 1901-Mar. 3, 1905		57, 58
do	Mar. 4, 1905-Mar. 3, 1909	26 Charles W. Fairbanks	59, 60
27 William H. Taft	Mar. 4, 1909-Mar. 3, 1913	27 James S. Sherman[10]	61, 62
28 Woodrow Wilson	Mar. 4, 1913-Mar. 3, 1921	28 Thomas R. Marshall	63, 64, 65, 66
29 Warren G. Harding[4]	Mar. 4, 1921-Aug. 2, 1923	29 Calvin Coolidge	67
30 Calvin Coolidge	Aug. 3, 1923-Mar. 3, 1925		68
do	Mar. 4, 1925-Mar. 3, 1929	30 Charles G. Dawes	69, 70
31 Herbert C. Hoover	Mar. 4, 1929-Mar. 31, 1933	31 Charles Curtis.	71, 72
32 Franklin D. Roosevelt	Mar. 4, 1933-Jan. 20, 1941	32 John N. Garner	73, 74, 75, 76
do	Jan. 20, 1941-Jan. 20, 1945	33 Henry A. Wallace	77, 78
do[4]	Jan. 20, 1945-Apr. 12, 1945	34 Harry S. Truman	79
33 Harry S. Truman	Apr. 12, 1945-Jan. 30, 1949		79, 80
do	Jan. 20, 1949-Jan. 20, 1953	35 Alben W. Barkley	81, 82
34 Dwight D. Eisenhower	Jan. 20, 1953-Jan. 20, 1961	36 Richard M. Nixon	83, 84, 85, 86
35 John F. Kennedy[4]	Jan. 20, 1961-Nov. 22, 1963	37 Lyndon B. Johnson	87, 88
36 Lyndon B. Johnson	Nov. 22, 1963-Jan. 20, 1965		88
do	Jan. 20, 1965-Jan. 20, 1969	38 Hubert H. Humphrey	89, 90
37 Richard M. Nixon	Jan. 20, 1969-Aug. 9, 1974	39 Spiro T. Agnew[11]	91, 92, 93
do		40 Gerald R. Ford	93
38 Gerald R. Ford	Aug. 9, 1974	41 Nelson A. Rockefeller (nom.)	

(1) Died Apr. 20, 1812. (2) Died Nov. 23, 1814. (3) Resigned Dec. 28, 1832, to become U. S. Senator. (4) Died in office. (5) Died Apr. 18, 1853. (6) Died Nov. 22, 1875. (7) Terms not consecutive. (8) Died Nov. 25, 1885. (9) Died Nov. 21, 1899. (10) Died Oct. 30, 1912. (11) Resigned Oct. 10, 1973.

Vice Presidents of the United States

The numerals given vice presidents do not coincide with those given presidents, because some presidents had none and some had more than one.

	Name	Birthplace	Yr.	Residence	Inaug.	Politics	Place of Death	Yr.	Age
1	John Adams	Quincy, Mass.	1735	Mass.	1789	Fed.	Quincy, Mass.	1826	90
2	Thomas Jefferson	Shadwell, Va.	1743	Va.	1797	Rep.	Monticello, Va.	1826	83
3	Aaron Burr	Newark, N.J.	1756	N.Y.	1801	Rep.	Staten Island, N.Y.	1836	80
4	George Clinton	Ulster Co., N.Y.	1739	N.Y.	1805	Rep.	Washington, D.C.	1812	73
5	Elbridge Gerry	Marblehead, Mass.	1744	Mass.	1813	Rep.	Washington, D.C.	1814	70
6	Daniel D. Tompkins	Scarsdale, N.Y.	1774	N.Y.	1817	Rep.	Staten Island, N.Y.	1825	51
7	*John C. Calhoun	Abbeville, S. C.	1782	S.C.	1825	Rep.	Washington, D. C.	1850	68
8	Martin Van Buren	Kinderhook, N.Y.	1782	N.Y.	1833	Dem.	Kinderhook, N.Y.	1862	79
9	Richard M. Johnson	Louisville, Ky.	1780	Ky.	1837	Dem.	Frankfort, Ky.	1850	70
10	John Tyler	Greenway, Va.	1790	Va.	1841	Whig.	Richmond, Va.	1862	71
11	George M. Dallas	Philadelphia, Pa.	1792	Pa.	1845	Dem.	Philadelphia, Pa.	1864	72
12	Millard Fillmore	Summerhill, N.Y.	1800	N.Y.	1849	Whig.	Buffalo, N.Y.	1874	74
13	William R. King	Sampson Co., N. C.	1786	Ala.	1853	Dem.	Dallas Co., Ala.	1853	67
14	John C. Breckinridge	Lexington, Ky.	1821	Ky.	1857	Dem.	Lexington, Ky.	1875	54
15	Hannibal Hamlin	Paris, Me.	1809	Me.	1861	Rep.	Bangor, Me.	1891	81
16	Andrew Johnson	Raleigh, N.C.	1808	Tenn.	1865	(x)	Carter Co., Tenn.	1875	66
17	Schuyler Colfax	New York City, N.Y.	1823	Ind.	1869	Rep.	Mankato, Minn.	1885	62
18	Henry Wilson	Farmington, N. H.	1812	Mass.	1873	Rep.	Washington, D.C.	1875	63
19	William A. Wheeler	Malone, N.Y.	1819	N.Y.	1877	Rep.	Malone, N.Y.	1887	68
20	Chester A. Arthur	Fairfield, Vt.	1830	N.Y.	1881	Rep.	New York City, N.Y.	1886	56
21	Thomas A. Hendricks	Muskingum Co., Ohio	1819	Ind.	1885	Dem.	Indianapolis, Ind.	1885	66
22	Levi P. Morton	Shoreham, Vt.	1824	N.Y.	1889	Rep.	Rhinebeck, N.Y.	1920	96
23	Adlai E. Stevenson[1]	Christian Co., Ky.	1835	Ill.	1893	Dem.	Chicago, Ill.	1914	78
24	Garret A. Hobart	Long Branch, N. J.	1844	N.J.	1897	Rep.	Paterson, N. J.	1899	55
25	Theodore Roosevelt	New York City, N. Y.	1858	N.Y.	1901	Rep.	Oyster Bay, N.Y.	1919	60
26	Charles W. Fairbanks	Unionville Centre, Ohio	1852	Ind.	1905	Rep.	Indianapolis, Ind.	1918	66
27	James S. Sherman	Utica, N. Y.	1855	N.Y.	1909	Rep.	Utica, N. Y.	1912	57
28	Thomas R. Marshall	N. Manchester, Ind.	1854	Ind.	1913	Dem.	Washington, D.C.	1925	71
29	Calvin Coolidge	Plymouth, Vt.	1872	Mass.	1921	Rep.	Northampton, Mass.	1933	60
30	Charles G. Dawes	Marietta, Ohio	1865	Ill.	1925	Rep.	Evanston, Ill.	1951	85
31	Charles Curtis	Topeka, Kan.	1860	Kan.	1929	Rep.	Washington, D.C.	1936	76
32	John Nance Garner	Red River Co., Tex.	1868	Tex.	1933	Dem.	Uvalde, Tex.	1967	98
33	Henry Agard Wallace	Adair County, Ia.	1888	Iowa	1941	Dem.	Danbury, Conn.	1965	77
34	Harry S. Truman	Lamar, Mo.	1884	Mo.	1945	Dem.	Kansas City, Mo.	1972	88
35	Alben W. Barkley	Graves County, Ky.	1877	Ky.	1949	Dem.	Lexington, Va.	1956	78
36	Richard M. Nixon	Yorba Linda, Cal.	1913	Calif.	1953	Rep.			
37	Lyndon B. Johnson	Johnson City, Tex.	1908	Tex.	1961	Dem.	San Antonio, Tex.	1973	64
38	Hubert H. Humphrey	Wallace, S. D.	1911	Minn.	1965	Dem.			
39	Spiro T. Agnew	Baltimore, Md.	1918	Md.	1969	Rep.			
40	Gerald R. Ford	Omaha, Neb.	1913	Mich.	1973	Rep.			

(*) John C. Calhoun resigned Dec. 28, 1832, having been elected to the Senate to fill a vacancy. (x) Andrew Johnson—a Democrat nominated by Republicans and elected with Lincoln on the National Union Ticket. (1) Adlai E. Stevenson, 23rd vice president, was grandfather of Democratic candidate for president, 1952 and 1956.

Presidents of the United States

No.	Name	Politics	Native State	Date Born	Inaug. at Age	Date of Death	Age at Death
1.	George Washington	Fed.	Va.	1732, Feb. 22	1789 ... 57	1799, Dec. 14	67
2.	John Adams	Fed.	Mass.	1735, Oct. 30	1797 ... 61	1826, July 4	90
3.	Thomas Jefferson	Dem.-Rep.	Va.	1743, Apr. 13	1801 ... 57	1826, July 4	83
4.	James Madison	Dem.-Rep.	Va.	1751, Mar. 16	1809 ... 57	1836, June 28	85
5.	James Monroe	Dem.-Rep.	Va.	1758, Apr. 28	1817 ... 58	1831, July 4	73
6.	John Quincy Adams	Dem.-Rep.	Mass.	1767, July 11	1825 ... 57	1848, Feb. 23	80
7.	Andrew Jackson	Dem.	S. C.	1767, Mar. 15	1829 ... 61	1845, June 8	78
8.	Martin Van Buren	Dem.	N. Y.	1782, Dec. 5	1837 ... 54	1862, July 24	79
9.	William Henry Harrison	Whig	Va.	1773, Feb. 9	1841 ... 68	1841, Apr. 4	68

No.	Name	Politics	Native State	Date Born	Inaug. at Age	Date of Death	Age at Death
10.	John Tyler	Whig	Va.	1790, Mar. 29	1841 . . 51	1862, Jan. 18	71
11.	James Knox Polk	Dem	N. C.	1795, Nov. 2	1845 . . 49	1849, June 15	53
12.	Zachary Taylor	Whig	Va.	1784, Nov. 24	1849 . . 64	1850, July 9	65
13.	Millard Fillmore	Whig	N.Y.	1800, Jan. 7	1850 . . 50	1874, Mar. 8	74
14.	Franklin Pierce	Dem	N.H.	1804, Nov. 23	1853 . . 48	1869, Oct. 8	64
15.	James Buchanan	Dem	Pa.	1791, Apr. 23	1857 . . 65	1868, June 1	77
16.	Abraham Lincoln	Rep	Ky.	1809, Feb. 12	1861 . . 52	1865, Apr. 15	56
17.	Andrew Johnson	(see note)*	N. C.	1808, Dec. 29	1865 . . 56	1875, July 31	66
18.	Ulysses Simpson Grant	Rep	Ohio	1822, Apr. 27	1869 . . 46	1885, July 23	63
19.	Rutherford Birchard Hayes	Rep	Ohio	1822, Oct. 4	1877 . . 54	1893, Jan. 17	70
20.	James Abram Garfield	Rep	Ohio	1831, Nov. 19	1881 . . 49	1881, Sept. 19	49
21.	Chester Alan Arthur	Rep	Vt.	1830, Oct. 5	1881 . . 50	1886, Nov. 18	56
22.	Grover Cleveland	Dem	N. J.	1837, Mar. 18	1885 . . 47	1908, June 24	71
23.	Benjamin Harrison	Rep	Ohio	1833, Aug. 20	1889 . . 55	1901, Mar. 13	67
24.	Grover Cleveland	Dem	N. J.	1837, Mar. 18	1893 . . 55	1908, June 24	71
25.	William McKinley	Rep	Ohio	1843, Jan. 29	1897 . . 54	1901, Sept. 14	58
26.	Theodore Roosevelt	Rep	N.Y.	1858, Oct. 27	1901 . . 42	1919, Jan. 6	60
27.	William Howard Taft	Rep	Ohio	1857, Sept. 15	1909 . . 51	1930, Mar. 8	72
28.	Woodrow Wilson	Dem	Va.	1857, Dec. 28	1913 . . 56	1924, Feb. 3	67
29.	Warren Gamaliel Harding	Rep	Ohio	1865, Nov. 2	1921 . . 55	1923, Aug. 2	57
30.	Calvin Coolidge	Rep	Vt.	1872, July 4	1923 . . 51	1933, Jan. 5	60
31.	Herbert Clark Hoover	Rep	Iowa	1874, Aug. 10	1929 . . 54	1964, Oct. 20	90
32.	Franklin Delano Roosevelt	Dem	N.Y.	1882, Jan. 30	1933 . . 51	1945, Apr. 12	63
33.	Harry S. Truman	Dem	Mo.	1884, May 8	1945 . . 60	1972, Dec. 26	88
34.	Dwight David Eisenhower	Rep	Tex.	1890, Oct. 14	1953 . . 62	1969, Mar. 28	78
35.	John F. Kennedy	Dem	Mass.	1917, May 29	1961 . . 43	1963, Nov. 22	46
36.	Lyndon Baines Johnson	Dem	Tex.	1908, Aug. 27	1963 . . 55	1973, Jan. 22	64
37.	Richard Milhous Nixon**	Rep	Cal.	1913, Jan 9	1969 . . 56		
38.	Gerald R. Ford	Rep	Neb.	1913, Jul. 14	1974 . . 61		

*Andrew Johnson—a Democrat, nominated vice president by Republicans and elected with Lincoln on National Union ticket.**Resigned Aug. 9, 1974.

Cabinets of the United States

Secretaries of State

The Department of Foreign Affairs was created by act of Congress July 27, 1789, and the name changed to Department of State on Sept. 15.

Presidents	Cabinet Officers	Home	Apptd.	Presidents	Cabinet Officers	Home	Apptd.
Washington	Thomas Jefferson	Va.	1789	Arthur	James G. Blaine	Me.	1881
"	Edmund Randolph		1794	"	F. T. Frelinghuysen	N. J.	1881
"	Timothy Pickering	Pa.	1795	Cleveland			1885
J. Adams			1795	"	Thomas F. Bayard	Del.	1885
"	John Marshall	Va.	1800	B. Harrison			1889
Jefferson	James Madison		1801	"	James G. Blaine	Me.	1889
Madison	Robert Smith	Md.	1809	"	John W. Foster	Ind.	1892
"	James Monroe	Va.	1811	Cleveland	Walter Q. Gresham	Ill.	1893
Monroe	John Quincy Adams	Mass.	1817	"	Richard Olney	Mass.	1895
J. Q. Adams	Henry Clay	Ky.	1825	McKinley			1897
Jackson	Martin Van Buren	N.Y.	1829	"	John Sherman	Ohio	1897
"	Edward Livingston	La.	1831	"	William R. Day		1898
"	Louis McLane	Del.	1833	"	John Hay	D. C.	1898
"	John Forsyth	Ga.	1834	T. Roosevelt			1901
Van Buren			1837	"	Elihu Root	N. Y.	1905
W. H. Harrison	Daniel Webster	Mass.	1841	"	Robert Bacon		1909
Tyler			1841	Taft			1909
"	Abel P. Upshur	Va.	1843	"	Philander C. Knox	Pa.	1909
"	John C. Calhoun	S. C.	1844	Wilson			1913
Polk			1845	"	William J. Bryan	Neb.	1913
"	James Buchanan	Pa.	1845	"	Robert Lansing	N. Y.	1915
Taylor			1849	"	Bainbridge Colby		1920
"	John M. Clayton	Del.	1849	Harding	Charles E. Hughes		1921
Fillmore			1850	Coolidge			1923
"	Daniel Webster	Mass.	1850	"	Frank B. Kellogg	Minn.	1925
"	Edward Everett		1852	Hoover			1929
Pierce	William L. Marcy	N. Y.	1853	"	Henry L. Stimson	N. Y.	1929
Buchanan			1857	F. D. Roosevelt	Cordell Hull	Tenn.	1933
"	Lewis Cass	Mich.	1857	"	F. R. Stettinius Jr.	Va.	1944
"	Jeremiah S. Black	Pa.	1860	Truman			1945
Lincoln			1861	"	James F. Byrnes	S. C.	1945
"	William H. Seward	N. Y.	1861	"	George C. Marshall	Pa.	1947
Johnson, A.			1865	"	Dean G. Acheson	Conn.	1949
Grant	Elihu B. Washburne	Ill.	1869	Eisenhower	John Foster Dulles	N. Y.	1953
"	Hamilton Fish	N. Y.	1869	"	Christian A. Herter	Mass.	1959
Hayes			1877	Kennedy	Dean Rusk	N. Y.	1961
"	William M. Evarts		1877	Johnson, L. B.			1963
Garfield			1881	Nixon	William P. Rogers	N. Y.	1969
"	James G. Blaine	Me.	1881	"	Henry A. Kissinger	Wash.D.C	1973

Secretaries of the Treasury

The Treasury Department was organized by act of Congress on Sept. 2, 1789.

Presidents	Cabinet Officers	Home	Apptd.	Presidents	Cabinet Officers	Home	Apptd.
Washington	Alexander Hamilton	N. Y.	1789	Madison	Albert Gallatin	Pa.	1809
"	Oliver Wolcott	Conn.	1795	"	George W. Campbell	Tenn.	1814
J. Adams			1797	"	Alexander J. Dallas	Pa.	1814
"	Samuel Dexter	Mass.	1801	"	William H. Crawford	Ga.	1816
Jefferson			1801	Monroe			1817
"	Albert Gallatin	Pa.	1801	J. Q. Adams	Richard Rush	Pa.	1825

Presidents	Cabinet Officers	Home	Apptd.	Presidents	Cabinet Officers	Home	Apptd.
Jackson	Samuel D. Ingham	"	1829	Cleveland	Daniel Manning	N. Y.	1885
"	Louis McLane	Del.	1831	"	Charles S. Fairchild	"	1887
"	William J. Duane	Pa.	1833	B. Harrison	William Windom	Minn.	1889
"	Roger B. Taney	Md.	1833	"	Charles Foster	Ohio	1891
"	Levi Woodbury	N. H.	1834	Cleveland	John G. Carlisle	Ky.	1893
Van Buren	"	"	1837	McKinley	Lyman J. Gage	Ill.	1897
W. H. Harrison	Thomas Ewing	Ohio	1841	T. Roosevelt	"	"	1901
Tyler	"	"	1841	"	Leslie M. Shaw	Ia.	1902
"	Walter Forward	Pa.	1841	"	George B. Cortelyou	N. Y.	1907
"	John C. Spencer	N. Y.	1843	Taft	Franklin MacVeagh	Ill.	1909
"	George M. Bibb	Ky.	1844	Wilson	William G. McAdoo	N. Y.	1913
Polk	Robert J. Walker	Miss.	1845	"	Carter Glass	Va.	1918
Taylor	William M. Meredith	Pa.	1849	"	David F. Houston	Mo.	1920
Fillmore	Thomas Corwin	Ohio	1850	Harding	Andrew W. Mellon	Pa.	1921
Pierce	James Guthrie	Ky.	1853	Coolidge	"	"	1923
Buchanan	Howell Cobb	Ga.	1857	Hoover	"	"	1929
"	Phillip F. Thomas	Md.	1860	"	Ogden L. Mills	N. Y.	1932
"	John A. Dix	N. Y.	1861	F. D. Roosevelt	William H. Woodin	"	1933
Lincoln	Salmon P. Chase	Ohio	1861	"	Henry Morgenthau Jr.	"	1934
"	William P. Fessenden	Me.	1864	Truman	Fred M. Vinson	Ky.	1945
"	Hugh McCulloch	Ind.	1865	"	John W. Snyder	Mo.	1946
Johnson, A.	"	"	1865	Eisenhower	George M. Humphrey	Ohio	1953
Grant	George S. Boutwell	Mass.	1869	"	Robert B. Anderson	Conn.	1957
Grant	William A. Richardson	Mass.	1873	Kennedy	C. Douglas Dillon	N. J.	1961
"	Benjamin H. Bristow	Ky.	1874	Johnson, L. B.	"	"	1963
"	Lot M. Morrill	Me.	1876	"	Henry H. Fowler	Va.	1965
Hayes	John Sherman	Ohio	1877	"	Joseph W. Barr	Ind.	1968
Garfield	William Windom	Minn.	1881	Nixon	David M. Kennedy	Ill.	1969
Arthur	Charles J. Folger	N. Y.	1881	"	John B. Connally	Tex.	1970
"	Walter Q. Gresham	Ind.	1884	"	George P. Shultz	Ill.	1972
"	Hugh McCulloch	"	1884	"	William E. Simon	N. J.	1974

Attorneys General

The office of attorney general was organized by act of Congress Sept. 24, 1789. The attorney general was made a member of the Cabinet in 1814. The Dept. of Justice was created June 22, 1870.

Presidents	Cabinet Officers	Home	Apptd.	Presidents	Cabinet Officers	Home	Apptd.
Washington	Edmund Randolph	Va.	1789	Hayes	Charles Devens	Mass.	1877
"	William Bradford	Pa.	1794	Garfield	Wayne MacVeagh	Pa.	1881
"	Charles Lee	Va.	1795	Arthur	Benjamin H. Brewster	"	1881
J. Adams	"	"	1797	Cleveland	Augustus Garland	Ark.	1885
Jefferson	Levi Lincoln	Mass.	1801	B. Harrison	William H. H. Miller	Ind.	1889
"	John Breckenridge	Ky.	1805	Cleveland	Richard Olney	Mass.	1893
"	Caesar A. Rodney	Del.	1807	"	Judson Harmon	Ohio	1895
Madison	"	"	1809	McKinley	Joseph McKenna	Cal.	1897
"	William Pinkney	Md.	1811	"	John W. Griggs	N. J.	1898
"	Richard Rush	Pa.	1814	"	Philander C. Knox	Pa.	1901
Monroe	"	"	1817	T. Roosevelt	"	"	1901
"	William Wirt	Va.	1817	"	William H. Moody	Mass.	1904
J. Q. Adams	"	"	1825	"	Charles J. Bonaparte	Md.	1906
Jackson	John McP. Berrien	Ga.	1829	Taft	George W. Wickersham	N. Y.	1909
"	Roger B. Taney	Md.	1831	Wilson	J. C. McReynolds	Tenn.	1913
"	Benjamin F. Butler	N. Y.	1833	"	Thomas W. Gregory	Tex.	1914
Van Buren	"	"	1837	"	A. Mitchell Palmer	Pa.	1919
"	Felix Grundy	Tenn.	1838	Harding	Harry M. Daugherty	Ohio	1921
"	Henry D. Gilpin	Pa.	1840	Coolidge	"	"	1923
W. H. Harrison	John J. Crittenden	Ky.	1841	"	Harlan F. Stone	N. Y.	1924
Tyler	"	"	1841	"	John G. Sargent	Vt.	1925
"	Hugh S. Legare	S. C.	1841	Hoover	William D. Mitchell	Minn.	1929
"	John Nelson	Md.	1843	F. D. Roosevelt	Homer S. Cummings	Conn.	1933
Polk	John Y. Mason	Va.	1845	"	Frank Murphy	Mich.	1939
"	Nathan Clifford	Me.	1846	"	Robert H. Jackson	N. Y.	1940
"	Isaac Toucey	Conn.	1848	"	Francis Biddle	Pa.	1941
Taylor	Reverdy Johnson	Md.	1849	Truman	Tom C. Clark	Tex.	1945
Fillmore	John J. Crittenden	Ky.	1850	"	J. Howard McGrath	R. I.	1949
Pierce	Caleb Cushing	Mass.	1853	"	J. P. McGranery	Pa.	1952
Buchanan	Jeremiah S. Black	Pa.	1857	Eisenhower	H. Brownell Jr.	N. Y.	1953
"	Edwin M. Stanton	Pa.	1860	"	William P. Rogers	Md.	1957
Lincoln	Edward Bates	Mo.	1861	Kennedy	Robert F. Kennedy	Mass.	1961
"	James Speed	Ky.	1864	Johnson, L. B.	"	"	1963
Johnson, A.	"	Ky.	1865	"	N. de B. Katzenbach	Ill.	1965
"	Henry Stanbery	Ohio	1866	"	Ramsey Clark	Tex.	1967
"	William M. Evarts	N. Y.	1868	Nixon	John N. Mitchell	N. Y.	1969
Grant	Ebenezer R. Hoar	Mass.	1869	"	Richard G. Kleindienst	Ariz.	1972
"	Amos T. Akerman	Ga.	1870	"	Elliot L. Richardson	Mass.	1973
"	George H. Williams	Ore.	1871	"	William B. Saxbe	Ohio	1974
"	Edwards Pierrepont	N. Y.	1875				
"	Alphonso Taft	Ohio	1876				

Secretaries of Agriculture

The Department of Agriculture was created by act of Congress May 15, 1862. On Feb. 8, 1889, its commissioner was renamed secretary of agriculture and became a member of the Cabinet.

Presidents	Cabinet Officers	Home	Apptd.	Presidents	Cabinet Officers	Home	Apptd.
Cleveland	Norman J. Colman	Mo.	1889	T. Roosevelt	James Wilson	Ia.	1901
B. Harrison	Jeremiah M. Rusk	Wis.	1889	Taft	"	"	1909
Cleveland	J. Sterling Morton	Neb.	1893	Wilson	David F. Houston	Mo.	1913
McKinley	James Wilson	Ia.	1897	"	Edward T. Meredith	Ia.	1920

Presidents	Cabinet Officers	Home	Apptd.	Presidents	Cabinet Officers	Home	Apptd.
Harding	Henry C. Wallace	Ia.	1921	Truman	Clinton P. Anderson	N. M.	1945
Coolidge			1923	"	Charles F. Brannan	Colo.	1948
Coolidge	Howard M. Gore	W. Va.	1924	Eisenhower	Ezra Taft Benson	Utah	1953
Coolidge	W. M. Jardine	Kan.	1925	Kennedy	Orville L. Freeman	Minn.	1961
Hoover	Arthur M. Hyde	Mo.	1929	Johnson, L. B.	"		1963
F. D. Roosevelt	Henry A. Wallace	Iowa	1933	Nixon	Clifford M. Hardin	Ind.	1969
"	Claude R. Wickard	Ind.	1940	"	Earl L. Butz	Ind.	1971

Secretaries of the Interior

The Department of Interior was created by act of Congress Mar. 3, 1849.

Presidents	Cabinet Officers	Home	Apptd.	Presidents	Cabinet Officers	Home	Apptd.
Taylor	Thomas Ewing	Ohio	1849	McKinley	Ethan A. Hitchcock	Mo.	1898
Fillmore	Thomas M. T. McKennan	Pa.	1850	T. Roosevelt	"		1901
"	Alex H. H. Stuart	Va.	1850	"	James R. Garfield	Ohio	1907
Pierce	Robert McClelland	Mich.	1853	Taft	Richard A. Ballinger	Wash.	1909
Buchanan	Jacob Thompson	Miss.	1857	"	Walter L. Fisher	Ill.	1911
Lincoln	Caleb B. Smith	Ind.	1861	Wilson	Franklin K. Lane	Cal.	1913
"	John P. Usher	"	1863	"	John B. Payne	Ill.	1920
Johnson, A.	"	"	1865	Harding	Albert B. Fall	N. M.	1921
"	James Harlan	Iowa	1865	"	Hubert Work	Colo.	1923
"	Orville H. Browning	Ill.	1866	Coolidge	"	Colo.	1923
Grant	Jacob D. Cox	Ohio	1869	"	Roy O. West	Ill.	1929
"	Columbus Delano	"	1870	Hoover	Ray Lyman Wilbur	Cal.	1929
"	Zachariah Chandler	Mich.	1875	F. D. Roosevelt	Harold L. Ickes	Ia.	1933
Hayes	Carl Schurz	Mo.	1877	Truman	"	Ill.	1945
Garfield	Sam. J. Kirkwood	Iowa	1881	"	Julius A. Krug	Wis.	1946
Arthur	Henry M. Teller	Colo.	1882	"	Oscar L. Chapman	Colo.	1950
Cleveland	Lucius Q. C. Lamar	Miss.	1885	Eisenhower	Douglas McKay	Ore.	1953
"	William F. Vilas	Wis.	1888	"	Fred A. Seaton	Nebr.	1956
B. Harrison	John W. Noble	Mo.	1889	Kennedy	Stewart L. Udall	Ariz.	1961
Cleveland	Hoke Smith	Ga.	1893	Johnson, L. B.	"		1963
"	David R. Francis	Mo.	1890	Nixon	Walter J. Hickel	Alaska	1969
McKinley	Cornelius N. Bliss	N. Y.	1897	"	Rogers C. B. Morton	Md.	1971

Secretaries of Health, Education and Welfare

The Department of Health, Education and Welfare was created by act of Congress Apr. 11, 1953.

Presidents	Cabinet Officers	Home	Apptd.	Presidents	Cabinet Officers	Home	Apptd.
Eisenhower	Oveta Culp Hobby	Tex.	1953	Johnson, L. B.	Anthony J. Celebreezze	Ohio	1963
"	Marion B. Folsom	N. Y.	1955	"	John W. Gardner	N. Y.	1965
"	Arthur S. Flemming	Ohio	1958	"	Wilbur J. Cohen	Mich.	1968
Kennedy	Abraham A. Ribicoff	Conn.	1961	Nixon	Robert H. Finch	Cal.	1969
Kennedy	Anthony J. Celebrezze	Ohio	1962	"	Elliot L. Richardson	Mass.	1970
				"	Casper W. Weinberger	Cal.	1973

Secretaries of Housing and Urban Development

The Department of Housing and Urban Development was created by act of Congress Sept. 9, 1965.

President	Cabinet Officers	Home	Apptd.	President	Cabinet Officers	Home	Apptd.
Johnson, L. B.	Robert C. Weaver	Wash.	1966	Nixon	George W. Romney	Mich.	1969
"	Robert C. Wood	Mass.	1968	"	James T. Lynn	Ohio	1973

Secretaries of Defense

The Department of Defense, originally designated the National military Establishment, was created Sept. 18, 1947. It is headed by the secretary of defense, who is a member of the president's cabinet.

The departments of the army, of the navy and of the air force function within the Department of Defense, and their respective secretaries are no longer members of the president's cabinet.

Presidents	Cabinet Officers	Home	Apptd.	Presidents	Cabinet Officers	Home	Apptd.
Truman	James V. Forrestal	N. Y.	1947	Kennedy	Robert S. McNamara	Mich.	1961
"	Louis A. Johnson	W. Va.	1949	Johnson, L. B.	"		1963
"	George C. Marshall	Pa.	1950	"	Clark M. Clifford	Md.	1968
"	Robert A. Lovett	N. Y.	1951	Nixon	Melvin R. Laird	Wisc.	1969
Eisenhower	Charles E. Wilson	Mich.	1953	"	Elliot L. Richardson	Mass.	1973
"	Neil H. McElroy	Ohio	1957	"	James R. Schlesinger	Va.	1973
"	Thomas S. Gates Jr.	Pa.	1959				

Not Members of the President's Cabinet

The Dept. of Defense created Sept. 18, 1947, consolidated the navy, army, air force into a single department.

Secretaries of the Air Force	Appointed
W. Stuart Symington	Sept. 18, 1947
Thomas K. Finletter	Apr. 24, 1950
Harold E. Talbot	Feb. 4, 1953
Donald A. Quarles	Aug. 12, 1955
James H. Douglas	Mar. 26, 1957
Dudley C. Sharpe	Dec. 10, 1959
Eugene M. Zuckert	Jan. 23, 1961
Dr. Harold Brown	July 10, 1965
Robert C. Seamans Jr.	Jan. 20, 1969

Secretaries of the Army	
Kenneth C. Royall	Sept. 18, 1947
Gordon Gray*	June 20, 1949
Frank Pace Jr.	Apr. 12, 1950

Earl D. Johnson (Acting)	Jan. 20, 1953
Robert T. Stevens	Feb. 4, 1953
Wilber M. Brucker	July 21, 1955
Elvis J. Stahr Jr.	Jan. 23, 1961
Cyrus R. Vance	May 21, 1962
Stephen Ailes	Jan. 20, 1964
Stanley R. Resor	June 17, 1965
Robert F. Froehlke	June 15, 1971
Howard H. Callaway	May 2, 1973

*In addition, Gordon Gray was acting secretary of the army from Apr. 28, 1949, and under secretary from May 25, 1949, until June 20, 1949.

Secretaries of the Navy	Appointed
John L. Sullivan	Sept. 18, 1947

Secretaries of the Navy (cont.)

Francis P. Matthews	May 25, 1949	
Dan A. Kimball	July 31, 1951	
Robert B. Anderson	Feb. 4, 1953	
Charles S. Thomas	May 3, 1954	
Thomas S. Gates Jr.	Apr. 1, 1957	
William B. Franke	June 1, 1958	
John B. Connally Jr.	Jan. 23, 1961	

Fred Korth	Dec. 11, 1961
Paul H. Nitze	Oct. 14, 1963
John T. McNaughton	June 6, 1967
Paul R. Ignatius	Aug. 4, 1967
John H. Chafee	Jan. 20, 1969
John W. Warner	Apr. 7, 1972
J. William Middendorf 2d	June 10, 1974

Secretaries of War

The War (and Navy) Department was created by act of Congress Aug. 7, 1789, and Gen. Henry Knox was commissioned secretary of war under that act Sept. 12, 1789.

Presidents	Cabinet Officers	Home	Apptd.
Washington	Henry Knox	Mass.	1789
"	Timothy Pickering	Pa.	1795
"	James McHenry	Md.	1796
J. Adams	"	"	1797
J. Adams	Samuel Dexter	Mass.	1800
Jefferson	Henry Dearborn	Mass.	1801
Madison	William Eustis	Mass.	1809
"	John Armstrong	N.Y.	1813
"	James Monroe	Va.	1814
"	William H. Crawford	Ga.	1815
Monroe	John C. Calhoun	S.C.	1817
J.Q. Adams	James Barbour	Va.	1825
"	Peter B. Porter	N.Y.	1828
Jackson	John H. Eaton	Tenn.	1829
"	Lewis Cass	Ohio	1831
"	Benjamin F. Butler	N.Y.	1837
Van Buren	Joel R. Poinsett	S.C.	1837
W.H. Harrison	John Bell	Tenn.	1841
Tyler	"	"	1841
"	John C. Spencer	N.Y.	1841
"	James M. Porter	Pa.	1843
"	William Wilkins	"	1844
Polk	William L. Marcy	N.Y.	1845
Taylor	George W. Crawford	Ga.	1849
Fillmore	Charles M. Conrad	La.	1850
Pierce	Jefferson Davis	Miss.	1853
Buchanan	John B. Floyd	Va.	1857
"	Joseph Holt	Ky.	1861
Lincoln	Simon Cameron	Pa.	1861
"	Edwin M. Stanton	Pa.	1862
Johnson, A.	"	"	1865
"	John M. Schofield	Ill.	1868

Presidents	Cabinet Officers	Home	Apptd.
Grant	John A. Rawlins	Ill.	1869
"	William T. Sherman	Ohio	1869
"	William W. Belknap	Iowa	1869
"	Alphonso Taft	Ohio	1876
"	James D. Cameron	Pa.	1876
Hayes	George W. McCrary	Iowa	1877
"	Alexander Ramsey	Minn.	1879
Garfield	Robert T. Lincoln	Ill.	1881
Arthur	"	"	1881
Cleveland	William C. Endicott	Mass.	1885
B. Harrison	Redfield Proctor	Vt.	1890
"	Stephen B. Elkins	W.Va.	1891
Cleveland	Daniel S. Lamont	N.Y.	1893
McKinley	Russel A. Alger	Mich.	1897
"	Elihu Root	N.Y.	1899
T. Roosevelt	"	"	1901
"	William H. Taft	Ohio	1904
"	Luke E. Wright	Tenn.	1908
Taft	Jacob M. Dickinson	"	1909
"	Henry L. Stimson	N.Y.	1911
Wilson	Lindley M. Garrison	N.J.	1913
"	Newton D. Baker	Ohio	1916
Harding	John W. Weeks	Mass.	1921
Coolidge	"	"	1923
"	Dwight F. Davis	Mo.	1925
Hoover	James W. Good	Ill.	1929
"	Patrick J. Hurley	Okla.	1929
F. D. Roosevelt	George H. Dern	Utah	1933
"	Harry H. Woodring	Kan.	1937
"	Henry L. Stimson	N.Y.	1940
Truman	Robert P. Patterson	N.Y.	1945
"	*Kenneth C. Royall	N.C.	1947

*Last member of the president's cabinet. The War Dept. Became the Dept. of the Army and is now a branch of the Dept. of Defense, created Sept. 18, 1947.

Secretaries of the Navy

The Navy Department was created by act of Congress Apr. 30, 1798.

Presidents	Cabinet Officers	Home	Apptd.
J. Adams	Benjamin Stoddert	Md.	1798
Jefferson	"	"	1801
"	Robert Smith	"	1801
Madison	Paul Hamilton	S.C.	1809
"	William Jones	Pa.	1813
"	Benjamin Williams Crowninshield	Mass.	1814
Monroe	"	"	1817
"	Smith Thompson	N.Y.	1818
"	Samuel L. Southard	N.J.	1823
J.Q. Adams	"	"	1825
Jackson	John Branch	N.C.	1829
"	Levi Woodbury	N.H.	1831
"	Mahlon Dickerson	N.J.	1834
Van Buren	"	"	1837
"	James K. Paulding	N.Y.	1838
W.H. Harrison	George E. Badger	N.C.	1841
Tyler	"	"	1841
"	Abel P. Upshur	Va.	1841
"	David Henshaw	Mass.	1843
"	Thomas W. Gilmer	Va.	1844
"	John Y. Mason	"	1844
Polk	George Bancroft	Mass.	1845
"	John Y. Mason	Va.	1846
Taylor	William B. Preston	"	1849
Fillmore	William A. Graham	N.C.	1850
"	John P. Kennedy	Md.	1852
Pierce	James C. Dobbin	N.C.	1853
Buchanan	Isaac Toucey	Conn.	1857

Presidents	Cabinet Officers	Home	Apptd.
Lincoln	Gideon Welles	Conn.	1861
Johnson, A.	"	"	1865
Grant	Adolph E. Borie	Pa.	1869
"	George M. Robeson	N.J.	1869
Hayes	Richard W. Thompson	Ind.	1877
"	Nathan Goff Jr.	W.Va.	1881
Garfield	William H. Hunt	La.	1881
Arthur	William E. Chandler	N.H.	1882
Cleveland	William C. Whitney	N.Y.	1885
B. Harrison	Benjamin F. Tracy	N.Y.	1889
Cleveland	Hilary A. Herbert	Ala.	1893
McKinley	John D. Long	Mass.	1897
T. Roosevelt	"	"	1901
"	William H. Moody	"	1902
"	Paul Morton	Ill.	1904
"	Charles J. Bonaparte	Md.	1905
"	Victor H. Metcalf	Cal.	1906
"	Truman H. Newberry	Mich.	1908
Taft	George von L. Meyer	Mass.	1909
Wilson	Josephus Daniels	N.C.	1913
Harding	Edwin Denby	Mich.	1921
Coolidge	"	"	1923
"	Curtis D. Wilbur	Cal.	1924
Hoover	Charles Francis Adams	Mass.	1929
F. D. Roosevelt	Claude A. Swanson	Va.	1933
"	Charles Edison	N.J.	1940
"	Frank Knox	Ill.	1940
"	James V. Forrestal	N.Y.	1944
Truman	"	"	1945

Secretaries of Commerce and Labor

The Dept. of Commerce & Labor, created by Congress Feb. 14, 1903, was divided by Congress Mar. 4, 1913, into separate Depts. of Commerce and Labor, the Secretary of each made a Cabinet member.

Secretaries of Commerce and Labor

Presidents	Cabinet Officers	Home	Apptd.
T. Roosevelt	Geo. B. Cortelyou	N.Y.	1903
"	Victor H. Metcalf	Cal.	1904
"	Oscar S. Straus	N.Y.	1906
Taft	Charles Nagel	Mo.	1909

Secretaries of Labor

Wilson	William B. Wilson	Pa.	1913
Harding	James J. Davis	Pa.	1921
Coolidge	"	"	1923
Hoover	"	"	1929
"	William N. Doak	Va.	1930

Secretaries of Labor (cont.)

Presidents	Cabinet Officers	Home	Apptd.
F. D. Roosevelt.	Frances Perkins.	N. Y.	1933
Truman	L. B. Schwellenbach.	Wash.	1945
"	Maurice J. Tobin.	Mass.	1949
Eisenhower.	Martin P. Durkin.	Ill.	1953
"	James P. Mitchell.	N. J.	1953
Kennedy.	Arthur J. Goldberg.	Ill.	1961
"	W. Willard Wirtz.	Ill.	1962
Johnson, L. B.	"	"	1963
Nixon.	George P. Shultz.	Ill.	1969
Nixon.	James D. Hodgson.	Cal.	1970
"	Peter J. Brennan.	N. Y.	1973

Secretaries of Commerce

Presidents	Cabinet Officers	Home	Apptd.
Wilson.	William C. Redfield.	N. Y.	1913
"	Josh. W. Alexander.	Mo.	1919
Harding.	Herbert C. Hoover.	Cal.	1921
Coolidge.	"	"	1923
"	William F. Whiting.	Mass.	1928

Hoover.	Robert P. Lamont.	Ill.	1929
"	Roy D. Chapin.	Mich.	1932
F. D. Roosevelt.	Daniel C. Roper.	S. C.	1933
"	Harry L. Hopkins.	N. Y.	1939
"	Jesse Jones.	Tex.	1940
"	Henry A. Wallace.	Ia.	1945
Truman.	"	"	1945
"	W. Averell Harriman.	N. Y.	1947
"	Charles Sawyer.	Ohio.	1948
Eisenhower.	Sinclair Weeks.	Mass.	1953
"	Lewis L. Strauss.	N. Y.	1958
"	Frederick H. Mueller.	Mich.	1959
Kennedy.	Luther H. Hodges.	N. C.	1961
Johnson, L. B.	John T. Connor.	N. J.	1965
"	Alex B. Trowbridge.	N. J.	1967
"	C. R. Smith.	N. Y.	1968
Nixon.	Maurice H. Stans.	Minn.	1969
"	Peter G. Peterson.	Ill.	1972
"	Frederick B. Dent.	S. C.	1973

Secretaries of Transportation

The Department of Transportation was created by act of Congress Oct. 15, 1966.

President	Cabinet Officer	Home	Apptd.	President	Cabinet Officers	Home	Apptd.
Johnson, L. B.	Alan S. Boyd.	Fla.	1966	Nixon.	John A. Volpe.	Mass.	1969
				"	Claude S. Brinegar.	Calif.	1973

Postmasters General were made members of the cabinet March 9, 1829, and 53 men held that rank before the organization of the U.S. Postal Service an independent agency July 1, 1971.

Wives and Children of the Presidents

Presidents*	Wife's Name	State	Born	Married	Died	Sons	Daughters
Washington.	Martha (Dandridge) Custis.	Va.	1732	1759	1802		
John Adams.	Abigail Smith.	Mass.	1744	1764	1818	3	2
Jefferson.	Martha (Wayles) Skelton.	Va.	1748	1772	1782	1	5
Madison.	Dorothea "Dolley" (Payne) Todd.	N. C.	1768	1794	1849		
Monroe.	Elizabeth Kortwright (1).	N. Y.	1768	1786	1830		
J. Q. Adams.	Louisa Catherine Johnson (2).	Md.	1775	1797	1852	3	1
Jackson.	Rachel (Donelson) Robards.	Va.	1767	1791	1828		
Van Buren.	Hannah Hoes.	N. Y.	1783	1807	1819	4	
William H. Harrison.	Anna Symmes.	N. J.	1775	1795	1864	6	4
Tyler.	Letitia Christian.	Va.	1790	1813	1842	3	4
"	Julia Gardiner.	N. Y.	1820	1844	1889	5	2
Polk.	Sarah Childress.	Tenn.	1803	1824	1891		
Taylor.	Margaret Smith.	Md.	1788	1810	1852	1	5
Fillmore.	Abigail Powers.	N. Y.	1798	1826	1853	1	1
"	Caroline (Carmichael) McIntosh.	N. J.	1813	1858	1881		
Pierce.	Jane Means Appleton.	N. H.	1806	1834	1863	3	
Lincoln.	Mary Todd.	Ky.	1818	1842	1882	4	
Johnson, Andrew.	Eliza McCardle.	Tenn.	1810	1827	1876	3	2
Grant.	Julia Dent.	Mo.	1826	1848	1902	3	1
Hayes.	Lucy Ware Webb.	Ohio.	1831	1852	1889	7	1
Garfield.	Lucretia Rudolph.	Ohio.	1832	1858	1918	4	1
Arthur.	Ellen Lewis Herndon.	Va.	1837	1859	1880	2	1
Cleveland.	Frances Folsom.	N. Y.	1864	1886	1947	2	3
Benjamin Harrison.	Caroline Lavinia Scott.	Ohio.	1832	1853	1892	1	1
"	Mary Scott (Lord) Dimmock.	Pa.	1858	1896	1948		1
McKinley.	Ida Saxton.	Ohio.	1847	1871	1907		2
Theodore Roosevelt.	Alice Hathaway Lee.	Mass.	1861	1880	1884		1
"	Edith Kermit Carow.	Conn.	1861	1886	1948	4	1
Taft.	Helen Herron.	Ohio.	1861	1886	1943	2	1
Wilson.	Ellen Louise Axson.	Ga.	1860	1885	1914		3
"	Edith (Bolling) Galt.	Va.	1872	1915	1961		
Harding.	Florence (Kling) De Wolfe.	Ohio.	1860	1891	1924		
Coolidge.	Grace Anna Goodhue.	Vt.	1879	1905	1957	2	
Hoover.	Lou Henry.	Iowa.	1875	1899	1944	2	
F. D. Roosevelt.	Anna Eleanor Roosevelt (1).	N. Y.	1884	1905	1962	4	1
Truman.	Bess Wallace.	Mo.	1885	1919			1
Eisenhower.	Mamie Geneva Doud (1).	Iowa.	1896	1916		1	
Kennedy.	Jacqueline Lee Bouvier (1).	N. Y.	1929	1953		1	1
Johnson, Lyndon.	Claudia Alta Taylor.	Tex.	1912	1934			2
Nixon, Richard.	Thelma Catherine Patricia Ryan.	Nev.	1912	1940			2
Ford, Gerald.	Elizabeth Bloomer Warren.	Ill.	1918	1948		3	1

*James Buchanan, 15 president, was unmarried. (1) Plus one infant, deceased. (2) Born London, father a Maryland citizen.

Biographies of U.S. Presidents

George Washington

George Washington, first president, was born Friday, Feb. 22, 1732 (Feb. 11, 1731, Old Style), the son of Augustine Washington and Mary Ball, at Wakefield on Pope's Creek, Westmoreland Co., Va. Col. John Washington, George's great-grandfather, came from Northamptonshire in 1657 or 1658; in 1665 he and an associate named Spencer bought 5,000 acres on the Potomac. George's father took the north 2,500 acres near Hunting Creek in 1735 and built a house in which George lived from 3 to 6 years of age; when 6 the family moved to Ferry farm, near Fredericksburg. His father died in 1743 when he was 11. He studied mathematics and surveying and when 16 went to live with his half brother Lawrence, who had inherited the Potomac farm and built Mount Vernon, the original house having burned. George surveyed the lands of William Fairfax on the Shenandoah, keeping a diary. He accompanied Lawrence to Barbados, West Indies, contracted small pox and was deeply scarred. Lawrence died in 1752 and George acquired his property by inheritance and purchase and added the 2,500 acres held by the Spencers. He valued land and when he died owned 70,000 acres in Virginia and 40,000 acres on the Great Kanawa and environs.

Washington's military service began in 1753 when Gov. Dinwiddie of Virginia made him lieutenant-colonel of militia. He clashed with the French and had to surrender Fort Necessity July 3, 1754. He was an aide to Braddock and helped organize the retreat after the fatal ambuscade of July 9, 1755. He helped take Fort DuQuesne from the French in 1758.

After his marriage to Martha Dandridge Custis, 1759, a widow, Washington lived at Mount Vernon, bred horses and cattle, raised fruit and practiced crop rotation. During the stamp act agitation, 1765, he supported the protesting Virginians. Although not at first for independence, he stood out against British exactions and took charge of the Virginia troops before war broke out. He was made commander-in-chief by the Continental Congress June 15, 1775, and took command at Cambridge July 3.

The successful issue of a war filled with hardships was largely due to his leadership. He was resourceful, a stern disciplinarian, and the one strong, dependable force for unity. He favored a federal government and became chairman of the Constitutional convention of 1787. He helped get the Constitution ratified and was unanimously elected President and inaugurated, April 30, 1789, on the balcony of New York's Federal hall at Broad and Wall Sts., now marked by his statue. In New York his mansion, near Franklin Sq., was the scene of formal dinners and levees. His pew in St. Paul's chapel is preserved.

His birthplace, Wakefield, was burned in 1780. On Feb. 22, 1932, a new Wakefield, built by donations, was dedicated as the George Washington Birthplace Monument, administered by the National Parks Service. The older Washingtons are buried there. It is 34 miles from Fredericksburg, Va., and 5 miles from Stratford Hall, birthplace of Robert E. Lee.

Although a Federalist, Washington made Thomas Jefferson secretary of state (resigned 1793). He was re-elected 1792, but refused to consider a 3d term and retired to Mount Vernon, 1797. He suffered acute laryngitis after a ride in snow and rain around his estate, was bled profusely, and died Dec. 14, 1799, aged 67. He was mourned here and abroad as one of the great men of his time. He was buried in a vault at Mount Vernon. (See article on Mount Vernon.) He willed Mount Vernon to his nephew, Bushrod Washington (1762-1829), associate justice, U. S. Supreme Court.

John Adams

John Adams, 2d president, Federalist, was born in Braintree (Quincy), Mass., Oct. 30, 1735 (Oct. 19, O.S.), the son of John Adams, a farmer, and Susanna Boylston of Brookline. He was a great-grandson of Henry Adams who came from England in 1636. He was graduated from Harvard, 1755, taught school, studied law. In 1765 he argued against taxation without representation before the royal governor. In 1770 he defended the British soldiers, who fired on civilians in the "Boston Massacre." He took part in the Provincial Congress of Massachusetts and the Continental Congress, seconded the independence resolution presented by Richard Henry Lee and with his cousin, Samuel Adams, signed the Declaration of Independence. He was a commissioner to France, 1778, with Benjamin Franklin and Arthur Lee; won recognition of the United States by The Hague, 1782; was first American minister to England, 1785-1788, and elected vice president with Washington, 1788 and 1792.

In 1796 Adams was chosen president by the electors, 71 to 68 so that opponents called him "president by 3 votes." The candidate with the second highest number of votes became vice president; this was Thomas Jefferson, his opponent. Intense antagonism to America by France caused agitation for war, led by Alexander Hamilton. Adams, breaking with Hamilton, opposed war but put the navy on a fighting basis. The U.S.S. Constitution, the United States, both 44 guns, and the Constellation, 36 guns, and armed merchantmen bagged 84 French ships in an undeclared war. To fight alien influence and muzzle criticism Adams supported the Alien and Sedition laws of 1798, which led to his defeat for reelection. He died July 4, 1826, on the same day as Jefferson, and was buried in the First Unitarian Church in Quincy, Mass.

Adams married Abigail Smith Nov. 23, 1744 (Nov. 12, O.S.). They had 2 daughters and 3 sons, one of whom, John Quincy Adams, became the 6th president.

Thomas Jefferson

Thomas Jefferson, 3d president, was born April 13, 1743 (Apr. 2, O. S.) at Shadwell, Va., the son of Peter Jefferson, a civil engineer of Welsh descent who raised tobacco, and Jane Randolph. Jefferson was an agrarian and an expansionist. Because he opposed the Federalists and centralization he was called a Republican, now synonymous with Democrat. His father died when he was 14, leaving him 2,750 acres and his slaves. Jefferson attended the College of William and Mary, 1760-1762, read classics in Greek and Latin and played the violin. In 1769 he was elected to the House of Burgesses. In 1770 he began building Monticello, near Charlottesville. In 1772 he married Martha Wayles Skelton. He was a member of the Virginia Committee of Correspondence and the Continental Congress and denied Britain's right to tax. Named a member of the committee to draw up a Declaration of Independence, he wrote the basic draft, 1776. He was a member of the Virginia House of Delegates, 1776-79, elected governor to succeed Patrick Henry, 1779, re-elected 1780, resigned, June 1781, amid charges of ineffectual military preparation. During his term he wrote the statute on religious freedom. In the Continental Congress, 1783, he drew up an ordinance for the Northwest Territory, forbidding slavery after 1800; its terms were put into the Ordinance of 1787. He was sent to Paris with Benjamin Franklin and John Adams to negotiate treaties of commerce, 1784; made minister to France, 1785, he made treaties with France and Prussia, studied architecture, gardening and the French Revolution, whose leaders consulted him.

Washington, appointed him secretary of state, 1789. Jefferson's strong faith in the consent of the governed, as opposed to executive control favored by Hamilton, secretary of the treasury, often led to conflict:

Dec. 31, 1793, he resigned. He was the Republican candidate for president in 1796; beaten by John Adams, he became vice president. He opposed Adams' alien and sedition laws with the Kentucky and Virginia resolutions, reiterating the basic rights of states. In 1800 Jefferson and Aaron Burr received equal votes for president, so the House of Representatives, with Hamilton's help, elected Jefferson, the first president to be inauguarated in Washington. Adams left town before the ceremony, but when Jefferson was re-elected in 1804 he voted for him. Jefferson canceled levees and titles and ignored diplomatic precedence. He turned Federalists out of office. He opposed a strong navy. By fighting those who feared to give power to the people he made democracy work. He considered John Marshall's Supreme Court reactionary. Big events of his administration were the Louisiana Purchase, 1803, and the Lewis and Clark Expedition. He established the University of Virginia and designed its buildings. After the Library of Congress was burned by the British he sold Congress some 6,000 vols. for $23,950. He was 6 ft. 2, temperate in debate, a deist in religion. He died July 4, 1826, on the same day as John Adams and was buried at Monticello, which, after various vicissitudes, passed to the Thomas Jefferson Memorial Foundation in 1923.

He married Martha Wayles Skelton, a widow, Jan. 1, 1772. They had one son and 5 daughters.

James Madison

James Madison, 4th president, Republican, was born Mar. 16, 1751 (Mar. 5 1750, O. S.) at Port Conway, King George Co., Va., the eldest of 12 children of James Madison and Eleanor Rose Conway. His great-grandfather, James Taylor (1674-1729), was also the great-grandfather of Zachary Taylor. Madison was graduated from Princeton, 1771, studied theology, 1772, sat in the Virginia Constitutional Convention, 1776, where his resolution on religious freedom was voted down; was a member of the Continental Congress and of the Annapolis convention, 1786, where he and Hamilton proposed the Constitutional Convention. He was chief recorder at that convention in 1787, and supported ratification in the Federalist papers, written with Hamilton and Jay. In 1785 he carried Jefferson's statute on religious liberty through the Virginia Assembly. He was elected to the House of Representatives in 1789, helped adopt the Bill of Rights and fought John Adams' alien and sedition laws. He favored agrarian policies with Jefferson and in 1801 became Jefferson's secretary of state. In 1803, when the Louisiana Purchase was consummated, he insisted on free navigation of the Mississippi, which he had already urged on Jay in 1780.

Elected president in 1808, Madison was a "strict constructionist," opposed to the free interpretation of the Constitution by te Federalists; he vetoed federal funds for state improvements, but changed in his second term. Madison inherited the conflict with Britain over its orders in council and its impressment of American seamen, which had led to Jefferson's embargo act and injured American commerce. He was reelected in 1812 by the votes of the agrarian South and recently admitted western states. Caught between British and French maritime restrictions, Madison drifted into war, declared June 18, 1812, unaware that Britain had canceled the orders 2 days before. While the war was inconclusive, it opened the way to peaceful negotiations. Madison successfully advocated a tariff to protect industry, a national system of roads and canals and a strong military organization. He retired in 1817 to his estate at Montpelier in Orange County, Va., built 1760, with a portico suggested by Jefferson. There he edited his famous papers on the Constitutional Convention. He became rector of the University of Virginia, 1826. He died June 28, 1836, and was buried near his home.

Madison married Dorothea "Dolley" Payne Todd, a widow, Sept. 15, 1794.

James Monroe

James Monroe, 5th president, Republican, was born April 28, 1758, in Westmoreland Co., Va., the son of Spence Monroe and Eliza Jones, who were of Scottish and Welsh descent, respectively. He attended the College of William and Mary, fought in the 3rd Virginia Regiment at White Plains, Brandywine, Monmouth, and was wounded at Trenton. He studied law with Thomas Jefferson, 1780, was a member of the Virginia House of Delegates and of Congress, 1783-86. He opposed ratification of the Constitution because it lacked a bill of rights; was U.S. Senator, 1790; minister to France, 1794-96, during which he improved relations with France, Spain and Algiers; four times governor of Virginia, 1799-1802, and 1811, Jefferson sent him to France as minister, 1803, to join R. R. Livingston in buying the isle of New Orleans from France and East and West Florida from Spain. Exceeding instructions, he signed a treaty for all of Louisiana. He was also sent to Madrid, 1804, and London, 1805, to settle disputes. He ran against Madison for president in 1808. He was chosen member of the Virginia Assembly, 1810-1811; secretary of state under Madison, 1811-1817; also secretary of war, Sept. 1814-Mar., 1815.

In 1816 Monroe was elected president; in 1820 reelected with all but one vote, this being cast for John Quincy Adams by William Plumer Sr. of New Hampshire. Although many historians have held that Plumer withheld his vote from Monroe so that only Washington would have been elected unanimously, Plumer himself said he voted for Adams because he had "discovered a want of foresight" in Monroe. Monroe's administration became the "Era of Good Feeling." He obtained the Floridas from Spain and suppressed the Seminoles; settled boundaries with Canada and eliminated border forts; supported the anti-slavery position that led to the Missouri Compromise. (In 1801 he had proposed settling Negro slaves in Africa. Monrovia, Liberia, was named for him.) In July, 1823, the U.S. served notice on Russia that it would oppose any Russian colony on this continent, after Russia had prohibited fishing on the northwest coasts. On Dec. 2, 1823, Monroe announced the doctrine that the U. S. would consider its safety endangered if European powers had authority on this hemisphere or attempted colonization. First half had been suggested by George Canning, British foreign minister, to curb Spain; U. S., rejecting proposal for joint declaration, issued it also as warning to Russia. Monroe owned Ash Lawn, 5 mi. from Charlottesville, Va., 1799-1825; inherited Oak Hill, Loudon Co., Va., from his uncle Joseph Jones, 1806. The mansion, replacing Jones' cottage, was designed by Jefferson and executed by James. Hoban, White House architect.

Monroe married Elizabeth Kortwright in 1786. They had a son who died in infancy and 2 daughters. Mrs. Monroe died in 1830 and he and the daughters moved to New York, were he died July 4, 1831.

John Quincy Adams

John Quincy Adams, 6th president, independent Federalist, was born July 11, 1767, at Braintree (Quincy), Mass., the son of John and Abigail Adams. His father was the 2nd president. He was educated in Paris, Leyden and Harvard, graduating in 1787. He served as American minister in the Netherlands, Berlin, St. Petersburg and London and helped draft the peace treaty of 1814. He had served as senator from 1803 to 1808 and his support of the Republican administration alienated the Federalists. President Monroe made him secretary of state, 1817, and he negotiated the cession of the Floridas from Spain, supported exclusion of slavery in the Missouri Compromise, and laid the base for the Monroe Doctrine, of which he, as much as Monroe, was the creator. In 1824 he was elected president by the House after he failed to win an Electoral College majority over Henry Clay and Andrew Jackson. His expansion of executive powers was strongly opposed and he was beaten in 1828 by Jackson. In 1831 he was sent to Congress as representative and served nine terms with distinction and independence. He fought slavery, opposed the annexation of Texas and the war with Mexico; was responsible for the Smithsonian Institution. He had a stroke in the House and died in the Speaker's room, Feb. 23, 1848.

Adams married Louisa Catherine Johnson on July 26, 1797. They had 3 sons and a daughter.

Andrew Jackson

Andrew Jackson, 7th president, originally a Jeffersonian-Republican later a Democrat, was born in the Waxhaws district, New Lancaster Co., S. C., Mar. 15, 1767, the posthumous son of Andrew Jackson, who came from County Antrim, Ireland with his wife, Elizabeth Hutchinson, and 2 sons, in 1765. At 13 young Andrew joined the militia in the Revolution and was captured; a British officer struck him with his sword when the boy refused to shine his boots. He read law in Salisbury, N. C., moved to Nashville, Tenn., speculated in land, married and raised cotton at the Hermitage, originally a log house. In 1796 he helped draft the Constitution of Tennessee and for one year occupied its one seat in the national House. He was in the Senate in 1797, and again in 1823. He defeated the Creek Indians at Horseshoe Bend, Ala., 1814, and as major general, U.S.A., drove the British out of Pensacola. With 6,000 backwoods fighters he defeated Packenham's 12,000 British troops at Chalmette, outside New Orleans, Jan. 8, 1815, losing only 7 to the British loss of 2,000. In 1818 he briefly invaded Spanish Florida to quell Seminoles and outlaws who harassed frontier settlements. In 1824 he ran for president against John Quincy Adams and was voted down by the House, though he had the most votes; in 1828 he carried everything, the West rising to support "Old Hickory" and a liberal land policy. He was a noisy debater and a duelist and introduced rotation in office called the "spoils system." He was suspicious of privilege; ruined the Bank of the United States by depositing federal funds with state banks. Though "Let the people rule" was his slogan, he at times supported strict contructionist policies against the expansionist West. He killed the Congressional caucus for nominating presidential candidates and substituted the national convention, 1832, when he was re-elected, with Martin Van Buren vice president. When South Carolina refused to collect imports under his protective tariff he ordered army and naval forces to Charleston. At the Jefferson Day dinner, 1830, he offered the toast: "Our Federal Union; it must be preserved." Vice President John C. Calhoun, exponent of state sovereignty, gave in reply the toast: "The Union — next to our liberty, most dear." Jackson recognized the Republic of Texas, 1836.

In 1791 Jackson married Rachel Donelson Robards who believed she had been divorced by Capt. Lewis Robards. But he did not actually obtain a divorce until 1793, after which the Jacksons were remarried. Mrs. Jackson died in 1828, shortly after Jackson's first election. He died at the Hermitage, June 8, 1845, and is buried there.

Martin Van Buren

Martin Van Buren, 8th president, Democrat, was born Dec. 5, 1782, at Kinderhook, N. Y., the son of Abraham Van Buren, a Dutch farmer, and Mary Hoes. He was surrogate of Columbia County, N. Y., state senator and attorney general and a law partner of Benjamin F. Butler in Albany. He was U. S. senator 1821, re-elected, 1827, elected governor of New York,

1828. He helped swing eastern support to Andrew Jackson in 1828 and was his secretary of state 1829-31. In 1832 he was elected vice president. He was a consummate politician, known as "the little magician," and influenced Jackson's policies. In 1836 he defeated William Henry Harrison for president by 170 to 73 electoral votes. He inaugurated the independent treasury system, and was the first advocate of mutual insurance of deposits by banks. He urged tariffs for revenue only and opposed internal improvements at national expense. His refusal to spend land revenues led to his defeat by Harrison in 1840. He lost the Democratic nomination of 1844 to Polk because he opposed annexation of Texas. In 1848 he ran for president on the Free Soil ticket and lost. He died July 24, 1862, at Kinderhook.

Van Buren married Hannah Hoes, a cousin, in 1807; she died in 1819. One of their sons, Abraham was secretary to the president. Abraham's wife Angelica Singleton, a cousin of "Dolley" Madison, was White House hostess during Van Buren's term.

William Henry Harrison

William Henry, Harrison, 9th president, Whig, who served only 31 days, was born in Berkeley, Charles City Co., Va., Feb. 9, 1773, the third son of Benjamin Harrison, signer of the Declaration of Independence. Educated at Hampden Sydney college, he later studied medicine under Dr. Benjamin Rush. Commissioned by Washington, he fought under Gen. Anthony Wayne at Fallen Timbers, 1794. He was secretary of the Northwest Territory, 1798; its delegate in Congress, 1799; first governor of Indiana Territory, and superintendent of Indian affairs. With 900 men he routed Tecumseh's Indians at Tippecanoe, Nov. 7, 1811. A major general, he defeated British and Indians at Battle of the Thames, Oct. 5, 1813. He served Ohio in Congress, 1816; as senator, 1824; was minister to Colombia. In 1840, when 68, he was elected president with John Tyler, 234 to 60, on a "log cabin and hard cider" slogan. He caught pneumonia during the inauguration and died April 4, 1841. He was buried in North Bend, Ohio.

Harrison married Anna Symmes in 1795. They had 6 sons. A grandson, Benjamin Harrison, became the 23d president.

John Tyler

John Tyler, 10th president, Independent Whig, was born Mar. 29, 1790, in Greenway, Charles City Co., Va., son of John Tyler and Mary Armistead. His father was governor of Virginia, 1808-11. Tyler was graduated from William and Mary, 1807; member of the House of Delegates, 1811; in Congress, 1816-21; in Virginia legislature, 1823-25; governor of Virginia, 1825-26; U. S. senator, 1827-36. In 1840 he was elected vice president and, on President Harrison's death, succeeded him. He favored pre-emption, allowing settlers to get government land; rejected a new bank bill and thus alienated Whig supporters except Daniel Webster, his secretary of state; refused to honor the spoils system. He signed the resolution annexing Texas, Mar. 1, 1845. He accepted renomination, 1844, but withdrew before election. He condemned South Carolina's nullification and secession and, as Virginia's commissioner to Buchanan, tried to keep Fort Sumter neutralized. He was president of the peace congress called in Washington by Virginia, 1861. After its failure he supported secession, sat in the provisional Confederate congress, became a member of the Confederate House, but died, Jan. 18, 1862, before it met. He was buried in Richmond.

Tyler first married Letitia Christian, in 1813; they had 3 sons and 4 daughters; she died in 1842. He married Julia Gardiner, of Gardiner's Is., N.Y., in 1844. They had 5 sons and 2 daughters.

James Knox Polk

James Knox Polk, 11th president, Democrat, was born in Mecklenburg Co., N. C., Nov. 2, 1795, the son of Samuel Polk, farmer and surveyor of Scotch-Irish descent, and Jane Knox. He went to Maury Co., Tenn., 1806; was graduated from the University of North Carolina, 1818; member of the Tennessee state legislature, 1823-25, known as "Napoleon of the Stump." He served in Congress 1825-39 and as speaker 1835-39. He supported Jackson and Van Buren, but was always expansionist. He was governor of Tennessee 1839-41, being defeated 1841, '43. In 1844, when both Clay and Van Buren announced opposition to annexing Texas, the Democrats made Polk the first dark horse nominee because he demanded control of all Oregon and annexation of Texas. He won 170 to 105. James Buchanan was his secretary of state. He reestablished the independent treasury system originated by Van Buren. His expansionist policy was opposed by Clay, Webster, Calhoun; he sent Zachary Taylor and an army to the Mexican border and when Mexicans attacked declared war existed. Abraham Lincoln, a Whig in Congress, opposed his war policy. Polk approved the acquisition of California, Utah and New Mexico (522,568 square miles) as part of America's "manifest destiny," but opposed retaining Mexico by force. He compromised on the Oregon boundary ("54-40 or fight!") by accepting the 49th parallel and giving Vancouver to the British. The Wilmot Proviso, outlawing slavery in new states, was debated in his term. Polk died in Nashville, June 15, 1849, and was buried on the capitol grounds there.

Polk married Sarah Childress on Jan. 1, 1824. They had no children.

Zachary Taylor

Zachary Taylor, 12th president, Whig, who served only 16 months, was born Nov. 24, 1784, in Orange Co., Va., the son of Richard Taylor, later collector of the port of Louisville, Ky. His grandfather and James Madison's paternal grandmother were brother and sister. Taylor enlisted 1806; was commissioned lieutenant by Jefferson, 1808; fought in the War of 1812, the Black Hawk War, 1832, and the Seminole war, 1837. He became known as Old Rough and Ready. He settled on a plantation near Baton Rouge, La. In 1845 Polk sent him to the Rio Grande; when the Mexicans attacked him, Polk declared war. Taylor was successful at Palo Alto and Resaca de la Palma, May 8 and 9, 1846; occupied Monterey. Polk made him major general but gave many of his troops to Gen. Winfield Scott at Vera Cruz. Taylor, with 5,000 men, defeated Santa Anna's 20,000 at Buena Vista, Feb. 22, 1847. He defeated Scott at the Whig convention, 1848; was elected president over Martin Van Buren with Millard Fillmore vice president. He resumed the spoils system and though once a slave-holder worked to have California admitted as a free state. He died of typhus July 9, 1850, and was buried near Louisville.

Taylor married Margaret Smith in 1810. They had one son and 5 daughters, one of whom, Sarah, married Jefferson Davis in 1835; she died a few months later.

Millard Fillmore

Millard Fillmore, 13th president, Whig, was born Jan. 7, 1800, in a log cabin on a Cayuga Co., N. Y., farm cleared in 1795 by his father, Nathaniel. He was apprenticed to a fuller and dyer; bought his freedom for $30 to study and became a teacher and postmaster in Buffalo, N. Y. He was counselor of the state Supreme Court, 1829; in the state Assembly, 1829-32; in Congress, 1833-35 and again 1837-43. He opposed the entrance of Texas as slave territory and voted for a protective tariff. He supported the appropriation of $30,000 for Morse's telegraph. In 1844 he was defeated for governor of New York. In 1848 he was elected vice president and succeeded as president July 10,

1850 after Taylor's death. Fillmore favored the Compromise of 1850 and signed the Fugitive Slave Law. His policies pleased neither expansionists nor slaveholders and he was not renominated in 1852. In 1856 he was nominated by the American (Know-Nothing) party and accepted by the Whigs, but defeated by Buchanan. He was chancellor of the University of Buffalo. He died in Buffalo, Mar. 8, 1874.

Fillmore first married Abigail Powers, in 1826 and they had one son and one daughter, Abigail died in 1853 and Fillmore married Caroline Carmichael McIntosh, a widow, in 1858. They had no children.

Franklin Pierce

Franklin Pierce, 14th president, Democrat, was born in Hillsboro, N. H., Nov. 23, 1804, the son of Benjamin Pierce, veteran of the Revolution and governor of New Hampshire, 1827. He attended Exeter and was graduated from Bowdoin, 1824. A lawyer, he served in the New Hampshire House, 1829-32; in Congress, supporting Jackson, 1833; U.S. Senator, 1837-42. He enlisted in the Mexican War, became brigadier general of volunteers and was wounded at Contreras. In 1852 Pierce was nominated on the 49th ballot over Cass, Douglas and Buchanan, defeating Gen. Winfield Scott, Whig. Though against slavery, Pierce was influenced by southern pro-slavery men (Jefferson Davis was his secretary of war) but he ignored the Ostend Manifesto that the U.S. either buy or take Cuba. He approved the Kansas-Nebraska Act, leaving slavery to popular vote ("squatter sovereignty"), 1854, and named a pro-slavery governor of Kansas. He signed a reciprocity treaty with Canada and approved the Gadsden Purchase from Mexico, 1853. He supported Commodore Matthew Perry's opening of Japan, 1854. Pierce died at Concord, N. H., Oct. 8, 1869.

Pierce married Jane Means Appleton. They had 3 children; all died in childhood.

James Buchanan

James Buchanan, 15th president, Federalist, later Democrat, was born of Scottish descent near Mercersburg, Pa., Apr. 23, 1791. He was a volunteer in the War of 1812; graduated from Dickinson, 1809; member, Pennsylvania legislature, 1814-16, Congress, 1820-31; Jackson's minister to Russia, 1831-33; U. S. Senator 1834-45. As Polk's secretary of state, 1845-49, he ended the Oregon dispute with Britain, supported the Mexican War and annexation of Texas. As minister to Britain, 1853, he signed the Ostend Manifesto, 1854, urging the U. S. to take Cuba. Nominated by Democrats over Pierce and Stephen A. Douglas, he was elected, 1856, over John C. Fremont (Republican) and Millard Fillmore (American Know-Nothing and Whig tickets). On slavery he favored popular sovereignty and choice by state constitutions; he accepted the pro-slavery Dred Scott decision as binding. His support of the pro-slavery Lecompton constitution for Kansas caused a break with Douglas Democrats. He denied the right of states to secede but wanted U. S. constitutional recognition of property rights in slaves and Federal action against fugitives. Buchanan refused demands of South Carolina for Federal property, but also refused to reinforce forts there until too late to help Fort Sumter. A strict constructionist, he desired to keep peace and found no authority for using force. He died at Wheatland, near Lancaster, Pa., June 1 1868, aged 77.

Buchanan was a bachelor. The mistress of the White House was the daughter of Buchanan's sister Jane, Harriet Lane, whose parents had died when she was a child.

Abraham Lincoln

Abraham Lincoln, 16th president, Republican, was born Feb. 12, 1809, in a log cabin on a farm then in Hardin Co., Ky., now in Larue. He was the son of

Thomas Lincoln (1778-1851), a descendant of Samuel Lincoln, who came from Hingham, England, 1637, settled at Salem and Hingham, Mass., and had 11 children. Thomas Lincoln, a carpenter, married Nancy Hanks, June 12, 1806. Nancy has been long believed to have been illegitimate, the "natural" daughter of Lucy and Thomas Hanks. But recent research by David S. Keiser of Elkins Park, Pa., strongly suggests that Nancy was not illegitimate but was actually the daughter of Mary Berry, who Keiser says was the wife of Thomas Hanks. Mary died when Nancy was 2 years old, Keiser says, and Lucy Hanks, a relative, took Nancy to her grandparents, who raised her.

Abraham had a sister, Sarah, born 1807, died 1828, and a brother Thomas, who died in infancy.

The Lincolns moved to Spencer Co., Ind., near Gentryville, when Abe was 7. Nancy died Oct. 5, 1818, aged 35. His father married Mrs. Sarah Bush Johnston, 1819; she had a favorable influence on Abe. In 1830 the family moved to Macon Co., Ill., where Abe and a cousin split 3,000 fence rails. In 1831 they moved to Coles Co. In New Salem, 1831-1837, Lincoln lost election to the Illinois General Assembly, 1832, but later won 4 times, beginning in 1834. He enlisted in the militia for the Black Hawk War, 1832. In New Salem he ran a store, 1833, surveyed land, 1834-36, was postmaster, 1833-36.

In 1837 Lincoln was admitted to the bar and became partner in a Springfield, Ill. law office. He began practice on 8th Judicial Circuit, 1839. He was a presidential elector, 1839, 1844, 1852, 1856. He failed of nomination for representative, 1843, but was elected to the 30th Congress, 1847. He opposed the Mexican War. He stumped New England for Zachary Taylor, 1848. He refused offices of secretary and governor of Oregon Territory, 1849. He opposed the Kansas-Nebraska Act and extension of slavery, 1854. When elected to the Illinois legislature, 1854, he declined in order to try for the Senate, but failed of election, 1855. He was proposed but not chosen for vice president at the first Republican convention, 1856, and he made 50 speeches for John J. Fremont, presidential nominee.

In 1858 Lincoln had Republican support in the Illinois legislature for the Senate but was defeated by Stephen A. Douglas, Dem., who had sponsored the Kansas-Nebraska Act. The issues were debated by Lincoln and Douglas Aug. 21-Oct. 15 at Ottawa, Freeport, Jonesboro, Charleston, Galesburg, Quincy and Alton, Ill.

Lincoln was nominated for president by the Republican party on an anti-slavery platform, at Chicago, May 18, 1860. He ran against Stephen A. Douglas, northern Democrat; John C. Breckinridge, southern pro-slavery Democrat; John Bell, Constitutional Union party. Lincoln got only 40% of the votes, but 180 electoral votes to 123. South Carolina seceded from the Union Dec. 20, 1860, followed in 1861 by 10 southern states.

Lincoln was inaugurated Mar. 4, 1861. Fort Sumter was attacked Apr. 12-14, and surrendered. Lincoln called for 75,000 volunteers Apr. 15, and 500,000 May 3. On Sept. 22, 1862, 5 days after the battle of Antietam, he annnounced that slaves in territory then in rebellion would be free Jan. 1, 1863, date of the Emancipation Proclamation. He reached the highest degree of eloquence at Gettysburg National Cemetery, Nov. 19, 1863.

Lincoln was re-elected, 1864, over Gen. Geo. B. McClellan, Democrat. Lee surrendered April 9, 1865. On April 14 (Good Friday) Lincoln was shot by actor John Wilkes Booth in Ford's Theater, Washington. He died the next day. His body lay in state in New York, Chicago and other cities before burial in Springfield, Ill. His estate reached $110,974, most of it saved from his annual salary of $25,000. His humanity, lofty concept of office and generous spirit made him the hero of the common man the world over.

Lincoln married Mary Todd in Springfield, Nov. 4, 1842. They had 4 sons.

Andrew Johnson

Andrew Johnson, 17th president, Democrat, was born in Raleigh, N. C., Dec. 29, 1808, the son of Jacob Johnson, porter at an inn and church sexton, and Mary McDonough Johnson, who had been a maid at the inn. His father died when he was 5. At 10 he was apprenticed to a tailor. At 16 he ran off to Greenville, Tenn. He became an alderman, 1828; mayor, 1830; state representative and senator, 1835-43; member of Congress, 1843-53; governor of Tennessee, 1853-57; U.S. Senator, 1857-62. He supported John C. Breckinridge against Lincoln in 1860. He had held slaves, but opposed secession and refused to follow Tennessee out of the Union. In March, 1862, Lincoln appointed him military governor of occupied Tennessee. In 1864 he was nominated for vice president with Lincoln on the National Union ticket to win Democratic support. He succeeded Lincoln as president April 15, 1865. In a controversy with Congress over the president's power over the South, he proclaimed, May 26, 1865, an amnesty to all Confederates except certain leaders if they would abolish slavery and ratify the 13th Amendment. States doing so added anti-Negro provisions that enraged Congress, which intended to enfranchise all Negroes and disenfranchise former Confederates. Congress restored military control over the South. When Johnson removed Edwin M. Stanton, secretary of war, without notifying the Senate, thus repudiating the Tenure of Office Act, the House impeached him for this and other reasons. He was tried by the Senate, which voted 35 for conviction, 19 for acquittal, lacking the two-thirds necessary to convict, May 26, 1868. He was a candidate before the next Democratic convention, but not nominated. He returned to the Senate in 1875, and in a strong speech defended his course. He supported the Lincoln policies, but his conciliatory attitude toward the South was fought by the radical Republicans. Johnson died July 31, 1875, and was buried at Greenville (now Greeneville), where his log cabin tailor shop and home are museums.

Johnson married Eliza McArdle in 1810. They had 3 sons and 2 daughters.

Ulysses S. Grant

Ulysses Simpson Grant, 18th president, Republican, was born at Point Pleasant, Ohio, Apr. 27, 1822, son of Jesse R. Grant, a tanner. The next year the family moved to Georgetown, Ohio. Grant's mother was Hannah Simpson. Grant was named Hiram Ulysses, but on entering West Point, 1839, his name was entered as Ulysses Simpson and he adopted it. He was graduated in 1843; and was 1st lieutenant and captain under Gens. Taylor and Scott in the Mexican War; resigned, 1854, worked in St. Louis until 1860, then went to Galena, Ill., where his father sold leather and hardware. He became colonel of the 21st Illinois Vols., 1861, then brigadier general; took Forts Henry and Donelson; was made major general of volunteers; fought at Shiloh. Took Vicksburg, became major general USA., and in March 1864, lieutenant general. He accepted Lee's surrender at Appomattox. In 1866 he was named a full general. President Johnson appointed Grant secretary of war when he suspended Stanton in defiance of the Senate, but Grant was not confirmed. He was nominated on the first ballot, May 30, 1868, and elected over Horatio Seymour, Democrat, 214 vs. 80 electoral votes. The 15th Amendment, amnesty bill and civil service reform were events of his administration. The Liberal Republicans opposed him with Horace Greeley, also Democratic nominee, 1872, but he was re-elected. An attempt by the Stalwarts (Old Guard) to nominate him in 1880 failed. In 1884 the collapse of Grant & Ward, investment house, left him penniless. He began his Personal Memoirs, writing while ill of cancer and completing them 4 days before his death at

Mt. McGregor, N.Y., July 23, 1885. The book realized over $450,000. Grant was buried in an imposing tomb on Riverside Drive, New York, where his wife also lies.

Grant married Julia Dent in 1848. They had 3 sons and one daughter.

Rutherford Birchard Hayes

Rutherford Birchard Hayes, 19th president, Republican, was born in Delaware, Ohio, Oct. 4, 1822, the posthumous son of Rutherford Hayes, a farmer, and Sophia Birchard. He was descended from Geoge Hayes, a Scot, who reached Windsor, Conn., in 1680. He was raised by his uncle Sardis Birchard, educated in Norwalk, Ohio, and Middletown, Conn., and graduated from Kenyon College, 1842, and Harvard Law school, 1845. He practiced law in Lower Sandusky, Ohio, now Fremont; was city solicitor of Cincinnati, 1858-61. He was major of the 23d Ohio Vols., wounded at South Mountain; became brigadier general and major general by brevet, 1864. He served in Congress 1864-67, supporting Reconstruction and Johnson's impeachment. He was elected governor of Ohio, 1867 and 1869; beaten for Congress 1872; re-elected governor, 1875. He supported the merit principle in appointments, economy, prison reform and public libraries. In 1876 he was nominated for president over James G. Blaine and believed he had lost to Samuel J. Tilden, Democrat, 184 to 163 electoral votes. But Zachariah Chandler, chairman of the Republican National Committee, relying on Republican domination of the South, urged the validity of contesting 22 electoral returns from Florida, South Carolina, Louisiana; also Oregon. Frauds in Louisiana injuring Tilden were permitted to stand. Promises to withdraw troops from the South were reported used to suborn Democrats. The election was judged by an Electoral Commission, appointed by Congress, 8 Republicans and 7 Democrats, who refused to "go behind state returns" and by strict party vote elected Hayes by 185 over 184. The withdrawal of troops followed, but handicapped Republican rule, and as Hayes proceeded to reform civil service he alienated political spoilsmen. He advocated repeal of the Tenure of Office Act that had led to Johnson's impeachment. He supported sound money and specie payments. Hayes died in Fremont, Ohio, Jan. 17, 1893.

Hayes married Lucy Webb in 1852. They had 7 sons and one daughter.

James Abram Garfield

James A. Garfield, 20th president, Republican, was born Nov. 19, 1831, in a log cabin at Orange, Cuyahoga Co., Ohio, the son of Abram and Eliza Ballou Garfield. His father, a canal contractor and farmer from New York, was descended from Edward Garfield, who reached Massachusetts Bay Colony in 1630 and helped found Watertown, Mass. James was the youngest of 4 children; his father died in 1833 and his mother supported them. He worked as a canal bargeman, farmer and carpenter; attended Western Reserve Eclectic, later Hiram College, and was graduated from Williams in 1856. He became professor of ancient languages and literature at Hiram, then principal. He was in the Ohio Senate in 1859. Anti-slavery and anti-secession, he volunteered for the war, became colonel of the 42nd Ohio Infantry and brigadier in 1862. He fought at Shiloh, was chief of staff for Rosecrans and was made major general for gallantry at Chickamauga. He entered Congress as a radical Republican in 1863; supported specie payment as against paper money (greenbacks). On the electoral commission in 1876 he voted for Hayes against Tilden on strict party lines. He was senator-elect in 1880 when he became the Republican nominee for president. He was chosen on the 36th ballot as a compromise over Gen. Grant, James G. Blaine and John Sherman. This alienated the Grant following but Garfield was elected and Blaine became his

secretary of state. On July 2, 1881, Garfield was shot by an unbalanced office-seeker, Charles J. Guiteau, while entering the old Baltimore & Potomac station in Washington. He died Sept. 19, 1881, at Elberon, N. J., and was buried in Cleveland, Ohio. Guiteau was hanged June 30, 1882.

Garfield married Lucretia Rudolph in 1858. They had 4 sons and one daughter.

Chester Alan Arthur

Chester A. Arthur, 21st president, Republican, was born at Fairfield, Vt., Oct. 5, 1830, the son of the Rev. William Arthur, from County Antrim, Ireland, and Malvina Stone Arthur, member of a New Hampshire family. He graduated at Union College, 1848, taught school at Pownall, Vt., studied law in New York. In 1853 he argued in a fugitive slave case that slaves transported through New York State were thereby freed; in 1855 he obtained a ruling that Negroes were to be treated the same as whites on street cars. He helped organize the New York State Militia, 1861; was made quartermaster general and equipped troops for the front. He was made collector of the Port of New York, 1871. In 1877 President Hayes, reforming the civil service, ordered Arthur's resignation; he refused because he was not personally culpable, but was removed, 1879. This made Senators Conkling, Platt and the New York machine stalwarts enemies of Hayes. Arthur and the stalwarts tried to nominate Grant, for a third term, 1880; when Garfield was nominated, Arthur received second place in the interests of harmony. On Sept. 19, 1881, Garfield died and Arthur became president. He supported civil service reform and the tariff of 1883; arranged an unratified canal treaty with Nicaragua. He was defeated for renomination by James G. Blaine, 1884, but supported Blaine. He died Nov. 18, 1886, and was buried in Albany, N. Y.

Arthur married Ellen Lewis Herndon in 1859. They had 2 sons and one daughter.

Grover Cleveland

(According to a ruling of the State Dept. Grover Cleveland is both the 22d and the 24th president, because his 2 terms were not consecutive. By individuals, he is only the 22d.)

Grover Cleveland, 22d and 24th president, Democrat, was born in Caldwell, N. J., Mar. 18, 1837, the son of Richard F. Cleveland, a Presbyterian minister, and Ann Neale, daughter of a Baltimore merchant who had come from Ireland. The future president was named Stephen Grover, but dropped the Stephen. He clerked in Clinton and Buffalo, N. Y., taught in the New York City Institution for the Blind; was admitted to the bar in Buffalo, 1859; became assistant district attorney, 1863; sheriff 1869; major, 1881; governor of New York, 1882. He was an independent, honest administrator who hated corruption. He was nominated for president over Tammany Hall opposition, 1884, defeating James G. Blaine, 219 to 182. He enlarged the civil service, vetoed many pension raids on the Treasury. In 1888 he was defeated by Benjamin Harrison, although his popular vote was larger. Re-elected over Harrison, 1892, by 277 to 145, he faced a money crisis brought about by lowering of the gold reserve, circulation of paper and exorbitant silver purchases under the Sherman act; he obtained repeal of the latter and a reduced tariff. An income tax was passed but declared unconstitutional by the Supreme Court, 1895. A severe depression and labor troubles racked his administration but he refused to interfere in business matters and rejected, as crackpot theory, Jacob Coxey's demand for work relief of $20,000,000 monthly. He broke the Pullman strike with troops to move the mail, 1894. He rejected the platform of W. J. Bryan's silver Democrats, 1896, and supported the gold Democrats, Palmer and Buckner. He died in Princeton, N. J., June 24, 1908.

Cleveland married Frances Folsom in the White House, June 2, 1886. They had 2 sons and 3 daughters.

Benjamin Harrison

Benjamin Harrison, 23d president, Republican, was born at North Bend, Ohio, Aug. 20, 1833. His great-grandfather, Benjamin Harrison, was a signer of the Declaration of Independence; his grandfather, William Henry Harrison, was 9th president; his father John Scott Harrison was a member of Congress, 1853-57. His mother was Elizabeth F. Irwin. He attended school in a log cabin on his father's farm; graduated from Miami University, 1852; was admitted to the bar, 1853, and practiced in Indianapolis, Ind. As a second lieutenant, he raised recruits and became colonel of the 70th Indiana Volunteer Infantry. He fought at Kenesaw Mountain, Peachtree Creek, Nashville, and in the Atlanta campaign. In 1865 he was made a brigadier general by brevet. He failed to be elected governor of Indiana, 1876; but became senator, 1881, and worked for the G. A. R. pensions vetoed by Cleveland. In 1888 he defeated Cleveland for president 233 to 168. He expanded the pension list greatly; suppressed the Louisiana lottery; signed the McKinley high tariff bill and the Sherman silver purchase act. He helped the admission of North and South Dakota, Montana, Washington, Idaho and Wyoming, Republican states. He was defeated for re-election, 1892. He represented Venezuela in arbitration with Great Britain in Paris, 1899. He died at Indianapolis, Mar. 13, 1901, and was buried there.

Harrison married Caroline Lavinia Scott in 1853; they had one son and one daughter. The first Mrs. Harrison died in 1892 and in 1896 Harrison married her niece, Mary Scott Lord Dimmock, a widow. They had one daughter.

William McKinley

William McKinley, 25th president, Republican, was born in Niles, Ohio, Jan. 29, 1843, the son of William McKinley, an iron manufacturer, and Nancy Allison McKinley, and was the 7th of 9 children. His father's family was Scotch-Irish from County Antrim; his great-grandfather fought in the American Revolution. McKinley attended school in Poland, Ohio, and Alleghany College, Meadville, Pa., and enlisted for the Civil War at 18 in the 23d Ohio, in which Rutherford B. Hayes was a major. He was a commissary sergeant at Antietam. He rose to captain and in 1865 was made major by brevet. He studied law in the Albany, N.Y., law school; opened an office in Canton, Ohio, in 1867, and campaigned for Grant and Hayes. From 1876 to 1890, excepting 1882, he served in the House of Representatives and led the fight for a high tariff to protect "infant industries" and with reciprocal trade agreements (McKinley bill, enacted Oct. 1, 1890).Defeated on the issue in 1890, he was elected governor of Ohio, 1891 and 1893. He received 182 ballots for president in the Republican convention that nominated Benjamin Harrison in 1892. In 1896 he was elected president on a protective tariff, sound money (gold standard) platform over William Jennings Bryan, Democratic proponent of free silver. Chief factor was the astute vote-getting of Senator Marcus S. Hanna. McKinley was reluctant to intervene in Cuba on grounds of humanity, but the loss of the battleship Maine at Havana crystallized opinion. He demanded Spain's withdrawal from Cuba; Spain agreed to arbitration and armistice but Congress announced state of war as of Apr. 21. (Peace signed Dec. 10). In the 1900 campaign he defeated Bryan's anti-imperialist arguments with the prestige of prosperity, "the full dinner pail" and the vigorous campaigning of Theodore Roosevelt, vice presidential nominee. McKinley was a Methodist, beloved for his conciliatory nature, but conservative on business issues. He abhorred violence. On Sept. 6, 1901, while welcoming citizens at the Pan-American Exposition,

Buffalo, N.Y., he was shot by Leon Czolgosz, an anarchist. He died Sept. 14. His last words were: "It is God's way. His will, not ours, be done." McKinley, his wife and infant daughters rest in an imposing tomb in Canton. His favorite flower, the red carnation, was made the state flower.

McKinley married Ida Saxton in 1871. They had 2 daughters; both died in childhood.

Theodore Roosevelt

Theodore Roosevelt, 26th president, Republican was born in New York City, Oct. 27, 1858, the son of Theodore Roosevelt, collector of the port, and Martha Bulloch, daughter of Maj. J. S. Bulloch, Roswell, Ga. Roosevelt was descended from Claes Martenszan van Rosenvelt, and his wife Janett, who reached New Netherland from Holland about 1650. Theodore was a fifth cousin of Franklin D. Roosevelt and an uncle of Mrs. Eleanor Roosevelt. His mother was of Scotch-Irish, Huguenot stock and a southern sympathizer. Roosevelt was graduated from Harvard, 1880, attended Columbia Law School briefly; sat in the New York State Assembly, 1882-84; ranched in North Dakota, 1884-86; failed of election as mayor of New York, 1886; member of U.S. Civil Service Commission, 1889; president, New York Police Board, 1895, supporting the merit system; assistant secretary of the Navy under McKinley, Apr. 19, 1897—May 10, 1898, during which he instituted naval target practice and instructed Commodore George Dewey to take Manila in the event of war with Spain. He organized the 1st U.S. Volunteer Cavalry (Rough Riders) as lieut. col.; led the charge up Kettle Hill at San Juan and was made colonel by brevet. Elected governor, New York, 1898-1900, he fought the spoils system and achieved taxation of corporation franchises. Drafted for vice president, 1900, he became nation's youngest president at 42 years, 10 mos., 18 days, when McKinley died at Buffalo, Sept. 14, 1901. As president he fought corruption of politics by big business; dissolved Northern Securities Co. and others for violating anti-trust laws; intervened in coal strike on behalf of the public, 1902; instituted the old Dept. of Commerce and Labor; obtained Elkins Law forbidding rebates to favored corporations, 1903; Hepburn Law regulating railroad rates, 1906; Pure Food and Drugs Act, 1906, Reclamation Act and employers' liability laws. He organized conservation, mediated the peace between Japan and Russia, 1905; won the Nobel Peace Prize. He was the first to use the Hague Court of International Arbitration. By recognizing the new Republic of Panama he made Panama Canal possible, appointed Col. Geo. W. Goethals head commissioner and began canal. He was re-elected 1904, with 336 electoral votes vs. 140.

In 1908 he obtained the nomination of William H. Taft, who was elected. Later, considering Taft inimical to liberal policies, he organized the Progressive party, June 22, 1912, and ran for president against Taft and Woodrow Wilson, splitting the Republicans and causing Wilson's election. He was shot during the campaign but recovered. He advocated recall of elected officials, referendum on legislation and recall of judicial decisions, which alienated conservatives. In 1916 he left the Progressives and supported Charles E. Hughes, Republican. A strong friend of Britain, he fought American isolation. In 1917 President Wilson refused to let him organize a division. He wrote on many topics—his Winning of the West is best known—was a naturalist and hunter and traced the River of Doubt in Brazil, 1913-14, now Rio Roosevelt. He seemed likely to be the GOP nominee for president in 1920 but he died Jan. 6, 1919, at Sagamore Hill, Oyster Bay, N.Y., now a national shrine, and was buried near the Roosevelt bird refuge there.

Roosevelt's first marriage, in 1880, was to Alice

Hathaway Lee, who died in 1884; they had one daughter. In 1886, he married Edith Kermit Carow; they had one daughter and 4 sons. All 4 served in World War I; one was killed and 2 wounded. The 3 left all served in World War II; 2 died of natural causes while on active duty.

William Howard Taft

William Howard Taft, 27th president, Republican, was born in Cincinnati, Ohio, Sept. 15, 1857, the son of Alphonso Taft and Louisa Maria Torrey. His father was secretary of war and attorney general in Grant's cabinet; minister to Austria and Russia under Arthur. Taft was graduated from Yale, 1878; Cincinnati Law School, 1880; became law reporter for Cincinnati newspapers; was assistant prosecuting attorney, 1881-83; assistant county solicitor, 1885; judge, Superior Court, 1887; U.S. solicitor-general, 1890; federal circuit judge, 1892. In 1900 he became head of the U.S. Philippines Commission and was first civil governor of the Philippines, 1901-04; secretary of war, 1904; provisional governor of Cuba, 1906. He was groomed for president by Theodore Roosevelt as an exemplary public servant and elected over W. J. Bryan, 1908. His administration dissolved Standard Oil and tobacco trusts; instituted Department of Labor; drafted direct election of senators and income tax amendments. His tariff and conservation policies angered progressives; though renominated he was fought by Theodore Roosevelt; the result was Wilson's election. Taft was president of the League to Enforce Peace, supporting the League of Nations. He was professor of consitutional law, Yale, 1913-21; Chief Justice of the United States, 1921-30; illness forced him to resign. He died in Washington, Mar. 8, 1930, and was buried in Arlington National Cemetery.

Taft married Helen Herron in 1886; they had 2 sons and a daughter.

Woodrow Wilson

Woodrow Wilson, 28th president, Democrat, was born at Staunton, Va., Dec. 28, 1856, as Thomas Woodrow Wilson, son of a Presbyterian minister, the Rev. Joseph Ruggles Wilson and Janet (Jessie) Woodrow, daughter of a Presbyterian minister. He was a grandson of James Wilson, a Presbyterian of Ulster who reached Philadelphia in 1807, became a printer and in 1808 married an Ulster Presbyterian girl, a shipmate. In his youth Wilson lived in Augusta, Ga., Columbia, S. C., and Wilmington, N. C. He attended Davidson College, 1873-74; was graduated from Princeton, A.B., 1879; A. M., 1882; read law at the University of Virginia, 1881; practiced law, Atlanta, 1882-83; Ph.D., Johns Hopkins, 1886. He taught history and political economy at Bryn Mawr, 1885-88; at Wesleyan, 1888-90; was professor of jurisprudence and political economy at Princeton, 1890-1910; president of Princeton, 1902-1910, during which he tried to introduce innovations of organization that were fought by the graduate dean and alumni; governor of New Jersey, 1911-13, during which he obtained a primary election law, an employers' liability law and other reforms. In 1912 he was nominated for president with the aid of William Jennings Bryan, who sought to block James "Champ" Clark and Tammany Hall. Wilson won the election because the Republican vote for Taft was split by the Progressives under Theodore Roosevelt.

Wilson protected American interests in revolutionary Mexico and fought for American rights on the high seas as the first World War opened. His sharp warnings to Germany led to the resignation of his secretary of state, Bryan, a pacifist, while his protests against British interference with American ships disturbed the Allies. In 1916 he was re-elected by a slim margin with the slogan, "He kept us out of war," over Charles Evans Hughes, who was strongly supported by Theodore Roosevelt. Wilson's offer to mediate in the war (Dec. 18, 1916) was rejected. When the Germans started unrestricted submarine warfare, contrary to pledges, he broke diplomatic relations. After 4 American ships had been sunk he asked a declaration of war against Germany; it was voted April 6, 1917.

Wilson kept tight personal control over all phases of diplomatic and military activity. He relied more on reports of his confidential agent in Europe, Col. E. M. House, than on Secretary of State Robert Lansing and the U.S. ambassadors. However, he backed Gen. John J. Pershing, U.S. commander in chief, Herbert Hoover, food administrator, and others who had his confidence.

Wilson proposed peace Jan. 8, 1918, on the basis of his Fourteen Points, a state paper with worldwide influence. Basic was his doctrine of self-determination, or consent of the governed, in which he opposed handing peoples from one sovereignty to another. He also demanded a league to enforce peace. The Germans overturned their monarchy and a new republic accepted his terms and an armistice, Nov. 11. But at the November elections, the Democrats lost control of Congress.

Wilson went to Paris to help negotiate the peace treaty, the crux of which he considered the League of Nations, also urged by ex-President Taft and Elihu Root. In the U.S. Senate, Henry Cabot Lodge, William E. Borah and Hiram Johnson demanded reservations that would not make the United States subordinate to the votes of other nations in case of war. Wilson refused to consider any reservations and toured the country to get support. At Pueblo, Colo., Sept. 25, 1919, he broke down and several days later suffered a stroke. An invalid for months, he clung to his executive powers while his wife and doctor sought to shield him from affairs which would tire him.

He was awarded the 1919 Nobel Peace Prize, but the treaty was rejected by the Senate, Mar. 1920, by 49 to 35 (29 being sufficient to kill it). He made a public appearance on the day of Harding's inauguration in 1921, and formed a law partnership with Bainbridge Colby, but did not practice. He died Feb. 3, 1924, and was buried in Washington Cathedral.

Wilson's first marriage, in 1885, was to Ellen Louise Axson, who died in 1914. They had 3 daughters. Wilson married Edith Bolling Galt, a widow, in 1915; they had no children.

Warren Gamaliel Harding

Warren Gamaliel Harding, 29th president, Republican, was born near Corsica, now Blooming Grove, Ohio, Nov. 2, 1865, the son of Dr. George Tyron Harding, a country physician, and Phoebe Elizabeth Dickerson. He attended Ohio Central College, Iberia, Ohio, 1879-82; worked on the Star, Marion, Ohio, 1884 and a few years later bought the paper with a friend's help for a reported $300. He was state senator, 1900-04; lieutenant governor, 1904-06; defeated for governor, 1910; chosen U.S. Senator, 1915. He was a regular, "Old Guard" Republican; supported Taft, opposed Federal control of food and fuel; voted for anti-strike legislation, woman's suffrage and the Volstead prohibition enforcement act over President Wilson's veto; and opposed the League of Nations. In 1920 he was nominated for president on the 10th ballot with Calvin Coolidge. The Republicans capitalized on war weariness and fear that Wilson's League of Nations would curtail U.S. sovereignty. They defeated the Democrats, James M. Cox and Franklin D. Roosevelt, 16,152,000 to 9,147,000. Harding stressed a return to "normalcy"; worked for tariff revision and repeal of excess profits and high income taxes. On announcing ratification of treaties with Germany, Austro-Hungary, Nov. 14, 1921, he declared war officially ended July 2, 1921. His cabinet included Charles Evans Hughes (state); Herbert Hoover (commerce); Andrew S. Mellon (treasury). Two appointees, Albert B. Fall (interior) and Harry Daugherty (attorney general), became involved in the Teapot Dome scandal that embittered Harding's last days. He called the International Conference on Limitation of Armaments, 1921-22. Returning from a trip to Alaska he became ill and died in San Francisco, Aug. 2, 1923. He was buried in Marion, Ohio.

In 1891 Harding married Florence Kling De Wolfe, who had divorced her first husband. The Hardings had no children.

Calvin Coolidge

Calvin Coolidge, 30th president, Republican, was born in Plymouth, Vt., July 4, 1872, the son of John Calvin Coolidge, a storekeeper, and Victoria J. Moor, and named John Calvin Coolidge. His paternal ancestors came from England to Watertown, later Cambridge, Massachusetts Bay Colony, in 1630. Coolidge was graduated at Amherst, 1895; admitted to the bar in Northampton, 1897; became city councilman, 1889; city solicitor, 1900-01; clerk of the courts, 1904; member of the lower Massachusetts house, 1907-08; mayor of Northampton, 1910-11; state senator, 1912-15; and president of Senate, 1914-15; lieutenant governor, 1916-18; governor, 1919; re-elected, 1920. In Sept., 1919, Coolidge attained national prominence by his action in the Boston police strike during which he declared: "There is no right to strike against the public safety by anybody, anywhere, anytime." This brought his name before the Republican convention of 1920, where he received 34 votes for president and was nominated for vice president by 674¼ votes. He succeeded to the presidency on Harding's death, Aug. 2, 1923, the oath being administered by his father, a justice of the peace, in his home in Plymouth, Aug. 3, and again Aug. 17 before Justice A. A. Hoehling of the Supreme Court of the District of Columbia. He opposed the League of Nations; approved the World Court; vetoed the soldiers' bonus bill, which was passed over his veto. In 1924 he was re-elected by a huge majority with 15,725,016 over John W. Davis, Democrat, 8,385,586, and Robert M. LaFollette, Progressive, 4,822,856. He reduced the national debt by $2 billion in 3 years. He opposed the McNary-Haugen farm bill and price fixing, and supported his secretary of state Frank B. Kellogg, in the Kellog-Briand often quoted, opposing reduction of Europe's war debt. "They hired the money, didn't they?" With Republicans eager to renominate him he announced Aug. 2, 1927: "I do not choose to run for president in 1928." He became a life insurance director and wrote syndicated articles. He died of a heart attack in Northampton Jan. 5 1933. He was buried on a Plymouth hillside.

Coolidge married Grace Ann Goodhue in 1905; they had 2 sons.

Herbert Hoover

Herbert Clark Hoover, 31st president, Republican, was born at West Branch, Iowa, Aug. 10, 1874, son of Jesse Clark Hoover, a blacksmith (1847-1880) and Hulda Randall Minthorn (1848-83). Ancestor Andrew Hoover came to Pennsylvania from the West German Palatinate, 1738. Hoover grew up in Indian Territory and Oregon, won A.B. in engineering at Stanford, 1891. Briefly with U.S. Geological Survey and western mines; then mining engineer in western Australia, Asia, Europe, Africa, America. While chief engineer, imperial mines, China, he directed food relief for victims of Boxer Rebellion, 1900. He became a world figure in relief work, distributing over $5 billion worth during 1914-1923. He directed American Relief Committee, London, 1914-15; U.S. Comm for Relief in Belgium, 1915-1919; U.S. Food Administrator, 1917-1919; American Relief Administrator, 1918-1923, feeding children in defeated nations; Russian Relief, 1918-1923; Interallied Food Council; Supreme Economic Council. As secretary of commerce, 1921-

28, he began regulation of radio and aviation, pushed research program for National Academy of Science; organized 7-state pact for Colorado River irrigation and Hoover (Boulder) Dam. Elected president over Alfred E. Smith, 1928, he started White House Conferences on child health and protection, and housing; supported conservation of forests, oil, resources; initiated Naval Conference, 1930; organized RFC, Home Loan Banks, expanded Farm Loan Banks. He gave his official salary to charities and underpaid help. President Truman made him coordinator of European Food Program, 1947, chairman of the Commission for Reorganization of the Executive Branch, 1947-49, and chairman of the 2d Commission on Reorganization, 1953-55. He founded the Hoover Institution on War, Revolution & Peace at Stanford University. He died in New York City, Oct. 20, 1964, and was buried at West Branch, Iowa, where his birthplace is now a memorial.

Hoover married Lou Henry in 1899. They had 2 sons.

Franklin D. Roosevelt

Franklin Delano Roosevelt, 32d president, Democrat, was born near Hyde Park, N.Y., Jan. 30, 1882, the son of James Roosevelt (died 1900) and Sara Delano (died 1941). His ancestor, Claes Martenszan van Rosenvelt, came to New Amsterdam from Holland about 1650. Claes' son Nicholas, a New York, alderman in 1700 and 1715, had a son Johannes, from whom Theodore Roosevelt was descended, and a son Jacobus, from whom Franklin D. Roosevelt was descened. Franklin was graduated at Harvard, 1904; attended Columbia Law School, was admitted to the bar. He went to the New York Senate from his Dutchess County district, 1910 and 1913. He voted for Woodrow Wilson at the 1912 Democratic convention; in 1913 Wilson made him assistant secretary of the Navy.

Roosevelt ran for vice president, 1920, with James Cox and was defeated. From 1920 to 1928 he was a New York lawyer and vice president of Fidelity & Deposit Co. In Aug., 1921, polio paralyzed his legs. He learned to walk with leg braces and a cane and established the Warm Springs, Ga., Foundation, for helping other victims.

Roosevelt presented the name of Alfred E. Smith to the Democratic conventions of 1924 in New York and 1928 in Houston, calling Smith the Happy Warrior. Smith was nominated in 1928 and defeated. Roosevelt was elected governor of New York, 1928 and 1930. In 1932 at Chicago W. G. McAdoo, pledged to John N. Garner, threw his votes to Roosevelt, who was nominated, alienating Smith. The financial crash, unemployment and the Democratic promise to repeal prohibition made his victory inevitable. He asked emergency powers, proclaimed the New Deal, and put into effect a vast number of administrative changes. Foremost was "pump priming," or use of public funds for relief and public works, resulting in deficit financing. He greatly expanded the controls of the central government over business and by an excess profits tax and pyramiding income taxes produced a redistribution of earnings on an unprecedented scale. The Wagner Act gave labor many advantages in organizing and collective bargaining. He was the last president inaugurated on Mar. 4 (1933) and the first inaugurated on Jan. 20 (1937).

Roosevelt was a tremendous worker and traveler despite physical handicaps. He was the first President to use radio for "fireside chats." When the Supreme Court nullified some New Deal laws; he sought power to "pack" the court with additional justices, but Congress refused to give him the authority. Court resignations soon enabled him to replace conservatives who had opposed him. He was the first president to break the 3d term tradition and was elected to a 4th term, 1944, despite failing health. The culminating event of his career was World War II. He was openly hostile to fascist governments before the war and gave Britain substantial support, such as exchanging 50 destroyers for air bases, before Pearl Harbor made the United States a belligerent. He wrote the principles of fair dealing into the Atlantic Charter, Aug. 14, 1941 (with Winston Churchill) and in the Four Freedoms (freedom of speech, of worship, from want, from fear) Jan. 6, 1941. He conferred with allied heads of state at Casablanca, Jan., 1943; Quebec, Aug., 1943; Teheran, Nov.-Dec., 1943; Cairo, Dec., 1943; Yalta, Feb., 1945. He died at Warm Springs, Ga., April 12, 1945, aged 63, and was buried on his Hyde Park estate, where his house and library are in the national care.

Roosevelt married Anna Eleanor Roosevelt (a 5th cousin who was a niece of Theodore Roosevelt) in 1905. They had 4 sons and 1 daughter and a child that died in infancy.

Harry S. Truman

Harry S. Truman, 33d president, Democrat, was born at Lamar, Mo., May 8, 1884, the son of John Anderson Truman and Martha Ellen Young. Four grandparents were born in Kentucky and moved to Missouri in the 1840s. The Trumans came from England, the president's mother's grandmother from Northern Ireland, while an ancestor of his maternal grandfather, Solomon Young, came from Germany. A family disagreement on whether Harry Truman's middle name was Shippe or Solomon, after names of two grandfathers, resulted in his using only S. for his middle initial. He was a Baptist.

He attended public schools in Independence, Mo., worked for the Kansas City Star, 1901, and as railroad timekeeper, and helper in Kansas City banks up to 1905. He joined the Missouri National Guard, 1905, and was rejected by West Point for defective eyesight. He ran his family's farm, 1906-17. He entered the Field Artillery School at Fort Sill, Okla., 1917; became 1st lieutenant, Battery F, and captain, Battery D, 129th Field Artillery, 35th Div., AEF. He served in the Vosges, Meuse-Argonne and St. Mihiel actions in World War I and was discharged as major, 1919. After the war he ran a haberdashery, became judge of Jackson Co. Court, 1922-24; attended Kansas City School of Law, 1923-25. He was defeated, then elected presiding judge.

Truman was elected U.S. Senator in 1934; reelected 1940. In 1944 with President Roosevelt's approval he was nominated for vice president and elected. On Roosevelt's death Apr. 12,1945, Truman was sworn in as president by Chief Justice Harlan F. Stone. In 1948 he was elected president as polls predicted his defeat.

Truman authorized the first use of the atomic bomb (Hiroshima and Nagasaki, Aug. 6 and 9, 1945), bringing World War II to a rapid end. He was responsible for creating NATO, the Marshall Plan (to restore Western Europe economically) and for what came to be called the Truman Doctrine (to aid nations such as Greece and Turkey, threatened by Russian or other communist takeover). He broke a Russian blockade of East Berlin with a massive airlift, 1948-49. When Communist North Korea invaded South Korea, June 1950, he won UN approval for a "police action" and sent in forces under Gen. Douglas MacArthur. When MacArthur sought to pursue North Koreans into Communist China, Truman removed him from command.

On the domestic front, Truman was responsible for higher-minimum-wage, increased-social-security and aid-for-housing law. His 1952 seizure of the nation's steel mills to avert a strike was ruled illegal by the Supreme Court; a strike followed but was settled in 3 weeks. Truman died Dec. 26, 1972, at his Independence, Mo., home at the age of 88.

He married Elizabeth Virginia Wallace in 1919. They had one daughter, Margaret.

Dwight David Eisenhower

Dwight David Eisenhower, 34th president, Republican, was born Oct. 14, 1890, at Denison, Tex., the son of David Jacob Eisenhower and Ida Elizabeth Stover Eisenhower. His paternal grandfather was descended from German Mennonites who left the Rhineland for Pennsylvania in the 1730s, moved to Kansas in 1878. His father met his mother at Lane University, a United Brethren college at Lecompton, Kan. When Dwight was 1 year old his parents moved to Abilene, Kan. He attended high school and in 1915 was graduated at West Point. He was a lieutenant colonel in charge of a tank corps at Camp Colt, Gettysburg, Pa., in 1918. He graduated from Infantry Tank School, 1922; Command and General Staff School 1926; Army War College, 1928; Army Industrial College, 1933. He was in the office of the Chief of Staff, 1933-35. He was on the American Military Mission to the Philippines, 1935-39 and during 4 of those years on the staff of Gen. MacArthur. He was chief of staff, 3rd Div., later 9th Corps, 1940-41, and of the 3rd Army, 1941, as brigadier general. After the Louisiana maneuvers he was made chief of the War Plans Div., War Dept. General Staff, and then became assistant chief of staff, Operations Div. and in June, 1942, lieutenant general. He was made Commander of Allied forces landing in North Africa Nov. 8, 1942, and advanced to full general in Feb., 1943, and Commander in Chief of Allied Forces in North Africa. He became Supreme Commander, Allied Expeditionary Forces Dec. 31, 1943, and as such led the Normandy invasion June 6, 1944. He was given the temporary rank of General of the Army Dec. 19, 1944, which was made permanent in 1946. On May 7, 1945, he received the surrender of the Germans at Rheims. He was in command of the U.S. Occupation Force in Germany in 1945, and returned to serve as Chief of Staff, Nov. 19, 1945, to Feb. 7, 1948. From June 7, 1948, to Jan. 19, 1953, he was president of Columbia University, but he took leave of absence Dec. 16, 1950, to serve as Supreme Allied Commander in Europe to organize NATO forces.

Eisenhower resigned from the Army in June, 1952, and was nominated for president by the Republicans at Chicago, July 11, 1952. He defeated Adlai E. Stevenson by 442 to 89 electoral votes, was inaugurated Jan. 20, 1953. He was renominated unanimously in San Francisco, Aug. 22, 1956, and defeated Stevenson by 457 to 74. He called himself a moderate, favored "free market system" vs. government price and wage controls; kept government out of labor disputes; reorganized defense establishment; promoted missile programs, including Polaris. With strong aid of John Foster Dulles, his secretary of state, he continued foreign aid; demanded unification of Germany by free elections; sped end of Korean fighting; supplied planes to anti-communist Guatemalan government; endorsed Formosa and SE Asia defense treaties; backed UN in condemning Anglo-French raid on Egypt; advocated "open skies" policy of mutual inspection to USSR. He sent U.S. troops into Little Rock, Ark., Sept., 1957, during the segregation crisis and ordered Marines into Lebanon July-Aug., 1958. Eisenhower's rank as General of the Army was restored by Congress and signed by President Kennedy Mar. 22, 1961.

In 1948, Eisenhower published *Crusade in Europe*, his war memoirs, which quickly became a best seller. His other published works included *Mandate for Change* (1962), *Waging Peace* (1965), *The White House Years*, and *At Ease: Stories I Tell My Friends* (1967). He was an enthusiastic golfer and painter.

During his retirement at his farm near Gettysburg, Pa., Eisenhower took up the role of elder statesman, counseling his 3 successors in the White House. He was hospitalized in early 1968 after his 4th heart attack and died Mar. 28, 1969, in Washington. He was buried in Abilene, Kan.

Eisenhower married Mamie Geneva Doud, July 1, 1916. They had 2 sons; the first died in infancy.

John F. Kennedy

John Fitzgerald Kennedy, 35th president, Democrat, was born May 29, 1917, in Brookline, Mass., the second of 9 children of Joseph P. Kennedy, financier who later became ambassador to Great Britain, and Rose Fitzgerald Kennedy. He entered Harvard, attended the London School of Economics briefly in 1935, received a B.S., *cum laude* from Harvard in 1940. He served in the U. S. Navy, 1941-1945, commanded a PT boat in the Solomons and won the Navy and Marine Corps medal and Purple Heart. He covered the Potsdam Conference and the start of the U. N. at San Francisco for International News Service. He served as Representative in Congress from Massachusetts, 1947-1953, defeated Henry Cabot Lodge for the Senate in 1952, was re-elected 1958. He nearly won the vice presidential nomination in 1956.

Kennedy won the Democratic nomination for president at Los Angeles, July 14, 1960. Sen. Lyndon B. Johnson (Tex.), was named for vice president. Kennedy defeated Richard M. Nixon, Republican, by the slim margin of 118,550 popular votes and an electoral vote of 303 to 219. He was the first Roman Catholic to be elected president.

President Kennedy's most important act was his successful demand Oct. 22, 1962, that the Soviet Union dismantle all missile bases in Cuba. He established a quarantine of arms shipments to Cuba and continued surveillance by air. He defied Soviet attempts to force the Allies out of Berlin. He made the steel industry rescind its price rise. He backed civil rights, a mental health program, arbitration of railroad disputes and expanded medical care for the aged. Astronaut flights and satellite orbiting were greatly developed during his less than 3 years tenure. He wrote *Profiles in Courage*, which won a Pulitzer prize, and *Why England Slept*. He turned the White House spotlight on the cultural arts.

On Nov. 22, 1963, Kennedy was assassinated in Dallas, Tex. On Nov. 25, a national day of mourning, he was buried in Arlington National Cemetery.

Kennedy married Jacqueline Lee Bouvier Sept. 12, 1953. They had 1 daughter and 1 son.

Lyndon Baines Johnson

Lyndon Baines Johnson, 36th president, Democrat, was born on a farm near Stonewall, Tex., Aug. 27, 1908, son of Sam Ealy and Rebekah Baines Johnson. His father and grandfather had served in the Texas legislature. His family moved to Johnson City in 1913, where he was graduated from the high school in 1924. He received a B.S. degree at Southwest Texas State Teachers College, 1930, attended Georgetown Univ., Law School, Washington, 1935. He taught public speaking in Houston High School, 1930-32; served as secretary to Rep. R. M. Kleberg, 1932-35. In 1935 President Roosevelt appointed Johnson Texas state administrator of the National Youth Administration. In 1937 Johnson won a contest to fill the vacancy caused by the death of a representative and in 1938 was elected to the full term; after which he returned for 4 terms. A member of the Naval Reserve, he was a lieutenant commander, U.S. Navy, 1941-42, winning the Silver Star for a flight over Japanese positions at New Guinea. He was elected U.S. senator 1948 by only 87 votes margin over Gov. Coke Stevenson of Texas; in 1954 he was reelected by a large majority. He became Democratic whip, 1951, and leader, 1953, at 44. Johnson was Texas' favorite son for the Democratic presidential nomination in 1956 and had strong support in the 1960 convention, when the nominee, John F. Kennedy, asked him to run for vice president. His campaigning helped overcome religious bias against Kennedy in the South.

Johnson took the oath of office as president at 2:30 p.m., CST, on Nov. 22, 1963, 99 min. after the death of President Kennedy. In filling out the Kennedy term Johnson worked hard for welfare legislation and signed acts for civil rights, anti-poverty and tax reduction and averted strikes on railroads. He was nominated for president and elected Nov. 3, 1964, by 486 electoral votes to 52. Overshadowing other developments during Johnson's first full term in the White House were the expansion of the war in Vietnam, the committing of more than 500,000 American servicemen to conflict, intensive bombing by U.S planes and mounting U.S. casualties.

In face of increasing division in the nation and in his own party over his conduct of the war, Johnson announced, on Mar. 31, 1968, "I shall not seek, and I will not accept the nomination of my party for another term as your president." Near the end of his tenure, he indicated that he felt his greatest achievement was the passage of the Voting Rights Act of 1965; his biggest disappointment was that "peace has eluded me."

Retiring to his LBJ Ranch near Johnson City, Tex., the former president wrote his memoirs, *The Vantage Point* (1971), and oversaw the construction of the Lyndon Baines Johnson Library on the campus of the University of Texas in Austin. President Johnson died of a heart attack on Jan. 22, 1973. He was buried on his ranch near the Pedernales River.

Johnson married Claudia Alta (Lady Bird) Taylor on Nov. 17, 1934. They had 2 daughters.

Richard Milhous Nixon

Richard Milhous Nixon, 37th president, Republican, was the only president to voluntarily resign without completing his elected term. He was born in the small farming community of Yorba Linda, Cal., Jan. 9, 1913, the 2d of the 5 sons of Francis Anthony and Hannah Milhous Nixon. In 1922, the family moved to Whittier, Cal., where the future president graduated from Whittier College in 1934. He attended Duke University Law School. After practicing law in Whittier and serving briefly in the Office of Price Administration in 1942, he entered the Navy, serving in the South Pacific, and was discharged as a lieutenant commander.

Nixon was elected to the House of Representatives from California's 12th Congressional District in 1946 and re-elected in 1948. He achieved prominence as the House Un-American Activities Committee member who forced the showdown that resulted in the Alger Hiss perjury conviction. In 1950 Nixon moved to the Senate by defeating Democrat Helen Gahagen Douglas in a bitter campaign in which he accused her of being "soft on communism."

Elected vice president in the Eisenhower landslides of 1952 and 1956, Nixon achieved more prominence in that position than had his predecessors.

With Eisenhower's endorsement, Nixon won the Republican presidential nomination in 1960. He was defeated by Democrat John F. Kennedy, returned to California, and 2 years later was defeated in his race for governor against Democratic incumbent Pat Brown.

Taking the "long hard road" of the presidential primaries in 1968, he won the presidential nomination easily on the first ballot and went on to defeat Democrat Hubert H. Humphrey.

The 1969-73 Nixon Administration saw remarkable developments in international affairs as Nixon became the first U.S. president to visit China and Russia. He and his foreign affairs advisor, Dr. Henry A. Kissinger, achieved a detente with China and a partial strategic arms limitation agreement with the Soviet Union. In addition, Nixon brought an end to the U.S. ground combat role in South Vietnam.

These diplomatic triumphs did not, however, overshadow the serious economic difficulties which confronted the nation. In Aug., 1971, faced with alarming trade and balance of payments deficits and continuing inflation, Nixon announced a "new economic policy," with wage and price controls at home and negotiations abroad leading to the devaluation of the dollar.

In the field of law, Nixon appointed 4 new Supreme Court Justices, including the Chief Justice, thus altering the Court's balance in favor of a more conservative view. A conservative trend on issues of public order was also observed.

By the summer of 1972, the peace movement had cooled, the economy showed signs of healthy growth, and a period of normal relations among the superpowers seemed at hand. On Aug. 22, a confident Republican party nominated Nixon for election to a 2d term as president.

Reelected in a massive landslide, in 1972, Nixon soon secured a ceasefire agreement in Vietnam and completed the withdrawal of all U.S. troops in spite of heavy fighting and U.S. bombing in Cambodia and continued sporadic conflict in South Vietnam.

On Jan. 11, 1973, the Nixon administration ended most mandatory wage and price controls and on Feb. 12 announced a further devaluation of the dollar. Inflation, however, continued at peak levels and the dollar came under heavy pressure in the world's gold markets.

Nixon's 2d term was cut short by "The Watergate Affair," a series of scandals beginning with the espionage burglary of Democratic party national headquarters in the Watergate office complex on June 17, 1972. The break-in was led by employees of Nixon's reelection campaign committee and former White House staff members. Investigations and press revelations exposed the existence of secret wiretapping and political espionage by White House aides dating back to May 1969, as well as an organized attempt to frustrate any investigation of these activities or of the Watergate break-in.

From the beginning, Nixon denied any White House involvement in the Watergate break-in. When White House personnel were implicated in the Spring of 1973, Nixon denied personal knowledge of either that involvement or of the subsequent cover-up.

On July 16, 1973, a White House aide, under questioning by the Senate Select Committee on Presidential Campaign Activities, revealed that most of Nixon's office conversations and telephone calls had been recorded by an automatic taping system. The ensuing year saw the most severe constitutional confrontation in the nation's history as the president claimed executive privilege to keep the tapes secret and the courts and Congress sought the tapes for the prosecution of criminal indictments against former White House aides and for a House inquiry into possible impeachment proceedings against Nixon.

The confrontation reached its first climax Oct. 10, 1973, in the "Saturday Night Massacre" when Nixon fired the special prosecutor assigned to Watergate matters and accepted the resignations of the attorney general and his deputy when they refused to go along with the firing. The public outcry which followed caused Nixon to appoint a new special prosecutor and to turn over to the courts a number of subpoenaed tape recordings. Public reaction also brought the initiation of a formal inquiry into possible impeachment by the House of Representatives.

The second climax came late in July 1974. On July 24, the Supreme Court ruled unanimously that Nixon's claim of executive privilege must fall before the special prosecutor's subpoenas of tapes relevant to criminal trial proceedings. At the same time, the court refused to rule on Nixon's claim that a grand jury erred in naming him an "unindicted co-conspirator" in the Watergate cover-up.

Later the same day, the House Judiciary Committee opened a public, televised debate on whether to recommend that the full House impeach the president. By July 30, the 38-member committee had recommended House adoption of 3 articles charging obstruction of justice (21 Dems., 6 Reps. voting in favor), abuse of power (21 Dems., 7 Reps.), and contempt of Congress for refusing to respond to commit-

tee subpoenas (19 Dems., 2 Reps.).

On Aug. 5, under pressure from his special legal counsel, Nixon released transcripts of 3 recordings of conversations held on June 23, 1972, 6 days after the Watergate break-in. These transcripts showed that Nixon had known of, approved and directed Watergate cover-up activities.

As his defenders in the House and Senate withdrew their support, Nixon's aides and top Republican leaders publicly and privately urged him to resign. He announced his resignation on nationwide television on Aug. 8 and left office at noon on Aug. 9. He retired to San Clemente, Cal., still facing possible criminal charges for conspiracy, obstruction of justice, violations of civil rights, tax fraud, and misuse of government and campaign funds.

Nixon married Themla Catherine Patricia "Pat" Ryan on June 21, 1940. They had 2 daughters.

Gerald Rudolph Ford

Gerald Rudolph Ford, 38th president, Republican, was born July 14, 1913, in Omaha, Neb., son of Leslie and Dorothy Gardner King, and was named Leslie Jr. When he was 2, his parents were divorced and his mother moved with the boy to Grand Rapids, Mich. There she met and married Gerald R. Ford, head of a paint company, who formally adopted the boy and gave him his own name.

In high school, young Gerald became a star football center, named to all-city and all-state teams; at the University of Michigan he played on the undefeated 1932 and 1933 teams and was named most valuable player on the 1934 team. He turned down a Green Bay Packers professional football bid and went to Yale Law School, working part-time as assistant football coach, boxing coach and professional model. He graduated in the top third of the 1941 law class.

He began practicing law in Grand Rapids, but in 1942, shortly after U.S. entry into World War II, he joined the Navy and served 47 months in the Pacific, leaving in 1946 as a lieutenant commander.

Back in Grand Rapids, he resumed his law practice and won several Chamber of Commerce awards for community work. Entering the 1948 GOP primary, he upset the incumbent congressman in Michigan's 5th District and won the November election. He continued to win elections, spending 25 years in the House of Representatives, 8 of them as Republican leader. He also served on the Warren Commission, which investigated the assassination of President Kennedy, and was co-author of a book on the commission's work.

As congressman and GOP leader, he was consistently conservative, opposing much social welfare legislation but giving support to final passage of civil rights bills. His colleagues described him as dogged, sincere, a man of modest tastes.

On Oct. 12, 1973, after Vice President Spiro T. Agnew pleaded "no contest" to charges of income tax fraud and resigned his office, House Minority Leader Ford was nominated by President Nixon to become the new vice president. It was the first use of the procedures set out in the 25th Amendment. The Senate approved the appointment Nov. 27 by a 92-3 vote; The House followed suit, 387-35, on Dec. 6 and Ford was sworn in as the nation's 40th vice president that same day. As vice president, he spent much of his time on speaking tours, seeking to soothe the divisiveness which gripped the nation in the wake of the Watergate scandals.

When President Nixon, facing probable impeachment, resigned Aug. 9, 1974, Ford was sworn in as president, the first to serve without being chosen by the American people in a national election.

On Oct. 18, 1948, Ford married Elizabeth Bloomer Warren, whose first marriage had ended in divorce. The Fords had 3 sons and one daughter.

(See Chronology for further developments.)

Longevity of Presidents of the U. S.
Source: Statistical Bulletin, Metropolitan Life

	Year of Birth	Age, 1st Inauguration	Age at Death	Expectancy after 1st Inaugural	Years Lived After First Inaugural Actual	Above Expected	Below Expected
George Washington	1732	57	67	17.1	10.6		6.5
John Adams	1735	61	90	14.4	29.3	14.9	
Thomas Jefferson	1743	57	83	16.4	25.3	8.9	
James Madison	1751	57	85	16.3	27.3	11.0	
James Monroe	1758	58	73	15.7	14.3		1.3
John Quincy Adams	1767	57	80	16.3	23.0	6.7	
Andrew Jackson	1767	61	78	13.5	16.3	2.7	
Martin Van Buren	1782	54	79	17.2	25.4	8.2	
William H. Harrison†	1773	68	68	9.4	.1		9.3
John Tyler	1790	51	71	19.2	20.8	1.6	
James K. Polk	1795	49	53	21.5	4.3		17.2
Zachary Taylor†	1784	64	65	12.8	1.3		11.5
Millard Fillmore	1800	50	74	20.7	23.7	2.9	
Franklin Pierce	1804	48	64	22.0	16.6		5.4
James Buchanan	1791	65	77	11.9	11.3		.6
Abraham Lincoln‡	1809	52	56	19.8	4.1		15.6
Andrew Johnson	1808	56	66	17.2	10.3		6.9
Ulysses S. Grant	1822	46	63	22.8	16.4		6.4
Rutherford B. Hayes	1822	54	70	18.0	15.9		2.1
James A. Garfield‡	1831	49	49	21.2	.5		20.7
Chester A. Arthur	1830	50	56	20.1	5.2		15.0
Grover Cleveland	1837	47	71	22.1	23.3	1.2	
Benjamin Harrison	1833	55	67	17.2	12.0		5.2
William McKinley‡	1843	54	58	18.2	4.5		13.6
Theodore Roosevelt	1858	42	60	26.1	17.3		8.8
William H. Taft	1857	51	72	20.3	.8		
Woodrow Wilson	1856	56	67	17.1	10.9		6.2
Warren G. Harding†	1865	55	57	18.1	2.4		15.6
Calvin Coolidge	1872	51	60	21.4	9.4		12.0
Herbert C. Hoover	1874	54	90	19.0	35.6	16.7	
Franklin D. Roosevelt†	1882	51	63	21.7	12.1		9.6
Harry S. Truman	1884	60	88	15.3	27.7	12.4	
Dwight D. Eisenhower	1890	62	78	14.7	16.2	1.4	
John F. Kennedy‡	1917	43	46	28.5	2.8		25.7
Lyndon B. Johnson	1908	55	64	19.3	9.2		10.1
Richard M. Nixon	1913	56		18.8			

†Died during tenure. ‡Assassinated.

Burial Places of the Presidents

G. Washington	1732-1799	Mt. Vernon, Va.
John Adams	1735-1826	Quincy, Mass.
T. Jefferson	1743-1826	Charlottesville, Va.
James Madison	1751-1836	Montpelier Station, Va.
James Monroe	1758-1831	Richmond, Va.
John Q. Adams	1767-1848	Quincy, Mass.
Andrew Jackson	1767-1845	Nashville, Tenn.
M. Van Buren	1782-1862	Kinderhook, N.Y.
W. H. Harrison	1773-1841	North Bend, Ohio
John Tyler	1790-1862	Richmond, Va.
James Knox Polk	1795-1849	Nashville, Tenn.
Zachary Taylor	1784-1850	Louisville, Ky.
Millard Fillmore	1800-1874	Buffalo, N.Y.
Franklin Pierce	1804-1869	Concord, N.H.
James Buchanan	1791-1868	Lancaster, Pa.
A. Lincoln	1809-1865	Springfield, Ill.
Andrew Johnson	1808-1875	Greeneville, Tenn.
Ulysses S. Grant	1822-1885	New York City
R. B. Hayes	1822-1893	Fremont, Ohio
J. A. Garfield	1831-1881	Cleveland, Ohio
C. A. Arthur	1830-1886	Albany, N. Y.
Grover Cleveland	1837-1908	Princeton, N.J.
B. Harrison	1833-1901	Indianapolis, Ind.
W. McKinley	1843-1901	Canton, Ohio
T. Roosevelt	1858-1919	Oyster Bay, N.Y.
William H. Taft	1857-1930	Arlington Nat'l. Cem'y.
Woodrow Wilson	1856-1924	Washington Cathedral
W. G. Harding	1865-1923	Marion, Ohio
Calvin Coolidge	1872-1933	Plymouth, Vt.
Herbert Hoover	1874-1964	West Branch, Iowa
F. D. Roosevelt	1882-1945	Hyde Park, N.y.
D.D. Eisenhower	1890-1969	Abilene, Kan.
J. F. Kennedy	1917-1963	Arlington Nat'l. Cem'y.
Harry S. Truman	1884-1972	Independence, Mo.
Lyndon B. Johnson	1908-1973	Stonewall, Texas

Religious Background of Presidents

Baptist: Harding, Truman.
Christian Church (Disciples of Christ): Garfield, Lyndon B. Johnson.
Congregationalist: Coolidge.
Episcopalian: Washington, Madison, Monroe, William Henry Harrison, Tyler, Taylor, Pierce, Arthur, Franklin D. Roosevelt, and Ford.
Jefferson, an Episcopal Church member, later became a deist, said he was a "disciple of the doctrines of Jesus," and commended Unitarianism.
Friends (Quakers): Hoover, Nixon.

Methodist: Polk, Andrew Johnson, Grant, McKinley.
Presbyterian: Jackson, Buchanan, Cleveland, Benjamin Harrison, Wilson, Eisenhower.
Lincoln attended Presbyterian services in Washington but was not a member. Hayes attended the Methodist Church, but never joined.
Reformed Dutch: Van Buren, Theodore Roosevelt.
Roman Catholic: Kennedy.
Unitarian: John Adams, John Quincy Adams, Fillmore, Taft.

How America Was Named

America was named for Amerigo Vespucci (1454-1512), an Italian reputed to have made 4 voyages to the New World (1497-1503). The German geographer, Martin Waldseemuller, first used America in a book published in 1507.

Law on Succession to the Presidency

If by reason of death, resignation, removal from office, inability, or failure to qualify there is neither a president nor vice president to discharge the powers and duties of the office of president, then the speaker of the House of Representatives shall upon his resignation as speaker and as representative, act as president. The same rule shall apply in the case of the death, resignation, removal from office, or inability of an individual acting as president.

If at the time when a speaker is to begin the discharge of the powers and duties of the office of president there is no speaker, or the speaker fails to qualify as acting president, then the president pro tempore of the Senate, upon his resignation as president pro tempore and as senator, shall act as president.

An individual acting as president shall continue to act until the expiration of the then current presidential term, except that (1) if his discharge of the powers and duties of the office is founded in whole or in part in the failure of both the president-elect and the vice president-elect to qualify, then he shall act only until a president or vice president qualifies, and (2) if his discharge of the powers and duties of the office is founded in whole or in part on the inability of the president or vice president, then he shall act only until the removal of the disability of one of such individuals.

If, by reason of death, resignation, removal from office, or failure to qualify, there is no president pro tempore to act as president, then the officer of the United States who is highest on the following list, and who is not under disability to discharge the powers and duties of president, shall act as president: the secretaries of state, treasury, defense; attorney general; secretaries of interior, agriculture, commerce, labor; health, education and welfare; housing and urban development; transportation.

(Legislation approved July 18, 1947; amended Sept. 9, 1965, and Oct. 15, 1966.)

Presidents' Original Paternal Ancestry

Dutch: Van Buren, Theodore Roosevelt, Franklin D. Roosevelt. German: Eisenhower. Swiss and Palatinate German: Hoover.

English: Washington, John Adams, Madison, John Quincy Adams, William Henry Harrison, Tyler, Taylor, Fillmore, Pierce, Lincoln, Andrew Johnson, Grant, Garfield, Cleveland, Benjamin Harrison, Taft,

Harding, Coolidge. English-French-German: L. B. Johnson. English-Scottish-Irish: Truman.

Irish: Kennedy, Nixon. Scottish: Monroe, Hayes. Scottish-Irish: Jackson, Polk, Buchanan, Arthur, McKinley, Wilson. Welsh: Jefferson (according to family tradition).

Revolutionary Calendar, 1775

1775 March 23   Patrick Henry delivers "Give me Liberty or give me Death" speech.

April 19   Paul Revere's ride and Battles of Lexington Green and Concord Bridge.

May 10   Ethan Allen captures Ft. Ticonderoga; 2nd Continental Congress meets in Philadelphia.

May 31   Mecklenburg County (S.C.) Resolutions declare suspension of royal government.

June 15   George Washington named commander-in-chief of Continental Army.

June 17   Battle of Bunker Hill; British win, but sustain heavy losses.

Sept. 2   George Washington authorizes formation of a navy.

Nov. 10   Continental Congress authorizes formation of marine corps.

Dec. 11   Battle of Great Bridge forces British to abandon Norfolk, Va.

Dec. 31   General Arnold's expedition against Quebec ends in defeat.

The Presidents of the Continental Congresses

Congress President	Date Elected	Meeting Place	Term
Peyton Randolph, Va. (1)	Sept. 5, 1774	Philadelphia	Sept. 5 to Oct. 26, 1774
Henry Middleton, S.C.	Oct. 22, 1774		
Peyton Randolph, Va.	May 10, 1775	Philadelphia	May 10, 1775 to Dec. 12, 1776
John Hancock, Mass.	May 24, 1775	Baltimore	Dec. 20, 1776 to Mar. 4, 1777
		Philadelphia	Mar. 5 to Sept. 18, 1777
		Lancaster, Pa.	Sept. 27, 1777 (one day)
Henry Laurens, S.C.	Nov. 1, 1777 (4)	York, Pa.	Sept. 30, 1777 to June 27, 1778
John Jay, N.Y.	Dec. 10, 1778	Philadelphia	July 2, 1778 to June 21, 1783
Samuel Huntington, Conn.	Sept. 28, 1779		
Thomas McKean, Del.	July 10, 1781		
John Hanson, Md. (2)	Nov. 5, 1781		
Elias Boudinot, N.J.	Nov. 4, 1782	Princeton, N.J.	June 30 to Nov. 4, 1783
Thomas Mifflin, Pa.	Nov. 3, 1783	Annapolis, Md.	Nov. 26, 1783 to June 3, 1784
Richard Henry Lee, Va.	Nov. 30, 1784	Trenton, N.J.	Nov. 1 to Dec. 24, 1784
		New York City	Jan. 11 to Nov. 4, 1785
John Hancock, Mass. (3)	Nov. 23, 1785	"	Nov. 7, 1785 to Nov. 3, 1786
Nathaniel Gorham, Mass.	June 6, 1786	"	Nov. 6, 1786 to Oct. 30, 1787
Arthur St. Clair, Pa.	Feb. 2, 1787	"	Nov. 5, 1787 to Oct. 21, 1788
Cyrus Griffin, Va.	Jan. 22, 1788	"	Nov. 3, 1788 to Mar. 2, 1789

(1) Resigned Oct. 2, 1774

(2) Titled "President of the United States in Congress Assembled," John Hanson is considered by some to be the first U.S. President as he was the first to serve under the Articles of Confederation. He was, however, little more than presiding officer of the Congress, which retained full executive power. He could be considered the head of government, but not head of state.

(3) Resigned May 29, 1786, never having served, because of illness.

(4) Articles of Confederation agreed upon, Nov. 15, 1777; last ratification from Maryland, March 1, 1781.

United States Government

The Ford Administration
As of September 1, 1974

Terms of office of the President and Vice President, from January 20, 1973 to January 20, 1977. No person may be elected President of the United States for more than two four-year terms.

PRESIDENT — Gerald R. Ford of Michigan. Receives salary of $200,000 a year taxable, and in addition an expense allowance, also taxable, of $50,000 to assist in defraying expenses resulting from his official duties. Also there may be expended not exceeding $40,000, nontaxable, a year for travel expenses and official entertainment. Congress in 1971 provided lifetime pensions of $60,000 a year, free mailing privileges, free office space, and up to $65,000 a year for office help for ex-Presidents and $20,000 annually for their widows.

VICE PRESIDENT — Salary $62,500 a year and $10,000 for expenses, all of which is taxable.

Order of succession to presidency see Pg. 766.

The Cabinet
(Salaries $60,000 each)

Secretary of State — Henry A. Kissinger, Wash., D.C.
Secretary of Treasury — William E. Simon, N.J.
Secretary of Defense — James R. Schlesinger, Va.
Attorney General — William B. Saxbe, Ohio
Secretary of Interior — Rogers C. B. Morton, Md.
Secretary of Agriculture — Earl L. Butz, Ind.
Secretary of Commerce — Frederick B. Dent, S.C.
Secretary of Labor — Peter J. Brennan, N.Y.
Secretary of Health, Education and Welfare — Caspar W. Weinberger, Calif.
Secretary of Housing and Urban Development — James T. Lynn, Ohio.
Secretary of Transportation — Claude S. Brinegar, Calif.

The White House Staff
1600 Pennsylvania Ave. NW 20500

Counsellor to the President — Robert Hartman.
Assistant to the President — Alexander M. Haig Jr.
Press Secretary to the President — Jerald F. terHorst.
General Counsel — Philip Buchen.
Personal Secretary to the President — Dorothy Downton.
Press Secretary for the First Lady — Helen Smith.
Physician to the President — Rear Admiral William M. Lukash, USN.
Chief Usher — Rex W. Scouten.

Executive Agencies

National Security Council — Assistant to the President for Natl. Security Affairs — Henry A. Kissinger.
Council of Economic Advisers — Herbert Stein.
Council on Environmental Quality — Dr. Russell W. Peterson, chmn.
Central Intelligence Agency — William Colby, dir.
Office of Management and Budget — Roy L. Ash.
Special Representative for Trade Negotiations — William Eberle.

Department of State
2201 C St. NW 20520

Secretary of State—Henry A. Kissinger.
Deputy Secretary—Robert S. Ingersoll, designate.
Under Secy. for Political Affairs—Joseph J. Sisco.
Under Secy. for Security Assistance—vacant.
Deputy Under Secretaries—vacant (for economic affairs), L. Dean Brown (for Management).
Ambassadors at Large—U. Alexis Johnson, Ellsworth Bunker, Robert J. McCloskey.
Counselor—Helmut Sonnenfeldt.
Legal Advisor—Carlyle E. Maw.
Director of Policy Planning Staff—Winston Lord.

Assistant Secretaries for:
Administration—John M. Thomas.
African Affairs—Donald B. Easum.
Congressional Relations—A. Linwood Holton.
Economic Affairs—Willis C. Armstrong.
Educational & Cultural Affairs—John Richardson.
European Affairs—Arthur A. Hartman.
East Asian & Pacific Affairs—Robert S. Ingersoll.
Internatl. Organiz. Affairs—William B. Buffum.
Inter-American Affairs—Jack B. Kubisch.
Near-Eastern & S. Asian Affairs—Alfred L. Atherton Jr.
Public Affairs—Carol C. Laise.
Bureau of Security & Consular Affairs—Barbara M. Watson.
Deputy Inspector General, Foreign Assistance—John P. Constanty.
Chief of Protocol—Ambassador Henry E. Catto.
Dir. General, Foreign Service—Nathaniel Davis.
Dir. of Intelligence & Research—William G. Hyland.
Dir. of Internatl. Scientific and Technological Affairs—Herman Pollack.
Dir. of Politico-Military Affairs—George S. Vest.
Insp. Gen. Foreign Service—James S. Sutterlin.
Foreign Service Inst.—Howard E. Sollenberger, dir.
Agency for Internatl. Development—Daniel Parker, admin.
Advisory Committee on Voluntary Foreign Aid—Margaret Hickey.
Action—Michael P. Balzano.
U.S. Rep. to the UN and Rep. in the Security Council—John Scali, ambassador.

Treasury Department
15th St. & Pennsylvania Ave. NW 20220

Secretary of the Treasury — William E. Simon.
Deputy Secy. of the Treasury — vacant.
Under Secy. for Monetary Affairs — Jack F. Bennett.
Under Secretary — Edward C. Schmults.
General Counsel — vacant.
Deputy Under Secretaries — Gerald L. Parsky, Frederick L. Webber.
Assistant Secretaries: — Frederic W. Hickman, David R. Macdonald, Warren F. Brecht, John M. Hennessy, Edgar R. Fiedler, John K. Carlock.
Special Assistants to the Secretary: — John L. Hart, Edward M. Roob.
Bureaus: —
Accounts — David Mosso, comm.
Alcohol, Tobacco and Firearms — Rex D. Davis, dir.
Consolidated Federal Law Enforcement Training Center — William B. Butler, director
Comptroller of the Currency — James E. Smith.
Customs — Vernon D. Acree, comm.
Engraving & Printing — James A. Conlon, director
Internal Revenue Service — Donald C. Alexander, comm.
Mint — Mrs. Mary T. Brooks, director
Public Debt — H. J. Hintgen, comm.
treasurer of the U.S. — Francine L. Neff
U.S. Savings Bonds — Jesse L. Adams Jr., acting natl. dir.
U.S. Secret Service — H. Stuart Knight, director.

Department of Defense
The Pentagon 20301

Secretary of Defense — James R. Schlesinger.
Deputy Secy. of Defense — William Clements Jr.
Dir. of Def. Research and Engineering — Dr. Malcolm R. Currie.
Asst. Secretaries of Defense:
Comptroller — Terrence E. McClary.
Health and Environment — James R. Cowan, M.D.
Installations & Logistics — Arthur I. Mendolia.
Intelligence — Albert C. Hall.

Internatl. Security — Robert Ellsworth, designate.
legislative Affairs — John M. Maury.
Manpower & Reserve — William K. Brehm.
Program Analysis & Evaluation — Leonard Sullivan Jr.
Public Affairs — Jerry W. Friedheim.
General Counsel — Martin R. Hoffmann.
Joint Chiefs of Staff, Chairman — Gen. George S. Brown, USAF.

Department of the Army
The Pentagon 20310

Secretary of the Army — Howard H. Callaway.
Under Secretary — Herman R. Staudt.
Assistant Secretaries for:—
Finance Management — Hadlai A. Hull.
Installations & Logistics — Eugene E. Berg.
Research & Development — Norman R. Augustine.
Manpower & Reserve Affairs — M. David Lowe.
Chief of Public Information — Maj. Gen. L. Gordon Hill Jr.
Chief of Staff — Gen. Creighton W. Abrams.
Comptroller of the Army — Lt. Gen. E.M. Flanagan Jr.
Surgeon General — Lt. Gen. Richard R. Taylor.
Adjutant General — Maj. Gen. Verne L. Bowers.
Inspector General — Lt. Gen. Herron N. Maples.
Chief of Engineers — Lt. Gen. W.C. Gribble Jr.
U.S. Women's Army Corps. — Brig. Gen. Mildred C. Bailey.
Nat. Guard Bureau — Maj. Gen. Francis S. Greenlief.
Chief Army Reserve — Maj. Gen. J. Milnor Roberts Jr.
U.S. Army Materiel Command — Gen. H.A. Miley Jr.
U.S. Army Forces Command—Gen. Walter T. Kerwin Jr.
U.S. Army Training and Doctrine Command — Gen. William E. DePuy.
Commanding Generals, U.S. Armies: —
1st, Fort Meade Md. — Lt. Gen. James G. Kalergis.
5th, Ft. Sam Houston Tex. — Lt. Gen. John J. Hennessey.
6th Presidio of San Francisco Calif. — Lt. Gen. Elvy B. Roberts.
Military Dist. of Washington — Maj. Gen. Frederic E. Davison.

Department of the Navy
The Pentagon 20360

Secretary of the Navy — J. Wm. Middendorf 2d.
Under Secretary — Vacant.
Assistant Secretaries for:
Financial Management — Vacant.
Installations & Logistics — Jack L. Bowers.
Manpower & Reserve Affairs — Joseph T. McCullen Jr.
Research & Development — David S. Potter.
Judge Advocate Gen. — R. Adm. Merlin H. Staring.
Chief of Naval Operations — Adm. James L. Holloway 3d.
Chief of Naval Materiel — Adm. I. C. Kidd Jr.
Bureau Chiefs:
Medicine & Surgery — V. Adm. Donald . Custis.
Naval Personnel — V. Adm. David H. Bagley.
Military Sealift Command — R. Adm. John D. Chase.
U.S. Marine Corps: —
Commandant — Gen. Robert E. Cushman Jr.
Asst. Commandant — Gen. Earl E. Anderson.
Dep. Chief of Staff for Installations & Logistics — Maj. Gen. E. J. Miller.
Dir. of Women Marines — Col. M.A. Brewer.
Commandants, Naval Districts: —
1st, Boston — R. Adm. Richard E. Rumble.
3rd, New York — R. Adm. Wm. M. Pugh 2d.
4th, Philadelphia — R. Adm. Joseph L. Coleman.
5th, Norfolk — R. Adm. Roy G. Anderson.
6th, Charleston — R. Adm. Graham Tahler.
8th, New Orleans — R. Adm. Robert E. Riera.
9th, Great Lakes — R. Adm. Warren H. O'Neil.
10th, Roosevelt Roads — R. Adm. James D. Ramage.
11th, San Diego — R. Adm. Fillmore B. Gilkeson.
12th, San Francisco — R. Adm. Martin D. Carmody.
13th, Seattle — R. Adm. Thomas E. Bass 3d.
14th, San Francisco — R. Adm. Richard A. Paddock.
15th, Balboa — R. Adm. Robert H. Blount.
Naval District, Wash., D.C. — R. Adm. Arthur G. Esch.

Department of the Air Force
The Pentagon 20330

Secretary of the Air Force — John L. McLucas.
Under Secretary — James W. Plummer.
Assistant Secretaries for: —
Research & Development — Walter B. LaBerge.

Installations & Logistics — Frank A. Shrontz.
Financial Management — William Woodruff.
Manpower & Reserve Affairs — David P. Taylor.
General Counsel — Jack L. Stempler.
Director of Information — Maj. Gen. Guy E. Hairston Jr., designate.
Dir. of Space Systems — Brig. Gen. John F. Julpa Jr.
Dir. of Special Projects — Brig. Gen. David D. Bradburn.
Chief of Staff — Gen. David C. Jones.
Vice Chief of Staff — Gen. Richard H. Ellis.
Chief, Natl. Guard Bureau — Maj. Gen. Francis S. Greenlief.
Chief of Air Force Reserves — Maj. Gen. Homer I. Lewis.
Surgeon General — Lt. Gen. Robert A. Patterson.
Judge Advocate — Maj. Gen. H.R. Vague.
Inspector General — Lt. Gen. G. W. Johnson.
Deputy Chiefs of Staff: —
Systems & Logistics — Lt. Gen. William Snavely.
Programs & Resources — Lt. Gen. James A. Hill.
Personnel — Lt. Gen. J. W. Roberts.
Research & Development — Lt. Gen. W. J. Evans.
Plans & Operations — Lt. Gen. Robert E. Huyser.
Aerospace Defense Command — Gen. Lucius D. Clay Jr.
Air Force Logistics — Gen. William V. McBride.
Air Force Systems — Gen. Samuel C. Phillips.
Air Training — Vacant.
Air University — Lt. Gen. F. Michael Rogers.
Hdgts. Command — Maj. Gen. M. R. Reilly.
Military Airlift — Gen. Paul K. Carlton.
Strategic Air — Gen. Russell E. Dougherty.
Tactical Air — Gen. Robert J. Dixon.
Alaskan Air — Maj. Gen. Jack K. Gamble.
U.S.A.F. Southern Command — Maj. Gen. Arthur G. Salisbury.
Pacific Air Forces — Gen. Louis L. Wilson Jr.
U.S.A.F. Europe — Gen. John W. Vogt.
U.S.A.F. Security Service — Maj. Gen. Howard P. Smith.
Air Force Communications Service — Maj. Gen. Donald L. Werbeck.

Department of Justice
Constitution Ave. & 10th St. NW 20530

Attorney General — William B. Saxbe.
Deputy Attorney General — Laurence H. Silberman.
Solicitor General — Robert H. Bork.
Assistant Attorneys General: —
Antitrust Division — Thomas E. Kauper.
Civil Division — Carla Hills.
Civil Rights Division — J. Stanley Pottinger.
Criminal Division — Henry E. Petersen.
Drug Enforcement Admin. — John R. Bartels Jr., admin.
Land & Natural Resources Division — Wallace Johnson.
Legal Counsel — Robert G. Dixon.
Office of Legislative Affairs — W. Vincent Rakestraw.
Office of Management & Finance — Glen E. Pommerening, acting.
Public Information — John W. Hushen, dir.
Tax Division — Scott P. Crampton.
Fed. Bureau of Investigation — Clarence M. Kelley.
Board of Immigration Appeals — M. A.Roberts.
Board of Parole — Maurice H. Sigler.
Bureau of Prisons — Norman A. Carlson.
Community Relations Ser. — Benjamin Holman, dir.
Immigration and Naturalization Service — Leonard F. Chapman, commissioner.
Law Enforcement Assistance Admin. — Donald Santarelli.
Pardon Attorney — Lawrence M. Traylor.

Department of the Interior
C St. between 18th & 19th Sts. NW 20240

Secretary of the Interior — Rogers C. B. Morton.
Under Secretary — John C. Whitaker.
Assistant Secretaries for: —
Fish, Wildlife, and Parks — Nathaniel P. Reed.
Energy & Minerals — vacant.
Land and Water Resources — Jack O. Horton.
Program Development & Budget — Royston C. Hughes.
Management — James T. Clarke, acting.
Congressional & Legislative Affairs — John H. Kyl.
Commissioner of Indian Affairs — Morris Thompson.
Bureau of Land Management — Curtis J. Berklund.
Bureau of Mines — Dr. Thomas J. Falkie.
Bureau of Outdoor Recreation — James G. Watt.
Bureau of Reclamation — Gilbert G. Stamm.
Bureau of Sport Fisheries & Wildlife — Lynn Greenwalt.
Geological Survey — V.E. McKelvey.

National Park Service — Ronald H. Walker.
Office of Coal Research — S. William Gouse, acting.
Office of Communications — Robert A. Kelly.
Office of Saline Water — J. W. Pat O'Meara.
Office of Solicitor — Kent Frizzell.
Office of Water Resources Research — Dr. Warren A. Hall, acting.

Department of Agriculture
14th St. & Independence Ave. SW 20250

Secretary of Agriculture — Earl L. Butz.
Under Secretary — J. Phil Campbell.
Conservation, Research & Education — Robert W. Long.
Internatl. Affairs & Commodity Programs — Clayton K. Yeutter.
Marketing & Consumer Services — Richard L. Feltner.
Rural Development — William Erwin.
Agricultural Economics — Don Paarlberg.
Public Affairs — Wayne E. Swegle.
Intergovernmental Affairs — R. B. Wilson.
Agric. Mktg. Service — Erwin L. Peterson, admin.
Agric. Stabilization & Conserv. Service — Kenneth Frick, admin.
Annimal & Plant Health Inspection Ser. — E. J. Mulhern.
Commodity Exch. Auth. — Alex C. Caldwell, admin.
Cooperative State Research Ser. — R. L. Lovvorn.
Econ. Research Service — Quentin M. West, admin.
Extension Service — Edward Kirby, admin.
Farmer Coop. Service — Ronald D. Knutson, admin.
Farmers Home Admin. — Frank B. Elliott, admin.
Fed. Crop Insurance Corp. — Melvin R. Peterson.
Food & Nutrition Ser. — Edward J. Hekman, admin.
Foreign Agric. Service — Raymond A. Ioanes, admin.
Forest Service — John R. McGuire, chief.
General Counsel — John A. Knebel.
Office of Investigation — John V. Graziano, dir.
Packers & Stockyards Admin.— Marvin McLain.
Rural Electrific. Admin. — David Hume, admin.
Soil Conservation Service — Kenneth E. Grant, Admin.
Statistical Reporting Service — Harry C. Trelogan.

Department of Commerce
14th St. between Constitution & E St. NW 20230

Secretary of Commerce — Frederick B. Dent.
Under Secretary—John K. Tabor.
Asst. Secretaries — Henry B. Turner, Robert J. Blackwell, Betsy Ancker-Johnson, C. Langhorne Washburn, Dr. Sidney L. Jones.
General Counsel — Karl E. Bakke.
Bureau of the Census — Vincent R. Barabba.
Bureau of Economic Analysis — George Jaszi.
Bureau of Internatl. Commerce — Marinus van Gessel.
Bureau of East-West Trade — Cyril E. Geacintov.
Bureau of Competitive Assessment and Business Policy — Vacant.
Natl. Oceanic & Atmospheric Admin. — Robert M. White, admin.
Natl Technical Info. Service — William t. Knox, dir.
Economic Develop. Admin. — William Blunt, acting.
Natl. Bureau of Standards — Dr. Richard Roberts.
Office of Minority Business Enterprise — Alex M. Armendaris, dir.
Office of Product Standards — Frank LaQue.
Office of Telecommunications — John M. Richardson, acting dir.
Office of Textiles — Arthur Garel, dir.
Social & Economic Statistics Admin. — Edward D. Failor, admin.
U.S. Patent Office — C. Marshall Dann, comm.
U.S. Travel Service — C. Langhorne Washburn.

Department of Labor
14th St. & Constitution Ave. NW 20210

Secretary of Labor — Peter J. Brennan.
Under Secretary — Richard F. Schubert.
Counselor to the Secretary — Donald F. Rodgers.
Asst. Secretary for Manpower — William H. Kolberg.
Asst. Secretary for Labor-Management Relations — Paul J. Fasser Jr.
Asst. Secretary for Occupational Safety & Health — John H. Stender.
Asst. Secretary for Employment Standards — Bernard E. DeLury.
Women's Bureau — Carmen R. Maymi, director.
Asst. Secretary for Policy, Evaluation & Research — Abraham Weiss.

Solicitor of Labor — William J. Kilberg.
Bureau of Labor Statistics — Julius Shiskin.
Dep. Under Secy. for Internatl. Affairs — Joel Segall.
Dep. Under Secy. for Legislative Affairs — Benjamin Brown.
Asst. Secretary for Admin. & Management — Fred G. Clark.
Director of Public Affairs — Kenneth Downs.
Office of Information, Publications & Reports — John Leslie, director.

Department of Health, Education and Welfare
330 Independence Ave. SW 20201

Secretary of H.E.W. — Caspar W. Weinberger.
Under Secretary — Frank Carlucci.
Assistant Secretaries for: —
  Administration and Management — John R. Ottina.
  Public Affairs — Lewis Helm.
  Health — Dr. Charles C. Edwards.
  Planning and Evaluation — William Morrill.
  Education — Virginia Y. Trotter.
  Human Development — Stanley B. Thomas.
  Legislation — Stephen Kurzman.
  Comptroller — John D. Young.
General Counsel — John D. Rhinelander.
Surgeon General, Public Health Ser. — vacant.
Center for Disease Control — Dr. David J. Sencer, dir.
Alcohol, Drug Abuse and Mental Health Admin. — Dr. Roger O. Egeberg, M.D.
Health Resources Admin. — Dr. Kenneth Endicott.
Health Services Admin. — Harold O. Buzzell.
Office for Civil Rights — Peter Holmes, dir.
Social and Rehabilitation Ser. — James S. Dwight.
Commissioners of: —
  Education — Terrel H. Bell.
  Social Security — James B. Cardwell.
  Food and Drug Admin. — Dr. Alexander M. Schmidt.
National Institutes of Health — Robert S. Stone, M.D., dir.
National Institute of Education — Dr. Thomas K. Glennan Jr.

Department of Housing and Urban Development
451 7th St. SW 20410

Secretary of Housing & Urban Development — James T. Lynn.
Under Secretary — James L. Mitchell.
Assistant Secretaries: —
  Administration — Thomas G. Cody.
  Community Planning & Development — David Meeker.
  Equal Opportunity — Gloria E. A. Toote.
  Housing Management — H. R. Crawford.
  Housing Production & Mortgage Credit — Sheldon B. Lubar.
  Policy Development & Research — Michael H. Moskow.
  Legislative Affairs — Sol Mosher.
President, Govt. Natl. Mortgage Assn. — Vacant.
Office of Public Affairs — William I. Greener Jr.
Office of International Affairs — L. Wayne Gertmenian.
General Counsel — Robert R. Elliott, designate.
Federal Insurance Administrator — George K. Bernstein.
Office of Interstate Land Sales Registration — George K. Bernstein, admin.
Inspector General — Charles G. Haynes.

Department of Transportation
400 7th St. SW 20590

Secretary — Claude S. Brinegar.
Under Secretary — John W. Barnum. 4
Assistant Secretaries — Robert H. Cannon, Benjamin O. Davis Jr., William S. Heffelfinger, Robert T. Monagan.
National Highway Traffic Safety Admin. — Dr. James B. Gregory.
Natl. Trans. Safety Board — John H. Reed.
U.S. Coast Guard Commandant — Adm. Owen W. Siler.
Federal Aviation Admin. — Alexander P. Butterfield.
Federal Highway Admin. — Norbert T. Tiemann.
Federal Railroad Admin. — John W. Ingram.
Urban Mass Transportation Admin. — Frank C. Herringer.
St. Lawrence Seaway Development Corp. — David W. Oberlin.

Judiciary of the United States
Data as of June 10, 1974
Justices of the United States Supreme Court

The Supreme Court comprises the Chief Justice of the United States and 8 Associate Justices, all appointed by the President with advice and consent of the Senate. Salaries: Chief Justice $62,500 annually, Associate Justice $60,000.

Name; apptd from / Chief Justices in italics	Service Term	Yrs.	Born	Died
John Jay, N. Y.	1789-1795	5	1745	1829
John Rutledge, S, C.	1789-1791	1	1739	1800
William Cushing, Mass.	1789-1810	20	1732	1810
James Wilson, Pa.	1789-1798	8	1742	1798
John Blair, Va.	1789-1796	6	1732	1800
James Iredell, N. C.	1790-1799	9	1751	1799
Thomas Johnson, Md.	1791-1793	1	1732	1819
William Paterson, N. J.	1793-1806	13	1745	1806
John Rutledge, S. C.	1795(a)	—	1739	1800
Samuel Chase, Md.	1796-1811	15	1741	1811
Oliver Ellsworth, Conn.	1796-1800	4	1745	1807
Bushrod Washington, Va.	1798-1829	31	1762	1829
Alfred Moore, N. C.	1799-1804	4	1755	1810
John Marshall, Va.	1801-1835	34	1755	1835
William Johnson, S. C.	1804-1834	30	1771	1834
Henry B. Livingston, N.Y.	1806-1823	16	1757	1823
Thomas Todd, Ky.	1807-1826	18	1765	1826
Joseph Story, Mass.	1811-1845	33	1779	1845
Gabriel Duval, Md.	1811-1835	22	1752	1844
Smith Thompson, N. Y.	1823-1843	20	1768	1843
Robert Trimble, Ky.	1826-1828	2	1777	1828
John McLean, Ohio.	1829-1861	32	1785	1861
Henry Baldwin, Pa.	1830-1844	14	1780	1844
James M. Wayne, Ga.	1835-1867	32	1790	1867
Roger B. Taney, Md.	1836-1864	28	1777	1864
Philip P. Barbour, Va.	1836-1841	4	1783	1841
John Catron, Tenn.	1837-1865	28	1786	1865
John McKinley, Ala.	1837-1852	15	1780	1852
Peter V. Daniel, Va.	1841-1860	19	1784	1860
Samuel Nelson, N. Y.	1845-1872	27	1792	1873
Levi Woodbury, N. H.	1845-1851	5	1789	1851
Robert C. Grier, Pa.	1846-1870	23	1794	1870
Benjamin R. Curtis, Mass.	1851-1857	6	1809	1874
John A. Campbell, Ala.	1853-1861	8	1811	1889
Nathan Clifford, Me.	1858-1881	23	1803	1881
Noah H. Swayne, Ohio.	1862-1881	18	1804	1884
Samuel F. Miller, Iowa.	1862-1890	28	1816	1890
David Davis, Ill.	1862-1877	14	1815	1886
Stephen J. Field, Calif.	1863-1897	34	1816	1899
Salmon P. Chase, Ohio.	1864-1873	8	1808	1873
William Strong, Pa.	1870-1880	10	1808	1895
Joseph P. Bradley, N. J.	1870-1892	21	1813	1892
Ward Hunt, N. Y.	1872-1882	9	1810	1886
Morrison R. Waite, Ohio.	1874-1888	14	1816	1888
John M. Harlan, Ky.	1877-1911	34	1833	1911
William B. Woods, Ga.	1880-1887	6	1824	1887
Stanley Matthews, Ohio.	1881-1889	7	1824	1889
Horace Gray, Mass.	1881-1902	20	1828	1902
Samuel Blatchford, N.Y.	1882-1893	11	1820	1893
Lucius Q.C. Lamar, Miss.	1888-1893	5	1825	1893
Melville W. Fuller, Ill.	1888-1910	21	1833	1910
David J. Brewer, Kan.	1889-1910	20	1837	1910
Henry B. Brown, Mich.	1890-1906	15	1836	1913
George Shiras Jr., Pa.	1892-1903	10	1832	1924
Howell E. Jackson, Tenn.	1893-1895	2	1832	1895
Edward D. White, La.	1894-1910	16	1845	1921
Rufus W. Peckham, N.Y.	1895-1909	13	1838	1909
Joseph McKenna, Calif.	1898-1925	26	1843	1926
Oliver W. Holmes, Mass.	1902-1932	29	1841	1935
William R. Day, Ohio.	1903-1922	19	1849	1923
William H. Moody, Mass.	1906-1910	3	1853	1917
Horace H. Lurton, Tenn.	1909-1914	4	1844	1914
Charles E. Hughes, N.Y.	1910-1916	5	1862	1948
Willis Van Devanter, Wyo.	1910-1937	26	1859	1941
Joseph R. Lamar, Ga.	1910-1916	5	1857	1916
Edward D. White, La.	1910-1921	10	1845	1921
Mahlon Pitney, N. J.	1912-1922	10	1858	1924
Jas. C. McReynolds, Tenn.	1914-1941	26	1862	1946
Louis D. Brandeis, Mass.	1916-1939	22	1856	1941
John H. Clarke, Ohio.	1916-1922	5	1857	1945
William H. Taft, Conn.	1921-1930	8	1857	1930
George Sutherland, Utah.	1922-1938	15	1862	1942
Pierce Butler, Minn.	1922-1939	16	1866	1939
Edward T. Sanford, Tenn.	1923-1930	7	1865	1930
Harlan F. Stone, N. Y.	1925-1941	16	1872	1946
Charles E. Hughes, N.Y.	1930-1941	11	1862	1948
Owen J. Roberts, Pa.	1930-1945	15	1875	1955
Benjamin N. Cardozo, N.Y.	1932-1938	6	1870	1938
Hugo L. Black, Ala.	1937-1971	34	1886	1971
Stanley F. Reed, Ky.	1938-1957	19	1884	—
Felix Frankfurter, Mass.	1939-1962	23	1882	1965
William O. Douglas, Conn.	1939	—	1898	—
Frank Murphy, Mich.	1940-1949	9	1890	1949
Harlan F. Stone, N. Y.	1941-1946	5	1872	1946
James F. Byrnes, S. C.	1941-1942	1	1879	1972
Robert H. Jackson, N.Y.	1941-1954	12	1892	1954
Wiley B. Rutledge, Iowa.	1943-1949	6	1894	1949
Harold H. Burton, Ohio.	1945-1958	13	1888	1964
Fred M. Vinson, Ky.	1946-1953	7	1890	1953
Tom C. Clark, Tex.	1949-1967	18	1899	—
Sherman Minton, Ind.	1949-1956	7	1890	1965
Earl Warren, Calif.	1953-1969	16	1891	1974
John Marshall Harlan, N.Y.	1955-1971	16	1899	1971
William J. Brennan Jr., N.J.	1956	—	1906	—
Charles E. Whittaker, Mo.	1957-1962	5	1901	—
Potter Stewart, Ohio.	1958	—	1906	—
Byron R. White, Colo.	1962	—	1917	—
Arthur J. Goldberg, Ill.	1962-1965	3	1908	—
Abe Fortas, Tenn.	1965-1969	4	1910	—
Thurgood Marshall, N.Y.	1967	—	1908	—
Warren E. Burger, Va.	1969	—	1907	—
Harry A. Blackmun, Minn.	1970	—	1908	—
Lewis F. Powell Jr., Va.	1971	—	1907	—
William H. Rehnquist, Ariz.	1971	—	1924	—

(a) Rejected Dec. 15, 1795.

U.S. Court of Customs and Patent Appeals
Washington, D.C. 20439 (Salaries, $42,500)

Chief Judge — Howard T. Markey.

Associate Judges — Giles S. Rich, Phillip B. Baldwin, Donald E. Lane, Jack R. Miller.

United States Custom Court
New York, N.Y. 10007 (Salaries, $40,000)

Chief Judge — Nils A. Boe.

Judges — Morgan Ford, Scovel Richardson, Frederick Landis, James L. Watson, Herbert N. Maletz, Bernard Newman, Edward D. Re, Paul P. Rao.

United States Court of Claims
Washington, D.C. 20005 (Salaries, $42,500)

Chief Judge — Wilson Cowen.

Associate Judges — Oscar H. Davis, Shiro Kashiwa, Robert L. Kunzig, Marion T. Bennett, Byron G. Skelton, Philip Nichols Jr.

United States Tax Court
Washington, D.C. 20004

Chief Judge — Howard A. Dawson Jr.

Judges — Arnold Raum, Bruce M. Forrester, Irene F. Scott, William M. Fay, William M. Drennen, Austin Hoyt, Theodore Tannenwald Jr., Charles R. Simpson, C. Moxley

Featherston, Leo H. Irwin, Samuel B. Sterrett, William Quealy, William A. Goffe, Cynthia H. Hall, Darrell D. Wiles.

U.S. Court of Appeals

(Salaries, $42,500. CJ means Chief Judge)

District of Columbia — David L. Bazelon, CJ; J. Skelly Wright, Carl McGowan, Edward Allen Tamm, Harold Leventhal, Spottswood W. Robinson III, Roger Robb, George E. MacKinnon, Malcolm Richard Wilkey; Clerk's office, Washington, D.C. 20001.

First Circuit (Me., Mass., N.H., R.I., Puerto Rico) — Frank M. Coffin, CJ; Edward M. McEntee, Levin H. Campbell; Clerk's Office, Boston 02109.

Second Circuit (Conn., N.Y., Vt.) — Irving R. Kaufman, CJ; Henry J. Friendly, Paul R. Hays, Wilfred Feinberg, Walter R. Mansfield, William H. Mulligan, James L. Oakes, William H. Timber; Clerk's Office, New York 10007.

Third Circuit (Del., N.J., Pa., Virgin Islands) — Collins J. Seitz, CJ; Francis L. Van Dusen, Ruggero J. Aldisert, Arlin M. Adams; John J. Gibbons, Max Rosenn, James Hunter 3d, Joseph F. Weis Jr., Leonard I. Garth; Clerk's Office, Philadelphia 19107.

Fourth Circuit (Md., N.C., S.C., Va., W.Va.) — Clement F. Haynsworth, Jr., CJ; Harrison L. Winter, J. Braxton Craven Jr., John D. Butzner Jr., Donald Russell, John A. Field Jr., H. Emory Widener Jr.; Clerk's Office, Richmond, Va. 23219.

Fifth Circuit (Ala., Fla., Ga., La., Miss., Tex., Canal Zone) — John R. Brown, CJ; John Minor Wisdom, Walter Pettus Gewin, Griffin B. Bell, Homer Thornberry, James P. Coleman, Irving L. Goldberg, Robert A. Ainsworth Jr., John C. Godbold, David W. Dyer, Bryan Simpson, Lewis R. Morgan, Charles Clark, Thomas G. Gee, Paul H. Roney; Clerk's Office, New Orleans, La. 70130.

Sixth Circuit (Ky., Mich., Ohio, Tenn.) — Harry Phillips, CJ; Paul C. Weick, George Clifton Edwards Jr., Anthony J. Celebrezze, John W. Peck, Wade H. McCree Jr., William E. Miller, Albert J. Engel, Pierce Lively; Clerk's Office, Cincinnati 45202.

Seventh Circuit (Ill., Ind., Wis.) — Luther M. Swygert, CJ; Thomas E. Fairchild, Walter J. Cummings, Otto Kerner, resigned 7/25/74, Wilbur F. Pell Jr., John Paul Stevens, Robert A. Sprecher; Clerk's Office, Chicago 60604

Eighth Circuit (Ark., Iowa, Minn., Mo., Neb., N.D., S.D.) — Pat Mehaffy, CJ; Floyd R. Gibson, Donald P. Lay, Gerald W. Heaney, Myron H. Bright, Donald R. Ross, Roy L. Stephenson, William H. Webster; Clerk's Office, St. Louis 63101.

Ninth Circuit (Ariz., Calif., Idaho, Mont., Nev., Ore., Wash., Alaska, Hawaii, Guam) — Richard H. Chambers, CJ; Charles M. Merrill, M. Oliver Koelsch, James R. Browning, Ben Cushing Duniway, Walter Ely, Shirley M. Hufstedler, Eugene A. Wright, Ozell M. Trask, Joseph T. Sneed, Herbert Y. C. Choy, J. Clifford Wallace, Alfred T. Goodwin; Clerk's Office, San Francisco 94101.

Tenth Circuit (Colo., Kan., N.M., Okla., Utah, Wyo.) — David T. Lewis, CJ; Delmas C. Hill, Oliver Seth, William J. Holloway Jr., Robert H. McWilliams, James E. Barrett, William E. Doyle; Clerk's Office, Denver, Colo. 80202.

U.S. District Courts

(Salaries, $40,000. CJ means Chief Judge)

Alabama — Northern: Frank H. McFadden, CJ; Sam C. Pointer Jr., James Hughes Hancock, J. Foy Guin Jr.; Clerk's Office, Birmingham 35203. **Middle:** Frank M. Johnson Jr., CJ; Robert E. Varner; Clerk's Office, Montgomery 36101. **Southern:** Virgil Pittman, CJ; William Brevard Hand; Clerk's Office, Mobile 36602.

Alaska — James A. Von der Heydt, CJ; Clerk's Office, Anchorage 99510.

Arizona — Walter Early Craig, CJ; James A. Walsh, C. A. Muecke, William P. Copple, William C. Frey; Clerk's Office, Phoenix 85025.

Arkansas — Eastern: J. Smith Henley, CJ; Oren Harris, Garnett Thomas Eisele; Clerk's Office, Little Rock 72203. **Western:** Paul X. Williams, CJ; Oren Harris, J. Smith Henley; Clerk's Office, Fort Smith 72902.

California—Northern: Oliver J. Carter, CJ; Albert C. Wollenberg, Lloyd H. Burke, Alfonso J. Zirpoli, Stanley A. Weigel, Robert F. Peckham, Robert H. Schnacke, Samuel Conti, Spencer M. Williams, Charles B. Renfrew; Clerk's Office, San Francisco 94102. **Eastern:** Thomas J. MacBride, CJ; M. D. Crocker, Philip C. Wilkins; Clerk's Office, Sacramento 95814. **Central:** Albert Lee Stephens Jr., CJ; Jesse W. Curtis, E. Avery Crary, Francis C. Whelan, Irving Hill, A. Andrew Hauk, William P. Gray, Warren J. Ferguson,

Manuel L. Real, Harry Pregerson, David W. Williams, Robert J. Kelleher, Wm. Matthew Byrne Jr., Lawrence T. Lyick, Malcolm M. Lucas; Clerk's Office, Los Angeles 90012. **Southern:** Edward J. Schwartz, CJ; Howard B. Turentine, Gordon Thompson Jr., Leland C. Nielsen, William B. Enright; Clerk's Office, San Diego 92101.

Colorado — Alfred A. Arraj, CJ; Fred M. Winner, Sherman G. Finesilver; Clerk's Office, Denver 80201.

Connecticut — M. Joseph Blumenfeld, CJ; T. Emmet Clarie, Robert C. Zampano, Jon O. Newman; Clerk's Office, New Haven 06505.

Delaware — James L. Latchum, CJ; Walter K. Stapleton; Clerk's Office, Wilmington 19899.

District of Columbia— John J. Sirica, CJ; George L. Hart Jr., William B. Jones, Howard F. Corcoran, Oliver Gasch, William B. Bryant, John Lewis Smith Jr., Aubrey E. Robinson Jr., Joseph C. Waddy, Gerhard A. Gesell, John H. Pratt, June L. Green, Barrington D. Parker, Charles R. Richey, Thomas A. Flannery; Clerk's Office, Washington 20001.

Florida—Northern: Winston E. Arnow, CJ; David L. Middlebrooks Jr.; Clerk's Office, Tallahassee 32302. **Middle:** George C. Young, CJ; Charles R. Scott, Ben Krentzman, Gerald B. Tjoflat, William Terrell Hodges, John A. Reed Jr.; Clerk's Office, Jacksonville 32201. **Southern:** Charles B. Fulton, CJ; William O. Mehrtens, C. Clyde Atkins, Joe Eaton, Peter T. Fay, James Lawrence King, Norman C. Roettger Jr.; Clerk's Office, Miami 33101.

Georgia — Northern: Newell Edenfield, CJ; Sidney O. Smith Jr., Albert J. Henderson Jr., William C. O'Kelley, Charles A. Moye Jr., Richard C. Freeman; Clerk's Office, Atlanta 30301. **Middle:** J. Robert Elliott, CJ; Wilbur D. Owens Jr.; Clerk's Office, Macon 31202. **Southern:** Alexander A. Lawrence, CJ; Anthony A. Alaimo; Clerk's Office, Savannah 31402.

Hawaii — Martin Pence, CJ; Samuel P. King; Clerk's Office, Honolulu 96801.

Idaho — Ray McNichols, CJ; J. Blaine Anderson; Clerk's Office, Boise 83702.

Illinois — Northern: Edwin A. Robson, CJ; Richard B. Austin, James B. Parsons, Hubert L. Will, Bernard M. Decker, Abraham L. Marovitz, William J. Lynch, Frank J. McGarr, Thomas R. McMillen, William J. Bauer, Richard W. McLaren, Philip Tone, Prentice H. Marshall; Clerk's Office, Chicago 60604. **Eastern:** Henry S. Wise, CJ; James L. Foreman; Clerk's Office, Danville 61832. **Southern:** Robert D. Morgan, CJ; Harlington Wood Jr.; Clerk's Office, Peoria 61601.

Indiana — Northern: George N. Beamer, CJ; Jesse E. Eschbach, Allen Sharp; Clerk's Office, Hammond 46325. **Southern:** William E. Steckler, CJ; Cale J. Holder, S. Hugh Dillin, James E. Noland; Clerk's Office, Indianapolis 46204.

Iowa — Northern: Edward J. McManus, CJ; William C. Hanson; clerk's Office, Cedar Rapids 52401. **Southern:** William C. Hanson, CJ; William C. Stuart; Clerk's Office, Des Moines 50309.

Kansas — Wesley E. Brown, CJ; George Templar, Frank G. Theis, Earl E. O'Connor; Clerk's Office, Wichita 67201.

Kentucky — Eastern: Bernard T. Moynahan Jr., CJ; Mac Swinford, Howard David Hermansdorfer; Clerk's Office, Lexington 40501. **Western:** James F. Gordon, CJ; Mac Swinford, Rhodes Bratcher, Charles M. Allen; Clerk's Office, Louisville 40202.

Louisiana — Eastern: Frederick J. R. Heebe, CJ; Herbert W. Christenberry, Edward J. Boyle Sr., Lansing L. Mitchell, Fred J. Cassibry, Alvin B. Rubin, James A. Comiskey, R. Blake West, Jack M. Gordon; Clerk's Office, New Orleans 70130. **Middle:** E. Gordon West; Clerk's Office, Baton Rouge 70801. **Western:** Edwin F. Hunter Jr., CJ; Richard J. Putnam, Nauman S. Scott; Clerk's Office, Shreveport 71161.

Maine — Edward Thaxter Gignoux; Clerk's Office, Portland 04112.

Maryland — Edward S. Northrop, CJ; Frank A. Kaufman, Alexander Harvey 2d, James R. Miller Jr., Joseph Young, Herbert F. Murray, C. Stanley Blair; Clerk's Office, Baltimore 21202.

Massachusetts — Andrew A. Caffrey, CJ; W. Arthur Garrity Jr., Frank J. Murray, Frank H. Freedman, Joseph L. Tauro, Walter Jay Skinner; Clerk's Office, Boston 02109.

Michigan — Eastern: Frederick W. Kaess, CJ; Stephen J. Roth, Damon J. Keith, Lawrence Gubow, Cornelia G. Kennedy, John Feikens, Philip Pratt, Robert E. deMasico, Charles W. Joiner, James Harvey; Clerk's Office, Detroit 48226. **Western:** Noel P. Fox, CJ; Clerk's Office, Grand Rapids 49502.

Minnesota — Edward J. Devitt, CJ; Earl R. Larson, Miles W. Lord; Clerk's Office, St. Paul 55101.

Mississippi — Northern: William C. Keady, CJ; Orma R. Smith; Clerk's Office, Oxford 38655. **Southern:** Dan M. Russell Jr., CJ; William Harold Cox, Walter L. Nixon Jr.; Clerk's Office, Jackson 39205.

Missouri — Eastern: James H. Meredith, CJ; John K. Regan, William R. Collinson, H. Kenneth Wangelin, John F. Nangle; Clerk's Office, St. Louis 63101. **Western:** William H. Becker, CJ; John W. Oliver, William R. Collinson, Elmo B. Hunter, H. Kenneth Wangelin; Clerk's Office, Kansas City 64106.

Montana — Russell E. Smith, CJ; James F. Battin; Clerk's Office, Great Falls 59401.

Nebraska — Warren K. Urbom, CJ; Robert V. Denney, Albert G. Schatz; Clerk's Office, Omaha 68101.

Nevada — Roger D. Foley, CJ; Bruce R. Thompson; Clerk's Office, Las Vegas 89101.

New Hampshire — Hugh H. Bownes; Clerk's Office, Concord 03301.

New Jersey — Mitchell H. Cohen, CJ; James A. Coolahan, Lawrence A. Whipple, George H. Barlow, Clarkson S. Fisher, Frederick B. Lacey, Vincent P. Biunno, Herbert J. Stern; Clerk's Office, Trenton 08605.

New Mexico — H. Vearle Payne, CJ; Howard C. Bratton, Edwin L. Mechem; Clerk's Office, Albuquerque 87103.

New York — Northern: James T. Foley, CJ; Edmund Port; Clerk's Office, Albany 12201. **Eastern:** Jacob Mishler, CJ; John R. Bartels, John F. Dooling Jr., Jack B. Weinstein, Anthony J. Travia, Orrin G. Judd, Mark A. Costantino, Edward R. Neaher; Clerk's Office, Brooklyn 11201. **Southern:** David N. Edelstein, CJ; Edward Weinfeld, Charles M. Metzner, Lloyd F. MacMahon, Dudley B. Bonsal, Harold R. Tyler Jr., Inzer B. Wyatt, John M. Cannella, Charles H. Tenney, Marvin E. Frankel, Constance Baker Motley, Milton Pollack, Morris E. Lasker, Murray I. Gurfein, Lawrence W. Pierce, Arnold Bauman, Lee P. Gagliardi, Charles L. Brieant Jr., Whitman Knapp, Charles E. Stewart Jr., Thomas P. Griesa, Robert L. Carter, Robert J. Ward, Kevin Thomas Duffy, William C. Conner, Richard Owen; Clerk's Office, New York City 10007. **Western:** John O. Henderson, CJ; Harold P. Burke, John T. Curtin; Clerk's Office, Buffalo 14202.

North Carolina — Eastern: Algernon L. Butler, CJ; John D. Larkins Jr., Franklin T. Dupree Jr.; Clerk's Office, Raleigh 27611. **Middle:** Eugene A. Gordon, CJ; Hiriam H. Ward; Clerk's Office, Greensboro 27402. **Western:** Woodrow Wilson Jones, CJ; James B. McMillan; Clerk's Office, Asheville 28802.

North Dakota — Paul Benson, CJ; Bruce M. Van Sickle; Clerk's Office, Bismarck 58501.

Ohio — Northern: Frank J. Battisti, CJ; Ben C. Green, Don J. Young, William K. Thomas, Thomas D. Lambros, Robert B. Krupansky, Nicholas J. Walinski, Leroy J. Contie Jr.; Clerk's Office, Cleveland 44114. **Southern:** Joseph P. Kinneary, CJ; Timothy S. Hogan, Davis S. Porter, Carl B. Rubin; Clerk's Office, Columbus 43215.

Oklahoma — Northern: Allen E. Barrow, CJ; Luther L. Bohanon, Frederick A. Daugherty; Clerk's Office, Tulsa 74103. **Eastern:** Frederick A. Daugherty, CJ; Luther L. Bohanon; Clerk's Office, Muskogee 74402. **Western:** Frederick A. Daugherty, CJ; Luther L. Bohanon, Stephen S. Chandler, Luther B. Eubanks; Clerk's Office, Oklahoma City 73102.

Oregon — Robert C. Belloni, CJ; James M. Burns, Otto R. Skopil Jr.; Clerk's Office, Portland 97207.

Pennsylvania — Eastern: John S. Lord 3d, CJ; Alfred L. Luongo, John Morgan Davis, A. Leon Higginbotham Jr.,

John P. Fullam, Charles R. Weiner, E. Mac Troutman, John B. Hannum, Daniel H. Huyett 3d, Donald W. VanArtsdalen, J. William Ditter Jr., Edward R. Becker, James H. Gorbey, Raymond J. Broderick, Clarence C. Newcomer, Clifford Scott Green, Louis Charles Bechtle, Herbert A. Fogel. Clerk's Office, Philadelphia 19107. **Middle:** Michael H. Sheridan, CJ; William J. Nealon Jr., R. Dixon Herman, Malcolm Muir; Clerk's Office, Scranton 18501. **Western:** Rabe Ferguson Marsh, CJ; Herbert P. Sorg, Edward Dumbauld, Louis Rosenberg, Gerald, J. Weber, William W. Knox, Hubert I. Teitelbaum, Barron P. McCune, Ralph F. Scalera; Clerk's Office, Pittsburgh 15230.

Rhode Island — Raymond J. Pettine, CJ; Edward William Day; Clerk's Office, Providence 02901.

South Carolina — J. Robert Martin Jr., CJ; Robert W. Hemphill, Charles E. Simons Jr., Solomon Blatt Jr., Robert F. Chapman; Clerk's Office, Columbia 29202.

South Dakota — Fred J. Nichol, CJ; Andrew W. Bogue; Clerk's Office, Sioux Falls 57102.

Tennessee — Eastern: Frank W. Wilson, CJ; Robert L. Taylor, C. G. Neese; Clerk's Office, Knoxville 37901. **Middle:** Frank Gray Jr., CJ; L. Clure Morton; Clerk's Office, Nashville 37203. **Western:** Bailey Brown, CJ; Robert M. McRae Jr., Harry W. Wellford; Clerk's Office, Memphis 38103.

Texas — Northern: William M. Taylor Jr., CJ; Sarah T. Hughes, Halbert O. Woodward, Eldon B. Mahon, Robert M. Hill; Clerk's Office, Dallas 75202. **Southern:** Ben C. Connally, CJ; Allen B. Hannay, Reynaldo G. Garza, James Noel Jr., John V. Singleton Jr., Woodrow B. Seals, Carl O. Bue Jr., Owen D. Cox; Clerk's Office, Houston 77061. **Eastern:** Joe J. Fisher, CJ; William Wayne Justice, William M. Steger; Clerk's Office, Beaumont 77704. **Western:** Adrian A. Spears, CJ; Dorwin W. Suttle, Jack Roberts, Ernest Guinn, John H. Wood Jr.; Clerk's Office, San Antonio 78298.

Utah — Willis W. Ritter, CJ; Aldon J. Anderson; Clerk's Office, Salt Lake City 84101.

Vermont — James S. Holden, CJ; Albert W. Coffrin; Clerk's Office, Burlington 05401.

Virginia — Eastern: Richard B. Kellam, CJ; Walter E. Hoffman, Robert R. Merhige Jr., John A. MacKenzie, Albert V. Bryan Jr.; Clerk's Office, Norfolk 23501. **Western:** James C. Turk, CJ; Ted Dalton; Clerk's Office, Roanoke 24006.

Washington — Eastern: Marshall A. Neill, CJ; William N. Goodwin; Clerk's Office, Spokane 99210. **Western:** William N. Goodwin, CJ; Walter T. McGovern, Morell E. Sharp; Clerk's Office, Seattle 98104.

West Virginia — Northern: Robert Earl Maxwell, CJ; Sidney L. Christie; Clerk's Office, Elkins 26241. **Southern:** Dennis Raymond Knapp, CJ; Sidney L. Christie, Kenneth K. Hall; Clerk's Office, Charleston 25329.

Wisconsin — Eastern: John W. Reynolds, CJ; Myron L. Gordon; Clerk's Office, Milwaukee 53202. **Western:** James E. Doyle; Clerk's Office, Madison 53701.

Wyoming — Ewing T. Kerr; Clerk's Office, Cheyenne 82001.

Territorial Courts

Canal Zone — Guthrie F. Crowe; Clerk's Office, Ancon.

Guam — Cristobal C. Duenas; Clerk's Office, Agana, 96910.

Puerto Rico — Jose Toledo, CJ; Hernan G. Pesquera; Clerk's Office, San Juan 00904.

Virgin Islands — Almeric L. Christian, CJ; Warren H. Young; Clerk's Office, Charlotte Amalie, St. Thomas 00801.

The Federal Judicial System

The federal judicial system begins with the District Court. There are 94 of these courts, at least one in each state and Washington, D.C. Called courts of general jurisdiction, they have power to determine the facts and pass judgment in criminal cases involving violations of federal law and in civil cases where the amount of the suit is $10,000 or more and the contending parties reside in different states. Other types of cases handled by District Courts include suits in admiralty (maritime matters involving navigational waters), bankruptcy, patents, trademarks and copyrights.

Equal to the District Courts are special courts which handle only certain issues: the U.S. Customs Court, the Tax Court, and the Court of Claims, which hears suits against the U.S. government.

These trial courts are responsible for finding the facts in a case and for applying the law to the facts found. Appellate courts, theoretically, do not review the trial court's findings of fact. The job of the appellate court is to decide whether the trial judge applied the law properly. If an appellate court decides that there was error in the application of the law, it can simply reverse the lower court's decision and end the case there. But it can also send the case back to the lower court for retrial or for other proceedings that may be appropriate.

The District Courts and special courts are trial courts. Above them are several levels of appellate courts. The U.S. Court of Appeals, often called circuit courts, sits in 10 judicial circuits and Washington, D.C. It hears appeals from the District Courts and the Tax Court, and will review decisions of federal administrative agencies if it appears that such decisions may be unreasonable or arbitrary. The U.S. Court of Customs and Patent Appeals hears appeals from the Customs Court.

Ultimately, all decisions of these courts can be reviewed by the U.S. Supreme Court, which is also the first court of appeal from the U.S. Court of Claims. Besides reviewing federal court decisions, the Supreme Court is empowered to hear suits between the states and to review state supreme court decisions if an issue of federal law or the Constitution is involved.

National Political Committees

As of May, 1974

Democratic Officers

Chairman—Robert S. Strauss.
Vice Chairmen—Basil Paterson, Caroline Wilkins.
Secretary—Dorothy V. Bush.
Treasurer—C. Peter McColough.
National Headquarters—1625 Massachusetts Ave., N.W., Washington, D.C. 20036.

Republican Officers

Chairman—George Bush.
Co-Chairman—Mrs. Mary Louise Smith.
Vice Chairmen—Ray C. Bliss, Mrs. Hope McCormick, Bernard M. Shanley, Mrs. J. William Marriott, Robert J. Shaw, Mrs. Paula F. Hawkins, George P. Stadelman, Mrs. Isabel C. Moberly.
Secretary—Mrs. Estelle Stacy Carrier.
Treasurer—O. C. Carmichael, Jr.
General Council—Harry S. Dent.
National Headquarters—310 First St., S.E., Washington, D.C. 20003.

Members of the Democratic National Committee

(as of June, 1974. * indicates state chairman)

Alabama
Albert Rains, Gadsden
Ruth Johnson Owens, Birmingham
*Robert S. Vance, Birmingham
Dot Little, Huntsville

Alaska
Clifford E. Warren, Anchorage
Bettye Fahrenkamp, Fairbanks
*Mellie Terwilliger, Tok
Dr. Alan Homay, Anchorage

Arizona
Sam Goddard, Phoenix
Ora DeConcini, Tucson
*Charles Pine, Phoenix
Barbara Jarvis, Globe

Arkansas
Charles Ward, Conway
Mrs. Jack Carnes, Camden
*Brad Jesson, Fort Smith
Nancy Balton, Osceola

California
*John Burton, Sacramento
Shirley Goldinger, Los Angeles
Ms. Wallace Albertson, Los Angeles
Wyanne Bunyan, Mill Valley
Mary Ledesma, Huntington Pk.
Jo Seidita, Northridge
Madeleine Russell, San Francisco
Richard Chavez, Keene
Dorman Commons, Fullerton
Leon Ralph, Sacramento
Marvin Shapiro, Los Angeles
Al Villa, Fresno

Colorado
Arnold Alperstein, Lakewood
Doris Banks, Denver
*Monte Pascoe, Denver
Betty Orten, Westminister

Connecticut
John Golden, New Haven
Beatrice Rosentha, Waterford
*John M. Bailey, Hartford
Katherine T. Quinn, Hartford
John J. Driscoll, Bridgeport

Delaware
Edward Davis, Wilmington
Rebecca Twilley, Dover
*Ernest Killen, Harrington
Gertrude Tharp, Lewes

District of Columbia
John Hechinger, Washington
Lillian Huff, Washington
*William Lucy, Washington
Barbara Morgan, Washington

Florida
Dr. T. Wayne Bailey, DeLand
Hazel Talley Evans, St. Petersburg
*Jon C. Moyle, W. Palm Beach
Ann M. Cramer, Miramar
Gov. Reubin Askew, Tallahassee
Norman Bie, Clearwater

Georgia
Carlton Hicks, Brunswick

Mayor Mary Hitt, Jesup
*Charles Kirbo, Atlanta
Connie Plunkett, Carrollton
Herbert Mabry, Atlanta

Hawaii
Leo B. Rodby, Wahiawa
Momi Minn Lee, Honolulu
*Minoru Hirabara, Kunia
Matilda Molina, Honolulu

Idaho
James Donart, Weiser
Carolyn Selander, Boise
*Howard Humphrey, Boise
Ms. Ione Rambeau, Lewiston

Illinois
*John P. Touhy, Chicago
S. Jeanne Wycoff, Aledo
Jane Byrne, Chicago
Margaret Gordon, Chicago
John Karns, Jr., Belleville
Cecil Partee, Chicago
John Rednour, Duquoin
Penny Lee Severns, Decatur

Indiana
Richard Stoner, Columbus
Katie Wolf, Reynolds
*Bill Trisler, Indianapolis
Judy Burton, Rochester
Rozelle Boyd, Indianapolis

Iowa
Robert D. Fulton, Waterloo
Dagmar Vidal, Hampton
*Tom Whitney, Des Moines
Jean Haugland, Lake Mills

Kansas
Tom Corcoran, Topeka
Nell Blangers, Salina
*Norbert Dreiling, Hays
Mary Allen, Topeka

Kentucky
Gov. Wendell Ford, Frankfort
Martha Layne Collins, Versailles
*William R. Sullivan, Frankfort
Marie Turner, Jackson

Louisiana
Leon Irwin III, New Orleans
Mary Lou Winters, Columbia
Phyllis Landrieu, New Orleans

Maine
George Mitchell, S. Portland
Nancy Chandler, South China
*Violet Pease, Augusta
David Bustin, Augusta

Maryland
Thomas Farrington, Upper Marlboro
Dr. Mildred Otenasek, Baltimore
*William James, Bel Air
Mrs. Lyn Clark, Kensington
Clarence Blount, Baltimore

Massachusetts
Jerome Grossman, Newton
Helen Rees, Brookline
*Charles Flatherty, Cambridge

Eva B. Hester, Clinton
Doris Kanin, Arlington
Dr. Jesse Parks, Springfield

Michigan
Coleman Young, Detroit
Helen Irving, Detroit
*Morley Winograd, Lansing
Olivia Maynard, Flint
Sam Fishman, Detroit
Neil Staebler, Ann Arbor
Shirley Robinson, Detroit

Minnesota
Earl Craig, Minneapolis
Koryne Horbal, Minneapolis
*Henry Fischer, Minneapolis
Ruth Cain, Minneapolis
Ann Ober, Lake Crystal

Mississippi
Charles Evers, Fayette
Patt Derian, Jackson
*Aaron Henry, Clarksdale
Kathleen Feyen, Greenwood

Missouri
Warren Hearnes, Charleston
Jean Briscoe, New London
*David Donnelly, Jefferson City
Ina Shaffrey, St. Louis
Kermit Lewis, Neosho

Montana
Leif Erickson, Helena
Gladys Makela, Helena
*John Bartlett, Whitefish
Ruth Carrington, Hysham

Nebraska
Thomas Kelley, Omaha
Frances Ohmstede, Guide Rock
*Richard White, Lincoln
Dorothy Ley, Wayne

Nevada
Grant Sawyer, Las Vegas
Virginia Catt, Las Vegas
*Phil Carlino, Las Vegas
Mrs. Didi Carson, Las Vegas

New Hampshire
Hugh Gallen, Littleton
Maria Carrier, Manchester
*David LaRoche, Manchester
Eileen Gonthier, Grasmere

New Jersey
Don Lan, Springfield
*James Dugan, Bayonne
Ann Campbell, Trenton
Anne Martindell, Princeton
Richard I. Samuel, Westfjeld
Nicholas Caputo, Newark

New Mexico
Rudy Ortiz, Albuquerque
Mrs. U. D. Sawyer, Crossroads
*Mike Anaya, Moriarty
Consuelo Kitzes, Santa Fe

New York
Basil Paterson, New York
Jean Angell, Ithaca
*Joseph Crangle, Buffalo

Mae Gurevich, New York
Patrick Cunningham, Bronx
Daniel Collins, Brooklyn
Lucille King, Rochester
Margaret Costanza, Rochester
Theodora Martinez, Brooklyn
Dominic Baranello, Medford
Robert Dryfoos, New York
Allard Lowenstein, Brooklyn

North Carolina
Dr. Engene Poston, Boiling Springs
Gladys Bullard, Raleigh
*James Sugg, Raleigh
Alfreda Webb, Greensboro
Howard Lee, Chapel Hill

North Dakota
Gorman King, Valley City
Bea Peterson, New England
*Richard Ista, Fargo
Florence Olson, Enderlin

Ohio
Joseph Cole, Cleveland
Carole McClendon, Cleveland
*William Lavelle, Athens
Esther Mayl, Kettering
Robert McAlister, Columbus
Ann Fleckner, Columbus
Doris Rankin, Cincinnati
Sen. Morris Jackson, Cleveland

Oklahoma
J. C. Cobb, Tishomingo
Edna Mae Phelps, Seminole
*Guy Thompson, Oklahoma City
Mrs. Lorray Dyson, Guthrie

Oregon
Blaine Whipple, Portland
Alice Corbett, Portland
*Caroline Wilkins, Corvallis
Dr. John Meyer, Canyonville

Pennsylvania
Robert Jones, Scranton
Rita Wilson Kane, Pittsburgh
*Dennis Thiemann, Harrisburg
C. Delores Tucker, Harrisburg
George Schwartz, Philadelphia
Michael Johnson, Harrisburg
Ann Jordan, Philadelphia
Barbara Altemus, Bethlehem
James Kelley, Greensburg

Rhode Island
Milton Stanzler, Providence
Mildred Nichols, Providence
*Charles T. Reilly, Barrington
Mary Whalen, Warwick

South Carolina
Robert McNair, Columbia
Barbara Sylvester, Florence
*Donald Fowler, Columbia
Alice Cicenia, Summerville

South Dakota
Frank Wallahan, Rapid City
Mary Wallner, Sioux Falls
*Charles Bellman, Pierre
Beverly Bruce, Mitchell

Tennessee
D. Bruce Shine, Kingsport
Jean Livingston, Chattanooga
*James R. Sasser, Nashville
Mrs. Claude Dodd, Ridgely

Texas
Jess Hay, Dallas
Jane Blumberg, Seguin
*Calvin Guest, Bryan
Barbara Jordan, Houston
Ms. Billie Carr, Houston
Hall Timanus, Houston
Joe J. Bernal, San Antonio

Utah
Wayne Black, Salt Lake City

Jean Westwood, West Jordan
*John Klas, Salt Lake City
Marion Peterson, Sahna

Vermont
Daniel O'Brien, S. Burlington
Margaret Hartigan, Burlington
*Phillip Hoff, Burlington
Margaret Lucenti, Barre

Virginia
George Rawlings Jr.,
  Fredericksburg
Ruth Harvey Charity, Danville
*Joseph Fitzpatrick, Norfolk
Jessie Rattley, Newport News
W. Pat Jennings, Washington, D.C.

Washington
Luke Graham, Seattle
Claudine Davis, Coulee City
*Neale Chaney, Seattle
Gladys Morgen, Spokane
Ed Claplanhoo, Neah Bay

West Virginia
Rudolph DiTrapano, Charleston
JoAnne Powell, Romney
*J. C. Dillon, Charleston
Jean Bailey, Pineville

Wisconsin
Donald Peterson, Eau Claire
Mary Lou Burg, Arlington, Va.
*M. William Gerrard, LaCrosse
Marge Pattison, Madison
Michael Bleicher, Madison

Wyoming
Jerry Housel, Cody
June Boyle, Laramie
*Don Anselmi, Rock Springs
Mariko Miller, Casper

Members of the Republican National Committee
(as of June, 1974. * indicates state chairman)

Alabama
Perry O. Hooper, Montgomery
Mrs. Jean Sullivan, Selma
*J. Richard (Dick) Bennett Jr.,
  Birmingham

Alaska
Eldon R. Ulmer, Anchorage
Mrs. John Holm, Fairbanks
*John B. (Jack) Coghill, Nenana

Arizona
John H. Haugh, Tucson
Mrs. William Crisp, Scottsdale
*Harry Rosenzweig, Phoenix

Arkansas
Odell Pollard, Searcy
Mrs. Leona A. Troxell, Rose Bud
*Jim Caldwell, Little Rock

California
William S. Banowsky, Malibu
Miss Janet Johnston, Winters
*Gordon Luce, San Diego

Colorado
Bill Daniels, Denver
Mrs. Daniel Gray, Denver
*Dwight A. Hamilton, Denver

Connecticut
John Alsop, Hartford
Mrs. Mary H. Boatwright,
  Stonington
*J. Brian Gaffney, Hartford

Delaware
Thomas B. Evans Jr., Wilmington
Mrs. Bruce F. Day, Wilmington
*Herman Brown, Dover

District of Columbia
Robert S. Carter, D.C.
Mrs. J. Willard Marriott, D.C.
*Edmond E. Pendleton, D.C.

Florida
William C. Cramer, Miami
Mrs. Paula F. Hawkins, Maitland

*L. E. Thomas, Panama City

Georgia
Nolan Murrah, Jr., Columbus
Mrs. Nora Allen, Albany
*Robert J. Shaw, Atlanta

Hawaii
Edward Brennan, Honolulu
Mrs. Kinau Boyd Kamalii,
  Honolulu
*Mrs. Max S. Coray, Honolulu

Idaho
David Little, Emmett
Mrs. Orriette Sinclair, Twin Falls
*Mrs. Gordon Miner, Wallace

Illinois
Cliffard D. Carlson, Geneva
Mrs. Hope McCormick, Chicago
*Don Adams, Springfield

Indiana
L. Keith Bulen, Indianapolis
Mrs. Nat Hill, Bloomington
*Thomas S. Milligan, Indianapolis

Iowa
Charles E. Wittenmeyer, Davenport
Mrs. Elmer M. Smith, Des Moines
*John C. McDonald, Des Moines

Kansas
McDill Boyd, Phillipsburg
Mrs. Richard D. Rogers, Manhattan
*Jack Ranson, Wichita

Kentucky
Edwin G. Middleton, Louisville
*Mrs. Harold B. Barton, Corbin
*Charles R. Coy, Richmond

Louisiana
John H. Cade, Jr., Alexandria
*Patricia Lindh, Baton Rouge
*James H. Boyce, Baton Rouge

Maine
Cyril M. Joly Jr., Waterville
*Mrs. Henrietta Page Crane,
  Rockland
*Harold L. Jones, Augusta

Maryland
Richard M. Allen, Salisbury
Miss Louise Gore, Potomac
*Edward P. Thomas Jr., Baltimore

Massachusetts
Bruce Crane, Dalton
Mrs. Henry Dunster Howe,
  Belmont
*William A. Barnstead, Allston

Michigan
Creighton Holden, St. Clair
Mrs. John Riecker, Midland
*William F. McLaughlin, Lansing

Minnesota
Rudy Boschwitz, Minneapolis
Mrs. Harold LeVander,
  So. St. Paul
*Robert J. Brown, St. Paul

Mississippi
Victor Mavar, Biloxi
Mrs. James F. Hooper, Columbus
*Clarke Reed, Greenville

Missouri
Lawrence K. Roos, Clayton
Mrs. M. Stanley Ginn, Columbia
*Albert L. Rendlen, Hannibal

Montana
William R. Mackay, Roscoe
Mrs. Isabel C. Moberly, Shelby
*Kenneth R. Neill, Great Falls

Nebraska
R. L. "Dick" Herman, Omaha
Mrs. Richard W. Smith, Lincoln
*William E. Barrett, Lexington

Nevada
William M. Laub, Las Vegas
Mrs. Marvin B. Humphrey, Reno

*Walter P. Casey, Jr., Las Vegas
New Hampshire
Robert P. Bass, Jr., Concord
Miss Victoria Zachos, Concord
*David Gosselin, Concord
New Jersey
Bernard M. Shanley,
Newark
Mrs. Katherine K. Neuberger,
Lincroft
*Webster B. Todd, Trenton
New Mexico
Robert C. Davidson, Albuquerque
Mrs. Edward J. Neff, Albuquerque
*Murray Ryan, Silver City
New York
George L. Hinman, New York
Mrs. Keith S. McHugh, New York
*Richard M. Rosenbaum, Albany
North Carolina
J.E. Broyhill, Lenoir
Mrs. Louis G. Rogers, Charlotte
*Thomas S. Bennett, Raleigh
North Dakota
Ben J. Clayburgh, Grand Forks
Mrs. Gerridee Wheeler, Bismarck
*Allan C. Young, Devils Lake
Ohio
Ray C. Bliss, Akron
Miss Martha C. Moore, Cambridge
*Kent B. McGough, Columbus
Oklahoma
Skip Healey, Davis

Mrs. Grace Boulton, Okla. City
*Clarence E. Warner, Okla. City
Oregon
George P. Stadelman, The Dalles
Mrs. Collis P. Moore, Moro
*Dave Green, Madras
Pennsylvania
Thomas B. McCabe, Philadelphia
Miss Sarah Ann Stauffer,
Lancaster County
*Richard C. Frame, Harrisburg
Rhode Island
Frederick Lippitt, Providence
Mrs. Donald T. Gibbs, Middletown
*Thomas E. (Tucker) Wright,
Providence
South Carolina
Hal C. Boyd, Spartanburg
Dr. Inez C. Eddings, Columbia
*Jesse Cooksey, Spartanburg
South Dakota
William Lenker, Sioux Falls
Mrs. Nora Hussey, Sturgis
*E. Steeves Smith, Mitchell
Tennessee
George E. Wilson Jr., Harriman
Mrs. Keith McCauley Spurrier,
Memphis
*S. L. (Kopie) Kopald Jr., Memphis
Texas
Fred Agnich, Dallas
Mrs. Richard D. Bass, Dallas
*Jack Warren, Tyler

Utah
Dr. Ernest L. Wilkinson, Provo
Mrs. Myrene Rich Brewer, Ogden
*T. William Cockayne, Salt Lake City
Vermont
Roland Q. Seward Sr.,
E. Wallingford
Mrs. Madeline Harwood,
Manchester
*Stewart A. Smith, Rutland
Virginia
William H. Stanhagan, Falls Church
Mrs. Cynthia S. Newman, Falls
Church
*Richard D. Obenshain, Richmond
Washington
Kenneth R. Nuckolls, Bellingham
Mrs. Naida Pithoud, Vancouver
*Ross E. Davis, Tukwila
West Virginia
Arch A. Moore Jr., Charleston
Mrs. Irvin Humphreys, Huntington
*Thomas E. Potter, Charleston
Wisconsin
Ody J. Fish, Hartland
Mrs. John Pfeifer, Green Bay
*David C. Sullivan, Milwaukee
Wyoming
Robert F. Gosman, Casper
Mrs. Estelle Stacy Carrier, Douglas
*Jack Speight, Cheyenne

Other Major Political Organizations

American Party
(PO Box 1098, Pigeon Forge, Tenn. 37863)
Chairman—Thomas J. Anderson.
Americans For Democratic Action
(1424 16th St., N.W., Washington, D. C. 20036)
National Chairman—Donald Frasher
National Director—Leon Shull
Chairman Exec. Comm.—Cushing Dolbeare
Comm. on Political Education, AFL-CIO
(AFL-CIO Building, 815 16th St., Wash., D.C. 20006)
Chairman—George Meany
Secretary-Treasurer—Lane Kirkland
National Director—Alexander E. Barkan
Conservative Party of the State of N.Y.
(468 ark Ave. So., New York, N.Y. 10016)
Chairman—J. Daniel Mahoney
Secretary—Henry S. Jorin Jr.
Liberal Party of New York State
(1560 Broadway, New York, N.Y. 10036)
Chairman—Donald S. Harrington
First Vice Chairman—David Dubinsky
Secretary & Exec. Director—Ben Davidson
Treasurer—William W. Cowan

National States' Rights Party
(P.O. Box 1211, Marietta, Ga. 30061)
Chairman—J. B. Stoner
Secretary—Edward R. Fields
Treasurer—Peter Xavier

Prohibition National Committee
(P. O. Box 2635, Denver, Colo. 80201)
National Chairman—Charles Wesley Ewing
Executive Secretary—Earl F. Dodge
National Secretary—Roger C. Storms

Social Democrats, U.S.A.
(1182 Broadway, New York, N.Y. 10001)
National Chairmen—Bayard Rustin, Charles S. Zimmerman
Honorary Chairmen—Darlington Hoopes, A. Philip Randolph
National Secretary—Joan Suall

Socialist Labor Party
In Minnesota: Industrial Gov't. Party
(116 Nassau St., Brooklyn, N.Y. 11201)
National Secretary—Nathan Karp

Socialist Workers Party
(14 Charles Lane, New York, N.Y.10014)
National Chairman Emeritus—James P. Cannon
National Secretary—Jack Barnes
Organization Secretary—Barry Sheppard

America's Third Parties

Since 1860, there have been only 4 presidential elections in which all third parties together polled more than 10% of the vote: the Populists (James Baird Weaver) in 1892, the National Progressives (Theodore Roosevelt) in 1912, the La Follette Progressives in 1924, and George Wallace's American Party in 1968. In 1948, the combined third parties (Henry Wallace's Progressives, Strom Thurmond's States Rights party or Dixiecrats, Prohibition, Socialists, and others) received only 5.75% of the vote. In most elections since 1860, fewer than one vote in 20 has been cast for a third party. The only successful third party in American history was the Republican party in the election of Abraham Lincoln in 1860.

Major Third Parties

Party		Election	Issues	Strength in
Anti-Masonic	Wm. Wirt	1832	Against secret societies and oaths	Pennsylvania Vermont
Free Soil	Martin Van Buren	1848	Anti-slavery	New York, Ohio
American (Know Nothing)	Millard Fillmore	1856	Anti-immigrant	Northeast, South
Greenback	Peter Cooper, James B. Weaver	1876 1880	For "cheap money", labor rights	National
Prohibition	(numerous)	1872—	Anti-liquor	National
Populist	James B. Weaver	1892	For "cheap money", end of national banks	South, West
Socialists	Eugene Debs, Norman Thomas	1900—	For public ownership	National
Progressive (Bull Moose)	Theo. Roosevelt	1912	Against high tariffs	Midwest, West
Progressive	Robt. LaFollette	1924	Farmer & labor rights	Midwest, West
States Rights	Strom Thurmond	1948	For segregation	South
Progressive	Henry Wallace	1948	Anti-Cold War	New York, California
American	George Wallace	1968	For states' rights	South

Speakers of the House of Representatives

Party designations: A, American; D, Democratic; DR, Democratic Republican; F, Federalist; R, Republican; W, Whig. *Served only one day.

Name	Party, State	Tenure	Name	Party, State	Tenure
Frederick A. C. Muhlenberg	F, Pa.	1789-1791	Galusha A. Grow	R, Pa.	1861-1863
Jonathan Trumbull	F, Conn.	1791-1793	Schuyler Colfax	R, Ind.	1863-1869
Frederick A. C. Muhlenberg	F, Pa.	1793-1795	*Theodore M. Pomeroy	R, N. Y.	1869-1869
Jonathan Dayton	F, N. J.	1795-1799	James G. Blaine	R, Me.	1869-1875
Theodore Sedgwick	F, Mass.	1799-1801	Michael C. Kerr	D, Ind.	1875-1876
Nathaniel Macon	DR, N. C.	1801-1807	Samuel J. Randall	D, Pa.	1876-1881
Joseph B. Varnum	DR, Mass.	1807-1811	Joseph W. Keifer	R, Ohio	1881-1883
Henry Clay	DR, Ky.	1811-1814	John G. Carlisle	D, Ky.	1883-1889
Langdon Cheves	DR, S. C.	1814-1815	Thomas B. Reed	R, Me.	1889-1891
Henry Clay	DR, Ky.	1815-1820	Charles F. Crisp	D, Ga.	1891-1895
John W. Taylor	DR, N. Y.	1820-1821	Thomas B. Reed	R, Me.	1895-1899
Philip P. Barbour	DR, Va.	1821-1823	David B. Henderson	R, Iowa	1899-1903
Henry Clay	DR, Ky.	1823-1825	Joseph G. Cannon	R, Ill.	1903-1911
John W. Taylor	D, N. Y.	1825-1827	Champ Clark	D, Mo.	1911-1919
Andrew Stevenson	D, Va.	1827-1834	Frederick H. Gillett	R, Mass.	1919-1925
John Bell	D, Tenn.	1834-1835	Nicholas Longworth	R, Ohio	1925-1931
James K. Polk	D, Tenn.	1835-1839	John N. Garner	D, Tex.	1931-1933
Robert M. T. Hunter	D, Va.	1839-1841	Henry T. Rainey	D, Ill.	1933-1935
John White	W, Ky.	1841-1843	Joseph W. Byrns	D, Tenn.	1935-1936
John W. Jones	D, Va.	1843-1845	William B. Bankhead	D, Ala.	1936-1940
John W. Davis	D, Ind.	1845-1847	Sam Rayburn	D, Tex.	1940-1947
Robert C. Winthrop	W, Mass.	1847-1849	Joseph W. Martin, Jr.	R, Mass.	1947-1949
Howell Cobb	D, Ga.	1849-1851	Sam Rayburn	D, Tex.	1949-1953
Linn Boyd	D, Ky.	1851-1855	Joseph W. Martin, Jr.	R, Mass.	1953-1955
Nathaniel P. Banks	A, Mass.	1856-1857	Sam Rayburn	D, Tex.	1955-1961
James L. Orr	D, S. C.	1857-1859	John W. McCormack	D, Mass.	1962-1971
William Pennington	R, N. J.	1860-1861	Carl Albert	D, Okla.	1971-

The Electoral College

The President and the Vice President of the United States are the only elective Federal officials not elected by direct vote of the people. They are elected by the members of the Electoral College, an institution that has survived since the founding of the nation despite repeated attempts in Congress to alter or abolish it. In the elections of 1824, 1876 and 1888 the Presidential candidate receiving the largest popular vote failed to win a majority of the electoral votes.

On Presidential election day, the first Tuesday after the first Monday in November of every fourth year, each state chooses as many electors as it has Senators and Representatives in Congress. In 1964 for the first time, as provided by the 23rd Amendment to the Constitution, the District of Columbia voted for 3 electors. Thus, with 100 Senators and 435 Representatives, there are 538 members of the Electoral College, with a majority of 270 electoral votes needed to elect the President and Vice President.

Political parties customarily nominate their lists of electors at their respective state conventions. An elector cannot be a member of Congress or any person holding Federal office.

Some states print the names of the candidates for President and Vice President at the top of the ballot while others list only the namews of the electors. In either case, the electors of the party receiving the highest vote are elected. The electors will meet on the first Monday after the second Wednesday in December in their respective state capitals or in some other place prescribed by State Legislatures. By long-established custom they vote for their party nominee, thus giving all the state's electoral votes to him, although the Constitution does not require them to do so. The only constitutional requirement is that at least one of the persons each elector votes for shall not be an inhabitant of that elector's home state.

Certified and sealed lists of the votes of the electors in each state are mailed to the President of the U. S. Senate. He opens them in the presence of the members of the Senate and House of Representatives in a joint session held on Jan. 6 (the next day if that falls on a Sunday), and the electoral votes of all the states are then counted. If no candidate for President has a majority, the House of Representatives chooses a President from among the three highest candidates, with all Representatives from each state combining to cast one vote for that state. If no candidate for Vice President has a majority, the Senate chooses from the top two, Senators voting as individuals.

United States Government Independent Agencies

Source: General Services Administration

Address: Washington, D. C. Location and zip codes of agencies in parentheses, as of May 20, 1974.

ACTION — Director: Michael P. Balzano Jr. (806 Connecticut Ave. NW, 20525).

Administrative Conference of the United States — Chmn. Antonin Scalia (2120 L St. NW, 20037).

American Battle Monuments Commission — Chmn. Mark Clark (2067 Tempo A, 20315).

Appalachian Regional Commission — Federal Cochairman: Donald W. Whitehead; state co-chairman: Gov. John C. West (1666 Connecticut Ave. NW, 20235).

Arms Control & Disarmament Agency — Director: Fred C. Ikle (Department of State Bldg., 20451).

Atomic Energy Commission — Dixy Lee Ray, chmn.; William A. Anders, William E. Kriegsman, Clarence E. Larson, William O. Doub (Wash., D.C. 20545).

Central Intelligence Agency — William Colby, director (Wash., D.C. 20505).

Civil Aeronautics Board — Chmn.: Robert D. Timm (1825 Connecticut Ave. NW, 20428).

Civil Service Commission — Robert E. Hampton, chmn.; Jayne B. Spain, vice chmn., (1900 E St. NW, 20415).

Commission On Civil Rights — Chmn.: Arthur S. Flemming (1121 Vermont Ave. NW, 20425).

Commission of Fine Arts — J. Carter Brown, chmn. (708 Jackson Pl. NW, 20006).

Environmental Protection Agency — Administrator: Russell E. Train (410 M St. SW, 20460).

Equal Employment Opportunity Commission — John H. Powell Jr., chmn. (1800 G St. NW, 20506).

Export-Import Bank of the United States — William J. Casey, pres. and chmn. (811 Vermont Ave. NW, 20571).

Farm Credit Administration — T. Carroll Atkinson, chmn. (490 L'Enfant Plaza West SW).

Federal Communications Commission — Commissioners: Richard Wiley, chmn.; Charlotte T. Reid, Robert E. Lee, Benjamin L. Hooks, 3 vacancies (1919 M St. NW, 20554).

Federal Deposit Insurance Corporation — Chairman: Frank Wille (550 17th St. NW, 20429).

Federal Home Loan Bank Board — Chairman: Thomas R. Bomar (101 Indiana Ave. NW, 20552).

Federal Maritime Commission — Helen D. Bentley, chmn. (1100 L St. NW, 20573).

Federal Mediation and Conciliation Service — Director: W. J. Usery (Dept. of Labor Bldg., 20427).

Federal Power Commission — John N. Nassikas, chmn.; Don S. Smith, vice chmn. (825 N. Capital St. NW, 20426).

Federal Reserve System — Chairman, board of governors: Arthur F. Burns (20th St. and Constitution Ave. NW, 20551).

Federal Trade Commission — Commissioners: Lewis A. Engman, chmn.; Paul Rand Dixon, Mayo J. Thompson, M. Elizabeth Hanford, vacancy (Pennsylvania Ave. at 6th St. NW).

Foreign Claims Settlement Comm. of the U. S. — J. Raymond Bell, chmn. (1111 20th St. NW, 20579).

General Accounting Office — Comptroller general of the U. S. Elmer B. Staats (441 G St. NW, 20548).

General Services Administration — Administrator: Arthur F. Sampson (18th and F Sts. NW, 20405).

Government Printing Office — Public printer: Thomas F. McCormick (North Capitol and H Sts. NW, 20401).

Indian Claims Commission — Jerome K. Kuykendall, chmn. (1730 K St. NW, 20006).

Inter-American Foundation — Chmn.: Augustin S. Hart Jr. (1515 Wilson Blvd., Rosslyn, Va. 22209).

Interstate Commerce Commission — Commissioners: George M. Stafford, chmn.; Willard Deason, Kenneth H. Tuggle, Rupert L. Murphy, Dale Hardin, Virginia Mae Brown, W. Donald Brewer, Robert C. Gresham, Charles L. Clapp, Alfred T. MacFarland, A. Daniel O'Neal (12th St. and Constitution Ave. NW, 20423).

Library of Congress — L. Quincy Mumford, Librarian (10 First St. SE, 20540).

National Academy of Sciences — **National Academy of Engineering** — **National Research Council** — **Institute of Medicine** — President: Philip Handler (2101 Constitution Ave. NW, 20418).

National Aeronautics and Space Administration — Administrator: James C. Fletcher (Washington, D. C. 20546).

National Credit Union Administration — Herman Nickerson Jr. administrator (2025 M St. NW, 20456).

National Foundation on the Arts and Humanities — Nancy Hanks, chmn. (arts); Ronald S. Berman, chmn. (humanities) (805 15th St. NW, 20506).

National Labor Relations Board — Chmn.: Edward B. Miller (1717 Pennsylvania Ave. NW, 20570).

National Mediation Board — George S. Ives, chmn. (1230 16th St. NW, 20036).

National Science Foundation — Director: H. Guyford Stever (1800 G St. NW, 20550).

Occupational Safety and Health Review Commission — Chmn.: Robert D. Moran (1825 K St. NW, 20006).

Overseas Private Investment Corporation — President: Marshall T. Mays (1129 20th St. NW, 20527).

Postal Rate Commission — Chairman: Fred B. Rhodes (2000 L St. NW, 20268).

Railroad Retirement Board — Chairman: James L. Cowen (Rm. 444, 425 13th St. NW, 20004), Main Office (844 Rush St., Chicago, Ill. 60611).

Renegotiation Board — Chairman: William S. Whitehead (2000 M St. NW, 20446).

Securities and Exchange Commission — Commissioners: Ray Garrett Jr., chmn.; A.A. Sommer Jr., Irving M. Pollack, Philip Loomis Jr., John R. Evans (500 N. Capitol St., 20549).

Selective Service System — Director: Byron V. Pepitone (1724 F St. NW, 20435).

Small Business Administration — Administrator: Thomas S. Kleppe (1441 L St. NW, 20416).

Smithsonian Institution — S. Dillon Ripley, secretary (1000 Jefferson Drive SW, 20560).

Tariff Commission, United States — Chairman: Catherine Bedell (8th and E Sts. NW, 20436).

Tennessee Valley Authority — Chairman, board of directors: Aubrey J. Wagner (New Sprankle Bldg., Knoxville, Tenn. 37901 and Woodward Bldg., 15th and H Sts. NW, Washington, D.C. 20444).

United States Information Agency — Director: James Keogh (1750 Pennsylvania Ave. NW, 20547).

United States Postal Service — E. T. Klassen, postmaster general (475 L'Enfant Plaza West SW, 20260).

Veterans Administration — Administrator: Donald E. Johnson (Vermont Ave. at H St. NW, 20420).

MEMORABLE DATES

Consult also Chronology, Aviation Records, Polar Explorations, Fast Ocean Passages, Train Records, Marine Disasters, Political Assassinations, Earthquakes, Fires, Tornadoes, Amendments to the Constitution, Noted Personalities, Astronomical Data, Space Exploration, Sporting Records and other classifications.

B. C.

3000

Indus Valley Civilization sites at Mohenjo-Daro and Harappa in West-Pakistan. Civilization had complex form of government, elaborate irrigation and drainage system, writing, well laid out streets, houses of several stories. Ended about **1500 B. C.**

Pyramids begun by kings of Egypt at Sakkara. Cheops built great pyramid at Giza; Chephren second largest. Sphinx built about **2900 B. C.**

c. 1792-1750

Hammurabi ruled Semitic kingdom of Babylon; wrote great code of laws. Ruled Canaan in days of Abraham.

c. 1450 or c. 1275

Moses led the Israelites out of Egypt.

1360

Ikhnaton introduced monotheistic worship of Aten, or sun, in Egypt. A successor, Tutankhamen revived polytheistic orthodoxy **1350 B. C.** Tutankhamen buried at Thebes **1344 B. C.**, tomb opened by Howard Carter and Lord Carnarvon **1923-24 A. D.**

1184

Troy fell to Greeks after 10-year siege, according to Homer. While poem is legendary, numerous battles were waged on site at northwest corner of Asia Minor, three miles from Hellespont (Dardanelles). Later town of Ilium was visited by Xerxes and exploited by Alexander the Great. Romans, glorifying their legendary descent from Aeneas, who escaped from Troy, built up Ilium.

In **1871 A. D.** Heinrich Schliemann, German archaeologist, excavated site of Troy on hill of Hissarlik and found deposits of 7 cities. Dorpfeld found two more. Schliemann identified second city with Homer's Troy, but objects found in sixth city correspond better with Greek remains of **1200 to 1100 B. C.** found at Agamemnon's Mycenae.

1000

On death of King Saul **c. 1000 B. C.** David became king of Israel, but for 7½ years ruled only the southern kingdom of Judah. Thereafter he ruled all Israel, made Jerusalem capital. Solomon, son of David and Bathsheba, ruled **c. 973-933 B. C.**

753

Romulus founded Rome, according to legend.

612

Babylonians destroyed Nineveh, Assyrian capital. Nebuchadnezzar's Babylonians defeated Egyptians at Carchemish **605 B. C.** Built hanging gardens. Destroyed Solomon's temple **589 B. C.**

563

Gautama (Sakyamuni) Buddha, "the Enlightened," born near Himalayas; died **483 B. C.**, aged 80. Taught that pain in life is caused by desire; if desire is overcome, pain ends.

551

Confucius (Latinized form of K'ung-fu-tze) Chinese social philosopher, born; died **478 B. C.**

490

King Darius' Persian army landed at Marathon to march on Athens. Athenian infantry numbering 10,-000 routed 30,000 Persians.

484-480

Persian King Xerxes assembled a great army at Sardis to invade Greece. His Phoenicians and Egyptians built two ship bridges across Hellespont from Abydos (Nagara) to Sestos, 2,000 yards long. One bridge of planks and dirt rested on 360 ships; the other on 314. Herodotus says army crossed for 7 days and 7 nights.

At Thermopylae 480 B.C., Leonidas and 300 Spartans, supported by 700 Thespians and 400 Thebans,

held off Persians in pass until overcome. Persians took Athens and Attica. Athenians under Themistocles destroyed Persian fleet at Salamis under eyes of Xerxes, won land battle. Rallying about 70,000 from Greek states, they routed Persians at Plataea **479 B. C.**

438

Parthenon completed at Athens, 101'4" by 228'2"; Doric columns 33' tall, roof height 60'. Ictinus and Callicrates, designers; Phidias, chief sculptor.

431

Peloponnesian War began between Athens and Sparta. War ended **404 B. C.** with Sparta victorious.

399

Socrates, Greek philosopher, condemned by Athenian state, drank hemlock (dropwort). Plato, his student, recorded 35 dialogues, great philosophical work. Dialogues recommended: Gorgias, Apology, Crito, Phaedo, Republic, Phaedrus, Banquet. Xenophon, another student, recorded memorabilia.

356

Alexander "The Great" of Macedon born. Ruthless and energetic military leader, defeated Persians at Granicus, Issus, Arbela; conquered Asia Mkinor and Egypt, burned Persian capital, Persepolis, carried war to the Punjab. Founder of Alexandria. Died of fever at Babylon **323 B. C.**

300

Invention of Mayan calendar in Yucatan (approximate date) giving solar year 365.24 days and lunar month 29.52 days. Considered more exact than older calendars of Babylon, Assyria, Egypt, Greece.

264

Rome began first Punic War against Carthage, rich commercial seaport on Bay of Tunis. In 241 B. C. Carthage ceded Sicily and Lipari Islands; in 239 B. C. Rome annexed Sardinia and Corsica.

218-146

Hannibal, young Carthaginian, in a campaign against Rome during the second Punic War, crossed from Spain to Italy via the Alps with 20,000 infantry, 6,000 cavalry, and about 40 elephants. Defeated Romans at Lake Trasimene 217 B. C. and Cannae 216 B. C. Victories nullified by Fabius, "the delayer," hence "Fabian retreat." War closed with defeat of Carthage in Africa by Publius Scipio 202 B. C. Hannibal, after career in Asia Minor, committed suicide in Bithynia upon betrayal to Romans, c. 183 B.C.

Third Punic War 149-146 B. C., ended with total destruction of Carthage. Later Roman colony built there; eventually destroyed by Saracens 698 A. D.

60-27

Julius Caesar formed first triumvirate with Pompey and Crassus 60 B. C.; defeated Helvetii, Belgae, 58-57 B. C.; entered Britain 55 and 54 B. C. Crossed river Rubicon to fight Pompey, defeated him at Pharsalus 48 B. C. Defeated Pharnaces at Zela, Asia Minor, 47 B. C., sent "veni, vidi, vici" message; "I came, I saw, I conquered," to Roman Senate. Lived with Cleopatra, queen of Egypt, in Rome 46-44 B. C. Was dictator but refused crown.

Caesar assassinated in Roman Senate by group led by Cassius and Brutus 44 B. C. Caesar's will made his grand-nephew, Gaius Octavius, successor; he formed new triumvirate, Octavius ruling West, Mark Antony East and Lepidus Africa. At Philippi 42 B. C. Antony defeated Cassius and Brutus, both committed suicide. Antony joined Cleopatra in Alexandria; had 3 sons. Octavius defeated their fleet at Actium 31 B. C.; they committed suicide. Octavius received title of Augustus (venerated) 27 B. C., called first Roman emperor. Pax Romana began. Roman advance into northern Europe ended 9 A. D. when Germans under

Arminius defeated Varus. Augustus died **14 A. D.**

4

Birth of Jesus Christ in Bethlehem.

1 B. C. and 1 A. D.

The year **1 B. C.** *is the first year before the beginning of the Christian era. The year* **1 A. D.** *is the first year of the Christian era.* **Jan. 1, 1 B. C.** *is just one year before* **Jan. 1, 1 A. D.** *The elapsed number of years between a date B. C. and the same date A. D. is one less than the sum of the years. The Christian era was calculated by the monk Dionysius Exiguus in the 6th century after Christ. He placed Jesus' birth on* **Dec. 25** *in the year* **753** *of Rome and decided* **754** *should be the first year of the Christian era. Biblical scholars find his calculations in error and place the birth of Jesus in the Roman year* **750** (4 B. C.) *or earlier.*

A. D.
The Christian Era
29

Crucifixion of Jesus in reign of Roman emperor Tiberius; Pontius Pilate procurator in Judea. The Roman Catholic church gives the date of the crucifixion as **April 7, 30 A. D.**

43

Roman Emperor Claudius subdued Britons; occupation of 300 years begun.

64

Persecution of Christians by Nero; burning of Rome. Apostles Paul and Peter martyred c. **67.**

70

Jerusalem destroyed by Titus. Christians persecuted, worship in catacombs of Rome.

79

Pompeii, Herculaneum and Stabii destroyed by eruption of Mt. Vesuvius.

180

Death of Marcus Aurelius; onset of Roman decline.

311

Emperor Galerius, on deathbed, agreed to tolerance of Christians, Emperor Constantine **313** promulgated Edict of Milan, made Christianity legal.

325

Council of Nicaea called by Constantine in Bithynia, Asia Minor, to get churchmen to define orthodox Christian belief. Divinity of Christ and Holy Trinity endorsed; minority view of Arius rejected.

330

Constantine dedicated Byzantium capital of Eastern Empire, henceforth called Constantinople, now Istanbul. Baptized a Christian on his deathbed by Eusebius **337.**

380

Theodosius, Roman emperor, made Christianity based on Nicene creed official religion, banned pagan gods.

410

Rome sacked by Alaric, the Goth; by Genseric, the Vandal, **455.**

432

Bishop Patrick, native of Severn valley, was missionary to Ireland; labored 30 years, converting natives to Christianity. In **563** Columba founded church on Iona. In **597** Augustine arrived, founded church at Canterbury.

449

Anglo-Saxon migrations from continent to Britain.

483

Justinian I, Byzantine emperor, born; died **65.** During reign had Tribonian prepare Justinian Code (Corpus Juris Civilis) which became basic Roman law used later as a model by many modern European states.

570

Mohammed, born in Mecca; hegira, flight from Mecca to Medina, July 16, 622 is beginning of Moslem calendar. Saracens crossed to Spain **711,** established Moorish kingdom, lasted until **1492.**

731

Great period of Mayan empire began; ended **987.**

732

Charles Martel, Frankish ruler, defeated 90,000 Moors at Tours, France; height of Moslem invasion of Western Europe.

800

Charlemagne, king of Franks, proclaimed Holy Roman Emperor by Pope Leo III on Christmas Day in St. Peter's. Charlemagne fought Saxons, Lombards, Saracens 30 years to Christianize them; extended empire from Atlantic to eastern boundaries of Hungary. Died **814,** aged 72, was buried in his cathedral at Aix.

1000

Leif Ericsson's Norsemen reach Vinland, land of grape vines. Variously identified as Labrador, New England coast and Martha's Vineyard.

1014

Brian Boru, Irish king, defeated Danes at Clontarf.

1027

New empire of Mayas extended north to Mexico. Disintegration accelerated by pestilence **1480.** Destruction of Tayasal, Guatemala, Itza capital, by Spanish governor of Yucatan in **1697** ended Mayan millennium.

1054

Final break between Eastern (Orthodox) and Western (Roman) church came when Pope Leo IX excommunicated Michael Cerularius and his followers. Eastern Orthodox Church became established religion of Russia under the Czars. Russian patriarchate formed **1589.**

1066

William of Normandy conquered England at Hastings **Oct. 14;** Harold, last Saxon king of England, slain.

1096

First crusade, preached by Peter of Amiens, supported by Pope Urban II, raised 100,000 men. Captured Jerusalem **1099,** Acre, **1104. Second, 1146,** lost Jerusalem to Saladin. **Third, 1189,** Richard I of England took Jaffa. **Fourth, 1200,** besieged Constantinople **1204. Fifth, 1216,** achieved 10-year truce. **Sixth, 1238,** lost ground. **Seventh, 1245,** led by Louis IX (St. Louis) of France who was captured **1250. Eighth, 1270,** led by Louis who died near Tunis **1270. Children's crusade, 1212,** 50,000 children (est.); most died of disease and hunger or were sold as slaves.

1162

Genghis Khan, Mongol chief, born; died **1227.** Captured Peking **1215,** defeated Russians **1223,** conquered most of Central Asia and massacred population of Herat, Afghanistan. By 1241 Mongols under Batu had burned Moscow and Kiev and invaded Poland, Hungary, and the Danube Valley.

1215

Magna Carta, the great charter of England, signed by King John at Runnymede at insistence of 2,000 English barons who refused to fight on foreign soil and demanded end of illegal levies by king. Charter guaranteed privileges of nobility, church free from secular interference, right of freemen to legal protection. Freemen were privileged class; common people were villein farmers, practically serfs. But 400 years later Edward Coke and Puritans demanded protection for the common people under these rights of freemen. Also invoked Clause 39, out of which trial by jury developed: It reads: *No freeman shall be taken or imprisoned, or dispossessed, or outlawed, or banished, or in any way destroyed, nor will we go upon him, nor send upon him, except by the legal judgment of his peers or by the law of the land.*

1271

Marco Polo started with father and uncle for Cathay (China), Mongol kingdom of Kublai Khan. Served under Khan, returned to Venice **1295.** Wrote Travels.

1274

Thomas Aquinas, Italian, greatest scholastic philosopher, died.

1300
Dante and Giotto flourished; dawn of Renaissance.

1309
Clement V, French pope, made Avignon seat of church; Urban V returned to Rome 1367, abandoned it; Gregory XI finally reentered St. Peter's 1377. During the Great Schism, 1378-1417, French and Italian factions chose popes for Avignon and Rome; breach healed by Martin V 1417.

1346
Battle of Crecy, France, Aug. 26. Edward III of England defeated larger French force of Philip VI; first use of English longbow in continental warfare.

1348
Black Death (bubonic plague) hit Venice, rapidly spreading to rest of Europe by 1349. An estimated one-fourth of European population killed.

1382
John Wycliffe, English forerunner of Reformation, directed translation of Vulgate Bible into English vernacular. Supported bill in parliament declaring it sinful for clergy to hold property. By elevating Scriptures above church authority he anticipated Lutheran doctrine by 150 years.

1415
John Huss, Bohemian preacher, follower of Wycliffe, agitator of ecclesiastic reforms, burned at stake in Constance July 6 for heresy after German Emperor Sigismund revoked his safe-conduct.

1429
Joan of Arc, Maid of Orleans, obeying "voices" of saints, rallied French against English, raised siege of Orleans, effected coronation of Charles VII at Rheims. Through carelessness or treachery she was captured by Burgundians May 24, 1430, and sold to English for 10,000 livres. Placed on trial before bishop of Beauvais at Rouen for magic, disobeying parents, wearing male attire, and heresy, she admitted all after 114 days to escape torture, but was given life imprisonment. Tricked to resume male attire, she was condemned to death and burned at Rouen by English May 30, 1431. Sentence revoked 25 years later.

1453
Constantinople captured by Ottoman Turks.
End of 100-years' war between England and France, begun 1338. England lost all except Calais which the French captured 1558.

1456
Johann Gutenberg (Gansfleisch) completed first Bible printed from movable type; 2 vols., folio, 42 lines, 2 columns to page. Printing took 5 years. Date established by note in Mazarin copy.

1457
Johann Fust and Peter Schoeffler produced first book printed in colors, and having printers' name, date and place, a Psalter.

1475
William Caxton printed first book in English, translation of a French history of Troy, at Bruges. He moved to Westminster, London, where he printed the first dated book in England 1477.

1492
Christopher Columbus, Genoese navigator, after years of agitation in Spain gained support of Queen Isabella for westward voyage. Left Palos Aug. 3 with Santa Maria, 100 tons, 52 men; Pinta 50 tons, 18 men; Nina, 40 tons, 18 men. On Oct. 12 at 2 a.m., Rodrigo de Triana on Pinta discovered land. Columbus landed on Guanahani, Bahamas, called it San Salvador. Discovered Cuba and Hispaniola (Haiti or San Domingo); built first fort, La Navidad, there. For later voyages see Index.

1497
John Cabot, Venetian employed by English, reached Canada. His son Sebastian joined second voyage 1498. English claim to Canada based on their discoveries.

Amerigo Vespucci, Italian-born Spanish navigator, asserted he reached American mainland (New World) a year before Columbus. Martin Wald-

seemuller of St. Die in book 1507 asked land be called America "because Americus discovered it."

1498
Savonarola, preached against luxury and power of clergy, burned as heretic in Florence May 23.
Vasco da Gama, Portuguese navigator, reached India, discovered all-sea route from W. Europe.

1506
Pope Julius II (della Rovere) started new St. Peter's; employed Michelangelo, Bramante, Raphael.

1509
Henry VIII became king of England. Defeated Scots at Flodden Field 1513. Named Defender of the Faith by Pope Leo X for attacking Luther 1521. When pope refused to annul his marriage to Catherine of Aragon for lack of male issue, Henry divorced Catherine, married Anne Boleyn 1533. Act of Supremacy abrogated pope's authority, made king head of church in England 1534. He ordered monasteries closed 1536.

Queen Anne Boleyn was tried for adultery on order of Henry VIII in 1536 and beheaded. Henry married Jane Seymour, who died 1537, after giving birth to son who became Edward VI in 1547. Henry married Anne of Cleves, divorced her 1540. Married Catherine Howard, beheaded 1542, then Catherine Parr 1543 who survived him.

1513
Juan Ponce de Leon, veteran of one Columbus voyage, discovered and named Florida.
Vasco Nunez de Balboa left Spanish town of Santa Maria la Antigua del Darien on Isthmus of Panama, discovered South Sea, later called Pacific by Magellan.

1517
Martin Luther, Augustinian monk, preached faith over works, attacked abuse of selling papal indulgences, posted 95 theses (propositions) on Wittenberg church-door Oct. 31. Diet of Worms, under Charles V Jan. 1521 ordered recantation. Luther, backed by German princes, refused; put Scriptures above papal authority. Translated Greek New Testament into German 1522. Became head of German evangelical movement, broke with Rome, married. Augsburg Confession, basic Lutheran creed, presented to diet there by Melanchthon 1530.

1519
Hernando Cortes began conquest of Mexico.

1520
Fernando Magellan discovered Strait of Magellan; killed in .Philippines 1521. His crew completed first circumnavigation of the world arriving in Spain Sept. 6, 1522. Voyage proved the world round, showed large proportion of water to land, and revealed the Americas to be a New World.

1524
Giovanni da Verrazano, Italian, explored New England coast for French, probably New York Bay.

1526
William Tyndale produced in Cologne first printed version of New Testament in English, suppressed in England. Tyndale executed for heresy Oct. 6, 1536, at Vilvarde, near Brussels.

1529
Turks failed in siege of Vienna; farthest Ottoman Turk expansion in Europe.

1531-35
Francisco Pizarro conquered Peru for Spain.

1534
John Calvin, French-born religious reformer, published his Institutes of the Christian Religion, influential Protestant doctrine. Rejected Lutheran doctrine of consubstantiation; believed in religious base of citizenship, original sin, infant damnation. Influence extended to Scottish Presbyterians, English and New England Puritans.

Jacques Cartier, sent by Francis I of France, in two voyages 1534-36 discovered St. Lawrence River, reached site of Montreal. Basis of French claims to Canada.

1535
Miles Coverdale published first complete Bible in

English. Also worked on first authorized Bible, "The Great Bible," completed **1539**. Other editions: Whittingham's New Testament, with Calvin's introduction **1557**; Geneva Bible **1560**; Bishop's Bible **1568**.

1540

Francisco Coronado, searching for gold and "seven cities of cibola," explored Southwest north of Rio Grande with 70 horse and 30 foot soldiers. Hernando de Alarcon discovered Colorado River. Don Garcia Lopez de Cardenas discovered Grand Canyon.

1541

Hernando de Soto discovered Mississippi River.

1545

Council of Trent, in Austrian Tyrol, urged on Pope Paul III by Emperor Charles V, to define Catholic dogma and remedy ecclesiastical abuses, opened **Dec. 13**; continued intermittently until **1563**; reiterated supreme papal authority, outlined Roman Catholic faith.

1555

Bishops Ridley and Latimer burned at Oxford **Oct. 16**; Archbishop Cranmer of Canterbury burned **Mar. 21, 1556**; 277 other religious leaders burned in attempt of Queen Mary Tudor to restore Catholic authority. Elizabeth became queen **1558**, made Anglican communion official church.

1560

Some 1200 Huguenots hanged at Amboise. Catherine de Medici, regent of France for son, Charles IX, by **Edict of January 1562**, granted Huguenots right to worship outside walled towns. Infraction of edict led to massacre of Huguenots at Vassy **Mar. 1, 1562**, beginning of 8 religious wars. Massacre of St. Bartholomew **Aug. 24, 1572**, encouraged by Charles IX on marriage of sister, Marguerite de Valois to Henry of Navarre (non-Catholic). Henry III, who caused assassination of Catholic leaders Duc de Guise and Cardinal of Lorraine, was himself murdered **Aug. 1, 1589**. Henry IV (of Navarre) first Bourbon king, promulgated **Edict of Nantes Apr. 13, 1598**, giving Huguenots and Catholics equality before law. Henry converted to Catholicism; assassinated **May 14, 1610**. Revocation of edict by Louis XIV **Oct. 23, 1685**, led to large Huguenot emigration to England and America.

1564

William Shakespeare born; traditional date **Apr. 23**; Baptismal record **Apr. 26**.

1565

St. Augustine, Florida, founded by Pedro Menendez, Spaniard. Attacked by Sir Francis Drake **1586**.

1568

Ivan the Terrible of Russia executed hundreds accused of plot to kill crown prince.

1579

Sir Francis Drake claimed California for Queen Elizabeth. Left metal plate found in Marin County **1936**.

1582

First Catholic New Testament in English issued at Rheims; Old Testament translated at Douai **1609**.

1587

Mary, Queen of Scots, executed for treason; actually was threat to throne of Queen Elizabeth.

Virginia Dare, first child born of English parents in the New World, on Roanoke Isl., N. C., **Aug. 18**, 7 days after **Sir Walter Raleigh's** second expedition with 117 persons landed. (First, **1585**, returned to England **1586**.) By **1590** all trace of settlement had vanished except for a tree inscribed enigmatically "Croatoan."

1588

Spanish Armada, 132 ships, 33,000 soldiers and crews, sent by Philip II of Spain against England, destroyed by Drake's attacks and storms **July 21-29**. Only 50 ships returned to Spain. Fading of Spanish power; flourishing of Elizabethan England.

1590

Edmund Spenser began The Faerie Queen. First Shakespeare poem Venus and Adonis registered **1593**. First play to appear in quarto Titus Andronicus registered **1594**. Romeo and Juliet performed **1597**.

1600

Shakespeare's most productive decade opened. Included Henry V, Midsummer Night's Dream, Twelfth Night, Merry Wives of Windsor, Hamlet, Othello, Macbeth, King Lear, Tempest, etc. Shakespeare retired to Stratford-on-Avon **1610**; died **Apr. 23, 1616**, the same date that **Cervantes** died. First folio of 36 plays published **1623**; second, **1632**; third, **1663**; fourth, **1675**.

1602

Capt. Bartholomew Gosnold, English navigator, landed on Cape Cod which he named.

1605

Gunpowder Plot of Guy Fawkes to blow up King James I and parliament foiled when 36 barrels of gunpowder were found in parliament's cellar **Nov. 4**.

1607

Capt. John Smith and 105 cavaliers in 3 ships landed at Virginia and started first permanent English settlement in New World at Jamestown **May 13**. Virginia was first of the 13 colonies.

1609

Henry Hudson, English explorer of Northwest Passage, employed by Dutch East India Co.; sailed sloop Half Moon into New York harbor **Sept.** and up river to Albany. In **1610**, in English ship Discovery, 55 tons, explored Hudson Bay. On return in **1611**, Hudson was put into open boat with his son and 8 others by mutinous sailors. All were lost.

Spaniards settled Santa Fe, N.M., erected presidio.

1611

King James version (authorized version) of English Bible published; ordered by James I in **1604** it reconciled earlier versions and became basic Protestant Bible.

1618

Thirty Years' War began in Bohemia between Catholic and Protestant armies; ended **1648** with Peace of Westphalia, Alsace given to France. Holland and Switzerland received independence.

Sir Walter Raleigh convicted of conspiring in **1603** to remove James I; beheaded **Oct. 29**.

1619

House of Burgesses, first representative assembly in New World, elected by popular vote **July 30** at Jamestown, established principle of self-government for royal colony.

First Negro laborers—indentured servants—in English N. American colonies, landed by Dutch at Jamestown, **August**.

1620

Plymouth Pilgrims, Puritan separatists from Church of England, some living in Leyden, Holland, since **1609** left Plymouth, England, **Sept. 16** in Mayflower, 101 passengers, 48 crew. Original destination Virginia, they reached Cape Cod **Nov. 9-19**, explored coast, landed **Dec. 21** (Dec. 11, Old Style) at Plymouth, so named for Plymouth Co. on map made **1614** by Capt. John Smith. Mayflower Compact, signed on shipboard, was agreement to form a local government and abide by its laws. Started first common house **Dec. 25**. Half of colony perished during hard winter.

Gov. Bradford's comment, "They knew they were pilgrims" later led them to be called Pilgrims, as distinct from Puritans of Massachusetts Bay Colony **1630**.

1624

Dutch landed 8 men from ship, New Netherland, on Manhattan **May**. Proceeded to Albany.

1626

Peter Minuit bought Manhattan from Manhattan Indians **May 6** for trinkets.

1636

Harvard College founded **Oct. 28**.

1638

Peter Minuit landed 2 shiploads of Swedes and Finns at site of Wilmington, Del.

1642

Great Rebellion of the Puritan Parliament against

the civil and religious policies of Charles I of England begins **July** after Charles rejects parliament's demands for control of militia and church affairs and for right to appoint and dismiss the king's ministers.

Oliver Cromwell led army of Roundheads for parliament, defeated Charles' Cavaliers at **Marston Moor 1644** and **Naseby 1645.** Charles was delivered to parliament by the Scots **1648.**

Galileo died, **Newton** was born 100 years after **Copernicus** published heliocentric theory. Galileo defended theory: "Holy Spirit intended to teach us in the Bible how to go to Heaven, not how the heavens go." But in **1616** the Inquisition at Rome declared the assertion of earth's motion to be heretical and placed works of Copernicus, **Kepler** and Galileo on the Index until **1822.**

1648

Taj Mahal outside Agra, India, completed by Mogul Emperor Shah Jehan in memory of his favorite wife Mumtaz Mahal. Begun in **1630.**

1649

Charles I condemned by House of Commons sitting as high court; beheaded **Jan. 30.**

Commonwealth ruled by Commons and Council of State (John Milton, Latin secretary) with Cromwell at head. Cromwell routed Scots at Worcester **1651.** Cromwell made protector for life, actually dictator, **1653.** Admiral Blake took Jamaica from Spain **1655.**

Cromwell died 1658. His son Richard resigned rule. Puritan government collapsed and parliament called Charles II.

1660

John Bunyan, a tinker, imprisoned at Bedford, England, **Nov.** for unlawful preaching; released **1672** after writing part of Pilgrim's Progress.

Restoration under Charles II "Merry Monarch." Charles' Cavalier parliament restored Anglican church and refused freedom of worship to dissenters, promised by king in Declaration of Breda.

1664

King Charles II ordered Col. Nicolls and 300 men to seize **New Netherland** (Manhattan and environs) from Dutch, granted territory to his brother James, Duke of York. Peter Stuyvesant, Dutch director-general, yielded peacefully; province of New Netherland and city of New Amsterdam became New York. The Dutch recaptured both **Aug. 9, 1673;** ceded all by treaty to Britain **Nov. 10, 1674.**

American Revolution and War of Independence;

Great Britain, after acquiring Canada from France in 1763, tightened up colonial administration in North America. The Thirteen Colonies, used to self-government, resented duties on commerce and objected to paying for troops now quartered among them. **The Sugar Act of 1764** placed duties on lumber, foodstuffs, molasses and rum. **The Stamp Act of 1765** required revenue stamps to help defray cost of royal troops. The colonists formed Sons of Liberty groups and rejected British goods. Nine colonies, led by New York and Massachusetts at **Stamp Act Congress** in New York **Oct. 7-25, 1765,** adopted Declaration of Rights opposing taxation without representation in parliament and trial without jury by admiralty courts. In the Virginia House of Burgesses, Patrick Henry warned King George III of consequences declaring, "If this be treason make the most of it." Parliament repealed Stamp Act on **Mar. 17, 1766.**

Townshend Acts of 1767 levied taxes on glass, painter's lead, paper and tea imports. In 1770 all duties except tax on tea were repealed, but principle of right to tax was maintained. British troops fired into a mob **Mar. 5, 1770,** killed 5 including Crispus Attucks, a Negro, reportedly leader of the group; later called the **Boston Massacre.** Tea ships of East India Co., turned back at Boston, New York, Philadelphia in May 1773. Cargo ship burned at Annapolis **Oct. 14.** Cargo thrown overboard at **Boston Tea Party Dec. 16.** Parliament ordered port closed until tea was paid for, sent 4 regiments to Boston, suppressed town meetings and elective representation in Massachusetts.

Samuel Adams, in Boston, began uniting patriot leaders by Committees of Correspondence. Virginia called for first **Continental Congress** in Philadelphia **Sept. 5-Oct. 26, 1774.** On **Mar. 23, 1775, Patrick Henry** addressed revolutionary convention, Richmond, Va., with famous exclamation: "Give me liberty or give me death!"

Battles of 1775

Paul Revere and **William Dawes** on night of **Apr. 18,** on horseback, alerted Samuel Adams and John Hancock at Lexington and others that 700 British were on way to **Concord** to destroy arms. At **Lexington, Mass., Apr. 19** Minutemen lost 8 killed, 10 wounded. On return from Concord the harassed British lost 273.

Col. Ethan Allen (joined by Col. Benedict Arnold) captured **Ft. Ticonderoga,** N. Y., **May 10;** also Crown Point. Colonials headed for Bunker Hill, fortified Breed's Hill, Charlestown, Mass., repulsed British under Gen. William Howe twice before retreating **June 17;** British casualties 1,000; called **Battle of Bunker Hill.** Continental Congress **June 15** named George Washington commander-in-chief; he took command in Cambridge **July 3.** Maj. Gen. Richard Mongomery led troops agains Canada via New York, captured **Montreal** Nov. 13, Col. Arnold marched via Maine wilderness attacked **Quebec** Dec. 30-31; Montgomery killed. Colonals returned to New York state June 1776.

Mecklenburg Declaration of Independence adopted at Charlotte, Mecklenburg County, N. C., **May 20** (a disputed ktradition).

Declaration of Independence

Virginia voted for independence May 15. In Continental Congress **June 7, 1776,** Richard Henry Lee (Va.) moved "that these united colonies are and of right ought to be free and independent states." Resolutions adopted July 2. **Declaration of Independence** July 4. See article.

Col. Moultrie's batteries at Charleston, S. C., repulsed British sea attack June 28. Washington, with 10,000 men lost **Battle of Long Island** to Howe and Gen. Sir Henry Clinton with 15,000 **Aug. 27,** evacuated New York.

Nathan Hale, 21, executed as spy, without trial, by British **Sept. 22.**

Washington repulsed Howe at **Harlem Heights** Sept. 16, retreated to White Plains, N. Y. Brig. Gen. Arnold's Lake Champlain fleet was defeated at **Valcour** Oct. 11, but British returned to Canada. Howe failed to destroy Washington's army at **White Plains** Oct. 28. Hessians captured **Ft. Washington,** Manhattan, and 3,000 men Nov. 16; **Ft. Lee,** N. J., **Nov. 18.**

Washington in New Jersey recrossed Delaware River **Dec. 25-26,** defeated 1,400 Hessians at **Trenton,** N. J., **Dec. 26.**

Brandywine and Saratoga, 1777

Washington defeated Lord Cornwallis at **Princeton** Jan. 3. Continental Congress adopted Stars and Stripes **June 14.** See Flag article. Maj. Gen. John Burgoyne with 8,000 from Canada captured Ft. Ticonderoga **July 6.** Brig. Gen. Nicholas Herkimer, to raise St. Leger's siege of **Ft. Stanwix,** routed Indians at **Oriskany,** N. Y. **Aug. 6.** Burgoyne's Hessians defeated by Brig. Gen. John Stark and the Green Mountain Boys at **Bennington,** Vt. **Aug. 16.** Arnold raised siege of Ft. Stanwix.

1665
Great Plague in London killed 68,000. In **1666** great fire destroyed 13,200 houses, 89 churches.

1676
Nathaniel Bacon led planters, oppressed by taxes, against Gov. Berkeley at Jamestown, burned town. Bacon died suddenly; 23 followers executed.

Bloody Indian war in New England ended Aug. 12. King Philip, Wampanog chief, and many Narragansett Indians killed.

1682
Robert Cavelier, Sieur de la Salle, took lower Mississippi River country for Louis XIV, called it Louisiana **Apr. 9.** Had built French outposts in Illinois. Established fort at Lavaca, Tex. **1684** with 400 men. Killed by his own men on Trinity River, Tex., **Mar. 19, 1687.**

1683
William Penn signed treaty with Indians.

1689
King William's War, British in America vs. French and Indians, began; ended **1697.**

1692
Witchcraft delusion at Salem (now Danvers, Mass.), inspired by preaching; 19 persons hanged, 1 man crushed to death. Executions in Europe of women for witchcraft between 1484 and 1782 believed to have reached 300,000. Last in England **1716,** in Scotland **1722.**

1696
Capt. William Kidd, American, hired by British king and nobles to fight pirates and take booty, became pirate. Returned to New York with treasure **1698,** buried it on Gardiner's Island. Arrested and sent to England for trial. He was hanged **1701.**

1704
Indians attacked Deerfield, Mass., Feb. 28-29, killed 40, carried off 100.

Gibraltar taken by Britain from Spain **July 24;** formally ceded by Treaty of Utrecht **1713.**

Boston News Letter, first regular newspaper, started by John Campbell, postmaster. Publick Occurences was suppressed after one issue **1690.**

1709
British-Colonial troops captured French fort, Port Royal, Nova Scotia, in Queen Anne's War **1701-13.** France yielded Nova Scotia by treaty **1713.**

1712
Slaves revolted in New York Apr. 6. Six committed suicide, 21 were executed. Second rising, **1741;** 13

Origins, Battles, Results, 1763-1783

Boys at **Bennington,** Vt. **Aug. 16.** Arnold raised siege of Ft. Stanwix.

Howe defeated Washington near **Brandywine Creek,** Pa., **Sept. 11** and occupied Philadelphia. Congress moved to Lancaster, Pa. Inconclusive battle of **Germantown,** Pa., **Oct. 4.** Washington's army wintered at **Valley Forge.**

Americans massed at Bemis Heights on Hudson River under Maj. Gen. Horatio Gates, attacked by Burgoyne **Sept. 19.** At **Freeman's Farm,** Gen. Arnold and Col. Daniel Morgan's riflemen repulsed British, inflicted great losses. Gen. Clinton took **Fts. Clinton** and **Montgomery** below West Point Oct. 6, but did not support Burgoyne. Americans beat back Burgoyne at Bemis Heights **Oct. 7** and cut off British escape route. Burgoyne surrendered 5,000 men at ,**Saratoga,** N. Y., **Oct. 17.**

Marquis de la Fayette (Lafayette), aged 20, made major general.

Articles of Confederation and Perpetual Union adopted by Continental Congress **Nov. 15.**

Help from France

France recognized independence of 13 Colonies, signed treaty of aid with Benjamin Franklin, Silas Deane, Arthur Lee on **Feb. 6, 1778.** Sent fleet under Adm. d'Estainr. British evacuated Philadelphia in consequence **June 18.** Washington harassed British at **Monmouth Court House,** N. J., **June 28.** Wyoming Massacre **July 3** in Pa. by British and Indian force. British overran Georgia in December.

George Rogers Clark who took **Cahokia** and **Kaskaskia** (Ill.) 1778, took **Vincennes** Feb. 1779. Maj. Gen. Anthony Wayne **July 15** stormed **Stony Point, GTsMson** son, but withdrew after victory.

John Paul Jones in Bonhomme Richard defeated Serapis on the Atlantic **Sept. 23, 1779.** French fleet and Maj. Gen. Benjamin Lincoln's men were repulsed at Savannah Oct. 9.

Benedict Arnold's Treason

Three Continental soldiers, Paulding, Williams and Van Wart captured Major John Andre, adjutant general of the British army, in disguise at Tarrytown, N. Y., **Sept. 23, 1780,** finding papers betraying West Point, signed by Gen. Arnold, in his socks. He had lost his way after rendezvous with Arnold at Haverstraw, N. Y. Arnold, informed of Andre's capture, escaped from headquarters in Highlands, near present Garrison, N. Y., by barge to British sloop Vulture off Verplanck's Point.

Andre was found guilty by board of American officers at Tappan, N. Y., hanged as spy Oct. 2. Washington refused to intercede. Arnold made brigadier general in British army; burned New London, Conn., 1781. His wife, Peggy Shippen of Philadelphia, adjudged innocent by Washington, since proved implicated. Arnold died in London. Andre's body removed to Westminster Abbey 1821.

Road to Yorktown

Charleston, S.C., fell to the British May 12, 1780, but a segment of Lord Cornwallis' forces led by Maj. Patrick Ferguson was defeated near **Kings Mountain,** N. C., **Oct. 7** by militiamen commanded by Cols. John Sevier, Isaac Shelby, William Campbell and Benjamin Cleveland. Operations in South under Cornwallis ¬d Col. B. Tarleton in 1781 were checked by Maj. Gen. Nathanael Greene and Brig. Gen. Daniel Morgan. **Cowpens,** S. C., **Jan 17** was a victory, but **Guilford Court House,** N. C., **Mar. 15** was a British gain. Greene's harassments caused Cornwallis to retire to Wilmington, N.C., and thence to **Yorktown, Va.**

While **Lafayette waited** near Yorktown, Adm. De Grasse landed 3,000 French and stopped Adm. Thomas Graves' British fleet in Hampton Roads. Adm. Barras joined De rasse. Washington and Rochambeau joined forces and left 2,000 men to mislead Sir Henry Clinton in New York, marched to Annapolis and took boats to James River near Williamsburg, arrived Sept. 26. When siege of Cornwallis began Oct. 6, British had 6,000. Americans 8,846, French 7,800. Clinton decided too late to relieve Cornwallis. Graves sailed from New York with 7,000 Oct. 17 too late to reach Cornwallis who surrendered **Oct. 19, 1781.**

Independence, 1782

A new British cabinet agreed to recognize independence **March 1782.** Preliminary agreement signed in Paris **Nov. 30;** treaty **Sept. 3, 1783.** Congress ratified it **Jan. 14, 1784.** Washington ordered army disbanded **Nov. 3, 1783.** British evacuated New York **Nov. 25.** Washington bade farewell to his officers at Fraunce's Tavern, New York, **Dec. 4;** resigned **Dec. 23,** retired to Mount Vernon, Va. *For casualties see Index.*

slaves hanged, 13 burned, 71 transported.

1720

"**Mississippi Bubble**." John Law, Scottish, comptroller of finance in France, issued paper currency without security to back trading scheme. On basis of wild stories of gold in Louisiana, shares reached $4,000 value before collapse. Provoked large immigration to Louisiana.

1728

Pennsylvania Gazette founded by Samuel Keimer in Philadelphia. Benjamin Franklin bought interest **1729.**

1735

Freedom of the press recognized in New York by acquittal of **John Peter Zenger,** editor Weekly Journal, on charge of libelling British governor Cosby by criticizing his conduct in office.

1740-1741

Capt. Vitus Bering, Dane employed by Russians, discovered Alaska.

1743

King George's War. British and colonials vs. French. Siege of Louisbourg, Cape Breton Isl. was led by Gov. William Shirley of Massachusetts. Surrendered to British **June 17, 1745.** Returned to France by Treaty of Aix la Chapelle **1748.**

1746

English defeated Scots at Culloden Moor, near Inverness, **Apr. 16,** routing Stuart pretender, Prince Charles. The last battle fought on British soil, it terminated attempts of Stuarts to recover the English throne.

1751

Publication of the Encylopedie began in France, great popularizer of the Enlightenment.

1752

Benjamin Franklin, flying kite in thunderstorm, proved lightning is electricity **June 15.**

Gregorian calendar adopted by Great Britain and American colonies, dropping 11 days after Sept. 2; next day Sept. 14.

1754

French and Indian War started after French occupied uncompleted British post, called it Ft. Duquesne (site of Pittsburgh). Col. George Washington with Virginia troops clashed with French at Great Meadows, dug in at Ft. Necessity; capitulated and withdrew **July 3, 1754.** Boston's 3,000 provincial troops took Nova Scotia French forts **June 16, 1755.** French and Indians ambushed Gen. William Braddock's expedition 10 mi. from Ft. Duquesne (now Braddock, Pa.) **July 9;** Braddock fatally wounded, 714 killed. Gen. Sir William Johnson defeated French and Indians under Baron Dieskau at Lake George **Sept. 8.** British moved Acadian French out of Canada **Nov.** Britain formally declared war **May 18, 1756.** Surrendered Ft. William Henry (Lake George) to Montcalm. Montcalm at Ft. Ticonderoga, N.Y., repulsed 17,000 British **July 8, 1758.** French gave up Louisburg, Ft. Frontenac, Ft. Duquesne in 1758; Niagara, Ticonderoga, Crown Point in 1759. British captured Quebec **Sept. 18, 1759** in battles in which Montcalm and Gen. James Wolfe (Br.) died. Peace signed **Feb. 10, 1763** (hence "Seven Years' War"). French lost Canada and American Midwest.

1755

Great earthquake in Lisbon, Portugal, **Nov. 1,** 60,-000 died; 12,000 in Fez, Morocco; half of Madeira leveled; 2,000 houses lost in Mitylene; Oporto, Braga, Malaga damaged.

Samuel Johnson issued English Dictionary.

1756

Black Hole of Calcutta. Nawab of Bengal, attacking British East India Co., threw 146 British prisoners into room less than 20 ft. square **June 20;** only 23 survived overnight. Lord Robert Clive with 3,000 British troops defeated the Nawab's force of 50,000 **June 1757.**

1769

Napoleon Bonaparte born Aug. 15 in Ajaccio, Corsica; died at Longwood, St. Helena, **May 5, 1821.**

1772

First Partition of Poland by Austria, Prussia and Russia. Second and third partitions of **1793** and **1795** erased Poland from map of Europe, not to re-emerge until after World War I.

1781

Bank of North America incorporated in Philadelphia **May 26.** First chartered bank, Bank of Pennsylvania **Mar. 1, 1780** operated 1782-1784.

1783

Massachusetts Supreme Court outlawed slavery because of the words in the state Bill of Rights "all men are born free and equal."

1784

First successful daily newspaper, Pennsylvania Packet & General Advertiser, formed from tri-weekly **Sept. 21.**

1785

First steamboat experiment by John Fitch. New Jersey granted him rights to rivers **1786.** Fitch demonstrated, 3 mile an hour, steamboat with 12 mechanical oars on Delaware River **Aug. 22, 1787.** Pennsylvania, Delaware, Virginia, New York gave him river rights **1787.** He operated steamboat between Trenton and Philadelphia **1790.** He died **1798.**

1786

Delegates from 5 states at Annapolis asked Congress to call convention in Philadelphia to write practical constitution for the 13 states.

1787

Shays' rebellion in Massachusetts, led by Capt. Daniel Shays; the attempt to seize U. S. Arsenal in Springfield failed **Jan. 25.**

Northwest Ordinance adopted **July 13** by Continental Congress made effective Ordinance of 1784 drafted by Jefferson. Determined government of **Northwest Territory** north of johio River, west of New York: 5,000 male voters could establish legislature; 60,000 inhabitants could get statehood. Guaranteed freedom of religion, support for schools, no slavery.

James Rumsey, encouraged by George Washington, ran steamboat with power pump on Potomac **Dec. 3** and **11.** Patented **1791.** He died **1792.**

Constitutional convention opened at Philadelphia **May 14** with George Washington presiding; Constitution adopted by delegates **Sept. 17;** Ratification by 9th state, New Hampshire, **June 21, 1788,** meant adoption.

1788

First British settlement in Australia, a penal colony at Port Jackson, now Sydney.

1789

George Washington chosen president by all electors voting (73 eligible, 69 voting, 4 absent); John Adams Vice President, 34 votes, **Feb.** First U. S. Congress called **Mar. 4,** at Federal Hall, New York; regular sessions began **Apr. 6.** Washington inaugurated there **Apr. 30.** Supreme Court created by Federal Judiciary Act **Sept. 24.**

The French Revolution began **June 20** when the delegates to the Third Estate (Commons) met on the tennis court and took an oath not to disband until the king had granted France a constitution; Paris mob stormed the Bastille **July 14** to capture ammunition; released 7 non-political prisoners. France was declared a limited monarchy under Louis XVI; Mirabeau died **Apr. 2, 1791;** the king and family arrested **June 21, 1791;** Revolutionary Tribunal set up on **Aug. 19, 1792;** National Convention opened **Sept. 17, 1792,** a republic was established on **Sept. 22.** King Louis was beheaded **Jan. 21, 1793;** the Reign of Terror began **May 31, 1793;** Charlotte Corday stabbed Marat **July 13, 1793;** the queen was beheaded **Oct. 16, 1793;** Danton **Apr. 5, 1794;** Robespierre **July 28, 1794.** Revolutionary Tribunal abolished **Dec. 15, 1794.** Moderate Directory of 5 men established to rule France **1795.**

Mutiny on the British ship Bounty Apr. 28; Capt. William Bligh and 18 sailors set adrift in a launch. They rowed 3,618 miles to Timor, near Java. The Bounty, in command of Fletcher Christian, rebel mate, sailed to Tahiti. Some of the crew and 18 Polynesians, includingg 12 women, went on to Pitcairn Isl., arriving in 1790. Vessel burned after food and tools were landed.

1791

Continued attacks on settlements north of Ohio River by Indians armed by British, led Washington to send Gen. Arthur St. Clair and Gen. Wilkinson to area with 1,400 men. St. Clair was surprised near Wabash River in Ohio **Nov. 4,** lost 630 killed.

1792-94

Gen. Anthony Wayne made commander, took 2 years to train American Legion. Established Ft. Washington (Cinncinnati), Ft. Recovery, O., **1793;** Ft. Greeneville, Ft. Deposit, Ft. Defiance, **1794.** Routed Indians (Ottawas, Shawnees, Miamis, Iroquois) with bayonets at Fallen Timbers on Maumee River **Aug. 20, 1794,** checked British at Ft. Miamis.

Whiskey Rebellion, west Pennsylvania farmers protested "discriminatory" whiskey tax of **1791,** was suppressed by 15,000 militiamen **Sept. 1794.** Alexander Hamilton used incident to establish authority of the new federal government in enforcing its laws.

1795

Gen. Wayne built Ft. Wayne; signed peace with Indians at Fort Greeneville.

Triple Alliance formed by Great Britain, Russia and Austria, **Sept. 28.**

U. S. bought peace from Algiers and Tunis by paying $800,000, supplying a frigate and annual tribute of $25,000 **Nov. 28.**

1796

Washington's Farewell Address as President delivered **Sept. 19.** Gave strong warnings against permanent alliance with foreign powers, partiality toward favorite nation, big public debt, large military establishment and devices of "small artful, enterprising minority" to control or change government; praised reciprocal checks of Constitution; stressed need for enlightened public opinion; declared "religion and morality lead to political prosperity."

Vaccination discovered by Edward Jenner **May 14,** announced **1798;** laid foundation for modern immunology.

1797

U. S. frigate United States launched at Philadelphia **July 10;** Constellation at Baltimore **Sept. 7;** Constitution (Old Ironsides) at Boston **Sept. 20.**

France ordered capture of all neutral ships carrying British cargoes.

1798

War with France threatened over French raids on U. S. shipping and rejection of U. S. diplomats. Congress voided all treaties with France, ordered Navy to capture French armed ships. Navy (45 ships) and 365 privateers captured 84 French ships. U. S. Constellation took French warship Insurgente 1799. Napoleon stopped French raids after becoming First Consul.

Napoleon invaded Egypt and won Battle of the Pyramids **July 1798;** Nelson destroyed French fleet **Aug. 1-2** in Aboukir Bay. Rosetta stone, found in Egypt by one of Napoleon's officers **1799,** contained 3 identical inscriptions in ancient Egyptian hieroglyphics, demotic (common) Greek and classical Greek. Jean Champollion, a young French scholar, compared these writings and deciphered ancient Egypt's hieroglyphics. Napoleon returned secretly to France **1799,** became First Consul **Nov. 9-10, 1799,** after coup d'etat.

1801

Tripoli declared war June 10 against U. S., which refused added tribute to commerce-raiding corsairs. U. S. frigate Philadelphia captured in Tripoli harbor **Oct. 1803** burned by Stephen Decatur **Feb. 16, 1804.** Expedition under William Eaton forced Tripoli to conclude peace **June 4, 1805.**

1803

Robert Emmet convicted of treason by British in Ireland; executed in Dublin **Sept. 19.**

Louisiana Purchase. President Jefferson sent James Monroe to Paris to join Robert R. Livingston, U. S. minister, in offering up to $10,000,000 for the isle of Orleans (New Orleans) and West Florida. Napoleon, who had recovered Louisiana from Spain by secret treaty, offered all of Louisiana for $11,250,-000 in bonds, plus $3,750,000 indemnities to American citizens with claims against France. U. S. took title **Dec. 20.**

1804

Lewis and Clark expedition ordered by President Jefferson to explore what is now northwest U. S. Started from St. Louis **May 14;** ended **Sept. 23, 1806.** An Indian woman named Sacagawea served as guide and interpreter.

Alexander Hamilton (ex-Secretary of the' Treasury) and Vice President Aaron Burr, after years of bitter political rivalry, fought a duel **July 11** on the Hudson Palisades, Weehawken, N.J. Hamilton was mortally wounded, died **July 12.**

Code Napoleon systematized French law under the auspices of Napoleon Bonaparte. It became a model for many countries.

John Stevens, of Hoboken, N.J., operated experimental steamboat with twin-screw propellers for 9 miles.

1805

Napoleon, emperor since **May 18, 1804,** defeated Austrians at Ulm **Oct. 17;** Russo-Austrians at Austerlitz "masterpiece of battles" **Dec. 2.** Dissolved Holy Roman Empire. Made brothers Joseph, king of Naples, Louis, king of Holland.

Lord Nelson defeated French-Spanish fleet at Cape Trafalgar **Oct. 21;** lost his own life.

1806

Napoleon defeated Prussians at Jena **Oct. 14.** In **1807** he defeated Russians at Eylau; signed peace of Tilsit with Czar Alexander I. Made brother Jerome king of Westphalia; allotted Finland to Russia.

1807

Robert Fulton made first practical steamboat trip on Clermont (open boat, 140 by 13 ft., 7 ft. draft, side paddle wheels). Left New York **Aug. 17,** reached Albany, 150 mi., in 32 hrs.

Aaron Burr was tried for treason in Richmond, Va., **May. 22.** Charged with "assembling an armed force . . . to seize the city of New Orleans . . . and to separate the western from the Atlantic states," he was acquitted **Sept. 1.** Chief Justice John Marshall sitting as U. S. Circuit Court judge ruled that treason must be attested to two witnesses. After trial Burr went to Europe to avoid prosecution on Hamilton murder charge.

1808-09

French occupied Madrid in March; Rome in April; Napoleon made brother Joseph king of Spain in Peninsular War begun by British **1808,** continued until **1814.** Napoleon defeated Austrians at Wagram **July 6, 1809.** Annexed Papal States.

Phoenix, world's first ocean-going steamboat, built by John Stevens, left New York for Philadelphia **June 8, 1809.**

1810

Napoleon annulled marriage with the Empress Josephine; married Austrian Archduchess Marie Louise in March.

1811

William Henry Harrison, of Indiana territory, defeated Indians under the Prophet, brother of Tecumseh, governor in battle of Tippecanoe **Nov. 7.**

1812

Napoleon invaded Russia June 22 with first modern conscript army of 500,000 men; Russians outnumbered 3 to 1, retreated and used "scorched earth" policy. Napoleon's army defeated Russians at Borodino **Sept. 7;** took Moscow **Sept. 14.** Moscow destroyed by fire; lacking shelter and supplies, Napoleon ordered retreat **Oct. 19.** Army suffered from cold, starvation and Cossack attacks; only 30,000 survived.

1813

Napoleon with 180,000 French decisively defeated at Leipzig by 200,000 allied Prussians, Austrians, Russians, under Austrian Gen. Schwartzenberg in Battle of the Nations **Oct. 16-19.**

1814

Allies entered Paris Mar. 21; Napoleon abdicated **Apr. 11;** Louis XVIII restored to throne, **May 3;** Congress of Vienna opened **Nov. 3.** Napoleon exiled to Elba.

1815

Napoleon re-entered France Mar. 1, assumed command, ruled 100 days, **Mar. 20-June 22.** Defeated at Waterloo, Belgium, **June 18,** by Duke of Wellington (British), Count von Blucher (Prussian) and allies. Deported to St. Helena; died there **May 5, 1821.**

Holy Alliance, formed by Russia, Austria and Prussia; signed in Paris **Sept. 26;** promulgated in Frankfort **Feb. 2, 1816** and acceded to 1818 by the rulers of Great Britain and France.

1817

Rush-Bagot treaty signed **Apr. 28-29** limited U. S., Canadian naval armaments on the Great Lakes.

1820

Henry Clay's Missouri Compromise bill passed by Congress **Mar. 3.** Slavery was allowed in Missouri, but not elsewhere west of the Mississippi River north of 36° 30′ Latitude (the southern line of Missouri). Repealed **1854.**

1822

Revolution in Portugal. Separation of Brazil which proclaimed independence **Sept. 7.** Dom Pedro was crowned emperor **Dec. 1;** abdicated **1831;** succeeded by his son. A republic proclaimed **1888.**

Mexico separates from Spain, made Iturbide emperor **May;** forms republic **Oct. 1823.**

1823

Monroe Doctrine declared **Dec. 2.**

Mississippi River first ascended by steamboat, the

War of 1812 Between United States and Great Britain

The War of 1812, coming only 30 years after the end of the Revolution, had 3 major causes: (1) Britain, blockading France, seized American ships trading with France; (2) Britain, refusing to recognize naturalized American sailors, seized 4,000 by 1810 and impressed two-thirds into British service; (3) British armed Indians who raided western border. H.M.S. Leopard attacked U.S. Chesapeake 1807, killed 3 Americans, seized 4. Under President Jefferson U.S., 1807 and 1809 stopped trade with Europe which ruined American shippers. Under President Madison 1810 trade with Britain only was stopped.

War might have been averted. The British raised the blockade for American ships **June 16, 1812,** but the news did not reach U.S. by **June 18** when Congress by a small majority voted a declaration of war. Congress voted to raise army from 11,744 to 44,500 and to use militia. The Navy had 20 major ships of 500 guns. The West favored war; New England opposed it. The British were handicapped by war with France.

War on Land

Americans made many blunders due to poor leadership and refusal of regulars to work with militia. Brig. Gen. William Hull surrendered Detroit Aug. 16, 1812 to Maj. Gen. Issac Brock. Maj. Gen. Stephen Van Rensselaer with 2,300 took Queenston Heights, Canada, Oct. 13, but retired when regulars did not support. Brig. Gen. William H. Harrison had 1,000 casualties near Ft. Malden. Brig. Gen. Zebulon M. Pike (disc. Pike's Peak) took York, (Toronto), Apr. 27, 1813, killed in explosion. Gen. Henry Dearborn **May 27** took **Ft. George** and **Queenston Heights** aided by amphibious assault led by Col. Winifred Scott and Master Commandant Oliver Hazard Perry. British defeated 2,000 Americans a few days later.

Battle of the Thames, Ontario, Can., **Oct. 5, 1813.** Harrison with 3,500 men took Ft. Malden, pursued British 85 mi. Cavalry charge by Kentucky riflemen routed British and Indians, killing Shawnee chief, Tecumseh. Detroit frontier was safe for U.S. In the fall both Brig. Gen. Wade Hampton with 4,000 and Maj. Gen. James Wilkinson, with 6,000 mismanaged attempts to invade Canada; Wilkinson was defeated at Ogdensburg. British recaptured Fts. George and Niagara, burned Buffalo; Americans burned Newark and Queenston.

Battle of Lundy's Lane. Brig. Gen. Winfield Scott led fighting of Brown's army at Lundy's Lane, on road to Burlington **July 25, 1814;** result a draw with heavy losses, Scott was wounded.

Burning of Washington. In August British landed 4,000 men under Adm. Sir George Cockburn and Maj. Gen. Robert Ross. At **Bladensburg, Md., Aug. 24, 1814** Ross routed 5,000 hastily assembled U S. troops, then burned Capitol and White House; Maryland militia stopped British **Sept. 12** from reaching Baltimore; Ross was killed.

Battle of New Orleans. Maj. Gen. Andrew Jackson, who had defeated the Creek Indians at Horseshoe Bend on the Tallapoosa Mar. 27, 1814, and captured British base at Pensacola, Fla., Nov., on Dec. 23 engaged 2,000 British east of New Orleans, then retired to earthworks built with cotton bales. **Jan. 8, 1815,** 5,300 British under Maj. Gen. Sir Edward Pakenham attacked American entrenchments at Chalmette. Jackson had 3,500, a reserve of 1,000, 20 guns and an armed schooner. British had over 2,000 casualties. Pakenham was killed; Americans lost 71. British withdrew and left by sea Jan. 18. On Feb. 8 they took Mobile. News came **Feb. 14** that a treaty of peace had been signed at Ghent **Dec. 24, 1814.** U. S. ratified it **Feb. 17, 1815.**

War at Sea

Brilliant American gunnery brought naval victories. USS Essex captured Alert Aug. 13, 1812. USS Constitution, 44 guns, Capt. Isaac Hull, destroyed Guerriere **Aug. 19;** thereafter nicknamed **Old Ironsides.** USS Wasp took Frolic **Oct. 18.** USS United States, Capt. Stephen Decatur defeated Macedonian off Azores Oct. 25. Constitution beat Java Dec. 29, 1812. USS Chesapeake captured by Shannon June 1, 1813; Capt. James Lawrence, dying, called out: "Don't give up the ship!" USS Enterprise took Boxer Sept. 5.

Battle of Lake Erie. Commodore Oliver H. Perry defeated British fleet near Put-in-Bay **Sept. 10, 1813.** Perry, transferred from disabled flagship Lawrence to Niagara during battle, sent message to Harrison: "We have met the enemy and they are ours: 2 ships, 2 brigs, 1 schooner, 1 sloop."

USS Essex, Capt. David Porter, first U. S. warship to sail around South America, was defeated off Valparaiso, Chile, Mar. 28, 1814.

Bombardment of Ft. McHenry, Baltimore, for 25 hours, **Sept. 13-14, 1814,** by British fleet failed. Francis Scott Key, on board ship, wrote words for Star Spangled Banner.

Battle of Lake Champlain. Commodore Thomas Macdonough defeated fleet of Sir George Prevost near Plattsburg Sept. 11, 1814 while Brig. Gen. Thomas Macomb held 4,500 ready to oppose 11,000. British withdrew to Canada.

U. S. frigate President was captured Jan. 1815. Constitution captured Cyane and Levant Feb. 20, 1815. Hornet captured Penguin Mar. 23.

The War of 1812 was costly, but inspired national unity, gave recognition to men of the western border, made Andrew Jackson a political power.

Virginia, as far as Fort Snelling, Minn., **Apr. 21-May 10, 729 miles.**

Gas vacuum (internal combustion) engine operated successfully by Samuel Brown in London.

1824

Simon Bolivar ruler of Venezuela, Colombia, Ecuador, Peru broke Spanish power in South America.

1825

Great Britain repeals laws against trade unions.

First railroad to use steam locomotive (on level grade only) Stockton & Darlington RR opened in England **Sept. 27** with Stephenson's engine "Locomotion." First public railroad to use steam exclusively for passenger and freight traffic, Liverpool & Manchester, opened **Sept. 15, 1830.**

Erie Canal opened, first boat left Buffalo **Oct. 26,** reached N.Y. City. **Nov. 4.** Canal cost $7,000,000, but cut travel time by one-third, shipping costs one-tenth; opened Great Lakes area, made N. Y. City chief Atlantic port.

First iron steamboat built in America, the Codorus, at York, Pa., by John Elgar.

1827

Slavery in New York state abolished **July 4.**

Steamship Curacao, first European built oceanic vessel to use steam power alone, crossed the Atlantic **April** from Antwerp to Paramaribo, Dutch Guiana. The Royal William launched in Montreal **Apr. 29, 1831** left there **Aug. 18, 1833,** crossed to Europe in 25 days using only steam.

1828

First passenger railroad in U. S., Baltimore & Ohio, was begun **July 4,** first 14 miles opened to horse-drawn railcar traffic **May 24, 1830.**

1830

Mormon church organized by Joseph Smith in Fayette, N. Y., **Apr. 6.**

Revolution in France. Charles X abdicated **Aug. 2** and was succeeded by the duke of Orleans as Louis Philippe I. There were revolts in Brunswick, Saxony and Belgium. Belgium became independent kingdom.

First regularly scheduled passenger train service in United States using steam power opened at Charleston on South Carolina Railroad **Dec. 25** with 3½-ton U. S.-built locomotive, Best Friend of Charleston.

1831

Nat Turner, a Negro slave from Virginia, led a band of men in a slave rebellion, killed 57 whites, in August. Army called in, Turner captured, tried and hanged.

1832

Black Hawk War (Ill.-Wis.) **Apr. - Sept.** pushed Sac & Fox Indians across Mississippi.

South Carolina convention passes **Ordinance of Nullification Nov. 1832** against permanent tariff protection policy, declaring that if the federal government attempted to enforce the tariff the state would consider itself no longer a member of the Union. Congress **Feb. 1833** passed a compromise tariff act, whereupon South Carolina repealed act.

British Reform Bill: Middle class enfranchised; step toward political democracy **Mar. 23.**

1833

Slavery in British Empire outlawed **Aug. 28** as of **Aug. 1, 1834.** About 700,000 were liberated at cost of £20,000,000. Slavery was abolished in Britain **June 22, 1772.** Slave trade was suppressed 1807.

Oberlin College, first in U. S. to adopt coeducation. Oberlin refused to bar students on account of race 1835.

1835

Texas proclaimed independence from Mexico in convention **Nov. 1,** provisional government formed. Stephen Austin and Sam Houston leaders.

Fire in New York City Dec. 16-17 destroyed 674 buildings.

Gold discovered on Cherokee land in Georgia. Indians forced to cede lands **Dec. 20** and to cross Mississippi.

1836

Texans besieged in Alamo (San Antonio) by Mexicans under Santa Anna **Feb. 23-Mar. 6;** garrison including William Travis, Jim Bowie and David Crockett died defending the fort. At San Jacinto **Apr. 21** Sam Houston and 800 Texans defeated 3,000 Mexicans. Santa Anna signed treaties ending hostilities, promised to recognize Texan independence but Mexican congress repudiated treaties.

Marcus Whitman, H. H. Spaulding and wives reached Fort Walla Walla on Columbia River, Oregon. First white women to cross plains.

Seminole Indians in Florida under Osceola began attacks **Nov. 1, 1836,** protesting forced removal. The unpopular 8-yr. war ended **Aug. 14, 1842;** Indians sent to Oklahoma. War was the most costly Indian war; 1,500 soldiers died, $30,000,000 spent.

1837

Victoria, 18, niece of William IV, became queen of England. Married her first cousin, German Prince Albert of Saxe-Coburg, **1840.** He died **1861.**

1838

The Great Western a steamship, 236 ft. long, 450 horsepower, 1,340 gross tons, left Bristol, England, **Apr. 8,** arrived in N. Y. City **Apr. 23.** The Sirius, 178 ft. long, 703 tons, left Liverpool **Mar. 28** and Queenstown **Apr. 4,** reached N. Y. City **Apr. 22,** using only steam power.

1839

Belgium and the kingdom of the Netherlands were separated by treaties signed by those two countries and by Great Britain, France, Austria, Prussia and Russia at London **Apr. 19.** To the treaties was annexed a document declaring Belgium independent and perpetually neutral.

Opium War broke out between China and Britain. China tried to prohibit opium trade in Canton. British resist and take Canton. War ended with Treaty of Nanking **Aug. 1842.**

1840

Antarctic was found to be a continent by Comdr. Charles Wilkes of first U. S. exploring expedition; named Wilkes Land **Jan.-Feb.**

1841

First emigrant train for California, 47 persons, left Independence, Mo., **May 1,** reached Stanislaus River, **Nov. 4.**

First passenger train on Erie R.R. **June 30.**

1842

First use of anaesthetic (sulphuric ether gas) by Dr. Crawford W. Long in Jefferson, Ga. Dr. William T. G. Morton, dentist, used ether for painless extraction of tooth **Sept. 30, 1846;** administered ether in tumor operation **Oct. 16, 1846** at Massachusetts General Hospital, Boston.

1844

First message over first telegraph line sent from U. S. Supreme Court room **May 24** to Baltimore by inventor **Samuel F. B. Morse: "**What hath God wrought!**"**

Joseph Smith, Mormon leader, and brother Hyrum killed in Carthage, Ill., jail by mob **June 27.**

1845

Texas voted for annexation to U. S. **July 4.** Congress admitted Texas as 28th state **Dec. 29.**

1846

Mexican War. President James K. Polk ordered Gen. **Zachary Taylor** to seize disputed Texan land settled by Mexicans. After border clash, U. S. declared war **May 13;** Mexico **May 23.**

Bear flag of Republic of California raised by American settlers at Sonoma **June 14.** Gen. John C. Fremont took charge **July 5.** Commodore J. S. Sloat took Monterey **July 7** declared California annexed to U.S. Commodore Robert Stockton succeeded Sloat, was ordered to recognize Gen. Kearny as governor and commander-in-chief in California. Kearny was defeated by Mexicans **Dec. 6,** retreated to San Diego.

Gen. Taylor defeated Mexicans at Buena Vista **Feb. 23, 1847.** Gen. Winfield Scott with 12,000 troops (est.)

took Vera Cruz **Mar. 27**; Mexico City **Sept. 14**, captured dictator Santa Anna. By treaty, **Feb. 1848** Mexico ceded claims to Texas, California, Arizona, New Mexico, Nevada, Utah, part of Colorado. U. S. assumed $3,000,000 American claims and paid Mexico $15,000,000.

Treaty with Great Britain June 15, set boundary in Oregon Territory at 49th parallel (extension of existing line). Water boundary settled 1873. Expansionists in U. S. seeking boundary farther north used slogan "54° 40' or fight!"

Mormons, after violent clashes with settlers over polygamy, left Nauvoo, Ill., for west under Brigham Young, settled **July 1847** at Salt Lake City, Utah.

1847

First adhesive U. S. postage stamps on sale **July 1**; Benjamin Franklin 5c, Washington 10c.

1848

Gold discovered Jan. 24 by James W. Marshall, who was erecting sawmill in partnership with Capt. John A. Sutter on American River, branch of the Sacramento, near Coloma, Calif. Small finds of gold were reported 45 mi. northwest of Los Angeles 1841-44.

Louis Philippe dethroned in France; Second Republic set up **Feb. 26.**

Major Events of Civil War, 1861-1865;

For origins of the Civil War see Confederate States and Secession.

South Carolina, Georgia, Alabama, Mississippi, Louisiana and Florida formed the Confederate States of America **Feb. 8.** Chose Jefferson Davis provisional president; were joined later by Texas, North Carolina, Arkansas, Virginia and Tennessee.

First Year of War — 1861

South Carolina, through Gen. Beauregard, demanded surrender of Ft. Sumter in Charleston harbor Apr. 11, Maj. Robert Anderson, USA, refused. Bombardment started at 4:30 a.m. **April 12.** Anderson surrendered **Apr. 14.**

President Lincoln called for 75,000 militia from states by quotas **April 15.**

Battle of Bull Run or Manassas. Brig. Gen. Irvin McDowell attacked Beauregard's forces on the Warrenton Road **July 21**, pushed them back to Henry House hill. Gen. Joseph E. Johnston's army from Winchester, including forces commanded by Brig. Gen. Thomas J. Jackson and Gen. E. Kirby Smith reinforced Confederates, and with help of Gen. Jubal Early's brigade routed Federals. Brig. Gen. B. E. Bee, CSA, said: "Look, there is Jackson standing like a stone wall!" McDowell had 28,455 troops, 18,500 engaged, 2,708 casualties; Confederates had 32,072 available, 18,000 engaged, 1,967 casualties. Congress **July 22** authorized 500,000 men for army.

Events of 1862

Forts Henry and Donelson — Maj. Gen. Henry W. Halleck, Western Dept., sent Brig. Gen. U.S. Grant with 17,000 on river craft against **Ft. Henry** on Tennessee River; it fell **Feb. 6.** Grant rushed troops across 10 mi. of bogs to **Ft. Donelson** on the Cumberland, sent his "unconditional surrender" message to Brig. Gen. Simon B. Buckner, CSA, who gave up with 11,500 **Feb. 16.**

Gen. Albert S. Johnston, CSA, with 40,000 men surprised Grant at **Shiloh** Church near **Pittsburg Landing,** Tenn. **Apr. 6;** Johnston was killed. Gen. Beauregard retreated Apr. 7 after Brig. Gen. Don Carlos Buell reinforced Grant with about 20,000. U.S. had 44,895 engaged, with 1,734 killed out of 13,047 casualties; CSA, 1,728 killed out of 10,699 casualties.

Fighting ships and gunboats under Flag Officer David G. Farragut, Commodore D. D. Porter, in Mississippi silenced **Chalmette** batteries; with Gen. Benjamin F. Butler took forts; **New Orleans** surrendered **Apr.** 25. Farragut made rear admiral.

Monitor and Merrimack — Confederates rebuilt scuttled US frigate Merrimack into ironclad Virginia. Sank Cumberland, USN, destroyed Congress, USN, at Hampton Roads, Va., **Mar.** 8. Three other U.S. ships ran aground including Minnesota. Monitor, flat-decked ironclad, 900 tons, 172 ft. long with revolving turret and 2 11-in. guns, built by John Ericsson at $275,000 cost; Lt. John L. Worden commander, crew of 58, badly damaged Virginia **Mar. 9.** After Union took Virginia's base, Confederates scuttled ship May 11.

Peninsular Campaign — McClellan moved Army of the Potomac by sea to Fort Monroe, Va., 70 mi. from Richmond. Confederates sent Stonewall Jackson up Shenandoah Valley to divert U.S. troops; Jackson lost at **Kernstown**, Va., but routed U.S. troops at **McDowell, Front Royal, Winchester, Cross Keys, Port Republic**, Mar. 23-June 9. McClellan's advance troops clashed with Maj. Gen. James Longstreet at **Williamsburg** May 5. On May 25, 2 U.S. corps crossed to south side of Chickahominy leaving 3 on north side. Gen. Joseph E. Johnston attacked south side May 30, **Battle of Fair Oaks or Seven Pines**, was replused. Johnston was wounded and Lee took over Army of Northern Virginia.

Gen. Lee started **Seven Days' Battles** at Mechanicsville June 26. McClellan withdrew to **Gaines Mill** (1st Cold Harbor) where Lee with 57,000 assaulted Brig. Gen. Fitz John Porter's 34,000 June 27. McClellan held off Lee at **Savage Station** June 29, **Frayser's Farm** or Glendale June 30; stopped Stonewall Jackson at **White Oak Swamp** June 30. At **Malvern Hill** July 1 Confederates had 5,000 casualties from U.S. guns. Despite this success McClellan withdrew army to Harrison's Landing. With over 115,000 men available against Confederates' 95,000, McClellan from June 25-July 1 had 1,734 killed, 8,062 wounded, 6,053 missing; CSA had 3,478 killed, 16,261 wounded, 875 missing. In July Halleck became general in chief. McClellan was succeeded by Maj. Gen. John Pope.

Second Bull Run (Manassas). Stonewall Jackson and Maj. Gen. A. P. Hill, CSA, attacked Maj. Gen. Nathaniel P. Banks (part of Maj. Gen. John Pope's Army of Virginia) at Cedar Mountain, Va., Aug. 9. Jackson destroyed Pope's supplies at **Manassas** Aug. 26. Major battle was fought **Aug. 30.** Pope was checked by Jackson and Longstreet, withdrew; was relieved.

Antietam (Sharpsburg). Lee with 50,000 crossed Potomac Sept. 4 to Frederick, Md., moved across South Mountain to Hagerstown, Md. McClellan, fought Longstreet and D. H. Hill at **South Mountain** Sept. 14, Lee dropped back to Antietam creek near Sharpsburg, Md., Sept. 15; Jackson took **Harpers Ferry** where only 1,300 cavalry of 12,000 USA escaped. McClellan attacked **Sept. 17;** stopped Lee, but failed to use reserve and let Lee withdraw across Potomac. U. S. had 70,000 engaged, 13,000 casualties; CSA had 50,000 engaged, 13,000 casualties.

Fredericksburg, Va. Lincoln relieved McClellan, gave Army of the Potomac to Maj. Gen. Ambrose E. Burnside. Burnside crossed Rappahannock, made frontal attacks on Marye's Heights above Fredericksburg **Dec. 13.** Lee, Longstreet and Jackson with 75,000 repulsed him. USA lost 12,653; CSA 5,377.

Preliminary proclamation, Sept. 22, by President Lincoln announced that **Jan. 1, 1863,** slaves would be declared free in territory then in rebellion.

Events of 1863

Lincoln's Emancipation Proclamation Jan. 1 declared free forever the slaves in Arkansas, Texas, Louisiana (certain parishes already occupied excepted); Mississippi, Alabama, Florida, Georgia, South Carolina, North Carolina, Tennessee and Virginia

In Austria **Ferdinand I** abdicated **Dec. 2** in favor of his nephew Franz Josef. In Hungary, freedom was declared under Louis Kossuth; revolts in Ireland, Lombardy, Venice, Denmark and Schleswig-Holstein.

Communist Manifesto written by Karl Marx (1818-1883) and Friedrich Engels (1820-1895); still the basic doctrine of communism.

1850

Senator Henry Clay's Compromise of 1850 passed; admitted California as 31st state **Sept. 9**, slavery forbidden; made Utah and New Mexico territories without decision on slavery; amended Fugitive Slave Law punishing those who aided fugitive and abolished jury trial for fugitive, ended slave trade in Dist. of Columbia.

Jenny Lind's first American concert at Castle Garden, New York City, **Sept. 11**; P. T. Barnum was manager.

Taiping Rebellion, led by Hung Hsiu-ch'uan, began in Kwangsi province, China. One of the largest civil wars in history, it resulted in the death of an estimated 20 to 40 million, devastated entire provinces and nearly toppled the Manchu dynasty. The Taiping movement, pseudo-Christian in nature, was finally suppressed **1864** by Tseng Kuo-fan with the help of

Emancipation and Lincoln's Assassination

(West Virginia and other portions excepted). About 3,000,000 slaves were thus declared free.

Chancellorsville, Va. —Maj. Gen. Joseph E. Hooker succeeded Burnside and with 90,000 available, attempted to envelop Lee **May 2**. Jackson led 32,000 around US Army, drove in right of Maj. Gen. O. O. Howard. Jackson wounded by own troops **May 2** died May 10; succeeded by Maj. Gen. J. E. B. Stuart. Maj. Gen. John Sedgwick forced Confederates out of Marye's Heights; was pushed back May 4. Against consensus Hooker withdrew across Rappahannock. US casualties 17,197; CSA 13,000. Lincoln called for 100,000 men for 6 months June 15.

Gettysburg — Lee with 76,224 and 272 guns, invaded Penn. Army of the Potomac had 115,256, about 90,000 effective, 362 guns. Lincoln gave Maj. Gen. George G. Meade top command June 28. 1st US Cavalry (Buford) pushed back at Gettysburg by Lt. Gen. A. P. Hill, CSA, **July 1**. Lt. Gen. Richard S. Ewell, CSA, forced US back to Cemetery Hill; Maj. Gen. Reynolds, USA, killed. U. S. took Culp's Hill, extended line to Round Top. Lee's attacks checked **July 2**. On **July 3** Maj. Gen. George E. Pickett, Maj. Gen. Isaac Trimble and Brig. Gen. James J. Pettigrew with 12,400 made assault on foot from Seminary Ridge vs. US center (Hancock); were repulsed with 4,500 casualties. Lee retreated into Virginia; Meade did not pursue. Losses: US, 3,155 killed, 14,529 wounded, 5,365 missing; CSA, 3,903 killed, 12,709 wounded, 5,425 missing. Many of the missing were prisoners. Total casualties estimated at 23,049 USA, 20,451 CSA.

Vicksburg — Gen. William T. Sherman took **Jackson**, Miss., May.14. Lt. Gen. John C. Pemberton, CSA, commanding 30,000 men was defeated at **Champion's Hill and Black River Bridge**, shut up in Vicksburg. He surrendered **July 4**; Grant paroled prisoners. Gen. Banks with 15,000 captured **Port Hudson** July 8, giving US control of Mississippi River.

Tennessee — Maj. Gen. William S. Rosecrans took **Chattanooga** Sept. 9. Braxton Bragg, CSA, drove him back to **Chickamauga**, but Maj. Gen. George H. Thomas checked Bragg **Sept. 18-20**; was called "Rock of Chickamauga." Grant made commander of all armies there. Hooker took **Lookout Mt.**, fought "Battle Above the Clouds" **Nov. 24**. Sherman and Thomas dislodged Bragg at **Missionary Ridge** Nov. 25. Bragg retreated to Georgia.

Events of 1864

Grant made general in chief Mar. 12. Sherman succeeded him in West. Draft for 500,000 men to serve 3 yrs. or duration begun **Mar. 10**; 200,000 more Mar. 14.

Rear Adm. David G. Farragut won naval battle **Mobile Bay** Aug. 5.

Wilderness, Spotsylvania — Bloody battles followed when Grant crossed the Rapidan and was attacked by Lee at **Wilderness** May 5. Grant attacked Lee at **Spotsylvania Court House** May 10 (2nd Wilderness). Maj. Gen. Franklin G. Barlow took Spotsylvania salient, including **Bloody Angle** May 12 (3rd Wilderness). U.S. killed and wounded May 5-12 est. 26,813; missing 4,183. Maj. Gen. Sheridan's caval-

ry defeated Maj. Gen. J. E. B. Stuart at **Yellow Tavern**, Va., May 11; Stuart was fatally wounded, died May 12 in Richmond.

Cold Harbor — Lee took strong position near the Chickahominy. Grant made frontal attacks June 3, lost 7,000 casualties in 30 minutes, 11,000 June 1-3.

USS Kearsarge — Capt. John A. Winslow, engaged **CSS Alabama**, Capt. Raphael Semmes, off Cherbourg, France, **June 19**; Alabama surrendered and sank.

Early vs. Sheridan — Lee sent Maj. Gen. Jubal A. Early to hold Shenandoah Valley. Sheridan defeated Early at **Winchester** Sept. 19, **Fisher's Hill** Sept. 22. Early surprised Wright at **Cedar Creek** Oct. 19; Sheridan's famous ride from Winchester rallied troops, brought victory.

Sherman's Campaign for Atlanta — Sherman defeated Johnston at **Resaca**, Ga., May 14-15. Hooker repulsed at **New Hope Church**, Ga., May 25. Johnston repulsed Sherman at **Kenesaw Mtn.** June 27 (U.S. casualties 3,000, CSA 600), evacuated post, was superseded by Gen. J. B. Hood, CSA, July 17. Lt. Gen. William J. Hardee, CSA, defeated at **Peach Tree Creek** July 20. Hardee defeated in battle of **Atlanta** July 22 by Gen. J. B. McPherson who was killed. Sherman occupied Atlanta **Sept. 2**, burned it **Nov. 15**, started **March to the Sea**, reached **Savannah** Dec. 21. Thomas defeated Hood at **Nashville**, Tenn.

Events of 1865

Confederates evacuated Columbia, S. C., and **Charleston**, S. C., Feb. 17. Cape Fear River forts captured Feb. 20-21. Brig. Gen. George A. Custer defeated Early at **Waynesboro**, Va., Mar. 2. Confederates evacuated **Petersburg** and **Richmond** Apr. 2-3. Lee surrendered 27,805 to Grant at **Appomattox Court House**, Va., **Apr. 9**. Johnston surrendered 31,243 to Sherman at **Durham Station**, N. C., **Apr. 18**.

Murder of Lincoln

Lincoln was shot by John Wilkes Booth, an actor, in Ford's Theatre, in Washington, D.C., **April 14**, died **April 15**. Booth died of a bullet wound **April 26** in burning barn, on a farm near Bowling Green, Va. Those hanged for complicity were Mrs. Mary E. Surratt, David E. Herold, George A. Atzerodt and Lewis Payne (Powell) **July 7**. Also convicted of conspiracy were Dr. Samuel A. Mudd, who set Booth's broken ankle, Samuel Arnold, Michael O'Laughlin, and Edward Spangler. All were sentenced to life imprisonment except Spangler, who received a 6-year sentence. They were sent to Dry Tortugas prison, off Key West, where O'Laughlin died during an 1867 outbreak of yellow fever. Dr. Mudd's unselfish services as a physician during the outbreak won him a pardon; Arnold and Spangler were freed with Dr. Mudd in 1869. John H. Surratt, son of Mary E., fled to Europe, was brought back, tried and freed. Booth's body was buried under the stone floor of a naval prison in Washington, D. C., later reburied in the Booth family plot in Baltimore.

Slavery was abolished by adoption of the 13th amendment to the U. S. Constitution **Dec. 18**.

the "Ever Victorious Army" of Gen. Charles G. (Chinese) Gordon.

1851
Gold found in Australia.
Cornerstones of wings of U. S. Capitol laid.
New York & Hudson River R.R., New York to Albany, opened **Oct.**

1852
Louis Napoleon crowned emperor of the French.
Uncle Tom's Cabin, by Harriet Beecher Stowe, published. •

1853
Commodore Matthew C. Perry, U.S.N., received by Lord of Toda, Japan, **July 14;** negotiated treaty to open Japan to U. S. ships. Ratified **Mar. 8, 1854.**
Crimean War. A dispute between Greek Orthodox and Roman monks over holy places held by Turkey in Palestine led Russian Czar Nicholas I to extend protection to Greeks. Turkey declared war **Oct. 4, 1853.** Britain and France, fearing expansion of Russia, declared war **May 28, 1854.** Russia occupied Moldavia and Wallachia. Fighting concentrated in the Crimea and included famous **Charge of the Light Brigade** at Balaklava **Oct. 25, 1854,** 400 out of 607 killed; Russian defeat at Inkerman **Nov. 5, 1854;** fall of Sebastopol **Sept. 11, 1855.** Sardinia sent 15,000 troops to Allies; Prussia and Sweden cooperated. **Florence Nightingale** established first dressing stations. By Treaty of Paris **Mar. 30, 1856,** Russia ceded part of Bessarabia to Moldavia, freed Danube for navigation. Black Sea closed to warships (repudiated 1870).

1854
Republican party started at Ripon, Wis., **Feb. 28;** first state organization, Jackson, Mich., **July 6.** Opposed Kansas-Nebraska Act (became law May 30) which left issue of slavery in Kansas and Nebraska to vote of settlers.
Henry D. Thoreau wrote Walden.

1855
Walt Whitman issued Leaves of Grass; Henry W. Longfellow wrote Song of Hiawatha.

1856
First railroad train crossed Mississippi River at Rock Island, Ill.—Davenport, Ia., **Apr. 21.**
Republican party's first nominee for president, John C. Fremont **June-Nov.,** defeated by James Buchanan. Abraham Lincoln made 50 speeches for Fremont.
Lawrence, Kan., sacked **May 21** by slavery party; abolitionist John Brown led anti-slavery men against Missourians at Osawatomie **Aug. 30.** Federal troops ousted Missourians.

1857
Dred Scott decision of U. S. Supreme Court, 6-3, that a Negro slave did not become free when taken into free state and had no rights as citizen. Abraham Lincoln denounced decision. Chief Justice Roger B. Taney delivered the court's opinion that the Missouri Compromise was unconstitutional. Minnesota outlawed slavery.
Great Mutiny in India (Sepoy Rebellion) began in Merrut **May 10** when Indian soldiers revolted against British officers. First major Indian rebellion against English rule, crushed **1858.** British East India Company abolished and India placed under crown rule as a result of mutiny.
John D. Lee, a Mormon, led raid against wagon train at Mountain Meadows **Sept. 11,** killed 120, spared only 17 children under 7. U. S. Army supplies burned. Government sent 6,000 troops to supress "rebellion." Mormon Church unjustly accused.

1858
First Atlantic cable completed by Cyrus W. Field **Aug. 5.** Queen Victoria and President Buchanan exchanged greetings, but cable failed **Sept. 1.** Field tried again in 1865, succeeded in 1866.
Lincoln-Douglas debates in Ill. Aug. 21-Oct. 15.

1859
Dixie composed by Daniel D. Emmett was first performed by him with Bryant's Minstrels at Mechanics Hall, N. Y. City **Apr. 4.**
First commercially productive oil well, drilled near Titusville, Pa., by Edwin L. Drake **Aug. 27,** started boom.
John Brown, abolitionist, with 21 men seized U. S. Armory at Harpers Ferry (then Va.) **Oct. 16.** U. S. Marines under Lt. Col. Robert E. Lee captured raiders, killed 11. One Marine and 5 civilians also killed. Brown was hanged for treason by Virginia **Dec. 2** as were 5 of his band, at Charlestown (now Charles Town, W. Va.).
Darwin's Origin of Species published. His theory of evolution caused revolution in scientific, philosophical and religious thinking.

1860
Abraham Lincoln, Republican, elected president by 1,866,452 popular and 180 electoral votes; Stephen A. Douglas had 1,375,157 and 12; John C. Breckinridge, 847,953 and 72; John Bell 590,631 and 39. Lincoln took office **Mar. 4, 1861.** Breckinridge and Bell supported secession.
First Pony Express between Sacramento, Calif., and St. Joseph, Mo., 1,980 miles apart, started from each place at 5 p.m., **Apr. 3;** 80 men each rode 75 miles on 429 horses changed every 10 miles. There were 190 relay stations. The service ended **Oct. 24, 1861** when first transcontinental telegraph line was completed.
Giuseppe Garibaldi led 1,000 volunteers to Sicily in **May** to unify Italy for force; deposed Francis II of Naples; hailed Victor Emmanuel of Sardinia as king of Italy.

1861-65—Civil War. See Article Pages 788-789

1861
Emancipation of Russian serfs by Czar Alexander II. Paved the way for later reforms by Alexander.

1863
Draft riots in N. Y. City killed an estimated 1,000 including Negroes who were hung by mobs **July 13-16.** Protested provision allowing money payment in place of military service. Property loss about $1,500,-000. Money payment in place of service ended **July 4, 1864.**

1864
Sand Creek massacre of Cheyenne and Arapaho Indians by Col. John M. Chivington **Nov. 29** in a surprise dawn raid by 900 cavalrymen who killed between 150-500 men, women and children; 9 soldiers died. These tribes were awaiting surrender terms when attacked.

1866
Ku Klux Klan formed secretly in South to terrorize Negroes who voted. Disbanded **1869.** Not to be confused with Ku Klux Klan, Inc. organized **1915.**
First post of the Grand Army of the Republic formed at Decatur, Ill., **Apr. 6.** First national encampment met **Nov. 2** in Indianapolis, Ind. For years this Union veterans organization was a political force in the nation. Last encampment held **Aug. 31, 1949** in Indianapolis, 6 of the 16 surviving veterans attended.

1867
Alaska sold to U. S. by Russia for $7,200,000 (2 cents an acre) **Mar. 30** through efforts of Sec. of State William H. Seward and Sen. Charles Sumner.
Emperor Maximillian of Mexico executed by Juarez party **June 19.** He was an Austrian archduke placed on throne **Apr. 10, 1864** by French.
Dominion of Canada established **July 1.**
Abolition of the Shogunate and restoration of the Mikado marked beginning of Meiji reforms that industrialized and modernized Japan; feudalism abolished **1871;** Constitution promulgated **1889.**

1868
The World Almanac, a publication of the New York World newspaper, appeared for the first time.
Thomas D'Arcy McGee, a "Father of Confedera-

tion," was shot in first Canadian political assassination.

President Andrew Johnson, blocked by Senate in attempt to remove Edwin M. Stanton, secretary of war, for opposing his policies, was impeached for violation of Tenure of Office Act by House; tried by Senate and acquitted **March-May**. Stanton resigned.

Memorial Day first observed officially **May 30** on order by Gen. John A. Logan, commander G.A.R.

1869

Financial "Black Friday" in New York **Sept. 24**; caused by gold corner.

Transcontinental railroad completed; golden spike driven at Promontory, Utah **May 10** marking the junction of Central Pacific and Union Pacific.

Woman's suffrage law passed in territory of Wyoming **Dec. 10**.

1870

Franco-Prussian War. Napoleon III, French emperor, tricked into declaring war on Prussia by Bismarck, Prussian chancellor, over Spanish succession issue; surrendered with large army at Sedan **Sept. 4**. Nationalists declared republic **Sept. 4**. Leon Gambetta, bitter-ender, escaped from Paris in balloon **Oct. 7** to carry on war.

The troops of Victor Emmanuel II, under Gen. Cadorna, took possession of Rome **Sept. 20** in the name of the kingdom of Italy. Rome and the rest of the Papal States then were annexed by a plebiscite, taken **Oct. 2**.

1871

Court of Arbitration awarded United States damages of $15,500,000 in gold against Britain because British equipped Alabama and 12 other Confederate raiders. After sinking 65 U.S. ships Alabama was destroyed by U.S.S. Kearsarge off Cherbourg **1864**.

William I of Hohenzollern proclaimed German emperor at Versailles **Jan. 18**. Paris "Red Republicans" organized commune **Mar. 18-May 29**; burned Hotel de Ville, Tuileries palace, executed 67 hostages. Communards overcome by French army; deaths est. 20,000.

Treaty of Frankfort ended Franco-Prussian War **May 23**. France ceded Alsace, most of Lorraine, paid 5 billion francs indemnity.

The Law of Guarantees, passed by the Italian Parliament **May 13**, granted the pope and his successors possession of the Vatican, the Lateran and the villa of Castel Gandolfo and a yearly allowance of 3,225,000 lire, or about $645,000. The money was not claimed.

Great fire destroyed Chicago Oct. 8-11; loss est. $196,000,000. Started in Mrs. O'Leary's barn, 558 De Koven St., by cow upsetting lantern, according to legend.

Henry M. Stanley sent by James Gordon Bennett, owner of New York Herald, to find David Livingstone, missionary, greeted him **Nov. 10** at Ujiji in Central Africa, now Tanzania, with "Dr. Livingstone, I presume?"

1872

Amnesty Act restores civil rights to citizens of the South **May 22** except 500-700 former Confederate leaders.

1873

Panic in New York City began with bank failures **Sept. 20**.

First U. S. postal card issued **May 1**.

1874

"Boss" William Tweed in N. Y. City, convicted of fraud **Nov. 19** and sentenced to 12 years in prison; the court released him from Blackwells Island prison **June 1875** on a technicality; he was committed to Ludlow St. jail in a civil suit, escaped **Dec. 4, 1875**, and went to Cuba, then to Spain; brought back to N.Y. City **Nov. 1876**; died in Ludlow St. jail **Apr. 12, 1878**.

1875

Congress passes first Civil Rights Act, Mar. 1, which guarantees equal rights to Negroes in public accommodations and jury duty. Act invalidated in **1883** by Supreme Court ruling that the federal government

can protect only political, not social, rights.

First Kentucky Derby held in **May** at Churchill Downs at Louisville, Ky.

Mary Baker Eddy publishes "Science and Health."

1876

Samuel J. Tilden, Democrat, received majority of 250,000 popular votes for President over Rutherford B. Hayes, Republican, and had 184 electoral votes against 163, with returns from South Carolina, Florida, Louisiana and Oregon, 22 electoral votes, in dispute. Bitter contest for delegates with charges of corruption; left issue to Congress, which appointed electoral commission, 8 Republicans, 7 Democrats, Hayes given Presidency by strict party vote.

Gen. George A. Custer and 264 soldiers of the 7th Cavalry killed **June 25** in "last stand," Battle of the Little Big Horn, Mont., in Sioux Indian War, by Indian tribes united by Sitting Bull; fighting led by Chiefs Gall and Crazy Horse.

James Butler (Wild Bill) Hickok, shot dead from behind by Jack McCall, a desperado, in Deadwood, S. D., **Aug. 2**. A vigilance committee acquitted McCall but the U. S. Court in Yankton, S. D.; found him guilty and he was hanged.

1877

Molly Maguires, Irish terrorist society in Pennsylvania, broken up by hanging of 11 leaders for murders.

1878

First commercial telephone exchange opened, New Haven, Conn., **Jan. 28, 1878**. First private exchange, used by physicians, reported in use **July 1877** at Hartford, Conn.

1879

F. W. Woolworth opened his first five-and-ten store in Utica, N. Y., **Feb. 22**.

Henry George published Progress & Poverty, advocating single tax on land.

1881

President James A. Garfield shot in Washington, D.C., **July 2**; died in Elberon, N. J., **Sept. 19**.

Federation of Organized Trades and Labor Unions formed **Aug. 2** at Terre Haute, Ind.; later joined with 25 independent unions to form the American Federation of Labor at Columbus, Ohio, **Dec. 1886**.

1882

Prof. Robert Koch announced, in Berlin, discovery of the tuberculosis germ **Mar. 24**.

Triple Alliance of Germany, Austria and Italy formed. Denounced by Italy **1914**.

1883

Brooklyn Bridge opened May 24; panic on it **May 30**, 12 trampled to death.

1884

Financial panic in New York **May 5-7**.

1885

Gen. Charles G. (Chinese) Gordon, British governor of the Sudan, was slain **Jan. 26** by a Moslem soldier, who stuck the head on a spear, at Khartoum. Several thousand whites were massacred by the Mahdi's troops. Gen. Kitchener defeated the Mahdi's army **Sept. 2, 1898**.

First electric street railway in United States opened in Baltimore by Leo Daft **Aug. 10**.

Canadian rebel Louis Riel hanged for treason at Regina, following crushing of Northwest Rebellion.

Last spike driven Nov. 7 in Canadian Pacific Railway at Craigellachie, British Columbia, completed Canadian transcontinental railway system.

1886

Haymarket riot, evening of **May 4**, followed bitter labor battles for 8-hour day in Chicago, attacks on strike-breakers, police violence and attempts of anarchists to incite workers. A bomb killed 7 police and wounded 66. Eight anarchists found guilty. Seven years later Gov. John P. Altgeld denounced trial as unfair.

Geronimo, Apache Indian, surrendered **Mar. 27** to U. S. Gen. George Crook in Sonora, Mex., but fled the next day and finally surrendered **Sept. 4** to U. S. Gen. Nelson A. Miles in Arizona.

Dr. Arthur Conan Doyle invented famous detective Sherlock Holmes, in story, A Study in Scarlet. Published in Beeton's Christmas Annual **1887**.

1887

Flood in Hwang-ho River, China; 900,000 persons perished.

Opera Comique in Paris burned **May 25**; 200 lives lost.

1888

Great blizzard in eastern U. S. **Mar. 11-14**; 400 deaths.

1889

Crown Prince Rudolf of Austria and Baroness Maria Vetsera found slain in his hunting lodge, Mayerling, near Vienna **Jan. 29**.

Johnstown, Pa., flood May 31; 2,200 lives lost.

Universal Exhibition in Paris **May 6-Nov. 6.** Eiffel Tower (984.25 ft.) opened. First automobile exhibited, a Benz.

Dom Pedro II, emperor of Brazil, forced off throne by planters after he freed slaves. Died in Paris **1891**; last emperor on American soil.

1890

First execution by electrocution; William Kemmler **Aug. 6** at Auburn Prison, Auburn, N.Y., for murder.

Battle of Wounded Knee, S. D., **Dec. 29**, the last major conflict between Indians and U. S. troops, occurred when a band of Sioux were captured and brought to Wounded Knee Creek where Col. J. W. Forsyth ordered them disarmed. Some Indians resisted sparking the battle which killed about 200 Indian men, women and children; 29 soldiers died, 33 wounded.

Castle Garden closed as immigration depot and Ellis Island opened **Dec. 31;** closed 1954.

1892

Homestead, Pa., strike at Carnegie steel mills, near Pittsburgh; conflict between 300 Pinkerton guards and strikers; 7 guards and 11 strikers and spectators shot to death, many wounded **July 6**.

1893

Ford's Theater building, Washington, D. C. where Lincoln was shot, used by Pension Bureau, collapsed **June 9** killing 22.

1894

Chinese-Japanese War began July 25; Battle of Yalu **Sept. 17**; Treaty of Shimonoseki **April 17, 1895** gave Japan the Liaotung Peninsula, Formosa and the Pescadores.

Jacob S. Coxey led 20,000 unemployed from the Midwest into Washington, D. C., **Apr. 29**. Coxey died **May 18, 1951**, aged 97.

Strike of employees of Pullman Co., South Chicago, Ill., June, led Eugene V. Debs to call sympathetic strike of American Railway Union. President Cleveland called out Federal troops over protest of Gov. Altgeld (Illinois). Debs and 3 others were imprisoned 6 months for contempt of court. Strike called off **Aug. 7**.

Thomas A. Edison's kinetoscope given first public showing at 1155 Broadway, New York City **Apr. 14**, was patented **1891** for U. S. only.

Capt. Alfred Dreyfus found guilty of betraying French army secrets **Dec. 22** in sensational frame-up; real culprit, Major Esterhazy, acquitted; Dreyfus condemned to Devil's Island, off French Guiana. Recalled for second trial by efforts of Emile Zola and Clemenceau; again condemned **Sept. 9, 1899**. Public clamor led to pardon **Sept. 19**. Further proofs of innocence led to complete rehabilitation **1906** with rank of major. He served as a lieut. colonel in World War I.

1895

Cuban Revolution resumed Feb. 20; Gen. Antonio Maceo, leader of the insurrection, was killed in action **Dec. 7, 1896**.

X-rays discovered by Wilhelm Konrad Roentgen, a German physicist; Nobel prize winner **1901**.

1896

President Cleveland intervened in boundary dispute between Venezuela and British Guiana on basis

---

Spanish-American War of 1898; United States Becomes Naval Power

Spanish misrule in Cuba led to repeated attempts by Cuban patriots to gain rights of citizenship, abolition of slavery, and finally independence. When South America broke from Europe in the 1820's pro-slavery influence in the U. S. blocked movements to free Cuba and Puerto Rico. But in 1852, President Fillmore refused to join Great Britain and France in guaranteeing Spanish authority in Cuba. In 1854, the Ostend Manifesto, written largely by James Buchanan, urged the U.S. to buy Cuba or seize it to abolish oppression. Grant's administration offered to buy Cuba, but Spain refused.

In Cuba revolts led by Narciso Lopez and Joaquin de Aguero, 1848-1851, were suppressed and the leaders executed. In 1868, a major revolt led by Carlos de Cespedes and Manuel de Quesada lasted 10 years. In 1873, the Virginius expedition, flying the American flag, was seized by the Spaniards, and Americans and Cubans aboard were shot. This did not stop supplying of arms from the U. S. In 1895, the insurrection had spread so widely under Generals Calixto Garcia, Maximo Gomez and Antonio Macea that Spain landed 150,000 troops, but by 1896 over half of the island was in the hands of the patriots. The U. S. offered to mediate but was repulsed. The country was laid waste by Spanish troops and the accounts of suffering increased sentiment in the U. S. in favor of a free Cuba.

The battleship Maine, Capt. Charles D. Sigsbee, sent to Havana in January on goodwill tour, was blown up **Feb. 15, 1898;** 264 men, 2 officers killed. U.S. inquiry, Capt. William T. Sampson, board pres., blamed external explosion **Mar. 2**. Spanish inquiry **Mar. 28** blamed internal explosion. Congress **Mar. 9** voted $50,000,000 for defense. President McKinley **Mar. 27** demanded Spain grant armistice for negotiation with Cuba via U. S., end relocation of noncom-

batants in special military enclaves. Spain **Mar. 31** offered to arbitrate Maine, end relocation, but wanted Cubans to ask for armistice. After appeal by foreign ministers Spain granted armistice **Apr. 9**. President **Apr. 11** asked Congress for authority to intervene in Cuba. Congress **Apr. 20-25** debated joint resolution recognizing independence of Cuba, asked Spain to withdraw and empowered president to enforce it; adopted it with statement war existed since **Apr. 21**. Spain declared war **Apr. 24**.

Commodore George Dewey, with 6 warships destroyed the Spanish fleet (10 ships) in Manila Bay **May 1**, occupied Cavite. Spain, 167 dead; U.S., 7 wounded. Marines landed at Guantanamo **May 11**. Maj. Gen. William R. Shafter landed 10,000 men at Daiquiri and Siboney, including 1st U. S. Volunteer Cavalry (Rough Riders) recruited by Lt. Col. Theodore Roosevelt, commanded by Col. Leonard Wood. Brig. Gen. H. W. Lawton, Brig. Gen. Adna R. Chaffee with 6,654 men attacked El Caney, defended by 500 Spaniards **July 1**. Maj. Gen. Joseph Wheeler, Brig. Gen. J. F. Kent carried San Juan Hill with 8,336, same day.

Admiral Cervera's fleet left Santiago harbor **July 3**, was destroyed by ships of acting Rear Adm. Sampson and Commodore Winfield S. Schley; 353 Spaniards killed, 151 wounded; 1 American killed. Santiago surrendered **July 17**. Maj. Gen. Nelson A. Miles took Puerto Rico **July 25-28**. Armistice signed **Aug. 12**. Peace treaty signed in Paris **Dec. 10** eliminated Spain from lands discovered by Columbus. U. S. acquired Puerto Rico, Guam and Philippines, paying $20,000,000 for all Spanish claims in latter; guaranteed Cuban independence (ratified **Feb. 6, 1899**). U. S. had treaty rights in Cuba until 1934; granted Philippine independence **July 4, 1946**.

of Monroe Doctrine; appointed arbitration commission which settled it **Feb. 2, 1897.**

Guglielmo Marconi received first wireless patent from Britain **June 2.**

William Jennings Bryan delivered "Cross of Gold" speech at Democratic National Convention in Chicago **July 8.** Bryan nominated for president but defeated by Republican William McKinley.

1897

Eugene V. Debs formed Social Democratic party.

1898

Radium discovered by Pierre Curie, Mme. Curie and G. Bemont in Paris.

1898—Spanish-American War.
See Article Page 792

1899

South African (Boer) War began **Oct. 11;** Ladysmith relieved **Feb. 28, 1900;** Pretoria fell **June 5, 1900;** war ended **May 31, 1902** with loss of independence of Boer republics, Transvaal and Orange Free State, now in Republic of South Africa. British losses: 5,773 killed; 16,171 dead of wounds or disease; 22,829 wounded. Boers engaged est. 65,000; losses unknown.

Filipino insurgents (est. 12,000 under arms) unable to get recognition of independence from U. S. started guerrilla war **Feb. 4.** Crushed with capture **Mar. 23, 1901** of leader, Emilio Aguinaldo, by Brig. Gen. Frederick Funston.

Open Door Policy of U. S. Secy. of State John Hay supported by 6 nations. Policy was to make China an open market for international commerce and to preserve its integrity as a nation.

Boxer anti-foreign uprising started in China: Westerners and westernized Chinese murdered.

1900

Carry Nation, Kansas anti-saloon agitator, began raiding with hatchet. Died **June 9, 1911.**

Boxers in China killed German minister **June 20.** Foreigners besieged in Peking legations. Relief expedition of 18,000 American, British, French, Japanese and Russian troops took Tientsin **July 13;** Peking **Aug. 14.** U. S. had 2,500 men under Maj. Gen. A. R. Chaffee. Germans arrived and Field Marshal Count Alfred von Waldersee led army of occupation. Russia refused to yield parts of Manchuria. Dowager empress of China accepted allied terms **Sept. 1901.** All except U. S. exacted large concessions and indemnity of $333,000,000 payable in 39 years. U. S. accepted $25,000,000; returned half in 1908 to provide student exchange fund.

Campaign to wipe out yellow fever in Cuba begun **June 26** by Drs. Walter Reed, Aristides Agramonte, Jesse Lazear and James Carroll.

Galveston hurricane and tidal wave **Sept. 8;** 5,000 lives estimated lost.

1901

President William McKinley was shot at the Pan-American Exposition in Buffalo, N. Y., **Sept. 6** by Leon Czolgosz, anarchist; died **Sept. 14.** Theodore Roosevelt, 42, became youngest U. S. President.

Marconi signalled letter "S" by wireless telegraph across Atlantic from Cornwall, England, to Newfoundland **Dec. 12.**

1902

Anglo-Japanese alliance formed **Jan. 30** to protect Japan against encroaching Russians.

Cuban Republic inaugurated. American occupation under Gen. Leonard Wood ended **May 20.**

First International Arbitration Court opened in The Hague, Holland, **October.**

1903

First automobile trip across U. S. from San Francisco to New York **May 23-Aug. 1.**

Henry Ford, having withdrawn from the Detroit Automobile Co. in 1901 organized Ford Motor Co.

Treaty between U. S. and Colombia to have U. S. dig Panama Canal signed **Jan. 22, 1903,** rejected by Colombia. Panama declared independence **Nov. 3;** recognized by President Theodore Roosevelt **Nov. 6.** *See Canal Zone and Panama.*

First successful flight in heavier-than-air mechanically propelled airplane by **Orville Wright** (1871-1948) **Dec. 17, 1903,** rising from base of Kill Devil Hill, 4 miles south of Kitty Hawk, N. C., 120 ft. in 12 sec., in 27 mph wind. Fourth flight same day by **Wilbur Wright** (1867-1912), 852 ft., in 59 sec. Plane patented **May 22, 1906.**

1904

Russo-Japanese War began **Feb. 6.** Port Arthur surrendered to Japanese **Jan. 2, 1905.** Peace treaty signed in U. S. Navy Yard, Portsmouth, N. H., **Sept. 5, 1905.**

New York subway opened **Oct. 27.**

1905

Russian revolution crushed by Czar Nicholas II. Resulted in creation of Duma (parliament) to placate liberals. First meeting of Duma **May 10;** dissolved **July.**

Norway dissolved union with Sweden.

1906

San Francisco earthquake and fire **Apr. 18-19.** Dead: 452. Loss: $350,000,000.

Harry K. Thaw, Pittsburgh millionaire, shot and killed Stanford White, famous architect, on the roof of Madison Square Garden, N.Y. (26th and Madison) **June 25** on ground of avenging honor of wife Evelyn Nesbit.

1907

Financial panic in the United States.

Standard Oil of Indiana fined $29,240,000 by Judge K. M. Landis in U. S. Court, Chicago, for accepting freight rebates **Apr. 3.** Set aside **July 22, 1908.** Railroads found guilty of giving rebates.

First round-world cruise of U. S. "great White Fleet"; 16 battleships, 12,000 men; exhibited U. S. naval strength.

1908

Chelsea, Mass. destroyed by fire; loss more than $6,000,000, **Apr. 12.**

1909

Admiral Robert E. Peary reached North Pole **Apr. 6** on sixth attempt, accompanied by Matthew Henson, Negro, and 4 Eskimos.

Louis Bleriot flew across the English Channel from Calais to Dover, 31. mi. in 37 min., **July 25.**

Budget in Britain: "Soak the rich" taxation financed social security measures.

1910

Boy Scouts of America incorporated **Feb. 8** following visit to England by William D. Boyce, Chicago publisher; while there he met Sir Robert Baden-Powell, founder of the Scouting movement, who inspired him to initiate the program in America.

Glenn H. Curtiss won $10,000 offered by the World, N. Y., for first continuous flight, Albany to New York, 137 mi., 152 min., **May 29.**

Dynamite explosion at Los Angeles Times **Oct. 1** caused fire killing 21 in labor dispute.

1911

Italian-Turkish war began **Sept. 29.** Italians made first combat use of aircraft in warfare; Libya acquired by Italy.

First transcontinental airplane flight (interrupted by landings) by C. P. Rodgers, New York to Pasadena, **Sept. 17-Nov. 5;** time in air 82 hr., 4 min.

Capt. Roald Amundsen, Norwegian explorer, reached South Pole **Dec. 14.**

Mexican Revolution. Porfirio Diaz, president of Mexico since 1877 (except 1880-84) resigned **May 25** after successful revolt by Francisco L. Madero who succeeded him. People living in poverty wanted restoration of communal lands (ejidos), better conditions. In 1912 Madero, supported by Gen. Huerta, put down revolts by Gens. Orozco, Reyes and Felix Diaz. In Feb. 1913 Reyes was killed; Huerta helped depose Madero. Madero, his brother and Vice President Suarez were murdered. President Wilson refused recognition to Huerta and "government by assassination." Venustiano Carranza, rallying Maderos, was opposed by Gen. Francisco (Pancho) Villa in north. When American sailors were arrested at Tampico **Apr. 9, 1914,** the U. S. sent Atlantic fleet to Vera Cruz. Marines landed and snipers killed 19. Brig. Gen. Frederick Funston was sent **Apr. 27.** Huerta resigned **July 14, 1914,** Carranza occupied Mexico City **Aug. 20.** Villa, supported by Zapata, forced Carranza to leave for Vera Cruz. U. S. recognized Carranza **Oct. 19, 1915,** placed embargo on arms to other generals. Villa raided Santa Isabel **Jan. 10,** killed 18; Columbus, N. M., **Mar. 9, 1916,** killed 17. Gen. John J. Pershing with 12,000 sent into Mexico **Mar. 15.** Fight at Parral and Chihuahua **Apr. 12.** Carranza's troops attacked **June 21.** U. S. troops withdrawn **Feb. 4, 1917.** Carranza called constitutional convention, **Feb. 15. 1917,** became legal president **May 1, 1917.** He restored some of the land, nationalized coal and oil, expropriated some foreign holdings. Discontent caused new uprising and he was ambushed and killed. Obregon became president **Dec. 1, 1920.** Villa was killed in ambush at Parral **July 20, 1923.**

Chinese Revolution led by Sun Yat-sen overthrew Manchu dynasty. Republic formed **Feb. 12, 1912;** Yuan shih-K'ai elected president **Feb. 15.**

Parliament Act of 1911 reduced the power of British House of Lords to a suspensory veto which could delay but not deny bills.

1912

Capt. Robert F. Scott and 4 companions reached South Pole **Jan. 17;** died on return journey.

White Star liner Titanic wrecked on maiden trip, from Southampton to N. Y. City, by iceberg off Newfoundland **Apr. 14-15;** U. S. reported 1,517 lost; British Board of Trade reported 1,503 lost. There were 2,307 persons aboard. The ship was 882½ ft. long, cost $7,500,000.

War in Balkans against Turkey by Montenegro, Bulgaria, Serbia and Greece **Oct. 8-Dec. 3.**

1913

Sixteenth Amendment effective **Feb. 25** empowered Congress to levy and collect income taxes.

Act creating Federal Reserve System became law **Dec. 23.**

Principal Events of World War I, 1914-1918;

Origins. Since the defeat of France by Prussia in 1870-71 major powers of Europe had kept peace by diplomatic negotiations and a balance of power. Triple Alliance, of Germany, Austria and Italy, was defensive, with reservations; Triple Entente was an understanding between Britain, France and Russia. Nationalist aspirations in the Balkans had resulted in several wasteful wars and Italy had fought with Turkey and Ethiopia. Austria annexed Bosnia. Herzegovina, former Turkish Balkan provinces in 1908. Russia backed Serbia's efforts to get a port on the Adriatic. Germany's industrial expansion led to building of powerful navy, which Britain matched two for one for its own security. Germany's universal military service led France to adopt three-year training.

On **June 28, 1914,** Archduke Francis Ferdinand, heir to Austrian throne, was assassinated, with his wife, by Gavrillo Princip, Bosnian Serb terrorist, in Sarajevo, Bosnia. Austria-Hungary, through Count Berchthold, Austrian foreign minister, made 10 demands on Serbia for suppression of anti-Austrian agitation. Serbia conceded all but two, which called for Austrian enforcement police inside Serbia. It asked reference to The Hague peace tribunal. Austria demanded all or nothing.

Russia, fearing Austrian action was aimed at Russia, supported Serbia. Germany backed Austria. Britain, France, Italy proposed mediation, Sir Edward Grey, British foreign minister, **July 26** proposed conference of four major powers; Germany refused to join.

Austria declared war on Serbia **July 28.** Germany, citing Russian mobilization, declared war on Russia **Aug. 1;** on France **Aug. 3.** Germans entered Belgium in violation of treaty, of which Britain was co-signer. Britain asked Germany to guarantee neutrality of Belgium by midnight **Aug. 4;** Germany refused; British declared war **Aug. 4.** Italy, declaring German aggression made Triple Alliance inoperative, proclaimed neutrality. Japan declared war on Germany **Aug. 23** because of Anglo-Japanese treaty on Far East. Turkey joined Central Powers **Nov. 23.**

Lord Kitchener became British secy. for war. Belgian forts at Liege stopped Germans until **Aug. 7,** delayed German schedule. Germans entered Brussels **Aug. 20;** pushed back British Expeditionary Force (Sir John French) at Mons **Aug. 23-24;** burned most of Louvain **Aug. 25.** Von Hindenburg and Ludendorff defeated Russians at Tannenberg, East Prussia, **Aug. 26-31;** at Masurain Lakes **Sept. 5-10.**

In first Battle of the Marne, Sept. 5-10, French under Joffre, Foch and Gallieni, stopped German advance of Von Kluck and Von Bulow toward Paris; forced them back to Aisne where trench warfare began. British repulsed Germans at **Ypres Oct. 16-Nov. 24.** Belgians lost Antwerp **Oct. 9.** Russians forced Austrians back in Galicia. Austrians took and lost Belgrade **Dec. 2-15.**

British bombarded Dardanelles forts **Nov. 3;** declared war on Turkey, annexed Cyprus **Nov. 5.** Japan took Tsingtao **Nov. 6.**

1915—Submarine War Begins

In 1915 the war became a desperate battle of attrition on land and sea. British sank Ger. cruiser Bluecher **Jan. 24.** Germany ordered submarine blockade of Britain to start **Feb. 18.** U. S. held Germany to "Strict accountability" for American losses. Germans used liquid fire in Vosges **Mar. 3.** Roving German cruiser Dresden sunk in Pacific **Mar. 15.** Three Br.-Fr. battleships sunk at Dardanelles **Mar. 18.** Germans sank Falaba **Mar. 28,** 1 American lost. Turks sank British battleship Lord Nelson **Apr. 6.** Germans introduced poison gas at **Ypres Apr. 22,** Canadians saved the line. Allies landed at **Gallipoli Apr. 25.** Germans torpedoed Gulflight, U. S. tanker, **Apr. 30,** 2 Americans lost.

German sub sank Cunard liner **Lusitania** off Old Head of Kinsale, Ireland, **May 7;** of 1,959 aboard, including 702 crew, 1,198, including 124 Americans, died. This started a series of protests by U. S. to Germany. Secy. of State William J. Bryan resigned **June 8;** considered Wilson's Lusitania note too severe. After sinking Arabic **Aug. 19** Germans agreed not to sink liners without warning, but U. S. considered promises inadequate. U. S. dismissed Austrian Ambassador Dumba and Germans Boy-Ed and Von Papen for illegal activities.

South Africans under Gen. Botha captured German S. W. Africa. Italy declared war on Austria-Hungary **May 23,** on Turkey **Aug. 20,** on Germany **Aug. 27.** Bulgaria declared war on Serbia **Oct. 14;** Allies against Bulgaria **Oct. 15-19.** Germans occupied Russian Baltic ports, took Vilna; Austrians occupied Serbia. Allies landed at Salonika **Oct. 5.** Sir John French replaced by Sir Douglas Haig on British front **Dec. 15.** Allies began evacuation of Gallipoli (Dardanelles) **Dec. 19.**

1916—Great Battles

Germany announced Feb. 10 that armed merchant ships would be considered warships and sunk without warning. U. S. retorted **Feb. 15** international law per-

1914

Ford Motor Co. raised basic wage rates from $2.40 for 9-hr. day to $5 for 8-hr. day, Jan. 5.

First ship passed through Panama Canal Aug. 15.

Second International Brussels meeting of International Socialist Bureau July. Members included 5 men later heads of governments: Lenin (Russia); Ebert (German Republic); Stauning (Denmark); Branting (Sweden); MacDonald (Britain).

1915

First telephone talk, New York to San Francisco, Jan. 25 by Alexander Graham Bell and Thomas A. Watson.

First successful wireless from moving Lackawanna train to station, Feb. 7.

Twenty-one Demands presented by Japan to China; asked for almost complete control of China.

1916

Gregory Rasputin, confessor to czarina, killed in Petrograd (Leningrad) December.

Bomb exploded during San Francisco Preparedness Day Parade July 22, killed 10, wounded 40. Thomas J. Mooney, 33, labor organizer; Mrs. Mooney; Warren K. Billings, shoe worker; Israel Weinberg; and Edward D. Nolan were charged with murder. Mooney was sentenced to death, Billings to life imprisonment; others went free. President Wilson interceded for Mooney, who got life imprisonment 1918. Mooney was pardoned by Gov. C. L. Olson Jan. 7, 1939; Billings freed Oct. 16, 1939.

Black Tom explosion at munitions docks in Jersey City, N. J., July 30; 2 killed, $40,000,000 damages; traced to German saboteurs.

1917

The 18th (Prohibition) Amendment to the Constitution was submitted to the states by Congress Dec. 18. The first state (Mississippi) ratified it Jan. 8, 1918, and Jan. 16, 1919, the 36th state (Nebraska) ratified it, whereupon, by proclamation of the Secretary of State Jan. 29, 1919, it became effective one year from that date, Jan. 16, 1920. By Feb. 25, 1919 the legislatures of 45 states had ratified it; the 46th state (New Jersey) ratified it March 9, 1922. It was not ratified by Connecticut and Rhode Island. The Volstead (Prohibition Enforcement) Act was passed by Congress Oct. 1919, was vetoed by President Wilson, passed over his

Why United States Intervened

mitted self-defense of commercial ships. Germans made huge effort vs. Verdun Feb. 21, took Ft. Douaumont Feb. 25. Germany declared war on Portugal Mar. 8. Russians invaded Persia Mar. 10. Wilson threatened Apr. 18-19 to break relations unless Germany revised sub warfare; Germany met most of U.S. demands.

Uprising in Ireland Apr. 24-May 1. Patrick Pearse et al, executed; Sir Roger Casement hanged Aug. 3. Britain adopted conscription May 24. Jutland naval battle May 31- June 1. British Admirals Jellicoe and Beatty lost 5 major cruisers, 8 destroyers, 6,091 men; German Admirals Scheer and von Hipper lost 2 major ships, also cruisers, German destroyers, 2,545 men. Battle of Ypres June 2. Lord Kitchener drowned when Hampshire sunk off Orkneys June 5. Battle of the Somme July 1-10; second battle July 11-Aug. 3. Romania joined Allies Aug. 16, was defeated by January, 1917. U. S. Nov. 29 protested deportation of Belgian workers into Germany.

Germany and its allies called for peace negotiations Dec. 12, 1916 to halt bloodshed. Germany told the Vatican it was fighting for the integrity of its frontiers and development in peaceful competition. On Dec. 18, 1916, President Wilson asked the belligerents to state their aims and terms; in order to end rival leagues he asked formation of a League of Nations and protection of "weak peoples." The Allies called the German offer "empty and insincere." They also told President Wilson they wanted "restorations, reparations, indemnities."

1917—U. S. Enters War

When Germany began unrestricted submarine war United States Feb. 3 broke relations, refused negotiations until order was rescinded. Wilson Feb. 26 asked Congress to order arming of merchant ships; when Senate refused Wilson armed them by executive order Mar. 12. Intercepted note of German foreign secy. Zimmerman to German minister in Mexico suggested Mexico be asked to enter war to recover U. S. Southwest Feb. 28. U. S. declared war on Germany Apr. 6, adopted selective conscription May 18, registered men aged 21-30 June 5. First of American Expeditionary Force (AEF) landed in France June 26; Gen. John J. Pershing, commander-in-chief, Adm. William S. Sims, chief Naval Operations, Europe. U.S. declared war on Austria-Hungary Dec. 7.

Collapse of Russian Empire. When Navy and Army revolted Mar. 11-15 Czar Nicholas II abdicated. Provisional govt. made Kerensky premier July 20. Offensive in Galicia failed. In April Germans moved Lenin and associates from Switzerland to Russia via Sweden to disrupt war. Bolshevists overthrew Kerensky Nov. 7, formed socialist republic of workers and peasants with Lenin president of Council of Commissars; made peace with Germany, Austria-Hungary, Bulgaria and Turkey at Brest-Litovsk Mar. 3, 1918. Russians withdrew from Lithuania, Estonia, Latvia, Ukraine, Poland, Finland, Aland Isls., Erivan, Kars, Batum.

Other Fronts. Huge losses by Allies at Vimy, Arras, Cambrai, Passchendaele, Verdun. Petain succeeded Nivelle as French commander-in-chief. British took Jaffa, Baghdad, Jerusalem. Germans forced Italians back to Piave, Brenta; sank many ships.

1918—Victory for U. S. & Allies

German submarine war, Feb. 1, 1917-Feb. 1, 1918, cost U. S. 69 ships (171,061 tons); U. S. seized 686,494 German-Austrian tonnage. British lost 1,169 ships. Allies & neutrals lost 6,617,000 tons.

President Wilson presented his 14 points for peace to Congress Jan. 8. Asked open diplomacy; freedom of seas; restoration of Alsace-Lorraine to France; independence for Poland and Austrian minorities; "a general association of nations" to guarantee political and economic independence.

Collapse of Russian front released German troops for powerful thrusts on West front. Battle of the Somme, Mar. 21-Apr. 6. Gen. Ferdinand Foch made supreme commander Mar. 26. Battle of the Aisne May 27-June 5; AEF took Cantigny May 28. Germans reached Marne, AEF fought at Chateau Thierry, Belleau Woods. German retreat began July 19. AEF took St. Mihiel salient Sept. 12-20, fought at Meuse-Argonne Sept. 20-Nov. 11. British broke Hindenburg line Sept. 27.

Bulgaria gave up Sept. 30, Czar Ferdinand abdicated. Turkish armistice Oct. 30. Italians defeated Austrians at Vittorio Veneto, Austria and Hungary formed separate republics Nov. 1, Austria surrendered Nov. 4.

Germans accepted President Wilson's terms and recalled submarines Oct. 20; U. S. troops reached Sedan Nov. 7; revolution in Kiel and Hamburg Nov. 7; Bavaria proclaimed a republic Nov. 8; Kaiser abdicated Nov. 9, fled to Holland. Armistice signed in Marshal Foch's railway coach, near Compiegne, France, Nov. 11; bugles sounded "cease firing" at 11 a.m. German fleet surrendered to British Nov. 21; AEF entered Mainz Dec. 6; crossed Rhine Dec. 13.

veto, in effect **Jan. 17, 1920.** New York, Montana and Wisconsin cancelled their enforcement acts by 1929. Franklin D. Roosevelt, 1932 presidential candidate, endorsed repeal; 21st Amendment repealed 18th, but guaranteed dry states against liquor importation, became law **Dec. 5, 1933.**

Balfour Declaration Nov. 2 favored establishment of a national homeland in Palestine for Jewish people.

1918

Romanovs killed. Czar Nicholas of Russia, the Empress Alexandra; the daughters, Olga, Tatiana, Marie, Anastasia; the son, Alexis; Prince Dolgorolkoff, Dr. Botkin, a lady-in-waiting and a nurse were shot by Bolshevist orders in Ekaterinburg **July 16;** also in Perm **July 12** the Bolshevists assassinated the Czar's brother, Grand Duke Michael and in Alapalievsky north of Ekaterinburg they killed the Grand Duke Sergius Mikhalilovitch, Igor and Ivan Constantinovich.

Influenza epidemic killed estimated 20,000,000 throughout world, 548,000 Americans.

1919

Rosa Luxemburg and Karl Liebknecht, leading German communists and founders of the Spartacus Party, shot and killed **Jan.** by soldiers who were taking them to prison.

Peace conference opened in Paris **Jan. 18;** treaty signed in palace at Versailles **June 28** between German representatives and Allied powers and U. S. President Wilson submitted treaty to Senate **July 10.** Ratified by Germany **July 10,** Britain **July 26,** Italy **Oct.7,** France **Oct.13,** Japan **Oct.27.** Not signed by China. Rejected by U.S. Senate **Nov. 19** which considered American sovereignty not properly safeguarded in League of Nations. Never ratified by U.S.

Three U.S. Navy seaplanes left Trepassy, Newfoundland, **May 16;** one, the NC-4, reached the Azores **May 17;** Lisbon **May 27;** Plymouth, England **May 31. John Alcock** and **A. W. Brown** made **June 14-15,** a non-stop air flight from Newfoundland to Ireland. A British dirigible, R-34, left Scotland **July 2** and descended in Mineola, N. Y., **July 6.** It left for England **July 10** and arrived there **July 13.** A round-trip transcontinental air race, New York to San Francisco, was won by **Lt. W.B. Maynard** and **Lt. Alex Pearson Oct. 8-18**.

1920

League of Nations began at Geneva, Switzerland, **Jan. 10;** dissolved **Jan. 10, 1946.**

Nicola Sacco, 29, shoe factory employee and radical agitator, and **Bartolomeo Vanzetti,** 32, fish peddler and anarchist, accused of killing two men in payroll holdup at South Braintree, Mass., **Apr. 15.** Found guilty **1921** they became objects of six-year campaign for release on grounds of want of conclusive evidence and prejudice of court. Appeals failing, they were executed at Charlestown, Mass., prison **Aug. 22, 1927.** Trial sharply criticized by Wickersham Commission on law procedure.

Wall St., New York City, bomb explosion, killed 30, injured 100; did $2,000,000 damage **Sept. 16.**

1921

Joint Congressional resolution declaring peace with Germany and Austria signed **July 2** by President Harding. Treaty signed **Aug. 25,** ratified by Senate **Oct. 18.**

Limitation of Armaments Conference met in Washington **Nov. 12, 1921-Feb. 6, 1922.** U. S., Britain, France, Italy, Japan agreed to curtail naval construction. Nine powers outlawed poison gas and restricted submarine attack on merchantmen. U. S., Britain, France, Japan agreed on integrity of China. Ratified **Aug. 5, 1925.**

1922

Roof of Knickerbocker (movie) Theatre collapsed in Washington, D. C., **Jan. 28;** 98 dead.

Violence during coal-mine strike at Herrin, Ill., **June 22-23** cost 36 lives, 21 non-union miners.

Fascist march on Rome Oct 30; Mussolini's power in Italy began.

1923

Occupation of Ruhr by French and Belgian troops to enforce reparations began **Jan. 11.**

First sound-on-film moving pictures "Phonofilm" was shown by Lee de Forest at Rivoli Theatre, New York City, beginning **Apr.**

Beer Hall Putsch in Munich led by Gen. Ludendorff and Adolf Hitler **Nov. 8-9.** Several supporters killed in street clashes. Ludendorff was arrested and paroled; Hitler was wounded. He was arrested **Nov. 12** and imprisoned at Landsberg where he wrote Mein Kampf.

1924

Dawes Reparation Plan accepted by Allies and Germany in London **Aug. 16:** Owen D. Young put in charge. French troops began evacuation of the Ruhr **Aug. 18.**

Nellie Taylor Ross elected governor of Wyoming **Nov. 9** after death of her husband **Oct. 2;** installed **Jan. 5, 1925.** First woman governor. Miriam (Ma) Ferguson was elected governor of Texas **Nov. 9;** installed **Jan. 20, 1925.**

1925

Floyd Collins unable to extricate himself from Sand Cave, near Cave City, Ky., which he discovered, died within 300 ft. of entrance **Feb.**

John T. Scopes was found guilty of having taught evolution in the Dayton (Tenn.) high school and was fined $100 and costs **July 24.** William Jennings Bryan, chief counsel for prosecution, died in Dayton **July 26.** Clarence Darrow, chief defense counsel, died **Mar. 13, 1938.** Scopes died **Oct. 21, 1970.** The last law prohibiting teaching evolution in U. S. public schools was ruled unconstitutional by the Mississippi Supreme Court **Dec. 2, 1970.**

Pickwick Club, Boston, collapsed **July 4;** 44 died.

By Treaty of Locarno Oct. 16 Germany agreed to demilitarization of Rhineland and security of Franco-German and Belgo-German frontiers.

1926

Dr. Robert H. Goddard demonstrated the practicality of rockets **Mar. 16** at Auburn, Mass., with the first liquid fuel rocket flight; the rocket traveled 184 feet in 2.5 seconds.

General strike paralyzed Britain **May 3-12.** Parliament passed act making general strike criminal conspiracy against nation.

Germany admitted to the League of Nations Sept. 8. Locarno treaties with Germany (1925) went into effect **Sept. 14.**

1927

About 1,000 U. S. Marines landed in China **Mar. 5** to protect property in civil war. U. S. and British consulates looted by nationalists **Mar. 24.**

Albert Snyder, art editor, killed **Mar. 20** by his wife, Ruth Brown Snyder, and Henry Judd Gray, corset salesmen. Both confessed and were executed at Sing Sing **Jan. 12, 1928.**

Capt. Charles A. Lindbergh, U. S. air mail pilot, left Roosevelt Field, L. I. N. Y., at 7:52 A. M., **May 20** alone in monoplane, Spirit of St. Louis, competing for Raymond Orteig's offer of $25,000 for first New York-Paris non-stop flight. Reached Le Bourget airfield, Paris, 5:21 P.M. (10:21 P.M. Paris time) **May 21,** 3,610 miles in 33 hrs. 29 mins., 30 secs. Returned on cruiser Memphis, U.S.N., with plane; welcomed by President Coolidge in Washington **June 11,** given rank of colonel. Tremendous ticker tape parade, N. Y. City **June 13.**

The Jazz Singer, Al Jolson, demonstrated part-talking pictures in New York City **Oct. 6.**

1928

The St. Francis water-supply dam, 40 miles north of Los Angeles, Calif., collapsed; 450 lives lost, 700 houses swept away **Mar. 13.**

First all-talking picture, Lights of New York, presented at Strand, N. Y. City, **July 6.**

Times Square subway wreck, N. Y. City (IRT line) **Aug. 24,** killed 18, injured 97.

Kellogg-Briand Peace Pact signed **Aug. 27** by 62 nations. Condemned the use of war as an instrument of national policy.

Dirigible Graf Zeppelin, Capt. Hugo Eckener, with 20 passengers and 38 crew, flew from Friedrichshafen, Germany to Lakehurst, N. J., **Oct. 11-15;** returned **Oct. 29-31.** Made round the world trip from Friedrichshafen with 20 passengers **Aug. 14-Sept. 4, 1929** via Tokyo, Los Angeles, Lakehurst, N. J.

Stalin issued **first 5 year plan:** Rapid, ruthless industrialization of Russian economy.

1929

"St. Valentine's Day massacre" in Chicago **Feb. 14;** gangsters killed 7 rivals.

The Papal State, extinct since **1870,** revived as State of Vatican City, at Rome **June 7.**

U. S. paper money one-third smaller in size went into circulation **July 10.**

Albert B. Fall, former Secretary of the Interior was convicted of accepting a bribe of $100,000 from Edward L. Doheny in the leasing of the Elk Hills **(Teapot Dome)** naval oil reserve. He was sentenced **Nov. 1** to $100,000 fine and a year in prison. He died **Nov. 30, 1944.**

Stock Market crash Oct. 29 marked end of postwar prosperity when 16 million shares changed hands, including unrestricted short selling. Decline in value estimated at $15 billion by end of 1929; stock losses for 1929-1931 estimated at $50 billion; worst American depression began.

1930

London Naval Reduction Treaty signed by U.S., Britain, Italy, France and Japan **Apr. 22;** in effect **Jan. 1, 1931.** Set proportional reductions of the navies of each country. Its terms expired **Dec. 31, 1936.**

Joseph F. Crater, a justice of the state Supreme Court in New York City, vanished **Aug. 6.**

1931

British Parliament enacted Statute of Westminster, giving legal status to declaration of Imperial Conference of 1926 proclaiming Britain and the dominions, including Canada, completely equal "in no way subordinate one to another."

Mukden Incident occurred **Sept. 18** when Japanese troops attacked Mukden garrison and then overran Manchuria. China protested to League of Nations.

1932

Japan sends troops into China Jan. 27 following murder of Japanese Buddhist priest in Shanghai **Jan. 15.**

Manchuria became Manchukuo (Japanese puppet state) **Feb. 18;** Henry Pu Yi, Manchu emperor who abdicated in 1912, installed as ruler **Mar. 9** at Changchun, called Hsingching.

Charles Lindbergh Jr. kidnaped **Mar. 1.**

Bonus March on Washington, **May 29** by World War I veterans demanding Congress pay their bonus in full. Army disbanded the marchers on President Hoover's orders.

1933

Adolf Hitler becomes German Chancellor **Jan. 30.**

German Reichstag building in Berlin was destroyed **Feb. 27** by fire believed set by Nazis. Marinus van der Lubbe, Dutch communist, found guilty; beheaded **Jan. 10, 1934** in Leipzig.

All banks in the United States were ordered closed by President Roosevelt **Mar. 6.**

Gold standard dropped by United States; announced by President Roosevelt on **Apr. 19** and ratified by Congress **June 5.**

Spain, by Parliamentary edict, May 17 disestablished the Church.

Germany quit the League of Nations Oct. 14 and withdrew from the disarmament conference.

President Roosevelt accorded diplomatic recognition to the Soviet Union **Nov. 16.**

Prohibition ended in the United States as Utah, 36th state, ratified 21st Amendment to Constitution **Dec. 5** repealed 18th (Prohibition) Amendment.

1934

The Dionne sisters, first quintuplets to survive beyond infancy, were born **May 28** in Callender, Ont., Canada; to Mr. and Mrs. Oliva Dionne.

President von Hindenburg of Germany died **Aug. 2. Adolf Hitler** consolidated offices of president and chancellor, became fuehrer.

Long March by Chinese Communists started **Oct.** Mao Tse-tung led 100,000 in 6,000-mile trek from south to north China; only 20,000 completed journey and reached Yenan **Oct. 1935.**

Italy refused to arbitrate disputes on Italian Somaliland border between Italian and Ethiopian troops, demanded reparations, apology **Dec. 19.**

1935

Hitler rejected Versailles Treaty, ordered conscription in Germany **Mar. 10.**

Will Rogers, 56, comedian, and Wiley Post, 36, aviator, were killed **Aug. 15** when Post's airplane crashed in a fog near Point Barrow, Alaska.

Social Security Act passed by Congress **Aug. 14.**

Ethiopia appealed to League of Nations against Italy. Italy invaded Ethiopia **Oct. 2-4.**

Economic sanctions against Italy went into effect **Nov. 18** supported by 52 nation-members of the League of Nations, and by one non-member Egypt. The sanctions ended **July 15, 1936.**

1936

King George V, 70, died Jan. 20 on his estate at Sandringham, England, and was succeeded by his eldest son, Prince of Wales, 42, who took the title of King Edward VIII. He abdicated **Dec. 11, 1936** and was succeeded by his brother, the Duke of York, who became King George VI. The ex-ruler was created Duke of Windsor with the title of "His Royal Highness" which was not extended to his wife. He gave up the throne, he said, because he could not marry "the woman I love," Mrs. Wallis Warfield of Baltimore, Md., who obtained a divorce **Oct. 27** in Ipswich, England, from Ernest A. Simpson, an insurance agent. The decree became absolute **May 3, 1937.** The couple was married **June 3, 1937** in Monts, France.

Reoccupation of demilitarized Rhineland zone, in violation of the Locarno pact, begun by German troops **May 7.**

Emperor Haile Selassie of Ethiopia escaped Italian advance by boarding British cruiser for Palestine **May 1.** Premier Mussolini of Italy announced end of war **May 5,** proclaimed annexation of Ethiopia with King Victor Emmanuel Emperor.

Revolt against Spain's Republican Government began **July 17** in Morocco and spread to Spain, included much of the army and air force and half of the navy; Jose Giral became Loyalist premier; **July 18** Loyalists defeated insurgents in Madrid and **July 19** insurgents gained control in Cadiz, Huelva, Seville, Cordoba and Granada; insurgents set up own government **July 24;** insurgents took Badajoz **Aug. 16;** began aerial bombing of Madrid **Aug. 24;** captured Irun **Sept. 4;** took San Sebastian and Toledo **Sept. 12;** Gen. Francisco Franco proclaimed head of the nationalist (insurgent) government **Oct. 1;** seige of Madrid begun by insurgents **Oct. 21;** Loyalist government moved from Madrid to Valencia, **Nov. 6.**

Japan and Germany signed an anti-Comintern pact **Nov. 25.** Italy joined **Nov. 6, 1937.**

1937

Spanish insurgents took Malaga **Feb. 8.** Warships of Great Britain, France, Italy and Germany **March 13,** began to police the coasts of Spain under the 27-nation neutrality agreement. Gen. Franco **Apr. 19** set up a one-party state, dissolving the Falange and Carlist organizations. New Loyalist government formed **May 17** under Premier Juan Negrin; Loyalists shifted government to Barcelona **Oct. 28;** insurgents proclaimed blockade of all Loyalist ports **Nov. 28.**

The army-supported Japanese Cabinet of Hayashi resigned **May.** Fighting in China, west of Peiping, was renewed by Japanese **July;** Tungchow was attacked **July 27;** the Japanese **July 29** bombed Tientsin destroying Nankai University; **Aug. 9** they took formal possession of Peiping.; **Aug. 11** they landed marines at Shanghai and shelled Nankow. Nanking, Canton and many other places in the eastern provinces of China were attacked by Japanese planes **Oct. 23**; Suiyuan Province declared independence from China. The Chinese abandoned Shanghai and the Japanese took control **Nov. 8**. Premier Chiang Kaishek moved to Hankow **Dec. 12**.

Japanese bombs sank the U. S. gunboat Panay **Dec. 12** with loss of 2 lives; and several American oil carriers (the captain of one died) on the Yangtze River above Nanking. The Japanese apologized and paid indemnity.

Hitler repudiated war guilt clause of Versailles Treaty **Jan. 30**. Treaty blamed Germany for World War I. Hitler stated that from this time onward Germany was free from obligations imposed upon her by the treaty.

Amelia Earhart Putnam, aviator, and co-pilot lost **July 2** near Howland Isl. in the Pacific.

Italy gave notice Dec. 11 of withdrawal from the League of Nations.

1938

Spanish insurgent planes from Majorca began daily

Principal Events of World War II, 1939-1945

Major Belligerents — German army invaded Poland **Sept. 1, 1939**; Norway and Denmark, **April 9, 1940**; the Netherlands, Belgium and Luxemburg, **May 10, 1940**. Occupied France (Vichy) signed an armistice with Germany **June 22, 1940**. Germany invaded Russia **June 22, 1941**, unoccupied France and Italy **Nov. 11, 1942**. Surrendered unconditionally **May 7, 1945** (May 6 EST). War with Germany formally declared ended by Britain, France, Australia, New Zealand on **July 9, 1951**; by U. S. **Oct. 19, 1951**.

Great Britain declared war on Germany Sept. 3, 1939, as did Australia and New Zealand. Union of South Africa declared war **Sept. 6**; Canada **Sept. 10**. Britain declared war on Italy **June 11, 1940**; on Finland, Hungary and Romania, **Dec. 7, 1941**; on Japan **Dec. 8, 1941**; on Bulgaria **Dec. 13, 1941**; on Thailand **Jan. 25, 1942**.

France declared war on Germany **Sept. 3, 1939**; on Italy **June 11, 1940**. Free French (De Gaulle) declared war on Japan **Dec. 8, 1941**.

Italy (Benito Mussolini, Duce) declared war on Great Britain and France **June 10, 1940**; on the U. S. **Dec. 11, 1941**. Surrendered unconditionally **Sept. 8, 1943**. Declared war against Germany **Oct. 13, 1943**, against Japan **July 14, 1945**. Signed treaty of peace **Feb. 10, 1947**, in Paris, with Britain, France, U. S. and USSR.

Japan invaded French Indo-China Sept. 22, 1940; attacked Pearl Harbor naval station and the Philippines by air **Dec. 7, 1941** and declared war on the United States, Great Britain, Australia, Canada, New Zealand and the Union of South Africa on **Dec. 7, 1941**; on the Netherlands **Jan. 11, 1942**. Japan accepted the Allied terms unconditionally **Aug. 14, 1945**; signed surrender terms **Sept. 1, 1945** (Sept. 2, Tokyo time) on board USS Missouri; signed treaty of peace with all big powers (except USSR) and a total of 49 nations at San Francisco **Sept. 8, 1951**.

Union of Soviet Socialist Republics (Russia) signed nonaggression pact with Germany **Aug., 1939**; invaded Poland, **Sept. 17, 1939**, and Finland, **Nov. 30, 1939**. Signed peace with Finland **Mar. 12, 1940**. Russia was invaded by Germany and Romania **June 22, 1941**. Finland declared war on Russia **June 25, 1941**. Armistice with Finland **Sept. 19, 1944**, peace treaty **Feb. 10, 1947**. Declared war on Japan **Aug. 8, 1945**, effective Aug. 9. Signed treaties of peace with Italy, Hungary, Romania, Bulgaria and Finland **Feb. 10, 1947**.

U. S. declared war on Japan Dec. 8, 1941. Germany and Italy declared war on U. S. **Dec. 11, 1941**. A few hours later U. S. declared war on Germany and Italy. Also Bulgaria, Hungary and Romania **June 5, 1942**; signed peace treaties with Italy, Bulgaria, Hungary and Romania **Feb. 10, 1947**; with Japan **Sept. 8, 1951**.

Retreat from Dunkirk by British Expeditionary Force took place **May 26-June 4**, 1940, when 900 vessels took 338,226 troops across the English Channel, 26,175 of them French.

Nazi bombing of Britain began **July 10, 1940** and reached its height **Sept. 7, Oct. 15** and **Dec. 29**. Coventry was damaged Nov. 14; Birmingham **Nov. 19-22**. Many London churches were burned **Dec. 29**. Desperate attacks on German aircraft by RAF stop-

ped threat of invasion. Of this defense Prime Minister Churchill said: "Never in the field of human conflict was so much owed by so many to so few."

Pearl Harbor. Over 100 Japanese planes attacked U. S. Pacific fleet (86 ships) anchored at Pearl Harbor, Hawaii on **Dec. 7, 1941** (7:55 a.m. Hawaiian time; 1:25 p.m. EST.) Totally lost battleship Arizona. Severely damaged: battleships Oklahoma, Nevada, California, West Virginia, 3 destroyers, 1 target ship, 1 minelayer. Damaged and repaired: battleships Pennsylvania, Maryland, Tennessee; cruisers Helena, Honolulu, Raleigh. Casualties: navy, 2,117 officers and men killed, 960 missing, 876 wounded; army, 226 officers and men killed, 396 wounded.

Planes Over Tokyo. Lt. Col. James H. Doolittle, with 16 B-25's and 79 pilots and crewmen, took off **Apr. 18, 1942**, from carrier Hornet, 688 mi. from Tokyo by sea; dropped 500-lb. bombs on Tokyo, Nagoya, Kobe. Eight airmen were captured off China coast; 3 were shot, others imprisoned. Total dead, 9. One plane landed near Vladivostok and was interned by Russians; the crew escaped to Iran.

Loss and recapture of Philippines. Manila and Cavite taken by Japan **Jan. 2, 1942**. Maj. Gen. Jonathan M. Wainwright commanded at Bataan, which was attacked by 200,000 Japanese **Jan. 10**. Gen. Douglas MacArthur ordered to leave Philippines, reached Australia **Mar. 17**, vowed, "I shall return." Wainwright defended Bataan until **Apr. 8, 1942**. Japan took 35,000 U. S. and Filipino troops prisoner, including 5,000 Marines, forced them into prison via the "Death March" of Bataan. Wainwright surrendered Corregidor **May 6** with 11,574 troops. Gen. MacArthur returned to the Philippines near Palo on Leyte, **Oct. 20, 1944**. U. S. entered Luzon via Lingayen Gulf **Jan. 9, 1945**. Manila was taken **Feb. 3**; Corregidor reoccupied **Feb. 16-Mar. 1**.

Germany attacked the Soviet Union June 22, 1941; took Minsk, Smolensk, Kiev, Kharkov, Orel; besieged Leningrad, fought a terrible battle in the ruins of Stalingrad **August 1942** and extended the German lines to the Caucasus Mts.; tide turned in **Nov. 1942**; the Russians encircled Stalingrad and the Nazi army there surrendered **Jan. 31, 1943**. Russian Army reached the Oder River **Feb. 1945**.

North African coast fight began **Aug. 6, 1941**, when Marshal Graziani led the Italians against the British with some success. The first counteroffensive in December relieved Tobruk, where British had held out 8 months. The British pushed the Germans under Rommel back to El Aghelia, but Rommel regained the lost ground. He captured Tobruk with its garrison of 25,000 British **June 21, 1942**, and pushed the British back to within 70 mi. of Alexandria. On **Oct. 23**, the British, heavily reinforced and under Lt. Gen. Bernard L. Montgomery, attacked Rommel at El Alamein and inflicted heavy losses on the Germans and Italians, routed them to Tunisia.

North African expedition by U. S. and Britain landed 150,000 American and 140,000 British troops on French North Africa **Nov. 8, 1942** (Nov. 7 EST), with Lt. Gen. Dwight D. Eisenhower, C-in-C. The Allies began campaign against Italy by seizing Pantelleria Isl. **June 11, 1943**. U. S. 7th Army under Maj. Gen.

bombing of Barcelona **Jan. 16.** Insurgent ship Baleares sunk off Cartagena **Mar. 6** by Loyalist forces. Insurgent air raids killed 1,000 in Barcelona **Mar. 7;** insurgents took Lerida cutting Loyalist Spain in two **Apr. 15.** Italy began token withdrawal of 10,000 troops **Oct. 10.** Insurgents began final campaign **Dec. 23** against Barcelona which fell **Jan. 26, 1939.**

Hitler invaded Austria Mar. 11. After resignation of Chancellor Kurt von Schuschnigg and President Wilhelm Miklas **Mar. 13** the new Chancellor, Arthur Seyss-Inquart, proclaimed the political and geo-

graphic union of Germany and Austria. This was ratified by a popular vote, excluding Jews, in Austria **Apr. 10.** The Italian Grand Council, headed by Premier Benito Mussolini, voted approval.

Douglas G. Corrigan of Los Angeles, flew from Brooklyn to Dublin **July 17-18.** Having no permit or passport, he jokingly said he flew the "wrong way."

At a conference in Munich, Bavaria, Britain and France yielded **Sept. 30** to Nazi demands for the cession of the Sudetenland to Germany by Czechoslovakia, thus ending a 15-day international crisis during

Summary of Aerial, Naval and Military Actions

George S. Patton Jr. and British-Canadian 8th Army landed on Sicily **July 10.** Mussolini was forced to resign **July 25** and escaped to German lines **Sept. 12.** The Italian mainland was invaded and Italy surrendered **Sept. 8,** 1943, but heavy fighting with Germans followed and they were not dislodged until spring of 1945.

Battle of the Coral Sea on **May 7-8, 1942,** took heavy toll of ships and planes on both sides, was first battle fought by naval planes from ships that had neither sight nor range of enemy. U. S. lost carrier (Lexington), 66 planes, 543 men; Japan lost 80 planes, 900 men. **Battle of Midway June 3-6, 1942,** U. S. lost 1 carrier (Yorktown), 1 destroyer, 150 planes, 307 men; Japan lost 4 carriers, 253 planes, 3,500 men. The Japanese navy halted their advance toward Australia and withdrew northward.

Guadalcanal, in the southern Solomon Islands, assaulted by U. S. Marines **Aug. 7, 1942,** in one of the most costly Allied Pacific campaigns, finally won by the Allies in **January 1943.**

Battle for Leyte Gulf, biggest naval action ever fought, occurred **Oct. 22-27, 1944,** in three engagements destroying Japanese naval power. Battles were fought in Surigao Strait, off Samar and off Cape Engano. Ships engaged: U. S. 166, Japanese 65. Airplanes: U. S. 1,280; Japanese 716. Losses for Philippine campaign — Japan: 3 large carriers, 3 light carriers, 1 escort carrier, 4 battleships, 14 cruisers, 32 destroyers, 11 submarines, total 68. U. S.: 1 light carrier, 3 escort carriers, 6 destroyers, 3 destroyer escorts, 1 high-speed transport, 7 submarines, total 21. U. S. lost 1 ship to a kamikaze (suicide) plane at Leyte and 5 in subsequent actions. Total airplane losses for Philippine campaign from Oct., 1944-Jan. 1945: Japan (est.) 7,000, including 722 kamikaze; U. S. 967.

D-Day: Invasion of France — Invasion of France by Allies **June 6, 1944.** About 1,000 planes and gliders dropped paratroopers on Cotentin Peninsula near Normandy, 5 a.m. London time. About 1,000 R.A.F., 1,400 U. S. bombers attacked installations. First assault troops landed 6:30 a.m. on beaches along line Carentan-Bayeux-Caen; U. S. on west, British-Canadians on east. Total Allied strength available 2,876,439, including 17 British divisions of which 3 Canadian; 20 U. S. divisions, 1 French, 1 Polish.

Gen. Dwight D. Eisenhower was Supreme Commander of Allied Expeditionary Forces:

British took Bayeux June 7; Carentan fell June 13; U. S. took Cherbourg June 27; British-Canadians took Caen July 9 after desperate fighting. Lt. Gen. George S. Patton Jr. with 3rd U. S. Army attacked south and west of St. Lo Aug. 1. Canadians took Falaise Aug. 16. German army routed Aug. 23 in the Argentan-Falaise gap by U.S.-Canadian armies and Allied aircraft. Allies were then free to overrun northern France and liberate Paris **Aug. 25.**

Allies invaded France Aug. 14-15, 1944, east of the mouth of the Rhone River with 1,000 ships (641 U. S., 316 British).

The Ardennes Bulge was a violent counter-attack by 15 German divisions (Gen. von Rundstedt commander-in-chief) launched **Dec. 16, 1944.** By Dec. 19 the 1st U. S. Army was pushed out of Germany and the Germans penetrated 60 mi. west of Celles, Belgium. Lt. Gen. Patton's 3rd U. S. Army rescued besieged Americans at Bastogne, Belgium, **Dec. 21** and Nazi drive was stopped by **Dec. 25.** Allies wiped out the Bulge by **Jan. 31, 1945.** Near Malmedy, Belgium, Germans shot captured American soldiers with machine guns and left them dead on the field. U. S. losses estimated at 40,000; Germans lost 220,000 dead and prisoners.

Rhine Crossing — On **Mar. 7, 1945,** the 9th Armored Div., 3rd Corps, First Army, found Ludendorff Bridge at Remagen on the Rhine intact; Gen. Eisenhower ordered Gen. Omar N. Bradley to put 5 divisions across; on 5th day army ceased using bridge, used Treadway floating bridge, built in 10 hr. 11 min.; Remagen bridge collapsed **Mar. 17.**

Iwo Jima assaulted by U. S. joint expeditionary force **Feb. 19, 1945,** with land action by U. S. Marines; invasion used 495 ships, including 17 aircraft carriers and 1,170 planes. U. S. troops engaged, 111,308, of which 75,144 were assault troops. Island was conquered by **Mar. 16.** U. S. lost 4,590 killed; Japanese deaths est. over 20,000.

Okinawa, principal Japanese base in the Ryukyu group, was invaded **Apr. 1, 1945,** in the final land campaign of the war. The troops used 1,300 vessels, including airplane carriers. After 83 days of fighting the end was marked by the formal suicide of the two Japanese generals. U. S. men engaged up to June 30, 1945, reached 176,491 army, 88,500 Marines, 18,000 navy. Japanese strength at start was 77,199. U. S. losses were 49,151 of which 12,520 were killed or missing, 36,631 wounded. The Japanese lost 110,071 killed, wounded and 7,400 prisoners.

U. S. lost 763 aircraft; Japan lost 7,830 of which 1,020 were destroyed on the ground. U. S. had 36 ships sunk, 369 damaged; Japan had 16 sunk, including the Yamato, world's largest battleship, full naval displacement 72,809 tons, 861 ft. long, 9 18-in. guns, 3,333 personnel. Hit by over 10 aerial torpedoes at Kyushu; 300 survived.

V-E Day — German armies began surrendering May 4, 1945. Unconditional surrender signed **May 7** at 2:41 a.m., French time, in Rheims Hq., designating cessation of operations May 9 at 12:01 a.m., London time (May 8, 6:01 p.m., Eastern U. S. War Time). Surrender also signed in Berlin. **May 8** celebrated as **V-E Day.**

Atomic Bombs — First atomic bomb ever used in war was dropped by U. S. plane **Aug. 6, 1945,** on Hiroshima, Japan (pop. 343,969). Second U. S. bomb dropped on Nagasaki (pop. 252,630) **Aug. 9, 1945.** Estimates of dead from bombs and radiation exposure vary: Hiroshima, 80,000 to over 200,000; Nagasaki, 39,000 to 74,000. Japan surrendered **Aug. 14.** Formal surrender aboard USS Missouri **Sept. 2, 1945,** Far Eastern Time, celebrated as **V-J Day.**

Consult Index for additional listings under World War II.

which British Prime Minister Neville Chamberlain made two flying visits to Chancellor Adolf Hitler. Premier Mussolini of Italy backed Hitler's territorial demands. Hitler signed a "peace declaration" with Britain **Sept. 30**, occupied Sudetenland **Oct. 1-10**. President Roosevelt asked Hitler to preserve the peace. Eduard Benes, president of Czechoslovakia, resigned **Oct. 5**.

About 4,000 sq. mi. of Czech land was awarded to Hungary **Nov. 2** by German-Italian arbitrators (Foreign Mins. Joachim von Ribbentrop and Galeazzo Ciano) meeting in Vienna. The area was populated by Hungarians. Cessions to Poland were agreed on between Prague and Warsaw.

1939

Uranium atom was first measured in U. S. at Columbia Univ. **Jan. 25**. In 1940, uranium 235, a rare isotope, proved to be prime fissionable form of uranium.

The Loyalist Spanish government surrendered Barcelona to the insurgents **Jan. 26**. Madrid surrendered **Mar. 24**; war ended **Mar. 29** with Franco victor.

The Republic of Czechoslovakia was dissolved **Mar. 14**; Hungarian troops seized Carpatho-Ukraine **Mar. 14**; Nazis occuped Bohemia and Moravia which became German protectorates **Mar. 16**.

Japanese troops in Manchukuo and Soviet and Mongol troops near Lake Bor began 6-month border fight **May 11**; 20,000 killed.

Germany and Italy signed 10-year military pact in Berlin **May 22**.

Nazi Germany and Soviet Union signed a 10-year non-aggression treaty **Aug. 24**.

N. Y. World's Fair opened **Apr. 30**, closed **Oct. 31**; reopened **May 11, 1940** and finally closed **Oct. 21**.

President Roosevelt proclaimed a limited national emergency **Sept. 8**, an unlimited emergency **May 27, 1941**. Both ended by President Truman **Apr. 28, 1952**.

**1939-1945 World War II
See Article Pages 798-799**

1940

Finnish-Russian peace signed in Moscow **Mar. 12**.

Estonia, Latvia and Lithuania annexed by Union of Soviet Socialist Republics **July 14**.

1941

The Four Freedoms termed essential by President Franklin D. Roosevelt in a speech to Congress **Jan. 6** were freedom of speech and expression, freedom of worship, freedom from want and freedom from fear.

United States Marines occupied Iceland **July 7** on invitation from that country.

The Atlantic Charter an 8-point joint U. S. - British declaration of principles, was issued by President Roosevelt and Prime Minister Winston Churchill **Aug. 14** after conference aboard a battleship off Newfoundland.

President Roosevelt and Secretary of State Hull **Nov. 17** received special Japanese envoys, Saburo Kurusu and Admiral Nomura, for conference on the Far East.

Japan attacked U. S. fleet at Pearl Harbor **Dec. 7** as first act of war. *See World War II.*

Hitler ordered policy of genocide as the "final solution" to the Jewish "problem." By end of war an estimated 4,500,000 to 6,000,000 Jews had been exterminated in Nazi concentration camps. Many other religious, ethnic and political groups were also persecuted.

1942

Fire swept through Cocoanut Grove, a Boston night club, **Nov. 28**, killing 491 and injuring scores.

First nuclear chain reaction (fission of uranium isotope, U-235) at Univ. of Chicago, under physicists Arthur Compton, Enrico Fermi, et al, **Dec. 2**.

1943

President Roosevelt signed June 10 the pay-as-you-go income tax bill. Starting **July 1** wage and salary

earners were subject to a 20% withholding tax.

Race riot in Detroit June 21; 34 dead, 700 injured. Riot in Harlem section of New York; 6 Negroes killed.

1944

Deadly coal fumes from locomotive in Italian railway tunnel near Balvana; killed 521, **Mar. 2**.

Ringling Brothers and Barnum & Bailey Circus fire in Hartford, Conn., caused a stampede in the main tent; 168 killed, 487 injured **July 6**.

1945

Yalta Conference met in the Crimea, USSR, **Feb. 3-11**. Pres. Roosevelt, Churchill, and Stalin; arranged to get Russia into war against Japan.

President Roosevelt, 63, died of cerebral hemorrhage in Warm Springs, Ga. **Apr. 12**.

Mussolini caught by partisans near Dongo on Lake Como while trying to get to Switzerland, executed **Apr. 28**.

Hitler committed suicide in ruined chancellery, Berlin, **Apr. 30**, with wife Eva Braun. Goebbels and wife poisoned children, committed suicide.

United Nations Conference on International Organization of 46 nations, San Francisco, opened **Apr. 25**; closed **June 26** with address by Truman and adoption of UN charter.

Potsdam, Germany, conference of President Truman, Stalin and Churchill **July 17-Aug. 2**. After **July 25** Attlee replaced Churchill.

First atomic bomb, produced at Los Alamos, N. M., exploded at Alamogordo, N. M., **July 16**. Bomb dropped on Hiroshima **Aug. 6**, on Nagasaki **Aug. 9**.

United States forces entered Korea south of 38^c parallel to displace Japanese **Sept. 8**.

Gen. Douglas MacArthur took over supervision of Japan **Sept. 9**.

Vidkun Quisling, pro-Nazi premier of Norway, executed by a firing squad in Oslo **Oct. 23**.

Nationalization of the Bank of France and four other major banks ordered by French **Dec. 2**.

1946

William Joyce, "Lord Haw Haw," broadcaster for Nazis, hanged in London for treason **Jan. 3**.

The first General Assembly of the United Nations opened in London **Jan. 10**.

League of Nations in Geneva, Switzerland, transfers physical assets to the United Nations **Apr. 18**.

Philippines given independence by. U. S. **July 4**; Manuel Roxas elected first president of new republic.

Twenty-two Nazi leaders convicted of war crimes **Sept. 30** by International Tribunal in Nuremberg. Eleven Nazis were sentenced to death by hanging **Oct. 1**. Hermann Goering committed suicide by poison in Nuremberg Prison, two hours before he was scheduled to be hanged **Oct. 15**. The 10 other top Nazis were hanged individually. They were: Hans Frank, Wilhelm Frick, Col. Gen. Alfred Jodl, Gestapo Chief Ernst Kaltenbrunner, Field Marshal Wilhelm Keitel, Alfred Rosenberg, Fritz Sauckel, Arthur Seyss-Inquart, Julius Streicher and Foreign Minister Joachim von Ribbentrop.

Others sentenced for war crimes: Gen. Anton Dostler, Nazi, hanged in Rome Dec. 1, 1945, for shooting 15 U. S. soldiers without trial; Joseph Kramer, "Beast of Belsen" and 10 others hanged Dec. 14, by British for atrocities at Belsen and Auschwitz concentration camps; Gen. Yamashita, Japanese commander in Philippines, hanged Feb. 23, 1946; Lt. Gen. Homma, who ordered Bataan death march, shot near Manila Apr. 3, 1946; Marshal Ion Antonescu, dictator of Romania, hanged June 1, 1946; Karl Hermann Frank, Nazi ruler in Czechoslovakia, hanged in Prague May 22 for ordering massacre of Lidice; 48 Nazi officers and guards hanged by the U. S. Army at Landsberg, Germany, May, 1947, for mass murders at Mauthausen camp.

President Truman proclaimed the cessation of hostilities of World War II **Dec. 31**.

1947

British Labor Government took possession of coal mines, cables and wireless communications **Jan. 1**.

Peace treaties for Hitler's European satellites, imposing $1.33 billion in reparations, signed **Feb. 10, 1947.**

Truman Doctrine. President Truman asked Congress to appropriate $400,000,000 for aid to Greece and Turkey to combat communism, **Mar. 12.** Approved **May 15.**

The United Nations Security Council voted unanimously **Apr. 2** to place under U. S. trusteeship the Pacific islands formerly mandated to Japan.

Taft-Hartley Labor Act approved by U. S. Senate, 68 to 24, **May 13.** The house concurred **June 4** by a vote of 320 to 79. The measure was vetoed by President Truman **June 20,** but the House overrode the veto, 331 to 83, on the same day. The Senate overrode the veto, 68-25, **June 23.**

Proposals known later as the Marshall Plan, under which the U. S. would extend financial aid to all European countries "willing to assist in the task of recovery," were made by Secy. of State George C. Marshall in a Speech **June 5** at Harvard University. Congress authorized the spending in the next 3½ years of some $12 billion on Marshall Plan aid, which was credited with restoring economic health to free Europe and halting the march of communism in those countries cooperating in the plan. The Marshall proposals set the pattern for the vast U. S. post-war program of foreign aid.

Hindu India and Moslem Pakistan, formerly British India, gained independence **Aug. 15.** Lord Louis Mountbatten was the last British Viceroy of India.

1948

British Labor Government nationalized railways **Jan. 1.**

Mohandas K. Gandhi, Hindu spiritual leader and champion of freedom for India, was shot and killed by a Hindu fanatic in New Delhi **Jan. 30.** Communal rioting took the lives of nearly 100 leaders and members of the Mahasabba, politico-religious group to which Gandhi's assassin belonged, **Jan. 30-Feb. 2.**

Czechoslovakia joined the communist block in Eastern Europe after President Benes yielded **Feb. 25** to an ultimatum to install a pro-Soviet Cabinet. He resigned **June 7;** succeeded by Klement Gottwald, communist. Benes died **Sept. 3.** Communists reported Jan Masaryk, Foreign Minister, committed suicide **Mar. 10.**

A land blockade of Berlin's Allied sectors was started **Apr. 1** by the Soviet Military Govt. which refused to permit U.S. and British supply trains to pass through the Soviet zone of Germany. This blockade and a Western counter-blockade were lifted **Sept. 30, 1949** after British and U. S. planes had airlifted 2,343,315 tons of food and coal into West Berlin.

Charter of the Organization of American States signed **Apr. 30** at 9th International Conference of American States at Bogota, Colombia.

The Free State of Israel was proclaimed in Tel Aviv **May 14** as the British evacuated Palestine. First de facto recognition came from the United States **May 14.** Soviet Russia granted recognition **May 17** of Israeli government's de jure (legal) authority in Jewish Palestine. Chaim Wiezmann elected president by the Constituent Assembly **Feb. 14, 1949.**

The Cominform (Communist Information Bureau) at a Prague meeting **June 28,** denounced Marshal Tito and other leaders of the Yugoslav Communist party as deserters from the Marxist-Leninist doctrine.

Alger Hiss, former State Department official, was indicted in New York City **Dec. 15** on two perjury charges after he had denied passing secret documents to Whittaker Chambers, a former magazine editor, for transmission to a communist spy ring. A jury failed to reach an agreement **July 8, 1949.** His second trial **Nov. 17, 1949-Jan. 21, 1950** ended with conviction on 2 counts and a sentence of 5 years in a federal prison. Appeals to higher courts were rejected and Hiss began his sentence **Mar. 22, 1951.** He denied all charges. He petitioned Federal Court, New York, for retrial on basis of new evidence of "forgery by typewriter" Jan. 24, 1952. Judge H. W. Goddard

denied it, July 22, 1952, Supreme Court on Apr. 27, 1953. He was released **Nov. 27, 1954.**

Former Premier Hideki Tojo and 6 other Japanese war leaders were hanged **Dec. 23** as war criminals.

Joseph Cardinal Mindszenty, Roman Catholic primate of Hungary, arrested by Communist government in Budapest on charges of treason, espionage and black market dealing **Dec. 27.** Convicted, given life imprisonment **Feb. 8, 1949.** All persons taking part in the cardinal's prosecution were excommunicated by Pope Pius XII. Mindszenty freed **Oct. 31, 1956;** after 15 years in U. S. Embassy in Budapest the cardinal left Hungary **Sept. 28, 1971** for West Europe.

1949

Mildred E. (Axis Sally) Gillars was convicted by a federal jury in New York City **Mar. 10** of treason in broadcasting Nazi propaganda during war. She received 10 to 30 years in prison. Freed **1961.**

North Atlantic Treaty adopted **Mar. 18** by U.S., Canada and 10 Western European nations, agreeing that "an armed attack against one or more of them in Europe and North America shall be considered an attack against all." Signed **Apr. 4** ratified by Senate **July 21.**

Ireland severed last ties with Britain by leaving Commonwealth, **Apr. 18.**

End of American A-bomb monopoly revealed by President Truman's announcement **Sept. 23** that an atomic explosion had occurred in the USSR.

Mrs. I. Toguri D'Aquino, (Tokyo Rose) of Japanese wartime broadcasts, was sentenced in San Francisco **Oct. 7** to 10 years in prison for treason. Paroled **1956.**

Eleven leaders of U. S. Communist party convicted **Oct. 14,** after 9-month trial in New York City, of advocating violent overthrow of U. S. Government. Federal Judge Harold R. Medina **Oct. 21** sentenced 10 defendants to 5 years in prison each and the 11th, a war veteran, to 3 years. U.S. Court of Appeals upheld conviction **Aug. 1, 1950.** Supreme Court upheld the conviction **June 4, 1951.** Seven surrendered **July 2, 1951;** of the other 4, hunted as fugitives, one, Gus Hall, was captured **Oct. 8, 1951,** and given 3 additional years. Robert G. Thompson was captured **Aug. 27, 1953.** Five defense lawyers, cited for contempt during the trial, received sentences ranging from 1 to 6 months **Apr. 24, 1952;** Supreme Court upheld sentences **Mar. 10, 1952.**

Nationalist China's government fled to Formosa **Dec. 7.** Chinese Communists took Yunnan and Kunming as Nationalists deserted.

1950

Great Britain recognized Communist China Jan. 6 one day after breaking diplomatic relations with Chiang Kai-shek's nationalist Chinese regime.

U.S. Jan. 14 recalled all consular officials from Communist China after the latter seized the American consulate general in Peiping.

Masked bandits robbed Brink's Inc., Boston express office, **Jan. 17** of $2,775,395.12, of which $1,218,211.29 was in cash. Solution announced 1956 by FBI; 8 men sentenced to life.

President Truman authorized AEC to produce the hydrogen bomb (H-bomb), **Jan. 31.**

Dr. Klaus J. E. Fuchs, German-born atomic research physicist at Harwell, England, pleaded guilty **Mar. 1** to violating the Official Secrets Act and received 14 years in prison. He had communicated valuable atomic information to Russian agents since 1942. At one time he worked at Los Alamos, N. M. Released **June 23, 1959.**

The Army seized all railroads Aug. 27, on orders of President Truman, to prevent a general strike after unions had rejected terms of an 18c an hour raise for yardmen but none for trainmen. Roads returned to owners **May 23, 1952** after signing of new labor contract.

In an attempt to kill President Truman, two members of a Puerto Rican nationalist movement tried to shoot their way into the President's house, Washington, **Nov. 1.** *See Assassinations.*

U. S. Dec. 8 banned shipments to Communist China

and to Asiatic ports trading with it.

Supreme Court ruled Dec. 11 that under the 5th amendment no one could be forced to testify against himself.

1951

Ilse Koch was sentenced to life imprisonment by a German court in Frankfort **Jan. 15** for inciting the murder of a Buchenwald prisoner.

With Sen. Estes Kefauver (D. Tenn.) as chairman, the Senate Committee to Investigate Organized Crime in Interstate Commerce exposed nationwide criminal organizations that reaped huge illegal profits, used these funds to enter legitimate businesses, influenced politicians and bought protection. Preliminary report **Feb. 28** said gambling took over $20 billion a year.

Julius Rosenberg, his wife, Ethel, and Morton Sobell, all U. S. citizens, were found guilty **Mar. 29** of conspiracy to commit wartime espionage. Rosenbergs sentenced to death, Sobell to 30 years; appeals denied. David Greenglass, brother of Mrs. Rosenberg and a state witness, received 15 years in prison. Rosenbergs executed at Sing Sing prison, Ossining, N.Y., **June 19, 1953.** Sobel, released **Jan. 14, 1969.**

President Truman relieved Gen. Douglas MacArthur of his command in the Far East **Apr. 11.** *See Korean War.*

European Coal and Steel Plan proposed by French Foreign Minister Robert Schuman **May 9.** British Labor Government rejected plan but 6 other nations, France, West Germany, Italy, Belgium, Netherlands, and Luxembourg agreed to conference. Treaty ratified **June 16, 1952.**

UN General Assembly voted arms embargo against Communist China **May 18.**

Tariff concessions by the U. S. to the Soviet Union, Communist China and all communist-dominated lands were suspended **Aug. 1.**

Transcontinental television inaugurated **Sept. 4** with President Truman's address at the Japanese Peace Treaty Conference in San Francisco.

Japanese Peace Treaty signed in San Francisco **Sept. 8** by U. S. and 48 other nations.

War between Germany and the U.S. formally ended **Oct. 19.** Great Britain and France ended war with Germany **July 9.**

1952

Queen Elizabeth II proclaimed queen of Canada **Feb. 6** marking first time monarch was specifically enthroned in name of Canada.

U. S. seizure of nation's steel mills was ordered by President Truman **Apr. 8** to avert a strike by 600,000 CIO United Steelworkers. Seizure was ruled illegal by the Supreme Court **June 2.** Strike followed **June 3,** was settled **July 24.**

First jetliner passenger service opened **May 2,** British DeHavilland Comet, London to Johannesburg, South Africa, 6,724 mi. in less than 24 hours.

Peace contract between West Germany, U.S., Great Britain and France was signed in Bonn **May 26.** Allied high commissions abolished.

Puerto Rico became an "associated free state" or commonwealth of the U. S. **July 25** after President Truman gave approval to a new constitution.

West Germany agreed Sept. 10 to pay Israel $822,000,000 over 12 to 14 years as indemnity for Nazi and anti-Semitic acts.

Britain successfully completed its first atomic test

Korean War and United States Intervention

Republic of Korea was invaded June 25, 1950 (June 24 EST) by over 60,000 North Korean troops spearheaded by over 100 Russian-built tanks. UN Security Council demanded cessation of hostilities and withdrawal to 38th parallel. On June 27, it asked UN members to help carry out its demand. President Truman, **June 27,** ordered Gen. of the Army Douglas MacArthur to aid South Korea and the U. S. 7th Fleet to protect Formosa against possible aggression and keep the Chinese Nationalist forces from attacking the mainland. Requested by the UN to name a commander, the President designated Gen. MacArthur **July 8, 1950.**

North Korean forces took Seoul, South Korean capital **June 29,** U. S. ground forces entered the conflict **June 30.** The President termed the intervention a "police action."

The war had three phases: (1) The North Korean drive was checked by U. S. and associated troops, with help of a brilliant landing by U. S. Marines at **Inchon Sept. 15. Pyongyang,** North Korean capital, was taken **Oct. 20,** U. S. 7th Division reached Manchurian border **Nov. 20.**

(2) Counter-attack by 200,000 Chinese Communist "volunteers," who crossed Yalu River **Nov. 26,** forced evacuation of 105,000 UN troops and 91,000 Korean civilians at Hungnam Dec. 24. The Chinese pushed across 38th parallel, drove 70 mi. into South Korea. The UN General Assembly, **Feb. 1,** named Communist China the aggressor in Korea. UN troops pushed Chinese back across parallel **Apr. 3,** stopped offensive by 600,000 Chinese **Apr. 22-30.**

(3) Removal of Gen. MacArthur from command **Apr. 11, 1951,** and start of negotiations for truce along 38th parallel **July 10, 1951.**

President Truman removed Gen. MacArthur from all Far East commands and replaced him with Gen. Matthew B. Ridgway, commander of 8th Army. MacArthur had wished to pursue Chinese across Yalu River to their air depots in Manchuria and on **Mar. 25** had threatened Communist China with air and naval

attack. He had been warned to clear all announcements of policy through Washington. The president opposed his views. A Senate inquiry **May 3-June 27, 1951,** found that MacArthur was not charged with insubordination, but had disregarded the president's order to clear policy statements through the Defense Department.

Cease fire and armistice talks began July 1951 and dragged on with numerous break-downs until **July 27, 1953** (July 26, EST) when armistice was signed, fighting ended 12 hrs. later. A military armistice commission supervised truce; 10 joint UN-Communist teams policed demilitarized zone; Neutral Nations Supervisory Commission watched military movements in ports; voluntary repatriation of prisoners was provided and Communists had privilege of interviewing prisoners refusing repatriation.

Prisoner repatriation began Aug. 6, 1953, at Panmunjom, ended **Sept. 6, 1953.** UN turned over 75,-799 prisoners (70,150 North Koreans and 5,640 Chinese). Communists released 12,760, including 7,850 South Koreans, 3,597 Americans, 945 Britons and 228 Turks. Maj.Gen. Dean was released Sept. 4.

The Supervisory Commission, made up of members from Czechoslovakia, Poland, Sweden and Switzerland, was reduced one-half in **Sept. 1955** on repeated complaints that the communist members were spying in South Korea. Repeated reports indicated that the North Koreans had violated many terms of the armistice, built numerous airfields and received naval vessels. The UN Command expelled the commission from South Korea in **June 1956,** on grounds that its Czech and Polish members and the North Korean government had frustrated the operation of the armistice agreement. The UN Command announced in **June 1957,** that it could no longer be bound by armistice provisions controlling importation of military equipment into Korea, but would modernize UN forces "to restore the relative balance of military strength that the armistice was intended to preserve."

off northwest Australia Oct. 3 detonating a bomb aboard a naval vessel.

First hydrogen device explosion Nov. 1 at AEC Eniwetok proving grounds in Pacific reported by witnesses but not officially confirmed for more than a year. President Eisenhower told Congress Feb. 2, 1954, that the 1952 test was "the first full-scale thermonuclear explosion in history . . . the first step in the hydrogen weapon program of the United States."

Alan Nunn May, British scientist who gave atom secrets to the USSR, was released from prison **Dec. 29,** after serving 6 yr. 8 mo. of his 10-yr. term.

1953

Joseph Stalin died Mar. 5. By 1955, Nikita Khrushchev emerged as dominant political leader of USSR.

Mau Mau or "Hidden Ones" of Kenya's Kikuyu tribe, formed to force whites from Kenya and to regain ancestral lands from government, climaxed sporadic violence **Mar. 26,** by murdering 71 and wounding 100 fellow Kikuyus who remained loyal to colonial government. Jomo Kenyatta, tribal leader, found guilty **Apr. 8** of organizing Mau Mau, sentenced to 7 years on **Dec. 12, 1963.** Kenya became independent and Jomo Kenyatta became prime minister and president **Dec. 12, 1964.**

Mount Everest was conquered May 29 by Edmund P. Hillary of New Zealand and Tensing Norkay, a Nepalese living in India.

Demonstration by workers in East Berlin against increased work quotas **June 16** erupted into an anticommunist riot by 20,000 to 50,000 people **June 17,** and became a general strike involving 200,000 in East Germany. Soviet troops quelled disturbances, killed 16.

Lavrenti P. Beria, chief of Soviet secret police, was dismissed **July 10** as an enemy of the people. He was executed **Dec. 23** along with 6 of his aides. Purge extended to Georgia, the Ukraine, Byelorussia and other Soviet states.

First USSR announcement of H-bomb explosion **Aug. 20;** AEC reported explosion occurred **Aug. 12.**

1954

Nautilus, first atomic-powered submarine, was launched at Groton, Conn., **Jan. 21.**

Five members of Congress were wounded in the House **Mar. 1** by 4 Puerto Ricans, one a woman, who fired pistols at random from a spectators' gallery, shouting for Puerto Rican independence. Representatives recovered, attackers imprisoned.

Dien Bien Phu, French military outpost in NW Vietnam, fell to the Vietminh army of Ho Chi Minh **May 7.**

Geneva Conference on Far Eastern Affairs was held **Apr. 26-July 21** by foreign ministers of 19 nations, including Communist China. Free elections in Korea foundered on communist objections to UN supervision. Armistice, effective **Aug. 11,** ended 7½ years of war in Indo-China with French withdrawal; Vietminh received 62,000 sq. mi. and 13,000,000 people in North Vietnam. Cambodia and Laos became independent countries.

Racial segregation in public schools was ruled unconstitutional in a unanimous decision of the Supreme Court **May 17.**

Southeast Asia Treaty Organization (SEATO) formed by collective defense pact signed in Manila **Sept. 8** by the U. S., Britain, France, Australia, New Zealand, Philippines, Pakistan and Thailand.

Agreement signed in Paris Oct. 23 provided for West German sovereignty, rearmament and entrance into NATO and the Western European Union.

Condemnation of Sen. Joseph R. McCarthy (R. Wis.) voted by Senate, 67-22, **Dec. 2** for contempt of a Senate elections subcommittee, for abuse of its members and for insults to the Senate during investigation **Apr. 22-June 17** of charges brought by the Dept. of the Army vs. Sen. McCarthy, growing out of the Senator's investigation of alleged subversive activities.

1955

Afro-Asian conference of 29 nations met in Ban-

dung, Indonesia, **Apr.** Conference gave expression to the new nationalism of developing nations.

Federal Republic of West Germany became a sovereign state **May 5** when ratifications were deposited in Bonn. U. S. completed ratification **Apr. 21.** President Eisenhower signed an order ending U. S. occupation but troops remained on a contractual basis.

The Warsaw Pact, a 20-yr. mutual defense treaty, was signed at Warsaw **May 14** by USSR, Albania, Bulgaria, Czechoslovakia, Hungary, Poland, Romania and East Germany.

A meeting of heads of state "at the summit" proposed by U. S., Great Britain and France, to the USSR, took place **July 18-23** in Geneva, Switzerland, with President Eisenhower top negotiator for the U.S. It was followed by a meeting of the foreign ministers **Oct. 27-Nov. 16** with Secy. of State Dulles acting for U. S.

Juan D. Peron, president and dictator of Argentina, was deposed **Sept. 19** after a military revolt begun **June 16** by naval and marine corps units. Maj. Gen. Eduardo Lonardi became provisional president **Sept. 23,** was displaced **Nov. 13** by a military junta which chose Maj. Gen. Pedro Aramburu provisional president.

Rosa Parks initiated the first nationally significant direct action by the Negro community **Dec.1** by refusing to give her seat to a white man on a bus in Montgomery, Ala. Bus segregation ordinance declared unconstitutional by a federal court following boycott and NAACP protest.

Merger of America's two largest labor organizations was effected **Dec. 5** under the name American Federation of Labor and Congress of Industrial Organizations. George Meany became president, Walter Reuther became vice president in charge of the industrial department. The merged AFL-CIO had a membership estimated at 15,000,000.

1956

At 20th Congress of Soviet Communist party in Moscow **Feb. 14-25** party chief Nikita S. Khrushchev and other leaders denounced Joseph Stalin, repudiated cruelties of Stalinism and proclaimed a policy of peaceful coexistence with the West. New party line helped to alienate Chinese communists and hasten Sino-Soviet split. U. S. State Dept. **June 4** published text of Khrushchev's 7-hr. secret speech.

Workers in Poznan, Poland, revolted June 28 against communist rule; uprising crushed with 44 killed, hundreds wounded.

Principles of Organization of American States outlined in Panama Declaration signed in Panama City **July 22** by President Eisenhower and heads of 18 other Western Hemisphere states.

Egypt seized Suez Canal July 26 under nationalization decree after President Gamal Abdel Nasser denounced Western withdrawal of proposed Aswan dam financing.

Army H21 helicopter landed in Washington, D. C., **Aug. 24** after first non-stop transcontinental helicopter flight—2,610 mi. in 37 hours.

First trans-Atlantic telephone cable system went into use **Sept. 25** between Clarenville, Newfoundland, and Oban, Scotland.

Polish Communist leaders Oct. 19-21 defied Kremlin leadership and elected Wladyslaw Gomulka to head more independent government.

Hungarian revolt against Soviet-dominated regime began **Oct. 23,** was crushed **Nov. 4** by Soviet armed forces.

Israel invaded Egypt's Sinai Peninsula Oct. 29. When Egypt rejected demand for cease-fire made by France and Britain, the two nations bombed Egypt by air **Oct. 31,** landed forces **Nov. 5-6.** U. S. condemned attack, supported cease-fire demand by UN. Egypt and Israel accepted cease-fire. Britain and France followed, fighting stopped **Nov. 7.**

UN established first international police force **Nov. 5** to supervise truce in Middle East.

1957

Britain set off its first hydrogen bomb in Pacific test **May 15.**

Soviet Union announced Aug. 26 that it had successfully tested an intercontinental ballistic missile.

Sen. Strom Thurmond (D. S.C.) held Senate floor for 24 hrs. 18 min., **Aug. 28-29,** eclipsing record filibuster of 22 hr. 26 min. set by Sen. Wayne Morse (D. Ore.) in 1953.

First underground nuclear explosion set off by Atomic Energy Commission in Nevada **Sept. 19.**

A Federal-state controversy over admission of Negroes to the previously all-white Central High School in Little Rock, Ark., reached a showdown **Sept. 4** when National Guardsmen ordered out by Gov. Orval Faubus (D.) barred 9 Negro students from entering the school. A conference between Faubus and President Eisenhower brought no tangible result but Faubus complied **Sept. 21** with a federal court order to remove the National Guardsmen. The Negroes entered school **Sept. 23** but were ordered to withdraw by local authorities because of fear of mob violence. President Eisenhower sent federal troops to Little Rock **Sept. 24** to enforce the federal court's order and the school began operation on an integrated basis.

First man-made satellite, Sputnik I, was launched by Soviet scientists **Oct. 4.** The 184-lb. sphere circled the earth about every 1½ hours in an ellipitcal orbit at altitudes ranging from some 140 miles to 560 miles above the earth. The Russians **Nov. 3** launched Sputnik II, weighing 1,120 lbs., carrying a live dog, Laika, as the world's first space passenger and orbiting the earth about every 103.7 minutes at altitudes ranging from some 160 miles to about 1,062 miles. Soviet authorities announced the dog's death **Nov. 10.** Sputnik I disintegrated **Jan. 4, 1958** and Sputnik II, **Apr. 14, 1958.**

1958

First U. S. earth satellite to go into orbit, Explorer I, launched by Army **Jan. 31** at Cape Canaveral, Fla.

Gen. Charles de Gaulle became French premier **June 1** averting threatened civil war; De Gaulle constitution, increasing power of executive, overwhelmingly adopted **Sept. 28.** De Gaulle elected **Dec. 21** as first president of 5th Republic.

Arab nationalist rebels seized Iraqi government **July 14,** killed King Faisal II, proclaimed republic. President Eisenhower sent U.S. marines to Lebanon **July 15** to forestall alleged effort by Soviet Union and United Arab Republic to engineer overthrow of Lebanon regime. Withdrawal of U. S. troops began **Aug. 12.**

Jet airliner passenger service across Atlantic was opened **Oct. 4** by British Overseas Airways Corp.

First domestic jet airline passenger service in U.S. opened by National Airlines **Dec. 10** between New York and Miami.

1959

Fidel Castro assumed power in Cuba following collapse of Fulgencio Batista's government **Jan. 1.**

St. Lawrence Seaway opened **Apr. 25;** was dedicated **June 26** by President Eisenhower and Queen Elizabeth II.

George Washington, first U.S. ballistic-missile submarine, launched at Groton, Conn., **June 9.**

N.S. Savannah, world's first atomic-powered merchant ship, launched **July 21** at Camden, N.J.

Soviet Premier Khrushchev paid unprecedented visit to U. S. **Sept. 15-27,** made transcontinental tour, conferred with President Eisenhower.

1960

A wave of sit-ins began **Feb. 1** when 4 Negro college students in Greensboro, N. C., refused to move from a Woolworth lunch counter when they were denied service. By Sept. 1961 more than 70,000 Negroes and white students had participated in sit-ins.

First French nuclear test explosion occurred **Feb. 13** in Sahara Desert.

Caryl Chessman, who had won 8 stays of execution since his 1948 conviction on robbery, kidnaping and attempted rape charges, was put to death **May 2** in the gas chamber at San Quentin prison, near San Francisco.

A U-2 reconnaissance plane of the U.S., piloted by Francis Gary Powers, was shot down in the Soviet Union **May 1.** Soviet Premier Khrushchev refused to participate in the Paris summit conference scheduled for **May 16** unless President Eisenhower apologized for U-2 flights over the USSR; the Big Four leaders went to Paris but the conference did not take place. Powers was freed **Feb. 10, 1962,** in exchange for convicted Soviet spy Rudolf Abel, who was serving a 30-year term imposed by U. S. in 1957.

Adolf Eichmann's capture in Argentina by Israeli agents announced **May 22;** former Nazi SS general accused of playing a major role in killing of millions of Jews. After 4-month trial in Jerusalem, sentenced by Israeli court **Dec. 15, 1961,** hanged for crimes against humanity **May 31, 1962.**

1961

The United States severed diplomatic and consular relations with Cuba **Jan. 3.**

Maj. Yuri Gagarin of the Soviet Union became **Apr. 12** the first human space traveler; he was launched into orbit from Siberia in a spacecraft called Vostok I and returned to earth after one circuit of the globe.

Invasion of Cuba "Bay of Pigs" Apr. 17 by Cuban exiles attempting to overthrow the regime of Premier Fidel Castro was repulsed.

Commander Alan B. Shepard Jr. was rocketed from Cape Canaveral, Fla., 116.5 miles above the earth in a Mercury capsule **May 5** in the first U. S. manned sub-orbital space flight; he landed safely in the Atlantic 302 miles away. **Capt. Virgil I. (Gus) Grissom** made a similar flight from Cape Canaveral **July 21.**

East Germany closed the border between East and West Berlin **Aug. 12-13** to stop the exodus of East Germans to the West; the East Germans built a wall dividing the city.

Dag Hammarskjold, Secy. General of the UN was killed in a plane crash near Ndola, Northern Rhodesia **Sept. 18.** U Thant of Burma was elected Acting Secy. General **Nov. 3.**

Nuclear blasts of 25 megatons and over 50 megatons, largest man-made explosions to date, were set off by the Soviet Union **Oct. 23** and **Oct. 30** respectively, despite world protests.

1962

Lt. Col. John H. Glenn Jr. became the first American in orbit **Feb. 20** when he circled the earth 3 times in the Mercury capsule Friendship 7.

A truce agreement Mar. 18 ended the 7-yr. Moslem revolt against French rule in Algeria. Algerians cast an overwhelming vote for independence in a referendum **July 1** and French President Charles de Gaulle declared the country independent **July 3.**

The 3d Soviet astronaut was sent into orbit **Aug. 11** and the 4th followed him into a nearly identical orbit **Aug. 12,** both descended **Aug. 15.** They were **Maj. Andrian G. Nikolayev,** who made a record 64 orbits of the earth, and **Lt. Col. Pavel R. Popovich,** who made 48 orbits.

The largest cash robbery to date in U. S. history occurred **Aug. 14** when a gang held up a U. S. mail truck near Plymouth, Mass., and stole $1,551,277.

A Soviet offensive buildup in Cuba was revealed to the American people **Oct. 22** by President Kennedy, who ordered a naval and air quarantine on shipment of offensive military equipment to the island. President Kennedy and Soviet Premier Khrushchev reached agreement **Oct. 28** on a formula to end the crisis. Kennedy said **Nov. 2** that Soviet missile bases in Cuba were being dismantled.

1963

The first woman space traveler, Soviet **Jr. Lt. Valentina V. Tereshkova** was launched into orbit in Vostok VI **June 16;** landed **June 19** after 48 orbits.

U.S. Supreme Court ruled, 8-1, **June 17** that state and local laws requiring recitation of the Lord's Prayer or Bible verses in public schools were unconstitutional.

A limited nuclear test-ban treaty was agreed upon **July 25** by the United States, the Soviet Union and Britain, barring all nuclear tests except those conducted underground. It became effective **Oct. 10.**

The biggest robbery to date occurred Aug. 8 when an armed holdup gang stole more than $7,000,000 (£2,500,000) in currency from a mail train near Cheddington, England. Some of the money was recovered.

Vietnam War and United States Intervention

American combat involvement in Vietnam for about 12 years made the Vietnam War the longest in U.S. history. U.S. interest in the area began when President Harry S. Truman **June 27, 1950,** sent a 35-man military advisory team to aid the French in their fight against communist forces in North Vietnam.

After the French stronghold of Dien Bien Phu fell to communist forces **May 8, 1954,** France and North Vietnam agreed at the Geneva Conference on Indochina, **May 8 to July 21,** to partition Vietnam pending reunification elections. President Dwight D. Eisenhower offered South Vietnam economic aid **Oct. 24, 1954,** and agreed to help train the South Vietnamese army **Feb. 12, 1955.** In July, the South Vietnamese government refused a North Vietnamese request to prepare for reunification elections on grounds that free elections would be impossible in North Vietnam.

North Vietnam announced **Dec. 1960** the formation of the National Liberation Front (Viet Cong) of South Vietnam; terrorism in the South increased. The number of U.S. military advisers in South Vietnam rose from about 2,000 in Dec. 1961 to over 15,000 by the end of 1963.

Ngo Dinh Diem, South Vietnam president since 1955, was assassinated during a military coup **Nov. 1, 1963.** Stable government did not return to South Vietnam until **June 1965,** when Gen. Nguyen Van Thieu assumed command of a military government.

The major American commitment in Vietnam began after the U.S. destroyers Maddox and C. Turner Joy were reportedly attacked **Aug. 2, 1964,** by North Vietnamese torpedo boats in the Gulf of Tonkin. The U.S. Congress **Aug. 7** passed the Gulf of Tonkin Resolution giving the president power to "take all necessary measures to repel any armed attack against the forces of the United States and to prevent further aggression." In **Feb. 1965,** President Johnson ordered continuous bombing raids over North Vietnam below the 20th parallel.

U.S. commanders were authorized to commit 23,-000 advisers to combat **June 8, 1965.** U.S. army, navy, air and marine forces committed in Vietnam reached 184,300 men by year's end. The U.S. began bombing strikes in the Hanoi-Haiphong area **June 29, 1966.** By Dec. 31, 1966, U.S. forces in Vietnam reached 385,300 men, not including some 60,000 men in the U.S. fleet and some 33,000 men stationed in Thailand.

The unconventional conflict in South Vietnam required the use of new ground warfare tactics. "Search and destroy" missions and "free-fire zones" for artillery were the most publicized of these new tactics because of their potential hazard to non-combatants. Armed helicopters were used extensively because of their mobility.

As the fighting and American casualties escalated, large scale protests against the war erupted in the U.S. Thousands of war protestors marched **Oct. 21-22, 1967,** in Washington, D.C., and hundreds were arrested when they stormed the Pentagon. Nevertheless, American troop strength climbed to 474,300 men in Dec., 1,500 more than peak U.S. strength in Korea during the Korean War.

In the **"Tet offensive" Jan. 30, 1968,** the Viet Cong attacked 30 provincial capitals in South Vietnam. The city of Hue was held by the Viet Cong for 25 days, with bitter street fighting ending **Feb. 24.** Saigon was heavily attacked and the U.S. Embassy was occupied for 6 hrs. Record casualties were suffered on both sides. President Johnson **Mar. 31** announced a bombing halt over 90% of North Vietnam and asked Hanoi for a peaceful response.

While the fighting continued, preliminary peace talks between the U.S. and North Vietnam opened in Paris **May 10.** In Chicago, police and troops clashed with 10,000-15,000 anti-war demonstrators during the Democratic National Convention **Aug. 26-29.**

Expanded peace talks, including representatives from South Vietnam and the Viet Cong, opened in Paris **Jan. 18, 1969.** American forces in South Vietnam reached a peak of 543,400 men in **Apr. 1969.** U.S. battle deaths **Apr. 3** totaled 33,641 men, surpassing by 12 those killed in the Korean War. Withdrawal of U.S. combat troops began **July 8, 1969,** and on **Nov. 3** President Nixon announced a Vietnamization policy which would transfer the fighting to South Vietnamese forces.

Protest in the U.S. continued, however, as hundreds of thousands of Americans demonstrated opposition to the Vietnam War **Oct. 15** in a nationwide "moratorium." Some 250,000 demonstrators gathered in Washington, D.C., **Nov. 15** in the largest anti-war protest in U.S. history.

As the Paris talks continued, U.S. and South Vietnamese forces invaded neutral Cambodia **Apr. 30, 1970,** to destroy communist supply bases in border area sanctuaries. On **May 4** at Kent State Univ. in Ohio, 4 students were slain and 9 wounded when National Guardsmen opened fire during a demonstration against the Cambodian incursion; 100 U.S. colleges were closed down to protest the Cambodian invasion and Kent State killings. A year later, during massive anti-war protests in Washington, D.C., between **May 3-5,** police arrested some 12,614 people, at least 7,000 of them on the first day — a record high for arrests in a civil disturbance in U.S. history.

President Nixon revealed **Jan. 25, 1972,** that secret peace negotiations had been conducted since the previous June by presidential adviser Henry A. Kissinger. In the biggest communist attack since 1968, North Vietnamese forces **Mar. 30** launched an offensive in force against South Vietnam through the demilitarized zone (DMZ) between the 2 Vietnams. Bombing of North Vietnam resumed **Apr. 15,** the first intensive bombing of the North since 1968. Quang Tri, capital city of South Vietnam's northernmost province, fell to Hanoi troops **May 1.** The mining of Haiphong and other North Vietnamese ports was ordered by President Nixon **May 8.** After initial setbacks, South Vietnamese troops brought the invasion to a halt.

The last U.S. combat troops left Vietnam Aug. 11. Hanoi announced **Oct. 26** that secret talks had achieved a tentative agreement. On **Nov. 1,** President Thieu denounced the proposed plan as a "surrender," and on **Dec. 18** President Nixon ordered the heaviest bombing of the war against North Vietnam. B-52 bombers were used for the first time against targets in Hanoi; some 15 were shot down by Hanoi's surface-to-air missiles.

Peace talks resumed **Jan. 8, 1973,** and President Nixon ordered a halt to all offensive military operations against North Vietnam **Jan. 15.** Peace pacts were formally signed in Paris **Jan. 27** by the U.S., North and South Vietnam, and the Viet Cong. A ceasefire began in Vietnam on **Jan. 28.** Between **Feb. 12 and Apr. 1,** 590 American POWs were released by North Vietnam. Some 1,359 Americans were reported missing in Indochina. The last American troops left Vietnam **Mar. 29,** officially ending any direct U.S. military role. U.S. combat deaths were counted at 46,079 as of **Aug. 25, 1973.** Total dead were estimated at some 2 million.

and over a dozen men were sentenced to long prison terms.

Washington demonstration by 200,000 persons **Aug. 28** in support of Negro demands for equal rights. Highlight was speech in which Dr. Martin Luther King said: "I have a dream that this nation will rise up and live out the true meaning of its creed, 'We hold these truths to be self evident: that all men are created equal'."

The South Vietnamese government of President Ngo Dinh Diem was overthrown **Nov. 1-2** in a coup by the armed forces. Diem and his brother, secret police chief Ngo Dinh Nhu, were captured and killed.

President John F. Kennedy was shot and fatally wounded by an assassin **Nov. 22** as he rode in a motorcade through downtown Dallas, Tex. Texas Gov. **John B. Connally Jr.**, riding in the same car, was also shot but not fatally injured. Vice President Lyndon B. Johnson was inaugurated President shortly afterward in Dallas. **Lee Harvey Oswald** was arrested and charged with the murder of the president. Oswald was shot and fatally wounded **Nov. 24** by **Jack Ruby** 52, a Dallas night club owner, who was convicted of murder **Mar. 14, 1964**, and was sentenced to death. The murder conviction was reversed by the Texas Court of Criminal Appeals. Ruby died of natural causes **Jan. 3, 1967** while awaiting re-trial.

1964

Pope Paul VI toured the Holy Land **Jan. 4-6**, the first pope to visit there since Christianity began, the first to travel by air, and the first to leave Italy in over 150 years.

Three civil rights workers were reported missing in Mississippi **June 22**. The bodies of Michael Schwerner, Andrew Goodman and James E. Chaney were found buried near Philadelphia, Miss., **Aug. 4**. Twenty-one white men were arrested. On **Oct. 20, 1967**, an all-white federal jury convicted 7.

The Warren Commission released **Sept. 27** a report containing the conclusion that Lee Harvey Oswald was solely responsible for the killing of Pres. Kennedy.

Soviet Premier Khrushchev was ousted as premier and Soviet Communist party chief **Oct. 14-15**. Aleksei N. Kosygin replaced him as premier and Leonid I. Brezhnev took over the party leadership.

Communist China conducted a successful test explosion of its first atomic bomb **Oct. 16**.

1965

A Selma to Montgomery, Ala., civil rights march was led by Dr. Martin Luther King Jr., **Mar. 21-25**. They started with 3,200 and swelled to 25,000. They were guarded along the way by 4,000 troops dispatched by Pres. Johnson.

U.S. armed forces sent to Dominican Republic to protect U.S. citizens and prevent a revolution **Apr. 28**. The Organization of American States **May 23** set up a peace-keeping force to maintain order.

Los Angeles riot by discontented Negroes living in the Watts area resulted in the death of 35 persons and property damage estimated at $200,000,000 **Aug. 11-16**.

Pope Paul VI visited N.Y. City **Oct. 4** and delivered a personal appeal for peace to the UN. It was the first time a pope had come to America.

Massive electric power failure blacked out most of northeastern U.S., parts of 2 Canadian provinces the night of **Nov. 9-10**. Approximately 80,000 sq. mi. with a population of 30,000,000 were affected. In N.Y. City over 800,000 were trapped in the subways for hours.

Independence proclaimed in Rhodesia by minority white regime **Nov. 11**.

1966

Kwame Nkrumah, president of Ghana since independence in 1957, was overthrown **Feb. 24**.

France withdrew all its armed forces from the integrated NATO military alliance **July 1**.

Medicare, government program to pay part of the medical expenses of citizens over 65, began **July 1**.

A sniper atop the Univ. of Texas tower in Austin, Tex., shot 44 persons **Aug. 1**, killing 14. Shot to death by police, the sniper was identified as Charles J. Whitman, 25, an honor student at the university. Police later found the bodies of his wife and his mother.

Edward Brooke (R. Mass.) elected **Nov. 8** as first Negro U.S. Senator in 85 years.

1967

Rep. Adam Clayton Powell (D. N.Y.) was denied **Mar. 1** his seat in 90th Congress because House of Representatives charged him with misuse of government funds and nepotism. Re-elected in 1968, he was seated by the 91st Congress but was fined $25,000 and stripped of his 22 years' congressional seniority. Died **Apr. 4, 1972**.

In 6-day Israeli-Arab war June 5-10, Israel smashed armed forces of United Arab Republic, Syria and Jordan; Israel captured territory 4 times its own area. A U.S. communications ship the U.S.S. Liberty, was attacked and heavily damaged by Israeli planes and torpedo boats **June 8** in international waters 15 miles north of the Sinai Peninsula. Thirty-four U.S. crewmen were killed and 75 wounded. Israel apologized for the attack, which it called accidental.

Pres. Johnson and Soviet Premier Aleksei Kosygin met **June 23 and 25** at Glassboro State College in N.J.; agreed not to let any crisis push them into nuclear war.

Black riots in Newark, N.J., July 12-17 killed some 26, injured 1,500, over 1,000 arrested. In Detroit, Mich., **July 23-30** at least 40 died, 2,000 injured and 5,000 left homeless by rioting, looting and burning in city's black ghetto. Quelled by 4,700 federal paratroopers and 8,000 National Guardsmen.

Thurgood Marshall sworn in **Oct. 2** as first black U.S. Supreme Court Justice. **Carl B. Stokes** (D. Cleveland) and **Richard G. Hatcher** (D. Gary, Ind.), elected first black mayors of major U.S. cities. **Nov. 7**.

Dr. Christiaan Barnard, Capetown, South Africa, performed first successful human heart transplant **Dec. 3** on Louis Washkansky, who lived for 18 days.

1968

U.S.S. Pueblo and 83-man crew seized in Sea of Japan **Jan. 23** by North Koreans; 82 men released **Dec. 22**.

White racism cited as chief cause of Negro violence in Kerner Commission report on civil disorders **Feb. 29**.

Pres. Johnson said Mar. 31 he would not seek or accept the Democratic party nomination for another term.

Rev. Dr. Martin Luther King Jr., 39, assassinated **Apr. 4** in Memphis, Tenn. Riots in Washington, D.C., caused Pres. Johnson to call out troops. By **Apr. 14** racial violence erupted in 125 cities in 29 states. James Earl Ray, an escaped convict, pleaded guilty to the slaying, was sentenced to 99 years.

Six New Left students' protest at Univ. of Nanterre, France, **May 2** grew into nearly a month of civil violence and by **May 24** 10,000,000 strikers paralyzed country. DeGaulle saved regime with broad reforms.

Sen. Robert F. Kennedy, 42 (D. N.Y.) shot **June 5** in Hotel Ambassador, Los Angeles, after celebrating Calif. and S.D. presidential primary victories. Died **June 6**. Sirhan Beshara Sirhan, a Jordanian Arab living in L.A., convicted of murder and sentenced to death.

Soviet Union and other Warsaw Pact nations invaded Czechoslovakia **Aug. 20-21** to crush Alexander Dubcek's liberal regime.

1969

Dwight D. Eisenhower, 78, 34th president of the U.S. and Supreme Allied Commander in Europe during World War II, died of coronary heart disease **Mar. 28**.

Unarmed U.S. reconnaissance plane, with 31 aboard, shot down by North Korean jets **Apr. 15** in the Sea of Japan about 100 miles from the mainland.

Charles de Gaulle resigned as president of France **Apr. 28** after losing a referendum by a narrow margin.

Supreme Court Justice Abe Fortas resigned **May 14**, the first judge to do so in the tribunal's history because of public pressure.

A car driven by Sen. Edward M. Kennedy (D. Mass.) plunged off a bridge into a tidal pool on Chappaquiddick Island, Mass., **July 18**. The body of Mary Jo Kopechne, a 28-year-old secretary, was found drowned, in the car.

U.S. astronaut Neil A. Armstrong, 38, commander of the Apollo 11 mission, became the first man to set foot on the moon **July 20**. After stepping onto the moon Armstrong said: "That's one small step for a man, one giant leap for mankind." Air Force Col. **Edwin E. Aldrin Jr.** accompanied Armstrong on the moon landing.

The Selective Service System held the first draft lottery since 1942 in Washington **Dec. 1** to set the order of selection for the draft in 1970.

1970

Joseph A. Yablonski, 59, United Mine Workers official, his wife, and their daughter were found shot to death **Jan. 5** in their Clarksville, Pa., home. Six persons were indicted by a federal grand jury in Cleveland on charges of conspiring to kill Yablonski.

The 31-month Nigerian civil war ended with the surrender **Jan. 12** of secessionist Biafra after a loss of about 2,000,000 lives.

The Supreme Court ordered 14 school districts in Alabama, Florida, Georgia, Louisiana, Mississippi and Texas **Jan. 14** to integrate some 300,000 pupils by **Feb. 1** reaffirming its 1969 "desegregate now" ruling.

A federal jury Feb. 18 found the defendants in the turbulent 21-week trial of the "Chicago 7" innocent of conspiring to incite riots during the 1968 Democratic National Convention. However, 5 were convicted of crossing state lines with intent to incite riots.

The United States cast its first veto in the UN Security Council **Mar. 17** when it joined Britain in rejecting a resolution calling on UN members to cut all communications with Rhodesia.

More than 6,000 New York City postmen, angry over Congressional delays in granting pay raises, walked off the job **Mar. 18** and began the first large-scale strike in the U.S. postal service's 195-year history.

Millions of Americans participated in anti-pollution demonstrations **Apr. 22** to mark the first Earth Day.

The first women generals in American history were named by President Nixon **May 15** when he promoted Col. Elizabeth P. Hoisington, director of the Women's Army Corps, and Col. Anna Mae Hays, chief of the Army Nurse Corps, to the rank of brigadier general.

The Norwegian explorer Thor Heyerdahl and a multi-national crew of 7 set sail from Morocco **May 17** in a frail papyrus boat, the Ra II, in an attempt to prove that ancient Egyptians could have reached the new world. The craft sailed into Bridgetown Harbor, Barbados, **July 12**.

An earthquake in Peru May 31 wiped out scores of cities and villages and left more than 50,000 dead, 20,000 missing and 150,000 to 200,000 injured. U.S. Geological Survey experts termed the disaster "the most destructive historic earthquake in the Western hemisphere."

A postal reform measure was signed by President Nixon **Aug. 12**, creating an independent U.S. Postal Service, thus relinquishing governmental control of the U.S. mails after almost two centuries. Began **July 1, 1971**.

Egypt's Pres. Gamal Abdel Nasser, 52, the most powerful leader in the Arab world, died in Cairo **Sept. 28**.

Salvador Allende Gossens, 62, first democratically elected Marxist head of government in the world, was sworn in as Chile's president **Nov. 3**.

Charles De Gaulle, 79, died of a heart attack in Colombey-les-Deux Eglises **Nov. 9**.

A cyclone and giant waves devastated a 2,338-square-mile area of Pakistan's Bay of Bengal coast **Nov. 13** in one of the worst disasters of modern times. An estimated 300,000 persons were killed.

1971

Charles Manson, 36, and 3 of his followers were found guilty **Jan. 26** of first degree murder in the brutal slaying in 1969 of actress Sharon Tate and 6 others. They were sentenced to death in the gas chamber.

A treaty prohibiting installation of nuclear weapons on the seabed beyond any nation's 12-mile coastal zone was signed by 63 nations **Feb. 11**.

A Constitutional amendment lowering the voting age to 18 in all elections was approved in the Senate by a vote of 94-0 **Mar. 10**. The proposed 26th Amendment received House approval by a 400-19 vote **Mar. 23**; Ohio ratified it on **June 30** making it a law.

Civil war between East and West Pakistan beginning **Mar. 25** brought death from war and starvation to hundreds of thousands and caused 9,000,000 refugees to pour into India.

A court-martial jury of 6 officers **Mar. 29** after 13-days deliberation, convicted Lt. William L. Calley Jr., of premeditated murder of 22 South Vietnamese men, women and children at My Lai on **Mar. 16** 1968. He was sentenced to life imprisonment **Mar. 31**. Sentence reduced to 20 years **Aug. 20** 1971 by Lt. Gen. Albert O. Conner.

Haiti's Francois (Papa Doc) Duvalier, 64, died **Apr. 21**. His son Claude, 19, succeeded him **Apr. 22**.

Amtrak, the nation's new rail passenger system, went into operation **May 1** with the goal to "get people back on trains."

Publication of classified Pentagon papers on the U.S. involvement in Vietnam was begun **June 13** by the New York Times. In a 6-3 vote, the U.S. Supreme Court **June 30** upheld the right of the New York Times and Washington Post to publish the documents under the protection of the First Amendment. Daniel Ellsberg, admitted leaker of the 47-volume Pentagon analysis, was arraigned **June 28** on charges of unauthorized possession of secret documents.

President Nixon began a sweeping new economic program **Aug. 15** calling for a 90-day wage, price and rent freeze, to be effective immediately. He also freed the dollar for devaluation against other currencies by cutting its tie with gold, and halted the conversion of foreign held dollars into gold.

More than 1,000 New York State troopers and police stormed the Attica State Correctional Facility where 1,200 inmates held 38 guards hostage **Sept. 13**, ending a 4-day rebellion in the maximum-security prison. Nine hostages and 28 convicts were shot to death in the assault.

Chile virtually expropriated the Anaconda and Kennecott copper mines **Sept. 28** when President Allende subtracted $774 million from proposed compensation for the U.S. owners. He claimed the deduction was for "excess profits" harvested by the U.S. firms over 16 years.

Communist China is granted UN membership when the General Assembly by a vote of 76 to 35, with 17 abstentions, adopted an Albanian resolution **Oct. 25** to seat Mao Tse-tung's communists and oust Chiang Kai-shek's nationalists.

India invaded Pakistan Dec. 3 in defense of splinter nation of Bangladesh, formerly East Pakistan. Following India's victory in the 14-day war, Shiek Mujibur Rahman, the father of the secessionist rebellion, became the prime minister of Bangladesh **Jan. 12**.

President Nixon announced Dec. 18 an 8.57% devaluation of the U.S. dollar to allow American goods to be more competitive in the world market, while raising the price of certain imports. The devaluation would be accomplished by a $3 increase in the price of gold, from $35 an ounce to $38.

1972

President Nixon arrived in Peking Feb. 21 for an 8-

day visit to China, which he called a "journey for peace." The unprecedented visit ended with a joint communique pledging that both powers would work for "a normalization of relations."

Author Clifford Irving and his wife admitted **Mar. 13** that his purported interviews with multi-millionaire Howard Hughes and his subsequent biography of Hughes were hoaxes.

By a vote of 84 to 8, the Senate approved **Mar. 22** a constitutional amendment banning legal discrimination against women because of their sex and sent the measure to the states for ratification.

Britain imposed direct rule over North Ireland **Mar. 30,** ending 51 years of semi-autonomous rule by the North Ireland government.

Canada's Prime Minister Pierre Trudeau and President Nixon **Apr. 13-15** signed a landmark treaty calling for a massive program to cleanse the Great Lakes of pollution.

J. Edgar Hoover, 77, director of the Federal Bureau of Investigation (FBI) for all of its 48 years, serving under 8 presidents, died **May 2.**

Alabama Gov. George C. Wallace, campaigning at a Laurel, Md., shopping center **May 15,** was shot and seriously wounded as he greeted a large, enthusiastic crowd. Arthur H. Bremer, 21, was sentenced **Aug. 4** to 63 years in prison for the shooting of Wallace and 3 bystanders.

In the first visit of a U.S. president to Moscow, President Nixon arrived **May 22** for a week of summit talks with Kremlin leaders which culminated in a landmark arms pact aimed at a standoff between the missile forces of the two nuclear giants.

The Environmental Protection Agency announced **June 14** a near-total ban on agricultural and other uses of the pesticide DDT, to become effective **Dec. 31.**

Five men were arrested June 17 for breaking into the offices of the Democratic National Committee in the Watergate office complex in Washington, D.C.

Hurricane Agnes hit Florida **June 19** and went on a 10-day rampage up 250 miles of eastern seaboard with winds and rains which unleashed "the most extensive" floods in the country's history, causing 118 deaths and more than $3 billion in property damage.

Atty. Gen. John N. Mitchell, confidant and campaign manager of President Nixon, quit **July 1** as chairman of the Committee to Re-elect the President.

The White House announced July 8 that the U.S. would sell the Soviet Union at least $750 million of American wheat, corn and other grains over a period of 3 years.

Less than two weeks after Sen. Thomas F. Eagleton received the Democrats' nomination for vice-president, he confirmed **July 25** reports that he had undergone electroshock treatment on two occasions in the 1960s. Eagleton withdrew as nominee **July 31.** R. Sargent Shriver was named as vice presidential candidate **Aug. 8.**

By a vote of 88 to 2, the Senate **Aug. 3** ratified the strategic arms treaty limiting the U.S. and Russia to two antiballistic missile sites each. In White House ceremonies **Oct. 3** President Nixon and Soviet Foreign Min. Andrei Gromyko signed and exchanged the final documents implementing the accords, which also limited the two powers' land-based and submarine-borne nuclear missile forces.

Eight Arab guerrillas, members of the Black September terrorist group, invaded the Israeli dormitory in the Olympics village in Munich early **Sept. 5** killing two members of the Israeli squad. Twenty-three hours later, after tense negotiations, 5 of the terrorists and 9 hostages were killed.

Japan's Prime Min. Kakuei Tanaka and China's Premier Chou En-lai terminated more than 40 years of enmity **Sept. 29** when they signed an accord to end the technical state of war existing between the two Asian powers since 1937, and renewed diplomatic relations.

In a final report of a 2-year investigation of the New York City Police Dept., Whitman Knapp, chairman of the probe, concluded **Dec. 28** that "a sizeable majority" of the city's police were involved in some sort of wrongdoing as of Oct. 1971.

Life ended publication with its **Dec. 29** issue after 36 years as the leading weekly pictorial magazine.

1973

Great Britain, Ireland and Denmark formally entered the European Common Market **Jan. 1.**

All mandatory wage and price controls were ended by President Nixon **Jan. 11,** some 17 months after their establishment under the Economic Stabilization Act.

All state laws that limited a woman's right to an abortion during the first 3 months of pregnancy were overturned **Jan. 22** by the U.S. Supreme Court in a 7-2 decision.

The end of the military draft was announced **Jan. 27** by Defense Secretary Melvin R. Laird.

U.S. Secy. of the Treasury George P. Shultz announced **Feb. 12** a 10% devaluation of the U.S. dollar against nearly all the major world currencies.

Former Illinois Gov. Otto Kerner was found guilty **Feb. 19** of 17 counts of conspiracy, accepting a bribe, income tax evasion, mail fraud and perjury.

Ending 20 years of war, the Laotian government and communist-led Pathet Lao announced **Feb. 21** that they had reached a cease-fire agreement.

Some 200-300 members of the militant American Indian Movement **Feb. 27** seized the trading post and church at historic Wounded Knee on the Oglala Sioux Reservation in South Dakota. The insurgents demanded that the U.S. Senate Foreign Relations Committee hold hearings on treaties made with Indians, and that the Senate start a "full-scale investigation" of government treatment of Indians. After numerous negotiation failures both sides signed an agreement **May 5** stipulating removal of government armored personnel carriers and concurrent surrender of weapons by the insurgent Indians. The hamlet was evacuated **May 8.**

Palestinian terrorists invaded a reception **Mar. 1** at the Saudi Arabian embassy in Khartoum, Sudan, and held 6 diplomats hostage. After a breakdown of negotiations between the gunmen and Sudanese government officials, the 8 Palestinians **Mar. 2** executed 2 U.S. envoys and a Belgian charge d'affaires.

James W. McCord, a key figure in the Watergate conspiracy, said **Mar. 23** in a letter to the court that he and others had been under "political pressure" to plead guilty and remain silent. He said there were others involved who had escaped indictment.

Government imposed ceilings on wholesale and retail prices for beef, pork and lamb for an indefinite period were announced by President Nixon **Mar. 29.**

Automobile makers Apr. 11 were given until 1976 to meet 1975 standards for reducing automotive emissions of hydrocarbons and carbon monoxide.

A 20-year, multibillion dollar chemical-fertilizer barter arrangement was signed **Apr. 12** by Armand Hammer, chairman of Occidental Petroleum Corp., and Soviet Deputy Foreign Trade Minister Nikolai Komarov.

President Nixon responded to the Watergate crisis in an address over radio and television **Apr. 30.** Although he himself had not played a role in the Watergate case, he said, he accepted, as "top man in the organization," full responsibility for those "people whose zeal exceeded their judgment." Earlier the same day 3 of his top aides resigned: chief of staff H. R. Haldeman, domestic affairs assistant John D. Ehrlichman and presidential counsel John W. Dean 3d. Atty. Gen. Richard G. Kleindienst also handed in his resignation.

The West German Bundestag ratified a treaty **May 11** establishing formal relations with the German

Democratic Republic in East Germany.

Presiding Judge William M. Byrne dismissed **May 11** all government charges of espionage, theft and conspiracy against Daniel Ellsberg and Anthony J. Russo Jr., the defendants in the 89-day Pentagon Papers trial. The decision precluded a retrial, but did not vindicate the defendants nor resolve the major constitutional issues in the controversial case. The crucial revelation leading to dismissal of the case came **Apr. 27** when Judge Byrne released a Justice Dept. memorandum stating that 2 of the convicted Watergate defendants, E. Howard Hunt and G. Gordon Liddy, had broken into the office of Ellsberg's psychiatrist with the intention of stealing Ellsberg's medical records. Byrne released E. Howard Hunt's grand jury testimony **May 14** in which Hunt stated that the White House had conceived the plot and supervised and paid for the break-in.

Hearings by the Senate Select Committee on Presidential Campaign Activities into the Watergate scandal opened in Washington, D. C.,**May 17** chaired by Sam J. Ervin (D.,N.C.) assisted by Howard H. Baker (R.,Tenn.).

President Nixon released a statement **May 22** in which he asserted that he made legitimate efforts to restrict investigation into some matters related to the Watergate affair because they impinged on national security. The president further stated that his concern over foreign policy leaks and the publication of the Pentagon Papers led to the establishment in 1971 of a small White House investigative unit, the "plumbers," supervised by John D. Ehrlichman.

Thomas Bradley defeated incumbent Sam Yorty **May 29** to become the first black mayor of Los Angeles.

Premier George Papadopoulos announced **June 1** that the military-led Greek government had abolished the monarchy and proclaimed a republic.

President Nixon set a freeze June 13 on all retail prices. The freeze included food prices but excluded rents, interest, dividends, and raw agricultural products.

The U.S. and USSR signed 9 agreements during Soviet Communist party General Secretary Leonid I. Brezhnev's **June 16-25** visit to the U.S. President Nixon and Brezhnev vowed **June 22** to avoid military confrontations which might lead the U.S. and the USSR into nuclear war with each other or with a 3d country. The agreement obliged the 2 nations to enter into immediate consultations if relations between them or between one of them and some other country "appear to involve risk of nuclear conflict." On **June 24** Brezhnev became the first Soviet leader to address the American people over television.

John Dean, former presidential counsel, **June 25** read a 6-hour statement in which he described a widespread cover-up of the Watergate conspiracy. He said the cover-up had spread from the White House staff and the Committee to Re-elect the President (CRP) to the Justice Dept. and to the "Oval Office" of the president.

Former President Juan D. Peron returned **June 20** to Argentina after almost 20 years of exile. He was re-elected president of Argentina **Sept. 23,** but died 9 months later on July 1, 1974.

The U.S. Supreme Court set new guidelines on obscenity **June 21** with decisions in 5 obscenity cases, all decided by a 5-4 vote. The rulings appeared to allow states to ban books, magazines, plays and motion pictures which are offensive to local community standards.

Nomination of Clarence M. Kelley as FBI director was approved by the Senate **June 27.**

The Federal Trade Commission July 9 charged 8 of the largest U.S. oil companies with conspiracy to monopolize the refining of petroleum products. The commission said the 23-year conspiracy had led to shortages of gasoline, forcing "substantially higher prices" on American consumers, and caused some independent petroleum marketers to close down.

The Senate Armed Service Committee July 16 began a probe into allegations that the U.S. Air Force had made secret B-52 bombing raids into Cambodia in 1969 and 1970. Defense Secretary James R. Schlesinger verified the secret raids **July 16** describing them as "fully authorized" and necessary for the protection of U.S. servicemen. The Defense Dept. disclosed **July 17** that some 3,500 secret bombing raids had been made over Cambodia in the 14-month period beginning Mar. 1969, while Cambodia was officially recognized as a neutral country.

Herbert Kalmbach, formerly personal attorney and fund raiser for President Nixon, told the Senate Watergate Committee **July 16** that through a series of clandestine meetings and telephone calls he had raised $220,000 for the 7 defendants in the Watergate trial, believing the money was intended for legal fees and support of the defendants' families.

White House tape recording of all conversation in the president's offices since Mar. 1971 was revealed by Alexander P. Butterfield, former presidential deputy assistant, in a surprise appearance before the Senate Watergate Committee **July 16.** On **July 23** citing separation of powers and executive privilege, President Nixon refused to release any tapes to Senate investigators.

Afghanistan was proclaimed a republic **July 17** following a coup d'etat by junior officers led by Lt. Mohammad Daud Khan, King Mohammad Zahir Shah's brother-in-law and cousin.

John Ehrlichman, former presidential adviser, told the Senate Watergate Committee **July 24** that John Dean's misleading information thwarted President Nixon's effort to give the nation a factual account of the Watergate conspiracy.

The largest multiple murder case in U. S. history was revealed by Elmer Henley, 17, and David Brooks, 18, who confessed to participation in torture slayings of 27 young men over a 3-year period. They were indicted in Houston, Tex., on murder charges **Aug. 14.** Police learned of the murders **Aug. 7** when Henley told them he had killed Dean Corll, 33, for whom he and Brooks had procured the victims.

The U. S. officially ceased bombing in Cambodia at midnight **Aug. 14** in accord with a June Congressional ruling. The bombing halt was preceded by several days of intensive bombing around Phnom Penh.

The Chinese Communist party held its 10th Congress **Aug. 24-28.** The Congress formally expelled the late Lin Piao, adopted a revised party constitution, selected a new Central Committee and approved a political report by Premier Chou En-lai. Chou emphasized that China considered the "socialist-imperialist" Soviet Union a greater threat than the U. S.

W. A. "Tony" Boyle, 71, former United Mine Workers president, was arrested and charged with murder **Sept. 6** in the slaying of Joseph A. Yablonski, his wife and daughter. The indictment charged Boyle had instigated a plan to assassinate Yablonski.

Forty-six years of civilian rule in Chile ended **Sept. 11** when a 4-man military junta overthrew President Salvador Allende Gossens in a violent military coup. Allende's Popular Unity Coalition was the world's first freely elected Marxist government.

Henry A. Kissinger's nomination as Secy. of State was confirmed **Sept. 21.**

President Nixon's 1972 campaign finance aides revealed **Sept. 28** that campaign fund raisers had collected a record $60.2 million.

The 4th and biggest Arab-Israeli War in 25 years erupted **Oct. 6** along the 103-mile-long Suez Canal and on the Golan Heights. The war began on the afternoon of Yom Kippur, the Jewish Holy Day of Atonement, and was marked by heavy troop and material losses on both sides. UN observers in the Middle East reported that Egyptian forces had crossed the Suez Canal at 5 points and that Syrian forces had attacked at 2 points on the Golan Heights. By **Oct. 11** the Egyptian army had established a bridgehead of about 60,000 men in the Sinai. The Egyptian army's advance was greatly aided by use of new Russian SAM-6 missiles which stymied the Israeli air offensive against the bridgehead.

After losing ground on both fronts Israel counterattacked. Israel claimed **Oct. 12** that its forces had pushed to within 18 miles of Damascus, despite the arrival of Iraqi and Jordanian forces on the Syrian front. Israel **Oct. 16** said it had sent a task force across the Suez Canal to attack Egyptian tanks, artillery and missile sites on the west bank. By **Oct. 24**, this Israeli force had isolated the city of Suez and the Egyptian 3d Army in Sinai.

Meeting at the special request of the U. S. and USSR, the UN Security Council in the early morning hours of **Oct. 22** passed, 14-0, a U.S.-USSR sponsored resolution calling for a cease-fire in place. Fighting continued until a 2d cease-fire went into effect **Oct. 24** with UN supervision.

A total ban on oil exports to the U. S. was imposed by Arab oil-producing nations **Oct. 19-21**. The ban was lifted Mar. 18, 1974.

The U. S. startled the international community **Oct. 25** by suddenly placing its military forces on a worldwide "precautionary alert." Secy. of State Henry A. Kissinger asserted that "ambiguous" signs that the USSR might intervene militarily in the Middle East had necessitated the alert. The crisis ended when the USSR and U. S. joined in a Security Council vote barring the superpowers from participation in a Middle East peace-keeping force. A 7,000-man UN peace-keeping force was approved **Oct. 27** for an initial period of 6 months.

Charles (Bebe) G. Rebozo, according to an **Oct. 9** New York Times report, told Senate Watergate investigators and the Internal Revenue Service that in 1969 and 1970 he had accepted $100,000 in cash from agents of Howard Hughes. He also told Senate investigators that he had kept the money, allegedly a campaign gift, in a safe deposit box for 3 years until he returned it early in 1973.

Vice President Spiro T. Agnew Oct. 10 resigned and pleaded "nolo contendere" to tax evasion on payments made to him by Maryland contractors. Agnew was sentenced to 3-years probation and fined $10,-000.

Violent student demonstrations, culminating in bloody clashes with troops **Oct. 14** forced the resignation of Thailand's Premier Thanom Kittikachorn.

Capturing 59% of the vote, Maynard Jackson, a 35-year-old attorney, **Oct. 16,** defeated incumbent Sam Massell to become the first black mayor of Atlanta, Ga.

Atty. Gen. Elliott Richardson resigned, and his deputy William D. Ruckelshaus and Watergate Special Prosecutor Archibald Cox were fired **Oct. 20** when Cox rejected an administration compromise on the disputed Watergate tapes and threatened to secure a judicial ruling that President Nixon was violating a court order to turn tapes over to Judge John Sirica.

A massive expression of public outrage was followed **Oct. 23** by an agreement among Congressional leaders that the House Judiciary Committee should inquire into the possible impeachment of President Nixon. Also on **Oct. 23,** the president's lawyer, C. A. Wright, announced that the disputed tapes would, after all, be turned over to the court. On **Oct. 30,** White House counsel J. Fred Buzhardt revealed that two of the tapes did not exist.

For events of 1974 and late 1973 see chronology.

---

100 Years Ago in the Almanac

For the first time since the Civil War, in 1874, the United States elected a Democratic House of Representatives with Democrats winning in traditional Republican strongholds such as Pennsylvania, Ohio and Massachusetts. Although Ulysses S. Grant had been re-elected overwhelmingly 2 years previously, the swing from Democrat to Republican reflected the gradual attrition of Republican strength during Grant's 2 Administrations. The Republicans, however, maintained control of the Senate where only one-third of the seats were up for election.

General parliamentary elections in Canada also produced a political turnabout. The Liberal victory came in the wake of the previous year's Pacific railroad scandal which had brought down Sir John Macdonald's government.

Scattered race riots marred national serenity in the U.S. in 1874. A band of disguised men, **Aug. 26,** removed 16 Negroes accused of shooting 2 white men from a Trenton, N.J., jail and shot them. Fifteen persons died, **Aug. 12,** when military forces suppressed a race riot in Austin, Miss. In Vicksburg, Miss., **Dec. 7,** an attempt to reinstate a carpetbag sheriff who had been forced to resign brought death to 75 Negroes.

Anti-Saloon Crusade

From January through March, Christian women crusaded against saloons in southern Ohio. They sang and prayed for their cause in the saloons and, when expelled, carried on their crusade outside. The National Women's Christian Temperance Union was organized, **Nov. 18-19,** in Cleveland, Ohio, as a "sober, second thought of the temperance crusade."

Abroad, the Conservatives overwhelmed the British general elections, gaining an 83-seat majority. Prime Minister W.E. Gladstone yielded to Benjamin Disraeli who formed the government for the second time in his career.

In July, Denmark granted Iceland self-government. Great Britain annexed the Fiji Islands in December.

France Steps into Indochina

France, **Mar. 15,** assumed a protectorate over Annam. In a treaty signed at Saigon, the Emperor of Annam was obliged to conform his foreign policy to that of France and to recognize French possession of Cochin China. In return, the French promised protection and suppression of piracy with French gunboats and officers. The emperor, however, systematically evaded the treaty provisions and began to appeal to China for aid against the French.

The protest of a new school of French painters against the official Salon of the French Academy, which had consistently rejected their works, culminated in 1874 in the independent First Impressionist Show. The name, "Impressionist," derived from Claude Monet's "Impression: Sunrise." Works by Paul Cezanne, Edgar Degas, and Camille Pissarro were also displayed in the show.

Literary highlights of 1874 included Thomas Hardy's "Far From the Madding Crowd," Mark Twain's "Life on the Mississippi," Victor Hugo's "Ninety-Three," and Stubbs' "Constitutional History of England."

Prominent contributions in music were Johann Strauss's "Die Fledermaus" and M.P. Moussorgsky's "Boris Gudonov" and "Pictures From an Exhibition."

The necrology for 1874 listed Millard Fillmore, the 13th president of the United States, and Charles Sumner, U.S. Civil War stateman and champion of the abolition of slavery.

The birth list was an impressive one, including Winston Churchill, Herbert Hoover, Robert Frost, W. Somerset Maugham, and Gertrude Stein.

Some Notable Marine Disasters Since 1868

(Figures Indicate Estimated Lives Lost)

1865, Apr. 27—Sultana; a Mississippi River steamer blew up; 1,400.

1868, Mar. 18—Magnolia; steamboat blew up on Ohio River; 80.

1868, Apr. 9—Sea Bird; steamer burned on Lake Michigan; 100.

1868, Dec. 4—United States and America; steamboats collided, burned, on Ohio River near Warsaw, Ill.; 72.

1869, Oct. 27—Stonewall; steamer burned on Mississippi River below Cairo, Ill.; 200.

1870, Jan. 24—Oneida; American ship sank in collision off Yokohama; 115.

1870, Jan. 28—City of Boston; American steamer of Inman Line vanished between New York and Liverpool; 191.

1871, July 30—Westfield; Staten Island ferryboat exploded in New York Harbor; 100.

1872, Nov. 7—Mary Celeste; American half-brig sailed from New York for Genoa; found abandoned in Atlantic 4 weeks later in mystery at sea; crew never heard from; loss of life unknown.

1873, Jan. 22—Northfleet; British steamer foundered off Dungeness, England; 300.

1873, Apr. 1—Atlantic; British (White Star) steamer wrecked off Nova Scotia; 547.

1873, Nov. 23—Ville de Havre; French steamer, New York to Havre, sank after collision with Loch Earn; 230.

1875, Nov. 7—Schiller; German mail steamer wrecked off Scilly Islands; 200.

1875, Nov. 4—Pacific; American steamer sank after collision off Cape Flattery; 236.

1875, Dec. 6—Deutschland; German steamer, Bremen to New York, wrecked at mouth of Thames; 157.

1877, Nov. 24—Huron; U. S. warship wrecked off North Carolina; 100.

1878, Jan. 31—Metropolis; American steamer wrecked off North Carolina; 100.

1878, Sept. 3—Princess Alice; British steamer sank after collision in Thames; 700.

1878, Dec. 18—Byzantin; French steamer sank after Dardanelles collision; 210.

1880, Nov. 24—Uncle Joseph; French steamer sank in collision off Spezzia, Greece; 250.

1881, May 24—Victoria; steamer capsized in Thames River, Canada; 200.

1883, Jan. 19—Cambria; German steamer hit iceberg in North Sea; 389.

1884, Jan. 18—City of Columbus; American steamer wrecked off Gay Head Light, Mass.; 103.

1887, Nov. 15—Wah Yeung; British steamer burned at sea; 400.

1887, Nov. 19—W. A. Scholten; Dutch steamer sank in English Channel collision; 134.

1890, Feb. 17—Duburg; British steamer wrecked, China Sea; 400.

1890, Mar. 1—Quetta; British steamer wrecked off Cape York, Australia; 124.

1890, Sept. 19—Ertogrul; Turkish frigate foundered off Japan; 540.

1891, Mar. 17—Utopia; British steamer sank in collision off Gibraltar; 574.

1892, Oct. 28—Roumania; British steamer wrecked off Portugal; 113.

1893, Feb. 8—Trinacria; British steamer wrecked off Spain; 115.

1895, Jan. 30—Elbe; German steamer sank in collision with British steamer Crathie in North Sea; 335.

1895, Mar. 11—Reina Regenta; Spanish cruiser foundered near Gibraltar; 400.

1898, Feb. 15—Maine; U. S. battleship blown up in Havana Harbor; 266.

1898, July 4—La Bourgogne, Cromartyshire; French steamer and British sailing ship collided off Nova Scotia; 560.

1898, Nov. 26—Portland; American steamer wrecked off Cape Cod; 157.

1900, June 30—Main, Bremen and Saale; German steamers destroyed in $10,000,000 dock fire at Hoboken, N. J.; 145.

1901, Feb. 22—Rio de Janeiro; American mail steamer wrecked in San Francisco Harbor; 128.

1903, June 7—Libau; French steamer sank in collision near Marseilles; 150.

1904, June 15—General Slocum; excursion steamer burned in East River, New York City; 1,030.

1904, June 28—Norge; steamer wrecked on Rockall Reef off Scotland; 590.

1906, Jan 22—Valencia; American steamer lost off Vancouver Island; 129.

1906, Aug. 4—Sirio; Italian steamer wrecked off Cape Palos, Spain; 350.

1907, Feb. 12—Larchmont; American steamer sank in Long Island Sound; 131.

1907, July 20—Columbia and San Petro; American steamers collided off California coast; 100.

1908, Mar. 23—Matsu Maru; Japanese steamer sank in collision near Hakodate, Japan; 300.

1909, Aug. 1—Waratah; British steamer, Sydney to London, vanished; 300.

1910, Feb. 9—General Chanzy; French steamer wrecked off Minorca, Spain; 200.

1911, Sept. 25—Liberte; French battleship exploded at Toulon; 285.

1912, Mar. 5—Principe de Asturias; Spanish steamer wrecked off Spanish coast; 500.

1912, Apr. 14-15—Titanic; British (White Star) liner hit iceberg in North Atlantic; 1,517.

1912, Sept. 28—Kichemaru; Japanese steamer sank off Japanese coast; 1,000.

1913, Mar. 1—Calvados; British steamer lost in Sea of Marmora, Turkey; 200.

1914, May 29—Empress of Ireland; Canadian steamer sank after collision with collier in St. Lawrence River; 1,024.

1915, May 7—Lusitania; British (Cunard Line) steamer torpedoed by German submarine, sank off Ireland; 1,198.

1915, July 24—Eastland; Excursion steamer capsized in Chicago River; 812.

1916, Feb. 26—Provence; French cruiser sank in Mediterranean; 3,100.

1916, Aug. 29—Hsin Yu; Chinese steamer sank off Chinese coast; 1,000.

1917, Dec. 6—Mont Blanc, Imo; French ammunition ship and Belgian steamer collided in Halifax Harbor; 1,600.

1918, Apr. 25—Kiang-Kwan; Chinese steamer sank in collision off Hankow; 500.

1918, July 6—Columbia; steamer sank in Illinois River at Wesley City; 87.

1918, July 12—Kawachi; Japanese battleship blew up in Tokayama Bay; 500.

1918, Oct. 25—Princess Sophia; Canadian steamer sank off Alaskan coast; 398.

1919, Jan. 17—Chaonia; French steamer lost in Straits of Messina, Italy; 460.

1919, Sept. 9—Valbanera; Spanish steamer lost off Florida coast; 500.

1921, Mar. 18—Hong Kong; steamer wrecked in South China Sea; 1,000.

1922, Aug. 26—Niitaka; Japanese cruiser sank in storm off Kamchatka, USSR; 300.

1923, Apr. 23—Mossamedes; Portuguese mail steamer went aground at Cape Frio, Africa; 220.

1924, Jan. 10—L-24; British submarine in collision off Portland, England; 48.

1924, Mar. 19—No. 43; Japanese submarine in collision off Sasebo, Japan; 49.

1925, Sept. 25—S-51; American submarine in collision with steamer City of Rome off Block Island, R. I.; 34.

1925, Nov. 11—M-1; British submarine in English Channel collision; 69.

1927, Oct. 25—Principessa Mafalda; Italian steamer blew up, sank off Porto Seguro, Brazil; 314.

1927, Dec. 17—S-4; American submarine in collision off Provincetown, Mass.; 40.

1928, Nov. 12—Vestris; British steamer sank in gale off Virginia coast; 113.

1932, Sept. 9—Observation; Steamboat carrying workmen to Rikers Island blew up in East River, N. Y. City; 72.

1934, Sept. 8—Morro Castle; American steamer, Havana to New York, burned off Asbury Park, N. J.; 125.

1939, May 23—Squalus; American submarine sank off Portsmouth, N. H.; 26.

1941, June 16—0-9; American submarine lost in test dive off Maine; 33.

1942, Feb. 18—Truxton and Pollux; American destroyer and cargo ship ran aground, sank off Newfoundland; 204.

1942, Oct. 2—Curacoa; British cruiser sank after collision with liner Queen Mary; 335.

1947, Jan. 19—Himera; Greek steamer hit a mine off Athens; 392.

1947, Apr. 16—Grandcamp; French freighter exploded in Texas City, Tex., Harbor, starting fires; 510.

1949, Sept. 17—Noronic; Canadian Great Lakes steamer burned at Toronto; 119.

1950, Jan. 12—Truculent; British submarine in Thames collision; 65.

1951, Apr. 16—Affray; British submarine lost in English Channel; 75.

1952, Apr. 26—Hobson and Wasp; American destroyer and aircraft carrier collided in Atlantic; 176.

1952, Sept. 24—La Sibylle; French submarine lost off Toulon; 48.

1953, Apr. 4—Dumlupinar and Naboland; Turkish submarine and Swedish steamer collided in Dardanelles; 81.

1953, Oct. 16—Leyte; U. S. aircraft carrier damaged by explosion below decks in Boston; 37.

1954, May 26—Bennington; U. S. aircraft carrier damaged by explosions, fire off Quonset Point, R. I.; 103.

1954, Sept. 26—Toya Maru; Japanese ferry sank in Tsugaru Strait, Japan; 1,172.

1956, July 26—Andrea Doria and Stockholm; Italian liner and Swedish liner collided off Nantucket; 51.

1957, July 14—Eshghabad; Soviet ship ran aground in Caspian Sea; 270.

1959, Jan. 30—Hans Hedtoft; Danish passenger-freighter hit iceberg, Greenland; 95.

1960, Dec. 19—Constellation; U. S. aircraft carrier burned in Brooklyn Navy Yard; 50.

1961, Apr. 8—Dara; Brit. liner burned in Persian Gulf; 212.

1961, July 8—Save; Portuguese ship ran aground off Mozambique; 259.

1963, Feb. 3—Marine Sulphur Queen; American tanker vanished in Gulf of Mexico; 39.

1963, Apr. 10—Thresher; U. S. Navy atomic submarine sank in North Atlantic; 129.

1964, Feb. 10—Voyager and Melbourne; Australian destroyer sank after collision with Australian aircraft carrier off New South Wales; 82.

1965, Nov. 13—Yarmouth Castle; Panamanian registered cruise ship burned, sank off Nassau; 89.

1966, Oct. 26—Oriskany; U. S. aircraft carrier caught fire, Gulf of Tonkin; 43.

1967, July 29—Forrestal; U. S. aircraft carrier caught fire off North Vietnam; 134.

1968, Jan. 25—Dakar; Israeli submarine vanished in Mediterranean; 69.

1968, Jan. 27—Minerve; French submarine vanished in Mediterranean; 52.

1968, May 21—Scorpion; U. S. nuclear submarine sank in Atlantic near Azores; 99.

1969, Jan. 14—Enterprise; U. S. aircraft carrier suffered fires and explosions off Hawaii; 27.

1969, June 2—Evans; U. S. destroyer cut in two by Australian carrier Melbourne, S. China Sea; 74.

1970, Mar. 4—Eurydice; French submarine sank in Medtierranean near Toulon; 57.

1970, Dec. 15—Namyong-Ho; South Korean ferry sank in Korea Strait; 308.

1971, May 22—Meteor; Norwegian cruise ship burned near Vancouver, B. C.; 32.

1972, May 11—Royston Grange and Tien Cheung; Brit. cargo and Liberian tanker collided River Plate, Argentina; 84.

1972, Nov. 15—Merlin; Greek troopship sank after colliding with tanker near Piraeus, Greece; 46.

1973, May 5—Three river boats collided near Dacca, Bangladesh; c. 250.

(See also Chronology)

Floods, Tidal Waves

Date, Location, Number of Deaths—See also Chronology

Year	Date	Location	Deaths	Year	Date	Location	Deaths
1887	. . . .	Hwang-ho Riv., China	900,000	1960	Oct. 10	East Pakistan	6,000
1889	May 31	Johnstown, Pa.	2,200	1960	Oct. 31	East Pakistan	4,000
1900	Sept. 8	Galveston, Tex.	5,000	1962	Feb. 17	German North Sea coast	343
1903	June 15	Heppner, Ore.	325	1962	Sept. 27	Barcelona, Spain	445
1911	. . . .	Yangtze River, China	100,000	1963	Oct. 9	Dam collapse, Vaiont, Italy	1,800
1913	Mar. 25-27	Ohio, Indiana	732	1965	June 11	Sanderson, Tex.	10
1913	Dec. 1-5	Brazos River, Tex.	177	1966	Nov. 4-6	Florence, Venice, Italy	113
1915	Aug. 17	Galveston, Tex.	275	1967	Jan. 18-24	Eastern Brazil	894
1927	. . . .	Mississippi River Valley	214	1967	Mar. 19	Rio de Janeiro, Brazil	436
1928	Mar. 13	Collapse of St. Francis		1968	Aug. 7-14	Gujarat state, India	1,000
		Dam, Santa Paula, Calif.	450	1968	Oct. 7	Northeastern India	780
1928	Sept. 13	Lake Okeechobee, Fla.	2,000	1969	Jan. 18-26	Southern California	91
1937	Jan. 22	Ohio, Miss. Valleys	250	1969	Mar. 17	Mundau Valley, Alagoas, Braz.	218
1939	. . . .	Northern China	200,000	1969	July 4	Northern Ohio	41
1947	. . . .	Honshu Island, Japan	1,900	1969	Oct. 1-8	Tunisia	500
1951	Aug.	Manchuria	1,800	1969	Aug. 25	Western Virginia	189
1953	Jan. 31	Western Europe	2,000	1969	Sept. 15	South Korea	250
1954	Aug. 17	Farahzad, Iran	2,000	1970	May 20	Central Romania	160
1955	Oct. 7-12	India, Pakistan	1,700	1970	July 22	Himalayans, India	500
1959	Nov. 1	Western Mexico	2,000	1971	Feb. 26	Rio de Janeiro, Brazil	130
1959	Dec. 2	Frejus, France	412	1972	June 9	Rapid City, S.D.	236
1960	May 23-24	Hawaii, Japan, Okinawa	237	1972	Aug. 7	5-week Philippines	454

Major Earthquakes

Date, Location, Number of Deaths—See also Chronology

Year	Place	Deaths	Year	Place	Deaths
1057	China, Chihli	25,000	1906	Aug. 16	Chile, Valparaiso	1,500
1268	Asia Minor, Silicia	60,000	1908	Dec. 28	Italy, Messina	75,000
1290	Sept. 27	China, Chihli	100,000	1915	Jan. 13	Italy, Avezzano	29,970
1293	May 20	Japan, Kamakura	30,000	1920	Dec. 16	China, Kansu	180,000
1531	Jan. 26	Portugal, Lisbon	30,000	1923	Sept. 1	Japan, Tokyo	143,000
1556	Jan. 24	China, Shensi	830,000	1932	Dec. 26	China, Kansu	70,000
1667	Nov.	Caucasia, Shemaka	80,000	1933	Mar. 10	Long Beach, Calif.	115
1693	Jan. 11	Italy, Catania	60,000	1935	May 31	India, Quetta	60,000
1737	Oct. 11	India, Calcutta	300,000	1939	Jan. 24	Chile, Chillan	30,000
1755	June 7	Northern Persia	40,000	1939	Dec. 27	Turkey, Erzincan	23,000
1755	Nov. 1	Portugal, Lisbon	60,000	1946	May 31	Eastern Turkey	1,300
1783	Feb. 4	Italy, Calabria	50,000	1946	Dec. 21	Japan, Honshu	2,000
1797	Feb. 4	Ecuador, Quito	41,000	1948	June 28	Japan, Fukui	5,131
1811	Dec. 16	U. S. New Madrid, Mo.		1949	Aug. 5	Ecuador, Pelileo	6,000
1822	Sept. 5	Asia Minor, Aleppo	22,000	1950	Aug. 15	India, Assam	1,500
1828	Dec. 28	Japan, Echigo	30,000	1953	Mar. 18	Northwestern Turkey	1,200
1868	Aug. 13-15	Peru and Ecuador	25,000	1954	Sept. 9-12	Northern Algeria	1,657
1875	May 16	Venezuela, Colombia	16,000	1956	June 10-17	Northern Afghanistan	2,000
1896	June 15	Japan, sea wave	22,000	1957	July 2	Northern Iran	2,500
1906	Apr. 18	Calif., San Francisco	452	1957	Dec. 4	Outer Mongolia	1,200

1957	Dec. 13.....	Western Iran..........	2,000
1960	Feb. 29.....	Morocco, Agadir........	12,000
1960	May 21-30...	Southern Chile........	5,700
1962	Sept. 1......	Northwestern Iran......	10,000
1963	July 26.....	Yugoslavia, Skopje.....	1,100
1964	Mar. 27.....	Alaska.................	131
1966	Aug. 19....	Eastern Turkey.........	2,529
1968	Aug. 31....	Northeastern Iran.......	11,588
1970	Mar. 28....	Western Turkey........	1,086
1970	May 31....	Northern Peru..........	66,794
1971	Feb. 9.....	Southern California.....	65
1972	Apr. 10....	Southern Iran..........	5,057
1972	Dec. 23....	Nicaragua.............	10,000

Fires
Date, Location and Number of Persons Killed—*See also Chronology*

1871	Oct. 8	Chicago, $196,000,000 loss......	250
1871	Oct. 9	Peshtigo, Wis., forest fire.........	1,182
1876	Dec. 5	Brooklyn (N.Y.) Theater........	295
1877	June 20	St. John, N.B., Canada.........	100
1881	Dec. 8	Ring Theater, Vienna............	850
1887	May 25	Opera Comique, Paris...........	200
1887	Sept. 4	Exeter, England, theater........	200
1894	Sept. 1	Hickley, Minn., forest fire........	413
1897	May 4	Charity bazaar, Paris...........	150
1900	June 30	Hoboken, N.J., docks...........	326
1902	Sept. 20	Church, Birmingham, Ala........	115
1903	Dec. 30	Iroquois Theater, Chicago........	602
1904	Feb. 7	Baltimore, Md.................	none
1908	Jan. 13	Rhoads Thea., Boyertown, Pa.....	170
1908	Mar. 4	School, Collinwood, Ohio........	176
1911	Mar. 25	Triangle factory, N.Y. City......	145
1914	June 26	1,000 bldgs., Salem, Mass.......	0
1918	Apr. 13	Norman, Okla., state hospital....	38
1918	Oct. 12	Cloquet, Minn., forest fire.......	400
1919	June 20	Mayaguez Theater, San Juan......	150
1923	May 17	School, Camden, S.C...........	76
1924	Dec. 24	School, Hobart, Okla...........	35
1929	May 15	Clinic, Cleveland, Ohio.........	125
1930	Apr. 21	Penitentiary, Columbus, Ohio.....	320
1931	July 24	Pittsburgh, Pa., home for aged....	48
1938	May 16	Atlanta, Ga., Terminal Hotel.....	35
1940	Apr. 23	Dance hall, Natchez, Miss.......	198
1942	Nov. 28	Cocoanut Grove, Boston........	491
1943	Sept. 7	Gulf Hotel, Houston...........	55
1944	July 6	Ringling Circus, Hartford.......	168
1946	June 5	LaSalle Hotel, Chicago.........	61
1946	Dec. 7	Winecoff Hotel, Atlanta........	119
1946	Dec. 12	New York, ice plant, tenement....	37
1949	Apr. 5	Hospital, Effingham, Ill........	77
1950	Jan. 7	Davenport, Ia., Mercy Hospital....	41
1953	Mar. 29	Largo, Fla., nursing home.......	35
1953	Apr. 16	Chicago, metalworking plant.....	35
1957	Feb. 17	Home for aged, Warrenton, Mo....	72
1957	Nov. 11	Niagara Falls, N.Y., tenement....	18
1958	Mar. 19	New York City loft building......	24
1958	Nov. 8	Tenement, Montreal, Can........	21
1958	Dec. 1	Parochial school, Chicago........	95
1958	Dec. 16	Store, Bogota, Colombia........	83
1959	Mar. 5	School near Little Rock, Ark......	24
1959	June 23	Resort hotel, Stalheim, Norway....	34
1960	Mar. 12	Pusan, Korea, chemical plant.....	68
1960	June 11	Liverpool, England, store........	22
1960	July 14	Mental hospital, Guatemala City...	225
1960	Nov. 13	Movie theater, Amude, Syria......	152
1961	Jan. 6	Thomas Hotel, San Francisco.....	20
1961	May 15	Tenement, Hong Kong..........	25
1961	Dec. 8	Hospital, Hartford, Conn........	16
1961	Dec. 17	Circus, Niteroi, Brazil..........	323
1963	May 4	Theater, Diourbel, Senegal.......	64
1963	Nov. 18	Surfside Hotel, Atlantic City, N.J..	25
1963	Nov. 23	Rest home, Fitchville, Ohio......	63
1963	Dec. 29	Roosevelt Hotel, Jacksonville, Fla..	22
1964	May 8	Apartment building, Manila.......	30
1964	Dec. 18	Nursing Home, Fountaintown, Ind.	20
1965	Mar. 1	Apartment, LaSalle, Canada......	28
1965	Dec. 20	Jewish center, Yonkers, N.Y......	12
1966	Mar. 11	Numata, Jap., 2 ski resorts.......	31
1966	Aug. 13	Melbourne, Austr., hotel........	29
1966	Sept. 12	Anchorage, Alaska, hotel........	14
1966	Oct. 17	N.Y. City bldg. (firemen)........	12
1966	Dec. 7	Erzurum, Turkey, barracks.......	68
1967	Feb. 7	Restaurant, Montgomery, Ala.....	25
1967	May 22	Store, Brussels, Belgium........	322
1967	July 16	State prison, Jay, Fla...........	37
1968	Jan. 9	Brooklyn, N.Y., tenement.......	13
1968	Feb. 11	Franklin, Pa., residence........	11
1968	Feb. 16	Moberly, Mo., tavern..........	12
1968	Feb. 26	Shrewsbury, England, hospital...	22
1968	May 11	Vijayawada, India, wedding hall ..	58
1968	Nov. 18	Glasgow, Scotland, factory......	24
1969	Jan. 26	Victoria Hotel, Dunnville, Ont....	13
1969	Feb. 25	Office building, N.Y. City.......	11
1969	Apr. 6	Tenement, Bridgeport, Conn......	11
1969	Dec. 2	Nursing home, Notre Dame, Can..	54
1970	Jan. 9	Nursing home, Marietta, Ohio.....	27
1970	Mar. 20	Hotel, Seattle, Wash...........	19
1970	Nov. 1	Dance hall, Grenoble, France.....	145
1970	Nov. 5	Nursing home, Pointes-aux-Trembles, Que....	17
1970	Dec. 20	Hotel, Tucson, Arizona.........	28
1971	Mar. 6	Psychiatric clinic, Burghoelzi, Switz...	28
1971	Apr. 20	Hotel, Bangkok, Thailand.......	24
1971	Apr. 25	Apt. building, Seattle, Wash......	12
1971	Oct. 19	Nursing home, Honesdale, Pa......	15
1972	July 5	Sherborne, England, hospital.,...	30
1973	Nov. 6	Fukui, Japan, train............	28
1973	Dec. 2	Seoul, Korea, theater..........	50
1973	Feb. 6	Paris, France, school..........	21

Major Railroad Wrecks in the United States
Source: Federal Railroad Admin., Office of Safety
Date, Location and Number of Persons Killed. *See also Chronology*

1876	Dec. 29	Ashtabula, Ohio...............	92
1880	Aug. 11	Mays Landing, N.J.............	40
1887	Aug. 10	Chatsworth, Ill...............	81
1888	Oct. 10	Mud Run, Pa.................	55
1896	July 30	Atlantic City, N.J.............	60
1903	Dec. 23	Laurel Run, Pa...............	53
1904	Aug. 7	Eden, Colo..................	96
1904	Sept. 24	New Market, Tenn............	56
1906	Mar. 16	Florence, Colo..............	35
1906	Oct. 28	Atlantic City, N.J.............	40
1906	Dec. 30	Washington, D.C..............	53
1907	Jan. 2	Volland, Kans...............	33
1907	Jan. 19	Fowler, Ind.................	29
1907	Feb. 16	New York City...............	22
1907	Mar. 23	Colton, Calif................	26
1907	July 20	Salem, Mich.................	33
1907	Sept. 15	Canaan, N.H................	24
1910	Mar. 1	Wellington, Wash.............	96
1910	Mar. 21	Green Mountain, Ia...........	55
1911	Aug. 25	Manchester, N.Y..............	29
1912	July 4	East Corning, N.Y............	39
1912	July 5	Ligonier, Pa.................	23
1913	Sept. 2	North Haven, Conn............	21
1914	Aug. 5	Tipton Ford, Mo..............	43
1914	Sept. 15	Lebanon, Mo................	28
1916	Mar. 29	Amherst, Ohio..............	27
1917	Feb. 27	Mount Union, Pa.............	20
1917	Sept. 28	Kellyville, Okla.............	23
1917	Dec. 20	Shepherdsville, Ky............	46
1918	June 22	Ivanhoe, Ind................	68
1918	July 9	Nashville, Tenn..............	101
1918	Nov. 2	Brooklyn, Malbone St. Tunnel....	97
1919	Jan. 12	South Byron, N.Y.............	22
1919	July 1	Dunkirk, N.Y................	12
1919	Dec. 20	Onawa, Maine...............	23
1921	Feb. 27	Porter, Ind.................	37
1921	Dec. 5	Woodmont, Pa...............	27
1922	Aug. 5	Sulphur Spring, Mo...........	34
1922	Dec. 13	Humble, Tex................	22
1923	Sept. 27	Lockett, Wyo................	31
1925	June 16	Hackettstown, N.J............	50
1925	Oct. 27	Victoria, Miss...............	21

1926	Sept. 5	Waco, Colo.	30
1928	Aug. 24	I. R. T. subway, N. Y., Times Sq.	18
1938	June 19	Saugus, Mont.	47
1939	Aug. 12	Harney, Nev.	24
1940	Apr. 19	Little Falls, N. Y.	31
1940	July 31	Cuyahoga Falls, Ohio	43
1943	Aug. 29	Wayland, N. Y.	27
1943	Sept. 6	Frankford Junction, Philadelphia	79
1943	Dec. 16	Bet. Rennert and Buie, N. C.	72
1944	July 6	High Bluff, Tenn.	35
1944	Aug. 4	Near Stockton, Ga.	47
1944	Sept. 14	Dewey, Ind.	29
1944	Dec. 31	Bagley, Utah.	50
1945	Aug. 9	Michigan, N. D.	34
1946	Apr. 25	Naperville, Ill.	45
1947	Feb. 18	Gallitzin, Pa.	24
1950	Feb. 17	Rockville Centre, N. Y.	31

1950	Sept. 11	Coshocton, Ohio	33
1950	Nov. 22	Richmond Hill, N. Y.	79
1951	Feb. 6	Woodbridge, N. J.	84
1951	Nov. 12	Wyuta, Wyo.	17
1951	Nov. 25	Woodstock, Ala.	17
1953	Mar. 27	Conneaut, Ohio	21
1956	Jan. 22	Los Angeles, Calif.	30
1956	Feb. 28	Swampscott, Mass.	13
1956	Sept. 5	Springer, N. M.	20
1957	June 11	Vroman, Colo.	12
1958	Sept. 15	Elizabethport, N. J.	48
1960	Mar. 14	Bakersfield, Calif.	14
1962	July 28	Steelton, Pa.	19
1966	Dec. 28	Everett, Mass.	13
1971	June 10	Salem, Ill.	11
1972	Oct. 30	Chicago, Ill.	45

World's worst wreck occurred Dec. 12, 1917, Modane, France, passenger train derailed, 543 killed.

Historic Assassinations Since 1865

1865—April 14. Abraham Lincoln, President of the United States, in Washington; died Apr. 15.

1881—Mar. 13. Alexander II, of Russia.—July 2. James A. Garfield, President of the United States, in Washington; died Sept. 19.

1893—Oct. 28. Carter H. Harrison, Mayor of Chicago.

1894—June 24. Marie Francois Sadi-Carnot, President of France.

1900—Jan. 30. William Goebel, Governor of Kentucky.—July 29. Humbert I, King of Italy.

1901—Sept. 6. William McKinley. President of the United States, in Buffalo; died Sept. 14. Leon Czolgosz executed for the crime Oct. 29.

1913—Feb. 23. Francisco I. Madero, President of Mexico and Jose Pino Suarez, the Vice-President.—Mar. 18. George, King of Greece.

1914—June 28. Archduke Francis Ferdinand of Austria-Hungary and his wife, Countess Sophie Chotek, Duchess of Hohenberg, in Sarajevo, Bosnia (later part of Yugoslavia), by Gavrillo Princip.

1916—Oct. 21. Karl Sturgkh, Austrian Premier.—Dec. 30. Grigori Rasputin, politically powerful Russian monk.

1918—July 12. Grand Duke Michael of Russia. at Perm.—July 16. Nicholas II, abdicated as Czar of Russia; his wife, the Czarina Alexandra; their son, Czarevitch Alexis, and their daughters, Grand Duchesses Olga, Tatiana, Marie, Anastasia, and 4 members of their household were murdered in cold blood by Bolsheviks at Ekaterinburg.

1920—May 20. Gen. Venustiano Carranza, President of Mexico, in Tiaxcaltenago.

1922—June 24. Walter Rathenau, German foreign minister.—Aug. 22. Michael Collins, Irish revolutionary.

1923—July 20. Gen. Francisco "Pancho" Villa, ex-rebel leader, in Parral, Mexico.

1928—July 17. Gen. Alvaro Obregon, President-elect of Mexico, in San Angel, Mexico.

1933—Feb. 15. In Miami, Fla., Joseph Zangara, anarchist, shot at President-elect Franklin D. Roosevelt, but a woman seized his arm, and the bullet fatally wounded Mayor Anton J. Cermak, of Chicago, who died Mar. 6. Zangara was electrocuted on Mar. 20, 1933.

1934—July 25. In Vienna, Engelbert Dollfuss, Chancellor of Austria, by Nazi, in the chancellery. Otto Planetta convicted and hanged.

1935—Sept. 8. U. S. Senator Huey P. Long, shot in Baton Rouge, La., by Dr. Carl Austin Weiss, who was slain by Long's bodyguards.

1940—Aug. 20. Leon Trotsky (Lev Bronstein), 63, exiled Russian war minister, near Mexico City. Killer, identified as Ramon Mercador del Rio, a Spaniard, served 20 years in Mexican prison.

1948—Jan. 30. Mohandas K. Gandhi, 78, shot in New Delhi, India, by Nathuran Vinayak Godse, 36.—Sept. 17. Count Folke Bernadotte, U.N. Mediator for Palestine, ambushed in Jerusalem.

1951—July 20. King Abdul ibn Hussein of Jordan.

1956—Sept. 21. Anastasio Somoza, President of Nicaragua, in Leon; died Sept. 29.

1957—July 26. President Carlos Castillo Armas of Guatemala, in Guatemala City by one of his own guards, who then committed suicide.

1958—July 14. King Faisal of Iraq; his uncle, Crown Prince Abdul Illah, and July 15, Premier Nuri as-Said, by rebels in Baghdad.

1959—Sept. 25. Prime Minister S. W. R. D. Bandaranaike of Ceylon, by Buddhist monk in Colombo.

1961—Jan. 17. Ex-Premier Patrice Lumumba of the Congo, ex-Youth Minister Maurice Mpolo and Senate Vice President Joseph Okito in Katanga Province.—May 30. Dominican dictator Rafael Leonidas Trujillo Molina shot to death by assassins near Ciudad Trujillo.

1963—Jan. 13. President Sylvanus Olympio of Togo, by ex-soldiers at Lome.—June 12. Medgar W. Evers, NAACP's Mississippi field secretary, in Jackson, Miss.—Nov. 1-2. President Ngo Dinh Diem of the Republic of Vietnam and his brother, Ngo Dinh Nhu, in a military coup.—Nov. 22. U. S. President John F. Kennedy fatally shot in Dallas, Tex.; accused Lee Harvey Oswald murdered while awaiting trial.

1965—Jan. 21. Irani Premier Hassan Ali Mansour fatally wounded by assassin in Teheran; 4 executed.—Feb. 21. Malcolm X, Negro nationalist, fatally shot in New York City; 3 sentenced to life.

1966—Sept. 6. Prime Minister Hendrik F. Verwoerd of South Africa stabbed to death in parliament at Capetown by drifter later ruled insane.

1968—Apr. 4. Rev. Dr. Martin Luther King Jr. fatally shot in Memphis, Tenn.; James Earl Ray sentenced to 99 years.—June 5. Sen. Robert F. Kennedy (D-N.Y.) fatally shot in Los Angeles; Sirhan Sirhan, resident alien, sentenced to death.

1969—Feb. 3. Eduardo Mondlane, leader of Mozambique Liberation Front, by explosive parcel in mail at Dar es Salaam, Tanzania.—July 5. Tom Mboya, Kenya's minister of economic planning and development, in Nairobi.—Oct. 17. A. A. Shermarke, President of Somalia, at Las Anos, Somalia.

1971—Nov. 28. Jordan Prime Minister Wasfi Tal, in Cairo, by Palestinian guerrillas.

1973—July 1. Col. Yosef Alon, an Israeli military attache, was shot to death at his home in Chevy Chase, Md.

Assassination Attempts

1910—Aug. 6. New York City Mayor Wm. J. Gaynor shot and seriously wounded by discharged city employee.

1912—Oct. 14. Former U. S. President Theodore Roosevelt shot and seriously wounded by demented man in Milwaukee.

1950—Nov. 1. In an attempt to assassinate President Truman, two men identified as members of a Puerto Rican nationalist movement—Griselio Torresola and Oscar Collazo—tried to shoot their way into

Blair House. Torresola was killed, and a guard, Pvt. Leslie Coffelt was fatally shot. Collazo, wounded, recovered and was tried and convicted Mar. 7, 1951 for the murder of Coffelt. His death sentence was commuted to life imprisonment by President Truman.

1970—Nov. 27. Pope Paul VI unharmed by knife-wielding assailant dressed as priest who attempted to attack him in Manila airport. Benjamin Mendoza, Bolivian, charged with attempted murder.

1972—May 15. George Wallace shot in Maryland.

1972—Dec. 7. Mrs. Ferdinand E. Marcos, wife of the Philippine president, was stabbed and seriously hurt in Pasay City, Philippines.

See also Chronology and Memorable Dates.

Major Kidnaping Crimes

Edward A. Cudahy Jr., 16, in Omaha, Neb., **Dec. 18, 1900.** Returned Dec. 20 after $25,000 paid. Pat Crowe confessed.

Robert Franks, 13, in Chicago, **May 22, 1924,** by two youths, Loeb and Leopold, who killed boy. Demand for $10,000 ignored. Loeb died in prison, Leopold paroled 1958, freed 1963.

Charles A. Lindbergh Jr., 20 mos. old, in Hopewell, N.J., **Mar. 1, 1932;** found dead May 12. Ransom of $50,000 was paid to man identified as Bruno Richard Hauptmann, 35, paroled German convict who entered U. S. illegally. Hauptmann passed ransom bill and $14,000 marked money was found in his garage. He was convicted after spectacular trial at Flemington, and electrocuted in Trenton, N. J., prison, Apr. 3, 1936.

William A. Hamm Jr., 39, in St. Paul, **June 15, 1933.** $100,000 paid. Alvin Karpis given life, paroled in 1969.

Charles F. Urschel, in Oklahoma City, **July 22, 1933.** Released July 31 after $200,000 paid. George (Machine Gun) Kelly and 5 others given life.

Edward G. Bremer, 37, St. Paul, Minn., **Jan. 17, 1934.** Released Feb. 7 after $200,000 paid. Two given life.

George Weyerhaeuser, 9, in Tacoma, Wash., **May 24, 1935.** Returned home June 1 after $200,000 paid. Kidnapers given 20 to 60 years.

Charles Mattson, 10, in Tacoma, Wash., **Dec. 27, 1936.** Found dead Jan. 11, 1937. Kidnaper asked $28,000, failed to contact.

Arthur Fried, in White Plains, N. Y., **Dec. 4, 1937.** Body not found. Two kidnapers executed.

Peter Levine, 12, in New Rochelle, N. Y., **Feb. 24, 1938.** Dismembered body found May 29.

Robert C. Greenlease, 6, son of a Kansas City, Mo., motor car dealer, taken from school **Sept. 28, 1953,** and held for $600,000. Body found Oct. 7, when Mrs. Bonnie Brown Heady and Carl A. Hall were arrested. They pleaded guilty and were executed Dec. 18.

Evelyn Smith, 23, in Phoenix, Ariz., **June 9, 1954.** Released unharmed June 10, after $75,000 was paid.

Peter Weinberger, 32 days old, Westbury, N. Y., **July 4, 1956,** for $2,000 ransom, not paid. Child found dead. Angelo John LaMarca, 31, convicted, executed.

Cynthia Ruotolo, 6 wks. old, taken from carriage in front of Hamden, Conn. store **Sept. 1, 1956.** Body found in lake.

Lee Crary, 8, in Everett, Wash., **Sept. 22, 1957,** for $10,000 ransom, not paid. Escaped after 3 days, led police to George E. Collins, convicted.

Eric Peugeot, 4, taken from playground at St. Cloud golf course, Paris, **Apr. 12, 1960.** Released unharmed 3 days later after payment of undisclosed sum to kidnaper who had demanded $100,000. Two sentenced to prison.

Frank Sinatra Jr., 19, from hotel room in Lake Tahoe, Calif., **Dec. 8, 1963.** Released Dec. 11 after his father paid $240,000 ransom. John W. Irwin, Barry W. Keenan and Joseph C. Amsler sentenced to prison; most of ransom recovered.

Daniel Jesse Goldman, 18, abducted **Mar. 18, 1966,** from his home near Bal Harbour, Fla.

Mrs. Betty Hill, 42, was held prisoner in her Boulder, Colo., home **Jan. 6, 1967,** by an intruder who released her shortly afterward when her husband paid $50,000 ransom.

Kenneth King, 11, was abducted from his bedroom in Beverly Hills, Calif., **Apr. 3, 1967,** but was freed unharmed 3 days later after his father paid $250,000 ransom.

Barbara Jane Mackle, 20, abducted **Dec. 17, 1968,** from Atlanta, Ga., motel, was found unharmed 3 days later, buried in a coffin-like wooden box 18 inches underground, after her father had paid $500,000 ransom; Gary Steven Krist sentenced to life, Ruth Eisenmann-Schier to 7 years; most of ransom recovered.

Anne Katherine Jenkins, 22, abducted **May 10, 1969,** from her Baltimore apartment, freed 3 days later after her father paid $10,000 ransom; Edward Lee Dull and Marie Calvert charged with crime.

Mrs. Roy Fuchs, 35, and 3 children held hostage two hours **May 14, 1969,** in Long Island, N. Y., released after her husband, a bank manager, paid kidnapers $129,000 in bank funds; 4 men arrested, ransom recovered.

C. Burke Elbrick, U. S. Amb. to Brazil, kidnaped by Brazilian revolutionaries in Rio de Janeiro **Sept. 4, 1969;** released 3 days later after Brazil yielded to kidnapers' demands by publishing manifesto and releasing 15 political prisoners.

Mrs. Mary Nelles, 26, abducted near Toronto, Canada, **Sept. 7, 1969;** freed unharmed after payment of $200,000 ransom; 5 sentenced to 10-15 years, ransom recovered.

Patrick Dolan 18, found shot to death near Sao Paulo, Brazil, **Nov. 5, 1969,** after he was kidnaped and $12,500 paid.

Sean M. Holly, U. S. diplomat, in Guatemala **Mar. 6, 1970;** freed two days later upon release of 3 terrorists from prison.

Lt. Col. Donald J. Crowley, U. S. air attache, in Dominican Republic **Mar. 24, 1970;** released after government allowed 20 prisoners to leave the country.

Count Karl von Spreti, W. German Ambassador to Guatemala, **Mar. 31, 1970;** slain after Guatemala refused demands for $700,000 and release of 22 prisoners.

Rudy W. Martinez, Guatemalan coffee exporter, by terrorists **Apr. 23, 1970;** released on payment of large ransom.

Pedro Eugenio Aramburu, former Argentine President, by terrorits **May 29, 1970;** body found July 17.

Ehrenfried von Holleben, W. German Ambassador to Brazil, by terrorists **June 11, 1970;** freed after release of 40 prisoners.

Fernando Londono y Londono, former Colombian Foreign Minister, by Colombian terrorists **July 9, 1970;** freed after family paid $200,000 ransom.

Daniel A. Mitrione, U. S. diplomat, **July 31, 1970,** by terrorists in Montevideo, Uruguay; body found Aug. 10 after government rejected demands for release of all political prisoners.

Aloysio Dias Gomide, Brazilian vice consul, in Montevideo, **July 31, 1970;** released Feb. 21, 1971, after wife paid ransom estimated at over $250,000.

Claude L. Fly, U. S. agronomist, by terrorists in Montevideo **Aug. 7, 1970;** released Mar. 2, 1971, after suffering illness.

James R. Cross, British trade commissioner, **Oct. 5, 1970,** by French Canadian separatists in Quebec; freed Dec. 3 after 3 kidnapers and relatives flown to Cuba by government.

Pierre Laporte, Quebec Labor Minister, by separatists **Oct. 10, 1970;** body found Oct. 18.

Eugen Beihl, W. German businessman, by Basque separatists, in San Sebastian, Spain, **Dec. 1, 1970;** released Dec. 25 unharmed.

Giovanni E. Bucher, Swiss Ambassador **Dec. 7, 1970,** by revolutionaries in Rio de Janeiro; freed Jan. 16, 1971, after Brazil released 70 political prisoners.

Geoffrey Jackson, British Ambassador, in Montevideo, **Jan. 8, 1971,** by Tupamaro terrorists. Held as ransom for the release of imprisoned terrorists, he was released Sept. 9, after the prisoners escaped.

Four U. S. airmen, in Ankara, by Turkish leftist terrorists on **Mar. 4, 1971.** $400,000 ransom was not paid, but they were released unharmed Mar. 8.

Ephraim Elrom, Israel consul general in Istanbul, **May 17, 1971.** Held as ransom for imprisoned terrorists, he was found dead May 23.

Mrs. Virginia Piper, 49, abducted **July 27, 1972,** from her home in suburban Minneapolis; found unharmed near Duluth two days later after her husband paid $1,000,000 ransom to the kidnapers.

See also Chronology.

Some Major Tornadoes Since 1925

Source: National Climatic Center, NOAA, Dept. of Commerce

Date			Place	Dead	Date			Place	Dead
1925	Mar.	18	Mo., Ill., Ind.	689	1952	Mar.	21	Ark., Mo., Tenn. (series)	208
1926	Nov.	25	Belleville to Portland, Ark.	53	1953	May	11	Waco, Tex.	114
1927	Apr.	12	Rock Springs, Tex.	74	1953	June	8	Flint to Lakeport, Mich.	116
1927	May	9	Arkansas, Poplar Bluff, Mo.	92	1953	June	9	Worcester and vicinity, Mass.	90
1927	Sept.	29	St. Louis, Mo.	72	1953	Dec.	5	Vicksburg, Miss.	38
1929	Apr.	25	S.E.-Central Ga.	40	1955	May	25	Udall, Kans.	80
1930	May	6	Hill & Ellis Co., Tex.	41	1957	May	20	Williamsburg, Kans. to Ruskin.	
1932	Mar.	21	Ala. (series of tornadoes)	268				Heights, Mo.	48
1936	Apr.	5	Tupelo, Miss.	216	1958	June	4	Northwestern Wisconsin	30
1936	Apr.	6	Gainesville, Ga.	203	1959	Feb.	10	St. Louis, Mo.	21
1938	Sept.	29	Charleston, S. C.	32	1960	May	5, 6	S. E. Oklahoma, Arkansas.	30
1942	Mar.	16	Central to N.E. Miss.	75	1965	Apr.	11	Ind., Ill., Mich., Wis.	271
1942	Apr.	27	Rogers & Mayes Co., Okla.	52	1966	Mar.	3	Jackson, Miss.	57
1944	June	23	Ohio, Pa., W. Va., Md.	150	1966	Mar.	3	Mississippi, Alabama.	61
1945	Apr.	12	Okla.-Ark.	102	1967	April	21	Illinois.	33
1946	Jan.	4	N. E. Texas	30	1968	May	15	Arkansas.	34
1947	Apr.	9	Texas, Okla. & Kans.	169	1969	Jan.	23	Mississippi.	32
1948	Mar.	19	Bunker Hill & Gillespie, Ill.	33	1970	Apr.	18	Texas Panhandle (series)	25
1949	Jan.	3	La. & Ark.	58	1970	May	11	Lubbock, Tex.	26
					1971	Feb.	21	Miss. delta.	110

Number of Tornadoes in U. S. Since 1924, Deaths

Year	No.	Deaths	Year	No.	Deaths	Year	No.	Deaths	Year	No.	Deaths
1924	130	376	1937	147	29	1950	199	70	1962	658	28
1925	119	794	1938	213	183	1951	272	34	1963	461	31
1926	111	144	1939	152	87	1952	236	230	1964	713	73
1927	163	540	1940	124	65	1953	437	516	1965	899	298
1928	203	92	1941	118	53	1954	549	35	1966	570	99
1929	197	274	1942	167	384	1955	593	125	1967	912	116
1930	192	179	1943	152	58	1956	532	83	1968	661	131
1931	94	36	1944	169	275	1957	864	191	1969	604	66
1932	151	394	1945	121	210	1958	565	66	1970	649	73
1933	258	362	1946	106	78	1959	589	58	1971	888	156
1934	147	47	1947	165	313	1960	618	47	1972	.84	27*
1935	180	70	1948	183	140	1961	682	51	1973	1109†	87
1936	151	552	1949	249	212				Total	19,921	10,582
									Average	343	182

*Record low; † Record High

Hurricanes, Typhoons, Blizzards, Other Storms

Date, Locations, Number of Deaths—See also Chronology
Names of hurricanes and typhoons in italics

1888	Mar. 11-14	Blizzard, East U.S.	400
1900	Sept. 8	Hurricane, Galveston, Tex.	6,000
1926	Sept. 16-22	Hurricane, Fla., Ala.	372
1926	Oct. 20	Hurricane, Cuba	600
1928	Sept. 12-17	Hurricane, W. Indies, Fla.	4,000
1930	Sept. 3	Hurricane, San Domingo	2,000
1938	Sept. 21	Hurricane, New England	600
1942	Oct. 15-16	Hurricane, Bengal, India.	11,000
1944	Sept. 12-16	Hurricane, N. C. to New England.	389
1953	Sept. 25-27	Typhoon, Vietnam, Japan	1,300
1954	Aug. 30	H. Carol, northeast U.S.	68
1954	Sept. 11	H. Edna, n.e. U.S., Canada	23
1954	Oct. 12-16	H. Hazel, east U.S., Haiti	347
1955	Aug. 12-13	H. Connie, Carolinas, Va., Md.	43
1955	Aug. 18-19	H. Diane, eastern U.S.	400
1955	Sept. 19	H. Hilda, Mexico.	200
1955	Sept. 22-28	H. Janet, Caribbean.	500
1956	Feb. 1-29	Blizzard, western Europe.	1,000
1957	June 27-30	H. Audrey, La., Tex.	430
1958	Feb. 15-16	Blizzard, n.e. U. S.	171
1959	Sept. 17-19	T. Sarah, Far East	2,000
1959	Sept. 26-27	T. Vera, Honshu, Japan	4,466
1960	Sept. 4-12	H. Donna, Caribbean, e. U. S.	148
1961	Sept. 11	H. Carla, Tex., La.	40
1961	Oct. 31	H. Hattie, Br. Honduras	400
1962	Feb. 17	Flooding, German North Sea Coast.	343
1962	Sept. 27	Flooding, Barcelona, Spain.	445
1963	May 28-29	Windstorm, E. Pakistan.	22,000
1963	Oct. 4-8	H. Flora, Cuba, Haiti.	6,000
1964	Oct. 4-7	H. Hilda, La., Miss., Ga.	38
1964	June 30	T. Winnie, N. Philippines	107
1964	Sept. 5	T. Ruby, Hong Kong and China.	735
1964	Sept. 14	Flooding, Central S. Korea.	563
1964	Nov. 12	Flooding, S. Vietnam.	7,000
1965	May 11-12	Windstorm, E. Pakistan.	17,000
1965	June 1-2	Windstorm, E. Pakistan.	30,000
1965	Sept. 7-10	H. Betsy, Fla., Miss., La.	74
1965	Dec. 15	Windstorm, E. Pakistan.	10,000
1966	June 4-10	H. Alma, Honduras, s.e. U. S.	51
1966	Sept. 24-30	H. Inez, Carib., Fla., Mex.	293
1967	July 9	T. Billie, Japan.	347
1967	Sept. 5-23	H. Beulah, Carib., Mex., Tex.	54
1967	Dec. 12-20	Blizzard, southwest U. S.	51
1968	Nov. 18-28	T. Nina, Philippines.	63
1969	Aug. 17-18	H. Camille, Miss., La.	258
1969	July 4-5	Flooding, wind and electrical storms, n. Ohio.	41
1970	July 30-Aug. 5	H. Celia, Cuba, Fla., Tex.	31
1970	Aug. 20-21	H. Dorothy, Martinique.	42
1970	Sept. 15	T. Georgia, Philippines.	300
1970	Oct. 14	T. Sening, Philippines.	583
1970	Oct. 15	T. Titang, Philippines.	526
1970	Nov. 13	Cyclone, East Pakistan.	300,000 or more
1971	Aug. 1	T. Rose, Hong Kong.	130
1972	June 19-29	H. Agnes, Fla. to N. Y.	118
1972	Dec. 3	T. Theresa, Philippines.	169

Explosions

Date, Location. Number of Deaths—See also Marine Disasters, Fires and Chronology

1910	Oct. 1	Los Angeles Times Bldg.	21
1913	Mar. 7	Dynamite, Baltimore harbor.	55
1915	Sept. 27	Gasoline tank car, Ardmore, Okla.	47
1917	Apr. 10	Munitions plant, Eddystone, Pa.	133
1917	Dec. 6	Halifax Harbor, Canada.	1,600
1918	July 2	Explosives, Split Rock, N. Y.	50
1918	Oct. 4	Shell plant, Morgan Station, N.J.	64
1919	May 22	Food plant, Cedar Rapids, Ia.	44
1920	Sept. 16	Wall Street, New York, bomb.	30
1924	Jan. 3	Food plant, Pekin, Ill.	42
1937	Mar. 18	New London, Tex., school	294
1940	Sept. 11	Hercules Powder, Kenvil, N. J.	51
1942	June 5	Ordnance plant, Elwood, Ill.	49
1944	Apr. 14	Bombay, India, harbor.	700
1944	July 17	Port Chicago, Calif., pier.	322
1944	Oct. 21	Liquid gas tank, Cleveland.	135

1947	Apr.	16	Texas City, Tex., pier............	561
1948	July	28	Farben works, Ludwigshafen, Ger.	184
1950	May	19	Munition barges, S. Amboy, N. J..	30
1956	Aug.	7	Dynamite trucks, Cali, Colombia.	1,100
1958	Apr.	18	Sunken munitions ship, Okinawa..	40
1958	May	22	Nike missiles, Leonardo, N. J....	10
1959	Apr.	10	World War II bomb, Philippines...	38
1959	June	2	Gas truck, Penn. Turnpike.......	10
1959	June	28	Rail tank cars, Meldrin, Ga.......	25
1959	Aug.	7	Dynamite truck, Roseburg, Ore....	13
1959	Nov.	2	Jamuri Bazar, India, explosives..	46
1959	Dec.	13	Dortmund, Ger., 2 apt. bldgs......	26
1960	Mar.	4	Belgian munition ship, Havana....	100
1960	Oct.	25	Gas, Windsor, Ont., store........	11
1962	Jan.	16	Gas pipeline, Alberta, Canada....	19
1962	Mar.	3	Gasoline truck, Syria...........	31
1962	Oct.	3	Telephone Co. office, N. Y. City..	23
1963	Jan.	2	Packing plant, Terre Haute, Ind...	16
1963	Mar.	9	Dynamite plant, So. Africa......	45
1963	Mar.	9	Steel plant, Belecke, W. Germany.	19

1963	Aug.	13	Explosives dump, Gauhiti, India..	32
1963	Oct.	31	State Fair Coliseum, Indianapolis.	73
1964	July	23	Bone, Algeria, harbor munitions..	100
1965	Mar.	4	Gas pipeline Natchitoches, La....	17
1965	Aug.	9	Missile silo, Searcy, Ark.......	53
1965	Oct.	21	Bridge, Tila Bund, Pakistan.......	80
1965	Oct.	30	Marketplace, Cartagena, Col.....	48
1965	Nov.	24	Armory, Keokuk, Iowa.........	20
1966	Oct.	13	Chemical plant, La Salle, Que....	11
1967	Feb.	17	Chemical plant, Hawthorne, N.J..	11
1967	Dec.	25	Apartment bldg., Moscow........	20
1968	Apr.	6	Sports store, Richmond, Ind......	43
1970	Apr.	8	Subway construction, Osaka, Japan........................	73
1970	Nov.	11	Oil well, Tulsa, Okla...........	9
1970	Dec.	11	Tavern building, N. Y. City......	9
1971	June	24	Tunnel, Sylmar, Calif..........	17
1971	June	28	School, fireworks, Pueblo, Mex...	13
1971	Oct.	21	Shopping center, Glasgow, Scot....	20
1973	Feb.	10	Liquified gas tank, Staten Is., N.Y.	40

Principal Mine Disasters in the U. S.
Source: Bureau of Mines

Note: Prior to 1968, only disasters with losses of 50 or more lives are listed; for 1968-72, all disasters in which 5 or more men are killed are listed. Only fatalities to mining company employees are included.

All Bituminous-coal mines unless otherwise designated

Date	Location	Killed	Date	Location	Killed
March 1855	Coalfield, Va................	55	3-2-1915	Layland, W. Va................	112
4-3-1867	Winterpock, Va..............	69	4-27-1917	Hastings, Colo................	121
9-6-1869[1]	Plymouth, Pa................	110	6-8-1917[2]	Butte, Mont.................	163
2-16-1883	Braidwood, Ill..............	69	8-4-1917	Clay, Ky....................	62
1-24-1884	Crested Butte, Colo..........	59	6-5-1919[1]	Wilkes-Barre, Pa............	92
3-13-1884	Pocahontas, Va..............	112	11-6-1922	Spangler, Pa................	77
1-27-1891	Mount Pleasant, Pa..........	109	11-22-1922	Dolomite, Ala...............	90
1-7-1892	Krebs, Okla.................	100	2-8-1923	Dawson, N. M...............	120
3-20-1895	Red Canyon, Wyo............	60	8-14-1923	Kemmerer, Wyo..............	99
6-28-1896[1]	Pittston, Pa................	58	3-8-1924	Castle Gate, Utah...........	171
5-1-1900	Scofield, Utah..............	200	4-28-1924	Benwood, W. Va.............	119
5-19-1902	Coal Creek, Tenn............	184	2-20-1925	Sullivan, Ind...............	52
7-10-1902	Johnstown, Pa...............	112	5-27-1925	Coal Glen, N. C.............	53
6-30-1903	Hanna, Wyo.................	169	12-10-1925	Acmar, Ala.................	53
1-25-1904	Cheswick, Pa...............	179	1-13-1926	Wilburton, Okla............	91
2-20-1905	Virginia City, Ala...........	112	11-3-1926[2]	Ishpeming, Mich............	51
1-29-1907	Stuart W. Va................	84	4-30-1927[2]	Everettville, W. Va..........	97
12-6-1907	Monongah, W. Va............	361	5-19-1928	Mather, Pa.................	195
12-16-1907	Yolande, Ala................	57	12-17-1929	McAlester, Okla............	61
12-19-1907	Jacobs Creek, Pa............	239	11-5-1930	Millfield, Ohio.............	79
3-28-1908	Hanna, Wyo.................	59	12-23-1932	Moweaqua, Ill..............	54
11-28-1908	Marianna, Pa...............	154	1-10-1940	Bartley, W. Va..............	91
12-29-1908	Switchback, W. Va...........	50	3-16-1940	St. Clairsville, Ohio........	72
1-12-1909	Switchback, W. Va...........	67	7-15-1940	Portage, Pa.................	63
11-13-1909	Cherry, Ill.................	259	5-12-1942	Osage, W. Va...............	56
1-31-1910	Primero, Colo...............	75	2-27-1943	Red Lodge, Mont............	74
5-5-1910	Palos, Ala..................	90	7-5-1944	Belmont, Ohio..............	66
10-8-1910	Starkville, Colo............	56	3-25-1947	Centralia, Ill...............	111
11-8-1910	Delagua, Colo...............	79	12-21-1951	West Frankfort, Ill..........	119
4-7-1911	Throop, Pa.................	72	3-6-1968[3]	Calumet, La................	21
4-8-1911	Littleton, Ala..............	128	8-7-1968	Greenville, Ky..............	9
12-9-1911	Briceville, Tenn............	84	11-20-1968	Farmington, W. Va..........	78
3-20-1912	McCurtain, Okla............	73	12-30-1970	Hyden, Ky.................	38
3-26-1912	Jed, W. Va.................	83	4-12-1971[3]	Rosiclare, Ill..............	7
4-23-1913	Finleyville, Pa.............	96	5-2-1972[2]	Kellogg, Idaho.............	91
10-22-1913	Dawson, N. M..............	263	7-22-1972	Blacksville, W. Va..........	9
4-28-1914	Eccles, W. Va..............	181	12-16-1972	Itmann, W. Va.............	5
10-27-1914	Royalton, Ill...............	52			

World's worst mine disaster killed 1,549 workers in the Honkeiko Colliery in Manchuria Apr. 25, 1942.
(1) Anthracite mine. (2) Metal mine. (3) Nonmetal mine.

Some Notable Aircraft Disasters Since 1937

Date	Aircraft	Site of accident	Deaths
1937 May 6	German zeppelin Hindenburg.......	Burned at mooring, Lakehurst, N. J..................	36[1]
1944 Aug. 23	U. S. Air Force B-24.............	Hit school, Freckelton, England...................	76[1]
1945 July 28	U. S. Army B-25................	Hit Empire State bldg., N.Y.C..................	14[1]
1949 Nov. 1	Eastern Air Lines DC-4...........	Rammed by Bolivian P-38, Wash., D.C...........	55
1950 June 24	Northwest Airlines DC-4..........	Exploded in storm over Lake Michigan...........	58
1951 Dec. 16	Miami Airlines C-46..............	Plunged into Elizabeth River, N. J..............	56
1952 Dec. 20	U. S. Air Force C-124............	Fell, burned, Moses Lake, Wash................	87
1953 Mar. 3	Canadian Pacific Comet jet........	Karachi, Pakistan..........................	11[2]
1953 June 18	U. S. Air Force C-124............	Crashed, burned near Tokyo..................	129
1955 Nov. 1	United Air Lines DC-6B..........	Exploded, crashed near Longmont, Colo.........	44[3]
1956 June 20	Venezuelan Super-Constellation.....	Crashed in Atlantic off Asbury Park, N. J.......	74
1956 June 30	TWA Super-Const., United DC-7....	Collided over Grand Canyon, Arizona..........	128
1957 Aug. 11	Maritime, Central Airways DC-4....	Crashed in swamp near Quebec................	79
1959 Feb. 3	Amer. Airlines Lockheed Electra....	Crashed in East River, New York City..........	65
1960 Feb. 25	USN transport & Arg. airliner.....	Collided in air near Rio de Janeiro............	61
1960 Mar. 17	Northwest Airlines Electra.........	Exploded over Tell City, Ind.................	63

Date	Aircraft	Location / Cause	Deaths
1960 July 27	Sikorsky S-58 helicopter	Crashed in Chicago suburbs	13[4]
1960 Dec. 16	United DC-8 jet, TWA Super-Constellation	Collided over New York City	134[5]
1961 Feb. 15	Sabena Airlines Boeing 707	Crashed at Berg, Belgium	73[1]
1961 Sept. 1	TWA Constellation	Crashed at Hinsdale, Ill.	78
1961 Sept. 10	President Airlines DC-6	Crashed at Shannon, Ireland	83
1961 Nov. 8	Imperial Airlines Constellation	Crashed near Richmond, Va.	77[4]
1962 Mar. 1	Amer. Airlines Boeing 707 jet	Crashed after takeoff, New York City	95
1962 Mar. 4	Br. Caledonian Airlines DC-7C	Crashed near Douala, Cameroun	111
1962 Mar. 16	Flying Tiger Super-Const.	Vanished in western Pacific	107
1962 June 3	Air France Boeing 707 jet	Crashed on takeoff from Paris	130
1962 June 22	Air France Boeing 707 jet	Crashed in storm, Guadeloupe, W. I.	113
1962 Nov. 27	Brazilian Varig Boeing 707 jet	Crashed and burned in Lima, Peru	97
1963 Feb. 1	Mid. E. Viscount, Turk. AF C-47	Collided over Ankara, Turkey	95
1963 June 3	Chartered Northw. Airlines DC-7	Crashed in Pacific off British Columbia	101
1963 Nov. 29	Trans-Canada Airlines DC-8F	Crashed after takeoff from Montreal	118
1963 Dec. 8	Pan American Boeing 707	Crashed near Elkton, Md.	82
1964 Feb. 26	Br. Eagle Bristol Britannia	Crashed near Innsbruck, Austria	83
1964 Mar. 1	Paradise Airline Constellation	Crashed in snow storm, Lake Tahoe, Calif.	85
1964 May 11	U.S. MATS C-135 Stratolifter	Crashed at Clark AB, Philippines	75
1965 Feb. 8	Eastern Air Lines DC-7B	Plunged into Atlantic after takeoff, New York	84
1965 May 20	Pakistani Boeing 720-B	Crashed at Cairo, Egypt, airport	121
1966 Jan. 24	Air India Boeing 707 jetliner	Crashed on Mont Blanc, France-Italy	117
1966 Feb. 4	All-Nippon Boeing 727	Plunged into Tokyo Bay	133
1966 Mar. 5	BOAC Boeing 707 jetliner	Crashed on Japan's Mount Fuji	124
1966 Apr. 22	Military-chartered Electra	Crashed in storm near Ardmore, Okla.	82
1966 Sept. 1	Britannia 102 turboprop	Crashed near Ljubljana, Yugoslavia	97
1966 Dec. 24	U. S. military-chartered, CL-44	Crashed into village in South Vietnam	129[1]
1967 Mar. 9	TWA DC-9, Beechcraft	Collided in air at Urbana, Ohio	26
1967 Apr. 20	Swiss Britannia turboprop	Crashed at Nicosia, Cyprus	126
1967 June 3	Chartered British DC-4	Crashed into Mont Canigou, France	88
1967 June 4	Chartered British Argonaut	Crashed at Stockport, England	72
1967 July 19	Piedmont Boeing 727, Cessna 310	Collided in air, Hendersonville, N. C.	82
1967 Oct. 12	British-Cypriot Mark IV Comet	Crashed into sea off Turkey	66
1967 Nov. 20	TWA Convair 880	Crashed in snowstorm at Cincinnati, Ohio	68
1967 Dec. 8	Peruvian Faucett DC-4	Crashed near Huanuco, Peru	66
1968 Apr. 20	S. African Airways Boeing 707	Crashed on takeoff, Windhoek, S. W. Africa	122
1968 May 3	Braniff International Electra	Crashed in storm near Dawson, Tex.	85
1968 Sept. 11	Air France Caravelle	Caught fire, crashed off Nice, France	95
1969 Mar. 16	Venezuelan DC-9	Crashed after takeoff from Maracaibo, Venezuela	155[7]
1969 Mar. 20	United Arab Ilyushin-18	Crashed at Aswan airport	87
1969 June 4	Mexican Boeing 727	Rammed into mountain near Monterrey, Mexico	79
1969 Sept. 9	Allegheny DC-9	Collided with student pilot's plane, Shelbyville, Ind.	83
1969 Nov. 20	Nigerian VC-10	Crashed near Iju, Nigeria	87
1969 Dec. 8	Olympia Airways DC-6B	Crashed near Athens in storm	93
1970 Feb. 15	Dominican DC-9	Crashed into sea on takeoff from Santo Domingo	102
1970 July 3	British chartered jetliner	Crashed near Barcelona, Spain	112
1970 July 5	Air Canada DC-8	Crashed near Toronto International Airport	108
1970 Aug. 9	Peruvian turbojet	Crashed after takeoff from Cuzco, Peru	101[1]
1970 Oct. 2	Chartered Martin 404	Crashed in Rocky Mts. near Silver Plume, Colo.	30[8]
1970 Nov. 14	Southern Airways DC-9	Crashed in mountains near Huntington, W. Va.	75[9]
1970 Dec. 31	Soviet Aeroflot Ilyushin 18	Crashed on takeoff, Leningrad	90
1971 May 23	Yugoslavian civil Tupolev-134a	Crashed on landing, Rijeka, Yugo.	78
1971 July 30	All-Nippon Boeing 727, Japanese Air Force F-86	Collided over Morioka, Japan	162[10]
1971 Aug.	Soviet Aeroflot Tupolev-104	Crashed at Irkutsk airport, USSR.	97
1971 Sept. 4	Alaska Airlines Boeing 727	Crashed into mountain near Juneau, Alaska	111
1972 Mar. 14	Danish Airliner	Crashed near Dubai, U. of A. Emirates	112
1972 Aug. 14	E. German Ilyushin-62	Crashed on take-off East Berlin	156
1972 Oct. 13	Aeroflot Ilyushin-62	E. German airline crashed near Moscow	176
1972 Dec. 4	Chartered Spanish airliner	Crashed on take-off, Canary Islands	155
1972 Dec. 29	Eastern Airlines Lockheed Tristar	Crashed on approach to Miami Int'l. Airport	100
1973 Jan. 22	Chartered Boeing 707	Burst into flames during landing, Kano Airport, Nigeria	176
1973 Apr. 10	British Vanguard turboprop	Crashed during snowstorm at Basel, Switzerland	104
1973 June 3	Soviet Supersonic TU-144	Exploded in air near Goussainville, France	14[11]
1973 July 11	Brazilian Boeing 707	Crashed on approach to Orly airport Paris	122
1973 July 23	Pan American Boeing 707	Crashed after takeoff from Papeete, Tahiti	68
1973 July 31	Delta Airlines jetliner	Crashed on landing in heavy fog at Logan Int'l. Airport, Boston	89
1973 Aug. 13	Spanish Caravelle jet	Exploded and crashed near La Coruna, Spain	85

(1) Including those on the ground and in buildings. (2) First fatal crash of commercial jet plane. (3) Caused by bomb planted by John G. Graham in insurance plot to kill his mother, a passenger. (4) First crash of commercial helicopter. (5) Including all 128 aboard the planes and 6 on ground. (6) Including 74 Army recruits. (7) Killed 84 on plane and 71 on ground. (8) Including 13 members of Wichita State U. football team. (9) Including 43 Marshall U. football players and coaches. (10) Airline-fighter crash, pilot of fighter parachuted to safety, was arrested for negligence. (11) First supersonic airliner crash killed 6 crewmen and 8 on the ground; there were no passengers.

Record Oil Spills, 1967-1971

Source: U. S. Geological Survey, Conservation Division

Name and Place	Date	Cause of Spill	Barrels
Tanker, Torrey Canyon, England	Mar. 18, 1967	Grounding	700,000
Tanker, World Glory, South Africa	June 13, 1968	Hull failure	322,000
Tanker, Atlantic Ocean	Mar. 27, 1971	Sinking	220,000
Tanker, Keo, Massachusetts	Nov. 5, 1969	Hull failure	210,000
Storage tank, Sewaren, N. J.	Nov. 1969	Tank failure	200,000
Pipeline, West Delta area, La.	Oct. 15, 1967	Anchor dragging	160,000
Tanker, Japan	Nov. 30, 1971	Tanker broke in half	149,080
Tanker, R. C. Stoner, Wake Island	Sept. 6, 1967	Grounding	143,300
Tanker, Andron, West African coast	May 5, 1968	Sinking	117,000

The Woman Worker: America's Unrecognized Resource
By Hana Umlauf

Do women really make less than men in jobs calling for the same skill, effort and time? Yes, definitely, reports the highest economic authority in the U. S. The President's Council of Economic Advisers estimates that, after adjusting for demand for or prestige of a particular job and its skill level, as well as education and training required and past work experience, women generally make less, "perhaps on the order of 20% less," than men.

Of the 42% of women workers who worked full-time in 1973 (50 to 52 weeks per year), only half earned at least $5,903. That figure represented 57.9% of the $10,202 median earnings of fully employed men.

In 1973, nearly 35 million women in the United States, 49% of all women over the age of 16, were working. They represented nearly 40% of the total working force of the U. S.

Although the greater number of women workers held white collar jobs, most held less skilled and lower paying jobs. Over $1/3$ of all women workers were found in the clerical category, 17% were service workers, and 14% were operatives, mainly in factories. Of the 15% holding professional or technical positions, 2 million were teachers.

In January 1973, then President Richard M. Nixon, in the first economic report ever to deal with the status of women, acknowledged that women had not made much progress in achieving job equality or equal pay since 1956. Despite increased consciousness-raising stemming from the feminist movement and some spectacular gains, the majority of women workers have made slow progress.

What Holds Women Back?

What's holding women back? Recent studies on the female executive point to some of the myths and assumptions about women which keep them from moving up and gaining top-ranking positions.

A survey published in the Sept./Oct. Harvard Business Review studied 20 major U. S. corporations which employ some 2 million people and discovered that women represented less than 1% of all the officials, managers and professionals. Cynthia Epstein, an associate professor of sociology at Queens College, who studied women's advance through corporate ranks, concluded, "Women are getting better salaries and titles, but not the top posts." Women seem to be falling into the same pattern which has befallen the black businessman. They attain middle management posts, but their advancement stops short of the executive suite where the final decision-making power lies.

Two women, Margaret Henning and Anne Jardim, both former faculty members of the Harvard Business School, have set out to deal with what they consider the behavioral differences between men and women that impede a women's progress in business. They maintain women do not know how to behave when they enter a male-dominated corporation. Unlike the women's movement, Henning and Jardim argue that women, not the men, must change.

Women in business, they say, are caught up in the "waiting to be chosen" syndrome. They wait to be given the positions and salaries they feel they deserve rather than demanding them. Women also assume that they will be tolerated only if they are superefficient. Consequently, women become experts in narrow areas rather than becoming managerial generalists. They also bear the brunt of the male assumption that women are more interested in their marriage or children than in their careers.

The root of the female mobility problem in business lies in childhood, according to Henning and Jardim. Unlike boys, in their early years women receive no environmental support from their peers to be aggressive. They are taught to be like their mothers, even though society considers mothers to be sec-

ond best. Therefore, women make negative assumptions about their place in the corporation, questioning their right to be there.

To deal with these behavioral problems, Jardim and Henning have developed 2 academic programs for women, both associated with Simmons College in Boston, Mass. The first, which began in September, 1974, is a graduate program leading to a degree in management. The second, financed through a foundation set up by the National Association of Bank Women, is an academic program for female bank executives leading to B.A. and M.A. degrees from Simmons.

Despite the slow rate of progress, women are making forward strides and their efforts are being gradually rewarded. A recent issue of the Gallagher Presidents' Report noted that although women currently comprise only 10% of the average company's executives, 3 in 5 corporation presidents say they plan to increase the number of female executives in their companies over the next 5 years.

Breakthrough in Banking Industry

Perhaps the greatest breakthrough for professional women in 1973 came in the banking industry. In response to a class action suit on behalf of its female employees, the Bank of America, the world's largest commercial bank, came through with a far-reaching settlement, which may well have vast ramifications throughout the banking industry.

The settlement provides for $10 million per year in salaries for women. The bank also promised to increase the overall proportion of women officers to 40% by the end of 1978, with 5% at the highest management level. Ten women were to be assigned immediately to the 250 positions in overseas branches staffed entirely by men.

Possibly the most impressive aspect of the settlement was the establishment of a $3.75 million trust fund to be used exclusively by women employees at all levels of the bank. The fund will provide for training, education and travel, sabbatical leaves and other "self-development" programs.

Women working for the federal government have also shown significant gains. Despite a general decline in federal jobs, the number of women employed full-time in white collar jobs (excluding the U. S. Postal Service) rose by 2,000 in 1973. Women held about 40.8% of the federal government's 1.4 million white collar jobs in October 1973.

Results of a survey of job categories showed women were moving upward in government jobs. The percentage of women in mid-level positions (GS-7 to GS-12) increased from 22% in 1972 to 23.4% in 1973, despite a 10,000 decrease in jobs for women and a 79,000 decrease in jobs for men. Women gained 41 jobs in the supergrade level while men lost 87 positions.

Few Women in Science and Engineering

Not all professions, however, are opening up to women to the same degree. According to a recent MIT report, careers in science and engineering are still extremely difficult for a woman to pursue. MIT attributes much of the problem to the persistence of sex-role stereotyping. From early on, teachers, employers and women themselves assume science and engineering are male areas. Currently, an estimated 1% of jobs in the 2 fields are held by women.

In May 1973, a workshop at MIT, sponsored by the Carnegie Corporation and the Alfred P. Sloan Foundation, brought together some 125 scholars, educators, industrialists to discuss women in science and technology. The report on their conference urged broad recruitment into industry of women in science-oriented school programs, and financial aid for training and retraining of women for technical jobs.

In the related field of medicine, women have been making steadier gains. In the past 3 years, the enrollment of women in medical schools has doubled from 3,894 or 9.6% to 7,824 or 15.4%.

Observers feel that the influx of women has already begun to change patterns long considered discriminatory in medical schools. Among them are medical school interviews, lecture hall humor, and laboratory participation long considered to carry sexist overtones. Also prevalent is the belief that the introduction of more women into medicine will bring greater flexibility to the profession, notably by injecting more emphasis on group rather than individual work.

Women On Increase in Unions

Organized labor is another area that has shown a marked increase in women: 330,000 new female union members between 1970 and 1972. In 1972, women accounted for 24.9% of national union and employee association membership.

In March, 3,000 of those women, representing 58 unions, formed a national Coalition of Labor Union Women. They pledged to improve the lives of working women by becoming activists on women's issues in their individual unions. Olga Madar, a vice president of the United Automobile Workers, was elected coalition president. Specific objectives outlined by the coalition included more aggressive organization of unorganized women (some 30 million or 85% of working women); positive union action against sex discrimination in pay, hiring, job classification and promotion; participation of women in policy-making positions within unions; and union support of legislation providing for child care facilities, "livable" minimum wages and improved maternity and pension benefits.

Access to apprenticeship programs in various trades, one means of upward mobility for women in union structure, has been sadly lacking. In 1973, the U.S. Department of Labor's Manpower Administration published a 3-year study entitled "Women in Apprenticeship—Why Not?" The study concluded that women should have their own apprenticeship outreach program, similar to those for minority youths in the construction trades.

The study, coordinated by Norma Briggs, included a demonstration project in the Fox River Valley area of east-central Wisconsin, chosen because it has many small and large businesses which use the apprenticeship system. A survey of 78 area businesses revealed that no women were included in the apprenticeship programs. "Unsuitable" conditions for women workers was the chief reason given. However, further study disclosed that many women, in spite of the "unsuitable" conditions, were working on an unskilled level without the pay or opportunities available to male apprentices.

According to Briggs, it became clear in interviews with male union members that "the typical union member's firm belief in equal pay and equality of opportunity was severely modified by his belief that men were the breadwinners, the serious workers, who should therefore get the opportunities when there are not enough to go around." It was also discovered that notices about apprenticeship openings were often posted in areas not accessible to women.

In June, Labor Secretary Peter J. Brennan announced a pilot project in 6 cities to expand women's opportunities in apprenticeship outreach programs. Each of the cities — Boston, New York City, Cleveland, Atlanta, Chicago, and Los Angeles — would also hold a conference on women in apprenticeship. Brennan said, "We are determined to find a place for the working women in apprenticeable occupations that have never before been considered usual 'women's work.'"

Federal Government Presses Equality

In the past year, the federal government took several steps forward in the battle against sex discrimination in employment. For one, the Census Bureau, in late 1973, revised its Occupational Classification System to eliminate the stereotyping of "men's" and "women's" jobs. The changes, mainly replacing the suffix "men" by "worker" or "operator," affected 52 of 441 job titles. The changes will be incorporated in the gathering and publication of future census statistics.

In early 1974, the New Comprehensive Employment and Training Act (CETA) specifically prohibited federal funding of any manpower programs that discriminate against women. The labor secretary is also authorized to cut off funds to any existing program which discriminates against women.

Also early in 1974, the Office of Federal Contract Compliance (OFCC) was reorganized to strengthen enforcement of equal opportunity regulations applying to federal contractors. Under the new organization an estimated 250,000 federal contractors and subcontractors must take affirmative action to recruit, hire, train, and promote women minority workers into jobs where they have been underutilized.

Women Office Holders

Currently, the picture is also bleak for women pursuing careers as public servants. Only 16 of 435 congressional representatives are women; only 26 women hold statewide offices of any kind and 441 women sit in state legislatures (about 6% of legislators).

However, the prospect for 1974, with more than 3,000 women running for local, state, and federal office, tripling the number of candidates in 1972, is encouraging. Given the Watergate scandal, the prevailing attitude is becoming "most men haven't done so good, why not give women a chance."

Pollster Peter Hart reports, "Women definitely are helped by the honesty issue." For one thing, no women were involved in the Watergate scandal, mostly because they are on the periphery of the political process.

Heading the slate of women candidates is Rep. Ella Grasso, the unanimous nominee of the Connecticut Democratic Party for that state's governorship. If elected, a likely event, she will be the first female governor to be elected in her own right and the nation's highest ranking woman official.

More dismal is the record of black women seeking public office. According to the Joint Center for Political Studies, sexism and racism are the dominant inhibiting factors. The majority of black women who do hold offices are on boards of education and in municipal offices. Only 17 black women hold county offices and 4 sit in Congress. The figures, small as they are, however, have doubled since 1969.

What's Needed in the Future?

Though gradual, the process of integration of women into better-paying skilled jobs is a fact. Observers note that a decade of legislation barring sex discrimination in employment must open up more diversified and higher skilled jobs for women. They point out that the key to equality in job opportunity and compensation is two-fold. First, women must rid themselves of longheld assumptions about a woman's role in the working world and set career goals commensurate with the full extent of their abilities. Research has shown that the process is not an easy one. It calls for job and career counseling as well as recognition on the part of management that women can play a vital and responsible role in the work force.

Second, proponents of equal opportunity argue that more and better training programs in diversified skills as well as education in management must be made accessible to women. Then, given the same advantages men have when they begin their careers, women could become an integral and equal segment of the working force in the United States.

SPORTS OF 1974

Olympic Games Records

The modern Olympic Games, first held in Athens, Greece, in 1896, were the result of efforts by Baron Pierre de Coubertin, a French educator, to promote interest in education and culture, also to foster better international understanding through the universal medium of youth's love of athletics.

His source of inspiration for the Olympic Games was the ancient Greek Olympic Games, most notable of the four Panhellenic celebrations. The games were combined patriotic, religious and athletic festivals held every four years. The first such recorded festival was that held in 776 B.C., the date from which the Greeks began to keep their calendar by "Olympiads," or four-year spans between the games.

The first Olympiad is said to have consisted merely of a 200-yard foot race near the small city of Olympia, but the games gained in scope and became demonstrations of national pride. Only Greek citizens — amateurs — were permitted to participate. Winners received laurel, wild olive and palm wreaths and were accorded many special privileges. Under the Roman emperors, the games deteriorated into professional carnivals and circuses. Emperor Theodosius banned them in 394 A.D.

Baron de Coubertin enlisted 9 nations to send athletes to the first modern Olympics in 1896; now more than 100 nations compete. Winter Olympic Games were started in 1924.

Sites and Unofficial Winners of Games

1896 Athens (U.S.)	1912 Stockholm (U.S.)	1936 Berlin (Germany)	1964 Tokyo (U.S.)
1900 Paris (U.S.)	1920 Antwerp (U.S.)	1948 London (U.S.)	1968 Mexico City (U.S.)
1904 St. Louis (U.S.)	1924 Paris (U.S.)	1952 Helsinki (U.S.)	1972 Munich (USSR)
1906 Athens (U.S.) unofficial	1928 Amsterdam (U.S.)	1956 Melbourne (USSR)	1976 Montreal (July 16-
1908 London (U.S.)	1932 Los Angeles (U.S.)	1960 Rome (USSR)	Aug. 1)

Olympic Games Champions 1896—1972

(*Indicates Olympic Record)

Track and Field—Men

60 Meter Run

1900	Alvin Kraenzlein, United States	7s*
1904	Archie Hahn, United States	7s*

100 Meter Run

1896	Thomas Burke, United States	12s
1900	Francis W. Jarvis, United States	10.8s
1904	Archie Hahn, United States	11s
1906	Archie Hahn, United States	11.2s
1908	Reginald Walker, South Africa	10.8s
1912	Ralph Craig, United States	10.8s
1920	Charles Paddock, United States	10.8s
1924	Harold Abrahams, Great Britain	10.6s
1928	Percy Williams, Canada	10.8s
1932	Eddie Tolan, United States	10.3s
1936	Jesse Owens, United States	10.3s
1948	Harrison Dillard, United States	10.3s
1952	Lindy Remigino, United States	10.4s
1956	Bobby Morrow, United States	10.5s
1960	Armin Hary, Germany	10.2s
1964	Bob Hayes, United States	10.0s
1968	Jim Hines, United States	9.9s*
1972	Valeri Borzov, USSR	10.1s

200 Meter Run

1900	J. W. B. Tewksbury, United States	22.2s
1904	Archie Hahn, United States	21.6s
1908	Robert Kerr, Canada	22.4s
1912	Ralph Craig, United States	21.7s
1920	Allan Woodring, United States	22s
1924	Jackson Scholz, United States	21.6s
1928	Percy Williams, Canada	21.8s
1932	Eddie Tolan, United States	21.2s
1936	Jesse Owens, United States	20.7s
1948	Mel Patton, United States	21.1s
1952	Andrew Stanfield, United States	20.7s
1956	Bobby Morrow, United States	20.6s
1960	Livio Berruti, Italy	20.5s
1964	Henry Carr, United States	20.3s
1968	Tommie Smith, United States	19.8s*
1972	Valeri Borzov, USSR	20s

400 Meter Run

1896	Thomas Burke, United States	54.2s
1900	Maxey Long, United States	49.4s
1904	Harry Hillman, United States	49.2s
1906	Paul Pilgrim, United States	53.2s
1908	Wyndham Halswelle, Great Britain, walkover.	50s
1912	Charles Reidpath, United States	48.2s
1920	Bevil Rudd, South Africa	49.6s
1924	Eric Liddell, Great Britain	47.6s
1928	Ray Barbuti, United States	47.8s
1932	William Carr, United States	46.2s
1936	Archie Williams, United States	46.5s
1948	Arthur Wint, Jamaica, B.W.I.	46.2s

1952	George Rhoden, Jamaica, B.W.I.	45.9s
1956	Charles Jenkins, United States	46.7s
1960	Otis Davis, United States	44.9s
1964	Michael Larrabee, United States	45.1s
1968	Lee Evans, United States	43.8s*
1972	Vincent Matthews, United States	44.7s

800 Meter Run

1896	Edwin Flack, Great Britain	2m. 11s
1900	Alfred Tysoe, Great Britain	2m. 1.4s
1904	James Lightbody, United States	1m., 56s
1906	Paul Pilgrim, United States	2m. 1.2s
1908	Mel Sheppard, United States	1m. 52.8s
1912	James Meredith, United States	1m. 51.9s
1920	Albert Hill, Great Britain	1m. 53.4s
1924	Douglas Lowe, Great Britain	1m. 52.4s
1928	Douglas Lowe, Great Britain	1m. 51.8s
1932	Thomas Hampson, Great Britain	1m. 49.8s
1936	John Woodruff, United States	1m. 52.9s
1948	Mal Whitfield, United States	1m .49.2s
1952	Mal Whitfield, United States	1m. 49.2s
1956	Thomas Courtney, United States	1m. 47.7s
1960	Peter Snell, New Zealand	1m. 46.3s
1964	Peter Snell, New Zealand	1m· 45.1s
1968	Ralph Doubell, Australia	1m. 44.3s*
1972	Dave Wottle, United States	1m .45.9s

1,500 Meter Run

1896	Edwin Flack, Great Britain	4m. 33.2s
1900	Charles Bennett, Great Britain	4m. 6s
1904	James Lightbody, United States	4m. 5.4s
1906	James Lightbody, United States	4m. 12s
1908	Mel Sheppard, United States	4m. 3.4s
1912	Arnold Jackson, Great Britain	3m. 56.8s
1920	Albert Hill, Great Britain	4m. 1.8s
1924	Paavo Nurmi, Finland	3m. 53.6s
1928	Harry Larva, Finland	3m.53.2s
1932	Luigi Beccali, Italy	3m. 51.2s
1936	Jack Lovelock, New Zealand	3m. 47.8s
1948	Henri Eriksson, Sweden	3m. 49.8s
1952	Joseph Barthel, Luxemburg	3m. 45.2s
1956	Ron Delaney, Ireland	3m. 41.2s
1960	Herb Elliott, Australia	3m. 35.6s
1964	Peter Snell, New Zealand	3m. 38.1s
1968	Kipchoge Keino, Kenya	3m. 34.9s*
1972	Pekka Vasala, Finland	3m. 36.3s

3,000 Meter Steeplechase

1920	Percy Hodge, Great Britain	10m. 2.4s
1924	Willie Ritola, Finland	9m. 33.6s
1928	Toivo Loukola, Finland	9m. 21.8s
1932	Volnari Iso-Hollo, Finland	10m. 33.4s
	(About 3450 mtrs. extra lap by error)	
1936	Volnari Iso-Hollo, Finland	9m. 3.8s
1948	Thure Sjoestrand, Sweden	9m. 4.6s

1952	Horace Ashenfelter, United States	8m. 45.4s
1956	Chris Brasher, Great Britain	8m. 42.2s
1960	Zdzislaw Krzyszkowiak, Poland	8m. 34.2s
1964	Gaston Roelants, Belgium	8m. 30.8s
1968	Amos Biwott, Kenya	8m. 51s
1972	Kipchoge Keino, Kenya	8m. 23.6s*

5,000 Meter Run

1912	Hannes Kolehmainen, Finland	14m. 36.6s
1920	Joseph Guillemot, France	14m. 55.6s
1924	Paavo Nurmi, Finland	14m. 31.2s
1928	Willie Ritola, Finland	14m. 38s
1932	Lauri Lehtinen, Finland	14m. 30s
1936	Gunnar Hooker, Finland	14m. 22.2s
1948	Gaston Reiff, Belgium	14m. 17.6s
1952	Emil Zatopek, Czechoslovakia	14m. 6.0s
1956	Vladimir Kuts, USSR	13m. 39.6s
1960	Murray Halberg, New Zealand	13m. 43.4s
1964	Bob Schul, United States	13m. 48.8s

Cross-Country

1912	Hannes Kolehmainen, Finland	45m. 11.6s

5 Mile Run

1906	H. Hawtrey, Great Britain	26m. 26.2s
1908	Emil Voigt, Great Britain	25m. 11.2s*

10,000 Meter Run

1912	Hannes Kolehmainen, Finland	31m. 20.8s
1920	Paavo Nurmi, Finland	31m. 45.8s
1924	Willie Ritola, Finland	30m. 23.2s
1928	Paavo Nurmi, Finland	30m. 18.8s
1932	Janusz Kusocinski, Poland	30m. 11.4s
1936	Ilmari Salminen, Finland	30m. 15.4s
1948	Emil Zatopek, Czechoslovakia	29m. 59.6s
1952	Emil Zatopek, Czechoslovakia	29m. 17.0s
1956	Vladimir Kuts, USSR	28m. 45.6s
1960	Pytor Bolotnikov, USSR	28m. 32.2s
1964	Billy Mills, United States	28m. 24.4s
1968	Naftali Temu, Kenya	29m. 27.4s
1972	Lasse Viren, Finland	27m. 38.4s*

Marathon

1896	Spyos Loues, Greece	2h. 55m. 20s
1900	Michael Teato, France	2h. 59m.
1904	Thomas Hicks, United States	3h. 28m. 53s
1906	W. J. Sherring, Canada	2h. 51m. 23.6s
1908	John J. Hayes, United States	2h. 55m. 18.4s
1912	Kenneth McArthur, South Africa	2h. 36. 54.8s
1920	Hannes Kolehmainen, Finland	2h. 32m. 35.8s
1924	Albin Stenroos, Finland	2h. 41m. 22.6s
1928	El Ouafl, France	2h. 32m. 57s
1932	Juan Zabala, Argentina	2h. 31m. 36s
1936	Kitei Son, Japan	2h. 29m. 19.2s
1948	Delfo Cabera, Argentina	2h. 34m. 51.6s
1952	Emil Zatopek, Czechoslovakia	2h. 23m. 03.2s
1956	Alain Mimoun, France	2h. 25m.
1960	Abebe Bikila, Ethiopia	2h. 15m. 15.2s
1964	Abebe Bikila, Ethiopia	2h. 12m. 11.2s*
1968	Mamo Wolde, Ethiopia	2h. 20m. 26.4s
1972	Frank Shorter, United States	2h. 12m. 19.7s

10,000 Meter Cross-Country

1920	Paavo Nurmi, Finland	27m. 15s*
1924	Paavo Nurmi, Finland	32m. 54.8s

1,500 Meter Walk

1906	George V. Bonhag, United States	7m. 12.6s

3,000 Meter Walk

1920	Ugo Frigerio, Italy	13m. 14.2

3,500 Meter Walk

1908	George Larner, Great Britain	14m. 55s

10,000 Meter Walk

1912	George Goulding, Canada	46m. 28.4s
1920	Ugo Frigerio, Italy	48m. 6.2s
1924	Ugo Frigerio, Italy	47m. 49s
1948	John Mikaelsson, Sweden	45m. 13.2s
1952	John Mikaelsson, Sweden	45m. 02.8s*

20,000 Meter Walk

1956	Leonid Spirine, USSR	1h. 31m. 27.4s
1960	Vladimir Golubnickiy, USSR	1h. 34m. 7.2s
1964	Kenneth Mathews, Great Britain	1h. 29m. 34.0s
1968	Vladimir Golubnichiy, USSR	1h. 35m. 58.4s
1972	Peter Frenkel, E. Germany	1h. 26m. 42.4s*

50,000 Meter Walk

1932	Thomas W. Green, Great Britain	4h. 50m. 10s
1936	Harold Whitlock Great Britain	4h. 30m. 41.4s
1948	John Lundgren, Sweden	4h. 41m. 52s
1952	Giuseppe Bordoni, Italy	4h. 28m. 07.8s
1956	Norman Read, New Zealand	4h. 30m. 42.8s

1960	Donald Thompson, Great Britain	4h. 25m. 30s
1964	Abdon Pamich, Italy	4h. 11m. 11.2s
1968	Christoph Hohne, E. Germany	4h. 20m. 13.6s
1972	Bernd Kannenberg, W. Germany	3h. 56m. 11.6s*

110 Meter Hurdles

1896	Thomas Curtis, United States	17.6s
1900	Alvin Kraenzlein, United States	15.4s
1904	Frederick Schule, United States	16s
1906	R. G. Leavitt, United States	16.2s
1908	Forrest Smithson, United States	15s
1912	Frederick Kelly, United States	15.1s
1920	Earl Thomson, Canada	14.8s
1924	Daniel Kinsey, United States	15s
1928	Sydney Atkinson, South Africa	14.8s
1932	George Saling, United States	14.6s
1936	Forrest Towns, United States	14.2s
1948	William Porter, United States	13.9s
1952	Harrison Dillard, United States	13.7s
1956	Lee Calhoun, United States	13.5s
1960	Lee Calhoun, United States	13.8s
1964	Hayes Jones, United States	13.6s
1968	Willie Davenport, United States	13.3s
1972	Rod Milburn, United Sates	13.2s*

200 Meter Hurdles

1900	Alvin Kraenzlein, United States	25.4s
1904	Harry Hillman, United States	24.6s*

400 Meter Hurdles

1900	J. W. B. Tewksbury, United States	57.6s
1904	Harry Hillman, United States	53s
1908	Charles Bacon, United States	55s
1920	Frank Loomis, United States	54s
1924	F. Morgan Taylor, United States	52.6s
1928	Lord Burghley, Great Britain	53.4s
1932	Robert Tisdall, Ireland	51.8s
1936	Glenn Hardin, United States	52.4s
1948	Roy Cochran, United States	51.1s
1952	Charles Moore, United States	50.8s
1956	Glenn Davis, United States	50.1s
1960	Glenn Davis, United States	49.3s
1964	Rex Cawley, United States	49.6s
1968	Dave Hemery, Great Britain	48.1s
1972	John Akii-Bua, Uganda	47.8s*

Standing High Jump

1900	Ray Ewry, United States	5ft. 5 in.
1904	Ray Ewry, United States	4ft. 11 in.
1906	Ray Ewry, United States	5ft. 1 5-8 in.
1908	Ray Ewry, United States	5ft. 2 in.
1912	Platt Adams, United States	5ft. 4 1-4 in.*

Running High Jump

1896	Ellery Clark, United States	5ft. 11 1-4 in.
1900	Irving Baxter, United States	6ft. 2 4-5 in.
1904	Samuel Jones, United States	5ft. 11 in.
1906	Con Leahy, Ireland	5ft. 9 7-8 in.
1908	Harry Porter, United States	6ft. 3 in.
1912	Almer W. Richards, United States	6ft. 4 in.
1920	Richard Landon, United States	6ft. 4 3-8 in.
1924	Harold Osborn, United States	6ft. 6 in.
1928	Robert W. King, United States	6ft. 4 3-8 in.
1932	Duncan McNaughton, Canada	6ft. 5 5-8 in.
1936	Cornelius Johnson, United States	6ft. 7.15-16 in.
1948	John L. Winter, Australia	6ft. 6 in.
1952	Walter Davis, United States	6ft. 8.32 in.
1956	Charles Dumas, United States	6ft. 11 1-4 in.
1960	Robert Shavlakadze, USSR	7ft. 1in.
1964	Valery Brumel, USSR	7ft. 1 7-8 in.
1968	Dick Fosbury, United States	7ft. 4 1-4 in.*
1972	Yuri Tarmak, USSR	7ft. 3 3-4 in.

Standing Broad Jump

1900	Ray Ewry, United States	10ft. 6 2-5 in.
1904	Ray Ewry, United States	11ft. 4 7-8 in.*
1906	Ray Ewry, United States	10ft. 10 in.
1908	Ray Ewry, United States	10ft. 11 1-4 in.
1912	Constantin Tsicilitras, Greece	11ft. 3-4 in.

Long Jump

1896	Ellery Clark, United States	20ft. 9 3-4 in.
1900	Alvin Kraenzlein, United States	23ft. 6 7-8 in.
1904	Myer Prinstein, United States	24ft. 1in.
1906	Myer Prinstein, United States	23ft. 7 1-2 in.
1908	Frank Irons, United States	24ft. 6 1-2 in.
1912	Albert Gutterson, United States	24ft. 11 1-4 in.
1920	Wm. Pettersson, Sweden	23ft. 5 1-2 in.
1924	DeHart Hubbard, United States	24ft. 5 1-8 in.
1928	Edward B. Hamm, United States	25ft. 4 3-4 in.
1932	Edward Gordon, United States	25ft. 3-4 in.
1936	Jesse Owens, United States	26ft. 5 5-16 in.
1948	William Steele, United States	25ft. 8 in.
1952	Jerome Biffle, United States	24ft. 10.03 in.
1956	Gregory Bell, United States	25ft. 8 1-4 in.

1960	Ralph Boston, United States	26ft. 7 3-4 in.
1964	Lynn Davies, Great Britain	26ft. 5 3-4 in.
1968	Bob Beamon, United States	29ft. 2 1-2 in.*
1972	Randy Williams, United States	27ft. 1-2 in.

400 Meter Relay

1912	Great Britain	.42.4s
1920	United States	.42.2s
1924	United States	41s
1928	United States	41s
1932	United States	40s
1936	United States	39.8s
1948	United States	40.3s
1952	United States	40.1s
1956	United States	39.5s
1960	Germany (U.S. diqual.)	39.5s
1964	United States	39.0s
1968	United States	38.2s*
1972	United States	38.2s*

1,600 Meter Relay

1908	United States	3m. 27.2s
1912	United States	3m. 16.6s
1920	Great Britain	3m. 22.2s
1924	United States	3m. 16s
1928	United States	3m. 14.2s
1932	United States	3m. 8.2s
1936	Great Britain	3m. 9s
1948	United States	3m. 10.4s
1952	Jamaica, B.W.I.	3m. 03.9s
1956	United States	3m. 04.8s
1960	United States	3m. 02.2s
1964	United States	3m. 00.7s
1968	United States	2m. 56.1s*
1972	Kenya	2m. 59.8s

Pole Vault

1896	William Hoyt, United States	10ft. 9 3-4 in.
1900	Irving Baxter, United States	10ft. 9.9 in.
1904	Charles Dvorak, United States	11ft. 6 in.
1906	Fernand Gouder, France	11ft. 6 in.
1908	A. C. Gilbert, United States	
	Edward Cook Jr., United States	12 ft. 2 in.
1912	Harry Babcock, United States	12ft. 11 1-2 in.
1920	Frank Foss, United States	13ft. 5 in.
1924	Lee Barnes, United States	12ft. 11 1-2 in.
1928	Sabin W. Carr, United States	13ft. 9 1-2 in.
1932	William Miller, United States	14ft. 1 7-8 in.
1936	Earle Meadows, United States	14ft. 3 1-4 in.
1948	Guinn Smith, United States	14ft. 1 1-4 in.
1952	Robert Richards, United States	14ft. 11 1-4 in.
1956	Robert Richards, United States	14ft. 11 1-2 in.
1960	Don Bragg, United States	15ft. 5 1-8 in.
1964	Fred Hansen, United States	16ft. 8 1-2 in.
1968	Bob Seagren, United States	17ft. 8 1-2 in.
1972	Wolfgang Nordwig, E. Germany	18ft. 1-2 in.*

16-Lb. Hammer Throw

1900	John Flannagan, United States	167ft. 4 in.
1904	John Flannagan, United States	168ft. 1 in.
1908	John Flannagan, United States	170ft. 4 1-4 in.
1912	Matt McGrath, United States	179ft. 7 1-8 in.
1920	Pat Ryan, United States	172ft. 5 5-8 in.
1924	Fred Tootell, United States	174ft. 10 1-8 in.
1928	Patrick O'Callaghan, Ireland	168ft. 7 3-8 in.
1932	Patrick O'Callaghan, Ireland	176ft. 11 1-8 in.
1936	Karl Hein, Germany	185ft. 4 3-16 in.
1948	Imre Nemeth, Hungary	183ft. 11 1-2 in.
1952	Jozsef Csermak, Hungary	197ft. 11.67 in.
1956	Harold Connolly, United States	207ft. 3 1-2 in.
1960	Vasily Rudenkov, USSR	220ft. 2 in.
1964	Romuald Klim, USSR	228ft. 9 1-2 in.
1968	Gyula Zsivotsky, Hungary	240ft. 8 in.
1972	Anatoli Bondarchuk, USSR	247ft. 8 1-2 in.*

Discus Throw

1896	Robert Garrett, United States	95ft. 7 1-2 in.
1900	Rudolf Bauer, Hungary	118ft. 2.9-10in.
1904	Martin Sheridan, United States	128ft. 10 1-2 in.
1906	Martin Sheridan, United States	136ft. 1-3 in.
1908	Martin Sheridan, United States	134ft. 2 in.
1912	Armas Taipale, Finland	148ft. 4 in.
	Both hands—Armas Taipale, Finland	271ft. 10 1-4 in.
1920	Elmer Niklander, Finland	146ft. 7 1-4 in.
1924	Clarence Houser, United States	151ft. 5 1-8 in.
1928	Clarence Houser, United States	155ft. 3 in.
1932	John Anderson, United States	162ft. 4 7-8 in.
1936	Ken Carpenter, United States	165ft. 7 3-8 in.
1948	Adolfo Consolini, Italy	173ft. 2 in.
1952	Sim Iness, United States	180ft. 6.85 in.
1956	Al Oerter, United States	184ft. 11 in.

1960	Al Oerter, United States	194ft. 2 in.
1964	Al Oerter, United States	200ft. 1 1-2 in.
1968	Al Oerter, United States	212ft. 6 1-2 in.*
1972	Ludvik Danek, Czech.	211ft. 3 1-2 in.

Standing Hop, Step and Jump

| 1900 | Ray Ewry, United States | 34ft. 8 1-2 in.* |
| 1904 | Ray Ewry, United States | 34ft. 7 1-4 in. |

Triple Jump

1896	James Connolly, United States	45 ft.
1900	Myer Prinstein, United States	47ft. 4 1-4 in.
1904	Myer Prinstein, United States	47 ft.
1906	P. G. O'Connor, Ireland	46ft. 2 in.
1908	Timothy Ahearne, Great Britain	48ft. 11 1-4 in.
1912	Gustaf Lindblom, Sweden	48ft. 5 1-8 in.
1920	Vilho Tuulos, Finland	47ft. 7 in.
1924	Archie Winter, Australia	50ft. 11 1-4in.
1928	Mikio Oda, Japan	49ft. 11 in.
1932	Chuhei Nambu, Japan	51ft. 7 in.
1936	Naoto Tajima, Japan	52ft. 5 7-8 in.
1948	Arne Ahman, Sweden	50ft. 6 1-4 in.
1952	Adhemar de Silva, Brazil	53ft. 2.59 in.
1956	Adhemar de Silva, Brazil	53ft. 7 1-2 in.
1960	Jozef Schmidt, Poland	55ft. 1 3-4 in.
1964	Jozef Schmidt, Poland	55ft. 3 1-2 in.
1968	Victor Saneyev, USSR	57ft. 3-4 in.*
1972	Victor Saneyev, USSR	56ft. 11 in.

16-Lb. Shot Put

1896	Robert Garrett, United States	36ft. 2 in.
1900	Robert Sheldon, United States	46ft. 3 1-8 in.
1904	Ralph Rose, United States	48ft. 7 in.
1906	Martin Sheridan, United States	40ft. 4.8 in.
1908	Ralph Rose, United States	46ft. 7 1-2 in.
1912	Pat McDonald, United States	50ft. 4 in.
	Both hands—Ralph Rose,	
	United States	90ft. 5 1-2 in.
1920	Ville Porhola, Finland	48ft. 7 1-8 in.
1924	Clarence Houser, United States	49ft. 2 3-8 in.
1928	John Kuck, United States	52ft. 3-4 in.
1932	Leo Sexton, United States	52ft. 6 3-16 in.
1936	Hans Woelke, Germany	53ft. 1 13-16 in.
1948	Wilbur Thompson, United States	56ft. 2 in.
1952	Parry O'Brien, United States	57ft. 1.43 in.
1956	Parry O'Brien, United States	60ft. 11 in.
1960	William Nieder, United States	64ft. 6 3-4 in.
1964	Dallas Long, United States	66ft. 8 1-2 in.
1968	Randy Matson, United States	67ft. 4 3-4 in.
1972	Wladyslaw Komar, Poland	69ft. 6 in.*

Discus Throw—Greek Style

| 1906 | Werner Jaevinen, Finland | 115ft. 4 in. |
| 1908 | Martin Sheridan, United States | 124ft. 8 in.* |

Javelin Throw

1906	Erik Lemming, Sweden	175ft. 6 in.
1908	Erik Lemming, Sweden	178ft. 7 1-2 in.
	Held in Middle—Erik Lemming,	
	Sweden	179ft. 10 1-2 in.
1912	Erik Lemming, Sweden	198ft. 11 1-4 in.
	Both hands, Julius Saaristo,	
	Finland	358ft. 11 7-8 in.
1920	Jonni Myyra, Finland	215ft. 9 3-4 in.
1924	Jonni Myyra, Finland	206ft. 6 3-4 in.
1928	Eric Lundquist, Sweden	218ft. 6 1-8 in.
1932	Matti Jarvinen, Finland	238ft. 7 in.
1936	Gerhard Stoeck, Germany	235ft. 8 5-16 in.
1948	Kaj T. Rautavaara, Finland	228ft. 10 1-2 in.
1952	Cy Young, United States	242ft. 0.79 in.
1956	Egil Danielsen, Norway	281ft. 2 1-4 in.
1960	Viktor Tsibulenko, USSR	277ft. 8 3-8 in.
1964	Pauli Nevala, Finland	271ft. 2 1-2 in.
1968	Yanis Lusis, USSR	295ft. 7 1-4 in.
1972	Klaus Wolferman, W. Germany	296ft. 10 in.*

Modern Pentathlon

1952	Lars Hall, Sweden	32 pts.
1956	Lars Hall, Sweden	4,843 pts.
1960	Ferenc Nemeth, Hungary	5,024 pts.
1964	Ferenc Torok, Hungary	5,116 pts.
1968	Bjoern Ferm, Sweden	4,964 pts.
1972	Andras Balczo, Hungary	5,412 pts.*

Decathlon

1912	Hugo Wieslander, Sweden	7,724.49 pts.
1920	Helge Loveland, Norway	6,804.35 pts.
1924	Harold Osborn, United States	7,710.775 pts.
1928	Paavo Yrjola, Finland	8,056.20 pts.
1932	James Bausch, United States	8,462.23 pts.
1936	Glenn Morris, United States	7,900 pts.
1948	Robert Mathias, United States	7,139 pts.
1952	Robert Mathias, United States	7,887 pts.
1956	Milton Campbell, United States	7,937 pts.
1960	Rafer Johnson, United States	8,392 pts.

1964 Willi Holdorf, Germany.....................7,887 pts.
1968 Bill Toomey, United States..................8,193 pts.
1972 Nikolai Avilov, USSR.......................8,454 pts.*
former point system, 1936-1960

Track and Field—Women

100 Meter Run
1928 Elizabeth Robinson, United States...........12.2s
1932 Stella Walsh, Poland.......................11.9s
1936 Helen Stephens, United States..............11.5s
1948 Francina Blankers-Koen, Netherlands........11.9s
1952 Marjorie Jackson, Australia................11.5s
1956 Betty Cuthbert, Australia..................11.5s
1960 Wilma Rudolph, United States...............11.0s*
1964 Wyomia Tyus, United States.................11.4s
1968 Wyomia Tyus, United States.................11.0s*
1972 Renate Stecher, E. Germany.................11.1s

200 Meter Run
1948 Francina Blankers-Koen, Netherlands........24.4s
1952 Marjorie Jackson, Australia................23.7s
1956 Betty Cuthbert, Australia..................23.4s
1960 Wilma Rudolph, United States...............24.0s
1964 Edith McGuire, United States...............23.0s
1968 Irene Szewinska, Poland....................22.5s
1972 Renate Stecher, E. Germany.................22.4s*

400 Meter Run
1964 Betty Cuthbert, Australia......................52s
1968 Colette Besson, France.........................52s
1972 Monika Zehrt, E. Germany......................51s*

800 Meter Run
1928 Linda Radke, Germany...................2m. 16.8s
1960 Ljudmila Shevcova, USSR.................2m. 4.3s
1964 Ann Packer, Great Britain...............2m. 1.1s
1968 Madeline Manning, United States........2m. 0.9s
1972 Hildegard Falck, W. Germany............1m. 58.6s*

1500 Meter Run
1972 Ludmila Bragina, USSR.....................4m. 1.4s*

400 Meter Relay
1928 Canada...48.4s
1932 United States..................................47.0s
1936 United States..................................46.9s
1948 Netherlands....................................47.5s
1952 United States..................................45.9s
1956 Australia......................................44.5s
1960 United States..................................44.5s
1964 Poland...43.6s
1968 United States..................................42.8s*
1972 West Germany...................................42.8s*

1600 Meter Relay
1972 East Germany...............................3m. 23s*

80 Meter Hurdles
1932 Mildred Didrikson, United States...........11.7s
1936 Trebisonda Villa, Italy....................11.7s
1948 Francina Blankers-Koen, Netherlands........11.2s
1952 Shirley Strickland de la Hunty, Australia..10.9s
1956 Shirley Strickland de la Hunty, Australia..10.7s

1960 Irina Press, USSR...........................10.8s
1964 Karin Balzer, Germany.......................10.5s
1968 Maureen Caird, Australia....................10.3s*

100 Meter Hurdles
1972 Annelie Ehrhardt, E. Germany...............12.6*

High Jump
1928 Ethel Catherwood, Canada................5ft. 3 in.
1932 Jean Shiley, United States.........5ft. 5 1-4 in.
1936 Ibolya Csak, Hungary....................5ft. 3 in.
1948 Alice Coachman, United States......5ft. 6 1-8 in.
1952 Esther Brand, South Africa........5ft. 5 3-4 in.
1956 Mildred L. McDaniel, United States.5ft. 9 1-4 in.
1960 Iolanda Balas, Romania...............6ft. 1-4 in.
1964 Iolanda Balas, Romania...........6ft. 2 7-8 in.*
1968 Miloslava Reskova, Czech........5ft. 11 3-4 in.
1972 Uirike Meyfarth, W. Germany......6ft. 2 3-4 in.

Discus Throw
1928 Helena Konopacka, Poland..........129ft. 11 7-8 in.
1932 Lillian Copeland, United States.......133ft. 2 in.
1936 Gisela Mauermayer, Germany......156ft. 3 3-16 in.
1948 Micheline Ostermeyer, France....137ft. 6 1-2 in.
1952 Nina Romaschkova, USSR..........168ft. 8 1-2 in.
1956 Olga Fikotova, Czechoslovakia...176ft. 1 1-2 in.
1960 Nina Ponomareva, USSR...........180ft. 8 1-4 in.
1964 Tamara Press, USSR.............187ft. 10 1-2 in.
1968 Lia Manolin, Romania...........191ft. 2 1-2 in.
1972 Faina Melnik, USSR................218ft. 7 in.*

Javelin Throw
1932 Mildred Didrikson, United States....143ft. 4 in.
1936 Tilly Fleischer, Germany.........148ft. 2 3-4 in.
1948 Herma Bauma, Austria..............149ft. 6 in.
1952 Dana Zatopekova, Czechoslovakia...165ft. 7 in.
1956 Inessa Janzeme, USSR..............176ft. 8 in.
1960 Elvira Ozolina, USSR..............183ft. 8 in.
1964 Mihaela Penes, Romania.........198ft. 7 1-2 in.
1968 Angela Nemeth, Hungary...........198ft. 1-2 in.
1972 Ruth Fuchs, E. Germany..........209ft. 7 in.*

Shot Put
1948 Micheline Ostermeyer, France.....45ft. 1 1-2 in.
1952 Galina Zybina, USSR..............50ft. 1 1-2 in.
1956 Tamara Tishkyevich, USSR...........54ft. 5 in.
1960 Tamara Press, USSR...............56ft. 9 7-8 in.
1964 Tamara Press, USSR...............59ft. 6 1-4 in.
1968 Margitta Gummel, E. Germany........64ft. 4 in.
1972 Nadezwda Chizhova, USSR..............69ft.*

Long Jump
1948 Olga Gyarmati, Hungary...........18ft. 8 1-4 in.
1952 Yvette Williams, New Zealand.....20ft. 5 3-4 in.
1956 E. Krzeskinska, Poland...........20ft. 9 3-4 in.
1960 Vyera Krepina, USSR.............20ft. 10 3-4 in.
1964 Mary Rand, Great Britain.........22ft. 2 1-4 in.
1968 V. Viscopoleanu, Romania........22ft. 4 1-2 in.*
1972 Heidemarie Rosendahl, W. Germany...22ft. 3 in.

Pentathlon
1964 Irina Press, USSR......................5,246 pts.
1968 Ingred Becker, W. Germany..............5,098 pts.
1972 Mary Peters, England...................4,801 pts.*

Swimming—Men

100 Meter Freestyle
1896 Alfred Hajos, Hungary.......................1:22.2
1904 Zoltan de Halomay, Hungary (100 yards).....1:02.8
1906 Charles Daniels, U.S........................1:13.0
1908 Charles Daniels, U.S........................1:05.6
1912 Duke P. Kahanamoku, U.S.....................1:03.4
1920 Duke P. Kahanamoku, U.S.....................1:01.4
1924 John Weissmuller, U.S........................59.0
1928 John Weissmuller, U.S........................58.6
1932 Yasuji Miyazaki, Japan.......................58.2
1936 Ferenc Csik, Hungary.........................57.6
1948 Wally Ris, U.S...............................57.3
1952 Clark Scholes, U.S...........................57.4
1956 Jon Henricks, Australia......................55.4
1960 John Devitt, Australia.......................55.2
1964 Don Schollander, U.S.........................53.4
1968 Mike Wenden, Australia.......................52.2
1972 Mark Spitz, U.S.............................51.2*

200 Meter Freestyle
1968 Mike Wenden, Australia......................1:55.2
1972 Mark Spitz, U.S............................1:52.8*

400 Meter Freestyle
1904 C. M. Daniels, U.S. (440 yards)............6:16.2
1906 Otto Sheff, Austria........................6:23.8
1908 Henry Taylor, Great Britain................5:36.8
1912 George Hodgson, Canada.....................5:24.4
1920 Norman Ross, U.S...........................5:26.8
1924 John Weissmuller, U.S......................5:04.2
1928 Albert Zorilla, Argentina..................5:01.6
1932 Clarence Crabbe, U.S.......................4:48.4
1936 Jack Medica, U.S...........................4:44.5
1948 William Smith, U.S.........................4:41.0
1952 Jean Boiteux, France.......................4:30.7
1956 Murray Rose, Australia.....................4:27.3
1960 Murray Rose, Australia.....................4:18.3
1964 Don Schollander, U.S.......................4:12.2
1968 Mike Burton, U.S...........................4:09.0
1972 Brad Cooper, Australia....................4:00.3*

1,500 Meter Freestyle
1908 Henry Taylor, Great Britain...............22:48.4
1912 George Hodgson, Canada....................22:00.0
1920 Norman Ross, U.S..........................23:23.2
1924 Andrew Charlton, Australia................20:06.6
1928 Arne Borg, Sweden.........................19:51.8
1932 Kasuo Kitamura, Japan.....................19:12.4
1936 Noboru Terada, Japan......................19:13.7
1948 J. P. McClane, U.S........................19:18.5
1952 Ford Konno, U.S...........................18:30.0
1956 Murray Rose, Australia....................17:58.9
1960 Jon Konrads, Australia....................17:19.6
1964 Robert Windle, Australia..................17:01.7
1968 Mike Burton, U.S..........................16:38.9
1972 Mike Burton, U.S.........................15:52.6*

400 Meter Medley Relay
1960	United States	4:05.4
1964	United States	3:58.4
1968	United States	3:54.9
1972	United States	3:48.2*

400 Meter Freestyle Relay
1964	United States	3:33.2
1968	United States	3:31.7
1972	United States	3:26.4*

800 Meter Freestyle Relay
1908	Great Britain	10:55.6
1912	Australia	10:11.6
1920	United States	10:04.4
1924	United States	9:53.4
1928	United States	9:36.2
1932	Japan	8:58.4
1936	Japan	8:51.5
1948	United States	8:46.0
1952	United States	8:31.1
1956	Australia	8:23.6
1960	United States	8:10.2
1964	United States	7:52.1
1968	United States	7:52.3
1972	United States	7:38.8*

100 Meter Backstroke
1904	Walter Brack, Germany (100 yds.)	1:16.8
1908	Arno Bieberstein, Germany	1:24.6
1912	Harry Hebner, U.S.	1:21.2
1920	Warren Kealoha, U.S.	1:15.2
1924	Warren Kealoha, U.S.	1:13.2
1928	George Kojac, U.S.	1:08.2
1932	Masaji Kiyokawa, Japan	1:08.6
1936	Adolph Kiefer, U.S.	1:05.9
1948	Allen Stack, U.S.	1:06.4
1952	Yoshi Oyokawa, U.S.	1:05.4
1956	David Thiele, Australia	1:02.2
1960	David Thiele, Australia	1:01.9
1968	Roland Matthes, E. Germany	58.7
1972	Roland Matthes, E. Germany	56.6*

200 Meter Backstroke
1964	Jed Graef, U.S.	2:10.3
1968	Roland Matthes, E. Germany	2:09.6
1972	Roland Matthes, E. Germany	2:02.8*

100 Meter Breaststroke
1968	Don McKenzie, U.S.	1:07.7
1972	Nobutaka Taguchi, Japan	1:04.9*

200 Meter Breaststroke
1908	Frederick Holman, Great Britain	3:09.2
1912	Walter Bathe, Germany	3:01.8
1920	Haken Malmroth, Sweden	3:04.4
1924	Robert Skelton, U.S.	2:56.6
1928	Yoshiyuki Tsuruta, Japan	2:48.8
1932	Yoshiyuki Tsuruta, Japan	2:45.4
1936	Tetsuo Hamuro, Japan	2:42.5
1948	Joseph Verdeur, U.S.	2:39.3
1952	John Davies, Australia	2:34.4
1956	Masura Furukawa, Japan	2:34.7
1960	William Mulliken, U.S.	2:37.4
1964	Ian O'Brien, Australia	2:27.8
1968	Felipe Munoz, Mexico	2:28.7
1972	John Hencken, U.S.	2:21.5*

100 Meter Butterfly
1968	Doug Russell, U.S.	55.9
1972	Mark Spitz, U.S.	54.3*

200 Meter Butterfly
1956	William Yorzyk, U.S.	2:18.6
1960	Michael Troy, U.S.	2:12.8
1964	Kevin J. Berry, Australia	2:06.6
1968	Carl Robie, U.S.	2:08.7
1972	Mark Spitz, U.S.	2:00.7*

200 Meter Individual Medley
1968	Charles Hickcox, U.S.	2:12.0
1972	Gunnar Larsson, Sweden	2:07.2*

400 Meter Individual Medley
1964	Dick Roth, U.S.A.	4:45.4
1968	Charles Hickcox, U.S.A.	4:48.4
1972	Gunnar Larsson, Sweden	4:32*

Springboard Diving
		Points
1904	Dr. G. E. Sheldon, U.S.	12 2-3
1906	Gottlob Walz, Germany	

1908	Albert Zuerner, Germany	85.5
1912	Paul Guenther, Germany	6
1920	Louis Kuehn, U.S.	6
1924	Albert White, U.S.	7
1928	Pete Desjardins, U.S.	185.04
1932	Michael Gallitzen, U.S.	161.38
1936	Richard Degener, U.S.	161.57
1948	Bruce Harlan, U.S.	163.64
1952	David Browning, U.S.	205.29
1956	Robert Clothworthy, U.S.	159.56
1960	Gary Tobian, U.S.	170.00
1964	Kenneth Sitzberger, U.S.	159.90
1968	Bernie Wrightson, U.S.	170.15
1972	Vladimir Vasin, USSR.	594.09

Platform Diving
1928	Pete Desjardins, U.S.	98.74
1932	Harold Smith, U.S.	124.80
1936	Marshall Wayne, U.S.	113.58
1948	Sammy Lee, U.S.	130.05
1952	Sammy Lee, U.S.	156.28
1956	Joaquin Capilla, Mexico	152.44
1960	Robert Webster, U.S.	165.56
1964	Robert Webster, U.S.	148.58
1968	Klaus Dibiasi, Italy	164.18
1972	Klaus Dibiasi, Italy	504.12

Water Polo
1900	Great Britain		1936	Hungary
1904	United States		1948	Italy
1908	Great Britain		1952	Hungary
1912	Great Britain		1956	Hungary
1920	Great Britain		1960	Italy
1924	France		1964	Hungary
1928	Germany		1968	Yugoslavia
1932	Hungary		1972	USSR

Swimming—Women
100 Meter Freestyle
1912	Fanny Durack, Australia	1:22.2
1920	Ethelda Bleibtrey, U.S.	1:13.6
1924	Ethel Lackie, U.S.	1:12.4
1928	Albina Osipowich, U.S.	1:11.0
1932	Helene Madison, U.S.	1:06.8
1936	Hendrika Mastenbroek, Holland	1:05.9
1948	G. M. Anderson, Denmark	1:06.3
1952	Katalin Szoke, Hungary	1:06.3
1956	Dawn Fraser, Australia	1:02.0
1960	Dawn Fraser, Australia	1:01.2
1964	Dawn Fraser, Australia	59.5
1968	Jan Henne, U.S.	1:00.0
1972	Sandra Neilson, U.S.	58.6*

200 Meter Freestyle
1968	Debbie Meyer, U.S.	2:10.5
1972	Shane Gould, Australia	2:03.6*

400 Meter Freestyle
1924	Martha Norelius, U.S.	6:02.2
1928	Martha Norelius, U.S.	5:42.8
1932	Helene Madison, U.S.	5:28.5
1936	Hendrika Mastenbroek, Holland	5:26.4
1948	Ann Curtis, U.S.	5:17.8
1952	Valerie Gyenge, Hungary	5:12.1
1956	Lorraine Crapp, Australia	4:54.6
1960	Chris von Saltza, U.S.	4:50.6
1964	Virginia Duenkel, U.S.	4:43.3
1968	Debbie Meyer, U.S.	4:31.8
1972	Shane Gould, Australia	4:19.0*

800 Meter Freestyle
1968	Debbie Meyer, U.S.	9:24.0
1972	Keena Rothhammer, U.S.	8:53.7*

400 Meter Medley Relay
1960	United States	4:41.1
1964	United States	4:33.9
1968	United States	4:28.3
1972	United States	4:20.7*

400 Meter Freestyle Relay
1912	Great Britain	5:52.8
1920	United States	5:11.6
1924	United States	4:58.8
1928	United States	4:47.6
1932	United States	4:38.0
1936	Holland	4:36.0
1948	United States	4:29.2

1952	Hungary	4:24.4
1956	Australia	4:17.1
1960	United States	4:08.9
1964	United States	4:03.8
1968	United States	4:02.5
1972	United States	3:55.2*

100 Meter Backstroke

1924	Sybil Bauer, U.S.	1:23.3
1928	Marie Braun, Holland	1:22.0
1932	Eleanor Holm, U.S.	1:19.4
1936	Dina Senff, Holland	1:18.9
1948	Karen Harup, Denmark	1:14.4
1952	Joan Harrison, South Africa	1:14.3
1956	Judy Grinham, Great Britain	1:12.9
1960	Lynn Burke, U.S.	1:09.3
1964	Cathy Ferguson, U.S.	1:07.7
1968	Kaye Hall	1:06.2
1972	Melissa Belote	1:05.8*

200 Meter Backstroke

1968	Pokey Watson, U.S.	2:24.8
1972	Melissa Belote, U.S.	2:19.2*

100 Meter Breaststroke

1968	Djurdjica Bjedov, Yugoslavia	1:15.8
1972	Cathy Carr, U.S.	1:13.6*

200 Meter Breaststroke

1924	Lucy Morton, Great Britain	3:32.2
1928	Hilde Schrader, Germany	3:12.6
1932	Clare Dennis, Australia	3:06.3
1936	Hideko Maehata, Japan	3:03.6
1948	Nelly Van Vliet, Holland	2:57.2
1952	Eva Szekely, Hungary	2:51.7
1956	Ursula Happe, Germany	2:53.1
1960	Anita Lonsbrough, Great Britain	2:49.5
1964	Galina Prozumenschikova, USSR	2:46.4
1968	Sharon Wichman, U.S.	2:44.4
1972	Beverly Whitfield, Australia	2:41.7*

200 Meter Medley

1968	Claudia Kolb, U.S.	2:24.7
1972	Shane Gould, Australia	2:23.1*

400 Meter Medley

1964	Donna De Varona, U.S.	5:18.7
1968	Claudia Kolb, U.S.	5:08.5
1972	Gail Neall, Australia	5:03.0*

100 Meter Butterfly

1956	Shelley Mann, U.S.	1:11.0
1960	Carolyn Schuler, U.S.	1:09.5
1964	Sharon Stouder, U.S.	1:04.7
1968	Lynn McClements, Australia	1:05.5
1972	Mayumi Aoki, Japan	1:03.3*

200 Meter Butterfly

1968	Ada Kok, Netherlands	2:24.7
1972	Karen Moe, U.S.	2:15.6*

Springboard Diving

		Points
1920	Aileen Riggin, U.S.	9
1924	Elizabeth Becker, U.S.	8
1928	Helen Meany, U.S.	78.62
1932	Georgia Coleman, U.S.	87.52
1936	Marjorie Gestring, U.S.	89.27
1948	Victoria M. Draves, U.S.	108.74
1952	Mrs. Patricia McCormick, U.S.	147.30
1956	Patricia McCormick, U.S.	142.36
1960	Ingrid Kramer, Germany	155.81
1964	Ingrid Engel-Kramer, Germany	145.00
1968	Sue Gossick, U.S.	150.77
1972	Micki King, U.S.	450.03

Platform Diving

		Points
1928	Elizabeth B. Pinkston, U.S.	31.60
1932	Dorothy Poynton, U.S.	40.26
1936	Mrs. Dorothy Poynton Hill, U.S.	33.93
1948	Victoria M. Draves, U.S.	68.87
1952	Mrs. Patricia McCormick, U.S.	79.37
1956	Mrs. Patricia McCormick, U.S.	84.85
1960	Ingrid Kramer, Germany	91.28
1964	Lesley Bush, U.S.	99.80
1968	Milena Duchkova, Czech	109.59
1972	Ulrika Knape, Sweden	390.00

Leading Olympic Game Medal Winners, 1896-1972

Nation	Gold	Silver	Bronze	Total
United States	583	412(a)	373	1368
Soviet Union	211	182	170	563
Great Britain	143	194	157	494
Sweden	123	124	156	403
Germany(b)	108	150	135	393
France	121	124	129	374
Italy	116	98	98	312
Hungary	102	90	105	297
Finland	83	70	97	250
Japan	65	60	51	176
Australia	63	52	61	176
Switzerland	37	53	48	138
The Netherlands	41	44	47	132
Denmark	28	48	48	124
Poland	30	33	60	123
Czechoslovakia	38	41	32	111
Canada	23	39	49	111
Norway	39	29	30	98
Greece	21	40	33	94
East Germany(b)	29	32	30	91
Belgium	20	37	30	87
Romania	18	22	32	72
Austria	15	23	30	68
West Germany(b)	18	21	26	65
South Africa	16	15	22	53
Bulgaria	13	25	15	53
Argentina	13	19	13	45
Turkey	23	12	7	42
Yugoslavia	12	15	9	36
Cuba	9	11	7	27
Iran	4	10	13	27
Mexico	6	9	10	25
New Zealand	12	2	10	24

(a) Refused Basketball Medal in 1972.
(b) East and West began competing separately in 1968

Winter Olympic Games Champions, 1924-1972

Sites and Unofficial Winners of Games

1924—Chamonix, France (Norway)
1928—St. Moritz, Switzerland (Norway)
1932—Lake Placid, N.Y. (U.S.)
1936—Garmisch-Partenkirchen (Norway)

1948—St. Moritz (Sweden)
1952—Olso, Norway (Norway)
1956—Cortina d'Ampezzo, Italy (USSR)
1960—Squaw Valley, Calif. (USSR)

1964—Innsbruck, Austria (USSR)
1968—Grenoble, France (Norway)
1972—Sapporo, Japan (USSR)
1976—Innsbruck, Austria, Feb. 4-15

Biathlon

	Time
1960—Klas Lestander, Sweden	1:33:21.6
1964—Vladimir Melanin, USSR	1:20:26.8
1968—Magnar Solberg, Norway	1:13:45.9
1972—Magnar Solberg, Norway	1:15:55.5

Biathlon Relay

	Time
1968—USSR, Norway, Sweden	2:13.02
1972—USSR, Finland, E. Germany	1:51.44

Bobsledding

4-Man Bob

(Driver in parentheses)

	Time
1924—Switzerland (Edward Scherrer)	5:45.54
*1928—United States (William Fiske)	3:20.5
1932—United States (Willaim Fiske)	7:53.68
1936—Switzerland (Pierre Musy)	5:19.85
1948—United States (Edward Rimkus)	5:20.1
1952—Germany (Andreas Ostler)	5:07.84
1956—Switzerland (Frank Kapus)	5:10.44
1964—Canada (Victor Emery)	4:14.46
1968—Italy (Eugenio Monti)	2:17.39
1972—Switzerland (Jean Wicki)	4:43.07

*Five-man bobsled

2-Man Bob

	Time
1932—U.S.A. (Hubert Stevens)	8:14.74
1936—U.S.A. (Ivan Brown)	5:29.29
1948—Switzerland (F. Endrich)	5:29.2
1952—Germany (Andreas Ostler)	5:24.54
1956—Italy (Dalla Costa)	5:30.14
1942—Great Britain (Antony Nash)	4:21.90
1968—Italy (Eugenio Monti)	4:41.54
1972—W. Germany (Wolfgang Zimmerer)	4:47.07

Figure Skating

Men's Singles

1908	Ulrich Sachow, Sweden
1920	Gillis Grafstrom, Sweden
1924	Gillis Grafstrom, Sweden
1928	Gillis Grafstrom, Sweden
1932	Karl Schaefer, Austria
1936	Karl Schaefer, Austria
1948	Richard T. Button, U.S.A.
1952	Richard T. Button, U.S.A.
1956	Hayes Alan Jenkins, U.S.A.
1960	David W. Jenkins, U.S.A.
1964	Manfred Schnelldorfer, Germany
1968	Wolfgang Schwartz, Austria
1972	Ondrej Nepela, Czechoslovakia

Women's Singles

1908	Madge Syers, Great Britain
1920	Magda Julin-Mauroy, Sweden
1924	Mrs. Heima von Szabo-Planck, Austria
1928	Sonja Henie, Norway
1932	Sonja Henie, Norway
1936	Sonja Henie, Norway
1948	Barbara Ann Scott, Canada
1952	Jeanette Altwegg, Great Britain
1956	Tenley E. Albright, U.S.A.
1960	Carol Heiss, U.S.A.
1964	Sjoukje Dijkstra, Holland
1968	Peggy Fleming, U.S.A.
1972	Beatrix Schuba, Austria

Pairs

1908	Anna Hubler & Heinrich Burger, Germany
1920	Ludovika & Walter Jakobsson, Finland
1924	Helene Engelman & Alfred Berger, Austria
1928	Andree Joly & Pierre Brunet, France
1932	Andree Joly & Pierre Brunet, France
1936	Maxie Herber & Ernest Baier, Germany
1952	Micheline Lannoy & Pierre Baugniet, Belgium
1952	Ria and Paul Falk, Germany
1956	Elizabeth Schwarz & Kurt Oppelt, Austria
1960	Barbara Wagner & Robert Paul, Canada
1964	Ludmila Beloussova & Oleg Protopopov, USSR
1968	Ludmila Beloussova & Oleg Protopopov, USSR
1972	Irina Rodnina & Alexei Ulanov, USSR

Alpine Skiing

Men's Downhill

	Time
1948—Henri Creiller, France	2:55.0
1952—Zeno Colo, Italy	2:30.8
1956—Anton Sailer, Austria	2:52.2
1960—Jean Vuarmet, France	2:06.0
1964—Egon Zimmermann, Austria	2:18.1
1968—Jean Claude Killy, France	1:59.85
1972—Bernhard Russi, Switzerland	1:51.43

Men's Giant Slalom

	Time
1952—Stein Eriksen, Norway	3:25.0
1956—Anton Sailer, Austria	3:00.1
1960—Roger Staub, Switzerland	1:48.3
1964—Francois Bonlieu, France	1:46.7
1968—Jean Claude Killy, France	3:29.28
1972—Gustavo Thoeni, Italy	3:09.62

Men's Slalom

	Time
1948—Edi Reinalter, Switzerland	2:10.3
1952—Othmar Schneider, Austria	2:00.0
1956—Anton Sailer, Austria	194.7 pts.
1960—Ernst Hinterseer, Austria	2:08.9
1964—Josef Stiegler, Austria	2:11.13
1968—Jean Claude Killy, France	1:39.73
1972—Francisco Fernandez Ochoa, Spain	1:09.27

Women's Downhill

	Time
1948—Hedi Schlunegger, Switzerland	2:28.3
1952—Trude Jochum-Beiser, Austria	1:47.1
1956—Madeline Bethod, Switzerland	1:40.7
1960—Heidi Biebl, Germany	1:37.6
1964—Christl Haas, Austria	1:55.3
1968—Olga Pall, Austria	1:40.87
1972—Marie Therese Nadig, Switzerland	1:36.68

Women's Giant Slalom

	Time
1952—Andrea Mead Lawrence, U.S.A.	2:06.8
1956—Ossi Reichert, Germany	1:56.5
1960—Yvonne Ruegg, Switzerland	1:39.9
1964—Marielle Goitschel, France	1:52.2
1968—Nancy Greene, Canada	1:51.97
1972—Marie Therese Nadig, Switzerland	1:29.90

Women's Slalom

	Time
1948—Gretchen Fraser, U.S.A.	1:57.2
1952—Andrea Mead Lawrence, U.S.A.	2:10.6
1956—Renee Colliard, Switzerland	112.3 pts.
1960—Anne Heggtveigt, Canada	1:49.6
1964—Christine Goitschel, France	1:35.11
1968—Marielle Goitschel, France	1:25.86
1972—Barbara Cochran, United States	91.24

Nordic Skiing

Men's Cross-Country Events
15 Kilometers (9.3 miles) or Equivalent

	Time
1924—Thorleif Haug, Norway	1:14:31
1928—Johan Grottumsbraaten, Norway	1:37:01
1932—Sven Utterstrom, Sweden	1:23:07
1936—Erik-August Larsson, Sweden	1:14:38
1948—Martin Lundstrom, Sweden	1:13:50
1956—Hallgeir Brenden, Norway	49:39.0
1960—Haakon Brusveen, Norway	51:55.0
1960—Haakon Brusveen, Norway	51:55.0
1964—Eero Mantyranta, Finland	50:54.1
1968—Harald Groenningen, Norway	47.54.2
1972—Sven-Ake Lundback, Sweden	45:28.2

(Note: Approx. 18-kilo course 1924-1952)

30 Kilometers (18.6 miles)

	Time
1956—Veikko Hakulinen, Finland	1:44:06.0
1960—Sixten Jernberg, Sweden	1:51:03.9
1964—Eero Mantyranta, Finland	1:30:50.7
1968—Franco Nones, Italy	1:35:39.2
1972—Vyacheslav Vedenin, USSR	1:36:31.1

50 Kilometers (31 miles)

	Time
1924—Thorleif Haug, Norway	3:44:32.0
1928—Per Erik Hedlund, Sweden	4:52:03.0

1932	Veli Saarinen, Finland	4:28.00.0
1936	Elis Viklund, Sweden	3:30:11.0
1948	Nils Karlsson, Sweden	3:47:48.0
1952	Veikko Hakulinen, Finland	3:33:33.0
1956	Sixten Jernberg, Sweden	2:50:27.0
1960	Kaleiv Hamalainen, Finland	2:59:06.3
1964	Sixten Jernberg, Sweden	2:43:52.6
1968	Ole Ellefsaeter, Norway	2:28:45.8
1972	Paal Tyldum, Norway	2:43:14.7

40 Kilometer Cross-Country Relay

		Time
1936	Finland, Norway, Sweden	2:41:33.0
1948	Sweden, Finland, Norway	2:32:08.0
1952	Finland, Norway, Sweden	2:20:16.0
1956	USSR, Finland, Sweden	2:15:30.0
1960	Finland, Norway, USSR	2:18:45.6
1964	Sweden, Finland, USSR	2:18:34.6
1968	Norway, Sweden, Finland	2:08:33.5
1972	USSR, Norway, Switzerland	2:04:47.9

15 Km. Cross-Country & Jumping

		Points
1924	Thorleif Haug, Norway	453.800
1928	Johan Grottumsbraaten, Norway	427.800
1932	Johan Grottumsbraaten, Norway	446.200
1936	Oddbjorn Hagen, Norway	430.300
1948	Heikki Hasu, Finland	448.800
1952	Simon Slattvik, Norway	451.621
1956	Sverre Stenersen, Norway	455.000
1960	Gerog Thoma, Germany	457.952
1964	Tormod Knutsen, Norway	469.280
1968	Franz Keller, W. Germany	449.04
1972	Ulrich Wehling, E. Germany	413.340

Ski Jumping (90 Meters)

		Points
1924	Jacob T. Thams, Norway	227.5
1928	Alfred Andersen, Norway	230.5
1932	Birger Ruud, Norway	228.0
1936	Birger Ruud, Norway	232.0
1948	Petter Hugsted, Norway	228.1
1952	A. Bergmann, Norway	226.0
1956	Antti Hyvarinen, Finland	227.0
1960	Helmut Recknagel, Germany	227.2
1964	Toralf Engan, Norway	230.7
1968	Vladimir Beloussov, USSR	231.3
1972	Wojiech Fortuna, Poland	219.9

Ski Jumping (70 Meters)

		Points
1964	Veikko Kankkonen, Finland	229.9
1968	Jiri Raska, Czech	216.5
1972	Yukio Kasaya, Japan	244.2

Women's Events
5 Kilometers (approx. 3.1 miles)

		Time
1964	Claudia Boyarskikh, USSR	17:50.5
1968	Toini Gustafsson, Sweden	16:45.2
1972	Galina Koulacova, USSR	17:00.5

10 Kilometers (6.2 miles)

		Time
1952	Lydia Wideman, Finland	41:40.0
1956	Lyubob Kosyreva, USSR	38:11.0
1960	Maria Gusakova, USSR	39:46.6
1964	Claudia Boyarskikh, USSR	40:24.3
1968	Toini Gustafsson, Sweden	36:46.5
1972	Galina Koulacova, USSR	34:17.8

15 Kilometer Cross-Country Relay

		Time
1956	Finland, USSR, Sweden	1:09:01.0
1960	Sweden, USSR, Finland	1:04:21.4
1964	USSR, Sweden, Finland	59:20.2
1968	Norway, Sweden, USSR	57:30
1972	USSR, Finland, Norway	48:46.1

Ice Hockey
(Three medal winners, in order)

1920	Canada, U.S.A. Czechoslovakia
1924	Canada, U.S.A., Great Britain
1928	Canada, Sweden, Switzerland
1932	Canada, U.S.A., Germany
1936	Great Britain, Canada, U.S.A.
1948	Canada, Czechoslovakia, Switzerland
1952	Canada, U.S.A., Sweden
1956	USSR, U.S.A., Canada
1960	U.S.A. Canada, USSR
1964	USSR. Sweden, Czechoslovakia
1968	USSR, Czechoslovakia, Canada
1972	USSR, U.S.A., Czechoslovakia

Luge
Men's Singles

		Time
1964	Thomas Kohler, Germany	3:25.77
1968	Manfred Schmid, Austria	2:52.48
1972	Wolfgang Scheidel, E. Germany	3:27.58

Men's Doubles

		Time
1964	Austria	1:41.62
1968	East Germany	1:35.85
1972	Italy, E. Germany (tie)	1:28.35

Women's Singles

		Time
1964	Ortun Enderlein, Germany	3:24.67
1968	Erica Lechner, Italy	2:28.66
1972	Anna M. Muller, E. Germany	2:59.18

Speed Skating
Men's Events
500 Meters

		Time
1924	Charles Jewtraw, U.S.A.	0:44.0
1928	Clas Thunberg, Finland &	
	Bernt Evensen, Norway (tie)	0:43.4
1932	John A. Shea, U.S.A.	0:43.4
1936	Ivar Ballangrud, Norway	0:43.4
1948	Finn Helgesen, Norway	0:43.1
1952	Kenneth Henry, U.S.A.	0:43.2
1956	Evgeniy Grishin, USSR	0:40.2
1960	Evgeniy Grishin, USSR	0:40.2
1964	R. Terrence McDermott, U.S.A.	0:40.1
1968	Erhard Keller, W. Germany	0:40.3
1972	Erhard Keller, W. Germany	0:39.4

1,500 Meters

		Time
1924	Clas Thunberg, Finland	2:20.8
1928	Clas Thunberg, Finland	2:21.1
1932	John A. Shea, U.S.A.	2:57.2
1936	Charles Mathiesen, Norway	2:19.2
1948	Sverre Farstad, Norway	2:17.6
1952	Hjalmar Anderson, Norway	2:20.4
1956	Evgeniy Grishin, USSR	2:08.6
1960	Roald Edgar Aas, Norway &	
	Evgeniy Grishin, USSR (tie)	2:10.4
1964	Ants Anston, USSR	2:10.3
1968	Cornelis Verkerk, Holland	2:03.4
1972	Ard Schenk, Netherlands	2:02.9

5,000 Meters

		Time
1924	Clas Thunberg, Finland	8:39.0
1928	Ivar Ballangrud, Norway	8:50.5
1932	Irving Jaffee, U.S.A.	9:40.8
1936	Ivar Ballangrud, Norway	8:19.6
1948	Reidar Liakleb, Norway	8:29.4
1952	Hjalmar Anderson, Norway	8:10.6
1956	Boris Shilkov, USSR	7:48.7
1960	Viktor Kosichkin, USSR	7:51.3
1964	Knut Johannesen, Norway	7:38.4
1968	F. Anton Maier, Norway	7:22.4
1972	Ard Schenk, Netherlands	7:23.6

10,000 Meters

		Time
1924	Julius Skutnabb, Finland	18:04.8
1928	Event not held, thawing of ice	
1932	Irving Jaffee, U.S.A.	19:13.6
1936	Ivar Ballangrud, Norway	17:24.3
1948	Ake Seyffarth, Norway	17:26.3
1952	Hjalmar Anderson, Norway	16:45.8
1956	Sigvard Ericsson, Sweden	16:35.9
1960	Knut Johannesen, Norway	15:46.6
1964	Jonny Nilsson, Sweden	15:50.1
1968	Johnny Hoeglin, Sweden	15:23.6
1972	Ard Schenk, Netherlands	15:01.3

Women's Events
500 Meters

		Time
1960	Helga Haase, Germany	0:45.9
1964	Lydia Skoblikova, USSR	0:45.0
1968	Ludmila Titova, USSR	0:46.1
1972	Anne Henning, U.S.A.	0:43.3

1,000 Meters

		Time
1960	Klara Guseva, USSR	1:34.1
1964	Lydia Skoblikova, USSR	1:33.2
1968	Carolina Geijssen, Holland	1:32.6
1972	Monika Pflug, W. Germany	1:31.4

1,500 Meters

		Time
1960	Lydia Skoblikova, USSR	2:52.2
1964	Lydia Skoblikova, USSR	2:22.6
1968	Kaija Mustonen, Finland	2:22.4
1972	Dianne Holurn, USSR	2:20.8

3,000 Meters

		Time
1960	Lydia Skoblikova, USSR	5:14.3
1964	Lydia Skoblikova, USSR	5:14.9
1968	Johanna Schut, Holland	4:56.2
1972	Stien Kaiser Baas, Netherlands	4:52.1

World Record Fish Caught by Rod and Reel

Source: Salt-Water: International Game Fish Association. Fresh-Water: Field & Stream Magazine. Records confirmed to June, 1974.

Salt Water Fish

The International Game Fish Assn. revised its standards for world records, effective July 1, 1970. Line samples and line tests are now required in order for a world record application to be recognized. Records listed below are based on the new standards.

Species	Weight	Length	Girth	Where caught	Date	Angler
Albacore	74 lbs. 13 oz.	4'2"	34³/₄"	Arguineguin, Canary Islands	Oct. 28, 1973	Olof Idegren
Amberjack	149 lbs.	5'11"	41³/₄"	Bermuda	June 21, 1964	Peter Simons
Barracuda, Great	83 lbs.	6''/₄"	29"	Lagos, Nigeria	Jan. 13, 1952	K. J. W. Hackett
Bass, Giant Sea	563 lbs. 8 oz.	7'5"	72"	Anacapa Island, California	Aug. 20, 1968	James D. McAdam, Jr.
Bass, Cal. White sea	83 lbs. 12 oz.	5'5¹/₂"	34"	San Felipe, Mexico	Mar. 31, 1953	L. C. Baumgardener
Bass, Channel	90 lbs.	4'7¹/₂''	38¹/₄"	Rodanthe, N.C.	Nov. 7, 1973	Elvin Hooper
Bass, Sea	8 lbs.	1'10"	19"	Nantucket Sound, Mass.	May 13, 1951	H. R. Rider
Bass, Striped	72 lbs.	4'6¹/₂"	31"	Cuttyhunk, Mass.	Oct. 10, 1969	Edward J. Kirker
Blackfish (or Tautog)	21 lbs. 6 oz.	2'7¹/₂'	23¹/₂"	Cape May, N.J.	June 12, 1954	R. N. Sheafer
Bluefish	31 lbs. 12 oz.	3'11"	23"	Hatteras Inlet, North Carolina	Jan. 30, 1972	James M. Hussey
Bonefish	19 lbs.	3'3⁵/₈''	17"	Zululand, S. Africa	May 26, 1962	Brian W. Batchelor
Bonito, Oceanic	39 lbs. 15 oz.	3'3"	28"	Walker Cay, Bahamas	Jan. 21, 1952	F. Drowley
	40 lbs.	3'2³/₄"	27¹/₂"	Baie du Tambeau, Mauritius	Apr. 19, 1971	Joseph R. P. Caboche, Jr.
Cobia	110 lbs. 5 oz.	5'3"	34"	Mombasa, Kenya	Sept. 8, 1964	Eric Tinworth
Cod	98 lbs. 12 oz.	5'3"	41"	Isle of Shoals, Mass.	June 8, 1969	Alphonse Bielevich
Dolphin	85 lbs.	5'9"	37¹/₂"	Spanish Wells, Bahamas	May 29, 1968	Richard Seymour
Drum, Black	111 lbs.	4'5¹/₂"	45³/₄"	Cape Charles, Va.	May 20, 1973	Betty V. Hall
Flounder, Summer	30 lbs. 12 oz.	3'2¹/₂"	30¹/₂"	Vina del Mar, Chile	Nov. 1, 1971	Augusto Nunez Moreno
Jewfish	680 lbs.	7'1¹/₂"	66"	Fernandina Beach, Fla.	May 20, 1961	Lynn Joyner
Kingfish	78 lbs. 12 oz.	5'5¹/₂"	30"	La Romana, Dominican Republic	Nov. 26, 1971	Fernando Viyella
Marlin, Black	1,560 lbs.	14'6"	81"	Cabo Blanco, Peru	Aug. 4, 1953	A. C. Glassell, Jr.
Marlin, Blue	845 lbs.	13'1"	71"	St. Thomas, Virgin Islands	July 4, 1968	Elliot J. Fishman
Marlin, Pacific Blue	1,153 lbs.	14'8"	73"	Guam	Aug. 21, 1969	Greg Perez
Marlin, Striped	415 lbs.	11'	52"	Cape Brett, N.Z.	Mar. 31, 1964	B. C. Bain
Marlin, White	159 lbs. 8 oz.	9'	36"	Pompano Beach, Fla.	Apr. 25, 1953	W. E. Johnson
Permit	50 lbs. 8 oz.	3'8³/₄"	33³/₄"	Key West, Fla.	Mar. 5, 1971	Marshall Earnest
Pollack	43 lbs.	4'	29"	Brielle, N.J.	Oct. 21, 1964	Philip Barlow
Rainbow Runner	30 lbs. 15 oz.	3'11"	22"	Kauai, Hawaii	Apr. 27, 1963	Holbrook Goodale
Roosterfish	114 lbs.	5'4''	33''	La Paz, Mex.	June 1, 1960	Abe Sackheim
Sailfish, Atlantic	123 lbs.	10'4''	32³/₄''	Walker Cay, Bahamas	Apr. 25, 1950	H. Teetor
Sailfish, Pacific	221 lbs.	10'9''	....	Santa Cruz Is.	Feb. 12, 1947	C. W. Stewart
Shark Blue	410 lbs.	11'6''	52"	Rockport, Mass.	Sept. 1, 1960	R. C. Webster
	410 lbs.	11'2''	52¹/₂''	Rockport, Mass.	Aug. 17, 1967	Martha Webster
Shark, Mako	1,061 lbs.	12'2''	79¹/₂''	Mayor Island, N.Z.	Feb. 17, 1970	James Penwarden
Shark, Man-Eater or White	2,664 lbs.	16'10''	9'6''	Cedunea, So. Australia	Apr. 21, 1959	Alfred Dean
Shark, Porbeagle	430 lbs.	8'	63''	Channel Island, Eng.	June 29, 1969	Desmond Bougourd
Shark, Thresher	729 lbs.	8'5''	61''	Mayor Island, N.Z.	June 3, 1959	Mrs. V. Brown
Shark, Tiger	1,780 lbs.	13'10¹/₂''	103''	Cherry Grove, S. C.	June 14, 1964	Walter Maxwell
Snook, or Robalo	52 lbs. 6 oz.	4'1¹/₂''	26''	Lapaz, Mexico	Jan. 9, 1963	Jane Haywood
Swordfish	1,182 lbs.	14'11¹/₂''	78''	Iquique, Chile	May 7, 1953	L. Marron
Tanguigue	81 lbs.	5'11¹/₂''	29¹/₄''	Karachi, Pakistan	Aug. 27, 1960	George E. Rusinak
Tarpon	283 lbs.	7'2¹/₂''	....	L. Maracaibo, Venezuela	Mar. 19, 1956	M. Salazar
Tuna, Allison (Yellowfin)	308 lbs.	7'	5'7''	San Benedicto Isl., Mexico	Jan. 18, 1973	Harold J. Tolson
Tuna, Atlantic Big-Eyed	321 lbs. 12 oz.	7'4³/₄''	58¹/₄''	Hudson Canyon, N. Y.	Aug. 19, 1972	Vito LaCaputo
Tuna, Pacific Big-Eyed	435 lbs.	7'9''	63¹/₂''	Cabo Blanco, Peru	Apr. 17, 1957	Dr. Russel Lee

Species	Weight	Length	Girth	Where caught	Date	Angler
Tuna, Blackfin	38 lbs.	3'3¹/₄''	28³/₄''	Bermuda	June 26, 1970	Archie L. Dickens
	38 lbs.	3'5''	28''	Islamorada, Fla.	May 21, 1973	Elizabeth Jean Wade
Tuna, Bluefin	1,065 lbs.	10'3''	96''	Cape Breton, N.S.	Nov. 19, 1970	Robert G. Gibson
Wahoo	149 lbs.	6'7³/₄''	37¹/₂''	Cat Cay, Bahamas	June 15, 1962	John Pirovano
Weakfish	19 lbs. 8 oz.	3'1''	23³/₄''	Trinidad, W. Indies	Apr. 13, 1962	Dennis Hall
Weakfish, Spotted	15 lbs. 3 oz.	2'10¹/₂''	20¹/₂''	Fort Pierce, Fla.	Jan. 13, 1949	C. W. Hubbard
	15 lbs. 6 oz.	2'9''	23³/₄''	St. Lucie River, Fla.	May 4, 1969	Michael Foremny
Yellowtail	111 lbs.	5'2''	38''	Bay of Islands, New Zealand	June 11, 1961	A. F. Plim

Freshwater Fish

Species	Weight	Length	Girth	Where caught	Date	Angler
Bass, Largemouth	22 lbs. 4 oz.	32¹/₂''	28¹/₂''	Montgomery Lake, Ga.	June 2, 1932	George W. Perry
Bass, Smallmouth	11 lbs. 15 oz.	27''	21²/₃''	Dale Hollow Lake, Ky.	July 9, 1955	David L. Hayes
Bass, Redeye	6 lbs. ¹/₂ oz.	20¹/₂''	15⁴/₅''	Hallawakee Creek, Ala.	Mar. 24, 1967	Thomas Sharpe
Bass, Rock	2 lbs. 2 oz.	13''	14''	Mille Coquin Lake, Mich.	Aug. 13, 1971	Richard M. Barta
Bass, White	5 lbs. 5 oz.	19¹/₂''	17''	Ferguson Lake, Calif.	March 8, 1972	Norman W. Mize
Bass, Yellow	2 lbs. 2 oz.	14''	13''	Lake Monona, Wis.	Jan. 18, 1972	James Thrun
Black Bullhead	8 lbs.	24''	17³/₄''	Lake Waccabuc, N. Y.	Aug. 1, 1951	Kani Evans
Bass, Spotted	8 lbs. 10¹/₂ oz.	23¹/₂''	19⁷/₈''	Smith Lake, Ala.	Feb. 25, 1972	Billy Henderson
Bluegill	4 lbs. 12 oz.	15''	18¹/₄''	Ketona Lake, Ala.	Apr. 9, 1950	T. S. Hudson
Bowfin	19 lbs. 12 oz.	39''		Lake Marion, S. C.	Nov. 5, 1972	M. R. Webster
Buffalo, Bigmouth	36 lbs. 8 oz.	41¹/₂''	27''	Cedar River, Iowa	Sept. 19, 1973	Ella Mae Pidima
Buffalo, Smallmouth	22 lbs. ¹/₂ oz.	33¹/₂''	22¹/₂''	Barbwell Creek, Wis.	May 25, 1973	Greg Hougelin
Carp	55 lbs. 5 oz.	42''	31''	Clearwater Lake, Minn.	July 10, 1952	Frank J. Ledwein
Catfish, Blue	97 lbs.	57''	37''	Missouri River, S. D.	Sept. 16, 1959	E. B. Elliott
Catfish, Channel	58 lbs.	47¹/₂''	29¹/₈''	Santee-Cooper Res., S. C.	July 7, 1964	W. B. Whaley
Catfish, Flathead	76 lbs.	53''	32''	Piedmont Lake, Ohio	July 12, 1972	Dale C. Yoho
Char, Arctic	Record being reviewed.					
Crappie, Black	5 lbs.	19¹/₄''	18⁶/₈''	Santee-Cooper Res., S. C.	Mar. 15, 1957	Paul E. Foust
Crappie, White	5 lbs. 3 oz.	21''	19''	Enid Dam, Miss.	July 31, 1957	Fred L. Bright
Dolly Varden	32 lbs.	40¹/₂''	29¹/₄''	L. Pend Oreille, Idaho	Oct. 27, 1949	N. L. Higgins
Drum, Freshwater	54 lbs. 8 oz.	31¹/₂''	29''	Nickajack Lake, Tenn.	Apr. 20, 1972	Benny E. Hull
Gar, Alligator	279 lbs.	93''	....	Rio Grande R., Texas	Dec. 2, 1951	Bill Valverde
Gar, Longnose	50 lbs. 5 oz.	72¹/₄''	22¹/₄''	Trinity River, Texas	July 30, 1954	Townsend Miller
Grayling, Arctic	Record being reviewed.					
Muskellunge	69 lbs. 15 oz.	64¹/₂''	31³/₄''	St. Lawrence River, N. Y.	Sept. 22, 1957	Arthur Lawton
Perch, White	4 lbs. 12 oz.	19¹/₂''	13''	Messalonskee Lake, Maine	June 4, 1949	Mrs. Earl Small
Perch, Yellow	4 lbs. 3¹/₂ oz.	....	....	Bordentown, N. J.	May, 1865	Dr. C. C. Abbot
Pickerel, Chain	9 lbs. 6 oz.	31''	14''	Homerville, Ga.	Feb. 17, 1961	Baxley McQuaig, Jr.
Pike, Northern	46 lbs. 2 oz.	52¹/₂''	25''	Sacandaga Res., N. Y.	Sept. 15, 1940	Peter Dubuc
Salmon, Atlantic	79 lbs. 2 oz.	....	....	Tana River, Norway	1928	Henrik Henriksen
Salmon, Chinook	92 lbs.	58¹/₂''	36''	Skeena River, B. C.	July 19, 1959	Heinz Wichmann
Salmon, Silver	31 lbs.	....	....	Cowichan Bay, B. C.	Oct. 11, 1947	Mrs. Lee Hallberg
Salmon, Landlocked	22 lbs. 8 oz.	36''	est. 20''	Sebago Lake, Maine	Aug. 1, 1907	Edward Blakely
Sauger	8 lbs. 12 oz.	28''	15''	Lake Sakakawea, N. D.	Oct. 6, 1971	Mike Fischer
Shad, American	9 lbs. 2 oz.	25''	17¹/₂''	Enfield, Conn.	Apr. 28, 1973	Edward P. Nelson

Species	Weight	Length	Girth	Where caught	Date	Angler
Sturgeon, White	360 lbs.	111''	86''	Snake River, Idaho	April 24,1956	Willard Cravens
Sunfish, Green	2 lbs.	11¼''	12½''	Salem, Ill.	May 15,1972	Kenneth Collier, Sr.
Sunfish, Redear	4 lbs. 8 oz.	16¼''	17¾''	Chase City, Va.	June 19,1970	Maurice E. Ball
Trout, Brook	14½ lbs.	31½''	11½''	Nipigon River, Ontario	July, 1916	Dr. W. J. Cook
Trout, Brown	39½ lbs.	....	....	Lock Awe, Scotland	1866	W. Muir
Trout, Cutthroat	41 lbs.	39''	....	Pyramid Lake, Nev.	Dec., 1925	J. Skimmerhorn
Trout, Golden	11 lbs.	28''	16''	Cook's Lake, Wyo.	Aug. 5, 1948	Charles S. Reed
Trout, Lake	Record being reviewed.					
Trout, Rainbow Stlhd. or Kamloops	42 lbs. 2 oz.	43''	23½''	Bell Island, Alaska	June 22,1970	David Robert White
Trout, Sunapee	11 lbs. 8 oz.	33''	17¼''	Lake Sunapee, N. H.	Aug. 1,1954	Ernest Theoharis
Walleye	25 lbs.	41''	29''	Old Hickory Lake, Tenn.	Aug. 1,1960	Mabry Harper
Warmouth	1 lb. 13 oz.	10¾''	12¼''	Cumberland County, Ill.	May 22, 1971	Wesley Mills
Whitefish, Lake	12 lbs. 9 oz.	32''	17⅛''	Great Slave L., N. W. T.	July 28, 1972	Eddie Drygeese
Whitefish, Mountain	5 lbs.	19''	14''	Athabasca R., Alberta	June 3, 1963	Orville Welch

Westminster Kennel Club

Year	Best-in-show	Breed	Owner
1964	Ch. Courtenay's Fleetfoot	Whippet	Mrs. Margaret P. Newcombe
1965	Ch. Charmichael's Fanfare	Scottish terrier	Mr. and Mrs. Charles C. Stalter
1966	Ch. Zeloy Mooremaides Magic	Wire Fox terrier	Marion G. Bunker
1967	Ch. Bardene Bingo	Scottish terrier	E. H. Stuart
1968	Ch. Stingray of Derryabah	Lakeland terrier	Mr. and Mrs. James A. Farrell Jr.
1969	Ch. Glamoor Good News	Skye terrier	Walter & Mrs. Adele F. Goodman
1970	Ch. Arriba's Prima Donna	Boxer	Dr. & Mrs. P. J. Pagano & Dr. Theodore S. Fickles
1971	Ch. Chinoe's Adamant James	English springer spaniel	Dr. Milton Prickett
1972	Ch. Chinoe's Adamant James	English springer spaniel	Dr. Milton Prickett
1973	Ch. Acadia Command Performance	Poodle	Mrs. Jo Ann Sering & Edward B. Jenner
1974	Ch. Gretchenhof Columbia River	German pointer	Dr. Richard Smith

Leonard Brumby, Sr. Memorial Trophy

Junior Winner at Westminster Kennel Club

1964—Clare Hodge, Byrn Mawr, Pa. **Breed**—Whippet.

1965—Jennifer Sheldon, Massapequa, N. Y. **Breed**—Afghan.

1966—Laura Swyler, Commack, N.Y. **Breed**—Dox.

1967—David L. Brumbaugh, Perry, Ga. **Breed**—Min. Schnauzer.

1968—Cheryl Baker, Kennesaw, Ga. **Breed**—Beagle.

1969—Charles Garvin, Columbus, Ohio. **Breed**—Dalmatian.

1970—Pat Hardy, Cincinnati, Ohio. **Breed**—Golden Retriever.

1971—Heidi Shellenbarger, Costa Mesa, Calif. **Breed**—Whippet.

1972—Deborah Dagny Von Aherns, Edison Township, N. J. **Breed**—Afghan.

1973—Teresa Nail, Ft. Worth, Texas. **Breed**—Doberman Pinscher.

1974—Leslie Church, St. Louis, Mo. **Breed**—Min. Schnauzer.

James E. Sullivan Memorial Trophy Winners

The James E. Sullivan Memorial Trophy, named after the former president of the AAU and inaugurated in 1930, is awarded annually by the AAU to the athlete who "by his or her performance, example and influence as an amateur, has done the most during the year to advance the cause of sportsmanship."

Year	Winner	Sport	Year	Winner	Sport	Year	Winner	Sport
1930	Bobby Jones	Golf	1944	Ann Curtis	Swimming	1959	Parry O'Brien	Track
1931	Barney Berlinger	Track	1945	Doc Blanchard	Football	1960	Rafer Johnson	Track
1932	Jim Bausch	Track	1946	Arnold Tucker	Football	1961	Wilma Rudolph Ward	Track
1933	Glenn Cunningham	Track	1947	John Kelly, Jr.	Rowing	1962	James Beatty	Track
1934	Bill Bonthron	Track	1948	Robert Mathias	Track	1963	John Pennel	Track
1935	Lawson Little	Golf	1949	Dick Button	Skating	1964	Don Schollander	Swimming
1936	Glenn Morris	Track	1950	Fred Wilt	Track	1965	Bill Bradley	Basketball
1937	Don Budge	Tennis	1951	Rev. Robert Richards	Track	1966	Jim Ryun	Track
1938	Don Lash	Track	1952	Horace Ashenfelter	Track	1967	Randy Matson	Track
1939	Joe Burk	Rowing	1953	Dr. Sammy Lee	Diving	1968	Debbie Meyer	Swimming
1940	Greg Rice	Track	1954	Mal Whitfield	Track	1969	Bill Toomey	Track
1941	Leslie Mac Mitchell	Track	1955	Harrison Dillard	Track	1970	John Kinsella	Swimming
1942	Cornelius Warmerdam	Track	1956	Patricia McCormick	Diving	1971	Mark Spitz	Swimming
1943	Gilbert Dodds	Track	1957	Bobby Joe Morrow	Track	1972	Frank Shorter	Track
			1958	Glenn Davis	Track	1973	Bill Walton	Basketball

National Duckpin Bowling Champions, 1974

Men's Singles—Smith Green, Providence, R.I. 489

Women's Singles—Lori Cabral, Providence, R.I. 432

Men's Doubles—Bob Burchard-Bob Devine, Providence,R.I.

. . . . 925

Women's Doubles—Nancy Gawor-Jean Stewart, Baltimore. 844

Men's Team—Marchone's Italian Del., Washington, D.C. . . . 2093

Women's Team—Scallops, Washington, D.C. 1899

Men's All Events—Basil Boone, Annapolis, Md. 1337

Women's All Events—Phyllis Rapson, Manchester, Conn. . . 1239

Mixed Doubles—Anita Rothman-Bill Mueller, Baltimore, Md. 862

Badminton Championships in 1974

U. S. National Championship
Hayward, Cal., Apr. 12-15, 1974

Men's Singles—Chris Kinard, Pasadena, Calif. def. Charles Coakley, Costa Mesa, Calif., 15-12, 15-8.
Ladies' Singles—Cindy Baker, Salt Lake City, Utah def. Pam Bristol, Flint, Mich., 11-8, 11-8.
Men's Doubles—Don Paup, Washington, D.C. & Jim Poole, Northridge, Calif. def. Mike Adams, Flint, Mich. & Tom Carmichael, Clarkson, Mich., 15-5, 15-4.
Ladies' Doubles—Pam Bristol & Diane Hales, Claremont, Calif. def. Ethel Marshall, Buffalo & Dot O'Neil, Norwich, Conn., 15-9, 15-7.
Mixed Doubles—Mike Walker, Alhambra, Calif. & Judiann Kelly,

Norwalk, Conn. def. Charles Coakley & Carlene Starkey, San Diego, 15-3, 2-15, 15-9.
Senior Men—Jim Poole def. Tom Heden, Millwood, N.Y., 15-6, 15-1.
Senior Men's Doubles—Bill Goodman, Wellesley, Mass. & Jim Poole def. Jim Hodgkins & Fred Trifonoff, Huntington Beach, Calif., 15-5, 15-2.
Senior Ladies' Doubles—Ethel Marshall & Bea Massman, Buffalo def. Joyce Jones, Seattle & Gloria Eli, Flint, Mich., 15-6, 15-0.

All-England Championships
Wembley, Eng., Mar. 20-23, 1974

Men's Singles—Rudy Hartono, Indonesia def. Punch Gunalan, Malaysia, 8-15, 15-9, 15-10.
Ladies' Singles—Hiroe Yuki, Japan def. Gillian Gilks, England, 11-6, 12-11.
Men's Doubles—Tjun & J. Wahjudi, Indonesia def. Christian & Sumirat, Indonesia, 15-8, 15-6.

Ladies' Doubles—Margaret Beck & Gillian Gilks, England def. Margaret Boxall & Sue Whetnall, England, 15-5, 18-14.
Mixed Doubles—J. Eddy & Sue Whetnall, England def. Derek Talbot & Gillian Gilks, England, 15-5, 7-15, 15-10.

Canadian Championships
Winnipeg, Manitoba, Mar. 26-31, 1974

Men's Singles—Jamie Paulson, Ontario def. Jamie McKee, Ontario, 15-3, 15-5.
Ladies' Singles—Jane Youngberg, B. C. def. Judy Rollick, B, C., 11-2, 12-10.
Men's Doubles—Raphi Kanchanaraphi, Ontario & Channarong

Ratanasuengsuang, Alberta def. Yves Pare, Quebec & Jamie Paulson, 15-4, 15-11.
Ladies' Doubles—Jane Youngberg & Barbara Welch, Ontario def. Mimi Nilsson & Judy Rollick, 15-14, 10-15, 15-14.
Mixed Doubles—Rolf Paterson & Mimi Nilsson def. Raphi Kanchanaraphi & Barbara Welch, 15-9, 15-11.

U. S. National Junior Championships
Seattle, Wash., Mar. 20-23, 1974

Boy's Singles—Pat Tryon, Wilmington, Del. def. Richard Williams, Phoenix, 15-9, 8-15, 15-7.
Girl's Singles—Madalene Steinbroner, Manhattan Beach, Calif., def. Barbie Bell, Flint, Mich., 11-4, 11-2.
Boy's Doubles—Guy Rittman, Warwick, R. I. & Peter Cornell, Philadelphia def. Bob Gilmour & Mike Kelly, Manhattan Beach, Calif., 17-16, 15-8.

Girl's Doubles—Carrie Morrison, Pt. Angeles, Wash. & Madalene Steinbroner def. Denis Corlett & Karan Bushman, Manhattan Beach, Calif., 15-10, 15-1.
Mixed Doubles—Mike Kelly & Madalene Steinbroner, def. Matt Fogarty, Duxbury, Maine & Sheri Jones, Seattle, Wash., 15-3, 9-15, 15-5.

Rodeo Championship Standings 1973
Source: Rodeo Cowboys Assn., Inc.

Event	Winner	Money Won	Event	Winner	Money Won
All Around	Larry Mahan, Dallas, Texas	$64,447	Calf Roping	Ernie Taylor, Hugo, Oklahoma	$38,772
Saddle Bronc	Bill Smith, Cody, Wyoming	26,069	Steer Wrestling	Bob Marshall, San Martin, Calif.	31,817
Bareback	Joe Alexander, Cora, Wyoming	37,021	Team Roping	Leo Camarillo, Donald, Oregon	20,693
Bullriding	Bobby Steiner, Austin, Texas	28,099	Steer Roping	Roy Thompson, Tulia, Texas	6,259

Rodeo Cowboy All Around Champions

Year	Winner	Money Won	Year	Winner	Money Won
1960	Harry Tompkins, Dublin, Texas	$32,522	1967	Larry Mahan, Brooks, Oregon	$51,996
1961	Benny Reynolds, Melrose, Mont.	31,309	1968	Larry Mahan, Salem, Oregon	49,129
1962	Tom Nesmith, Bethel, Okla.	32,611	1969	Larry Mahan, Brooks, Oregon	57,726
1963	Dean Oliver, Boise, Idaho	31,329	1970	Larry Mahan, Brooks, Oregon	41,493
1964	Dean Oliver, Boise, Idaho	31,150	1971	Phil Lyne, George West, Texas	49,245
1965	Dean Oliver, Boise, Idaho	33,163	1972	Phil Lyne, George West, Texas	60,852
1966	Larry Mahan, Brooks, Oregon	40,358	1973	Larry Mahan, Dallas, Texas	64,447

World Pocket Billiards Champions

1931—Ralph Greenleaf	1944—Willie Mosconi	1963—Luther Lassiter
1932—Ralph Greenleaf	1945—Willie Mosconi	1964—Luther Lassiter, Arthur Cranfield
1933—Erwin Rudolph	1946—Irving Crane	1965—Joe Balsis
1934—Erwin Rudolph	1947—Willie Mosconi	1966—Luther Lassiter
1935—Andrew Ponzi	1948—Willie Mosconi	1967—Luther Lassiter
1936—James Caras	1949—James Caras	1968—Irving Crane
1937—Ralph Greenleaf	1950—Willie Mosconi	1969—Ed Kelly
1938—James Caras	1951—Willie Mosconi	1970—Irving Crane
1939—James Caras	1952—Willie Mosconi	1971—Ray Martin
1940—Andrew Ponzi	1953—Willie Mosconi	1972—Irving Crane
1941—Willie Mosconi, Erwin Rudolph	1954—none	1973—Lou Butera
1942—Irving Crane	1955—Irving Crane, Willie Mosconi	1974—Ray Martin
1943—Andrew Ponzi	1956-62—none	

National Basketball Association, 1973-74

Eastern Conference

Atlantic Division

Club	W.	L.	Pct.	G.B.
Boston Celtics	56	26	.683	—
New York Knickerbockers	49	33	.598	6½
Buffalo Braves	42	40	.512	14
Philadelphia 76's	24	58	.293	31½

Central Division

Club	W.	L.	Pct.	G.B.
Capital Bullets	46	35	.568	—
Atlanta Hawks	35	47	.427	11½
Houston Rockets	32	50	.390	14½
Cleveland Cavaliers	29	53	.354	17½

Western Conference

Midwest Division

Club	W.	L.	Pct.	G.B.
Milwaukee Bucks	59	23	.720	—
Chicago Bulls	54	28	.659	5
Detroit Pistons	53	29	.646	6
K. C. - Omaha Kings	33	49	.402	26

Pacific Division

Club	W.	L.	Pct.	G.B.
Los Angeles Lakers	47	35	.573	—
Golden State Warriors	44	38	.537	3
Seattle SuperSonics	37	45	.451	10
Phoenix Suns	30	52	.366	17
Portland Trail Blazers	27	55	.329	20

NBA Playoffs

Eastern Division—Boston defeated Buffalo 4 games to 2. New York defeated Capital 4 games to 3. Boston defeated New York 4 games to 1.

Western Division—Chicago defeated Detroit 4 games to 3. Milwaukee defeated Los Angeles 4 games to 1. Milwaukee defeated Chicago 4 games to 0.

Championship—Boston defeated Milwaukee 4 games to 3.

Final Statistics

Individual Scoring Leaders
(Minimum 65 Games Played)

	G.	FG.	FT.	Pts.	Avg.
McAdoo, Buffalo	74	901	459	2261	30.6
Maravich, Atlanta	76	819	469	2107	27.7
Jabbar, Milwaukee	81	948	295	2191	27.0
Hudson, Atlanta	65	678	295	1651	25.4
Goodrich, Los Ang.	82	784	508	2076	25.3
Barry, Golden State	80	796	417	2009	25.1
Tomjanovich, Hou.	80	788	385	1961	24.5
Petrie, Portland	73	740	291	1771	24.3
Haywood, Seattle	75	694	373	1761	23.5
Havlicek, Boston	76	685	346	1716	22.6
Lanier, Detroit	81	748	326	1822	22.5
Wicks, Portland	75	685	314	1684	22.5
Chenier, Capital	76	697	274	1668	21.9
Carr, Cleveland	81	748	279	1775	21.9
B. Love, Chicago	82	731	323	1765	21.8
Hayes, Capital	81	689	357	1735	21.4
Carter, Philadelphia	78	706	254	1666	21.4
Frazier, New York	80	674	295	1643	20.5
Russell, Golden St.	82	738	208	1684	20.5
Murphy, Houston	81	671	310	1652	20.4
T. VanArsdale, Phil.	78	614	298	1526	19.6

Field Goal Leaders
(Minimum 560 Attempts)

	FGM.	FGA.	Pct.
McAdoo, Buffalo	901	1647	.547
Jabbar, Milwaukee	948	1759	.539
Tomjanovich, Houston	788	1470	.536
Murphy, Houston	671	1285	.522
Beard, Golden State	316	617	.512
Ray, Chicago	313	612	.511
Nelson, Boston	364	717	.508
Hairston, Los Angeles	385	759	.507
Lanier, Detroit	748	1483	.504
Dandridge, Milwaukee	583	1158	.503

Free Throw Leaders
(Minimum 160 Attempts)

	FTM.	FTA.	Pct.
DiGregorio, Buffalo	174	193	.902
Barry, Golden State	417	464	.899
Mullins, Golden State	168	192	.875
C. Walker, Chicago	439	502	.875
Bradley, New York	146	167	.874
Murphy, Houston	310	357	.868
Snyder, Seattle	194	224	.866
Goodrich, Los Angeles	508	588	.864
F. Brown, Seattle	195	226	.863
McMillian, Buffalo	325	379	.858

Rebound Leaders
(Minimum 70 Games)

	G.	Off.	Def.	Tot.	Avg.
Hayes, Capital	81	334	1109	1463	18.1
Cowens, Boston	80	264	993	1257	15.7
McAdoo, Buffalo	74	281	836	1117	15.1
Jabbar, Milwaukee	81	287	891	1178	14.5
Thurmond, Gold St.	62	249	629	878	14.2
Hairston, Los Ang.	77	335	705	1040	13.5
Haywood, Seattle	75	318	689	1007	13.4
Lacey, KC-Omaha	79	293	762	1055	13.4
Lanier, Detroit	81	269	805	1074	13.3
Ray, Chicago	80	283	692	977	12.2
Heard, Buffalo	81	270	677	947	11.7
D. Smith, Houston	79	259	664	923	11.7

Blocked Shots
(Minimum 70 Games)

	G.	No.	Avg.
E. Smith, Los Angeles	81	393	4.85
Jabbar, Milwaukee	81	283	3.49
McAdoo, Buffalo	74	246	3.32
Lanier, Detroit	81	247	3.04
Hayes, Capital	81	240	2.96
Thurmond, Golden State	62	179	2.89
Heard, Buffalo	81	230	2.84
Lacey, KC-Omaha	79	184	2.33
Ray, Chicago	80	173	2.16
G. T. Johnson, Golden St.	66	124	1.88
Haywood, Seattle	75	106	1.41

Steals
(Minimum 65 Games)

	G.	No.	Avg.
Steele, Portland	81	217	2.68
Mix, Philadelphia	82	212	2.59
R. Smith, Buffalo	82	203	2.48
Hudson, Atlanta	65	160	2.46
Sloan, Chicago	77	183	2.38
Gilliam, Atlanta	62	134	2.16
Barry, Golden State	80	169	2.11
Chenier, Capital	76	155	2.04
Van Lier, Chicago	80	162	2.03
Frazier, New York	80	161	2.01

Assists
(Minimum 70 Games)

	G.	No.	Avg.
DiGregorio, Buffalo	81	663	8.2
Murphy, Houston	81	603	7.4
Wilkens, Cleveland	74	522	7.1
Frazier, New York	80	551	6.9
Bing, Detroit	81	555	6.9
Van Lier, Chicago	80	548	6.9
Robertson, Milwaukee	70	446	6.4
Barry, Golden State	80	484	6.1
Havlicek, Boston	76	447	5.9

NBA Champions 1947-1974

Year	Regular Season Eastern Conference	Western Conference	Playoffs Winner	Runner-Up
1947	Washington	Chicago	Philadelphia	Chicago
1948	Philadelphia	St. Louis	Baltimore	Philadelphia
1949	Washington	Rochester	Minneapolis	Washington
1950	Syracuse	Minneapolis	Minneapolis	Syracuse
1951	Philadelphia	Minneapolis	Rochester	New York
1952	Syracuse	Rochester	Minneapolis	New York
1953	New York	Minneapolis	Minneapolis	New York
1954	New York	Minneapolis	Minneapolis	Syracuse
1955	Syracuse	Ft. Wayne	Syracuse	Ft. Wayne
1956	Philadelphia	Ft. Wayne	Philadelphia	Ft. Wayne
1957	Boston	St. Louis	Boston	St. Louis
1958	Boston	St. Louis	St. Louis	Boston
1959	Boston	St. Louis	Boston	Minneapolis
1960	Boston	St. Louis	Boston	St. Louis
1961	Boston	St. Louis	Boston	St. Louis
1962	Boston	Los Angeles	Boston	Los Angeles
1963	Boston	Los Angeles	Boston	Los Angeles
1964	Boston	San Francisco	Boston	San Francisco
1965	Boston	Los Angeles	Boston	Los Angeles
1966	Philadelphia	Los Angeles	Boston	Los Angeles
1967	Philadelphia	San Francisco	Philadelphia	San Francisco
1968	Philadelphia	St. Louis	Boston	Los Angeles
1969	Baltimore	Los Angeles	Boston	Los Angeles
1970	New York	Atlanta	New York	Los Angeles

Year	Atlantic	Central	Midwest	Pacific	Winner	Runner-Up
1971	New York	Baltimore	Milwaukee	Los Angeles	Milwaukee	Baltimore
1972	Boston	Baltimore	Milwaukee	Los Angeles	Los Angeles	New York
1973	Boston	Baltimore	Milwaukee	Los Angeles	New York	Los Angeles
1974	Boston	Capital	Milwaukee	Los Angeles	Boston	Milwaukee

NBA Scoring Leaders

Year	Scoring Champion	Pts.	Avg.	Year	Scoring Champion	Pts.	Avg.
1947	Joe Fulks, Philadelphia	1,389	23.2	1962	Wilt Chamberlain, Philadelphia	4,029	50.4
1948	Max Zaslofsky, Chicago	1,007	21.0	1963	Wilt Chamberlain, San Francisco	3,586	44.8
1949	George Mikan, Minneapolis	1,698	28.3	1964	Wilt Chamberlain, San Francisco	2,948	36.5
1950	George Mikan, Minneapolis	1,865	27.4	1965	Wilt Chamberlain, San Fran., Phila.	2,534	34.7
1951	George Mikan, Minneapolis	1,932	28.4	1966	Wilt Chamberlain, Philadelphia	2,649	33.5
1952	Paul Arizin, Philadelphia	1,674	25.4	1967	Rick Barry, San Francisco	2,775	35.6
1953	Neil Johnston, Philadelphia	1,564	22.3	1968	Dave Bing, Detroit	2,142	27.1
1954	Neil Johnston, Philadelphia	1,759	24.4	1969	Elvin Hayes, San Diego	2,327	28.4
1955	Neil Johnston, Philadelphia	1,631	22.7	1970	Jerry West, Los Angeles	2,309	31.2
1956	Bob Pettit, St. Louis	1,849	25.7	1971	Lew Alcindor, Milwaukee	2,596	31.7
1957	Paul Arizin, Philadelphia	1,817	25.6	1972	Kareem Abdul-Jabbar (Alcindor), Milwaukee	2,822	34.8
1958	George Yardley, Detroit	2,001	27.8	1973	Nate Archibald, Kansas City-Omaha	2,719	34.0
1959	Bob Pettit, St. Louis	2,105	29.2	1974	Bob McAdoo, Buffalo	2,261	30.6
1960	Wilt Chamberlain, Philadelphia	2,707	37.9				
1961	Wilt Chamberlain, Philadelphia	3,033	38.4				

NBA All-Star Team, 1974

Position	First Team	Second Team
Forward	John Havlicek, Boston	Elvin Hayes, Capital
Forward	Rick Barry, Golden State	Spencer Haywood, Seattle
Center	Kareem Abdul-Jabbar, Milwaukee	Bob McAdoo, Buffalo
Guard	Walt Frazier, New York	Dave Bing, Detroit
Guard	Gail Goodrich, Los Angeles	Norm Van Lier, Chicago

NBA All-Defensive Team

Position	First Team	Second Team
Forward	Dave DeBusschere, New York	Bob Love, Chicago
Forward	John Havlicek, Boston	Elvin Hayes, Capital
Center	Kareem Abdul-Jabbar, Milwaukee	Nate Thurmond, Golden State
Guard	Norm Van Lier, Chicago	Don Chaney, Boston
Guard	Walt Frazier, New York (tie)	Jim Price, Los Angeles (tie)
	Jerry Sloan, Chicago (tie)	Dick Van Arsdale, Phoenix (tie)

1974 NBA Player Draft

The following are the first round picks of the National Basketball Assn.

Portland — Bill Walton, UCLA.
Philadelphia — Marvin Barnes, Providence.
Seattle (from Cleveland) — Tom Burleson, North Carolina State.
Phoenix — John Shumate, Notre Dame.
Houston — Bobby Jones, North Carolina.
Kansas City-Omaha — Scott Wedman, Colorado.
Atlanta — Tom Henderson, Hawaii.
Cleveland (from Seattle) — Campy Russell, Michigan.
Buffalo — Tom McMillen, Maryland.

Atlanta (from New Orleans) — Mike Sojourner, Utah.
Golden State — Keith Wilkes, UCLA.
Los Angeles — Brian Winters, South Carolina.
Washington — Len Elmore, Maryland.
Chicago (from New York) — Maurice Lucas, Marquette.
Detroit — Al Eberhard, Missouri.
Chicago — Cliff Pondexter, Long Beach State.
Boston — Glen McDonald, Long Beach State.
Milwaukee — Gary Brokaw, Notre Dame.

Podoloff Cup Winners

Kareem Abdul-Jabbar of the Milwaukee Bucks was selected as the winner of the Maurice Podoloff Cup (named after the former league commissioner) for Most Valuable Player in the NBA for the 1973-74 season.

1956—Bob Pettit, St. Louis
1957—Bob Cousy, Boston
1958—Bill Russell, Boston
1959—Bob Pettit, St. Louis
1960—Wilt Chamberlain, Philadelphia
1961—Bill Russell, Boston
1962—Bill Russell, Boston
1963—Bill Russell, Boston
1964—Oscar Robertson, Cincinnati

1965—Bill Russell, Boston
1966—Wilt Chamberlain, Philadelphia
1967—Wilt Chamberlain, Philadelphia
1968—Wilt Chamberlain, Philadelphia
1969—Wes Unseld, Baltimore
1970—Willis Reed, New York
1971—Lew Alcindor, Milwaukee
1972—Kareem Abdul-Jabbar (Alcindor), Milwaukee
1973—Dave Cowens, Boston
1974—Kareem Abdul-Jabbar. Milwaukee

NBA Rookie of the Year Awards

1954—Don Meineke, Ft. Wayne
1955—Ray Felix, Baltimore
1956—Maurice Stokes, Rochester
1957—Tom Heinsohn, Boston
1958—Woody Sauldsberry, Phil.
1959—Elgin Baylor, Minnesota
1960—Wilt Chamberlain, Philadelphia

1961—Oscar Robertson, Cincinnati
1962—Walt Bellamy, Chicago
1963—Terry Dischinger, Chicago
1964—Jerry Lucas, Cincinnati
1965—Willis Reed, New York
1966—Rick Barry, San Francisco
1967—Dave Bing, Detroit

1968—Earl Monroe, Baltimore
1969—Wes Unseld, Baltimore
1970—Lew Alcindor, Milwaukee
1971—Dave Cowens, Boston;
        Geoff Petrie, Portland (Tie)
1972—Sidney Wicks, Portland
1973—Bob McAdoo, Buffalo
1974—Ernie DiGregorio, Buffalo

Sports Arenas

The seating capacity of sports arenas can vary depending on the event being presented. The figures below are the normal seating capacity for basketball. (*) indicates hockey seating capacity.

Name and location

Ak-Sar-Ben Coliseum, Omaha, Neb................*6,000
Alexander Memorial Coliseum, Atlanta........... 6,996
Allen County Mem., Ft. Wayne...................*8,025
Amarillo Civic Center, Texas.................... 5,001
American Royal Bldg., Kansas City...............*6,122
Astrodome, Houston............................ 19,000
Astrohall, Houston............................. 10,000
Atlantic City Audit., Atlantic City, N. J........... 40,000
Baltimore Civic Center............... 13,043-*11,329
Bismarck Coliseum, No. Dakota.................. 7,000
Boston Arena..................................*6,000
Boston Garden...................... 15,314-*15,003
Buffalo Memorial Auditorium......... 17,300-*15,845
Capital Center, Wash., D. C......... 17,500-*16,926
Charlotte Coliseum.................. 11,666-*9,575
Chicago Stadium.................... 17,374-*18,000
Cincinnati Gardens................. 11,650-*10,606
Cleveland Arena.................... 11,000-*9,300
Cobo Arena, Detroit................ 11,055-*10,500
Convention Center, San Antonio................. 10,146
Convention Hall, Philadelphia...................*9,500
Cow Palace, San Francisco...................... 14,500
Crosby Kemper Memorial Audit., Kansas City..... *16,500
Dallas Memorial Auditorium..................... 8,088
Dallas State Fair Coliseum......................*7,490
Denver Auditorium Arena........................ 6,985
Denver Coliseum...............................*9,038
Dorton Arena, Raleigh, N. C..................... 8,058
Duluth Arena Auditorium........................ 6,919
Eastern States Coliseum, Springfield, Mass.......*5,934
Edmonton Coliseum............................*16,000
Edmonton Gardens, Alberta, Canada.............*5,800
Fairgrounds Coliseum, Indianapolis.............. 9,479
Freedom Hall, Louisville, Ky.................... 16,933
Greensboro Coliseum................ 15,500-*13,280
Halifax Forum, Nova Scotia......................*5,206
Hampton Roads Coliseum, Virginia.......... 10,000-*7,771
Hara Arena, Dayton............................*5,600
HemisFair Arena, San Antonio.................. 10,146
Hershey (Pa.) Sports Arena......................*7,259
Hobart Arena, Troy, Ohio....................... 6,000
Hofheinz Pavilion, Houston..................... 10,218
International Amphitheatre, Chicago............. 9,000
Jacksonville Coliseum..........................*7,900
Kiel Auditorium, St. Louis...................... 10,574
Kitchener Memorial Auditorium, Ontario.........*6,250
Las Vegas Convention Center.................... 9,000
Long Beach Arena, Calif........................ 11,168
Los Angeles Forum.................. 17,505-*16,005
Los Angeles Sports Arena............... 15,333-*11,325
Louisville Convention Center................... 5,833
Lubbock Municipal Coliseum, Texas............. 10,400
Macon Coliseum...............................*8,000
Madison Square Garden, New York....... 19,694-*17,500
Maple Leaf Gardens, Toronto........... 17,000-*16,316
McElroy Auditorium, Waterloo, Iowa............. 7,200
Memorial Arena, Victoria, B. C..................*5,021
Met. Sports Center, Bloomington, Minn..........*15,067

Name and location

Miami Beach Convention Hall Annex............. 9,500
Mid-South Coliseum, Memphis.................. 10,945
Milwaukee Arena.............................. 10,938
Mobile Municipal Auditorium................... 13,100
Monroe Civic Center, Monroe, La............... 8,000
Montreal Forum..............................*18,350
Moody Coliseum, Dallas........................ 9,500
Municipal Auditorium, Kansas City.............. 9,929
Nashville Municipal Auditorium................. 8,000
Nassau Coliseum, Uniondale, N. Y.... 16,000-*14,665
New Orleans Municipal Auditorium.............. 9,100
Norfolk Scope, Va..................... 10,600-*9,364
Oak Creek Ice Arena, Des Moines................*4,400
Oakland Coliseum Arena.............. 13,961-*12,500
Oakland Auditorium........................... 6,500
Oklahoma City Myriad.........................*13,400
Olympia, Detroit.............................*14,200
Olympic Auditorium, Los Angeles............... 10,500
Omaha Civic Auditorium....................... 9,144
The Omni, Atlanta.................. 16,818-*15,278
Onondaga County Audit., Syracuse...............*6,300
Ottawa Civic Center...........................*9,355
Pacific Coliseum, Vancouver...................*15,569
Penn Palestra, Philadelphia.................... 9,200
Philadelphia Civic Center......................*9,100
Pittsburgh Civic Arena.........................*13,650
Providence Civic Center.............. 11,619-*10,108
Portland Memorial Arena............. 11,815-*10,500
Quebec Coliseum.............................*10,000
Reynolds Coliseum, Raleigh, N. C............... 12,400
Richmond Coliseum, Virginia........... 10,700-*9,674
Rhode Island Auditorium, Providence............*5,175
Rivergate Auditorium, New Orleans............. 9,200
Roanoke Coliseum, Virginia.................... 10,100
Rochester (N.Y.) Memorial Arena................*7,010
St. Louis Arena...............................*18,006
St. Paul Civic Center, Minn....................*16,180
Salt Palace, Salt Lake City........... 12,201-*12,000
Sam Houston Arena, Houston.......... 8,925-*9,300
San Diego Intl. Sports Arena...................*13,600
San Francisco Civic Auditorium................. 7,500
Seattle Coliseum................... 14,065-*12,300
Spectrum, Philadelphia.............. 17,156-*17,000
Springfield Civic Center........................*7,466
Tarrant County Convention Center, Ft. Worth...... 13,500
Tingley Coliseum, Albuquerque................. *12,000
Toledo Sports Arena...........................*6,200
Tulsa Civic Center............................*6,923
Uline Arena, Washington, D. C.................. 11,000
Varsity Arena, Toronto.........................*9,300
Veterans Memorial Audit., Des Moines........... 15,000
Veterans Memorial Coliseum, New Haven.........*8,808
Veterans Memorial Coliseum, Phoenix..... 12,721-*12,600
Walker Sports Arena, Muskegon.................*5,700
Will Rogers Coliseum, Ft. Worth, Texas..........*6,800
Windsor Arena, Ontario........................*5,200
Winnipeg Arena..............................*11,000
Winston-Salem Coliseum....................... 9,020

American Basketball Association, 1973-74

Eastern Division

Club	W.	L.	Pct.	G.B.
New York Nets	55	29	.655	—
Kentucky Colonels	53	31	.631	2
Carolina Cougars	47	37	.560	8
Virginia Squires	28	56	.333	27
Memphis Tams	21	63	.250	34

Western Division

Club	W.	L.	Pct.	G.B.
Utah Stars	51	33	.607	—
Indiana Pacers	46	38	.548	5
San Antonio Spurs	45	39	.536	6
San Diego Conquistadors (a)	37	47	.440	14
Denver Rockets	37	47	.440	14

(a) Won playoff game with Denver for fourth place.

ABA Playoffs

Eastern Division—New York defeated Virginia 4 games to 1. Kentucky defeated Carolina 4 games to 0. New York defeated Kentucky 4 games to 0.

Western Division—Utah defeated San Diego 4 games to 2. Indiana defeated San Antonio 4 games to 3. Utah defeated Indiana 4 games to 3.

Championship—New York defeated Utah 4 games to 1.

Final Statistics

Individual Scoring
(Minimum of 1,000 Points)

	G.	FG.	FT.	Pts.	Avg.
Erving, New York	84	897	454	2299	27.3
McGinnis, Indiana	80	784	488	2071	25.8
Issel, Kentucky	83	826	457	2118	25.5
Gervin, San Antonio	74	664	378	1730	23.3
Wise, Utah	82	712	396	1826	22.2
Lamar, San Diego	84	617	272	1713	20.3
Johnson, San Diego	84	657	199	1690	20.1
Carter, Virginia	80	529	392	1546	19.3
Thompson, Memphis	78	529	410	1498	19.2
Simpson, Denver	75	595	208	1404	18.7
Gilmore, Kentucky	84	621	326	1568	18.6
Calvin, Carolina	83	488	490	1496	18.0
Dampier, Kentucky	84	555	238	1492	17.7
Boone, Utah	84	581	300	1480	17.6
J. Jones, Utah	83	583	229	1395	16.8
Paultz, New York	77	519	222	1260	16.3
Kenon, New York	84	589	156	1334	15.8
Silas, San Antonio	84	486	349	1321	15.7
R. Jones, San Antonio	78	497	186	1219	15.6

Three-point field goals — Erving 17, McGinnis 5, Issel 3, Gervin 8, Wise, 2, Lamar 69, Johnson 59, Carter 32, Thompson 10, Simpson 2, Calvin 10, Dampier 48, Boone 6, R. Jones 13.

Two-Point Percentage
(Minimum of 200 Made)

	FGM.	FGA.	Pct.
Nater, San Antonio	467	845	.553
J. Jones, Utah	583	1059	.551
Owens, Carolina	442	837	.528
Chones, Carolina	535	1015	.527
Grant, San Diego	356	677	.526
Beaty, Utah	417	795	.525
Eakins, Virginia	445	855	.520
Beck, Denver	425	822	.517
Erving, New York	897	1742	.515
Irvine, Virginia	242	470	.515

Three-Point Percentage
(Minimum of 20 Made)

	FGM.	FGA.	Pct.
Dampier, Kentucky	48	124	.387
Keller, Indiana	50	131	.382
R. Brown, Indiana	56	155	.361
Combs, Memphis	52	147	.354
Carter, Virginia	32	93	.344
Beasley, Utah	22	64	.344
Roche, Kentucky	36	105	.343
Buse, Indiana	36	107	.336
Shepherd, San Diego	65	202	.322

Free Throws
(Minimum of 135 Made)

	FTM	FTA	Pct.
J. Jones, Utah	229	259	.884
Calvin, Carolina	490	560	.875
Boone, Utah	300	343	.875
Johnson, San Diego	199	235	.847
Carter, Virginia	392	466	.841
Roche, Kentucky	148	177	.836
Dampier, Kentucky	238	286	.832

Assists
(Minimum of 200)

	G.	A.	Avg.
Smith, Denver	76	619	8.1
C. Williams, Kentucky	90	557	6.1
Dampier, Kentucky	84	473	5.6
R. Taylor, Virginia	80	416	5.2
J. Jones, Utah	83	429	5.1
Erving, New York	84	434	5.1
Thompson, Memphis	78	396	5.0
Boone, Utah	84	417	4.9

Rebounds
(Minimum of 500)

	G.	Off.	Def.	Tot.	Avg.
Gilmore, Kentucky	84	478	1060	1538	18.3
McGinnis, Indiana	80	422	775	1197	14.9
C. Jones, S. Diego	79	322	773	1095	13.8
Nater, San Antonio	79	286	712	998	12.6
Daniels, Indiana	76	247	638	885	11.6
Kenon, New York	84	375	587	962	11.4
Erving, New York	84	263	636	899	10.7
Issel, Kentucky	83	346	501	847	10.2
Paultz, New York	77	211	571	782	10.1

Blocked Shots

	G.	No.
C. Jones, San Diego	79	316
Gilmore, Kentucky	84	287
Erving, New York	84	204
Hillman, Indiana	83	177
Keye, Denver	79	149
Paultz, New York	77	147

Steals

	G.	No.
McClain, Carolina	84	250
R. Taylor, Virginia	80	215
Erving, New York	84	190
Caldwell, Carolina	79	170
Gale, New York	80	167
McGinnis, Indiana	80	159
B. Taylor, New York	75	154

ABA Champions

	Regular Season		Playoffs	
Year	Eastern Division	Western Division	Winner	Runner-Up
1968	Pittsburgh	New Orleans	Pittsburgh	New Orleans
1969	Indiana	Oakland	Oakland	Indiana
1970	Indiana	Denver	Indiana	Los Angeles
1971	Virginia	Indiana	Utah	Kentucky
1972	Kentucky	Utah	Indiana	New York
1973	Carolina	Utah	Indiana	Kentucky
1974	New York	Utah	New York	Utah

ABA All-Star Team, 1974

Position	First Team	Second Team
Forward	Julius Erving, New York	Dan Issel, Kentucky
Forward	George McGinnis, Indiana	Willie Wise, Utah
Center	Artis Gilmore, Kentucky	Swen Nater, San Antonio
Guard	Jimmy Jones, Utah	Louie Dampier, Kentucky
Guard	Mack Calvin, Carolina	Ray Boone, Utah

ABA Most Valuable Player & Rookie of Year

Year	MVP	Rookie
1968	Connie Hawkins, Pittsburgh	Mel Daniels, Indiana
1969	Mel Daniels, Indiana	Warren Armstrong, Oakland
1970	Spencer Haywood, Denver	Spencer Haywood, Denver
1971	Mel Daniels, Indiana	Dan Issel, Kentucky & Charlie Scott (tie)
1972	Artis Gilmore, Kentucky	Artis Gilmore, Kentucky
1973	Billy Cunningham, Carolina	Brian Taylor, New York
1974	Julius Erving, New York	Swen Nater, San Antonio

ABA Scoring Leaders

Year	Scoring Champion	Pts.	Avg.	Year	Scoring Champion	Pts.	Avg.
1968	Connie Hawkins, Pittsburgh	1,875	26.7	1972	Charlie Scott, Virginia	2,524	34.5
1969	Rick Barry, Oakland	1,190	34.0	1973	Julius Erving, Virginia	2,268	31.9
1970	Spencer Haywood, Denver	2,519	29.9	1974	Julius Erving, New York	2,299	27.3
1971	Dan Issel, Kentucky	2,480	29.8				

Basketball Hall of Fame
Springfield, Mass.

The Naismith Memorial Basketball Hall of Fame was incorporated in 1959 to serve as a memorial to James Naismith, who invented the game of basketball for students of the School for Christian Workers (now Springfield College) in December, 1891, at Springfield, Mass. The following persons have been enshrined in the Basketball Hall of Fame for outstanding contributions to basketball:

Players

Beckman, John
Borgmann, Bennie
Cousy, Robert J.
Davies, Robert
DeBernardi, Forrest
Dehnert, Henry G.
Endacott, Paul
Foster, Harold
Friedman, Max
Gruenig, Robert
Hanson, Victor
Holman, Nat
Hyatt, Charles
Kurland, Robert
Lapchick, Joe
Luisetti, Angelo
McCracken, Branch
McCracken, Jack
Macauley, C. Edward
Mikan, George L.
Murphy, Charles
Page, H. O. "Pat"
Pettit, Robert L.
Phillip, Andy

Roosma, Col. John S.
Russell, John
Schayes, Dolph
Schmidt, Ernie
Schommer, John J.
Sedran, Barney
Steinmetz, Christian
Thompson, John A.
Wachter, Edward A.

Coaches

Auerbach, Arnold J.
Blood, Ernest A.
Cann, Howard G.
Carlson, Dr. H. Clifford
Carnevale, Ben
Dean, Everett S.
Diddle, Edgar A.
Drake, Bruce
Gill, Amory T.
Hobson, Howard A.
Iba, Henry P.
Julian, Alvin F.
Keaney, Frank W.
Keogan, George E.
Lambert, Ward L.

Loeffler, Kenneth D.
Lonborg, Arthur
Meanwell, Dr. Walter E.
Rupp, Adolph F.
Sachs, Leonard D.
Wooden, John R.

Contributors

Allen, Dr. Forrest C.
Bee, Clair F.
Brown, Walter A.
Bunn, John W.
Douglas, Robert L.
Fisher, Harry
Gootlieb, Edward
Gulick, Dr. Luther H.
Hickox, Edward J.
Hinkle, Paul D.
Irish, Ned
Jones, R. William
Mokray, William G.
Morgan, Ralph
Morgenweck, Frank
Naismith, Dr. James
O'Brien, John J.

Olsen, Harold G.
Podoloff, Maurice
Porter, H. V.
Ripley, Elmer
St. John, Lynn W.
Saperstein, Abe
Schabinger, Arthur A.
Stagg, Amos Alonzo
Taylor, Charles H.
Tower, Oswald
Trester, Arthur L.
Wells, W. R. Clifford

Referees

Kepbron, George T.
Hoyt, George
Kennedy, Matthew P.
Quigley, Ernest C.
Tobey, David
Walsh, David H.

Teams

First Team
Original Celtics
Buffalo Germans
Renaissance

Lacrosse Championships in 1974
Source: Jack Kelly, The Lacrosse Newsletter

NCAA University Champions — Johns Hopkins University.
NCAA College Division Champions — Towson State College, Md.
U.S. Intercollegiate Lacrosse Association Champion — Johns Hopkins Univ.
National Club Lacrosse Association Champion — Long Island A.C., Garden City, N.Y.
South Atlantic Division Champion — Washington & Lee.
Ivy League Champion — Cornell Univ.
Independent Division — Hobart College
Midwest Division — Bowling Green Univ.
Colonial Division — Boston State Univ.
New England Intercollegiate Champion — University of Massachusetts.
Rocky Mountain Champion — Air Force Academy.
Florida Open Champion — Pensacola Naval Air Station.

NCAA University Championship
at Rutgers University Stadium, New Brunswick, N. J. June 1, 1974 — Johns Hopkins 17, Maryland 12.
NCAA Semi-finals —
Maryland 19, Cornell 10; Johns Hopkins 12, Wash. & Lee 12.

NCAA Quarter-finals —
Maryland 12, Rutgers 6; Cornell 15, Virginia 8; Washington & Lee 11, Navy 9; Johns Hopkins 18, Hofstra 10.
NCAA College Division Championship
at Cortland, N. Y., May 25, 1974 — Towson State (Md.) 18, Hobart 17.
Junior College Championship
at Farmingdale, N. Y., May 11, 1974 — Nassau C. C. 13, Farmingdale State Ag. & Tech 6.
1974 USILA University All-America Team

Goalie — Skeet Chadwick (Washington & Lee)
Defense — Mike Farrell (Maryland)
Defense — Boo Smith (Virginia)
Defense — John Lawlor (Navy)
Midfield — Frank Urso (Maryland)
Midfield — Rick Kowalchuk (Johns Hopkins)
Midfield — Ted Bauer (Washington & Lee)
Midfield — Skip Lichtfuss (Washington & Lee)
Attack — Jack Thomas (Johns Hopkins)
Attack — Jim Trenz (Cornell)
Attack — Barry Robertson (Virginia)

Hockey Champions in 1973-74

National Hockey League

Final Standings

East Division Club	W.	L.	T.	Pts.	GF	GA	West Division Club	W.	L.	T.	Pts.	GF	GA
Boston	51	17	9	113	349	221	Philadelphia	50	16	12	112	273	164
Montreal	45	24	9	99	293	240	Chicago	41	14	23	105	272	164
N.Y. Rangers	40	24	14	94	300	251	Los Angeles	33	33	12	78	233	231
Toronto	35	27	16	86	274	230	Atlanta	30	34	14	74	214	238
Buffalo	32	34	12	76	242	250	Pittsburgh	28	41	9	65	242	273
Detroit	29	39	10	68	255	319	St. Louis	26	40	12	64	206	248
Vancouver	24	43	11	59	224	296	Minnesota	23	38	17	63	235	275
N.Y. Islanders	19	41	18	56	182	247	California	13	55	10	36	195	342

Leading Scorers

Player—Club	G.	Goals	Asts.	Pts.	Player—Club	G.	Goals	Asts.	Pts.
Esposito, Boston	78	68	77	145	Park, Rangers	78	25	57	82
Orr, Boston	74	32	90	122	Hextall, Minnesota	78	20	62	82
Hodge, Boston	76	50	55	105	F. Mahovlich, Montreal	71	31	49	80
Cashman, Boston	78	30	59	89	Mikita, Chicago	76	30	50	80
Clarke, Philadelphia	78	35	52	87	Redmond, Detroit	76	51	26	77
Martin, Buffalo	78	52	34	86	Gilbert, Rangers	75	36	41	77
Apps, Pittsburgh	75	24	61	85	MacLeish, Philadelphia	78	32	45	77
Sittler, Toronto	78	38	46	84	Martin, Chicago	78	30	47	77
MacDonald, Pittsburgh	78	43	39	82	Dionne, Detroit	74	24	53	77

Club Scoring Leaders

Atlanta

Player	G.	Goals	Asts.	Pts.
Tom Lysiak	77	19	45	64
Al McDonough	72	24	31	55
Bobby Leiter	78	26	26	52
Larry Romanchych	73	22	29	51
Jacques Richard	78	27	16	43

Boston

Player	G.	Goals	Asts.	Pts.
Phil Esposito	78	68	77	145
Bobby Orr	74	32	90	122
Ken Hodge	76	50	55	105
Wayne Cashman	78	30	59	89
John Bucyk	78	31	44	75

Buffalo

Player	G.	Goals	Asts.	Pts.
Richard Martin	78	52	34	86
Rene Robert	76	21	44	65
Don Luce	75	26	30	56
Jim Lorentz	78	23	31	54
Gilbert Perreault	55	18	33	51

California

Player	G.	Goals	Asts.	Pts.
Joey Johnston	78	27	40	67
Ivan Boldirev	78	25	31	56
Walt McKechnie	63	23	29	52
Reg Leach	78	22	24	46
Gary Croteau	75	14	21	35

Chicago

Player	G.	Goals	Asts.	Pts.
Stan Mikita	76	30	50	80
Pit Martin	78	30	47	77
Jim Pappin	78	32	41	73
Dennis Hull	74	29	39	68
Dick Redmond	76	17	42	59

Detroit

Player	G.	Goals	Asts.	Pts.
Marcel Dionne	74	24	53	77
Mickey Redmond	76	51	26	77
Red Berenson	76	24	42	66
Guy Charron	77	25	30	55
Nick Libett	67	24	24	48

Los Angeles

Player	G.	Goals	Asts.	Pts.
Butch Goring	70	28	33	61
Juha Widing	71	27	31	58
Bob Berry	77	23	33	56
Bob Nevin	78	20	30	50
Frank St. Marseille	78	14	36	50

Minnesota

Player	G.	Goals	Asts.	Pts.
Dennis Hextall	78	20	62	82
Bill Goldsworthy	74	48	26	74
Danny Grant	78	29	35	64
Jean Paul Parise	78	18	37	55
Fred Stanfield	74	16	28	44

Montreal

Player	G.	Goals	Asts.	Pts.
Frank Mahovlich	71	31	49	80
Yvan Cournoyer	67	40	33	73
Pete Mahovlich	78	36	37	73
Jacques Lemaire	66	29	38	67
Guy Lafleur	73	21	35	56

N. Y. Islanders

Player	G.	Goals	Asts.	Pts.
Denis Potvin	77	17	37	54
Bill Harris	78	23	27	50
Ralph Stewart	67	23	20	43
Ed Westfall	68	19	23	42
Bob Nystrom	77	21	20	41

N. Y. Rangers

Player	G.	Goals	Asts.	Pts.
Brad Park	78	25	57	82
Rod Gilbert	75	36	41	77
Pete Stemkowski	78	25	45	70
Jean Ratelle	68	28	39	67
Walt Tkaczuk	71	21	42	63

Philadelphia

Player	G.	Goals	Asts.	Pts.
Bobby Clarke	78	35	52	87
Rick MacLeish	78	32	45	77
Bill Barber	75	34	35	69
Ross Lonsberry	75	32	19	51
Gary Dornhoefer	57	11	39	50

Pittsburgh

Player	G.	Goals	Asts.	Pts.
Syl Apps	75	24	61	85
Lowell MacDonald	78	43	39	82
Jean Pronovost	77	40	32	72
Ron Schock	77	14	29	43
Ron Stackhouse	69	6	29	35

St. Louis

Player	G.	Goals	Asts.	Pts.
Garry Unger	78	33	35	68
Pierre Plante	78	26	28	54
Greg Polis	78	22	25	47
Glen Sather	71	15	29	44
Wayne Merrick	64	20	23	43

Toronto

Player	G.	Goals	Asts.	Pts.
Darryl Sittler	78	38	46	84
Norm Ullman	78	22	47	69
Paul Henderson	69	24	31	55
Dave Keon	74	25	28	53
Ron Ellis	70	23	25	48

Vancouver

Player	G.	Goals	Asts.	Pts.
Andre Boudrias	78	16	59	75
Dennis Ververgaert	78	26	31	57
Don Lever	78	23	25	48
Gerry O'Flaherty	78	22	20	42
Jocelyn Guevremont	72	15	24	39

Leading Goalies

Goalie—Club	G.	GA.	SO.	Avg.	Goalie—Club	G.	GA.	SO.	Avg.
Bernie Parent, Phila.	73	136	12	1.89	Rogie Vachon, Los Ang.	65	175	5	2.80
Tony Esposito, Chicago.	70	141	10	2.04	Michel Larocque, Mont.	27	69	0	2.89
Doug Favell, Toronto	32	79	0	2.71	Gilles Gilbert, Boston.	54	158	6	2.95
Wayne Thomas, Montreal.	42	111	1	2.76	Dave Dryden, Buffalo.	53	148	1	2.97
Dan Bouchard, Atlanta.	46	123	5	2.77	Ed Giacomin, Rangers.	56	168	5	3.07

Stanley Cup Playoff Results

Philadelphia defeated Atlanta 4 games to 0.
Chicago defeated Los Angeles 4 games to 1.
Boston defeated Toronto 4 games to 0.
New York defeated Montreal 4 games to 2.

Philadelphia defeated New York 4 games to 3.
Boston defeated Chicago 4 games to 2.
Philadelphia defeated Boston 4 games to 2.

Conn Smythe Trophy (MVP in Playoffs)

1965—Jean Beliveau, Montreal
1966—Roger Crozier, Detroit
1967—Dave Keon, Toronto

1968—Glenn Hall, St. Louis
1969—Serge Sevard, Montreal
1970—Bobby Orr, Boston

1971—Ken Dryden, Montreal
1972—Bobby Orr, Boston
1973—Yvan Cournoyer, Montreal
1974—Bernie Parent, Philadelphia

Stanley Cup Champions

1928—New York	1940—New York	1952—Detroit	1964—Toronto
1929—Boston	1941—Boston	1953—Montreal	1965—Montreal
1930—Montreal	1942—Toronto	1954—Detroit	1966—Montreal
1931—Montreal	1943—Detroit	1955—Detroit	1967—Toronto
1932—Toronto	1944—Montreal	1956—Montreal	1968—Montreal
1933—New York	1945—Toronto	1957—Montreal	1969—Montreal
1934—Chicago	1946—Montreal	1958—Montreal	1970—Boston
1935—Montreal Maroons	1947—Toronto	1959—Montreal	1971—Montreal
1936—Detroit	1948—Toronto	1960—Montreal	1972—Boston
1937—Detroit	1949—Toronto	1961—Chicago	1973—Montreal
1938—Chicago	1950—Detroit	1962—Toronto	1974—Philadelphia
1939—Boston	1951—Toronto	1963—Toronto	

Hockey Trophy Winners

Ross Trophy Leading Scorer	Norris Trophy Best Defenseman	Calder Trophy Best Rookie
1974—Phil Esposito, Boston	Bobby Orr, Boston	Denis Potvin, N.Y. Islanders
1973—Phil Esposito, Boston	Bobby Orr, Boston	Steve Vickers, N.Y. Rangers
1972—Phil Esposito, Boston	Bobby Orr, Boston	Ken Dryden, Montreal
1971—Phil Esposito, Boston	Bobby Orr, Boston	Gil Perreault, Buffalo
1970—Bobby Orr, Boston	Bobby Orr, Boston	Tony Esposito, Chicago
1969—Phil Esposito, Boston	Bobby Orr, Boston	Danny Grant, Minn.
1968—Stan Mikita, Chicago	Bobby Orr, Boston	Derek Sanderson, Boston
1967—Stan Mikita, Chicago	Harry Howell, N.Y. Rangers	Bobby Orr, Boston
1966—Bobby Hull, Chicago	Jacques Laperriere, Montreal	Brit Selby, Toronto
1965—Stan Mikita, Chicago	Pierre Pilote, Chicago	Roger Crozier, Detroit
1964—Stan Mikita, Chicago	Pierre Pilote, Chicago	Jacques Laperriere, Montreal

Hart Trophy M.V.P.	Vezina Trophy Leading Goalie	Lady Byng Trophy Sportsmanship
1974—Phil Esposito, Boston	Tony Esposito, Chi., Bernie Parent, Phil.	John Bucyk, Boston
1973—Bobby Clarke, Philadelphia	Ken Dryden, Montreal	Gilbert Perreault, Buffalo
1972—Bobby Orr, Boston	Esposito, Smith, Chicago	Jean Ratelle, N.Y. Rangers
1971—Bobby Orr, Boston	Giacomin, Villemure, New York	John Bucyk, Boston
1970—Bobby Orr, Boston	Tony Esposito, Chicago	Phil Goyette, St. Louis
1969—Phil Esposito, Boston	Hall, Plante, St. Louis	Alex Delvecchio, Detroit
1968—Stan Mikita, Chicago	Worsley, Vachon, Montreal	Stan Mikita, Chicago
1967—Stan Mikita, Chicago	Hall, De Jordy, Chicago	Stan Mikita, Chicago
1966—Bobby Hull, Chicago	Hodge, Worsley, Montreal	Alex Delvecchio, Detroit
1965—Bobby Hull, Chicago	Sawchuck, Bower, Toronto	Bobby Hull, Chicago
1964—Jean Beliveau, Montreal	Charlie Hodge, Montreal	Ken Wharram, Chicago

1974 Final Standings

American League

North Division

	W	L	T	F	A	Pts.
Rochester	42	21	13	296	248	97
Providence	38	26	12	330	244	88
Nova Scotia	37	27	12	263	223	86
New Haven	35	31	10	291	275	80
Boston	23	40	13	239	297	59
Springfield	21	40	15	251	327	57

South Division

	W	L	T	F	A	Pts.
Baltimore	42	24	10	310	232	94
Hershey	39	23	14	320	241	92
Cincinnati	40	25	11	273	233	91
Richmond	22	40	14	248	320	58
Jacksonville	24	44	8	244	334	56
Virginia	22	44	10	216	307	54

Western League

	W	L	T	F	A	Pts.
Phoenix	43	32	3	300	273	89
Salt Lake	41	33	4	356	297	86
San Diego	40	33	5	278	281	85

	W	L	T	F	A	Pts.
Portland	39	33	6	292	258	84
Seattle	32	42	4	288	319	68
Denver	28	50	0	249	335	56

Central League

	W	L	T	F	A	Pts.		W	L	T	F	A	Pts.
Oklahoma City	36	25	11	280	230	83	Ft. Worth	30	28	14	237	241	74
Omaha	34	23	15	259	217	83	Tulsa	28	31	13	233	239	69
Dallas	29	26	17	220	227	75	Albuquerque	16	40	16	188	263	48

Oklahoma City awarded first place with more wins.

Ontario Major League

	W	L	T	F	A	Pts.		W	L	T	F	A	Pts.
Kitchener	43	18	9	377	229	95	Ottawa	30	31	9	293	277	69
St. Catharines	41	23	6	358	278	88	Toronto	29	31	10	318	304	68
Peterborough	35	21	14	255	230	84	Sault	24	40	6	295	352	54
London	36	27	7	282	250	79	Kingston	20	43	7	256	378	47
Sudbury	31	26	13	298	288	75	Hamilton	16	49	5	221	376	37
Oshawa	33	29	8	283	275	74							

Western Canada League

Eastern Division

	W	L	T	F	A	Pts.
Regina	43	14	11	377	225	97
Flin Flon	34	21	13	322	259	81
Swift Current	35	24	9	340	306	79
Saskatoon	30	29	9	283	272	69
Brandon	27	37	4	305	348	58
Winnipeg	23	38	7	258	338	53

Western Division

	W	L	T	F	A	Pts.
Calgary	41	18	9	329	236	91
New Westminster	36	21	11	284	251	83
Medicine Hat	29	31	8	305	314	66
Edmonton	25	36	7	252	302	57
Victoria	22	40	6	259	336	50
Kamloops	13	49	6	248	375	32

National Hockey League Amateur Draft, 1974

First Round Selections

NHL Team	Player	Position	1973-74 Team
1-Washington	Greg Joly	Defense	Regina
2-Kansas City	*Wilf Paiement	R. Wing	St. Catharines
3-California	**Rick Hampton	Defense	St. Catharines
4-N.Y. Islanders	Clark Gillies	L. Wing	Regina
5-Montreal	Cam Connor	L. Wing	Flin Flon
6-Minnesota	*Doug Hicks	Defense	Flin Flon
7-Montreal	Doug Risebrough	Center	Kitchener
8-Pittsburgh	*Pierre Larouche	Center	Sorel
9-Detroit	Bill Lochead	L. Wing	Oshawa
10-Montreal	Rick Chartraw	Defense	Kitchener
11-Buffalo	*Lee Fogolin	Defense	Oshawa
12-Montreal	**Mario Tremblay	R. Wing	Montreal
13-Toronto	**Jack Valiquette	Center	Sault
14-N.Y. Rangers	**Dave Maloney	Defense	Kitchener
15-Montreal	Gord McTavish	Center	Sudbury
16-Chicago	**Grant Mulvey	R. Wing	Calgary
17-California	Ron Chipperfield	Center	Brandon
18-Boston	Don Larway	R. Wing	Swift Current

*18 Year Olds   **17 Year Olds

Players in the Hockey Hall of Fame

S. G. (Sid) Abel
John J. (Jack) Adams
C. J. S. (Syl) Apps
Donald Bain
Hobart (Hobey) Baker
Martin (Marty) Barry
Jean Beliveau
Clint (Benny) Benedict
Douglas (Doug) Bentley
Max Bentley
Hector (Toe) Blake
Richard (Dickie) Boon
Emile (Butch) Bouchard
Frank Boucher
George (Buck) Boucher
Russell Bowie
Frank Brimsek
H. L. (Punch) Broadbent, M.M.
Walter (Turk) Broda
Billy Burch
H. H. (Harry) Cameron
Francis (King) Clancy
Aubrey (Dit) Clapper
Sprague Cleghorn
Neil Colville
Charles Conacher
Alex Connell
William (Bill) Cook
Art Coulter
W. M. (Bill) Cowley
Samuel R. (Rusty) Crawford
John P. (Jack) Darragh
Allan (Scotty) Davidson
Clarence (Hap) Day
Cyril (Cy) Denneny
Charles G. Drinkwater

Tommy Dunderdale
William (Bill) Durnan
Mervyn (Red) Dutton
Cecil H. (Babe) Dye
Arthur Farrell
Frank Foyston
Frank Fredrickson
W. A. (Bill) Gadsby
Charles (Chuck) Gardiner
Herbert Gardiner
James H. (Jimmy) Gardner
Bernard (Boom Boom) Geoffrion
Edward (Eddie) Gerard
H. L. (Billy) Gilmour
E. R. (Ebbie) Goodfellow
F.X. (Moose) Goheen
Michael (Mike) Grant
Wilfred (Shorty) Green
Silas (Si) Griffis
Joseph (Joe) Hall
George Hainsworth
Doug Harvey
George Hay
W.M. (Riley) Hern
Bryan Hextall
Harry (Hap) Holmes
Thomas (Tom) Hooper
G. R. (Red) Horner
Gordon Howe
Sydney (Syd) Howe
John B. (Bouse) Hutton
Harry Hyland
James Dickenson Irvin
H. (Busher) Jackson
Ernest (Moose) Johnson
I. W. (Ching) Johnson

T. C. (Tom) Johnson
Aurel Joliat
Gordon (Duke) Keats
Leonard (Red) Kelly
Theodore (Teeder) Kennedy
Elmer James Lach
Edouard (Newsy) Lalonde
J. B. (Jack) Laviolette
Hugh Lehman
Percy LeSueur
R. B. T. (Ted) Lindsay
Duncan (Mickey) MacKay
Sylvio Mantha
Joseph Malone
John (Jack) Marshall
Fred (Steamer) Maxwell
Frank McGee
W. G. (Billy) McGimsie
George McNamara
Dickie Moore
Patrick (Paddy) Moran
H. W. (Howie) Morenz
William (Billy) Mosienko
Frank Nighbor
Reginald Noble
Harold (Harry) Oliver
Lester Patrick
Thomas (Tom) Phillips
Didier (Pit) Pitre
Walter (Babe) Pratt
Joseph (Joe) Primeau
Harvey Pulford
Frank Rankin
Chuck Rayner
Kenneth (Ken) Reardon
Maurice (The Rocket) Richard

George Richardson
Gordon Roberts
Arthur H. Ross
Blair Russell
Ernie Russell
J. D. (Jack) Ruttan
T. G. (Terry) Sawchuk
Fred Scanlan
Milt Schmidt
David (Sweeney) Schriner
Earl Walter Seibert
Oliver Seibert
Edward William Shore
Albert (Babe) Siebert
H. J. (Bullet Joe) Simpson, M.M.
Alfred (Alf) Smith
Reginald (Hooley) Smith
Tommy Smith
Russell (Barney) Stanley
John (Black Jack) Stewart
Nelson Stewart
Bruce Stuart
Horace (Hod) Stuart
Fred (Cyclone) Taylor, OBE
Harry J. Trihey
Cecil (Tiny) Thompson
Georges Vezina
John (Jack) Walker
Martin Walsh
Harry E. Watson
Harry Westwick
R. C. (Cooney) Weiland
Fred Whitcroft
Gordon (Phat) Wilson
Roy Worters

World Hockey Association

Final Standings

East Division

	P	W	L	T	F	A	Pts.
New England	78	43	31	4	291	260	90
Toronto	78	41	33	4	304	272	86
Cleveland	78	37	32	9	266	264	83
Chicago	78	38	35	5	271	273	81
Quebec	78	38	36	4	306	280	80
Jersey	78	32	42	4	268	312	68

West Division

	P	W	L	T	F	A	Pts.
Houston	78	48	25	5	318	219	101
Minnesota	78	44	32	2	332	273	91
Edmonton	78	38	37	3	267	269	79
Winnipeg	78	34	29	5	263	296	73
Vancouver	78	27	50	1	281	342	55
Los Angeles	78	25	53	0	239	340	50

WHA Playoff Results

Houston defeated Winnipeg 4 games to 0.
Minnesota defeated Edmonton 4 games to 1.
Chicago defeated New England 4 games to 3.
Toronto defeated Cleveland 4 games to 1.

Houston defeated Minnesota 4 games to 2.
Chicago defeated Toronto 4 games to 3.
Houston defeated Chicago 4 games to 0.

Final Scoring

Player, Club	G.	A.	Pts.	Player, Club	G.	A.	Pts.
Mike Walton, Minnesota	57	60	117	Gary Jarrett, Cleveland	31	40	71
Andre Lacroix, Jersey	31	80	111	Marc Tardif, Los Angeles	40	30	70
Gordie Howe, Houston	31	69	100	Tom Webster, New England	43	26	69
Bobby Hull, Winnipeg	53	42	95	Larry Pleau, New England	26	43	69
Wayne Connelly, Minnesota	42	53	95	Jim Harrison, Edmonton	24	45	69
Wayne Carleton, Toronto	37	55	92	Gary Veneruzzo, Los Angeles	39	29	68
Danny Lawson, Vancouver	50	38	88	Robert Guindon, Quebec	31	37	68
Bryan Campbell, Vancouver	27	61	88	Claude St.-Sauveur, Vancouver	38	30	68
Serge Bernier, Quebec	37	49	86	Andre Gaudette, Quebec	24	44	68
Larry Lund, Houston	33	53	86	Gavin Kirk, Toronto	20	48	68
Frank Hughes, Houston	42	42	84	Kevin Morrison, Jersey	24	43	67
Ralph Backstrom, Chicago	33	50	83	Don Burgess, Vancouver	30	36	66
Andre Hinse, Houston	24	56	80	J.-P. Leblanc, Los Angeles	20	46	66
Mark Howe, Houston	38	41	79	Wayne Dillon, Toronto	30	35	65
George Morrison, Minnesota	26	49	75	Rejean Houle, Quebec	27	35	62
Chris Bordeleau, Winnipeg	26	49	75	Ron Ward, LA-Cleveland	33	28	61
Ron Climie, Edmonton	38	36	74	Guy Trottier, Toronto	26	35	61
Fran Huck, Winnipeg	26	48	74	Rick Sentes, Toronto	26	34	60
Rosaire Paiement, Chicago	30	43	73	Michel Parizeau, Quebec	26	34	60
John French, New England	24	48	72	Al Karlander, New England	20	40	60

WHA All-Star Team, 1974

Position	First Team	Second Team
Goal	Gerry Cheevers, Cleveland	Don McLeod, Houston
Defense	Allan Hamilton, Edmonton	J. C. Tremblay, Quebec
Defense	Paul Shmyr, Cleveland	Rick Ley, New England
Center	Andre Lacroix, Jersey	Bryan Campbell, Vancouver
Right Wing	Gordie Howe, Houston	Mike Walton, Minnesota
Left Wing	Bobby Hull, Winnipeg	Wayne Carleton, Toronto

NHL All-Star Team, 1974

Position	First Team	Second Team
Goalie	Bernie Parent, Philadelphia	Tony Esposito, Chicago
Defense	Bobby Orr, Boston	Barry Ashbee, Philadelphia
Defense	Brad Park, New York	Bill White, Chicago
Center	Phil Esposito, Boston	Bobby Clarke, Philadelphia
Right Wing	Ken Hodge, Boston	Mickey Redmond, Detroit
Left Wing	Rick Martin, Buffalo	Wayne Cashman, Boston

Canadian Intercollegiate Athletic Union Champions

Basketball

1968	Waterloo Lutheran
1969	Windsor
1970	British Columbia
1971	Acadia
1972	British Columbia
1973	St. Mary's
1974	Guelph

Football

1967	Alberta
1968	Manitoba
1969	Manitoba
1970	Western Ontario
1971	Western Ontario
1972	Alberta
1973	St. Mary's

Soccer

1972	Alberta
1973	Loyola

Swimming and Diving

1967	Toronto
1968	Toronto
1969	Toronto
1970	Toronto
1971	Toronto
1972	McGill
1973	Toronto
1974	Toronto

Volleyball

1968	Ottawa
1969	Winnipeg
1970	Montreal
1971	Winnipeg
1972	Winnipeg
1973	Winnipeg
1974	Winnipeg

Wrestling

1969	O.Q.A.A.
1970	Alberta
1971	Alberta
1972	Alberta
1973	Assoc. Champion
1974	Assoc. Champion

Hockey

1963	McMaster
1964	Alberta
1965	Manitoba
1966	Toronto
1967	Toronto
1968	Alberta
1969	Toronto
1970	Toronto
1971	Toronto
1972	Toronto
1973	Toronto
1974	Waterloo

Speed Ice-Skating Championships in 1974

National Outdoor Championships
Lake Como, Minn., Jan. 26-27, 1974

Senior Men
1/6 Mile—Les Barczewski. Time—0:24.35.
440 Yds.—Les Barczewski. Time—0:33.82.
880 Yds.—Les Barczewski. Time—1:10.81.
3/4Mile—M. Passarella. Time—2:05.07.
1 Mile—B. Jacquin. Time—2:52.69.
Champion—Les Barczewski & M. Passarella.

Senior Women
1/6 Mile—Nancy Class. Time—0:27.06.
440 Yds.—N. Thorne. Time—0:39.07.
880 Yds.—Kris Garbe. Time—1:29.80.
3/4 Mile—Kris Garbe. Time—2:15.58.
1 Mile—Nancy Class. Time—3:16.75.
Champion—Kris Garbe.

North American Outdoor Championships
Alpena, Mich., Feb. 2-3, 1974

Senior Men
220 Yds.—Les Barczewski. Time—0:19.3.
440 Yds.—Les Barczewski. Time—0:37.5.
880 Yds.—S. Grunnet. Time—1:22.5.
3/4 Mile—S. Grunnet. Time—2:02.9.
1 Mile—Rich Wurster. Time—2:49.
5 Miles—Rich Wurster. Time—15.:24.1.
Champion—S. Grunnet

Senior Women
220 Yds.—Nancy Class. Time—0:21.3.
440 Yds.—Nancy Class. Time—0:41.2.
880 Yds.—Nancy Class. Time—1:49.3.
3/4 Mile—Kris Garbe. Time—2:39.8.
1 Mile—Kris Garbe. Time—3:42.1.
Champion—Nancy Class.

National Indoor Championships
Mt. Prospect, Ill., March 16-17, 1974

Senior Men
440 Yds.—Bill Lanigan. Time—0:39.
880 Yds.—R. Rattray. Time—1:18.6.
3/4 Mile—A. Karras. Time—2:02.
1 Mile—R. Rattray. Time—2:45.9.
2 Miles—Bill Lanigan. Time—5:55.1.
Champion—R. Rattray.

Senior Women
440 Yds.—P. Hartrich. Time—0:44.3.
880 Yds.—P. Hartrich. Time—1:26.9.
3/4 Mile—P. Hartrich. Time—2:10.8.
1 Mile—P. Hartrich. Time—3:01.2.
Champion—P. Hartrich.

North American Indoor Championships
Quebec, March 23-24, 1974

Senior Men
400 Meters—Les Barczewski. Time—0:38.5.
800 Meters—Bill Lanigan. Time—1:18.
1,000 Meters—Bill Lanigan. Time—1:39.3.
1,500 Meters—Bill Lanigan. Time—2:32.
3,000 Meters—Bill Lanigan. Time—5:22.3.
Champion—Bill Lanigan

Senior Women
400 Meters—Michele Conroy. Time—0:41.8.
800 Meters—Michele Conroy. Time—1:24.6.
1,000 Meters—P. Hartrich. Time—1:46.2.
1,500 Meters—P. Hartrich. Time—2:48.8.
Champion—Michele Conroy.

Figure Skating Champions

National Champions   World Champions

Year	Men	Women	Men	Women
1951	Richard Button	Sonya Klopfer	Richard Button, US.	Jeannette Altwegg, Eng.
1952	Richard Button	Tenley Albright	Richard Button, U.S.	Jacqueline du Bief, France
1953	Hayes Jenkins	Tenley Albright	Hayes Jenkins, U.S.	Tenley Albright, U.S.
1954	Hayes Jenkins	Tenley Albright	Hayes Jenkins, U.S.	Gundi Busch, Germany
1955	Hayes Jenkins	Tenley Albright	Hayes Jenkins, U.S.	Tenley Albright, U.S.
1956	Hayes Jenkins	Tenley Albright	Hayes Jenkins, U.S.	Carol Heiss, U.S.
1957	Dave Jenkins	Carol Heiss	Dave Jenkins, U.S.	Carol Heiss, U.S.
1958	Dave Jenkins	Carol Heiss	Dave Jenkins, U.S.	Carol Heiss, U.S.
1959	Dave Jenkins	Carol Heiss	Dave Jenkins, U.S.	Carol Heiss, U.S.
1960	Dave Jenkins	Carol Heiss	Alain Giletti, France	Carol Heiss, U.S.
1961	Bradley Lord	Laurence Owen	none	none
1962	Monty Hoyt	Barbara Roles Pursley	Don Jackson, Canada	Sjoukje Dijkstra, Neth.
1963	Tommy Litz	Lorraine Hanlon	Don McPherson, Canada	Sjoukje Dijkstra, Neth.
1964	Scott Allen	Peggy Fleming	Manfred Schnelldorfer, Germany	Sjoukje Dijkstra, Neth.
1965	Gary Visconti	Peggy Fleming	Alain Calmat, France	Petra Burka, Canada
1966	Scott Allen	Peggy Fleming	Emmerich Danzer, Austria	Peggy Fleming. U. S.
1967	Gary Visconti	Peggy Fleming	Emmerich Danzer, Austria	Peggy Fleming, U.S.
1968	Tim Wood	Peggy Fleming	Emmerich Danzer, Austria	Peggy Fleming, U.S.
1969	Tim Wood	Janet Lynn	Tim Wood, U.S.	Gabriele Seyfert, E. Ger.
1970	Tim Wood	Janet Lynn	Tim Wood, U.S.	Gabriele Seyfert, E. Ger.
1971	John Misha Petkevich	Janet Lynn	Ondrej Nepela, Czech.	Beatrix Schuba, Austria
1972	Ken Shelley	Janet Lynn	Ondrej Nepela, Czech.	Beatrix Schuba, Austria
1973	Gordon McKellen, Jr.	Janet Lynn	Ondrej Nepela, Czech.	Karen Magnussen, Canada
1974	Gordon McKellen, Jr.	Dorothy Hamill	Jan Hoffman, E. Germany	Christine Errath, E. Germany

Canadian National Figure Skating Champions

Year	Men	Women	Year	Men	Women
1957	Charles Snelling	Carole Jane Pachl	1966	Donald Knight	Petra Burka
1958	Charles Snelling	Marg. Crosland	1967	Donald Knight	Valerie Jones
1959	Donald Jackson	Marg. Crosland	1968	Jay Humphrey	Karen Magnussen
1960	Donald Jackson	Wendy Griner	1969	Jay Humphrey	Linda Carbonetto
1961	Donald Jackson	Wendy Griner	1970	David McGillivray	Karen Magnussen
1962	Donald Jackson	Wendy Griner	1971	Toller Cranston	Karen Magnussen
1963	Donald McPherson	Wendy Griner	1972	Toller Cranston	Karen Magnussen
1964	Charles Snelling	Petra Burka	1973	Toller Cranston	Karen Magnussen
1965	Donald Knight	Petra Burka	1974	Toller Cranston	Lynn Nightingale

National Football League
Final 1973 Standings

American Conference

Eastern Division

Club	W.	L.	T.	Pct.	Pts.	Opp.
Miami	12	2	0	.857	343	150
Buffalo	9	5	0	.643	259	230
New England	5	9	0	.357	258	300
New York	4	10	0	.286	240	306
Baltimore	4	10	0	.286	226	341

Central Division

Club	W.	L.	T.	Pct.	Pts.	Opp.
Cincinnati (a)	10	4	0	.714	286	231
*Pittsburgh	10	4	0	.714	347	210
Cleveland	7	5	2	.571	234	255
Houston	1	13	0	.071	199	447

Western Division

Club	W.	L.	T.	Pct.	Pts.	Opp.
Oakland	9	4	1	.679	292	175
Denver	7	5	2	.571	354	296
Kansas City	7	5	2	.571	231	192
San Diego	2	11	1	.179	188	386

National Conference

Eastern Division

Club	W.	L.	T.	Pct.	Pts.	Opp.
Dallas (b)	10	4	0	.714	382	203
*Washington	10	4	0	.714	325	198
Philadelphia	5	8	1	.393	310	393
St. Louis	4	9	1	.321	286	365
New York	2	11	1	.179	226	362

Central Division

Club	W.	L.	T.	Pct.	Pts.	Opp.
Minnesota	12	2	0	.857	296	168
Detroit	6	7	1	.464	271	247
Green Bay	5	7	2	.429	202	259
Chicago	3	11	0	.214	195	334

Western Division

Club	W.	L.	T.	Pct.	Pts.	Opp.
Los Angeles	12	2	0	.857	388	178
Atlanta	9	5	0	.613	318	224
San Francisco	5	9	0	.357	262	319
New Orleans	5	9	0	.357	163	312

(a)Clinched first place on basis of better conference record than Pittsburgh.
(b)Clinched first place on basis of most points scored in head-to-head competition against Washington.
*Clinched wild card playoff spot.
AFC playoffs — Miami 34, Cincinnati 16; Oakland 33, Pittsburgh 14; Miami 27, Oakland 10.
NFC playoffs — Dallas 27, Los Angeles 16; Minnesota 27, Washington 20; Minnesota 27, Dallas 10.
Championship game — Miami 24, Minnesota 7.

Miami Defeats Minnesota in Super Bowl

The Miami Dolphins defeated the Minnesota Vikings, 24-7 to win the 1974 Super Bowl game. The Dolphins by winning their second straight Super Bowl equaled the feat of the Green Bay Packer teams of 1967 and 1968. The game was played Jan. 13, 1974 at Rice Stadium, Houston, before a crowd of 68,142 plus an estimated 60 million television viewers.

Score by Quarters

Miami	14	3	7	0—24
Minnesota	0	0	0	7— 7

Scoring

Miami—Csonka 5 run (Yepremian kick).
Miami—Kiick 1 run (Yepremian kick).
Miami—Field goal Yepremian 28.
Miami—Csonka 2 run (Yepremian kick).
Minnesota—Tarkenton 4 run (Cox kick).

Team Statistics

	Minnesota	Miami
First downs	14	21
Rushes-Yardage	24-72	53-196
Passing yardage	166	63
Return yardage	0	30
Passes	18-28-1	6-7-0
Punts	5-42.2	3-39.6
Fumbles-Lost	2-1	1-0
Penalties-Yardage	7-65	1-4

Attendance—68,142.

Individual Statistics

Miami rushing — Csonka, 33 for 145 yards; Morris, 11 for 34; Kiick, 7 for 10; Griese, 2 for 7.
Minnesota rushing — Reed, 11 for 32 yards; Foreman, 7 for 18; Tarkenton, 4 for 17; Marinaro, 1 for 3; Brown, 1 for 2.
Miami passing — Griese, 6 of 7 for 73 yards.
Minnesota passing — Tarkenton, 18 of 28 for 182 yards (one intercepted).
Miami pass receiving — Warfield, 2 for 33 yards; Mandich, 2 for 21; Briscoe, 2 for 19.
Minnesota pass receiving — Voight, 3 for 46 yards; Gilliam, 4 for 44; Marinaro, 2 for 39; Foreman, 5 for 27; Brown, 1 for 9; Lash, 1 for 9; Kingsriter, 1 for 9; Reed, 1 for minus 1.

Super Bowl

Year	Winner	Loser	Site
1967	Green Bay Packers, 35	Kansas City Chiefs, 10	Los Angeles Coliseum
1968	Green Bay Packers, 33	Oakland Raiders, 14	Orange Bowl, Miami
1969	New York Jets, 16	Baltimore Colts, 7	Orange Bowl, Miami
1970	Kansas City Chiefs, 23	Minnesota Vikings, 7	Tulane Stadium, New Orleans
1971	Baltimore Colts, 16	Dallas Cowboys, 13	Orange Bowl, Miami
1972	Dallas Cowboys, 24	Miami Dolphins, 3	Tulane Stadium, New Orleans
1973	Miami Dolphins, 14	Washington Redskins, 7	Los Angeles Coliseum
1974	Miami Dolphins, 24	Minnesota Vikings, 7	Rice Stadium, Houston

Jim Thorpe Trophy Winners

The winner of the Jim Thorpe Trophy, named after the athletic great, is picked by Murray Olderman of Newspaper Enterprise Assn. in a poll of players from the 26 NFL teams. It goes to the most valuable NFL player and is the oldest and highest professional football award.

Year	Player and Team
1955	Harlon Hill, Chicago Bears
1956	Frank Gifford, N. Y. Giants
1957	John Unitas, Baltimore Colts
1958	Jim Brown, Cleveland Browns
1959	Charley Conerly, N. Y. Giants
1960	Norm Van Brocklin, Philadelphia Eagles
1961	Y. A. Tittle, N. Y. Giants
1962	Jim Taylor, Green Bay Packers
1963	(tie) Jim Brown, Cleveland Browns and Y. A. Tittle, N. Y. Giants
1964	Lenny Moore, Baltimore Colts
1965	Jim Brown, Cleveland Browns
1966	Bart Starr, Green Bay Packers
1967	John Unitas, Baltimore Colts
1968	Earl Morrall, Baltimore Colts
1969	Roman Gabriel, Los Angeles Rams
1970	John Brodie, San Francisco
1971	Bob Griese, Miami
1972	Larry Brown, Washington
1973	O. J. Simpson, Buffalo

National Football League

Year	Winners (W-L-T) (East)	Winners (W-L-T) (West)	Playoff
1933	New York Giants (11-3-0).........	Chicago Bears (10-2-1)...........	Chicago Bears 23, New York 21
1934	New York Giants (8-5-0).........	Chicago Bears (13-0-0)...........	New York 30, Chicago Bears 13
1935	New York Giants (9-3-0).........	Detroit Lions (7-3-2).............	Detroit 26, New York 7
1936	Boston Redskins (7-5-0).........	Green Bay Packers (10-1-1).......	Green Bay 21, Boston 6
1937	Washington Redskins (8-3-0).....	Chicago Bears (9-1-1)...........	Wash. 28, Chicago Bears 21
1938	New York Giants (8-2-1).........	Green Bay Packers (8-3-0)........	New York 23, Green Bay 17
1939	New York Giants (9-1-1).........	Green Bay Packers (9-2-0)........	Green Bay 27, New York 0
1940	Washington Redskins (9-2-0).....	Chicago Bears (8-3-0)...........	Chicago Bears 73, Wash. 0
1941	New York Giants (8-3-0).........	Chicago Bears (10-1-1) (A).......	Chicago Bears 37, New York 9
1942	Wash. Redskins (10-1-1).........	Chicago Bears (11-0-0)..........	Wash. 14, Chicago Bears 6
1943	Wash. Redskins (6-3-1) (A)......	Chicago Bears (8-1-1)...........	Chicago Bears 41, Wash. 21
1944	New York Giants (8-1-1).........	Green Bay Packers (8-2-0)........	Green Bay 14, New York 7
1945	Wash. Redskins (8-2-0)..........	Cleveland Rams (9-1-0)..........	Cleveland 15, Washington 14
1946	New York Giants (7-3-1).........	Chicago Bears (8-2-1)...........	Chicago Bears 24, New York 14
1947	Philadelphia Eagles (8-4-0) (A)..	Chicago Cardinals (9-3-0).......	Chicago Cardinals 28, Phila. 21
1948	Philadelphia Eagles (9-2-1).....	Chicago Cardinals (11-1-0)......	Phila. 7, Chicago Cardinals 0
1949	Philadelphia Eagles (11-1-0)....	Los Angeles Rams (8-2-2)........	Philadelphia 14, Los Angeles 0
1950	Cleveland Browns (10-2-0) (A)...	Los Angeles Rams (9-3-0) (A)....	Cleveland 30, Los Angeles 28
1951	Cleveland Browns (11-1-0).......	Los Angeles Rams (8-4-0)........	Los Angeles 24, Cleveland 17
1952	Cleveland Browns (8-4-0)........	Detroit Lions (9-3-0) (A)........	Detroit 17, Cleveland 7
1953	Cleveland Browns (11-1-0).......	Detroit Lions (10-2-0)..........	Detroit 17, Cleveland 16
1954	Cleveland Browns (9-3-0)........	Detroit Lions (9-2-1)...........	Cleveland 56, Detroit 10
1955	Cleveland Browns (9-2-1)........	Los Angeles Rams (8-3-1)........	Cleveland 38, Los Angeles 14
1956	New York Giants (8-3-1).........	Chicago Bears (9-2-1)...........	New York 47, Chicago Bears 7
1957	Cleveland Browns (9-2-1)........	Detroit Lions (8-4-0) (A)........	Detroit 59, Cleveland 14
1958	New York Giants (9-3-0) (A).....	Baltimore Colts (9-3-0).........	Baltimore 23, New York 17 (B)
1959	New York Giants (10-2-0)........	Baltimore Colts (9-3-0).........	Baltimore 31, New York 16
1960	Philadelphia Eagles (10-2-0)....	Green Bay Packers (8-4-0).......	Philadelphia 17, Green Bay 13
1961	New York Giants (10-3-1)........	Green Bay Packers (11-3-0)......	Green Bay 37, New York 0
1962	New York Giants (12-2-0)........	Green Bay Packers (13-1-0)......	Green Bay 16, New York 7
1963	New York Giants (11-3-0)........	Chicago Bears (11-1-2)..........	Chicago 14, New York 10
1964	Cleveland Browns (10-3-1).......	Baltimore Colts (12-2-0)........	Cleveland 27, Baltimore 0
1965	Cleveland Browns (11-3-0).......	Green Bay Packers (10-3-1) (A)..	Green Bay 23, Cleveland 12
1966	Dallas Cowboys (10-3-1).........	Green Bay Packers (12-2-0)......	Green Bay 34, Dallas 27

(A) Won divisional playoff. (B) Won at 8:15 sudden death overtime period.

Year	Conference	Division	Winners (W-L-T)	Playoffs
1967.......	East...........	Century	Cleveland (9-5-0)...........	Dallas 52, Cleveland 14
		Capitol	Dallas (9-5-0)	
	West..........	Central	Green Bay (9-4-1)...........	Green Bay 28, L. A. 7
		Coastal.....	Los Angeles (11-1-2) (A).....	Green Bay 21, Dallas 17
1968.......	East...........	Century	Cleveland (10-4-0)...........	Cleveland 31, Dallas 20
		Capitol	Dallas (12-2-0)	
	West..........	Central	Minnesota (8-6-0)...........	Baltimore 24, Minnesota 14
		Coastal.....	Baltimore (13-1-0)..........	Baltimore 34, Cleveland 0
1969.......	East...........	Century	Cleveland (10-3-1)...........	Cleveland 38, Dallas 14
		Capitol	Dallas (11-2-1)	
	West..........	Central	Minnesota (12-2-0)..........	Minnesota 23, Los Angeles 20
		Coastal.....	Los Angeles (11-3-0)........	Minnesota 27, Cleveland 7
1970.......	American......	Eastern......	Baltimore (11-2-1)..........	Baltimore 17, Cincinnati 0
		Central......	Cincinnati (8-6-0)...........	Oakland 21, Miami 14
		Western......	Oakland (8-4-2)...........	Baltimore 27, Oakland 17
	National.......	Eastern......	Dallas (10-4-0).............	Dallas 5, Detroit 0
		Central......	Minnesota (12-2-0).........	San Francisco 17, Minnesota 14
		Western......	San Francisco (10-3-1)......	Dallas 17, San Francisco 10
1971.......	American......	Eastern......	Miami (10-3-1)............	Miami 27, Kansas City 24
		Central......	Cleveland (9-5-0)...........	Baltimore 20, Cleveland 3
		Western......	Kansas City (10-3-1)........	Miami 21, Baltimore 0
	National.......	Eastern......	Dallas (11-3-0)............	Dallas 20, Minnesota 12
		Central......	Minnesota (11-3-0).........	San Francisco 24, Washington 20
		Western......	San Francisco (9-5-0).......	Dallas 14, San Francisco 3
1972.......	American......	Eastern......	Miami (14-0-0)............	Miami 20, Cleveland 14
		Central......	Pittsburgh (11-3-0).........	Pittsburgh 13, Oakland 7
		Western......	Oakland (10-3-1)..........	Miami 21, Pittsburgh 17
	National.......	Eastern......	Washington (11-3-0)........	Washington 16, Green Bay 3
		Central......	Green Bay (10-4-0).........	Dallas 30, San Francisco 28
		Western......	San Francisco (8-5-1).......	Washington 26, Dallas 3
1973.......	American......	Eastern......	Miami (12-2-0)............	Miami 34, Cincinnati 16
		Central......	Cincinnati (10-4-0).........	Oakland 33, Pittsburgh 14
		Western......	Oakland (9-4-1)...........	Miami 27, Oakland 10
	National.......	Eastern......	Dallas (10-4-0)............	Dallas 27, Los Angeles 16
		Central......	Minnesota (12-2-0).........	Minnesota 27, Washington 20
		Western......	Los Angeles (12-2-0).......	Minnesota 27, Dallas 10

American Football League

Year	Eastern Division	Western Division	Playoff
1960	Houston Oilers (10-4-0).............	L. A. Chargers (10-4-0)...............	Houston 24, Los Angeles 16
1961	Houston Oilers (10-3-1).............	San Diego Chargers (12-2-0)..........	Houston 10, San Diego 3
1962	Houston Oilers (11-3-0).............	Dallas Texans (11-3-0).............	Dallas 20, Houston 17 (b)
1963	Boston Patriots (8-6-1) (a).........	San Diego Chargers (11-3-0)........	San Diego 51, Boston 10
1964	Buffalo Bills (12-2-0).............	San Diego Chargers (8-5-1).........	Buffalo 20, San Diego 7
1965	Buffalo Bills (10-3-1).............	San Diego Chargers (9-2-3).........	Buffalo 23, San Diego 0
1966	Buffalo Bills (9-4-1).............	Kansas City Chiefs (11-2-1)........	Kansas City 31, Buffalo 7
1967	Houston Oilers (9-4-1).............	Oakland Raiders (13-1-0)...........	Oakland 40, Houston 7
1968	New York Jets (11-3-0).............	Oakland Raiders (12-2-0) (a)...........	New York 27, Oakland 23
1969	New York Jets (10-4-0).............	Oakland Raiders (12-1-1)...............	Kansas City 17, Oakland 7 (c)

(a) won divisional playoff (b) won at 2:45 of second overtime. (c) K. C. def. Jets to make playoffs.

National Football Conference Leaders
(National Football League, 1962-1969)

Passing

Year	Player	Atts.	Com.	YG	TD
1962	Bart Starr, Green Bay	285	178	2,438	9
1963	Y. A. Tittle, N. Y. Giants	367	221	3,145	14
1964	Bart Starr, Green Bay	272	163	2,144	4
1965	Rudy Bukich, Chicago	312	176	2,641	9
1966	Bart Starr, Green Bay	251	156	2,257	3
1967	Sonny Jurgensen, Washington	508	288	3,747	16
1968	Earl Morrall, Baltimore	317	182	2,909	17
1969	Sonny Jurgensen, Washington	422	274	3,102	15
1970	John Brodie, San Francisco	378	223	2,941	24
1971	Roger Staubach, Dallas	211	126	1,882	15
1972	Norm Snead, N. Y. Giants	325	196	2,307	17
1973	Roger Staubach, Dallas	286	179	2,428	23

Pass-Receiving

Year	Player	Ct.	YG	TD
1962	Bobby Mitchell, Washington	72	1,384	11
1963	Bobby Conrad, Cards, St. Louis	73	967	10
1964	Johnny Morris, Chicago	93	1,200	10
1965	Dave Parks, San Francisco	80	1,344	12
1966	Charlie Taylor, Washington	72	1,119	12
1967	Charlie Taylor, Washington	70	990	9
1968	Clifton McNeil, San Francisco	71	944	7
1969	Dan Abramowicz, New Orleans	73	1,015	7
1970	Dick Gordon, Chicago	71	1,026	13
1971	Bob Tucker, Giants	59	791	4
1972	Harold Jackson, Philadelphia	62	1,048	4
1973	Harold Carmichael, Philadelphia	67	1,116	9

Scoring

Year	Player	TDs	PAT	FG	Pts.
1962	Jim Taylor, Green Bay	19	0	0	114
1963	Don Chandler, New York	0	52	18	106
1964	Lenny Moore, Baltimore	20	0	0	120
1965	Gale Sayers, Chicago	22	0	0	132
1966	Bruce Gossett, Los Angeles	0	29	28	113
1967	Jim Bakken, St. Louis	0	36	27	117
1968	Leroy Kelly, Cleveland	20	0	0	120
1969	Fred Cox, Minnesota	0	43	26	121
1970	Fred Cox, Minnesota	0	35	30	125
1971	Curt Knight, Washington	0	27	29	114
1972	Chester Marcol, Green Bay	0	29	33	128
1973	David Ray, Los Angeles	0	40	30	130

Rushing

Year	Player	YG	Atts.	TD
1962	Jim Taylor, Green Bay	1,474	272	19
1963	Jimmy Brown, Cleveland	1,863	291	12
1964	Jimmy Brown, Cleveland	1,446	280	7
1965	Jimmy Brown, Cleveland	1,544	289	17
1966	Gale Sayers, Chicago	1,231	229	8
1967	Leroy Kelly, Cleveland	1,205	235	11
1968	Leroy Kelly, Cleveland	1,239	248	16
1969	Gale Sayers, Chicago	1,032	236	8
1970	Larry Brown, Washington	1,125	237	5
1971	John Brockington, Green Bay	1,105	216	4
1972	Larry Brown, Washington	1,216	285	8
1973	John Brockington, Green Bay	1,144	265	3

American Football Conference Leaders
(American Football League, 1962-1969)

Scoring

Year	Player	TDs	PAT	FG	Pts.
1962	Gene Mingo, Denver	4	32	27	137
1963	Gino Cappelletti, Boston	2	35	22	113
1964	Gino Cappelletti, Boston	7	36	25	155
1965	Gino Cappelletti, Boston	9	27	17	132
1966	Gino Cappelletti, Boston	6	35	16	119
1967	George Blanda, Oakland	0	56	20	116
1968	Jim Turner, N. Y. Jets	0	43	34	145
1969	Jim Turner, N. Y. Jets	0	33	32	129
1970	Jan Stenerud, Kansas City	0	26	30	116
1971	Garo Yepremian, Miami	0	33	28	117
1972	Bobby Howfield, N. Y. Jets	0	40	27	121
1973	Roy Gerela, Pittsburgh	0	36	29	123

Rushing

Year	Player	YG	Atts.	TD
1962	Cookie Gilchrist, Buffalo	1,096	214	13
1963	Clem Daniels, Oakland	1,098	214	3
1964	Cookie Gilchrist, Buffalo	981	230	6
1965	Paul Lowe, San Diego	1,121	222	7
1966	Jim Nance, Boston	1,458	299	11
1967	Jim Nance, Boston	1,216	269	7
1968	Paul Robinson, Cincinnati	1,023	238	8
1969	Dick Post, San Diego	873	182	6
1970	Floyd Little, Denver	901	209	3
1971	Floyd Little, Denver	1,133	284	6
1972	O. J. Simpson, Buffalo	1,251	292	6
1973	O. J. Simpson, Buffalo	2,003	332	12

Passing

Year	Player	Atts.	Com.	YG	TD
1962	Len Dawson, Dallas	310	189	2,749	17
1963	Tobin Rote, San Diego	287	170	2,510	17
1964	Len Dawson, Kansas City	354	199	2,879	18
1965	Jack Hadl, San Diego	348	174	2,798	21
1966	Len Dawson, Kansas City	284	159	2,527	10
1967	Daryle Lamonica, Oakland	425	220	3,228	20
1968	Len Dawson, Kansas City	224	131	2,109	9
1969	Greg Cook, Cincinnati	197	106	1,854	11
1970	Daryle Lamonica, Oakland	356	179	2,516	22
1971	Bob Griese, Miami	263	145	2,089	19
1972	Earl Morrall, Miami	150	83	1,360	11
1973	Ken Stabler, Oakland	260	163	1,997	14

Pass-Receiving

Year	Player	Ct.	YG	TD
1962	Lionel Taylor, Denver	77	908	4
1963	Lionel Taylor, Denver	78	1,101	10
1964	Charlie Hennigan, Houston	101	1,561	8
1965	Lionel Taylor, Denver	85	1,131	6
1966	Lance Alworth, San Diego	73	1,383	13
1967	George Sauer, N. Y. Jets	75	1,189	6
1968	Lance Alworth, San Diego	68	1,312	10
1969	Lance Alworth, San Diego	64	1,003	4
1970	Marlin Briscoe, Buffalo	57	1,036	8
1971	Fred Biletnikoff, Oakland	61	929	9
1972	Fred Biletnikoff, Oakland	58	802	7
1973	Fred Willis, Houston	57	371	1

1974 NFL Player Draft

The following are the first round picks of the National Football League.

Team	Player	Pos.	College	Team	Player	Pos.	College
1—Dallas	Ed Jones	DE	Tenn. State	14—Denver	Randy Gradishar	LB	Ohio State
2—San Diego	Bo Matthews	RB	Colorado	15—San Diego	Don Goode	LB	Kansas
3—N. Y. Giants	John Hicks	OT	Ohio State	16—Kansas City	Woody Green	RB	Arizona St.
4—Chicago	Waymond Bryant	LB	Tenn. State	17—Minnesota	Fred McNeill	LB	UCLA
5—Baltimore	John Dutton	DT	Nebraska	18—Buffalo	Reuben Gant	TE	Oklahoma St.
6—N. Y. Jets	Carl Barzilauskas	DT	Indiana	19—Oakland	Henry Lawrence	OT	Florida A & M
7—St. Louis	J. V. Cain	TE	Colorado	20—Chicago	Dave Gallagher	DT	Michigan
8—Detroit	Ed O'Neil	LB	Penn St.	21—Pittsburgh	Lynn Swann	WR	USC
9—San Francisco	Wilbur Jackson	RB	Alabama	22—Dallas	Charley Young	RB	No. Carolina St.
10—San Francisco	Bill Sandifer	DT	UCLA	23—Cincinnati	Bill Kollar	DT	Montana State
11—Los Angeles	John Cappelletti	RB	Penn St.	24—Baltimore	Roger Carr	WR	Louisiana Tech
12—Green Bay	Barty Smith	RB	Richmond	25—Minnesota	Steve Riley	OT	USC
13—New Orleans	Rick Middleton	LB	Ohio State	26—Miami	Donald Reese	DE	Jackson State

1973 NFL Individual Leaders

National Conference

Passing*

	Att.	Comp.	Pct. Comp.	Yards Gained	TD. Passes	Longest	Int.	Avg.Yds. Gained
Staubach, Dallas	286	179	62.6	2428	23	53	15	8.49
Tarkenton, Minnesota	274	169	61.7	2113	15	54	7	7.71
Hadl, Los Angeles	258	135	52.3	2008	22	69	11	7.78
Gabriel, Philadelphia	460	270	58.7	3219	23	80	12	7.00
Kilmer, Washington	227	122	53.7	1656	14	64	9	7.30
Hart, St. Louis	230	120	52.2	1786	10	57	8	7.77
Lee, Atlanta	230	120	52.2	1786	10	57	8	7.77
Jurgensen, Washington	145	87	60.0	904	6	36	5	6.23
Johnson, New York	177	99	55.9	1279	7	48	8	7.23
Munson, Detroit	185	95	51.4	1129	9	54	8	6.10
Manning, New Orleans	267	140	52.4	1642	10	65	12	6.15
Douglass, Chicago	174	81	46.6	1057	5	63	7	6.07
Spurrier, San Francisco	157	83	52.9	882	4	58	7	5.62
Brodie, San Francisco	194	98	50.5	1126	3	66	12	5.80
Snead, New York	235	131	55.7	1483	7	46	22	6.31

Scorers—Kicking

	XP—XPA	FG—FGA	Pts.
Ray, Los Angeles	40—42	30—47	130
Mike-Mayer, Atlanta	34—34	26—38	112
Dempsey, Philadelphia	34—34	24—40	106
Gossett, San Francisco	26—26	26—33	104
Knight, Washington	37—37	22—42	103
Bakken, St. Louis	31—31	23—32	100
Fritsch, Dallas	43—43	18—28	97
Cox, Minnesota	33—33	21—35	96
Marcol, Green Bay	19—20	21—35	82

Scorers—Touchdowns

	Tot.	Rush.	Pass.	Ret.	Pts.
Brown, Washington	14	8	6	0	84
Anderson, St. Louis	13	10	3	0	78
Jackson, Los Angeles	13	0	13	0	78
Ray, Atlanta	11	9	2	0	66
Ron Johnson, New York	9	6	3	0	54
Gilliam, Minnesota	9	1	8	0	54
Carmichael, Philadelphia	9	0	9	0	54
V. Washington, San Fran.	8	8	0	0	48
Garrison, Dallas	8	6	2	0	48

Pass Receiving

	No.	Yds.	Avg.	TDs.
Carmichael, Philadelphia	67	1116	16.7	9
Taylor, Washington	59	801	13.6	7
Young, Philadelphia	55	854	15.5	6
Tucker, New York	50	681	13.6	5
Sullivan, Philadelphia	50	322	6.4	1
Kwalick, San Francisco	47	729	15.5	5
Herrmann, New York	43	520	12.1	2
Gilliam, Minnesota	42	907	21.6	8
Bulaich, Philadelphia	42	403	9.6	3

Rushing

	Att.	Yds.	Avg.	TDs.
Brockington, Green Bay	265	1144	4.3	3
Hill, Dallas	273	1142	4.2	6
McCutcheon, Los Angeles	210	1097	5.2	2
Hampton, Atlanta	263	997	3.8	4
Sullivan, Philadelphia	217	968	4.5	4
Ron Johnson, New York	260	902	3.5	6
Brown, Washington	273	860	3.2	8
Bertelsen, Los Angeles	206	854	4.1	4
Foreman, Minnesota	182	801	4.4	4
Taylor, Detroit	176	719	4.1	5

American Conference

Passing*

	Att.	Comp.	Pct. Comp.	Yards Gained	TD. Pass	Long	Int.	Avg.Yds. Gained
Stabler, Oakland	260	163	62.7	1997	14	80	10	7.68
Griese, Miami	218	116	53.2	1422	17	46	8	6.52
Anderson, Cincinnati	329	179	54.4	2428	18	78	12	7.38
Johnson, Denver	346	184	53.2	2465	20	62	17	7.12
Woodall, New York	201	101	50.2	1228	9	56	8	6.11
Plunkett, New England	376	193	51.3	2550	13	64	17	6.78
Livingston, Kansas City	145	65	44.8	916	6	48	7	6.32
Domres, Baltimore	191	93	48.7	1153	9	66	13	6.04
Bradshaw, Pittsburgh	180	89	49.4	1183	10	67	15	6.57
Phipps, Cleveland	299	148	49.5	1719	9	51	20	5.75
Pastorini, Houston	290	154	53.1	1482	5	50	17	5.11
Fouts, San Diego	194	87	44.8	1126	6	69	13	5.80
Ferguson, Buffalo	164	73	44.5	939	4	42	10	5.73

Scorers—Touchdowns

	Tot.	Rush.	Pass.	Ret.	Pts.
Little, Denver	13	12	1	0	78
Simpson, Buffalo	12	12	0	0	72
Warfield, Miami	11	0	11	0	66
Morris, Miami	10	10	0	0	60
Shanklin, Pittsburgh	10	0	10	0	60
Moses, Denver	9	1	8	0	54
Curtis, Cincinnati	9	0	9	0	54
Clark, Cincinnati	8	8	0	0	48

Pass Receiving

	No.	Yds.	Avg.	TDs.
Willis, Houston	57	371	6.5	1
Podolak, Kansas City	55	445	8.1	0
Rucker, New England	53	743	14.0	3
Biletnikoff, Oakland	48	660	13.8	4
Curtis, Cincinnati	45	843	18.7	9
Siani, Oakland	45	742	16.5	3
Clark, Cincinnati	45	347	7.7	0
Barkum, New York	44	810	18.4	6

*At least 140 attempted passes needed to qualify. Leader based on percentage of completions — touchdown passes — interceptions — and average yards.

American Conference (Con't)

Scorers—Kicking	XP—XPA	FG—FGA	Pts
Gerela, Pittsburgh	36—37	29—43	123
Yepremian, Miami	38—38	25—37	113
Turner, Denver	40—40	22—33	106
Blanda, Oakland	31—31	23—33	100
Muhlmann, Cincinnati	31—32	21—31	94
Stenerud, Kansas City	21—23	24—38	93
Cockroft, Cleveland	24—24	22—31	90
Leypoldt, Buffalo	27—27	21—30	90
Howfield, New York	27—27	17—24	78

Rushing	Att.	Yds.	Avg.	TDs
Simpson, Buffalo	332	2003	6.0	12
Csonka, Miami	219	1003	4.6	5
E. Johnson, Cincinnati	195	997	5.1	4
Clark, Cincinnati	254	988	3.9	8
Little, Denver	256	979	3.8	12
L. Mitchell, Baltimore	253	963	3.8	2
Morris, Miami	149	954	6.4	10
Hubbard, Oakland	193	903	4.7	6
Boozer, New York	182	831	4.6	3
Podolak, Kansas City	210	721	3.4	3

1973 NEA All-NFL Team

First Team	Offense	Second Team
John Gilliam, Minnesota	Wide Receiver	Paul Warfield, Miami
Harold Jackson, Los Angeles	Wide Receiver	Harold Carmichael, Philadelphia
Art Shell, Oakland	Tackle	Rayfield Wright, Dallas
George Kunz, Atlanta	Tackle	Ron Yary, Minnesota
Larry Little, Miami	Guard	Gene Upshaw, Oakland
Joe Scibelli, Los Angeles	Guard	Reggie McKenzie, Buffalo
Bob Johnson, Cincinnati	Center	Jack Rudney, Kansas City
Riley Odoms, Denver	Tight End	Charley Young, Philadelphia
Fran Tarkenton, Minnesota	Quarterback	John Hadl, Los Angeles
O. J. Simpson, Buffalo	Running Back	Larry Csonka, Miami
John Brockington, Green Bay	Running Back	Lawrence McCutcheon, Los Angeles
Garo Yepremian, Miami	Kicker	Roy Gerela, Pittsburgh

First Team	Defense	Second Team
Bill Stanfill, Miami	End	John Zook, Atlanta
Alan Page*, Minnesota	End	Elvin Bethea, Houston
Joe Greene, Pittsburgh	Tackle	Paul Smith, Denver
Mike Reid, Cincinnati	Tackle	Manny Fernandez, Miami
Lee Roy Jordan, Dallas	Middle Backer	Willie Lanier, Kansas City
Dave Wilcox, San Francisco	Linebacker	Jack Ham, Pittsburgh
Chris Hanburger, Washington	Linebacker	Ted Hendricks, Baltimore
Willie Brown, Oakland	Corner Back	Lem Barney, Detroit
Mel Renfro, Dallas	Corner Back	Clarence Scott, Cleveland
Dick Anderson, Miami	Safety	Jake Scott, Miami
Bill Bradley, Philadelphia	Safety	Ken Houston, Washington
Ray Guy, Oakland	Punter	Jerrell Wilson, Kansas City

*Page is normally a defensive tackle

George Halas Trophy Winners

The Halas Trophy, named after football coach George Halas, is awarded annually to the outstanding defensive player in football in a poll conducted by Newspaper Enterprise Assn. of NFL players.

1966—Larry Wilson, St. Louis
1967—Deacon Jones, Los Angeles
1968—Deacon Jones, Los Angeles
1969—Dick Butkus, Chicago
1970—Dick Butkus, Chicago
1971—Carl Eller, Minnesota
1972—Joe Greene, Pittsburgh
1973—Alan Page, Minnesota

Canadian Football League
1973 Final Standings

Eastern Conference	W.	L.	T.	PF	PA	PTS.
Ottawa	9	5	0	275	234	18
Toronto	7	5	2	265	231	16
Montreal	7	6	1	273	238	15
Hamilton	7	7	0	304	263	14

Western Conference	W.	L.	T.	PF	PA	PTS.
Edmonton	9	5	2	329	284	20
Saskatchewan	10	6	0	360	287	20
British Columbia	5	9	2	261	328	12
Calgary	6	10	0	214	368	12
Winnipeg	4	11	1	267	315	9

East Semifinal—Montreal 32, Toronto 10 (20 minute overtime).
West Semifinal—Saskatchewan 33, British Columbia 13
East Final—Ottawa 23, Montreal 14
West Final— Edmonton 25, Saskatchewan 23

Canadian Football League (Grey Cup)

Winners of Eastern and Western divisions meet in championship game for Grey Cup (donated by Governor-General Earl Grey in 1909). Canadian football features three downs, 110-yard field, and each team can have 12 players on field at one time.

1948—Calgary Stampeders 12, Ottawa Rough Riders 7
1949—Montreal Alouettes 28, Calgary Stampeders 15
1950—Toronto Argonauts 13, Winnipeg Blue Bombers 0
1951—Ottawa Rough Riders 21, Saskatchewan Roughriders 14
1952—Toronto Argonauts 21, Edmonton Eskimos 11
1953—Hamilton Tiger-Cats 12, Winnipeg Blue Bombers 6
1954—Edmonton Eskimos 26, Montreal Alouettes 25
1955—Edmonton Eskimos 34, Montreal Alouettes 19
1956—Edmonton Eskimos 50, Montreal Alouettes 27
1957—Hamilton Tiger-Cats 32, Winnipeg Blue Bombers 7
1958—Winnipeg Blue Bombers 35, Hamilton Tiger-Cats 28
1959—Winnipeg Blue Bombers 21, Hamilton Tiger-Cats 7
1960—Ottawa Rough Riders 16, Edmonton Eskimos 6
1961—Winnipeg Blue Bombers 21, Hamilton Tiger-Cats 14
1962—Winnipeg Blue Bombers 28, Hamilton Tiger-Cats 27
1963—Hamilton Tiger-Cats 21, British Columbia Lions 10
1964—British Columbia Lions 34, Hamilton Tiger-Cats 24
1965—Hamilton Tiger-Cats 22, Winnipeg Blue Bombers 16
1966—Saskatchewan Roughriders 29, Ottawa Rough Riders 14
1967—Hamilton Tiger-Cats 24, Saskatchewan Roughriders 1
1968—Ottawa Rough Riders 24, Calgary Stampeders 21
1969—Ottawa Rough Riders 29, Saskatchewan Roughriders 11
1970—Montreal Alouettes 23, Calgary Stampeders 10
1971—Calgary Stampeders 14, Toronto Argonauts 11
1972—Hamilton Tiger-Cats 13, Saskatchewan Rough Riders 10
1973—Ottawa Rough Riders 22, Edmonton Eskimos 18

All-Time Pro Football Records

Leading Lifetime Rushers (As of Sept. 14, 1974)

Player	League	Yrs.	Att.	Yards	Avg.	Player	League	Yrs.	Att.	Yards	Avg.
Jim Brown	NFL	9	2,359	12,312	5.2	Floyd Little	AFL-NFL	7	1,399	5,566	4.0
Joe Perry	AAFC-NFL	16	1,929	9,723	5.0	Mike Garrett	AFL-NFL	9	1,308	5,481	4.2
Jim Taylor	NFL	10	1,941	8,597	4.4	Dick Bass	NFL	10	1,218	5,417	4.4
Leroy Kelly	NFL	10	1,727	7,274	4.2	Jim Nance	NFL-AFL	7	1,341	5,401	4.0
John Henry Johnson	NFL-AFL	13	1,571	6,803	4.3	Hugh McElhenny	NFL	13	1,124	5,231	4.7
Don Perkins	NFL	8	1,500	6,217	4.1	O.J. Simpson	AFL-NFL	5	1,108	5,174	4.7
Ken Willard	NFL	9	1,582	5,930	3.7	Lenny Moore	NFL	12	1,069	5,174	4.8
Steve Van Buren	NFL	8	1,320	5,860	4.3	Ollie Matson	NFL	14	1,170	5,173	4.4
Bill Brown	NFL	13	1,630	5,797	3.5	Larry Csonka	AFL-NFL	6	1,089	5,151	4.7
Rick Casares	NFL-AFL	12	1,431	5,797	4.1	Clem Daniels	AFL-NFL	9	1,146	5,138	4.5

Most Yards Gained, Season—2,003, O.J. Simpson, Buffalo Bills, 1973.
Most Yards Gained, Game—250, Orban (Spec) Sanders, New York Yankees vs. Chicago Rockets, Oct. 24, 1947; O.J. Simpson, Buffalo vs. New England, Sept. 16, 1973.
Most games, 100 Yards or more, Season—11, O.J. Simpson, Buffalo Bills, 1973.
Most Games, 100 Yards or more, Career—58, Jim Brown, Cleveland Browns, 1957-1965.
Most Touchdowns Rushing, Career—106, Jim Brown, Cleveland Browns, 1957-1965.
Most Touchdowns Rushing, Season—19, Jim Taylor, Green Bay Packers, 1962.
Most Touchdowns Rushing, Game—6, Ernie Nevers, Chicago Cardinals vs. Chicago Bears, Nov. 8, 1929.
Most Rushing Attempts, Season—332, O.J. Simpson, Buffalo Bills, 1973.
Most Rushing Attempts, Game—39, O.J. Simpson, Buffalo Bills vs. Kansas City, Oct. 29, 1973.
Longest run from Scrimmage—97 yds., Andy Uram, Green Bay vs. Chicago Cardinals, Oct. 8, 1939; Bob Gage, Pittsburgh vs. Chicago Bears, Dec. 4, 1949. (Both scored touchdown.)

Leading Lifetime Passers (Minimum 1500 attempts)

Player	League	Yrs.	Att.	Comp.	Yds.	Pts.*	Player	League	Yrs.	Att.	Comp.	Yds.	Pts.*
Otto Graham	AAFC-NFL	10	2,626	1,464	23,584	86.8	Don Meredith	NFL	9	2,308	1,170	17,199	74.7
Len Dawson	NFL-AFL	17	3,366	1,905	26,043	83.4	Y.A. Tittle	AAFC-NFL	17	4,395	2,427	33,070	74.4
Sonny Jurgensen	NFL	17	4,095	2,326	31,039	82.3	Earl Morrall	NFL	18	2,593	1,326	20,087	74.1
Fran Tarkenton	NFL	13	4,449	2,459	33,248	80.5	Daryle Lamonica	AFL-NFL	11	2,592	1,285	19,119	73.5
Bart Starr	NFL	16	3,149	1,808	24,718	80.3	Frank Albert	AAFC-NFL	7	1,564	831	10,795	73.5
Johnny Unitas	NFL	18	5,186	2,830	40,239	78.2	Bob Griese	AFL-NFL	7	1,761	929	12,341	73.1
Frank Ryan	NFL	13	2,133	1,090	16,042	77.7	John Brodie	NFL	17	4,491	2,469	31,548	72.3
Roman Gabriel	NFL	12	3,773	1,975	25,442	75.7	Billy Wade	NFL	13	2,523	1,370	18,530	72.2
Norm Van Brocklin	NFL	12	2,895	1,553	23,611	75.3	Sammy Baugh	NFL	16	2,995	1,693	21,886	72.0
Sid Luckman	NFL	12	1,744	904	14,686	75.3	Milt Plum	NFL	13	2,419	1,306	17,536	71.9

*Rating points based on performances in the following categories: Percentage of completions, percentage of touchdown passes, percentage of interceptions and average gain per pass attempt.

Most Yards Gained, Season — 4,007, Joe Namath, New York Jets, 1967.
Most Yards Gained, Game — 554, Norm Van Brocklin, Los Angeles vs. N.Y. Yankees, 1951 (27 completions in 41 attempts).
Most Touchdowns Passing, Career — 290, John Unitas, Baltimore Colts, 1956-1973.
Most Touchdowns Passing, Season — 36, George Blanda, Houston Oilers, 1961, and Y.A. Title, New York Giants, 1963.
Most Touchdowns Passing, Game — 7, Sid Luckman, Chicago Bears vs. New York Giants, Nov. 14, 1943; Adrian Burk, Philadelphia Eagles vs. Washington Redskins, Oct. 17, 1954; George Blanda, Houston Oilers vs. New York Titans, Nov. 19, 1961; Y.A. Tittle; New York Giants vs. Washington Redskins, Oct. 28, 1962. Joe Kapp, Minnesota Vikings vs. Baltimore Colts, Sept. 28, 1969.
Most Passing Attempts, Season — 508, Sonny Jurgensen, Washington Redskins, 1967 (288 completions).
Most Passing Attempts, Game — 68, George Blanda, Houston Oilers vs. Buffalo Bills, Nov. 1, 1961 (37 completions).
Most Passes Completed, Season — 288, Sonny Jurgensen, Washington Redskins, 1967 (508 attempts).
Most Passes Completed, Game — 37, George Blanda, Houston Oilers vs. Buffalo Bills, Nov. 1, 1964 (68 attempts).
Most Consecutive Passes Completed — 15, Len Dawson, Kansas City Chiefs vs. Houston Oilers, Sept. 9, 1967; Joe Namath, N.Y. Jets vs. Miami (12), Oct. 22, 1967; vs. Boston (3), Oct. 22, 1969.

Leading Lifetime Receivers

Player	League	Yrs.	No.	Yds.	Avg.	Player	League	Yrs.	No.	Yds.	Avg.
Don Maynard	AFL-NFL	14	633	11,834	18.7	Boyd Dowler	NFL	12	474	7,270	15.4
Ray Berry	NFL	13	631	9,275	14.7	Pete Retzlaff	NFL	11	452	7,412	16.4
Lionel Taylor	AFL	9	567	7,195	12.7	Carroll Dale	NFL	14	438	8,271	18.9
Lance Alworth	AFL-NFL	11	542	10,266	18.9	Jackie Smith	NFL	11	434	7,188	16.6
Charlie Taylor	NFL	10	528	7,470	14.1	Mike Ditka	NFL	12	427	5,812	13.6
Bobby Mitchell	NFL	11	521	7,954	15.3	Bobby Joe Conrad	NFL	12	422	5,902	14.0
Billy Howton	NFL	12	503	8,459	16.8	Charley Hennigan	AFL	7	410	6,823	16.6
Tom McDonald	NFL	12	495	8,410	17.0	Fred Biletnikoff	AFL-NFL	9	408	6,512	16.0
Don Hutson	NFL	11	488	7,991	16.4	Billy Wilson	NFL	10	407	5,902	14.4
Art Powell	AFL-NFL	10	479	8,046	16.8	Jim Phillips	NFL	10	401	6,044	15.1

Most Yards Gained, Season — 1,746, Charley Hennigan, Houston Oilers, 1961.
Most Yards Gained, Game — 303, Jim Benton, Cleveland Rams vs. Detroit Lions, Nov. 22, 1945 (10 receptions).
Most Pass Receptions, Season — 101, Charley Hennigan, Houston Oilers, 1964.
Most Pass Recptions, Game — 18, Tom Fears, Los Angeles Rams vs. Green Bay Packers, Dec. 3, 1950 (189 yards).
Most Consecutive Games, Pass Receptions — 96, Lance Alworth, San Diego Chargers, 1962-1969.
Most Touchdown Passes, Career — 99, Don Hutson, Green Bay Packers, 1935-1945.
Most Touchdown Passes, Season — 17, Don Hutson, Green Bay Packers, 1942; Elroy Hirsch, Los Angeles Rams, 1951; Bill Groman, Houston Oilers, 1961.
Most Touchdown Passes, Game — 5, Bob Shaw, Chicago Cardinals vs. Baltimore Colts, Oct. 2, 1950.
Most Consecutive Games, Touchdown Passes — 11, Elroy Hirsch, Los Angeles Rams, 1950-1951; Buddy Dial, Pittsburgh 57-60.

Miscellaneous Records

Most Fumbles, Season — 16, Don Meredith, Dallas Cowboys, 1964.
Most Fumbles, Game — 7, Len Dawson, Kansas City Chiefs vs. San Diego Chargers, Nov. 15, 1964.
Longest Run With Recovered Fumble — 104 yds., Jack Tatum, Oakland Raiders vs. Green Bay Packers, Sept. 24, 1972.
Longest Winning Streak (Regular Season) — 17 games, Chicago Bears, 1933-1934.
Longest Undefeated Streak. (Includes Tie Games) — 29 games, Cleveland Browns, 1947-1949 (Won 27, Tied 2).
Most Seasons, Active Player — 24, George Blanda, Chicago Bears, 1949-1958; Houston Oilers, 1960-1966 and Oakland, 67-73.

Leading Lifetime Scorers

Player	League	Yrs.	TD	PAT	FG	Total	Player	League	Yrs.	TD	PAT	FG	Total
George Blanda	NFL-AFL	24	9	855	311	1,842	Don Hutson	NFL	11	105	172	7	823
Lou Groza	AAFC-NFL	21	1	810	264	1,608	Pete Gogolak	AFL-NFL	9	0	323	163	812
Gino Cappelletti	AFL	11	42	350	176	1,130	Jan Stenerud	AFL-NFL	7	0	233	179	770
Fred Cox	NFL	11	0	384	230	1,074	Paul Hornung	NFL	9	62	190	66	760
Jim Bakken	NFL	12	0	369	212	1,005	Jim Brown	NFL	9	126	0	0	756
Jim Turner	AFL-NFL	10	0	333	220	993	Tom Davis	NFL	11	0	348	130	738
Sam Baker	NFL	15	2	428	179	977	Mike Clark	NFL	10	0	325	133	724
Bruce Gossett	NFL	10	0	349	208	973	Lenny Moore	NFL	12	113	0	0	678
Lou Michaels	NFL	13	1	386	187	955*	Ben Agajanian	AAFC-NFL					
Bobby Walston	NFL	12	46	365	80	881		AFL	13	0	343	104	655
*Includes safety.							Gordy Soltau	NFL	9	25	284	70	644

Most Points, Season — 176, Paul Hornung, Green Bay Packers, 1960 (15 TD's, 41 PAT's, 15 FG's).
Most Points, Game — 40, Ernie Nevers, Chicago Cardinals vs. Chicago Bears, Nov. 28, 1929 (6 TD's, 4 PAT's).
Most Touchdowns, Season — 22, Gale Sayers, Chicago Bears, 1965 (14 rushing, 6 pass receptions, 1 punt return, 1 kickoff return).
Most Touchdowns, Game — 6, Ernie Nevers, Chicago Cardinals vs. Chicago Bears, Nov. 28, 1929 (6 rushing); Dub Jones, Cleveland Browns vs. Chicago Bears, Nov. 25, 1951 (4 rushing, 2 pass receptions); Gale Sayers, Chicago Bears vs. San Francisco 49ers, Dec. 12, 1965 (4 rushing, 1 pass reception, 1 punt return).
Most Points After Touchdown, Season — 64, George Blanda, Houston Oilers, 1961 (65 attempts).
Most Consecutive Points After Touchdown — 234, Tommy Davis, San Francisco 49ers, 1959-1965.
Most Field Goals, Game — 7, Jim Bakken, St. Louis Cardinals vs. Pittsburgh Steelers, Sept. 24, 1967.
Most Field Goals, Season — 34, Jim Turner, New York Jets, 1968 and 1969.
Most Field Goals Attempted, Season — 49, Bruce Gossett, Los Angeles Rams, 1966; Curt Knight, Washington Redskins, 1971.
Most Field Goals Attempted, Game — 9, Jim Bakken, St. Louis Cardinals vs. Pittsburgh Steelers, Sept. 24, 1967 (7 successful).
Most Consecutive Field Goals — 16, Jan Stenerud, Kansas City Chiefs, Nov. 2, 1969, Dec. 7, 1969.
Most Consecutive Games, Field Goal — 31, Fred Cox, Minnesota Vikings, 1968-1970.
Longest Field Goal — 63 yds., Tom Dempsey, New Orleans Saints vs. Detroit Lions, Nov. 8, 1970.
Highest Field Goal Completion Percentage, Career (400 attempts) — 66.1, Jan Stenerud, Kansas City Chiefs, 1967-1973 (179 FG's in 271 attempts).
Highest Field Goal Completion Percentage, Seaon (20 attempts) — 88.5, Lou Groza, Cleveland Browns, 1953 (23 FG's in 26 attempts).

Pass Interceptions

Most Passes Had Intercepted, Game — 8, Jim Hardy, Chicago Cardinals vs. Philadelphia Eagles, Sept. 24, 1950 (39 attempts).
Most Passes Had Intercepted, Season — 42, George Blanda, Houston Oilers, 1962 (418 attempts).
Most Passes Had Intercepted, Career — 276, George Blanda, Chicago Bears, 1949-1958; Houston Oilers, 1960-1966; Oakland Raiders, 1967-1972 (4,000 attempts).
Most Consecutive Passes Attempted Without Interception — 294, Bart Starr, Green Bay Packers, 1964-1965.
Most Interceptions By, Season — 14, Dick Lane, Los Angeles Rams, 1952.
Most Interceptions By, Career — 79, Emlen Tunnell, New York Giants, 1948-1958; Green Bay Packers, 1959-1961.
Most Consecutive Games, Passes Intercepted By — 8, Tom Morrow, Oakland Raiders, 1962 (4), 1963 (4).
Most Touchdowns Scored via Pass Interceptions, Lifetime — 9, Ken Houston, Houston Oilers, 1967 (2); 1968 (2); 1969; 1971 (4).

Punting

Highest Punting Average, Career (300 Punts) — 45.10, Sam Baugh, Washington Redskins, 1937-1952 (338 Punts).
Highest Punting Average, Season (20 Punts) — 51.3, Sam Baugh, Washington Redskins, 1940 (35 Punts).
Highest Punting Average, Game (4 Punts) — 59.4 Sam Baugh, Washington Redskins vs. Detroit Lions, Oct. 27, 1940 (5 punts).
Longest Punt — 98 yds., Steve O'Neal, New York Jets, vs. Denver Broncos, Sept. 21, 1969.

Kickoff Returns

Most Yardage Returning Kickoffs, Career — 6,502 Ron Smith, Chicago Bears, 1965; Atlanta Falcons, 1966-67; Los Angeles Rams, 1968-69; Chicago Bears, 1970-72, San Diego Chargers, 1973.
Most Yardage Returning Kickoffs, Season — 1,317, Bobby Jancik, Houston Oilers, 1963.
Most Yardage Returning Kickoffs, Game — 294, Wally Triplett, Detroit Lions vs. Los Angeles Rams, Oct. 29, 1950 (4 returns).
Most Touchdowns Scored via Kickoff Returns, Career — 6, Ollie Matson, Chicago Cardinals, 1952 (2), 1954, 1956, 1958 (2); Gale Sayers, Chicago Bears, 1965, 1966 (2), 1967 (3); Travis Williams, Green Bay Packers, 1967 (4),1969, Los Angeles Rams, 1971.
Most Touchdowns Scored via Kickoff Returns, Season — 4, Travis Williams, Green Bay Packers, 1967; Cecil Turner, Chicago Bears, 1970.
Most Touchdowns Scored via Kickoff Returns, Game — 2, Tim Brown, Philadelphia Eagles vs. Dallas Cowboys, Nov. 6, 1966; Travis Williams, Green Bay Packers vs. Cleveland Browns, Nov. 12, 1967.
Most Kickoff Returns, Career — 256, Ron Smith, Chicago Bears, 1965; Atlanta Falcons, 1966-67; Los Angeles Rams, 1968-69; Chicago Bears, 1970-72, San Diego Chargers, 1973.
Most Kickoff Returns, Season — 47, Odell Barry, Denver Broncos, 1964.
Longest Kickoff Return — 106 yds., Al Carmichael, Green Bay Packers vs. Chicago Bears, October 7, 1956 (scored touchdown); Noland Smith, Kansas City vs. Denver, Dec. 17, 1967 (scored touchdown).

Punt Returns

Most Yardage Returning Punts, Career — 2,209, Emlen Tunnell, New York Giants, 1948-1958; Green Bay Packers, 1959-1961.
Most Yardage Returning Punts, Season — 612, Rodger Bird, Oakland Raiders, 1967.
Most Yardage Returning Punts, Game — 205, George Atkinson, Oakland Raiders vs. Buffalo Bills, Sept. 15, 1968.
Most Touchdowns Scored via Punt Returns, Career — 8, Jack Christiansen, Detroit Lions, 1951 (4); 1952 (2), 1954, 1956.
Most Punt Returns, Career — 258, Emlen Tunnell, New York Giants, 1948-1958; Green Bay Packers, 1959-1961.
Most Punt Returns, Season — 53, Alvin Haymond, L. A. Rams, 1970.
Most Punt Returns, Game — 9, Rodger Bird, Oakland Raiders vs. Denver Broncos, Sept. 10, 1967.
Longest Punt Return — 98, Gil LeFebvre, Cincinnati Reds vs. Brooklyn Dodgers, Dec. 3, 1933 (scored touchdown); Charle West, Minnesota Vikings vs. Washington Redskins, Nov. 3, 1968 (scored touchdown).

Pro Football Attendance

Pro Football's all-game attendance, including pre-season and post-season games, rose to an all-time high of 15,500,586 in 1973. The paid attendance during the regular 1973 season was 10,730,933 for a per game average of 58,961, a 2.73% increase over the previous year.

Federal legislation required clubs to make available for local telecast any game sold out 72 hours prior to kickoff. During the regular season, 9.48% of tickets sold were not used. In 1972, when local games were blacked out, 5.98% of the tickets sold were not used.

Pro Football's Hall Of Fame

Canton, Ohio

Raymond Barry	Bill George	Bobby Layne	Jim Parker
Cliff Battles	Otto Graham	Vince Lombardi	Joe Perry
Sammy Baugh	Red Grange	Sid Luckman	Pete Pihos
Chuch Bednarik	Lou Groza	Link Lyman	Hugh (Shorty) Ray
Bert Bell	Joe Guyon	Tim Mara	Dan Reeves
Charles Bidwell	George Halas	Gino Marchetti	Andy Robustelli
Jim Brown	Ed Healey	George Marshall	Art Rooney
Paul Brown	Mel Hein	Ollie Matson	Joe Schmidt
Tony Canadeo	Pete Henry	George McAfee	Ernie Stautner
Joe Carr	Arnold Herber	Hugh McElhenny	Ken Strong
Guy Chamberlin	Bill Hewitt	John (Blood) McNally	Joe Stydahar
Jack Christiansen	Clarke Hinkle	Mike Michalske	Jim Thorpe
Dutch Clark	Elroy Hirsch	Wayne Millner	Y. A. Tittle
Jim Conzelman	Cal Hubbard	Marion Motley	George Trafton
Art Donovan	Lamar Hunt	Bronco Nagurski	Charlie Trippi
Paddy Driscoll	Don Hutson	Greasy Neale	Emlen Tunnell
Bill Dudley	Walt Kiesling	Ernie Nevers	Clyde (Bulldog) Turner
Turk Edwards	Frank (Bruiser) Kinard	Leo Nomellini	Norm Van Brocklin
Tom Fears	Curly Lambeau	Steve Owen	Steve Van Buren
Dr. Daniel Fortmann	Dick (Night Train) Lane	Clarence (Ace) Parker	Bob Waterfield
			Alex Wojciechowicz

World Horseshoe Pitching Champions

Year	Champion	W.	L.	Ringer %	Year	Champion	W.	L.	Ringer %
1964	Harold Reno, Sabina, Ohio	32	3	84.1	1970	Dan Kuchcinski, Erie, Pa.	34	1	84.9
1965	Elmer Hohl, Wellesley, Ont.	32	3	84.6	1971	Curt Day, Frankfort, Ind.	35	0	85.0
1966	Curt Day, Frankfort, Ind.	26	2	86.6	1972	Elmer Hohl, Wellesley, Ont.	33	2	86.0
1967	Dan Kuchcinski, Erie, Pa.	34	1	84.4	1973	Elmer Hohl, Wellesley, Ont.	32	3	83.5
1968	Elmer Hohl, Wellesley, Ont.	35	0	88.5	1974	Curt Day, Frankfort, Ind.	32	3	81.8
1969	Dan Kuchcinski, Erie, Pa.	35	0	84.7					

Year	Ladies Champion	Ringer %	Junior Champion	Ringer %
1966	Vicki Winston, Lamonte, Mo.	72.5	Mark Seibold, Huntington, Ind.	75.6
1967	Vicki Winston, Lamonte, Mo.	73.6	Farron Eisemann, Riverton, Wyo.	73.6
1968	Lorraine Thomas, Lockport, N.Y.	74.6	Farron Eisemann, Riverton, Wyo.	78.5
1969	Vicki Winston, Lamonte, Mo.	79.6	Mark Seibold, Huntington, Ind.	83.7
1970	Ruth Hangen, Buffalo, N.Y.	72.0	Bill Holland, Indianapolis, Ind.	79.2
1971	Ruth Hangen, Buffalo, N.Y.	73.4	Walter Ray Williams, Eureka, Calif.	86.3
1972	Ruth Hangen, Buffalo, N.Y.	76.6	Walter Ray Williams, Eureka, Calif.	89.2
1973	Ruth Hangen, Getzville, N.Y.	79.6	Jeffrey Williams, Eureka, Calif.	85.5
1974	Lorraine Thomas, Lockport, N.Y.	80.2	Doug Kienia, Kittery, Maine	81.2

National AAU Weightlifting Championships

York, Pa. June 8-9, 1974
(Competition consisted of 2 lifts—snatch and clean and jerk)

Flyweight (114 lbs.) — Joel Eiddel, Dewar, Ia.,430 lbs.

Bantamweight (123 lbs.) — Sal Dominguez, York Barbell Club, 485 lbs.

Featherweight (132 lbs.) — Roman Mielec, York Barbell Club, 512¹/₂ lbs.

Lightweight (148 lbs.) — Dan Cantore, San Francisco, 633³/₄ lbs.

Middleweight (165 lbs.) — Fred Lowe, York Barbell Club, 672¹/₂ lbs.

Light Heavyweight (181 lbs.) — Tom Hirtz, 678¹/₄ lbs.

Middle Heavyweight (198 lbs.) — Phil Grappaldi, York Barbell Club, 718 lbs.

Heavyweight (242 lbs.) — Al Feuerbach, San Jose, Calif., 759 lbs.

Super Heavyweight — James Gargano, Los Angeles YMCA, 759 lbs.

National Amateur Bicycle Championships in 1974

Detroit, Mich. (Road); North Brook, Ill. (Track); July 27-Aug. 3, 1974
Road Races

Senior Men—John Allis, Massachusetts.
Junior Men — David Mayer - Oakes, Texas.
Senior Women — Jane Robinson, Washington.
Intermediate Boys — Bruce Donaghy, New Jersey.
Veterans — Jim Meyers, California.

Senior Men 1000 Meter — Steve Woznick, New Jersey.
Senior Women Sprints — Sue Novarra, Michigan.
Senior Women 3000 Meter Pursuit — Mary Jane Reoch, Pennsylvania.
Junior Men — Gilbert Hatton, California.
Intermediate Boys — Bruce Donaghy, New Jersey.
Intermediate Girls — Dana Scruggs, Indiana.
Midget Boys — Italo Bastinelli, New Jersey.
Midget Girls — Amy Johnson, Michigan.
4000 Meter Team Pursuit — Ralph Therrio, David Mulica, Ron Skarin, Les Luczy, Southern California.

Track Races

Senior Men Sprints — Steve Woznick, New Jersey.
Senior Men 4000 Meter Pursuit — Ralph Therrio, California.
Senior Men 10 Mile — Ralph Therrio, California.

Tour de France Bicycle Race

Eddy Merckx of Belgium won the 1974 Tour de France bicycle race for the fifth time in 1974. The 3,840 kilometer race lasted 21 days and was worth over $40,000 to the winner.

Soap Box Derby, 1974

Curt Yarborough of Elk Grove, Calif., the 11-year-old brother of the 1973 champion, won the 37th All-American Soap Box Derby at Akron, Ohio on Aug. 17. The winner raced down the 950 ft. Derby Downs hill in 27.15 seconds. First prize was a $3,000 scholarship.

Annual Results of Major Bowl Games

Rose Bowl, Pasadena

1902—Michigan 49, Stanford 0
1916—Wash. State 14, Brown 0
1917—Oregon 14, Pennsylvania 0
1918-19—Service Teams
1920—Harvard 7, Oregon 6
1921—California 28, Ohio State 0
1922—Wash. & Jeff. 0, California 0
1923—So. California 14, Penn State 3
1924—Navy 14, Washington 14
1925—Notre Dame 27, Stanford 10
1926—Alabama 20, Washington 19
1927—Alabama 7, Stanford 7
1928—Stanford 7, Pittsburgh 6
1929—Georgia Tech 8, California 7
1930—So. California 47, Pittsburgh 14
1931—Alabama 24, Wash. State 0
1932—So. California 21, Tulane 12
1933—So. California 35, Pittsburgh 0
1934—Columbia 7, Stanford 0
1935—Alabama 29, Stanford 13

1936—Stanford 7, So. Methodist 0
1937—Pittsburgh 21, Washington 0
1938—California 13, Alabama 0
1939—So. California 7, Duke 3
1940—So. California 14, Tennessee 0
1941—Stanford 21, Nebraska 13
1942—Oregon St. 20, Duke 16
(at Durham)
1943—Georgia 9, UCLA 0
1944—So. California 29, Washington 0
1945—So. California 25, Tennessee 0
1946—Alabama 34, So. California 14
1947—Illinois 45, UCLA 14
1948—Michigan 49, So. California 0
1949—Northwestern 20, California 14
1950—Ohio State 17, California 14
1951—Michigan 14, California 6
1952—Illinois 40, Stanford 7
1953—So. California 7, Wisconsin 0
1954—Mich. State 28, UCLA 20

1955—Ohio State 20, So. California 7
1956—Mich. State 17, UCLA 14
1957—Iowa 35, Oregon St. 19
1958—Ohio State 10, Oregon 7
1959—Iowa 38, California 12
1960—Washington 44, Wisconsin 8
1961—Washington 17, Minnesota 7
1962—Minnesota 21, UCLA 3
1963—So. California 42, Wisconsin 37
1964—Illinois 17, Washington 7
1965—Michigan 34, Oregon St. 7
1966—UCLA 14, Mich. State 12
1967—Purdue 14, So. California 13
1968—Southern Cal. 14, Indiana 3
1969—Ohio State 27, Southern Cal 16
1970—Southern Cal 10, Michigan 3
1971—Stanford 27, Ohio State 17
1972—Stanford 13, Michigan 12
1973—So. California 42, Ohio State 17
1974—Ohio State 42, So. California 21

Orange Bowl, Miami

1933—Miami (Fla.) 7, Manhattan 0
1934—Duquesne 33, Miami (Fla.) 7
1935—Bucknell 26, Miami (Fla.) 0
1936—Catholic U. 20, Mississippi 19
1937—Duquesne 13, Miss. State 12
1938—Auburn 6, Mich. State 0
1939—Tennessee 17, Oklahoma 0
1940—Georgia Tech 21, Missouri 7
1941—Miss. State 14, Georgetown 7
1942—Georgia 40, TCU 26
1943—Alabama 37, Boston Col. 21
1944—LSU 19, Texas A&M 14
1945—Tulsa 26, Georgia Tech 12
1946—Miami (Fla.) 13, Holy Cross 6

1947—Rice 8, Tennessee 0
1948—Georgia Tech 20, Kansas 14
1949—Texas 41, Georgia 28
1950—Santa Clara 21, Kentucky 13
1951—Clemson 15, Miami (Fla.) 14
1952—Georgia Tech 17, Baylor 14
1953—Alabama 61, Syracuse 6
1954—Oklahoma 7, Maryland 0
1955—Duke 34, Nebraska 7
1956—Oklahoma 20, Maryland 6
1957—Colorado 27, Clemson 21
1958—Oklahoma 48, Duke 21
1959—Oklahoma 21, Syracuse 6
1960—Georgia 14, Missouri 0

1961—Missouri 21, Navy 14
1962—LSU 25, Colorado 7
1963—Alabama 17, Oklahoma 0
1964—Nebraska 13, Auburn 7
1965—Texas 21, Alabama 17
1966—Alabama 39, Nebraska 28
1967—Florida 27, Georgia Tech 12
1968—Oklahoma 26, Tennessee 24
1969—Penn State 15, Kansas 14
1970—Penn State 10, Missouri 3
1971—Nebraska 17, Louisiana St. 12
1972—Nebraska 38, Alabama 6
1973—Nebraska 40, Notre Dame 6
1974—Penn State 16, Louisiana St. 9

Sugar Bowl, New Orleans

1935—Tulane 20, Temple 14
1936—TCU, 3, LSU 2
1937—Santa Clara 21, LSU 14
1938—Santa Clara 6, LSU 0
1939—TCU 15, Carnegie Tech 7
1940—Texas A&M 14, Tulane 13
1941—Boston Col. 19, Tennessee 13
1942—Fordham 2, Missouri 0
1943—Tennessee 14, Tulsa 7
1944—Georgia Tech 20, Tulsa 18
1945—Duke 29, Alabama 26
1946—Oklahoma A&M 33, St. Mary's 13
1947—Georgia 20, No. Carolina 10
1948—Texas 27, Alabama 7

1949—Oklahoma 14, No. Carolina 6
1950—Oklahoma 35, LSU 0
1951—Kentucky 13, Oklahoma 7
1952—Maryland 28, Tennessee 13
1953—Georgia Tech. 24, Mississippi 7
1954—Georgia Tech 42, West Virginia 19
1955—Navy 21, Mississippi 0
1956—Georgia Tech 7, Pittsburgh 0
1957—Baylor 13, Tennessee 7
1958—Mississippi 39, Texas 7
1959—LSU 7, Clemson 0
1960—Mississippi 21, LSU 0
1961—Mississippi 14, Rice 6

1962—Alabama 10, Arkansas 3
1963—Mississippi 17, Arkansas 13
1964—Alabama 12, Mississippi 7
1965—LSU 13, Syracuse 10
1966—Missouri 20, Florida 18
1967—Alabama 34, Nebraska 7
1968—LSU 20, Wyoming 13
1969—Arkansas 16, Georgia 2
1970—Mississippi 27, Arkansas 22
1971—Tennessee 34, Air Force 13
1972—Oklahoma 40, Auburn 22
1972 (Dec.)—Oklahoma 14, Penn State 0
1973 (Dec.)—Notre Dame 24, Alabama 23

Cotton Bowl, Dallas

1937—TCU 16, Marquette 6
1938—Rice 28, Colorado 14
1939—St. Mary's 20, Texas Tech 13
1940—Clemson 6, Boston Col. 3
1941—Texas A&M 13, Fordham 12
1942—Alabama 29, Texas A&M 21
1943—Texas 14, Georgia Tech 7
1944—Randolph Field 7, Texas 7
1945—Oklahoma A&M 34, TCU 0
1946—Texas 40, Missouri 27
1947—Arkansas 0, LSU 0
1948—So. Methodist 13, Penn State 13
1949—So. Methodist 21, Oregon 13

1950—Rice 27, No. Carolina 13
1951—Tennessee 20, Texas 14
1952—Kentucky 20, TCU 7
1953—Texas 16, Tennessee 0
1954—Rice 28, Alabama 6
1955—Georgia Tech 14, Arkansas 6
1956—Mississippi 14, TCU 13
1957—TCU 28, Syracuse 27
1958—Navy 20, Rice 7
1959—TCU 0, Air Force 0
1960—Syracuse 23, Texas 14
1961—Duke 7, Arkansas 6
1962—Texas 12, Mississippi 7

1963—LSU 13, Texas 0
1964—Texas 28, Navy 6
1965—Arkansas 10, Nebraska 7
1966—LSU 14, Arkansas 7
1967—Georgia 24, So. Methodist 9
1968—Texas A&M 20, Alabama 16
1969—Texas 36, Tennessee 13
1970—Texas 21, Notre Dame 17
1971—Notre Dame 24, Texas 11
1972—Penn State 30, Texas 6
1973—Texas 17, Alabama 13
1974—Nebraska 19, Texas 3

Sun Bowl, El Paso

1936—Hardin Simmons 14, New Mex. St. 14
1937—Hardin-Simmons 34, Texas Mines 6
1938—West Virginia 7, Texas Tech 6
1939—Utah 26, New Mexico 0
1940—Catholic U. 0, Arizona St.0
1941—Western Reserve 26, Arizona St. 13
1942—Tulsa 6, Texas Tech 0
1943—Second Air Force 13,
Hardin-Simmons 7
1944—Southwestern (Tex.) 7,
New Mexico 0
1945—Southwestern (Tex.) 35, U. of Mex. 0
1946—New Mexico 34, Denver 24
1947—Cincinnati 38, Virginia Tech 6

1948—Miami (O.) 13, Texas Tech 12
1949—West Virginia 21, Texas Mines 12
1950—Texas Western 33, Georgetown 20
1951—West Texas St. 14, Cincinnati 13
1952—Texas Tech 25, Col. Pacific 14
1953—Col. Pacific 26, Miss. Southern 7
1954—Texas Western 37, Miss. Southern 14
1955—Texas Western 47, Florida St. 20
1956—Wyoming 21, Texas Tech 14
1957—Geo. Washington 13, Tex. Western 0
1958—Louisville 34, Drake 0
1959—Wyoming 14, Hardin-Simmons 6
1960—New Mexico St. 28, No. Texas St. 8
1961—New Mexico St. 20, Utah State 13

1962—Villanova 17, Wichita 9
1963—West Texas St. 15, Ohio U. 14
1964—Oregon 21, So. Methodist 14
1965—Georgia 7, Texas Tech 0
1966—Texas Western 13, TCU 14
1967—Wyoming 28, Florida St. 20
1968—UTex El Paso 14, Mississippi 7
1969—Auburn 34, Arizona 10
1969—(Dec. 20) Nebraska 45, Georgia 6
1970—Georgia Tech. 17, Texas Tech. 9
1971—LSU 33, Iowa State 15
1972—North Carolina 32, Texas Tech 28
1973—Missouri 34, Auburn 17

Gator Bowl, Jacksonville

1946—Wake Forest 26, South
    Carolina 14
1947—Oklahoma 34, N.C. State 13
1948—Maryland 20, Georgia 20
1949—Clemson 24, Missouri 23
1950—Maryland 20, Missouri 7
1951—Wyoming 20, Wash. & Lee 7
1952—Miami (Fla.) 14, Clemson 0
1953—Florida 14, Tulsa 13
1954—Texas Tech 35, Auburn 13

1955—Auburn 33, Baylor 13
1956—Vanderbilt 25, Auburn 13
1957—Georgia Tech 21, Pittsburgh 14
1958—Tennessee 3, Texas A&M 0
1959—Mississippi 7, Florida 3
1960—Arkansas 14, Georgia Tech 7
1961—Florida 13, Baylor 12
1962—Penn State 30, Georgia Tech 15
1963—Florida 17, Penn State 7
1964—No. Carolina 35, Air Force 0

1965—Florida St. 36, Oklahoma 19
1966—Georgia Tech 31, Texas Tech 21
1967—Tennessee 18, Syracuse 12
1968—Penn State 17, Florida St. 17
1969—Missouri 35, Alabama 10
1969—(Dec. 27) Florida 14, Tenn. 13
1971—Auburn 35, Mississippi 28
1972—Georgia 7, N. Carolina 3
1973—Auburn 24, Colorado 3
1973—(Dec.)—Texas Tech 28, Tenn. 19

Astro-Bluebonnet Bowl, Houston

1959—Clemson 23, TCU 7
1960—Texas 3, Alabama 3
1961—Kansas 33, Rice 7
1962—Missouri 14, Georgia Tech 10
1963—Baylor 14, LSU 7

1964—Tulsa 14, Mississippi 7
1965—Tennessee 27, Tulsa 6
1966—Texas 19, Mississippi 0
1967—Colorado 31, Miami (Fla.) 21
1968—SMU 28, Oklahoma 27

1969—Houston 36, Auburn 7
1970—Oklahoma 24, Alabama 24
1971—Colorado 29, Houston 17
1972—Tennessee 24, Louisiana St. 17
1973—Houston 47, Tulane 7

Liberty Bowl, Memphis

1959—Penn State 7, Alabama 0
1960—Penn State 41, Oregon 12
1961—Syracuse 15, Miami 14
1962—Oregon 6, Villanova 0
1963—Miss. State 16, N. C. State 12

1964—Utah 32, West Virginia 6
1965—Mississippi 13, Auburn 7
1966—Miami (Fla.) 14, Va. Tech 7
1967—N. C. State 14, Georgia 7
1968—Mississippi 34, Va. Tech 17

1969—Colorado 47, Alabama 33
1970—Tulane 17, Colorado 3
1971—Tennessee 14, Arkansas 13
1972—Georgia Tech 31, Iowa State 30
1973—No. Carolina St. 31, Kansas 18

Peach Bowl, Atlanta

1968—LSU 31, Florida St. 27
1969—West Virginia 14, S. Carolina 3

1970—Arizona St. 48, N. Carolina 26
1971—Mississippi 41, Georgia Tech. 18

1972—N. Carolina State 49, W. Va. 13
1973—Georgia 17, Maryland 16

College Football Conference Champions

Atlantic Coast
1960—Duke
1961—Duke
1962—Duke
1963—No. Carolina St.,
    No. Carolina
1964—No. Carolina St.
1965—Duke
1966—Clemson
1967—Clemson
1968—No. Carolina St.
1969—So. Carolina
1970—Wake Forest
1971—North Carolina
1972—North Carolina
1973—No. Carolina St.

Ivy League
1960—Yale
1961—Columbia, Harvard
1962—Dartmouth
1963—Dartmouth, Princeton
1964—Princeton
1965—Dartmouth
1966—Dartmouth, Harvard, Princeton
1967—Yale
1968—Yale, Harvard
1969—Princeton, Dartmouth, Yale
1970—Dartmouth
1971—Dartmouth Cornell
1972—Dartmouth
1973—Dartmouth

Big Eight
1960—Missouri
1961—Colorado
1962—Oklahoma
1963—Nebraska
1964—Nebraska
1965—Nebraska
1966—Nebraska
1967—Oklahoma
1968—Kansas, Oklahoma
1969—Missouri, Nebraska
1970—Nebraska
1971—Nebraska
1972—Nebraska
1973—Oklahoma

Big Ten
1960—Minn., Iowa
1961—Ohio State
1962—Wisconsin
1963—Illinois
1964—Michigan
1965—Michigan St.
1966—Michigan St.
1967—Indiana, Purdue, Minn.
1968—Ohio State
1969—Michigan, Ohio State
1970—Ohio State
1971—Michigan
1972—Ohio State, Michigan
1973—Ohio State, Michigan

Mid-America
1960—Ohio Univ.
1961—Bowling Green
1962—Bowling Green
1963—Ohio Univ.
1964—Bowling Green
1965—Bowling Green, Miami
1966—Miami, Western Mich.
1967—Toledo, Ohio Univ.
1968—Ohio Univ.
1969—Toledo
1970—Toledo
1971—Toledo
1972—Kent State
1973—Miami

Missouri Valley
1960—Wichita
1961—Wichita
1962—Tulsa
1963—Cincinnati, Wichita
1964—Cincinnati
1965—Tulsa
1966—No. Texas, Tulsa
1967—North Texas
1968—Memphis State
1969—Memphis State
1970—Louisville
1971—Memphis State
1972—Louisville, W. Texas,
    Drake
1973—No. Texas St., Tulsa

Southeastern
1960—Mississippi
1961—Alabama, Louisiana St.
1962—Mississippi
1963—Mississippi
1964—Alabama
1965—Alabama
1966—Alabama, Georgia
1967—Tennessee
1968—Georgia
1969—Tennessee
1970—Louisiana State
1971—Alabama
1972—Alabama
1973—Alabama

Southwest
1960—Arkansas
1961—Texas, Arkansas
1962—Texas
1963—Texas
1964—Arkansas
1965—Arkansas
1966—Southern Methodist
1967—Texas A & M
1968—Texas, Arkansas
1969—Texas
1970—Texas
1971—Texas
1972—Texas
1973—Texas

Pacific Eight
1960—Washington
1961—UCLA
1962—Southern Calif.
1963—Washington
1964—Oregon St., Southern Calif.
1965—UCLA
1966—Southern Calif.

1967—Southern Calif.
1968—Southern Calif.
1969—Southern Calif.
1970—Stanford
1971—Stanford
1972—Southern Calif.
1973—Southern Calif.

Southern
1960—VMI
1961—Citadel
1962—VMI
1963—Virginia Tech
1964—West Virginia
1965—West Virginia
1966—E. Carolina,
    William & Mary

1967—West Virginia
1968—Richmond
1969—Richmond, Davidson
1970—William & Mary
1971—Richmond
1972—East Carolina
1973—East Carolina

AAU Volleyball Championships in 1974

The Michiana Volleyball Club of Chicago won the 1974 National AAU Senior Volleyball Championship by defeating Outrigger "AA", 15-11, 10-15, and 15-11 in Dallas, Texas on May 12, 1974. The women's championship was won by a Dallas Athletic Club entry.

College Football

University Division

Team	Nickname	Team Colors	Conference	Coach	1973 Record (W-L-T)
Air Force	Falcons	Blue & Silver	Independent	Ben Martin	6-4-0
Alabama	Crimson Tide	Crimson & White	Southeastern	Paul Bryant	11-1-0
Appalachian State	Mountaineers	Black & Gold	Southern	Jim Brakefield	3-7-1
Arizona State	Sun Devils	Maroon & Gold	Western Athletic	Frank Kush	11-1-0
Arizona	Wildcats	Red & Blue	Western Athletic	Jim Young	8-3-0
Arkansas	Razorbacks	Cardinal & White	Southwest	Frank Broyles	5-5-1
Army	Cadets	Black, Gold, Gray	Independent	Homer Smith	0-10-0
Auburn	Tigers	Orange & Blue	Southeastern	Ralph Jordan	6-6-0
Baylor	Bears	Green & Gold	Southwest	Grant Teaff	2-9-0
Boston College	Eagles	Maroon & Gold	Independent	Joseph Yukica	7-4-0
Bowling Green	Falcons	Orange & Brown	Mid-American	Don Nehlen	7-3-0
Brigham Young	Cougars	Royal Blue & White	Western Athletic	LaVell Edwards	5-6-0
Brown	Bruins	Brown & Cardinal	Ivy	John Anderson	4-3-1
California	Golden Bears	Blue & Gold	Pacific-8	Mike White	4-7-0
Cincinnati	Bearcats	Red & Black	Independent	Tommy Mason	4-7-0
Citadel	Bulldogs	Blue & White	Southern	Bobby Ross	3-8-0
Clemson	Tigers	Purple & Orange	Atlantic Coast	Jim Parker	5-6-0
Colgate	Red Raiders	Maroon	Independent	Neil Wheelwright	5-5-0
Colorado State	Rams	Green & Gold	Western Athletic	Sarkis Arslanian	5-6-0
Colorado	Buffaloes	Silver & Gold	Big Eight	Bill Mallory	5-6-0
Columbia	Lions	Blue & White	Ivy	Bill Campbell	1-7-1
Cornell	Big Red	Carnelian & White	Ivy	Jack Musick	3-5-1
Dartmouth	Big Green	Dartmouth Green	Ivy	Jack Crouthamel	6-3-0
Davidson	Wildcats	Red & Black	Southern	Ed Farrell	2-8-0
Dayton	Flyers	Red & Blue	Independent	Ron Marciniak	5-5-1
Drake	Bulldogs	Blue & White	Missouri Valley	Jack Wallace	2-9-0
Duke	Blue Devils	Blue & White	Atlantic Coast	Mike McGee	2-8-1
East Carolina	Pirates	Purple & Gold	Southern	Pat Dye	9-2-0
Florida State	Seminoles	Garnet & Gold	Independent	Darrell Mudra	0-11-0
Florida	Gators	Orange & Blue	Southeastern	Doug Dickey	7-5-0
Fresno State	Bulldogs	Cardinal & Blue	Pacific	J. R. Boone	2-9-0
Furman	Paladins	Purple & White	Southern	Art Baker	7-4-0
Georgia Tech	Yellow Jackets	Old Gold & White	Independent	Pepper Rodgers	5-6-0
Georgia	Bulldogs	Red & Black	Southeastern	Vince Dooley	7-4-1
Harvard	Crimson	Crimson	Ivy	Joe Restic	7-2-0
Hawaii	Rainbows	Green & White	Independent	Larry Price	9-2-0
Holy Cross	Crusaders	Royal Purple	Independent	Ed Doherty	5-6-0
Houston	Cougars	Scarlet & White	Southwest	Bill Yeoman	11-1-0
Idaho	Vandals	Silver & Gold	Big Sky	Ed Troxel	4-7-0
Illinois	Fighting Illini	Orange & Blue	Big Ten	Bob Blackman	5-6-0
Indiana	Fightin' Hoosiers	Cream & Crimson	Big Ten	Lee Corso	2-9-0
Iowa State	Cyclones	Cardinal & Gold	Big Eight	Earle Bruce	4-7-0
Iowa	Hawkeyes	Old Gold & Black	Big Ten	Bo Commings	0-11-0
Kansas State	Wildcats	Purple & White	Big Eight	Vince Gibson	5-6-0
Kansas	Jayhawks	Crimson & Blue	Big Eight	Don Fambrough	7-4-1
Kent State	Golden Flashes	Blue & Gold	Mid-American	Don James	9-2-0
Kentucky	Wildcats	Blue & White	Southeastern	Fran Curci	5-6-0
Lamar	Cardinals	Red & White	Southland	Vernon Glass	5-5-0
Long Beach State	Forty Niners	Brown & Gold	Pacific Coast	Wayne Howard	1-9-1
Louisiana State	Fighting Tigers	Purple & Gold	Southeastern	Charles McClendon	9-3-0
Louisville	Cardinals	Red, Black, White	Missouri Valley	T. W. Alley	5-6-0
Marshall	Thundering Herd	Green & White	Independent	Jack Lengyel	4-7-0
Maryland	Terps	Red & White	Atlantic Coast	Jerry Claiborne	8-4-0
Memphis State	Tigers	Blue & Gray	Independent	Fred Pancoast	8-3-0
Miami (Fla.)	Hurricanes	Orange, Green, White	Independent	Pete Elliott	5-6-0
Miami (Ohio)	Redskins	Red & White	Mid-American	Dick Crum	11-0-0
Michigan State	Spartans	Green & White	Big Ten	Dennie Stolz	5-6-0
Michigan	Wolverines	Maize & Blue	Big Ten	Bo Schembechler	10-0-1
Minnesota	Gophers	Maroon & Gold	Big Ten	Cal Stoll	7-4-0
Mississippi State	Bulldogs	Maroon & White	Southeastern	Bob Tyler	4-5-2
Mississippi	Rebels	Red & Blue	Southeastern	Ken Cooper	6-5-0
Missouri	Tigers	Old Gold & Black	Big Eight	Al Onofrio	8-4-0
Navy	Midshipmen	Navy Blue & Gold	Independent	George Welsh	4-7-0
Nebraska	Cornhuskers	Scarlet & Cream	Big Eight	Tom Osborne	9-2-1
New Mexico State	Aggies	Crimson & White	Missouri Valley	Jim Bradley	5-6-0
New Mexico	Lobos	Cherry & Silver	Western Athletic	Bill Mondt	4-7-0
North Carolina State	Wolfpack	Red & White	Atlantic Coast	Lou Holtz	9-3-0
North Carolina	Tar Heels	Blue & White	Atlantic Coast	Bill Dooley	4-7-0
Northern Illinois	Huskies	Cardinal & Black	Mid-American	Jerry Ippoliti	6-5-0
North Texas State	Mean Green	Green & White	Missouri Valley	Hayden Fry	5-5-1
Northwestern	Wildcats	Purple & White	Big Ten	John Pont	4-7-0
Notre Dame	Fighting Irish	Gold & Blue	Independent	Ara Parseghian	11-0-0
Ohio State	Buckeyes	Scarlet & Gray	Big Ten	Woody Hayes	10-0-1
Ohio Univ.	Bobcats	Green & White	Mid-American	Bill Hess	5-5-0
Oklahoma State	Cowboys	Orange & Black	Big Eight	Jim Stanley	5-4-2
Oklahoma	Sooners	Crimson & Cream	Big Eight	Barry Switzer	10-0-1
Oregon State	Beavers	Orange & Black	Pacific-8	Dee Andros	2-9-0
Oregon	Ducks	Green & Yellow	Pacific-8	Don Read	2-9-0
Pacific	Tigers	Orange & Black	Pacific Coast	Chester Caddas	7-2-1
Penn State	Nittany Lions	Blue & White	Independent	Joe Paterno	12-0-0
Pennsylvania	Red & Blue	Red & Blue	Ivy	Harry Gamble	6-3-0

Team	Nickname	Team Colors	Conference	Coach	1973 Record (W-L-T)
Pittsburgh	Panthers	Old Gold & Navy Blue	Independent	John Majors	6-5-1
Princeton	Tigers	Orange & Black	Ivy	Bob Casciola	1-8-0
Purdue	Boilermakers	Old Gold & Black	Big Ten	Alex Agese	5-6-0
Rice	Owls	Blue & Gray	Southwest	Al Conover	5-6-0
Richmond	Spiders	Red & Blue	Southern	Jim Tait	8-2-0
Rutgers	Scarlet Knights	Scarlet	Independent	Frank Burns	6-5-0
San Diego State	Aztecs	Scarlet & Black	Independent	Claude Gilbert	9-1-1
San Jose State	Spartans	Gold & White	Pacific Coast	Darryl Rogers	5-4-1
South Carolina	Fighting Gamecocks	Garnet & Black	Independent	Paul Dietzel	7-4-0
Southern California	Trojans	Cardinal & Gold	Pacific-8	John McKay	9-2-1
Southern Illinois	Salukis	Maroon & White	Independent	Doug Weaver	3-7-1
Southern Methodist	Mustangs	Red & Blue	Southwest	Dave Smith	6-4-1
Southern Mississippi	Golden Eagles	Black & Gold	Independent	P. W. Underwood	6-4-1
Stanford	Cardinals	Cardinal & White	Pacific-8	Jack Christiansen	7-4-0
Syracuse	Orangemen	Orange	Independent	Frank Maloney	2-9-0
Tampa	Spartans	Red, Gold, Black	Independent	Denny Fryzel	8-3-0
Temple	Owls	Cherry & White	Independent	Wayne Hardin	9-1-0
Tennessee	Volunteers	Orange & White	Southeastern	Bill Battle	8-4-0
Texas A & M	Aggies	Maroon & White	Southwest	Emory Bellard	5-6-0
Texas Christian	Horned Frogs	Purple & White	Southwest	Jim Shofner	3-8-0
Texas Tech	Red Raiders	Scarlet & Black	Southwest	Jim Carlen	11-1-0
Texas	Longhorns	Orange & White	Southwest	Darrell Royal	8-3-0
Toledo	Rockets	Blue & Gold	Mid-American	Jack Murphy	3-8-0
Tulane	Green Wave	Olive Green & Sky Blue	Independent	Bennie Ellender	9-3-0
Tulsa	Golden Hurricane	Blue, Crimson, Gold	Missouri Valley	F. A. Dry	6-5-0
UCLA	Bruins	Navy Blue & Gold	Pacific-8	Dick Vermeil	9-2-0
Utah State	Aggies	Navy Blue & White	Independent	Phil Krueger	7-4-0
Utah	Utes	Crimson & White	Western Athletic	Tom Lovat	7-5-0
U Texas Arlington	Mavericks	Royal Blue & White	Southland	Bud Elliott	4-6-0
U Texas El Paso	Miners	Orange & White	Western Athletic	Gil Bartosh	0-11-0
Vanderbilt	Commodores	Black & Gold	Southeastern	Steve Sloan	5-6-0
Villanova	Wildcats	Blue & White	Independent	Jim Weaver	3-8-0
VMI	Keydets	Red, White, Yellow	Southern	Bob Thalman	3-8-0
Virginia Polytechnic Inst.	Gobblers	Orange & Maroon	Independent	Jimmy Sharpe	2-9-0
Virginia	Cavaliers	Orange & Blue	Atlantic Coast	Sonny Randle	4-7-0
Wake Forest	Demon Deacons	Old Gold & Black	Atlantic Coast	Chuck Mills	1-9-1
Washington State	Cougars	Crimson & Gray	Pacific-8	Jim Sweeney	5-6-0
Washington	Huskies	Purple & Gold	Pacific-8	Jim Owens	2-9-0
Western Michigan	Broncos	Brown & Gold	Mid-American	Bill Doolittle	6-5-0
West Texas State	Buffaloes	Maroon & White	Missouri Valley	Gene Mayfield	2-9-0
West Virginia	Mountaineers	Old Gold & Blue	Independent	Bobby Bowden	6-5-0
Wichita State	Shockers	Gold & Black	Missouri Valley	Jim Wright	4-7-0
William & Mary	Indians	Green, Gold, Silver	Southern	Jim Root	6-5-0
Wisconsin	Badgers	Cardinal & White	Big Ten	John Jardine	4-7-0
Wyoming	Cowboys	Brown & Yellow	Western Athletic	Fritz Shurmur	4-7-0
Yale	Bulldogs	Yale Blue	Ivy	Carmen Cozza	6-3-0

Selected College Division Teams

Team	Nickname	Team Colors	Conference	Coach	Record
Akron	Zips	Blue & Gold	Independent	Jim Dennison	6-5-0
Alabama A & M	Bulldogs	Maroon & White	Southern IAC	Louis Crews	5-5-0
Alma	Scots	Maroon & Cream	Michigan	Phil Brooks	5-4-0
Arkansas State	Indians	Scarlet & Black	Southland	Bill Davidson	6-4-0
Austin Peay	Governors	Scarlet & White	Ohio Valley	Jack Bushofsky	2-8-0
Baldwin-Wallace	Yellow Jackets	Brown & Gold	Ohio	Lee J. Tressel	6-3-0
Ball State	Cardinals	Cardinal & White	Independent	Dave McClain	5-5-1
Boise State	Broncos	Orange & Blue	Big Sky	Tony Knap	9-2-0
Boston Univ	Terriers	Scarlet & White	Yankee	Paul Kemp	3-7-0
Bridgeport	Purple Knights	Purple & White	Independent	Ray Murphy	9-1-0
Bucknell	Bisons	Orange & Blue	Independent	Fred Prender	3-4-2
Butler	Bulldogs	Blue & White	Indiana	Bill Sylvester	5-5-0
Case Western	Spartans	Blue & Gray	Presidents' Athletic	Flory Mauriocourt	0-9-0
Chico State	Wildcats	Cardinal & White	Far Western	Dick Trimmer	7-3-0
Coast Guard	Cadets	Blue & White	Independent	Otto Graham	8-2-0
Coe	Kohawks	Crimson & Gold	Midwest	Wayne Phillips	8-1-0
Colby	Mules	Blue & Grey	Maine	Richard McGee	1-7-0
Colorado Western	Mountaineers	Crimson & Slate	Rocky Mountain	William Noxon	6-3-0
Connecticut	Huskies	Blue & White	Yankee	Larry Naviaux	8-2-1
C.W. Post	Pioneers	Green & Gold	Met. Intercollegiate	Dom Anile	10-1-0
Defiance	Yellow Jackets	Purple & Gold	Hoosier-Buckeye	Dick Snyder	7-2-0
Delaware	Fightin' Blue Hens	Blue & Gold	Independent	Harold Raymond	8-3-0
Denison	Big Red	Red & White	Ohio	Keith Piper	3-5-1
De Pauw	Tigers	Old Gold & Black	Indiana	Tom Mont	6-3-0
Doane	Tigers	Orange & Black	Nebraska Inter.	Ray Best	7-2-1
Findlay	Oilers	Orange & Black	Hoosier-Buckeye	Byron E. Morgan	1-9-0
Grambling	Tigers	Black & Gold	Southwestern	Eddie Robinson	9-2-0
Heidelberg	Student Princes	Red, Orange & Black	Ohio	Pete Riesen	6-3-0
Idaho State	Bengals	Orange & Black	Big Sky	Bob Griffin	2-9-0
Illinois State	Redbirds	Red & White	Independent	Gerry Hart	5-6-0
Jackson State	Tigers	Blue & White	Southwestern	Robert Hill	9-2-0
Kalamazoo	Hornets	Orange & Black	Michigan	Ed Baker	4-4-0
Kenyon	Lords	Purple & White	Ohio	Philip Morse	5-4-0
Knox	Siwash	Purple & Gold	Midwest	Albert Reilly	6-2-1
Lafayette	Leopards	Maroon & White	Independent	Neil Putnam	6-3-1
Lawrence	Vikings	Navy & White	Midwest	Ron Roberts	4-4-0
Lehigh	Engineers	Brown & White	Independent	Fred Dunlap	7-3-1

Team	Nickname	Team Colors	Conference	Coach	1973 Record (W-L-T)
Los Angeles Cal State.	Diablos.	Black & Gold.	Pacific Coast.	Jim Williams.	5-6-0
Louisiana Tech.	Bulldogs.	Red & Blue.	Southland.	Maxie Lambright.	9-1-0
Maine.	Black Bears.	Blue & White.	Yankee.	Walt Abbott.	3-7-0
Massachusetts.	Minutemen.	Maroon & White.	Yankee.	Richard MacPherson.	6-5-0
McNeese State.	Cowboys.	Blue & Gold.	Southland.	Jack Doland.	7-3-0
Michigan Tech.	Huskies.	Silver & Gold.	Northern.	Jim Kapp.	5-4-1
Middlebury.	Panthers.	Blue & White.	Independent.	Mickey Heinecken.	7-1-0
Middle Tenn.	Blue Raiders.	Blue & White.	Ohio Valley.	Bill Peck.	4-7-0
Monmouth.	Fighting Scots.	Crimson & White.	Midwest.	Bill Reichow.	6-1-1
Montana State.	Bobcats.	Blue & Gold.	Big Sky.	Sonny Holland.	7-4-0
Montana.	Grizzlies.	Cooper, Silver, Gold.	Big Sky.	Jack Swarthout.	4-6-0
Moorhead State.	Dragons.	Scarlet & White.	Northern.	Ross Fortier.	6-4-0
Morgan State.	Bears.	Blue & Orange.	Mid-Eastern.	Nathaniel Taylor.	6-3-0
Mt. Union.	Purple Raiders.	Purple & White.	Ohio.	Ken Wable.	3-6-0
Muhlenberg.	Mules.	Cardinal & Gray.	Middle Atlantic.	Frank Marino.	7-1-1
Nebraska Wesleyan.	Plainsmen.	Yellow & Brown.	Nebraska IAC.	Harold Chaffee.	4-3-1
New Hampshire.	Wildcats.	Blue & White.	Yankee.	William Bowes.	4-5-0
No. Carolina A & T.	Aggies.	Blue & Gold.	Mid-Eastern.	Hornsby Howell.	4-6-1
North Dakota State.	Bison.	Yellow & Green.	North Central.	Ev Kjelbertson.	8-2-0
North Dakota.	Sioux.	Green & White.	North Central.	Jerry Olson.	6-4-0
Northern Arizona.	Lumberjacks.	Blue & Gold.	Big Sky.	Ed Peasley.	4-6-0
Northern Michigan.	Wildcats.	Old Gold & Green.	Independent.	Gil Krueger.	2-7-1
Ohio Northern.	Polar Bears.	Burnt Orange, Black.	Independent.	A. Wallace Hood.	2-7-0
Ohio Wesleyan.	Battling Bishops.	Red & Black.	Ohio.	Jack Fouts.	3-5-1
Olivet.	Comets.	Cardinal & White.	Michigan.	Douglas Kay.	6-3-0
Portland State.	Vikings.	Green & White.	Independnet.	Ron Stratten.	1-10-0
Puget Sound.	Loggers.	Green, Gold, Blue.	Independent.	Paul Wallrof.	7-3-0
Redlands.	Bulldogs.	Maroon & Gray.	So. Calif.	Frank Serrao.	8-1-0
Rhode Island.	Rams.	Blue & White.	Yankee.	Jack Gregory.	5-2-2
Ripon.	Redmen.	Crimson & White.	Midwest.	William Connor.	5-3-1
Rochester.	Yellow Jackets.	Yellow, Blue.	Independent.	Peter Stark.	6-3-0
St. Cloud State.	Huskies.	Red & Black.	Northern.	Mike Simpson.	4-6-0
St. Lawrence.	Larries.	Scarlet & Brown.	ICAC.	Ted Stratford.	5-3-0
St. Norbert.	Knights.	Green & Gold.	Independent.	Howie Kolstad.	4-5-0
St. Olaf.	Lions.	Black & Gold.	Midwest.	Tom Porter.	5-4-0
Santa Clara.	Broncos.	Cardinal & White.	Independent.	Pat Malley.	4-6-0
Slippery Rock.	Rockets.	Green & White.	Pennsylvania.	Bob Di Spirito.	7-2-0
So. Carolina State.	Bulldogs.	Garnet & Blue.	Mid-Eastern.	Willie Jeffries.	7-2-1
So. Dakota State.	Jackrabbits.	Yellow & Blue.	North Central.	John Gregory.	5-5-1
South Dakota.	Coyotes.	Vermillion & White.	North Central.	Joe Salem.	8-2-0
Southern Oregon.	Red Raiders.	Red & Black.	Evergreen.	Scott Johnson.	6-3-0
SW Louisiana.	Ragin'Cajuns.	Vermilion & White.	Southland.	Augie Tammariello.	0-10-0
Swarthmore.	Little Quakers.	Garnet.	Middle Atlantic.	Lewis Elverson.	0-7-0
Tennessee Tech.	Golden Eagles.	Purple & Gold.	Ohio Valley.	Don Wade.	2-8-1
Texas Southern.	Tigers.	Maroon & Gray.	Southwestern.	Roderick Page.	4-6-1
Thiel.	Tomcats.	Blue & Gold.	President's Athletic.	James McCullough.	6-2-1
Trenton State.	Lions.	Blue & Gold.	New Jersey State.	Fred O'Conner.	7-3-0
Tufts.	Jumbos.	Blue & Brown.	Independent.	Paul Pawlak.	1-7-0
Tuskegee.	Golden Tigers.	Old Gold, Crimson.	Independent.	Haywood Scissum.	7-4-0
Upsala.	Vikings.	Blue & Gray.	Middle Atlantic.	John Hooper.	0-8-0
Valparaiso.	Crusaders.	Brown & Gold.	Indiana.	Norm Amundsen.	6-5-0
Vermont.	Catamounts.	Green & Gold.	Yankee.	Carl Falivene.	3-6-0
Wabash.	Little Giants.	Scarlet & White.	Indiana.	Frank Navarro.	5-5-0
Wash. & Jeff.	Presidents.	Red & Black.	Presidents Athletic.	Pat Mondock.	2-7-0
Wash. & Lee.	Generals.	Royal Blue, White.	College Athletic.	William McHenry.	2-7-0
Wayne State.	Tartars.	Green & Gold.	Independent.	Dick Lowry.	5-4-1
Weber State.	Wildcats.	Purple & White.	Big Sky.	Dick Gwinn.	3-8-0
Wesleyan.	Cardinals.	Red & Black.	Little Three.	Bill Macdermott.	3-5-0
Western Illinois.	Leathernecks.	Purple & Gold.	Independent.	Brodie Weston.	7-4-0
Western Kentucky.	Hilltoppers.	Red & White.	Ohio Valley.	Jimmy Feix.	10-0-0
Wilkes.	Colonels.	Navy & Gold.	Middle Atlantic.	Roland Schmidt.	5-3-0
Williams.	Ephmen.	Purple.	Little Three.	Robert Odell.	6-2-0
Wittenberg.	Tigers.	Red & White.	Ohio.	Dave Maurer.	9-0-0
Wooster.	Fighting Scots.	Black, Old Gold.	Ohio.	Robert O'Brien.	5-3-0
Youngstown State.	Penguins.	Red & White.	Independent.	Rey Dempsey.	4-6-0

National College Football Champions

The NCAA recognizes as unofficial national champion the team selected each year by the AP (poll of writers) and the UPI (poll of coaches). When the polls disagree both teams are listed. The AP poll originated in 1936 and the UPI poll in 1950.

1936 Minnesota	1945 Army	1954 Ohio State, UCLA	1964 Alabama
1937 Pittsburgh	1946 Notre Dame	1955 Oklahoma	1965 Alabama, Mich. State
1938 Texas Christian	1947 Notre Dame	1956 Oklahoma	1966 Notre Dame
1939 Texas A&M	1948 Michigan	1957 Auburn, Ohio State	1967 Southern Calif.
1940 Minnesota	1949 Notre Dame	1958 Louisiana State	1968 Ohio State
1941 Minnesota	1950 Oklahoma	1959 Syracuse	1969 Texas
1942 Ohio State	1951 Tennessee	1960 Minnesota	1970 Nebraska, Texas
1943 Notre Dame	1952 Michigan State	1961 Alabama	1971 Nebraska
1944 Army	1953 Maryland	1962 Southern Calif.	1972 Southern Calif.
		1963 Texas	1973 Notre Dame, Alabama

College Football Stadiums

School	Capacity	School	Capacity
Alabama Univ. of (Denny Stad.) University, Ala.	58,000	New Mexico St. U. (Aggie Memorial Stad.).	16,000
Arizona State Univ. (Sun Devil), Tempe	51,000	New Mexico, Univ. Stad., Albuquerque.	30,000
Arizona, Univ. of (Arizona Stad.) Tucson.	40,000	North Carolina St. U. (Carter Stad.), Raleigh.	41,000
Arkansas, Univ. of (Razorback Stad.) Fayetteville.	48,000	North Carolina, Univ. of (Kenan Stad.).	47,000
Auburn Univ (Cliff Hare Stad.), Auburn, Ala.	62,291	Northern Illinois Univ. Stad., DeKalb.	20,257
Ball State Univ. Stad., Muncie, Ind.	16,000	North Texas St. Univ. (Fouts Field), Denton	20,280
Baylor Univ., Waco, Texas	50,000	Northwestern Univ. (Dyche Stad.), Evanston, Ill.	55,000
Boston Coll. (Alumni Stad.), Boston, Mass.	32,000	Notre Dame Stad., South Bend, Ind.	59,075
Boston Univ. (Nickerson Field), Boston.	15,000	Ohio State Univ. (Ohio Stad.), Columbus.	84,000
Bowling Green State Univ. (Doyt Perry Field).	23,272	Ohio U. (Don Peden Stad.), Athens.	17,550
Brigham Young Univ. (Cougar Stad.), Utah.	30,000	Oklahoma State (Lewis Stad.), Stillwater.	52,000
Brown Stad., Providence, R. I.	17,851	Oklahoma, Univ. of (Memorial Stad.), Norman.	63,500
Bucknell (Memorial Stad.), Lewisburg, Pa.	17,500	Old Dominion Univ. (Foreman Field), Norfolk.	32,000
Butler Univ. (Butler Bowl), Indianapolis, Ind.	19,500	Oregon St. Univ. (Parker Stad.), Corvallis.	41,000
Calif., Univ. of (Memorial Stad.), Berkeley.	77,000	Oregon, Univ. of (Autzen Stad.), Eugene.	41,097
Catholic Univ. (The Stadium), Wash., D.C.	18,000	Pacific, Univ. of the (Knoles Stad.), Calif.	33,790
Central Mich. Univ. (Shorts Stad.), Mt. Pleasant.	20,000	Penn. State Univ. (Beaver Stad.).	57,500
Cincinnati, Univ. of (Nippert), Ohio.	25,692	Penn., Univ. of (Franklin Field), Phila.	60,546
Citadel (Johnson Hagood Stadium), Charleston.	22,500	Pittsburgh, Univ. of (Pitt. Stad.), Pa.	57,331
Clemson Univ. (Memorial Stad.), S.C.	43,451	Princeton, (Palmer Mem. Stad.), Princeton, N.J.	45,725
Colorado St. Univ. (Hughes Stad.), Ft. Collins.	30,000	Purdue, (Ross-Ade Stad.), Lafayette, Ind.	69,250
Colorado, Univ. of (Folsom Field), Boulder.	50,126	Rice Stad., Houston, Texas.	72,500
Columbia Univ. (Baker Field), N.Y., N.Y.	32,000	Rutgers Stad., New Brunswick, N.J.	23,000
Conn., Univ. of (Memorial Stad.), Storrs.	15,200	San Jose St. Coll. (Spartan Stad.).	35,000
Cornell (Schoellkopf Crescent), Ithaca, N.Y.	34,000	So. Carolina, Univ. of (Williams-Brice), Columbia.	54,564
Dartmouth Coll. (Memorial), Hanover, N.H.	20,816	So. Illinois Univ. (McAndrew), Carbondale.	15,000
Delaware, Univ. of (Delaware Stad.), Newark.	21,919	So. Mississippi, Univ. of (Faulkner Field).	36,000
Denver Stad., Univ. of.	27,500	Southwestern La., (Cajun Field), Lafayette, La.	23,000
Drake Stad., Des Moines, Iowa.	18,500	Stanford Stad., Stanford, Calif.	86,352
Duke Univ., (Wade Stad.), Durham, N.C.	45,000	Syracuse Univ. (Archbold Stad.).	35,000
E. Carolina (Ficklen Stad.), Greenville.	20,000	Tampa, Univ. of (Tampa Stad.), Fla.	47,000
Eastern Kentucky (Hanger Stadium), Richmond.	20,000	Temple Stad., Phil.	20,547
Eastern Mich. Univ. (Rynearson), Ypsilanti.	17,000	Tenn. State (Hale), Nashville.	16,000
Florida State, (Campbell Stad.), Tallahassee.	40,500	Tenn. Tech. Univ. (Overall Field), Cookeville.	16,000
Florida, Univ. of (Florida Field), Gainesville.	63,364	Tenn., Univ. of (Neyland Stad.), Knoxville.	71,166
Georgia Inst. of Tech. (Grant Field), Atlanta.	58,120	Texas A. & I. Univ. (Javelina Stad.), Kingsville.	17,000
Georgia, Univ. of (Sanford Stad.), Athens.	59,200	Texas A. & M. Univ. (Kyle Field).	48,000
Grambling Coll. (Memorial Stad.), La.	15,400	Texas Christian Univ. (Carter Stad.), Ft. Worth.	46,000
Harvard Stad., Boston, Mass.	37,289	Texas Tech. Univ. (Jones Stad.), Lubbock.	47,000
Hawaii, Univ. of (Honolulu Stad.).	23,000	Texas, Univ. of (Memorial), Austin.	81,000
Holy Cross (Fitton Field), Worcester, Mass.	25,000	Texas, El Paso (Sun Bowl).	30,000
Idaho Stad., Univ. of, Moscow.	23,000	Toledo, Univ. of (Glass Bowl), Ohio.	18,210
Illinois, Univ. of (Memorial Stad.), Urbana.	71,229	Trinity Univ. (Alamo Stad.), San Antonio, Tex.	22,500
Indiana St. (Memorial Stad.), Terre Haute.	20,500	Tulane Stad. (Sugar Bowl), New Orleans, La.	80,985
Indiana Univ. (Memorial Stadium), Bloomington.	52,354	Tulsa, Univ. of (Skelly), Tulsa, Okla.	40,235
Iowa State Univ. (Clyde Williams Stad.).	35,000	U. S. Air Force Acad. (Falcon Stad.), Colo.	49,068
Iowa, Univ. of (Kinnick Stad.), Iowa City.	60,200	U. S. Military Academy (Michie Stad.).	41,428
Kansas State Univ. Stad., Manhattan.	42,000	U. S. Naval Academy (Navy-Marine Corps Mem. Stad.),	
Kansas, Univ. of (Memorial), Lawrence.	51,500	Annapolis, Md.	28,000
Kent State Univ. (Memorial), Kent.	28,415	Utah State Univ. (Romney Stad.), Logan.	20,000
Kentucky, Univ. of (Commonwealth), Lexington.	58,000	Utah, Univ. of (Ute Stad.), Salt Lake City.	30,000
Lamar Univ. (Cardinal Stad.), Beaumont, Tex.	17,150	Vanderbilt, (Dudley Stad.), Nashville.	34,000
Lehigh Univ. (Taylor Stad.), Bethlehem, Pa.	17,000	Va. Poly Inst. (Lane Stad.), Blacksburg.	35,000
Louisiana Tech. Univ. (Joe Aillet Stad.), Ruston.	23,000	Virginia, Univ. of (Scott Stad.), Charlottesville.	25,000
La. State Univ. (Tiger), Baton Rouge.	67,510	Wake Forest (Groves Stad.), Winston-Salem, N.C.	30,275
Marshall Univ. (Fairfield Stadium), Huntington.	16,500	Washington State Univ. (Clarence D. Martin).	22,600
Maryland, Univ. of (Byrd), College Park.	35,000	Washington, Univ. of (Husky Stad.), Seattle.	58,946
Mass., Univ. of (Alumni Stad.), Amherst.	17,000	Weber St., Coll. Stad., Ogden, Utah.	18,000
Memphis State (Memphis Memorial).	50,164	West Texas State Univ. (Kimbrough), Canyon.	20,500
Miami Univ. (Miami Field), Oxford, Ohio.	14,900	West Virginia Univ. (Mountaineer Field).	37,000
Michigan State Univ. (Spartan Stadium).	76,000	Western Illinois Univ. (Hanson Field), Macomb.	18,000
Michigan, Univ. of (Mich. Stad.), Ann Arbor.	101,710	Western Kentucky Univ. (L. T. Smith Stad.).	19,250
Middle Tenn. St. Univ. (Jones Field).	15,000	Western Mich. Univ. (Waldo Stad.), Kalamazoo.	24,500
Minnesota, Univ. of (Memorial Stad.).	56,725	Wichita State, (Cessna Stadium).	30,500
Mississippi St. Univ. (Scott Field).	35,000	William & Mary, Coll. of (Cary Stad.).	15,000
Mississippi, Univ. of (Hemingway Stad.).	34,500	Wisconsin, Univ. of (Camp Randall).	77,280
Missouri, Univ. of (Memorial Stad.), Columbia.	55,000	Wyoming, Univ. of (Memorial) Laramie.	23,000
Nebraska, Univ. of (Memorial Stad), Lincoln.	73,621	Xavier (Corcoran Field), Cincinnati.	15,000
		Yale Bowl, New Haven, Conn.	70,874

Outland Awards

Honoring the outstanding interior lineman selected by the Football Writers' Association of America.

Year	Player, College, Pos.	Year	Player, College, Pos.	Year	Player, College, Pos.
1946	George Connor, Notre Dame, T	1956	Jim Parker, Ohio State, G	1966	Loyd Phillips, Arkansas, T
1947	Joe Steffy, Army, G	1957	Alex Karras, Iowa, T	1967	Ron Yary, Southern Cal, T
1948	Bill Fischer, Notre Dame, G	1958	Zeke Smith, Auburn, G	1968	Bill Stanfill, Georgia, T
1949	Ed Bagdon, Michigan St., G	1959	Mike McGee, Duke, T	1969	Mike Reid, Penn State, DT
1950	Bob Gain, Kentucky, T	1960	Tom Brown, Minnesota, G	1970	Jim Stillwagon, Ohio State, LB
1951	Jim Weatherall, Oklahoma, T	1961	Merlin Olsen, Utah State, T	1971	Larry Jacobson, Nebraska, DT
1952	Dick Modzelewski, Maryland, T	1962	Bobby Bell, Minnesota, T	1972	Rich Glover, Nebraska, MG
1953	J. D. Roberts, Oklahoma G	1963	Scott Appleton, Texas, T	1973	John Hicks, Ohio State, G
1954	Bill Brooks, Arkansas, G	1964	Steve Delong, Tennessee, T		
1955	Calvin Jones, Iowa, G	1965	Tommy Nobis, Texas, G		

College Football Coach of the Year

(Football Writers Assn.)

Year	Coach	School	Year	Coach	School
1946	Earl Blaik	Army	1960	None picked.	
1947	H. O. (Fritz) Crisler	Michigan	1961	Paul (Bear) Bryant	Alabama
1948	Bennie G. Oosterbaan	Michigan	1962	John McKay	USC
1949	Charles B. (Bud) Wilkinson	Oklahoma	1963	Darrell Royal	Texas
1950	Charles Caldwell	Princeton	1964	Ara Parseghian	Notre Dame
1951	Charles (Chuck) Taylor	Stanford	1965	Tommy Prothro	UCLA
1952	Clarence L. (Biggie) Munn	Mich. State	1966	Tom Cahill	Army
1953	James M. Tatum	Maryland	1967	John Pont	Indiana
1954	Henry R. (Red) Sanders	UCLA	1968	Woody Hayes	Ohio State
1955	Hugh Duffy Daughety	Mich. State	1969	Bo Schembechler	Michigan
1956	Bowden Wyatt	Tennessee	1970	Alex Agase	Northwestern
1957	Woody Hayes	Ohio State	1971	Bob Devaney	Nebraska
1958	Paul E. Dietzel	LSU	1972	John McKay	USC
1959	Ben Schwartzwalder	Syracuse	1973	Johnny Majors	Pittsburgh

Heisman Trophy Winners

The Heisman Trophy is named after John Heisman, football coach and athletic director of the Downtown Athletic Club. Awarded annually to the nation's outstanding college football player.

1935	Jay Berwanger, Chicago, HB	1948	Doak Walker, SMU, HB
1936	Larry Kelley, Yale, E	1949	Leon Hart, Notre Dame, E
1937	Clinton Frank, Yale, QB	1950	Vic Janowicz, Ohio State, HB
1938	David O'Brien, Tex. Christian, QB	1951	Richard Kazmaier, Princeton, HB
1939	Nile Kinnick, Iowa, QB	1952	Billy Vessels, Oklahoma, HB
1940	Tom Harmon, Michigan HB	1953	John Lattner, Notre Dame, HB
1941	Bruce Smith, Minnesota, HB	1954	Alan Ameche, Wisconsin, FB
1942	Frank Sinkwich, Georgia, HB	1955	Howard Cassady, Ohio St., HB
1943	Angelo Bertelli, Notre Dame, QB	1956	Paul Hornung, Notre Dame, QB
1944	Leslie Horvath, Ohio State, QB	1957	John Crow, Texas A & M, HB
1945	Felix Bianchard, Army, FB	1958	Pete Dawkins, Army, HB
1946	Glenn Davis, Army, HB	1959	Billy Cannon, La. State, HB
1947	John Lujack, Notre Dame, QB	1960	Joe Bellino, Navy, HB

1961	Ernest Davis, Syracuse, HB
1962	Terry Baker, Oregon State, QB
1963	Roger Staubach, Navy, QB
1964	John Huarte, Notre Dame, QB
1965	Mike Garrett, USC, HB
1966	Steve Spurrier, Florida, QB
1967	Gary Beban, UCLA, QB
1968	O. J. Simpson, USC, RB
1969	Steve Owens, Oklahoma, RB
1970	Jim Plunkett, Stanford, QB
1971	Pat Sullivan, Auburn, QB
1972	Johnny Rodgers, Nebraska, RB-R
1973	John Cappelletti, Penn State, RB

Table Tennis Championships in 1974

44th U.S. National Open

Oklahoma City, Okla. May 23-26, 1974

Men's Singles—Kjell Johanssen, Sweden.
Women's Singles—Yukie Ohzeki, Japan.
Mixed Doubles—Nobuhiko Hasegawa & Tazauko Abe, Japan.
Women's Doubles—Ann-Christine Hellman & Birgitta Issen, Sweden.
Men's Doubles—Stellan Bengtseon & Kjell Johanssen, Sweden.
Senior Singles—Tim Boggan, Merrick, N.Y.
Senior Doubles—William Sharpe & George Reeker, Philadelphia, Pa.

Junior Under 17—Roger Sverdlik, Rockville Centre, N.Y.
Under 17 Doubles—Rick Seemiller, Pittsburgh & Mike Veillette, Rochester, Mich.
Girls Under 17—Mariann Demonkes, Quebec.
Girls Under 17 Doubles—Mariann Demonkes & Biruta Plucas, Toronto.
Men's Team—Sweden.
Women's Team—Japan.

33rd Annual Canadian International

Toronto, Ont. Aug. 31-Sept. 2, 1974

Men's Singles—Dan Seemiller, Pittsburgh.
Women's Singles—Mariann Demonkes, Chateauguy, Quebec.
Mixed Doubles—Errol Caetano & Violetta Nesukaitis, Toronto.
Women's Doubles—Sue Hildebrandt, Warren, Mich. & Shirley Gore, Montreal.

Men's Doubles—George Brathwaithe, Brooklyn, N.Y. & Dan Seemiller, Pittsburgh.
Senior Singles—Bernard Bukiet, N.Y., N.Y.
Esq. Singles—Max Marinko, Toronto.
Jr. Singles—Mike Veillette, Rochester, Mich.
Boys—Mike Stern, Maplewood, N.J.

Black Sports Hall of Fame

(Chosen by Black Sports magazine)

Baseball	Basketball	Football	Track & Field
Henry Aaron	Elgin Baylor	Jim Brown	Cleveland Abbot
Roy Campanella	Wilt Chamberlain	Dr. Brud Holland	Bob Beamon
Roberto Clemente	Chuck Cooper	Herb McDonald	Alice Coachman
Martin Dihigo	Dr. E. B. Henderson	Marion Motley	Harrison Dillard
Larry Doby	Bill Russell	Fritz Pollard	Rafer Johnson
Josh Gibson	Jack Twyman	Paul Robeson	Ralph Metcalfe
		Buddy Young	Jesse Owens
Monte Irvin	**Boxing**		Eulace Peacock
Willie Mays			Wilma Rudolph
Minnie Minoso	Muhammad Ali	**Golf**	Willye White
Satchel Paige	Henry Armstrong	Charlie Sifford	
Branch Rickey	Joe Frazier		
Jackie Robinson	Joe Louis	**Tennis**	**Historians**
	Ray Robinson	Althea Gibson	Morris Levitt
	Jose Torres	Dr. Robert Johnson	

American Bowling Congress Championships, 1974

Indianapolis, Ind.

Regular Division

Individual

1. Gene Krause, Cleveland, Ohio. 247, 257, 269—773.
2. Rik Krecow, Cleveland, Ohio. 235, 279, 257—771.
3. Earl Stutz Jr., Norfolk, Va. 270, 237, 248 —755.
Runners-up—Gary Cunningham, Syracuse, N.Y. 754; Frank Celebra, Kenosha, Wis. 750; John Sudduth, Warrentown, Va. 739; James Rae, South Bend, Ind. 733; Jim Fedigan, Rochester, N. Y. 730; Robert Hemmelgarn, Celina, Ohio 724; Larry Wisenhall, York, Pa. 723.

All-Events

1. Bob Hart, Detroit, Mich. 687, 702, 698—2087.
2. Jimmy Doolen, Wichita Falls, Tex. 731, 665, 676—2072.
3. Marvin Stoudt, Lebanon, Pa. 629, 735, 700—2064.
Runners-up—Bill Hohensee, Albany, N.Y. 2058; Mike Heffner, Chicago, Ill. 2053; Gary Niemczyk, St. Paul, Minn. 2052; Ray Williams, Detroit, Mich. 2050; Bill Gaume, Kent, Ohio 2019; Frank Williams, Rolla, Mo. 2016; Tom Martenson, Rockford, Ill. and John Denton, Lawton, Okla. 2014.

Doubles

1. Chuck Sunseri, Detroit, Mich. 238, 255, 244—717; Bob Hart, Detroit, Mich. 238, 269, 195—702. Aggregate—1419.
2. Norman Eckert, Harrisburg, Pa. 231, 237, 170—638; Marvin Stoudt, Lebanon, Pa. 210, 246, 279—735. Aggregate—1373.
3. Bob Shoemaker, Harrisburg, Pa. 247, 206, 189—642; Calvin Yohe, Harrisburg, Pa. 257, 203, 268—728. Aggregate—1370.
Runners-Up—Fred Hansen-Mike Heffner, Chicago, Ill. 1369; Lew Magas-Rich Skufca, Cleveland, Ohio 1367; Jerry Ward-Bob Kuhl, Cleveland, Ohio 1365; Rod Toft-Dan Brick, St. Paul, Minn. 1361; Leonard Gross-Tom Ryan, Cambridge, Ohio 1355; Tom Suchan-Bill Gaume, Kent, Ohio 1346; Carl Martin-Melvin Johnson, Des Moines, Iowa 1338.

Teams

1. Olympia Beer, Omaha, Neb.—Gary Wilson 146, 216, 215—577; Jim Rood 186, 287, 255—728; Robert Lane 158, 205, 211 —574; Tom Kelly 173, 192, 279—644; Boyd Hayden 205, 247, 211—663. Aggregate—3186.
2. Coon Brothers, Detroit, Mich.—Richard Beattie 178, 204, 232—614; Tom Vallone 210, 202, 200—612; Hal Jolley 206, 199, 201—606; Don Wray 201, 187, 190—572; Ray Williams 223, 225,300. Aggregate—3158.

Classic Division

Individual

1. Ed DiTolla, Hackensack, N.J. 266, 269, 212—747.
2. Bud Tufts Jr., Miamisburg, Ohio 245, 203, 278—726.
3. Paul Colwell, Tucson, Ariz. 247, 223, 245—715.
Runners-up—Pete Tountas, Tucson, Ariz. 713; Fred Borden, Akron, Ohio 710; Charles Venable, Brooklyn, N.Y. and Dave Juric, Hammond, Ind. 708; Darrell Bowie, Tacoma, Wash., Ron Stromfeld, Columbus, Ohio and Dick Weber Sr., St. Louis, Mo. 706.

All-Events

1. Jim Godman, Vero Beach, Fla. 731, 749, 704—2184.
2. Roy Buckley, Columbus, Ohio 717, 688, 698—2103.
3. Paul Colwell, Tucson, Ariz. 689, 671, 715—2075.
Runners-up—Mickey Higham, Kansas City, Mo. 2066; Bill Spigner, Hamden, Conn. 2065; Ed DiTolla, Hackensack, N.J. 2042; Nick Francis, Folsom, Pa. 2030; Tye Critchlow, Claremont, Calif. 2016; Dick Weber Jr., St. Louis, Mo. 2012; Charles Venable, Brooklyn, N.Y. 2006.

Doubles

1. Bob Perry, Paterson, N.J. 215, 183, 268—666; Tye Critchlow, Claremont, Calif. 223, 234, 226—693. Aggregate—1359.
2. Bus Oswalt, Muncie, Ind. 243, 214, 247—704; Bob Perry, Muncie, Ind. 175, 225, 247—647. Aggregate—1351.
3. Roy Buckley, Columbus, Ohio 235, 249, 204—688; Carmen Salvino, Chicago, Ill. 259, 160, 235—654. Aggregate—1342.
Runners-up—Don McCune-Jim Stefanich, Joliet, Ill. 1338; Gary Mage-Earl Anthony, Seattle, Wash. 1329; Bob Fitt-Rick Minier, Akron, Ohio and Dale Mani-Bob Buchanon, Canton, Ohio 1326; Bobby Cooper, Dallas and George Pappas, Charlotte, N.C. and Jay Robinson-Gary Dickinson, Ft. Worth, Tex. 1324; John Denton-Bob McGregor, Lawton, Okla. and Don Carter-Jim Godman, Miami, Fla. 1317.

Teams

1. Ebonite, Hopkinsville, Ky.—Don Carter 169, 187, 219—575; Ray Bluth 200, 247, 224—671; Johnny Guenther 215, 210, 222 —647; Bob Strampe 183, 201, 225—609; Jim Godman 232, 212, 171—615. Aggregate—3117.
2. Munsingwear, Minneapolis, Minn.—Roy Buckley 226, 246, 217—689; Norm Meyers 227, 209, 204—640; Barry Asher 202, 205, 213—620; Bud Horn 216, 201, 192—609; Nelson Burton Jr. 192, 181, 185—558. Aggregate—3116.

Other Bowling Championships in 1974

4th U. S. Open—New York, N. Y., Feb. 10-16—Larry Laub, San Francisco, Calif. Average 223, prize $8,000. Women—Irving, Tex., May 13-16—Pat Costello, Union City, Calif. Average 202, prize $6,000.
National Intercollegiate Championships, Indianapolis, Ind., April 7—Doubles—Jerry Novosel, Penn State and Richard Ficken, Maryland. Singles—Richard Chang. UCLA. All events—

Ralph Welborn, Mt. Hood, Ore.
Invitational Bowling Tournament of the Americas—Miami, Fla., July 14-20—Men's Doubles, Ron Woolet-Bob Hart, U. S.; Singles, Alfonso Rodriguez, Mexico; All Events—Bob Hart, U.S. Women's Doubles, JoAnne Rogalski-Mary Lou Graham, U.S.; Singles, Mary Lou Graham, U.S.; All Events, Mary Lou Graham, U.S.

Masters Bowling Tournament Champions

Year	Winner	Runner-up	W.L.	Avg.
1962	Bill Golembiewski, Detroit, Mich.	Ron Winger, Los Angeles, Calif.	7-0....	223-12
1963	Harry Smith, St. Louis, Mo.	Bobby Meadows, Dallas, Tex.	7-0....	219-3
1964	Billy Welu, St. Louis, Mo.	Harry Smith, Baltimore, Md.	7-0....	227
1965	Billy Welu, St. Louis, Mo.	Don Ellis, Houston, Tex.	9-1....	202-12
1966	Bob Strampe, Detroit, Mich.	Al Thompson, Cleveland, Ohio.	7-0....	219-8
1967	Lou Scalia, Miami, Fla.	Bill Johnson, New Orleans, La.	7-0....	216-9
1968	Pete Tountas, Tucson, Ariz.	Buzz Fazio, Detroit, Mich.	9-1....	220-15
1969	Jim Chestney, Denver, Colo.	Barry Asher, Costa Mesa, Calif.	10-1...	223-2
1970	Don Glover, Bakersfield, Calif.	Bob Strampe, Detroit, Mich.	9-1....	215-10
1971	Jim Godman, Lorain, Ohio.	Don Johnson, Akron, Ohio.	9-1....	229-8
1972	Bill Beach, Sharon, Pa.	Jim Godman, Lorain, Ohio.	8-1....	220-27
1973	Dave Soutar, Gilroy, Calif.	Dick Ritger, Hartford, Wisc.	7-0....	218-61
1974	Paul Colwell, Tucson, Ariz.	Steve Neff, Sarasota, Fla.	7-0....	234-17

All-Time Records for League and Tournament Play

Type of record	Holder of record	Year	Score	Competition
High team total	Budweiser Beer, St. Louis, Mo.	1958	3,858	League
High team game	Hook Grip Five, Lodi, N.J.	1950	1,342	League
High doubles total	Nelson Burton Jr., Billy Walden, St. Louis.	1970	1,614	Tournament
High doubles game	Tom Dern-Ron Spohn, Columbus, Ohio.	1965	587	League
High individual total	Albert Brandt, Lockport, N.Y.	1939	886	League
High all events score	Frank Benkovic, Milwaukee, Wis.	1932	2,259	Tournament

Record Averages for Consecutive Tournaments

No. in row	Name of record holder	Span	Games	Average
Two	Steve Nagy, Cleveland, Ohio.	1951-52	18	224.09
Three	Steve Nagy, Cleveland, Ohio.	1952-53	27	221.02
Four	Bob Strampe, Detroit, Mich.	1964-67	48	215.40
Five	Bob Strampe, Detroit, Mich.	1964-68	57	215.28
Ten	Bob Strampe, Detroit, Mich.	1961-70	111	211.10

Official Records of Annual ABC Tournaments

Type of record	Holder of record	Year	Score
High team total	Ace Mitchell Shur-Hooks, Akron, Ohio	1966	3,357
High team game	Falstaff Beer, San Antonio, Texas.	1958	1,226
High doubles score	John Klares-Steve Nagy, Cleveland, Ohio	1952	1,453
High doubles game	John Gworek-Henry Krnidowski, Buffalo, N.Y.	1946	544
High singles total	Lee Jouglard, Detroit, Mich.	1951	775
High all events score	Jim Godman, Vero Beach, Fla.	1974	2,184
High team all events	Falstaff Beer, St. Louis, Mo.	1958	9,608
High life-time pin total	Bill Doehrman, Ft. Wayne, Indiana	1908 to 1974	104,090

Bowlers With Six or More Sanctioned 300 Games

Elvin Mesger, Sullivan, Mo.	26	Howard Holmes, Los Angeles	8	Salvatore Bivona, Paterson, N.J.	6
George Billick, Old Forge, Pa.	17	Casey Jones, Plymouth, Wisc.	8	Lou Campi, Dumont, N.J.	6
Dick Weber, St. Louis	16	Russell Field, San Jose, Calif.	8	Ed Davis, Milford, N.J.	6
Al Faragalli, Wayne, N.J.	14	Roger Fink, Lodi, Calif.	8	Don Dubro, St. Louis, Mo.	6
Don Carter, Tarzana, Calif.	13	George Pappas, Charlotte, N.C.	8	*Bill Flynn, Cleveland	6
Dave Soutar, Gilroy, Calif.	13	Dennis Wright, Milwaukee	8	Sam Garofalo, St. Louis.	6
Ray Bluth, St. Louis, Mo.	12	Ray Eklund, Milwaukee	8	Joe Joseph, Lansing, Mich.	6
Walter Ward, Cleveland.	12	Walter King, Detroit, Mich.	8	Pete Kozloski, Plains, Pa.	6
*Hank Marino, Milwaukee	11	Junie McMahon, Lodi, N.J.	8	Vince Lucci, Trenton, N.J.	6
Frank Clause, Old Forge, Pa.	11	Joe Donato, Schenectady, N.Y.	7	Steve Nagy, Cleveland.	6
Ed Lubanski, Detroit, Mich.	11	Eddie Botten, Union City, N.J.	7	Frank Pollak, Pittsburgh.	6
Pat Patterson, St. Louis.	11	Dick Hoover, Akron.	7	Robert Pinkalla, Milwaukee	6
Don Johnson, Akron.	10	Ken McKenzie, Dallas	7	Harold Schaeffer, St. Louis.	6
Boss Bosco, Akron.	9	Ray Schanen, Milwaukee.	7	Harry Smith, Redwood City, Calif.	6
Al Savas, Milwaukee.	9	Wayne Pinkalla, Milwaukee	7	Bob Strampe, Detroit, Mich.	6
Lou Foxie, Paterson, N.J.	9	George Pappas, Charlotte	7	Jerry Thrap, St. Louis, Mos.	6
Jerry Woji, Stockton, Calif.	9	Bob Ramirez, Los Angeles	7	George Tomek, Plymouth, Pa.	6
Norm Meyers, St. Louis	9	Don McCune, Munster, Ind.	7	Stephen Tomek, Plymouth, Pa.	6
Tom Hennessey, St. Louis, Mo.	9	Bud Horn, Los Angeles	7	William Capleton, Prospect Park, N.J.	6

*Bowled two 300 games in official 3-game-series.

PBA Winter Tour, 1974

Date	Event	Winner	Winner's Share
Jan. 1-5.	Midas Open, Oakland, Calif.	Dick Ritger	$14,000
Jan. 8-12.	Don Carter Classic, Los Angeles	Larry Laub	7,500
Jan. 15-19.	Showboat International, Las Vegas.	Jim Stefanich	14,000
Jan. 22-26.	King Louie Open, Kansas City, Mo.	George Pappas	6,000
Jan. 29-Feb. 2.	Cleveland Open.	Larry Laub	7,000
Feb. 5-9.	Fair Lanes Open, Baltimore.	Dick Ritger.	7,500
Feb. 10-16.	BPAA U.S. Open, New York.	Larry Laub	8,000
Feb. 19-23.	Winston-Salem Open.	Ed Ressler	14,000
Feb. 28-Mar. 2.	STP Classic, Miami, Fla.	Alex Seymore	10,000
Mar. 5-9.	New Orleans Lions Open.	Paul Colwell.	6,000
Mar. 12-16.	Lincoln-Mercury Open, Denver.	Johnny Guenther	10,000
Mar. 19-23.	Miller High Life Open, Milwaukee.	Johnny Guenther	10,000
Mar. 26-30.	Ebonite Open, Toledo, Ohio.	Wayne Zahn	10,000
Apr. 1-6.	Firestone Tournament of Champions, Akron, Ohio.	Earl Anthony	25,000

Leading PBA Averages in 1973

	Name, City	Tournaments	Games	Pinfall	Average
1.	Earl Anthony, Tacoma, Wash.	29	915	197,456	215.799
2.	Barry Asher, Costa Mesa, Cal.	30	999	214,456	214.671
3.	Don McCune, Munster, Ind.	33	1124	240,850	214.279
4.	Roy Buckley, Columbus, O.	30	980	208,445	212.699
5.	Jay Robinson, Los Angeles.	32	1031	218,703	212.333
6.	Gary Dickinson, Ft. Worth, Tex.	31	1014	215,195	212.224
7.	Dick Ritger, Hartford, Wis.	27	986	209,234	212.205
8.	Don Johnson, Akron, O.	31	949	201,192	212.002
9.	Dennis Swayda, Phoenix, Ariz.	31	1024	216,794	211.713
10.	Johnny Guenther, Seattle, Wash.	17	499	105,509	211.441
11.	Jim Godman, Lorain, O.	26	850	179,639	211.340
12.	Nelson Burton Jr., St. Louis, Mo.	19	499	105,432	211.287
13.	Mike McGrath, St. Louis, Mo.	29	884	186,442	210.907
14.	Matt Surina, Longview, Wash.	31	941	198,395	210.834
15.	Marty Piraino, Syracuse, N.Y.	15	369	77,783	210.794
16.	Bobby Cooper, Dallas, Tex.	30	899	189,226	210.485
17.	Paul Colwell, Tucson, Ariz.	32	1031	216,967	210.443
18.	John Handegard, Eugene, Ore.	33	1017	213,735	210.162
19.	Carmen Salvino, Chicago, Ill.	27	815	171,136	209.983
20.	Larry Laub, San Francisco, Cal.	22	655	137,507	209.934
21.	Mark Roth, Brooklyn, N.Y.	22	672	141,049	209.894
22.	Gus Lampo, Endicott, N.Y.	20	553	115,961	209.694
23.	Dick Weber, St. Louis, Mo.	20	650	136,169	209.491
24.	Dave Davis, Atlanta, Ga.	32	947	198,189	209.281
25.	Jim Stefanich, Joliet, Ill.	32	947	198,189	209.281

Leading PBA Averages by Years

Year	Player	Tournaments	Average	Year	Player	Tournaments	Average
1962 —	Don Carter, St. Louis, Mo.	25	212.844	1968 —	Jim Stefanich, Joliet, Ill.	33	211.895
1963 —	Billy Hardwick, Louisville, Ky.	26	210.346	1969 —	Billy Hardwick, Louisville, Ky.	33	212.957
1964 —	Ray Bluth, St. Louis, Mo.	27	210.512	1970 —	Nelson Burton, Jr., St. Louis, Mo.	32	214.908
1965 —	Dick Weber, St. Louis, Mo.	19	211.895	1971 —	Don Johnson, Akron, O.	31	213.977
1966 —	Wayne Zahn, Atlanta, Ga.	27	208.663	1972 —	Don Johnson, Akron, O.	30	215.290
1967 —	Wayne Zahn, Atlanta, Ga.	29	212,142	1973 —	Earl Anthony, Tacoma, Wash.	29	215.799

PBA Leading Money Winners

Total winnings are from PBA, ABC Masters and BPAA All-Star tournaments only, and do not include numerous other tournaments nor earnings from special television shows and matches.

Year	Player	Total	Year	Player	Total	Year	Player	Total
1959	Dick Weber	$ 7,672	1964	Bob Strampe	$33,592	1969	Billy Hardwick	$64,160
1960	Don Carter	22,525	1965	Dick Weber	47,674	1970	Mike McGrath	52,049
1961	Dick Weber	26,280	1966	Wayne Zahn	54,720	1971	Johnny Petraglia	85,065
1962	Don Carter	49,972	1967	Dave Davis	54,165	1972	Don Johnson	56,648
1963	Dick Weber	46,333	1968	Jim Stefanich	67,375	1973	Don McCune	69,000

The $100,000 Firestone Tournament of Champions

This is professional bowling's richest tournament and has been held each year since its inception in 1965, in Akron, Ohio, the home of the Professional Bowlers Association. First prize is $25,000.

Year	Winner	Year	Winner	Year	Winner	Year	Winner
1965	Billy Hardwick	1967	Jim Stefanich	1969	Jim Godman	1972	Mike Durbin
1966	Wayne Zahn	1968	Dave Davis	1970	Don Johnson	1973	Jim Godman
				1971	Johnny Petraglia	1974	Earl Anthony

Women's International Bowling Congress Champions

Year	Individual	All Events	Two-Woman Teams	Five-Woman Teams
1968	Norma Parks, Raytown, Md. 691	Janice Reichley, Waco, Tex. 1,889	Pauline Stickler-Mary Lou Graham, Miami. 1,250	Hudepohl Beer, Cincinnati. 2,923
1969	Joan Bender, Arvada, Colo. 690	Helen Duval, Berkeley, Calif. 1,927	Gloria Bouvia, Portland, Ore.-Judy Cook, Grandview, Mo. 1,315	Fitzpatrick Chevrolet, Concord, Calif. 2,986
1970	Dorothy Fothergill, N. Attleboro, Mass. 695	Dorothy Fothergill. 1,984	Gloria Bouvia, Portland, Ore.-Judy Cook, Kansas City, Mo. 1,256	Parker-Fothergill Pro Shop, Cranston, R.I. 3,034
1971	Mary Scruggs, Richmond, Va. 698	Lorrie Koch, Carpentersville, Ill. 1,840	Dorothy Fothergill, N. Attleboro, Mass.-Mildred Martorella, Rochester, N.Y. 1,263	Koenig & Strey Real Estate, Wilmette, Ill. 2,891
1972	D. D. Jacobson, Playa Del Rey, Calif. 737	Mildred Martorella, Rochester, N.Y. 1,877	Judy Roberts-Betty Remmick, Denver, Lakewood, Colo. 1,247	Angeltown Creations, Placentia, Calif. 2,838
1973	Bobbie Buffaloe, Costa Mesa, Calif. 706	Toni Calvery, Midwest City, Okla. 1,910	Dorothy Fothergill, N. Attleboro, Mass.-Mildred Martorella, Rochester, N.Y. 1,238	Fitzpatrick Chevrolet, Concord, Calif. 2,897
1974	Shirley Garms, Lake Island, Ill. 702	Judy Cook Soutar, Kansas City, Mo. 1,944	Jane Leszczynski, Milwaukee-Carol Miller, Waukesha, Wisc. 1,313	Kalicak International Construction, Kansas City, Mo. 2,973

Records of 300 Games in WIBC Sanctioned Play

1973-74—Irene Arslan, Sunnyvale, Calif.; Nancy Bassett, Salina, Kan.; Leemoi Bekey, San Rafael, Calif.; Josephine Borges, Oakland, Calif.; Lydia Brewer, LaMirada, Calif.; Judith Chapman, Littleton, Colo.; Ferne Crawford, Philadelphia, Pa.; Ethel Dezell, Staples, Minn.; Mary Ickes, Woodville, Ohio; Barbara Kaufold, Butler, Pa.; Nell Kleinschmidt, Mt. Carmel, Ill.; Betty Morris, Stockton, Calif.; Lou Lane, Austin, Texas; Patsy Lynn, Spokane, Wash.; Lupe McCabe, Fresno, Calif.; Cindy Pearl, Louisville, Ky.; Roslyn Stewart, Detroit, Mich.; Mel Williams, Fayetteville, N.C.; Jacqueline Wissler, Reading, Pa.

1972-73—Betty Geisler, San Antonio, Texas; Helen Gilkerson, Lexington, Ky.; Connie Graham, Victorville, Calif.; Rita Justice, Wilmington, Del.; Barbara Keicher, Depew, N.Y.; Cindy Kimbirauskas, Lansing, Mich.; Joan Lilly, Convington, Ky.; Paula Martin, Houston, Texas; Phyllis Max, Toledo, Ohio; Nancy Mazzier, Weed, Calif.; Dorothy McMullen, Madison, Ill.; Jean Nash, Toledo, Ohio; Marge Pacanowski, Westfield, N.Y.;

Ann Poisguy, Oregon, Ohio; Joan Ray, Yuma, Ariz.; Barbara Skokan, Perth Amboy, N.J.; Gaylene Suedbeck, Slayton, Minn.; Katherine Thompkins, Seattle, Wash.; Val Tridico, Mansfield, Ohio; Bonnie Triptow, Taylorsville, Utah; Geneva Tucker, Nashville, Tenn.; Jeannine Williams, Fremont, Calif.; Kenda Williams, Amarillo, Texas; Susan Zaluk, Garwood, N.J.

1971-72—Marilyn Bourbonais, Wauwatosa, Wis.; Bernita Cade, Mahomet, Ill.; Barbara Fincel, Phoenix, Ariz.; Sharon Gilder, Richmond, B.C., Canada; Arlene Hardebeck, Covington, Ky.; Maureen Harris, Madison, Wis.; Mona Jackson, Houston, Texas; Pat Jinks, Houston, Texas; Linda Kaiser, Springfield, Mo.; Marge Lewandowski, Sterling Heights, Mich.; Betty Mivelaz, Tujunga, Calif.; Esmeralda Munden, Honolulu, Hawaii; Vickie Myers, Sunland, Calif.; Nicola Petersen, El Paso, Texas; Helen Radtke, Massillon, Ohio; Dorothy Rumple, Rockford, Ill.; Beverly Russell, Sturgis, S.D.; Elizabeth Welch, Nyack, N.Y.; Diane Wilhelm, Cincinnati, Ohio; Jean Worthy, Norwalk, Calif.

World Track and Field Records

As of Sept., 1974
*Indicates pending record; a number of new records await confirmation

Men

Running

Event	Record	Holder	Country	Date	Where made
100 yds.	9.1 s.	Bob Hayes	U.S.A.	June 21, 1963	St. Louis, Mo.
		James Hines	U.S.A.	May 13, 1967	Houston, Tex.
		Charlie Greene	U.S.A.	June 15, 1967	Provo, Utah
		John Carlos	U.S.A.	May 10, 1969	Fresno, Calif.
		Harry Jerome	Canada	July 15, 1966	Edmonton Canada
		Willie McGee	U.S.A.	May 8, 1970	Houston
		Steve Williams	U.S.A.	May 12, 1973	Fresno, Calif.
	*9.0 s.	Ivory Crockett	U.S.A.	May 11, 1974	Knoxville, Tenn.
220 yds.	19.5 s.	Tommie Smith	U.S.A.	May 7, 1966	San Jose, Calif.
220 yds.	20.0 s. (Turn)	Tommie Smith	U.S.A.	May 11, 1966	Sacramento, Calif.
440 yds.	44.5	John Smith	U.S.A.	June 26, 1972	Eugene, Ore.
880 yds.	*1 m., 43.9 s.	Rick Wohlhuter	U.S.A.	June, 1974	Los Angeles
1 mile	3 m., 51.1 s.	Jim Ryun	U.S.A.	June 23, 1967	Bakersfield. Calif.
2 miles	8 m., 13.8 s.	Brendon Foster	Gt. Britain	Aug. 27, 1973	....
3 miles	12 m., 47.8 s.	Emiel Puttemans	Belgium	Sept. 20, 1972	Brussels
6 miles	26 m., 47.0 s.	Ron Clarke	Australia	July 14, 1965	Oslo, Norway
10 miles	46 m., 04.2 s.	Willy Polleunis	Belgium	Sept. 20, 1972	Brussels
15 miles	1 hr., 12 min., 48.2 s.	Ron Hill	Gt. Britain	July 21, 1965	Bolton, Eng.

Running — Metric Distances

100 meters	9.9 s.	Jim Hines	U.S.A.	June 20, 1968	Sacramento
		Charlie Greene	U.S.A.	June 20, 1968	Sacramento
		Ronnie Smith	U.S.A.	June 20, 1968	Sacramento
		Jim Hines	U.S.A.	Oct. 14, 1968	Mexico City
		Eddie Hart	U.S.A.	July 1, 1972	Eugene, Ore.
		Reynaud Robinson	U.S.A.	July 1 1972	Eugene, Ore.
		Steve Williams	U.S.A.	June 22, 1974	Los Angeles
200 meters	19.5 s.	Tommie Smith	U.S.A.	May 7, 1966	San Jose, Calif.
200 meters	19.8 s. (Turn)	Tommie Smith	U.S.A.	Oct. 16, 1968	Mexico City
		Donald Quarrie	Jamaica	Aug. 3, 1971	Cali, Colombia
400 meters	43.8 s.	Lee Evans	U.S.A.	Oct. 18, 1968	Mexico City
800 meters	1 m., 43.7 s.	Marcello Fiasconaro	Italy	June 27, 1973	Milan, Italy
1,000 meters	*2 m., 13.9 s.	Rick Wohlhuter	U.S.A.	July 30, 1974	Oslo, Norway
1,500 meters	3 m., 33.1 s.	Jim Ryun	U.S.A.	July 8, 1967	Los Angeles
	*3 m., 32.2 s.	Filbert Bayi	Tanzania	Feb. 2, 1974	Christchurch, N. Z.
2,000 meters	4 m., 56.2 s.	Michel Jazy	France	Oct. 12, 1966	Saint Maur, France
3000 meters	*7 m., 35.2 s.	Brendon Foster	Gt. Britain	Aug. 3, 1974	Gateshead, Eng.
5,000 meters	13 m., 13 s.	Emiel Puttemans	Belgium	Sept. 20, 1972	Brussels
10,000 meters	27 m., 31 s.	Dave Bedford	Gr. Britain	July 13, 1973	London
20,000 meters	57 m., 44.4 s.	Gaston Roelants	Belgium	Sept. 20, 1972	Brussels
25,000 meters	1 hr., 15 m., 22.6 s.	Ron Hill	Gr. Britain	July 21, 1965	Bolton, Eng.
30,000 meters	1 hr., 31 m., 30.4 s.	Jim Alder	Gr. Britain	Sept. 5, 1970	London
3,000 meter stpl	8 m., 14 s.	Ben Jipcho	Kenya	June 27, 1973	Helsinki

Hurdles

120 yards	13.0 s.	Rod Milburn	U.S.A.	June 25, 1971	Eugene, Ore.
		Rod Milburn	U.S.A.	June 20, 1973	Eugene, Ore.
220 yards	21.9 s.	Don Styron	U.S.A.	Apr. 2, 1960	Baton Rouge
440 yards	48.8 s.	Ralph Mann	U.S.A.	June 20, 1970	Des Moines, Iowa
110 meters	13.1 s.	Rod Milburn	U.S.A.	July 6, 1973	Zurich
		Rod Milburn	U.S.A.	July 22, 1973	Siena, Italy
200 meters	21.9 s.	Don Styron	U.S.A.	Apr. 2, 1960	Baton Rouge
200 meters	22.5 s.	Martin Lauer	W. Germany	July 7, 1959	Zurich, Switz.
	(Turn)	Glenn Davis	U.S.A.	Aug. 20, 1960	Berne, Switz.
400 meters	47.8 s.	John Akii-Bua	Uganda	Sept. 2, 1972	Munich

Relay Races

440 yds. (4x110) (2 turns)	38.6 s.	USC (McCullough, Kuller, Simpson, Miller)	U.S.A.	June 17, 1967	Provo, Utah
880 yds. (4x220)	1 m., 21.7 s.	Texas A&M (Rogers, Woods, M. Mills, C. Mills)	U.S.A.	Apr. 24, 1970	Des Moines, Iowa
1 mile (4x440)	3 m., 02.8 s.	National Team (Yearwood, Bernard, Roberts, Mottley)	Trinidad & Tobago	Aug.13,1966	Kingston, Jamaica
2 miles (4x880)	7 mi., 10.4 s.	Chicago TC (Bach, Sparks, Paul, Wohlhuter)	U.S.A.	May, 1973	Durham, N.C.
4 miles (4x1) (mile)	16 m., 02.8 s.	New Zealand Nat'l. Team	New Zealand	Feb. 3, 1972	Auckland, N.Z.

Relay Races—Metric Distances

400 mtrs.	38.2 s.	Nat'l. Team (Greene, Pender, R. Smith, Hines)	U.S.A.	Oct. 20, 1968	Mexico City
		Nat'l. Team (Black, Taylor, Tinker, Hart)	U.S.A.	Sept. 10, 1972	Munich
800 mtrs. (4x200)	1 mi., 21.5 s.	National Team (Ossola, Obeti, Benedetti, Mennea)	Italy	July 21, 1972	Barletta

1,600 mtrs. (4x400)	**2 m., 56.1 s.**	Nat'l. Team (Matthews, Freeman, James, Evans)	U.S.A.	Oct. 20, 1968	Mexico City
3,200 mtrs. (4x800)	**7 m., 08.6 s.**	Nat'l. Team (Kinder, Adams, Bogatzki, Kemper)	W. Germany	Aug. 13, 1966	Wiesbaden

Field Events

High Jump	**7 ft. 6³/₄ in.**	Dwight Stones	U.S.A.	July 14, 1973	Munich
Long Jump	**29 ft., 2¹/₄ in.**	Bob Beamon	U.S.A.	Oct. 18, 1968	Mexico City
Triple Jump	**57 ft., 2³/₄ in.**	Victor Saneyev	USSR	Oct. 17, 1972	Sukhumi, USSR
Pole Vault	**18 ft., 5³/₄ in.**	Bob Seagren	U.S.A.	July 2, 1972	Eugene, Ore.
16 lb. shot put	***72 ft., 2³/₄ in.**	George Woods	U.S.A.	Feb. 8, 1974	Los Angeles
Discus throw	**229 ft., 9¹/₂ in.**	Jay Silvester	U.S.A.	June 10, 1971	Ystad, Sweden
Javelin throw	**308 ft., 8 in.**	Klaus Wolfermann	W. Germany	May 5, 1973	W. Germany
16 lb. hammer throw	***251 ft., 6 in.**	Alexei Spiridonov	USSR	Sept. 11, 1974	Munich
Decathlon	**8,454 pts.**	Nikolai Avilov	USSR	Sept. 8, 1972	Munich

Walking

20 miles	**2 h., 31 m., 33.0 s.**	Anatoliy Vedjakov	USSR	Aug. 23, 1958	Moscow, USSR
30 miles	**3 h., 51 m., 48.6 s.**	Gerhard Weidner	W. Germany	Apr. 8, 1973	
2 hours	**26,911 meters**	Karl-Heinz Stadtmuller	E. Germany	Apr. 16, 1972	Berlin
30 km	**2 h., 14 m., 45.6 s.**	Karl-Heinz Stadtmuller	E. Germany	Apr. 16, 1972	Berlin
50 km	**4 h., 00 m., 27.2 s.**	Gerhard Weidner	W. Germany	Apr. 8, 1973	

Women

Running

100 yards	**10.0 s.**	Chi Cheng	Taiwan	June 13, 1970	Portland, Ore.
220 yards	**22.6 s.**	Chi Cheng	Taiwan	July 3, 1970	Los Angeles
440 yards	**52.2 s.**	Kathy Hammond	U.S.A.	Aug. 12, 1972	
880 yards	**2 m., 02.0 s.**	J. Pollock	Australia	July 5, 1967	Sweden
		*Madeline Manning Jackson	U.S.A.	May 14, 1972	Philadelphia
1 mile	**4 m., 29.5 s.**	Paolo Cacchi	Italy	Aug. 8, 1973	
60 meters	**7.2 s.**	Betty Cuthbert	Australia	Feb. 27, 1960	Australia
		Irina Bochkaryova	USSR	Aug. 28, 1960	Moscow
100 meters	**10.8 s.**	Renate Stecher	E. Germany	July 20, 1973	Dresden
200 meters	***22 s.**	Irena Szewinska	Poland	June 13, 1974	Potsdam
400 meters	***49.9 s.**	Irena Szewinska	Poland	June 22, 1974	Warsaw
800 meters	**1 m., 57.5 s.**	Svetla Zlateva	Bulgaria	Aug. 24, 1973	...
1500 meters	**4 m., 01.4 s.**	Ludmila Bragina	USSR	Sept. 9, 1972	Munich
3000 meters	**9 m., 9 s.**	Paola Pigni	Italy	May 11, 1972	Formia, Italy

Hurdles

100 meters	**12.5 s.**	Annelie Ehrhardt	E. Germany	June 15, 1972	Potsdam
		Pamela Ryan	Australia	June 28, 1972	Warsaw
200 meters	**25.7 s.**	Pamela Ryan	Australia	Nov. 25, 1971	Melbourne
400 meters	**57.3 s.**	Maria Sykora	Austria	June, 1973	Frankfurt

Field Events

High jump	***6 ft. 4³/₄ in.**	Rosemarie Witschas	E. Germany	Sept. 8, 1974	Rome
Shot put	**60 ft.**	Nadezwda Chizhova	USSR	Sept. 7, 1972	Munich
Long jump	**22 ft., 5¹/₄ in.**	Heide Rosendahl	W. Germany	Sept. 3, 1970	Turin, Italy
Discus throw	***229 ft., 4 in.**	Faina Melnik	USSR	May, 1974	Prague
Javelin	**213 ft., 5 in.**	Ruth Fuchs	E. Germany	June 11, 1972	...
Pentathlon	**4,932 pts.**	Burglinde Pollak	E. Germany	Sept. 22, 1973	...

Relay Races

400 mtrs. (4x100)	***42.5 s.**	National Team	E. Germany	Sept.8, 1974	Rome
800 mtrs. (4x200)	**1 m., 33.8 s.**	Nat'l. Team (Tranter, James, Simpson, Peal)	Gt. Britain	Aug. 24, 1968	London
880 yds. (4x220)	**1 m., 35.8 s.**	(Hoffman, Boyle, Kilborn, Lamy)	Australia	Nov. 9, 1969	Brisbane, Aust.
1,600 mtrs. (4x400)	**3 m., 23.0 s.**	Nat'l. Team	E. Germany	Sept. 10, 1972	Munich
1 mile (4x440)	**3 m., 33.9 s.**	(Hammond, Fergerson, Manning-Jackson, Edwards)	U.S.A.	Aug. 12, 1972	

World High Jump Records

Year	Jumper	Height	Year	Jumper	Height
1912	George Horine, U.S.	6-7	1960	John Thomas, U.S.	7-1¹/₂
1914	Edward Beeson, U.S.	6-7¹/₄	1960	John Thomas, U.S.	7-1³/₄
1924	Harold Osborn, U.S.	6-8¹/₄	1960	John Thomas, U.S.	7-2
1933	Walter Marty, U.S.	6-8¹/₂	1960	John Thomas, U.S.	7-3³/₄
1934	Walter Marty, U.S.	6-9	1961	Valery Brumel, USSR	7-3³/₄
1936	C. Johnson, U.S.	6-10³/₄	1961	Valery Brumel, USSR	7-4¹/₄
1936	D. Albritton, U.S.	6-9³/₄	1961	Valery Brumel, USSR	7-4¹/₂
1937	Mel Walker, U.S.	6-10¹/₂	1962	Valery Brumel, USSR	7-5
1941	Lester Steers, U.S.	6-11	1962	Valery Brumel, USSR	7-5¹/₄
1953	Walter Davis, U.S.	6-11¹/₂	1963	Valery Brumel, USSR	7-5³/₄
1956	Charles Dumas, U.S.	7-0¹/₂	1971	Pat Matzdorf, U.S.	7-6¹/₄
1957	Y. Stepanov, USSR	7-1*	1973	Dwight Stones, U.S.	7-6¹/₂

*Made with built-up shoe.

67th Annual Millrose Games

New York, N.Y., Jan. 25, 1974

60 Yds.—Herb Washington, E. Lansing, Mich. **Time—0:06.1.**
60 Yd. High Hurdles—Larry Shipp, LSU. **Time—0:06.9.**
500 Yds.—Maurice Peoples, Arizona St. **Time—0:57.6.**
Mel Sheppard 600 Yds.—Stan Vinson, Eastern Mich. **Time —1:11.2.**
Charles Howe Half-Mile—Rick Wohlhuter, U. of Chicago TC. **Time—1:50.8.**
Mike Devaney 1,000 Yds.—Lennox Steward, N.Y. Pioneer Club. **Time—2:09.5.**

Wanamaker Mile—Tony Waldrop, North Carolina. **Time— 3:59.7.**
Shot Put—George Woods, Pacific Coast Club. 68 ft. 11½ in.
Pole Vault—Casey Carrigan, Pacific Coast Club. 17 ft.
Women's 60 Yds.—Mattline Render. **Time—0:07.3.**
Women's 600 Yds.—Brenda Nichols, Atoms TC. **Time— 1:24.**
Women's 1,000 Yds.—Mary Decker, Blue Angels TC. **Time —2:27.4.**

6th U.S. Olympic Invitation Track Meet

New York, N.Y., Feb. 8, 1974

50 Meters—Mike McFarland, Chicago TC. **Time—0:05.7.**
55 Meter Hurdles—Rod Milburn, Baton Rouge TC. **Time— 0:06.8.**
400 Meters—Fred Sowerby, Sports International. **Time— 0:48.3.**
500 Meters—Howard Brock, Seton Hall. **Time—1:04.6.**
800 Meters—Brian McElroy, New York AC. **Time—1:51.1.**
1,000 Meters—Cliff Bruce, Manhattan College. **Time— 2:27.8.**
1,500 Meters—Byron Dyce, Florida TC. **Time—3:40.7.**

1,500 Meter Walk—Dave Romansky. **Time—6:05.4.**
3,000 Meters—Denis Fikes, Penn. **Time—8:05.8.**
Pole Vault—Reinhard Kuretzky, W. Germany. 16 ft. 4 in.
High Jump—Chris Dunn, New York AC. 7 ft. 1 in.

Women's Events

50 Meters—Mattline Render, PAL. **Time—0:06.3.**
400 Meters—Brenda Nichols, Atoms TC. **Time—0:56.4.**
800 Meters—Svetla Elateva, Bulgaria. **Time—2:06.**
Ms. Metric Mile (1,500 Meters)—Francie Larrieu, Pacific Coast Club. **Time—4:18.3.**

San Francisco Examiner Games

San Francisco, Calif., Feb. 1, 1974

60 Yds.—Steve Williams, San Diego St. **Time—0:06.1.**
60 Yd. Hurdles—Charles Rich, Cal International. **Time— 0:07.1.**
440 Yds.—Carl Lawson, Idaho St. **Time—0:50.1.**
600 Yds.—Marcello Fiasconaro, Italy. **Time—1:10.4.**
One Mile—Fannie Van Ziil, South Africa. **Time—4:01.3.**

2 Miles—Mirus Yifter, Ethiopia. **Time—8:43.4.**
Shot Put—George Woods, Pacific Coast Club. 70 ft. 4½ in.
Long Jump—Stan Whitley, Cal International. 25 ft. 4 in.
Pole Vault—Kjell Isaksson. 17 ft. 3 in.
High Jump—Reynaldo Brown. 7 ft. 2 in.

Toronto Star—Maple Leaf Indoor Games

Toronto, Ont., Feb. 15, 1974

50 Yds.—Herb Washington, E. Lansing, Mich. **Time—0:05.1.**
50 Yd. Hurdles—Willie Davenport, Baton Rouge, La. **Time— 0:05.9.**
600 Yds.—Maurice Peoples, Arizona St. **Time—1:11.**
1,000 Yds.—Rick Wohlhuter, Chicago. **Time—2:05.9.**
One Mile—John Hartnett, Villanova. **Time—3:59.6.**
3 Miles—Dick Taylor, New Zealand. **Time—13:08.**
High Jump—Kestutis Sapka, USSR. 7 ft. 2 in.
Pole Vault—Kjell Isaksson, Sweden. 17 ft. 6 in.

Women's Events

50 Yds.—Raelene Boyle, Australia. **Time—0:05.7.**
50 Yd. Hurdles—Patty Johnson, La Jolla, Calif. **Time— 0:06.5.**
600 Yds.—Yvonne Saunders, Guelph, Ont. **Time—1:18.4.**
800 Meters—Liliana Tomova, Bulgaria. **Time—2:07.6.**
1,500 Meters—Francie Larrieu, Calif. **Time—4:12.2.**

AAU Indoor Track and Field Championships

New York, N.Y., Feb. 22, 1974

60 Yds.—Herb Washington, Ann Arbor, Mich. **Time—0:06.6.**
60 Yd. High Hurdles—Tom Hill, U.S. Army. **Time—0:06.9.**
600 Yds.—Wesley Williams, San Diego TC. **Time—1:11.3.**
1,000 Yds.—Rick Wohlhuter, U. of Chicago TC. **Time— 2:06.8.**
One Mile—John Walker, New Zealand. **Time—4:01.6.**
3 Miles—Dick Taylor, New Zealand. **Time—13:08.6.**
2 Mile Walk—Larry Walker, Beverly Hills Striders. **Time— 13:24.**
Sprint Medley Relay—Adelphi. **Time—2:07.4.**
35 Lb. Weight Throw—Jacques Paul Accambray, Kent St. 70 ft. 6 in.
Triple Jump—Milan Tiff, Beverly Hills Striders. 54 ft.
Long Jump—Jerry Proctor, Beverly Hills Striders. 25 ft. 10 in.
Shot Put—Terry Albritton. 69 ft. ¾ in.
Pole Vault—Vic Diaz, Beverly Hills Striders. 17 ft. 8 in.
High Jump—Tom Woods, Oregon St. 7 ft. 2 in.

Women's Events

60 Yds.—Theresa Montgomery, Tennessee St. **Time— 0:06.7.**
60 Yd. High Hurdles—Patty Johnson, La Jolla TC. **Time— 0:07.7.**
220 Yds.—(tie) Theresa Montgomery & Linda Cordy, Atoms TC. **Time—0:25.**
440 Yds.—Brenda Nichols, Atoms TC. **Time—0:56.1.**
880 Yds.—Mary Decker, Blue Angels. **Time—2:07.1.**
One Mile—Robin Campbell, Sports International. **Time— 4:50.7.**
One Mile Walk—Susan Brodock, Rialton Round Runners. **Time—7:28.6.**
One Mile Relay—Atoms TC. **Time—4:00.5.**
Shot Put—Maren Seidler, Mayor Daley's Youth Fdn. 54 ft. 4 in.
Long Jump—Martha Watson, Lakewood International. 20 ft. 9½ in.
High Jump—Joni Huntley, Oregon TC. 6 ft.

10th Annual NCAA Indoor Track and Field Championships

Detroit, Mich., March 9, 1974. Sponsored by the Detroit News

60 Yds.—Cliff Outlin, Auburn. **Time—0:06.**
60 Yd. High Hurdles—Danny Smith, Florida State. **Time— 0:07.2.**
440 Yds.—Larance Jones, Northeast Missouri. **Time—0:48.6.**
600 Yds.—Stan Vinson, Eastern Michigan. **Time—1:10.1.**
880 Yds.—Reggie Clark, William & Mary. **Time—1:52.2.**
One Mile—Tony Waldrop, North Carolina. **Time—3:59.5.**
2 Miles—John Hartnett, Villanova. **Time—8:33.6.**

3 Miles—John Ngeno, Washington St. **Time—11:20.8.**
Distance Medley Relay—Missouri. **Time—9:45.**
Pole Vault—Larry Jessee, Texas, El Paso. 16 ft. 6 in.
35 Lb. Weight Throw—Jacques Accambray, Kent State. 71 ft. 10¾ in.
Shot Put—Hans Hoglund, Texas, El Paso. 67 ft. 7¼ in.
Long Jump—Kingsley Adams, Colorado. 25 ft. 3¾ in.
Triple Jump—Tom Haynes, Middle Tennessee St. 54 ft. 6¾ in.

National AAU Outdoor Track and Field Championships
Los Angeles, Calif., June 21-22, 1974

100 Meters — Steve Williams, unattached. **Time — 0:09.9.**
200 Meters — Don Quarrie, Beverly Hills Striders.
Time—0:20.5.
400 Meters — Maurice Peoples, DC Striders. **Time — 0:45.2.**
800 Meters — Rich Wohlhuter, Univ. of Chicago TC.
Time — 1:43.9.
1,500 Meters — Rod Dixon, New Zealand. **Time — 3:37.5.**
5,000 Meters — Dick Buerkle, NYAC. **Time — 13.33.4.**
10,000 Meters — Frank Shorter, Florida TC. **Time — 28:16.0.**
110 Meter High Hurdles — Charles Foster, N.C. Central. **Time
— 0:13.4.**
400 Meter Intermediate Hurdles — Jim Bolding, unattached.
Time — 0:48.9.

3,000 Meter Steeplechase — Jim Johnson, Club Northwest.
Time — 8:28.8.
Triple Jump — John Craft, Univ. of Chicago TC. 54 ft. 4³/₄ in.
Pole Vault — Dave Roberts, Gulf Coast TC. 17 ft. 6 in.
High Jump — Dwight Stones, Pacific Coast TC. 7 ft. 3³/₄ in.
Long Jump — Bouncy Moore, unattached. 26 ft. 5²/₄ in.
Shot Put — Al Feuerbach, Pacific Coast Club. 70 ft. 9³/₄ in.
Javelin — Sam Colson, unattached. 280 ft. 8 in.
Hammer — Steve DeAutremont, Beverly Hills Striders. 226 ft. 6
in.
Discus — John Powell, San Jose. 214 ft. 11 in.
5,000 Meter Walk — John Knifton, NYAC. **Time — 22:23.0.**

Women's AAU Outdoor National Track and Field Championships
Bakersfield, Calif., June 28-29, 1974

100 Yds. — Renaye Bowen, Lakewood Intl. **Time—0:10.4.**
100 Meter Hurdles — Patty Johnson, La Jolla TC. **Time—
0:13.2.**
220 Yds. — Alice Annum, Sports Intl. **Time—0:23.1.**
440 Yds. — Debra Sapenter, Prairie View. **Time—0:52.2.**
400 Meter Hurdles — Andrea Bruce, Prairie View. **Time—
0:59.7.**
880 Yds. — Mary Decker, unattached. **Time—2:05.2.**
One Mile Walk — Sue Brodock, Rialto Roadrunners. **Time—
7:29.7.**
One Mile — Julie Brown, Los Angeles TC. **Time—4:45.1.**

2 Miles — Lynn Bjorkland, Duke City Dashers. **Time—10:11.1.**
440 Yd. Relay — Texas Women's Univ. **Time—0:45.6.**
One Mile Relay — Sports International. **Time—3:39.6.**
Shot Put — Maren Seidler, Mayor Daley YF. 54 ft. 3 in.
Javelin — Kathy Schmidt, Los Angeles TC. 203 ft. 2 in.
High Jump — Joni Huntley, Oregon TC. 6 ft.
Long Jump — Martha Watson, Lakewood Intl. 21 ft. 3¹/₂ in.
Discus — Joan Pavelich, La Jolla TC. 173 ft. 11 in.
Team Scoring — Sports International, 56 pts.; Prairie View, 45
pts.; Los Angeles TC, 45 pts.

National Interscholastic Outdoor Track and Field Records

Source: National Federation of State High School Associations. Records approved to Oct., 1974

Event	Record	Holder	School	Site and year
100 yds.	0:09.3	William Gaines	Clearview Regional H.S., Mulica Hill, N.J.	Highland Park, N.J., 1967
		Gregory Edmond	Ball H.S., Austin, Tex.	Austin, Tex., 1974
220 yds.	0:20.2	Forrest Beaty	Herbert Hoover H.S., Glendale, Calif.	Chaffey, Calif., 1961
440 yds.	0:45.8	Ronald E. Ray	Ferguson H.S., Newport News, Va.	Charlottesville, Va., 1972
880 yds.	1:48.8	Richard J. Joyce	Sierra H.S., Whittier, Calif.	Bakersfield, Calif., 1965
1 mile	3:58.3	James Ryun	Wichita East H.S., Wichita, Kan.	Wichita, Kan., 1965
2 mile	8:41.5	Steve Prefontaine	Marshfield High School, Coos Bay, Ore.	Corvallis, Ore., 1969
120 yd. high hurdles	0:13.5	Richmond Flowers, Jr.	Sidney Lanier H.S., Montgomery, Ala.	Mobile, Ala., 1965
		William Tipton	Central H.S., Pontiac, Mich.	Saginaw, Mich., 1967
		Randall L. Lightfoot	Plainview H.S., Plainview, Texas	Austin, Tex., 1971
		Steve Caminiti	Crespi Carmelite H.S., Encino, Calif.	Encino, Calif., 1964
180 yd. low hurdles	0:18.1	Donald Castronovo	Oceanside H.S., Oceanside, N.Y.	Ithaca, N.Y., 1964
		Earl McCullouch	Polytechnic H.S., Long Beach, Calif.	Norwalk, Calif., 1964
High jump	7 ft. 7³/₄ in.	Mark Wilson	Monte Vista H.S., Danville, Calif.	Fresno, Calif., 1974
Long jump	25 ft. 9¹/₂ in.	Gerald Hardeman	Edison H.S., Fresno, Calif.	Porterville, Calif., 1972
Pole vault	16 ft. 7 in.	Casey Carringan	Orting High School, Orting, Wash.	Bellingham, Wash., 1969
		Robert Pullard	Los Angeles H.S., Los Angeles, Calif.	Los Angeles, Calif., 1969
Triple jump	52 ft. 6¹/₄ in.	David Tucker	San Joaquin Mem. H.S., Fresno, Calif.	Bakersfield, Calif., 1970
Shot put (12 lbs.)	72 ft. 3¹/₄ in.	Sam Walker	W. W. Samuell H.S., Dallas, Tex.	Corpus Christi, Tex., 1968
Discus	201 ft. 3 in.	Christopher James Adams	Los Altos H.S., Los Altos, Calif.	Berkeley, Calif., 1970
Javelin	254 ft. 11 in.	Russell Francis	Pleasant Hill H.S., Pleasant Hill, Ore.	Pleasant Hill, Ore., 1971
440 yd. relay	0:40.2	Delley, G. Pouncy, J. Pouncy, Shaw	Lincoln High School, Dallas, Tex.	Austin, Texas, 1970
880 yd. relay	1:25.4	Jackson, James, Reed, Hill	White Plains (N.Y.) H.S.	Jamaica, N.Y., 1966
1 mile relay	3:11.8	Bouche, Bradley, Brents, Morton	Memorial H.S., Houston, Texas	Baytown, Texas, 1967
		Anderson, Black, Tompkins, Thompson	Killian High School, Miami, Fla.	Gainesville, Fla., 1969
2 mile relay	7:41.9	Mentz, Jakosa, Bowman, Grant	Proviso West H.S., Hillside, Ill.	Glen Ellyn, Ill., 1965
Sprint Medley Relay (1 mile)	3:23.3	Corson, Brake, Brents, Morton	Memorial H.S., Houston, Texas	Houston, Texas, 1967

Evolution of the World Record for the One Mile Run

The table below shows how the world record for the one-mile has been lowered in the past 110 years.

Time	Individual	Year	Time	Individual	Year
4:56	Charles Lawes, Britain	1864	4:07.6	Jack Lovelock, New Zealand	1933
4:36.5	Richard Webster, Britain	1865	4:06.8	Glen Cunningham, U. S.	1934
4:29	William Chinnery, Britain	1868	4:06.4	Sydney Wooderson, Britain	1937
4:28.8	W. C. Gibbs, Britain	1868	4:06.2	Gunder Haegg, Sweden	1942
4:26	Walter Slade, Britain	1874	4:06.2	Arne Andersson, Sweden	1942
4:24.5	Walter Slade, Britain	1875	4:04.6	Gunder Haegg, Sweden	1942
4:23.2	Walter George, Britain	1880	4:02.6	Arne Andersson, Sweden	1943
4:21.4	Walter George, Britain	1882	4:01.6	Arne Andersson, Sweden	1944
4:19.4	Walter George, Britain	1882	4:01.4	Gunder Haegg, Sweden	1945
4:18.4	Walter George, Britain	1884	3:59.4	Roger Bannister, Britain.	1954
4:18.2	Fred Bacon, Scotland	1894	3:58	John Landy, Australia.	1954
4:17	Fred Bacon, Scotland	1895	3:57.2	Derek Ibbotson, Britain.	1957
4:15.6	Thomas Conneff, U.S.	1895	3:54.5	Herb Elliott, Australia.	1958
4:15.4	John Paul Jones, U.S.	1911	3:54.4	Peter Snell, New Zealand	1962
4:14.6	John Paul Jones, U. S.	1913	3:54.1	Peter Snell, New Zealand	1964
4:12.6	Norman Taber, U. S.	1915	3:53.6	Michel Jazy, France.	1965
4:10.4	Paavo Nurmi, Finland	1923	3:51.3	Jim Ryun, U. S.	1966
4:09.2	Jules Ladoumegue, France	1931	3:51.1	Jim Ryun, U. S.	1967

78th Annual Boston Marathon

Neil Cusack of Ireland covered the traditional distance of 26 miles 385 yards in 2 hours 13 minutes 39 seconds to win the 1974 Boston Marathon. The leading finishers and their times follow:

1—Neil Cusack, E. Tennessee State 2:13:39
2—Thomas Fleming, New York A.C. 2:14.25
3—Jerome Drayton, Toronto.................. 2:15.40
4—Lucian Rosa, Selon, Wis.................. 2:15.53
5—Vilho Paajanen, Finland.................. 2:16.15
6—Steven Hohe, Twin Cities T.C............. 2:17:44
7—Robert Moore, Toronto................... 2:16:45
8—Ronald Wayne, Oregon T.C. 2:16:58
9—Bernard Allen, Maryland................. 2:17:02
10—Carl Hatfield, W. Virginia T.C. 2:17:36
11—John Vitale, New Haven T.C. 2:18:54

12—Daniel W. Moynihan, Tuft 2:19:13
13—Reid Harter, Santa Monica T.C. 2:19:15
14—William Rodgers, Gr. Boston T.C. 2:19:34
15—Heinz Kubelt, West Germany............2:19:50

Women's Division

1—Mrs. Michiko Gorman, L.A.............. 2:47:11
2—Christa Koff'schlager, W. Germany 2:53:00
3—Mrs. Nina Kuscsik, Suffolk A.C. 2:55:24
4—Manuela Preuss, West Germany 2:58:46
5—Kathy Switzer, New York................3:01:38

National Skeet Shooting Association World Championships, 1974

San Antonio, Texas, July 26-Aug. 2, 1974

All-Around Championship—550 Targets

Champion — Noel Winters, Baltimore, Md., 548.
Woman — Karla Roberts, Bridgeton, Mo., 542.
Junior Woman — Marina Pakis, Hot Springs, Ark., 523.
Junior Boy — Mike Schmidt, Prior Lake, Minn., 544.
Veteran — George Vicknair, Baton Rouge, La., 533.
Sub-senior — Sam Caradonna, Warren, Mich., 542.
Senior — Paul Dublin, Jacksonville, Tex., 534.
Collegiate — Tito Killian, San Antonio, Tex., 547.

12-Gauge—250 Targets

Champion — Tito Killian, San Antonio, Texas, 250.
Woman — Karla Roberts, Bridgeton, Mo., 249.
Junior Woman — Marina Pakis, Hot Springs, Ark., 242.
Junior Boy — Mike Schmid , Prior Lake, Minn., 249.
Veteran — Henry Alcus, New Orleans, La., 248.
Sub-senior — John Kujawa, South Bend, Ind., 250.
Senior — Loyd Huval, Baton Rouge, La., 249.
Collegiate — Tito Killian, 250.

20-Gauge—100 Targets

Champion — Terry Nichols, Shelton, Conn., 100.
Woman — Cathy Kaufman, San Antonio, Texas, 99.
Junior Woman — Marina Pakis, Hot Springs, Ark., 98.
Junior Boy — Bobby Utting, Rush, N.Y., 100.

Veteran — Milton Terrill, San Francisco, Calif., 97.
Sub-senior — Ains Borsum, Baldwin, Mich., 100.
Senior — Paul Dublin, Jacksonville, Texas, 99.
Collegiate — Terry Nichols, 100.

28-Gauge—100 Targets

Champion — Dennis Thomas, Scottsdale, Ariz., 100.
Woman — Karla Roberts, Bridgeton, Mo., 98.
Junior Woman — Marina Pakis, Hot Springs, Ark., 94.
Junior Boy — Mike Schmidt, Prior Lake, Minn., 100.
Veteran — Henry Alcus, New Orleans, La., 99.
Sub-senior — John Kujawa, South Bend, Ind., 100.
Senior — George Martin, Detroit, Mich., 98.
Collegiate — Kevin Gordon, Missoula, Mont., 100.

.410 Gauge—100 Targets

Champion — Kenny Barnes, Bakersfield, Calif., 100.
Woman — Jackie Ramsey, San Antonio, Texas, 99.
Junior Woman — Marina Pakis, Hot Springs, Ark. 89.
Junior Boy — Breck Chaisson, Houma, La., 99.
Veteran — George Vicknair, Baton Rouge, La., 94.
Sub-senior — Murray Jackson, Conway, S.C., 98.
Senior — R. H. Snyder, Middlefield, Ohio, 96.
Collegiate — Jackie Ramsey, 99.

National Skeet Shooting Association International Championships

Virginia Beach, Va., July 5-7, 1974

Championship—200 Targets

Champion — Mike Ward, U. S. Army, Ft. Benning, Ga., 195.
Runner-up — Pat Whitaker, U. S. Army, Ft. Benning, Ga., 194.
Woman — Claudia Butler, Virginia Beach, Va., 176.

Junior — Thomas Fellers, Morganville, N.J., 161.
Senior — John St. Lawrence, Louisville, Ky., 173.

National AAA Judo Championships in 1974

Men

139 Lb. Class — Katsuji Nerio, California.
154 Lb. Class — Pat Burris, Anaheim, Calif.
176 Lb. Class — Irwin Cohen, Chicago, Ill.
205 Lb. Class — Steve Cohen, Chicago, Ill.
Heavyweight — Jack Anderson, Minnesota.
Open Class — Jimmy Wooley.
Overall Championship — Irwin Cohen.

Women

105 Lb. Class — Kay Hummer, New Jersey
120 Lb. Class — Diane Pierce, Minnesota.
135 Lb. Class — Margaret Thornton, Indianapolis, Ind.
150 Lb. Class — Bonnie Korte.
165 Lb. Class — Chris Penich, Hollywood, Calif.
Open Class — Marie Brazil, New York, N.Y.
Overall Championship — Marie Brazil.

Boxing Champions by Classes

As of Sept. 15, 1974

Heavyweight.	George Foreman, Hayward, Calif.	Lightweight (135 lbs.).	Roberto Duran, Panama
Light-Heavyweight (175 lbs.)	Vacant	Junior Lightweight (130 lbs.)	Ben Villaflor, Philippines
Middleweight (160 lbs.). . . .	Carlos Monzon, Argentina	Featherweight (126 lbs.). . .	Ruben Olivares, Mexico
Welterweight (147 lbs.). . . .	Jose Napoles, Mexico City	Bantamweight (118 lbs.). . .	Soo Hawn Hong, South Korea
Jr. Welterweight (140 lbs.) . .	Antonio Cervantes, Colombia	Flyweight (112 lbs.).	Chartchai Chionoi, Thailand

Ring Champions by Years

*Abandoned title

Heavyweights

1882-1892	John L. Sullivan (A)
1892-1897	James J. Corbett (B)
1897-1899	Robert Fitzsimmons
1899-1905	James J. Jeffries (C)
1905-1906	Marvin Hart
1906-1908	Tommy Burns
1908-1915	Jack Johnson
1915-1919	Jess Willard
1919-1926	Jack Dempsey
1926-1928	Gene Tunney*
1928-1930	Vacant
1930-1932	Max Schmeling
1932	Jack Sharkey
1933	Primo Carnera
1934	Max Baer
1935-1936	James J. Braddock
1937-1949	Joe Louis*
1949-1951	Ezzard Charles
1951-1952	Joe Walcott
1952-1956	Rocky Marciano*
1956-1959	Floyd Patterson
1959	Ingemar Johansson
1960-1962	Floyd Patterson
1962-1963	Sonny Liston
1964-1967	Cassius Clay* (Muhammad Ali) (D)
1970-1973	Joe Frazier
1973	George Foreman

(A) London Prize Ring (bare knuckle champion).

(B) First Marquis of Queensberry Champion.

(C) Jeffries abandoned the title (1905) and designated Marvin Hart and Jack Root as logical contenders and agreed to referee a fight between them, the winner to be declared champion. Hart defeated Root in 12 rounds (1905) and in turn was defeated by Tommy Burns (1906) who immediately laid claim to the title. Jack Johnson defeated Burns (1908) and was recognized as champion. He clinched the title by defeating Jeffries in an attempted comeback (1910).

(D) Title declared vacant by the World Boxing Assn. and other groups in 1967 after Clay's refusal to fulfill his military obligation.

Light Heavyweights

1903	Jack Root, George Gardner
1903-1905	Bob Fitzsimmons
1905-1912	Philadelphia Jack O'Brien*
1912-1916	Jack Dillon
1916-1920	Battling Levinsky
1920-1922	Georges Carpentier
1922-1923	Battling Siki
1923-1925	Mike McTigue
1925	Paul Berlenbach (outpointed McTigue)
1926-1927	Jack Delaney* (outpointed Berlenbach)
1927-1929	Tommy Loughran* (outpointed McTigue)
1930-1934	Maxey Rosenbloom (outpointed Jimmy Slattery recognized as champion in N.Y.
1934-1935	Bob Olin (N.Y.)
1935-1939	John Henry Lewis*
1939	Melio Bettina
1939-1941	Billy Conn*
1941	Anton Christoforidis (won NBA title)
1941-1948	Gus Lesnevich, Freddie Mills
1948-1950	Freddie Mills
1950-1952	Joey Maxim
1952-1960	Archie Moore
1961	Harold Johnson (NBA); Archie Moore (N.Y.)
1962-1963	Harold Johnson
1963-1965	Willie Pastrano
1965-1966	Jose Torres
1966-1968	Dick Tiger
1968-1974	Bob Foster*

Middleweights

1884-1891	Jack "Nonpareil" Dempsey
1891-1897	Bob Fitzsimmons*
1897-1907	Tommy Ryan*
1907-1908	Stanley Ketchel, Billy Papke
1908-1910	Stanley Ketchel
1911-1913	Vacant
1913	Frank Klaus, George Chip
1914-1917	Al McCoy
1917-1920	Mike O'Dowd
1920-1923	Johnny Wilson
1923-1926	Harry Greb
1926-1931	Tiger Flowers, Mickey Walker
1931-1932	Gorilla Jones (NBA), Ben Jeby (New York)
1932-1937	Marcel Thil
1938	Al Hostak (NBA), Solly Krieger (NBA) Fred Apostoli (New York).
1939-1940	Al Hostak (NBA).
1939	Fred Apostoli, N.Y.; Ceferino Garcia, N.Y.
1940	Tony Zale (NBA), Ken Overlin (New York)
1941	Tony Zale (NBA), Billy Soose (New York)*
1942-1947	Tony Zale
1947-1948	Rocky Graziano
1948	Tony Zale, Marcel Cerdan
1949	Marcel Cerdan, Jake LaMotta
1950	Jake LaMotta
1951	Ray Robinson; Randy Turpin; Ray Robinson
1952	Ray Robinson*
1953-1955	Carl (Bobo) Olson
1955-1957	Ray Robinson
1957	Gene Fullmer, Ray Robinson, Carmen Basilio
1958	Carmen Basilio, Ray Robinson
1959	Gene Fullmer (NBA); Ray Robinson, N.Y.
1960	Gene Fullmer (NBA); Paul Pender (New York and Mass.)
1961	Gene Fullmer (NBA); Terry Downes (New York, Mass., Europe)
1962	Gene Fullmer, Dick Tiger (NBA); Paul Pender (New York and Mass.)*
1963	Dick Tiger (universal).
1963-1965	Joey Giardello
1965-1966	Dick Tiger
1966-1967	Emile Griffith
1967	Nino Benvenuti
1967-1968	Emile Griffith
1968-1970	Nino Benvenuti
1970	Carlos Monzon

Welterweights

1892-1894	Mysterious Billy Smith
1894-1896	Tommy Ryan
1896	Kid McCoy (outgrew class)
1900	Mysterious Billy Smith, Rube Ferns Matty Matthews
1901	Matty Matthews, Rube Ferns
1901-1904	Joe Walcott
1904-1906	Dixie Kid, Joe Walcott, Honey Mellody
1907-1911	Mike Sullivan
1911-1915	Vacant
1915-1919	Ted Lewis, Jack Britton
1919-1922	Jack Britton
1922-1926	Mickey Walker
1926	Pete Latzo
1927-1929	Joe Dundee
1929	Jackie Fields
1930	Jackie Fields, Jack Thompson, Tommy Freeman
1931	Freeman, Thompson, Lou Brouillard
1932	Jackie Fields
1933	Young Corbett, Jimmy McLarnin
1934	Barney Ross, Jimmy McLarnin
1935-1938	Barney Ross

1938-1940	Henry Armstrong
1940	Fritzi Zivic
1941-1946	Fred Cochrane
1946-1946	Marty Servo*; Ray Robinson (A)
1946-1950	Ray Robinson*
1951	Johnny Bratton (NBA): Kid Gavilan
1951-1954	Kid Gavilan
1954-1955	Johnny Saxton
1955	Tony De Marco: Carmen Basilio
1956	Carmen Basilio, Johnny Saxton, Carmen Basilio
1957	Carmen Basilio*
1958-1960	Virgil Akins: Don Jordan
1960	Benny Paret
1961	Emile Griffith, Benny Paret
1962	Benny Paret, Emile Griffith
1963	Luis Rodriguez, Emile Griffith
1964-1966	Emile Griffith*
1966-1969	Curtis Cokes
1969-1970	Jose Napoles, Billy Backus
1971	Jose Napoles

(A) Robinson gained the title by defeating Tommy Bell in an elimination agreed to by the NY Commission and the N.B.A. Both claimed Robinson waived his title when he won the middleweight crown from LaMotta in 1951. Gavilan defeated Bratton in an elimination to find a successor.

Lightweights

1896-1899	Kid Lavigne
1899-1902	Frank Erne
1902-1908	Joe Gans
1908-1910	Battling Nelson
1910-1912	Ad Wolgast
1912-1914	Willie Ritchie
1914-1917	Freddie Welsh
1917-1925	Benny Leonard*
1925	Jimmy Goodrich, Rocky Kansas
1926-1930	Sammy Mandell
1930	Al Singer, Tony Canzoneri
1930-1933	Tony Canzoneri
1933-1935	Barney Ross*
1935-1936	Tony Canzoneri
1936-1938	Lou Ambers
1938	Henry Armstrong
1939	Lou Ambers
1940	Lew Jenkins
1941-1943	Sammy Angott
1943	Beau Jack (New York), Bob Montgomery, Beau Jack (New York)
1944-1947	Bob Montgomery (New York) S. Angott (NBA), J. Zurita (NBA)
1945-1951	Ike Williams (NBA: later universal)
1951-1952	James Carter
1952	Lauro Salas, James Carter
1953-1954	James Carter
1954	Paddy De Marco; James Carter
1955	James Carter; Bud Smith
1956	Bud Smith, Joe Brown
1956-1962	Joe Brown
1962-1965	Carlos Ortiz
1965	Ismael Laguna
1965-1968	Carlos Ortiz
1968-1969	Teo Cruz
1969-1970	Mando Ramos
1970	Ismael Laguna
1970-1972	Ken Buchanan
1972	Roberto Duran

Featherweights

1892-1900	George Dixon (disputed)
1900-1901	Terry McGovern, Young Corbett*
1901-1912	Abe Attell
1912-1923	Johnny Kilbane
1923	Eugene Criqui, Johnny Dundee
1923-1925	Johnny Dundee*
1925-1927	Kid Kaplan*
1927-1928	Benny Bass, Tony Canzoneri
1928-1929	Andre Routis
1929-1932	Battling Battalino*
1932-1934	Tommy Paul (NBA)
1933-1936	Freddie Miller
1936-1937	Petey Sarron
1937-1938	Henry Armstrong*
1938-1940	Joey Archibald (B)
1940-1941	Harry Jeffra
1941	Joey Archibald, Chalky Wright
1941-1942	Chalky Wright
1942-1948	Willie Pep
1948-1949	Sandy Saddler
1949-1950	Willie Pep
1950-1957	Sandy Saddler*
1957-1959	Hogan (Kid) Bassey

1959-1963	Davey Moore
1963-1964	Sugar Ramos
1964-1969	Vicente Saldivar*
1969	John Famechon
1970	Vincente Saldivar
1970-1972	Kuniaki Shibata
1972	Clemente Sanchez*
1974	Ruben Olivares

(B) After Petey Scalzo knocked out Archibald (Dec. 5, 1938) in an overweight match and was refused a title bout, the NBA named Scalzo champion. The NBA title succession was: Petey Scalzo, 1938-1941: Richard Lemos, 1941: Jackie Wilson, 1941-1943: Jackie Callura, 1943: Phil Terranova, 1943-1944: Sal Bartolo, 1944-1946.

Bantamweights

1890-1892	George Dixon*
1892-1894	Vacant
1894-1899	Jimmy Barry*
1899-1900	Terry McGovern*
1901-1902	Harry Harris*
1902-1903	Harry Forbes
1903-1904	Frankie Neil
1904	Joe Bowker*,
1905-1907	Jimmy Walsh*
1907-1910	Vacant
1910-1914	Johnny Coulon
1914-1917	Kid Williams
1917-1920	Pete Herman
1920-1921	Joe Lynch
1921	Pete Herman, Johnny Buff
1922	Johnny Buff, Joe Lynch
1922-1924	Joe Lynch
1924	Abe Goldstein, Eddie Martin
1925	Eddie Martin, Charley (Phil) Rosenberg
1925-1926	Charley (Phil) Rosenberg
1927-1928	Bud Taylor* (NBA only)
1929-1935	Al Brown
1935-1936	Baltazar Sangchili
1936	Tony Marino, Sixto Escobar
1937	Sixto Escobar, Harry Jeffra
1938-1940	Sixto Escobar*
1941-1942	Lou Salica
1942-1947	Manuel Ortiz
1947	Harold Dade, Manuel Ortiz
1948-1950	Manuel Ortiz
1950-1952	Vic Toweel
1952-1954	Jimmy Carruthers*
1954-1956	Robert Cohen
1956-1957	Mario D'Agata
1957-1959	Alphonse Halimi
1959-1960	Jose Becerra*
1961-1965	Eder Jofre
1965-1968	Fighting Harada
1968-1969	Lionel Rose
1969-1970	Ruben Olivares
1970-1971	Chuchu Castillo
1971-1972	Ruben Olivares
1972	Rafael Herrera
1972-1973	Enrique Pinder
1973	Romero Anaya, Arnold Taylor
1974	Soo Hawn Hong

Flyweights

1916-1923	Jimmy Wilde
1923-1925	Pancho Villa
1925-1927	Fidel La Barba*
1927-1929	Vacant
1929	Emile Pladner
1930	Midget Wolgast (N.Y.); Frankie Genaro (NBA)
1931-1932	Young Perez
1932-1935	Jackie Brown
1935-1938	Benny Lynch*
1939-1941	Peter Kane*
1941-1943	Vacant
1943-1947	Jackie Patterson
1947-1950	Rinty Monaghan*
1950	Terry Allen
1950-1952	Dado Marino
1952-1954	Yoshio Shiraj
1954-1960	Pascual Perez
1960-1962	Pone Kingpetch
1962-1963	Fighting Harada
1963	Pone Kingpetch, Hiroyuki Ebihara
1964-1965	Pone Kingpetch
1965-1966	Salvatore Berruni
1966	Walter McGowen
1966-1969	Chartchai Chionoi
1969	Efren Torres
1970-1973	Erbito Salvarria
1973	Venice Borkorsor*
1974	Chartchai Chionoi

History of Heavyweight Championship Bouts
*Title Changed Hands

1889—July 8—John L. Sullivan beat Jake Kilrain, 75 rounds, Richburg, Miss. (Last championship bare knuckles bout.)

***1892**—Sept. 7—James J. Corbett defeated John L. Sullivan, 21 rounds, New Orleans. (Used big gloves for first time.)

1894—Jan. 25—James J. Corbett ko'd Charley Mitchell, 3 rounds, Jacksonville, Fla.

***1897**—March 17—Bob Fitzsimmons defeated James J. Corbett, 14 rounds, Carson City, Nev.

***1899**—June 9—James J. Jeffries beat Bob Fitzsimmons, 11 rounds, Coney Island, N.Y.

1899—Nov. 3—James J. Jeffries beat Tom Sharkey, 25 rounds, Coney Island, N.Y.

1900—May 11—James J. Jeffries knocked out James J. Corbett, 23 rounds, Coney Island, N.Y.

1901—No. 15—James J. Jeffries, ko'd Gus Ruhlin, 5 rounds, San Francisco.

1902—July 25—James J. Jeffries knocked out Bob Fitzsimmons, 8 rounds, San Francisco.

1903—Aug. 14—James J. Jeffries knocked out James J. Corbett, 10 rounds, San Francisco.

1904—Aug. 26—James J. Jeffries knocked out Jack Monroe, 2 rounds, San Francisco.

***1905**—James J. Jeffries retired, July 3—Marvin Hart knocked out Jack Root, 12 rounds, Reno. Jeffries refereed and presented the title to the victor. Jack O'Brien also claimed the title.

***1906**—Feb. 23—Tommy Burns defeated Marvin Hart, 20 rounds, Los Angeles.

1906—Nov. 28—Philadelphia Jack O'Brien and Tommy Burns, 20 rounds, draw, Los Angeles.

1907—May 8—Tommy Burns defeated Jack O'Brien, 20 rounds, Los Angeles.

1907—July 4—Tommy Burns knocked out Bill Squires, 1 round, Colma, Cal.

1907—Dec. 2—Tommy Burns knocked out Gunner Moir, 10 rounds, London.

1908—Feb. 10—Tommy Burns knocked out Jack Palmer, 4 rounds, London.

1908—March 17—Tommy Burns knocked out Jem Roche, 1 round, Dublin.

1908—April 18—Tommy Burns knocked out Jewey Smith, 5 rounds, Paris.

1908—June 13—Tommy Burns knocked out Bill Squires, 8 rounds, Paris.

1908—Aug. 24—Tommy Burns knocked out Bill Squires, 13 rounds, Sydney, New South Wales.

1908—Sept. 2—Tommy Burns knocked out Bill Lang, 2 rounds, Melbourne, Australia.

***1908**—Dec. 26—Jack Johnson stopped Tommy Burns, 14 rounds, Sydney, Australia. Police halted contest.

1909—May 19—Jack Johnson and Jack O'Brien, 6 rounds, draw, Philadelphia.

1909—June 30—Jack Johnson and Tony Ross, 6 rounds, draw, Pittsburgh, Pa.

1909—Sept. 9—Jack Johnson and Al Kaufman, 10 rounds, no decision, San Francisco.

1909—Oct. 16—Jack Johnson knocked out Stanley Ketchell, 12 rounds, Colma, Cal.

1910—July 4—Jack Johnson knocked out Jim Jeffries, 15 rounds, Reno, Nev. (Jeffries came back from retirement.)

1912—July 4—Jack Johnson won on points from Jim Flynn, 9 rounds, Las Vegas, N.M. (contest stopped by police).

1913—Nov. 28—Jack Johnson knocked out Andre Spaul, 2 rounds, Paris.

1913—Dec. 9—Jack Johnson and Jim Johnson, 10 rounds, draw, Paris. (Bout called a draw when Jack Johnson declared he had broken his arm.)

1914—June 27—Jack Johnson won from Frank Moran, 20 rounds, Paris.

***1915**—April 5—Jess Willard knocked out Jack Johnson, 26 rounds, Havana, Cuba.

1916—March 25—Jess Willard and Frank Moran, 10 rounds (no decision), New York City.

***1919**—July 4—Jack Dempsey knocked out Jess Willard, Toledo, O. (Willard failed to answer bell for fourth round.)

1920—Sept. 6—Jack Dempsey knocked out Billy Miske, 3 rounds, Benton Harbor, Mich.

1920—Dec. 14—Jack Dempsey knocked out Bill Brennan, 12 rounds. New York City.

1921—July 2—Jack Dempsey knocked out George Carpentier, 4 rounds, Boyle's Thirty Acres, Jersey City, N.J. (Carpentier had held the so called white heavyweight title since July 16, 1914, in a series established in 1913, after Jack Johnson's exile in Europe late in 1912.)

1923—July 4—Jack Dempsey won on points from Tom Gibbons, 15 rounds, Shelby, Mont.

1923—Sept. 14—Jack Dempsey knocked out Luis Firpo, 2 rounds, New York City.

***1926**—Sept. 23—Gene Tunney beat Jack Dempsey, 10 rounds, decision, Philadelphia.

1927—Sept. 22—Gene Tunney beat Jack Dempsey, 10 rounds, decision, Chicago.

1928—July 26—Gene Tunney knocked out Tom Heeney, 11 rounds, Yankee Stadium, New York; soon afterward he announced his retirement.

***1930**—June 12—Max Schmeling of Germany defeated Jack Sharkey in fourth round when Sharkey fouled Schmeling in a bout which was generally considered to have resulted in the election of a successor to Gene Tunney, New York.

1931—July 3—Max Schmeling knocked out Young Stribling, 15 rounds, Cleveland.

***1932**—June 21—Jack Sharkey defeated Max Schmeling, 15 rounds, decision, New York City.

***1933**—June 29—Primo Carnera knocked out Jack Sharkey, six rounds, New York City.

1933—Oct. 22—Carnera defeated Paulino Uzcudun, 15 rounds, Rome.

1934—March 1—Primo Carnera defeated Tommy Loughran in 15 rounds, Miami.

***1934**—June 14—Max Baer knocked out Primo Carnera, eleven rounds, New York City.

***1935**—June 13—James J. Braddock defeated Max Baer, 15 rounds, New York City.

***1937**—June 22—Joe Louis knocked out James J. Braddock, 8 rounds, Chicago.

1937—Aug. 30—Joe Louis defeated Tommy Farr, 15 rounds, decision, New York City.

1938—Feb. 23—Joe Louis knocked out Nathan Mann, 3 rounds, New York City.

1938—April 1—Joe Louis knocked out Harry Thomas, 5 rounds, New York City.

1938—June 22—Joe Louis knocked out Max Schmeling, one round, New York City.

1939—January 25—Joe Louis knocked out John H. Lewis, 1 round, New York City.

1939—April 17—Joe Louis knocked out Jack Roper, 1 round, Los Angeles.

1939—June 28—Joe Louis knocked out Tony Galento, 4 rounds, New York City.

1939—September 20—Joe Louis knocked out Bob Pastor, 11 rounds, Detroit, Mich.

1940—February 9—Joe Louis defeated Arturo Godoy, 15 rounds, decision, New York City.

1940—March 29—Joe Louis knocked out Johnny Paychek, 2 rounds, New York City.

1940—June 20—Joe Louis knocked out Arturo Godoy, 8 rounds, New York City.

1940—Dec. 16—Joe Louis knocked out Al McCoy, 6 rounds, Boston.

1941—Jan. 31—Joe Louis knocked out Red Burman, 5 rounds, New York City.

1941—Feb. 17—Joe Louis knocked out Gus Dorzaio, 2 rounds, Philadelphia.

1941—March 21—Joe Louis knocked out Abe Simon, 13 rounds, Detroit, Mich.

1941—April 8—Joe Louis knocked out Tony Musto, 9 rounds, St. Louis, Mo.

1941—May 23—Joe Louis beat Buddy Baer, 7 rounds, Washington, D. C., on a disqualification.

1941—June 18—Joe Louis knocked out Billy Conn, 13 rounds, New York City.

1941—Sept. 29—Joe Louis knocked out Lou Nova, 6 rounds, New York City.

1941—Jan 9—Joe Louis knocked out Buddy Baer, 1 round, New York City.

1942—March 27—Joe Louis knocked out Abe Simon, 6 rounds, New York City.

1946—June 19—Joe Louis knocked out Billy Conn, 8 rounds, New York City.

1946—Sept. 18—Joe Louis knocked out Tami Mauriello, 1 round, New York City.

1947—Dec. 5—Joe Louis defeated Joe Walcott in a 15-round bout by a split decision, New York City.

1948—June 25—Joe Louis knocked out Joe Walcott, 11 rounds, New York City.

***1949**—June 22—Following Joe Louis' retirement Ezzard Charles defeated Joe Walcott by a unanimous decision, 15 rounds, Chicago, Ill (N.B.A. recognition only).

1949—Aug. 10—Ezzard Charles knocked out Gus Lesnevich, seven rounds, New York City.

1949—Oct 14—Ezzard Charles knocked out Pat Valentino, eight rounds, San Francisco (clinched American title).

1950—Aug. 15—Ezzard Charles knocked out Freddy Beshore, 14 rounds, Buffalo, N.Y.

1950—Sept. 27—Ezzard Charles defeated Joe Louis in latter's attempted comeback, 15 rounds. New York City (universal recognition).

1950—Dec. 5—Ezzard Charles knocked out Nick Barone, 11 rounds, Cincinnati, Ohio.

1951—Jan. 12—Ezzard Charles knocked out Lee Oma, 10 rounds, New York, N.Y.

1951—March 7—Ezzard Charles outpointed Joe Walcott, 15 rounds, Detroit, Mich.

1951—May 30—Ezzard Charles outpointed Joey Maxim, light. heavyweight champion, 15 rounds, Chicago.

*1951—July 18—Joe Walcott knocked out Ezzard Charles, 7th round, Pittsburgh, Pa.

1952—June 5—Joe Walcott outpointed Ezzard Charles, 15 rounds, Philadelphia, Pa.

*1952—Sept. 23—Rocky Marciano knocked out Joe Walcott, 13th round, Philadelphia, Pa.

1953—May 15—Rocky Marciano knocked out Joe Walcott, first round, Chicago, Ill.

1953—Sept. 24—Rocky Marciano knocked out Roland LaStarza, 11th round, Polo Grounds, New York, N.Y.

1954—June 17—Rocky Marciano outpointed Ezzard Charles, 15 rounds, Yankee Stadium, New York, N.Y.

1954—Sept. 17—Rocky Marciano knocked out Ezzard Charles, 8th round, Yankee Stadium, New York, N.Y.

1955—May 16—Rocky Marciano knocked out Don Cockell, 9th round, Kezar Stadium, San Francisco, Calif.

1955—Sept. 21—Rocky Marciano knocked out Archie Moore, 9th round, Yankee Stadium, N.Y. Marciano retired undefeated, Apr. 27, 1956.

*1956—Nov. 30—Floyd Patterson knocked out Archie Moore, 5th round, Chicago, Ill.

1957—July 29—Floyd Patterson knocked out Hurricane Jackson, 10th round, Polo Grounds, New York, N.Y.

1957—Aug. 22—Floyd Patterson knocked out Pete Rademacher, 6th round, Seattle, Wash.

1958—Aug. 18—Floyd Patterson ko'd Roy Harris, 12th round, Los Angeles, Calif.

1959—May 1—Floyd Patterson knocked out Brian London, 11 rounds, Indianapolis, Ind.

*1959—June 26—Ingemar Johansson, Sweden, ko'd Floyd Patterson, 3rd round, Yankee Stadium, New York City.

*1960—June 20—Floyd Patterson knocked out Ingemar Johansson, 5th round, Polo Grounds, New York, N.Y. (First heavyweight in boxing history to regain title.)

1961—Mar. 13—Floyd Patterson knocked out Ingemar Johansson, 6th round, Convention Hall, Miami Beach, Fla.

1961—Dec. 4—Floyd Patterson knocked out Tom McNeeley, 4th round, Toronto, Ont. Canada.

*1962—Sept. 25—Sonny Liston knocked out Floyd Patterson, first round, Comiskey Park, Chicago, Ill.

1963—July 22—Sonny Liston knocked out Floyd Patterson, first round, Las Vegas, Nevada.

*1964—Feb. 25—Cassius Clay knocked out Sonny Liston, 7th round, Miami Beach, Fla.

1965—May 25—Cassius Clay knocked out Sonny Liston, first round, Lewiston, Maine.

1965—Nov. 11—Cassius Clay knocked out Floyd Patterson, twelfth round, Las Vegas, Nev.

1966—Mar. 29—Cassius Clay outpointed George Chuvalo, 15 rounds, Toronto, Ont.

1966—May 21—Cassius Clay knocked out Henry Cooper, sixth round, London, Eng.

1966—Aug. 6—Cassius Clay knocked out Brian London, third round, London, Eng.

1966—Sept. 10—Cassius Clay knocked out Karl Mildenberger, twelfth round, Frankfurt, Germany.

1966—Nov. 14—Cassius Clay knocked out Cleveland Williams, third round, Houston, Tex.

1967—Feb. 6—Cassius Clay outpointed Ernie Terrell, 15 rounds, Houston, Tex.

1967—March 22—Cassius Clay knocked out Zora Folley, seventh round, New York. Clay was stripped of his title by the WBA and others for refusing military service.

*1970—Feb. 16—Joe Frazier knocked out Jimmy Ellis, fifth round, New York.

1970—Nov. 18—Joe Frazier knocked out Bob Foster, second round, Detroit.

1971—Mar. 8—Joe Frazier outpointed Cassius Clay (Muhammad Ali), 15 rounds, New York, N.Y.

1972—Jan. 15—Joe Frazier knocked out Terry Daniels, fourth round, New Orelans.

1972—May 25—Joe Frazier knocked out Ron Stander, fifth round, Omaha.

*1973—Jan. 22—George Foremen knocked out Joe Frazier, second round, Kingston, Jamaica.

1973—Sept. 1—George Foreman knocked out Joe Roman, first round, Tokyo.

1974—Mar. 3—George Foreman knocked out Ken Norton, second round, Caracas.

Major Professional Boxing Bouts

Oct., 1973 — Oct., 1974 *Championship Bout

Date	Winner	Loser	Result	Site
Oct. 21	Muhammad Ali	Rudi Lubbers	D-12	Jakarta
Oct. 24	Jimmy Ellis	Al Jones	KO-7	Atlanta
Nov. 13	Joe Burger	Mac Foster	D-10	London
Nov. 13	Chris Finnegan	Mike Quarry	D-10	London
*Dec. 1	Bob Foster	Pierre Fourie	D-15	Johannesburg
Dec. 14	Jerry Quarry	Earnie Shavers	KO-1	New York
		1974		
Jan. 28	Muhammad Ali	Joe Frazier	D-12	New York
Jan. 29	Fernando Cabanela	Chartchai Chionoi	D-10	Honolulu
*Feb. 9	Carlos Monzon	Jose Napoles	KO-7	Paris
Feb. 11	Tony Mundine	Manuel Fierro	KO-6	Brisbane, Aust.
Mar. 2	Pierre Fourie	Mike Quarry	D-10	Johannesburg
Mar. 5	Ruben Olivares	Art Hafey	D-12	Inglewood, Calif.
*Mar. 16	Roberto Duran	Esteban DeJesus	KO-11	Panama City
Mar. 16	Luis Faustino	Roberto Davila	D-12	Son Paulo, Brazil
Mar. 18	Roger Menetrey	Billy Backus	D-12	Paris
Mar. 19	Ron Lyle	Oscar Bonavena	D-12	Denver
*Mar. 26	George Foreman	Ken Norton	KO-2	Caracas
Apr. 8	Willie Moore	Stanley Haywood	KO-7	Philadelphia
*Apr. 27	Chartchai Chionoi	Fritz Chervet	D-15	Zurich
May 1	Ken Buchanan	Antonio Puddu	KO-6	Sardinia
May 27	Rodrigo Valdez	Benny Briscoe	KO-7	Monte Carlo
June 4	Oscar Alvardo	Koichi Wajima	KO-15	Tokyo
June 17	Joe Frazier	Jerry Quarry	KO-5	New York
*June 17	Bob Foster	Jorge Ahumada	Draw	Albuquerque
*July 3	Soon Hwan Hong	Arnold Taylor	D-15	Durban, S.A.
*July 9	Ruben Olivares	Zensuke Utagawa	KO-7	Inglewood, Calif.
July 16	Ron Lyle	Jimmy Ellis	D-12	Denver
July 30	Jorge Ahumada	Angel Oquendo	D-12	New York
*Aug. 3	Jose Napoles	Hedgemon Lewis	KO-9	Mexico City
*Aug. 25	Ben Villaflor	Yasutsune Uyehara	KO-2	Honolulu
Sept. 4	Chuck Wepner	Terry Hinke	KO-11	Salt Lake City
Sept. 7	Bobby Chacon	Alfredo Marcano	KO-9	Los Angeles
Oct. 1	Shoji Oguma	Betulio Gonzales	D-15	Tokyo
Oct. 1	John Conteh	Jorge Ahumada	D-15	Wembley, Eng.

Golf Records

United States Amateur

Year	Winner	Year	Winner	Year	Winner	Year	Winner
1900	Walter Travis	1919	Davidson Herron	1937	John Goodman	1958	Charles Coe
1901	Walter Travis	1920	Chick Evans, Jr.	1938	Willie Turnesa	1959	Jack Nicklaus
1902	Louis James	1921	Jesse Guilford	1939	Bud Ward	1960	Deane Beman
1903	Walter Travis	1922	Jess Sweetser	1940	Dick Chapman	1961	Jack Nicklaus
1904	Chandler Egan	1923	Max Marston	1941	Bud Ward	1962	Labron Harris, Jr.
1905	Chandler Egan	1924	Bob Jones	1942-45	(Not Played)	1963	Deane Beman
1906	Eben Byers	1925	Bob Jones	1946	Ted Bishop	1964	Bill Campbell
1907	Jerome Travers	1926	George Von Elm	1947	Skee Riegel	1965	Robert Murphy, Jr.
1908	Jerome Travers	1927	Bob Jones	1948	Willie Turnesa	1966	Gary Cowan
1909	Robert Gardner	1928	Bob Jones	1949	Charles Coe	1967	Bob Dickson
1910	William Fownes, Jr.	1929	Harrison Johnston	1950	Sam Urzetta	1968	Bruce Fleisher
1911	Harold Hilton	1930	Bob Jones	1951	Billy Maxwell	1969	Steve Melnyk
1912	Jerome Travers	1931	Francis Ouimet	1952	Jack Westland	1970	Lanny Wadkins
1913	Jerome Travers	1932	Ross Somerville	1953	Gene Littler	1971	Gary Cowan
1914	Francis Ouimet	1933	George Dunlap, Jr.	1954	Arnold Palmer	1972	Vinnie Giles
1915	Robert Gardner	1934	Lawson Little	1955	Harvie Ward	1973	Craig Stadler
1916	Chick Evans, Jr.	1935	Lawson Little	1956	Harvie Ward	1974	Jerry Pate
1917-18	(Not Played)	1936	John Fischer	1957	Hillman Robbins		

Women's United States Amateur

Year	Winner	Year	Winner	Year	Winner	Year	Winner
1900	Frances Griscom	1919	Alexa Stirling	1937	Mrs. J.A. Page	1958	Anne Quast
1901	Genevieve Hecker	1920	Alexa Stirling	1938	Patty Berg	1959	Barbara McIntire
1902	Genevieve Hecker	1921	Marion Hollins	1939	Betty Jameson	1960	JoAnne Gunderson
1903	Bessie Anthony	1922	Glenna Collett	1940	Betty Jameson	1961	Anne Q. Decker
1904	Georgiana Bishop	1923	Edith Cummings	1941	Mrs. Frank New	1962	JoAnne Gunderson
1905	Pauline Mackay	1924	Mrs. D. C. Hurd	1942-45	(Not Played)	1963	Anne Q. Welts
1906	Harriot Curtis	1925	Glenna Collett	1946	Babe Zaharias	1964	Barbara McIntire
1907	Margaret Curtis	1926	Mrs. G. Stetson	1947	Louise Suggs	1965	Jean Ashley
1908	Kate Harley	1927	Mrs. M. Horn	1948	Grace Lenczyk	1966	JoAnne Carner
1909	Dorothy Campbell	1928	Glenna Collett	1949	Dorothy Porter	1967	Lou Dill
1910	Dorothy Campbell	1929	Glenna Collett	1950	Beverly Hanson	1968	JoAnne Carner
1911	Margaret Curtis	1930	Glenna Collett	1951	Dorothy Kirby	1969	Catherine Lacoste
1912	Margaret Curtis	1931	Helen Hicks	1952	Jackie Pung	1970	Martha Wilkinson
1913	Gladys Raven Scroft	1932	Virginia Van Wie	1953	Mary Faulk	1971	Laura Baugh
1914	Mrs. H. A. Jackson	1933	Virginia Van Wie	1954	Barbara Romack	1972	Mary Budke
1915	Mrs. C. H. Vanderbeck	1934	Virginia Van Wie	1955	Pat Lesser	1973	Carol Semple
1916	Alexa Stirling	1935	Glenna C. Vare	1956	Marlene Stewart	1974	Cynthia Hill
1917-18	(Not Played)	1936	Pamela Barton	1957	JoAnne Gunderson		

United States Open

Year	Winner	Year	Winner	Year	Winner	Year	Winner
1895	Horace Rawlings	1914	Walter Hagen	1934	Olin Dutra	1956	Cary Middlecoff
1896	James Foulis	1915	Jerome Travers*	1935	Sam Parks, Jr.	1957	Dick Mayer
1897	Joe Lloyd	1916	Chick Evans*	1936	Tony Manero	1958	Tommy Bolt
1898	Fred Herd	1917 -1918	(Not played)	1937	Ralph Guldahl	1959	Billy Casper
1899	Willie Smith	1919	Walter Hagen	1938	Ralph Guldahl	1960	Arnold Palmer
1900	Harry Vardon	1920	Edward Ray	1939	Byron Nelson	1961	Gene Littler
1901	Willie Anderson	1921	Jim Barnes	1940	Lawson Little	1962	Jack Nicklaus
1902	L. Auchterlonie	1922	Gene Sarazen	1941	Craig Wood	1963	Julius Boros
1903	Willie Anderson	1923	Bob Jones*	1942 -45	(Not played)	1964	Ken Venturi
1904	Willie Anderson	1924	Cyril Walker	1946	Lloyd Mangrum	1965	Gary Player
1905	Willie Anderson	1925	Willie MacFarlane	1947	L. Worsham	1966	Billy Casper
1906	Alex Smith	1926	Bob Jones*	1948	Ben Hogan	1967	Jack Nicklaus
1907	Alex Ross	1927	Tommy Armour	1949	Cary Middlecoff	1968	Lee Trevino
1908	Fred McLeod	1928	John Farrell	1950	Ben Hogan	1969	Orville Moody
1909	George Sargent	1929	Bob Jones*	1951	Ben Hogan	1970	Tony Jacklin
1910	Alex Smith	1930	Bob Jones*	1952	Julius Boros	1971	Lee Trevino
1911	John McDermott	1931	Wm. Burke	1953	Ben Hogan	1972	Jack Nicklaus
1912	John McDermott	1932	Gene Sarazen	1954	Ed Furgol	1973	Johnny Miller
1913	Francis Ouimet*	1933	John Goodman*	1955	Jack Fleck	1974	Hale Irwin

*Amateur

U. S. Women's Open Golf Champions

Year	Winner	Year	Winner	Year	Winner	Year	Winner
1948	Mrs. M. D. Zaharias	1955	Fay Crocker	1962	Murie Lindstrom	1969	Donna Caponi
1949	Louise Suggs	1956	Mrs. K. Cornelius	1963	Mary Mills	1970	Donna Caponi
1950	Mrs. M. D. Zaharias	1957	Betsy Rawls	1964	Mickey Wright	1971	JoAnne Gunderson Carner
1951	Betsy Rawls	1958	Mickey Wright	1965	Carol Mann		
1952	Louise Suggs	1959	Mickey Wright	1966	Sandra Spuzich	1972	Susie Maxwell Berning
1953	Betsy Rawls	1960	Betsy Rawls	1967	Catherine Lacoste (a)	1973	Susie Maxwell Berning
1954	Mrs. M. D. Zaharias	1961	Mickey Wright	1968	Susie Maxwell Berning	1974	Sandra Haynie

(a) Amateur

Canadian Open Golf Champions

Year	Winner	Year	Winner	Year	Winner	Year	Winner
1942	Craig Wood	1951	Jim Ferrier	1959	Doug Ford	1967	Billy Casper
1943-44	(Not played)	1952	John Palmer	1960	Art Wall, Jr.	1968	Bob Charles
1945	Byron Nelson	1953	Dave Douglas	1961	Jacky Cupit	1969	Tommy Aaron
1946	George Fazio	1954	Pat Fletcher	1962	Ted Kroll	1970	Kermit Zarley
1947	Bobby Locke	1955	Arnold Palmer	1963	Doug Ford	1971	Lee Trevino
1948	C.W. Congdon	1956	Doug Sanders	1964	Kel Nagle	1972	Gay Brewer
1949	E.J. Harrison	1957	George Bayer	1965	Gene Littler	1973	Tom Weiskopf
1950	Jim Ferrier	1958	Wes Ellis, Jr.	1966	Don Massengale	1974	Bobby Nichols

Professional Golf Tournaments in 1974
Men

Date	Event	Winner	Score	Prize
Jan. 7	Bing Crosby Tournament, Pebble Beach, Calif.	Johnny Miller	208	$27,500
Jan. 13	Phoenix Open	Johnny Miller	271	30,000
Jan. 20	Dean Martin-San Diego Open	Johnny Miller	272	30,000
Jan. 28	Andy Williams-San Diego Open	Bobby Nichols	275	34,000
Feb. 3	Hawaiian Open, Honolulu	Jack Nicklaus	271	44,000
Feb. 10	Bob Hope Desert Classic, Palm Springs, Calif.	Hubert Green	341	32,048
Feb. 17	Glen Campbell-Los Angeles Open	Dave Stockton	276	30,000
Feb. 24	Jackie Gleason Inverrary Tournament, Ft. Lauderdale	Leonard Thompson	278	52,000
Mar. 3	Citrus Open, Orlando, Fla.	Jerry Heard	273	30,000
Mar. 10	Doral-Eastern Open, Miami	Brian Allin	272	30,000
Mar. 17	Greater Jacksonville Open, Fla.	Hubert Green	276	30,000
Mar. 24	Heritage Golf Classic, Hilton Head Island, S.C.	Johnny Miller	276	40,000
Mar. 31	Greater New Orleans Open	Lee Trevino	267	30,000
Apr. 7	Greater Greensboro (N.C.) Open	Bob Charles	270	44,066
Apr. 14	Masters Tournament, Augusta, Ga.	Gary Player	278	35,000
Apr. 21	Monsanto Open, Pensacola, Fla.	Lee Elder	*274	30,045
Apr. 28	Tournament of Champions, Carlsbad, Calif.	Johnny Miller	280	40,000
Apr. 28	Tallahassee (Fla.) Open	Allen Miller	274	18,000
May 6	Byron Nelson Classic, Dallas	Brian Allin	269	30,045
May 12	Houston Open	Dave Hill	276	30,000
May 19	Colonial National Tournament, Ft. Worth, Tex.	Rod Curl	276	50,000
May 26	Danny Thomas-Memphis Classic	Gary Player	273	35,000
June 2	Kemper Open, Charlotte, N.C.	Bob Menne	*270	50,000
June 9	IVB-Philadelphia Classic	Hubert Green	271	30,000
June 16	U.S. Open, Mamaroneck, N.Y.	Hale Irwin	287	35,000
June 23	American Golf Classic, Akron, Ohio	Jim Colbert	*281	34,000
June 30	Western Open, Oak Brook, Ill.	Tom Watson	287	40,000
July 6	Milwaukee Open	Ed Sneed	276	25,000
July 14	Quad Cities Open, Bettendorf, Iowa	Dave Stockton	271	20,000
July 21	B.C. Open, Endicott, N.Y.	Richie Karl	*273	30,000
July 28	Canadian Open, Toronto	Bobby Nichols	270	40,000
Aug. 4	Pleasant Valley Classic, Sutton, Mass.	Vic Regalado	278	40,000
Aug. 11	PGA Championship, Clemmons, N.C.	Lee Trevino	276	45,000
Aug. 18	Sammy Davis Jr.-Greater Hartford Open	Dave Stockton	268	40,000
Aug. 25	Westchester Classic, Harrison, N.Y.	Johnny Miller	268	50,000
Sept. 2	Tournament Players Championship, Marietta, Ga.	Jack Nicklaus	272	50,000
Sept. 8	Southern Open, Columbus, Ga.	Forrest Fezler	271	20,000
Sept. 9	World Series of Golf, Akron, Ohio	Lee Trevino	*139	50,000
Sept. 15	World Open, Pinehurst, N. C.	Johnny Miller	*281	60,000
Sept. 22	Ohio Kings Island Open, Mason, Ohio	Miller Barber	277	30,000

Women

Date	Event	Winner	Score	Prize
Feb. 3	Burdines Tournament, Miami, Fla.	Sandra Palmer	*215	$4,950
Feb. 10	Women's Classic, Port St. Lucie, Fla.	Gail Denenberg	71	15,000
Feb. 17	Naples Tournament, Naples, Fla.	Carol Mann	209	5,400
Mar. 3	Orange Blossom Classic, St. Petersburg, Fla.	Kathy Whitworth	209	4,250
Mar. 10	S&H Green Stamp Tournament, Houston	Carol Mann	219	20,000
Mar. 17	Bing Crosby Tournament, Guadalajara, Mexico	Jane Blalock	215	4,240
Apr. 21	Colgate-Dinah Shore Winners Circle Tournament	Jo Ann Prentice	*289	32,000
Apr. 28	Birmingham Classic, Birmingham, Ala.	Jane Blalock	211	5,000
May 5	Lady Tara Open, Atlanta	Sandra Spuzich	*219	5,000
May 12	American Defender Classic, Raleigh, N.C.	Jo Ann Prentice	137	5,000
May 26	Hoosier Classic, Plymouth, Ind.	JoAnne Carner	213	5,000
June 2	Baltimore Tournament, Baltimore	Judy Rankin	144	5,700
June 9	Desert Classic, Las Vegas	JoAnne Carner	284	20,000
June 16	Medina Open, Medina, Ohio	Sandra Haynie	*215	5,700
June 23	LPGA Championship, Sutton, Mass.	Sandra Haynie	288	7,000
June 30	Peter Jackson Classic, Montreal	Carole Jo Skala	208	12,000
July 7	Niagara Frontier Tournament, Grand Island, N.Y.	Sue Roberts	213	5,000
July 14	Columbus Classic, Columbus, Ohio	Sharon Miller	211	5,700
July 21	Women's U.S. Open, La Grange, Ill.	Sandra Haynie	295	6,073
July 28	Wheeling Tournament, Wheeling, W. Va.	Carole Jo Skala	212	5,000
Aug. 4	George Washington Tournament, Horsham, Pa.	Sandra Haynie	213	5,700
Aug. 18	St. Paul Open, St. Paul, Minn.	JoAnne Carner	212	5,000
Aug. 25	National Jewish Hospital Open, Golden, Colo.	Sandra Haynie	213	5,000
Sept. 8	Dallas Civitan Tournament, Dallas	JoAnne Carner	217	5,700

*Won Playoff.

British Open Golf Champions

Year	Winner	Year	Winner	Year	Winner	Year	Winner
1906	James Braid	1925	Jim Barnes	1940-45	(Not played)	1960	Kel Nagle
1907	Arnaud Massy	1926	Bob Jones	1946	Sam Snead	1961	Arnold Palmer
1908	James Braid	1927	Bob Jones	1947	Fred Daly	1962	Arnold Palmer
1909	J. H. Taylor	1928	Walter Hagen	1948	Henry Cotton	1963	Bob Charles
1910	James Braid	1929	Walter Hagen	1949	Bobby Locke	1964	Tony Lema
1911	Harry Vardon	1930	Bob Jones	1950	Bobby Locke	1965	Peter Thomson
1912	Ted Ray	1931	Tommy Armour	1951	Max Faulkner	1966	Jack Nicklaus
1913	J. H. Taylor	1932	Gene Sarazen	1952	Bobby Locke	1967	Roberto de Vicenzo
1914	Harry Vardon	1933	Denny Shute	1953	Ben Hogan	1968	Gary Player
1915-19	(Not played)	1934	Henry Cotton	1954	Peter Thomson	1969	Tony Jacklin
1920	George Duncan	1935	Alf Perry	1955	Peter Thomson	1970	Jack Nicklaus
1921	Jock Hutchison	1936	Alf Padgham	1956	Peter Thomson	1971	Lee Trevino
1922	Walter Hagen	1937	T. H. Cotton	1957	Bobby Locke	1972	Lee Trevino
1923	Arthur Havers	1938	R. A. Whitcombe	1958	Peter Thomson	1973	Tom Weiskopf
1924	Walter Hagen	1939	Richard Burton	1959	Gary Player	1974	Gary Player

Masters Golf Tournament Champions

Year	Winner	Year	Winner	Year	Winner	Year	Winner
1934	Horton Smith	1946	Herman Keiser	1956	Jack Burke	1966	Jack Nicklaus
1935	Gene Sarazen	1947	Jimmy Demaret	1957	Doug Ford	1967	Gay Brewer, Jr.
1936	Horton Smith	1948	Claude Harmon	1958	Arnold Palmer	1968	Bob Goalby
1937	Byron Nelson	1949	Sam Snead	1959	Art Wall, Jr.	1969	George Archer
1938	Henry Picard	1950	Jimmy Demaret	1960	Arnold Palmer	1970	Billy Casper
1939	Ralph Guldahl	1951	Ben Hogan	1961	Gary Player	1971	Charles Coody
1940	Jimmy Demaret	1952	Sam Snead	1962	Arnold Palmer	1972	Jack Nicklaus
1941	Craig Wood	1953	Ben Hogan	1963	Jack Nicklaus	1973	Tommy Aaron
1942	Byron Nelson	1954	Sam Snead	1964	Arnold Palmer	1974	Gary Player
1943-1945 (Not played)		1955	Cary Middlecoff	1965	Jack Nicklaus		

Professional Golfers' Association Championships

Year	Winner	Year	Winner	Year	Winner	Year	Winner
1916	Jim Barnes	1932	Olin Dutra	1947	Jim Ferrier	1961	Jerry Barber
1919	Jim Barnes	1933	Gene Sarazen	1948	Ben Hogan	1962	Gary Player
1920	Jock Hutchison	1934	Paul Runyan	1949	Sam Snead	1963	Jack Nicklaus
1921	Walter Hagen	1935	Johnny Revolta	1950	Chandler Harper	1964	Bob Nichols
1922	Gene Sarazen	1936	Denny Shute	1951	Sam Snead	1965	Dave Marr
1923	Gene Sarazen	1937	Denny Shute	1952	James Turnesa	1966	Al Geiberger
1924	Walter Hagen	1938	Paul Runyan	1953	Walter Burkemo	1967	Don January
1925	Walter Hagen	1939	Henry Picard	1954	Melvin Harbert	1968	Julius Boros
1926	Walter Hagen	1940	Byron Nelson	1955	Doug Ford	1969	Ray Floyd
1927	Walter Hagen	1941	Victor Ghezzi	1956	Jack Burke	1970	Dave Stockton
1928	Leo Diegel	1942	Sam Snead	1957	Lionel Hebert	1971	Jack Nicklaus
1929	Leo Diegel	1944	Bob Hamilton	1958	Dow Finsterwald	1972	Gary Player
1930	Tommy Armour	1945	Byron Nelson	1959	Bob Rosburg	1973	Jack Nicklaus
1931	Tom Creavy	1946	Ben Hogan	1960	Jay Hebert	1974	Lee Trevino

British Amateur Golf Champions

Year	Winner	Year	Winner	Year	Winner	Year	Winner
1930	Bobby Jones (U.S.)	1940-45 (Not played)		1955	Joseph Conrad (U.S.)	1965	Mike Bonallack
1931	E. Martin-Smith	1946	James Bruen	1956	John Beharrell	1966	Bobby Cole
1932	J. De Forest	1947	Willie Turnesa	1957	Reid Jack	1967	Bob Dickson (U.S.)
1933	Michael Scott	1948	Frank Stranahan (U.S.)	1958	Joseph Carr	1968	Mike Bonallack
1934	Lawson Little (U.S.)	1949	Sam McCready	1959	Deane Beman (U.S.)	1969	Mike Bonallack
1935	Lawson Little (U.S.)	1950	Frank Stranahan (U.S.)	1960	Joseph Carr	1970	Mike Bonallack
1936	H. Thompson	1951	Dick Chapman (U.S.)	1961	Michael Bonallack	1971	Steve Melnyk (U.S.)
1937	Robert Sweeny	1952	Harvie Ward (U.S.)	1962	Richard Davies (U.S.)	1972	Trevor Homer
1938	C. Yates (U.S.)	1953	Joseph Carr	1963	Michael Lunt	1973	Dick Siderowe (U.S.)
1939	Alex Kyle	1954	Doug Bachli	1964	Gordon Clark	1974	Trevor Homer

Professional Golfers' Association Hall of Fame

Established in 1940 to honor those who have made outstanding contributions to the game by their lifetime playing ability.

Anderson, Willie	Dutra, Olin	Hutchison, Jock, Sr.	Runyan, Paul
Armour, Tommy	Evans, Chick	Jones, Bob	Sarazen, Gene
Barnes, Jim	Farrell, Johnny	Little, W. Lawson	Shute, Denny
Brady, Mike	Ghezzi, Vic	Mangrum, Lloyd	Smith, Alex
Burke. Billy	Guldahl, Ralph	McDermott, John	Smith, Horton
Cooper, Harry	Hagen, Walter	McLeod, Fred	Smith, MacDonald
Cruickshank, Bobby	Harbert, M. R. (Chick)	Nelson, Byron	Snead, Sam
Demaret, Jimmy	Harper, Chandler	Ouimet, Francis	Travers, Jerry
Diegel, Leo	Harrison, E. J.	Picard, Henry	Travis, Walter
Dudley, Edward	Hogan, Ben	Revolta, Johnny	Wood, Craig

PGA Leading Money Winners

Year	Player	Dollars	Year	Player	Dollars	Year	Player	Dollars
1945	Byron Nelson	52,511	1955	Julius Boros	65,121	1965	Jack Nicklaus	140,752
1946	Ben Hogan	42,556	1956	Ted Kroll	72,835	1966	Billy Casper	121,944
1947	Jimmy Demaret	27,936	1957	Dick Mayer	65,835	1967	Jack Nicklaus	188,988
1948	Ben Hogan	36,812	1958	Arnold Palmer	42,407	1968	Billy Casper	205,168
1949	Sam Snead	31,593	1959	Art Wall, Jr.	53,167	1969	Frank Beard	175,223
1950	Sam Snead	35,758	1960	Arnold Palmer	75,262	1970	Lee Trevino	157,037
1951	Lloyd Mangrum	26,088	1961	Gary Player	64,540	1971	Jack Nicklaus	244,490
1952	Julius Boros	37,032	1962	Arnold Palmer	81,448	1972	Jack Nicklaus	320,542
1953	Lew Worsham	34,002	1963	Arnold Palmer	128,230	1973	Jack Nicklaus	308,362
1954	Bob Toski	65,819	1964	Jack Nicklaus	113,284			

LPGA Leading Money Winners

Year	Winner	Dollars	Year	Winner	Dollars	Year	Winner	Dollars
1952	Betsy Rawls	14,505	1960	Louise Suggs	16,892	1967	Kathy Whitworth	32,937
1953	Louise Suggs	19,816	1961	Mickey Wright	22,236	1968	Kathy Whitworth	48,379
1954	Patty Berg	16,011	1962	Mickey Wright	21,641	1969	Carol Mann	49,152
1955	Patty Berg	16,492	1963	Mickey Wright	31,269	1970	Kathy Whitworth	30,235
1956	Marlene Hagge	20,235	1964	Mickey Wright	29,800	1971	Kathy Whitworth	41,181
1957	Patty Berg	16,272	1965	Kathy Whitworth	28,658	1972	Kathy Whitworth	65,063
1958	Beverly Hanson	12,629	1966	Kathy Whitworth	33,517	1973	Kathy Whitworth	82,854
1959	Betsy Rawls	26,774						

PGA Career Money Winners
(as of Jan., 1974)

Player	Dollars	Player	Dollars	Player	Dollars
Jack Nicklaus	2,012,068	Tom Weiskopf	884,640	Tommy Aaron	691,660
Arnold Palmer	1,633,651	Frank Beard	879,519	Gay Brewer	656,181
Billy Casper	1,421,502	Miller Barber	827,343	Bob Goalby	609,384
Lee Trevino	1,069,441	George Archer	787,189	Bruce Devlin	598,729
Bruce Crampton	1,065,709	Doug Sanders	760,937	Dave Stockton	592,926
Gary Player	984,350	Bobby Nichols	741,211	Bert Yancey	589,807
Julius Boros	926,310	Dave Hill	718,379	Don January	586,372
Gene Littler	921,275	Dan Sikes	716,437	Chi Chi Rodriguez	583,321

Ryder Cup Matches

United States vs. Great Britain Professional (biennial)
Series Standing, United States 16, Great Britain 3, 1 Tie

Series Record	Series Record
1953—United States 6¹/₂; Great Britain 5¹/₂	1965—United States 19¹/₂; Great Britain 12¹/₂
1955—United States 8; Great Britain 4	1967—United States 23¹/₂; Great Britain 8¹/₂
1957—Great Britain 7; United States 4	1969—United States 16; Great Britain 16
1959—United States 8¹/₂; Great Britain 3¹/₂	1971—United States 18¹/₂; Great Britain 13¹/₂
1961—United States 14¹/₂; Great Britain 9¹/₂	1973—United States 10; Great Britain 13
1963—United States 23; Great Britain 9	

International Walker Cup Golf Match

United States vs. Great Britain — Men's Amateur (Biennial)
Series Standing — United States 21, Great Britain 2, 1 tie

Year	Series Record	Year	Series Record
1953	United States 9; Great Britain 3	1965	United States 11; Great Britain 11
1955	United States 10; Great Britain 2	1967	United States 13; Great Britain 7
1957	United States 8; Great Britain 3	1969	United States 10; Great Britain 8
1959	United States 9; Great Britain 3	1971	Great Britain 13; United States 11
1961	United States 11; Great Britain 1	1973	United States 14; Great Britain 10
1963	United States 9; Great Britain 3		

International Curtis Cup Golf Match

United States vs. Great Britain — Women's Amateur (Biennial)
Series Standing — United States 14, Great Britain 2, 2 ties

Year	Series Record	Year	Series Record
1952	Great Britain 5; United States 4	1964	United States 10¹/₂; Great Britain 7¹/₂
1954	United States 6; Great Britain 3	1966	United States 13; Great Britain 5
1956	Great Britain 5; United States 4	1968	United States 10¹/₂; Great Britain 7¹/₂
1958	Great Britain 4¹/₂; United States 4¹/₂	1970	United States 11¹/₂; Great Britain 6¹/₂
1960	United States 6¹/₂; Great Britain 2¹/₂	1972	United States 10; Great Britain 8
1962	United States 8; Great Britain 1	1974	United States 13; Great Britain 5

U.S. National Fencing Champions in 1974

Men's Foil—Heik Hambarzumian, Letterman General Hospital, Calif.
Men's Epee—Daniel Cantillon, Fencing Academy of Michigan
Men's Sabre—Peter Westbrook, New York Fencer's Club
Women's Foil—Gay Jacobsen, Halberstadt Fencers Club, Calif.
Women's Foil Team—Salle Santelli, N.Y.
Men's Foil Team U.S. Marine Corps.
Men's Epee Team—Mori Fencing Academy, Calif.
Men's Sabre Team—New York Athletic Club, N.Y.

Intercollegiate Rowing Association Regatta
Onondage Lake, Syracuse, N. Y. (Three miles)

Year	Winner	Time	Year	Winner	Time	Year	Winner	Time
1956	Cornell	16:22.4	1963	Cornell	17:24.0	1969	Penn (A).	6:30.4
1957	Cornell	15:26.6	1964	California (A)	6:31.1	1970	Washington (A)	
1958	Cornell	17:12.1	1965	Navy	16:51.3	1971	Cornell (A).	6:06.0
1959	Wisconsin	18:01.7	1966	Wisconsin	16:03.4	1972	Penn (A).	6:22.6
1960	California	15:57.0	1967	Penn	16:13.9	1973	Wisconsin (A).	6:21.0
1961	California	16:49.2	1968	Penn(A)	6:15.6	1974	Wisconsin (A).	6:33.0
1962	Cornell	17:02.9						

(A) Race at 2,000 meters.

National Rowing Championships, 1974

Elite Quarter-Mile Singles—Jim Dietz, New York AC.
Senior Singles—Bill Stout, Long Beach RA.
Senior Four With Coxswain—Vesper BC.
Elite Four—Vesper and New York AC.
Senior Pair—Univ. of Western Ontario.
Elite Double—New York AC.

Senior Eight—Vesper BC.
Elite Pair With Coxswain—Vesper BC.
Elite 155-Lb. Double—Undine BC.
Elite 155-Lb. Four—Vesper BC.
Elite 155-Lb. Pair—New York AC.

Shuffleboard Championships in 1974

National Singles Championship, St. Petersburg, Fla., March 4-6 — Men's Open, Bailee Stepp, St. Petersburg, Fla.; Men's Closed, Willard Bowen, Boynton Beach, Fla.; Women's Open, Audrie Haley, Bradenton, Fla.; Women's Closed, Lucy Magee, St. Petersburg.
National Doubles Championship, Mid Florida Lakes, Fla., Jan. 21-23 — Men's Doubles, Merritt Gordon, St. Petersburg and Jason Badee, Lakeland, Fla. Women's Doubles, Kate

Gruber, Lakeland and Marie Sutton, Bradenton, Fla.
Summer National Championships, Lakeside, Ohio, July 22-27 — Men's Open, Lary Faris, Lakeside, Ohio; Men's Closed, Charles McGee, Miami, Fla.; Women's Open, Mildred Davis, Palmetto, Fla.; Women's Closed, Pat Hill, Orlando, Fla. Men's Doubles, Charles McGee and George Frye, Toledo, Ohio; Women's Doubles, Kay Smock, Miami, Fla. and Marie Sutton.

1974 Water Ski Champions

32nd Annual National Water Ski Championships
Callaway Gardens, Ga. August 21 - 25, 1974

Men's Overall — Ricky McCormick, Hialeah, Fla., 2,623 points.
Men's Slalom — Kris LaPoint, Castro Valley, Calif., 52 buoys.
Men's Tricks — Russ Stiffler, Upland, Calif., 5,370 points.
Men's Jumping — Mike Suyderhoud, Petaluma, Calif., 160 feet.
Women's Overall — Liz Allan Shetter, Groveland, Fla., 2,975 points.
Women's Slalom — Liz Allan Shetter, 53 buoys.
Women's Tricks — Liz Allan Shetter, 4,130 points.
Women's Jumping — Liz Allan Shetter, 125 feet.
Senior Men's Overall — Dr. J. D. Morgan, Key West, Fla., 3,208 points.
Senior Men's Slalom — Tommy Wycoff, Connelly Springs, N.C., 49 buoys.
Senior Men's Tricks — Bob Abbott, Akron, Ohio, 3,890 points.
Senior Men's Jumping — Nito Quitevis, St. Paul, Minn., 120 feet.
Senior Women's Overall — Barbara Cleveland, Hawthorne, Fla., 3,799 points.
Senior Women's Slalom — Barbara Heddon, Lake Wales, Fla., 45 buoys.
Senior Women's Tricks — Barbara Cleveland, 3,880 points.

Senior Women's Jumping — Barbara Cleveland, 104 feet.
Boy's Overall — Lucky Lowe, Birmingham, Ala., 2,416 points.
Boy's Slalom — Bill Chisnell, Pontiac, Mich., 44¹/₂ buoys.
Boy's Tricks — Tony Cecil, Jr., Louisville, Ky., 4,230 points.
Boy's Jumping — Lucky Lowe, 125 feet.
Girl's Overall — Camille Duvall, Greenville, S.C., 2,777 points.
Girl's Slalom — Camille Duvall, 45 buoys.
Girl's Tricks — Jayne Henley, St. Louis, Mo., 3,280 points.
Girl's Jumping — Carrie Pawinski, Mukwonago, Wisc., 101 feet.
Junior Boy's Overall — Sammy Duvall, Greenville, S.C., 3,987 points.
Junior Boy's Slalom — Mark Scharosch, Napa, Calif., 50 buoys.
Junior Boy's Tricks — Sammy Duvall, 3,570 points.
Junior Boy's Jumping — Rick Anderson, Anderson, S. C., 103 feet.
Junior Girl's Overall — Tish Fain, Clemson, S. C., 2,626 points.
Junior Girl's Slalom — Tish Fain, 40 buoys.
Junior Girl's Tricks — Terri Olson, Gobles, Mich., 1,960 points.
Junior Girl's Jumping — Tish Fain, 84 feet.

16th Annual Masters Tournament
Callaway Gardens, Ga., July 13 - 14, 1974

Men's Overall — George Athans, Quebec, Canada, 2,635 points.
Men's Slalom — Mark Crone, Shapleigh, Maine, 50 buoys.
Men's Tricks — Ricky McCormick, Hialeah, Fla., 5,030 points.
Men's Jumping — Wayne Grimditch, Pompano Beach, Fla., 170 feet.

Women's Overall — Liz Allan Shetter, Groveland, Fla., 2,677 points.
Women's Slalom — Liz Allan Shetter, 51¹/₂ buoys.
Women's Tricks — Maria Victoria Carrasco, Caracas, Venezuela, 5,040 points.
Women's Jumping — Linda Leavengood Giddens, Eastman, Ga., 114 feet.

National Roller Skating Championships, 1974

Lincoln, Nebr.

Men Singles — Darryl Bayles, Delanco, N.J.
Ladies Singles — Natalie Dunn, Bakersfield, Calif.
Junior Men Singles — Royce Miller, Houston, Texas
Junior Ladies Singles — Lisa Bergin, Ft. Worth, Texas
Senior Dance — John LaBriola & Debra Coyne, Whittier, Calif.
Junior Dance — Brad Byrd & Doria Priest, Whittier, Calif.
Esquire Dance — Donald Benson & Phyllis Benson, Norwood, Maine.
Senior Men Figures — Keith King, E. Meadow, N.Y.
Senior Ladies Figures — Natalie Dunn, Bakersfield, Calif.
Junior Men Figures — LeRoy Hicks, Whittier, Calif.
Junior Ladies Figures — Leigh Ann Davis, Richardson, Texas
Senior Mixed Pairs — Mark Revere & Darlene Waters, Pontiac, Mich.

Junior Mixed Pairs — Pat Jones & Robbie Coleman, Memphis, Tenn.

Speed Events

Senior Men — Chris Snyder, Springfield, Mo.
Senior Ladies — Robin Wilcock, Thousand Oaks, Calif.
Junior Men — Tim Small, Ft. Lauderdale, Fla.
Junior Ladies — Mara Jones, Tacoma, Wash.
Senior Two-Man Relay — Tim Small & Tom Small, Ft. Lauderdale, Fla.
Senior Two-Lady Relay — Dana Jones & Mara Jones, Tacoma, Wash.

Trapshooting Championships in 1974
Source: Trap & Field Magazine

75th Grand American Tournament
Vandalia, Ohio, Aug. 15-24, 1974

Grand American Handicap

Men — John Steffen, Minnetonka, Minn.		99x100
Women — Georgie McCown, Newman, Ill.		99x100
Juniors — Randy Voss, LeSueur, Minn.		98x100
Sub-Juniors — Charles Bradley, Vest, Ky.		97x100
Veterans — A. J. Meyer, Elba, N. Y.		96x100
Industry — Tom Garrigus, Hillsboro, Ore.		95x100
Past Winner Trophy — Charles Harvey, Oskaloosa, Ia.		97x100
Jimmy Robinson Trophy to High Canadian — Frank Myslik Jr., Brampton, Ont.		96x100

Clay Target Championship

Men — Hiram Bradley, Vest, Ky.		200x200
Women — Dolores Hendersched, White Haven, Pa.		198x200
Juniors — Leo Harrison III, Hannibal, Mo.		198x200
Sub-Juniors — James Linke, Woonsocket, S. D.		198x200
Veterans — Walter Johnson, Inglewood, Calif.		198x200
Industry — Tom Garrigus, Hillsboro, Ore.		198x200

Doubles Championship

Men — Steve Carmichael, Kansas City, Mo.		100x100
Women — Susan Nattrass, Edmonton, Alta.		95x100
Juniors — Leo Harrison III, Hannibal, Mo.		96x100
Sub-Juniors — Eugene Leoni Jr., Ambler, Pa.		97x100

Veterans — Henry Austin, Champagne, Ill.		90x100
Industry — Lee Davidson, Tipp City, Ohio		96x100

Champion of Champions

Men — Bueford Bailey, Big Springs, Neb.		100x100
Women — Susan Nattrass, Edmonton, Alta.		100x100
Juniors — Percy Talkington, New Martinsville, West Virginia		99x100

High-Over-All

Men — Britt Robinson, Tahoka, Tex.		971x1000
Women — Susan Nattrass, Edmonton, Alta.		938x1000
Juniors — Doug Davidson, Devils Lake, N. D.		951x1000
Sub-Juniors — David Craite, Grosse Point Farms, Mich.		936x1000
Veterans — Vic Reinders, Waukesha, Wisc.		934x1000
Industry — Tom Garrigus, Hillsboro, Ore.		951x1000

All-Around Championship

Men — Steve Carmichael, Kansas City, Mo.		395x400
Women — Barbara Renfro, Dillon, Mont.		379x400
Juniors — Randy Voss, LeSueur, Minn.		389x400
Sub-Juniors — Eugene Leoni Jr., Ambler, Pa.		385x400
Veterans — Vic Reinders, Waukesha, Wisc.		378x400
Industry — Tom Garrigus, Hillsboro, Ore.		386x400

Contract Bridge Championships in 1973-74

Winners of Major Events at 3 ACBL National Tournaments
Fall 1973 — Spring and Summer 1974

Source: American Contract Bridge League

Fall Nationals
Las Vegas, Nev., Dec. 7-16, 1973; attendance, 13,464 tables.

Reisinger Board-a-Match Teams — Peter Weichsel, Alan Sontag, New York, N.Y.; Larry Cohen, Dr. Richard Katz, Los Angeles, A. E. "Bud" Reinhold, Highland Park, Ill.
Blue Ribbon Pairs — Kit Woolsey, Washington, D.C.; Steve Robinson, Alexandria, Va.
Life Master Men's Pairs — Norman Kay, Narberth, Pa.; Edgar Kaplan, New York, N.Y.

Life Master Women's Pairs — June Deutsch, Frieda Arst, Chicago, Ill.
Mixed Pairs — Bernard Chazen, Fort Lee, N.J.; Marilyn Johnson, Houston, Texas.
Most Master Points for the Tournament — Larry Cohen, Los Angeles, 207 Master Points.

Spring Nationals
Vancouver, B.C., March 22-31, 1974; attendance 8,329 tables.

Vanderbilt Knockout Teams — Joseph Silver, Eric Kokish, Montreal; Robert Crossley, David Crossley, San Rafael, Calif.
Men's Teams — Ronald Andersen, Parsippany, N.J.; Merle Tom, Cedar Grove, N.J.; Hugh MacLean, Minneapolis, Minn.; Mark Feldman, Brighton, Maine; Stephen Goldstein, New York, N.Y.
Women's Teams — Marilyn Johnson, Houston, Texas; Dorothy Truscott; Jacqui Mitchell, Gail Moss, New York, N.Y.; Mary

Jane Farell, Beverly Hills, Calif.; Emma Jean Hawes, Fort Worth, Texas.
Men's Pairs — George Steiner, George Slemmons, Bellevue, Wash.
Women's Pairs — Jan Stansby, Oakland, Calif.; Pat Leary, Livermore, Calif.
Most Master Points for Tournament — Ronald Andersen, Parsippany, N.J., 250 Master Points.

Summer Nationals
New York City, July 11-23, 1974; attendance, 15,310 tables.

Spingold Knockout Teams — Steve Goldberg, Marietta, Ga.; Lou Bluhm, Richard Shepherd, Atlanta, Ga.; Larry Gould, Decatur, Ga.
Grand National Teams — John Swanson, Culver City, Calif.; Paul Soloway, Dr. Richard Katz, Larry Cohen, Edwin Kantar, William Eisenberg, Los Angeles.
Master Mixed Teams — Edith Kemp, Jerome Yavitz, Miami

Beach, Fla.; Rita Seamon, William Seamon, North Miami, Fla.
Life Master Pairs — G. Robert Nail, Houston, Texas; Gerald Michaud, Wichita, Kansas.
Senior and Advanced Senior Master Pairs — Dale Beers, Springfield, Pa.; David Silberstein, East Haddam, Conn.
Most Master Points for the Tournament — Richard Shepherd, Atlanta, Ga. 161.84 Master Points.

1974 World Championships

World Team Champions — Italy, Giorgio Belladonna, Benito Garozzo, Pietro Forquet, Benito Bianchi. (Sandro Salvetti, non-playing captain).
Mixed Pairs — Switzerland, Tony Trad and Loula Gordon.
Mixed Teams — United States, Robert Lipsitz, Peggy Lipsitz, Steve Parker, Jo Morse, Steve Robinson.

Ladies Pairs — Great Britain, Rixi Markus and Fritzi Gordon.
Open Pairs — United States, Robert Hamman and Robert Wolff.
Venice Challenge Cup — United States, Dorothy Truscott, Emma Jean Hawes, Carol Sanders, Betty Ann Kennedy, Bette Cohn, Marietta Passell, (Ruth McConnell, non-playing captain).

Chess

Chess dates back to antiquity. Its exact origin is unknown. The strongest players of their time, and therefore regarded by later generations as world champions, were Francois Philidor, France; Alexandre Deschappelles, France; Louis de la Bourdonnais, France; Howard Staunton, England; Adolph Anderssen, Germany and Paul Morphy, United States. In 1866 Wilhelm Steinitz of Austria defeated Adolph Anderssen and claimed the title of World Champion. The official world champions, since the title was first used follow:

1866-1894 Wilhelm Steinitz, Vienna	1935-1937 Dr. Max Euwe, Holland	1958-1959 Mikhail Botvinnik, USSR
1894-1921 Dr. Emanuel Lasker, Berlin	1937-1946 Dr. Alexander A. Alekhine,	1960-1961 Mikhail Tal, USSR
1921-1927 Jose R. Capablanca, Havana	Paris	1961-1963 Mikhail Botvinnik, USSR
1927-1935 Dr. Alexander A. Alekhine,	1948-1957 Mikhail Botvinnik, USSR	1963-1969 Tigran Petrosian, USSR
Paris	1957-1958 Vassily Smyslov, USSR	1969-1972 Boris Spassky, USSR
		1972 Bobby Fischer, U.S.

United States Champions

1852-1862 Paul Morphy	1894-1897 Jackson Showalter	1944-1946 Arnold S. Denker	1962	Larry Evans
1871-1887 George Mackenzie	1897-1906 Harry Nelson	1946 Samuel Reshevsky	1963-1967	Bobby Fischer
1887-1892 Max Judd	Pillsbury	1948 Herman Steiner	1968	Larry Evans
1892-1894 Simon Lipschultz	1906-1909 Jackson Showalter	1951-1953 Larry Evans	1969-1971	Samuel Reschevsky
1894 Jackson Showalter	1909-1936 Frank J. Marshall	1954 Arthur B. Bisguier	1973	Robert Byrne
1894 Albert B. Hodges	1936-1944 Samuel Reshevsky	1958-1961 Bobby Fischer	1974	Walter Browne

America Casting Assn. Combined Championships in 1974

Toronto, Ontario, Aug. 7-11, 1974

Men
Grand All Around Champion — Steve Rajeff, San Francisco, Calif.
Anglers All Around Champion — Steve Rajeff.
All Accuracy — Steve Rajeff, 584 pts.
All Distance — Steve Rajeff, 5,246 ft.
Distance Plugs — Steve Rajeff, 3,485 ft.
Distance Flies — Steve Rajeff, 1,761 ft.
Accuracy Plugs — Steve Rajeff, 289 pts.
Accuracy Flies — Steve Rajeff, 295 pts.

Women
All Accuracy — Ann Strobel, New Orleans, La., 537 pts.
Accuracy Plugs — Cecilia Stahl, St. Louis, Mo., 266 pts.
Accuracy Flies — Pauline Cathcart, LaCanada, Calif., 277 pts.

Intermediates
All Accuracy — Tim Rajeff, San Francisco, Calif., 538 pts.
Accuracy Flies — Tim Rajeff, 259 pts.
Accuracy Flies — Tim Rajeff, 279 pts.

Sports on Television

Source: A. C. Nielsen

	Average Audiences			Distribution of Total Viewers		
	Percent Households	Percent Men	Total Viewers (000)	Percent Men	Percent Women	Percent Non-Adults
Football 1973-'74						
Super Bowl	41.6	38.1	50,670	48	30	22
ABC-NFL	20.7	18.7	23,150	52	30	18
CBS-NFL	15.4	13.1	16,220	51	27	22
NBC-NFL	14.6	12.7	15,080	54	27	19
Coll. All-Stars/Bowls	18.3	19.8	26,600	47	32	21
NCAA	12.2	9.8	12,520	50	29	21
NBC—Baseball						
World Series	30.7	24.5	34,750	45	38	17
All-Star	23.8	20.8	27,600	48	32	20
Playoffs	15.0	9.8	14,680	43	41	16
Reg. Season	9.3	6.8	9,020	48	33	19
Basketball						
NBA	10.0	8.7	11,180	50	28	22
NCAA/NIT	8.8	DATA NOT AVAILABLE				
ABA	3.4	2.2	3,660	38	29	33
Bowling	8.9	5.9	9,690	39	39	22
Hockey						
NHL	5.6	4.2	5,850	46	33	21
WHA	2.1	1.5	2,450	40	31	29
CBS—Horse Racing						
Triple Crown	16.3	11.3	17,480	41	41	18
CBS Races	5.8	2.5	4,710	33	39	28
ABC—Auto Racing	11.1	5.2	8,640	38	32	30
ABC—Boxing	5.2	4.3	5,110	53	29	18
Multi-Sports Series						
Wide World of Sports	10.7	8.7	12,570	44	30	26
American Sportsman	9.1	7.2	9,830	46	29	25
CBS Sports Spectacular	5.9	4.7	6,950	43	36	21
Golf						
Tournaments	7.8	6.6	8,830	48	38	14
CBS Golf Classics	3.8	2.8	4,070	43	33	24
Tennis						
Riggs-King Special	28.5	21.9	37,170	38	44	18
Tournaments	4.5	2.7	4,060	42	38	20
CBS Tennis Classic	4.3	3.1	4,700	42	36	22
Super Stars	10.9	9.9	14,330	43	25	32
World Cup Skiing	5.2	DATA NOT AVAILABLE				

Curling Events in 1974

The Douglas Medal, St. Andrews Golf Club, Jan. 2-5, Schenectady CC, Chick Hequembourg, skip. **The Griffith Medal,** N.Y. Caledonian CC, Joe Milano, skip. **The Williamson Medal,** CC of New York, Jim Walker, skip.
    Granite State Trophy, Nashua, N. H., Jan. 9-12, Weston CC, J. Cawley, skip. **Patterson Medal,** Winchester CC, C. Reeves,

skip. **The Merrick Bowl,** Nashua CC, R. Bickford, skip.
    New Hampshire State Trophy, Feb. 13-16, Winchester CC, C. Reeves, skip. **Mt. Washington Bowl,** Florenville N.B., M. McAloon, skip. **Gate City Medal,** Sussex, N.B., E. Jorgenson, skip.

World Champions

Year	Country & Skip	Year	Country & Skip	Year	Country & Skip
1964	Canada (Lyall Dagg)	1968	Canada (Ron Northcott)	1972	Canada (Orest Melesnuk)
1965	United States (Bud Somerville)	1969	Canada (Ron Northcott)	1973	Sweden (Kjell Oscarius)
1966	Canada (Ron Northcott)	1970	Canada (Don Duguid)	1974	United States (Bud Somerville)
1967	Scotland (Chuck Hay)	1971	Canada (Don Duguid)		

Polo Records

National Open Tournament

1964	Oak Brook 10, Solo Cup Crescents 9
1965	Oak Brook 11, Bunn Tyco Chicago 5
1966	Tulsa 10, Fountain Grove 5
1967	Bunntyco-Oakbrook 8, Milwaukee 2
1968	Midland 9, Milwaukee 0
1969	Tulsa Green Hill 11, Milwaukee 10
1970	Tulsa Green Hill 9, Oak Brook 5
1971	Oak Brook 8, Green Hill Farm 7
1972	Milwaukee 9, Tulsa 5
1973	Oak Brook 9, Willow Bend 4
1974	Milwaukee 7, Houston 6

Silver Cup

1964	Oak Brook 8, Tulsa 5
1965	Santa Barbara-Oak Brook 7, Milwaukee 2
1966	Sunny Climes 9, Oak Brook 7
1967	Milwaukee 11, Keswick-Blue Ridge 7
1968	Oak Brook 12, Keswick Sunny Climes 9
1969	Oak Brook 7, Milwaukee 6
1970	Oak Brook 9, Tulsa Green Hill 7

1971	Green Hill Farm 8, Milwaukee 6
1972	Red Doors Farm 10, Sun Ranch 6
1973	Houston 6, Willow Bend 4

Intercollegiate Championship

1964	Yale 12, Cornell 9
1965	Yale 12, Cornell 3
1966	Cornell 12, Yale 10
1967	Yale 12, Cornell 11
1968	Yale 17, Cornell 13
1969	Yale 17, Cornell 16
1970	Yale 22, Cornell 10
1971	Yale 12, Virginia 11
1972	Univ. of Conn. 17, Univ. of Virginia 15
1973	Univ. of Conn. 19, Univ. of Virginia 10
1974	Univ. of Conn. 18, Cornell 16

Other Tournaments

Gold Cup — Milwaukee 9, Houston 8.
America Cup — Boca Raton 7, Milwaukee 5.
Butler National Hdcp --- Milwaukee 11, Tulsa 6.
Delegate's Cup — Oak Brook 6, Chattanooga 5.

Professional Sports Directory

Baseball

Commissioner's Office
15 W. 51st St.
New York, N.Y. 10019

National League

National League Office
Mills Bldg.
220 Montgomery St.
San Francisco, Calif. 94104

Atlanta Braves
PO Box 4064
Atlanta, Ga. 30302

Chicago Cubs
Wrigley Field
Chicago, Ill. 60613

Cincinnati Reds
100 Riverfront Stadium
Cincinnati, Ohio 45202

Houston Astros
Astrodome
Houston, Texas 77001

Los Angeles Dodgers
Dodger Stadium
1000 Elysian Park Ave.
Los Angeles, Calif. 90012

Montreal Expos
PO Box 500, Station R
Montreal, Quebec

New York Mets
William A. Shea Stadium
Roosevelt Ave. & 126th St.
Flushing, N.Y. 11368

Philadelphia Phillies
Philadelphia Veterans Stadium
Broad St. & Pattison Ave.
Philadelphia, Pa. 19148

Pittsburgh Pirates
600 Stadium Circle
Pittsburgh, Pa. 15212

St. Louis Cardinals
Busch Memorial Stadium
250 Stadium Plaza
St. Louis, Mo. 63102

San Diego Padres
9449 Friars Rd.
San Diego, Calif. 92120

San Francisco Giants
Candlestick Park
San Francisco, Calif. 94124

American League

American League Office
520 Boylston St.
Boston, Mass. 02116

Baltimore Orioles
Memorial Stadium
Baltimore, Md. 21218

Boston Red Sox
24 Jersey St.
Boston, Mass. 02215

California Angels
Anaheim Stadium
2000 State College Blvd.
Anaheim, Calif. 92806

Chicago White Sox
White Sox Park
Dan Ray & 35th St.
Chicago, Ill. 60616

Cleveland Indians
Municipal Stadium
Cleveland, Ohio 44114

Detroit Tigers
Tiger Stadium
Detroit, Mich. 48216

Kansas City Royals
Harry S. Truman Sports Complex
PO Box 1969
Kansas City, Mo. 64141

Milwaukee Brewers
Milwaukee County Stadium
Milwaukee, Wisc. 53246

Minnesota Twins
Metropolitan Stadium
8001 Cedar Ave.
Bloomington, Minn. 55420

New York Yankees
Parks Administration Bldg.
Flushing, N.Y. 11368

Oakland A's
Oakland-Alameda County
  Coliseum
Oakland, Calif. 94621

Texas Rangers
Arlington Stadium
PO Box 1111
Arlington, Texas 76010

Basketball

National Basketball Assn.

League Office
2 Pennsylvania Plaza
Suite 2010
New York, N.Y. 10001

Atlanta Hawks
100 Techwood Drive
Atlanta, Ga. 30303

Boston Celtics
North Station
Boston, Mass. 02114

Buffalo Braves
Memorial Auditorium
Buffalo, N.Y. 14202

Capital Bullets
Capital Centre
Largo, Md. 20780

Chicago Bulls
Sheraton Chicago Hotel
505 North Michigan Ave.
Chicago, Ill. 60611

Cleveland Cavaliers
3717 Euclid Ave.
Cleveland, Ohio 44115

Detroit Pistons
Cobo Arena
Detroit, Mich. 48226

Golden State Warriors
556 Golden Gate Ave.
San Francisco, Calif. 94102

Houston Rockets
3930 Kirby Drive
Houston, Texas 77006

Kansas City-Omaha Kings
210 W. 14th St.
Kansas City, Mo. 64105
1804 Capitol Ave.
Omaha, Nebr. 68102

Los Angeles Lakers
The Forum
3900 W. Manchester Blvd.
or PO Box 10
Inglewood, Calif. 90306

Milwaukee Bucks
901 West 4th St.
Milwaukee, Wisc. 53203

New Orleans Jazz
Braniff Place Hotel
1500 Canal St.
New Orleans, La. 70140

New York Knickerbockers
Madison Square Garden Center
4 Pennsylvania Plaza
New York, N.Y. 10001

Philadelphia 76ers
The Spectrum
Philadelphia, Pa. 19148

Phoenix Suns
PO Box 1369
Phoenix, Ariz. 85001

Portland Trail Blazers
Lloyd Bldg.
700 NE Multnomah St.
Portland, Ore. 97232

Seattle SuperSonics
221 West Harrison
Seattle, Wash. 98119

American Basketball Assn.

League Office
1700 Broadway
New York, N.Y. 10019

Denver Nuggets
1108 15th St.
Denver, Colo. 80202

Indiana Pacers
Market Square Center
Indianapolis, Ind. 46204

Kentucky Colonels
Executive Inn
Louisville, Ky. 40213

Memphis Sounds
1000 Early Maxwell Blvd.
Memphis, Tenn. 38104

New York Nets
One Old Country Rd.
Carle Place, N.Y. 11590

St. Louis Spirits
5050 Oakland Ave.
St. Louis, Mo. 63110

San Antonio Spurs
Hemissair Arena
PO Box 530
San Antonio, Texas 78292

San Diego Conquistadors
3500 Sports Arena Blvd.
San Diego, Calif. 92110

Utah Stars
Salt Palace
Stars Ave. & W. Temple
Salt Lake City, Utah 84101

Virginia Squires
Norfolk Scope
Norfolk, Va. 23510

Football

National Football League

NFL League Office
410 Park Avenue
New York, N.Y. 10022

Atlanta Falcons
521 Capitol Ave. SW
Atlanta, Ga. 30312

Baltimore Colts
Executive Plaza
Hunt Valley, Md. 21031

Buffalo Bills
1 Bills Drive
Orchard Park, N.Y.14127

Chicago Bears
173 W. Madison St.
Chicago, Ill. 60602

Cincinnati Bengals
200 Riverfront Stadium
Cincinnati, Ohio 45202

Cleveland Browns
Cleveland Stadium
Cleveland, Ohio 44114

Dallas Cowboys
6116 North Central Expressway
Dallas, Texas 75206

Denver Broncos
5700 Logan St.
Denver, Colo. 80216

Detroit Lions
1401 Michigan Ave.
Detroit, Mich. 48216

Green Bay Packers
1265 Lombardi Ave.
Green Bay, Wisc. 54303

Houston Oilers
6910 Fannin
Houston, Texas 77025

Kansas City Chiefs
1 Arrowhead Drive
Kansas City, Mo. 64129

Los Angeles Rams
10271 W. Pico. Blvd.
Los Angeles, Calif. 90064

Miami Dolphins
330 Biscayne Blvd.
Miami, Fla. 33132

Minnesota Vikings
7110 France Ave. So.
Edina, Minn. 55435

New England Patriots
Schaefer Stadium
Foxboro, Mass. 02035

New Orleans Saints
944 St. Charles Ave.
New Orleans, La. 70130

New York Giants
10 Columbus Circle
New York, N.Y. 10019

New York Jets
595 Madison Ave.
New York, N.Y.10022

Oakland Raiders
7811 Oakport St.
Oakland, Calif. 94621

Philadelphia Eagles
Veterans Stadium
Philadelphia, Pa. 19148

Pittsburgh Steelers
Three Rivers Stadium
Pittsburgh, Pa. 15212

St. Louis Cardinals
200 Stadium Plaza
St. Louis, Mo. 63102

San Diego Chargers
9449 Friars Road
San Diego, Calif. 92120

San Francisco 49ers
1255 Post St.
San Francisco, Calif. 94109

Washington Redskins
PO Box 17247
Dulles Intl. Airport
Washington, D.C. 20041

World Football League

League Office
4299 MacArthur Blvd.
Newport Beach, Calif. 92660

Birmingham Americans
PO Box 2431
Birmingham, Ala. 35203

Chicago Fire
1580 N. Northwest Hwy.
Park Ridge, Ill. 60068

Detroit Wheels
144 Lafayette West
Detroit, Mich., 48228

Florida Blazers
4045 Orange Blossom Trail
Orlando, Fla. 32809

The Hawaiians
233 Keawe St.
Honolulu, Hawaii 96813

Houston Texans
Box 1365
Houston, Texas 77001

Jacksonville Sharks
Gulf Life Tower
Jacksonville, Fla. 32207

Memphis Southmen
1835 Union Avenue
Memphis, Tenn. 38104

New York Stars
415 Madison Ave.
New York, N.Y. 10017

Philadelphia Bell
220 S. Broad St.
Philadelphia, Pa. 19102

Portland Storm
401 SW 11th St.
Portland, Ore. 97205

Southern Calif. Sun
2000 State College Blvd.
Anaheim, Calif. 92806

Hockey

National Hockey League

League Office
920 Sun Life Bldg.
Montreal, 110, Quebec

Atlanta Flames
100 Teckwood Dr., NW
Atlanta, Ga. 30303

Boston Bruins
150 Causeway St.
Boston, Mass. 02114

Buffalo Sabres
Memorial Auditorium
Buffalo, N. Y. 14202

California Golden Seals
Oakland-Alameda County
Coliseum
303 Hegenberger Rd.
Oakland, Calif. 94621

Chicago Black Hawks
1800 W. Madison St.
Chicago, Ill. 60612

Detroit Red Wings
5920 Grand River
Detroit, Mich. 48208

Kansas City Scouts
Crosby Kemper Memorial Arena
Genesee St.
Kansas City, Mo. 64102

Los Angeles Kings
3900 W. Manchester Blvd.
Inglewood, Calif. 90306

Minnesota North Stars
7901 Cedar Avenue
Bloomington, Minn. 55420

Montreal Canadiens
2313 St. Catherine St., West
Montreal, 108, Quebec

New York Islanders
1155 Conklin St.
Farmingdale, N. Y. 11735

New York Rangers
Madison Square Garden
4 Pennsylvania Plaza
New York, N. Y. 10001

Philadelphia Flyers
The Spectrum
Pattison Place
Philadelphia, Pa. 19148

Pittsburgh Penguins
Civic Arena
Pittsburgh, Pa. 15219

St. Louis Blues
5700 Oakland Ave.
St. Louis, Mo. 63110

Toronto Maple Leafs
60 Carlton St.
Toronto, Ont.

Vancouver Canucks
Pacific Coliseum
100 North Renfrew St.
Vancouver 6, B.C.

Washington Capitals
Capital Center
Landover, Md. 20786

World Hockey Assn.

League Office
1010 North Main St.
Santa Ana, Calif. 92701

Chicago Cougars
111 E. Wacker Drive
Chicago, Ill. 60601

Cleveland Crusaders
2923 Streetsboro Rd.
Richfield Township, Ohio 44286

Edmonton Oilers
MacDonald Hotel
Edmonton, Alberta

Houston Aeros
810 Bagby St.
Houston, Texas 77002

Indianapolis Racers
151 N. Delaware St.
Indianapolis, Ind. 46204

Michigan Stags
30100 Telegraph Road
Birmingham, Mich. 48010

Minnesota Fighting Saints
St. Paul Civic Center
St. Paul, Minn. 55102

New England Whalers
1 Civic Center Plaza
Hartford, Conn. 06101

Phoenix Roadrunners
Valley Center
Phoenix, Ariz. 85073

Quebec Nordiques
Exhibition Grounds
Quebec 3, Que.

San Diego Mariners
3500 Sports Arena Blvd.
San Diego, Calif. 92110

Toronto Toros
238 Bloor St., W.
Toronto, Ont.

Vancouver Blazers
Pacific Coliseum
Vancouver, B.C.

Winnipeg Jets
Winnipeg Arena
Winnipeg, Man.

Rifle and Pistol Individual Championships in 1974
Source: National Rifle Association of America

National Rifle & Pistol Championships (Outdoor, Conventional)

Pistol — SFC Hershel L. Anderson, USA, Ft. Benning, Ga., 2657-150X.
Civilian Pistol — Robert L. Settle, Biscayne Park, Fla., 2607-100X.
Woman Pistol — SFC Barbara J. Hile, USA, Ft. Benning, Ga., 2562-75X.
Senior Pistol — Gil Hebard, Knoxville, Ill., 2568-78X.
Police Pistol — Jerry L. Wilder, Remington, Ind., 2599-97X.
Smallbore Rifle Prone — Maj. Presley W. Kendall, USA, Carlisle, Ky., 6389-500X.
Woman Smallbore Rifle Prone — Lisa S. Helbing, Ft. Worth, Tex., 6376-509X.
Junior Smallbore Rifle Prone — Robert L. DeHart, Coral Gables, Fla., 6381-455X.
Civilian Smallbore Rifle Prone — Thomas J. Whitaker, Belmont, Calif., 6386-548X.
Smallbore Rifle Position — Maj. Lones W. Wigger, Jr., Ft. Benning, Ga., 3131-179X.
Woman Smallbore Rifle Position — Gloria K. Parmentier, Alexandria, Va., 3093-144X.
Civilian Smallbore Rifle Position — William P. Schweitzer, Lancaster, Pa., 3112-179X.
Senior Smallbore Rifle Position — Robert A. Makielski, Michawaka, Ind., 3072-125X.

Junior Smallbore Rifle Position — Dale A. Cox, Fairfax, Va., 3097-130X.
High Power Rifle — Jack P. Sicola, Santa Cruz, Calif., 1564-59X.
Match Rifle Service — Sgt. Paul C. Laberge, NGUS, Shelburne, Vt., 1506-32X.
Match Rifle Senior — Harold V. Slocum, Oakville, Conn., 1519-30X.
Match Rifle Woman — Betty J. Swarthout, Westland, Mich., 1483-32X.
Match Rifle Junior — Gary E. Tubb, Canadian, Tex., 1554-52X.
Match Rifle Collegiate — G. David Tubb, Canadian, Tex., 1559-55X.
Service Rifle Champion — Sgt. Daniel Sanchez, USMC, Norfolk, Va., 1558-46X.
Service Rifle Civilian — Richard C. Whiting, Waldorf, Md., 1519-27X.
Service Rifle Woman — PN3 Mary B. Feeney, USN, San Diego, Calif., 1507-22X.
Service Rifle Junior — John T. McNally, Ft. Meade, Md., 1476-24X.
Service Rifle Senior — MSG Gerritt H. Stekeur, NGUS, Latham, N. Y., 1538-43X.
Service Rifle Collegiate — William W. Safranek, Ft. Meade Md., 1496-22X.

U. S. NRA International Shooting Championships

English Match — PFC Victor Auer, USAR, Hollywood, Calif., 1783.
Smallbore 3-Position — Capt. Lanny Bassham, USA, Columbus, Ga., 3464.
Air Rifle — Capt. Lanny Bassham, USA, Columbus, Ga., 382.
Ladies Air Rifle — Sue Ann Sandusky, Ft. Worth, Tex., 368.
Junior Air Rifle — Janet Hays, Cincinnati, Ohio, 375.
Free Rifle, 300 Meter — Capt. Lanny Bassham, 3428.
Running Boar — Lt. Louis Theimer, USA, Columbus, Ga., 1675.
Running Boar Mixed Speed — Lt. Louis Theimer, 373.
Rapid Fire Pistol — PFC Melvin Makin, Salem, Ore., 1753.
Air Pistol — SFC Hershel Anderson, USA, Columbus, Ga., 388.
Ladies Air Pistol — SFC Barbara J. Hile, USA, Columbus, Ga., 376.
Junior Air Pistol — Victor Arambula, Commerce, Calif., 342. .
Center Fire Pistol — SFC Bonnie D. Harmon, USA, Columbus, Ga., 1776.
Ladies Smallbore Pistol — SFC Barbara J. Hile, 1745.

Ladies Standard Pistol — SFC Barbara J. Hile, 1669.
Standard Pistol — SFC Bonnie D. Harmon, 1715.
Free Pistol — SFC Hershel L. Anderson, USA, Columbus, Ga., 1672.
Ladies Standard Rifle Prone — Lt. Diana Zimmerman, USA, Columbus, Ga., 1761.
Standard Rifle 3-Position — Capt. Margaret Murdock, USAR, Topeka, Kan., 1727.
Clay Pigeon — Walter Zobell, Jackson, Montana, 294.
Ladies Clay Pigeon — Audrey Grosch, Minneapolis, 277.
Junior Clay Pigeon — Gary Rainey, Carlyle, Ill., 278.
International Skeet — John Satterwhite, USA, Issaqush, Wash., 296.
Ladies International Skeet — Claudia Butler, Virginia Beach, Va., 268.
Junior International Skeet — Bradley Simmons, Tyler, Tex., 288.

National Indoor Rifle & Pistol Championships

Conventional Rifle — William R. Rigby, Greenbelt, Md., 799.
Conventional Rifle Woman — Karen E. Monez, San Leandro, Calif., 798.
International Rifle — Capt. John H. Writer, USAR, Clarendon Hills, Ill., 596.
International Rifle Women — Capt. Margaret Murdock, USAR, Topeka, Kan., 587.
Conventional Pistol — SFC Bonnie D. Harmon, USA, Ft. Benning, Ga., 886.
Conventional Pistol Woman — SFC Barbara J. Hile, USA, Ft. Benning, Ga., 874.
International Pistol — SFC Hershel L. Anderson, USA, Ft. Benning, Ga., 573.
International Pistol Woman — Sharon Best, USA, Ft. Benning, Ga., 520.

National Intercollegiate Rifle & Pistol Championships

Conventional Rifle — Wanda R. Oliver, E. Wash. St., 300.
Conventional Rifle Woman — Wanda R. Oliver, 300.
Conventional Rifle ROTC — Wanda R. Oliver, 300.
International Rifle — Thomas E. Wassom, E. Tenn. St., 585.
International Rifle Woman — Wanda R. Oliver, 579.
International Rifle ROTC — Stephen B. Baumeister, Kemper Mil. Acad., 581.

Conventional Pistol — John S. Miller, Calif. St. Univ., 866.
Conventional Pistol Woman — Elizabeth C. Gathright, Univ. of Virginia, 824.
International Pistol — Stepehen C. Goldstein, MIT, 531.
International Pistol Woman — Elizabeth C. Gathright, 509.
International Pistol ROTC — Michael G. Woodcock, Colorado Coll., 521.

USLTA National Champions

Men's Singles

Year	Champion	Final Opponent	Year	Champion	Final Opponent
1920	Bill Tilden	William Johnston	1948	Pancho Gonzales	Eric Sturgess
1921	Bill Tilden	Wallace Johnston	1949	Pancho Gonzales	F. R. Schroeder, Jr.
1922	Bill Tilden	William Johnston	1950	Arthur Larsen	Herbert Flam
1923	Bill Tilden	William Johnston	1951	Frank Sedgman	E. Victor Seixas, Jr.
1924	Bill Tilden	William Johnston	1952	Frank Sedgman	Gardnar Mulloy
1925	Bill Tilden	William Johnston	1953	Tony Trabert	E. Victor Seixas, Jr.
1926	Rene Lacoste	Jean Borotra	1954	E. Victor Seixas, Jr.	Rex Hartwig
1927	Rene Lacoste	Bill Tilden	1955	Tony Trabert	Ken Rosewall
1928	Henri Cochet	Francis Hunter	1956	Kenneth Rosewall	Lewis Hoad
1929	Bill Tilden	Francis Hunter	1957	Malcolm Anderson	Ashley Cooper
1930	John Doeg	Francis Shields	1958	Ashley Cooper	Malcolm Anderson
1931	H. Ellsworth Vines	George Lott	1959	Neale A. Fraser	Alejandro Olmedo
1932	H. Ellsworth Vines	Henri Cochet	1960	Neale A. Fraser	Rod Laver
1933	Fred Perry	John Crawford	1961	Roy Emerson	Rod Laver
1934	Fred Perry	Wilmer Allison	1962	Rod Laver	Roy Emerson
1935	Wilmer Allison	Sidney Wood	1963	Rafael Osuna	F. A. Froehling, 3d
1936	Fred Perry	Don Budge	1964	Roy Emerson	Fred Stolle
1937	Don Budge	Baron G. von Cramm	1965	Manuel Santana	Cliff Drysdale
1938	Don Budge	C. Gene Mako	1966	Fred Stolle	John Newcombe
1939	Robert Riggs	S. Welby Van Horn	1967	John Newcombe	Clark Graebner
1940	Don McNeill	Robert Riggs	1968	Arthur Ashe	Tom Okker
1941	Robert Riggs	F. L. Kovacs	1969	Rod Laver	Tony Roche
1942	F. R. Schroeder, Jr.	Frank Parker	1970	Ken Rosewall	Tony Roche
1943	Joseph Hunt	Jack Kramer	1971	Stan Smith	Jan Kodes
1944	Frank Parker	William Talbert	1972	Ilie Nastase	Arthur Ashe
1945	Frank Parker	William Talbert	1973	John Newcombe	Jan Kodes
1946	Jack Kramer	Thomas Brown, Jr.	1974	Jimmy Connors	Ken Rosewall
1947	Jack Kramer	Frank Parker			

Men's Doubles

Year	Doubles Champions	Year	Doubles Champions
1920	William Johnston and Clarence Griffin	1948	Gardnar Mulloy and William Talbert
1921	Bill Tilden and Vincent Richards	1949	John Bromwich and William Sidwell
1922	Bill Tilden and Vincent Richards	1950	John Bromwich and Frank Sedgman
1923	Bill Tilden and Brian Norton	1951	Frank Sedgman and Kenneth McGregor
1924	Howard Kinsey and Robert Kinsey	1952	Mervyn Rose and E. Victor Seixas, Jr.
1925	R. Norris Williams and Vincent Richards	1953	Rex Hartwig and Mervyn Rose
1926	R. Norris Williams and Vincent Richards	1954	E. Victor Seixas, Jr. and Tony Trabert
1927	Bill Tilden and Francis Hunter	1955	Kosei Kamo and Atsushi Miyagi
1928	George Lott and John Hennessey	1956	Lewis Hoad and Kenneth Rosewall
1929	George Lott and John Doeg	1957	Ashley Cooper and Neale Fraser
1930	George Lott and John Doeg	1958	Hamilton Richardson and Alejandro Olmedo
1931	Wilmer Allison and John Van Ryn	1959	Neale A. Fraser and Roy Emerson
1932	H. Ellsworth Vines and Keith Gledhill	1960	Neale A. Fraser and Roy Emerson
1933	George Lott and Lester Stoefen	1961	Dennis Ralston and Chuck McKinley
1934	George Lott and Lester Stoefen	1962	Rafael Osuna and Antonio Palafox
1935	Wilmer Allison and John Van Ryn	1963	Dennis Ralston and Chuck McKinley
1936	Don Budge and C. Gene Mako	1964	Dennis Ralston and Chuck McKinley
1937	Baron G. von Cramm and Henner Henkel	1965	Roy Emerson and Fred Stolle
1938	Don Budge and C. Gene Mako	1966	Roy Emerson and Fred Stolle
1939	Adrian Quist and John Bromwich	1967	John Newcombe and Tony Roche
1940	Jack Kramer and Frederick Schroeder, Jr.	1968	Robert Lutz and Stan Smith
1941	Jack Kramer and Frederick Schroeder, Jr.	1969	Fred Stolle and Ken Rosewall
1942	Gardnar Mulloy and William Talbert	1970	Pierre Barthes and Nicki Pilic
1943	Jack Kramer and Frank Parker	1971	John Newcombe and Roger Taylor
1944	Don McNeill and Robert Falkenburg	1972	Cliff Drysdale and Roger Taylor
1945	Gardnar Mulloy and William Talbert	1973	John Newcombe and Owen Davidson
1946	Gardnar Mulloy and William Talbert	1974	Bob Lutz and Stan Smith
1947	Jack Kramer and Frederick Schroeder, Jr.		

Men's Indoor Champions

Year	Singles	Doubles	Year	Singles	Doubles
1962	Chas. McKinley	R. Laver-C. McKinley	1969	Stan Smith	Stan Smith-Robert Lutz
1963	Dennis Ralston	D. Ralston-C. McKinley	1970	Ilie Nastase	Stan Smith-Arthur Ashe
1964	Chas. McKinley	M. Santana-J. L. Arilla	1971	Clark Graebner	Juan Gisbert-Manuel Orantes
1965	Jan Erik Lundquist	D. Ralston-C. McKinley	1972	Stan Smith	Andres Gimeno-Manuel Orantes
1966	Charles Pasarell	Robert Lutz-Stan Smith	1973	Jimmy Connors	Juan Gisbert-Jurgen Fassbender
1967	Charles Pasarell	Arthur Ashe-Charles Pasarell	1974	Jimmy Connors	None
1968	Cliff Richey	Thomas Koch-Tom Okker			

Women's Indoor Champions

Year	Champion	Doubles Champions	Year	Champion	Doubles Champions
1962	Carole Wright	Ruth Jeffery & Belmar Gunderson	1969	Mary Ann E. Curtis	Mary Ann Eisel &
1963	Carol Hanks	Carol Hanks & Mary Ann Eisel			Valerie Ziegenfuss
1964	Mary Ann Eisel	Mary Ann Eisel & Katharine Hubbell	1970	Mary Ann E. Curtis	Peaches Bartkowicz &
1965	Nancy Richey	Carol Hanks Aucamp &			Nancy Richey
		Mary Ann Eisel	1971	Billie Jean King	Billie Jean King & Rosemary Casals
1966	Billie Jean King	Billie Jean King & Rosemary Casals	1972	Virginia Wade	Rosemary Casals & Virginia Wade
1967	Billie Jean King	Carol Hanks Aucamp &	1973	Evonne Goolagong	Olga Morozova & Marina Kroskina
		Mary Ann Eisel	1974	Billie Jean King	None
1968	Billie Jean King	Billie Jean King & Rosemary Casals			

Women's Singles, Doubles, Mixed Doubles

Year	Singles Champions	Doubles Champions	Mixed Doubles Champions
1935	Helen Jacobs	Helen Jacobs & Mrs.Sarah P. Fabyan	Mrs. Sarah P. Fabyan & Enrique Maier
1936	Alice Marble	Mrs. M. G. Van Ryn & Carolin Babcock	Alice Marble & C. Gene Mako
1937	Anita Lizana	Mrs. Sarah P. Fabyan & Alice Marble	Mrs. Sarah P. Fabyan & Don Budge
1938	Alice Marble	Alice Marble & Mrs. Sarah P. Fabyan	Alice Marble & Don Budge
1939	Alice Marble	Alice Marble & Mrs. Sarah P. Fabyan	Alice Marble & Harry Hopman
1940	Alice Marble	Alice Marble & Mrs. Sarah P. Fabyan	Alice Marble & Robert Riggs
1941	Mrs. Sarah P. Cooke	Mrs. S. P. Cooke & Margaret Osborne	Mrs. Sarah P. Cooke & Jack Kramer
1942	Pauline Betz	A. Louise Brough & Margaret Osborne	A. Louise Brough & Frederick Schroeder
1943	Pauline Betz	A. Louise Brough & Margaret Osborne	Margaret Osborne & William Talbert
1944	Pauline Betz	A. Louise Brough & Margaret Osborne	Margaret Osborne & William Talbert
1945	Sarah P. Cooke	A. Louise Brough & Margaret Osborne	Margaret Osborne & William Talbert
1946	Pauline Betz	A. Louise Brough & Margaret Osborne	Margaret Osborne & William Talbert
1947	A. Louise Brough	A. Louise Brough & Margaret Osborne	A. Louise Brough & John Bromwich
1948	Mrs. Margaret O. du Pont	A. Louise Brough & Mrs. M. O. du Pont	A. Louise Brough & Thomas Brown, Jr.
1949	Mrs. Margaret O. du Pont	A. Louise Brough & Mrs. M. O. du Pont	A. Louise Brough & Eric Sturgess
1950	Mrs. Margaret O. du Pont	A. Louise Brough & Mrs. M. O. du Pont	Mrs. M. O. du Pont & Kenneth MacGregor
1951	Maureen Connolly	Doris Hart & Shirley Fry	Doris Hart & Frank Sedgman
1952	Maureen Connolly	Doris Hart & Shirley Fry	Doris Hart & Frank Sedgman
1953	Maureen Connolly	Doris Hart & Shirley Fry	Doris Hart & E. Victor Seixas, Jr.
1954	Doris Hart	Doris Hart & Shirley Fry	Doris Hart & E. Victor Seixas, Jr.
1955	Doris Hart	A. Louise Brough & Mrs. M. O. du Pont	Doris Hart & E. Victor Seixas, Jr.
1956	Shirley J. Fry	A. Louise Brough & Mrs. M. O. du Pont	Mrs. M. O. duPont & Kenneth Rosewall
1957	Althea Gibson	A. Louise Brough & Mrs. M. O. du Pont	Althea Gibson and Kurt Nielsen
1958	Althea Gibson	Darlene Hard & Jeanne Arth	Mrs. M. O. du Pont & Neale Fraser
1959	Maria Bueno	Darlene Hard & Jeanne Arth	Mrs. M. O. du Pont & Neale Fraser
1960	Darlene Hard	Darlene Hard & Maria Bueno	Mrs. M. O. du Pont & Neale Fraser
1961	Darlene Hard	Darlene Hard & Lesley Turner	Margaret Smith & Robert Mark
1962	Margaret Smith	Maria Bueno & Darlene Hard	Margaret Smith & Fred Stolle
1963	Maria Bueno	Margaret Smith & Robyn Ebbern	Margaret Smith & Kenneth Fletcher
1964	Maria Bueno	Billie Jean Moffit & Karen Susman	Margaret Smith & John Newcombe
1965	Margaret Smith	Carole C. Graebner & Nancy Richey	Margaret Smith & Fred Stolle
1966	Maria Bueno	Maria Bueno & Nancy Richey	Donna Floyd Fales & Owen Davidson
1967	Billie Jean King	Rosemary Casals & Billie Jean King	Billie Jean King & Owen Davidson
1968	Virginia Wade	Maria Bueno & Margaret S. Court	Mary Ann Eisel & Peter Curtis
1969	Margaret Smith Court	Francoise Durr & Darlene Hard	Margaret S. Court & Marty Riessen
1970	Margaret Smith Court	M. S. Court & Judy Tegart Dalton	Margaret S. Court & Marty Riessen
1971	Billie Jean King	Rosemary Casals & Judy Tegart Dalton	Billie Jean King & Owen Davidson
1972	Billie Jean King	Francoise Durr & Betty Stove	Margaret S. Court & Marty Riessen
1973	Margaret Smith Court	Margaret S. Court & Virginia Wade	Billie Jean King & Owen Davidson
1974	Billie Jean King	Billie Jean King & Rosemary Casals	Pam Teeguarden & Geoff Masters

NCAA Tennis Champions

Year	Singles	College	Doubles	College
1964	Dennis Raltson	So. California	Dennis Ralston & Bill Bond	So. California
1965	Arthur Ashe	UCLA	Arthur Ashe & Ian Crookenden	UCLA
1966	Charles Pasarell	UCLA	Charles Pasarell & Ian Crookenden	UCLA
1967	Bob Lutz	So. Calif.	Stan Smith & Bob Lutz	So. Calif.
1968	Stan Smith	So. Calif.	Stan Smith & Bob Lutz	So. Calif.
1969	Joaquin Loyo Mayo	So. Calif.	Joaquin Loyo Mayo & Marcelo Lara	So. Calif.
1970	Jeff Borowiak	UCLA	Pat Cramer & Luis Garcia	Miami (Fla.)
1971	Jimmy Connors	UCLA	Jeff Borowiak & Haroon Rahim	UCLA
1972	Dick Stockton	Trinity (Tex.)	Sandy Mayer & Roscoe Tanner	Stanford
1973	Sandy Mayer	Stanford	Sandy Mayer & Jim Delaney	Stanford
1974	John Whitlinger	Stanford	John Whitlinger & Jim Delaney	Stanford

Clay Court Champions

Year	Champion	Year	Champion	Year	Champion	Year	Champion
1951	Tony Trabert	1957	E. Victor Seixas, Jr.	1963	Chuck McKinley	1969	Zeljko Franulovic
1952	Arthur Larsen	1958	Bernard Bartzen	1964	Dennis Ralston	1970	Cliff Richey
1953	E. Vic Seixas, Jr.	1959	Bernard Bartzen	1965	Dennis Ralston	1971	Zeljko Franulovic
1954	Bernard Bartzen	1960	Barry MacKay	1966	Cliff Richey	1972	Bob Hewitt
1955	Tony Trabert	1961	Bernard Bartzen	1967	Arthur Ashe	1973	Manuel Orantes
1956	Herbert Flam	1962	Chuck McKinley	1968	Clark Graebner	1974	Jimmy Connors

Davis Cup International Tennis—Challenge Round

Year	Winner	Loser	Score	Year	Winner	Loser	Score	Year	Winner	Loser	Score
1900	U.S.	Brit. Isles	3-0	1927	France	U.S.	3-2	1953	Australia	U.S.	3-2
1902	U.S.	Brit. Isles	3-2	1928	France	U.S.	4-1	1954	U.S.	Australia	3-2
1903	British	U.S.	4-1	1929	France	U.S.	3-2	1955	Australia	U.S.	5-0
1904	British	Belgium	5-0	1930	France	U.S.	4-1	1956	Australia	U.S.	5-0
1905	British	U.S.	5-0	1931	France	Gt. Britain	3-2	1957	Australia	U.S.	3-2
1906	British	U.S.	5-0	1932	France	U.S.	3-2	1958	U.S.	Australia	3-2
1907	Australasia	British	3-2	1933	Gt. Britain	France	3-2	1959	Australia	U.S.	3-2
1908	Australasia	U.S.	3-2	1934	Gt. Britain	U.S.	4-1	1960	Australia	Italy	4-1
1909	Australasia	U.S.	3-2	1935	Gt. Britain	U.S.	5-0	1961	Australia	Italy	5-0
1911	Australasia	U.S.	5-0	1936	Gt. Britain	Australia	3-2	1962	Australia	Mexico	5-0
1912	British	Australasia	3-2	1937	U.S.	Gt. Britain	4-1	1963	U.S.	Australia	3-2
1913	U.S.	British	3-2	1938	U.S.	Australia	3-2	1964	Australia	U.S.	3-2
1914	Australasia	U.S.	3-2	1939	Australia	U.S.	3-2	1965	Australia	Spain	4-1
1919	Australasia	British	4-1	1940-1945 (Not played)				1966	Australia	India	4-1
1920	U.S.	Australasia	5-0	1946	U.S.	Australia	5-0	1967	Australia	Spain	4-1
1921	U.S.	Japan	5-0	1947	U.S.	Australia	4-1	1968	U.S.	Australia	4-1
1922	U.S.	Australasia	4-1	1948	U.S.	Australia	5-0	1969	U.S.	Romania	5-0
1923	U.S.	Australasia	4-1	1949	U.S.	Australia	4-1	1970	U.S.	W. Germany	5-0
1924	U.S.	Australasia	5-0	1950	Australia	U.S.	4-1	1971	U.S.	Romania	3-2
1925	U.S.	France	5-0	1951	Australia	U.S.	3-2	1972	U.S.	Romania	3-2
1926	U.S.	France	4-1	1952	Australia	U.S.	4-1	1973	Australia	U.S.	5-0

British (Wimbledon) Champions

Inaugurated 1877

Year	Men's Singles	Women's Singles	Year	Men's Singles	Women's Singles
1946	Yvon Petra	Pauline Betz	1961	Rod Laver	Angela Mortimer
1947	Jack Kramer	Margaret Osborne	1962	Rod Laver	Karen Hantze Susman
1948	Bob Falkenburg	A. Louise Brough	1963	Chuck McKinley	Margaret Smith
1949	Fred R. Schroeder	A. Louise Brough	1964	Roy Emerson	Maria Bueno
1950	Budge Patty	A. Louise Brough	1965	Roy Emerson	Margaret Smith
1951	Dick Savitt	Doris Hart	1966	Manuel Santana	Billie Jean King
1952	Frank Sedgman	Maureen Connolly	1967	John Newcombe	Billie Jean King
1953	Victor Seixas	Maureen Connolly	1968	Rod Laver	Billie Jean King
1954	Jaroslav Drobny	Maureen Connolly	1969	Rod Laver	Ann Jones
1955	Tony Trabert	A. Louise Brough	1970	John Newcombe	Margaret S. Court
1956	Lewis Hoad	Shirley Fry	1971	John Newcombe	Evonne Goolagong
1957	Lewis Hoad	Althea Gibson	1972	Stan Smith	Billie Jean King
1958	Ashley Cooper	Althea Gibson	1973	Jan Kodes	Billie Jean King
1959	Alex Olmedo	Maria Bueno	1974	Jimmy Connors	Chris Evert
1960	Neale Fraser	Maria Bueno			

National Junior Tennis Champions

Junior Singles
1968 Bob McKinley
1969 Eric Van Dillen
1970 Brian Gottfried
1971 Raul Ramirez
1972 Patrick DuPre
1973 Billy Martin
1974 Ferd Taygan

Junior Doubles
1968 Bob McKinley and F. D. Robbins
1969 Richard Stockton and Eric Van Dillen
1970 Brian Gottfried and Alex Mayer, Jr.
1971 Jim Delaney and Chip Fisher
1972 Steve Mott and Brian Teachar
1973 Billy Martin and Trey Waltke
1974 Francisco Gonzalez and Rocky Maguire

Boys' 16 Singles
1968 Jimmy Connors
1969 James Hagey
1970 Freddy DeJesus
1971 Billy Martin
1972 Bill Maze
1973 Ben McKnown
1974 Walter Redondo

Boys' 16 Doubles
1968 James Hagey and Robert Kreiss
1969 James E. Delaney, 3rd, and Chip Fisher
1970 Freddy DeJesus and John Whitlinger
1971 Billy Martin and Trey Waltke
1972 Bruce Manson and Perry Wright
1973 Nial Brash and Matt Mitchell
1974 Jeff Robbins and Van Winitsky

Girls' 18 Singles
1968 Kristy Pigeon
1969 Sharon Walsh
1970 Sharon Walsh
1971 Chris Evert
1972 Ann Kiyomura
1973 Carrie Fleming
1974 Rayni Fox

Girls' 18 Doubles
1968 Kristy Pigeon and Denise Carter
1969 Gail Hansen and Patty Ann Reese
1970 Kristien Kemmer and Nancy Ornstein
1971 Janet Newberry and Eliza Pande
1972 Marita Redondo and Laurie Tenney
1973 Susan Boyle and Kathy May
1974 Anne Bruning and Barbara Hallquist

Girls' 16 Singles
1968 Janet Newberry
1969 Eliza Pande
1970 Chris Evert
1971 Carrie Fleming
1972 Marita Redondo
1973 Betsy Nagelson
1974 Zenda Leiss

Girls' 16 Doubles
1968 Kristine Kemmer and Janet Newberry
1969 Chris Evert and Susan Epstein
1970 Barbara Downs and Ann Kiyomura
1971 Ann Kiyomura and Marita Redondo
1972 Jeanne Evert and Kathy Kendall
1973 Susan Mehmedbasich and Robin Tenney
1974 Sherry Acker and Anne Smith

Tennis Championships in 1974

Australian Open (Melbourne) — Men's Singles: Jimmy Connors; Men's Doubles: Case and Masters; Women's Singles: Evonne Goolagong; Women's Doubles: Goolagong and Michel.

Italian Open (Rome) — Men's Singles: Bjorn Borg; Men's Doubles: Ramirez and Gottfried; Women's Singles: Chris Evert; Women's Doubles: Evert and Morozova.

French Open (Paris) — Men's Singles: Bjorn Borg; Men's Doubles: Crealy and Parun; Women's Singles: Chris Evert;

Women's Doubles: Navratilova and Molina.

Virginia Slims of Newport — Singles: Chris Evert; Doubles: Heldman and Chanfreau.

Women's Collegiates — Singles: Jane Stratton; Doubles: Ann Lebedeff and Karen Reinke.

Federation Cup — Women's teams of all nations — Final Round — Australia defeated U.S. 2-1.

Tennis Prize Money Winners, 1973

	Men			Women	
1.	Ilie Nastase, Romania	$228,750	1.	Margaret Court, Australia	$180,058
2.	Stan Smith, United States	204,225	2.	Chris Evert, United States	142,949
3.	Tom Okker, Netherlands	173,500	3.	Rosemary Casals, United States	89,625
4.	Jimmy Connors, United States	156,400	4.	Evonne Goolagong, Australia	75,029
5.	John Newcombe, Australia	133,050	5.	Billie Jean King, United States	69,675
6.	Arthur Ashe, United States	127,850	6.	Virginia Wade, England	62,019
7.	Rod Laver, Australia	120,125	7.	Kerry Melville, Australia	59,672
8.	Ken Rosewall, Australia	110,950	8.	Nancy Gunter, United States	43,112
9.	Manuel Orantes, Spain	97,175	9.	Helga Masthoff, West Germany	38,035
10.	Brian Gottfried, United States	87,850	10.	Betty Stove, Netherlands	33,475

World Team Tennis

The Denver Racquets won the 1974 World Team Tennis Championship by defeating the Philadelphia Freedoms in two straight matches, 27-21, 28-24. Andrew Pattison of Denver was voted the most valuable player.

World Championship Tennis, 1974

Date	Event, City	Singles Winner	Doubles
Jan. 21-27	U.S. Pro Indoor Championships (all groups), Philadelphia	Rod Laver	Pat Cramer-Mike Estep

Red Group

Jan. 28-Feb. 3	Fidelity, Richmond, Va.	Ilie Nastase	Nikki Pilic-Phil Dent
Feb. 11-17	Rothmans International, Toronto	Tom Okker	Raul Ramirez-Tony Roche
Feb. 25-Mar. 3	Saga Bay Classic, Miami	Cliff Drysdale	John Alexander-Phil Dent
Mar. 13-17	Xerox Classic, Washington, D.C.	Ilie Nastase	Bob Hewitt-Frew McMillan
Mar. 25-31	Algemene Bank Nederland, Rotterdam	Tom Okker	Bob Hewitt-Frew McMillan
Apr. 1-7	Pool-Data Pro Championships, Munich	Frew McMillan	Bob Hewitt-Frew McMillan
Apr. 8-14	Marlboro Classic, Monte Carlo	Andrew Pattison	John Alexander-Phil Dent
Apr. 15-23	Clows Classic, Johannesburg	Andrew Pattison	Bob Hewitt-Frew McMillan

Green Group

Feb. 11-17	Astor Cup, Bologna	Arthur Ashe	Ove Bengtson-Bjorn Borg
Feb. 18-24	Rothmans International, Wales & London	Bjorn Borg	Ove Bengtson-Bjorn Borg
Feb. 25-Mar. 3	Winston Indoor Classic, Barcelona	Arthur Ashe	Arthur Ashe-Roscoe Tanner
Mar. 11-17	Copersucar Uniao, Sao Paulo	Bjorn Borg	Adriano Panatta-Ion Tiriac
Mar. 25-31	Kemper International Desert Classic, Palm Desert	Rod Laver	Jan Kodes-Vladimir Zednik
Apr. 8-14	Kawasaki Classic, Tokyo	Rod Laver	Ray Moore-Onny Parun
Apr. 15-21	River Oaks-American General, Houston	Rod Laver	Colin Didley-Rod Laver
Apr. 22-28	United Bank Classic, Denver	Roscoe Tanner	Arthur Ashe-Roscoe Tanner

Blue Group

Feb. 4-10	Raymond Jones Classic, St. Petersburg	John Newcombe	Owen Davidson-John Newcombe
Feb. 18-24	WCT for CHILD, Nassau, N.Y.	Stan Smith	Jeff Borowiak-Dick Crealy
Feb. 25-Mar. 3	Michelob Pro-Celebrity, La Costa	John Newcombe	Clark Graebner-Charlie Pasarell
Mar. 25-31	Peachtree Corners—1st National Bank Classic, Atlanta	Dick Stockton	Bob Lutz-Stan Smith
Apr. 1-7	Hibernia Bank Classic, New Orleans	John Newcombe	Bob Lutz-Stan Smith
Apr. 8-14	The Classic, Orlando	John Newcombe	Owen Davidson-John Newcombe
Apr. 15-21	NCNB Classic, Charlotte	Jeff Borowiak	Buster Mottram-Raul Ramirez
Apr. 22-28	Holton Classic, St. Louis	Stan Smith	Ismail El Shafei-Brian Fairlie

WCT Final Championship Summaries

Singles Quarterfinals

Smith defeated Laver 6-7, 6-4, 6-4, 7-5
Newcombe defeated Okker 6-3, 6-3, 6-2
Kodes defeated Nastase 7-6, 6-1, 7-5
Borg defeated Ashe 7-5, 6-4, 7-6

Semifinals

Newcombe defeated Smith 6-1, 3-6, 7-6, 6-2
Borg defeated Kodes 4-6, 6-4, 6-3, 6-2

Third Place

Smith defeated Kodes 6-4, 7-6

Finals

Newcombe defeated Borg 4-6, 6-3, 6-3, 6-2

Doubles Quarterfinals

Davidson/Newcombe defeated Graebner/Pasarell 7-5, 7-6, 6-2
Lutz/Smith defeated Alexander/Dent 7-6, 6-3, 6-3
Ashe/Tanner defeated Case/Masters 7-6, 3-6, 7-6, 7-5
Hewitt/McMillan defeated Bengston/Borg 6-4, 7-6, 3-6, 6-3

Semifinals

Davidson/Newcombe defeated Lutz/Smith 6-4, 6-4, 6-7, 7-6
Hewitt/McMillan defeated Ashe/Tanner 7-5, 6-4, 6-4

Finals

Hewitt/McMillan defeated Davidson/Newcombe 6-2, 6-7, 6-1, 6-2

The America's Cup

Competition for the America's Cup grew out of the first contest to establish a world yachting championship, one of the carnival features of the London Exposition of 1851. The race, open to all classes of yachts from all over the world, covered a 60-mile course around the Isle of Wight, the prize was a cup worth about $500, donated by the Royal Yacht Squadron of England, known as the "America's Cup" because it was first won by the United States yacht America. Successive efforts of British and Australian yachtsmen have failed to win the famous trophy, which remains in the United States.

On Sept. 17, 1974, the 66-foot 12-Meter yacht Courageous won a fourth straight victory over the Australian challenger, Southern Cross, to keep the symbol of world sailing supremacy in the United States. In four races, Southern Cross lost to Courageous by a total of 18 minutes 51 seconds. The U.S. yacht was designed by Olin Stephens and skippered by Ted Hood.

Winners of the America's Cup

1851	America	1901	Columbia defeated Shamrock II, England, (3-0)
1870	Magic defeated Cambria, England, (1-0)	1903	Reliance defeated Shamrock III, England, (3-0)
1871	Columbia (first three races) and Sappho (last two races) defeated Livonia, England, (4-1)	1920	Resolute defeated Shamrock IV, England, (3-2)
		1930	Enterprise defeated Shamrock V, England, (4-0)
1876	Madeline defeated Countess of Dufferin, Canada, (2-0)	1934	Rainbow defeated Endeavour, England, (4-2)
1881	Mischief defeated Atalanta, Canada, (2-0)	1937	Ranger defeated Endeavour II, England, (4-0)
1885	Puritan defeated Genesta, England, (2-0)	1958	Columbia defeated Sceptre, England, (4-0)
1886	Mayflower defeated Galatea, England, (2-0)	1962	Weatherly defeated Gretel, Australia, (4-1)
1887	Volunteer defeated Thistle, Scotland, (2-0)	1964	Constellation defeated Sovereign, England, (4-0)
1893	Vigliant defeated Valkyrie II, England, (3-0)	1967	Intrepid defeated Dame Pattie, Australia, (4-0)
1895	Defender defeated Valkyrie III, England, (3-0)	1970	Intrepid defeated Gretel, II, Australia, (4-1)
1899	Columbia defeated Shamrock, England, (3-0)	1974	Courageous defeated Southern Cross, (4-0)

Auto Racing

Indianapolis 500 Winners

Year	Winner	Chassis	Engine	MPH	Gross	Runner up
1940	Wilbur Shaw	Maserati	Maserati	114.277	$85,525	Rex Mays
1941	Floyd Davis, Mauri Rose	Wetteroth	Offenhauser	115.117	90,925	Rex Mays
1946	George Robson	Adams	Sparks	114.820	115,450	Jimmy Jackson
1947	Mauri Rose	Deidt	Offenhauser	116.338	137,425	Bill Holland
1948	Mauri Rose	Deidt	Offenhauser	119.814	171,075	Bill Holland
1949	Bill Holland	Deidt	Offenhauser	121.327	179,050	Johnnie Parsons
1950	Johnnie Parsons	Kurtis Kraft	Offenhauser	124.002(a)	201,135	Bill Holland
1951	Lee Wallard	Kurtis Kraft	Offenhauser	126.244	207,650	Mike Nazaruk
1952	Troy Ruttman	Kuzma	Offenhauser	128.922	230,100	Jim Rathmann
1953	Bill Vukovich	Kurtis Kraft 500A	Offenhauser	128.740	246,300	Art Cross
1954	Bill Vukovich	Kurtis Kraft 500A	Offenhauser	130.840	269,375	Jim Bryan
1955	Bob Sweikert	Kurtis Kraft 500C	Offenhauser	128.209	270,400	Tony Bettenhausen
1956	Pat Flaherty	Watson	Offenhauser	128.490	282,052	Sam Hanks
1957	Sam Hanks	Epperly	Offenhauser	135.601	300,252	Jim Rathmann
1958	Jimmy Bryan	Epperly	Offenhauser	133.791	305,217	George Amick
1959	Rodger Ward	Watson	Offenhauser	135.857	338,100	Jim Rathmann
1960	Jim Rathmann	Watson	Offenhauser	138.767	369,150	Rodger Ward
1961	A. J. Foyt	Watson	Offenhauser	139.130	400,000	Eddie Sachs
1962	Rodger Ward	Watson	Offenhauser	140.293	426,152	Len Sutton
1963	Parnelli Jones	Watson	Offenhauser	143.137	494,031	Jim Clark
1964	A. J. Foyt	Watson	Offenhauser	147.350	506,625	Rodger Ward
1965	Jim Clark	Lotus	Ford	151.388	628,399	Parnelli Jones
1966	Graham Hill	Lola	Ford	144.317	691,809	Jim Clark
1967	A. J. Foyt	Coyote	Ford	151.207	737,109	Al Unser
1968	Bobby Unser	Eagle	Offenhauser	152.882	809,627	Dan Gurney
1969	Mario Andretti	Hawk	Ford	156.867	805,127	Dan Gurney
1970	Al Unser	P. J. Colt	Ford	155.749	1,000,002	Mark Donohue
1971	Al Unser	P. J. Colt	Ford	157.735	1,001,604	Peter Revson
1972	Mark Donohue	McLaren	Offenhauser	163.465	1,011,846	Al Unser
1973	Gordon Johncock	Eagle	Offenhauser	159.014(b)	1,006,105	Billy Vukovich
1974	Johnny Rutherford	McLaren	Offenhauser	158.589	1,015,686	Bobby Unser

(a) 345 miles. (b) 332.5 miles. Race Record—163.465 MPH, Mark Donohue, 1972.

1974 Indianapolis 500 Standings

1—Johnny Rutherford, Fort Worth, Tex., McLaren-Offy, 200 laps, 158.589 miles per hour average.
2—Bobby Unser, Albuquerque, N. M., Eagle-Offy, 200 laps.
3—Bill Vukovich, Fresno, Calif., Eagle-Offy, 199 laps.
4—Gordon Johncock, Phoenix, Ariz., Eagle-Offy, 199 laps.
5—David Hobbs, Upper Boddington, England, McLaren-Offy, 196 laps.
6—Jim McElreath, Arlington, Tex., Eagle-Offy, 195 laps.
7—Pancho Carter, Huntington Beach, Calif., Eagle-Offy, 191 laps.
8—Bob Harkey, Indianapolis, Eagle-Foyt, 190 laps.
9—Lloyd Ruby, Wichita Falls, Tex., Eagle-Offy, 187 laps.
10—Jerry Grant, Irvine, Calif., Eagle-Offy, 175 laps.
11—John Martin, Long Beach, Calif., McLaren-Offy, 169 laps.
12—Tom Bigelow, Whitewater, Wis., Vollstedt-Offy, 162 laps.
13—Bill Simpson, Hermosa Beach, Calif., Eagle- Offy, 162 laps.
14—Mike Hiss, Tustin, Calif., McLaren-Offy, 159 laps.
15—A. J. Foyt Jr., Houston, Coyote-Foyt, 141 laps, transmission trouble.

World's Land Speed Records—Evolution of the Mile Record

Date	Driver	Car	MPH	Date	Driver	Car	MPH
12/18/98	Chassenloup-Laubat	Jeantaud	39.24	4/22/28	Keech	White Triplex	207.552
4/29/99	Jenatzy	Jamais Contente		3/11/29	Seagrave	Irving-Napier	231.446
		Jenatzy	65.79	2/ 5/31	Campbell	Napier-Campbell	246.086
11/17/02	Augieres	Mars	77.13	2/24/32	Campbell	Napier-Campbell	253.96
11/ 5/03	Duray	Gabron-Brillie	84.73	2/22/33	Campbell	Napier-Campbell	272.109
12/30/04	Barras	Darracq	109.65	9/ 3/35	Campbell	Bluebird Spl.	301.13
1/25/05	Bowden	Mercedes	109.75	11/19/37	Eyston	Thunderbolt #1	311.42
1/26/06	Marriott	Stanley (Steam)	127.659	9/16/38	Eyston	Thunderbolt #1	357.5
3/16/10	Oldfield	Benz	131.724	8/23/39	Cobb	Railton	368.9
4/23/11	Burman	Benz	141.732	9/16/47	Cobb	Railton-Mobil	394.2
2/12/19	DePalma	Packard	149.875	8/ 5/63	Breedlove	Spirit of America	407.45
4/27/20	Milton	Dusenberg	155.046	10/27/64	Arfons	Green Monster	536.71
4/28/26	Parry- Thomas	Thomas Spl.	170.624	11/15/65	Breedlove	Spirit of America	600.601
3/29/27	Seagrave	Sunbeam	203.790	10/23/70	Gary Gabelich	Blue Flame	622.407

World Grand Prix Champions

Year	Driver	Year	Driver	Year	Driver
1950	Nino Farina, Italy	1958	Mike Hawthorne, England	1966	Jack Brabham, Australia
1951	Juan Fangio, Argentina	1959	Jack Brabham, Australia	1967	Denis Hulme, New Zealand
1952	Alberto Ascari, Italy	1960	Jack Brabham, Australia	1968	Graham Hill, England
1953	Alberto Ascari, Italy	1961	Phil Hill, United States	1969	Jackie Stewart, Scotland
1954	Juan Fangio, Argentina	1962	Graham Hill, England	1970	Jochen Rindt, Austria
1955	Juan Fangio, Argentina	1963	Jim Clark, Scotland	1971	Jackie Stewart, Scotland
1956	Juan Fangio, Argentina	1964	John Surtees, England	1972	Emerson Fittipaldi, Brazil
1957	Juan Fangio, Argentina	1965	Jim Clark, Scotland	1973	Jackie Stewart, Scotland

U.S. Auto Club National Champion

Year	Driver	Year	Driver	Year	Driver	Year	Driver
1950	Henry Banks	1956	Jimmy Bryan	1962	Rodger Ward	1968	Bobby Unser
1951	Tony Bettenhausen	1957	Jimmy Bryan	1963	A. J. Foyt	1969	Mario Andretti
1952	Chuck Stevenson	1958	Tony Bettenhausen	1964	A. J. Foyt	1970	Al Unser
1953	Sam Hawks	1959	Rodger Ward	1965	Mario Andretti	1971	Joe Leonard
1954	Jimmy Bryan	1960	A. J. Foyt	1966	Mario Andretti	1972	Joe Leonard
1955	Bob Sweikert	1961	A. J. Foyt	1967	A. J. Foyt	1973	Roger McCluskey

Grand Prix for Formula 1 Cars, 1974

Grand Prix	Winner, Car
Argentine	Denis Hulme, McLaren
Austrian	Carlos Reutemann, Brabham
Belgian	Emerson Fittipaldi, McLaren
British	Jody Scheckter, Tyrrell-Ford
Brazilian	Emerson Fittipaldi, Tyrrell-Ford
Canadian	Emerson Fittipaldi, McLaren-Ford
Dutch	Niki Lauda, Ferrari
French	Ronnie Peterson, JPS-Lotus

Grand Prix	Winner, Car
German	Clay Regazzon. Ferrari
Italian	Ronnie Peterson, Lotus
Monte Carlo	Ronnie Peterson, Lotus
South African	Carlos Reutemann, Brabham BT44
Spanish	Niki Lauda, Ferrari
Swedish	Jody Scheckter, Tyrrell-Ford
United States	Carlos Reutemann, Brabham-Ford

NASCAR Racing in 1974
Winston Cup Grand National Races

Date	Race & Site	Winner	Car	Money Won
Jan. 26	Winston Western 500, Riverside, Calif.	Cale Yarborough	Chevrolet	$16,325
Feb. 17	Daytona 500, Daytona Beach, Fla.	Richard Petty	Dodge	34,100
Feb. 24	Richmond 500, Richmond, Va.	Bobby Allison	Chevrolet	6,330
Mar. 3	Carolina 500, Rockingham, N.C.	Richard Petty	Dodge	15,025
Mar. 17	Southeastern 500, Bristol, Tenn.	Cale Yarborough	Chevrolet	6,655
Mar. 24	Atlanta 500, Atlanta, Ga.	Cale Yarborough	Chevrolet	15,560
Apr. 7	Rebel 500, Darlington, S.C.	David Pearson	Mercury	16,075
Apr. 21	Gwyn Staley 400, No. Wilkesboro, N.C.	Richard Petty	Dodge	6,250
Apr. 28	Virginia 500, Martinsville, Va.	Cale Yarborough	Chevrolet	18,000
May 5	Winston 500, Talladega, Ala.	David Pearson	Mercury	20,285
May 11	Music City USA 420, Nashville Tenn.	Richard Petty	Dodge	5,990
May 19	Mason-Dixon 500, Dover, Del.	Cale Yarborough	Chevrolet	15,300
May 26	World 600, Charlotte, N.C.	David Pearson	Mercury	25,900
June 9	Tuborg 400, Riverside, Calif.	Cale Yarborough	Chevrolet	14,925
June 16	Motorstate 400, Irish Hills, Mich.	Richard Petty	Dodge	14,190
July 4	Firecracker 400, Daytona Beach, Fla.	David Pearson	Mercury	16,850
July 14	Volunteer 500, Bristol, Tenn.	Cale Yarborough	Chevrolet	5,725
July 20	Nashville 420, Nashville Tenn.	Cale Yarborough	Chevrolet	6,025
July 28	Dixie 500, Atlanta, Ga.	Richard Petty	Dodge	16,350
Aug. 4	Purolator 500, Pocono, Pa.	Richard Petty	Dodge	14,000
Aug. 11	Talladega 500, Talladega, Ala.	Richard Petty	Dodge	21,465
Aug. 25	Yankee 400, Brooklyn, Mich.	David Pearson	Mercury	15,265
Sept. 2	Southern 500, Darlington, S.C.	Cale Yarborough	Chevrolet	25,000
Sept. 8	Capital City 500, Richmond, Va.	Richard Petty	Dodge	6,740
Sept. 15	Delaware 500, Dover, Del.	Richard Petty	Dodge	15,175
Sept. 22	Wilkes 400, No. Wilkesboro N.C.	Cale Yarborough	Chevrolet	7,275
Sept. 29	Old Dominion 500, Martinsville Va.	Earl Ross	Chevrolet	14.300

Daytona 500 Winners

Year	Driver (Car)	Avg. MPH	Year	Driver (Car)	Avg. MPH
1959	L. Petty (Oldsmobile)	135.521	1967	M. Andretti (Ford)	146.926
1960	J. Johnson (Chevrolet)	124.740	1968	C. Yarborough (Mercury)	143.251
1961	M. Panch (Pontiac)	149.601	1969	L. Yarborough (Ford)	160.875
1962	F. Roberts (Pontiac)	152.529	1970	P. Hamilton (Plymouth)	149.601
1963	T. Lund (Ford)	151.566	1971	R. Petty (Plymouth)	144.456
1964	R. Petty (Plymouth)	154.334	1972	A. J. Foyt (Mercury)	161.550
(a)1965	F. Lorenzen (Ford)	141.539	1973	R. Petty (Dodge)	157.205
(b)1966	R. Petty (Plymouth)	160.627	(c)1974	R. Petty (Dodge)	140.894

(a)322.5 miles because of rain. (b)495 miles because of rain. (c)450 miles.

1974 Leading Daytona 500 Finishers

Driver—Car	Laps	Purse	Driver—Car	Laps	Purse
1—Richard Petty, Dodge	200	$36,650	6—Donnie Allison, Chevrolet	199	$7,150
2—Cale Yarborough, Chevrolet	200	18,250	7—Darrell Waltrip, Chevrolet	199	5,900
3—Ramo Stott, Chevrolet	200	11,300	8—Bobby Isaac, Chevrolet	198	6,825
4—Coo Coo Marlin, Chevrolet	200	8,350	9—Dick Brooks, Dodge	197	5,050
5—A. J. Foyt, Chevrolet	199	8,465	10—Walter Balpard, Chevrolet	197	4,910

Grand National Champions (NASCAR)

Year	Driver (Car)	Year	Driver (Car)	Year	Driver (Car)
1949	R. Byron (Oldsmobile)	1957	E. Baker (Chevrolet)	1965	N. Jarrett (Ford)
1950	W. Rexford (Oldsmobile)	1958	L. Petty (Oldsmobile)	1966	D. Pearson (Dodge)
1951	H. Thomas (Ply.-Hudson)	1959	L. Petty (Olds.-Plymouth)	1967	R. Petty (Plymouth)
1952	T. Flock (Hudson)	1960	R. White (Chevrolet)	1968	D. Pearson (Ford)
1953	H. Thomas (Hudson)	1961	N. Jarrett (Chevrolet)	1969	D. Pearson (Ford)
1954	L. Petty (Chrysler)	1962	J. Weatherly (Pontiac)	1970	B. Isaac (Dodge)
1955	T. Flock (Chrysler)	1963	J. Weatherly (Pontiac-Mercury)	1971	R. Petty (Plymouth)
1956	E. Baker (Chrysler-Dodge)	1964	R. Petty (Plymouth)	1972	R. Petty (Plymouth)

Motorcycle Racing
Grand National Champion

Year	Champion	Year	Champion	Year	Champion	Year	Champion
1950	Larry Headrick	1956	Joe Leonard	1962	Bart Markel	1968	Gary Nixon
1951	Bobby Hill	1957	Joe Leonard	1963	Dick Mann	1969	Mert Lawwill
1952	Bobby Hill	1958	Carroll Resweber	1964	Roger Reiman	1970	Gene Romero
1953	Bill Tuman	1959	Carroll Resweber	1965	Bart Markel	1971	Dick Mann
1954	Joe Leonard	1960	Carroll Resweber	1966	Bart Markel	1972	Mark Brelsford
1955	Brad Andres	1961	Carroll Resweber	1967	Gary Nixon	1973	Ken Roberts

Power Boat Racing Champions
APBA Gold Cup Race

Year	Boat	Owner	Driver	Winner's fastest heat	Site
1959	Maverick	W. T. Waggoner, Jr.	Bill Stead	106.278	Seattle, Wash.
1961	Miss Century 21	Willard Rhodes	Bill Muncey	102.399	Reno, Nev.
1962	Miss Century 21	Willard Rhodes	Bill Muncey	101.446	Seattle, Wash.
1963	Miss Bardahl	Ole Bardahl	Ron Musson	114.650	Detroit, Mich.
1964	Miss Bardahl	Ole Bardahl	Ron Musson	108.104	Detroit, Mich.
1965	Miss Bardahl	Ole Bardahl	Ron Musson	110.655	Seattle, Wash.
1966	Tahoe Miss	Harrah's	Mira Slovak	97.861	Detroit, Mich.
1967	Miss Bardahl	Ole Bardahl	Bill Schumacher	104.691	Seattle, Wash.
1968	Miss Bardahl	Ole Bardahl	Bill Schumacher		Detroit, Mich.
1969	Miss Budweiser	Bernard Little & Tom Friedkin	Bill Sterett	103.587	San Diego, Calif.
1970	Miss Budweiser	Hydroplanes, Inc.	Dean Chenoweth	101.848	San Diego, Calif.
1971	Miss Madison	Miss Madison, Inc.	Jim McCormick	101.522	Madison, Ind.
1972	Atlas Van Lines	Atlas Van Lines	Bill Muncey	103.547	Detroit, Mich.
1973	Miss Budweiser	Hydroplanes, Inc.	Dean Chenoweth	104.046	Tri-Cities, Wash.
1974	Pay'N Pak	David J. Heerensperger	George Henley	112.056	Seattle, Wash.

Skiing in 1974
World Alpine Ski Championships

Men's Downhill—David Zwilling, Austria. **Time—1:56.98.**
Men's Slalom—Gustavo Thoeni, Italy. **Time—109.98 sec.**
Men's Giant Slalom—Gustavo Thoeni. **Time—3:07.92.**
Women's Downhill—Annemarie Proell-Moser, Austria. **Time—1:50.84.**

Women's Slalom—Hanni Wenzel, Lichtenstein. **Time—94.63 sec.**
Women's Giant Slalom—Fabienne Serrat, France. **Time—1:43.18.**

World Nordic Ski Championships
Falun, Sweden

Men's 15 km Cross-Country—Magne Myromo, Norway. **Time—41:39.10.**
Men's 30 km Cross-Country—Thomas Magnusson, Sweden. **Time—1:33:41.41.**
Men's 50 km Cross-Country—Gerhard Grimmer, E. Germany. **Time—2:19:45.56.**
Men's Nordic Combined (15 km Cross-Country and jumping)—Ullrich Wheling, E. Germany. **421.14 pts.**

Men's 70 Meter Ski Jump—Hans Georg Aschenbach, E. Germany. **248.9 pts.**
Men's 90 Meter Ski Jump—Hans Georg Aschenbach. **240.4 pts.**
Women's 5 km Cross-Country—Galina Kulakova, USSR. **Time—15:17.42.**
Women's 10 km Cross-Country—Galina Kulakova. **Time—31:25.79.**

The World Cup Winners

Men	Women
1967—Jean Claude Killy, France	1967—Nancy Greene, Canada
1968—Jean Claude Killy, France	1968—Nancy Greene, Canada
1969—Karl Schranz, Austria	1969—Gertrud Gabi, Austria
1970—Karl Schranz, Austria	1970—Michele Jacot, France
1971—Gustavo Thoeni, Italy	1971—Annemarie Proell, Austria
1972—Gustavo Thoeni, Italy	1972—Annemarie Proell, Austria
1973—Gustavo Thoeni, Italy	1973—Annemarie Proell, Austria
1974—Piero Gros, France	1974—Annemarie Proell-Moser, Austria

Stadiums

For stadiums that house a major league baseball team and college stadiums see index.

Name and location	Capacity
American Legion Memorial, Charlotte, N.C.	22,315
Arrowhead Stadium, Kansas City, Mo.	78,034
Balboa Stadium, San Diego, Calif.	34,500
Bowman Grey Stad., Winston-Salem, N.C.	16,841
Buffalo War Memorial Stadium	46,206
Columbus (Ga.) Memorial Stadium	35,000
Cotton Bowl, Dallas, Texas	72,000
Downing Stadium, New York, N.Y.	27,000
Empire Stadium, Vancouver	32,759
Franklin Field, Philadelphia	60,658
Gator Bowl, Jacksonville, Fla.	70,000
Halawa Stadium, Hawaii	50,000
Honolulu Stadium	25,000
John F. Kennedy Stadium, Philadelphia	90,000
Robert F. Kennedy Memorial Stadium, Wash., D.C.	53,041
Kentucky Exposition Stadium, Louisville	21,000
Kezar Stadium, San Francisco	59,636
Ladd Memorial Stadium, Mobile, Ala.	40,605
Lambeau Field, Green Bay, Wis.	56,263
Legion Field, Birmingham, Ala.	72,000
Long Beach (Calif.) Veterans Memorial	15,000
Los Angeles Memorial Coliseum	90,000
Memphis Memorial Stadium	50,000
Mile High Stadium, Denver	51,706
Mississippi Memorial Stadium, Jackson	46,000
Orange Bowl, Miami, Fla.	80,010
Ottawa Stadium, Ottawa, Canada	27,872
Portland Civic Stadium	33,000
Rich Stadium, Buffalo, N.Y.	80,020
Richmond (Va.) City Stadium	22,000
Roanoke (Va.) Victory Stadium	30,000
Roosevelt Stadium, Jersey City	25,000
Rose Bowl, Pasadena, Calif.	100,570
Rubber Bowl, Akron, Ohio	35,007
Schaefer Stadium, Foxboro, Mass.	60,999
Sicks Stadium, Seattle	24,420
Soldier Field, Chicago	55,701
Sugar Bowl, New Orleans, La.	80,982
Sun Bowl, El Paso, Texas	30,000
Tampa Stadium, Tampa, Fla.	45,005
Texas Stadium, Dallas	65,111
Wood Memorial Stadium, Sioux Falls, S.D.	10,000

Longest Softball Game

History's longest softball game was played by 50 teams from New Jersey who played a 685 inning game in 123 hours and 42 minutes at Parsipanny, N. J. The game ended on Labor Day, 1974, and was sponsored by the Muscular Dystrophy Contributions Marathon.

College Basketball

Final Standings in 1973-74 Season. *Won Playoff.

Ivy

	Conference Games		All Games	
	W	L	W	L
Pennsylvania	13	1	21	6
Brown	11	3	17	9
Princeton	11	3	16	10
Harvard	9	5	11	13
Yale	5	9	8	16
Columbia	4	10	5	20
Dartmouth	2	12	4	22
Cornell	1	13	3	23

Middle Atlantic

East

	W	L	W	L
*St. Joseph's	5	1	19	11
LaSalle	5	1	18	10
Temple	4	2	16	9
American U.	4	2	16	10
Drexel	2	4	15	9
Hofstra	1	5	8	16
West Chester	0	6	11	15

West

	W	L	W	L
Rider	8	2	13	13
Lafayette	7	3	17	9
Delaware	7	3	15	11
Gettysburg	4	6	15	10
Bucknell	2	8	8	16
Lehigh	2	8	3	21

Yankee

	W	L	W	L
Massachusetts	11	1	21	5
Connecticut	9	3	19	8
New Hampshire	8	4	16	9
Rhode Island	6	5	11	14
Vermont	3	9	9	17
Boston U.	2	9	9	16
Maine	2	10	14	10

Atlantic Coast

	W	L	W	L
N.C. State	12	0	30	1
North Carolina	9	3	22	6
Maryland	9	3	23	5
Virginia	4	8	11	16
Clemson	3	9	14	12
Wake Forest	3	9	13	13
Duke	2	10	10	16

Southeastern

	W	L	W	L
Vanderbilt	15	3	23	5
Alabama	15	3	22	4
Tennessee	12	6	17	9
Mississippi	9	9	15	10
Florida	9	9	15	11
Kentucky	9	9	13	13
Miss. State	8	10	16	10
Louisiana St.	6	12	12	14
Auburn	5	13	10	16
Georgia	2	16	6	20

Southern

	W	L	W	L
Furman	11	1	22	9
Richmond	10	4	16	12
Davidson	7	3	18	9
East Carolina	8	6	13	12
Wm. & Mary	5	6	9	18
Citadel	4	9	10	14
VMI	3	9	6	18
Appalachian	1	11	5	20

Ohio Valley

	W	L	W	L
Austin Peay	10	4	17	10
Morehead St.	10	4	17	9
Middle Tenn.	9	5	18	8
Western Ky.	8	6	15	10
Murray St.	6	8	12	13
Eastern Ky.	6	8	8	15
Tenn. Tech	4	10	7	18
East Tenn.	3	11	8	18

Mid-Eastern

	W	L	W	L
U. Md. E. Shore	11	1	27	2
Morgan St.	11	1	28	5
N.C. A&T	7	5	16	10
Delaware St.	5	7	18	11
Howard U.	4	8	11	15
S.C. State	2	10	13	15
N.C. Central	2	10	5	16

Big Ten

	W	L	W	L
*Michigan	12	2	22	5
Indiana	12	2	23	5
Purdue	10	4	21	9
Wisconsin	8	6	16	8
Mich. State	8	6	13	11
Minnesota	6	8	12	12
Iowa	5	9	8	16
Ohio State	4	10	9	15
Northwestern	3	11	9	15
Illinois	2	12	5	18

Mid-American

	W	L	W	L
Ohio U.	9	3	16	11
Toledo	8	4	19	9
Bowling Green	7	5	15	11
Central Mich.	6	6	14	12
Miami, O.	6	6	13	13
Western Mich.	5	7	13	13
Kent State	1	11	9	17
Ball State	—	—	14	12
Northern Ill.	—	—	8	17
Eastern Mich.	—	—	8	18

Ohio

	W	L	W	L
Wittenberg	10	2	22	4
Muskingum	10	2	16	6
Ohio Northern	10	3	18	7
Capital	8	4	16	7
Mount Union	8	5	17	9
Marietta	7	5	13	10
Wooster	7	6	13	10
Heidelberg	7	6	10	13
Otterbein	6	6	11	12
Denison	5	8	10	12
Oberlin	3	8	9	12
Kenyon	3	9	9	13
Baldwin-Wallace	2	11	4	19
Ohio Wesleyan	1	12	2	17

Indiana

	W	L	W	L
Evansville	10	2	19	9
Butler	9	3	14	12
St. Joseph's	8	4	20	10
Valparaiso	8	4	15	11
Ind. Central	5	7	15	11
Wabash	1	11	7	18
DePauw	1	11	5	20

Big Eight

	W	L	W	L
Kansas	13	1	23	7
Kansas St.	11	3	19	8
Oklahoma	9	5	18	8
Nebraska	7	7	14	12
Iowa State	6	8	15	11
Colorado	4	10	9	17
Okla. State	3	11	9	17
Missouri	3	11	12	14

Missouri Valley

	W	L	W	L
Louisville	11	1	21	7
Bradley	9	3	20	8
Tulsa	7	6	18	8
New Mexico St.	7	6	14	11
Wichita St.	6	7	11	15
West Texas St.	5	8	11	15
North Texas St.	4	8	13	13
St. Louis	4	8	9	16
Drake	3	9	13	13

Southwest

	W	L	W	L
Texas	11	3	12	15
Texas Tech	10	4	17	9
So. Methodist	10	4	15	12
Texas A&M	7	7	15	11
Arkansas	6	8	10	16
Baylor	5	9	12	13
Rice	5	9	11	17
Texas Christian	2	12	8	17
Houston	—	—	17	9

Southland

	W	L	W	L
Arkansas St.	4	0	17	8
UTex. Arlington	2	2	7	18
Lamar	0	4	6	19
McNeese St.	—	—	20	5
Louisiana Tech	—	—	8	13

Southwestern

	W	L	W	L
Jackson St.	11	1	22	6
Alcorn A&M	10	2	22	6
Southern U.	8	4	17	13
Texas Southern	5	7	15	13
Grambling	5	7	16	11
Miss. Valley	3	9	8	17
Prairie View	0	12	0	17

Western

	W	L	W	L
New Mexico	10	4	22	7
Utah	9	5	22	8
Arizona	9	5	19	7
Arizona St.	9	5	18	9
UTex. El Paso	8	6	18	7
Brigham Young	6	8	11	15
Colo. State	5	9	12	14
Wyoming	0	14	4	22

Big Sky

	W	L	W	L
*Idaho St.	11	3	20	8
Montana	11	3	18	8
Weber St.	8	6	14	12
Gonzaga	7	7	13	13
Boise St.	6	8	12	14
Idaho	5	9	12	14
Montana St.	5	9	11	15
Northern Ariz.	3	11	6	20

Pacific — 8

	W	L	W	L
UCLA	12	2	26	4
Southern Cal	11	3	24	5
Oregon	9	5	15	11
Washington	7	7	16	10
Oregon St.	6	8	13	13
Stanford	5	9	11	14
California	3	11	9	17
Wash. State	3	11	8	21

West Coast

	W	L	W	L
San Francisco	12	2	19	9
Seattle	11	3	15	11
UN Las Vegas	10	4	20	6
Loyola, Cal.	6	8	13	14
St. Mary's	5	9	15	13
UN Reno	4	10	11	15
Pepperdine	4	10	8	18
Santa Clara	4	10	8	19

Pacific Coast

	W	L	W	L
Long Beach St.	12	0	24	2
L.A. State	8	4	17	10
UC Santa Barbara	7	5	16	10
Fresno St.	5	7	16	9
Pacific	4	8	14	12
San Diego St.	4	8	7	19
San Jose St.	2	10	11	15

Major Basketball Independents

East	W	L
Providence	28	4
Pittsburgh	24	4
St. John's	20	7
Syracuse	19	7
Boston College	21	9
Rutgers	18	8
Manhattan	18	9
St. Bonaventure	17	9
Fairfield	17	9
Colgate	15	10
Seton Hall	16	11
George Washington	15	11
St. Francis, Pa.	15	11
Canisius	14	12
Penn State	14	12
Northeastern	12	11
Long Island Univ.	13	12
Georgetown	13	13
Duquesne	12	12
Niagara	12	14
Fairleigh Dickinson	11	14
Navy	9	13

	W	L
West Virginia	10	15
St. Peter's	8	18
Fordham	8	17
Holy Cross	8	18
Villanova	7	19
Army	6	18
Buffalo	5	20

South	W	L
UNC Charlotte	22	4
South Carolina	22	5
South Alabama	22	6
Georgia Southern	19	7
Va. Commonwealth	17	7
Florida St.	18	8
Jacksonville	20	10
Mercer	16	8
Stetson	17	9
Memphis St.	19	11
NE Louisiana	16	10
Virginia Tech	13	13
Tulane	12	14

	W	L
South Florida	11	14
Southern Miss.	11	15
Samford	6	20
Georgia Tech	5	21
Georgia St.	1	25

Midwest	W	L
Notre Dame	26	3
Marquette	26	5
Southern Ill.	19	7
Cincinnati	19	8
Dayton	20	9
Illinois St.	17	9
Detroit	17	9
Marshall	17	9
DePaul	16	9
UW Milwaukee	14	12
Indiana St.	12	14
Loyola, Ill.	12	14
Xavier	8	18
Cleveland St.	6	20

Missouri Valley	W	L
Oral Roberts	23	6
Creighton	23	7
Oklahoma City	13	13

Southwest		
Pan American	13	9
Hardin-Simmons	11	14
Houston Baptist	9	19

Rocky Mountain		
Utah State	16	10
Air Force	11	13
Denver	11	15

Pacific Coast		
Hawaii	19	9
Portland St.	16	11
Portland	15	11

NCAA Individual Statistics, 1973-74

Scoring

	G	FG	FT	Pts.	Avg.
Fogle, Canisius	25	326	183	835	33.4
King, Pan American	22	257	167	681	31.0
Williams, Austin Peay	25	272	143	687	27.5
Stewart, Richmond	25	269	125	663	26.5
Thompson, N.C. State	31	325	155	805	26.0
Bullington, Ball St.	26	255	154	664	25.5
Oleynick, Seattle	26	249	155	653	25.1
Outlaw, N.C. A&T	26	265	117	647	24.9
Biles, Tulsa	26	257	127	641	24.7
Shumate, Notre Dame	29	281	141	703	24.2
Coleman, Murray St.	25	260	82	602	24.1
McCants, Oral Roberts	29	304	89	697	24.0
Coulter, Morehead St.	25	237	122	596	23.8
McDermott, St. Fran. NY	24	224	123	571	23.8
Norman, Arizona	26	264	90	618	23.8
Burden, Utah	30	288	136	712	23.7
Russell, Michigan	27	254	132	640	23.7
Johnson, Denver	26	244	120	608	23.4
Sellers, Rutgers	26	227	148	602	23.2
Dark, Va. Commonwealth	24	245	65	555	23.1
Bailey, Fresno St.	24	238	77	553	23.0
Malone, Southern Miss	26	228	141	597	23.0
Luckett, Ohio U.	27	254	109	617	22.9
Robinson, Texas	26	255	75	585	22.5
Tolson, Arkansas	21	204	64	472	22.5
Tyson, Eastern Mich.	26	252	79	583	22.4

Field Goal Percentage
(Minimum five field goals per game)

	G	FG	FGA	Pct.
Fleming, Arizona	26	136	204	.667
Walton, UCLA	27	232	349	.665
Cox, Mississippi	25	152	242	.628
Shumate, Notre Dame	29	281	448	.627
Skinner, Massachusetts	26	196	316	.620
Carroll, Howard U.	25	205	332	.617
Fry, Miss. State	26	141	233	.605
Morgan, Samford	25	214	354	.605
Garrett, Purdue	30	276	465	.594

	G	FG	FGA	Pct.
C. Pondexter, Long Beach	25	167	283	.590
Wilson, Boise St.	26	153	260	.588
Meriweather, Southern Ill.	26	233	396	.588
Gray, Long Beach St.	26	174	296	.588
Bullock, Texas Tech	26	229	390	.587

Free Throw Percentage
(Minimum three free throws per game)

	G	FT	FTA	Pct.
Medlock, Arkansas	26	87	95	.916
Snow, Tennessee	26	81	91	.890
Ferrell, Marshall	26	128	145	.883
Compton, Vanderbilt	28	89	102	.873
Kruger, Kansas St.	27	122	140	.871
Cook, Memphis St.	28	119	138	.862
Johnson, Denver	26	120	140	.857
Palubinskas, LSU	26	121	142	.852
Cosey, West Texas St.	26	80	95	.851
Bullington, Ball State	26	154	183	.842
Dunleavy, South Carolina	27	97	116	.836
Burden, Utah	30	136	163	.834
Sylvester, Dayton	29	90	108	.833
Arizin, William & Mary	27	119	143	.832

Rebounds

	G.	No.	Avg.
Barnes, Providence	32	597	18.7
McCullough, Pan American	22	358	16.3
Robinson, Kent State	26	423	16.3
Campion, Manhattan	27	419	15.5
Padgett, UN Reno	26	395	15.2
McKinney, Baylor	25	375	15.0
Meriweather, Southern Ill.	26	387	14.9
Walton, UCLA	27	398	14.7
Elmore, Maryland	28	412	14.7
Warner, Maine	24	350	14.6
Hopson, Oklahoma St.	26	375	14.4
Price, St. Bonaventure	26	374	14.4
deVries, Illinois St.	26	373	14.3
Mosley, Seton Hall	21	299	14.2

College Basketball Coach of the Year

(United Press International)

Year	Winner, College
1952—Dudley Moore, LaSalle
1953—Branch McCracken, Indiana
1954—Dudley Moore, LaSalle
1955—Phil Woolpert, San Francisco
1956—Phil Woolpert, San Francisco
1957—Frank McGuire, North Carolina
1958—Tex Winter, Kansas State
1959—Adolph Rupp, Kentucky

Year	Winner, College
1960—Pete Newell, California
1961—Fred Taylor, Ohio State
1962—Fred Taylor, Ohio State
1963—Ed Jucker, Cincinnati
1964—John Wooden, UCLA
1965—Dave Strack, Michigan
1966—Adolph Rupp, Kentucky
1967—John Wooden, UCLA

Year	Winner, College
1968—Guy Lewis, Houston
1969—John Wooden, UCLA
1970—John Wooden, UCLA
1971—Al McGuire, Marquette
1972—John Wooden, UCLA
1973—John Wooden, UCLA
1974—Digger Phelps, Notre Dame

NCAA Basketball Champions

Year Champion	Year Champion	Year Champion	Year Champion
1939—Oregon	1948—Kentucky	1957—North Carolina	1966—Texas Western
1940—Indiana	1949—Kentucky	1958—Kentucky	1967—UCLA
1941—Wisconsin	1950—CCNY	1959—California	1968—UCLA
1942—Stanford	1951—Kentucky	1960—Ohio State	1969—UCLA
1943—Wyoming	1952—Kansas	1961—Cincinnati	1970—UCLA
1944—Utah	1953—Indiana	1962—Cincinnati	1971—UCLA
1945—Oklahoma A&M	1954—La Salle	1963—Loyola (Chi.)	1972—UCLA
1946—Oklahoma A&M	1955—San Francisco	1964—UCLA	1973—UCLA
1947—Holy Cross	1956—San Francisco	1965—UCLA	1974—No. Carolina State

National Invitation Tournament Champions

Year Champion	Year Champion	Year Champion	Year Champion
1938—Temple	1948—St. Louis	1957—Bradley	1966—Brigham Young
1939—Long Island Univ.	1949—San Francisco	1958—Xavier (Ohio)	1967—Southern Illinois
1940—Colorado	1950—CCNY	1959—St. John's	1968—Dayton
1941—Long Island Univ.	1951—Brigham Young	1960—Bradley	1969—Temple
1942—West Virginia	1952—LaSalle	1961—Providence	1970—Marquette
1943—St. John's	1953—Seton Hall	1962—Dayton	1971—North Carolina
1944—St. John's	1954—Holy Cross	1963—Providence	1972—Maryland
1945—DePaul	1955—Duquesne	1964—Bradley	1973—Virginia Tech
1946—Kentucky	1956—Louisville	1965—St. John's	1974—Purdue
1947—Utah			

NCAA College Division Basketball Champions

Year Champion	Year Champion	Year Champion	Year Champion
1957—Wheaton	1962—Mt. St. Mary's	1967—Winston-Salem	1971—Evansville
1958—South Dakota	1963—South Dakota St.	1968—Kentucky Wesleyan	1972—Roanoke
1959—Evansville	1964—Evansville	1969—Kentucky Wesleyan	1973—Kentucky Wesleyan
1960—Evansville	1965—Evansville	1970—Philadelphia Textile	1974—Morgan State
1961—Wittenberg	1966—Kentucky Wesleyan		

Major-College Records

(Restricted to games between four-year colleges.)

Career Scoring Averages

Player, Team	Last Year	Games	FG	FT	Pts.	Avg.
Pete Maravich, LSU	1970	83	1,387	893	3,667	44.2
Austin Carr, Notre Dame	1971	74	1,017	526	2,560	34.6
Oscar Robertson, Cincinnati	1960	88	1,052	869	2,973	33.8
Calvin Murphy, Niagara	1970	77	947	654	2,548	33.1
Frank Selvy, Furman	1954	78	922	694	2,538	32.5
Rick Mount, Purdue	1970	72	910	503	2,323	32.3
Darrell Floyd, Furman	1956	71	868	545	2,281	32.1
Nick Werkman, Seton Hall	1964	71	812	649	2,273	32.0
Willie Humes, Idaho St.	1971	48	565	380	1,510	31.5
Elgin Baylor, Col. Idaho-Seattle	1958	80	956	588	2,500	31.3
William Averitt, Pepperdine	1973	49	615	311	1,541	31.4
Dwight Lamar, SW Louisiana	1973	112	1,445	603	3,493	31.2
Elvin Hayes, Houston	1968	93	1,215	454	2,884	31.0
Bill Bradley, Princeton	1965	83	856	791	2,503	30.2

Season Averages

Player, Team	Year	Games	FG	FT	Pts.	Avg.
Pete Maravich, LSU	1970	31	522	337	1,381	44.5
Pete Maravich, LSU	1969	26	433	282	1,148	44.2
Pete Maravich, LSU	1968	26	432	274	1,138	43.8
Frank Selvy, Furman	1954	29	427	355	1,209	41.7
Johnny Neumann, Mississippi	1971	23	366	191	923	40.1
Billy McGill, Utah	1962	26	394	221	1,009	38.8
Calvin Murphy, Niagara	1968	24	337	242	916	38.2
Austin Carr, Notre Dame	1970	29	444	218	1,106	38.1
Austin Carr, Notre Dame	1971	29	430	241	1,101	38.0
Rick Barry, Miami (Fla.)	1965	26	340	293	973	37.4
Elvin Hayes, Houston	1968	33	519	176	1,214	36.8
Howard Komives, Bowling Green	1964	23	292	260	844	36.7
Dwight Lamar, SW Louisiana	1972	29	429	196	1,054	36.3

Single-Game Scoring

Player, Team (Opponent)	Year	Pts.	Player, Team (Opponent)	Year	Pts.
Selvy, Furman (Newberry)	1954	100	Floyd, Furman (Morehead St.)	1955	67
Mikvy, Temple (Wilkes)	1951	73	Maravich, LSU (Tulane)	1969	66
Maravich, LSU (Alabama)	1970	69	Handlan, W. & Lee (Furman)	1951	66
Murphy, Niagara (Syracuse)	1969	68	Zawoluk, St. John's (St. Peter's)	1950	65

Individual Records, Season

Field Goal Percentage	Alcindor, UCLA, 1967	667	Rebounds	Dukes, Seton Hall, 1953	734
	Martens, Ab. Christian, 1972	667	Field Goals Attempted	Maravich, LSU, 1970	1,168
Free Throw Percentage	Boyer, Arkansas, 1962	933	Free Throws Attempted	Selvy, Furman, 1954	444
Rebounds Per Game	Slack, Marshall, 1955	25.6			

Major League Pennant Winners, 1901-1974

National League

American League

Year	Winner	Won	Lost	Pct.	Manager	Year	Winner	Won	Lost	Pct.	Manager
1901	Pittsburgh	90	49	.647	Clarke	1901	Chicago	83	53	.610	Griffith
1902	Pittsburgh	103	36	.741	Clarke	1902	Philadelphia	83	53	.610	Mack
1903	Pittsburgh	91	49	.650	Clarke	1903	Boston	91	47	.659	Collins
1904	New York	106	47	.693	McGraw	1904	Boston	95	59	.617	Collins
1905	New York	105	48	.686	McGraw	1905	Philadelphia	92	56	.622	Mack
1906	Chicago	116	36	.763	Chance	1906	Chicago	93	58	.616	Jones
1907	Chicago	107	45	.704	Chance	1907	Detroit	92	58	.613	Jennings
1908	Chicago	99	55	.643	Chance	1908	Detroit	90	63	.588	Jennings
1909	Pittsburgh	110	42	.724	Clarke	1909	Detroit	98	54	.645	Jennings
1910	Chicago	104	50	.675	Chance	1910	Philadelphia	102	48	.680	Mack
1911	New York	99	54	.647	McGraw	1911	Philadelphia	101	50	.669	Mack
1912	New York	103	48	.682	McGraw	1912	Boston	105	47	.691	Stahl
1913	New York	101	51	.664	McGraw	1913	Philadelphia	96	57	.627	Mack
1914	Boston	94	59	.614	Stallings	1914	Philadelphia	99	53	.651	Mack
1915	Philadelphia	90	62	.592	Moran	1915	Boston	101	50	.669	Carrigan
1916	Brooklyn	94	60	.610	Robinson	1916	Boston	91	63	.591	Carrigan
1917	New York	98	56	.636	McGraw	1917	Chicago	100	54	.649	Rowland
1918	Chicago	84	45	.651	Mitchell	1918	Boston	75	51	.595	Barrow
1919	Cincinnati	96	44	.686	Moran	1919	Chicago	88	52	.629	Gleason
1920	Brooklyn	93	60	.604	Robinson	1920	Cleveland	98	56	.636	Speaker
1921	New York	94	56	.614	McGraw	1921	New York	98	55	.641	Huggins
1922	New York	93	61	.604	McGraw	1922	New York	94	60	.610	Huggins
1923	New York	95	58	.621	McGraw	1923	New York	98	54	.645	Huggins
1924	New York	93	60	.608	McGraw	1924	Washington	92	62	.597	Harris
1925	Pittsburgh	95	58	.621	McKechnie	1925	Washington	96	55	.636	Harris
1926	St. Louis	89	65	.578	Hornsby	1926	New York	91	63	.591	Huggins
1927	Pittsburgh	94	60	.610	Bush	1927	New York	110	44	.714	Huggins
1928	St. Louis	95	59	.617	McKechnie	1928	New York	101	53	.656	Huggins
1929	Chicago	98	54	.645	McCarthy	1929	Philadelphia	104	46	.693	Mack
1930	St. Louis	92	62	.597	Street	1930	Philadelphia	102	52	.622	Mack
1931	St. Louis	101	53	.656	Street	1931	Philadelphia	107	45	.704	Mack
1932	Chicago	90	64	.584	Grimm	1932	New York	107	47	.695	McCarthy
1933	New York	91	61	.599	Terry	1933	Washington	99	53	.651	Cronin
1934	St. Louis	95	58	.621	Frisch	1934	Detroit	101	53	.656	Cochrane
1935	Chicago	100	54	.649	Grimm	1935	Detroit	93	58	.616	Cochrane
1936	New York	91	62	.597	Terry	1936	New York	102	51	.667	McCarthy
1937	New York	95	57	.625	Terry	1937	New York	102	52	.662	McCarthy
1938	Chicago	89	63	.586	Hartnett	1938	New York	99	53	.651	McCarthy
1939	Cincinnati	97	57	.630	McKechnie	1939	New York	106	45	.702	McCarthy
1940	Cincinnati	100	53	.654	McKechnie	1940	Detroit	90	64	.584	Baker
1941	Brooklyn	100	54	.649	Durocher	1941	New York	101	53	.656	McCarthy
1942	St. Louis	106	48	.688	Southworth	1942	New York	103	51	.669	McCarthy
1943	St. Louis	105	49	.682	Southworth	1943	New York	98	56	.636	McCarthy
1944	St. Louis	105	49	.682	Southworth	1944	St. Louis	89	65	.578	Sewell
1945	Chicago	98	56	.636	Grimm	1945	Detroit	88	65	.575	O'Neill
1946	St. Louis	98	58	.628	Dyer	1946	Boston	104	50	.675	Cronin
1947	Brooklyn	94	60	.610	Shotton	1947	New York	97	57	.630	Harris
1948	Boston	91	62	.595	Southworth	1948	Cleveland	97	58	.626	Boudreau
1949	Brooklyn	97	57	.630	Shotton	1949	New York	97	57	.630	Stengel
1950	Philadelphia	91	63	.591	Sawyer	1950	New York	98	56	.636	Stengel
1951	New York	98	59	.624	Durocher	1951	New York	98	56	.636	Stengel
1952	Brooklyn	96	57	.627	Dressen	1952	New York	95	59	.617	Stengel
1953	Brooklyn	105	49	.682	Dressen	1953	New York	99	52	.656	Stengel
1954	New York	97	57	.630	Durocher	1954	Cleveland	111	43	.721	Lopez
1955	Brooklyn	98	55	.641	Alston	1955	New York	96	58	.623	Stengel
1956	Brooklyn	93	61	.604	Alston	1956	New York	97	57	.630	Stengel
1957	Milwaukee	95	59	.617	Haney	1957	New York	98	56	.636	Stengel
1958	Milwaukee	92	62	.597	Haney	1958	New York	92	62	.597	Stengel
1959	Los Angeles	88	68	.564	Alston	1959	Chicago	94	60	.610	Lopez
1960	Pittsburgh	95	59	.617	Murtaugh	1960	New York	97	57	.630	Stengel
1961	Cincinnati	93	61	.604	Hutchinson	1961	New York	109	53	.673	Houk
1962	San Francisco	103	62	.624	Dark	1962	New York	96	66	.593	Houk
1963	Los Angeles	99	63	.611	Alston	1963	New York	104	57	.646	Houk
1964	St. Louis	93	69	.574	Keane	1964	New York	99	63	.611	Berra
1965	Los Angeles	97	65	.599	Alston	1965	Minnesota	102	60	.630	Mele
1966	Los Angeles	95	67	.586	Alston	1966	Baltimore	97	63	.606	Bauer
1967	St. Louis	101	60	.627	Schoendienst	1967	Boston	92	70	.568	Williams
1968	St. Louis	97	65	.599	Schoendienst	1968	Detroit	103	59	.636	Smith

National League

Year	East Winner	W.	L.	Pct.	Manager	West Winner	W.	L.	Pct.	Manager	Playoff Winner
1969	N.Y. Mets	100	62	.617	Hodges	Atlanta	93	69	.574	Harris	New York
1970	Pittsburgh	89	73	.549	Murtaugh	Cincinnati	102	60	.630	Anderson	Cincinnati
1971	Pittsburgh	97	65	.599	Murtaugh	San Francisco	90	72	.556	Fox	Pittsburgh
1972	Pittsburgh	96	59	.619	Virdon	Cincinnati	95	59	.617	Anderson	Cincinnati
1973	N.Y. Mets	82	79	.509	Berra	Cincinnati	99	63	.611	Anderson	New York
1974	Pittsburgh	88	82	.543	Murtaugh	Los Angeles	102	60	.630	Alston	Los Angeles

American League

	East				West					Playoff
Year	Winner	W.	L.	Pct.	Manager	Winner	W.	L.	Pct.	Manager	Winner

Year	Winner	W.	L.	Pct.	Manager	Winner	W.	L.	Pct.	Manager	Winner
1969	Baltimore......	109	53	.673	Weaver	Minnesota......	97	65	.599	Martin	Baltimore
1970	Baltimore......	108	54	.677	Weaver	Minnesota......	98	64	.605	Rigney	Baltimore
1971	Baltimore......	101	57	.639	Weaver	Oakland........	101	60	.627	Williams	Baltimore
1972	Detroit.........	86	70	.551	Martin	Oakland........	93	72	.600	Williams	Oakland
1973	Baltimore......	97	65	.599	Weaver	Oakland........	94	68	.580	Williams	Oakland
1974	Baltimore......	91	71	.562	Weaver	Oakland........	90	72	.556	Dark	Oakland

All-Star Baseball Games, 1933-1974

Year	Winner	Score	Location	Year	Winner	Score	Location
1933	American	4-2	Chicago	1956	National	7-3	Washington
1934	American	9-7	New York	1957	American	6-5	St. Louis
1935	American	4-1	Cleveland	1958	American	4-3	Baltimore
1936	National	4-3	Boston	1959	National	5-4	Pittsburgh
1937	American	8-3	Washington	1959	American	5-3	Los Angeles
1938	National	4-1	Cincinnati	1960	National	5-3	Kansas City
1939	American	3-1	New York	1960	National	6-0	New York
1940	National	4-0	St. Louis	1961	National(3)	5-4	San Francisco
1941	American	7-5	Detroit	1961	Called-Rain	1-1	Boston
1942	American	3-1	New York	1962	National(3)	3-1	Washington
1943*	American	5-3	Philadelphia	1962	American	9-4	Chicago
1944*	National	7-1	Pittsburgh	1963	National	5-3	Cleveland
1945	(not played)			1964	National	7-4	New York
1946	American	12-0	Boston	1965	National	6-5	Minnesota
1947	American	2-1	Chicago	1966	National(3)	2-1	St. Louis
1948	American	5-2	St. Louis	1967	National(4)	2-1	Anaheim
1949	American	11-7	New York	1968*	National	1-0	Houston
1950	National(1)	4-3	Chicago	1969	National	9-3	Washington
1951	National	8-3	Detroit	1970*	National(2)	5-4	Cincinnati
1952	National	3-2	Philadelphia	1971*	American	6-4	Detroit
1953	National	5-1	Cincinnati	1972*	National	4-3	Atlanta
1954	American	11-9	Cleveland	1973*	National	7-1	Kansas City
1955	National(2)	6-5	Milwaukee	1974*	National	7-2	Pittsburgh

1. 14 innings. 2. 12 innings. 3. 10 innings. 4. 15 innings. * Night game.

Cy Young Award Winners

Year	Player, Club	Year	Player, Club	Year	Player, Club
1956	Don Newcombe, Dodgers	1965	Sandy Koufax, Dodgers	1970	(NL) Bob Gibson, Cardinals
1957	Warren Spahn, Braves	1966	Sandy Koufax, Dodgers		(AL) Jim Perry, Minn.
1958	Bob Turley, Yankees	1967	(NL) Mike McCormick, Giants	1971	(NL) Ferguson Jenkins, Chicago
1959	Early Wynn, White Sox		(AL) Jim Lonborg, Red Sox		(AL) Vida Blue, Oakland
1960	Vernon Law, Pirates	1968	(NL) Bob Gibson, Cardinals	1972	(NL) Steve Carlton, Philadelphia
1961	Whitey Ford, Yankees		(AL) Dennis McLain, Tigers		(AL) Gaylord Perry, Cleveland
1962	Don Drysdale, Dodgers	1969	(NL) Tom Seaver, New York	1973	(NL) Tom Seaver, New York
1963	Sandy Koufax, Dodgers		(AL) McLain, Det., Cuellar, Balt.		(AL) Jim Palmer, Baltimore
1964	Dean Chance, Angels				

Baseball Stadiums
National League

		Home Run Distances (in ft.)			Seating
Team	Stadium	LF	Center	RF	Capacity
Atlanta Braves	Atlanta Stadium	330	402	330	52,870
Chicago Cubs	Wrigley Field	355	400	353	37,741
Cincinnati Reds	Riverfront Stadium	330	404	330	51,726
Houston Astros	Astrodome	330	400	330	44,500
Los Angeles Dodgers	Dodger Stadium	330	395	330	56,000
Montreal Expos	Jarry Park	340	420	340	28,000
New York Mets	Shea Stadium	341	410	341	55,300
Philadelphia Phillies	Veterans Stadium	330	408	330	56,581
Pittsburgh Pirates	Three Rivers Stadium	340	410	340	50,235
St. Louis Cardinals	Busch Memorial Stadium	330	404	330	50,100
San Diego Padres	San Diego Stadium	330	410	330	47,634
San Francisco Giants	Candlestick Park	335	410	335	58,000

American League

Team	Stadium	LF	Center	RF	Capacity
Baltimore Orioles	Memorial Stadium	309	410	309	52,137
Boston Red Sox	Fenway Park	315	420	302	33,379
California Angels	Anaheim Stadium	333	402	333	43,200
Chicago White Sox	White Sox Park	352	400	352	46,550
Cleveland Indians	Municipal Stadium	320	400	320	76,977
Detroit Tigers	Tiger Stadium	340	440	325	54,220
Kansas City Royals	Royals Stadium	330	410	330	40,762
Milwaukee Brewers	Milwaukee County Stadium	320	402	315	47,611
Minnesota Twins	Metropolitan Stadium	346	425	330	45,921
*New York Yankees	Yankee Stadium	301	461	296	65,010
Oakland A's	Oakland-Alameda County Coliseum	330	400	330	50,000
Texas Rangers	Arlington Stadium	330	400	330	35,698

*Yankees played at Shea Stadium in 1974.

1974 Little League World Series

The 28th Little League World Series was won by Taiwan for the fourth year in a row as they defeated Red Bluff (Calif.) by a score of 12-1 on Aug. 24, 1974, at Williamsport, Pa.

Home Run Leaders

National League		American League	
Year	**HR.**	**Year**	**HR.**
1918 Gavvy Cravath, Phil.	8	1918 Babe Ruth, Boston; Tilly Walker, Phil.	11
1919 Gavvy Cravath, Phil.	12	1919 Babe Ruth, Boston.	29
1920 Cy Williams, Phil.	15	1920 Babe Ruth, New York.	54
1921 George Kelly, New York.	23	1921 Babe Ruth, New York.	59
1922 Rogers Hornsby, St. Louis.	42	1922 Ken Williams, St. Louis.	39
1923 Cy Williams, Phil.	41	1923 Babe Ruth, New York.	41
1924 Jacques Fournier, Brooklyn.	27	1924 Babe Ruth, New York.	46
1925 Rogers Hornsby, St. Louis.	39	1925 Bob Meusel, New York.	33
1926 Hack Wilson, Chicago.	21	1926 Babe Ruth, New York.	47
1927 Hack Wilson, Chi; Cy Williams, Phil.	30	1927 Babe Ruth, New York.	60
1928 Hack Wilson, Chi.; Jim Bottomley, S.L.	31	1928 Babe Ruth, New York.	54
1929 Charles Klein, Phil.	43	1929 Babe Ruth, New York.	46
1930 Hack Wilson, Chicago.	56	1930 Babe Ruth, New York.	49
1931 Charles Klein, Phil.	31	1931 Babe Ruth, Lou Gehrig, New York.	46
1932 Charles Klein, Phil.; Mel Ott, N.Y.	38	1932 Jimmy Foxx, Phil.	58
1933 Charles Klein, Phil.	28	1933 Jimmy Foxx, Phil.	48
1934 Collins, S.L.; Mel Ott, N.Y.	35	1934 Lou Gehrig, New York.	49
1935 Walter Berger, Boston.	34	1935 Jimmy Foxx, Phil., Hank Greenberg, Det.	36
1936 Mel Ott, New York.	33	1936 Lou Gehrig, New York.	46
1937 Mel Ott, N.Y.; Joe Medwick, S.L.	31	1937 Joe DiMaggio, New York.	46
1938 Mel Ott, New York.	36	1938 Hank Greenberg, Detroit.	58
1939 John Mize, St. Louis.	28	1939 Jimmy Foxx, Boston.	35
1940 John Mize, St. Louis.	43	1940 Hank Greenberg, Detroit.	41
1941 Dolph Camilli, Brooklyn.	34	1941 Ted Williams, Boston.	37
1942 Mel Ott, New York.	30	1942 Ted Williams, Boston.	36
1943 Bill Nicholson, Chicago.	29	1943 Rudy York, Detroit.	34
1944 Bill Nicholson, Chicago.	33	1944 Nick Etten, New York.	22
1945 Tommy Holmes, Boston.	28	1945 Vern Stephens, St. Louis.	24
1946 Ralph Kiner, Pittsburgh.	23	1946 Hank Greenberg, Detroit.	44
1947 Ralph Kiner, Pitts.; John Mize, N.Y.	51	1947 Ted Williams, Boston.	32
1948 Ralph Kiner, Pitts.; John Mize, N.Y.	40	1948 Joe DiMaggio, New York.	39
1949 Ralph Kiner, Pittsburgh.	54	1949 Ted Williams, Boston.	43
1950 Ralph Kiner, Pittsburgh.	47	1950 Al Rosen, Cleveland.	37
1951 Ralph Kiner, Pittsburgh.	42	1951 Gus Zernial, Chicago-Philadelphia.	33
1952 Ralph Kiner, Pittsburgh; Hank Sauer, Chicago	37	1952 Larry Doby, Cleveland.	32
1953 Ed Mathews, Milwaukee.	47	1953 Al Rosen, Cleveland.	43
1954 Ted Kluszewski, Cincinnati.	49	1954 Larry Doby, Cleveland.	32
1955 Willie Mays, New York.	51	1955 Mickey Mantle, New York.	37
1956 Duke Snider, Brooklyn.	43	1956 Mickey Mantle, New York.	52
1957 Hank Aaron, Milwaukee.	44	1957 Roy Sievers, Washington.	42
1958 Ernie Banks, Chicago.	47	1958 Mickey Mantle, New York.	42
1959 Ed Mathews, Milwaukee.	46	1959 Rocky Colavito, Cleveland,	
1960 Ernie Banks, Chicago.	41	Harmon Killebrew, Washington.	42
1961 Orlando Cepeda, San Francisco.	46	1960 Mickey Mantle, New York.	40
1962 Willie Mays, San Francisco.	49	1961 Roger Maris, New York.	61
1963 Hank Aaron, Milwaukee;		1962 Harmon Killebrew, Minnesota.	48
Willie McCovey, San Francisco.	44	1963 Harmon Killebrew, Minnesota.	45
1964 Willie Mays, San Francisco.	47	1964 Harmon Killebrew, Minnesota.	49
1965 Willie Mays, San Francisco.	52	1965 Tony Conigliaro, Boston.	32
1966 Hank Aaron, Atlanta.	44	1966 Frank Robinson, Baltimore.	49
Willie McCovey, San Francisco.	44	1967 Carl Yastrzemski, Boston;	
1967 Hank Aaron, Atlanta.	39	Harmon Killebrew, Minn.	44
1968 Willie McCovey, San Francisco.	36	1968 Frank Howard, Wash.	44
1969 Willie McCovey, San Francisco.	45	1969 Harmon Killebrew, Minn.	49
1970 Johnny Bench, Cincinnati.	45	1970 Frank Howard, Wash.	44
1971 Willie Stargell, Pittsburgh.	48	1971 Bill Melton, Chicago.	33
1972 Johnny Bench, Cincinnati.	40	1972 Dick Allen, Chicago.	37
1973 Willie Stargell, Pittsburgh.	44	1973 Reggie Jackson, Oakland.	32
1974 Mike Schmidt, Philadelphia.	36	1974 Dick Allen, Chicago.	32

All-time Major League Record (154-game Season)—60—Babe Ruth, New York Yankees (A), 1927. **(162-game Season)—61**—Roger Maris, New York Yankees, 1961. Prior to the 1931 season a batted ball that bounced into the stands was a home run (now a ground-rule double). None of Babe Ruth's record 60 homers bounced into the stands.

Runs Batted In Leaders

National League		American League	
Year	**RBI**	**Year**	**RBI**
1938 Joe Medwick, St. Louis.	122	1938 Jimmy Foxx, Boston.	175
1939 Frank McCormick, Cinn.	128	1939 Ted Williams, Boston.	145
1940 John Mize, St. Louis.	137	1940 Hank Greenberg, Detroit.	150
1941 Dolph Camilli, Brooklyn.	120	1941 Joe DiMaggio, New York.	125
1942 John Mize, New York.	137	1942 Ted Williams, Boston.	137
1943 Bill Nicholson, Chi.	128	1943 Rudy York, Detroit.	118
1944 Bill Nicholson, Chi.	122	1944 Vern Stephens, St. Louis.	109
1945 Dixie Walker, Brooklyn.	124	1945 Nick Etten, New York.	111
1946 Enos Slaughter, St. Louis.	130	1946 Hank Greenberg, Detroit.	127
1947 John Mize, New York.	138	1947 Ted Williams, Boston.	114
1948 Stan Musial, St. Louis.	131	1948 Joe DiMaggio, New York.	155
1949 Ralph Kiner, Pittsburgh.	127	1949 Ted Williams, Vern Stephens, Boston.	159
1950 Del Ennis, Philadelphia.	126	1950 Walt Dropo, Vern Stephens, Boston.	144
1951 Monte Irvin, New York.	121	1951 Gus Zernial, Chi.-Phila.	129
1952 Hank Sauer, Chicago.	121	1952 Al Rosen, Cleveland.	105
1953 Roy Campanella, Brooklyn.	142	1953 Al Rosen, Cleveland.	145
1954 Ted Kluszewski, Cincinnati.	141	1954 Larry Doby, Cleveland.	126
1955 Duke Snider, Brooklyn.	136	1955 Ray Boone, Detroit, Jack Jensen, Boston.	116
1956 Stan Musial, St. Louis.	109	1956 Mickey Mantle, New York.	130
1957 Hank Aaron, Milwaukee.	132	1957 Roy Sievers, Washington.	114

1958	Ernie Banks, Chicago	129
1959	Ernie Banks, Chicago	143
1960	Hank Aaron, Milwaukee	126
1961	Orlando Cepeda, San Francisco	142
1962	Tommy Davis, Los Angeles	153
1963	Hank Aaron, Milwaukee	130
1964	Ken Boyer, St. Louis	119
1965	Deron Johnson, Cincinnati	130
1966	Hank Aaron, Atlanta	127
1967	Orlando Cepeda, St. Louis	111
1968	Willie McCovey, San Francisco	105
1969	Willie McCovey, San Francisco	126
1970	Johnny Bench, Cincinnati	148
1971	Joe Torre, St. Louis	137
1972	Johnny Bench, Cincinnati	125
1973	Willie Stargell, Pittsburgh	119
1974	Johnny Bench, Cincinnati	129

1958	Jack Jensen, Boston	122
1959	Jack Jensen, Boston	112
1960	Roger Maris, New York	112
1961	Roger Maris, New York	142
1962	Harmon Killebrew, Minn.	126
1963	Dick Stuart, Boston	118
1964	Brooks Robinson, Baltimore	118
1965	Rocky Colavito, Cleveland	108
1966	Frank Robinson, Baltimore	122
1967	Carl Yastrzemski, Boston	121
1968	Ken Harrelson, Boston	109
1969	Harmon Killebrew, Minn.	140
1970	Frank Howard, Wash.	126
1971	Harmon Killebrew, Minn.	119
1972	Dick Allen, Chicago	113
1973	Reggie Jackson, Oakland	117
1974	Jeff Burroughs, Texas	118

Batting Champions

	National League				American League		
Year	Player	Club	Pct.	Year	Player	Club	Pct.
1907	Honus Wagner	Pittsburgh	.350	1907	Ty Cobb	Detroit	.350
1908	Honus Wagner	Pittsburgh	.354	1908	Ty Cobb	Detroit	.324
1909	Honus Wagner	Pittsburgh	.339	1909	Ty Cobb	Detroit	.377
1910	Sherwood Magee	Philadelphia	.331	1910	Ty Cobb	Detroit	.385
1911	Honus Wagner	Pittsburgh	.334	1911	Ty Cobb	Detroit	.420
1912	Henry Zimmerman	Chicago	.372	1912	Ty Cobb	Detroit	.410
1913	Jacob Daubert	Brooklyn	.350	1913	Ty Cobb	Detroit	.390
1914	Jacob Daubert	Brooklyn	.329	1914	Ty Cobb	Detroit	.368
1915	Larry Doyle	New York	.320	1915	Ty Cobb	Detroit	.369
1916	Hal Chase	Cincinnati	.339	1916	Tris Speaker	Cleveland	.386
1917	Edd Roush	Cincinnati	.341	1917	Ty Cobb	Detroit	.383
1918	Zack Wheat	Brooklyn	.335	1918	Ty Cobb	Detroit	.382
1919	Edd Roush	Cincinnati	.321	1919	Ty Cobb	Detroit	.384
1920	Rogers Hornsby	St. Louis	.370	1920	George Sisler	St. Louis	.407
1921	Rogers Hornsby	St. Louis	.397	1921	Harry Heilmann	Detroit	.394
1922	Rogers Hornsby	St. Louis	.401	1922	George Sisler	St. Louis	.420
1923	Rogers Hornsby	St. Louis	.384	1923	Harry Heilmann	Detroit	.403
1924	Rogers Hornsby	St. Louis	.424	1924	Babe Ruth	New York	.378
1925	Rogers Hornsby	St. Louis	.403	1925	Harry Heilmann	Detroit	.393
1926	Eugene Hargrave	Cincinnati	.353	1926	Henry Manush	Detroit	.378
1927	Paul Waner	Pittsburgh	.380	1927	Harry Heilmann	Detroit	.398
1928	Rogers Hornsby	Boston	.387	1928	Goose Goslin	Washington	.379
1929	Lefty O'Doul	Philadelphia	.398	1929	Lew Fonseca	Cleveland	.369
1930	Bill Terry	New York	.401	1930	Al Simmons	Philadelphia	.381
1931	Chick Hafey	St. Louis	.349	1931	Al Simmons	Philadelphia	.390
1932	Lefty O'Doul	Brooklyn	.368	1932	Dale Alexander	Det.-Bos.	.367
1933	Charles Klein	Philadelphia	.368	1933	Jimmy Foxx	Philadelphia	.356
1934	Paul Waner	Pittsburgh	.362	1934	Lou Gehrig	New York	.363
1935	Arky Vaughan	Pittsburgh	.385	1935	Buddy Myer	Washington	.349
1936	Paul Waner	Pittsburgh	.373	1936	Luke Appling	Chicago	.388
1937	Joe Medwick	St. Louis	.374	1937	Charlie Gehringer	Detroit	.371
1938	Ernie Lombardi	Cincinnati	.342	1938	Jimmy Foxx	Boston	.349
1939	John Mize	St. Louis	.349	1939	Joe DiMaggio	New York	.381
1940	Debs Garms	Pittsburgh	.355	1940	Joe DiMaggio	New York	.352
1941	Pete Reiser	Brooklyn	.343	1941	Ted Williams	Boston	.406
1942	Ernie Lombardi	Boston	.330	1942	Ted Williams	Boston	.356
1943	Stan Musial	St. Louis	.357	1943	Luke Appling	Chicago	.328
1944	Dixie Walker	Brooklyn	.357	1944	Lou Boudreau	Cleveland	.327
1945	Phil Cavarretta	Chicago	.355	1945	George Stirnweiss	New York	.309
1946	Stan Musial	St. Louis	.365	1946	Mickey Vernon	Washington	.353
1947	Harry Walker	Philadelphia	.363	1947	Ted Williams	Boston	.343
1948	Stan Musial	St. Louis	.376	1948	Ted Williams	Boston	.369
1949	Jackie Robinson	Brooklyn	.342	1949	George Kell	Detroit	.343
1950	Stan Musial	St. Louis	.346	1950	Billy Goodman	Boston	.354
1951	Stan Musial	St. Louis	.355	1951	Ferris Fain	Philadelphia	.344
1952	Stan Musial	St. Louis	.336	1952	Ferris Fain	Philadelphia	.327
1953	Carl Furillo	Brooklyn	.344	1953	Mickey Vernon	Washington	.337
1954	Willie Mays	New York	.345	1954	Roberto Avila	Cleveland	.341
1955	Richie Ashburn	Philadelphia	.338	1955	Al Kaline	Detroit	.340
1956	Hank Aaron	Milwaukee	.328	1956	Mickey Mantle	New York	.353
1957	Stan Musial	St. Louis	.351	1957	Ted Williams	Boston	.388
1958	Richie Ashburn	Philadelphia	.350	1958	Ted Williams	Boston	.328
1959	Hank Aaron	Milwaukee	.355	1959	Harvey Kuenn	Detroit	.353
1960	Dick Groat	Pittsburgh	.325	1960	Pete Runnels	Boston	.320
1961	Roberto Clemente	Pittsburgh	.351	1961	Norm Cash	Detroit	.361
1962	Tommy Davis	Los Angeles	.346	1962	Pete Runnels	Boston	.326
1963	Tommy Davis	Los Angeles	.326	1963	Carl Yastrzemski	Boston	.321
1964	Roberto Clemente	Pittsburgh	.339	1964	Tony Oliva	Minnesota	.323
1965	Roberto Clemente	Pittsburgh	.329	1965	Tony Oliva	Minnesota	.321
1966	Matty Alou	Pittsburgh	.342	1966	Frank Robinson	Baltimore	.316
1967	Roberto Clemente	Pittsburgh	.357	1967	Carl Yastrzemski	Boston	.326
1968	Pete Rose	Cincinnati	.335	1968	Carl Yastrzemski	Boston	.301
1969	Pete Rose	Cincinnati	.348	1969	Rod Carew	Minnesota	.332
1970	Rico Carty	Atlanta	.366	1970	Alex Johnson	California	.328
1971	Joe Torre	St. Louis	.363	1971	Tony Oliva	Minnesota	.337
1972	Billy Williams	Chicago	.333	1972	Rod Carew	Minnesota	.318
1973	Pete Rose	Cincinnati	.338	1973	Rod Carew	Minnesota	.350
1974	Ralph Garr	Atlanta	.353	1974	Rod Carew	Minnesota	.364

Most Valuable Player Awards
Baseball Writers' Assn.

National League			American League		
Year	Player	Club	Year	Player	Club
1931—Frank Frisch		St. Louis	1931—Lefty Grove		Philadelphia
1932—Charles Klein		Philadelphia	1932—Jimmy Foxx		Philadelphia
1933—Carl Hubbell		New York	1933—Jimmy Foxx		Philadelphia
1934—Dizzy Dean		St. Louis	1934—Mickey Cochrane		Detroit
1935—Gabby Hartnett		Chicago	1935—Henry Greenberg		Detroit
1936—Carl Hubbell		New York	1936—Lou Gehrig		New York
1937—Joe Medwick		St. Louis	1937—Charley Gehringer		Detroit
1938—Ernie Lombardi		Cincinnati	1938—Jimmy Foxx		Boston
1939—Bucky Walters		Cincinnati	1939—Joe DiMaggio		New York
1940—Frank McCormick		Cincinnati	1940—Hank Greenberg		Detroit
1941—Dolph Camilli		Brooklyn	1941—Joe DiMaggio		New York
1942—Mort Cooper		St. Louis	1942—Joe Gordon		New York
1943—Stan Musial		St. Louis	1943—Spurgeon Chandler		New York
1944—Martin Marion		St. Louis	1944—Hal Newhouser		Detroit
1945—Phil Cavarretta		Chicago	1945—Hal Newhouser		Detroit
1946—Stan Musial		St. Louis	1946—Ted Williams		Boston
1947—Bob Elliott		Boston	1947—Joe DiMaggio		New York
1948—Stan Musial		St. Louis	1948—Lou Boudreau		Cleveland
1949—Jackie Robinson		Brooklyn	1949—Ted Williams		Boston
1950—Jim Konstanty		Philadelphia	1950—Phil Rizzuto		New York
1951—Roy Campanella		Brooklyn	1951—Yogi Berra		New York
1952—Hank Sauer		Chicago	1952—Bobby Shantz		Philadelphia
1953—Roy Campanella		Brooklyn	1953—Al Rosen		Cleveland
1954—Willie Mays		New York	1954—Yogi Berra		New York
1955—Roy Campanella		Brooklyn	1955—Yogi Berra		New York
1956—Don Newcombe		Brooklyn	1956—Mickey Mantle		New York
1957—Henry Aaron		Milwaukee	1957—Mickey Mantle		New York
1958—Ernie Banks		Chicago	1958—Jackie Jensen		Boston
1959—Ernie Banks		Chicago	1959—Nellie Fox		Chicago
1960—Dick Groat		Pittsburgh	1960—Roger Maris		New York
1961—Frank Robinson		Cincinnati	1961—Roger Maris		New York
1962—Maury Wills		Los Angeles	1962—Mickey Mantle		New York
1963—Sandy Koufax		Los Angeles	1963—Elston Howard		New York
1964—Ken Boyer		St. Louis	1964—Brooks Robinson		Baltimore
1965—Willie Mays		San Francisco	1965—Zoilo Versalles		Minnesota
1966—Roberto Clemente		Pittsburgh	1966—Frank Robinson		Baltimore
1967—Orlando Cepeda		St. Louis	1967—Carl Yastrzemski		Boston
1968—Bob Gibson		St. Louis	1968—Denny McLain		Detroit
1969—Willie McCovey		San Francisco	1969—Harmon Killebrew		Minnesota
1970—Johnny Bench		Cincinnati	1970—John (Boog) Powell		Baltimore
1971—Joe Torre		St. Louis	1972—Vida Blue		Oakland
1972—Johnny Bench		Cincinnati	1972—Dick Allen		Chicago
1973—Pete Rose		Cincinnati	1973—Reggie Jackson		Oakland

Rookie of the Year Award (Baseball Writers Assn.)

1947—Combined Selection—Jackie Robinson, Brooklyn, 1b
1948—Combined Selection—Alvin Dark, Boston, N. L. ss

National League

Year	Winner	Year	Winner	Year	Winner
1949—Don Newcombe, Brooklyn, p		1958—Orlando Cepeda, S. F., 1b		1966—Tommy Helms, Cinn., 2b	
1950—Sam Jethroe, Boston, of		1959—Willie McCovey, S. F., 1b		1967—Tom Seaver, N. Y., p	
1951—Willie Mays, N. Y., of		1960—Frank Howard, Los Angeles, of		1968—Johnny Bench, Cinn., c	
1952—Joe Black, Brooklyn, p		1961—Billy Williams, Chicago, of		1969—Ted Sizemore, L. A., 2b	
1953—Jim Gilliam, Brooklyn, 2b		1962—Ken Hubbs, Chicago, 2b		1970—Carl Morton, Mont., p	
1954—Wally Moon, St. Louis, of		1963—Pete Rose, Cinn., 2b		1971—Earl Williams, Atl., c	
1955—Bill Virdon, St. Louis, of		1964—Richie Allen, Phil., 3b		1972—Jon Matlack, N. Y., p	
1956—Frank Robinson, Cinn., of		1965—Jim Lefebvre, L. A., 2b		1973—Gary Matthews, S. F., of	
1957—Jack Sanford, Phil., p					

American League

Year	Winner	Year	Winner	Year	Winner
1949—Roy Sievers, St. Louis, of		1958—Albie Pearson, Wash., of		1966—Tommie Agee, Chicago, of	
1950—Walt Dropo, Boston, 1b		1959—Bob Allison, Wash., of		1967—Rod Carew, Minn., 2b	
1951—Gil McDougald, N. Y., 3b		1960—Ron Hansen, Balt., ss		1968—Stan Bahnsen, N. Y., p	
1952—Harry Byrd, Phil., p		1961—Don Schwall, Boston, p		1969—Lou Piniella, K. C., of	
1953—Harvey Kuenn, Detroit, ss		1962—Tom Tresh, N. Y., if-of		1970—Thurman Munson, N. Y., c	
1954—Bob Grim, N. Y., p		1963—Gary Peters, Chicago, p		1971—Chris Chambliss, Cleve., 1b	
1955—Herb Score, Cleveland, p		1964—Tony Oliva, Minn., of		1972—Carlton Fisk, Bos., c	
1956—Luis Aparicio, Chicago, ss		1965—Curt Blefary, Balt., of		1973—Al Bumbry, Balt., of	
1957—Tony Kubek, N. Y., if-of					

Triple Crown Winners
Players leading league in batting, runs batted in and homers

Year	Player & Team	Year	Player & Team
1909	Ty Cobb, Detroit Tigers	1937	Joe Medwick, St. Louis Cardinals
1912	Heinie Zimmerman, Chicago Cubs	1942	Ted Williams, Boston Red Sox
1922	Rogers Hornsby, St. Louis Cardinals	1947	Ted Williams, Boston Red Sox
1925	Rogers Hornsby, St. Louis Cardinals	1956	Mickey Mantle, New York Yankees
1933	Jimmy Foxx, Philadelphia Athletics	1966	Frank Robinson, Baltimore Orioles
1933	Chuck Klein, Philadelphia Phillies	1967	Carl Yastrzemski, Boston Red Sox
1934	Lou Gehrig, New York Yankees		

Major League No-Hit Games Since 1960
Complete Nine-inning Games

Year Pitcher, Club	Opposition	Score
1960—Don Cardwell, Chicago	St. Louis	4-0
1960—Lew Burdette, Milwaukee	Philadelphia	1-0
1960—Warren Spahn, Milwaukee	Philadelphia	4-0
1961—Warren Spahn, Milwaukee	San Francisco	1-0
1962—Bo Belinsky, Los Angeles	Baltimore	2-0
1962—Earl Wilson, Boston	Los Angeles	2-0
1962—Sandy Koufax, Los Angeles	New York	5-0
1962—Bill Monbouquette, Boston	Chicago	1-0
1962—Jack Kralick, Minnesota	Kansas City	1-0
1963—Sandy Koufax, Los Angeles	San Francisco	8-0
1963—Don Nottebart, Houston	Philadelphia	4-1
1963—Juan Marichal, San Francisco	Houston	1-0
1964—Ken Johnson, Houston	Cincinnati	0-1
1964—Sandy Koufax, Los Angeles	Philadelphia	3-0
1964—Jim Bunning (1), Philadelphia	New York	6-0
1965—Jim Maloney(2), Cincinnati	New York	0-1
1965—Jim Maloney (3), Cincinnati	Chicago	1-0
1965—Sandy Koufax (1), Los Angeles	Chicago	1-0
1965—Dave Morehead, Boston	Cleveland	2-0
1966—Sonny Siebert, Cleveland	Washington	2-0
1967—S. Barber, Stu Miller (4), Baltimore	Detroit	0-2
1967—Don Wilson, Houston	Atlanta	2-0
1967—Dean Chance, Minnesota	Cleveland	2-1
1967—Joe Horlen, Chicago	Detroit	4-0
1968—Tom Phoebus, Baltimore	Boston	6-0
1968—Jim Hunter (1), Oakland	Minnesota	4-0
1968—George Culver, Cincinnati	Philadelphia	6-1
1968—Gaylord Perry, San Francisco	St. Louis	1-0
1968—Ray Washburn, St. Louis	San Francisco	2-0
1969—Bill Stoneman, Montreal	Philadelphia	7-0
1969—Jim Maloney, Cincinnati	Houston	10-0
1969—Don Wilson, Houston	Cincinnati	4-0
1969—Jim Palmer, Baltimore	Oakland	8-0
1969—Ken Holtzman, Chicago	Atlanta	3-0
1969—Bob Moose, Pittsburgh	New York	4-0
1970—Dock Ellis, Pittsburgh	San Diego	2-0
1970—Clyde Wright, California	Oakland	4-0
1970—Bill Singer, Los Angeles	Philadelphia	5-0
1970—Vida Blue, Oakland	Minnesota	6-0
1971—Ken Holtzman, Chicago	Cincinnati	1-0
1971—Rick Wise, Philadelphia	Cincinnati	4-0
1971—Bob Gibson, St. Louis	Pittsburgh	11-0
1972—Burt Hooton, Chicago	Philadelphia	4-0
1972—Milt Pappas, Chicago	San Diego	8-0
1972—Bill Stoneman, Montreal	New York	7-0
1973—Steve Busby, Kansas City	Detroit	3-0
1973—Nolan Ryan, California	Kansas City	3-0
1973—Nolan Ryan, California	Detroit	6-0
1973—Jim Bibby, Texas	Oakland	6-0
1973—Phil Niekro, Atlanta	San Diego	9-0
1974—Steve Busby, Kansas City	Milwaukee	2-0
1974—Dick Bosman, Cleveland	Oakland	4-0
1974—Nolan Ryan, California	Minnesota	4-0

(1) Perfect game. (2) Maloney pitched ten hitless innings, then allowed two hits in the eleventh. (3) Ten innings. (4) Barber pitched 8²/₃ innings, Miller ¹/₃ of an inning.

Major League Perfect Games

Year Player	Clubs	Score	Year Player	Clubs	Score
1904 Cy Young	Boston vs. Phil. (AL)	3-0	1956 Don Larson (b)	N.Y. Yankees vs. Brooklyn	2-0
1908 Addie Joss	Cleveland vs. Chicago (AL)	1-0	1964 Jim Bunning	Phil. vs. N.Y. Mets (NL)	6-0
1917 Ernie Shore (a)	Boston vs. Wash. (AL)	4-0	1965 Sandy Koufax	Los Angeles vs. Chic. (NL)	1-0
1922 Charles Robertson	Chicago vs. Detroit (AL)	2-0	1968 Jim Hunter	Oakland vs. Minn. (AL)	4-0

(a) Babe Ruth, the starting pitcher, was ejected from the game after walking the first batter. Shore replaced him, and the base-runner was out stealing. Shore retired the next 26 batters. (b) World Series.

Ryan's Fastball Clocked

Nolan Ryan of the California Angels twice threw a ball 100.9 mph in a game against the Tigers on Aug. 20, 1974. The entire game was clocked by infra-red radar. Ryan broke Bob Feller's 28 year-old record of 98.6 mph.

American Legion Junior Baseball World Champions

Year Winner	Year Winner	Year Winner	Year Winner
1959—Detroit, Mich.	1963—Long Beach, Calif.	1967—Tuscaloosa, Ala.	1971—West Covina, Calif.
1960—New Orleans, La.	1964—Upland, Calif.	1968—Memphis, Tenn.	1972—Baldwin, Mo.
1961—Phoenix, Ariz.	1965—Charlotte, N.C.	1969—Portland, Oregon	1973—Puerto Rico
1962—St. Louis, Mo.	1966—Oakland, Calif.	1970—West Covina, Calif.	1974—Puerto Rico

Robinson Named First Black Manager

Frank Robinson became the first black man to manage a major league baseball team when he was selected to manage the Cleveland Indians for the 1975 season. Robinson, the only player to win the Most Valuable Player Award in both the National and American league, will also be an active player.

National League Records, 1974

Final Standings

Eastern Division	W.	L.	Pct.	G.B.
Pittsburgh	88	74	.543	—
St. Louis	86	75	.534	1½
Philadelphia	80	82	.494	8
Montreal	79	82	.491	8½
New York	71	91	.438	17
Chicago	66	96	.407	22

Western Division	W.	L.	Pct.	G.B.
Los Angeles	102	60	.630	—
Cincinnati	98	64	.605	4
Atlanta	88	74	.543	14
Houston	81	81	.500	21
San Francisco	72	90	.444	30
San Diego	60	102	.370	42

National League Playoffs

Oct. 5—Los Angeles 3, Pittsburgh 0.
Oct. 6—Los Angeles 5, Pittsburgh 2.
Oct. 8—Pittsburgh 7, Los Angeles 0.

Oct. 9—Los Angeles 12, Pittsburgh 1.
(Los Angeles won 3-of-5 series, 3-1)

*Rookie   †Bats—Pitches Lefthanded   ‡Switch Hitter

Club Batting

Club	Pct.	AB	R.	H.	HR.	SB
Pittsburgh	.274	5702	751	1560	114	55
Los Angeles	.272	5557	798	1511	139	149
St. Louis	.265	5620	677	1492	83	172
Houston	.263	5489	653	1441	110	108
Philadelphia	.261	5494	676	1434	95	115
Cincinnati	.260	5535	776	1437	135	146
Montreal	.254	5343	662	1355	86	124
San Francisco	.252	5482	634	1380	93	107
Chicago	.251	5574	669	1397	110	78
Atlanta	.248	5533	661	1375	120	72
New York	.235	5468	572	1286	96	43
San Diego	.229	5415	541	1239	99	85

Club Pitching

Club	ERA	G.	IP	H.	R.	BB	SO
Los Angeles	2.97	162	1465	1272	561	464	943
Atlanta	3.05	163	1474	1343	563	488	772
Cincinnati	3.41	163	1466	1364	631	536	875
New York	3.42	162	1470	1433	646	504	908
Houston	3.47	162	1451	1396	632	601	738
St. Louis	3.48	161	1473	1399	643	616	794
Pittsburgh	3.49	162	1466	1428	657	543	721
Montreal	3.60	161	1429	1340	657	544	822
San Francisco	3.78	162	1439	1409	723	559	756
Philadelphia	3.91	162	1447	1394	701	682	892
Chicago	4.28	162	1466	1593	826	576	895
San Diego	4.58	162	1446	1536	830	715	857

Individual Batting

Leaders—450 or More At Bats

Player—Club	Pct.	AB	R.	H.	HR.	RBI	SB
Garr, Atlanta†	.353	606	87	214	11	54	26
Oliver, Pittsburgh†	.321	617	96	198	11	85	10
*Gross, Houston†	.314	127	447	51	116	2	34	2
Buckner, Los Angeles†	.314	580	83	182	7	58	31
*Madlock, Chicago	.313	453	65	142	9	54	11
Zisk, Pittsburgh	.313	536	75	168	17	100	1
Garvey, Los Angeles	.312	642	95	200	21	111	5
*McBride, St. Louis†	.309	559	81	173	6	56	30
Smith, St. Louis‡	.309	517	79	160	23	100	4
Brock, St. Louis†	.306	635	105	194	3	48	118

Individual Pitching

Leaders—162 or More Innings

Pitcher—Club	W.	L.	ERA	G.	IP	H.	BB	SO
Capra, Atlanta	16	8	2.28	39	217	163	84	137
P. Niekro, Atlanta	20	13	2.38	41	302	249	88	195
Matlack, New York†	13	15	2.41	34	265	221	76	195
Marshall, Los Angeles	15	12	2.42	106	208	191	56	143
Messersmith, Los Ang.	20	6	2.59	39	292	227	94	221
McGlothen, St. Louis	16	12	2.70	31	237	212	89	142
Barr, San Francisco	13	9	2.74	44	240	223	47	84
Rooker, Pittsburgh†	15	11	2.77	33	263	228	83	139
Dierker, Houston	11	10	2.89	33	224	189	82	150
Caldwell, San Fran.†	14	5	2.95	31	189	176	63	83

Individual Batting (over 100 at-bats)   Individual Pitching (over 50 innings)

*Rookie   †Bats—Pitches Lefthanded   ‡Switch Hitter

Atlanta Braves

Batting	Pct.	G.	AB	R.	H.	HR.	RBI	SB
Garr†	.353	143	606	87	214	11	54	26
Aaron	.268	112	340	47	91	20	69	1
Perez	.260	127	447	51	116	2	34	2
Baker	.256	149	574	80	147	20	69	18
Johnson	.251	136	454	56	114	15	62	1
Murrell	.248	73	133	11	33	2	12	0
*Office†	.246	131	248	20	61	3	31	5
Evans†	.240	160	571	99	137	25	79	4
*Correll	.238	73	202	20	48	4	29	0
Lum†	.233	106	361	50	84	11	50	0
Tepedino†	.231	78	169	11	39	0	15	1
Robinson	.230	145	452	52	104	0	29	11
Oates†	.223	100	291	22	65	1	21	2
Casanova	.202	42	104	5	21	0	8	0
*Foster	.196	72	112	16	22	1	5	1

Pitching	W.	L.	ERA	G.	IP	H.	BB	SO
House†	6	2	1.92	56	103	74	27	64
Capra	16	8	2.28	39	217	163	84	137
P. Niekro	20	13	2.38	41	302	249	88	195
*Leon	4	7	2.64	34	75	68	14	38
Morton	16	12	3.14	38	275	293	89	113
Reed	10	11	3.39	28	186	171	41	78
Krausse	4	3	4.16	29	67	65	32	27
Harrison	6	11	4.71	20	126	148	49	46

Chicago Cubs

Batting	Pct.	G.	AB	R.	H.	HR.	RBI.	SB
*Madlock	.313	128	453	65	142	9	54	11
Monday†	.294	142	538	84	158	20	58	7
Cardenal	.293	143	542	75	159	13	72	23
Williams†	.280	117	404	55	113	16	68	4
Morales	.273	151	534	70	146	15	82	2
*Thornton	.261	107	303	41	79	10	46	2
Kessinger‡	.259	153	599	83	155	1	42	7
Mitterwald	.251	78	215	17	54	7	28	1
Grabarkewitz	.226	87	155	28	35	2	14	4
*Swisher	.214	90	280	21	60	5	27	0
*Sperring	.206	42	107	9	22	1	5	1
*Ward†	.204	92	137	8	28	1	15	0
*Rosello	.203	62	148	9	30	0	10	1
Harris‡	.195	62	200	18	39	0	11	9
Fanzone	.190	65	158	13	30	4	22	0
*LaCock†	.182	35	110	9	20	1	8	0

Pitching	W.	L.	ERA	G.	IP	H.	BB	SO
*Zamora	3	9	3.11	56	84	82	19	38
Bonham	11	22	3.85	44	243	246	109	191
Frailing†	6	9	3.89	55	125	150	43	71
*Todd	4	2	3.89	43	88	82	41	42
Stone	8	6	4.13	38	170	185	64	90
*Dettore	3	5	4.15	16	65	64	31	43
Reuschel	13	12	4.29	41	241	262	83	160
LaRoche†	5	6	4.79	49	92	103	47	49
Hooton	7	11	4.81	48	176	214	51	94
Burris	3	5	6.60	40	75	91	26	40

Cincinnati Reds

Batting

Batting	Pct.	G.	AB	R.	H.	HR.	RBI	SB
Morgan†	.293	149	512	107	150	22	67	58
Rose‡	.284	163	652	110	185	3	51	2
Concepcion	.281	160	594	70	167	14	82	41
Driessen†	.281	150	470	63	132	7	56	10
Geronimo†	.281	150	474	73	133	7	54	9
Bench	.280	160	621	108	174	33	129	5
Perez	.265	158	596	81	158	28	101	1
Foster	.264	106	276	31	73	7	41	3
*Griffey†	.251	88	227	24	57	2	19	9
Crowley†	.240	84	125	11	30	1	20	1
Plummer	.225	50	120	7	27	2	10	1
Rettenmund	.216	80	208	30	45	6	28	5
Chaney†	.200	117	135	27	27	2	16	1

Pitching

Pitching	W.	L.	ERA	G.	IP	H.	BB	SO
C. Carroll	12	5	2.14	57	101	96	30	46
Gullett†	17	11	3.04	36	243	201	88	183
Norman†	13	12	3.15	35	186	170	68	141
Borbon	10	7	3.24	73	139	133	32	53
Kirby	12	9	3.27	36	231	210	91	160
Nelson	4	4	3.39	14	85	67	35	42
*T. Carroll	4	3	3.69	16	78	68	44	37
Billingham	19	11	3.95	36	212	233	664	103
Hall†	3	1	4.08	40	64	54	30	48

Houston Astros

Batting

Batting	Pct.	G.	AB	R.	H.	HR.	RBI	SB
*Gross†	.314	156	589	78	185	0	36	12
Watson	.298	150	524	69	156	11	67	3
M. May†	.289	127	405	47	117	7	54	0
*Milbourne	.279	112	136	31	38	0	9	6
Helms	.279	137	452	32	126	5	50	5
Cedeno	.269	160	610	95	164	26	102	57
L. May	.268	152	556	59	149	24	85	1
Rader	.257	152	533	61	137	17	78	7
Metzger‡	.253	143	572	66	145	0	30	9
*C. Johnson	.228	83	171	26	39	10	29	0
Edwards†	.222	50	117	8	26	1	10	1
*Howard‡	.216	64	111	19	24	2	5	4

Pitching

Pitching	W.	L.	ERA	G.	IP	H.	BB	SO
Forsch	8	7	2.80	70	103	98	37	48
Dierker	11	10	2.89	33	224	189	82	150
Wilson	11	13	3.07	33	205	170	100	112
Roberts†	10	12	3.44	34	204	216	65	72
*Cosgrove†	7	3	3.50	45	90	76	39	47
Griffin	14	10	3.54	34	211	202	89	110
Scherman†	2	5	4.13	53	61	67	26	35
Richard	2	3	4.15	15	65	58	36	42

Los Angeles Dodgers

Batting

Batting	Pct.	G.	AB	R.	H.	HR.	RBI	SB
Buckner†	.314	145	580	83	182	7	58	31
Garvey	.312	156	642	95	200	21	111	5
Crawford†	.295	139	468	73	138	11	61	7
Wynn	.271	150	535	104	145	32	108	18
Russell	.269	160	553	61	149	5	65	14
Lopes	.266	145	530	95	141	10	35	59
Yeager	.266	94	316	41	84	12	41	2
Cey	.262	159	577	88	151	18	97	1
Ferguson	.252	111	349	54	88	16	57	2
Paciorek	.240	85	175	23	42	1	24	1
Joshua†	.234	81	124	11	29	1	16	3

Pitching

Pitching	W.	L.	ERA	G.	IP	H.	BB	SO
*Zahn†	3	5	2.03	21	80	78	16	33
Marshall	15	12	2.42	106	208	191	56	143
Messersmith	20	6	2.59	39	292	227	94	221
John†	13	3	2.59	22	153	133	42	78
Sutton	19	9	3.23	40	276	241	80	179
Downing†	5	6	3.67	21	98	94	45	63
Rau†	13	11	3.73	36	198	191	70	126
Hough	9	4	3.75	49	96	65	40	63

Montreal Expos

Batting

Batting	Pct.	G.	AB	R.	H.	HR.	RBI	SB
Jorgensen†	.310	131	287	45	89	11	59	3
Davis†	.295	153	611	86	180	12	89	25
Bailey	.280	152	507	69	142	20	73	4
Singleton‡	.276	148	511	68	141	9	74	5

(Montreal con't.)

Batting

Batting	Pct.	G.	AB	R.	H.	HR.	RBI	SB
*Foote	.262	125	420	44	110	11	60	2
Foli	.254	121	441	41	112	0	39	8
Breeden	.247	79	190	14	47	2	20	0
Fairly†	.245	101	282	35	69	12	43	2
Lintz‡	.238	113	319	60	76	0	20	50
*Cox	.220	77	236	29	52	2	26	2
Frias	.214	75	112	12	24	0	7	1
Woods	.205	90	127	15	26	1	12	6

Pitching

Pitching	W.	L.	ERA	G.	IP	H.	BB	SO
*Murray	1	1	1.03	32	70	46	23	31
Taylor	6	2	2.17	61	108	101	25	43
Carrithers	5	2	3.00	22	60	56	17	31
*DeMola	1	0	3.10	25	58	46	21	47
*Montague	3	4	3.14	46	83	73	38	43
*Blair	11	7	3.27	22	146	113	72	76
Torrez	15	8	3.58	32	186	184	84	92
Walker	4	5	3.82	33	92	96	28	70
Renko	12	16	4.03	37	228	222	81	138
Rogers	15	22	4.46	38	254	255	80	154
McAnally	6	13	4.47	25	129	126	56	79

New York Mets

Batting

Batting	Pct.	G.	AB	R.	H.	HR.	RBI	SB
Kranepool†	.300	94	217	20	65	4	24	1
Jones	.282	124	461	62	130	13	60	3
Millan	.268	136	518	50	139	1	33	5
Staub†	.258	151	561	65	145	19	78	2
Grote	.257	97	319	25	82	5	36	0
Milner†	.252	137	507	70	128	20	63	10
Hahn	.251	110	323	34	81	4	28	2
Harrelson‡	.227	106	331	48	75	1	13	9
Garrett†	.224	151	522	55	117	13	53	4
Hodges†	.221	59	136	16	30	4	14	0
Martinez	.219	116	334	32	73	2	43	3
Boswell†	.216	96	222	19	48	2	15	0
Dyer	.211	63	142	14	30	0	10	0
Schneck†	.205	93	254	23	52	5	25	4

Pitching

Pitching	W.	L.	ERA	G.	IP	H.	BB	SO
Matlack†	13	15	2.41	34	265	221	76	195
Seaver	11	11	3.20	32	236	199	75	201
Koosman†	15	11	3.36	35	265	258	85	188
Sadecki†	8	8	3.41	34	103	107	35	46
*Apodaca	6	6	3.50	35	103	92	42	54
Aker	2	2	3.57	41	58	50	23	25
Miller	2	2	3.58	58	78	89	39	35
Parker	4	6	3.92	40	131	145	46	58
McGraw†	6	11	4.15	41	89	96	32	54

Philadelphia Phillies

Batting

Batting	Pct.	G.	AB	R.	H.	HR.	RBI	SB
Montanez†	.304	143	527	55	160	7	79	3
Cash	.300	162	687	89	206	2	58	20
Johnstone†	.295	64	200	30	59	6	30	5
Schmidt	.282	162	568	108	160	36	116	23
Bowa‡	.275	162	669	97	184	1	36	39
Luzinski	.272	85	302	29	82	7	48	3
Unser†	.264	142	454	72	120	11	61	6
Anderson	.251	145	395	35	99	5	34	2
Boone	.242	146	488	41	118	3	52	3
Hutton†	.240	96	208	32	50	4	33	2
Robinson	.236	100	280	32	66	5	29	5
Brown	.232	70	168	19	39	7	19	0

Pitching

Pitching	W.	L.	ERA	G.	IP	H.	BB	SO
Lonborg	17	13	3.21	39	283	280	70	121
Carlton†	16	13	3.22	39	291	249	136	240
Schueler	11	16	3.72	44	203	202	98	109
Ruthven	9	13	4.01	35	213	182	116	153
Scarce†	3	8	5.01	58	70	72	33	50
Twitchell	6	9	5.22	25	112	122	65	72

Pittsburgh Pirates

Batting

Batting	Pct.	G.	AB	R.	H.	HR.	RBI	SB
Oliver†	.321	147	617	96	198	11	85	10
Zisk	.313	149	536	75	168	17	100	1
Stargell†	.301	140	508	90	153	25	96	0
Stennett	.291	157	673	84	196	7	56	8
Hebner†	.291	146	550	97	160	18	68	0
Sanguillen	.287	151	596	77	171	7	68	2

(Pittsburgh con't.)

Batting	Pct.	G.	AB	R.	H.	HR.	RBI	SB
Parker†	.282	73	220	27	62	4	29	3
Kirkpatrick†	.247	116	271	32	67	6	38	1
*Taveras	.246	126	333	33	82	0	26	13
Robertson	.229	91	236	25	54	16	48	0
Clines	.225	107	276	29	62	0	14	14
*Mendoza	.221	91	163	10	36	0	15	1

Pitching	W.	L.	ERA	G.	IP	H.	BB	SO
Hernandez†	5	2	2.74	58	69	68	18	33
Rooker†	15	11	2.77	33	263	228	83	139
Ellis	12	9	3.15	26	177	163	41	91
Brett†	13	9	3.30	27	191	192	52	96
Giusti	7	5	3.31	64	106	101	40	53
Kison	9	8	3.49	40	129	123	57	71
Reuss†	16	11	3.50	35	260	259	101	105
*Demery	6	6	4.26	19	95	95	51	51
*Morian	0	3	4.29	39	65	54	48	38

St. Louis Cardinals

Batting	Pct.	G.	AB	R.	H.	HR.	RBI	SB
*McBride†	.309	150	559	81	173	6	56	30
Smith‡	.309	143	517	79	160	23	100	4
Brock†	.306	153	635	105	194	3	48	118
Torre	.282	147	529	59	149	11	70	1
Simmons‡	.272	152	599	66	163	20	103	0
Reitz	.271	154	579	48	157	7	54	0
Hunt	.263	127	426	67	112	0	26	2
Cruz†	.261	107	161	24	42	5	20	4
Sizemore	.250	129	504	68	126	2	47	8
Tyson	.223	151	422	35	94	1	37	4
Melendez	.218	83	124	15	27	0	8	2
McCarver†	.217	74	106	13	23	0	11	0

Pitching	W.	L.	ERA	G.	IP	H.	BB	SO
Garman	7	2	2.63	64	82	66	27	45
McGlothen	16	12	2.70	31	237	212	89	142
*Forsch	7	4	2.97	19	100	84	34	39
Hrabosky†	8	1	2.97	65	88	71	38	82
Folkers†	6	2	3.00	55	90	65	38	57
Curtis†	10	14	3.78	33	195	199	83	89
Osteen†	9	11	3.80	31	161	184	58	51
Gibson	11	13	3.83	33	240	236	104	129
Siebert	8	8	3.83	28	134	150	51	68
Foster	7	10	3.89	31	162	167	61	78

San Diego Padres

Batting	Pct.	G.	AB	R.	H.	HR.	RBI	SB
Grubb†	.286	140	444	53	127	8	42	4
Tolan†	.266	95	357	45	95	8	40	7
Winfield	.265	145	498	57	132	20	75	9
Beckert	.256	64	172	11	44	0	7	0
McCovey†	.253	128	344	53	87	22	63	1
Thomas‡	.247	141	523	48	129	3	41	7
Hilton	.240	74	217	17	52	1	12	3
Hernandez	.232	147	512	55	119	0	34	37
Kendall	.231	141	424	32	98	8	45	0
Gaston	.213	106	267	19	57	6	33	0
Colbert	.207	118	368	53	76	14	54	10
Roberts	.167	113	318	26	53	5	18	2

Pitching	W.	L.	ERA	G.	IP	H.	BB	SO
*Freisleben	9	14	3.65	33	212	194	112	131
*Spillner	9	11	4.01	30	148	153	70	95
*Tomlin†	2	0	4.34	47	58	59	30	29
Jones†	8	22	4.46	40	208	217	78	124
Romo	5	5	4.58	54	71	78	37	36
Greif	9	19	4.66	43	226	244	94	137
*Hardy	9	4	4.68	76	102	129	44	57
Corkins	2	2	4.82	25	56	53	32	41
Palmer	2	5	5.67	22	73	68	59	52
Arlin	1	7	5.91	16	64	85	37	18

San Francisco Giants

Batting	Pct.	G.	AB	R.	H.	HR.	RBI	SB
Rader†	.291	113	323	26	94	1	26	1
Matthews	.287	154	561	87	161	16	82	11
Maddox	.284	135	538	74	153	8	50	21
*Miller	.278	73	198	19	55	0	16	1
Goodson†	.272	98	298	25	81	6	41	1
*Ontiveros‡	.265	120	343	45	91	4	33	0
Rudolph	.259	57	158	11	41	0	10	0
Bonds	.256	150	567	97	145	21	71	41
Speier	.250	141	501	55	125	9	53	3
Fuentes‡	.249	108	390	33	97	0	22	7
Thomasson†	.244	120	315	41	77	2	29	7
Arnold	.241	78	174	22	42	1	26	1
Kingman	.223	121	350	41	78	18	55	8
Phillips†	.219	100	283	19	62	2	20	4

Pitching	W.	L.	ERA	G.	IP	H.	BB	SO
Barr	13	9	2.74	44	240	223	47	84
Williams	1	3	2.79	39	100	93	31	48
Caldwell†	14	5	2.95	31	189	176	63	83
Sosa	9	7	3.48	68	101	94	45	48
*D'Acquisto	12	14	3.77	38	215	182	124	167
*Halicki	1	8	4.26	16	74	84	31	40
Moffitt	5	7	4.50	61	102	99	29	49
Bradley	8	11	5.17	30	134	152	52	72
Bryant†	3	15	5.60	41	127	142	68	75

Major League Baseball Attendance

National League

Club	1974	1973	Increase Decrease
Atlanta	981,085	800,655	+180,430
Chicago	1,015,859	1,351,705	−335,846
Cincinnati	2,164,248	2,017,601	+146,647
Houston	1,090,728	1,394,004	−303,276
Los Angeles	2,632,754	2,136,192	+496,562
Montreal	1,019,134	1,246,863	−227,729
New York	1,709,309	1,912,390	−203,081
Philadelphia	1,808,693	1,475,934	+332,759
Pittsburgh	1,110,565	1,319,913	−209,348
St. Louis	1,838,459	1,574,046	+246,413
San Diego	1,075,401	611,826	+463,575
San Francisco	520,081	834,193	−314,112
Totals	**16,966,316**	**16,675,322**	**+290,994**

American League

Club	1974	1973	Increase Decrease
Baltimore	959,051	958,667	+384
Boston	1,563,307	1,481,002	+82,305
California	917,030	1,058,206	−141,176
Chicago	1,163,010	1,302,527	−139,517
Cleveland	1,111,895	615,107	+496,788
Detroit	1,243,090	1,724,146	−481,056
Kansas City	1,172,892	1,345,341	−172,449
Milwaukee	955,731	1,092,158	−136,427
Minnesota	662,401	907,499	−245,098
New York	1,272,860	1,262,103	+10,757
Oakland	812,475	1,000,763	−188,288
Texas	1,193,903	686,085	+507,818
Totals	**13,027,645**	**13,433,604**	**−405,959**

Major League Attendance Records

All-time Season Records, Both Leagues — 30,122,191 in 1973.
All-time Season Record, One Club — 2,755,184 — Los Angeles Dodgers, 1962.
Record Attendance, World Series — 420,784 — 1959 Series between Los Angeles Dodgers and Chicago White Sox.
Record Attendance, World Series Game — 92,706 — fifth game, 1959 Series, Los Angeles, Oct. 6.
Record Attendance, Regular Season Game — 84,587 — Municipal Stadium, Cleveland, Sept. 12, 1954, in doubleheader between the Indians and Yankees. (Not including pass list of 1,976.)
Attendance, Regular-Season Single Game — 78,672 — Los Angeles Memorial Coliseum, April 18, 1958, in opening game between Los Angeles Dodgers and San Francisco Giants.

American League Records, 1974

Final Standings

Eastern Division

	W.	L.	PCT.	G.B.
Baltimore	91	71	.562	—
New York	89	73	.549	2
Boston	84	78	.519	7
Cleveland	77	85	.475	14
Milwaukee	76	86	.469	15
Detroit	72	90	.444	19

Western Division

	W.	L.	PCT.	G.B.
Oakland	90	72	.556	—
Texas	84	76	.525	5
Minnesota	82	80	.506	8
Chicago	80	80	.500	9
Kansas City	77	85	.475	13
California	68	94	.420	22

American League Playoffs

Oct. 5—Baltimore 6, Oakland 3.
Oct. 6—Oakland 5, Baltimore 0.
Oct. 8—Oakland 1, Baltimore 0.

Oct. 9—Oakland 2, Baltimore 1.
(Oakland won 3-of-5 series, 3-1)

*Rookie †Bats—Pitches Lefthanded ‡ Switch Hitter

Club Batting

Club	Pct.	AB	R.	H.	HR.	SB
Texas	272	5449	690	1482	99	113
Minnesota	272	5632	673	1530	111	74
Chicago	268	5577	684	1492	135	64
Boston	264	5499	696	1449	109	104
New York	263	5524	671	1451	101	53
Kansas City	259	5582	667	1448	89	146
Baltimore	256	5535	659	1417	116	145
Cleveland	255	5474	662	1395	131	79
California	254	5401	618	1372	95	120
Detroit	247	5568	620	1375	131	67
Oakland	247	5331	689	1315	132	164
Milwaukee	244	5472	647	1335	120	106

Club Pitching

Club	ERA	G.	IP	H.	R.	BB.	SO.
Oakland	2.95	162	1440	1322	551	430	754
Baltimore	3.27	162	1474	1393	612	480	700
New York	3.31	162	1455	1402	623	528	829
Kansas City	3.51	162	1472	1477	662	482	731
California	3.52	163	1439	1339	657	649	986
Minnesota	3.64	163	1455	1436	669	513	934
Boston	3.72	162	1455	1462	661	463	751
Milwaukee	3.76	162	1458	1475	660	493	621
Cleveland	3.80	62	1446	1419	694	479	650
Texas	3.82	161	1434	1423	698	449	871
Chicago	3.94	163	1466	1470	721	548	826
Detroit	4.16	162	1456	1443	768	621	869

Individual Batting

Leaders—450 or More At Bats

Player—Club	Pct.	AB	R.	H.	HR.	RBI	SB
Carew, Minnesota†	.364	599	86	218	3	55	38
Orta, Chicago†	.316	525	73	166	10	67	9
McRae, Kansas City	.310	539	71	167	15	88	11
Piniella, New York	.305	518	71	158	9	70	1
Maddox, New York	.303	466	75	141	3	45	6
Randle, Texas‡	.302	520	65	157	1	49	26
Burroughs, Texas	.301	554	84	167	25	118	2
Yastrzemski, Boston†	.301	515	93	155	15	79	12
R. Allen, Chicago	.301	462	84	139	32	88	7

Individual Pitching

Leaders—162 or More Innings

Pitcher—Club	W.	L.	ERA	G.	IP	H.	BB	SO.
Hunter, Oakland	25	12	2.49	41	318	268	46	143
G. Perry, Cleveland	21	13	2.52	37	322	230	99	216
Hassler, California†	7	11	2.61	23	162	132	79	76
Blyleven, Minnesota	17	17	2.66	37	281	244	77	249
Fitzmorris, Kansas City	13	6	2.79	34	190	189	63	53
Jenkins, Texas	25	12	2.83	41	328	286	45	225
Ryan, California	22	16	2.89	42	333	221	202	367
Tiant, Boston	22	13	2.92	38	311	281	82	176
Kaat, Chicago†	21	13	2.92	42	277	263	63	142
J. Perry, Cleveland	17	12	2.96	36	252	242	64	71

Individual Batting (over 100 at-bats) Individual Pitching (over 50 innings)
*Rookie †Bats-Pitches lefthanded ‡Switch hitter

Baltimore Orioles

Batting	Pct.	G.	AB	R.	H.	HR.	RBI	SB
Davis	.289	158	626	67	181	11	84	6
Robinson	.288	153	553	46	159	7	59	2
Baylor	.272	137	489	66	133	10	59	29
Powell†	.265	110	344	37	91	12	45	0
Grich	.261	160	582	92	152	19	82	17
Blair	.261	151	552	77	144	17	62	27
Williams	.254	118	413	47	105	14	52	0
Coggins†	.243	113	411	53	100	4	32	26
Northrup†	.243	105	383	43	93	12	45	0
Oliver	.243	119	379	23	92	8	59	3
Cabell	.241	80	174	24	42	3	17	5
Bumbry†	.233	94	270	35	63	1	19	12
Belanger	.225	155	493	54	111	5	36	17
*Fuller	.222	64	189	17	42	7	28	1
Etchebarren	.222	62	180	13	40	2	15	1
Hendricks†	.208	66	159	18	33	3	8	0

Pitching	W.	L.	ERA	G.	IP	H.	BB.	SO
Jackson†	6	4	2.55	49	67	48	22	56
Reynolds	7	5	2.74	54	69	75	14	43
*Garland	5	5	2.97	20	91	68	26	40
Grimsley†	18	13	3.07	40	296	267	76	158
Cuellar†	22	10	3.11	38	269	253	86	106
Palmer	7	12	3.27	26	179	176	69	84
Hood†	1	1	3.58	20	57	47	20	25
McNally†	16	10	3.58	39	259	260	81	111
Alexander	6	9	4.03	30	114	127	43	40
Jefferson	1	0	4.42	20	57	55	38	31

Boston Red Sox

Batting	Pct.	G.	AB	R.	H.	HR.	RBI	SB
Yastrzemski†	.301	148	515	93	155	15	79	12
Fisk	.299	52	187	36	56	11	26	5
*Burleson	.284	114	384	36	109	4	44	3
Evans	.281	133	463	60	130	10	70	4
Cooper†	.275	121	414	55	114	8	43	2
Beniquez	.267	106	389	60	104	5	33	19
Petrocelli	.267	129	454	53	121	15	76	1
Griffin	.266	93	312	35	83	0	33	2
Miller†	.261	114	280	41	73	5	22	13
Montgomery	.252	88	254	26	64	4	38	3
Carbo†	.249	117	338	40	84	12	61	4
Guerrero	.246	93	284	18	70	0	23	3
Carter	.246	56	126	14	31	5	20	1
*Blackwell‡	.246	44	122	9	30	0	8	1
Harper	.237	118	443	66	105	5	24	28
McAuliffe†	.210	100	272	32	57	5	24	2
Johnson	.171	110	351	30	60	13	43	2

Pitching	W.	L.	ERA	G.	IP	H.	BB.	SO
Tiant	22	13	2.92	38	311	281	82	176
Drago	7	10	3.48	33	176	165	56	90
Lee†	17	15	3.51	38	282	320	67	95
Moret†	9	10	3.75	31	173	158	79	111
Sequi	6	8	4.00	58	108	106	49	76
Cleveland	12	14	4.32	41	221	234	69	103
Marichal	5	1	4.89	11	57	61	14	21

California Angels

Batting	Pct.	G.	AB	R.	H.	HR.	RBI	SB
Rivers†	.285	118	466	69	133	3	31	30
*Nettles†	.274	56	175	27	48	0	8	20
Lahoud†	.271	127	325	46	88	13	44	4
*Bochte†	.270	57	196	24	53	5	26	6
Stanton	.267	118	415	48	111	11	52	10
Valentine	.261	117	371	39	97	3	39	8
Lienas	.261	72	138	16	36	2	17	0
Doyle†	.260	147	511	47	133	1	34	6
*Doherty†	.256	74	223	20	57	3	15	2
Rodriquez	.253	140	395	48	100	7	36	4
*Chalk	.252	133	465	44	117	5	31	10
Schaal	.236	65	199	13	47	3	24	2

Pitching	W.	L.	ERA	G.	IP	H.	BB	SO
Hassler†	7	11	2.61	23	162	132	79	76
Ryan	22	16	2.89	42	333	221	202	367
Singer	7	4	2.97	14	109	102	43	77
*Tanana†	14	19	3.11	39	269	262	77	180
*Figueroa	2	8	3.69	25	105	119	36	49
Lange	3	8	3.79	21	114	111	47	57
Lockwood	2	5	4.33	37	81	81	32	39
Stoneman	1	8	6.10	13	59	78	31	33

Chicago White Sox

Batting	Pct.	G.	AB	R.	H.	HR.	RBI	SB
Orta†	.316	139	525	73	166	10	67	9
Allen	.301	128	462	84	139	32	88	7
Henderson‡	.292	162	602	76	176	20	95	12
Muser†	.291	103	206	16	60	1	18	1
Kelly†	.281	122	424	60	119	4	21	18
*Dent	.274	154	496	55	136	5	45	3
Herrmann†	.259	107	367	32	95	10	39	1
Sharp†	.253	100	320	45	81	4	24	0
May†	.249	149	551	66	137	8	58	8
Melton	.242	136	495	63	120	21	63	3
Hairston‡	.229	45	109	8	25	0	8	0
*Downing	.225	108	293	41	66	10	39	0
Santo	.221	117	375	29	83	5	41	0

Pitching	W.	L.	ERA	G.	IP	H.	BB	SO
B.Johnson	10	4	2.73	18	122	105	32	76
Kaat†	21	13	2.92	42	277	263	63	142
Wood†	20	19	3.60	42	320	305	80	169
Forster†	7	8	3.33	59	134	120	48	105
Gossage	4	6	4.15	39	89	92	47	64
Pitlock†	3	3	4.42	40	106	103	55	68
Bahnsen	12	15	4.17	38	216	230	110	102

Cleveland Indians

Batting	Pct.	G.	AB	R.	H.	HR.	RBI	SB
McCraw†	.294	101	231	38	68	6	34	2
Gamble†	.291	135	454	74	132	19	59	5
Ellis	.285	128	477	58	136	10	64	1
Hendrick	.279	139	495	65	138	19	67	6
Spikes	.271	155	568	63	154	22	80	10
Brohamer†	.270	101	315	33	85	2	30	2
Bell	.262	116	423	51	111	7	46	1
Robinson	.245	144	477	81	117	22	68	5
Lowenstein†	.242	140	508	65	123	8	48	36
Duffy	.233	158	549	62	128	8	48	7
Lee†	.233	79	232	18	54	5	25	3
Hermoso	.221	48	122	15	27	0	5	2
Alvarado	.210	69	124	13	26	0	12	1
Duncan	.200	136	425	45	85	16	46	0
Lis	.200	81	150	20	30	6	19	1
Torres‡	.187	108	150	19	28	3	12	2

Pitching	W.	L.	ERA	G.	IP	H.	BB	SO
G. Perry	21	13	2.52	37	322	230	99	216
J. Perry	17	12	2.96	36	252	242	64	71
*Buskey	2	7	3.36	55	99	103	36	43
Bosman	7	5	4.11	25	127	126	29	56
R. Johnson	3	4	4.38	14	72	75	37	36
Peterson†	9	14	4.39	32	160	200	39	57
Kline	5	10	4.64	20	97	96	36	23
Beene	4	4	4.66	38	83	77	28	45
Wilcox	2	2	4.69	41	71	74	24	33

Detroit Tigers

Batting	Pct.	G.	AB	R.	H.	HR.	RBI	SB
Horton	.298	72	238	32	71	15	47	0
Freehan	.297	130	445	58	132	18	60	2
Oglivie†	.270	92	252	28	68	4	29	12
Kaline	.262	147	558	71	146	13	64	2
*LeFlore	.260	59	254	37	66	2	13	23
Sutherland	.254	149	619	60	157	5	49	1

(Detroit con't.)	Pct.	G.	AB	R.	H.	HR.	RBI	SB
Moses	.237	74	198	19	47	4	19	0
*Lane	.233	50	103	16	24	2	9	2
N. Cash†	.228	53	149	17	34	7	12	1
Nettles†	.227	43	141	20	32	6	17	3
Rodriguez	.222	159	571	54	127	5	49	2
Brinkman	.221	153	502	55	111	14	54	2
Stanley	.221	99	394	40	87	8	34	5
Sharon	.217	60	129	12	28	2	10	4

Pitching	W.	L.	ERA	G.	IP	H.	BB	SO
Hiller†	17	14	2.64	59	150	127	62	134
*Lemanczyk	2	1	3.99	22	79	79	44	52
Lolich†	16	21	4.15	41	308	310	78	202
Coleman	14	12	4.31	41	286	272	158	177
Fryman†	6	9	4.31	27	142	120	67	92
Ray	1	3	4.50	28	52	49	29	26
LaGrow	8	19	4.67	37	216	245	80	85
Slayback	1	3	4.75	16	55	57	26	23
Walker†	5	5	4.99	28	92	100	54	52

Kansas City Royals

Batting	Pct.	G.	AB	R.	H.	HR.	RBI	SB
McRae	.310	148	539	71	167	15	88	11
Otis	.284	146	552	87	157	12	73	18
*Brett‡	.282	133	457	49	129	2	47	8
Pinson†	.276	115	406	46	112	6	41	21
Rojas	.271	144	542	52	147	6	60	8
Wohlford	.271	143	501	55	136	2	44	16
*Solaita‡	.268	96	239	31	64	7	30	0
Healy	.252	139	445	59	112	9	53	16
*Cowens	.242	110	269	28	65	1	25	5
Mayberry†	.234	126	427	63	100	22	69	4
Patek	.225	149	537	72	121	3	38	33
White	.221	99	204	19	45	1	18	3
Martinez	.215	43	107	10	23	1	8	0
Cepeda	.215	33	107	3	23	1	18	1
Scheinblum‡	.174	46	109	8	19	0	4	0

Pitching	W.	L.	ERA	G.	IP	H.	BB	SO
Bird	7	6	2.74	55	92	100	27	62
Fitzmorris	13	6	2.79	34	190	189	63	53
Mingori†	2	3	2.82	36	67	53	23	43
Dal Canton	8	10	3.14	31	175	135	82	96
Busby	22	14	3.39	38	292	284	92	198
McDaniel	1	4	3.53	38	107	109	24	47
Pattin	3	7	4.00	25	117	121	28	50
Briles	5	7	4.02	18	103	118	21	41
Splittorff†	13	19	4.10	36	226	252	75	90

Milwaukee Brewers

Batting	Pct.	G.	AB	R.	H.	HR.	RBI	SB
Money	.283	159	629	85	178	15	65	9
Scott	.281	158	604	74	170	17	82	9
Briggs†	.253	154	554	72	140	17	73	9
*Yount	.250	107	344	48	86	3	26	7
*Moore	.245	72	204	17	50	0	19	3
T. Johnson†	.245	93	245	25	60	0	25	4
Mitchell	.243	88	173	27	42	5	20	7
Porter†	.241	131	432	59	104	12	56	8
Berry	.240	98	267	21	64	1	24	3
Hegan†	.235	107	243	24	57	9	41	1
May†	.226	135	477	56	108	10	42	4
Coluccio	.223	138	394	42	88	6	31	15
Garcia	.199	141	452	46	90	12	54	8

Pitching	W.	L.	ERA	G.	IP	H.	BB	SO
Murphy	10	10	1.90	70	123	97	51	47
Sprague	7	2	2.39	20	94	94	31	57
Champion	11	4	3.61	31	162	168	49	60
Rodriguez	7	4	3.62	43	112	97	51	58
Slaton	13	16	3.92	40	250	254	102	126
*Kobel†	6	14	3.99	34	169	166	54	74
Colborn	10	13	4.06	33	224	230	60	83
Wright†	9	20	4.42	38	232	264	54	64
*Travers†	2	3	4.92	23	53	59	30	31

Minnesota Twins

Batting	Pct.	G.	AB	R.	H.	HR.	RBI	SB
Carew†	.364	153	599	86	218	3	55	38
Hisle	.286	143	510	68	146	19	79	12
Oliva†	.285	127	459	43	131	13	57	0
Brye	.283	135	488	52	138	2	41	1
Braun†	.280	129	453	53	127	8	40	4
Soderholm	.276	141	464	63	128	10	51	7
Darwin	.264	152	575	67	152	25	94	1
Borgmann	.252	128	345	33	87	3	45	2
Thompson	.250	97	264	25	66	4	25	1
Terrell‡	.245	116	229	43	56	0	19	3
*Kusick	.239	76	201	36	48	8	26	0
Bourque†	.225	96	160	11	36	2	24	0
Killebrew	.222	122	333	28	74	13	54	0
*Gomez	.208	82	168	18	35	0	3	2

(Minnesota con't.)

Pitching	W.	L.	ERA	G.	IP	H.	BB	SO
Campbell	8	7	2.63	63	120	109	55	89
Blyleven	17	17	2.6(	37	281	244	77	249
Goltz	10	10	3.26	28	174	192	45	89
Decker	16	14	3.29	37	249	234	97	158
Butler†	4	6	4.09	26	99	91	56	79
*Albury†	8	9	4.12	32	164	159	80	85
Burgmeier†	5	3	4.50	50	92	92	26	34
Corbin	7	6	5.30	29	112	133	40	50

New York Yankees

Batting	Pct.	G.	AB	R.	H.	HR.	RBI	SB
Blomberg†	.311	90	264	39	82	10	48	2
Piniella	.305	140	518	71	158	.9	70	1
Maddox	.303	137	466	75	141	3	45	6
Johnson	.287	124	481	60	138	5	43	20
White‡	.275	136	473	68	130	7	43	15
Murcer†	.274	156	606	69	166	10	88	14
Alomar‡	.261	122	333	47	87	1	28	8
Munson	.261	144	517	64	135	13	60	2
Michael‡	.260	81	177	19	.46	0	13	0
Chambliss†	.255	127	467	46	119	6	50	0
Mason‡	.250	152	440	41	110	5	37	1
Nettles†	.246	155	566	74	139	22	75	1
Dempsey	.239	43	109	12	26	2	12	1
Sudakis†	.232	89	259	26	60	7	39	0
Gonzalez	.204	60	142	12	29	1	9	1

Pitching	W.	L.	ERA	G.	IP	H.	BB	SO
L yet	9	3	1.66	66	114	93	43	89
Gura†	5	1	2.41	8	56	54	12	17
Wallace†	6	0	2.42	23	52	42	35	34
Upshaw	1	6	3.04	43	68	63	28	34
Dobson	19	15	3.07	39	281	282	75	157
May†	8	5	3.19	35	141	104	58	102
Stottlemyre	6	7	3.58	16	113	119	37	40
Medich	19	15	3.60	38	280	275	91	154
Tidrow	12	12	4.16	37	210	226	66	108
Woodson	2	3	5.07	13	55	64	16	24

Oakland A's

Batting	Pct.	G.	AB	R.	H.	HR.	RBI	SB
Rudi	.293	148	593	73	174	22	99	2
Campaneris	.290	134	527	77	153	2	41	34
Jackson†	.289	148	506	90	146	29	93	25
*C. Washington†	.285	73	221	16	63	0	19	6

(Oakland con't.)

	Pct.	G.	AB	R.	H.	HR.	RBI	SB
Alou	.268	96	220	13	59	2	15	0
North‡	.260	149	543	79	141	4	33	54
Bando	.243	146	498	84	121	22	103	2
Holt†	.234	109	239	25	56	0	16	0
Mangual	.233	115	365	37	85	9	43	3
Green	.213	100	287	20	61	2	22	2
Tenace	.211	158	484	71	102	26	73	2
Kubiak‡	.209	99	220	22	46	0	18	1
Fosse	.196	69	204	20	40	4	23	1
Haney	.165	76	121	12	20	2	3	1

Pitching	W.	L.	ERA	G.	IP	H.	BB	SO
Lindblad†	4	4	2.05	45	101	85	30	46
Hunter	25	12	2.49	41	318	268	46	143
Fingers	9	5	2.65	76	119	104	29	95
*Abbott	5	7	3.00	19	96	89	34	37
Holtzman†	19	17	3.07	39	255	273	51	117
Hamilton†	7	4	3.15	29	117	104	48	69
Blue†	17	15	3.26	40	282	246	98	174
Odom	1	5	3.83	34	87	85	52	52
Knowles†	3	3	4.25	45	53	61	35	18

Texas Rangers

Batting	Pct.	G.	AB	R.	H.	HR.	RBI	SB
*Hargrove†	.323	131	415	57	134	4	66	0
Randle‡	.302	151	520	65	157	1	49	26
Burroughs	.301	152	554	84	167	25	118	2
Tovar	.292	138	562	78	164	4	58	13
Spencer†	.278	118	352	36	98	7	44	1
Fregosi	.261	78	230	31	60	12	34	0
Harrah	.260	161	573	79	149	21	74	15
Grieve	.255	84	259	30	66	9	32	0
*Sundberg	.247	132	368	45	91	3	36	2
Nelson	.236	121	474	71	112	3	42	25
Lovitto‡	.223	113	283	27	63	2	26	6
Sims†	.198	44	121	8	24	3	8	0

Pitching	W.	L.	ERA	G.	IP	H.	BB	SO
Foucault	8	9	2.25	69	144	123	40	106
Jenkins	25	12	2.83	41	328	286	45	225
J. Brown	13	12	3.57	35	217	219	74	134
Hargan	12	9	3.95	37	187	202	48	98
Hands	6	5	4.19	37	129	141	28	78
Clyde†	3	9	4.38	28	117	129	47	52
Bibby	19	19	4.74	41	264	255	113	149

Leading Pitchers. Earned-Run Average

Based on 10 complete games through 1950 then 154 innings until A. L. expanded in '61, N. L. in '62, then 162 innings.

National League

Year	Pitcher, Club	G	IP	ERA
1950	Jim Hearn, St. L.-N. Y.	22	134	2.49
1951	Chet Nichols, Boston	33	156	2.88
1952	Hoyt Wilhelm, New York	71	159	2.43
1953	Warren Spahn, Milwaukee	35	266	2.10
1954	John Antonelli, New York	39	259	2.29
1955	Bob Friend, Pittsburgh	44	200	2.84
1956	Lew Burdette, Milwaukee	39	256	2.71
1957	Johnny Podres, Brooklyn	31	196	2.66
1958	Stu Miller, San Francisco	41	182	2.47
1959	Sam Jones, San Francisco	50	271	2.82
1960	Mike McCormick, San Fran.	40	253	2.70
1961	Warren Spahn, Milwaukee	38	263	3.01
1962	Sandy Koufax, Los Angeles	28	184	2.54
1963	Sandy Koufax, Los Angeles	40	311	1.88
1964	Sandy Koufax, Los Angeles	29	223	1.74
1965	Sandy Koufax, Los Angeles	43	336	2.04
1966	Sandy Koufax, Los Angeles	41	323	1.73
1967	Phil Niekro, Atlanta	46	207	1.87
1968	Bob Gibson, St. Louis	34	305	1.12
1969	Juan Marichal, San Francisco	37	300	2.10
1970	Tom Seaver, New York	37	291	2.81
1971	Tom Seaver, New York	36	286	1.76
1972	Steve Carlton, Philadelphia	41	346	1.98
1973	Tom Seaver, New York	36	290	2.07
1974	Buzz Capra, Atlanta	39	217	2.28

American League

Year	Pitcher, Club	G	IP	ERA
1950	Early Wynn, Cleveland	32	214	3.20
1951	Saul Rogovin, Det.-Chi.	27	217	2.78
1952	Allie Reynolds, New York	35	244	2.07
1953	Ed Lopat, New York	25	178	2.43
1954	Mike Garcia, Cleveland	45	259	2.64
1955	Billy Pierce, chicago	33	206	1.97
1956	Whitey Ford, New York	31	226	2.47
1957	Bobby Shantz, New York	30	173	2.01
1958	Whitey Ford, New York	30	219	2.01
1959	Hoyt Wilhelm, Baltimore	32	226	2.19
1960	Frank Baumann, Chicago	47	185	2.68
1961	Dick Donovan, Washington	23	169	2.40
1962	Hank Aguirre, Detroit	42	2`6	2.21
1963	Gary Peters, Chicago	41	243	2.33
1964	Dean Chance, Los Angeles	46	278	1.56
1965	Sam McDowell, Cleveland	42	274	2.17
1966	Gary Peters, Chicago	29	204	2.03
1967	Joe Horlen, Chicago	35	258	2.06
1968	Luis Tiant, Cleveland	34	258	1.60
1969	Dick Bosman, Washington	31	193	2.19
1970	Diego Segui, Oakland	47	162	2.56
1971	Vida Blue, Oakland	39	312	1.82
1972	Luis Tiant, Boston	43	179	1.91
1973	Jim Palmer, Baltimore	38	296	2.40
1974	Catfish Hunter, Oakland	41	318	2.49

ERA is computed by multiplying the number of earned runs allowed by 9, then dividing by the number of innings pitched.

Aaron Passes Ruth in Lifetime Home Runs

Shortly after the start of the 1974 baseball season, Henry Aaron of the Atlanta Braves hit his 714th and 715 home run to equal and pass the major league lifetime home run record of the immortal Babe Ruth. Because they played in different eras, it is not possible to compare the two baseball greats as home run hitters. Below is the major league record of both men.

Henry Louis (Hank) Aaron
Born, Mobile, Alabama, February 5, 1934.
Bats Right.   Throws Right.   Height, 6 feet.   Weight, 180 pounds.

Year Club League	Pos.	g.	ab	r.	h.	2b	3b	hr.	rbi	sb	Avg.
1954 Milwaukee...... NL	OF	122	468	58	131	27	6	13	69	2	.280
1955 Milwaukee...... NL	OF-2B	153	602	105	*189	*37	9	27	106	3	.314
1956 Milwaukee...... NL	OF	153	609	106	*200	*34	14	26	92	2	*.328
1957 Milwaukee (a)... NL	OF	151	615	*118	198	27	6	*44	*132	1	.322
1958 Milwaukee...... NL	OF	153	601	109	196	34	4	30	95	4	.326
1959 Milwaukee...... NL	OF-3B	154	629	116	*223	46	7	39	123	8	*.355
1960 Milwaukee...... NL	OF-2B	153	590	102	172	20	11	40	*126	16	.292
1961 Milwaukee...... NL	OF-3B	*155	603	115	197	*39	10	34	120	21	.327
1962 Milwaukee...... NL	OF-1B	156	592	127	191	28	6	45	128	15	.323
1963 Milwaukee...... NL	OF	161	631	*121	201	29	4	*44	*130	31	.319
1964 Milwaukee...... NL	OF-2B	145	570	103	187	30	2	24	95	22	.328
1965 Milwaukee...... NL	OF	150	570	109	181	*40	1	32	89	24	.318
1966 Atlanta........ NL	OF-2B	158	603	117	168	23	1	*44	*127	21	.279
1967 Atlanta........ NL	OF-2B	155	600	*113	184	37	3	*39	109	17	.307
1968 Atlanta........ NL	OF-1B	160	606	84	174	33	4	29	86	28	.287
1969 Atlanta........ NL	OF-1B	147	547	100	164	30	3	44	97	9	.300
1970 Atlanta........ NL	OF-1B	150	516	103	154	26	1	38	118	9	.298
1971 Atlanta........ NL	1B-OF	139	495	95	162	22	3	47	118	1	.327
1972 Atlanta........ NL	1B-OF	129	449	75	119	10	0	34	77	4	.265
1973 Atlanta........ NL	OF-1B	120	392	84	118	12	1	40	96	1	.301
1974 Atlanta........ NL	OF-1B	112	340	47	91	16	0	20	69	1	.268
Major League Totals		**3,076**	**11,628**	**2,107**	**3,600**	**600**	**96**	**733**	**2,202**	**240**	**.309**

Championship Series

	g.	ab	r.	h.	2b	3b	hr.	rbi	sb	Avg.
1969 Atlanta......... NL OF	3	14	3	5	2	0	3	7	0	.357

World Series Record

		g.	ab	r.	h.	2b	3b	hr.	rbi	sb	Avg.
1957 Milwaukee...... NL	OF	7	28	5	11	0	1	3	7	0	.393
1958 Milwaukee...... NL	OF	7	27	3	9	2	0	0	2	0	.333
World Series Totals ..		**14**	**55**	**8**	**20**	**2**	**1**	**3**	**9**	**0**	**.364**

(a) Selected most valuable player in National League for 1957. * Led league.

George Herman (Babe) Ruth
Born, Baltimore, Md., Feb. 6, 1895. Died Aug. 16, 1948 in New York
Batted and Threw Left Handed. Height 6 ft. 2 in. Weight 215 lbs.

Year Club League	Pos. (b)	g.	ab	r.	h.	2b	3b	hr.	rbi	sb	Ave.
1914 Boston........ AL	P-OF	5	10	1	2	1	0	0	2	0	.200
1915 Boston........ AL	P-OF	42	92	16	29	10	1	4	21	0	.315
1916 Boston........ AL	P-OF	67	136	18	37	5	3	3	15	0	.272
1917 Boston........ AL	P-OF	52	123	14	40	6	3	2	12	0	.325
1918 Boston........ AL	P-OF	95	317	50	95	26	11	*11	66	6	.300
1919 Boston........ AL	P-OF	130	432	*103	139	34	12	*29	396	2	.315
1920 New York...... AL	P-OF	142	458	*158	172	36	9	*54	*137	14	.376
1921 New York...... AL	P-OF	152	540	*177	204	44	16	*59	*170	17	.378
1922 New York...... AL	OF	110	406	94	128	24	8	35	96	2	.315
1923 New York...... AL	OF	152	522	*151	205	45	13	*41	*130	17	.393
1924 New York...... AL	OF	153	529	*143	200	39	7	*46	121	9	*.378
1925 New York...... AL	OF	98	359	61	104	12	2	25	66	2	.290
1926 New York...... AL	OF	152	495	*139	184	30	5	*47	*155	11	.372
1927 New York...... AL	OF	151	540	*158	192	29	8	*60	164	7	.356
1928 New York...... AL	OF	154	536	*163	173	29	8	*54	*142	4	.323
1929 New York...... AL	OF	135	499	121	172	26	6	*46	154	5	.345
1930 New York...... AL	P-OF	145	518	150	186	28	9	*49	153	10	.359
1931 New York...... AL	OF	145	534	149	199	31	3	*46	163	5	.373
1932 New York...... AL	OF	132	457	120	156	13	5	41	137	2	.341
1933 New York...... AL	OF-P	137	459	97	138	21	3	34	103	4	.301
1934 New York...... AL	OF	125	365	78	105	17	4	22	84	1	.288
1935 Boston........ NL	OF	28	72	13	13	0	0	6	12	0	.181
Major League Totals		**2,502**	**8,399**	**2,174**	**2,873**	**506**	**136**	**714**	**2,216**	**123**	**.342**

(b) Played a limited number of games at first base. * Led league.

World Series Record

	g.	ab	r.	h.	2b	3b	hr.	rbi	sb	Avg.
1915 Boston........ AL	1	1	0	0	0	0	0	0	0	.000
1916 Boston........ AL	1	5	0	0	0	0	0	0	0	.000
1918 Boston........ AL	3	5	0	1	0	1	0	2	0	.200
1921 New York...... AL	6	16	3	5	0	0	1	4	2	.313
1922 New York...... AL	5	17	1	2	1	0	0	1	0	.118
1924 New York...... AL	6	19	8	7	1	1	3	3	0	.368
1926 New York...... AL	7	20	6	6	0	0	4	5	1	.300
1927 New York...... AL	4	15	4	6	0	0	2	7	1	.400
1928 New York...... AL	4	16	9	10	3	0	3	4	0	.625
1932 New York...... AL	4	15	6	5	0	0	2	6	0	.333
World Series Totals	**41**	**129**	**37**	**42**	**5**	**2**	**15**	**33**	**4**	**.326**

World Series, 1974
Composite Box Score
Oakland A's

	G	AB	R	H	2B	3B	HR	RBI	BB	SO	BA	PO	A	E	FA
Jim Holt, ph-1b	4	3	0	2	0	0	0	2	0	0	.667	1	0	0	1.000
Claudell C. Washington, rf-ph-cf-lf	5	7	1	4	0	0	0	0	1	1	.571	3	0	0	1.000
Ken Holtzman, p	2	4	2	2	1	0	1	1	1	1	.500	0	3	0	1.000
Campy Campaneris, ss	5	17	1	6	2	0	0	2	0	2	.353	6	16	2	.917
Joe Rudi, lf-1b	5	18	1	6	0	0	1	4	0	3	.333	28	0	0	1.000
Reggie Jackson, rf	5	14	3	4	1	0	1	1	5	3	.286	6	1	1	.875
Gene Tenace, 1b	5	9	0	2	0	0	0	0	3	4	.222	20	1	0	1.000
Ray Fosse, c	5	14	1	2	0	0	1	1	1	5	.143	27	1	0	1.000
Sal Bando, 3b	5	16	3	1	0	0	0	2	2	5	.063	2	10	0	1.000
Bill North, cf	5	17	3	1	0	0	0	0	2	5	.059	17	0	1	.944
Jesus Alou, ph	1	1	0	0	0	0	0	0	0	1	.000	0	0	0	.000
Angel Mangual, ph	1	1	0	0	0	0	0	0	0	1	.000	0	0	0	.000
Rollie Fingers, p	4	2	0	0	0	0	0	0	0	1	.000	0	1	0	1.000
Catfish Hunter, p	2	2	0	0	0	0	0	0	0	2	.000	1	1	0	1.000
Vida Blue, p	2	4	0	0	0	0	0	0	0	4	.000	0	3	0	1.000
Dick Green, 2b	5	13	1	0	0	0	0	1	1	4	.000	15	14	1	.967
Herb Washington, pr	3	0	0	0	0	0	0	0	0	0	.000	0	0	0	.000
Larry Haney, c	2	0	0	0	0	0	0	0	0	0	.000	6	0	0	1.000
Dal Maxvill, 2b-pr	2	0	0	0	0	0	0	0	0	0	.000	0	0	0	.000
Blue Moon Odom, p	2	0	0	0	0	0	0	0	0	0	.000	0	0	0	.000
Total	5	142	16	30	4	0	4	14	16	42	.211	132	51	5	.973

Los Angeles Dodgers

	G	AB	R	H	2B	3B	HR	RBI	BB	SO	BA	PO	A	E	FA
Andy Messersmith, p	2	4	0	2	0	0	0	0	0	2	.500	1	4	1	.833
Tom Paciorek, pr-ph	3	2	1	1	1	0	0	0	0	0	.500	0	0	0	.000
Steve Garvey, 1b	5	21	2	8	0	0	0	1	0	3	.381	34	3	0	1.000
Steve Yeager, c	4	11	0	4	1	0	0	1	1	4	.364	32	4	1	.973
Willie Crawford, ph-rf	3	6	1	2	0	0	1	1	0	0	.333	1	0	0	1.000
Bill Buckner, lf	5	20	1	5	1	0	1	1	0	1	.250	11	0	0	1.000
Bill Russell, ss	5	18	0	4	0	1	0	2	0	2	.222	4	11	1	.938
Jim Wynn, cf	5	16	1	3	1	0	1	2	4	4	.188	5	0	0	1.000
Ron Cey, 3b	5	17	1	3	0	0	0	0	3	3	.176	5	9	1	.933
Joe Ferguson, rf-c	5	16	2	2	0	0	1	2	4	6	.125	14	1	2	.882
Dave Lopes, 2b	5	18	2	2	0	0	0	0	2	4	.111	19	9	0	1.000
Al Downing, ph	1	1	0	0	0	0	0	0	0	1	.000	0	0	0	.000
Leondaus Lacy, ph	1	1	0	0	0	0	0	0	0	0	.000	0	0	0	.000
Don Sutton, p	2	3	0	0	0	0	0	0	0	2	.000	0	2	0	1.000
Von Joshua, ph	4	4	0	0	0	0	0	0	0	0	.000	0	0	0	.000
Mike Marshall, p	5	0	0	0	0	0	0	0	1	0	.000	0	4	0	1.000
Rick Auerbach, pr	1	0	0	0	0	0	0	0	0	0	.000	0	0	0	.000
Jim Brewer, p	1	0	0	0	0	0	0	0	0	0	.000	0	0	0	.000
Charlie Hough, p	1	0	0	0	0	0	0	0	0	0	.000	0	0	0	.000
Total	5	158	11	36	4	1	4	10	16	32	.228	126	50	6	.967

Pitching Summary
Oakland

	G	GS	CG	IP	H	R	ER	BB	SO	HB	WP	W	L	Pct.	ERA
Blue Moon Odom	2	0	0	$1\frac{1}{3}$	0	0	0	1	2	0	0	1	0	1.000	0.00
Catfish Hunter	2	1	0	$7\frac{2}{3}$	5	1	1	2	5	0	0	1	0	1.000	1.17
Ken Holtzman	2	2	0	12	13	3	2	4	10	0	1	1	0	1.000	1.50
Rollie Fingers	4	0	0	$9\frac{1}{3}$	8	2	2	2	6	1	0	1	0	1.000	1.93
Vida Blue	2	2	0	$13\frac{2}{3}$	10	5	5	7	9	0	0	0	1	.000	3.29
Total	5	5	0	44	36	11	10	16	32	1	1	4	1	.800	2.05

Saves—Fingers 2, Hunter

Los Angeles

	G	GS	CG	IP	H	R	ER	BB	SO	HB	WP	W	L	Pct.	ERA
Charlie Hough	1	0	0	2	0	0	0	1	4	0	1	0	0	.000	0.00
Jim Brewer	1	0	0	$\frac{1}{3}$	0	0	0	0	1	0	0	0	0	.000	0.00
Mike Marshall	5	0	0	9	6	1	1	1	10	0	0	0	1	.000	1.00
Al Downing	1	1	0	$3\frac{2}{3}$	4	3	1	4	3	0	0	0	1	.000	2.45
Don Sutton	2	2	0	13	9	4	4	3	12	1	1	1	0	1.000	2.77
Andy Messersmith	2	2	0	14	11	8	7	7	12	1	1	0	2	.000	4.50
Total	5	5	0	42	30	16	13	16	42	2	3	1	4	.200	2.79

Save—Marshall

Composite Score by Innings

Oakland	1	2	3	1	1	4	1	1	2	—16
Los Angeles	0	1	0	2	1	4	0	1	2	—11

Umpires—Gorman (NL), Kunkel (AL), Harvey (NL), Denkinger (AL), Olsen (NL) and Luciano (AL).
Official Scorers—Jack Herman, St. Louis Globe-Democrat; Gordon Verrell, Long Beach Press-Telegram; Ron Bergman, Oakland Tribune, and Charley Feeney, Pittsburgh Post-Gazette.

A's Defeat Dodgers in Five Games

The Oakland A's became world baseball champions for the third straight year by defeating the Los Angeles Dodgers in the 1974 world series 4 games to 1.

1974 World Series Box Scores

First Game

Dodger Stadium, Los Angeles, Oct. 12

Oakland	ab	r	h	bi		Los Angeles	ab	r	h	bi
Campaneris, ss.	2	1	1	1		Lopes, 2b	5	1	0	0
North, cf	2	0	0	0		Buckner, lf	5	0	2	0
Bando, 3b	4	0	0	0		Wynn, cf	4	1	1	1
Jackson, rf	3	1	1	1		Garvey, 1b	5	0	2	0
C.Washington, rf.	0	0	0	0		Paciorek, pr	0	0	0	0
Rudi, lf	4	0	2	0		Ferguson, rf	3	0	0	0
Tenace, 1b.	3	0	1	0		Cey, 3b	3	0	1	0
Fosse, c.	3	0	0	0		Russell, ss	4	0	1	0
Green, 2b.	3	0	0	0		Yeager, c	3	0	1	0
Holt, ph	1	0	0	0		Crawford, rf	1	0	1	0
Maxvill, ss	0	0	0	0		Messersmith, p.	3	0	2	0
Holtzman, p	1	1	1	0		Joshua, ph	1	0	0	0
Fingers, p.	2	0	0	0		Marshall, p	0	0	0	0
Hunter, p.	0	0	0	0						
Total	**28**	**3**	**6**	**2**		**Total**	**37**	**2**	**11**	**1**

Oakland . . . . 0 1 0 0 1 0 0,1 0—3
Los Angeles . . . . 0 0 0 0 1 0 0 0 1—2

Errors — Campaneris, Jackson, Cey. Double plays — Oakland 1, Los Angeles 1.Left on base — Oakland 6, Los Angeles 12. Two-base hits — Holtzman. Home runs — Jackson (1), Wynn (1). Sacrifices — Campaneris 2, North, Tenace.

	ip	h	r	er	bb	so
Holtzman	4 1/3	7	1	0	2	3
Fingers (W, 1-0)	4 1/3	4	1	1	1	3
Hunter	1/3	0	0	0	1	
Messersmith (L, 0-1)	8	5	3	2	3	8
Marshall	1	1	0	0	1	1

Save — Hunt (1). Hit by pitch — by Fingers (Ferguson). Wildpitch — Messersmith. Time of game — 2:43. Attendance — 55,974.

How runs were scored — one in A's second: Jackson hit a home run.

One in A's fifth: Holtzman doubled and went to third on a wild pitch. Holtzman scored on a squeeze bunt by Campaneris.

One in Dodgers fifth: Lopes was safe on an error. Buckner singled, Lopes scoring on an outfield error.

One in A's eighth: Campaneris singled and was sacrificed to second. Campaneris scored on Cey's throwing error.

One in Dodger's ninth: Wynn hit a home run.

Second Game

Dodger Stadium, Los Angeles, Oct. 13

Oakland	ab	r	h	bi		Los Angeles	ab	r	h	bi
Campaneris, ss.	4	0	1	0		Lopes, 2b	4	0	0	0
North, cf	4	0	0	0		Buckner, lf	4	0	0	0
Odom, p.	0	0	0	0		Wynn, cf	3	0	0	0
Bando, 3b	3	1	0	0		Garvey, 1b	4	1	2	0
Jackson, rf	3	1	2	0		Ferguson, rf	3	1	1	2
Rudi, lf	4	0	1	2		Cey, 3b	3	1	0	0
H. Washington, pr	0	0	0	0		Russell, ss	3	0	1	0
Tenace, 1b.	3	0	0	0		Yeager, c	3	0	2	1
Fosse, c.	2	0	0	0		Sutton, p.	2	0	0	0
Alou, ph	1	0	0	0		Marshall, p	0	0	0	0
Haney, c	0	0	0	0						
Mangual, ph.	1	0	0	0						
Green, 2b.	2	0	0	0						
Holt, ph	1	0	1	0						
Maxvill, 2b.	0	0	0	0						
Blur, p	2	0	0	0						
C. Washington, cf	1	0	1	0						
Total	**31**	**2**	**6**	**2**		**Total**	**29**	**3**	**6**	**3**

Oakland . . . . 0 0 0 0 0 0 0 0 2—2
Los Angeles . . . . 0 1 0 0 0 2 0 0 x—3

Errors—Russell. Double plays— Los Angeles 2. Left on base —Oakland 5, Los Angeles 6. Two-base hits — Campaneris, Jackson. Home run—Ferguson 1. Stolen base—Ferguson. Sacrifice—Sutton.

	ip	h	r	er	bb	so
Blue (L, 0-1)	7	6	3	3	2	5
Odom	1	0	0	0	1	2
Sutton (W, 1-0)	8	5	2	2	2	9
Marshall	1	1	0	0	0	2

(Second game continued)

Save—Marshall 1. Hit by pitch—by Sutton (Bando). Wild pitch —Sutton. Time of game—2:40. Attendance—55,989.

How runs were scored—One in Dodger second: Cey walked. Russell singled Yeager singled, scoring Cey.

Two in Dodger sixth: Garvey singled. Ferguson hit a home run.

Two in A's ninth: Bando was hit by a pitch. Jackson doubled. Rudi singled, scoring Bando and Jackson.

Third Game

Oakland-Alameda County Stadium, Oct. 15

Los Angeles	ab	r	h	bi		Oakland	ab	r	h	bi
Lopes, 2b	3	0	2	0		North, cf	4	1	1	0
Buckner, lf	4	1	1	1		Campaneris, ss	4	0	2	1
Wynn, cf	4	0	1	0		Bando, 3b	3	1	0	0
Garvey, 1b	4	0	1	0		Jackson, rf	3	0	0	0
Crawford, rf	4	1	1	1		C. Washington, rf.	0	0	0	0
Ferguson, c	3	0	0	0		Rudi, lf	4	0	1	1
Auerbach, pr	0	0	0	0		Tenace, 1b	2	0	1	0
Cey, 3b	4	0	0	0		H.Washington, pr	0	0	0	0
Russell, ss	5	0	1	0		Holt, 1b	0	0	0	0
Downing, p.	1	0	0	0		Fosse, c.	4	0	0	0
Brewer, p.	0	0	0	0		Green, 2b.	3	1	0	0
Lacy, ph.	1	0	0	0		Hunter, p.	2	0	0	0
Hough, p.	0	0	0	0		Fingers, p	0	0	0	0
Joshua, ph.	1	0	0	0						
Marshall, p	1	0	0	0						
Total	**33**	**2**	**7**	**2**		**Total**	**29**	**3**	**5**	**2**

Los Angeles . . . . 0 0 0 0 0 0 0 1 1—2
Oakland . . . . 0 0 2 1 0 0 0 x—3

E—Ferguson 2, Green, Campaneris. DP—Oakland 3. LOB—Los Angeles 6, Oakland 8. 2B—Campaneris. HR—Buckner (1), Crawford (1). SB—Lopes 2, Jackson. S—Hunter.

	ip	h	r	er	bb	so
Downing (L, 0-1)	3 2/3	4	3	1	4	3
Brewer	1/3	0	0	0	0	1
Hough	2	0	0	0	1	4
Marshall	2	1	0	0	0	1
Hunter (W, 1-0)	7 1/3	5	1	1	2	4
Fingers	1 2/3	2	1	1	0	1

WP—Hough. Time—2:35. Attendance—49,347.

How runs were scored — Two in A's third: North singled. Campaneris grounded out, North going to third. Bando walked. Jackson reached first on an infield error, North scoring. Rudi singled scoring Bando.

One in A's fourth: Green walked. Hunter sacrificed Green to second. Campaneris singled scoring Green.

One in Dodgers eighth: Buckner hit a home run.

One in Dodgers ninth: Crawford hit a home run.

Fourth Game

Oakland-Alameda County Coliseum, Oct. 16

Los Angeles	ab	r	h	bi		Oakland	ab	r	h	bi
Lopes, 2b	4	0	0	0		Campaneris, ss	3	0	0	0
Buckner, lf	4	0	1	0		North, cf	3	1	0	0
Wynn, cf	3	0	1	0		Bando, 3b	3	1	1	1
Garvey, 1b	4	1	2	0		Jackson, rf	3	1	1	0
Ferguson, rf	3	1	0	0		Rudi, lf	3	0	0	0
Cey, 3b	4	0	1	0		C. Washington,lf.	3	1	2	0
Russell, ss	4	0	1	2		Tenace, 1b	0	0	0	0
Yeager, c	3	0	1	0		Fosse, c.	2	0	1	0
Joshua, ph	1	0	0	0		Holt, ph	1	0	1	2
Messersmith, p.	1	0	0	0		H. Washington, pr	0	0	0	0
Paciorek, ph.	1	0	0	0		Haney, c	0	0	0	0
Marshall, p	0	0	0	0		Green, 2b.	2	0	0	0
						Holtzman, p	3	1	1	1
						Fingers, p	0	0	0	0
Total	**32**	**2**	**7**	**2**		**Total**	**26**	**5**	**7**	**5**

Los Angeles . . . . 0 0 0 2 0 0 0 0 0—2
Oakland . . . . 0 0 1 0 0 4 0 0 x—5

(Fourth game continued)

Error—Messersmith. Double plays—Los Angeles 2, Oakland 1. Left on base—Los Angeles 6, Oakland 4. 2 base hits—Buckner, Yeager, Wynn. 3 base hit—Russell. Home run—Holtzman.

	ip	h	r	er	bb	so
Messersmith (L, 0-2)....	6	6	5	5	4	4
Marshall.............	2	1	0	0	0	2
Holtzman (W, 1-0).....	7²/₃	6	2	2	2	7
Fingers..............	1¹/₃	1	0	0	0	2

Save—Fingers (1). Hit by pitcher—by Messersmith (Campaneris). Wild pitch—Holtzman. Time of game—2:17. Attendance—49,347.

How runs were scored—One in A's third: Holtzman hit a home run.

Two in Dodgers fourth: Garvey singled. Ferguson walked. Russell tripled scoring Garvey and Ferguson.

Four in A's sixth: North walked. North went to second on an error by the pitcher on an attempted pickoff. Bando singled scoring North. Jackson walked. Rudi sacrificed the runners to second and third. C. Washington walked. Holt singled scoring Bando and Jackson. C. Washington scored on an infield out.

Fifth Game

Oakland-Alameda County Coliseum, Oct. 17

Los Angeles	ab	r	h	bi	Oakland	ab	r	h	bi
Lopes,2b......	2	1	0	0	Campaneris, ss..	4	0	2	0
Buckner, lf......	3	0	1	0	North, cf........	4	1	0	0
Wynn, cf.......	2	0	0	1	Bando, 3b.......	3	0	0	1
Garvey, 1b......	4	0	1	0	Jackson, rf......	2	0	0	0
Ferguson, rf....	4	0	1	0	Rudi, 1b........	3	1	2	1
Cey, 3b........	3	0	0	0	C.Washington, lf..	3	0	1	0
Russell, ss.....	3	0	0	0	Fingers, p.......	0	0	0	0
Crawford, ph....	1	0	0	0	Fosse, c........	3	1	1	1
Yeager, c......	2	0	0	0	Green, 2b.......	3	0	0	0
Joshua, ph......	1	0	0	0	Blue, p.........	2	0	0	0
Sutton, p.......	1	0	0	0	Odom, p........	0	0	0	0
Paciorek, ph....	1	1	1	0	Tenace, 1b......	1	0	0	0
Marshall, p......	0	0	0	0					
Total.......	27	2	5	2	**Total**........	28	3	6	3

Los Angeles.............. 0 0 0   0 0 2   0 0 0—2
Oakland................. 1 1 0   0 0 0   1 0 x—3

Errors—Yeager, North. Double plays—Oakland 1. Left on base—Los Angeles 6, Oakland 3. Two-base hits—Paciorek.

Home runs Fosse (1), Rudi (1). Stolen bases—North, Campaneris. Sacrifice—Buckner. Sacrifice flies—Bando, Wynn.

	ip	h	r	er	bb	so
Sutton...............	5	4	2	2	1	3
Marshall (L, 0-1)........	3	2	1	1	0	4
Blue................	6²/₃	4	2	2	5	4
Odom (W, 1-0)...........	¹/₃	0	0	0	0	0
Fingers..............	2	1	0	0	1	0

Save — Fingers (2). Time of game — 2:23. Attendance — 49,-347.

How runs were scored — One in A's first: Campaneris singled. North forced Campaneris at second. North stole second and went to third on a bad throw. Bando hit a sacrifice fly scoring North.

One in A's second: Fosse hit a home run.

Two in Dodgers sixth: Paciorek doubled. Lopes walked. Buckner sacrificed the runners to second and third. Wynn hit a sacrifice fly scoring Paciorek. Garvey singled scoring Lopes.

One in A's seventh: Rudi hit a home run.

World Series Results, 1903-1974

1903 Boston AL 5, Pittsburg NL 3
1904 No Series
1905 New York NL 4, Philadelphia AL 1
1906 Chicago AL 4, Chicago NL 2
1907 Chicago NL 4, Detroit AL 0, 1 tie
1908 Chicago NL 4, Detroit AL 1
1909 Pittsburgh NL 4, Detroit AL 3
1910 Philadelphia AL 4, Chicago NL 1
1911 Philadelphia AL 4, New York NL 2
1912 Boston AL 4, New York NL 3, 1 tie
1913 Philadelphia AL 4, New York NL 1
1914 Boston NL 4, Philadelphia AL 0
1915 Boston AL 4, Philadelphia NL 1
1916 Boston AL 4, Brooklyn NL 1
1917 Chicago AL 4, New York NL 2
1918 Boston AL 4, Chicago NL 2
1919 Cincinnati NL 5, Chicago AL 3
1920 Cleveland AL 5, Brooklyn NL 2
1921 New York NL 5, New York AL 3
1922 New York NL 4, New York AL 0, 1 tie
1923 New York AL 4, New York NL 2
1924 Washington AL 4, New York NL 3
1925 Pittsburgh NL 4, Washington AL 3
1926 St. Louis NL 4, New York AL 3

1927 New York AL 4, Pittsburgh NL 0
1928 New York AL 4, St. Louis NL 0
1929 Philadelphia AL 4, Chicago NL 1
1930 Philadelphia AL 4, St. Louis NL 2
1931 St. Louis NL 4, Philadelphia AL 3
1932 New York AL 4, Chicago NL 0
1933 New York NL 4, Washington AL 1
1934 St. Louis NL 4, Detroit AL 3
1935 Detroit AL 4, Chicago NL 2
1936 New York AL 4, New York NL 2
1937 New York AL 4, New York NL 1
1938 New York AL 4, Chicago NL 0
1939 New York AL 4, Cincinnati NL 0
1940 Cincinnati NL 4, Detroit AL 3
1941 New York AL 4, Brooklyn NL 1
1942 St. Louis NL 4, New York AL 1
1943 New York AL 4, St. Louis NL 1
1944 St. Louis NL 4, St. Louis AL 2
1945 Detroit AL 4, Chicago NL 3
1946 St. Louis NL 4, Boston AL 3
1947 New York AL 4, Brooklyn NL 3
1948 Cleveland AL 4, Boston NL 2
1949 New York AL 4, Brooklyn NL 1
1950 New York AL 4, Philadelphia NL 0

1951 New York AL 4, New York NL 2
1952 New York AL 4, Brooklyn NL 3
1953 New York AL 4, Brooklyn NL 2
1954 New York NL 4, Cleveland AL 0
1955 Brooklyn NL 4, New York AL 3
1956 New York AL 4, Brooklyn NL 3
1957 Milwaukee NL 4, New York AL 3
1958 New York AL 4, Milwaukee NL 3
1959 Los Angeles NL 4, Chicago AL 2
1960 Pittsburgh NL 4, New York AL 3
1961 New York AL 4, Cincinnati NL 1
1962 New York AL 4, San Francisco NL 3
1963 Los Angeles NL 4, New York AL 0
1964 St. Louis NL 4, New York AL 3
1965 Los Angeles NL 4, Minnesota AL 3
1966 Baltimore AL 4, Los Angeles NL 0
1967 St. Louis NL 4, Boston AL 3
1968 Detroit AL 4, St. Louis NL 3
1969 New York NL 4, Baltimore AL 1
1970 Baltimore AL 4, Cincinnati NL 1
1971 Pittsburgh NL 4, Baltimore AL 3
1972 Oakland AL 4, Cincinnati NL 3
1973 Oakland AL 4, New York NL 3
1974 Oakland AL 4, Los Angeles NL 1

World Series Attendance and Receipts Since 1953

Year	Clubs	G.	Attendance	Receipts	Year	Clubs	G.	Attendance	Receipts
1953	N.Y.(A)-Brooklyn (N).....	6	307,350	1,779,269	1964	St. Louis (N)-N.Y. (A)....	7	321,807	2,243,187
1954	New York (N)-Cleve. (A)..	4	251,507	1,566,203	1965	L.A. (N)-Minn. (A).......	7	364,326	2,975,041
1955	Brooklyn (N) N.Y. (A).....	7	362,310	2,337,515	1966	L.A. (N)-Balt. (A) **.....	4	220,791	2,047,142
1956	N.Y. (A)-Brooklyn (N)....	7	345,903	2,173,254	1967	St. Louis (N)-Bos. (A)....	7	304,085	2,350,607
1957	Milw. (N)-N.Y. (A).......	7	394,712	2,475,978	1968	St. Louis (N)-Det.-(A)....	7	379,670	3,018,113
1958	N.Y. (A)-Milw. (N).......	7	393,909	2,397,223	1969	N.Y. Mets (N)-Balt. (A)...	5	272,378	2,857,782
1959	L.A. (N)-Chicago (A)*....	6	420,784	2,626,973	1970	Balt. (A)-Cinn. (N)......	5	253,183	2,599,170
1960	Pitts. (N)-N.Y. (A).......	7	349,813	2,230,627	1971	Balt. (A)-Pitts. (N).......	7	351,091	3,787,694
1961	N.Y. (A)-Cincinnati (N)...	5	223,247	1,480,095	1972	Oak. (A)-Cinn. (N).......	7	363,149	3,954,542
1962	N.Y. (A)-San Fran. (N)...	7	376,864	2,878,891	1973	Oak.-(A)-N.Y. Mets (N)...	7	359,489	3,923,968
1963	L.A. (N)-N.Y. (A)........	4	247,279	1,995,190	1974	Oak.(A)-L.A. (N)........	5	260,004	3,007,194

Receipts do not include fees for radio and television rights. *Attendance record. **Receipts record for 4-game Series.

Members of National Baseball Hall of Fame and Museum

The shrine of organized baseball, dedicated June 12, 1939 is located in Cooperstown, N.Y.

Alexander, Grover Cleveland
Anson, Cap
Appling, Lucius B.
Baker, Home Run
Bancroft, Dave
Barrow, Edward G.
Beckley, Jake
Bell, Cool Papa
Bender, Chief
Berra, Yogi
Bottomley, Jim
Boudreau, Lou
Bresnahan, Roger
Brouthers, Dan
Brown (Three Finger), Mordecai
Bulkeley, Morgan C.
Burkett, Jesse C.
Campanella, Roy
Carey, Max
Cartwright, Alexander
Chadwick, Henry
Chance, Frank
Chesbro, John
Clarke, Fred
Clarkson, John
Clemente, Roberto
Cobb, Ty
Cochrane, Mickey
Collins, Edward T.

Collins, James
Combs, Earle
Comiskey, Charles A.
Conlan, Jocko
Connolly, Thomas H.
Coveleski, Stan
Crawford, Sam
Cronin, Joe
Cummings, Candy
Cuyler, Kiki
Dean, Dizzy
Delahanty, Ed
Dickey, Bill
DiMaggio, Joe
Duffy, Hugh
Evans, Billy
Evers, John
Ewing, Buck
Faber, Urban
Feller, Bob
Flick, Elmer H.
Ford, Whitey
Foxx, James E.
Frick, Ford
Frisch, Frank
Galvin, Pud
Gehrig, Lou
Gehringer, Charles
Gibson, Josh

Gomez, Lefty
Goslin, Goose
Greenberg, Hank
Griffith, Clark
Grimes, Burleigh
Grove, Lefty
Hafey, Chick
Haines, Jessee
Hamilton, Bill
Harridge, Will
Hartnett, Gabby
Heilmann, Harry
Hooper, Harry
Hornsby, Rogers
Hoyt, Waite
Hubbell, Carl
Huggins, Miller
Irvin, Monte
Jennings, Hugh
Johnson, Byron
Johnson, Walter
Keefe, Timothy
Keeler, William
Kelley, Joe
Kelly, George
Kelly, King
Klem, Bill
Koufax, Sandy
Lajoie, Napoleon

Landis, Kenesaw M.
Leonard, Buck
Lyons, Ted
Mack, Connie
Mantle, Mickey
Manush, Henry
Maranville, Rabbit
Marquard, Rube
Mathewson, Christy
McCarthy, Joe
McCarthy, Thomas
McGinnity, Joe
McGraw, John
McKechnie, Bill
Medwick, Joe
Musial, Stan
Nichols, Kid
O'Rourke, James
Ott, Mel
Paige, Satchel
Pennock, Herb
Plank, Ed
Radbourne, Charlie
Rice, Sam
Rickey, Branch
Rixey, Eppa
Robinson, Jackie
Robinson, Wilbert
Roush, Edd

Ruffing, Red
Ruth, Babe
Schalk, Ray
Simmons, Al
Sisler, George
Spahn, Warren
Spalding, Albert
Speaker, Tris
Stengel, Casey
Terry, Bill
Thompson, Sam
Tinker, Joe
Traynor (Pie), Harold J.
Vance, Dazzy
Waddell, Rube
Wagner, Honus
Wallace, Roderick
Walsh, Ed
Waner, Lloyd
Waner, Paul
Ward, John
Weiss, George
Welch, Mickey
Wheat, Zach
Williams, Ted
Wright, George
Wright, Harry
Wynn, Early
Young, Cy
Youngs, Ross

All-Time Home Run Leaders

Player	HR.	Player	HR.	Player	HR.	Player	HR.
Hank Aaron	733	Duke Snider	407	Hank Greenberg	331	Rudy York	277
Babe Ruth	714	Al Kaline	399	Roy Sievers	318	Roger Maris	275
Willie Mays	660	Frank Howard	382	Dick Allen	309	Vic Wertz	266
Frank Robinson	572	Orlando Cepeda	379	Al Simmons	307	Bobby Thomson	264
Harmon Killebrew	559	Norm Cash	377	Carl Yastrzemski	303	Brooks Robinson	258
Mickey Mantle	536	Rocco Colavito	374	Rogers Hornsby	302	Bob Allison	256
Jimmy Foxx	534	Gil Hodges	370	John (Boog) Powell	301	Jim Wynn	255
Ted Williams	521	Ralph Kiner	369	Chuck Klein	300	Joe Gordon	253
Ed Mathews	512	Joe DiMaggio	361	Robert Johnson	288	Larry Doby	253
Ernie Banks	512	John Mize	359	Hank Sauer	288	Vada Pinson	252
Mel Ott	511	Yogi Berra	358	Del Ennis	288	Fred Williams	251
Lou Gehrig	493	Willie Stargell	346	Frank Thomas	286	Leon Goslin	248
Stan Musial	475	Ron Santo	342	Ken Boyer	282	Vernon Stephens	247
Willie McCovey	435	Joe Adcock	336	Ted Kluszewski	279	Hack Wilson	244

1974 Amateur Softball Association Champions

Division	National Champion	Division	National Champion
Men's Fast Pitch	Guanella Bros., Santa Rosa, Calif.	Men's Industrial Slow Pitch	Aetna Life & Casualty,
Women's Fast Pitch	Raybestos Brakettes, Stratford,		Charlotte, N.C.
	Conn.	16" Slow Pitch	Strikers, Chicago, Ill.
Men's Open Slow Pitch	Howard Furniture, Denver, N.C.	National Church	St. Martins, St. Louis, Mo.
Women's Slow Pitch	North Miami Dots, Miami, Fla.	Industrial "A"	Sears, Bloomington, Minn.
		Class A Girls	Seaman's IGA, Athens, Ohio

National AAU Gymnastic Championship

Billings, Montana, Apr. 26-28, 1974

Men

Vaulting — John Crosby, NYAC.
Floor Exercise — John Crosby.
Side Horse — Percival, Oregon Gym Club.
Still Rings — Robert Rice, NYAC.
Parallel Bars — Yoshi Hayasaki.
Horizontal Bars — Yoshi Hayasaki.
All-Around — Yoshi Hayasaki.

Women

Balance Beam — Ann Carr, Manettes.
Uneven Parallel Bars — Joan Moore Rice, Manettes.
Vaulting — Mysiak, So. Conn.
Floor Exercise — Joan Moore Rice.
All-Around — Joan Moore Rice.

29th Annual National Field Archery Assn. Championships

Golden, Colorado, July 22-26, 1974

Freestyle

Senior Men — Frank Miller.
Professional Men — Gale Cavallin, Costa Mesa, Calif.
Open Men — Tim Moyer, Glendora, Calif.
Amateur Men — Terry Ragsdale, White Oak, Texas.
Professional Women — Ginger McClintock, Penngrove, Calif.
Open Women — Barbara Morris, Frankfort, Ky.
Amateur Women — Kathy Cramberg, Dallas City, Ill.

Freestyle - Limited

Professional Men — Bill Connally, LaPorte, Texas.
Open Men — Walter Kop, N. Babylon, New York.
Amateur Men — Richard Johnson, Webster, Mass.

Professional Women — Carole Pfohl, Newburgh, Ind.
Open Women — Lois Inskeep, Tucson, Ariz.
Amateur Women — Irene Lorensen, Phoenix, Ariz.

Barebow

Open Men — David Hughes, Irving, Texas.
Amateur Men — Mike Flier, Pekin, Ill.
Open Women — Janis Beverly, Americus, Ga.
Amateur Women — Betty Selkirk, Canton, Ill.

Bowhunter

Open Men — Cal Vogt, Canoga Park, Calif.
Amateur Men — Charles Maloney, Bolingbrook, Ill.
Open Women — Anita LaComb, Lakewood, Colo.

Trotting and Pacing Records

Source: Larry Evans, United States Trotting Association. Records to Jan., 1974.

Trotting Records

Asterisk (*) denotes record was made in a race. Times — seconds in fifths.

One Mile Records (Mile Track)

All-age — 1:54.4 — Nevele Pride, Indianapolis, Ind., Aug. 31, 1969.

Two-year-old — *1:58.2 — Nevele Pride, Lexington, Ky., Oct. 4, 1967.

Three-year-old — *1:56.2 — Super Bowl, Du Quoin, Ill., Aug. 30, 1972.

(Half-Mile Track)

All-age — *1:56.4 — Nevele Pride, Saratoga Springs, N.Y., Sept. 6, 1969.

Two-year-old — *2:00.1 — Ayres, Delaware, Ohio, 1963.

Three-year-old Colt — *1:58.3 — Songcan, Delaware, Ohio, 1972.

Odd Distances

1-1/16 Miles — *2:05.3 — Senator Frost, Inglewood, Calif., Oct. 17, 1959.

1-1/16 Miles, Half-mile Track — *2:07.2 — Nevele Pride, Westbury, N.Y., 1969.

1-3/16 Miles — *2:22.4 — Scotch Victor, Inglewood, Calif., Nov. 6, 1954.

1¼ Miles — *2:30.3 — Pronto Don, Inglewood, Calif., Nov. 24, 1951.

1¼ Miles, Half-mile Track — *2:31.2 — Speedy Scot, Westbury, N.Y., 1964; Noble Victory, Westbury, N.Y., 1966.

1½ Miles — 3:02.1 — Greyhound, Indianapolis, Ind., Sept. 14, 1937.

1½ Miles, Half-mile Track — 3:05.2 — Snow Speed, Yonkers, N.Y., 1969.

2 Miles — 4:06 — Greyhound, Indianapolis, Ind., Sept. 19, 1939.

2 Miles, Half-mile Track — *4:10.4 — Pronto Don, Westbury, N.Y., Sept. 13, 1951.

Fastest Two Heats — *1:57.2; *1:56.3 — Nevele Pride, Indianapolis, Aug. 31, 1968.

Fastest Two Heats, Half-Mile Track — *1:58.4, *2:00.3 — Speedy Rodney, Goshen, N.Y., 1966.

Pacing Records

One Mile Records (Mile Track)

All-age — 1:52 — Steady Star, Lexington, Ky., Oct. 1, 1971.

Two-year-old — *1:56.1 — Ricci Reenie Time, Lexington, Ky., 1972.

Three-year-old — 1:54 — Steady Star, Lexington, Ky., Oct. 7, 1970.

(Half-Mile Track)

All-age — 1:55.3 — Adios Butler, Delaware, Ohio, Sept. 21, 1961; Albatross, Delaware, Ohio, 1972.

Two-year-old — *1:58.4 — Columbia Hanover, Yonkers, N.Y., Nov. 8, 1969; J. R. Skipper, Delaware, Ohio, 1972.

Three-year-old — 1:56.3 — Strike out, Delaware, Ohio, 1972.

Odd Distances

1¼ Miles — *2:30.2 — Dr. Stanton, Arcadia, Calif., May 15, 1948.

1¼ Miles, Half-mile Track — *2:29.3 — Irvin Paul, Westbury, N.Y., Sept. 1, 1962.

1-1/16 Miles — *2:03.1 — Adios Vic, Inglewood, Calif., Oct. 23, 1965.

1-1/16 Miles, Half-mile Track — *2:06 — Albatross, Westbury, N.Y., 1972.

1¼ miles — 2:09.1 — True Duane, Hollywood Park, 1966.

1½ Miles — *3:05.2 — Right Time, Inglewood, Calif., 1961; and K. D. Senator, E. Boston, Mass., 1963.

1½ Miles, Half-mile Track — *3:02.3 — Overcall, Westbury, N.Y., June 5, 1969.

2 Miles — 4:17 — Dan Patch, Macon, Ga., 1903.

2 Miles, Half-mile Track — *4:08.4 — Irvin Paul, Yonkers, N.Y., June 28, 1962.

Fastest Two Heats — *1:54.4, 1:54.4 — Albatross, Lexington, Ky., Oct. 2, 1971.

The Hambletonian
(3-year-old trotters) Du Quoin, Ill.

Year	Winner	Best Time	Value	Year	Winner	Best Time	Value
1940—Spencer Scott	2:02	$43,658	1958—Emily's Pride	1:59 4-5	$106,719
1941—Bill Gallon	2:05	38,729	1959—Diller Hanover	2:01 1-5	125,284
1942—The Ambassador	2:04	38,954	1960—Blaze Hanover	1:59 3-5	144,590
1943—Volo Song	2:02 1-2	42,298	1961—Harlan Dean	1:58 2-5	131,573
1944—Yankee Maid	2:04	33,577	1962—A.C.'s Viking	1:59 3-5	116,312
1945—Titan Hanover	2:04	50,190	1963—Speedy Scot	1:58	115,549
1946—Chestertown	2:02 1-2	50,905	1964—Ayres	1:56 4-5	115,281
1947—Hoot Mon	2:00	46,267	1965—Egyptian Candor	2:04 3-5	122,245
1948—Demon Hanover	2:02	59,941	1966—Kerry Way	1:58 1-5	122,540
1949—Miss Tilly	2:01 2-5	69,791	1967—Speedy Streak	2:00	122,650
1950—Lusty Song	2:02	75,209	1968—Nevele Pride	1:59 2-5	116,190
1951—Mainliner	2:02 3-5	95,263	1969—Lindy's Pride	1:57 3-5	124,910
1952—Sharp Note	2:02 3-5	87,637	1970—Timothy T.	2:00 1-5	143,630
1953—Helicopter	2:01 3-5	117,118	1971—Speedy Crown	1:57 2-5	128,770
1954—Newport Dream	2:02 3-5	106,830	1972—Super Bowl	1:56 2-5	119,090
1955—Scott Frost	2:00 3-5	86,863	1973—Flirth	1:57 1-5	144,710
1956—The Intruder	2:01 3-5	98,591*	1974—Christopher T.	1:58 3-5	160,150
1957—Hickory Smoke	2:00 1-5	111,126			

Little Brown Jug
(Three-Year-Old Pacers)

Year	Winner	Winning Driver	Purse	Year	Winner	Winning Driver	Purse
1952	Meadow Rice	Wayne Smart	$60,463	1964	Vicar Hanover	Billy Haughton	$66,590
1953	Keystoner	Frank Ervin	54,972	1965	Bret Hanover	Frank Ervin	71,447
1954	Adios Harry	Morris MacDonald	69,332	1966	Romeo Hanover	George Sholty	74,616
1955	Quick Chief	Billy Haughton	66,608	1967	Best of All	James Hackett	84,778
1956	Noble Adios	John Simpson, Sr.	52,666	1968	Rum Customer	Billy Haughton	104,226
1957	Torpid	John Simpson, Sr.	73,528	1969	Laverne Hanover	Billy Haughton	109,731
1958	Shadow Wave	Joe O'Brien	65,252	1970	Most Happy Fella	Stanley Dancer	100,110
1959	Adios Butler	Clint Hodgins	76,582	1971	Nansemond	Herve Filion	102,944
1960	Bullet Hanover	John Simpson, Sr.	66,510	1972	Strike Out	Keith Waples	104,916
1961	Henry T. Adios	Stanley Dancer	70,069	1973	Melvin's Woe	Joe O'Brien	120,000
1962	Lehigh Hanover	Stanley Dancer	75,038	1974	Armbro Omaha	Billy Haughton	132,630
1963	Overtrick	John Patterson, Sr.	68,294				

Leading Drivers

Year	Races Won		Grand Circuit		Money Won	
1957.	Bill Haughton	156	John Simpson	$367,670	Bill Haughton	$586,950
1958.	Bill Haughton	176	Joe O'Brien	267,342	Bill Haughton	816,659
1959.	William Gilmour	165	Joe O'Brien	263,636	Bill Haughton	711,435
1960.	Del Insko	156	Del Miller	338,594	Del Miller	567,282
1961.	Bob Farrington	201	Jimmy Arthur	248,211	Stanley Dancer	674,723
1962.	Bob Farrington	203	Stanley Dancer	306,454	Stanley Dancer	760,343
1963.	Donald Busse	201	Ralph Baldwin	299,899	Bill Haughton	790,086
1964.	Bob Farrington	312	Stanley Dancer	269,080	Stanley Dancer	1,051,538
1965.	Bob Farrington	310	Joe O'Brien	304,791	Bill Haughton	889,943
1966.	Bob Farrington	283	George Sholty	293,531	Stanley Dancer	1,218,403
1967.	Bob Farrington	277	Bill Haughton	448,294	Bill Haughton	1,305,773
1968.	Herve Filion	407	Bill Haughton	448,040	Bill Haughton	1,654,172
1969.	Herve Filion	394	Bill Haughton	489,495	Del Insko	1,635,463
1970.	Herve Filion	486	Stanley Dancer	439,019	Herve Filion	1,647,837
1971.	Herve Filion	543	Stanley Dancer	462,694	Herve Filion	1,915,945
1972.	Herve Filion	605	Bill Haughton	416,626	Herve Filion	2,473,265
1973.	Herve Filion	445	Bill Haughton	456,192	Herve Filion	2,233,302

Harness Horse of the Year

1947 — Victory Song	1954 — Stenographer	1961 — Adios Butler	1968 — Nevele Pride
1948 — Rodney	1955 — Scott Frost	1962 — Su Mac Lad	1969 — Nevele Pride
1949 — Good Time	1956 — Scott Frost	1963 — Speedy Scot	1970 — Fresh Yankee
1950 — Proximity	1957 — Torpid	1964 — Bret Hanover	1971 — Albatross
1951 — Pronto Don	1958 — Emily's Pride	1965 — Bret Hanover	1972 — Albatross
1952 — Good Time	1959 — Bye Bye Byrd	1966 — Bret Hanover	1973 — Sir Dalrae
1953 — Hi Lo's Forbes	1960 — Adios Butler	1967 — Nevele Pride	

"Parked Out" Computations

Harness Racing mathematicians have compiled these figures on the added distance in each mile that a horse travels when "parked out" (racing outside another horse, five feet out from the point at which the track is measured).

½ mile track (4 turns to mile) . . . . 62.832 feet   ¾ mile track with chute, and mile track (2 turns to mile) 31.416 feet
⅝ mile track (3 turns to mile) . . . . 47.124 feet

The World Cup

The World Cup, emblematic of international soccer supremacy, was won by West Germany on July 7, 1974, with a 2-1 victory over the Netherlands. By winning the championship, West Germany became the fourth host country to emerge as champion since the trophy was put up in 1930. The next World Cup will be held in 1978 in Argentina. Winners and sites of previous World Cup play follow:

Year	Winner	Site	Year	Winner	Site
1930	Uruguay	Uruguay	1958	Brazil	Sweden
1934	Italy	Italy	1962	Brazil	Chile
1938	Italy	France	1966	England	England
1950	Uruguay	Brazil	1970	Brazil	Mexico City
1954	W. Germany	Switzerland	1974	W. Germany	W. Germany

North American Soccer League Final Standings

Northern Division	W.	L.	Tie Win	Bonus* Points	Total*	Central Division	W.	L.	Tie Win	Bonus* Points	Total*
Boston	10	9	1	31	94	Dallas	9	8	3	37	100
Toronto	9	10	1	30	87	St. Louis	4	15	1	27	54
Rochester	8	10	2	23	77	Denver	5	15	0	19	49
New York	4	14	2	28	58						
Eastern Division						**Western Division**					
Miami	9	5	6	35	107	Los Angeles	11	7	2	38	110
Baltimore	10	8	2	39	105	San Jose	9	8	3	40	103
Philadelphia	8	11	1	23	74	Seattle	10	7	1	32	101
Washington	7	12	1	25	70	Vancouver	5	11	4	28	70

*Total Points — Win, 6 pts.; Tie-win (win on tie-breaker), is 3 pts.; Loss, 0 pts. Bonus Points — one point is awarded for each goal scored up to a maximum of three per team per game. Playoff winner — Los Angeles.

Top Scorers

Player (Team)	G	A	Pts.	Player (Team)	G	A	Pts.
Paul Child (San Jose)	15	6	36	Ilija Mitic (Dallas)	10	1	21
Peter Silvester (Baltimore)	14	3	31	John Coyne (Dallas-Boston)	7	7	21
Douglas McMillan (Los Angeles)	10	10	30	Archie Roboostoff (San Jose)	6	8	20
John Rowlands (Seattle)	10	8	28	Jim Fryatt (Philadelphia)	8	4	20
Steven David (Miami)	13	0	26	Alvin Henderson (Baltimore)	7	6	20
David Butler (Seattle)	10	2	22	Frank Large (Baltimore)	9	2	20
Randy Horton (New York)	9	4	22	Gary Darrell (Washington)	9	2	20
Andy Provan (Philadelphia)	9	3	21				

Top Goalkeepers

Goalkeeper (Team)	Min.	Goals	Avg.	Goalkeeper (Team)	Min.	Goals	Avg.
Barry Watling (Seattle)	1800	16	0.80	Bob Rigby (Philadelphia)	1800	22	1.10
Ian McKechnie Boston)	1280	13	0.94	Ken Cooper (Dallas)	1800	22	1.10

World Swimming Records

As of Oct. 1, 1974

Effective June 1, 1969, FINA will recognize only records made over a 50-meter course.

Men's Freestyle

Distance	Time	Holder	Country	Where made	Date
100 Meters	0:51.22	Mark Spitz	U.S.A.	Munich	Sept. 3, 1972
200 Meters	1:51.66	Tim Shaw	U.S.A.	Concord, Calif.	Aug., 1974
400 Meters	3:54.69	Tim Shaw	U.S.A.	Concord, Calif.	Aug. 22, 1974
800 Meters	8:17.6	Stephen Holland	Australia	Brisbane, Aust.	Aug. 5, 1973
1,500 Meters	15:31.75	Tim Shaw	U.S.A.	Concord, Calif.	Aug., 1974

Men's Breaststroke

100 Meters	1:03.88	John Hencken	U.S.A.	Concord, Calif.	Aug. 1974
200 Meters	2:18.21	John Hencken	U.S.A.	Concord, Calif.	Aug., 1974

Men's Butterfly

100 Meters	0:54.27	Mark Spitz	U.S.A.	Munich	Aug. 31, 1972
200 Meters	2:00.07	Mark Spitz	U.S.A.	Munich	Aug. 28, 1972

Men's Backstroke

100 Meters	0:56.30	Roland Matthes	E. Germany	Moscow	Apr. 8, 1972
200 Meters	2:01.87	Roland Matthes	E. Germany	Belgrade, Yugo.	Sept. 6, 1973

Men's Individual Medley

200 Meters	2:06.32	David Wilkie	Scotland	Vienna	Aug., 1974
400 Meters	4:28.89	Steve Furniss	U.S.A.	Concord, Calif.	Aug., 1974
		Andras Hargitay	Hungary	Vienna	Aug. 20, 1974

Men's Freestyle Relays

400 M. (4x100)	3:25.17	Nat'l Team (Coan, Montgomery Bottom, Hickcox)	U.S.A.	Concord, Calif.	Aug., 1974
800 M. (4x200)	7:33.22	Nat'l Team (Krumpholz, Backhaus, Klatt, Montgomery)	U.S.A.	Belgrade, Yugo.	Sept. 7, 1973

Men's Medley Relays

400 M. (4x100)	3:48.16	Nat'l Team (Stamm, Bruce, Spitz, Heidenreich)	U.S.A.	Munich	Sept. 4, 1972

Women's Freestyle

100 Meters	0:56.96	Kornelia Ender	E. Germany	Vienna	Aug., 1974
200 Meters	2:02.94	Shirley Babashoff	U.S.A.	Condord, Calif.	Aug., 1974
400 Meters	4:15.77	Shirley Babashoff	U.S.A.	Concord, Calif.	Aug. 22, 1974
800 Meters	8:47.66	Jo Harshbarger	U.S.A.	Concord, Calif.	Aug., 1974
1,500 Meters	16:33.95	Jenny Turrall	Australia	Concord, Calif.	Aug., 1974

Women's Breaststroke

100 Meters	1:12.28	Renate Vogel	E. Germany	Concord, Calif.,	Aug. 1974
200 Meters	2:34.99	Carla Linke	E. Germany	Vienna	Aug., 1974

Women's Butterfly

100 Meters	1:01.88	Rosemarie Kother	E. Germany	Concord, Calif.	Aug., 1974
200 Meters	2:13.76	Rosemarie Kother	E. Germany	Belgrade, Yugo.	Sept. 8, 1973

Women's Backstroke

100 Meters	1:02.98	Ulrika Richter	E. Germany	Concord, Calif.	Aug., 1974
200 Meters	2:17.35	Ulrika Richter	E. Germany	Vienna	Aug. 25, 1974

Women's Individual Medley

200 Meters	2:20.51	Ulrika Tauber	E. Germany	Vienna	Aug., 1974
400 Meters	4:52.42	Ulrika Tauber	E. Germany	Vienna	Aug. 21, 1974

Women's Freestyle Relays

400 M. (4x100)	3:51.99	Nat'l Team (Heddy, Marshall, Peyton, Babashoff)	U.S.A.	Concord, Calif.	Aug., 1974

Women's Medley Relays

400 M. (4x100)	4:13.78	Nat'l Team	E. Germany	Vienna	Aug., 1974

National AAU Outdoor Diving Championships

Decatur, Ala., Aug. 14-17, 1974

Men
One-Meter — Tim Moore.
Three-Meter — Keith Russell.
Ten Meter Platform — Keith Russell.

Women
One-Meter — Cynthia Potter.
Three-Meter — Christine Loock.
Ten Meter Platform — Teri York.

Swimming Events in 1974
NCAA Championships
Long Beach, Calif., Mar. 28-30, 1974

50 Yd. Freestyle—John Trembley, Tennessee. **Time**—0:20.23.
100 Yd. Freestyle—Joe Bottom, USC. **Time**—0:45.06.
200 Yd. Freestyle—Jim Montgomery, Indiana. **Time**—1:39.19.
500 Yd. Freestyle—John Naber, USC. **Time**—4:26.85.
1,650 Yd. Freestyle—Jack Tingley, USC. **Time**—15:29.28.
100 Yd. Butterfly—John Trembley. **Time**—0:48.72.
200 Yd. Butterfly—Robin Backhaus, Washington. **Time**—1:47.04.
100 Yd. Backstroke—John Naber. **Time**—0:50.52.
200 Yd. Backstroke—John Naber. **Time**—1:48.95.
100 Yd. Breaststroke—David Wilkie, Miami of Florida. **Time**—0:56.62.

200 Yd. Breaststroke—John Hencken, Stanford. **Time**—2:01.74.
200 Yd. Individual Medley—Steve Furniss, USC. **Time**—1:51.52.
400 Yd. Freestyle Relay—Indiana. **Time**—3:00.35.
800 Yd. Freestyle Relay—Indiana. **Time**—6:40.32.
1-Meter Diving—Tim Moore, Ohio State. 494.25 pts.
3-Meter Diving—Richard McAllister, Air Force Academy. 526.-41 pts.
Team Champion—1. USC, 339 pts.; 2. Indiana, 338 pts.; 3. Tennessee, 250 pts.

National AAU Short Course Championship
Dallas, Texas, Apr. 10-13, 1974

Men

100 Yd. Freestyle—Joe Bottom, USC. **Time** — 0:44.84.
200 Yd. Freestyle—Kurt Krumpholtz, Santa Clara SC. **Time** — 1:39.47.
500 Yd. Freestyle—Tim Shaw, Long Beach. **Time** — 4:23.50.
1,650 Yd. Freestyle — Mike Bruner, Pacific AC. **Time** — 15:15.33.
100 Yd. Backstroke — John Naber, USC. **Time** — 0:50.41.
200 Yd. Backstroke — John Naber. **Time** — 1:49.70.
100 Yd. Breaststroke — John Hencken, Santa Clara SC. **Time** — 0:55.50.
200 Yd. Breaststroke — Rick Colella, Totem Lake ST. **Time** — 2:01.42.
100 Yd. Butterfly — Steve Baxter, Santa Clara SC. **Time** — 0:49.51.
200 Yd. Butterfly — Robin Backhaus, Washington. **Time** — 1:47.27.
200 Yd. Individual Medley — Lee Engstrand, Tennessee. **Time** — 1:51.28.
400 Yd. Individual Medley — Rick Colella, Totem Lake ST. **Time** — 3:57.19
400 Yd. Freestyle Relay — USC. **Time** — 3:02.16.
800 Yd. Freestyle Relay — USC. **Time** — 6:41.24.
400 Yd. Medley Relay — USC. **Time** — 3:20.87.
Team Championship — USC, 564 pts.; Univ. of Washington, 347 pts.; Santa Clara SC, 229 pts.

Diving

One-Meter Springboard — Tim Moore, Columbus, Ohio, 517.-65 pts.
Three-Meter Springboard — Phil Boggs, U.S. Air Force, 547.-20 pts.
Ten-Meter Platform — Steve McFarland, Univ. of Miami, 486.21 pts.

Women

100 Yd. Freestyle — Kathy Heddy, Central Jersey. **Time** — 0:50.89.
200 Yd. Freestyle — Shirley Babashoff, Mission Viejo. **Time** — 1:48.79.
500 Yd. Freestyle — Shirley Babashoff. **Time** — 4:47.34.
1,650 Yd. Freestyle — Karen Hazen, Arden Hills. **Time** — 16:28.37.
100 Yd. Backstroke — Linda Stimpson, Lakewood AC. **Time** — 0:57.30.
200 Yd. Backstroke — Wendy Cook, Canadian Dolphins. **Time** — 2:04.00.
100 Yd. Breaststroke — Marcia Morey, Decatur SC. **Time** — 1:05.53.
200 Yd. Breaststroke — Lynn Colella, Totem Lake ST. **Time** — 2:19.77.
100 Yd. Butterfly — Peggy Tosdal, Mission Viejo. **Time** — 0:55.91.
200 Yd. Butterfly — Valerie Lee, Mission Viejo. **Time** — 2:00.84.
200 Yd. Individual Medley — Kathy Heddy, Central Jersey. **Time** — 2:05.06.
400 Yd. Individual Medley — Jenni Franks, Wilmington, Del. **Time** — 4:26.22.
400 Yd. Freestyle Relay — Mission Viejo. **Time** — 3:29.22.
800 Yd. Freestyle Relay — Mission Viejo. **Time** — 7:30.73.
400 Yd. Medley Relay — Santa Clara SC. **Time** — 3:54.2.
Team Championship —Santa Clara SC, 323 pts.; Mission Viejo, 258 pts.; Jack Nelson SC, 182 pts.

Diving

One-Meter Springboard — Christine Loock, SMU, 459.09 pts.
Three-Meter Springboard — Jenni Chandler, Pt. Aquarius, Atlanta, 459.33 pts.
Ten-Meter Platform — Janey Ely, Bryan Robbins Divers, Dallas, 327.75 pts.

National AAU Long Course Championship
Concord, Calif., Aug. 22-25, 1974

Men

100 Meter Freestyle—Tom Hickcox, Phoenix, Ariz. **Time**—0:52.164.
200 Meter Freestyle—Tim Shaw, Long Beach, Calif. **Time**—1:51.66.
400 Meter Freestyle—Tim Shaw. **Time**—3:54.69.
1,500 Meter Freestyle—Tim Shaw. **Time**—15:31.752
100 Meter Backstroke—John Naber, Menlo Park, Calif. **Time**—0:58.12.
200 Meter Backstroke—John Naber. **Time**—2:03.53.
100 Meter Butterfly—Mike Bottom, Santa Clara, Calif. **Time**—0:55.50.
200 Meter Butterfly—Mike Bruner, Stockton, Calif. **Time**—2:01.69.
100 Meter Breaststroke—John Hencken, Santa Clara, Calif. **Time**—1:04.38.
200 Meter Breaststroke—John Hencken. **Time**—2:18.93.
200 Meter Individual Medley—Steve Furniss, Huntington Beach, Calif. **Time**—2:08.263.
400 Meter Individual Medley—Steve Furniss. **Time**—4:30.56.
400 Meter Medley Relay—Santa Clara SC. **Time**—3:50.23.
400 Meter Freestyle Relay—Gatorade SC. **Time**—3:30.468.
800 Meter Freestyle Relay—Long Beach SC. **Time**—7:36.62.
Team Champion—Santa Clara SC.

Women

100 Meter Freestyle—Kim Peyton, Portland, Ore. **Time**—0:58.224.
200 Meter Freestyle—Shirley Babashoff, Mission Viejo, Calif. **Time**—2:02.947.
400 Meter Freestyle—Shirley Babashoff. **Time**—4:15.77.
1,500 Meter Freestyle—Jenny Turrall, Sydney, Australia. **Time**—16:33.947.
100 Meter Backstroke—Margie Moffitt, Fairfax, Va. **Time**—1:04.68.
200 Meter Backstroke—Wendy Cook, Vancouver, B.C. **Time**—2:18.81.
100 Meter Butterfly—Deena Deardurff, Cincinnati. **Time**—1:02.77
200 Meter Butterfly—Valerie Lee, Mission Viejo, Calif. **Time**—2:16.52.
100 Meter Backstroke—Marcia Morey, Decatur, Ill. **Time**—1:14.19.
200 Meter Backstroke—Marcia Morey. **Time**—2:39.90.
200 Meter Individual Medley—Kathy Heddy, Summit, N.J. **Time**—2:22.477.
400 Meter Individual Medley—Jenni Franks, Wilmington, Del. **Time**—5:00.51.
400 Meter Medley Relay—Lakewood AC. **Time**—4:24.76.
400 Meter Freestyle Relay—Mission Viejo. **Time**—3:58.10.
800 Meter Freestyle Relay—Mission Viejo. **Time**—8:30.23.
Team Champion—Mission Viejo.

Kentucky Derby, 3 Year Olds

Churchill Downs, Louisville, Ky.

Inaugurated 1875, Distance 1 1/4 miles; 1 1/2 miles until 1896

Year	Winner	Jockey	Wt.	Second	Winner's Share	Time
1901	His Eminence	J. Winkfield	117	Sannazarro	$4,850	2:07.3-4
1902	Alan-a-Dale	J. Winkfield	117	Inventor	4,850	2:08.3-4
1903	Judge Himes	H. Booker	117	Early	4,850	2:09
1904	Elwood	F. Prior	117	Ed Tierney	4,850	2:08.1-5
1905	Agile	J. Martin	122	Ram's Horn	4,850	2:10.3-4
1906	Sir Huon	R. Troxer	117	Lady Navarre	4,850	2:08.4-5
1907	Pink Star	A. Minder	117	Zal	4,850	2:12.3-5
1908	Stone Street	A. Pickens	117	Sir Cleges	4,850	2:15.1-5
1909	Wintergreen	V. Powers	117	Miami	4,850	2:08.1-5
1910	Donau	F. Herbert	117	Joe Morris	4,850	2:06.2-5
1911	Meridian	G. Archibald	117	Governor Gray	4,850	2:05
1912	Worth	C. H. Shilling	117	Duval	4,850	2:09.2-5
1913	Donerail	R. Goose	117	Ten Point	5,475	2:04.4-5
1914	Old Rosebud	J. McCabe	114	Hodge	9,125	2:03.2-5
1915	Regret*	J. Notter	112	Pebbles	11,450	2:05.2-5
1916	George Smith	J. Loftus	117	Star Hawk	16,600	2:04.3-5
1917	Omar Khayyam	C. Borel	117	Ticket	9,750	2:04
1918	Exterminator	W. Knapp	114	Escoba	14,700	2:10.4-5
1919	Sir Barton	J. Loftus	112	Billy Kelly	20,825	2:09.4-5
1920	Paul Jones	T. Rice	126	Upset	30,375	2:09
1921	Behave Yourself	C. Thompson	126	Black Servant	38,450	2:04.1-5
1922	Morvich	A. Johnson	126	Bet Mosie	46,775	2:04.3-5
1923	Zev	E. Sande	126	Martingale	53,600	2:05.2-5
1924	Black Gold	J. D. Mooney	126	Chilhowee	52,775	2:05.1.5
1925	Flying Ebony	E. Sande	126	Captain Hal	52,950	2:07.3-5
1926	Bubbling Over	A. Johnson	126	Bagenbaggage	50,075	2:03.4-5
1927	Whiskery	L. McAtee	126	Osmand	51,000	2:06
1928	Reigh Count	C. Lang	126	Misstep	55,375	2:10.2-5
1929	Clyde Van Dusen	L. McAtee	126	Naishapur	53,950	2:10.4-5
1930	Gallant Fox	E. Sande	126	Gallant Knight	50,725	2:07.3-5
1931	Twenty Grand	C. Kurtsinger	126	Sweep All	48,725	2:01.4-5
1932	Burgoo King	E. James	126	Economic	52,350	2:05.1-5
1933	Brokers Tip	D. Meade	126	Head Play	48,925	2:06.4-5
1934	Cavalcade	M. Garner	126	Discovery	28,175	2:04
1935	Omaha	W. Saunders	126	Roman Soldier	39,525	2:05
1936	Bold Venture	I. Hanford	126	Brevity	37,725	2:03.3-5
1937	War Admiral	C. Kurtsinger	126	Pompoon	52,050	2:03.1-5
1938	Lawrin	E. Arcaro	126	Dauber	47,050	2:04.4-5
1939	Johnstown	J. Stout	126	Challedon	46,350	2:03.2-5
1940	Gallahadion	C. Bierman	126	Bimelech	60,150	2:05
1941	Whirlaway	E. Arcaro	126	Staretor	61,275	2:01.2-5
1942	Shut Out	W. D. Wright	126	Alsab	64,225	2:04.2-5
1943	Count Fleet	J. Longden	126	Blue Swords	60,275	2:04
1944	Pensive	C. McCreary	126	Broadcloth	64,675	2:04.1-5
1945	Hoop, Jr.	E. Arcaro	126	Pot o' Luck	64,850	2:07
1946	Assault	W. Mehrtens	126	Spy Song	96,400	2:06.3-5
1947	Jet Pilot	E. Guerin	126	Phalanx	92,160	2:06.3-5
1948	Citation	E. Arcaro	126	Coaltown	83,400	2:05.2-5
1949	Ponder	S. Brooks	126	Capot	91,600	2:04.1-5
1950	Middleground	W. Boland	126	Hill Prince	92,650	2:01.3-5
1951	Count Turf	C. McCreary	126	Royal Mustang	98,050	2:02.3-5
1952	Hill Gail	E. Arcaro	126	Sub Fleet	96,300	2:01.3-5
1953	Dark Star	H. Moreno	126	Native Dancer	90,050	2:02
1954	Determine	R. York	126	Hasty Road	102,050	2:03
1955	Swaps	W. Shoemaker	126	Nashua	108,400	2:01.4-5
1956	Needles	D. Erb	126	Fabius	123,450	2:03.2-5
1957	Iron Liege	W. Hartack	126	Gallant Man	107,950	2:02.1-5
1958	Tim Tam	I. Valenzuela	126	Lincoln Road	116,400	2:05
1959	Tomy Lee	W. Shoemaker	126	Sword Dancer	119,650	2:02.1-5
1960	Venetian Way	W. Hartack	126	Bally Ache	114,850	2:02.2-5
1961	Carry Back	J. Sellers	126	Crozier	120,500	2:04
1962	Decidedly	W. Hartack	126	Roman Line	119,650	2:00.2-5
1963	Chateaugay	B. Baeza	126	Never Bend	108,900	2:01.4-5
1964	Northern Dancer	W. Hartack	126	Hill Rise	114,300	2:00
1965	Lucky Debonair	W. Shoemaker	126	Dapper Dan	112,000	2:01.1-5
1966	Kauai King	D. Brumfield	126	Advocator	120,500	2:02
1967	Proud Clarion	R. Ussery	126	Barbs Delight	119,700	2:00.3-5
1968	Dancer's Image (A)	R. Ussery	126	Forward Pass	122,600	2:02.1-5
1969	Majestic Prince	W. Hartack	126	Arts and Letters	113,200	2:01.4-5
1970	Dust Commander	M. Manganello	126	My Dad George	127,800	2:03.2-5
1971	Canonero II	G. Avila	126	Jim French	145,500	2:03.1-5
1972	Riva Ridge	R. Turcotte	126	No Le Hace	140,300	2:01.4-5
1973	Secretariat	R. Turcotte	126	Sham	155,050	1:59.2-5
1974	Cannonade	A. Cordero	126	Hudson County	274,000	2:04

(A) Dancer's Image was disqualified from purse money by order of the Churchill Downs stewards after tests disclosed that he had run with a pain-killing drug, phenylbutazone, in his system. All wagers were paid on Dancer's Image. Forward Pass was awarded first place money.

The Kentucky Derby has been won five times by two jockeys, Eddie Arcaro, 1938, 1941, 1945, 1948 and 1952; and Bill Hartack, 1957, 1960, 1962, 1964 and 1969; and three times by each of three jockeys, Isaac Murphy, 1884, 1890 and 1891; Earle Sande, 1923, 1925 and 1930, and Willie Shoemaker, 1955, 1959, 1965. *Regret only filly ever to win the Derby.

Preakness
Inaugurated 1773; 13-16 miles, 3 year olds Pimlico, Baltimore, Md.

Year	Winner	Jockey	Weight	Second	Winning Share	Time
1935	Omaha	W. Saunders	126	Firethorn	$25,325	1:58.2-5
1936	Bold Venture	G. Woolf	126	Granville	27,325	1:59
1937	War Admiral	C. Kurtsinger	126	Pompoon	45,600	1:58.2-5
1938	Dauber	M. Peters	126	Cravat	51,875	1:59.4-5
1939	Challedon	G. Seabo	126	Gilded Knight	53,710	1:59.4-5
1940	Bimelech	F. A. Smith	126	Mioland	53,230	1:58.3-5
1941	Whirlaway	E. Arcaro	126	King Cole	49,365	1:58.4-5
1942	Alsab	B. James	126	Requested		
				Sun Again	58,175	1.57
1943	Count Fleet	J. Longden	126	Blue Swords	43,190	1:57.2-5
1944	Pensive	C. McCreary	126	Platter	60,075	1:59.1-5
1945	Polynesian	W. D. Wright	126	Hoop Jr.	66,170	1:58.4-5
1946	Assault	W. Mehrtens	126	Lord Boswell	96,620	2:01.2-5
1947	Faultless	D. Dodson	126	On Trust	98,005	1:59
1948	Citation	E. Arcaro	126	Vulcan's Forge	91,870	2:02.2-5
1949	Capot	T. Atkinson	126	Palestinian	79,985	1:56
1950	Hill Prince	E. Arcaro	126	Middleground	56,115	1:59.1-5
1951	Bold	E. Arcaro	126	Counterpoint	83,110	1:56.2-5
1952	Blue Man	C. McCreary	126	Jampol	86,135	1:57.2-5
1953	Native Dancer	E. Guerin	126	Jamie K.	65,200	1:57.4-5
1954	Hasty Road	J. Adams	126	Correlation	91,600	1:57.2-5
1955	Nashua	E. Arcaro	126	Saratoga	67,550	1:54.3-5
1956	Fabius	W. Hartack	126	Needles	84,250	1:58.2-5
1957	Bold Ruler	E. Arcaro	126	Iron Liege	65,250	1:56.1-5
1958	Tim Tam	I. Valenzuela	126	Lincoln Road	97,900	1:57.1-5
1959	Royal Orbit	W. Harmatz	126	Sword Dancer	136,200	1:57
1960	Bally Ache	R. Ussery	126	Victoria Park	121,000	1:57.3-5
1961	Carry Back	J. Sellers	126	Globemaster	126,200	1:57.3-5
1962	Greek Money	J. L. Rotz	126	Ridan	135,800	1:56.1-5
1963	Candy Spots	W. Shoemaker	126	Chateaugay	127,500	1:56.1-5
1964	Northern Dancer	W. Hartack	126	The Scoundrel	124,200	1:56.4-5
1965	Tom Rolfe	R. Turcotte	126	Dapper Dan	128,100	1:56.1-5
1965	Kauai King	D. Brumfield	126	Stupendous	129,000	1:55.2-5
1967	Damascus	W. Shoemaker	126	In Reality	141,500	1:55.1-5
1968	Forward Pass	I. Valenzuela	126	Out of the Way	142,700	1:56.4-5
1969	Majestic Prince	W. Hartack	126	Arts and Letters	129,500	1:55.3-5
1970	Personality	E. Belmonte	126	My Dad George	151,300	1:56.1-5
1971	Canonero II	G. Avila	126	Eastern Fleet	137,400	1:54
1972	Bee Bee Bee	E. Nelson	126	No Le Hace	135,300	1:55.3-5
1973	Secretariat	R. Turcotte	126	Sham	129,900	1:54.2-5
1974	Little Current	M. Rivera	126	Neopolitan Way	156,000	1:56.3-5

Belmont Stakes
Elmont, N. Y. Inaugurated 1867; 1½ Miles, 3 year olds

Year	Winner	Jockey	Weight	Second	Winning Share	Time
1935	Omaha	W. Saunders	126	Firethorn	$35,480	2:30.3-5
1936	Granville	J. Stout	126	Mr. Bones	29,800	2:30
1937	War Admiral	C. Kurtsinger	126	Sceneshifter	38,020	2:28.3-5
1938	Pasteurized	J. Stout	126	Dauber	34,530	2:29.2-5
1939	Johnstown	J. Stout	126	Belay	37,020	2:29.3-5
1940	Bimelech	F. A. Smith	126	Your Chance	35,030	2:29.3-5
1941	Whirlaway	E. Arcaro	126	Robert Morris	39,770	2:31
1942	Shut Out	E. Arcaro	126	Alsab	44,520	2:29.1-5
1943	Count Fleet	J. Longden	126	Fairy Manhurst	35,340	2:28.1-5
1944	Bounding Home	G. L. Smith	126	Pensive	55,000	2:32.1-5
1945	Pavot	E. Arcaro	126	Wildlife	52,675	2:30.1-5
1946	Assault	W. Mehrtens	126	Natchez	75,400	2:30.4-5
1947	Phalanx	R. Donoso	126	Tide Rips	78,900	2:29.2-5
1948	Citation	E. Arcaro	126	Better Self	77,700	2:28.1-5
1949	Capot	T. Atkinson	126	Ponder	60,900	2:30.1-5
1950	Middleground	W. Boland	126	Lights Up	61,350	2:28.3-5
1951	Counterpoint	D. Gorman	125	Battlefield	82,000	2:29
1952	One Count	E. Arcaro	126	Blue Man	82,400	2:30.1-5
1953	Native Dancer	E. Guerin	126	Jamie K.	82,500	2:28.3-5
1954	High Gun	E. Guerin	126	Fisherman	89,000	2:30.4-5
1955	Nashua	E. Arcaro	126	Blazing Count	83,700	2:29
1956	Needles	D. Erb	126	Career Boy	83,600	2:29.4-5
1957	Gallant Man	W. Shoemaker	126	Inside Tract	77,300	2:26.3-5
1958	Cavan	P. Anderson	126	Tim Tam	73,440	2:30.1-5
1959	Sword Dancer	W. Shoemaker	126	Bagdad	93,525	2:28.2-5
1960	Celtic Ash	W. Hartack	126	Venetian Way	96,785	2:29.3-5
1961	Sherluck	B. Baeza	126	Globemaster	104,900	2:29.1-5
1962	Jaipur	W. Shoemaker	126	Admiral's Voyage	109,550	2:28.4-5
1963	Chateaugay	B. Baeza	126	Candy Spots	101,700	2:30.1-5
1964	Quadrangle	M. Ycaza	126	Roman Brother	110,850	2:28.2-5
1965	Hail to All	J. Sellers	126	Tom Rolfe	104,150	2:28.2-5
1966	Amberoid	W. Boland	126	Buffle	117,700	2:29.3-5
1967	Damascus	W. Shoemaker	126	Cool Reception	104,950	2:28.4-5
1968	Stage Door Johnny	H. Gustines	126	Forward Pass	117,700	2:27.1-5
1969	Arts and Letters	B. Baeza	126	Majestic Prince	104,050	2:28.4-5
1970	High Echelon	J. L. Rotz	126	Needles N Pens	115,000	2:34
1971	Pass Catcher	W. Blum	126	Jim French	97,710	2:30.2-5
1972	Riva Ridge	R. Turcotte	126	Ruritania	93,950	2:28
1973	Secretariat	R. Turcotte	126	Twice A Prince	90,120	2:24
1974	Little Current	M. Rivera	126	Jolly Johu	101,970	2:29.1-5

Major Stakes Races, 1974

Event	Track	Added Value	Winner	Dist. Furl.	Time: Seconds in Fifths	Jockey
			3 Year Olds and Up			
Bowling Green Hdcp.	Belmont	$ 50,000	Take Off	12	2:26.2	R. Turcotte
Brooklyn Hdcp.	Aqueduct	100,000	Forego	9½	1:54.4	H. Gustines
Californian Stakes.	Hollywood	100,000	Quack	8½	1:40.1	D. Pierce
Carter Hdcp.	Belmont	75,000	Forego	7	1:22.1	H. Gustines
Century Hdcp.	Hollywood	100,000	Big Whippendeal.	11	2:13.3	M. Rivera
Excelsior Hdcp.	Aqueduct	50,000	Everton, 2nd	9	1:49	M. Castaneda
Governor Stakes.	Belmont	100,000	Big Spruce	9	1:46.1	M. Hole
Grey Lag Hdcp.	Aqueduct	75,000	Prove It	10	2:00.1	J. Velasquez
Gulfstream Hdcp.	Gulfstream	100,000	Forego	10	1:59.4	H. Gustines
Haskell Hdcp.	Monmouth	100,000	True Knight	10	2:02	M. Rivera
Hialeah Turf Cup.	Hialeah	100,000	Big Whippendeal.	12	2:16.1	M. Rivera
Hollywood Gold Cup.	Hollywood	125,000	Tree of Knowledge.	10	1:59.4	W. Shoemaker
Marlboro Cup.	Belmont	250,000	Big Spruce	9	1:46.3	M. Hole
Metropolitan Hdcp.	Belmont	100,000	Arbees Boy	8	1:34.2	E. Maple
Pan American Hdcp.	Gulfstream	100,000	London Company.	12	2:26.2	A. Cordero
Santa Anita Hdcp.	Santa Anita	150,000	Prince Dantan	10	2:03.3	R. Turcotte
Suburban Hdcp.	Aqueduct	100,000	True Knight	10	2:01.2	A. Cordero
Trenton Hdcp.	Garden State	100,000	True Knight	10	2:06	A. Cordero
U. N. Hdcp.	Atlantic City	100,000	Halo	9½	1:56.4	J. Velasquez
William DuPont Hdcp.	Delaware	50,000	Forage	8½	1:42.5	J. Vasquez
Whitney Stakes.	Saratoga	50,000	Tri Jet	9	1:47	L. Pincay
Woodward Stakes.	Belmont	100,000	Forego	12	2:27.2	H. Gustines
			3 Year Olds and Up, Fillies and Mares			
Beldame Stakes.	Belmont	100,000	Desert Vixen	9	1:46.3	L. Pincay
Diana Hdcp.	Saratoga	50,000	Fairway Flyer	9	1:47.1	J. Velasquez
The Matchmaker.	Atlantic City	100,000	Desert Vixen	9½	1:55.1	L. Pincay
Muskett Hdcp.	Belmont	50,000	Desert Vixen	8	1:34.3	L. Pincay
Vanity Hdcp.	Hollywood	100,000	Tallahto	9	1:47	L. Pincay
			3 Year Olds			
Belmont Stakes.	Belmont	125,000	Little Current	12	2:29.1	M. Rivera
Blue Grass Stakes.	Keeneland	50,000	Judger	9	1:49.1	L. Pincay
Dwyer Hdcp.	Aqueduct	75,000	Hatchet Man	10	2:01.1	R. Turcotte
Flamingo.	Hialeah	100,000	Bushongo	9	1:49	D. Macbeth
Florida Derby.	Gulfstream	150,000	Judger	9	1:49	L. Pincay
Illinois Derby.	Sportsman's Park	100,000	Sharp Gary	9	1:50	G. Gallitano
Jerome Hdcp.	Aqueduct	50,000	Stonewalk	8	1:34	A. Cordero
Jersey Derby.	Garden State	100,000	Better Arbitor.	9	1:50.2	C. Barbera
Kentucky Derby.	Churchill Downs	125,000	Cannonade	10	2:04	A. Cordero
Ohio Derby.	Thistledown	100,000	Stonewalk	9	1:53.1	M. Rivera
Preakness.	Pimlico	150,000	Little Current	9½	1:54.3	M. Rivera
Santa Anita Derby.	Santa Anita	125,000	Destroyer	9	1:48.4	I. Valenzuela
Travers Stakes.	Saratoga	100,000	Holding Pattern.	10	2:05.1	M. Miceli
Wood Memorial.	Aqueduct	50,000	Flip Sal.	9	1:51.2	A. Cordero
(2 Divisions)		50,000	Rube The Great.	9	1:49.3	M. Rivera
			3 Year Olds, Fillies			
Alabama Stakes.	Saratoga	50,000	Quaze Quilt	10	2:03.2	H. Gustines
Coaching Club American Oaks.	Belmont	100,000	Chris Evert	12	2:28.4	J. Velasquez
Hollywood Oaks.	Hollywood	75,000	Miss Musket	9	1:47.4	L. Pincay
Kentucky Oaks.	Churchill Downs	50,000	Quaze Quilt	8½	1:46.3	Gavidia
Mother Goose Stakes.	Belmont	75,000	Chris Evert	9	1:48.3	J. Velasquez
			2 Year Olds			
Arlington-Wash. Futurity.	Arlington	150,000	Greek Answer	6½	1:17.4	M. Castaneda
Champagne Stakes.	Belmont	125,000	Foolish Pleasure.	8	1:36	J. Vasquez
Cowdin Stakes.	Belmont	50,000	Foolish Pleasure.	7	1:22.3	J. Vasquez
Hopeful Stakes.	Saratoga	60,000	The Bagel Prince.	6½	1:16.4	A. Cordero
(2 Divisions)		60,000	Foolish Pleasure.	6½	1:16	B. Baeza
Kindergarten Stakes.	Liberty Bell	100,000	Master Derby	6	1:11.4	J. Espinosa
Sapling.	Monmouth	100,000	Foolish Pleasure.	6	1:10.2	J. Vasquez
			2 Year Olds, Fillies			
Lassie Stakes.	Arlington	100,000	Hot N Nasty.	6	1:11.2	....
Frizette Stakes.	Belmont	100,000	Molly Ballintine.	8	1:37	L. Pincay
Sorority Stakes.	Monmouth	100,000	Ruffian	6	1:09	J Vasquez
Spinway Stakes.	Saratoga	50,000	Ruffian	6	1:08.3	V. Bracciale

Leading Money-Winning Horses

(As of Jan. 1974.) †Filly

Horse, Year Foaled	Sts.	1st	2nd	3rd	Dollars	Horse, Year Foaled	Sts.	1st	2nd	3rd	Dollars
Kelso, 1957	63	39	12	2	1,977,896	Dr. Fager, 1964	22	18	2	1	1,022,642
Round Table, 1954	66	43	8	5	1,749,869	Swoon's Son, 1953	51	30	10	3	970,605
Buckpasser, 1963	31	25	4	1	1,462,014	Roman Brother, 1961	42	16	10	5	943,473
Nashua, 1952	30	22	4	1	1,288,565	Stymie, 1941	131	35	33	28	918,485
Carry Back, 1958	62	21	11	11	1,241,165	T. V. Lark, 1957	72	19	13	6	902,194
Damascus, 1964	32	21	7	3	1,176,781	†Shuvee, 1966	44	16	10	6	890,445
Cougar, 2nd, 1966	50	20	7	17	1,162,725	Swaps, 1952	25	19	2	2	848,900
Secretariat, 1970	19	14	3	1	1,155,893	Nodouble, 1965	42	13	11	5	846,749
Fort Marcy, 1964	75	21	18	14	1,109,791	Sword Dancer, 1956	39	15	7	4	829,610
Citation, 1945	45	32	10	2	1,085,760	Candy Spots, 1960	22	12	5	1	824,718
Riva Ridge, 1969	28	16	3	1	1,077,027	Mongo, 1959	46	22	10	4	820,766
Native Diver, 1959	81	37	7	12	1,026,500	Armed, 1941	81	41	20	10	817,475

Annual Leading Jockey—Money Won

Year	Jockey	Dollars	Year	Jockey	Dollars	Year	Jockey	Dollars
1941	Meade, D.	398,627	1952	Arcaro, E.	1,859,591	1963	Shoemaker, W.	2,526,925
1942	Arcaro, E.	481,949	1953	Shoemaker, W.	1,784,187	1964	Shoemaker, W.	2,649,553
1943	Longden, J.	573,276	1954	Shoemaker, W.	1,876,760	1965	Baeza, B.	2,582,702
1944	Atkinson, T.	899,101	1955	Arcaro, E.	1,864,796	1966	Baeza, B.	2,951,022
1945	Longden, J.	981,977	1956	Hartack, W.	2,343,955	1967	Baeza, B.	3,088,888
1946	Atkinson, T.	1,036,825	1957	Hartack, W.	3,060,501	1968	Baeza, B.	2,835,108
1947	Dodson, D.	1,429,949	1958	Shoemaker, W.	2,961,693	1969	Valasquez, J.	2,542,315
1948	Arcaro, E.	1,686,230	1959	Shoemaker, W.	2,843,133	1970	Pincay, L. Jr.	2,626,526
1949	Brooks, S.	1,316,817	1960	Shoemaker, W.	2,123,961	1971	Pincay, L. Jr.	3,784,377
1950	Arcaro, E.	1,410,160	1961	Shoemaker, W.	2,690,819	1972	Pincay, L. Jr.	3,225,827
1951	Shoemaker, W.	1,329,890	1962	Shoemaker, W.	2,916,844	1973	Pincay, L. Jr.	4,093,492

Annual Leading Money-Winning Horses

Year	Horse	Dollars	Year	Horse	Dollars	Year	Horse	Dollars
1941	Whirlaway	272,386	1952	Crafty Admiral	277,225	1963	Candy Spots	604,481
1942	Shut Out	238,872	1953	Native Dancer	513,425	1964	Gun Bow	580,100
1943	Count Fleet	174,055	1954	Determine	328,700	1965	Buckpasser	568,096
1944	Pavot	179,040	1955	Nashua	752,550	1966	Buckpasser	669,078
1945	Busher	273,735	1956	Needles	440,850	1967	Damascus	817,941
1946	Assault	424,195	1957	Round Table	600,383	1968	Forward Pass	546,674
1947	Armed	376,325	1958	Round Table	662,780	1969	Arts and Letters	555,604
1948	Citation	709,470	1959	Sword Dancer	537,004	1970	Personality	444,049
1949	Ponder	321,825	1960	Bally Ache	455,045	1971	Riva Ridge	503,263
1950	Noor	346,940	1961	Carry Back	565,349	1972	Droll Roll	471,633
1951	Counterpoint	250,525	1962	Never Bend	402,969	1973	Secretariat	860,404

Triple Crown Turf Winners, Owners and Jockeys

(Kentucky Derby, Preakness and Belmont Stakes)

Year	Horse	Owner	Jockey	Year	Horse	Owner	Jockey
1919	Sir Barton	J. K. L. Ross	J. Loftus	1943	Count Fleet	Mrs. J. D. Hertz	J. Longden
1930	Gallant Fox	W. Woodward	E. Sande	1946	Assault	R. J. Kleberg	W. Mehrtens
1935	Omaha	W. Woodward	W. Sanders	1948	Citation	Warren Wright	E. Arcaro
1937	War Admiral	S. D. Riddle	C. Kurtsinger	1973	Secretariat	Meadow Stable	R. Turcotte
1941	Whirlaway	Warren Wright	E. Arcaro				

Queen's Plate

The Queen's Plate (known as the King's Plate during reign of male), Canada's most famous thoroughbred race, is the oldest continuously run stakes race in North America. Originated in 1860 over 1⅛ miles (now 1¼ miles) for 3-year-olds, Canadians-foaled, race is staged under Royal tutelage for trophy and 50 gold sovereigns plus purse. Trophy is not a plate but a foot-high gold cup valued at $5,000. However, race is identified as a plate race because of 17th Century English tradition of awarding plates.

Year	Winner, Jockey	Time	Dollars	Year	Winner, Jockey	Time	Dollars
1952—	Epigram, G. Robillard	1:58.3-5	17,022	1964—	Northern Dancer, W. Hartack	2:02.1-5	49,234
1953—	Canadian, E. Arcaro	1:52.1-5	20,592	1965—	Whistling Sea, T. Inouye	2:03.4-5	47,852
1954—	Collisteo, C. Rogers	1:52	22,452	1966—	Titled Hero, A. Gomez	2:03.3-5	52,173
1955—	Ace Marine, G. Walker	1:52.2-5	25,514	1967—	Jammed Lovely, J. Fitzsimmons	2:03	51,821
1956—	Canadian Champ, D. Stevenson	1:55	25,430	1968—	Merger, W. Harris	2:05.2-5	53,641
1957—	Lyford Cay, A. Gomez	2:03.3-5	26,210	1969—	Jumping Joseph, A. Gomez	2:04.1-5	55,022
1958—	Caledon Beau, A. Coy	2:04.1-5	26,151	1970—	Almoner, S. Hawley	2:04.4-5	57,395
1959—	New Providence, R. Ussery	2:04.4-5	51,767	1971—	Kennedy Road, S. Hawley	2:03	54,388
1960—	Victoria Park, A. Gomez	2:02	42,750	1972—	Victoria Song, R. Platts	2:02	56,143
1961—	Blue Light, H. Dittfach	2:05	46,475	1973—	Royal Chocolate, T. Colangelo	2:08	80,697
1962—	Flaming Page, J. Fitzsimmons	2:04.3-5	51,225	1974—	Amber Herod, R. Platts	2:09.1-5	96,541
1963—	Canebora, M. Ycaza	2:04	54,850				

Quarter Horse Racing

The richest horse race in the world, the All American Futurity is run each Labor Day at Ruidoso Downs, New Mexico. It is open to 2-year-old Quarter Horses. The distance of the event was 400 yards through 1972; 440 yards starting in 1973.

Year	Winner	Weight	Time	Value to Winner	Jockey	Owner
1960	Tonto Bars Hank	119	20.2	$65,122	C. Perner	Milo and C. G. Whitcomb
1961	Pokey Bar	119	20.1	101,212	K. Chapman	Hugh Huntley
1962	Hustling Man	119	20.3	96,425	C. Detiege	J. B. Ferguson
1963	Goetta	116	20.40	127,500	C. Smith	Hugh Huntley
1964	Decketta	119	20.30	134,030	B. Morris	W. W. Wilson
1965	Savannah Jr.	120	20.30	192,730	J. Wallace	J. R. and R. E. Cates
1966	Go Dick Go	119	20.27	198,300	B. Nesmith	Joe V. Leitner
1967	Laico Bird	119	20.11	228,300	B. Harmon	F. H. Jones Jr.
1968	Three Oh's	119	20.06	160,372	J. Nicodemus	Donald G. Strole
1969	Easy Jet	119	20.46	159,840	W. Lovell	Walter Merrick
1970	Rocket Wrangler	119	20.09	178,488	J. Nicodemus	John R. Adams
1971	Mr. Kid Charge	120	19.65	200,841	J. Cox	Will F. Whitehead
1972	Possumjet	119	20.04	336,629	P. Herrera	Jack Byers
1973	Time To Thinkrich	120	21.58	330,000	J. Watson	Vessels Stallion Farm
1974	Easy Date	120	21.60	330,000	D. Knight	Walter Merrick

Chronology of Year's Events

Reported Month by Month in 3 Categories: National, International, and General —Nov. 1,1973, to Nov. 1, 1974

NOVEMBER, 1973
National

Saxbe, Jaworski Nominated—President Richard M. Nixon announced, **Nov. 1,** that he would nominate William B. Saxbe (R-Ohio) as his 4th Attorney General. Coincidentally, Acting Attorney General Robert H. Bork announced that, with the president's approval, he had nominated Leon Jaworski, a conservative Texas Democrat, as the new Special Watergate Prosecutor. The nomination came with the understanding that Jaworski would have "complete freedom" to investigate administration wrongdoing. Bork confirmed that, "Should he (Jaworski) disagree with a decision of the Administration with regard to the release of Presidential documents, there will be no restrictions placed on his freedom of action." The president also agreed that Jaworski would not be dismissed without approval of a substantial majority of 8 Congressional leaders to be designated by Bork.

Segretti Sentenced—U.S. District Court Judge Gerhard A. Gesell, **Nov. 5,** sentenced Donald H. Segretti to 6 months in prison for his efforts to disrupt the 1972 Democratic presidential primary election in Florida. Charges included circulating a phony letter accusing Senators Hubert H. Humphrey and Henry A. Jackson of sexual misconduct. Sources close to Watergate prosecutors reported, **Nov. 26,** that Segretti said it had been President Nixon's former appointments secretary Dwight L. Chapin who had first alerted him to expect a phone call from E. Howard Hunt, who allegedly, from February 1972 until the Watergate break-in, became Segretti's contact on covert activities. Chapin was indicted **Nov. 29,** on 4 charges of perjury in connection with his statements before the Watergate grand jury dealing with his association with Segretti.

Congress Overrides War Powers Bill Veto—The House and Senate, **Nov. 7,** voted, 284-135 and 78-15 respectively, to override President Richard M. Nixon's veto on the war powers bill. The action was the first success of 9 attempts in 1973 to override presidential vetos. The bill, which became law immediately, curbs the president's power to commit armed forces to hostilities abroad without Congressional approval. The White House called the vote a serious undermining of "this nation's ability to act decisively and convincingly in times of international crisis."

Nixon Launches Public Offensive—At the beginning of November, President Richard M. Nixon launched a counter-offensive against severe decline in public confidence in his leadership. From **Nov. 9** to **15,** he scheduled meetings with GOP Congressional leaders, which drew mixed reviews. On **Nov. 12,** Nixon met with 6 southern Democratic senators. On **Nov. 13** and **15,** he held meetings with 15 Republican senators. Nixon, **Nov. 15,** told a convention of the National Association of Realtors that he would not resign saying, "As far as the President of the United States is concerned, he hasn't violated his trust and he isn't going to violate his trust now." The President carried his offensive to the south, **Nov. 17-20,** with a series of public appearances. Addressing newspaper editors at Disney World, Fla., Nixon said, **Nov. 17,** that the "people have got to know whether or not their President is a crook—well, I'm not a crook."

Watergate Defendants Sentenced—U.S. District Court Judge John J. Sirica, **Nov. 9,** sentenced 6 of the defendants in the Watergate break-in case. E. Howard Hunt received 2½ to 8 years in jail and a $10,000 fine for his role in planning the break-in. Sirica gave lesser terms to those who carried out the plan: 1 to 5 years for James W. McCord Jr., 1 to 4 years for Frank A. Sturgis, Eugenio R. Martinez, and Virgilio R. Gonzalez, and 18 months to 6 years for Bernard L. Barker. The 7th Watergate defendant, G. Gordon Liddy, had already been sentenced to a maximum of 20 years reflecting his refusal to cooperate with the prosecution. All 6 could have been sentenced up to 20 years but, according to Sirica, received "the lowest minimum I thought justified under the circumstances of this case."

Oil Executives Admit Illegal Campaign Contributions—Gulf Oil Corporation, the Ashland Oil Company, and 2 top executives of each pleaded guilty, **Nov. 13,** to making illegal contributions of $100,000 apiece with corporate funds to President Richard M. Nixon's 1972 re-election campaign. Both corporations were fined $5,000 and their executives, Gulf Vice President Claude C. Wild and Ashland Board Chairman Orin E. Atkins, were fined $1,000 each. Both Atkins and Wild, **Nov. 14,** told the Senate Watergate Committee that, upon being told by Commerce Secretary Maurice A. Stans that such a contribution was expected from all major corporations, they had secretly arranged to have the funds drawn from foreign subsidiaries. Representatives of 3 other large corporations, American Airlines, Braniff International, and the Goodyear Tire and Rubber Co., **Nov. 15,** told the Senate Watergate Committee they had similarly channeled cash through foreign countries to hide illegal use of corporate funds for the Nixon re-election fund.

Cox Dismissal Ruled Illegal—U.S. District Court Judge Gerhard A. Gesell ruled, **Nov. 14,** that the dismissal of Watergate Special Prosecutor Archibald Cox had violated a Justice Department regulation. Such an action is prohibited according to the Justice Department "except for extraordinary improprieties" of which Cox was not accused. Acting Attorney General Robert H. Bork dismissed Cox on Oct. 20, 1973, upon the request of President Richard M. Nixon. The court decision did not order reinstatement of Cox. Cox said he would not seek to regain his position because legal claims would only divert attention from a vigorous investigation of the Watergate scandal being conducted by Leon Jaworski, the new special prosecutor.

Nixon Signs Alaska Pipeline Bill—President Richard M. Nixon, **Nov. 16,** signed into law the controversial bill to build a 789-mile pipeline from Prudhoe Bay on Alaska's North Slope to the warm water port of Valdez. Nixon hailed the bill as the first step to make the U.S. wholly self-sufficient for its energy supplies by 1980. The House, **Nov. 12,** had approved the bill, 361-14, and the Senate had followed suit, **Nov. 13,** in a 80-5 vote. In final form, the bill contained a provision barring court review of the environmental impact bill.

Gap in Nixon-Haldeman Tape Disclosed—The White House disclosed, **Nov. 21,** that there was an 18½-minute gap in the subpoenaed tape of a Nixon-Haldeman conversation on June 20, 1972, 3 days after the Watergate break-in. Presidential Counsel J. Fred

Buzhardt said White House tests could not provide any explanation for the gap which did contain "an audible tone," but no conversation. The president's personal secretary Rose Mary Woods, in testimony **Nov. 26** and 27, stated that, through carelessness, she might have caused part of the gap. The White House maintained it did not discover until Nov. 14, 1973, that the Nixon-Haldeman meeting was one of the subpoenaed tapes, thereby explaining the delay in disclosure of the gap. Judge John J. Sirica immediately ordered the subpoenaed tapes to be turned over to him for safekeeping.

Stock Market Dips to Lowest in 11 Years—Reflecting fears that the energy crisis might lead to recession in 1974, the Dow Jones Industrial average, **Nov. 26**, fell 29.05 points. The drop, in which all 30 blue chip stocks showed a decline, was the largest single-day break since **May 28, 1962**, following President John F. Kennedy's confrontation with the steel industry. The market had also declined considerably **Nov. 10** with a 24.4 drop and **Nov. 19** when it dropped 28.67 points.

Krogh Pleads Guilty—Egil Krogh Jr., the former head of the "plumbers," the White House special investigation unit, pleaded guilty, **Nov. 30**, to civil rights violations in connection with the Sept. 1971 burglary of the office of Daniel Ellsberg's psychiatrist. In return for the guilty plea and Krogh's promise to cooperate with the Watergate special prosecutor, U.S.District Court Judge Gerhard A. Gesell dropped additional charges of perjury before the Watergate grand jury. State charges against Krogh in California arising from the break-in were also dropped.

International

U.S., Egypt Renew Official Ties— Egyptian President Anwar el-Sadat and U.S. Secretary of State Henry A. Kissinger announced, **Nov. 7**, in Cairo that their 2 countries had agreed to resume diplomatic relations and would exchange ambassadors within 10 days to 2 weeks. Official relations had been severed **June 6, 1967**, when Egyptians charged U.S. aircraft were aiding Israeli forces in the Middle East war. Hermann F. Eilts, formerly ambassador to Saudi Arabia, was named U.S. ambassador to Egypt and Ashraf Ghorbal was named to the Washington embassy.

Israel, Egypt Solidify Cease-fire, Exchange Prisoners — Climaxing military negotiations at Kilometer 101 on the Suez-Cairo Road, Israel and Egypt, **Nov. 11**, signed a U.S.-sponsored exchange-of-POW'S agreement. After resolving a cease-fire line dispute which threatened the agreement, both nations, **Nov. 15**, began the exchange of prisoners. Both sides agreed to discuss their return to positions held on **Oct. 22**, to allow supplies to flow to the city of Suez and Egyptian forces on the eastern bank of the Suez Canal, and to replace Israeli checkpoints on the Suez-Cairo Road with UN checkpoints. The exchange of prisoners, 241 Israelis and 8,301 Egyptians, was completed **Nov. 22**. Israeli-Egyptian military talks on disengagement broke down **Nov. 29** with both sides claiming they had no new proposals to make and could not accept existing ones. No new date for talks was set. Israeli and Egyptian forces exchanged heavy machine gun and mortar fire less than 2 miles from the negotiation site at Kilometer 101. According to Israeli sources, the talks broke down over Egyptian demands that Israeli troops return to positions held **Oct. 22** on the west bank of the Suez and pull back 20 to 23 miles from the eastern side of the Suez Canal. Egyptians said stalling and backtracking by Israeli negotiators had precipitated the breakdown.

Kissinger Confers With Chinese Leaders — Capping 3½ days of discussions with top Chinese leaders, U.S. Secretary of State Henry A. Kissinger, **Nov. 14**, publicly stated that "no matter what happens in the United States in the future" its policy toward China would remain constant. Kissinger, **Nov. 11**, had conferred for 2¾ hours with Communist party chairman Mao Tse-tung in what the Chinese press called a

---

Nixon Requests Emergency Energy Measures

As the United States faced a widening shortage of crude oil and refinery products exacerbated by the Arab oil boycott, President Richard M. Nixon, **Nov. 7**, went on nationwide television to ask Congress for an emergency energy act and outlined various conservation proposals, including the institution of year-round day-light savings time. He also asked for a relaxation of environmental standards on a case-by-case basis and for approval and funding of increased exploration, development and production of naval petroleum reserves.

The president concluded the 25-minute energy message on a personal note. Admitting that it had been a very difficult year, Nixon spoke directly to those who had suggested that he resign. "I have no intention," Nixon stated, "of walking away from the job I was elected to do."

On **Nov. 8**, Nixon followed up his television appeal with a request to Congress for a bi-partisan move to enact emergency legislation before Congress recessed at the end of December. The Senate passed the National Emergency Energy Act on **Nov. 19**. House passage of the bill was delayed until after the Thanksgiving recess.

As the energy situation worsened, President Nixon, **Nov.25**, again over nationwide television, issued orders for a series of "strong, effective countermeasures" to cut energy consumption. A 15% nationwide reduction in delivery of gasoline by refiners to whole-salers and retailers headed the list. The cut, Nixon said, would enable refiners to concentrate on production of heating oil.

The president also asked gasoline station owners to cease selling gas on Sundays. The measure would be voluntary pending Congressional approval of the National Energy Emergency Act. Nixon said he would also impose, pending Congressional approval, a national speed limit of 50 mph for cars and 55 mph for trucks and buses.

In the area of heating oil, Nixon asked for 15% reduction in residential use, 10% in industrial use and 25% reduction in store and other commercial use. Jet fuel supplies, the president said, would be cut an additional 15%, bringing the total in reductions to 25%.

In summing up, Nixon sounded a recurring note in his assessment of the U.S.'s energy posture in the coming years: "In the last third of this century, our independence will depend on maintaining and achieving self-sufficiency in energy."

In further energy developments, President Nixon, **Nov. 28**, signed into law the Emergency Petroleum Allocation Act of 1973. Under the law, the government would, within 30 days, set up allocation, or supply-management, programs for crude oil and refinery products to combat discrimination against particular regions or independent refiners and distributors.

"friendly" atmosphere. Kissinger also conferred extensively with Premier Chou En-lai. In their first meeting, **Nov. 10,** he told Chou that the U.S. was determined "to complete the process" of normalizing relations with China as quickly as possible. In an official communique issued **Nov. 14,** both sides agreed to "continue their efforts to promote normalization of relations."

Coalition Government for North Ireland—Seven weeks of stormy negotiations between Britain's Secretary of State for Ulster William Whitelaw and Northern Ireland political leaders culminated, **Nov. 21,** in a compromise plan to create an 11-man executive body in which Protestants and Catholics would share power. Whitelaw, **Nov. 22,** disclosed to the House of Commons that 6 seats in the cabinet would go to the Unionist party, which represents about half of the Protestant seats in the Assembly, 4 seats to the Social Democratic and Labor party, which represents the Catholics, and 1 seat to the small nonsectarian Alliance party. The cabinet would also include 4 nonvoting members. Unionist party leader Brian Faulkner would head the body and Social Democratic and Labor leader Gerald Fitt would become deputy chief. The body would be entrusted with all of Northern Ireland's affairs except security, justice, foreign relations, and some financial matters.

Military Coup Deposes Greek President—Following weeks of student-worker riots, Greek President George Papadopoulos was deposed and placed under house arrest, **Nov. 25,** in a bloodless military coup. The new military leaders imposed a 24-hour curfew in Athens and Salonika. First Army commander Lieut. Gen. Phaidon Gizikis replaced Papadopoulos as president. Premier Spyros Markenzinis and his civilian cabinet were replaced with a new 17-man civilian cabinet headed by Adamantios Androutspoulos, a former cabinet member under Papadopoulos. Also dismissed were the armed forces commander in chief and chiefs of the army, air force and Athens police. Official communiques from the military leaders behind the coup said they had acted because Papadopoulos had been moving too quickly toward the restoration of democracy, thereby leading Greece toward "chaos and catastrophe." They also proclaimed Papadopoulos had failed to achieve the objectives of the 1967 revolution to cleanse public life and create conditions for a return to a healthy parliamentary life. They announced they had the support of all of the armed forces. The guiding force behind the coup was reported to be military police chief Brig. Gen. Dimitrios Ioannidis. The deposed president's problems had climaxed, **Nov. 17,** when he was forced to call in tank troops to help police dislodge about 2,000 students who had clashed with police after seizing the Athens Polytechnic University campus. The students, joined by some 200 building workers, had demanded the overthrow of the government.

Arab Extremists Hijack Dutch Jet—Three gunmen who identified themselves as members of the Arab Nationalist Youth for Liberation of Palestine, **Nov. 25,** hijacked a KLM jumbo jet in flight over the Middle East. The plane, carrying 247 passengers and 18 crew members, was enroute from Amsterdam to Tokyo. After following a checkered course through the Middle East, the hijackers finally surrendered the plane and remaining 11 hostages, **Nov. 28,** in Dubai in return for safe-conduct guarantees. The extremists had freed 247 passengers and 8 stewardesses in exchange for 2 hostages and a load of fuel, **Nov. 27,** in Valletta, Malta, after negotiations with the Dutch government ended in an agreement not to send arms to Israel or allow Jewish emigrants from the Soviet Union or military volunteers to leave the Netherlands for Israel. The Dutch government maintained that the agrement would have no impact on existing policies.

Arabs Hold Summit—Completing a 3-day summit held in Staoeli, Algeria, 15 Arab heads of state together with Palestinian leaders, **Nov. 28,** issued a communique announcing an embargo on oil exports to Portugal, Rhodesia and South Africa. The conference also agreed on continued embargo of countries supporting Israel and continued reduction of oil production until the revenues dropped to ¼ of oil revenues in 1972. The conference supported the continued use of oil as an economic weapon to create international pressure for Israeli withdrawal from all occupied Arab territories.

General

Indictments in Insurance Scandal — A Los Angeles federal grand jury indicted, **Nov. 1,** 20 former executives and employees of the Equity Funding Corporation of America and 2 of the company's former auditors in an alleged swindle involving $120 million in bogus assets and some 60,000 fictitious life insurance policies. Heading the list in the 105-count indictment were Equity's former president and chairman Stanley Goldbaum and former executive vice presidents Fred Levin and Samuel B. Lowell. All defendants were charged with conspiracy to commit securities fraud, filing false documents with the Securities and Exchange Commission, bank fraud, interstate transportation of counterfeit securities, and electronic eavesdropping.

Nine Slain in California— In the 6th mass murder in California in the past 4 years, 9 persons were found dead, **Nov. 7,** in the Lodi, Calif.- ranch-style home of Walter Parkin. The dead, all bound and shot in the head, included Parkin, his wife, 2 children, a babysitter, and her boyfriend, parents and brother. The killings were believed to be connected with a burglary of the store Parkin operated in Victor, 2 miles east of Lodi. Police, **Nov. 8,** apprehended 2 fugitives, Douglas Gretzler, 22, of New York City, and Willie Luther Steelman, 28, of Lodi, in connection with the slayings. Both were also wanted on a 2-count murder charge in Phoenix, Ariz.

Disasters — At least 127 men were missing and feared dead, **Nov. 7,** when a cyclone slammed into a 22-boat fishing fleet in the Bay of Bengal . . . Fire raged for 8 hours in a Kumamoto, Japan, department store, **Nov. 29,** killing 107 persons and injuring at least 100 others.

DECEMBER 1973

National

Love Quits in Energy Shake-up—Former Colorado Governor John A. Love resigned, **Dec. 3,** as the administration's energy "czar." Love's resignation upstaged White House plans, disclosed **Dec. 1,** to announce the creation of a Federal Energy Administration to be headed by Deputy Treasury Secretary William E. Simon. Although the White House plan kept Love "on the team," Love said he was being shunted aside in the shakeup. President Richard M. Nixon, **Dec. 4,** formally appointed Simon as the new "energy czar." Simon would remain deputy treasury secretary as well as gain cabinet rank as a counselor to the president. Nixon also announced that he was creating by executive order a new Federal Energy Office and that the Federal Energy Administration which Simon would eventually head would be established later by statute.

Truckers Protest Fuel Crisis — Protesting rising fuel costs and government-imposed reductions in highway speed limits, independent truckers, **Dec. 4-7,** blocked key U.S. highways in Pennsylvania, Ohio, West Virginia, Connecticut, and Delaware. On **Dec. 5,** when the protest had escalated to paralyzing proportions, Teamster officials and representatives of the National Association of Truck Stop Operators, although they had disavowed the protest action, asked for meetings with President Richard M. Nixon to discuss the truckers' grievances. Transportation Secretary Claude S. Brinegar appealed for an end to the protest and promised an immediate investigation of alleged price gouging and a review of diesel fuel allocations to truck stops. Independent truckers took further action, **Dec. 13-14,** in a 2-day strike initiated by Michael Parkhurst, a former driver and editor of *Overdrive Magazine,* an independent anti-Teamster publication based in Los Angeles. Although planned as a peaceful protest in which drivers would leave their rigs at home rather than block highways, reports of violence, chiefly in the Pennsylvania and Ohio area, vandalism and intimidation marred the action.

Ford Confirmed as VP—Following an affirmative 387 to 35 House vote, Gerald R. Ford was sworn in **Dec. 6,** as the 40th vice president of the United States. The Senate, **Nov. 27,** had approved the nomination, 92 to 3. In a brief speech following the ceremony, Ford pledged his full "support and loyalty" to the president and bid a "fond good-by" to his colleagues in the House. The confirmation followed weeks of exhaustive hearings and debate which had produced few surprises. The House, **Dec. 6,** chose John J. Rhodes (R-Ariz.) by acclamation to succeed Ford as minority leader of the House.

Nixon Discloses Financial Records—To clear up doubts and misinformation about his personal finances, President Richard M. Nixon, **Dec. 8,** made public his financial file, including income tax forms from his first 4 years in office. He acknowledged, however, that the disclosures might lead to "more questions and controversies." According to the disclosed records, Nixon had become a millionaire during his term in office by tripling his net worth although his $200,000-a-year salary and $50,000 expense account were virtually his only sources of income. The records also revealed that in 3 years, because of various deductions and exemptions, Nixon had paid taxes equivalent to those levied against an income of only $15,000 a year. The president acknowledged the controversial nature of 2 tax decisions which had led to his reduced taxes. One decision involved a large deduction based on the president's gift of his vice-presidential papers to the National Archives. The second controversy centered on whether Nixon had realized capital gains on the sale of property in California. The president said he would abide by the decision of the Congressional Joint Committee on Internal Revenue Taxation as to whether he owed additional taxes. Wilbur D. Mills (D., Ark.), chairman of the Joint Committee, announced, **Dec. 12,** that the committee had decided to investigate all aspects of Nixon's tax returns during his term in office rather than focus on the 2 controversial returns.

Simon Outlines Fuel Allocation—Energy chief William E. Simon, **Dec. 12,** outlined broad fuel allocations plans "to insure equitable distribution at the wholesale level" during the winter months. According to the plan, scheduled to go into effect **Dec. 27,** priority for the rights to gasoline was given to the Defense Department; essential community services

such as firefighting and health care; farming; manufacturing; passenger and freight transportation; mail delivery; and energy production, especially fuel for electric utilities. Users of heating oil and diesel fuel were divided into 2 categories. In the first, public passenger transportation and energy producers were alloted 100% of their 1972 consumption while health care and other vital community users received 110%. In the 2nd category, including industry, manufacturing, farming, food processing, and cargo and mail handling, users were allocated rights to 110% of 1972 consumption. All other users were awarded 100% of 1972 consumption.

Saxbe Confirmed as Attorney General—The Senate voted 75-10, **Dec. 17,** to confirm Sen. William B. Saxbe (R., Ohio) as attorney general. In confirmation hearings before the Senate Judiciary Committee, Saxbe stated, **Dec. 12,** that he would "vigorously support" the special Watergate prosecutor in his investigation of whether "high crimes and misdemeanors" had been committed by the White House.

Rockefeller Resigns—After 15 years as governor of the state of New York, Nelson A. Rockefeller, **Dec. 18,** resigned his office in order to pursue a new national role. Lt. Governor Malcolm Wilson succeeded Rockefeller. Denying that he was resigning to make his 4th try for the presidency, Rockefeller said he felt he could perform a greater public service as head of 2 national commissions, the National Commission on Water Quality and the new National Commission on Critical Choices for Americans.

GAO Issues Report on Nixon Residences—The General Accounting Office's private report on federal spending at President Richard M. Nixon's private residences, issued **Dec. 18,** called for Congressional action toward closer control and public disclosure of such expenditures in the future. The report placed total spending at the residences at San Clemente, Calif., and Key Biscayne, Fla., at $1.4 million. This figure did not include spending at both sites for office complexes and military communications and other support systems which brought the total to $10 million. Although most of the expenses did actually involve presidential protection, the GAO reported that some governmental expenditures were questionable and perhaps should have been paid for by the president.

Sirica Upholds Privilege Claims on Tapes—U.S. District Court Judge John J. Sirica, **Dec. 19,** ruled that President Richard M. Nixon's claims of executive privilege on parts of 3 presidential tapes sought by the special Watergate prosecution were, with minor exceptions, valid. Sirica stated that, after listening to the tapes, he had determined that the parts under contention were not relevant to the Watergate case. The ruling covered portions of Nixon's June 20, 1973, conversations with advisers John D. Ehrlichman and H.R. Haldeman which came after the disputed 18-minute gap and part of Nixon's Sept. 15, 1973, conversation with John W. Dean 3rd. As Sirica handed down the decision, lawyers for the Senate Watergate Committee served the White House with subpoenas covering nearly 500 presidential tape recordings and documents.

Nixon OKs Gas and Oil Price Rise—In a brief White House appearance, President Richard M. Nixon announced, **Dec. 19,** that he would allow increases in the price of oil and gasoline. In a surprise move, Nixon also submitted a proposal for a "windfall profits" tax on oil producers. Responding immediately to the president's announcement, the Cost of Living Council authorized a price increase of $1 per barrel for crude oil and estimated the increase would cause the cost of gasoline and heating oil to rise 2.3 cents per gallon, bringing average gasoline price to 44.6 cents per gallon and average heating oil price to 30.7 cents per gallon. The president explained that the "windfall profits" tax would be an excise-type levy to be placed on crude oil prices that rose above a certain base and would not apply to the refining and marketing phases of the oil business.

Congress Fails to Pass Energy Measure—The 93rd Congress adjourned, **Dec. 22**, without passing emergency legislation. The move left the president without sweeping powers to impose gasoline rationing, ban Sunday sales of gasoline, and impose other energy conservation measures. A controversial windfall profits provision, which would have required price rollbacks in cases where it could be proven that a seller in any sector of the petroleum industry had made "windfall profits" due to the energy crisis, presented the chief stumbling block to the bill's passage. Faced with White House pressure and a filibuster led by oil state senators, the Senate, **Dec. 21**, passed, in a 52-8 vote, a modified version, stripped of the windfall profits provision. The House, however, rejected the compromise version by a 219-to-34 vote. House members expressed anger that the Senate had capitulated to pressure from the Federal Energy Office and a small group of senators. President Nixon, **Dec. 22**, issued a conciliatory statement in which he acknowledged the difficulty in reaching agreement on complex legislation.

International

Accord Reached on Ulster—Talks held at Sunningdale, England, between British Prime Minister Edward Heath, Irish Republic Prime Minister Liam Cosgrave, and members of the new executive body for British-controlled Northern Ireland culminated, **Dec. 9**, in an agreement on sweeping proposals for the future of Ulster. Both Great Britain and the Republic of Ireland promised to make pledges, to be deposited at the United Nations, concerning the status of Northern Ireland. UN supervision would give the pledges international status, thereby placing their observance under the jurisdiction of the International Court of Justice. Ireland pledged that the current status of Northern Ireland could not be changed except by majority decison in Northern Ireland. Britain pledged to create no obstacles should a majority in Northern Ireland decide to join an united Ireland. The agreement also established a Council of Ireland to serve as a link between the government of the Republic of Ireland and Northern Ireland's executive body. The council membership, to consist of 7 members of each, would concern itself with "executive" functions as yet undefined. The accord was acclaimed in both London and Dublin **Dec. 10**.

Venezuelan Election—In a 4-million voter turnout, Venezuelans, **Dec. 9**, electel Social Democrat Carlos Andres Perez to a 5-year term as president. On the key issue of oil production, Perez, **Dec. 12**, promised to meet "international commitments" on oil deliveries during his administration, but said he did not feel obliged to increase oil production. Although he stressed that Latin America had a right to be resentful of U. S. President Richard M. Nixon's Latin American policy, he said Venezuela would not take part in a "generalized strategic hatred" of the United States government.

Heath Sets 3-Day Week—As energy shortages caused by slowdowns by coal, railway, and electrical workers continued to plague the British economy, Prime Minister Edward Heath, **Dec. 13**, imposed a 3-day week, effective Jan. 1, 1974, on the greater part of British industry. On **Dec. 17**, the British government abandoned its goal of economic growth for a policy geared toward economic survival. The new policy centered on the largest budget cut in British history, restrictions on consumer credit and additional taxes on high-income earners and some real estate developers. Further restrictions included a ban on television broadcasting after 10:30 p.m.

EEC Summit Stresses Unity—Leaders of the 9 member nations of the European Economic Community opened a 2-day summit, **Dec. 14**, with the approval of a statement on "European identity." The statement stressed independence yet maintained that close ties with the U. S. were "mutually beneficial" and did not hinder EEC efforts to establish a distinct entity for itself. The foreign ministers of 4 Arab countries, Algeria, Tunisia, the Sudan, and United Arab Emirates, unexpectedly confronted the meeting with a message that the EEC nations would have to take a stronger pro-Arab position if they wanted to end the Arab oil squeeze. After bitter argument, the meeting ended, **Dec. 15**, with a 9-nation agreement to face the oil crisis together and a call for Israel to withdraw from Arab territories held since the 1967 war. West German Chancellor Willy Brandt said the EEC leaders had succeeded in speaking with "a single European voice" but that "a very difficult period lay ahead."

Massacre at Rome Airport—Five armed Palestinian guerrillas, **Dec. 17**, hurled incendiary bombs at a Pan Am jetliner at Rome's international airport, killing 20 persons aboard. Two others were killed as the gunmen hijacked a Lufthansa jetliner, taking hostages along with them. After being refused permission to land in Beirut, the plane made brief stopovers in Athens and Damascus and, **Dec. 18**, continued to Kuwait where the hijackers released 12 hostages and surrendered in return for "free passage" to an unknown destination. One report said that while in radio communication with Greek authorities at the Athens airport, the Palestinians had demanded the release of 2 Arab terrorists held since an August attack on Athens airport. To force their demands, the guerrillas killed one hostage and dumped his body before leaving Athens. The Kuwaiti government said, **Dec. 19**, that it had no plans "at the moment" to try the 5 hijackers.

Spanish Premier Assassinated—Heir apparent to Generalissimo Francisco Franco, 70-year-old Spanish Premier Louis Carrero Blanco was assassinated, **Dec. 20**, in Madrid. ETA, an outlawed Basque terrorist group, claimed credit for the killing which was said to be revenge for the killing of 9 Basque militants by the government. Rightist extremists marred the funeral procession, **Dec. 21**, shouting insults at the Catholic church, castigating the government's weakness in dealing with "reds," and calling for an army takeover. Spanish security police, **Dec. 22**, named 6 members of the most aggressive wing of the ETA as responsible for the assassination. On **Dec. 28**, 4 alleged members of the ETA denied the 6 named were responsible and told French newsmen the commando unit responsible for the assassination was "in a safe place" and ready to strike again against fascist power. Franco, **Dec. 28**, named Interior Minister Carlos Arias Navarro as the new premier. On **Dec. 30**, in his first public appearance since the assassination, Franco told the nation that the attack had strengthened the country's institutions and united Spaniards.

Mideast Conference in Geneva—After several days' delay, the Arab-Israeli peace conference opened, **Dec. 21**, in Geneva, Switzerland. Syria did not attend. The first round of talks ended Dec. 22

with a quick agreement to move "forthwith" toward talks on the separation of Egyptian and Israeli forces along the Suez Canal. These talks between Israeli and Egyptian generals began in Geneva, **Dec. 26**, under the auspices of the Middle East conference.

Japanese Declare Economic Emergency—As part of a government effort to combat rising inflation and the oil shortage, the Japanese cabinet, **Dec. 22**, approved an "austerity" budget for 1974. The budget called for the smallest annual increase in spending in 4 years. Coincidentally, Premier Kakuei Tanaka declared an economic "state of emergency" and cut oil and electricity supplies for industry by 20 per cent, effective Jan. 1, 1974. However, on **Dec. 26**, the oil cutback was suspended in view of the Dec. 25 decision by Arab oil producers to increase oil output in January.

Arabs Increase Oil Flow and Double Prices—Meeting in Kuwait for 2 days, Arab oil ministers, Dec. 25, decided to increase by 10 per cent the flow of oil, effective Jan. 1, to most countries, excluding the United States and the Netherlands which would remain under embargo. The decision cancelled the **Dec. 9** announcement of a further 5 per cent reduction in oil flow during January. The decision, however, did not affect the Arab oil producers' **Dec. 23** announcement of a doubling in the price of Persian Gulf crude oil.

Labor Party Loses Seats in Israeli Election—In Israeli parliamentary elections, Premier Golda Meir's Labor party lost ground, **Dec. 31**, to the Likud, a coalition of right-wing parties. The Labor party, however, still seemed certain to dominate the next government. Official election results, released **Jan. 8**, showed that Mrs. Meir's Labor alignment had won 51 of 120 seats in the Knesset, the Israeli parliament, representing a loss of 5 seats. The Likud gained 7 seats for a total of 39.

General

Contempt Ruling in "Chicago 7" Case—Defendants in the "Chicago 7" conspiracy trial, David T. Dellinger, Jerry Rubin, and Abbie Hoffman, were found guilty, **Dec. 4**, along with their defense attorney William M. Kuntsler, of contempt in the 1969-70 trial. The ruling was made by U.S. District Court Judge Edward T. Gignoux, a Maine judge appointed by the Supreme Court to try the case. Rennard C. Davis, Thomas E. Hayden, and attorney Leonard Weinglass were acquitted of contempt charges. The other 2 "Chicago 7" defendants, John Froines and Lee Weiner, had been freed from further prosecution **Nov. 3**. Stating that the defendants had been sufficiently punished by the contempt ruling and jail terms previously served, Judge Gignoux, **Dec. 6**, did not impose sentence. He cited the improper behavior of the original trial judge, Julius J. Hoffman, as a major factor in his decision.

Getty Grandson Returned—J. Paul Getty 3rd, the 17-year-old grandson of oil billionaire J. Paul Getty, was found, **Dec. 15**, at a deserted service station in Southern Italy, 5 months after his kidnapping in Rome. According to reports, Getty was freed by his kidnappers after his family, **Dec. 12**, handed over a ransom of $2.8 million. Negotiations between the family and Getty's kidnappers had intensified after the Rome newspaper Il Messagero had received a letter containing a severed human ear and lock of reddish brown hair allegedly belonging to Getty. Italian police stated that the kidnappers were believed to be associated with the Mafia.

Boyle Pleads Not Guilty—Former United Mine Workers Pres. W.A. Boyle pleaded not guilty, **Dec. 22**, to 3 counts of murder in connection with the 1969 slaying of the Joseph Yablonski family. After the plea, Boyle was returned to Springfield, Mo., to begin serving a 3-year sentence for making illegal political contributions with union funds.

Disasters—A chartered Caravelle twin-engine jet crashed in the Rif Mountains in Morocco, Dec. 23, killing all 106 persons aboard, most of them Moroccans returning home for the holidays . . . An overloaded ferryboat capsized in the Pacific Ocean off the coast of Ecuador, killing nearly 200 persons **Dec. 24**.

JANUARY 1974

National

Nixon Rejects Watergate Committee Subpoenas—Pres. Richard M. Nixon, **Jan. 4**, refused to comply with subpoenas from the Senate Watergate Committee for more than 500 tape recordings and documents. Nixon told Watergate Committee Chairman Sam J. Ervin that such a response "would unquestionably destroy any vestige of confidentiality of presidential communications, thereby irreparably impairing the constitutional functions of the office of the presidency." Chief committee counsel Samuel Dash said the committee would not seek to enforce the subpoenas pending the outcome of the court case involving an earlier subpoena for 5 tapes.

Nixon Issues Papers on Milk Fund, ITT—Pres. Richard M. Nixon, **Jan. 8**, issued 2 papers dealing with his involvement in 1971 in administration decisions related to an increase in federal price supports for milk and an anti-trust suit against ITT. In the milk case, Nixon said he had taken "traditional political considerations" relating to the needs of farm states into account in ordering the increase, but termed "utterly false" the contention he had granted favors to milk producers or ITT in return for campaign contributions. In the ITT anti-trust case, the president said he had intervened because he felt the suits were based on the philosophy that "bigness per se" is bad, a philosophy with which he disagreed. Nixon said he had been unaware of an ITT pledge to fund the Republican National Convention when he intervened. Although the milk decision had been "totally proper," the president admitted that he had been aware of the milk industry's plans to contribute up to $2 million to his re-election campaign at the time of his decision. Nixon also cited intensive Congressional pressure and the economic merits of the case itself as factors in his decision. On **Jan. 11**, in a brief filed in federal court, lawyers for consumer crusader Ralph Nader argued that a tape recording of a Nixon conversation with dairy industry representatives negated the White House contention Nixon had not mentioned campaign contributions and that his remarks could be construed as thanks for financial support.

Military Spy Ring Disclosed—The New York Times disclosed, **Jan. 11**, that according to well-informed sources, the White House "plumbers" had discovered, late in 1971, evidence that a "ring" of military officers, some of them assigned to the National Security Council, had passed secret information about U.S. diplomatic initiatives to Pentagon officials. David R. Young Jr., who headed the inquiry, had concluded, according to the sources, that secret information from Henry A. Kissinger's office had been leaked to Adm. Thomas A. Moorer, chairman of the Joint Chiefs of Staff. Moorer, **Jan. 14**, termed the allegation "ludicrous." The White House inquiry apparently stemmed from the December 1971 publication of

NSC documents on the India-Pakistan war by Jack Anderson and spread to investigation of possible widespread military spying. No formal charges were filed, but as many as 6 military men connected with the NSC were reassigned, including Rear Adm. Robert O. Welander then serving as liaison officer between the Joint Chiefs of Staff and the NSC. Also implicated was Welander's chief aide, Yeoman 1.C. Charles E. Radford. The White House, **Jan. 15,** minimized the story, describing the affair as simply a case of a young Navy yeoman who "was told to keep his eyes open and who went ape."

Experts Report on Tape Gap—A court-appointed panel of 6 technical experts reported, **Jan. 15,** that at least 5 separate erasures and re-recordings had caused the 18½-minute gap on one of the tapes Pres. Richard M. Nixon had turned over to the Senate Watergate Committee. The experts concluded that the gap, on a tape of the President's June 20, 1972 conversation with then chief of staff H.R. Haldeman, could not have been caused by a single accidental pressing of a wrong button, as the White House had contended. Although the panel report did not state whether or not the erasures had been made deliberately, under questioning by Assistant Special Watergate Prosecutor Richard Ben-Veniste, the panel agreed that their evidence would be "consistent" with results that would be found if the attempt had been deliberate.

Oil Companies Report Huge Profits—Scoring gains chiefly in overseas profits, major oil companies showed a sharp rise in earnings in the 4th quarter of 1973 during the Arab oil embargo. Exxon, **Jan. 23,** announced profits were up 59% over the same period in 1972. Mobil announced, **Jan. 24,** a 68% increase in profits for the same period; Texaco earnings were up 70% and Ashland profits were up 52% for the last quarter. Only Shell Oil showed a decline of 1.5% in profits during the last quarter although full year figures showed a 27% gain.

Krogh Sentenced—U.S. District Court Judge Gerhard A. Gesell, **Jan. 24,** sentenced Egil Krogh Jr., former head of the White House "plumbers" unit, to 6 months in prison on a charge of conspiracy against the rights of citizens in the burglary of the office of Dr. Daniel Ellsberg's psychiatrist. Krogh, who insisted he had received no specific instruction or authority regarding the burglary from Pres. Nixon, said he would begin in depth discussion with the Watergate prosecutor in the following week. He had refused to speak before because he did not want his statements to affect his sentencing. Krogh maintained that he alone was responsible for his "terrible mistake" and "repulsive conduct."

Nixon Issues Energy Message—Pres. Richard M. Nixon, **Jan. 23,** proposed to Congress more stringent taxation on foreign profits of oil companies and a 2-year delay on stricter emissions standards for automobiles. The president's tax proposal called for the elimination of the 22% depletion allowance for foreign crude oil production. Nixon emphasized the importance of increased domestic energy production if the U.S. was to be independent of foreign suppliers by 1980. He placed secondary importance on conservation, although he suggested that Congress require labels be placed on automobiles and major appliances indicating how much energy they consume. Nixon also called again for the enactment of a "windfall profits" tax on crude oil prices. Nixon further recommended the speeding up of licensing and construction of nuclear power plants, more federal money for urban transportation and expanded leasing of the outer continental shelf for oil and gas exploration.

Porter Pleads Guilty—Former Scheduling Director for the Committee to Re-elect the President Herbert L. Porter, **Jan. 29,** pleaded guilty to a charge of lying to the FBI during an early investigation of the Watergate scandal. He was sentenced Apr. 11, to 15 months in prison. The sentence, except for 30 days, was immediately suspended.

Nixon Offers 10-Point Program—In his nationally televised State of the Union message and accompanying 22,000-word statement to Congress, Pres. Richard M. Nixon, **Jan. 30,** presented a 10-point program to check inflation, lessen the energy crisis, enhance world peace, and institute domestic reforms in the areas of health, welfare, and transportation. The president also pledged that he would not resign, saying, "One year of Watergate is enough." Recognizing the "special responsibility" of the House Judiciary Committee and its impeachment investigation, Nixon promised he would cooperate with the committee, but would be limited by the precedent set by every other president "by never doing anything that weakens the office of the Presidency or weakens the ability of Presidents of the future." The president's 10 goals included a continued policy of detente with the great powers and a "lasting peace" in the Middle East, a check in rising prices without recession, and new initiatives in world trade. The president also promised a new system of comprehensive health insurance which would guarantee high quality care to every American, "a crucial breakthrough" in public transportation, federal aid to education reforms, and a "new road toward reform of the welfare system." Nixon also disclosed that the executive budget for fiscal year 1975 would be set at $304.4 billion, an increase of $29.7 billion over the previous year.

International

Violence Greets Tanaka Tour—Riots aimed at "Japanese imperialism" marred Japanese Premier Kakuei Tanaka's 5-nation, 10-day tour of Southeast Asia, **Jan. 7-17.** Some 2,000 anti-Japanese students accosted Tanaka, **Jan. 9,** in Bangkok, Thailand, with signs decrying "economic imperialism." The low-point of the tour came, **Jan. 15,** in Jakarta, Indonesia, when demonstrations claimed the lives of 8 persons. Anti-Japanese sentiment spurred attacks on Japanese property, leading to the burning of hundreds of cars and the cancellation of Tanaka's program. Indonesian President Suharto offered regrets over the events at a dinner given in Tanaka's honor. Bands of students, some 500 strong, continued to roam the city, **Jan. 16,** hurling insults at the Japanese.

Crackdown on Opposition in South Korea—Following Pres. Park Chung Hee's **Jan. 8** decrees aimed at curbing political opposition, the South Korean government, **Jan. 12,** detained at least 6 opposition leaders and assigned police to accompany more than 20 others on a 24-hour-a-day basis. Among those detained were 4 members of the National Assembly, including the president of one opposition party and the vice president of the other. The first of the 2 **Jan. 8** decrees, both directed against mounting opposition to Park's consitution adopted under martial law in 1972, prohibited attempts to oppose, deny or repeal the constitution or any actions barred by the emergency measures. The 2d decree established emergency courts-martial to deal with violations of the first decree. Those violating the first measure would be subject to arrest, trial and imprisonment up to 15 years. Despite the decrees, a group of 30 civic and religious leaders continued their campaign to collect a million signatures for a petition demanding a "democratic" constitution.

Faulkner Steps Down From Party Post—Brian Faulkner, **Jan. 7**, stepped down as leader of the Unionists, Northern Ireland's largest Protestant party. Faulkner's resignation came on the heels of the **Jan. 4** 454-to-374 vote by the Unionist ruling council against the creation of a Council of Ireland, a consultative body that would provide links with the Irish Republic. The vote represented a setback for Faulkner's policy of moderation. Faulkner, however, maintained that he would continue as head of the new Protestant-Catholic coalition which had assumed power **Jan. 1** in accord with the Sunningdale agreement the previous December. The moderate-hardliner split was underlined, **Jan. 22**, when militants led by Rev. Ian Paisley, of the Democratic Unionist Party, disrupted the first session of Northern Ireland's provincial assembly to be attended by the Protestant-Catholic coalition. On **Jan. 23**, 20 anti-coalition members, led by Rev. Paisley, walked out of the assembly to protest the coalition.

French Float Franc—Finance Minister Giscard d'Estaing announced, **Jan. 19**, that France would float the franc for 6 months, thereby undertaking a de facto devaluation. The decision broke up the Common Market's monetary agreement of March 1973, which had set narrow limitations on exchange rate variations between EEC countries. The French move would allow for a free float without regard for the other EEC currencies. Giscard d'Estaing said the move was necessary to protect French gold reserves, threatened by escalating petroleum prices, and because "there is no chance that the international monetary system will be reformed in 1974 or 1975." By **Jan. 21**, the remaining EEC members which had participated in the joint float agreement announced they would maintain the joint float.

China Expels 5 Soviets—Mainland China expelled 5 Soviet citizens, including 3 members of the Soviet embassy and 2 of their wives, **Jan. 19**, on charges of espionage. A Chinese Foreign ministry note, published by Hsinhua, the official Chinese press agency, stated that the Soviets were caught on the outskirts of Peking in the act of making contact with Chinese agents for the purpose of a mutual transfer of espio-

nage and counterrevolutionary documents and equipment. In retaliation, the USSR, **Jan. 21**, ousted a young Chinese diplomat on charges of spying and issued a strong protest, citing in particular the "barbarous" 4-day detention of the 5 Soviet citizens. The Chinese, **Jan. 23**, published the confession of a Chinese alleged to be the Soviet agent involved with the 5 ousted Soviets.

China Seizes Paracels—After 2 days of fierce fighting with South Vietnamese troops, **Jan. 19-20**, the mainland Chinese took complete control of the disrupted Paracel Islands. One American and 150 South Vietnamese were either killed or captured as a result of the hostilities. The longstanding dispute between China and Vietnam over the islands, a desolate archipelago believed to have oil deposits, was renewed, **Jan. 11**, when China reclaimed sovereignty. Subsequently, a group of Chinese fishermen landed on Robert Island and planted a Chinese flag. South Vietnam responded, **Jan. 16**, to what they called "a threat to peace and security in the area" by sending 6 gunboats into the area, followed **Jan. 18** by 30 Navy commandos who forced the Chinese fishermen off the island. With MIG support, a Chinese force of 600 men, **Jan. 19**, overwhelmed the South Vietnamese forces.

General

Arrests in Foster Slaying—Oakland police, **Jan. 11**, arrested Joseph M. Remiro, a 27-year-old Vietnam war veteran and political activist, for the November 1973 murder of Oakland School Superintendent Marcus A. Foster. The .38 caliber gun used in the Foster killing was found in Remiro's possession. Police said they had also uncovered what appeared to be the headquarters of the Symbionese Liberation Army, the underground group which had claimed responsibility for the killing. On **Jan. 24**, police also charged Russell Little, another arrested SLA member, in the Foster killing.

Arrests in Getty Kidnaping—Three men said to have underworld connections in southern Italy were arrested, **Jan. 16**, on charges of having kidnaped J. Paul Getty 3d. It was also reported that Italian police had recovered part of $2.8 million ransom said to have been paid for Getty's release. Police said they were seeking a 4th man in the case.

Israel, Egypt Reach Agreement To Separate Forces Along Suez Canal

Egypt and Israel, **Jan. 17**, announced simultaneously in Jerusalem, Cairo, and Washington that they had agreed to separate their military forces along the Suez Canal. Signed **Jan. 18** by the Israeli and Egyptian chiefs of staff on the Cairo-Suez Road, the agreement was reached chiefly through the mediation of U.S. Secretary of State Henry A. Kissinger who shuttled continuously, **Jan. 11-17**, between Jerusalem and Aswan.

U.S. officials in Israel, **Jan. 17**, disclosed that another agreement, the "United States proposal," had also been reached. The details of the second agreement which defined the limitation of troops and arms in the area were kept secret. The second agreement was signed, **Jan. 18**, by Egyptian Pres. Anwar Sadat in Cairo and Israeli Premier Golda Meir in Jerusalem.

The troop separation agreement called for Israeli forces to abandon their bridgehead on the western bank of the Suez Canal and to withdraw forces to a 5- to 7½-mile zone 14 to 20 miles east of the canal and west of Gidi and Mitla Passes. The accord called for

Egyptian forces to remain on the east bank in a 5- to 7½-mile zone. The United Nations Emergency Force would patrol a buffer zone 3½- to 5-miles wide between the Egyptian and Israeli forces. The disengagement process was to be completed within 40 days.

In Washington, U.S. Pres. Richard M. Nixon, **Jan. 17**, told the American people, "We in the United States can be proud of the role that has been played by Secretary Kissinger and his colleagues in working to bring the parties together."

Following a 9-hour debate centering on opposition charges the agreement was one-sided, the Israeli parliament, **Jan. 22**, approved the accord by a vote of 76 to 35.

On **Jan. 24**, Israeli forces began formal withdrawal of forces from their bridgehead on the western bank which they had occupied since the Oct. 24, 1973 cease-fire. On **Jan. 28**, Israeli forces lifted their siege of the city of Suez and evacuated the surrounding area. The separation of forces was completed ahead of schedule on **Mar. 4**.

Disasters—At least 100 persons were feared dead, **Jan. 5**, when a ferry sank in strong winds and high seas in the central Philippines . . . A Turkish airliner crashed and burst into flames on takeoff from the military airport at Izmir, **Jan. 27**, killing 63 of the 73 persons aboard . . . A Pan Am Boeing 707 crashed, **Jan. 31**, in Pago Pago, American Samoa, leaving 96 of the 101 persons aboard dead.

FEBRUARY
National

Nixon Predicts Severe Inflation—Pres. Richard M. Nixon, **Feb. 1**, in his annual Economic Message to Congress, predicted severe inflation with little or no economic growth in the months immediately ahead. However, he predicted better times in the second half of the year. Nixon stated that, despite continued inflation, he would continue a policy of progressive removal of wage controls to restore the flexibility needed for efficiency and expansion in a period of economic strain. On **Feb. 4**, Nixon sent a $304.4 billion budget to Congress which aides said he would "bust" with more spending if needed to check a serious slump in the economy.

SLA Kidnaps Patricia Hearst—Covering their escape with a barrage of rifle fire, 2 black men and one white woman, **Feb. 4**, kidnaped Patricia Hearst, the 19-year-old granddaughter of William Randolph Hearst, from her Berkeley apartment. The Symbionese Liberation Army, the group which had claimed responsibility for the death of Oakland school superintendent Marcus A. Foster, stated, **Feb. 7**, in a letter to Berkeley radio station KPFA, that they were holding Patty Hearst. On **Feb. 12**, the SLA demanded that Patty's father, San Francisco Examiner editor and president Randolph A. Hearst, give $230-million worth of free food to the poor as evidence of good faith in negotiating for his daughter's release. The demand was accompanied by a tape of Patty's voice pleading for her father's cooperation. On the same tape, SLA leader "Field Marshal" Cinque, addressing Hearst as "the corporate chairman of a fascist media empire of the ultra right," told him he was "quite willing to carry out the execution of your daughter to save the life of starving men, women, and children of every race." Hearst, **Feb. 13**, rejected the demand as impossible and promised a counter plan in 24 to 48 hours. On **Feb. 18**, Hearst announced he was prepared to put up $2 million — $500,000 of his own money and the rest from the Hearst Foundation — for food to open up negotiations for the return of his daughter. Disclosing the details of his plan, Hearst, **Feb. 19**, said the food distribution would be handled by an experienced staff and supervised by representatives of the poor. SLA leader Cinque, **Feb. 21**, called the $2-million offer insufficient and demanded $4 million more. He threatened to cut off communications if the demand were not met in 24 hours. On **Feb. 22**, the Hearst Corporation offered $4 million if Patty were released. Meanwhile, in East Oakland, fistfighting accompanied the first food deliveries under the Hearst plan. After a lapse in communication, Patty, in a taped message **Mar. 9**, said not enough was being done to bring about her release. SLA leaders also criticized the quality of food being distributed by Hearst. On **Mar. 11**, Hearst announced he would try to meet demands for better food and, on **Mar. 25**, the program resumed with the distribution of top quality groceries. On **Mar. 26**, the food program ran out of money. It would be resumed with an additional $4

million if Patty were released unharmed, Hearst said.

Moorer Recommended Radford Court Martial—Jt. Chiefs of Staff Chairman Adm. Thomas H. Moorer told reporters, **Feb. 6**, after secret testimony before the Senate Armed Services Committee, that he had twice recommended that Yeoman 1.C. Charles E. Radford be court martialed for leaking National Security Council documents to the press in 1971 and twice had been overruled by civilian authorities. Previously, in a **Jan. 30** letter to committee chairman John C. Stennis, Moorer conceded he had twice received documents Radford had "retained" from the President's top security advisers. On **Feb. 8**, Radford told The New York Times he had stolen hundreds of NSC documents at the behest of Adms. Rembrandt C. Robinson and Robert O. Welander, both former liaison officers between the Jt. Chiefs of Staff and the NSC. The documents had subsequently been forwarded to Moorer's office. In testimony before the Senate Armed Services committee, Welander, **Feb. 21**, denied having ever "ordered or directed" Radford to pilfer highly classified documents. On **Feb. 20**, Radford had testified to the contrary and, although he did not submit direct evidence, said he "assumed" and "believed" Moorer had received the purloined materials.

Impeachment Inquiry Begins—The House, **Feb. 6**, voted, 410 to 4, to grant broad constitutional power to the Judiciary Committee to pursue its impeachment inquiry. The decision empowered the panel to subpoena anyone, including the president, with evidence pertinent to the investigation. On **Feb. 7**, the Senate Watergate Committee, in an unanimous vote, decided to turn over all its investigative files to the House Judiciary Committee. On **Feb. 25**, the Judiciary Committee sent a request to the White House for some 700 pages of documents and 17 tape recordings necessary for its impeachment inquiry. The request was for materials already provided to Watergate Special Prosecutor Leon Jaworski.

Pact Reached in Truckers' Strike—As the work stoppage by independent truck drivers protesting high fuel costs was beginning to affect supplies of consumer goods, prices and employment, negotiators reached an agreement with the government **Feb. 7**. The agreement included a 6% surcharge on freight rates, immediately approved by the ICC, to cover increased fuel costs. An order, on **Feb. 5**, by Pres. Richard M. Nixon for a month-long freeze on diesel fuel prices had failed to sway the striking drivers. By **Feb. 11**, most truckers were back on the road. The violence-marred 11-day strike took a toll of 2 lives and scores of injured.

Jaworski, Nixon Face Clash Over More Tapes—Watergate Special Prosecutor Leon Jaworski stated, **Feb. 14**, in a letter to the Senate Judiciary Committee, that Pres. Richard M. Nixon had refused on **Feb. 13** to turn over a large number of additional tapes and documents needed for the Watergate investigations. Jaworski said he could return indictments without the materials, but that they were important for a complete and thorough investigation. On **Feb. 15**, the White House announced Nixon wanted to avoid another "point of confrontation" with Jaworski and had instructed attorney James D. St. Clair to continue discussion with Jaworski on the matter.

Gasoline Shortage Grows—As complaints from motorists, gasoline station owners, and state officials about gas shortages and government handling of the problem mounted, Federal Energy Office Administrator William Simon, **Feb. 19**, ordered emergency allocations of 84 million gallons of gasoline to 20 states. On **Feb. 14**, FEO Deputy Administrator John C. Sawmill had sent experts to 20 states suffering severe gasoline shortages to study a possible revision of the allocation system. By **Feb. 15**, 7 states and the District of Columbia had implemented a form of rationing based on odd and even numbered license plates. On **Feb. 16**, FEO had allowed a 1% hike in gas prices for stations whose allocations had been reduced at least 15% from the 1972 base level.

Watergate Committee Ends Public Hearings—The Senate Watergate Committee decided, **Feb. 19**, to continue the remainder of its investigation behind closed doors in order not to interfere with the impeachment process of the House Judiciary Committee or criminal cases initiated by the Watergate special prosecutor. The Senate later extended the life of the committee to May 28 during which time the committee would continue to investigate allegations, pursue its court case for additional White House tapes and prepare its final report. On **Feb. 25**, the panel appealed a **Feb. 8** ruling by U.S. District Court Judge Gerhard A. Gesell dismissing a suit to obtain 5 White House tapes. Gesell had ruled that the "blazing atmosphere" of the committee's hearings might be harmful to criminal prosecution.

GOP Suffer Congressional Losses—A Democrat, Richard F. VanderVeen, **Feb. 19**, defeated Robert VanderLaan, a Republican, in a Michigan Congressional contest to fill Vice President Gerald R. Ford's seat. Viewing the election as a gauge of Nixon's standing among orthodox Middle West Republicans, Ford said he was "very disappointed by the results." In his campaign, VanderVeen had tried to turn the contest into a referendum on whether Pres. Nixon should resign. In a private meeting with the President, **Feb. 20**, Ford said the Watergate scandal had been responsible, in part, for the loss. Earlier in the month, John P. Murtha, a Democrat and Vietnam veteran, had, **Feb. 5**, defeated Harry M. Fox in a Pennsylvania Congressional by-election, ending 24 years of Republican domination in that district.

Nixon Bars Appearance at Ehrlichman Trial—Pres. Richard M. Nixon, **Feb. 25**, cited constitutional grounds in his refusal to appear as a witness at the California burglary and conspiracy trial of John D. Ehrlichman. He had been summoned at Ehrlichman's request. Nixon stated that the president "cannot sacrifice the compelling and real 'interests' of over 200 million Americans to satisfy the possible interests of any one individual."

Kalmbach Pleads Guilty—Pres. Richard M. Nixon's personal lawyer and chief fundraiser, Herbert W. Kalmbach, **Feb. 25**, pleaded guilty to charges that he had helped to run an illegal Congressional campaign committee in 1970 and promised a contributor an ambassadorship in return for $100,000. In a letter filed with U.S. District Judge John J. Sirica, Watergate Special Prosecutor Leon Jaworski indicated Kalmbach had been allowed to plead guilty to technical campaign violations in exchange for cooperation and full disclosure of "all relevant information and documents" in the Watergate case. All other potential charges against him were dropped.

Impeachable Charges Debated—In a news conference on **Feb. 25**, Pres. Richard M. Nixon stated that the House could not impeach him unless it presented evidence that he had violated criminal law. He also disclosed that he had refused on constitutional grounds a request that he testify before the Watergate grand jury. Nixon's statement on impeachment came in response to a 49-page advisory report by the bipartisan

legal staff for the impeachment inquiry issued **Feb. 21**. The report described impeachment as a remedy against "constitutional wrongs that subvert the structure of government, or undermine the integrity of office and even the Constitution itself." The president's attorneys, under the direction of James St. Clair, **Feb. 28**, presented the White House position on the nature of presidential impeachment. The report stated "a president may only be impeached for indictable crimes" and those crimes must be of "a very serious nature" and "committed in one's governmental capacity."

International

British Miners Strike, Heath Calls Election—Following weeks of fruitless negotiations between the British government and the coal miners' union, union members voted overwhelmingly, **Feb. 4**, to go on strike to support their pay demands. The strike vote followed failure to agree on a **Jan. 30** proposal by Prime Minister Edward Heath that miners accept the standing 16.5% pay increase and await the finding of an impartial board on additional pay boosts. On **Feb. 7**, Heath decided to take the issue to the people and called for a general election on **Feb. 28**, 16 months earlier than required. He made a last minute appeal to miners to delay the strike until after the election, but the appeal was rejected Feb. 8. Amid fears that the strike would have a devastating affect on the already-battered economy, coal miners began their nationwide strike **Feb. 10**. On **Feb. 12**, union leaders rejected the offer of a group of unidentified industrialists to supplement the miners' pay pending a Pay Board decision on wage increases. The miners, **Feb. 13**, announced a total ban on replenishing diminishing coal stocks at power plants and other unions offered support by refusing to transport coal. The Pay Board disclosed, **Feb. 22**, that due to an error in official calculations of wages, miners were actually earning 8% to 10% less than average industrial laborers rather than 2% to 3% less as the government had contended.

Iran, Iraq Clash—Baghdad radio reported, **Feb. 10**, that Irani forces backed by armor and artillery had provoked clashes with Iraqi forces on their mutual border near Badra. Iraq reported 70 Iranian killed and one Iraqi dead and 22 wounded in the clashes. They claimed the Iranians were amassing more troops near the border and flying jet fighters deep into Iraqi air space. Iran, **Feb. 11**, charged Iraqi aggression in the clashes and reported 41 Iranians had been killed and 81 wounded and 22 Iraqis killed. Iran demanded compensation for the Iranian victims and punishment for those responsible.

Rebel Attack Kills 200 in Cambodia—Heavy shelling of Pnom Penh by Cambodian rebels, **Feb. 11**, killed nearly 200 civilians and wounded as many. Renewed shelling, **Feb. 16**, took 8 more lives and left 25 wounded. Earlier, U.S. President Richard M. Nixon vowed, in a letter to Cambodian Pres. Lon Nol published **Feb. 2**, that the U.S. would continue the "maximum possible assistance to his government."

Solzhenitsyn Exiled to West—The Soviet Union, **Feb. 13**, stripped Nobel Prize-winning author Alexander Solzhenitsyn of his citizenship and deported him to West Germany. He was accused of "performing systematically actions that are incompatible with being a citizen." Although Solzhenitsyn had long been an outspoken critic of the Soviet government, the final move in a month-long campaign against him stemmed from the **Dec. 28** publication in Paris of Solzhenitsyn's Gulag Archipelago, an expose of the

Soviet prison system. Pravda, in a major attack on **Jan. 14,** had charged the book was "stuffed with cynical falsifications, concocted to serve the forces of imperialist reaction." Solzhenitsyn snapped back, **Jan. 18,** that the campaign against his book revealed the USSR's "animal fear of exposure" and accused critics of maliciously distorting the book. Solzhenitsyn was arrested by force **Feb. 12,** after he and his wife had refused 2 summons for him to meet with state investigators. In his first interview since exile, Solzhenitsyn, **Feb. 18,** in Zurich, Switzerland, vowed to continue to work in exile and said he had as much right to live on Russian soil as those who had physically thrown him out. On Mar. 12, he announced that he would settle in Zurich and, on **Mar. 29,** he was reunited with his family. They had been allowed to leave the USSR without losing their citizenship and also to bring out the author's personal archives.

Oil-consuming Nations Confer—A conference of the U.S. and 13 major oil-consuming nations in Washington, D.C., **Feb. 13,** adopted a U.S. proposal for international cooperation to combat the world energy crisis. France objected strongly to 4 of the 17 points in the proposal. French Foreign Minister Michel Jobert protested that the conference had been ill-conceived and ill-planned and that the U.S. had used energy matters as a "pretext" to strengthen its influence in Europe. The French objected to a comprehensive action program to deal with all facets of the energy situation, the formation of a coordinating group of senior officials to develop an action program, the establishment of a coordinating group to prepare for a conference of oil-producing and oil-consuming nations as soon as possible, and the adoption of financial and monetary measures to avoid "competitive depreciation and the escalation of restrictions on trade and payment or disruptions in external borrowing." Despite French objections, U.S. Secretary of State Henry A. Kissinger expressed optimism that France would continue to participate in the follow-up meeting of oil consumers and producers.

Latin American Foreign Ministers Meet—U.S. Secretary of State Henry A. Kissinger, **Feb. 21,** opened a 3-day conference with 24 Latin American and Caribbean foreign ministers with a call for the creation of a new "Western Hemisphere community." Although the conference rejected the appeal for a new community, the members, **Feb. 23,** charted a "new relationship" setting up an informal framework for continuing high-level discussions, or, if necessary, negotiations on troublesome issues.

U.S., Egypt Resume Relations—Ending a 7-year breach, the U.S. and Egypt, **Feb. 28,** announced that they would immediately resume diplomatic relations. The decision followed a meeting between Egyptian Pres. Anwar Sadat and U.S. Secretary of State Henry A. Kissinger.

General

Long Island Physician Acquitted—After a 55-minute jury deliberation, Dr. Vincent A. Montemarano, **Feb. 5,** was found not guilty in the death of Eugene Bauer, a terminally-ill cancer patient at the Nassau County Medical Center in New York. In the case, originally termed a mercy killing but later characterized by the prosecuting district attorney as a "murder of convenience," Montemarano was accused of injecting a fatal dose of potassium chloride into the patient to avoid a return later in the evening to pronounce the patient dead. In the highly emotional trial — 2 prosecution witnesses broke down on the

stand — the defense, which never conceded that the injection had been made, sought to prove the patient could have died from any one of several causes.

Skylab 3 Crew Returns Safely—In a smooth Pacific splashdown, **Feb. 8,** the Skylab 3 astronauts completed man's longest space flight after 84 days, 1 hour, 17 minutes in space. The crew — Marine Lt. Col. Gerald P. Carr, Dr. Edwin G. Gibson, and Air Force Lt. Col. William R. Pogue — experienced dizziness on return but were soon pronounced fit and in better physical shape than the 2 previous Skylab crews. Their fitness was ascribed, at least in part, to a more vigorous physical exercise program. The astronauts had circled the earth a record 1,214 times and traveled a record 34½ million miles. During the flight, the crew observed and photographed the comet Kohoutek, overcame a failure in the gyroscope system, and operated several experimental processes for making metal alloys and ultrapure crystals for electronics in the weightless environment of space. With an array of telescopes, they observed the sun for a total of 338 hours. Except for the planned joint U.S.-USSR manned space flight in 1975, Skylab 3 was the last scheduled U.S. space mission until the 2-stage shuttle rocket currently being developed begins operations in 1979 or later.

Atlanta Editor Abducted—The self-proclaimed "American Revolutionary Army," **Feb. 20,** abducted J. Reginald Murphy, the 40-year-old editorial-page editor of the Atlanta Constitution, from his home in Atlanta. The abductors, describing themselves as rightist revolutionaries, **Feb. 21,** demanded $700,000 in ransom and called for the resignation of the nation's top elected officials followed by new elections. After 49 hours in captivity, Murphy was freed unharmed, **Feb. 22,** after the Constitution paid the ransom. On **Feb. 23,** police recovered most of the $700,000-ransom after arresting William A.H. Williams, a 33-year-old construction contractor and ex-convict, and his wife. Police said, **Feb. 24,** the kidnaping appeared to be the work of a single individual, Williams, who had earlier been involved in a $300,000 oil hoax in Miami.

Hijacker Kills 2, Then Himself—In an attempted hijacking of a Delta Airlines jet at Baltimore-Washington airport, Samuel Joseph Byck, **Feb. 22,** fatally shot the plane's co-pilot and an airport policeman. During the attempt, he was wounded by another policeman and then killed himself. The hijack attempt was the first in 13 months, following the government-ordered screening of all passengers by electronic weapons detectors.

Disasters—A 25-minute fire caused by an air-conditioner short circuit, **Feb. 1,** burned the upper floors of the 25-story Crensul Investment Bank in Sao Paulo, Brazil, claiming 189 lives . . . At least 60 were dead and more than 100,000 homeless, according to reports, **Feb. 17,** in severe flooding in 3 northwestern provinces of Argentina.

MARCH
National

GOP Loses 3rd Congressional Race — Democrat Thomas A. Luken narrowly defeated his Republican opponent, Willis D. Gradison Jr., **Mar. 5,** in a special election in Ohio's 1st Congressional District. The district had gone Democratic only 3 other times in this century.

Nixon Concedes Hush Money Knowledge — At a nationally televised news conference, Pres. Richard M. Nixon, **Mar. 6,** denied that on Mar. 21, 1973 he had approved the payment of hush money or granting of clemency to the defendants in the Watergate break-in. He conceded, however, that the taped conversation of the meeting in question might be subject to other interpretations. On Aug. 15, 1973, Nixon had told the nation that on Mar. 21, 1973 John Dean had told him money had been paid for defense fees and support of the defendants' families, but not to procure their silence. Nixon now admitted the question of hush money had come up, but that he had clearly stated, "It is wrong, that's for sure."

Jaworski Tapes Go To Impeachment Inquiry — Presidential Counsel James D. St. Clair, **Mar. 6,** announced that Pres. Richard M. Nixon would turn over to the Judiciary Committee all the tapes and materials which the White House had previously delivered to Watergate Special Prosecutor Leon Jaworski. He added that the president would be willing to submit to written questions from the committee and, if necessary, to an interview at the White House by a small number of committee members. Nixon, at his **Mar. 6** news conference, called his decision "a very forthcoming offer." However, the Judiciary Committee disclosed, **Mar. 7,** that St. Clair had informed them the president would not comply with requests for further materials not bearing directly on the Watergate cover-up. The committee decided to defer a subpoena on an outstanding request for 6 tapes not bearing directly on the cover-up. On **Mar. 12,** it was disclosed the Judiciary Committee had requested 42 more White House tapes, beyond the outstanding request for 6 tapes, covering 6 different areas. Presidential Press Secretary Ron Ziegler said, **Mar. 12,** that it would be constitutionally irresponsible for the White House to give the House panel all the information it was seeking. On **Mar. 27,** Ziegler suggested that some of the 42 tapes might not exist.

Nixon Vetoes Emergency Energy Bill — Pres. Richard M. Nixon, **Mar. 6,** vetoed the emergency energy bill. His veto was promptly sustained when the Senate vote to override, 58-40, fell 8 votes short of the needed 2/3's majority. Nixon said the bill threatened "to undo the progress we have already made" and to create "a host of new problems." Nixon objected chiefly to the bill's provision for a rollback in crude oil prices. The end result of a rollback, according to Nixon, would be reduced energy supplies, longer gasoline lines, and increased unemployment. The bill had also provided authorization for the establishment of gas rationing and benefits for workers losing their jobs because of "energy-related" conditions.

Six Indicted in Ellsberg Break-in — A Washington, D.C., federal grand jury, **Mar. 7,** indicted John D. Ehrlichman, Charles W. Colson, G. Gordon Liddy, Bernard L. Barker, Eugenio R. Martinez, and Felipe Diego in the 1971 break-in at the Beverly Hills, Calif., office of Dr. Lewis Fielding, Dr. Daniel Ellsberg's former psychiatrist. E. Howard Hunt, Egil Krogh Jr., and David R. Young Jr., all members of the "plumbers," the White House special investigations unit, were named as unindicted co-conspirators. All 9 were charged with violating Dr. Fielding's civil rights by working together to "oppress, threaten and intimidate" him by secretly entering his office "without legal process, probable cause, search warrant or other lawful authority." According to the indictment, the burglary was initiated, with Ehrlichman's approval "on assurance it is not traceable," to obtain Ellsberg's psychiatric files. Ehrlichman was also charged with 4 other counts, 3 for lying under oath to a grand jury and one for making false statements to the FBI. California charges against Ehrlichman, Young, and Liddy arising from the Ellsberg break-in were dropped, **Mar. 13,** by Los Angeles Superior Court Judge Gordon Ringer. However, a perjury charge against Ehrlichman before a Los Angeles grand jury was allowed to stand.

Nixon Urges Campaign Reform — Pres. Richard M. Nixon, **Mar. 8,** in a message to Congress and a radio speech, presented proposals to clean up political

Former Nixon Aides Indicted on Cover-up Charges; Sealed Report on Nixon Goes to Judiciary Panel

In an historic indictment, 7 former White House and presidential campaign aides were charged, **Mar. 1,** with conspiracy in the cover-up of the Watergate scandal in a 15-minute session in the courtroom of U.S. District Judge John J. Sirica. Never before had so many trusted advisers of a U.S. president been charged in a single indictment.

Those indicted were: former White House Chief of Staff H. R. Haldeman for conspiracy, obstruction of justice, and 3 counts of perjury; former Attorney General and Presidential Campaign Director John N. Mitchell for conspiracy, obstruction of justice, false statements to the FBI, false testimony to a grand jury, and perjury; former Presidential Assistant for Domestic Affairs John D. Ehrlichman for conspiracy, obstruction of justice, false statements to the FBI, and false statements to a grand jury; former Special Presidential Counsel Charles W. Colson for conspiracy and obstruction of justice; former campaign aide Robert C. Mardian for conspiracy; former attorney for the Committee to Re-elect the President Kenneth W. Parkinson for conspiracy and obstruction of justice; and former Haldeman aide Gordon C. Strachan for conspiracy, obstruction of justice, and false statements to a grand jury.

The chief charge in the conspiracy, which had continued "up to and including" that day, was that all 7 "and other persons to the grand jury known and unknown did combine, conspire, and confederate and agree" to make false statements to the FBI and CIA and to prevent them from transacting their official business "honestly and impartially."

All told, the indictment included 24 separate counts alleging destruction of evidence, making false statements, and making payments to as well as giving assurances of clemency to the defendants in the Watergate break-in case.

The grand jury also handed over to Judge Sirica a sealed envelope and a bulky briefcase of data reportedly dealing with Pres. Richard M. Nixon's role in the Watergate case. Well-informed sources reported, **Mar. 2,** that the grand jury had decided Nixon had been involved in the cover-up. However, unable to indict him, they had decided to urge the court to turn over their conclusions to the impeachment inquiry.

All 7 indicted Nixon aides pleaded not guilty **Mar. 9.**

Judge Sirica ordered, **Mar. 18,** that the sealed report and accompanying material, which he made clear dealt with Nixon's acts "in his public capacity" during the period under investigation, be given to the House Judiciary Committee for its impeachment inquiry. The White House, represented by James D. St. Clair, raised no objection. The Court of Appeals, **Mar. 21,** refused an appeal by attorneys for Strachan and Haldeman to block the delivery of the report to the House. On **Mar. 27,** the report was delivered to the House Judiciary Committee.

campaigns. Nixon stated that full disclosure of private political contributions was the most important of all reforms. To simplify the contribution process, Nixon called for one fund-raising committee and a single bank account per candidate, and no cash contributions above $50. He suggested a $3,000 limit per contributor for House and Senate candidates and a $15,000-limit per contributor in presidential campaigns. Nixon also expressed strong opposition to public financing of campaigns, calling it "a raid on the public treasury." Senate Republican leader Hugh Scott and Sen. Edward M. Kennedy disagreed with Nixon's attack on public campaign financing. Common Cause, the citizen's lobby, issued a statement saying Nixon's 1972 campaign "constitutes the greatest case ever made for controlling campaign finance abuses through public financing of elections.

Buckley Asks Nixon Resignation — Long-time staunch presidential supporter Sen. James L. Buckley of New York, **Mar. 19,** asked for the resignation of Pres. Richard M. Nixon as the "one way and one way only by which the crisis can be resolved, and the country pulled out of the Watergate swamp." In Chicago, on **Mar. 15,** Nixon had again brushed aside talk of resignation as "an easy cop-out." Buckley was the first conservative Republican in Congress to call for the president's resignation.

Nixon Eases Energy Restrictions — Following the **Mar. 18** lifting of the Arab oil embargo, Pres. Richard M. Nixon, **Mar. 19,** said he was easing some restrictions on energy consumption, among them the ban on Sunday gasoline sales. He flatly ruled out compulsory rationing of gasoline. He also said he had ordered Federal Energy Office Administrator William E. Simon to increase fuel allocations to the industrial and agricultural sectors to insure they would have "the necessary energy to operate at full capacity."

Eight Indicted in Kent State Slayings — One present member and 7 former members of the Ohio National Guard were indicted, **Mar. 29,** by a federal grand jury in Cleveland, O., on charges of violating the rights of 4 Kent State University students who were killed and 9 who were wounded in May 1970 during demonstrations protesting the U.S. invasion of Cambodia. The grand jury, however, did not find any evidence of conspiracy.

Nixon Yields on Jaworski Subpoena — Pres. Richard M. Nixon agreed, **Mar. 29,** to turn over to Special Watergate Prosecutor Leon Jaworski materials he had subpoenaed **Mar. 15.** Although the nature of the contents was not disclosed, reports **Mar. 30** said the subpoena had sought information on campaign contributions.

International

Heath Resigns, Wilson Forms New Government — Failing to form a coalition with Jeremy Thorpe's Liberal party, British Prime Minister Edward Heath resigned, **Mar. 4,** clearing the way for Labor party leader Harold Wilson to form Britain's first minority cabinet in 45 years. Heath had declined to resign, **Mar. 1,** after neither his Conservative party nor the opposition Labor party had attained a majority in general elections held **Feb. 28.** Wilson named his new cabinet, **Mar. 5,** and immediately tackled the government's crippling 3-week dispute with striking coal miners over wage increases. With the expectation of Wilson's support, the Pay Board proposed raises of about 35%, more than twice what Heath had offered before his resignation. After 12 hours of talks, miners, **Mar. 6,** accepted the 35% increase, which according to estimates, would cost the government some $230 million per year. On **Mar. 7,** Wilson ended

the 3-day work week which had been necessitated by the nationwide coal strike. Wilson, **Mar. 11,** ended a 4-month state of emergency imposed Nov. 13, signifying the government no longer needed extraordinary powers to deal with Britain's economic situation.

Selassie Pledges Democratic Government — Under pressure from mutinous army troops and a threatened workers' strike, Ethiopian Emperor Haile Selassie, **Mar. 5,** agreed to a constitutional convention to create a new system of elected democratic government. Spread of a military mutiny in Asmara, Ethiopia's 2nd largest city, had forced the resignation of Selassie's cabinet, **Feb. 28,** and Selassie had appointed a new premier **Mar. 1.** Pressure on Selassie, grew, **Mar. 7,** when workers struck for 16 demands including a $1.50 per day minimum wage, pension plans and a social security system. The strike was called off, **Mar. 10,** when the unions won concessions on their demands, among them a compromise that a new minimum wage would be fixed after a 2-month "cooling-off" period.

Meir Forms Cabinet, Ends Political Stalemate — Ending 9 weeks of domestic political stalemate, Israeli Premier Golda Meir, **Mar. 6,** formed a new coalition cabinet. Included were Defense Minister Moshe Dayan and Communications Minister Shimon Peres, both of whom reversed decisions not to serve unless the cabinet included the right-wing Likud. The Israeli parliament, **Mar. 10,** supported the new government with a 62-to-46 vote of confidence. Premier Meir, angered by severe criticism from both the right and left in parliament, had stunned her Labor party and country, **Mar. 3,** with a decision to withdraw from government. Under pressure from Labor party colleagues, she had reversed her decision **Mar. 4.**

Military Rebellion in Portugal Fails — A brief military rebellion in Portugal in support of 2 dismissed generals failed, **Mar. 16,** when it found itself without support. The crisis began **Mar. 14,** when Lisbon dismissed Defense Staff Chief Gen. Francisco de Costa Gomes and his deputy, Gen. Antonio de Spinola, for advocating a change in Portuguese policy toward her African territories. Spinola, supported by Costa, had proposed ending the wars against African guerrillas in favor of offering Mozambique, Angola, and Portuguese Guinea equal status with Portugal in a proposed federation. A state of alert was imposed, **Mar. 16,** and 33 military officers were arrested.

Arabs End Oil Embargo — Seven of the 9 Arab oil-producing nations agreed, **Mar. 18,** at a Vienna meeting of the Organization of Petroleum Exporting Countries, to lift the embargo they had imposed against the United States in October 1973. Libya and Algeria did not vote with the majority. Algeria said she was lifting the embargo provisionally until June 1, the date scheduled for a Cairo meeting of Arab oil ministers to review the oil situation. The embargo would continue against Denmark and the Netherlands, designated as "unfriendly" nations. Saudi Arabia, **Mar. 18,** immediately pledged to increase production by 1 million barrels a day, all of which would go to the U.S. market. However, despite appeals from consumer nations, the OPEC members had decided, **Mar. 17,** not to roll back oil prices.

Royal Kidnap Attempt Fails — Ian Ball, 26, **Mar. 20,** fired several shots at a car carrying Princess Anne and her husband, Capt. Mark Philips, in an attempted kidnaping in London. Although the royal couple escaped unharmed, 4 others, the Princess's bodyguard, chauffeur, a uniformed policeman, and a passerby, were seriously injured. The police, **Mar. 21,** arrested Ball and said they believed the attack had been a "one-man" operation without political motivation. A letter to Queen Elizabeth demanding about $4.8 million in ransom was found in the defendant's car. The government announced that new measures would be taken shortly to protect the royal family.

Kissinger, Brezhnev Confer — U.S. Secretary of State Henry A. Kissinger returned to the U.S., **Mar. 28**, following 3 days of talks in Moscow with Communist Party Secretary Leonid Brezhnev and other Soviet officials, without the "concrete progress" he had predicted, **Mar. 24**, on his arrival in Moscow. He had hoped to achieve a "conceptual breakthrough" which would lead to a Soviet-American agreement on strategic arms limitations. The final communique stated that both sides would pursue "the established policy aimed at making the process of improving Soviet-American relations irreversible." Plans for President Richard M. Nixon's June visit to Moscow remained unchanged.

General

L. I. Boy Kidnaped —Eight-year-old John Calzadilla of Dix Hills, N.Y., kidnaped near his home, **Mar. 6**, was released unharmed, **Mar. 8**, at a restaurant in Secaucus, N. J., after his father had delivered a $50,-000 ransom. The FBI, **Mar. 12**, arrested 3 persons, 2 of them brothers of the father's former wife, in Miami in connection with the case. Five others, including 4 teenagers, had already been charged.

Japanese WW II Survivor Surrenders — Lt. Hiroo Onoda, 52, a Japanese soldier missing in the Philippines since the end of World War II, was found, **Mar. 10**. In an informal surrender, he presented his sword to Maj. Gen. Jose Rancudo, the commander of the Philippine Air Force. He said he had not emerged before because his last order had been to continue guerrilla warfare. On **Mar. 12**, amidst a tremendous outpouring of patriotic emotion, he returned to his native Japan.

Philadelphia Police Found Corrupt — The Pennsylvania Crime Commission, in a 1,404-page report, charged, **Mar. 10**, that police corruption in Philadelphia was "ongoing, widespread, systematic and occurring at all levels of the police department." The report also charged the office of Philadelphia Mayor Frank L. Rizzo and the police department had tried to block the 18-month-long investigation.

Wife of Minnesota Banker Abducted — The wife of Gunnar Kronholm, a St. Paul, Minn., bank president, was abducted, **Mar. 15**, from her home. Mrs. Kronholm was released unharmed, **Mar. 18**, after the payment of a $200,000 ransom. James William Johnson, a local contractor, was arrested and charged with the kidnaping. Police reported, **Mar. 26**, that they had recovered all but $80 of the ransom.

Disasters — In the worst air disaster in history, all 345 persons aboard died, **Mar. 3**, when a Turkish DC-10 crashed in the forest of Ermenonville, 26 miles northeast of Paris. . . . An estimated 2,000 to 5,000 Brazilians were killed in severe floods and rains which ended **Mar. 29**. Worst hit was Tubaro in Southern Brazil where as many as 1,000 persons died.

APRIL
National

Nixon Agrees to Pay Back Taxes — The White House announced, **Apr. 3**, that Pres. Richard M. Nixon would pay $432,787.13 in back taxes plus interest for the years 1969 through 1972. The figure was based on an IRS report of an investigation of Nixon's tax returns. The total came to about $465,000. The President's decision came shortly after the release of a staff report of the Joint Committee on Internal Revenue Taxation placing Nixon's tax delinquency for the same years at $476,431. A White House spokesman said that although Nixon's tax attorneys felt they could make a strong case against the findings, the President had said, when he asked for the investigation, he would abide by the decision and was so doing. The committee staff report found underpayment in 5 categories of taxable income Nixon should have reported and 6 categories of deductions to which he had not been entitled. The report, however, made no allegation of fraud because, it stated, this was an issue which might come up before the impeachment inquiry. The committee staff discovered improprieties in nearly all the controversial areas the President had asked them to look into, including a $482,018 charitable deduction for his vice-presidential papers and failure to report capital gains on 2 real estate sales. The report also disclosed some new matters — failure to report as taxable income certain expenditures made from public funds for his family's, not the public's, benefit. These included improvements on the Nixon homes at San Clemente and Key Biscayne, personal travel, and $5,391 for a "masqued ball" for his daughter Tricia in 1969. The impeachment inquiry began immediately to study the committee's report, apparently with the intention of focusing on whether Nixon's treatment of his tax liabilities had diminished public respect for the presidency.

Patty Hearst Avows SLA Membership — Patricia Hearst, kidnapped by the Symbionese Liberation Army **Feb. 5**, announced, in a recorded message, **Apr. 3**, that she had rejected an offer of freedom from the SLA and chosen to join the underground terrorist group to fight for "the freedom of the oppressed people." On **Apr. 15**, she was identified as one of 9 participants in a San Francisco, Calif., bank robbery. FBI study of the photographs from the robbery, however, concluded that she may have acted under duress. Identifying herself as "Tania," Patty Hearst, **Apr. 24**, denied, again via a tape recorded message, that she had been coerced to participate in the robbery. A federal warrant was issued for her arrest as a material witness in the robbery. Her parents continued to insist their daughter had been coerced.

California Lt. Governor Indicted — The Watergate grand jury, **Apr. 3**, indicted Ed Reinecke, Lt. Governor of California, on 3 counts of lying to the Senate Judiciary Committee. The charges stemmed from the committee's Mar.-Apr. 1972 investigations into possible political influence in the settlement of 3 anti-trust suits against ITT.

Chapin Convicted — Dwight L. Chapin, formerly appointments secretary to Pres. Richard M. Nixon, was convicted by a U.S. District Court in Washington, D.C., **Apr. 5**, of 2 counts of lying to a Watergate grand jury. He was found guilty of lying about his relationship with Donald H. Segretti who had pleaded guilty to political "dirty tricks" in the 1972 presidential campaign. Chapin was sentenced, **May 15**, to 10 to 30 months in prison.

GOP Loses 4th Congressional Race — Democrat J. Bob Traxler, **Apr. 16**, defeated James M. Sparling Jr., in a special election in Michigan's 8th Congressional District. Traxler, the first Democrat elected in that district since 1932, had campaigned against Pres. Richard M. Nixon in an attempt to make election into a referendum on Nixon's performance in office. Nixon had campaigned for Sparling in Michigan.

Nixon Restructures Treasury Post, Names Simon — Pres. Richard M. Nixon, **Apr. 17**, named William E.

Simon, the administrator of the Federal Energy Office, to replace George P. Shultz, who had resigned, **Mar. 14,** as Secretary of the Treasury. Simon would not, unlike Shultz, be the over-all director of economic policy for the administration. Nixon said he himself would take a more active role in economic policy formulation and succeed Shultz as chairman of the Council on Economic Policy. John C. Sawhill was named to succeed Simon as FEO administrator.

Jaworski Subpoenas More Tapes — U.S. District Court Judge John J. Sirica, in response to an appeal from Watergate Special Prosecutor Leon Jaworski, **Apr. 18,** issued a subpoena to Pres. Richard M. Nixon for tapes and records of 64 White House conversations. Jaworski had argued he needed the materials — all but one, conversations between Nixon and his former top aides — for use in the trial of the cover-up case.

Mitchell, Stans Acquitted — Former Attorney General John N. Mitchell and former Commerce Secretary Maurice H. Stans were acquitted, **Apr. 28,** by a federal district court in New York City, of all charges they had attempted to impede a Securities and Exchange Commission investigation of financier Robert L. Vesco in return for a secret $200,000 cash contribution to Pres. Richard M. Nixon's 1972 presidential campaign. Both had been directors of that campaign. The 18-count indictment had charged Mitchell and Stans with conspiracy, obstruction of justice, and perjury for attempting to block the SEC investigation into Vesco's mutual funds dealings and then lying to a grand jury about their roles. Interviewed after the verdict, the jurors said they had not believed the key government witnesses, chief among whom were former Presidential Counsel John W. Dean 3rd and SEC Chairman G. Bradford Cook. The verdict was seen as a boost for Nixon's anti-impeachment campaign, particularly for bringing into ques-

tion the credibility of Dean, Pres. Nixon's chief accuser.

International

French President Dies — Following a year of speculation about his health, Georges Pompidou, the 18th president of the modern French republic, died **Apr. 2.** He had succeeded Charles de Gaulle almost 5 years before. Alain Poher, the centrist president of the Senate, was officially named acting president **Apr. 3.** Even as Pompidou was quietly buried Apr. 4 at a village cemetery at Orvillers, the race for president began with the announced candidacies of 2 former premiers, Jacques Chaban Delmas and Edgar Faure. The date of a new election was set for May 5. Heads of state and government from more than 50 countries, including U.S. Pres. Richard M. Nixon, gathered, **Apr. 6,** at Notre Dame Cathedral in Paris to pay their last respects to Pompidou.

Coalition Cabinet Formed in Laos — A coalition government of neutralists, rightists, and pro-communist Pathet Lao was established, **Apr. 5,** in Laos, a result of the Feb. 1973 Laotian cease-fire agreement. Souvanna Phouma, premier of the preceding Vientiane government of neutralists and rightists, remained as premier of the coalition government and Phouma's half-brother, Pathet Lao leader Prince Souphanouvong, became president of the National Political Council, an advisory body to the cabinet. The new cabinet, consisting of 5 members each from the Vientiane and Pathet Lao factions, and 2 ministers agreeable to both sides, was installed, **Apr. 6,** in Vientiane.

Prisoner Dispute on Subcontinent Resolved — India, Pakistan, and Bangladesh, **Apr. 9,** signed an agreement settling a 3-year dispute on Pakistani POWs taken in the 1971 India-Pakistan war. According to the agreement, made public **Apr. 10,** all 195 Pakistani POWs facing charges of murder and rape in

---

Nixon Issues 1,200 Pages of Tape Transcripts; House Judiciary Committee Charges Noncompliance

Assuring a nationwide television audience that he had "nothing to hide," Pres. Richard M. Nixon, **Apr. 29,** disclosed that he would turn over to the House Judiciary Committee and make public 1,200 pages of edited transcripts of White House conversations relating to Watergate. The transcripts included, according to the president, "all the relevant portions of all the subpoenaed conversations that were recorded and related to Watergate or the cover-up." Nixon conceded that while the transcripts would clear him, they would embarrass him and stir up new controversy.

As a measure of authenticity, Nixon invited Judiciary Committee Chairman Peter W. Rodino Jr. and Edward Hutchinson, the committee's top Republican, to come to the White House to listen to the tapes.

Nixon's decision came in response to an **Apr. 11** subpoena issued by the Judiciary Committee for tapes and records of 42 White House conversations. The transcripts, although massive in extent, did not include 11 of those conversations or supplementary notes and Dictabelts also under subpoena. In a party-line split, the committee, in a 20-18 vote, **May 1,** decided to send Nixon a letter stating that, by offering transcripts in lieu of tapes, Nixon had failed to comply with the committee's subpoena. The decision followed a disclosure by committee counsel John M. Doar that the transcripts were, at least in part, "not accurate."

Released **Apr. 30,** the transcripts were liberally sprinkled with "unintelligibles," "inaudibles," and "expletives deleted." In his television address, Nixon stated the transcripts showed that he did not become aware of the cover-up until Mar. 21, 1973, that he ruled out clemency for E. Howard Hunt, and acted quickly to discover the truth once he was informed of the cover-up. He also stated that some people could find the evidence of the transcripts ambiguous.

As political leaders studied the transcripts, criticism of Nixon snowballed. Senate Republican leader Hugh Scott said, **May 7,** the transcripts portrayed "deplorable, disgusting, shabby immoral performances" by all those involved, including the president. House Republican leader John J. Rhodes agreed and Republican Senator Charles H. Percy added "shocking" to the list of descriptive adjectives.

Subsequently, on **July 9,** the Judiciary Committee released 8 transcripts of White House conversations which, in many cases, showed variations from the White House versions. Included was a side-by-side comparison of the 2 versions which, in nearly all cases, indicated the White House version had put Nixon in a better light. The committee version indicated the president had been pleased with John Dean's work and that certain Nixon comments could suggest his knowledge and sanction of a cover-up, as well as his acquiescence to "hush money" payments to the Watergate defendants.

Bangladesh would be repatriated and Bangladesh agreed to drop the trials as an "act of clemency." Pakistan also stated that it "condemned and deeply regretted any crimes that may have been committed" by its forces during the 1971 conflict. In a partial easing of the problem of the Bihari minority, the agreement stated that Pakistan would accept more than the 140,000 Biharis it had originally proposed to receive. The agreement opened up the way for normal relations on the subcontinent. India and Pakistan immediately agreed to work out plans to resume communication and travel links as well as trade, economic, and cultural ties.

Israeli Premier Resigns — Israeli Premier Golda Meir resigned, **Apr. 10**, bringing down her month-old coalition cabinet. Deep divisions within her Labor party came to a head over the report of an official commission, issued **Apr. 2**, which placed the primary blame for Israeli unpreparedness in the 1973 October War on the military command, not the government. Both the right and left attacked the report, **Apr. 3**, as too lenient on Meir and Defense Secretary Moshe Dayan, bringing calls for Dayan to step down and take responsibility for setbacks during the early part of the war. A Labor party deadlock over whether Dayan should resign led to Meir's decision to step down. The Labor party, **Apr. 21**, overcame pressure for immediate elections and, **Apr. 23**, chose Itzhak Rabin, the commander of Israeli forces in the 1967 Arab-Israeli war, to form a new coalition government.

Arab Guerrillas Attack Israeli Town — Three Arab guerrillas, **Apr. 11**, attacked a 4-story residential building in the Israeli border town of Qiryat Shemona, killing 18 persons, mostly women and children. The Lebanese-based Marxist Popular Front for the Liberation of Palestine took responsibility for the raid and, **Apr. 12**, announced that the attack on Qiryat Shemona had been aimed at sabotaging upcoming Middle East peace negotiations at Geneva. In retaliation, Israeli forces, **Apr. 12**, raided several southern Lebanese border towns, attacking homes allegedly belonging to Arab guerrilla sympathizers. On **Apr. 13**, Israeli Defense Minister Moshe Dayan warned Lebanon that if it failed to police Arab guerrillas, Israel would continue its punitive raids into Lebanon.

Egypt Ends Reliance on USSR Arms — Egyptian Pres. Anwar Sadat disclosed, **Apr. 18**, that Egypt had decided to abandon its 18-year reliance on the Soviet Union for arms supplies. For the past 6 months, the Soviet Union had put off Egyptian requests for more Soviet weapons. On **Apr. 21**, Sadat explained that Egypt had found unacceptable the USSR's use of weapons and ammunition supply as an "instrument of policy leverage" to influence Egyptian action.

Military Deposes Portuguese Government — Calling themselves the Movement of Armed Forces, rebel army officers, **Apr. 25**, took control of the Portuguese government and pledged to bring democracy to Portugal and peace to its African territories. The virtually bloodless coup ended more than 40 years of civilian dictatorship. The take-over began before dawn when army units moved into Lisbon and seized a radio station and key ministries. After an attempt to resist with the aid of Republican National Guard units, Premier Marcello Caetano surrendered in the late afternoon. Gen. Antonio de Spinola emerged as the effective leader of the new government, a 7-man military junta. In a television broadcast, Spinola promised elections for a new president and national assembly. He also announced a program of political action including the abolition of censorship, freedom of political association, freedom of assembly, and the abolition of the security police. Official decrees issued **Apr. 29** officially dismantled the ousted dictatorship and proclaimed amnesty for all political prisoners.

General

QE II Disabled off Bermuda — Enroute from New York City to St. Thomas in the Virgin Islands, the Queen Elizabeth II, **Apr. 1**, encountered boiler problems and stalled off the coat of Bermuda. She drifted for 36 hours until engineers gave up efforts at emergency repairs. All 1,648 passengers, in ebullient spirits, were transferred, **Apr. 3**, to a Norwegian cruise ship, the Sea Venture, for transport back to New York.

Boyle Convicted — Deposed mine workers' Pres. W. A. Boyle was found guilty, **Apr. 11**, of 3 counts of first-degree murder. He was convicted of ordering the 1969 death of reformist union rival Joseph A. Yablonski, and Yablonski's wife and daughter. The conviction carried a mandatory life imprisonment sentence.

Rep. Chisholm Exonerated — Rep. Shirley Chisholm (D-N.Y.), **Apr. 23**, was virtually absolved by the Justice Department of charges she and her campaign committee had mishandled funds in her 1972 presidential campaign. The charges of violations of the federal disclosure law had been brought the previous fall by the General Accounting Office.

Art Treasures Stolen in Ireland — Five armed thieves led by a young woman, **Apr. 26**, stole 19 art masterpieces valued at $20 million from the Blessington, Ireland, home of millionaire Alfred Beit. Included were works by Goya, Reubens, and Vermeer. The head of a Dublin art gallery received a ransom note, **May 3**, demanding the transfer of 4 convicted IRA guerrillas from a London jail to Northern Ireland and a ransom of about $1.2 million. On **May 4**, police raided a cottage in southern Ireland and recovered the stolen paintings. They also arrested Bridget Rose Dugdale, a former university lecturer and the daughter of a millionaire, who was charged, **May 6**, with armed theft and the possession of explosives and firearms.

Disasters— The worst tornado disaster in 49 years claimed at least 310 lives and caused damage exceeding $1 billion, **Apr. 3**, in an area reaching from Michigan to Georgia. Worst hit was Xenia, Ohio, where 35 persons were reported killed and half the town destroyed . . . A DC-4 carrying gold miners on their way home from Malawi crashed, **Apr. 4**, in Francistown, Botswanna, killing 77 persons . . . At least 100 were feared dead, **Apr. 14**, when 2 motor launches collided on the Rupsa River in Bangladesh . . . All 107 persons aboard died, **Apr. 23**, when a Pan Am 707 crashed in the mountainous regions of Bali in Indonesia . . . At least 250 persons were dead and more than 500 missing, **Apr. 25**, after landslides wiped out 3 villages in the Peruvian Andes.

MAY
National

Agnew Disbarred — The Maryland Court of Appeals, **May 2**, unanimously ordered that former Vice President Spiro T. Agnew be disbarred in view of his plea, the previous August, of *nolo contendere* to a tax evasion charge. Agnew's defense attorneys had argued in favor of suspension rather than disbarment. Judge J. Dudley Briggs said, in the court's opinion, "It is difficult to feel compassion for an attorney who is so morally obtuse that he consciously cheats for his own pecuniary gain that government he has sworn to serve, completely disregards the words of the oath he uttered when first admitted to the bar, and absolutely fails to perceive his professional duty to act honestly in all matters."

Impeachment Hearings Open — The House Judiciary Committee's long-awaited hearings to consider a recommendation to impeach Pres. Richard M. Nixon opened **May 9.** In an 18-minute public session, the committee members pledged to use the "awesome" power of impeachment wisely. After a brief procedural debate, the committee went into closed session to hear evidence gathered by the committee staff in 6 areas of possible impeachable offense by the president. In the evidentiary phase of the inquiry which concluded **June 21,** the panel heard evidence on the Watergate break-in and aftermath, the Watergate cover-up, Nixon administration involvement in the Ellsberg break-in, alleged White House use of IRS for political benefit, Nixon's personal tax situation, and the 1969 secret bombing of Cambodia. Special presidential counsel James D. St. Clair sat in on all the sessions.

Resignation Pressure Increases — In the wake of resignation rumors flooding Washington and mounting pressure from Republican leaders and conservative newspapers for resignation, White House Press Secretary Ron Ziegler, **May 10,** announced Pres. Richard M. Nixon was "up to the battle" and had no intention of resigning. On **May 9,** House Republican leader John J. Rhodes, noting calls for Nixon's resignation from conservative voices such as the Chicago Tribune, the Omaha World-Herald, and the Hearst newspaper chain, had urged Nixon to consider resignation. On **May 11,** Nixon's daughter, Julie Eisenhower, indicated her father had told the family he would not resign as long as one member of the Senate supported him. This was the first indication Nixon considered it possible he might be impeached by the House.

Kleindienst Pleads Guilty — Former Attorney General Richard G. Kleindienst pleaded guilty, **May 16,** in a Washington, D.C., federal district court, to a misdemeanor charge he had refused to testify accurately and fully before a Congressional committee investigating administration handling of an ITT antitrust settlement. Kleindienst became the first U.S. attorney general to be convicted of a criminal offense. The charge stemmed from Kleindienst's testimony at Senate Judiciary Committee hearings on his nomination to succeed John N. Mitchell as attorney general. In return for the misdemeanor plea, Watergate Special Prosecutor Leon Jaworski agreed not to bring perjury charges against the former attorney general.

6 SLA Members Killed in Shootout — Hundreds of heavily armed police, **May 17,** laid siege to the Los Angeles, Calif., hideout of suspected Symbionese Liberation Army fugitives. The gun battle and ensuing fire left 6 dead. Patricia Hearst who had been kidnaped by the SLA in February was not, according to reports **May 18,** in the hideout. Medical examiners identified the bodies as Donald D. Defreeze, alias SLA leader General Field Marshal Cinque, Nancy Ling Perry, William L. Wolfe, Patricia Soltyski, Angela Atwood, and Camilla Hall. In related developments the FBI, **May 19,** identified Patty Hearst as one of 3 participants in a **May 16** holdup of a sporting goods store and classified her as "an armed and dangerous fugitive." On **May 21,** the FBI charged Patty with kidnaping, armed robbery, and assault with a deadly weapon.

Magruder Sentenced — Jeb Stuart Magruder, formerly deputy director of the Committee to Re-elect the President was sentenced, **May 21,** by U.S. District Court Judge John J. Sirica to a minimum of 10 months to 4 years in prison for his role in the Watergate break-in and cover-up. Sentencing had been delayed since Magruder's guilty plea, in August 1973, in order to evaluate his cooperation with Watergate prosecutors.

Nixon Rejects 2 House Subpoenas — Pres. Richard M. Nixon stated, May 22, that he would not comply with 2 subpoenas, issued by the House Judiciary Committee **May 15,** for Watergate-related tapes and documents. He further said that he would reject all future subpoenas. In a letter to Committee Chairman Peter W. Rodino, Nixon said the panel already had all the information it needed for its impeachment inquiry and its "constantly escalating requests" for more material would only prolong the impeachment process. He added that compliance would "constitute such a massive invasion into the confidentiality of Presidential conversation that the institution of the Presidency itself would be fatally compromised." Rodino termed Nixon's response "a very grave matter" and implied that the panel could consider the refusal grounds for impeachment.

Bumpers Defeats Fulbright — A virtual unknown until 1968 when he won the Arkansas governorship, Dale Bumpers, May 28, defeated Senate Foreign Relations Committee Chairman J. W. Fulbright in Arkansas' Democratic primary for the Senate. Bumpers carried an almost 2 to 1 margin against the incumbent, who was running for his 6th term.

Supreme Court to Decide on Tape Request — The Supreme Court, May 31, agreed to make a quick decision on Pres. Richard M. Nixon's claim of executive privilege to withhold tapes of 64 White House conversations subpoenaed by Watergate Special Prosecutor Leon Jaworski. The court, thereby, allowed Jaworski to bypass the Court of Appeals to expedite a decision on the critical issue. On **May 20,** U.S. District Court Judge John J. Sirica had rejected an attempt by special presidential counsel James D. St. Clair to quash the subpoena. Sirica had also criticized the president's attempt to abridge the independence of the special prosecutor as a violation of the law and of Nixon's own assurances of independence.

Spy Scandal Forces Brandt Resignation — West German Chancellor Willy Brandt resigned, **May 6,** taking responsibility for "negligence" that allowed an East German spy to become a member of his staff. The arrest and confession of Brandt's aide for party affairs, Gunter Guillaume, had been disclosed **Apr. 25.** Brandt asked Foreign Minister Walter Scheel to fill his place until parliament elected a new chancellor. In a televised speech, **May 8,** Brandt told the stunned German people that he had resigned because of indications his private life would be drawn into speculation about the case. The Social Democrats chose Finance Minister Helmut Schmidt to succeed Brandt, **May 7.** Schmidt was elected by the parliament, **May 16,** and sworn in as West Germany's 5th postwar chancellor. Walter Scheel was elected, **May 15,** to the ceremonial post of president in a show of solidarity between his Free Democrats and Brandt's Social Democrats.

Trudeau Government Falls — Canadian Prime Minister Pierre Elliott Trudeau's minority Liberal party government fell, **May 8,** when it lost a vote of confidence in the House of Commons over its budgetary policies. The leftist New Democratic party, which had supported Trudeau in past votes, joined the Progressive Conservatives in the 137-123 no-confidence vote. The opposition charged Trudeau's budget failed to come to grips with escalating inflation.

25 Israelis Die in Arab Terrorist Attack — Israeli troops, **May 15**, stormed a school building in the northern Israeli town of Maalot where 3 Arab terrorists were holding about 90 students hostage in return for the release of 20 Arab commandos held in Israel. All 3 guerrillas, 21 of the students, and one Israeli soldier were dead as a result of the attack. Earlier in the day, the guerrillas had burst into a Maalot apartment, killing a family of 3. In heavy reprisal raids, **May 16** and **17**, Israeli planes bombed and strafed Palestinian refugee camps and suspected guerrilla hideouts in Lebanon, with casualties placed at 21 dead and 134 injured. The Popular Democratic Front for the Liberation of Palestine announced the commando raid had been aimed against U.S. Secretary of State Henry A. Kissinger's peace mission in the Middle East. At a state funeral for the slain Israelis, mourners, screaming "Revenge, revenge," focused their rage at the Israeli government's failure to curb Arab terrorists.

India Explodes Nuclear Device — Becoming the 6th member of the nuclear nations club, India, **May 18**, conducted a successful test of a powerful nuclear device. The test, "a peace nuclear explosive experiment" according to India's Atomic Energy Commission, was conducted underground at a depth of more than 330 feet. The Canadian government, which had given aid to India's nuclear energy program, protested, **May 20**, that the test violated a 1971 understanding on peaceful nuclear use and, **May 22**, suspended further aid to India's atomic energy program. On **May 22**, India expressed surprise at adverse criticism and affirmed that her new technology would be developed solely for peaceful purposes.

Giscard d'Estaing Wins in France — Conservative Valery Giscard d'Estaing, **May 19**, won a narrow victory, 50.66% of the votes, over his socialist opponent, Francois Mitterrand, in the runoff election for the French presidency. Mitterrand and Giscard d'Estaing had emerged, **May 5**, as the 2 top contenders for the presidency with 42% and 33% of the first ballot vote, respectively. Giscard d'Estaing, the finance minister under the Pompidou government, had promised social reform and new faces in the government. On **May 27**, he named Jacques Chirac, a Gaullist and former interior minister, as premier and, **May 28**, presented his cabinet, characterized by nonpolitical specialists. On **May 29**, at his first cabinet meeting, Giscard d'Estaing prohibited all government wiretapping and ordered the destruction of files from all previous taps. He also pledged to develop France "as a country of political and intellectual asylum."

India Crushes Rail Strike — Weakened by mass arrests of union leaders and workers, India's 20-day railway strike collapsed **May 28**. Union leaders who had been demanding increased wages and an annual bonus conceded that the arrests — estimated at 20,000 to 50,000 — had crushed the strike. Prime Minister Indira Gandhi who had refused to negotiate until the strike call was withdrawn argued that the government could not meet union demands which would cost the government $700 million per year. Losses in production and trade disruption during the strike were estimated at between $1.5 and $2 billion.

Ulster Strike Ends in British Direct Rule — The British government **May 29**, again assumed direct rule of Northern Ireland following the collapse, **May 28**, of the 5-month-old Protestant-Catholic coalition government. A 14-day strike led by the Ulster Workers Council in protest over the establishment of an All-Ireland Council had brought Northern Ireland to a virtual economic standstill. The formation of the council had been agreed upon last December by Britain, the Irish Republic, and Northern Ireland's moderate Roman Catholic and Protestant leaders. The UWC, having achieved at least one goal — the fall of the executive coalition government — ended the strike **May 29**. The UWC, however, failed to achieve another main objective, a British promise to call new elections after the period of direct rule.

Israel, Syria Sign Disengagement Accord — Following intensified fighting in March along the Golan Heights and 32 days of intensive shuttle diplomacy by U.S. Secretary of State Henry A. Kissinger, Israel and Syria, **May 31**, signed an agreement in Geneva disengaging forces on the Golan Heights. It was the first armistice between the 2 countries since the 1948 Israeli war for independence. According to the agreement and accompanying map released **May 30**, Israel agreed to give up Syrian territory captured during the October 1973 war, plus a strip on the Golan Heights seized during the 1967 war. Military forces would be limited to either side of a ¼-mile neutral buffer zone manned by the United Nations Disengagement Observer Force. Prisoners-of war would be returned within 24 hours of the signing of the agreement. The United States, reportedly, gave both Israel and Syria unpublished assurances concerning its understanding on some points of the accord, including agreement to conduct aerial reconnaissance to assure implementation of the accord and to support Israeli retaliation for Palestinian commando raids. It was also reported that the breakthrough leading to the agreement had, in part, come with secret assurances by Syria, given to Israel through Kissinger, that Palestinian guerrillas would not be infiltrated into Israel from Syria.

General

Franklin National Discloses Losses — For the first time since the 1930s Depression, a major bank, Franklin National Bank, announced, **May 12**, it would not pay regular quarterly dividends. The bank also revealed that it had lost as much as $39 million in foreign currency trading because an employee had "operated beyond his authority and without the bank's knowledge." The Federal Reserve announced immediately that it was prepared to advance funds to meet the bank's liquidity problems. The New York Clearing House Assn. announced, **May 25**, that 11% of the bank's deposits, $325 million, had been withdrawn since the disclosure. On **June 20**, the bank revealed that its foreign exchange losses had in fact amounted to $62.6 million, some $25 million more than it had first indicated.

4 Indicted in "Zebra" Killings — A California state grand jury, **May 16**, indicted 4 Black Muslims for murdering 3 white persons and conspiring to kill others at random. The 3 murders were among the 12 apparently motiveless "Zebra" killings committed during the previous 5 months. San Francisco Mayor Joseph L. Alioto had heightened controversy surrounding the case, **Apr. 29**, with a statement that a statewide ring called the "Death Angels" was responsible for the 12 killings and perhaps some 80 others committed since 1971. Both federal and local enforcement officials had stated there was no evidence for Alioto's contention.

Helicopter Hijacked to Pan Am Building — Claiming affiliation with the Jewish Defense League, 21-year-old David Kamaiko, **May 24**, hijacked a helicopter from a New York City heliport, seizing the pilot, whom he later shot, and a hostage. He demanded $2 million to be delivered by a bikini-clad girl. He said the money would be used to buy guns for the JDL, but the JDL denied any knowledge of him. Kamaiko was captured by police after he landed on the Pan Am Building in mid-Manhattan.

Disasters — Some 250 persons drowned, **May 1,** when a motor launch capsized in waters off Bangladesh. . . . Reports, **May 1,** placed the death toll at 200 in floods and landslides in Brazil.

JUNE
National

Colson Pleads Guilty — Once known as the tough-talking hatchet man on the presidential staff, former counsel Charles W. Colson pleaded guilty, **June 3,** to attempting to obstruct justice and influence the trial of Dr. Daniel Ellsberg. In return for the one-count indictment, Colson agreed to cooperate with Watergate Special Prosecutor Leon Jaworski. Jaworski agreed to drop criminal charges of conspiracy against Colson for alleged involvement in the Watergate cover-up and participation in the Ellsberg break-in. Colson had recently converted to evangelical christianity. Sen. Harold E. Hughes, a confidante and spiritual associate, said Colson "wants to be free so he can go and tell the whole story to the Rodino committee." On **June 21,** U.S. District Court Judge Gerhard A. Gesell sentenced Colson to 1 to 3 years in prison and imposed a $5,000 fine. At the sentencing, Colson expressed regret and contrition for his offense. He also stated that Pres. Richard M. Nixon had urged him "on numerous occasions" to commit the acts for which he was being jailed. However, he said he was confident the president had acted in what he believed to be the national interest. He confessed that he had failed the president because, "I never really questioned whether what he wanted done was right or wrong." The House Judiciary Committee announced that Colson's statements made it imperative he be called as a witness in the impeachment inquiry.

Kleindienst Sentence Suspended — Former Attorney General Richard G. Kleindienst, who had pleaded guilty in May to misleading a Senate committee investigating the ITT case, **June 7,** was given a suspended sentence by U.S. District Court Judge George L. Hart. The sentence, the minimum under law, was 30 days in prison and a $100 fine. Judge Hart, describing Kleindienst as a man of "highest integrity" but with "a heart that is too loyal," placed the former attorney general on one-month unsupervised probation.

Nixon Rejects House Subpoena — Moving closer to a constitutional conflict with Congress, Pres. Richard M. Nixon, **June 10,** rejected a House Judiciary Committee subpoena for 45 Watergate-related conversations. In his 4th refusal of a House subpoena, Nixon again said he would refuse to comply with all further subpoenas. On **June 24,** in an attempt to accelerate the impeachment inquiry, the impeachment panel issued what it described as its 4 final subpoenas for 49 more White House conversations.

Kissinger Threatens to Resign — In an extraordinary news conference, **June 11,** in Salzburg, Austria, Secretary of State Henry A. Kissinger threatened to resign unless allegations he participated in "illegal and shady" wiretapping activity were cleared up. Kissinger's threat came in response to a **June 8** report from unidentified Congressional sources and ensuing "innuendos" that Kissinger's National Security Council office had been more directly involved in 1969-71 federal wiretapping of 13 newsmen and 4 federal officials than Kissinger had lead senators to believe in his 1973 confirmation hearings. Kissinger had testified that he had only supplied to the FBI the names of those with access to sensitive information. The reports alleged Kissinger had instigated the taps. Obviously hurt and angry, Kissinger said that he had asked the Senate Foreign Relations Committee to reopen its investigation of the matter. The committee unanimously accepted the request. Congressional members and government officials rallied, **June 12,** in support of Kissinger urging him not to resign. Both Senate Democrats and Republicans introduced a resolution expressing high regard for the Secretary of State. Presidential counselor Dean Burch charged the House Judiciary Committee, now allegedly out of Chairman Peter W. Rodino's control, had leaked derogatory information about Kissinger. Rodino denied the charge. Former FBI Acting Director William D. Ruckelshaus who had investigated the wiretapping earlier, said, **June 16,** that Kissinger's role was "pretty much as he's described it."

Nixon, Ehrlichman Battle Over Access to Files — U.S. District Court Judge Gerhard A. Gesell formally announced, **June 14,** that Pres. Richard M. Nixon had agreed to give former aide John D. Ehrlichman sufficient access to his own White House files and ordered that Ehrlichman stand trial **June 26** with 3 other defendants in the 1971 Ellsberg break-in. Gesell had, **June 11,** ordered a separate, delayed trial for Ehrlichman because of the president's "resistence to lawful trial subpoenas" by Ehrlichman for direct access to his own personal notes. The Watergate prosecution, **June 12,** had asked Gesell to reconsider his order, arguing the delay might result "in perhaps no trial at all." The controversy had begun **June 4,** when White House spokesmen said the materials would have to be screened and extraneous matters removed before the notes could be turned over. Gessel's decision came after a compromise worked out with presidential counsel J. Fred Buzhardt Jr. in which, after assuring Gesell, to his satisfaction, that the notes were extraneous to the issue of Ehrlichman's guilt or innocence, the White House dropped its claim of executive privilege.

Top Court to Rule on Co-conspirator Charge — The Supreme Court, **June 15,** agreed to decide whether the Watergate grand jury had the right to name Pres. Richard M. Nixon a co-conspirator in the Watergate cover-up without indicting him. In accepting the president's appeal, the Supreme Court decided to make the decision part of its consideration of the presidential tape case brought by Watergate Special Prosecutor Leon Jaworski. The disclosure of the grand jury's action, previously a matter of speculation came, **June 6,** from special presidential counsel James D. St. Clair in response to an inquiry on a report published in the Los Angeles Times.

Kalmbach Sentenced — Herbert W. Kalmbach, formerly personal attorney to Pres. Richard M. Nixon and a major campaign fundraiser for Nixon in 1972, was sentenced, **June 17,** to 6 to 8 months in prison and fined $10,000. He had pleaded guilty in February to operating an illegal campaign committee for Congressional candidates in the 1970 election.

Nixon Health Cited — Giving credence to speculation on the president's health, the White House announced, **June 24,** that Pres. Richard M. Nixon had suffered from phlebitis, an inflammation in the leg veins, before and during his trip to the Middle East. White House physician, Dr. Walter K. Tkach reported that the president was now in good health.

Mother of Dr. King Slain — Alberta Williams King, the 69-year-old mother of Dr. Martin Luther King Jr., was shot and killed, **June 30,** while playing the organ in Atlanta's Ebenezer Baptist Church. A church deacon was also killed and a young worshiper was wounded. Marcus Wayne Chenault, 23, of Dayton, Ohio, was charged with murder and assault and indicted **July 9.** The FBI concluded, **July 4,** that Chenault had acted alone and "not in concert with others." Chenault was convicted, **Sept. 12,** and sentenced to die in the electric chair on Nov. 8.

International

Servan-Schreiber Dismissed in A-Test Dispute—French Pres. Valery Giscard d-Estaing, **June 9,** dismissed his Minister of Reform, Jean-Jacques Servan-Schreiber, over his public criticism of a **June 8** government decision to hold more nuclear tests in the South Pacific. In a news conference earlier in the day, Servan-Schreiber charged that the military had presented the decision, made by the old Pompidou government, as a *fait accompli* and not open to further discussion.

Rumor Government Regains Support—After the **June 10** resignation of Premier Mariano Rumor's 3-party government over disagreement on how to deal with Italy's economic crisis, the Rumor government, **June 19,** won a new lease on life. In the breakthrough, the 4 parties that had originally supported the government reached an accord on an economic austerity program. The Chamber of Deputies, **June 28,** in a 326-255 vote of confidence, authorized the government to raise $5 billion in new taxes during the next 12 months. Emergency decrees, issued **July 6,** to implement the austerity program included a surtax on automobiles, an increase in the value-added tax, increased property tax, and increases in gasoline prices.

6 Israelis Dead in Separate Arab Raids—Expressing their "reaction to President Nixon's visit to the Arab world," 4 Arab guerrillas, **June 13,** attacked the Shamir kibbutz in northern Israel, killing 3 women. The guerrillas were killed in an ensuing battle with the men of the kibbutz. They carried leaflets indicating they had intended to seize hostages as barter for the release of 100 Palestinian guerrillas in Israeli jails. In a separate incident **June 24,** 3 Arab terrorists attacked a small apartment house in the northern Israeli resort town of Nahariya, killing 3 civilians before being slain in a gunfight with Israeli soldiers. One Israeli soldier was also killed and 5 wounded. In a surprise announcement **June 25,** Al Fatah, the largest and most moderate Palestinian resistance organization, took responsibility for the attack. The attack was seen as a signal Al Fatah and other moderate Palestinian groups were now committed to the simultaneous use of diplomacy and violence to gain admission to the Geneva talks on peace in the Middle East.

U. S. President Visits Middle East—Returning to Washington after a 5-nation tour of the Middle East, Pres. Richard M. Nixon, **June 19,** said a "profound and lasting change has taken place in that part of the world." Obviously buoyed by enthusiastic receptions he had received from the Arab people and leaders, Nixon concluded, "where there was no hope for peace there is now hope." On the first leg of his journey, **June 12-14,** Nixon spent 3 days in Egypt and held intensive meetings with Egyptian Pres. Anwar Sadat. To facilitate the Middle East peace negotiations, Sadat and Nixon agreed, **June 13** to hold a series of bilateral meetings involving the Arab countries, the USSR, and the U.S. before the next round of Geneva talks. On **June 14,** the U.S. and Egypt announced, as part of a sweeping declaration of friendship and cooperation, the U. S. had agreed to provide Egypt with nuclear technology to be used for peaceful

means. On Nixon's stop in Saudi Arabia, King Faisal, **June 14,** warned Nixon there could not be real peace in the Middle East until all occupied Arab territories had been liberated and the people of Palestine regained their rights and were free to return to their homes. On **June 16,** Pres. Nixon and Syrian Pres. Hafez al-Assad announced that their 2 countries would resume diplomatic relations, which had been broken since the 1967 Arab-Israeli war. Both described the decision as the first step toward a lasting Middle East peace. Upon arrival in Israel, **June 16,** Nixon encountered the first signs of hostility when demonstrators made references to his Watergate problems. In an extensive communique, Nixon, **June 16,** assured Israel of long-term military and economic assistance from the U.S. and indicated the 2 nations would soon cooperate, with some technological aid and a supply of nuclear fuel coming from the U.S. In Jordan, on the last leg of Nixon's Middle East journey, the U.S. and Jordan, **June 18,** agreed to form a joint Jordanian-American commission to review cooperation between the 2 countries on a regular basis.

News Media Curbed in Portugal — The provisional Portuguese government, **June 22,** placed strict restrictions on all news media. The restrictions, to be administered by a 7-man military committee, covered the press, radio, television, theater, and films. According to the new restrictions, discussion and criticism of political and religious doctrines and public administration would be legitimate but could not offend the government or take the form of inciting military disobedience, strikes or unauthorized demonstrations.

Sudan Frees Terrorists — Sudanese Pres. Gaafar al-Nimeiry announced, **June 24,** that he would turn over to the Palestine Liberation Organization the 8 Arab guerrillas who had killed 2 American diplomats and one Belgian in the March 1973 attack on the Saudi Arabian embassy in Khartoum. Convicted **June 23,** the 8 terrorists had been sentenced to life imprisonment. Nimeiry had commuted the sentence to 7 years before making his decision to free them. The U.S., **June 25,** issued a strongly-worded protest and recalled its ambassador. According to the U.S. State Department, the 8 terrorists were jailed, **June 28,** upon their arrival in Egypt.

NATO Leaders Sign Declaration — Following months of strained U.S.-European relations, the leaders of the 15-member North Atlantic Treaty Organization, in Brussels, **June 26,** signed a declaration on Atlantic Relations. The declaration to guide NATO through the next 25 years had been approved, **June 19,** in Ottawa, by the foreign ministers of the member-nations. The declaration affirmed wider and more intimate consultation on common problems, including those outside the alliance area. U.S. Pres. Richard M. Nixon told his NATO allies that the U.S. would maintain its forces in Europe "if there is a similar effort by our allies." He also pledged not to reduce U.S. forces unless there were a reciprocal action by the Soviet Union. Nixon, in Brussels on his way to meet with Soviet leader Leonid I. Brezhnev, pledged to consult with the allies both before and after his Moscow talks.

France, Iran Sign Massive Agreement — France and Iran, **June 27,** reached agreement on a massive 10-year development program, amounting to $4 billion. Included was a provision for the sale to Iran of five 1,000-megawatt nuclear reactors worth $1.1 billion. Iran's promise to advance $1 billion to the Bank of France and to pay for 3/4's of the reactors in 5 years would substantially ease France's critical balance-of-payment problem.

General

Kidnaping of Irish Couple Linked to IRA — Kidnapers who abducted the Earl and Countess of Donoughmore, **June 4**, from their mansion 90 miles from Dublin, Ireland, released the couple, **June 9**, because convicted members of the IRA in English prisons had given up their hunger strike. The prisoners had refused to eat unless they were transferred to prisons in Northern Ireland. The kidnapers had made no ransom demand.

Panovs Go to Israel — Following a 2-year struggle over free emigration, Soviet authorities, **June 7**, decided to allow Valery Panov and his wife Galina Ragozina, formerly dancers with Leningrad's Kirov Ballet, to emigrate to Israel. They had lost their positions with the ballet 2 years before when they applied for visas to Israel. Upon arrival in Tel Aviv, the Panovs, **June 15**, said they intended to resume ballet training.

Attorneys in Manson Trial Indicted — Chief Prosecutor Vincent T. Bugliosi and defense attorney David Shinn, both participants in the 1970 murder trial of Charles Manson, were indicted in Los Angeles, **June 28**, on 3 counts each of perjury. They were accused of perjury in denying they had violated a gag rule that prohibited participants in the Manson trial from discussing the case with the press, specifically in denying they were sources for Los Angeles reporter William Farr. Farr had written an exclusive article stating the Manson group had planned a series of murders other than those for which they were being tried. Farr had already served 46 days in jail for refusing to reveal his sources before a grand jury.

Disasters — A Colombian airliner crashed, **June 9**, into mountains near Cucuta, Colombia, killing 43 persons . . . Tropical storm Dinah lashed the island of Luzon in the Philippines, **June 11**, leaving 71 persons dead . . . At least 200 persons died in a landslide, **June 28**, 95 miles east of Bogota, Colombia.

JULY

National

Gurney Charged With Extortion — A Jacksonville grand jury, **July 10**, indicted Florida Sen. Edward J. Gurney, along with 6 other men, on charges of running an influence peddling and extortion racket for the past 3½ years. According to the indictment, Gurney offered to exert pressure on the Department of Housing and Urban Development to secure housing contracts and mortgage insurance for Florida contractors and real estate developers. In exchange, it was charged, Gurney received at least $223,000 for use as "personal, political, and travel expenses" and operations of his Washington and Florida office since 1970. Thirty-nine real estate developers were named as unindicted co-conspirators. Gurney, who maintained he was absolutely innocent, **July 23**, abandoned his re-election campaign in order to prepare his defense.

Ehrlichman Guilty in Ellsberg Break-in — Former Nixon aide John D. Ehrlichman and 3 others were found guilty, **July 12**, of conspiring to violate the civil rights of Dr. Lewis Fielding of Beverly Hills, Calif., formerly pyschiatrist to Dr. Daniel Ellsberg, discloser of the "Pentagon Papers." The others were G. Gordon Liddy, Bernard L. Barker, and Eugenio R. Martinez, all members of the "plumbers," the White House special investigations unit. Ehrlichman was also found guilty on 3 counts of making false statements. One charge — making false statements to the FBI — was thrown out. **July 22**, by U.S. District Court Judge Gerhard A. Gesell as inapplicable to Ehrlichman's case. Striking at the heart of Ehrlichman's defense, Gerhard had charged the jury that Ehrlichman need not have specifically authorized a "break-in" or "illegal entry" to be found guilty, but merely a "convert operation" which led to an intrusion by governmental agents into "an area which one would normally expect to remain private." On **July 31**, Gesell sentenced Ehrlichman to 20 months to 5 years in jail for what he called "a shameful episode in the history of this country." Liddy was sentenced to one to 3 years in prison to be served concurrently with his sentence for participation in the Watergate break-in. Gesell gave Barker and Martinez suspended sentences and placed them on 3-year probation. He said they had been duped by high government officials and had been sufficiently punished.

Watergate Committee Issues Final Report — The Senate Select Committee on Presidential Campaign Activities, which had come to be known as the Watergate Committee, **July 13**, issued its final report on the committee's investigation into the Watergate scandal and other abuses related to the 1972 presidential campaign. "If our free institutions are to survive," the committee concluded, campaign practices "must be effectively supervised and enforcement of the criminal laws vigorously pursued against all offenders — even those of high estate . . ." The 2,250-page report, covering 17 months of investigation, was drawn chiefly from testimony before the committee and documents which had been previously published. The report contained no specific accusations because, according to the report, the panel's work had not been conducted "to determine the legal guilt or innocence of any person or whether the president should be impeached." The report did put forth 35 legislative proposals for a sweeping overhaul of campaign practices. The proposals included the creation of an independent and permanent office of "public attorney" to investigate alleged wrongdoing in cases of conflict of interest in the executive branch; a federal elections commission with supervisory and enforcement powers; restrictions on domestic intelligence activities by the White House staff; and limits on campaign contributions. With the exception of 2 members — Daniel K. Inouye (D-Ha.) and Joseph M. Montoya (D-N.Mex.) — the committee expressed opposition to public financing of federal election campaigns as a threat to free expression.

Supreme Court Rules Against Nixon — In an historic 8-0 decision, the Supreme Court ruled, **July 24**, that Pres. Richard M. Nixon had to give up "forthwith" the tapes and document relating to 64 White House conversations sought by Watergate Special Prosecutor Leon Jaworski for use in the cover-up trial. On a secondary issue — whether the grand jury had the right to name Nixon an unindicted co-conspirator in the cover-up — the court ruled that the question was irrelevant and said that it should not have agreed to review it. The historic event, the first time the court had deliberated a criminal case in which a president was actually accused of participating in a conspiracy, had begun **July 8** with 3 hours of debate on the questions. Presidential counsel James D. St. Clair had argued that compliance with the Jaworski subpoena would seriously weaken the presidency. He also argued that because the issues were inavoidably intertwined with the impeachment inquiry, the court should not even consider the case in such a "political context." Jaworski, in his argument, attacked Nixon's claim of executive privilege, saying constitutional government would be in serious jeopardy if no one, not even the Supreme Court, could limit the authority of the president. In its unanimous decision, the Supreme Court affirmed that the judicial branch decides the law and that the executive branch must abide by its determination. Justice William H. Rehnquist had disqualified himself on the grounds he had served under former Attorney General John N. Mitchell, one of the defendants in the cover-up trial. Eight hours later, St. Clair announced that Nixon would obey the court's decision "in all respects." He indicated, however, that the response would be delayed as the White House began the "time-consuming process" of reviewing the tapes and preparing an index and analysis. However, under pressure from U.S. District Court Judge John J. Sirica, who was to receive the tapes, St. Clair agreed to turn over the first batch of 20 "priority" conversations on **July 30.**

Supreme Court Rules on Busing — The Supreme Court, **July 25,** in a 5-to-4 decision, all but banned busing of children for the purpose of desegregation. The court struck down a plan to desegregate the predominantly black Detroit school system by merging it with predominantly white neighboring districts. In the majority opinion, Chief Justice Warren E. Burger, argued that illegal segregation in a city school system could not be eased by combining it with predominantly white suburbs, even if it was the only apparent way to achieve social balance. Justice Thurgood Marshall, in the dissenting opinion, charged the majority with "emasculation of our constitutional guarantee of equal protection" and termed the decision "a giant step backward" in school desegregation.

Reinecke Found Guilty — A Washington D.C., federal jury, **July 27,** convicted Calif. Lt. Gov. Ed Reinecke of lying to the Senate Judiciary Committee about an ITT pledge to help finance the 1972 Republi-

---

House Judiciary Committee Votes Three Articles of Impeachment, Charges Obstruction of Justice, Abuse of Power, Contempt of Congress

Following almost 6 months of investigation, the House Judiciary Committee, in nationally-televised hearings held **July 24-30,** recommended 3 articles of impeachment to the full house. The first article, voted 27-11, **July 27,** charged Pres. Richard M. Nixon had personally engaged in a "course of conduct" designed to lead to obstruction of justice in the Watergate scandal. Article II, approved 28 to 10, **July 27,** charged Nixon had "repeatedly" failed to carry out his constitutional oath in a series of alleged abuses of power. On **July 30,** in a narrow 21-17 vote, the committee approved a 3rd article which accused the president of unconstitutional defiance of committee subpoenas. (See Index for complete Articles of Impeachment.)

Before recessing on **July 30,** the impeachment panel voted down 2 additional impeachment articles. One, defeated in a 26-12 vote, charged Nixon with conducting a secret bombing campaign in Cambodia beginning in 1969. The other, also defeated 26-12, charged Nixon with misconduct based on underpayment of federal income taxes and acceptance of government-paid improvements on his personal homes.

Hampered by 2 bomb threats and the harsh glare of television camera lights, the committee, **July 24,** began its public debate, the last working session in a reluctant, yet deliberate, process leading to a recommendation on impeachment.

By the end of the 10 hours of preliminary debate **July 25,** all question of whether the committee's work would end in a bipartisan split had disappeared. As the members described the agony of their soulsearching to their constituencies, via television, it became apparent the committee would recommend impeachment in a strong bipartisan vote.

As debate on Article I began **July 26,** the pro-impeachment members doggedly outlined 9 elements in their charge of presidential obstruction of justice. The anti-impeachment faction, led vociferously by Rep. Charles W. Sandman, argued the charge lacked specificity and that the president deserved to know the exact details of his alleged offenses. As the debate often grew harsh, pro-impeachment representatives insisted that the evidence, though circumstantial, was overwhelming and argued that general charges would make it feasible to introduce later evidence not yet on hand.

Although the result was obvious to all beforehand,

the affect of the final vote on **July 27,** was stunning. A hush fell over the hot, crowded committee room as 27 representatives answered "aye" to charges Nixon had obstructed justice.

Debate, **July 29,** on Article II, though lacking the earlier drama, continued to be intensive. Rep. Charles E. Wiggins argued the article, which outlined presidential abuse of power, represented a "step toward a parliamentary system of government" by making the president accountable for his actions after the fact. Rep. Joshua Eilberg characterized the pro-impeachment sentiment when he said, "The Nixon White House made secret police a reality in America."

On **July 30,** in debate on Article III, anti-impeachment members gained support in their argument that the contempt of congress charge constituted "political overkill." Nevertheless, pro-impeachment representatives, arguing failure to hold Nixon in contempt would destroy the only safety valve in the constitution to protect against an irresponsible president, carried the vote.

Preceding the public hearings, the impeachment committee, in closed sessions **July 3-17,** had taken testimony from Alexander P. Butterfield, John W. Dean 3d, Charles W. Colson, Herbert W. Kalmbach, and Henry E. Peterson. Special presidential counsel James D. St. Clair was present at the hearing and was given an opportunity to question witnesses.

On **July 19,** John M. Doar, majority counsel to the impeachment inquiry, urged the committee to recommend impeachment and submitted 29 potential articles of impeachment. Minority counsel Albert E. Jenner supported Doar's recommendation. Committee Republicans, **July 21,** replaced Jenner with assistant counsel Sam Garrison. Jenner remained on the committee as an assistant to Doar.

The mood of the impending hearings was set, **July 23,** on the eve of the debate, when Rep. Lawrence J. Hogan, a conservative Maryland Republican, announced that he would vote for impeachment because Nixon had lied repeatedly about Watergate.

Beginning **July 11,** the Judiciary Committee released over 30 massive volumes of evidence based on its investigation. The evidence took the form of statements of information and supporting documents. Also included was rebuttal information prepared by St. Clair.

can National Convention. Reinecke charged the conviction was a "gross miscarriage of justice" and his attorney James E. Cox said he would file post-trial motions for mistrial and dismissal of the indictment. On **Oct. 2**, Reinecke resigned his California office and received an 18-month suspended sentence.

Connally Indicted for Bribery — The Watergate grand jury, **July 29**, indicted former Treasury Secretary John B. Connally on 5 counts involving acceptance of a bribe, perjury, and conspiracy to obstruct justice. The charges alleged he had received $10,000 in cash payments from the Associated Milk Producers, Inc. in return for his recommendations in 1971 to raise federal milk price supports. Also indicted was Jake Jacobsen, the attorney for the dairy group and longtime friend of Connally. On **July 31**, Harold S. Nelson, the former general manager of the Associated Milk Producers, Inc., pleaded guilty to conspiring to bribe Connally. He also admitted to conspiracy in connection with illegal corporate campaign contributions to a long list of public officials, including senators Hubert H. Humphrey and Edmund S. Muskie. Humphrey's former press secretary Norman Sherman and aide John Valentine had been charged, **July 30**, by the Watergate Special Prosecutor with having helped the Associated Milk Producers, Inc. make illegal contributions to Humphrey's campaign and others.

International

Peron Dead at 78 — Argentinian Pres. Juan Domingo Peron, one of the most remarkable and controversial figures in Latin American history, died, **July 1**, at the age of 78. His vice president and wife, Isabel Peron, immediately succeeded Peron, becoming the first woman chief of state in America. Isabel Peron had received full presidential powers, **June 29**, following official disclosure of the seriousness of Peron's illness. Military, political, labor, and business leaders gave immediate and full expressions of support to the politically-inexperienced new leader. Huge emotional crowds, **July 2**, thronged to mourn Peron and see the cortege carrying his body from the presidential palace to the Metropolitan Cathedral where a mass was offered. On **July 8**, Isabel Peron vowed to follow her husband's policies "without an iota of change" and announced that workers would get a bonus of one month's pay to compensate for rising prices and the prohibition on strikes.

U.S., Turkey in Opium Dispute — The Turkish government, **July 1**, announced a decision to permit again the cultivation and sale of opium policies. The U.S., **July 6**, called back its ambassador, William F. Macomber Jr., for consultations. As part of a 1971 U.S.-Turkey agreement, Turkey agreed, in return for a U.S. pledge to give Turkey $35.7 million over a 4-year period, to ban the cultivation and sale of poppies, then the main source of illegal heroin in the U.S. On **July 2**, U.S. State Department had said it would not give Turkey the remaining $20 million. Turkey maintained that the sale would be strictly controlled and directed only to the international pharmaceutical market and, **July 7**, seeking to avoid a serious showdown, said it would accept any U.S. aid in controlling the poppy flow. On **July 8**, in both the House and Senate, bills to suspend all military and economic aid to Turkey were introduced. Turkish Foreign Minister Turan Gunes said, **July 10**, that even if aid were cut off, Turkey would not change the status of U.S. military bases maintained in Turkey under NATO. He warned, however, that such a move might cause an "unstoppable wave" of adverse opinion among Turkish politicians and the public.

USSR Interrupts U.S. Broadcasts — On **July 2**, while U.S. Pres. Richard M. Nixon was in the USSR for summit talks, the Soviet TV station in Moscow blocked out broadcasts by the 3 major U.S. television networks on Soviet dissident activities. The broadcasts included reports on physicist Andrei Sakharov's hunger strike on behalf of political prisoners. Despite a statement that "hot-headed" technicians had been told not to interrupt transmissions, American broadcasts on Sakharov were again blocked **July 3**. CBS White House correspondent Robert Pierpoint charged the actions were an apparent violation of an agreement that Moscow would allow transmission of any and all news relating to the summit talks. Soviet television officials took the position that there was no relation between the summit talks and the broadcasts.

Moscow Summit Fails to produce Breakthrough — Following 5 days of discussion, U.S. Pres. Richard M. Nixon and Soviet Communist Party leader Leonid I. Brezhnev, **July 3**, signed a number of limited nuclear agreements in Moscow. The documents fell short of the hoped for breakthrough on a permanent agreement to limit offensive nuclear weapons. Obviously disappointed, Brezhnev had said, **July 2**, that the accords "could probably have been wider." The 2 leaders did commit their countries to negotiating a new interim accord covering both qualitative and quantitative limitations on strategic nuclear weapons up to 1985. They also negotiated accords on limiting underground tests of nuclear weapons and committing each nation to a single are for deployment of antiballistic missiles. On **June 28** and **29**, Brezhnev and Nixon signed several agreements on cultural, scientific, and economic cooperation which augmented accords signed in 1972. U.S. Secretary of State Henry A. Kissinger said, **July 4**, in Paris, that the talks had faltered over difficulty in agreeing on a balance between missile totals and warhead totals — currently, the USSR leads in missiles while the U.S. holds the edge in warheads. A **July 7** front-page editorial in Pravda, the communist party organ, rebutted some western assessments of the summit, saying the complex of agreements "signifies an essential movement forward on the path of strengthening peace and mutual trust."

Military Tightens Grip on Ethiopia — Ethiopian Emperor Haile Selassie, **July 3**, acceded to 3 proposals put forth by the military, including amnesty for political prisoners and immediate institution of constitutional reforms. The army's 4th division had taken virtual control of Addis Ababa, **June 28**, and begun a new series of arrests of prominent officials. By **July 16**, the arrests numbered 80, including Defense Minister Lt. Gen. Abebe Abye. On **July 9**, the army issued guidelines for the future government. According to the 13-point manifesto, Selassie would remain as Emperor, but with reduced powers, and the military would assume a major role in cabinet decisions. Premier Endalkachew, accused by the military of responsibility in government failure to institute reforms, was ousted **July 22**.

Cabinet Collapses in Portugal — The 2-month-old cabinet of Portuguese leader Gen. Antonio da Spinola collapsed, **July 9**, when Premier Adelino da Palma Carlos and 4 other centrist ministers resigned. The resignations came when the military-dominated Council of State refused Palma Carlos the additional powers he felt he needed to effectively control the cabinet, plagued by increasing dispute between leftists and conservatives. On **July 11**, Spinola dismissed the rest of the cabinet and, **July 13**, named Col. Vas dos Santos Goncalves, an army engineer, as the new premier. On **July 17**, Spinola named a new cabinet in which half the posts went to military officers, most of whom belonged to the Armed Forces Movement which had overthrown the Caetano dictatorship in April.

Franco Delegates Powers — Hospitalized for treatment of phlebitis complicated by internal bleeding, Spain's Francisco Franco, **July 19**, delegated his powers as ruler to his designated successor, Juan Carlos de Borbon. He interrupted his dominion over the Spanish people for the first time in 35 years. By **July 23**, doctors reported that Franco had fully recov-

ered and would soon begin a long vacation. On **Sept. 2**, Franco again assumed full power as chief of state.

Tanaka Loses Strength — Continuing a decade-long decline in conservative strength, Premier Kakuei Tanaka's Liberal-Democrats suffered a considerable loss, **July 8**, in elections for the upper house of the Japanese parliament. Although Tanaka's party was reduced to 126 seats in the 252-seat house, it would continue to control it with the support of at least 2 independent conservatives.

Trudeau Wins Majority — Winning substantial gains all across Canada, Prime Minister Elliott Pierre Trudeau's Liberal party, **July 8**, increased its

---

Makarios Ousted on Cyprus; Turkish Army Invades Island; Greek Junta Quits

Led by 650 Greek officers, the Cypriot National Guard, **July 15**, in a violent coup, overthrew the government of Archbishop Makarios. Major fighting took place in Nicosia between the rebels and the pro-Makarios tactical reserve police. Fighting was also reported in Limassol, Larnaca, and Famagusta. Contrary to early reports that he had been slain, Makarios fled to Paphos, then Malta, and finally, **July 17**, flew to London to rally international support. In a radio broadcast from Paphos, Makarios charged the Greek military junta was behind the coup.

Nikos Giorgiades Sampson, a publisher and former terrorist, was named to succeed Makarios. Although a fervent supporter of EOKA-B, a pro-enosis (union with Greece) guerrilla group, Sampson was reported to have pledged to maintain an independent Cyprus. Earlier in July, Makarios had demanded the Greek military government recall the Greek officers assigned to the Cypriot National Guard, charging they were aiding the pro-enosis EOKA-B which was dedicated to overthrowing him.

The British government, one of the guarantors with Greece and Turkey of an independent Cyprus, urged Turkey and Greece to exercise restraint in the "potentially explosive" situation. Turkey announced it would not "accept any fait accompli" in Cyprus and expressed concern for the Cypriot Turkish minority, 18% of the Cypriot population. Premier Bulent Ecevit charged the coup constituted an intervention in Cyprus by Greece. Greece termed the coup the internal affair of an independent state. However, both Greece and Turkey were reported to have deployed their forces in a demonstration of military power.

As fighting continued, **July 16**, the UN Security Council met to consider the coup, but failed to act. The U.S. engaged in intensive diplomatic exchanges with Greece and Turkey to keep "a very dangerous situation" under control. London became the center of diplomatic negotiations as British Prime Minister Harold Wilson and Foreign Secretary James Callaghan met with Makarios and Ecevit, **July 17**, in an attempt to ease the tense situation.

On **July 18**, bowing to pressure from the other NATO nations, Greece agreed to gradually replace the 650 Greek officers in the Cypriot National Guard. The decision fell short of Turkey's demand for complete withdrawal of the officers.

As intensive diplomatic efforts faltered and Greece continued to reject immediate withdrawal of Greek officers, Turkey, early **July 20**, invaded Cyprus, ostensibly to protect the Turkish Cypriote minority.

At the end of the day's heavy fighting between Turkish forces and Greeks and Greek Cypriots, Turkey had established a beachhead on the northern coast and secured an inland corridor to Nicosia.

Fighting was also reported between the Turkish and Greek Cypriot communities in Nicosia. Heavy casualties were reported on both sides. Greece immediately ordered a general mobilization and moved troops to her short eastern border with Turkey. The Greek government pledged to meet "expansionist Turkish acts" at any cost."

Heavy fighting continued **July 21** with little change in battle lines. A naval clash between Greece and Turkey in the Mediterranean ended with Turkish claims it had halted a Greek landing on Cyprus.

Following intensive negotiations headed by Britain and the United States, Greece and Turkey accepted an uneasy UN-sponsored cease-fire effective **July 22** and agreed to meet in Geneva for talks on the Cyprus problem.

Discredited by its participation in the Cyprus crisis and faced with the awesome possibility of war with Turkey, the Greek military government, **July 23**, turned control of Greece over to civilian leaders. As the Greek people rejoiced, shouting "Demokratia," former Premier Constantine Karamanlis returned from self-imposed exile in Paris to be sworn in as the new head of state.

The civilian government immediately removed press censorship and, on **July 24**, pledged every decree violating the rights of citizens would be abolished. The new government also announced the release of all political prisoners and amnesty for all political crimes.

On Cyprus, strongman Sampson, **July 23**, ceded the presidency to Glafkos Clerides, the widely respected president of the House of Representatives. Sampson said that since his primary mission — the overthrow of the "personal rule" of Makarios — had been accomplished, it was time to turn the presidency over to a man with acknowledged negotiating skill. On the same day the new Athens government recognized Makarios as the legal leader of Cyprus, Clerides, **July 24**, warned that it would be very unwise for Makarios to return to Cyprus.

The Greek, British, and Turkish foreign ministers, **July 25**, began talks in Geneva on a solution of the Cyprus problem. Following initial disagreement and a temporary breakdown in talks, Greece, Turkey, and Great Britain, **July 30**, signed a standstill cease-fire on Cyprus to end fighting which had continued after the UN-sponsored cease-fire went into effect **July 22**. The agreement provided for further negotiaitons, to begin **Aug. 8**, on political problems on Cyprus. The accord also met Turkey's demand to retain its forces on Cyprus until an acceptable agreement would be reached. The 3 powers also agreed that the UN would patrol a buffer zone established between Greek and Turkish Cypriot lines.

strength from a minority to a majority in parliament in national elections. The Liberal party would hold 141 seats in the new 264-member House of Ocmmons. (For additional details, see page 497.)

General

Maheu Wins Hughes Defamation Suit — A Los Angeles, Calif., federal court jury decided, **July 1**, t lat Robert A. Maheu had been damaged by defaming statements made by his former employer, billionaire Howard R. Hughes. Maheu had demanded $17.3 million in damages because Hughes had said in a telephone news conference that he had dismissed Maheu because "he stole me blind." The money value of the damage was to be determined at a later hearing set for October.

Soviet Ballet Star Stays in Canada — The Canadian Ministry of Immigration, **July 2**, granted a special permit to Kirov ballet star Mikhail Baryshnikov to stay in Canada for one year. Baryshnikov had defected to the West, **June 29**, while appearing in Toronto as a guest star with the Bolshoi Ballet. In an interview, **July 4**, Baryshnikov stated he had defected for artistic and prsonal reasons, not pokitical ones.

Armed Convicts Seize Hostages in Washington — Two armed convicts, Frank Gorham Jr. and Otis D. Wilkerson, **July 11**, seized control of the basement cellblock of the U.S. courthouse in Washington D.C., taking 7 persons hostage. After the failure of negotiations with police and court officials to obtain free passage out of the U.S. in exchange for the 7 hostages, the convicts quietly surrendered **July 15**. The 7 hostages had managed to escape **July 14**.

Henley Convicted in Texas Mass Murders — Elmer Wayne Henley, an 18-year-old high school dropout, was convicted by a San Antonio, Tex., jury, **July 15**, of murdering 6 youths. Though accused of participating in sexual tortures and murders of at least 26 teen-aged boys, he had named the 6 youths in a written confession following his arrest in August 1973. He was sentenced, **Aug. 8**, to 6 consecutive 99-year terms, the harshest sentence allowed under Texas law.

Rep. Brasco Convicted — Rep. Frank J. Brasco, D-N.Y., was convicted, **July 19**, of conspiracy to take bribes in return for procuring a Post Office contract for a Mafia-controlled truck company. His first trial resulted in a hung jury. The one-count indictment charged that Brasco and his uncle, Joseph Brasco, now deceased, had conspired to receive $27,500 in 1968 to win a mail-hauling contract for a truck company owned by John A. Masiello, identified by federal authorities as a major Mafia figure in Westchester Co., N.Y.

Disasters — In her sweep across most of Japan and part of South Korea, typhoon Gilda left at least 108 persons dead and caused $334 million in damage, according to reports **July 11** . . . A bus collided with a truck, **July 28**, 250 miles south of Belem, Brazil, leaving at least 69 persons dead and 10 seriously injured.

AUGUST
National

Milk Co-op Fined—U.S. District Court Judge George L. Hart, **Aug. 1**, fined Associated Milk Producers Inc., the nation's largest dairy cooperative, the maximum amount of $35,000 following a guilty plea to a 6-count criminal information alleging conspiracy and illegal campaign giving in 1968, 1970, and 1972. The dairy co-op had requested leniency because the offense was a "cavalier violation" of a widely disregarded law. According to the information, recipients, all of whom denied knowledge of the donor, included

former Pres. Richard M. Nixon who received $100,-000 in 1969, in what AMPI officials had described as an effort to "make peace" with the incoming administration. Other recipients included Sen. Hubert H. Humphrey, Sen. Edmund S. Muskie, and Rep. Wilbur D. Mills, all Democrats. In further milk fund developments, former Humphrey press secretary Norman Sherman and aide Jack Valentine, **Aug. 12**, pleaded guilty to charges of aiding and abetting illegal corporate donations by the milk producers to political campaigns. The donations, according to the criminal information filed by the Watergate Special Prosecutor's office, had gone to Humphrey's 1972 presidential campaign and to other Democratic campaigns, including that of South Dakota Sen. James Abzourek.

Dean Sentenced—Former presidential counsel John W. Dean 3rd was sentenced, **Aug. 2**, by U.S. District Court Judge John J. Sirica to a minimum of one year and a maximum of 3 years in prison for his confessed role in the Watergate cover-up. At the sentencing, Dean asked for "compassion" and "understanding," saying he had tried to "right the wrong" he had committed. Dean had pleaded guilty in a special arrangement with the Watergate prosecution whereby in return for Dean's cooperation the prosecution would not press other potential charges. Although Dean had originally sought total immunity, the prosecution had found evidence against him not covered by previous grants of immunity and had been able to persuade Dean to plead guilty to one charge of conspiracy to obstruct justice.

Senate Panel Clears Kissinger—The Senate Foreign Relations Committee, **Aug. 6**, unanimously concluded that Secretary of State Henry A. Kissinger had not misled the committee about his role in the wiretapping of 17 government officials and newsmen from 1969 to 1971. In June, Kissinger had threatened to resign unless he were cleared of allegations he had misrepresented his role during confirmation hearings on his nomination as Secretary of State. The report concluded "that there were no contradictions between what Dr. Kissinger told the committee last year and the totality of new information available." The report also stated that if, at the time of the hearings, it had known what it now did, the committee would nonetheless have reported favorably on Kissinger's nomination. Reports from the State Department noted Kissinger was "gratified" and no longer saw any reason for resignation.

Connally and Jacobsen Plead—Former Treasury Secretary John B. Connally pleaded not guilty, **Aug. 9**, before U.S. District Court Judge George L. Hart Jr., to charges he had accepted a bribe, perjury, and conspiracy to obstruct justice in connection with an effort to raise federal milk price supports. On **Aug. 7**, Jake Jacobsen, the attorney for the Associated Milk Producers Inc., had pleaded guilty to bribing Connally. At the arraignment, Jacobsen said he had paid Connally a total of $10,000 in milk co-op funds in return for Connally's recommendation in March 1971 for the price increase.

Ford Attacks Inflation—In his first appearance as president before a joint session of Congress, Gerald R. Ford, **Aug. 12**, called inflation "public enemy number one" and asked for bipartisan restraint in government spending. In response to a recent Congressional proposal, Ford offered to preside over a domestic "summit meeting" to devise a bipartisan approach to creating economic growth and stability. He also called for reactivation of the Cost of Living Council to monitor wages and prices. Ford, **Aug. 13**, met with AFL-CIO Pres. George Meany, an infrequent White House visitor during the previous administration, to request the federation's cooperation to stimulate economic growth. On **Aug. 24**, Ford signed a bill establishing the Council on Wage and Price Stability, which he promised would not be a preliminary step to reintroducing a system of mandatory price and wage controls. He also warned that the council could not be expected to provide "an instant answer or immediate panacea" for inflation. Ford further promised that he would keep government spending under $300 billion for fiscal year 1975.

Access to Nixon Tapes Debated—Based on a "formal" although unwritten decision by presidential counsels James D. St. Clair and J. Fred Buzhardt, White House spokesmen said, **Aug. 14**, that tapes of former Pres. Richard M. Nixon's conversations were his personal property and would be returned to his control. On **Aug. 16**, acting through his new counsel Philip W. Buchen, appointed **Aug. 15**, Pres. Gerald R. Ford ordered that the Nixon White House tapes and documents be held in White House custody until all legal issues involving the Watergate affair were re-

solved. White House sources reported that Ford had been upset that Buzhardt and St. Clair had made their decision without consulting Watergate Special Prosecutor Leon Jaworski.

Ford Favors Limited Amnesty—In a surprise announcement, Pres. Gerald R. Ford, **Aug. 19**, told the convention of Veterans of Foreign Wars in Chicago that he favored "leniency" for the nation's estimated 50,000 military draft evaders, as a move to "bind up the nation's wounds." He also named former Indiana Rep. Richard L. Roudebush as the new administrator of the Veterans Administration. The Ford announcement on amnesty reversed a policy which had been steadfastly held by his predecessor, Richard M. Nixon. Although he would continue to oppose "unconditional blanket amnesty," Ford ordered a study to find a way young men who had refused to fight in the Vietnam war could "work their way back" to full citizenship. He disclosed he had directed Attorney General William B. Saxbe and Defense Secretary James R. Schlesinger to report to him by Sept. 1 on the status of men charged with draft eva-

Nixon Resigns as 37th U.S. President; Ford Takes Over in Smooth Transition

Following a week of dramatic developments which almost totally eroded his Congressional support, Pres. Richard M. Nixon, **Aug. 9**, resigned as the 37th president of the United States. He was the first president to resign in U.S. history. Shortly afterward, Gerald Rudolph Ford was sworn in as the 38th U.S. president.

The turning point came **Aug. 5**, when Nixon, under pressure from his counsel James D. St. Clair, released 3 transcripts of June 23, 1972 conversations with former chief of staff H.R. Haldeman along with an admission he had made "a serious act of omission" in his previous accounts of the Watergate cover-up. Nixon admitted that the transcripts showed that, on June 23, just 6 days after the Watergate break-in, he had originated plans to have the FBI halt its probe of the break-in for political as well as national security reasons. He admitted that he had kept the evidence from his lawyer, his staff, and his supporters on the House Judiciary Committee. Still maintaining that he would not resign, Nixon said that, although it was "virtually a foregone conclusion" that the House would impeach him, he hoped the Senate would look at all the evidence "in perspective" and would vote to acquit him. (For excerpts from Nixon's admission and the transcripts, see pp. 00-00.)

Nixon's Congressional support, which had slipped perceptibly since the House Judiciary Committee had voted 3 articles of impeachment, caved in almost immediately. Within 48 hours of Nixon's admission, the 10 Judiciary Committee members who had voted against all the articles of impeachment had reversed their positions, on the basis of the new evidence, and announced they would vote to impeach on Article I in the House. However, even as estimates of Nixon's support in the Senate dwindled to 20 votes, the president, **Aug. 7**, met with his cabinet to say that he would not resign, but would remain in office until the impeachment process ran its course.

However, pressure to resign, from the White House staff led by Gen. Alexander M. Haig Jr. and Congressional leaders, mounted. Three Republican leaders, Senators Hugh Scott and Barry Goldwater and House Minority Leader John J. Rhodes, met, **Aug. 7**, for 30 minutes with Nixon. Scott told the president that the situation "is very gloomy on Capitol Hill," and Goldwater informed Nixon that he had no more than 15 of the 34 votes needed to avoid conviction in the Senate.

Finally, on the evening of **Aug. 8**, following a day in which he was described as having serenely applied himself to the schedule of a busy president, Nixon, in a 16-minute television address, announced that he would resign the next day. Speaking calmly, without the often bitterness and combative language of previous statements, Nixon said he hoped his departure would start a "process of healing that is so desperately needed in America." While not referring specifically to the Watergate affair, Nixon acknowledged that some of his judgments as president may have been wrong. He cited his lack of Congressional support as a major reason for his decision to resign.

Shortly afterward, Ford, in a brief statement to the press, praised Nixon for "one of the greatest personal decisions on behalf of all of us as Americans." He also announced that Secretary of State Henry A. Kissinger had agreed to stay on with the Ford administration.

On the morning of **Aug. 9**, Nixon bid a tearful farewell to the remnants of his broken administration, telling them, "Always remember, others may hate you, but those who hate you don't win unless you hate them — and then you destroy yourself." At 11:35 a.m., he handed his resignation to Secretary of State Kissinger and boarded a plane for San Clemente, Calif.

At 12:03 p.m. Supreme Court Chief Justice Warren E. Burger administered the oath of office to Gerald R. Ford. Stressing his awareness that he had become the first president not to be elected to office, Ford pledged to conduct an administration of "openness and candor." Stating that "our long national nightmare is over," Ford called upon the nation to "bind up the internal wounds of Watergate. His voice breaking, he also asked the nation to pray for his predecessor, that the man "who had brought peace to millions" might "find it for himself."

Delving into the process of transition of power, Ford named a 4-member committee — former Pennsylvania Gov. William W. Scranton, NATO Ambassador Donald M. Rumsfeld, Interior Secretary Rogers C.B. Morton, and John O. Marsh, a member of his vice presidential staff — to oversee the transition and make recommendations on staff changes. He also named Detroit Press Washington columnist J.F. terHorst as his press secretary.

sion on desertion. In response to Ford's position, Ray Soden, National Commander of the 1.8 million-member VFW, stated that the group would remain opposed to any kind of amnesty. Generally, draft dodgers and evaders showed little enthusiasm for Ford's conciliatory move. They had consistently argued that they accept nothing short of unconditional amnesty and viewed the idea of forced service as an implication they had done something wrong. On **Aug. 31**, Ford met with Saxbe and Schlesinger who proposed that returning draft evaders and deserters perform some sort of alternate public service, as well as swear some type of oath of allegiance. Ford asked for additional information from the 2 cabinet members before making his decision.

U.S. Ambassador Slain on Cyprus—On **Aug. 19**, in the midst of a demonstration in Nicosia staged by Greek Cypriots to express bitterness at their defeat by Turkish forces armed with U.S. weapons, U.S. Ambassador Rodger P. Davies was shot and killed. Also killed was an embassy secretary who rushed to his aid. Warrants were issued for 3 persons, **Aug. 20**, in connection with the killing. Police said that the juxtaposition of the demonstration and the shooting suggested both had been planned.

Rockefeller Nominated As Vice President—Ending 12 days of extensive speculation, Pres. Gerald R. Ford, **Aug. 20**, named former New York Gov. Nelson A. Rockefeller as his choice for vice president. With few exceptions, the choice was widely applauded in Congress. In the nomination speech, Ford said he regarded Rockefeller as "a good partner for me" and "a good partner for our country and the world." Ford noted that because he had ascended to the presidency without being elected, he had consulted a broad spectrum of his party — all Republican Congressmen, all Republican governors, and members of the Republican National Committee — before making his decision. Rockefeller, in response, praised Ford for reawakening "faith and hope" in the American people and said he was optimistic about the long-term future. A few hours later, Rockefeller went to Capitol Hill to confer with Sen. Howard W. Cannon and Rep. Peter W. Rodino, the chairmen of the 2 Congressional committees which would conduct the confirmation hearings.

Impeachment Inquiry Issues Final Report—The House of Representatives, **Aug. 20**, without fanfare or debate, passed a resolution, 412-3, accepting the report of the Judiciary Committee on its impeachment inquiry. The report, had Richard M. Nixon not resigned the presidency, would have been the basis for impeachment proceedings in the House and trial by the Senate. The resolution commended the committee for its "conscientious and capable effort" and called the inquiry "full and complete." The 528-page report, published **Aug. 22**, contained the evidence on which the 3 articles of impeachment against Nixon had been voted, personal statements by all the committee members except Chairman Peter W. Rodino, and majority and minority opinions on each of the articles. In the section on Article I which alleged Nixon had participated in a criminal conspiracy to cover-up the Watergate break-in, the 11 representatives who had originally dissented, cited the new evidence released by Nixon on **Aug. 5**, which had caused them to reverse their positions. In a signed statement, they declared that Nixon had not been "hounded from office" by his critics, but rather that Nixon "had imprisoned the truth about his role in the Watergate cover-up so long and so tightly within the solitude of his Oval Office that it could not be unleashed without destroying his Presidency." (For further excerpts from the report, see pp. 35-40.)

Cover-up Trial Delayed—Reversing an earlier decision, U.S. District Court Judge John J. Sirica, **Aug. 22**, accepted a U.S. Court of Appeals recommendation that he postpone the Watergate cover-up trial for 3 weeks. It had been scheduled for Sept. 9. Watergate Special Prosecutor Leon Jaworski had asked for more time for "all parties" to review the recently surrendered White House tapes and to resolve the legal status of former Pres. Richard M. Nixon in the case. On **Aug. 29**, Nixon was served a subpoena, initiated by former aide John D. Ehrlichman, to appear in his defense at the trial.

Steinbrenner Fined—George M. Steinbrenner, an industrialist and principal owner of the New York Yankees, **Aug. 30**, was fined $15,000 by a U.S. District Court in Cleveland, Ohio, on charges of making illegal corporate campaign contributions to former Pres. Richard M. Nixon and several Democratic Congressmen. He had pleaded guilty to the charge **Aug. 23**. The American Shipbuilding Co., of which Steinbrenner is chairman, was also fined $20,000 for 2 violations of federal campaign laws. According to sources, members of the Watergate Special Prosecutor's staff were incensed at the light sentence for what they considered the strongest case of campaign violation abuse under investigation.

International

Greece Restores 1952 Constitution—Premier Constantine Karamanlis' civilian government, **Aug. 1**, restored the 1952 Greek constitution which had been abolished in 1968 by a referendum following the 1967 military coup. The government stipulated that legislative power would be vested in the cabinet and the government would retain the right to rule by decree until a Constitutional Assembly was held. Constitutional provisions relating to the monarchy were temporarily suspended and executive powers vested in the presidency, thus postponing the controversial decision of whether deposed King Constantine would be recalled from exile. On **Aug. 21**, King Constantine said he would be willing to accept severe restrictions on the monarchy in return for an opportunity to return to Greece. He said he favored a role similar to the monarchs of Scandinavia and Britain. Meanwhile, the civilian government continued its purge of military elements associated with the junta which had ruled since 1967. On **Aug. 19**, the Supreme Council of National Defense, dominated by civilian cabinet officers, fired 10 key generals and appointed new generals to top service posts.

Turkey Divides Cyprus, Declares Cease-fire—Halting an intensive drive begun **Aug. 14**, Turkish military forces completed a division of Cyprus, **Aug. 16**, declared a unilateral cease-fire, and announced readiness to resume talks in Geneva with Britain and Greece on the political future of Cyprus. Turkish Premier Bulent Ecevit declared that Turkey was now in a position "where the foundations have been laid for a new federal state of Cyprus in which the rights and security of the Turkish Cypriots would be guaranteed." Fighting actually continued until **Aug. 18** when the cease-fire took hold with Turkey in control of about 40% of the island. The military offensive had begun following the breakdown of the Geneva talks. Turkey had refused to grant a 36-hour recess to allow Greek Cypriot representatives to consult with their government on a Turkish proposal to divide Cyprus into a number of separate communities under Greek Cypriot and Turkish Cypriot administration. The Geneva talks had begun early in August to attempt to draw cease-fire lines between the combatants in accord with the **July 30** cease-fire agreement. During that time, Turkish forces, meeting no effective opposition from Greek Cypriot forces, had continued to advance across Cyprus. In reaction to Turkey's renewed military advances, Greece, Aug. 14, had withdrawn her military forces from NATO, blaming the NATO allies for failing to stop Turkish aggression. However, on **Aug. 15**, Greek Premier Constantine Karamanlis told the Greek people that Greece would not go to war over Cyprus. Armed opposition was impossible, Karamanlis said, by reason of distance as well as the fact of Turkey's overwhelming military advantage. On Aug. 16, Karamanlis rejected Turkey's proposal to resume peace talks and also rejected an invitation to go to the U.S. to discuss the Cyprus crisis with Pres. Gerald R. Ford. Referring to Turkey's military division of Cyprus, he emphatically stated that it would be naive for anyone to think Greece would "negotiate under pressure of a fait accompli." As the month continued, efforts to renew peace talks bogged down. On Aug. 24, Greek Foreign Minister George Mavros announced acceptance of a USSR proposal for a 15-nation conference to find a political solution for the Cyprus crisis and for withdrawal of all foreign troops. However, Turkey, Aug. 27, rejected the Soviet plan and called for Greece to resume negotiations at Geneva "without delay." Some progress, however, was made, Aug. 26, when UN Secretary General Kurt Waldheim, after separate meetings, brought together Cypriot Pres. Glafkos Clerides, Greek, and Vice President Rauf Denktash, Turkish, for their first meeting since the breakdown of the Geneva talks. Waldheim arranged for the 2 to hold future weekly meetings to discuss humanitarian problems.

Assassination Attempt Kills Park's Wife—A bullet intended for South Korean Pres. Park Chung Hee, **Aug. 15**, struck and killed his wife. Park had been delivering a Liberation Day speech in Seoul. The assailant was tentatively identified as Mun Se Kwang, a Korean living in Japan. On Aug. 17, investigators charged that the assassination attempt had been ordered by North Korean Pres. Kim Il Sung. On Aug. 20, Park accepted the resignations of 2 high officials who took responsibility for the assassination attempt. They were Pak Chung Gyu, Park's long-time confidant and bodyguard, and Home Minister Hong Jong Chul whose ministry included the police assigned to guard the president.

Selassie Stripped of Some Powers—Strengthening their grip on Ethiopia, the armed forces, **Aug. 16**, stripped 82-year-old Emperor Haile Selassie of more of his powers. As a squadron of jets flew over Addis Ababa and tanks, armored cars, and troop carriers paraded through the streets, the military abolished the emperor's crown council, court of justice, and military council. Arrests of Selassie's closest associates continued, Aug. 9-17, bringing the total to over 150.

South Korean President Rescinds Emergency Decrees—South Korean Pres. Park Chung Hee, Aug. 23, lifted 2 politically repressive decrees in what appeared to be the first move to ease the campaign he had conducted against political opponents since January. The first decree, imposed Jan. 8, had forbidden all discussion, criticism, and demands for revision of the 1972 constitution, which gives the president unlimited power. The second, dating to Apr. 3, barred all dissent against the government and its policies, with penalties ranging from 5 years imprisonment to death. Two decrees remained: one establishing secret courts-martial and permitting arrests without warrants and another cutting taxes for low income persons and raising taxes on luxury goods. Over 100 persons, many of them students charged with advocating the overthrow of the government, had been arrested and convicted under the rescinded decrees.

Portugal Begins Dissolution of African Empire—Ending more than 11 years of fighting, Portugal, Aug. 26, signed an agreement in Algiers with representatives of the African Party for the Independence of Guinea-Bissau and the Cape Verde Islands granting independence to Portuguese Guinea, effective Sept. 10. A de facto cease-fire had existed since shortly after the April military coup in Portugal. In the agreement, Portugal promised to remove by Oct. 31 all troops from the territory, to be called Guinea-Bissau. The accord also provided for a referendum to be held at a future unspecified date on the future of the Cape Verde Islands, administered as part of Portuguese Guinea. The referendum decision, a compromise by the African rebels who had demanded the islands be part of the new republic, had opened the way for the agreement.

Terrorists Kidnap Former Mexican Leader—A band of 4 armed terrorists, Aug. 28, kidnapped J. Guadalupe Zuno Hernandez, the 83-year-old father-in-law of Mexican Pres. Luis Echeverria Alvarez. A political power in Mexico for a half century, Zuno was formerly governor of Jalisco state and founder of the University of Guadalajara. On Aug. 29, the Mexican government, following a policy established by Pres. Echeverria after the 1973 kidnapping of U.S. General Consul Terrence G. Leonhardy, refused to negotiate with the terrorists. Released unharmed Sept. 8, Zuno criticized his son-in-law's government for allowing "itself to come under the control of the reactionary forces of the world."

UN Population Conference Meets—Ending a 10-day meeting in Bucharest, Romania, the United Nations World Population Conference, consisting of some 1,250 delegates from 135 nations, Aug. 30, adopted a vaguely-worded Plan of Action to curb world population growth. Approved by acclamation after extensive revisions sought chiefly by the underdeveloped nations, the action plan did not set any national or international goals or focus on the question of overpopulation potentially overtaxing the world's food supply and other resources. Rather, the 108-item, 10,000-word program suggested that proper policies, formulated by nations individually could substantially reduce the world's current 2% population growth rate. The plan stressed that population control be subordinated to social and economic development policies which were deemed the key to solving population problems. The conference also stressed equality of women in all walks of life and suggested the affluent nations of the world reduce consumption of world resources in the name of "international equity." On many occasions, the conference had been interrupted by political digressions, namely attacks by China against the 2 superpowers, the U.S. and USSR, as "chief culprits" behind the poverty of the underdeveloped world.

Bonn Makes Loan to Italy—West German Chancellor Helmut Schmidt and Italian Premier Mariano Rumor announced, Aug. 31, that West Germany had agreed to grant a $2 billion credit to Italy to bail the country out of its financial crisis. Schmidt said he would also support a plan for a European Common Market loan to Italy. The $2-billion loan was aimed at strengthening Italy's lira, battered by a huge balance-of-payments deficit.

General

4 Die in Texas Prison Escape Attempt—Four persons, 2 inmates and 2 of their hostages, died, Aug. 3, in a shoot-out during an escape attempt at the state penitentiary in Huntsville, Tex. Three armed inmates, including the dead men, Fred Gomez Carrasco and Rudolpho Dominguez, had held 12 prison employees and fellow prisoners hostage in the penitentiary library for 11 days in an attempt to bargain for their freedom. A preliminary autopsy, **Aug. 5**, indicated the 2 inmates had killed themselves. However, after the official report, **Aug. 28**, that Carrasco and Dominguez had been killed by law officers in what was ruled a justifiable homicide, Tex. Gov. Dolph Briscoe, **Aug. 29**, ordered a special court inquiry into the incident.

Soviet Mountaineers Perish—A Japanese-American mountain climbing team, **Aug. 8**, discovered 7 frozen bodies of a team of 8 Soviet women mountain climbers on an expedition in the Soviet Pamirs. The 8th woman was believed to have been blown over a summit ridge. The women had been attempting to traverse the 23,400-ft. Mt. Lenin, when they were caught in a severe snowstorm and perished **Aug. 7**.

GM Agrees to Rollback Prices—Under pressure from Pres. Gerald R. Ford, the General Motors Corporation announced, **Aug. 21**, that it was lowering to 8.5% its previously announced 9.5% increase in prices for 1975 models.

2nd Soviet Space Link-Up Fails—Following up the successful docking of the USSR's Soyuz 14 with the orbiting space station Salyut 3 in July, Soyuz 15 abruptly ended its mission **Aug. 28**, after an apparent failure to achieve a link-up with Salyut 3. The Soyuz missions were being conducted to test equipment in preparation for the 1975 joint Soviet-American docking of a Soyuz with a U.S. Apollo spaceship.

Disasters—As month-long flooding brought on by torrential monsoons began to subside in Bangladesh, **Aug. 12**, a death toll of at least 2,500 persons was reported. Waters had covered 20,000 of the nation's 55,000 square miles. Cholera was reported spreading widely in the wake of the floods. . . . An Air-Mali airliner crashed, **Aug. 12**, near Ouagadougou, Upper Volta, killing 47 persons. . . Of 50 persons aboard, 49 died, **Aug. 14**, when a Venezuelean airliner crashed on the Caribbean island of Margarita during a violent rainstorm. . . At least 78 persons were reported dead and more than a million homeless, **Aug. 21**, as flood waters began to recede in central Luzon in the Philippines. . . A train derailed, **Aug. 30**, in the main railroad station in Zagreb, Yugoslavia, leaving 150 persons dead.

SEPTEMBER
National

Ford Makes Appointments — In the first major change in a key post under his administration, Pres. Gerald R. Ford, **Sept. 4**, named National Republican Committee Chairman George Bush as his envoy to China, replacing David K. E. Bruce. Ford appointed Louise Smith to fill Bush's post. Previously serving as a co-chairman of the Republican National Committee, Smith became the first woman to head the Republican party. On **Sept. 16**, Ford nominated his chief of staff, Gen. Alexander M. Haig Jr., as Supreme Allied Commander of NATO, effective Dec. 15. Effective Nov. 1, Haig would also serve as Commander of U. S. Force in Europe. To succeed Haig, Ford, **Sept. 24**, named NATO ambassador Donald Rumsfeld to be an assistant to the president with cabinet rank. Rumsfeld would be in charge of administration and coordination.

CIA Role in Chile Probed — According to reports released, **Sept. 7**, by The New York Times, CIA director William E. Colby testified in Congressional hearings last April that the Nixon administration had authorized the spending of more than $8 million for covert CIA activities in Chile from 1970 to 1973 to make it impossible for socialist Pres. Salvador Allende Gossens to govern. According to Colby, the operations were considered a test of the technique of using heavy cash funding to bring down a government antagonistic to the United States. He also testified that all of the opeations had been approved by Henry A. Kissinger's 40 Committee, a secret high-level intelligence panel. On **Sept. 8**, Massachusetts Rep. Michael J. Harrington called for full-scale public hearings on the matter and said he would formally ask the House Foreign Relations Committee to summon Kissinger and Colby to testify. On **Sept. 14**, it was reported by well-informed sources that Kissinger had directed a far-reaching program by the Nixon administration to curtail economic aid and credits to Chile before Allende's election. On **Sept. 16**, again in reports in The New York Times, former Chilean Ambassador Edward M. Korry stated that, in fact, during Allende's first year of rule, the U. S. had pursued "an extraordinary soft line" and had tried to develop a "modus vivendi" with Allende's socialist government. Also on **Sept. 16**, Pres. Gerald R. Ford, at his first news conference, supported clandestine use of the CIA "to help implement foreign policy and protect national security." He acknowledged CIA activities had been conducted because "there was an effort being made by the Allende government to destroy opposition news media, both the writing press as well as the electronic press, and to destroy opposition political parties." In response to the multiplying allegations about the CIA's role in Chile, the Senate Foreign Relations Committee, **Sept. 17**, ordered an inquiry to study available evidence that official testimony on these activities had been misleading. On **Sept. 19**, as intelligence sources revealed the CIA had secretly financed striking labor unions and trade groups in Chile for more than 18 months before Allende's overthrow, Kissinger told the Senate Foreign Relations Committee that CIA activities had been authorized to keep alive political parties and the news media, never to subvert the Allende government.

Ford Announces Amnesty Program—Pres. Gerald R. Ford proposed, **Sept. 16**, to offer conditional amnesty to those Vietnam era draft evaders and military deserters who would be willing to work up to 2 years in public service jobs. The announcement of the plan had been delayed from its scheduled Sept. 10 date because Ford had been tied up with his decision to grant former Pres. Richard M. Nixon an unconditional pardon. Although, he said, the "serious offenses" of draft evasion and military desertion need not "be condoned," Ford, sounding a favorite theme, continued, "reconciliation calls for an act of mercy to bind the nation's wounds and heal the scars of divisiveness." Under his "earned re-entry program," Ford established a 9-member presidential clemency board to review cases of those who had already been convicted or punished for desertion or draft evasion. The board would be headed by former New York State Sen. Charles E. Goodell and include Notre Dame Pres. Rev. Theodore M. Hesburgh, a proponent of unconditional amnesty. Military deserters and draft evaders who had not been punished or convicted would have until Jan. 31, 1975, to turn themselves into authorities, to reaffirm their allegiance to the U.S., and to agree to spend up to 2 years in public service jobs, ranging from hospital attendants to conservationists. The length of alternative service would be decided by the parent service on a case-by-case basis. On **Sept. 17**, the government ordered he release from prison of about 95 draft evaders on 30-day furloughs while the clemency board reviewed their cases under Ford's program. On **Sept. 18**, government officials said that thousands of military deserters would be allowed to return and receive undesirable discharges without performing any alternative service. Officials maintained this action was not a loophole in the Ford plan but had been taken into consideration by the Pentagon, which did not want to take deserters back into the military. On the weekend of **Sept. 22**, a group representing exile organizations in Canada, France, and Britain, agreed unanimously to condemn the Ford program. By the end of October, only 1,481 out of an estimated 12,500 military deserters had applied for amnesty and 500 of these were already in military custody. Of an estimated eligible 6,800 draft evaders, only 66 had surrendered. Only 560 of some 213,000 convicted evaders and deserters had applied to the Clemency Review Board for a review of their cases.

Price Index Rises 1.3%—During the month of August, according to figures released **Sept. 20**, the Consumer Price Index rose 1.3%, the largest monthly increase since 1947, with the exception of periods immediately following lifting of price freezes. The only exception to a general rise in prices for food, consumer goods, and services was a decrease in gasoline prices. The 1.3% increase brought the price index to 150.2 against its 1967 base of 100.

Ford, Kissinger Warning on High Oil Prices—In separate speeches, both Pres. Gerald R. Ford and Henry A. Kissinger, **Sept. 23**, issued warnings that continued high prices set by oil-producing nations imperiled the world economy and could lead to a "breakdown of world order and safety." Addressing the 9th World Energy Conference in Detroit, Mich., Ford said the U.S. recognized the need of oil producers to develop their own economies, but "that sovereign nations cannot allow their policies to be dictated, or their fate decided, by artificial [price] rigging and distortion of world commodity markets." Kissinger, giving a gloomy assessment of the world situation to the UN General Assembly, implied that if U.S. cooperation to help nations like Saudi Arabia and Iran to diversify their economies failed to ease the oil price situation, the U.S. might be forced to change its policy. Arab nations reacted angrily to the remarks, charging the U.S. was waging a war of nerves against the Arab countries.

Kennedy Pulls Out of Presidential Race—Sen. Edward M. Kennedy, **Sept. 23**, announced that he would not seek the Democratic nomination for president in 1976. Kennedy, who had been the acknowledged

Ford Pardon For Former President Greeted by Widespread Criticism

Early Sunday morning, a time not generally associated with major political announcements, Pres. Gerald R. Ford, **Sept. 8**, announced that he was granting an unconditional pardon to former Pres. Richard M. Nixon for all federal crimes that he " committed or may have committed or taken part in" while serving as president. Nixon issued a statement from San Clemente, Calif., saying he accepted the pardon and that he had been "wrong in not acting more decisively and more forthrightly in dealing with Watergate."

Shortly thereafter, White House Press Secretary J. F. terHorst resigned his post as a matter of conscience in protest over the pardon. TerHorst specifically cited the "injured" reputations and families of former Nixon aides who were either indicted or in prison for Watergate-related cases. Deputy Press Secretary John W. Hushen replaced terHorst as acting press secretary. Democrats vociferously joined in terHorst's protest, expressing dismay and disapproval of the decision.

In issuing the pardon, Ford said he intended the action to spare the former president and the nation further punishment in the Watergate scandals. Ford further said that his decision was based on the fact that "many months and perhaps more years will have to pass" before Nixon could obtain a fair trial. Additionally, in a comment not included in his original statement, Ford said it was common knowledge that allegations and accusations hanging over Nixon were "threatening his health." (For the text of the pardon and excerpts from Ford's accompanying statement, see p. 40.)

Presidential counsel Philip W. Buchen explained that Ford's "act of mercy" had been made without any demands on Nixon and without consultation with Watergate Special Prosecutor Leon Jaworski who was responsible for prosecuting the Watergate Case. Jaworski announced that he would not contest the pardon.

Buchen also announced that the Ford administration had come to an agreement with Nixon on the custody of the former president's papers and tapes.

According to the agreement signed **Sept. 6**, in San Clemente, the materials would be preserved for 3 years for possible use in court cases arising out of the Watergate scandals. After 3 years, Nixon could destroy any or all of the tapes. All the tapes were to be destroyed on Sept. 1, 1984 or at Nixon's death, if it occurred prior to that date.

Reports, **Sept. 9**, from reliable sources, suggested Nixon's ultimately successful attempts to beat back demands for a revealing statement on his Watergate role had delayed the granting of the pardon. To clarify the issue of whether Nixon's acceptance of the pardon implied guilt, Buchen, **Sept. 10**, said granting a pardon "can imply guilt — there is no other reason for granting a pardon." He added that he had told Ford a pardon carried an implication of guilt and that had not deterred him.

Following the pardon decision, a barrage of widespread criticism from all over the country began to pour into the White House. Criticism was spurred by reports, **Sept. 10**, that Ford was considering a pardon for all those convicted or accused of crimes in Watergate and related scandals. Solid bipartisan opposition to a blanket pardon led to a Ford decision, announced **Sept. 12**, not to pardon any of the Watergate defendants until the judicial process was completed in each case.

Speculation that Nixon's health was instrumental in the pardon decision was accelerated, **Sept. 16**, despite continued White House denials, by reports Ford's chief of staff, Gen. Alexander M. Haig Jr., had told the president, on **Aug. 29**, that without an unconditional pardon it might be too late to avert "a possible personal and national tragedy" of Nixon's complete physical and mental collapse.

A battery of questions about the pardon greeted Ford, **Sept. 16**, at his first news conference. Ford adamantly insisted that he had made "no deal" with Nixon before his resignation in the matter of granting a pardon. He did, however, concede that the "antagonism" to his decision had stunned him, but not swayed his belief it had been correct.

frontrunner for the nomination, said, "I simply cannot do that to my wife and children and the other members of my family." He added that the decision was "firm, final and unconditional." In addition to his own children, Kennedy is surrogate father to the children of his dead brothers, John F. Kennedy and Robert F. Kennedy. Kennedy's decision broke open the Democratic field, pointing to an open convention in 1976.

Nixon Enters the Hospital—Former Pres. Richard M. Nixon, **Sept. 23**, entered Memorial Hospital Center in Long Beach, Calif., for extensive tests and treatment of a flare-up of the phlebitis from which he had suffered during his Middle East trip. Former Nixon physician Maj. Gen. Walter Tkach had reported, **Sept. 14**, that Nixon had suffered a new attack of phlebitis in his left leg; however, despite the advice of his doctors and family, Nixon had refused to enter the hospital. The state of Nixon's health had become the subject of wide speculation since Pres. Gerald R. Ford, in granting an unconditional pardon to Nixon, **Sept. 8**, had alluded to Nixon's weakening health.

Rockefeller Confirmation Hearings Held—The Senate Rules Committee, **Sept. 23-26**, held public hearings on the nomination of Nelson A. Rockefeller as vice president. At the opening of the hearings which focused on the vast Rockefeller family fortune, Rockefeller said he hoped the "myth or misconception" about that fortune and its influence would be "exposed and dissipated." Rockefeller revealed that the total of his wealth and that of his wife and children was $218 million, mostly held in trusts. He said his net worth was $62.5 million and that his yearly income over the past 10 years had averaged $4.6 million before taxes. He further said that during his lifetime he had paid $69 million in taxes, but had paid nothing in 1970. Rockefeller's most vigorous interrogator was Virginia Sen. Robert C. Byrd who challenged Rockefeller on the issue that his wealth posed a problem of undue power.

Calley Conviction Overturned—U.S. District Court Judge J. Robert Elliott, **Sept. 25**, in Columbus, Ga., overturned the conviction of Lt. William L. Calley Jr. in the 1968 massacre of civilians in Mylai, South Vietnam. He ordered Calley released "forthwith" from the military prison at Ft. Leavenworth. In the decision, Elliott ruled that "massive adverse pretrial publicity" had made a fair trial impossible. He also contended the charges in the case had been "improperly drawn and illegally used," and that Calley had been denied the right to call certain witnesses. The Army said it would not comply with the order for release and would appeal the decision to a higher court.

Pell and Javits Go to Cuba — Against the expressed wishes of the State Department, Sen. Jacob K. Javits and Sen. Claiborne Pell, both members of the Senate Foreign Relations Committee, **Sept. 27**, flew for a weekend visit to Cuba. They were preceded by a chartered plane carrying 28 reporters and photographers. On **Sept. 28**, the senators met with Cuban Foreign Minister Raul Roa and Pres. Osvaldo Dorticos Torrado to discuss the possibility of renewing U. S.-Cuban ties broken since 1961. After meeting for 3 hours with Cuban Premier Fidel Castro, the senators said they believed Castro was "interested — that is our impression — in working toward better relations with the United States, a normalization of relations."

White House Holds Economic Summit — Pres. Gerald R. Ford, **Sept. 28**, ended a 2-day national conference on inflation by saying he would move quickly to present "a coherent and consistent" policy to fight "stagflation," the joint threat of inflation and economic recession. He also announced the creation of an Economic Policy Board to consolidate and coordi-

nate the administration's economic efforts. Treasury Secretary William E. Simon was named to chair the board. Ford also established a White House Labor-Management Committee and named Princeton University economics professor Albert Rees to head his newly established Council on Wage and Price Stability. The inflation conference had nearly collapsed as Democratic Congressional leaders and labor representatives had attacked administration economic policy. Earlier in the month, in preparation for the inflation conference, Ford had met separately with leading economists, labor leaders, businessmen, and others, in give-and-take sessions for ideas to battle inflation and economic recession.

International

U. S., East Germany Establish Relations — The United States and East Germany, **Sept. 4**, established diplomatic relations. The U. S. was the last major western national to recognize East Germany since it emerged from virtual international isolation 3 years ago. The U. S. named John Sherman Cooper, former Republican senator from Kentucky, ambassador to East Berlin and Rolf Sieber, a 44-year-old professor of economics, was named ambassador to the U. S. Diplomatic recognition was negotiated by East German Foreign Ministry official Herbert Suss and U. S. Assistant Secretary for European Affairs Arthur A. Hartman. Establishment of relations had been made possible when East Germany had agreed to hold future discussions on the possible compensation of Jewish victims of Nazism.

Mozambique Pact Reached — Portuguese Foreign Minister Mario Soares and Samora Machel, leader of the Front for the Liberation of Mozambique (Frelimo), **Sept. 7**, signed an agreement, in Lusaka, Zambia, providing for a provisional Mozambique government headed by Frelimo until formal independence set for June 25, 1975. A cease-fire ending the 10-year-war in the country also went into effect. A few hours later, white settlers in protest of the pact seized control of the radio station in Lourenco Marques and brought commercial life to a halt. The white backlash movement, calling itself the Movement for a Free Mozambique, formally urged Portuguese officials to modify the agreement, asserting control should not be given to Frelimo without a test of popular sentiment. However, failing to get support from the Portuguese armed forces, the white settlers' resistence collapsed **Sept. 10**. The interim government was installed, **Sept. 20**.

Ethiopian Emperor Deposed — Culminating a process begun last February, the Ethiopian armed forces, **Sept. 12**, peacefully deposed 82-year-old Emperor Haile Selassie. Selassie, formerly hailed as the "Lion of Judah," had ruled Ethiopia for 58 years. The Armed Forces Committee, which over the past months had stripped Selassie of his powers, did not declare an end to the monarchy, but called for the return of the emperor's partially-paralyzed son, 57-year-old crown prince Asfa Wossen, to be crowned as figurehead king with no powers. The coordinating committee also announced that a provisional government headed by Lt. Gen. Aman Michael Andom would rule until elections could be held. The committee dissolved parliament, banned all strikes and unauthorized demonstrations, and proclaimed a domestic program based on equality for all Ethiopians and priority for land reform. On **Sept. 18**, the provisional military government announced the time was not acceptable for a civilian government, but, faced with mounting demands, announced, **Sept. 22**, the formation of a 48-member civilian advisory board.

Terrorists Seize French Embassy — Three armed members of the Japanese Red Army terrorist organization, **Sept. 13**, seized part of the French embassy in The Hague, Netherlands, taking 9 hostages, including Count Jacques Senard, the French ambassador. They threatened to kill the hostages one by one unless a comrade identified as Yutaka Furuya were freed from prison in France. Although Furuya was immediately flown to The Hague, negotiations stalled until **Sept. 17**, when the terrorists released their hostages and, taking Furuya with them, flew to an undisclosed destination. The French government also paid a $300,000 ransom. On **Sept. 18**, the 4 terrorists landed in Damascus, Syria, and turned themselves, as well as the ransom, over to the Palestine Liberation Organization.

Soviet Art Show Disrupted—Soviet vigilantes, **Sept. 15**, using bulldozers and dump trucks, broke-up an outdoor exhibition of nonconformist Soviet art as it was being set up on a vacant lot and seized some of the paintings. Two water trucks chased a fleeing crowd of some 100 persons, including artists, western correspondents, and diplomats. Three American journalists were struck. The 13 organizers of the exhibit, claiming Moscow authorities had told them the lot was available, sent a written protest to the Communist Party Politburo protesting lawlessness, arbitrary misuse of force, and violation of their constitutional rights. On **Sept. 16**, a Moscow municipal court imposed 15-day prison terms and fines on 5 of the organizers on charges of petty hooliganism for resisting the vigilantes. Oskar Rabin, one of the sentenced artists, said the group would attempt to hold the same show in the same place on Sept. 29. Authorities, **Sept. 18**, returned 10 of the 18 seized paintings, but said they would bar further shows. On **Sept. 20**, in a reversal, Moscow authorities said the artists could hold a show in 8 days, on a Saturday, in woods near Ismailovsky Park. The artists, **Sept. 22**, rejected the proposal saying they wanted to hold their show on Sunday when more people would be free to attend. On **Sept. 24**, Moscow authorities yielded and, **Sept. 29**, more than 10,000 people attended the first officially-sanctioned show of modern art in the USSR since the avantgarde movement of the 20s.

South Korea, Japan Settle Dispute—The Japanese government, **Sept. 19**, offered South Korea both written and oral expressions of regret, settling a diplomatic dispute which had arisen over the **Aug. 15** assassination attempt on South Korean Pres. Park Chung Hee. Park's wife was killed in the attempt. The Japanese embassy in Seoul had been the target of South Korean demonstrations Sept. 6-12. At a rally on **Sept. 9**, 15 persons had cut off their little fingers to rally anti-Japanese sentiment. Demonstrators charged Japan was not cooperating with the investigation of the assassination attempt.

Prisoners Exchanged on Cyprus—Cypriot Pres. Glafkos Clerides, representing the Greek community, and Vice President Rauf Denktash, leader of the Turkish Cypriots, **Sept. 20**, agreed to exchange all prisoners captured during the recent war on Cyprus. According to the agreement, about 5,000 prisoners would be released at the places of their choice. Previously, the 2 leaders, **Sept. 12**, had agreed on a partial exchange of all ill, wounded, and under-18-year-old prisoners of war. The talks, arranged by UN Secretary General Kurt Waldheim, almost collapsed when Denktash, **Sept. 2**, had cancelled the first meeting following discovery of a mass grave containing the bodies of 84 Turkish Cypriots. He had charged that Greek Cypriot soldiers had committed "mass murder" of Turkish civilians. The Clerides government had denied such murders had been committed.

Dominican Terrorists Seize Hostages—Armed terrorists, identified as Dominican leftists, **Sept. 27**, seized Barbara A. Hutchison, director of the U.S. Information Service in the Dominican Republic, in Santo Domingo, and then seized the Venezuelan embassy, taking 7 more hostages. Proclaiming themselves "The Freedom Movement of 12th January," the 7 terrorists announced they had planted bombs in the embassy and would blow it up unless the U.S. paid $1 million in ransom and 38 prisoners were released from Dominican jails. One hostage escaped **Sept. 28**. As terrorists continued the seige, the Dominican left, **Oct. 1**, denied all association with the terrorists. On **Oct. 7**, Dominican Pres. Joaquin Balaguer offered the terrorists safe conduct out of the country in return for the hostages. The terrorists, **Oct. 9**, freed the remaining hostages and immediately flew to Panama where they had been promised asylum.

Spinola Resigns in Portugal—Gen. Antonio de Spinola, provisional president of Portugal, resigned **Sept. 30**. Three other conservative members of the 7-man ruling junta who had been linked by leftists to an alleged right-wing plot against the provisional government also resigned. The unexpected move left the government chiefly in the hands of leftist military officers and civilians. The Portuguese left had won a major victory, **Sept. 28**, by forcing Spinola and his conservative supporters to cancel a mass demonstration in Lisbon. However, leftists and Spinola had come to a truce, **Sept. 29**, on measures to strengthen the democratization process. Gen. Francisco da Costa Gomes, head of the armed forces and close associate of Spinola, replaced the president.

General

Busing Protested in Boston — Violent protest, centered at Boston's South Boston High School, **Sept. 12**, marked the start of the city's busing program to integrate its public schools. Five youths were arrested for disorderly conduct, including rock throwing. Fear of violence and a boycott called by white parents kept attendance at South Boston High at 100 out of 1,500 enrolled pupils. Federal District Judge W. Arthur Garrity had ordered the busing last June after having found the school system to be deliberately segregated. Other areas of Boston where violence had been expected remained quiet, although system-wide attendance was found to be about 65% of normal. After the first day's incidents, Mayor Kevin H. White ordered police escorts for the school buses involved in the busing plan.

Wounded Knee Defendants Freed — U. S. District Court Judge Fred. J. Nichol, **Sept. 16**, dismissed all charges against Dennis J. Banks and Russell C. Means, leaders of the 1973 Indian takeover of Wounded Knee, S. Dak. The 2 defendants faced 3 counts of assault on government officials, one of conspiracy, and one of larceny. In the dismissal, Nichol berated the prosecution, the Justice Department, and particularly the FBI for their handling of the case. The FBI, which earlier in the trial had been shown to lie and suborn perjury, Nichol said, "has certainly deteriorated."

Fifi Batters Honduras — In a sweep across Nicaragua, Honduras, El Salvador, Guatemala, and Belize before dying down over southeastern Mexico, Hurricane Fifi, **Sept. 19-20**, wreaked havoc in Honduras. According to official Honduran estimates, 7,000-8,000 persons were killed and some 300,000 left homeless in ensuing floods and landslides. As the U. S. and many other nations and international relief organizations flew in donations of food, medicine, clothing, and other supplies, Honduran officials, **Sept. 22**, ordered mass cremations to stem epidemics and further deaths. Hardest hit was Choloma, 12 miles north of San Pedro Sula, where 2,700 of the town's 5,000 people were reported dead. However, on **Sept. 25**, the U. S. Army disaster unit, which had come to aid the devastated country, announced that, based on "confirmed deaths and reliable sources," only about 1,000 persons had died in all of Honduras.

Disasters — A U. S.-bound TWA airliner crashed, **Sept. 8**, in the stormy Ionian Sea off Greece, killing all 80 persons aboard . . . Attempting to land at Charlotte, N.C., an Eastern Airlines DC-9, **Sept. 11**, crashed into nearby woods, killing 69 of the 82 persons aboard . . . All 70 persons aboard died when an Air Vietnam Boeing 727 exploded during a hijacking attempt, **Sept. 15**, near a provincial air field on the South Vietnamese coast.

OCTOBER
National
Watergate Cover-up Trial Opens — The trial of 5 former aides of Richard Nixon accused of covering up the Watergate scandal began **Oct. 1**, in Washington, D.C. Facing charges including conspiracy, obstruction of justice, and perjury were former domestic affairs assistant John D. Ehrlichman, former chief of staff H. R. Haldeman, former Attorney General John N. Mitchell, former Mitchell assistant Robert C. Mardian, and former attorney for the Committee to Re-elect the President Kenneth W. Parkinson. The presiding judge, John J. Sirica, **Sept. 30**, ordered a separate trial for a 6th defendant, Gordon C. Strachan, formerly aide to Haldeman, because his case had become involved in a legal tangle. On **Oct. 11**, a jury of 3 men and 9 women was impaneled and sequestered for the duration of the trial. The special Watergate prosecution opened its case, **Oct. 14**, charging former Pres. Richard M. Nixon had held a "multitude of meetings" in April 1973 and 1974 to devise "scenarios" and "lines" for handling the Watergate situation and for sacrificing some persons to the prosecution to save others.

Soviet Grain Sales Halted — Treasury Secretary William E. Simon announced, **Oct. 4**, that the administration had put a hold on 2 contracts for sales of 125 million bushels of grain to the USSR. The action was explained as an anti-inflation move to discourage speculation in grain markets at a time when U.S. crop prospects had been damaged by bad weather. All major grain-exporting would, according to the announcement, be informed that no major contracts could be signed in the future without specific prior approval of the White House.

Ford Delivers Economic Plan — Urging a "new mobilization" against inflation, Pres. Gerald R. Ford, **Oct. 8**, proposed a broad, basically conservative, program to deal with the nation's sagging economy. Ford said that if inflation were not whipped, it would "destroy our country, our homes, our liberties, our property and finally our national pride — as surely as any well-armed war-time enemy." Ford's program included a one-year 5% tax surcharge on corporate and individual incomes, exempting families with a gross income less than $15,000. Ford said that, with Congressional agreement, he would keep federal spending below $300 billion for fiscal year 1975. To deal with inflation casualties, Ford proposed additional benefits for those who had exhausted regular unemployment benefits.

Jaworski Quits — Watergate Special Prosecutor Leon Jaworski, **Oct. 12**, announced that he was resigning effective Nov. 1. Taking pains to make clear his resignation was in no way associated with Pres.

Gerald R. Ford's unconditional pardon of former Pres. Richard M. Nixon, Jaworski said he believed the work of the Watergate special prosecution was largely completed. He recommended Deputy Special Prosecutor Henry S. Ruth Jr. be named as his successor. On **Oct. 26**, Ruth was sworn in as the 3rd Watergate special prosecutor.

Rockefeller Discloses Money Gifts — On **Oct. 5**, vice-presidential nominee Nelson Rockefeller disclosed he had made gifts of $50,000 to Henry A. Kissinger, $86,000 to a former Republican New York state chairman, and an unspecified amount, later disclosed to be $625,000 for Dr. William J. Ronan, chairman of the Port Authority of New York and New Jersey. On **Oct. 11**, Rockefeller made public a list of 20 others to whom he had given a total of approximately $2 million over the past 17 years. On **Oct. 14**, Rockefeller took full responsibility for a derogatory biography about Arthur J. Goldberg, published in 1970 when they were rivals for the New York governorship.

Compromise Reached on Aid to Turkey—Ending a month-long deadlock with the administration, Congress, **Oct. 17**, passed compromise legislation which would continue aid to Turkey until Dec. 10. Pres. Gerald R. Ford had twice before vetoed similar legislation to cut off aid to Turkey. In the compromise, Ford reluctantly agreed to accept the legislation, an appropriations bill with provisions dealing with aid to Turkey. Under the provisions, military aid to Turkey would be cut off after Dec. 10 and resumed only when the president certified that Turkey was in compliance with U.S. foreign aid laws barring offensive use of American weapons and that "substantial progress" had been made toward a Cyprus settlement. The president could also continue or restore aid if he found it would "further negotiations for a peaceful solution of the Cyprus conflict."

Compromise on Soviet Trade Reached—Sen. Henry M. Jackson, **Oct. 18**, made public an exchange of letters between himself and Secretary of State Henry A. Kissinger disclosing a compromise to provide trade benefits to the USSR in return for a substantial relaxation of Soviet emigration policies. Opening the way for passage of a long-sought omnibus trade bill, Jackson said he had received assurances that the compromise could lead to annual emigration of at least 60,000 Jews and others from the Soviet Union.

Tape Accord Delayed—U.S. District Court Judge Charles R. Richey, **Oct. 21**, issued a temporary restraining order barring the Ford administration from carrying out its agreement with former Pres. Richard M. Nixon on his White House tapes and papers. Richey ordered that all the materials he held at the White House and released only in response to subpoenas. He further said that Nixon would only gain access to the materials "for the sole purpose of preparing to testify in the Watergate (cover-up) criminal trial." In arguments before Richey, Nixon attorney Herbert J. Miller disclosed that the "death clause" providing for destruction of the materials upon Nixon's death would not become effective for 5 years.

Ford Makes Changes in Energy Team—Pres. Gerald R. Ford, **Oct. 29**, announced the forced resignation of Federal Energy Administrator John C. Sawhill. Andrew E. Gibson, who served as Maritime Administrator and as assistant secretary of commerce for domestic and international business in the first Nixon administration, was named to replace Sawhill. Ford also named Dixie Lee Ray, chairman of the now defunct Atomic Energy Commission, to the new post of assistant secretary of state for oceans and national environmental and scientific affairs; Robert C. Seamans Jr. to head the new Energy Research and Development Administration, which will take over the research work of the AEC and other agencies; and former astronaut William A. Anders as chairman of the new Nuclear Regulatory Commission, which will take over the AEC's responsibility for regulating peaceful uses of nuclear power. Ford said, "This is a new team that will be in charge of the energy program" under Interior Secretary Rogers C.B. Morton, who also heads the new Energy Resources Council.

Nixon Undergoes Surgery—Intensive internal bleeding, 6 hours after surgery to combat a potentially lethal blood clot in the left leg, **Oct. 29**, sent former Pres. Richard M. Nixon into shock for 3 hours. After a team of physicians and intensive care nurses applied countershock measures, Nixon returned to a stable vascular condition; he remained on the hospital's "critical list." Nixon had re-entered Memorial Hospital Medical Center in Long Beach, Calif., **Oct. 23**, because of complications in his phlebitis condition. He underwent surgery to place a plastic clamp on a vein in his pelvis to prevent a clot in his upper thigh from breaking loose and moving through his heart to lodge in either lung. On **Oct. 31**, Nixon showed improvement, but remained on the critical list.

International

Labor Victor In British Elections—Following a 3-week campaign in which voters voiced disenchantment with almost every political party, Harold Wilson's Labor party, **Oct. 10**, won a slim e-seat majority in Great Britain's 635-seat House of Commons. The majority had eluded Wilson in February's parliamentary election. Edward Heath's Conservative party lost 20 seats and Jeremy Thorpe's Liberal party lost 2 seats.

New Oil Discoveries in Mexico — Mexican oil officials, **Oct. 15**, confirmed reports that new discoveries of large deposits of oil had been made in the southeast part of Mexico. However, they maintained early reports suggesting reserves of up to 20 billion barrels of oil had been exaggerated. They estimated crude oil exports would rise from 35,000 barrels daily to about 137,000 barrels a day by 1975. On **Oct. 21**, Mexican Pres. Luis Echeverria Alvarez, meeting with U.S. Pres. Gerald R. Ford on both sides of the U.S.-Mexican border near Nogales, Ariz., said the oil would be put on the world market when developed.

Kissinger Confers in Moscow — Having completed 4 days of talks with top Soviet leaders, U.S. Secretary of State Henry A. Kissinger, **Oct. 27**, said the 2 countries had moved considerably closer to a formula for limiting offensive strategic weapons. "We're aiming for a strategic arms limitation agreement during 1975," said Kissinger, "and I think there is a reasonable chance." However, no details on the talks were made available. On **Oct. 26**, Kissinger and Communist party leader Leonid A. Brezhnev had announced that Pres. Gerald R. Ford would meet with Brezhnev in November in the Vladivostok area. The meeting would be held in preparation for a general summit next summer.

Arab Nations Support PLO — Meeting in Rabat, Morocco, the heads of state of 20 Arab nations, **Oct. 28**, including Jordan's King Hussein, unanimously called for the creation of an independent Palestinian state "on any Palestinian land that is liberated" from Israeli occupation. The Arab leaders also recognized Palestine Liberation Organization leader Yasir Arafat as the "sole legitimate representative of the Palestinian people." Also on **Oct. 29**, during the final moments of the conference, the Arab nations agreed on a 4-year multi-billion-dollar program to aid the PLO and Egypt, Syria, and Jordan — the 3 countries bordering on Israel. The funds would be provided by the Arab oil-producing countries. Earlier in the month the UN General Assembly had voted, **Oct. 14**, to give the PLO a voice at its meetings.

U.S. Pledges Grain to India — Following a meeting between U.S. Secretary of State Henry A. Kissinger and senior Indian officials, it was announced, **Oct. 29**, that the U.S. would supply at least 500,000 tons of grain at reduced prices to India. A joint U.S.-India communique following Kissinger's 3-day visit underlined the "broadening" relationship between India and the U.S.

General

Franklin National Declared Insolvent, Sold—In the largest bank failure in U.S. history, Franklin National Bank, **Oct. 8**, was declared insolvent and sold to the European-American Bank and Trust Co., a New York-chartered entity owned by the 6 of Europe's largest banks. Depositors were told they would suffer no losses and there would be no interruption of services to the public. The Securities and Exchange Commission, **Oct. 17**, filed fraud charges against 9 former officers, directors, and employees of the bank and its parent company, the Franklin National Corp.

Ford Busing Comment Angers Boston Mayor— Speaking about the Boston school desegregation order which had spurred violence in that city since the beginning of September, Pres. Gerald R. Ford, **Oct. 9**, said he had "consistently opposed" forced busing to achieve racial balance. He added that he deplored the violence that had occurred and called upon Boston citizens to respect the law. Mayor Kevin H. White, **Oct. 10**, accused Ford of having "fanned the flames of resistance" to school integration and of possibly having endangered the lives of Boston schoolchildren. Persistent violence and resistance, including a one-day system-wide boycott, had led to an **Oct. 8** request by White for federal marshals. When refused, White, **Oct. 9**, readied some 300 state police and 100 Metropolitan District Commission police to enforce the law. As the situation intensified, Mass. Gov. Francis W. Sargent, **Oct. 15**, asked Ford to send federal troops and mobilize National Guard units. On **Oct. 16**, the Pentagon placed units of the 82nd Airborne Division at Ft. Bragg on "increased readiness" for use if needed. On **Oct. 31**, federal district Judge W. Arthur Garrity signed a "final order" instructing the Boston School Committee to develop a city wide school integration plan by **Dec. 16**. The plan, effective next fall, would replace the interim court-ordered plan for desegregation currently under way. At month's end violence and tension had eased substantially.

Ali Regains Title—Muhammad Ali became the second man in boxing history to regain the world heavyweight championship, **Oct. 30**, when he knocked out George Foreman in the eighth round of their early morning bout at Kinshasa, Zaire. The 32-year old Ali was considered the underdog in the match with the younger, more powerful Foreman. The crowd of nearly 60,000 was clearly rooting for Ali, chanting "Ali, bomaye" meaning "Ali, kill him." Ali, once known as Cassius Clay, had been stripped of his heavyweight crown in 1967 by the World Boxing Assn. and other groups for refusing to enter military service.

Laws Passed, Bills Vetoed During 93d Congress, 2d Session (1974)

The 93d Congress convened for its 2d session Jan. 21, 1974. Major bills passed and signed into law by either President Nixon or President Ford, as well as other actions during the session, included:

Signed by Nixon

OMB Confirmations. Required that future appointments of directors and deputy directors of the Office of Management and Budget be confirmed by the Senate (signed Mar. 2).

Minimum Wage Raised. Provided the basic minimum wage would rise from $1.60 to $2 May 1, 1974; to $2.10 Jan. 1, 1975, and $2.30 Jan. 1, 1976. Slightly delayed pay rises were set for farm workers and some others. Coverage was extended to an additional 7 million workers in federal, state and local government, domestic service, chain stores (Apr. 8).

FEA Established. A Federal Energy Administration was created with powers to fix gasoline allotments, ban prohibitive profits and develop export-import policies (May 7).

Mail Hikes Postponed. Put off until 1979 rate increases on newspapers, magazines, books, records, etc. scheduled for 1976; and from 1981 to 1987 for non-profit organizations (June 30).

Budget Reform. Curbed the president's power to impound appropriated funds by requiring Congressional agreement; also changed beginning of fiscal year from July 1 to Oct. 1 starting 1976 (July 12).

Aid to Cattlemen. Provided $2 billion in government-backed emergency loans to livestock producers (July 26).

Signed by Ford

Gold Ownership. Decreed an end, as of Dec. 31, 1974, to the 40-year ban on sale or purchase of gold by private citizens (Aug. 14).

Education and Busing. Provided $25.2 billion over 4 years in aid to elementary and secondary schools; placed restrictions on busing for desegregation, prohibiting it beyond the school next closest to a student's home except by court determination that it was necessary (Aug. 21).

Housing Aid. Provided $11.1 billion over 3 years for locally-administered community development grants to replace Model Cities and Urban Renewal programs, rent subsidies for low-income families, loans to developers of housing for the aged and handicapped, and experimental cash housing allowances for poor persons (Aug. 22). (See Housing Aid below also.)

Wage-Price Stability. Created a monitoring agency as sought by Ford, the Council on Wage and Price Stability (Aug. 24).

Pension Reform. Established federal standards for existing private pension plans including employes' eligibility, vesting and funding benefits, a government guarantee corporation, and tax deductions for those outside plans who set up their own. (Sept. 2).

Standard Time Restored. Amended 1973 law that set up year-long daylight saving (to save energy); provided return to standard time Oct. 27, 1974 to Feb. 23, 1975 (Oct. 5).

Election Finance Reform. Provided for public financing of presidential elections with each major party candidate getting $20 million (from voluntary $1 checkoffs on federal income tax returns); placed limits on amounts Senate and House candidates may spend; set limit of $25,000 an individual may contribute to all federal candidates and organizations in an election year (Oct. 15).

Railroad Pensions. Congress overrode a Ford veto and passed into law (360-12 in the House, 72-1 in the Senate) a railroad retirement bill providing $285 million annually for 25 years to prop up pensions to retired railroadmen (Oct. 16).

Housing Aid. Provided $3 billion to finance up to 100,000 new homes through government purchase of mortgages to aid the housing industry (Oct. 18).

Turkey Aid "Cutoff." After 2 successive attempts to cut off aid to Turkey had been vetoed by Ford, compromise legislation was signed by him (Oct. 18); it allowed military aid to Turkey to continue to Dec. 10 providing Turkey did not send U.S.-supplied war implements to Cyprus; after Dec. 10 it would be cut off until the president certified no U.S. weapons were being used offensively and substantial progress had been made toward a Cyprus agreement.

Ford Defeated on Pay Hikes

The Senate, 64-35, rejected a plea by President Ford to postpone for 3 months a 5.52% pay increase for 3.6 million federal employes; the Senate action, Sept. 19, allowed the increases to go into effect as scheduled Oct. 1. The president had sought the delay as an anti-inflation move.

Vetoes by Ford

In addition to veto actions on aid to Turkey and railroad pensions (see both above), Ford also:

Vetoed a freedom-of-information bill which had a provision that a petitioner could ask a federal judge to decide whether specific classified information on foreign policy or national defense should be made public (Oct. 17).

Vetoed a pay hike for U.S. marshals (Aug. 13).

Vetoed an animal health research bill (Aug. 13).

Vetoes by Nixon

Vetoed an emergency energy bill which provided authority for gasoline rationing and a rollback of prices (Mar. 6).

Vetoed a $13.5 billion appropriations bill providing funds for the Agriculture Department and several agencies, saying it exceeded his 1975 budget limit by $540 million (Aug. 8).

Things Congress Didn't Do

Because of a filibuster, the Senate again failed to ratify the 25-year-old UN agreement to outlaw genocide. The vote was 7 short of the two-thirds necessary to cut off the filibuster (Feb. 6).

Another Senate filibuster killed a proposal, already passed by the House, to set up a consumer protection agency. The proposal, at issue for 5 years, failed this time on a 64-34 vote to close debate, 2 votes short of the needed two-thirds (Sept. 19).

Attempts, started 100 years ago, to have the U.S. convert to the metric system, failed again when the House voted down a voluntary, 10-year conversion plan, 240-153 (May 7).

A national health insurance bill, despite an urgent appeal from Ford to pass such a measure, was suddenly abandoned by the House Ways and Means Committee (Aug. 22).

A tax reform amendment which would have cut taxes on low and middle incomes and raised them for many businesses, including the oil industry, failed when backers could not stop a filibuster, getting only a 48-50 vote, far from two-thirds, on a motion to close debate (June 26).

Major Decisions of the U.S. Supreme Court, 1974

The U.S. Supreme Court ruled 6-3, that a grand jury may legally use illegally obtained evidence as a basis for questioning witnesses (Jan. 8, 1974).

The court also:

Held, 5-4, that a state may not require political parties to take loyalty oaths (Jan. 9).

Ruled that public school systems cannot force a female teacher to take maternity leave "before a firm date in the last few weeks of pregnancy (Jan. 21).

Unanimously held that San Francisco public schools must provide English language instruction to Chinese-speaking pupils (Jan. 21).

Refused to review the conviction of Arthur Bremer in the shooting of Alabama Gov. George C. Wallace. (Feb. 19).

Liddy Disbarred

Disbarred G. Gordon Liddy, convicted in the Watergate burglary, from practicing before it (Feb. 25).

Ruled, 8-1, that a conscientious objector, although he did 2 years of civilian service, is not entitled to veterans educational benefits (Mar. 4).

Held, 6-3, that cable TV companies don't have to pay copyright fees to networks whose material they retransmit to subscribers (Mar. 4).

Declared unconstitutionally vague, 6-3, a Massachusetts law which made it a crime to treat the U.S. flag "contemptuously"; in this case a man wearing a flag sewn onto his pants (Mar. 25).

Unanimously struck down a California law requiring political candidates to pay filing fees (Mar. 26).

Upheld, 7-2, a Belle Terre, N.Y., village ordinance barring occupancy of one-family houses by more than 2 people who are not related; the zoning law was aimed at "groupers" and communes (Apr. 1).

Upheld, 6-3, the 1970 Bank Secrecy Act, turning down claims that it unconstitutionally invaded the privacy of depositors by requiring banks to report certain domestic and foreign money transactions.

Unanimously refused to review a lower court ruling which rejected charges that then-president Nixon ordered the 1973 Cambodia bombing illegally, without Congressional authorization (Apr. 15).

Kent Parents Can Sue

Held, 8-0, that parents of 3 Kent State Univ. students killed in 1970 had a right to bring suit against the then governor and officers of the Ohio National Guard, declaring states and officials do not have immunity from suits in cases where deprivation of federal rights is claimed (Apr. 17).

Refused, 8-0, to re-examine a Memphis school desegregation plan which transferred some black pupils to all-white schools but kept 40% of black pupils in all-black schools to save money by limiting busing (Apr. 22).

Let stand a lower court decision upholding a Massachusetts state contract requiring builders to use all possible means to employ minorities in at least 20% of jobs in all categories (Apr. 22).

Refused to decide, 5-4, in the Marco DeFunis - University of Washington Law School case, whether the school could give admission preference to blacks with lower academic and test records over whites with higher records (Apr. 23).

Upheld, 6-3, a Florida law giving widows, but not widowers, a $500 property tax exemption on the grounds that women have greater difficulty coping financially than do men after the death of a spouse (Apr. 23).

Unanimously held that a number of narcotics sellers were illegally convicted in 1970 on wiretap evidence authorized by the attorney general's executive assistant instead of the attorney general (May 13).

Upheld, 5-4, a Louisiana law permitting a seller of installment goods to get a court order to repossess them when payments are overdue, without hearing or notice to the buyer (May 13).

Let stand a lower court decision barring the University of Mississippi from interfering with publication of an English department magazine containing words school officials considered obscene (May 13).

Unanimously ruled that a Colorado state inspector who stepped onto a factory's land to make visual tests for air pollution had a right to do so (May 20).

Ruled, 6-3, that a person bringing a class action suit must notify all identifiable members of the class potentially benefited, no matter what the cost of doing so (May 28).

Let stand a decision declaring unconstitutionally broad and general a Louisiana obscenity law barring lewd and indecent publications (May 28).

Equal Pay for Women

Upheld, 5-3, a 10-year-old federal law requiring employers to pay women equal wages with men for equal work; it was the court's first action on the law (June 3).

Let stand a decision that James Earl Ray, convicted killer of the Rev. Dr. Martin Luther King Jr., could have a hearing on his claim that his lawyers advised him to plead guilty so as to increase their income from a book (June 3).

Agreed to decide whether the Watergate grand jury had the right to name Richard Nixon, then president, as an unindicted co-conspirator in the Watergate cover-up (June 15). But on July 24 the court ruled, 8-0, it should not have agreed to the review and left Nixon's name in the indictment.

Ruled, 6-3, that California can deny illness disability payments to women with normal pregnancies (June 17).

Unanimously held that the movie "Carnal Knowledge" was not obscene and that jurors may apply their own "community standards" in dealing with obscenity cases (June 24).

Upheld, 5-4, the federal law under which an advertisement for an illustrated version of a presidential commission's report on obscenity was barred from the mails (June 24).

Unanimously declared an unconstitutional restriction on freedom of the press a Florida law requiring newspapers to print replies from political candidates criticized in the papers (June 25).

Nixon Must Give Up Tapes

Ruled, 8-0, that then-president Nixon would have to surrender tape recordings and other data on 64 White House conversations for use as evidence in the Watergate cover-up trial of former subordinates (July 24).

Held, 5-4, that busing pupils across school district lines between a black inner city (Detroit) and white suburbs was improper and contrary to the tradition of local school control (July 25).

Refused to overturn the conviction of a Russian spy, letting stand a lower court decision that the president may order wiretaps, without court warrants, to obtain foreign espionage information, as long as the taps are reasonable (Oct. 15).

Declined to review a decision upholding the N.Y. City Transit Authority's right to fire a member of its police force who violated regulations by growing a goatee (Oct. 15).

Vital Statistics

Source: Division of Vital Statistics, National Center for Health Statistics, Public Health Service

First Half-Year, January-June 1974

Births

During the first half of 1974 there were 1,510,000 live births, about 2% fewer than for the first half of 1973. The birth rate for this period was 14.4 per 1,000 population compared with 14.8 for the corresponding period in 1973, and the fertility rate was 66.2 births per 1,000 women 15-44 years of age, compared with 68.9 for the earlier period.

Marriages

Provisional data for the first half of 1974 indicate that the marriage rate may be declining from the 1972-1973 level, the highest level reached since 1950.

In the first half of 1974, 36,000 fewer marriages were performed than in the first half of 1973. The marriage rate for the period was 9.8 per 1,000 population a decline of 3.9% from the rate for the first half of 1973.

Divorces

The number of divorces and annulments granted during the 6 months ending with June was up about 6.0%, to 476,000, from the corresponding period in 1973. The rate was 4.5 per 1,000 population, up from 4.3 for the first half of 1973, a 4.7% increase.

Deaths

The death rate for the first half of 1974 was 9.4, as compared with 9.8 for the same period in 1973.

During January-May 1974 the rates for the following causes of death were significantly lower when compared with the same period a year earlier: hyperplasia of prostate decreased 44.4%, infections of the kidney decreased 22.6%, and influenza and pneumonia were down 22.3%. There were no significant increases during January-May 1974.

Provisional Statistics
12 months ending with June 1974

	Number		Rate*	
	1974	1973	1974	1973
Live births	3,112,000	3,191,000	14.8	15.3
Deaths	1,950,000	1,974,000	9.3	9.4
Natural increase	1,162,000	1,217,000	5.5	5.9
Marriages	2,241,000	2,286,000	10.6	10.9
Divorces	940,000	873,000	4.5	4.2
Infant deaths	53,100	57,800	17.1	18.1
Population base (in millions)			210.7	209.9

*Per 1,000 population

Annual Report for the Year 1973 (Provisional Statistics)

The birth rate for 1973 — 15.0 per 1,000 population — declined to a record low level for the United States in a period that witnessed the number of marriages continuing to rise, but at a decreasing rate. The provisional vital statistics summarized here show that births exceeded deaths by 1,164,000.

In 1973 the number of live births in the United States declined to an estimated 3,141,000, about 4 percent fewer than the number estimated for 1972. The birth and fertility rates declined to record low levels in 1973. The birth rate was 15.0 per 1,000 population and the fertility rate was 69.3 births per 1,000 women 15-44 years of age. These rates were 4 and 6 percent lower, respectively, than in 1972.

Although these rates are at record low levels, the population grew by 1,164,000 persons during 1973 as a result of natural increase, the excess of births over deaths. These declines were more than enough to offset a 2-percent increase in the number of women in the childbearing ages (assumed to be 15-44 years), resulting in a decline of about 115,000 births.

Deaths

There were approximately 1,977,000 deaths to residents of the United States during 1973, 15,000 more than in 1972. However, the provisional death rate for 1973 was 9.4 per 1,000 population, the same as the rate recorded for 1972. In 1973 there were approximately 55,300 infant deaths resulting in an estimated infant mortality rate of 17.6 per 1,000 live births. This was the lowest annual rate ever recorded in the United States and represents a decrease of 4.9 percent from the estimated rate of 18.5 in 1972. The infant mortality rate was a record low for every month in 1973 except February. Both the neonatal (under 28 days) and the postneonatal (28 days to 11 months) mortality rates declined in 1973 with the neonatal rate showing a proportionately greater decline than the postneonatal rate. The estimated expectation of life at birth in 1973 was 71.3 years for the total population, the highest life expectancy ever attained in the United States.

Marriages and Divorces

During 1973 approximately 2,277,000 marriages were performed in the United States, about 8,000 more than in 1972, or an increase of less than 0.5 percent. The provisional marriage rate remained the same for 1973 as for 1972, 10.9 per 1,000 population. The number of marriages increased in 34 states and declined in 16 and the District of Columbia.

Both the number and the rate of divorces and annulments granted in the United States continued to increase in 1973. The provisional number of divorces granted was 913,000. This represented an increase of 74,000 or 9 percent over the number of divorces granted in 1972. The divorce rate was 4.4 per 1,000 population, the highest national rate ever reported and 10 percent above the 1972 rate. The previous all-time peak of 4.3 per 1,000 population occurred in 1946. When comparing 1973 with 1963, the divorce rate nearly doubled. The average annual increase was around 5 percent for the years 1963 to 1968 and a little over 8 percent from 1968 to 1973.

Births and Deaths in the United States

Data refer only to events occurring within the United States, including Alaska beginning in 1959 and Hawaii in 1960. Excludes fetal deaths. Rates per 1,000 population enumerated as of April 1 for 1955, and 1960; estimated as of July 1 for all other years. (P) Provisional.

	Births				Deaths			
			Totals				Totals	
Year	Males	Females	Number	Rate	Males	Females	Number	Rate
1955	2,073,719	1,973,576	4,047,295	24.6	872,638	656,079	1,528,717	9.3
1960	2,179,708	2,078,142	4,257,850	23.7	975,648	736,334	1,711,982	9.5
1965	1,927,054	1,833,304	3,760,358	19.4	1,035,200	792,936	1,828,136	9.4
1970	1,915,378	1,816,008	3,731,386	18.4	1,078,478	842,553	1,921,031	9.5
1971	1,822,910	1,733,060	3,555,970	17.2	1,077,332	850,210	1,927,542	9.3
1972(P)	NA	NA	3,256,000	15.6	1,095,310	866,640	1,962,000	9.4
1973(P)	NA	NA	3,141,000	15.0	1,097,830	879,090	1,977,000	9.4

Births and Deaths by States

Source: Division of Vital Statistics, National Center for Health Statistics.

States	Births 1973	Births 1972	Deaths 1973	Deaths 1972	States	Births 1973	Births 1972	Deaths 1973	Deaths 1972
Alabama	59,760	61,869	35,604	34,313	Montana	11,189	11,361	6,763	6,847
Alaska	6,640	6,797	1,457	1,492	Nebraska	22,899	23,500	15,150	15,615
Arizona	37,980	37,258	17,238	16,082	Nevada	8,800	8,793	4,524	4,460
Arkansas	32,687	32,985	21,881	21,571	New Hampshire	11,077	11,294	7,700	7,482
California	300,637	303,542	174,297	167,979	New Jersey	93,478	97,529	67,824	66,974
Colorado	39,345	39,869	19,060	18,453	New Mexico	20,643	20,589	8,129	7,994
Connecticut	36,342	39,130	26,778	26,490	New York	241,349	254,431	179,448	182,570
Delaware	8,222	8,867	5,137	5,153	North Carolina	85,772	89,491	48,027	47,345
Dist. of Col.	19,919	21,579	9,769	10,393	North Dakota	10,376	10,577	6,003	5,819
Florida	107,879	108,985	90,251	85,396	Ohio	160,946	170,347	101,087	102,164
Georgia	90,048	84,337	40,402	44,189	Oklahoma	39,770	41,246	26,720	25,967
Hawaii	15,334	15,324	4,594	4,487	Oregon	31,731	32,303	20,915	20,289
Idaho	13,996	13,828	6,290	6,114	Pennsylvania	154,560	164,742	126,895	127,051
Illinois	166,844	175,604	107,871	108,894	Rhode Island	12,659	13,495	9,496	9,601
Indiana	84,388	87,191	49,761	48,622	South Carolina	47,787	49,007	24,580	23,587
Iowa	39,303	41,383	29,193	29,799	South Dakota	10,545	10,728	6,558	7,078
Kansas	30,610	31,637	22,106	21,922	Tennessee	68,484	69,752	42,383	41,610
Kentucky	55,663	55,419	34,447	33,857	Texas	218,200	219,822	103,228	99,971
Louisiana	65,887	68,611	35,272	34,314	Utah	27,958	27,934	7,685	7,571
Maine	15,314	15,892	10,906	11,174	Vermont	6,305	7,180	4,440	4,451
Maryland	47,349	51,059	32,191	32,826	Virginia	68,980	71,939	40,540	40,199
Massachusetts	74,777	79,522	62,214	63,037	Washington	45,447	47,148	30,532	29,881
Michigan	140,731	147,187	77,427	77,923	West Virginia	28,146	29,679	20,248	20,739
Minnesota	54,273	56,629	34,571	34,991	Wisconsin	62,584	64,142	41,491	42,088
Mississippi	44,399	45,449	23,766	23,218	Wyoming	5,912	5,814	3,020	2,999
Missouri	71,496	74,981	53,433	52,653	Total	3,141,000	3,256,000	1,977,000	1,962,000

Marriages, Divorces and Rates in the United States

Source: Division of Vital Statistics, National Center for Health Statistics.

Data refer only to events occurring within the United States, including Alaska beginning with 1959 and Hawaii with 1960. Rates per 1,000 population.

Year	Marriages[1] No.	Rate	Divorces[2] No.	Rate[3]	Year	Marriages[1] No.	Rate	Divorces[2] No.	Rate[3]
1890	570,000	9.0	33,461	0.5	1940	1,595,879	12.1	264,000	2.0
1895	620,000	8.9	40,387	0.6	1945	1,612,992	12.2	485,000	3.5
1900	709,000	9.3	55,751	0.7	1950	1,667,231	11.1	385,144	2.6
1905	842,000	10.0	67,976	0.8	1955	1,531,000	9.3	377,000	2.3
1910	948,166	10.3	83,045	0.9	1960	1,523,000	8.5	393,000	2.2
1915	1,007,595	10.0	104,298	1.0	1965	1,800,000	9.3	479,000	2.5
1920	1,274,476	12.0	170,505	1.6	1970	2,179,000	10.7	715,000	3.5
1925	1,188,334	10.3	175,449	1.5	1971	2,196,000	10.6	768,000	3.7
1930	1,126,856	9.2	195,961	1.6	1972(p)	2,269,000	10.9	839,000	4.0
1935	1,327,000	10.4	218,000	1.7	1973(p)	2,277,000	10.9	913,000	4.0

(1) Includes estimates and marriage licenses for some states for all years. (2) Includes reported annulments. (3) Divorce rates for 1945, based on population including armed forces overseas. (p) Provisional.

Marriages and Divorces by States 1973[1]

Source: Division of Vital Statistics National Center for Health Statistics

(Divorces include reported annulments) [1] Provisional.

State	Marriages	Divorces	State	Marriages	Divorces	State	Marriages	Divorces
Alabama	48,178	21,273	Louisiana	39,469	NA	Oklahoma	41,053	20,523
Alaska	3,836	2,056	Maine	11,997	4,680	Oregon	19,596	11,917
Arizona	26,022	NA	Maryland	48,171	14,165	Pennsylvania	101,183	30,497
Arkansas	26,075	17,205	Massachusetts	46,213	14,469	Rhode Island	7,698	2,409
California	170,173	117,677	Michigan	94,974	26,046	South Carolina	55,961	7,903
Colorado	27,262	14,189	Minnesota	32,878	10,962	South Dakota	12,312	1,808
Connecticut	25,959	7,890	Mississippi	28,889	11,081	Tennessee	56,326	22,122
Delaware	4,272	2,187	Missouri	53,755	22,023	Texas	151,167	64,759
Dist. of Col.	5,665	2,975	Montana	7,812	3,779	Utah	14,818	5,270
Florida	88,838	56,021	Nebraska	13,770	5,071	Vermont	4,986	2,146
Georgia	66,972	23,975	Nevada	102,866	8,550	Virginia	58,336	16,151
Hawaii	9,758	3,964	New Hampshire	9,615	3,364	Washington	42,040	21,785
Idaho	12,268	4,477	New Jersey	59,308	21,761	West Virginia	18,152	7,286
Illinois	120,606	45,323	New Mexico	15,136	6,179	Wisconsin	40,097	11,642
Indiana	61,144	NA	New York	155,807	47,460	Wyoming	5,048	2,224
Iowa	27,629	9,176	North Carolina	47,299	18,648			
Kansas	24,686	10,566	North Dakota	5,745	1,383	Total	2,277,000	913,000
Kentucky	37,102	12,783	Ohio	103,754	48,907			

Wedding Anniversaries

The traditional names for wedding anniversaries go back many years in social usage. As such names as wooden, crystal, silver and golden were applied it was considered proper to present the married pair with gifts made of these products or of something related. While the list of permissible gifts is extensive, gifts are most appropriate when retaining a suggestion of the originals. Thus the wooden anniversary may call for anything of wood, including furniture, but as the years mount the gifts become more valuable until the 60th or diamond anniversary, calls for diamonds. The traditional list follows, with a few allowable revisions in parentheses.

1st—Paper	6th—Iron	11th—Steel	20th—China	45th—Sapphire
2nd—Cotton	7th—Wool, copper	12th—Silk	25th—Silver	50th—Gold
3rd—Leather	8th—Bronze	13th—Lace	30th—Pearl	55th—Emerald
4th—Linen, (silk)	9th—Pottery, (china)	14th—Ivory	35th—Coral	60th—Diamond
5th—Wood	10th—Tin, (aluminum)	15th—Crystal	40th—Ruby	

Leading Causes of Death
United States: 1972 Estimates

Source: National Center for Health Statistics, U.S. Public Health Service, HEW & The American Heart Association

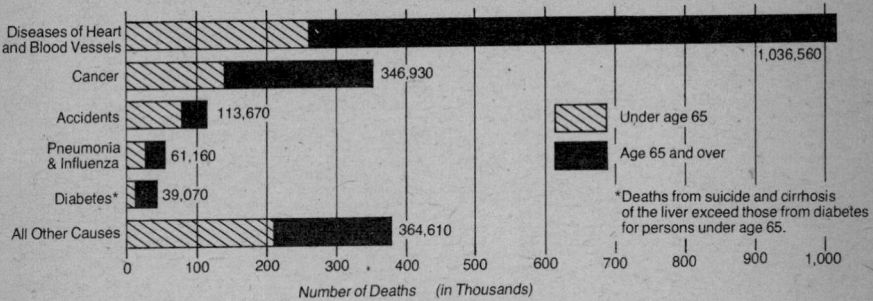

- Diseases of Heart and Blood Vessels — 1,036,560
- Cancer — 346,930
- Accidents — 113,670
- Pneumonia & Influenza — 61,160
- Diabetes* — 39,070
- All Other Causes — 364,610

Under age 65 / Age 65 and over

*Deaths from suicide and cirrhosis of the liver exceed those from diabetes for persons under age 65.

Number of Deaths (in Thousands)

Warning Signs
Source: American Heart Association.

Of Heart Attack
—Prolonged, oppressive pain or unusual discomfort in the center of the chest
—Pain may radiate to the shoulder, arm, neck or jaw
—Sweating may accompany pain or discomfort
—Nausea and vomiting may also occur
—Shortness of breath may accompany other signs
The American Heart Association advises immediate action at the onset of these symptoms. The Association points out that over half of heart attack victims die before they reach the hospital and that the average victim waits 3 hours before seeking help.

Of Stroke
—Sudden temporary weakness or numbness of face or limbs
—Temporary loss of speech, or trouble speaking or understanding speech
—Temporary dimness or loss of vision, particularly in one eye
—An episode of double vision
—Unexplained dizziness or unsteadiness
—Change in personality, mental ability
—New or unusual pattern of headaches

Major Risk Factors

Blood pressure—systolic pressure under 120 is normal; systolic pressure over 150
= 2 times the risk of heart attack
= 4 times the risk of stroke

Cholesterol—level under 194 is normal; level of 250 or over
= 3 times the risk of heart attack or stroke

Cigarettes—with non-smoking considered normal; smoking one pack a day
= 2 times the risk of heart attack
= 5 times the risk of stroke

Cardiovascular Disease Statistical Summary
Source: National Center for Health Statistics, U.S. Public Health Service
(1972 estimates)

Prevalence —28,410,000 Americans have some form of heart and blood vessel disease:
—Hypertension — 22,950,000 (1 in 6 adults)
—Coronary heart disease — 3,940,000
—Rheumatic heart disease — 1,730,000
—Stroke— 1,680,000
Mortality — 1,036,560 in 1972 (53% of all deaths); 1975 estimate — 1,054,500 (52%) — 25% of those killed by cardiovascular disease are under 65 years of age.
Heart Attack — 683,100 deaths in 1972.
—3,940,000 persons have had heart attacks or angina pectoris.
—350,000 per year die before they get to the hospital; average victim waits 3 hours before seeking help.
Stroke — 210,050 deaths in 1972.
—1,680,000 are afflicted with symptoms of stroke.
Hypertension (high blood pressure)
—22,950,000 adults have it; only 50% know it.

—only 25% of victims are under treatment.
—only 12.5% of victims have it under control.
—easily detectable and usually controllable.
Rheumatic Heart Disease — afflicts 100,000 children; 1,680,000 adults.
—14,090 deaths in 1972.
Congenital Heart Defects — 25,000 annually born with heart defects.
—infant deaths are about 8,000 a year.
Coronary Care Units (CCU) — about 4,500 (66%) of U.S. general hospitals have coronary care capability.
—1,800 hospitals have full-scale CCU's.
Costs —$20 billion annually (American Heart Association estimate for 1975).
—$2.7 billion for doctors and nurses.
— 6.9 billion for hospitals and nursing homes.
— .7 billion for medicine.
— 1.1 billion for research and Miscellaneous.
— 8.6 billion in lost income of victims.

Deaths and Death Rates for Selected Causes*

Source: Division of Vital Statistics, National Center for Health Statistics.
Rates per 100,000 population

1973* Cause of death	Number	Rate	1973* Cause of death	Number	Rate
All causes	1,977,000	942.1	Acute bronchitis and bronchiolitis	810	0.4
Enteritis and other diarrheal diseases	2,370	1.1	Influenza and pneumonia	61,160	29.1
Tuberculosis, all forms	3,870	1.8	Influenza	4,970	2.4
Syphilis and its sequelae	410	0.2	Pneumonia	56,190	26.8
Other infective and parasitic diseases	3,350	1.6	Bronchitis, emphysema, and asthma	30,280	14.4
Malignant neoplasms, including			Chronic and unqualified bronchitis	5,810	2.8
neoplasms of lymphatic and			Emphysema	22,540	10.7
hematopoietic tissues	353,440	168.4	Asthma	1,930	0.9
Diabetes mellitus	36,450	17.4	Peptic ulcer	7,830	3.7
Meningitis	1,600	0.8	Hernia and Intestinal obstruction	6,710	3.2
Major cardiovascular diseases	1,073,460	494.4	Cirrhosis of liver	33,630	16.0
Diseases of heart	754,460	359.5	Cholelithiasis, cholecystitis and cholangitis	3,280	1.6
Active rheumatic fever and chronic			Nephritis and nephrosis	7,740	3.7
rheumatic heart disease	13,580	6.5	Infections of Kidney	6,100	2.9
Hypertensive heart disease with or			Hyperplasia of prostate	1,700	0.8
without renal disease	7,810	3.7	Congenital anomalies	13,940	6.6
Ischemic heart disease	682,910	325.4	Certain causes of mortality in early infancy	31,030	14.8
Chronic disease of endocardium and			Symptoms and ill-defined conditions	38,310	18.3
other myocardial insufficiency	4,870	2.3	All other diseases	112,700	53.7
All other forms of heart disease	39,900	19.0	Accidents	115,040	54.8
Hypertension	8,010	3.8	Motor vehicle accidents	55,690	26.5
Cerebrovascular diseases	214,650	102.3	All other accidents	59,350	28.3
Arteriosclerosis	33,430	15.9	Suicide	24,440	11.6
Other diseases of arteries,			Homicide	19,700	9.4
arterioles, and capillaries	26,910	12.8	All other external causes	5,370	2.6

Due to rounding estimates of death, figures may not add to total. *Provisional.
Data based on a 10% sampling of all death certificates for a 12 month (Jan.-Dec.) period.

Principal Types of Accidental Deaths

Source: Division of Vital Statistics, National Center for Health Statistics,
Data for 1971 are National Safety Council estimates

Year	All types	Motor vehicle	Falls	Burns	Drowning	Firearms	Machinery	Poison gases	Other poisons
1960	93,806	38,137	19,023	7,645	6,529	2,334	1,951	1,253	1,679
1965	108,004	49,163	19,984	7,347	6,799	2,344	2,054	1,526	2,110
1969	116,000	56,000	18,000	7,000	7,200	2,400	....	1,600	2,700
1970	115,000	54,600	16,900	6,700	6,400	2,400	....	1,600	3,700
1971	113,000	54,400	16,800	6,800	6,000	2,400	....	1,600	3,800
1972	115,000	56,300	16,700	6,700	6,200	2,400	....	1,700	3,700
1973	117,000	55,800	16,900	6,400	8,700	2,700	....	1,500	3,700

Death Rates per 100,000 Population

Year	All types	Motor vehicle	Falls	Burns	Drowning	Firearms	Machinery	Poison gases	Other poisons
1960	52.1	21.2	10.6	4.2	3.6	1.3	1.1	0.7	0.9
1965	55.7	25.4	10.3	3.8	3.5	1.2	1.1	0.8	0.1
1969	57.4	27.7	8.9	3.5	3.6	1.2	NA	0.8	1.3
1970	56.4	26.9	8.3	3.3	3.1	1.2	....	0.8	1.8
1971	55.0	26.4	8.3	3.3	2.9	1.1	....	0.8	1.8
1972	55.4	27.0	8.0	3.2	3.0	1.2	....	0.8	1.8
1973	55.8	26.6	8.1	3.0	4.1	1.3	....	0.7	1.8

Accidental Injuries by Severity of Injury

1973* Severity of Injury	Total*	Motor-Vehicle	Work	Home	Public Non-Motor-Vehicle
All Injuries*	11,600,000	2,050,000	2,500,000	4,150,000	3,000,000
Deaths	117,000	55,800	14,200	26,000	25,000
Nonfatal injuries	11,500,000	2,000,000	2,500,000	4,100,000	3,000,000
Permanent impairments*	420,000	170,000	90,000	110,000	70,000
Temporary total disabilities	11,100,000	1,850,000	2,400,000	4,000,000	2,900,000

Certain Costs of Accidental Injuries, 1973 ($ billions)

	Total*	Motor-Vehicle	Work	Home	Public Non-Motor-Vehicle
Total*	$26.2	$13.9	$6.4	$3.4	$3.2
Wage loss	13.3	6.6	2.9	2.1	2.3
Medical expense	5.4	1.7	1.6	1.3	0.9
Insurance admin. Costs	7.5	5.6	1.9	...	...

*Duplication between motor-vehicle, work and home are eliminated in total.

Birth Stones

Source: Retail Jewelers of America, Inc.

Month	Ancient	Modern	Month	Ancient	Modern	Month	Ancient	Modern
January	Garnet	Garnet	May	Agate	Emerald	September	Chrysolite	Sapphire
February	Amethyst	Amethyst	June	Emerald	Pearl, Moonstone or Alexandrite	October	Aquamarine	Opal or Tourmaline
March	Jasper	Bloodstone or Aquamarine	July	Onyx	Ruby	November	Topaz	Topaz
April	Sapphire	Diamond	August	Carnelian	Sardonyx or Peridot	December	Ruby	Turquoise or Zircon

The term precious stones actually applies only to diamonds, rubies, sapphires and emeralds. All others are semiprecious. Precious gems are minerals brought to perfection by the lapidary's art. The pearl, often a gem of great value, is not a precious stone.

Average Future Lifetime in United States

Source: Division of Vital Statistics, National Center for
Health Statistics, 1973 Data

Age Interval	Number Living[1]	Avg. Life Expect.	White Male	White Female	Average remaining lifetime[2] All Others Male	Average remaining lifetime[2] All Others Female
0-1	100,000	71.3	68.4	76.1	61.8	69.9
1-5	98,243	71.6	68.6	76.1	62.7	70.9
5-10	97,929	67.8	64.9	72.3	59.1	67.2
10-15	97,718	63.0	60.0	67.4	54.3	62.3
15-20	97,523	58.1	55.1	62.5	49.4	57.4
20-25	96,961	53.4	50.6	57.6	44.9	52.6
25-30	96,244	48.8	46.1	52.8	40.8	47.9
30-35	95,565	44.1	41.4	48.0	36.7	43.3
35-40	94,771	39.5	36.8	43.2	32.5	38.8
40-45	93,716	34.9	32.2	38.5	28.5	34.4
45-50	92,074	30.5	27.8	33.9	24.8	30.3
50-55	89,543	26.2	23.6	29.4	21.3	26.4
55-60	85,837	22.3	19.7	25.2	18.2	22.7
60-65	80,390	18.6	16.3	21.1	15.4	19.3
65-70	72,911	15.2	13.2	17.2	13.0	16.1
70-75	63,362	12.1	10.4	13.6	10.6	13.2
75-80	50,981	9.5	8.1	10.4	9.0	11.2
80-85	36,156	7.3	6.2	7.9	7.8	9.2
85 and up	21,947	5.4	4.7	5.7	6.0	7.2

(1.) Of 100,000 born alive, number living at beginning of age interval. (2) Average number of years of life remaining at beginning of age interval.

Years of Life Expected at Birth

Year	Total	Male	Female	Year	Total	Male	Female
1973[1]	71.3	67.6	75.3	1960	69.7	66.6	73.1
1972[1]	71.2	67.4	75.2	1950	68.2	65.6	71.1
1971	71.1	67.4	75.0	1940	62.9	60.8	65.2
1970	70.8	67.1	74.6	1930	59.7	58.1	61.6
1969	70.5	67.0	74.3	1920	54.1	53.6	54.6
1965	70.2	66.8	73.7	1910	47.3	46.3	48.3

Based on Death-Registration States 1900-1925, and United States 1930-1973. (1.) Provisional.

Purchases and Ownership of Life Insurance in U.S. and Assets of U.S. Life Insurance Companies

Legal Reserve Life Insurance Companies
Source: Division of Statistics & Research, Institute of Life Insurance
In millions of dollars.

Year	Purchases of Life Insurance Ordinary	Group	Industrial	Total	Insurance in Force Ordinary	Group	Industrial	Credit	Total	Assets
1940	7,022	747	3,318	1,087	79,346	14,938	20,866	380	115,530	30,802
1950	18,260	6,237	5,492	29,989	149,116	47,793	33,415	3,844	234,168	64,020
1960	56,183	15,328	6,906	78,417	341,881	175,903	39,563	29,101	586,448	119,576
1965	89,643	52,867*	7,302	149,812*	499,638	308,078	39,818	53,020	900,554	158,884
1970	138,356	68,939*	6,612	213,907*	734,730	551,357	38,644	77,392	1,402,123	207,254
1971	143,480	55,313	7,651	206,444	792,318	589,883	39,202	81,931	1,503,334	222,102
1972	156,859	59,953	7,394	224,206	853,911	640,689	39,975	93,410	1,627,985	239,730
1973	176,289	66,653	7,606	250,548	928,192	708,322	40,632	101,154	1,778,300	252,436

*Includes Servicemen's Group Life Insurance $27. 4 billion in 1965 and $16.8 billion in 1970.

Canadian Motor Vehicle Traffic Deaths

Source: Statistics Canada

Province	Number 1972	Number 1971	Province	Number 1972	Number 1971
Total	6,237	5,573	Ontario	1,891	1,769
			Manitoba	186	181
Newfoundland	118	87	Saskatchewan	251	218
Prince Edward Island	51	30	Alberta	450	461
Nova Scotia	244	224	British Columbia	680	636
New Brunswick	223	214	Yukon	8	14
Quebec	2,129	1,730	Northwest Terr.	6	9

Physical Growth Range for Children from 1 to 18 Years*

Source: U.S. Public Health Service, H.E.W.

Age	Shortest 5%	Median Height	Tallest 5%	Lightest 5%	Median Weight	Heaviest 5%
			Boys			
1	28.4	30.2	32.0	18.7	23.3	27.8
2	32.1	34.6	37.1	23.3	28.3	33.3
3	35.3	37.8	40.3	27.1	32.5	37.9
4	38.3	40.8	43.3	30.0	36.1	42.2
5	40.3	43.4	46.4	33.0	40.3	47.6
6	42.8	45.9	49.0	36.0	44.7	53.4
7	44.8	48.1	51.4	40.3	50.9	61.5
8	46.9	50.5	54.1	44.4	57.4	70.4
9	48.8	52.8	56.8	48.0	64.4	80.4
10	50.6	54.3	59.2	51.4	71.4	91.4
11	51.9	56.4	60.9	53.3	78.9	102.5
12	53.5	58.6	63.7	60.0	86.0	113.5
13	55.2	61.3	67.4	65.3	98.6	131.9
14	57.5	64.1	70.7	75.5	111.8	148.1
15	61.0	66.9	72.8	88.0	124.3	160.6
16	63.8	68.9	74.0	97.8	133.8	169.8
17	65.2	69.8	74.4	106.5	139.8	174.0
18	65.9	70.2	74.5	110.3	144.8	179.3
			Girls			
1	27.6	29.4	31.2	17.4	21.7	26.0
2	31.6	33.8	36.0	22.3	27.1	31.9
3	35.3	37.5	39.7	26.3	32.3	38.3
4	38.1	40.7	43.3	28.8	36.1	43.4
5	40.6	43.4	46.2	32.2	40.9	49.6
6	42.8	45.9	49.0	35.5	45.7	55.9
7	44.5	47.8	51.1	38.3	51.0	63.7
8	46.4	50.0	53.6	42.0	57.2	72.4
9	48.2	52.2	56.2	45.1	63.6	82.1
10	49.9	54.5	59.1	48.2	71.0	95.0
11	51.9	57.0	62.1	55.4	82.0	108.6
12	54.1	59.5	64.9	63.9	94.4	124.9
13	57.1	62.2	66.8	72.8	105.5	138.2
14	58.5	63.1	67.7	83.0	113.0	144.0
15	59.5	63.8	68.1	89.5	120.0	150.5
16	59.8	64.1	68.4	95.1	123.0	150.1
17	60.1	64.2	68.3	97.9	125.8	153.7
18	60.1	64.4	68.7	96.0	126.2	156.4

*This table simply gives a general picture for American children. When used as a standard, the individual variation in children's growth should not be overlooked. In most cases the height-weight relationship is probably a more valid index of weight status than a weight-for-age assessment.

Average Weight of Americans by Height and Age

Source: Society of Actuaries; based on a 4-year study of 5,000,000 persons

The figures represent weights in ordinary indoor clothing and shoes, and heights with shoes.

Height	Men 20-24	25-29	30-39	40-49	50-59	Height	Women 20-24	25-29	30-39	40-49	50-59
5'0''.........	122	128	131	134	136	4'10''........	102	107	115	122	125
5'1''.........	125	131	134	137	139	4'11''........	105	110	117	124	127
5'2''.........	128	134	137	140	142	5'0''.........	108	113	120	127	130
5'3''.........	132	138	141	144	145	5'1''.........	112	116	123	130	133
5'4''.........	136	141	145	148	149	5'2''.........	115	119	126	133	136
5'5''.........	139	144	149	152	153	5'3''.........	118	122	129	136	140
5'6''.........	142	148	153	156	157	5'4''.........	121	125	132	140	141
5'7''.........	145	151	157	161	162	5'5''.........	125	129	135	143	148
5'8''.........	149	155	161	165	166	5'6''.........	129	133	139	147	152
5'9''.........	153	159	165	169	170	5'7''.........	132	136	142	151	156
5'10''........	157	163	170	174	175	5'8''.........	136	140	146	155	160
5'11''........	161	167	174	178	180	5'9''.........	140	144	150	159	164
6'0''.........	166	172	179	183	185	5'10''........	144	148	154	164	169
6'1''.........	170	177	183	187	189	5'11''........	149	153	159	169	174
6'2''.........	174	182	188	192	194	6'0''.........	154	158	164	174	180
6'3''.........	178	186	193	197	199						
6'4''.........	181	190	199	203	205						

Pedalcycle Accidents

Since 1935, the number of pedalcycle-motor-vehicle deaths have more than doubled. The number of pedalcycles in use has increased twenty-fold since 1935; so the death rate in 1973 was about one-tenth the rate in 1935. The proportion of deaths occurring to young adults and adults has steadily increased since 1960. Persons 15 years of age and older accounted for more than one-half the deaths in 1973 compared to one-fifth in 1960.

The Nation's Hospitals

Source: American Hospital Association

In 1973, there were 7,123 hospitals in the United States registered by the American Hospital Association. These institutions had about 1.53 million beds and reported admitting some 31.7 million in-patients. About $36.3 billion was spent to provide services for both in-patients and outpatients, or a cost of $173 per resident of the nation.

	Hospitals		Beds		Average Daily Census		Admissions		Expenses ($1,000)	
	Fed.	Non.-Fed.	Fed.	Non-Fed.	Fed.	Non-Fed.	Fed.	Non-Fed.	Fed.	Non-Fed.
Alabama	8	144	2,992	24,072	2,367	18,705	35,658	605,111	$ 60,207	$ 433,346
Alaska	10	16	761	917	486	541	21,751	30,218	22,852	27,781
Arizona	18	60	1,725	8,913	1,264	6,578	45,399	293,514	52,924	296,970
Arkansas	4	91	2,054	9,081	1,777	6,782	23,020	352,282	42,099	188,006
California	34	612	13,112	109,866	9,750	76,859	209,523	2,978,191	412,324	3,457,758
Colorado	6	91	2,305	12,269	1,809	9,029	40,511	407,441	63,118	343,369
Conn.	5	63	1,061	20,181	788	16,312	14,306	424,785	35,523	564,536
Delaware	2	12	406	4,409	287	3,836	6,277	68,659	9,792	92,893
Dist. of Col.	4	17	5,744	6,306	4,756	4,930	34,127	184,427	128,307	248,626
Florida	15	193	4,327	46,721	3,368	35,694	49,427	1,198,430	147,592	1,043,463
Georgia	10	166	3,317	29,448	2,566	23,767	49,427	771,883	80,287	591,371
Hawaii	1	30	750	4,665	497	3,309	20,735	88,527	21,269	98,660
Idaho	2	50	212	3,579	161	2,428	3,998	116,710	6,320	74,674
Illinois	10	288	7,283	77,575	6,028	60,795	70,632	1,850,551	163,181	2,086,662
Indiana	6	130	2,357	34,294	1,887	26,687	20,168	805,552	43,447	691,522
Iowa	3	144	1,765	19,713	1,281	13,412	14,424	515,095	40,695	371,817
Kansas	8	155	2,297	16,548	1,840	11,912	27,224	404,730	52,045	318,824
Kentucky	6	126	2,730	17,662	2,042	13,907	40,530	563,256	65,235	372,635
Louisiana	8	150	2,785	24,255	2,075	18,231	49,148	642,160	68,396	462,783
Maine	2	50	889	7,155	719	5,283	6,387	155,534	14,962	134,170
Maryland	11	72	3,695	27,494	2,788	22,669	47,954	461,480	112,011	652,270
Mass.	9	196	4,517	51,453	3,718	40,209	35,293	923,286	96,281	1,420,975
Michigan	9	238	2,902	53,886	2,391	42,963	28,829	1,297,847	69,393	1,535,947
Minnesota	5	188	1,998	31,234	1,629	22,473	18,758	681,522	49,052	612,969
Mississippi	5	107	1,810	15,211	1,540	11,941	26,858	396,770	40,092	222,677
Missouri	8	149	3,439	33,545	2,623	26,347	51,072	820,780	80,116	730,150
Montana	6	60	391	3,932	304	2,471	9,001	130,951	10,390	75,737
Nebraska	5	101	1,048	10,413	824	7,084	19,765	269,980	27,648	210,145
Nevada	4	20	269	2,884	200	2,050	6,360	91,527	10,383	82,024
New Hamp.	2	34	288	6,220	223	4,808	5,186	124,499	9,184	100,363
New Jersey	4	137	3,456	45,171	2,785	35,843	34,734	946,572	66,128	1,060,157
New Mexico	12	46	1,133	5,343	815	3,656	32,360	146,827	33,002	107,514
New York	17	398	11,172	164,029	9,174	136,252	93,655	2,657,910	260,852	4,479,524
N. Carolina	9	152	3,474	31,159	2,717	24,596	50,765	788,963	79,670	589,260
N. Dakota	5	57	421	5,356	329	3,663	13,123	123,149	10,973	84,149
Ohio	6	233	5,000	69,865	4,006	55,827	39,082	1,665,498	110,963	1,613,553
Oklahoma	12	133	1,460	16,329	1,025	11,874	38,310	439,523	47,739	305,016
Oregon	2	84	961	11,202	807	7,878	12,456	335,857	25,362	265,279
Penn.	13	303	7,616	97,951	6,254	77,162	48,733	1,760,209	151,212	2,056,553
Rhode Island	3	19	650	7,291	505	6,312	12,699	134,517	20,147	183,330
So. Carolina	7	85	2,059	17,579	1,607	13,860	47,226	395,371	53,965	263,531
So. Dakota	10	53	1,314	4,816	1,036	3,280	19,553	114,284	23,206	67,919
Tenn.	5	156	3,150	29,561	2,658	23,622	34,736	759,350	66,450	572,172
Texas	28	538	8,673	68,729	7,075	50,834	147,546	1,986,468	213,942	1,426,236
Utah	3	35	618	4,210	439	3,059	9,653	167,361	17,975	117,560
Vermont	1	20	200	4,020	150	3,184	3,145	75,192	5,992	73,244
Virginia	11	118	4,539	32,837	3,540	27,696	70,885	665,982	115,771	572,848
Washington	11	118	3,154	14,326	2,213	9,604	47,577	508,803	82,411	397,507
West Va.	6	78	1,328	14,872	1,112	11,696	17,143	361,151	32,630	249,199
Wisconsin	3	182	2,040	31,756	1,728	23,322	21,346	745,910	59,217	705,414
Wyoming	3	28	611	2,174	489	1,365	4,818	62,427	10,891	33,143
Totals	**397**	**6,726**	**142,258**	**1,392,468**	**112,452**	**1,076,597**	**1,865,127**	**32,487,022**	**$3,523,633**	**$32,766,231**

Canadian General and Allied Special Hospitals

1972	Hospitals			Beds			Admissions			Expenses ($1,000)*
	Pub.	Priv.	Fed.	Pub.	Priv.	Fed.	Pub.	Priv.	Fed.	Pub.
Canada	1,051	112	97	141,074	4,896	7,522	3,593,922	29,869	64,346	$2,784,090
Nfld.	47	—	—	3,000	—	—	83,946	—	—	54,287
P.E.I.	9	—	—	751	—	—	23,127	—	—	9,859
N.S.	47	—	2	4,839	—	547	134,498	—	4,253	92,360
N.B.	40	—	—	4,449	—	—	119,377	—	—	75,868
Quebec	185	51	9	37,288	2,811	1,558	755,463	14,780	5,173	796,834
Ontario	233	57	13	49,022	2,006	1,841	1,321,452	14,163	14,866	1,069,300
Manitoba	85	1	16	6,318	50	689	183,783	250	6,758	120,727
Sask.	140	—	3	7,591	—	113	217,140	—	2,787	105,370
Alberta	145	—	8	14,025	—	880	357,141	—	11,572	212,148
B.C.	114	2	3	13,572	16	1,501	393,041	546	9,255	2,244,915
Yukon	—	—	6	—	—	160	—	—	4,004	—
N.W.T.	6	1	37	219	13	233	4,954	130	5,678	2,422

*Private and Federal Hospitals do not submit Financial Returns.

How to Obtain Birth, Marriage, Death Records

The United States Government has published a series of inexpensive booklets entitled Where to Write for Birth & Death Records; Where to Write for Marriage Records; Where to Write for Divorce Records; Where to Write for Birth and Death Records of U.S. Citizens who were born or died outside of the U. S. and birth certifications for alien children adopted by U. S. citizens; You May Save Time Proving Your Age and Other Birth Facts. They tell where to write to get a certified copy of or original vital record. Supt. of Documents, Government Printing Office, Washington, D. C. 20402.

Nursing Care Homes in United States

Source: Division of Health Resources Statistics, National Center for Health Statistics

State	Nursing Care Homes				Personal Care homes with nursing care		Personal Care and domiciliary care homes	
	Homes	Beds	Residents	Full-time Personnel	Homes	beds	Homes	Beds
Total...............	12,871	917,707	824,038	567,717	3,568	192,347	5,565	91,544
Alabama............	178	12,546	11,439	8,419	11	859	3	34
Alaska.............	7	478	379	371	1	175	—	—
Arizona............	65	4,554	4,042	2,733	9	375	8	291
Arkansas...........	201	14,118	12,977	6,575	15	728	2	207
California..........	1,373	104,297	86,332	62,102	462	17,473	2,442	24,212
Colorado...........	166	13,511	12,293	8,070	26	2,397	20	541
Connecticut........	246	18,474	17,593	10,935	36	1,628	98	1,815
Delaware...........	27	1,302	1,175	956	5	541	2	35
District of Columbia..	34	2,038	1,904	1,851	27	583	12	153
Florida.............	290	29,104	23,494	16,697	41	4,090	42	2,677
Georgia............	247	20,469	18,953	11,836	25	2,098	11	242
Hawaii.............	27	1,641	1,543	1,250	35	286	70	364
Idaho..............	53	3,569	3,151	1,993	5	179	6	165
Illinois............	574	44,438	40,840	29,941	238	15,236	234	7,197
Indiana............	403	25,658	23,168	17,168	72	5,431	47	1,449
Iowa...............	437	22,347	20,093	12,170	146	7,967	164	3,471
Kansas............	247	14,166	12,963	9,235	174	7,043	59	659
Kentucky..........	139	9,051	7,706	7,937	144	7,365	61	2,206
Louisiana..........	193	13,732	12,547	6,930	13	665	6	213
Maine.............	144	5,400	5,059	3,606	44	876	100	1,115
Maryland...........	157	13,008	12,217	8,601	28	1,620	10	61
Massachusetts......	643	39,309	37,274	21,327	170	7,501	147	2,877
Michigan...........	419	36,834	34,473	25,641	72	4,655	71	1,795
Minnesota..........	380	31,608	29,175	15,274	95	7,146	118	2,389
Mississippi.........	108	6,305	5,541	3,732	16	593	10	217
Missouri...........	355	25,162	22,229	15,094	94	5,818	45	1,042
Montana...........	61	3,368	3,157	2,201	27	894	15	197
Nebraska..........	150	10,775	9,730	5,576	73	3,820	30	507
Nevada............	21	1,033	840	877	1	50	21	358
New Hampshire.....	97	4,591	4,255	2,684	28	627	15	242
New Jersey.........	297	22,454	20,205	15,742	64	3,456	205	4,865
New Mexico........	35	2,259	1,765	1,775	8	794	17	246
New York..........	589	57,906	55,145	51,008	178	14,396	329	8,810
North Carolina......	148	8,326	7,380	8,632	285	7,115	410	3,776
North Dakota.......	50	3,828	3,603	2,521	28	1,520	31	846
Ohio...............	940	46,923	42,377	28,630	158	10,551	93	2,050
Oklahoma..........	369	24,451	21,771	11,722	23	1,891	19	561
Oregon............	197	12,880	11,925	7,074	43	2,984	71	1,307
Pennsylvania.......	547	43,451	39,581	29,942	143	12,674	63	1,566
Rhode Island.......	91	4,798	4,496	2,573	30	800	64	913
South Carolina......	99	6,455	5,687	4,023	8	805	11	216
South Dakota.......	85	4,917	4,674	2,689	37	1,747	31	378
Tennessee..........	194	11,050	9,448	6,767	20	1,570	20	1,697
Texas..............	799	61,505	53,267	31,860	92	7,543	46	1,764
Utah...............	78	3,133	2,913	1,929	55	1,442	9	194
Vermont...........	55	2,263	2,052	1,569	17	317	29	430
Virginia............	154	10,326	9,272	7,961	62	3,115	119	2,237
Washington........	287	23,060	20,325	11,270	60	4,123	38	1,381
West Virginia.......	57	2,504	2,338	2,445	23	647	44	701
Wisconsin..........	356	30,973	28,028	15,668	98	5,965	36	710
Wyoming...........	20	1,359	1,244	735	3	173	11	165

Active Federal and Non-Federal Doctors by States

(as of Dec. 31, 1971)

Source: Division of Health Resources Statistics, National Center for Health Statistics

	Total	Non-Fed.	Fed.		Total	Non-Fed.	Fed.		Total	Non-Fed.	Fed.
All areas....	322,288	[2]293,029	[2]29,199	Kansas......	2,788	2,484	304	N. D........	635	557	78
United States	316,545	290,381	26,164	Kentucky....	3,506	3,205	301	Ohio........	14,409	13,811	598
Alabama.....	3,284	2,981	303	Louisiana....	4,683	4,292	391	Oklahoma...	2,786	2,478	308
Alaska.......	353	226	127	Maine.......	1,133	1,050	83	Oregon......	3,080	2,941	139
Arizona......	2,895	2,440	455	Maryland....	9,535	7,168	2,367	Pa..........	18,235	17,419	816
Arkansas....	1,878	1,698	180	Mass.......	12,427	11,531	896	R. I.........	1,603	1,433	170
California....	39,926	36,329	3,597	Michigan....	11,270	10,882	388	S. C........	2,670	2,312	358
Colorado.....	4,291	3,729	562	Minnesota...	5,950	5,540	410	S. D........	598	504	94
Connecticut..	5,895	5,648	247	Mississippi..	1,986	1,744	242	Tennessee...	4,977	4,614	363
Delaware....	772	721	51	Missouri....	6,201	5,839	362	Texas.......	14,783	12,768	2,015
D of C.......	4,028	2,933	1,095	Montana....	778	713	65	Utah........	1,600	1,479	121
Florida......	10,207	9,180	1,027	Nebraska....	1,780	1,642	138	Vermont.....	804	770	34
Georgia.....	5,538	4,872	666	Nevada.....	578	527	51	Virginia......	6,502	5,482	1,020
Hawaii......	1,222	1,129	93	N. H........	1,025	968	57	Washington..	5,382	4,763	619
Idaho.......	709	655	54	New Jersey..	10,791	10,261	530	W. Va.......	1,917	1,790	127
Illinois......	16,006	15,008	998	New Mexico..	1,385	1,130	255	Wisconsin...	5,536	5,272	264
Indiana......	5,318	5,126	192	New York....	43,651	41,833	1,818	Wyoming....	353	316	37
Iowa.......	2,932	2,795	137	N. C........	5,954	5,393	561	Puerto Rico..	2,632	2,479	153
								Outlying areas	3,051	169	2,882

(1) Excludes 3,207 physicians with addresses unknown. (2) Includes 2,771 Federal M.D.s overseas not distributed by location.

Transportation Accident Death Rates

Source: National Safety Council

Kind of Transportation Passenger Deaths in 1972	Passenger Miles	Passenger Deaths	Rate Per 100,000,000 Pass. Miles	1970-1972 Aver. Death Rate
Automobiles and taxis..................	1,940,000,000,000	33,700	1.70	1.80
Automobiles on turnpikes...............	53,000,000,000	550	1.04	1.04
Buses...............................	72,000,000,000	170	0.24	0.20
Railroad passenger trains..............	9,100,000,000	6	0.07	0.28
Scheduled air transport planes (domestic)......	139,900,000,000	128	0.10	0.12

(1) Drivers of passenger automobiles are considered passengers.

Selected Statistics on State and County Mental Hospitals

Source: National Institute of Mental Health

Year	Total Admitted[1]	Net Releases[2]	Deaths in Hospital	Residents End of Year	Expense Per Patient[3]
1955	178,003	NA	44,384	558,922	$1,116.59
1960	234,791	NA	49,748	535,540	1,702.41
1969	379,838	373,287	35,962	373,984	4,593.61
1970	393,174	394,627	30,804	338,592	5,435.38
1971	414,926	418,750	26,835	308,024	6,420.79
1972	390,000*	401,567	23,282	275,995	7,576.24
1973	377,020*	386,962	19,899	248,562	9,207.92

*Includes estimates. NA Not available. (1) Excludes transfers.
(2) Net releases alive from hospital is computed by subtracting returns from long-term leave from the total discontinuations.
(3) Per average daily resident patient population.

Patients in State and County Mental Hospitals

Source: National Institute of Mental Health. Average Daily Census 1973

State	Number	State	Number	State	Number	State	Number
UNITED STATES		Hawaii	179	Mississippi	4,181	Oregon	1,433
TOTAL	252,607	Idaho	246	Missouri	5,173	Pennsylvania	19,195
Alabama	4,360	Illinois	10,786	Montana	1,085	Rhode Island	1,650
Alaska	149	Indiana	6,043	Nebraska	914	South Carolina	5,369
Arizona	715	Iowa	1,101	Nevada	352	South Dakota	968
Arkansas	528	Kansas	1,550	New Hampshire	1,458	Tennessee	4,972
California	9,246	Kentucky	1,159	New Jersey	11,827	Texas	9,799
Colorado	1,254	Louisiana	3,521	New Mexico	408	Utah	274
Connecticut	3,360	Maine	1,331	New York	46,136	Vermont	649
Delaware	1,195	Maryland	6,169	North Carolina	5,840	Virginia	8,358
District of Columbia	2,994	Massachusetts	8,522	North Dakota	650	Washington	1,914
		Michigan	8,567	Ohio	12,834	West Virginia	3,480
Florida	7,334	Minnesota	4,229	Oklahoma	2,788	Wisconsin	7,205
Georgia	8,821					Wyoming	336

The above data was based on reports of the 334 State and county hospitals. The full-time personnel was estimated at 225,227 and the expenditures $2,325,986. The average daily expenditures per patient based on the resident patient population of hospitals reporting expenditures was $25.20.

Estimated Patient Care Episodes in Psychiatric Facilities

Source: National Institute of Mental Health

		Inpatient Services				Outpatient Psychiatric Services	Community Health Centers[2]
Year	All Facilities	All	State and County	Private*	General	VA	
1971	4,038,143	1,721,389	745,259	126,600	542,642	176,800	1,693,848	622,906
1969	3,572,822	1,678,371	767,115	123,850	535,493	186,913	1,603,303	291,148
1967	3,139,742	1,659,391	801,354	124,258	578,513	128,196	1,383,000	97,351
1965	2,636,525	1,565,525	804,926	125,428	519,328	115,843	1,071,000	—
1955	1,675,352	1,296,352	818,832	123,231	265,934	88,355	379,000	—

*Includes estimates of episodes of care in residential treatment centers for emotionally disturbed children.

Patients in Canadian Mental Hospitals

Average Patients Per Day, 1972

	Mental	Psychiatric	Retardates	Emotionally Disturbed Children	Other	Total Private	Total Mental Hospital
Can	29,375	1,152	16,327	126	1,987	930	49,897
Nfld	696	—	—	—	—	—	696
P.E.I.	272	—	19	—	—	—	291
N.S.	789	500	—	—	—	—	1,289
N.B.	1,180	—	141	—	—	—	1,321
Que	12,166	151	3,398	—	410	—	16,125
Ont	8,637	343	6,326	110	107	858	16,381
Man	1,155	35	1,200	—	—	—	2,390
Sask	446	61	1,341	—	—	—	1,848
Alta	1,828	—	2,244	16	378	—	4,466
B.C.	2,206	62	1,656	—	1,092	72	5,088

Annual Fire Losses in the United States

Source: National Insurance Actuarial and Statistical Assn.

Year	Loss	Year	Loss	Year	Loss	Year	Loss
1940	285,878,697	1960	1,107,824,000	1969	1,952,022,000	1972	2,304,000,000
1945	484,274,000	1965	1,455,631,000	1970	2,264,000,000	1973	2,639,000,000
1955	885,218,000	1968	1,829,922,000	1971	2,316,000,000	1974 (6 mo.)	1,582,000,000

Marriage Information—Canada

Source: Compiled from information provided by the various Provincial Government departments and agencies concerned. (As of June, 1974)

Marriageable age, by provinces, for both males and females with and without consent of parents or guardians. In some provinces, the court has authority, given special circumstances, to marry young couples below the minimum age. Most provinces waive the blood test requirement and the waiting period varies across the provinces.

Province	With consent		Without consent		Blood test		Wait for License	Wait after License
	Men	Women	Men	Women	Other Province Required	Other Province Accepted		
Newfoundland.....	—	—	19	19	—	—	—	—
Prince Edward Island	16	16	18	18	Yes	Yes	5 days	None
Nova Scotia.......	(1)	(1)	19	19	None	None	5 days	None
New Brunswick.....	14-18	14-18	18+	18+	None	None	5 days	None
Quebec..........	14	12	18	18	None	—	—	None
Ontario..........	14	14[2]	18	18	None	—	None[3]	3 days
Manitoba.........	16	16	18	18	Yes	Yes	None	24 hours
Saskatchewan.....	15	15	18	18	Yes	Yes	5 days	None
Alberta..........	18—	18—	18+	18+	Yes[4]	Yes[5]	None[6]	None
British Columbia....	16[7]	16[7]	19	19	None	None	2 days[8]	None
Yukon Territory.....	15	15	19	19	None	None	None	24 hours
Northwest Territories	15	15	19	19	None	Yes	None	None

(1) There is no statutory minimum age in the Province. Anyone under the age of 19 years must have consent for marriage, and no person under the age of 16 years may be married without authorization of a Family Court Judge and in addition must have the necessary consent of the parent or guardian.

(2) Women under 14 years also require a medical certificate as to necessity of marriage to prevent illegitimacy of offspring.

(3) Special requirements applicable to non-residents.

(4) Applies only to applicants under 60 years of age.

(5) This is upon filing of negative lab report indicating blood test was taken within 14 days preceding date of application for license.

(6) Exception where consent is required by mail; depending receipt of divorce documents, etc.

(7) Persons under 16 years of age (no minimum age specified) may also be married if they have obtained, in addition to the usual consent from parents or guardian, an Order from a Judge of the Supreme or County Court in this Province.

(8) Including day of application, e.g., a license applied for on a Monday cannot be issued until Wednesday.

Grounds for Divorce in Canada

Source: Government of Canada Divorce Act

The grounds for divorce in Canada are the same for all the provinces and its territories. There are two categories of offence.

A. Marital Offence
  Adultery
  Sodomy
  Bestiality
  Rape
  Homosexual act
  Subsequent marriage
  Physical cruelty
  Mental cruelty
B. Marriage Breakdown by Reason of:—

Imprisonment for aggregate period of not less than 3 years
Imprisonment for not less than 2 yrs. on sentence of death or sentence of 10 yrs. or more
Addiction to alcohol
Addiction to narcotics
Whereabouts of spouse unknown
Non-consummation
Separation for not less than 3 yrs.
Desertion by Petitioner for not less than 5 years
Residence time: Domicile in Canada
Time between interlocutory and final decree: normally 3 months before final can be applied for.

Canadian Active Civilian Physicians, 1973

Source: Department of National Health and Welfare.

Province	Number	Ratio to Pop.
Newfoundland......................	542	1:996
Prince Edward Island...............	105	1:1105
Nova Scotia......................	1,157	1:700
New Brunswick....................	677	1:972
Quebec..........................	9,886	1:618
Ontario..........................	13,707	1:586
Manitoba.........................	1,597	1:629
Saskatchewan.....................	1,152	1:786
Alberta..........................	2,526	1:674
British Columbia...................	4,040	1:586
Yukon...........................	18	1:1111
Northwest Territories...............	29	1:1310
Canada..........................	**35,436**	**1:629**

Marriage Information

Source Compiled by William E. Mariano: Council on Marriage Relations, Inc.,
110 East 42 St., New York, N. Y. 10017 (as of Nov. 1, 1974)

Marriageable age, by states, for both males and females with and without consent of parents or guardians. But in most states, the court has authority, in an emergency, to marry young couples below the ordinary age of consent, where due regard for their morals and welfare so requires. In many states, under special circumstances, blood test and waiting period may be waived.

State	With consent Men	With consent Women	Without consent Men	Without consent Women	Blood test Required	Blood test Other state accepted*	Wait for license	Wait after license
Alabama (b)	17	14	21	18	Yes	Yes	None	None
Alaska	18	16	21	18	Yes	No	3 days	None
Arizona	16²	16	18	18	Yes	Yes	None	None
Arkansas	17	16⁴	21	18	Yes	No	3 days	None
California	—²	—²	18	18	Yes	Yes	None	None
Colorado	16	16	18	18	Yes	. . . . .	None	None
Connecticut	16	16(q)	18	18	Yes	Yes	4 days	None
Delaware	—(q)	16⁴	18	18	Yes	Yes	None	24 hrs. (c)
District of Columbia	18	16	21	18	Yes	Yes	3 days	None
Florida	18	16	21	21	Yes	Yes	3 days	None
Georgia	18	16	19	19	Yes	Yes	None (b)	None (o)
Hawaii	17(e)	16	20	18	Yes	Yes	None	None
Idaho	16	16	18	18	Yes	Yes	None (p)	None
Illinois (a)	—(e)	15(e)	21	18	Yes	Yes	None	None
Indiana	17	17	18	18	Yes	No	3 days	None
Iowa	18	16	18	18	Yes	Yes	3 days	None
Kansas	—(e)²	—(e)²	18	18	Yes	Yes	3 days	None
Kentucky	18	16	18	18	Yes	No	3 days	None
Louisiana (a)	18	16	18	18	Yes	No	None	72 hours
Maine	16	16	18	18	No	No	5 days	None
Maryland	18	16	21	18	None	None	48 hours	None
Massachusetts	—²	—²	18	18	Yes	Yes	3 days	None
Michigan (a)	—	16	18	18	Yes	No	3 days	None
Minnesota	—	16(e)	18	18	None	. . . . .	5 days	None
Mississippi (b)	17	15	21	21	Yes	. . . . .	3 days	None
Missouri	15	15	21	18	Yes	Yes	3 days	None
Montana	—²	—²	19	19	Yes	Yes	5 days	None
Nebraska	18	16	19	19	Yes	Yes	5 days	None
Nevada	—	16	18	18	None	None	None	None
New Hampshire (a)	14(e)	13(e)	18	18	Yes	Yes	5 days	None
New Jersey (a)	—	16	18	18	Yes	Yes	72 hours	None
New Mexico	16	16	21	21	Yes	Yes	None	None
New York	16	14	18	18	Yes	No	None	24 hrs.(h)
North Carolina (a)	16	16	18	18	Yes	Yes	None	None
North Dakota (a)	—²	15	18	18	Yes	. . . . .	None	None
Ohio (a)	18	16	18	18	Yes	Yes	5 days	None
Oklahoma	18	15	21	18	Yes	No	None (f)	* *
Oregon	18(e)	15(e)	18	18	Yes	No	7 days	None
Pennsylvania	16	16	18	18	Yes	Yes	3 days	None
Rhode Island (a) (b)	18	16	18	18	Yes	No	None	None
South Carolina	16	14	18	18	None	None	24 hrs.	None
South Dakota	18	16	18	18	Yes	Yes	None	None
Tennessee (b)	16	16	21	21	Yes	Yes	3 days	None
Texas	16	16	18	18	Yes	Yes	None	None
Utah (a)	16	14	21	18	Yes	Yes	None	None
Vermont (a)	18	16	18	18	Yes	. . . . .	None	5 days
Virginia (a)	18	16	18	18	Yes	Yes	None	None
Washington	17	17	18	18	(d)	. . . . .	3 days	None
West Virginia	18²	16	18	18	Yes	No	3 days	None
Wisconsin	18	16	18	18	Yes	Yes	5 days	None
Wyoming	18	16	21	21	Yes	Yes	None	None
Puerto Rico	16	16	21	21	(f)	None	None	None
Virgin Islands	16	14	21	18	None	None	8 days	None

Many states have additional special requirements; contact individual state.
(a) Special laws applicable to non-residents. (b) Specials laws applicable to those under 21 years; Alabama; bond required if male is under 21, female under 18. (c) 24 hours if one or both parties resident of state; 96 hours if both parties are non-residents. (d) None, but male must file affidavit. (e) Parental consent plus Court's consent required. (f) None, but a medical certificate is required. (g) Wait for license from time blood test is taken; Arizona, 48 hours. (h) Marriage may not be solemnized within 10 days from date of blood test. (j) If either under 21; Idaho, 3 days; Oklahoma, 72 hrs. (x) May be waived. (l) 3 days if both applicants are under 18 or female is pregnant. (2) Statute provides for obtaining license with parental or court consent with no stated minimum age. (3) If either party is under 18, 3 days. (4) Under 16, with parental and court consent. Delaware; Female under 18.(o) All those between 19-21 cannot waive 3 day waiting period. (p) If either under 18— wait full 3 days. (q) If under stated age court consent required.

Grounds for Divorce

Source: Compiled by William E. Mariano; Council on Marriage Relations, Inc., 110 East 42nd Street, New York, N.Y. 10017. Persons contemplating divorce should study latest decisions or secure legal advice before initiating proceedings since different interpretations or exceptions in each case can change the conclusion reached.

*Exceptions are to be noted.

State	Cruelty	Desertion	Non-support	Alcohol	Felony	Impotency	Pregnancy at marriage	Drug addiction	Fraudulent contract	Other causes	Residence time	Time between interlocut'y and final decrees
Alabama	X	X	X	X	X	X	X	X		Q-K-W-F-MM	1 year*	None-R
Alaska	X	/X		x	X	X		X		F-K-B	1 year	None
Arizona										QQ	90 days	None
Arkansas	X	X	X	X	X	X				B-Y-K-DD	3 months*	None
California	X	X	X	X	X	X				K-K-K	6 months	6 months
Colorado										QQ	90 days	None
Connecticut	X	X	X	X	X				X	K-F-QQ	3 years*	None
Delaware		X	X	X	X					F-K-Y-DD-FF	2 years	3 months
Dist. of Columbia		X			X					Y-Z	1 year	None
Florida										QQ-K	6 months	None
Georgia	X	X		X	X	X	X	X	X	K-M-AA-QQ	6 months	
Hawaii										QQ	6 months	'
Idaho	X	X	X	X	X					QQ	1 year	
Illinois	X	X		X	X	X				X-K	6 weeks	None
Indiana					X	X					1 year*	None
Iowa										K-QQ	6 months	None
Kansas	X	X	X	X	X	X			X	MM	1 year*	None-S
Kentucky										K-F-CC	6 months	None-T
Louisiana										QQ	180 days	None
Maine	X	X	X	X	X				X	X-Z	6 months	None
Maryland		X			X	X				X-KK	1 year	None
Massachusetts	B	X	X	X	X				X	Y-K-W	2 years*	6 mos.
Michigan			X							MM	1 year*	None
Minnesota		X								MM	1 year*	None
Mississippi	X	X		X	X	X	X	X		K-W-OO	1 year*	None-T
Missouri										K-M-DD	1 year*	None-U
Montana	X	X	X	X	X					QQ	1 year	None*
Nebraska										K-KK	1 year	6 months
Nevada	X	X	X	X	X					QQ	6 weeks	None
New Hampshire	X	X	X	X	X	X				K-Y	1 year*	None
New Jersey	X	X		X						D-GG-HH-II-KK	1 year*	None
New Mexico	X	X	X	X						NN-K-Y	1 year*	None
New York	X	X		X						F	6 months	None
North Carolina	X	X								X-Z*	1 year	
North Dakota	X	X			X	X				Q-K-X	6 months	None
Ohio	X	X	X	X	X	X				K-KK	1 year	None
Oklahoma	X	X	X	X	X	X			X	BB-CC-DD	1 year	None
Oregon	X	X							X	F-K-BB-CC	6 months	None
Pennsylvania	X	X		X	X	X			X	KK	6 months*	90 days
Rhode Island	X	X	X	X	X	X				B-M-DD-K-Y	1 year*	None
South Carolina	X	X	X	X					X	H-X	2 years*	6 months
South Dakota	X	X	X	X	X				X	Y	1 year	None
Tennessee	X	X	X	X	X	X				K	1 year*	None
Texas	X	X		X	X					A-DD-EE	6 months*	None-T
Utah	X	X	X	X	X	X				K-X-F-PP	1 year	None-T
Vermont	X	X	X							W-K	3 months	3 mos.*
Virginia		X			X	X		X		Y-K	6 htnths	3 mos.-O*
Washington									X	J-B-X	1 year	None-U*
West Virginia	X	X	X	X	X			X		B-K-Y-KK	6 months	None
Wisconsin	X	X	X	X	X					X-K	2 years*²	None
Wyoming	X	X	X	X	X	X	X			Y-Z-K	6 months	None-T

(1.) Determined by court order. (2.) No minimum residence required in adultery cases. (3.) Or 5 days after action is set for trial, whichever is sooner. (4.) Except one year when defendant is a non-resident, or personal service of a summons is impossible. (A) Violence. (B) Indignities. (C) Loathsome disease. (D) Joining religious order disbelieving in marriage. (E) Unchaste behavior after marriage. (F) Incompatibility. (H) Any gross misbehavior or wickedness. (I) Wife being a prostitute. (J) Husband being a vagrant. (K) 5-yrs. insanity; permanent insanity in Utah: incurable insanity in Calif. Exceptions 1 yr. Wis.; 18 mos. Alaska; 2 yrs. Ga.,Ha., Ind., N.J., Nev., Ore., Wash., and Wyo.; 3 yrs. Ark., N.C., Fla., Tex., Minn., Colo., Kan., Hawaii, Md., Miss., W. Va.; 6 yrs. Idaho. (M) Consanguinity. (N) In cruelty cases, one yr. to remarry. (O) Plaintiff, 6 mos.; defendant 2 yrs. to remarry. (P) If guilty spouse is sentenced to infamous punishment. (Q) Crime against nature. (R) Sixty days to remarry. (S) One year to remarry; Hawaii one year with minor child. Except Iowa, 90 days. (T) Six months to remarry; in Kan. 60 days. (U) Adultery cases, remarriage in discretion of court. (W) Separation for 2 yrs. after decree for same in Ala. and Minn.;3 yrs. in Utah; 4 yrs. in N.J.; 18 mos. in N.H.; 5 yrs. in Md. (X) Separation, no cohabitation—5 yrs., Exceptions La., Va., Wyo. W.Va. 2 yrs.; Tex. and Maine 3 yrs.; N.C. 1 yr. and R.I. 10 yrs. (Y) Separation, no cohabitation—3 years. Exceptions: Vt., Wash., 2 yrs.; Del., Md., N.J., N.Y., and 18 mos.; D.C. and Wis. 1 yr.; (Z) Separation for 2 yrs. after decree for Dist. of Col.; 1 yr. for N.Y., Wis. and La. (AA) Mental incapacity at time of marriage. (BB) Procurement of out-of-state divorce. (CC) Gross neglect of duty. (DD) Bigamy. (EE) Attempted homicide. (FF) Plaintiff under age at time of marriage. (GG) Treatment which injures health or endangers reason. (HH) Wife without state for 10 yrs. (II) Wife in state 2 yrs.; husband never in state and has intent to become citizen of foreign country. (JJ) Seven years absence. (KK) Irreconcilable differences. (LL) Life sentence dissolves marriage. (MM) Breakdown of marriage with no reasonable likelihood of preservation. (NN) Deviate sexual conduct. (OO) Course of conduct detrimental to the marriage relationship of party seeking divorce. (PP) Incompatibility without regard to fault. (QQ) Marriage irretrievably broken.

Adultery is either grounds for divorce or evidence of irreconcilable differences and a breakdown of the marriage in all states. The plaintiff can invariably remarry in the same State where he or she procured a decree of divorce for annulment. Not so the defendant, who is barred in certain States for some offenses. After a period of time has elapsed even the offender can apply for special permission. The U.S. Supreme Court in a 5 to 4 opinion, ruled April 18, 1949, that one sided quick divorces could be challenged as illegal if notice of the action was not served on the divorced partner within the divorcing States, excepting where the partner was represented at the proceedings. **Enoch Arden Laws.** Disappearance and unknown to be alive—Conn. 7 years absence; N. H., 2 years; N. Y., 5 years (called dissolution); Vt., 7 years.

Motor Vehicle Traffic Deaths by States

Source: State traffic authorities

Place of accidents	Number 1973	1972	Mil. death rate* 1973	1972	Place of accidents	Number 1973	1972	Mil. death rate* 1973	1972
Total U.S.*	55,800	56,600	4.3	4.5	Montana	323	395	5.8	7.3
Alabama	1,235	1,248	6.2	6.0	Nebraska	433	485	3.9	4.5
Alaska	76	59	4.7	3.9	Nevada	267	259	6.4	6.7
Arizona	958	807	5.9	5.5	New Hampshire	145	179	2.8	3.5
Arkansas	672	764	5.0	6.0	New Jersey	1,355	1,314	2.8	2.8
California	4,905	4,996	3.8	3.9	New Mexico	638	587	6.7	6.6
Colorado	672	738	4.1	4.6	New York	3,082	3,197	4.6	4.3
Connecticut	516	467	2.8	2.6	North Carolina	1,889	1,976	5.3	5.8
Delaware	129	132	3.6	3.8	North Dakota	208	208	4.8	5.1
District of Columbia	76	73	2.5	2.5	Ohio	2,342	2,451	3.6	3.9
Florida	2,660	2,498	4.5	4.5	Oklahoma	797	843	3.7	4.1
Georgia	1,904	1,885	5.3	4.7	Oregon	635	734	4.0	4.8
Hawaii	136	146	3.4	3.9	Pennsylvania	2,223	2,352	3.3	3.5
Idaho	349	348	6.5	6.6	Rhode Island	131	122	2.4	2.5
Illinois	2,367	2,254	3.9	3.8	South Carolina	967	1,099	4.7	5.6
Indiana	1,605	1,555	4.1	4.2	South Dakota	286	294	5.6	5.8
Iowa	813	873	4.1	4.6	Tennessee	1,427	1,414	4.9	5.1
Kansas	623	666	4.1	4.6	Texas	3,692	3,688	4.6	4.8
Kentucky	1,117	1,093	4.6	4.7	Utah	361	382	5.0	5.7
Louisiana	1,158	1,161	6.0	6.2	Vermont	154	151	4.7	4.7
Maine	247	258	3.6	3.8	Virginia	1,220	1,256	3.5	3.8
Maryland	821	813	3.2	3.7	Washington	775	852	3.3	3.8
Massachusetts	1,010	991	3.4	3.3	West Virginia	478	523	4.7	5.3
Michigan	2,213	2,258	3.8	3.9	Wisconsin	1,156	1,168	4.0	4.2
Minnesota	1,024	1,031	4.1	4.1	Wyoming	192	197	5.6	5.8
Mississippi	883	922	6.4	7.0					
Missouri	1,448	1,474	4.7	5.0	Puerto Rico	568	550	7.5	8.2

* The mileage death rate is the number of deaths per 100,000 vehicle-miles.

Deaths in Civil Aviation Accidents

Source: National Safety Council

Year	Total deaths*	Scheduled flights (passengers) — Domestic No.	Rate**	International No.	Rate**	General aviation No.	Rate**
1960	1,286	297	0.93	10	0.12	787	24
1965	1,279	205	0.38	21	0.12	1,029	21
1970	1,454	0	0.00	2	0.01	1,310	20
1971	1,608	174	0.16	0	0.00	1,405	21
1972	1,581	160	0.13	0	0.00	1,400	20
1973	1,627	128	0.10	69	0.19	1,340	20

*Includes some deaths not shown separately—crew members in scheduled operations and persons not in planes killed in airplane accidents. Excludes deaths in military plane accidents.
**Rates are the number of deaths per 100,000,000 passenger miles. (1) (NSC estimate) Pilots and other crew members are considered passengers for general aviation only.

Accidental Deaths by Age, Sex, and Type

Source: National Safety Council

Age and Sex	All Types	Motor-Vehicle	Falls	Drowning	Fires, Burns*	Ingest. of Food, Object	Fire-arms	Poison (solid, liquid)	Poison by Gas	% Male All Types
All Ages	114,638	54,633	16,926	7,860	6,718	2,753	2,406	3,679	1,620	70%
Under 5	6,594	1,915	340	890	848	906	93	226	34	58%
5 to 14	8,203	4,159	196	1,550	609	122	413	44	58	69%
15 to 24	24,336	16,720	425	2,330	385	166	726	1,010	384	80%
25 to 34	12,842	7,686	391	810	437	133	377	677	242	80%
35 to 44	11,137	5,760	720	710	566	195	272	517	231	77%
45 to 54	12,415	5,913	1,163	660	889	303	230	486	250	73%
55 to 64	11,749	5,186	1,679	460	943	315	174	355	200	72%
65 to 74	10,644	4,084	2,565	280	951	280	75	210	123	63%
75 & over	16,624	3,179	9,444	150	1,077	333	46	153	96	46%
Age unknown	94	31	3	20	13	0	0	1	2	78%
Sex										
Male	79,756	39,274	8,734	6,673	3,988	1,654	2,060	2,369	1,193	
Female	34,882	15,359	8,192	1,187	2,730	1,099	346	1,310	427	
Per cent male	70%	72%	52%	85%	59%	60%	86%	64%	74%	

††Data are for 1970, latest official figures.

Accidental Deaths by Month and Type, 1970 and 1973

Month	1973 Totals	1970 Details by Type ALL TYPES	Motor-Vehicle	Falls	Drowning	Fires, Burns*	Ingest. of Food, Object	Fire-arms	Poison (solid, liquid)	Poison by Gas
All Months	117,000	114,638	54,633	16,926	7,860	6,718	2,753	2,406	3,679	1,620
January	8,900	9,177	3,684	1,688	210	1,039	240	208	320	313
February	8,000	8,229	3,744	1,407	220	828	237	152	222	181
March	9,350	8,732	4,165	1,370	370	720	204	179	237	207
April	9,000	8,735	4,094	1,309	570	603	215	169	278	111
May	10,200	9,906	4,741	1,341	1,080	439	220	148	324	98
June	11,000	10,064	4,739	1,338	1,360	304	229	171	319	55
July	11,350	10,695	4,837	1,406	1,590	338	227	153	327	58
August	11,000	10,894	5,208	1,446	1,240	314	242	193	341	51
September	10,300	9,428	4,876	1,322	550	307	206	175	320	41
October	10,000	9,510	5,079	1,363	260	432	250	233	318	135
November	9,250	9,491	4,668	1,410	30	634	246	359	315	178
December	8,650	9,777	4,798	1,526	180	760	237	266	358	192
Average	9,750	9,553	4,553	1,411	655	560	229	201	307	135

Source: NCHS and NSC.   *Includes deaths resulting from conflagration regardless of nature of injury.
†Includes drowning in water transport accidents. Some totals partly estimated.

U.S. Building Fire Losses By Causes

Source: National Fire Protection Assn. Copyright 1974

These estimated figures are intended to show the relative order of magnitude of fire losses by cause, and to indicate year-to-year trends. While they are reasonable approximations based on experience in typical states, they should not be taken as exact records for each class. The figures by themselves do not show the relative safety in use of various types of materials, devices, fuels, or services, and they should not be used for that purpose.

Cause	No. of Fires	Estimated Loss
Heating and Cooking Equipment	165,800	$ 189,700,000
Equipment defective or misused	97,500	$126,800,000
Chimneys and flues	23,900	17,700,000
Hot ashes and coals	6,500	3,700,000
Combustibles near heaters and stoves	37,900	41,500,000
Smoking-Related	115,200	100,700,000
Electrical	170,700	331,500,000
Wiring and general equipment	106,700	213,300,000
Motors and appliances	64,000	118,200,000
Trash burning	35,200	2,400,000
Flammable Liquids[1]	67,300	61,200,000
Open Flames and Sparks[1]	70,000	99,500,000
Sparks and embers	6,500	7,000,000
Welding and cutting	9,800	34,400,000
Friction, sparks from machinery	16,200	17,100,000
Thawing pipes	5,500	11,100,000
Other open flames	32,000	29,900,000
Lightning	21,600	41,900,000
Children and Fire	70,800	76,300,000
Exposure	25,200	23,200,000
Incendiary and Suspicious	94,300	320,000,000
Spontaneous Ignition	14,900	25,500,000
Gas Fires and Explosions[1]	9,600	23,400,000
Explosions from Fireworks, Explosives	4,300	5,200,000
Miscellaneous Known Causes	70,500	191,400,000
Unknown Causes	150,500	1,045,300,000
TOTAL BUILDING FIRES	1,085,900	$2,537,200,000

[1]Does not include fires originating in heating and cooking equipment.

INTERPOL (International Criminal Police Organization)

The United States is one of 114 countries that are members of INTERPOL, the International Criminal Police Organization. United States participation in INTERPOL was authorized by Congress in 1958. Because of the Treasury Dept.'s activities in the suppression of counterfeiting, smuggling and the narcotics traffic, all of which have international ramifications, that department was designated as U. S. representative to INTERPOL.

Each member nation has one vote at a general assembly of INTERPOL held annually at a site chosen by the delegates at the previous year's assembly. The chairman of the U. S. delegation attending such meetings is the Assistant Secretary of the Treasury (Enforcement and Operations).

INTERPOL dates from 1914, but World War I brought suspension of all its activities until 1923. The organization's first constitution was drawn up in that year. Files on international criminals were built up gradually to a point where their value to the police of member nations became apparent. During World War II the files disappeared from Vienna, where the General Secretariat of INTERPOL was located.

The organization was reconstituted at the end of World War II. The General Secretariat was moved to Paris and is now located in the Parisian suburb of Saint-Cloud. The Secretariat functions as a central depository for fingerprints, photographs and other records of international criminals. It also operates an internationel radio network to 41 of the member countries.

Interpol does not employ any investigators as such. Foreign requirements for investigation are referred to the National Central Bureaus, the offices established in each country to liaison Interpol affairs. Scotland Yard is the National Central Bureau for the United Kingdom; the Surete in France; the Questore in Italy; the Melbourne City Police in Australia serve as the National Central Bureaus for those countries.

In the United States all inquiries, both domestic and foreign, are channeled through the National Central Bureau at the Treasury Dept. in Washington. Unless foreign requirements for investigation in the United States involve Federal jurisdiction or interest, they are referred to local and state police agencies for investigation. All U.S. enforcement agencies may call upon Interpol Washington for investigation in other member countries.

Locations of Federal Detention Areas

Source: U.S. Bureau of Prisons

Penitentiaries: Atlanta, Ga.; Leavenworth, Kan.; Lewisburg, Pa.; McNeil Island, Wash.; Marion, Ill.; Terre Haute, Ind. **Reformatories:** El Reno, Okla.; Petersburg, Va.; Women, Alderson, W.Va. **Medical center:** Springfield, Mo.; Hospital; Maintenance unit. **Prison camps:** Eglin Air Force Base, Florida; Montgomery, Ala.; Safford, Ariz.; Allenwood, Pa. **Correctional Institutions:** Danbury, Conn.; La Tuna, Tex.; Lompoc, Cal.; Texarkana, Tex.; Milan, Mich.; Tallahassee, Fla.; Seagoville, Tex.; Terminal Island, Cal.; Sandstone, Minn.; Ft. Worth, Tex. **Detention headquarters center:** New York City; Florence, Ariz. **Institutions for juvenile and youth offenders:** Ashland, Ky.; Englewood, Col.; Morgantown, W. Va. **Community Treatment Centers:** Detroit, Mich.; Chicago, Ill.; Los Angeles, Cal.; Kansas City, Mo.; Atlanta, Ga.; Houston, Tex.; Oakland, Cal.; New York City; Dallas, Tex.

Total Arrest Trends by Sex — 1972-73

Source: Federal Bureau of Investigation, Uniform Crime Reports — 1973

Offense charged	Males				Females			
	Total		Under 18		Total		Under 18	
	1973	Percent change 1972-73	1973	Percent change 1972-73	1973	Percent change 1972-73	1973	Percent change 1972-73
Total[1]	5,212,599	+3.3	1,274,978	+6.1	945,915	+4.5	355,744	+.5
Murder and nonneglig. manslaughter	11,760	+9.4	1,315	+4.8	2,077	+1.5	127	—
Neglig. manslaughter	2,470	+1.0	306	+53.0	323	+2.9	21	−58.0
Forcible rape	18,387	+12.0	3,632	+13.4	—	—	—	—
Robbery	92,190	+4.3	31,372	+12.9	6,679	+5.2	2,340	−4.3
Aggravated assault	126,717	+11.1	21,286	+7.4	19,306	+10.0	3,626	+1.9
Burglary — breaking or entering.	284,679	+10.4	154,885	+16.6	16,244	+14.3	8,330	+21.3
Larceny — theft	420,049	+1.7	211,032	−1.8	193,885	+7.7	85,891	+3.0
Auto theft	106,622	+5.2	60,554	+10.1	6,747	+9.0	3,995	+13.8
Other assaults	229,227	+1.8	41,347	+4.8	36,248	+.8	10,420	−6.5
Arson	9,408	+11.1	5,645	+12.7	1,179	+28.7	539	+13.5
Forgery and counterfeiting	29,090	−1.2	3,239	+16.4	10,688	+8.2	1,224	+11.0
Fraud....................	54,805	+5.2	2,266	+12.8	24,808	+10.8	768	+8.6
Embezzlement	4,037	+19.2	333	+21.5	1,269	+37.5	82	+28.1
Stolen property offenses	60,020	+4.5	20,921	+15.7	6,725	+9.2	1,856	+26.2
Vandalism	106,039	+4.3	74,070	+1.8	8,906	+2.0	5,440	−1.7
Weapons; carrying, possessing, etc.	102,605	+7.7	17,040	+12.3	8,912	+15.8	962	+17.3
Prostitution and commercialized vice...................	10,761	+9.2	444	+23.7	31,953	+7.7	1,293	+40.4
Other sex offenses (except forcible rape).	43,364	+5.2	8,287	+2.5	3,648	−7.0	1,198	−13.1
Narcotic drug laws.	394,327	+20.6	98,753	+39.8	66,604	+11.6	21,864	+25.9
Gambling.................	49,116	−13.2	1,373	−.5	4,706	−12.2	102	+61.9
Offenses against family, children .	35,698	−2.2	622	+28.8	3,729	−4.4	257	+11.3
Driving under the influence.....	576,252	+18.6	7,976	+29.8	45,124	+22.5	610	+41.5
Liquor laws...............	146,021	−3.0	55,893	+5.3	25,761	−.2	13,904	+5.1
Drunkenness...............	1,053,579	−4.6	28,526	−6.0	82,282	−4.7	4,706	−13.2
Disorderly conduct	363,186	+1.0	81,786	−3.6	79,716	+15.9	17,943	−8.9
Vagrancy.................	31,487	−2.1	4,739	−7.5	16,897	−11.6	1,090	−10.4
All other offenses (except traffic)	682,900	−3.1	169,553	−.9	125,607	−2.6	51,268	−6.8

[1] Totals will not add due to deletion of several minor arrest categories.

Canada: Criminal Offenses and Crime Rate

Source: Statistics Canada

	1972 Actual Offenses	Rate	1973 Actual Offenses	Rate	Percent change in rate
Murder.	478	2.2	474	2.1	−4.5
Attempted Murder	412	1.9	482	2.2	16.0
Manslaughter...........................	50	0.2	85	0.4	68.5
Rape..................................	1,286	5.9	1,522	6.9	17.3
Other Sexual Offenses	9,595	44.0	9,969	45.3	3.0
Wounding..............................	1,706	7.8	1,858	8.4	8.0
Assaults (Not indecent).................	85,239	390.6	88,072	400.2	2.4
Total-Crimes of Violence	**98,766**	**452.4**	**102,462**	**463.7**	**2.5**
Robbery...............................	11,839	54.3	12,376	56.2	3.6
Breaking and Entering....................	191,088	875.7	189,608	861.5	−1.6
Theft, Motor Vehicle.....................	70,421	322.7	69,214	314.5	−2.6
Theft Over $200	149,409	684.7	60,496	274.9	−59.9
Theft $200 and Under.....................	314,501	1441.3	405,385	1841.9	27.8
Have Stolen Goods	13,858	63.5	13,766	62.5	−1.5
Frauds................................	68,792	315.3	70,228	319.1	1.2
Total-Property Crimes.................	**819,908**	**3757.5**	**821,073**	**3730.5**	**−0.7**
Prostitution.	2,183	10.0	3,505	15.9	59.2
Gaming and Betting......................	3,126	14.3	2,821	12.8	−10.5
Offensive Weapon.......................	7,528	34.5	8,733	39.7	15.0
Other Criminal Code.....................	259,416	1188.9	326,035	1481.3	24.6
Arson and Attempted Arson...............	2,732	12.5	2,630	11.9	−4.6
Total-Other Crimes	**274,985**	**1260.2**	**343,724**	**1561.7**	**23.9**
Total Criminal Code	**1,193,659**	**5467.9**	**1,267,259**	**5735.6**	**4.9**
Federal Statutes........................	39,796	182.4	43,054	195.6	7.3
Provincial Statutes	318,564	1459.9	337,145	1531.8	4.9
Municipal By-Laws.......................	73,667	337.6	73,958	336.0	−0.5
Addicting Opiate-Like Drugs	3,234	14.8	3,822	17.4	17.2
Cannabis (Marihuana)....................	20,606	94.4	42,989	195.3	106.8
Controlled Drugs	1,717	7.9	2,087	9.5	20.5
Restricted Drugs........................	3,259	14.9	4,209	19.1	28.0

Federal Bureau of Investigation

The Federal Bureau of Investigation (FBI) is an activity of the Department of Justice, and is located at 9th St. and Pennsylvania Ave., Washington, D. C., 20535. It investigates all violations of Federal laws except those specifically assigned to some other agency by legislative action, such violations including counterfeiting, and internal revenue, postal and customs violations. It also investigates espionage, sabotage, treason and other matters affecting internal security, as well as kidnaping, transportation of stolen goods across state lines, interstate traffic in prostitution and violations of the Federal bank and atomic energy laws.

The FBI collects and classifies police and crime reports for the nation. While this division is of great usefulness in detecting criminals, it serves a wider purpose in recording the fingerprints of many other citizens who voluntarily make this record.

The FBI has 59 field divisions in the principal cities of the country. Consult telephone directories for location and phone numbers.

An applicant for the position of Special Agent of the FBI must be at least 23 and under 36 years old and graduate of a state-accredited resident law school or from a resident four-year college with a major in accounting with at least one year of practical accounting and/or auditing experience. In addition, applicants with a four-year resident college degree with a major in certain areas or 3 years specialized experience of a professional, executive, or complex investigative nature are presently being considered on a limited basis. An agent gets 14 weeks of training, during which he learns techniques of investigation and arrest and recognition of evidence.

Clarence M. Kelley, former FBI agent and professional law enforcement officer, became Director on July 9, 1973.

U. S. Govt. Crime Reports
Source: Federal Bureau of Investigation

Offense	1973 est.	Percent over[1] 1972	1968
Murder	19,510	+4.5	+34.8
Forcible rape	51,000	+9.0	+54.8
Robbery	382,680	+1.3	+39.2
Assault	416,270	+6.2	+39.7
Burglary	2,540,000	+7.2	+31.4
Larceny	4,304,400	+3.9	+18.9
Auto theft	923,600	+3.9	+12.9
Total	8,638,400	+4.9	+23.5

[1]Percent by which the rate of crime per 100,000 population increased in 1973 over 1972 and 1968.

Crime in the U.S. Increases 5.7% in 1973

Crime in the U.S., as measured by the Crime Index offenses, increased by 5.7% in 1973 over 1972. Violent crimes were up 4.9%, with forcible rape reports up 9.2% (partly, perhaps, because of a greater willingness of victims to report the crime), while aggravated assault (assault with a dangerous weapon including the fists) was up 7%. Murders increased 5.2% and robberies were up 2.1%. Property crimes went up 5.8%, with burglaries increasing by 8% and larceny and auto theft up 4.7% each. Serious crime in cities of 250,000 or more people was up only 1%, while crime in suburban areas grew by 9%.

Crime Index Trends by Geographic Regions
1973 over 1972
(rates per 100,000 population)

Region[1]	Total	Violent	Property	Murder	Forcible Rape	Robbery	Assault	Burglary	Larceny	Auto Theft
Northeast	+4.6	+0.9	+5.1	+ 4.1	+11.7	-3.7	+ 7.1	+4.6	+4.6	+ 7.5
North Central	+6.3	+5.6	+6.4	+11.8	+10.4	+1.0	+10.1	+9.0	+5.7	+ 3.5
South	+7.2	+4.9	+7.5	+ 1.6	+ 9.7	+8.7	+ 2.5	+9.8	+6.4	+ 6.4
West	+1.0	+5.3	+0.6	+ 1.3	+ 3.8	+3.3	+ 7.3	+4.7	-1.0	- 2.4

[1]Northeast includes New England, New Jersey, New York and Pennsylvania; North Central extends west through Nebraska and includes Missouri; South extends from Delaware, Maryland and West Virginia to Oklahoma and Texas.

Crime Rates by States
Source: Federal Bureau of Investigation, Uniform Crime Reports — 1973
(Rates per 100,000 population)

	Total	Violent	Property	Murder	Rape	Robbery	Assault	Burglary	Larceny	Auto Theft
Alabama	2,512.3	350.1	2,162.2	13.2	21.2	79.4	236.3	882.0	1,053.1	227.2
Alaska	4,943.3	384.5	4,558.8	10.0	44.5	67.0	263.0	1,167.3	2,865.5	526.1
Arizona	6,703.9	479.9	6,224.0	8.1	31.0	147.3	293.6	1,958.3	3,720.1	545.6
Arkansas	2,538.9	289.9	2,249.0	8.8	19.5	71.5	190.0	801.0	1,315.7	132.3
California	6,304.9	565.8	5,739.1	9.0	40.6	240.4	275.8	1,979.6	3,123.6	635.9
Colorado	5,495.8	414.0	5,081.9	7.9	38.7	162.9	204.4	1,598.8	2,910.6	572.5
Connecticut	3,664.4	208.7	3,455.7	3.3	11.1	84.2	110.1	1,029.3	1,909.7	516.7
Delaware	4,582.6	350.8	4,232.6	5.9	15.8	90.3	238.0	1,219.4	2,526.4	486.8
Florida	5,960.3	604.6	5,355.7	15.4	31.9	222.3	335.0	1,857.2	3,048.6	499.9
Georgia	3,430.3	412.4	3,017.9	17.4	25.8	158.1	211.1	1,268.8	1,390.7	358.4
Hawaii	4,958.8	155.6	4,803.1	5.3	20.2	83.7	46.5	1,535.5	2,830.8	436.9
Idaho	3,457.8	164.3	3,293.6	2.6	14.2	26.9	120.5	848.8	2,237.8	207.0
Illinois	4,324.9	555.9	3,769.1	10.4	24.0	272.8	248.7	1,025.1	2,236.2	507.7
Indiana	3,533.6	247.5	3,286.1	7.2	21.0	106.1	113.2	962.2	1,952.6	371.4
Iowa	2,831.6	102.3	2,729.3	2.2	11.3	32.9	55.9	634.0	1,904.6	190.7
Kansas	3,513.8	217.5	3,296.3	6.0	18.0	78.1	115.3	1,030.5	2,055.3	210.5
Kentucky	2,265.3	220.1	2,045.2	9.7	16.3	85.1	109.1	679.7	1,139.2	226.2
Louisiana	3,402.9	425.6	2,977.3	15.4	22.2	138.6	249.3	962.1	1,690.4	324.9
Maine	2,544.4	113.7	2,430.6	2.1	7.8	20.7	83.1	857.3	1,401.2	172.7
Maryland	4,791.4	641.1	4,150.3	11.3	27.8	301.6	300.4	1,144.6	2,457.9	547.8
Massachusetts	4,521.0	351.9	4,169.1	4.4	16.3	182.0	149.3	1,330.3	1,729.2	1,109.6
Michigan	5,489.4	585.2	4,904.2	12.1	35.1	282.7	255.2	1,584.6	2,771.3	548.3
Minnesota	3,535.6	177.7	3,357.8	2.7	14.9	88.7	71.5	1,016.4	2,004.7	336.7
Mississippi	1,926.3	339.1	1,587.2	16.1	17.1	46.8	259.1	593.8	879.7	113.8
Missouri	4,141.4	408.7	3,732.8	9.0	28.2	193.4	178.1	1,234.8	2,052.6	445.4

(continued)

(continued)	Total	Violent	Property	Murder	Rape	Robbery	Assault	Burglary	Larceny	Auto Theft
Montana	3,395.3	167.4	3,227.9	6.0	16.4	36.3	108.7	755.6	2,241.7	230.5
Nebraska	2,811.2	185.4	2,625.8	4.3	16.5	62.5	102.1	637.4	1,685.7	302.7
Nevada	6,632.1	572.1	6,060.0	12.2	46.0	262.0	251.8	2,149.8	3,299.1	611.1
New Hampshire	2,329.3	82.0	2,247.3	2.1	9.5	13.3	57.1	685.0	1,373.3	189.0
New Jersey	4,082.5	391.9	3,690.6	7.4	18.8	206.2	159.4	1,244.5	1,873.4	572.7
New Mexico	4,707.9	454.3	4,253.5	11.4	32.1	125.9	284.9	1,432.1	2,485.7	335.7
New York	4,306.7	731.2	3,575.5	11.1	26.1	439.6	254.4	1,296.7	1,671.5	607.2
North Carolina	2,811.9	437.8	2,374.0	13.0	16.1	71.4	337.4	892.0	1,308.2	173.8
North Dakota	2,078.4	60.8	2,017.7	0.8	7.3	7.3	45.3	383.4	1,502.8	131.4
Ohio	3,495.9	291.7	3,204.1	7.3	21.4	143.5	119.5	943.0	1,884.3	376.9
Oklahoma	3,466.4	246.2	3,220.2	6.6	20.0	68.2	151.4	1,163.9	1,745.2	311.1
Oregon	5,297.1	292.7	5,004.4	4.9	29.3	99.4	159.0	1,607.7	2,988.5	408.2
Pennsylvania	2,458.8	262.5	2,196.3	6.3	14.9	135.3	106.0	766.6	1,069.9	359.8
Rhode Island	4,678.3	282.5	4,395.8	3.4	8.3	97.0	173.8	1,189.1	2,312.3	894.3
South Carolina	3,327.0	394.6	2,932.4	14.4	22.5	79.2	278.6	1,194.3	1,492.1	246.0
South Dakota	2,175.8	126.9	2,048.9	3.8	12.8	24.7	85.5	498.7	1,406.0	144.2
Tennessee	3,060.1	358.0	2,702.1	13.2	26.9	130.5	187.5	1,009.8	1,362.2	330.1
Texas	4,046.2	381.5	3,664.7	12.7	25.5	142.1	201.1	1,266.4	2,051.1	347.2
Utah	4,247.1	208.5	4,038.6	3.2	22.9	62.6	119.8	989.3	2,748.1	301.2
Vermont	2,498.1	70.5	2,427.6	2.2	11.2	8.8	48.3	801.5	1,489.9	136.2
Virginia	3,238.7	285.7	2,953.0	8.5	20.7	101.0	155.5	825.8	1,859.1	268.1
Washington	5,089.9	271.5	4,818.5	4.0	26.2	96.3	145.0	1,540.4	2,902.4	375.7
West Virginia	1,471.5	123.7	1,347.8	5.7	9.3	27.9	80.8	415.8	824.9	107.1
Wisconsin	3,176.9	115.4	3,061.5	2.6	10.8	48.7	53.3	710.6	2,122.0	228.9
Wyoming	3,413.0	216.1	3,196.9	6.8	15.6	32.9	160.9	699.7	2,282.7	214.4

Reported Crime in Metropolitan Areas, 1973

Source: Federal Bureau of Investigation, Uniform Crime Reports—1973

The 27 Standard Metropolitan Statistical Areas listed below are those which appear most frequently among the top 30 cities in per capita reported crime rate for each of 7 kinds of major crime: the 5 listed below plus forcible rape and aggravated assault.

The rates are for reported crimes only; they are not an accurate index of crimes actually committed. In many metropolitan areas an unknown number of crimes go unreported by victims. This is especially true of the crimes of rape, burglary and larceny. Additionally, figures are often distorted for political reasons.

The number in parentheses following the city name indicates the number of categories (including forcible rape and aggravated assault) in which the city appears among the top 30.

The numbers in parentheses following crime rate figures give that city's rank in that category of crime. If no number appears, the city is not among the top 30 in that category. The cities are listed in order of their violent crime rate.

| Metropolitan Areas | Total[1] | Rate per 100,000 population | | Murder[3] | Robbery | Burglary | Larceny | Auto Theft |
		Violent[2]	Property[3]					
New York City, N.Y. (5)	5,457.5	1,204.9 (1)	4,252.6	17.5(16)	747.0 (1)	1,691.3	1,656.5	904.8 (6)
Miami, Fla.(4)	6,726.8(12)	947.8 (2)	5,779.0(25)	15.7	382.0 (6)	1,919.9(28)	3,181.0	678.1(26)
Baltimore, Md.(3)	5,545.6	916.2 (3)	4,629.4	15.4	458.7 (3)	1,351.1	2,636.3	642.1(29)
Los Angeles-Long Beach, Cal.(5)	6,628.5(13)	837.9 (4)	5,790.6(24)	12.4	370.6 (7)	2,187(11)	2,723.9	879.1 (8)
Detroit, Mich.(4)	6,098.3	821.5 (5)	5,276.8	19.3(10)	470.3 (2)	1,661.4	2,731.9	883.4 (7)
Albuquerque, N.M.(5)	6,966.4(10)	726.2 (9)	6,240.2(12)	12.6	271.3(21)	2,231.0 (8)	3,468.7(23)	540.5
Las Vegas, Nev.(5)	7,526.3 (4)	709.9(10)	6,816.5 (5)	15.0	352.8(10)	2,639.1 (1)	3,413.4(26)	763.9(15)
Orlando, Fla.(3)	6,404.3(23)	696.0(11)	5,708.4(29)	12.7	199.1	2,051.4(15)	3,158.8	498.2
Saginaw, Mich.(4)	6,617.1(14)	688.1(12)	5,929.0(20)	16.9(19)	307.1(16)	1,936.1(25)	3,778.8(11)	214.1
Baton Rouge, La.(3)	6,362.7(25)	686.6(13)	5,676.1	15.9(28)	163.1	2,018.7(20)	3,157.3	500.1
San Francisco-Oakland, Cal.(5)	7,277.8 (6)	683.6(14)	6,594.2 (7)	10.9	353.3 (9)	2,205.6 (9)	3,643.0(17)	745.6(16)
Daytona Beach, Fla.(4)	7,861.4 (2)	668.2(15)	7,193.1 (2)	10.6	283.3(19)	2,634.1 (2)	4,130.6 (3)	428.5
Jacksonville, Fla.(3)	5,861.8	668.0(17)	5,193.9	19.8 (7)	260.9(24)	1,888.6	2,897.0	408.3
Gainesville, Fla.(5)	6,575.8(17)	657.6(20)	5,918.3(21)	17.4(17)	170.9	2,050.4(16)	3,477.2(21)	390.7 *
New Orleans, La.(3)	4,778.2	657.2(21)	4,121.0	21.6 (2)	324.7(11)	1,337.0	2,063.9	720.2(18)
Fayetteville, N.C.(3)	3,884.5	646.4(22)	3,238.1	16.1(25)	180.6	1,517.7	1,478.5	241.9
W.Palm Beach-Boca Raton, Fla.(3)	7,125.2 (8)	634.8(25)	6,490.4 (9)	17.8(14)	171.5	2,243.2 (7)	3,838.8 (8)	408.3
Memphis, Tenn.(4)	5,597.1	619.8(29)	4,977.3	18.7(12)	307.9(15)	1,901.4(29)	2,633.7	442.2
Atlanta, Ga.(4)	5,273.4	616.3(30)	4,657.2	21.8 (1)	315.2(12)	2,003.8(21)	2,077.4	575.9
Ann Arbor, Mich.(4)	7,746.9 (3)	601.0	7,146.0 (3)	4.6	186.5	2,417.2 (4)	4,264.3 (2)	464.5
Phoenix, Ariz.(4)	8,165.2 (1)	569.0	7,596.2 (1)	8.3	187.1	2,509.6 (3)	4,394.2 (1)	692.4(23)
Ft. Lauderdale-Hollywood, Fla.(5)	7,519.8 (5)	542.4	6,977.4 (4)	16.7(21)	271.2(22)	2,144.2(12)	4,120.3 (4)	712.8(21)
Denver-Boulder, Colo.(5)	6,584.6(15)	519.9	6,064.8(14)	10.0	233.2(29)	1,996.4(22)	3,272.1(30)	796.3(13)
Stockton, Cal.(4)	6,819.4(11)	455.6	6,363.8(10)	16.3(24)	198.4	2,031.4(17)	3,703.2(14)	629.2(30)
Fresno, Cal.(3)	7,214.5 (7)	450.8	6,763.7 (6)	9.6	206.7	2,383.8 (6)	3,553.3(19)	826.6(12)
Santa Cruz, Cal.(4)	6,489.1(19)	436.2	6,052.9(15)	20.3 (5)	67.4	2,123.2(13)	3,495.7(20)	434.1
Santa Rosa, Cal.(3)	6,464.3(20)	331.4	6,132.9(13)	6.8	72.3	2,022.2(19)	3,649.2(16)	461.6

[1]Other metro areas among the top 30 in total reported crime (preponderantly property crime) are Reno, Nev. (9); Sarasota, Fla. (16); Bakersfield, Cal. (18); Modesto, Cal. (21); Kalamazoo, Mich. (22); Tucson, Ariz. (24); Riverside-San Bernardino-Ontario, Cal. (26); Eugene-Springfield, Ore.(27); Portland, Ore. (28); San Jose, Cal. (29); and Sacramento, Cal. (30).

[2]Violent crime includes murder and non-negligent manslaughter, forcible rape, robbery and aggravated assault. Other metro areas in the top 30 in reported violent crime are Paterson-Clifton-Passaic, N.J. (6); Chicago (7); Columbia, S.C. (8); Little Rock, Ark. (15); Flint, Mich. (18); Trenton, N.J. (19); Waco, Tex. (23); Washington, D.C. (24); Tallahassee, Fla. (26); Lafayette, La. (27); Greensboro-Winston-Salem-High Point, N.C. (28).

[3]Property crime includes burglary, larceny and auto theft. Other metro areas among the top 30 in reported property crime are Reno, Nev. (8); Sarasota, Fla. (11); Bakersfield, Cal. (16); Modesto, Cal. (17); Tucson, Ariz. (18); Eugene-Springfield, Ore. (19); San Jose, Cal. (22); Kalamazoo, Mich. (23); Portland, Ore. (26); Sacramento, Cal. (27); Riverside-San Bernardino-Ontario, Cal. (28); Yakima, Wash. (30).

[4]Of the top 30 cities in murder all but 7 are in the South. In fact, of the 83 southern cities included in the FBI crime report, 58 had murder rates higher than that of the country as a whole.

Reported Crime, 1972-73, by Size of Place

Source: Federal Bureau of Investigation, Uniform Crime Reports - 1973

Population group (1973 estimates)	Grand Total	Violent crime	Property crime	Murder-non-neg man-slaughter	Forcible Rape	Robbery	Aggra-vated Assault	Burglary	Auto theft
Total All Agencies: 6,615 agencies; total population 172,639,000									
1972.	7,306,145	746,462	6,559,683	16,169	41,364	353,224	335,705	2,079,546	805,713
1973.	7,667,612	778,804	6,888,808	17,128	45,167	358,038	358,471	2,230,714	835,948
Percent change. . . .	+4.9	+4.3	+5.0	+5.9	+9.2	+1.4	+6.8	+7.3	+3.8
Total Cities: 4,804 cities; total population 122,368,000									
1972.	6,116,375	650,563	5,465,812	13,151	32,812	329,400	275,200	1,664,903	710,695
1973.	6,370,032	673,843	5,696,189	14,054	36,177	332,434	291,178	1,774,846	731,651
Percent change. . . .	+4.1	+3.6	+4.2	+6.9	+10.3	+0.9	+5.8	+6.6	+2.9
54 cities over 250,000; population 41,649,000									
1972.	2,689,833	419,118	2,270,715	8,503	19,463	243,484	147,668	772,860	401,185
1973.	2,718,825	418,502	2,300,323	8,953	20,968	239,314	149,267	801,327	404,778
Percent change. . . .	+1.1	-0.1	+1.3	+5.3	+7.7	-1.7	+1.1	+3.7	+.9
97 cities, 100,000 to 250,000; population 13,952,000									
1972.	821,725	68,023	753,702	1,555	3,878	29,587	33,003	234,435	92,713
1973.	858,892	74,313	784,579	1,634	4,389	31,733	36,557	252,045	95,576
Percent change. . . .	+4.5	+9.2	+4.1	+5.1	+13.2	+7.3	+10.8	+7.5	+3.1
259 cities, 50,000 to 100,000; population 18,088,000									
1972.	856,717	58,475	798,242	1,106	3,506	24,257	29,606	223,208	87,015
1973.	893,014	64,617	828,397	1,154	4,108	25,811	33,544	238,109	89,136
Percent change. . . .	+4.2	+10.5	+3.8	+4.3	+17.2	+6.4	+13.3	+6.7	+2.4
490 cities, 25,000 to 50,000; population 17,265,000									
1972.	708,688	45,181	663,507	841	2,485	17,434	24,421	178,148	63,956
1973.	766,116	50,407	715,709	932	2,824	19,132	27,519	196,100	69,270
Percent change. . . .	+8.1	+11.6	+7.9	+10.8	+13.6	+9.7	+12.7	+10.1	+8.3
1,207 cities, 10,000 to 25,000; population 19,276,000									
1972.	675,667	37,913	637,754	755	2,260	10,452	24,446	167,377	45,345
1973.	736,696	42,650	694,046	879	2,554	11,869	27,348	187,315	50,417
Percent change. . . .	+9.0	+12.5	+8.8	+16.4	+13.0	+13.6	+11.9	+11.9	+11.2
2,697 cities under 10,000; population 12,137,000									
1972.	363,745	21,853	341,892	391	1,220	4,186	16,056	88,875	20,481
1973.	396,489	23,354	373,135	502	1,334	4,575	16,943	99,950	22,474
Percent change. . . .	+9.0	+6.9	+9.1	+28.4	+9.3	+9.3	+5.5	+12.5	+9.7
Suburban Area: 2,817 agencies; population 58,643,000									
1972.	1,942,987	130,427	1,812,560	2,720	9,819	41,478	76,410	565,220	167,888
1973.	2,116,212	145,897	1,970,315	2,956	10,525	45,545	86,871	624,421	184,014
Percent change. . . .	+8.9	+11.9	+8.7	+8.7	+7.2	+9.8	+13.7	+10.5	+9.6
Rural Area: 1,389 agencies; population 20,653,000									
1972.	299,152	25,819	273,333	1,243	2,270	3,382	18,924	117,546	15,941
1973.	327,824	27,019	300,805	1,245	2,395	3,596	19,783	127,536	18,291
Percent change. . . .	+9.6	+4.6	+10.1	+.2	+5.5	+6.3	+4.5	+8.5	+14.7

858 Law Enforcement Officers Killed 1964-1973

Souce: Uniform Crime Reports (FBI)

1. Responding to disturbance calls. 125
2. Burglaries in progress or pursuing suspect. 61
3. Robberies in progress or pursuing suspect. 166
4. Attempting other arrests. 209
5. Civil disorders. 11
6. Handling, transporting, custody of prisoners. 38
7. Investigating suspicious persons and circumstances. 60
8. Ambush. 69
9. Unprovoked mentally deranged. 38
10. Traffic stops. 81

Geographically for the period of 1964-1973 the 858 officers who were slain in line of duty were divided in this fashion: Northeast 132; North Central 215; South 357 and West 154.

Police Roster

Police officers and civilian employees in large cities as of Oct. 31, 1973

City	Officers	Civilian	City	Officers	Civilian	City	Officers	Civilian
Anchorage, Ala.	105	47	Indianapolis, Ind. . . .	1,100	200	Philadelphia, Pa. . . .	8,026	928
Atlanta, Ga.	1,458	199	Jacksonville, Fla. . . .	770	397	Phoenix, Ariz.	1,307	265
Baltimore, Md.	3,571	628	Jersey City, N.J.	1,041	35	Pittsburgh, Pa.	1,551	30
Birmingham, Ala. . . .	637	121	Kansas City, Mo. . . .	1,310	371	Portland, Ore.	714	236
Boise, Idaho	122	39	Little Rock, Ark.	268	63	Rochester, N.Y.	632	104
Boston, Mass.	2,565	278	Los Angeles, Cal. . .	7,134	2,541	Sacramento, Cal. . . .	521	134
Bridgeport, Conn. . .	457	20	Louisville, Ky.	757	196	St. Louis, Mo.	2,218	653
Buffalo, N.Y.	1,359	139	Memphis, Tenn.	1,170	292	St. Petersburg, Fla. .	410	224
Chicago, Ill.	13,415	1,460	Miami, Fla.	764	200	San Antonio, Tex. . .	1,040	194
Cincinnati, Ohio. . . .	1,125	261	Milwaukee, Wisc. . . .	2,128	190	San Bernardino,		
Cleveland, Ohio. . . .	2,437	(a)	Minneapolis, Minn. . .	850	91	Cal.	205	50
Columbus, Ohio. . . .	1,106	220	Nashville, Tenn.	784	148	San Diego, Cal.	1,014	257
Dallas, Tex.	1,929	621	Newark, N.J.	1,501	329	San Francisco, Cal. .	1,958	360
Denver, Col.	1,297	313	New Orleans, La. . . .	1,343	458	San Jose, Cal.	654	136
Detroit, Mich.	5,575	702	New York, N.Y.	29,861	4,427	Santa Ana, Cal.	225	83
Ft. Worth, Tex.	656	153	Norfolk, Va.	510	94	Seattle, Wash.	1,138	256
Fresno, Cal.	312	81	Oakland, Cal.	722	270	Stockton, Cal.	203	44
Gary, Ind.	394	55	Oklahoma City,			Tampa, Fla.	598	127
Hartford, Conn.	505	80	Okla.	621	96	Toledo, Ohio.	764	72
Honolulu, Hawaii . . .	1,403	319	Omaha, Nebr.	575	125	Tucson, Ariz.	484	144
Houston, Tex.	2,184	334	Pasadena, Cal.	202	70	Washington, D.C. . . .	4,937	665

POSTAL INFORMATION
United States Postal Service

The Postal Reform Act, creating a government-owned postal service under the Executive branch and replacing the old Post Office Department, was signed into law by President Nixon on Aug. 12, 1970. The service officially came into being on July 1, 1971.

The new U.S. Postal Service is governed by an 11-man Board of Governors. Nine members are appointed to 9-year terms by the President with Senate approval. These 9, in turn, choose a Postmaster General, who is no longer a member of the President's Cabinet. The Board and the new Postmaster General choose the 11th member, who serves as Deputy Postmaster General. A new Postal Rate Commission of 5 members, appointed by the President, recommends postal rates to the governors for their approval.

The first Postmaster General under the new system was Winton M. Blount. He resigned Oct. 29, 1971, and was replaced by his deputy, E. T. Klassen, Dec. 7, 1971.

United States Domestic Rates (as of Sept. 15, 1974)
First Class

Letters written, and matter sealed against inspection, 10ᶜ for each ounce or fraction.
U.S. Postal cards; single 8ᶜ; double 16ᶜ; private post cards, same.

First class includes written matter, namely letters, postal cards, post cards (private mailing cards) and all other matter wholly or partly in writing, whether sealed or unsealed, except manuscripts for books, periodical articles and music, manuscript copy accompanying proofsheets or corrected proofsheets of the same and the writing authorized by law on matter of other classes. Also matter sealed or closed against inspection. Bills and statements of accounts.

Greeting Cards

May be sent first class or single piece third class.

Airmail

Air postal or post card 11ᶜ each, letters and packages (up to 9 ounces) 13ᶜ an ounce. Business reply cards are 13ᶜ each. Business reply envelopes not over 2 ounces, 13ᶜ per ounce plus 2ᶜ per piece, weight over 2 ounces, 13ᶜ an ounce plus 6ᶜ per piece. Over 9 ounces priority mail rates plus 6ᶜ per piece. This is in the U. S. its territories and possessions, also to Armed Forces outside the U. S. when addressed APO or FPO, New York, N. Y., San Francisco, Calif. or Seattle, Wash. May be certified, registered, sent C.O.D. or special delivery.

Second Class

Single copy mailings by general public 8ᶜ for first 2 ounces and 2ᶜ for each additional ounce or the 4th class rate, whichever is lower. There are special rates for publications, newspapers and bulk mailing, consult local postmasters for rates and permit.

Third Class

Third Class (limit up to but not including 16 ounces): Mailable matter not in 1st and 2nd classes.

Single mailing: Greeting cards (sealed or unsealed), small parcels, printed matter, booklets and catalogs. 10ᶜ the first 2 ounces and 8 cents for each 2 ounces for pieces 4 ounces through 15.9 ounces.

Bulk material: Books, catalogs of 24 pages or more, seeds, cuttings, bulbs, roots, scions and plants; subject to a minimum rate, consult postmaster.

Other matter: Newsletters, shoppers' guides, advertising circulars. Subject to a minimum rate for which Post Office should be consulted. Separate rates for some nonprofit organizations. Bulk mailing fee, $30 per calendar year. Apply to postmaster for permit.

Parcel Post—Fourth Class

Fourth Class or Parcel Post (16 ounces and over): Merchandise, printed matter, etc., may be sealed.

On parcels weighing less than 10 lbs. and measuring more than 84 inches, but not more than 100 inches in length and girth combined, the minimum postal charge shall be the zone charge applicable to a 10-pound parcel.

Priority Mail

First-class mail of more than 12 ounces and airmail of more than 9 ounces have been merged into a "Priority Mail (Heavy Pieces)" service. First-class and airmail weighing up to one pound is charged $1.25 or $1.30 depending on destination zone. The most expeditious handling and transportation available will be used for fastest delivery.

Forwarding Addresses

The law that increased postal rates established the return address service for all classes of mail. (First time for first-class mail.) The mailer, in order to obtain a forwarding address, must endorse the envelope or cover "Address Correction Requested." The destination post office then will determine whether a forwarding address has been left on file and provide it for a fee of 10ᶜ.

Special Handling

Third and Fourth class parcels will be handled and delivered as expeditiously as practicable (but not special delivery) upon payment, in addition to the regular postage: Up to 2 lbs., 25ᶜ; over 2 lbs. and up to 10 lbs., 35ᶜ; over 10 lbs., 50ᶜ. Such parcels must be endorsed, Special Handling.

Special Delivery

First class mail up to 2 lbs., 60ᶜ, over 2 lbs. and up to 10 lbs., 75ᶜ; over 10 lbs. 90ᶜ. All other classes up to 2 lbs. 80ᶜ, over 2 and up to 10 lbs., 90ᶜ, over 10 lbs. $1.05.

Priority Mail

Air Parcel Post (over 9 ounces to 70 lbs.): Packages not to exceed 100 inches in length and girth combined, including written and other matter of the first class, whether sealed or unsealed, fractions of a pound being charged as a full pound. Thirteen cents an ounce or fraction for all domestic air mail up to and including 8 ounces regardless of distance or zone.

Rates according to zone apply between the U.S. and Puerto Rico and Virgin Islands.

Parcels weighing less than 10 pounds, measuring over 84 inches but not exceeding 100 inches in length and girth combined are chargeable with a minimum rate equal to that for a 10 pound parcel for the zone to which addressed.

Zones	To 1 lb.	1¹/₂	2	2¹/₂	3	3¹/₂	4	4¹/₂	5
1, 2, 3	$1.25	$1.50	$1.75	$1.93	$2.11	$2.29	$2.47	$2.65	$2.83
4	1.25	1.54	1.83	2.03	2.23	2.43	2.63	2.83	3.03
5	1.25	1.60	1.95	2.17	2.39	2.61	2.83	3.05	3.27
6	1.30	1.68	2.06	2.31	2.56	2.81	3.06	3.31	3.56
7	1.30	1.75	2.20	2.48	2.76	3.04	3.32	3.60	3.88
8	1.30	1.82	2.34	2.65	2.96	3.27	3.58	3.89	4.20

Postal Union Mail Special Services

Registration. — Available to practically all countries. Fee 95c. The maximum indemnity payable—generally only in case of complete loss (of both contents and wrapper) — is $13.07. To Canada only the fees are 95c and $1.25, providing indemnity for loss up to $100 to $200, respectively.

Return receipt. — Fee is 15c when the receipt is requested at time of mailing, requested after mailing 25c.

Special delivery. — Available to most countries. Consult post office. Fees: For post cards, letter mail, and airmail "other articles," 60c up to 2 pounds; over 2 to 10 pounds, 75c; over 10 pounds, 90c. For surface "other articles," 80c, 90c and $1.05, respectively.

Special handling. — Entitles AO *surface* packages to priority handling between mailing point and U.S. point of dispatch. Fees: 25c for packages to 2 pounds, 35c for packages over 2 pounds to 10 pounds, and 50c for packages over 10 pounds.

Airmail — There is daily air service to practically all countries.

Marking. — An article intended for special delivery service must have affixed to the cover near the name of the country of destination "EXPRESS" (Special Delivery) label, obtainable at the post office, or it may be marked on the cover boldly in red "EXPRESS" (Special Delivery).

Prepayment of replies from other countries. A mailer who wishes to prepay by letter from another country may do so by sending his correspondent one or more international reply coupons, which may be purchased at United States post offices. One coupon should be accepted in any country in exchange for stamps to prepay a surface letter of the first unit of weight to the U.S.

Registry. All mailable matter prepaid with postage at the first-class or airmail rate may be registered. The mailer is required to declare the value of mail presented for registration.

Insurance is applicable to 3d and 4th class matter. Matter for sale addressed to prospective purchasers who have not ordered it or authorized its sending will not be insured.

C.O.D.: Unregistered — is applicable to 3d and 4th class matter and sealed domestic mail of any class bearing postage at the 1st class rate. Such mail must be based on bona fide orders or be in conformity with aagreements between senders and addresses. Registered-For details consult postmaster.

Certified mail service is available for any matter having no intrinsic value on which 1st class or air mail postage is paid. Receipt is furnished at time of mailing and evidence of delivery obtained. The fee is 30c in addition to postage. Return receipt, restricted delivery and special delivery are available upon payment of additional fees. No indemnity.

Money Orders

Amount	Domestic	Foreign
$0.01 to $10.00............	25c	45c
10.01 to 50.00............	35c	65c
50.01 to 100.00............	40c	75c

Individual Piece Mailings
(Fourth Class Catalogs)

Weight lbs.	Local	1&2	3	Zones 4	5	6	7	8
1.5	$0.34	.41	.42	.44	.46	.48	.51	.55
2	.35	.43	.44	.47	.49	.52	.56	.61
2.5	.36	.45	.46	.50	.53	.56	.61	.67
3	.38	.47	.49	.52	.56	.61	.66	.73
3.5	.39	.49	.51	.55	.60	.65	.71	.79
4	.40	.51	.53	.58	.63	.69	.77	.86
4.5	.41	.52	.55	.61	.66	.73	.82	.92
5	.42	.54	.57	.63	.70	.77	.87	.98
6	.45	.58	.62	.69	.77	.86	.97	1.10
7	.47	.62	.66	.74	.83	.94	1.07	1.22
8	.50	.66	.71	.80	.90	1.03	1.17	1.34
9	.52	.70	.75	.85	.97	1.11	1.28	1.47
10	.54	.73	.79	.91	1.04	1.19	1.38	1.59

Zone Mileage

1	UP to 50	3	150-300	5	600-1,000	7	1,400-1,800
2	50-150	4	300-600	6	1,000-1,400	8	over, 1,800

Registered Mail

Indemnity to $100	$0.95
100.01 to 200	1.25
200.01 to 400	1.55
400.01 to 600	1.85
600.01 to 800	2.15
800.01 to 1,000	2.45
1,000.01 to 2,000	2.75
2,000.01 to 3,000	3.05
3,000.01 to 4,000	3.35
4,000.01 to 5,000	3.65
5,000.01 to 6,000	3.95
6,000.01 to 7,000	4.25
7,000.01 to 8,000	4.55
8,000.01 to 9,000	4.85
9,000.01 to 10,000	5.15

Consult postmaster for registry rates above $10,000.

Insured Mail

$0.01 to $15...............................	$0.20
15.01 to 50	.30
50.01 to 100	.40
100.01 to 150	.50
150.01 to 200	.60

Return receipts for over $15 from 15c to 25c.

C.O.D. Mail
Consult postmaster for fees and conditions of mailing.

Parcel Post Rate Schedule

1 lb., not exceeding	Local	1 & 2	3	Zones 4	5	6	7	8
2	$0.61	$0.72	$0.75	$0.83	$0.92	$1.02	$1.12	$1.21
3	.65	.78	.83	.92	1.04	1.18	1.32	1.45
4	.69	.84	.90	1.01	1.16	1.33	1.51	1.69
5	.73	.90	.98	1.10	1.28	1.49	1.71	1.93
6	.77	.96	1.05	1.19	1.40	1.64	1.90	2.17
7	.81	1.02	1.13	1.28	1.52	1.80	2.10	2.41
8	.85	1.08	1.20	1.37	1.64	1.95	2.29	2.65
9	.89	1.14	1.28	1.46	1.76	2.11	2.49	2.89
10	.93	1.20	1.35	1.55	1.88	2.26	2.68	3.13
11	.97	1.26	1.43	1.64	2.00	2.42	2.88	3.37
12	1.01	1.32	1.50	1.73	2.12	2.57	3.07	3.61
13	1.05	1.38	1.58	1.82	2.24	2.73	3.27	3.85
14	1.09	1.44	1.65	1.91	2.36	2.88	3.46	4.09
15	1.13	1.50	1.73	2.00	2.48	3.04	3.66	4.33
16	1.17	1.56	1.80	2.09	2.60	3.19	3.85	4.57
17	1.21	1.62	1.88	2.18	2.72	3.35	4.05	4.81
18	1.25	1.68	1.95	2.27	2.84	3.50	4.24	5.05
19	1.29	1.74	2.03	2.36	2.96	3.66	4.44	5.29
20	1.33	1.80	2.10	2.45	3.08	3.81	4.63	5.53

(Consult postmaster for parcels over 20 pounds or measuring more than 72 inches, length and girth.)

Special Fourth-Class Rate
(limit 70 lbs.)

First pound or fraction 18c; 8c for each additional pound or fraction. Only following specific articles: books 24 pages or more, at least 22 of which are printed consisting wholly of reading matter or scholarly bibliography containing no advertisement other than incidental announcements of books; 16 millimeter films in final form (except when mailed to or from commercial theaters); printed music in bound or sheet form; printed objective test materials; sound recordings, playscripts and manuscripts for books, periodicals and music; printed educational reference charts; loose-leaf pages and binders therefor consisting of medical information for distribution to doctors, hospitals, medical schools and medical students. Package must be marked "Special 4th-Class Rate" stating item contained.

Library Rate (limit 70 lbs.)

First pound or fraction 6c; each additional pound or fraction 3c. Books when loaned or exchanged between schools, colleges, public libraries and certain non-profit organizations; books, printed music, bound academic theses, periodicals, sound recordings, other library materials, museum materials (specimens, collections), scientific or mathematical kits, instruments or other devices; also catalogs, guides or scripts for some of these materials. Must be marked "Library Rate".

Post Office-Authorized 2-Letter State Abbreviations

Gradually replacing the traditional abbreviations for the states of the United States are the two-letter ones approved by the Post Office Department when it introduced the ZIP Code in 1963. The official list follows, including the District of Columbia, Guam, Puerto Rico and the Virgin Islands (all capital letters are used):

Alabama	AL	Kentucky	KY	Ohio	OH
Alaska	AK	Louisiana	LA	Oklahoma	OK
Arizona	AZ	Maine	ME	Oregon	OR
Arkansas	AR	Maryland	MD	Pennsylvania	PA
California	CA	Massachusetts	MA	Puerto Rico	PR
Colorado	CO	Michigan	MI	Rhode Island	RI
Connecticut	CT	Minnesota	MN	South Carolina	SC
Delaware	DE	Mississippi	MS	South Dakota	SD
Dist. of Col.	DC	Missouri	MO	Tennessee	TN
Florida	FL	Montana	MT	Texas	TX
Georgia	GA	Nebraska	NE	Utah	UT
Guam	GU	Nevada	NV	Vermont	VT
Hawaii	HI	New Hampshire	NH	Virginia	VA
Idaho	ID	New Jersey	NJ	Virgin Islands	VI
Illinois	IL	New Mexico	NM	Washington	WA
Indiana	IN	New York	NY	West Virginia	WV
Iowa	IA	North Carolina	NC	Wisconsin	WI
Kansas	KS	North Dakota	ND	Wyoming	WY

Also approved for use in addressing mail are the following abbreviations:

Alley	Aly	Drive	Dr	Plaza	Plz
Arcade	Arc	Expressway	Expy	Point	Pt
Avenue	Ave	Extended	Ext	Road	Rd
Boulevard	Blvd	Extension	Ext	Rural	R
Branch	Br	Freeway	Fwy	Square	Sq
Bypass	Byp	Gardens	Gdns	Street	St
Causeway	Cswy	Grove	Grv	Terrace	Ter
Center	Ctr	Heights	Hts	Trail	Trl
Circle	Cir	Highway	Hwy	Turnpike	Tpke
Court	Ct	Lane	Ln	Viaduct	Via
Courts	Cts	Manor	Mnr	Vista	Vis
Crescent	Cres	Place	Pl		

Commemorative Stamps and Regular Postal Issues 1974

Date		Commemorative Stamp	Value	From
Jan	2	International Airmail - Mt. Rushmore	26c	Rapid City, SD
Jan	4	Zip Code	10c	Washington, DC
Jan	4	Aerogramme	18c	Atlanta, GA
Jan	4	Airmail Postal Card	11c	State College, PA
Jan	4	International Postal Card	12c	Miami, FL
Jan	4	International Airmail Postal Card	18c	Miami, FL
Jan	11	International Airmail - Statue of Liberty	18c	Hempstead, NY
Jan	23	Elizabeth Blackwell	18c	Geneva, NY
Mar	11	Veterans	10c	Washington, DC
Mar	26	Robert Frost	10c	Derry, NH
Apr	4	NATO Aerogramme	18c	Washington, DC
Apr	18	Preserve the Environment	10c	Spokane, WA
May	4	Horse Racing	10c	Louisville, KY
May	14	Skylab	10c	Houston, TX
June	6	Universal Postal Union	10c	Washington, DC
June	13	Mineral Heritage (Block of 4 stamps)	10c	Lincoln, NE
June	15	Kentucky's 1st Settlement	10c	Harrodsburg, Ky
July	4	Bicentennial-Continental Congress (Block of 4 Stamps)	10c	Philadelphia, PA
Aug	5	Jefferson Stamps Booklet	13c, 10c	Oakland, CA
Aug	6	Chautauqua (Rural America)	10c	Chatauqua, NY
Aug	16	Kansas Wheat (Rural America)	10c	Hillsboro, KS
Aug	31	Tennis Envelope	10c	Forest Hills, NY
Sept	23	Energy Conservation	10c	Detroit, MI
Oct	10	Legend of Sleepy Hollow	10c	North Tarrytown, NY
Oct	12	Retarded Children Can Be Helped	10c	Arlington, TX
Oct.	23	2 Christmas Stamps — Altarpiece, Currier & Ives scene	10c ea.	New York City, NY

Postal Receipts at Large Cities

Fiscal Year	Boston	Chicago	Detroit	L.A.	New York	Phila.	St. Louis	Wash. D.C.
1970	$92,510,086	290,705,477	70,606,905	144,894,554	471,130,333	102,137,637	62,909,460	80,965,864
1971	95,205,407	292,558,518	70,256,324	149,063,344	359,170,452	107,122,556	65,104,974	84,053,982
1972	109,178,539	332,951,729	85,997,396	172,644,940	395,523,484	120,055,844	73,246,822	99,980,611
1973	114,159,472	339,770,450	84,358,518	172,365,582	392,348,195	120,173,378	75,342,257	103,152,177

Other Cities, for Fiscal Year 1973: Atlanta, $94,932,131; Baltimore, $59,316,991; Cincinnati, $49,284,583; Cleveland, $71,116,670; Columbus, $51,305,084; Dallas, $90,863,971; Denver, $51,855,326; Houston, $73,204,191; Indianapolis, $48,974,228; Kansas City, $58,207,336; Minneapolis, $73,176,918; Pittsburgh, $53,987,020; San Francisco, $88,347,608; Seattle, $46,135,613.

Post Offices in the United States

As of June 30, 1974, there was a total of 31,000 post offices throughout the U.S. and Possessions. Of this number 5,407 were First Class; 7,477 Second Class; 12,233 Third Class; and 5,883 Fourth Class.

Surface Mail, Air Mail, Parcel Post International Rates

Aerogrammes — 18 cents each to all countries.
Air Mail Post Cards (single) — 18 cents to all countries except Canada and Mexico (11c)

Country	Ordinary surface mail (not over 1 oz.)	Air Service Letters and letter pkgs. (per ½ oz.)	Other Articles First 2 oz.	Other Articles Each add'l 2 oz. or fraction	Parcel Post First 4 oz.	Parcel Post Each add'l 4 oz. or fraction	Surface Parcel Post First 2 lbs.	Surface Parcel Post Each add'l pound or fraction	Max. wt. for parcel post (surface or air) lbs.
Afghanistan	.18	.26	.70	.35	2.53	.96	1.55	.45	22
Albania	.18	.26	.60	.24	2.68	.63	1.55	.45	22
Algeria	.18	.26	.60	.24	2.18	.64	1.55	.45	44
Andorra	.18	.26	.60	.24	2.25	.56	1.55	.45	44
Angola	.18	.26	.70	.35	2.36	.81	1.55	.45	22
Anguilla	.18	.21	.50	.13	1.43	.29	1.55	.45	22
Antigua	.18	.21	.50	.13	1.43	.29	1.55	.45	22
Argentina	.18	.21	.60	.24	1.98	.86	1.55	.45	22
Aruba	.18	.21	.50	.13	1.67	.36	1.40	.40	44
Ascension Isl.	.18	.21	.60	.24	(4)	—	1.55	.45	22
Australia	.18	.26	.70	.35	2.11	.97	1.55	.45	44
Austria	.18	.26	.60	.24	2.17	.59	1.55	.45	44
Azores	.18	.26	.60	.24	1.57	.45	1.55	.45	22
Bahamas	.18	.21	.50	.13	1.76	.21	1.40	.40	22
Bahrein	.18	.26	.70	.35	1.95	.83	1.55	.45	22
Barbados	.18	.21	.50	.13	1.53	.41	1.40	.40	22
Barbuda	.18	.21	.50	.13	1.43	.29	1.40	.40	22
Belgium	.18	.26	.60	.24	1.94	.53	1.55	.45	44
Bermuda	.18	.21	.50	.13	1.52	.38	1.40	.40	33
Bhutan	.18	.26	.70	.35	(4)	—	...	...	(5)
Bolivia	.18	.21	.60	.24	1.99	.55	1.55	.45	44
Bonaire	.18	.21	.50	.13	1.67	.36	1.40	.40	44
Botswana	.18	.26	.70	.35	2.14	1.02	1.55	.45	22
Brazil	.18	.21	.60	.24	2.37	.63	1.55	.45	44
Br. Honduras	.18	.21	.50	.13	1.72	.37	1.55	.45	44
Br. Virgin Isl.	.18	.21	.50	.13	1.43	.29	1.40	.40	22
Brunei	.18	.26	.70	.35	2.42	1.18	1.55	.45	22
Bulgaria	.18	.26	.60	.24	1.73	.60	1.55	.45	22
Burma	.18	.26	.70	.35	2.66	1.15	1.55	.45	22
Burundi	.18	.26	.70	.35	2.22	.86	1.55	.45	22
Cambodia	.18	.26	.70	.35	(4)	—	1.55	.45	22
Cameroon	.18	.26	.70	.35	2.25	.74	1.55	.45	22
Canada[3]	.10	.13	(6)	—	(6)	—	1.40	.40	35
Cape Verde Isl.	.18	.26	.70	.35	2.19	.65	1.55	.45	22
Cen. Africa Rep.	.18	.26	.70	.35	2.22	.86	1.55	.45	44
Ceylon	.18	.26	.70	.35	2.68	1.03	1.55	.45	22
Chad	.18	.26	.70	.35	2.22	.86	1.55	.45	44
Chile	.18	.21	.60	.24	2.35	.71	1.55	.45	22
China Rep.	.18	.26	.70	.35	1.98	.84	1.55	.45	44
China, Cont.[7]	.18	.26	.70	.35	2.48	1.10	1.55	.45	44
Colombia	.18	.21	.60	.24	2.30	.40	1.55	.45	44
Comoro Isl.	.18	.26	.70	.35	2.52	1.15	1.55	.45	44
Congo (Brazza.)	.18	.26	.70	.35	2.22	.86	1.55	.45	44
Corsica	.18	.26	.60	.24	2.40	.53	1.55	.45	44
Costa Rica	.18	.21	.50	.13	1.66	.34	1.40	.40	44
Cuba	.18	.21	.50	.13	(4)	—	...	...	(5)
Curacao	.18	.21	.50	.13	1.67	.36	1.40	.40	44
Cyprus	.18	.26	.70	.35	2.32	.68	1.55	.45	22
Czechoslovakia	.18	.26	.60	.24	1.75	.61	1.55	.45	44
Dahomey	.18	.26	.70	.35	1.90	.68	1.55	.45	44
Denmark	.18	.26	.60	.24	1.72	.58	1.55	.45	44
Dominica	.18	.21	.50	.13	1.92	.38	1.40	.40	22
Dominican R.	.18	.21	.50	.13	1.80	.29	1.40	.40	44
Ecuador	.18	.21	.60	.24	2.24	.38	1.55	.45	44
El Salvador	.18	.21	.50	.13	1.78	.35	1.40	.40	44
Equatorial Guinea	.18	.26	.70	.35	2.27	.98	1.55	.45	44
Estonia[2]	.18	.26	.70	.35	2.29	.76	1.55	.45	44
Ethiopia	.18	.26	.70	.35	2.28	.88	1.55	.45	44
Faeroe Isl.	.18	.26	.60	.24	1.72	.58	1.55	.45	44
Falkland Isl.	.18	.21	.60	.24	2.41	.68	1.55	.45	22
Fiji Islands	.18	.26	.70	.35	2.25	.72	1.55	.45	44
Finland	.18	.26	.60	.24	1.75	.63	1.55	.45	44
France— incl. Monaco	.18	.26	.60	.24	2.40	.53	1.55	.45	44
French Guiana	.18	.21	.60	.24	1.76	.45	1.55	.45	44
Fr. Polynesia	.18	.26	.70	.35	2.17	.61	1.55	.45	44
Fr. Ter. Afars, Issas	.18	.26	.70	.35	2.33	.83	1.55	.45	44
Gabon Rep.	.18	.26	.70	.35	2.22	.86	1.55	.45	44
Gambia	.18	.26	.70	.35	1.92	.61	1.55	.45	22
Germany, incl. Saar.	.18	.26	.60	.24	1.69	.56	1.55	.45	44
Ghana	.18	.26	.70	.35	2.35	.74	1.55	.45	22
Gibraltar	.18	.26	.60	.24	1.74	.60	1.55	.45	22
Gilbert & Ellice	.18	.26	.70	.35	2.14	.80	1.55	.45	22
Great Britain	.18	.26	.60	.24	1.67	.53	1.55	.45	22
Greece	.18	.26	.60	.24	2.11	.67	1.55	.45	22
Greenland	.18	.26	.60	.24	1.89	.75	1.55	.45	44
Grenada	.18	.21	.50	.13	1.92	.38	1.40	.40	22
Guadeloupe	.18	.21	.50	.13	1.61	.29	1.40	.40	44

Country	Ordinary surface mail (not over 1 oz.)	Letters and letter pkgs. (per 1/2 oz.)	Air Service Other Articles First 2 oz.	Each add'l. 2 oz. or fraction	Parcel Post First 4 oz.	Each add'l 4 oz. or fraction	Surface Parcel Post First 2 lbs.	Each add'l pound or fraction	Max. wt. for parcel post (surface or air) lbs.
Guatemala	.18	.21	.50	.13	2.02	.37	1.40	.40	44
Guinea	.18	.26	.70	.35	1.98	.77	1.55	.45	44
Guyana	.18	.21	.60	.24	1.95	.40	1.55	.45	22
Haiti	.18	.21	.50	.13	1.81	.28	1.40	.40	44
Honduras	.18	.21	.50	.13	1.72	.37	1.40	.40	¹44
Hong Kong	.18	.26	.70	.35	2.13	1.00	1.55	.45	22
Hungary	.18	.26	.60	.24	1.74	.61	1.55	.45	44
Iceland	.18	.26	.60	.24	2.14	.45	1.55	.45	44
India	.18	.26	.70	.35	2.15	1.02	1.55	.45	¹44
Indonesia	.18	.26	.70	.35	2.80	1.22	1.55	.45	22
Iran	.18	.26	.70	.35	2.15	.77	1.55	.45	44
Iraq	.18	.26	.70	.35	2.40	.76	1.55	.45	44
Ireland (Eire)	.18	.26	.60	.24	1.66	.53	1.55	.45	22
Israel	.18	.26	.70	.35	2.36	.73	1.55	.45	22
Italy	.18	.26	.60	.24	2.12	.63	1.55	.45	44
Ivory Coast	.18	.26	.70	.35	1.98	.76	1.55	.45	44
Jamaica	.18	.21	.50	.13	1.90	.26	1.40	.40	22
Japan	.18	.26	.70	.35	1.76	.64	1.55	.45	22
Jordan	.18	.26	.70	.35	2.19	.72	1.55	.45	22
Kenya	.18	.26	.70	.35	2.36	.88	1.55	.45	22
Korea (Rep. of)	.18	.26	.70	.35	1.81	.68	1.55	.45	22
No. Korea¹	.18	.26	.70	.35	(4)	....	....	....	(5)
Kuwait	.18	.26	.70	.35	1.92	.80	1.55	.45	44
Laos	.18	.26	.70	.35	2.70	1.10	1.55	.45	22
Latvia²	.18	.26	.70	.35	2.29	.76	1.55	.45	44
Lebanon	.18	.26	.70	.35	2.19	.72	1.55	.45	¹44
Leeward Islands	.18	.21	.50	.13	1.43	.29	1.40	.40	22
Lesotho	.18	.26	.70	.35	2.14	1.02	1.55	.45	22
Liberia	.18	.26	.70	.35	1.80	.67	1.55	.45	22
Libya	.18	.26	.60	.24	2.17	.68	1.55	.45	44
Liechtenstein	.18	.26	.60	.24	1.92	.54	1.55	.45	44
Lithuania²	.18	.26	.70	.35	2.29	.76	1.55	.45	44
Luxembourg	.18	.26	.60	.24	1.99	.52	1.55	.45	44
Macao	.18	.26	.70	.35	2.58	1.00	1.55	.45	22
Madagascar	.18	.26	.70	.35	2.49	.98	1.55	.45	22
Madeira Isl.	.18	.26	.60	.24	1.69	.58	1.55	.45	22
Malawi	.18	.26	.70	.35	2.14	1.00	1.55	.45	22
Malaysia	.18	.26	.70	.35	2.60	1.14	1.55	.45	22
Maldives, Rep. of	.18	.26	.70	.35	2.89	1.04	1.55	.45	22
Mali	.18	.26	.70	.35	2.79	.66	1.55	.45	44
Malta	.18	.26	.60	.24	2.10	.63	1.55	.45	22
Martinique	.18	.21	.50	.13	1.61	.29	1.40	.40	44
Mauritania	.18	.26	.70	.35	1.90	.63	1.55	.45	44
Mauritius	.18	.26	.70	.35	2.42	1.04	1.55	.45	22
Mexico	.10	.13	.50	.13	1.42	.28	1.40	.40	44
Montserrat	.18	.21	.50	.13	1.43	.29	1.55	.45	22
Morocco	.18	.26	.60	.24	2.12	.63	1.55	.45	44
Nauru (Rep.)	.18	.26	.70	.35	2.11	.97	1.55	.45	22
Nepal	.18	.26	.70	.35	2.14	1.02	1.55	.45	44
Netherlands	.18	.26	.60	.24	1.90	.53	1.55	.45	44
Neth. Antilles	.18	.21	.50	.13	1.67	.36	1.40	.40	44
Nevis	.18	.21	.50	.13	1.43	.29	1.40	.40	22
New Caledonia	.18	.26	.70	.35	2.26	.75	1.55	.45	44
New Guinea	.18	.26	.70	.35	2.19	1.06	1.55	.45	22
New Hebrides	.18	.26	.70	.35	2.13	.75	1.55	.45	44
New Zealand	.18	.26	.70	.35	2.40	.86	1.55	.45	22
Nicaragua	.18	.21	.50	.13	1.67	.34	1.40	.40	44
Niger	.18	.26	.70	.35	2.78	.64	1.55	.45	44
Nigeria	.18	.26	.70	.35	2.53	.75	1.55	.45	22
Norway	.18	.26	.60	.24	1.72	.58	1.55	.45	44
Oman, Sultanate of	.18	.26	.70	.35	1.95	.83	1.55	.45	22
Outer Mongolia	.18	.26	.70	.35	(4)	....	1.55	.45	(5)
Pakistan	.18	.26	.70	.35	2.79	.98	1.55	.45	22
Palestine	.18	.26	.70	.35	2.36	.73	1.55	.45	11
Panama	.18	.21	.50	.13	2.01	.36	1.40	.40	¹70
Papua	.18	.26	.70	.35	2.19	1.06	1.55	.45	22
Paraguay	.18	.21	.60	.24	1.99	.54	1.55	.45	44
Peru	.18	.21	.60	.24	2.32	.48	1.55	.45	44
Philippines	.18	.26	.70	.35	2.44	.94	1.55	.45	¹44
Pitcairn	.18	.26	.70	.35	2.33	.83	1.55	.45	22
Poland	.18	.26	.60	.24	2.10	.60	1.55	.45	44
Portugal	.18	.26	.60	.24	1.65	.51	1.55	.45	22
Portugese E. Af.	.18	.26	.70	.35	2.76	1.03	1.55	.45	22
" Timor	.18	.26	.70	.35	2.93	1.38	1.55	.45	22
" W. Africa	.18	.26	.70	.35	2.36	.81	1.55	.45	22
Qatar	.18	.26	.70	.35	1.95	.83	1.55	.45	22
Reunion	.18	.26	.70	.35	2.33	1.02	1.55	.45	44
Rhodesia	.18	.26	.70	.35	2.14	1.00	1.55	.45	22
Romania	.18	.26	.60	.24	1.95	.63	1.55	.45	22
Rwanda	.18	.26	.70	.35	2.22	.86	1.55	.45	22
Ryukyu	.18	.26	.70	.35	1.76	.64	1.55	.45	22
Sabah	.18	.21	.50	.13	1.67	.36	1.55	.45	44
St. Christopher	.18	.21	.50	.13	1.92	.38	1.40	.40	22
St. Eustatius	.18	.21	.50	.13	1.67	.36	1.40	.40	44

Country	Ordinary Surface mail (not over 1 oz.)	Letters and letter pkgs. (per ½ oz.)	Air Service — Other Articles — First 2 oz.	Air Service — Other Articles — Each add'l. 2 oz. or fraction	Air Service — Parcel Post — First 4 oz.	Air Service — Parcel Post — Each add'l 4 oz. or fraction	Surface Parcel Post — First 2 lbs.	Surface Parcel Post — Each add'l pound or fraction	Max. wt. for parcel post (surface or air) lbs.
St. Helena	.18	.26	.70	.35	2.42	.98	1.55	.45	22
St. Lucia	.18	.21	.50	.13	1.92	.38	1.40	.40	22
St. Pierre, Miquelon	.18	.21	.50	.13	1.38	.28	1.40	.40	44
St. Vincent	.18	.21	.50	.13	1.92	.38	1.40	.40	22
Santa Cruz Isl.	.18	.26	.70	.35	2.50	1.12	1.55	.45	22
Saudi Arabia	.18	.26	.70	.35	2.50	.80	1.55	.45	22
Senegal	.18	.26	.70	.35	1.88	.60	1.55	.45	22
Seychelles	.18	.26	.70	.35	2.04	.90	1.55	.45	44
Sierra Leone	.18	.26	.70	.35	2.49	.65	1.55	.45	22
Singapore	.18	.26	.70	• .35	2.60	1.14	1.55	.45	22
Solomon Isl.	.18	.26	.70	.35	2.51	1.12	1.55	.45	22
Somali Rep.	.18	.26	.70	.35	'2.60	.91	1.55	.45	22
South Africa	.18	.26	.70	.35	2.14	1.02	1.55	.45	22
Spain	.18	.26	.60	.24	2.25	.56	1.55	.45	'44
Sp. W. Africa	.18	.26	.70	.35	2.26	.65	1.55	.45	'44
Sudan	.18	.26	.70	.35	2.52	.81	1.55	.45	22
Surinam	.18	.21	.60	.24	1.80	.42	1.55	.45	44
Sweden	.18	.26	.60	.24	1.72	.58	1.55	.45	44
Switzerland	.18	.26	.60	.24	1.92	.54	1.55	.45	44
Syria	.18	.26	.70	.35	1.99	.74	1.55	.45	'44
Tanzania	.18	.26	.70	.35	2.41	.92	1.55	.45	22
Thailand	.18	.26	.70	.35	2.64	.94	1.55	.45	22
Togo	.18	.26	.70	.35	2.07	.76	1.55	.45	44
Tonga	.18	.26	.70	.35	1.88	.75	1.55	.45	22
Trinidad, Tobago	.18	.26	.50	.13	1.91	.36	1.40	.40	22
Tristan da Cunha	.18	.26	.70	.35	2.28	.97	1.55	.45	22
Tunisia	.18	.26	.60	.24	2.11	.60	1.55	.45	44
Turkey	.18	.26	.60	.24	1.82	.68	1.55	.45	44
Turks Islands	.18	.21	.50	.13	1.81	.26	1.40	.40	22
Uganda	.18	.26	.70	.35	2.36	.88	1.55	.45	22
USSR²	.18	.26	.70	.35	2.29	.76	1.55	.45	44
United Arab Emir.	.18	.26	.70	.35	1.95	.83	1.55	.45	44
UAR (Egypt)	.18	.26	.60	.24	1.87	.74	1.55	.45	44
Upper Volta	.18	.26	.70	.35	2.19	.71	1.55	.45	44
Uruguay	.18	.21	.60	.24	2.36	.72	1.55	.45	44
Vatican City	.18	.26	.60	.24	1.95	.59	1.55	.45	44
Venezuela	.18	.21	.60	.24	2.18	.34	1.55	.45	44
Vietnam, Rep. of	.18	.26	.70	.35	2.65	1.04	1.55	.45	44
North Vietnam	.18	.26	.70	.35	(4)				(5)
Western Samoa	.18	.26	.70	.35	2.18	.64	1.55	.45	22
Windward Isl.	.18	.21	.50	.13	1.92	.38	1.40	.40	22
Yemen	.18	.26	.70	.35	2.26	.88			22
Yugoslavia	.18	.26	.60	.24	1.75	.63	1.55	.45	44
Zaire	.18	.26	.70	.35	2.22	.86	1.55	.45	44
Zambia	.18	.26	.70	.35	2.14	1.00	1.55	.45	22

(1.) Restrictions apply; consult post office. (2.) To facilitate distribution and delivery, include "Union of Soviet Socialist Republics" or "USSR" as part of the address. (3.) Small packets weight limit one pound. (4.) No air parcel post service. (5.) No surface parcel post service. (6.) No airmail AO or parcel post to Canada; prepare and prepay all airmail packages as letter mail. (7.) The Continental China Postal authorities will not deliver articles unless addressed to show name of the country as "People's Republic of China"; also, acceptable spelling of capital is "Peking."

International Mails
Weight and Dimensional Limits and Surface Rates
For air rates and parcel post see pages 972-974

Letters and letter packages: All written matter or correspondence recordings, must be sent as letter mail. Weight limit: 4 lbs. to all countries except Canada, which is 60 lbs. Surface rates: Canada and Mexico 10ᶜ per oz. to 12 oz.: over 12 oz. to 1 lb. $1.30; over 1 lb. to 1½ lbs., $1.82; over 1½ lbs. to 2 lbs., $2.34; over 2 to 2½ lbs., $2.65; 2½ to 3 lbs., $2.96; 3 to 3½ lbs., $3.27; 3½ to 4 lbs., $3.58. To Canada only: Over 4 to 4½ lbs., $3.89; 4½ to 5 lbs., $4.20; over 5 lbs., 62ᶜ each pound or fraction; to all other countries, 18ᶜ for first ounce; 1 oz. to 2 oz., 31ᶜ, 2 oz. to 4 oz., 41ᶜ, 4 oz. to 8 oz., 92ᶜ, 8 oz. to 16 oz., $1.74; 16 oz. to 32 oz., $2.89; 32 oz. to 64 oz., $4.62. Air rates: Canada and Mexico 13ᶜ per oz.; Central and South America, Caribbean Islands, Bahamas, Bermuda and St. Pierre, 21ᶜ a half oz.; all other countries 26ᶜ a half oz.; aerogrammes, 18ᶜ.

Post cards. Surface rates to Canada and Mexico, 8ᶜ; to all other countries, 12ᶜ. By air, Canada and Mexico, 11ᶜ; to all other countries, 18ᶜ. Maximum size permitted, 6 x 4¼ in.; minimum, 5½ x 3½.

Printed matter. To Canada and Mexico, 10ᶜ first 2 oz., 6ᶜ each additional oz. or fraction; to other countries 10ᶜ for first 2 oz. or fraction, 16ᶜ for 2 to 4 oz., 32ᶜ for 4 to 8 oz., 56ᶜ for 8 oz. to 1 lb., 85ᶜ for 1 to 2 lbs., $1.16 for 2 to 4 lbs. To countries admitting regular prints over 4 lbs. 58ᶜ for each additional 2 lbs. or fraction. (Consult post office for rates and conditions applying to certain publications mailed by the publishers or by registered news agents.) Book weight limits for most countries is 11 lbs; for exceptions see below.

Exceptional weight limits for printed matter. Printed matter may weigh up to 22 lbs. to Bolivia, Brazil, Chile, Colombia, Costa Rica, Cuba, Dominican Republic, Ecuador, El Salvador, Guatemala, Haiti, Honduras, Mexico, Nicaragua, Panama, Paraguay, Peru, Spain (including Balearic Islands, Canary Islands and Northern Africa).

Matter for the blind. Surface rate free; air rates to Canada 13ᶜ per oz. (For all other countries, consult postmaster.) Weight limit 15 lbs.

Small packets. Postage rates for small items of merchandise and samples are lower than for letter packages or parcel post; weight limits up to 2 lbs. Surface rates: Canada and Mexico, 10ᶜ first 2 oz. and 6ᶜ each additional 2 oz. or fraction. All other countries, for 4 oz. or less 18ᶜ; 4 to 8 oz. 35ᶜ; 8 oz. to 1 lb., 58ᶜ; 1 to 2 lbs., $1.04. Air rates: Canada, 13ᶜ per oz. For other rates, see schedule "Air Service Other Articles" under heading of International Rates for Ordinary Surface Mail, Air Mail and Surface Parcel Post, pages 972-975.

Canadian Postal Rates
Domestic Mail

First class mail costs 8c for the first oz.; between 1 and 2 oz., 14c; between 2 and 4 oz. 20c; between 4 and 8 oz., 32c; between 8 and 12 oz., 44c and between 12 oz. and a pound, 54c. Postcards 7c. Third class mail costs 6c for first 2 ounces and 3c for first 2 ounces and 3c each additional 2 oz. or fraction. All domestic first class mail not heavier than 66 lbs. and exceeding certain sizes is carried by air if it will speed delivery.

International

All mail up to 8 oz. travels by air. An air mail sticker or the word "air mail" must be on the envelope. Cost is 15c for first oz., between 1 and 2 oz., 30c; between 2 and 4 oz., 40c and between 4 and 8 oz., 90c. Postcards 10c. Aerogrammes 15c.

To the United States, its Territories and Possessions: Air mail 10c each oz. (maximum 25 lbs.) Postcards 10c each by air mail. Surface letter mail is 8c for first oz., between 1 and 2 oz., 14c; between 2 and 4 oz., 20c; between 4 and 8 oz. 32c and between 8 oz. and a lb., 54c. Surface postcards are 8c. Printed papers are 6c up to 2 oz., between 2 and 4 oz., 9c; between 4 and 8 oz., 15c and between 8 oz. and a lb., 27c. Small packets are delivered in a speedier and alternative surface to the Parcel Post for a charge of 9c up to 4 oz., between 4 and 8 oz., 15c and 8 oz. to a lb., 27c.

United Nations Postage Stamps Issued in 1974

UN stamps in United States denominations, valid for postage only on mail deposited at UN Headquarters, New York, and UN stamps in Swiss denominations, valid for postage only on mail deposited at the United Nations Office, Geneva, are available at face value from the UN Postal Administration in New York and Geneva and through sales agencies around the world. They may be obtained by mail or automatically through the Customer Deposit Account service, both in New York and Geneva. Revenue from the sale of UN stamps for postage purposes goes to the U.S. Postal Service and the Swiss PTT, respectively; from philatelic sales, revenue goes to the UN.

Date	Stamp	Value
11 Jan.	ILO Headquarters	10c, 21c
22 Mar.	UPU Centenary	10c
6 May	Brazilian Peace Mural	10c, 18c
10 June	Definitives	2c, 10c, 18c
16 Sept.	Air Mails	13c, 18c, 26c
18 Oct.	World Population Year	10c, 18c
22 Nov.	Law of the Sea	10c, 26c

International Parcel Post
For rates see pages 972-974

General dimensional limits—Greatest length, 3½ feet; greatest length and girth combined, 6 feet.

Prohibited articles. Before sending goods abroad the mailer should satisfy himself that they will not be confiscated or returned because their importation is prohibited or restricted by the country of address.

Packing. Parcels for transmission overseas should be even more carefully packed than those intended for delivery within the continental United States. Containers should be used which will be strong enough to protect the contents from the weight of other mails, from pressure and friction, climatic changes, and repeated handlings.

Sealing. Registered or insured parcels must be sealed. To some countries the sealing of ordinary (unregistered and uninsured) parcels is optional, and to others compulsory. Consult post office.

Customs declarations, and other forms. A parcel post sticker, and at least one customs declaration giving a complete description of the contents, are required for each parcel mailed to another country.

Metric Conversion Chart—Approximations

Symbol	When You Know	Multiply By	To Find	Symbol
		Length		
mm	millimeters	0.04	inches	in
cm	centimeters	0.4	inches	in
m	meters	3.3	feet	ft
m	meters	1.1	yards	yd
km	kilometers	0.6	miles	mi
		Area		
cm²	square centimeters	0.16	square inches	in²
m²	square meters	1.2	square yards	yd²
km²	square kilometers	0.4	square miles	mi²
ha	hectares (10,000m2)	2.5	acres	
		Mass (weight)		
g	grams	0.035	ounce	oz.
kg	kilograms	2.2	pounds	lb
t	tonnes (1000kg)	1.1	short tons	
		Volume		
ml	milliliters	0.03	fluid ounces	fl oz
l	liters	2.1	pints	pt
l	liters	1.06	quarts	qt
l	liters	0.26	gallons	gal
m³	cubic meters	35	cubic feet	ft³
m³	cubic meters	1.3	cubic yards	yd³
		Temperature (exact)		
°C	Celsius temp.	9/5 (+32)	Fahrenheit temp.	°F
		Temperature (exact) to Metric		
°F	Fahrenheit temp.	—32 5/9 of remainder	Celsius temp.	°C

Symbol	When You Know	Multiply By	To Find	Symbol
		Length		
in.	inches	*2.5	centimeters	cm
ft	feet	30	centimeters	cm
yd	yards	0.9	meters	m
mi	miles	1.6	kilometers	km
		Area		
in²	square inches	6.5	sq. centimeters	cm²
ft²	square feet	0.09	square meters	m²
yd²	square yards	0.8	square meters	m²
mi²	square miles	2.6	sq. kilometers	km²
	acres	0.4	hectares	ha
		Mass (weight)		
oz	ounces	28	grams	g
lb	pounds	0.45	kilograms	kg
	short tons (2000 lb)	0.9	tonnes	t
		Volume		
tsp	teaspoons	5	milliliters	ml
tbsp	tablespoons	15	milliliters	ml
fl oz	fluid ounces	30	milliliters	ml
c	cups	0.24	liters	l
pt	pints	0.47	liters	l
qt	quarts	0.95	liters	l
gal	gallons	3.8	liters	l
ft³	cubic feet	0.03	cubic meters	m³
yd³	cubic yards	0.76	cubic meters	m³

*1 in=2.54 cm (exactly)

QUICK REFERENCE INDEX

First Class Postal Rates in Brief

United States Domestic

Letters—10c per ounce or fraction thereof, limit 12 ounces.
Air Mail Letters—13c an ounce or fraction thereof; limit 9 ounces. Includes mail to Armed Forces outside U.S. when addressed APO or FPO, New York, N.Y., San Francisco, Calif., or Seattle, Wash.
Postal Cards—8c each (up to 4½ x 6 in.) Double cards, 16c. Private cards, 16c.
Air mail post cards—11c each.

United States International

Letters—(1) Canada and Mexico, 10c per ounce to 12 ounces; over 12 ounces to 1 pound, $1.30; over 1 pound to 1½ pounds, $1.82; over 1½ to 2 pounds, $2.34; over 2 to 2½ pounds, $2.65; over 2½ to 3 pounds, $2.96; over 3 to 3½ pounds, $3.27; and over 3½ to 4 pounds, $3.58. TO CANADA ONLY: Over 4 to 4½ pounds, $3.89; over 4½ to 5 pounds, $4.20; over 5 pounds, 62c each additional pound or fraction.
(2) Countries other than Canada and Mexico, 1 ounce, 18c; over 1 to 2 ounces, 31c; over 2 to 4 ounces, 41c; over 4 to 8 ounces, 92c; over 8 ounces to 1 pound, $1.74; over 1 to 2 pounds, $2.89; and over 2 to 4 pounds, $4.62.
Air Mail Letters—(1) Canada and Mexico, 13c per ounce. (2) Cen. America, S. America, the Caribbean Is., Bahamas, Bermuda and St. Pierre and Miquelon, 21c per half ounce. (3) All other countries, 26c per half ounce.
Aerogrammes—To all countries, 18c each.
Postal cards—To Canada and Mexico 8c each. To all other countries, 12c each.
Air mail post cards—To Canada and Mexico 11c each, to other countries 18c each.

Canada

Domestic—1 oz., 8c; 1-2 oz., 14c; 2-4 oz., 20c; 4-8 oz., 32c; 8-12 oz., 44c; 12 oz.-1 lb., 54c. **Postcards 7c.**
International—Letters to U.S.: by air, 10c each oz.; surface—same as domestic first class, except: 8 oz.-1 lb., 54c; 1-2 lb., $1.50; 2-4 lb., $3.00. **Letters other than to U.S.:** 1 oz., 15c; 1-2 oz., 30c; 2-4 oz., 40c; 4-8 oz., 90c. **Postcards 10c.**
Aerogrammes 15c.